Artist's rendition of Canada as seen from far
above Central America. Projection courtesy
M. Feuchtwanger and S.L. Pattison,
Department of Geography, Simon Fraser
University. Artwork by Michael J. Lee.

THE
CANADIAN
ENCYCLOPEDIA

SECOND EDITION

VOLUME III

Min – Sta

Hurtig Publishers
Edmonton

Hurtig Publishers Ltd.
10560 – 105 Street
Edmonton, Alberta
Canada T5H 2W7

Every attempt has been made to identify and credit sources for
photographs. The publisher would appreciate receiving
information as to any inaccuracies in the credits for
subsequent editions.

Canadian Cataloguing in Publication Data

Main entry under title:
The Canadian Encyclopedia

Editor in Chief: James H. Marsh.

ISBN 0-88830-326-2 (set) –ISBN 0-88830-327-0
(v. 1). –ISBN 0-88830-328-9 (v. 2). –ISBN
0-88830-329-7 (v. 3). –ISBN 0-88830-330-0 (v.4)

1. Canada–Dictionaries and encyclopedias.
I. Marsh, James H.
FCwe.C36 1985   971'.003'21   C84-091250-1
F1006.C36 1985

Designed, typeset and manufactured
in Canada

Minting From 1858 to 1907 most issues of Canadian COINS were struck at the Royal Mint in London, Eng, with additional issues from the Heaton Mint of Birmingham. The Royal Mint in Ottawa was opened in 1908 as a branch of the Royal Mint in London, and operated as such until 1931.

When the Dominions were made equal with Great Britain by the Statute of Westminster, the Ottawa mint became independent and was renamed the Royal Canadian Mint. It operated as a branch of the Department of Finance until 1969, when it became a crown corporation. Today the Royal Canadian Mint strikes coins for foreign countries as well as for Canada. Since 1965 a branch mint at Hull, Qué, has produced special issues and sets for collectors. Since 1974 the mint that opened at Winnipeg, Man, has shared with Ottawa the production of the nation's coinage.

To make coins, metal ingots are rolled into sheets of the proper thickness, from which the blanks are cut. The blanks are cleaned, polished and sent to the coining room, where they are struck by dies. A die is developed by a lengthy and painstaking process. A master punch is first produced by means of a reducing machine. A model in hard plastic, about 20 cm in diameter, is scanned by a tracer at one end of the machine. At the other end, a cutter duplicates the movements of the tracer and cuts the design in reduced size on a steel block about 7.5 cm in diameter. A second reducing machine then scans the block and reproduces the design, in the intended size of the coin, onto another steel block. This final reduction, the master punch, is used to sink the master matrix.

Details lacking in the master punch are punched into the matrix, which is used to produce the working punches. The working punches are then used to sink the working dies, which strike the coinage. Since 1945 all coinage dies have been chromium plated in order to give longer die life and a better finish to coins.

R.C. WILLEY

Minto, NB, Village, pop 3197 (1986c), 3399 (1981c), inc 1962, named for the eighth governor general of Canada, the earl of MINTO, in 1904 when the construction of the railway opened the area. It is located 56 km N of Fredericton in the Minto coalfields, which has produced 36 million tons of coal in the century since 1886, and continues to produce at the rate of 600 000 per annum. Reserves are estimated at 18 million t. The first coal mines in Canada operated here, with coal being shipped to Boston in 1639, but it was not until 1825 that coal was mined regularly.

Because the seams of coals are near the surface, mechanical mining was not introduced until 1905. Underground mining was carried out from 1930 to 1971, but with most of the coal about 8 m below the surface, strip mining is more economical and is the only method employed today. Labour problems and a strike in 1937 were resolved the following year by new provincial legislation. For New Brunswick, the village is unusually cosmopolitan. The area is a single resource centre with neither forestry or agriculture possible because of the soil quality.

BURTON GLENDENNING

Minto, Gilbert John Murray Kynynmond Elliot, 4th Earl of, soldier, governor general of Canada 1898-1904, viceroy of India 1905-10 (b at London, Eng 9 July 1845; d at Minto Castle, near Hawick, Scot 1 May 1914). Lord Melgund (his title before succeeding to the earldom) served as military secretary to Gov Gen marquess of LANSDOWNE, 1883-85, and as F.D. MIDDLETON's chief of staff during the NORTH-WEST REBELLION. In

1898 he became governor general; his term was marked by controversy and political strife. He was inexperienced in government, distrustful of politicians and determined to play an active part in Canadian public life, and his criticism of his government's handling of the SOUTH AFRICAN WAR crisis, his interest in reforming the Canadian Militia and his support for Joseph Chamberlain's imperial preference campaign all caused tension. More positively, he attempted to forge closer ties between French and English Canadians, to preserve the written and material record of Canada's past, to promote sports (the Minto Cup in lacrosse) and to protect Canada's northern miners and native peoples from the neglect and mismanagement of government.

CARMAN MILLER

Reading: Carman Miller, *The Canadian Career of the Fourth Earl of Minto* (1980).

Mirabel, Qué, City, pop 13 875 (1986c), 14 080 (1981c), inc 1971, located some 55 km NW of Montréal, is one of Québec's youngest cities and also one of its most extended (covering some 750 km²). It was created in Jan 1979 through the arbitrary merger of 14 existing municipalities whose lands had been expropriated in Mar 1969 for the construction of the new international airport for Montréal, since named "Mirabel" in honour of a little hamlet that has now disappeared. The dismemberment of this ancient land and its new orientation has completely changed the regional structures and habits of its population. The airport, linked to Montréal by the Laurentian Autoroute, is in the centre of town. The region's economy still depends on agriculture.

GILLES BOILEAU

Miramichi Lumber Strike began 20 Aug 1937 when 1500 millworkers and longshoremen along the Miramichi R in northern New Brunswick struck 14 lumber firms for increased wages, shorter working hours and union recognition. The strike was organized by the NB Farmer-Labour Union, an unaffiliated trade union that had been formed just prior to the strike by Gregory McEachreon, a local merchant. The provincial government was petitioned by the union to intervene in the dispute under its recently enacted fair wage legislation, but the government refused to do so unless the men first returned to work. The strike ended on Aug 31 with a compromise settlement worked out by mediators. The Miramichi lumber strike and the strike in the MINTO coalfields in Oct 1937 forced the province to re-evaluate its

Earl of Minto, governor general of Canada 1898-1904 (*courtesy National Archives of Canada/C-51950*).

labour relations policy and consequently to introduce new labour legislation in 1938.

PATRICK BURDEN

Miramichi River, 220 km long from Juniper, NB, to the Gulf of ST LAWRENCE, arises in central NB. Its 2 branches, the SW and NW Miramichi, join at Beaubears I, near NEWCASTLE, NB. Seaward from here, and throughout the open shallow Inner Bay, river water forms a fresh, less dense layer on top of saltier denser water. This is the picturesque Miramichi Estuary formed some 4000 years ago when currents and waves built a barrier of sand islands across the drowned, ice-deepened valley in the soft sandstones and shales of Pennsylvanian age. The effect of the sea is felt 65 km inland at Redbank as a regular rise and fall in the river flow.

Early view of the Miramichi River from Beaubears I, where the 2 branches of the river meet (*courtesy New Brunswick Museum*).

Since their settlement by ACADIANS after the fall of LOUISBOURG and by English lumbermen, later turned shipbuilders, the scenic shores have been the focus of the dual economic life of fishing and forestry. Besides the legendary ATLANTIC SALMON run – the foremost in eastern N America before its devastation by overfishing, pollution and unknown causes – smelt, gaspereau, shad, eel, herring, mackerel and lobsters are exploited. Formerly, extensive log rafts plied the river's waters; now major forest industries at CHATHAM and Newcastle depend on the Miramichi for shipping and effluent disposal. The spirit and independence of the Miramichi inhabitants are characterized by their survival, sometimes immersed to their necks in river water, of the Great Miramichi Fire (1825) in which 200 people died and almost one-quarter of NB's forests were burned. The obverse side of this individualism is the salmon poaching notorious along the length of the river. The name, which may be the oldest recorded name of native origin in Canada, may come from the Montagnais word for "country of the Micmac."　　　KATE KRANCK

Miron, Gaston, poet, publisher (b at Ste-Agathe-des-Monts, Qué 8 Jan 1928). Miron spent the period 1947-53 discovering through everyday events the values of his province — its landscapes, people, heritage, social conditions and politics. In 1953 he and a few friends founded the Montréal publishing house L'Hexagone, and he continued his explorations of contemporary society. His poetry, for a long time oral, has been published in *L'Homme rapaillé* (1970) and *Contrepointes* (1975) and has captured an international audience. His poems are rooted in the here and now, but they remain faithful to Québec's ancestral language, customs and usages, crystallizing isolated images: the man we meet on the street and whom we find in ourselves; the man committed to a political struggle; the collective and social individual caught up in a common destiny; and the land. Through these themes, his writing exalts and reconciles opposing elements in a time frame that is repetitive but that tends towards an ultimate transcendence. The poetry is dense and measured.

Miron was the first poet to show the Quebecer as he is. He had a definite influence on poetry of the 1960s and 1970s and he awakened the N American and European reader to a particular and universal anthropological reality.

EUGÈNE ROBERTO

Mirvish, Edwin, theatrical producer, entrepreneur (b at Colonial Beach, Virginia 24 July 1914). He came to Canada in 1923. Mirvish is well known for "Honest Ed's" discount department store and the 4 restaurants he operates in Toronto. He has long been involved with theatrical production. In 1962 he bought the Royal Alexandra Theatre in Toronto and in 1982 he purchased the famous Old Vic Theatre in London, Eng, which he refurbished and restored to its former splendour. With his son, David, he has presented such noteworthy productions at the Old Vic as the premiere of the musical *Blondel*; the Stratford, Canada, production of *The Mikado* and Michael Bogdanov's modern interpretation of Shakespeare's *Henry IV, Parts I & II* and *Henry V*. Among his many honours are the Canada Medal and Officer of the Order of Canada. He has received honorary LLD's from Trent U and U of Waterloo.　　　JAMES DeFELICE

Miscou Island, 64 km², comprises the most eastern part of Gloucester County, NB, on the W side of the Gulf of St Lawrence and at the entrance to CHALEUR BAY. The island is characterized by white sandy beaches, spruce trees, deep-sea fishing, lakes and salt lagoons, and a lighthouse at the northern tip, Miscou Pt. Originally inhabited by

the MICMAC, it was discovered by Jacques CARTIER in 1534. Populated by settlers from France and the Channel Islands (hence its unique "patois" of Old French), the island passed to Britain in 1763. Its name derives from the Micmac *susqu* meaning "boggy marsh" or "low land."　　　DAVID EVANS

Miscouche, PEI, pop 677 (1986c), 752 (1981c), situated 62 km E of Charlottetown. Miscouche is a derivation of a Micmac word meaning "grassy lands." An inland community, Miscouche is located in an agricultural area. It was originally settled by Acadians from Malpeque Bay in 1727. In the early 1800s, Scottish settlers then immigrated to Miscouche. Today, the town is chiefly a residential community. Much of the population is either retired or employed in Summerside or at CFB Summerside. On the main route to Acadian PEI, Miscouche has benefited from tourism. One of the town's main landmarks is the Miscouche Museum.　　　W.S. KEIZER

Miss Canada The representation of Canada as a sweet but coy young lady was a Victorian convention that was abandoned about the time of WWII. A popular depiction of Miss Canada was in winter garb – wearing skates, an overcoat, a tuque and a sash. At other times she was shown royally resisting the blandishments of a conniving Uncle Sam, symbolic of the US, siding instead with a portly John Bull, representative of Great Britain. Miss Canada is also a title awarded annually since 1946, on the basis of beauty, talent, personality, etc to contestants with regional titles by the Miss Canada Pageant.　　　JOHN ROBERT COLOMBO

Mission, BC, District Municipality, pop 21 985 (1986c) 20 056 (1981c), inc 1969, area 25 333 ha, is located on the N bank of the FRASER R, 70 km by road E of Vancouver. An Oblate priest, Father Fourquet, established a mission on the present site 1860-61. Large-scale development began after the CPR was completed (1885) and a bridge built across the Fraser (1891). A community known as Mission Junction sprang up and was incorporated as the village of Mission in 1922. The surrounding countryside was established as the Corporation of the District of Mission in 1892. In 1969 the Corporation and the village were amalgamated to form the present municipality, which has 2 main communities, Mission and Hatzic, and 4 smaller ones: Steelhead, Stave Falls, Silverdale and Ruskin. Hatzic, to the E of Mission, is mainly residential and is separated from Mission by land owned by the province as part of the agricultural land reserve. Mission's economy is based on lumbering, manufacturing, dairying and fruit and vegetable growing. A major landmark is the Benedictine monastic complex, Westminster Abbey, moved to Mission from Burnaby in 1954.　　　ALAN F.J. ARTIBISE

Missions and Missionaries In New France as elsewhere the christianization of the native Indian population was an ostensible motive for European occupation, and trading companies and governors were under official pressure to provide it. The actual work was left largely to religious orders and societies. JESUITS entered Acadia in 1611, RÉCOLLETS the St Lawrence Valley and the Huron country in 1615, while Capuchins, SULPICIANS, and priests of the Society of Foreign Missions were later active. Missions were eventually established in all areas penetrated by the French, including the Iroquois country and extending to James Bay, the western Great Lakes and beyond. The most celebrated of these was the Huron mission, which was reopened by the Jesuits in 1634 and came to an end in 1649-50 when the Iroquois destroyed the Huron Confederacy and killed Jean de BRÉBEUF and several other missionaries (*see* STE MARIE AMONG THE HURONS).

The British Conquest of 1759-60 cut off the supply of recruits to French agencies, and Protestants were slow to show interest in Indian missions. The first successful effort, that of Methodists among the Mississauga of Upper Canada from 1823, was made possible by the emergence of a corps of native missionaries among whom Peter JONES (Kahkewaquonaby) and John SUNDAY (Shah-wun-dais) were most prominent. Anglicans and MORAVIANS were also active, and in 1843 the Jesuits entered the province. In western Canada the leading agencies have been the Church Missionary Society (Anglican) from 1820, the Wesleyan (later Canadian) Methodists from 1840, the Oblates of Mary Immaculate (Roman Catholic) from 1845, the Presbyterians from 1866 and the United Church of Canada from 1925. Among the Inuit the Moravians, in Labrador from 1771, have been followed by the CMS and the Oblates. While a large measure of paternalism has marked all of these missions, emphasis now is on encouraging the active participation of native Christians. In recent years many new missions have been opened, most conspicuously by Pentecostals and other conservative evangelicals.

Providing religious services to white settlers also called for missionary effort. The French orders and societies that worked among the Indians also served the colonists of New France. Some leading Protestant organizations were the Society for the Propagation of the Gospel (Anglican), the Glasgow Colonial Society (Church of Scotland), the Colonial Missionary Society (Congregational) and the American Home Missionary Society (Congregational/Presbyterian). American preachers founded Methodist and Baptist churches in central Canada, while the Methodists of the Atlantic provinces received missionaries mainly from England. Roman Catholic missions, both white and Indian, were generously subsidized by the Society for the Propagation of the Faith, founded at Lyon in 1822.

Before the middle of the 19th century, Canadian churches were sponsoring missionaries overseas. In 1845 Richard Burpee went to India with support from Maritime Baptists, and in 1846 the tiny Presbyterian Church of Nova Scotia agreed to send John Geddie to the New Hebrides. By the end of the century practically all Canadian Protestant churches supported missions overseas; that of the Methodists in west China grew to be the largest Protestant mission anywhere. The Sudan Interior Mission, a nondenominational faith mission officially organized at Toronto in 1898, was probably the largest of all Protestant missionary organizations at the time of its merger with the Andes Evangelical Mission to form the Society of International Missionaries. Since WWII Roman Catholics and conservative evangelicals have overtaken the larger Protestant churches in the scale of their missionary operations. Meanwhile the latter have moved toward a relation of equal partnership with overseas churches, and much of their work is carried on in co-operation with such international agencies as the World Council of Churches.　　　JOHN WEBSTER GRANT

Mississauga, Ont, City, pop 374 005 (1986c), 315 056 (1981c) located 20 km W of TORONTO on Lake Ontario. Originally called Toronto Township, its present name is derived from the original inhabitants, the Mississauga, a band of the OJIBWA, who had migrated from the upper Great Lakes region by the early 18th century. The Mississauga developed a partnership with unlicensed French fur traders at the mouth of a waterway known as Rivière du Crédit. The lower Credit R valley remained the domain of the Mississauga until British authorities purchased the surrounding land in 1805. In the following year, LOYALISTS as well as American and British immigrants began to settle along Dundas Street and along the lakeshore W of the Credit R. The steady influx of farmers into the area by 1818 prompted the colonial administration to purchase the remainder of the Mississauga Tract, which included the northern part of Toronto Township. By 1826 the Mississauga had been resettled on a reserve north of the mouth of the Credit where they remained until 1847 when the provincial government moved them to the Grand River Reserve.

When incorporated in 1850 Toronto Township had a population of about 7500. In the absence of adequate roads, the inhabitants of the township came to identify more strongly with the local villages and hamlets. For example, Cooksville and Dixie were farm service centres along Dundas Street; Erindale, Streetsville and Meadowvale were millsites on the Credit R; Port Credit, Clarkson and Malton were railway stations.

Toronto Township's rural landscape and its role as an agrarian hinterland remained relatively unaltered until after WWI when the advent of the automobile and paved roads encouraged residents from Toronto to move to cheaper premises in the surrounding "suburbs." From a sprawling "bedroom" community of little more than 15 000 people in 1945, Toronto Township was dramatically transformed into a conglomeration of planned residential and industrial subdivisions, high-rise apartments and office complexes, shopping centres, multilane highways and Canada's busiest airport. With its population reaching 100 000 in 1968, Toronto Township became the Town of Mississauga and was incorporated as a city in 1974. Although it is rapidly emerging as the leading commercial and industrial centre in the expanding urban frontier W of Toronto, Mississauga continues its struggle to build a civic identity in the shadow of a giant metropolitan neighbour and in the face of a tradition of local village identification. The recently completed Mississauga Civic Centre is expected to develop into the new downtown core for Canada's fastest-growing city. ROGER E. RIENDEAU

Mistassini, Qué, Town, pop 6734 (1986c), 6682 (1981c), inc 1976, is located on the Rivière Mistassini, to the N of Lac SAINT-JEAN. Mistassini in Cree means "great stone." Settlement dates from 1892, when the Trappist fathers from OKA came to found a monastery in the forests N of Lac Saint-Jean. The monks also built a flour mill and a sawmill. Mistassini is a small service centre for surrounding parishes. Its population grew with the construction of the Dolbeau paper mill (1927) and power stations on the Péribonka R (1954-60). The town's growth forced the monastery to move to the nearby countryside (1979). Each Aug Mistassini holds its Blueberry Festival, honouring the small, blue fruit found in such abundance in the district. MARC ST-HILAIRE

Mistassini, Lac, 2336 km², elev 372 m, max length 159 km, is located in central Québec, 360 km E of JAMES BAY and 220 km NW of Lac SAINT-JEAN. Fed by numerous small lakes and streams, it drains to the W, via Lakes Mesgouez and Némiscau, following the course of the Rivière de RUPERT. It is the largest natural lake in the province. A series of rocky island ridges virtually divide it into 2 separate lakes. It is surrounded by black and white spruce, white birch, poplar, larch, jackpine and balsam fir, which support a fairly extensive logging industry. The waters of the lake contain whitefish, pike, gray and lake trout, and freshwater seals have been reported. The caribou have been overhunted, but moose are still frequently seen. The area has also been overtrapped, and the populations of fox, otter, lynx, marten, mink and beaver have been seriously reduced. The lake was

discovered by Abbé Charles ALBANEL in 1672, and was long a centre of the FUR TRADE. It still has a trading post, a Church of England mission and a Cree reservation. Geologist Albert Peter LOW wintered at the lake in 1884-85 and surveyed it June-July 1885. Today the area is famous for its production of blueberries, contributing greatly to the annual Canadian harvest. The name derives from the Cree word *mista-assini*, meaning "great stone." DAVID EVANS

Mistletoe family, Loranthaceae, includes about 30 genera and over 1000 species. It is predominantly tropical but has members in temperate regions. Plants are mostly small shrubs, parasitic on gymnosperms and woody flowering plants. They are attached to hosts, drawing nutrients from them through modified roots (haustoria). Severe infestations may produce abnormal growth of branches, called "witches' brooms." Flowers are small, usually greenish and, in N American species, unisexual. Fruits, fleshy berries with shelled seeds, are eaten by birds, which wipe the seeds from their beaks onto trees or deposit them in droppings. The only Canadian genus, *Arceuthobium*, comprises about 10 species, 4 of which are native to Canada. Three tend to parasitize particular trees: *A. americanum*, pine; *A. douglasii*, Douglas fir; *A. pusillum*, spruce. Only *A. campylopodum* has several hosts. *A. pusillum* occurs in the East, the others in the West. Most mistletoes are leafy and often evergreen, but *Arceuthobium* species have leaves reduced to scales, thus appearing leafless. The genus is unique in the explosive discharge of seeds from fruits. Some western Indian groups ate boiled berries, and used "leaf tea" for contraception. Some species may be toxic to livestock. Familiar mistletoe, *Viscum album*, is native to Europe, Africa and Asia. It has long been associated with ancient Celtic religious ceremonies, and its modern use as a Christmas decoration may derive from this. *See also* PLANTS, NATIVE USES.

Mitchell, Charles Alexander, scientist, veterinarian, medical historian (b at Clarksburg, Ont 9 Aug 1891; d at Ottawa 8 July 1979). After graduating from the Ontario Veterinary Coll, Toronto, in 1915, he worked for the Dominion Dept of Agriculture 1914-57 and was Dominion Animal Pathologist 1944-57. Author of numerous articles, he was internationally recognized for his secret work on animal diseases during WWII. A strong supporter of organized VETERINARY MEDICINE, Mitchell was closely involved in the formation of regional and national veterinary associations and local medical study groups. In addition he researched and reported on many aspects of Canadian veterinary and medical history. Late in life he became director of research 1958-72 at Ottawa Civic Hospital. From 1958 to 1970 he was also associate professor in the Faculty of Medicine at U of Ottawa. J.F. FRANK

Mitchell, Humphrey, electrician, trade unionist, politician (b at Old Shoreham, Eng 9 Sept 1894; d at Ottawa 1 Aug 1950). After serving in the Royal Navy in WWI, Mitchell settled in Hamilton, Ont, to work as an electrician. He served 2 years as president and 22 as secretary of the Hamilton and District Trades and Labor Council and chaired the Ontario executive of the TRADES AND LABOR CONGRESS OF CANADA. He was elected city alderman (1929-31) and in a 1931 by-election won a seat in the House of Commons. Although an independent labourite, he refused to join the new CCF and eventually gravitated towards the Liberals. After his defeat in the 1935 general election, he entered the federal Department of Labour; he later headed a number of wartime commissions and boards on labour mat-

ters. From 1941, just before he regained a parliamentary seat, until his death he was minister of labour under KING and ST. LAURENT. The introduction of new compulsory collective-bargaining legislation during his tenure laid the basis for Canada's postwar industrial-relations system. CRAIG HERON

Mitchell, James, lawyer, politician, premier of NB (b at Scotch Settlement, York County, NB 16 Mar 1843; d at St Stephen, NB 15 Dec 1897). Mitchell was a prominent lawyer in St Stephen and during the early years of his career was also inspector of schools for Charlotte County. A Liberal MLA from 1882 to 1897, he served as provincial surveyor general, commissioner of agriculture, receiver general and provincial secretary before becoming premier in 1896. Poor health forced him to retire in 1897 after 15 uneventful months, and his administration accomplished little of lasting significance. ARTHUR T. DOYLE

Popular singer and songwriter Joni Mitchell (*courtesy WEA Canada/photo by Norman Seeff*).

Mitchell, Joni, stage name of Roberta Joan Anderson, pop singer, songwriter (b at Fort Macleod, Alta 7 Nov 1943). Initially a folksinger in Calgary and Toronto, Mitchell moved to the US in 1966, eventually settling near Los Angeles. Widely influential as a lyric stylist, her songs "Urge for Going," "The Circle Game" and "Both Sides Now" were popular in recordings by other artists. Through 14 albums from 1968 (eg, *Blue, Court and Spark, Hejira, Dog Eat Dog*) she outstripped her folk beginnings and, with her collaboration in 1978 with Charles Mingus (*Mingus*), reached into jazz. Her album *Clouds* received a Grammy Award in 1969. MARK MILLER

Mitchell, Ken, playwright, novelist, short story writer, poet, actor, teacher, scriptwriter (b at Moose Jaw, Sask 13 Dec 1940). Mitchell grew up on a farm near Moose Jaw, and attended U Sask, Regina; while a student, he began to write stories and radio plays for the CBC. After receiving his MA in 1967, he joined that university's English department, where he continues to teach. An ardent supporter of prairie culture, Mitchell helped found the Saskatchewan Writers' Guild in 1969; edited the anthology *Horizon: Writings of the Canadian Prairie* (1977); wrote the screenplay for *The*

Hounds of Notre Dame (1980); and produced a critical study of his literary antecedent, Sinclair ROSS (*Sinclair Ross: A Reader's Guide*, 1981). A prolific, humorous storyteller, Mitchell succeeds particularly well in his story collection *Everybody Gets Something Here* (1977), in his entertaining novels *Wandering Rafferty*, (1972), *The Meadowlark Connection: A Saskatchewan Thriller* (1975), *The Con Man* (1979) and in his anthology of selected works, *Ken Mitchell Country* (1985). Believing that Canadians need to know more about their heroes, and possessing a keen ear for dialogue, Mitchell has turned naturally to play writing. Several of his plays, including *The Medicine Line* (1976), *The Shipbuilder* (1979) and *Tommy*, (1986), as well as *Davin: The Politician* (1979) and the much-acclaimed country western *Cruel Tears* (1977), retain a strong prairie flavour. Mitchell has subsequently extended his range to China in *The Great Cultural Revolution* (1980) and *Gone the Burning Sun* (1985), a one-man show based on the life of Dr Norman BETHUNE, which toured China in 1987. *Through the NanDa Gate* (1986) is a poetic/photographic account of Mitchell's teaching experiences in mainland China.

DONNA COATES

Mitchell, Peter, lawyer, politician, Conservative premier of NB 1866-67 (b at Newcastle, NB 4 Jan 1824; d at Montréal 25 Oct 1899). A colourful swashbuckler, Mitchell became a celebrity as Canada's first minister of fisheries but died bitter and unrewarded. He entered politics in 1856 and, as a strong supporter of Confederation, became premier of NB in 1866 through a fluke. In the Senate 1867-72 and elected to the Commons in 1872, he was Sir John A. MACDONALD's minister of fisheries 1867-73 and proved himself both innovative and aggressive. He created an international incident when Canadian gunboats seized American fishermen in Canadian waters. The PACIFIC SCANDAL ended Mitchell's influence, though he remained in politics for several years and purchased the *Montreal Herald*. His self-esteem increased, as did his unreliability. He drifted to the Liberals, nursing grievances against Macdonald and others.

CARL M. WALLACE

Mitchell, William Ormond, novelist, dramatist (b at Weyburn, Sask 13 Mar 1914). In his treatment of prairie settings and language, W.O. Mitchell has depicted the West in fiction and influenced many later writers. He studied at U of Man and U of A. In 1944, after teaching 2 years, he settled in High River, Alta, where he remained until 1968 except for 3 years as fiction editor at MACLEAN'S (1948-51). After 1968 he was writer-in-residence at the Banff Centre, U of C, U of A and Massey Coll, Toronto. He was at U Windsor 1978-87 and now lives in Calgary.

In 1947 Mitchell achieved instant recognition with the publication of his classic WHO HAS SEEN THE WIND. The novel examines the initiation of the boy Brian into the meaning of birth and death, life, freedom and justice. The children and the eccentrics, the ever-drunken Ben and the madman Saint Sammy, are the most vivid characters. Mitchell portrays the beauty and power of the prairie and the wind, symbolizing God. Allan KING directed the feature film based on the novel (1977). Mitchell's second novel *The Kite* (1962) is also concerned with life and mortality. Here Mitchell combines comic anecdotes with a more archetypal theme of the quest that ends in celebration and immortality. *The Vanishing Point* (1973) was a reworking of an early unpublished novel. Set on the Paradise Valley Reserve, its theme is the resolution of alienation; it is an affirmation of racial and personal interconnectedness. His novel *How I Spent My Summer Holidays*

W.O. Mitchell, author of *Who Has Seen the Wind*, a novel that portrays the prairies (*photo by Peter Paterson*).

(1981) returns to the theme of initiation, but the vision is much darker. Hugh leaves childhood innocence to pass into a world of betrayal, guilt, repression and violence. In the end, the old man Hugh is left only with knowledge. His latest novel, *Since Daisy Creek* (1984), is a contemporary Canadian *Moby Dick*. Mauled by a magnificent grizzly, Colin Dobbs, a failed novelist, suffers mental as well as physical scars, and seeks to heal himself through writing. The salty Dobbs and his feisty daughter Annie are Mitchell's most vivid characters since Daddy Sherry.

Mitchell also wrote many plays for radio and TV. The popular *Jake and the Kid* (1961) originated in stories written for *Maclean's*; the series ran weekly on CBC Radio 1950-56. Around the hired man and the adolescent Kid, Mitchell wove the adventures of the community of Crocus, Sask. The eccentric characters, tall tales and local dialect added to the audience's enjoyment. The series was televised in 1961. The early radio plays *The Devil's Instrument* (1949) and *The Black Bonspiel of Wullie MacCrimmon* (written 1951, publ 1965) were later revised as full-length plays; the latter was staged in 1979 by Theatre Calgary as were *The Kite* (1981) and 2 plays written for the stage, *Back to Beulah* (which won the Chalmers Award, 1976) and *For Those in Peril on the Sea* (1982). These plays were published in *Dramatic W.O. Mitchell* (1982). Mitchell also experimented with a musical, *Wild Rose*, in 1967. In 1973 Mitchell became a Member of the Order of Canada. He has been awarded several honorary degrees and was the director of the Writing Division, Banff Centre 1975-85.

CATHERINE MCLAY

Reading: M. Peterman, "W.O. Mitchell," *Profiles in Canadian Literature* (1980).

Mite, common name for some members of order Acari, a large, diverse group of tiny ARACHNIDS. Worldwide, about 30 000 species of mites have been described, of an estimated 250 000; in Canada, about 2000 of an estimated 10 000. Mites may exceed INSECTS in numbers of individuals: up to 1 million mites, representing some 100 species, may occur in one square metre of forest soil and litter in Canada. The earliest fossils are 380 million years old. Mite remains of present-day genera are commonly found in pieces of 80 to 100-million-year-old amber from Canada, Mexico and Europe. As their common name indicates, "mites" are unusually small; most range from 0.1 to 10 mm. Mites come in all colours; many are dull, but some, especially water mites, are bright red, blue or green. Like spiders, mites lack well-defined abdominal segments, but unlike spiders their abdomen is not separated from

the rest of the body by a narrow waist. Mites grow by gradual metamorphosis: egg, 6-legged larva, 1-3, 8-legged nymphal stages and 8-legged adult. Mites and TICKS are the most ubiquitous single animal group, living in nearly every terrestrial and aquatic habitat, including the sea. Mites may disperse by air currents or by birds, mammals and flying insects. Many have developed nonpredacious feeding habits, eg, feeding on bacteria, yeasts, fungi, algae, mosses and higher plants. Others parasitize insects and vertebrates (except fish), some being found in secretive spots, eg, inside bird quills, under lizard scales, in lungs of seals, and in human facial pores. Mites are both destructive and useful. Herbivorous spider mites are pests of various crops, forest trees and ornamentals. Some eriophyid mites, also herbivorous, form galls or transmit plant viruses, including wheat streak mosaic in Canada. Mites cause great economic losses in stored grain, other food and organic products. House dust mites concentrate allergenic materials. Other mites, eg, chiggers, mange and scabies mites, are important parasites and sometimes transmit human and livestock diseases. Some species are beneficial as predators of herbivorous mites; others feed on weeds. The importance of oribatid mites in decomposing and recycling organic matter in soil is just beginning to be understood.

EVERT E. LINDQUIST

Mitel Corporation, *see* ELECTRONICS INDUSTRY.

Mladenovic, Milos, professor, editor (b S of Belgrade, Serbia 1903; d at Montréal 4 Oct 1984). With degrees in law and commerce from Belgrade and a doctorate from the Sorbonne, he joined McGill's history department in June 1950. He introduced courses on eastern European, USSR and Byzantine history and also lectured on the Soviet legal system. He examined the history of war as part of "the general historical process," stressing above all the reciprocal influences of social structure and the forms taken by military conflict. Mladenovic devoted the greater part of his life to his graduate students, who published a festschrift in his honour in 1969, *Eastern Europe: Historical Essays*, and a symposium of essays, *War and Society in the 19th Century Russian Empire* (1972). At one time in the 1970s, 7 departments of history, 2 of political science and one of Byzantine studies were chaired by his former students. From 1964 to 1974 he was editor of *The New Review*, the only scholarly journal in Canada devoted to eastern European history. He published many books, articles and reviews in English, French, German and Serbian.

J.L. BLACK

Moberly, Walter, civil engineer (b at Steeple Aston, Eng 15 Aug 1832; d at Vancouver 14 May 1915). He came to Canada as a child and studied in Canada W, later moving to BC. In 1859 he was appointed superintendent of public works and in 1862 was involved in the construction of the Yale-Cariboo wagon road (*see* CARIBOO ROAD). He was assistant surveyor general of BC 1864-66 and then spent 4 years in the US. In 1871 he was in charge of surveys for the route of the CPR through the Rocky Mts and was the discoverer of EAGLE PASS. He published his reminiscences, *The Rocks and Rivers of British Columbia*, in 1885.

ERIC J. HOLMGREN

Moccasin Though they were of 2 major types, there were as many kinds of moccasins distributed throughout N America as there were tribes who manufactured them. Moccasins found in the Arctic and on the Plains are hard soled, consisting of a deerskin upper sole sewn to a heavier and stiffer bottom sole. Soft-soled moccasins, made from a single piece of hide, are characteristic of the Subarctic, the northern prairies and north-

Huron moccasins (*courtesy National Museums of Canada/Canadian Museum of Civilization/S77-1857*).

eastern N America. The soft-soled variety have a wider distribution and are more efficient for use with SNOWSHOES. RENÉ R. GADACZ

Mockingbird, common name for some members of the THRASHER family (Mimidae). The northern mockingbird (*Mimus polyglottos*), the only mockingbird in Canada, is a rare, permanent resident across Canada and is slowly extending its range northward. Grey above, greyish white below, its white wing patches and white outer tail feathers are conspicuous in flight. Its loud, musical, repetitive song is often given at night and includes mimicked vocalizations of other birds. Northern mockingbirds inhabit dense thickets and woodland edge, maintaining territories year-round, defending food sources in winter. Breeding occurs May-July; clutches contain 4-5 eggs. J.C. BARLOW

The northern mockingbird (*Mimus polyglottos*) is a rare resident of Canada (*artwork by Claire Tremblay*).

Moffat Communications Limited, controlled by Randall L. Moffat, owns and operates radio stations in Vancouver, Calgary, Edmonton,

Moose Jaw-Regina, Winnipeg and Hamilton. The company also owns CKY-TV, the CTV-network affiliate in Winnipeg, which extends service to 97% of Manitoba's population. Moffat's 80%-owned CABLE-TELEVISION company, Winnipeg Videon Inc, provides service to over 145 874 households. The company also owns over 85% of 2 cable-television systems in the US. Profits in 1987 were $5.1 million, with revenues of $63.8 million. PETER S. ANDERSON

Mohawk, the most eastern member of the IROQUOIS Confederacy, resided in 3 principal villages ("castles") on the banks of the Mohawk R. In 1609 and 1610 they were defeated by their northern neighbours, assisted by CHAMPLAIN. Mohawk hostilities were then channelled eastward, where they drove the Mahicans out of the Mohawk Valley and gained access to the Dutch traders of Ft Orange (now Albany, NY). By 1640 they had exhausted beaver stocks in their own country and turned to plundering fur fleets coming to trade with the French. A truce between New France and the Mohawk was arranged in 1645. Isaac JOGUES attempted to establish a Jesuit mission in their country but was suspected of witchcraft and killed. Shortly afterward the Mohawk and SENECA combined to drive the HURON from their homeland.

The French burned the Mohawk villages in the autumn of 1666 and then made peace. The JESUITS established a mission and encouraged their converts to move to the St Lawrence, away from English influence, where settlements were established in the 1670s. War broke out, and the Mohawk towns were burned in 1693, with some of the Catholic Mohawk aiding the French against their kinsmen. The entire Iroquois Confederacy negotiated treaties of peace and neutrality with both the French and English in 1701.

In 1710, 3 Mohawk chiefs and a Mahican journeyed to London where they were presented to Queen Anne. To counteract French Jesuit influence, Anglican missionaries were promised to the Mohawk, and the queen presented communion silver for a chapel. Catholic Mohawk from the St Lawrence played an active role as French allies, participating in the destruction of Deerfield, Mass, in 1704 and Groton, Mass, in 1707.

During the 18th century the Mohawk, now living in 2 principal towns, became surrounded by white settlers. They adopted the housing styles of their neighbours and were closely tied to the British administration; the Indian superintendent, Sir William JOHNSON, married a Mohawk, Mary BRANT. Johnson used Mohawk warriors in the final French-English conflict for possession of the continent. Johnson died before the outbreak of the American Revolution. The Mohawk joined that struggle in 1777, under the leadership of Joseph BRANT who had just returned from England. Brant and his Mohawk frequently defeated the Americans but were forced to flee their homes, which were confiscated and used by the rebel settlers.

After the war, Brant and his followers settled on the Grand R on a grant secured for them by Gov Frederick HALDIMAND (now the Six Nations Reserve). Other Mohawk, under John DESERONTYON, settled on the Bay of Quinte. The Mohawk were largely Anglican, and the Queen Anne communion silver was divided between the 2 reserves. The Mohawk who settled in Ontario and those on the St Lawrence became increasingly incorporated into the white man's world. Mohawk from Caughnawaga outside Montréal established a reputation as boatmen and were recruited to ferry Gen Garnet WOLSELEY's army up the Nile in 1884-85 (*see* NILE EXPEDITION). In later years, men from this same reserve established a reputation as structural-steel workers.

Over 3000 Mohawk continue to speak their native language. Some of them returned to the HANDSOME LAKE RELIGION and established longhouse congregations at Caughnawaga in the 1920s and St Regis (Akwasasne) in the 1930s. Residents of both these communities had been Roman Catholic for some 250 years. *See also* NATIVE PEOPLE: EASTERN WOODLANDS; IROQUOIS WARS; and general articles under NATIVE PEOPLE.
 THOMAS S. ABLER

Reading: B.G. Trigger, ed, *Handbook of North American Indians*, vol 15: *Northeast* (1978).

Moisie, Rivière, 410 km long, rises in eastern Québec from Lac Opocopa and flows S to the ST LAWRENCE R. With a DRAINAGE BASIN of 19 200 km² and a mean discharge of 490 m³/s, it is the river of greatest volume along the middle N Shore of the St Lawrence. Its current is swift and its rapids are numerous. The deep, rugged valley is lined with spruce, fir, birch, aspen and pine. It is one of the best salmon and trout rivers in eastern N America. The HBC has a trading post at the village of Moisie at the river's mouth, some 20 km E of Sept-Îles. The name possibly derives from a Montagnais personal name. JAMES MARSH

Mold, or mould, term for woolly or cottony growths produced by FUNGI, and for species causing these growths. Molds are numerous and common Canadian species have worldwide distributions. Maximum species numbers and growth rates occur under warm, humid conditions, but some molds grow slowly at -20°C, while others continue growing at +60°C. Mold consists of hyphae (filaments), masses of which are called mycelia. Vegetative mycelium develops in organic material or soil; visible mold consists of fertile hyphae and spore-producing structures. Materials in which hyphae grow are digested (decayed) and the fungus absorbs products as nutrients. Decay, an essential natural process, causes deterioration of foods, textiles and structural materials. In addition to causing spoilage, some molds produce poisonous substances (mycotoxins) that render foods unsafe. Mycotoxins may be carcinogenic. Mold infections cause skin diseases (eg, ringworm and athlete's foot). Severe systemic infections (mycoses) are common in some regions. Hay fever may be caused by airborne mold spores. Domesticated and wild animals and birds are subject to similar afflictions. Molds infect and kill insects and cause many plant diseases; some water molds cause fatal fish and crustacean infections. Common blue and green molds, which cause spoilage of fruits, vegetables and jams, are mostly species of *Penicillium* and *Aspergillus*. Some species of these genera are important in industrial production of antibiotics, citric and gluconic acids, etc. Blue cheeses owe their distinctive flavour to species of *Penicillium*. Molds related to black bread mold and *Aspergillus* species are used in production of some Asian foods (eg, tofu, tempeh, saki and soy sauce). R. J. BANDONI

Mole, common name for 20-29 species of predominantly burrowing insectivores of family Talpidae, restricted to Eurasia and N America. Six species occur in Canada. Moles have cylindrical bodies; dense, velvetlike fur; pointed, mobile snouts (with fingerlike appendages in the starnosed mole); minute eyes and external ears greatly reduced or lacking. The 5-toed feet show varying degrees of adaptation for swimming (Old World water moles) or burrowing. Moles usually mate in spring; gestation lasts 4-6 weeks; litters average 2-5 young. They may live 3-4 years. Canadian species are largely subterranean, preying mainly on soil invertebrates. They may eat their own weight in food daily. Shrew, coast and Townsend's moles (*Neurotrichus gibbsii, Scapanus* *orarius, S. townsendii*, respectively) live in extreme southwestern BC; eastern mole (*S. aquaticus*) in Essex County, Ont; hairy-tailed mole (*Parascalops breweri*) in forests of Ont and Qué; and the somewhat aquatic star-nosed mole (*Condylura cristata*) from the Maritimes to Man and N to the boreal forest. C.G. VAN ZYLL DE JONG

Molecular Biology, subdiscipline of BIOCHEMISTRY that studies the structure, synthesis and degradation of macromolecules (ie, very large molecules) found in living cells, their metabolic regulation (how they are interrelated and balanced during synthesis and degradation) and their expression (how the GENETIC code operates and is controlled through structural interrelationships). Macromolecules include the nucleic acids DNA (deoxyribonucleic acid) and RNA (ribonucleic acid), proteins (including enzymes), carbohydrates, and complexes of carbohydrates and proteins and lipids (soluble cellular fats and waxes) and proteins. The term was used by Oswald T. Avery in the late 1940s and was early equated with the study of nucleic acids. As a result of their work on bacteria, Canadian researchers Avery and Colin M. MacLeod and American Maclyn McCarty were the first to provide firm evidence that DNA was the genetic material in the cell (1944).

The structure of DNA is a double helix, first described in 1953 by Nobel laureates (1962) J.D. Watson (an American who had been influenced by Avery's work) and British researcher Francis Crick. The double helix is composed of 2 antiparallel chains of sugar-phosphate "backbones" with complementary pairs of nucleic-acid bases in the centre. American biochemist Erwin Chargaff's observation of base pairing was important to Watson and Crick's discovery, as were the X-ray diffraction studies of British biophysicist Rosalind Franklin. Just before the elucidation of the structure of DNA by Watson and Crick, G. Wyatt (now at Queen's University) described 5-methylcytosine, the first modified base found in DNA molecules, and confirmed base pairing and the base composition of a number of DNAs. DNA was postulated as the template for RNA synthesis by French biochemists Jacques Monod and François Jacob (Nobel Prize, 1965). RNA synthesis is called transcription; protein synthesis from the RNA transcript is called translation. Once the protein is translated, depending on the type of cell, it can then undergo a series of changes (eg, addition of carbohydrate or lipid) to make the complex proteins that are part of many cells.

A large part of research in molecular biology has been undertaken on viruses, the simplest of life forms, because they have no complex cellular structure or cell membrane. Some of the earliest basic studies on viral systems were made by Canadian researcher Felix d'Herelle, who independently discovered bacteriophages (bacterial viruses). Viruses are composed either of DNA or RNA with associated proteins, and thus can be used as model systems for examining replication (DNA synthesis), transcription (RNA synthesis) and translation (protein synthesis). Bacteriophages were the first to be examined in detail. DNA synthesis is best understood in these viruses mainly because of studies led by American biochemist A. Kornberg (Nobel Prize, 1959). More recently, eukaryotic viruses (ie, those that attack nucleated cells) have been used. The virus can be considered a microcosm of the cells and tissues of animals and its molecular biology is controlled by mechanisms analogous to those in cells. Viruses that have RNA as their genetic material are called retroviruses; some retroviruses have been implicated in human CANCER. However, most viruses that attack eukaryotic cells are DNA viruses.

Molecular biology has expanded as a result of the application of recombinant DNA techniques (ie, GENETIC ENGINEERING), following the isolation of restriction enzymes in 1970 by American biochemist Hamilton Smith (Nobel Prize, 1978). Restriction enzymes cut DNA molecules at specific sites (base sequences). Joining enzymes can link together the DNA fragments. These enzymes were used to join different DNA molecules together in gene-splicing experiments to form recombinant molecules, first on bacterial cells and viruses. In 1977 the first recombinant molecules composed of mammalian DNA inserted into bacterial elements called plasmids were constructed. Plasmids are particles found in some bacterial cells that contain DNA, but they are not part of the chromosomal apparatus of the bacterium. The next important discovery was of "gene splicing" ie, the RNA synthesized from the DNA of eukaryotic cells can be much larger than the final messenger RNA product, because those segments of the RNA product that are not necessary to code for the protein message are cut out, and the remaining RNA spliced together.

This work was followed by the development of powerful, fast and relatively easy methods for determining the base sequence of DNA, ie, the order of the base components in DNA. Two laboratories, those of Walter Gilbert in Cambridge, Massachusetts, and Fred Sanger in Cambridge, England, developed different methods. Gilbert, Sanger and Californian Paul Berg (who performed the first cloning experiments) received a Nobel Prize in 1980. The advent of these technologies has led to a complete change in classical and molecular genetics. The ability to explain clinical observations at the level of the DNA molecule has led to a better understanding of many hereditary diseases. Changes in the DNA at the base sequence level cause differences in the messenger RNA sequence which, when translated into protein, result in the wrong protein being made or in an altered protein, leading to a dysfunction characteristic of the GENETIC DISEASE. Many genetic concepts have been revised; eg, multiple gene copies have been proven to exist for many proteins.

Concurrent with the studies on nucleic acids have been studies on proteins and their interaction with each other and with nucleic acids. Studies by Ptashne at Harvard and Anderson at Alberta have provided the first understanding of the molecular mechanisms of protein – DNA interaction in the process of transcriptional control of one bacteriophage gene.

Canadians have played an important part in the development of molecular biology. Gobind KHORANA, who received the Nobel Prize for the first chemical synthesis of a nucleic-acid molecule in 1968, started his work at the British Columbia Fisheries Research Laboratories, Vancouver. Khorana's many students include G. Tener (UBC), who developed a chromatographic column for separating nucleic acids over a range of sizes, an innovation that has had tremendous methodological impact on molecular biology; and M. Smith (UBC), who was a member of Sanger's laboratory when the first DNA virus molecule was sequenced in 1977. Groups are now undertaking research in molecular biology in all major Canadian universities (within laboratories in Faculties of Medicine and Science), in the BIOTECHNOLOGY companies located in most provinces, and in many federal and provincial laboratories. *See also* NATIONAL RESEARCH COUNCIL OF CANADA; RESEARCH, PROVINCIAL ORGANIZATIONS.

JOHN H. SPENCER

Molecules in Interstellar Space Atoms had been detected in the interstellar medium by 1921 and, between 1936 and 1942, C.S. BEALS, then at the Dominion Astrophysical Observatory (DAO), Victoria, and Adams and Dunham in the US, detected optical transitions of the molecules CH, CN and CH$^+$ in interstellar space. Andrew MCKELLAR (DAO) found that the CN molecule showed evidence of an excitation of 2.3 K. This temperature was not understood at the time but is now known to result from microwave cosmic background radiation.

In 1963 the first detection of a molecule (the hydroxyl radical OH) at centimetre-wavelength radio frequencies was made by Weinreb, Barrett, Meeks and Henry of the Massachusetts Institute of Technology. The detection at millimetre wavelengths of the more complicated molecule ammonia (NH$_3$), by Townes, Welch and their collaborators at Berkeley in 1968, led to a flurry of further discoveries. Using earth-satellite Copernicus, Lyman Spitzer, Jr, and his co-workers at Princeton detected molecules in the ultraviolet. About 53 molecules have been detected, many by US astronomers using the Kitt Peak (Arizona) millimetre-wave telescope. When fully explored, using SPACE TECHNOLOGY, the infrared region is expected to produce a rich yield of new molecules.

Spectra from interstellar molecules give a wide variety of information about the interstellar medium and have shown that a significant fraction of the medium is clumped into molecular clouds, ranging from less than 100 times the mass of the SUN to a million solar masses. Within these clouds the visible stars in the GALAXY are formed. Molecular radiation provides information about the temperature, density and velocities within the clouds, and the clouds themselves are being used to map the structure of our galaxy. Improvements in the sensitivity and angular resolving power of telescopes have allowed detection of radiation from molecular clouds in several nearby galaxies. When larger millimetre-wave telescopes, now being constructed, are operational, research opportunities will be even greater.

Radiation detected from interstellar molecules usually arises from changes in a molecule's state of rotation. Substitution of an isotopic species of one of the atoms in the molecule (which produces a significant change in the rotation speed) is therefore easy to detect. This technique allows measurement of isotope ratios of several common atoms (eg, hydrogen, carbon, oxygen, nitrogen, sulphur) in a number of clouds throughout the galaxy; these studies have indicated that, apart from anomalies in the region of the galactic centre, the isotopic composition of the rest of the galaxy (including our solar system) appears to be fairly uniform.

Canadians have made significant contributions to the search for new interstellar molecules. In the early 1970s the molecules HCN and HC$_3$N were detected, the latter by UBC graduate Barry Turner, working at the National Radio Astronomy Observatory in Virginia. This sequence was greatly extended by a group of Canadian radio astronomers from the Herzberg Institute of Astrophysics (named for Gerhard HERZBERG, 1971 recipient of the Nobel Prize in chemistry for his study of the spectra of molecules). Inspired by T. Oka, the principal investigators were Lorne Avery, Norm Broten and John MacLeod who, with the British spectroscopist Harry Kroto, used the 46 m telescope at ALGONQUIN PROVINCIAL PARK to discover successively the molecular sequence HC$_5$N, HC$_7$N, HC$_9$N. Subsequently, another team at the same institute detected HC$_{11}$N, at present the heaviest interstellar molecule detected. Scientists are now trying to establish the existence in interstellar space of the simplest amino acid, glycine, which is a building block of DNA and therefore of life forms. WILLIAM SHUTER

Molinari, Guido, painter (b at Montréal 12 Oct 1933). He studied briefly at the School of Design at the Montreal Museum of Fine Arts (1950-51), and began making drawings and paintings combining automatic methods with a disciplined approach. He was a leader in the development of a rigorous colour abstraction in Montréal. Characteristic of his paintings in the 1960s were vertical, hard-edged bands of colour. Pictorial space in these paintings was created by the spectator's perception of the shifting and mixing of the colours. More recently, colour in his work has been reduced to very dark values, and rather than narrow bands, the paintings are divided into 2 to 5 large vertical sections. In 1956 Molinari was a founding member of the Association des artistes non-figuratifs de Montréal. He exhibited at the Biennale in Venice in 1968, where he was awarded the David E. Bright Foundation prize. In 1977 he participated in the Paris Biennale, and in 1980 he was awarded the Paul-Émile BORDUAS prize by the Québec government. Molinari teaches at Concordia U and has exerted a powerful influence on younger artists, through his teaching, his theoretical writing and his opinions, firmly held and strongly stated.   MARILYN BURNETT

Reading: D. Burnett, *Quantificateur* (1979); P. Théberge, *Guido Molinari*, (1976).

Mollusc, soft-bodied, usually shelled INVERTE-BRATE belonging to one of the largest animal phyla (Mollusca) with some 100 000 living and about 35 000 FOSSIL species. Molluscs are found on land and in salt and fresh water, and include SNAILS, ABALONE, CLAMS, MUSSELS, OCTOPUSES and SQUID. Molluscs range from some of the smallest invertebrates (snails and clams, measured in millimetres) to the largest (giant squid, up to 15-20 m long). The group is characterized by a muscular foot on which the animals creep; a calcareous shell secreted by the underlying fleshy mantle; and a feeding structure, the radula, consisting of a membrane, bearing sharp cusps, thrusting out from the mouth (found in all major groups except Bivalvia). Food particles (plant or animal tissue) are rasped on the inward or return stroke and are borne into the gullet and through the alimentary tract in grooves lined with cilia (hairlike projections). Bivalves feed mainly on waterborne food particles, captured by a mucus-filtering system formed from the gills. Mollusc shells consist of calcium carbonate crystals (sometimes with magnesium carbonate) interspersed in an organic framework. The mineralized shells have left a rich fossil history dating back to the earliest evidence of animal life. The ancestral mollusc is thought to have been a small, creeping, bilaterally symmetrical inhabitant of ocean shallows, bearing a shield-shaped shell. It ate fine algae scraped from rocks. Seven major classes of living molluscs evolved: Monoplacophora, Polyplacophora (chitons) and Gastropoda (snails) most closely resemble the primitive form; Aplacophora, Scaphopoda (tuskshells), Bivalvia (clams) and Cephalopoda (octopuses) represent more radical divergences from the ancestral type. Molluscs, because of their diverse and often beautiful shell shapes, accessibility, and importance as food and disease vectors, have played important cultural and economic roles in human history. Malacology studies the diversity, classification and EVOLUTION of molluscs. A brief discussion of the 7 major molluscan classes follows.

Monoplacophora, small class comprising some 7 species in genus *Neopilina;* no Canadian species are known. First discovered live in 1952 from deep-dredge collections off the Pacific coast of Costa Rica, these small (0.3-3 cm long) animals were hitherto known only from fossils of the Cambrian period (570-505 million years ago).

Their primitive features, eg, single, shield-shaped shell (hence, name Monoplacophora), poorly developed head, and repetitive systems of paired kidneys, gills and foot retractor muscles, suggest that Monoplacophora represent one of the earliest molluscan groups. They are adapted for life at great depths and eat unicellular plants and animals and sponge material grazed from the sea bottom.

Polyplacophora, the chitons, marine class comprising some 600 living species, ranging from a few centimetres or less to over 30 cm long. The name, meaning "bearer of many plates," refers to the 8 distinctive, overlapping shell-plates. The protective shell and broad, adhesive foot permit life on rocks in wave-disturbed intertidal zones. They eat unicellular algae, scrapings from seaweeds and occasionally animal matter. The poorly developed head, rudimentary nervous system, primitive larval form and multiple gills suggest that chitons diverged early from the main line of molluscan evolution. The gum-boat chiton (*Cryptochiton*) of the Canadian West Coast is one of the world's largest chitons.

Gastropoda, the largest molluscan class, with 75 000 living and about 15 000 fossil species, includes some of the most common invertebrates: limpets, abalones, PERIWINKLES, conchs, WHELKS, SLUGS and snails. Gastropoda are harvested and cultured for food worldwide. Certain freshwater snails are important disease vectors, acting as intermediate hosts for liver and blood flukes that parasitize humans (eg, schistosomiasis). Snail shells are prized for their form and beauty. Gastropods occupy more habitats and represent more species than any other molluscan class. This extensive adaptive radiation was made possible through 3 major changes from the molluscan ancestral plan: development of a complex head with elaborate receptors and nervous system; coiling of shell; and torsion, involving a 180° twisting of the shell and visceral mass over the lower body section. Coiling and torsion evolved independently. Coiling probably preceded torsion, converting the ancestral shell from a simple, flattened shield to a fully protective retreat. The earliest form of coiled shell (found only in extinct species) was planospiral, ie, each spiral lying outside of the preceding one in the same plane (eg, like a coiled rope). This large, unwieldy and probably unbalanced shell was improved by evolution of asymmetrical coiling about a central axis. The new shell had its centre of gravity squarely over the body midline. The outward projection of the largest whorl of the shell creates the mantle cavity (lined with the shell-secreting membrane), which houses gills and sensory equipment for testing water quality and receives discharge of kidneys, gonads and rectum.

Torsion, thought to have occurred after the evolution of a planospiral shell, formed the gut and nervous system into a U-shape and brought the mantle cavity from its posterior position to an anterior one. Torsion occurs in the larval stage of living gastropods. Its significance in gastropod evolution is disputed. Some argue its importance to larvae (protective withdrawal into mantle cavity); others, to adults (enhanced respiratory stream). An important consequence of the shifting of the mantle cavity to the front was the potential for fouling the head region with rectal and kidney wastes. The solution, involving redirection of water flow for respiration, resulted in considerable modifications of shell design. For example, the perforated shells of abalone and keyhole limpets allow a unidirectional flow of water through the mantle cavity: in over the head, past the gills, then past the rectal and kidney outlets, exiting via the shell holes.

Gastropods are separated into 3 subclasses.

Prosobranchia, the largest, is mainly marine and includes gastropods having full torsion, eg, limpets, abalones, whelks, periwinkles and conchs. Among members of this subclass exploitation of habitats and food types has been extensive; some even live as parasites. Foodstuffs include dead organic material, microscopic phytoplankton, seaweeds and animal prey (including fish). In snails the food-procuring device is the radula, which in cone shells has evolved into poisonous barbs that can be thrust into prey. Therefore, certain cone shells can be highly toxic to humans. The second subclass, Opisthobranchia, is almost entirely marine, with some 1100 species including sea slugs, sea hares, sea butterflies and bubble shells. Opisthobranchs have undergone detorsion in their evolution, shifting the mantle cavity to the side. Associated with this has been a tendency towards reduction or loss of shell and mantle cavity, and a loss of gills. Shell loss may have led to evolution of defences characteristic of opisthobranchs, eg, ability to swim, acid secretion, protective internal spines (spicules), camouflage coloration, and secondhand use of stinging cells seized intact from coelenterate prey. The third subclass, Pulmonata [Lat, "lung"], probably evolved from the Prosobranchia. Pulmonates include some 20 000 species of land snails and slugs, freshwater snails, and a few marine snails, having in common a loss of gills and conversion of mantle cavity into a lung. This highly successful group includes numerous crop and garden pests.

Aplacophora, obscure class of shell-less Mollusca (aplacophora means lacking shell) comprising some 250 living species. Aplacophorans live in marine bottom sediments or on hydroids and soft corals throughout the oceans. These small (up to 5 cm long), worm-shaped animals have a vestigial head and archaic nervous system; shell, mantle and foot are absent. Aplacophorans are largely predators or scavengers and use the radula to procure food. Their evolutionary position among molluscs is unclear, as the extent of their primitiveness or specialization is unknown. Aplacophorans superficially resemble polyplacophorans; therefore, the 2 groups are sometimes combined in a separate taxon, Amphineura.

Scaphopoda, small class of burrowing marine molluscs, the tusk or tooth shells, comprising some 350 living species. The shell, ranging from less than 1 cm to 5-6 cm long, is cylindrical and resembles an elephant's tusk, open at both ends. The animal lies buried in sediment with the smaller, posterior end of shell near the surface of the substratum. A ventilating current circulates through the shell, exiting from the hole at the posterior tip. Scaphopods eat microscopic organisms collected by small tentacles. Tusk shells, specifically genus *Dentalium,* were prized as ornaments and were used as a medium of exchange by Northwest Coast Indians.   THOMAS CAREFOOT

Bivalvia, also called Pelecypoda ("hatchet-foot") or Lamellibranchia ("comb-shaped gills"). The class includes clams, mussels, SCALLOPS, OYSTERS and shipworms, and is exclusively aquatic. Approximately 12 000 species are known. In Canada there are 415 marine and about 200 freshwater species. Bivalves are used for food and were important to coastal native peoples. They now support fishing and AQUACULTURE on the Atlantic and Pacific coasts. Bivalves provide mother-of-pearl and freshwater and marine pearls. Most Canadian bivalves are 1-10 cm long, but species shorter than 1 mm and longer than 1 m are known. A hinged shell, consisting of 2 calcareous valves (half-shells) joined by a hinge ligament on the back, is characteristic of the group. The hinge region frequently has interlocking teeth that align the valves. Many bivalves have 1 or 2 protruding tubes (siphons) for entry and exit of water. The head is reduced as sensory functions are located on external body parts. Gills are small in groups that feed by sorting food from sediment, big in those that pump large volumes of water to trap suspended food particles. Gills may be minute or entirely replaced by a muscular flap used to catch small prey. The foot is used for locomotion and especially for digging, but may be absent in adults of sedentary forms. The sexes are usually separate, but some species are hermaphroditic. Alteration of sex, depending on age or external conditions, occurs in several groups. Fertilization is usually external and development occurs in the plankton. A number of species living in cold, boreal or deep water brood the young within the shell or in a specially constructed pouch. The nervous system is simple, consisting of 3 pairs of interconnected ganglia (nerve masses). Specialized sensory organs include statocysts that monitor position; complex eyes on the mantle margins or siphons in some groups; and other organs sensitive to vibration. The alimentary system includes a stomach with complex ciliary sorting mechanisms that communicate with complex digestive diverticula (glandular tubes or sacs). Many groups possess a crystalline style (secreted, translucent rod), in the midgut or in a separate pouch, that aids in digestion. The intestine may be short or coiled. The alimentary system may be reduced or entirely absent. Scallops and a few other groups can swim briefly to avoid enemies, but the enclosing shell enforces sedentary habits (eg, lying on or buried in sediment, attaching to solid objects or boring). This life mode has limited the adaptive potential to minor structural changes; however, bivalves have been a successful group from earliest times. Frequently they occur in large numbers, and the filtering forms are an important link between the planktonic (drifting) and benthic (bottom-dwelling) communities. Their origin is unknown and their classification subject to change. Five living subclasses and 12 orders are recognized. FRANK R. BERNARD

Cephalopoda ("head-foot") Extensive modification of the molluscan head-foot resulted in the cephalopod's characteristic parrotlike beak, surrounded by a ring of grasping appendages: 8 sucker-covered arms for the octopods, 8 arms and 2 tentacles with suckers or hooks for squid and CUTTLEFISH, and 60-94 simple arms in the primitive chambered or pearly nautilus. Of the 650 living cephalopod species, only 3 species of genus *Nautilus* have external shells. These are the last living tetrabranchiates (4-gilled cephalopods), although thousands of shelled Nautiloidea and Ammonoidea from the Paleozoic (between 570 and 225 million years ago) and Mesozoic (between 225 and 65 million years ago) are known from fossils. The hollow shells provided buoyancy and protection, but modern dibranchiate (2-gilled) cephalopods have given them up, apparently for flexibility and speed. These predatory, marine carnivores have little in common, externally, with other molluscs. Their shell-less muscular mantles work as pumps to force water through a funnellike tube that can be aimed in any direction. This jet-propulsion system provides for high-speed swimming with rapid direction changes, comparable to that of fish. Their swimming manoeuvres, complex arm movements, rapid colour changes and sophisticated camera eyes (resembling human eyes) require the most complex nervous systems in the invertebrate world. Only birds and mammals have larger brains relative to body size. Octopuses, sometimes called devil fishes, are easily trained and have been studied as examples of how animals learn. Squid, too, are important for research; their giant nerve cells were a key to understanding the electrophysiological basis of nerve function.

Although most of the world's cephalopods are tropical or subtropical, 46 species occur along Canada's coasts. This limited variety is made up for by size and quantity. Specimens of the giant squid or kraken (*Architeuthis dux*) found in Newfoundland, have reached nearly 20 m long (including tentacles) and may weigh up to 454 kg. Giant squid are the largest invertebrates known. On the Pacific coast, *Octopus dofleini*, the world's largest octopod, may exceed 80 kg. This octopus is fished commercially, as are 3 species of squid: *Loligo opalescens* in the West, *Loligo pealei* and *Illex illecebrosus* in the East. The arrow squid, *I. illecebrosus*, is famed for its exploits on Newfoundland's "squid jigging grounds." It was originally caught as cod bait, but annual catches of 410 t make this a major fishery in its own right, and one of the world's largest cephalopod FISHERIES. Dried or frozen, this "fish bait" is considered a delicacy in Oriental and Mediterranean markets. When cooked quickly, it is tender and has a delicate flavour resembling that of shrimp and scallops. Cephalopods are one of the largest, underused food resources. Deep-sea cephalopods are a major food for many whales. It has been estimated that sperm whales alone consume some 800 million t annually, over 10 times man's total annual fish catch. Cephalopod fisheries are particularly attractive because most cephalopods grow rapidly, spawning and dying after only 1-2 years. R.K. O'DOR

Reading: R.D. Barnes, *Invertebrate Zoology* (1980); Arthur H. Clarke, *Freshwater Molluscs of Canada* (1981).

Molluscan Resources Although Canada's coastline is extensive and contains many diverse molluscan species, the resource is economically relatively small. In 1985 about 69 213 t valued at $83 million were taken. SCALLOPS and SQUID from the Atlantic coast were the dominant species, accounting for 95% by weight and 97% by value of all molluscs from both coasts. There is no molluscan fishery in arctic waters. In Canada most molluscs are fished rather than cultured. For most species the short growing season results in growth rates too slow for profitable culture. The OYSTER is the only species now cultured in some quantity, although MUSSEL culture is beginning. Expanded production of both is possible but, in general, the potential for molluscan AQUACULTURE in Canada is not great. The occurrence of paralytic shellfish poison can limit the use of some species. The toxin derives from poisonous planktonic dinoflagellates on which bivalves feed. Although harmless to molluscs, it can be fatal to humans. Also fatal is the toxin domoic acid which caused a ban on Atlantic shellfish in late 1987 after 100 people became ill and at least 2 died after eating poisoned mussels from PEI. Except for scallop and partially for squid, most species are fished for or cultured by individual fishermen or families. Native people fish certain species (eg, CLAMS) commercially and for food. Federal and provincial governments participate in regulation as well as controlling factors such as sanitation, pollution, lands and marketing. Jurisdictions differ from province to province as a result of agreements developed through the years. Scallops are fished by vessels 20-30 m long, pulling drags over the bottom in depths up to 100 m. The centre of the fishery is on GEORGES BANK, ownership of which was contested by Canada and the US until Oct 1984, when the International Court at The Hague awarded the easternmost one-sixth, rich in scallops and groundfish, to Canada. It is unlikely that production can be increased beyond the level of past catches. Only the adductor mussel is used, sold fresh or frozen. On the Atlantic coast, oysters are cultured in shallow waters below the low-tide mark. Oyster ground is leased from the federal government and planted with oyster seed collect-

ed by various means. Oysters are marketed in the shell, usually by the dozen, and are eaten raw. On the Pacific coast the oyster industry uses a Japanese species that normally grows in intertidal areas. These zones are leased from the provincial government. Oysters are shelled and sold by volume of meat. Clams occur in both intertidal and subtidal areas and are fished by hand and by mechanical harvesters. Some are sold fresh but most are canned. A number of commercial species occur on both coasts and the fishery is regulated by season, quota or size. ABALONE live in rocky subtidal areas of the Pacific coast and are fished by divers. The catch is regulated by size and area quota. Most abalone are sold frozen to Japan. The centre of squid production is Newfoundland where they are fished by jigs and nets. Squid are used for bait and exported to Japan for food. D.B. QUAYLE

	Atlantic		Pacific	
Species	Live Weight (1000s of t)	Value (Millions$)	Live Weight (1000s of t)	Value (Millions$)
Clams	7.7	7.2	8.3	8.1
Oysters	2.1	2.1	3.4	2.6
Abalone	—	—	0.04	0.4
Scallop	47.2	62.2	—	—
Squid	0.4	0.1	—	—

Canadian Mollusc Production, 1985
(Source: Dept of Fisheries and Oceans, Ottawa, 1987)

Molson, Eric Herbert, industrial capitalist (b at Montréal 16 Sept 1937). Molson was educated at Bishop's, Princeton and McGill. In 1960 he entered the family-founded company, Molson Breweries of Canada, as an apprentice brewer, became assistant brewmaster 1962, brewmaster 1966, VP 1970 and president 1980. In June 1982 he became deputy chairman of the board of The Molson Companies Ltd, of which he and his family control a majority of the voting shares.
JORGE NIOSI

Molson, John, brewer, banker, steamship builder (b at Spalding, Eng 28 Dec 1763; d at Île Ste-Marguerite, Qué 11 Jan 1836). Orphaned as a child, he attended private boarding schools, immigrated to Canada in 1782, and in 1786 used his parents' legacy to become sole owner of a small brewery in Montréal. He had the business sense to exploit Montréal's growth as entrepôt in the fur

Portrait of John Molson, 1810, artist unknown, from London, Eng (*courtesy Molson Breweries of Canada Ltd*).

trade and commercial base for developing the hinterland of Upper Canada. In 1816 he took his 3 sons into partnership, including John MOLSON, Jr, as John Molson and Sons. He used cash payments from brewing to finance banking activities and build a steamboat line operating between Montréal and Québec City. In 1809 he had his own steamboat, the ACCOMMODATION, built at Montréal with an engine constructed at the Forges St-Maurice. He also entered the lumber business during the building boom of the early 1800s, built a hotel and in 1821 established the colony's first distillery and financed the CHAMPLAIN AND SAINT LAWRENCE RAILROAD, the first railway in Canada. Molson introduced the early steam engine to Montréal industry and became a close friend of James Watt, Sr. He sat in the House of Assembly of Lower Canada 1816-20, became president of the Bank of Montreal in 1826, and in 1832 was appointed a member of the Legislative Council of Lower Canada, where he upheld the interests of English-speaking businessmen amid the emerging discontent of French Canadians. Molson must be counted among the most prominent entrepreneurs in Canada during the first third of the 19th century.   ALBERT TUCKER

Reading: M. Denison, *The Barley and the Stream* (1955); S.E. Woods, Jr, *The Molson Saga 1763-1983* (1983).

Molson, John, Jr, brewer, entrepreneur in banking, transportation and utilities (b at Montréal 14 Oct 1787; d there 12 July 1860), eldest son of John MOLSON the elder, whose deputy he was from 1807 to 1835. In 1836 after the death of his father, he sold his 25% interest in the Molson brewing and distilling operations to his 2 brothers, Thomas and William. He was then able to concentrate on his other positions, such as first president of the CHAMPLAIN AND SAINT LAWRENCE RAILROAD (1836), founding president of the City Gas Co (1837) which brought gas lighting to Montréal, and director of the Bank of Montreal (1824-53). In partnership with his brother William he founded Molson Bank (1854). Like his brothers, he was known also for his philanthropy in Montréal's civic life, contributing generously to McGill U and serving as governor of the Montréal General Hospital.   ALBERT TUCKER

Molson Companies Limited, is one of Canada's oldest companies. Established in Montréal in 1786, it was incorporated in 1930 as Molson's Brewery Ltd, then became Molson Breweries Ltd in 1962 and Molson Industries Ltd in 1968; it adopted its present name in 1973. These name changes reflect the changing nature of the company. From 1967 onward the company acquired interests in numerous business enterprises, and it is now a diversified Canadian corporation. Today, its principal businesses are brewing (Molson Breweries of Canada Ltd), retail merchandising (Beaver Lumber Company Ltd and Lighting Unlimited Corp Ltd), and marketing of specialty chemicals (Diversey Corp). It owns 9 breweries in 7 provinces, markets more than 3000 cleaning and sanitizing products in over 100 countries, and is the major Canadian retailer of lumber, building materials and related hardgoods. As of 1987 the company had annual revenues of $2.3 billion (ranking 52nd in Canada), assets of $1.2 billion (ranking 82nd), and 11 400 employees. Control of the corporation remains in the hands of the founding Molson family.

Molson Prize, annual awards funded from the income of a $1 million endowment given to the CANADA COUNCIL by the Molson Family Foundation "to encourage Canadians of outstanding achievement in the fields of the Arts, the Humanities or the Social Sciences to make further contributions to the cultural or intellectual heritage of

Molson Prize Recipients 1970-87

1970	Jean-Paul Audet (scholar)
	Morley Callaghan (writer)
	Arnold Spohr (dir Royal Winnipeg Ballet)
1971	Northrop Frye (literary scholar)
	Duncan Macpherson (cartoonist)
	Yves Thériault (writer)
1972	Maureen Forrester (contralto)
	Rina Lasnier (poet)
	Norman McLaren (filmmaker)
1973	John James Deutsch (economist)
	Alfred Pellan (painter)
	George Woodcock (writer)
1974	Celia Franca (dancer, dir of Nat Ballet)
	W.A.C.H. Dobson (scholar)
	Jean-Paul Lemieux (painter)
1975	Alex Colville (painter)
	Pierre Dansereau (ecologist)
	Margaret Laurence (writer)
1976	Denise Pelletier (actress)
	Jon Vickers (tenor)
	Orford String Quartet
1977	John Hirsch (theatre director)
	Bill Reid (sculptor and carver)
	Jean-Louis Roux (actor and theatre director)
1978	Gabrielle Roy (novelist)
	George Story (lexicographer)
	Jack Shadbolt (painter)
1979	Jean Duceppe (actor)
	Betty Oliphant (dir Nat Ballet School)
	Michael Snow (painter)
1980	Michel Brault (filmmaker)
	Lois Marshall (singer)
	Robert Weaver (editor, radio producer)
1981	Margaret Atwood (writer)
	Marcel Trudel (historian)
	John Weinzweig (composer)
1982	Gilles Vigneault (singer)
	Louis-Edmond Hamelin (geographer)
	Jack McClelland (publisher)
	Allan C. Cairns (political scientist)
1983	Brian Macdonald (choreographer)
	Francess Halpenny (gen editor, DCB)
1984	James G. Eayrs (political scientist)
	Marcel Dubé (dramatist)
1985	Ronald Melzack (psychologist)
	Gaston Miron (writer)
1986	William Dray (philosopher/historian)
	J. Mavor Moore (playwright, actor, dir)
1987	Yvette Brind'Amour (actress)
	Marc-Adélard Tremblay (anthropologist)

Canada." The laureates are chosen by the chairman and president of the Canada Council in consultation with a jury chosen from across Canada. The selectors have attempted to choose laureates who are close to the peak of an outstanding career and the terms provide that no individual may be awarded the prize more than once. The first prizes given in 1964 were $15 000 each; the amount was increased to $25 000 in 1982 and to $50 000 in 1983. One prize was awarded annually until 1982, and 2 since; but 4 were given in 1982 to celebrate the Council's 25th anniversary.

Molybdenum (Mo), silver-grey metallic element with an unusually high melting point (2610°C). It is an important alloying element in iron, steels and specialty alloys and is used frequently in combination with other ferrous additives. The molybdenum content in these products ranges from a fraction of 1% to as much as 20%. A commonly used refractory (heat-resistant) metal, molybdenum is also used in catalysts, dyes and pigments. In IRON AND STEEL manufacture, the addition of molybdenum imparts hardness, strength and corrosion resistance and improves weldability. The principal mineral source of molybdenum, molybdenite (molybdenum disulphide, MoS_2), may be used as a solid lubricant and as an additive to greases and oils. About 58% of world output comes from primary molybdenum mines; the balance is a by-product of copper mining. Canada is one of the largest producers of molybdenum, sharing the honour with the US, Chile and the USSR. Estimated 1986 Canadian production was 12 914 t. About 97% of Canada's output is produced in BC, the remainder in Québec. Canada consumes about 10% of this output and exports the balance, mostly to the European Economic Community and Japan. Molybdenum contributed about 0.02% of the GDP in 1986. It is third (after copper and gold) in value among metals in BC. *See also* MINERAL RESOURCES.   D.G. FONG

Monarch Butterfly, is the only BUTTERFLY of the family Danaidae (order Lepidoptera) found in Canada. It is possibly the best-known, most publicized migratory butterfly on Earth. Visiting every province and territory, it is only numerous where the host plant MILKWEED (*Asclepias* spp.) grows. Its large size and slow, sailing flight makes it a familiar butterfly of such areas. The spring migration northwards into Canada is accomplished by the progressive advancement of successive generations. The legendary fall migration southwards is undertaken by adults of the final summer brood. Monarchs born W of the Rockies overwinter in California; those from central and eastern N America in central Mexico. After 40 years of research, the first Mexican wintering site was discovered in 1974 by Frederick Urquhart of U of T.

Monarchs were originally thought to contain a poison absorbed from their caterpillars' host plant. This was said to protect them from predation. Recent research on monarchs congregating at the Mexican wintering grounds suggests that only certain species of milkweed contain these deadly cardiac glycosides. Therefore, butterflies originating from caterpillars reared on nonpoisonous milkweeds, eg, common milkweed (*A. syriaca*) and showy milkweed (*A. speciosa*) are no longer thought toxic.   BERNARD S. JACKSON

Monarchism is based on ancient principles favouring a symbolic leader, state traditions, nonpartisan public relations and modern principles of parliamentary democracy. Canada, an autocratic monarchy before RESPONSIBLE GOVERNMENT was established, has become a constitutional monarchy in which the sovereign, GOVERNOR GENERAL and LIEUTENANT-GOVERNORS act on ministerial advice. Constitutional monarchy helps resolve the problem of ensuring that politicians can be elected, criticized, defeated and held responsible and accountable, a difficult feat if symbolism and administration are combined in one person. Executive functions are divided among the sovereign, governor general and lieutenant-governors, who exercise symbolic and decorative duties relating to public relations for the state, formal powers (eg, assenting to legislation) used on ministerial advice, and emergency powers for unusually serious constitutional crises such as electoral deadlock. The PRIME MINISTER, as partisan government leader, is not given formal powers of his own by the Constitution Acts; he advises on the use of the CROWN's powers as first minister responsible to Parliament. This combination, at federal and provincial levels, of reigning without governing and governing without reigning has worked comparatively well in Canada. With both levels of government sovereign in exercising their allotted powers (*see* DISTRIBUTION OF POWERS and CONSTITUTIONAL LAW), the monarch is the only official associated with all the state's powers and is therefore the focus of authority at a modest cost to Canada, which contributes nothing towards the Queen's maintenance and comparatively little to that of her representatives.

The Atlantic provinces, Ontario and BC have traditionally supported the Crown. Attitudes on the Prairies towards the Crown have been recently affected by Prairie discontent with Ottawa, by the influence of American preference for a congressional as opposed to a parliamentary system and by a long series of partisan patronage appointments to governorships by one party during 50 of the last 60 years. Québec enthusiastically supported the monarchy until about 1955 when the Crown became a factor in arguments about nationalist symbolism. Nevertheless, the Crown was strongly entrenched in the Constitution in 1982 by a formula requiring the support of Parliament and all 10 provincial legislatures before its status could be altered.

Monarchism concerns ways of governing as well as forms of government. Canada's monarch and governors, monarchal in theory for constitutional reasons, are democratic in their ways of governing, while many presidents elsewhere have become, in practice, absolute monarchs. Ironically, even Canadian premiers may be said to have acted occasionally as absolute monarchs. The governments of premiers W. ABERHART (Alta), M. DUPLESSIS (Qué), M. HEPBURN (Ont) and J. SMALLWOOD (Nfld) were one-man enterprises. The misunderstanding about monarchism has resulted largely from the troublesome Canadian weakness of maintaining high-profile premiers in office for excessively long periods and of one-party dominance and patronage overshadowing the Crown and submerging the Opposition. Indeed, monarchism as a way of governing is inevitable in some form in every political system; the main questions concern its type – absolute or constitutional. FRANK MacKINNON

Reading: Frank MacKinnon, *The Crown in Canada* (1976).

Monashee Mountains are a 400 km long ridge in southern BC. To the W they merge with the Okanagan and Shuswap highlands; their eastern boundary is the S-flowing COLUMBIA R. The name, meaning peaceful mountain, was given by a Scottish prospector. The border area around ROSSLAND, Grand Forks and Greenwood was settled in the 1890s and has had prosperous periods of copper mining and smelting. PETER GRANT

Monck, Charles Stanley, 4th Viscount in the Irish peerage and **1st Baron** in the UK peerage, governor general of BNA, 1861-67, governor general of Canada and PEI, 1867-68 (b in Templemore, Tipperary, Ire 10 Oct 1819; d at his Irish residence, Charleville, Enniskerry 29 Nov 1894). Monck was educated at Trinity Coll, Dublin, and then called to the Irish Bar at King's Inn in 1841. An Irish peer from 1849, he represented Portsmouth as a Liberal in the House of Commons and served as a lord of the Treasury. Appointed governor general of BNA in 1861, Monck displayed considerable diplomatic skill in dealing with the serious Canadian-American tensions of the day. A keen advocate of the defence and political consolidation of BNA, Monck was one of the architects of the GREAT COALITION, devised to carry CONFEDERATION, and he worked assiduously to overcome opposition to Confederation in NS and NB. As a mark of favour, the British government extended his term so that he might become the first governor general of Canada. RIDEAU HALL was purchased during his term to serve as official viceregal residence. From 1874 to 1892 he served as lord lieutenant of Dublin County, Ire. CARMAN MILLER

Monckton, Robert, British army officer (b in Yorkshire, Eng 24 June 1726; d at London, Eng 21 May 1782). Monckton arrived in Nova Scotia in 1752 and took part in the establishment of LUNENBURG in 1753. Two years later he engineered the first British success of the SEVEN YEARS' WAR when he captured FT BEAUSÉJOUR (NB) in June, and that fall he supervised the deportation of the ACADIANS. Lieutenant-governor of NS from Dec 1755, in 1758 Monckton raided Acadian settlements on the Saint John R. The following year he took part in the siege of Québec as second-in-command to James WOLFE. Wounded on the Plains of Abraham, he left Québec in Oct for further service in the southern colonies and the West Indies, where he stayed until 1763. A competent and humane soldier, Monckton was briefly considered for the command in N America, but never returned. By the time of his death, he had become a lieutenant-general. STUART SUTHERLAND

Moncton, NB, City, pop 55 468 (1986c), 54 743 (1981c), inc 1890, is situated in eastern NB on a bend of the Petitcodiac R. Its first settlers, who were of German origin, called their community The Bend. The modern name, first used in the 1860s, honours Robert MONCKTON, a British commander who became lieutenant-governor of Nova Scotia. Today, almost one-third of the population claims French as a mother tongue; the remainder is English speaking.

History Moncton's early prosperity was intimately linked to SHIPBUILDING. The turning point in its economic history was the establishment of a shipyard by George and Joseph Salter in 1849. By 1850 the shipping trade had become important enough that Moncton was made a port of entry. The town was incorporated in 1855 and that same year the first bank, the Westmorland Bank, was established. The decline of wooden ships wreaked disaster on Moncton. The bank collapsed and Moncton lost its status as an incorporated town in 1862. The beginnings of a new era, however, came with the railway, especially in the post-Confederation period when Moncton became the headquarters of the shops for the INTERCOLONIAL RY and a booming railway centre.

Economy It is the railway industry for which the city is best known today. Moncton is often referred to as "The Hub of the Maritimes" because all railway lines in and out of the Maritimes must pass through it. The CNR is the city's largest nongovernment employer and has played a vital part in the well-being of Moncton.

Townscape Moncton is home to UNIVERSITÉ DE MONCTON, a French-language university established in 1963. It also has the distinction of having the first law school in the world teaching common law in the French language. Sites of interest in Moncton include Magnetic Hill, where cars appear to coast uphill, and the tidal bore, which features some of the highest tides in the world. SHEVA MEDJUCK

Monetary Policy refers to any of a number of government measures undertaken to affect financial markets and credit conditions with the ultimate objective of influencing the overall behaviour of the economy. In Canada, monetary policy is the responsibility of the BANK OF CANADA, a federal crown corporation that implements its policy decisions largely through its ability to alter the Canadian money supply. The money supply is that portion of the financial wealth of Canadian households which has sufficient liquidity to be considered money. At the least it includes coin, currency, and chequing-account deposits in chartered banks, all of which have perfect liquidity in that they represent, at face value, an immediate means of payment for purchases made. Some economists broaden the money-supply definition by including additional chartered-bank deposits (eg, savings accounts) or deposits in other financial institutions such as trust companies or credit unions.

The Bank of Canada is not able to control the money supply directly, because the deposit portion of the money supply results from decisions made within the private BANKING system. By taking deposits from individual Canadian households and firms and then lending these funds, the

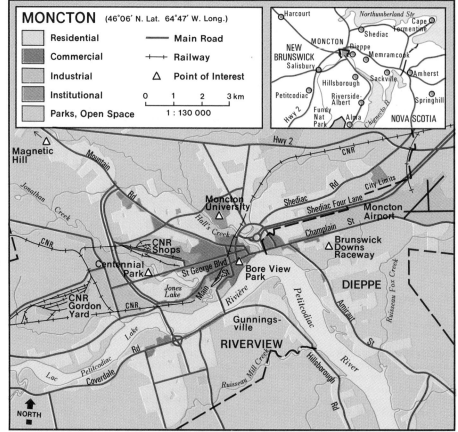

MONCTON (46°06' N. Lat. 64°47' W. Long.)

Residential — Main Road
Commercial +—+ Railway
Industrial △ Point of Interest
Institutional 0 1 2 3 km
Parks, Open Space 1 : 130 000

NORTH

commercial banks, in essence, "create" money because, in theory, the new funds will be redeposited in the banking system. However, the money-creation powers of the commercial banks are constrained by 2 factors. First if INTEREST yields on other financial assets rise, Canadians will probably choose to hold a relatively smaller portion of their wealth as coin, currency and (largely low-yield) money deposits. Second, the banks are limited in loan expansion by the need to retain reserves (basically cash in the vault, and deposits of the individual banks at the Bank of Canada) to meet possible withdrawal needs. By altering interest rates and the level of banking reserves, or both, the Bank of Canada can manipulate the money supply indirectly with a high degree of precision (particularly over periods of 3 to 6 months or longer).

One method of manipulating the money supply, termed open-market operations, involves the trading of Canadian government securities in the secondary bond and treasury bill markets. A purchase of government bonds by the Bank of Canada represents an immediate increase in the stock of money held by the general public, raises banking system reserves, and therefore has a multiplied indirect effect on the total money supply. The added demand for bonds also puts downward pressure on bond yields and hence on the overall level of interest rates. Through a sequence of opposite effects, a sale of bonds will decrease the money supply and raise interest rates. The Bank of Canada can also affect interest rates and banking-system reserves by altering the BANK RATE (ie, the interest rate paid by the chartered banks on loans made to them by the Bank of Canada). However, since March 1980, the Bank of Canada has abandoned the bank rate as a formal policy tool and instead has allowed it to float passively one-quarter of 1% above the rate paid on 90-day treasury bills.

Control of the money supply is a powerful tool for influencing the general behaviour of the Canadian ECONOMY. For example, stimulative monetary policy (ie, a higher rate of money-supply expansion) will put downward pressure on interest rates, strengthen business investment and housing demand, and hence raise the overall level of demand in the economy. During a cyclical downturn, when there is heavy unemployment and idle plant capacity, this stronger demand should in theory lead to a rise in output and increased jobs. Reduced money growth, on the other hand, acts as a restraining force on the economy – causing upward pressure on interest rates and reducing both investment and total demand. At a time of high INFLATION, such restraint will help reduce price and wage increases.

Because of the strong links between Canadian and American financial markets, monetary policy also has a major impact on the Canadian-US dollar EXCHANGE RATE. If Canadian monetary policy is significantly more expansionary than US policy, the value of the Canadian dollar will tend to depreciate in relation to the US dollar. A more contractionary Canadian policy will result in the reverse effect.

Yet, despite its important effects, monetary policy also has limitations. It cannot, for example, simultaneously stimulate economic demand to reduce unemployment and restrain demand to combat inflation. Nor can the Bank of Canada increase money growth rates to reduce interest rates below US levels while at the same time successfully stabilizing the Canadian-US exchange rate. Therefore, monetary policy decisions often require painful choices ("trade-offs"). Sometimes these trade-offs involve conflicts between the short-term and long-term effects of a particular policy. For example, a sustained rise in money-supply growth may cause an initial increase in both jobs and production, but eventually it will lead to a correspondingly higher inflation rate with little or no permanent effect on employment or output. Similarly a major reduction in the rate of money-supply expansion ultimately will reduce even strongly entrenched inflation, but this accomplishment may take several years during which output and employment both fall. These intertemporal conflicts can be complicated by a third limitation – ignorance – for there are still many unresolved questions concerning the mechanisms whereby changes in monetary policy affect the economy, the nature of the interrelations between real and financial variables, and the exact determinants of wage- and price-setting decisions. Finally, monetary policy is restricted by the impact of other government actions, especially FISCAL POLICY, ie, decisions about government expenditures and taxation. Fiscal policy also influences overall economic demand, and if fiscal and monetary policy are not co-ordinated, they can work at cross-purposes. In Canada the minister of finance and the governor of the Bank of Canada consult regularly. Furthermore, since 1961 there has been an explicit agreement that if any irreconcilable conflict between the 2 arises, the governor must either follow the written (and publicly released) directive of the minister or resign his office. Nonetheless, there is also a strong tradition that, except in such acute circumstances, the Bank of Canada should be able to set an independent monetary policy, free from political pressures. Therefore the potential for conflicting policies does exist.

The creation of monetary policy is often a highly contentious issue. Disagreements sometimes occur because of differing factual judgements about current economic circumstances (eg, whether or not a recession has started), or because of conflicting value judgements (eg, whether it is more unfair to have inflation erode the value of fixed pensions or to have recession cause the loss of jobs). Frequently, however, debate reflects broad conceptual differences about the appropriate strategy for monetary policy. Although there are many alternative (and intermediate) viewpoints, 2 general approaches can be distinguished.

Keynesianism   Although considerably modified and refined by his followers, English economist John Maynard Keynes's concepts of the use of monetary and fiscal policy, developed during the GREAT DEPRESSION, remain highly influential (*see* KEYNESIAN ECONOMICS). Keynesians place considerable stress on the many influences that tend to destabilize the economy, including shifts in business and consumer confidence, dynamic investment cycles, and international trade, financial and price shocks. Keynesian policy, therefore, tends to be highly activist or discretionary, in the sense that the nature of monetary (and fiscal) actions alters significantly in response to perceived or anticipated shifts in overall economic circumstances. Carried to its logical limit such continual policy shifts are sometimes referred to as "fine tuning."

Keynesians recognize the risk that the policy chosen may sometimes worsen rather than improve economic performance. Some Keynesians, therefore, cautiously argue that while major cyclical swings should be countered by an appropriate policy change, minor fluctuations should be largely ignored. As a group, however, Keynesians are especially concerned that complete failure to react to economic downturns could lead to episodes of prolonged and severe economic stagnation – characterized by falling output and high unemployment – which can and should be avoided. In his original analysis, Keynes argued principally for discretionary fiscal rather than monetary policy. His followers now generally believe that both tools are powerful and both should be actively used.

Monetarism   The most important distinguishing characteristic of monetarists is their strong skepticism about the use of discretionary monetary policy to offset business-cycle fluctuations. Instead they advocate a neutral policy in which money-supply growth rates would be set and maintained at low levels, regardless of economic circumstances. Monetarists dispute the claim that the economy is inherently unstable, arguing that steady money growth coupled with automatic stabilizing influences in the private sector (and possibly automatic fiscal-policy stabilizers) will keep fluctuations to modest proportions. Secondly, they maintain that changes in monetary policy are unlikely to be effective in reducing output and employment oscillations and may actually accentuate them. The existence of potentially long and uncertain lags between the implementation and impact of a policy change is one important element in this argument. Finally, monetarists are concerned about the effect political pressures may have on the choice of a monetary policy. They assert that in practice Keynesian monetary policy will be too stimulative, aiming at immediate employment and output gains and ignoring the potential for higher inflation in the long run.

In the 1960s and early 1970s, the Keynesian approach was dominant, and the generally strong economic performance of the Canadian economy and many other economies was attributed, in part, to the implementation of Keynesian monetary and fiscal policy. However, the frequent bouts of double-digit inflation from the mid-1970s through the early 1980s, coupled with new theoretical analysis by a number of monetarists, greatly increased the influence of monetarist ideas on both academic economists and central bankers, including the Bank of Canada. Currently, many economists would accept elements of both Keynesian and monetarist analysis, while at the same time acknowledging that considerable further research needs to be done on both the nature and impact of monetary policy.

RONALD G. WIRICK

Reading: D. Bond, R. Shearer and J. Chant, *The Economics of the Canadian Financial System* (4th ed, 1983).

Money consists of anything that is generally accepted for the settlement of debts or purchase of goods or services. The evolution of money as a system for regulating society's economic transactions represented a significant advancement over earlier forms of exchange based on BARTER, a transaction in which goods and services are exchanged for other goods or services rather than money (today, barter is sometimes used as a form of tax evasion and in trade between nations). Money has at least 3 functions: it serves as a medium of exchange; a measure by which prices, debts and wages are expressed; and a store of value. These functions are interdependent, although some theorists (eg, Keynesians, Marxists) stress that money must have intrinsic value (eg, GOLD or SILVER) that represents labour, while others (eg, monetarists) emphasize that the most important characteristic of money is its acceptability as a means of exchange.

In many ancient societies gold and silver served as money. They had intrinsic value, were easily portable and divisible, and were indestructible. Gold and silver coins were minted by the STATE (*see* COINAGE). The 17th-century development of goldsmith BANKING in Europe marked the transition to paper money. Goldsmiths issued paper bills backed by the gold in their vaults. During the 18th and 19th centuries, European states established central banks to regulate their monetary systems; by the turn of this century most states had taken over the issuance of paper money backed by bullion. Today, however, none of the major state currencies is officially backed by bullion (see GOLD STANDARD).

Canada's first paper money was playing cards, specially cut and signed by the governor and issued in 1685 to supplement the chronically short supply of French and Spanish silver coins then used as the main medium of exchange in New France (see PLAYING-CARD MONEY). The playing cards had no intrinsic value but their inscribed value was supposedly guaranteed by the colonial government. In an attempt to pay for the Seven Years' War the government then issued vast amounts of paper money, the worth of which it could not guarantee. The result was rampant INFLATION.

After the Conquest (1759-60), the British introduced sterling and for almost a century pounds, shillings and pence were official money in Canada. In practice this meant setting a sterling value for the various kinds of money in existence. The Spanish dollar was rated at 5 shillings, which meant there were 4 to the pound, a value first established by Halifax merchants. Dollar banknotes were printed, including a $4 denomination to conform to the official value of the pound, a value which made it different from the British pound. British money never became dominant, however, and a hodgepodge of money circulated in Canada in the first half of the 19th century, including Nova Scotia provincial money, American dollars, Spanish dollars, American gold coins and "army bills" used by the British forces to buy supplies in the War of 1812. The use of the army money accustomed Canadians to reliable paper money.

The decision to reject British money and adopt a decimal system like that in the US was made in the 20 years before Confederation. In 1858 a law required that accounts of the government of the Province of Canada be kept in dollars instead of pounds. At the same time, the government began to issue its own money to circulate alongside the bills issued by the BANK OF MONTREAL and other banks. In the first decades after Confederation, most Canadians simply assumed that a dollar was a dollar, whether it was issued by the government in Washington or Ottawa or by a bank. Canada's monetary system always paralleled that of the US, with some notable differences. In 1870 the Dominion government issued SHINPLASTERS (25-cent government notes) to counteract the effect of an overabundance of American silver coinage in Canada that was worth only 80¢ against the Canadian dollar at that time. The American and Canadian dollars first diverged seriously in the period of high inflation that followed WWI (see EXCHANGE RATES). The Canadian dollar dropped to 84¢ US in 1920, but quickly recovered and was steady at about 100 cents in the last half of the 1920s. With the Great Depression, the Canadian dollar dropped to about 80¢ US, a record low until recent times, but the dollar recovered before the economy and was as high as $1.04 US in the mid-1930s. During WWII, the value of the Canadian dollar was fixed at about 91¢ US. From 1952 to 1962, when the Canadian dollar was allowed to "float" rather than having a fixed value in American dollars, it was often worth more than the US dollar because of the flood of American investment in Canada. A dollar crisis hit Canada in the midst of the 1962 federal election campaign and the dollar was pegged at 92.5¢ US. In 1970 the Canadian dollar was again set free to float and quickly rose to be worth more than the US dollar, but this strength was deceptive and the 1976 election of the Parti Québécois in Québec triggered a fall which took it to an historic low point of 69¢ US on 4 Feb 1986, it has since recovered from that point.

The 1970s revived interest in the old idea that inflation was essentially caused by too much money and attempts were made to try and limit the money supply in the economy (see MONETARY POLICY). The money supply (total amount of money) includes cash, bank deposits, deposits in financial institutions, certain kinds of short-term notes and sometimes credit cards. The Bank of Canada has several operational definitions of the money supply. M-1 (currency in circulation outside of the chartered banks, ie, the actual cash in people's pockets and bank deposits that can be withdrawn without notice) is the most narrow definition. However, it does not correspond to the US definition of M-1 (in Canada, M-1B, which equals the Canadian M-1 plus chequable savings deposits, is the equivalent of the US M-1). The Bank of Canada had tried prior to 1982 to regulate the supply of M-1 (which amounted at that time to about $30 billion, $13 billion of which was currency) to restrain the money supply in an attempt to lower inflation, but the introduction of computer banking made it difficult to determine if M-1 could accurately measure the existing money supply. The next widest definition of money supply, M-2, includes M-1B, nonchequing personal term and savings deposits and some corporate chequable and nonchequable notice deposits. Canadian M-2, which was close to $190 billion in the late 1980s, corresponds to the American M-2. The broadest definition of money supply is M-3; it consists of M-2 and nonpersonal term deposits, including certificates of deposit held by business corporations. M-3 amounted to $230 billion in the late 1980s. The total money supply consists of M-3 plus Government of Canada deposits in chartered banks.

Canada's monetary system is of course linked to the international monetary system, which underwent a serious crisis in the early 1980s. This crisis was manifested in high rates of inflation, even hyperinflation in many countries, high interest rates, erratic gold and silver prices and a Third World debt problem of seemingly unmanageable proportions.

The process of monetary evolution which began several thousand years ago is still under way. The exact direction it will take is impossible to predict, but some elements of the functions of money as a store of value, measure of value and medium of exchange will be retained.

D. McGILLIVRAY

Monk, Lorraine, née Spurrell, photography curator, author (b at Montréal). She was educated at McGill (BA, MA). As executive producer of the Still Photography Division of the NATIONAL FILM BOARD OF CANADA 1960-80, Monk was instrumental in making the division a national cultural force, collecting, preserving, exhibiting and publishing contemporary Canadian PHOTOGRAPHY. In 1967 she inaugurated "The Photo Gallery" in Ottawa, the first gallery in the country devoted to contemporary Canadian photography. She also produced countless exhibitions and audiovisual presentations, as well as many photographic books, such as *Canada: A Year of the Land* (1967), which won major awards for printing excellence, *The Female Eye* (1975), *Canada* (1975), which won the silver medal at the Leipzig International Book Fair, and *Between Friends* (1976), which won the gold medal at the Leipzig International Book Fair. After leaving the NFB, she has continued to organize photo exhibitions and to produce books, such as *Canada with Love* (1982). She has worked tirelessly to establish the Canadian Museum of Photography, which held its first exhibition in Toronto in 1987. Monk received the Centennial Medal (1967) and is an Officer of the Order of Canada.

LOUISE ABBOTT

Monk, Maria, (b at St-Jean-sur-Richelieu, Qué 1817 to Scottish parents; d half-mad in the prison on Blackwell's I [Welfare I] 1849), author of *The Awful Disclosures of the Hôtel Dieu Nunnery of Montreal*. A difficult child, her mother sent her to a Montréal shelter in 1834, from which, pregnant, she was expelled the following year. Having fled to the US, she became the centre of the nativist anti-Catholic controversy upon the publication of the book she wrote describing the horrors she suffered while a nun in Hôtel-Dieu in Montréal. The success of the book set off a furious debate between its partisans and adversaries. William L. Stone went to Montréal to get to the bottom of it and visited the Hôtel-Dieu: it became evident that Maria Monk had never set foot in the place. Stone's refutation and the publication of sworn testimonies gathered in Montréal put an end to the credibility of Monk's pamphlet though not to its distribution: 300 000 copies were circulated before the American Civil War. PHILIPPE SYLVAIN

Monroe, Walter Stanley, businessman, politician (b at Dublin, Ire 14 May 1871; d at St John's 6 Oct 1952). He was Newfoundland's eighteenth prime minister, June 1924-Aug 1928; his newly constituted party swept to power, ending Albert HICKMAN's brief prime ministership. A well-established and successful businessman, Monroe had served for a short time in William WARREN's Cabinet before that administration was replaced by Hickman's. In May 1924 Monroe was chosen as leader of a new alliance, the Liberal-Conservatives, which defeated Hickman in the June election. During Monroe's term, in spite of deepening financial difficulties, there was some industrial expansion and the long-fought LABRADOR BOUNDARY DISPUTE was settled. In Aug 1928 he passed the leadership to his cousin Frederick ALDERDICE and returned to his business concerns.

ROBERT D. PITT

Mont-Joli, Qué, Town, pop 6670 (1986c), 6359 (1981c), inc 1945, is located 30 km NE of RIMOUSKI at the entrance to the Matapédia Valley. The development of a transportation infrastructure was the most important factor in the area's urbanization, beginning with the construction of the INTERCOLONIAL RY, which reached Mont-Joli in 1874. Further growth resulted from the establishment of train-repair yards. The headquarters of the Canada and Gulf Terminal Ry (linking Mont-Joli and Matane) located in the village in 1910. These developments led to the opening of a foundry that produced railway equipment. WWII saw the arrival of a military airport, firing range and bombing school; this centre has become the present regional airport. The government of Maurice DUPLESSIS built a sanitarium here. One of the first radio stations in Québec opened here in 1922. Today, Mont-Joli has become a service town, and transportation plays a lesser role.

ANTONIO LECHASSEUR

Mont Ste-Anne, Qué, provincial park created in 1969, is located 40 km E of QUÉBEC CITY. Part of the LAURENTIAN HIGHLANDS, its flattened summit (815 m) dominates the N shore of the St Lawrence R. Mont Ste-Anne is internationally known for its SKIING facilities, and World Cup races have been held there since 1971. Downhill skiers enjoy over 50 km of both gentle and steep runs. The area is superbly equipped, with ski jumps, 90 km of illuminated and patrolled ski trails, and a 10 km snowshoe trail. A year-round chair lift takes people to the summit and its outstanding view of the river, its islands and the S shore. The park is a pleasant summer recreation spot with walking trails, bicycle and jogging paths, an 18-hole golf course and camping facilities.

CLAUDINE PIERRE-DESCHÊNES

Mont St-Hilaire Nature Conservation Centre, administered by MCGILL UNIVERSITY, comprises Mont St-Hilaire (one of the 10 Monteregian Hills located 35 km E of Montréal), which rises 400 m above the Richelieu R and covers 11 km². The mountain was formed by the intrusion, some 100 million years ago, of igneous rock into sedimentary layers that have since been removed by erosion processes, including glaciation. The mountain's several peaks surround Lac Hertel (0.3 km²), which is drained by a small stream. Variations in altitude and climate produce a pattern of vegetation dominated by forests of pine, oak, maple, beech and birch. Animal species include 41 species of mammal (eg, skunk, fox, raccoon, porcupine, muskrat, squirrel, deer) and some 178 species of bird (eg, pileated woodpecker, warbler, hawk, Canada goose). Indians used the mountain until the 1700s, when French settlers began exploiting its timber and waterpower resources. After 1844, the Campbell family developed it as a tourist resort until 1913, when it was bought by Brig A.H. GAULT. He protected its natural qualities and in 1958 bequeathed it to McGill. Since then it has been managed for conservation, scientific research, education and recreation. In 1960 it became a migratory BIRD SANCTUARY and in 1978 was recognized by UNESCO as Canada's first Biosphere Reserve. The public has year-round access to the western, 6 km² nature-centre zone which includes 24 km of trails.   JOHN S. MARSH

Mont Sorrel, an important feature on the S shoulder of the Ypres Salient, captured by German forces on 2 June 1916 from the 3rd Division of the Canadian Corps. Maj-Gen M.S. Mercer, commanding the division, was killed and Brig-Gen V.A.S. Williams, commanding the 8th Brigade, was taken prisoner, the highest-ranking Canadians to be killed and captured during WORLD WAR I. An immediate counterattack that night failed but stemmed any further German advance. A more deliberate counterattack recaptured Mont Sorrel on June 12. Between June 2 and 14 the Canadians lost some 8000 men and the Germans nearly 6000.   BRERETON GREENHOUS

Montagnais-Naskapi live in the eastern and northern portions of the Québec-Labrador Peninsula. They call themselves, and in Labrador are called, Innu ("person"), and are divided into many regional groups (eg, *Uashau Innuts* – the Sept-Îles band). The terms "Montagnais" (French for "mountain people") and "Naskapi" (origin uncertain) both appeared in French 17th-century missionary sources. These terms have been used to refer to different groups over time. By the late 19th century "Naskapi" had acquired the connotation of the far northern "unchristianized" group (the native term is *Mushuau Innuts* – "Barren Land People"), while the group known as "Montagnais" primarily inhabited the forest. The total population is now approximately 9000.

The Montagnais-Naskapi are descended from populations that came to Québec-Labrador thousands of years ago. Although they briefly fought INUIT, IROQUOIS, MICMAC and ABENAKI, they were not a warlike group, and at least some hostility was a side effect of European contact. In the TADOUSSAC region they played an important role in early Canadian history as military allies of the French in wars with the British and their Indian allies (*see* IROQUOIS WARS); CHAMPLAIN formed an alliance with one group in 1608. They also established one of the first known game preserves, and for some years attempted to keep both Europeans and other Indians away from their grounds.

For 2 centuries the FUR TRADE was the focus of their relations with Europeans. Trade at the Gulf of St Lawrence posts was a monopoly of the Crown, first of France and later of Britain, and

Montagnais Indians making a birchbark canoe *c*1870, near La Malbaie, north shore of the St Lawrence R (*courtesy National Gallery of Canada*).

was leased to private traders. By the mid-1800s most areas were overtrapped, and the Montagnais needed assistance from missions and the government to survive. Soon commercial forestry increased their difficulties, and they were excluded from salmon rivers which were leased.

Prior to the 1800s most contacts between the Barren Ground subgroup and Europeans were indirect, by trade through neighbouring CREE and Montagnais intermediaries. Life depended on the movements of the Barren Ground CARIBOU. There was a special caribou hunt leader (*Atik Utshimau*) but his authority lasted only for the hunt. Starting in 1830, the HUDSON'S BAY COMPANY opened posts in this northern region, supplied first from Fort Chimo and later from North West River, Labrador. The fur trade had disastrous results, because trapping did not fit with nomadic caribou hunting. Large numbers of people died, some of starvation and others from disease. By the 1950s a still unsettled Barren Ground group was trading at Fort Chimo; sick and starving, they were finally persuaded by the government to settle at the new mining town of SCHEFFERVILLE, Qué, while another group settled at Davis Inlet, Labrador.

Although there are strong pressures to abandon the nomadic life – most recently, their perceived threat from low level military training flights over their territory – some Montagnais-Naskapi spend part of the winter hunting. Game animals are caribou (for the eastern and northern area), moose (for the west), beaver, bear, lake fish and salmon. The people depend on their ability to travel, using the CANOE in summer, and SNOWSHOES and TOBOGGANS in winter. European items, such as flour, guns and even SNOWMOBILES, are fitted into an essentially native way of life.

The Montagnais-Naskapi developed an intellectually rich tradition on a modest material base. Every part of the caribou was used; the skin was decorated with painted or quill designs to make clothing of many kinds. Drums accompanied sacred singing. A caribou shoulder-blade, burned in a prehunt ritual, was believed to foretell the location of game. This belief in animal spirits played a major role in the hunt. Status was gained mainly through the ability to make gifts of meat to others. After the hunt a ceremonial feast of bone fat, *makushan*, was held. Much of the ancestral religion is recorded in legends. The language is part of the Algonquian family and was one of the

first in N America into which Christian texts were translated.

In the early 1970s the Montagnais-Naskapi organized themselves politically, with the Conseil Attikameg-Montagnais in Québec, the Naskapi Montagnais Innu Assn in Labrador, and the Naskapi of Schefferville. In 1975 this last group was excluded from the Agreement in Principle leading to the JAMES BAY AGREEMENT but negotiated a separate agreement, which provides them with a new village N of Schefferville. The other groups are pressing the government for settlement of their LAND CLAIMS. New creative expressions, such as the books of the first Montagnais author, An Antane Kapesh, and recordings by singers such as Phillip MacKenzie, have recently appeared, showing that the culture continues to adapt. *See also* NATIVE PEOPLE: SUBARCTIC and general articles under NATIVE PEOPLE.   ADRIAN TANNER

Reading: G. Henriksen, *Hunters in the Barrens: The Naskapi on the Edge of the White Man's World* (1973); F.G. Speck, *Naskapi: The Savage Hunters of the Labrador Peninsula* (1977); L.M. Turner, *Indians and Eskimos in the Quebec-Labrador Peninsula: Ethnology of the Ungava District* (1894, repr 1979).

Montague, PEI, Town, pop 1994 (1986c), 1957 (1981c), inc 1917, located 45 km SE of Charlottetown, is a picturesque community divided by the Montague R. Until incorporation, the town was known as Montague Bridge. While the original settlement date is unknown, in 1840 the townsite was occupied by 4 partly cleared farms. Situated on a navigable river that flows into the NORTHUMBERLAND STR, Montague began developing around the mid-19th century as a commercial and shipbuilding centre. Economic ties with the surrounding fertile agricultural region sustained Montague when the shipbuilding industry died later in that century. While it still lacks an industrial base, the town has experienced renewed prosperity with the agricultural revitalization that began in the 1960s. Out-of-province investment has started tobacco farms and rejuvenated the mixed- and dairy-farming industries. Montague is the commercial centre of SE Kings County.   W.S. KEIZER

Montcalm, Louis-Joseph de, Marquis de Montcalm, military officer (b at Candiac, France 28 Feb 1712; d at Québec City 14 Sept 1759). Montcalm entered the army at age 9 and served with distinction. In 1756 he was promoted *maréchal de camp* and replaced Baron Dieskau as commander of French troops in N America. He arrived in Québec 13 May 1756 under orders that he was subordinate to VAUDREUIL, the governor general of NEW FRANCE. Vain and contemptuous of

Marquis de Montcalm, commander of the French forces during the Seven Years' War (*courtesy National Archives of Canada/C-27665*).

colonial authorities and their preference for guerrilla tactics, he developed open hostility to Vaudreuil and labelled the whole administration corrupt. He captured Ft William Henry (Aug 1757), and in July 1758 he conducted a successful defence against a British attack on Ft Carillon. His dispatches to France showed his own efforts to best effect and were critical of Vaudreuil. He was appointed 20 Oct 1758 lieutenant-general – the second-highest rank in the French army. In May 1759 Gen James WOLFE and Vice-Adm Charles Saunders appeared before Québec. In Sept a series of errors by the French allowed Wolfe to scale the riverbank and land some 4500 men on the PLAINS OF ABRAHAM, less than 2 km from the city. Wolfe's position was threatening but precarious and Montcalm chose the one course of action that could have brought defeat: on the morning of Sept 13 he hastily rushed his troops into battle. The French were routed and Montcalm received a mortal wound from which he died the next morning. Historians have long been at odds with the assessment on the plaque on the Plains of Abraham of the "gallant, good and great" man. He won some notable victories but suffered the greatest defeat in Canadian military history. *See also* SEVEN YEARS' WAR.　　IAN CASSELMAN

Reading: Guy Frégault, *La Guerre de la conquête 1754-60* (1955, trans *Canada: The War of the Conquest* 1969); C.P. Stacey, *Quebec, 1759* (1959).

Montcalm Construction Case (1979) *Montcalm Construction Inc v Minimum Wage Commission et al* was concerned with whether or not provincial labour laws applied to the employees of a construction company that had a contract with the federal government to build the landing strips at Mirabel Airport on land belonging to the Crown in right of Canada. The Supreme Court of Canada decided that while aeronautics fell within federal jurisdiction, the salaries paid by an independent business are so far removed from aerial navigation and use of an airport that the power to regulate the matter could not form an integral part of the primary jurisdiction of Parliament over aeronautics or be tied to the development of a federal operation. The court also ruled that federal lands are not extraterritorial enclaves within provincial boundaries and that valid and generally relevant provincial laws apply to them.
　　GÉRALD-A. BEAUDOIN

Montenegrins, *see* YUGOSLAVS.

Montferrand, Jos, French Canadian of legendary strength who lived in the Ottawa-Montréal region in the early 19th century. He fought many famous boxers of his day, but was best known for protecting local Frenchmen from English troublemakers, once taking on 20 single-handedly. Exploits of extraordinary strength attributed to him include pointing with a plow to give someone directions and leaping so high in a dance that he left the print of his heel on the hotel ballroom ceiling. Tales of the legendary Joe Mufferaw, strongman of the Ottawa Valley were based on Montferrand. Tales of Mufferaw's power were tempered by his gentle kindness. Anonymous or inexplicable events are often attributed to "Who else but Joe Mufferaw?"
　　NANCY SCHMITZ AND CAROLE H. CARPENTER

Montgomery, Lucy Maud, writer, diarist (b at Clifton, PEI 30 Nov 1874; d at Toronto 24 Apr 1942). Raised in Cavendish, PEI, and educated at Prince of Wales Coll (PEI) and Dalhousie, Montgomery was earning money from her pen by the late 1890s. In 1908 her first novel, ANNE OF GREEN GABLES, became an instant best-seller. In 1911 Montgomery married the Rev Ewan Macdonald and moved permanently to Ontario. She published 7 sequels to *Anne,* the autobiographical *Emily* trilogy and 2 well-received novels for adults. During her lifetime, she published 22 books of fiction, a serialized version of her life, a book of poetry, and approximately 450 poems and 500 short stories. At her death, she left 10 volumes (over 5000 pages) of unpublished personal diaries (1889-1942) – an outstanding record of social history and of a remarkable woman's life. These journals are now being edited; volume I appeared in 1985 and volume II in 1987.

Writing for a popular market that demanded "happy endings," Montgomery nevertheless managed to depict an infinite number of human frailties, but she softened these with her natural wit, her benevolent view of mankind and her use of the romance structure. Her ear for dialogue, together with her insight into human nature and her choice of universal themes, has made her Canada's most enduring literary export, and red-haired "Anne" has become a world-famous literary character.　　MARY RUBIO

Lucy Maud Montgomery, author of *Anne of Green Gables* (*courtesy Public Archives of PEI*).

Montizambert, Frederick, physician, public-health official (b at Québec, Canada E 3 Feb 1843; d at Ottawa 2 Nov 1929). Montizambert practised in Québec before entering the Canadian public-health service in 1866. In 1899 he became director general of public health and sanitary adviser to the Government of Canada. He supervised the federal government's disorganized and dispersed health services, published articles on sanitation and studied the use of chaulmoogra oil in the treatment of leprosy. He was a member of many health and medical organizations in Canada, Britain, the US and France.
　　JANICE DICKIN McGINNIS

Montmagny, Qué, City, pop 11 958 (1986c), inc 1845, located on the S shore of the St-Lawrence R, 50 km downriver from Québec City at the junction of the St-Nicholas R and the Rivière du Sud. In a very picturesque setting, Montmagny is a port and manufacturing centre producing such goods as household appliances and wood products. It is well served by highway, rail and ferry transportation. The city is named for Charles Huault, Sieur de MONTMAGNY, the second governor of New France. Jacques CARTIER passed Montmagny and its many offshore islands in 1535 and noted its beautiful surroundings. In 1646 a seigneury containing the area was granted to Huault, although permanent European habitation did not begin until the 1670s. Montmagny was a thriving pulp and paper centre at the time of its official founding, although this and the river transportation industries were severely affected by the Great Depression. Recently, the tourist industry has grown in importance.　　SERGE DURFLINGER

Montmagny, Charles Huault de, called Onontio by the Indians, governor of NEW FRANCE (b in France *c*1583; d on Île St-Christophe, W Indies *c*1653). Montmagny succeeded CHAMPLAIN in 1636 and was governor and lt-general of New France until 1648. His primary concern was defence of the fledgling colony; he worked to lay out and fortify Québec C and give some protection to Trois-Rivières. In 1641 the IROQUOIS WARS broke out, and Montmagny built Ft Richelieu (at Sorel, Qué) to counter the threat. In 1647 the establishment of a council (forerunner of the SOVEREIGN COUNCIL) placed some curbs on the exercise of his powers as governor.
　　MARY McDOUGALL MAUDE

Montmorency, Qué, a village located 12 km E of QUÉBEC CITY, is now part of the municipality of Beauport (pop 62 869, 1986c). The famous 76 m MONTMORENCY FALLS were named in 1603 by Samuel de CHAMPLAIN in honour of the duc de Montmorency, later the viceroy of New France. Gen James WOLFE's troops were defeated on 31 July 1759 on the cliffs of the falls near Courville. The manor, built in 1781 by Frederick HALDI-MAND, govenor general in chief of Canada, known as "Kent House," was inhabited 1791-94 by the duke of Kent, father of Queen Victoria. By the late 19th century, a large textile factory founded in 1889, Montmorency Cotton, located near the falls and served by the CPR, employed most of the local population. It became Dominion Textile in 1905 and still operates. In recent years, after its fusion with Beauport, the area has been turning into a residential suburb of Québec City.　　CLAUDINE PIERRE-DESCHÊNES

Montmorency Falls, located 10 km E of Québec City at the mouth of the Rivière Montmorency, where it empties into the St Lawrence R, is the highest waterfall in the province of Québec and the ninth-highest in Canada. The Rivière Montmorency rises in the provincial Parc des Laurentides N of Québec City and courses 100 km before reaching the St Lawrence. The 76 m cataract (some 22 m higher than Niagara Falls) forms a spectacular cascade as it joins the waters N of the Île d'Orléans. Whether seen from the base or the crest, or from the 1737 m suspension bridge that joins the N shore of the St Lawrence to the Île d'Orléans, the waterfall has captivated visitors

The 84 m cliff over which the Rivière Montmorency falls is literally the exposed edge of the Canadian Shield (*courtesy Ron Redfern, Random House Inc*).

since the days of Samuel de CHAMPLAIN. In wintertime the spray from the waterfall creates a "sugarloaf" cone of ice, often 30 m or more in height. Tobogganing down the cone was a popular 19th-century pastime. The nearby community of MONTMORENCY takes its name from the waterfall. The town's industries are fueled by the hydroelectric power developments at the waterfall, and Québec City is provided with power and light from the same source.

The waterfall was first noted by Jean Fonteneau *dit* Alfonse (who served as pilot in the 1542 expedition of Sieur de ROBERVAL) in his *Cosmographie*. In 1613 Champlain named the waterfall after Henri II, duc de Montmorency, governor of Languedoc and admiral of France, who served as viceroy of New France 1620-25. In July 1759, during the campaign to take all French possessions in Canada, British forces landed near the base of the waterfall and established a fortified camp on the heights to the E. The ensuing Battle of Montmorency (31 July 1759) saw the British, under General James WOLFE, repulsed and forced to evacuate their positions by French forces sent from Québec City. A plaque commemorating this historic event is at the Montmorency church. An enduring tourist attraction over the years, the waterfall has observation points and picnic areas at both its base and crest.   DAVID EVANS

Montréal, located in southwestern Québec, is the metropolis of the province and was the most populous city in Canada for a century and a half. Situated on Île de Montréal, the largest in the Hochelaga Archipelago, at the confluence of the ST LAWRENCE and OTTAWA rivers, it occupies a strategic location on one of the world's greatest rivers, at the heart of a hydrographical system covering all of eastern N America. A major industrial centre, commercial and financial metropolis, railway and maritime bridgehead, and home of francophone culture in N America, Montréal is one of the world's great cities and enjoys international acclaim.

Since 1870 the urbanized area has been steadily overflowing the limits of the city proper, despite numerous annexations of suburban municipalities. In 1986 the census metropolitan area included approximately 100 different municipalities, the largest being Montréal-Nord (90 303); La Salle (75 947); Saint-Léonard (76 299) and Saint-Laurent (67 002) on Île de Montréal; Laval (268 335) and Repentigny (40 778) N of Île de Montréal; and Longueuil (125 441) and Saint-Hubert (66 218) on the S shore.

Settlement Montréal had difficult beginnings. The initial objective of evangelizing the Indians

proved utopian and had to be largely abandoned. In settling on Île de Montréal, MAISONNEUVE and his group of 4 dozen colonists were caught in a storm of conflict between Indian tribes for control of the fur supply. A permanent state of war with the Iroquois marked the early decades of the colony's existence (*see* IROQUOIS WARS). The French military intervention of 1665-66 eased tensions in Montréal somewhat, but it was not until the conclusion of the peace treaty with the Iroquois in 1701 that the climate became more relaxed.

Development While QUÉBEC CITY was the administrative capital and the main port where exchanges took place with France, Montréal was a city of the interior, soon to become the great centre of the FUR TRADE, from which the COUREURS DE BOIS, VOYAGEURS and the famous explorers, such as LA SALLE, DULHUT, d'IBERVILLE and LA VÉRENDRYE, set out. They established a network of trading posts to secure furs for Montréal and methodically explored the N American continent from the Gulf of Mexico to the Rockies. Relying upon the labour of the Indians, the fur trade did not provide much employment in Montréal itself. Strong dependence on this single activity and the weakness of the region's agriculture explain why population growth in Montréal was slow. At the end of the 17th century, the city had just over 1000 inhabitants, rising to approximately 5500 in 1789. In addition to the voyageurs and the coureurs de bois, religious institutions made their presence felt in the life of the community. Among these was the Order of Saint-Sulpice, which held Île de Montréal *en seigneurie* for close to 200 years from its seminary building, providing it with priests for the parish church. Built in 1685, the seminary building still stands today on the Place d'Armes.

After the British conquest (the city surrendered in 1760), Montréal's economy continued to depend entirely on the fur trade for several decades. Scottish merchants – Alexander MACKENZIE, the FROBISHER brothers, Simon MCTAVISH, Duncan, Simon and William MCGILLIVRAY, to name only the best known – took the place of francophone merchants. The Scots combined their interests to create the NORTH WEST CO to compete more effectively with the HUDSON'S BAY CO for control of the fur trade of the Northwest. Despite the disadvantage of distance, the Montréal-based firm prospered

Plan of Montréal, 1759 (*courtesy National Archives of Canada/Cartographic and Architectural Archives Div/H3/340*).

until it was assimilated by its rival in 1821. The fur trade had played an important role in establishing Montréal's hegemony over the interior. From the end of the 18th century, the city's growth depended increasingly on the settlement of the rural hinterland, both on the plain outside Montréal and in Ontario. The large influx of emigrants from the British Isles, which began in 1815, accelerated the settlement process. By the 1820s its population outnumbered that of Québec City and it had clearly asserted itself as the metropolis. In 1825 Montréal already had 22 540 inhabitants; there were 44 591 in 1844. A dynamic merchant class, engaged in the import and export trade, succeeded the fur-trade magnates. This group created the BANK OF MONTREAL in 1817 and the Committee of Trade in 1822, invested in maritime shipping and, in 1836, began to invest in railways.

Large-scale immigration enabled the residents of British origin to become the majority in the city around 1831. Conflict between French and English and struggles for representative government marked the 1830s and resulted in the REBELLIONS OF 1837. The defeat of the PATRIOTES gave a political victory to the new anglophone bourgeoisie and after 1840 the francophone leaders had no choice but to agree to co-operate with them. During the following years, fundamental changes took place in transportation and industry. Expansion of the St Lawrence canal system and the deepening of the channel to Québec City made Montréal the principal seaport. Railway construction, particularly of the GRAND TRUNK RY, made the city the hub of the railway system. Finally the process of industrialization, begun around the middle of the century, was to alter the city's face completely. After depending for generations on trade and commerce for its livelihood, Montréal was becoming a major industrial centre.

Montréal grew rapidly 1850-1914. The population increased to 467 986 in 1911 (528 397 including the suburbs). The city proper overflowed its boundaries and quickly reached the cities in the suburbs, annexing 22 between 1883 and 1918. Industrial growth attracted those in search of employment. French Canadians living in rural areas poured into the city to join the urban proletariat and from 1867 Francophones were again in the majority. Immigration increased dramatically at the turn of the century and Montréal became a more cosmopolitan city. The settlement of the Canadian West was also important for the city's development. The CANADIAN PACIFIC RY established its head office here in the 1880s. Much western grain

Population: 1 054 420 (1986c), 1 018 609 (1981cA);
  2 921 357 (1986 CMA), 2 862 286
  (1981 ACMA)
Rate of Increase (1981-86): City -.3%; CMA 2.1%
Rank in Canada: Second (by CMA)
Date of Incorporation: 1832
Land Area: City 176.90 km²; CMA 3508.89 km²
Elevation: 200 m (Mount Royal)
Climate: Average daily temp, July 20.9°C, Jan -10.2°C;
  Yearly precip 946.2 mm; Hours of sunshine
  2054 per year

View of Montréal harbour from the Customs House,
1878-80 (*courtesy Notman Photographic Archives*).

was shipped through the port of Montréal, which was considerably enlarged at the beginning of the 20th century. Montréal was then indisputably the metropolis of Canada, and St-James Street was the country's financial centre. Toronto, however, was a powerful rival, and in the long run benefited more from western settlement; eventually (around 1970) it took Montréal's place as Canada's centre of economic activity, largely because of its proximity to a larger population in the US.

After WWI, Montréal saw another period of growth, based on industry, trade, finance and transportation. In 1931 the population of the city and suburbs reached over one million. But the GREAT DEPRESSION brought this period of expansion to a halt and caused grave social hardship. At the Depression's height, in Feb 1934, there were 62 000 unemployed in the city, with 240 000 receiving government assistance. The city administration ran into debt because of huge relief expenses and was placed under trusteeship by the provincial government in the early 1940s.

WWII stimulated production and employment and helped restore prosperity. The 1950s and 1960s saw strong growth, supported by a new wave of immigrants and a large exodus of inhabitants from rural areas. This growth was especially apparent in the suburbs, where many new cities sprang up. The downtown area was completely transformed, and in the process the working classes, longtime residents of the area, had to move elsewhere. Under the leadership of Mayor-Jean DRAPEAU, Montréal embarked upon great

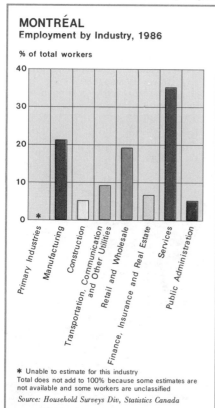

MONTRÉAL
Employment by Industry, 1986

% of total workers

* Unable to estimate for this industry
Total does not add to 100% because some estimates are
not available and some workers are unclassified

Source: Household Surveys Div, Statistics Canada

projects, several on an international scale: the Métro (begun 1966), the International World Exposition (EXPO 67), the 1976 Summer Olympic Games and the Floralies Internationales (1980). The earlier projects were undertaken during a period of relative prosperity, but a decline became more pronounced in the 1970s. Slow growth, combined with the decision of many large firms to move their corporate headquarters to Toronto, caused the city to lose its prominent position, and it was relegated to the level of Canada's second-largest agglomeration. Montréal remained nevertheless a great city and experienced a renewed vitality in the mid-1980s. The city proper has a population of 1 million, compared to the city proper of Toronto, which has 610 000.

Cityscape Mount Royal, a small mountain of volcanic origin (elev about 250 m), dominates Montréal's landscape. Its graduated terraces mark the city's elevations and also determined its settlement pattern for many years. After a trial period at Pointe-à-Callière, Montréal's founder, Maisonneuve, moved to the elevated site (25 m) he had chosen farther from the river near Place D'Armes. This was to be the site of Vieux ("Old") Montréal, enclosed for many years by a wall, erected at the beginning of the 18th century and demolished in the early 19th century. Few visible traces of the early French settlement remain. With a dozen or so exceptions (Seminary, 1685; Château Ramezay, 1705), the old buildings still in existence date from the 19th century; the area's wealthy residents have made way for stores, warehouses and office buildings. For a long time, downtown Montréal was confined to this area, centered around Notre-Dame and St-Jacques streets. Since 1960, however, the downtown has expanded considerably, and a second pole of activity, to the NW, has grown up along Dorchester Blvd (renamed Réne-Lévesque Blvd in 1987), which is lined with skyscrapers. The most famous is the cruciform PLACE VILLE MARIE (45 storeys), inaugurated 1962. This expansion led to the remodelling of the city. Many buildings with historical value were demolished, ancient residential areas were radically altered and thousands of low-income residents were displaced, as was always the case in such actions in the 1950s and 1960s.

Around this downtown core are residential districts with the highest density of dwellings in the city, dating from the beginning of the century. The houses, built in rows, generally have 2 or 3 storeys and much-celebrated outdoor stairways, a trademark of Montréal architecture of this period. On the higher slopes of Mount Royal nestle the well-to-do areas, the cities of Westmount and Outremont in particular. At the mountain's summit are a park and 2 cemeteries. Farther away are the newer districts built just after the war, such as Ahuntsic on the Rivière des Prairies. The density of dwellings is not as high here as in the older sectors. Finally, the vast suburban areas developed in the late 1950s are characterized by the N American-style single-family residence. They cover the western and eastern ends of the island and overflow onto the Île Jésus (Laval) and the N shore, as well as onto the vast S shore, the home of more than half a million people.

The Montréal landscape is circumscribed by the majestic St Lawrence to the S and the Rivière des Prairies, skirting the N side of the island. Numerous bridges connect the different areas; 14 have been built for automobiles, 7 for railways and one for both uses. In the middle of the St Lawrence is Île Ste-Hélène, a park for many years, which was enlarged as one-third of the site for Expo 67, where the annual exhibition Man and His World was held for years and where the La Ronde amusement park continues to attract over 1 million visitors each summer. Next to it is the man-made Île Notre-Dame, built for Expo 67, which housed Floralies International (1980); it is now a park. Farther east the imposing shape of the Olympic Stadium (1976) dominates the district of Maisonneuve.

Population Since the mid-19th century, Montréal has had 3 distinct decades of rapid growth: 1851-61, 1901-11 and 1951-61. Since 1966 the number of city inhabitants has declined while the population in the suburbs has increased. In 1931, 80% of the metropolitan area population lived in Montréal proper; in 1981 this figure was 35%. The early city limits, established 1792, remained the same for almost a century. After 1883 the annexation of suburban municipalities began. From 1883 to 1918, 22 were annexed; since 1963, 4 more have been added.

Demographic growth has largely been the result of an influx of people from outside the city.

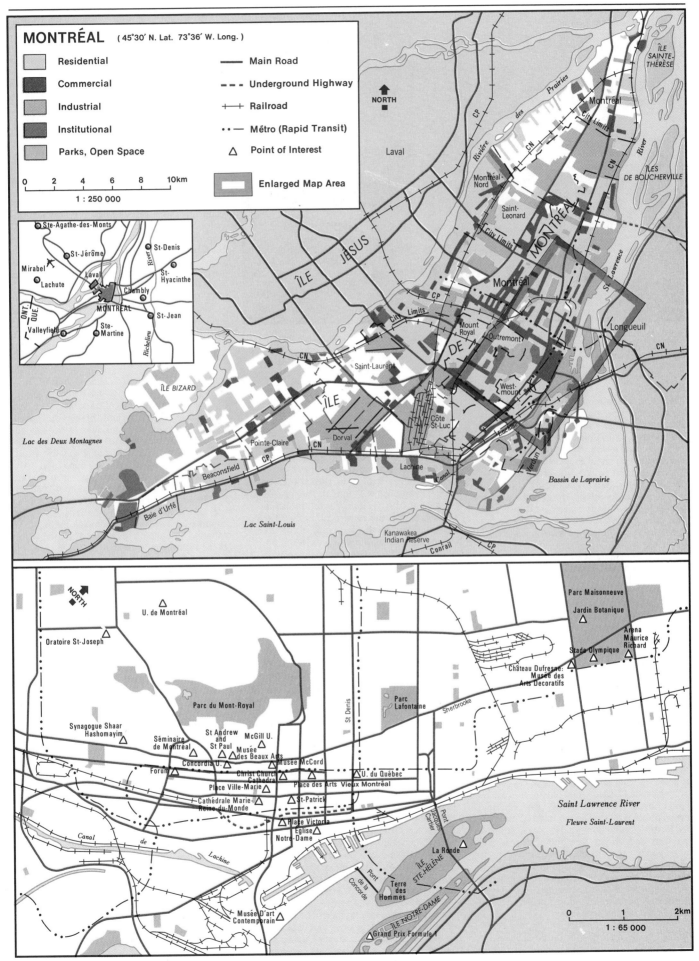

MONTRÉAL (45°30′ N. Lat. 73°36′ W. Long.)

Residential	Main Road
Commercial	Underground Highway
Industrial	Railroad
Institutional	Métro (Rapid Transit)
Parks, Open Space	△ Point of Interest
	Enlarged Map Area

0 2 4 6 8 10km
1 : 250 000

Ste-Agathe-des-Monts
St-Jérôme
St-Denis
Mirabel
Lachute
Laval
St-Hyacinthe
Chambly
MONTRÉAL
ONT. QUE.
Valleyfield
Ste-Martine
St-Jean
Richelieu

ÎLE BIZARD
Lac des Deux Montagnes
ÎLE
Pointe-Claire
Dorval
Beaconsfield
Baie d'Urfé
Lac Saint-Louis
Kanawakea Indian Reserve
Conrail

Laval
NORTH
Rivière des Prairies
CP
CN
ÎLE SAINTE-THÉRÈSE
Montréal City Limits
Montréal-Nord
Saint-Leonard
CN
ÎLES DE BOUCHERVILLE
Montréal
MONTRÉAL
City Limits
Mount Royal
Outremont
Longueuil
St-Lawrence River
CN
ÎLE JÉSUS
CP
City Limits
Saint-Laurent
Westmount
DE
Côte St-Luc
Lachine Canal
Verdun
Lachine
Bassin de Laprairie

Lower map (1 : 65 000)

NORTH
U. de Montréal
Oratoire St-Joseph
Parc du Mont-Royal
Synagogue Shaar Hashomayim
Séminaire de Montréal
St Andrew and St Paul
McGill U.
Musée des Beaux Arts
Concordia U.
Musée McCord
Forum
Christ Church Cathedral
Place Ville-Marie
Place des Arts
U. du Québec
Cathédrale Marie-Reine-du-Monde
St-Patrick
Place Victoria
Église Notre-Dame
Canal de Lachine
Pont de la Concorde
Musée D'art Contemporain
Pont Jacques Cartier
Terre des Hommes
ÎLE STE-HÉLÈNE
La Ronde
ÎLE NOTRE-DAME
Grand Prix Formule 1
St Denis
Parc Lafontaine
Sherbrooke
Parc Maisonneuve
Jardin Botanique
Arena Maurice Richard
Stade Olympique
Château Dufresne: Musée des Arts Decoratifs
Vieux Montréal
Saint Lawrence River
Fleuve Saint-Laurent

0 1 2km
1 : 65 000

Aerial view of Montréal, showing Île Ste-Hélène and the Jacques Cartier Bridge across the St Lawrence R in the foreground (*courtesy SSC Photocentre/photo by Michel Gagné*).

The periods of most rapid growth coincided with the arrival of large numbers of immigrants. The most significant growth, however, was a result of internal migration. British living in Québec rural areas returned to the city, as did an even more significant number of French Canadians. After the war, natural growth was also a major contributing factor. In 1981 natives of other countries accounted for 16% of the metropolitan area population. Most Montréalers are natives of the province. After Paris, Montréal has long been described as the largest French-speaking city in the world.

During the greater part of the 19th century, 98% of Montréal's population was of French or British descent. The British were in the majority 1831-67; the French Canadians then regained first place and have since held this position. At the turn of the century, contingents of JEWS from eastern Europe began to arrive, commencing the process of ethnic diversification which accelerated during the 20th century. By 1981 French Canadians formed 66% of the CMA population; the British formed 11%; and other ethnic groups formed 20%. The major ones are ITALIAN or Jewish groups, but many different ethnic groups are represented in Montréal. Some of them (GERMANS, POLES, UKRAINIANS, DUTCH) have been in Montréal longer than others. Groups from Southern Europe (GREEKS and PORTUGUESE), Asia and the West Indies arrived since the late 1950s. In addition to these groups, 3% of the population is listed as being of multiple ethnic origin.

Economy and Labour After having an economy based on the fur trade for 150 years, Montréal evolved into a diversified commercial metropolis, focusing on both international trade in basic products and on the distribution of manufactured goods. From the mid-19th century, industry played a growing role, and in the 20th century the services sector expanded with the rise of financial institutions, universities, engineering firms, etc. Today, trade, industry and services are the main economic activities.

Since the 1960s significant industrial decentralization was directed towards the suburbs, but the industrial sector remains important in Montréal. The principal manufacturing industries include food and beverages, clothing, metal products, transportation materials and equipment, and chemical products. Automation brought a drop in manufacturing employment. In 1986, Statistics Canada estimated that only 20.7% of employable workers in the metropolitan area were directly involved in manufacturing. Administrative work and management functions employed 31.4%, the services sector 34.6%.

Transportation Montréal has long been a key seaport in eastern N America. Before the opening of the ST LAWRENCE SEAWAY in 1959, all goods destined for or coming from the Great Lakes had to be transshipped at Montréal. The constant improvement of navigation above and below the city began with the construction of the Lachine Canal (1825) and the deepening of the channel between Montréal and Québec (1851). Port facilities now extend over 24 km and include 117 berths, which accommodated more than 3000 ships in 1984. Long a major Canadian grain-exporting centre, Montréal's port has 4 grain elevators with a total capacity of 550 000 t. In recent years the handling of containers has played an increasing role, and 5 terminals have been equipped for this purpose.

Montréal is also closely associated with the history of Canadian railways. The hub of the great transcontinental systems, it is at the head of major lines running S into the US. Canada's main railway companies, CN and CP, have their headquarters here, as does Air Canada. Montréal's 2 international airports are Dorval for Canadian and American domestic flights, and Mirabel for international flights. Saint-Hubert airport is used mainly by private and military aircraft. Interconnecting expressways, built mostly in the 1960s, crisscross the city and connect with numerous intercity highways. The public bus and subway systems are under the jurisdiction of the Société de transport de la communauté urbaine de Montréal. The Montréal Métro, inaugurated in 1966, glides quietly underground on rubber tires. Successive extensions brought its length in 1988 to 62 km and the number of stations to 65.

Government and Politics Montréal was first granted its charter in 1832. From 1796 municipal affairs had been administered by magistrates not accountable to citizens for their actions. In 1836, with the provincial legislature out of session because of political unrest in Lower Canada, the city charter was not renewed, and the magistrates resumed their role. The city was granted a new charter in 1840. In 1851 election of the mayor was extended to the people, though only property owners and certain tenants had this privilege. In its first decades the council resembled a private club for important Montréal businessmen.

In the late 19th century, poor administration and corruption at city hall led some businessmen to form reformist groups. After a public inquiry, the provincial government created a Board of Control (4 elected members), limiting councillors' responsibilities in the general administration. Financial difficulties led the Québec government in 1918 to set up a 5-member administrative commission, with full powers to put the city back on its feet. In 1921 city council regained its powers, and in 1940 it was reformed: one-third of the 99 councillors were elected by property owners, another third by property owners and tenants, and one-third were appointed by public bodies such as the Chamber of Commerce and the universities. The last category was abolished in 1960, and it was not until 1970 that the councillors and mayor were elected by universal suffrage.

In the 20th century, Montréal politics have been dominated by populist mayors who have held office for several terms: Médéric Martin (1914-24, 1926-28); Camillien HOUDE (1928-32, 1934-36, 1938-40, 1944-54), nicknamed "Mr Montréal," and Jean Drapeau (1954-57 and 1960-86). Drapeau's Parti civique de Montréal (fd 1960) transformed civic political customs, until then practised by somewhat lax interest groups and numerous independent councillors. The Parti civique has held the majority of seats on council, lending cohesion and continuity to the city administration. During the 1970s citizens' committees, trade-union militants and progressive associations combined forces in opposition. The Montréal Citizens Movement challenged the Parti civique and finally won the election of 1986 under the leadership of Jean Dore. Mayor Drapeau was known for his grandiose projects. A veritable commercial traveller, he promoted the image of Montréal throughout the world. The soaring cost of the 1976 Olympic facilities tarnished his image for some and brought a halt to such lavish spending. During the last few years of his mandate, the city administration concentrated more on the quality of urban life and the environment.

Montréal and the suburban cities have long disputed the sharing of costs and responsibilities for urban development. Since 1970 all municipalities on the island have been represented in the Montréal Urban Community, a public association with island-wide responsibilities, including police protection, urban planning, sewage treatment services and antipollution activities. Representatives of Montréal proper have a majority of seats on council and on the Urban Community executive.

Cultural Life The presence of a strong francophone population gives Montréal a distinctive character among large N American cities. It is the main centre of expression and diffusion of the French Canadian culture, as well as the meeting place between the French and American cultures. The anglophone minority also has its particular cultural institutions here.

Montréal is an important university centre, with 2 French-speaking universities – UNIVERSITÉ DE MONTRÉAL and UNIVERSITÉ DU QUÉBEC à Montréal – and 2 English-speaking universities – MCGILL and CONCORDIA. The Québec National Library, located here, has copies of all works published in the province. The municipal library has an important collection of Canadiana (Salle Gagnon). The MUSÉE DES BEAUX-ARTS (museum of fine arts), established over a century ago, contains a general collection; the MUSÉE D'ART CONTEMPORAIN collects the works of 20th-century artists. The

Place des Arts, Montréal (*photo by Bill Brooks/Masterfile*).

McCord Museum specializes in ethnology and the history of Canada. The centre for performing arts is PLACE DES ARTS (with 3 concert halls), where the ORCHESTRE SYMPHONIQUE DE MONTRÉAL performs. There are also a number of theatre companies in the city.

The MONTREAL CANADIENS are the city's most famous professional sports team. They have won the STANLEY CUP more often than any other team and are one of sport's most enduring dynasties. The MONTREAL EXPOS play in the National Baseball League and the MONTREAL ALOUETTES played in the CFL until 1987. The city hosts the annual Canadian Grand Prix, Formula 1, automobile race. Montréal is also a centre for international competitions in amateur sports, the most famous held so far being the 1976 Summer Olympics. The Montréal International Marathon is run annually in Sept.   PAUL-ANDRÉ LINTEAU

Montreal Alouettes, FOOTBALL team. Founded in 1868, the Montreal Football Club was Canada's first organized football team. A later merger with the Montreal Amateur Athletic Assn produced the MAAA Winged Wheelers, who competed in the Big Four (Interprovincial Rugby Union) until 1936 – defeating Regina in the 1931 GREY CUP. In 1946 Lew Hayman established the Montreal Alouettes. They won the 1949 Grey Cup (defeating the CALGARY STAMPEDERS) and, led by quarterback Sam ETCHEVERRY, made 3 successive Grey Cup appearances (all losses to the EDMONTON ESKIMOS) from 1954 to 1956. Etcheverry finally won his Grey Cup in the 1970 game, coaching the Alouettes to victory over Calgary. They faced Edmonton in the final in 1974, 1975 and 1977-1979, winning Grey Cups in 1974 and 1977 under Marv Levy. In 1977 the Alouettes moved into Montréal's Olympic Stadium (58 367 seats) and enjoyed several years success. In 1981 Vancouver entrepreneur Nelson Skalbania purchased the team, brought in several high-priced American players and the following year declared the team bankrupt. It was bought by Charles Bronfman and the name was changed to Concordes, but it continued to lose millions of dollars. It was turned over to former Eskimo general manager Norm Kimball in 1987. The name reverted to Alouettes again, but the team was disbanded before the season began.   WILLIAM HUMBER

Montreal and Lachine Railroad began operations 19 Nov 1847 between Bonaventure Station in Montréal and the St Lawrence R. Built to bypass the LACHINE rapids, it was 12 km long. The railway merged with the Lake St Louis and Province Railway in 1850, taking the name Montreal and New York Railroad. In 1857 it amalgamated with the CHAMPLAIN AND SAINT LAWRENCE RAILROAD under the name Montreal and Champlain Railroad. It was eventually absorbed by the GRAND TRUNK RAILWAY.   JAMES MARSH

Montreal Canadiens, one of the 4 teams that formed the NATIONAL HOCKEY LEAGUE in 1917. The original franchise was granted to J. Ambrose O'Brien in 1909 and the team played its first game 5 Jan 1910. The team was officially named Le Club athlétique canadien in 1911 and was composed entirely of francophone players until the 1912-13 season. Led by Newsy LALONDE, Jack Laviolette and goalie Georges VÉZINA, the Canadiens won their first STANLEY CUP 1915-16. The team early on established its reputation for flair, speed and offensive power; in addition to Joe MALONE and Aurèle JOLIAT, it had in Howie MORENZ the most exciting player of the 1920s and 1930s. The Canadiens won the Stanley Cup 1923-24, 1929-30 and 1930-31, but not again until 1943-44 and 1945-46 when the explosive Maurice RICHARD, goalie Bill DURNAN, Toe BLAKE and Elmer Lach joined the team. The victory in 1952-53 marked the seventh in the Canadiens' history to that point, and in 1955-56 the team began an era of success unmatched in the history of professional hockey. The team won 5 straight Stanley Cups to 1959-60, 4 out of 5 from 1964-65 to 1968-69, again in 1970-71 and 1972-73, and another 4 straight 1975-76 to 1978-79 – an amazing record of 15 Stanley Cups in 24 years. In the same 24-year span, the team finished first in its division 17 times. Individual stars of the period, including Jacques PLANTE, Doug HARVEY, Jean BELIVEAU, Bernie GEOFFRION, Henri RICHARD, Ken DRYDEN, Larry ROBINSON, Jacques Lemaire, Guy Lapointe, Serge Savard and Guy LAFLEUR, amassed an impressive array of individual awards, including the VÉZINA TROPHY (14 times), JAMES NORRIS TROPHY (9 times), ART ROSS TROPHY (8 times) and HART TROPHY (6 times).

The Canadiens moved into the Montreal Forum in 1924 (rebuilt in 1968 at a cost of $10 million) and are currently owned by Brasserie Molson du Canada Ltée. Throughout its history the Canadiens have been a symbol of pride and excellence for the sporting public of Québec, although they now share the avid hockey fans of Québec with QUEBEC NORDIQUES. The Canadiens won their 23rd Stanley Cup in the 1985-86 season, setting a new record for professional sports championships.   JAMES MARSH

Montreal Expos The first Canadian team admitted to BASEBALL's National League, the Expos began play in 1969 at Jarry Park in Montréal's north end. The team's principal owner, Charles Bronfman, hired John McHale to oversee the club's operation. The Expos moved to Olympic Stadium in 1977, and in 1979 achieved their first winning season with a record of 96-65, finishing 2 games behind the Pittsburgh Pirates. Memorable moments in the team's history include Bill Stoneman's "no-hitters" in 1969 and 1972, the Expos winning the National League's Eastern division pennant in 1981, and the selection of Gary Carter, Andre Dawson, Al Oliver, Tim Raines and Steve Rogers to play in both the 1982 and 1983 All-Star games. Between 1979 and 1983 the Expos attracted over 2 million fans annually, except for the strike-shortened 1981 season, and in that 5-year period earned the best overall winning percentage (.548) in the National League. The team remained competitive in the mid- and late 1980s, finishing only 4 games out of first place in 1987.   WILLIAM HUMBER

Montreal International Competition/Concours International de Montréal, annual music competition held in Montréal for outstanding young musicians from around the world. The organization was incorporated in 1963 with Wilfrid PELLETIER as honorary president and the first competition was held in 1965. Alternating among piano, violin and voice, each competition is restricted to performers 16-30 years of age (piano and violin) and 20-35 (voice). There are 2 preliminary rounds and a final round in which the ORCHESTRE SYMPHONIQUE DE MONTRÉAL often takes part. The rigorous admission standards and the high quality of its juries have made the competition one of the most prestigious in the world. The prize money ($10 000 first prize) and opportunities for performances with leading Canadian orchestras have attracted superb young musicians. Among contestants who have gone on to highly successful careers are Gidón Kremer (2nd, violin, 1969), Ivo Pogorelic (1st, piano, 1980) and Sandra Graham (2nd, voice, 1985). A special prize is awarded to the best interpreter of a new work by a Canadian composer, especially commissioned for the competition. *See also* MUSIC AWARDS AND COMPETITIONS.

Montréal Riots, the most spectacular moment of which was the burning of the Parliament building on 25 Apr 1849, occurred during a serious

The Burning of Parliament (1849), painting attributed to Joseph Légaré. It is thought that rioters, furious at the passing of the Rebellion Losses Bill, broke the gas mains and that the resulting leak led to the flames (*courtesy McCord Museum/McGill University*).

economic and political crisis in the Province of Canada. After 1848 the Reformers had formed the government; relegated to the Opposition, the Tories, who were largely Anglophones and supported British rule and economic links with Britain, felt threatened by the French Canadian influence in government. Resentment was felt most keenly in Montréal, the capital city, where the population was half English speaking, half French speaking.

In Feb and Mar 1849 when the LAFONTAINE-BALDWIN ministry passed the REBELLION LOSSES BILL, the opposition violently denounced the Act. On Apr 25, at the Tories' instigation, crowds of protesters opposed Gov Gen Lord ELGIN's sanction of this law; they threw stones and rotten eggs at his carriage. That evening, public protest turned into a riot: the mob invaded Parliament and set fire to the building. The riots involved thousands of people, lasted 2 days and included attacks on the private property of several Reform leaders, including LaFontaine and HINCKS. But Lord Elgin's endorsement of the majority decision in Parliament – in effect an affirmation of RESPONSIBLE GOVERNMENT – won the approval of most of the people and of the British government. Less than a month after the riots, however, it was decided that the seat of government should no longer be Montréal, which was considered too susceptible to ethnic tensions.   JEAN-PAUL BERNARD

Montreal Standard began as a Saturday newspaper in 1905, an attempt to create a Canadian version of the *Illustrated London News*. The initial object was to provide a serious yet lively look at the week's events through photographs and news stories. During WWI in particular, and to a lesser extent during WWII, this format was both popular and successful. Over time, the *Standard* became less news oriented and more a feature-filled weekly, with comics, recipes and fiction jostling for space with advertising and illustrations. The original broadsheet format changed to tabloid size, but by the beginning of the 1950s *Montreal Standard* seemed out of date. In 1951 its publishers conceived the idea of WEEKEND MAGAZINE, and the *Standard*'s staff was absorbed into the new periodical. *See also* NEWSPAPERS.   J.L. GRANATSTEIN

Montreal Symphony Orchestra, *see* ORCHESTRE SYMPHONIQUE DE MONTRÉAL.

Montrose, BC, Village, pop 1183 (1986c), 1245 (1981c), inc 1956, located in the W Kootenay district of southeastern BC. It is situated on a wide bench along Beaver Cr, just E of the creek's junction with the Columbia R, about 5 km SE of the smelter city of TRAIL. The village was named by Trail lawyer A.G. Cameron after his hometown in Scotland.   JOHN STEWART

Monts, Pierre Du Gua de, explorer, trader, colonizer (b at Saintonge, France c1558; d in France 1628). A founder of the earliest permanent French settlements in N America and a close associate of Samuel de CHAMPLAIN, de Monts exerted great influence during the first 2 decades of the 17th century. His first visit to Canada was probably made in 1600 with Pierre Chauvin de Tonnetuit, and in 1603 he received royal patents for the colonization, commercial exploitation and government of Acadia. In 1604 he established a settlement on the Île Ste-Croix (Dochet I). Forced by climate and disease to move to PORT-ROYAL in 1605, the colony survived and prospered until the revocation of de Monts's fur-trading monopoly in 1607 forced its temporary abandonment. By then de Monts had returned to France and turned his attention to the St Lawrence Valley. Although he never visited N America again, he sent Champlain to found a trading post at Québec in 1608, thus playing a leading role in establishing it as a con-

tinuing French settlement. De Monts pursued his commercial interests in Canada until 1617, when he retired to the Ardennes.   JOHN G. REID

Monument A monument is normally a free-standing, large-scale structure, often artistically embellished, which has as its primary function the commemoration of persons, events or concepts believed to have sufficient importance to merit a public, visible and permanent tribute.

Pre-Confederation Prior to Confederation, 1867, only a small number of major public monuments were erected. The majority of these were dedicated either to monarchs (Louis XIV at Québec City in 1686, and George III at Montréal in 1773), or to military heroes, such as the column dedicated to Lord Nelson (Montréal, 1809), the obelisk jointly commemorating WOLFE and MONTCALM (Québec City, 1828), and the imposing memorial to Sir Isaac BROCK (Queenston Heights, UC, first built c1830). Not all, however, have survived intact: the monument to George III, for example, was apparently deliberately destroyed c1775. The first monument to Brock was tampered with twice by saboteurs linked to the Rebellions of 1837, the second time seriously: the damage done to the monument in 1840 by an explosive device led to its eventual rebuilding in 1853.

Confederation to Centennial (1867-1967) In the 100 years following Confederation, the focus of the monument shifted still further toward the commemoration of specific persons, especially those who had shaped both the political and the cultural history of Canada. In cities across the country, as well as in the federal and provincial capitals, monuments were erected to such diverse figures as early explorers and prime ministers, pioneer settlers and provincial premiers, and outstanding citizens from varying walks of life. Along with this change of focus came a change of format: the predominantly architectural monuments of the pre-Confederation era gradually ceded place (though never entirely) to bronze statuary, while professionally trained sculptors, increasingly Canadian-born, gradually supplanted the military officers, engineers and architects who had designed the earlier memorials. An attempt was even made to create a Canadian version of the Statue of Liberty: when plans for a colossal "Angel of Welcome and Peace" at Québec C failed, the federal government erected instead an imposing monument of Madeleine de Verchères at Verchères, Qué, intended both to greet and to inspire new immigrants to Canada as they arrived by the St Lawrence River.

The War Memorial By far the most ubiquitous monument in Canada is the memorial dedicated to the war dead of WWI. Although monuments had been erected earlier to the North-West Rebellion and the South African War, they were often elaborate in design and few in number, while after WWII peacetime facilities for the living, such as memorial arenas, were often preferred as tributes. (One of the notable exceptions is the Ottawa Memorial, erected by the Commonwealth War Graves Commission in memory of the airmen who died in WWII, and for whom there is no known grave.) In contrast, the memorials erected in cities and towns across Canada to the fallen of WWI are both more numerous and more widely varied in form. They range from a simple cairn or cut-stone cenotaph to memorial arches, gates and towers, and from memorial avenues of trees to winged female figures extending laurel wreaths of victory to the uniformed soldiers below. The most common memorial, however, is that of the single soldier of bronze or stone, often sited near the railway station from which so many young men left.

Brock's monument, Queenston Heights, commemorating the battle in which Sir Isaac Brock was killed (*courtesy Environment Canada, Parks*).

The first Brock's monument, Queenston, UC, c1830 (*courtesy National Archives of Canada/C-12618*).

The Monument in Transition (1967 to the present) While some traditional monuments were still erected during the 1960s and 1970s, such as the statues of Louis St. Laurent in Ottawa and Queen Elizabeth II in Winnipeg, there was a greater tendency to innovate with both style and meaning. On occasion, the more experimental artistic

Monument to Sir Arthur Doughty, Dominion archivist, Ottawa (*courtesy National Capital Commission/photo by T. Atkinson*).

Sir John A. Macdonald monument, Ottawa (*courtesy National Capital Commission/photo by T. Atkinson*).

styles then being used in much PUBLIC ART and outdoor SCULPTURE were adapted to commemorative purposes (with varying degrees of public acceptance), as in the monuments to Louis RIEL in Regina and Winnipeg, or in the series of special markers erected by Environment Canada, Parks to such figures as Vilhjalmur STEFANSSON (Arnes, Man), the Rt Hon Alexander MACKENZIE (Sarnia, Ont) or Captain George VANCOUVER (Vancouver). In other instances, a new type of monument flourished: while large in scale and symbolic in purpose, they are usually brightly coloured, have easily identifiable motifs, and are made of unusual materials (examples would include the Pysanka at Vegreville, Alta, and the Canada Goose at Wawa, Ont). In the 1980s, however, another trend emerged, with the erection of such monuments as the Guelph fountain

Nelson's monument, Jacques Cartier Square, photo taken in 1914 (*courtesy Notman Photographic Archives*).

in honour of "The Family" or the Ottawa portrait statues of John DIEFENBAKER and Terry FOX. Many Canadian communities expressed their desire to honour traditional values once again in traditional ways. *See also* HISTORIC SITE.

TERRY G. GUERNSEY

Reading: M. Baker, *Symbol in Stone, Manitoba's Third Legislative Building* (1986); F. Bayer, *The Ontario Collection* (1984); Canada, NCC, *Statues of Parliament Hill* (1986); H.F. Wood and J. Swettenham, *Silent Witnesses* (1974); Québec, Assemblé nationale, *L'Hôtel du parlement* (1986).

Moodie, Susanna, nee Strickland, author, settler (b at Bungay, Eng 6 Dec 1803; d at Toronto 8 Apr 1885). Susanna was the youngest in a literary family of whom Catharine Parr TRAILL and Samuel Strickland are best known in Canada. Her struggles as a settler, progressive ideas, attachment to the "best" of contemporary British values, suspicion of "yankee" influence in Canada, and her increasingly highly regarded book, ROUGHING IT IN THE BUSH, have made her a legendary figure in Canada.

From comfortable beginnings Susanna and her sisters became precociously engaged in writing, partly for economic reasons, after their father's death in 1818. They produced work for children, for gift books and for ladies' periodicals. Susanna wrote sketches of Suffolk life for *La Belle Assemblée* 1827-28, prefiguring the style and method of her later, best-known book. She moved to London in 1831, where she continued an association begun earlier with the Anti-Slavery Soc, meeting her future husband, John Wedderburn Dunbar Moodie, at the home of the society's secretary. For the society she wrote 2 antislavery tracts, *The History of Mary Prince, a West Indian Slave* (1831) and *Negro Slavery Described by a Negro* (1831), establishing her humanitarianism and sensitivity to the range of character and moral outlook among "respectable" people. *Enthusiasm: and Other Poems* (1831) also reveals a writer engaged in serious ideas. After her marriage in 1831, she and her husband emigrated with their first child (of 6) in July 1832 largely for financial reasons – Dunbar Moodie being a half-pay officer and Mrs Moodie being without wealth. Arriving in the Cobourg area of Upper Canada, they attempted to farm in 2 different locations over the next 7 years. Unsuccessful, they removed to Belleville in 1840 after Dunbar Moodie was appointed sheriff of Victoria Dist. Emigration and the pioneering years, however, provided Mrs Moodie with material for the *Literary Garland* (Montréal) – material later incorporated in *Roughing It* and drawn upon for her novel *Flora Lyndsay*.

In Belleville Mrs Moodie wrote and published a good deal, much of her output romantic fiction set outside Canada. During 1847-48 she and her husband edited and wrote for the *Victoria Magazine*, intending to supply good literature for the mechanic class – skilled and semiskilled workers. She published *Roughing It in the Bush* in 1852, *Life in the Clearings* in 1853 and *Flora Lyndsay* in 1854 – all 3 concerned with Canada. It is often (incorrectly) remarked that she wrote documentary realism for the British market and romantic adventure for the Canadian market. In fact, she published both in both countries and in the US, but England provided her with more opportunity to publish than Canada did.

Roughing It in the Bush is her best-known and best work. It combines her steadfast moral vision, her fascination with differences in character, a willingness to reveal personal weakness and inexperience, considerable psychological insight and a generous measure of wit and playfulness. Together with its sequel, *Life in the Clearings*, it has formed the basis of her reputation.

Louis Riel monument, Regina (*courtesy Government of Saskatchewan*).

Mrs Moodie lived in or near Belleville until the death of her husband in 1869, from which time she lived chiefly in Toronto until her own death.

R.D. MATHEWS

Moody, Richard Clement, royal engineer (b in Barbados, British W Indies 13 Feb 1813; d at Bournemouth, England 31 Mar 1887). Educated at the Royal Military Academy at Woolwich, Eng, he obtained a commission in the Corps of Royal Engineers and was posted to St Vincent, W Indies (1831); served as the first governor of the Falkland Is (1841-49); commanded the Royal Engineers at Newcastle upon Tyne and served in Malta where he was promoted lt-col (1855). He was appointed commander of the British Columbia Detachment, Royal Engineers, in 1858 and chief commissioner of lands and works and lt-gov of the new crown colony of British Columbia in 1859. The Royal Engineers, established for

Susanna Moodie author of the classic *Roughing It in the Bush*, published 1852 (*courtesy National Archives of Canada/C-7043*).

military, practical and scientific purposes, policed the goldfields in the interior, surveyed townsites, constructed roads and selected New Westminster as the colony's first capital. In 1863, the Royal Engineers were disbanded and Moody returned to England. DENNIS F.K. MADILL

Moon, natural satellite of Earth, with a mean diameter of 3476 km and a mass of 7.28 x 10^{22} kg (1.23% of Earth's mass). Three moons of Jupiter and one of Saturn are larger; the planet Pluto is smaller. The moon's mean distance from Earth is 384 500 km in an orbit that requires 29.5306 days from one New Moon to the next. The moon shines only by reflected sunlight, appearing as a crescent when it is within 90° of the sun. Except near New Moon, it is second only to the sun in brightness. Tidal effects of Earth have forced the moon's rotation to match its (the moon's) orbital period; hence, one side of the moon always faces Earth and only 59% of its surface is visible. Because it is so close, the moon's influence exceeds the sun's as the cause of TIDES on Earth. The moon has been important in religion and art from earliest times and was the basis of the lunar calendar.

The dark grey lunar surface reflects only 7% of the sunlight it receives (comparable to the reflectivity of black soil). The moon is dominated by thousands of craters, ranging from microscopic pits to gigantic Clavius, diameter 230 km. Water appears to be absent from the moon and the maria (lunar seas) are large lava-flooded craters. Maria and almost all small craters are now known to have been formed by the impact of meteorites (or COMETS) and the mountain chains surrounding some maria are parts of the craters' rim structures. Other surface features include rilles, long cracks or valleys which are typically 100 km long, 1-3 km wide and several hundred metres deep. Rilles are interpreted as tension cracks resulting from the cooling of surface layers. Crater chains consist of small craters (normally along a rille) caused by venting of gas from the interior.

For most people the highlight of the space program was the landing of Apollo 11 ASTRONAUTS on the moon on 20 July 1969. The landing followed a series of unmanned missions by the US and the USSR which provided close-ups of the moon's surface, including pictures of the far side, which is also covered with craters but is deficient in maria. Six American landings and several Soviet probes returned lunar soil and rocks for intensive study. The landings confirmed the absence of both a lunar atmosphere and a magnetic field; chemical studies of the rocks showed that the moon contains less metal than Earth and is deficient in volatile material. The formation ages of the rocks are between 3.1 and 4.42 billion years, which accord with current estimates of the age of the solar system (nearly 4.6 billion years). The maria were flooded 3.1-3.8 billion years ago, filling pre-existing impact basins with younger rocks. Records from seismic instruments left on the moon indicate a small core with an outer fluid layer, surrounded by a mantle and crust.

Historically, there are 3 main theories of the moon's origin: it was split off from Earth, shortly after Earth's formation (fission theory); it resulted from the capture by Earth of one or more bodies that had formed elsewhere in the solar system; Earth and moon were assembled in the same region as a double planet. A new theory has developed close to 2 decades after the return of lunar samples. Known as the large impactor hypothesis, it suggests that the moon formed early in solar system history as the result of a collision between the Earth and another object of mass at least one-tenth of Earth's. In this theory the moon is composed mainly of material from the impactor, heated by the collision, and the theory appears to

Dora Mavor Moore visiting a class of young students at the New Play Society school, Toronto, 1957 (*courtesy National Archives of Canada/PA-137084/Walter Curtin*).

explain dynamical peculiarities of the Earth-moon system as well as chemical anomalies revealed by study of moon rocks.

Although lunar research has not been a major activity of Canadian scientists, several important contributions have occurred. An extensive program of impact-crater studies initiated by C.S. BEALS at the Dominion Observatory, Ottawa, involved analysis of both lunar and terrestrial craters. In his later years, Beals studied the relative ages of some lava surfaces by counting the frequencies of small craters on photographs obtained from lunar orbit. Geological studies of moon rocks were conducted in government laboratories in Ottawa and the evidence for ancient lunar magnetic fields was found by David W. Strangway (currently at UBC) while working in the US. Lunar craters are normally named after deceased scientists, and 10 Canadians are among those honoured in this fashion: Oswald T. Avery, Sir Frederick BANTING, C.S. Beals, C.A. CHANT, Reginald Alworth Daly, J.S. FOSTER, F.S. HOGG, Andrew MCKELLAR, R.M. PETRIE and J.S. PLASKETT.
IAN HALLIDAY

Moore, Brian, writer, journalist (b at Belfast, N Ire 25 Aug 1921). Twice winner of the Gov Gen's Award for fiction, he is one of the most accomplished and innovative of 20th-century novelists, giving a painstaking, ironically humorous portrayal of characters at the point of change. In the earlier, "Irish" novels, eg, *The Lonely Passion of Judith Hearne* (1955) and *The Feast of Lupercal* (1957), his forlorn characters struggle in vain to break from their environments. Each of his novels explores the confrontation of past and present on different terms and from the perspective of individually realized characters and examines the consciousness of characters who conjure into fictional reality apparitions from the past. His later works include *The Luck of Ginger Coffey* (1960, Gov Gen's Award), *Catholics* (1972), *The Great Victorian Collection* (1975, Gov Gen's Award), *The Mangan Inheritance* (1979) and *The Color of Blood* (1987). He also wrote *The Revolution Script* (on the kidnapping of James Cross by the FLQ in Oct 1970) and the film script of Alfred Hitchcock's *Torn Curtain*. He lived in Canada 1948-58 and now resides in California, maintaining his Canadian citizenship. GERALD LYNCH

Reading: H. Dahlie, *Brian Moore* (1969); J. Flood, *Brian Moore* (1974).

Moore, Dora Mavor, actress, teacher (b at Glasgow, Scot 8 Apr 1888; d at Toronto 15 May 1979). After studying elocution at Toronto's Margaret Eaton School of Expression, she became the first Canadian to graduate from London's Royal Academy of Dramatic Art. She made her professional debut in 1912 in Ottawa, with the Colonial Stock Co, and then joined Ben Greet's Pastoral Players in New York, performing Shakespeare on their CHAUTAUQUA tours. She was with Greet again in 1918, playing Viola in *Twelfth Night* at London's "Old Vic." Returning to Toronto to raise 3 sons, she plunged into teaching and directing amateurs. In 1938 she founded the Village Players which toured Shakespeare to schools. It was the prototype for her nonprofit, professional New Play Society which played 10 seasons (1946-56) and produced 72 plays, 47 of which were original. As well as its annual satiric revue *Spring Thaw*, which delighted audiences for 25 years (1948-73), the NPS ran a theatre school (1950-68) which survived the demise of the producing company. Moore was instrumental in bringing Tyrone GUTHRIE to the STRATFORD FESTIVAL. Toronto's annual theatre awards have been named in her honour. DAVID GARDNER

Moore, Keith Leon, anatomist (b at Brantford, Ont 5 Oct 1925). Educated at Western (PhD, 1954), he joined the staff at U of Man in 1956. In 1965 he became professor of anatomy and head of the department there and in 1976 assumed the same positions at U of T, and later became associate dean, Faculty of Medicine at U of T. Internationally recognized for his research in genetics, embryology and teratology, he has served as president of the Canadian Assn of Anatomists and as chairman of the board of the Canadian Federation of Biological Societies. Among the widely adopted textbooks he has written are *The Developing Human* (1973, 3rd ed 1982), *Before We Are Born* (1974, 2nd ed 1983) and *Clinically Oriented Anatomy* (1980). A fellow of the International Academy of Cytology and of the Royal Soc of Medicine, he has received awards both for his publications and teaching, including the 1984 J.C.B. Grant Award of the Canadian Assn of Anatomists.
T.V.N. PERSAUD

Moore, James Mavor, actor, playwright, producer, professor, public servant (b at Toronto 8 Mar 1919), son of Dora Mavor MOORE. An artistic polymath, Mavor Moore was born into a distinguished academic and theatrical family. Educated at the U of T schools, he graduated from U of T in 1941. He became a feature producer for CBC radio and after serving in army intelligence during WWII, returned to the CBC as chief producer for the new International Service and briefly for the Pacific Region in Vancouver. In 1946 he returned to Toronto where he helped launch the New Play Society, seedbed of Canada's postwar professional theatre. During the same period he served as a writer, director or producer for UN radio and TV in New York. In 1950 he became chief producer of television for the CBC, a post he held until 1954, all the while continuing his own theatrical writing and composing. He is perhaps best known for the annual revue *Spring Thaw* (est 1948), which he produced to 1966, and for his opera librettos (including that for Harry SOMERS's opera *Louis Riel*). Moore began to teach at York in 1970 and served the Canada Council as chairman through difficult financial and political times from 1979 to 1983, when he was succeeded by Maureen FORRESTER. He continued to write a column for the *Globe and Mail* on cultural matters. In 1986 he was awarded the Molson Prize.   J.L. GRANATSTEIN

Moore, Thomas Albert, Methodist minister, moderator of United Church of Canada (b at Acton, Canada W 29 June 1860; d at Toronto 31 Mar 1940). After his ordination in 1884, Moore served several Ontario congregations before becoming secretary of the General Conference of the Methodist Church 1906-25 and secretary of the General Council of the United Church 1925-36. A member of the Methodist Church's union committee, he was elected moderator of the UNITED CHURCH OF CANADA in 1932. Moore's managerial skills and evangelistic enthusiasm made him a leader in the fight for social improvement. An honoured and respected spokesman for religious and secular institutions, he toured and preached for religious renewal and moral reform.
   NEIL SEMPLE

Moore, Tom, carpenter, trade-union leader (b at Leeds, Eng 1878; d at Ottawa 6 July 1943). Arriving in Canada in 1909, Moore practised his trade in Niagara Falls, Ont, and served in the carpenters' union as both local official and general organizer for eastern Canada 1911-18. In 1918 he was elected president of the TRADES AND LABOR CONGRESS OF CANADA at the head of a slate that opposed radical tendencies in the Canadian labour movement, especially those in western Canada that would form the ONE BIG UNION the next year. He held that office until 1935 and again 1938-43. He served on royal commissions on industrial relations in 1919 and on employment and social insurance in the 1930s. His position also won him a seat at the Int Labour Organization in the 1920s and at other international labour conferences.
   CRAIG HERON

Moores, Frank Duff, merchant, politician, 2nd premier of Newfoundland 1972-79 (b at Carbonear, Nfld 18 Feb 1933). In 1968 Moores won the federal seat of Bonavista-Trinity-Conception for the Progressive Conservative Party and in 1970 became the leader of the Newfoundland PC Party. The Oct 1971 election ended in a near tie between the Liberals and Conservatives. In Jan 1972, when Liberal Prem SMALLWOOD resigned, Moores was asked to form a new government. He went on to win the 1972 and 1975 elections. In contrast to Premier Smallwood, who followed policies of centralization and industrialization, Moores emphasized rural development and re-source control. In 1979 he retired from politics to re-enter private business. In 1983 he was a prominent organizer of the successful PC leadership campaign of Brian MULRONEY and served in Ottawa as adviser to Mulroney when he became PM. In 1987 Moores was chairman of Government Consultants International, a large and powerful lobbying group.   MELVIN BAKER

Moose (*Alces alces*), largest living member of the DEER family (Cervidae). Cows may weigh up to 490 kg and, in Alaska, bulls may reach 600 kg. More commonly, females weigh about 350 kg, bulls about 400 kg. Moose have a black coat; long, stiltlike legs for wading through deep snow; a humped back; a long face with an overhanging upper lip, large ears and a dewlap of skin (bell) hanging from the throat. Their distribution extends from Nfld (introduced), through NS and NB, W to BC and N to Alaska. Called elk in Europe, they range across the USSR and Scandinavia. Bulls have long, horizontally spreading, palmate antlers, which begin to grow in Apr. Antlers, which remain velvet-covered until Aug and early Sept when they are used for fighting during the breeding season, Sept-Oct, are shed Dec-Feb. In breeding season, cows are vocal; hunters can attract bulls by imitating the female call. Females can breed at 16-18 months and reproduce until 18-20 years old. Calves, often twins, are born in late May and early June. Newborns are an unspotted, light red to reddish brown colour. Cows will defend young calves against both wolves and humans. Moose inhabit deciduous-coniferous forests across Canada; recently, they have extended their range beyond the treeline. In winter moose occupy forests where snow levels are reduced. They browse birch, aspen and willow twigs and, in summer, frequent lakes to eat aquatic vegetation, at times submerging completely. After forest fires, moose seek new deciduous growth in regenerating forests. They may damage young conifers by trampling saplings and browsing the growing ends. The moose population is limited by wolf predation, HUNTING and starvation of calves in deep-snow winters.   A.T. BERGERUD

Moose Factory, Ont, UP, located on an island in the Moose R, 24 km from JAMES BAY and opposite MOOSONEE. Founded (1672-73) by Charles Bayly, it was the HBC's second post and the first English settlement in what is now Ontario. Originally called Moose Fort, it was captured (1686) by the French in a daring overland attack led by de TROYES. It was returned to the HBC 1713 and trading activities resumed 1730. Among the restored buildings at this historic site is the blacksmith's shop (1740), likely the oldest wooden building in Ontario. The altar cloth and liturgical vestments at St Thomas's Anglican Church (1864) are of moosehide. The island is home to a Cree band.
   JAMES MARSH

Moose Jaw, Sask, City, pop 35 073 (1986c), 33 941 (1981c), inc 1903, is located 160 km N of the US border. The city lies in a sheltered valley at the confluence of the Moose Jaw R and Thunder Cr. The city's colourful name is likely based on Indian sources and was perhaps first applied to a local creek that supposedly resembled the outline of a moose's jawbone; another explanation is that it comes from a Cree word for "warm breezes." An agricultural service centre, it is the province's third-largest city. Moose Jaw is governed by a mayor and 10 aldermen elected at large. The city's growth was closely tied to the expansion of cereal agriculture. Though it became an important retail, wholesale and industrial centre, Moose Jaw never rivalled nearby REGINA (65 km to the E), which shared the same tributary area. Its greatest periods of growth were from 1911 to 1921 when the population increased 40%, the 1940s with an increase of 17%, and the 1950s with an increase of 36%. For decades the sprawling CPR shops and marshalling yards dominated the urban landscape and remained the lifeblood of Moose Jaw's economy. The CPR's presence was diminished in the mid-1950s with the conversion to diesel locomotives, but has recently been revived with a large repair shop. CFB Moose Jaw, first established as a training facility in 1941, is now the city's largest employer. The majority of the population is native-born and British in origin. People of German, Scandinavian and Ukrainian origin form the largest non-British elements. The 5 largest religious denominations are United Church, Roman Catholic, Anglican, Lutheran and Presbyterian.

CFB Moose Jaw, the largest jet-training base in Canada, has a military population of 4500 service, including dependents, and 350 civilian personnel. Moose Jaw is located on the Trans-Canada Hwy, the CPR main line and a branch line of the CNR, and is served by 2 bus lines. Crescent Park, in the heart of the city, is 11 ha in extent and includes the Public Library, the Art Museum and

In summer, moose frequent lakes to eat aquatic vegetation (*photo by Stephen J. Krasemann/DRK Photo*).

a swimming pool and other recreational facilities. Moose Jaw's educational facilities include the Saskatchewan Technical Institute. The city is served by one English-language TV station, a radio station and a daily newspaper, the Moose Jaw *Times-Herald*.   J. WILLIAM BRENNAN

Moose River, 80 km long, is formed by the confluence of the Mattagami and the Missinaibi rivers. About 55 km downstream, it is joined by the Abitibi R, then by the N French R, and flows NE to discharge into the bottom of JAMES BAY in northern Ontario. With its tributaries it drains most of the northeastern part of the province. Once well travelled by fur traders, the river valley today is the site of mining, pulp and paper, and hydroelectric developments. MOOSE FACTORY, Ontario's oldest trading post (est 1672-73), is located on an island in the river's mouth, opposite the mainland village of MOOSONEE, Ontario's only saltwater port. The Ontario Northland Ry links these settlements to the S.   DANIEL FRANCIS

Moosomin, Sask, Town, pop 2257 (1986c), inc 1887, is located in southeastern Saskatchewan 15 km W of the Manitoba border. When the CPR entered the North-West Territories in 1882 Moosomin quickly established itself as one of the leading towns on the prairies. Prior to the development of branch lines it served an area extending from the Qu'Appelle to the Souris rivers in southeastern Saskatchewan. The community continues as an important service and judicial centre.
                    DON HERPERGER

Moosonee, Ont, UP, pop 216 (1986c), 1433 (1981c), located on the Moose R, 25 km from JAMES BAY. The old fur-trade post, MOOSE FACTORY, lies on an island nearby. The site was chosen in 1931 as the northern terminus of the Ontario Northland Ry, which follows an old Indian canoe route along the Abitibi and Moose rivers; the railway was built in 1932. The name was derived from the Cree name for Moose River Factory, and was used in this spelling for an Anglican diocese founded 1872. Moosonee is Ontario's only saltwater port, but high hopes for its prosperity were never realized. Many of the local Indian population are employed as guides for the tourists and hunters who ride the "Polar Bear Express" from COCHRANE.   JAMES MARSH

Moraine, landform composed of an accumulation of sediment deposited by or from a GLACIER and possessing a form independent of the terrain beneath it. Moraines are composed primarily of till, an unsorted mixture of clay, silt, sand, pebbles, cobbles and boulders deposited directly from a glacier. Moraines are classified according to their form, origin and position (*see* GLACIATION). End (terminal), lateral, medial and recessional moraines, composed of ridges of till, are commonly associated with valley glaciers in mountainous areas. Well-developed examples are present on or near the Athabasca Glacier in JASPER NATIONAL PARK. The ice sheets that covered much of Canada during the ICE AGE produced end, recessional, interlobate, hummocky (knob and kettle) and cross-valley moraines in many parts of the country. Interlobate moraines, such as the Oak Ridges moraine N of Toronto, were formed be-

tween 2 advancing tongues of an ice sheet. Hummocky moraines, composed of irregularly spaced knobs and mounds of till formed by melting glaciers, cover much of the Canadian prairie. Cross-valley moraines were formed at or near the margin of a glacier terminating in a lake or ocean. Good examples are found along the shores of Hudson Bay and in Labrador.   N.W. RUTTER

Moravians, as commonly used in the English-speaking world, refers to members of the Moravian Church, formally known as the Unitas Fratrum (United Brethren). Claiming adherence to the world's oldest Protestant Church, they trace their pre-Reformation origins to the teachings of Jan Hus, who was burned at the stake by Roman Catholic persecutors in 1415. His followers, who were eventually driven underground and scattered throughout Europe, included a small group of people who moved to a remote part of Moravia and, in 1457, founded the Unitas Fratrum. In the early 18th century, Moravians established a headquarters at Herrnhut (Lord's Watch), now in E Germany. Under the guidance of a Saxon nobleman, Count Nikolaus von Zinzendorf, they embarked on a foreign mission program which eventually led them to many countries, including Canada. With financial assistance from their congregations in Britain, they established the first mission among the Inuit of N America at NAIN, Labrador, in 1771. A few decades later Moravian missionaries from the US founded an Indian mission in Upper Canada, at Fairfield on the Thames R. The Moravian Indians at Fairfield, and later New Fairfield (also called Moraviantown) were Delaware who had been earlier converted in Pennsylvania and Ohio. Although the mission at New Fairfield was transferred to the Canadian Methodist Episcopal Church in 1902, Moravian congregations are still active in Labrador. In addition, there are now 8 congregations in Alberta and one in Vancouver, consisting mostly of descendants of German-speaking emigrants from 19th-century Russia.   J. GARTH TAYLOR

Moraviantown, Battle of (sometimes called Battle of the Thames) 5 Oct 1813. Following the American naval victory under Cdr Oliver H. Perry in the battle on Lake Erie at PUT-IN-BAY on 10 Sept 1813, the entire western peninsula of Upper Canada was in danger of falling into enemy hands. Maj-Gen Henry PROCTOR, who commanded all British and Canadian forces west of Burlington, was short of supplies and decided to retreat up the River Thames. After a slow and disorderly withdrawal, he took his stand near Moraviantown. The tired and dispirited British line broke early in the battle, leaving the Indians under TECUMSEH, who was killed, to fend for themselves. To the Indians, Proctor's actions confirmed their worst fears about the lack of resolution and commitment by their longtime ally, King George III. Proctor, court-martialed and suspended from rank and pay for 6 months, never held an important command again. Fortunately for UC, the invading American army returned to Detroit before it could exploit the strategic possibilities of its victory on the Thames. *See also* WAR OF 1812.   CARL A. CHRISTIE

Morawetz, Oskar, composer (b at Svetla, Czechoslovakia 17 Jan 1917). Recognized as a leading composer from the mid-1940s when he won national awards for his first 2 compositions in 1944-45, Morawetz remains one of Canada's most frequently performed composers. He came to Canada in 1940 and studied at U of T; in composition, however, he is self-taught. Romantic by temperament, he has always avoided writing music that "cannot be felt but needs explanation con-

As recorded in the calligraphy of moraines which stripe its melting surface, the Lowell Glacier is formed at the confluence of several dozen smaller glaciers (*photo by J.A. Kraulis*).

sisting of mathematical formulas." Lyrical melody, lively rhythm, secure polyphony and innovative exploitation of instrumental colour are hallmarks of his style. Graceful works in a happy vein, such as *Carnival Overture* (1946) and *Overture to a Fairy Tale* (1956), are typical of Morawetz's early music. Among his best known and most highly regarded compositions are *Piano Concerto No 1* (premiered by Zubin Mehta with Anton KUERTI 1963), *Sinfonietta for Winds and Percussion* (selected in 1966 for the Critics Award, Cava dei Trirena, Italy), *Memorial to Martin Luther King* (solo cello and orchestra, commissioned by Mstislav Rostropovich 1968), *From the Diary of Anne Frank* (soprano and orchestra, 1970) and *Psalm 22* (voice and orchestra, premiered by Maureen Forrester 1984). Some of his shorter works have become standard repertoire internationally. In 1983 the CBC issued an anthology of his music. In 1987 he became the first composer to be awarded the Order of Ontario. By 1988 more than 120 orchestras, led by such conductors as Kurt Masur, Andrew Davis and Charles Dutoit, have performed his works.   BARCLAY McMILLAN

Morden, Man, Town, pop 5004 (1986c), 4579 (1981c), inc 1903, is located 105 km SW of Winnipeg and 20 km N of the international boundary. The area contains fossils of prehistoric wildlife and the ancient sites of Mound Builders, and has received European and Métis explorers, traders and buffalo hunters. Ontarians homesteaded here 1874; Jewish and Mennonite settlers followed. The Morden townsite – named for Alvey Morden, an early settler – was established by the CPR 1881-82, and by 1885 had a thriving business community. The region is well suited to agriculture. A federal research station at Morden is the main prairie centre for horticultural and special crops research. Morden is the major service centre for the region. It has several industries, including farm implement, clothing and kitchen products manufacturers and an epoxy plant. It is the only Canadian site of commercial production of bentonite clay.   D.M. LYON

Morel, François, composer, pianist, professor, conductor (b at Montréal 14 Mar 1926). He was one of the few composers to have received his education entirely in Québec, and he studied with, among others, Claude CHAMPAGNE and Jean PAPINEAU-COUTURE. His composing career began with *Antiphonie* (1953). With other musicians, including Serge GARANT, he presented ground-breaking concerts of contemporary music during the mid-1950s. He worked for several years for Radio-Canada as a composer of incidental music, and as musical adviser, researcher and program host. In all his work, he paid particular attention to rhythmic pulse and orchestration. In 1980 the Concours international de musique de Montréal commissioned *Melisma* from him. Morel's other works include *L'Étoile noire, Radiance, Aux marges du silence* and *L'Oiseau-demain*. In the early 1980s, he stopped writing incidental music to devote himself increasingly to conducting. He is chairman of Éditions Québec-Musique and founder and artistic director of the group Bois et cuivres du Québec. HÉLÈNE PLOUFFE

Morenz, Howarth William, Howie, hockey player (b at Mitchell, Ont 21 Sept 1902; d at Montréal 8 Mar 1937). He played junior hockey in Stratford, Ont, and joined MONTREAL CANADIENS in 1923. A swift skater, deft stickhandler and prolific scorer, he was a popular idol in Montréal. He helped stir interest in hockey in the US and was traded to Chicago Black Hawks (1934) and then New York Rangers before returning to Montréal (1936). He died as a result of injuries suffered in a game on 28 Jan 1937. His death was mourned across Canada, and thousands filed past his bier, placed dramatically at centre ice in the Montréal Forum. Morenz scored 270 goals and 467 points in 14 seasons, led the NHL in scoring in 1928 and 1931 and won the HART TROPHY (most valuable player) in 1928, 1931 and 1932. JAMES MARSH

Howie Morenz, the most exciting hockey player of his era, died as a result of complications from injuries suffered in a game (*courtesy National Archives of Canada/C-29495/Jurotsky, Toronto*).

Morgan, Henry, merchant, founder of Canada's oldest department store (b at Saline, Scot 1819; d at Montréal 12 Dec 1893). After apprenticing in a Scottish wholesale house, Morgan came to Canada 1845 and opened a dry-goods store with David Starke Smith on St Joseph Street (now Notre Dame) in Montréal. When Smith retired in 1852 Morgan was joined by his brother James and the firm became Henry Morgan & Co. By 1874 the store employed 150 clerks with each department responsible for its own management, buying and overhead expenses. The business moved several times until in 1891 it found its final location in a large new building at the top of Beaver Hall Hill on St Catherine Street – a move regarded by the Montréal mercantile community as a commercial

catastrophe and an unwelcome invasion of a select residential neighbourhood. Convinced that Montréal would expand northward from the waterfront, Morgan was vindicated when his competitors followed him to what would become Montréal's main shopping area. In the 1950s, branches of Morgan & Co were opened in many large centres in Ontario and Québec, and a Morgan continued to head the company until it merged with the HBC in 1960. JOY L. SANTINK

Morgentaler, Henry, physician, abortion advocate (b at Lodz, Poland 19 Mar 1923). The son of Jewish socialist activists killed in the Holocaust, Morgentaler survived Auschwitz and Dachau, arriving in Canada in 1950. He began a general practice in medicine in Montréal in 1955 but by 1969 was devoting all his energies to family planning. He was one of the first Canadian doctors to perform vasectomies, insert IUDs and provide contraceptive pills to the unmarried. As president of the Montréal Humanist Fellowship he urged the Commons Health and Welfare Committee in 1967 to repeal the law against ABORTION.

To draw attention to the safety and efficacy of clinical abortions, Morgentaler in 1973 publicized the fact that he had successfully carried out over 5000 abortions. When a jury nevertheless found him not guilty of violating article 251 of the Criminal Code the Québec Court of Appeal (in Feb 1974), in an unprecedented action, quashed the jury finding and ordered Morgentaler imprisoned. Though this ruling was upheld by the Supreme Court a second jury acquittal led Ron Basford, minister of justice, to have a Criminal Code amendment passed, taking away the power of appellate judges to strike down acquittals and order imprisonments. After a third jury trial led to yet another acquittal all further charges were dropped. In Nov 1984 Morgentaler and 2 associates were acquitted of conspiring to procure a miscarriage at their Toronto clinic. The Ontario government appealed the acquittal; the accused appealed to the Supreme Court of Canada, which struck down the law in early 1988 on the basis that it conflicted with rights guaranteed in the Charter. The treatment of Morgentaler has focused attention on legal procedures as well as on the issue of abortion. ANGUS MCLAREN

Morice, Father Adrien Gabriel, Oblate missionary (b in Mayenne Départment, France 27 Aug 1859; d at St-Boniface, Man 21 Apr 1938). He joined the Oblate Order in 1879 before coming to Victoria, BC, in 1880. Ordained priest in 1882, he served as a missionary at the Stuart Lake mission at Fort St James in the northern interior of BC from 1885 until 1905. He was then transferred to St-Boniface, Man, where he died. An atypical missionary, he became a clergyman-historian and is best known for his *History of the Northern Interior of British Columbia* (1904), his magnum opus, *The Carrier Language* (2 vols, 1932), and the compilation of the first comprehensive map of the north-central interior of BC (1907).
DENNIS F.K. MADILL

Reading: David Mulhall, *Will to Power: The Missionary Career of Father A.G. Morice* (1986).

Morin, Augustin-Norbert, lawyer, politician, judge (b at St-Michel-de-Bellechasse, LC 13 Oct 1803; d at Ste-Adèle, Canada E 27 July 1865). Morin was without oratorical talent and seemed dimmed by his associates, the brilliant speakers L.J. PAPINEAU and L.H. LAFONTAINE, but it was he who assured the continuity of French Canadian political claims for a quarter century as a member of the Assembly of Lower Canada from 1830 and of the Province of Canada in 1841 and 1842-55. He formed a ministry with Francis HINCKS 1851-54 and with Sir Allan MACNAB in 1854-55. Morin

drafted the 92 Resolutions adopted in 1834 by the Assembly, presenting the members' grievances and arguing for an elected Legislative Council (achieved in 1856) and RESPONSIBLE GOVERNMENT (achieved 1848). In 1852 Morin became the first dean of the Faculty of Law of the new UNIVERSITÉ LAVAL, which he had helped found. In 1854 he managed to achieve abolition of the seigneurial regime. He sat as judge of the Superior Court 1855-59 when he became a member of the commission that drafted the first CIVIL CODE of Lower Canada. Morin also founded the newspaper *La Minerve* in 1826 and contributed to it for 10 years. He acquired land N of Montréal where he experimented with several crops, notably potatoes.
JEAN-MARC PARADIS

Morin, Claude, professor, politician (b at Montmorency, Qué 16 May 1929). A Laval professor 1956-63, he became after 1960 one of the most influential advisers to Jean LESAGE's administration. He was considered one of the prime thinkers behind the QUIET REVOLUTION and held the positions of economic adviser (1960-63), deputy minister of federal-provincial affairs (1963-67) and deputy minister of intergovernmental affairs (1967-71). He resigned after political disagreements with Robert BOURASSA's government to become professor at the École nationale d'administration publique, UQ, and in 1972 joined the Parti Québécois. He was defeated in the riding of Louis-Hébert in 1973 but elected in 1976. As minister of intergovernmental affairs for the PQ government (Nov 1976 to Jan 1982) Morin was a principal architect of the electoral strategy that brought the party to power and of its strategy for the referendum on SOVEREIGNTY-ASSOCIATION and for constitutional negotiations with the federal government (1976-81). He resigned in Jan 1982 over a dispute with René LÉVESQUE concerning the direction the PQ was taking on sovereignty-association, returning to his academic career. DANIEL LATOUCHE

Morin, Jacques-Yvan, professor, politician, nationalist (b in Québec c15 July 1931). He undertook graduate studies in law at McGill U, Cambridge and Harvard. He was admitted to the Québec Bar in 1953 and became professor of international and constitutional law at U de M in 1958. He focused his attention on international law, the nature of FEDERALISM and was involved in the arbitration of numerous labour disputes in Québec. Between 1964 and 1968 he was a member of the Cour international d'arbitrage at the Hague, Netherlands, as well as several other associations dealing with international legal issues. In 1964 Morin began advocating a highly decentralized form of federalism for Canada, a genuine "confederation". He presided over the Etats généraux du Canada français between 1966 and 1969, and the Mouvement national des Québécois, championing the ideology SOVEREIGNTY-ASSOCIATION advocated by the PARTI QUÉBÉCOIS. He ran unsuccessfully as a PQ candidate in the 1970 election but was elected in 1973 to the National Assembly where he was leader of the Opposition for the Parti Québécois. Following the PQ victory in Nov 1976, Morin was appointed vice-premier. Between 1976 and 1985, he headed up several ministries, including those of education, 1976-80, cultural and scientific development, 1980-82 and intergovernmental affairs, 1982-85. He retired from active politics in 1985 to pursue his scholarly interests. M.D. BEHIELS

Morin, Léo-Pol, pianist, music critic, teacher, composer (as James Callihou) (b at Cap-St-Ignace, Qué 13 July 1892; d in an accident near Lac Marois, N of Montréal 29 May 1941). An ambassador for the French music of his era, he also contributed to the growth of Canadian music. After studying in Québec C and Montréal, he won the Prix d'Europe (1912) and continued his training in Paris. He returned to Canada in 1914 and devoted himself to teaching and concert performances. In 1918 he was one of the founders of Le NIGOG, a music, literature and fine-arts review. During a second stay in Europe (1919-25), he toured with Ravel (1923); in 1928 he played in a concert given by Ravel in Montréal. Morin first wrote on music for *La Patrie* (1926-29), then made weekly contributions to *La PRESSE* (1929-31) and *Le Canada* (1933-41). He wrote several harmonizations for folk songs.   HÉLÈNE PLOUFFE

Morin, Paul, lawyer, poet and translator (b at Montréal 6 Apr 1889; d at Beloeil, Qué Sept 1963). Admitted to the Québec Bar in 1910, Morin decided to study COMPARATIVE LITERATURE at the Sorbonne, Paris. His doctoral thesis on Henry Wadsworth Longfellow was published in 1913. After briefly teaching literature at McGill (1914-15) and in the US (1915-18), Morin went on to become secretary at the École des beaux-arts, Montréal (1922-30) and, after 1930, a court translator. His translation of Longfellow's *Evangeline* appeared in 1924. In Morin's first collection of poems, *Le Paon d'émail* (1911), he most closely followed the Parnassian school, emphasizing the description of scenes and works of art, full of mythological and literary allusions. In his second collection, *Poèmes de cendre et d'or* (1922), for which he won the Prix David, he achieved greater technical perfection and displayed a more personal style. His last collection, *Géronte et son miroir*, appeared in 1960. His poetry, in sparkling images, was witness to his great concern for form and lasting fascination with other places, real or imaginary.   NICOLE BOURBONNAIS

Morine, Sir Alfred Bishop, lawyer, public figure (b at Port Medway, NS 31 Mar 1857; d at Toronto 18 Dec 1944). Morine's first career was editing newspapers, first in NS and after 1883 at St John's. Journalism launched him into Newfoundland politics, and politics into law. Beginning in 1886, he represented Bonavista in the Assembly for 20 years; he held several portfolios in the late 1890s and became a paid advocate for the Reid Newfoundland Co. In 1898 he was publicly embarrassed and forced to resign because of blatant conflict of interest. From 1906 to 1912 Morine established a Toronto law practice, lost his second mainland bid for election, and chaired the Public Service Commission of Canada (1911-12). He again became MHA for Bonavista 1914-19 and was also minister of justice 1919 and government leader in the legislative council 1924-28. From 1928 he resided in Toronto, writing on Newfoundland affairs and occasionally giving causes such as Confederation his elder statesman's support. He was a leading spokesman for Newfoundland on the FRENCH SHORE question and was an example of the toleration that the public showed to corrupt politicians. He was knighted in 1928.   M. MacLEOD

Morinville, Alta, Town, pop 5364 (1986c), inc 1901, is located on the CNR, 41 km NW of Edmonton. Settlement in the area, known as Grand Brûlé, was first encouraged by the Oblate fathers, and in 1891, Abbé Jean-Baptiste Morin brought in a party of "colons" from Québec and the US. That year, a chapel was built 3 km W of the present townsite, and in 1894 it was moved to within the townsite. The arrival of the railway in 1905 brought further growth, and in 1911 Morinville became a town. It remains the centre of a rich mixed-farming district and the home of many commuters to Edmonton. Coal deposits and later oil and gas discoveries have added to

this economy. Trappings of Franco-Alberten culture are also much in evidence, including the St-Jean-Baptiste Church, built in 1907, which dominates the skyline.   DAVID LEONARD

Moriyama, Raymond, architect, planner (b at Vancouver 11 Oct 1929). Educated at U of T and McGill, Moriyama began to practise architecture in Toronto in 1958; in 1969 he went into partnership with Ted Teshima. Moriyama is noted as a designer of monumental civic buildings in which the space pleases the public for whom the buildings are intended, an achievement not always realized in architecture today. His buildings include the ONTARIO SCIENCE CENTRE (1969), Scarborough Civic Centre (1973) and the Metropolitan Toronto Library (1977). His projects, however, have ranged from the design of a Japanese ceremonial bell, the Goh Ohn bell (awarded the Gov Gen's Medal for Architecture, 1982), to a vast planning project in Saskatchewan's Meewasin Valley. In 1988 Moriyama was designing the Canadian embassy in Tokyo, Japan, and the North York City Centre in Ontario. He became an Officer of the Order of Canada in 1985.   SUSAN FORD

Scarborough Civic Centre (1973) designed by Raymond Moriyama (*courtesy Moriyama & Teshima/Lenscape Inc*).

Mormon Church, fd 1830 in upstate New York. The Church of Jesus Christ of Latter-day Saints, by far the largest Mormon denomination, is the only one of significance in Canada. Its members regard it as the ancient church of Christ, destroyed through apostasy but restored by divine revelation. Unlike Catholics and Protestants, Latter-day Saints accord sacred value to a continuing record of revelations received through church leaders, as well as to the Bible; and they accepted the *Book of Mormon* as the inspired translation of accounts concerning immigrant descendants of the House of Israel in the Western Hemisphere and of a visit to their descendants by the resurrected Christ shortly before his ascension. The centrality of families to Morman belief is witnessed by their rejection of original sin, believing instead that God married Adam and Eve in the Garden of Eden and that their sin, willful disbelief, led to the expulsion from the Garden. Sacred temple rituals which link family generations are performed by the living on behalf of predeceased relatives, thus ensuring a perpetuation of generations in eternity. Through family units and impeccable living (sanctification), they believe that man may become deified, as their Father in Heaven is. In their concern for relations between the living and the dead, they have developed immense genealogical records.

Growing rapidly, the original Mormon religious community moved westward. After the 1844 assassination of founder Joseph Smith Jr, its main body was forced by religious persecution to make an arduous journey from Illinois to Utah under Brigham Young. In Utah the doctrine of polygyny, openly adopted, brought Mormons into conflict with American authorities until the practice was officially abandoned in 1890.

From its earliest years the LDS Church had sought converts in British North America. Smith undertook his only foreign missionary work in Upper Canada, and Young was among the first missionaries to go there. Most Canadian converts journeyed S and W to join other Mormons in Illinois, and then in Utah. By the 1880s, church leaders had come to see the Canadian West as suitable for colonization and as a refuge, at least for fugitive polygamists. In 1887 the first Mormon settlers, led by Charles Ora Card, arrived in the North-West Territories [Alberta] and established CARDSTON. After polygyny ceased to be an issue, the LDS Church sent other immigrants to southern Alberta. They developed the region's first major irrigation system and established the sugar beet industry there. By 1910, when Mormon immigration to Canada had almost ceased, Latter-day Saints formed a majority of the rural population S and SW of Lethbridge, as they do now. While the greater number of Canada's 113 000 Mormons (1987) reside in cities, Cardston retains its significance as the site of Canada's only Mormon temple, although construction of a new temple in the Toronto area is expected to be completed by spring 1988.
  KEITH PARRY

Reading: A History of the Mormon Church in Canada (1968); Thomas F. O'Dea, *The Mormons* (1957).

Morning Glory family (Convolvulaceae), containing 1200 species of herbaceous plants, is represented in Canada by cultivated common morning glory (*Ipomoea purpurea*) and 3 related species; 11 species of climbing, parasitic dodders (genus *Cuscuta*); and 5 species of bindweed (*Convolvulus*). Common morning glory, less popular as a garden ORNAMENTAL than formerly, persists as a weed or in waste places. Native to tropical America, it is closely related to the sweet potato. Dodders are leafless, vinelike annuals without chlorophyll. They have orange or reddish threadlike stems that encircle stems of herbs and shrubs and attach themselves by suckers that tap the host plant for water and nutrients. Once suckers are operational, dodders' roots disappear. Two bindweeds are important weeds in Canada. Field bindweed (*C. arvensis*), a European perennial found across Canada (except possibly Newfoundland and PEI), twines counterclockwise around crop and other plants, and spreads by seeds and underground roots. The white or slightly pink flowers are about 2.5 cm across. Hedge bindweed (*C. sepium*), similar in appearance, has flowers up to 5 cm across.
  PAUL B. CAVERS

Moroni, David Lee, dancer, teacher, director (b at Ottawa 14 Mar 1938). As founding principal of the Royal Winnipeg Ballet School's professional division, Moroni has made a significant contribution to the quality of dance education in Canada and has helped raise the technical standard of the company itself, into which many of his students have graduated. Moroni trained in Ottawa with Nesta Toumine and danced in her local company before joining the ROYAL WINNIPEG BALLET in 1964 where he became a principal dancer in 1966 and associate artistic director in 1976. In 1970 he retired from dancing to head the company school's newly established professional program. Under the particular tutelage of the great Russian teacher Vera Volkova, Moroni was able to develop a successful academic regime, of which celebrated ballerina Evelyn HART is the most distinguished product.
  MICHAEL CRABB

Morrice, James Wilson, painter (b at Montréal 10 Aug 1865; d at Tunis, Tunisia 23 Jan 1924). Morrice was one of the earliest Canadian mod-

J.W. Morrice, *The Ferry, Québec* (c1909), oil on canvas. Morrice's winter paintings of Québec are distinctively Canadian in their cold light and stark forms (*courtesy National Gallery of Canada*).

ernist painters and the first Canadian to achieve widespread acceptance abroad. Born of a wealthy and strictly Presbyterian merchant family, he showed an early interest in painting. His father wanted him to enter law and, after studying at U of T and Osgoode Hall, he was called to the Ontario Bar in 1889, but never practised. Montréal dealer William Stewart advised him to study abroad and Sir William VAN HORNE, recognizing his talent, persuaded his father to finance his art studies in Europe. He began his studies at the Académie Julian in Paris in 1890 but soon sought individual masters, first the Barbizon painter Henri Harpignies, then the American painter James McNeill Whistler. But it was in Venice, which he visited with Maurice CULLEN in 1896, that the peculiar light effects changed his perception and set him on his course as a painter.

Morrice never returned to live in Canada, but each year until his father died in 1914 he visited and painted the extraordinary winter sketches and pictures of Québec City and its environs that represent the Canadian side of his work. Paris remained for many years the centre of his world. He became one of the Left Bank expatriate painters and writers, and frequented cafés such as the Chat Blanc in Montparnasse, where he associated with Whistler and Charles Conder and English writers Arnold Bennett and Somerset Maugham, who portrayed him as a minor character in their books. They record his wit, his bibulous geniality, and his habit of making quick oil studies on small wood panels. These sketches were always the start of Morrice's paintings. He made hundreds, some later worked up into canvases. At first he was influenced by the late Impressionists, notably Bonnard and Vuillard, but from about 1909, when he met Henri Matisse, he moved towards the Fauves, with their more violent colouring and their stronger and more rhythmical composition. At the same time he visited N Africa. There, and in the Caribbean, to which he first travelled in 1915, he encountered the clear, strong tones of his later palette. Yet

even at its most opulent, his painting was never strident in colour; it never lost his special delicacy and translucency.

The years of WWI were particularly disruptive. The Paris café life dwindled away; he went to London but found the climate difficult. He spent a period as a Canadian war artist and in this role painted a most uncharacteristic work – a mural of an endless line of soldiers marching through the mud of a battlefield. When the war ended, he spent more of his time in countries where the warmth was kind to his health and the colours and light inspired him as a painter. He was critically ill at Montreux, Switzerland, in 1922; when he went on to N Africa the rumour reached Paris that he was dead, and in 1923 some friends organized a retrospective exhibition. He died in reality a few months later.

Morrice's fame in his native country was almost entirely posthumous. Though he was a member of the short-lived Canadian Art Club, 1907-15, and was elected to the Royal Canadian Academy in 1913, he was mainly appreciated by a few fellow painters, and it was not until after his death that the first major exhibitions of his work were held in Canada. In Europe, however, he began to gain recognition in the early 1900s. In Paris, he exhibited regularly at the modernist Salon d'Automne, of which he became a vice-president. The more advanced French painters accepted him, and before Canadian galleries were acquiring his paintings on any scale, Morrice's work was moving into the great European public collections.

Morrice was a painter who bestrode 2 worlds. His work finds a place in the European modernist tradition and his tropical paintings have an exoticism of colour and spirit that few Canadian painters paralleled until recently. Yet his winter paintings of Québec, which include among them some of his most famous canvases, such as *The Ferry, Québec*, and *The Ice Bridge*, are so distinctive in their cold light and stark forms that one cannot think of them as anything but Canadian. They are among the first truly great Canadian paintings. GEORGE WOODCOCK

Morris, Man, Town, pop 1613 (1986c), 1570 (1981c), inc 1883, is located at the confluence of the Red and Morris rivers, 55 km S of Winnipeg.

First called Scratching River and later named after Alexander MORRIS, Manitoba's second lieutenant-governor, it was the site of fur-trade rivalries in the early 1800s and later a landmark for cart brigades moving between St Paul, Minn, and the RED RIVER COLONY. By the early 1870s Ontarians were homesteading in the area. Morris soon became a busy stagecoach stop between Fargo, N Dak, and Fort Garry. Like other Manitoba towns, it was caught up in the competition for a rail line, offering a substantial bonus to attract the CPR 1882-83. By 1884-85 the town had collapsed under its debt load; it only recovered in the mid-1890s.

The Red and Morris rivers have greatly affected the town, especially during floods in l950, 1966 and 1979. Morris is a trade centre for a prosperous grain-growing region and has several industries. Tourism has become important with development of the "Big M" – the Manitoba Stampede and Agricultural Exhibition held in July. D.M. LYON

Morris, Alexander, politician (b at Perth, Ont 17 Mar 1826; d at Toronto 28 Oct 1889). Educated at Glasgow U, Queen's and McGill, Morris was law clerk to John A. MACDONALD in whose Cabinet he later (1869) served in as minister of inland revenue. Morris shared the imperialist sentiments of the business class and in his pamphlet *Nova Britannia* spoke enthusiastically of confederation and Canada's western destiny. Appointed chief justice of Manitoba in 1872, he became lt-gov (1873-78) and lt-gov of the North-West Territories (1872-76). He brought some harmony to an unsettled province, introduced responsible government and established U of Manitoba. His greatest passion was Indian affairs; the peaceful transfer of most of western Canada was due in part to his diplomacy and patience in the negotiations of Treaties 3, 4, 5 and 6. The major weakness of his administration was his inability to preserve Métis lands. Morris later served in the Ontario legislature (1878-86), wrote a history of the treaties and continued his life work in the Presbyterian Church. He was a governor of both McGill and Queen's.

JEAN FRIESEN

Morris, Alwyn, canoeist (b at Montréal 22 Nov 1957). He won the K-1 1000 m and K-1 500 m junior national championships in 1977 and was the 1977 recipient of the Tom Longboat Award for top N American Indian athlete. With Hugh FISHER he won a gold medal in the K-2 1000 m (time 3:24.22) and a bronze in the K-2 500 m (1:35.41) at the 1984 Los Angeles Olympics.

JAMES MARSH

Morris, Clara, stage name of Clara Morrison, née La Montagne, actress, author (b at Toronto 17 Mar c1848; d at New Canaan, Conn 20 Nov 1925), dubbed "the Queen of Melodrama" for her ability to move an audience to tears. Taken to Cleveland as a child, she was a "ballet-girl" in 1860. By 1869 she was a leading lady in Cincinnati and she played Halifax in 1870 before being discovered that Sept in New York by Augustin Daly. She was an overnight triumph in Wilkie Collins's *Man and Wife* and a sensational success as Camille and mad Cora in *L'Article 47*. Eventually ill health curtailed her appearances. She wrote 3 vols of reminiscences, *Life on the Stage* (1901), *Stage Confidences* (1902) and *Life of a Star* (1906), as well as several novels and volumes of stories. DAVID GARDNER

Morris, Edward Patrick, 1st Baron Morris, politician, prime minister of Newfoundland (b at St John's 8 May 1859; d at London, Eng 24 Oct 1935). Morris was elected to the Newfoundland Assembly in 1885. In 1889 he joined Sir William

WHITEWAY's Liberal Cabinet. He was especially important to the party as a senior Roman Catholic politician with immense influence in St John's. Morris's relationship with Robert BOND, who succeeded to the Liberal leadership in 1897, was uneasy. They split in 1898 but reunited in 1900 to take power from the Tories. Morris became minister of justice in Bond's Cabinet but, urged on by Bond's opponents, resigned in 1907 and in 1908 formed the People's Party, which won the 1909 election. Morris had no clear policy other than to keep himself in power, and his government was tainted by accusations of conflict of interest. His popularity waned during WWI as the Opposition capitalized on discontent caused by profiteering and mismanagement. Having formed the first National Government in 1917, Morris retired early 1918 to England, where he was raised to the peerage.

J.K. HILLER

Morris, Joseph, labour organizer (b in Lancashire, Eng 14 June 1913). He immigrated to Vancouver I where he worked as a woodcutter. He organized for the International Woodworkers of America and rose through the ranks to become president of Local 1-80 (1948) and regional president (1953-62). He was then elected executive VP of the CANADIAN LABOUR CONGRESS until in 1974 he became the congress's president. Morris viewed work in the labour movement as a battle for small gains. Under his leadership, the CLC in 1976 issued a "manifesto" favouring tripartite decision making, and opposed wage controls in a "national day of protest" – the largest organized demonstration in Canadian history. In 1977 Morris was elected chairman of the International Labor Organization. He retired from the congress presidency in 1978. In 1984 he became a Companion of the Order of Canada; and since then Morris has served on the boards of a number of organizations.

LAUREL SEFTON MACDOWELL

Morris, Patrick, merchant, shipowner, politician and officeholder (b at Waterford, Ire 1789; d at St John's 22 Aug 1849). Morris came to St John's around 1804 to work as a clerk in the merchant fishery and within 6 years he had accumulated enough expertise, capital and connections with the predominantly Catholic Irish clientele to enter trade on his own account. From its inception Morris's trade centered on the transportation of fishing servants and salt provisions from his native Waterford, and return cargoes of dried cod and train oil. His trade grew rapidly, resulting in the purchase of 4 oceangoing vessels 1814-25, and expanded along the S shore of St John's, by 1820 heavily Irish, and the populous Conception Bay. He also entered the seal fishery. In 1832, for example, he sent 6 schooners with 132 men to the ice and exported over 10 000 pelts to London.

Throughout his long political career he championed the rights of the poor and disadvantaged, especially the poor immigrant Irish of St John's. In 1820 he was chairman of the St John's Committee of Inhabitants, a group of leading citizens pursuing political and juridical reform. His efforts were rewarded with the judicature Act of 1824 and a local legislature in 1832. Morris served on more than a dozen committees in St John's and was a juror, justice of the peace, member of the House of Assembly, and in 1840, colonial treasurer. Morris was head of a political and commercial clan probably unprecedented among the immigrant Irish in Canada. A dozen of his kinsmen were merchants or agents in St John's; 6 were members of the assembly; 5 of the council, virtually the only Catholics to be so honoured up to the 1850s. JOHN MANNION

Morris, William, businessman, politician (b at Paisley, Scot 31 Oct 1786; d at Montréal 29 June 1858). Elected to the legislative assembly of Upper Canada (Ontario) in 1820 and raised to the legislative council in 1835, Morris was a leading conservative whose political championship of the Presbyterian Church of Canada, which he helped found in 1831, made him a bitter opponent of John STRACHAN and his followers. He fought successfully on behalf of his church for a share of the CLERGY RESERVES and was instrumental in the establishment of Queen's College (Queen's U) in 1841 as a rival to the Anglican-dominated King's College (U of T). A supporter of Gov Gen METCALFE in the crisis of 1843, Morris served as receiver general (1844-47) and president of the executive council (1846-48) before ill health forced his withdrawal from politics.

HARRY BRIDGMAN

Morrison, Donald, outlaw (b near Megantic [Lac-Mégantic], Canada E c1858; d at Montréal 19 June 1894). He was the son of Scottish settlers, grew up near Lk Mégantic and spent several years working as a cowboy in western Canada and the US. In 1886 he became involved in a financial dispute which resulted in the loss of the family farm to Maj Malcolm McAulay. Believing he had been cheated by the wealthy and influential McAulay, he harassed the new owners, and a special constable, Lucius (Jack) Warren, was engaged to arrest him. On 22 June 1888 Morrison shot and killed Warren in Megantic. After evading capture for some months, largely through the assistance of sympathetic Scottish farmers, he was apprehended on 21 Apr 1889, tried and sentenced to 18 years hard labour. Broken by prison life, he refused food and medication, and died of consumption within 5 years. He became a legendary figure in the Scottish settlements of eastern Québec. His story is romanticized in a poem by Oscar Dhu [Angus Mackay], *Donald Morrison, the Canadian Outlaw* (1892), and is the subject of a fictional account by Bernard Epps, *The Outlaw of Megantic* (1973).

EDWARD BUTTS

Reading: M. Robin, *The Bad and the Lonely* (1976); C. Wallace, *Wanted: Donald Morrison* (1977).

Morrison, James, "J.J.," salesman, farmer, farm leader (b near Arthur, Canada W 25 July 1861; d at Toronto 17 Mar 1936). He attended business college in Toronto during 1885 and worked as a salesman until 1900 when he returned to the family farm. He became active in local educational and farm issues as a member of the Patrons of Industry and joined the Ontario Grange in 1907. In 1914 he helped plan the development of the United Farmers of Ontario (secretary 1914-33) and the United Farmers Cooperative Company (secretary 1914-35). Morrison organized the delegation of 3000 Ontario farmers that marched on Ottawa in 1918 to protest the government's CONSCRIPTION policy. He also played a crucial role in the Progressive victory in Ontario in 1919, although he declined the premiership in favour of E.C. DRURY. Because he thought the Progressive movement should remain exclusively a farmers' movement, Morrison soon disagreed vigorously with Drury's approach; his obstructionism contributed significantly to the Drury government's defeat in 1923.

IAN MACPHERSON

Morrison, Mary Louise, soprano (b at Winnipeg 9 Nov 1926). Studies at the Royal Conservatory of Music brought Morrison to Toronto, where she began her career as an opera singer, appearing with the Canadian Opera Co and on the CBC. She also appeared frequently as soloist with choirs and orchestras in works of the stan-

dard repertoire. Morrison is best known, however, as a dedicated interpreter of 20th-century music. She has sung in numerous premieres of Canadian works, many of which, in recognition of her exceptional ability to make avant-garde music enjoyable to audiences, have been specially written for her. Much of her contemporary music performance in Canada and abroad has been undertaken as a member of the Lyric Arts Trio.

BARCLAY MCMILLAN

Morrisseau, Norval, artist (b at Sand Point Reserve, near Beardmore, Ont 14 Mar 1932). He is a self-taught artist of Ojibwa ancestry (his Ojibwa name means "Copper Thunderbird") and he originated the pictographic style, or what is referred as "Woodland Indian art," "legend painting" or "x-ray art." This style is a fusion of European easel painting with Ojibwa MIDEWIWIN Society scrolls and pictography of rock paintings. Introduced to the Canadian public at the Pollock Gallery, Toronto, in 1962, Morrisseau was the first Indian to break through the Canadian professional white-art barrier. Throughout the 1960s Morrisseau's pictographic style grew in popularity and was often perceived by other Cree, Ojibwa and Ottawa artists as a tribal style, to be adapted for their own cultural needs. By the 1970s younger artists painted exclusively in his genre. For Morrisseau, the 1970s saw him struggling to reconcile native and Christian religions in his art and personal life. Combining his Ojibwa heritage, instilled in him by his maternal grandfather, Moses Nanakonagos, with the religion Eckankar, his works during the 1980s have become more focused on spiritual elements. Morrisseau continues to study Ojibwa shamanistic practices, which he believes elevates his work to a higher plane of understanding.

TOM HILL

Reading: Elizabeth McLuhan and Tom Hill, *Norval Morrisseau and the Emergence of the Image Makers* (1984).

Norval Morrisseau, *Indian Vision, Man* (nd), tempera on paper. Morrisseau has struggled to reconcile native and Christian religions in his art (*courtesy Glenbow Museum, Calgary*).

Morrow, Patrick Alan, photographer, mountaineer (b at Invermere, BC 18 Oct 1952). His abilities as an adventure photographer led to a position on the 1982 Canadian MOUNT EVEREST

EXPEDITION, and on Oct 7 of that year he became the second Canadian to reach the top of the world. (Teammate Laurie SKRESLET was first.) On Mt Everest, he realized he had stood atop 3 continents – N America, S America and Asia – and during the next 4 years he climbed to the highest points of Europe, Africa, Antarctica and Australasia, reaching his final summit in May 1986. American businessman Dick Bass claimed mountaineering's "grand slam" before Morrow, but while Bass used Australia's Mt Kosciusko as one of his 7 targets, Morrow included all of Australasia in his continental definition, and thus he climbed Carstensz Pyramid in Irian Jaya, a peak nearly twice as high as Kosciusko. He was made a Member of the Order of Canada in 1987.

BART ROBINSON

Morse, Eric, promoter of wilderness travel by canoe in Canada (b at Naini Tal, India 27 Dec 1904; d at Ottawa 18 Apr 1986). Oriented from youth toward CANOEING, he undertook long river journeys with influential persons from 1951. In Ottawa from 1942, with the RCAF, as national secretary UN Assn in Canada, then as national director, Assn of Canadian Clubs he introduced his friends to canoeing on nearby waterways. Blair FRASER and Omond SOLANDT went on his first long journey; Pierre Elliott TRUDEAU went with him in 1966. Morse retraced FUR TRADE ROUTES – the subject of his classic book *Fur Trade Routes of Canada* – then explorers' routes. He traversed the Barren Lands from Hudson Bay to Alaska until 1977. For this pioneer work his name was given in 1985 to a river running into the Back R at Garry Lake. His canoeing memoirs, *Whitewater Saga* (1987), were published posthumously by his wife.

COURTNEY C.J. BOND

Mortality, *see* POPULATION.

Mortgage, a legal paper in which borrowers agree to surrender their property to a lender if they do not pay back the money they owe, with INTEREST. If the property is easily movable, eg, a car or a boat, the deal is called a chattel mortgage, but most mortgages involve real estate and are called collateral mortgages. The ordinary way to buy a house in Canada is to raise most of the money by a mortgage loan on the house itself because if the borrowers fail to make their mortgage payments the lender can foreclose the mortgage and take the house and sell it (*see* BANKING). Lenders try not to write a mortgage for more than the property will bring when sold. Sometimes there is more than one mortgage on the same property, in which case, if the borrower fails to repay, the holder of the first mortgage recovers all his money before the holder of a second mortgage recovers any. As a result, interest rates on second and third mortgages are high. Under the National Housing Act, first passed in 1938 and much amended since, the federal government insures mortgages on moderately priced new houses, cutting the risk and so lowering the interest rate. Mortgages not guaranteed under the NHA – which includes most mortgages on the resale of older homes – are called conventional mortgages. In the 1950s and 1960s, most mortgages lasted 20 or 30 years. Lenders ceased offering such long-term mortgages in the 1970s when interest rates rose rapidly. Most mortgages are now due in one, 3 or 5 years, although even the 5-year mortgages were rare in the early 1980s when interest rates climbed to more than 21%. Banks, forbidden to lend mortgage money before 1954, had written about 37% of the more than $144-billion worth of mortgages that were outstanding in the late 1980s.

DON McGILLIVRAY

Morton, William Lewis, historian, professor (b at Gladstone, Man 13 Dec 1908; d at Medicine

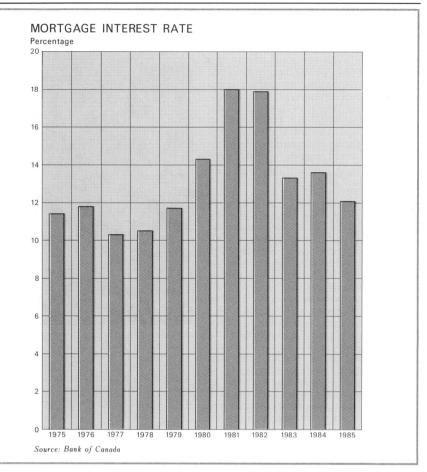

MORTGAGE INTEREST RATE
Percentage
Source: Bank of Canada

Hat, Alta 7 Dec 1980). Educated at U of Man and Oxford, Morton combined a lengthy career as a professor of history at U of Man and Trent U with a record of distinguished publications. By the 1950s he had become one of Canada's best-known and most accomplished historians. In his writings he consistently sought to combine his commitment to regional distinctiveness with his concern for elucidating the nature of the Canadian identity, particularly as it was shaped and structured by imperial links with France and England. Among his many books, conservative in tone and interpretation, are *The Progressive Party in Canada* (1950), winner of the Gov Gen's Award for nonfiction; *Manitoba: A History* (1957) and *The Canadian Identity* (1961). *The Critical Years* (1964) was one volume in the Canadian Centenary Series, of which Morton was executive editor. "History is not an academic mystery," he once wrote. "It's what the community thinks about itself, how it sorts out ideas."

A.B. McKILLOP

Mosaic (1967-), a quarterly magazine devoted to "the comparative study of literature and ideas," founded at U of Manitoba under the editorship of Kenneth McRobbie. It publishes only critical and interpretive essays. Each issue is now devoted to a single scholarly theme, eg, "From an Ancient to a Modern Theatre"; "The Novel and Its Changing Forms"; "The Eastern European Imagination in Literature." An unusual feature of *Mosaic* is that many issues are republished in book form.

GEORGE WOODCOCK

Mosher, Aaron Roland, trade unionist (b in Halifax County, NS 10 May 1881; d at Ottawa 26 Sept 1959). In 1907 Mosher led Halifax freight-shed employees on strike. In 1908, when the Canadian Brotherhood of Railway Employees (CBRE) was founded, Mosher was elected its first president, a position he held until 1952. Under his leadership CBRE became the largest Canadian transport-workers' union. As a national industrial union, it embraced employees who were outside the jurisdiction of the craft railway brotherhoods. CBRE briefly affiliated with the Trades and Labor Congress but was expelled at the insistence of a competing international union. Mosher became Canada's foremost exponent of national unionism. In 1927 he became president of the new All-Canadian Congress of Labour. When it was succeeded by the CANADIAN CONGRESS OF LABOUR (1940), Mosher retained the presidency. During WWII, as a labour representative on several government committees, he favoured collective-bargaining legislation and opposed wartime wage controls.

LAUREL SEFTON MacDOWELL

Mosquito [Span, "little fly"], a fragile, long-legged FLY of order Diptera, family Culicidae. About 3000 species are known worldwide, at least 74 in Canada. Only females seek blood meals; both sexes feed on nectar. All mosquitos have a long, slender proboscis (beak), a pair of slender, fifteen-segmented antennae, and densely scaled wing veins. The female proboscis has 6 long, pointed stylets that enter the victim's skin in rapid succession. The female may take 3 times her own weight in blood, using it for egg production. Eggs are laid on water or moist soil. Those laid on soil may hatch after flooding or may remain dormant until the next spring. Eggs deposited in water habitats subject to drying, eg, shallow pools or water-filled containers, can resist desiccation for weeks or months. All larvae are aquatic and, except for a few predaceous species, feed on detritus and micro-organisms. Pupae are active, but non-feeding. Adult life averages 3 weeks in summer, but Canadian species that overwinter as adults in protected places may live 8-9 months. One species may overwinter as larvae in water-filled leaves of purple PITCHER PLANT. In some areas of

Canada, these larvae may be ice-bound for 6-7 months. Most species are tropical. They are feared as transmitters of malaria, filariasis and dengue fever (affecting about 0.5 billion people annually). In Canada, mosquitos transmit human and equine encephalitis viruses and the NEMATODE causing dog heartworm. In northern boreal forests, mosquitos are serious INSECT PESTS of people and animals. Their bites cause considerable irritation and result in significant blood loss. Mosquitos present a barrier to northern development by reducing hours spent outdoors for industrial and recreational purposes.   R.A. BRUST

Reading: D.M. Wood, P.T. Dang and R.A. Ellis, *The Mosquitoes of Canada* (1979).

Moss, small terrestrial plant, usually less than 10 cm tall, that lacks true conducting tissues (xylem, phloem) and has a dominant gametophyte (sexual) generation. Mosses are the largest and most highly developed group of division Bryophyta (which also includes LIVERWORTS and hornworts). Bryophytes are sometimes known as the "amphibians of the plant world" because of their dependence on water for sexual reproduction. Mosses show alternation of generations, ie, have 2 phases in the life cycle. These are the free-living, perennial gametophyte (the typical green moss plant), and the short-lived sporophyte (asexual generation), which remains dependent on the gametophyte. The sporophyte produces spores that are wind dispersed. Some spores germinate into new gametophyte plants. Gametophyte plants produce sex cells (eggs, sperm) that undergo fertilization to produce another sporophyte. The gametophyte has rhizoids (rootlike structures that attach the plant to its substrate), a simple or branched stem, and small leaves (mostly only one cell thick). The sporophyte has a foot embedding it into the gametophyte and a spore capsule usually borne on a stalk (seta). Some mosses reproduce asexually by gemmae (small groups of cells produced on the gametophyte tissues) or by bulbils (small, deciduous shoots) found in leaf axils. Most mosses can also reproduce by fragmentation, ie, the breaking off of almost any plant part, which then grows into a new plant. Lacking true conducting tissues, mosses mostly absorb water directly through the stem and leaves. Many botanists believe that mosses evolved from primitive vascular plants (ie, those having true conducting tissues). Others argue that they developed from some green algal ancestor. Mosses are thought to be a reduced group, which lost much evolutionary potential by having a dominant gametophyte generation and by lacking specialized conducting tissues (a factor limiting size).

Mosses occur in several growth forms, the more common being turfs, cushions, mats and wefts. Individual plants are usually closely associated and several hundreds may be found in a single turf or cushion. Mosses grow in many places but prefer moist, shady habitats. A few are aquatic (especially water mosses, genus *Fontinalis*); some grow in very dry places (especially granite mosses, *Andreaea*). Common growth surfaces include rocks, trees, rotten wood, humus and soil. The presence of copper mosses may indicate high levels of heavy metals in the substrates. Dung mosses grow only on dung or other nitrogen-rich substrates. PEAT mosses (genus *Sphagnum*) accumulate into deposits that may be several hundred metres thick. Peat is used in horticulture and as fuel. Mosses, an important part of the ground cover in the boreal coniferous forests, are also a conspicuous part of arctic TUNDRA or mountain vegetation. Some mosses are good pioneer colonizers and quickly invade bare or disturbed soil,

Haircap moss (*Polytrichum piliferum*) (*photo by Mary W. Ferguson*).

consolidating it by their dense, turflike growth. There are over 10 000 species worldwide of which about 1250 occur in N America. Individual parts of Canada have fewer species (eg, 466 species in Alberta, 445 in Newfoundland, 430 in Ontario). Mosses thrive in humid climates, and coastal parts of Canada have a greater diversity than the interior parts.   GUY R. BRASSARD

Moth, common name for insects that, with BUTTERFLIES, constitute the order Lepidoptera. Probably over 100 000 species of moths exist worldwide, several thousand in Canada. Moths are distinguished from butterflies by having threadlike or feathery antennae. Most are nocturnal. They vary in size from adults of some leaf miners, with wings spreading little more than 3 mm, to the Asian atlas moth, spreading 20 cm. The related cecropia moth, spreading 12 cm, is Canada's largest. Most moths have mouthparts modified into a coiled proboscis (tongue) for extracting nectar from blossoms.

Moths have 4 developmental stages: egg, larva, pupa and adult. Moth larvae, called caterpillars, are usually plant feeders. Most consume leaves; others feed on roots (eg, ghost moth larvae), bore into tree trunks (carpenter worms), feed beneath the surface of leaves, stems or bark thus forming tunnels (leaf, stem or bark miners), or bore into fruits or seeds (codling moth larvae). In many species, larvae live in shelters formed by rolling and tying leaves together (leaf rollers); others build portable cases in which to live (bagworms). Pupae are usually contained in a cocoon, or in a cell in the soil. Although most moth larvae are solitary, some live in colonies, eg, webworms and tent caterpillars. The American tent caterpillar is a periodic pest in fruit-growing areas of eastern Canada. Larvae spin a silken nest in which they congregate when not feeding. Forest tent caterpillars, which feed on broad-leafed trees, do not form an actual nest, but gather in a mass in crotches of tree branches. In some years, forest tent caterpillars are numerous enough to damage large tracts of broad-leafed trees.

One family (Sphingidae) of large moths attracts popular interest. It includes hawk or sphinx moths, distinguished by long, narrow wings and rapid flight. Although primarily nocturnal, they often fly at dusk and greatly resemble hummingbirds as they hover, feeding. Larvae of 2 species, tobacco and tomato hornworms, are occasional crop pests. Another family (Tortricidae) of much smaller moths includes economically important species. The codling moth, a pest of apples, bores into fruit, making it inedible. Spruce budworm, the primary problem of Canada's FOREST industry, sometimes destroys vast acreages of conifers. One of the largest families (Noctuidae) includes the owlet moths (millers) and many economically important larvae (eg, cutworms). Cutworms hide in the surface layer of soil in daytime and feed on young plants at night, often severing stems at the surface. Several pest species occur in Canada, pale western, red-backed and black cutworms being among the most important. The armyworm, another chronic pest, derives its name from larvae that march en masse from one stand of grain to another. Another group of Noctuidae contains species that bore into flowers and fruits (eg, corn earworm, tobacco budworm). Larvae of

The cecropia moth, Canada's largest, has a wingspan of 12 cm (*photo by Mary W. Ferguson*).

Luna moth *(Actius luna)* *(photo by Bill Ivy)*.

another large family (Geometridae) are called geometers or inchworms, from their form of locomotion. This family includes pest species responsible for defoliation of trees (eg, spring and fall cankerworms). Clothes moths, which occur worldwide, are carried from house to house on clothing or other articles of animal origin. Their natural food is hair, wool, feathers, etc.

D.F. HARDWICK

Motherwell, William Richard, agrarian activist, politician (b at Perth, Canada W 6 Jan 1860; d at Regina 23 May 1943). An early homesteader in Saskatchewan, he was a cofounder 1901 of the Territorial Grain Growers' Assn, which under his leadership exacted legislation to curb monopolistic practices by line elevator companies and the CPR. Appointed Saskatchewan's first minister of agriculture in 1905, he was a tireless advocate of techniques that enabled the dry belt to be cultivated effectively; he also helped establish the College of Agriculture. A LAURIER Liberal, he resigned in 1918, largely in opposition to the provincial party's support of CONSCRIPTION. Between 1921 and 1930 he served twice as federal minister of agriculture under PM Mackenzie KING and initiated important national measures to increase farm production. *See also* MOTHERWELL HOMESTEAD.

LYLE DICK

Motherwell Homestead, near Abernethy, Sask, for over 60 years the residence of William R. MOTHERWELL. He homesteaded in what is now Saskatchewan in 1882. The HOMESTEAD is an excellent example of the Ontario settlers' approach to farmstead design and scientific agriculture in the PRAIRIE WEST. To separate the principal functional elements, Motherwell divided the farmstead into 4 quadrants – domestic, garden, water supply and barnyard. To provide protection from the elements, an attractive landscape and a means for trapping snow for spring meltwater, he designed an elaborate shelterbelt system. By building an Ontario-style house and barn, and landscaping a lawn-tennis court and ornamental plantings, Motherwell recreated the feeling of a rural Ontario estate. In 1966 the Canadian government designated the homestead a national HISTORIC SITE, and by 1983 had restored it to commemorate Motherwell's career and the history of scientific agriculture in western Canada.

LYLE DICK

Motorcycle Racing takes a variety of forms, each with its own rules and specialized equipment. The best known is road racing, in which cyclists race in categories, usually related to engine size, over special circuits or on public highways closed for the occasion. Motocross is conducted on a closed circuit over rough, cross-country terrains and natural obstacles. Dirt-track races are run at speedway tracks. Other forms include time trials, hill climbing, sprints, endurance runs and ice racing. The Canadian Motorcycle Assn was formed in 1946 to organize competition when motorcycling became a popular competitive sport. In 1967 Canada hosted a World Championship Road Race for the first time and a Canadian team participated in the international Six-Day Trials, the "Olympics of Motorcycling." Mike Duff placed second on the Grand Prix circuit in the 1960s. In 1972 John Williams, of Markham, Ont, won the World B Division Hill-Climbing Championship.

BARBARA SCHRODT

Motto The heraldic practice of affixing an inscription, expressive of an appropriate sentiment, to a coat of arms or a crest has been honoured by the Dominion of Canada and 8 of the 10 provinces. Neither territory has a motto, but many municipalities have mottoes of their own.

The motto of the Dominion of Canada is A MARI USQUE AD MARE which is officially translated "From Sea to Sea" and "D'un océan à l'autre." A listing of the provinces and their official mottoes and translations is as follows. Alberta: *Fortis et Liber* ("Strong and free"); British Columbia: *Splendour Sine Occasu* ("Splendour without diminishment"); Manitoba: no official motto; New Brunswick: *Spem Reduxit* ("Hope was restored"); Newfoundland: *Quaerite Prime Regnum* ("Seek ye first the Kingdom of God"); Nova Scotia: *Munit Haec et Altera Vincit* ("One defends and the other conquers"); Ontario: *Ut Incepit Fidelis Sic Permanet* ("Loyal it began, loyal it remains"); Prince Edward Island: *Parva Sub Ingenti* ("The small under the protection of the great"); Québec: *Je me souviens* ("I remember"); Saskatchewan: no official motto. The motto of the city of Ottawa is "Advance – Ottawa – En Avant."

JOHN ROBERT COLOMBO

Mount Allison University, Sackville, NB, was established in 1839 by a local merchant, Charles Frederick Allison. Mount Allison was a boys' academy owned and operated by the METHODIST Church but open to all denominations. It opened in 1843, and a branch institution for girls was added in 1854. It attained degree-granting status in 1858, at which time it was referred to as Mount Allison College. Teaching began in 1862 and the first 2 degrees were granted in 1863. In 1875 the college conferred on Grace Annie LOCKHART the first baccalaureate awarded to a woman in the British Empire and in 1882 granted to Harriet Starr Stewart the first bachelor of arts degree awarded to a woman in Canada. In 1886 the charter of the college was amended and the name became University of Mount Allison College, the word "College" gradually and unofficially being dropped over the years.

Mount Allison is primarily an undergraduate university, awarding degrees in arts, science, music, fine arts, commerce and education, and certificates in engineering, secretarial studies and bilingualism. Although the university is no longer church controlled, it retains close ties with the UNITED CHURCH. Over the years it has preserved the character of a compact scholarly community. By combining a manageable size with excellent facilities (many of the buildings have been constructed since 1960) Mount Allison seeks to provide the best in undergraduate instruction to a largely residential student body. Forty Rhodes scholars have graduated since 1900. Admission is selective, with all programs generally receiving more qualified applicants than can be accepted. In 1985-86 full-time undergraduate enrolment was 1734.

Mount Assiniboine Provincial Park (est 1922, 386 km²), area of mountain peaks, alpine meadows and lakes dominated by Mt ASSINIBOINE (about 35 km S of BANFF, Alta). The park, which is mainly above 1500 m, has a score of peaks exceeding 2700 m, numerous small lakes (notably Lk Magog), and some underground streams in KARST areas. Mammals include wapiti, moose, mule deer, mountain goats, bighorn sheep, bear, wolf, ground squirrel, coyote, porcupine; 66 bird species have been observed (eg, Canada jay, ptarmigan, waterfowl, golden eagles). The area was explored in the early 1800s and brought to public attention in the 1880s by G.M. DAWSON, who named Mt Assiniboine after the Indians who had hunted the area for generations. The Alpine Club of Canada promoted recreation in the area and was instrumental in establishing the park, which was expanded in 1973. Today the park is used mainly for hiking, climbing, horseback riding and cross-country skiing. There are few facilities other than a lodge and cabins at Lk Magog, primitive campsites and trails. Access is mainly on foot or horseback from the Sunshine Village ski area, Spray Reservoir or Highway 93.

JOHN S. MARSH

Mount Carleton Provincial Park (est 1962, 174 km²), comprising part of the Central Highlands of NB, is located 43 km by road ESE of St Quentin. The highlands are complex geologically. Mt Carleton, focus of the park and the highest peak (820 m) in the Atlantic provinces, is a monadnock of resistant rock left after erosion produced the surrounding valleys and lakes. The varied habitat is dominated by conifers and deciduous species (eg, beech, maple, birch, ash). Mammals include moose, deer and beaver; fish are abundant. Canoe routes of Indians and French missionaries traversed the area, which was initially exploited for lumber. Tourists subsequently established fish and game clubs. The area has continued to be popular for canoeing, fishing, camping, hiking and, in winter, cross-country skiing and snowmobiling. Two roads provide access but are sometimes impassable because of adverse weather conditions.

JOHN S. MARSH

Mount Edziza Provincial Park (est 1972, 2300 km² ha) comprises part of the Tahltan Highlands, between the Stikine and Iskut rivers in BC. The nearest community is Telegraph Creek, 20 km NW of the park. The area is a volcanic wilderness that, according to Indian legend and scientific research, has been geologically active within the last few hundred years. Some 30 cinder cones dominate the park landscape, the highest of which, Mt Edziza, rises to 2787 m. Around it is a 640 km² lava plateau. To the S are the older, brilliantly coloured and glacially eroded Spectrum Mts. The area experiences great temperature variations, and snow may persist on the peaks throughout summer. Wildlife includes mountain goats, stone sheep and, at lower elevations, mountain caribou, grizzly bear and moose. In the late 1800s, a trail was built across the southern part of what is now the park, through Raspberry Pass, to allow construction of a telegraph line that would link N America, Asia and Europe. Abandoned poles and derelict cabins can still be found along this route. All access to this wilderness is by rough trails that require visitors to be experienced and fully self-sufficient.

JOHN S. MARSH

Mount Everest Expedition The highest mountain in the world at 8847.7 m, Mt Everest lies on the border between Nepal and Tibet. It was first climbed in 1953 by New Zealander Edmund Hillary and Sherpa Tenzing Norgay. Since that time, Everest has been attempted by mountaineers from many nations. In 1982 the Canadian Mt Everest Expedition took up the challenge, under the sponsorship of Air Canada. The team consisted of 20 Canadians, under Bill March of Calgary, and 39 Nepalese Sherpas.

Preparations for the climb took 5 years and involved over 100 Canadian companies, who provided nearly 20 tonnes of equipment and food. Special equipment had to be designed and manufactured, including tents made of "bulletproof" nylon. Over 6000 man-days of food was packed in Canada into daily ration boxes for carrying up the mountain. In addition, preparations were made to send TV signals back to Canada using 3 satellites. (This was the first "live" TV coverage of an Everest expedition.) After a 240 km hike from Katmandu, capital city of Nepal, the expedition arrived at the base of Everest on 15 Aug 1982. Over the next 2 weeks rapid progress was made through the terrifying Icefall and into the Western Cwm ("valley"). By the end of Aug the route had been pioneered to Camp 2 at 6545 m. However, on Aug 31 tragedy struck when a huge avalanche fell across the route in the Icefall, killing 3 Sherpas. Two days later a collapsing ice tower killed cameraman Blair Griffiths.

This double blow stopped the expedition, sending half the team home, and it was 2 weeks before the climb could proceed. On Sept 22 the climbers established Camp 2 and started work on the upper mountain. Camp 3 was established at 7155 m, and on Oct 4 the final Camp 4 was occupied on the South Col at 7980 m. On Oct 5 the first summit team of 32-year-old Laurie SKRESLET of Calgary and Sherpas Sundgare and Lhakpa Dorje left the South Col camp at 4 AM and reached the summit at 9:15 AM after a rapid ascent. Two days later, the summit was reached a second time by 29-year-old Pat MORROW of Kimberley, BC, and Sherpas Pema Dorje and Lhakpa Tshering. The Canadian expedition thus placed 2 Canadians and 4 Sherpas on the summit of Everest on its first attempt in a year marked by very bad weather. JOHN AMATT

Mount Orford Park, Qué, est 1938, is a provincial park located near MAGOG. The 57 km² park runs along the base of Mounts Orford (881 m) and Chauve (599 m), which lie on the lower Appalachian plateau and are separated from each other by the Rivière-aux-Cerises as it cuts diagonally across the park. The escarpments of the 2 main massifs have made possible the development of a celebrated downhill ski area and the park's huge hydrographic network is ideal for water sports, especially on Stukely and Fraser lakes. The abundant and varied vegetation is part of the Laurentian maple groves. The fauna include a major deer ground and an impressive beaver colony. The JEUNESSES MUSICALES DU CANADA established the Orford Art Centre, a music camp and cultural centre, in 1951. The centre's concert hall, a 500-seat amphitheatre, opened in 1960, and 2 modern residences were added in 1970. The ORFORD STRING QUARTET was formed by 4 students in 1965. CLAUDINE PIERRE-DESCHÊNES

Mount Pearl, Nfld, Town, pop 20 293 (1986c), 17 487 (1981cA), inc 1955, is situated just SW of ST JOHN'S. Originally known as Mount Cochrane, it was an estate awarded to British naval officer James Pearl in 1834 by Gov Cochrane. The estate was subdivided at Pearl's death in 1840. In this century Mount Pearl was the site of Marconi's first experiment in transoceanic wireless telegraphy. Glendenning's Farm, part of the original estate and a government demonstration farm in the 1930s, was the site of an airfield used by aviation pioneers. A popular summer resort in the 1930s, Mount Pearl was developed as an urban centre by the 1950s. A number of large subdivisions were built in the 1960s and the town grew as a dormitory community, which eventually included in its boundaries Newtown and Donovans, a large industrial park. Apart from local services, Mount Pearl depends on the industrial park and the neighbouring city of St John's for most of its commerce and employment.
JANET E.M. PITT AND ROBERT D. PITT

Mount Revelstoke National Park (est 1914) is a place of contrasting landscape, varying from rain forests and lush alpine meadows to barren, rocky ridges and GLACIERS. The jagged spires of the Selkirk Range are the backdrop for this 263 km² park. Grizzly bear and caribou range throughout, while mountain goats frequent the rocky bluffs. Alpine meadows feature pika, hoary marmot and golden-mantled ground squirrel, often under the gaze of the golden eagle. Between Oct and June the park is covered in a thick blanket of snow, but in the brief summer, meadows glow with the blossoms of lupine, aster and Indian paintbrush. The park offers primitive backcountry campsites. Private campgrounds are located nearby on the TRANS-CANADA HIGHWAY. See also PARKS, NATIONAL.
LILLIAN STEWART

Mount Saint Vincent University, Halifax, was founded in 1873 by the Sisters of Charity of Saint Vincent de Paul as a women's academy. After 1914 post-secondary education was provided by affiliation with DALHOUSIE UNIVERSITY. Mount Saint Vincent achieved degree-granting status in 1925, becoming the first independent college for women in the Commonwealth. It was totally burned in 1951, but reconstruction was immediate. It continued to offer secondary education along with its post-secondary programs and consequently remained Mount Saint Vincent College until becoming a university in 1966. It is now a liberal arts and science facility directed by the Sisters of Charity. While 17% of the student population is now male, the university still retains its primary objective of providing an environment and opportunity for the higher education of women, within the Roman Catholic tradition. The university offers degree programs in arts, business administration, child study, education, home economics, public relations, science and secretarial arts; diploma programs in executive, legal and medical secretarial studies; a certificate program in gerontology and both a certificate and a diploma in business administration. Master of Arts degrees are offered in the fields of education, school psychology and home economics. LOIS KERNAGHAN

Mount Tremblant Provincial Park, the first in Québec, was established in 1894 and occupies 1248 km² of the LAURENTIAN HIGHLANDS about 125 km NW of Montréal. Geologically, the park includes the very old igneous rocks of the Canadian SHIELD and, in the S, the younger sedimentary rocks of the ST LAWRENCE LOWLANDS, all of which have been glaciated. Two regions can be identified, the massif in the S, rising to Mt TREMBLANT (968 m), and the northern Great Lakes area, averaging 500 m in elevation. The park contains a major hydrographic network of lakes, rivers and waterfalls, including the watersheds of the rivers St-Maurice, Matawin and L'Assomption. The rich vegetation varies with altitude but includes maples, birches and conifers. The abundant fauna includes moose, bear, fox, hare, beaver, many amphibians, 193 species of birds and 36 species of fish (notably trout). The area was used for logging and gradually became popular for summer and winter recreation. The park was reorganized in 1981 into 4 recreation zones accessible by highway, and 3 roadless nature preservation zones. Mount Tremblant is noted for its ski resort.
JOHN S. MARSH

Mount Uniacke, UP, pop 1364 (1986c), 1145 (1981c), is located in central NS 35 km W of HALIFAX, on the highest point between YARMOUTH and Halifax. Rivers flow from here S to the Atlantic and N into MINAS BASIN. In 1784 Richard John UNIACKE, attorney general of NS, 1797-1830, was granted 400 ha on the Windsor road. He named the home that he built on that land Uniacke House after the home of his Irish grandfather. It was frequented by Halifax high society and visited by the elite of England, such as Edward, Duke of Kent, father of Queen Victoria. Now owned by the NS government, it is considered perhaps the most interesting example of colonial architecture in Canada. In 1865 gold was discovered at Mount Uniacke and from 1866 to 1910 the mines were worked. Other industries of this village are lumbering and limited farming. In the past 20 years its population has grown considerably owing to its low tax base and its easy commuting distance to Halifax. JEANNIE PETERSON

Mountain, native group living on the Mackenzie Mt slopes down to the MACKENZIE R. Historically, various small groups using the eastern slopes of the mountain range have been called Mountain and have traded at all the posts between Ft Liard and Ft Good Hope. Those Mountain trading into Ft Norman since the 1820s have maintained their identity while most others have gradually merged with the native populations using other trading posts along the Mackenzie R. The Mountain are Athapaskan speakers and their language is closely related to HARE and BEARLAKE. Historically, the name was probably appropriate for all natives in this region, including the Goat and NAHANI. Most information comes from those who continue to trade and live at Ft Norman.

Although the Mountain have exploited a large expanse of the Mackenzie Mts, from the Redstone R north to the Mountain R, their estimated population (1827-1971) has been less than 150. During the 19th century and aboriginally (according to their own accounts), the Mountain were fearful of and sometimes hostile to all native groups on the western slopes of the mountains. After the KLONDIKE GOLD RUSH (1897-98), increased contact with Yukon natives gradually reduced apprehensions and some settled and married into Yukon native groups. There is no evidence in oral tradition of hostile encounters with the Indians of the eastern region although contact was infrequent before the FUR TRADE.

The Mountain were almost totally dependent on moose, woodland caribou, mountain goats and Dall sheep. Population cycles or variations in migratory routes sometimes made it necessary to survive on the previous season's caches. This environment was often abundant, but during a bad winter, entire family bands could starve. The area is not rich in fur-bearing animals valuable in the fur trade. Most trade was in dried meat, grease and hides. In the late 19th century the Mountain developed the mooseskin boat – framed with green spruce wood and covered with raw moosehides sewn together. The boats were usually 12-18 m long and greatly increased the amount of trade goods that could be transported, although they were only functional for the trip down the rivers; people and dogs had to ascend the mountains by foot. This was often done in both spring and fall until the 1940s when dry meat and grease were no longer acceptable trade items. By mid-20th century the Mountain had made Ft Norman their permanent location. They now share their hunting, trapping and fishing areas with other native peoples in the Ft Norman area.
BERYL C. GILLESPIE

Reading: Handbook of North American Indians, vol 6: Subarctic, ed, J. Helm (1981).

Mountain, landform with steep sides and narrow summit area that rises prominently above adjacent land. A mountain is higher than a hill and smaller in area than a plateau, but the distinction is relative, depending more on relief (vertical distance from summits to valleys) than on size or elevation (vertical distance above mean sea level). Volcanic mountains or VOLCANOES are built by the accumulation of lava and solid ejecta from a volcanic vent. Erosional mountains are remnants of once larger uplands that have been dissected by streams or glaciers (*see* GLACIATION). Tectonic mountains have been elevated by crustal disturbances such as folding, faulting or plutonic activity (*see* PLATE TECTONICS). Most mountains are the product of several processes and their form depends on age, rock type and climate, which influence the type, extent and rate of EROSION. Mt Everest (elevation 8847.7 m), in the Himalayas, is the highest point on the Earth. The highest mountain in Canada is Mt LOGAN (elevation 5950 m) in the St Elias Mountains (*see* ST ELIAS, MOUNT) of the YT. The mountains having the greatest relief on the Earth are the volcanoes of oceanic islands, which rise from the deep ocean floor, eg, Mauna Kea, the highest mountain in Hawaii, which extends 9752 m from the ocean floor. *See also* GEOLOGICAL REGIONS. J.G. SOUTHER

Mountain, Jacob, first Anglican bishop of Québec (b at Thwaite Hall, Norfolk, Eng 1 Dec 1749; d at Québec City 16 June 1825). After graduation from Cambridge and 7 years of parish work, Mountain was appointed bishop of the new diocese of Québec in 1793. His episcopate coincided with the Napoleonic struggle and, largely because of the British government's preoccupation with it, Mountain was unable either to persuade those in authority to organize an effective church establishment in Québec or to subject the Roman Catholic Church to a form of government control, policies that he understood had been formulated and pursued after the cession of 1763. Yet Mountain accomplished much. In his episcopate 60 churches were built, including a stone cathedral in Québec City. He vigorously defended his church's claim to the CLERGY RESERVES. Between 1815 and 1825, a period of heavy immigration, he opened 35 missions. His clergy increased from 9 to 60, and he was able to augment their scanty stipends. He encouraged a new school system in Lower Canada and obtained a charter for McGill. Under pioneer conditions he made 8 laborious tours of the Canadas, going as far as Sandwich [Windsor].

A splendid preacher, Mountain was respected by colleagues in the Executive and Legislative councils of Lower Canada, with whom he was not always in agreement. He was not without his critics. The Roman Catholic hierarchy was apprehensive of his efforts to elevate the status of his church. Several governors and British colonial secretaries found his repeated demands difficult and even some of his clergy considered him more fitted for an English rather than a colonial see. But, aided by clergy and laity and with assistance from government and especially from the Society for the Propagation of the Gospel, he laid strong church foundations on which his successors, including his son George, later bishop of Montréal and third bishop of Québec, were able to build. T.R. MILLMAN

Reading: T.R. Millman, *Jacob Mountain, First Lord Bishop of Québec* (1947).

Mountain Ash (*Sorbus*), genus of small trees or shrubs of the rose family (Rosaceae), consisting of perhaps 100 species distributed in temperate Eurasia and N America. Plants are deciduous, lack thorns, and have simple or pinnate (feather-

Snowy mountain ash (*Sorbus decora*), with flowers and fruit. The small red fruits are much sought after by birds (*artwork by Claire Tremblay*).

like) leaves with 9-11 leaflets. Creamy white flowers form large, flat-topped clusters. Small, red, applelike fruits are much sought after by birds. There are 4 species native to Canada, usually found in moist woods: 2 eastern (*S. americana, S. decora*) and 2 western (*S. scopulina, S. sitchensis*). The introduced European mountain ash or rowan (*S. aucuparia*) is grown as an ORNAMENTAL from the Queen Charlotte Is to Newfoundland, and often escapes, appearing native. In some reference works, *Sorbus* is included in the genus *Pyrus* (pear). Berries and bark were used as medicine by N American Indians. The wood is easily bent and was used for CANOE frames and snowshoes. Mountain ash is not a true ASH.

Mountain Avens, common name for dwarf, trailing or mat-forming shrubs in genus *Dryas* of the rose family (Rosaceae). The genus includes about 4 species found mainly at higher altitudes of the Northern Hemisphere. Three are native to Canada. Furry, evergreen leaves, a single decorative flower and a mat-forming ability make mountain avens popular for rock gardens. They may be grown from cuttings, tuft division and from seed, particularly in sandy soil. The very hardy species *D. integrifolia* was chosen (1957) as the floral emblem of the NWT, where it is abundant and blooms June-July. It grows on rocky, barren slopes in the mountains of BC and Alberta, and throughout the territories and the arctic archipelago. This species has a corolla of white petals with a yellow centre. *See also* PROVINCIAL FLORAL EMBLEMS. CÉLINE ARSENEAULT

Three species of mountain avens are found in Canada, including the hardy species *Dryas integrifolia*, the floral emblem of the NWT (*photo by Mary W. Ferguson*).

Mountain Beaver (*Aplodontia rufa*), most primitive living member of order RODENTIA. Unlike true BEAVER, mountain beaver has no close living relative. It resembles a tailless muskrat and has a thick-set, heavy body, small ears and eyes, forefeet equipped with long, strong, curved claws for digging, and dense, short, grizzled brown fur. Adult males average 850 g in weight, females 775 g. Mountain beavers breed once annually (Feb-Mar), have a gestation period of 28-30 days and bear 2-3 young. They inhabit moist coniferous forests of the Cascade Mts from southwestern BC to central California. The mountain beaver digs a burrow system in damp, porous soil near streams. Burrow tunnels are 10-25 cm in diameter and 25-150 cm underground. Although several burrow systems may be adjacent, giving the appearance of a colony, the animals are by nature solitary. They do not hibernate and, in winter, eat conifer needles, leaves, tender twigs and bark, often climbing 2.5 m up shrubs and trees to clip branches. In summer they prefer sword ferns, bracken, leaves and various herbaceous plants. They can cause extensive damage by girdling young conifers and shrubs and by eating vegetable crops in gardens. R. BOONSTRA

Mountain Goat (*Oreamnos americanus*), even-toed, hoofed mammal of the cattle family (Bovidae), derived during the ice ages from the primitive Asiatic goat-antelopes. It is not a true goat but belongs to a tribe ancestral to sheep and goats. The mountain goat, largest and most cold-hardy species of its tribe, is widely distributed in the Canadian western mountains. Adapted to life on steep cliffs where footholds are often covered by snow or ice, it is a slow, methodical climber and compensates for a narrow habitat with wide food habits. Males may exceed 125 kg; females weigh about 15% less. Adult females with kids dominate all other goats, including the largest males. In hard winters such females evict other goats from choice habitat; in mild winters goats remain gregarious. Both sexes have short, curved horns that can inflict severe damage in rare but vicious fights. Male goats are protected by an exceptionally thick hide that, during mating season, swells on the haunches to a thickness exceeding 2 cm.

Mountain goat (*Oreamnos americanus*), the largest and most cold-hardy species of its tribe, is widely distributed in the mountains of western Canada (*photo by Wayne Lankinen/DRK Photo*).

Goats have thin, fragile skulls and do not clash head on. Adult males avoid combat if possible, relying on elaborate dominance displays. They normally withdraw from aggressive females. Males are dominant only at the peak of the mating season. Afterwards, they leave the female ranges or are evicted. One, rarely 2, kids are born in June and are carefully guarded by females. Mountain goats are adversely affected by disturbances and can be easily overhunted, but are rarely preyed on by natural predators.

VALERIUS GEIST

Mountain Range, a linear arrangement of mountain peaks and ridges surrounded by adjacent lower land or clearly separated from adjacent ranges by intervening valleys. The mountains of a range are commonly related to a single geological structure or rock formation. A group of related peaks with a circular rather than linear arrangement is called a massif. An array of mountain ranges, massifs and other topographic elements of related origin comprise a mountain system, and several systems a CORDILLERA. The Cordillera of western N America extends from Mexico to Alaska and includes about 20 mountain systems each composed of many mountain ranges. The Earth's major mountain systems lie along the margins of crustal plates where concentrated tectonic forces have caused uplift, deformation and igneous activity (*see* GEOLOGICAL PROCESSES; PLATE TECTONICS). Individual mountain ranges may be formed by volcanic eruptions or, more commonly, by differential EROSION of an uplifted terrane. When rapid uplift is accompanied by slow erosion, a plateau results. If erosion keeps pace with uplift, streams and GLACIERS erode away less competent rock, leaving more resistant rock standing as mountain ranges between the valleys. The long, narrow ranges of the ROCKY MOUNTAIN system of western Canada reflect the structure of resistant beds of folded and faulted sedimentary strata; the broader ranges and massifs of the Coast Range of BC were etched by water and glacier ice from an uplifted, granitic terrane of more uniform resistance to erosion. The relief and ruggedness of a mountain range depend on its age. The precipitous, very young ranges of the St Elias Mountains in the southwestern YT, where rapid uplift is still proceeding, include the highest individual peaks in Canada. Uplift of the somewhat less rugged Rocky Mts began to decline after an episode of deformation about 70 million years ago. The subdued topography of the ancient Appalachian Mts is the result of erosion during the 150 million years since the last major uplift and deformation in eastern Canada. Submarine mountain ranges, which rise from the ocean floor along mid-ocean ridges, such as the mid-Atlantic Ridge and East Pacific Rise, are of volcanic origin. On the moon and on planets that have little atmosphere, such as Mercury and Mars, circular or crescent-shaped mountain ranges around impact craters have survived for hundreds of millions of years without being destroyed by erosion. *See also* GEOLOGICAL REGIONS; VOLCANO.

J.G. SOUTHER

Mountain Sheep, highly successful, medium-sized, even-toed mammals of the cattle family (Bovidae), genus *Ovis*, comprising some 37 races in Eurasia and southern N America. SHEEP colonized N America during the last glaciation but remained rare until after the extinction of many large American mammals, about 11 000 years ago. In Canada, 2 species, each with 2 races, are recognized. Bighorns (*O. canadensis*) include the California bighorn in the arid ranges of southcentral BC and the larger Rocky Mountain bighorn in the Canadian Rockies. Thinhorn or Dall sheep (*O. dalli*) occur in the Territories and in northern BC. One race, black Stone sheep (*O. d. stonei*), is confined to Canada. Many sheep are glacier followers, doing best in cool, dry, sunny mountains within sight of snowfields. They vary greatly in size, reflecting the quality of their habitat. Large bighorn males (6 years or older) weigh about 110-120 kg in autumn; large females, 60-70 kg. Thinhorns weigh about 20% less. Fully grown males carry the largest horns relative to body size of horned mammals. These may measure over 115 cm, and weigh 10-12 kg. Horns are used like sledgehammers in fighting, as shields, and as symbols of rank among older males. A single lamb is born in late May or early June. In Canada, sheep are not endangered and respond well to wildlife management.

VALERIUS GEIST

The thinhorn, or Dall, sheep (*Ovis dalli*), found in the territories and northern BC (*photo by Stephen J. Krasemann/DRK Photo*).

Mountaineering is the practice of climbing in mountainous terrain for pleasure or research. Although it is usually associated with dangerous assaults of formidable summits, there are several elements to the activity, each often pursued for its own sake. Many people restrict their mountaineering to hikes in the lower regions of the mountains; others specialize in steep rock climbing, whether it be a 5 m boulder or a 1000 m cliff; others prefer climbing snow and ice; and yet others combine all 3 elements to stand atop the great alpine peaks of the world.

People have climbed mountains for centuries, either for religious reasons or simply to see the surrounding land better, but mountaineering as recreation is less than 150 years old. Towards the middle of the 18th century, European naturalists turned their attention to the glaciers of the Chamonix Valley of France, and their studies, combined with the Victorian era's interest in natural phenomena, gave birth to a general fascination with mountains. The earliest climbs in the mid-European Alps, such as Mont Blanc in 1786, were undertaken in the name of science, but by the early decades of the 19th century the Germans, French and Swiss were pursuing summits simply for pleasure. It remained for the British, however, to popularize the sport. During mountaineering's golden age – the years between 1854, when Alfred Wills climbed Switzerland's Wetterhorn, and 1865, when the combined teams of Edward Whymper and Rev Charles Hudson conquered the Matterhorn – more than 60 of the most difficult, spectacular climbs in the Alps were made for the first time, primarily by British climbers.

Within 15 years of the Matterhorn ascent, all the Alps of consequence had been scaled, and mountaineers began to look for new challenges. Some tackled more difficult routes up mountains previously ascended, and others explored new mountain ranges – the Andes of S America, the Caucasus of Russia, the Himalayas, the mountains of Africa and the western mountains of N America. The completion of the CPR in 1885 opened the SELKIRK MTS and the ROCKY MTS of Canada, and they became the first ranges on the continent to be systematically explored for their mountaineering potential. Glacier House, below ROGERS PASS in the Selkirks, was an internationally recognized meeting place for climbers in the late 1880s and early 1890s, but its popularity was soon overshadowed by LAKE LOUISE in the Rockies. To promote mountaineering in the western ranges, the CPR employed Swiss climbing guides for its clientele from 1899 to 1912. The ALPINE CLUB OF CANADA, modelled after Britain's prestigious Alpine Club (1850), was formed 1906 and published its first journal the next year.

Most of the early climbing in the Selkirks and Rockies was done by British members of the Alpine Club or by American members of the Appalachian Mountaineering Club of Boston. Phillop Abbot, a young lawyer, was climbing with a party from the AMC in 1895 when he fell from the icy flanks of Mt Lefroy above Lk Louise to become N America's first mountaineering casualty. Landmark climbs of the early years include Mt Sir Donald in 1890, Mt Temple in 1894, Mt Lefroy in 1897 and Mt ASSINIBOINE in 1901. Mt ROBSON, at 3954 m the loftiest of the Rockies, was not successfully climbed until 1913, after attempts by 5 separate parties dating from 1908.

Although the Rockies have remained internationally popular with climbers to the present day, the quest for new terrain carried climbers throughout Canada's North and West in the 1920s. In 1924, inspired by a daring British attempt on Mt Everest, the Alpine Club of Canada sponsored a climb of 5950 m Mt LOGAN, the highest elevation of Canada and second highest of the continent. In May 1925 a team of climbers under Albert H. MAC-CARTHY entered the St Elias Mts on the boundary between Alaska and the Yukon Territory. After 2 months among the highest, most glaciated mountains in N America, the men emerged to say they had reached the summit on the afternoon of June 23. Two years later, a first attempt was made on Mt WADDINGTON, at 4019 m the most impressive peak of the COAST MTS of BC. Despite repeated assaults, however, the summit remained untouched until 1936, when 2 Americans inched their way up the S face, at that time the hardest rock climb in N America.

Marmolata, Pigeon and Snowpatch spires, left to right, in the Purcell Mts, BC (*photo by Pat Morrow*).

Towards the summit of the Bugaboo Spire in the Purcell Mts, BC (*photo by Pat Morrow*).

Although Canada's mountains have been internationally famous for decades, Canada has produced few international mountaineers. During the late 1950s and early 1960s, however, many fine British- and European-born climbers settled in Canada, and under their tutelage a core of excellent Canadian climbers has emerged. Using refined climbing techniques and modern technological aids, the new generation has been quick to attempt increasingly difficult climbs on well-known mountains – winter ascents of the great N walls of the Rockies, or the knife-edge ridges and soaring buttresses of Mt Logan, for example – or untried peaks in places as far-flung as BAFFIN and ELLESMERE islands. Canadian centres of mountaineering activity include Montréal, Ottawa, Toronto, Thunder Bay, Calgary, Edmonton, Banff, Vancouver and Vancouver I, all of which are members of the Alpine Club of Canada. Climbers are rapidly extending the limits of both rock and waterfall ice climbing.

Canadians are also beginning to make their presence felt abroad. In 1977 the First Canadian Himalayan Expedition successfully negotiated Mt Pumori (7131 m), and in 1981 another team struggled to the summit of Dhaulagiri to become the first Canadians to stand atop an 8000 m peak. The most ambitious undertaking of the early 1980s, however, came in late Aug 1982, when a team of climbers, under Bill March of Calgary, left Katmandu, Nepal, bound for Mt Everest. More than a month later, on Oct 5, Laurie SKRESLET of Calgary became the first Canadian to stand on top of the world's highest mountain, followed 2 days later by Pat MORROW of Kimberley, BC. Members of that expedition returned to the Himalayas in subsequent years to attempt ambitious climbs on, among other peaks, Makalu (8490 m) and Kanchenjunga (8598 m). In May 1987 the 12-person non-Sherpa-supported Canadian Everest Light Expedition put 2 more Canadians, Dwayne CONGDON and Sharon WOOD, on top of Everest via the challenging West Ridge. Later that year, a contingent of 5 Québec climbers joined mountaineers from Poland and England to attempt the first winter ascent of K2, an endeavour considered by many to be mountaineering's greatest

contemporary challenge. *See also* MOUNT EVEREST EXPEDITION.   BART ROBINSON

Reading: R.W. Clark, *Men, Myths and Mountains* (1976); Chris Jones, *Climbing in North America* (1976).

Mouse, common name for several RODENTS of suborder Myomorpha, 11 species of which are found in Canada. Six are New World mice of the Cricetidae family: western harvest mouse, *Reithrodontomys megalotis;* DEER MOUSE, *Peromyscus maniculatus;* Cascade deer mouse, *P. oreas;* Sitka mouse, *P. sitkensis;* white-footed mouse, *P. leucopus;* and northern grasshopper mouse, *Onychomys leucogaster.* Four belong to the Dipodidae family: Pacific, western, meadow and woodland jumping mice (*Zapus trinotatus, Z. princeps, Z. hudsonius* and *Napaeozapus insignis,* respectively). One species of the Old World Muridae family, the house mouse (*Mus musculus),* was introduced by the first colonists. The familiar field mouse is actually the meadow VOLE. The western harvest mouse is the smallest, only 13 cm long including the tail. The largest, the western jumping mouse, measures 25 cm. Meadow jumping mice, deer mice and house mice are common throughout Canada. Sitka mice occur on the smaller Queen Charlotte Is. Cascade deer mice are limited to southern interior BC. Other species inhabit larger areas but are also limited to specific regions. Mice occur in forest and field but habitat varies with species. Most mice are primarily granivorous; in contrast, northern grasshopper mice are insectivorous. All mice are nocturnal. Some species remain active throughout winter, while others hibernate. House mice reproduce throughout the year, but most species are sexually active only from spring to autumn, generally producing several litters during the period. Mice are prey for various birds, mammals and snakes. Although certain species do not affect the economy, other granivorous species damage crops and reforestation projects.   JEAN FERRON

Mousseau, Jean-Paul-Armand, artist (b at Montréal 1 Jan 1927). After studying painting and interior decoration (1941-46), he studied under Paul-Émile BORDUAS (1946-51). In 1946 he joined Borduas and 5 students in the first group exhibition of abstract art held in Montréal. He was one of 16 to sign the REFUS GLOBAL (1948) and participated in all AUTOMATISTE exhibitions. During the mid-1950s he became interested in experimental work having elements in common with what the PLASTICIEN group was doing. By the mid-1960s, however, he had abandoned painting. His long-held belief that art must not be isolated from daily life led him into designing costumes, jewellery and posters, as well as into theatrical and interior design, sculpture and mural designs. In his 1961-62 murals for Hydro-Québec (Montréal) he used such nontraditional media as fibreglass, plastic resin and neon lighting, Mousseau being one of the most daring exploiters of new media and techniques during the early 1960s. He has concentrated on collaborating with architects, and his courses taught at the U de Québec à Montréal and at U Laval have explored the integration of colours, textures, materials and lighting into architecture.   BRIAN FOSS

Mousseau, Joseph-Alfred, lawyer, journalist, writer, politician, judge, premier of Québec 1882-84 (b at Berthier-en-Haut, LC 18 July 1838; d at Montréal 30 Mar 1886). Mousseau was admitted to the bar in 1860 and practised civil and criminal law for 20 years, becoming QC in 1873. Co-founder of both *Le Colonisateur* in 1867 and *L'Opinion publique* in 1870 and a supporter of CONFEDERATION in 1867, he won the federal riding of Bagot for the Conservative Party in 1874. He was re-elected in 1878 and became head of the

Executive Council on 8 Nov 1880 and, on May 20, secretary of state. In July 1882 he agreed to exchange positions with J.A. CHAPLEAU, thus becoming premier of Québec. After 2 years of division and strife within the Conservative Party, he resigned at the request of the federal leaders and became a puisne judge of the superior court for the district of Rimouski.   ANDRÉE DÉSILETS

Mowachaht ("people of the deer") a NOOTKA Indian tribe of NOOTKA SOUND, Vancouver I. They are also known as the Nootka, which is also the ethnolinguistic name for many tribes with similar languages and culture on the west coast of Vancouver I. The Mowachaht formerly consisted of 2 independent tribal groups that amalgamated as a result of disease and prolonged warfare in the historic period. Their traditional territories include the outer coast of Nootka I, Nootka Sound, Tahsis Inlet and Tlupana Inlet. Tribal villages were Yuquot and Coopte. Archaeological investigations reveal that Yuquot has been occupied by native people for at least 4300 years.

Prior to the formation of the Mowachaht, the tribal group at Yuquot was the first Nootkan people to have extensive contact with Europeans. They traded sea otter pelts with Capt James COOK in 1778, and controlled all native trade with his ships. Cook's crew found that the sea otter pelts could be sold for great profit in China, and a maritime FUR TRADE in sea otter pelts began in 1785. Yuquot, known as Nootka and Friendly Cove, soon became a major trading centre. The Yuquot, led by Chief MAQUINNA, controlled the trade at Nootka Sd, and became wealthy and powerful. In 1789 a Spanish expedition built a military post at Yuquot, and seized British trading ships, resulting in the NOOTKA SOUND CONTROVERSY. By the mid-1790s the trade declined at Nootka Sd. This may have influenced Maquinna to capture the trading ship *Boston* in 1803, ending the sea otter trade at Nootka Sd.

Reduction from prolonged warfare and European-introduced diseases caused many of the groups to amalgamate. In the 19th century the 2 tribal groups of Tahsis and Tlupana Inlets joined, forming the Mowachaht. In the 20th century they were joined by the Muchalaht, whose band officially merged with the Mowachaht band. Today the Mowachaht live at the village of Ahaminaqus, near Gold River, and at Yuquot.   JOHN DEWHIRST

Mowat, Farley, author (b at Belleville, Ont 12 May 1921). Mowat has been writing since his pre-teens. He recalls composing "mostly verse" while living with his family in Windsor (1930-33) and then publishing a regular column based on his observations of birds in the *Star-Phoenix* after his family moved to Saskatoon. He studied at U of T; on a field trip as a student biologist he became outraged at the problems of the Inuit, all of which he attributed to white misunderstanding and exploitation. His observations led to his first book, *People of the Deer* (1952), which made him an instant, albeit controversial, celebrity. Twenty-six books followed, many of which argued similar positions; in consequence, his works are bitterly attacked by some, highly praised by others; few readers remain neutral. He is reputed Canada's most widely read author; his books have been published in over 40 countries.

Mowat is considered a "natural" storyteller; he is also a brilliant stylist. No matter what the context, his narratives and anecdotes are fast-paced and compelling; his tone is graceful, personal, and conversational. Commitments to ideals inspire verbal fireworks; enthusiasms evoke poetic descriptions and vivid images; antipathies produce ridicule, lampoons and at times, evangelical condemnation. Most works are autobiographi-

By the time his 25th book appeared in 1979, Farley Mowat was reputedly Canada's most widely read author (*photo by Ron Watts/First Light*).

cal: *The Dog Who Wouldn't Be* (1957) and *Owls in the Family* (1961) are comic recollections of his youth; *The Regiment* (1961) and *And No Birds Sang* (1979) deal with his WWII experiences. Three books centre on his 8-year residency in Burgeo, Nfld: *The Rock Within the Sea* (1968) presents his seafaring neighbours as heroic because uncorrupted by modern technology; *The Boat Who Wouldn't Float* (1969) reflects his later disillusion; *A Whale for the Killing* (1972) transforms the wanton shooting of a trapped whale into a symbolic tragedy. His more recent *Sea of Slaughter* (1984) chronicles the destruction of species in the N Atlantic. The highly ironic *My Discovery of America* (1985) speculates on the reasons he was denied admission to the US for a lecture tour, and his *Virunga: The Passion of Dian Fossey* (1987) is a biography of the well-known primatologist.

Mowat's only novels are for juveniles. *Lost in the Barrens* (1956) won the Gov Gen's Award and is a masterpiece which incorporates many of the themes central to his adult works. On the surface an adventure story, its structure is allegorical: 2 youths — a Toronto-bred Caucasian and a Cree Indian — are able to survive an arctic winter for a time by sharing their skills, but eventually their insufficient knowledge of the North nearly dooms them; they can be rescued only by an Inuit boy whose knowledge supplements their own. GERALD J. RUBIO

Mowat, Sir Oliver, politician, premier of Ontario 1872-96 (b at Kingston, Upper Canada 22 July 1820; d at Toronto 19 Apr 1903). Mowat was privately educated in Kingston before becoming John A. MACDONALD's first articled law student. He was admitted to the bar in 1841 and quickly became a successful equity lawyer in Toronto. Mowat was brought up a Conservative, but as an adult opted for the Reform Party. After a brief interlude in Toronto municipal politics he sat in the Assembly of the Province of Canada 1858-64 where he was a prominent Reform leader. He served as provincial secretary in the brief administration of George BROWN and A.A. DORION in 1858, was postmaster general in the John Sandfield MACDONALD-Dorion regime in 1863-64, and returned to that portfolio during the GREAT COALITION of 1864. Mowat, as an active participant in the QUEBEC CONFERENCE, was a FATHER OF CONFEDERATION. In Nov 1864 he was appointed chancellor of Ontario, a post he held until 1872 when he succeeded Edward BLAKE as premier. He served as premier and attorney general until 1896 when he was appointed to the Senate and became federal minister of justice. Knighted in 1892, he left Ottawa in 1897 to become lt-gov of Ontario.

Mowat's greatest contribution was made as premier. A skilful electoral politician, he built a pragmatic and moderate Liberal Party, representative of all Ontario – Protestant and Catholic, rural and urban. Under Mowat's leadership, Ontario came of age economically, socially and politically. Agriculture was modernized, the importance of industry recognized, educational and scientific areas cultivated, urban problems addressed and trade unions accepted as part of the society. Substantial government regulation became part of Ontario life and numerous social programs were introduced. Mowat and his government also contributed to the definition of Canadian FEDERALISM. He was Canada's first important provincial-rights advocate and, through a series of successful legal and political battles with John A. Macdonald and the federal Conservative government, altered Macdonald's concept of Canada as a highly centralized state with the provinces weak and dependent. Moreover, Mowat and his colleagues established Ontario as the dominant province within Confederation. Ontario's resources were increased by expansion into northern territories and its boundaries substantially enlarged after a protracted dispute with the federal government. Good management of the key economic sectors of agriculture, industry and resources made it the richest province, and it is fair to describe Mowat's tenure of office as the era of the emergence of modern Ontario. DONALD SWAINSON

Muchalaht, a NOOTKA Indian tribe on the west coast of Vancouver I. Their traditional territories include Muchalat Inlet and the Gold R valley. Their main villages were Cheeshish and Ahaminaquus. The Muchalaht, unlike most Nootka, did not have access to the outer coast, and adapted to riverine and inland environments. Rich salmon streams, elk and deer were important for subsistence. After decimation by prolonged warfare they merged with the MOWACHAHT in the 19th century. In the early 20th century, a Muchalaht man inherited the Maquinna title of first chief of the Mowachaht, and the remaining Muchalaht moved to the Mowachaht village of Yuquot. In the 1950s the Muchalaht Band formally amalgamated with the Mowachaht (then Nootka) Band. JOHN DEWHIRST

Muhlstock, Louis, painter (b at Narajow, [Poland] 23 Apr 1904), best known as a painter of the Depression. Muhlstock came to Montréal in 1911 and worked for his family's fruit-importing firm. He took art lessons at night and from 1928 to 1931 studied in France. After 1931 he taught drawing at his Montréal studio and also drew unemployed men in nearby Fletcher's Field, capturing the spirit of the times in sensitive drawings in chalk or charcoal often done on wrapping paper. He evoked his east-end neighbourhood in vibrant street scenes from the market on St Lawrence-Main or shadowed yards. During WWII he sketched riveters at the Montréal shipyards, shown as *War Workers, 1945*. Muhlstock received recognition in 1937 from Douglas DUNCAN of the Picture Loan Soc, Toronto. During the 1950s and 1960s he held one-man shows at the Montreal Museum of Fine Arts and Waddington Galleries; in 1972 at the Verdun Cultural Centre. In 1976

Oliver Mowat, shown in 1869, was Ontario's premier (1872-96) during the emergence of modern Ontario (*courtesy National Archives of Canada/PA 28973*).

the Windsor Art Gallery exhibited "45 Years of Muhlstock"; in 1978 he showed at Place des Arts, and in 1986 Concordia U showed "New Theme and Variations." By this time Muhlstock's work was entirely abstract. ANNE MCDOUGALL

Mukherjee, Bharati, novelist, short-story writer (b at Calcutta, India 27 July 1940). Educated in India (BA U of Calcutta 1959, MA U of Baroda 1961) and the US (MFA 1963, PhD 1969, U of Iowa), Mukherjee emigrated from the US to Canada in 1966 but returned to the US in 1980 because she found that Canadian attitudes to East Indians — particularly East Indian women — had grown increasingly intolerant. Her fiction powerfully and sensitively evokes the cultural tensions and torn identities that her East Indian protagonists suffer both in N America and in India as they lived amidst the disjunctions of 2 very separate worlds and world views. Mukherjee has taught at Marquette (1964-65), U of Wisconsin (1965), McGill (1966-78), Skidmore College and currently, Montclair State College. Her first novel, *The Tiger's Daughter* (1972), was followed by *Wife* (1975). Mukherjee's acclaimed joint autobiographical account of her year in India – *Days and Nights in Calcutta*, written with her husband, writer Clark BLAISE – appeared in 1977, and her finest work to date, the book of short stories, *Darkness*, was published in 1985. With Blaise, she has completed *The Sorrow and the Terror*, an exploration of the 1985 Air India crash. NEIL BESNER

Mukluk, a watertight boot of INUIT manufacture, suitable for walking on the TUNDRA. The sole is made of sealskin and is sewn to tops of caribou skin. Sinew thread, used in a blind stitch passing only halfway through the skin, makes watertight seams. In winter and in cold weather several pairs are worn simultaneously. RENÉ R. GADACZ

Mullock, John Thomas, Roman Catholic bishop (b at Limerick, Ire 27 Sept 1807; d at St John's 29 Mar 1869). Consecrated bishop in 1847, Mullock came to Newfoundland as coadjutor in 1848. Two years later he became bishop of Newfoundland and directed the affairs of the church energetically for 20 years. He completed the cathedral, founded a new palace episcopal library, established St Bonaventure's College and 2 convents for the Presentation and Mercy Sisters, increased the number of priests and in 1856 divided the island into 2 dioceses. Involved in early attempts to develop steam, sail and cable communications in Newfoundland, he originated the idea of a transatlantic telegraph cable link from N America to Europe. His political support of the Liberals under P.F. LITTLE and John KENT was controversial, and his intervention in the 1861 election ultimately led to the decline of his influence. A scholar of wit and eloquence, he wrote many lectures and pamphlets.   J. ROGERS

Mulock, Sir William, lawyer, educator, Cabinet minister, provincial court justice (b at Bond Head, Canada W 19 Jan 1844; d at Toronto 1 Oct 1944). In Parliament from 1882 to 1905, Mulock was postmaster general (1896-1905) under LAURIER. He organized the federal Dept of Labour, becoming its first minister (1900-05) and bringing W.L. Mackenzie KING into public life as deputy minister. He negotiated an intergovernmental agreement to establish a telecommunications cable linking Canada, Australia and New Zealand and was instrumental in joining Canada and the UK through radio (1903). Advocating government ownership of Bell Telephone, he chaired the 1905 parliamentary inquiry into telephones until he was appointed chief justice of the Exchequer Division of the Supreme Court of Ontario (1905); he was chief justice of Ontario 1923-36. As vice-chancellor of U of T (1881-1900), he was the primary force in federating denominational and professional colleges into the expanded, co-operative university. He served as chancellor from 1924 to 1944.   ROBERT E. BABE

Mulroney, Martin Brian, lawyer, politician, prime minister of Canada (b at Baie-Comeau, Qué 20 Mar 1939). The son of Irish immigrants, Mulroney's father was an electrician, anxious that his children escape the paper mill that dominated BAIE-COMEAU. Brian attended the private St Thomas High School in Chatham, NB, and then St Francis Xavier U in Antigonish, NS, where he studied political science, joined the campus Conservative club, and was prime minister in the Combined Atlantic Universities Parliament. He worked for John DIEFENBAKER's successful leadership campaign in 1956. Smooth beyond his years, fluently bilingual and gregarious, Mulroney returned to Québec in 1961, receiving a law degree at Laval. He joined a major Montréal law firm (now Ogilvy-Renault) in 1964, soon specializing in labour negotiations for concerns such as Iron Ore Company of Canada and POWER CORPORATION OF CANADA. His father died in 1965, and Mulroney took on heavy family responsibilities. Later, in 1973, he married Mila Pivnicki. In 1974-75 he won public attention as an articulate and hard-hitting member of the Cliche Commission on violence and corruption in the construction industry in Québec. By now he was the leading Conservative organizer and fund-raiser in the province. Despite never having run for office, he was a strong candidate for the leadership of the federal party in 1976, finally being eliminated on the third ballot. He became VP of Iron Ore Company in 1976; as president 1977-83 he emphasized management-labour relations and was able, at the end of his term, to close the company's operation in SCHEFFERVILLE, Qué, without serious political repercussions. Mulroney again ran for the PC leadership in 1983, a low-key effort in response to charges that his 1976 campaign had been too slick and showy. He beat Joe CLARK on the final ballot: 1584 votes to 1325. As leader of the Opposition and MP for Central Nova in 1983-84, he proved a skilful manager, concentrating on healing party wounds and building a solid electoral machine. Moderate and conciliatory by nature, he called

Martin Brian Mulroney
Eighteenth Prime Minister of Canada

Birth: 20 Mar 1939, Baie-Comeau, Qué
Father/Mother: Ben/Mary Irene O'Shea
Father's Occupation: Electrician
Education: St Francis Xavier; U Laval
Religious Affiliation: Roman Catholic
First Occupation: Lawyer
Last Private Occupation: Executive
Political Party: Progressive Conservative
Period as PM: 17 Sept 1984-
Ridings: Central Nova 1983-84;
          Manicouagan 1984-
Marriage: 26 May 1973 to Mila Pivnicki (b 1953)
Children: 3 boys, 1 girl

(photo 1983 by Ron Watts/First Light)

for a strengthened private sector and less government intervention in the economy, minority French-language rights, and closer Canadian-American and federal-provincial relations. In the general election of 1984 he ran an almost flawless campaign against PM John TURNER's Liberals and won 211 seats, the largest number in Canadian history. Mulroney, who had always emphasized the importance of Québec to the Conservatives, captured the seat of Manicouagan, his home riding. The party took 58 of its seats in the province, the breakthrough that Mulroney had promised would take place under his leadership. He was sworn in as the 18th prime minister on 17 Sept 1984. The first 2 years of Mulroney's administration were marked by indecision and scandals in his Cabinet, but by spring 1987 he continued with his initiative for a FREE TRADE agreement with the US, reached in Oct of that year. One of his major accomplishments was the negotiation of the MEECH LAKE ACCORD, which, if ratified by the provinces, would finally bring Québec into the constitutional agreement.   NORMAN HILLMER

Multiculturalism, as a term, first came into vogue in the 1960s to counter "biculturalism," a term popularized by the Royal Commission on BILINGUALISM AND BICULTURALISM. It has to a considerable extent replaced the term "cultural pluralism," although that term is still favoured in Québec. Its use has spread from Canada to many countries, notably Australia. The term is used in at least 3 senses: to refer to a society that is characterized by ethnic or cultural heterogeneity; to refer to an ideal of equality and mutual respect among a population's ethnic or cultural groups; and to refer to government policy proclaimed by the federal government in 1971 and subsequently by a number of provinces. In Dec 1987 the Conservative government tabled a bill to introduce the Canadian Multiculturalism Act, which set forth the government's multiculturalism policy: "to recognize all Canadians as full and equal participants in Canadian society."

It was with the advent of the British in the 18th century, the gold rushes of the 19th century, and the settlement of the West in the late 19th and early 20th century that Canada became one of the world's main immigrant-receiving societies, a position it retained through the 1920s and after WWII (*see* IMMIGRATION; IMMIGRATION POLICY). Except in French Canada, ethnic and cultural groups were, ideally, to be assimilated by the English majority. This ideal was replaced first by the ideal of the "melting-pot," ie, the creation of a new ethnic or cultural group out of the combined elements in the population, and then by the ideal of the "mosaic," ie, the collaboration of all ethnic and cultural groups, which would nevertheless retain their distinctive characteristics. The mosaic was the precursor of multiculturalism.

It was only after the turbulent 1960s that the provincial and federal governments adopted explicit policies of multiculturalism, although, in the first decade, the federal government allotted these policies far less money than the policy of French-English bilingualism, which had been formalized 2 years earlier. Federally, there has been a minister responsible for multiculturalism since 1972, and since 1973 there has been a Canadian Multiculturalism Council and a Multiculturalism Directorate within the Dept of the Secretary of State.

Government policies of multiculturalism have been viewed with hostility and suspicion by many. French Canadians and others have regarded them as injurious to the French Canadian position as one of the 2 linguistic communities of which Canada is composed; some scholars have decried them as a means of buttressing Anglo-Saxon dominance, by diverting the efforts of the non-French and the non-English from political and economic affairs into cultural activities and excluding other ethnic groups from power and influence; some spokesmen from ethnic groups have viewed government multiculturalism policies as unacceptable substitutes for substantial aid; many have considered them bribes for "the ethnic vote."

The hostility and suspicion against multiculturalism have resulted from ambiguities in policy statements and in the term multiculturalism (it has been pointed out that a curious presumption of "multiculturalism" is that ethnic groups are outside the mainstream of society, whereas they can be more accurately described as cultural fractions that integrate unequally to form Canadian society). Social scientists have not adequately classified and communicated to politicians, bureaucrats and the public the subtle but necessary distinctions between cultural and structural assimilation, culture and ethnic group, etc.

Multicultural policies in the 1970s may not have met the needs of immigrants, especially the growing numbers belonging to "visible minorities," designed as they were for long-established ethnic groups of European background. Nonetheless, the introduction of the term and what has been called the multicultural movement have been important in calling attention to an important type of diversity within society and in engendering political recognition of it.   JEAN BURNET

Reading: J. Dahlie and L. Fernando, eds, *Ethnicity, Power and Politics in Canada* (1981); H. Palmer, ed, *Immigration and the Rise of Multiculturalism* (1975).

Multinational Corporation, business entity under common ownership or management control that operates in different countries. The parent and each of the subsidiaries are established under the laws and practices of the countries where they are located. The corporations are multinational in their geographic scope, but not in the sense that there is some multinational authority which permits them to operate. Of the top 100 industrial multinationals in the world, almost half have US parent companies, and about a third are in the PETROLEUM INDUSTRY; 8 of the 10 largest are in the oil industry and 2 are in the AUTOMOBILE INDUSTRY. The largest Canadian multinational in Canada, GENERAL MOTORS OF CANADA LTD, is the fourth largest company in the world.

Multinationals have come under scrutiny in Canada and elsewhere for their economic, political, social and cultural impact on host countries. Less developed countries argue that they have traded political independence for economic and cultural dependence. Politically, there is concern over the extent to which multinational corporations are used as instruments of foreign policy by the governments of countries where parent companies are located. Foreign multinationals have set up subsidiaries in Canada, but Canadian multinationals have also established subsidiaries abroad, and this has been a growing trend in the mid-1980s, especially in the US. The FOREIGN INVESTMENT REVIEW AGENCY, created by the Trudeau government to screen new foreign investments, was replaced by the Investment Act to encourage foreign investment in Canada. Although government policies can alter the way multinational corporations behave, their presence will persist because of their flexibility in adapting to changing circumstances. *See also* FOREIGN OWNERSHIP.   C.J. MAULE

Reading: I.A. Litvak and C.J. Maule, *The Canadian Multinationals* (1981).

Multiple Sclerosis Society of Canada, a nonprofit voluntary agency, was founded in 1948 to fund medical research into multiple sclerosis (MS), the most common disease of the central nervous system affecting young adults in Canada. It has since broadened its mandate to include provision of services to people who have multiple sclerosis and their family members and to educate the public and health-care professionals about this, as yet, incurable disease. In 1966, the Canadian organization helped found the International Federation of Multiple Sclerosis Societies. Headquartered in Toronto, the MS Society has 7 regional offices and approximately 100 chapters with a total of 25 000 members. The society has been instrumental, through its own funding and by urging increased government financial support, in advancing the development of multiple sclerosis research in Canada.

DEANNA GROETZINGER

Mumming, a performance by actors (mummers) in disguise, forms part of a worldwide cultural phenomenon of great complexity. The immediate origin of, and the closest analogies to, the principal Newfoundland mumming practices are found in Ireland and the UK. Many mummers' plays were in the hero-combat tradition of English folk plays and presented variations on a typical fourfold action: the presentation of the characters (eg, St George, the Doctor, Alexander, Sir Guy, the Turkish Knight and others); the combat between one or more antagonists; the cure or resurrection of a slain champion; and the collection of money by performers.

Two practices associated with mumming, the house visit with the performance of a play and the formal outdoor procession or parade, are richly documented from 19th-century sources. After WWI, however, these performances were discontinued, though not forgotten, until their revival by professional actors in the early 1970s, following scholarly research on the tradition. The parade had been a familiar event of the Christmas season as early as 1812, especially in St John's,

with elaborately costumed and disguised figures making their way through the streets, flanked by agile fools and "ownshooks" ("female" fools) armed with inflated bladders with which to thrash spectators. A type of performance (a combat or dialogue) was sometimes included at some point in the procession. This public form of mumming, even the wearing of disguise outdoors, was banned under an Act of the Legislative Assembly in 1861 because of the occasional disturbance and violence, but the ban was not effective.

The house visit during the Twelve Days of Christmas by mummers, or "jannies," is particularly common in Newfoundland and is similar to activities by "guisers" in northern England and Scotland, "skaklers" in Shetland, "belsnickles" in the German tradition in both NS and Virginia, and "naluyuks" in Labrador. When small groups of people appear at neighbourhood houses and seek admission, there is a reversal of normal modes of behaviour: reversal of sex (through costume disguise); of speech (the mummers' characteristic ingressive speech); of social role (the host is on the defensive); and of behavioural norms (the visitors are boisterous, uninhibited). At the centre of this form of mumming is the attempt by the host(s) to identify the disguised figures; the unveiling of the identified visitors; and the offering of refreshment. This less formal mumming tradition is still widespread in Newfoundland; it has been documented by folklorists and studied by anthropologists.   GEORGE M. STORY

Reading: H. Halpert and George M. Story, eds, *Christmas Mumming in Newfoundland* (1969).

Municipal Administration The activities of locally elected municipal councils are administered by officials and employees organized into municipal public-service departments (*see* MUNICIPAL GOVERNMENTS). The link between policy-making and administration is often supplied through committees of council, each of which reviews the activities of the department related to it and makes recommendations to council. Each department head is usually accountable to at least one committee. Other municipal administrative structures include boards of control, in some Ontario cities; boards of commissioners, in some western cities, under which each commissioner is responsible for a group of departments and all are collectively responsible to the municipal council for the entire municipal administration; and chief administrative officers accountable to the municipal council for the co-ordination of all municipal departments. Variations of these structures exist across Canada. Another structure is an executive committee selected by and from within the municipal council to exercise responsibilities similar to a board of control.

All Canadian municipalities elect, on an at-large basis, a mayor (or reeve in the case of some rural municipalities) who presides at council meetings and who can also make recommendations to council. In Canada, any leadership role that a mayor may exercise is dependent largely on the power of personality and not on powers assigned to this office.

Because most municipalities are organized departmentally by function (eg, public works, finance, personnel, parks) there may be a proliferation of 15 or more departments, which does not facilitate planning and co-ordination. Departments are therefore sometimes grouped together, ie, departments responsible for activities such as social services, parks, recreation, might constitute a community-services group, while those responsible for providing support services, eg, finance, personnel, information processing, might be grouped under management services.

Where such groupings are established, each department reports to a general director or commissioner responsible for the group.

Municipal governments have a major responsibility in the area of collective bargaining, because most municipal employees are organized. Major bargaining units include white collar and technical employees, skilled and unskilled labour, police, fire and transit workers.

Municipal budget preparation differs from that of other governments in that a balanced budget must be prepared annually. A deficit budget is not permissible; while municipal governments may borrow for capital works, provision must be made annually for the repayment of capital and interest. When expenditure estimates have been determined, all revenues other than those derived from property taxation are then calculated; the difference between this total and the expenditure estimates must then be made up by property TAXATION. The scale of expenditures therefore has a direct impact on the property-tax rate established annually.

The most difficult and controversial of municipal responsibilities involves the planning and regulation of land use. While most of this is undertaken by the municipal planning department, many other departments are also involved in the planning process, much of which must be conducted in accordance with procedures established in provincial planning legislation.

T.J. PLUNKETT

Municipal Finance is concerned with the revenues and expenditures of municipalities. Revenues are secured from local taxes (*see* TAXATION) and other local revenues and from provincial and federal grants. Property taxes include taxes for both general municipal purposes and schools, which in some provinces are levied directly by SCHOOL BOARDS and in others by the municipalities. Likewise, government grants include grants for education as well as for general municipal purposes. Taxes levied on "real property" (land and buildings) are the traditional and principal source of municipal tax revenue. The accuracy of the assessment of the value of real property is of paramount importance, especially in ensuring the equitable treatment of taxpayers in each municipality and, because many provincial grants are related to assessment, in ensuring equitable treatment of citizens in different municipalities. The principal basis of assessment is market value of property. Because of the importance and difficulty of establishing accurate and uniform assessments, all provinces have in recent years either assumed complete responsibility for assessment or imposed careful supervision over municipal assessment.

Most provinces provide either for a "homestead" provincial rebate to property taxpayers or for a property tax credit linked to provincial personal income tax, the former to reduce the burden, the latter to reduce the regressiveness of the property tax. Property tax exemptions are commonly granted for churches and other charitable organizations and in some provinces partial exemptions are granted for widows and the aged. Special assessment taxes are levied as supplementary charges for local improvements, eg, sidewalks, usually based on frontage of lots. Business taxes, calculated on such bases as rental value, floor space and real property assessment, are levied on occupants of business properties. Provincial and federal grants in lieu of taxes are paid on provincial and federal real property. Local nontax revenue derives from sales of services, eg, water, and from licences and fees, fines and penalties. Taxes on personal property and poll taxes, once quite general, have

Estimated General Revenue and Expenditure
of Municipal Governments, All Provinces 1985
(Source: *Canadian Tax Foundation,
Provincial and Municipal Finances*)

Revenue	*Millions$*	*Percent*
Property and related taxes	14 924	37.1
Other taxes	64	0.2
Revenue from sales and service	4 152	10.3
Other own source revenue	1 970	1.9
Intergovernmental transfers		
General purpose		
From provinces	1 757	4.4
Other	540	1.3
Specific purpose		
From provinces	16 676	41.4
Other	174	0.4
Total	40 261	100.0
Expenditure		
Education	17 427	41.4
Transportation and communications	4 133	9.8
Protection	3 471	8.3
Debt charges	3 089	7.3
Health	2 423	5.8
Social services	1 558	3.7
Other	9 963	23.7
Total	42 068	100.0

been abolished in most provinces, although the poll tax is still used in Newfoundland and is authorized in Saskatchewan municipalities but not applied. Ninety percent of the transfers (grants) from provincial and federal governments are special purpose (conditional) grants for such activities as education and social services; the remaining 10% are general purpose (unconditional), although these proportions differ widely from province to province. These transfers are meant principally to ease the property tax burden and to equalize it among municipalities.

Borrowing is typically for capital assets and the debt is amortized approximately over the life of the asset. Municipalities are not generally allowed to run deficits in their operating budgets. Although many municipalities still borrow in their own right, there is a trend towards consolidated borrowing by a provincial agency on their behalf to ensure more favourable interest rates and better debt management. While elementary and secondary education is still the principal local expenditure, provincial governments are increasingly assuming these costs, either by grants or, as in NB and PEI, by accepting complete responsibility for education.

Municipalities have long agitated for access to income and sales tax bases to reduce their dependence on the property tax, but because of the difficulties of administering these other taxes at the local level, the uneven yields per capita they would produce for the municipalities and the reluctance of the provinces to add another layer of such levies, the provinces have preferred to share revenues from these sources by means of grants. Manitoba and BC, however, now earmark a small part of their receipts from personal and corporate income taxes for their municipalities.

JOHN F. GRAHAM

Municipal Government, local government created by the provinces to provide services that can be more effectively handled under local control. It is responsible for the administration of CITIES, TOWNS and municipalities. Municipal governments make policy, raise revenue and ensure the implementation or administration of policy. The first 2 tasks are the responsibility of the municipal council, elected locally, which is expected to act as a local legislature. Under the CONSTITUTION ACT, 1982, the powers of municipal governments are determined by provincial gov-

ernments, but their performance is assessed by the electorate in regular elections. The administration is handled by the municipal PUBLIC SERVICE, made up of officials and employees appointed by the council and organized into departments. The necessary link between policy-making and administration is supplied in most municipal governments by a council or committee system, in which a municipal council establishes a series of committees to direct and control the municipal public service. The number of committees created by municipal governments depends on local circumstances and priorities. Each committee, made up of a specified number of council members, reviews the activities of the departments related to it and makes recommendations to the municipal council. The head of each municipal department is usually accountable to one committee and perhaps several, depending upon departmental responsibilities. Committees can sometimes recommend actions in one area that might conflict with another area of municipal responsibility; they also tend to fragment municipal decision making and administration. Many municipal governments, particularly in the larger cities, have either abandoned or modified this system. At least 4 other structures have evolved, for example the council-board of control and the council-executive committee co-ordinate arrangements at the political level, ie, the municipal council, while the council-chief administrative officer and the council-board of commissioners are responsible for similar arrangements at the administrative level. The board of control structure derived from experiments by US municipal reformers in the latter part of the 19th century. Adopted by the city of Toronto, it was made mandatory under The Municipal Act of Ontario for all cities in that province over 100 000 in population, although an amendment now permits municipal councils to abandon it.

Several large cities, notably Toronto, Ottawa, Hamilton and Windsor, have given up this structure after several decades. The board of control comprises the mayor as chairman and a number of controllers, elected city-wide, who are also full members of the municipal council. Other members of council are usually elected to represent wards. Under The Municipal Act a board of control is assigned executive powers, including preparation of the annual estimates, amendment of contracts, and nomination and dismissal of officials and employees. Boards of control have been criticized for their tendency to create 2 categories of council member: controllers elected at large and aldermen elected on a ward basis. Moreover, it was difficult for council to overturn a financial recommendation of the board except by a two-thirds majority vote of council. In the city of Toronto the board of control was eventually replaced by an executive committee selected from within the council. While this committee exercises powers similar to that of the former board of control, it is more directly accountable to the council, which controls its membership. Boards of control have existed in Ontario for most of this century but have not been adopted elsewhere in Canada. Council-executive committees have long existed in Montréal and Québec City, and a variant of them was established recently in Winnipeg.

The council-chief administrative officer (CAO) may also be known as city or municipal manager, city administrator or city commissioner. Largely a modified version of the council-manager system popular in the US, the CAO system is based on business organization. The municipal council, like a corporate board of directors, is concerned only with policy, while the

city manager, appointed by the council, has exclusive responsibility for and is accountable to the council for administration. Although some municipal governments in Canada now have managers, many have appointed an official as CAO with general responsibility for directing and co-ordinating the work of the municipal public service. As a result, municipal councils have often abolished committees, or council acts as a committee of the whole to receive reports from the CAO and other officials. Alternatively, councils have reduced the number of committees to which the CAO reports.

The council-board of commissioners arrangement evolved in western Canada, particularly in Edmonton, Calgary and Winnipeg. Instead of a single chief administrator, a management group of commissioners is appointed, one of whom is the chief commissioner. Each commissioner is responsible for a broad range of interrelated responsibilities. Heads of departments are accountable to the commissioners who as a board are collectively responsible to the municipal council for the entire municipal public service. Variants of these structures and combinations of them also exist. Winnipeg has an executive committee with a board of commissioners responsible to it; Québec City has an executive committee with a city manager accountable to it; and London employs a board of control with a CAO responsible to it.

Municipal structures also include a number of special purpose bodies usually established as local boards or commissions by provincial governments, although the extent of their use varies considerably, including, among others, library boards, utility commissions, transit authorities, parks and police commissions. Provincial statutes outline the procedures for the appointment of members. Most of these groups enjoy varying degrees of independence from municipal jurisdiction, although municipalities must provide a considerable proportion of their funds. Because these bodies fall under the control of both the provincial and municipal governments, it is difficult for the public to know just who is responsible and for what.

In contrast to the practice in some US cities in which duties such as budget formation and appointment of certain administration officers are the responsibility of the mayor, the significance of this office in Canada stems more from its high profile, although a mayor with a forceful personality may also be a strong leader. Variously described as "the chief officer," "the chief executive officer" or "the head of council" in provincial statutes, the mayor has little power independent of the municipal council. All provinces provide that the mayor shall be elected at large, and Canadian mayors generally are expected to preside at all council meetings, are ex officio members of all committees and can make recommendations to the municipal council.

Intergovernmental Relations The relationship between a province and its municipalities is one of superior and subordinates. Provincial governments legislate the duties of municipal governments and are responsible for their well-being. Some of the responsibilities assigned to municipal governments, such as the exercise of planning powers and MUNICIPAL FINANCE, are regulated by the provinces. The relationship between municipalities and the federal government is relatively unimportant. Federal programs that affect municipalities are generally handled through federal-provincial agreements.

Annexation and Amalgamation The extension of municipal boundaries by the annexation of peripheral rural areas is usually justified on the grounds that urban physical services such as water, sewerage facilities and roads can be provided more readily by the urban municipality than the rural area. When a major city is encircled by several smaller municipalities, or when 2 municipalities have developed side by side and share a common boundary, separate municipal jurisdictions complicate the provision of necessary services over the entire area and the need to secure orderly and planned development. This problem is sometimes solved by amalgamation, the consolidation of municipalities into a single municipal entity. Decisions about annexation or amalgamation can only be made by the provincial government. Because both usually provoke controversy, most provinces have established a procedure of hearings held by ADMINISTRATIVE TRIBUNALS such as the Ont Municipal Board, the Local Authorities Board in Alta or the Municipal Commission in Qué. In some circumstances a province may establish a special investigating commission to study the matter and make a recommendation. In large metropolitan areas where several municipal governments operate and outright amalgamation is almost impossible, some provinces have established METROPOLITAN GOVERNMENTS or REGIONAL GOVERNMENTS or districts. T.J. PLUNKETT

Municipal Loan Fund, Canada West, est 10 Nov 1852, created largely by Francis HINCKS, co-premier of the Province of Canada, whose government's central policy was railway development. Hincks permitted municipalities to borrow on the province's credit to invest in important works; the fund itself would be created by anticipated municipal repayments to the province. By 1855, encouraged by promoters who predicted that railway-inspired development would generate the extra wealth needed to repay loans, 47 communities in Canada W, some mere villages, had borrowed over $7 million, at least 80% for investment in local and branch line railways. Only a few railways proved economically viable. Laws passed late in 1854 cut off new borrowing, provided for repayment of some of the province's outlay from delinquent municipalities' shares in revenues from the secularized CLERGY RESERVES, and gave Lower Canadian municipalities access to a "fund" of equal value (of which only about $1.8 million had actually been borrowed when the whole scheme was terminated in 1859). Rates of repayment, never high, plummeted in the 1857-58 depression, and by 1862 arrears of interest had added another $3 million to the deficit. Thereafter the history of the fund merges with that of the Canadian PUBLIC DEBT.
DOUGLAS McCALLA

Municipal-Provincial Relations Municipalities in Canada are similar to provincial governments in a number of important respects. Their governing bodies are democratically elected; they have the power to tax and to legislate (bylaws, ordinances); they provide a wide range of public services and facilities; and they make public policy (eg, land-use planning).

Municipalities are unlike provincial governments as far as important aspects of constitutional status are concerned. The provinces derive their powers from the Constitution and hence their permanence and autonomous jurisdiction are guaranteed. Municipalities, on the other hand, draw their powers from provincial law, which can be changed simply by a majority vote of the legislature. These powers are usually set out in a Municipal Act which applies to all municipalities within one province. Some cities (eg, Vancouver, Saint John, Halifax) have a city charter, which is a separate Act of the legislature applying only to one city and providing powers that may differ in some respects from those contained in a Municipal Act.

Municipalities can usually exercise only those powers delegated to them by a provincial government. The province retains the right to change municipal boundaries, to abolish individual municipalities (as New Brunswick and Ontario have done), to alter municipal financial resources and to withdraw old powers or grant new ones. The province makes some powers mandatory and some permissive.

The autonomy of municipalities is severely restricted. For example, many municipal bylaws require provincial approval to become effective; municipal borrowings for capital projects are strictly controlled by the province's Ministry of Municipal Affairs or by a provincially appointed municipal board; many local planning decisions can be appealed to a provincial agency; and many local powers apply only to a shared provincial-municipal jurisdiction (eg, the environment). The limited autonomy of municipal governments raises questions about the democratic accountability of LOCAL GOVERNMENTS. They are accountable both to their own electorates and to provincial authorities, but in degrees that vary among provinces and even within some of them.

The relationship between municipalities and their respective provincial governments is not an easy one. Many municipal politicians are resentful about their lack of autonomy, and many provincial ministers and bureaucrats think of municipalities as just another interest group seeking to pressure the province into particular policy decisions. The special status of municipalities as governments elected on a universal franchise is well understood by ministers and officials of Municipal Affairs departments, but their colleagues in other departments or in Cabinet have their own vested interests in budgetary and jurisdictional decisions, which lead them to minimize the importance of municipal affairs.

Municipalities have come together in voluntary associations in their attempt to support the municipal interest in provincial policymaking. There is one such association for BC, Nova Scotia, PEI, Newfoundland and, as of 1982, Ontario. Québec and the Prairie provinces each had 2 such associations. New Brunswick has one association for cities, one for towns and one for villages. A national association, the Federation of Canadian Municipalities, exists to relate to the federal government.

A major concern of these associations is to secure a better financial arrangement for municipalities. Local revenue is mainly derived from property taxes and grants from the provinces. These grants are on average 80% conditional. The conditions sometimes induce municipalities to make choices that meet provincial policy goals at the expense of local goals. The property tax is generally seen as the most regressive of all the major tax fields in the country. Further, it does not grow with the economy or inflation as do sales and income taxes. Hence municipal leaders resent being limited to this particular tax field.

In several provinces, regular consultative meetings are held between the responsible minister and representatives of municipal associations. However, although the minister often uses the language of partnership, it is a very unequal partnership indeed. Sometimes there are promises of consultation before any provincial action affecting municipalities is taken, but when an election looms or the economy declines, such promises may well be forgotten. Because of the inferior constitutional position of municipalities, their most important powers are those of organization and persuasion. The powers of law and money, however, are on the provincial side.
ALLAN O'BRIEN

Munitions and Supply, Department of, Canada's principal agency for co-ordinating domestic industry during WORLD WAR II. It was decided that a civilian department should control the production of munitions for Canada and its allies, and accordingly Parliament passed the Munitions and Supply Act in Sept 1939 and brought it into force on 9 Apr 1940. The department's only minister was C.D. HOWE, who furnished dynamic, aggressive leadership, as well as significant political clout. Besides producing ARMAMENTS through its production branches, the department regulated scarce supplies held to be essential to war production, such as gasoline and silk (used for parachutes). To avoid creating a big bureaucracy, the department established crown corporations such as Victory Aircraft (bombers), POLYMER (artificial rubber) and Research Enterprises (high technology). The department was dissolved at the end of WWII with a highly successful record.
ROBERT BOTHWELL

Munk, Jens Eriksen, explorer (b at Barbo, Norway 3 June 1579; d at Copenhagen, Denmark 3 or 24 June 1628). Instructed by King Christian IV of Denmark to search for a NORTHWEST PASSAGE, he set out with 2 ships May 1619. After detours into Frobisher Bay and Ungava Bay he entered Hudson Bay Aug 25. He was forced to winter at the estuary of the CHURCHILL R, and by spring 61 of his men had succumbed to scurvy. Munk and 2 other survivors struggled home, reaching Norway 21 Sept 1620. He published an account of his voyage in 1624. Relics of his stay have been found at Pt Churchill.
JAMES MARSH

Munro, Alice, short-story writer (b at Wingham, Ont 10 July 1931). Munro's early years were spent in western Ontario. She met her first husband, James Munro, at the U of Western Ontario, and after 2 years of university she moved with him to Vancouver. In 1963 she helped establish Munro's Books, and in 1972 she returned to Ontario where she married Gerald Fremlin in 1976. She was awarded the Gov Gen's Award for *Dance of the Happy Shades* (1968) and *Who Do You Think You Are?* (1978), which was also runner-up for the Booker Prize. She is also the recipient of the Canadian Booksellers Assn International Book Year Award for *Lives of Girls and Women* (1971), the Canada-Australia Literary Prize (1977), and the first winner of the Marian Engel Award (1986). The strength of her fiction arises partially from its vivid sense of regional focus, most of her stories being set in Huron County, Ont, as well as from her sense of the narrator as the intelligence through which the world is articulated. Her theme has often been the dilemmas of the adolescent girl coming to terms with family and small town. Her more recent work has addressed the problems of middle age, of women alone and of the elderly. Characteristic of her style is the search for some revelatory gesture by which an event is illuminated and given personal significance. In *Lives of Girls and Women* each story is organized around a metaphor whose function is to draw all the elements of the various fictional sequences into a radiant centre. Thus the death of the protagonist's Uncle Craig that occurs in "Heirs of the Living Body" is related to other deaths and envisioned as part of natural process, such that the protagonist's mother can announce that "'Uncle Craig doesn't have to be Uncle Craig! Uncle Craig is flowers!'" He, like all of Munro's characters, shares one living body, although the connections might not always be perfectly clear. The implicit connection that does not always lead to epiphanic discovery is more apparent in *The Moons of Jupiter* (1982), for here relationships are suggested but the threads of attachment are not always unravelled.

The strength of Alice Munro's fiction lies in its vivid sense of place, as well as in her sense of the narrator as the intelligence through which the world is articulated (*photo by Larry Dillon*).

It is sometimes remarked that Munro's fiction is nearer to autobiography than fiction. In defence of *Lives of Girls and Women*, which is most frequently identified as being modelled on her life, Munro has asserted it is "autobiographical in form but not in fact." The distinction is perhaps not persuasive, but the charge is difficult to evade, for Munro's ear for the local speech has an absolute pitch and her narrators as filters of past and present possess an intelligence that makes one feel that if it is not her life being told, then it is ours. In many ways, furthermore, *Who Do You Think You Are?* may be considered a mature sequel to *Lives*, tracing the pattern, at least, of Munro's move to the west coast and back. *Dance of the Happy Shades* and *Something I've Been Meaning to Tell You* (1974), while containing some material that overlaps with experience drawn from the author's life, are carefully sequenced collections of short stories. Her most recent collection, *The Progress of Love* (1986), is a distillation of all her work so far, exploring with increased profundity the problems of time and the narrator's relation to it, in a prose that is perfectly instinct with wonder and compassion. E.D. BLODGETT

Munsinger Affair Between 1958 and 1961 Pierre SÉVIGNY, John DIEFENBAKER's associate minister of national defence, had an affair with Gerda Munsinger, a German immigrant. Acting on information from American sources, the RCMP warned Justice Minister Davie FULTON that Munsinger was a prostitute and a security risk. Fulton told Diefenbaker, who reprimanded Sévigny. Munsinger returned to Germany while Sévigny remained in the Cabinet. The affair meant nothing to anyone except the principals until Liberal Justice Minister Lucien Cardin, angered by Conservative taunts about security leaks, raised Munsinger's name 4 Mar 1966 in the Commons. The press revelled in Canada's first major parliamentary sex scandal. A royal commission criticized Diefenbaker's leniency but found no security breach. JOHN ENGLISH

Murder and Manslaughter, *see* HOMICIDE.

Murdoch, Beamish, lawyer, politician, author (b at Halifax 1 Aug 1800; d at Lunenburg, NS 9 Feb 1876). Already a successful lawyer when he was elected to the Nova Scotia Assembly in 1826, Murdoch lost his seat in 1830. A graceful essayist, widely published in leading journals of the time, he also wrote more substantial works, the most important of which is his *Epitome of the Laws of Nova Scotia* (1832-33), a unique work which earned him fame as "Nova Scotia's Blackstone" and which is still a primary source for historians. Murdoch returned to public life in 1841 when he was appointed clerk of the Board of Education

where he laboured tirelessly to establish a uniform provincial school system. Appointed recorder of Halifax in 1852, he retired in 1860, after which he published his *History of Nova Scotia* (1865-67). D.H. BROWN

Murdoch, James Young, lawyer, mining executive (b at Toronto 29 July 1890; d there 18 Apr 1962). A graduate of Osgoode Hall, Murdoch practised mining law in the Toronto firm Holden and Murdoch 1913-62; he was created KC in 1929. He drafted the incorporation of NORANDA MINES LTD and served as its first president 1923 to 1956, when he became chairman. Murdoch expanded and diversifed Noranda's original copper-mining interest in Québec through various investments. In WWII he held senior positions in 2 wartime crown corporations, was president of the National War Services Funds Advisory Board, chairman of the National War Services Committee of the YMCA and was awarded an OBE. Murdochville, Qué, was named after him in 1952, and for his contribution to the mining industry in Canada he received the Canadian Institute of Mining and Metallurgy's Blaylock Medal. JOSEPH LINDSEY

Murdoch Case, Supreme Court of Canada case (1975) involving matrimonial property law. Historically, wives could only own property by having it placed in their names or by providing all or part of its purchase price. No allowance was made for indirect contributions by them towards property acquisition or for their role in nurturing the family. In *Murdoch* the court decided that a wife who had helped run the family ranch had done "just about what the ordinary rancher's wife does" and had no right to a share in it. The outcry from women's groups produced reforms in provincial matrimonial property laws across Canada. Mrs Murdoch did obtain a lump sum of secured maintenance under the Federal Divorce Act. ALASTAIR BISSETT-JOHNSON

Murdochville Strike On 10 Mar 1957 the 1000 workers of Gaspé Copper Mines, Murdochville, Qué, struck for the right to unionize. The conflict lasted 7 months and ended in defeat for the miners. Moreover, a 15-year judicial battle finally awarded the company $1.5 million in damages from the United Steelworkers of America ("Métallos" in Québec). Murdochville was a COMPANY TOWN belonging to Gaspé Copper Mines, a subsidiary of the Noranda Mines empire. The company refused to recognize the miners' union (Métallos were affiliated with the Québec Federation of Labour, est Feb 1957) and used strikebreakers, along with provincial police dispatched by Prem Maurice DUPLESSIS, to subdue the strikers. This intervention by the state precipitated considerable violence. The strike led to joint action by the QFL and the Canadian Catholic Federation of Labour (*see* CONFEDERATION OF NATIONAL TRADE UNIONS), yet this common front, despite its immense potential, was seriously hampered by dissent within the QFL. The strike has often been called a turning point in QFL history; in fact it was the most dramatic episode in 12 years of effort leading to the 1965 unionization of Murdochville miners. GUY BÉLANGER

Murphy, Emily, née Ferguson, pen name Janey Canuck, writer, journalist, magistrate, political and legal reformer (b at Cookstown, Ont 14 Mar 1868; d at Edmonton 27 Oct 1933). Born into a prominent Ontario legal family, Murphy moved W in 1903 with her husband Arthur Murphy, an Anglican minister and entrepreneur, and their 2 daughters. A prolific contributor of book reviews and articles to Canadian magazines and newspapers, she adopted the pen name Janey Canuck and published 4 very popular books of

personal sketches: *The Impressions of Janey Canuck Abroad* (1901), *Janey Canuck in the West* (1910), *Open Trails* (1912) and *Seeds of Pine* (1914).

First in Swan R, Man, and then in Edmonton, where she lived from 1907, Murphy combined family life, writing and a multitude of reform activities in the interests of women and children. In 1911, responding to persistent public pressure organized by Murphy, the Alberta legislature passed a DOWER ACT protecting a wife's right to a one-third share in her husband's property. Murphy was also prominent in the suffrage movement, as well as a longtime executive member of the CANADIAN WOMEN'S PRESS CLUB (president 1913-20), the NATIONAL COUNCIL OF WOMEN OF CANADA, the FEDERATED WOMEN'S INSTITUTES OF CANADA (first national president) and over 20 other professional and volunteer organizations.

A self-taught legal expert, in 1916 she was appointed police magistrate for Edmonton and then Alberta, the first woman magistrate in the British Empire. Exposed to a succession of cases involving prostitution and juvenile offenders, she became an implacable enemy of narcotics, which she blamed for much organized crime and for victimizing the defenceless. *The Black Candle* (1922) by "Judge Murphy" was an expansion of articles published in *Maclean's* magazine describing in lurid detail the evils of the drug trade; her exposé led to laws governing narcotics that remained unaltered until the late 1960s.

Challenged on her first day on the bench by a lawyer who asserted that as a woman she was not a person in the eyes of British law, Murphy soon embarked on a decade-long campaign to have women declared legal "persons" and therefore eligible for appointive positions, including the Senate. With the support of 4 other Alberta women, Henrietta EDWARDS, Louise MCKINNEY, Nellie MCCLUNG and Irene PARLBY, she carried the PERSONS CASE to the Privy Council in Britain, which ruled in a celebrated judgement in 1929 that women were indeed persons under the BNA Act. The long-sought Senate appointment eluded Murphy, however, and she died in Edmonton of diabetes in 1933. SUSAN JACKEL

Reading: C. Mander, *Emily Murphy, Rebel* (1986).

Emily Murphy was prominent in the suffrage movement and in 1916 became the first woman magistrate in the British Empire (*courtesy Glenbow Archives, Calgary*).

Murphy, Harvey, trade unionist (b Poland 1900; d Toronto 30 Apr 1977). Of Polish-Jewish origin, Murphy (his adopted name) grew up in a working-class milieu in Ontario, joined the COM-MUNIST PARTY OF CANADA in the 1920s, and became perhaps the most influential communist in the Canadian trade-union movement in the 1940s. He played a leading role in the militant Mine Workers Union of Canada 1932-35, and took direction of the Canadian district of the International Union of Mine, Mill and Smelter Workers (Mine-Mill) in 1943. Its giant locals at Sudbury and Trail were key centres of the struggle over "red" unionism during the Cold War years; Murphy was a colourful and resourceful foe of anti-communist forces. He was less successful as the alleged "commissar" of the BC Federation of Labour, which he was very largely responsible for rechartering after 22 years of inactivity in 1944, but from which he was purged in 1948. Sudbury miners, excepting the members of still-active Local 598, joined the United Steel Workers of America after the failure of the 1958 strike, but Trail remained loyal to Murphy and Mine-Mill until the merger of 1966. Murphy's part in those negotiations is generally regarded as the beginning of a historic reconciliation between left-wing unionists and mainstream Canadian labour in the 1960s and early 1970s.   ALLEN SEAGER

Murray, Alexander, geologist, explorer (b at Crieff, Scot 2 June 1810; d there 18 Dec 1884). Murray served in the Royal Navy 1824-35, and then in 1837 immigrated with his young bride to Woodstock, Upper Canada. Their arrival coincided with the 1837 Rebellion; he served in the naval brigade that destroyed US steamer CAROLINE. The Murrays returned to England in 1841, the same year the Canadian Parliament authorized a geological survey of the United Provinces. Learning of this, Murray studied geology. He received an appointment in 1842-43 to the Geological Survey of Great Britain. When William LOGAN was appointed director of the GEOLOGICAL SURVEY OF CANADA, he selected Murray as an assistant. In May 1843 the Murrays returned to Canada. In 1851 he discovered the petroleum seepages near Black Creek, Canada West, which later became the location of the world's first drilled oil well; in 1856 he identified the first known nickel mineralization in the Sudbury Basin. Murray practically single-handedly mapped the geology of Canada West as recorded in *Geology of Canada* (1863). In 1864 he became first director of the Geological Survey of Newfoundland, at a time when the Island was virtually unexplored. Despite being crippled by an injury, within 10 years Murray had completed a topographical and geological map of the Island and co-published a report entitled *Geological Survey of Newfoundland* (1881), which showed that mineral, timber and agricultural resources were present in the interior.
RICHARD DAVID HUGHES

Murray, Anne (married name Langstroth), pop singer (b at Springhill, NS 20 June 1945). Canada's most successful pop performer of the 1970s, Murray was noticed first for her recording "Snowbird" (1970) after minor exposure on CBC TV from Halifax. With her personable alto, wholesome presence and stylistic versatility, she enjoyed great record success ("Danny's Song," "You Needed Me," "I Just Fall in Love Again," etc) and expanded her concert and TV itinerary to include pop and country music audiences. She has received many Juno Awards and several (US) Grammy Awards and in 1985 was made Companion of the Order of Canada.   MARK MILLER

Murray, George Henry, lawyer, politician, premier of NS (b at Grand Narrows, NS 7 June 1861;

d at Montréal 6 Jan 1929). Murray's unbroken 27 years in power (1896-1923) is a British Empire and Commonwealth record. Leadership of the NS Liberal Party fell to Murray when W.S. FIELDING entered the LAURIER Cabinet in 1896. Always cautious, Murray practised a form of brokerage politics, trying both to avoid controversy and to appeal to every constituency. His government continued Fielding's commitment to railway consolidation and road and bridge construction, encouraged agricultural and technical education, took some initial steps in improving the public health system, and co-operated with the federal government in prosecuting the war. His administration's more significant accomplishments included the legislation of PROHIBITION in 1906, the introduction of workers' compensation in 1916, the extension of the vote to women in 1918 and the development of the NS Power Commission in 1919. Faced with postwar economic dislocation, industrial collapse and the continuing mistrust of the province's working class, Murray retired in Jan 1923.   COLIN D. HOWELL

Murray, Gordon, surgeon (b at Stratford, Ont 29 May 1894; d at Toronto 7 Jan 1976). Murray's medical training was interrupted in 1917 when he became an artillery man and went overseas to fight at Ypres, the Somme and Vimy Ridge. Reaching the rank of sergeant major, he finished his medical training in 1921 and trained in anatomy and surgery in London. He was registrar at the London Hospital and acquired his FRSC London. In 1928 Murray returned to Toronto where he eventually joined the staff of the General Hospital and conducted imaginative and stimulating work in experimental surgery. His most notable work was with the anticoagulant drug Heparin: using it in many different exemplary applications he was one of the first in the world to demonstrate its use in patients in the prevention of thrombosis and embolism and in maintaining patency following arterial suture and vein grafts to arteries. As well, he developed the first "artificial kidney" to be used successfully in N America, and implanted the first successful homograph valve in the descending aorta of a human. The author of over 90 articles and 3 books, he delivered many scientific papers around the world. He was awarded the Gairdner Foundation International Annual Award in 1964 and became a Companion of the Order of Canada in 1967.

Murray, James, military officer, colonial administrator, first British governor of Québec (b at Ballencrieff, Scot 21 Jan 1721/22; d at Beauport House, near Battle, Eng 18 June 1794). Murray commanded a battalion in the siege of LOUISBOURG in 1758, and was one of James WOLFE's 3 brigadiers at Québec. After the Battle of the PLAINS OF ABRAHAM he remained in command of the city, facing undefeated French forces up the St Lawrence R. In Apr 1760 the Duc de LÉVIS advanced on Québec. Murray's garrison, weakened by disease, attacked near Ste-Foy, but was driven back into the city and besieged until British warships arrived (*see* Battle of STE-FOY). In Oct 1760 Murray was appointed military governor of the District of Québec and in Nov 1763 governor of the province. He was sworn in as the first civil governor 10 Aug 1764. A member of the landed gentry, he supported the agrarian, French-speaking inhabitants over the newly arrived, English-speaking merchants. He was reluctant to call a legislative assembly, promised in the ROYAL PROCLAMATION OF 1763, because he feared that Canadians would be barred from it on religious grounds. His willingness to allow French law and custom in the courts further alienated the merchants and led to his recall in Apr 1766 and he left Canada in June. Though charges were dismissed,

Portrait of Gen James Murray by an unknown artist, *c*1770-80 (*courtesy National Portrait Gallery, London*).

he did not return to Canada though he retained nominal governorship until Apr 1768. Nevertheless, his administrative arrangements for government were institutionalized in the QUEBEC ACT and were a factor in preventing Québec from becoming the 14th rebellious colony. From 1774 to 1782 Murray was lt-gov and later governor of Minorca, where he directed a spirited, though unsuccessful, defence against a Franco-Spanish besieging force.   O.A. COOKE

Murray, James Alexander, businessman, politician, premier of NB (b at Moncton, NB 9 Nov 1864; d at Sussex, NB 16 Feb 1960). A respected politician and forceful speaker, Murray represented Kings County 1908-20. He was a member and president of the Executive Council of NB and minister of agriculture, before becoming premier in 1917 for the shortest term in provincial history. His government was defeated at the polls less than a month later.
ARTHUR T. DOYLE

Murray, Sir John, oceanographer (b at Cobourg, Canada W 3 Mar 1841; d at Kirkliston, Scot 16 Mar 1914). At 17, Murray moved to Scotland, the ocean voyage inspiring him in his lifelong career. After attending U of Edinburgh, he became naturalist to the CHALLENGER EXPEDITION (1872-76), during which he mapped much of the ocean floor of the world and became expert at classifying sediments and determining their origins. Other expeditions included one to Spitsbergen in 1868 and a survey of freshwater lochs in Scotland, published in 6 vols. After the death of *Challenger* expedition leader C.W. Thomson, Murray edited most of the resulting 50 vols (1882-95), and wrote the 2-vol summary (1895). Other contributions included a theory on the origin of coral reefs, a textbook on OCEANOGRAPHY with Johan Hjort (1912) used for about 30 years, and a popular account (1913). His 1888 estimates of proportions of various depths of ocean floor still generally hold. He was knighted in 1898.
MARTIN K. MCNICHOLL

Murray, John Clark, philosopher (b at Thread and Tannahill, Scot 19 Mar 1836; d at Montréal 20 Nov 1917). Murray's career as a philosopher began in 1862 at Queen's in Kingston, Ont. Ten years later he accepted a position as professor of logic at McGill and remained there until he retired in 1903. His commitment to the PHILOSOPHY of Sir William Hamilton shifted radically after a time in Canada, and his Hegelian inclinations resulted in 2 works on philosophical psychology: *A Handbook of Psychology* (1885) and *Introduction to Psychology* (1904). All things exhibited a rational unity for Murray and reason was the crucial factor in his theory of human nature. In 1887 he wrote a manuscript, unpublished until 1982, entitled *The Industrial Kingdom of God,* which made a plea for social and economic reform and proposed a co-operative society based on Christian principles of freedom, equality and justice for all people.

Murray was scholarly, but not a recluse. He fought a long battle for women's political and educational rights. His public lectures, newspaper articles and contributions to popular journals made him widely known. Murray's Scottish determination and sense of public duty had an impact, not only on his students, among whom were author and poet William D. LIGHTHALL and Stephen LEACOCK, but also on the developing Canadian culture. His books *A Handbook of Christian Ethics* (1908) and *An Introduction to Ethics* (1891) and his social-gospel novel *He That Had Received the Five Talents* (1904) spell out his moral theory. He was a fellow of the Royal Soc of Canada and a Canadian philosopher who truly practised what he preached.
ELIZABETH A. TROTT

Murray, John Wilson, police detective (b at Edinburgh, Scot 25 June 1840; d at Toronto 12 June 1906). Called the "Great Canadian Detective," Murray was a pioneer of scientific crime investigation. He was one of the first to utilize forensic science and information obtained through autopsies. His painstaking method of reconstructing crimes and cross-checking statements and evidence to the smallest detail was both innovative and effective.

Originally trained as a sailor in the US Navy, Murray became a detective during the Civil War and was instrumental in thwarting an attempt by Canadian-based Confederates to seize a US warship on Lake Erie. After working as a detective for the Canadian Southern Ry he was invited by Attorney General Sir Oliver Mowat to become provincial detective of Ontario. He accepted the post in 1875 and held it for 31 years. In that period he solved hundreds of crimes, including the famous J.R. BIRCHALL murder case. His *Memoir,* originally published in 1904, is a colourful collection of his most notable cases. EDWARD BUTTS

Murray, Leonard Warren, naval officer (b at Granton, NS 22 June 1896; d at Derbyshire, Eng 25 Nov 1971). Murray joined the navy in 1911, served in WWI and by 1939 was deputy chief of the naval staff. In WWII he held a series of important operational commands culminating in that of commander in chief, Canadian Northwest Atlantic, in Apr 1943. The only Canadian to command a theatre of war, Murray was forced into early retirement (formally Mar 1946) by his supposed failure to curb the excesses of his sailors during the VE-DAY RIOTS in Halifax. In Sept 1945 he left for England, where he was called to the bar in 1949. MARC MILNER

Murray, Lowell, politician, senator (b at New Waterford, NS 26 Sept 1936). A master of the political backrooms, Murray was educated at St Francis Xavier and Queen's universities. He was chief of staff to justice minister E. Davie FULTON, to Senator Wallace MCCUTCHEON and to Conservative Leader Robert STANFIELD, and then he served as Premier Richard HATFIELD's deputy minister in NB. A longtime friend and close ally of Joe CLARK, Murray served as the Progressive Conservative Party's national campaign chair from 1977 to 1979 and 1981 to 1983, and Clark

made him a senator in 1979. After Brian Mulroney took the leadership, Murray successfully made the transition, and as minister of state for federal-provincial relations served as Ottawa's chief negotiator to the provincial capitals. Much of the credit for the MEECH LAKE ACCORD of 1987 belongs to his patient preparatory work. He became Leader of the Government in the Senate 30 June 1986. J.L. GRANATSTEIN

Murray, Margaret Teresa, "Ma," née Lally, newspaper publisher (b at Windy Ridge, Kansas 3 Aug 1888; d at Lillooet, BC 25 Sept 1982). She came to Canada in 1912, worked for a Vancouver weekly, and then married the editor, George Matheson Murray. They bought a small magazine, subsequently going from one publishing venture to another. In 1933 Mrs Murray started the *Bridge River-Lillooet News*; in 1944, the *Alaska Highway News*. Famous for her pungent editorials on politics, economics and morals, she delighted and infuriated with her acid, earthy wit, most points emphasized with "and that's fur damshur." She declared, "The state of politics in Canada is as low as a snake's belly in Arkansas, but a snake there never go so low that he didn't have a pit to hiss in." Whether threatened with lawsuits or horsewhipping, she took it all in stride, replying, "It's a poor turkey who can't pack a few lice." JEAN O'CLERY

Acerbic newspaper publisher "Ma" Murray, famous for her pungent editorials (*courtesy Provincial Archives of British Columbia/60425*).

Murray, Robert, sculptor (b at Vancouver 2 Mar 1936). His abstract metal SCULPTURE, constructed of simple geometric forms using industrial materials and methods, shares important stylistic characteristics with the work of British sculptor Anthony Caro, but it was influenced chiefly by American sculptors David Smith and Barnett Newman. In 1960 Murray moved to New York and established a close relationship with Newman, whom he had met the previous year at U of Saskatchewan's summer school at Emma Lake. Beginning in the 1960s with a fountain sculpture for Saskatoon's city hall, Murray has produced public sculptures for sites throughout Canada and the US. His early work was noted for its clear, open relationships with characteristics of contemporary minimalism, but since the mid-1970s he has developed a more lyrical vocabulary of curved, folded and twisted forms. His sculptures are unified by a smooth painted finish, often in saturated colours. ROALD NASGAARD

Robert Murray, *Saginaw* (1979), aluminum painted red (*courtesy Gallery One*).

Murray, Walter Charles, educator (b at Studholm, NB 12 May 1866; d at Saskatoon 24 Mar 1945). A philosophy professor at UNB and Dalhousie, Murray became president of UNIVERSITY OF SASKATCHEWAN in 1908, a position he held for 29 years. He advocated nondenominationalism and centralization in higher education, along with political neutrality and practical service to the community. At a time of controversy over agricultural education, Murray successfully steered U of Sask towards integrating agriculture with other fields of study. He encouraged the affiliation of religious and junior arts colleges with the provincial university, developed agriculture and extension departments, and established university control over instruction and examinations in the professional fields of law, pharmacy, engineering, accounting, education and medicine. Murray served on a number of government commissions on education. MAUREEN AYTENFISU

Murre, medium-sized member of the AUK family. Murres weigh 900-1000 g and are up to 46 cm long. Plumage is dark brown to black above, pure white below. Like all auks, murres come to land only to breed. Murres occur in cooler waters of the N Pacific and N Atlantic oceans and adjacent parts of the Arctic Ocean. There are 2 species: common murre (*Uria aalge*) breeds primarily in boreal and low arctic waters; thick-billed murre (*U. lomvia*) breeds farther N in high arctic waters. Murres often breed in dense colonies on coastal cliffs and islands, laying a single, large egg on bare rock ledges on the cliff face or surface. They first breed when 5 years old. Incubation, shared by both parents, takes 32-34 days. In Canada, both species are most abundant on the Atlantic coast. Small numbers of common murres breed in BC; thick-bills in the western Arctic. Almost 90% of eastern N American common murres breed in Newfoundland with about 67% (400 000 pairs) at FUNK I. Breeding distribution of thick-bills is also restricted; most breed at 11 sites in the eastern Arctic. The thick-billed murre population in eastern Canada totals 1 454 000 pairs, representing the entire population in eastern N America and 75% of all thick-bills breeding in the western N Atlantic. Numbers of both species have been seriously reduced over the last century because of habitat disturbance, hunting, oil pollution and probably fisheries development. D.N. NETTLESHIP

Murrell, John, playwright, director, actor (b at Colorado Springs, Col 15 Oct 1945). He came to Canada in 1968 and settled permanently in Calgary in 1970, graduating from U of Calgary in drama. His first play, *Haydn's Head* won a provincial competition in 1971, but not until *Power in the Blood* won the Clifford E. Lee Award in 1975 did Murrell begin to write full time. He was appointed playwright-in-residence at Calgary's Alberta Theatre Projects, which premiered the prairie history plays *A Great Noise, A Great Light* (1976), about William ABERHART and the Depression, and his most popular play with Canadian audiences, *Waiting for the Parade* (1977), which features 5 Calgary women coping alone during WWII. Murrell's most successful play, *Memoir* (1978), an exploration of actress Sarah Bernhardt's final days, has been translated into 15 languages and performed in 26 countries, earning him an international reputation. *Farther West* (1982), a shocking play about a doomed prostitute's quest for freedom, for which he also wrote the brief musical score, and *New World* (1984), a witty comedy focusing on a bizarre family reunion, are his most challenging works to date. Murrell has also achieved prominence as a translator. In 1985, he was appointed head of the Banff Playwright's Colony, a position he still holds.   DONNA COATES

Muscular Dystrophy Association of Canada (MDAC) fd 1954 by a group of parents who had children with muscular dystrophy. Now a national voluntary health organization with 11 offices across Canada, MDAC is dedicated to fighting over 40 different neuromuscular disorders which incapacitate, generally through severe muscle wasting. The association's first mandate is to fund medical research projects aimed at finding a cure for muscular dystrophy and related neuromuscular disorders. Anyone who has been diagnosed as having a neuromuscular disorder may become a client and begin to benefit from the many direct services available. The equipment program helps people with the loan, purchase and general maintenance of necessary items such as wheelchairs. A chapter program offers peer support while members enjoy recreational, educational and fund-raising activities. An extensive network of medical, government and support services contacts also ensures that all the client's needs are met. The association conducts many fund-raising events throughout the year, including the Canadian portion of the Jerry Lewis Labour Day Telethon.

Musée d'art contemporain de Montréal, opened in March 1965 in a temporary location in Place Ville-Marie, with a world-class exhibition of work by French painter Georges Rouault. The museum then moved to Château Dufresne in east-end Montréal, opening in July 1965 with a major exhibit, Artistes de Montréal, while the gardens simultaneously presented an international sculpture symposium. After 1967, the government moved the museum to the Galérie internationale pavilion built for Expo 67. Guy Robert, its original director, resigned in protest since this change distanced and isolated the museum from the public to whom it was supposed to present current living art.

Initially the permanent collection benefited from personal gifts by artists and collectors, to which were added gifts from art galleries, associations, companies, groups and foundations, so that the collection had works dating from the turn of the century to the present day. In 1973 the National Museums of Canada made a major donation of works by painter Paul-Émile BORDUAS, which were then given their own permanent hall.   MICHEL CHAMPAGNE

Musée des beaux-arts de Montréal (Montreal Museum of Fine Arts) This first and oldest of Québec museums was established in 1847, originally under the name of Montreal Society of Artists. Around 1860 it became the Art Assn of Montreal and finally in 1948-49 the association formed a new corporation under its present name. In 1972 it became a semi-public institution, largely funded by grants from different government levels.

First installed in a building on Phillips Square, the museum moved in 1912 to a new building on Sherbrooke St. Architects Edward and W.S. Maxwell conceived the plan in neoclassical style, much in vogue at that time. In 1976 a new wing by architect Fred LEBENSOLD was opened. During its long history the museum has continually been enriched by numerous gifts, most of them prestigious donations from the great families of Montréal. The collection includes international and Canadian works in all styles, all eras, and includes Inuit, Mexican, Peruvian and Polynesian works. Many works from lost civilizations, pieces of decorative art and furniture of the era round out its vast range of world art. Since 1909 the museum has had a remarkable room devoted to drawings and prints.
          MICHEL CHAMPAGNE

Musée du Québec, officially opened in June 1933, although the bill which created the museum had been passed in 1922. The present building is the work of architect Wilfrid Lacroix, who gave it neoclassical symmetry, and sculptor Émile Brunet who created its bronze main door, the ornamental façade and the bas-reliefs on the frieze. The museum had 3 original objectives: to provide a home for the provincial archives, the museum of natural sciences and the fine-arts museum. Over the years it developed its collections through the acquisition of remarkable and representative works of the evolution of the arts in French Canada. Little by little, it began concentrating exclusively on the fine arts, leaving to other institutions the job of conserving the national archives and the natural history collections.

Today the Musée du Québec exhibits important and prestigious works covering all ages and different artistic styles of Québec. Along with its modern and contemporary Canadian art, it has gold jewellery and a fine print and drawing room. It plays a major role through its educational services, library and documentation centre.
          MICHEL CHAMPAGNE

Museum Policy has to do with the legislative, financial and administrative arrangements made by governments to establish and support museums, and also with the decisions taken by each individual museum to establish its own role in the community. The internationallly accepted definition of a museum, in turn, is "a non-profitmaking, permanent institution in the service of society and of its development, and open to the public, which acquires, conserves, researches, communicates and exhibits, for the purposes of study and enjoyment, material evidence of man and his environment."

There are many kinds of museum, but to be a museum an institution must have an organized collection. It may specialize in subjects as different as fur trading or fossils or modern art. Zoos collect animals, aquariums collect fish and botanical gardens collect plants, but they are all museums. From the collections, we can learn about the cultures of people living now and their development from the past, and about our natural and physical environment and its evolution from the past. We can understand something of how our ancestors saw their world, and of the world they saw.

Not only are they different in their subject matter, but Canadian museums are very different in their scale and sponsorship. They range from very small community museums showing the pioneer history of the locality, to specialized museums concerned with particular industries, organizations, arts or sports, to major government institutions which for some subjects provide the most authoritative reference collections in the world. Some museums are housed in log cabins, fortresses, office foyers or convents; a few are in very impressive buildings designed for the purpose. There are probably about 2500 of them in Canada, but 90% of the public collections are held in about 60 of the largest ones.

Most museums were established and are operated by groups of citizens interested in preserving and making available evidence of the past. The oldest is probably the New Brunswick Museum, founded in 1842, sharing the honour with the GEOLOGICAL SURVEY OF CANADA which established its museum (later to evolve into the NATIONAL MUSEUM OF NATURAL SCIENCES) in the same year. During this period, governments typically provided support grudgingly if at all; there was very little official interest or involvement except where government research agencies, like the GSC, built up reference collections almost as a by-product of their other scientific work. On the initiative of the then governor general, the marquess of LORNE, the NATIONAL GALLERY OF CANADA was established in 1880, but did not have its own Act of Parliament until 1913, and will not be adequately housed until 1988. Provincial governments were equally diffident, and for practical purposes municipal governments took no interest at all. By mid-century, many Canadian museums had been established and had grown into dynamic institutions, but this largely reflected the dedication of private citizens, rather than of governments at any level. In official thinking, there was no significant museum policy.

Since WWII, and particularly since Centennial in 1967, official attitudes have become much more supportive, no doubt largely in response to changes in public attitudes to science, the arts, culture and heritage. The factors entering into these changes apply with different weights to different types of museum, levels of government and regions of the country, but a few of them may be summarized.

Centennial certainly increased public interest in Canadian heritage. This factor bears most strongly on the establishment and expansion of specialized and local history museums. People realized that the Canadian confederation had not only survived but had grown and prospered spectacularly during its first century, and there was a sense throughout the country that evidence of this accomplishment should be preserved and made available to those building the next century. The establishment or improvement of museums seemed an appropriate way to do this, and governments responded with technical advice, encouragement and partial funding. Corporations and industrial associations also saw specialized museums as an appropriate way to celebrate the success of the country and their own part in it. This trend did not disappear after Centennial; in 1986, the federal National Museums Task Force estimated that 50 new museums a year are inaugurated in Canada. Museum policy has been in part a response to such popular initiatives.

During the same postwar period, the cultural diversity of Canada has been recognized. The various communities that make up our society – regional, ethnic, religious, indigenous, linguistic and others – have reasonably expected to find their traditions represented in our cultural institutions, including both general and specialized museums. History museums and art galleries are the targets here. There remains much to be accomplished, but progress is evident. Governments are taking the social diversity of Canada more fully into account, both through encouraging specialized museums and by responding more sensitively to pluralist concerns within their own institutions.

Another recent element has been the often reluctant recognition that this is a period in human history when some understanding of science is necessary for everyone and when, for the Canadian community, our capability in science will determine our future. These considerations bear particularly on museums of natural science and of science and technology where, despite the contributions of the National Museum of Natural Science, the NATIONAL MUSEUM OF SCIENCE AND TECHNOLOGY and the ONTARIO SCIENCE CENTRE, Canadians have not been well served.

There are at least 2 dimensions to this. One has to do with the "popularization of science": the principle that scientific knowledge is interesting and accessible to everyone, if it is presented in ways that everyone can grasp. Science museums excel at this. Unfortunately in Canada only 3 or 4 have this mandate, and although they draw more visitors than the other museums in the same cities, similar opportunities are not available to people in other parts of the country.

The other dimension has to do with museum collections as scientific resources in themselves. This can involve any museum, but particularly natural science museums. In the natural sciences, and especially the biological sciences, the identification of specimens is of critical importance. This relates directly, for example, to studies of the effects of pesticides or acid rain or other environmental contaminants. The organized reference collections held by museums provide the only standard against which new discoveries or unexpected mutations can be assessed. Governments in Canada have been slow to recognize the role of museums as research resources. The National Museum of Natural Sciences is authoritative in some areas, as is the ROYAL ONTARIO MUSEUM and the Jardin botanique de Montréal, but in the battle for budget the scientists typically find it difficult to hold their own with the departments of the museum responsible for direct services to the visiting public.

In recognizing the need for museum policies governments are not, of course, influenced entirely by concern with the arts and sciences in themselves. In particular, in the past half-century, TOURISM has become an increasingly important industry in Canada, and a high proportion of museum visitors are tourists. People tend to postpone museum visits when they are at home, but take advantage of the fleeting opportunity when they travel. Museums are accordingly seen as cost-effective tourist attractions, and this provides an economical incentive for government support, which may complement the cultural and scientific objectives.

While the reasons may vary among regions and from one museum to another, governments of all levels have accordingly been brought to take a much more active interest in museums in recent years, and museum policies have been developed in the federal and all provincial governments and in some municipalities. The change in attitude is illustrated by the fact that in 1968 only one provincial government (Québec) had a minister with serious responsibility for museum affairs; 10 years later, no provincial government was without such a minister.

Policies differ in detail in each jurisdiction but all of them make a primary distinction between those collections which are owned by the govern-

ment, those which are owned by municipalities or nonprofit institutions like museum societies, and those which are in private hands. In the nature of things, with the passage of time and whether intended or not, governments accumulate a great many things which turn out to be museum material. The collections of the Canadian Postal Museum in Ottawa, and the Royal Canadian Mounted Police Museum in Regina are examples. As good stewards, governments have increasingly recognized that they have a responsibility to conserve and organize the collections they own, and to encourage the public to visit them.

For the nonprofit museums that they do not own, the federal and provincial governments provide modest financial support through various granting programs, as well as professional advice and assistance in technical aspects of museum management including, for example, help with the preservation and conservation of the collections (*see* CONSERVATION OF MOVABLE CULTURAL PROPERTY). Often, this assistance is channelled through national or provincial museum associations, which provide essential support especially to small local museums. Government programs also encourage the organization and circulation of travelling exhibitions, so that people in one part of the country may have opportunities to experience the cultural heritage of other regions.

For that important part of our heritage in private hands, there is not very much that governments can, or perhaps should, do. Through a system of export permits supported by purchase grants, the federal Cultural Property Export and Import Act of 1977 has been effective in assisting public collections to acquire important artifacts if and when the private owner decides to sell, but in general governments have not become involved.

The most important federal government collections are held by 4 institutions: the National Gallery of Canada (fine arts), the CANADIAN MUSEUM OF CIVILIZATION (human history and pre-history), the National Museum of Natural Sciences (all of nature except man), and the National Museum of Science and Technology. By the National Museums Act of 1968, these 4 were brought within a single corporation which subsequently assumed responsibility also for the Canadian Conservation Institute, the Canadian Heritage Information Network and a number of programs providing financial support to nonprofit museums across the country. Over the years, this consolidation proved difficult to operate effectively, and in 1987 the government announced its intention to re-establish the 4 museums as operationally independent institutions, and to assume direct responsibility within the Department of Communications for federal assistance to other museums.

Canadian museums are recent arrivals on the international scene. The major collections in other countries, especially in Europe, include works of art and other valuable and interesting objects accumulated over centuries of imperial, religious or dynastic history. One of the continuing policy issues in Canada turns on how far we should go in trying to build up similar collections, necessarily through the purchase of increasingly scarce and expensive items from abroad, instead of concentrating on our own natural history and our own much shorter recorded social and artistic traditions. The reasons for stressing Canada are obvious, but there is also a case for building international collections, especially in the fine arts. Many of the roots of Canadian painting and sculpture and applied arts are in "older" nations, and contemporary work in this country is part of the world scene. This line of argument holds that museums — art museums in particular — should encour-

age Canadians to experience the global and historic dimensions of our modern civilization without having to travel abroad. On the other hand, museums in other countries cannot be expected to specialize in Canadian art; this must be done in Canada or not at all. In addition, classic works of earlier centuries are very costly. Buying them, on those rare occasions when they come on the market, means that much less contemporary Canadian work can be acquired.

A second range of policy issues involves collections of artifacts, often representing the cultures of the original peoples of Canada, which are held by major history museums. Some of these collections, including, for example, material confiscated early in the century from West Coast POTLATCH ceremonies, were acquired in circumstances which are now recognised as odious. Others were accumulated perfectly legitimately, at a time when their long-term significance was recognised only by a few specialists; if they had not been collected, most of them would almost certainly have disappeared. In light of their cultural and sometimes spiritual significance for the people who keep alive the traditions that produced them, should they now be sent back?

There is probably no categorical answer, which explains why this remains a policy issue. Many of the articles are now very fragile, and they are less likely to disintegrate in good facilities under professional care. Large integrated collections also offer better opportunities for research, and accordingly for developing a fuller understanding of the cultures they represent. On the other hand, large institutions do not have an unblemished record for careful custody, and scholarly interests are not the only values involved. Satisfactory permanent homes for articles on long-term loan from the Canadian Museum of Civilization have been arranged in Thunder Bay, Yellowknife and elsewhere, and it is likely that similar agreements will be reached in the future, case by case.

A third policy issue — and the one which preoccupies museum trustees and directors more than any other — turns quite simply on money. Not only is there never enough, which is normal, but what money there is cannot always be devoted to the most pressing purposes. Raising money is never easy, but generally speaking it is easier to raise money for new museums, new buildings and impressive special exhibitions than it is for the humdrum, essential work of keeping the doors open, and conserving and presenting the existing collections for current audiences and future generations. Every year, more material is probably lost through disintegration than is gained through acquisitions. A good case can be made not only for better funding but also for changing the financial policy emphasis from capital to operations, which would suggest slowing down the rate of establishment of new museums and of expansions, in favour of better conservation and presentation of the collections already held. This issue appears differently to museum trustees and professionals on the one hand, and to politicians and their officials on the other, and no doubt public opinion will determine the outcome.

Ultimately, museum policy is an aspect of PUBLIC POLICY, and like all public policy it will finally be set not by deliberations in boardrooms and government offices but by what the public wants and is prepared to pay for. Canadian museums are good museums, and can be much better museums, but whether they achieve their potential depends finally on how much the public comes to care about the values they represent.

DAVID W. BARTLETT

False chantarelle *(Hygrophoropsis aurantiaca)*. Chantarelles are one of the relatively few wild mushrooms that Canada harvests commercially *(photo by Tim Fitzharris)*.

Bear's head hydnum *(Hericium ramosum) (photo by Mary W. Ferguson)*.

Oyster mushroom *(Pleurotus ostreatus)* is being cultivated commercially in Ontario and on an experimental basis in Québec *(photo by Mary W. Ferguson)*.

Fly agaric mushroom *(Amanita muscaria)* showing its distinctive red cap. Muscarine, which is present in small quantities in fly amanita, can be a fatal poison *(photo by Tim Fitzharris)*.

Mushroom and Puffball, fleshy, spore-bearing fruitbodies produced by many club FUNGI (Basidiomycetes) and a few sac fungi (Ascomycetes). Such fungi may be saprophytes, living on and causing decay of organic matter; symbionts, living in association with tree roots to their mutual advantage; or occasionally plant parasites. In soil-inhabiting species, mycelium (mass of filaments forming the vegetative body of the fungus) grows indefinitely; fruitbodies are produced when conditions are favourable. Rings of fruitbodies (eg, fairy rings) mark the location of buried mycelium. Rings expand annually and ages can be estimated from annual diameter increase. Some rings are over 500 years old. Mushroom species in Canada exceed 3000; of these many also occur on other continents.

Mycologists (biologists studying fungi) do not distinguish mushrooms from toadstools, although the latter term is popularly used for poisonous types. Related species may differ markedly in edibility and no simple tests exist for identifying edible types. Identifying features are macroscopic or microscopic. For specialists, microscopic features are most significant, eg, shape of spore-bearing cells, size and other features of spores and microscopic fruitbody structure. Macroscopic characteristics include fruitbody shape and colour, presence or absence of ring (annulus) and cup (volva), form of spore-producing layer (hymenium) and spore-print colour.

Annulus and Volva In the button stage, the cap and stalk of a mushroom are joined by a membrane (veil) that ruptures as growth occurs, preparatory to spore dispersal. As the destroying angel (common in eastern Canada) develops, remnants of 2 membranous veils are left as a ring on the stalk and a cup at the stalk base. Fly agaric or fly amanita has a bright red cap with warts (also veil remnants) and a ring; its cup consists of irregular ridges around the swollen stalk base. Mushrooms may have only the ring or only the cup; many have neither.

Hymenium Gill fungi, such as market mushrooms and amanitas, produce spore-bearing cells on surfaces of structures called gills. Pore fungi (eg, boletes) have pores (tubules) instead of gills. The hymenium of hedgehog mushrooms is borne on teeth; that of crested coral mushroom covers branch surfaces. The morels and potentially poisonous false morels produce spores in sacs (asci) on the outer cap surface. All of these have exposed spores, but puffball spores are enclosed in the fruitbody. Gemmed puffballs become dry at maturity, a pore develops at the top and the fruitbody functions as a bellows when struck (eg, by water drops).

Spore-Print Colour Spore masses, shown in spore prints, are white in amanitas and fairy-ring mushroom; chocolate brown in market mushrooms; yellowish, pinkish, rusty brown or black in other species.

Mushroom poisonings are caused by several toxins. Amanitas and some galerinas produce heat-stable amatoxins and phallotoxins, which induce symptoms felt only after 4-48 hours. Also potentially fatal, with a delay of up to 2 weeks before symptoms appear, are the orellanins produced by some Cortinarii. False morels produce a potent toxin (monomethylhydrazine) which is lost if the mushrooms are thoroughly cooked. Muscarine, present in small quantities in fly amanita, is abundant in some inocybes and clitocybes, poisoning by which may cause death; appropriate treatment neutralizes poison. Mild poisoning (diarrhea, etc) occurs with ingestion of numerous other mushrooms.

Commercial exploitation of wild mushrooms is not extensive in Canada, but a few are harvested and sold. Pine mushrooms (Canadian matsu-take) and chanterelles are exported. *See also* MUSHROOM CULTIVATION.   R.J. BANDONI

Reading: O. Miller, *Mushrooms of North America* (1980).

Mushroom Cultivation The mushroom cultivated on a large scale in Canada is *Agaricus bisporus* (also called *A. brunnescens*). The most commonly grown strains have white caps, less common strains are cream and brown. Small quantities of *A. bitorquis* (a related white species) are also grown. *Agaricus*, first cultivated in France in the 17th century, was grown by E. Cauchois in 1877 in Québec.

Nutrients for *Agaricus* are usually provided by horse-manure composted with straw and nitrogen-rich additives (eg, chicken manure, brewer's grains, ammonium nitrate, etc). Gypsum is added for texture. Composting is initiated by watering a horse-manure mixture stacked in long piles (2.0-2.4 m high, 1.8-2.2 m wide) on a concrete floor outdoors. Piles are turned mechanically 4 times during a 2-week period. Water may be added at each turn or less often, depending on the season. The temperature inside the piles rises to 70-75°C through the action of bacteria and fungi, which decompose plant and animal matter and convert inorganic to organic nitrogen compounds, providing nutrients for the mushrooms. Trays (1.2x1.8 m) or long shelves, arranged in tiers in dark mushroom houses, are filled with a layer (20 cm) of cooled compost. During the subsequent "cook-out" process, continuing microbial activity raises the temperature to about 45°C and, after 1-3 days, steam is let into the houses for several hours allowing pasteurization to occur (60°C), thus killing parasites. The compost is left for 5-12 days (at about 50°C), during which "conditioning period" micro-organisms produce more nutrients. The compost is then cooled to about 25°C. Mushroom spawn, prepared under sterile conditions by allowing vegetative mushroom mycelium to grow into cereal grains, is inserted into the compost and spread over the surface. The mycelium penetrates the compost in about 2 weeks. Compost is then covered (cased) with a 2-3 cm layer of pasteurized loam topsoil, or a deeper layer of sphagnum moss or peat mixed with soil (acid peat is neutralized with hydrated lime or limestone). The casing layer is watered and the mycelium grows through it. Beds are cooled by ventilation to about 20°C, stimulating formation of young mushrooms (pinheads) in about 4 days. They are harvested when caps are about 2-8 cm. At 7-11-day intervals new crops ("flushes" or "breaks") appear, one batch of compost yielding up to 7 crops. Strict sanitation is maintained and PESTICIDES are used because *Agaricus* is susceptible to attack by viruses, bacteria, microscopic FUNGI, nematodes and mushroom fly larvae.

Mushrooms are the most valuable Canadian vegetable crop. In 1986 Canadian production of *Agaricus* was 51 429 t ($136.3 million), of which 36 242 t were sold fresh (most of the remainder being canned). Ontario produced about half; BC almost 27%; Québec, Alberta, the Maritimes and Manitoba, the remainder. In 1985 per capita consumption was 1.48 kg. On a small scale, 2 edible mushrooms are cultivated commercially on wood: *Lentinus edodes,* known by Japanese name Shiitake, in Ontario and BC, and the oyster mushroom, *Pleurotus ostreatus,* in Ontario and, at least experimentally, in Québec. HANS E. GRUEN

Reading: F.J. Ingratta and T.J. Blom, *Commercial Mushroom Growing* (1980); N.W. Tape, *How to Grow Mushrooms* (1980).

Music, Profession of Professional musicians are those who through their skill, training and commitment are able to earn a living as musicians. They may be teachers, performers or non-performers, and their specialty may be popular, classical, military or religious music. Musicians are often active in more than one occupation at a time, particularly in teaching combined with other musical activities. The largest group of professional musicians is teachers working in schools, conservatories and universities, as music therapists and as coaches of singing and instrumental groups. Teaching, especially if associated with an institution, provides the most stable income and working conditions for a musician, though schoolteachers usually require a university degree or college diploma. At the conservatory and university level, exceptionally talented musicians may not need certification.

Competition is greatest among performers, whether ensemble or solo instrumentalists and vocalists or conductors. Artists perform only a few hours each week as far more time is spent in practice, rehearsal and, if on tour, travel. Experience in performance is included in all music training at the post-secondary level for popular or classical music. While it is possible to obtain good training in Canada (see MUSIC EDUCATION), most musicians seeking a virtuoso career will study abroad. Canada does not have a national school of music similar to those in ballet and theatre. Nonperforming professional musicians include composers, musicologists, ethnomusicologists, music librarians and archivists; journalists and editors; instrument builders, repair craftsmen and tuners; and music producers for radio, TV and recordings. Certain administrators in music schools, unions, performing rights societies, artist management and record companies, as well as technicians such as engineers in recording studios, may be trained musicians.

The cost of preparing for a career in music can be high, involving lessons, instruments and equipment, travel, promotion and management. Most musicians begin music study in their pre-teen years, though a talented person can make a later start. Income for the independent performer is often irregular and unpredictable. There are few fringe benefits and a musician in poor health cannot work. Musicians can be subject to arbitrary and unfair decisions by employers and as a group are poorly represented politically. Some areas of performance are highly stressful. Many of these unfavourable working conditions have been improved through the efforts of music unions and professional organizations for teachers, organists and composers. The American Federation of Musicians of the US and Canada (AF of M) negotiates union agreements with the CBC, CTV, NFB, the recording industry and companies producing commercials in which music is used, and its local branches negotiate with individual symphony orchestras and concert halls. The Union des artistes (UDA; French language) and the Assn of Canadian Television and Radio Artists (ACTRA; English language) protect members' rights and fees on radio, TV and the recording industry; and Canadian Actors' Equity Assn protects live-stage performers.

Before the early 1800s most musicians for whom there is documentation in Canada were connected to the church. During the 19th century, the church, the military, private teaching studios, instrument building and the music trade were the main sources of income, though most musicians combined 2 or more of these activities. Not until the mid-20th century was it possible for musicians to earn a living in one specialized field, as careers opened up in CBC broadcasting, symphony orchestras and schoolteaching. Opportunities for professional musicians expanded following the establishment of the CANADA COUNCIL and various provincial arts councils, although the

amount of government funding is diminishing.

Women have been active in the profession since at least the middle of the 19th century. It is likely that they were the bulwark of private teaching in the years after Confederation and appeared early as instrumentalists in orchestras. In spite of its disadvantages, the profession of music continues to attract participants. It is a challenging, creative career with scope for personal growth and satisfaction. See also CHAMBER MUSIC; COUNTRY AND WESTERN MUSIC; FOLK MUSIC; JAZZ; MUSIC BROADCASTING; MUSIC CRITICISM; MUSICAL INSTRUMENTS; MUSICOLOGY; OPERA; ORCHESTRAL MUSIC; POPULAR MUSIC; RECORDING INDUSTRY; RELIGIOUS MUSIC; SONGS AND SONG WRITING; and individual entries for organizations and groups.   CHRISTOPHER WEAIT

Music Awards and Competitions Music awards are given on a noncompetitive basis or are won in competition. Noncompetitive music awards recognize outstanding accomplishment, merit, leadership or generosity. Recipients may be part of a larger group honoured by government institutions (the Order of Canada, the Alberta Achievement Awards); they may be winners of prizes or trophies given specifically to members of the music community by musical clubs, professional organizations or businesses associated with music (the Canadian Music Council Medal or the Juno Awards); they may be given a monetary award by a foundation established to commemorate the work of a celebrated Canadian musician (the Glenn Gould Prize); or they may be the object of salutatory awards made by schools (honorary degrees). Winners are usually chosen by a specially appointed jury or awards committee. Noncompetitive music awards can also take the form of scholarships, bursaries, fellowships or study grants, as established by individuals, businesses, foundations, music clubs, educational institutions or professional music organizations.

Competitive music awards can be divided into several categories: those given at competitive festivals, or in performance, conducting or composition competitions. Some provide honours only and others give monetary awards. Competitive festivals provide opportunities for young musicians to compete against their peers and profit from the experience of public performance and the advice of the judges. Some competitive festivals award medals and trophies to prizewinners.

Performance competitions usually involve participation at the advanced-student or young professional level. Winners are chosen by an appointed jury. In addition to a monetary prize, there are rewards such as national recognition by press coverage of the competition, possible offers of recording contracts and invitations to perform for radio or TV or with major orchestras, choirs or concert groups. These competitions are sometimes held publicly in concert halls (the MONTREAL INTERNATIONAL COMPETITION) or on radio (the CBC Radio Talent Competition, formerly the CBC Talent Festival and successor to "Opportunity Knocks"). Conducting competitions are recent in Canada. They are sponsored by foundations, schools or conservatories to honour a well-known conductor who has shown particular interest in young musicians wishing to perform as conductors (the Heinz Unger Award). As well as offering a prize, usually money, these competitions provide a showcase for conductors to demonstrate their skills before representatives of community orchestras needing energetic and ambitious conductors. Composition competitions have increased greatly during the last 30 years. Sponsored by both the CBC and various corporations, as well as by musical organizations across Canada, composition competitions usually offer a cash prize for the winning composer,

and the public performance and sometimes the recording of the successful composition, usually by a major orchestra, choir, ensemble or soloist. In recent years an increasing number of music prizes and awards have been established by corporations. To facilitate this, the Council for Business and the Arts was established (1974). Also, corporations offer cash prizes and awards for specific accomplishments such as orchestras performing the most Canadian works in a season. For a listing of music awards and competitions consult the ENCYCLOPEDIA OF MUSIC IN CANADA.
                                                        MABEL H. LAINE

Music Broadcasting is the transmission of music via AM and FM radio and television networks and stations and by satellite. All transmission modes have French and English services and operate through privately and publicly owned systems. The FM stereo network is one of the world's largest high-quality music networks. In general, radio has been more important than TV for music broadcasting. The development of music broadcasting in Canada falls into 4 periods: pre-1936 (to the establishment of CBC); 1936-52 (to the introduction of TV); 1952-75 (to the pan-Canada FM stereo network); 1975 to the present.

Canada's contribution to BROADCASTING is noteworthy. Montréal's XWA (now CFCF) was one of the first stations in the world (May 1920) to offer regular, scheduled broadcasts. On 1 July 1927, the Diamond Jubilee of Canada's Confederation, a transcontinental network was inaugurated with a daylong broadcast, mostly of music. In the early 1920s the Canadian National Railways, under its president Sir Henry THORNTON, built radio studios in several centres across the land. In the mid-1920s complete Gilbert and Sullivan operas were studio broadcast, as was an ambitious series, "The Music Makers." In 1927 the famed HART HOUSE STRING QUARTET travelled coast to coast for (and on) the CNR, broadcasting recitals of Beethoven quartets. In 1929 the new network began N America's first series of radio symphony concerts, by members of the TORONTO SYMPHONY under Luigi von Kunits. The CPR had also begun to broadcast concerts, but the Depression in the 1930s ended the railways' involvement in national broadcasting. Between 1932 and 1936 Canadian public radio was developed by the Canadian Radio Broadcasting Commission under the Toronto critic Hector CHARLESWORTH. It was hastily organized and not well supported by the federal government.

In 1936 the CANADIAN BROADCASTING CORPORATION was founded and by the 1940-41 season CBC radio, operating nationally, regionally and locally, and in 2 language services, had presented some 600 symphonic broadcasts (many from the US), 2000 broadcasts of chamber music and 45 full-opera broadcasts (including the Metropolitan Opera, still broadcasting today). In 1942 the CBC commissioned from Healey WILLAN and John COULTER the radio opera *Transit Through Fire*, and 3 years later, the opera *Deirdre of the Sorrows*.

In this period Canadian programs were heard over the US Mutual, NBC and CBS networks. This was a time of much original live broadcasting, including the talent hunts ("Singing Stars of Tomorrow" from 1943, "Opportunity Knocks" from 1947) and many amateur-hour programs. Between 1944 and 1962 the CBC operated an alternative English-language network, the Dominion. Toronto's CJBC was owned by the CBC, but all other stations were privately owned affiliates. Alternative programming was mostly lighter than that of the trans-Canada network, though the Toronto and Montréal Symphony orchestras performed on Dominion on Tuesday nights followed by "CBC Concert Hall." In that period the CBC maintained studio orchestras in Halifax, Québec, Montréal, Toronto, Winnipeg and Vancouver, providing welcome employment for local musicians. By the late 1940s the CBC was the largest single employer of musicians in N America. Music broadcasting ranged from symphonic and opera to light and popular. Private stations broadcast local musicians and many pop singers and instrumentalists owed their first encouragement to radio broadcasts. In general, the most intensive music broadcasting was from the CBC.

In Sept 1952 the CBC inaugurated its television broadcasting. In those first years CBC TV was inventive and adventurous. Major opera and dance productions were mounted by Franz Kraemer, Vincent Tovell and Norman CAMPBELL in Toronto, and Pierre MERCURE in Montréal (whose French-network series "L'Heure du concert" was among the most remarkable ever produced on this continent). As costs mounted and the CBC was forced to economize by buying imported programs, Canadian TV production dwindled, especially in music programs, though the occasional special made its mark, such as Norman Campbell's 1966 National Ballet production of Prokofiev's Cinderella, or Harry SOMERS's opera Louis Riel produced by Franz Kraemer in 1969.

Although large audiences enjoyed the TV medium and private radio narrowed its perspectives, music on CBC Radio continued to flourish in the period from 1952 to 1975. The jazz and popular stylings of Phil NIMMONS (Toronto), Neil CHOTEM (Montréal) and Lance Harrison (Vancouver) were widely appreciated. Chamber music broadcasts also abounded. The CBC Symphony Orchestra, N America's only radio symphony orchestra, was active from 1952 to 1964 and featured many modern works, with special attention to Canadian composers. The Orchestra's growing reputation drew Igor Stravinsky to Toronto in the early 1960s for his 80th birthday celebration. This was a period of exceptional support for Canadian composers, through performances of their works, commissions and the engagement of John BECKWITH, Somers, Norma BEECROFT, Mercure and François MOREL as commentators. The English network began to produce its own series of stereo discs, first for broadcast use but later for sale.

After 1975 the increasing use of disc and tape wrought profound changes in the pattern of music broadcasting. The live or studio broadcast gave way to the varied program package, held together by a program host. The radio networks were reorganized in the mid-1970s and for the first time a fully national FM stereo network of high technical quality was inaugurated. AM retained its policy of providing programming for a general audience and FM was mostly music, largely non-pop though with some serious jazz. At first the schedule was perhaps 75% records, rarely Canadian. By the 1980s, however, CBC programmers had begun once more to diversify their formats, reviving "live-to-air" techniques for special events and in other ways projecting music as an art.

There was much live broadcasting of local origin, but after the early 1950s private radio settled comfortably into the "top 40" and foreign records, effectively preventing it from contributing to the development of music in Canada. One private-sector initiative of special note was the Canadian Talent Library, initiated and developed by Lyman Potts for the Standard Broadcasting syndicate. The Library recorded discs for broadcast only, featuring Canadian performers and much original Canadian composition.

By the early 1970s the regulatory CANADIAN RADIO-TELEVISION AND TELECOMMUNICATIONS COMMIS-SION (CRTC) had laid down new rules governing community service and Canadian content, which stimulated Canadian recordings and pop groups. New Canadian stars emerged (Anne MURRAY, Bruce COCKBURN, Burton CUMMINGS, the GUESS WHO) retracing a similar development already far advanced in Québec, where chansonniers (Gilles VIGNEAULT, Pauline JULIEN and Robert CHARLEBOIS) had for years been accorded star status.

During WWII the federal government established its International Service (mostly shortwave radio), supervised by the Dept of External Affairs but operated by the CBC. In 1968 the service came under full CBC responsibility and was renamed Radio Canada International in 1972. The IS/RCI made and distributed internationally hundreds of recordings. By 1977, RCI had begun its Anthology series, each a package of several discs of the music of a Canadian composer.

Music broadcasting has been crucial to the vitality of music in Canada. New technologies and changing tastes will affect form and style, but broadcasting will still play a leading role in bringing music to the public. See also POPULAR MUSIC.   KEITH MACMILLAN

Music Composition The repertoire of works composed in Canada in the traditions of Western art music goes back about 300 years; but by far its largest part belongs to the post-WWII period.

The late-17th-century "Prose de la Sainte-Famille," a long plainchant preserved in several manuscript copies in Québec City, is original both in text and music. The attribution of the music to a native-born priest, Charles-Amador Martin (1648-1711), is an attractive possibility, though not fully proven. This piece, though not nearly as early as the earliest compositions from New Spain, does antedate the earliest known by composers of New England. In the early 1980s a large number of previously unknown musical manuscripts, particularly those of the so-called Montreal Organ Book (1724; facsimile ed, 1981), revealed anonymous choral and organ-solo compositions of the early 18th century, some of which may be by local composers.

In the century preceding Confederation, the annals of urban musical life in many parts of Canada illustrate the versatility of pioneering professionals, who typically led choirs as well as chamber, wind and orchestral ensembles; handled sales of instruments and sheet music; taught music both privately and in schools; organized musical performances; and in almost all cases composed at least a modest quantity of new pieces. With the gradual flowering of a Canadian music-publishing industry after 1840, much of this literature followed the prevailing markets of sentimental and patriotic songs, dance music, piano variations on favourite melodies, and sacred music. But there was also a respectable and growing production of works in larger forms. Historical published (and occasionally also unpublished) Canadian music has been made more accessible through the series The Canadian Musical Heritage (Ottawa, from 1984), of which 7 vols had appeared by mid-1987, with several more in preparation.

The part-time composers of this period were nonetheless often quite skilled. Many came to Canada from other countries: Joseph QUESNEL (1746-1809), Charles Wugk Sabatier (1819-62) and Antoine Dessane (1826-73) from France; Stephen Codman (1796-1852) from England; James Paton Clarke (1808-77) and G.W. Strathy (1818-90) from Scotland; Frederic Glackemeyer (1751-1836) and T.F. Molt (1796-1856) from Germany; Stephen Humbert (1767-1849) and Mark Burnham (1791-1864) from the US.

Gifted native-born Canadians included J.-C. Brauneis, Jr (1814-71), Ernest GAGNON, Calixa LAVALLÉE, and Romain-Octave Pelletier (1843-1927). Achievements of unusual interest include the operetta Colas et Colinette (1789, text and music by Quesnel), one of the earliest N American works in this genre; Humbert's anthems and fuguing tunes, based on then current New England models; Dessane's imposing concerted church-music settings (he had been one of the last pupils of Cherubini); and the song cycle Lays of the Maple Leaf (1853) by Clarke. Indigenous references in subject or text are rare; the Clarke work is a notable exception; others include J.J. Perrault's Messe de Noël (1861), introducing folksong motives from French-speaking Canada, and Gagnon's "Stadaconé" (1858), a piano piece evocative of Amerindian rhythms.

Lavallée was the most versatile and prolific Canadian composer of the later 19th century, rarely overstepping convention but possessing a strong melodic sense and an extensive vocabulary of harmonies and colours. Some of his songs, and especially his works for solo piano (eg, "Le Papillon," "L'Oiseau-mouche") enjoyed an international vogue and have been successfully revived along with larger works such as his concert overture La Rose nuptiale and his operetta The Widow. Canadians know him best as the composer of "O Canada."

Among composers active between Confederation and WWI, most were native Canadians: eg, Joseph Vézina (1849-1924), Guillaume Couture (1851-1915), Alexis Contant (1858-1918), Wesley Octavius Forsyth (1859-1937), and Clarence Lucas (1866-1947). But this era also saw a large influx of professional musicians from Britain, many of whom were influential in teaching composition as well as in composing, especially for chorus; Charles A.E. HARRISS (1862-1929) and J. Humfrey Anger (1862-1913) are leading examples. Large choral-orchestral pieces now appeared more frequently, among them Arthur E. Fisher's The Wreck of the Hesperus (1893), Harriss's Torquil (1894), Contant's Caïn (1905) and Couture's Jean le Précurseur (1909), as well as orchestral works like Lucas' concert overture Macbeth (1900) and, less often, extended chamber works like Contant's Trio (1907). The favoured stage form was romantic or parodistic operetta rather than full-scaled opera. Themes were often frankly escapist, but indigenous situations inspired both Oscar Telgmann's Leo, the Royal Cadet (1889, still among the longest-running of Canadian operettas) and Vézina's Le Fétiche (1912, a fictionalization of French-Indian conflict).

In the interwar period, prominent composers were the native Canadians Rodolphe Mathieu (1890-1962), Claude CHAMPAGNE (1891-1965), and Ernest MACMILLAN (1893-1973), and the British-born Healey WILLAN (1880-1968) and Alfred Whitehead (1887-1974). MacMillan, best known as a conductor, produced one of the first Canadian string quartets (1921), and Willan what may be the first symphonies (no 1, 1936; no 2, 1948). The music of this group reflects, particularly around 1930, a strong interest in local folk music as material for compositional development. It also shows greater technical assurance than the music of earlier generations, but perhaps only in works such as Mathieu's Trio (1922) and the later works of Champagne (Quartet, 1954; Altitude, 1959) do international styles of 20th-century music show a marked influence. Willan had the longest and most productive career of any Canadian composer to date, covering almost a 70-year time-span and touching on almost all standard forms including symphony, concerto, opera, chamber music, organ and choral music and songs. His choral works, effectively combining classic a-cappella textures and an English-romantic harmonic idiom, drew wide international notice.

A few of Willan's students went on to composing careers which relate to his outlook (Godfrey Ridout, 1918-84; Robert Fleming, 1921-76). Champagne was also a widely respected teacher. But the period 1935-50 was one of generational confrontation: younger composers by and large rejected their seniors' work, and asserted new emphases. They regarded composing as a central professional activity, adopted current international idioms, turned to US rather than British or Continental-European schools for their training, established a new teacher-pupil tradition in Canada, and – most importantly – produced a substantial and vital new repertoire of musical works. The national cultural stirrings of the 1950s coincided with the rise of these figures (Murray Adaskin, b 1906; Jean Coulthard, b 1908; Barbara Pentland, b 1912; Violet Archer and John Weinzweig, both b 1913; and Jean Papineau-Couture, b 1917) and their students (Harry Freedman, b 1922; Harry Somers, b 1925; Clermont Pépin and François Morel, both b 1926; Pierre Mercure and John Beckwith, both b 1927; and Serge Garant, 1929-86) and with the arrival of important immigrant practitioners (Otto Joachim, b 1910, in Canada from 1949; Oskar MORAWETZ, b 1917, in Canada from 1940; Istvan Anhalt, b 1919, in Canada from 1949; Talivaldis Kenins and Udo Kasemets, both b 1919 and in Canada from 1951; and Sophie-Carmen ECKHARDT-GRAMATTÉ, 1899-1974, in Canada from 1953). The spirit of the epoch was further reflected in the founding of a professional association, the Canadian League of Composers (1951) and a support organization, the Canadian Music Centre (1959), in policies favouring contemporary works in CBC broadcasts and recordings, and in increased acceptance of creative music as a major subject in Canadian conservatories and university music departments.

This was a favourable climate for the maturation of a younger group, born in the 1930s, among whom are some of Canada's best-known composers – Gilles Tremblay, b 1932; R. Murray Schafer, b 1933; André Prévost, b 1934; Jacques Hétu, b 1938; Micheline Coulombe Saint-Marcoux, 1938-85; and Bruce Mather, b 1939. Among a large number whose work captured attention after 1967 (ie, composers born since 1940) may be mentioned Brian Cherney, b 1942; John Hawkins and John Rea, both b 1944; Donald Steven, b 1945; Michel Longtin, b 1946; Walter Boudreau and Barry Truax, both b 1947; Claude Vivier, 1948-83; Denis Lorrain and Stephen Gellman, both b 1948; Chan Ka-Nin and Alexina LOUIE, both b 1949; John Burke, b 1951; Serge Arcuri, b 1954; Denys Bouliane, b 1955; and Robert Rosen, b 1956. Seasoned composers born abroad who have settled in Canada since the later 1960s include Rudolf Komorous, Lothar Klein, Bengt Hambraeus, James Tenney, Michael Colgrass, Alcides Lanza, and Peter Paul Koprowski.

The repertoire which took shape in the 1950s exhibited many new features: for example, the pastoral strain in Coulthard; the amiable neoclassicism of Adaskin's scores; original approaches to abstract structuring, pursued with intensity especially by Pentland and Papineau-Couture. The 1960s, buoyant decade of the national centennial, saw a remarkable flourishing of compositions exploring new directions such as chance music, electronics and theatricalism. With major scores such as Mercure's *Triptyque* (1959) and *Lignes et points* (1963-64), Joachim's *Contrasts* (1967), and Somers' *Five Concepts*

(1961) and *Stereophony* (1963, for an orchestra deployed around the auditorium on various levels), the range of Canadian orchestral expression became considerably broadened. The latter's work in particular has continued to combine fullness of structure with a personal expressiveness touching on anguish in the soliloquies of *Louis Riel* (1967) and in the *Shaman's Song* (1983) or on sensuousness mixed with humour in *Love-in-Idleness* (1976, based on a scene from *A Midsummer Night's Dream*).

Weinzweig's works for solo instruments and orchestra (3 concertos, 8 divertimenti) have resulted from a close study of instrumental idioms. His music is characteristically lean-textured and often contains jazz, blues and swing inflections (*Refrains* for double bass and piano, 1976, and *Out of the Blues* for wind ensemble, 1981, are typical). In his work since 1970, dadaistic and quotational elements occur. Sensitivity to percussion colours is a feature of the music of Tremblay and Mather. Both excel in chamber works of mixed instrumentation. The former's preoccupation with an almost pantheistic symbolism (eg, in *Solstices*, 1971, and *Compostelle I*, 1978) may be traced to the influence of his teacher, Olivier Messiaen. Since the mid-1970s, Mather has concentrated on works calling for microtonal tunings (*Musique pour Champigny*, 1978; *Barbaresco*, 1984). Kasemets holds an independent avant-garde position; virtually his entire production since the early 1960s consists of happenings and mixed-media schemes rather than conventional musical "works."

Canadian research in electro-acoustic music has been internationally recognized from the pioneer inventions and compositions of Hugh LeCaine (1914-77) to the work of Anhalt, Joachim, Schafer, Saint-Marcoux, Truax and many others. In the theatre sphere, apart from incidental music by specialists such as Louis APPLEBAUM (b 1918), Gabriel Charpentier (b 1925) and Gary Kulesha (b 1954), the repertoire includes ballets by Freedman (*Rose Latulippe, Five over Thirteen, Oiseaux exotiques*), Somers (*House of Atreus*), Garant (*Findings*, based on his *Offrande I*) and Klein (*Canadiana*), and operas by Charles Wilson (*Heloise and Abelard*), Somers (*Louis Riel, The Death of Enkidu*), Beckwith (*The Shivaree*) and Vivier (*Kopernicus*).

Charpentier's cycle of 10 mini-operas, *A Night at the Opera*, like Schafer's more cosmic music dramas, *Patria* and *The Greatest Show on Earth*, had been produced only in part by 1987; however, the latter's *Apocalypsis, The Princess of the Stars* and *Ra* had all received full productions revealing a powerful mingling of operatic with ritualistic and earth-art elements. Historical reference and quotation, encountered in Schafer, Beckwith and others, become crucial factors in Rea's chamber work *Com-possession*, where dancing, electronics and live-instrumental sounds from past and present blend to evoke the spells of tarantulism.

The association of music with social comment is seen in Weinzweig's *Wine of Peace* and *Dummiyah*; in Pentland's *News*; in several works by Morawetz, notably *Memorial to Martin Luther King* and *From the Diary of Anne Frank*; and in Prévost's *Second Quartet ("Da Pacem")* and *Ahimsâ*.

Overt Canadianism is exemplified in works connected with Canadian history or environment or visual art, or based on Canadian literary texts. Examples are Schafer's youthful *Brébeuf*, set to portions of Brébeuf's journals; Morel's *Boréal* and *L'Etoile noire*, the latter based on a famous Borduas canvas; works by Weinzweig, Garant and others employing Inuit and Indian sources; Freedman's impressionistic *Images* and *Klee Wyck*; and Anhalt's unique music dramas –

half cantata, half documentary/pageant – *Foci, La Tourangelle* and *Winthrop*. The last 2 works delve into the meaning of cultural transplantation (from Old World to New), with a resourceful fusion of images drawn from the lives of particular early immigrants (*see* MUSIC HISTORY).

In the 1980s there was a renewal of interest in orchestral music, with highlights ranging from Pépin's *Fifth Symphony* (like his *Third*, inspired by astronomy) and Kenins' *Seventh* (with mezzo-soprano solo), to Garant's taut and austere *Plages* and Cherney's *... into the distant stillness ...* Especially formidable dimensions were undertaken in Rosen's *From Silence* (1982-83) and Gellman's *Universe Symphony* (1985) with their large forces, seriousness of tone, and Ivesian breadth and density. Recent works by Longtin, Hawkins and others sounded a call for renewal of classic key-centered forms (Longtin's deliberate homage in *Autour d'Ainola*, 1986, was to Sibelius; that of Hawkins, in *Breaking Through*, 1982, to Weill) – to which several younger composers seemed responsive. In Canada as elsewhere, the visual-art revival of representation after abstraction is paralleled in creative music by a revival of tonalism after serialism. In works such as Louie's *Music for a Thousand Autumns* and Vivier's *Siddartha*, non-western and even animalistic influences arise. A US observer, Stephen Young, singled out the last 2 composers during a 1987 address on recent Canadian music, finding in their scores "a kind of spirituality that may be unique." Young added, "Canadians have triumphed over their own world view of insecurity [in] a spiritual journey that, like the Rastafarian inner fire, cannot be taken from them by any who would seek to dominate, be it the cold, the US, or their own sense of inferiority."

The music-publishing industry in Canada, though thriving in earlier days, could not expand sufficiently to cope with the serious works of the post-WWII period. Efforts in the 1960s by G. Ricordi (Canada) Ltd, Leeds Music (Canada) and especially BMI Canada Ltd through its *Canavangard* series, and in the 1980s by Les Éditions Doberman in Québec, gave published status to only a fraction of the successful concert repertoire produced – making the collection of the Canadian Music Centre an indispensable source for performers and students. However, the growth in production of serious-music recordings in the country has provided a fairer degree of accessibility. Major projects include Radio Canada International's *Anthology of Canadian Music*, a series of over 30 single-composer albums, and the catalogue of Centrediscs, an offshoot of the Canadian Music Centre.

Since the mid-1960s, larger Canadian cities have witnessed the growth of concert societies devoted to contemporary music, in which the work of local composers has received special, sometimes exclusive, attention. If large operatic and symphonic companies are like public art museums in their historical view, these new-music organizations may be compared to small independent galleries covering the contemporary scene. The oldest is the still-active SOCIÉTÉ DE MUSIQUE CONTEMPORAINE DU QUÉBEC, founded by Serge GARANT and others in 1966. Commissioning programs have provided a further boost to the composing profession, increasingly since about 1960. Whereas in the 1950s one rarely heard a new work which had been commissioned, in the 1980s one rarely hears one which has not been. The CBC's commissioning policies already created precedents in this regard in the 1940s; now the arts councils, as well as soloists, ensembles and concert-giving societies, have all become familiar sources of support for new compositions.

Though newer and less widely publicized than the Governor General's Awards for literature, the Jules Léger Prize for chamber music parallels them in one area of composition for which Léger (founder of the prize during his term as governor general) had special fondness. Past winners are Schafer, 1978; Mather, 1979; Garant, 1980; Rea, 1981; Boudreau, 1982; Hawkins, 1983; Cherney, 1985; Longtin, 1986; and Bouliane, 1987. More general recognition attaches to the Canadian Music Council's "Composer of the Year" citations, inaugurated in 1977 and awarded to Schafer, 1977; Tremblay, 1978; Freedman, 1980; Vivier, 1981; Bouliane, 1983; Archer, 1984; Beckwith, 1985; Louie, 1986; and Gellman, 1987. JOHN BECKWITH

Music Criticism Serious music criticism in Canada has existed only since the late 19th century. It takes the form of concert and record reviews written for publications and, in a few instances, longer articles in books. Prior to 1867, few commentaries about concerts were judgemental. Instead, articles simply reported on a social event, briefly commenting upon the performers, the staging and audience. Because concerts were so rare, any performance was appreciated and treasured. In the 1870s a limited critical awareness began to emerge as touring companies regularly made circuits through Canada and audiences could now compare the standards of local and visiting musicians. When choral societies and symphony orchestras were formed in major cities, regular concert seasons set the stage for critical assessments. Unfortunately, criticism was generally delegated to a local music teacher or amateur musician who avoided writing anything critical about concerts in the community. Newspaper reporters assigned the task often had little musical knowledge. Notable exceptions in French Canada were Guillaume COUTURE (*La Minerve, Revue de Montréal, La Patrie, Montréal Star*) and in the early 20th century Léo-Pol MORIN (*La Patrie, La Presse, Le Canada*), both of whom demanded higher performance standards and changes in repertoire. Their English Canada counterparts, Hector CHARLESWORTH (*Saturday Night*) and Augustus Bridle (*Toronto Daily Star*), also wrote critical reviews and assessed, for the first time, Canada's composers. J.D. LOGAN in 1917 attempted the first examination of the foundations of criticism in Canada in an essay on the aims, methods and status of aesthetic criticism. Such philosophical considerations of music criticism have been rare and in more recent times have usually been part of symposia or annual conferences.

Musical reporting now appears regularly in newspapers and some magazines in most major cities and large towns. With the growth of interest in POPULAR MUSIC and JAZZ, the media have created entertainment sections that include regular reviews and feature articles about the music scene and recordings, although discussions of new compositions and newly published scores are rare. Writers active across Canada in the 20th century include Thomas Archer, Claude Gingras, Eric McLean and Gilles Potvin in Montréal; Léo Roy in Québec; Jacob Siskind in Montréal and Ottawa; Augustus Bridle, Hector Charlesworth, John BECKWITH, William Littler, John Kraglund and Kenneth Winters in Toronto; Lorne Betts in Hamilton; Loretta Thistle in Ottawa; A.A. Alldrick and S.R. Maley in Winnipeg; Stanley Bligh, Max Wyman and Ida Halpern in Vancouver. Writers on jazz and popular music include Ritchie York, Bob Smith, Peter Goddard, Mark Miller, John Norris and Gilles Archambault. FREDERICK HALL

Music Education in Canada has progressed from rustic beginnings in the colonial period to the present time when music training is available both for amateurs and professionals, and, indeed, is an increasingly important facet of general education. Historically the main branches of music education can be identified as private teaching, school instruction (public and private), and music in higher education. However, music education in the 1980s has evolved into a sophisticated complex of activities involving institutions, professional organizations, government agencies and cultural groups.

Colonial Period to 1918 Missionaries and military personnel furnished early forms of musical activity. As permanent settlements developed, church choirs and bands, however informal and unsophisticated, became the wellsprings from which a vigorous musical life emerged. Religious orders provided most of the instruction in French Canada, with the result that music was closely associated with convent schools and other church institutions. Their contribution in English-speaking regions should also be recognized, particularly that of the Irish orders in Newfoundland. French and English origins of Canadian culture account for much of the diversity in music education. For example, solfège in Québec was based on the fixed doh system of continental Europe whereas the movable doh tradition in English Canada had its roots in Britain. Early American influences can be seen in the singing schools of Upper Canada where Protestant churches were prevalent.

Egerton RYERSON listed vocal music as a subject in the common schools of Upper Canada in 1846 and has been considered the champion of school music ever since. As chief superintendent of education, he formulated his educational plan after extensive travel to Britain, Europe and the US, where school systems had introduced singing on the strength of Pestalozzi's educational theories.

The question of "who should teach school music" and what training they should receive was never resolved satisfactorily. Ryerson attempted to provide such training within his Normal School, but the most successful results in the schools were achieved in cities such as Hamilton and London, Ont, and Ottawa where trained musicians were hired. As the population increased, these special music teachers assumed the role of supervisors and were expected to conduct in-service programs for the regular teachers. Generally, rote singing was the main activity although more competent teachers also taught sight reading and voice culture; written examinations suggest a certain preoccupation with the rudiments. Achievement in music was dependent upon the expertise and interest of the individual teachers; consequently the outcome was uneven from school to school. By the late 1880s enthusiasm for John Curwen's Tonic Sol-fa system had been transplanted to Canada by British immigrants such as A.T. Cringan who taught in the Toronto schools. Their missionary spirit was heightened in a controversy over a proposal to sanction a rival American method. Music in the rural schools was neglected or often nonexistent, but in the cities music supervisors mounted massed concerts and demonstrations to display their accomplishments, especially on the occasions of royal visits or Empire Days. These events were characterized by the singing of patriotic airs and a certain amount of flag waving. In the Prairie provinces, where there was an influx of European peoples, school officials encouraged the use of national songs in their zeal to Canadianize the population. Too often music in the schools relied upon these utilitarian benefits rather than on a sound educational philosophy.

In the late 19th century, music was an important subject in ladies' colleges and finishing schools, but the general curriculum for boys was tailored to university entrance and professional careers and usually did not include music. Later on, when girls attended regular high schools, the curriculum retained its commitment to the interests of the university and, consequently, music was not able to achieve any major status in secondary education.

A colourful array of private teachers in the 19th century free-lanced as organists, band conductors and music dealers; teaching was just one facet of their endeavours in a society which revelled in amateur artistic pursuits. The appellation "Professor" was common among these versatile entrepreneurs, some of whom left a trail of bad debts or were otherwise involved in social scandal. The more pretentious female teachers advertised themselves as "Madame" and, flaunting their superior European training, often claimed to be schooled in foreign languages. Such idiosyncrasies aside, even though much of the teaching was of a dubious standard, there were some outstanding individuals, most of whom gravitated to the cities.

Apart from degrees awarded to James Paton CLARKE and George William Strathy, BMus and DMus degrees were not granted in Canadian universities until the 1880s. In the British tradition, they were extramural programs administered through syllabi and examinations in theoretical subjects without regular instruction being given. These early beginnings did not establish music as a discipline in higher education.

The turn of the century brought a profusion of conservatories, although many were merely glorified studios and relatively few enjoyed any permanence or prestige. The major conservatories affiliated with universities in an arrangement whereby the former gave instruction and the latter conducted examinations. By the early years of the 20th century the Associated Boards of the Royal Schools of Music (England), the McGill Conservatorium and the Toronto Conservatory had established their examinations on a national scale. They served private teachers well through their graded syllabi and examination standards. The competitive festival movement, which had its origin in Edmonton (1908), also stimulated private instruction. After 1890, women's musical clubs became the patrons of music by sponsoring recitals and providing scholarships.

1919-45 The Toronto Conservatory became a Canadian mecca for musicians during the principalship of Sir Ernest MACMILLAN, 1926-42 (*see* ROYAL CONSERVATORY OF MUSIC OF TORONTO). The number of local conservatories decreased but several remained as centres of musical life in their respective regions: Halifax Conservatory, Mount Allison Conservatory, McGill Conservatorium, Regina College Conservatory, Alberta College Music Centre (Edmonton) and Mount Royal College Conservatory (Calgary). Although teachers from overseas dominated the scene, gradually more Canadians came to the fore – yet most of them still went abroad for advanced study.

The player piano and phonograph enhanced the place of music in the home, and in a striking way the growth of radio broadcasting increased the potential for American influence on Canadian society. Therefore, the establishment of CBC radio in 1936 was as vital to the cultural unity of the nation as railways had been for economic development in the 1880s (*see* BROADCASTING, RADIO AND TELEVISION).

In order to improve professional standards, private teachers formed organizations, first in the cities and then province wide. In 1935 the 4 western associations took the initial step towards a national organization (which became the Canadian Federation of Music Teachers' Assns in 1961) at a conference in Vancouver; Ontario joined in 1942 and others followed in due course. Another example of western initiative was the founding of the Western Board of Music (1936), a co-operative venture involving the universities and provincial departments of education in the 3 Prairie provinces.

Significant changes in general education owe their existence to the child development movement in the US and the focus in educational psychology on the growth of the individual. The specific changes in music were related to the "song method," with less emphasis on reading skills and the paramount importance of music appreciation.

Teachers could obtain learning materials from the Victor Talking Machine Co or tune in to radio programs prepared especially for schools (see EDUCATIONAL BROADCASTING). In practice, "progressive education" was not accomplished in the way it was idealized. Many classroom teachers dabbled in the "new," while the old generation of music specialists continued to stress basic skills. Inconsistent results in elementary grades reflected the inadequate training in normal schools, but in several provinces summer music sessions helped to improve the situation.

In some places music introduced as an option in junior high schools eventually led to its acceptance in secondary schools, but in most cases music was extracurricular. Glee clubs, orchestras and operettas became a tradition long before music teachers as such were appointed.

Music in the Protestant schools of Québec paralleled progress in Ontario, but in the Catholic schools the situation was static. Recognizing the need for improvement, in 1934 the Montréal Catholic School Commission appointed Claude CHAMPAGNE as director of music education.

Between the wars some universities retained their extramural degrees but, with few exceptions, music in higher education did not expand rapidly even where faculties of music were established – at Toronto (1918) and McGill (1920) or at Laval, where a school of music was created (1922). However, in the 1930s the Carnegie Foundation of New York financed record collections in many universities, a chair in music at U of Saskatchewan, and an expansion of extension programs at U of Alberta which led to the founding of the BANFF CENTRE FOR CONTINUING EDUCATION. Through a Carnegie grant, Ernest Hutcheson examined the need for advanced training at U of T (1937). When recommendations of that report were finally implemented (1946), it represented a landmark in Canadian music education.

Since 1946 The remarkable growth of music education since WWII can be attributed to developments in higher education and secondary schools, particularly in the field of instrumental music. The creation of the CANADA COUNCIL (1957) added further momentum through its sustained support of the arts, nurturing vital areas of Canadian culture on a general level.

U of T was at the heart of this cultural transformation. Advanced training was offered in the conservatory's newly created Senior School (1946), which featured an opera division that ultimately led to the CANADIAN OPERA COMPANY. At the same time, the Faculty of Music introduced a degree in school music to prepare specialists for secondary schools. Under the leadership of MacMillan, Arnold WALTER gave direction to these programs with insight and vision. Among the students enrolled were many returned servicemen, and from this nucleus came a new generation of Canadian performers, composers and teachers.

The school music degree was based on American patterns – a combination of practical and theoretical music with courses in the liberal arts.

Of faculty members recruited from the US, Robert Rosevear and Richard Johnston were strongly committed to music education. Concurrent with developments at the university, Brian McCool of the Ontario Dept of Education effectively promoted programs in the schools. In order to meet the demand, the department's summer school certificated a multitude of the instrumental teachers who had performing experience but little if any university education. Consequently, there have been marked philosophical differences in the ranks of Ontario's teachers.

Across the country the climate was conducive to change; instrumental music was already emerging in the high schools of Montréal and parts of BC. Consequently, by the 1960s similar developments in other regions demonstrated the need for specialized teachers and, in time, most universities either created new music departments or expanded their course offerings. This unprecedented growth in higher education necessitated the recruitment of additional faculty but since Canada had produced few students with graduate qualifications, universities turned primarily to American personnel to fill these positions.

The province of Québec experienced its own profound change in the late 1960s when the Parent Report, followed by the Rioux Report, led to a comprehensive plan for music at all levels within a modernized educational system. Based primarily on N American models, these revisions brought Québec into closer line with other provinces.

Québec's unique venture was founded as the Conservatoire de musique et d'art dramatique in 1942 by Wilfrid PELLETIER. Pelletier strengthened the influence of this institution even further after he became director of music, Ministère des affaires culturelles du Québec, in 1961. The CONSERVATOIRE DE MUSIQUE DU QUÉBEC consists of 7 teaching institutions throughout the province. By basing admission on competition and training professional musicians through specialized, cost-free institutions, the Conservatoire has given Québec a system of professional training unmatched in any other province.

Individual instruction, in both private and institutional settings, has been influenced by the growth of applied music in higher education, particularly in the appointment of distinguished performers and artists-in-residence. To some extent, this has checked the predilection of Canadians to study abroad.

The recent flowering of summer schools, institutes and special projects has stimulated a more competitive milieu for aspiring professionals, including opportunities at regional and local levels. The National Youth Orchestra, JEUNESSES MUSICALES, Banff Centre, CBC Talent Festivals, National Competitive Festival of Music, to name only a few, have become familiar names to Canadians. Nevertheless, it is evident that the quality of individual instruction in private domiciles and commercial studios associated with music dealers is still inconsistent.

Elementary school music has retained close ties to the song method with an increasing interest in Canadian folk songs (see FOLK MUSIC). Listening, rhythmic, and creative elements are also integrated into eclectic curricula. Since the 1960s, Orff and Kodály programs have flourished in a number of Canadian schools where specialized teachers have been used. Nevertheless, Canada has not taken full advantage of these international systems because music instruction is usually left to classroom teachers.

There is a diversity of choral, instrumental and general programs in junior-high and secondary

schools. Many of them are performance-oriented with a continuing stake in the competition festival, but philosophically there has been a trend towards a more balanced curriculum in order to foster aesthetic sensitivity. In the 1960s the John Adaskin Project addressed the lack of contemporary music in schools. This dialogue between composers and teachers, enhanced later by the books of R. Murray SCHAFER, proved to be a catalyst for creative approaches and alternatives. Recent excursions into new areas of folk, contemporary and popular culture have raised concerns within the profession, especially where traditional priorities have been threatened in a rapidly changing society.

One measure of maturity in Canadian music education has been evidenced by the formation of its professional organizations: Canadian Music Educators' Assn (1959), Canadian Federation of Music Teachers' Assns (1961), Canadian University Music Society (1965, originally Canadian Assn of University Schools of Music) and Fédération des associations de musiciens éducateurs du Québec (1966). Through professional development and publications, they provide valuable leadership and, in 1978, co-operated in hosting the World Congress of the International Society for Music in Education, held in London, Ont. On that occasion delegates from around the world became more aware of our cultural achievements and, for the first time, music education in Canada came into an international limelight. *See also* MUSIC HISTORY. J. PAUL GREEN

Reading: Encyclopedia of Music in Canada (1981); H. Kallmann, *A History of Music in Canada, 1534-1914* (1960); A. Walter, ed, *Aspects of Music in Canda* (1969).

Music History Music has had a home in N America for the thousands of years that Indians and Inuit have lived on this continent. Their music, however, enters recorded history only with early 17th-century European observers such as Marc LESCARBOT, Father Paul LE JEUNE and Father Gabriel Sagard, who were as fascinated by the exotic sounds and sights of native music making as they were ill equipped to describe and analyse it. Skilled investigators such as Franz BOAS, Ernest GAGNON and Alexander T. Cringan appeared only in the late 19th century, and another 50 years passed before composers integrated elements of native music into some of their works.

Since colonization began in the 17th century, the mainstream of musical development has been little affected by native music. The original settlers transplanted their songs, dances and religious chants, and successive waves of immigrants reinforced old-world traditions. The import of printed music, of teachers and of touring star performers, followed later by recorded and broadcasted music, has shaped taste and has by its weight stifled or at least retarded original expression. Music in Canada has paralleled the basic European style periods from the baroque to the classical, romantic and contemporary, usually lagging behind by a few decades. The attempt to transplant Old World patterns in a sparsely populated country with widely separated settlements could never be quite successful, however. The system of patronage and the professional resources for grand opera, symphony orchestras and other sophisticated manifestations of music were wanting; European-trained Canadian and immigrant musicians, settling down to their careers, were cut off from new developments in composition and therefore stagnated. In turn, adventurous young musicians sought their models from among foreign composers: until the middle of the 20th century the influence from outside has nearly always outweighed the influence from one Canadian generation to another. Imperceptibly, however, the Canadian environment began to assert its influence, first of all in the popular sphere. Song texts were adapted to local conditions and new ones invented; dance tunes were exchanged by French and Irish Canadians; amateurs and professionals outdid each other in writing patriotic music in the 1850-1920 era; and N American social dances came to be preferred to European genres. Such institutions as the competition festival, the "local centre" examination supervised by a conservatory or examination board, the touring company, the annual conference of specific branches of the profession and the network broadcasting system – all these are typically and congenially Canadian ways of sharing artistic experiences and exchanging ideas. From the "history of music in Canada," nourished from the outside, we are moving to a "Canadian music history," growing from within through the individuality of our musicians, the quality of our institutions, and the strength of our COMMUNICATIONS systems.

To the Fall of New France Written contemporary records of music in NEW FRANCE are few. Most consist of incidental references in the diaries and travel accounts of explorers and the reports of missionaries to their superiors in Europe. They begin with Jacques CARTIER's mention of the singing of the mass at Brest (Bonne Espérance Harbour) on 14 June 1534 and of the playing of the "trumpets and other musical instruments" at HOCHELAGA [Montréal] a year later. In the following century the missionaries regularly translated religious texts into verses in native tongues, since singing proved a useful handmaid in their efforts to convert the Indians to Catholicism.

As early as the 1630s French and Indian children at Québec City were taught to sing and play European instruments. Viols, violins, guitars, transverse flutes, drums, fifes and trumpets are among the instruments named in early accounts, but it would be wrong to conclude that all were cultivated continuously in New France.

By 1661 the Jesuit chapel at Québec City had an organ, and the parish church received one in 1663; 60 years later a craftsman, Paul-Raymond Jourdain, was engaged to do extensive repair and construction work. There hardly was a need for professional musicians – at least Bishop LAVAL seems to have been concerned less with training in church music than in the decorative arts – but some priests applied their talent or European training to take charge of the musical aspect of divine service (acting as *grand chantre*) or to play the organ. A French-born priest, René Ménard, composed motets around 1640, and the second Canadian-born priest, Charles-Amador Martin, is credited with the plainchant music for the Prose "Sacrae familiae felix spectaculum" (about 1700) in celebration of the Holy Family feastday. Early literature contains other references to religious composition, but "composing" may have meant simply selecting music for the service or writing the words. Surviving copies of early 18th-century editions of motets, masses and cantatas by de Bournonville, Campra, Morin and other French composers make it reasonable to conclude that skilful part-singing was practised. Similar evidence for instrumental performance is provided by the 1980 discovery of a manuscript volume with nearly 400 keyboard pieces brought to Montréal (where the first organ was installed about 1700) by Jean Girard in 1724 (*see* RELIGIOUS MUSIC).

Though it is unlikely that formal concerts were held, some of the administrators and explorers participated in music. Louis JOLLIET, the explorer, played the organ at church; Jacques RAUDOT, the intendant, encouraged vocal and instrumental performance; and one of his successors, Claude-

Thomas DUPUY owned a library of operatic scores. Although contemporary documentation is sparse, modern research has established that everyday life in New France abounded in yet another genre of music: the hundreds of French folksongs that preserved memories of the homeland, made hard work go faster and provided rhythm for dancing, accompanied perhaps by a fiddle, a drum or at least hand-clapping and foot-stomping (*see* FOLK MUSIC). Thus, musical life in colonial Canada was diversified from the beginning, even though outside the church it lacked any formal organization.

Urban Musical Life, 1750-1830 Vigorous immigration to the area between the Atlantic Ocean and Lk Huron and the stationing of British military bands in garrison towns were among the factors generating a more intensive and organized musical life in the second half of the 18th century. Our knowledge owes much to the introduction of the printing press to Canada (Halifax 1751), for in due time NEWSPAPERS began to announce concerts and carry advertisements for teachers and merchants. This information is supplemented by occasional references in travel literature, more often than not commenting on the French Canadians' love of dancing and singing. The singing of the VOYAGEURS was especially admired.

The regimental bands, featuring perhaps a dozen woodwind and brass instruments, entertained at parades, participated in festive ceremonies and played minuets and country dances at suppers and balls. A "Concert Hall" existed in Québec City by 1764 and subscription concerts by 1770, given, one may presume, by band players and skilled amateurs. Programs for the Québec City and Halifax concerts of the 1790s reveal orchestral and chamber music by Handel, J.C. Bach, Haydn, Mozart and Pleyel. Not until recent times was new music introduced to Canada more quickly. Beginning with the *Padlock* by Dibdin (Québec City, 1783), ballad and comic operas were heard in Halifax, Montréal and Québec City in performances by strolling actor-singers, often assembled in the US from among European artists but occasionally staged by resident amateurs, such as in Montréal's Théâtre de société, founded in 1789. One of that group's offerings was a light opera, *Colas et Colinette* (1790), with words and music by Louis-Joseph QUESNEL. The vocal parts of this work and those for Quesnel's *Lucas et Cécile* survive, but the music of John Bentley's pantomime *The Enchanters* (Montréal, 1786) and of his *Ode* marking the establishment of Upper and Lower Canada in 1791 is lost.

In the late 18th and early 19th centuries, the only way to make a living from music was to be a jack-of-all-trades: performer on several instruments, bandleader, teacher, repairer of instruments, importer of printed music and composer of marches, dances or church music for special occasions. Such versatile musicians were Frederick Glackemeyer, Jean-Chrysostome Brauneis, Sr, and Theodore F. Molt, from Germany; Guillaume Mechtler from Belgium; Louis Dulongpré (also a painter) from France; and Bentley and Stephen Codman from England. From the US came singing teachers – itinerant like the portrait painters and companies of actors – to teach the rudiments of notation and choral singing in "singing schools" set up in a community for a few weeks or months and ending with a concert. This movement spread west from the Maritimes after about 1800 and for over 100 years contributed to the improvement of church choirs. As a rule, until the mid-19th century, only the larger Anglican and Catholic churches could afford organs and skilled musicians; elsewhere a bass fiddle, serpent or bassoon might "give out" the hymn tune; yet other denominations frowned on elaborate mu-

sic. Church music also received an impetus with the publication of liturgical and hymn collections. *Le Graduel romain* (1800, Catholic), the first music printed in Canada, *Union Harmony* (1801, Methodist) and *The Colonial Harmonist* (interdenominational, 1832) are the oldest, respectively, from Québec, NB and Ontario.

The Victorian Age The inventions of the steamship and the railway, the growth of towns into cities with a prospering middle class, and the establishment of Responsible Government all helped in the 1840s to usher in the age of musical pioneering, the period when the foundations were laid for the institutions and relationships of present-day musical life. Beginning with the English singer John Braham in 1841, famous artists appeared in Canada: the violinists Ole Bull and Henri Vieuxtemps, the singer Jenny Lind and the pianist Sigismond Thalberg had all, by 1858, delighted audiences and set norms for resident artists to strive for. There were many musicians who took up the challenge through dedicated work in the cause of good music in good performance. In setting up teaching studios, in training their church choirs to appear in concerts and, together with other singers and with instrumentalists, to form "philharmonic societies" or "musical unions," in opening music stores and publishing firms, they drew on an abundance of natural talent and a thirst for "the finer things in life." The obstacles were many: the vanity of the newly prosperous merchant class was revealed in the shallowness of its taste; rivalries between musicians, dearth of performers on certain instruments and poor audience support made all musical enterprises precarious.

While a few of the first Canadian-born professional musicians were able to make decent livings at home – eg, the bandmaster Charles Sauvageau, the teacher Jean-Chrysostome Brauneis, Jr, and the church musician Jean-Baptiste Labelle – those who craved major careers in music had of necessity to seek them abroad, and indeed the exceptionally gifted found them, including Joseph B. Sharland, a music educator in Boston; Hugh A. Clarke, a professor at U of Pennsylvania; Samuel P. Warren, a virtuoso organist living in New York; Calixa LAVALLÉE, composer of Canada's national anthem ("O Canada"), who found success as a pianist and composer in Boston; Solomon Mazurette, who lived as a pianist in Detroit; and, perhaps the most outstanding of all, Emma Lajeunesse, the great soprano who, under the name ALBANI, became Canada's first world-famous musician. Many skilled musicians from Europe assumed Canadian roles as teachers, organists and leaders of musical societies, among them James P. CLARKE in Toronto, Antoine DESSANE in Québec City, Gustave Smith in Ottawa, Frederick Herbert Torrington in Montréal and later Toronto, and Frantz JEHIN-PRUME, primarily a violinist, in Montréal.

Among the earliest musical societies were the New Union Singing Society (1809) of Halifax; the Québec Harmonic Society (1820); the singers and band of the Children of Peace at Sharon, UC, proof of how strong leadership could make music flourish in a small village community; the York [Toronto] Band (1824); and the Philharmonic Society of Saint John, NB (1824). When the West was opened to colonization, the speed of musical development was telescoped, and societies were formed in the earliest years of many settlements. Victoria had a Philharmonic Society in 1859; Calgary and Winnipeg had bands in the 1870s, and concerts were given in Regina and Saskatoon in the 1880s. After Confederation every city and town had a number of societies, usually built around the core of a choir, and assisting orchestras were formed for special concerts with the help of band players, music teachers and amateurs. The largest and most enduring were the Toronto (1872-94) and Montréal (1875-99) Philharmonic societies, under the principal leadership of Torrington and Guillaume COUTURE, respectively, and the Septuor Haydn (1871-1903), a Québec City instrumental group led by Arthur Lavigne. Programs ranged from the haphazard assortment of band overtures, piano solos, national songs and choral pieces (the "grand concert of vocal and instrumental music") to oratorio performances and concert performances of operas (eg, *Messiah*, *The Creation*, *The Flying Dutchman*, and Beethoven's *Symphony No 9*). For OPERA, Canadians depended mainly on visiting troupes, although, sporadically, amateur performances were staged locally, and the Holman English Opera Troupe resided in Toronto and London, Ont, for some years. Instead of the ballad operas of the 18th century, the repertoire now embraced Italian and French grand opera. From rare performances of truncated versions accompanied by a handful of instrumentalists about the mid-century, opera became a frequent entertainment by professional companies, including those from New York C, by the end of the Victorian era. "Opera houses" opened in every community from Vancouver to Yarmouth, NS, but in general, except for Toronto's MASSEY HALL (1894), concert halls were inadequate.

On the popular level, orally transmitted folk songs yielded increasingly to fashionable ballads and dances (waltzes, quadrilles, gallops, polkas) propagated by imported printed music. However, there was a countercurrent in Québec, where songs like "À la claire fontaine" and "Vive la Canadienne" were quasi-national hymns, and where new patriotic songs such as "Un Canadien errant" (words 1842) and "Le Drapeau de carillon" (1858) gained wide popularity. Ernest GAGNON's collection *Chansons populaires du Canada* (1865-67) helped some 100 songs to a new life by bringing them to the attention of city folk and sophisticated musicians. Gagnon himself arranged folk tunes for choir, and Ontario composer Susie F. Harrison utilized such material in her *Trois Esquisses canadiennes* (1859) and her opera *Pipandor*, as did several foreign composers, eg, Sir Alexander Mackenzie in his *Canadian Rhapsody* (about 1905) for orchestra. James P. Clarke successfully captured a Canadian flavour in his group of songs *Lays of the Maple Leaf* (1853), but the bulk of composers accepted without question the stylistic trends current during their student years in Paris or Leipzig in both the concert and the popular genres. Most of the surviving Canadian compositions of the Victorian era were intended for the immediate needs of churches, bands, dance halls, patriotic rallies and the ever-growing number of parlour pianists and singers. Rarely did such music rise above the level of competence and prettiness, but it matched the average music in these genres produced in other countries. Couture's *Rêverie* (1875), W.O Forsyth's *Suite* (1888) and Clarence Lucas's *3 Shakespeare overtures* (about 1899) are among the rare orchestral works. Given the local resources, there was a greater incentive to write cantatas and light operas. Landmarks were Charles W. Sabatier's *Cantata in Honour of the Prince of Wales* (1860), J.B. Labelle's *Cantate: La Confédération* (about 1867), Lavallée's US-produced light operas *The Widow* (1881) and *TIQ* (*The Indian Question/Settled at Last*, publ 1883), Oscar F. Telgmann's "Canadian military opera" *Leo the Royal Cadet* (1889), which had over 150

performances, J.J. Perrault's *Messe de Noël* (1859-65) and Charles A.E. HARRISS's dramatic legend *Torquil* (publ 1896).

Progress in performance and composition was accompanied by the development of instrument building, music publishing and MUSIC EDUCATION. The making of pianos and pipe and reed organs began in the second decade of the 19th century in small workshops by German and US craftsmen and became a major industry by the end of the century, while violin making remained a cottage industry (*see* MUSICAL INSTRUMENTS). Important names were Samuel R. Warren and CASAVANT FRÈRES in pipe-organ building, T.A. Heintzman in piano manufacturing (*see* HEINTZMAN AND CO), and the Lyonnais family in violin building. R.S. Williams & Sons and Whaley, Royce & Co Ltd were among the largest instrument dealer-manufacturers.

Following the publication of church-music volumes (*see* HYMNS), music was printed in newspapers (1831) and periodicals, and after 1839 it appeared on its own, as sheet music. Dance music, marches and parlour pieces for the piano and songs made up the bulk of publications, but cantatas and light operas also found their way into print. Canadian works and foreign compositions were about equal in number. A. and S. Nordheimer, Arthur Lavigne, A.J. Boucher and Whaley, Royce & Co Ltd were among the most active companies. There were no public or university music libraries, but musical societies built collections of musical literature for their own members.

Music was introduced as an activity in many public schools after the middle of the 19th century; Alexander T. Cringan was one of its principal pioneers, and the Petit Séminaire de Québec had a school orchestra as early as 1833. King's College (later U of T) granted James P. Clarke a Bachelor of Music degree in 1846, and George W. Strathy received a Doctor of Music from the U of Trinity College (Toronto) in 1858, but only late in the century did several universities establish degree examinations, leaving the teaching to conservatories. The conservatories, of which the Toronto Conservatory (1886) soon became the leading institution, provided individual lessons (*see* ROYAL CONSERVATORY OF MUSIC).

Flourishing and Transition, 1900-40 Grandeur – an expression of wealth and power – was a universal characteristic of the turn of the century, and it showed itself in musical life as well. Compositions such as *Caïn* (1905) by Alexis Contant and *Jean le Précurseur* (publ 1914) by his fellow Montréaler Guillaume Couture were oratorios with full orchestra on a scale never before attempted in Canada. Joseph Vézina, bandmaster in Québec City, produced 3 comic operas. In 1903 C.A.E. Harriss organized the Cycle of Musical Festivals of the Dominion of Canada, which involved over 4000 singers and instrumentalists in 15 communities from Halifax to Victoria. Choirs of hundreds of singers coexisted in the large cities, and Toronto came to be called the "choral capital of North America" largely because of its TORONTO MENDELSSOHN CHOIR founded by A.S. VOGT. Montréal boasted an ambitious Montréal (later National) Opera Company (1910-13; 1913-14), and visiting companies presented such giant works as *Tristan und Isolde*, *Parsifal*, the *Ring* cycle and *Otello*, though these were exceptional. For orchestral fare even the large cities depended on visiting ensembles, usually from the northern US, that would accompany Canadian oratorio choirs and present programs of their own. However, Québec City, Montréal, Toronto, Halifax and Calgary established semiprofessional orchestras (*see* ORCHESTRAL MUSIC). Piano companies flourished as never before (*see* PIANO MANUFACTURING) and Émile

Berliner, inventor of the disc recording, established his gramophone business in Montréal, Conservatories mushroomed and examination boards were set up, the Académie de musique de Québec (1868), the Associated Board (British, operating in Canada from 1895 to 1953), the Dominion College of Montréal and the Toronto Conservatory, among others. After years of insular development, Canadians were able to find out about musical life in each other's cities from such periodicals as *Le Passe-Temps* (1895-1935, 1945-49), *Canadian Music Trades Journal* (1900-33) and *Musical Canada* (1906-33).

WWI produced a spate of patriotic songs, but it decimated orchestras, choirs and many other enterprises. After the war the era of active music making waned under the impact of the new technologies of recorded and radio-transmitted sound (*see* MUSIC BROADCASTING). Imports again dominated the market, filling homes with US popular and European concert music, providing only a modest outlet for Canadian performers and composers. In combination with the Great Depression, this shift caused a decline in the instrument industry and an employment crisis for musicians. There were significant new developments, however. Faculties or schools of music were established at the universities of Toronto (1918), McGill (1920) and Laval (1922). Orchestras, few of which had survived the war, were re-established, or new ones were founded, notably in Toronto (1922), Montréal (1930 and 1934) and Vancouver (1930; *see* TORONTO SYMPHONY; ORCHESTRE SYMPHONIQUE DE MONTRÉAL; VANCOUVER SYMPHONY), and broadcast studios employed musicians for musical and dramatic programs. Orchestras, choirs and solo performers could now be heard on networks across the country and in communities where concert facilities did not exist. Representative ensembles, in addition to the orchestras, were the Elgar Choir of BC, based in Vancouver, the Bach-Elgar Choir of Hamilton, the Toronto Mendelssohn Choir, the Arion Male Voice Choir of Victoria, the Schubert and Canadian Choirs of Brantford, the Winnipeg Male Voice Choir, the Disciples de Massenet of Montréal, the Dubois and HART HOUSE STRING QUARTETS of Montréal and Toronto, respectively, and the Société canadienne d'opérette of Montréal and its successor, Variétés lyriques. Recitals were fostered, in particular by the women's musical clubs. Famous popular groups were The DUMBELLS, a vaudeville troupe born in the trenches of WWI; Guy LOMBARDO and his Royal Canadians, a dance band that moved to the US; and the Bytown Troubadours, a male quartet. The western provinces found a congenial outlet for musical energies in the competition festivals. These were begun in Edmonton in 1908 and in the 1980s still bring thousands of children and music lovers together to match skills and take advice from visiting adjudicators (*see* MUSIC AWARDS AND COMPETITIONS).

The period between the wars also produced the first musician of national stature, Sir Ernest MACMILLAN, the only Canadian musician to have been knighted. Other musicians who achieved national or international recognition included, in chronological order, the singers Marie Toulinguet, Rodolphe PLAMONDON, Béatrice LA PALME, Edward JOHNSON, Louise Edvina, Florence Easton, Pauline DONALDA, Eva Gauthier, Sarah Fischer, Frances James and Raoul JOBIN; the organist Lynnwood Farnam; the pianists Emiliano Rénaud, Mona Bates, Léo-Pol MORIN, Ernest Seitz, Ellen Ballon and Muriel Kerr; the violinists Kathleen PARLOW and Frederick Grinke; the orchestra conductors Luigi von Kunits, Wilfrid PELLETIER, Reginald Stewart, Geoffrey WADDINGTON and Jean-Marie BEAUDET; the choirleaders Herbert A. Fricker, Bruce Carey and Charles Goulet; the bandmasters John Slatter, Charles O'Neill and J.J. Gagnier; and the carillonneur Percival PRICE.

The field recording, archival deposit and publication of folk and aboriginal music by Marius BARBEAU, W. Roy Mackenzie, Helen CREIGHTON and others resulted in the discovery and preservation of an unsuspected wealth of traditional music and local compositions. The series of folk arts and handicrafts festivals organized by J.M. Gibbon for the CPR from 1927 to 1934 (especially in Québec City and Banff) promoted public awareness of folk music and stimulated arrangements and new compositions by W.H. Anderson, Claude CHAMPAGNE, Hector Gratton, Alfred La Liberté, MacMillan, Oscar O'Brien, Léo Roy, Alfred Whitehead, Healey WILLAN and others. A foundation of regional folk idioms was widely believed to be the precondition for a distinctive Canadian music. However, although Champagne's *Suite canadienne* and MacMillan's *Two Sketches for Strings* have become Canadian classics, the majority of compositions were international in orientation. Anglo-Canadian composers and teachers of the craft, such as Douglas CLARKE, MacMillan, Leo Smith, Whitehead and Willan, were steeped in turn-of-the-century aesthetics and usually in British church traditions. On the whole, French Canadians such as Champagne, Laliberté, Rodolphe MATHIEU and Morin represented more modern influences, ranging from Scriabin to Debussy. Mathieu and Colin McPhee, who later investigated the music of Bali, were among the few exploring contemporary techniques. The majority of compositions were songs, choral settings and short piano pieces. Symphonies, string quartets and cantatas were usually written as degree exercises, but at least one composer, Willan, wrote in nearly all forms, from ballad and radio operas to symphonies, from organ pieces to choral music.

The teaching content at universities and conservatories and the concert repertoire were conservative, but to audiences in Canada the bulk of Bach, Mozart, Brahms and Debussy was still music to become familiar with. Without doubt, however, the dearth of pioneers for the radical new music of the day did delay the development of composers and audiences considerably.

Expansion since WWII, 1940-84 A swift expansion, almost an "explosion," of musical activity occurred in the 1940s. Subsequent progress has been nothing short of spectacular, retarded only slightly by the economic austerity of the 1970s and 1980s. It manifested itself in the emergence of world-rank performers and ensembles, of a large number of professional composers, and in the import, and assimilation by audiences, of a diversifed literature of new and old music from many parts of the world, offered in abundance in splendid new concert halls and arts centres, at festivals, and on recordings and broadcasts (*see* RECORDING INDUSTRY). This growth has been concomitant with a new pride in Canadian achievement and a conscious will to establish and maintain a cultural identity. It has been nurtured by enriched school music programs, the development of facilities for advanced education and scholarly research, and by new communications technologies. It has been built with the help of nationwide organizations setting standards, co-ordinating resources, promoting talent, protecting legal interests and lobbying governments. Agitation throughout the arts community has been largely responsible for new patterns of financial support for the arts from governmental agencies – foremost the CANADA COUNCIL – and, to a lesser degree, from private sources. Direct support is given through subsidies of various kinds (*see* ARTS FUNDING), and indirect support through quotas set on the Canadian content of concert series and broadcasts.

Before WWII there had been a few national music organizations (all named here by their latest name only), Composers, Authors and Publishers Assn of Canada (CAPAC, 1925), the Canadian Band Directors' Assn (1931) and the Canadian Federation of Music Teachers' Assns (1935). Later ones include Performing Rights Organization of Canada (PROCan, 1940), the umbrella organization the Canadian Music Council (1945), the CANADIAN LEAGUE OF COMPOSERS (1951), the CANADIAN MUSIC CENTRE (1959), the Canadian Music Educators' Assn (1959), the Canadian University Music Society (1965), the Assn of Canadian Orchestras (1972), and others for folk music, music libraries, music publishers, record producers and other special concerns.

The improvement of music education began with the establishment of the CONSERVATOIRE DE MUSIQUE DU QUÉBEC by the province of Québec in 1942, first in Montréal and later in 7 centres, and the creation of courses at the U of T for professional performers and school music educators (1946). The number of university music departments has grown from a handful in the 1930s to over 30. New research facilities include electronic music studios, folk and native music archives at the CANADIAN MUSEUM OF CIVILIZATION, U Laval and elsewhere, and the national collection of musical Canadiana at the NATIONAL LIBRARY OF CANADA (1970). The National Youth Orchestra (1960) provides experience for a young elite of instrumentalists, while JEUNESSES MUSICALES DU CANADA (1949) and CAMMAC (Canadian Amateur Musicians/Musiciens amateurs du Canada) (1953) and numerous summer music camps appeal to the wide range of music lovers. Music information and discussion has been fostered by such periodicals as *The Canadian Music Journal* (1956-62), *Opera Canada* (est 1960) and *The Canada Music Book* (1970-76). The ENCYCLOPEDIA OF MUSIC IN CANADA (1981, French ed 1983) bears witness to the growing interest in the history and current state of music in Canada.

The intensity and diversity of musical performance has assumed staggering proportions, whether one thinks of the 100 professional or community orchestras, the opera companies of Toronto (CANADIAN OPERA COMPANY), Montréal (Opéra du Québec, followed by Opéra de Montréal), Vancouver, Edmonton, Calgary (Southern Alberta Opera Assn), Winnipeg (Manitoba Opera Assn) and elsewhere, the chansonnier and *boîte à chansons* phenomenon of the 1960s, the summer FESTIVALS, the rock bands or the broadcast fare (*see* POPULAR MUSIC). Only a few highlights may be listed. The CBC had its golden age of music in the 1950s with its own symphony orchestra and opera company and its "L'Heure du concert" (French TV), but has since turned from a prime producer of music programs into a channel for programs originating in concert halls. Festivals have included those in Montréal (1936-65), STRATFORD, Ont (est 1953), Vancouver (1955-68), Ottawa (NATIONAL ARTS CENTRE, est 1971), as well as giant celebrations during EXPO 67 in Montréal and the 150th anniversary of the city of Toronto in 1984. International acclaim has been won by such groups as the ORFORD STRING QUARTET (1965), the FESTIVAL SINGERS OF CANADA (1954-79), the CANADIAN BRASS QUINTET (1970), the GUESS WHO rock band (1965-75) and others (*see* CHAMBER MUSIC). The main cities have ensembles for the performance of medieval and renaissance music on authentic instruments and also societies for the most recent music, notably the Société de musique contemporaine du Québec of Montréal (1966).

Individual performers of world repute include the singers Maureen FORRESTER, Lois MARSHALL, Louis QUILICO, Léopold SIMONEAU, Teresa STRATAS and Jon VICKERS (*see* SINGING); the pianists Glenn GOULD, Anton KUERTI, André Laplante and Ronald Turini; the violinists Ida HAENDEL and Steven STARYK; the cellists Lorne Munroe and Zara Nelsova; the harpsichordist Kenneth GILBERT; and the JAZZ musicians Maynard FERGUSON (trumpet) and Oscar PETERSON (piano). Mireille Lagacé and Hugh McLean are among the best organists; Alberto Guerrero, Lyell Gustin, Yvonne Hubert and Lubka Kolessa have been renowned piano teachers; and the list could be continued for many other disciplines. Canadian conductors of the period include John AVISON, Mario BERNARDI, Alexander BROTT and Boris BROTT, Victor FELDBRILL, Pierre HÉTU, Elmer ISELER, as well as many outstanding immigrants. Rika Maniates is one of several fine musicologists (*see* MUSICOLOGY); Edith FOWKE and Conrad Laforte are distinguished folk song scholars. Nicholas Goldschmidt (festivals), Gilles Lefebvre (Jeunesses musicales) and Arnold WALTER (education) have been organizers on the grand scale. Popular and folk singer-songwriters have included Paul ANKA, Edith Butler, Félix LECLERC, Monique LEYRAC, Gordon LIGHTFOOT, Alan Mills, Joni MITCHELL, Anne MURRAY and Gilles VIGNEAULT.

The breakthrough in composition that occurred about the middle of the century was 3 pronged: it established composition as a primary musical occupation; it introduced the teaching of contemporary techniques to the classroom, and it ended Canadian isolation from the avantgarde of Western music. Internationalism and diversity ruled as composers caught up with 12-tone technique, neoclassicism, electronic sound and other developments (*see* ELECTROACOUSTIC MUSIC). Many young Canadians polished their art in Paris, Rome or Darmstadt; some 3 dozen studied with the celebrated teacher Nadia Boulanger. Barbara PENTLAND, John WEINZWEIG and Jean PAPINEAU-COUTURE became leaders of the "radical" wing, Weinzweig and Papineau-Couture also the first 2 presidents of the Canadian League of Composers, and teachers of great influence. Listing composers by their teachers can be misleading, since the relationship may have been short or long, may have influenced technique or style, and may have been superseded by stronger influences. To list composers by labels of style ignores the process of maturing. Therefore a chronological list within the most recent areas of activity will suffice. To indicate the variety of influences, the countries of birth of adult immigrants are given, and to show the variety of genres, specialties are named.

Atlantic Provinces: Janis Kalnins (Latvia).

Québec: Otto Joachim (Germany), Maurice Blackburn (film), Alexander Brott, Gabriel CHARPENTIER, François MOREL, Clermont PÉPIN, Pierre MERCURE, Bengt Hambraeus (Sweden), Serge GARANT, Roger Matton, Gilles TREMBLAY, André Prévost, Alain Gagnon, Jacques Hétu, Micheline Coulombe SAINT-MARCOUX, Bruce MATHER, Brian Cherney and Claude Vivier.

Ontario: Keith Bissell, Lucio Agostini (radio drama), John Weinzweig, Eldon Rathburn (film), Samuel Dolin, Oskar MORAWETZ (Czechoslovakia), Louis APPLEBAUM (film), Godfrey RIDOUT, Udo KASEMETS (Estonia), Talivaldis Kenins (Latvia), István ÁNHALT (Hungary), Robert FLEMING (film), Harry FREEDMAN, Harry SOMERS, John BECKWITH, Lothar Klein (Germany), R. Murray SCHAFER, Norma BEECROFT and Srul Irving Glick.

Manitoba: S.C. ECKHARDT-GRAMATTÉ (raised in France and Germany) and Robert Turner.

Alberta: Violet ARCHER, Malcolm Forsyth, Richard Johnston (US) and Gerhard Wuensch (Austria).

British Columbia: Murray ADASKIN, Jean Coulthard, Barbara Pentland, Rudolf Komorous (Czechoslovakia), Michael C. Baker and Barry Truax.

Considering the variety of genres, techniques and styles embodied in the works of these and many other Canadian composers, can one detect distinct regional or national traits? Some critics have drawn parallels between lonely scenery and stark climate and the austere vocabulary of certain composers; others deny such parallels. Folk idioms, historical subject matter (as in Somers's opera *Louis Riel*) and the blending of pioneer-age music with modern techniques (as in certain Beckwith works) also provide means towards distinctiveness. A close awareness of our "soundscapes" has led Schafer to some original experiments. To shake off international influences would be pointless and impossible; gradually Canadian music will be shaped by composers who, like other Canadians, are products of Canadian society and react to their environment in ways that are subtly different from those of others. Among these composers there will be, if there are not already, a few of such talent and individuality that their music will determine what is called Canadian. HELMUT KALLMANN

Reading: W. Amtmann, *Music in Canada 1600-1800* (1975) and *La Musique au Québec 1600-1875* (1976); J. Beckwith and K. MacMillan, eds, *Contemporary Canadian Composers* (1975); I. Bradley, ed, *A Selected Bibliography of Musical Canadiana* (rev 1976); M. Calderisi, *Music Publishing in the Canadas, 1800-1867/L'Édition musicale au Canada, 1800-1867* (1981); *Encyclopedia of Music in Canada* (1981); C. Ford, *Canada's Music: An Historical Survey* (1982); Helmut Kallmann, *A History of Music in Canada 1534-1914* (1960); E. MacMillan, ed, *Music in Canada* (1955); *Music Directory Canada '84* (1984); G. Proctor, *Canadian Music of the Twentieth Century* (1980) and *Sources in Canadian Music* (2nd ed, 1979); S. Sadie, ed, *The New Grove Dictionary of Music and Musicians* (1980); Soeurs de Ste-Anne, eds, *Dictionnaire biographique des musiciens canadiens* (1935); K. Toomey and S. Willis, eds, *Musicians in Canada* (1981); A. Walter, ed, *Aspects of Music in Canada* (1969); *Aria* (est 1979); *The Canadian Composer/Le Compositeur canadien* (est 1965); *The Canadian Music Journal* (1956-62); *The Music Scene/La Scène musicale* (est 1967); *Musical Canada* (1906-33); *The Musical Journal* (1887-90?); *Musicanada* (1967-70, est 1976); *Opera Canada* (est 1960).

Music Publishing The earliest music printing and publishing in Canada was undertaken by newspaper and book publishers rather than music companies. In 1800, 1801 and 1802 John Neilson, publisher of the *Quebec Gazette/La Gazette de Quebec*, issued *Le Graduel (Processional* [sic], *Vespéral) romain*, volumes of plainchant, and by Confederation, 1867, some 50 volumes of church music and 30 subsequent editions had contributed to religious worship and musical literacy. By the same date, a dozen songbooks and pedagogical works – beginning with T.F. Molt's bilingual *Elementary Treatise on Music/Traité élémentaire de musique* – had been issued. Sheet music publishing developed more slowly. Neilson's effort to engrave Louis-Joseph QUESNEL's *Colas et Colinette* in 1807-09 faltered at the proof stage, and no copy is extant of *The Berlin Waltz* which the piano builder and music engraver Frederick Hund advertised in the *Quebec Mercury* in 1818. Individual pieces occasionally appeared in newspapers (1831) and magazines (1833) but sheet music publishing did not come into its own until 1840. The firms were importers of music and instruments; publishing usually was a sideline. A & S Nordheimer (Toronto, 1844) and A.J. Boucher (Montréal, 1865) survived into the 20th century. Other pioneers included Henry Prince in Montréal, E.G. Fuller in Halifax, Peter Grossman in Hamilton, the book and directory publisher Lovell in Montréal, and the book-

sellers J & A McMillan in Saint John, NB. The majority of mid- and late-19th-century sheet music publications were dances, marches and salon pieces for keyboard, and patriotic songs and parlour ballads. Choral and educational music was rare but, surprisingly, vocal scores of cantatas, operettas and similar works, from 50 to several hundred pages in length, were numerous. In addition to Canadian compositions, publishers issued foreign music in licensed and, sometimes, private editions. The most active period of Canadian music publishing lasted from about 1890 to 1920. The largest list was that of Whaley, Royce & Co (Toronto, 1888), others included Arthur Lavigne (Québec, 1868, publisher of the first edition of "O Canada"), J.-E. Bélair (*Le Passe-Temps*) (Montréal, 1895), J.L. Orme & Son (Ottawa, 1866), I. Suckling & Sons (Toronto, c1875), Strange & Co (Toronto, c1881), Anglo-Canadian Music Company (Toronto, 1885) and H.H. Sparks Music Co (Toronto, c1900). Not only the tunes and song texts, but the titles and cover illustrations of early Canadian sheet music provide an interesting mirror of taste and social life. An anthology of such music is being compiled by the Canadian Musical Heritage Society (1982).

Despite the Depression and the competition of recordings, music publishing moved forward in the decades between the world wars. Movies stimulated a mass market for licensed Canadian editions of pop songs and the competition festival and school music movements created a demand for choral and educational music. Representative of this new emphasis were the catalogues of Frederick Harris Music Co (Oakville, Ont, 1910), Waterloo Music Co (Waterloo, Ont, 1921) and Gordon V. Thompson (Toronto, 1932), all still in business, and the now defunct Éditions A. Fassio (Le Parnasse musical) (Lachute, Qué, 1933), Canadian Music Sales (Toronto, late 1920s) and Western Music Co (Vancouver, 1930). Several large international firms established branches in Toronto, including Boosey & Hawkes (1935), Oxford University Press (music department 1939), Chappell & Co (1946) and G. Ricordi & Co (1954). Most companies issued a modest amount of concert music by contemporary Canadians, especially BMI (now PRO) Canada, the performing rights society, but its publishing branch (1947) was taken over by Berandol Music Ltd in 1969. After a great expansion during the 1950s a retrenchment followed, although educational and choral music publishing continue to flourish.

Recordings had become the prime means of disseminating pop music, and for economic reasons – huge outlays and few performances – publishers could not cope with the increasing trend towards orchestral writing by concert music composers. In the concert field the solution was the establishment in 1959 of the Canadian Music Centre/Centre de musique canadienne, a nonprofit organization which lends or sells scores reproduced from manuscript and rents orchestral parts. However the young firms of Doberman (St-Nicolas, Qué) and Éditions J Ostiguy (St-Hyacinthe, Qué) are issuing many contemporary works and some composers have adopted self-publishing. A new type of music "publisher" has also appeared, one who licenses recording and other rights for popular music but rarely prints sheet music. The Canadian Music Publishers Association/Association canadienne des éditeurs de musique (1949) is the industry's umbrella organization; individual firms are affiliated with the performing rights organizations CAPAC and PRO Canada. The largest collection of Canadian music publications is that of the Na-

tional Library of Canada. Copyright entries have been listed by the government since 1868; full bibliographical details have been given in the National Library's monthly *Canadiana* since 1953. HELMUT KALLMANN

Reading: M. Calderisi, *Music Publishing in the Canadas, 1800-1867/L'Édition musicale au Canada, 1800-1867* (1981); *Encyclopedia of Music in Canada* (1981); L. Jarman, ed, *Canadian Music: A Selected Checklist 1950-73/La musique canadienne; une lists sélective 1950-73* (1976); National Library of Canada, *Canadiana* (est 1951).

Musical Instruments Canadian musical instruments have had a successful but specialized history. There has been little industrial or private manufacture of brass, woodwind or percussion instruments, which have been imported from other countries. The making of violins has flourished periodically, and the artistic traditions of the 19th-century Québec violin-making families Lyonnais, Martel, Lavallée and Bayeur have recommenced with the opening in 1979 of a school of stringed-instrument making in Québec by Sylvio de Lellis and Lamarre. The vogue for free-bass accordion playing, fostered since the 1960s, has been supplied by imported instruments. Individual enterprise founded unique companies such as the Stoermer Bell Foundry (Breslau, Ont, 1931) and Norman Acoustic Guitars (La Patrie, Qué, 1972).

Through the dynamism and integrity of personal and family establishments, and the reliable quality of their products, the PIANO and the organ have been the principal musical instruments of Canadian manufacture for both national consumer markets and international export. The piano was fashionable and popular before WWI in parlours, officers' clubs, church halls, schools, pioneer homesteads and gold-rush saloons. The zealous religious conviction that partially motivated the settlement of Canada was given musical expression through the organ. Canadian-made harmoniums (reed organs) were popular from about 1870 to 1910.

A post-depression slump was followed by a rise to a second sales peak, about 11 000 in 1986, but thereafter the piano industry suffered a dramatic decline, marked by successive financial failures and mergers until by 1987 no pianos were manufactured in Canada. In contrast, even pipe organ companies, headed by individual builders (such as Brunzema, Guilbaut-Thérien, Kney, Létouneau, Wilhelm and Wolff), have held their own internationally; by the beginning of the 1980s, through the maintaining of fine craftsmanship and the reliance on national products for certain components CASAVANT FRÈRES of St-Hyacinthe, Qué, has developed an output of which 80% was exported, with 18 installations in Japan alone.

Canadian forests have provided timber suitable for the manufacture of keyboard and stringed instruments that could function in the nation's climate. The availability of excellent wood has been a factor in attracting skilled craftsmen to this country, such as viola maker Otto Erdész who established a shop in Toronto in 1975. There is a developing interest in the construction of replicas or personal interpretations of medieval, Renaissance and baroque instruments. The new violin and bow specialists, harpsichord makers (Albarda, Kater, Redsell and Turner) and experts in the fashioning of lutes, viols and other early stringed instruments (Allworth, Philpot and Schreiner) have revived a positive attitude to the craft and a personal pride in home industry reminiscent of the original 19th-century workshops of Theodore Heintzman and Joseph Casavant. High-quality acoustic GUITARS are produced in limited numbers by craftsmen such as Frank Gay, Jean Larrivée and Pat Lister in different centres across Canada.

Collections Canadian-made musical instruments, in various states of playing condition, may be seen in pioneer villages, forts and museums of local historical societies. The sound of the 19th-century Québec violin makers is lost, with only a few examples remain in private ownership. Working examples remain of early organ builders Samuel Warren (Chambly, 1854), Louis Mitchel (Vaudreuil, 1871), Casavant Frères (Lacolle, 1885) and Napoléon Déry (St Roch-des-Aulnaies, 1874). Listed in the *Encyclopedia of Music in Canada* are 23 public and private collections of instruments, of Canadian and international provenance. The largest holding is that of the Royal Ontario Museum, based on the R.S. Williams Collection. Over 1000 instruments are divided among its Far Eastern, Ethnology and European departments. Native Canadian and non-Western instruments are found in the UBC Museum of Anthropology (Vancouver), the Provincial Museum of BC (Victoria), the Glenbow-Alberta Institute (Calgary), the Robertson Collection (Regina) and the Canadian Museum of Civilization (Ottawa).   WALTER H. KEMP

Musical Theatre includes pageants such as Augustus Bridle's *Heart of the World* (1927); spectacles like those at the CANADIAN NATIONAL EXHIBITION, beginning with *Ivanhoe* (1906); OPERA; operetta, especially the ever-popular Gilbert and Sullivan repertoire; masques such as F.A. DIXON and Arthur Clappé's *Canada's Welcome* (1879); Broadway-style book shows and revues, composed of songs and comic sketches. The first theatrical performance in Canada, LE THÉÂTRE DE NEPTUNE EN LA NOUVELLE FRANCE (1606) by Marc LESCARBOT, used music. Another early work, Joseph Quesnel's *Colas et Colinette* (1790) was a "comedy with ariettas." In the later 19th century most plays written to be performed were burlesques, parodies with original lyrics set to borrowed melodies. Local amateurs appeared in burlesques such as *'Our Boys' in the Riel Rebellion* in Halifax, *Dolorsolatio* in Montréal, *Ptarmigan* in Hamilton and *The Tricky Troubadour* in Winnipeg. In the 1880s E.A. McDowell's professional company toured the country with William H. Fuller's *H.M.S. Parliament*, a satirical version of *H.M.S. Pinafore*. Although vaudeville was popular until the 1920s, it was dominated by Americans. Talented Canadians such as Eva Tanguay and May Irwin had to emigrate to achieve stardom.

Canadians excelled at writing revues. The DUMBELLS, Canada's famous soldier entertainers of WWI, continued to perform through the 1920s. In the 1930s groups such as Toronto's Arts and Letters Club and the Winnipeg Press Club presented evenings in sophisticated satire, while workers' theatres staged more biting revues such as *We Beg to Differ* in Montréal and the "Beer and Skits" shows in Winnipeg (*see* THEATRE, HISTORY). Gratien GÉLINAS's annual *Fridolinons!* revues entertained Québec audiences from 1938 to 1946 with the views of a cocky kid in a Montreal Canadiens' sweater. The annual satirical revue *Spring Thaw* was first produced by Toronto's New Play Society in 1948 under the direction of Mavor MOORE. Twenty-four consecutive editions of *Spring Thaw* used skits and comic songs to help Canadians laugh at themselves. *My Fur Lady* (1957), a McGill University show that toured Canada, was similar to *Spring Thaw*, but had a tenuous plot. *My Fur Lady* featured several songs by Galt MacDermot, who later composed the music for *Hair*. In the 1960s Toronto's Theatre in the Dell and Old Angelo's became the first of many licensed cabarets to open across Canada offering light, intimate, small-cast professional entertainment. Many cabarets are based on the work of one composer (eg, *Oh Coward*, a pastiche of Noël

Coward's songs) or on similar types of songs (eg, *Flicks*, film music, and *Blue Champagne*, songs of the 1940s). Successful original cabarets have included *Sweet Reason*, David Warrack's *Oops!* and *Tease for Two*, Jacqueline Barrette's *Heureux celui qui Meurt*, Clémence Desrocher's Québec revues such as *La Grosse Tête* and Mark Shekter's and Charles Weir's *Toronto Toronto*.

While most Canadian theatres, including Winnipeg's Rainbow Stage, which specializes in musicals, prefer to present Broadway musicals, Canadians continue to write book musicals. Mavor Moore tried to establish a Canadian musical theatre in the 1950s by writing shows such as *Sunshine Town*, which was based upon the work of Stephen LEACOCK. Then Moore helped found the CHARLOTTETOWN SUMMER FESTIVAL in 1964, which his successor Alan LUND dedicated to Canadian musicals. Charlottetown's most widely produced musical has been *Anne of Green Gables* (Norman Campbell/Donald HARRON), both nationally and internationally (London, Eng, 1969; Osaka, Japan, 1970; on Broadway, 1971-1972). Also popular have been *Johnny Belinda* (John Fenwick/Mavor Moore), *The Legend of the Dumbells*, which used the troupe's original songs, and the mini-musical for 4 performers, *Eight to the Bar* (Joey Miller/Stephen Witkin). Some of Canada's finest young musicians have written for the Charlottetown Festival: Jim Betts (*On a Summer's Night*), David Warrack (*Windsor*) and Cliff Jones (*Kronborg: 1582*, a rock version of *Hamlet*). Jones's other Charlottetown shows have been *The Rowdyman*, based on Gordon PINSENT's book, and the mini-musical, *Love in the Back Seat*, which was later staged at the Citadel Theatre in Edmonton. The Citadel also premiered Jones's *Hey Marilyn!* an opulent tribute to American film star Marilyn Monroe.

While the Charlottetown Summer Festival was concentrating on Broadway-style musicals, many Canadian writers and composers explored alternative forms; eg, Tom Hendry and Stanley Silverman's *Satyricon* (Stratford, 1969), which was a lush extravaganza; Hendry and Stephen Jack's *Gravediggers of 1942*, a chilling evocation of the DIEPPE raid; Jacques Languirand and Gabriel Charpentier's *Klondyke*, a Brechtian view of the gold rush; Robert and Elizabeth Swerdlow's *Justine*, a counterculture allegory; George Walker and John Roby's *Rumours of our Death*, a bizarre comedy; and Phil Schreibman, Gordon Stobbe and Nancy White's *I Wanna Die in Ruby Red Tap Shoes*, a song-and-dance perspective on Canadian theatre. Saskatoon's Persephone Theatre had an unexpected hit with *Cruel Tears*, based on *Othello*, written by Ken Mitchell and the bluegrass band Humphrey and the Dumptrucks. One of the most spectacular contemporary musicals in Québec has been *Starmania*, a rock fantasy by Michel Berger and Luc Plamondon.

Vancouver composer, lyricist and librettist John GRAY has become Canada's dominant personality in musical theatre on the basis of 3 consecutive successful mini-musicals: *Eighteen Wheels*, a trucker's musical; *Billy Bishop Goes to War*, a one-man *tour de force* about the WWI flying ace; and *Rock and Roll*, an ironic commentary on the faded dreams of a popular small-time, small-town band. Writers like Gray, who in 1982 formed themselves into the Guild of Canadian Musical Theatre Writers (which grew out of workshops conducted in Toronto by Broadway's Lehman Engel), are continuing the challenging task of developing a distinctively Canadian musical theatre.   ROSS STUART

Musicology is the study of the historical development of Western art music, folk and traditional music (ethnomusicology) and aspects of music in

Anne of Green Gables, the Charlottetown Festival's most widely produced musical, has also appeared in London, Eng; Osaka, Japan; and on Broadway (*photo by Barrett and MacKay/Masterfile*).

acoustics, aesthetics, psychology and sociology. As an academic discipline it was introduced to Canada in 1954 when U of T appointed Harvey J. Olnick to organize a course for the Master of Music degree. By 1987, 37 Canadian universities offered undergraduate instruction in musicology and ethnomusicology; 15 universities had graduate programs at the master's level, and 7 offered doctoral programs for musicology, ethnomusicology, composition, music education and performance.

Canadian musicologists make considerable contributions as participants, officers and organizers for international societies. Since there is as yet no national society, musicological papers are presented at the Canadian University Music Society (CUSM), the Association pour l'avancement de la recherche en musique du Québec (ARMuQ), Canadian Folklore Society and other professional groups sponsored by the Canadian Learned Societies.

There are few outlets for scholarly articles on music in Canadian journals. Present publications are the *Canadian Folk Music Journal*, *Studies in Music from the University of Western Ontario* and CUSM *Review/Revue*. Canadian musicologists publish frequently in international journals and encyclopedias. Through these articles and monographs Canadians – including Gaston Allaire, Terence Bailey, Dimitri Conomos, Robert Falck, Bryan Gillingham, Andrew Hughes and Maria Rika Maniates on medieval and Renaissance music; Mary Cyr, Kenneth GILBERT and Hugh McLean on baroque/classical topics; and H. Robert Cohen, Donald McCorkle, Zoltan Roman and Alan Walker on more recent subjects – have contributed significantly to knowledge of Western art music.

Only brief, generally regional, surveys of Canadian music appeared before Helmut KALLMANN's *A History of Music in Canada 1534-1914* (1960). This pioneer publication was followed by Willy Amtmann's study of music under the French regime, *Music in Canada 1600-1800* (1975), and George Proctor's *Canadian Music of the Twentieth Century* (1980). The establishment of the CANADIAN MUSIC CENTRE in 1959 and the music division at the NATIONAL LIBRARY OF CANADA in 1970 facilitated the compilation of the ENCYCLOPEDIA OF MUSIC IN CANADA (1981). In 1982 the first complete overview in book form, Clifford Ford's *Canada's Music: An Historical Survey*, was published, and the Canadian Musical Heritage Society began publishing scholarly editions of early Canadian music in 1983. Individual researchers concentrated on specific areas to compile material from newspapers and periodicals: Phyllis Blakeley and Timothy McGee on NS; Nancy Vogan and J. Russell Harper on NB; William Bartlett on PEI; France

Malouin-Gélinas and Juliette Bourassa-Trépanier on Québec City; J. Antonio Thompson on Trois-Rivières; Peter Slemon and Lyse Richer-Lortie on Montréal; Beverley Cavanagh, Frederick Hall, Elaine Keillor and William Lock on various cities in Ontario; Carl Morey on Toronto; Norman Draper and Norman John Kennedy on Calgary; Wesley Berg on Edmonton and Dale McIntosh on Victoria. Antoine Bouchard and John S. McIntosh have investigated the development of organ building, and Dorith Cooper the history of opera. Helmut Kallmann in particular has done the basic research and collecting of resources that have made Canadian studies in music history possible as an academic subject. At American and Canadian universities, theses have appeared on various genres of Canadian compositions and, more specifically, on individual composers such as W.H. Anderson, Gena Branscombe, Claude CHAMPAGNE, Jean Coulthard, S.C. ECKHARDT-GRAMATTÉ, Robert FLEMING, Bruce MATHER, Rodolphe MATHIEU, Colin McPhee, Léo-Pol MORIN, Jean PAPINEAU-COUTURE, Barbara PENTLAND, Godfrey RIDOUT, Harry SOMERS, John WEINZWEIG and Healey WILLAN. In 1975 the Canadian Music Centre initiated its series of monographs on individual Canadian composers with Brian Cherney's *Harry Somers.*

In ethnomusicology, Mieczyslaw Kolinski developed cross-cultural analytical procedures that had considerable influence internationally and Jean-Jacques Nattiez developed a methodology based on semiology. With Charles Boiles, Nattiez published a history of the discipline to the mid-1970s in *Musique en jeu* (Sept 1977). The first ethnomusicology studies done by Canadians occurred after the pioneer works by Theodore Baker (1882), Carl Stumpf (1886) and Franz BOAS (1888), which included studies of some Indian and Inuit music. James TEIT and Alexander T. Cringan began making cylinders of BC tribes and Iroquois, respectively, in the 1890s. In the 20th century, anthropologists and musical scholars, including Marius BARBEAU, have concentrated on Indian/Inuit music to define the musical style of various cultures, including the Eastern Woodlands area, Plains Indians and North Pacific Coast. Only recently has musical research been done on the Montagnais/Naskapi, Athapaskan and Plateau tribal music, and in 1987 no comparative survey of Indian musical styles existed other than the brief section in Timothy McGee's *The Music of Canada* (1985). The research on Inuit music saw much activity in the 1970s after the initial investigations of Boas, Knud Rasmussen, Diamond JENNESS and Helen Roberts (*see* articles under NATIVE PEOPLE).

In the FOLK MUSIC studies of French, English and other ethnic groups in Canada, folklorists have concentrated on the history, diffusion and variants of individual songs rather than the musical styles involved. Marius Barbeau of the Museum of Man and Carmen Roy, the first director of the Museum's Canadian Centre for Folk Culture Studies, collected thousands of Franco-Canadian folk songs. Conrad Laforte of the Archives de folklore, Laval U, tackled the problem of cataloguing these songs with a classification system based on poetic structure. Germain Lemieux, a notable collector in Ontario, became director of the Institut de folklore (now Centre franco-ontarien de folklore), U de Sudbury, in 1959. Acadian studies initially begun by Anselme Chiasson and continued by Charlotte Cormier are centered at U Moncton. Thousands of Anglo-Canadian songs have been collected by W. Roy Mackenzie, Gerald S. Doyle, Helen CREIGHTON, Louise Manny and Kenneth Peacock in the eastern provinces. Much research is being done at the Folklore and Language Archive at Memorial U under Neil Rosenberg. In 1957 Edith FOWKE began collecting

in Ontario and has published many of the more than 1000 songs she has amassed. West of Ontario, Barbara Cass-Beggs, Margaret A. MacLeod, Tim Rogers and Philip Thomas have been the principal researchers. Of about 60 ethnic groups whose music has been collected in Canada, notable studies have been done on the DOUKHOBORS (Kenneth Peacock), Koreans (Bang-song Song) and UKRAINIANS (Robert Klymasz) (*see* FOLKLORE).

In ACOUSTICS, Oswald Michaud of Montréal and R.W. BOYLE of Alberta, later of the National Research Council, were pioneers. In 1948 Jean PAPINEAU-COUTURE gave the first course that directly related acoustics to musical composition. The Canadian project most prominent in research on the interaction of sound waves and people is the WORLD SOUNDSCAPE PROJECT at Simon Fraser U. In aesthetics, the first Canadian to promote new theories is R. Murray SCHAFER, in *The New Soundscape* (1969). M.R. Maniates has written on French musical aesthetics and mannerism, and Geoffrey Payzant is completing a reassessment and translation of the writings of Eduard Hanslick. Schafer has published studies on the aesthetic views of E.T.A. Hoffmann and Ezra Pound.

Experimental aesthetics and psychophysics have been the areas of greatest interest for Canadians involved with the psychology of music. Rodolphe Mathieu began musical-aptitude tests at the Canadian Institute of Music (Montréal) in 1930, and in 1935 the first courses in the psychology of music at the Maritime Academy of Music (Halifax) were given by Cyril Cornelius O'Brien. Although psychology departments in universities have carried out studies in music education, more research has been done on the perception of musical stimuli of pitch structure, order and tone sequences in music and various aspects of "absolute pitch." In experimental aesthetics, D.E. Berlyne, F.G. Hare and J.B. Crozier have explored arousal theory and information theory as related to music, and Paul Pedersen and David Rosenboom have applied psychophysical research to music composition. In the relatively new field of the sociology of music, John Shepherd has been a pioneer with his publications *Whose Music? A Sociology of Musical Languages* and *Written to Order: A Survey of Tin Pan Alley (1900-1950).*

ELAINE KEILLOR

Reading: M.R. Maniates, "Musicology in Canada, 1963-1979," *Acta Musicologica* 53 (1981).

Muskeg [Algonquian, "grassy bog"], term describing a type of landscape, environment, vegetation and deposit. It attained widespread use in the 1950s during northward expansion of resource development. Peatland and organic terrain are equivalent terms generally referring to northern landscapes characterized by a wet environment and vegetation (eg, black spruce muskeg) botanically classified as mire (subdivided into bogs and fens). Muskeg defies precise scientific definition. It may cover large areas (Hudson Bay Lowland) or occur as small, isolated pockets. Muskeg produces PEAT deposits of variable thicknesses and types because of incomplete decomposition of plant matter in the wet, acid environment. The particular vegetation and hydrological patterns allow recognition of different muskeg types by REMOTE SENSING. Most peat and muskeg in Canada is less than 10 000 years old and occurs in areas covered by the last GLACIATION. Peat accumulation rates and the distribution of muskeg are dependent on climate conditions and controlled by CLIMATE CHANGES. In northern regions, muskeg and PERMAFROST are closely associated and can present difficult engineering problems. No comprehensive, Canada-wide survey of muskeg has been made, but various estimates indicate that Canada may have more muskeg (over 1 295 000

km^2) than any other country. Because of its importance to wildlife, WATER resources and the northern environment, muskeg is no longer considered wasteland. When managed properly, organic soils on peat have excellent capability for agriculture and forestry. Peat products have long-established uses in horticulture, and there is renewed interest in peat as an alternate ENERGY source. Peat provides raw materials for the CHEMICAL INDUSTRY (resins, waxes, paints, etc) and can serve as an efficient filter for some HAZARDOUS WASTES. *See also* SWAMP, MARSH AND BOG; VEGETATION REGIONS.
J. TERASMAE

Reading: N.W. Radforth and C.O. Brawner, eds, *Muskeg and the Northern Environment in Canada* (1977).

Muskellunge (*Esox masquinongy*), large, predaceous, soft-rayed, freshwater fish occurring naturally only in eastern N America. The largest member of the PIKE family (Esocidae), it has an oval body and a duck-billed snout with large teeth. The single dorsal fin, anal fin and caudal fin are close together. Muskellunge are distinguished by a pattern of dark markings on a light background, 6-10 pores on the underside of each lower jaw, and the absence of scales from lower portions of cheeks and gill covers. Although individuals exceeding 1.8 m and 45 kg were once known, most modern specimens are much smaller (70-120 cm, 3-16 kg). Muskellunge prefer clean, cool, weedy waters. In Canada, they occur from Québec to eastern Manitoba. Other common names include musky, lunge and maskinonge. One of the most prized Canadian fishes, it is sought for its aerial acrobatics and hard fight, and also because anglers hope to establish a new record by catching one exceeding 32 kg.
E.J. CROSSMAN

Muskoka Lakes, 3 interconnected lakes — Rosseau, Joseph and Muskoka — in the picturesque Ontario vacation land E of Georgian Bay. Lk Muskoka is fed from the E by the 2 branches of the Muskoka R, the N branch rising in lakes Vernon and Fairy at HUNTSVILLE and the S in Lake of Bays. Lk Muskoka is connected to Lk Rosseau by the Indian R, and Lk Rosseau to Lk Joseph by the St Joseph R. A lock at Port Carling and a canal at Port Sandfield enable watercraft to

Muskoka Lakes region, Ontario. The scenic splendour of the area has attracted visitors for over 100 years (*photo by J.A. Kraulis*).

cruise among the lakes. The whole system drains from Lk Muskoka into Georgian Bay via Moon R (sometimes called Muskoka R). The name "Muskoka" is likely a corruption of "Misquuckkey," an Algonquin chief whose name appears on 2 treaties surrendering the area to Britain Nov 1815. Samuel de CHAMPLAIN (1616) and John Graves SIMCOE (1793) traversed the region, and David THOMPSON searched the area (1837) for a practical route from the Ottawa R to Georgian Bay.

Muskoka was opened to settlement when the Free Land Grant Act (1868) made land available, but although movement within the area was easy, a trip to Muskoka was an ordeal until the railway arrived in 1875. There is some arable land interspersed among the rock and forest, but farming has not been successful, accounting for less than 4% of employment in the area. The lumber industry was active during the late 19th and early 20th centuries, but is only of local importance today. The permanent population is about 40 150, with major concentrations at Huntsville, GRAVENHURST and Bracebridge. The scenic splendour and recreational attraction of the forests and lakes brought visitors from the growing cities of southern Ontario in Victorian times. The early focus of recreation was the resort hotel, replete with dance halls, croquet lawns, tennis courts, etc. There were about 30 establishments by 1879 and there are now 435. The first summer cottages appeared in the late 19th century on western Lk Joseph. At first the preserve of the wealthy, the area now has roughly 20 000 vacation homes, about half of them owned by Toronto residents. Access today is by paved highways north from Toronto. JAMES MARSH

Muskox (*Ovibos moschatus*), shaggy, horned mammal of the cattle family (Bovidae); occurs naturally only in Canadian arctic tundra (mainland and arctic islands) and in Greenland. Muskoxen are related to wild SHEEP and GOATS. They have humped shoulders and short legs, stand about 130 cm high, and weigh 180-270 kg. Muskoxen live in small herds in summer and larger groups (60 or more) in winter. Herds are loosely organized but a dominance hierarchy is present among bulls, cows and subadults. Synchronized cycles of alternating feeding and rumination keep the constantly moving animals together. Females produce a single calf in Apr-June. Though suckling may continue throughout their first year, calves begin feeding on plants within a few weeks of birth. The playful calves spend most of their time together, returning to the mothers

Muskox (*Ovibos moschatus*). The shaggy mammal, related to wild sheep and goats, occurs naturally only in the Canadian Arctic and Greenland (*photo by Fred Bruemmer*).

only for suckling, travel or safety. When confronted by wolves or humans, muskoxen line up facing attackers, pressed tightly together with calves wedged in between. If surrounded, they form a solid ring and may charge out at the enemy. When harassed they stampede, sometimes leaving behind stragglers that are more easily killed by wolves. In midsummer the thick layer of insulating underwool is shed, giving muskoxen a very shaggy appearance. Prolonged courtship begins in late July as bulls assess the females' reproductive state. In Aug, courtship with increasing contact leads to successful mating. Males may challenge the dominant bull for herd leadership. After exchanging deep, roaring bellows, opponents show the broad bases of their horns and rub the preorbital glands against their forelegs in a ritualized display. They then back up and gallop forward to meet in a series of head-on clashes. Head-to-head scuffling may then determine the winner. Muskoxen dig craters in the snow with the forehooves to reach winter forage. Dominant herd members displace others from craters already dug. A wind-hardened crust is broken by pounding with the chin. In severe storms, muskoxen remain lying down for extended periods. Unusual snow conditions can lead to extensive deaths by starvation. Overhunting by explorers, fur traders and whalers led to a ban on HUNTING from 1917 to 1970. Muskoxen were protected further in 1927 with establishment of the Thelon Game Sanctuary. Inuit and sports hunting is now permitted in some areas. Muskox habitats are affected by resource exploration and development, and there are few places in Canada where muskoxen and their habitat are fully protected. DAVID R. GRAY

Muskrat (*Ondatra zibethicus*), a fairly large rodent common to the wetlands and waterways of N America (*photo by Tim Fitzharris*).

Muskrat (*Ondatra zibethicus*), fairly large RODENT common throughout much of N America in wetlands and waterways where water 1-2 m deep supports rooted vegetation and does not freeze to the bottom. It was introduced to Eurasia around 1905. Muskrats are brown, chunky in appearance, and 40-63 cm long, with a distinctive, laterally flattened, sparsely haired tail contributing 18-25 cm. Adults weigh 0.5-1.8 kg. Large hindfeet and slightly webbed toes are edged with short, stiff hairs (swimming fringes). Four incisors cut and hold plant food and 12 cheek teeth grind it. Paired glands beneath the tail base produce musk for marking territories. Two or three litters of 5-7 (range 1-11) young are born Apr-Aug. In marshes muskrats build domelike houses of vegetation up to 1.2 m high and 1.8 m across; in ponds and streams they dig bank burrows. They swim and dive well and eat many kinds of aquatic plants, especially cattails. In winter they eat in "push-ups," minihouses over plunge-holes in the ice, where they can be trapped. Mink are their most important nonhuman predators. Their durable pelts are an important source of income

for Canadian trappers. Muskrats occasionally damage banks and dams. Wildlife biologists manage muskrat populations for sustained yields by improving habitat and regulating harvests. Muskrat numbers decline drastically every 6-10 years, because of infectious diseases and breeding failures. DONALD A. SMITH

Muslims, *see* ISLAM.

Musquodoboit Harbour, NS, UP, pop 832 (1986c), 936 (1981c), located 40 km NE of HALIFAX, takes its name from the Micmac, meaning "rolling out in foam" or "suddenly widening out after a narrow entrance at its mouth." The Musquodoboit Valley, comprising the communities of Upper, Middle and Centre Musquodoboit, was mostly settled by LOYALISTS and second-generation "planters" from TRURO. Industries today include lumbering, and harvesting and exporting Christmas trees, an industry begun in the 1930s. Still an agricultural area today, farming is mainly devoted to raising livestock. Gold mines opened in nearby Caribou Mines, Mooseland and Moose River Gold Mines brought prosperity to the valley as it developed service industries. LIMESTONE extraction is now a major industry, and the valley is known for its good hunting and fishing. JANICE MILTON

Mussallem, Helen Kathleen, nursing educator (b at Prince Rupert, BC). After beginning her career as a staff nurse at the Vancouver General Hospital, she served overseas during WWII as a lieutenant in the Royal Canadian Army Medical Corps. A graduate of Columbia University's Teacher's College, she was an instructor, then director of education, at the VGH School of Nursing. Active throughout her career in nursing education, she served as executive director of the Canadian Nurses' Assn 1963-81. She received several awards and citations for her work as a nursing educator both in Canada and abroad where she advised international organizations such as the International Council of Nurses and the World Health Organization. In 1969 she was made an Officer in the Order of Canada and in 1981 received the Florence Nightingale Medal – the highest award of the International Red Cross. A recent publication is *Changing Roles of Professional Organizations* (1986). DANIEL FRANCIS

Mussel, bivalve (hinged shell) MOLLUSC of either the marine order Mytiloida or the freshwater superfamily Unionacea. Mussels, prized worldwide for food, are the *moule* of French cuisine. Marine mussels are elongated by enlargement of the posterior end. They are found attached to a support by byssal threads (filaments secreted by the mollusc) or partially buried. The blue, bay or common mussel (*Mytilus edulis*) occurs on Canada's East and West coasts and is the only mussel of commercial interest in this country. Recent AQUACULTURE operations in the Maritimes have been successful. In 1985, 696 t were produced annually on both coasts. Two other mussels provide a recreational fishery and have potential for development: sea mussels (*M. californianus*), found on the exposed West Coast, and horse mussels (*Modiolus modiolus*), present in deeper waters of the Pacific and Atlantic coasts. In late 1987 a ban on East Coast mussels was the result of some 100 people becoming ill and at least 2 dying from eating Maritime mussels. The demoic acid toxin was responsible. FRANK R. BERNARD

Mustard, *see* OILSEED CROPS; VEGETABLE.

Mutchmor, James Ralph, Presbyterian and United Church minister (b at Providence Bay, Manitoulin I, Ont 22 Aug 1892; d at Toronto 17 May 1980). After serving in an artillery battery in WWI, he resumed his theological studies and from 1920 to 1936 served churches in Winnipeg's north end. In 1937 he moved to Toronto as associate secretary, and from 1938 to 1963 as secretary, of the Board of Evangelism and Social Service and crusaded against drinking, gambling and social immorality. He was elected moderator of the United Church in 1962. A humanitarian and an able administrator, he led several delegations to the government demanding improved social conditions. He published his memoirs, entitled *Mutchmor*, in 1965. NEIL SEMPLE

Mutual Aid, the principal economic means by which Canada assisted its allies with food, raw materials and munitions from May 1943 until the end of WORLD WAR II. The Mutual Aid Board, chaired by C.D. HOWE, supervised all Allied purchases in Canada and allocated over $2-billion worth of Canadian production without charge, most of it going to Britain and the Commonwealth. An act of enlightened self-interest, it adhered to the fundamental principle that there should be no war debts that would burden postwar trade. Mutual Aid and the BILLION DOLLAR GIFT were unpopular measures, but they provided the financial basis for Canadian war production, which was the key to Canada's wartime prosperity and perhaps its most significant contribution to the victory. HECTOR M. MACKENZIE

Mutual Funds, open-ended investment institutions that raise capital by issuing shares to investors. In contrast to closed-end funds, mutual funds do not have fixed capitalizations. They issue shares to investors continuously and are ready to redeem outstanding shares on demand. In principle, the types of securities in mutual-fund portfolios can vary widely, but in practice a particular fund's portfolio is determined by the proffered investment objectives of the fund; some specialize in fixed-income securities, some in Canadian equities, some only in foreign securities, gold, securities of new ventures or securities of corporations in a particular industry.

Mutual funds are managed professionally by federally or provincially chartered management (investment advisory) corporations or by trust companies. Many firms will manage and distribute shares of only one mutual fund but on average a Canadian firm manages 4 different funds. The firms receive compensation in the form of management fees, calculated as a percentage of the net asset value of the fund (the difference between the market values of its assets and liabilities). In addition, some funds levy sales (load) charges at the time of purchase. The selling price of the shares of a fund with a load charge (usually 10%) is calculated by dividing the fund's net asset value per share by one minus the percent load charge. For example, if a fund levies an 8% sales charge and its net asset value per share is $5, the fund's shares will be sold at $5.43 = $5 ÷ (1 - 0.08). When shareholders sell shares in the fund, they will be redeemed at the prevailing net asset value per share. Most Canadian funds do not charge redemption fees.

Mutual funds are subject to provincial securities acts as are any fund's investment objectives and policies. In the 1970s the total asset growth of mutual funds declined as a result of the introduction of capital-gains tax; competition took the form of increased mortgage holdings, pension funds and corporate bonds. S.M. TINIC

Mycorrhizae, symbiotic associations between plant roots and FUNGI, are thought to occur on roots of 95% of all SEED PLANTS. They are probably essential to the survival in nature of both partners. The plant derives an enhanced ability to absorb essential minerals and greater resistance to root diseases. The fungus obtains sugars directly from its partner, without competition from other micro-organisms. Mycorrhizae occur in several forms that differ in benefits conferred upon plants and fungi involved. The most widespread, endomycorrhizae, occur in about 90% of seed plants and involve approximately 50 species of fungi, thought to belong to the Zygomycotina. In these associations, the fungus invades cells of the root cortex (outer layer) and there forms swellings (vesicles) or highly branched and shrublike appendages (arbuscules). Less widespread types of mycorrhizae, restricted primarily to orchids and members of the heath family, resemble endomycorrhizae but involve Ascomycotina and Basidiomycotina. Ectomycorrhizae, which involve 5000-6000 species of fungi, occur on relatively few plants, mainly trees of pine, birch, willow and oak families. In ectomycorrhizae, the fungus forms a thick sheath around the root, often increasing its diameter several times; filaments penetrate between, but do not enter, root cells. In Canada ectomycorrhizae reach a particularly high level of development. Most Canadian forests are dominated by trees forming ectomycorrhizae and, during wet seasons, mycorrhizal fungi produce large numbers of MUSHROOMS.

Mycorrhizae are thought to enhance a plant's ability to absorb phosphorus. The role of nitrogen in mycorrhizal physiology is less well understood. Endomycorrhizae are thought to use simple sources of nitrogen. Ectomycorrhizae, able to absorb more complex forms of nitrogen, are thought to compete with soil microorganisms for nitrogen locked in leaf litter. Orchid and heath mycorrhizae may be the most efficient in extracting complex nitrogen compounds. Mycorrhizae are under study by researchers in forestry and agriculture worldwide. Tree seedlings inoculated with selected ectomycorrhizal fungi have been found to have improved survival rates and field growth, and the practice may prove especially effective in areas where natural mycorrhizal levels are low. The manipulation of endomycorrhizae in agricultural practice shows great promise and eventually may eliminate heavy use of fertilizers. At present, however, the inability to grow endomycorrhizal fungi in laboratories has hindered attempts to produce adequate amounts of inoculum. The Jardin botanique, Montréal, and U Laval, Québec City, intend to begin production of maple seedlings inoculated with mycorrhizae, which will allow the trees to grow in nutrient-poor soils. DAVID MALLOCH

Myers, Barton, architect (b at Norfolk, Va 6 Nov 1934). He immigrated to Canada in 1968 to join the Faculty of Architecture at U of T. He was principal of the firm of Diamond and Myers until 1975, then founded Barton Myers Associates with offices in Toronto and Los Angeles. He is an original designer with a strong sense of context and heritage; his projects include the CITADEL THEATRE and the Housing Union Building (HUB) at U of A in Edmonton, Sherbourne Lanes housing in Toronto and the Seagram Museum in Waterloo, Ont. Shortly after winning the competition to design additions to the Art Gallery of Ontario in 1987, he closed his Toronto office and moved permanently to Los Angeles. LEON WHITESON

Mynarski, Andrew Charles, gunner (b at Winnipeg 14 Oct 1916; d at Cambrai, France 12 June 1944). He was mid-upper gunner of a Lancaster bomber that caught fire. Though free to jump, he persisted in trying to save a trapped comrade. His parachute and clothing caught fire and he died from his burns, though his comrade miraculously survived the plane crash. Mynarski was awarded the VICTORIA CROSS posthumously for his effort to save another's life. JAMES MARSH

Mysteries, *see* POPULAR LITERATURE.

Nahani, also Nahanni, is an Athapaskan word that, with various spellings, has been used to designate native groups in BC, the NWT and the YT. It is considered to be an inaccurate and inappropriate name for any specific group or for any cultural-linguistic grouping. European fur traders and explorers began to use the term Nahani in the early part of the 19th century, often in reference to an Indian group that was not in direct contact with them and only vaguely known from Indian reports. In the 20th century the term was gradually replaced by more accurate designations, although the Canadian government still used Nahani in the 1970s for the languages of 3 Yukon groups in the Whitehorse, Ross R and Liard R areas. These peoples have been identified as Southern TUTCHONE and KASKA speakers. *See also* NATIVE PEOPLE: SUBARCTIC.   BERYL C. GILLESPIE

Nahanni Butte, NWT, UP, is located on the N side of the SOUTH NAHANNI R near its junction with the LIARD R, 507 air km SW of YELLOWKNIFE. Named after the NAHANI people, the tiny Slavey DENE community is the access point for NAHANNI NATIONAL PARK (est 1972). The area has been haunted for some 60 years by rumours of a lost gold mine, and 25 deaths and mysterious disappearances have been reported. The site became settled 25 years ago when the government relocated people from a settlement at Netla River, 24 km away.   ANNELIES POOL

Nahanni National Park (est 1972) is over 4700 km² of rugged mountains, wild rivers and luxurious hot springs stretched along the SOUTH NAHANNI R in the SW corner of NWT. Tales of lost gold mines and hidden tropical valleys lured prospectors in the early 1900s. Many disappeared without trace in the harsh land and, when 2 headless corpses were discovered, stories of fierce mountain men spread. No one found gold or tropical valleys, but prospectors did discover a land of incomparable beauty. The South Nahanni R twists for more than 320 km through the PARK, crashing through 3 immense canyons over 1000 m deep, plummeting 90 m over Virginia Falls, rushing past boiling hot springs, icy caves, soaring mountains and seething rapids. The vegetation is characterized by boreal and alpine species. Frequent, extensive fires have marked much of the forest.

Spectacular Virginia Falls on the South Nahanni R in Nahanni National Park, NWT (*courtesy Environment Canada, Parks/Prairie & Northern Region*).

The park's 32 mammal species include Dall sheep, moose, woodland caribou and grizzly bear. Peregrine falcons, trumpeter swans and golden eagles are among the 120 species of birds recorded. The adventures experienced by the gold seekers can be recaptured by visitors canoeing, hiking or wilderness camping. Essential services and facilities are available in Fort Simpson, NWT. The park is a UNITED NATIONS WORLD HERITAGE SITE.
                                      LILLIAN STEWART

Nain, Nfld, Town, pop 1018 (1986c), 938 (1981c), inc 1970, is the most northerly community on the Labrador coast. It was given its name when chosen by the MORAVIANS in 1771 as their first mission. Until the 20th century the mission served as a permanent trading base for trappers, hunters and fishermen who followed ancient seasonal migration routes. The mission members, the only permanent European settlers, ran the store and trading post until 1926, when the HBC assumed its operation. In the 1940s this store passed to the Newfoundland government; the International Grenfell Assn and the Labrador E Integrated School Board took over the medical and educational services. The main industry is fishing, with the main species, arctic char, salmon, cod and scallops being processed at the local plant. CN Marine operates a coastal boat service and there is year-round air service. The modern town has been settled year-round since the 1950s, its population being augmented by the resettlement of the former Moravian missions of Nutak and Hebron.
                    JANET E.M. PITT AND ROBERT D. PITT

Naismith, James A., physician, educator, inventor of BASKETBALL (b at Almonte, Canada W 6 Nov 1861; d at Lawrence, Kansas 28 Nov 1939). Orphaned at age 8, Naismith returned to Almonte High School at age 20 to complete his education. He showed prowess in athletics at McGill, and in Dec 1891, as a young instructor at the YMCA International Training School at Springfield, Mass (now Springfield College), he invented the game of basketball. At 37, Naismith graduated from the Gross Medical School of Colorado U with a medical degree. He was associated with U Kansas for some 40 years as professor, physician and director of physical education and published several books on sport. At 64 he became an American citizen. Basketball has achieved a worldwide popularity.
                                      FRANK T. BUTLER

Nakamura, Kazuo, painter (b at Vancouver 13 Oct 1926). After studying at Toronto's Central Technical School (1948-51), Nakamura became a member of PAINTERS ELEVEN. His paintings, first of rectangular block structures recalling the prairies, and then of white oil paint over string laid horizontally on canvas, as in *Infinite Waves* (1957), had a simpler structure and coloration (mostly monochrome) than the work of the Eleven. Like Jock MACDONALD's painting, Nakamura's often concerned the new science, time and space. For this reason he is sometimes considered to have been the most advanced member of the group. He himself characterized his work as more geometric than hard-edge. His nature and landscape paintings, done at the same time as his abstractions, were equally general in tone. As part of Nakamura's explorations, he investigated number structure, the most complex field of mathematics, equating it with the structure of forms.
                                      JOAN MURRAY

Naked Poems, by Phyllis WEBB (1965), is one of the most influential works of its time, for it suggested a new vision of the book-length poem which profoundly affected a number of poets in the following literary generations. Full of lyric intensity yet transcending mere lyric posturing, *Naked Poems* is Canada's first masterpiece of process poetics, a series of precisely crafted minimal texts which remain open to the possibilities of what the third section calls the "Non Linear." In this gestational long poem, sexual and writerly desire are interrogated and integrated in a manner new to Canadian poetry.   DOUGLAS BARBOUR

Nakusp, BC, Village, pop 1410 (1986c), 1495 (1981c), located on the E shore of Upper Arrow Lake in the West Kootenay district of south-eastern BC. The region was settled during the mining boom of the 1890s and early 1900s. As well, settlers engaged in mixed farming and a prosperous lumber industry developed. Nakusp was an important landing for the various paddlewheel steamboats that served the industries and settlers along the Arrow Lakes until the 1950s. After that, the village and area went into some decline but have recovered in recent years. The forest industry remains important today and tourism has increased greatly with a new highway and free ferry connecting the area with the Trans-Canada Highway at Revelstoke 104 km N. The nearby Nakusp Hot Springs are open year-round.   JOHN STEWART

Names At common law a person's surname is a question of custom and repute only; it can be changed at will provided it is not done for a fraudulent purpose. Married women are not obliged to take their husbands' names. Provincial laws, typically called Vital Statistics Act (governing the naming of children at birth) and the Change of Name Act, have supplemented or supplanted the common law. Legitimate children generally have to be registered within a specified period from birth in the father's surname. Illegitimate children are registered in the mother's name unless the father agrees in writing to the child taking his name. Change of Name statutes document a legal change of name. If adults change their names, the consent of a spouse to a change of name affecting both partners is necessary. Divorced women can revert legally to their original names. To change children's names, the consent of one or both parents, and sometimes of the child (if over 14 years of age), may be required. Under Québec law spouses retain their own names for legal purposes. Children take the family name of one or both parents.

ALASTAIR BISSETT-JOHNSON

Nanabozo (Nanabozho or Nanabush), a mythological culture hero found in the cosmological traditions of the Algonquian tribes of central and eastern Canada. He is the impersonation of life, with the power to create life in others. He appears as diverse personalities which represent the various phases and conditions of the life cycle. In some myths Nanabozo creates animals and causes plants and roots to grow so men can eat. He plays a dual role in mythology, both as benefactor to the Indian and as a prankish and obscene fool.

RENÉ R. GADACZ

Nanaimo, BC, City, pop 49 029 (1986c), 47 069 (1981c), inc 1874, is located on the E coast of VANCOUVER I, 110 km N of Victoria and 27 km W of Vancouver, across the Str of Georgia. It is situated on a narrow coastal plain; a few areas in the city have elevations of 290 m. Nanaimo is surrounded by good agricultural land and rich timber resources. Its excellent deep harbour has made it an important distribution and regional centre. Also, it is the axis of several transportation routes: the Esquimalt and Nanaimo Ry; the Trans-Canada and Island hwys; and ferry services to and from the mainland. With its beautiful natural setting, mild climate and beaches, parks and nearby camping sites, the city is an important tourist centre. Nanaimo was dedicated as the "Harbour City" by Prince Charles and his wife Diana in 1986. It is governed by a mayor and 8 aldermen, but shares some responsibilities with the regional district of Nanaimo (est 1967). Nanaimo's most noted annual event is the "bathtub weekend," when "tubbers" from around the world race across the Str of Georgia to Vancouver in motor-powered bathtubs.

History The Coast SALISH Indians were the region's first inhabitants. The Spanish explorers Galiano and Valdés came in the 1790s. The HBC established a fortified post 1849, and the discovery of COAL in 1852 led to permanent settlement. In 1854, 24 families arrived from England to settle in Colvile Town, the name first given the settlement, after Andrew Colvile, governor of the HBC. In 1862 the Vancouver Coal Mining and Land Co bought out the HBC mines and expanded operations. Completion of the Esquimalt to Nanaimo Ry (1886) spurred development. The city grew with its increasing coal output. Production from the 3 main seams in the area reached its peak in 1923 when over 1 million tonnes were mined. Once the easily accessible coal was mined, however, it became increasingly dangerous and expensive to extract the fuel and by the early 1950s the city turned to forest products.

Economy Nanaimo has used its good harbour for trading, servicing and distribution industries. Fishing and lumbering have also grown since the 1950s. The Port of Nanaimo has 3 deep-sea berths, and the BC and CP Ry ferries have docks at Nanaimo. Duke Point Industrial Park, when completed, will focus on forest products and re-

lated industries. Nanaimo is one of a few resource towns that have achieved transformation to a diversified regional centre.

Cityscape The Hudson's Bay Co fort, built in 1853, is the oldest preserved HBC fort in Canada and houses a museum. Central Nanaimo's street pattern is based on a century-old radial pattern of streets converging on the waterfront and central business district. Until the 1950s Nanaimo was a city of contrasts – coal-mine officials and entrepreneurs built large homes in certain areas while the miners lived in "stark frame company houses" on the waterfront or on company lands outside the city.

ALAN F.J. ARTIBISE

Reading: E.B. Norcross, ed, *Nanaimo Retrospective: The First Century* (1979).

Nanisivik, NWT, Settlement, pop 315 (1986c), 261 (1981c), is located on the S shore of Strathcona Sound on the BORDEN PENINSULA of BAFFIN I, 1650 air km NE of Yellowknife. The mining community is the home of Nanisivik Mines, which produces cadmium, lead, silver and zinc. Opened in 1974, the mine today employs Inuit as well as southern workers on a rotations system. The area has historically never been inhabited by Inuit and is devoid of wildlife, while vegetation is scarce.

ANNELIES POOL

Nanogak, Agnes, graphic artist (b on Baillie Is, NWT 12 Nov 1925). She is known for her energetic and colourful depictions of traditional myths and legends. Her works have figured prominently in every print collection published by the Holman artists' co-operative since 1967. Daughter of William Natkutsiak (Billy Banksland) who came from Alaska to the Canadian Arctic with the explorer Vilhjalmur STEFANSSON, since 1937 Nanogak has made her home in Holman, NWT, where she married William Goose, raised a large family and developed her artistic career. Her narrative prints and drawings evoke a rich variety of stories reflecting the Alaskan roots of her father and the Mackenzie Delta/Copper Eskimo culture of her mother and husband. Both artist and storyteller, Nanogak has illustrated 2 books of Inuit stories, *Tales from the Igloo,* ed and trans by Maurice Metayer (1972), and *More Tales from the Igloo* (1986).

MARIE ROUTLEDGE

Nanticoke, Ont, City, pop 20 202 (1986c), 19 816 (1981c), located on the N shore of Lk Erie, 58 km SW of Hamilton. It was incorporated in 1974 by the amalgamation of 7 municipalities, one of which was Nanticoke, an Indian word meaning "crooked or winding," referring to a nearby creek. Although basically an agricultural community of 65 588 ha, it has a growing heavy industrial sector, including a massive Steel Co of Canada complex and a Texaco Canada oil refinery. Ontario Hydro has located a generating station here – one of the world's largest coal-burning plants. See also ELECTRIC-POWER GENERATION.

DANIEL FRANCIS

Napoleonic Wars When Napoleon made himself master of France in 1799, revolutionary upheavals had destroyed *privilege* – barriers of geography and class which prevented the authority of the central government from falling equally upon all. Thus Napoleon was able to consolidate the physical, human and especially the fiscal resources of the nation and to launch an unprecedented campaign of conquest in which the military effectiveness of the "modern" state overwhelmed traditionally organized opponents. Only Britain, Portugal and Russia refused to succumb, and their resistance led to his defeat in 1814-15.

In Europe the Napoleonic Wars produced irreversible political, social and legal changes; however, Britain's mastery of the oceans was unbreakable, and as Napoleon attempted with some success to close the European continent to Britain – both as a market and as a source of supply – the significance of the wars overseas is more practical than doctrinal. The Napoleonic regime could do little in the Americas to implement the anti-slavery resolutions of earlier revolutionary governments, and full emancipation came only in the mid-19th century. For many years the British blockade cut off the Spanish-American colonies from their colonial master and made them dependent upon English trade for European goods, certainly contributing to their successful struggle for independence in the early 19th century. And faced with the mounting financial pressures of incessant warfare, in 1803 Napoleon sold to the US the Louisiana Territory, the whole western drainage basin of the Mississippi R, thus precluding a French West in that part of N America. For Canada, the greatest impact of the wars was a stimulus to the export economy. Fundamental was the British navy's need for a secure source of timber, the American Revolution having left the supply from the former Atlantic colonies uncertain and the French wars having closed the Baltic. The result was an enormous development of the

---

Nanisivik, on the S shore of Baffin Island, is one of the most northerly mining communities in the world. Nanisivik Mines produces cadmium, lead, silver and zinc (*photo by Karl-Heinz Raach*).

Canadian forest industry, especially in New Brunswick, accompanied by some growth of the trade in grain.

The Napoleonic Wars, during which both sides infringed the rights of neutrals, also produced a secondary struggle called the WAR OF 1812 between the US and Britain. Various issues, aggravated by British IMPRESSMENT of American seamen, led the young US to attempt expeditions against Canada, seen by Americans as campaigns of liberation but by Canadians as invasions; this struggle was ended in 1815 without significant results, though it was followed in 1817 by the RUSH-BAGOT AGREEMENT demilitarizing the Great Lakes – the basis of future agreements peacefully regulating the entire Canadian-American border.

In sum, the revival of French political and military power produced no notable reawakening of francophone assertiveness overseas, though one might note the foundation in Lower Canada of the first French-language newspaper, *Le Canadien*, in 1806. The Napoleonic Wars seem not to have challenged seriously the British domination of the Atlantic established in 1763.

G.A. ROTHROCK

Nares, Sir George Strong, naval officer, arctic explorer (b at Aberdeen, Scot 24 Apr 1831; d at Surbiton, Scot 15 Jan 1915). As a mate on HMS *Resolute* 1852-54 he helped to haul sledges in the search for Sir John FRANKLIN. After extensive hydrographical service in southern seas, he commanded the scientific arctic expedition of 1875-76. HMS *Discovery* and *Alert* wintered separately. Lt P. Aldrich explored the northern coast of Ellesmere I. Cdr A.H. Markham's heavy sledges reached a record 83°20′26″ N despite frequent ice ridges. The Admiralty investigated the unexpected outbreak of scurvy, but despite this Nares later rose to vice-admiral. C.S. MACKINNON

Narwhal (*Monodon monoceros*), once known as sea unicorn, is a toothed WHALE of arctic seas. It is best known for its straight, tightly spiraled tusk, which is one of 2 fully developed teeth in the upper jaw and projects through the lip, reaching 3 m in length. The tusk, found in adult males and, rarely, females is of unknown function. Double-tusked narwhals occur occasionally. Narwhals grow to a maximum length of 4.8 m (excluding tusk). Narwhals have no dorsal fin. Body colour is grey at birth, almost black in juveniles, and mottled black and white in adults. Old individuals can be almost completely white, with dark patches confined to the dorsal surface. The narwhal's distribution, centered in Davis Str, Baffin Bay and Lancaster Sound, also includes Hudson Str, Hudson Bay, Foxe Basin and waters surrounding most of the Canadian ARCTIC ARCHIPELAGO. Another population occurs in the Greenland Sea. Traditionally, narwhals were hunted by native people in Canada and Greenland, primarily for meat, oil, sinew and muktuk (skin and adhering blubber). A market for narwhal ivory developed during the Middle Ages in Europe and the Far East. Today, Inuit hunt partly for muktuk and partly to supply a trophy market. The ice-adapted narwhal is rarely found far from pack ice. It survives in the pack by using narrow cracks and small pools of open water, and eats mainly small fish, squid and crustaceans. In 1985, the narwhal population inhabiting Lancaster Sound was estimated at 18 000-30 000 animals.

R. REEVES AND E.D. MITCHELL

Nash, Cyril Knowlton, journalist, broadcasting executive (b at Toronto 18 Nov 1927). After a few years as a teenaged sportswriter and pulp fiction editor in Toronto, Nash achieved professional credentials as a journalist in 1947 when he joined the British United Press Service as a bureau

manager. Financial security and the opportunity for travel came 1951-58 when he was director of information for the International Federation of Agricultural Producers, based in Washington. From 1958 to 1969, as a free-lance writer-broadcaster in Washington, he reported the tumultuous events of the Kennedy-Johnson administrations for the CBC and a number of Canadian newspapers. In 1969, tempted by the opportunity to help reform the corporation's public affairs programming, Nash accepted the position of director of television information programs on the CBC. Since 1978 he has been the CBCs chief correspondent and anchor on *The National* (the latter until he stepped down in late 1987). He has published *History on the Run* (1984), *Times to Remember: A Canadian Photo Album* (1986) and *Prime Time at Ten: Behind the Camera Battles of Canadian TV Journalism* (1987). STANLEY GORDON

Naskapi, *see* MONTAGNAIS-NASKAPI.

Nass River, 380 km long, rises in the northern interior of BC and flows generally SW, draining approximately 20 700 km², to reach the Pacific at Portland Inlet. Its major tributaries are the Bell-Irving, Meziadin and Cranberry rivers. The name comes from a Tlingit word meaning "food depot," referring to the biological productiveness of the river. Its annual eulachon run in particular attracted Indians from afar who traded with the resident Nishga, today still the main inhabitants of the Nass Valley. While the lower valley is an important timber-production area, and many traditional resource-harvesting practices have altered as a result, the Nishga still adhere closely to a complex system of land ownership and title throughout the entire area (*see* LAND CLAIMS). There are 4 villages, all Nishga, along the river – New Aiyansh, Canyon City, Greenville and Kincolith. Recent lava flows are a feature of the valley near New Aiyansh and play an important role in Nishga history. According to Nishga sources, some 2000 people were killed by volcanic flows in the late 1700s.

ROSEMARY J. FOX

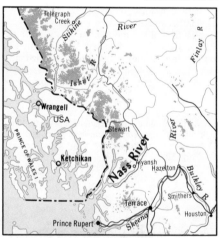

Nathanson, Nathan Louis, businessman (b at Minneapolis, Minn 24 May 1886; d at Toronto 27 May 1943). He purchased his first theatre in Toronto in 1916 and in 1920 sold a chain of theatres to Adolph Zucker's Paramount Pictures (US), becoming president of Paramount's newly formed Canadian subsidiary, Famous Players. The 1923 takeover of Allen Brothers Theatres established the predominance of Famous Players in Canadian film exhibition. Directly and through subsidiaries, Famous Players also dominated FILM DISTRIBUTION to Canadian theatres. Covertly, in the late 1930s, Nathanson began acquiring theatres on his own and making other arrangements with the intent of establishing his own theatre chain.

He resigned from Famous Players in 1941 to join his son Paul in Odeon Theatres. A confidant of C.D. HOWE, Nathanson was appointed to the original board of governors of the CBC in 1936, becoming VP of the board in 1940. ROBERT E. BABE

National Action Committee on the Status of Women is an action-oriented organization made up of about 543 member groups from all over Canada. Started in 1971 with 30 groups, it is the largest umbrella organization of women's groups in Canada (1987). It focuses mainly on pressuring the federal government to make changes that will improve the STATUS OF WOMEN on equal pay, native women's rights, pensions and other matters, but supports provincial and local issues as well. Policy is set at the annual general meeting. The executive is elected from the membership and is volunteer. DORIS ANDERSON

National Archives of Canada, until 1987 Public Archives of Canada, is one of Canada's oldest and most important archival institutions. As the national keeper of Canada's documentary unpublished records, the National Archives houses material from many sources, relating to all aspects of Canadian life. An order-in-council (1872) appointed an officer in the Dept of Agriculture to be responsible for historical documents of national significance. This marked the beginning of Canada's first federal ARCHIVES. In 1903, the head of the archives was given the additional responsibility of selecting and preserving valuable records of the federal government. An Act of Parliament (1912) transformed the archives into a separate department, the Public Archives.

Collections now comprise millions of documents, such as copies of early French and British records relating to the colonial regime in Canada, files from all federal government departments and agencies, as well as rare books, maps and atlases, medals and photographs. Correspondence and other papers of individuals and private societies, films, TV programs, sound recordings and computer-generated records are also included. The archives preserves these materials and provides consultation facilities to make them accessible to researchers from government, universities, the media, or citizens interested in history and genealogy. To reach the general public, the archives produces brochures, slides, microfiches and reference books, and organizes exhibitions that highlight its diverse holdings and illustrate the country's development. The archives also plays an important role in government administration by assisting federal departments and agencies in using efficient records management systems, in ensuring that papers created in the course of administration are systematically destroyed when no longer needed, and that valuable documents are preserved and eventually transferred to its permanent collections.

Individuals who made significant contributions while holding the position of Dominion Archivist include Arthur G. DOUGHTY (1904-35), Gustave LANCTOT (1937-48) and W. Kaye LAMB (1948-69). The title was dropped in 1987, and in that year the archives were administered by National Archivist Jean-Pierre Wallot and his assistant Michael Swift.

NATIONAL ARCHIVES OF CANADA

National Arts Centre, Ottawa, is the most prestigious and beautiful performing arts complex in Canada. Designed by Fred LEBENSOLD, the Centre consists of a 2236-seat opera house, a 969-seat theatre, a 350-seat studio and a 150-seat salon. The National Arts Centre Act (1966) called on the Centre "to develop the performing arts in the National Capital Region and to

Façade of National Arts Centre (Ottawa), designed by Fred Lebensold (*courtesy Environment Canada, Parks/Heritage Recording Services*).

assist the CANADA COUNCIL in the development of the performing arts elsewhere in Canada." Since its opening in June 1969 under director general G. Hamilton Southam, the NAC has been a major national and international showcase for Canadian theatre, opera, music and dance. It has also been a focus of controversy because of its large operating budget. Construction, originally estimated at $9 million, mushroomed to over $46 million. Though financed in part by the Dept of the Secretary of State, the NAC has never enjoyed the full political and financial support needed to carry out its ambitious national bicultural objectives. While the National Arts Centre Orchestra, under former conductor Mario BERNARDI, achieved an international reputation, the English- and French-language theatre companies made only limited national tours and failed to win consistent critical and popular acclaim. In 1983 opera production and the annual summer Festival Ottawa were suspended and in 1984 the English-language theatre company was disbanded. Approximately 900 performances are held throughout the year before 700 000 people. In Sept 1987 Gabriel Chmura was appointed music director and conductor.   ANTON WAGNER

National Assembly (Assemblée Nationale), unicameral provincial legislature of Québec. Following the abolition of the legislative council of Québec in 1968, the legislative assembly became the National Assembly. It includes all provincially elected members of the governing and opposition parties. Its procedures are comparable to those of the federal Parliament.   RÉJEAN PELLETIER

National Association of Women and Law held its founding convention in Winnipeg in 1975. The present membership is composed of approximately 1000 women lawyers, law students and professionals in related fields. Its objects are education to promote understanding of feminist legal issues; research to examine laws, policies and proposed reforms; and action to eliminate sexual discrimination. NAWL also promotes information exchange through its newsletter and affiliation with other women's groups. It is concerned with a broad range of feminist legal issues and has specifically involved itself with the reform of the CRIMINAL CODE on sexual assault and with the lobby on the equality provisions in the CANADIAN CHARTER OF RIGHTS AND FREEDOMS.
JANICE DICKIN MCGINNIS

National Atlas of Canada The *Atlas of Canada* (1906), published by the Dept of the Interior, was one of the world's first national atlases. A second edition similar in style and content was published in 1915, as a collection of small-scale thematic maps dealing with relief, geology, communications, forests, population origin and density, major political boundaries, and plans of principal cities. No new edition appeared until 1958 when, stimulated by the International Geographical Union and the Canadian Social Science Research Council, the Dept of Mines and Technical Surveys published 110 sheets in a loose-leaf binding. In their entirety they show the nature, extent and use of the physical resources of Canada, and their effect on the economy and society of the country. An edition in French was also produced for the first time. Between 1969 and 1973 a fourth edition, titled *The National Atlas of Canada*, was published and in 1974 for the first time a commercial publisher, Macmillan Co of Canada, entered into a joint publishing venture with the Dept of Energy, Mines and Resources to issue a conventionally bound version of the atlas, in both English and French editions. The fifth edition, begun in 1978, is an ongoing series of unbound, large-format sheets, including some thematic packages which can be replaced with new printings. A new edition is planned for 1990.
N.L. NICHOLSON

National Ballet of Canada, founded 1951, is the country's largest professional dance company, with more than 60 dancers. It performs a majority of the full-evening story ballets that have survived from the 19th century as well as selections from its large accumulated repertoire of 20th-century works. Ballets by many of the century's leading choreographers such as George Balanchine, Frederick Ashton, Antony Tudor, Kenneth MacMillan and Glen Tetley who, as artistic associate, created an original work for the company. Other Canadian choreographers have been included in the company's repertoire, notably David ADAMS and Grant STRATE in the 1950s and 1960s and Anne Ditchburn, James KUDELKA and Constantin PATSALAS during the late 1970s and early 1980s. Despite the large quantity of contemporary choreography it performs, the company's artistic character and public image is best defined by its lavish productions of such enduring full-length classics as *Giselle, La Fille mal gardée, Swan Lake* and *The Sleeping Beauty*.

The Toronto-based company was founded by Celia FRANCA under the auspices of a group of local ballet enthusiasts. Despite its title, the company

never received an official "national" mandate. Franca and her board of directors decided independently to give the company a national base by drawing its dancers from across Canada and by undertaking costly and extensive Canadian tours. Franca also believed that only by staging the classics could the dancers be properly developed and finally judged by internationally accepted standards of excellence. The NATIONAL BALLET SCHOOL, fd in 1959, has played a major role in helping the company to meet these standards.

Though the company's early years were plagued by financial problems that restricted its range of activities, it went on tour within Canada and the US and has since performed in many European countries, Mexico and Japan; US and England. In 1964 it adopted the 3200-seat O'Keefe Centre in Toronto as the site for its hometown performances; and as well-equipped theatres were built across Canada, the company expanded to fill their stages with large-scale productions. Apart from Franca, a number of figures have played significant roles in the company's development. Erik BRUHN, who was artistic director in 1983-1986, had been closely associated with the company for the preceding 19 years as guest artist, teacher and producer.

Rudolf Nureyev, who first danced with the company in 1965, returned in 1972 to stage his spectacular version of *The Sleeping Beauty*. Nureyev is widely credited with having advanced the company's standards of performance, with promoting the careers of Karen KAIN, Frank AUGUSTYN and Veronica TENNANT, and with attracting to it a larger measure of international attention. Alexander Grant, artistic director 1976-83, increased the number of annual performances, placed renewed emphasis on developing Canadian choreographers and improved the opportunities for younger dancers, particularly the men. Bruhn's directorship was marked by increased efforts to attract first-rate choreography from leading international choreographers and to answer criticisms of excessive artistic conservatism in the company by introducing more modernistic works. His blueprint for the company's development continues with the appointment of Valerie Wilder, who danced with the company 1970-78, and Lynn Wallis as associate artistic directors after Bruhn's death. See also BALLET.   MICHAEL CRABB

Reading: K. Bell and C. Franca, *The National Ballet of Canada* (1978); A. Oxenham with Michael Crabb, *Dance Today in Canada* (1977); H. Whittaker, *Canada's National Ballet* (1967).

National Ballet School, based in Toronto, is an independent, private residential and day school for students from grades 5 through 12. It offers an integrated program of academic studies and dance instruction for about 150 full-time students, designed to provide a balanced education for those contemplating a professional dance career. In addition to its regular program, the school offers a teacher-training course. Students who have graduated from grade 12 may continue to receive ballet instruction if necessary to prepare them for admission to a performing company. Auditions for admission are held annually in major centres across Canada. Students from abroad are also occasionally accepted.

The school was founded in 1959 as a necessary adjunct to the NATIONAL BALLET OF CANADA. Although many of its graduates still join that company, the school has for most of its existence operated as an independent institution under the direction of its founding principal, Betty OLIPHANT. It is widely regarded as one of the world's leading ballet schools. Its students have distinguished themselves as prizewinners in a number of prestigious international ballet competitions and its graduates, among them such renowned artists as Veronica TENNANT, Karen KAIN, Frank AUGUSTYN, Kevin Pugh and Martine van Hamel, are to be found in leading dance companies around the world. MICHAEL CRABB

National Bank of Canada, with head offices in Montréal, is a Canadian chartered bank which commenced operations in 1979 as a result of the merger between the Banque Canadienne Nationale (fd 1859 as the Banque National; merged 1924 with Banque d'Hochelaga and new name adopted 1925) and The Provincial Bank of Canada (fd 1861). In 1981 it purchased Laurentide Mortgage Corporation, which specialized in mortgage loan operations, and several active subsidiaries of Laurentide Financial Corporation. In 1986 it took over the Mercantile Bank of Canada. Today, it conducts a general banking business and offers related financial services at over 600 branches and offices throughout Canada. As of Oct 1986 it had revenue of $2.8 billion, assets of $27.9 billion (ranking 6th among financial institutions in Canada) and 11 274 employees. DEBORAH C. SAWYER

National Capital Commission is a federal crown agency. It was created by the 1958 National Capital Act to prepare plans for and assist in the development, conservation and improvement of the National Capital Region so that the nature and character of the capital of Canada would be in accord with its national significance. The NCC, and its predecessor bodies since 1899, have had substantial powers of expropriation. Today, some 30% of the urbanized part of the 4662 km² of the National Capital Region (NCR) is federal property. The NCR has no judicial significance. It is not a federal district with powers of its own, and therefore the federal government has jurisdiction only over the lands it owns. In the 50s, 60s and 70s, the NCC implemented a plan prepared by a French urbanist, Jacques Gréber, at the request of the then PM Mackenzie KING. The plan's emphasis was placed on highlighting the beautiful natural setting of the capital and on co-ordinating the improvement of the local infrastructure. In May 1986, Cabinet approved a new mandate for the NCC. This mandate is based on 3 elements: the capital as Canada's meeting place, the capital as a tool to communicate Canada to Canadians, and the capital as an environment within which the national treasures will be safeguarded and preserved. In approving this new mandate, the government recognized that the capital no longer requires the degree of physical development that it did in the early years of its evolution. For that reason, the commission was requested to de-emphasize its involvement in the development of regional infrastructure in favour of acting as catalyst and co-ordinator of the cultural dimension of the capital. The commission has 20 members, drawn from across Canada, with each province represented. Its committees meet periodically, but its autonomy is limited; almost all decisions reside

A ski trail within the National Capital Region (*courtesy Department of Regional Industrial Expansion.*)

with the federal government. The operating budget in 1986-87 was about $45 million, and capital expenditures $40 million. MARC LAMONTAGNE

National Council of Women of Canada (NCWC), founded in 1893 as part of Canada's first feminist wave, is a member of the International Council of Women. Led by its first president, Lady ABERDEEN, the NCWC became the champion of women and children. NCWC recruits have been overwhelmingly urban, anglophone and middle class. A conservative leadership delayed adoption of a suffrage platform until 1910. A federal structure with local councils and nationally organized societies has moderated policy and contributed to the NCWC's influence as a lobbyist. In the 1960s it called for a royal commission on the STATUS OF WOMEN; in the 1980s it demanded the entrenchment of women's rights in the Constitution. VERONICA STRONG-BOAG

National Defence, Department of, created 1 Jan 1923, the result of the amalgamation of the departments of Naval Services and Militia and Defence, and the Air Board. Intended primarily as an economy measure, but also to improve the co-ordination of national security policy, the formation of a single department brought the Royal Canadian Navy, the Militia (later Canadian Army) and the Canadian Air Force (later Royal Canadian Air Force) under one minister. Efforts to integrate the 3 service headquarters failed. WWII saw a major expansion and restructuring of the department. Although individual service departments were not created in law, a minister of national defence for air was appointed in May 1940 and a minister of national defence for naval services in July. In practice this meant that there were 3 separate ministries. Following demobilization, departmental organization reverted in 1946 to prewar form.

In an attempt to end triplication of effort, certain support services common to all branches were integrated over the next few years, and in 1951 a chairman, chiefs of staff, was appointed to co-ordinate training and operations among the 3 services. Integration followed in 1964, when one chief of the defence staff replaced the individual service chiefs; on 1 Feb 1968 these 3 services were unified into the Canadian ARMED FORCES. In Oct 1972 the civilian and military branches in Ottawa were merged into the single National Defence Headquarters. Senior appointments in DND are filled by both civilians and serving officers. The governor general, as the sovereign's representative, is commander in chief of the Canadian Armed Forces. The minister, deputy minister and chief of the defence staff (senior military adviser to the minister) are assisted by their staff at NDHQ. The vice chief of the defence staff is both head of his own division of the staff and the senior staff officer to the whole headquarters. Assistant deputy ministers may be either military or civilian. Including uniformed and civilian personnel, DND has been the largest government department since 1945, while its operating budget has consistently been among the 3 highest. STEPHEN HARRIS AND O.A. COOKE

National Development in the Arts, Letters and Sciences, Royal Commission on (Massey-Lévesque Commission), established by order-in-council 8 April 1949, was the broadest investigation of its kind ever undertaken in Canada. Its 5 commissioners were Vincent MASSEY (chairman), Henri Lévesque (co-chairman), Arthur Surveyer, a Montréal engineer, Norman MACKENZIE, president of UBC, and Hilda NEATBY, historian. Its final report was submitted 1 June 1951 and its recommendations covered all aspects of education, culture and the mass media.

The commission's work was pursued against the backdrop of a major transition in Canadian cultural affairs. Although the country's prewar cultural life was primarily focused on amateur, community-oriented, voluntary activities, the commission foresaw that these activities were giving way to a more urban, impersonal and national orientation; the overall character of the final report is a strange mixture of mourning for an age that was rapidly passing and of excitement at the new era of professional "mass culture" that lay ahead. It is generally believed that the commission's most important accomplishments were the ultimate establishment of arms-length federal support for the arts through the CANADA COUNCIL and the creation of the NATIONAL LIBRARY OF CANADA. It may be, however, that its most enduring legacies are the very high standards of analysis and writing that it set, standards that have not been surpassed by any of its successors. *See also* ARTS FUNDING; EDUCATION. RICHARD STURSBERG

National Energy Board, est 1959 under the National Energy Board Act. The 9-member board is responsible for regulation of oil, gas and electrical industries and for advising the government on matters concerned with the development and use of energy resources. The regulatory role encompasses the granting of permission for the construction of interprovincial PIPELINES, authorization of pipeline crossings, pipeline safety, regulation of pipeline tolls and tariffs, licences authorizing the export of oil, gas and electric power and control of exports of refined oil products. It has administered the National Oil Policy (1961-74) and the NATIONAL ENERGY PROGRAM. Over the years, the board's advisory role has declined in importance as the federal government has come to rely increasingly on the Dept of Energy, Mines and Resources for energy policy. The board is formally constituted as a court of record.

National Energy Program (NEP) was introduced on 28 Oct 1980 as part of the first Liberal budget after the 1980 election. Coming in the wake of the 160% increase in world oil prices in 1979-80 and the prolonged stalemate between the federal government and Alberta over energy pricing and revenue-sharing, the NEP was a unilateral attempt by the federal government to achieve 3 objectives: energy security, by which was meant oil self-sufficiency; a redistribution of wealth towards the federal government and consumers; and a greater Canadian ownership of the oil industry. To reach these objectives, the government adopted a wide-ranging set of measures. Among these measures were grants to encourage oil drilling in remote areas; grants to consumers to convert to gas or electric heating; new taxes on the oil industry; an expanded role for the Crown Corporation PETRO-CANADA; and a 25% government share of all oil and gas discoveries offshore and in the North. These measures were all promised on the expectation that the world oil price would continue to rise indefinitely. When it did not (the price started to fall in 1982), any justification for these interventional policies evaporated and the NEP itself was shown to have been ill conceived.

The NEP, one of the most sweeping government policies ever undertaken in Canada, was dismantled by the Progressive Conservatives after their 1984 election victory. Although the NEP did reduce Canadian dependence on oil and foreign ownership of the oil industry, its chief legacy was one of distrust of the federal government by the western provinces. *See also* ENERGY POLICY. FRANÇOIS BREGHA

National Farmers Union, fd 1969, voluntary organization of farm families. The NFU is democratically structured to assure members full control at all levels. Objectives include the betterment of the social and economic status of farmers through education, legislation and agricultural marketing structures, and reduction of costs and service charges. As a general farm organization, the NFU promotes policies that will resolve conflicts of interest between regions and between producers of various commodities. Incorporated through a 1970 Act of Parliament, the NFU was founded in July 1969 through an amalgamation of provincial farm unions in Ontario, Manitoba, Saskatchewan and BC. It also has members in both the Maritimes and Alberta. *See also* CO-OPERATIVE MOVEMENT.   STUART A. THIESSON

National Film Board of Canada, est 1939, was the principal focus for Canadian FILM activity for the first 2 decades of its history. The NFB has pioneered developments in social documentary, animation, documentary drama and direct cinema; and it has been a continuing initiator of new technology. Its films have won hundreds of international awards. The NFB was founded 2 May 1939 under the terms of the National Film Act and following a report on government film activities by John GRIERSON, who was appointed the first film commissioner in Oct 1939. The Act was revised in 1950, primarily to separate the NFB from direct government control; this revised Act includes the NFB's mandate to interpret Canada to Canadians and other nations. The NFB was originally designed as a modestly staffed advisory board, but the demands of wartime production, together with Grierson's personality, led to a shift into active production by absorbing (1941) the Canadian Government Motion Picture Bureau (formerly the Exhibits and Publicity Bureau, est 1919). By 1945 it had grown into one of the world's largest film studios with a staff of 787. More than 500 films had been released (including 2 propaganda series, *The World in Action* and *Canada Carries On,* shown monthly in Canadian and foreign theatres); an animation unit had been set up, nontheatrical distribution circuits were established and many young Canadian filmmakers trained.

Grierson resigned in 1945 and was replaced by his deputy, Ross McLean, who faced considerable difficulties in the postwar years. Budgets and staff were reduced and the NFB came under attack for allegedly harbouring left-wing subversives and as a monopoly that threatened the livelihood of commercial producers. McLean's replacement (1950), Arthur IRWIN, calmed the storm, initiated a new National Film Act, restructured the NFB along modern bureaucratic lines and planned to move the NFB from Ottawa to Montréal (completed 1956 under Irwin's successor, Albert TRUEMAN). Also during the postwar decade, production expanded into new areas: the first dramatic films were made, new techniques explored in animation, and the information film and production for TV initiated. Filmmakers paid more attention to style and technical polish, and new approaches emerged, more intimate in tone than the didactic approach of the war years. These were clearly evident in the films of one production group, Unit B, headed by Tom Daly, whose work led in the late 1950s to the world's first consistent use of direct cinema in the *Candid Eye* TV series. In Québec the NFB was viewed for some years as a federalist agency that denied Québec's cultural aspirations. French-language production was minimal until the late 1950s when the demands of TV and the move to Montréal provided catalysts for expansion. Many young Québec filmmakers were hired who were to play seminal roles in the flowering of Québec cinema in the 1960s, both within and outside the NFB. These filmmakers refused to ac-

cept the anglophone domination of the NFB's administration.

After a series of protests, the appointment of the first French-speaking commissioner, Guy Roberge, initiated a series of changes that culminated (1964) in a total separation of production along linguistic lines.

Women filmmakers made major contributions during the war years but were then virtually absent from active production until the early 1970s. Encouraged by such series as *En tant que femmes* and *Working Mothers*, and the development of Studio D under Kathleen SHANNON, women have since made significant contributions both as directors and technicians. Native peoples objected for many years to the folkloric and condescending images of themselves projected in NFB films. Only in the late 1960s, in such programs as *Challenge for Change*, did a truer portrait emerge. At the same time, Indians and Inuit were given access to NFB equipment to produce their own films. This initial impetus towards an increasing accessibility to the means of production was continued through the 1970s as the NFB established regional production centres across Canada. Animation has always been an NFB priority and, though the work of such pioneers as Norman MCLAREN is widely recognized, it has been the continuing commitment to encourage new talent that has maintained the vigour of this section and made it one of the most admired in the world (*see* FILM ANIMATION).

Production of dramatic feature films for theatrical release began in 1963-64 and has continued, despite debate about the appropriateness of such production within a state institution. Many NFB feature films have won international awards and have had wide release; since 1984 these have notably included a number of intensely realistic social dramas and comedies produced with modest budgets. The growth of the commercial film industry in the late 1960s and the expansion of film production within the CBC effectively eliminated the NFB from its once dominant position in Canadian film. But it has continued to attract talented new filmmakers, to emphasize high qualities of production, and to maintain its position as the world's most widely respected national film agency.   PETER MORRIS

Reading: D.B. Jones, *Movies and Memoranda* (1982); James Rodney, *Film as a National Art: NFB of Canada and the Film Board Idea* (1977).

National Gallery of Canada in Ottawa has the most distinguished collection of Canadian and European paintings in the country. When the marquis of LORNE was governor general he encouraged the foundation of the Royal Canadian Academy of Arts and the National Gallery of Canada, and presided over an exhibition of works by future members of the RCA on 6 March 1880 (*see* PAINTING). At first the gallery was a collection of the diploma works of academicians, supplemented by occasional gifts. It was only in 1913, with the adoption by Parliament of an Act to incorporate the National Gallery, the appointment of a board of trustees headed by Sir Edmund WALKER, and the confirmation by the board of the 1910 appointment of Eric Brown as director, that the National Gallery could claim even the ambition of equalling other national galleries throughout the British Empire.

Both Walker and Brown were interested in Canadian art. Even before Tom THOMSON died in 1917, for example, the gallery had bought his work. Subsequent curators, such as Robert H. Hubbard, J. Russell Harper, Jean-René Ostiguy, Jean Trudel, Dennis Reid and Charles Hill have built up a representative selection of both historical and contemporary Canadian art. Sculpture

The new National Gallery building, designed by Moshe Safdie, under construction in 1987 (*photo by Jim Merrithew*).

and the decorative arts have also been acquired. The gallery has received gifts from many patrons, including J.M. MacCallum, Vincent Massey, Douglas Duncan, Mr and Mrs Harry Jackman and Henry Birks.

To provide a context for Canadian art, the gallery in 1907 began to buy European art from the end of the Middle Ages to our time. Even with the limited funds available before WWII, important works were purchased, such as paintings by Piero di Cosimo, Bronzino, Canaletto, Monet and Degas. After 1945 purchases were made from the Prince of Liechtenstein, including a Rembrandt, a Rubens and 2 Chardins, and from the Vollard Estate, among them paintings by Cézanne and pastels by Degas. In recent years a few pieces of decorative art and major pieces of SCULPTURE, including marbles by Puget, Bernini and Canova, have been added to the collection. Sir Edmund Walker, a print collector himself, encouraged the development of a prints and drawings collection. This tradition was continued under Kathleen M. Fenwick, curator from 1928 to 1968. In 1967 a PHOTOGRAPHY section was established, with James Borcoman as curator.

The National Gallery of Canada has always had a sense of national responsibility. By 1914 it was sending exhibitions and making extended loans to other museums across the country. It sponsors Canadian art abroad through the Venice Biennale and other exhibitions in places as distant as Tel Aviv and Peking. Gallery research, in conservation and the history of art, is exemplary. All media – exhibitions, film, television, radio – have been used to communicate with Canadians about gallery collections and Canadian art.

In 1968 the National Gallery was incorporated as part of the NATIONAL MUSEUMS OF CANADA, and in 1982 the Canada Museums Construction Corporation was established to provide the gallery with a home. After more than a century in borrowed space, the gallery will finally have a building of its own. The new building, designed by Moshe SAFDIE, will officially open 21 May 1988 in Ottawa. As of 21 Sept 1987 the director of the National Gallery was Shirley Thomson.

JEAN SUTHERLAND BOGGS

Reading: Jean Sutherland Boggs, *The National Gallery of Canada* (1971); R.H. Hubbard, National Gallery of Canada, *Catalogue of Paintings and Drawings,* (3 vols, 1951-60).

National Health and Welfare, Department of, est 1944 by the federal Department of National Health and Welfare Act. It was originally formed in 1919 as the Department of Health, which was merged with the Department of Soldiers' Civil Re-establishment to form the Department of Pensions and National Health in 1928. It has charge of matters relating to the promotion and preservation of the health, social security and social welfare of Canadians and is responsible for investigation and research into public health and welfare, inspection and medical care of immigrants and seamen and supervision of public-health facilities. Other programs include the CANADA PENSION PLAN, FAMILY ALLOWANCES and Old-Age Security, Vocational Rehabilitation and New Horizons. The NATIONAL COUNCIL OF WELFARE and the MEDICAL RESEARCH COUNCIL report to the minister. The department's estimated 1987-88 budget was estimated at $29.2 million.

National Hockey League, established at Montréal 26 Nov 1917. The original teams were MONTREAL CANADIENS, Montreal Wanderers, Ottawa Senators and Toronto Arenas; Québec held a franchise but decided not to operate that season. In the next 25 years the league underwent numerous changes in composition, scheduling and playoff format. Boston Bruins were the first American club to join (1924); by 1926, 6 of the 10 teams were from the US. In 1942 there were 6 teams left (Montreal, TORONTO MAPLE LEAFS, Boston, Chicago Black Hawks, Detroit Red Wings and New York Rangers) and the league remained unchanged until 1967 when 6 new US-based teams were added (California – later Oakland – Seals, Los Angeles Kings, Minnesota North Stars, Philadelphia Flyers, Pittsburgh Penguins and St Louis Blues). Buffalo Sabres and VANCOUVER CANUCKS joined in 1970 and Atlanta Flames and New York Islanders in 1972. The number of teams reached 18 by 1974 (with the addition of Kansas City Scouts and Washington Capitals) – of which only 3 were based in Canada. One team folded in 1978 but Hartford Whalers, EDMONTON OILERS, QUEBEC NORDIQUES and WINNIPEG JETS joined the following year after the collapse of the WORLD HOCKEY ASSN. The Atlanta franchise moved to Calgary (*see* CALGARY FLAMES), bringing the number of NHL teams in Canada to 7. The majority of players in the NHL are still recruited from Canadian junior hockey, although the number of players from Sweden, Finland, Czechoslovakia and the US has increased dramatically.

The NHL has failed to win large TV contracts in the US and it has been criticized for having a playoff system that eliminates only 5 of 21 teams after an 80-game schedule, but it remains the premier professional HOCKEY league in the world. The STANLEY CUP, awarded exclusively to NHL teams since the 1926-27 season, is emblematic of the world professional championship. *See also* CANADA CUP. JAMES MARSH

National Holidays As with most countries, Canada's national holidays mark religious, quasi-religious or patriotic occasions. Statutory holidays are established by Act of Parliament and are observed, without fail, by federal employees and by most Canadians although increasingly, statutory holidays are becoming days for shopping and for large sales. Canadian statutory holidays are as follows: New Year's Day; Good Friday; Easter Monday; Victoria Day; Canada Day (formerly called Dominion Day); Labour Day; Thanksgiving Day; Remembrance Day; and Christmas Day.

The derivation of the 3 Christian holidays needs no explanation. New Year's Day, Jan 1, marks the beginning of the new year. VICTORIA DAY (variously known as May 24th, the Queen's Birthday, EMPIRE DAY or Commonwealth Day) is celebrated in all provinces except Québec (where it is celebrated on the Fête de Dollard) on the Monday before May 25 and has been a national holiday since 1901. Traditionally, cottages are opened for the summer and gardens planted on this weekend, and the day is still celebrated in some parts of the country with fireworks displays. Canada Day, July 1, commemorates the day on which Canadian CONFEDERATION came into existence in 1867. Originally celebrated in rather quiet – and hence very Canadian – ways, Canada Day is now the occasion for elaborate cultural and entertainment spectacles, paid for by the federal government to foster Canadian nationalism.

LABOUR DAY is celebrated on the first Monday in Sept, once again providing an occasion for a long summer weekend. The day honours the contribution of organized labour and has been celebrated since at least 1872 and as a statutory holiday since 1894. Labour Day is usually celebrated with large parades and union picnics. Thanksgiving Day, which provides another long weekend, is observed on the second Monday in October (unlike the holiday in the US which falls on the last Thursday in Nov) and celebrates the harvest season. The statutory holiday began in 1879, almost certainly as an imitation of the American celebration, but earlier in the year as a recognition of the shorter growing season in Canada.

REMEMBRANCE DAY is observed on Nov 11, the day of the armistice that ended the Great War in 1918. Usually celebrated with ceremonies at cenotaphs in towns and villages and at the National Cenotaph in Confederation Square, Ottawa, the day is marked by a moment of silence at 11 AM and by gatherings or parades of veterans of the world wars and the Korean conflict.

A substantial number of holidays are celebrated in the provinces. Boxing Day, Dec 26, is becoming almost universally observed as a day to recover from the exertions of the Christmas season. Civic Holiday, variously called Heritage Day in Alberta and Saskatchewan and Simcoe Day in Ontario, is also celebrated in Manitoba and the NWT and gives a long weekend at the beginning of Aug. Quebeckers celebrate Fête nationale du Québec on June 24. Newfoundland observes St Patrick's Day, St George's Day, Discovery Day, Memorial Day (July 1) and Orangemen's Day. *See also* RELIGIOUS FESTIVALS. J.L. GRANATSTEIN

National Income, strictly, is a money measure of the incomes received or accruing to residents of a country as owners of the agents of production, during a specified period of time. National income includes wages, rents, interest and profits, not only in the form of cash payments, but as income from contributions made by employers to pension funds, income of the self-employed, and undistributed business profits.

In market economies such as Canada's, the measures of national income include (with some exceptions) only those economic activities in which goods or services are sold in markets; the few exceptions ("imputed values") are illustrated by the inclusion in the estimates of a rental income for owner-occupied homes, and by the inclusion in the income of farmers of an estimate of the value of the produce from their own farms consumed by the farm families themselves. At the same time, official and nearly all private estimates do not include anything for the value of all of the services performed in the household by the unpaid homemaker (*see* HOUSEWORK). This large omission is serious if national income is being used to measure the well-being of a country's

National Income and Gross National Product, Canada, 1986 (Billion$)	
Wages, salaries and supplementary labour income	267.278
Military pay and allowances	2.957
Corporation profits before taxes less dividends paid to nonresidents	17.929
Interest and miscellaneous investment income	57.327
Accrued net income of farm operators from farm production	5.400
Net income of nonfarm unincorporated business, including rent	32.753
Inventory valuation adjustment	-7.335
Net national income at factor cost	376.309
Indirect taxes, less subsidies	53.794
Capital consumption allowances	57.465
Residual error of estimate	0.840
GDP at market prices	488.408

people. As it stands, this measure of national income is exactly equivalent to what the net production of goods and services would sell for on the market if there were nothing else added to the prices of goods and services; it is therefore a measure of the net value of products measured at factor cost. However, the prices at which goods are exchanged in markets do include indirect taxes such as sales taxes and customs duties. In the national accounts, these taxes and the allowances for depreciation and obsolescence may be added to the net national income at factor cost to obtain the measure "gross national product at market prices."

In Canada, official national income estimates are prepared by Statistics Canada. By collecting a wide range of economic and other statistical data, Statistics Canada incidentally obtains information useful in estimating national income and related items in the system of national accounts; when necessary, it conducts surveys specifically designed to elicit data for national income estimates. In addition, it can obtain information provided to other public bodies, eg, tabulations prepared from both personal and corporate income-tax returns.

The components of national income given in the official accounts partly depend on the available data. Wages and salaries paid to hired workers (the largest component) are shown because they can be obtained from data sources such as the census of manufactures, reports filed by financial institutions, and income-tax returns. Similarly, estimates of property income, the recompense for the productive services of capital goods, natural resources and entrepreneurship, are obtained from much the same sources and are shown in interest and rental income and corporation profits. Net interest and dividends paid to residents of other countries are not included. Incomes of unincorporated self-employed persons must be otherwise estimated. Incomes of farmers are estimated by subtracting from the receipts from sales of farm products the expenses incurred in production; the resulting farm income is a mixture of labour income (for the work of the farmer and his unpaid family), and of property income. Incomes of other unincorporated businesses, eg, those engaged in the professions, and in merchandising or service industries, are calculated in the same way, or, in some instances, from income-tax tabulations.

The indirect taxes and capital consumption allowances (depreciation) added to national income to yield GDP are derived respectively from government records and from business and other records; some imputation of depreciation is necessary in certain cases, eg, those involving government-owned buildings and owner-occupied housing.

The national accounts include 4 main categories of expenditure: consumer purchases; purchases of new capital goods by businesses, governments and persons; government purchases; and net exports of goods and services. The measure of these expenditures reflects the prices actually paid for goods and services. The expenditure on capital goods also includes both the component of capital expenditure that just makes up for capital consumption and the net addition to the capital stock. The sum of these expenditures is gross national expenditure.

Gross domestic product (as opposed to GNP), is a money measure of the value of all goods and services produced in Canada regardless of the fact that some of the income generated in their production may belong to residents of other countries. GNP is a measure of the goods and services that are available to residents of Canada. The former exceeds the latter to the extent that interest and dividends paid abroad exceed those received from abroad.

The UN has encouraged its members to prepare uniform national income calculations, but comparisons of the resulting per capita national incomes must be interpreted with care for 3 reasons. First, the exchange rates used to put such measures into a common currency, so that the comparisons can be made, reflect the comparative prices in each currency only of goods that are traded internationally (comparative prices of untraded goods may not be at all well reflected in exchange rates); second, the size of nonmarket production and hence the portion of production that is not measured in national income estimates vary greatly among countries (typically, less-developed countries have relatively large nonmarket sectors of production); third, patterns of consumption vary greatly among countries and comparisons of money incomes may not reflect the effect of these variations on a population's well-being. Comparisons are also made intertemporally for a single country. National income and related estimates are usually calculated first in the prices of the period (most commonly a year) to which they apply. For year-to-year comparisons, the aggregates, usually the national expenditure estimates, are deflated by price indices to remove the effects of price change from the changes in the aggregate production; they are then said to be measured in constant prices, ie, the prices of a particular year.　　　　　　M.C. URQUHART

National Indian Brotherhood, *see* ASSEMBLY OF FIRST NATIONS.

National Library of Canada was established by the National Library Act (1953) as a federal government department to collect, preserve and promote the printed heritage of Canada, and to assist in developing and making accessible library services and resources in Canada. The Library collects books, periodicals, newspapers, microforms, sound recordings and other materials which are published in Canada, about Canada or written by Canadians. Legal deposit regulations in the National Library Act require that Canadian publishers deposit 1 or 2 copies of new books (depending on the price) and other materials with the Library. Selected foreign publications in the humanities and social sciences are also available, and the total collections number about 3 million items. The Library has the largest collections in the world of Canadian music (printed and recorded), Canadian newspapers and official publications of the federal and provincial governments. It also houses collections of rare Canadian books, manuscripts of Canadian authors, and theses

(microfilmed for preservation, sale or loan) from most Canadian universities. The Library's collections and its reference, advisory and locations services are available to all Canadians, who may visit its building in Ottawa or have another library contact the National Library.

Through a number of programs, the Library also endeavours to assist Canadian libraries in providing their services to Canadians. It maintains a central catalogue of the holdings of Canadian libraries, and publishes the national bibliography (*Canadiana*) as well as many other bibliographies, catalogues and technical reports. The sharing of library resources via the latest computer and telecommunication technologies is promoted through the Library's participation in national and international activities aimed toward standardization. Within Canada, the Library co-ordinates and promotes a network of Canadian libraries which may share resources through such means as a computer-based system of interlibrary loan. The Library is directed by the National Librarian (W.K. LAMB 1953-68; G. SYLVESTRE 1968-83; M. Scott 1984-), assisted by an advisory board composed of librarians, scholars and other interested individuals from all parts of Canada.　　MARIANNE SCOTT AND GUY SYLVESTRE

National Museum of Man, *see* CANADIAN MUSEUM OF CIVILIZATION.

National Museum of Natural Sciences (NMNS) The origins of the NMNS may be found in the GEOLOGICAL SURVEY OF CANADA (1842) and the NATIONAL MUSEUMS OF CANADA. In 1956 Natural and Human History branches were established that were to become the NMNS and CANADIAN MUSEUM OF CIVILIZATION (CMC, formerly National Museum of Man) under the National Museums Act of 1968, which established the National Museum of Canada, a crown corporation reporting to the minister of communications. In 1987 the minister announced the federal government intention to dissolve the corporation and establish the national museums as independent, autonomous institutions. Following a major renovation of the Victoria Memorial Museum in the early 1970s, only the permanent galleries of the NMNS and CMC remained in the building, with staff and collections being dispersed throughout the National Capital Region. After the 1988-89 relocation of the CMC to a new site in Hull, Qué, the NMNS expects to expand its exhibitions throughout the building's 8000 m² of available space. The NMNS is a component of the National Museums of Canada, a crown corporation reporting to the minister of communications.

The collections of the museum are its prime asset and their scientific, heritage and commercial value are irreplaceable. Although used in exhibits, they are much more than display collections for they contain the essential standards against which all biological and geological research is conducted. These specimens are the definitive proof of the existence, variation and distribution of animals, plants and minerals in time and space. Curators, while collecting for the national collections, played an important role in exploring western Canada and, in more recent times, the Arctic. Notable were John MACOUN, who made valuable botanical studies of the Prairies in the 1870s; Percival Algernon TAVERNER, whose ornithological research culminated in the classic *Birds of Canada*, published in 1934; Charles Mortram STERNBERG, who collected more dinosaur fossils than any other individual, mostly from the Alberta Badlands; and Alf Erling PORSILD, an authority on the alpine and arctic plants of N America and Greenland.

The NMNS maintains collections of vascular plants, mosses, bryophytes, lichens, algae, birds,

mammals, film and audio records of bird and mammal behaviour, reptiles, amphibians, fishes, invertebrate animals (notably molluscs, polychaetes and crustaceans), minerals, gemstones, rocks, vertebrate fossils (notably dinosaurs and Quaternary mammals), and fossil spores and plants. The majority of these collections are the most complete of their kind in the world. The museum also houses a collection of natural history art, and collections of mounted birds and mammals that are available with specimens and models for exhibit and education programs. In total, the NMNS collections, soon to be rehoused in a new curatorial complex, contain over 2.5 million accessioned specimen lots that include about 5 million species. Approximately 100 000 specimens are added to the collections annually, with most collected by staff. An arctic research station is maintained on BATHURST I to support field projects.

Among the museum's first public successes were an exhibition of economically valuable minerals for the 1851 Great Exhibition in London and the instigation of specimen loans for schools in 1874. Currently, there are 8 exhibition galleries that average one-half million visitors annually, and more than 70 travelling exhibits that circulate to institutions throughout Canada and abroad are produced each decade. Innovative education programs continue to be an essential component of exhibitions, with theatre, film, workshops, field trips and other media being used to meet the needs of special audiences such as preschool children, the aged and the handicapped. A natural history information service is available to the public. The National Museum of Natural Sciences published 2 scientific series, *Syllogeus* and *Publications in Natural Sciences*, in addition to trade publications which have included such national best-sellers as *The Birds of Canada* by W. Earl Godfrey.

The museum is organized into 3 curatorial research divisions (Botany, Zoology, and Earth Sciences), 4 public programming divisions (Exhibits, Design and Technical Operations, Education, Outreach), an administration sector and a directorate. In 1988 the NMNS had a budget of $13.5 million and a full-time staff of 215. *See also* MUSEUM POLICY.　　　　　RIDGELEY WILLIAMS

Reading: A.F. Key, *Beyond Four Walls: The Origins and Development of Canadian Museums* (1973).

National Museum of Science and Technology (NMST) had its roots in the GEOLOGICAL SURVEY OF CANADA museum (1842), renamed the National Museum of Canada in 1927. In 1966 a separate Science and Technology Branch was created, under its own director, and small collections of artifacts which had been under the trusteeship of other branches of the National Museum were transferred to it. In Apr 1967 a warehouse on the outskirts of Ottawa was put at its disposal and the museum was opened to the public on 16 Nov 1967. The following year it became the NMST, a part of the NATIONAL MUSEUMS OF CANADA.

The National Museum of Science and Technology collects and preserves objects and data relating to scientific and technological history and development in Canada, carries out research, and sponsors exhibits and public programs. Major subject areas include pure science (mathematics, physics, chemistry), astronomy, transportation, communication, agriculture, forestry, fishing, extractive industries, industrial technology, energy, aviation and space, marine technology, fire technology, graphic arts technology, medical technology and photography. Collections total approximately 20 000 artifact lots with 60 000 individual objects, and 80 000 photos as well as associated archival material.

The National Aviation Museum, an autonomous submuseum of the NMST, is considered to have one of the world's finest aeronautical collections. In 1986 it had 151 000 visitors and in 1988 a new building was opened to house the historic aircraft and aero-engines assembled from the Canadian Armed Forces, the Canadian War Museum and the first National Aviation Museum, augmented by 30 aircraft since 1967. The new facility provides aerotechnology and chronological displays of aircraft, a mock control tower, and permanent restoration and collections storage space. WWI aircraft demonstrations by museum staff at airshows and exhibitions across the country are very popular.

The museum's OBSERVATORY houses Canada's largest refracting telescope, obtained from the Dominion Observatory, which is used for education programs. In 1986 astronomy evenings and telescope viewing attracted 3617 visitors. Monthly skysheets were distributed to 25 000 readers, and the monthly Stargazing column was published by 40 newspapers across Canada. Other public programming activities include artifact demonstrations, regional science fairs, special tours and films, travelling exhibits and publications. Exhibits, both continuing and temporary, use innovative design and display methods and stress visitor participation. As part of its program in 1987-88 the NMST co-operated in joint projects: with CP, on a temporary and travelling exhibit "Well done in Every Way"; with the National Archives on the history of newscasting in Canada; and with Canadian Engineers and Associates of Science and Technology for a holography exhibit entitled "Images in Time and Space."

NMST has been in the forefront of developing modern museum practices, with experiments in the use of computers, in registration procedures, traffic management studies, analysis of visitor patterns, and the use of the outdoor surroundings of the museum as a technology park. Its expertise in restoration of heavy objects, particularly those in transportation, has been made available to museums both nationally and internationally.

DAVID M. BAIRD

National Museums of Canada was the collective title of the NATIONAL GALLERY OF CANADA, CANADIAN MUSEUM OF CIVILIZATION, NATIONAL MUSEUM OF NATURAL SCIENCES and NATIONAL MUSEUM OF SCIENCE AND TECHNOLOGY, joined in a single corporation with the Canadian Conservation Institute, the Museum Assistance Program, the National Museum Library, and a range of museums' support and administrative units. Together, the museums collected and conserved data and artifacts, particularly in relation to the Canadian heritage; conducted research in their various disciplines; sponsored publications as well as public programs and exhibits both in Ottawa and across the country; aided and advised institutions and individuals abroad; and assisted and partly funded galleries and museums within Canada.

The NMC Corporation owed its origin to many factors, including a desire for more dynamic leadership and to simplify the procedure of reporting to government, but also to augment the role of the museums nationally and thereby attract more funding to the institutions. Several resignations and feuds inside the National Museum during the 1950s and 1960s also attracted unwelcome attention, which was increased when a long-delayed new building was again postponed in 1967. In Nov 1967 Secretary of State Judy LAMARSH introduced a bill in the House of Commons providing for the reorganization of the federal government's cultural repositories into one corporation. Despite some vociferous objections, the National Gallery was embedded in the new entity, while the former National Museum was divided into 3 parts. Within the corporation, the 4 directors reported to a new board of trustees, who, with a secretary general, supervised the National Museums, in conjunction with special advisory committees for each museum or gallery. The National Museums Act took effect on 1 Apr 1968.

A further change occurred in 1972 when Gérard PELLETIER, as secretary of state, announced a new policy intended to strengthen the role of the national museums within Canada. A Museum Assistance Program was established to furnish subsidies to regional and local museums, and other central services were expanded to help local collections unable to afford elaborate and expensive equipment and highly trained personnel (see CONSERVATION OF MOVABLE CULTURAL PROPERTY). The effect was most beneficial, although critics noted that subsidies, once started, tended to become permanent as local museums integrated them into their budgets. It also proved impossible, in the long run, to accommodate every museum and every purpose in the subsidy program.

Although much progress was made in rehabilitating the central museum facilities during the 1970s, it remained true that new buildings were a relatively low priority of government, with the effect that museum facilities were dispersed all over the Ottawa region, sometimes in highly inappropriate quarters and locations. The style in which the museums and the National Gallery were administered varied according to the particular board and secretary general. Relations between the board and the secretaries general were not always smooth, and in case of conflict it was still necessary, as it had been before 1968, to appeal to the attention of an often busy and preoccupied minister. While, in the early 1980s, money was finally made available for new National Museum of Man (now Canadian Museum of Civilization), National Gallery and National Aviation Museum buildings, direction of their construction was assigned to a new CROWN CORPORATION, the Canada Museums Construction Corporation. In retrospect, it appears that the attempt to distance the National Museums from the public service, which seemed so promising in 1967-68, was not entirely successful, whereas the attempt to broaden the museums' national service, and therefore their political support, was achieved at the cost of postponing necessary improvements at the centre. It was, in short, a very Canadian compromise. This unsatisfactory compromise was finally resolved in 1988 by the abolition of the NMC. The result of this new development was, however, uncertain.

ROBERT BOTHWELL

National Policy, tariff protection for Canadian manufacturers, the rallying cry of Sir John A. MACDONALD's Liberal-Conservative Party in its successful 1878 general election campaign. Alexander MACKENZIE's Liberal Party, in office 1873-78, adhered to a policy of tariffs for revenue purposes – around 20% CUSTOMS duties on manufactured goods – despite the depression of the 1870s and the failure of the government's 1874-75 attempt to negotiate a RECIPROCITY agreement with the US. Macdonald's National Policy became a public issue after the Liberal government failed to raise the tariff in the 1876 budget. It was set in motion in the budget of 14 Mar 1879 after consultation with business interests. It was intended to be a nationalistic policy which would broaden the base of the Canadian economy and restore the confidence of Canadians in the development of their country. That the National Policy would also assist in the development of a group of wealthy businessmen who could be counted on to contribute generously to the Conservative Party was another factor that Macdonald acknowledged. The tariff on most foreign manufactured goods was increased, affording substantial protection to Canadian manufacturers. Equally important to the manufacturers were the reduced customs duties on the necessary raw materials and semi-processed products, which lowered their costs of production.

Over time the National Policy took on a broader meaning in Conservative Party rhetoric, which tended to equate the National Policy with its larger development policies: the CANADIAN PACIFIC RAILWAY (1880s); western settlement (the DOMINION LANDS Act of 1872 and immigration policy); harbour development; and the subsidization of fast steamship service to Europe and Asia to facilitate the export of Canadian products. It became the centrepiece of Conservative Party policy for decades, being espoused by R.B. BENNETT in the 1930s as fervently as it was by Macdonald in the 1880s. Macdonald's last election, in 1891, was fought in defence of his National Policy. Sir Wilfrid LAURIER's Liberal government, 1896-1911, adopted the PROTECTIONIST principles if not the rhetoric of the National Policy tariff and kept its general tariff at similarly protectionist rates. Even the Laurier government's famous reciprocity agreement with the US in 1911 made only a few concessions on import duties on manufactured goods; the bulk of the agreement abolished duties on natural products, and customs duties were lowered on a restricted list of manufactured goods. But this alarmed manufacturers enough to swing their support back to the Conservatives in the 1911 general election. Campaigning on the argument that a mature economy had developed under the National Policy, that reciprocity threatened the Canadian economy, and that the choice before the electors was "whether the spirit of Canadianism or of Continentalism shall prevail on the northern half of this continent," Robert BORDEN's Conservatives swept to victory, bringing a continuance of the National Policy. See also CONTINENTALISM; NATIONALISM; ECONOMIC NATIONALISM.

ROBERT CRAIG BROWN

Reading: Robert Craig Brown, *Canada's National Policy, 1883-1900* (1964); V.C. Fowke, *The National Policy and the Wheat Economy* (1957); P. Russell, "The National Policy, 1879-1979," *Jnl of Canadian Studies* 14 (1979).

National Research Council of Canada (NRC), federal CROWN CORPORATION responsible to Parliament, through the minister of state for science and technology. The NRC was formed in 1916 as the Honorary Advisory Council for Scientific and Industrial Research. It immediately funded research committees for special needs, offered science fellowships at Canadian universities, and carried out a research inventory (the first statistical review of Canadian scientific manpower and budgets). Early plans to found an NRC national laboratory at Ottawa were not authorized until 1928. During the presidency of H.M. TORY (1923-35), laboratory staff reached 153, including 54 scientists and research engineers, all but one of whom were employed on industrial or applied research. Tory's successor, Gen A.G.L. MCNAUGHTON, enlarged the staff to 300 and prepared the NRC laboratories for their central role in war research (from medicine and food packaging to weapons and synthetic fuels). Under C.J. MACKENZIE, president from 1939 to 1952, NRC staff reached 2000 and was reorganized to provide a stronger foundation in basic (pure) SCIENCE. Pres E.W.R. STEACIE (1952-62) established the principle that NRC extramural budgets for university grants and fellowships should rise to match the intramural budget ($21.5 million in 1962-63) and initiated the Industrial Research Assistance Program for extramural grants to private industry (see INDUSTRIAL RESEARCH AND DEVELOPMENT).

Many of the NRC's functions have been "spun off" to separate bodies. For example, the council was the government's general adviser on SCIENCE POLICY from 1916 until the Science Secretariat was created in 1964. Laboratory activities initiated by the NRC and delegated to separate bodies include military research (to the DEFENCE RESEARCH Board, 1947), atomic research (to ATOMIC ENERGY OF CANADA LTD, 1952), medical research grants (to the MEDICAL RESEARCH COUNCIL, 1966), and university grants and scholarships (to the NATURAL SCIENCES AND ENGINEERING RESEARCH COUNCIL, 1978).

Structure and Functions In the 1987-88 fiscal year the National Research Council had a total staff of 3228 (including 1102 scientists and research engineers) and a total budget of $451 million. The 14 laboratory divisions were organized in 3 functional groups: Biotechnology and Chemistry, Physical Sciences and Engineering, and Technology Transfer (comprising the Industrial Research Assistance Programme).

Since about 1920, continuing extramural activities have included dozens of Associate Committees on special problems, from tuberculosis to railways, from tribology (the science of lubrication and friction) to the National Fire Code. The NRC represents Canada in several international bodies and co-ordinates multilateral special projects, such as the Canada-France-Hawaii astronomical OBSERVATORY and the Tri-University Meson Facility in Vancouver. The NRC library, founded in 1924, became the national science library in 1957 and, in 1974, was renamed the Canada Institute for Scientific and Technical Information. CISTI collects all the world's major scientific journals for the main branches of science and engineering and a selection of others, totalling 30 586 current serials and more than 10 000 defunct serials in 1985-86. That fiscal year 325 377 items were supplied or copied by Interlibrary Loan and 377 091 computer searches for scientific information were carried out. The NRC founded the *Canadian Journal of Research* in 1929. It now publishes 13 scientific journals. The NRC no longer subsidizes others' journals, since this function has been transferred to the Natural Sciences and Engineering Research Council which supports approximately 30 Canadian research journals. Since 1929, it has also maintained a technical information service for industry. Now the Field Advisory Service of the Industrial Research Assistance Programme, it answered some 25 000 inquiries in 1986-87, mostly from medium- and small-sized manufacturers.

DONALD J.C. PHILLIPSON

Reading: W. Eggleston, *National Research in Canada: The NRC 1916-1966* (1978); M. Thistle, *The Inner Ring: The Early History of the National Research Council of Canada* (1966).

National Resources Mobilization Act, was passed 21 June 1940 by Parliament. It represented the government's response to the public clamour for a more effective Canadian war effort that arose in the wake of the stunning German victories in Belgium and France. The Act enabled the government to requisition the property and services of Canadians for home defence. An earlier promise made by PM Mackenzie King in 1939 not to introduce CONSCRIPTION for overseas service was honoured, but it was reversed in Aug 1942 following the national plebiscite of Apr 1942. The amended NRMA permitted the sending of conscripts overseas in addition to the existing regular volunteer forces. The NRMA was important politically as it attested to the government's determination to intensify the war effort. It tended to appease the conscriptionists without antagonizing the anti-conscriptionists. In military affairs the Act created a duality in Canada's military that was to last until the war's end. It also resulted in the training of a large body of men for military duty. From 1940 to 1944 close to 60 000 NRMA soldiers ("zombies") volunteered for general service, and several thousand more were sent to the front after the use of conscripts for overseas service actually began late in 1944. N.F. DREISIGER

National Transcontinental Railway was a government-built railway from Winnipeg, via Sioux Lookout, Kapuskasing, Cochrane and Québec City, to Moncton. In Oct 1903 the government of Wilfrid Laurier committed itself to the construction of a third transcontinental railway, despite the existence of the CANADIAN PACIFIC RY and CANADIAN NORTHERN RY. Its purpose was to provide western Canada with direct rail connection to Canadian Atlantic ports, and to open up and develop the northern frontiers of Ontario and Québec. The government came to an arrangement with the GRAND TRUNK RY whereby its totally owned subsidiary, the Grand Trunk Pacific Ry Co, would build the western section (Winnipeg to the Pacific), while the government itself would build the eastern section (Winnipeg to Moncton) and eventually turn it over to the GTPR for operation.

Construction, administered by 4 government-appointed commissioners, significantly exceeded estimates, but the last spike was driven on 17 Nov 1913, completing the eastern section except for the QUÉBEC BRIDGE. The NTR was never incorporated and the financial problems of the GTPR prevented it from taking over the NTR as agreed. It remained under government management until 1918 when operations were entrusted to the recently nationalized Canadian Northern Railway. In 1923 it became a part of the Canadian National Railways. T.D. REGEHR

Reading: A.W. Currie, *The Grand Trunk Railway of Canada* (1957); G.R. Stevens, *Canadian National Railways,* Vol 2 (1962).

National War Labour Board, est 1941 with 5 regional boards to enforce the Canadian government's program of wage stabilization in the volatile wartime economy. The first chairman was Humphrey MITCHELL, later also minister of labour. In early 1943, strong pressures created by a steel strike and worker agitation led to his replacement by Justice C.P. McTague. McTague had broad powers to deal with labour militancy and, unlike Mitchell, he was not identified with partisan politics. PM Mackenzie King instructed him to recommend modifications to the Wage Stabilization Order and to draft a labour-relations code. McTague and his colleague on the board, lawyer Joseph Cohen, had strong personal and political disagreements that resulted in separate reports being presented in Aug 1943. Cohen was dismissed, but McTague's report considerably affected government policy. McTague recommended that the board should have the authority to adjust wages that had been held down unfairly by the government and that family allowances might be considered as an alternative policy if it appeared that wage adjustment would be inflationary. The government eventually adopted both recommendations. McTague's wartime labour code took form on 17 Feb 1944. It defined the right of labour to organize and established a system for defining and certifying bargaining units. It formed the basis for the postwar Canadian system of LABOUR RELATIONS. The board's authority declined soon afterwards, when McTague resigned to become a Conservative candidate. JOHN ENGLISH

Nationalism is the doctrine or practice of promoting the collective interests of the national community or STATE above those of individuals, regions, special interests or other nations. In the arts, nationalism is the expression of, or the appeal for, distinctive national styles. Although its historic origins are diverse, in its modern forms nationalism is a product of the late 18th and 19th centuries, particularly of the American and French revolutions and the unification movements in Germany and Italy. Emulating the European and American models, national movements of self-determination and liberation have, over the past 200 years, transformed nationalism into a worldwide political and cultural phenomenon. In the first 25 years after WWII, 66 new nations were created.

In Europe nationalist thought has contained a central (though often merely implicit) notion of racial superiority which has frequently been expressed in the display and use of military force. In contrast, US nationalism blossomed from the romantic conception of a free people joined together under God to create a new and perfect union, free forever from European sins and weaknesses. Nationalism does not necessarily have a particular ideological slant, but varies from right to left on the political spectrum; its flavour and content depend upon the historical circumstances.

Canada came to consciousness in a period when world war had undermined European power and discredited European nationalism and when the national power and influence of the US had spread throughout the world. In the Western world, the 2 wars, which were widely attributed to the excesses of nationalism, have contributed (along with liberal and Marxist historical thought) to strong antinationalist and internationalist reactions. Since 1945, Canadians have been divided about the Canadian variety of nationalism. Their federal governments, reflecting this confusion, have varied from the antinationalist to the nationalist — with incongruous results. The postwar prime minister most committed in rhetoric to the defence of national interests, John DIEFENBAKER, was probably the least effective in that defence; the PM most ardently opposed in principle to nationalism, Pierre Elliott TRUDEAU, zealously defended a nationalist ENERGY POLICY.

National sentiment developed slowly after confederation, reflecting the strengths of provincialism and, in English-speaking Canada, the overriding sense of membership in the British Empire. There were glimmerings of nationalism in the CANADA FIRST movement of the 1870s and among writers of the 1890s. By 1911 Canada's nationalist dilemmas were becoming evident when the Laurier government was defeated over its modestly independent naval policy and a scheme of reciprocity with the United States, through a combination of anti- and pro-imperialist and anti-American opponents.

The country's participation in WWI did most to create a sense of distinct nationhood. The aftermath of WWI brought a surge of cultural nationalism, centered in Toronto and reflected in the painting of the GROUP OF SEVEN, in the founding of the CANADIAN FORUM, and the literary commentary of William Arthur DEACON in SATURDAY NIGHT magazine. Political nationalism, under the guidance of the Liberal government of W.L. Mackenzie KING, was directed against the fading symbols of colonial ties with Great Britain. This anticolonial nationalism met no resistance from Great Britain, but it conflicted with the attachment many English-speaking Canadians felt for British symbols, an attachment most persistently expressed politically through the CONSERVATIVE PARTY. WWII thrust Canada, willy-nilly, into close military and economic integration with the US, which seriously undermined the possibility of independent Canadian nationhood. By 1945 the federal Liberal government and its influential senior civil service were inclined to believe that the country had passed beyond the era of nationalism into internationalism (in diplomacy) and CONTINENTALISM (in economic and cultural relations with the US), a condition considered blessed. In his last years of power, however, King sometimes brooded about the dangers of this absorption, and dreamed of independence. But, after the spring of 1946, COLD WAR hysteria caused King, as well as most Canadian politicians and their followers, to suppress such ideas.

Canadian national consciousness and the articulation of national interests were unexpectedly placed in suspension for a decade. English-speaking Canada was absorbed in economic development and Québec remained enveloped in its past. A vast and generally comfortable cultural and economic invasion from the south took place with the country's tacit consent. Only very tentative nationalist alarms could be sounded in this atmosphere of approval. The first of these in the postwar period was the Report of the Massey Royal Commission on NATIONAL DEVELOPMENT IN THE ARTS, LETTERS AND SCIENCES (1951). It noted that the Canadian community faced not only dispersal in a vast landscape, but "influences from across the border as pervasive as they are friendly." In education, book publishing, magazine publishing, filmmaking, and radio the commission surveyed the American influences on Canadian life and warned of "the very present danger of permanent dependence." Its nationalist program for containing the cultural challenge was increasingly accepted by the Liberal government of the early 1950s, while the same government maintained its indifference to any measures of ECONOMIC NATIONALISM. The Gordon Royal Commission on CANADA'S ECONOMIC PROSPECTS warned in 1956 of the potential dangers of economic subordination to the US and offered a mildly nationalist program of countermeasures. It was ignored by the ST. LAURENT administration. In view of the growth of direct US investment in Canada (*see* FOREIGN INVESTMENT), and Liberal encouragement of it, both the Conservative and CO-OPERATIVE COMMONWEALTH FEDERATION (CCF) opposition parties spoke in nationalist tones before the 1957 general election that brought the Conservatives to power. But in 6 years the Diefenbaker government could not work out a coherent cultural or economic program and continued, in practice, to promote economic and military integration with the US, while at the same time antagonizing the US administration with its defiant manner.

The Conservative defeat of 1963 brought a reformed Liberal Party to power under Lester B. PEARSON. In the beginning the Pearson government was dominated by the nationalist economic views of the minister of finance, Walter GORDON, a dissenting and atypical member of the Toronto business establishment. Gordon's program for gentle patriation of the economy suffered setbacks in Parliament and in party caucus almost immediately, but measures to limit foreign ownership of newspapers, magazines, radio and television were adopted in 1965, and the CANADA DEVELOPMENT CORPORATION was eventually established. After 1965 the Pearson government retreated into quietism and came to terms with the opponents of nationalist policy in the business community. The Report of the Watkins Task Force on FOREIGN OWNERSHIP AND THE STRUCTURE OF CANADIAN INDUSTRY (1968) was officially ignored, as had been the Gordon Report. The government's renewed antinationalism was reinforced by the accession in 1968 of Pierre Trudeau, whose dogmatic opposition to nationalism was the product of his experiences in Québec under DUPLESSIS and his interpretation of European history.

The relative failure of Canadian nationalist policies in the 1960s and the evidence of overwhelming American influence in Canada stimulated the growth of a variety of popular nationalist organizations and activities in English-speaking Canada from 1968 onwards. The COMMITTEE FOR AN INDEPENDENT CANADA, led by Walter Gordon, Abraham Rotstein, Mel Hurtig, Peter NEWMAN and others, lobbied during the 1970s for a range of nationalist policies. The WAFFLE group sought to stiffen the nationalist backbone of the NEW DEMOCRATIC PARTY but was eventually defeated and dispersed. The Public Petroleum Association incorporated nationalists from both movements in its campaign for repatriation of the oil industry. A select committee of the Ontario legislature on economic and cultural nationalism, a national commission on Canadian Studies at the university level led by T.H.B. Symons, and various commissions on national identity in the media were active in the early 1970s. During its MINORITY GOVERNMENT 1972-74, the federal Liberal government conceded to evidence of increasing popular support for nationalist policies by creating the FOREIGN INVESTMENT REVIEW AGENCY and PETRO-CANADA, although both organizations lacked any clear direction from the Cabinet during their early years.

The nationalist movement in English-speaking Canada was weakened in the 1970s by an unreconciled division over attitudes to Québec nationalism. One element, while sympathetic to the cultural and linguistic aspirations of the Québecois, regarded Québec nationalism as a subversive force threatening the integrity of Canada. Another element saw it, on the contrary, as a potential complement to Canadian nationalism, to be emulated by English-speaking Canadians. The division has lasted into the 1980s, when both Québec and Canadian nationalism seem to have lost their popular momentum. Following the Liberal Party's defeat in 1979, the Conservatives under Joe CLARK adopted a generally antinationalist stance favouring appeasement of MULTINATIONAL CORPORATIONS and the provinces, but the stance was uncertain and was incoherently applied in policy. The government's early parliamentary defeat precipitated the election campaign of 1980, during which Trudeau and Marc LALONDE, in response to what they perceived as the forces of national disintegration in Québec and the West, adopted strong nationalist-centralist attitudes that led, on their return to power, to a drive for unilateral patriation of the Constitution and to the NATIONAL ENERGY PROGRAM of Nov 1980. This new Trudeau nationalism was blunt and heavy-handed, aimed at undercutting the growing power of the provinces rather than promoting national objectives for their own sake. It promoted strong responses from the provinces and from international business, who were able to appeal both to an unusual Canadian sense of fair play and to strong latent distaste for the prime minister's style. In the face of this opposition, the government's constitutional policy was adjusted to meet some provincial objections (though not those of Québec); and the energy policy was modified.

In the fall of 1982 the FEDERAL CULTURAL POLICY REVIEW COMMITTEE (Applebaum-Hébert) completed the first comprehensive survey of federal cultural policy since Massey's 1951 Royal Commission Report on Arts, Letters and Sciences. This review lacked the clear national vision and impact of the Massey Report. While it reflected the vastly expanded range of Canadian cultural enterprise in the intervening years, and contained over 100 policy recommendations, its proposals for retrenchment in the NATIONAL FILM BOARD and the CBC gave the Canadian cultural community confusing signals about national policy.

The Progressive Conservative government of Brian MULRONEY, elected in September 1984, adopted a policy of general reconciliation with the US which led to comprehensive FREE TRADE negotiations in 1986 and 1987, and a series of Canadian capitulations to American interests. Its persistence in an antinationalist approach to the US was unprecedented, and prompted the revival of a nationalist opposition (*see*, eg, COUNCIL OF CANADIANS).

Since 1945 the provinces, with only occasional exceptions (particularly Saskatchewan under the NDP's Allan BLAKENEY from 1971-82), have followed open-door economic policies in competitive pursuit of foreign investment, regarding Ottawa's intermittent ventures into economic nationalism as misguided or worse. In the 1970s, however, the resource-rich provinces at last began to retrieve substantial shares of the economic rents formerly lost to the multinationals, but they typically did so in the name of provincial rather than national interests.

Canadian interests and the expression of national sensibility have been relegated to the margins of Canadian public life because of the overwhelming influences of American business and American culture in Canada and of the pressures of provincialism. Policies of national self-protection accepted as normal and uncontroversial in other industrial countries have been regarded with widespread alarm and disapproval in Canada. Efforts to sustain the Canadian arts have always been faced with the mass-marketing advantages of American competitors, whose products spill over the border, and with the dispiriting effects of rapid changes in technology that frequently render regulation obsolete. Nationalism in Canada, under the persistent barrages of the provincial governments, the business community, and the American private lobbies, administrations and media, has remained defensive and apologetic, rarely aggressive and never expansionist. It has become tenacious, but it remains the precarious nationalism of a diverse community that is still only dimly aware of itself, existing always in the American shadow and beset by doubt. *See also* FRENCH CANADIAN NATIONALISM; ECONOMIC NATIONALISM; REGIONALISM.   DENIS SMITH

Reading: D. Cameron, *Nationalism, Self-Determination and The Quebec Question* (1974); W.L. Gordon, *A Choice For Canada* (1966); G. Grant, *Lament For A Nation* (1965); L. LaPierre, *If You Love This Country* (1987); K. Levitt, *Silent Surrender* (1970); Denis Smith, *Gentle Patriot* (1973).

Nationalist League, fd in Montréal 1 Mar 1903, during renewed British IMPERIALISM, increased anglophone aggressiveness towards Francophones and growing Canadian INDUSTRIALIZATION. Comprising a few largely unknown journalists and lawyers, including Olivar Asselin (president), Omer Héroux (secretary) and Armand Lavergne, the league sought to spread the nationalist views of its indisputable mentor, Henri BOURASSA. Its program focused on achieving a purely Canadian NATIONALISM and was based on 3 points: autonomy of Canada in the British Empire and the provinces in Confederation; respect for Canadian duality; and establishment of uniquely Canadian economic and cultural policies. The league had no clearly defined structure and had few members. After a promising beginning, when it launched the weekly *Le Nationaliste* and organized public meetings featuring Bourassa, it almost disappeared in 1906.

The league then inspired the "nationalist movement." The nationalists were stubbornly doctrinal, tireless opponents of the governments in power and fervent participants in Québec electoral politics. But because it was poorly organized, elitist and too closely associated with Bourassa, the "nationalist movement" gradually declined after the 1912 provincial election without having attained its major objectives. *See also* FRENCH CANADIAN NATIONALISM.   RÉAL BÉLANGER

Nationalization, the takeover of ownership and control of a privately owned enterprise by the STATE. States have traditionally taken private property for public purposes, eg, land for construction of roads; but this "right of eminent domain" is in contrast to nationalization, which is often carried out in pursuit of economic, social or political policies, eg, to increase Canadian ownership in the petroleum industry through the takeover of foreign oil companies by the federal crown corporation PETRO-CANADA. Whether it is justified for pragmatic reasons, eg, the provision of an essential service, or for broader collectivist goals, such as ECONOMIC NATIONALISM, nationalization infringes on the liberal tenets of the security of property and reliance on the market. The state uses or threatens to use its power to obtain property either by expropriation, with or without compensation, or by acquiring property in a sale by using pressure and excluding other purchasers. Although compensation may be prompt and fair, the threat of coercion may reduce the value of property, and the state always claims to be the final arbiter.

When a state nationalizes the holdings of foreign investors, the position of Western industrialized countries (especially the US) is that nationalization is only justified after prompt and adequate compensation, determined by an impartial authority. However, developing countries, in which there is often great resentment of foreign control, argue that states have perpetual sovereignty over their own resources and have the right to nationalize in order to further economic self-determination and economic development. They claim that nationalization and compensation are subject only to the laws of the nationalizing country – a position embodied in resolutions of the UN General Assembly, including Resolution 1803 of Dec 1962. Nonetheless, nationalization is usually accompanied by compensation in recognition of fairness and of the need to maintain the confidence of foreign investors.

Although Canada generally supports the ideology of free enterprise, the concern about extent of foreign ownership and control of Canadian resources prompted nationalizations during the 1970s, particularly by NEW DEMOCRATIC PARTY governments in BC, which between 1972 and 1974 nationalized a number of firms in the forest-products industry; and the NDP government in Saskatchewan which in 1975 announced that it would nationalize at least 50% of the potash industry. Throughout the decade, the federal Liberal government proposed "Canadianization" of the oil industry, a policy which culminated in the NATIONAL ENERGY PROGRAM of 1980. Canadianization does not necessarily mean nationalization, since it includes the purchase of foreign firms by private Canadian companies. Moreover, state control was achieved by purchase, involving little coercion. Nonetheless, critics claimed that government measures distorted market values and resulted in inappropriate compensation.

The spate of nationalizations and a general reaction against the increasing role of the state in the economy resulted in a countermovement to reduce government involvement and to denationalize or "privatize" government enterprises. The movement to return operations, especially commercial functions, to the private sector found its fullest expression in the United Kingdom where the Conservative government of Margaret Thatcher has conducted an ambitious privatization program since 1979.

In Canada, the privatization of the BC Resources Investment Corp by the BC Social Credit government attracted considerable attention. Privatization initiatives continued at the provincial level, most dramatically in British Columbia in 1987 when the Social Credit government under William VANDER ZALM announced a broad program to transfer functions from the government to the private sector.

Federally, privatization was espoused by the short-lived Progressive Conservative government of Joe CLARK, but its commitment to privatize Petro-Canada contributed to its defeat in 1980. However, the election in 1984 of a new Progressive Conservative government under Brian MULRONEY marked a return of the objective of privatization. The government established a privatization secretariat to select companies for and to carry out privatization, either by sale of the company to an existing private-sector entity, or by general sale of shares to the public. Between 1984 and 1988 a number of crown entities were privatized, including Canadian Arsenals Limited, CANADAIR, DE HAVILLAND, and Teleglobe Canada.   J. DONNER

Native Council of Canada Up to the 1950s, MÉTIS interests were represented by a variety of local political organizations and activists (*see* Louis RIEL; Gabriel DUMONT; James BRADY; Malcolm NORRIS). In 1961 the National Indian Council was founded as an umbrella group for Métis and Indian concerns. When these 2 groups proved politically incompatible, the Council split in 1968 to form the Canadian Métis Society (since 1970 the Native Council of Canada) to represent Métis and nonstatus interests and the National Indian Brotherhood (now ASSEMBLY OF FIRST NATIONS) to represent status Indians. The NCC is composed of provincial and territorial organizations, usually called native councils or Métis and nonstatus Indian associations. The NCC holds an annual assembly at which member organizations are represented, and is governed by a board of directors, consisting of presidents of the member associations, and an executive elected by the assembly. It is funded almost entirely by the federal government's Native Citizens' Directorate. The Constitutional Review Commission also receives federal funds to participate in the FIRST MINISTERS CONFERENCES on ABORIGINAL RIGHTS.

The number of persons represented by the NCC has been a matter of controversy. The NCC asserts there are one million Métis and nonstatus persons, but Statistics Canada data from the 1981 census gives much lower figures and the 1986 data is not yet available. The 1985 changes in the Indian Act restored Indian status to many women and their children as well as to enfranchised veterans. The decrease in the number of nonstatus Indians will not necessarily reduce membership in the NCC which has tended to organize around urban locals. Many of the people whose status was restored through the 1985 amendments may not gain effective access to reserve lands, while others will continue to live in the city for their own reasons. The long-run effect of the 1985 amendments will likely focus on the needs of the rapidly growing native population in most urban areas across Canada.

NCC policy operates around the premise of Métis nationalism within the Canadian context and the deeply felt sense of Indianness among the nonrecognized native people. It asserts that these groups have the right to define themselves historically and culturally, and to improve their position in modern Canadian society. NCC rests its demands on aboriginal rights (as mentioned in the Constitution) as well as on needs, and seeks a special relationship for Métis and nonstatus Indi-

ans with the federal government. *See also* NATIVE PEOPLE, POLITICAL ORGANIZATION AND ACTIVISM.   MICHAEL POSLUNS

Native-French Relations Breton and Norman fishermen came into contact with the Algonkian peoples of the northeast at the beginning of the 16th century, if not earlier, as they put into natural harbours and bays to seek shelter from storms and to replenish water and food supplies. There is some indication that these first contacts with native inhabitants were not always friendly. A few individuals were kidnapped and taken to France to be paraded at the court and in public on state and religious occasions. Also, precautions seem to have been taken to hide the women inland when parties landed from ships engaged in cod fishing or walrus hunting. On the other hand, there were also mutually satisfactory encounters as barter took place. The natives brought furs and hides in exchange for beads, mirrors, little bells and trinkets of aesthetic and perhaps spiritual value. Both sides seemed content with this growing exchange. Soon the natives exacted goods of more materialistic value, eg, needles, knives, kettles, woven cloth, while the French displayed an insatiable desire for well-worn beaver cloaks.

In the 16th century, the French, like their western European neighbours, proceeded to lay claim to lands "not possessed by any other Christian prince" on the theory that these were uninhabited, or at least uncultivated, and needed to be brought under Christian dominion. The royal commission to ROBERVAL for the St Lawrence region, dated 15 Jan 1541, and LA ROCHE's commission for Sable I in 1598 enjoined acquisition either by voluntary cession or conquest.

By the early 17th century, as the FUR TRADE expanded and Catholic missionary work was seriously contemplated, a policy of pacification emerged. The fact that the French chose to colonize along the Bay of Fundy marshlands and the St Lawrence Valley, from which the original Laurentian Iroquois had disappeared by 1580, meant that no native peoples were displaced to make way for colonists. This peaceful cohabitation remained characteristic of relations up to the fall of ACADIA (1710) and of NEW FRANCE (1760). Beyond the Acadian farmlands and the Laurentian seigneurial tract the native peoples on their ancestral lands continued to be fully independent, following their traditional life-style and customs. Royal instructions to Gov Courcelles in 1665 had emphasized that "the officers, soldiers and all His Majesty's adult subjects treat the Indians with kindness, justice and equity, without ever causing them any hurt or violence." Furthermore, it was ordered that no one was to "take the lands on which they are living under pretext that it would be better and more suitable if they were French."

Royal instructions in 1716 not only required peaceful relations with the native peoples in the interests of trade and missions but also forbade the French from clearing land and settling west of the Montréal region seigneuries. In the PAYS D'EN HAUT care was taken to obtain permission from the natives before establishing a trading post, fort, mission station or small agricultural community such as Detroit or in the Illinois country. Following a conference with 80 Iroquois delegates at Québec in the autumn of 1748, Gov La Galissonière and Intendant Bigot reaffirmed that "these Indians claim to be and in effect are independent of all nations, and their lands incontestably belong to them." Nevertheless, France continued to assert its sovereignty and to speak for the "allied nations" at the international level. This sovereignty was exercised against European rivals through the allied "nations," not at their expense through the suppression of local customs and independence. The native peoples accepted this protectorate because it offered them external support while permitting them to govern themselves and pursue their traditional ways. The Micmac, and later the Abenaki, accepted the Catholic religion, even in the absence of large-scale sustained evangelization, as a confirmation of their alliance and brotherhood with the French and resistance to Anglo-American incursions. When the Micmac eventually were forced to sign a treaty of peace and friendship with the British authorities at Halifax in 1752, the Abenaki who had taken refuge in Canada rebuffed the official delegate of the governor at Boston.

Beginning their apostolic labours in Acadia in 1611 and in Canada in 1615, Catholic MISSIONARIES dreamed of a rapid conversion of native peoples and even wondered if they might not be descendants of the Ten Lost Tribes of Israel. Traditional Micmac and Montagnais hospitality dictated that the itinerant missionaries be well received. Soon evangelization efforts were centered on the sedentary, horticultural and strategically located HURON confederacy (*see* STE MARIE AMONG THE HURONS). But factionalism arising out of favouritism shown to converts and the EPIDEMICS which decimated the population almost brought the mission to a close. On two occasions the Jesuits were spared execution or exile on charges of witchcraft only by French threats to cut off the trade on which the Huron had become dependent. Following the dispersal of the Huron in 1648-49, the missionaries turned to other groups in the Great Lakes basin, including the IROQUOIS confederacy, but they never enjoyed great success. Most natives assumed a tolerant dualism: "you can have your ways and we will have ours for every one values his own wares."

More success was achieved on the *réductions*, or reserves as they came to be known, established within the seigneurial tract of New France. In 1637 the seigneury of Sillery near Québec was designated a *réduction* for some Montagnais encamped nearby as well as all nomadic northern hunters who would take up agriculture under Jesuit tutelage. Although the Montagnais did not remain long, some Abenaki refugees came to settle, and finally Huron who escaped from the Iroquois conquest of their country. Eventually there were reserves near each of the 3 French bridgeheads of settlement: Lorette near Québec for the Huron; Bécancour and Saint-François near Trois-Rivières for the Abenaki; Kahnawaké near Montréal for the Iroquois and Lac-des-Deux-Montagnes for both Algonquins and Iroquois. These reserves were relocated from time to time at ever greater distances from the principal towns not only because of soil exhaustion but also because of the desire of the missionaries to isolate the native converts from the temptations of alcohol, prostitution and gambling. The Kahnawaké reserve, with the connivance of certain Montréal merchants, became an important link in an illicit trade with Albany and New York. Those who came to live on reserves were motivated by religious ideals and the need to escape persecution or encroachment on their lands, but in time the economic advantages to be reaped were not inconsiderable. It was often on the reserves that canoemen, scouts and warriors were recruited for trade and war. The products of the field and the hunt, as well as the manufacture of canoes, snowshoes and moccasins found a good outlet on the Québec market.

Official French objectives had been to christianize and *francisize* the natives in order to attain the utopian ideal of "one people." The church through itinerant missions, education of a native élite in France, reserves and boarding schools

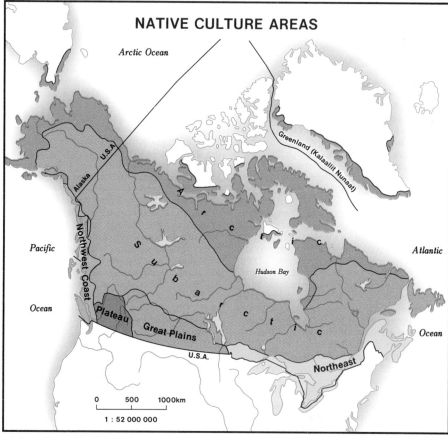

NATIVE CULTURE AREAS

Arctic Ocean

Greenland (Kalaallit Nunaat)

U.S.A.

Alaska

Northwest Coast

Pacific

Ocean

A r c t i c

S u b a r c t i c

Hudson Bay

Atlantic

Plateau

Great Plains

U.S.A.

Northeast

Ocean

0   500   1000km

1 : 52 000 000

tried to achieve this objective but in the end it was clear that the natives would not abandon their culture, even when converted. It was the missionaries who, like the fur traders, learned the native languages and adopted native survival techniques.

Racial intermarriage, or *métissage*, traced its origin to the casual encounters, almost exclusively between native women and Frenchmen deprived of European spouses, beginning with the fishermen and sailors along the Atlantic seaboard, and spreading into the hinterland as traders and interpreters, later unlicensed COUREURS DE BOIS, and finally garrison troops came into contact with the interior tribes. VOYAGEURS and canoemen travelling to and from the upper country of Canada in the interests of the fur trade acquired the services of native women to make and break camp, cook, carry baggage and serve as mistresses. Many of these unions became longlasting and were recognized locally as legitimate *à la façon du pays*. Canon law forbade the marriage of Catholics with pagans, so missionaries often had to instruct and baptize adults and children and then regularize such unions. In 1735 Louis XV forbade most mixed marriages; nevertheless the rise of MÉTIS communities in the Great Lakes basin, particularly along Lake Superior, indicated the prevalence of the practice.

Warfare was an aspect of native life in which the French soon became involved. Most of the tribes remained steadfastly attached to and loyal to France through to PONTIAC's rising in 1763, with the exception of the Iroquois, Fox and Sioux. Champlain, by supporting his Algonkian and Huron trading partners in 1609, earned the long-lasting enmity of the Iroquois. The French were unable to save the Huron from destruction at their hands in 1648-49, nor were they able to stop Iroquois incursions into their own or their western allies' territories until the peace of Montréal, 1701 (*see* IROQUOIS WARS). The Fox became hostile in 1712 and were the objects of several

military expeditions before their dispersal in 1730. The Sioux also often attacked France's trading partners and allies before agreeing to a general peace settlement in 1754. Canadian militiamen and native auxiliaries distinguished themselves also in expeditions to aid Louisiana against the Chickasaws and the Natchez.

France spent large sums of money for the annual distribution of the "King's presents" to the allied nations. In addition, the Crown issued clothing, weapons and ammunition to native auxiliaries, paid for their services, and maintained their families when the men were on active duty. The natives were judged invaluable for guiding, scouting and surprise raiding parties. Their war aims and practices, including scalping and platform torture, were not interfered with as they generally fought alongside the French as independent auxiliaries. In defeat, the French remembered them, obtaining in the terms of capitulation (1760) that they be treated as soldiers under arms, that they "be maintained in the Lands they inhabit," and that they enjoy freedom of religion and keep their missionaries. *See also* NATIVE WHITE RELATIONS.   CORNELIUS J. JAENEN

Native People The native peoples of Canada are considered under 6 subheadings: Arctic, Eastern Woodlands, Northwest Coast, Plains, Plateau and Subarctic. Cross references are provided to entries on tribal groups and to thematic articles on native peoples.

Arctic

Territory and Natural Environment The INUIT have enjoyed almost exclusive occupation of the Canadian Arctic, those inland and coastal areas N of the TREELINE. In areas close to the treeline, Inuit and Indians have traditionally occupied similar environments (though rarely at the same time) and have hunted and fished similar game species. The arctic regions are characterized by long daylight hours in summer, with moderate temperatures.

Etching (c 1824) of a group of Inuit by Capt G.F. Lyon. Inuit skilfully made clothing and footwear from animal skins. The parka usually consisted of an inner and outer jacket of caribou fur, and the footwear was of sealskin (*courtesy National Archives of Canada/C-25703*).

Winters are long and cold, and at more northerly locations there is a midwinter period when the sun is entirely absent. Plant cover may be continuous, especially in well-watered locations, although rocky outcrops and barren dry areas are common. Trees are entirely lacking in the Arctic, though low shrubby plants occur, including several varieties bearing edible berries. Landforms are variable, from lake-studded lowlands to glacier-strewn alpine areas.

Major Language and Tribal Groups There are 8 main Inuit tribal groups in Canada, the LABRADOR, UNGAVA, BAFFIN ISLAND, IGLULIK, CARIBOU, NETSILIK, COPPER and Western Arctic Inuit (*see* NATIVE PEOPLE, DEMOGRAPHY). The Western Arctic Inuit (or Inuvialuit) are recent immigrants, or their descendants, from Alaska, taking the place of the MACKENZIE INUIT, who were decimated by several smallpox and influenza EPIDEMICS at the turn of the century. The SADLERMIUT, in northwestern Hudson Bay, died out following contact early this century (*see* NATIVE PEOPLE, HEALTH).

All of the Canadian Inuit speak one language, Inuktitut or Eskimo-Aleut, though there are 6 different dialects (*see* NATIVE PEOPLE, LANGUAGES). However, because of improved travel opportunities and the development of Inuit-language radio and TV programming, language differences are diminishing (*see* COMMUNICATIONS IN THE NORTH; NATIVE PEOPLE, COMMUNICATIONS). Traditionally, there was no written language, but after contact with missionaries, writing systems were widely adopted. Since 1920 the adult literacy rate has been almost 100%.

Historical Summary The first sustained contact with outsiders occurred between Moravian missionaries and Labrador Inuit in the late 18th century. Fleeting trade contacts were established at a few other locations in the Arctic, but most contact occurred nearly a century later. During the latter half of the 19th century, explorers and commercial whalers introduced various trade items to the Inuit, though it was only following the end of commercial whaling, at the time of WWI, that trading posts became more or less permanently established in the arctic regions. Mission stations and police posts were also established during this period. Following WWII there was an intensification of government activity, including the establishment of schools, nursing stations, airports and communication installations, and housing programs in the newly established settlements and hamlets.

Traditional Culture Inuit tribal groups in traditional times contained 500-1000 members. The most important social and political unit was the regional BAND, several of which together constituted the larger tribal group within which marriages occurred and all members spoke a similar

dialect. Regional bands would congregate for short periods, customarily during the winter months, when people would gather in sealing camps. During the rest of the year, they lived in smaller bands, often composed of 2 to 5 families. Each household generally consisted of a married couple and their children, though elderly or unmarried relatives might also be present. Many economic and social activities involved interhousehold co-operation, and widespread sharing was, and still is, a predominant characteristic of Inuit social life. Most families who chose to live together were closely related, with leadership of the group generally assumed by the oldest active male member.

Marriage was nearly universal among Inuit and customarily took place in early adulthood; it was usual for the young couple to reside close to the parents of one or the other spouse. Many households included adopted children, an indication of the high value accorded children. Children were an important means of establishing valued interfamily relationships through adoption, betrothal, adult-child relationships established at birthing ceremonies, and naming practices. The family was an important economic unit, relying on a decided division of responsibilities among all household members, including children and elderly relatives.

Most Inuit groups based their economy on sea-mammal hunting. In summer and fall many groups hunted caribou or moved to favoured coastal locations to hunt and fish a variety of game species. Fishing and food gathering (for bird eggs, shellfish and berries) were important seasonal activities, as were hunts for polar bear and whale. Though high value was placed on fresh food, quantities were also stored for future use. Drying, and caching in cool areas, were common techniques, although several special techniques (such as storing in oil) were also used.

The traditional technology was based on locally available materials, principally bone, horn, antler, ivory, stone and animal skins. In some areas grass or baleen was used for basketry, wood substituted for bone, native copper for antler or bone, and bird or fish skins for animal skins. Use was made of special parts of animals, eg, sinew, intestine and bladders. The improvising abilities of Inuit are well known today, and

Inuit with traditional summer dwelling and kayak at Peel River, NWT, 1901 (*courtesy National Archives of Canada/PA-124050/C.W. Mathers Coll*).

Coronation Gulf eskimo putting sinew backing on bow (*courtesy Department Library Services, American Museum of Natural History*).

many Inuit inventions are considered technological masterpieces. The domed snowhouse (IGLOO), the toggling harpoon head and the KAYAK are noteworthy examples. There was an understandable relationship between location of settlements and seasonably available food resources. The composition of settlements might change periodically in response to social needs and desires to interact with kinsmen residing elsewhere. Many hunting methods became more effective when several hunters worked co-operatively, eg, during winter seal hunting.

Sleds and skin-covered boats were universally employed by Inuit, though regional variations in both design and use were common. Dogs historically served as hunting animals and were used to locate seals under the sea ice or to hold bears or muskoxen at bay. They were also used as pack animals in the summer. Men used single-seat kayaks for hunting sea mammals and for hunting caribou in rivers and lakes. In Alaska, large skin-covered UMIAKS were used for whale hunting, although in the Canadian Arctic (and Greenland) such boats were more usually used by women to transport households from place to place.

The skin tent, often with a short ridgepole, was generally made from dehaired sealskins and weighted down along the ground with rocks. Among the Caribou Inuit, the tent was often conical in shape, and constructed from dehaired caribou skins. Tents were used when suitable snow was not available for snowhouses, or when away from the sites of sod and stone-walled houses.

Snowhouse design was variable. At winter settlements the main living chamber could be quite large, perhaps 4 m in diameter and almost 3 m high. In addition, there were chambers for storage and an entrance passage, and often extra living chambers attached to the side. In some regions it was customary to line the walls with caribou skins for insulation. Most snowhouses had a snow sleeping platform and a window (made from clear lake ice) set into the roof (*see* HOUSE). Smaller, less elaborate snowhouses are still commonly used during winter travelling. In the western Arctic, where driftwood logs occur, permanent dwellings were constructed for winter use. Windows in this case were made from translucent animal-skin parchment.

Inuit skilfully manufactured footwear and clothing from locally obtained and prepared animal skins. Even though parkas, gloves and boots followed a similar basic design, regional variations in pattern and technique persisted. For most Inuit groups, footwear was made from the skin of 2 different species of seal, either haired (for winter use) or hairless (for spring and summer use); the latter were entirely waterproof. In some areas caribou skin replaced sealskin, especially for winter boots. The parka traditionally consisted of an inner and outer jacket, usually of caribou fur. Among some groups, sealskin parkas were commonly worn in spring through autumn, and caribou fur was preferred for winter clothing. Women's clothing was often more elaborate than men's, with a voluminous hood on the tailed and aproned parka. Infants were carried in a pouch against the woman's back, not in the hood. There was little bodily adornment, though women's facial tattooing was practised.

Birth was associated with several socially significant rituals. Among some groups, in addition to an attending midwife, there was another adult who served as the child's ritual sponsor, assuming responsibilities for the child's moral upbringing. Throughout life, special terms of address were used, and in the case of a boy, his first killed game animals, and in the case of a girl, her first sewn items, were presented to this adult. Naming occurred at birth and had special significance, as Inuit names included part of the identity and character of the name bearer. Betrothal of children could occur at any time, even before birth. Young people promised to each other used a special form of address, and their families related in ways appropriate to the future relationship. There were many rituals associated with hunting, although these are becoming less common. Animal bones or ceremonial bundles, and ceremonies involving self-induced trance, were used to foretell future events. Marriage, an exceptionally stable institution among Inuit, was customarily preceded by a period of trial marriage. Polygamy, and more rarely polyandry, also occurred, but were not common practices.

In the 20th century, Inuit have universally embraced CHRISTIANITY, and a large number of communities are now served by ordained Inuit clergy or trained catechists. Prior to missionary activity,

Indian Encampment on Lake Huron (c1845-50) by Paul Kane depicts the characteristic birchbark dwellings and canoes of the Ojibwa (*courtesy Art Gallery of Ontario*).

Inuit religious leaders were shamans who often underwent lengthy and arduous training. Shamans were intermediaries between the Inuit and the various spiritual forces that influenced human affairs. Inuit life in pre-Christian days required strict adherence to various prohibitions and rules of conduct, so that the role of the SHAMAN was usually to determine transgressors and to prescribe appropriate atonement (*see* NATIVE PEOPLE, RELIGION). Early missionary activity was similarly constituted, with many new rules and prohibitions introduced and penitence demanded after sinning.

Young Inuit were expected to learn by example, through close association with adults. Desire to be praised by respected elders and to attain social competence were strong incentives for young people to join adult society (*see* NATIVE PEOPLE, EDUCATION). Many of the values and beliefs of the society were demonstrated implicitly in behaviour; eg, the constant sharing of food and other commodities was a manifestation of the value of generosity and co-operation and a negation of stinginess, greediness or selfishness. Reinforcements of these lessons were contained in the stories that elders enjoyed telling, especially to children (*see* INUIT MYTH AND LEGEND).

The traditional musical instrument was the drum, up to 1 m in diameter, made by stretching a skin membrane across a wooden hoop. Among Western Arctic Inuit, several sitting drummers usually accompanied one or several dancers, whereas elsewhere in the Canadian Arctic drumming was an individual performance at which the drummer stood and chanted, swaying rhythmically with the drum beat. Following contact with outsiders, instruments such as concertinas, accordians, violins, harmonicas and, more recently, guitars became widespread. Square dancing, often in extended and intricate performances without a caller, was very popular. "Throat singing" occurred among some groups, usually performed by 2 women producing a wide range of sounds from deep in the throat and thorax.

Decorative arts were associated with skin sewing, or were inscribed on utensils. Recent innovations in INUIT ART, eg, soapstone carving, printmaking and wall hangings, stem from traditional skills, sometimes using new materials or

techniques. Skills in creating string figures, and other games that develop memory, manual dexterity and patience, continue to be practised.

Culture Change Since contact with outsiders, many changes in Inuit society and culture have occurred. The early adoption of iron tools, firearms, cloth and wooden boats altered or replaced certain material items. Adoption of Christianity has resulted in the loss of many traditional religious ideas and practices, and Canadian law has been superimposed on customary law in areas concerned with marriage, dispute settlement and game management (*see* NATIVE PEOPLE, LAW). Even the language has changed, with English words replacing numerals above 6 (though the Inuit words for 10 and 20 are still retained). However, many material items cannot be satisfactorily replaced; among these are harpoons used in marine mammal hunting, sealskin boots and caribou parkas required for winter hunting, snowhouses and sleds used in winter travelling, and the techniques of preparing animal skins and sewing skin clothing. Important elements of the value system also resist change, including traditional child-rearing practices, concerns about environmental matters, the continued survival of the Inuit language and culture, and respect for individual autonomy (*see* INUIT CO-OPERATIVES).

In the early 1970s a national organization, the INUIT TAPIRISAT OF CANADA, was established to protect Inuit cultural and individual rights. The organization created several agencies in response to expressed needs. An Inuit Language Commission, for example, was formed to seek the best means of ensuring the increased use of Inuktitut for governmental, educational and communications purposes, and a Land Claims Office was established to research and negotiate Inuit LAND

Narwhal (*Monodon monoceros*), adult male. Payer Harbour, northwest Greenland c1902; photograph by Admiral Robert E. Peary (*courtesy Edward P. Stafford/National Geographic Society*).

Beaded hat (*courtesy Royal Ontario Museum*).

CLAIMS. Many of these issues, such as protection of the arctic environment, are international in scope. Therefore, an international Inuit organization, the Inuit Circumpolar Conference, was formed with committees seeking to strengthen pan-Inuit communication, cultural and artistic activities, and international co-operation in environmental protection. This organization has affiliation with numerous international bodies, including the United Nations, thereby ensuring that Inuit concerns become widely understood throughout the world.   MILTON M.R. FREEMAN

Eastern Woodlands

Territory and Natural Environment The Canadian Eastern Woodlands are part of a larger biotic region that extends SW to Illinois and E to coastal N Carolina. The deciduous forests of southern Ontario, the St Lawrence lowlands and coastal Atlantic provinces phase N into the mixed deciduous-coniferous canopy of the Canadian SHIELD in the W and the Appalachian uplands in the E.

Except in the Atlantic provinces, the Great Lakes-St Lawrence watershed provided access to water transportation to all Eastern Woodland peoples. Climate and soil conditions allowed peoples S of upland regions to grow corn, beans and SQUASH; by far the largest portion of their diet consisted of products of their extensive fields. The white-tailed deer was perhaps the most important game animal in Indian subsistence except in the N, where moose and caribou were found. Seals were hunted by some coastal peoples. Inland, freshwater fish, and along the seaboard eels, molluscs and crustaceans, were taken. Waterfowl and land birds were seasonally important in some areas. During the historic period, fur bearers, especially BEAVER, were significant to the Indian economy. A variety of berries, nuts, tubers and plants was collected, and some groups harvested maple and birch sap and WILD RICE.

Major Language and Tribal Groups Eastern Woodland Indians spoke languages belonging to 2 unrelated families, Iroquoian and Algonquian. At the onset of the historic period, Iroquoians occupied much of southern Ontario, northern Ohio, Pennsylvania and New York, and the St Lawrence Valley as far E as the Québec City area. Algonquian groups extended from Lk Superior N of Lk Huron to the Ottawa Valley, thence E through New England and the Atlantic provinces to the coast. Iroquoian peoples included Erie (S of Lake Erie), NEUTRAL (Grand R-Niagara R area), Wenro (E of Niagara R), Five Nations IROQUOIS – SENECA, CAYUGA, ONONDAGA, ONEIDA, MOHAWK (Genesee R to Mohawk R and N to the Adirondack Mts), HURON – 5 tribes (Georgian Bay to Lk Simcoe), PETUN – (SE of Georgian Bay) and St Lawrence Iroquoians (Montréal to Québec City). Algonquian peoples included OJIBWA (Lk Superior to northeastern Georgian Bay), OTTAWA (Manitoulin I and Bruce Pen), Nipissing (Lk Nipissing area), ALGONQUIN (Ottawa R and tributaries), ABENAKI (Vermont, NH, western Maine and southeastern Québec), MALISEET (St Lawrence Valley S to Bay of Fundy, eastern Maine and western NB) and MICMAC (southeast Gaspé Pen, eastern NB, PEI and NS).

The speakers of Iroquoian languages belong to 2 branches, a southern one composed of Cherokee, and a northern branch that includes all of the tribes noted above. The languages of the Canadian Iroquoians (the St Lawrence Iroquoians, the Huron, Petun and Neutral) are now all extinct, and the 6 Iroquoian languages spoken in Canada today (Mohawk, Oneida, Onondaga, Cayuga, Seneca, Tuscarora) were brought by groups of

immigrants (LOYALISTS) from New York state. Within the Canadian Eastern Woodlands there are 2 branches of the Algonquian family, Central Algonquian (Ojibwa, Ottawa, Nipissing and Algonquin) and Eastern Algonquian (Abenaki, Micmac and Maliseet). Languages within each branch show a high degree of mutual intelligibility, with the Central Algonquian forming dialect chains (*see* NATIVE PEOPLE, LANGUAGES).

Historical Summary Although the NORSE seem to have made sporadic visits to the eastern seaboard between the 10th and 14th centuries, major European influences were initiated by fishermen to the Grand Banks – who also began trading for furs in the early 16th century just prior to Jacques CARTIER's contacts with Micmac and St Lawrence Iroquois in 1534-35. During the late 16th century the FUR TRADE expanded to involve, either directly or indirectly, most Eastern Woodland peoples. During this period the St Lawrence Iroquoians deserted their longtime homelands and, although there is debate as to whether its origin is precontact or postcontact, the famed Iroquois Confederacy became prominent.

By the early 17th century there were European settlements on Sable I (temporary), at Tadoussac, briefly on the St Croix R in Maine, and at PORT-ROYAL in the Annapolis Valley. In 1609 Henry HUDSON explored the New England coast and the river named after him, while Samuel de CHAMPLAIN accompanied a MONTAGNAIS war party against the Mohawk near Lk Champlain, an event that marked the beginning of European participation in the almost continuous intertribal hostilities that lasted for a century. By 1624, when the Dutch established New Amsterdam [New York], fur bearers had been largely exterminated along the Atlantic coast. During the first half of the 17th century, European epidemics (*see* NATIVE PEOPLE, HEALTH) and warfare drastically reduced Indian populations, and subsistence cycles of hunter-gatherers were disrupted. Dependency relationships developed when a variety of European trade items replaced aboriginal ones, and new forms of territoriality and leadership emerged. In New England the Pequot War (1637) and King Philip's War (1675-76) led to population shifts clearing the way for European settlement. Some Abenaki moved to St Francis near the St Lawrence after about 1660. In the Great Lakes area, the Five Nations Iroquois intensified their attack on other Iroquoians and Algonquians during the 1640s and 1650s, forcing many peoples to flee from their homelands (*see* IROQUOIS WARS). Remnant groups of Huron, Petun, Neutral and Erie fled W and became known as Wyandot. One group of Huron settled at Lorette near Québec City. The Five Nations Iroquois, reduced by warfare and disease, replenished their numbers by adopting war captives and refugees. During the late 17th century, as Iroquois power began to wane, Ojibwa and Algonquin expanded into southern Ontario; their descendants occupy reserves there today. In 1722 the Iroquois accepted the Tuscarora, a northern Iroquoian-speaking people who had fled north from the Carolinas. Following this addition, the confederacy was often called the Six Nations, although the Tuscarora were never politically equal to the 5 founding nations.

Throughout the first half of the 18th century most Algonquians of the Eastern Woodlands supported the French and supplied them with furs in exchange for European commodities. Except for a group of Mohawk who had settled near Montréal, the majority of the Iroquois were allied with the British. At the time of the SEVEN YEARS' WAR and after the fall of NEW FRANCE to the British in 1759-60, Ottawa and Ojibwa, dis-

Maydoc-Gun-Kungee, an Ojibwa painted by artist Paul Kane (*courtesy Royal Ontario Museum*).

pleased with new policies, temporarily captured Detroit and Michilimackinac. Most Algonquians, however, supported the British cause during the AMERICAN REVOLUTION, but the struggle split the loyalties of the New York state Iroquois, many of whom subsequently moved to lands granted to them by the British in southern Ontario. Members of all the Six Nations Iroquois settled along the Grand R, and some Mohawk settled at the Bay of Quinte. Land cessions in New York, a growing dependency on whites, and general demoralization stimulated a revitalization movement in 1799 led by the Seneca prophet Handsome Lake. The new religion spread to other Iroquois communities in the US and Canada (*see* HANDSOME LAKE RELIGION). After the WAR OF 1812 some Ojibwa, Ottawa and Potawatomi moved from the US to the Georgian Bay area. A portion of the Oneida settled on the Thames R. During the first half of the 19th century, reserves were surveyed for Algonquians along Georgian Bay, the Robinson-Huron and Robinson-Superior treaties of 1850 enfranchising most Algonquians in Ontario. In the Atlantic provinces some 60 Micmac reserves were established (*see* INDIAN RESERVE; INDIAN TREATIES).

As white settlements throughout the Eastern Woodlands grew larger and more numerous, hunting and gathering by various Algonquians waned in importance. Small-scale horticulture, often the result of missionary influences, increasingly supplemented a diet which came to include store foods as well as locally obtained fish and game. Some Indians were employed by Euro-Canadians in such activities as lumbering, mining and the fur trade, or as part-time labourers.

On reserves, an elected system of chiefs and councillors replaced traditional political institutions, except among some Iroquois whose confederate chiefs filled political offices. At Six Nations the traditional system was formally replaced by an elected system in 1924, but the old confederate system often continued in opposition to the elected officers and the federal government that failed to recognize it.

By the 20th century the majority of Eastern Woodland Indians had adopted Christianity, albeit sometimes only nominally. Many Iroquois continued to practise the Longhouse religion of Handsome Lake. Dependency on government sources of economic support, owing to few employment opportunities or inadequate training,

Cradle board (*courtesy Royal Ontario Museum*).

resulted in poverty on most reserves not situated near large urban centres. Following the GREAT DEPRESSION of the 1930s, many Indians moved to urban centres in Canada and the US to work, and many more have since done so. Often they make frequent trips to the reserve and, when not employed or after retirement, return. After about 1960 new government-sponsored job programs on reserves and the revitalizaton of old arts and crafts lessened economic dependency. Health clinics and modern medical treatment have resulted in dramatic population growth so that many tribal groups are now numerically larger than at the time of contact (*see* NATIVE PEOPLE, DEMOGRAPHY). By 1986 there were 33 209 Iroquoians on 8 reserves in Canada, including 1890 Huron at Lorette. Some 12 459 Micmac are affiliated with 25 reserves in the Atlantic provinces and 1048 Abenaki with the St Francis reserve. The number of other Algonquians residing in the Canadian Eastern Woodlands is difficult to determine since not all are registered Indians associated with reserves. A figure of 50 000, however, seems reasonable.

Traditional Culture Iroquoian: All Iroquoians relied primarily on cultivated corn, beans and squash. Fishing, hunting and gathering supplemented domestic crops. Men cleared forest areas while women planted and harvested and made pottery. The Huron exchanged corn for fish and hides with Nipissing. Crop storage permitted sedentary and often palisaded settlements varying from small hamlets with a few families to towns where as many as 2500 persons resided. Population density was high, reaching a peak of perhaps 24 persons per km² (60 persons per sq mile) among the Huron. Although estimates vary, there may have been from 70 000 to 90 000 northern Iroquoians at contact.

A typical village contained a large number of elm- or cedar-bark longhouses. Each LONGHOUSE sheltered several related families. Residence in these households was matrilocal; ie, upon marriage a man would move into his wife's longhouse. As well, descent, inheritance and succession followed the female line. One or more households formed a matrilineage. Several lineages composed an exogamous clan designated by a particular totem emblem (crest). Tribes appear to have been composed of from 3 to 10 clans

whose members were scattered in several villages. Among some groups, clans were divided into 2 categories or moieties. Clan mates, regardless of village, and among the Five Nations even through tribal affiliation, considered themselves to be siblings.

Most Iroquoian peoples possessed both civil chiefs and war chiefs. The Five Nations Confederacy had a council of 50 permanent and hereditary offices which has survived in modified form to the present. Among the Five Nations, condolence ceremonies commemorate deceased confederacy chiefs, replace them and bestow on the successors the honorary names associated with the office. The Huron had a similar political system.

All groups possessed religious specialists (SHAMAN), engaged in seasonal rituals often associated with crop harvests and held periodic feasts (*see* NATIVE PEOPLE, RELIGION). The Huron held elaborate FEASTS OF THE DEAD, usually at the time when villages were to be moved to new locations. The bones of dead relatives were gathered and placed in mass graves (ossuaries) with grave goods. The Five Nations had a number of medicine societies focused on curing, the best known being the FALSE FACE SOCIETY. During performances members wore elaborately carved wooden masks.

Algonquian: Horticulture as a subsistence activity was either absent or marginal among most Eastern Woodland Algonquians. Ottawa, Algonquin, Abenaki and Maliseet grew some crops; the Ojibwa and Micmac grew none, and the Nipissing traded fish for Huron corn. Hunting and fishing provided the bulk of the food. Deer, bear, moose, caribou and even seals, porpoises and whales were harvested in areas where they could be found. Bows, arrows, lances, traps, snares and deadfalls were used in hunting, and hooks, weirs, leisters and nets were employed to procure fish. In the Great Lakes area wild rice was harvested in the early fall, and maple or birch sap was collected in the early spring. Meat was either boiled or roasted for immediate consumption or smoke-dried for future use. A seasonal round of activities tended to inhibit a strictly sedentary existence, although the abundance of certain food, especially fish, and some horticulture permitted a greater degree of sedentation than among Subarctic peoples farther north. Dwellings were smaller and

Haida village on the Queen Charlotte Is, BC (*courtesy Geological Survey of Canada/255*).

less permanent than among Iroquoians, varying from conical birchbark TIPIS to domed WIGWAMS or rectangular structures that housed several families. Village size varied seasonally, with the largest population concentrations occurring in summer. Some Ottawa and Abenaki villages may have numbered 300 persons. Unlike the Iroquoians who travelled mainly on land or in crude elm-bark CANOES, the Algonquians made gracile birchbark canoes. In winter they used SNOWSHOES, sleds and TOBOGGANS. Trade and visiting appear to have been common activities among adjacent Algonquian peoples.

The aboriginal population of the different Algonquian groups is difficult to estimate owing to postcontact movements and the effects of diseases. There may have been 15 000 to 20 000 Central Algonquians in Canada and an equal number of Eastern Algonquians either in Canada or whose descendants later moved to Canada. More research is required before these estimates can be refined.

Prior to European intervention, the largest political unit among most Woodland Algonquians appears to have been the band-village, there being no confederacies of village chiefs. Each BAND or band-village appears to have possessed at least one chief or headman, whose position was usually hereditary within the male line. Patrilineal groups designated by an animal totem seem to have been characteristic of all peoples. Village-band territories were not strictly demarcated, and all members had equal access to basic subsistence resources. While intertribal feuds may have occurred, it is doubtful that warfare was conducted on the same scale as that which characterized the early historic period.

The most important religious figure was the shaman, who engaged in curing and performed magical rites to ward off evil spirits such as WINDIGO and to appease or locate game. Impersonal powers pervaded the universe, and Algonquians made no conceptual distinction between the human and animal worlds. Seasonal rituals and feasts were held, as well as rituals associated with birth, puberty and death. The vision quest associated with the acquisition of a personal supernatural guardian helper existed among all groups. Central Algonquians held Feasts of the Dead that were similar but not identical to those of the Huron. During the 17th century these feasts attracted large numbers of persons, often from

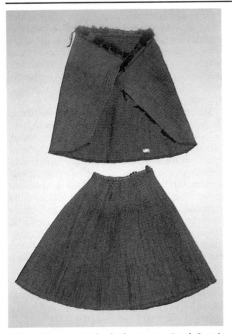

Skirt and cape of cedar bark (*courtesy Royal Ontario Museum*).

several tribes. Because quantities of goods were given away and the names of new chiefs raised, they came to resemble the Northwest Coast funerary POTLATCH.

Culture Change There has been considerable culture change among all Eastern Woodland groups. Hunting, gathering and fishing have become marginal subsistence activities except among some Micmac, for whom fishing has remained significant. Agriculture, altered by new technologies, crops and rules regarding the sexual division of labour, declined as reserve populations grew, lands were partitioned, and new job opportunities arose. Such traditional foods as corn bread and corn soup are still eaten, and tobacco continues to be grown for ritual purposes. Different reserve populations and different groups on the same reserve represent varying degrees of acculturation and assimilation (*see* NATIVE PEOPLE, SOCIAL CONDITIONS). Some Algonquians still maintain an essentially animistic world view, while Iroquois following the Longhouse religion adhere to modified aboriginal beliefs and principles. Traditional beliefs and values tend to remain strongest among those who regularly speak the native language. A revitalization of selected aspects of traditional cultures, not only arts and crafts (*see* INDIAN ART) but also dances and rituals, as well as a greater political awareness, have served to reinforce identity and esteem after over 3 centuries of cultural erosion.

CHARLES A. BISHOP

Northwest Coast

Territory and Natural Environment The Canadian portion of the Northwest Coast is a region of extremes in topography, from wide beaches to deep fjords and snowcapped mountains. Temperatures are moderate, the Jan mean above freezing and July less than 18°C. The northern coast and outer islands receive 155-655 cm of rain annually, and the protected south coast 65-175 cm, mostly in winter. Heavy coniferous forests thrive, and beaches and streams are lined with dense undergrowth.

In the precontact period, food was plentiful: black-tailed deer, bear, elk and mountain goat were available locally, and sea mammals (seals and porpoises) as well as vast quantities of fish and shellfish were found everywhere. Most im-

portant were the great runs of PACIFIC SALMON, which arrived in regular annual migrations and were eaten fresh or dried for year-round use.

Major Language and Tribal Groups Of all the aboriginal regions in Canada, the Northwest Coast exhibits most diversity in language. The Inland TLINGIT of the northwest tip of BC and the southwest Yukon are an interior branch of the Tlingit of the south Alaska coast. On the QUEEN CHARLOTTE IS are HAIDA. Both Tlingit and Haida are language isolates, unique languages with no proven relationship to any other. Along the Nass and Skeena rivers and adjacent coast are people speaking 3 languages of the TSIMSHIAN language family, which may be remotely related to several other language families, collectively called Penutian, spoken from Oregon southward. Strung along the coast from Tsimshian territory to NE Vancouver I are Haisla (KITAMAAT), Heiltsuk (BELLA BELLA), Oowekyala (Rivers Inlet) and Kwakwala (Southern KWAKIUTL). They in turn are related to Westcoast (NOOTKA) and Nitinat, languages spoken on the west coast of Vancouver I and Makah on Cape Flattery in Washington. All of these languages belong to the Wakashan language family. The remaining coastal people of BC speak languages of the large Salishan family. In the north, surrounded by Heiltsuk and Haisla, are the BELLA COOLA. In Georgia Strait, below the Southern Kwakiutl, are speakers of 7 mutually unintelligible Coast Salish languages: Comox, Pentlatch (extinct) and Sechelt, together referred to as NORTHERN GEORGIA STRAIT COAST SALISH, and Squamish, Halkomelem, Nooksack (now only in Washington state) and Straits Salish, together called CENTRAL COAST SALISH.

In summary, there are 19 mutually unintelligible languages spoken on the Northwest Coast of BC, and these in turn belong to 5 separate units among which no relationship has yet been clearly established (*see* NATIVE PEOPLE, LANGUAGES).

Historical Summary Although the earliest settlement of the Northwest Coast occurred probably 10 000 years ago (*see* PREHISTORY), the first contact with Europeans came late in the 18th century, when Spanish and British explorers opened the way for traders seeking rich stocks of sea-otter pelts. All tribes eagerly adopted firearms, iron tools and other European goods, but permanent trading posts awaited establishment of a series of forts by the HUDSON'S BAY CO, which by 1850 controlled the trade.

Discovery of gold on the Fraser R in 1857 brought a rush of miners and settlers to the newly established colonies (*see* GOLD RUSHES). Towns were few, but Indians were attracted to them

from afar for trade goods. Contagious diseases, particularly smallpox, wrought havoc among the Indians, who were reduced to a minority within the population by 1885.

Gov James DOUGLAS made a few small treaties with Indian villages on Vancouver I between 1850 and 1859 (*see* INDIAN TREATIES). This recognition of Indian title was less clear when BC entered Confederation in 1871. Commissions were established in 1876 and 1912 and charged with creating and confirming INDIAN RESERVES. Neither commission had authority to make treaties or deal definitively with Indian grievances. Though reserves were imposed unilaterally and did not always meet Indian requests, they did provide minimal protection for many village sites as the influx of strangers continued.

The unsettled land question and government oppression, including an anti-POTLATCH clause in the INDIAN ACT in 1884, led to protests by local groups. Organized pan-tribal associations emerged later with formation of the Allied Tribes of British Columbia in 1915 and the Native Brotherhood of British Columbia in 1931.

From earliest contact with outsiders, coastal Indians traded willingly and worked as labourers, boatmen and house servants. Those living in dispersed locations with viable subsistence economies were ideal seasonal workers in the early stages of resource development. However, as mechanization and centralization of the fish and timber industries proceeded, participation of Indians as workers and independent small producers diminished. Resource industries still dominate Indian occupational patterns, but by the 1960s unemployment and underemployment in coastal communities was chronic.

Traditional Culture Throughout the Northwest Coast the material bases of life were similar. Carpentry was men's work, and with blades of stone and shell, wooden wedges and stone hammers they fashioned the myriad items of everyday use. Huge winter dwellings of post-and-beam structure covered by split cedar planks were created in distinct regional styles. So too were dugout CANOES, which provided transportation along rapid streams and on the open sea.

It fell mainly to women to spin twine required for fishnets and lines and to weave items from cedar bark and roots – large storage containers,

Interior of a Clallam Winter Lodge (c 1851-56), oil on canvas, by Paul Kane. Huge winter dwellings of post-and-beam construction were created in distinct regional styles – in this case a Salishan people (*courtesy National Gallery of Canada/John Evans, 1959*).

open-work collecting baskets and exquisite, finely decorated hats. Mats fashioned from cedar bark or rushes provided furnishings and lined houses for additional warmth. Women also twined cedar-bark skirts and cloaks for everyday wear. Elaborately decorated CHILKAT BLANKETS of twined cedar bark and mountain-goat wool were worn on special occasions by people in northern tribes. Among Coast Salish, mountain-goat wool supplemented by dog wool was twilled into heavy blankets with decorative borders. These were items of daily wear in cold weather. Everywhere on the coast, fur cloaks supplemented this simple stock of clothing.

Fishing, hunting and gathering were the means of subsistence on the Northwest Coast. Resources from the sea were of first importance. Fishing devices were adapted to suit specific conditions of sea and stream and local occurrence of fish species; techniques included trolling and jigging with baited hooks, harpooning and spearing, use of nets and construction of tidal traps, or weirs, in streams. Land mammals were taken with bow and arrow, snares, deadfalls and nets; sea mammals with harpoons at sea and with clubs or nets wherever animals came ashore. The abundant waterfowl fell prey to a variety of ingenious nets. Gathering of shellfish, berries, edible roots, bulbs and green shoots provided additional nutritious foods. None of these varied resources was evenly distributed in all regions, and coastal tribes followed a pattern of moving or dispersing from winter villages to outlying sites as the season came round for each resource, and then returning to the main base.

While fishing and hunting were mainly the work of men, and women did most gathering of plant and beach foods, the division of labour was complementary and often co-operative. Both men and women made the tools necessary for work. Because almost all foods were produced at times in quantities greater than immediate need, they were preserved. Men did most of the initial production of fish and game, but women did the cooking and preservation (see SMOKEHOUSE).

The primary unit of society everywhere on the Northwest Coast was a large group of kinsmen who usually shared a common ancestor. Among northern peoples, membership in the kin group was passed down through women, but in the south membership could be claimed through either the male or the female lines. In both areas the result was a core of close kin with in-married spouses living together in a house or house cluster under the direction and guidance of capable leaders. These leaders held formal titles or prominent names hereditary within the family line and acted as managers of family property, including nonmaterial possessions such as names, ritual performances, special songs or secret knowledge. The foundation, however, was ownership of real property such as house sites, berry patches, hunting territory, seal rookeries and fish-trap sites. While some territory and waters were open to general use, more productive harvesting places were privately owned.

Real property, combined with skilful management of family labour and individually owned capital equipment, enabled kin groups and their chiefs to achieve high productivity and accumulate tangible wealth. Property was the basis and vehicle of the Northwest Coast system of rank and class. In some tribes there was precise status with internal ranking; in others, flexible categories. An upper-lower distinction of some form was universal, as was the institution of SLAVERY. Slaves were acquired in war or by purchase and, although they lived in owners' houses, lacked full civil rights and were required to perform menial chores.

Fishhooks in composite shot (*courtesy Royal Ontario Museum*).

Villages were always close to navigable water, with houses ranged parallel to the beach facing the water. Although united by kinship, dialect and common interest in territory, villages had no government except that effected by powerful lineages. During the early historic period, among Coast Tsimshian and Northern Westcoast (Nootka), strong village leaders emerged and began to extend their influence through the confederation of villages. These alliances were the only form of tribal organization. Feuding occurred in response to injury or trespass, and occasionally escalated into warfare. Acquisition of property, including slaves, was also a motivation for conflict. The small size and divisiveness of village units, and the practice of restituting wrongs with gifts, helped to limit the scale of warfare.

High-ranking individuals from separate kin groups and villages found common cause in class membership and ritual associations, often termed secret societies. Most important of all were bonds of marriage and gift exchanges which accompanied them. Marriages were contracted between people of different kin groups, often in widely separated villages. In order to validate lineage rights and maintain class position, assemblies of people from many kin groups were convened to witness claims. Guests were fed and given gifts at these potlatches. Barter and trade occurred, but gifts and feasts were major means of distribution and exchange.

All tribes conducted serious religious rites in winter and viewed summer as more appropriate for games, feasts and naming activities. There was no strict segregation of the sacred and secular, as the sacred was implicit in all thought and action. Belief in potent spirits identified with animate objects and forms was fundamental. Spirits could interfere in human affairs, but by self-purification an individual might induce them to become personal helpers. They were a source of power for religious practitioners or shamans, but also endowed ordinary folk with special competence or good fortune, and in some areas became hereditary privileges. This awareness of power in the animate, nonhuman sphere was consistent with widespread use of prayers and welcoming ceremonies to foster the annual runs of fish.

The course of each person's life brought changes of status as puberty was attained, names received or marriage made. Taboos and elaborate ritual and feasting accompanied these events. Illness, while associated with physical causes, was also ascribed to soul loss or intervention of spirit forces, and shamans were called upon for diagnosis and corrective treatment. All tribes believed in life after death and in ghosts that could be harmful to the living. Funeral and memorial ritual served to separate the living and the dead and to sustain, honour and placate the dead.

Music and decorative arts were associated with both sacred and secular activities. Spirit helpers conferred songs, and secret society or family tra-

dition was transmitted through songs which often accompanied masked re-enactments of mythic events. There were songs for all occasions – soothing infants, playing games, expressing love and sorrow. The voice was the only melodic instrument, although a variety of percussive devices, whistles and horns was used as accompaniment.

Sculptural and decorative art was also part of daily life, applied to tools, houses, baskets, clothing and items associated with the supernatural. Wood sculpture and painting, notably TOTEM POLES, are the most renowned features of Northwest Coast culture. Archaeological evidence suggests that art has a long history in the area and that regional styles share basic similarities of form with an earlier tradition. In the N the art is highly formalized and often depicts family crests on property. Wakashan sculptors excelled in creating masks for dramatic performances. The Salish put emphasis on religious implements with little concern for crests. In all areas ownership of sculptural and decorative art was indicative of wealth and denoted class position (see NORTHWEST COAST INDIAN ART).

Culture Change Though early acceptance of European clothing and tools brought visible changes to Northwest Coast cultures, villages, often on ancient sites, still retain their original orientation to the sea and traditional foods are favoured in the diet. Enforced Westernization was the policy of missionaries and government administrators until recent times. Compulsory education in centrally located boarding schools, where native speech was forbidden, had devastating effects on community structure, Indian socialization and languages. Several Northwest Coast languages now have only a few fluent speakers and are in danger of extinction, despite efforts to reverse the trend with formal language-teaching programs. Pentlatch, for example, is already extinct.

Despite the ban on the potlatch from 1884 to 1951, feasts and ceremonial exchanges, especially among the Southern Kwakiutl, never completely ceased and have experienced revival in recent decades. The few Coast Salish villages where spirit dancing survived have served as centres for a dramatic religious revival that has continued to attract followers. These institutions remain private to the Indian communities, where they strengthen Indian identity and self-esteem (see SHAKER RELIGION).

The population of Northwest Coast tribes has continued to increase since a low point in 1915. In 1985 there were about 40 000 registered Indians and perhaps as many again who are nonregistered descendants of coastal tribes. Isolated villages have lost residents as unemployment and educational opportunity induced people to move to urban centres. More than 40% of the registered population are off-reserve residents.

Northwest Coast Indians have remained steadfast in objecting to policy and practice that have reduced ABORIGINAL RIGHTS and left LAND CLAIMS unsettled (see NATIVE PEOPLE, GOVERNMENT POLICY). They have been strong supporters of provincial and national Indian associations.   MICHAEL KEW

Plains

Territory and Natural Environment The Plains Indian culture area extended from southern Manitoba and the Mississippi R westward to the Rocky Mts, and from the N Saskatchewan R south into Texas. This was a region of continental climate – hot and dry summers and very cold winters. High grass covered the rolling prairies in the east; short grasses, sage and cacti the arid high plains to the west. Flat land and rolling hills ex-

Assiniboine Hunting Buffalo (nd), oil on canvas, by Paul Kane. The Plains Indians buffalo hunt was greatly facilitated by the acquisition of the horse (*courtesy National Gallery of Canada*).

tend in all directions. Flowing eastward, rivers have cut deeply into the land, and provide practically all the scarce available water. Tree growth on the high plains is restricted to these valleys, becoming rapidly more noticeable toward the margins of the area.

Plains Indian culture was based primarily on the immense herds of BISON or buffalo which roamed over and fed upon these grasslands until the early 1880s. Bison herds shared these resources with pronghorn antelopes, elk, mule deer, jack rabbits, prairie dogs and a range of small herbivores, grouse, prairie chicken, geese, ducks and cranes. This wildlife was preyed upon by wolves, coyotes, grizzly bear, mountain lion, eagles, other birds of prey and man.

Major Language and Tribal Groups The languages spoken by the various Plains tribes belong to 6 linguistic families, of which 3 were represented on the Canadian Plains. Algonquian languages were spoken by the BLACKFOOT, Gros Ventre (Atsina), Plains CREE and Plains OJIBWA; Siouan languages were those of the ASSINIBOINE, STONEY and DAKOTA Sioux. Athapaskan was spo-

Cree pipe stem bearer by artist Paul Kane (*courtesy Royal Ontario Museum*).

ken by the SARCEE. Languages from 2 families were as divergent as German is from Chinese, and within each family languages were as different as English from Dutch. This linguistic diversity and the high mobility of the nomadic population on the Plains encouraged the development of communication by means of hand gestures or sign language (*see* NATIVE PEOPLE, LANGUAGES).

Before epidemics in the early 1800s reduced the population, the northern Plains Indians numbered an estimated 33 000. Tribal populations in that region ranged from about 700 for the Sarcee to about 15 000 for the 3 Blackfoot tribes.

Historical Summary Small bands of nomadic hunters roamed the Plains some 10 000 years ago (*see* PREHISTORY). Most of these people, however, slowly drifted southward to be succeeded by other migrants. About 200 AD a horticultural population from the Mississippi Valley spread northwestward, ultimately reaching, temporarily, the southern parts of Saskatchewan and Alberta (*see* CLUNY EARTHLODGE VILLAGE). They settled in semipermanent villages near their gardens along the rivers. Through their contacts with more elaborate cultures in southeastern N America, these gardeners played an important role in the northwestern expansion of certain religious ideas and rituals. The prehistoric hunters and gardeners established the general cultural patterns basic to the Plains Indian culture of the historic period.

Spanish colonists from Mexico introduced horses to the southern Plains in the 16th century. By intertribal trade and raiding, the animals spread northward, reaching the Canadian Plains by the 1730s. The use of horses altered hunting techniques and enabled the people to transport larger and more comfortably furnished dwellings. Their obvious improvement of the life of the nomadic hunters caused the development of HORSE raiding as the most common form of intertribal warfare. Warfare was a dangerous game, as ritualized as medieval knighthood in Europe, with social prestige and wealth as its goals. Small war parties would raid enemy territory, run off the horses and sometimes kill a few people.

At approximately the same period that horses were moving north, fur traders arriving from the East introduced firearms. From 1730 to 1870 the Plains Indians played an important role in the FUR TRADE, which in turn profoundly changed their way of life. Adjusting their hunting to the demands of the traders, the Indians gradually

gave up their original independence for the amenities offered by the fur trade.

Traditional Culture Women gathered edible roots and berries whenever they were available but the main source of food came from hunting by the men, especially buffalo hunting. The Plains Cree and Plains Ojibwa added fish to the diet, but fish was unimportant elsewhere on the Plains. Animal-skin disguises were used to get close enough to the game for the effective use of bows and arrows. Buffalo herds were driven into pounds or corrals and killed, or were stampeded over steep cliffs (*see* BUFFALO HUNT). While acquisition of the horse greatly facilitated buffalo hunting, muzzle-loading guns proved inferior to bow and arrows, which were given up only after shorter breechloaders were introduced by the 1860s.

When men hunted, women were busy processing the results of this activity, particularly in preserving (through drying) foods. Some meat was cooked and eaten immediately, but most was sliced and sun-dried for the winter, or ground and mixed with fat and berries to make PEMMICAN. Buffalo hides were used for robes, tent covers, MOCCASINS and shields; tools and utensils were made of the bison's horns, hooves, hair, tail, bones and sinew; buffalo dung was used as a fuel on the treeless plains. Skins of antelope and elk were preferred in the manufacture of clothing: breechcloth, leggings and shirts for men, long dresses and leggings for women.

The family property was transported on a TRAVOIS (a triangular frame of poles) dragged along by dogs. Travois also provided the framework of the conical dwelling called TIPI, which was covered with buffalo skins sewn together. After the introduction of the horse, larger travois and tipi were constructed. SNOWSHOES were used during the winter by some tribes on the northern Plains.

Many utilitarian articles manifested the rich yet tribally distinct artistic temperament of the Plains Indians. They ranged from skin tattoos, clothing painted or embroidered with dyed porcupine quills, paintings on tipi covers, shields and rawhide containers, carvings on wooden bowls, horn spoons and stone pipes, the extensive use of feathers in ceremonial regalia, to large boulder monuments laid out on the ground (*see* INDIAN ART). Certain individuals were known and approached for their exceptional ability in a specific craft, but, even for them, craft production was not an exclusive occupation. Most of the colourfully decorated Plains Indian artifacts seen in museums were made by women. Men produced equipment for the hunt, war and ceremonies.

The adjustment of the native way of life to the natural environment, and in particular to the movements of the buffalo herds, was reflected in their social organization. Most tribes consisted of loosely organized and independent bands. Band chiefs had the respect and support of their follow-

Medicine bundle (*courtesy Royal Ontario Museum*).

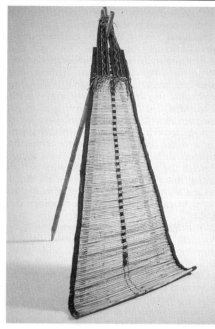

Backrest (*courtesy Royal Ontario Museum*).

ers as long as they were successful in the quest for food and in defence against enemy attacks. Chiefs were advisers rather than rulers; their decisions were based on unanimous approval reached in the council of elders. Public shame and ridicule were the principal means of social discipline. Most of the year the bands moved around independently of each other. In lean periods even the band might have to split up into smaller groups that would have a better chance of finding sufficient food.

Only in midsummer, when the buffalo were concentrated in large herds, would the bands come together for a few weeks in one large tribal encampment. Then the people joined in the celebrations of their ceremonial and military societies, which were the principal means of tribal cohesion. After the performance of the SUN DANCE and possibly a tribal buffalo drive, the bands separated again; in the fall they moved to well-protected campsites in river valleys, foothills and parklands, where they spent the winter.

Religious ideas and practices permeated all aspects of daily life. Fundamental to Plains Indian religion was the belief that animals and other natural phenomena possessed spiritual power that could, under proper circumstances, be manipulated to personal advantage. The individual seeking such power went to a lonely spot where he fasted and prayed until a spiritual guardian appeared to him in a dream (vision quest). The difference between ordinary men and ritual leaders was a gradually developing one, primarily based upon the amount of spiritual power acquired either by personal visions or by ritualized purchase from other individuals. Mystical experiences gave rise to cults that either disappeared when the initiator died, or became increasingly popular. All tribal rituals had their origins in such cults.

Culture Change The normally slow and gradual rate of societal change accelerated rapidly for the Plains Indians after they came into contact with European civilization. Though distinctly native in character, historic Plains Indian culture would have been impossible without the European horse and the European trader. The introduction of metalwares made native pottery, stone chisels and arrowheads obsolete in the mid-18th century; glass beads gradually replaced quillwork after 1830; cloth became as common as skin for cloth-

ing after 1850. For more than a century the fur trade was the sole medium of contact between Euro-Canadian society and the northern Plains Indians.

During this period the native people were generally free to accept or reject whatever the European had to offer, and as such the fur trade provided a measure of adjustment that prepared the Indians for the more intensive culture change later forced upon them. The MÉTIS, descendants of European-Indian parents, trace their origins to the early trading period. However, the fur trade did not bring only greater material wealth; epidemic diseases of European origin swept the northern Plains in 1781, 1819, 1837, 1845, 1864 and 1869 (*see* NATIVE PEOPLE, HEALTH). Each time thousands of Indians died, and the survivors were left with their world views and beliefs undermined. During this period the consumption of alcohol became widespread, particularly after the arrival of American whisky traders in the 1860s (*see* NATIVE PEOPLE, SOCIAL CONDITIONS). In these years also, the depletion of the buffalo herds became noticeable, owing to indiscriminate overhunting for profit, especially after the completion of a transcontinental railway in the US.

In response to the increasing violence in the region, the newly formed North-West Mounted Police came west in 1874 and enforced law and order within a short time. However, they could neither halt the disappearance of the buffalo herds nor stop the settlers from establishing farms and villages all over the plains. In 1870 the federal government purchased the North-West from the HUDSON'S BAY CO, and, in a series of treaties between 1871 and 1877, the government secured land cessions from the Indians (*see* INDIAN TREATIES). In 1880 the total population of the Canadian plains reached 120 000, in which the approximately 30 000 Indians had become a minority. Most Indians were then living on reserves (*see* INDIAN RESERVE), where government agents tried to introduce them to new means of subsistence, primarily agriculture. Years of scarcity and starvation followed, in which the people depended upon the frequently inadequate rations of the government. Throughout this difficult period of social and economic adjustment, missions of various Christian denominations played a major role in providing a new education system, frequently acting as mediators between the natives and white society.

Some of these churches initially supported Indian leaders in their efforts to create provincial native organizations through which they could articulate their social and economic needs. Starting in the 1920s, these organizations struggled against government harassment and native apathy, slowly lifting the oppressive paternalism of government policy. After WWII the activities of native organizations increased, forcing the federal government to take its responsibilities more seriously. On the reserves, various economic programs have been initiated and government agents have increasingly transferred their administrative responsibilities to elected chiefs and tribal councils. Accurate population numbers are hard to obtain, but in 1986 there were at least 65 000 Indians living on the Canadian plains: about 16 000 in southern Alberta, about 20 000 in southern Saskatchewan; and about 28 000 in southern Manitoba.   TED J. BRASSER

Plateau

Territory and Natural Environment The Plateau culture area is named after the geographically defined Columbian Plateau. In Canada this area consists of the high plateau between the BC coast range of mountains and the Rockies. Scholars

Ju-Ah-Kis-Gaw [Ojibwa] Woman with her Child in a Cradle (1835), oil on canvas by George Catlin (*courtesy National Museum of American Art, Smithsonian Institution/gift of Mrs Joseph Harrison, Jr*).

over the years have suggested a variety of northern borders for the Plateau culture area. In 1932 Diamond JENNESS referred to this area as "The Cordillera," extending as far N as TAHLTAN territory. Other scholars have taken the SEKANI homeland or CARRIER country as the limit. The most recent anthropological consensus affiliates all of these peoples with the subarctic cultural area and uses the northern boundary of Shuswap territory as the northern border of the Plateau.

Hot, dry summers and cold winters are typical throughout the Plateau. This climate creates an environment well suited to mule and white-tailed deer, caribou, black bear, grizzly bear, elk and mountain sheep, as well as smaller animals, including coyote, fox, lynx, wolf, raccoon, porcupine, marten, weasel, beaver, marmot and hare. The major rivers supported annual runs of PACIFIC SALMON and other fish, which were the mainstay of subsistence.

Major Language and Tribal Groups The linguistic families represented by this culture area in Canada are the Athapaskan (NICOLA-SIMILKAMEEN, now extinct), Salishan (Interior Salish — Shuswap, Lillooet, Thompson, Okanagan; *see* SALISH, INTERIOR) and Kutenai (KOOTENAY) (*see* NATIVE PEOPLE, LANGUAGES).

Historical Summary Archaeologists postulate that about 9000-10 000 years ago, not long after the glaciers from the most recent ice age receded, the BC Plateau was populated by native people who had migrated northward from more southerly areas of this same Plateau, where the glaciers had receded earlier (*see* PREHISTORY). Gradually there emerged a culture adapted to the forested mountains, sage- and cactus-covered hills, and riverine resources of the area.

The Plateau's abundant natural resources were the major stimulus that attracted non-Indians to this area. At first it was furs — the lure of furs brought the explorer Alexander MACKENZIE into contact with the Northern Shuswap people in 1793, and David THOMPSON into Kootenay country in 1807. In 1808 Simon FRASER explored the river that now bears his name. All of these explorers were received hospitably by the Plateau Indians. One chief took Fraser by the arm and directed him to shake hands with every one of the 1200 Indians assembled at Lytton to meet him.

By the 1820s, fur-trading posts were established throughout the Plateau. With the introduction of firearms and metal implements, the hunting of fur-bearing animals became much more efficient, and soon their numbers dwindled. At the same time, diseases such as measles, influenza and smallpox swept through the native settlements, killing thousands of Indian people.

Gold was the impetus for the next wave of non-Indians to overrun the Plateau. The discovery of gold in 1857 on the Fraser R attracted almost 30 000 fortune seekers of many ethnic backgrounds (*see* GOLD RUSHES). Not surprisingly, violence erupted immediately. In an effort to restore peace and protect Indian lands from further encroachment, the new governor of BC, James DOUGLAS, began working out a policy of native rights. He decided the best way to handle the problem of land ownership was to extinguish Indian rights to their lands through treaties and compensation. The native people would then live on INDIAN RESERVES. On the Canadian Plateau, NO INDIAN TREATIES were signed and no compensation was paid, although reserves were surveyed and allotted. By the late 1880s all of the Plateau Indian peoples had been assigned to live on scattered, small reserves.

Traditional Culture We have only an incomplete record of what Plateau life was like before it was affected by the presence of Euro-Canadians. When the first detailed studies of these people were made in the late 1880s and early 1900s, the traditional ways had already changed dramatically. The summation that follows from the works of pioneer ethnographers James TEIT, Franz BOAS, George Mercer DAWSON and Charles HILL-TOUT, supplemented by the work of contemporary researchers, reflects our gaps in knowledge of traditional Plateau life.

In this region groups of related people worked and travelled together in the spring, summer and fall, then joined with other such groups to winter in relatively permanent winter villages. Plateau society was egalitarian and communal in most respects, although men were the major decision makers. Within each village there were a number of chiefs or headmen who organized economic activities; eg, there was a salmon chief for fishing, and so on. The advice of these men was taken seriously, but every adult male took part in gatherings to discuss the general concerns of the group. There were no formal councils; when confronted with an issue affecting the group at large, a man invited other males to discuss it. Often it was the advice of the old people or the most experienced that was accepted.

The division of labour was based on gender. Men were responsible for hunting, trapping, fishing and manufacturing implements from bone, wood and stone, and also for warfare. Women's responsibilities included preparing food for meals and for winter storage, harvesting plants, maintaining the home and caring for small children. There was little formal specialization of roles. Those men who had acquired certain physical and spiritual abilities during their adolescent training became "professional" hunters of bear and mountain goat. All men were expected to be competent deer hunters. Land and its resources were considered communal property, with a few exceptions. Some salmon-fishing stations were owned by individuals, while others were owned collectively by resident or village groups. Hunting grounds and root-harvesting grounds were generally open to all those who spoke the same language, and consent to use these areas was sometimes extended to others.

Food was shared liberally among all villagers. At public salmon-fishing stations, a weir or net was used to catch fish for the entire village, and men with harpoons caught fish for their individu-

Kee-A-Kee-Ka-Sa-Coo-Way, "the man that gives the war whoop," head chief of the Cree, painted by artist Paul Kane (*courtesy Royal Ontario Museum*).

al families' needs. As the Plateau economy was based on hunting, fishing and gathering, all seasonal and unreliable activities, much time and effort was spent smoking food or drying it for storage. The entire community, children and adults, was involved in this activity.

Food was not always plentiful – there were occasions when the salmon runs failed, certain animals were not available, or root and berry crops did not materialize. At such times the people had to travel farther and work harder to survive. Each spring the appearance of the first run of salmon and the first fruits or berries was celebrated with a special ceremony.

Transportation on the Plateau was by means of dugout CANOES made from red cedar or cottonwood, or bark canoes from white pine or birch. SNOWSHOES were commonly used – their designs were specially suited to the varying conditions of snow and terrain. In early times dogs were used as pack animals as well as in hunting deer. By the 1730s the HORSE was introduced into the Canadian Plateau from farther S and dramatically improved the mobility of native peoples. It is likely that the Kootenay were the first Plateau group in Canada to obtain horses.

The 3 main house types found on the Plateau were the semisubterranean pit house, the tule-mat lodge and the TIPI. The pit house most often consisted of a circular excavated pit protected by a conical roof of poles covered with brush and earth. Variation was found from area to area – the pit could be circular or square, the roof conical, pyramidical or almost flat, and the entrance either a hole (which also served as an exit for smoke) in the centre of the roof or a door at the side of the roof. Sometimes tunnels acted as entrances or connected several pit houses together. Although pit houses were most commonly used as winter dwellings, recent information suggests they were sometimes used at other times of the year.

Lodges covered with bark, or mats of tule or grass, were employed throughout the Plateau. There were 3 main ground plans: rectangular, parallel sides with rounded ends, or rectangular with one end rounded. For winter use these lodges were banked around their bases with dirt and snow. One or more fires were positioned in the centre of the lodge. In the Kootenay area of the Plateau, hide-covered tipis were used in addition to the other dwelling types. The Kootenay tipi was of the 4-pole-foundation type, with

about 15 supplementary poles. Lean-tos of poles and brush were also used for shelters at temporary camps. Other structures included a SWEAT LODGE for men and a menstrual isolation place for women. Traditional-style dwellings were generally last used in the Canadian Plateau around the mid- to late 1880s, although in some areas their use extended into the early 1900s.

Plateau peoples felt a deep connection with the inanimate beings that inhabited their environment. Everything around them was imbued with special powers, even rocks and trees. This spiritual relationship with nature permeated all aspects of daily life (*see* NATIVE PEOPLE, RELIGION). During adolescence, every individual underwent special training to receive guardian-spirit power from a nature-helper. The spirit came to the person when he or she was in a trancelike state, told the recipient how to use the gift, and provided a "power song." Shamans who trained longer and more intensively received special powers enabling them to cure the sick or cause harm to others and were both respected and feared. They used their guardian-spirit powers in curing performances (*see* SHAMAN).

The Winter Guardian Spirit Dance, the major ceremony of most Plateau peoples in the US, was practised in Canada mainly by the Okanagan. The dance was likely celebrated in former times by the Shuswap, Thompson and Lillooet as well, although in a slightly different manner. Some Canadian Okanagan people still participate in winter dances today in both BC and the US. The winter dance was hosted by shamans, who used the occasion to communicate their spirit powers in public. After one or several nights of dancing and administering to the needs of the sick, the host or hostess presented the guests with gifts. Other Salishan groups in the Plateau held similar ceremonies, marked by the singing of spirit songs, at any time of the year.

Among the Kootenay, a ceremony was held which united a spirit power and its possessor for such purposes as predicting future events and finding lost objects. This ceremony, along with the SUN DANCE, points to the relationship of the Kootenay people with the Plains Indians.

Clothing for the Plateau peoples was sewn from the tanned hides of animals and woven from local grasses or from the pounded bark of bushes. MOCCASINS were common; most often they were made from deer hide, but occasionally from salmon skin. Winter clothing consisted of the thick skins of fur-bearing animals. Among some groups clothing was decorated with dentalia shells, ochre paint, porcupine quills or native-made beads or seeds. Mats and baskets woven for utilitarian purposes were often beautiful as well. Tattooing and nose and ear piercing were common but not universal.

Songs were important in traditional Plateau life, and were used by individuals to summon religious and magical powers. Singing was sometimes accompanied by bird-bone flutes, rattles of deer hooves, and sticks being struck on boards, but mainly by hide-covered wooden-frame drums. One type of song still known and widely performed today is the stick-game song, sung while playing an indigenous gambling game involving 2 opposing teams.

The extensive Plateau oral literature that once occupied the long winter evenings now fills only the pages of books. A complex cycle of tales, frequently with humorous and bawdy episodes, involved the trickster-creator known as Coyote.

Culture Change Hudson's Bay Co officials and early missionaries tried to introduce literacy and calendars to the Plateau peoples, but it was a Catholic missionary, Father LE JEUNE, who had the most success. Contemporary attempts to teach

Kutchin man's summer costume of tanned caribou skin decorated with beads, dentalia (highly prized shells obtained in trade with Northwest Coast tribes) and red ochre (*courtesy National Museums of Canada/Canadian Museum of Civilization/K75-954*).

native people to write the various Plateau languages have not yet proved as successful as Le Jeune's work at the turn of the century, when more than 2000 Interior Salish became literate.

For a time, Plateau groups universally adopted CHRISTIANITY, but there has been a resurgence of the old religions. Since the establishment of INDIAN RESERVES in the late 1800s, Plateau Indians have played a major role in struggles relating to native LAND CLAIMS in BC. The influential Indian organization, the Allied Tribes of British Columbia, was initiated at Spences Bridge in the Canadian Plateau in 1915 by several Interior Salish Indians assisted by ethnographer James Teit. This organization was active for 12 years.

Since the early 1970s some younger Plateau Indians have made a conscious attempt to reinterpret traditional ways, resulting in a "pan-Indian" native movement that is becoming more widespread (*see* PAN-INDIANISM). The mid- to late 1970s saw the establishment of powerful Indian tribal councils in the Canadian Plateau, organized along linguistically defined lines and consisting of several bands. Both the bands and the tribal councils are strong advocates of Indian government, economic development of reserve lands, educational opportunities for Indians, cultural and linguistic survival, and equitable settlement of the long-standing land-claims issues with both federal and provincial governments.

DOROTHY KENNEDY AND RANDY BOUCHARD

Subarctic

Natural Environment The area of Subarctic cultures lies largely within the 5 million km² zone of northern or boreal coniferous forest that extends from the arctic tundra to the mountains, plains or deciduous forest in the S and across N America from Labrador nearly to the Bering Sea. Three-quarters of the area lies on the Canadian

Shield, Hudson Bay and Mackenzie R lowlands. It is dotted with many lakes and crossed by innumerable rivers. The rest consists of western mountain ranges, plateaus and the Yukon R lowlands. Winters are long and harsh but forest cover and snow provide shelter for people and animals. Temperatures often reach −50°C in winter but can rise to 35°C in summer.

Mammals commonly found in the area are moose, caribou, black bear, Dall sheep (northwestern mountains), beaver, hare ("rabbit") and either marmot or groundhog, which were important for materials and subsistence; and wolverine, otter, marten, mink, weasel, muskrat, lynx, wolf, coyote, fox and others which, together with some of the subsistence species, provided furs for trade. Muskoxen, bison and wapiti also were available at a few localities. Fish abound in the rivers and lakes, and include several species of whitefish, pike, lake trout, grayling and suckers in the arctic drainage and salmon in the Pacific and, to a lesser extent, Atlantic drainages. Migratory waterfowl pass through the Subarctic seasonally in great numbers.

Major Languages and Tribal Groups Most peoples of the Eastern Subarctic speak languages of the Algonquian family; those of the Western Subarctic, Athapaskan languages. Northern Subarctic Algonquians, including the ATTIKAMEK and MONTAGNAIS-NASKAPI of Québec and Labrador, speak dialects of the Cree language, and Algonquians to the south of them speak dialects of Ojibwa. The BEOTHUK of Newfoundland spoke a language of uncertain affinity. Linguists have identified more than 20 different Northern Athapaskan languages within the Western Subarctic, including Alaska (*see* NATIVE PEOPLE, LANGUAGES).

Most Indians of the Subarctic were not organized politically as tribes, but they can be divided into named groups of people, members of contiguous bands (local populations exploiting defined territories) who spoke the same language dialect and were related by kinship and common traditions. Within each of the 2 major language families, neighbouring groups often shared similar ways of life. Perhaps because the Western Subarctic is physically more diverse than the East, there was more linguistic and cultural diversity among the Athapaskans than the Algonquians.

Historical Summary Contact with Europeans changed Subarctic cultures profoundly. The effects of contact differed according to time and place. Early contact during the 17th century

Dogrib Indians at Great Slave Lake unloading a canoe (*courtesy Provincial Archives of Alberta/E. Brown Coll/B779*).

Model of skin boat (canoe) (*courtesy Royal Ontario Museum*).

caused extensive migration of Subarctic people such as the CREE and brought about new and different intertribal relationships. The 19th century was characterized by direct contact between native people and Europeans engaged in the FUR TRADE. Different tribes experienced the effects of contact with greater or lesser severity. In Newfoundland, loss of habitat and killing by whites led to complete extinction of the native Beothuk by 1829. By contrast, the neighbouring Montagnais-Naskapi (Innu) developed a trapping economy and systematic trade relations with Europeans. They adapted successfully to contact conditions because Europeans needed them to trap furs and had no immediate use for their hunting territories. Other Indians such as the Cree became fur-trade middlemen between the HUDSON'S BAY CO and Subarctic Athapaskans to the west. Following Alexander MACKENZIE's voyages of exploration along the Peace and Mackenzie rivers beginning in 1789, the rival NORTH WEST CO established trading posts that gave its traders direct contact with the Athapaskans. In 1821 these posts were taken over by the HBC, which has remained an important influence in the area.

The 20th century has increasingly seen a period of resource development in the North and the movement of non-natives into the Subarctic. These conditions have motivated contemporary Subarctic natives to press for LAND CLAIMS settlements and increased control over their own affairs.

Traditional Culture All natives of the Subarctic lived by hunting, fishing, trapping and gathering wild plants. Indigenous farming was not practical within their territory (crops successfully grown in the North today did not reach contiguous areas until after European contact). Men did most of the big-game hunting, while women snared hare, fished, cut and dried meat, and processed hides.

Beaver tail snowshoes (*courtesy Royal Ontario Museum*).

Some hunting techniques such as drives and the construction and operation of corrals involved most adult members of a BAND (*see* BUFFALO HUNT).

Since game animals were thinly distributed over vast territories in the boreal forest, or were available only locally or seasonally, Subarctic human population densities were among the lowest in the world. Some scholars estimate that the entire area may have supported as few as 60 000 people, although others believe that before the introduction of European diseases, populations could have been larger.

Subarctic natives typically lived in local bands of 25-30 people. Each band moved frequently from one place to another within a well-defined territory as game supplies changed from season to season and from year to year. A group's size and the nature of its annual economic cycle were strongly influenced by the availability of local resources. The TUTCHONE, Athapaskans of the Yukon Plateau, and others west of the Rocky Mts, gathered along rivers during the summer to catch and dry salmon. The CHIPEWYAN, Athapaskans living north of Lk Athabasca, moved to the edge of the barren grounds to follow the caribou herds. Montagnais and Naskapi spent their summers near the Atlantic, Gulf of St Lawrence or James Bay coasts and their winters inland. A single band often did not have exclusive access to its territory since adjacent bands frequently obtained hunting rights, especially if they faced food scarcity, or certain peripheral areas were used in common. However, rich sites such as lakes or rivers where fish could be taken regularly were usually exploited by the same band year after year. During the summer, when food was abundant, several local bands often resided together.

Most Subarctic bands did not have formal chiefs before European contact. People aligned themselves with persons who manifested leadership abilities and took the initiative for undertaking specific tasks such as trading, war or communal hunting, including the necessary prior preparations. Aside from the prestige and respect this brought them, their authority did not generally extend beyond these tasks. White fur traders, however, attempted to establish chiefs and to endow them with considerable power, in order to have better control of the Indian population tied to the trading post.

Most adult men and women had a part in making decisions that affected the band. Families or individuals who did not agree with a particular decision were free to join another band or camp, or to act on their own for a time. Subarctic people were noted for the value they placed on personal autonomy as well as for the flexibility of their social organization. These characteristics helped them respond to the opportunities and limitations of their environment.

Ties of kinship, reckoned primarily matrilineally among Pacific drainage Athapaskans, bilaterally among those of the Mackenzie drainage, and both bilaterally and patrilineally among the Algon-

quian speakers, joined people together. Normally, people who had regular contacts used kinship terms, in part structured according to generation (eg, the eldest people become grandfather or grandmother), to address and refer to one another. Kinship relations often determined membership in groups and regulated marriages. In addition, tribes west of the Mackenzie R were organized into clans, and also in some cases by dual divisions (moieties) adopted from West Coast tribes. These divisions served primarily to insure hospitality and protection to clan members who might be visiting from other camps or tribes, to fulfil certain largely ceremonial obligations to the opposite division, eg, cremation and/or burial of the dead and reciprocal feasts, and to regulate marriage through the requirement of clan exogamy.

Since their food quest necessitated mobility, natives of the Subarctic had limited material possessions. They travelled light and preferred to make heavier tools and implements as they were needed rather than carry them from place to place. Success in hunting depended on accurate knowledge of animal behaviour. Children were taught to be self-reliant, observant and resourceful. They were expected to learn the habits of game animals and to find their way through large areas of difficult terrain. They were assisted in these skills by listening to long hours of practical narrative accounts and mythological tales and by learning special trapping and hunting songs and innumerable riddles. Those who made stupid mistakes from failure to be observant were the butt of ridicule.

Northern forest Indians made summer MOCASINS, leggings, shirts and coats of soft tanned hides from which the hair had been removed by scraping. Unique among the Athapaskans was the short V-tailed summer slipover caribou skin shirt, highly ornamented with dyed porcupine quills, dentalium and beads made from seeds (later glass, trade beads). This exquisite shirt was worn with trousers with moccasins attached. For wear during the coldest months, rabbit skins were cut into strips, twisted and woven into parkas and sleeping robes, and 2-piece suits were made from caribou hides with the hair left on and turned inside. Several different styles of moccasins lined with rabbit skin or dried grass were used.

Hunting implements included bows, various types of arrows, and a variety of ingenious traps, snares, deadfalls, and such devices as the caribou drift fence and pound. People caught fish with dip and gill nets, traps, spears, and hook and line. They dried berries in the fall or stored them in baskets in pits in the ground. Often the berries were mixed with fat and fish to make "Eskimo ice cream" in the far northwest, or were mixed with pounded dried meat and grease to make PEMMICAN. Women were skilled in preparing meat for drying, hide tanning and sewing, making cooking and storage containers of skins, birchbark or coiled spruce root basketry, and making fishnets from willow baste or babiche.

Men made SNOWSHOES, TOBOGGANS, sleds and hunting implements. Survival depended on being able to travel long distances. Snowshoes were essential for winter travel. Heavy loads were transported on toboggans and, in the far northwest, sleds pulled both by dogs and people. Aboriginally, few dogs were available for traction. During the summer, people and their belongings were moved along rivers and lakes by canoe.

Because of their mobile existence, northern forest people built shelters constructed of easily transported bark or skin covers and of locally available materials. Dwellings varied considerably depending on local materials and traditions, but in all areas they were designed to be heated and lit by a single fire. They did not usually ac-

commodate more than 2 families. Among the northern OJIBWA, summer dwellings were bark TIPIS or dome-shaped lodges also covered with birchbark. Many of the Arctic drainage Athapaskans lived in conical shelters covered with hides, similar to the Plains tipi. Among the KUTCHIN and HAN of the Yukon, as well as in northern Alaska, the conical tent was replaced by a domed or hemispherical one. Double lean-to structures covered with hides and brush also were used in the Arctic (Mackenzie) drainage and the northwestern mountain and plateau region. At fishing camps in the Cordillera there were unchinked "smokehouses" that resembled roughly built log cabins. In order to provide added warmth in winter dwellings, the hair was left on the hide coverings of conical and domed tents which, although bulky, nevertheless were portable. Some Athapaskans of the Mackenzie District and Cordillera as well as Indians of the eastern Subarctic wintered in conical log structures chinked with moss and partially covered with dirt and snow. The Han near Dawson, as well as many Alaskan groups, built rectangular pit houses that were heavily banked with turf to withstand the cold, while far to the south in BC, groups such as the CHILCOTIN made pit houses similar to those used in the Plateau.

Considerable effort was taken to cache food and equipment not needed for the season at hand, in specially prepared pits, strong cribbed and conical structures and cairns, or on racks and platforms in trees.

Myths and legends taught about a time when animals had great power and could assume human form. Many Subarctic people tell stories about a "culture hero," the first person to become powerful. For them, power and knowledge were one. They said someone with power "knows something." The culture hero demonstrated the personal knowledge and self-reliance that were recognized as important survival skills, and could outwit evil medicine persons and overcome dangerous animals of the myth time, and thus make the world a safer place in which humans could live. Beliefs about the interdependence of people and nature, embodied in myth, helped Subarctic natives interpret their environment.

Religious leaders were people who used their powers for the benefit of others, though to some people they sometimes used their power for evil. Among many Algonquians, these SHAMANS, or medicine people, conducted the SHAKING TENT ceremony in which distant spirits of people or animals were conjured for curing and prophecy in a special tipi. Elsewhere, shamans performed under a blanket or dressed in a special manner as a signal of their office. Western Athapaskan medicine men and women charged high prices for their services and asserted prerogatives or took liberties among their people, for which reason some of them were feared and hated. Among the Naskapi, certain men and women told about the trail ahead by scapulamancy, a form of divination done by interpreting the pattern of cracks on a caribou shoulder blade heated by fire. The BEAVER of the Peace R region had prophets called Dreamers – people who had experienced death and flown like swans to a spirit land beyond the sky. They were healers and leaders in religious dances based on songs they brought back from their journeys to heaven. Like many other Subarctic people, they sang to the accompaniment of single-headed hand drums. Most people, however, had certain varying amounts of medicine power. In addition, there was a body of belief and practices, proscriptions (taboos), prescriptions and minor rituals which existed apart from shamanism, divination and curing. Among these customs were the special observances taken prior to and

Cree camp on the prairie, south of Vermilion, Alta, Sept 1871. The conical tipi was covered with buffalo skins (*courtesy National Archives of Canada/PA-5181*).

after killing animals, as in bear ceremonialism and that attendant to the deaths of humans.

Culture Change Contact with Europeans presented a challenge to native peoples of the Subarctic. Many quickly became dependent on trade goods such as guns, knives, axes, cooking pots and clothing, and eventually food, since they turned from harvesting animals for food and skins to trapping those species desired in European markets. Bands moved to within travelling distance of trading posts, and the traders endeavoured to control the Indians. Trading chiefs who could negotiate with the Europeans became as important as the earlier hunt leaders. The fur trade had a considerable impact on Subarctic ecology. Many species of game and fur-bearing animals were depleted. European diseases such as smallpox, tuberculosis, measles and influenza killed large numbers of people (*see* NATIVE PEOPLE, HEALTH). Other people died of starvation during periods of disease and game scarcity. Native people adopted many elements of CHRISTIANITY but also retained many of their own spiritual traditions, sometimes covertly. The ability to assimilate new techniques and ideas is a typical attribute of the Subarctic native culture.

In modern times, large-scale resource development and settlement of the North by large numbers of outsiders have threatened the native economy of trapping and subsistence hunting. In 1975 the Grand Council of the Cree signed the James Bay and Northern Québec Agreement accepting compensation for social and ecological impacts of the James Bay Hydroelectric Project (*see* JAMES BAY AGREEMENT). Many Cree continued to hunt and trap on their land. Natives of the western Subarctic in the District of Mackenzie, organized politically into the DENE NATION, are seeking a settlement that recognizes their right to a certain degree of self-determination within the Canadian national context.   ROBIN RIDINGTON

Reading: H.A. Dempsey, *Indian Tribes of Alberta* (1978); P. Drucker, *Indians of the Northwest Coast* (1955); W. Duff, *The Indian History of British Columbia* (1964); L.M. and J.R. Hanks, *Tribe Under Trust: A Study of the Blackfoot Reserve of Alberta* (1950); H.B. Hawthorn et al, *The Indians of British Columbia* (1958); D. Jenness, *The Indians of Canada* (1932); T. McFeat, ed, *Indians of the North Pacific Coast* (1966); D.G. Mandelbaum, *The Plains Cree* (1979); R.B. Morrison and C.R. Wilson, *The Native Peoples: The Canadian Experience* (1987); A. Ray, *Indians in the Fur Trade* (1974); V.F. Ray, *Cultural Relations in the Plateau of Northwestern America* (1939); W.C. Sturtevant, gen ed, *Handbook of North American Indians*, vol 15: *Northeast*, ed, B.G. Trigger (1978) and vol 6: *Subarctic*, ed, J. Helm (1981), other volumes are forthcoming; J.W. Vanstone, *Atha-*

paskan Adaptations: Hunters and Fishermen of the Subarctic Forests (1974); M. Zaslow, ed, *A Century of Canada's Arctic Islands 1880-1980* (1981).

Native People, Communications After the late 19th century a few periodicals were published for native audiences by non-Indian missionary organizations, notable examples being the Chinook-language *Kamloops Wawa* (1891-1905) and the Inuktitut-language Oblate publications of the 1940s and 1950s. Among the few purely Indian journals was the Hagersville, Ont, *Indian* (1885-86). Native journalism in Canada is not well documented, except for the Indian impersonators Grey Owl (A.S. BELANEY) and Buffalo Child Long Lance (*see* LONG LANCE, BUFFALO CHILD) who published extensively on native issues in the 1920s and 1930s.

Rapid progress in communications technology in the 1960s, coupled with increased exposure to radio, TV and newsprint, has caused INDIAN, INUIT and MÉTIS leaders to become more aware of the power of mass communications as a means of influencing the political process. Convinced that the mass media was intended for the non-native audience and controlled by non-native interests, many native organizations, at the BAND, provincial and national levels, started to publish their own newsletters and newspapers in the 1970s. These publications were concerned mainly with advocacy on native issues, with little space allotted to news or human-interest features. Many later publications reflect a wider range of interests.

In the mid-1960s, working with seed money from the province of Alberta, Eugene Steinhauer, a Cree who later became president of the Indian Assn of Alberta, purchased a tape recorder and some rudimentary editing equipment and started producing news and public-affairs items for broadcast on the CBC outlets in Alberta. By 1968 Steinhauer's one-man communications operation had become the Alberta Native Communications Society, a nonprofit organization funded by the province and the federal secretary of state, which eventually expanded beyond radio into TV production and the publication of a tabloid newspaper, *The Native People* (1968-82). It took as its slogan, "From Smoke Signals to Satellites." Other native communications societies, all funded at least in part by the secretary of state through the Native Communications program, and some partially funded by provinces, sprang up in various parts of Canada.

By 1987 there were 16 native communications societies: Indian News Media Inc (Stand Off, Alta); Aboriginal Multi-Media Society of Alberta (Edmonton); Aboriginal Radio and Television Society (ARTS; Lac La Biche, Alta); Native Communications Society of British Columbia (Vancouver); Ye Sa To Publications Native Communi-

cations Society (Whitehorse, YT); Inuvialuit Communications Society (Inuvik), Native Communications Society of the Western Northwest Territories (Yellowknife) and Okalakatiget Society (Iqaluit); Okaalakatigik Society (Nain, Labrador); Native Communications Inc (Thompson, Man); Wa Wa Tay Native Communications Society (Sioux Lookout, Ont); Taqramiut Nipingat Inc (Dorval, Qué), Société de Communications Attikamek Montagnais (SOCAM; Village des Hurons, Qué) and James Bay Cree Communications Society (Val D'Or, Qué); Saskatchewan Native Communications and Whetamatouin Corporation (Regina); and Native Communications Society of NS (Membertou Reserve, Sydney). The secretary of state had plans for expansion of its native communications program to include societies in other parts of Canada where native people expressed an interest and capability to operate a society.

From its inception, the secretary of state program was based on the principle that the societies should serve both status and nonstatus audiences and should not be controlled or unduly influenced by native political organizations, extending the "free and independent" press tradition of the non-native society. This principle was accepted by some native leaders, but strongly rejected by others. This rejection was particularly strong in Saskatchewan and NB, where most native leaders adopted the position that there could be no native communications societies unless they were part of or strongly influenced by the native political organizations and served separate status or nonstatus audiences.

Casual or unlicensed broadcasting in native languages had been carried out since the earliest days of northern radio. Perhaps one of the most important developments in native communications in the early 1980s was a decision by the CRTC to license the Inuit Broadcasting Corp in Frobisher Bay [IQALUIT] to produce television programs for the mainly Inuit audience in northern Québec and the eastern Arctic and to link them via the CBC's satellite channel. Another development was the licensing of CANCOM, a privately owned satellite transmission company, to provide satellite television and radio service to "underserved" areas (*see* COMMUNICATIONS IN THE NORTH; SATELLITE COMMUNICATIONS). As of 1987 native communications groups in various northern locations have established native radio networks which use satellite distribution.

ROBERT J. RUPERT

Native People, Demography Although estimates vary of the native population of Canada at the time of the arrival of Europeans, anthropologists give a tentative figure of about 350 000. Thereafter, the number of native people declined dramatically owing to disease, starvation and warfare. By 1867, it is thought that between 100 000 and 125 000 Indians remained in what is now Canada, along with approximately 10 000 MÉTIS and half-breeds in Manitoba and 2000 Inuit in the Arctic. The native population of Canada continued to decline until 1920 (*see* NATIVE PEOPLE, HEALTH). Since then, however, it has increased at a rate faster than that of the general population. The annual INDIAN population growth rate, eg, peaked in the late 1950s at slightly under 4% (the postwar Indian "baby-boom"), and since then has gradually declined to about 1.5%.

In 1986, according to Statistics Canada, there were in Canada approximately 331 000 Indians, 27 000 Inuit, and 398 000 Métis and people of mixed native origin, comprising a total aboriginal population of 756 000, or 3% of Canada's total population. While generally accurate, these figures are based on only a 20% sample of the Canadian population, rather than a complete census. In addition, incomplete enumeration of many Indian reserves and communities in 1986 prevented government demographers from developing more precise statistical data.

Native people comprise 59% of the total population of the NWT and 21% in the Yukon. Among the provinces, native people account for 9% of the population in Manitoba, 8% in Saskatchewan, 5% in Alberta and BC, and 1-2% in the eastern and Atlantic provinces. Ontario, however, has the greatest number of native people (180 000), followed by BC (136 000), Alberta (113 000), Manitoba (93 000), Québec (89 000) and Saskatchewan (78 000).

The Department of INDIAN AFFAIRS AND NORTHERN DEVELOPMENT estimates, based on 1980 census figures, that of the total Indian population of Canada, 65% live in rural or remote areas of the country and 35% live in urban or semiurban areas. The proportions are comparable for the Métis and nonstatus Indian population. Among the provinces, BC, Saskatchewan and Manitoba have the highest proportion of native people living in rural or remote areas, while Ontario, Québec and the Atlantic provinces have the highest proportion living in urban and semiurban areas. Inuit, Indians and Métis in the Yukon and NWT live almost entirely in rural and remote regions.

Since the mid-1960s an increasing number of native people have moved away from their reserves (Indians) or home communities – usually to urban centres. This migration stems primarily from the lack of economic opportunity in or near INDIAN RESERVES and native communities. According to 1986 census figures, approximately 35% of the total Indian population now lives off-reserve, compared to just 18% in 1960. Inuit communities are relatively stable in comparison to native communities in southern Canada. DAN GOTTESMAN

Reading: T. Berger, Northern Frontier, Northern Homeland (1977); H. Hawthorne, A Survey of the Contemporary Indians of Canada (1966-67); Indian Conditions: A Survey (1980); Statistics Canada, Population by Aboriginal Origins Showing Single and Multiple Origins, On and Off Indian Reserves and Settlements, for Canada, Provinces and Territories, 1986 (1987).

Native People, Economic Conditions

Aboriginal economies were based primarily on *sharing* (a familistic, egalitarian pooling of resources) in the 26 simple or BAND-level societies to the north; on *reciprocity* (a calculated, give-and-take exchange) in the 17 intermediate or "tribal" level societies to the south; and on *redistribution* (a centralized and politically organized administration of the economy) in all 11 developed chiefdoms of the Northwest Coast. These highly ranked Pacific Coast societies did buy and sell slaves, who made up about 10% of the population. No native societies had true money, or any medium of exchange with high "liquidity," by which one thing such as coins could buy a wide variety of goods and services. There were no true markets where prices were primarily set by the supply and demand of goods. There was no such thing as employment for wages. During the FUR-TRADE period, however, the elements of a barter/wage economy infiltrated many native communities. In 1981 only about 38% of status Indians over 15 years of age were "employed," in the sense of working for a monetary income, compared to 60% of the general population over 15.

To the degree that native people in Canada today participate in their aboriginal economic heritage, they have problems in integrating with the general Canadian economy. A native trying to get into business has to learn details of a new and complex system involving such things as accounting, bidding, contracts, licences, loans, unions and taxes. The "unemployment rate," those seeking wage employment and unable to get it, was 17% among status Indians and 7% in the general population in 1981.

Three factors have been particularly important in patterning modern native economies: the specific evolutionary heritage of each of the surviving traditional societies; the extent to which individuals were drawn in the past into the money, market and wage economy; and the federal governments's role in the support and administration of the economies of native communities.

In general the more socially and politically complex aboriginal societies adapted most successfully, at time of contact, with the non-native economy, and this holds true of their participation in the modern economy. Natives with a heritage that goes back to the chiefdoms of BC or to the southern tribes, such as the BLACKFOOT, MOHAWK or HURON, have higher incomes than the INUIT, DENE and northern Algonquian peoples with a band heritage. Historical differences in participation in the modern economy have shown up in the same societies; the CREE and OJIBWA, eg, who moved onto the prairies with the fur trade, made economic advances over those who remained in their homelands in northern Québec and Ontario. This economic boom made Cree and Ojibwa the largest and second-largest native societies in Canada, respectively.

After WWII, and especially in the 1960s, the federal government began to play a more active role in the delivery of social, educational and economic development services to native communities (*see* NATIVE PEOPLE, GOVERNMENT PROGRAMS). The annual federal expenditures on native programs were estimated (1983) to be $2.6 billion ($1.9 billion on status Indians), with the following approximate distribution: community affairs 35%, education 32%, health 13%, administration 6%, economic development 5%, employment 5%, policy and research 1%, and other areas including housing, native associations and sports 3% (*see* NATIVE PEOPLE, SOCIAL CONDITIONS).

The greatest economic advantage that native people have is that they do not pay income tax, provincial tax or certain excise taxes when they reside and work on their reserves. In some respects the 592 INDIAN bands are like municipalities in that they have many powers of self-administration. They may levy property taxes or manage businesses that can operate on reserves without paying taxes. Most of the costs of education, health and welfare on the reserves are paid for by the federal government.

Native people are caught in a swirl of choices. In the traditional communities, a high value is placed on such noneconomic values as the maintenance of proper family and social relations and a tolerant acceptance of individual life-styles, often with strong elements of aesthetics and spirituality. Natives often live in a material state that most Canadians would despise and call "poverty." Native politicians play up this sympathy for native poverty to win material programs for their communities, but most natives have visited the cities of Canada and still prefer to live in their own rural communities (*see* NATIVE PEOPLE, DEMOGRAPHY).

We expect that all people who choose to live in rural areas will have fewer modern conveniences than urban people simply because of the high costs of delivering those services to highly scattered locations. In Canada about 60% of all houses in rural, summer cottage and remote bush areas have running water, sewage disposal and indoor plumbing, but only about 40% of the native houses in rural and remote communities have all these facilities. A DIAND survey found that 38% of reserve housing was overcrowded.

Part of the answer to this discrepancy is that there are many very remote native communities: 48% of the band areas are "remote" or "inaccessible," which means that they cannot be reached by roads – only by foot trails, by water or by aircraft; 23% are considered rural; and only 29% are semiurban or urban.

The land base of the 2284 Indian reserves and settlements tends to be quite small (12.6 million ha in 1985), so the native population has few resources to work with. The land base is only about 7.6 ha (19 acres) per status Indian in Canada in 1985 (350 000 status Indians and 2 649 000 ha), compared with 62 ha per status person for Indians in the US. The average size of a Canadian Indian reserve is 1100 ha or 4.3 square miles. Most of the land is suitable only for primary production such as fishing and forestry. About 20% of Indian land has good agricultural potential, but this land is located largely in southern Canada where natives already have access to other forms of employment.

Statistics for the 1981 labour force indicate a high level of dependency and a level of wage employment that is only half that of the national average. A significant number of natives still harvest fish and game for subsistence purposes in the traditional style. Native people are strongly represented in outdoor and seasonal work, though these occupations pay less than such indoor and year-round work as professional, technical, managerial, clerical, sales and service occupations. The average 1980 income of native people was $8600; the national average was $13 100.

Occupational Representation	Indians	National
Fishermen, trappers, hunters	17%	1%
Farmers and farm workers	19%	12%
Loggers	12%	2%
Labourers	14%	6%
Other, mostly indoor work	38%	79%

The low incomes, poverty and unemployment of native people are, to a considerable degree, the result of cultural heritage, choice of occupation and residence far from the main centres of the economy; by comparison, racial discrimination and level of education are secondary factors. Almost all native people complete elementary school, most have some secondary education, and a small percentage are going on to complete college or university (*see* NATIVE PEOPLE, EDUCATION). On average, the formal education of native adults is only about 2 years below the national average; and the gap is closing, with non-native rural students and native students spending roughly the same number of years in school. The 1981 census found that 28.7% of the native population had a high school or higher level of education. Anti-Indian discrimination is not generally severe enough to influence economic matters except in some communities in the Prairie provinces and northern Ontario.

Indications of a prosperous future are seen in several current Indian enterprises. There is a national distribution of small businesses in native communities – retail stores, beauty salons and barber shops, laundromats, tourist camps and leasing of cottage lots; in Québec, manufacturing of canoes and lacrosse sticks, a fish-packing plant, a shopping centre, and the high-steel construction work of the Mohawks; in Ontario, manufacturing of shoes and fur coats, an industrial park, a ski resort, a large cranberry farm and over 125 tons of WILD RICE production per year; in Manitoba, 2 bush airlines, a shopping centre and honey production; in Saskatchewan, farming and ranching; in Alberta, the Sawridge Motor Hotel in Jasper, manufacturing prefabricated houses, petroleum production and cattle ranching; in BC, fish farming and packing, forestry and lumber milling, mining services and office rentals; in the NWT, Inuit Development Corporation investments in mining, a hotel and office buildings. There are over 750 successful Indian businesses in Canada, many started with loans from DIAND's Indian Economic Development Fund or the newer (1983), native managed, Native Economic Development Program. Although many of these enterprises are heavily subsidized by government and band funds, they are hopeful signs of the growth of a native entrepreneurial system.

The national unemployment rate for adult Métis and nonstatus Indians is around 32%. Those who are employed have an average income 16% lower than the national average. They live generally in the same regions as Indians, with a greater tendency for urbanization. Eight Métis communities in 5 areas in Alberta live on provincially established reserves and are involved in fishing, farming and logging. In some provinces the Métis have separate rights and regulations from other native people. Alberta and the NWT, eg, permit them to do general subsistence fishing, and Ontario and NB have special Métis provisions for certain fishing areas.

In Ontario there are 50 000-90 000 culturally active Métis and nonstatus Indians, depending upon the criteria used. In 1978-79 a core of 5444 politically active Métis in 66 communities was surveyed and it was found that 23% of the adults in the work force were unemployed, about 3 times the provincial unemployment rate at the time. However, 60% owned their own home, which is just slightly lower than the Ontario general rate of 66%, and housing facilities were found to be fairly good for a largely rural population: 94% had electricity, 85% had running water and 82% had sewers.

The arctic economy is still primarily based on government programs, such as those of northern development and defence. For example, an oil pipeline constructed from Zama, Alta, to Norman Wells on the Mackenzie River employed over 100 northern natives. The sale by Inuit of sculptures, prints, tailored clothing and furs has also become important in their economy (*see also* INUIT CO-OPERATIVES). JOHN A. PRICE

Reading: John A. Price, *Indians of Canada: Cultural Dynamics* (1988).

Native People, Education Traditional education among most INDIAN and INUIT was by observation and practice, family and group socialization, oral teachings, and participation in tribal ceremonies and institutions. With these methods children learned the values, skills and knowledge considered necessary for adult life. This style of education continues today, but its importance to many Indians has been overshadowed during the past 350 years by the introduction of a formal European-American classroom style of education.

Formal European education of Indian children began in the early 1600s in New France, in mission schools operated by French religious orders such as the Recollets, Jesuits and Ursulines. These schools established a pattern of church involvement in Indian education that dominated until after WWII. The major goals of these mission schools were the "civilization" and Christianization of Indians. In the late 1700s and early 1800s Protestant churches also became active in the education of Indian children in what is now Canada. From 1763 to 1830 the imperial government dealt with "Indian Affairs" through the military; provision for education for native peoples was minimal. After 1830, when administration was transferred to the secretary of state for the colonies, some money was diverted to education by means of donations to church organizations. This funding allowed the building of schools on some reserves. During this same period various colonies began to provide limited resources for the education of tribal groups within their boundaries.

From the 1830s the churches, mainly the Roman Catholic and Anglican denominations, in co-operation with the colonial governments and later the federal government, began to establish residential (boarding) schools for Indians. By 1900 there were 64 residential schools in Canada. Staffed by missionary teachers who gave vocational and manual as well as religious instruction, these schools were seen as the ideal system for educating Indians because they removed children from the influences of traditional family life. They complemented the prevailing policy of assimilating Indians into white society. Indian parents saw residential schools as necessary evils; necessary because many Indians saw Christianity as a new and positive force in their lives, or because they recognized the need for European skills; but evil because they removed children from their homes and family ties. Most Indians regarded the regime in residential schools as harsh and cruel: children were physically punished for disobedience, and most school staffs forbade the use of native languages by students and made the children feel ashamed of their native identity.

After 1867, education for native peoples fell into 2 categories: education for status Indians became a federal responsibility under the constitution and the treaties; that for nonstatus Indians, Inuit and MÉTIS a provincial or territorial responsibility. By 1900 there were some 226 federally funded day schools in INDIAN RESERVES; the majority of teachers were missionaries and the curriculum included a large proportion of religious instruction. By the 1930s the curriculum began to be more closely patterned on that of the non-Indian provincial schools.

By 1940 statistics revealed that few status Indian children were benefiting from their formal education experiences. Many children were repeating 3 or 4 grades in elementary school, and only a small percentage were graduating from elementary school and going on to high school. During the 1940s the federal government, in co-operation with provincial education authorities, established a policy of integration: federal funds would be provided to enable Indian students to attend provincial elementary and high schools. The expectation was that by removing Indian students from the poorly staffed, inadequately equipped, heavily church-oriented day schools, assimilation would be accelerated and the performance of students improved. Enrolments in provincial schools rose rapidly and by 1960 there were about 10 000 Indian students attending off-reserve provincial schools. Numerous problems became evident in the program, which led to its reevaluation by Indian parents and political leaders. Although the qualifications of provincial teachers were superior, they lacked specialized training to teach Indian students. Indian parents criticized the removal of children to boarding homes as well as the daily commuting by bus to attend provincial schools. Most Indian students were not achieving success: in 1967 only 200 Indian students were enrolled in Canadian universities out of a total native student population of some 60 000.

In 1972 the National Indian Brotherhood produced a policy on Indian education, "Indian Control of Indian Education," which was subsequently adopted by the Dept of Indian Affairs and Northern Development (DIAND) as federal policy. It identified the importance of local community control to improve education, the need for more Indian teachers, the development of rel-evant curricula and teaching resources in Indian schools, and the importance of language instruction and native values in Indian education. Since the presentation of this policy several changes have occurred. By 1983 over 200 schools on reserves were managed entirely or in part by band councils. Over 80 reserve schools offer native-language classes, and 38% of native children attending school are given some form of native-language instruction. Several programs to increase the number of native teachers have been established in universities in Ontario, Manitoba, Saskatchewan, Alberta, BC and NB. In an effort to improve teaching materials for and about native people, DIAND and the Canadian Museum of Civilization have co-operated in the preparation of dictionaries, grammars and reading texts.

Trent U in Peterborough, Ontario, was the first Canadian university to establish a native studies program, followed since 1969 by similar programs in 9 other universities. A unique approach to post-secondary education is under way at U of Regina, where an Indian Cultural College is part of the university federated system. In 1976, as a result of the JAMES BAY AGREEMENT, the largest Indian-controlled school board in Canada, the Cree School Board, was created.

Although some Inuit were educated in mission schools in Labrador as early as the 1790s, formal education for Inuit began on a national scale only in the 1950s with the construction of elementary and residential schools throughout major settlements in the Arctic. The decrease in residential schools in the Arctic paralleled the decrease in residential schools for Indians and led to a school-construction program by the federal government in most Inuit villages by 1970. Inuit education programs, unlike those in Indian and other schools for natives, identify Inuktitut, the Inuit language, as the language of instruction for part or all of the primary grades. In spite of this pedagogical innovation, education for Inuit has been impeded by problems similar to those encountered by other native students.

Statistics are not available for Métis and nonstatus Indian students, but studies generally indicate that, owing to poor socioeconomic conditions and the absence of any specific provincial or federal responsibility for their education, they suffer consequences similar to other native people in their attempt to receive a formal education.

For native people to benefit from their formal education, several changes are necessary. Indian bands, through local or regional education authorities, will have to exercise more control of education policies, budgeting, teacher hiring and school programs. Teaching resources and curricula will need to incorporate and reinforce the culture and values that native children acquire within the family. Education at the local and urban levels will need to expand options in technical and vocational programs. Greater consideration must be given to instructing native children in the primary grades in the language of the home and community, particularly in areas where the native language is in danger of becoming extinct (*see* NATIVE PEOPLE, LANGUAGES). It is clear from past experience that efforts to alienate native people from their culture have not promoted learning in the formal education process. HARVEY McCUE

Readings: National Indian Brotherhood, *Indian Control of Indian Education* (1972); Jerry Pacquette, *Aboriginal Self Government and Education in Canada* (1986).

Native People, Government Policy For the most part, government policy towards native people has meant INDIAN policy. The INUIT were barely touched by government until the 1940s, while special responsibility for MÉTIS and nonstatus Indians has been largely denied. The early history of Indian policy in Canada is characterized by the presence of both France and Britain as colonizing powers. Post-Confederation policy was largely based on the Upper Canadian model, although with significant regional differences.

The very scientific and social revolution that made European expansion overseas possible made it more difficult for Europeans to coexist with the preindustrial peoples they encountered throughout the world. The European technological society sought to conquer nature and shed traditional values – in sharp contrast with native cultures, which were based on extremely close relationships with nature and on strong reliance on tradition. When the 2 societies had to share the same territory, the differing outlooks were irreconcilable. European states attempted to solve the problem by assuming dominance. They claimed by right of "discovery" the less populated lands around the world and declared indigenous people living there to be subject to the colonizing power. However, the material and practical dependence of the Europeans who first came to N America upon the more numerous and better-adapted native people led to Indian-white trading and military alliances. During the period of alliances, which lasted until the early 19th century, Indian policy was diplomatic and military in orientation because native people were considered in some sense to constitute sovereign and independent nations (*see* NATIVE PEOPLE, LAW).

French contacts with Indians involved trade, war and missionary work. Official French policy had 2 objectives: to evangelize the Indians and to assimilate them into French society. Although a few Indian groups settled on church-controlled agricultural reserves near the French, the vast majority continued to live apart as independent nations. By the 1690s, the failure of large-scale assimilation of Indians was accepted even by missionaries and government officials. Fur traders had always discouraged it as being bad for trade (*see* FUR TRADE). Since the French settlements did not expand extensively into Indian territory and displace the inhabitants, the French never recognized formally that Indians had rights in the land and no land cession treaties were ever made. The more populous English colonies, however, expanded towards the West. Although some of them had made treaties with the Indians whom they displaced, they posed a constant threat to neighbouring tribes.

Conflicting alliances between native groups and Europeans dated from the early 17th century when Samuel de CHAMPLAIN built an alliance with the HURON and hence alienated the Huron's enemies, the IROQUOIS. Throughout the next 2 centuries the French and British each attracted Indian allies in their competition for trade, land and empire in N America. With the collapse of French imperial power after the SEVEN YEARS' WAR (1756-63), France's erstwhile Indian allies faced the threat of unobstructed British expansion. Indian resistance was expressed in a series of risings associated with the OTTAWA chief, PONTIAC. The Imperial authorities responded by issuing in the ROYAL PROCLAMATION OF 1763 an assurance to the Indians that they would not be disturbed in their territories beyond the settled colonies. Indian land could only be surrendered to the Crown and at a general assembly of Indians. This principle formed the basis of the later treaty system.

Within 20 years, the successful revolt of Britain's Thirteen Colonies revived alliances as Indian nations vainly strove to protect their territory from American expansion. Britain willingly used their assistance in its own diplomatic and military endeavours to protect its Canadian conquests. Indian support proved valuable to the British in the WAR OF 1812. This twilight of the alliance period overlapped with the beginning of the second stage of Indian policy extending through Confederation to the mid-20th century. Its characteristic features were the imposition by European governments of treaties, reserves and paternalistic social policies, all intended to promote Indian assimilation to the general population. As land was needed for settlement in Upper Canada, treaties were made to "extinguish" ABORIGINAL RIGHTS to the soil according to the principles of the Royal Proclamation of 1763. By contrast, land-cession treaties were not made in the older colonies of the Maritimes or in Québec even when new areas were opened to settlement.

As the non-Indian population increased, Indians ceased to be treated as independent nations and were settled on reserves (*see* INDIAN RESERVE). There, Indian "bands" were organized under the supervision of Indian Dept superintendents or agents. No longer military diplomats, but local managers of reserve land and BAND affairs, they encouraged Indians to farm, become self-supporting by nontraditional means, and generally live like the surrounding population. Schools and churches were usually provided. These activities were organized by a civilian Indian Dept, which replaced the military authority in 1830. The establishment of common property in reserves and band funds, special legislation and treaty rights led to the development of the legal concept of Indian status. Some persons of Indian ancestry – the Métis and nonstatus Indians – never qualified for Indian status or lost it in a variety of ways. Apart from land or scrip grants and special hunting rights for Métis in certain areas, the government has denied any special responsibility towards these people. They are, however, mentioned in the new CONSTITUTION ACT, 1982. The ultimate goal of Indian policy in most of the post-Confederation period was to eliminate all Indian status by assimilating Indians and encouraging them to apply for ENFRANCHISEMENT. This legal process has never been popular with Indians and has failed in its overall objective.

At Confederation, responsibility for Indians was allocated to the central government in Ottawa. This did not affect the general direction of Indian policy, which remained largely unchanged until at least the mid-20th century. As the Dominion prepared for the settlement and development of new territories, the treaty system continued to be used as an expansionist arm of Indian policy. Where the land was not yet wanted, Indians were left without treaties. This situation has given rise to comprehensive LAND CLAIMS in northern Canada. While the federal government made treaties on the Prairies where it controlled the land, it could not do so in BC where there was also a provincial interest in Indian lands. Hence, aboriginal rights and a unique type of reserve claim remain to be settled there. The distinctive course of Québec policy led to the special arrangements embodied in the JAMES BAY AGREEMENT. The administrative arm of Indian policy also continued with little change after Confederation. The Indian Dept became a federal office in 1868 and has continued under various titles until the present day. Indian legislation was consolidated into one INDIAN ACT in 1876. The diversity among Indian people and the regions of Canada, combined with the differences in historical experience, however, led to variations in regional administration. In the more settled regions, Indian administration was linked by the common goals of interim protection and ultimate assimilation. In the remoter regions, prudence and economy dictated neglect.

A 1939 court decision ruled that Inuit were a federal responsibility, but they have not been subject to the Indian Act. Separate programs of economic development and services were applied to them, especially since the 1950s as development increasingly invaded their homeland and disrupted their way of life.

Prior to WWII, Indian policy was made by government without consulting Indians and with little public attention. By the 1940s this began to change. Indians became politically more active and less willing to accept their marginal position in society or to have others make decisions for them. Public opinion became more informed and disturbed about Indian poverty and marginality. Policy reflected this changing situation through new and expanded programs. The government sought to promote economic development and to provide equality of services to Indians, particularly through agreements with the provinces.

The Indian Act was revised in 1951, but the quickened pace of change soon required a further revision. Consultation meetings (1968-69) with Indian representatives created the expectation of participation in the proposed revision. Indians made it clear that they wanted their special rights honoured and their land and treaty claims settled before Indian Act revision. Indian expectations were dashed with the release of the government's policy proposals (White Paper) in June 1969, which seemed to ignore all of their stated priorities. The proposals suggested a phased abolition of the Indian Dept and of the Indian Act within 5 years, eliminating Indian status. The importance of Indian treaties and aboriginal claims was downplayed. The Indian response to the proposed government policy was hostile and sustained. A comprehensive network of Indian political organizations was formed and made counter-proposals of their own concerning a wide range of claims. The government, facing an awakened public conscience, retreated from its proposals and then provided funding to support Indian efforts to clarify their demands. Indian people nevertheless remain suspicious that the White Paper policies remain the goals of government even yet.

Since the White Paper, Indian political activity has greatly increased awareness of Indian problems and goals among the general public and the Indian population itself. Most Indian political organizations with whom governments deal obtain their support and validity from a strong community base. An experienced Indian leadership has emerged capable of meeting the government's stated willingness to negotiate issues. At the insistence of native people, a section was inserted in the Constitution Act, 1982, which affirms existing aboriginal and treaty rights and which includes within the definition of "aboriginal peoples of Canada" the Indians, Inuit and Métis. However, the meaning of the section remains largely undefined and is a matter of controversy amongst first ministers and native leaders. On a related issue, the House of Commons Special Committee on Indian Self-Government (the Penner Committee) released a report in 1983 recommending that Indian communities be given the opportunity to work out new forms of band government to replace the present limited structures under the Indian Act. Recognizing that Indian nations were self-governing before the period of dependency and paternalism, the report recommended the establishment of Indian governments as another order of government separate from the federal and provincial. Consequently, a self-government branch was established within the Dept of Indian and Northern Affairs to work on community-based self-government initiatives. So far, a municipal model has been agreed upon and enacted for the Sechelt Band of BC, while some bands are working for more autonomy within the Indian Act. However, the more innovative goals set out in the Penner Report have not yet been achieved. JOHN LEONARD TAYLOR

Reading: H. Cardinal, *The Unjust Society* (1969); P.A. Cumming and N.H. Mickenberg, *Native Rights in Canada* (2nd ed, 1972); J.E. Hodgetts, *Pioneer Public Service* (1955); C.J. Jaenen, *Friend and Foe: Aspects of French-Amerindian Cultural Contact in the Sixteenth and Seventeenth Centuries* (1976); R.J. Surtees, *The Original People* (1971); B.G. Trigger, *The Indians and the Heroic Age of New France* (1977); L.F.S. Upton, *Micmacs and Colonists: Indian-White Relations in the Maritimes, 1713-1867* (1979); S.M. Weaver, *Making Canadian Indian Policy* (1981).

Native People, Government Programs In Canada, government programs for native people have been implemented by the federal government and some of the provinces. Historically the Government of Canada has recognized special program responsibilities and obligations only toward status Indians (*see* INDIAN), and INUIT. MÉTIS and nonstatus Indians have been denied federal government recognition as native people with special rights. Their needs have been left to be met by whatever programs provincial governments might implement from time to time. Limited federal funding of Métis and nonstatus Indian organizations for political and cultural development finally began in 1970, but economic, social and health programs for these native people remain with the provinces or do not exist at all.

Since Confederation, the INDIAN ACT has been the major piece of legislation through which the federal government has defined its administration of Indians and Indian lands. From the 19th to the mid-20th century, Canada's Indian policy had twin contradictory goals: protection of Indians from white society and assimilation of Indians into white society. These goals were implemented by the government through a program of strong managerial control which, by the 1960s, led to much public criticism. These goals were expressed in political, economic and cultural programs aimed at destroying the traditional basis of Indian life. An integral part of this exercise was the ENFRANCHISEMENT, or loss of legal Indian identity, of over 20 000 Indians between 1876 and 1974 by the government. Enfranchisement, along with the denial of native recognition and rights to the Métis, created a native population abandoned to the fate of assimilation.

In practice, a substantial shift in federal policy and program orientation has occurred since the early 1950s. Native cultures are allowed free expression; native political organizations are recognized and funded; Indian bands and Inuit organizations have taken over responsibility for some government program administration; residential schools and missionary teachers have given way to a mixed system of federal, provincial and Indian/Inuit-run schools funded by the Dept of INDIAN AFFAIRS AND NORTHERN DEVELOPMENT (DIAND); the paternalistic role of Indian agents and bureaucrats has become a technical and professional role, but not to the extent that Indians prefer.

In spite of these improvements, some attitudes and practices have changed very little. The Canadian government continues to minimize its responsibilities and obligations toward Indians and other native people and, consequently, seeks to transfer to provincial or Indian BAND authorities its expenditures on programs and services. In 1978-79 total federal expenditures for Indians amounted to $829 million, or only 1.7% of the federal government's annual budget – a percentage unchanged between 1970 and 1980. (Total expenditures for non-Indian native programs amounted to an additional $40.5 million.) Growth in Indian and Inuit Affairs Program (IIAP) expenditures for Indian programs and services, 1970-80, was two-thirds less than the growth in expenditures for non-Indian social programs in Canada. In real terms, IIAP expenditures for Indians during this time period increased by approximately 15% per capita, whereas federal expenditures for non-Indians grew by 128% per capita. All the while, by the government's own reckoning, socioeconomic conditions in Indian communities are actually growing worse.

Compounding the problem of Indian and native program underfunding is the allocation of scarce funds within the IIAP budget to various types of programs. Approximately 94% of all IIAP appropriations are directed to "maintenance and remedial programs." In contrast, about 6% of the budget is directed to job-creation and economic development initiatives. In 1978-79, 22.3% of the IIAP budget went for social assistance, while only 6.6% went for economic development. In 1981-82, the figures were 27% and 7.5%, respectively. Outside of education the greatest proportion of program funds goes to what can only be described as welfare programs.

In addition to the programs of DIAND, the Canadian government provides funding, services and programs to native people through 5 other federal departments. These include National Health and Welfare, Secretary of State, Regional Industrial Expansion, Employment and Immigration, and the Canada Mortgage and Housing Corporation. According to DIAND, federal expenditures on all native programs amounted to approximately $2.8 billion in 1985-86, an increase of 75% since 1975-76. These figures, however, do not substantially alter the breakdown of IIAP expenditures as outlined above.

In addition to DIAND programs, the following departments and programs are in place.

Health Since 1945, public health services have been provided to Indian bands by the Medical Services Branch of National Health and Welfare, with DIAND funding program administration at the band level. Increasingly, public health programs, health liaison workers and public health nurses are being managed by Indian band health committees. In 1985-86, Indian health care expenditures amounted to $342 million.

Housing DIAND funds the construction of houses on-reserve, the purchase of houses off-reserve, road construction, water, sewer and electrical services. However, the role of CMHC in funding on-reserve housing is increasing. Under its rural native housing and rehabilitation programs, CMHC accepts Indian bands, tribal councils, Métis, and nonstatus Indian and Inuit organizations as nonprofit housing societies for funding purposes. DIAND and CMHC funding for housing was $410 million in 1985-86.

Education DIAND provides comprehensive support for the education of Indian children through secondary school. Schools on-reserve are run by the department or by Indian bands directly; off-reserve, provincial schools receive tuition subsidies from the department for each Indian student enrolled. Support for Indian students in university and professional programs was provided but suspended in 1985. Overall, in 1985-86, DIAND expenditures for education amounted to $595 million.

Social Support With provincial support unavailable to status Indians (except in Ontario), DIAND provides social assistance to those in need of basic income support. This funding is usually administered directly by Indian bands. In addition, child-care, adult-care and counselling services are sometimes purchased for Indians by DIAND from provinces. In 1985-86, DIAND spent $345 million on social support programs.

Economic and Employment Development The economic development of Indian communities is supported primarily by DIAND, DRIE and Canadian Employment and Immigration Commission (CEIC). DIAND provides nonrepayable grants to cover basic economic development project costs, as well as loans for additional capital needs. DRIE, through Special Agricultural and Rural Development Act grants and other agreements, funds various sorts of Indian and native economic development projects. CEIC, through its Canada Works, Manpower Training and Youth Employment programs, provides short-term jobs, vocational training and employment services for native people. Overall expenditures on native economic and employment development in 1985-86 were $346 million.

Communications The Native Citizens Directorate of Secretary of State supports native newspapers, newsletters, and radio and television programming through its Native Communications Program and its Northern Native Broadcast Access Program.

Political Organizations The Native Citizens Directorate of Secretary of State, through its Native Representative Organizations Program, funds basic organizational, administrative and developmental costs for national and provincial native associations and organizations.

Cultural and Urban Support DIAND and the Native Citizens Directorate fund cultural development programs, Indian-operated cultural centres, native women's organizations, native artists and cultural projects. The NCD also funds a network of native FRIENDSHIP CENTRES, which provide cultural support, social and informational services to native people in urban centres.

Land Claims Through its research branch, DIAND funds research into treaty rights and LAND CLAIMS undertaken by Indian bands, tribal councils or provincial organizations.

Indian-Government Consultations Regional, provincial and national native organizations have received funding in the past from DIAND and Secretary of State to assist in preparing for meetings and negotiations on major policy developments, such as revising the Indian Act and patriation and amendment of the Constitution. Funding continues on a limited meeting-by-meeting basis.

Decisions on what programs and services to provide to native people and at what levels they should be funded are primarily influenced by the overall political and economic agenda of the federal government. Native priorities and needs are an important, but secondary, influence on policy and program development. Increasingly, native people are demanding the right to design and implement their own programs to make them effective in meeting their needs. DAN GOTTESMAN

Reading: J.E. Chamberlin, *The Harrowing of Eden* (1975); DIAND, *Indian Conditions: A Survey* (1980) and *Information: Federal Programs and Service to Aboriginal People* (1987); H. Hawthorne, *A Survey of the Contemporary Indians of Canada* (1966-67); *Indian Self-Government in Canada: Report of the Special Committee* (1983); Thalassa Research Associates, *The Economic Foundation of Indian Self-Government* (1983); S.M. Weaver, *Making Canadian Indian Policy* (1981).

Native People, Health From the 16th to the 19th century, both permanent and seasonal (whalers, fishermen, fur traders) immigrants to Canada brought with them infections that had long been established in the Old World but were rare or nonexistent among the native populations of N America. Lack of acquired resistance caused minor viral infections, such as "colds," as well as measles, influenza and smallpox to become deadly EPIDEMICS, spreading in waves through the Indian and Inuit tribes, reducing most groups to a fraction of their original number and wiping some out completely. Those not killed by acute viral epidemics suffered from depressed immunity against other infections for a period of weeks or months. Tuberculosis became the "white death," the main scourge in the S and E from the mid-18th century and in the W and N since 1850.

Exposure to infection was increased by crowding on reservations and permanent settlements with poor housing, sanitation and water supply (*see* NATIVE PEOPLE, SOCIAL CONDITIONS). Resistance to disease was further lowered by famines or malnutrition resulting from loss of traditional food supplies and by alcohol abuse. The continued physical and sociocultural decline was such that Diamond JENNESS wrote in the early 1930s that most Indian and Inuit groups in Canada would disappear as distinct peoples within a few decades.

The numerical decline came to a halt for southern Canadian Indians in the 1920s and 1930s and for Indians and Inuit of northern Canada after WWII. Gradually acquired resistance to the new infections, improved medical care, effective drug treatment, and massive efforts by the Canadian government to improve housing, sanitation and nutrition on INDIAN RESERVES and in northern settlements helped to turn the tide and save most native tribes from complete physical extinction – the fate of their brethren in Newfoundland (BEOTHUK) and Southampton I (SADLERMIUT). Indians and Inuit became in the 1950s and 1960s the fastest growing sector of the Canadian population by a natural increase, respectively, of 3% and 4% annually, thereby regaining and in recent years exceeding numbers estimated to have existed in precontact times (*see* NATIVE PEOPLE, DEMOGRAPHY). In the mid-1980s, infant mortality rates per 1000 were 18.2 and 34.5 for Indians and Inuit, compared to 18.7 per 1000 for other Canadians. Life expectancy doubled for Canadian Indians between 1950 and 1969, when the gap in relation to other Canadians had narrowed to approximately 10 years.

The physical, mental and social well-being of modern Indians and Inuit is not the success story that these biostatistics might suggest. While acute and chronic infections have been effectively eliminated as main causes of death, an increasing proportion of deaths are now caused by violence, suicides and accidents, most of them related to alcohol abuse. The majority of these accidents kill and cripple adolescents and young adults, and grave concern is expressed by natives and non-natives about this indirect "genocidal" process. In recent years, this extraordinary high loss of life has interrupted and partly reversed some of the previous gains in life expectancy.

Less dramatic, but also of increasing danger for the well-being of Indians and Inuit, is the loss of their previously superb physical fitness and the emergence of insidious diseases of modern man such as obesity, gallbladder problems, sugar-diabetes, high blood pressure, heart infarcts and other arteriosclerotic diseases.　　OTTO SCHAEFER

Native People, Languages As nearly as can be determined, 53 distinct indigenous languages are spoken in Canada. These languages fall into 11 separate families. Three of the families consist of only a single language, for which the term *isolate* is used. Of the remaining 8 families, some are groupings of languages as closely related as those comprising the Romance, Germanic or Slavic families of Indo-European, while others are more ramified groupings on the order of Indo-European as a whole. In a few cases the indigenous language families of Canada and the rest of N America have been found to be genetically related, although far more proposals of relationship have been advanced than have actually been proven. In the light of present knowledge the majority of indigenous language families of N America appear to be as independent from one another as Indo-European is from Uralic, Sino-Tibetan or Japanese. N America is unquestionably one of the most complex linguistic regions in the world.

NATIVE LANGUAGE FAMILIES FROM THE 16th TO 18th CENTURIES

Arctic Ocean

Greenland (Kalaallit Nunaat)

Alaska (U.S.A.)

Eskimo-Aleut

Athapaskan

Tlingit

Haidan

Tsimshian

Pacific Ocean

Wakashan

Salishan

Kutenaian

Siouan U.S.A.

Atlantic

Algonquian

Hudson Bay

Iroquoian

Atlantic Ocean

0　500　1000km

1 : 52 000 000

Many of the 53 indigenous languages of Canada are spoken in several more or less mutually intelligible dialects, particularly when the language is distributed over a large area. Thus, Cree is a single language spoken in 6 recognized dialects (Plains, Swampy, Northern, Woods, Moose and East) in dozens of communities and reserves from the Rockies across central Canada and well into Québec; and Ojibwa, whose local dialect variants go by such names as Ottawa, Mississauga, Chippewa, Algonquin and Saulteaux, is found in many communities throughout central Canada. Such dialects grade into one another to form chains whose members may approach mutual unintelligibility at the geographic extremes. Nevertheless, these chains are considered single languages for purposes of classification. Cree and Ojibwa are 2 of the 9 Algonquian family languages spoken in Canada; some of these and still others are spoken in the US. In the early 1980s there were an estimated 154 000 speakers of Canadian indigenous languages, a figure which suggests that slightly less than one native person in 2 then retained knowledge of his mother tongue.

Indigenous Language Families of Canada 1986
(Source: Statistics Canada, Catalogue 93-102)

Family/Isolate	Approx Number of Speakers in Canada	Language Spoken in Canada (with principal dialects in parentheses)
Algonquian	116 800	9 languages in Canada: Abenaki (Western dialect), Blackfoot, Cree (Plains, Swampy, Northern, Woods, Moose and East dialects), Delaware (Munsee dialect), Maliseet, Micmac, Montagnais-Naskapi, Ojibwa (Algonquin, Ottawa [Odawa], Mississauga, Chippewa, Saulteaux dialects), Potawatomi
Athapaskan (Northern)	17 100	15 languages in Canada: Beaver, Carrier, Chilcotin, Chipewyan, Dogrib, Han, Hare, Kaska, Kutchin, Sarcee, Sekani, Slave, Tagish, Tahltan, Tutchone
Eskimo-Aleut	22 200	1 language in Canada: Inuktitut (as many as 6 dialects)
Haida	200	Language isolate (Skidegate and Masset dialects)
Iroquoian	500	6 languages in Canada: Mohawk (2 dialects), Oneida, Onondaga, Cayuga (2 dialects), Seneca, Tuscarora
Kutenai	200	Language isolate
Salishan	1 900	10 languages in Canada comprising Coast and Interior divisions, each with further subdivisions: Bella Coola, Comox (Sliammon), Halkomelem (several dialects), Lillooet, Okanagan (2 dialects), Sechelt, Shuswap, Squamish, Straits (several dialects), Thompson
Siouan	2 400	1 language in Canada: Dakota (Santee, Teton or Lakota, and Assiniboine dialects)
Tlingit	300	Language isolate (inland dialect spoken in Canada)
Tsimshian	1 200	3 languages, all in Canada: Coast Tsimshian, Nass-Gitksan, Southern Tsimshian
Wakashan	1 400	5 languages in Canada belonging to North and South Branches: Haisla, Heiltsuk, Kwakwala [Kwakiutl], Nitinat, Nootka
Not stated	11 300	

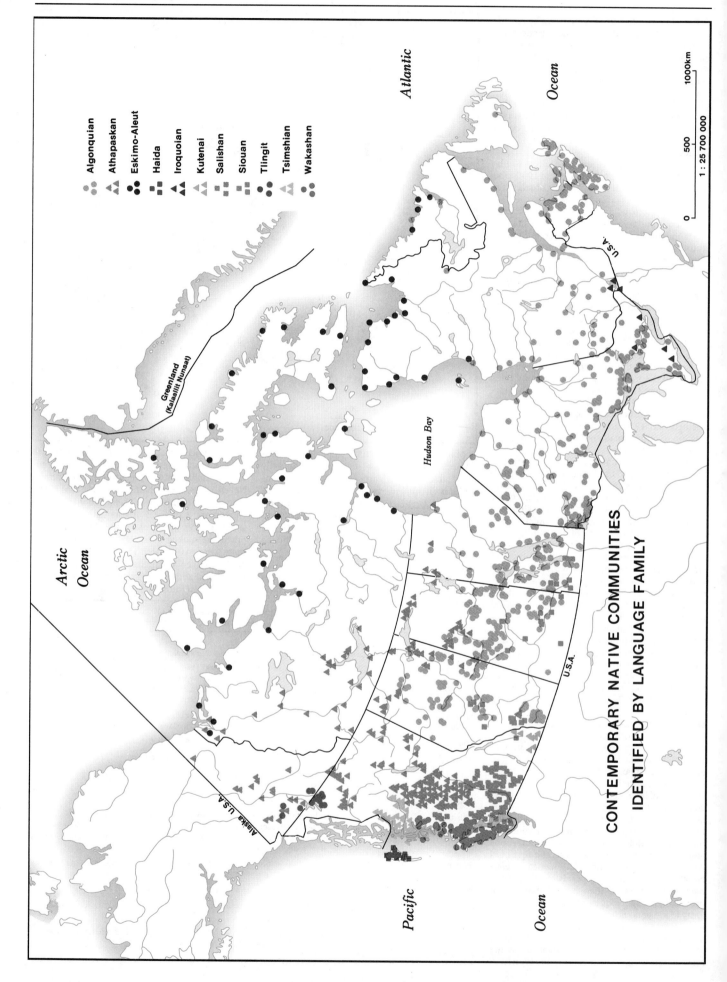

CONTEMPORARY NATIVE COMMUNITIES
IDENTIFIED BY LANGUAGE FAMILY

Algonquian
Athapaskan
Eskimo-Aleut
Haida
Iroquoian
Kutenai
Salishan
Siouan
Tlingit
Tsimshian
Wakashan

1 : 25 700 000

1000km
500
0

Atlantic
Ocean

Arctic
Ocean

Pacific
Ocean

Greenland
(Kalaallit Nunaat)

Hudson Bay

U.S.A.

Alaska U.S.A

The Status of Proposed Distant Genetic Relationships of Canadian Indigenous Language Families

Family	Proposed Larger Group Affiliations	Stocks, Families or Isolates Included	Status of Groupings and Links in Current Research
Algonquian	Algonquian-Ritwan (Algic)	Algonquian + Ritwan (Wiyot and Yurok of NW California)	Widely accepted as established. Wiyok and Yurok may not form a separate subgroup as the term Ritwan implies.
	Algonquian-Wakashan	Algic (as above) + Mosan (Wakashan, Salishan and, in the US, Chimakuan) + Kutenai + possibly Beothuk (the extinct language of Newfoundland)	The overall hypothetical construct considered doubtful; some links (Kutenai with Salishan and/or Algonquian) considered possible. Link with Beothuk now discounted
	Macro-Algonquian (Algonquian-Gulf)	Algic + Gulf grouping in SE US (Muskogean, Natchez, Tunica, Chitimacha, Atakapa)	The status of the Gulf grouping uncertain, that of the larger construct even more so
Athapaskan	Athapaskan-Eyak	Athapaskan (Northern, Pacific and Southern) + Eyak (Alaska)	Widely accepted as established
	Na-Dene	Athapaskan-Eyak + Haida + Tlingit	Tlingit possibly remotely related to Athapaskan-Eyak, Haida now thought not to be. No relationship yet found between Haida and Tlingit
Eskimo-Aleut		Eskimo-Aleut + Chukotan (Siberia)	The connection with Chukotan, now generally accepted, makes Eskimo-Aleut the only indigenous language family of N America with a proven Old World connection
Haida	Na-Dene	See Athapaskan	See Athapaskan
Iroquoian	Macro-Siouan	Iroquoian + Siouan + Caddoan (central US)	The Iroquoian-Siouan link is firmer than the postulated Siouan-Caddoan and Iroquoian-Caddoan links
Kutenai	Algonquian-Wakashan	See Algonquian	See Algonquian
Salishan	Mosan	See Algonquian	See Algonquian
Siouan	Macro-Siouan	See Iroquoian	See Iroquoian
Tlingit	Na-Dene	See Athapaskan	See Athapaskan
Tsimshian	Penutian	15 families and isolates mostly found in California and Oregon	Penutian grouping postulated but not proven. The relationship with outliers such as Tsimshian especially tenuous
Wakashan	Mosan	See Algonquian	See Algonquian

Geographic Distribution of Canadian Indigenous Language Families Not one of the Canadian indigenous language families falls exclusively within Canada and most of them straddle the US-Canadian border. Eskimo-Aleut extends not only into the US (Alaska) but also into Siberia on the west and Greenland on the east.

Within Canada, the indigenous language families concentrate in the West. Except for Eskimo-Aleut, whose Eskimo branch stretches across the entire Canadian Arctic, only 2 language families are found east of Lk Winnipeg, Algonquian and Iroquoian, and only the latter is found exclusively beyond this point. Siouan, Algonquian and Northern Athapaskan are present in the prairies, although the latter 2 belong primarily to the Boreal Forest area; and Northern Athapaskan and Tlingit are spoken in a number of communities in the BC interior. Along the West Coast and its inland waterways are found large numbers of Salishan, Tsimshian, Wakashan and Haida communities. The isolate Kutenai is located in southeastern BC near the lake and river of that name (Kootenay). Eight of the 11 language families are spoken within BC alone. This concentration of families has suggested to students of Indian history that the West is a linguistically old area and the most likely staging area for successive migrations of speakers to the south and east, a view which accords quite well with archaeological and ethnological findings. By contrast, central and eastern Canada are dominated by the Algonquian family and particularly by the 2 languages Cree and Ojibwa. This situation suggests far more recent language spread relative to the West.

Classification of Indigenous Languages Linguistic classification involves both the question of internal relationships among members of the same family, and the question of external links between families in still larger groupings, termed *stocks* or *superstocks* depending upon how comprehensive they are. While the membership within families of all of the 53 languages spoken in Canada today is well known and adequately established, higher order groupings of families into stocks are far less certain. It is an interesting feature of the development of linguistic research in N America that students of Amerindian languages were once considerably more daring about external classification than they are now.

The high-water mark of indigenous language classification was achieved by Edward SAPIR in a famous paper published in the *Encyclopaedia Britannica* in 1929, a paper which set the directions of indigenous language research for decades afterwards and which still provokes lively discussion. In this classification the numerous families of N America were first grouped into 12 middle-level stocks considered reasonably assured, and then – far more speculatively – into 6 far-reaching superstocks considered possible though far from proven. All but one of the Canadian indigenous language families were subsumed under 4 superstock headings: Algonquian-Wakashan (Algonquian, Kutenai, Wakashan, Salishan, plus 3 families in the US); Na-Dene (Athapaskan, Haida and Tlingit); Penutian (centered in California and Oregon, with Tsimshian as the sole Canadian member); Hokan-Siouan (numerous families in the western US and some in Mexico, with the Siouan and Iroquoian families spilling over into Canada). One family, Eskimo-Aleut, was regarded then, as today, as constituting a separate stock. In recent decades there has been a steady retreat from this and other massively integrative classificatory schemes, back at least to the middle-level stocks. In some cases additional middle- or lower-level links have been proposed even as the higher order links have come undone through continuing research. Thus, Eyak, a language isolate in Alaska, joined with Athapaskan during the same recent period that saw the dismantling of the Na-Dene superstock as a whole; and the link between Siouan and Iroquoian, while problematic, is on firmer footing today than in 1929, although little remains of Sapir's Hokan-Siouan superstock in which both families were originally placed.

The Structural Diversity of Indigenous Languages Early descriptions of the indigenous languages of N America tended to cast all of them in the same mold as "polysynthetic" or "holo-phrastic" in order to capture a tendency found in a number of them toward great complexity of the word, particularly the verb. It was found that many of the formal elements expressed in familiar European languages by separate words or word endings were, in the majority of Amerindian languages, combined as chains of prefixes or suffixes surrounding basic roots, or both. Certainly there are families such as Eskimo-Aleut, Iroquoian and Algonquian where the term polysynthesis can be said to characterize the verb, but such general typological labels leave a spurious impression of structural uniformity and obscure important differences sometimes found even among languages belonging to the same family. Moreover, there are Amerindian languages which are as "analytic" as English, and others which are as "inflective" as Latin and Greek, so that it is impossible to speak of all the indigenous languages of this hemisphere as fitting a single structural type or set of types.

In addition, virtually every grammatical category known from the languages of the Old World (systems of person, case, number, gender, tense, mode, aspect, voice) is found among the languages of N America, and there are some unusual categories which have been the focus of considerable interest in indigenous language research: verb stems to denote categories of shape and motion, sets of demonstratives to indicate whether an object mentioned by the speaker is visible or invisible to him, verb modes to indicate whether what the speaker is saying can be verified from his immediate experience, even different sets of numerals to count different classes of objects. One particular line of research, which has developed around the so-called world-view problem, has attempted to determine if, and how, such categories influence habitual thought patterns among speakers.

Amerindian languages exhibit great diversity in their sound systems. In some families, such as Iroquoian and Eskimo-Aleut, the inventory of basic sounds is limited; in others, such as those located in the Plateau and on the Pacific coast, the inventories of basic sounds, particularly in consonant series, are quite large.

MICHAEL K. FOSTER

Reading: L. Campbell and M. Mithun, eds, *The Languages of Native America* (1979); J.K. Chambers, ed, *The Languages of Canada* (Part 1: "The Native Languages") (1979); Michael K. Foster, "Canada's First Languages," *Language and Society* 7 (1982), 7-16; [Map of] "Indian and Inuit Communities and Languages," *National Atlas of Canada*, 5th ed (1980); *International Journal of American Linguistics*; T.A. Sebeok, ed, *Linguistics in North America* (1973).

Native People, Law Owing to Canada's complex social and constitutional history, the special legal rights of Canada's native peoples vary from one part of the country to another and in their application to different groups. Today there are no longer special disabilities attached to native status. Earlier rules (eg, those preventing Indian people from voting or leaving their reserves without permission) have been repealed; other discriminatory laws are unlikely to be enforced (eg, DRYBONES CASE). The one thing native people cannot legally do is bargain away their ABORIGINAL RIGHTS, treaty rights or reserved lands to anyone other than the Crown in right of Canada. Generally, native people have the same legal rights as other Canadians and may be able to claim special rights by virtue of their native status which is a complex issue.

Native Status Section 35 of the CONSTITUTION ACT, 1982, defines "the aboriginal peoples of Canada" as the INDIAN, INUIT and MÉTIS peoples. Historical and legal differences of the past, however, complicate the question of definition and this problem is aggravated today because the 3 groups do not share equal rights, nor does the federal government accept equal responsibility in dealing with them.

In early times, people who followed the Indian way of life were accepted as Indians. Not until 1850 was a bloodline requirement prescribed in Lower Canada to define who could occupy Indian reserve lands. Since Confederation, federal law has created an elaborate system of status and band membership for Indians. 1985 amendments to the INDIAN ACT dramatically changed these historic rules, which had been widely criticized.

The federal government determines Indian status under its own rules which no longer exclude women marrying non-Indians. Status is neither gained nor lost through marriage. Band membership will be determined by the same rules unless Bands enact their own membership codes. And Band Councils can now enact residency by-laws. The old pattern of determining status, Band membership and residency rights by the same set of rules is now subject to variation across the country.

The courts have held that Parliament's power in relation to "Indians" includes legislative control over Eskimos or Inuit, but there is no "Inuit Act," possibly because there have not been "Inuit reserves" to regulate. Inuit status is likely to be defined legally as LAND CLAIMS are negotiated and the question of "beneficiaries" is addressed. For northern Québec Inuit this process was accomplished by an initial enrolment of beneficiaries with future additions on the basis of descent, marriage or adoption.

Métis, however, is a term of uncertain application, used variously to describe everyone of mixed native/non-native blood, or those who took land scrip rather than treaty (see INDIAN TREATIES); those entitled to Métis lands under the MANITOBA ACT, 1870; those registered under the Alberta Métis Betterment Act; or the francophone segment of the mixed-blood communities of the Northwest. Depending on which definition is used and through how many generations it is extended, estimates of the Métis population range from 100 000 to one million. Generally, no continuing Métis rights are recognized under federal law, and in the constitutional discussions in 1984 federal government representatives took the position that Métis, unlike Indians and Inuit, were not under federal legislative jurisdiction. Some provincial laws do make special provisions for Métis communities within their boundaries. If Parliament does have parallel jurisdiction over Métis and their lands, these provisions could generate constitutional confusion.

Land Rights of Native People Parliament also has the power to make laws in relation to "lands reserved for the Indians," and the federal government has the power to bargain with native groups for the release of native land rights. Under Canadian CONSTITUTIONAL LAW, once such a release is given those lands are subject to the general provincial ownership of crown lands and natural resources and the federal government loses all rights to deal with such lands on behalf of the natives. Even the clear provisions of the Indian Act dealing with federal management of surrendered Indian reserve lands cannot operate unless there is a federal-provincial agreement in place concerning the status of the surrendered lands.

Such agreements have been made with NS, NB, Ontario and BC, and by the Statute of Westminster, 1931, which affects Alberta, Saskatchewan and Manitoba. There are no special arrangements with Québec, PEI or Nfld; none are required for the territories which are under federal jurisdiction.

The land rights of native peoples are largely undefined, but they have been described as "usufructuary," referring to a Roman law right to use land owned by another; in this case it is the native right to use lands technically owned by the Crown. Native rights to land as defined by the Indian Act are communal in nature, belonging to the group rather than the individual member, and cannot be bargained away except by the group to the Crown in right of Canada (see INDIAN RESERVE).

Laws of General Application Native people are subject to the general law of the land, together with other Canadians, unless there is some aboriginal, treaty or other provision affording special protection. If a law conflicts with native life-style or culture, and there is no special protection, the courts will apply that law to natives.

Laws of general application can be provincial laws or federal statutes such as the Criminal Code or the Fisheries Act. Under s88 of the Indian Act, however, provincial laws cannot be applied to limit Indian treaty rights. The courts have yet to determine whether federal laws will be able to limit aboriginal and treaty rights recognized under the Constitution in 1982; federal laws could do so prior to that date.

Hunting and Fishing Rights Many of the Indian treaties included promises that hunting and fishing would not be disturbed. In those areas where there are such treaties, the courts have held that hunting and fishing can be regulated by the federal government, as they have been by the Fisheries Act and the Migratory Birds Convention Act. In the Prairie provinces, in order to consolidate treaty promises, the BNA Act, 1930, guaranteed Indians the right to hunt and fish for food, free of provincial regulation, on unoccupied crown lands and other lands to which they have a right of access. Métis have failed in their attempt to claim these rights.

Where there are no treaty rights, however, as in most of BC, provinces can regulate native hunting and fishing. It is not clear, however, that a province could do so if an aboriginal right to hunt on traditional land is established in a non-treaty area. In the territories there are special legal exemptions permitting Indians and Inuit to hunt for food.

Legal Status of Native Communities While native rights are regarded as communal, the formal legal status even of Indian bands is not clearly defined in Canadian law: bands may not be able to sue or be sued in their own names or limit financial liability for debts to communal assets. Some groups avoid this by incorporation, a legal procedure to acquire certain rights and immunities; others avoid incorporation because it entails the loss of tax exemptions relating to Indian status.

Inuit and Métis groups have incorporated political and development associations (see NATIVE PEOPLE, POLITICAL ORGANIZATION AND ACTIVISM) and formed co-operatives (see INUIT CO-OPERATIVES), but do not as communities have statutory powers under federal law. Indian bands and BAND councils are given limited powers under the Indian Act. One of the goals of Indian self-government is to enhance and to recognize constitutionally the legal rights and powers of bands.

Customary and Cultural Practices Canadian law has recognized certain native traditions. One example is the early recognition courts gave to customary marriages, although without a parallel recognition of customary divorce. The Indian Act refers to "customary adoptions," without explanation, and the courts have recognized these adoptions not only in Indian, but also in Inuit communities, on the basis of recognition of indigenous customary law. Similarly, because the election provisions of the Indian Act are not mandatory, band leadership chosen by customary means can exercise the statutory powers of a chief and council.

It is likely that the catalogue of legally recognized customary practices will increase in future. The CANADIAN CHARTER OF RIGHTS AND FREEDOMS, for example, refers to customary language rights, and these rights may apply to native languages.

Taxation Under the Indian Act the interest of an Indian or a band in reserve lands, and the personal property of Indians or bands situated on a reserve, are exempt from taxation. Complex questions have arisen in applying this provision to sales and income taxes. The federal government takes the position that income taxes are not payable by Indians if their income is payable on a reserve. Federal sales tax, which is a hidden tax, is generally paid by all native people regardless of where they live. The same is true of provincial sales taxes in most jurisdictions, although some provinces recognize specific exemptions for reserve residents or for on-reserve purchases by Indians.

There is no special exemption from customs and excise duties, notwithstanding provision in JAY'S TREATY (1794) and the Treaty of GHENT (1814) that Indians could cross the Canada-US border freely with their goods. In the *Francis* Case (1956) the Supreme Court of Canada held that these were not Indian treaties and that, while they were international treaties, they had not been given legislative force within Canada.

Native groups can be expected to advocate extended tax exemptions in the course of constitutional and land-claims negotiations.

Equality before the Law Democratic theories of majority rule and equality before the law often give insufficient regard to minority rights, and this inherent tension has found its way into native cases. The 1960 CANADIAN BILL OF RIGHTS affirmed the right to equality before the law and, in the DRYBONES CASE, the Supreme Court of Canada held that an Indian had been unfairly discriminated against on the basis of race by being convicted under an Indian Act provision that made it an offence for an Indian to be intoxicated off reserve. The Indian Act provision, which imposed slightly heavier penalties, was struck down since it denied the accused equality before the law.

In a later case, the court did not apply the Canadian Bill of Rights. Its decision in the LAVELL CASE (1973) was based on reasoning that if the court struck down a discriminatory membership provision of the Act, it might effectively repeal the whole statute that discriminates on the basis of race. The court's decision in *Lavell* was widely criticized. This potential conflict between minority rights and equality before the law is apparent in the Canadian Charter of Rights and Freedoms, where specific provision is made that none of the guarantees, including that of equality before the law, shall be construed so as to diminish aboriginal or treaty rights.

Summary Following the Constitution Act, 1982, the constitutionally recognized legal rights

Jim Igloliarte, Inuk judge at Nain, Labrador (*photo by Karl-Heinz Raach*).

of native peoples are of 3 types: those determined to be "existing" for the purposes of constitutional protection; those acquiring constitutional protection by way of land-claims settlements; and those given constitutional or statutory recognition as the result of negotiations between native groups and governments. *See also* ROYAL PROCLAMATION.

WILLIAM B. HENDERSON

Reading: P. Cumming and N. Mickenberg, *Native Rights in Canada* (2nd ed, 1972); K. Lysyk, "The Unique Constitutional Position of the Canadian Indian," *Canadian Bar Review* 45 (1967); D. Sanders, "Indian Hunting and Fishing Rights," *Saskatchewan Law Review* 38 (1973-74); J.C. Smith, "*Regina* v. *Drybones* and Equality before the Law," *Canadian Bar Review* 49 (1971); W.S. Tarnopolsky, "The Canadian Bill of Rights and the Supreme Court Decisions in *Lavell* and *Burnshine*: A Retreat from *Drybones* to Dicey?" *Ottawa Law Review* 7 (1975).

Native People, Political Organization and Activism Political activism among Canada's Indians since the latter part of the 19th century has largely reflected their attempts to organize political associations beyond the BAND level in order to pursue their common interests. One of the earliest of these Indian associations, the Grand General Indian Council of Ontario, was the outcome of missionaries' efforts to establish a council of OJIBWA nations prior to Confederation. In existence from the 1870s until 1938, the council pursued a cautious and conciliatory course in its dealings with federal Indian administrators. The Plains CREE, in contrast, in the 5 years prior to the NORTH-WEST REBELLION of 1885, began to form a political alliance to force the federal government to honour what Indians viewed as treaty commitments (*see* INDIAN TREATIES). Though limited in scope and largely unintended, Indian participation in the rebellion pre-empted a previously scheduled gathering of Indian leaders from across the Prairies to decide how they might best press for desired changes in federal Indian policy and administration. The rebellion led to a tightening of government control of reserves and further erosion of Indian autonomy. While political organization and activism were severely constrained by the terms of the INDIAN ACT and by the fact that most Indians were not entitled to vote in federal and provincial elections until after WWII, the struggle to realize their various aims continued.

In the 1890s the Nishga in BC began their campaign to obtain government recognition of their aboriginal land rights, while in 1906 the chief of the Capilano Band travelled to England to place a LAND CLAIMS petition before King Edward VII. A new organization, the Allied Tribes of British Columbia, was formed in 1915 in an unsuccessful attempt to force a judicial decision on land claims by the British Privy Council. Following the government's rejection of the Allied Tribes' land claims in 1927, the organization folded, only to be

succeeded in 1931 by the Native Brotherhood of British Columbia, an organization that arose out of Indian labour-oriented activities in coastal industry.

Attempts to create a national political organization for Indians first began in Ontario and Québec during WWI when the American-based Council of Tribes began a short-lived but energetic campaign to expand into Canada. In 1918 the League of Indians of Canada was formed in Ontario by F.O. Loft, a returning veteran and member of the Six Nations Reserve who advocated resolution of a set of grievances common to Indians across Canada: loss of reserve lands and the failure to recognize aboriginal land rights; restriction of native people's hunting and trapping rights; educational policies and administrative practices that sought to eliminate Indian languages and customs; and the generally poor economic and health conditions on reserves. Loft's efforts in the early 1920s to bring western Indians into the league were surprisingly effective, despite the opposition he encountered from senior officials of the Dept of Indian Affairs who attempted, among other measures, to revoke his legal status as an INDIAN. In view of the difficulties of uniting geographically separated and ethnically, linguistically and religiously divided bands in a national Indian organization, the league's eventual failure was less remarkable than its initial success.

During the late 1930s and 1940s there was an increase in native political organization, especially at the regional and provincial levels, with the formation, for example, of the Indian Assn of Alberta and the Saskatchewan Indian Assn in 1944. The creation of the North American Indian Brotherhood in 1945 by Andrew PAULL, a BC Indian leader, was another attempt to establish a national organization of Canadian Indians, but it failed, partly because of the suspicion it was an organization primarily for Catholic Indians.

Public concern over the anomalous social, economic and legal status of Indians in Canada led to the convening of special parliamentary inquiries into the administration of Indian Affairs 1946-48 and 1959-61. Both inquiries prompted the formation of a number of associations that sought to speak on behalf of regional and provincial Indian constituencies. In Saskatchewan, for example, the merger during the 1940s and 1950s of a number of small organizations, including the Protective Assn for Indians and their Treaties, the Saskatchewan Indian Assn, the Union of Saskatchewan Indians, and the Queen Victoria Treaty Protective Assn, led to the creation of the Federation of Saskatchewan Indians, an association which since the late 1950s has served as the principal representative organization of Indians in that province.

The extension of the federal franchise to Indians in 1960 and of the provincial franchise to Indians in Alberta in 1965 and Québec in 1969 erased a major political distinction between Indians and other Canadians. Nevertheless, many Indians were and continue to be reluctant to exercise their right to vote partly for fear of compromising their special legal and constitutional status. Since 1962 a steadily declining proportion of eligible Indian voters has cast ballots in federal elections; by 1979 their rate of participation in federal elections was less than half that of non-Indians. Participation in Indian band elections, however, remains at a high level, suggesting a lack of faith on the part of Indians that normal federal and provincial political channels and processes can satisfy their interests.

The federal government's 1969 proposals to abolish both the Indian Act and the Dept of Indian Affairs and to transfer administrative responsibility for Indians to provincial governments sparked

a dramatic increase in the scope and intensity of political organization and activism among Canada's native peoples. Opposition to the government's proposals led in the early 1970s to the creation of several new provincial associations and the transformation of some existing ones into active political organizations that began to receive political recognition from governments as the appropriate representatives of their people. Provincial and territorial associations also received public funds to operate a variety of research, liaison and service programs on behalf of native peoples. The special legal and administrative interests of registered Indians led them in most cases to keep their organizations separate from those established by the MÉTIS and nonstatus Indians.

Beyond the provincial level, the National Indian Brotherhood (which became the ASSEMBLY OF FIRST NATIONS representing 90% of chiefs across Canada in 1980) and the NATIVE COUNCIL OF CANADA (representing Métis and nonstatus Indians) pursued changes in government policies with respect to ABORIGINAL RIGHTS, economic development, education and many other fields (*see* NATIVE PEOPLE, GOVERNMENT PROGRAMS). Between 1978 and 1982 Indian, Métis and nonstatus organizations, along with the INUIT TAPIRISAT OF CANADA, intervened in the repatriation of the Canadian constitution in order to ensure legal enshrinement of their aboriginal rights. Since the 1970s Canadian native leaders have also become leading participants in international minority-indigenous-peoples organizations such as the Inuit Circumpolar Conference and the World Council of Indigenous People, founded at a conference in Pt Alberni, BC, in 1975, whose international secretariat was located in Lethbridge, Alta, and moved to Ottawa in 1984.

In addition to native people's involvement in provincial, national and international representative organizations, a variety of other, often short-lived, special interest groups have appeared: Canadian Indian Youth Council (1960s), Saskatchewan Native Youth Movement (1970s), Calgary Urban Indian Treaty Alliance (early 1970s), Canadian Native Communications Society (1960s-1970s), Indian Rights for Indian Women (1970s) and National Native Women's Assn of Canada (1970s). The National Alliance for Red Power (1960s, early 1970s) and the American Indian Movement (1970s), organizations that advocated more radical programs of action than those adopted by officially recognized provincial and territorial organizations, also received limited support from native people within Canada.

The political activism of Canada's native peoples since WWII has afforded them increasingly greater access to various levels of political decision making and has substantially altered some aspects of their situation. Notwithstanding the election of native candidates to parliament, provincial legislatures and territorial councils on several occasions, however, native activism has for the most part been conducted outside the bounds of electoral politics. Since 1969 considerable effort has gone into establishing communication channels and negotiating mechanisms to facilitate dealings between native peoples and governments. The leaders of native organizations have also discovered a number of effective political tactics, including the use of the mass media to communicate their concerns to potentially sympathetic non-native audiences in Canada and elsewhere in the world who may in turn apply pressure on Canadian political leaders.

Native leaders have tended to eschew threats of violence but have become adept at mounting symbolic protests; one example was the mounting of the "Constitutional Express" that took large numbers of native people to Ottawa by train during the constitutional negotiations so they might personally convey their opposition to the government's position. Yet while native political organizations have become publicly prominent and have succeeded in changing government policy in a number of fields, their dependence on government financing serves indirectly to limit their political autonomy. Nevertheless, limited autonomy has been a feature of the political situation of native peoples for more than 100 years.

In coming years, native political organizations will be confronted both by internal and external challenges. Native people represent only a small minority within the overall population of Canada. The political influence that native leaders have exercised during the past 2 decades to persuade governments to extend special treatment to their people has been largely contingent upon a general level of affluence and tolerance within Canadian society. How native people will be treated by governments in the future remains to be seen. Equally important, however, will be the determination of native people at the community level to insist that their organizations continue to defend the political values and objectives that have long guided political organizations and activism among indigenous peoples in Canada.

NOEL DYCK

Reading: A.L. Getty and A.S. Lussier, eds, *As Long as the Sun Shines and Water Flows: A Reader in Canadian Native Studies* (1983); DIAND, *Indian Conditions: A Survey* (1980); G. Manuel and M. Posluns, *The Fourth World: An Indian Reality* (1974); E.P. Patterson, *The Canadian Indian* (1972); A. Tanner, ed, *The Politics of Indianness: Case Studies of Native Ethnopolitics in Canada* (1983); D. Whiteside, *Historical Development of Aboriginal Political Associations in Canada,* 1 (1973).

Native People, Religion Indian and Inuit religions consist of a complex set of social and cultural customs for dealing with the sacred and the supernatural. There are rich traditions of religious mythology and ceremonial in most areas. Spectacular religious manifestations are found on the Northwest Coast (Kwakiutl, Haida, Tsimshian), the northern Great Plains (Blackfoot, Peigan, Blood, Sarcee) and the Central and Eastern Woodlands (Ojibwa, Cree, Huron, Iroquois). In general, the subarctic Athapaskan groups and the arctic Inuit have less elaborate religious ceremonials, but are rich in mythic tradition (*see* INUIT MYTH AND LEGEND).

While their mythologies defy simple classification, 3 main types of myths, features of which often occur in combination, are particularly important in the religion of native peoples. The first group consists of creation myths that describe the origins of the cosmos and the interrelations of its elements. Here belong the Earth Diver myth, in which either the Great Spirit or the Transformer dives or orders other animals to dive into the primeval water to bring up mud, out of which he fashions the Earth (Eastern Woodlands, Northern Plains); the Trickster myths, which frequently but not always represent the Transformer as a comical character who steals light, fire, water, food, animals or even mankind and loses them or sets them loose to create the world as it is now (RAVEN among the Bella Coola, Tsimshian, Haida; Hare, NANABOZO or Nanabush among the Ojibwa; Frog in the Columbian Plateau; Coyote among the Blackfoot); and the Culture Hero myths, in which the Transformer appears as a human being of supernatural powers who brings the world into its present form by heroic feats (GLOOSCAP of the Micmac, Maliseet, Abenaki). Especially in the Columbian Plateau and the Great Plains, there are said to be 2 Transformers (more precisely, a Transformer and a companion who is a brother, sister or other relative). They try to outdo each

other in feats of strength, ability or cunning that result in the formation of the world as it now exists.

Many myths tell of the origin of the moon, the sun and the stars. In these myths there is usually a tension between the heavenly bodies; eg, the cool moon by night is said to be necessary to counteract the burning of the Earth and the killing of people by the heat of the sun. An Inuit myth tells of the sun and moon as brother and sister, but since they have engaged in incest in their human lives they are doomed to eternal separation. Among many forms of myth about human origins are those that tell of the Transformer changing various animals into people. Others tell of the origin of death. The second group of myths include the institutional myths, which tell of the origins of religious institutions, such as the SUN DANCE (northern Plains), sacred MEDICINE BUNDLES (Blackfoot, Cree, Ojibwa, Iroquois), winter ceremonies (Coast Salish, Nootka, Kwakiutl) and the Green Corn Ceremonial (Iroquois; *see also* FALSE FACE SOCIETY).

Where there is a belief that primordial times were very different from the present, the pattern in which the ancient mythic beings arranged their social and religious institutions becomes the norm for people now. Myths of the third group, the ritual myths, serve as detailed texts for the performance of ceremonials and rituals by which cosmic order is dramatically represented (Plains Sun Dance, Ojibwa MIDEWIWIN ritual and the Iroquois Green Corn Ceremonial). Fertility, birth, initiation and death rites are often clearly stipulated in mythology. Shamanic performances may also be described (*see* SHAMAN). Ceremonials are often preceded by stringent purification rites, such as sweat baths (eg, Salish, Blackfoot, Eastern Woodlands), fasting and sexual abstinence (*see* SWEAT LODGE). Feasting is a common feature of ceremonial performance.

The use of hallucinogenic drugs such as peyote appears to be limited and relatively recent in religious observances among Canadian native people, although trance states seem to be reasonably common (eg, in Salish winter dancing, shamanic performances among many groups, and perhaps in the SHAKING TENT rituals).

Some myths appear to have lost their religious sacredness and, while considered to be basically true accounts of true mythic beings, have become folktales recounted for entertainment or instruction. All religious myths and many folktales have a moral or ethical dimension in which behaviour patterns are prescribed, prohibited, commended or condemned.

Myths of the Orpheus type are prominent in the Eastern Woodlands (Huron, Ojibwa, Montagnais-Naskapi, Iroquois, Ottawa), the Northwest Coast (Salish, Kwakiutl, Nootka, Haida, Tsimshian, Tlingit) and the Columbian Plateau (Thompson, Okanagan, Carrier; Salish, Interior). They tell of the Culture Hero or other prominent religious figure making a perilous journey to the realm of the dead to bring back a deceased loved one. These myths contain detailed characterizations of the land of the dead, and are important to an understanding of such diverse phenomena as the Plains Ghost Dance, concepts of the soul and many aspects of shamanism.

Among societies that have practised agriculture at some time in their history, many groups believe in a senior Great Spirit or Great Mystery (*Wakan Tanka* of the Plains societies and *Kitchi Manitou* of the eastern Algonquians). In general, supernatural mystery or power is called *Orenda* by the Iroquois, *Wakan* by the Plains peoples and MANITOU by the Algonquian societies, and is potentially beneficent, though it can be dangerous if treated carelessly or with disrespect. This mystery

or power is a property of the spirits, but it also adheres to the Transformer, Trickster, Culture Hero, or spirit figures. Shamans, prophets and ceremonial performers are endowed with it. The spirits of all living things are powerful and mysterious, as are many natural phenomena and ritually significant places. Ritual objects such as rattles, drums, MASKS, medicine bundles and ritual sanctuaries are filled with mystery (*see* CALUMET; MEDICINE WHEELS).

Most Northwest Coast groups consider time to be divided into the present and a remote mythological period when things were different from now, and believe that the state of things in the present was brought into being by the Transformer. Concepts of the future are developed principally as they refer to the death of the individual and his afterlife. The world of the dead is usually believed to lie at a great distance from the world of the living, often beyond a great river, on islands far out at sea, in the remote mountains or in the underworld. It can only be reached after a difficult journey by the dead, or a perilous one for the living (eg, shamans, the spirit figures of the Orpheus myth). The world is believed to have a circular surface covered with a domelike overworld. These levels are joined by a "cosmic axis" which may be represented by a "world tree," a "rainbow bridge" or the "backbone of the worlds" (the Milky Way). Religious myths of the Star Husband (Temagami Ojibwa), the Chain of Arrows (Tlingit) or the Stretching Tree (Chilcotin) tell of contacts made between humans and the world beyond via this axis. Ceremonially, such elements as columns of smoke, central house posts or the central pole of the Sun Dance lodge represent this axis. Whirlpools or caves may represent the way to the underworld. Many groups tell of a primeval sea or world deluge. Most recognize at least 6 cardinal directions (the 4 corners of the world, plus the zenith and the nadir). Northwest Coast societies such as the Kwakiutl divide the year into 2 major seasons: the summer ("profane") time and the winter ("supernatural") time, in which most religious ceremonials take place. Agricultural societies such as the Iroquois have more complex ceremonial calendars organized around the harvest times of various food plants, with a life-renewal ceremonial usually held in midwinter.

A key concept among Indian and Inuit societies is the notion of the Guardian of the Game, a supernatural person who is said to control or hold stewardship over one or all of the animal species, especially those hunted by man. Typical examples are to be found in the Bear ceremonial of the Abenaki and Montagnais-Naskapi, the Spirit of the Buffalo in Plains societies, and Sedna the sea goddess and Guardian of the Seals among the Inuit.

Of several religious figures, shamans are the most notable. They function as healers, prophets, diviners and custodians of religious mythology, and are often the officiants at religious ceremonies. In some societies, all these functions are performed by the same person; in others shamans are specialists. Healing practitioners may belong to various "orders," as in the Midewiwin or Great Medicine Society of the Ojibwa, or to secret or closed societies (Kwakiutl, Blackfoot). The Ojibwa Midewiwin was a closed society containing 4 (sometimes 8) orders of men and women who could be consulted at any time of sickness or communal misfortune and who performed the annual Midewiwin world-renewal ceremonial in late summer. Shamans were co-ordinators of the Plains Sun Dance (Blackfoot, Sarcee), which was also a world-renewal ceremonial. Closed, or even secret, shamanic societies played an important role in the Winter Ceremonial of the Kwakiutl,

Giver of Life by Jessie Oonark (*courtesy Sanavik Co-operative, Baker Lake, NWT*).

Nootka and other Northwest Coast societies. Shamans were associated with powers generally thought to be beneficial to the community, but were believed in some cases to use their powers for sorcery. Shaman-prophets and diviners were concerned with predicting the outcome of the hunt, relocating lost objects and determining the root causes of communal discontent and ill will. Blackfoot, Cree, Ojibwa and other societies had diviners who made their prophecies (perhaps in trance states) in the dramatic Shaking Tent ceremony. Shamans in Cree, Blackfoot and Ojibwa societies were custodians of the sacred medicine bundles containing objects and materials endowed with great mystery and power.

Natural causes were recognized for many diseases, especially physically curable ones; others were commonly believed to be the result of intrusion into the body of objects placed there by sorcerers. The shaman-healer's treatment of such diseases was dictated by his tutelary spirit, but usually consisted of the shaman ritually sucking the disease agent out of the body, brushing it off with a bird's wing, or drawing it out with dramatic gestures.

Illness could also result from "spirit loss." The shaman-healer's action was then directed to recovering the patient's spirit (either his soul or his guardian spirit power, or both) and reintroducing it to the body. Personal or communal disorders were often held to be the result of disrespectful behaviour toward game animals, tribal sacred objects or natural phenomena.

The Guardian Spirit Quest once occurred throughout most of the tribal groups of Canada; it is undergoing a revival in Northwest Coast tribal religions, especially among the Coast Salish. Males, especially at puberty but also at other times of life, made extended stays in remote areas while fasting, praying and purifying themselves by washing in streams and pools. The goal was to seek a vision of, or an actual encounter with, a guardian spirit – very frequently an animal, but also a mythological figure. Establishment of contact with a guardian spirit was held to make an individual healthy, prosperous and successful, particularly in hunting and fishing. The guardian spirit could be hinted at (Salish) or even directly represented or dramatized (Kwakiutl) in songs, masks, TOTEM POLES, house paintings, facial and body painting, or in personal religious regalia.

Seasonal ceremonials and "life-crisis" rituals are very common. Among the seasonal rituals are "firstfruits" and harvest ceremonies, and New Year life- and creation-renewal rites (Ojibwa Midewiwin ceremony, Plains Sun Dance, First Salmon rites of the Northwest Coast). Among the life-crisis rituals are ceremonies at birth or the giving of a name, at puberty, marriage and death, all of which are normally accompanied by some solemnity. The 17th-century Huron Feast of the Dead may have incorporated features of both seasonal and life-crisis rituals.

Contact with European religious systems has produced several types of religious reactions among native peoples, although it has brought change in some way to all aboriginal religious forms. Some Indian religions eventually rejected European forms and turned to "nativistic movements," which seek to revive previous religious practices and beliefs (eg, the Iroquois HANDSOME LAKE RELIGION). "Syncretistic religions" seek to combine traditional native forms with European observances (eg, the SHAKER RELIGION of the Salish area and the Native American Church of the Plains). Other religious movements radically opposed European forms (eg, the 19th-century Ghost Dance of the Sioux and other Plains tribes).

Indian and Inuit religious institutions should be understood in the context of the kinship, political and social-control institutions with which they are intricately interrelated. DEREK G. SMITH

Reading: F. Boas, *Kwakiutl Ethnography* (1966); I. Goldman, *The Mouth of Heaven* (1975); A. Hultkrantz, *Belief and Worship in Native North America* (1981), *Prairie and Plains Indians* (1973) and *The Religions of the American Indians* (1982); P. Radin, *The Trickster* (1956); C.E. Schaeffer, *Blackfoot Shaking Tent* (1969); S. Thompson, *Tales of the North American Indians* (1966); R. Underhill, *Red Man's Religion* (1965); E.H. Waugh and K. Dad Prithipaul, *Native Religious Traditions* (1979).

Native People, Social Conditions The social conditions of native people in Canada are affected by the federal Dept of INDIAN AFFAIRS AND NORTHERN DEVELOPMENT (DIAND), the various native organizations and the BAND administration of INDIAN RESERVES. The minister of Indian affairs and northern development has responsibility for exercising the duties and functions of the INDIAN ACT on behalf of the federal government. Indian organizations are representative associations at the national, provincial and tribal or band levels and often have mandates that include the improvement of social conditions both on and off reserves. The band administration, as the elected body, has direct responsibility for the operation of the

reserve and the social conditions of its members.

Nonstatus Indians and MÉTIS are not subject to the Indian Act, and therefore are not eligible for assistance by DIAND (*see* INDIAN). Legally the provinces are responsible for social assistance for these groups. They obtain some support from the federal Dept of the Secretary of State and have national, provincial and local associations that are concerned with their social conditions. INUIT, although not covered under the Indian Act, were included in the term "Indian" in the CONSTITUTION ACT, 1867, and are thus subject to federal responsibility. They receive assistance from DIAND, and from the provincial governments of the NWT, Québec and Newfoundland.

Social conditions of Canada's native people must be discussed as a set of interconnected phenomena including geographical location, income level and cultural factors. Place of residence may be an isolated northern community or reserve and for others a large urban centre. There has been a major shift of natives to urban centres over the last 20 years, particularly among young (under 40) southern natives. The Clatworthy Study (1981) reported that over 1000 natives moved to Winnipeg each year. In the Far North, Inuit live in settlements ranging from a few dozen people to several thousand in size, although many still depend to a large extent on trapping, hunting and fishing. Over 50% of food is "country" food, harvested directly by native people.

Employment rates for natives are the lowest of any ethnic group, income per family often falling at or below one-half of that of the general city population. The 1981 census showed that social assistance in the form of government transfer payments was 10% of the income of nonstatus Indians and 27% of the income of reserve status Indians. Population increase of Indians is reported at 53% in the period 1961-81. Although no accurate figures are available for the Métis and nonstatus Indians, it is thought to be about the same. The Inuit population increase in that period was 115%. This increase has resulted in greater demands for social assistance, health services and jobs (*see* NATIVE PEOPLE, GOVERNMENT PROGRAMS).

Cultural factors interact significantly with social conditions. They may support and protect the family, or they may limit its success and be viewed as obstacles in the process of acculturation. Perhaps the most debated of the cultural patterns is the importance placed upon sharing. Historically, sharing was necessary to survival: a successful hunter shared food with the group and could expect others to share with him. In the contemporary cash economy and nuclear family, sharing can create problems; a family living in a small apartment is disrupted if another moves in to share the proceeds of income and living quarters.

Housing Adequate housing in native communities and Indian reserves continues to be a major problem. 22% of registered Indian private dwellings are crowded, with more than one person per room; on reserves the figure is 33%. Over 50% of dwellings on reserves lack central heating, and nearly one third have no bathroom. Houses built on reserves in the past were often shoddily constructed. In the 1980s there were improvements. About 30% of the current housing stock was built between 1982 and 1987, and another 35% renovated. The average number of inhabitants per house has declined from 5.9 in 1977 to 4.8 in 1987. Inuit housing is largely supplied by governments of each jurisdiction on a rental basis keyed to income. Although early housing was inadequate, new designs have been developed in consultation with Inuit.

Utility services in native communities and Indian reserves, with the exception of electricity, are far below the national average. Running water is found in only about 50% of Indian homes, with greater percentages in the Maritimes, Québec, Ontario, Alberta and BC and less in Saskatchewan, Manitoba and in the North. Sewage service is also lacking in over half of the Indian homes (55%), distribution being similar to that of running water. Most arctic communities have trucked water and sewage systems, and many have "utilidors," encased above-ground piped water and sewage services.

Inadequate fire protection for Indians living on reserves is related to the extremely high rate of fire deaths. This rate in 1982 was 23 per 100 000, as compared to the national level of 2.4 per 100 000. In 1975 about 11% of the bands owned and operated their own fire-protection units; an additional 20% were dependent on outside municipal units under contract. Many arctic settlements have small water trucks and pumps, but few have formal fire-protection equipment.

Road construction on Indian reserves has increased in recent years; in 1977-78, for example, 360 km of new road and over 640 km of reconstructed road were completed. This increase appears to be related to resource development.

Health Life expectancy of Indians of both sexes at birth increased by 3 years by 1981; it is now 62.4 years for men and 68.9 years for women, about 10 years less than the Canadian average. Native death, illness and accident rates were 3 times the national average in 1982, reflecting poor health conditions such as inadequate nutrition, housing, sewage disposal, potable water supplies and access to health services. The leading causes of death among registered Indians that year were injury and poisoning. The suicide rate was nearly 3 times that of the general population – 5 times among young adults. Deaths of Indians under 45 are caused mainly by violence – motor vehicle accidents, suicides, burns and fire, firearms and drowning. It is estimated that 50-60% of accidents and deaths are alcohol-related. There have been marked improvements, however, in Indian health in the past generation, because of better control of infectious disease. Better prenatal care and improved health conditions are lowering infant mortality, though in 1982 it was nearly twice that of the general population. Between 1960 and 1982 the infant mortality rate for Indians fell from 79 per 1000 to 17 (the figures for the general population are 27 and 9.1) (*see* NATIVE PEOPLE, HEALTH).

Antisocial Behaviour The incidence of crime among the native populations of Canada is several times that of the general population. Crime, however, is not an isolated phenomenon: it is related to poverty, crowding, alcohol and cultural disintegration. It is estimated that over half of all crimes committed by natives are alcohol related. Native representation in penitentiaries in 1977 was 280 per 100 000, as compared to the non-native figure of 40 per 100 000. Prison rates are highest on the Prairies and in the North (over 40% of inmates are natives), followed by Alberta and BC (under 30%), and lowest in the Atlantic and central provinces (under 10%). Natives commit different crimes from whites and are more likely to be involved in violent offences against other persons than against property. They tend to be given shorter sentences than non-natives, which may reflect an understanding of the social conditions by the courts or the fact that the violence is of a more minor kind. Arctic correctional facilities emphasize traditional activities such as seal hunting and other innovative measures. The rapid increase in natural-resources employment for Inuit during the 1970s seems to have contributed to an increase in alcohol problems and related offences such as assaults. Increasingly, native people play an active role in their own policing services. Inuit-

operated alcoholism-prevention and -treatment programs combat what Inuit see as a critical problem. In the 1970s and 1980s Indians began to develop their own police forces. RCMP and other police forces have added native constables to their staffs, and native communities have upgraded both local constable skills and equipment.

The Indian juvenile delinquency rate is alarmingly high in Canada: 353 per 100 000, as compared to the national average of 128 per 100 000. This rate in part reflects the fact that fewer native juveniles are let off with a warning (15%) as compared to non-native (46%). The difference is still significant, even when the number of warnings is taken into consideration, and probably reflects the number of children living in care outside their homes, social conditions of their home communities, and the breakdown of the traditional family unit and support group. It seems unlikely that the crime and juvenile delinquency rates for natives will improve before major changes are made in the social conditions of native communities.

Family Life The average on-reserve Indian family is larger (4.5 members) than the average Canadian family (3.2 members). The largest families are on reserves in Manitoba and Saskatchewan (4.7 members). Off-reserve Indian families are not much larger than those of the general population. Single parent families are twice as common among Indians as among the general population; on reserves, 75% are headed by women; off reserves, 90%.

The number of children taken into care by social agencies increased fivefold between 1962 and 1977, a result of increased migration to urban areas and attendant social problems, notably alcohol abuse, the decline in the effectiveness of extended families under rapidly changing conditions, and the extension of non-native child-care agency services to Indians on reserves. Native groups, both Indian and Métis, have responded by developing their own agencies, and in the early 1980s Indian organizations contracted with DIAND and the provincial governments to assume responsibility for dependent and neglected children. The rate of adoption of native children by non-native – over 80% of such adoptions – is expected to drop, and Child and Family Services has attempted to locate and return to native communities many of the children previously placed in non-native homes; the courts, however, have considered continuity of placement in a stable situation to be more important than cultural factors. The number of children in care will also likely decline, given the native emphasis on treatment within the family rather than the non-native stress on apprehension and agency guardianship. The Inuit adoption rate has always been high, ranging from 15% to 70% of children born in arctic communities, because of the desire of older people for children, and the extended-family recognition of responsibility. Since the 1950s, traditional Inuit adoption practices have been formally recognized by the courts. ART BLUE

Reading: DIAND, *Indian Conditions: A Survey* (1980); H.B. Hawthorn, *A Survey of the Contemporary Indians of Canada* (1966-67); N.H. Lithwick et al, *An Overview of Registered Indian Conditions in Canada* (1986); J.A. Price, *Indians of Canada: Culture Dynamics* (1979).

Native People, Urban Migration Native people are the most rural ethnic population in Canada and there are strong antiurban, prorural traditions within native society. One-half of a million native people are tied to the bush and rural country by heritage, by inalienable rights in a rural land base, and by a broad range of community services paid for by the federal government. These conditions are supported by the CONSTITUTION ACT, 1982, a legal guarantee that is unique in the world

for an aboriginal population with a predominantly hunting heritage (*see* ABORIGINAL RIGHTS).

The modern market system and other features of Canadian culture have penetrated most native communities to such an extent that the traditional subsistence way of life is being redefined as socially inferior, as "unemployment" and "poverty." Thus, with the added factors of an increase in native population and the depletion of game in some areas, people leave hunting, fishing and fur trapping to find "real employment" and the more materialistic way of life in the towns.

A semiurban life in large villages was indigenous among the agricultural HURON and IROQUOIS in the E and the coastal SALISH, NOOTKA, KWAKIUTL and TSIMSHIAN in BC. This heritage prepared people from these societies to live in cities somewhat better than natives with a seminomadic hunting heritage. Some 11% of the population of registered INDIAN bands have become urbanized because they are located adjacent to or within urban centres. The general level of urbanization of a province also affects the urbanization of the Indians who live there. Thus the level of off-reserve migration is high in Ontario and BC, moderate in the Prairies and low in Québec, the Maritimes and the NORTH. The high rates of migration have come from the Indian bands that are of smaller size, that have a tradition of working off the reserve, and that have poor on-reserve opportunities, higher education levels, more racially integrated schools and a poorly developed BAND government.

While 30% of the status Indians officially live off the reserve, in fact the figure seems to be about 40%: 16% rural nonreserve, 12% in towns and small cities and 12% in cities greater than 100 000 in population. The expansion of medical, educational, housing and business services on reserves has supported the desire to maintain at least a nominal residence on a reserve. Also, there is a potential population of 76 000 women and their children who lost Indian status through marriage and can now be reinstated through Bill C-31 of 1985. Many of these people are also trying to be accepted by their ancestral bands and to re-establish residences on reserves. This is producing a minor urban-to-reserve migration. The 1981 census found 173 370 people had a significant "self-identity" as MÉTIS or nonstatus Indians (which is more relevant than the broader category of Indian biological heritage). These native people had a similar rural-urban distribution to the off-reserve status Indians.

In moving off the reserve the Indian is leaving the jurisdiction where services are supported primarily by the Dept of INDIAN AFFAIRS AND NORTHERN DEVELOPMENT (DIAND), and moving into the jurisdiction of dozens of other federal and provincial agencies. All the federal ministries, except Defence and External Affairs, had Indian programs in 1983, and some 21% of the $2.6 billion federal budget for native programs was spent outside DIAND. The Secretary of State, in particular, funds off-reserve Indian programs, providing several million dollars annually to support native political associations, urban Indian FRIENDSHIP CENTRES across the country, women's associations, and social and cultural associations (*see* NATIVE PEOPLE, GOVERNMENT PROGRAMS). The urban Indian centres provide valuable social functions and help to integrate the diverse social services available to Indians in cities. The Ontario Task Force on the Needs of Native People in an Urban Setting (1981) surveyed 232 people across the province in educational, political and social service positions, 87% of them native, 65% female and 53% with a university degree. Their ranking of the 10 most important services currently available to urban native people was as follows: drug and alcohol therapy; education; cultural aware-

Features of Indian Life in Four Cities, 1979 (percent)

	Vancouver	Edmonton	Winnipeg	Toronto
Return home regularly	66	72	81	85
Speak an Indian language	62	70	73	62
Membership in an Indian organization	26	9	25	22
Education of grade 10 or higher	59	33	37	52
Receive social assistance	15	64	46	39

ness; employment and housing; family and children's services; justice and social welfare; youth services; recreation; women's services, health care and nutrition; and senior citizen's services.

Indian women tend to go further in school and take lower paying but steadier jobs than the men, and make up 54% of the urban Indian migrants nationally. A 1978 survey by the Ontario Native Women's Assn of 1094 Indian women showed only slight differences in the activities and attitudes of the women who lived on and those who lived off reserves. Most of the off-reserve Indians live in towns and the smaller range of cities, and continue to maintain strong kinship and friendship ties with those who live on reserves.

Social-workers' statistics often make urban Indian life look bleak and depressing, and ignore the warmth, humour and good times of daily life. Toronto, for example, had 11 375 native people (1981 census) scattered across the metropolitan area from a wide range of tribal backgrounds and income levels. An important cultural creativity can be seen in the new kind of Indian society that is developing in urban Canada. The evolution of urban Indian institutions (Québec has a unique, more assimilating, urban pattern) has generally been in 4 stages: urban bar cliques and welfare services provided by non-Indians; normal family-oriented kinship-friendship networks as the Indians themselves take over social services such as court work, therapy for alcoholics, and social work with poor single-parent families; an elaboration of artistic, educational, political, recreational and religious voluntary associations; and the development of academic and professional services by Indians. While it is normal to find elements of all stages present in a single city, one stage will usually be predominant at any particular time. Individual Indian migrants make an easier adjustment when they migrate to cities with a more mature Indian ethnic institutional system.

Studies across the country show that Indians usually make an initial urban migration to find a job when they are young. At first they correspond and return regularly to their reserves for visits and vacations, but gradually they settle into a stable life with a job, family and house in the city and make fewer return visits. Successful urban adaptations are related to several factors: the cultural background of individuals according to the traditional evolutionary level of their native social heritage; historical elements such as the length and intensity of white contact; the urban proximity of their communities; the local quality of white receptivity such as the extent of anti-Indian racism; and the maturity of urban Indian ethnic institutions in the city they move to.

A regional ranking of successful urban adaptations starts high with Québec, where few Indians leave reserves but are relatively well received when they do move; next are southern Ontario, southern Alberta and Vancouver, which are high on evolutionary level, urban proximity and mature ethnic institutions; then BC, the Yukon, the NWT and the Maritimes; and finally, northern Alberta, Saskatchewan, Manitoba and northern Ontario, which have the poorest urban adaptations on account of widespread anti-Indian RACISM, simply organized band societies, low urban proximity and relatively immature urban Indian ethnic institutions.

Urbanization across the Arctic, from Siberia to Greenland, has been a process of concentration from hundreds of very small seminomadic aboriginal hunting groups into dozens of permanent villages, and a few large towns such as INUVIK and Frobisher Bay (*see* IQALUIT). Since INUIT, mixed-bloods and whites must live co-operatively in the same communities, people get to know each other and there is less racial prejudice and discrimination than in the northern part of the Prairie provinces, where Indians and Métis tend to live in reserves or other communities segregated from the white towns. Social problems in the Arctic tend to develop in the large towns, or where there is a high turnover of workers in boom town conditions, as at TUKTOYAKTUK, the base for the oil exploration in the Beaufort Sea.   JOHN A. PRICE

Reading: R. Breton and G. Grant, eds, *The Dynamics of Government Programs for Urban Indians in the Prairie Provinces* (1984); John A. Price, *Native Studies: American and Canadian Indians* (1978).

Native-White Relations Europeans first visited N America in their quest for fishing grounds. By the late 17th century they had penetrated into the northern half of the continent in search of furs. Over several centuries and across half a continent, many kinds of individual and group relations between native people and whites were established. The situations of contact changed over time, the pattern of change from S to N and from E to W reflecting the movement of Europeans. The BEOTHUK and the MICMAC were among the first Indians of Canada to meet the Europeans. The Beothuk, a small group, were treated as enemies and as wild animals to be destroyed. They responded with resistance and flight. Most were killed or died off as a result of economic, social and physical disruption of their lives. The Micmac, however, became allies and partners of the French (*see* NATIVE-FRENCH RELATIONS).

Peaceful and friendly relations, linked to common goals such as the FUR TRADE, were maintained when they suited the needs of the parties involved. These ties sometimes led to marriages and personal friendships and to greater cultural understanding. When there was no basis for co-operation and material aid, there was likely to be competition, friction and violence. Prejudices and stereotypes were aggravated and reinforced by economic conditions and the desire by the whites to acquire more and more Indian land. The fur trade, at which the native people were adept because of the nature of their economy and technical skills, dramatically affected the organization of Indian societies. In exchange for pelts, the Europeans offered new, decorative and often useful goods, eg, weapons and utensils that were longer lasting and more efficient than some of the native people's own stone, bone and hide artifacts.

Like the Indians, the Inuit generally received the Europeans with an initial attitude of curiosity and cordiality. The Inuit had their earliest European contact with explorers (in the 16th century) and whalers (by the early 18th century). Inuit hunted food for the whalers and were hired as sailors and harpooners, and they traded pelts for European goods. European diseases, introduced first by whalers, spread among the Inuit in epidemic proportions. By the late 19th and early 20th centuries whalers had depleted the whale population, first in the eastern Arctic waters and then in the western Arctic. By this time the Inuit in those areas had become dependent on European trade goods.

The experience of each people that came into contact with the Europeans was unique, but the overall effect of such contact was similar. The technology and economy of native culture began to change even before face-to-face contact had taken place, because the items that the Europeans traded frequently preceded the Europeans themselves. Native people moved from their aboriginal territory to pursue the pelt-bearing animals, and this altered their economy and sometimes led to conflict with the previous occupants of an area. Native people also became overspecialized in their economic dependence on the fur trade and European goods, neglecting their aboriginal technology and in some cases their traditional food base. When the fur trade moved deeper into the interior, it left the native people dependent upon European goods and upon new forms of employment, eg, as canoeists, mercenaries, food suppliers, guides and translators. As the traditional economic base deteriorated, many native people became destitute. At the same time, disease decimated their populations. The HURON and PETUN populations were reduced by 50% in one decade (1630s) as a result of EPIDEMICS. The HAIDA on the Queen Charlotte Islands declined from a population of about 8000, in the early 19th century, to about 800 by the late 19th century.

From the mid-17th century to the late 19th century, this population decline led many Europeans to believe that native people would disappear. The autonomy of the native people first in the economic and technological spheres, then in the social, political, demographic, religious and even artistic spheres, was increasingly eroded as the Indians moved from a position of collaboration and partnership with the fur traders to a condition of dependence and then subjection. Missionaries, messianic religions and revitalization movements contributed to or reflected the collapse of traditional systems of social and religious organization. Cultural survival was sought in Indian-based religions, some of which borrowed and adapted elements of CHRISTIANITY. Responses to the missionary appeal varied among native people from acceptance to rejection; some native people believed the power of the newcomer might be drawn upon by the Indians.

By the middle or late 19th century, relations between Indians and Europeans had entered a new phase because hundreds of thousands of Europeans had settled in the Maritimes and in central Canada. The new dominant economy – agriculture – pushed the Indians to the sidelines and backwaters of social and economic life. In the same year as the ROYAL PROCLAMATION OF 1763, PONTIAC organized an armed resistance of more than a dozen tribes in the Ohio Valley and Great Lakes area against the British takeover from the French after the SEVEN YEARS' WAR and the encroachment of British colonial settlers across the Appalachian Mountains. TECUMSEH, like Pontiac, tried to resist white settlement, but after the WAR OF 1812 the Great Lakes Indians were no longer important military or economic allies. As the European population became a larger and larger majority, European culture came to dominate N America.

The Royal Proclamation gave the imperial government the sole right to alienate lands from the Indians and initiated the procedure of signing land-surrender treaties between the British and Indians in N America. In the late 18th and early 19th centuries, there followed, in Upper Canada [southern Ontario], a series of land surrender treaties that confined Indians to small holdings and made large tracts of land available to settlers. Indians were relieved of their lands, through treaties of land surrender, through designation of reserves, and through expropriations of reserve lands. In the Maritimes, Québec, most of BC, the Yukon and parts of the northern territories,

The Red Lake chief making a speech to the governor of Red River at Ft Douglas, 1825; coloured lithograph by Peter Rindisbacher. Most Indian groups continued to live as independent nations into the 19th century. Fur traders discouraged assimilation as being bad for trade (*courtesy National Archives of Canada/C-1939*).

where treaties were not signed, the Indians were nevertheless obliged to give up large areas of land. It is very doubtful that Indians and whites had the same understanding of the land surrender treaties. In most Indian cultures, land was not regarded as a commodity that could be bought and sold. Evidence from Indian testimony shows that Indians understood these agreements to be matters of sharing, of friendship, of mutual respect, and not final and irrevocable sales of land. On the European side, however, these treaties were regarded as legal purchases of land, with attending obligations such as the provision of annual payments, farm supplies, medical aid and so forth.

Throughout the 19th century, federal legislation shaped the life of native people. In 1876 the INDIAN ACT was passed, consolidating previous legislation and more clearly defining and confining the native people. Public and legal affairs of status Indians were governed by successive amendments and a new Indian Act in 1951. Bands were assigned reserve lands, which constituted the remains of the vast homelands once held by the native people. These reserves were to be training grounds for assimilating the native peoples into the general society. At the same time, the Indians were to be removed from the influences that were judged as "undesirable" and submitted to controlled culture change toward "civilization" and self-sufficiency.

Like the Indians of the Prairie provinces, the MÉTIS also experienced the effects of the flood of European settlers. Their efforts to resist this threat resulted in the RED RIVER REBELLION and NORTH-WEST REBELLION. Their resistance was crushed after brief outbreaks of war and their political leader, Louis RIEL, was convicted of treason and executed (1885). In the late 20th century, paralleling some of the more recent Indian movements, the Métis have begun to reassert their identity.

From the early 19th century, government has pursued a policy of encouraging the assimilation of the native people. European colonizers regarded Indian culture as "backward," "stagnant," "primitive" and "inferior" to European culture. The policy of assimilation would, it was thought,

remedy the situation. Indians who seemed to accept programs for cultural change were seen as "progressives"; those who resisted were "conservatives." The enfranchisement system removed an Indian from this group; in exchange for citizen status and voting privileges Indian status was lost. In the late 19th century and early 20th century, Indian administrators interfered increasingly in the everyday affairs of reserve life. Indian landholdings came to be seen as an impediment to "progress" and "development," and this justified the expropriation of reserve lands, especially those close to urban settlements.

To ensure their own survival, Indian leaders have frequently made compromises with the Europeans. CROWFOOT expressed his appreciation for aid given the Blackfoot and signed Treaty No 7 (1877) as a means of further protection. Chief Herbert Wallace, a Port Simpson Tsimshian of the early 20th century, credited the missionaries with assisting the Indians to understand better their own LAND CLAIMS and land rights. At that time the Nishga renewed their land protest with the Nishga Petition (1913).

By the late 20th century some of the most acculturated Indian leaders had also become the most insistent critics of the poor treatment accorded Indians and advocates of greater concern for the survival of Indian traditions as well as political and economic rights. The White Paper of 1969, which threatened Indian survival, and to which Indian spokesmen such as Harold CARDINAL responded vigorously, changed the course of Indian protest. New Indian organizations sprang into existence and existing organizations were rekindled with enthusiasm.

Pan-Indianism has been fostered to a degree by the meeting of peoples of various tribes and cultures in the cities and as a result of a common language, residential schools (before the second half of the 20th century) and increased physical mobility. One of the most exciting adaptive possibilities lies in the Northwest Territories where, unlike most of Canada, native peoples constitute the majority of the population.

Since 1971, the year the Inuit national organization, the INUIT TAPIRISAT OF CANADA, was formed, Inuit have also made a greater effort to gain control over their own affairs. Leaders have emerged from among a generation of younger people more familiar with the culture of southern Canada, but determined to preserve and develop Inuit land and culture. The native people, though socially,

culturally and economically exploited by centuries of relations with non-natives, have survived as a people. They now demand greater control of and participation in all the spheres of public affairs that govern them. *See also* NORTH and various entries under NATIVE PEOPLE.   E.P. PATTERSON

Reading: E.P. Patterson, *The Canadian Indian* (1972).

NATO (North Atlantic Treaty Organization), est 1949, was Canada's first peacetime military alliance, placing the nation in a defensive military arrangement with the US, Britain and the nations of western Europe. In 1947 there was much concern in Ottawa as the Soviet Union created a buffer zone in eastern Europe between itself and W Germany. The USSR was apparently pursuing a policy of aggressive military expansion at home and subversion abroad, and there was real fear that France or Italy might become communist (*see* COLD WAR). The problem was complicated by what Ottawa saw as a resurgent isolationism in the US, an unwillingness by Congress to pick up the international burdens that France and Britain, both weakened by WWII, could no longer bear. The answer seemed to lie in an arrangement that would link the democracies on both sides of the Atlantic into a defensive alliance, thus securing western Europe from attack while involving the US firmly in world affairs. An extra advantage for Ottawa was that such an arrangement would bind together all of Canada's trading partners, and it thus suggested potential economic benefits.

The initial public expression of this thinking was that of Escott REID, Dept of External Affairs, at the COUCHICHING CONFERENCE on 13 Aug 1947. Other Canadians, including Reid's minister, Louis ST. LAURENT, picked up the idea, and it was soon being discussed in Washington and London. Secret talks between the British, Americans and Canadians followed, and these led to formal negotiations for a broader alliance in late 1948. Canada's representative was Hume WRONG, ambassador to the US and a hardheaded realist. Wrong believed any treaty should be for defence alone, a view popular among the other participants. But Ottawa had grander visions, and L.B. PEARSON and Reid pressed him to argue for the inclusion of a clause calling for the elimination of economic conflicts among the parties. Despite misgivings, Wrong secured the inclusion of Article II, the "Canadian article." Regrettably, little came of it.

The treaty was signed 4 Apr 1949, but it was largely a paper alliance until the KOREAN WAR. That led the NATO states to build up their forces, and for Canada this had major consequences: a huge budget increase and the first stationing of troops abroad in peacetime. The Canadian contribution was small, but its quality was widely considered to be second to none. Nonetheless, high costs and the nuclear arms given the forces in 1963 worried critics. After a major review of foreign policy, the Trudeau government decided in 1969 to cut the Canadian contribution drastically, reducing the army and air elements. Although in the 1980s Canadian troops continued in Europe in these diminished numbers, and although a new Soviet truculence raised concerns, the Canadian commitment of arms and men to the alliance remained substantially lower than other NATO partners wished.   J.L. GRANATSTEIN

Reading: E. Reid, *Time of Fear and Hope* (1977).

Nattrass, Susan Marie, trapshooter (b at Medicine Hat, Alta 5 Nov 1950). She has dominated her sport. By 1981 she had been women's world champion 6 times (setting several records in the process) and was the perennial Canadian and N American champion. In the 1976 Montréal Olympics, she was the first woman to compete in the trapshooting event in Olympic history. In 1981 Nattrass won the LOU MARSH TROPHY as Canada's athlete of the year and was awarded the Order of Canada. She placed 3rd in the 1986 world championships. Nattrass has been inducted into both the Alberta and Canada sports halls of fame, and in 1987 she received the Silver Ribbon Award from Edmonton mayor Laurence Decore.

GERALD REDMOND

Natural Resources, *see* RESOURCES.

Natural Resources Transfer Acts, 1930 Under these 3 Acts – one each for Manitoba, Saskatchewan and Alberta – the federal government turned over to the Prairie provinces the jurisdiction that it had exercised over the crown lands and natural resources of the region since its purchase from the Hudson's Bay Co in 1870. The federal government had believed that it must control the land and resources to enable it to oversee the national goal of quickly populating the PRAIRIE WEST, making it productive and integrating it into the national economy. This became a popular grievance in the West, where federal control appeared to relegate the provinces to second-class status in confederation, and to result in the subordination of regional concerns to national goals. The Natural Resources Transfer Acts thus were very popular in the West, for they at last recognized equality of jurisdiction for all Canadian provinces.   D.J. HALL

Natural Sciences and Engineering Research Council, est 1978 as a crown corporation, reports to Parliament through the Ministry of State for Science and Technology. It comprises a president, a vice-president and 20 members representing Canadian universities, industry and labour. It was established to promote science and engineering outside the health sciences and it also responds to the minister's requests for advice on specific research.

Nault, André, Métis leader (b at Point Douglas, Red River Colony 1829; d at St Vital, Man 1924). Although a kinsman of Louis RIEL and always considered a Métis, Nault was not of mixed blood. Interference with his hay privileges by surveyors provoked the first armed resistance in the North-West in 1869. During the rebellion of 1870 he was in charge of the party that seized Ft Garry, and he sat on the council that condemned Thomas SCOTT on 3 Mar 1870. Nault commanded the firing squad the next day. Chased across the border and left for dead by Orangemen shortly after the Canadian takeover, Nault returned to St Vital and in 1873 was arrested with Ambroise Lépine for Scott's murder. Unlike Lépine he was not tried and was pardoned as part of the general amnesty of 1875.   J.M. BUMSTED

Nault, Fernand, stage name of Fernand-Noël Boissonneault, dancer, choreographer, teacher, director (b at Montréal 27 Dec 1921). As resident choreographer of Les GRANDS BALLETS CANADIENS Nault has created a succession of highly theatrical ballets which have greatly contributed to the company's popularity. Trained in Canada, the US and Europe, he danced with American Ballet Theatre 1944-65 and was also a company ballet master from 1958. His lengthy association with Les Grands Ballets Canadiens began in 1965 and he has variously held the positions of associate director 1967-74, director of schools 1974-76 and resident choreographer. Nault was guest choreographer of the Colorado Ballet 1978-81 and its artistic director 1981-82. He has been awarded the Order of Canada (1977), the Prix du Québec (1984) and the Prix Denise-Pelletier (1984).   MICHAEL CRABB

Naval Aid Bill As early as 1909 the Conservative Party believed that Canada should contribute "emergency" funds to help the Royal Navy maintain its superiority over the German navy. In Mar 1912 the RN required more "dreadnought" battleships. After consulting with Winston Churchill, First Lord of the ADMIRALTY, in July 1912, PM BORDEN agreed to provide up to $35 million for 3 dreadnoughts. Payment was authorized by the Naval Aid Bill, introduced by Borden in Dec. The Liberals resisted bitterly, angered by Borden's neglect of the Canadian navy (est 1910 by the NAVAL SERVICE ACT). The Conservatives carried the bill on 15 May 1913 only by imposing CLOSURE on debate for the first time in Canadian history. However, the Liberal majority in the Senate defeated the bill 2 weeks later. WWI began before Borden could do anything more about naval policy.   ROGER SARTY

Naval Service Act established the Royal Canadian Navy, 4 May 1910. The Act proposed a small navy under the control of the Canadian government, with emergency provision for transfer to the British ADMIRALTY. PM Wilfrid LAURIER had been under increasing pressure from the British government and Canadian imperialists to contribute directly to the Royal Navy, in the face of a growing challenge from the German navy. The Act was bitterly opposed by French Canadian nationalists, led by Henri BOURASSA, who opposed deeper involvement in imperial affairs. Laurier's compromise placated neither group, severely reduced his support in Québec, and ultimately contributed to his defeat in 1911. The navy survived, although it entered WWI with only 2 warships, the RAINBOW and the *Niobe*. *See also* ARMED FORCES.

ROGER SARTY

Navigation may be defined as the science of finding one's way between 2 points. However, the term is now used most commonly in the context of aviation or marine travel as in navigating an aircraft or navigating a ship across the ocean. Navigation requires establishing one's position and the measurement of motion relative to the Earth's surface, and the development of this science is intimately connected with the history of man's efforts to travel the seas, which was in turn driven by the twin forces of world exploration and mercantile expansion.

Evidence suggests that the Phoenicians, Arabs and ancient Greeks were familiar with the use of nighttime positions of stars and constellations to aid in marine navigation, but this knowledge was lost to Europeans in the Dark Ages and only regained after about the year 1000 from the Arabs. Several native Pacific cultures also made use of these techniques. Until the reintroduction of this concept, navigation techniques used in Europe usually relied on staying within sight of land and using "Portolan charts," showing the shape of coastlines and the location of each harbour.

The translation of Ptolemy's *Geography* around 1409 began a revolution in navigation and introduced to Europe the concept of dividing the Earth's surface into a grid of east-west and north-south lines of latitude and longitude. Latitude, or north-south position, could be determined from the angle of a known star or the sun at its highest point above the horizon, referring to celestial tables developed by astronomers; but longitude (the east-west position) required knowledge of the time at which a star sighting was taken. This in turn spurred the development of accurate time-pieces, or chronometers. Thus, the development of timekeeping, navigation, astronomy and map-making are all closely intertwined.

While celestial navigation is still taught to ships officers, modern aids to navigation are now relied upon extensively in both air and marine modes. For mariners, these range from satellite systems through radio position measuring systems, such

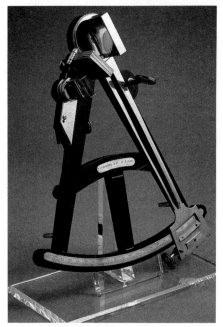

English sextant, *c*1790-1810, a navigational instrument which aided sailors in ascertaining latitude and longitude (*courtesy Royal Ontario Museum*).

English Hadley quadrant (an instrument for measuring altitudes) marked by Spencer, Browning and Rust, London, *c*1790-1810. A quadrant usually had a plumb line or spirit level for fixing the vertical or horizontal direction (*courtesy Royal Ontario Museum*).

Arnold 176: chronometer (an instrument for measuring time) used by George Vancouver when exploring the Pacific Northwest, 1791-1795 (*courtesy Vancouver Maritime Museum*).

as "LORAN-C," now in extensive use in N America, to the more conventional aids, such as LIGHT-HOUSES, buoys and shore beacons. In Canada, aids to navigation are provided by the CANADIAN COAST GUARD for the benefit of all types of users from pleasure craft to large container ships. Air navigation aids are provided by Transport Canada.

Because of its long history, marine navigation normally has priority over other uses of the water and approval for the construction of works which could obstruct marine navigation is also required from the Canadian Coast Guard.

MICHAEL A.H. TURNER

Navigation Acts, a complex set of British laws dating from 1651 and 1660, regulating British and later imperial shipping and trade to foster economic and naval power (*see* MERCANTILISM). They governed ownership and crew nationality of vessels trading to Britain and her colonies, and the acceptability of routes and commodities. They were used to try to link British North America economically with the West Indian colonies; more generally, trade among BNA colonies and theirs with Britain had to be conducted in British or colonial vessels. Trade on the Great Lakes did not entirely fit the system; enforcement was lax before 1815 and by 1822 legislation permitted cross-lake trade in many commodities. Following repeal of the CORN LAWS in 1846, Canadians resentfully denounced the Acts as a burden. They were repealed in 1849 as part of Britain's overall movement to free trade.

DOUGLAS MCCALLA

Navy, *see* ARMED FORCES: NAVY.

Navy Island, Ont, 130 km², the only Canadian island in the NIAGARA R, is owned by the federal government and managed by the Niagara Parks Commission; access is solely by boat. So named because its timber was used to build British naval vessels in the mid-1760s, it was briefly occupied by insurgents during the REBELLIONS OF 1837-38. By the 1880s it contained a summer resort hotel, orchards and farm buildings. It was proposed as the site for a permanent United Nations headquarters in 1945, but remains an isolated, uninhabited wilderness reserve rarely visited except for summer camping. JOHN N. JACKSON

Navy League of Canada, a volunteer organization fd 1918 under federal charter, but tracing its origins to branches of the British Empire Navy League established in Canada from 1895. The league's central function is the promotion of Canada's maritime interests, and it has consistently supported expansion of the merchant marine. The league provided seamen's comforts during wartime and has been active in youth training. Boy's Naval Brigades (now called Sea Cadets) were begun in 1903, and after 1945 training was extended to girls and preadolescents (Navy League Cadets). *See also* CADETS; ARMED FORCES.

MARC MILNER

Neal, William Merton, "Billy," railway executive (b at Toronto 20 June 1886; d at Longbow Lk, Ont 19 Oct 1961). Neal entered the CPR's service in 1902, qualifying as a stenographer in Winnipeg 2 years later. Most of his experience was in the West, although he was on loan as general secretary to the Canadian Ry Board during WWI. He succeeded D.C. COLEMAN as general manager of the western lines in 1934 and became a VP in 1942. Neal, who hired Grant MCCONACHIE as his assistant in Winnipeg, ceaselessly promoted McConachie's interests and also those of CP Air. The federal government was determined to force CPR to divest itself of its air subsidiary at the end of the war, but Neal, whose relations with C.D. HOWE were excellent, persuaded it otherwise and the

airline survived. Neal was president and chairman of CPR for just over a year before being obliged to resign because of ill health.

ROBERT BOTHWELL

Neatby, Hilda Marion, educator (b at Sutton, Eng 19 Feb 1904; d at Saskatoon 14 May 1975), sister of Kenneth NEATBY. Best known as author of *So Little for the Mind* (1953), a critique of Canadian education, Neatby was also an influential member of the Massey Commission (*see* NATIONAL DEVELOPMENT IN THE ARTS, LETTERS AND SCIENCES, ROYAL COMMISSION ON), a historian of Québec and a professor at U of Sask. In her 1953 study, Neatby called for a return to basics in primary education and an emphasis on traditional education for the best students in high school. She presented her ideas forcefully. These were strongly criticized by educational bureaucrats and widely debated throughout Canada. She published *Quebec, The Revolutionary Age, 1760-1791* (1966). The following year she became a Companion of the Order of Canada. MICHAEL HAYDEN

Neatby, Kenneth William, agricultural scientist (b at Sutton, Eng 30 Mar 1900; d at Ottawa 27 Oct 1958), brother of Hilda NEATBY. Son of an English doctor who immigrated to Saskatchewan in 1906, Neatby joined the Winnipeg Rust Laboratory as a wheat geneticist in 1926, and in 1933 discovered how to forecast rust resistance in new wheat hybrids. He taught at U of A 1935-40 and then spent 6 years as farm liaison agent for a wheat wholesaler. After becoming director of the Dept of Agriculture's science service in 1946 he doubled its size and tripled its budget, laying the foundation for a new research branch that was formally created some months after his death. The dept's Neatby Building, housing 125 laboratories, commemorates him.

DONALD J.C. PHILLIPSON

Nechako River rises in the COAST MTS in W-central BC and flows E to form a principal tributary of the FRASER R. Because of massive damming of its headwaters, it is no longer possible to give its length or tell exactly where it used to rise. Since the 1950s its headwaters have been backed up into the huge Nechako Reservoir behind Kenney Dam, and two-thirds of this flow is diverted W to provide power for aluminum production at KITIMAT. The river drains 46 000 km² (14 000 km² above the dam). Its principal tributaries are the Cheslatta, Nautley and Stuart rivers. James Mc-Dougall of the NWC was the first non-native to reach the Nechako (1806), called *Incha-Khoh* ("big river") by the local CARRIER Indians. In 1807 Simon FRASER established Fort George (now PRINCE GEORGE) at the Nechako-Fraser confluence. Fur traders in the valley were followed in the late 19th century by prospectors heading for the Omineca and Klondike goldfields, and by workers on the Yukon telegraph line. Homesteaders came to farm in the early 20th century. Today the river valley supports an economy based on farming, forestry and mining. The Nechako and its tributaries are also important salmon-spawning streams. Diversion and regulation of the river for power generation caused the displacement of native and non-native people in the 1950s and adversely affected salmon stocks. ROSEMARY J. FOX

Neel, Louis Boyd, conductor, administrator, lecturer, surgeon (b at Blackheath [London], Eng 19 July 1905; d at Toronto 30 Sept 1981). In 1932, while maintaining a busy surgical practice in London, Neel formed the Boyd Neel Orchestra, a chamber ensemble of 17 string players performing and recording contemporary music as well as the established repertoire. A surgeon in the British navy in WWII, he organized concerts for

the armed forces. He guest-conducted most important symphony orchestras and opera companies before coming to Toronto as dean of the ROYAL CONSERVATORY OF MUSIC (1953-71). He conducted the CBC Symphony Orchestra (1953-64), founded and conducted the Hart House Orchestra (1954-71) and conducted the Mississauga Symphony Orchestra (1971-78). Awarded honorary degrees from the Royal Academy of Music and U of T, he was a Commander of the British Empire. His memoirs, *My Orchestras and Other Adventures: The Memoirs of Boyd Neel*, were published in 1985.

MABEL H. LAINE

Neepawa, Man, Town, pop 3314 (1986c), 3425 (1981c), inc 1883, on the fertile beautiful plains, is 175 km NW of Winnipeg. Neepawa, a native term for "plenty," is a service centre for surrounding grain and livestock farms. Homesteading began in the 1870s. The townsite was established in 1880-81, competing against MIN-NEDOSA as regional centre. The Manitoba and North Western Railway arrived in 1883, followed by a Canadian Northern line in 1902. Early economic activity included wheat marketing, services, grain milling, wood and marble works, a roundhouse, a brick yard and a creamery. Salt refining, to tap natural brines, began in the 1920s and was revived in 1932, operating under a succession of owners until 1970. During WWII, Neepawa had an elementary air-training school. Contemporary activity includes integrated boiler and pork operations, and timber preservation. Birthplace of author Margaret LAURENCE and pioneer music educator Eva Clare, Neepawa hosts the annual Manitoba Holiday Festival of the Arts. D.M. LYON

Nègres blancs d'Amérique (1968), a Marxist analysis of Québec history and a program for the future, written under the guise of autobiography by Pierre Vallières while he was confined in a Manhattan jail for FLQ activities. It dramatizes his impoverished, frustrated childhood during the DUPLESSIS era as the son of working-class parents in Longueuil-Annexe; his checkered career as a philosophy student, office worker, Franciscan postulant, writer and friend of the poet Gaston MIRON and of the intelligentsia associated with CITÉ LIBRE, PARTI PRIS and Le DEVOIR; and his "conversion" to MARXISM and FLQ involvement following a trip to France and Spain. To Vallières, Québec's working class reveals the characteristics of a colonized people; "white niggers" denotes a condition of being which he felt could be altered only through violent revolution. The work was revised and expanded in 1969, and it was translated in 1971 as *White Niggers of America*.

MICHÈLE LACOMBE

Neilson, John, journalist, politician (b at Balmaghie, Scot 17 July 1776; d at Québec C 1 Feb 1848). At the age of 21, Neilson succeeded his brother Samuel at the helm of the bilingual *Quebec Gazette*, which he ran for 50 years. Although of conservative views, he championed the cause of the French Canadians, and from 1818 to 1833 was an elected member of the Assembly of Lower Canada. On 2 occasions, in 1823 and 1828, he travelled to London to protest successfully against a proposed union of Lower and Upper Canada. Around 1831, he began to dissociate himself from L.-J. PAPINEAU and his party, but in 1838 he resumed his vigorous opposition to the union of the 2 Canadas. Re-elected to the legislature in 1841, he was made Speaker of the Assembly in 1844.

GISÈLE VILLENEUVE

Nelles, Percy Walker, naval officer (b at Brantford, Ont 7 Jan 1892; d at Victoria 13 June 1951). Nelles achieved his first command, HMS *Dragon*, in 1929 and 2 years later took over HMCS *Sague-*

nay, the first warship built specifically for Canada. As chief of the naval staff 1934-44, he was instrumental in the navy's survival of the Depression and the architect of its phenomenal wartime growth. An able, if colourless, administrator, Nelles was sent to London in Jan 1944 as liaison officer following a bitter break with naval minister A.L. MACDONALD over the handling of naval expansion. He retired in Jan 1945.

MARC MILNER

Nelligan, Émile, poet (b at Montréal 24 Dec 1879; d there 18 Nov 1941). A romantic, Parnassian and symbolist, Nelligan was an outstanding turn-of-the-century writer. Except for a few summer vacations in Cacouna and a sea voyage about which little is known, Nelligan spent his entire life in Montréal. He attended the École Olier 1886-90, Mont Saint-Louis 1890-93 and the Petit Séminaire de Montréal 1893-96. In Sept 1896 he enrolled in the Collège Sainte-Marie, which he left in Mar 1897. He became friendly with Louis Dantin and Arthur de Bussières, and on 10 Feb 1897 he was elected a member of the École littéraire de Montréal and began writing poetry with increasing ardour.

His first poem, "Rêve fantasque," had been published in *Le Samedi* on 13 June 1896, under the pseudonym of Émile Kovar. Other poems appeared in *Le Monde illustré, Alliance nationale* and *Le Petit Messager du Très-Saint-Sacrement.* In the course of his reading, he discovered Lamartine, Hugo and Millevoye, Verlaine, Baudelaire and Pierre Dupont, Rodenback and Rolliant, Catule Mendès, Heredia and Leconte de Lisle, and other Parnassian and symbolist poets such as Sully Prudhomme, Théodore de Banville, Albert Samain and Arthur Rimbaud. He was fascinated by the dark world of Edgar Allan Poe.

Nelligan recited his poems brilliantly at the 4 sessions of the École littéraire de Montréal. At the last meeting, held in the Château de Ramezay on 26 May 1899, he performed a forceful reading of his "Romance du vin," which, with his unforgettable "Vaisseau d'or," has contributed to his almost legendary fame. On 9 Aug 1899, exhausted, ill and on the verge of insanity, Nelligan was taken to the Retraite Saint-Bénoît; in 1925 he was transferred to the Hôpital Saint-Jean-de-Dieu, where he remained until his death.

Poet Émile Nelligan (1904), whose sad and nostalgic poetry has given him almost legendary status in Québec literature (*courtesy National Archives of Canada/C-88566/ Laberge/Gill Coll*).

Nelligan's work, which includes some 170 poems, sonnets, rondels, songs and prose poems, is strikingly lyrical. The poet's voice is sad and nostalgic, oscillating between the theme of the passage of time and a hallucinatory vision of the world. Conveyed through traditional prosody, Nelligan's imagery often attains the symbolic. His work was collected by Louis Dantin and published in 1904. Three subsequent editions were issued in 1925, 1932 and 1945. In 1952 Luc Lacourcière published a critical edition of the work, which was reprinted in 1958, 1966 and 1974. Two deluxe editions appeared in 1967 and 1979. *See also* LITERATURE IN FRENCH; POETRY IN FRENCH.

PAUL WYCZYNSKI

Nelligan, Kate, actress (b at London, Ont 16 Mar 1951). She studied at York U and received her drama training at the Central School of Speech in London, Eng. She made her London debut as Jenny in *Knuckle* by David Hare, in whose work she has become most associated. In 1978 she played Susan Traherne in Hare's *Plenty* at the National Theatre, repeating the role in New York in 1982. Other significant roles include Ellie Dunn in *Heartbreak House* at the Old Vic (1975); Marianne in *Tales from the Vienna Woods* at the National (1977) and Rosalind in *As You Like It* at Stratford (1977). She joined the American Repertory Theatre in Cambridge, Mass, in 1984 to play Josie in Eugene O'Neill's *Moon For the Misbegotten*. Nelligan has been highly praised for her roles in such television productions as "Thérèse Raquin" and Hare's "Dreams of Leaving," and in the feature films *The Romantic Englishwoman* (1975), *Dracula* (1979), *Eye of the Needle* (1980), *Without a Trace* (1982) and *Eleni* (1985).

JAMES DEFELICE

Nelson, BC, City, pop 8113 (1986c), 9143 (1981c), inc 1897, named after Hugh Nelson, lt-gov of BC, overlooks the W arm of Kootenay Lk, 660 km E of Vancouver. The prehistoric boundary of the Interior SALISH and the KOOTENAY is nearby. In 1887 Silver King Mine on Toad Mt led to rapid growth in Nelson. The first railway in the Kootenay reached here in 1892; the Spokane Falls and Northern Ry (Burlington Northern) followed in 1894. Nelson soon became a transfer point for lake traffic and, with completion of the Crow's Nest Pass Ry and the Kettle Valley line (1898), developed as a railway maintenance and service centre.

A copper and lead smelter operated in Nelson 1896-1907. Disease virtually eliminated fruit farming between 1920 and 1950. Nelson remains the administrative and wholesale distribution centre for the Kootenay region. Logging and sawmilling have been intermittently important; the plywood plant was closed in 1982 but the site was bought in 1986 by a company planning to build a sawmill. The closure of Notre Dame U was mitigated by the establishment of the David Thompson University Center, which closed in 1984 but was reopened in Sept 1987 as David Thompson College offering a full coeducational (residential or day) program for grades 9 to 12.

WILLIAM A. SLOAN

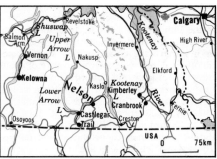

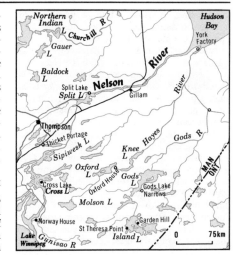

Nelson River, 644 km long, flows NNE out of Playgreen Lk, at the NW tip of Lk Winnipeg. It spills out into a number of lakes, including Cross, Sipiwesk, Split and Stevens, flowing E from the latter into Hudson Bay. Its main tributaries are the Burntwood R, on which THOMPSON, Man, is located, and the Grass R. Sir Thomas BUTTON wintered at its mouth 1612 and named it for Robert Nelson, a ship's master who died there. The entrance to the river became the scene of a bitter struggle for the fur trade, and YORK FACTORY was established at Marsh Point, a peninsula separating the Nelson and HAYES R. However, the Hayes, not the Nelson, became the main route inland. The Nelson takes an often turbulent course through the granitic SHIELD; as the last link in the long SASKATCHEWAN R system and as a conduit for the waters of the Red and Winnipeg rivers as well, it has a mean flow at its outlet of 2066 m^3/s. Today the Nelson's drop and huge volume are exploited for hydroelectric power. The largest developments are Kettle Rapids, built 1970-74 (1272 MW), Long Spruce, built 1977-79 (980 MW), and Kelsey, built 1960-72 (224 MW), to provide power for nickel smelters at Thompson.

JAMES MARSH

Nematoda, phylum of unsegmented, cylindrical worms; approximately 30 000 species are known. Nematodes exhibit both radial and bilateral symmetry. The smallest adults are under 0.25 mm long; the largest (whale parasites) may exceed 9 m. Nematodes are pseudocoelomate, ie, have an unlined space between the body wall and digestive tract. Flexible cuticle covers the fluid-filled body. The digestive tract (a muscular, glandular esophagus and simple intestine) extends from mouth to anus. The mouth may contain elaborate, cuticular (horny) teeth, plates or a hollow spear. Circulatory and respiratory systems are absent. Sexes are separate. All nematodes, regardless of habitat or life-style, possess similar life cycles: 4 larval stages, each separated by a molt in which old cuticle is shed and replaced, precede the adult stage. Molts may be the only indication of development since larvae may be superficially identical to adults. Most nematodes are free-living scavengers, herbivores or predators, in soil, fresh water or salt water. Parasitic species living in plants or animals are less common but more notorious. The golden nematode has decimated potato crops in Newfoundland and southern Vancouver I. Others cause serious damage to timber, field and greenhouse crops. Trichina worm in pigs or bears and dog round worm are familiar animal parasites. Virtually every animal can be infected with several species. Nematodes have been classified variously as an order, class or phylum, and were once considered a class of phylum Aschelmintha.

T.F. MACE

Nepheline Syenite, white to whitish grey, medium-grained IGNEOUS ROCK. It consists of nepheline, potash and soda feldspar and accessory magnesium and iron-rich minerals. The Canadian nepheline syenite industry began in 1932 with the staking of claims on Blue Mt near Peterborough, Ont. A long period of persistent efforts in technical and market research and in development was necessary to establish this unique industry. The use of nepheline syenite as a raw material for glass, ceramic and filler industries was first developed in Canada, which was the world's only producer for many years. Over the years, nepheline syenite has become preferred to feldspar as a source of alumina and alkalis for glass manufacture. It promotes more rapid melting at lower temperatures, thus reducing energy consumption, lengthening the life of the furnace and improving yield and quality of glass. The material is used in ceramic glazes and enamels and in fillers in paints, papers, plastics and foam rubber. A growing market is developing in the white-ware industry where the material is used as a body and a glaze ingredient for bathroom fixtures, vitreous enamels, china, ovenware, electric porcelain and ceramic artwares. The 2 Canadian nepheline syenite operations are located at Blue Mt, Ont. Other occurrences have been identified but these are either too high in iron content or too variable in chemical composition for exploitation. Nepheline syenite occurs in southern BC, in the Bancroft area of Ontario and in southern Québec, but none of these deposits is, as yet, of economic significance. Extraction in the Blue Mt area is by open pits. Ore is hauled to the mill where it is put through a magnetic separation circuit to remove iron-bearing minerals. The mill produces several grades of nepheline syenite, based on grain size and iron content, to meet a wide variety of markets. Shipments in 1986 were 485 000 t, worth $20.4 million (down from 1981 shipments of 605 000 t, worth about $18 million). Canada exports 70% of its production; about 90% to the US. *See also* METALLURGY.   J.Y. TREMBLAY

Neptune Theatre, in Halifax, named after Canada's first theatrical production (Marc LESCARBOT's Théâtre de Neptune, 1606) opened on 1 July 1963 in a 525-seat former vaudeville house. Tom Patterson, founder of the STRATFORD FESTIVAL, and Leon Major, Neptune's founding artistic director, with the support of the CANADA COUNCIL, had visited Halifax in 1962 to explore the possibility of establishing a professional theatre there. The response was positive and, with dedicated support from the community, the theatre was obtained and renovations were undertaken.

The first company in Canada to engage its artists and technicians on a 52-week basis and to adopt the repertory system, Neptune attracted directors such as George McCowan and Mavor MOORE. But within 4 years, the company was in grave financial difficulties and was rescued by the provincial and municipal governments. In 1978, when the theatre was in trouble again because of a decline in subscriptions, actor John NEVILLE was appointed artistic director. Within 5 years, Neptune's deficit had been eliminated and the number of season-ticket holders had doubled. In addition to traditional offerings, Neville presented plays by Canadians such as Rick SALUTIN and John GRAY. Tom Kerr was artistic director, 1983-86 and Richard Ouzounion since then.

Nesbitt, Arthur Deane, businessman (b at Montreal 16 Nov 1910; d there 22 Feb 1978). Educated as an engineer at McGill, where he first took up flying, Nesbitt joined the RCAF in 1939 and fought with distinction (winning the DFC) in No 1 Fighter Squadron 1940-41. He subsequently commanded No 111 Squadron in the Aleutian campaign 1941-42 and No 114 Spitfire Wing and No 143 Typhoon Wing in the North-West Europe campaign 1944-45. He retired in 1945 as a group captain. Nesbitt was president and latterly also chairman of Nesbitt, Thomson, the investment dealership begun by his father, 1952-77, playing a significant role in the underwriting of a host of Canadian companies. His dynamic part in the birth of TRANSCANADA PIPELINES is celebrated in William Kilbourn's *Pipe Line* (1970); he served on the board of TCPL for many years, and on those of other major concerns as well. An active athlete throughout his life, he died shortly after a skiing accident left him almost completely paralyzed.
                                                NORMAN HILLMER

Netball is a ball-goal game, played chiefly in English-speaking countries by girls and women, with 2 teams of 7 players. As in BASKETBALL, the aim is to score goals by throwing the ball into a ring attached to a 10-foot (3.05 m) pole. Players may not run with the ball, and are restricted to prescribed areas of the court. After the early form of basketball was introduced into England in 1895, it was modified as a sport for girls. Netball spread throughout the Commonwealth and was introduced in Canada in the early 1960s, the first games being played in Montréal in 1962. The Canadian Amateur Netball Assn was formed in 1973 and the first national championship was held in 1975. World tournaments are held every 4 years; Canada placed 11th out of 22 countries in 1979, 12th in 1983, and 10th in 1987. Netball will be the official demonstration sport at the Commonwealth Games in 1990. In Canada it is played mainly in NS, Qué, Ont, Alta and BC.
                                                BARBARA SCHRODT

Netsilik Inuit (or Netsilingmiut) are one of several groups of INUIT who live on the Arctic coast of Canada W of Hudson Bay. When visited by the Greenlandic explorer Knud Rasmussen in 1923, the 259 Netsilingmiut were scattered throughout a territory of about 103 600 km² between Committee Bay, Victoria Strait and Somerset I. Until recently they were nomadic hunters. Their name means "people of the place where there is seal" and probably derives from the name of a lake, Netsilik (Seal), on BOOTHIA PENINSULA. The Netsilingmiut traditionally lived in small shifting family groups with simple nonhierarchical social organization. There was no formal government and no institutionalized group relationships. They hunted seal, caribou, muskoxen and occasionally polar bear, and fished for salmon, trout and char. By ingenious technology, they converted the bones, skins and flesh of these animals, as well as stone, snow and ice, into all the necessary survival materials.

The Netsilingmiut speak a dialect of Inuktitut, the language spoken by Inuit from northern Alaska to eastern Greenland. The Netsilingmiut had a detailed knowledge of an enormous expanse of territory. They sometimes spent several years on journeys to the coast of Hudson Bay and to the Thelon R, where they obtained knives, needles, wood for sledges and KAYAKS, and, early in the 20th century, firearms.

White men first entered Netsilik territory early in the 19th century, some in search of a NORTHWEST PASSAGE from the Atlantic to the Pacific; others in search of the remains of the FRANKLIN Expedition. Explorers were a second source of goods from the outside world. A third source appeared in 1923, when the first HBC post was established on KING WILLIAM I. The HBC was followed in the 1930s by missionaries, then by the RCMP; and in the 1950s the process of change accelerated with the establishment of schools and nursing stations. Today, most Netsilingmiut live in or near the settlements of Spence Bay and Pelly Bay on Boothia Peninsula, and Gjoa Haven on King William I. They are Christian, many speak English and Inuktitut, and their life is heavily influenced by southern goods, services and institutions. Many of their values and ways of relating to one another remain Inuit. *See also* NATIVE PEOPLE: ARCTIC.
                                                JEAN L. BRIGGS

Reading: Asen Balikci, *The Netsilik Eskimo* (1970).

Nettiling Lake, 5530 km², elev 29 m, max length 123 km, is located toward the S end of BAFFIN I, in the Great Plain of the Koukdjuak, about 110 km SW of AUYUITTUQ NATIONAL PARK, 160 km W of Pangnirtung and 280 km NW of the IQALUIT [Frobisher Bay] settlement. The third-largest lake of the Far North and tenth largest in Canada, it is fed by AMADJUAK LK and several other small lakes and streams. The largest lake on Baffin I, it is dotted by numerous islands and contains 3 bays: Mirage, Camsell and Burwash. It empties into FOXE BASIN from its W shore via the very shallow Koukdjuak R.   DAVID EVANS

Neuroscience is the study of the structure and function of the nervous system. It includes a number of subfields such as neuroanatomy, neurochemistry, neuropharmacology, neurophysiology and the study of brain mechanisms in behaviour (neuroethology, neuropsychology, psychobiology and psychopharmacology). In addition, the medical fields of neurology, neurosurgery and PSYCHIATRY are closely related to that of neuroscience.

Anatomical investigations of the nervous system have revealed the existence of specialized cells or neurons, which occur in vast numbers, in a great variety of shapes, sizes and functions, and form interconnected systems of enormous complexity. A British scientist, C.S. Sherrington, first understood that one neuron can influence the activity of a second neuron primarily via a specialized area of contact which he referred to as a synapse. Subsequent work has revealed that synaptic transmission is usually the result of the release of a chemical substance (a neurohumor or neurotransmitter) which acts on specialized macromolecules (receptors) located in the membrane of the recipient neuron. It is of historical interest that some essential features of this concept were originally proposed in 2 papers published by a Canadian, F.H. Scott, in 1905 and 1906. However, Scott's ideas were too far in advance of the times and were ignored. The chemical nature of synaptic transmission did not become generally accepted until several decades later.

Modern research has shown that there are many chemically distinctive neurotransmitters. As a result, it is possible to alter the operation of specific types of synapses by the administration of drugs that alter the release or the effect of specific neurotransmitters. Great practical importance attaches to this fact since it makes possible the pharmacological treatment of disorders of the nervous system. It also provides the basis for the widespread non-medical use of drugs that alter various aspects of the brain's function in a selective manner.

The establishment of the Montreal Neurological Institute (MNI) at McGill U in 1934, with Wilder PENFIELD as its first director, had a major effect on the development of neuroscience in Canada. The MNI, together with related departments at McGill and U de Montréal made Montréal known worldwide for research and teaching in neuroscience and for the study and treatment of disorders of the nervous system. Scientists and physicians trained in Montréal, and subsequently established eminent careers elsewhere in Canada and the world. For example, David Hubel, a Canadian-born US citizen who was educated at Harvard University and subsequently took up a position there, was awarded the Nobel Prize in 1981 for his studies on brain mechanisms in vision.

The MNI became especially well known for the advances made by Penfield and H. Jasper in the diagnosis, classification and treatment of epilepsy. The identification of the role of γ-aminobutyric acid (GABA), now believed to be the major inhibitory transmitter in the brain with a role in conditions as diverse as epilepsy and in the effect of anti-anxiety drugs, was made at the MNI by A.W. Bazemore, K.A.C. Elliott and E. Florey in 1957. The discoveries that Parkinson's disease was due to a deficiency of dopamine, an important neurotransmitter, and that the symptoms of the disease could be dramatically reversed by treatment with L-dopa, a compound from which the brain can manufacture dopamine, were made almost simultaneously 1960-62 by A. Barbeau, G.F. Murphy and T.L. Sourkes in Montréal and by O. Hornykiewicz and his colleagues in Vienna.

Work by H. Jasper, K. Krnjevic, H. MacIntosh and J.H. QUASTEL of McGill and J. Szerb of Dalhousie provided much of the basis of our present understanding of the action of another neurotransmitter, acetylcholine, in the brain. This work has recently assumed considerable practical importance as a result of the demonstration by British and American investigators that Alzheimer's disease is associated with a severe loss of acetylcholine-containing neurons in the brain.

The establishment of brain-behaviour research in Canada was due, in large part, to D.O. HEBB of McGill. Work in Hebb's laboratory demonstrated the important role played by ordinary environmental stimulation in the development and maintenance of normal brain function. One of Hebb's students, B. Milner, carried out a series of studies at the MNI which demonstrated the localization of various mental abilities in different parts of the cerebral cortex. An especially notable finding was the profound disturbance of memory resulting from injury to the hippocampal formation and amygdala. In 1953 J. Olds and P.M. Milner, working in Hebb's laboratory, discovered that animals would voluntarily deliver electrical stimulation to certain parts of their own brain when enabled to do so by means of an implanted electrode. It is widely believed that this phenomenon establishes that the localization of motivation and pleasure exists in the brain.

At the present time, research in neuroscience is undergoing an explosive development everywhere in the developed world. Every large Canadian university has programs in neuroscience fields in several academic departments. The US-based Society for Neuroscience has well over 600 Canadian members. New technology such as computerized tomography, magnetic resonance imaging and positron-emission tomography now permit non-invasive investigation of the living human nervous system at a level of detail which was unimaginable a few years ago. It is reasonable to expect great improvements in our understanding of the nervous system and our ability to treat diseases of the nervous system in the coming decades. C.H. VANDERWOLF

Neutral in the early 17th century lived in the Hamilton-Niagara district of SW Ontario and in New York state. They spoke an Iroquoian language and were known to the HURON as the *Attiwandaronk*, meaning "people whose speech is awry or a little different." In 1615 Samuel de CHAMPLAIN misnamed them "la Nation neutre" since they were then at peace with the Five Nations and the Huron. The Neutral numbered about 40 000 and had an army of 4000 to 6000

warriors prior to the smallpox EPIDEMICS of 1638-40. They lived in LONGHOUSES in about 40 settlements that included large palisaded towns, villages and smaller specialized seasonal hamlets distributed around the Niagara Peninsula and along the Niagara Escarpment. The main concentration of settlements was within a 32 km radius of Hamilton, Ont.

The Neutral had trading and war alliances with surrounding Iroquoian-speaking peoples, particularly the PETUN, Huron, Wenro, Kakwa, Erie, Andaste and probably some of the Five Nations of IROQUOIS. They were also allied with the OTTAWA against the Algonquian-speaking Mascouten of Michigan and Ohio. The Mascouten were longstanding, bitter enemies, and in 1643 the Neutral army captured and brought back 800 prisoners, both male and female, torturing some of them.

They relied upon horticultural crops of corn, beans and SQUASH, as well as on considerable hunting of deer, raccoon, black bear and the now extinct passenger pigeon. Their diet was augmented by fishing and nut collecting, and tobacco was cultivated for ritual and trade purposes. The men were heavily tattooed and in summer wore little if any clothing. They were extremely proficient at knapping chert arrowheads and scrapers, and the women made pottery, though it was gradually replaced by European copper containers. Such trade items were often included in their cemeteries as grave goods.

It has been suggested that unlike other contemporaneous Northeastern Iroquoians, the Neutral had developed politically beyond the confederacy level. Their powerful war chieftain Souharissen, with 10 Neutral tribes united under his rule, had far more political power than those of other groups whose chiefs had little real control over their tribesmen. The capital town Ounontisaston (9.6 km SE of present-day Brantford) was visited by the French Recollet priest Joseph de la Roche Daillon in 1626, and 14 years later by Jesuits Jean de BRÉBEUF and Joseph Marie Chaumonot. In 1650-51 the Iroquois dispersed and destroyed the Neutral as a cultural entity. *See also* NATIVE PEOPLE: EASTERN WOODLANDS and general articles under NATIVE PEOPLE. WILLIAM C. NOBLE

Reading: B.G. Trigger, ed, *Handbook of North American Indians,* vol 15: *Northeast* (1978).

Neville, John, actor, director, producer (b at London, Eng 2 May 1925). He began a distinguished career as a classical actor in Great Britain in 1947 and became associate producer of the Nottingham Playhouse Company in 1961 and its joint theatre director 1963-67. Neville came to Canada in 1972. As artistic director of the CITADEL THEATRE, Edmonton, 1973-78, he improved public support and the artistic stature and scope of the theatre. From 1978 to 1983 he served as artistic director of the NEPTUNE THEATRE, Halifax, where he again doubled subscriptions and toured productions to smaller communities. He made his critically acclaimed acting debut at the STRATFORD FESTIVAL as Don Armado in *Love's Labour's Lost* in 1983, repeating the role in 1984. Neville became the artistic director of the Stratford Festival in 1985, succeeding John HIRSCH, and helped restore the financial stability and artistic stature of the Festival. In 1987 his appointment as artistic director was extended through the 1989 season. ANTON WAGNER

New, Chester William, university teacher, historian, biographer (b at Montréal 9 Oct 1882; d at Hamilton, Ont 31 Aug 1960). Raised and educated in Hamilton, New was a graduate of U of T and McMaster. Ordained a Baptist minister, he served a brief pastorate before embarking on graduate work in history, some at Oxford and in Germany

but the bulk of it at U of Chicago. His first teaching post was at Manitoba's Brandon College, then an affiliate of McMaster. In 1920 he joined the latter as professor of history and department head, a position he occupied until he retired in 1951. His colourful teaching style, renowned absentmindedness, and keen backing of intercollegiate athletics endeared him to generations of students. Apart from his widely used high-school history textbooks his best-known works were *Lord Durham* and *Henry Brougham* (published posthumously). He was a fellow of the RSC. CHARLES M. JOHNSTON

New Brunswick is one of 3 provinces collectively known as the "Maritimes." Joined to Nova Scotia by the narrow Chignecto Isthmus and separated from Prince Edward Island by the Northumberland Str, NB forms the land bridge linking this region to continental N America. It is bounded in the N by Québec and in the W by the US (Maine), and its history has often been influenced by the activities of these powerful neighbours. Successively part of an Algonquian cultural area, of French ACADIA, and of British Nova Scotia, it achieved separate colonial status only after the arrival of LOYALIST refugees from the AMERICAN REVOLUTION.

In 1784 the British divided Nova Scotia at the Chignecto Isthmus, naming the W and N portion New Brunswick after the German duchy of Brunswick-Lunenburg, which was also ruled at the time by King George III of England. NB was one of the 4 original provinces, its entry being essential to CONFEDERATION. Its influence declined sharply with the rise of the West and the central cities; yet it has survived a series of economic crises to develop progressive communities with enviable life-styles. The return of Acadians expelled during the SEVEN YEARS' WAR (1756-63) and the immigration of francophones from Québec created tensions between the 2 language groups. The trend in recent years has been towards tolerance and an increasing acceptance of duality in public institutions. NB is now the only officially bilingual province in Canada.

Land and Resources

The area of New Brunswick is 73 436 km². The principal regional divisions are the watershed of the Bay of FUNDY, centering on the SAINT JOHN R valley, and the N and E shores. The Saint John R offered early access to much of the best farmland and timber resources of the province. Occupied by the descendants of Loyalists and other immigrants from Great Britain and the United States, the valley has been inhabited mainly by Protestants who, until the 1960s, tended to dominate the government, and the educational and commercial institutions of the province. The residents of north and east shores, living in coastal fishing villages and interior lumbering settlements along the rivers, have been separated physically from the valley communities by uplands and belts of forest, and separated culturally by their predominantly French language and Catholic religion.

The 2 major divisions include several sub-regions. In the NW the French-speaking population of Madawaska County, closer to Québec and conscious of common interests with neighbouring Americans, talk of a "republic of Madawaska." Residents of Carleton and Victoria counties on the upper Saint John have a sense of community based on their virtual monopoly of the potato industry and strengthened by their strong commitment to evangelical religions. In the SW at the mouth of the Bay of Fundy lies Charlotte County, distinguished in part by its fisheries, including a unique sardine fishery, and by strong tourist and

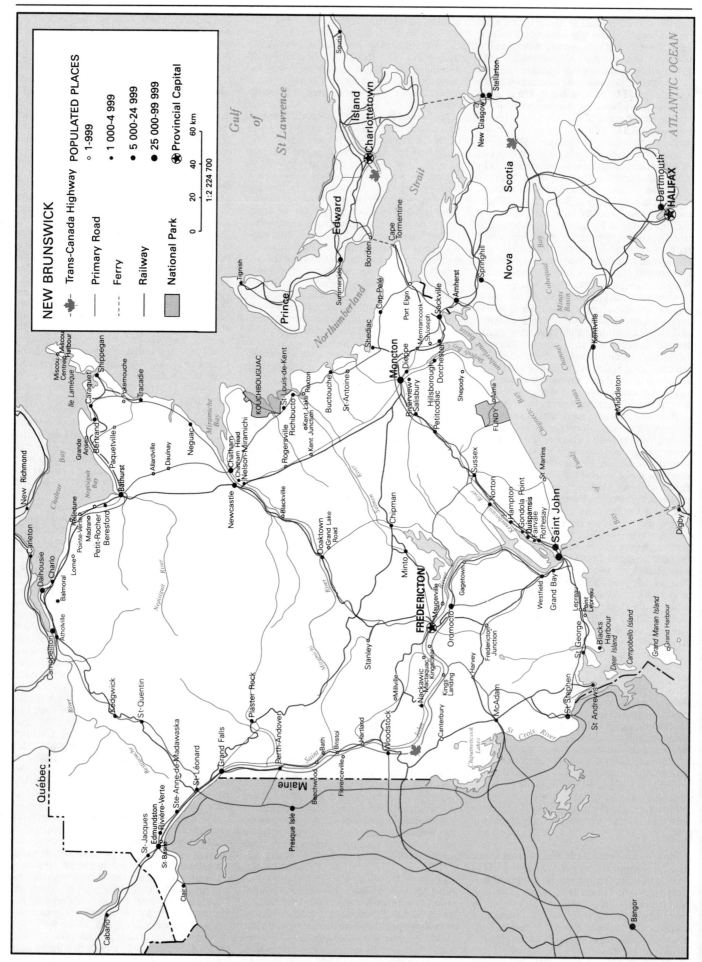

NEW BRUNSWICK

Trans-Canada Highway　POPULATED PLACES
- 1-999
- 1 000-4 999
- 5 000-24 999
- 25 000-99 999
- ⊛ Provincial Capital

Primary Road

Ferry

Railway

National Park

1:2 224 700

0　20　40　60 km

New Brunswick

Capital: Fredericton
Motto: Spem Reduxit ("Hope was restored")
Flower: Purple violet
Largest Cities: Saint John, Moncton, Fredericton, Bathurst, Edmundston, Campbellton
Population: 709 442 (1986c); rank eighth, 2.8% of Canada; 49.4% urban; 50.6% rural; 9.8 per km² density; 1.9% increase from 1981-86; 4.8% increase from 1976-86
Languages: English 63.6%; French 31.8%; Other 1.1%; 3.5% English plus one or more languages
Entered Confederation: 1 July 1867
Government: Provincial – Lieutenant-Governor, Executive Council, Legislative Assembly of 58 members; federal – 10 senators, 10 members of the House of Commons
Area: 73 436 km², including 1344 km² of inland water; 0.7% of Canada
Elevation: Highest point – Mount Carleton (820 m); lowest point – sea level along northern and eastern coasts
Gross Domestic Product: $8.1 billion (1986)
Farm Cash Receipts: $226.4 million (1986)
Value of Fish Landings: $94.1 million (1986)
Electric Power Produced: 11 422 GWh (1985)
Sales Tax: 11% (1987)

other ties with the US. There is another division at the head of Fundy, where Albert and Westmorland counties encompass an anglophone population conscious of its central location in a Maritime region, while the Acadian community of Westmorland and Kent counties aspires to the leadership of the French in the province. An anomaly in the regional division is the Miramichi section of Northumberland County, which as a traditionally English-speaking, mixed Catholic and Protestant area, bisects the Acadian community of the northern and eastern shores. In the N, Gloucester and to a lesser degree Restigouche counties form a heartland of Acadian culture.

Geology New Brunswick's rock foundation was largely formed in the Paleozoic era, 570 to 245 million years ago. It was part of a geological formation extending from the southeastern US to Newfoundland. Much of the rock in northern and western NB was created through ocean deposits of the Ordovician period (505-438 million years ago). These rocks were folded, intruded with granites, and overlain with lavas which reflected sporadic volcanic activity throughout the Paleozoic era. They contain the zinc-lead-copper deposits of the Bathurst to Newcastle area. Folding, faulted movements and volcanic activity reached a climax over 350 million years ago in what has been called the Acadian Orogeny. Much of the base of the central and eastern parts of the province originated in the later Carboniferous period (ending 286 million years ago) with the rocks formed in rivers, swamps and shallow basins. These included red, green and grey sandstones, some of which are coal-bearing, and conglomerates and isolated deposits of limestone, gypsum, salt and oil-bearing shales.

Surface New Brunswick topography is characterized by northern uplands, rising to 820 m and mountainous in appearance, gently rolling hills in the centre and E, sharp hills on the southern coast sloping down to tidal marshes and a lowland plain in the SE. The soils tend to be thin and acidic over the uplands, deeper but frequently poorly drained and acidic in the centre and W, and rocky in portions of the S. The best soils tend

to lie in intervale lands along the rivers. The upper Saint John is flanked by low plateaus of well-drained sandy loam with good lime content – excellent for growing potatoes. The finely textured soils of the Fundy lowlands are also suitable for agriculture. Whatever their agricultural deficiencies, NB soils do grow trees. Only 7% of the province is cleared land; 2% is covered with water; and 2% is regarded as barren wasteland, leaving almost 90% of the province under forest cover. Of this, 38% is softwood, 14% is hardwood and the remaining 48% is mixed, with softwood predominating in about half. Spruce and fir are the leading softwoods, followed in importance by cedar and white pine. Jack pine, red pine, hemlock and larch are also present. The hardwoods are led by red and sugar maples, poplar, white and yellow birch and beech in that order, with occasional ash, elm, hop hornbeam and red oak.

Water No part of New Brunswick is more than 180 km from the ocean, the principal means of early transportation. An extensive river system brought access well into the interior of the province, permitting early development of the timber trade and dictating patterns of settlement. The largest cities are located on the rivers, as are most of the towns and villages. Lakes are common in the S, with the largest, Grand Lk, more than 30 km in length.

Climate New Brunswick's climate tends to be continental, though tempered by proximity to the ocean. It is harshest in the NW where more than one-third of precipitation comes as snow, and temperatures are several degrees colder than the central interior. Coastal communities are several degrees warmer in winter and slightly cooler in summer, with annual snowfalls of only 15% to 20% of precipitation. The average frost-free period varies from about 100 days in the NW to 125 along the Fundy coast.

Resources The forest is the province's greatest natural resource, supporting lumbering, pulp and paper, hunting and fishing as well as the tourist industry. Second in importance are mineral deposits, which include the base metals near Bathurst in the N, potash deposits near Sussex in

the S, significant coal reserves in the area of Grand Lk, oil shales in Westmorland County and recent gold discoveries along the Bay of Fundy. Third comes agriculture, with substantial potato production on the northern Saint John, and dairy and mixed farming largely in the river valleys. Fisheries rank fourth with ground fish, lobster, crab and herring taken from the Bay of Fundy, Northumberland Str and eastern shore fisheries. Both agriculture and fisheries support a substantial food-processing industry. The rivers, especially the Saint John in utilities at Mactaquac, Beechwood and Grand Falls, have yielded significant portions of the province's energy needs. Still to be assessed is the energy potential of the Bay of Fundy tides which rise from 4.6 m at the entrance to over 16 m at the head of the bay. Fish and game offer a recreational resource to resident and visiting sportsmen. Trout are caught throughout the province; bass and pickerel are available in southern lakes. In 1984, 42 228 bright salmon were taken by 16 119 licensed anglers and 113 991 licensed hunters reported a white-tailed deer kill of 26 016. Bear, rabbit, ducks, geese and ruffed grouse are also hunted. A limited kill of moose is permitted. In recent years winter angling has been developed in 135 lakes and ponds. In 1984 3634 licensed trappers took furs (muskrat, beaver, raccoon, marten, fox, mink, coyote, bobcat, fisher, otter and lynx) valued at approximately $1 million.

Conservation Forest conservation efforts by provincial and federal governments have included forest inventories in 1958, 1968 and 1979, active suppression of forest fires, aerial attacks on the spruce budworm, replanting of forests and the maintenance of numerous game reserves. The most recent inventory reported a sharp reduction in burnt-over areas, a significant increase in reforestation (the Department of Natural Resources reported planting 30 million seedlings on crown lands in 1985 and making available another 2 million for small freehold owners from provincial nurseries at Kingsclear, Madran and St Paul de Kent), but an overall decline of approximately 5% in merchantable softwood. The decline was attributed to higher levels of harvest and the ravages of the spruce budworm. Shortages were also reported in hardwood available for veneer and sawlogs. The budworm, a moth whose larvae in summer months devour the needles of spruce and fir, did serious damage to provincial forests in the 1920s and then departed, and since 1952 the province has met a later outbreak with aerial spraying of pesticides which killed a portion of the budworms and their natural predators. However, the budworm's persistence as well as the potential damage to human health by the spray present the province with an acute dilemma.

In the 1970s salmon angling improved markedly with the federal ban on commercial salmon fishing. The war continues against poaching with the arming of wardens, the tagging of legally caught salmon, and jail sentences and vehicle confiscation for night hunters. Attempts to protect fish and game, and to assert an overriding provincial jurisdiction have brought wardens into conflict with Indians trying to defend traditional treaty and aboriginal fishing and hunting rights. The federal Department of Fisheries attempts to protect fishing stocks by the rotation of lobster seasons, by limiting commercial fishing licences and placing quotas on particular species, and by the division of fishing grounds.

People

New Brunswick's initial European settlers were Acadian French who, with the use of dikes, farmed the marshlands of the Chignecto Isthmus

Near Bath in the Saint John Valley (*courtesy Tourism New Brunswick*).

and part of the northern shore of the Bay of Fundy. Following their expulsion (1755 onwards) their lands were taken by Protestant settlers from New England (*see* PLANTERS), Pennsylvania and Yorkshire, Eng. When the Acadians tried to return after the Peace of Paris, 1763, some were granted land in the Memramcook area and some found employment in fishing stations from the Gaspé to Cape Breton. When the Loyalists arrived, most of the Acadians on the lower Saint John pushed up the river to Ste-Anne-de-Madawaska. The Loyalist exiles, approximately 14 000 in number, penetrated the interior largely by way of the Saint John R. Essentially a cross section of society in the Thirteen Colonies, they included a very few college graduates and Anglican clergy and close to 1000 blacks, most of them slaves of wealthy Loyalists but some, perhaps a third, Loyalists in their own right. About 200 blacks later left for Sierra Leone and the remainder were joined by refugee blacks from the WAR OF 1812. Although the Loyalists overwhelmed the perhaps 3000 residents of NB on their arrival, they too were diluted in the first half of the 19th century by immigrant waves of SCOTS and IRISH who found employment in a burgeoning lumber industry. Forced to compete with cheap immigrant labour, older settlers frequently left. In the depression of the traditional timber and SHIPBUILD-ING economy in the 1880s, it was the turn of the Irish and Scots to seek employment elsewhere. The growth of cities outside the region and the collapse of the new industrial economy in the 1920s continued to drain the population of most of its natural increase. Acadians, who were more resistant to economic pressures to leave, and were bolstered by immigration from Québec, consolidated their hold on the northern counties as railways opened new lands for colonization. The trend to urbanization changed NB from more than two-thirds rural before 1941 to predominantly urban by 1971. Then came a reversal as the officially designated urban population dropped from 62% to 49.4% by 1986, owing to a resumption of migration from the region as well as a residential move to the suburbs, which had been made attractive by improved services, cheaper land and lower taxes.

Urban Centres New Brunswick's chief metropolitan area is SAINT JOHN (pop 121 265, CMA). A leading centre of British North America in the mid-19th century, the city owed its importance to the timber trade (made accessible by its river) and to its ice-free port, which supplied the estuary and dominated shipping and shipbuilding on the Bay of Fundy. Saint John's metropolitan pretensions were flawed by its failure to secure the provincial capital or the university and undermined by NB's entry into a nation whose interests were continental rather than maritime. Saint John's current urban status is largely industrial, based on an oil refinery, pulp and paper mills, a nuclear power plant, dry dock facilities and a major container port. Second in importance as a metropolitan region is MONCTON (pop 102 084, CMA), which has long owed its importance to transportation and distribution facilities (headquarters of the Atlantic division of the CNR and a trucking centre). It is also the traditional headquarters for the Acadian media and financial institutions and in the 1960s became the site of a provincial francophone university. Ranking third as a metropolitan centre FREDERICTON (pop 65 768, CMA) gained its importance from Saint John's deficiencies – the provincial government and university. When the civil service and universities mushroomed in the 1960s and early 1970s, so did Fredericton. A neighbouring town, OROMOCTO (pop 9656), the headquarters for CFB GAGETOWN, reflects in its growth and decline the shifting status of the Canadian Armed Forces. BATHURST (pop 34 895, CMA), EDMUNDSTON (pop 22 614, CMA) and CAMPBELLTON (pop 17 418, CMA; 14 867 in NB, 2551 in Qué) emerged as largely single-industry towns when NB made the transition from sawlogs to pulp and paper manufacture. With base-metal mining, a zinc reduction mill, and with an ice-free port at nearby Belledune, Bathurst is now becoming the industrial leader of the N.

Labour Force By occupation New Brunswick's labour force breaks down as follows: managerial and professional, 26.7%; clerical, 15.7%; sales, 9.4%; service, 15.7%; primary occupations, 5.3%; processing, 12.4%; construction, 7.1%; transportation, 4.5%; material handling, 3.4%. Service industries are the principal employers ac-

counting for almost 57% of jobs available. Utilities at 8.6% and public administration at 8.6% make the non-goods-producing sector responsible for 75% of jobs. The primary industries of forestry, mining, fisheries and agriculture provide the base for most of the 13.4% of positions in manufacturing.

New Brunswick's potential labour force of persons over 15 years totalled 546 000 in June 1987. The official participation rate of 61.9% was 6% under the national average. The rate was much higher in the 25-to-44 age brackets, approximating 92% for men and 67% for women. Participation rates were highest, approaching national levels, in the Saint John R valley and lowest (just over 50%) in the northern counties of Gloucester, Northumberland and Restigouche. Participation rates correlated with difficulty in entering the labour force. Unemployment was highest in the northern counties. From 1981 to 1986 NB's unemployment rate, despite a 5% growth in jobs over that period, averaged nearly 15%, approximately 6% above the national level, although since 1985 the economy has surged and unemployment has dropped to just over 13%. Traditionally, young New Brunswickers have emigrated to find employment. Not since Confederation has the province held its entire natural increase and the 1960s recorded a net loss of 59% "going down the road." Emigration declined in the 1970s as the first half of the decade saw New Brunswickers return, though the second half saw a resumption of the exodus, when Alberta replaced Toronto as a principal attraction. This trend continued until 1983 when the Alberta economy weakened and New Brunswickers again returned home. Ontario's strong economic showing in 1985 and 1986 again served to lure young New Brunswickers away from their home province.

Language Of the total population of 709 442, 63.6% gave their mother tongue as English and 31.8% French in the census of 1986. Another 4095 cited European languages, 1350 Asian. Approximately 7100 were native Indians. Provincial language legislation is intended to provide equality between the 2 official languages. Institutional backing for the language legislation is provided by 2 parallel educational systems, including a French university with its own law school and other professional schools, and by the hiring of specially trained court interpreters, the creation of unilingual French schools wherever the lure of playground English seemed too strong, and the construction of French cultural centres in Fredericton, Saint John and Newcastle.

The children of the province's 3983 Micmac and 3152 Maliseet attend regular provincial schools. Indians receive other provincial services, including medical treatment, foster care for children, and forestry protection and roads for the 15

Le Village Acadien at Caraquet, NB, preserves traditional Acadian buildings (*photo by Malak, Ottawa*).

Gross Domestic Product - New Brunswick 1986 at Factor Cost ($Millions)	
Agriculture	120.6
Forestry	172.8
Fishing	42.9
Mining	255.2
Manufacturing	1125.2
Construction	591.6
Utilities	359.6
Goods Producing	2666.8
Transportation and Communication	863.0
Wholesale and Retail Trade	894.4
Finance, Insurance and Real Estate	1055.6
Community, Business and Personal Service	1771.3
Public Administration and Defence	866.5
Service Producing	5449.7

occupied reserves – all at federal expense. Indians are exempt from the 11% sales tax but pay other provincial taxes. The province supports Indian athletic events and has adopted a policy of affirmative action in assisting Indians to obtain jobs. The province, to date, has refused to recognize the land claims of the Union of New Brunswick Indians.

Ethnicity The population of French origin grew dramatically after Confederation; from 44 907 or 15.72% in 1871 to 24.15% in 1901 and 33.56% in 1931. By the latter decade the figures for those of French origin and those giving French as their mother tongue (32.67%) had begun to diverge, suggesting a degree of assimilation. The gap had widened by 1961 when 38.82% gave French as their ethnic origin compared with 35.21% as their mother tongue. In 1971, following a period of declining birthrates, figures for ethnic origin dropped to 37% and for mother tongue to 34%. In the 1986 census, 31.8% of the population of New Brunswick reported French as a mother tongue. The Acadian population appears to have stabilized. Other ethnic groups in 1871 included 29.27% English, 35.24% Irish and 14.31% Scots. These were highly represented in the emigration patterns of the depression of the 1880s and in subsequent rural depopulation. By 1971 only 57.6% of New Brunswickers gave their ethnic origin as British. Relative changes were also suggested by the rise of the percentage of French origin in the Roman Catholic Church from 46.8% in 1871 to 72.4% in 1961. Other New Brunswick ethnic groups in 1971 included Germans, 7350; Dutch, 4475; Scandinavians, 2985; Asians, 1400; Italians, 970; Jews, 765; Ukrainians, 525; and Poles, 450.

Religion In 1971, 52.2% of New Brunswickers professed adherence to the Roman Catholic Church. Of these 68.2% were of French origin inhabiting the northern and eastern shores. Of the remainder almost half resided in Saint John. Of the leading Protestant denominations, Baptists accounted for 14%; United, 13.4%; Anglican, 10.9%; Pentecostal, 2.7%; and Presbyterians, 2.1%. The Anglicans were concentrated in the lower Saint John R valley. Baptists and Pentecostals were strong in the so-called bible belt from Victoria and Carleton E to Albert and Westmorland. The United Church, bearing both Methodist and Presbyterian traditions, was scattered throughout the English-speaking sections. Other religious groups included Salvation Army (2185), Lutheran (1880), Jewish (850), Ukrainian Catholic (700), Greek Orthodox (375), with "others" listed in the census totalling 11 885 and an identical number listed as having no religious affiliation.

Economy

Since the early 19th century timber has dominated the New Brunswick economy. The province, like the Maritime region as a whole, underwent severe economic dislocation in the latter half of the 19th century as a declining ship-building industry, stagnant timber markets and increased tariffs struck hard at the outports. New railways and the rise of manufacturing towns failed to compensate for losses in the older industries. The 1920s saw a decline of the industrial towns, as their industries were closed down after takeovers by central Canadian competitors or were adversely affected by national policies and hindered from competing in national markets.

By the 1930s pulp and paper mills had surpassed lumber in importance and their rise encouraged the development of hydroelectricity. Nevertheless, farm and fishing activity declined and emigration rates remained high in succeeding decades. Government campaigns for economic development in the 1960s and early 1970s, although not always successful, have seen the expansion of forest industries, the advent of a new and important mining industry, modernization of fisheries and farming, increased manufacturing based largely on local resources and the cultivation of tourism.

Agriculture The vicissitudes of agriculture in New Brunswick, as elsewhere in Canada, reflect a relative decline in the value of agricultural products and the abandonment of near-subsistence farming by rural people drawn to the attractions of a consumer economy. Although total production remained stationary, farm holdings declined from 31 899 in 1941 to 3554 in 1986; improved land went from 350 000 ha to 168 913 ha; and direct agricultural employment dropped from 26 834 in 1951 to an estimated 6000 in 1986. Meanwhile, the numbers employed in the processing and transportation of agricultural produce has grown to an estimated 18 000.

POTATOES, especially seed potatoes, are the province's chief agricultural export and account for 20% of the national total. Production is concentrated along the upper Saint John R valley with Carleton and Victoria counties accounting for approximately 80% of the crop and Madawaska another 15%. Dairy production is most important in Kings, Westmorland and York counties where farmers supply the 3 major cities. Potatoes and dairy products together account for 44% of the province's farm income; beef, poultry

and hogs make up another 31.5% and field crops 7.5% (fruit 3% and vegetables 4.5%); eggs (6%) and maple products (2.5%) round out the total. Producers are organized under a dozen boards that market milk, turkeys, eggs, hogs, cream, chickens, apples, some forest products and bedding plants.

Industry The non-goods-producing industries of New Brunswick account for two-thirds of the province's Gross Domestic Product, about 5% higher than the national average, and yield over 70% of the total wages and salaries. Of 267 000 jobs in 1986, 23 000 were in transportation, communication and other utilities; 11 000 in finance, insurance and real estate; 89 000 in community, business and personal services, including educational and medical services; 51 000 in retail and wholesale trade, of which the annual retail value exceeds $2 billion, and 23 000 in public administration and defence exclusive of crown corporations. Included in public administration were over 4000 military personnel, chiefly located at CFB Gagetown, a training base for land forces, and at an air force base near Chatham.

The tourist industry in 1985 yielded revenues estimated at $450 million (up from $257 million in 1980) and accounted for over 15 000 "man years" of employment. To such attractions as Saint John's reversing falls, the potted-plant-shaped rocks on Albert County's Fundy coast, the tidal bore of the Bay of Fundy, and rugged forest and coastal scenery, the provincial government added highly successful recreations of historical communities: a Loyalist settlement, KINGS LANDING, near Fredericton and the Acadian Village at CARAQUET; the government has also created or drawn attention to more than 60 museums, restored fortifications and other sites of historic interest around the province including a new archaeological site at Mud Lake Stream.

Two major national parks, Fundy near Alma and Kouchibouguac near Richibucto, are complemented by 57 provincial parks, only 3 of which operate year-round. Attendance at the parks in 1985 exceeded 2.5 million visits. The parks encourage tourists to pause in their tours of the Maritime region and they enhance the quality of life for local residents.

Manufacturing industries are largely based on the processing of primary products produced locally. One-third of their net value of production is

Along with dairy products, potatoes account for 44% of NB's farm income (*photo by Karl Sommerer*).

related to the forest industry. Food and beverage processing, notably the McCain enterprises at Florenceville and Grand Falls, ranks 2nd in gross value of factory shipments. The Irving oil refinery in Saint John, Brunswick Mining and Smelting in Bathurst, and the Saint John Shipbuilding & Dry Dock Co Ltd are the other large producers. A $3-billion contract for the building of patrol frigates for the Canadian navy was awarded to a Saint John firm in 1983, and in late 1987 the federal government announced that all 6 of a batch of navy patrol frigates were to be built in Saint John for a total injection of $814 million. Significant too are chemical products, the processing of non-metallic minerals, metal fabricating and printing and publishing. Altogether in 1986 manufacturing employed 41 000 in approximately 1450 firms with an annual output valued at $4.5 billion. Over 900 have fewer than 25 employees. Ninety percent of all firms are owned locally while only 4%, accounting for 8% of the jobs, are foreign owned.

The construction industry employed 17 000 in 1986 and represented an investment of over $1 billion. For most of the decade the nuclear plant at Point Lepreau was the largest project. By the end of 1986 major construction activity included the modernization of pulp and paper plants, continued potash developments near Sussex, the NB Electric Power Commission's new Chatham Generating Station and shipyard expansion at the port of Saint John.

Mining Mining was traditionally of scant importance in New Brunswick. The gypsum, granite and grindstones included among 19th-century exports were largely of local significance. Although coal led to a rapid development of the Grand Lk region, especially with the arrival of the railway in 1903, that area never yielded enough to make the province self-sufficient. With coal's loss of status to oil and hydroelectricity, coal mining had come to a virtual halt by the mid-1960s. The energy crises of the early and mid-1970s led to coal's recovery through strip-mining, but by then coal was upstaged by mineral developments in the NE. The discoveries of extensive base-metal reserves in the Bathurst-Dalhousie region in the 1950s have raised the mining industry to a position of major importance. By 1981 the value of NB's mineral output exceeded half a billion dollars and in 1986 directly employed over 4000 men. NB's zinc production was 16% of the national total; silver 16%, lead 25% and copper 9%; and antimony and bismuth were 85% and 67% respectively. Expansion continues with potash developments near Sussex and gold discoveries near the Bay of Fundy. The growth of the mining industry has brought development into the poorest section of the province and has largely justified in economic terms the upgraded transportation, education, health and other services launched in the 1960s program of equal opportunity.

Forestry The forest which now covers almost 90% of the province has traditionally dominated the New Brunswick economy. Accessible rivers and a British preferential tariff led to the rapid development of the timber industry early in the 19th century as the white pine was slashed for British marine and domestic needs. Closely integrated with the TIMBER TRADE was a widely diffused shipbuilding industry which both absorbed forest products and facilitated their access to markets. In the mid-19th century, forest products accounted for more than 80% of the province's exports. The timber trade had declined by the end of the century and the province lost markets from a shrinking West Indian economy, new American tariffs and fresh competition from W coast timber. These problems were only partially alleviated in the rise by the late 1920s of a vigorous pulp and paper

industry. By the mid-1980s the forest industry accounted for over 15% of the jobs in the province, 60% of provincial exports and over one-quarter of goods produced. Pulp consumed 80% of the timber harvested with the remainder going for lumber and similar products. Lumber mills tended to be small, with a majority contributing only 5% of production. Pulp mills demanding large capital outlays and a large work force have been major factors in the urban development of the province. Three pulp mills, controlled by the IRV-ING GROUP interests, at or near Saint John, produce sulphate pulp, newsprint, tissue and materials for corrugated cardboard cartons. Mills at Newcastle and South Nelson produce sulphate pulp and pulp and paper respectively. Consolidated Bathurst's mill at Bathurst produces sulphate pulp and corrugated medium. The New Brunswick International Paper Company operates a newsprint mill at Dalhousie, and Fraser's Incorporated, a member of the Noranda group, has plants near Campbellton and Edmundston. Others include a hardwood pulp mill at Nackawic and a paper bag company at Barker's Point.

Of the 6 million ha of productive forestland, 52% is privately owned. The remaining 48% owned by the Crown has traditionally been leased to the larger firms. The 32% of woodland held in small parcels has supplied an important source of income for farmers and fishermen. The forest industry has also been the inspiration for a forest management school at Fredericton, a forestry faculty at U of New Brunswick, and for federal and provincial research laboratories in the province. The recognition of the potential limits of resources for which many are competing has led governments to abandon the leasing of crown lands in favour of long-term guarantees of timber to major producers.

Fisheries The fisheries of New Brunswick account for about 18% of the production of the Canadian E coast fisheries. In decline until the 1960s, the industry was revived by a modernization of methods and vessels. Additional enthusiasm was generated by expectations of a 200-mile (370 km) limit, finally asserted in 1977. Recent years have seen a decline in volume associated with a general reduction of fish stocks, although prices rose sharply in the late 1970s. The main fishing areas are the Gulf of St Lawrence, Northumberland Str and the Bay of Fundy. In 1986 the total value of the catch was $94.1 million by 6500 fishermen operating almost 4000 vessels. In processed value, lobster led the way at $32.2 million; crab was second at $17.3 million, herring was third at $10.7 million and scallop and cod followed with values of $5.8 and $4.7 million respectively. Exports accounted for almost half of the production with 61% going to the US, 3.7% to Europe and 7.7% to Central America. Exports to Japan increased in the period 1981 to 1985 from negligible to $56.5 million (21.7% of the total). The fish-processing industry employs over 10 000 workers in 130 plants in the province.

Finance Most financial institutions, such as banks and trust and insurance companies, are local branches of central Canadian firms. Among the few exceptions are local credit unions and the Compagnie assomption mutuelle d'assurance-vie, largely an Acadian institution with its headquarters at Moncton.

Transportation Far from central markets and with their chief city aspiring to national port status, New Brunswickers have traditionally shown great concern about transportation. They have protested disproportionately high railway freight-rate increases, loss of regional autonomy in the federally owned Intercolonial Railway and a failure to channel Canada's winter trade through Canadian ports. In 1927 their region

won a partial victory in the Maritime Freight Rates Act, which provided for statutory reductions in freight rates. In that year they created the Maritime Freight Rates Commission (now the Atlantic Provinces Transportation Commission) at Moncton, as a permanent watchdog of regional interests in transportation policy. In 1969 the Maritime Freight Rates Act was repealed in favour of one creating a regional committee to administer transportation subsidies to encourage industrial development. By then transportation had become much more complex as highway trucking surpassed the railways in the carriage of freight. Airplanes and buses carried the bulk of public passengers. The advent of containerized traffic, for which the ice-free facilities of the port of Saint John were particularly well suited, encouraged a renewed struggle for enhanced status as a national port. Currently, New Brunswick has 2 major railway systems: the CPR which runs through the US state of Maine and whose eastern terminus is Saint John, and the CNR whose regional headquarters is Moncton and main terminus is Halifax. Passenger service operated for the 2 lines by the crown corporation VIA RAIL has been reduced to a train a day from and to central Canada, and rail-liner service between Fredericton, Saint John, Moncton and Campbellton.

Saint John, Moncton and Fredericton have major airports with sophisticated navigational aids. Other licensed public airports include Charlo, St Léonard, Edmundston, Woodstock, Bathurst, Pokemouche, Chatham and St Stephen. Service to central Canada is provided by Air Canada and Eastern Provincial Airways. The latter provides a network of flights within the province and region. There are also over 2 dozen landing strips maintained for forest protection or private use.

SMT, an Irving-owned firm, supplies the major bus service within the province, connecting with Acadian at Amherst, NS, Voyageur at Edmundston, and Greyhound at St Stephen. During recent years, aided by federal and provincial funds, municipally owned urban transit has been maintained in Saint John, Moncton and Fredericton. There are also several local bus lines.

Saint John is the major port with year-round service for containerized and bulk traffic. Its busy season has traditionally been the winter, when the St Lawrence R is frozen over. It is served by 9 container shipping lines with access to ports in over 100 countries. Conventional steamship services are provided monthly and bimonthly by 22 lines to most regions of the world. Ten other ports dot the NB shoreline, of which Caraquet is an important fishing centre, Chatham-Newcastle an outlet for fish and timber exports, and Belledune the major outlet for the base-metal industry.

Energy New Brunswick was better off than its Maritime and New England neighbours at the end of the cheap oil era signalled by the OPEC cartel and the shortages of 1973-74 and 1979-80. The publicly owned New Brunswick Power Commission had built, with federal assistance, a major dam on the Saint John R near Fredericton which had more than doubled the province's electrical capacity from that source. Limited coal reserves in the Grand Lk area proved accessible to strip-mining. In 1970 the NB government had already committed the province to nuclear energy through the construction of a Candu reactor at Point Lepreau. By 1985 the proliferation of electrical generation capacity combined with a federal program to convert homes from oil to electrical heating resulted in a significant decline in the demand for oil and natural gas. Electricity is now the primary source of energy in the province.

The major producers of energy are the Irving refinery at Saint John, whose capacity is approximately double the province's requirements, and the NB Electric Power Commission, which maintains major oil-fired thermal units at Coleson Cove and Courtney Bay, and 2 largely coal-fired units at Grand Lk and Dalhousie. The major sources of hydro are the Mactaquac, Beechwood and Grand Falls utilities. A trade-off exists as oil and nuclear-generated electricity exported to Maine virtually equals the hydroelectricity imported from Québec. The Point Lepreau nuclear reactor delivers 5.355 million megawatt hours (or about 50% of normal provincial generation) operating at 90% capacity. Half of this is committed to sale in the US to recover costs of construction which greatly exceeded estimates. Additional power projects under consideration include a second nuclear reactor and a natural gas pipeline through the Maritimes. Construction is currently underway at NBEPC Chatham Generating Station, a federally funded research and development project, designed to test a system to reduce sulphur emissions from a coal-fired electrical generation plant.

Government and Politics

New Brunswick's titular head of state is the LIEUTENANT-GOVERNOR. Appointed by the federal government and officially representing the Queen, his duties are largely ceremonial. Power resides with the premier, the leader of the party or coalition having a majority of support in the 58-seat elected legislative assembly. The premier presides over a Cabinet, each member of which normally heads a provincial department or, in one case, a crown corporation, the NB Electric Power Commission. The assembly, elected for no more than a 5-year mandate, is ordinarily sovereign within its spheres of responsibility. These spheres were originally outlined in the BNA Act (CONSTITUTION ACT, 1867), and have been subject to subsequent amendment and judicial interpretation; the province is also subject to the CANADIAN CHARTER OF RIGHTS AND FREEDOMS. Women achieved the provincial vote in 1919, but were not entitled to run for provincial office until 1934. They currently hold 3 seats in the assembly and 2 positions in the Cabinet.

The courts of New Brunswick have been in a period of transition. The basic structure was a Supreme Court (divided between Appeals and Queen's Bench), county courts, and courts presided over by provincial magistrates. Under the BNA Act the first 2 levels were appointed and paid for by the federal government; the third by the provinces who were responsible for the "administration" of justice. In 1979, with federal co-operation, the county or district courts were amalgamated with courts of Queen's Bench. Recently, through a family division of the Queen's Bench, NB has been experimenting with an integrated family and juvenile court system. Under the Official Languages Act, French and English were guaranteed judicial services in their own languages. Since 1967 an ombudsman has investigated citizens' complaints against public agencies and officials.

Local Government As part of its so-called "equal opportunity" reforms of the 1960s, the Liberal government of Louis ROBICHAUD abolished the 15 county councils and restricted the responsibilities of the city, town and village councils largely to services for property. Municipal taxes were limited to a percentage of the actual market value of real property in each community. Provincial "equalization" payments assist the poorer municipalities. Property services for rural areas are supplied directly by the province.

Federal Representation In federal politics New Brunswick has traditionally had one representative in the Cabinet and 10 seats in the Senate. It now has 10 seats in the House of Commons; an

Lieutenant-Governors of New Brunswick 1867-1987

Name	Term
Charles Hastings Doyle	1867
Francis Pym Harding	1867-68
Lemuel Allan Wilmot	1868-73
Samuel Leonard Tilley	1873-78
Edward Barron Chandler	1878-80
Robert Duncan Wilmot	1880-85
Samuel Leonard Tilley	1885-93
John Boyd	1893
John James Fraser	1893-96
Abner Reid McClelan	1896-1902
Jabez Bunting Snowball	1902-07
Lemuel John Tweedie	1907-12
Josiah Wood	1912-17
Gilbert White Ganong	1917
William Pugsley	1917-23
William Freeman Todd	1923-28
Hugh Havelock McLean	1928-35
Murray MacLaren	1935-40
William George Clark	1940-45
David Lawrence MacLaren	1945-58
J. Leonard O'Brien	1958-65
John Babbitt McNair	1965-68
Wallace Samuel Bird	1968-71
Hédard J. Robichaud	1971-82
George Francis Gillman Stanley	1982-87
Gilbert Finn	1987-

actual decline of 5 seats since Confederation owing to a reduction in the province's population as a percentage of the Canadian total. Occasionally, it has been able to enhance its influence through co-operation with NS and PEI, although these have experienced a similar decline.

Regional Government Efforts at co-operation for internal development and external influence were formalized in the Council of Maritime Premiers in 1973. In quarterly meetings of the premiers and in agencies such as the Maritime Provinces Higher Education Commission, the 3 provinces sought to establish regional co-operation, possibly moving towards political union, although this is no longer a goal. Although failures to agree on initial plans for energy, constitutional reform and regional development disappointed many regionalists, co-operation has been achieved in more than 40 other areas.

Public Finance In 1986 ordinary revenues totalled $2.6 billion. Major sources included taxes on individual income (15.1%), corporate income (3.2%), fuel (3.3%) and real property (8.6%). The provincial personal income tax rate of 55.5% of federal basic tax is, along with the corporate income tax, collected by the federal government for the province. The NB sales tax of 11% exempts clothing, footwear, and equipment used in manufacturing. Approximately one-quarter of total provincial revenues comes from federal equalization payments – a plan intended to help poorer provinces maintain a basic standard of services. About 10% is derived from federal payments in support of established programs, such as hospital insurance, medicare and post-secondary education. Major expenditures include health and social services (34.0%), education (21.5%), municipalities (8.5%) and service of public debt (13.8%). Expenditures for physical assets such as bridges, highways, schools and hospitals are considered capital expenditures and are financed through borrowing. In 1986 these totalled $280 million, of which 55% went for roads and bridges and 25% for schools and hospitals.

Health Although New Brunswick was the first province to establish a department of health, economic difficulties saw its services lag far behind most other provinces until the late 1960s. Today the province is divided into 7 health regions with major regional hospitals at Saint

John, Fredericton, Moncton and Bathurst, and 2 under construction at Campbellton and Edmundston. These are supplemented by 33 smaller institutions. Psychiatric care is offered in the home, in chronic care hospitals at Saint John and Campbellton, and in units of the regional hospitals. Hospital and other medical services are provided without premiums under the nationally integrated programs. Small user fees were introduced in 1983. A provincial plan aids people over 65 in the payment of prescription drugs. Over 4000 senior citizens receive care in the 64 provincially subsidized nursing homes. Public health services include nursing, inspection, control of communicable diseases, maternal and child health care, home care, nutrition, tuberculosis control and the operation of a home dialysis program.

Politics Since 1900, when party affiliation had solidified, New Brunswick has had a balanced 2-party system. However, in the Oct 1987 election the Liberals swept the House, an almost unprecedented event in Canadian history. Third parties have fared poorly in provincial politics, despite a United Farmers' Party which won 6 seats in 1920, the CCF which captured 11% of the vote in 1944, the Parti Acadien which made a strong showing in 2 constituencies in 1978, and the NDP which raised its share of the popular vote to 10.2% in 1982 and elected one candidate as well as another in a by-election in 1984. Excepting a lone Progressive elected in 1921, third parties have done little better at the federal level.

The outstanding issues in provincial politics have involved ethnicity and regional disparity. The growth of the population of French origin from 15.7% in 1871 to 38.8% by 1961 has underlain a persistent agitation by Acadian leaders for representation and influence commensurate with numbers and led to the formation of a separatist political party, the Parti Acadien. Politicians have occasionally exploited tensions between the 2 linguistic groups, but the winning party has traditionally been that which has been able to win a substantial share of support from both. The election in 1960 of the venturesome young Acadian premier, Louis J. Robichaud, in a conjunction of circumstances conducive to change, contributed to economic and linguistic reforms so rapid and

Premiers of New Brunswick 1866-1987

Name	Party	Term
Peter Mitchell		1866-67
Andrew Rainsford Wetmore		1867-70
George Luther Hatheway		1871-72
George Edwin King		1872-78
John James Fraser		1878-82
Daniel Lionel Hanington		1882-83
Andrew George Blair	Liberal	1883-96
James Mitchell	Liberal	1896-97
Henry Robert Emmerson	Liberal	1897-1900
Lemuel John Tweedie	Liberal	1900-07
William Pugsley	Liberal	1907
Clifford William Robinson	Liberal	1907-08
John Douglas Hazen	Conservative	1908-11
James Kidd Flemming	Conservative	1911-14
George Johnson Clarke	Conservative	1914-17
James Alexander Murray	Conservative	1917
Walter Edward Foster	Liberal	1917-23
Peter John Veniot	Liberal	1923-25
John Babbington Macaulay Baxter	Conservative	1925-31
Charles Dow Richards	Conservative	1931-33
Leonard Percy de Wolfe Tilley	Conservative	1933-35
A. Allison Dysart	Liberal	1935-40
John Babbitt McNair	Liberal	1940-52
Hugh John Flemming	Conservative	1952-60
Louis Joseph Robichaud	Liberal	1960-70
Richard B. Hatfield	Conservative	1970-87
Frank Joseph McKenna	Liberal	1987-

fundamental as to be called revolutionary. The Acadians gained most from the program of equal opportunity, which redistributed incomes from urban centres to a poverty-stricken north, pressed ahead with projects for economic development, and proposed language services to both peoples along the lines of the federal Royal Commission ON BILINGUALISM AND BICULTURALISM. Of critical importance to the program's success was the simultaneous attack on regional disparity by federal governments. Despite the opposition of prominent corporations and conservatives appalled at the pace of change, Robichaud remained in power for the decade. Nor did his successor, Conservative and Protestant Richard HATFIELD, seek to reverse the trend. Indeed, so enthusiastically did his government implement changes along the lines of the program that his party made increasing inroads in Acadian constituencies, defusing the Parti-Acadien's bid for a separate Acadian province. The drive for economic development slowed by the end of the 1970s, owing more in part to the decline of interest by federal governments than to public criticism of spectacular failures, such as the Bricklin sports car.

Under Hatfield's successor, the Liberal Frank McKenna, the province's outlook seemed promising. Especially encouraging was the award of a huge navy patrol frigate-building contract from the federal government, announced in late 1987.

Education

The educational institutions of Loyalist New Brunswick began with a strong Anglican bias which stimulated the proliferation of other denominational schools and colleges. The Common Schools Act of 1871, which established free public schools, virtually excluded the Catholics. A later compromise permitted teaching by members of religious orders and religious instruction after school hours. Education, however, remained a flashpoint of tension among religious and language groups in the province.

Administration The educational reforms of the 1960s relieved municipalities of their responsibilities for education and sought full educational services for both French and English in their own languages. The 12 grades of elementary and high school are administered in 41 school districts by local school boards but are financed by the province. Parallel systems for each language group report to 2 deputy ministers acting for the Dept of Education. While the Dept of Community Colleges assumes responsibility for community colleges and adult continuing education programs, the universities and the Maritime Forest Ranger School are under the jurisdiction of the Maritime Higher Education Commission, an agency designed by the Council of Maritime Premiers to rationalize higher education offerings and facilities throughout the region. The NB School of Fisheries and the NB Craft School are the responsibilities of other provincial departments. Aid for post-secondary students is provided through provincially administered, partially forgivable, interest-free loans.

Institutions In 1986-87 the francophone system served 46 318 students in 154 schools under 15 school boards. The anglophone system served 92 705 students in 280 schools under 26 school boards. There were 10 community colleges with 3946 students enrolled in French-language programs and 8043 in English. Anglophone university programs served a total of 13 390 students in 1985-86 at UNIVERSITY OF NEW BRUNSWICK (Fredericton and Saint John); at Catholic-affiliated SAINT THOMAS, which shared library and sports facilities of the Fredericton campus; and at United Church-affiliated MOUNT ALLISON UNIVERSITY (Sackville). In 1985-86 francophone programs served a total of

New Brunswick Fashionables, at Fredericton (1834), lithograph by J.N. Giles. Fredericton was the early political and social capital of NB (*courtesy National Archives of Canada/C-10546*).

6049 students at UNIVERSITÉ DE MONCTON and affiliated centres in Edmundston and Shippegan. Recent trends have included pressure for unilingual schools and school boards by Francophones, the emergence of a burgeoning French-immersion program in the anglophone system (which included 15 206 students in 96 schools in 1986-87) and the establishment of private schools by evangelical denominations. Traditional Anglican boarding schools are Rothesay Collegiate and Netherwood School for Girls, both at Rothesay.

Cultural Life

Bliss CARMAN, Sir Charles G.D. ROBERTS, A.G. BAILEY, Desmond PACEY, W.S. MacNutt, Alden NOWLAN and Antonine MAILLET are a few of the New Brunswick literary and historical figures of international repute. Prominent artists have included John Hammond, Miller Brittain, Alex COLVILLE, Jack Humphrey and Lawren P. Harris. An early interest in science and its practical application was evident in pioneering programs in engineering and forestry at UNB and in the work of the Natural History Society of Saint John. That this tradition continues is indicated by recent reports of breakthroughs in "bionic" artificial limbs and in natural methods of insect control. Fredericton in the 1870s and Saint John by the turn of the century seemed to produce environments particularly suited to creative endeavour. From the 1920s private patrons such as J.C. Webster of Shediac and Lord Beaverbrook (formerly Max AITKEN of Newcastle) helped develop institutional bases for creativity and for popular education through museums, art galleries, playhouses and universities.

Arts In recent decades the universities have been centres of literary and artistic endeavour. Mount Allison is famous for its artists and musicians. UNB has developed journals of national stature in the literary FIDDLEHEAD and the historical *Acadiensis*. The U of Moncton has become a centre of research in Acadian studies. Acadian choirs have gained an international reputation for excellence. Theatre New Brunswick, a professional theatre company based in Fredericton, offers live theatre in the towns and cities of the province. There are 6 public art galleries. More than 250 authors belong to the NB authors association. Although the region lacks an effective scholarly press, local publishers produce popular works of fiction, humour, folklore and family and community history.

Communication Daily newspapers include the Saint John *Telegraph-Journal*, the Fredericton *Gleaner* and the Moncton *Times-Transcript* (all owned by the Irving interests), *L'Acadie Nouvelle* and *Le Matin*. Until its recent bankruptcy, the French-language *L'Evangeline* was the daily voice of Acadians in the province. A senior Canadian magazine, the *Atlantic Advocate*, is published in Fredericton.

The province receives 3 major TV sources, the CBC, CTV and Radio-Québec. Cable television (which carries the major American networks, the public television channel of the U of Maine, and FM radio) is available in urban centres. Several Pay TV channels have recently begun service. The CBC radio offers 10 outlets in French and 16 in English. Over 400 000 telephones are operated in the province by the NB Telephone Co Ltd, a Bell-dominated company integrated with the TransCanada telephone system.

Historic Sites New Brunswick has 2 public archives and 3 university archives, 2 historical settlements, a national historic park, a share in 2 international historic parks, 21 museums, 13 military restorations or other historic buildings open to the public and over 1000 buildings designated of historical interest.

The New Brunswick Museum in Saint John has been an exhibitor of natural history and a collector of newspapers, public French-immersion records and genealogical records for over 50 years. Since 1967 the Provincial Archives of NB in Fredericton has been the depository of government records, collections of public and private papers and other historical and genealogical materials. Kings Landing, the restoration of a Loyalist settlement up the river from Fredericton, is a spectacular attempt to bring history alive to visitors through the activities of a 19th-century village. The Acadian Village at Caraquet is a recreation of life in another cultural tradition. FT BEAUSÉJOUR, a national historic park located near the NS border (near Sackville), is a restoration of a significant French fort of the mid-18th century. Roosevelt Summer Home and Park on CAMPOBELLO ISLAND run by a joint Canadian-American Commission includes the Franklin D. Roosevelt summer estate and neighbouring houses, and offers luxury accommodation for small conferences. Recently a second international park has been designated on Saint Croix I, the site of Champlain's first settlement in N America. Heritage societies have been active in Fredericton, St John, St Andrews, Chatham-Newcastle and Albert County. Concerns have involved the preservation of city cores and neighbourhoods, covered bridges and buildings of historical significance.

Lumber at Saint John, NB, 1890 (*courtesy National Archives of Canada/PA-117982/Isaac Erb*).

History

The first settlers of New Brunswick were the Micmac whose communities spread from NS and PEI to the S coast of the Gaspé peninsula. From the early 16th century they had developed contacts with the Europeans and established a trade which made them dependent on European technologies and victims of European diseases. The Micmac had long followed a pattern of seasonal migration from hunting grounds in the wooded uplands in winter to gatherings on the shore in summer for shellfishing and social congress. The Maliseet were more direct victims of European expansion. Pushed from their homes in New England, they had found refuge along the Saint John R in the 17th century.

Exploration When the French attempted settlement, first at the mouth of the ST CROIX R in 1604 and later at PORT-ROYAL, they were welcomed by the Micmac who taught them how to survive. After the French had shifted their interest to Québec, the Indians helped a few young men who remained, including Charles de Saint-Étienne de LA TOUR, to establish a fur trade on the Saint John R. The death of Isaac de RAZILLY in 1635, leader of a revived settlement at Port-Royal, occasioned a feudalistic struggle over trade and territory between La Tour, Charles de MENOU d'Aulnay and Nicolas DENYS. On d'Aulnay's death in 1650, La Tour regained control of the Saint John and Denys recovered a fishing and trading post at Miscou harbour and built another at Nipisiquit (Bathurst). After an extensive career in trade and fisheries along the coast of ACADIA, Denys returned to Nipisiquit in 1668 to write an historically important description of Acadia before returning to France in 1671 to have the volume published. The Saint John R valley remained Indian territory from which the French launched raids against New England in the 1690s, helping to create a deep-seated and persistent hostility to the French presence in Acadia.

Settlement Meanwhile the tiny settlement begun at Port-Royal flourished, spreading around the Bay of Fundy to include the Chignecto Isthmus and Shepody on the N shore. The Acadians developed a unique society characterized by a diking technology which enabled them to farm the marshes left by the Bay of Fundy's tides. Their society was also characterized by neglect from the French authorities, and this encouraged the development of a tightly knit and independent community. Caught in imperial struggle between British and French, most were expelled by the British in 1755 or later and scattered throughout the Thirteen Colonies or were returned to France. Those who returned after the Treaty of PARIS (1763) found their lands occupied by several thousand immigrants, largely from New England. Some received grants of land in the Memramcook area, some squatted along the Saint John R and some found employment with the Robin brothers of Jersey in the Channel Is, who in 1764 began to establish fishing stations along the coast from Gaspé to Cape Breton I. After the American Revolution, approximately 14 000 Loyalist refugees came to the N shore of the Bay of Fundy, established the city of Saint John and settled the Saint John and St Croix river valleys. A few penetrated other parts of the province. Hungry for jobs and conscious of their isolation from Halifax, they petitioned for separate colonial status, which was granted in 1784.

Development Napoleon's continental blockade, which in 1809 cut Britain off from traditional timber supplies from the Baltic region, led to a deliberate effort through protective timber tariffs to foster the colonial industry as a dependable source. Blessed with rivers which made accessible rich stands of spruce and pine, NB's squared-timber trade boomed for half a century. Timber became a source of development leading to new settlement and giving its own peculiar cast to the economy and to politics and society. Population grew from perhaps 25 000 to almost 200 000 by mid-century. Indeed governments and historians have been critical of the province's excessive reliance on this single, highly volatile staple. Booms and slumps tended to bankrupt the settler reliant on timber, and many settlers were reduced to wage labour status, dependent on a few influential entrepreneurs in each region. Associated with the timber industry was wooden shipbuilding, whose production sites dotted the coast and rivers of the province and by mid-century turned out over 100 vessels a year, both for export and for the use of the merchants of Saint John.

New Brunswick industries, helped by the Crimean War and American Civil War, and by a RECIPROCITY treaty with the US in natural products, weathered the crisis of the British abandonment of the timber tariffs and NAVIGATION ACTS in the late 1840s. But the conjunction of blows which afflicted NB's economy after Confederation, of which the NATIONAL POLICY of protective tariffs was but one, proved more permanently damaging. The reciprocity treaty was cancelled, timber resources became less merchantable, and the wooden vessels lost in their competition with steam-driven, iron-hulled ships. New Brunswickers by the thousand left the declining ports and timber towns to find employment in the US.

Some New Brunswick entrepreneurs were quick to make the transition to a national, continental economy. Confederation brought the INTERCOLONIAL RAILWAY to NB by 1876 and the CPR reached Saint John in 1889. Merchants, lumbermen and shipbuilders tended to transfer their capital to iron foundries, textile mills, sugar refineries and other secondary industries whose growth was fostered by the tariff. But eventually many of the new industries, scattered through the province, were taken over by the larger and better capitalized industries of central Canada. The classic pattern emerged of takeover, failure to modernize, closure and the exploitation of the market from expanding plants in central Canada. The postwar recession of the 1920s saw the continued decline of traditional industries, and the virtual collapse of a manufacturing sector further undercut by adverse federal policies in tariffs and transportation. Investigation of Maritime problems by a federal royal commission and attempted remedial action were largely negated as NB plunged with the rest of the world into the Depression of the 1930s. Several decades of economic stagnation reduced NB to a standard of living much lower than the national average. National policies served to increase the disparity, as the tariff (or, during WWII, federal investment) created and maintained a manufacturing sector in central Canada. Meanwhile, Maritime governments lacked the money to maintain essential services. By 1940 NB's expenditures on education and health services were slightly over half of the national average; its illiteracy and infant mortality rates were the highest in the country. Despite the recognition of the Rowell-Sirois Report on DOMINION-PROVINCIAL RELATIONS (1940) of the need for a fairer distribution of the tax revenues from a national economy, the adjustment grants which the commissioners recommended for the poorer provinces were not adopted until the early 1960s.

The nature of NB's disparity was twofold: the extreme disparity of standards of living compared with other provinces; and the internal disparity between the urban sections of the largely English S and the rural sections of the largely French N. The attack on both proceeded simultaneously. Within the province, the government moved behind a slogan of "equal opportunity" to provide greater equality in services. Acting on the recommendations of the 1963 Byrne Commission, the Robichaud administration proceeded with more than 125 pieces of legislation to alter radically the division in responsibilities between provincial and county or municipal units of government. Acting on the principle that the provincial government should maintain services to people, the government took responsibility for educational, medical, judicial and social assistance services. To the municipalities it left services to property such as water, sewer, fire protection and local police services. Taxes were to be assessed province wide on the actual market value of property.

Along with the rationalization in services went a determined effort at economic development. The optimism of the 1960s persuaded both federal and provincial governments that the chronic disparity of province and region could be overcome through industrialization. Federal-provincial attempts at rural development, government investments in electricity generation, mining, forestry, fishery and secondary manufacturing, the building of major highways through the N of the province, and the use of transportation subsidies to help NB products reach national markets were all part of a federal-provincial effort to push the province's standard of living closer to the national average. To a large degree such efforts have been successful. Social and educational services are now on a par with the rest of the country. A well-trained civil service has helped primary industries modernize in a transitional period when the failure to do so would have meant collapse. A favourable infrastructure and direct assistance reversed a pattern of decline in secondary industry.

Nevertheless the province's improved standard of living rests upon a fragile base. The enthusiasm for industrial development by federal governments slowed in the 1970s amid spectacular failures and the jealousies of other regions. Governments have found the maintenance of fiscal transfers less controversial – transfers which in any case return to the centre in the purchase of consumer goods. Of critical importance are the indirect transfers which accompany such traditional welfare-state programs as old-age pensions and unemployment insurance. No less important are the direct EQUALIZATION PAYMENTS and grants for established programs, which in 1986 accounted for one-third of the ordinary revenues. As past victims and beneficiaries, New Brunswickers have a vital interest in the continuing evolution of the Canadian constitution.   ERNEST R. FORBES

Reading: A.G. Bailey, *Culture and Nationality* (1972); R.J. Bryn and R.J. Sacouman, eds, *Underdevelopment and Social Movements in Atlantic Canada* (1977); J. Daigle, ed, *The Acadians of the Maritimes: Thematic Studies* (1982); J. Fingard, *Jack in Port: Sailortowns of Eastern Canada* (1982); Ernest R. Forbes, *The Maritime Rights Movement 1919-1927: A Study in Canadian Regionalism* (1979); W.S. MacNutt, *New Brunswick: A History 1784-1867* (1963); G.A. Rawlyk, *Nova Scotia's Massachusetts, 1630 to 1784* (1973); S.A. Saunders, *Economic History of the Maritime Provinces* (1939); W.A. Spray, *The Blacks in New Brunswick* (1972); H.G. Thorburn, *Politics of New Brunswick* (1961); R.A. Tweedie, F. Cogswell and W.S. MacNutt, eds, *Arts in New Brunswick* (1967); L.F.S. Upton, *Micmacs and Colonists: Indian-White Relations in the Maritimes, 1713-1867* (1979); E.C. Wright, *The Loyalists of New Brunswick* (1955); G. Wynn, *Timber Colony: A Historical Geography of Early Nineteenth Century New Brunswick* (1981). *See also* the journal *Acadiensis*.

New Brunswick Research and Productivity Council (NBRPC), research organization established by a provincial Act as a crown corporation in 1962. NBRPC initially encouraged university-based research in industrial and scientific technology through grants-in-aid. This phase ended in 1965 when it commenced research for provincial and other Canadian and international industrial and government clients. NBRPC gained an international reputation for expertise in computer-assisted manufacturing and extractive metallurgy (eg, through development of a specialized sulphation roast process). In 1981 a Council of Maritime Premiers Committee on Research and Development advocated a co-operative expansion with the NOVA SCOTIA RESEARCH FOUNDATION CORPORATION to serve the entire region. Research is conducted by staff (about 100 people) under an executive director, primarily in laboratories at UNIVERSITY OF NEW BRUNSWICK, Fredericton. Additional facilities include a provincially sponsored Manufacturing Design Centre (a joint venture with a number of universities and colleges). Research into the economic feasibility of a technique developed in 1985 at Chatham for extracting minerals from low-yield deposits is continuing at Fredericton. Funding is through industrial and government contracts, with ongoing federal and provincial grants.   MARTIN K. MCNICHOLL

New Brunswick School Question On 17 May 1871 the New Brunswick government passed the Common Schools Act to strengthen and reform the school system. At the same time, however, it abandoned an informal system of separate schools that had grown up since the 1850s. There was an outcry from NB's Roman Catholics, and various remedies were proposed or attempted: DISALLOWANCE, resolutions in the Canadian House of Commons, the courts. None worked. The 1871 Act, though it violated familiar conventions, did not violate Section 93 of the BRITISH NORTH AMERICA ACT. Two cases made that clear: *Ex parte Renaud* at the NB Supreme Court, 1873, and *Maher* v *The Town of Portland* at the JUDICIAL COMMITTEE OF THE PRIVY COUNCIL in London, 1874. The Jan 1875 Caraquet riots, in which 2 people were shot and killed, showed strongly the need for accommodation on the school issue; amendments somewhat improving the Catholic position were then made to the Act. But NB did not get real separate schools; it got an informal system, not unlike that in Nova Scotia.   P.B. WAITE

New Caledonia ("New Scotland"), a name given in 1806 to the central and highland plateau area of BRITISH COLUMBIA by Simon FRASER, a partner, trader and explorer in the NORTH WEST CO. Fraser had never been to Scotland, but the BC interior reminded him of his mother's descriptions of the Scottish Highlands. New Caledonia became a trading department or district for the NWC, and had its headquarters at Ft St James, built in 1806 on Stuart Lk. Nearby were Forts Fraser and George, the latter at the junction of the Nechako and Fraser rivers, from which Fraser began his celebrated exploration of the river, named after him, that drained New Caledonia to the S. Other names for the central interior appeared on maps at this time: the Americans called it Oregon; Capt George VANCOUVER called it New Hanover; and British fur trader James Colnett called it North West Georgia. However, the NWC's dominance of the FUR TRADE of the BC interior, until the 1821 merger with the HUDSON'S BAY CO, assured the continuance of the name New Caledonia.

In 1858 legislation was introduced to create a crown colony to bring British law and authority to an area undergoing a GOLD RUSH and rapid population expansion. Colonial Secretary Sir Edward Bulwer-Lytton called the region New Caledonia; however, the French possessed a S Pacific colony called New Caledonia, and to avoid confusion or resentment the name was changed to British Columbia. Queen Victoria made this choice, and New Caledonia became British Columbia on 2 Aug 1858. Thereafter the earlier term gradually disappeared from general use.   BARRY M. GOUGH

New Democratic Party (NDP), founded in Ottawa in 1961 at a convention uniting the CO-OPERATIVE COMMONWEALTH FEDERATION (CCF), affiliated unions of the CANADIAN LABOUR CONGRESS (CLC) and New Party clubs, is a democratic socialist party (*see* SOCIAL DEMOCRACY) and a member of the Socialist International.

The party has had 3 leaders: T.C. DOUGLAS (1961-71), David LEWIS (1971-75) and Ed BROADBENT (1975). In the 9 elections since its birth, the NDP has received the following percentages of votes in federal elections: 13.5% (1962), 13.1% (1963), 17.9% (1965), 17.0% (1968), 17.7% (1972), 15.4% (1974), 17.9% (1979), 19.8% (1980), 18.8% (1984). While this is an increase compared to the CCF, the federal NDP has yet to form the national government. Because of the electoral system, the NDP, like the CCF before it, has consistently received a smaller percentage of the seats in Parliament (8.7%) than its percentage vote (16.8%). In the 1984 election the NDP won 30 seats, a number increased by 3 by-election victories in 1987. Federally the NDP has made the greatest impact during MINORITY GOVERNMENT situations. While the West provided the highest level of voting support, individual memberships and MPs for the party, a majority of NDP votes come from central Canada (largely Ontario). The NDP, like the CCF, has been unable to elect an MP from Québec, although one former Québec Conservative MP defected to the NDP in 1986, but soon left in 1987. Nevertheless, the party enjoyed unprecedented popularity in the province in 1987.

The CCF-NDP has formed governments in BC (1972-75), Saskatchewan (1944-64, 1971-82), Manitoba (1969-77, 1981) and the Yukon Territory (1985). It has served as the Official Opposition in Alberta, Ontario and Nova Scotia.

In domestic affairs, the NDP is committed to a moderate form of SOCIALISM and a mixed economy. It favours government planning and public ownership (eg, CROWN CORPORATIONS, co-operatives), where necessary, to provide jobs and services. The CCF-NDP has always been a forceful exponent of such SOCIAL SECURITY measures as universal medical care, old-age pensions, workers' compensation and unemployment insurance as a means to reduce class inequalities. As the official political voice of labour, the NDP has encouraged trade-union organization. In recent years, the party has favoured industrial democracy and workers' control in the factories. While the CCF advocated strong, federal government, the NDP has been more receptive to provincial rights.

In foreign policy, the NDP, like the CCF, has manifested strong pacifist tendencies. While this pacifism moderated somewhat in the 1950s and early 1960s, the party currently opposes Canada's involvement in NATO and NORAD and calls for Canada to become a nuclear-free zone. The party is critical of the high rate of foreign, particularly American, ownership of Canadian industry. Largely because of NDP pressure, recent Liberal governments introduced such nationalist measures as the National Energy Program (NEP) and the Foreign Investment Review Agency (FIRA). The NDP opposed the FREE TRADE accord with the US sponsored by the Conservatives in 1987.

While the party has always proposed an evolutionary form of socialism, a persistent minority endeavours to push the party further left. The WAFFLE, the most famous faction, ceased its operations within the NDP in 1972 only to be replaced by another "left-caucus." While the NDP led national public opinion polls for much of 1987 in federal elections to date the NDP still remained stalled as a third party and was engaged in discussions about the appropriate role of social democracy and of KEYNESIAN ECONOMICS, a debate to which Jim Laxer contributed with his controversial 1983 report. In an effort to alleviate fears among the Canadian public of the growth of big government, the NDP has increasingly advocated more decentralist proposals.   ALAN WHITEHORN

Reading: I. Avakumovic, *Socialism in Canada* (1978); S. Knowles, *The New Party* (1961); D. Lewis, *The Good Fight* (1981); L. McDonald, *The Party that Changed Canada* (1987); T. McLeod and I. McLeod, *Tommy Douglas: The Road to Jerusalem* (1987); D. Morton, *The New Democrats 1961-1986* (1986); M. Oliver, ed, *Social Purpose for Canada* (1961).

New Denver, BC, Village, pop 596 (1986c), 642 (1981c), inc 1929, is located near the NE end of Slocan Lk, 48 km W, 116 km N of Nelson. Eli Carpenter, discoverer of Slocan Lk, wintered there in 1891. The site was first called Eldorado, then New Denver (1892), after Denver, Colo. The first newspaper in Slocan, called *The Ledge*, was published there by R.T. Lowery. New Denver was an early service centre for mines and the nearby towns of Three Forks, Sandon, Cody, Silverton and Slocan City. Mining declined after WWI, and by WWII 1500 relocated JAPANESE formed the bulk of the population. After the war, Japanese from other relocation centres moved here, and small-scale mining was supplemented by logging. The creation of Valhalla Wilderness Park, together with the magnificent scenery and surrounding ghost towns, give New Denver an optimistic future as a tourist centre.

WILLIAM A. SLOAN

New France France was a colonial power in N America from the early 16th century, the age of great European discoveries and fishing expeditions, to the early 19th century, when Napoléon Bonaparte sold Louisiana to the US. From the founding of Québec in 1608 to the ceding of Canada to Britain in 1763, France placed its stamp upon the history of the continent, much of whose lands – including ACADIA, the vast territory of Louisiana and the Mississippi Valley – lay under its control. The populations it established, especially in the St Lawrence Valley, are still full of vitality today.

France became interested in the New World later than the other Western Christian powers – England, Spain and Portugal – and after the trips made by Christopher Columbus in 1492, John CABOT in 1497 and the CORTE-REAL brothers in 1501 and 1502. In 1524 Giovanni VERRAZZANO followed the eastern shore of America from Florida to Newfoundland. Jacques CARTIER then made 3 voyages of discovery for France. He took possession of the territory in the name of the king of France by planting a cross on the shores of the Gaspé in 1534. The next year he sailed up the St Lawrence R and visited Indian settlements at Stadacona [Québec] and Hochelaga [Montréal]. He spent the winter at Stadacona, where 25 of his men died of scurvy, and returned to France in 1536.

In 1541-42 he returned, establishing a short-lived colony, which he called "Charles-bourg-Royal," at the mouth of the Rivière du Cap-Rouge near Stadacona. Religion gave the impetus to his voyages, but economic motives were even more obvious. The hope of finding a NORTHWEST PASSAGE to the Indies and the fabled Kingdom of the Saguenay was constantly stressed. Cartier brought back to France some minerals from this final voyage which he thought were gold and diamonds, but were only iron pyrite and quartz (*see* DIAMONDS OF CANADA). After these initial disappointments France turned its attention elsewhere and ignored the distant land until the end of the century.

Meanwhile, some Frenchmen had shown sustained interest in the region's FISHERIES. There are reports of BASQUE, Breton and Norman fishermen on the GRAND BANKS as early as the first decade of the 16th century. Each year more ships – a dozen or so in the decade 1520-30, about 100 by mid-century – made fishing trips. By 1550 fishermen were drying their catch on the shores, making contact with the Indians and taking furs back to France. In the 1580s, ship owners were leaving

Paysanne in the time of New France, *c*1650, by Henri Beau (*courtesy National Archives of Canada/C-1248*).

fishing for the FUR TRADE, an activity which was to draw Frenchmen far into the continent.

In 1608 Samuel de CHAMPLAIN, considered the founder of New France, erected a *habitation* (building) at Québec. He continued Cartier's dream of finding an opening to the Indies, pursued the commercial interests of the businessmen, his sponsors, and followed the king's wishes. The settlement responded to economic demands: go out to the fur-rich areas, forge close contact with native suppliers and try to obtain the right of exploitation. The scale of the operation made it necessary to form private companies.

The colony's administration, 1608-63, was entrusted to these commercial companies, which were formed by merchants from various cities of France. Succeeding companies promised to settle and develop the French land in America in return

for exclusive rights to its resources. The COMPAGNIE DES CENT-ASSOCIÉS, created by the great minister of Louis XIII, Cardinal de Richelieu, ran New France 1627-63, either directly or through subsidiary companies. It did not achieve the desired results. In 1663 the population numbered scarcely 3000 people, 1175 of them Canadian-born. Less than 1% of the granted land was being exploited. Of the 5.4 million livres' worth of possible annual resources enumerated by Champlain in 1618 – eg, fish, mines, wood, hemp, cloth and fur – only fur yielded an appreciable return, and it was irregular and disappointing.

Nor was evangelization among the natives flourishing. During its first half-century, New France experienced an explosion of missionary fervour, as demonstrated by the number and zeal of its apostles, inspired by the Catholic Counter-Reformation (*see* CATHOLICISM). In 1634 the Jesuits renewed the mission of STE MARIE AMONG THE HURONS in the western wilds. VILLE-MARIE, which became Montréal, was the work of mystics and the devoted. But the missionaries managed to convert very few Indians.

Various political and military events hindered colonization efforts. The alliances formed by Champlain made enemies of the Iroquois. Québec fell to the freebooting KIRKE brothers in 1629. The Iroquois nations grew belligerent as soon as the country was returned to France in 1632. Between 1648 and 1652 they destroyed HURONIA, a hub of French commercial and missionary activity. Attacks on the very heart of the colony demonstrated that the colony's survival was in doubt (*see* IROQUOIS WARS).

In 1663 Québec was just a commercial branch operation: the fur trade was opposed to agriculture, cross-cultural contact meant war and disease for the natives, the French population was small, and the administration of the colony by commercial exploiters was a disaster. The company relinquished control of the colony to the king. Under Louis XIV New France flourished. He made the colony a province of France, giving it a similar hierarchical administrative organization. He watched over its settlement, extended its territory and allowed its enterprises to multiply. However, he had first to guarantee the peace.

Under the marquis de Tracy, the CARIGNAN-SALIÈRES REGIMENT built forts, ravaged Iroquois villages and demonstrated French military power.

Champlain's rendering of the Québec habitation, from *Les Voyages* (1613) (*courtesy National Library of Canada/ Rare Book Division*).

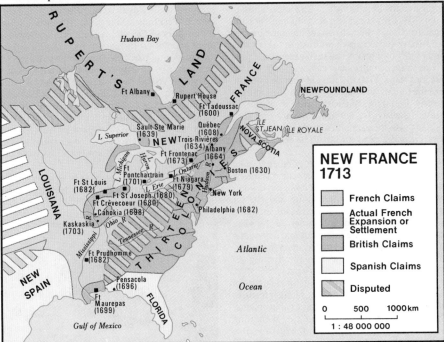

The habitant of New France had greater independence than his counterpart in France (*courtesy National Archives of Canada/C-866*).

The Iroquois made peace, and 400 soldiers stayed in the colony as settlers. The king also had 850 young women sent out as brides-to-be, and quick marriages and families were encouraged. When the offspring of these FILLES DU ROI came of age 20 years later, the demographic situation had changed. In 1663 there had been one woman to every 6 men; now the sexes were roughly equal in number. The colony thereafter replenished 95% of its numbers through childbirth.

Under the authority of Jean-Baptiste Colbert, comptroller general of finances and then navy minister (*see* MINISTÈRE DE LA MARINE), colonial administration was entrusted to a GOUVERNEUR (for military matters and external relations) and an INTENDANT (for justice, civil administration and finances – ie, all civil aspects of colonial administration). The SOVEREIGN COUNCIL (Superior Council after 1703) acted as a court of appeal and registered the king's edicts.   The imperialism of Louis XIV, the pacification of the Iroquois and the need to rebuild the network of fur-trade treaties led to renewed EXPLORATIONS into the Great Lakes and Mississippi regions by such exceptional people as François DOLLIER DE CASSON, Louis JOLLIET, Jacques MARQUETTE and the Cavelier de LA SALLE. But the Indian wars started again in 1682 and the colony found new heroes, such as Pierre Le Moyne d'IBERVILLE. Political, military and missionary activity, combined with economic factors, created a need for furs to be acquired from the Indian nations.

Intendant Jean TALON, with Colbert's solid backing and other favourable circumstances, started a vigorous development program. In addition to watching over agriculture and the fur trade, Talon began ventures such as shipbuilding, trade with the West Indies, commercial crops like flax and hemp, fishing industries and a brewery. But by the time he left in 1672, economic circumstances had changed and virtually nothing remained of these premature initiatives.

It is difficult to identify the major elements of this nascent society. For Acadia, familiar features are the quality of its agricultural establishments, the importance of fishing and the alternating British and French regimes. In the St Lawrence Valley, farmers, though in the majority, were still

clearing the land. Craftsmen no longer had the support of major enterprises. Fur traders were being squeezed by increasingly difficult regulations and economic circumstances, yet they provided the colony's only exports. Military officers, thanks to the introduction of coin currency and the presence of opportunities to flaunt themselves, enjoyed some prestige by entering into business and being in the governor's entourage. The seigneur had little revenue and took his standing from his title and the exercise of functions entirely unrelated to the land (*see* SEIGNEURIAL SYSTEM). Social mobility was still possible and caused categories and groups to mingle, but there were 2 worlds: the city and the country.

New France reached its greatest territorial extent at the start of the 18th century. About 250 people lived in a dozen settlements in Newfoundland, and there were about 1500 in Acadia. Several hundred lived around the mouth of the Mississippi and around the Great Lakes. People from the St Lawrence Valley lived on the shoreline of Labrador as fishermen. The Saguenay R Basin (the King's Domain) had a few trading posts. Canada had about 20 000 inhabitants, most of them farmers scattered along a ribbon of settlement between the 2 urban centres of Québec and Montréal. In the West, a series of trading posts and forts dotted the communication lines. Finally, in the 1740s, the LA VÉRENDRYE family carried the exploration of the continent right to the foothills of the Rockies.

Despite this expansion, New France has been described as a "colossus with feet of clay." The British American colonies were 20 times as populous and felt themselves encircled and at risk. Through the Treaty of UTRECHT of 1713, which ended the WAR OF THE SPANISH SUCCESSION, France yielded Newfoundland, the Acadian peninsula, Hudson Bay and supremacy in trade over the Iroquois to the English. Furthermore the early 18th century brought a major economic crisis in the colony. Its main export item was hit by a European sales slump, declining quality and less attractive returns.

Recovery was slow, but the economy experienced an unprecedented boom during the long period of peace, 1713-44. France built an imposing fortress at LOUISBOURG to protect its fishing zones, land and commercial trade with the colony. After 1720 agricultural surpluses were exported to Île Royale (Cape Breton I) and the French West Indies. Some 200 seigneurs lived in the territory of Canada. A high birthrate led to a rapid population increase, which in turn led to the creation of parishes. Despite the strictures of MERCANTILISM, 2 major industries were established: the FORGES SAINT-MAURICE and royal shipbuilding. In 1735 a road linked Québec City and Montréal for the first time. Yet the fur trade still accounted for 70% of the colony's exports. And peace was being used to prepare for war: 80% of the colony's budgets (which never equalled the sums spent on the king's amusements) went for

A view of the Intendant's Palace by Richard Short (*courtesy National Archives of Canada/C-360*).

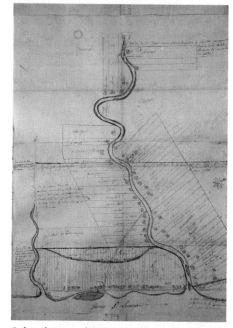

Cadastral survey of Batiscan, a seigneury belonging to the Jesuits, 1725. In the mid-18th century one-third of the Canadian population lived on seigneuries belonging to religious institutions (*courtesy Centre des archives d'outre-mer, Aix-en-Provence, Recensements, G^1 461*).

military expenses. Much more was spent on constructing European-style FORTIFICATIONS than on strengthening alliances with the Indian nations.

Colonial society, influenced by the French elite that led it, modelled itself on the mother country, yet increasingly grew apart from it because of the colony's small population and very different, land-based, economic and geographic circumstances. Nobles, the middle class, military officers, seigneurs, civil administrators and traders formed a high society which was extremely sensitive to the favours of the colonial authorities. Eighty percent of the population lived on and by the land. Each generation produced new pioneers who cleared and settled land, acclimatized themselves, managed some new territory and came to know their neighbours. The acquisition of this territory in America by the descendants of Frenchmen was characterized by the importance of the land, of inheritance, of economic independence and of analysed social relationships.

But France felt that New France cost much and yielded little. The expensive but inconclusive WAR OF THE AUSTRIAN SUCCESSION, which ended in 1748, saw the destruction of French overseas trade by Britain. The SEVEN YEARS' WAR found France on the defensive against England, now an aggressive maritime power. The British colonies, with 2 million inhabitants, were pitted against a mere 70 000 French colonists, a sign of the very limited success of French colonization in N America. After some spectacular military successes, the result of strategy well adapted to the local terrain, France fell back on the defensive. On 13 Sept 1759 the troops of Gen James WOLFE defeated those of the marquis de MONTCALM in the Battle of the PLAINS OF ABRAHAM near Québec City. Montréal fell the next year. France yielded its colony to England in the Treaty of PARIS (1763). It was the end, or nearly so, of French political power in America – but not of French presence. France left a great legacy to America: the Canadiens. They refused assimilation and affirmed their existence. Protected by their language, religion and institutions, concentrated in a limited geographic area, difficult to penetrate, they devel-

oped a way of life, social customs and attitudes of their own. Having become Québecois, they continued to strive to develop their nationality.
JACQUES MATHIEU

Reading: W.J. Eccles, *France in America* (1972); G.F.G. Stanley, *New France, The Last Phase* (1968); M. Trudel, *Introduction to New France* (1968) and *The Beginnings of New France* (1973).

New Glasgow, NS, Town, pop 10 022 (1986c), 10 464 (1981c), inc 1875, is located on the East R of Pictou, 15 km SE of PICTOU; it is the largest municipal unit and centre of an urban community of 4 towns – Trenton, New Glasgow, Stellarton, Westville – and the trading centre for the farming, lumber and fishing counties of Pictou, Antigonish and Guysborough. It was settled originally by Scottish pioneers, but local industries brought tradesmen from European countries whose descendants have blended with the original Scottish populace. Its location at the head of the tidewater made it the trading centre of the surrounding pioneering agricultural area. The era of wooden shipbuilding 1826-1880s and the development of coal created an industrial complex which in 1883 broadened into the opening of the first steelmaking plant in Canada, the Nova Scotia Steel Co. The steel company's forged and rolled products supplied central Canadian manufacturers, particularly for farm implements and railway construction. Railway freight car construction began in 1913 and continues. Growth continued through WWI, followed by decline because of the advantage in freight costs held by central Canadian manufacturers. Population growth over 6 decades has been very slow, from 8917 in 1921. Pulp processed from the local softwood stand and the manufacture of automobile and truck tires have maintained the labour force despite the near total abandonment of the coal industry in the New Glasgow area.
JAMES CAMERON

New Hamburg, Ont, UP, pop 3682 (1986c), 3923 (1981c), is located midway between KITCHENER and STRATFORD in the midst of a prosperous rural countryside (populated partly by Old Order Mennonite and Amish, who settled the area in the 1830s. At first called simply Hamburg, after the port of departure of many German emigrants in the 19th century, it was a result of the railway boom created by the expansion of the GRAND TRUNK RY in 1857 and of the influx of German immigrants in the mid-19th century. The sixth generation of pioneer farmers of German origin remains on the land, and the settlement today is primarily an agricultural service centre. Population growth after the 1850s was slow until after WWII. New Hamburg is known widely for its annual Ontario Mennonite Relief Sale of traditional handicrafts. In 1973 it was reorganized within the Regional Municipality of Waterloo and reverted to the status of a settlement within the Township of Wilmot.
KEN McLAUGHLIN

New Left, an international political movement of the 1960s, mainly of youth and students, which originated in the "Ban the Bomb" movement of the late 1950s. It expanded to include issues such as the VIETNAM WAR, Third World liberation struggles, women's liberation, education, ecology, and popular culture. Critical of the Old Left (SOCIAL DEMOCRACY and MARXISM-Leninism) and its alienating hierarchical, centralized and bureaucratic structures, the New Left proposed local control of the political process, accessibility to political and social institutions and participatory democracy. Critical as well of modern capitalism, the New Left advocated confrontations with that system by dissident intelligentsia and workers, and by the poor, blacks, natives and ethnic minorities. It included sup-

porters of every position between nonviolent civil disobedience and libertarian socialism. In Canada, the ideas of the New Left were argued about and practised by the Student Union for Peace Action, the Canadian Union of Students, Students for a Democratic University and the Union générale des étudiants de Québec – highly decentralized organizations that were active on a regional, even local, basis. Also active in the debates were *Our Generation* and *Canadian Dimension* magazines. Among issues raised by the Canadian New Left were nuclear disarmament, community organizing, the "multiversity," American control of the economy, the composition of the working class, Québecois separatism and sexual inequality.

After the OCTOBER CRISIS (1970) the New Left fell into disarray, although it was also weakened by the incursion of government-sponsored groups (eg, The Company of Young Canadians, which was established to support, encourage and develop programs of social and economic reform); by failure to link up with working-class organizations and by the lack of a sustained program and strategy for social change. In the 1970s many adherents entered the women's liberation movement, the PARTI QUÉBÉCOIS and various Marxist-Leninist groups. New Left ideas have been revived in the antinuclear movement.
MYRNA KOSTASH

New Liskeard, Ont, Town, pop 5286 (1986c), 5551 (1981c), inc 1903, located on the NW end of Lk TIMISKAMING, 157 km NW of North Bay. The history of this agrarian community at the mouth of Wabi Cr dates back to 1892 when the Ontario government first opened up the area to settlement. The agricultural potential of the Little Clay Belt, a 56 km strip of land stretching to the NW, quickly attracted farmers from "Old" Ontario. First known as Liskeard (after Liskeard, Eng), the name was changed by postal authorities to New Liskeard to avoid confusion with Lisgar, Leskard in Durham County. By 1896 a thriving village had come into existence. Its role as service centre to the surrounding farming community was assured by the arrival of the Temiskaming and Northern Ontario Ry (ONTARIO NORTHLAND) in 1905, and its growth in the 20th century was shaped by the varying fortunes of agriculture. Since 1966 it has been the site of a college of agricultural technology.
MATT BRAY

New Provinces: Poems of Several Authors
(1936). This was – albeit of modest scope – a milestone selection of modernist Canadian verse. Under the anonymous editorship of F.R. SCOTT, who was variously assisted by A.J.M. SMITH and Leo KENNEDY this project took 4 years of negotiation and pleading on the part of Scott before it was finally published by the Macmillan Co of Canada. The anthology features the work of 4 Montréal poets (A.M. KLEIN, Leo Kennedy, A.J.M. Smith, F.R. Scott) and 2 from Toronto (E.J. PRATT and R. FINCH), and with its modest "Preface" establishes the modernists' claim on the attention of the Canadian reader. The original preface, written by an aggressively minded Smith, had been rejected by the publisher as being too impatient with traditional Canadian poetry. The "Rejected Preface" was resurrected in 1964, and was made an important feature of the new edition of *New Provinces* published in 1976.
MICHAEL GNAROWSKI

New Religious Movements, unorthodox, splinter religions that are usually outgrowths of ancient religious traditions. The complexity of the subject and a desire for objectivity have led scholars to prefer this expression to the popular term "cult," which has become associated with the 1978 mass suicide of People's Temple members in Jonestown, Guyana, and with other dangerous

practices. In the sociology of religion, "church," "sect" and "cult" have specialized meanings identifying specific types of religious movements; "cult" suggests an intellectually inclined, mystically oriented group rather like the QUAKERS. A theological definition identifies cults as groups that deviate from some traditional standard of Christian orthodoxy. Thus, Roman Catholics might argue that Baptists constitute a cult. Yet, as a result of media coverage, "cult" has come to refer to groups such as the Unification Church ("Moonies") and the International Society for Krishna Consciousness (Hare Krishna, or ISKCON).

The Jonestown tragedy distorts discussion about new religions. Few people realize that the Jonestown group was both religious and political. Jim Jones was a minister in a traditional Christian denomination, but his group was a political co-operative with strong socialist ideas. Most members of the new religions are well educated and relatively affluent young Caucasians often recruited as individuals, but the people at Jonestown were generally ill-educated, poor, black Americans often recruited as families. The social differences between the new religions and the People's Temple are so great that few meaningful comparisons can be made.

Sociologists David G. Bromley and Anson D. Shupe argue that most people react unfavourably towards the new religions because of "media hype," and that actual membership in N American new religious movements is low. Sociologist Reginald Bibby discovered that only about 1% of Canadians have even a strong interest in new religious movements (1983 and 1987); more significantly, only a fraction of 1% have any actual group involvement. Daniel G. Hill, commissioned by the Ontario government to study the "cult problem," agrees, citing a Toronto magazine which claimed that the Hare Krishnas had 10 000 members in Toronto when they had only 80 full-time members. It is difficult to give accurate membership figures for most new religions. The groups and their critics both tend to exaggerate their numbers. Hare Krishna in Toronto claims about "80 full-time members" and "5000 part-time or associates who attend services." The latter figure appears impressive, but includes anyone who visits the temple or an organized meeting, and a minority of the East Indian community who find in the movement an opportunity to continue traditional religious practices. What is perhaps most deceiving is the large number of groups, most of them relatively small. Richard Bergerson counted some 300 religious or para-religious groups in Québec, but the 1981 census indicates that over 88% of Quebecers are Roman Catholic. Nor is geographical distribution necessarily broad: most of Québec's non-Catholics are found in Montréal.

How many people belong to the more controversial new religions in Canada? Estimates show about 450 Hare Krishna members; 350-650 Unification Church members; 250 Children of God; about 700 full-time Scientologists and 15 000 taking Scientology courses; and over 200 000 who had been initiated into Transcendental Meditation (TM). However, if membership in new religions is small, the number of people holding nontraditional religious views and likely to have participated in the new movements is relatively high. Bibby's research indicates that 28% of Canadians have some interest in yoga; 21% in TM; 45% in astrology; and 69% in ESP. About 13% believe in reincarnation. Frederick Bird and Bill Reimer found that 32% of their sample of adult students in Montréal had participated at some time in activities organized by new religions, but they emphasize the difference between occasional participation and full membership. It may be that a market exists for new religious movements to fulfil needs that are not met by traditional churches. But by 1988 no group had fully established itself in Canadian society, although some groups, such as ISKCON and TM, have established rural communities and own property. It appears that, after sampling various groups, many people will not join any, commonly reverting to Protestant or Roman Catholic affiliations, or occasionally turning to such traditional movements as the Mormons or the more conservative Christian churches.

When placed in historical context the new religious movements may appear less strange. Modern society is called a "secular society," in which RELIGION and the sacred play little official role. Many provinces exclude religion from the curriculum in public schools, thus suggesting an attitude that religion is essentially unimportant. Hence, when young people turn to religion in any significant way their actions are seen as odd and needing explanation.

Traditionally, society's values have been based on religious values. Before the rise of CHRISTIANITY many different religions competed for the hearts and minds of the people. Even after Christianity became accepted as the religion of Europe there were periods of religious renewal and revival that produced many new varieties of Christianity. Perhaps the best known of these periods was the 16th-century Reformation.

Many theories exist as to why new religions grow. Some people posit tension and social unrest, whereas others stress religious reactions to dead orthodoxies. But the rise of new religions is not new, and by examining past examples we can discover patterns that help us understand the present better. Thus, although groups such as the METHODISTS and MORMONS began as suspect movements and encountered strong opposition, we know today that they did not cause society to disintegrate and that over time their practices were influenced by, and helped form, social attitudes in a positive way.

Identifying the New Religions The popularity of new religions is constantly changing and new groups continually appear. In the mid-1960s TM was growing rapidly; in the early 1970s it was the Divine Light Mission; in the mid-1970s the Unification Church; and in the early 1980s Rajneeshism. Each movement went through a period of rapid growth and then spectacular decline. Hence, a means of identifying groups generally is more valuable than an elaborate enumeration of new religions and their particular beliefs. To identify specific groups, one must recognize the existence of central experiences that may be generally labelled "spiritual." These include dreams, visions, precognition, ESP, a sense of awe, a sense of a presence, ghosts, dread, etc. They occur in all religious traditions. Specific traditions give them explicit interpretations in their own teachings. Thus, in the HINDU tradition Indian villagers see visions of Krishna, in Roman Catholicism the Virgin Mary may appear to the devoted, and in some newer groups spacemen reveal spiritual truths. In each case a system of thought is used to make sense out of strange experiences.

Three main systems of interpretation mold the teachings and practices of the new religious movements. The traditional Western systems originated with the religion of the ancient Hebrews and express themselves through JUDAISM, Christianity and ISLAM. This type of religion, which has distinctive ideas about God, creation and the nature of humanity, may be called the Abramic tradition because its member religions all recognize Abraham as their founding father. The second type of system is that which in its

many forms has the practice of meditation or yoga at its core. It finds expression in Hinduism, BUDDHISM, Jainism and SIKHISM. The third religious type is that in which religious thought is expressed in technical and scientific language. Religions of this type are truly new religions which openly proclaim their modernity and boast of their superiority. Some are forms of gnosticism that claim both Jewish and Greek roots, but whose schools employ much modern psychology. Another manifestation of modernity can be found in the Human Potential Movement, which includes client cults in which individuals seek to transform themselves through training and participation in various groups, encounters and techniques. Although these systems can be isolated, syncretism (the combination of differing beliefs and traditions) makes any summary of individual movements difficult. One can begin to categorize different new religions by their heritage and their rhetoric. The Unification Church is primarily Abramic although influenced by Korean philosophies. Hare Krishna is yogic, and Scientology is a religion of modernity. The classifications do not explain the religions, but help to identify them and assist the observer to analyse and understand their dynamics and theological patterns. The groupings should be seen as dynamic models to assist understanding, not as static analyses of beliefs. Members of new religions must be recognized to be on individual spiritual quests. A person may join the Unification Church essentially because of a vivid experience that that church appears able to explain. As the members' understanding of Unification thought grows, their essential allegiance to the group may then change from a reliance upon experience to a commitment to the beliefs of the group's development of Abramic concepts. In time, through study, this commitment to Abramic themes may lead the convert out of the group in search of a more traditional interpretation of the Abramic tradition.

Why and How People Join Social and psychological needs vary from person to person. New religions meet many of these, but so do golf clubs, traditional churches, theatrical groups, political movements and a host of other social organizations. The new religions seem to meet 2 requirements especially well: giving meaning and purpose to life, and taking "spiritual" experience seriously.

Few Canadians seem to be on a quest for life's meaning and most seem content with their immediate goals. Yet most people have wondered at some time about the purpose or meaning of existence. If during one such time of conscious reflection a person meets members of a new religious movement who claim to have found the answer to his or her questions, he or she may be tempted to investigate and perhaps join that movement. Beyond merely puzzling over life's meaning, many people have "spiritual" experiences, including unusual feelings and sensations ranging from out-of-the-body experiences to ESP and mystical visions. According to Bibby, some 58% of Canadians think they have had premonitions and 51% claim to have experienced mental telepathy. Research in Britain indicates that these and other apparently inexplicable occurrences are far more common than is usually thought. Yet our secular culture regards such experiences as at best "odd" and at worst evidence of psychological illness. Naturally, few people are willing to talk openly about them. However, members of the new religions take such experiences very seriously and not only interpret them, but actually encourage people to talk about and reflect on them. By supplying meaning to everyday life and offering explanations for unusual experiences, the new religions are able to present potential con-

verts with a comprehensive world view that is self-authenticating. Thus the new religion holds out to the convert insights and psychological supports that make membership attractive.

Recruitment generally proceeds primarily along friendship networks; members bring their friends into the groups. This theory of interaction is clearly illustrated in a classic paper by J. Loflund and R. Stark, "Becoming a World-Saver: A Theory of Conversion to a Deviant Perspective" (*American Sociological Review*, 1965). Once initial contact has been established, existing members become the candidate's new friends and friendship ties are strengthened and extended. The importance of friendship in this process becomes obvious when one considers the response of outsiders to a new religion. Usually, family members or old friends warn the new or potential convert against the group. Such warnings normally strengthen rather than weaken the cause of the new religion, because they are perceived not as criticism of the religion but as uninformed criticism of one's friends. Also, most religious groups teach that the outside world is under the influence of evil powers which will do everything possible to prevent potential converts from accepting the truth.

Brainwashing-Deprogramming Controversy One major reason for interest in the new religions in the 1970s was the claim that "cults recruit members by brainwashing techniques." This was supported by lurid autobiographical stories along with TV and radio interviews given by people who claimed to have "escaped" from the cults through deprogramming. Theoretical support came from Flo Conway and Jim Siegleman, authors of *Snapping* (1978), in which a theory of personality change is proposed to explain why people join the new religions. The authors intended their work to include not only the Unification Church, but also all "born-again" or EVANGELICAL Christians, and to show that William Sargent's *Battle for the Mind* (1957), their theoretical base, is a study of Christian conversion generally. The assumption behind the theory is that the human mind is like a computer and that people, because they can be programmed, are not responsible for their actions.

Snapping, and Josh Freed's *Moonwebs* (1981) – a sensational account of life among the Moonies – and other books support the practice of forcible deprogramming. This involves kidnapping members of religious groups and holding them prisoner until, through a combination of kindness, love, criticism and fear, members "break" and renounce their membership. This practice is clearly illegal and has many implications for civil religious liberties. Deprogramming has not been restricted to members of the new religions: in the US, Roman Catholics, Anglicans, Baptists, members of feminist groups and others have been deprogrammed because their views offended other family members. In Calgary and Montréal, widespread publicity surrounded the kidnapping and attempted deprogramming of Unification Church members. The Montréal case became the basis of the 1982 film *Ticket to Heaven*. Ontario's Hill Commission, however, spoke out strongly against kidnapping, and concluded that, if cults practise mind control and brainwashing, the evidence shows that they are not very successful. Deprogramming therefore appears unnecessary.

University of Toronto psychiatrist Saul V. Levine has argued that even when the deprogramming "succeeds" it usually creates severe mental problems. For deprogramming to work, people must be convinced that they were victims who joined the religion against their will through a process of brainwashing which removed from them all responsibility for their actions. The result is that they can never be sure that they are not being trapped again by a brainwashing technique of which they are unaware. An acute sense of dependency and self-doubt is created. By contrast, people who voluntarily leave new religions after participation retain their psychological integrity and self-respect. They may consider themselves fools for joining, but they have no fear of being trapped again.

Considerable evidence exists that membership in the new religions depends on individual free choice. Strong social pressures may be exerted by some groups, but such pressures are essentially no different from those of more traditional religious groups or other voluntary associations. Moreover, most people who join new religions soon leave by choice. British sociologist Eileen Barker's study of Unification Church recruiting techniques showed that, although many people accepted invitations to the church for several weeks, at the end of a year only 4% of those contacted became members. Similar work by others indicates equally high dropout rates from all new religious movements.

New Religions of Canadian Origin Although not usually recognized as a new religious movement, the Latter Rain Movement, which originated in North Battleford, Sask, in 1948, may be the most influential Canadian contribution to modern religion. Essentially a PENTECOSTAL revival movement, Latter Rain spread from a Foursquare Gospel church through evangelical Christianity worldwide. Many contemporary practices of CHARISMATIC Christianity, such as "singing in tongues," gained popularity as a result of this movement, which produced hundreds of new independent evangelical churches. Most have remained essentially orthodox, but some developed unusual beliefs and practices. Today, in Canada, the most prolific of new religions are continental in nature and not essentially Canadian. Evangelical groups which attempt to recreate biblical Christianity are the most common. These are usually orthodox and generally accepted by other Christians. But a significant minority adopt social and theological beliefs that place them on the fringe of orthodoxy. Others, such as the Local Church, the Way and the Children of God, have been rejected by other Christians and have become centres of controversy.

Probably considered the most notorious is the Children of God, or "the Love Family." The group originated with David Berg, a Pentecostal evangelist, as a California "Jesus people" group in 1968. Berg's movement arrived in 1971 in Vancouver, where it grew relatively rapidly. Berg changed his name to Moses David and claimed to receive "revelations" from God that included visions of the end of Western society. Eventually the group formed a series of colonies that went underground as a result of adverse publicity and the exposure of their allegedly perverse sexual practices. At its height the Children of God had around 8000 members. In 1983 it likely had under 2000 worldwide, with about 50 in Canada.

A fascinating precursor of the new religions may be found in the Aquarian Foundation, established in BC in the late 1920s by the infamous BROTHER TWELVE. Based largely on the teachings of THEOSOPHY, the group had a spectacular rise and equally dramatic decline; Brother Twelve's vicious exploitation of his disciples, and his debasement of the spiritual principles upon which the group was founded, led to the break-up of his colony in the early 1930s.

A uniquely Canadian movement is the Kabalarian Philosophy. Founded in Vancouver in 1930 by Alfred J. Parker (1897-1964), it blends Eastern and Western thinking, and teaches an understanding of mind and cycles based on mathematics. Its practices include vegetarian diets and physical exercises similar to those of yoga. Another important group in BC is the Emissaries of Divine Light, based at One Hundred Mile House. It encourages highly respectable forms of living and is essentially Eastern in orientation.

In Alberta there are several fundamentalist Mormon groups. These usually assert that the Utah Church of Jesus Christ of the Latter-day Saints has deviated from the true Mormon doctrine by rejecting the practice of polygamy. Like charismatic Christians they thrive on prophetic revelations and a literal interpretation of the Scriptures. Although not a new religion, an important movement that originated in Saskatchewan is Ex-Mormons for Jesus, an organization of fundamentalist Christians. They are similar to the Toronto-based Committee on Mind Abuse (COMA) and other anticult organizations across Canada. These groups are united by the belief that cults are bad and that action is needed to fight them. Bromley and Shupe in *The New Vigilantes* (1980) claim that in their social organization such movements are similar to the new religions (*see* MORMON CHURCH). In Québec the Apostles of Infinite Love began in the 1950s after its founder, a former Catholic priest, moved from France. He ordained a Québecois, Gaston Tremblay, as Pope Jean Grégoire XVII, and in spite of his 2-year sentence for forcible detention of 3 children, the group expanded to over 30 monasteries in Canada and the US.

The New Age Movement In the early 1980s various writers began discussing what they called "the new age movement." Foremost among these was Marilyn Ferguson whose book, *The Aquarian Conspiracy* (1980), became a best-seller. It was not until Jan 1987, however, that the concept of the new age really gained widespread popularity, as a result of the television miniseries *Out on a Limb*, which widely illustrated actress Shirley MacLaine's spiritual autobiography and quickly established her as the leading theologian of popular religion.

MacLaine and like-minded members of the new age movement do not belong to easily identified religious groups. Rather, they share common beliefs such as reincarnation, and they rely heavily on the insights of "trans-channellers" who are, in fact, a modernized form of spiritualist medium. The popularity of new age religion in the 1980s supports sociologist Reginald Bibby's view that the late 20th century will see a proliferation of individualized religions offering partial solutions to a variety of personal problems in a supermarket-type religious atmosphere.

I. HEXHAM, R.F. CURRIE, J.B. TOWNSEND

Spiritualism

Although formal spiritualism has existed for over 125 years, it should be considered within an examination of new religious movements because of a revival of interest in N America. Modern spiritualism developed in the 19th century within a spiritual and mystic resurgence based on such influences as earlier mysticism, Emanuel Swedenborg's writings, New Thought, Rosicrucianism and N American Indian SHAMANISM and spiritism. Andrew Jackson Davis and Phineas P. Quimby were especially important mid-19th-century influences. Through the work of 18th-century Austrian physician F.A. Mesmer, trance and clairvoyance had become familiar. In 1848 Margaretta and Kate Fox in Hydesville, NY, began to communicate with a spirit by rappings. Mediumistic circles soon spread throughout the US. The movement arrived in Canada by 1850 and quickly spread through the country; it was taken to Britain in 1852. The dissemination of the spiritualist system is simple: all that is required to begin a group is a person with mediumistic abilities.

There are 7 principles to which most Canadian spiritualists subscribe: the fatherhood of God (not a person but the creative universal spirit); the brotherhood of man; communication of spirits and ministry of angels; the continuous existence of the human soul; personal responsibility (including free will); compensation and retribution hereafter for all good and evil deeds done on Earth; and the eternal progress open to every human soul. There is no belief in an eternal hell — every soul can progress. Some spiritualists believe in reincarnation. These principles also imply that the living have both a physical and a spiritual body. Based on these principles are 2 propositions: the survival of the individual personality, or spirit, after death, and the concern of the spirit world for the living and the ability to communicate with the living. The objective of spiritualism is scientific verification of these 2 propositions rather than simple belief that they are true. This is accomplished, spiritualists believe, at each service by spirits' communications to the living through mediums or by spiritual/psychic healing. A particular group may emphasize messages or healing; healing seems to be more important in western Canada than in Ontario, but the result is the same: verification of survival after death.

Spiritualists believe that everyone has at least one spirit "guide," who is around to aid, protect and instruct, and that mediums have special abilities, in altered states of consciousness or trance, to communicate with their guides and move spiritually into an alternative reality where time and space do not exist as we know them. The medium may clairvoyantly be able to see glimpses of the future or the past. The guides allow other spirits to contact the medium who then acts as the agent through whom messages are passed from the spirit world to the living. Early spiritualism emphasized such physical "proofs" of spirit communication as table rappings by spirits, materialization of spirits, levitation and other phenomena presumably from the spirit world. Although these sometimes occur in modern séances, they are not an important element of the current movement.

Spiritual/psychic healing differs from faith healing in that faith healing occurs in churches, is performed by clergy, normally requires some faith on the part of the sick person, and frequently claims instantaneous cures. Spiritual/psychic healing is done by laity who are often affiliated with an organized spiritualist church, and is often done in a private home. It requires no faith on the part of the patient, and rarely produces instantaneous cures. Healing requires a series of treatments. Further, spiritualist/psychic healers insist that their patients continue traditional treatments with their doctors. Healing is thus an adjunct rather than an alternative to medical therapies.

A healer believes that spirits work through him or her to send "energy" to the patient. The healer is merely an "instrument" through which the spirit world acts. A treatment is usually accomplished in 10-15 minutes by the healer's entering a semitrance and either touching the patient's body or holding the hands about 2-4 cm from the body, directing the healing energies through the hands.

Believers often organize into churches loosely structured around a mediumistic or charismatic leader, but they remain individualist in belief. The 2 kinds of groupings are religious services, held in a church, and psychic development circles, usually held in a home. The church service is composed of hymn singing, a sermon, messages from the spirit world and healing. Organization is egalitarian, with many members taking part in the service as healers, speakers or mediums. The circles are groups of about 10 who meet regularly to communicate with the spirit world, to send healing energies to persons not present and to develop their psychic and mediumistic abilities. The use of Ouija boards and similar mechanisms to contact spirits is discouraged because it might possibly allow the "lower spirits" to come, and this would be harmful.

Many Canadian spiritualists attend "camps" in the US, where formal classes are held in healing, mediumship and aspects of the belief system, and a minister's or healing certificate may be obtained. Spiritualism is primarily an urban, middle-class phenomenon. Spiritualists are not marginal to society, but participate actively in community affairs; their activities are tolerated by society and generally ignored by traditional churches. Women are equal with men and often take a lead in a spiritual activity. Children are not deliberately drawn into membership: it is necessary to keep a balance between the mystical and the real world, a distinction that might be difficult for a young child. Visitors are warmly welcomed, but no pressure is exerted to join the organization or to accept particular beliefs. Some spiritualists estimate that there are 800-1000 spiritualists in Canada in the 1980s, but only about one-third are active. Although there have been a number of important spiritualists in Canada, the most prominent was PM Mackenzie KING. J.B. TOWNSEND

Reading: W.S. Bainbridge and R. Stark, "Church and Cult in Canada," *The Canadian Journal of Sociology* 7, 4 (1982); R. Bergeron, *Le Cortège des fous de Dieu* (1982); R.W. Bibby, "Religionless Christianity," *Social Indicators Research* 13, 1 (1983) and *Fragmented Gods* (1987); F. Bird and B. Reimer, "Participation Rates in New Religious Movements," *Journal for the Scientific Study of Religions* 21, 1 (1982); D.G. Bromley and A.D. Shupe, *Strange Gods* (1982); M.D. Bryant, ed, *Religious Liberty in Canada* (1979); R.S. Ellwood, Jr, *Religious and Spiritual Groups in Modern America* (1973); A. Hardy, *The Spiritual Nature of Man* (1971); D.G. Hill, *Study of Mind Development Groups, Sects and Cults in Ontario* (1980); Irving Hexham and Carla Poewe, *Understanding Cults and New Religions* (1986); W.R. Martin, *The Kingdom of Cults* (1965) and *The New Cults* (1980); G.K. Nelson, *Spiritualism and Society* (1969); J.T. Richardson, "People's Temple and Jonestown," *Journal for Scientific Study of Religion* 19, 3 (1980).

New Waterford, NS, Town, pop 8326 (1986c), 8805 (1981c), inc 1913, is located about 6 km NW of Glace Bay and 23 km NNE of Sydney in the industrial Cape Breton region. New Waterford is a coal-mining settlement fallen on difficult times. Formerly known as Barrachois, (from *barachois,* meaning sandbar, lagoon or pond), its present name is likely derived from the Irish seaport and shiretown of Waterford, from which many early settlers came. Coal mining in the vicinity began as early as 1854 at Lingan and later at Low Point in 1865. The giant Dominion Coal Co commenced operation at Barrachois in 1907; several other large mines opened before WWI. This expansion drew a largely Catholic but ethnically mixed society (Irish, Scottish, English and eastern Europeans) to the many company houses of this single-enterprise community. The miners have since faced many hardships, including the great CAPE BRETON STRIKES of the 1920s, but particularly the closure of the mines during the 1960s and 1970s. Some miners commute to Glace Bay, but others have turned to different occupations and seek limited work opportunities throughout industrial Cape Breton. L.D. McCANN

New Westminster, BC, City, inc 1860, pop 39 972 (1986c), 38 550 (1981c), is located on the N bank of the FRASER R, 20 km E of Vancouver. Surveyed by the Royal Engineers and named by Queen Victoria, "The Royal City" was established

in 1859 by Gov James DOUGLAS as the capital of BC. Few colonial era buildings survived a fire in 1898 but one, the Captain William Irving House (1862-64), is now the city's historic centre.

History New Westminster never displaced its great rival, Victoria, as the commercial metropolis of the Fraser R and Cariboo goldfields. Then, in 1867, the Legislative Council chose Victoria as the permanent capital of the recently united colonies of BC and Vancouver I. Although New Westminster secured a CPR branch line in 1886, the completion of the main line to Vancouver in 1887 further relegated it to secondary rank. Nevertheless the city remained an important freshwater port, a major lumber producer, a salmon-canning centre, a commercial centre for the Fraser Valley and an administrative and service headquarters with such institutions as the County Court, the BC Penitentiary, the Provincial Mental Hospital and the Royal Columbian Hospital. The city also secured rail links to the US via the Great Northern Ry and Fraser River Ry Bridge (1904); to the eastern Fraser Valley via the BC Electric Ry (1910); and to eastern Canada via the CNR (1915). Population growth has been uneven. Rising during the CPR boom from 1500 (1881) to 6678 (1891), the population remained steady until it doubled to 13 199 during the boom decade 1901-11. It then rose gradually to 42 835 in 1971 but has since declined. New Westminster has been known for such figures as John Robson, BC premier and founder of the *British Columbian* newspaper (1861-1983), and for the national success of its lacrosse teams. The city is home of the CANADIAN LACROSSE HALL OF FAME.

Economy Although the once-famous salmon-canning industry has gone, the forestry industry remains important, employing over 40% of the manufacturing work force in local mills producing lumber, shingles, plywood, and pulp and paper for local consumption and export. Nevertheless the number of industrial plants has declined in the past decade; much retailing has moved to suburban municipalities, and the Fraser R Harbour Commission has transferred most of the port activity to the river's S side and to Annacis Island. Increasingly, the city is becoming a residential centre marked by apartment buildings rather than single-family dwellings, a trend which may grow with the completion of the Automated Light Rapid Transit line to Vancouver and the proposed redevelopment of the waterfront for housing and commercial purposes. PATRICIA E. ROY

Pattullo Bridge, New Westminster, BC (*courtesy Elliott and Nicole Bernshaw/Bernshaw Photography*).

Newcastle, NB, Town, pop 5804 (1986c), 6280 (1981c), inc 1899, is located below the juncture of the NW and SW branches of the MIRAMICHI R. The shire town of Northumberland County 1786-1967, it was probably named for Thomas Pelham-Holles, duke of Newcastle and PM of England. Two Scots, William Davidson and John Cort, settled the area in 1765, drawn by the potential of the salmon fishery. They were followed

by some LOYALISTS and many Scottish and Irish immigrants. In 1825 a great fire devastated the Miramichi area and laid waste Newcastle and nearby Douglastown. Only 12 of Newcastle's 260 buildings escaped the flames. The fire put an end to the masting industry, but shipbuilding, the fisheries and lumbering became significant industries afterwards and the latter 2 are still important. Newcastle is a busy port, exporting wood pulp and wood products. The town's most famous "son" was Max AITKEN, later Lord Beaverbrook, who later became the province's greatest benefactor. WILLIAM R. MacKINNON

Newcastle, Ont, 1985, OMD, pop 34 073 (1986c), Regional Municipality of Durham, formed 1974 by amalgamation of the village of Newcastle, Bowmanville, Clarke and Darlington Townships and the Police Village of Orono. It is located on the north shore of Lake Ontario 80 km east of Toronto. The name Newcastle was granted by the post office in 1845 causing some confusion as another townsite to the east had adopted the same name. Initially the town was outstripped by nearby Bond Head, but in 1849 Daniel MASSEY bought out his partner F.R. Vaughan and moved his foundry to Newcastle. Eventually it would become one of the largest farm machinery manufacturers in the world. In 1851 Bond Head and Newcastle merged under the latter name: the other Newcastle became Port of Brighton. In the 19th century Newcastle was a major port for both lake freight and passenger traffic but railway competition and American tariffs ended this. Newcastle was also the site of one of the world's first fish hatcheries (est 1868). In the 20th century Newcastle is a tourism centre and serves as home for many residents who work in Oshawa or east Toronto. Besides members of the Massey family, other notables include Joseph Atkinson, eventually owner of the Toronto *Star* and founder of the Atkinson Charitable Foundation. GERALD STORTZ

Newcombe, Howard Borden, geneticist (b at Kentville, NS 19 Sept 1914). After studying at Acadia and McGill and wartime service in the Royal Navy, he worked with M. Demerc at Cold Spring Harbor Laboratory, NY. In 1947 he moved to the Chalk River Laboratory of ATOMIC ENERGY OF CANADA LTD. In 1949 he provided proof for the occurrence of spontaneous, undirected mutations in bacteria. This work eliminated the last vestiges of Lamarckism from biology and contributed greatly to the subsequent explosive development of molecular genetics. In 1957 he turned his attention to vital statistics and health records for analytical studies in demographic genetics. He pioneered computer-assisted "record linkage" techniques in epidemiology. He was a founder of the Genetics Soc of Canada and in 1963 was elected a fellow of the Royal Society of Canada. ROBERT H. HAYNES

Newfie Bullet An affectionate but ironic name informally applied to the transinsular Newfoundland passenger railway in its latter days. A narrow-gauge train, winding 900 km around lakes and mountains from St John's to Channel-Port aux Basques (track completed in 1898), the Newfie Bullet was not noted for its speed. In the late 1960s CNR replaced the subsidized passenger service with a bus service. ROBERT D. PITT

Newfoundland, the youngest of the Canadian provinces, joined Confederation at midnight on 31 Mar 1949. Some portion of the coast of this easternmost part of Canada was assuredly one of the first parts of the continent seen by Europeans. Tenth-century Viking explorers from Iceland and Greenland saw Labrador and settled briefly in the northern part of the Island of Newfoundland. In the late 15th century the GRAND BANKS SE of New-

Newfoundland

Capital: St John's
Motto: Quaerite Prime Regnum Dei ("Seek ye first the Kingdom of God")
Flower: Pitcher plant
Largest Cities: St. John's, Corner Brook
Population: 568 349 (1986c); rank ninth, 2.2% of Canada; 58.9% urban; 41.1% rural; 1.5 per km² density; 0.1% increase from 1981-86; 1.9% increase from 1976-86
Languages: English 98.6%; French 0.4%; Other 0.7%; 0.3% English plus one or more languages
Entered Confederation: 31 Mar 1949
Government: Provincial – Lieutenant-Governor, Executive council, House of Assembly of 52 members; federal – 6 senators, 7 members of the House of Commons
Area: 404 517 km², including 34 032 km² of inland water; 4.1% of Canada
Elevation: Highest point – Mount Caubvick, Torngat Mountains (1652 m); lowest point – sea level along coasts
Gross Domestic Product: $5.470 billion (1986)
Farm Cash Receipts: $45.2 million (1986)
Value of Fish Landings: $163 million (1986); $215 million (1987e)
Electric Power Produced: 41 387 GWh (1985)
Sales Tax: 12% (1987)

foundland were known to Basque, French and Portuguese fishermen. Since the time of King Henry VII of England, who on 10 Aug 1497 awarded John CABOT £10 for finding "the new isle," the Island has been referred to as Terra Nova, but more commonly in the English-speaking world as Newfoundland. The French call it Terre-Neuve; the Spanish and Portuguese still call it Terra Nova. The LABRADOR part of the province may have received its name from the Portuguese designation, "Terra del Lavradors." CAPE SPEAR, near St John's, is the easternmost point of the province and thus, excepting Greenland, of N America. From Cape Spear across the Atlantic to the nearest point in Ireland it is nearly 3000 km. Winnipeg, in mid-Canada and Miami in the southeastern US are farther away – 3100 km and 3400 km, respectively. The southern coast of the province lies astride lat 47° N, but Cape Chidley on the northernmost tip of Labrador is just N of 60° N, giving the province a total north-south extent of just over 1800 km. The land and freshwater area is 404 517 km², of which 292 218 km² are in Labrador and 112 299 km² are on the Island. Newfoundland is the seventh-largest Canadian province. Neighbouring NS, NB and PEI are smaller, and even their combined area is less than that of Newfoundland, which is slightly larger than Japan.

Land and Resources

The province is physically divided into 2 major units of unequal area, the much larger unit being the mainland territory of Labrador to the N and the smaller unit the Island of Newfoundland to the S. Within each there are distinct variations in the physical characteristics of the environment and in the occurrence and availability of natural resources and corresponding variations in the nature and pattern of human settlement.

Distinctive subregions within each major unit can be outlined. In Labrador there are 3 such regions: a northern coastal region, ruggedly mountainous, deeply fjorded and growing only ground-level subarctic vegetation, with very little settlement; a southern coastal region with a rugged, barren foreshore and a forested hinter-

land, with light to moderate settlement; and the bulk of the vast interior, which comprises a well-forested, dissected plateau, where settlement is concentrated in a few large towns.

On the Island of Newfoundland there are 4 distinct regions, the W coast, the interior, the NE coast and the S coast. The W coast is dominated by the table-topped Long Range Mts, which rise to 722 m. They are bordered in places by a narrow, well-forested coastal plain and are frequently penetrated by glacially deepened valleys and by several large, fjordlike bays, the largest of which are the Bay of Islands and Bonne Bay. There is almost continuous settlement in the bays and coves along this coast and there is some interior settlement in the Codroy Valley to the south and around Deer Lk, which lies on a small plain within the mountain range. The interior is a plateaulike region with frequent undulations in the terrain representing the ridges and slopes of the watersheds carved out by the major stream systems; 4 large rivers, EXPLOITS, GANDER, HUMBER and Terra Nova, drain most of the area. The region supports extensive forest stands, particularly on the gentle slopes of the major watersheds. Settlements are widely separated and most of the population is concentrated in a few large towns associated with forest or mineral-resource use and with transportation services. The NE coast, with its numerous bays, islands and headlands, fronts on the Atlantic Ocean from the Great Northern Peninsula to the AVALON PENINSULA. Inland sections of this region are generally well forested, but exposed headlands and offshore islands have low, scrubby vegetation. The region has a shoreline typical of land that was submerged by glaciation and in places rebounded after the ice caps melted. Thus, there are innumerable bays, coves, islands and fjords, which often provide excellent harbours. It is also an area that can annually expect to be blocked by arctic drift ice throughout the winter and early spring. Settlement has developed along the shores of most of the bays and on some offshore islands. The S coast region coincides with the whole southern portion of the Island of Newfoundland. This coast also has the deeply embayed characteristics of a submerged shore-

line. It is not blocked by arctic drift ice, although in some years parts of the eastern Avalon Peninsula as far S as St John's may be cut off for a few days. In inland areas the topography is generally hilly and rugged and much land is covered by shallow bogs and heathy vegetation. On the gentle slopes of the major river systems and in the interior of the Avalon Peninsula there is good forest vegetation.

Geology Labrador occupies the easternmost section of the Canadian SHIELD and comprises mostly tough, ancient Precambrian igneous and metamorphic rocks. There are some areas of softer sedimentary rocks, notably in the W in a formation called the Labrador Trough – within which lie some of the most extensive iron-ore deposits in N America. The interior region is plateaulike, on average about 450 m above sea level and greatly dissected by large, E-flowing rivers, such as the CHURCHILL R and its tributaries, which cut through the eastern rim of the saucer-shaped Shield to discharge into the Labrador Sea. This rim is largely mountainous, especially in the N, where the TORNGAT MOUNTAINS rise to over 1500 m. The highest peak is Mount Caubvick at 1652 m.

The Island of Newfoundland is part of the Appalachian system and displays in its major bays, peninsulas, river systems and mountain ranges the typical SW to NE alignment. Rocks are more varied on the Island than in Labrador. Continental drifting, followed by frequent periods of crustal deformation and interspersed by long periods of erosion and deposition, have combined to produce this great variety in types and ages. The oldest rocks are Precambrian and occur in the E, in and around the Avalon and Burin peninsulas; they are mostly folded sedimentary rocks, but in a few areas later intrusions have solidified into volcanic rocks. Small remnants of gently sloping Cambrian and Ordovician sedimentary rocks occur in pockets along the coast. The most significant are in Conception Bay, where the Ordovician rocks that form BELL I contain layers of hematite iron ore with estimated reserves of billions of tonnes. The central and western portions of the Island are underlaid by a great variety of Paleozoic rocks of sedimentary, igneous and metamorphic origin, within which crustal deformation has been generally severe. Long periods of

Mountain stream in the Torngat Mts of Labrador (*photo by John Foster/Masterfile*).

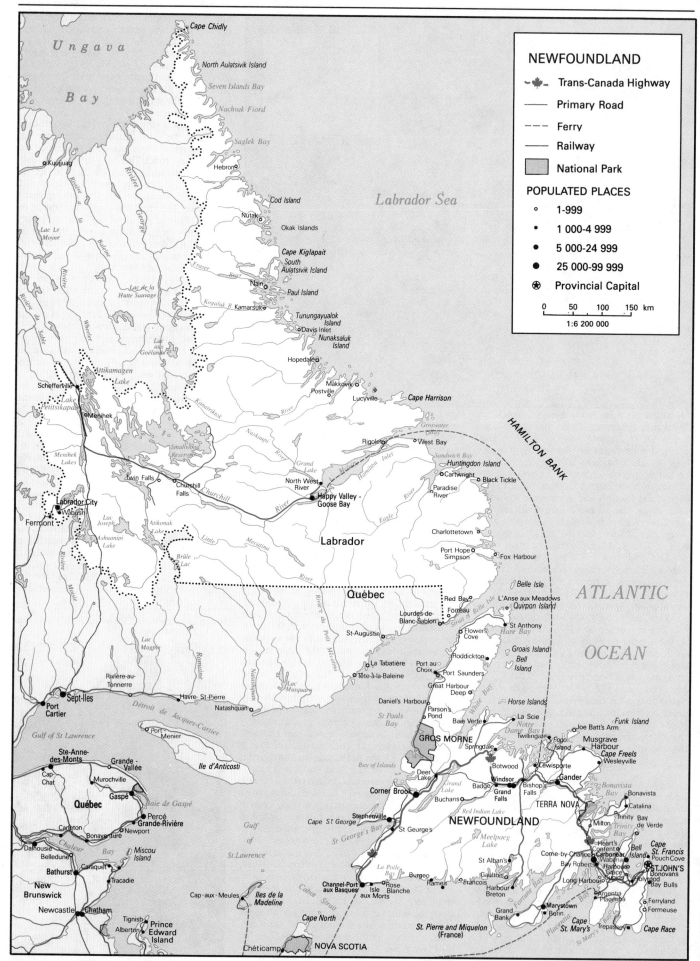

François, an outport on Newfoundland's southern coast (*photo by John deVisser*).

erosion following periods of uplift have left a polycyclical landscape with the remnants of old erosion surfaces displayed in the plateaulike interior and on the flat-topped mountains of the Long Range. There is a mineralized belt in these Paleozoic rocks, stretching from an area on the S coast just E of CHANNEL-PORT AUX BASQUES to the general area of western Notre Dame Bay on the NE coast, within which occur ores containing copper, lead, zinc, gold and silver. Through the years many deposits have been mined or quarried on a small scale and for brief periods. Around Buchans to the W of Red Indian Lk, significant deposits of ore have supported a large mining operation since 1928, and a large asbestos quarry has operated near Baie Verte on the NE coast since 1963. Significant deposits of gold have recently been found in several areas with the Hope Brook mine near Cinq Cerf opening in 1987. The youngest and least-disturbed rocks of this Paleozoic series lie in and around the coastal plain on the W coast. These are Mississippian and Pennsylvanian and contain much limestone and gypsum, both of which are quarried. There are a few coal deposits and signs of petroleum, but nothing of commercial value has been discovered. Parallel to the E coast of the Island, under the ocean, extensive deposits of Cretaceous rock appear to stretch the length of the Grand Banks. Drilling from offshore rigs has proved the presence of enormous reserves of petroleum and natural gas in this area. Development will depend on the economic and technical feasibility of operations under adverse weather and iceberg conditions.

Surface All areas of the province show the effects of continental GLACIATION during the Pleistocene era, whose last stages are now dated to 7000 years ago. Moving ice sheets scoured and sculpted the surface. Most of the unconsolidated parent material beneath present-day soils consists of glacial debris or marine sediments, the latter now exposed owing to postglacial uplift. The interior regions of both Labrador and the Island are strewn with lakes and covered with moraines, and give evidence of an immense ice cap, which initially moved radially outward from a centre W of Labrador, but in the later periods of the Pleistocene broke down into smaller, separate ice caps

with centres in Labrador, the W-central Island and the Avalon Peninsula. Most coastal regions are fjorded where the ice channeled down the valleys of the preglacial fluvial system. The longest and most steep-sided FJORDS occur in northern Labrador and around the Great Northern Peninsula of the Island, but there are few places where this scouring effect from ice movement is absent. Most bays have been deepened and are often fjordlike in character. Many places in the N of the Island and in Labrador show, because of postglacial uplift, raised shorelines and large stretches of marine sediments. The most striking and extensive marine deposits are those in the remnants of raised deltas that occur around St George's Bay and around Happy Valley-Goose Bay in Labrador at the mouth of the Churchill R. Coastal features, such as offshore islands, spits, tombolos and bay-mouth bars (*barachoix*), which are typical of a submerged shoreline, are common throughout the S and SE coastal regions.

Soils are generally coarse and immature. In northern Labrador and in high places throughout the province, because of coolness and exposure, vegetation is either entirely lacking or is only of the subarctic, lichen tundra ground-level variety. In the interior regions where surface deposits are deep, such as on the watersheds of the Churchill, Exploits, Humber and Gander rivers, there are excellent forest stands. Extensive bogland has developed in the many hollows of this glaciated landscape. The forest is made up of several of the species common to the boreal forest that stretches across northern N America. Black spruce predominates, especially in open stands and where forest has regenerated after fire. Close forest is most common and here black spruce and balsam fir are dominant, the ratio varying with the site type; balsam fir regenerates more successfully in places that have been clear-cut. Subdominants are represented by larch, pine and such typical boreal deciduous species as paper birch, aspen, alder, pin cherry and mountain ash. Many of the nonforested areas support ground-level, mossy plants, some of which are food for wildlife, and some, such as the blueberry, partridge berry and bakeapple ("cloudberry"), which can be gathered for human consumption.

Water Through scouring and deposits, glaciation left a pockmarked landscape capable of storing vast quantities of water in thousands of lakes, ponds and bogs. Many of the ponds are shallow, but many of the lakes are large, old valleys deepened by glacial scouring and dammed by glacial deposits. In interior Labrador hundreds of lakes have been combined by means of canals, dikes and dams, to create a 5698 km² reservoir (roughly one-third the size of Lk Ontario) behind the huge hydro development of CHURCHILL FALLS. Because of the moist climate and plentiful snowfall, the water table is high in all areas, usually lakes are full and rivers flow perennially. There is naturally some seasonal fluctuation and occasionally very wet or dry years, but there are rarely shortages of water for domestic or industrial use.

Climate varies considerably throughout the province. Interior Labrador has a continental climate, but the southeastern areas around the Burin and Avalon peninsulas are marine. The transitional variation makes it difficult to designate specific climatic regions, but certain generalizations can be made. The climate of northern Labrador is truly subarctic in that there is generally coolness and dryness throughout the year. Winters are very cold with mean temperatures averaging -20°C, and summers are cool, July mean temperatures averaging 5-10°C. These temperatures are recorded at sea level, and the high land in the Torngat Mts would be even colder. Precipitation is low, annually averaging only 46 cm at

Cape Chidley, of which 50% falls as snow. The winters of interior Labrador are extremely cold, with mean temperatures for Jan of between -18°C and -23°C; summers are warm, with mean temperatures for July of between 13°C and 17°C. The lowest temperature for the province was recorded in western Labrador at -51°C and the highest at Goose Bay at 38°C. In coastal areas the modifying influence of the ocean reduces the temperature range between summer and winter. In southern Labrador coastal regions are cold in winter and cool in summer, and interior regions are often severely cold in winter but warm in summer. On the Island there is a similar though not so marked difference between coastal and inland regions. The mean Jan temperature at St John's is -4°C, while the July mean is 15°C. Inland, for most locations, the midwinter mean is between -6°C and -10°C, and the midsummer mean is 13° to 16°C.

Precipitation varies in a NW to SE direction. Average annual precipitation around the Avalon and Burin peninsulas is over 140 cm, and the amount decreases northwestward to amounts around 40-60 cm in Labrador. Precipitation is fairly even every month, but in northern locations about half falls as snow, and in the milder SE snowfall is only about 12%. In any one year great variations may be experienced, depending largely on the paths taken by the storms that cross N America from W to E. When the path is northerly, mild winters with little snow result, but when southerly, there may be a severe, cold and snowy winter. Frequent storms mean frequent windy weather and high average velocities. Coastal waters are often hazardous for small craft. The mixing of the air masses off the Labrador Current and the Gulf Stream frequently creates fogs on the Grand Banks and in eastern and southern coastal areas, particularly in spring and early summer.

Resources and Conservation The economy of Newfoundland is heavily dependent on natural resources. After its discovery around 1497, the Island depended on cod fishing for nearly 400 years, until the forest and mineral resources began to be exploited.

Forests The variation in climate and in the nature of the terrain dictates a similar variation in the nature of vegetation and growth rates. Generally the well-drained lowlands have the best forest growth, and there are sufficient timber stands to constitute an important resource. Initially the forests were used for building, fencing, fuel and boatbuilding and for shore structures related to the fishery, which made a small dent in the forest resource near coastal settlements. Since the turn of the 20th century, the increased value of lumber and pulpwood has led to penetration and exploitation of the interior. Much timber has been cut and regrowth is generally good although loss through FOREST FIRES and insect infestation has been at times severe.

Minerals Minerals of economic interest occur in many areas. Those in the mineralized belt of the Island (mostly the base metals, copper, lead and zinc) are mined at Buchans, Daniel's Harbour and near Baie Verte, when market conditions permit. Elsewhere, iron ore from hematite is mined in western Labrador, asbestos is quarried at Baie Verte, gypsum near St George's, pyrophyllite (aluminum silicate) near Foxtrap, Conception Bay South, and limestone near Corner Brook. Other mineral deposits, which have been or may be mined, include fluorspar at St Lawrence, iron ore on Bell Island, gold, copper, barite, uranium and limestone in various places, and the important offshore oil and gas reserves.

Fishery Perhaps the greatest and most permanent resource is the fish population of the waters surrounding the province. Groundfish, such as cod, grey sole, flounder, redfish and turbot, are plentiful on the banks and at times in all inshore areas. Surface-dwelling fish, such as caplin, squid, herring and mackerel, thrive in some areas, and migrating salmon are caught both at sea and in the larger rivers. Trout are plentiful in lakes, ponds and rivers and lobster and crabs in the shallow southern waters.

Hydroelectricity Large natural reservoirs on the Labrador plateau and interior Island have presented opportunities for the large-scale development of HYDROELECTRICITY. In Labrador, 5225 MW have been developed at Churchill Falls and there is a potential for a further 2000-3000 MW, mostly on the lower Churchill R. On the Island about 1255 MW have been developed and a further potential remains untapped.

Conservation Since most of the interior of the province is relatively uninhabited, there is ample space and a suitable habitat for wildlife, some species of which constitute an important resource. There is a greater variety in Labrador than on the Island. Among large game are several species of caribou, moose, black bear and, in northern coastal areas, polar bear. There are many small, fur-bearing animals; the most important are beaver, fox, lynx, rabbit, otter and muskrat. Some are trapped for the value of their pelts or for food and some are hunted annually by licensed sportsmen. In many coastal areas colonies of millions of seabirds nest annually, primarily gulls, gannets, murres, kittiwakes and puffins. Sanctuaries to protect these birds have been declared at Gannet I off the Labrador coast, on FUNK ISLAND and Gull I off the E coast of the Avalon Peninsula and at Cape St Mary's on the S coast. GROS MORNE NATIONAL PARK preserves a spectacular natural region on the W coast and TERRA NOVA NATIONAL PARK on the E coast. There are also 76 provincial parks, a wilderness area in the central Avalon Peninsula and another in the south-central interior.

People

A small percentage of the population is aboriginal. The Island's only indigenous people, the BEOTHUK, are now extinct. There are a few thousand INUIT and N American Indians (MONTAGNAIS-NASKAPI) living mostly in Labrador and maintaining their original languages and some of their ancient cultures. MICMAC, living mainly on the Island's S coast, in the Conne R area, are engaged in LAND CLAIM disputes with the provincial government. Elsewhere the population is of European origin, the majority descended from immigrants from SW England and S Ireland. On the W coast of the Island there are pockets of people of French descent (mostly ACADIAN) and some SCOTS whose ancestors were from Cape Breton, NS. Religious affiliation closely follows ethnic

Premiers of Newfoundland 1949-87

	Party	Term
Joseph R. Smallwood	Liberal	1949-72
Frank D. Moores	Conservative	1972-79
A. Brian Peckford	Conservative	1979-

St John's, the capital and largest city of Newfoundland, named for the presumed date of discovery on the Feast of St John the Baptist in June 1497 (*photo by Bill Brooks/ Masterfile*).

origin. Most of those of IRISH and French descent are Roman Catholic and those of English origin are Anglican, United Church, Pentecostal, Salvation Army or Seventh-Day Adventists.

Settlement by Europeans proceeded slowly and reflected the dominance of the fisheries. Early settlers paid little attention to the soil or lack of amenities and settled on the shoreline in bays and coves close to the inshore and offshore fishing grounds, primarily on the E coast. Settlement gradually spread and became permanent. The first centres developed around St John's and Conception Bay, then generally along the E and S coasts.

Fish were caught in summer, cured with salt, sun dried and shipped back to Europe in the fall. Inevitably centres of trade and commerce evolved, such as St John's, Harbour Grace, Trinity and Bonavista, and economic ties with the mother country were gradually relinquished. The livelihood of the population depended almost entirely on the vicissitudes of the fishery. New arrivals were few and out-migration to more promising N American areas was constant. The number of settlers grew slowly from about 12 000 in 1763 to about 200 000 in 1891.

In the late 19th and early 20th centuries some diversification in the economy created greater stability. Iron-ore mines were opened on Bell Island in Conception Bay in 1894 and pulp and paper manufacture was started at Grand Falls in 1910. In 1925 a second pulp and paper mill was built in CORNER BROOK on the W coast, and in 1928 the mining of base metals was initiated at Buchans. A transinsular railway, begun in 1881 with several spur lines, contributed to the gradual improvement in economic conditions, and in 1935 the population numbered approximately 290 000. The Great Depression of the early 1930s was keenly felt, but ironically WWII brought an unprecedented prosperity, mainly because of employment provided by the construction and maintenance of large defence bases at St John's, Gander, Goose Bay, Stephenville and Argentia. There was only limited postwar prosperity, and by a referendum the people voted to join the Canadian Confederation in 1949. Benefits in the form of generous welfare payments, pensions and numerous other allowances, as well as the postwar marketing boom, kept the economy buoyant throughout the 1950s. The transition to provincial status was not painless, but most Newfound-

landers, especially the young, are proud to be part of Canada. Over 60% of the 568 349 residents of the province in 1986 were born after the entry into Confederation.

The distribution of people changed markedly over the century since the 1880s. When the cod fishery was the only important occupation, nearly all settlement was coastal. Most villages were small and the few large towns owed their size to their role as centres of trade and commerce. As other resources were developed, the mining towns, such as Wabana and Buchans, and pulp and paper towns, such as Corner Brook and Grand Falls, emerged. In the 1950s the centres of Labrador City and Wabush grew rapidly with the development of the iron-ore mines in western Labrador. Incidental to this diversification in the economy a pattern of centralization evolved. Opportunity in the fishery became limited because of the shifting emphasis from numerous small-boat operators to offshore trawlers and the switch from sun-cured, salted fish to fresh-frozen fish in modern plants. A subsequent population movement resulted in the demise of many of the small "outports" and the growth in the size and importance of centres with facilities for fish processing and with access to provincial transportation and communications networks.

In 1986, 59% of the population lived in incorporated towns. About 10% of the LABOUR FORCE was engaged in primary occupations (fishing, mining, logging and farming). About 13% was engaged in manufacturing and processing, each largely associated with the fishery, pulp and paper, and mining industries. The majority are in professional, clerical and other service-related occupations.

Economy

Once wholly dependent upon the fishery, the economy now includes mining and mineral processing, manufacture based on forest resources and the provision of services and government in centres of trade, commerce, transportation and communication. Transfer payments to areas of regional disparity and other federal government benefits are of paramount importance. The province is generously endowed with natural resources and given a favourable economic climate and clever management could prosper on its own merit. Periodically, development of each resource in turn has proved beneficial to both primary and secondary producers. It is anticipated that the development of offshore oil and natural gas will positively influence the province's economy, but true prosperity will occur only when all resources are developed concurrently and successfully (*see* REGIONAL ECONOMICS).

Gross Domestic Product - Newfoundland 1986 at Factor Cost ($Millions)	
Agriculture	24.9
Forestry	57.4
Fishing	133.9
Mining	478.1
Manufacturing	503.6
Construction	446.3
Utilities	288.2
Total	1932.4
Transportation and Communication	535.5
Wholesale and Retail Trade	573.8
Finance, Insurance and Real Estate	478.1
Community, Business and Personal Service	1198.5
Public Administration and Defence	752.3
Total	3538.1

Agriculture Agriculture has been of very minor importance in Newfoundland because of the poor soil and adverse climate. Less than 0.01% of the land in the province is farmed – about half of it being confined to the northern Avalon Peninsula. Nevertheless, there are scattered pockets of fertile land and conditions are suitable for the growth of hay and pasture crops. Root crops such as potatoes, turnips and cabbage are produced in significant quantities, and in some places livestock, particularly cattle and sheep, are raised on natural pastures. Swine and poultry production is important, as is dairy farming around St John's and Corner Brook. The province is almost self-sufficient in egg production.

There are about 4876 ha of land in crops and 3821 ha in pasture (1986 census). 1986 yields show harvests of potatoes totalling 3.3 million kg on 500 ha, turnips totalling 3.26 million kg on 162 ha and cabbage totalling 2.3 million kg on 109 ha. Beets, carrots, lettuce, savory, strawberries, chard, broccoli and brussels sprouts are grown in small quantities in small market gardens. Over 1 million kg of wild blueberries are packed for export annually. There are roughly 4400 head of dairy cattle, producing 17 000 kL of milk, 1000 head of beef cattle and 1500 calves. About 16 500 pigs are raised and slaughtered annually. There are about 3400 head of sheep, just over 400 000 layer chickens, producing 8.5 million dozens of eggs, and nearly 5 million broilers. Other than blueberries, all agricultural production is consumed locally and over 80% of the meat, fruit and vegetables are imported. Studies have shown that the mineral and organic soils (bogs) could provide all the food needed by the present population (except the major grains and tropical and subtropical fruits), but whether such an achievement would be economically feasible has not yet been established.

Industry The most significant industrial activities based on local raw materials are the numerous processing plants for fresh-frozen and salted codfish, the pulp and paper mills, and the particle-board mill at Donovans, near St John's. Industries using local materials, but on a much smaller scale, are small boatbuilding yards, lumber mills, door and window construction, the canning of seafood and wild berries, and some homecraft industries producing souvenirs.

Large manufacturing concerns using imported materials are the phosphorus plant at Long Harbour on the Isthmus of Avalon, the steel-shipbuilding plant at Marystown, the paint-manufacturing plant at St John's and numerous small plants producing staples such as bread, biscuits, margarine, ice cream, soft drinks, beer and other items, whose reputations give them a competitive advantage over imports. The tourist industry is small but has great potential. The province offers unique scenery and excellent parks, motels, hotels and historic sites, which survive mainly through local use aided by provincial and federal funds. Remoteness from the mainland and the increasing cost of travel has made progress slow.

Mining In recent years Newfoundland has mined, on average, about 20 million t of ore valued in 1986 at $764 million, down from $869 million in 1985 and employing around 3200 people. Over 90% of the exported mineral product is from the twin communities of Wabush and Labrador City in western Labrador. Here, IRON ORE is quarried and concentrated (being low grade with about 20-30% iron content). Some ore is pelletized to provide a finished product that is carried S by rail to Sept-Îles, Qué, and thence through the Great Lakes-St Lawrence Waterway to smelters and steel mills around the Great Lakes. Poor markets for iron ore in the early 1980s curtailed production and jobs were lost. The copper-lead-zinc mine at Buchans, operating since 1928, has little ore and few employees remain; at its peak it produced over 50 000 t of concentrate annually, with an average value of $35 million. An asbestos mine at Baie Verte on the NE coast has a fluctuating output, annually producing between 13 000 t and 89 000 t. Other mining operations are small. A new gold mine opened at Cinq Cerf in 1987. There is a pyrophyllite quarry at Foxtrap, Conception Bay S, that employs a few dozen people. Otherwise activity is sporadic and confined to the quarrying of limestone for cement near Corner Brook, and gypsum for plasterboard at Flat Bay near St George's. The iron mines at Wabana on Bell I closed in 1966 for lack of markets for that type of ore, although there are billions of tonnes in reserve. The fluorspar mine at St Lawrence on the foot of the Burin Peninsula closed in 1978. Efforts to redevelop the property began in 1983 and production again resumed in 1987. The demand for brick for local building supports a small brickmaking industry at Milton, on Trinity Bay, where there are deposits of suitable clay and shale.

Forestry The principal use of the forest is for the production of newsprint. The mills at Corner Brook, Stephenville and Grand Falls together use an average just short of 2 million m³ (68% of the provincial forest output), which has had a value in recent years of just over $300 million when converted to newsprint. The market for newsprint is highly competitive, and the periodic shutdown of plants or the reduction of staff for weeks and even months has been commonplace. In 1986 about 6000 people were employed in logging, wood manufacturing, sawmills, and the pulp and paper industry. Use of modern machinery means fewer jobs for loggers. Wood is delivered to the mills more often by road and rail than by the spring drive on streams and major rivers. In recent years there has been serious loss of good wood because of insect infestation, particularly by the spruce budworm. For the present there is an overabundance of wood, but the infestation has alerted foresters to the need for better harvesting techniques and they now have a planned program of reforestation. In addition to newsprint, a significant portion of the forest product is taken for fuel (20%), lumber, poles, fencing and mining timber. There are few large sawmills but many small ones. Total annual production has declined from over 100 000 m³ in 1980 to around 75 000 m³ in 1984; this supplies about one-half of the provincial requirements.

Fisheries Before 1930 the fishing industry concentrated on the production and sale of salted and sun-cured COD. The main markets were Mediterranean and Caribbean countries. The advent of quick-freezing and of boats capable of transporting the frozen product to market radically changed the industry. Year by year the percentage of salted cod produced and sold declined, whereas the percentage of fresh-frozen fish species such as cod, turbot, plaice and redfish increased, and the principal market shifted to the US. The fishing industry has changed constantly from that time, partly in response to innovations and the modernization of fishing techniques, but also as a result of market variations, competition and the fluctuations of supply and demand. Today, fish companies are found on all coasts, relying on the catches of their own large, deep-sea trawlers, which bring a variety of fish from the banks, and on the small catches of the still numerous inshore fishermen. The latter use gill nets, cod traps and baited lines and operate from medium-sized boats (long-liners) or from small trap boats or even dories. Since they operate near the shore and have limited range, their catch fluctuates. A few still prepare sun-cured salt cod, for which there is a good market, but most dried salt cod is now produced mechanically by large plants. Changes in the fishery since 1930 have meant more employment on shore in the processing plants and fewer men to secure the catch. Communities with large plants have grown markedly in size and importance although, as mainly one-industry towns, their future is insecure. In many settlements along the coast fishermen augment their income seasonally by catching lobster, salmon, caplin, herring, mackerel, squid, eels, scallops and crab totalling up to 100 000 t and with a landed value of nearly $50 million. In recent years a ready market has emerged for species or fish roe that previously were ignored; E European, Portuguese and Japanese ships annually purchase large quantities of squid, caplin and roe. Despite the emergence of new export markets, the US continues to be the largest market for Newfoundland fish, accounting for 18% of the province's total exports of all products in 1986. On average, 500 000 metric t of fish, with a landed value of around $200 million, are taken annually by the 13 000 full-time and another 13 000 part-time fishermen. The total processed value is now over $700 million, owing mainly to the increases in the price of cod. The offshore catch by trawlers usually amounts to two-fifths of the total and is made up mainly of cod, plaice and grey sole, redfish, turbot and herring. The inshore catch is two-thirds cod.

In 1984 many of the fishing companies faced receivership because of heavy debts incurred during a period of poor markets, overproduction and overexpansion. An agreement was reached between the 2 levels of government and the banks whereby a new supercompany, Fisheries Products International Ltd, was formed through the amalgamation of all the former large companies. The success of the restructured fishery has in 1985 resulted in the return of FPI to the private sector (*see* FISHERIES HISTORY).

Finance The province is served by all the major Canadian banking houses, trust companies, insurance brokers and loan companies. Most regional head offices are in St John's, but there are branches in all the larger towns in all regions. There are 14 credit unions, 19 consumer co-operatives, 19 housing co-ops and 13 producer co-ops. The CO-OPERATIVE MOVEMENT has had its ups and downs.

Some fishermen's producer co-ops are very successful and a few consumer co-operative enterprises in large centres have profitable supermarket outlets. Private enterprise is encouraged, especially in resource-oriented areas, and government loans and grants are commonly used in small-business enterprises, such as fishing, sawmilling, farming and small-boat building.

Transportation In the early years of settlement all transportation was by boat or, in the N in winter, by dog team. The establishment of railways, roads and airports brought changes. The transinsular railway from St John's to Channel-Port aux Basques was started in the 1880s and quickly developed branch lines to Argentia in Placentia Bay, Bay de Verde in Conception Bay, Trepassey in the southern Avalon, and Bonavista. Branches were later built to Lewisporte on Bay of Exploits and to Stephenville. The line now operated by CN is narrow gauge and primitive, but it provided an essential service and fostered development across the Island throughout the first half of the 20th century. It was especially valuable to northern communities that were icebound for much of the winter. The railway is declining in importance and now carries mostly freight, and nearly all branch lines are closed or plan to close. There were also a number of small private or company-owned railways, such as the Grand Falls Central. The ultramodern Labrador and Québec North Shore Railway (LQNS) transports ore from Ungava and western Labrador, running from Schefferville, Qué, through Labrador, to Sept-Îles, Qué, on the Gulf of St Lawrence, with an important branch line to Wabush and Labrador City.

Highway development was rudimentary up to 1949. Roads were local, narrow and generally unpaved. A continual road-building and -improving program since the 1950s has provided an Island-wide road network, which is mostly paved and includes the TRANS-CANADA HIGHWAY from St John's to Channel-Port aux Basques. Few communities are isolated. A few important offshore islands have ferry service. Several important offshore islands, eg, Random, Twillingate and Greenspond, are now linked by causeways. In Labrador there is only a short road link between the communities on the Strait of Belle Isle and an interior road from Goose Bay westward through Churchill Falls to the LQNS Railway. The Newfoundland section of another road, linking Wabush and Labrador City with the Québec highway system, to give the majority of the Labrador population year-round land access to the rest of Canada, has been completed.

BUSH FLYING has been important in Newfoundland since the 1920s, and some isolated areas still rely on ski- or float-equipped small aircraft or helicopter service for mail and emergencies. The number of landing strips increases annually and many areas can now rely on regular service. There are large airports at St John's, Gander, Deer Lk, Stephenville, Goose Bay and Labrador City; national and regional airlines provide regular scheduled service to and from these points.

The strategic location of Newfoundland made it a logical point for the initial attempts to cross the Atlantic by air. The first successful flight was that made by Alcock and Brown 14-15 June 1919 from St John's to Clifton, Ireland, in a 2-motor biplane. There were many subsequent crossings from Newfoundland in the 1920s and 1930s, culminating with the ferrying of thousands of bombers from Gander to England during WWII (*see* FERRY COMMAND); there was also flying-boat service from Botwood, and regular transatlantic air service via Gander in the prejet era.

Steamship Service Steamship service supplies Labrador coastal communities throughout the summer. There is also some coastal trade by sea around the Island, restricted in winter to the S coast because of arctic drift ice. Ferry service between Channel-Port aux Basques and N Sydney, Cape Breton I, operates daily year-round; and there is a CN Marine ferry service between N Sydney, NS, and Argentia three days a week, June-Sept. Mineral products, processed fish and newsprint are exported mostly in the summer

from centres near the plants such as Corner Brook, Botwood and Long Harbour, and from larger towns with fish plants. Most imported products arrive by ship through Channel-Port aux Basques, Corner Brook, St John's and Goose Bay, and are distributed throughout the province by rail and road. In the far N, SNOWMOBILES have largely replaced dog teams in providing transport for hunters and trappers.

Energy Energy resources in the form of hydropower are abundant, especially in Labrador. The province uses only a fraction of its potential energy. On the Island all industrial and domestic needs are currently met by 1255 MW provided by hydro sources and 550 MW from thermal sources. Some projects to help alleviate the high cost of power on the Island include using wood waste and peat in industrial and institutional furnaces. Most of the huge amount of power generated at CHURCHILL FALLS in Labrador is exported to Québec. The resale of this power by HYDRO-QUÉBEC at enormous profits has always irked the Newfoundland government. An attempt to circumvent the contract with Hydro-Québec by enacting legislation authorizing withdrawal of water rights was declared illegal by the Supreme Court of Canada in May 1984.

Government and Politics

The provincial legislature of Newfoundland (officially called the House of Assembly) has 52 members elected from single-member districts. As in other provinces it is modelled on the British parliamentary system. The formal head of government and representative of the Crown is the LIEUTENANT-GOVERNOR who is appointed by the prime minister for a period of at least 4 years. The statutory life of the House of Assembly cannot exceed 5 years. The PREMIER and actual head of government is usually the leader of the political party holding the majority of seats in the legislature. The CABINET, comprising the ministers of all government departments, is chosen by the premier from his caucus. Areas of provincial and federal jurisdiction are specified in the CONSTITUTION ACT, 1867. The provincial judicial system includes the Newfoundland Supreme Court, 7 district courts and 18 provincial courts. The Supreme Court is divided into a Trial Division with a chief justice and 6 associate justices, an Appeals Division with a chief justice and 8 associate justices. There is also a Unified Family Court where cases are heard by a single justice. All these justices are federal appointees. The Supreme Court Trial Division sits in St John's but goes on circuit to areas with no local courts. Each of the 7 district courts is located in one of the 7 federal electoral districts and is federally administered. The 18 provincially funded and administered courts are located in major communities throughout the province.

Local Government Local government in Newfoundland bears little resemblance to that found elsewhere in Canada. The pattern of isolated coastal settlement precluded the establishment of a county or township system and generally retarded the initiation of local government. St John's, the first municipality, was incorporated as a town in 1888 and received its city charter in 1921. Local government came much later to other large centres. It was not until the post-WWII period that incorporation became common, in fact until 1938 St John's was the only incorporated place in Nfld. Many communities have chosen to remain free from local taxes, building codes and other regulations and forgo the benefits of incorporation, such as road repair, garbage collection and street lighting. At present, out of over 800 communities, less than half have any form of local government. There are 2 cities, ST

JOHN'S and CORNER BROOK, one metropolitan area surrounding St John's, 168 towns, 140 communities and 110 local service districts (LSDs), the latter 2 usually representing groups of communities. Town and community councils have limited taxing authority and can provide few local services. Major works are often mainly financed by the provincial Department of Municipal Affairs, and the provincial government funds health, education, police, highway maintenance and other services.

Federal Representation The TERMS OF UNION under which Newfoundland entered Confederation in 1949 stipulated that the province would be represented federally by 6 members of Parliament (later increased to 7) and 6 senators. Traditionally, at least one Newfoundland MP is appointed to the Cabinet. Several have made a mark in the high-profile portfolios of finance and external affairs, but in general the small representation gives the province limited clout in national decision making.

Public Finance Newfoundlanders endure the highest provincial tax rates in Canada. The 1987 budget estimated that almost one-third of the province's revenue would come from retail sales tax, which is 12%, and from personal income tax. Despite this high taxation rate, the government still receives about half its revenue from federal transfer payments and equalization grants. For 1987 this amounted to over $1.1 billion. Education and health, at 23.2% and 21.9% respectively, are the areas of greatest expenditure. Provincial debt charges account for over 18%.

Health In the 1987-88 fiscal year the provincial government budgeted over $500 million for health care – one-fifth of total expenditures. Under the Medical Care Act of 1969, most health-care services are free to residents of the province. The foundations of the health-care system lie in the cottage hospital system and the International Grenfell Association facilities. The cottage hospital system, initiated by the Commission Government in 1936, was designed to bring a high standard of health care to outport residents. Small hospitals were constructed in central locations around the Island, but their number has been reduced in favour of larger regional hospitals. The International Grenfell Association, founded by Sir Wilfred GRENFELL in the early 1900s and centered in St Anthony, has provided essential health-care services to inhabitants of the northern areas, particularly coastal Labrador. The General Hospital in St John's is the largest and best-equipped hospital; it is part of the Health Science Centre on the Memorial U campus, which also includes a Faculty of Medicine and a school of nursing.

Politics Newfoundland's colourful political history began in 1832, with the granting of representative government. A governor and council, appointed by the British government, held most of the power. A House of Assembly was elected by the people by open ballot. Legislation had to pass both chambers. This unworkable form of government was replaced, by popular demand in 1855, with RESPONSIBLE GOVERNMENT based on the British parliamentary system. In 1934, following the onset of the Great Depression and while saddled with crushing debts, the "Dominion" reverted to crown colony status and was governed by a commission consisting of a British governor and 3 commissioners and 3 Newfoundlanders, all appointed by the British government. From 1832 to 1933 no enduring political party with a strongly defined political ideology emerged. The "Liberal," "Conservative" or "People's" parties were in fact loose coalitions of individual politicians and special-interest groups. Religion, ethnicity and social status were strong factors in early politics.

For example, the Catholic "Liberal" Party in the mid-1800s was dedicated to advancing the interests of Newfoundland's Irish community. Parties also coalesced around issues such as Confederation with Canada, the building of a railway and fishermen's interests versus those of the fish merchants. The campaign for Confederation that culminated successfully in 1949 was led by Joseph R. SMALLWOOD, a journalist, radio broadcaster and businessman. In 2 general referenda, Newfoundlanders voted by a narrow margin to join Canada. A lieutenant-governor was appointed and Smallwood was asked to form an interim government. In the new province's first general election and the first election since 1932 Smallwood's Liberals took 22 seats, the Conservatives 5 and an Independent 1. The split represented not only the outports versus St John's but the confederates against the anticonfederates.

Present-day elections show that this old hostility is all but dead. Smallwood's Liberals dominated Newfoundland's politics throughout the 1950s and 1960s. Weakened by conflicts between the premier and some powerful Cabinet ministers and by adverse reactions in the press, the Liberals lost the election of 1972. The Progressive Conservative Party took office, led by Frank MOORES until 1979, when the leadership passed to Brian PECKFORD, the former minister of mines and energy in the Moores administration. In 1982 Peckford led his party to a landslide victory, winning 44 of the legislature's 52 seats. The remaining 8 seats were held by Liberals. In 1985 Peckford won a reduced majority, obtaining 36 seats to the Liberals' 15; the first NDP was elected in Newfoundland history. In the early 1980s relations between the Newfoundland government and the federal government were strained because of disputes over the ownership of offshore resources, over the sale of hydropower in Labrador and over the restructuring of the N Atlantic fishing industry. A change in government in Ottawa produced considerably better relations between Newfoundland and the federal government. By late 1987, when some provinces were uncertain about free trade with the US, Peckford came out in strong support of the Mulroney government's initiatives in that direction.

Education

History The first Newfoundland schools were organized by the Church of England's missionary Society for the Propagation of the Gospel in Foreign Parts (SPG), which funded a school in Bonavista in the 1720s. Later in the 18th century the SPG operated schools in St John's and in several of the larger outports. They were apparently open to children of all denominations. A variety of schools were organized in the early 19th century, the most significant being those operated by the Newfoundland School Society. Established in 1823 with a special concern for educating Newfoundland's poor, by the early 1840s this society had nondenominational schools in many towns and outports. The 1836 Education Act represented the first direct government involvement with education; funds were distributed among the societies promoting education and nondenominational boards of education were established. By 1843 the education grant had more than doubled and was divided between Roman Catholic and Protestant school boards. The Protestant grant eventually was distributed among several Protestant denominations. Post-Confederation amalgamation occurred among several Protestant school systems, but government-funded, church-administered education survives today. The denominational education system was protected in the Terms of Union (1948).

Map of Newfoundland (1775) based mainly upon the surveys of Captain James Cook during the 1760s (*courtesy National Archives of Canada/NMC-52301*).

Administration Excepting a few small private institutions, Newfoundland's 607 schools are administered by regional denominational school boards. Representatives of each denomination and of the provincial Department of Education make up a Council of Education, responsible for many overall policy decisions. In 1986-87 the education budget was $410 million. In 1986 there were 8050 teachers serving 139 900 students in grades from kindergarten to grade 12.

Institutions MEMORIAL UNIVERSITY OF NEWFOUNDLAND, founded in 1925 as Memorial University College, was made the province's only university by a special Act of the House of Assembly (1949). Located on the northern outskirts of St John's, Memorial had 9714 full-time and 4092 part-time students in 1985-86. Sir Wilfred Grenfell College, a 2-year college located at the Corner Brook campus of Memorial, was established in 1975. In many of its larger centres Newfoundland has post-secondary vocational schools, including the College of Fisheries, Navigation, Marine Engineering and Electronics, and the College of Trades and Technology, both in St John's, and the Bay St George Community College on the W coast.

Cultural Life

The ancestors of most Newfoundlanders came from SE Ireland or SW England and brought with them distinct and enduring cultures. This heritage, shaped by centuries of Newfoundland's isolated, maritime way of life, has produced a vibrant, distinctive culture, expressed in dialects, crafts, traditions, cooking, art, music and writing. Old World influences have generally been replaced by those of the New World, a gradual pro-

cess accelerated by Confederation and more recently through mass communications, but much of the province's distinctiveness persists. Newfoundlanders are increasingly appreciative of their unique heritage, as shown by the many successful folk festivals and heritage societies. The various levels of government have supported efforts to preserve and enhance Newfoundland's historic culture. The provincial government, primarily through its Department of Culture, Recreation and Youth, supports a provincial museum and the provincial archives in St John's, as well as smaller museums elsewhere in the province and a network of arts and culture centres in major centres. Memorial U, through its art gallery, its extension service and the work of various faculties, has served the province well.

Arts Without neglecting universal concerns and techniques, many Newfoundland artists practise distinctive Newfoundland art forms and use local themes. Poets such as E.J. PRATT, painters such as David BLACKWOOD and Christopher and Mary PRATT, theatre groups such as the Mummers Troupe (*see* MUMMING), novelists such as Percy Janes and journalists such as Ray Guy have drawn inspiration from their Newfoundland homes. Writers and musicians traditionally had to go outside the province for quality production and publishing; several local companies now provide these artists with excellent facilities.

Communications The first newspaper published in Newfoundland was the weekly St John's *Royal Gazette* (1807). By the 1830s several weekly and biweekly newspapers were established in St John's and in the major outports. They were highly politicized, reflecting and perhaps aggravating the political, religious and social tensions that periodically upset 19th-century Newfoundland. Among Newfoundland's first daily newspapers were the *Daily Ledger* (est 1859), the *Morning Chronicle* (est 1861), the *St. John's Free Press and*

Town and harbour of St John's, 1831, aquatint by William Eager (*courtesy National Archives of Canada C/41605*).

Daily Advertiser (est 1877) and the St John's *Evening Telegram* (est 1879). In 1987 the province had 3 daily newspapers, the *Evening Telegram* and the Corner Brook *Western Star*, both part of the Thomson newspaper chain, and the locally owned St John's *Daily News*. Fourteen weekly regional newspapers, all English language, are also published. Newfoundland's first public radio stations began operation in St John's in the 1920s. By the 1930s radio stations were broadcasting throughout the Island. In Apr 1949 the CBC began its Newfoundland operation and initiated FM broadcasting in 1975. The province's first TV station, CJON, was opened in 1955; originally a CBC affiliate, it became associated with the national CTV network in 1964 after the CBC opened its own St John's TV studios. Cable TV on the Island dates from 1977, although it is still unavailable outside major centres. Poor reception and limited program choice are continuing sources of frustration to the residents of more isolated areas.

Historic Sites Federal assistance is generous in the establishment and maintenance of historic sites. Newfoundland's rich, colourful history is honoured in several national historic parks, including SIGNAL HILL overlooking St John's harbour, site of one of the last French-English battles in N America; Castle Hill, near Placentia, commemorating the French fishing and military presence in Newfoundland; Cape Spear, site of one of Canada's oldest surviving lighthouses and the most easterly point in N America; PORT AUX CHOIX, site of ancient Maritime Archaic and Indian cultures; and L'ANSE AUX MEADOWS, the sole confirmed Viking site in N America, which was declared a UNESCO WORLD HERITAGE SITE in 1978. The Basque Whaling Archaeological site at RED BAY in Labrador is the only fully preserved Basque whaling vessel from the 16th century.

History

People have lived in the area covered by the modern province since at least 7000 BC. Archaeological research suggests that the Maritime Archaic people were present from at least that time. There is much evidence of INUIT presence before the European occupation, especially in northern areas, and of N American Indians both on the Island and in Labrador. The Island Indians, the Beothuk, were periodically encountered by European settlers. The best known were 2 women, Mary March (DEMASDUIT) and SHAWNANDITHIT, who were captured in 1819 and brought to St John's. They soon died, presumably of European diseases. Very little is known about Beothuk society and even less about Beothuk history.

Exploration At the end of the 10th century, NORSE, including LEIF ERICSSON, made several voyages of exploration from Greenland to overseas lands to the W and SW, and established a temporary settlement at L'Anse aux Meadows on the Great Northern Peninsula of the Island. In 1497

John Cabot, a Venetian navigator, sailed on a voyage of discovery for Henry VII of England and discovered new lands, which are believed to have been between NS and Labrador and included a "new isle." In 1500 the Portuguese explorer Gaspar CORTE-REAL made a more thorough exploration and named several bays and capes along the E coast of the Island. In 1535-36 Jacques CARTIER demonstrated that Newfoundland was an island by sailing through Cabot Strait as well as the Strait of Belle Isle. In the 15th and 16th centuries, Basque, Portuguese, Spanish, French and English fished the waters around Newfoundland and Labrador. The English brought the fish home or sold it to Spain, Portugal or France. The French fished mainly in northern areas. Some Spanish ships were engaged in whaling from ports in southern Labrador, and traces of their shore operations and wrecks of their ships are now being researched.

Settlement In 1583 Sir Humphrey GILBERT, with a charter from Elizabeth I of England to start a colony in N America, despite finding St John's harbour filled with ships from Spain and Portugal, claimed the adjacent territory for England. Following this declaration, apparently accepted by all except the French, the waters around Nfld came under the control of the merchants from SW England, who are often referred to as the West Country Merchants or the Merchant Adventurers. They dominated trade in the area by demanding and receiving virtually exclusive rights to the prolific offshore fishing grounds. They periodically succeeded in persuading British monarchs and parliaments to enact laws that would discourage and even forbid permanent settlement in Newfoundland; however, colonies were begun on the Avalon Peninsula throughout the early 1600s by several Englishmen with direct royal permission. John GUY established settlers at Cupids (then called Cupers Cove) in Conception Bay in 1610 and later Sir William VAUGHAN, Lord Falkland, Sir George CALVERT (Lord Baltimore) and Sir David KIRKE made similar attempts, particularly at FERRYLAND on the E coast. Their efforts were frustrated by the W Country Merchants, the French (who had granted the Island to the Compagnie des Cents-Associés in 1627) and the lack of protection against the prevalent PIRACY. In 1634, under Charles I, the First Western Charter decreed that the captain of the first British vessel arriving in a Newfoundland harbour each spring would be admiral and governor of the harbour for that season. In effect he had dictatorial powers, and in the interest of his sponsoring W Country Merchants he often took harsh measures to discourage settlement. House burning, lashings and even hangings were common. In 1699 William III gave permission for additional settlement and limited some of the powers of the fishing admirals, but improvement was slight and those who dared to winter over risked losing all their possessions and even their lives. In the 17th century the French, who were already well established on the mainland, claimed Newfoundland and set up a colony at Placentia on the S of the Avalon Peninsula in the 1660s. Under Pierre Le Moyne d'IBERVILLE, they destroyed most of the settlements on the E coast of the Island and claimed St John's. Under the Treaty of UTRECHT, 1713, the French lost all the territory they had gained on the Island, but retained exclusive fishing rights on the N shore from Cape Bonavista to Point Riche.

The lot of the determined settlers improved a little during the 18th century. In 1729, because of complaints against the fishing admirals, the first naval governor, Capt Henry Osborne, was appointed to take charge during the summer fishing season. He established 6 districts with 17 justices of the peace and 13 constables and to some degree

counteracted the power of the W Country Merchants. Settlers still suffered; the Irish were particularly badly treated and one governor tried to ship them all back home. Following continued complaints to the British Crown, a civil court was established in 1791 for one year with John Reeves as magistrate. In 1792 a supreme court of criminal judicature was created with John Reeves acting as chief justice, ending the rule of the admirals and of the naval governors' courts.

During the SEVEN YEARS' WAR, 1756-63, the French reclaimed many settlements, including St John's, but British forces under Alexander Colville and William Amherst recaptured the area. By the Treaty of PARIS, 1763, Britain regained most of the territory taken by France, but the fishing rights on the FRENCH SHORE were confirmed and France was awarded the islands of SAINT-PIERRE AND MIQUELON. During the latter part of the 18th century, Britain was at war not only with France, but also with the American colonists and with Spain and Holland. Immigration to Newfoundland was still not encouraged, but ironically, because of a prosperous trade in fish and the need for fishermen, settlement proceeded virtually unhindered; by 1827 the population was over 60 000.

Development Once a significant permanent population was established, petitions for better government and local representation increased. Dr William Carson and Patrick Morris, through a campaign of pamphlets and petitions to Britain, succeeded in having representative government established in 1832, with the objective to obtain RESPONSIBLE GOVERNMENT and full colonial status which was finally achieved in 1855. Settlement proliferated throughout the 19th century. The salt-cod fishery was the principal occupation and the mainstay of the economy, and there was some logging, mining and agriculture. In the late 1800s the transinsular railway began to open up the interior, and goods and services became accessible to many parts formerly isolated in winter. Representatives of the various Newfoundland governments attended the CONFEDERATION conferences, but they chose not to join, despite substantial support of the movement.

When the French fishing rights were revoked in 1904, the northern and western coasts were available for settlement. Until about 1925 the economy was based on the primary industries – fishing, mining, and pulp and paper – but debts incurred through building railways and supporting a regiment in WWI, coupled with the Great Depression after 1929, produced bankruptcy and government collapse. Newfoundland was forced to beg Britain for assistance and eventually reassumed colonial status under a COMMISSION OF GOVERNMENT. The economy recovered remarkably towards the end of the 1930s, mainly because of increasing demand for products of the sea, mines and forests, and because of increased activity in defence-based construction in anticipation of WWII. During the war many young people joined the armed forces overseas, and at home there was full employment. The US, Canada and Britain established several army bases, 2 large naval bases and 5 airports in Newfoundland. Gander was the largest and most important airport because of its role in the transatlantic Ferry Command. When the Commission Government was dissolved in 1949 it had cleared all debts and left a surplus of over $40 million. After WWII a national convention was elected to debate the question of Newfoundland's future and to make recommendations. It was decided to hold a referendum through which the people would make a choice between the Commission Government, Confederation with Canada, or a return to responsible government and Dominion status. The referendum proved inconclusive except that Newfoundlanders were unwilling to retain the Commission Government. A second referendum with the options of Confederation or Dominion was then held. An intensive campaign ensued between the confederates, led by Joseph R. Smallwood, and the anticonfederates, which the confederates won by a narrow margin, 52% to 48%. Canada accepted Newfoundland at midnight on 31 March 1949 and Smallwood became premier of the first provincial government.

The next 2 decades witnessed dramatic and substantial changes in the economy and in the life-style of Newfoundlanders. The fishing industry was revolutionized as dozens of fresh-fish processing plants were established on all coasts and as they gradually all but replaced the old method of the family-run enterprise of catching, salting and sun-curing cod for sale to Caribbean and Mediterranean areas. Draggers operating offshore on the Banks, and smaller boats in the nearshore and inshore waters, could now catch a variety of species for delivery to the plants, where the fish were quick frozen for new markets, chiefly in the US. The number of fishermen declined greatly and opportunity for shore work in the plants increased. The pulp and paper mills at Corner Brook and Grand Falls substantially increased production, and mines at Buchans, St Lawrence and Wabana worked to capacity. New industries were launched with government backing and although most failed – including the huge oil refinery at Come by Chance, a steel mill, a rubber-goods plant, a leather-products plant and a knitting mill – a few succeeded, notably the plasterboard mill and cement plant at Corner Brook, the particle-board mill near St John's and the phosphorus plant at Long Harbour, Placentia Bay. The huge iron-ore mines of western Labrador came into production in the 1950s. Since WWII many people have moved from small communities to large towns and growth centres. As chances for local employment have diminished, young people have left at an annual rate of about 5000. With opportunities accessible through cheap transportation by land, air and sea, they have moved on, most to central or western Canada. The population that was 289 588 in 1935 had risen to 568 349 in 1986, but growth has slowed and there is evidence of a levelling off.

The impact of the economic recession of the late 1970s and early 1980s was keenly felt in Newfoundland, although there was no comparison with the desperate conditions of the Great Depression in the early 1930s. Unemployment insurance, old-age pensions, social assistance and other benefits of the welfare state ensured decent living and health standards. High unemployment has most severely affected the young; it is hoped that intensified vocational and technical training programs will prepare the new generation for the anticipated resurgence in the economy with offshore oil development. The Hibernia field, described as huge and possibly larger than the North Sea deposits, is still being tested; when it is developed, many small industries and servicing enterprises could profit. Decisions of the Supreme Courts of Newfoundland and of Canada in 1983 and 1984 declared that ownership of offshore resources (specifically the Hibernia oil field) was federal. On 11 Feb 1985 an agreement was signed between the Newfoundland government and the new federal Conservative administration, giving Ottawa and St John's "joint say over offshore oil and gas management" and allowing "the province to tax the resources as if they were on land." Exports remain of vital importance to the economy: by 1987-88, for example, some 80% of the province's fish went to the US. The reliance on exports may have been a key factor in the premier's strong support for the federal government's free trade initiatives with the US.
W.F. SUMMERS

Reading: D. Alexander, "Newfoundland's Traditional Economy and Development to 1934," *Acadiensis* (Spring 1976); J.K. Hiller and P. Neary, eds, *Newfoundland in the Nineteenth and Twentieth Centuries* (1980); H. Horwood, *Newfoundland* (1969); H. Ingstad, *Westward to Vinland* (1969); J. Mannion, ed, *The Peopling of Newfoundland* (1977); S.J.R. Noel, *Politics in Newfoundland* (1970); F.W. Rowe, *Education and Culture in Newfoundland* (1976) and *A History of Newfoundland and Labrador* (1980); J.R. Smallwood, ed, *Encyclopedia of Newfoundland and Labrador*, vols I & II (1981) and *The Book of Newfoundland*, vols I-VI (1967); W.F. Summers and M.E. Summers, *Geography of Newfoundland* (1965); J.A. Tuck, *Aboriginal Inhabitants of Newfoundland's Great Northern Peninsula* (nd) and *Newfoundland and Labrador Prehistory* (1976).

Newfoundland Acts In 1699 the first legislation regarding NEWFOUNDLAND was passed in the British Parliament. Formally An Act to Encourage the Trade to Newfoundland, it is better known in Newfoundland as King William's Act or The Newfoundland Act. Like previous ORDERS-IN-COUNCIL, the Act was more concerned about visiting fishermen than settlers. Despite population increases during the 18th century, settlers continued to be governed by FISHING ADMIRALS (captains of West Country ships) and justices of the peace or magistrates, all under the jurisdiction of the naval convoy commodores who spent the summers supervising the fishery.

Between 1756 and 1800, European wars slowed settlement in Newfoundland and lessened the demand for some measure of self-government. The following 3 decades saw rapid growth and a vociferous demand, headed by William CARSON and Patrick MORRIS, for REPRESENTATIVE GOVERNMENT. This was aided by the British reform movement: it was not mere coincidence that the bill giving Newfoundland representative government was introduced into the British Parliament on the day that the Reform Bill received royal assent, 7 June 1832.

Representative government, consisting of an elected assembly and an appointed council, proved to be unworkable and was modified by the Aug 1842 Newfoundland Act, which integrated council with the assembly. In 1847 a new Act in effect revived the council and made it an upper house. But nothing short of RESPONSIBLE GOVERNMENT, as established in Nova Scotia and Canada in 1848, would satisfy the people. Following disputes between local factions and between Newfoundland and Britain, responsible government was awarded in 1855. It remained until Nov 1933 when, facing bankruptcy, Newfoundland asked Britain to suspend its constitution. The 1933 Newfoundland Act made this possible. In 1949 Newfoundland became a province and again enjoyed the privileges and responsibilities of democratic government.
F.W. ROWE

Newfoundland Bill The people of NEWFOUNDLAND rejected CONFEDERATION in 1867, choosing to remain a British colony until 1948, when a majority of voters indicated their willingness to join Canada. The 2 governments negotiated the Terms of Union, which, following a request from the Canadian Parliament, were incorporated by the British Parliament into the BRITISH NORTH AMERICA ACT, thus becoming part of the Canadian Constitution. Newfoundland (including LABRADOR) became a province on 31 Mar 1949.
F.W. ROWE

Newfoundland Loggers' Strike began 31 Dec 1958 when hundreds of loggers employed by Anglo-Newfoundland Development Co at Grand Falls struck for wage increases and for improvements in living conditions at wood camps. The AND Co was determined not to settle with the loggers' union, the International Woodworkers of America. The IWA and its charismatic leader, H. Landon Ladd, had been invited to Newfoundland in 1956 by loggers who wanted it to replace the weak and ineffective Newfoundland Loggers' Association. The company, the NLA executive and Newfoundland's media fought the IWA's raid on the NLA membership, portraying its organizers as violent radicals. The IWA counterattacked in full-page newspaper ads and radio broadcasts. Newfoundland public opinion gradually went against the IWA while most loggers voted to have it as their union. For 6 weeks the strike was a normal labour dispute, but public opposition to the IWA reached such a pitch that on 12 Feb 1959 Prem Joseph SMALLWOOD intervened. He declared he would drive the IWA out of Newfoundland and had the legislature pass a law stripping the IWA of its legal bargaining rights. The CANADIAN LABOUR CONGRESS, the International Labour Organization and much of the Canadian media community condemned Smallwood for "his attempt to destroy free trade unionism." But in Newfoundland public support for the legislation grew when on Mar 10 a policeman was killed in a confrontation with picketers. Smallwood replaced the IWA with the government-sponsored Newfoundland Brotherhood of Wood Workers. The loggers quickly signed a contract with AND almost identical to the one proposed by the IWA, thus ending the strike. Two years later, Smallwood turned the NBWW over to the United Brotherhood of Carpenters and Joiners. The CLC suspended the UBCJ for its collusion with Smallwood, but the suspension was ineffective. Against the will of the loggers, the UBCJ became their official bargaining agent. Smallwood and the paper companies had successfully driven the IWA from Newfoundland.
BILL GILLESPIE

Newfoundland Resettlement Program From the time that Newfoundland was first settled, people have moved in search of good fishing grounds, land sites or new employment. When fishing grounds became crowded or, in more recent times, as the inshore fishery declined, people left their former homes in search of better opportunities in other Newfoundland settlements or in Canada and the US, greatly reducing the populations of some communities and leaving others completely abandoned.

Although between 1946 and 1954 an estimated 49 communities were abandoned without government assistance, in 1953 the Newfoundland Dept of Welfare began a centralized program in response to a perceived need to assist and accelerate the process. The program offered small amounts of financial relocation assistance to each household in communities where health, educational and other facilities were lacking or inadequate and where every household had agreed to move. This scheme, which moved 110 communities, marked the beginning of government-assisted resettlement in Newfoundland and Labrador.

The Newfoundland Resettlement Program, which succeeded the Centralization Program, was a joint federal-provincial operation. From 1967 to 1975, it provided money to people in about 150 communities and also increased the amount available for assistance from $400 to $1000 or more depending on household size, and decreased the proportion of assenting households required from 100% to 75%. A federal-provincial resettlement committee approved the move of each household to designated "growth centres," 77 of Newfoundland's larger communities ostensibly selected because they offered more social and economic opportunities.

The resettlement program, now abandoned, is generally viewed as a failure. Despite the superior social services of growth centres, especially in education, many new industries failed and resettled workers were displaced from their traditional livelihoods in the fishery. Social dislocation and alienation arose from poor social and economic integration within new communities. With the rebuilding of the inshore fishery, some fishermen and their families, particularly in Placentia Bay, have returned without government assistance to resume their livelihood seasonally or year-round in formerly resettled communities. Reunions are often held in these and other abandoned places to mark the passing of a way of life. ROBERT D. PITT

Newlove, John, poet, editor (b at Regina 13 June 1938). Newlove is noted for his "direct and visually precise" style, in which most of the traditional signs of poetry – simile and metaphor, overt symbolism, rhyme and heightened language – seldom appear, yet which is intensely rhythmic, full of punning turns and wry modulations of tone. He has unsentimentally explored the existential roots of contemporary despair, yet alongside his evocations of loss, self-hatred and self-pity, envy and anger, his poems offer moments of compassion, ecstasy and, occasionally, even pure joy. Overemphasis on the fear and loathing in his poems ignores the rich wit, irony and humour, the affirmations to be found in the scrupulous honesty of his bare-bones poetic. In the early 1960s, Newlove left the Prairies for Vancouver where he read and studied his craft. Within a few years, his poetry of drifters in contemporary space and historical time had gained him a reputation as a major chronicler of loss and alienation. From poems concerned with personal history in *Moving in Alone* (1965), he moved to poems about Canadian history, of where "we are in truth, whose land this is and is to be," notably in the encounter with native culture in *Black Night Window* (1968), and then to poems on human history, especially the history of war and cruelty in *Lies* (1972), which won the Gov Gen's Award. He moved to Toronto in the late 1960s to work as an editor. In the 1970s, he became a free-lance editor and writer-in-residence at various institutions across the country. *The Fat Man: Selected Poems* appeared in 1977 and a long philosophical poem, *The Green Plain*, in 1981. In 1986 he published his first collection of new poems since *Lies*. *The Night the Dog Smiled* (1986) confirms his profound talent while expanding the range and generosity of his vision. DOUGLAS BARBOUR

Newman, Leonard Harold, geneticist (b at Merrickville, Ont 31 Aug 1881; d at Ottawa 16 Jan 1978). From 1905 to 1923 Newman was secretary of the government-sponsored Canadian Seed Growers' Association, founded by J.W. ROBERTSON to improve agriculture by encouraging farmers to breed better strains of crop plants. He took advanced training in genetics in Sweden and succeeded Charles SAUNDERS as Dominion Cerealist in 1923. Newman's duties included licensing cereal varieties for growing in Canada and he regularly attended fall fairs to talk to farmers and explain official policies. Able to identify almost any variety of wheat he might be shown, he enjoyed challenging farmers to stump him. In 1948 he retired to the family farm settled by his grandfather, one of Colonel BY's officers, on the Rideau R and became an enthusiastic local historian.
DONALD J.C. PHILLIPSON

Newman, Peter Charles, journalist, author, newspaper and magazine editor (b at Vienna, Austria 10 May 1929). Originally named Peta Karel Neuman by his secularized Jewish parents, he came to Canada as a refugee in 1940. Envisaging a business career for his son, Newman's father enrolled him in 1944 as a "war guest" boarder at

Upper Canada College where he met members of the Canadian establishment whose lives he would later document. Once he mastered English, Newman began writing, first for the University of Toronto newspaper, then for the FINANCIAL POST in 1951. By 1953 he was Montréal editor of the *Post*, a position he held for 3 years before returning to Toronto to be assistant editor, then Ottawa columnist, at MACLEAN'S. In Ottawa, Newman produced his masterly popular political chronicle of John DIEFENBAKER, *Renegade in Power: The Diefenbaker Years* (1963). Five years later, he published a similar, but less successful, study of Lester PEARSON, *The Distemper of Our Times* (1968).

The following year he became editor-in-chief at the Toronto *Star* (later publishing some of his best journalism in *Home Country: People, Places and Power Politics*, 1973) and changed his focus from politicians to members of the Canadian business establishment. In *Flame of Power* (1959), he assembled 11 profiles of the first generation of Canada's business magnates; next he explored the lives of those who currently wielded financial power in popular studies such as his 2-volume *The Canadian Establishment* (1975, 1981), *The Bronfman Dynasty* (1978) and *The Establishment Man: A Portrait of Power* (1982). His books have sold a perhaps unprecedented 1 million copies in Canada and he has had a profound effect on political reporting and business journalism, making them more personalized and evocative. He was editor of *Maclean's* where for a decade (1971-82) he worked to transform the magazine from a monthly to a weekly with a Canadian slant on international and national events. In 1982 he resigned to work on a 3-volume history of the Hudson's Bay Co. Two volumes have been published (*Company of Adventurers*, 1985, and *Caesars of the Wilderness*, 1987). A fourth book, to accompany the volumes, is to contain the maps, charts and diagrams. ELSPETH CAMERON

Newmarket, Ont, Town, pop 34 923 (1986c), 29 753 (1981c), inc 1880, located on the Holland R with easy access to the Don and Humber rivers, 25 km N of Metro Toronto. It was a natural site for a "new market" to serve surrounding settlements as well as fur traders and Indians bound for Toronto. The informal name stuck, and the town is still a market for the produce of Holland Marsh. Lt-Gov John Graves SIMCOE invited the Society of Friends (QUAKERS) to settle the area. Led by Timothy Rogers they arrived in 1801. Their meeting house (*c*1810) on Yonge St, now a historic site, was the first religious building erected by settlers N of York. The families of Elisha Beman and Christopher Robinson (father of John Beverley ROBINSON) dominated early settlement. (The spot was called Beman's Corners originally.) W.L. MACKENZIE had strong support in the region, and Samuel LOUNT was one of its Reform martyrs. Tanning and office furniture were once important manufacturing concerns. Newmarket is a regional centre and residential community, the seat of the York regional government and home of Pickering College, a Quaker foundation for boys. Robert SIMPSON and a partner opened his first store in the village. K.L. MORRISON

News Agencies Canadian newspapers and broadcast stations depend heavily on news agencies for a regular supply of news from outside their immediate geographical area. One-third to one-half of news and editorial content comes from news agencies, also called wire services or press associations. Material has traditionally been delivered to newspapers by leased teletype circuits. Some equipment for this transmission has the capability of producing punched tapes which can be fed directly into automatic typesetters. Larger newspapers now receive agency copy

more quickly through direct computer-to-computer linkups. Broadcasters can receive both print and voice reports.

Most dailies and broadcasters obtain the report of the CANADIAN PRESS (CP). United Press International, a US-based private company, maintains a small subscriber list and staff in Canada. The major domestic broadcast agencies are Broadcast News, a CP subsidiary, Standard Broadcast News, and CKO Newsradio. TV networks use international agencies such as Visnews. Supplemental services offer alternative news reports and a wide array of interpretive and background material. Widely circulated are Southam News Service and the services of large US newspapers such as the *New York Times, Washington Post* and *Los Angeles Times.* The Associated Press (US), Reuters (British) and Agence France-Presse connect with the CP through exchange agreements. PETER JOHANSEN

Newspapers Canada's first newspaper, John Bushell's *Halifax Gazette*, began publication in 1752. Like most colonial newspapers in N America, it was an adjunct of a commercial printing operation. Moreover, it was dependent on the printing and patronage largesse of the colonial government. This reliance on revenues from sources other than readers – from governments, political parties and ADVERTISING – would remain a characteristic of Canadian newspapers.

There were no newspapers in New France, in part because of the opposition of French officialdom to the establishment of printing presses in the colony. The British Conquest, and the termination of the SEVEN YEARS' WAR in 1763, brought a trickle of printers from the American colonies. In 1764, 2 Philadelphia printers, William Brown and Thomas Gilmore, began the bilingual *Quebec Gazette* at Québec City. In 1785 Fleury Mesplet, a French printer who had been jailed because of his attempts to persuade Québec to join the American Revolution, started publication of the *Montréal Gazette*. In 1793, under the auspices of Upper Canada's first governor, a Québec printer started the *Upper Canada Gazette* at Newark [Niagara-on-the-Lake], the first newspaper in what is now Ontario. Like the *Halifax Gazette*, these first papers – operating in colonies where populations were low – remained utterly dependent upon government patronage. In Upper Canada, William Lyon MACKENZIE pressed the Assembly to subsidize the province's first paper mill, in part to ensure a source of newsprint for his journal – a telling example that the close relationship between newspapers and government patronage held even for a democratic firebrand.

The development of legislative assemblies in British N America encouraged political factions. At the same time, particularly in Halifax, Saint John, Montréal, Kingston and York [Toronto], a merchant class, with an interest both in reading commercial intelligence and in advertising, was growing. Weekly newspapers sprouted up, allied with political movements and the various mercantile and agricultural interests. In Lower Canada, the Québec City *Mercury* (1805) and the Montréal *Herald* (1811) became mouthpieces for the province's English-speaking merchants, while *Le Canadien* (1806) and *La Minerve* (1826) spoke for the rising French Canadian professional interests. In Upper Canada, William Lyon Mackenzie used his *Colonial Advocate* (1824) to argue the cause of Reformers in general and farmers in particular against the dominant professional and mercantile groups. In the Maritimes, newspapers such as Joseph HOWE's *Novascotian* (1824) of Halifax also worked to challenge the authority of colonial oligarchies.

Newspapers, Politics and the State By the early decades of the 19th century, most newspapers were allied with either the Reform (now Liberal) or Conservative Party. These early newspapers were by no means simple tools of the parties they claimed to support but rather were organs of specific leaders or factions within the parties. Thus the Toronto *Globe* (1844) was a personal organ of its publisher, the Reform politician George BROWN. The Toronto *Mail* (1872), while set up to act as spokesman for the whole Conservative Party, was quickly captured by the dominant faction led by John A. MACDONALD.

Moreover, it was not unusual for an organ to deviate from the party line. The *Mail*, for example, broke with the Macdonald Conservatives in the 1880s, forcing the party to set up the *Empire* in 1887. The relative independence of newspapers from political parties and governments varied from place to place. But in general, newspapers had more potential for independence from parties as their revenues from circulation and advertising grew. While they may not have been tools of the parties, newspapers remained closely tied into political factions well into the 20th century. The TORONTO STAR was reorganized in 1899 by a business consortium anxious to obtain an organ for the new Liberal prime minister, Wilfrid LAURIER. The Ontario Conservatives purchased the Toronto *News* in 1908 to act as a party organ. During the first decade of the 20th century the Calgary *Herald* used the organizational apparatus of the Alberta Conservative Party to sell subscriptions. As late as the 1930s, most major Québec newspapers were tied into patronage from the ruling government.

In part, the politicization of newspapers continued because readers demanded partisanship. POLITICS was a serious matter in 19th-century Canada; newspapers were expected to have views. Thus occurred the phenomenon of the 2-newspaper town. By 1870 every town large enough to support one newspaper supported 2 – one Liberal and one Conservative. As well, newspapers have never cut themselves off completely from government patronage. Since 1867 the federal government has subsidized newspaper publishers by granting them special postal rates. Canada's first international wire service, Canadian Associated Press (1903), was subsidized by the federal government, as was the domestic news co-operative, CANADIAN PRESS, during the initial years after its founding in 1917.

The relationship between Canadian newspapers and the STATE has also had a darker side. Early publishers who were considered overly critical of government actions could and did find themselves in jail. Libel and criminal libel laws were used to silence bothersome editors. In the 20th century, state action was aimed primarily at leftwing newspapers. The COMMUNIST PARTY OF CANADA found itself proscribed and its publications banned at various times. The Québec government of Maurice DUPLESSIS (1936-39 and 1944-59) used its PADLOCK ACT to shut down what it considered to be communist newspapers. Limited CENSORSHIP was imposed by the federal government in 1970, following the kidnapping of 2 men during the OCTOBER CRISIS.

The Rise of Advertising While partisanship remained, the financial dependence of newspapers on governments and political parties did decline throughout the 19th century. The reason has to do with the economics of newspaper publishing and with overall economic development. Newspapers faced high overhead costs, ie, newspapers were forced to incur the same initial outlays for equipment, typesetting and editorial matter whether they printed one copy or a run of 10 000. In the 1860s, when daily circulations were usually under 5000, these overhead costs were covered by party or government patronage. But as population expanded and literacy increased, publish-

ers were able to spread these overhead costs over more readers. In addition, as a newspaper's circulation increased, merchants became more interested in it as an advertising medium. With productive capacity increasing in all industries, advertising – as a means of persuading people to buy the massive volume of goods being produced – became crucial. Early advertisers were wholesalers trying to catch the attention of other merchants, but by the 1880s retail advertising, aimed at a mass market, was dominant. By 1900 consumers were flooded with newspaper advertisements calling upon them to purchase such things as soap, patent medicines or electric belts. Big-city dailies were earning between 70% and 80% of their revenues from advertising.

Technological developments in the newspaper industry, and in the economy as a whole, hastened the trend to large-circulation, advertising-based newspapers. The spread of the TELEGRAPH during the 1850s and the laying of the Atlantic cable in 1866 increased the availability of world news to newspapers, but at the same time increased their overhead costs of production. By the 1880s, high-speed web presses and stereotyping allowed newspapers to expand their circulations in order to earn more revenue to cover these costs. In 1876 the combined circulation of daily newspapers in the 9 major urban centres was 113 000. Seven years later, it had more than doubled. Railway building, from the mid-19th century onwards, put more of the population within reach of daily and weekly newspapers. By the 1890s, typecasting machines such as the linotype were allowing daily newspapers to expand their size from the standard 4-, 8- or 12-page format to 32 or 48 pages (*see* PRINT INDUSTRY). This greatly increased the amount of advertising space available. At the same time, the development of newsprint manufactured from wood pulp provided a cheap source of supply to newspapers. The price of newsprint plummeted from $203/ton in 1873 to $50/ton in 1900.

Daily Newspapers Early newspapers were weeklies, although a few might be published 2 or 3 times a week. Canada's first daily newspaper, the Montréal *Daily Advertiser*, began in 1833, only to go bankrupt within a year. Daily publication began in earnest in the 1840s when 2 other Montréal newspapers, the *Gazette* and *Herald*, decided to publish each day during the busy commercial season of the summer. Population growth, increased literacy and urbanization hastened the transformation from weekly to daily journalism. In 1873 there were 47 dailies in Canada; by 1900 the country boasted 112 daily newspapers. The major dailies, in turn, used the mails and the railway system to blanket the countryside with their weekly editions and, by the 20th century, with special weekend supplements such as the Toronto STAR WEEKLY or Montréal *Family Herald*.

Newspapers, first weeklies and later dailies, sprang up in the West as white settlement increased. Victoria's *British Colonist* began publication in 1858, the *Manitoba Free Press* (*see* WINNIPEG FREE PRESS) in 1872, the *Saskatchewan Herald* in 1878, and the Edmonton *Bulletin* in 1880.

The growth of a new working class in the larger cities, particularly Toronto and Montréal, encouraged new kinds of newspapers with more emphasis on local news, mass circulation, classified advertisements and (in some cases) muckraking. These newer papers, which sold for a penny a copy (a half or a third of the price of the older established dailies), included Montréal's *La* PRESSE (1884) and *Star* (1869); Toronto's *Telegram* (1876), *News* (1881), *World* (1880) and *Star* (1892); and the Hamilton *Herald* (1889). The older established papers also increased circulation to attract the new classes of readers. In Toronto in

1872 each family bought, on average, one newspaper; by 1883 the average Toronto family was purchasing 2 newspapers each day.

However, in the province of Québec as a whole, newspaper growth was initially hampered by a low literacy rate. In 1871 only 50% of Québec's French-speaking adults could read and write, compared to 90% for all Ontario adults. Unique to Québec though were daily newspapers devoted to religious ends, such as the ultramontane Roman Catholic *Le Nouveau Monde* (1867) and the Protestant *Daily Witness* (1860). In Québec, newspapers allied to the church, to nationalism and to the cause of French Canada flourished well into the 20th century. In 1910 nationalist Henri Bourassa founded *Le* DEVOIR to promote Québec interests. Papers such as *Le Devoir*, though small in terms of circulation, remained influential among the Québec intelligentsia (*see* FRENCH CANADIAN NATIONALISM).

Labour daily newspapers have been uncommon in Canada. The *Toronto Star* was started by striking printers in 1892, with the backing of the local trade union movement; but within a year it had gone bankrupt and passed out of labour hands. In 1948 the Winnipeg *Citizen* began publication with labour backing; starved for capital, it too went out of business in a year.

The number of daily newspapers peaked at 138 in 1913. By then, the pressures to curb competition and concentrate ownership had already begun. Within each town and city, newspapers vied with each other to expand circulation and thus capture advertising. The competition was costly. Losers merged with stronger papers or went out of business. In Toronto, for instance, the *Mail* and the *Empire* merged in 1895; the resultant *Mail and Empire* merged with the *Globe* in 1936 (*see* GLOBE AND MAIL). By 1949, 4 formerly independent Halifax newspapers – the *Herald*, *Chronicle*, *Mail* and *Star* – had merged into one operation with 2 daily editions. The growth of radio in the 1930s and television in the 1950s broke the print monopoly over advertising. By 1953 there were only 89 daily newspapers in the country. By 1986 that number had climbed to 110. However, by the late 1980s, only 8 Canadian cities were served by 2 or more separately owned daily newspapers. With political partisanship becoming less important to readers, the system of the 2-newspaper town had broken down (*see* LAW AND THE PRESS; MEDIA OWNERSHIP).   THOMAS WALKOM

Contemporary By the late 1980s daily newspapers were a diminished but still major part of the Canadian mass-media industry. Most newspapers belonged, individually or through chains, to conglomerate enterprises with large holdings in other media or nonmedia businesses. Some leading publishers were again diversifying, this time into the new electronic print medium: either online services for access on office or home computers, or videotex services for access on adapted television terminals with key pads. The Toronto *Globe and Mail*, for example, had established the Info Globe online service with a database of the newspaper's contents over a number of years. SOUTHAM INC, owners of the Southam chain of newspapers, and TORSTAR CORP, owners of the *Toronto Star*, had formed Infomart, a videotex marketing organization prominent in the development of the Canadian TELIDON system; the *Star* later dropped out. *Le* SOLEIL of Québec City and *La Presse* of Montréal were early participants in videotex trials. The *London Free Press* was a pioneer in the use of videotex for informational advertising in shopping centres.

Electronic print was expected to start cutting into the newspapers' advertising revenue, and possibly their readership base, as the technology developed to provide flat, portable terminals and higher definition print and graphics. However, the convenience of the daily newspaper as a comprehensive source of news, general information and entertainment, with readability, portability and flexibility, appeared likely to sustain it for a long period. Many of the early electronic print services were big losers; improvements in the technology were introduced more slowly than many firms had expected.

Newspapers were studied by the 1969-70 Senate Special Committee on Mass Media, under the chairmanship of Senator Keith DAVEY, and by the 1980-81 Royal Commission on Newspapers, whose members were chairman Tom KENT, Laurent Picard and Borden Spears. Both studies dwelt on the extent of concentration of newspaper ownership and the diminution of newspaper competition, the Kent commission stressing the conglomeration of newspapers with other types of business. Both studies maintained that freedom of the press embodied the principle of widespread dissemination of information and opinion from a diversity of sources, and that this could be injured by excessive concentration of the press. The Davey recommendation that the federal government establish a Press Ownership Review Board to curb newspaper mergers was unheeded. The Kent recommendation that newspaper owners should not also be permitted to hold radio and TV broadcasting licences in the same market was accepted in principle by the Trudeau government; it was given only limited application by the CRTC and was dropped by the Mulroney government. Ottawa also put pressure on newspapers to belong to press councils. By the late 1980s press councils were functioning in all provinces except Saskatchewan. The Kent recommendations to reduce the worst cases of concentration and to offset the effects of conglomeration by measures to provide for journalistic independence and public accountability were not accepted. They were strongly opposed by the proprietors as an alleged interference with press freedom.

Mergers and closings of big-city dailies in the 20th century contrasted with the emergence of new dailies, as small towns grew into cities. An important new development since 1960 has been the appearance of tabloid newspapers in the larger metropolitan areas. Until their arrival, nearly all big-city dailies were newspapers, or mergers of newspapers, already established by the turn of the century. The tabloids repeated the strategy of Canada's first mass-circulation dailies in the late 19th century (*La Presse* in Montréal and the *Star* in Toronto) of appealing to the "lowbrow" audience. The pioneer of tabloids in Canada was Pierre PÉLADEAU, with the extraordinarily successful *Le Journal de Montréal* and *Le Journal de Québec* in the 1960s. The Toronto *Sun,* rising out of the ashes of the Toronto *Telegram* in 1971, repeated this success in English Canada – adding right-wing populism to the tabloid formula of sex, sin and sport – and expanded into a chain including sister "Suns" in Edmonton and Calgary. The other main innovation in newspaper marketing occurred at the up-scale end of the market in 1980 and succeeding years when the Toronto *Globe and Mail,* now owned by the THOMSON GROUP as part of its takeover of FP Publications, made use of the new technology of telematics to publish a national edition. This edition is transmitted via satellite for printing at plants in Atlantic, central and western Canada (*see* SATELLITE COMMUNICATIONS).

These various developments provided Canadians, depending on where they lived, with roughly 4 types of daily newspaper: (1) the up-scale, national daily, represented by the Toronto

The paper boy was a common sight on city corners in the late 19th and early 20th centuries (*courtesy Archives of Ontario*).

Globe and Mail in English and *Le Devoir* of Montréal in French; (2) the down-scale tabloids; (3) small-city dailies, such as the Thomson papers dating from before 1980 and the smaller Desmarais papers in French; and (4) middle-market omnibus dailies, the largest circulation group, existing as monopolies in most larger cities, competing with tabloids in others. Those dailies were typified by Southam newspapers such as the Calgary *Herald* or Montréal *Gazette* in English, and UNIMÉDIA's *Le Soleil* of Québec City in French. A fifth category consists of Chinese-language dailies, the Toronto *Chinese Express* and *Shing Wah Daily News* and the Vancouver *Chinese Voice* and *Chinese Times.*

The daily circulation of all 110 Canadian dailies in 1986 was 5 583 782. The Kent Commission reported in 1981 that Toronto, Montréal and Vancouver accounted for 44% of national circulation. Circulation per capita had kept slightly ahead of general population growth over the previous decade. A market survey showed that 80% of the adult population reported reading at least 3 or 4 issues of a daily newspaper each week. Regular newspaper reading came close to matching the proportion of the population that could get prompt newspaper delivery, with readership a little lower in French Canada than in English.

The Kent Commission reported that the French-language market accounted for 18% of national circulation, spread among 11 newspapers: 9 published in Québec, one in Ottawa and one in Moncton. Ninety percent of French circulation was accounted for by 3 chains: Pierre Péladeau's QUEBECOR INC (with about half of the chain circulation), Paul DESMARAIS's Gesca (*see* POWER CORP) and Jacques Francoeur's UniMédia.

In the English-language market, Kent reported, 59% of circulation was accounted for by the Southam (32.8) and Thomson (25.9) chains, and other ownership groups brought chain circulation to 74% of the total. Concentration in this market was heightened in 1981 when Torstar Corp added a second chain of Toronto-area weeklies to the one it already owned, and again in 1982 when the MACLEAN HUNTER media group obtained control of the Toronto *Sun* chain. By 1986 Southam, with 15 papers, accounted for 28% of the English-language market and Thomson, with 39 papers, for 20%.

Taking both French and English markets together, only a quarter of the number of newspapers and less than a quarter of circulation was in the hands of independents, and several of these – eg, *Toronto Star, London Free Press* – belonged to multimedia conglomerates. Concentration was reflected regionally by the fact that in all but 3 provinces (Ontario, Québec and NS), single chains controlled two-thirds or more of provincial circulation. Figures prepared by Statistics Canada showed the following percentages of national circulation controlled by the 4 largest owners in Canada: in 1950, 37.2%; 1955, 34.3%; 1960, 35.7%; 1965, 43.6%; 1970, 52.9%; 1975, 62.7%; 1980, 65.1% and 1986, 67%. A further concentrative factor contributing to homogeneity in Canadian JOURNALISM was the common ownership by the daily newspaper proprietors of the dominant news agency, the Canadian Press, which was also a major supplier of news to radio and TV stations.

The Kent Commission found that the economics of the newspaper industry are conducive both to reduction of competition in local markets and to concentration of ownership. Newspapers derive about 80% of their revenue from selling 50% to 60% of their space to advertisers, and

The newsroom of the *Globe and Mail* in 1938 (*courtesy the* Globe and Mail).

Newspaper Circulations (1986)
(Source: Canadian Advertising Rates and Data: The Media Authority Catalogue)

City	Newspaper	Circulation
Vancouver	Sun	Mon-Thurs 229 692; Fri 273 616; Sat 280 456
Vancouver	Province	Mon-Sat 175 262; Sun 223 301
Victoria	Times-Colonist	Mon-Sat 77 698; Sun 75 442
Calgary	Herald	Mon-Thurs & Sat 134 417; Fri 175 174; Sun 119 395
Calgary	Sun	Mon-Fri 73 416; Sun 88 138
Edmonton	Journal	Mon-Thurs & Sat 160 934; Fri 195 438; Sun 142 466
Edmonton	Sun	Mon-Fri 83 503; Sun 115 578
Regina	Leader-Post	70 082
Saskatoon	Star-Phoenix	59 785
Winnipeg	Free Press	Mon-Fri 170 443; Sat 231 667; Sun 147 567
Winnipeg	Sun	Mon-Fri 47 526; Sun 57 309
Hamilton	Spectator	142 606
London	Free Press	126 971
Ottawa	Citizen	Mon-Fri 184 724; Sat 238 461
Ottawa	Le Droit	Mon-Fri 37 437; Sat 42 506
Toronto	Globe and Mail	318 300 (Ont 229 700, Alta 21 600, BC 24 700; Qué 12 400; NS 8000)
Toronto	Star	Mon-Fri 525 669; Sat 802 397; Sun 531 341
Toronto	Sun	Mon-Fri 286 883; Sun 456 245
Montréal	Le Devoir	Mon-Fri 29 528; Sat 33 001
Montréal	Gazette	Mon-Fri 199 204; Sat 271 203
Montréal	Le Journal de Montréal	Mon-Fri 317 024; Sat 354 505; Sun 338 369
Montréal	La Presse	Mon-Fri 191 698; Sat 303 201; Sun 139 059
Québec	Le Journal de Québec	Mon-Fri 103 127; Sat 106 350; Sun 91 553
Québec	Le Soleil	Mon-Fri 116 688; Sat 145 545; Sun 92 753
Fredericton	Gleaner	27 799
Moncton	Times-Transcript	45 346
Saint John	Telegraph-Journal	32 465 morning; Sat 62 360 (affiliated)
Saint John	Evening Times-Globe	32 198 evening
Halifax	Chronicle-Herald	80 274 morning (affiliated)
Halifax	Mail-Star	57 870 evening
Charlottetown	Guardian and Patriot	18 182 morning; 5 677 evening
St John's	Telegram	Mon-Fri 38 392; Sat 54 003

only about 20% of their revenue from selling newspapers to readers. Advertisers in most markets can reach readers more cheaply through one newspaper than through 2 or more. Thus, head-to-head competition between the same type of newspapers has disappeared from most cities, and a limited variety of newspapers is only possible where the market is large enough to be segmented into distinct audiences. At the same time, the high capital cost of starting or re-equipping a newspaper, combined with the economies to be realized through skilled central management, have favoured chains over independents. Once a newspaper's monopoly is established in a market, or a segment of a market, a paper has proved to be more profitable than the average business. Such newspapers serve as cash sources to develop other enterprises in a conglomerate.

The hometown nature of the daily newspaper remains its strongest characteristic. Even with the relatively recent development in Canada of market segmentation and a metropolitan pattern of journalism, the national or regional paper must retain a firm base in the metropolis where it is published. Opinion surveys show that although audiences prefer TV for national and world news, and generally find TV the most believable medium, they still read the daily newspaper for local and regional coverage. On the average, two-thirds or more of a newspaper's editorial budget is spent in-house, rather than for outside news services and features. Newspapers try to develop a sense of common interest and common cause with their readers.

National coverage in Canadian newspapers has improved in depth and scope since the 1960s, owing largely to the efforts of the Canadian Press, Southam News, the Toronto *Globe and Mail* and the *Toronto Star* to provide stronger Ottawa and interregional coverage. International news coverage by Canadian journalists has gradually been extended, urged on by criticism in both the Davey and Kent reports. In public-affairs coverage, which continues to be the newspaper's primary social responsibility, the press has felt increasingly bound to follow the scenarios of TV, the preferred medium of the politicians, particularly at the national level and in the larger provinces. Most studies of newspaper content have concluded that newspaper journalism continues to play a strong role in setting the agenda for public debate by establishing news priorities.

As the number of big-city dailies declined and the remaining newspapers tended to drop unprofitable out-of-town circulation, community newspapers enjoyed a boom. From 1971 to 1980 aggregate weekly circulation of community newspapers increased from 3.8 million to 8.8 million, or from about one-eighth to more than one-quarter of aggregate weekly circulation of the daily newspapers.

During this period there was a steady trend toward concentration of ownership of community newspapers into chains, and of ownership by the proprietors of dailies. Statistics Canada reported that by 1985 total circulation of community papers stood at 9.5 million. This figure includes both French and English papers, as well as bilingual papers, mainly in Québec, with a total circulation of 2.8 million and ethnic weeklies with a total circulation of 954 000. Many community newspapers are distributed free and rely entirely on advertising for revenue.

Advertising expenditures, on which the media are so dependent, were estimated as follows in 1986: daily newspapers, 22.7%; weeklies, 5.6%; general magazines, 4.3%; television, 16.6%; radio, 9.1%; other print (chiefly direct mail and catalogue), 23.7%; and outdoors 7.3%. Thus, daily newspapers had succeeded in retaining one of the largest shares, but had to be considered in combination with community newspapers in order to outdo the combination of TV and radio. Daily newspaper advertising revenues reached $1.5 billion in 1986, up from $987 million in 1980, which was nearly double the 1974 amount. Thus, revenues continued to increase tremendously after the 1980 closings that had precipitated the appointment of the Kent Commission.

Responding to market opportunities, daily newspapers have shown a trend in the larger cities from afternoon to morning (or all-day) publication, and to publishing Sunday editions. The dailies appear to have consolidated a place for themselves alongside the other media, helped somewhat by the fragmentation of radio and TV audiences owing to the multiplication of stations and channels, although competition for the advertising dollar remains intense.

The possibility that electronic print services will take away some of the informational advertising in which newspapers are strongest appears to be one of the chief threats to which newspapers will have to respond in the long run. *See also* MAGAZINES. TIM CREERY

Reading: P. Audley, *Canada's Cultural Industries* (1983); Canada, Royal Commission on Newspapers, *Report* (1981); Canada, Senate Special Committee on the Mass Media, *Report* (1970); J. Hamelin and A. Beaulieu, "Aperçu du journalisme québecoise d'expression française," *Recherches sociographiques* (1966); W.H. Kesterton, *A History of Journalism in Canada* (1967); P. Rutherford, *The Making of the Canadian Media* (1978) and *A Victorian Authority* (1982).

Newt, *see* SALAMANDER.

Newton, Lilias, née Torrance, portrait painter (b at Montréal 3 Nov 1896; d there 10 Jan 1980). A witty and sophisticated portrait painter, Newton studied in London, Paris and Montréal. She joined the Beaver Hall Hill Group in 1920 and was elected associate member of the Royal Canadian Academy of Arts in 1923 and member in 1937 (its third woman member). A founding member of the Canadian Group of Painters (1933), she taught at the Musée des beaux-arts de Montréal (1937-40). Her portraits hang in most universities and many boardrooms; pictures of 4 notable colleagues – A.Y. JACKSON, Lawren HARRIS, Edwin HOLGATE, and Arthur LISMER – are at the National Gallery. Her work is distinguished by fresh colour, vigorous composition and sharp insight. Informal portraits of her son Forbes and of friends show great charm and rapport. In 1956 she painted the official portraits of Queen Elizabeth and Prince Philip for Rideau Hall. ANNE McDOUGALL

Newton, Margaret, plant pathologist (b at Montréal 20 Apr 1887; d at Victoria 6 Apr 1971), sister of Robert NEWTON. While still a student at McGill, Margaret Newton worked on the first scientific survey of wheat rust in Canada, following the epidemic of 1916, and joined the Dominion Rust Research Laboratory, Winnipeg, on its creation. Her research in association with J.H. CRAIGIE is summarized in T. JOHNSON's *Rust Research in Canada* and I.L. Conners's *Plant Pathology in Canada*. Newton was possibly the first Canadian woman to undertake a lifelong research career. She never married and reportedly would work until near exhaustion – and then relax by foreign travel or strenuous canoe expeditions. In 1922 she was invited to the Soviet Union to discuss her work with wheat rust. She became an FRCS in 1942 and received the Flavelle Medal in 1948. She retired owing to ill health, perhaps caused by 25 years of exposure to rust-disease spores. A women's residence hall at U Vic is named in her memory. DONALD J.C. PHILLIPSON

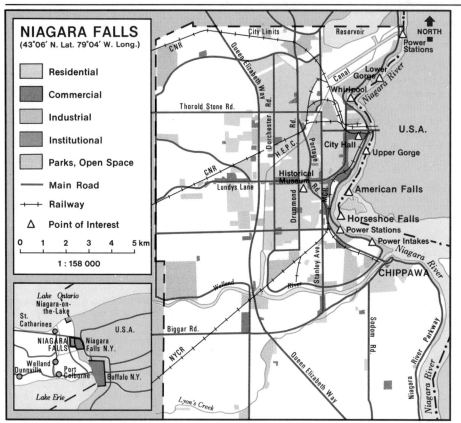

NIAGARA FALLS
(43°06' N. Lat. 79°04' W. Long.)

- Residential
- Commercial
- Industrial
- Institutional
- Parks, Open Space
- —— Main Road
- +—+ Railway
- △ Point of Interest

0 1 2 3 4 5 km

1 : 158 000

Newton, Robert, plant biochemist, university president (b at Montréal 7 Feb 1889; d at Laguna Hills, Calif 22 Nov 1985), brother of Margaret NEWTON. He was one of 5 children; all, including 2 girls, became scientists, 4 with PhD qualifications. After service in WWI (MC 1917), Newton became professor of field crops at U of A, whose president H.M. TORY became chairman of the NATIONAL RESEARCH COUNCIL in 1923. Newton's research was focused on wheat: winter hardiness, drought resistance and resistance to rust. He became Tory's chief adviser on agricultural science, served as director of the NRC's Division of Biology and Agriculture (1932-40), and succeeded Tory as chairman of the influential Grain Research Committee. His best university students were sent abroad to earn PhD degrees in the world's leading institutions and came home to constitute the core of the NRC's biology staff. Newton returned to Edmonton in 1940 and was president of U of A 1941-50.   DONALD J.C. PHILLIPSON

Niagara Escarpment, in its Ontario portion, is 725 km long, covering 1923 km², with a maximum height of 335 m. An escarpment may be defined as a steep rock face of great length formed by an abrupt termination of strata. The Niagara Escarpment adds a unique visual quality to Ontario's landscape as it crosses the province from QUEENSTON, on the NIAGARA R, through HAMILTON, Milton, Orangeville, COLLINGWOOD, OWEN SOUND and Tobermory to MANITOULIN I and ST JOSEPH I. It marks part of the shore of an ancient sea centered in Michigan, which extended W from Rochester, NY, across Ontario to Michigan, then down the W side of Lk Michigan into Wisconsin. Water erosion and glaciation molded its striking features. Historically, the escarpment's waterfalls, forests and rocks provided power and building materials for a young province. In time, however, its archaeological sites, rich fauna and flora, and outstanding potential for recreation – such as hiking on the BRUCE TRAIL, skiing and nature study – created a demand for measures to preserve its scenic splendour. To resolve the complicated jurisdic-

tion of municipalities, regions, counties and conservation authorities, the Niagara Escarpment Commission produced a plan to preserve the escarpment's ecological integrity and a Niagara park system of 116 units.   RAYMOND N. LOWES

Reading: William Gillard and Thomas Tooke, *The Niagara Escarpment* (1975).

Niagara Falls, Ont, City, pop 72 107 (1986c), 70 960 (1981c), inc 1904. Its fame and name are based on the resplendent NIAGARA FALLS on the NIAGARA R, but its growth has combined tourism with railhead developments and with manufacturing (including electrochemicals and abrasives) based on readily available hydroelectric power. The earliest hotel was built in 1822, and by the

1850s several small communities had developed around the attractions of the falls and the historic battlefield of LUNDY'S LANE. The first bridge was built across the gorge in 1848 and in 1853 the GREAT WESTERN RY arrived, establishing a railhead near the Whirlpool Rapids Bridge of today. The community of Drummondville was settled in 1800 near the future Lundy's Lane battlefield. Clifton was established in 1832 near the falls, and a third community, Elgin, grew up where the first bridge was built over the gorge in 1848. In 1856 the villages of Clifton and Elgin were incorporated as the town of Clifton, which became the town of Niagara Falls in 1881. Meanwhile in 1881, Drummondville became the *village* of Niagara Falls. The confusion ended in 1904 when the town and village of the same name were incorporated as the city of Niagara Falls (pop 7000). The Township of Stanford joined the city in 1963 and in 1973 under regional government the village of Chippawa became part of the larger city. The first power companies began operation in 1905 and 1906, and Sir Adam Beck No 1 was the largest powerhouse in the world at the time of its completion in 1921. Sir Adam Beck No 2 (1223 MW) was eventually opened in 1954. Both developments required massive diversions of water, through both canals and tunnels, from the falls into the powerhouses.

The falls became known in Europe and the US through the paintings and descriptions of visitors in the early 19th century, but full-scale development of tourism came after the 1850s with the arrival of the Great Western Ry in 1853 and in the 1920s with the automobile. In 1885 the provincial government established Queen Victoria Park in contrast to the jumbled, carnival atmosphere of earlier times. In the 1930s Sir Harry OAKES bought the sites of the 2 largest hotels and donated them to the Niagara Parks Commission, making possible a well-designed open space around the falls. The city contains probably the longest strip of motels in the world, along Hwy 20 from the E, and scenic towers ring the falls. Annual visitors are estimated at 12 to 14 million.   JOHN N. JACKSON

Reading: G. Siebel, ed, *Niagara Falls, Canada* (1967).

Niagara Falls, spectacular waterfall in the NIAGARA R, is the world's greatest waterfall by volume. It is split in 2 by Goat I. The American Falls are 64 m high and 305 m wide, with a flow of 14 million litres of water per minute. The Canadian, or Horseshoe, Falls are 54 m high and 675 m wide, with a flow of 155 million litres. The falls were formed some 10 000 years ago as retreating glaciers exposed the NIAGARA ESCARPMENT, divert-

Wide-angle photograph showing the American Falls on the left and Canadian Falls on the right, and the *Maid of the Mist* (photo by John deVisser).

Niagara Falls (1799), watercolour by E. Henn. The falls have been a source of inspiration to visitors for centuries (*courtesy Royal Ontario Museum*).

ing the waters of Lk ERIE, which formerly drained S, northward into Lk ONTARIO. The falls have eroded the soft shale and limestone of the escarpment some 1.2 m per year and now stand 11 km from their place of origin at present-day QUEENSTON. The falls were understandably of spiritual significance to the Indians, and "Niagara," meaning "thunder of water," is said to be the last remaining word of the NEUTRAL.

The awesome spectacle was first described by Louis HENNEPIN, who saw the falls in 1678, calling them "a vast and prodigious Cadence of Water." Among those who tried to describe their effect was Charles Dickens, who wrote, "I seemed to be lifted from the earth and to be looking into Heaven." With tourism, which began in the 1800s, came daredevils who defied the falls in barrels, boats and rubber balls. The most celebrated was Blondin who performed on a tightrope over the gorge (1859). Stunting was outlawed in 1912. To save the area from hucksters and speculators, Ontario created Queen Victoria Park in 1887 – Canada's first provincial park. Millions of tourists visit the area every year, viewing the falls from several towers, a tunnel beneath Horseshoe Falls, an aerocar over the whirlpool and the *Maid of the Mist*, a boat that carries sightseers to the foot of the falls. International agreements control the diversion of water for hydroelectric power. The Niagara Diversion Treaty (1950) stipulated that a minimum flow be reserved for the falls and that the rest be divided equally between Canada and the US. In Canada water is diverted from the Niagara R above the falls and fed into the turbines of Sir Adam Beck Generating Stations No 1 and No 2 by canals and tunnels.   JAMES MARSH

Niagara Historic Frontier, stretching about 50 km along both sides of the Niagara R from Lk Ontario to Lk Erie, is dotted with HISTORIC SITES and cairns. This region was first the home of various Iroquoian and Algonquian peoples. The French arrived in the late 17th century, and tangible evidence remains at Ft Niagara (near Youngstown, NY), which surrendered to British and colonial forces in July 1759. During the AMERICAN REVOLUTION and the WAR OF 1812, Ft Niagara was the scene of considerable military activity.

On the west (Canadian) side of the river, across from Ft Niagara, stand Ft George, Ft Mississauga and Butler's Barracks, all under the auspices of Parks Canada. Ft George, built in 1796, was structurally altered before the War of 1812. Captured by the Americans in a fierce battle on 27 May 1813, it was retaken by British troops that Dec. By war's end it was tumbling into ruins. In 1937 the Niagara Parks Commission funded Ft George's reconstruction according to the original plans of the Royal Engineers. The site was transferred to the federal government in 1969 and established in 1977 as Fort George National Historic Park.

Battlefield sites such as QUEENSTON HEIGHTS, Stoney Creek and LUNDY'S LANE commemorate the people and events of the War of 1812. As well, FORT ERIE, built in 1764 and now administered by the St Lawrence Parks Commission, was an active site from the time of PONTIAC to Confederation.   ROBERT S. ALLEN

Niagara-on-the-Lake, Ont, Town, pop 12 494 (1986c), 12 186 (1981c), located where the Niagara R enters Lk Ontario. It was settled by LOYALISTS who had served in Butler's Rangers and was named Newark and made capital of UPPER CANADA by John Graves SIMCOE. The name "Niagara" was taken when the capital moved to York, and it was changed (*c*1900) to the present name to avoid confusion with NIAGARA FALLS (19 km S). In May 1813 the Americans captured nearby Ft George, occupied the town that summer and burned it in Dec. Its heyday was the 1850s, when it was connected to Toronto by steamer and to Buffalo, NY, by railway. However, increased use of the WELLAND CANAL and removal of the county seat to ST CATHARINES arrested growth. Camp Niagara (est 1871) trained militia and regulars to 1966. Regional government merged the town and township under one name (1970). Tourism, fruit growing and yacht building are chief industries. Steamer and rail connections had ceased by 1960, victims of the automobile.

Niagara-on-the-Lake is one of the best-preserved early 19th-century towns in N America. Many impressive, neoclassical and Georgian homes still exist here: Clench House (*c*1824); Kirby House (*c*1815), once the home of William KIRBY; McFarland House and Field House (both *c*1800) on the Niagara Pkwy; and Willowbank (1835) in Queenston. St Andrew's Church (1831) is perhaps the finest example of Greek Revival in Ontario. Butler's Barracks (post-1815), the Niagara Apothecary (1820) and Ft George (1796-99) have been restored. A number of resi-

dents have designated their homes under the Ontario Heritage Act and the town council has designated the downtown area as a Heritage District. The Niagara Historical Museum (1907) displays Loyalist artifacts. The SHAW FESTIVAL was held at the Court House (built 1847) before opening its own theatre in 1973. Niagara-on-the-Lake is a premier tourist attraction and an architectural and historical treasure.   JOHN L. FIELD

Reading: John L. Field, ed, *Bicentennial Stories of Niagara-on-the-Lake* (1981); Peter J. Stokes, *Old Niagara on the Lake* (1971).

Niagara Peninsula lies between Lakes ONTARIO and ERIE and the NIAGARA R in SW Ontario. As the river is also the international boundary, the peninsula has played a frontier role since 1783. Physically, it includes 2 contrasting plains separated by the NIAGARA ESCARPMENT. The Ontario Plain, with fertile, sandy soils and a favourable climate, contains the Niagara Fruit Belt, where much of Canada's soft fruits and vines are grown. The wooded slopes of the escarpment, an abrupt rise of some 60 m, are etched deeply by gorges with falls at their head, most notably at NIAGARA FALLS, and are quarried for limestone. The Erie Plain, with bedrock closer to the surface, is less productive than its northern counterpart; the soils are poorly drained clay, and the climate is wetter, with shorter frost-free periods.

Subregions in the peninsula provide a rich variation of detail: shoreline bluffs along Lk Ontario, with ponded river estuaries behind sandbars; the shoreline of glacial Lk Iroquois across the Ontario Plain; the Short Hills embayment in the escarpment, with steep-sided slopes; a kame at Fonthill, the highest point of the peninsula; the buried St Davids Gorge, the plugged channel of an ancestral Niagara R; marsh areas, including peat bogs, on the southern plain; the slender Onondaga Escarpment inland from Lk Erie; and limestone headlands alternating with sandy bays along Lk Erie.

Settlement has responded to this diverse terrain. Indian villages followed the escarpment, and many trails became roads. Permanent settlement arose during the 1780s with the influx of LOYALISTS. NIAGARA-ON-THE-LAKE was established temporarily as the first capital of Upper Canada, QUEENSTON and Chippawa as portage terminals, and Fort George and FORT ERIE as garrisons commanding entry to the Niagara R. Immigrants first settled the Niagara R frontage and the Ontario Plain, then the Erie Plain. Townships, surveyed with 40 ha lots, had a road in front of each concession and between every other lot. Mills developed where rivers crossed the escarpment or could be dammed for water power, and accordingly, services arose at several "corners" accessible from nearby communities.

The expanding economy was disrupted severely by American invasion during the WAR OF 1812, and by an aftermath of border mistrust. W.L. Mackenzie and some of his supporters found refuge across the border during the REBELLION OF 1837, and FENIAN raids were launched from the American side in the 1860s. Matters changed, however, with interlinking rail and highway bridges, the substantial introduction of American-owned industries, and the development of the Lk Erie shoreline under American seasonal cottage and recreational properties.

As the Niagara R was unnavigable, the WELLAND CANAL was constructed across the peninsula to provide through transport by water to the continental interior. First opened in 1829 but continually enlarged, the canal had water power available at every lock, where streams were crossed, and from hydraulic raceways. A line of new settlement was added to the peninsula: ST CATHAR-

INES became an industrial town; Port Dalhousie and PORT COLBORNE grew as ports; and THOROLD and WELLAND were founded, together with Port Robinson and Allanburg on the main canal and Wainfleet and Dunnville on the feeder canal.

Eventually, Niagara-on-the-Lake lost its premier position, and the county functions of the town were transferred successively to Dunnville, Welland and St Catharines.

Railways strengthened existing settlements. Routes constructed during the 1850s along the 2 lakeshores, the Niagara R and the Welland Canal were augmented by 2 southern routes during the 1870s and a transverse HAMILTON-Buffalo line in the 1890s. Settlement expanded at border crossing points, especially Clifton (now Niagara Falls) at the Suspension Bridge and Victoria (Bridgeburg, now Fort Erie) at the International Bridge. Welland, at the hub of the peninsula, expanded "Where Rails and Water Meet" (its civic motto), as did Merritton. Railways also encouraged the emergence of fruit farming, which replaced wheat and mixed farming N of the escarpment; cottage and recreational developments along the shoreline of Lk Erie; and tourism at Niagara Falls. St Catharines became a spa, and religious campgrounds were introduced at Niagara-on-the-Lake, Niagara Falls, Crystal Beach and Grimsby Beach.

The infrastructure was again strengthened through hydroelectric developments at Niagara Falls, and at DeCew Falls (St Catharines) from the Welland Canal. As generating stations, storage reservoirs and power-transmission lines were added to the landscape, towns obtained a new impetus for expansion. Major industries developed, expecially along the Welland Canal in St Catharines, Thorold, Welland and Port Colborne, and at Niagara Falls and Chippawa on the Niagara River.

By 1986 the Niagara Regional Municipality housed 370 132 persons. The principal industries include automotive parts, chemical and electrical products, metal fabrication, primary metals, pulp and paper, shipbuilding, and food and drink, including wineries. St Catharines is the principal service centre.

An extensive interurban streetcar network connecting the towns was replaced by highway improvements, especially the QUEEN ELIZABETH WAY (opened 1939) through the fruit belt to Fort Erie in the 1930s. Outward sprawl from its own towns and sporadic growth into the peninsula from the W now present severe problems. The annual loss of agricultural land on the most productive soil in Canada is severe; external shopping centres have denuded the historic urban cores of much retailing strength; and the escarpment as a vital scenic landscape is threatened by linear developments. Conservation, urban quality and respect for the environment have become major issues, together with the economic future of old, established manufacturing industries.

JOHN N. JACKSON

Reading: John N. Jackson and John Burtniak, *Railways in the Niagara Peninsula* (1978).

Niagara River, 55 km long, issues from Lk ERIE and flows N over NIAGARA FALLS to Lk ONTARIO. The upper section is navigable to a series of rapids above the falls, and in fact the first ship built on the Great Lakes, LA SALLE's GRIFFON, was built here. The river is extremely deep, and beneath the falls flows through a spectacular gorge. Its average flow at Queenston is 5760 m³/s – greater than the Fraser, Columbia or Nelson. It is crossed by several bridges, notably the Peace (1927) at FT ERIE and the Rainbow (1941), which connects the cities of NIAGARA FALLS, Ont, and Niagara Falls, NY.

JAMES MARSH

Nichol, Barrie Phillip, "bp Nichol," writer, sound poet, editor, teacher (b at Vancouver 30 Sept 1944). bp Nichol is recognized as one of Canada's leading experimental writers. He first achieved international recognition for concrete poetry in the 1960s and he has published and recorded his work in many different places and ways. He has performed sound poetry as one of the group The Four Horsemen and in solo concerts, and he has explored theoretical possibilities in the Toronto Research Group; he has published a wide range of poetry and prose in books and pamphlets. In 1970 he won the Gov Gen's Award for poetry. All Nichol's writing forms a unity, but his long ongoing poem, *The Martyrology* (1972-), is the central work. Major critical works are Stephen SCOBIE's *bp Nichol: What History Teaches* (1984) and *Read the Way He Writes: A Festschrift for bp Nichol* (1986).

DOUGLAS BARBOUR

Nichol, Robert, businessman, politician, militia officer (b at Dumfries, Scot *c* 1774; d near Queenston, UC 3 May 1824). A successful merchant in Norfolk County, UC, he was elected to the House of Assembly in 1812, 1816 and 1820. During the WAR OF 1812 he served as quartermaster general of militia. Mercurial and capricious, he led the opposition in the Assembly after 1817, though often working closely with the administration and criticizing unrelentingly "the base and wicked Executive." He was an early promoter of canals, and his Assembly report on the resources of the province defined for a generation a strategy for economic development. Nichol described himself with detachment as "more of the Epicurean than Stoic" with "not sufficient stability." ROBERT L. FRASER

Nicholas, Cynthia, "Cindy," marathon swimmer (b at Toronto 20 Aug 1957). She began competitive swimming in 1963, in Scarborough, Ont, and set several Canadian age-group records, mostly in the butterfly stroke. Her first marathon achievement was a 1974 Lk Ontario crossing that bettered all previous records – for both men and women. In 1977 she became the first woman to complete a double crossing of the English Channel, taking 10 hours off the previous mark. In 1979 she won the title "Queen of the Channel," for her 6th crossing; by 1982 she had completed 19 crossings, including five 2-way trips. She also set record times in Chaleur Bay swims, and was the 1976 women's world marathon swimming champion. Nicholas was named Canadian female athlete of the year in 1977 and is a Member of the Order of Canada. BARBARA SCHRODT

Nicholls, Sir Frederic, capitalist, business lobbyist (b in England 23 Nov 1856; d at Battle Creek, Mich 25 Oct 1921). Nicholls played a crucial role in promoting early manufacturing in Canada. Educated as an electrical engineer in Germany, he came to Canada in 1874. A Conservative in politics, he was active in creating the NATIONAL POLICY in the late 1870s. He was the founder and editor (until 1893) of the *Canadian Manufacturer*, and prominent in Toronto press, yachting and charitable organizations. Nicholls was one of the first to exploit the possibilities of electric energy in Canada. In 1891 his Toronto Incandescent Light Co first brought commercial electric LIGHTING to the city, and soon enjoyed a monopoly over the city's electric lighting and power needs. He went on to develop the power-generating potential of NIAGARA FALLS with the Electrical Development Co, and the manufacture of electric equipment with the Canadian General Electric Co. In 1896 he was president of the National Electric Light Assn of America. After the rise of the "people's power" movement in Ontario in the 1900s, Nicholls found much less scope for private power development. He was

later involved in numerous Canadian-incorporated utility companies in South and Central America and the Caribbean. In 1917 he was appointed to the Canadian Senate.

DUNCAN MCDOWALL

Reading: H.V. Nelles, *The Politics of Development* (1974).

Nichols, Jack, painter (b at Montréal 16 Mar 1921). Nichols taught himself to draw with the encouragement of Louis MUHLSTOCK in Montréal and the instruction of F.H. VARLEY in Ottawa (1936-40). He was commissioned to paint for the Canadian merchant marine in 1943 and was appointed a navy war artist in 1944. He crossed the Channel on D-Day (6 June) with the British and painted the Normandy landings and actions near Brest. His subjects were always servicemen engaged in their everyday activities. Nichols followed Carl SCHAEFER in winning the Guggenheim Fellowship for creative painting (1947-48). After the war he taught at UBC and at U of T. In his day he was famous for his melancholy, nostalgic drawings and lithographs. JOAN MURRAY

Nichols, Joanna Ruth, children's writer (b at Toronto 4 Mar 1948). In *A Walk Out of the World* (1969) and *The Marrow of the World* (1972), Nichols portrays the adventures of children transported to alternate universes. The latter was Canadian Children's Book of the Year. In *Ceremony of the Innocence* (1969), an adolescent must resolve conflicting feelings towards her father. *Song of the Pearl* (1976) treats the moral growth of Margaret who, after her death, examines her behaviour in earlier incarnations, while *The Left-Handed Spirit* (1978) recounts the young heroine's discovery of her special healing powers.

JON C. STOTT

Nicholson, Francis, soldier, governor of NS (b at Downholme, Eng 12 Nov 1655; d at London, Eng 5 Mar 1727/28). He led 2 unsuccessful attacks on Canada via the Hudson R and Lk CHAMPLAIN (1709 and 1711). In 1710, he captured PORT-ROYAL with 500 marines and a flotilla under Commodore George Martin. He was made governor of Nova Scotia and Placentia in 1712, but spent only Aug to Oct 1714 in the new colony. Nicholson was recalled and dismissed, ostensibly for maladministration. JAMES MARSH

Nicholson, John Robert, lawyer, public servant, politician (b at Newcastle, NB 1 Dec 1901; d at Vancouver 8 Oct 1983). In 1941 Nicholson was called to Ottawa to the Dept of Munitions and Supply by C.D. HOWE. He helped organize Polymer Corp and remained there after the war, becoming executive VP. He joined Brazilian Traction (BRASCAN) in 1952 and later helped reorganize the BC Liberal Party. Elected MP in 1963, he held various posts until becoming lt-gov of BC (1968-73). ROBERT BOTHWELL

Nickel (Ni), the 24th most abundant element in the Earth's crust, comprises about 0.008% of crustal rocks. Nickel is malleable and ductile. Its high melting point (1455°C), strength and hardness make it desirable for many technical applications. It takes a high polish and in alloys provides strength and resistance to corrosion and heat. Possibly its earliest use was as an unknown element in an ancient Chinese white metal alloy (*paktong*) used in tableware, candlesticks and other ornamental and household articles. The Swedish scientist Axel Cronstedt discovered the existence of nickel in 1751. The major contemporary use for nickel, as an alloying element in stainless steel, consumes nearly 50% of the total supply. Other major uses are in high-nickel alloys, foundry steel and electroplating. The presence of nickel and copper MINERALS near the present city of SUDBURY, Ont, was known as early as 1856, but it was not until 1883, during construction of the Canadian Pacific Railway, that the significance of the discovery was recognized. By 1890 most ore bodies in the district, comprising the world's largest source of nickel, had been located.

Canada has been the world's largest producer for several decades but its share of world production has declined from 76% in 1950 to about 25% in 1984. In 1986 total Canadian nickel production was 180 599 t valued at $1.075 billion. Other major producers are the USSR, New Caledonia and Australia. Principal markets for Canadian nickel are the US and western Europe. Canada's domestic market accounts for less than 2% of world consumption. The principal Canadian producers are INCO LTD and Falconbridge Ltd. Inco operated mines at Sudbury, Ont, and at THOMPSON, Man. Falconbridge operated mines at Sudbury. All Canadian mines are based on sulphide ores. Most nickel mines in Canada are underground, but some are also open cast. After the ore is broken, it is sent to the concentrator where it is crushed and the sulphide minerals concentrated by flotation. The concentrate is smelted to produce nickel matte, which is sent to a refinery where cathodes, anodes, pellets and other products are made. *See also* COINAGE.   R.G. TELEWIAK

Nickinson, John, soldier, actor-manager (b at London, Eng 2 Jan 1808; d at Cincinnati, Ohio 9 Feb 1864). He stimulated the development of theatre in Toronto and was father of an acting family. He joined the 24th Regiment at age 15 and was posted to Québec C and Montréal where he performed with the garrison amateurs, notably at Montréal's Theatre Royal in 1833. Discharged in 1836, he played his first professional season in Albany, moving in 1837 to New York, where he specialized in dialect comedy. He established a pattern of playing winter seasons in New York and summers in Canada often as an actor-manager. In 1851 Nickinson put together his own company, loosely built around his acting family (Charlotte Morrison, Eliza Peters, Virginia Marlowe, Isabella Walcot and John Jr), and toured the Great Lakes and Lower Canada. Between 1853 and 1858 he successfully ran Toronto's Royal Lyceum Theatre, eventually turning it over to his son-in-law, Owen Marlowe. He acted briefly in New York before stage-managing Pike's Opera House in Cincinnati. His daughter, Charlotte Morrison (d 1910) managed the stock company for Toronto's Grand Opera House 1874-79.   DAVID GARDNER

Nicol, Eric, humorist, playwright, journalist (b at Kingston, Ont 28 Dec 1919). Nicol was raised in Vancouver and has long written a column for the Vancouver *Province* which has provided a foundation for his many humorous collections, such as *Girdle Me a Globe* (1957, Leacock Medal for Humour). These works are characterized by verbal shenanigans put in service to play up the foibles of middle-class, urban family life, with occasional diversions into history as it is popularly misunderstood. Nicol is a jack-of-all-trades, having produced everything from *Vancouver* (1970), a lively history of the city, to *A Scar is Born* (1968), an account of the unsuccess on Broadway of one of his many stage plays. He has written many radio plays and TV scripts, as well as on professional sports (eg, *The Joy of Hockey,* 1978). He frequently works in close collaboration with cartoonists. Recent work includes *The U.S. or US – What's the Difference, Eh?* (1986, with illustrations by Dave Moore).

Nicola-Similkameen were an enclave of Athapaskans living in the Nicola and Similkameen river valleys of S-central BC (and, marginally, N-central Washington state), surrounded by Interi-

or Salish (*see* SALISH, INTERIOR). One theory regarding Nicola-Similkameen settlement in this area suggests they originated from a Chilcotin Athapaskan war party that stayed and intermarried with the Thompson and Okanagan Interior Salish in the mid-1700s. Another suggests that the Nicola-Similkameen had a long history in this area, having moved from a more northerly Athapaskan homeland many hundreds of years ago, but archaeological data have not supported this theory.

The few words of Nicola-Similkameen that have been recorded suggest that this language was related to Chilcotin, about 250 km to the N, but analysis of artifacts from archaeological excavations indicates that Nicola-Similkameen PREHISTORY is closely linked with that of the neighbouring Lillooet, Thompson and Okanagan areas. By the early 1900s few people remained who spoke the Nicola-Similkameen language, as it had become secondary to the languages of those who now occupied their territory – the Thompson and Okanagan. The Nicola-Similkameen language is now extinct. The last person who had even a partial knowledge of this language died around 1940. However, there are still some geographical place-names both in the Nicola and Similkameen river valleys that are recognized by Interior Salish as being in the Nicola-Similkameen language, and some Thompson and Okanagan people are aware of their Nicola-Similkameen ancestry.

Very little information concerning Nicola-Similkameen culture has been recorded. They, like their Interior Salish neighbours, generally lived in semisubterranean dwellings (pit houses) during the winter and in tule-mat lodges at other times of the year. The Nicola-Similkameen subsisted primarily on lake fishing. Salmon were obtained mainly through trade, as anadromous fish were not available either in the Nicola R or along the entire length of the Similkameen R. The Nicola-Similkameen diet was supplemented by elk, deer and small game, as well as vegetal foods.

Thompson and Okanagan encroachment into Nicola-Similkameen territory was the result of several factors, perhaps the most important being the introduction of the HORSE to the Plateau area in the 18th century. The horse extended travel for the purposes of trade and food harvesting, with the result that Thompson and Okanagan peoples came to utilize areas occupied by the Nicola-Similkameen. By the mid-1800s the Nicola-Similkameen were under the influence of the Thompson and Okanagan. Epidemic diseases, intermarriage with the Interior Salish, and the increasing presence of non-Indians further hastened the demise of the Nicola-Similkameen in the latter half of the 19th century. *See also* NATIVE PEOPLE: PLATEAU and general articles under NATIVE PEOPLE.
    DOROTHY KENNEDY AND RANDY BOUCHARD

Reading: F. Boas, "Fifth Report on the Indians of British Columbia," *British Association for the Advancement of Sciences, Annual Report* (1895); G.M. Dawson, "Notes on the Shuswap People of British Columbia," *Transactions of the Royal Society of Canada* 9(2), (1891).

Nicolet, Qué, Town, pop 5065 (1986c), 4880 (1981c), inc 1872, is situated some 3 km from the mouth of the Rivière Nicolet at the eastern end of Lac St-Pierre. Named for Champlain's associate, Jean NICOLLET, it grew slowly from its founding in the early 1700s. Although situated on a vast plain, Nicolet has taken a particular shape. Long blocked to the N by private institutional holdings and to the S by agricultural land, it grew only eastward, along the river and was thus subject to springtime flooding and often suffered from landslides. In the early 19th century it became a major agricultural town and an

important crossroads for the townships of the S shore. With its economic activity based on the forest and dairy industries and retail commerce, Nicolet was increasingly the centre for back-country agricultural parishes. This was the town's golden age: several religious communities settled there and a diocese was formed in 1877. Its population at the time of the 1891 census was 2518. In the 20th century, however, Nicolet failed to establish a viable industrial structure to match the economic growth in its hinterland. DRUMMONDVILLE, VICTORIAVILLE, Plessisville, Princeville and SHERBROOKE all industrialized with the help of American and British capital. Nicolet lost the title of regional capital and its intellectual and religious roles replaced its commercial one. Today, it is a small service centre.
    RICHARD CHABOT

Nicollet de Belleborne, Jean, interpreter, explorer (b at Cherbourg, France *c*1598; d at Sillery, Qué 27 Oct 1642). Like BRÛLÉ he lived among the Indians to learn their languages, spending 2 years on Allumette I with the Algonquin and later staying with the Nipissing, 1620-29. He was the first European to explore the American Northwest on a fruitless search for the MER DE L'OUEST which took him to Green Bay and the Fox and Illinois rivers. He finally settled at Trois-Rivières, Qué, where he continued to act as an interpreter. On a mission to save an Iroquois prisoner, his shallop was overturned and he drowned. His "memories" recounting life among the Nipissing have come down to us in the JESUIT RELATIONS. JAMES MARSH

Nielsen, Erik Hersholt, politician (b at Regina 24 Feb 1924). He flew in 101 Squadron in WWII, winning the DFC for "courage and devotion to duty," and rejoined the RCAF, 1946-51, as a legal officer while earning a law degree at Dalhousie. He opened a law practice in Whitehorse in 1952 and was elected Conservative MP for the Yukon in 1957. Tenacious and combative in the House, he built a reputation based upon tough cross-examination of Liberal ministers, knowledge of parliamentary practice and loyalty to party and leader. He was minister of public works in the CLARK government 1979-80, deputy Opposition House leader 1980-81 and Opposition House leader 1981-83. After Clark's resignation as party leader, Nielsen was interim national head of the PCs, 2 Feb-11 June 1983. Brian MULRONEY named him deputy leader of the national PC Party in 1983, deputy prime minister and president of the Privy Council in 1984, and minister of national defence in 1985. He became a target of Opposition attacks in the House for his alleged stonewalling tactics and penchant for secrecy and was dropped from Cabinet in June 1986. He resigned his seat in Jan 1987 and became president of the Canadian Transport Commission. NORMAN HILLMER

Nighthawk, medium-sized bird of the goatsucker family (Caprimulgidae) characterized by a very short, exceptionally wide bill, enhanced by a ring of projecting bristles, possibly used to capture insects in flight. Nighthawks have large eyes; small, weak feet; long, pointed wings; and soft plumage of mottled blacks, browns, greys and whites. Most active at twilight and night, they spend the day perched lengthways along a limb or fallen log, take cover in a natural cavity, or on the ground, camouflaged by their plumage. Nighthawks are known for their seemingly erratic wing beats, for regularly repeating nonvarying calls for extended periods, and for producing a booming sound with their wing feathers during steep, high-speed dives. Common nighthawk (*Chordeiles minor*), occurring throughout all but arctic Canada, prefers to deposit its 2 eggs on open ground. Whip-poor-will (*Caprimulgus vociferus*)

of eastern and central Canada lays 2 eggs on the forest floor and forages near the ground. Common poorwill (*Phalaenoptilus nuttallii*) inhabits semiarid areas in southern BC and occasionally Alberta, laying 2 white eggs on bare ground, often under a shrub. This was the first bird species known to hibernate. When disturbed at the nest, these birds often hiss, snakelike, and feign injury.
PHILIP H.R. STEPNEY

Nightshade, common name for several plants of nightshade family (Solanaceae); properly, refers only to certain species of genus *Solanum*. Seven species of *Solanum* occur in Canada, of which only *S. carolinense* (horse or ball nettle), found in southern Ontario, is native. The most familiar nightshade is *S. dulcamara*, climbing nightshade or European bittersweet, found across Canada. It is an attractive vine with potatolike, purple or blue flowers and glossy, poisonous, red berries. Common, deadly or black nightshade (*S. americanum*) is poisonous to humans, and to browsing animals and poultry, causing similar symptoms in each (particularly paralysis and stupefaction). It need not be fatal, depending on amount ingested and maturity of plant. Tubers of cultivated POTATO (*S. tuberosum*) are poisonous if they become green from exposure to sun and their foliage is toxic to ruminants. The family is important as a source of food, drugs and ORNAMENTAL plants, and also contains many other POISONOUS PLANT members: belladonna or "deadly nightshade" (*Atropa belladonna*), not native to N America, is a garden plant with poisonous black berries; thornapples (jimsonweeds or Jamestownweeds, genus *Datura*), ornamentals with showy flowers, contain poisonous alkaloids in all parts; TOMATO vines (*Lycopersicon esculentum*) are poisonous when grazed by cattle; TOBACCO (*Nicotiana*) contains the toxic alkaloid, nicotine. JOHN M. GILLETT

Nigog, Le, arts magazine fd 1918 in Montréal by architect Fernand Préfontaine, writer Robert de Roquebrune and musician Léo-Pol MORIN. It was the brainchild of Préfontaine, who held a salon for cultivated friends at his Westmount home. Some of them, like Préfontaine himself, had been so impressed by their experience of Parisian artistic life that they came home determined to do something about a Québec which they found intellectually behind the times. The resulting review, *Le Nigog* (named for an instrument used by Indians to spear salmon), sought to educate French Canadians about contemporary art and literature and attracted some 30 collaborators, including 5 Anglophones, to its team. The editors won themselves immediate enemies when they proclaimed the primacy of form over subject matter as the condition of a universal art. Regionalists were horrified: the formalist claim destroyed the serenity with which they had supported the thinking of the establishment. The torture, however, lasted only one year and 12 issues (408 pages). The venture, which had opened up new horizons to Québec youth, gave early expression in French Canada to the views of the French modernists. *See also* LITERARY PERIODICALS IN FRENCH.
ARMAND AND BERNADETTE GUILMETTE

Nijinsky, champion colt by NORTHERN DANCER (b 1967). Bred in Oshawa, Ont, by E.P. TAYLOR's stables, Nijinsky was sold as a yearling and trained in Ireland. Winning 11 of his 13 races, including the Irish Sweeps Derby, he was the first horse in 35 years to win the English triple crown. Nijinsky has been second only to his father in his role as stud. In 1985, a one-year-old son of Nijinsky (grandson of Northern Dancer) was sold for $US 13.1 million – a record price for thoroughbreds. The horse was later named Seattle Dancer.
JAMES MARSH

Nile Expedition In early 1884 British Gen Charles Gordon went to the Sudan to rescue Egyptian garrisons cut off by a Muslim uprising led by the Mahdi; but he allowed himself to become trapped in the capital, Khartoum. In Mar 1884 Britain organized a rescue expedition under Garnet WOLSELEY, who had commanded the Anglo-Canadian force sent in 1870 to put down the RED RIVER REBELLION. Wolseley believed the Nile R offered the only reliable route to Khartoum and that Canadian VOYAGEURS could help ensure passage of a large expedition.

On the clear understanding that the 386 "voyageurs" (most of them in fact lumbermen) were volunteers in British pay, PM Macdonald's government did not obstruct recruitment by Gov Gen Marquess LANSDOWNE. For 6 months the recruits helped row, paddle, pole and drag the expedition's boats up the Nile, but in vain. Two days before the expedition sighted Khartoum on 26 Jan 1885, the city had fallen to Mahdists. Gordon had been killed. The expedition failed in its main purpose, but for Canadians it was an exotic opportunity to prove themselves against others from all over the growing British Empire.
ROY MACLAREN

Nimmons, Philip Rista, jazz musician (b at Kamloops, BC 3 June 1923). Nimmons formed his big band, Nimmons 'N' Nine (later Nimmons 'N' Nine Plus Six), in Toronto in 1953, after classical studies at the Juilliard School, New York (clarinet), and the Royal Conservatory of Music, Toronto (composition). The band was enlarged to 16 musicians in 1965 and made several more albums, including recordings of Nimmons most ambitious works, *Atlantic Suite* (1974), *Transformations* (1975) and *Invocation* (1976). Extremely popular through regular CBC broadcasts and concert tours, the band was active only sporadically by 1980. Long involved in music education, Nimmons's began teaching at U of T in 1973, and has helped establish jazz programs elsewhere. His recent work includes *Skyscape: Sleeping Beauty and the Lions* for concert band, which premiered at Expo 86.
MARK MILLER

Nine-Hour Movement, international workers' attempt to secure shorter working days; in Canada, Jan-June 1872. Beginning in Hamilton, the demand for the 9-hour day (some workers were expected to labour as long as 12 hours) spread quickly to Toronto and Montréal, gathering support in Ontario towns from Sarnia to Perth. Echoes were heard as far E as Halifax. For the first time Canadian labour organized a unified protest movement, developed tactics of resistance, and cultivated articulate working-class leaders. Nine-Hour leagues united union and non-union workers, and in May labour representatives formed the Canadian Labor Protective and Mutual Improvement Association. Some newspapers popularized labour's causes. In Mar-Apr an unsuccessful Toronto printers' strike reminded labour that employers were strongly antagonistic to workers' initiatives and that trade unions were actually illegal in Canada. On May 15 Hamilton's "nine-hour pioneers" defied opposition with a procession of 1500 workers. Skilled, respectable craftsmen emerged as labour leaders. James Ryan, a Great Western Railway machinist-engineer recently arrived in Canada, was Hamilton's central figure. In Toronto his counterpart was cooper John HEWITT, and in Montréal, James Black.

Although some groups won concessions, the movement was unsuccessful. Employer hostility helped its defeat, as did the waning of post-Confederation prosperity. Equally significant were divisions within the working class. Women and the unskilled figured peripherally at best, ensuring

that the struggle touched certain sectors more fully than others. All this, in conjunction with the apparent failure of militant strikes and workplace action to win decisive victories for workers, fed the attempt to secure rights politically through LABOUR LAW.

The Nine-Hour Movement was not an utter failure. Its struggle in 1872 indicated that labour had a public presence and that its interests, institutions and political stance reflected its unique social position and economic needs. It represented a necessary, if ambiguous, beginning in labour's capacity for self-government. The right to associate in trade unions was obtained. Working-class activists won major concessions immediately after 1872: repeal of repressive legislation, passage of laws strengthening workers' hands against employers, and franchise extension. The nine-hour pioneers gave way to the CANADIAN LABOR UNION.
BRYAN D. PALMER

Niosi, Bert (Bartolo), bandleader (b at London, Ont 10 Feb 1909; d at Mississauga, Ont 3 Aug 1987). He was known as "Canada's King of Swing" during his residency (1932-50) at the Palais Royale dance hall in Toronto. He joined CBC radio's "Happy Gang" (1952-59) and served as musical director (conductor, arranger) for several CBC TV series, including "The Tommy Hunter Show" (1965-76). Niosi was most notably a clarinetist and alto saxophonist, but he also played trumpet and trombone with his dance band. Two brothers were also dance band and radio musicians: Joe (1906-77), a bassist, and Johnnie (1914-65), a drummer. MARK MILLER

Nipawin, Sask, Town, pop 5488 (1986c), 4376 (1981c), inc 1937, is located 200 km NE of Saskatoon. The town is named for a height on the SASKATCHEWAN R just upstream from the present townsite (in Cree, "place where one stands"), which commanded a wide view of plain and river and served as a popular lookout point for the Indian bands that frequented the area. Nipawin is situated at a point on the Saskatchewan R where the prairie and woodland meet. Camping, fishing and other recreational activities are popular and 2 regional parks are located in the area. The soil to the S of the town is rich, and crops grown in the region include wheat, oats, barley, alfalfa and canola.
DON HERPERGER

Nipigon, Lake, 4848 km², elev 320 m, 165 m deep, located in northwestern Ontario, 100 km NE of THUNDER BAY, drains S into Lk SUPERIOR through the Nipigon R. The name may be derived from the Ojibwa *Animi-bee-gong* ("continuous water"). In the 18th century, the Cree who occupied the area were gradually displaced by the present inhabitants, the Ojibwa. European visitors included RADISSON and DES GROSEILLIERS (1659-60), Father Allouez (1667) and DULHUT, who in 1684, in response to competition from the HBC, built Ft La Tourette on the NE shore of the lake. Later posts were established by the NWC

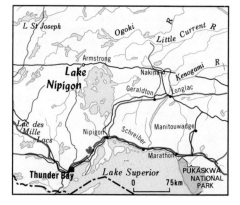

and HBC, but none grew into major settlements. With its limited population, unspoiled environment and abundant fish and wildlife, the area is ideal for outdoor recreation. The lake, the fourth largest in Ontario, supports a small commercial fishery and the adjacent forests supply pulpwood for mills in Red Rock and Thunder Bay. Since 1940 water has been transferred S from the AL-BANY R watershed, via the Ogoki Diversion, into Lk Nipigon, increasing its natural capacity and allowing the generation of 266 000 kW from 3 hydroelectric plants on the Nipigon R.

DAVID D. KEMP

Nipissing, Lake, 831 km², elev 196 m, fifth-largest in Ontario excluding the GREAT LAKES, is located 50 km NE of GEORGIAN BAY. Its name derives from an Indian word meaning "little water." Lk Nipissing runs in an E-W direction to a length of 80 km. Because it parallels the prevailing winds, navigation is frequently treacherous. It is comparatively shallow (about 10 m in most places) and is consequently well aerated, which is conducive to healthy plant and fish life. Dozens of rivers and streams drain into Lk Nipissing, the largest being the Sturgeon R. Historically its 2 most important outlets were the Mattawa R, which links it to the the OTTAWA R system, and the FRENCH R, which issues from its SW end, draining into Georgian Bay. Along this Ottawa-N Georgian Bay route travelled the early French explorers – the first being Étienne BRÛLÉ in 1610 – tracing a path followed by fur traders for the next 200 years. Permanent settlement around the lake dates from 1874 at Nipissing village in the SE and from 1882 at NORTH BAY when the CPR reached its NE shore. From the 1880s through to WWI Lk Nipissing was a major transportation route for settlers and lumbering, as steamships plied it regularly. Since then it has served mainly as a tourist and recreation waterway.

MATT BRAY

The shore of Lake Nipissing, Ont. The lake was on the main fur-trade route (*photo by John deVisser*).

Nishga The Nishga (or Nisga'a) were the original occupants of the Nass R valley of northwestern BC. They continue to live along the Nass, from which their name derives, in 4 villages: New Aiyansh, Kincolith, Greenville and Canyon City. Their language, Nass-Gitksan (with 3 surviving forms: Nishga, Eastern and Western GITKSAN), is related within the Tsimshian language family to Coast TSIMSHIAN. The Nishga are also held to be distantly related to the Penutian peoples of Oregon and California. Nishga life represented the sophisticated NORTHWEST COAST culture patterns, with monumental cedar carving (TOTEM POLES and other large figures, plank houses, canoes, etc), balanced reliance upon hunting, fishing and gathering, and the socially complex pageantry of the POTLATCH feast. Many aspects of this traditional life continue, although adapted to the occupations and technology of the contemporary Canadian economy. Every Nishga belongs to a descent group, or phratry, an aspect of individual identity which, like the rights to names, songs and dances,

is inherited through the maternal line. The Nishga language has been gradually replaced in use by English, but is now being taught as a subject in district schools. Once almost completely discontinued, the Nishga carving tradition has been revitalized, and Nishga totem poles now stand in Chicago, Phoenix and Vancouver, as well as on the banks of the Nass (primarily the work of Nishga carver Norman Tait and his associates).

In 1912 the Nishga were the first native group to initiate a legally constituted LAND CLAIM action against the Canadian government. The Nishga have always been at the front of the land-claims movement. Claiming continuing aboriginal rights to their traditional lands, they went to court in 1969 (*see* CALDER CASE, 1973) for a declaration that their title had never been surrendered by treaty or otherwise extinguished. Dismissed in BC courts, their contention was finally taken to the Supreme Court of Canada, where the notion of an aboriginal title was supported, but no agreement was reached as to how these rights might be evaluated or extinguished. An extensive Nishga land-claims case awaits adjudication. The federal government has agreed to settle aboriginal claims, while the BC government denies the existence of aboriginal rights or any obligation to negotiate a settlement of native claims.

J.V. POWELL AND VICKIE D. JENSEN

Niven, Frederick John, journalist, novelist (b at Valparaiso, Chile 31 Mar 1878; d at Vancouver 30 Jan 1944). Niven is best known for his novels of Scotland and Scots in Canada. Raised and educated in Scotland, Niven wrote about Canada for British papers after an 1899-1900 trip to BC. From 1908 he produced over 30 novels, 3 of which are not only considered his best work but are often thought of as an historically authentic trilogy of western settlement: *The Flying Years* (1935), *Mine Inheritance* (1940) and *The Transplanted* (1944) present Canada's development from the beginnings of the Selkirk settlement to WWII. Niven settled near Nelson, BC, after 1920.

TERRENCE CRAIG

Niverville, Louis de, painter (b at Andover, Eng 7 June 1933). Self-taught, Niverville worked 1957-63 as a graphic designer for the Canadian Broadcasting Corporation in Toronto alongside Dennis BURTON and Graham COUGHTRY. The turning point in his work, when he considers he really started to paint, was in 1966-67 with a mural for Expo Theatre in Montréal. After that he developed a formidable technique, particularly with collage, to express an astonishing, visionary world often wrought from childhood memories. Niverville's work is characterized by fresh and provocative thought. He directs his dreams, orchestrating their curious juxtapositions, strange happenings and colours into his paintings.

JOAN MURRAY

Nixon, Harry Corwin, politician, premier of Ontario (b at St George, Ont 1 Apr 1891; d there 22 Oct 1961). He won acclaim for his political longevity, spending 42 years as an Ontario MPP. Elected among the UNITED FARMERS OF ONTARIO in 1919, he eventually led that group's remnant into farmer Mitchell HEPBURN's revitalized Liberal Party and to the first Liberal victory in a quarter century (1934). Throughout Hepburn's regime, Provincial Secretary Nixon's stability helped balance the premier's mercurial temperament and after "Mitch" and his chosen successor, Gordon D. CONANT, resigned, the party chose Nixon as leader and thus premier (May 1943). An election followed 3 months later, and voters ousted the Liberals. Nixon continued to represent his rural constituency until his death.

BARBARA A. McKENNA

Nobbs, Percy Erskine, architect (b at Haddington, Scot 11 Aug 1875; d at Montréal 5 Nov 1964). As director 1903-10 and then professor of design (until 1940) at McGill School of Architecture, Nobbs was an important force in early Canadian architectural education. His training under Scottish Arts and Crafts architect Robert Lorimer led him to pioneer study of Canada's vernacular architecture, which he regarded as the key to functional, environmentally sensitive modern design. His works include notable buildings and extensions at McGill, numerous commissions in the Montréal region, and the development plan (with Frank Darling) and early academic buildings at the University of Alberta. SUSAN WAGG

Reading: Susan Wagg, *Percy Erskine Nobbs* (1982).

Nobel Prizes, endowed by Alfred Nobel (1833-96), the Swedish inventor of dynamite, were created in 1901. Five were awarded annually, one for each of physics, chemistry, medicine or physiology, literature and peace, until 1969 when a prize for economics was endowed by the Swedish state bank. Nobel prizes constitute a medal accompanied by a cash award; they are often shared by 2 or 3 winners. The 3 prizes for science, awarded by the scientific academies of Sweden, are generally considered the world's highest scientific accolade. Canadians have won 3: F.H. BANTING and J.J.R. MACLEOD were awarded the physiology/ medicine prize in 1923, and Gerhard HERZBERG and John POLANYI the chemistry prizes in 1971 and 1986, respectively.

Lists of prize-winners are convenient indicators of national standing in science. Literature prizes, nominally for "idealistic" writing, have a similar function, although awarded on more subjective grounds than those for science (where research citations indicate an individual's worldwide reputation). For example, the 1986 prize awarded Wole Soyinka was widely considered as appropriate recognition by Europe of African or Nigerian contributions to world culture. In this vein Canadian literature, increasingly recognized since the 1960s, may expect such an accolade reasonably soon. Irving LAYTON and Robertson DAVIES are known to have been proposed. Nominations may be made by many people, eg, university professors, to the Swedish Academy that awards the prizes.

Nobel Peace Prizes, awarded by the Norwegian Parliament, are more explicitly political, and have been awarded to institutions, eg, the Red Cross and UNICEF, as well as to individuals. L.B. PEARSON was awarded the Nobel Peace Prize in 1957 for diplomatic solutions to the SUEZ CRISIS of 1956. No Canadian has been awarded a Nobel prize for economics.

Nobel prizes acquired their political character in 1936, when a Peace prize was awarded to Karl von Ossietzky, a German citizen then in a concentration camp. Adolf Hitler decreed that no German should accept a Nobel prize. Three German scientists awarded prizes in 1938 and 1939 were presented with their medals (but not the cash) after the war. A number of individuals have refused Nobel prizes, eg, Boris Pasternak (literature, 1958), Jean-Paul Sartre (literature, 1964) and Le Duc Tho (peace, 1973). Nobel prizes for science are generally considered nonpolitical and none have been refused. DONALD J.C. PHILLIPSON

Reading: Harriet Zuckerman, *Scientific Elite: Nobel Prizes in the United States* (1977).

Noble, Charles Sherwood, agriculturist, industrialist (b at State Centre, Iowa 16 May 1873; d at Lethbridge, Alta 5 July 1957). He developed the Noble Blade, a cultivator that gave dryland farmers everywhere their first sure method of protecting soil from wind erosion. He homesteaded at Knox, N Dak, in 1896 and at Claresholm, Alta, in 1902. In 1909 he purchased 2024 ha near Lethbridge and founded the town of Nobleford. He farmed 13 134 ha by 1918 but lost everything to drought and depression in 1922. In the 1920s and 1930s he and several neighbours experimented with soil conservation methods, including the blade cultivator. Noble took the best of these ideas, patented a blade support system, and manufactured the Noble Blade, which cut off weeds below the soil surface, leaving the stubble undisturbed. He was named an MBE (1943) and received an LLD from U of A (1952).

ALEX JOHNSTON

Noise, unwanted or unmusical sounds, especially those that are random or irregular. The attitude that noise is not conducive to the well-being of sentient creatures is as old as history. The Babylonian story of the Flood, as recorded at about the time of Hammurabi (2000 BC), attributes the event to the anger of the gods over the noise of men. Egyptian priest Ipu-ner lamented, "Noise passes through the land leaving a trail of sadness." In his ethical directives to doctors, Hippocrates (400 BC) stated, "Noise must be avoided and kept well removed from the sick." Some of the sources of noise in those times may be gleaned from the history of Sybaris, a Greek colony in southern Italy (600 BC), where noisy trades, such as blacksmithing and stonemasonry, were prohibited within city walls. Impact noises were evidently the Sybarites' main concern. This was not the case in Imperial Rome where the main noise came from traffic. In that walled city of one million people, traffic congestion was so great that goods vehicles were allowed on the streets only at night. The continual movement of steel-rimmed wheels on stone-paved streets created a clatter that caused Marcus Martial (80 AD) to complain: "I have Rome right beside my bed at night." In England in the days of Henry VIII, the method of maintaining "the peace, quiet, rest and tranquility of the citizens" was still primarily by prohibiting certain noisy activities at least during resting hours (9 PM to 4 AM). Carts using the streets daily within the city of London could not "have wheels shod with iron, but bare, under pain of six shillings."

One problem that inhibited noise control before the 20th century was the inability to measure noise levels. The ear is an unreliable measuring instrument, a problem further complicated by the ability to become habituated to frequent or regular background sounds. Electronic amplifiers solved the problem and made sound-level meters convenient and reasonably standardized, allowing correlations between exposure to noise levels and quantitatively measured effects on people. "Boilermaker's ears," a loss of hearing resulting from long-term exposure to extreme noise, had long been recognized but, in the middle of this century, a more general relation was established between noise exposure and hearing loss. Subjective reactions (eg, annoyance) have yielded to ever-improved methods of measurement. Sound-level meters are calibrated in decibels (db) and have weighting networks discriminating against certain frequencies. For example, the A-weighting network, most widely used in dealing with human response, gives less weight to low frequencies because they produce less annoyance, hearing loss, etc.

Noise levels may be divided into 3 ranges according to their effects on people. Zero decibels is the approximate threshold of hearing. Levels of 0-40 db are generally judged as quiet and annoy only if they contain strong tone components. Those between 40 and 80 db may be a nuisance, depending on their nature and the conditions under which they occur. For example, the level of conversational speech at a distance of 30 cm averages about 60 db. A full orchestra may play for extended periods at 80 db and well above that for brief periods, yet we willingly pay for exposure to it. Nuisance noises generally occur outdoors in urban and suburban environments and are the subject of noise bylaws. Significant causes include car traffic, which is all-pervasive, truck and public transportation traffic (road and rail), which is more restricted, and air traffic, which is usually more localized but can have adverse effects even far from civilization. An important part of nuisance noise may come from air conditioners, lawnmowers, snowblowers, etc. These noises are annoying because they may startle and distract, and interfere with understanding speech or with rest and sleep. The limit set by bylaws for environmental noise may vary from a low of 40 db in suburban, purely residential areas at night, to a high of 75 db in a purely industrial area during the day.

Distance can be a very effective protection from environmental noise: in a uniform atmosphere, each time the distance doubles, the noise from a single source is reduced by 6 db. For example, most passenger cars travelling at 60 km per hour produce a noise level of 65 db at 15 m, 59 db at 30 m and 53 db at 60 m. Unfortunately, distance often cannot be controlled at will. Distance is the primary means of keeping air-traffic noise down in residential areas. Buildings, rock formations and forests act as noise barriers, most effective at short distances. House design can affect noise levels in the indoor environment: maximum wall attenuation (about 45 db), double windows with forced ventilation and sound-absorbing materials inside the house all help reduce noise. Noise levels of 80-120 db are uncommon in our environment, but are common in some industries and at airports.

Noise may cause physiological damage, especially to the inner ear; duration of exposure is fundamentally important. The Canadian government (like most other Western governments) has set a limit of 90 db to the noise level to which unprotected industrial workers may be constantly exposed during a working day. Many governments set this limit at 85 db. For higher levels, permissible exposure time is lower. Exposure without protection to levels above 115 db is usually not permitted. Noise levels above 120 db are rare except near powerful sources such as jet or rocket engines. Sound may be felt at 120 db; it will cause pain in the ears at 130 db. At 160 db, or higher, combustible sound-absorbing materials may be ignited by the heat into which the sound energy is transformed. White noise, which has nearly uniform energy distribution over the audible frequency range, is often used to mask low-level noise with annoying characteristics. It may also be used to mask low-level speech from neighbouring areas, thus preventing distraction and ensuring privacy. White noise is not usually effective when the offending noise is above about 40 db. Humans are not the only animals to suffer from excessive noise. For example, in wild bird populations, noises in the 40-80 db range may interfere with nesting success. Even normally acceptable sounds may be a source of debilitating stress, eg, birds may desert their breeding territories in response to excessive playbacks of territorial songs.

In comparison with other countries, Canada has little noise abatement legislation and the legislation that exists is aimed primarily at private individuals. Such laws as do exist to regulate various kinds of noise pollution are controlled by different levels of government. Noise from traffic, industry, etc, is regulated by municipal governments. Ottawa was the first Canadian city to pass a quantitative noise bylaw (1970). Aircraft noise is controlled by the Air Services Division of the federal Department of Transport. Canadian airports that have noise abatement policies for aircraft takeoffs and landings include Montréal International, Toronto-Lester B. Pearson International and Winnipeg International. No regulations exist to control small plane or helicopter noise. Partial curfews (affecting flights from midnight to 7 AM) are in place at Montreal and Toronto airports. WORKERS' COMPENSATION boards have authority to investigate industrial noise.

A great deal of research has been done at the NATIONAL RESEARCH COUNCIL OF CANADA on reducing noise at the source; for example, noise in suction rolls (eg, in paper mills) may be reduced by designing quiet drilling patterns. Attempts to block sound once it is produced resulted in development of hearing protectors with liquid-filled cushions, which are used at airports around the world.

Controlling noise in the community by community and road design and by legislation has received a great deal of attention, as has the transmission of sound under the complex conditions prevailing in the real world. The effects of various levels of noise on sleep characteristics have been studied for about 15 years. University of Toronto Institute of Aerospace Studies has been involved in examining AERODYNAMIC noise, both at boundary layers and in jets. At McMaster U, the chief effort in this field has been on community reaction to traffic noise.

G.J. THIESSEN

Reading: Environmental Health Directorate, *Noise Hazard and Control* (1979). G.J. Thiessen and T.S.W. Embleton, *Elements of Noise Control in Community Planning* (1987).

Non-Medical Use of Drugs, Royal Commission on the (LeDain Commission), was appointed 29 May 1969 and published 4 reports 1970-73. Chaired by Gerald LeDain, the commission investigated the role governments and courts should play in prohibiting and regulating the use and distribution of drugs (particularly opiate and marijuana but also alcohol, barbiturates, amphetamines and others) used for nonmedical purposes. The inquiry was commissioned when nonmedical drug use was in part symbolic of a more widespread controversy over life-styles and political participation, and it operated in an atmosphere of controversy. It broadened its interpretation of its mandate to include a discussion of the social values promoting drug use. Hearings were held across Canada, sometimes in camera with drug users, sometimes in coffee houses. The testimony of those affected by governmental and court actions was greatly emphasized. The final report (1973) contained extensive scientific documentation and recommended that policies should be adopted to discourage nonmedical drug use and that sanctions should be tailored to fit the crime. The inquiry did not recommend decriminalization of nonmedical drugs, although one of the 2 dissenting commissioners did. Most of the recommendations have not been legislated, but in enforcing existing legislation, the courts have followed the direction advocated by the inquiry. *See also* DRUG USE, NONMEDICAL.

LIORA SALTER

Non-Partisan League, an agrarian protest movement imported into Canada from N Dakota in 1915. The league became a political force in the Prairie provinces after its 1916 victory in the N Dakota state election. A number of leading urban radicals, including J.S. WOODSWORTH, William IRVINE and Salem BLAND, provided organizational assistance. The league hoped to replace the party system with a form of direct democracy where

CABINET domination of the legislature would be replaced by control of MLAs by their individual constituencies. Issues were to be decided on their merits rather than as a result of partisan difference. Although the league itself had disappeared as a political force by 1921, its influence continued to be felt in western Canada. Farmers, partly won over by its rhetoric, became more class conscious, and the old party system was swept away by a succession of new groups, the PROGRESSIVES, the UNITED FARMERS OF ALBERTA, SOCIAL CREDIT and the CO-OPERATIVE COMMONWEALTH FEDERATION.

J.T. MORLEY

Nonsuch, vessel which set out for HUDSON BAY from Gravesend, Eng, 3 June 1668, with Sieur DES GROSEILLIERS and a small crew and anchored off the mouth of the RUPERT R on Sept 29. A second sailing vessel, the *Eaglet*, with Pierre RADISSON aboard, was forced to turn back. The 2 French traders had persuaded Prince Rupert and several English investors to finance the voyage to prove that the vast fur resources of interior N America could be tapped via Hudson Bay. The *Nonsuch*'s crew wintered in James Bay and reached England on 10 Oct 1669 with a cargo of furs that the press reported "made them some recompense for their cold confinement." The charter for the HUDSON'S BAY COMPANY was granted on 2 May 1670.

In 1968 a replica of the *Nonsuch* was built in England to honour the 300th anniversary of the voyage. It was shipped to Montréal in 1970 and displayed on the Great Lakes and Pacific coast before being installed in a specially built museum in Winnipeg. The replica is considered to be the most accurate reconstruction of a 17th-century ship.

JAMES MARSH

Nonsuch, replica (1968) of the ship that in 1668 carried Sieur des Groseilliers on his historic voyage into Hudson Bay. It is housed in the Manitoba Museum (*courtesy Manitoba Museum of Man and Nature*).

Noorduyn Norseman The first bush plane of all-Canadian origin, it was designed after consultations with bush pilots and built in Montréal by R.B.C. (Bob) Noorduyn. It was a rugged, single-engined craft, with the large cabin, loading door and high wing that were prime requirements for bush aircraft. It first flew Nov 1935, and over 900 were built in all, many seeing service in the RCAF and 7 other air forces. Amphibious and capable of landing or taking off in tight spots, it became a standard workhorse of the Canadian North. In 1982, 41 were still registered in Canada; 4 are in museums.

JAMES MARSH

Nootka ("It goes around") is the popular but erroneous name for the score of ethnically related tribes along the Pacific coast of Vancouver I and around Cape Flattery (US). Locally, "Nootka" misnames only NOOTKA SOUND and its Mowach'at̲h̲ people. The island groups are also popularly termed "Westcoast" and those of the cape, "Makah," a Straits Salish word. In 1978 NUU-CHAH-NULTH ("All along the mountains"), was officially adopted by the Westcoast tribes as their name. *Aht* is another superseded anthropological

Interior of habitation at Nootka Sound, by John Webber, coloured pen and ink, 1778 (*courtesy Peabody Museum, Harvard University/T325*).

designation taken from the suffix "at̲h̲" ("people of") on the tribal names. "Nitinat" refers only to the Nitinat Lake tribes.

Linguistically, Nootka is one of the 2 main divisions of the Wakashan family, the other being Kwakiutl. Its dialects (and tribes) are Northern Nootka (Ch'i:qtlis'at̲h̲, Qa:'yo:kw'at̲h̲, 'I:ḥatis'at̲h̲, Noch'a:l—'at̲h̲, Mowach'at̲h̲, Machl—'at̲h̲, Central Nootka (Hucaubvrishkwi:'at̲h̲, Mano:his'at̲h̲, 'O:ts'o:s'at̲h̲, 'A:ho:s'at̲h̲, Qil—tsama'at̲h̲, Tla'o:kwi'at̲h̲, Yo:lo'il—'at̲h̲, T'okw'a:'at̲h̲, Hucaubvro:choqtlis'at̲h̲, Ts'isha:'-at̲h̲, Ho:pach'as'at̲h̲, Ho:'i:'at̲h̲), Nitinat (Di:ti:d'a:'tx̲, Tl—o:'o:ws'a:tx̲, Qwa:badow'a:'tx̲, P'a:chi:-d'a:'tx̲), Makah (Q'widishch'a:'at̲h̲) and Ozette ('Osi:l—'a:'tx̲). Speakers of Nitinat, Makah and Ozette can grasp the Northern and Central Nootka dialects, but not vice versa.

The Nootka date back at least 4000 years in their land. Territories were defined by tribe, but in total stretched from Cape Scott (N Vancouver I) to past Ozette Lk (Washington state) in the S. Relations were generally friendly with the culturally and linguistically related KWAKIUTL on the NW, but less so with the more alien Coast Salish groups to the E and S. Trade and intermarriage occurred in all directions. White contact dates from PERÉZ HERNÁNDEZ's visit in 1774, and the initial focus was the sea-otter trade. Acquisition of guns intensified warfare, with well-armed Nootka groups such as the Mowach'at̲h̲, 'A:ho:sat̲h̲ and Tla'o:kwi'at̲h̲ nearly exterminating others such as the Machl—'at̲h̲, 'O:ts'o:s'at̲h̲ and T'ok'wa:'at̲h̲. Introduced diseases and alcohol so reduced and debilitated the Nootkans that in the second half of the 19th century colonialization was almost unopposed. Population, estimated at 30 000 at first contact, plunged to only about 2000 in the 1930s. In 1986 there were about 5000. No land surrender was signed on Vancouver I, but in the late 19th century small INDIAN RESERVES were demarcated with a total area only half that of the Cape Flattery Reservation established in the US by treaty in 1855 (*see* INDIAN TREATIES). Curtailment of hunting and fishing, including prohibition of the vital salmon weir traps, deprived Nootkans of their traditionally rich economic base.

Nootkans were accomplished woodworkers, outstanding products being fine cedar CANOES and big multifamily houses (*see* HOUSE; NORTHWEST COAST INDIAN ART). Hunting/fishing gear and techniques were refined. Fish (particularly salmon and halibut), sea mammals and shellfish, were mainstays of their diet, supplemented by fowl,

deer, elk, bear and plant foods. Clothing was comparatively uncomplicated. The seasonal round involved moving by large canoes between winter concentrations in sheltered inlets and smaller summer camps scattering to the outside coast. WHALING with harpoons and floats was a cultural highlight, both economically important and prestigious. Spirit powers were believed to animate all things, and power seeking was common. Any undertaking was prepared for by secret purificatory rituals entailing bathing and scrubbing in cold waters.

Society was closely ranked, with a continuous gradation from chiefs to commoners and a slave class of war captives. Descent was traced through both male and female connections. Property rights were keenly held, including intangibles such as names, songs and stories. Chiefs owned most of the rights and were wealthy. Intensive ceremonialism occasioned frequent feasting and entertainment with song, dance, contests and theatricals (*see* POTLATCH). Especially elaborate celebrations were the Wolf Ritual cycle of a general secret society, girls' puberty rites and marriage. A zestful sense of life prevailed by the sea.

Historically the Mowach'at̲h̲ provided the setting for the NOOTKA SOUND CONTROVERSY, 1789-94, with Chief MAQUINNA (actually M'okwina) their leading participant. In 1811 Chief Wi:kinanish of the Tla'o:kwi'at̲h̲ took the TONQUIN after provocation. In 1864 the Ahousat captured the schooner *Kingfisher*, and a punitive expedition was sent

Woman of Nootka Sound, by John Webber, pencil or pen and ink, 1778 (*courtesy Peabody Museum, Harvard University/T326*).

against them – the Denman naval expedition. The Bering Sea fur sealing, about 1870 to 1911, was carried out by Nootkans transported there with their canoes. In the 1980s they live mainly by fishing and logging. Traditional culture and language are weakened, but a strong native identity persists. *See also* NATIVE PEOPLE: NORTHWEST COAST and general articles under NATIVE PEOPLE.   E.Y. ARIMA

Reading: E.Y. Arima, *The West Coast Nootka People* (1983).

Nootka, an historic fur-trading centre at Friendly Cove, NOOTKA SOUND, on the W coast of Vancouver I, BC. The name is a European misnomer given to the Nootka Indian village of Yuquot ("windy place"). Archaeological investigations show that it has been occupied for more than 4000 years. First prolonged contact between Indians and Europeans on the NORTHWEST COAST took place at Yuquot with the arrival of Capt James COOK in 1778. As a result of trading sea otter pelts with the Cook expedition, Yuquot became known as a friendly village with large quantities of furs. A maritime fur trade began in 1785, and Nootka soon became the main port of call on the Northwest Coast. Spain established a military post, San Lorenzo de Nutka, at Yuquot 1789-95. The fur trade declined in the 1790s and essentially ended at Nootka Sound by 1800 owing to the extermination of the sea otter. Yuquot was the summer village of the Mowach'ath, and is still occupied today.   JOHN DEWHIRST

Nootka Sound, BC, is an inlet on VANCOUVER I'S western coast, 270 km NW of VICTORIA. From a cluster of forested islands near the mouth of the sound, 3 deep inlets (Tahsis, Tlupana and Muchalat) penetrate inland. One of these reaches 65 km inland to Strathcona Provincial Park, another to the sawmilling community of Tahsis. The first inhabitants of the region were the NOOTKA, who made their living by hunting and fishing. They were the only Canadian Indians to specialize in WHALING and were the first in BC to meet Europeans. The coastal environment was particularly bountiful in fish of many varieties, and the semisedentary Nootka developed an elaborate culture.

The sound was likely first explored by James COOK in 1778, although PERÉZ HERNÁNDEZ had approached it 4 years earlier. Cook first called the inlet King George's Sound, then Nootka Sound thinking this was its Indian name. Soon after, the region became a centre of trade and then of competition among Russia, Britain and Spain. In 1789 a Spanish force occupied the sound and built a fort; 2 months later a British force arrived and a quarrel developed. In the ensuing NOOTKA SOUND CONTROVERSY, Spain eventually agreed to a convention (1794) according to which both nations were free to navigate and fish in the Pacific, to trade and establish settlements. At first the Nootka prospered from the sea-otter fur trade that followed European explorations, but the introduction of diseases such as smallpox virtually wiped them out. The main Indian settlement at Yuquot ("windy place") is still important for the remaining Nootka, many of whom work in pulp mills at Gold River and CAMPBELL RIVER. *See also* NORTHWEST COAST.   ALAN F.J. ARTIBISE

Nootka Sound Controversy, involved the competing claims of Spain and Britain for control of trade and navigation on the NORTHWEST COAST and in the Pacific Ocean, 1789-94. Spain claimed the Pacific as its exclusive territory by right of the Treaty of Tordesillas (1494). Britain argued that navigation was open to any nation, and territorial claims had to be backed by effective occupation. In July 1789 Esteban MARTÍNEZ, Spanish commandant at NOOTKA SOUND, seized several British merchant ships. John MEARES, part owner of these

ships, reported the seizure to his government in his *Memorial* of 30 Apr 1790. Britain demanded compensation and threatened war, but Spain declined to pay compensation and prepared for war, hoping its long-standing Bourbon ally, France, would provide assistance. France, undergoing revolution, refused. Under the terms of 3 conventions Spain was obliged to accede to British requests and compensate the British for their losses. Under the third Nootka Convention (11 Jan 1794) Spain and Britain recognized each other's rights of trade at Nootka Sd and in other Pacific coast areas not already controlled by Spain. Subjects of either nation could erect temporary buildings at Nootka, but not permanent garrisons or factories. Neither nation could claim exclusive sovereignty. Nootka Sd was to be maintained as a free port by Spain and Britain, and to be open to other nations. On 28 Mar 1795 both countries completed their withdrawal from Nootka Sd. The controversy ended in symbolic victory for British mercantile and political interests.

BARRY M. GOUGH

NORAD (North American Air Defence Agreement), announced on 1 Aug 1957; renamed North American Aerospace Defence Command in 1981, it integrates the air-defence forces of the US and Canada under a joint command at Colorado Springs, Colo. The agreement has occasionally been a focus of controversy. PM John DIEFENBAKER and Minister of National Defence George PEARKES, just installed in office, hastily accepted the advice of the Canadian military and agreed to integrate the RCAF with the USAF for the air defence of the continent. The decision was taken without adequate preparation (the formal signing did not take place until 12 May 1958, one indication of subsequent concerns), and the government was roasted for its haste by the Liberal Opposition, who themselves would almost certainly have accepted a similar agreement had the 1957 election result turned out differently.

Technically the agreement has been a success, co-ordinating 2 air forces in a difficult task and keeping Canadian airmen in touch with doctrine and policy – and keeping them flying. But because the concurrence of the 2 governments is required before formal alerts or action, there has been difficulty, most notably in 1962 during the CUBAN MISSILE CRISIS. The Americans went on standby alert as soon as the crisis was apparent, but the Diefenbaker government delayed for a period of days, angering the Kennedy administration and provoking much criticism in Canada. The matter was complicated by the fact that the BOMARC MISSILES at the 2 Canadian Bomarc bases had no nuclear warheads, another consequence of divisions in Cabinet; and the Bomarc itself was greatly resented by partisans of the CF-105 AVRO ARROW aircraft, which had been cancelled by the government 3 years earlier in a decision that some (unfairly) blamed on NORAD.

NORAD has been kept in place by successive governments. The renaming of the command in 1981 reflected a new emphasis on defence and warning against missiles, and the advent of Cruise missiles increased NORAD's necessity. The Canadian government recognized this in 1985 by deciding to upgrade the North Warning System. In 1987 the Canadian component consisted of CF-18 interceptor aircraft and, as from the beginning, a Canadian as the deputy commander at Colorado Springs.   J.L. GRANATSTEIN

Reading: C. Gray, *Canadian Defence Priorities* (1972); J.T. Jackel, *No Boundaries Upstairs: Canada, the US and the Origins of North American Air Defence* (1987).

Noranda Mines Limited, with head offices in Toronto, is a multinational, multi-product com-

pany. The company was incorporated in 1964 as an amalgamation of Geco Mines Ltd (incorporated in 1953) and Noranda Mines Limited (incorporated in 1922 to acquire mining claims in Ontario and Québec from a private syndicate). The company grew through acquisitions in mining and related industries, and today it is a diversified natural-resource company. Its principal activities are in mining, manufacturing and forest products, with its subsidiary, Noranda Sales Corporation Ltd, handling worldwide sales. Noranda Mines has properties in Canada, the US and overseas, including S America and Australia. In 1986 it had sales or operating revenue of $3.5 billion (ranking 24th in Canada), assets of $5.9 billion (ranking 15th) and 47 600 employees. Brascade Resources holds 46% of the shares.

DEBORAH C. SAWYER

Nordicity, concept developed in Canada from the 1960s that refers to the perceived state or degree of "northernness" of high-latitude regions. Depending on the area under consideration, nordicity may be determined by CLIMATE, BIOGEOGRAPHY, GEOGRAPHY, psychology or other factors. The concept deals with questions such as how severe is the northern zone of Canada? How has this frigid periphery of N America been perceived? To understand these questions it is necessary to recognize that the NORTH has cultural as well as physical dimensions. Objective, calculated geographic nordicity expresses a certain image of this cold region, but cannot account for all the different perceptions of those who live there.

Definitions of the North are primarily dependent on the criteria chosen to make up the definition. Originally the Arctic was defined simply as a region of polar night or day, with a frozen subsoil and without trees or agriculture. The nordicity concept developed a more encompassing definition which included physical and human geography. A nordic index was devised for calculating and quantifying the number of "polar values" (called VAPO) and establishing the nordicity of a space or phenomenon. This index is based on 10 criteria, each expressed on a scale of 0-100. The criteria include one locational variable and 5 natural and 4 human factors. For location, 45° N lat is assigned 0 VAPO; 90° N, 100 VAPO. Summerheat values range from more than 150 days above 5.6°C, 0 VAPO, to 0 days, 100 VAPO. Similarly, with annual cold, 550 degree days below 0°C is assigned 0 VAPO; 6650 days, 100 VAPO. The human factors are more difficult to quantify but, for example, degree of economic activity ranges from "interregional centre with multiple services, heavy investment," assigned 0 VAPO, to "no production, none foreseen," 100 VAPO. A table outlining these variables allows an arithmetic evaluation of the nordic character of cold regions and facilitates understanding of the factors most im-

Nordicity Compared by Polar Value (VAPO) Criteria

Nordic Criterion	Schefferville, Qué	Verkhoianski, USSR[1]	Keewatin, NWT[2]
Latitude	21	44	42
Summer heat	37	62	60
Annual cold	42	100	75
Types of ice	60	90	75
Total precipitation	0[3]	90	90
Plant cover	40	40	80
Accessibility by land	20	50	100
Air service	20	40	100
Resident population	20	50	90
Economic activities	35	65	100
Total[4]	295	631	812

[1] Considered the pole of coldness in the Northern Hemisphere
[2] Interior portion
[3] Too much precipitation to fit concept of nordic aridity
[4] For comparison, the North Pole has 1000 VAPO

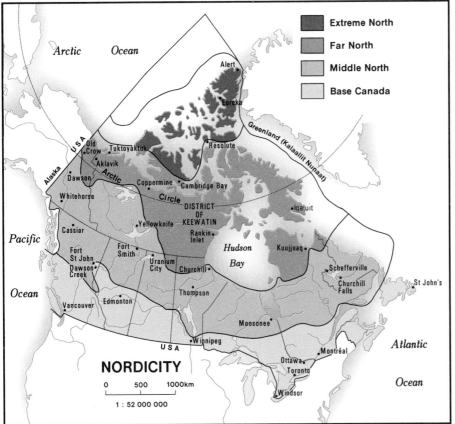

NORDICITY

Extreme North
Far North
Middle North
Base Canada

0   500   1000km

1 : 52 000 000

Arctic Ocean

Alert

Eureka

Greenland (Kalaallit Nunaat)

Resolute

USA
Old
Crow
Tuktoyaktuk
Aklavik
Alaska
Dawson
Whitehorse
Arctic
Coppermine
Cambridge Bay
Circle
DISTRICT
OF
KEEWATIN
Cassier
Yellowknife
Rankin
Inlet

Iqaluit

Pacific
Fort
St John
Fort
Smith
Uranium
City
Churchill
Hudson
Bay
Kuujjuaq

Ocean
Dawson
Creek
Thompson
Churchill
Falls
Scheffervile
St John's

Vancouver
Edmonton

Moosonee

Winnipeg
USA
Atlantic

Ottawa
Montréal
Toronto
Ocean

Windsor

---

portant to this evaluation. Another useful tool is the *isonord*, a line on a map joining points that have equal polar values.

This evaluation process provides information for the task of fixing the southern limit of the North. Formerly, that limit was determined by a single factor, eg, an isotherm (10°C in July), a latitude (often the ARCTIC CIRCLE), an administrative boundary (60°N lat), or a topographic feature (Hudson Str). No one factor is now considered definitive, but nordicity does increase abruptly above isonord 200, suggesting a fundamental break running across Canada. This isonord runs along the southern edge of Long Range in Newfoundland, sweeps along the lower Côte-Nord and Minganie and runs N of the Saguenay depression in Québec and Lake of the Woods, Ont. It passes through Lk Winnipegosis, Man, and touches Montreal Lk, Sask. In Alberta, it runs N of the agricultural area of the Peace R country to the oil and gas fields of Fort St John, BC. In BC, the CORDILLERA complicates the determination of the true North. Pockets of discontinuous PERMAFROST lodge in the summits of peaks in southern parts of the province; temperate conditions are found in the bottoms of northern valleys. However, considering all criteria and despite the anomalies, the boundary of the cordilleran North can be fixed between 53° and 55°.

The nordicity index and the zones that it defines can have several uses. Apart from setting the North's southern limits, it allows subdivision of the polar world itself into zones. Moreover, it has been used for the classification of documents, construction of a scale of workers' allowances, analysis of the evolution through time of tourist potential, estimation of the cost of services, and for a study by the Fisheries Board of Canada. This index would provide a more realistic basis for determining royalty zones in the development of northern PETROLEUM than does the simple division by latitude now used.

Canada's ecological limit has been fixed by the federal government at 200 nautical miles (370

km) from shore in the Arctic Ocean. Thus the nordic political territories include parts of 7 provinces, the YT and the NWT. Including the waters within the North and the oceanic water belt, the nordic space occupies about 70% of Canada's territory. This seems a more exact estimate than the official 39%, which includes only the landmasses and fresh waters of the YT and the NWT. Inside this immense zone (one-third water), the population in 1971 was less than 300 000 resident inhabitants, a demographic mass comparable to that of Alaska and Iceland; by 1990 the population is expected to be 400 000. Canada's nordicity is more severe than that of Scandinavia or even Siberia, a fact that discourages settlement. The Canadian North consists of hundreds of small settlements scattered over a territory larger than Europe. A web of technical and social services keeps these isolated worlds in touch with the South.

Northern Zones

The idea that the North could be divided into broad East-West bands appeared repeatedly in works of the mid-19th century. For example, in 1832 Joseph Bouchette divided western Canada as follows: everything S of 56° N lat, everything between 56° and 65°, everything from 65° to the Arctic Ocean. Thematic divisions between boreal forest and TUNDRA, between subarctic and arctic, between seasonal and permanent pack ice, between regions of partial and total light, between Indian and Inuit lands, all reflect other zonal gradations. The regional subdivisions of the North include 3 major regions of about 1 million km² each, the boundaries of which do not follow lines of latitude.

Middle North Bounded by isonords 200 and 500 VAPO, the region has a subarctic climate, stretches from Labrador to the YT and includes many lakes and bogs. It has been the domain of pioneering thrusts, of "vertical" corridors for the extraction of MINERAL RESOURCES and the production of HYDROELECTRICITY. The Middle North in-

cludes about 90% of the North's permanent inhabitants. About 85% of the Middle North lies within provincial boundaries, a fact that receives insufficient political attention. Examples of mid-nordic nordicity include Churchill, Man, 450 VAPO; Dawson City, YT, 435; Yellowknife, NWT, 390; Cassiar, BC, 377; Labrador Sea, Nfld, 297; Red Lake, Ont, 220.

Far North spans the area between 500 and 800 VAPO. Natural factors (eg, limited summer heat, tundra landscape) and human factors (eg, presence of Inuit and rarity of major RESOURCE exploitation) again combine to express a total zonal situation. Being partly composed of interconnected bodies of water, the Far North allows a certain amount of penetration by boat in summer. Since only about 25 000 inhabitants live in this quarter of the Canadian landmass, the ecumene of primary activity is extremely extensive. The Far North is an arctic land that has few residential oases and is economically very weak. Its population, unlike that of the Middle North, consists mostly of indigenous people. Examples of this nordicity include Resolute, NWT, 775 VAPO; Old Crow, YT, 624; Hudson Bay (centre), 622; Aklavik, NWT, 511.

Extreme North This hypernorthern region, which covers less than 10% of Canada's landmass, includes heavily iced marine waters with a nordicity in the 850 VAPO range. It is a region of ice (on land, at sea and in the depths). The Extreme North is almost devoid of settlements, with the exception of a few white outposts such as Alert (NWT). Government expenditure is usually larger than private. Alert has 878 VAPO; Eureka, NWT, 857; the Barnes Ice Cap, 804.

Historic Nordicity

Like any region defined by natural and psychological factors (the latter heavily influencing settlement), the North has varied in size over its history. Even if, in the course of a generation, the boundaries of permafrost, sea ice and boreal forest barely change, the factors involved in settlement and abandonment of habitations, in economic development and in the creation of mental perspectives are constantly evolving. At the beginning of the Age of Discovery, Canada was considered all north because of the severe winter conditions. As Morris Zaslow has noted: "In the immediate post-Confederation period, anything beyond Lake Nipissing was termed North." In Québec and central Labrador, iron-ore exploration and hydroelectric development have caused this outland to lose some of its former polaricity. According to the nordic index, in 1941 the future site of Schefferville, Qué, had 533 VAPO; 25 years later, 295. Settlement caused its denordification. Thus, in the last century, as a result of a redefinition of zones, the real Canadian North has become less widespread and the average nordicity of the country has become lower. A quantitative denordification of approximately 25% has occurred.

Between 1881 and 1971, the resident population of the North multiplied sevenfold (43 060-292 702). The present nordic space, especially the Middle North, has been overrun by Canadian and foreign immigrants, but this penetration has been uneven in time and space. The movement had begun by 1881 (census year). At that time, the future province of Newfoundland/Labrador accounted for more than half of all the whites resident in the Canadian North. By 1910, 8000-10 000 northerners (whites and Amerindians) lived in the NWT, the YT, Manitoba, Ontario and Québec, but the influx only became important in the course of the 20th century. Between 1911 and 1941 settlement patterns once again modified the regional pattern. As a result of mineral exploration and agricultural development along the pioneer fringes of western Canada, Alsama (Alta-Sask-Man) had 50% of the nordic population and became the main nordic mega-region; Manitoba stood first among the provinces. Since the mid-20th century, a strong natural increase in the indigenous population and increases in governmental administration and oil exploration have caused an increase in Canada's northern population. Thus, the YT, the NWT and Newfoundland/Labrador have experienced increased growth percentages. In 1971 Alsama was still first, followed by the territories (counted as one). BC, Ontario and Québec accounted for only 22% of the nordic population of the country.

Developmental Nordicity

The North has known at least 5 developmental visions since Martin FROBISHER's mining projects of the 16th century. An initial period of optimism, based on the hope of discovering a NORTHWEST PASSAGE, ended when that proved unprofitable. The resulting view, that the North was almost totally useless, led to suggestions that nordic lands should be sold or given away. A more recent political vision is of the North as an unlimited reservoir of natural resources. The final visions are an ideology of nondevelopment ("Freeze the Arctic") and one of integrated planning that respects nordic culture.

At least 2 categories of nordicities of exploitation must be identified: nordicity of use and normative nordicity. The first can be seen inductively through examination of the activities of entrepreneurs and employers who lack specialized training for work in the North. Clearly, the nordicity of use has influenced economic and political growth both in private and government frameworks. Many activities in the North seem to have been determined by southern Canadian interests, by federal jurisdiction over the territories, and by the inadequate appreciation of Amerindian ethnicity. These activities have resulted in exploitation poorly adjusted to northern conditions. Normative nordicity, corresponding to the vision of an ideal and theoretical good, is based on the triple principle of cultural, ecological and regional respect for the North. Its objective is a coherent plan, not a laisser-faire philosophy. These 2 developmental nordicities are widely separated ideologically. Happily, this gulf has been somewhat diminished by a series of measures: recognition of certain Amerindian rights (eg, in the JAMES BAY AGREEMENT); development technologies that increasingly respect arctic regions (CONSTRUCTION, resource extraction, TRANSPORTATION); changes in administrative policies; educational programs that are more appropriate to northern cultures; Amerindian political activity. Thanks to an increasingly developed multidisciplinary study of all aspects of the North, a new political economy of the North with a nationalist tone and a new GEOPOLITICS encompassing Canada as a whole are developing. The process of the entry of the North into Canadian affairs is far from complete. *See also* RESOURCE MANAGEMENT. LOUIS-EDMOND HAMELIN

Reading: Louis-Edmond Hamelin, *Nordicité canadienne* (1975, rev 1980, tr *Canadian Nordicity: It's Your North, Too,* 1979).

Normal Schools were first established by provincial departments of education in mid-19th-century British N America, as institutions to train teachers for the rapidly expanding tax-supported public education systems of the day. The term "normal" derived from France's École normale supérieure of the 1790s, and implied that teaching methods used therein would become the norm for all schools within the government's jurisdiction. For a century or more, Canadian normal schools remained under the direct control of provincial departments of education, and were criticized for strict adherence to established and prescribed methods of instruction. Alberta in 1945 was the first province to transfer teacher training from normal schools to university faculties of education. Other provinces followed suit, though a few provincially controlled normal schools, renamed teachers' colleges, still survive in Canada. ROBERT M. STAMP

Norman, E. Herbert, diplomat, scholar (b at Karuizawa, Japan 1 Sept 1909; d at Cairo, Egypt 4 Apr 1957); he studied at U of T and Harvard, and, having joined the Dept of External Affairs, was posted to Japan, 1940-42. In 1946 he returned there with the Allied occupation's Office of Counter Intelligence, and published extensively on Japan. His career was blighted by charges that he had been a Communist during the 1930s. The charges were true enough, but Minister of External Affairs Lester B. PEARSON affirmed his confidence in Norman, kept him in the diplomatic service, and sent him as ambassador to Egypt. When the US Senate again publicized charges that Norman was a security risk, he committed suicide. ROBERT BOTHWELL

Norman Wells, NWT, Settlement, pop 627 (1986c), 420 (1981c), is located on the N bank of the MACKENZIE R, 145 km S of the ARCTIC CIRCLE and 684 air km NW of YELLOWKNIFE. It was the first settlement in the NWT to be established entirely as a result of nonrenewable-resource development. During WWII an oil pipeline was built between Norman Wells and Whitehorse, YT; it was abandoned after the war. Oil and gas fields in the area produce over a million barrels of crude oil per year, and the community is a major supplier of fuel to northerly locations, as well as a transportation centre for air and river traffic. In the spring of 1985, the Norman Wells pipeline, linking Norman Wells to the south, was completed. ANNELIES POOL

Norman Wells, NWT. The pipeline, dredge, trench and work camp are visible *(photo by Jim Merrithew).*

Normandy Invasion On 6 June 1944, after almost a year of special assault and combined operations training, the 3rd Canadian Infantry Division (Maj-Gen R.O.D. Keller) and the 2nd Canadian Armoured Brigade (Brig R.A. Wyman) were part of the Allied forces which attacked the Normandy coast of France in Operation *Overlord.* Landing on "Juno" Beach, between Vaux and St Aubin-sur-Mer, the Canadians penetrated about 9 km inland by the end of D-Day. Beating back enemy counterattacks during the next several days, the Canadians continued to thrust inland against growing opposition, aided by highly effective tactical air support. Supported by British formations on either flank, a lodgement area was gained and additional formations reinforced the assault forces. In the Canadian sector the 2nd Canadian Infantry Division (Maj-Gen C. FOULKES)

and 4th Canadian Armoured Division (Maj-Gen G. Kitching) arrived to form the Second Canadian Corps under Lt-Gen G.G. SIMONDS. With these and additional forces, the First Canadian Army (Lt-Gen H.D.G. CRERAR) took over command of the eastern part of the Allied front.

During June and July the Canadians fought a number of battles to seize enemy positions. Carpiquet, Caën, Vaucelles, Bourguébus Ridge and Verrières Ridge were some of the major areas where heavy fighting took place. During late July and Aug while the Canadian and British forces held most of the German formations on the eastern sector, the American Army broke the German line at St-Lô. The possibility of a massive pincer movement to encircle the German armies in Normandy was presented to the Allied commanders. The Canadian Army was ordered to launch several massive armoured and infantry attacks towards Falaise. After a series of fierce battles, Falaise was seized on Aug 16, and in the final attack on Trun and Chambois, Canadians and Poles met with American forces to complete the pincer movement. This ended the Normandy Campaign. The pursuit of the enemy into Belgium and the Netherlands began. Canadian forces suffered 18 444 casualties during the Normandy fighting. The 1st Canadian Parachute Battalion, which fought under British command, lost over 300 officers and men in their operations. *See also* WORLD WAR II. *See* map on p 1507. R.H. ROY

Noronic, Great Lakes steamer of the Canada Steamship Lines Ltd, built at Pt Arthur, Ont, in 1913. It was consumed by fire in Toronto at dockside on 17 Sept 1949. There was a tragic delay in summoning the fire department and 118 people died. *See also* DISASTERS. JAMES MARSH

Norquay, John, politician, premier of Manitoba, 1878-87 (b near St Andrews, Man 8 May 1841; d at Winnipeg 5 July 1889). One of Red River's most distinguished sons, Norquay successfully moved from the fur trade and the river lot into modern business and politics after Manitoba entered Confederation. His great-grandmother was a native woman and his paternal ancestors were jacks-of-all-trades at fur-company posts. He was one of the best students in Red River schools and was successively a teacher, farmer and fur trader between 1857 and 1870, when he

John Norquay, Manitoba's only premier of mixed European and native ancestry *(courtesy Provincial Archives of Manitoba/N5781).*

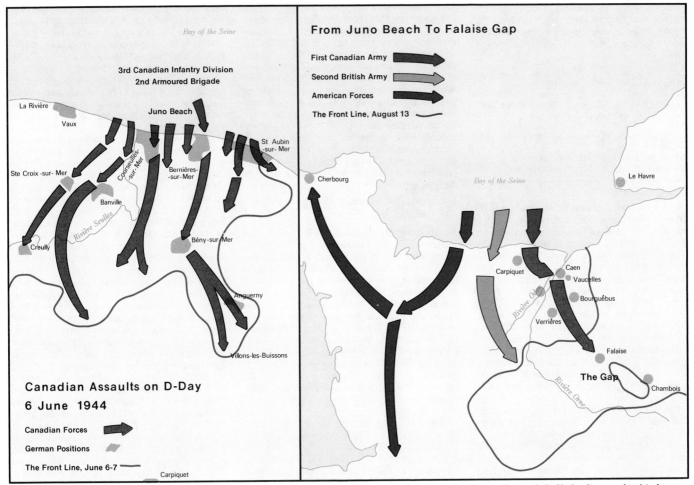

From Juno Beach To Falaise Gap

First Canadian Army
Second British Army
American Forces
The Front Line, August 13

3rd Canadian Infantry Division
2nd Armoured Brigade

Juno Beach

Bay of the Seine

La Rivière
Vaux
Ste Croix -sur- Mer
Courseulles-sur-Mer
Banville
Bernières-sur-Mer
St Aubin -sur- Mer
Rivière Seulles
Creully
Bény-sur-Mer
Anguerny
Villons-les-Buissons

Canadian Assaults on D-Day
6 June 1944

Canadian Forces
German Positions
The Front Line, June 6-7
Carpiquet

Cherbourg
Bay of the Seine
Le Havre
Carpiquet
Caen
Vaucelles
Bourguébus
Verrières
Rivière Orne
Falaise
The Gap
Chambois
Rivière Orne

was elected to Manitoba's first legislature. He rose quickly to prominence in the House, was a Cabinet minister (1871-74, 1875-78), and became premier upon the retirement of R.A. DAVIS on the basis of his strong following among "old" (pre-1870) settlers and French-speaking Manitobans.

The Norquay government successfully extended Manitoba's boundaries and secured larger federal subsidies, but it eventually foundered upon Canada's railway policy. Caught between PM John A. MACDONALD's guarantee of a CPR freight monopoly and Manitoban demands for rail competition, Norquay chose to fight Ottawa in 1887 by building a railway to the US. Macdonald intervened and, by an apparent double cross, precipitated a financial scandal and the collapse of the Norquay ministry. Though he briefly led a small opposition to the new GREENWAY government, Norquay's sudden death in 1889 prevented him from restoring his reputation in Canadian public life.

Norquay was widely liked in Manitoba. His name has been kept alive not only because he was the province's only premier of mixed European and native ancestry but because of his amiable disposition and considerable talents.

GERALD FRIESEN

Norris, Hannah Maria, Baptist missionary (b at Canso, NS 30 Nov 1842; d at Toronto 14 Sept 1919). Though baptized a Congregationalist as a child, Hannah was raised in a strong Baptist community and eventually received adult baptism in that church. In 1869 Norris determined to go to Burma as a missionary and appealed to the Baptist women of NS to support her plans. On 18 June 1870 in Canso the first Canadian woman's missionary aid society was formed for this purpose. Other locals were set up, and in 1884 the Woman's Baptist Missionary Union of the Maritime

provinces was organized, an example followed elsewhere in Canada and by many other denominations. Norris went to Burma and eventually married the Rev W.F. Armstrong. She became committed to building a school for all nationalities in Rangoon, and travelled widely in search of funds for this project. She remained in Burma until 1919 when she returned to Canada.

WENDY L. MITCHINSON

Norris, Leonard Matheson, editorial cartoonist, illustrator (b at London, Eng 1 Dec 1913). Norris immigrated to Port Arthur [Thunder Bay], Ont, as a child, studied for a year at the ONTARIO COLLEGE OF ART and worked as an advertising artist, 1938-40. After army service he became an art director for MACLEAN HUNTER LTD and in 1950 editorial cartoonist for the Vancouver *Sun*, where he remained until his retirement in 1978. More a social than a political cartoonist, Norris uses the technique of English cartoonist Carl Giles, drawing ordinary people in commonplace domestic situations to express his middle-class, conservative message. In 1974 he was elected to the Royal Canadian Academy of Arts. Norris's reputation extends well beyond BC and Canada; annual collections of his work have sold over 250 000 copies.

JOHN H. THOMPSON

Norris, Malcolm Frederick, Métis leader (b at St Albert, Alta 25 May 1900; d at Calgary 5 Dec 1967). Widely recognized as one of this century's most important and charismatic MÉTIS leaders, Norris was born into one of Edmonton's founding families but rejected privilege to fight racial discrimination. A brilliant orator in English and Cree and a consummate Métis politician, he was a key figure in the Association des Métis d'Alberta et des Territoires du Nord Ouest, the Indian Assn of Alberta and the Métis Assn of Saskatchewan.

Outspoken on behalf of Indians and Métis, he was active in the CCF and in the Communist Party, promoting reforms for native people. A tireless and militant democrat and protagonist in many battles with government, he warned native leaders to avoid the dependency of government funding, a warning today regarded as prophetic.

MURRAY DOBBIN

Norris, Tobias Crawford, politician, premier of Manitoba (b at Brampton, Canada W 5 Sept 1861; d at Toronto 29 Oct 1936). Although his name has been virtually forgotten, Norris was a towering political figure in Manitoba early in the 20th century. Originally a homesteader, he gradually moved into professional auctioneering and was well known across western Canada. Elected an MLA in 1896, Norris led the Liberal Party in Manitoba 1910-26, serving as premier 1915-22. During his term of office his government dealt with wartime conditions and the return to peace. The Norris government has been called "the centre of reform activity in Canada" for its time. It was responsible for TEMPERANCE legislation, female suffrage, compulsory education, workman's compensation and minimum-wage legislation, as well as the establishment of a public-nursing system, rural farm credit, regulation of industrial conditions, and a mother's allowance for widowed dependent mothers. Under Norris, road construction and public-works programs were expanded at the same time that the province was brought out of debt. After his retirement from politics in 1928 he served on the Board of Ry Commissioners until his death. J.M. BUMSTED

Norse Voyages In mid-985 or mid-986 an Icelandic flotilla led by ERIC THE RED set out to colonize SW Greenland. Near summer's end BJARNI HERJOLFSSON, a trader, belatedly sailed to join them

Norse Voyages

Voyage	Oleson[1]	Gathorne-Hardy[2]	Greenlanders' Saga	Eric the Red's Saga
Bjarni	986	986	985	–
Leif	1001-02	1002-03	1003-04	1000
Thorvald	1004-06	1004-07	1005-06	–
Thorstein	1007	1008	1007	1001
Karlsefni	1011-13	1020-23	1009-11	1003-06
Freydis	1014-15	c1024	1012-13	–

[1] Tryggvi Oleson, *Early Voyages and Northern Approaches* (1963)

[2] G.M. Gathorne-Hardy, *The Norse Discoverers of America* (1921)

but was blown far off course. He coasted N to the latitude of southern Greenland, then turned E to complete his intended voyage, becoming the first European of certain record to have reached the American mainland. His landfall was probably eastern or northeastern Newfoundland, from which he coasted N at least to the termination of Labrador. The more southerly lands he found were well forested. About the turn of the century Eric's eldest son, LEIF ERICSSON, decided to exploit Bjarni's discovery. Sailing to the region of Bjarni's landfall, he wintered in a protected harbour while his men cut a cargo of vines, valued as fasteners in shipbuilding, and timber. His camp was the genesis of the legendary *Vinland*, which historians have variously located from Florida to Hudson Bay.

About 1004 a colonizing venture consisting of 160 people in 4 ships, with domestic animals, including cattle, sailed from Greenland under Icelander Thorfinnr KARLSEFNI. The flotilla evidently crossed Davis Str at its narrowest point to Baffin I, then coasted southwards. Landings were made and the regions named according to their nature: *Helluland* ("rocky land") accurately describes the mountainous Baffin I and Labrador coasts S nearly to Nain, whereas *Markland* ("wooded land") correctly describes the balance of the Labrador coast.

The expedition may have been seeking Leif's Vinland but, if so, was unsure of its location. A camp was established at *Straumfiord* (Str of Belle Isle), probably at Épaves Bay on the northern tip of Newfoundland (*see* L'ANSE AUX MEADOWS) where traces of sod-walled structures believed to be of Norse provenance have been excavated. The expedition wintered there, but in the spring several parties set off to look for Vinland or some comparable settlement site. One, commanded by Thorvaldr Ericsson, reconnoitred W along the N shore of the Gulf of St Lawrence, perhaps as far as Sept-Îles. Most members of the expedition, under Karlsefni, sailed southwards along the W coast of Newfoundland and located a promising settlement site which they called Hop, probably near present-day St Paul's Bay. Here the cattle were put out to pasture and houses were built. Early the following spring the settlement was visited by INUIT. A conflict, for which the Norse were evidently responsible, ensued and several settlers were killed. The remainder returned to Straumfiord.

That summer Karlsefni again explored southwards and again met and fought with natives, apparently Indians. Meanwhile, Ericsson reconnoitred the Labrador coast N to Lk Melville, where he fought with Inuit and was himself killed. By early autumn, about 1006, the Norse had concluded that they could not maintain a settlement in the new lands and the survivors began departing for Greenland and Iceland.

Documentation of this early period, eg, in the medieval *Greenlanders' Saga* and *Eric the Red's*

Saga, is surprisingly full, but after about 1007 only fragmentary references are to be found. Nevertheless, we know that as late as 1349 Greenlanders were still voyaging to Markland for timber; and the archaeological work of T.E. Lee in Ungava indicates a major Norse presence there, perhaps as late as the mid-14th century. It is unreasonable to believe that the continuity of the Norse voyages and discoveries was ever seriously sundered or that they were unknown to the N European maritime community. The Greenland and Iceland Norse deserve full recognition, not only for having made the first known European exploration of Canada, but for having lit the way for the great age of western exploration which began in the 15th century. FARLEY MOWAT

Reading: Helge Ingstad, *Westward to Vinland* (1969); Farley Mowat, *Westviking* (1965).

North, in strictly geographic terms, refers to the immense hinterland of Canada that lies beyond the narrow strip of the country in which most Canadians live and work, but generally refers to the NORTHWEST TERRITORIES and the YUKON. The North is a varied land, with mighty rivers, forested plains, "great" lakes that extend from the Mackenzie Valley to the edge of the Canadian SHIELD, an inland sea (Hudson Bay), the beaches, bars and islands of the arctic coast and the arctic seas themselves, in winter covered by ice and snow, in summer by floating fields of ice. Immense flocks of birds migrate to the Arctic each summer; other wildlife includes whales, walrus, narwhals, seals and caribou – the staple of the native peoples.

Biologists divide the North into 2 great regions, called "biomes," comprising the boreal forest and the TUNDRA. The boreal forest, characterized by spruce trees and MUSKEG, is a broad band of coniferous forest extending across Canada from Newfoundland to Alaska. The tundra, which reaches from the boreal forest northward to the Arctic Ocean and comprises 20% of Canada's landmass, is treeless and is sometimes called "the barrens," although it includes landscapes as varied and beautiful as any in Canada – plains, mountains, hills, valleys, rivers, lakes and sea coasts.

The tundra and the boreal forest meet along the TREELINE, a transitional zone usually many kilometres wide. This very important biological boundary, which separates forest and tundra, also separates the traditional lands of the Indians and the INUIT. The treeline may also be viewed as the southern limit of the Arctic, the boundary between the Arctic and the Subarctic. Arctic or Subarctic, however, the region is one of great climatic contrasts. In midsummer it is never dark, but in midwinter the only daylight is a combined sunset and sunrise. Although summer can be pleasantly warm, with temperatures in excess of 20°C, the season is short and the weather often raw and damp. Both rainfall and snowfall are light. Because, in the true Arctic, precipitation is as low as that in the driest parts of the Canadian prairies, the Arctic may be described as semidesert. It is remarkable, therefore, that the land surface in summer is predominantly wet and swampy and dotted with innumerable shallow ponds, fens and water-filled frost cracks. In southern Canada the ground freezes in the winter, but downward from the surface, and thaws completely again in the spring. In the subarctic and arctic regions, frost has penetrated below the maximum depth of summer thaw and a layer of frozen ground called PERMAFROST remains permanently beneath the surface. The seasonally thawed active layer of the soil holds the water, like a sponge, from rain and melting snow, which cannot drain through the frozen ground. The combination of climate and topography in the northern biomes have pro-

duced unique plant and animal populations. The species that thrive in the North are tough, in order to survive, but they are also vulnerable. Because of the fragility of this region, it would not be difficult to cause irreparable injury to the environment and to the peoples who depend upon it.

Peoples of the North It is not always easy to remember, on a flight over the unbroken boreal forest, the tundra or the sea ice, that the Canadian North has been inhabited for many thousands of years. The populations that have occupied this great area were never large, but their skills as travellers and hunters made it possible for them to make use of virtually all the land without altering the environment. Because of extremely slow rates of plant growth and decay, signs of ancient occupation – old house remains, tent rings, fire-cracked rocks – are visible almost everywhere and it is not difficult for archaeologists to find, on or close to the surface, a wealth of artifacts and other evidence revealing the richness, diversity and breadth of aboriginal society.

The Inuit (formerly known as Eskimos) occupy the shores of the Arctic Ocean and of Hudson Bay. Although the Inuit speak closely related dialects of the same language, regionally there are differences among them reflected in technology and social organization that even today complicate anthropological generalizations. The Inuit themselves perceive important differences between their various groups; the Inuvialuit of the Mackenzie Delta see themselves as distinct from the COPPER INUIT, their neighbours to the E and the Copper Inuit – or Qurdlurturmiut – emphasize that they are unlike the NETSILIK, the Aivilim or the IGLOOLIK, who live still farther E. And within each of these broad groups finer divisions and distinctions exist, reflecting different patterns of land use and of changes in dialect and hunting techniques.

The Indians of the Mackenzie Valley are part of the Athapaskan group and regard themselves, notwithstanding dialectical variation in their languages, as "the people," the DENE. The Indians of the Yukon are largely Athapaskan, yet these northern Indians are by no means all the same, for they speak several languages – KUTCHIN (sometimes called Loucheux), NAHANI, TAGISH, HARE, SLAVEY, DOGRIB and CHIPEWYAN.

The native peoples came originally from Asia, crossing the land bridge over the Bering Strait during the last ice age (*see* BERINGIA; PREHISTORY). The Athapaskan Indians arrived 10 000 to 15 000 years ago, eventually to occupy large tracts of land, including the Mackenzie Valley and the Yukon. The Inuit arrived about 4000 years ago, spreading throughout the Arctic, including all the coastal areas, practically all of the islands of the Arctic Archipelago to the Ungava Peninsula and as far E as the Gulf of St Lawrence and Newfoundland. The Dene were established in the forestlands of northern Canada and the Inuit inhabited the northern rim of the New World at least 5000 years before Martin FROBISHER made his landfall off Baffin Island in 1576 or Samuel HEARNE reached the Arctic coast in 1772.

Although for both the Inuit and the Dene the dog team was the usual means of travel and the caribou the principal source of food and winter clothing, each of these peoples had its own way of hunting, of raising children and of regarding the environment and the spiritual powers they believed were integral to their world. Their respective knowledge of the land and of its life constitute distinctive ethnoscientific traditions.

During the past 160 years, the MÉTIS have also been categorized as northern native peoples. The first Métis who moved into the North in the early 19th century settled around Great Slave Lake; they trace their ancestry to the unions between French COUREURS DE BOIS and Indian women in

Polaris Mine, Little Cornwallis Island, NWT. It is natural to think of developing the North and extracting its resources, but large-scale economic development may have serious repercussions for the native population (*photo by Karl-Heinz Raach*).

the early days of the fur trade. In the aftermath of the NORTH-WEST REBELLION of 1885, many Métis moved north and settled in the Mackenzie Valley. Other Métis, sometimes called "country-born," are the descendants of unions between Hudson's Bay Company men – mainly of Scottish origin – and Dene women. The children of these unions usually intermarried with the original Dene inhabitants, so close family ties exist between the Métis and the Dene.

Future of the North The issues that concern the North today result from the presence of the white man, whose advent was spearheaded by the explorers and fur traders seeking to extend the fur-trade empire. The explorers and fur traders were followed by clergy, who were followed by representatives of government. The pattern of historical development in every region of Canada was reflected in the North, with one difference. The opening of the prairies by the construction of the CPR was followed by agricultural settlement, the establishment of many centres of white population and widespread diffusion of European language and culture. In the North, however, where agricultural settlement is out of the question, it is nonrenewable resources, eg, gold, silver, lead, zinc, copper and oil and natural gas, that have spurred economic development. These industries do not promote widespread white settlement, but rather "instant" towns, eg, Faro in Yukon and Pine Point in the NWT, with imported labour forces.

A large part of the white population is transient; even government employees are likely to regard their service in the North as a tour of duty limited to a few years. The native people therefore constitute, in the NWT, a majority of permanent residents, and in Yukon a very substantial minority. These facts bear significantly on the future of the North, for they make possible what was not possible when the West was opened up – the preservation of the great herds of migratory animals, the development of the native economy, and the establishment of political institutions that fully recognize the special place of the native peoples.

The northern economy is mixed. The people living there have traditionally depended on renewable resources, eg, hunting, trapping and fishing for employment. The mining industry largely employs white people, as does the oil and gas industry, although the latter has also sought to employ native people. The federal and the territorial governments are now the largest employers of both white and native people. The North is perceived as Canada's last frontier. It is natural to think of developing it, of subduing the land, and extracting its resources to fuel Canada's industry.

Because many people are committed to the view that the economic future of the North depends solely on large-scale industrial development, policies concerning the North have often weakened or destroyed that sector of the economy based on renewable resources and those who earned a living by hunting, trapping and fishing have been regarded as unemployed. These policies have brought serious pressures to bear on the native population, many of whom, if they continue to live on the renewable resources, may experience relative poverty and suffer the loss of a productive way of life. If they relinquish traditional ways of life, which are considered culturally important and a source of self-respect, then the devaluation of that way of life can have widespread and dismaying consequences.

The Inuit, the Dene and the Métis say the North is their homeland; they do not oppose industrial development in the North; they believe, however, that they are entitled to a measure of control over the pace of such development and a share in the wealth it may create. In their view, these goals will only be achieved if new political institutions that truly reflect the interests of the native peoples are established in the North. This implies a new set of political and economic priorities for northern development. It depends on the recognition of native LAND CLAIMS, for it is through their claims that the

The North is an immense, varied land. Shown here are Sugarloaf Mts, Carcajou Range, NWT (*photo by Hans Blohm/Masterfile*).

native people seek to preserve their languages, their art, their culture, their values – their very identity.

Development of the North need not be defined exclusively in terms of large-scale, capital-intensive technology. The possibilities of the renewable resource sector need not be ignored, eg, the fish and mammal resources of the NWT can provide sufficient protein for a human population in that region 2 to 4 times the present size. Development might also include a greatly expanded program of wildlife management and a carefully regulated harvest, with active involvement of native people. At the same time there is no reason why native people cannot enjoy access to the economy of the dominant society.

The Dene, the Inuit and the Métis are advancing proposals for new political arrangements in Yukon and the NWT. Whatever the outcome of these proposals, they are evidence of a renewed determination – and a new capacity – on the part of native people in the North to defend what they believe is their right to a future of their own.

Canadians share a mass culture with the US but it is Canada that has a distinct northern geography and special concern for the North. Canada's achievements in the development of the North are in many ways unsurpassed, eg, the exploration and mapping of the Arctic by land and sea, the development of fur-collecting posts, the mining industry's discovery of uranium off the shores of Great Bear Lake in the 1930s and its extraction of iron ore from the arctic islands in the 1980s. The Canadian oil and gas industry and its engineers lead the world in the development of technology for the recovery of oil and gas in arctic waters. Progress tends to be equated only with industrial and technological advancement. Ultimately the form that northern development takes – political, social and economic – will reflect the beliefs that Canadians hold about the kind of society they want to build. In the North, however, the questions beneath the surface of our national life cannot be avoided. For many Canadians these questions make the North not simply a geographical area but a state of consciousness.

T.R. BERGER

North Battleford, Sask, City, pop 14 876 (1986c), inc 1913, is located on the N bank of the N Saskatchewan R at its junction with the Battle R 140 km NW of Saskatoon. In 1905 the main line of the CANADIAN NORTHERN RY worked its way across much of Saskatchewan. It had been anticipated that the line would be surveyed through the existing town of Battleford, but the railway crossed the river 5 km NW of the former territorial capital. A new townsite, named North Battleford, was laid out in 1905. The community grew rapidly with many businesses and residents abandoning the older community and moving to the new rail centre. By 1913 North Battleford was granted city status. Growth was slow until the end of WWII, but the population doubled in the following decade. The city is a key distribution and receiving centre for northwestern Saskatchewan's rich mixed farming, lumbering and fishing area.

DON HERPERGER

North Bay, Ont, City, pop 50 623 (1986c), 51 268 (1981c), inc 1925, located on a northern bay of Lk NIPISSING, at the junction of Hwys 11 and 17, some 360 km N of Toronto and 340 km NW of Ottawa. Traditional "Gateway to the North," the city is administrative seat for the Dist of Nipissing. North Bay lies roughly along the "Nipissing Route" where the FUR TRADE portage of La Vase connected the waters of Trout Lk and the Ottawa and Mattawa rivers with Lk Nipissing, the French R and Georgian Bay. Its development awaited the slow progression of settlement up the Ottawa

Valley and from southern Ontario which was initiated by the arrival of the CPR (1882). Later rail connections were made to Toronto (1886) and to the resource areas northward (1904). Town status was achieved in 1891, and by 1914 North Bay was a regional supply centre and key rail point. It did not "boom" in the manner of many northern centres, but it also avoided the "bust" cycle so intimately associated with such resource-based growth. The city's geographically advantageous position has aided a variety of economic endeavours. It remains a major fur centre, and its wild-fur auctions are among the largest in the world. Wood and wood products remain important. Recently a variety of processing and general manufactures have supplemented traditional industries. North Bay also benefits from income generated by a military base and, more so, from an important tourist industry focused on scenic Lk Nipissing and the "Near North" regions. North Bay's population is largely of British origin with a strong French Canadian presence and notable elements of Dutch, Italian, Scandinavian and German stock – all enjoying the convenience of a prosperous urban life with proximity to the "Near North."   PETER KRATS

Reading: W.K.P. Kennedy, *North Bay: Past, Present Prospective* (1961).

North Cape, also called North Pt, is the northern extremity of PEI, dividing NORTHUMBERLAND STR from the Gulf of St Lawrence proper. From the shoreline a low cliff of PEI's characteristic red sandstone leads to shallow water, with irregular reefs extending N and E to North Point Reef 8 km offshore. North Point Light, beamed from a 19 m white octagonal tower, and a light and whistle buoy 2.8 km N of the cape are important aids to navigation. Principal occupations are fishing and agriculture. Silver fox farms were also common here until the demise of the industry in the late 1930s.   P.C. SMITH

North Pole, Earth's northernmost geographic point, located at the northern end of the Earth's axis. The pole lies in the Arctic Ocean more than 7200 km N of ELLESMERE ISLAND, at a point where the Arctic Ocean is 4087 m deep and usually covered with drifting pack ice. The pole experiences 6 months of complete sunlight and 6 months of night each year; from it, all directions are south. Because the Earth's surface areas near the N and S poles receive the sun's rays at the most slanted angle, they absorb the least heat. Centrifugal force causes Earth to bulge outwards at the equator; hence, it is slightly flattened at the poles. However, during the International Geophysical Year (1957-58) it was found that Earth is very slightly pear shaped, with the North Pole at the smaller end. This bulge (about 15 m high) covers millions of square kilometres around the pole.

The North Pole did not become a goal of ARCTIC EXPLORATION until fairly late; the few early expeditions that tried to reach it were looking for a polar route to the East rather than for the pole itself. W.E. PARRY left Spitsbergen to try to reach the pole in 1827 and attained 82°45'; further expeditions, American and British, took place in the 1860s and 1870s. It is widely accepted today that the pole was first reached by the American explorer Robert E. Peary, who started from Ellesmere I on 1 Mar 1909. With Peary on his final dash were his dog driver Matthew Henson and 4 Inuit. It is claimed that they arrived at the pole on Apr 6 and remained there 30 hours. A competing claim was made by F.A. Cook, a former traveller with Peary, who said he had reached the pole on 21 Apr 1908 and had remained there 2 days. The controversy still continues, but Peary's claim seems the more valid and has been accepted by the US Congress and geographical institutions in many countries. In 1926 Richard E. Byrd and Floyd Bennett made the first airplane flight over the pole; in the same year, it was reached by dirigible by the international team of Roald AMUNDSEN, Lincoln Ellsworth and Umberto Nobile. The pole was visited by the US nuclear submarine *Nautilus* in 1958.

Since 1907 various Canadians have invoked what is known as the "sector principle" as a possible legal basis to a claim for sovereignty in the polar region. By this claim Canada would have jurisdiction over a wedge-shaped segment between the line of longitude 60° W of Greenwich (N from a point on the meridian that is near Ellesmere I) and the meridian 141° W of Greenwich (forming the border between the YT and Alaska); these meridians converge (as do all meridians of the Northern Hemisphere) at the North Pole. The theory has not received general acceptance as a legal basis for a claim. *See also* GEOMAGNETIC POLE.
HUGH N. WALLACE

Reading: A. Cooke and C. Holland, *The Exploration of Northern Canada, 500 to 1920* (1978); M. Zaslow, ed, *A Century of Canada's Arctic Islands* (1981).

North-South Institute, a nonprofit corporation est (1976) to conduct professional and policy-relevant research on Canada's relations with the developing world. The institute organizes seminars and publishes research reports, an annual *Review/Outlook* and newsletters on topics such as Canadian foreign policy, trade and adjustment, Third World debt and development assistance programs. The institute has published in-depth assessments of Canadian aid in 4 countries, and in 1988 published a major study of Canadian nongovernmental organizations. NSI has received major funding from the Donner Canadian Foundation and CIDA. Headquartered in Ottawa, it is governed by a board of directors.
GREGORY WIRICK

North Sydney, NS, Town, pop 7472 (1986c), 8820 (1981c), inc 1885, is situated in industrial Cape Breton on the N side of Sydney Harbour. Unlike many communities in this region, the town economy is fairly diversified but focuses on its seaport function. Micmac occupied "Gwesomkeak" for centuries. Early settlers were LOYALISTS, but many Scots arrived in the early 19th century, followed by the famine Irish. The town's port function grew after 1827 when the General Mining Assn began coal mining at nearby Sydney Mines and built a railway linking the 2 communities. Shipping and shipbuilding also prospered through the mid-19th century. Local firms, such as Archibald and Co, broadened their marine activities to include sealing, deep-sea fishing and international trade. North Sydney was established as the terminus of a ferry service between Newfoundland and Canada in 1898, a function now maintained by CN Marine (since early 1987, Marine Atlantic). Also important today are several large fish-processing plants and the servicing of offshore fishing fleets. The Northside Industrial Park is jointly operated by the towns of North Sydney and Sydney Mines; the first industry to locate here is a division of Magna International Ltd.   L.D. McCANN

North Vancouver, BC, City (pop 35 698, 1986c, 33 952, 1981c) and District (pop 68 241, 1986c, 65 367, 1981c), is located in southwestern BC, adjacent to the city of VANCOUVER. Situated on the N shore of Burrard Inlet, N Vancouver extends from the Capilano R on the W to beyond Deep Cove on the E. The north shore mountains – such as Crown, Grouse, Seymour, Hollyburn and, highest and most famous, the Lions – form a scenic backdrop. The city of North Vancouver is surrounded by the Dist of North Vancouver (area 17 819 ha) except at the waterfront. Elevations in the area range from sea level to 1400 m. The district (inc 1891) is governed by a mayor and 6 aldermen, as is the city (inc 1907), which is centered on Lonsdale Avenue.

History The rich forests on the N shore of Burrard Inlet first attracted settlers to the area. In 1862 T.W. Graham and Co acquired a 194 ha timber stand in what is now North Vancouver, and timber was soon shipped from the quickly erected Pioneer Mills. A small waterfront mill town developed into the largest settlement on the inlet. An American, Sewell P. Moody, bought Pioneer Mills in 1872 and gave his name to the settlement of Moodyville. In 1886 the N shore became North Vancouver after Vancouver was incorporated. The Second Narrows Railway Bridge, completed in 1925, provided a fixed rail and vehicle link with Vancouver; Lions Gate Bridge (1938) provided a second link; and Second Narrows Vehicle Bridge (c1959) provided the third link.

Economy North Vancouver is an important shipping port for lumber, ore and grain, and has numerous manufacturing establishments and shipyards – the RCMP schooner ST. ROCH was built here 1928. Versatile Pacific Co Ltd is one of the largest shipyards in Canada. The extension of the Pacific Great Eastern Ry (now BC Ry) from Squamish in the 1950s increased the city's importance as a transshipment point. Tourists are attracted by the facilities for fishing, sailing, skiing and mountain climbing in the area's 75 parks. In Capilano Canyon Park, the famous Capilano Suspension Bridge, 70 m above the river, stretches 137 m across the canyon. Cleveland Dam, north of the park, releases most of the water for Greater Vancouver consumption from Capilano Lk. In the eastern part of the Dist is Mt Seymour Provincial Park.

Cityscape North Vancouver is a popular residential and tourist area. Attractions include Lonsdale Quay Market and Waterfront Park, Grouse Mountain Skyride, Capilano Salmon Hatchery, Capilano College, the Museum and Archives, Presentation House and, most recently, the addition of a wilderness regional park (Lynn Creek Headwaters Park).   ALAN F.J. ARTIBISE

North West Company, a major force in the FUR TRADE from the 1780s to 1821. Managed primarily by Highland SCOTS who migrated to Montréal after 1760, or came as LOYALISTS escaping the American Revolution, it also drew heavily on Canadien labour and experience. The name first described Montréal traders who in 1776 pooled resources to reduce competition among themselves and to resist inland advances of the HUDSON'S BAY COMPANY. In 1779 a new temporary organization took the name. Its 16 shares were held by 9 partnerships including business leaders Simon McTAVISH, Isaac Todd and James McGILL, and several experienced winterers in the Indian country. A 1780 reorganization joined McTavish, the FROBISHER brothers, the McGills and the Ellices, with Peter POND as their agent in the Athabasca country.

Pond's inland encounter with opposition trader Jean-Étienne Waddens and the latter's murder in Mar 1782, along with increased American and HBC competition, clarified the need for a more unified, formal and permanent organization. In the winter of 1783-84, the NWC therefore became an enduring multiple partnership controlled by the Frobishers and Simon McTavish, with annual trade valued at about £100 000. A

Armorial bearings of the North West Company (*courtesy National Archives of Canada*).

powerful rival remained, however. Gregory, McLeod and Co backed John Ross and other traders not included in the NWC, and intense rivalry ensued 1784-87. Pond was again linked with murder – that of Ross in Athabasca. Coalition was again the answer, and in mid-1787 the NOR'WESTERS and Gregory, McLeod amalgamated. Dominated by the Montréal firm of McTavish, Frobisher, and Co, dynamic entrepreneurs thus came together – men such as the MCGILLIVRAYS and, from the ranks of their former rivals, Roderick McKenzie and Alexander MACKENZIE. While McTavish and Frobisher handled Montréal affairs, Alexander Mackenzie led inland expansion. The Athabasca trade was reorganized with a new base, Ft Chipewyan on Lk Athabasca. A far-flung system of canoe brigades, provisioned by PEMMICAN from the plains, furnished transport and brought out up to 20 000 MADE BEAVER annually. It also gave Mackenzie the support needed to explore the Mackenzie R to its mouth in 1789.

During 1790-91, McTavish attempted unsuccessfully to have Britain end the HBC monopoly. Later efforts to lease transit rights from the HBC through its depots on Hudson Bay were rebuffed as well. The only remaining option was to intensify direct rivalry with the "English," who were extending their own network of inland posts. Through the 1790s the Nor'Westers prevailed. Their control of over two-thirds of the Canadian fur trade by 1795 was complemented by Mackenzie's reaching the Pacific overland in July 1793. Potential rivals in Montréal were muted by a 1792 agreement to co-operate.

In 1794 JAY'S TREATY settled the boundary between US and British territory, challenging the Montréalers' access to Detroit, Lk Michigan, the depot of Grand Portage on Lk Superior and the SW trade beyond. Reorganization in 1795 accommodated Montréal interests who, displaced from the south, sought a place in the northern trade. But NWC winterers, notably Alexander Mackenzie, were aggrieved at their standing in the company. In 1797, Forsyth, Richardson, and Co, which had remained outside the 1795 agreement, began to back the winterers, and in 1798 formed the New North West or XY COMPANY. Joined by Alexander Mackenzie in 1800 (after his NWC commitment ended), the XY Co opposed the NWC from the Great Lakes to Athabasca. Simon McTavish's death, however, enabled reconciliation and the merger of the firms in Nov 1804.

Meanwhile, NWC-HBC confrontations increased. NWC acquisition of Québec's KING'S POSTS extended the company's activities as far as Lk Mistassini, inland from Hudson Bay. During 1803 to 1806, the Nor'Westers maintained a base on James Bay, and although this enterprise proved unprofitable, rivalry intensified elsewhere. In EXPLORATION, the NWC kept the upper hand, with Duncan McGillivray, David THOMPSON and Simon FRASER crossing the Rocky Mts and the latter 2 reaching the Pacific. When Thompson reached the Columbia R mouth in July 1811, he encountered a new post which had been erected by the American John Jacob Astor's PACIFIC FUR COMPANY. Isolated from its source of support by the WAR OF 1812, Astoria was sold to the Nor'-Westers in Oct 1813. It was returned to the Americans by the Treaty of GHENT. Two new NWC western trade districts proved profitable for some years, but hopes to develop a China trade and a liaison with the EAST INDIA CO bore little fruit.

One factor limiting such developments was a deteriorating situation east of the Rockies. The HBC posed trade challenges and, with the earl of SELKIRK, was planning an agricultural colony in an area pivotal to the Nor'Westers' transportation and provisioning networks. NWC attempts to block the plan by buying up HBC stock in London and by discouraging prospective colonists in Scotland failed. The stage was thus set for a series of bitter and costly clashes at RED RIVER COLONY, FORT WILLIAM and elsewhere. The SEVEN OAKS INCIDENT, 19 June 1816, was the worst event in a conflict neither side could win. From 1815 to 1819, repeated clashes and seizures of men and goods in Athabasca exacerbated bad feeling. In June 1819, 7 NWC partners and numerous men were seized by a HBC force under William Williams, the new governor in chief of RUPERT'S LAND, at the Grand Rapid of the Saskatchewan R. Both the prestige of the Nor'Westers and their business that year were thus impaired, despite successes in impeding the inland activities of HBC officers John Clarke and Colin Robertson.

By 1820, strong forces were building towards a resolution of the conflict. NWC partners, concerned about their future, varied in their support for William McGillivray's aggressive measures against the HBC. Splits between the WINTERING PARTNERS and the Montréal agents deepened. Their partnership agreement would expire in 1821, and clearly its terms would need radical revision. Britain was drawn into the broader NWC-HBC struggle, as each company lobbied for official support. The COLONIAL OFFICE wished the restoration of peace and a settlement of the serious territorial and legal issues which reached beyond the conflict and were aggravated by it. In 1821 a parliamentary Act granted exclusive trade to the HBC and to William and Simon McGillivray and Edward ELLICE of the NWC, in an effort to placate all parties by devising coalition, not amalgamation. A Deed Poll designated 53 field officers, 32 NWC and 21 HBC, as shareholding chief factors and chief traders, under the charge of HBC governors William Williams and George SIMPSON, the latter a newcomer. The name, charter and privileges of the old HBC provided a foundation for the new firm, while the Nor'Westers' skills and experience contributed a scope and dynamism that served the company well.

JENNIFER S.H. BROWN

Reading: Jennifer S.H. Brown, *Strangers in Blood* (1980); M.W. Campbell, *The North West Company* (1957); E.E. Rich, *The Fur Trade and the Northwest to 1857* (1967); W. Stewart Wallace, ed, *Documents Relating to the North West Company* (1934).

North-West Mounted Police, a paramilitary police force est 1873 to maintain law and order, and to be a visible symbol of Canadian sovereignty, in the newly acquired North-West Territories (including present-day Alberta and Saskatchewan). The NWMP helped Indians make the transition to INDIAN RESERVES after treaties were signed and assisted incoming settlers. "Royal" was added to its name in 1904, and in 1920 the RNWMP merged with the DOMINION POLICE to form the ROYAL CANADIAN MOUNTED POLICE.

North Yukon National Park, *see* KLUANE NATIONAL PARK.

North-West Rebellion, 1885, culmination of the discontent of the MÉTIS, Indians and white settlers which had not abated since the RED RIVER REBELLION of 1869-70. The Plains Indians – CREE, BLACKFOOT, BLOOD, PIEGAN, SAULTEAUX – had been reduced to near starvation by the virtual disappearance of the buffalo. In 1880 Cree chief BIG BEAR worked for an Indian confederacy and found an ally in CROWFOOT, leading chief of the Blackfoot. A series of confrontations between destitute Indians and Indian Dept employees over rations threatened to break into open violence. The Métis had found transition from hunting to farming difficult and by 1884 had grown desperate that their rights would ever be recognized. A delegation brought Louis RIEL back from exile in the US and on July 8 he held his first public meeting in Canada since 1870, urging all dissatisfied people in the North-West to unite and press their case on Ottawa. The white settlers also had grievances. Those who had settled along the Saskatchewan R in anticipation of the railway were disturbed that the CPR had chosen a more southerly route. John A. Macdonald's Conservative government failed to address the grievances of all 3 groups.

In the fall of 1884 Riel prepared a petition and urged the Métis, English half-breeds and white settlers to sign it. At St Laurent [Sask] on 8 Mar 1885 a meeting passed a 10-point "Revolutionary Bill of Rights" which asserted Métis rights of possession to their farms and made other demands. On Mar 18 and 19, the Métis formed a provisional government and an armed force at Batoche, with Riel president and Gabriel DUMONT military commander. Prisoners were taken in the Batoche area and, in anticipation of a police advance, Métis forces occupied the community of DUCK LAKE, midway between Batoche and Ft Carlton. In the morning of Mar 26, the NWMP, augmented by citizen volunteers to a total strength of 100, moved towards Duck Lake under Superintendent Lief CROZIER. A large Métis and Indian force met them on the Carlton Trail near the village. A parlay ended in confusion and the police and volunteers fired at their enemy hidden in a large hollow north of the road and in a cabin to the south. The battle ended shortly after with the police and volunteers retreating to Ft Carlton. Nine volunteers and 3 police were killed. Five Métis and one Indian died. Riel persuaded the rebel soldiers not to pursue the retreating force and the Métis returned to Batoche. The police evacuated Ft Carlton and retired to Prince Albert.

The Ottawa government's reaction was astonishingly swift, considering that the CPR north of Lk Superior was not completed. There were only a few hundred full-time soldiers in Canada but militia mobilization began Mar 25, the day before the Duck Lake battle. CPR manager William VAN HORNE quickly arranged for Canadian troops to be transported across the gaps, enabling them to reach Qu'Appelle by Apr 10. In less than a month, almost 3000 troops had been transported west; most were Ontario militia units but the force included 2 Québec battalions and one from Nova Scotia. From the West came about 1700 of the eventual total of just over 5000 that Major-General Frederick MIDDLETON commanded.

The rebel victory at Duck Lake encouraged a

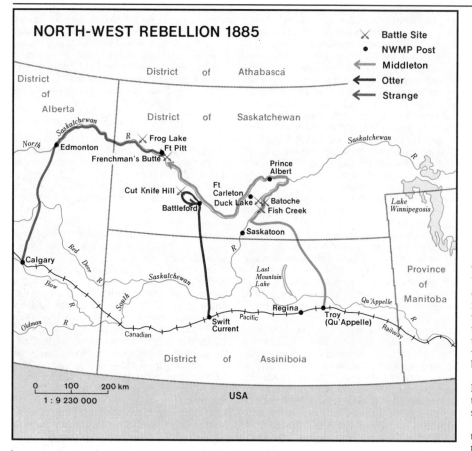

NORTH-WEST REBELLION 1885

District of Athabasca

District of Alberta

District of Saskatchewan

District of Assiniboia

✕ Battle Site
● NWMP Post
← Middleton
← Otter
← Strange

Edmonton
North Saskatchewan R
R
✕ Frog Lake
Ft Pitt
Frenchman's Butte
Cut Knife Hill ✕
Ft Carleton
Duck Lake ✕
Battleford
Prince Albert
✕ Batoche
✕ Fish Creek
Saskatchewan R
Lake Winnipegosis
Saskatoon
Calgary
Red Deer R
Bow R
South Saskatchewan R
Oldman R
Last Mountain Lake
Regina
Troy (Qu'Appelle)
Qu'Appelle R
Swift Current
Pacific
Canadian
Railway
Province of Manitoba

USA

0   100   200 km
1 : 9 230 000

large contingent of Cree to move on Battleford from reserves to the west. Residents of the area flocked to the safety of Ft Battleford. On Mar 30, Assiniboines south of Battleford killed 2 whites and joined the Cree forces. Terrified settlers huddled in Ft Battleford for almost a month as the Cree and Assiniboine organized a huge war camp to the west.

Big Bear had been the last plains chief to take treaty, and in 1885 he was still resisting taking a reserve, still agitating for a better deal. As a result, his band included some of the more militant Plains Cree. The government took a hard line with Big Bear's band, cutting off rations to force them to settle. By the spring of 1885, it was almost inevitable that Big Bear's band at Frog Lake, north of modern-day Lloydminster, would clash violently with the government. On the night of Apr 1, warriors of Big Bear's band took prisoner several whites and Métis. Shortly after church on Sunday, Apr 2, war chief Wandering Spirit shot and killed Sub-Indian Agent Thomas Quinn. Chief Big Bear tried to stop the violence but the warriors took their own initiative from their war chief and killed 2 priests, the government farming instructor, an independent trader, a miller and 3 other men. Several people were spared, including the widows of 2 of the dead men (see FROG LAKE INCIDENT).

Gen Middleton's original plan was simple. He wanted to march all his troops north from the railhead at Qu'Appelle to Batoche. But the killings at Frog Lake and the "siege" of Battleford forced him to send a large group under Lt-Col William OTTER north from a second railhead at Swift Current to relieve Battleford. Pressure from Alberta led to the creation of a third column at Calgary under Maj-Gen Thomas Bland STRANGE.

On Apr 14, the Frog Lake Cree besieged Ft Pitt, on the N Saskatchewan R just east of the modern Alberta-Saskatchewan border. On Apr 15, after a policeman died in a small skirmish, the Cree allowed the NWMP detachment to flee downriver.

Middleton set off on the 50 km march to Batoche from Clarke's Crossing on the S Saskatchewan R on Apr 23. About 900 men, including 2 artillery batteries, were split into 2 groups, one for each side of the river. The Métis were determined to fight but differed about where to make a stand. Riel wanted to concentrate all efforts on defending Batoche; Dumont favoured a more forward position. Dumont won the argument and on Apr 12, with about 150 Métis and Indians, prepared an ambush at Tourond's Coulee, which the government soldiers would know as FISH CREEK, 20 km S of Batoche on the east side of the S Saskatchewan. As Middleton's scouts approached the coulee early on Apr 24, the rebels opened fire. Until mid-afternoon, Middleton's soldiers tried unsuccessfully to drive Dumont's men from the ravine and suffered heavy casualties, 6 killed and 49 wounded. The rebels had only 4 killed. It took most of the day for Middleton to get the troops from the west bank across the river on a makeshift ferry and they arrived too late to take part in the fighting. At the end of the day, both commanders decided to pull back. The Métis had held their

ground and Middleton's advance was stopped.

On May 1, Col Otter moved west from Battleford with 300 men and early on May 2 they confronted the Cree and Assiniboine force just west of CUT KNIFE CREEK, 40 km from Battleford. The Indians had enormous advantages of terrain, virtually surrounding Otter's force on an inclined, triangular plain. Cree war chief Fine Day deployed his soldiers highly successfully in wooded ravines. After about 6 hours of fighting, Otter retreated. Casualties would have been very high as the militia recrossed the creek had not Chief POUNDMAKER persuaded the Indians not to pursue the soldiers. Eight of Otter's force died; 5 or 6 Indians were killed. Otter's foray against the Indians violated the spirit of Gen Middleton's orders and the setback prompted Middleton to wait 2 weeks for reinforcements before resuming his march toward Batoche. On the morning of May 9, his forces attacked the carefully constructed defences at the southern end of the Batoche settlement. The steamer *Northcote*, transformed into a gunboat, attempted to attack the village from the river, but the Métis lowered the ferry cable, incapacitating the boat. After a brief, intense conflict in the morning, the cautious Middleton kept the attackers at a discreet distance from the enemy positions. In the afternoon, after failing to make headway against the entrenched enemy, the troops built a fortified camp just south of Batoche.

The next 2 days, May 10 and 11, were essentially repeats of the first. The troops marched out in the morning, attacked the Métis lines with little success and retired to their camp at night. On May 12, Middleton tried a co-ordinated action from the east and south but the southern group failed to hear a signal gun and did not attack. In the afternoon, apparently without specific orders, 2 impetuous colonels led several militia units in a charge. The rebels, weary and short of ammunition, were overrun. Eight of Middleton's force died during the Battle of Batoche. The general later reported that 51 rebels were killed, but that number seems high. Riel surrendered on May 15; Dumont fled to Montana.

During the Battle of Batoche, Gen Strange was resting his Alberta Field Force at Edmonton after a hard march from Calgary. The column left Edmonton on May 14 and on May 28 they caught up to the Frog Lake Indians, dug in at the top of a steep hill near a prominent landmark known as FRENCHMAN'S BUTTE, 18 km NW of Ft Pitt. Direct advance against the entrenched Indians would have been very difficult and Strange's scouts found no practical way around the Cree positions. They fired at each other from long range for several hours before both sides retreated.

Big Bear (front row, second from left) and Poundmaker (front row, far right) shown at their 1885 trials (*courtesy Glenbow Archives, Calgary*).

Rocky Mountain Ranger militia – en route from Fort Macleod to Medicine Hat [Alta], 1885 – extreme right, John "Kootenai" Brown, scout (*courtesy National Archives of Canada/C-18974A*).

The last shots of the rebellion were fired on June 3 at Loon Lake, 40 km north of Frenchman Butte, where a few mounted men under NWMP Supt Sam STEELE skirmished with the retreating Frog Lake Cree. None of Steele's men was killed but 4 Indians died, including a prominent Woods Cree chief.

Chief Poundmaker and the Battleford area Indians had surrendered to Gen Middleton on May 26 at Battleford. At the end of May, Big Bear was the only important rebel still at large. Gen Middleton's pursuit of Big Bear was so cumbersome that the soldiers never did find him. The Frog Lake Indians released their white prisoners on June 21 and Big Bear surrendered to the Mounted Police on July 2 at Ft Carlton. Before the first of Aug, almost all of the militia were home.

The rebellion had not been a concerted effort by all groups in the North-West. Even most Métis communities stayed out of the fighting. The people of the South Branch communities, centered at Batoche, had been the principal combatants. The Plains Cree of Big Bear's band had participated, but the neighbouring Woods Cree had not. Some Cree from the Batoche area fought with the Métis, as did Dakota from a reserve from south of present-day Saskatoon. The Blackfoot had remained neutral, the Blood refusing to abandon their traditional animosity towards the Cree. Almost every white settler had rallied to the government cause, despite the fact that their vocal agitation before the shooting started had helped to create the environment that had made the rebellion possible.

As the soldiers left the West, Louis Riel's trial for high treason began at Regina. Riel demanded a political trial. His lawyers failed in their attempt to convince the jury that Riel's religious and political delusions made him unaware of the nature of his acts, largely because Riel was so eloquent in his address to the jury on July 31. The law provided no alternative to the death penalty, and on Sept 18 Riel was sentenced to be hanged.

The government arrested many people on the lesser charge of treason-felony. W.H. JACKSON, Riel's personal secretary, was acquitted by reason of insanity. Most of the provisional government council pleaded guilty and received sentences ranging from conditional discharges to 7 years in penitentiary. Chiefs Poundmaker and Big Bear were tried and sentenced to 3 years in jail. Several other Indians from Batoche, Frog Lake and Battleford were sentenced to various terms after treason-felony convictions. Dakota chief White Cap was the only major native political leader acquitted of treason-felony. Eleven Indians were convicted of murder as a result of the Frog Lake "massacre" and other killings carried out during the rebellion.

Riel's execution was postponed 3 times: twice to allow appeals to higher courts, then for a fuller medical examination of his alleged insanity. The appeals failed and the medical commission report was ambiguous. The federal government could have commuted the death sentence and the decision to "let the law take its course" was purely political. Riel was hanged at Regina 16 Nov 1885.

French Canadians supported the campaign to suppress the rebellion, but there was widespread outrage in Québec over Riel's execution that did not abate over time. Wilfrid Laurier's passionate denunciation of the government's action was a major step forward in his career. On Nov 26, 8 Indians, including Frog Lake war chief Wandering Spirit, were hanged at Battleford. Three other convicted murderers had their sentences commuted. All the rebels sentenced to jail were released early. Gabriel Dumont, among others, eventually returned from the US under the terms of a general amnesty.

The rebellion had profound effects on western Canada. It was the climax of the federal government's efforts to control the native and settler population of the West. Indians who had thought themselves oppressed after the treaties of the 1870s became subjugated, administered people. The most vocal members of the Métis leadership had either fled to Montana or were in jail. It took native peoples of western Canada many decades to recover politically and emotionally from the defeat of 1885.   BOB BEAL AND ROD MACLEOD

Reading: Bob Beal and Rod Macleod, *Prairie Fire* (1984); George F.G. Stanley, *The Birth of Western Canada* (1936); Desmond Morton, *The Last War Drum* (1972).

North-West Schools Question, a conflict between church and state for control of education in the North-West Territories (now Saskatchewan and Alberta). In 1875 the federal NORTH-WEST TERRITORIES ACT introduced the principle of SEPARATE SCHOOLS for Protestant (mostly anglophone) and Roman Catholic (mostly francophone) religious groups in the region. In 1884 the first local school legislation created 2 denominational school systems under one Board of Education with autonomous Protestant and Catholic sections. As the Protestant majority grew, legislative and administrative measures by 1892 had transformed denominational schools into a system of state-controlled "national" or public schools, with a few separate schools in which the religious influence became minimal. In 1894 Catholic appeals to the federal government for more control over education failed.

The issue was revived in 1904-05 during negotiations for provincial autonomy for Alberta and Saskatchewan. Early in 1905, amidst national controversy, Minister of the Interior Clifford SIFTON resigned in protest against a vague school clause in the AUTONOMY BILLS. Deep feelings, especially in Ontario and Québec, severely tested Canadian unity and threatened to split the Liberal Party. A compromise clause proposed by Sifton after his resignation was accepted by PM Laurier to avoid the impending split; the clause, which became part of the new provinces' constitutions, preserved the educational conditions of 1892. With the bishop of St Albert, Émile Legal, unwilling to follow his metropolitan, Adélard Langevin of St-Boniface, into opposition, and with the Liberals in firm control of the first elections in the new provinces, the question quickly disappeared as a national issue. *See also* MANITOBA SCHOOLS QUESTION; NEW BRUNSWICK SCHOOL QUESTION; ONTARIO SCHOOLS QUESTION; SEPARATE SCHOOL. M.R. LUPUL

North-West Territories Act The original Act of 1875 established permanent institutions of government for the Territories, as well as amending and consolidating the diverse legislation pertaining to the region. Under the Temporary Government Act of 1869, renewed annually, the region formerly known as "Rupert's Land and the North-Western Territory," acquired from the HUDSON'S BAY COMPANY in 1870, was governed by an appointed lieutenant-governor and council. The 1875 Act provided for the gradual addition of elected members to the council as the increase in the population warranted it; when there were 21 elected members, the appointive members would be dropped. The Act also covered real estate, wills, rights of married women, the administration of justice and the prohibition of intoxicants. Perhaps most controversial was section 11, intended to establish and guarantee Protestant and Roman Catholic schools; debate over the resulting NORTH-WEST SCHOOLS QUESTION climaxed during passage of the AUTONOMY BILLS of 1905.

By amendment in 1877 French and English were given equal status in the government and courts of the region. In 1891 the Territorial legislature was empowered to "regulate its proceedings" and promptly discarded the official use of French.

In 1888 the federal government established a legislative assembly of 25, elective except for 3 nonvoting legal advisers. In 1891 the assembly was made wholly elective, and in 1897 a full Cabinet government was granted. Although eventually given the forms and many of the responsibilities of provincial government, the local government was never given control of public lands and natural resources, or a wide tax base; nor was adequate compensation provided by Ottawa to meet the demands for local services. This fueled the autonomy movement leading to provincial status for Alberta and Saskatchewan in 1905.

In 1912 the Act (now the Northwest Territories Act) was amended to take into account the region's more restricted size and population, and government by appointed officials was restored. In 1951 elective members were added to the council, and by 1966 they constituted a majority of the council. That year 2 federal constituencies were created. The following year the commissioner and Territorial administration were moved from Ottawa to Yellowknife, and by 1970 the government once again had powers superficially similar to those of provincial governments. In 1975 the assembly was made fully elective, and it chose some of its members to sit on the executive council; but the commissioner and 2 appointed assistants who also sat on the council continued to have great influence on local government policy, and were ultimately responsible to Ottawa, not to the elected assembly.   DAVID J. HALL

North-West Territories, 1870-1905 Rupert's Land and the North-Western Territory were acquired by Canada from the Hudson's Bay Co on 15 July 1870. A small province of Manitoba was created on the same date; the remaining new territory, stretching W to British Columbia and N to the Arctic Ocean, would be governed directly by the federal government and be known as the North-West Territories; in the early years, it would also include much of northern present-day Ontario and Québec.

The boundaries of the region were subject to frequent change. The region N and sometimes E of Manitoba was established as the District of Keewatin in 1876. The boundaries of Manitoba were changed in 1877, and enlarged in 1881 and 1912. Yukon Territory was created in 1898; and the provinces of Alberta and Saskatchewan created in 1905. Internally, 4 administrative districts were created in 1882: Assiniboia, Saskatchewan, Alberta and Athabaska. It was into these districts, in the southern portion of the Territories, that the great bulk of the settlement population would flow, and consequently on which most government attention was focused prior to 1905.

The region was first governed under "an Act for the Temporary Government of Rupert's Land and the North-Western Territory when united with Canada," passed in 1869. It provided a provisional government by a federally appointed lieutenant-governor and council, which governed initially from Winnipeg. In 1875 the NORTH-WEST TERRITORIES ACT provided a new framework: the governor and council would now operate from a territorial capital (first Battleford, then Regina), and as the settlement population increased, elected members would be added, until a territorial assembly which was substantially elective was created in 1888.

Despite the trappings of representative government, the region remained firmly under the control of the federal government. Ottawa negotiated the INDIAN TREATIES and administered subsequent native policy. It controlled the public lands and natural resources of the region throughout the period. It carefully controlled expenditure of the annual federal grant to the Territories, which comprised the bulk of government funds available for necessary public works such as roads, schools and bridges. Federal goals were clear: the region was to be developed in the national interest. Most of the 25 million acres (c 10.1 million ha) of land that went to support construction of the CPR, for example, came from the North-West Territories. Immigration and settlement were also promoted for reasons of national as well as regional development.

However well intentioned the federal government might have been, it was remarkably insensitive to the needs and desires of the western population. The most dramatic result of the grievances of Indians and Métis was the NORTH-WEST REBELLION of 1885. But the white population was also incensed over protective tariffs, exorbitant freight rates, centrally controlled land policy and niggardly federal grants. The belated creation of 4 parliamentary seats for the Territories, effective in the 1887 election, changed nothing. The result was agitation led by F.W.G. HAULTAIN for more control in the hands of the locally elected assembly. Granting of responsible government in 1897 did not solve the basic problems of a territorial government with insufficient powers and resources to cope with the needs of a rapidly expanding settlement population. Demands for provincial autonomy were finally met in 1905 with the creation of Alberta and Saskatchewan. *See also* PROVINCIAL GOVERNMENT; TERRITORIAL EVOLUTION.   DAVID J. HALL

Reading: Gerald Friesen, *Prairie Road* (1984); J.A. Lower, *Western Canada* (1983).

Northcott, Ronald Charles, curler (b at Innisfail, Alta 31 Dec 1935). Northcott began curling in Vulcan, Alta, in 1950 and was vice-skip on the 1953 Alberta High School champions. He joined the Calgary Curling Club in 1958, and between 1961 and 1978 competed in 9 Alberta championships. Northcott represented Alberta at 6 Canadian championships (Briers) and won Canadian and world championships in 1966, 1968 and 1969; he was also all-star Brier skip in each of those years. Voted Calgary's athlete of the year in 1966 and 1968, he received the Order of Canada in 1976.   RAY KINGSMITH

Northern Dancer, racehorse (b at Oshawa, Ont 27 May 1961). Bred at E.P. TAYLOR's National Stud Farm, Northern Dancer was unsold as a yearling, but as a 2-year-old won the Remsen Stakes, NY, the Flamingo and Florida derbies, and the Summer Stakes, Coronation Futurity and Carleton Stakes in Canada. Northern Dancer was the first Canadian-bred horse to win the Kentucky Derby (1964) and went on to win the Preakness, finish third in the Belmont and win the QUEEN'S PLATE. Known for his stamina, Northern Dancer was also very fast – only Secretariat has bettered his Kentucky Derby record of 2 minutes flat for the $1\frac{1}{4}$-mile course. Retired to stud, Northern Dancer became the leading sire of stakes winners (about 125 by 1987) in this century, including Epsom Derby winners NIJINSKY and The Minstrel.   JAMES MARSH

Northern Georgia Strait Coast Salish At the time of European contact in the 1790s, the people inhabiting the coast of BC in the northern Strait of GEORGIA area were the Pentlatch, the Comox and the Sechelt. Their languages are identified by these same names and belong to the Coast Salish division of the Salishan language family. In the early 1800s the Pentlatch, who lived along the E coast of Vancouver I from the vicinity of Kye Bay in the N to the approximate area of Parksville in the S suffered greatly from disease and from Indian raiding parties from the W coast of the island. Gradually the Pentlatch became absorbed by their northern neighbours, the Comox. The last speaker of the Pentlatch language died in 1940.

The Comox of Vancouver I were also the victims of tribal hostilities in the early 1800s. Their northern neighbours, the Lekwiltok, began to expand southward, displacing the Island Comox from their territory that extended from around Salmon R to Kye Bay (*see* KWAKIUTL).

The remaining Island Comox descendants live on the Comox Indian Reserve, with a population of about 120. Through intermarriage, the people living at Comox adopted both the ceremonials and the language (called Kwakwala) of the Lekwiltok. The Island Comox dialect of the Comox language is almost completely lost.

The Comox-speaking Coast Salish people along the eastern shore of the northern Georgia Strait fared better. Sometimes referred to as Mainland Comox, they are composed of the Homalco, Klahoose and Sliammon, living in the area from Bute Inlet in the N to Stillwater in the S. Formerly the Homalco and Klahoose occupied the protected waters of Bute and Toba inlets, respectively, as well as the adjacent islands. By the late 1800s, when INDIAN RESERVES were established, their main villages were located at Church House near the entrance to Bute Inlet, the present home of about 10 Homalco, and at Squirrel Cove on Cortes I, the home of about 30 Klahoose. Since most Homalco and Klahoose, along with the Sliammon, live on the reserve at the mouth of Sliammon Cr (N of Powell River), formerly a traditional Sliammon village and now a modern one of about 550, the term Sliammon is commonly used to designate all 3 of these groups. The Sechelt, who traditionally occupied Jervis Inlet, both sides of the Sechelt Pen and the adjacent islands, number 640 and live on reserves adjacent to the town of Sechelt.

Like other northwest coast Indians, the northern Georgia Strait Coast Salish had access to a wealth of natural resources, including the 5 species of PACIFIC SALMON, rockfish, seals, shellfish, deer, mountain goats, bear and migratory birds. Vegetable foods provided the necessary complement to fish and meat. An inventory of a traditional HOUSE would indicate that the giant western red cedar was the most versatile of plant materials. Its strong, easily split wood was used for making house planks, dugout CANOES, boxes, barbecuing sticks, drying racks and bowls. Western red cedar inner bark was pounded until soft and used for mats, ropes, clothing and ceremonial costumes. The art of cedar-root basketry is still practised by some women. *See also* NATIVE PEOPLE: NORTHWEST COAST and general articles under NATIVE PEOPLE.

DOROTHY KENNEDY AND RANDY BOUCHARD

Reading: H. Barnett, *The Coast Salish of British Columbia* (1975); Dorothy Kennedy and Randy Bouchard, *Sliammon Life, Sliammon Lands* (1983).

Northern Lights, or aurora borealis, dynamic displays of multicoloured luminosity appearing in the day or night sky in high latitudes in the Northern Hemisphere. At any instant of time, the auroras are arrayed along a band (the auroral oval) with the North GEOMAGNETIC POLE near its centre. The band is normally about 500-1000 km wide, its average position in Canada being over Yellowknife, NWT, to the West, and Grande rivière de la Baleine, Qué, to the East. During intense activity the oval may expand as far S as Miami, Florida (Aug 1972), and beyond. The luminosity can fluctuate violently, particularly near local midnight when explosive bursts of activity called substorms are triggered. Auroras originate in the ionosphere, the upper atmosphere, 100-300 km above the Earth's surface. They are caused primarily by energized electrons (1-20 kilo-electron volts) which are accelerated towards the ionosphere from a region 5000-10 000 km above the Earth's surface. These energetic electrons bombard the upper atmosphere and "excite" atmospheric constituent particles. When these particles return to less excited states, they give off light. Green or red light comes from excited atomic oxygen; purple light from excited molecular nitrogen.

Current theory states that the energy driving auroras is obtained from the solar wind, a gas composed primarily of protons and electrons, blowing away from the SUN at supersonic velocities of 300-1000 km/s (*see* PHYSICS). The solar magnetic field is embedded in the gas and is pulled by the wind deep into interplanetary space. The wind interacts with the Earth's magnetic field, distorting it to form the magnetosphere (ie, the comet-shaped cavity,

Ultraviolet auroral emissions photographed by the Canadian imager aboard the Swedish Viking satellite. In this false colour picture, red regions represent the most intense auroras, particularly brilliant in the night sky over NE Canada. The island of Greenland is shown in outline, top and centre (*courtesy the Viking Images Team*).

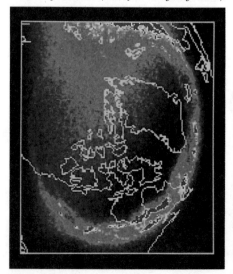

blunt end towards the sun, carved in the interplanetary medium by the Earth's magnetic field). The magnetosphere is broken near each pole by a cleft region. Some solar-wind plasma, slowed and heated by interaction with the magnetosphere, enters the cleft region and penetrates directly to the ionosphere causing the dayside auroras. However, most of the particles leaking into the magnetosphere are trapped behind the Earth, and through processes analogous to convection end up flowing towards the Earth. Some of these particles are accelerated into the nightside ionosphere causing brilliant auroras. The amount of energy leaking into the magnetosphere is regulated predominantly by the strength of the interplanetary magnetic field and its direction in relation to the Earth's magnetic field lines at the outer boundary of the magnetosphere. Activity also varies with sunspot and solar-flare occurrence. Parallel phenomena in the Southern Hemisphere are known as the aurora australis.

Auroras are the visible portion of the dissipation of the energy which has entered the magnetosphere from the solar wind. This energy is also dissipated through ohmic heating (ie, heat generated by electric current flow through a resistor). This process involves giant currents, sometimes in excess of one million amperes, which flow through the resistive ionosphere in the region of luminous auroras. These currents create magnetic fields which can make compass needles show direction incorrectly and which can cause surges in power lines resulting in electric-power outages.

The northern lights have haunted the imaginations of spectators for centuries. To the Inuit, the *arsaniit* are the sky people enjoying a ball game. Some Indians view the lights as ancestral spirits dancing before the Great Spirit. Recently, Canadian researchers placed an ultraviolet imager aboard the Swedish Viking satellite and succeeded in obtaining a global view of the auroras and in following their rapid time variations. GORDON ROSTOKER

Northern Railway of Canada The railway was designed to link the 3 lakes for which it was originally named – the Ontario, Simcoe and Huron Railway. It opened May 1853 when the locomotive *Toronto* (made in Toronto) hauled the first steam train in present-day Ontario from Toronto to Mitchell's Corners (present-day Aurora). The line was soon extended to Bradford and Allandale and by 1855 the entire stretch to COLLINGWOOD was completed, including a branch to Lk SIMCOE. The railway made Collingwood a prosperous transshipment point from the midwestern US and tapped the rich timber reserves of Simcoe County. It was largely responsible for the hegemony TORONTO managed to establish over the northern hinterland, but was a financial failure itself. On the verge of bankruptcy, it was reorganized 1858 as the Northern Ry of Canada. Branches were built from Collingwood to Meaford (1872), Allandale to Gravenhurst (1875), and eventually to Huntsville and North Bay. It merged with the Hamilton and North Western Ry (1879) and was taken over by the GRAND TRUNK RAILWAY in 1888, later becoming part of the CN system. JAMES MARSH

Northern Review, literary magazine appearing irregularly, 1945-56, edited by John SUTHERLAND. It represented the end of the era when Montréal was the leading centre of modern Canadian POETRY IN ENGLISH. It arose from the merger of the earlier rivals, *Preview* and *First Statement*. *Preview* was founded in Mar 1942 by a group including Patrick Anderson, the journal's driving spirit, and F.R. SCOTT; later P.K. PAGE and A.M. KLEIN joined the editorial group. *Preview*'s orientation was cosmopolitan; its members looked largely towards the English poets of the 1930s for inspiration. *First Statement* was founded in Sept 1942 by Suther-

land, who was soon joined by Irving LAYTON and Louis DUDEK. Its writers attacked the "colonialism" of *Preview* and advocated a poetry related to local conditions and ways of speech; this meant that in practice they looked to American models, notably Ezra Pound and William Carlos Williams. First Statement Press also published poetry chapbooks, and when the rival magazines submerged their differences and united in *Northern Review,* the press continued, publishing books by Layton, Anderson, Anne WILKINSON and Raymond SOUSTER. The group that originally embarked on *Northern Review* included Scott, Klein, Layton, Anderson, Page, A.J.M. SMITH, Dorothy LIVESAY and Ralph GUSTAFSON, but in 1947 several members of the board resigned over a controversial review Sutherland published without consulting his associates. In 1948 Layton left, and the review became largely an expression of Sutherland's increasingly conservative attitude, though it still attracted good writers, including Mavis GALLANT, Brian MOORE, Marshall MCLUHAN and George WOODCOCK. It came to an end with Sutherland's death in 1956. GEORGE WOODCOCK

Northern Telecom Limited, *see* ELECTRONICS INDUSTRY.

Northumberland Strait is a tidal water body between PEI and the coast of eastern NB and northern NS, extending 225 km WNW to ESE from Cap-Lumière, NB, to Cape George, NS, with a width of 4-17 km. It is 68 m deep at its eastern end but less than 20 m over a large central area. Preglacial and glacial valleys eroded into red sandstone and siltstone lead from both ends into the floor of the Gulf of ST LAWRENCE. The retreat of glacial ice from the strait and surrounding area about 13 000 years ago was followed by flooding by the sea. Soon after, isostatic uplift excluded the sea from the central area, which became an isthmus joining opposite coasts. By 5000 years ago, the rising sea level had flooded this link, establishing the strait, which has been slowly deepening.

A generally shallow depth causes strong tidal currents, water turbulence and a high concentration of suspended red silt and clay, which led early French colonists to name the strait "la mer rouge." Shallowness is also largely responsible for the warmest summer water temperature in eastern Canada (July, 16°C) and a consequent concentration of summer tourist activity, as well as a prolific shellfish and lobster fishery. Equable climate and extensive tillable soils form the basis for mixed agriculture and vegetable growing (particularly potatoes) on both coasts. The strait is crossed by 2 ferries – Cape Tormentine, NB, to Borden, PEI, and Caribou Ferry, NS, to Wood I, PEI. In Nov 1987, the federal government issued a call for tenders for a proposed bridge or tunnel to be constructed across the 14 km width of strait from Cape Tormentine to Borden, and in Jan 1988 about 60% of PEI voters favoured the possibility of establishing a fixed link. The strait's coastal areas were settled by ACADIAN French from the early 16th century, and by English, LOYALISTS and SCOTS in the 18th century. The principal coastal towns are CHARLOTTETOWN and SUMMERSIDE, PEI; PICTOU, NS; and SHEDIAC and Richibucto, NB. The strait was named for HMS *Northumberland*, flagship of Admiral Colville. I.A. BROOKES

Northwest Coast, the name given by 18th-century navigators and traders to the great arc of Pacific coast and offshore islands stretching from present-day northern California to an ill-defined point along the Alaska coast – at Prince William Sound or even Cook Inlet. Modern anthropologists identify the native culture of the NW Coast as that, within rough limits, between Yakutat Bay, SE Alaska, and Trinidad Bay or Cape Mendocino,

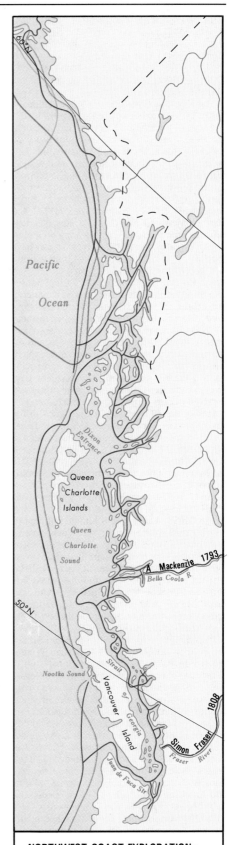

NORTHWEST COAST EXPLORATION: RUSSIAN & BRITISH

——	Bering, Vitus (Rus) 1741
——	Chirikov, Aleksei (Rus) 1741
———	Cook, James (Br) 1778-79
———	Vancouver, George (Br) 1792; 1793; 1794

Calif. Along this narrow coastal belt the Indians developed high levels of civilization based upon the sea's plentiful resources. Warmed by the N Pacific Current and deluged along most of its length by heavy annual precipitation, the NW Coast produces dense coniferous forests and abundant vegetation.

The NW Coast was one of the last temperate ocean frontiers to be explored and settled by Europeans. Despite the attractions of the N Pacific as the western end of a possible NORTHWEST PASSAGE, the region remained isolated. Distance, the limitations of shipbuilding technology and Spain's jealous control over most of the N and S American littoral prevented intrusion by all but the most hardy. Apocryphal voyages by Lorenzo Ferrer Maldonado (1588), Juan de FUCA (1592) and Bartholomew de Fonte (1640) confused cartographers, who prepared charts bearing no resemblance to reality. In 1579 Francis DRAKE may have reached 48° N lat before returning southward to the approximate latitude of present-day San Francisco and then crossing the Pacific, but his exact northernmost location remains a matter of conjecture. In 1602 Sebastian Vizcaíno discovered Monterey Bay for Spain and sailed to about 43° N lat. Until the 18th century, however, Spain was occupied with its earlier conquests and remained content to claim rather than to explore the coastline. Although one Spanish transpacific galleon crashed at present-day Nehalem Bay, Ore, in the latter 17th century, none of its crew survived to carry word back to Mexico.

During the 18th century interest grew in the unexplored N Pacific. Russian expansion into Siberia resulted in expeditions by Vitus BERING to Bering Str (1728) and in 1741 by Bering and Aleksei Chirikov to the NW Coast around 55° N lat. Rumours of this activity impelled the Spanish Crown to order voyages northwards from Mexico. In 1774 Juan Pérez Hernández reached about 55° N. He touched at the Queen Charlotte Is and at Nootka Sd (Vancouver I) but did not land to take possession for Spain. In 1775 a new expedition under Bruno de Hezeta and Juan Francisco de la BODEGA Y QUADRA sailed northwards to investigate the Russian presence. Bodega and Quadra reached about 58°30' N lat and discovered Bucareli Bay, Prince of Wales I. Spain dispatched another major expedition in 1779, but government secrecy prevented information on the NW Coast from reaching the public.

The challenge to Spain came from Britain rather than Russia. In 1777-78, James COOK crossed the Pacific via the Sandwich Is [Hawaii] to the NW Coast. Cook was to search for a Northwest Passage and to explore the unknown coastline. He spent nearly a month at Nootka Sd before continuing northward to Alaska and the Aleutian Is. Later in Macau and Canton, Cook's men discovered a potentially lucrative trade in the sea-otter pelts they had obtained on the NW Coast. The publication of Cook's voyage abruptly ended the coast's isolation. After 1785 commercial expeditions from London, Bombay, Calcutta, Macau and American ports such as Boston opened the maritime FUR TRADE. By 1792 there were at least 21 trading vessels on the coast. Trading captains included George Dixon, John MEARES and Charles William Barkley. The trade in sea-otter pelts had begun in 1786; it reached its apogee in the 1790s before declining after 1812.

The Spaniards were ignorant about the burgeoning maritime fur trade until 1788, when they renewed their own voyages to check Russian encroachments southward from Alaska. Esteban José MARTÍNEZ discovered 6 Russian posts in Alaska and, after hearing from the traders that Russian ships would soon occupy Nootka Sd, he persuaded the Mexican viceroy to authorize a

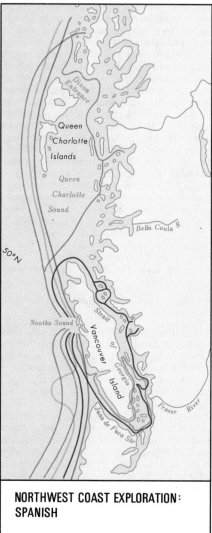

NORTHWEST COAST EXPLORATION: SPANISH

——— Pérez Hernández, Juan 1774

——— Bodega y Quadra, Juan Francisco de la 1775

——— Eliza, Francisco de 1790

——— Alcalá Galiano and Valdés 1792

——— Caamaño, Jacinto 1792

voyage to occupy the sound for Spain. In 1789 Martínez arrived there and found British and American vessels. His seizure of the British vessels sparked the NOOTKA SOUND CONTROVERSY, a clash of imperial interests which almost precipitated a European conflict. However, 3 Nootka Conventions provided for a peaceful sharing of the northern ports and resources. Spain withdrew in 1795, abandoning the fur trade to the British and Americans. Meanwhile, scientific expeditions of the Comte de Lapérouse (1786, France), George VANCOUVER (1792-94, Britain), Alejandro MALASPINA (1791, Spain) and the SUTIL AND MEXICANA (1792, Spain) explored the resources and indigenous inhabitants of the NW Coast.

The major impact of the maritime fur trade was to introduce the coastal Indians to firearms, metal tools and manufactured items. The European traders employed some violence and also introduced alcohol and diseases, but the nature of the fur harvest meant that they did not create permanent shore bases. Even before the beginning of the 19th century, however, some observers noted a decline in the number of sea otters and predicted the demise of the trade. This fact, combined with resistance from the Chinese (the major market), reduced the coast's appeal.

The coast's isolation was not to return. In July 1793, Alexander MACKENZIE of the NORTH WEST

COMPANY arrived overland down the Bella Coola R to Pacific tidewater. In 1808 Simon FRASER descended the river that was to carry his name, and in 1811 David THOMPSON reached the mouth of the Columbia R. There he discovered that American traders from John Jacob Astor's PACIFIC FUR COMPANY had arrived by sea to construct Astoria. With the amalgamation in 1821 of the NWC and the HUDSON'S BAY COMPANY, the European presence ceased to be transitory. In 1821 Russia claimed the coast southwards to 51° N lat as its territory, but British and American protests led to the 1825 settlement of the ALASKA BOUNDARY at 54°40'. To compete with the maritime fur traders, the HBC built a string of permanent forts. After negotiation of the OREGON TREATY in 1846, the HBC's far western interests centered on Vancouver I, which became a colony in 1849. Although there was subsequent competition between the fur traders and settlers, the latter won out. With the emergence of colonies and boundary agreements separating the Russian, British, American and Spanish (later Mexican) spheres, the Northwest Coast as a concept ceased to exist except as a historical memory. *See also* SPANISH EXPLORATION. CHRISTON I. ARCHER

Reading: G. Barratt, *Russia in Pacific Waters, 1715-1825* (1981); W.L. Cook, *Flood Tide of Empire* (1973); R. Fisher, *Contact and Conflict* (1977); Barry M. Gough, *Distant Dominion* (1980).

Northwest Coast Indian Art More than 4000 years ago Indians of the BC coast (and adjacent areas of Washington and southeastern Alaska) developed artistic traditions that are heralded throughout the world for their imaginative and stylistic qualities. Objects made in these traditions are so highly formalized and distinctive that once some of the basic principles have been grasped, they can be easily identified. The "formline" is the primary design element on which Northwest Coast art depends; it is the positive delineating force of the painting, relief or engraving. Formlines are continuous, flowing, curvilinear lines that turn, swell and diminish in a prescribed manner. They are used for figure outlines, internal design elements, and in abstract compositions.

While native people in general do not make a distinction between what is art and what is not, nor do they have a term which corresponds to the English word "art," Northwest Coast Indian people consider recognition of meaning and form traditions to be most important. Throughout the region, special objects were made originally for the purpose of displaying certain inherited privileges and rights of their owners. Although ways of reckoning kinship vary between groups, people claiming common descent also claim rights to ancestrally derived territories, spirit powers, names, songs, dances, crests and other "properties" that both contain and display their family's wealth and identity.

Potlatches are events of great pomp and formality arranged to celebrate the handing down of names, rights and privileges from one generation to the next. These privileges, together with the associated artifacts, are publicly displayed and their transfer committed to the collective memory of the potlatching community. Another defining feature of the POTLATCH is the distribution of wealth objects (and money in more recent times) by the host group to the guests, who include people from other villages and tribes. Acceptance of gifts constitutes validation by the guests that the host group is transferring its inheritance in the approved manner.

Crests, or heraldic art, are objects associated with the potlatch. A crest itself is a concept, usually but not always referring to animals (both natural and imaginary, eg, thunderbirds), which is given a conventionalized representation. Details

Haida argillite dish, 27 x 22 cm, attributed to Charles Edenshaw. Haida carvers began working argillite early in the 19th century (*courtesy UBC Museum of Anthropology*).

of the crest images vary widely, according to personal and stylistic preferences. Not all animal representations in Northwest Coast art are crests. Common crest-bearing artifacts are totem poles, painted housefronts and screens (room dividers), ceremonial robes and headdresses, staffs, feast dishes, spoons and ladles. Crests are jealously guarded possessions – they are a legacy from the ancestors, acquired in myth time from supernatural animals or images of supernaturals, to be held in perpetuity by their descendants. To display a crest of another group is an insult to the integrity and identity of that group.

Winter Dances (now held throughout the year) are elaborately staged performances featuring masked dancers and ingenious mechanical devices that create illusions of death and resurrection and other astounding manifestations of supernatural power and presences. In this context, animal representations, most notably MASKS, are related to but conceptually distinct from the potlatch proper. During these initiation rituals, encounters with supernatural powers occur, either as spirit possession or theatrical simulation (the distinction is not always clear to observers).

Shamanic Art Scholars believe that the winter dances developed out of an ancient guardian spirit complex, most highly developed among shamans (mystic healers). The visionary experience is de-

Haida rattle (pre-1880), wood, 25.3 x 12.6 cm (*courtesy UBC Museum of Anthropology*).

scribed as the appearance of an animal spirit helper or guardian in a dream or trance. From them, the dreamer drew knowledge and special powers. Northwest Coast shamans used special objects, often made of wood, ivory or bone, in which their spirit helpers were commemorated. These objects include amulets, soul catchers (carved tubular objects believed to be containers for lost souls) and Janus-faced globular shaman's rattles, which are among some of the great masterworks of Northwest Coast art (*see* SHAMAN).

Artists

Northwest Coast societies were unique in aboriginal Canada in that they sustained a group of professional male artists who were largely freed from the general food quest by the support of wealthy patrons who commissioned works for potlatches and winter dances. It appears that while most men made objects for personal and family use, the specialists were responsible for the exceptional art objects preserved and treasured in museums. Such artists were trained from youth as apprentices by master artists who, in most cases, were their uncles or fathers. As well as making the objects, they were responsible for the stagecraft

Tlingit basket, spruce root, 16 x 14.3 cm (*courtesy UBC Museum of Anthropology*).

involved in ritual use. While all women wove (basketry and textiles), some women past their child-rearing years specialized as did their male counterparts.

Women's Art In weaving, all of the techniques found elsewhere in N America were used, except true loom (heddle) weaving. The Inland TLINGIT excelled in false embroidery; the HAIDA in "self-designed" twined spruce-root hats; the Coast SALISH in cherry-bark imbrication on coiled baskets; and the NOOTKA (Westcoast) women in twined cedar-bark hats with onion-shaped tops, overlaid with strands of beargrass woven in conventionalized whale-hunting scenes.

An exceptional formline weaving technique was developed in the north, becoming a specialty of the Chilkat Tlingit in the 19th century. Chilkat blankets are the highest-valued examples of the weaver's art, worn by chiefs as far south as the Southern KWAKIUTL. The warps are shredded cedar bark twisted with mountain goats' wool; the wefts are pure wool. The warps were hung from a horizontal bar and the double weft strands were twined across them. Designs were made in formline crest designs, copied from patterned boards painted by men (*see* CHILKAT BLANKET).

The Coast Salish made twill-plaited blankets in geometric designs out of goat wool, cattail fluff and (reportedly) the hair of a small fluffy dog, extinct since early contact times. With the introduction of domestic sheep around 1850 and of

Chilkat blanket collected from the Haida (pre-1870), wool and cedar bark trimmed with otter fur; yellow, black, blue, white; 158 x 132 cm (*courtesy UBC Museum of Anthropology*).

Scottish knitting techniques, Coast Salish women began producing knitted Cowichan sweaters, which have since become a successful cottage industry. Basketmaking has continued with some vitality among the Coast Salish and Westcoast women, and is being revived among the TSIMSHIAN and Haida. Woven blankets were replaced by Hudson's Bay Co woolen blankets – both for dancing and as potlatch gifts. Crest designs were sewn on woolen blankets in buttons, shells, and appliqué.

Men's Art Men worked a variety of materials – wood, stone, horn, copper, bone, antler, leather, ivory and abalone shells – since aboriginal times; silver, gold and bronze in historic times, and works on paper and canvas in recent years. Knives, adzes, chisels, gouges and awls were made of stone, shell and beaver teeth, and hafted with sculptural forms. Metal was especially sought after from Europeans, and in the 19th century native paints were replaced by Western products.

Containers – bowls, dishes, boxes, chests, ladles, canoes – are a specialty. Boxes are made by a kerfing technique in which a single board is steamed and bent in 3 corner folds with a bottom and fourth corner attached by pegs. Stone, wooden and shell dishes and bowls are carved in animal shapes.

Styles

A series of conventions in Northwest Coast art permits the parts of animals to represent the entire creatures – eg, a raven's beak, beaver's teeth,

The Raven and the First Men (1980), contemporary yellow cedar Haida sculpture by Bill Reid, 210 x 180 cm (*courtesy UBC Museum of Anthropology*).

Tsimshian soul catcher (*c*1890), wood, 16 x 7 x 3 cm. Northwest Coast shamans used these objects to commemorate their spirit helpers (*courtesy UBC Museum of Anthropology*).

whale's flukes. Two animals frequently share a single body, or a single animal is split at the face or along the backbone to create 2 bilaterally symmetrical profiles; animal parts are rearranged from their biological locations; some are placed inside other animals, or intertwined with them. All these conventions create great formal and iconographic complexities.

Most obviously in the winter dances, but also widely recognizable in other Northwest Coast iconography, is the theme of transformation or metamorphosis between beings of the land, sea and sky, and ultimately between the domains of the living and the dead. A special type of transformation mask has double faces operated by strings so that an outer (usually animal) face opens to reveal a human face within. Masks frequently have movable eyes, jaws and other parts.

Three major styles have been identified – Northern, Central and Southern, corresponding to the major cultural divisions which are used by anthropologists:

The Northern Province, composed of Tlingit, Haida, Tsimshian, Niska, Gitksan and Northern Kwakiutl, exhibits a defining style of 2-dimensional painting, engraving and shallow relief carving based on a formline aesthetic. Formline compositions in the 19th century were most highly developed on housefronts, screens and chiefs' chests. The works of individual 19th-century masters of the formline aesthetic are being identified according to art historical principles by modern scholars.

Formline painting was based on a 3-colour scheme of primary black lines (aboriginally, charcoal and lignite), secondary red lines (ochres) and tertiary blue-green elements (copper minerals). Pigments were mixed with a medium derived from dried salmon eggs and paintbrushes were made of porcupine hairs. Designs were rendered freehand, although templates were frequently used for the recurring ovoid shapes.

A northern painting style was highly developed at contact, in which painted designs extended to the limits of the field (varying according to the object being decorated). All of the constituent elements in these designs harmonize according to a subtle and sophisticated aesthetic.

Sculpted formlines also occur as surface decoration on northern sculpture, including totem poles, headdresses, masks, rattles, canoes, canoe paddles, staffs, and various forms of bowls, dishes and boxes. Early in the 19th century, Haida carvers began working a soft, black shale (argillite) in order to make curios for sailors and traders, and later for settlers and tourists. Argillite carvings are still made in the Queen Charlotte Is, although the technical mastery of the early pieces has not yet been recovered in modern times.

The Central Province By 1880, elements of northern formline painting had been incorporated by the Southern Kwakiutl and Westcoast people, who adapted them to a prehistoric Old Wakashan

style encountered by Captain James COOK a century earlier. The Westcoast people developed a new and distinctive combination of formlines, geometric and naturalistic elements. The Kwakiutl continued to evolve an exuberant, colourful and flamboyant manner all their own. In the early 20th century they added orange, yellow and green paint to the repertoire. The BELLA COOLA borrowed many stylistic and ceremonial elements from their Kwakiutl neighbours, creating a style easily recognized by the heavy and bulbous features of its masks, and the typical use of a medium blue paint.

The Southern Province Painting and relief carving in the Coast Salish area is geometric – circles, chevrons, crescents, rows of dots, triangles and T-shapes. In recent years, scholars have noticed that these elements revealed a negative (recessed) formline-type design which is considered by some to be possibly ancestral to the northern formline tradition. Strong, simplified human and animal sculptures – house pots, coffins, grave posts, and a single-mask type, the protruding-eye Sxayxway – were also made. The Southern tradition barely survived into the 20th century, although it too has enjoyed a revival since the 1970s.

European Contact

After millenia of what appears to be continuous development, native artistic traditions and society were severely disrupted by European contact which, from the native point of view, amounted to an invasion. Although in the first century of white intrusion, native art and culture flourished under the stimulus of money, the FUR TRADE, new metal tools and other aspects of European technology, the native population became decimated and demoralized by alcoholism and disease, by white schools for native children, by political and religious suppression of the potlatch and by other forms of colonial oppression. By 1910 the traditional social structure and belief system was in such severe dislocation that white observers predicted its complete collapse and the inevitable assimilation of a remnant population into Canadian society. Except for a handful of Southern Kwakiutl artists who maintained their skills through traditional apprentice training, the great artistic tradition developed over 3000 years degenerated into souvenir production for infrequent tourists. It

looked like the end of one of humankind's most distinctive cultural achievements.

The Contemporary Revival In 1958 Haida carver Bill REID and Nimpkish carver Douglas Cranmer began recreating traditional Haida houses and totem poles for UBC Museum of Anthropology. Reid has since become the acknowledged leader of the Northwest Coast artistic revival. By the 1980s there were an estimated 200 men (and a few women) seriously engaged in artistic production in all the former styles. A sizable collector's market has developed around their work, and some experts believe that certain new pieces achieve the technical skill of 19th-century masters. Native artists such as Charlie Edenshaw, Robert DAVIDSON, Joe DAVID, Norman Tait, Douglas Cranmer and Tom Hall were becoming cultural leaders, using their skills as artists to fan the dying embers of traditional custom and belief. *See also* INDIAN ART; PICTOGRAPHS AND PETROGLYPHS.

MARJORIE M. HALPIN

Reading: M. Barbeau, *Totem Poles* (1950) and *Haida Carvers in Argillite* (1957); F. Boas, *Primitive Art* (1927, repr 1955); R.L. Carlson, ed, *Indian Art Traditions of the Northwest Coast* (1983); P. Gustafson, *Salish Weaving* (1980); Marjorie M. Halpin, *Totem Poles: An Illustrated Guide* (1981); A. Hawthorn, *Art of the Kwakiutl Indians* (1967); B. Holm, *Northwest Coast Indian Art: An Analysis of Form* (1965); P.L. MacNair, A.L. Hoover and K. Neary, *The Legacy: Continuing Traditions of Canadian Northwest* (1980); C. Samuel, *The Chilkat Dancing Blanket* (1982); D. Shadbolt, *Bill Reid* (1987).

Northwest Passage The search for a water route through the Arctic, N of the Canadian mainland, to the supposed wealth of the Far East was a chapter of frustrations in the history of EXPLORATION in Canada. For over 300 years, after it was realized that N America blocked the route to the Orient, expeditions probed the inhospitable sea and land environments seeking a commercial route to the Pacific. Martin FROBISHER (1576) and later John DAVIS (1585) reported the barren obstacle of Baffin I, but noted ice-blocked westward-leading passages N and S of the large island. Exploration in the

Map of the "North and Polar Regions," 1598, showing W. Barents's explorations (Davis Strait is seen in the upper-left portion). The 300-year search for a route through these northern waters was a long chapter of frustration in the history of exploration (*courtesy National Archives of Canada/NMC-21063*).

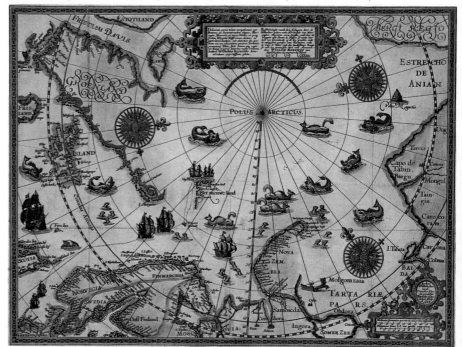

early 17th century was sidetracked into the broad opening of Hudson Str, but no sea routes were found W of Hudson Bay.

In 1819 Edward PARRY, in command of ships of the British navy, explored the opening N of Baffin I and W of Lancaster Sd to Melville I. This route through Viscount Melville Sd is the widest passage through the arctic islands, but Parry reported it blocked by eastward-moving heavy ice floes even in Aug. After 1829 John ROSS confirmed the extension of Boothia Peninsula N from the mainland, which blocked any sea route through that part of the central Arctic, but he missed the narrow opening through Bellot Str. The many expeditions after 1845 in search of the lost Sir John FRANKLIN finally defined the coastal outlines of most of the arctic islands and reported an uncertain ice-free period for ships of only 1-2 months in Aug and Sept. In 1853-54 Robert MCCLURE became the first person to traverse a route from W to E, partly by sledge over the sea ice from Banks I to near Devon I. As a result of the natural environmental information accumulated, commercial shipping had no further interest in the passage. The Hudson's Bay Co continued to use part of the water route to its posts around Hudson Bay. Otto SVERDRUP confirmed that there was no sea passage through the islands NW of Lancaster and Viscount Melville sounds 1898-1902.

The Northwest Passage was finally traversed 1903-06 by Norwegian adventurer Roald AMUNDSEN in his tiny ship, *Gjoa*. He travelled W and S of Lancaster Sd through Peel Sd and along the western Arctic coast through Queen Maud and Coronation gulfs. His western exit from the Arctic was simply a feasible route out of the area rather than a planned attempt to traverse the Northwest Passage. The first W to E passage by the RCMP vessel ST. ROCH under Henry LARSEN followed a similar route through the relatively shallow channels along the mainland coast 1940-42. Larsen left the central Arctic through Bellot Str and travelled N and E of Baffin I. During the summer of 1944 the *St. Roch* became the first to traverse the passage from E to W in a single year, using a new route W of Lancaster Sd, S through Prince of Wales Str between Banks and Victoria islands, and along the northern Alaska coast. Finally, in 1954, the first ship to achieve the passage from W to E in a single year was the Canadian government icebreaker *Labrador*. In 1969 the American oil tanker *Manhattan*, with the assistance of the Canadian icebreaker *John A. Macdonald*, traversed the Northwest Passage from E to W. The Northwest Passage again was the focus of national attention in the mid-to late 1980s when, as a result of the American *Polar Sea* traversing it, the question of ARCTIC SOVEREIGNTY arose. In early 1988 Canada and the US reached an agreement to permit US icebreakers access to arctic waters, including the Northwest Passage, on a case-by-case basis. The agreement, however, did not settle the question of sovereignty. *See also* ARCTIC EXPLORATION.   J. LEWIS ROBINSON

Reading: J. Honderich, *Arctic Imperative: Is Canada Losing the North* (1987); L.H. Neatby, *In Quest of The North West Passage* (1958).

Northwest Staging Route, an air route from Edmonton, over NW Canada to Fairbanks, Alaska, planned before WWII by Canada, developed and built by Canada and the US 1940-44. Costing about $75 million, it was usable in daylight by 1941, proving invaluable for the support of defence projects in the northwest and for delivering aircraft to Alaska and to the Soviet Union. Major landing fields in Canada included Grande Prairie, Fort St John, Fort Nelson, Watson Lake and Whitehorse. About 450 aircraft per month traversed the route in 1943.   KENNETH S. COATES

Northwest Territories

Capital: Yellowknife
Motto: None
Flower: Mountain avens
Largest Urban Centres: Yellowknife, Inuvik, Hay River, Iqaluit, Fort Smith, Rankin Inlet
Population: 52 238 (1986c); rank eleventh, 0.21% of Canada; 46.3% urban; 53.7% rural; 0.016 per km² density; 14.2% increase from 1981-86
Language: 53.6% English; 2.5% French; 27.8% Inuktitut; 16.1% Other (1986)
Entered Confederation: 15 July 1870
Government: Territorial — Commissioner, Executive Council, Legislative Assembly of 24 members; federal — one senator, 2 members of the House of Commons; the Minister of Indian Affairs and Northern Development may direct the Commissioner in the administration of the territory
Area: 3 379 684 km², including 133 294 km² of inland water; 33.9% of Canada
Elevation: Highest point — Mount Sir James MacBrien (2762 m); lowest point — sea level at Arctic shore
Gross Domestic Product: $1.67 billion (Yukon and NWT) (1986)
Value of Mineral Production: $503.065 million (1982); $789.8 million (1986)
Electric Power Generated: 451 GWh
Sales Tax: None (1987)

Northwest Territories (NWT) The name was originally applied to the territory acquired in 1870 from the HBC and Great Britain — RUPERT'S LAND and the North-Western Territory – which lay NW of central Canada. In 1880 Great Britain also transferred to Canada the arctic islands, N of the mainland, thereby adding to the territories. Large portions of NWT were subsequently removed to create the provinces of Manitoba (1870), Saskatchewan (1905) and Alberta (1905); the Yukon T (1898); and to add to the areas of Manitoba (1880, 1912), Ontario (1912) and Québec (1912). Even so, it constitutes the largest political subdivision within Canada (33.9% of the national area) and the northernmost landmass extending to within 800 km of the North Pole. Its enormous distances, northern location and sparse population impart distinctive characteristics.

Land and Resources

The NWT includes a mainland portion lying W of Hudson Bay-Foxe Basin and S of the BEAUFORT SEA and other arctic marine waters to the E. North of the mainland the Arctic Archipelago includes a great number of islands of varying size and complexity. The more westerly part of the mainland forms the Mackenzie Valley area, a subarctic region contrasting with the arctic mainland area that lies E and N of the TREELINE and is sometimes known as the Barren Lands. This vegetation division corresponds to a cultural division of the native peoples, with the Inuit occupying the Arctic and the Indians, or Dene, the Subarctic. The greater economic development and larger population of the subarctic Mackenzie Valley also set it apart from the arctic mainland.

Arctic Archipelago Although 60°N is the southern boundary of the NWT, all islands in James and Hudson bays and in HUDSON STRAIT, as well as those farther N, are included within the territories. Eighteen of the islands are larger than Canada's smallest province and the largest, BAFFIN I, is more than twice the size of Great Britain. Islands lying N

of the straits W from LANCASTER SOUND are known as the QUEEN ELIZABETH IS. Geologically, the islands of the Archipelago range from ancient Precambrian (Baffin I, eastern DEVON I and SE ELLESMERE I) through progressively younger formations to the NW. The eastern islands are mountainous and average 1800-2100 m, with Mt Barbeau (2616 m) in northernmost Ellesmere I the highest peak in the Archipelago. Permanent ice caps cover much of the eastern islands, and magnificent fjords occur in the coastal section. Canada's (and the world's) first arctic national park was established on eastern Baffin I in 1972 (AUYUITTUQ NATIONAL PARK). The central islands are plateaulike, while those in the NW and SW are mainly lowland plains. Severe climate and PERMAFROST result in very poor soil development. Vegetation is tundra, varying from low bush to grass, but it may be lacking in some sectors.

Ice covers all the surrounding seas for much of the year, and never disappears from around the northwesternmost islands, severely limiting navigation. Long, cold winters are characteristic of all the NWT. The SE sector of the Archipelago is not as cold, however, because of its proximity to the open waters of the N Atlantic, and with its higher elevation, it receives higher precipitation than elsewhere in the Arctic, which overall is among the driest areas of Canada. The Archipelago differs from the other 2 regions of the NWT in that summers remain cool, averaging only 4°C in July over most of the area because of the surrounding cold waters. The great contrast between the long days of summer and the short (even nonexistent) days of winter reflects the high latitude.

Marine biotic resources (whales, seals, fish) supplemented by caribou have traditionally supported the INUIT, along with trapping (white fox) in the first half of the 20th century. Commercial whaling by whites almost exterminated whales by c1910, though limited hunting by natives continues, eg, in the Mackenzie Delta. Polar bear skins and fox pelts still provide some income for the Inuit. The greatest postwar resource development has been

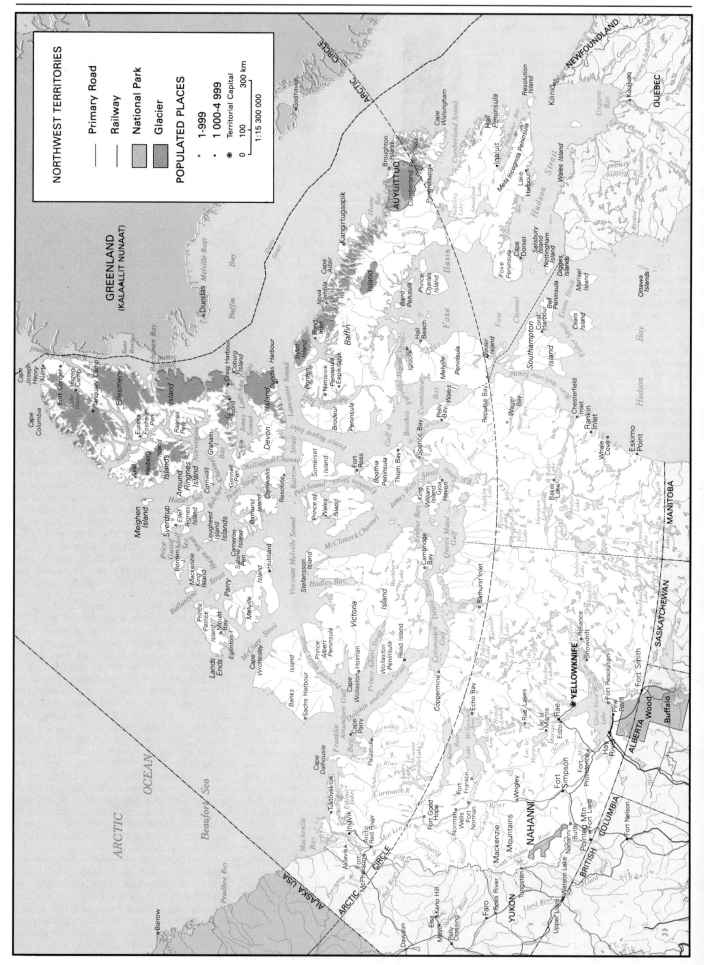

NORTHWEST TERRITORIES

— Primary Road
— Railway
National Park
Glacier

POPULATED PLACES
○ 1–999
• 1 000–4 999
⊛ Territorial Capital

1:15 300 000
0 100 300 km

in minerals, with 2 lead-zinc mines now in production in the Archipelago: Nanisivik at Strathcona Sound in N Baffin I, and Polaris on Little Cornwallis I. More widespread activity has resulted from the search for oil and natural gas in the NW Queen Elizabeth Is. Proven reserves of oil now are sufficient enough that Panarctic Oil and Gas has constructed a production site at Bent Horn on Cameron I and ships the oil by tanker to E Canada. Exploratory drilling for oil continues, especially offshore in the Beaufort Sea. This greatly increased resource development has aroused great concern for the fragile arctic ENVIRONMENT among both the native peoples and conservationists. The Lancaster Sound area and Polar Bear Pass on BATHURST I are especially sensitive areas.

Arctic Mainland The Canadian SHIELD makes up the arctic mainland. Pleistocene ice sheets polished its surface, stripping away surface material down to the bedrock. In places boulders and meltwater-sorted sands and gravels remain from the melting ice. Overall it is a gently undulating rocky surface of low elevation, with a bewildering maze of rivers and irregular lakes. As in the Archipelago, true soil is generally absent. Vegetation is also the tundra type, usually including considerable shrubs. In sheltered places, as along inland water courses, stunted trees may extend out from the forested lands on the S and W. Climatically as well as in location the arctic mainland lies between the Arctic Archipelago and the Mackenzie Valley, with more severe winter temperatures and higher summer temperatures than the former because of its continental location. BAKER LK, for example, W of Hudson Bay, has a mean daily temperature of -33.0°C in January and 11.0°C in July, with a mean total precipitation of 235 mm.

The greatest single natural resource of the region for the native peoples has been the migratory barren land CARIBOU, which swarmed in enormous herds to summer in this region. In this century caribou numbers fluctuated dramatically because of changes in hunting pressure and wolf abundance. Declines had serious repercussions for local residents here, resulting in the movement of the Caribou Eskimos of the Ennadai Lake area to the W coast of Hudson Bay. By 1985, caribou numbers were again large and most herds were increasing. In 1927 the Thelon Game Sanctuary was established along the THELON R W of Baker Lake to protect MUSKOXEN, which are also found near Bathurst Inlet and in the Arctic Archipelago. As in the Arctic Archipelago, marine biotic resources and trapping still provide some support for the Inuit, but most now are permanent residents in settlements and seek additional sources of income. A nickel mine at RANKIN INLET, in operation from 1957 to 1962, provided some employment before closing. In 1981 an Inuit-run corporation co-operated in the opening of a new gold mine at Cullaton Lk, 1300 km N of Winnipeg. Some residents from western settlements are employed in the oil and gas search, while exploration for uranium W of Baker Lake and development of gold-bearing properties W of Whale Cove currently provide some employment. There has been some development in recent years of tourist facilities for fishermen, bird watchers and photographers. Concerns have been voiced about the impact of large-scale resource development on the local environment, on the traditional native way of life and on native LAND CLAIMS.

Mackenzie Valley Area Geologically this area ranges from the Canadian Shield on its eastern margin, through younger Palaeozoic and Mesozoic sedimentary formations in sequence to the W. GREAT BEAR LK (31 300 km²) and GREAT SLAVE LK (28 600 km²) lie along the contact line of the Shield, which here often exceeds 300 m of relief. Much of the Mackenzie Valley area consists of the narrowing northward extent of the level continental Interior Plains, with occasional level-bedded hill areas a few hundred metres above the general surface. In the W it rises abruptly into the mountainous terrain of the rugged Cordillera region with peaks of over 2700 m. The area is integrated by the MACKENZIE R and its tributaries, whose total drainage area (1.8 million km²) and system length (4241 km) are the largest and longest in Canada.

Only the northernmost part of the area falls within the continuous permafrost zone, unlike the other two regions of the NWT. Almost all falls within the discontinuous zone where permafrost is widespread if not universal. The Mackenzie Valley area lies within the subarctic boreal forest zone, where spruce, pine, birch, larch and poplar are common. Extensive areas of poor drainage occur, especially on the plains, as a result of permafrost and continental glaciation. These result in string bogs and muskeg. Temperature ranges are greater in the Mackenzie Valley than in the other 2 regions. At Fort Good Hope a maximum of 35°C has been recorded and a low of -61.7°. In January the average mean temperature is approximately -30°C and somewhat milder temperatures can occur briefly throughout the winter. More importantly the summers are normally warmer in the Mackenzie Valley, with July's mean usually 16°C. Precipitation, including snowfall, is significantly higher than for most of the Arctic.

Hunting, fishing and trapping have been traditional activities for the native Indian population, and the FUR TRADE supported the earliest white presence. Moose, caribou, bear, beaver, fox, muskrat and migratory birds continue to be important, but the major resource base since the 1930s has been minerals. Though radium and uranium production from Port Radium on Great Bear Lk has now ended, silver continues to be produced in the area. The economically recoverable reserves of lead-zinc at Pine Point on the S side of Great Slave Lake have been mined out, and milling of ore will cease in 1988. The tungsten mine at Tungsten near the Yukon border was closed in 1986. Oil continues to be produced in the Mackenzie Valley at NORMAN WELLS, Canada's pioneer (1921) northern oilfield, though the focus of recent oil and gas search has now moved northwards. A commercial fishery operates at Hay River on Great Slave Lk. Limited commercial use has been made of forests because of remoteness from markets and slow growth rates.

The potential hydro power resources of the NWT have been estimated at about 15 000 MW, of which 10 200 MW are within the Mackenzie Valley area. The series of rapids on the SLAVE R near the Alberta boundary has attracted attention for possible hydroelectric power generation (up to 2000 MW), but such a project would have serious repercussions for wildlife and in any event must await development of southern markets for electricity. WOOD BUFFALO NATIONAL PARK, straddling the Alberta boundary, is Canada's largest national park (over 44 840 km²). It was established in 1922 to protect the only herd of wood bison in the wild state, and also contains several thousand plains buffalo and the summer nesting grounds of the nearly extinct whooping cranes. Concern for environmental disruption by large projects in the Mackenzie Valley and the Arctic was demonstrated in the 1970s, when the Berger enquiry into a MACKENZIE VALLEY PIPELINE resulted in its delay until native land claims and environmental issues were resolved.

People

A northward extension of the fur trade led to the first white presence in the NWT in the late 18th and early 19th centuries as posts were established down the Mackenzie Valley. Missions arrived in the latter part of the 19th century, and the RCMP and other representatives of the federal government in the present century. Mineral and transportation developments in the 1930s marked the beginning of a more significant white influx. In the arctic regions, the remoteness made access more difficult, and fur trade posts were not established there until the 20th century. Permanent settlements were not established in the Queen Elizabeth Is until after WWII.

Urban Centres

There are 64 communities in the Northwest Territories. The most populous of the small urban centres are located in the Mackenzie Valley area. Yellowknife is the largest city (pop 11 753). It began as a gold-mining centre and became territorial capital in 1967. Fort Smith (pop 2460) was the major administrative centre within the territories until 1967 and is still important as a regional centre. Hay River (pop 2964) is a transportation and fishing centre. Pangnirtung (pop 1004, 1986c) on Baffin I, adjacent to Auyuittuq, National Park, has growing importance as a tourist centre. Rae-Edzo (pop 1378), the largest Dene community in the NWT, is an administrative centre for the Dogrib people. Fort Simpson (pop 987), once the centre of the fur trade, is located at the confluence of the Liard and Mackenzie rivers. Inuvik (pop 3389) is the major administrative and transportation centre for the western Arctic, as is IQALUIT [Frobisher Bay] (pop 2947) for the eastern Arctic. Rankin Inlet (pop 1374) is the regional administrative centre for the Keewatin. Also in the Keewatin, Eskimo Point (pop 1189) was an Inuit summer camp until the 1900s and still relies largely on hunting and fishing. Baker Lake (pop 1009) is the only inland Inuit community. Cambridge Bay (pop 1002) is the territorial regional headquarters for the Kitikmeot region. Coppermine (pop 888) residents derive employment from oil, gas and mine exploration and development. Most settlements consist of only a few hundred.

Ethnicity

Native people represent 58% of the population, whereas white residents account for 42%. Almost all of the latter group are found in the Mackenzie Valley, mainly in the larger settlements. The 43.9% of the population speaking languages other than English or French is a reflection of the multiplicity of native cultures that prevails in the NWT. About two-thirds of Canada's 23 000 Inuit live in the NWT, entirely in the arctic regions where they constitute the majority of population. The numerous different Indian cultural groups of the Mackenzie Valley area, included within the Dene or Athapascan linguistic group, total about 11 000. The Métis (approximately 2600) usually have been included in the latter figure, but are stressing their own separate identity as a fourth major ethnic element in the NWT. All 3 native groups are increasingly active politically.

Growth Rate Because of the small total population, external policy and economic conditions have significant impact. Growth has been erratic since 1966, reflecting the administrative transfer from Ottawa to Yellowknife, and the fluctuating interest in mineral resource development. The birthrate remains one of the highest in Canada, however (in 1985, 28.4 per 1000 population), but creates pressure for employment.

Economy

Primary resource extraction always has been the foundation of the NWT economy. Furs, the original base, are now of much less importance. Commercial WHALING disappeared early in this century. From the 1930s minerals have become the most important economic base for the NWT, with all other economic activities except service, far behind.

Agriculture Agriculture is of negligible significance in the NWT. The warm summers of the Mackenzie Valley have encouraged speculation on its potential for agriculture, and there have been impressive crop tests recorded at favourably located experimentation stations. However, small markets, summer drought and limited good soils create serious obstacles, and improved transportation service often makes it cheaper to bring in agricultural products from the S. Only a few market gardens operate in the Hay River valley.

Mining In 1985 metal mining production in the NWT was valued at $722 million: 60% from zinc, 8% from lead, 26% from gold, 1% from silver and 5% from tungsten. Though only 5% of the total value was contributed by tungsten, the NWT has traditionally provided almost 100% of Canada's production of that mineral until low metal prices forced closure of the mine in 1986. Mining employs about 2000 people, or about 15% of the work force of the territories, and provides significant employment in related service activities, such as mining exploration. Except for the production of gold bullion, no smelting of minerals occurs in the territories, however, as concentrates are shipped elsewhere.

The only producing oilfield in the NWT until 1985 was at Norman Wells, and the oil is also refined locally. Production of approximately 3000 barrels daily from 50 wells has recently increased, with an $800-million expansion, to 25 000 barrels a day, which is piped S to Alberta. Tankers carry the 100 000 m³/yr production from Bent Horn on Cameron I to Montréal. A small gas field at Pointed Mountain in the SW near the NWT-Yukon-BC border pipes gas southward. The ongoing search for additional sources of oil and natural gas reflects Canada's hopes for national self-sufficiency in these fuels and for greater employment opportunities for northerners. The AMAULIGAK field in the Beaufort Sea has reserves estimated at 127 million m³. If world oil prices continue to recover, the Amauligak field might go into production in the 1990s. In addition to the 2 main arctic exploration areas (Beaufort Sea and NW Queen Elizabeth Is), the search now includes DAVIS STRAIT and NW Baffin.

Hunting and Trapping Hunting and trapping are more important in the daily lives of NWT residents than statistics might suggest. Although a large percentage of the 5000 residents holding general hunting and trapping licences are only part-time hunters and trappers, many of the people living in smaller communities earn most of their living by hunting, trapping and fishing. In addition to the fur value obtained ($3.3 million in 1984-85), the meat is a major item in the local diet. Since 1974 the territorial government has assisted those wishing to make a living off the land through the establishment of outpost camps. There are 54 permanent camps and about the same number of temporary sites at present, with a population of approximately 1200.

Fishing and Forestry The commercial fishery operates both summer and winter on Great Slave Lk. The annual limit is set at 1.7 million kgs but the catch is usually well under this. Whitefish and lake trout are the most important catch. Smaller quantities are also produced by other subarctic lakes, though Great Bear Lk is restricted to sport fishing. Arctic char supports some commercial fishery in such arctic communities as Cambridge Bay, Pelly Bay, Paulatuk and Rankin Inlet. Some 70 000 m³ of timber was cut in the Mackenzie Valley in 1985-86; lumber accounted

for 37 372 m³, fuel wood 32 374 m³ and roundwood 839 m³.

Tourism Tourism provides increasing economic benefits to the NWT, with visitors arriving by road via the MACKENZIE HIGHWAY system and the DEMPSTER HIGHWAY in the W. Fly-in sport fishing lodges and wilderness camps are served out of Yellowknife, Iqaluit, etc. The 3 national parks in the NWT attract visitors despite their distance from southern Canada: Auyuittuq is administered from Pangnirtung, Wood Buffalo from Ft Smith and NAHANNI from Ft Simpson. In 1979 Nahanni was declared a UN WORLD HERITAGE SITE. In 1986 the Ellesmere Island National Park Reserve was created on the N edge of Ellesmere Island and will become a full-fledged national park when land claims in the area are settled.

Arts and Crafts A vigorous arts and crafts program among the native people has been developed within the past 2 decades and now generates several million dollars annually. More than one-sixth of the native population is engaged seasonally in this activity. Inuit prints and sculpture have established an international reputation and are a major source of employment in Cape Dorset, Holman Island, Baker Lake and other communities. Most are handled through local co-operatives, which now number 46 in the NWT with a membership of over 5000. They operate a variety of services, including hotels, restaurants and retail stores and are the largest employers of native people in the North.

Transportation

Transportation in the NWT must cope with enormous distances, severe climatic conditions and the small, scattered population. It is remarkable that the NWT is so well served, and the high costs can be appreciated. Commercial water transportation still operates during the summer on the Mackenzie. A modern diesel tug and barge fleet is based at Hay River, with a secondary base at the mouth of the Mackenzie at Tuktoyaktuk, the only reliably sheltered harbour on the shallow western coast. The coastal communities from Tuktoyaktuk eastwards as far as the Boothia Peninsula are served by tug and dual-purpose barge, though often the short ice-free season may restrict such service to a single call. Eastern Arctic communities are served by vessels operating out of Churchill, Montréal and Halifax, with regular annual visits as far N as RESOLUTE but including some icebreaker escorted trips to Winter Harbour on Melville Peninsula.

Since WWII a limited road network has been extended northwards into the Mackenzie Valley. Highways are mainly all-weather gravel roads and include several important river ferry links. The total length is about 2200 km. The Mackenzie and Yellowknife highways now link Hay River and Yellowknife to the road system of NW Alberta. Extensions from Hay River tie in Pine Point and Ft Smith. A northward extension down the Mackenzie Valley ends at Wrigley, N of Fort Simpson. The Liard Highway completed in 1984, tying Ft Simpson to the ALASKA HIGHWAY. Inuvik and other Mackenzie Delta communities are now linked to Dawson, YT, by the Dempster Highway, making it almost possible to reach the shores of the Arctic Ocean by road. "Winter roads" exist seasonally over frozen lakes to some isolated communities and mines and are of very significant economic importance. The former Great Slave Lk Ry, now a branch of CNR's Peace River Division, extends 696 km N from Grimshaw, Alta, to Hay River and is the only railway in the NWT. A spur eastwards serves Pine Point and permits shipment south of lead-zinc concentrates, the primary reason for its construction in 1964. The railway also led to Hay

Airport at Spence Bay, NWT. Much of the North relies on air transport for supplies (*photo by Sherman Hines/Masterfile*).

River's development as the major river transportation centre because of its transshipment advantages, thus displacing the earlier all-water Slave R route via Ft McMurray, Alta. Aircraft often are the only practical method of transportation in the NWT, particularly in the Arctic. There are 184 airfields in the territories (serving most NWT communities with populations over 100), 14 of which are operated by Transport Canada as licensed airports. Regularly scheduled airline service is provided from southern Canadian cities into the larger communities as far N as Resolute. The main southern airports serving the NWT are Edmonton to the Mackenzie Valley area and to Resolute, Montréal to the Eastern Arctic and to Resolute, and Winnipeg to Yellowknife and Rankin Inlet and Iqaluit. An east-west service links Yellowknife and Iqaluit, one through Rankin Inlet, the other along the Arctic coast. Almost all communities, including the northernmost arctic settlements, now have local air service available, while nonscheduled charter aircraft bush planes operate from the larger centres to any point in the territories, even to the North Pole. It is interesting to note that in 1985, 18% of the total energy consumed in the NWT was aviation and turbo fuel.

Energy

Heating is a major cost for northerners, given the long, severe winters and the transportation costs. Energy needs for most settlements are provided by fuel oil and thermal power generation. In most of the territories hydro power is nonexistent. The Northern Canada Power Commission provides over 90% of all power in Canada's northern territories. In the NWT its installed capacity is 161 MW, with 115 MW thermal and 46 MW hydro, just the reverse of the relative proportions in the YT. At the present time hydro plants operate only N and S of Great Slave Lk: along the Snare R (23 600 kW) for the Yellowknife area, and at Twin Gorges on the Taltson R (20 800 kW) for the Pine Point area.

Government and Politics

From 1905 until after WWII the government of the NWT was carried on by the appointed commissioner and council, composed entirely of senior civil servants based in Ottawa. Beginning in 1951, elected members were added gradually to the previously all-appointed council until it became a fully elected body in 1975. Until 1963 the commissioner was a deputy minister in the federal department in charge of the administration of YT and NWT in addition to other major responsibilities. In 1964 the first full-time commissioner was appointed to a separate territorial office. In 1967 the seat of territorial government was moved to Yellowknife and the commissioner relocated there with the nucleus of what has become a territorial public service. The federal Northwest Territories Act contains the written

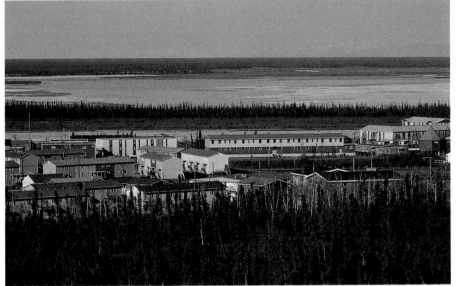

Inuvik, NWT, some 1086 km NW of Yellowknife, is the administrative and communications centre of the lower Mackenzie and the largest settlement N of the Arctic Circle (*photo by John Reeves/Masterfile*).

Northwest Territories	
Lieutenant–Governors	*Term*
William McDougall	1869-70
Adams George Archibald	1870-72
Francis Godschall Johnson	1872
Alexander Morris	1872-76
David Laird	1876-81
Edgar Dewdney	1881-88
Joseph Royal	1888-93
Charles Herbert Mackintosh	1893-98
Malcolm Colin Cameron	1898
Amédée Emmanuel Forget	1898-1904
	(office abolished in 1905)

Commissioners	*Term*
Part–time commissioners only, Ottawa residents	1905-63
Bent Gestur Sivertz	1963-67
Stuart Milton Hodgson (first NWT resident commissioner)	1967-79
John Havelock Parker	1979-

constitution and defines the powers of the territorial government. The territorial assembly consists of 24 elected members, one of whom it chooses to preside as Speaker. A unique feature of the assembly currently is that the majority of members are native people: 8 Inuit, 4 Dene, 3 Métis and 9 non-natives.

The chief executive officer for the territories is the commissioner, appointed by the federal government, who is required to administer the territories under instructions from the minister of Indian affairs and northern development. The government leader serves as chairman of the executive assembly, whose members are chosen by the legislative assembly from among its members. The role of the commissioner is changing as elected executive members assume increasing departmental and executive functions. Each member of the executive committee is responsible for one or more territorial government departments. The NWT elects 2 members to the Canadian Parliament and also has one representative in the Senate.

Judiciary The territorial judiciary comprises a Court of Appeal consisting of 18 justices appointed by the governor-general, 2 resident supreme court judges based in Yellowknife and 26 other judges from the provinces, 5 resident territorial judges (3 in Yellowknife, 1 in Hay River and 1 in Iqaluit), and 108 justices of the peace (56 of native origin) living in various communities. Judges and justices of the peace are appointed by the commissioner on the advice of the Judicial Council of the NWT. The judge of the supreme court of the NWT is ex officio judge in the YT, and vice versa. Court sessions are held in Yellowknife and on regular court circuits throughout the territories.

Local Government For administrative purposes the NWT is divided into 5 regions: Ft Smith Region (based in Ft Smith), Inuvik Region (Inuvik), Keewatin Region (Rankin Inlet), Kitikmeot Region (Cambridge Bay) and Baffin Region (Iqaluit, including all of the Queen Elizabeth Is). Decentralization and devolution recently have been increasing the importance of the regions. The fostering of development of local government to provide local decision making has been hampered by the small size of many of these communities and by their remoteness and limited local

economic resources. At present there are 42 incorporated municipalities in the NWT, of which 8 are tax-based: the city of Yellowknife; the towns of Inuvik, Hay River, Iqaluit, Ft Smith, Pine Point; and the villages of Ft Simpson and Norman Wells. There are 34 hamlets, 10 settlements and 12 unorganized communities.

Health Until the Northern Health Services was established by the federal government in 1954, health services in the territories were provided principally by church agencies. Since then they have been broadened to make available facilities that are similar to those elsewhere in Canada.

The territorial government has been assuming more responsibility in recent years. Modern hospitals are located in Yellowknife, Hay River, Ft Smith, Ft Simpson, Inuvik and Iqaluit, with lesser facilities including 40 nursing stations scattered over the territories. Dental care is available in Yellowknife, Hay River, Inuvik, Ft Smith and Iqaluit, and from government-employed full-time dentists and dental therapists located throughout the NWT.

Baffin Island in the Northwest Territories is more than twice the size of Great Britain (*photo by Sherman Hines/Masterfile*).

Politics Although candidates for the 2 NWT seats in the federal Parliament represent traditional political parties, this is not true for the territorial legislature, which operates on a "no political party" consensus basis. Two major issues occupy territorial residents currently: native land claims and political status. Though the Dene signed treaties with the federal government in the past, they dispute that land title was involved and, except for one at Hay River, reserves do not exist. The Dene, along with the Inuit and the Métis, are urgently seeking land claims settlement.

The federal government quickly accepted and implemented many of the recommendations of the 1966 Carrothers Commission on the development of government in the NWT. It is on record as supporting the move towards full responsible government. At present, however, it retains control of territorial resource revenues and the territorial government is dependent on the federal for the bulk of its finances (71% of government revenues). Whether resource revenues in future will be transferred or shared is a controversial issue. The 1980 Drury Commission endorsed the existing government and recommended that greater authority be transferred to it and to the communities. A further political issue is whether the territories will evolve into full provinces as residents wish, or into something else because of the partic-

Climate	Aklavik	Resolute	Yellowknife	Frobisher Bay	Baker Lake
Mean Daily Temp, Jan (C)	-28.6	-32.6	-28.6	-26.2	-33.0
Mean Daily Temp, July (C)	13.8	4.3	16.0	7.9	11.0
Mean Daily Temp, Year (C)	-8.9	-16.4	-5.6	-8.9	-12.2
Mean Total Precip, Year (mm)	205.5	136.4	250.0	415.2	234.6
Mean Snowfall, Year (cm)	99.1	78.7	119.4	247.2	100.0
Mean Duration of Sunshine, Year (hrs)	1909	1475	1435		
Mean Days with Fog, Year	11	49	19	20	
Thunderstorms per Year	1	1	5	1	
Mean Frost-Free Period (days)	77	9	108	59	

(Table titled "Northwest Territories")

ular problems (including huge costs). In a 1982 plebiscite a majority voted in favour of dividing the NWT. In Feb 1985 the new Conservative government endorsed the plan to divide the NWT into 2 independent jurisdictions – Nunavut in the east, composed of a primarily Inuit population, and a western territory, which may be called "Denendeh," composed of Dene, Métis, some Inuit and whites. Nevertheless some difficult issues remain to be resolved before the plan can be implemented, in particular the actual boundary line, which would separate the 2 new territories. The parties involved reached a tentative boundary agreement early in 1987, but this agreement failed before the final plebiscite could be held. In addition, legislation is going to be introduced to make English, French and the aboriginal dialects all official languages in the NWT.

Education

Until the end of WWII education was provided mainly by church missions, with students usually housed in nearby residences in a few larger centres. Beginning in 1959, a massive development program was initiated by the federal government and was transferred to the territorial government in 1969. Some 72 government-operated schools now exist, with 770 teachers and 13 300 students enrolled (compared with 6000 in 1962). A complete range of modern facilities are available up to the completion of secondary schooling, and the NWT has developed its own curriculum supplemented by the curriculum of the province of Alberta. Junior college and vocational training in the territories is supplied through programs offered by Arctic College, from campuses at Ft Smith, Iqaluit and Inuvik, and through extension services to other communities throughout the NWT. Programs are available, particularly geared to the needs of the area. Special efforts are made to encourage active local native participation in education programs, through further decentralization and local input to programs, through increased use of native languages and the use of local classroom assistants and the establishment of locally elected boards of education.

Cultural Life

Interest in native cultures in the NWT has de-

Archer Fiord, Ellesmere Island, NWT. Navigation along the arctic coast is severely limited much of the year by ice (*photo by P. Sutherland*).

veloped with government encouragement. In addition to assistance to arts and crafts programs, the knowledge of elderly native peoples is being tapped for the schools and being recorded for the future. Native cultural programs are active, and native-language centres have been established in several communities. The ARCTIC WINTER GAMES, held every 2 years since 1970, include a variety of traditional native games as well as more widely known sports, drawing competitors from the NWT, Yukon and Alaska. The Prince of Wales Northern Heritage Centre with its museum and archives is a major centre of public information and research in the NWT. Other community museums, historical societies and heritage groups operate within the territories.

Communications

Seven weekly newspapers are published regularly in the NWT and a general publisher is located in Yellowknife. In 1958 the CBC established a Northern Service to meet the special needs of northerners, native and non-native. Radio broadcasts are made in 10 native languages and dialects, as well as in English and French, and include local community as well as network programs. Relay transmitter stations and microwave systems help offset the great distances. Satellite channels now make it possible to transmit radio and TV programs into the most remote northern communities; all of the more than 60 centres with populations over 150 receive radio and TV. A second, commercial service offering as great a variety of programs as anywhere on the continent began in 1982. Two TV stations are located in Yellowknife and one in Iqaluit. Telephone and telegraph services link nearly all communities.

Historic Sites

Active archaeological surveys are providing greater knowledge about the early native peoples in the Subarctic and the Arctic. Such surveys have also provided evidence recently of Viking presence in the Eastern Arctic. Many historic sites are associated with the fur trade in the Subarctic, and with exploration for the NORTHWEST PASSAGE and the lost Franklin Expedition. These sites are now protected by law against vandalism and looting.

History

A variety of aboriginal cultures existed in the area before the arrival of the whites, based upon the nomadic hunting and fishing economies of the Inuit in the Arctic, and of the Dene in the Subarctic. Within the latter Athapaskan linguistic family, some 7 dialectical groups existed: Chipewyan, Yellowknife, Slave, Dogrib, Hare, Nahanni and Kutchin.

Exploration The first known white explorers to visit today's NWT were the Vikings, who sailed to the Eastern Arctic from their Greenland settlements (*c*1000 AD). In 1576 Martin FROBISHER was the first of a series of European explorers seeking the Northwest Passage, but by the early 16th century the severe ice conditions and the limitations of the ships checked much farther

advance. In 1770-71 Samuel HEARNE of the HBC made a remarkable overland trip from Churchill through the arctic mainland to the COPPERMINE R, but though the company used the Hudson Bay route, its interests were farther inland on the continent. Alexander MACKENZIE of the NWC pushed N from Ft Chipewyan on Lk Athabasca in 1789 to discover and follow the Mackenzie R to its mouth. Fur-trade posts were soon established along his route and in tributary areas, and were subsequently taken over by the HBC. Later exploration in the Arctic Archipelago focused on a renewed search for a Northwest Passage in the first part of the 19th century, and on attempts to reach the geographic North Pole in the latter part. The disappearance of Sir John FRANKLIN's 1845 expedition led to the addition of much map information by the search expeditions and included the traverse of the elusive passage in 1853 by MCCLURE (though the first traverse by ship was in 1903-04 by AMUNDSEN). Later British and American expeditions proceeding up the E coast of Ellesmere I explored the eastern Queen Elizabeth Is. The Norwegian explorer Otto SVERDRUP discovered most of the remaining islands to the NW at the turn of the 20th century, with Vilhjalmur STEFANSSON completing discoveries 1913-18.

Settlement The fur-trade posts provided the only nuclei of white settlement in the NWT until relatively recently. Missions were established near the posts along the Mackenzie in the latter part of the 19th century. Federal presence was represented in these small settlements after the turn of the century by the RCMP, by Royal Canadian Corps of Signals radio stations and by other agencies. Strategic water transportation sites, such as Ft Smith and Tuktoyaktuk, provided other attractions for limited settlement. Because of its easier accessibility and more varied resources, more incomers trickled into the Mackenzie Valley than the Arctic. Beginning in the 1930s mineral exploration aided by the bush pilots and their improved aircraft resulted in a significant influx of newcomers, even into the Arctic mainland. However, actual mine development is restricted to the Mackenzie area.

Development In recent decades major change and development in the NWT have resulted from international and national political events, widespread social change, large-scale resource demands and the availability of improved technology. As early as WWII the impact of international hostilities was felt in Mackenzie Valley settlements through the CANOL PROJECT and in the southern part of the Eastern Arctic through the North East Staging Route airports. The Cold War caused Dew Line radar stations to be built across the Arctic and contributed to the introduction of the first permanent settlements in the Queen Elizabeth Is as part of the Joint Arctic Weather Stations project (*see* HIGH ARCTIC WEATHER STATIONS). The federal government assumed increased responsibility with the creation (1953) of the Department of Northern Affairs and National Resources (now the Department of Indian Affairs and Northern Development). Major improvements were made in health services, housing, education facilities and communications to bring them more into line with those of southern Canada. More recently much of this responsibility has been delegated to the territorial government. Government services are now more numerous throughout northern settlements and occasionally provide the greatest source of local employment. As a result, most northern residents now live in permanent settlements for most of the year. The voracious demand for minerals and fuels along with improvements in mining and transportation technology have made northern resources economically attractive, and resource development is necessary to provide employment; but there is also a responsibility to protect the environment for native people and their traditional way of life and to protect wilderness habitats for future generations.

WILLIAM C. WONDERS

Reading: T. R. Berger, *Northern Frontier, Northern Homeland* (1976); L.-E. Hamelin, *Canadian Nordicity: It's Your North, Too* (1979); D.H. Pimlott, et al, eds, *Arctic Alternatives* (1973); K.J. Rea, *The Political Economy of the Canadian North* (1968); W.C. Wonders, ed, *The North* (1972); M. Zaslow, *The Opening of the Canadian North, 1870-1914* (1971), and ed, *A Century of Canada's Arctic Islands, 1880-1980* (1981).

Norway House, Man, consists of 2 closely related communities along Little Playgreen Lk and the E channel of the Nelson R, 30 km N of Lk Winnipeg and 460 km N of Winnipeg. The Norway House Indian Reserve, pop 2559 (1986cA; 1812, 1981c), with Rossville as its centre, is under the jurisdiction of the federal Dept of Indian and Northern Affairs, as well as an elected band chief and council. The nonreserve community (556, 1986c), under the provincial Dept of Northern Affairs, has a mayor and 6 councillors.

Located at the junction of several water routes, screened by a rocky shoulder from Little Playgreen Lk, Norway House was a hub of the HUDSON'S BAY COMPANY's fur-trade and supply lines, and an administrative centre for Rupert's Land. Three HBC posts were built in the area 1801-26, the last being at the site of the present community. Named after Norwegian axemen who were hired to open land communications from YORK FACTORY, Norway House was known for its fishing, hunting and for the production of YORK BOATS. Settlers from the RED RIVER COLONY found temporary refuge here in 1815 and 1816-17 after they were attacked by forces of the rival North West Co. Rev James EVANS, a Methodist, established a mission nearby in 1840 with 2 Indian associates. The original HBC warehouse, gateway and powder magazine have been preserved, and Norway House is still an active HBC centre. Commercial fishing, services and trapping are the mainstays of the local economy.

D.M. LYON

Situated north of Lk Winnipeg, Norway House (shown 1925) quickly became the centre of the Hudson's Bay Co's transport system. The neat wooden buildings ranged in a square are typical of 19th-century trading-post architecture (*courtesy Provincial Archives of Manitoba/ N10120*).

Norwegians Some 500 years before Columbus landed on a Caribbean island, displaced Norsemen discovered and attempted a settlement on Canada's shores (*see* NORSE VOYAGES; ICELANDERS). Nordic sagas helped Helge Ingstad, a Norwegian explorer and writer, to discover an ancient Norse site at L'ANSE AUX MEADOWS on the northern tip of Newfoundland in the 1960s – the earliest known site of European settlement in America. Norwegians were active in Canadian waters again at the end of the 19th century, with Fridtjof Nansen as the pioneer of major Norwegian expeditions. Otto SVERDRUP charted many of the arctic islands

and discovered AXEL HEIBERG, AMUND RINGNES and ELLEF RINGNES islands – all named for his Norwegian sponsors. Norwegian Roald AMUNDSEN navigated the last unsailed link in the NORTHWEST PASSAGE. It was not until 1930 that Norway recognized Canadian sovereignty in the Arctic. Henry A. LARSEN, of Norwegian birth, was the first Canadian to travel the Northwest Passage.

Permanent Norwegian migration to N America began in 1825 when the first shipload of Norwegians arrived in New York. In the next 75 years some 500 000 Norwegians landed at Québec, for this was the shortest corridor to the central American states. In spite of efforts by Canada, very few remained because of Canada's restrictive land policies at that time. Not until the turn of the century did Norwegians accept Canada as a land of the second chance.

Migration and Settlement Major settlements by Norwegians in the Canadian West occurred between 1886 and 1929, a span of time that can be roughly divided into 3 periods of 15 years each. In the first period, from 1886 to the turn of the century, the building of the CPR and the opening up of the West to homesteaders brought Norwegian settlers, and a Norwegian colony was established in Calgary in connection with the Eau Claire Lumber Mill. Second, from 1900 to 1914, there was a great influx of Norwegians from both the US and Norway (18 790 from Norway). Third, from 1914 to 1929, 21 574 Norwegians arrived from Norway. The 1931 census reported 93 243 people of Norwegian descent in Canada. Of these, 39 241 were born in Canada, 32 551 in Norway and 21 451 in the US. The GREAT DEPRESSION and WWII reduced the flow of Norwegian immigrants to 1376 from 1930 to 1945. From 1945 to 1959, 9196 arrived, but between 1960 and 1975 only 4615. Currently, the number of immigrants from Norway is very low and shows signs of decreasing. The 1986 census estimated that there were 61 575 Canadians of Norwegian origin.

Social and Cultural Life In Canada, Norwegians established their own ethnic and religious associations. Because Norwegian settlements in Canada began as extensions of their experiences in America, their major social organizations were generally continental institutions. This is still true of the Sons of Norway lodges, which were originally established in Minneapolis in 1895. The ethnic paper *Noørrana*, founded in 1910 in Winnipeg, is still published in Vancouver and has some 4000 subscribers.

In 1941, of Norwegians in Canada, 84.7% adhered to the Lutheran Church, 5.4% the United Church of Canada, 2.6% the Anglican, 1.5% the Presbyterian and 5.8% miscellaneous groups. In 1967 the Evangelical Lutheran Church, of Norwegian background, became an autonomous Canadian synod. Those of Norwegian background are a diminishing minority because of continuing church mergers.

Because most of the early immigrants were literate and Lutheran, they placed high value on a Christian education for their children. Most Norwegian settlements not only promoted local summer parochial schools but conducted confirmation classes beyond the regular Sunday school. The Norwegian Lutherans established Camrose Lutheran College in 1911, Outlook College in 1915. Then, in co-operation with other Lutheran synods, they founded the Canadian Lutheran Bible Institute in 1932 and Luther Theological Seminary in 1939.

Maintaining Group Identity Over the years, assimilation was promoted by the numerical superiority and dominance of an Anglo-Canadian culture, the levelling influence of the public school system, the decreasing migration from Norway, the readiness of Norwegians to speak English and

to marry into other groups, their readiness to accept Canadian citizenship and their above-average educational status, which opened doors to advancement in urbanized society. Nevertheless, a distinctive cultural identity is still maintained in the homes of Norwegian Canadians where traditions are centered on festivals and foods. Ethnic clubs and societies promote charter tours to Norway so that recent generations may become aware of their distinctive heritage. Norwegian ethnicity, far from dying out, has recently reasserted itself. Language classes in Norwegian are again popular, and even the third and fourth generations are discovering the distinctiveness of their roots.

Well-known Canadians of Norwegian descent include skier Anne HEGGTVEIT and figure skater Karen MAGNUSSEN.

GULBRAND LOKEN

Reading: Gulbrand Loken, *From Fjord to Frontier: A History of the Norwegians in Canada* (1980).

Nor'Wester, shortened version of North-Wester (variously spelled); historically, a NORTH WEST COMPANY agent, WINTERING PARTNER or servant; a trader or *engagé* who winters in the hinterland; or a veteran of these experiences. In the plural the term may refer to the NWC itself. A native or resident of the Northwest Territories, usually non-Indian, may be called a Nor'Wester, but in the literature of the FUR TRADE the term is usually associated with the NWC and its members.

JEAN MORRISON

Notary In common-law provinces persons admitted to the bar are sworn as notaries public. Other persons may be so commissioned by the LIEUTENANT-GOVERNOR upon the recommendation of the ATTORNEY GENERAL. A notary may draw and issue deeds, contracts and other commercial instruments and is a commissioner for taking affidavits. In Québec the legal profession is divided into "notaires" and "avocats." Notaires draft or receive acts and contracts that need authentication, an important aspect of Qué CIVIL LAW. They are not involved in matters where a dispute exists between the parties as to law or facts.

K.G. MCSHANE

Notley, Walter Grant, political leader (b at Didsbury, Alta 19 Jan 1939; d near High Prairie, Alta 19 Oct 1984). He was raised on a farm and shortly after graduating from U of A (1961) was hired as provincial secretary of the newly formed provincial New Democratic Party. In 1968 he was elected Alberta leader of the party, which at that time held no seats in the legislature. After 3 unsuccessful attempts to win a seat, he won the new riding of Spirit River-Fairview in 1971, holding it for the rest of his life. He was a one-man caucus for 11 years and won respect for his parliamentary skills and knowledge of the issues. He became Leader of the Official Opposition in Alberta after the NDP elected a second member in 1982. When the Alberta government reduced oil shipments to central Canada in protest against the National Energy Program, Notley was the only Alberta legislator to oppose the move. He then participated actively in the constitutional debate of 1980-81, criticizing the extreme views of both the federal and Alberta governments. Notley died in an aircraft accident.

GARTH STEVENSON

Notman, William, photographer (b at Paisley, Scot 8 Mar 1826; d at Montréal 25 Nov 1891). He immigrated to Canada in 1856 and found employment with a Montréal wholesale drygoods company. He had learned the daguerreotype process in Scotland and set up a photographic studio in Montréal. He rapidly gained prominence because of his superb portraits, the basis of attracting customers from all classes – from royalty to tradesmen. In 1858 he was commissioned by the Grand Trunk Ry to photograph the construction of Montréal's remarkable Victoria Bridge.

Notman's staff (55 in the 1870s) included apprentice photographers. He established 14 branch studios in eastern Canada and the US, all managed by his trainees. Notman won many medals for his work in exhibitions at home and abroad. To meet the demand for landscapes and other views, he sent his photographers across Canada, recording the construction of the CPR, the rise of the western cities, the life of the plains and coastal Indians, the lumber trade of the Ottawa Valley, East Coast fishing, rural activities and the bustle of the cities. Notman also became famous for the composite photographs of the snowshoe and curling clubs produced by his studio. These large creations were made up of 300 or more individual photographs, cut out and pasted onto a painted background.

Always community minded, Notman was involved in art associations, church societies, sports clubs and other Montréal organizations. He was also a backer of the Windsor Hotel and co-partner in large holdings in Longueuil, where he had a summer home. Of his 7 children, all 3 boys became photographers. William McFarlane NOTMAN, his eldest son, took over the business at his death. The Notman collection, containing over 400 000 photographs, plus office records and family correspondence, forms part of the collections of the Notman Photographic Archives housed in the McCord Museum of McGill U.   STANLEY G. TRIGGS

Notman, William McFarlane, photographer (b at Montréal 1 Nov 1857; d there 1 May 1913). At age 15 he started to work for his father, photographer William NOTMAN, and was made a partner in the business at about age 25. His portraits – of rural people at daily tasks and of well-dressed urban notables – are sensitive and powerful, and his skill in portraying the Canadian landscape was outstanding. Notman made 8 trips to western Canada 1884-1909 to photograph along the CPR line, documenting the early growth of towns and capturing dramatic views of the Rockies and Selkirks. He accompanied the 1901 royals tour of the Duke and Duchess of York from Québec C to Victoria. Notman also photographed extensively in Murray Bay, Tadoussac, Lac Saint-Jean and the Eastern Townships. In 1908 he made a steamer voyage around Newfoundland, photographing the ports of call.   STANLEY G. TRIGGS

Notre Dame Bay, 6000 km², is a large inlet of the Atlantic Ocean on the NE coast of Newfoundland. It contains many islands and its shores are indented by numerous coves and smaller embayments. One of Newfoundland's main rivers, the EXPLOITS, flows into the bay, carrying large quantities of timber from the interior as far as the pulp and paper mills at GRAND FALLS. The principal activity on the bay is fishing, with important commercial catches of cod, capelin and lobster. LEWISPORTE, a busy commercial port on the Bay of Exploits, is also the headquarters of the highly successful bluefin-tuna sportfishing on Notre Dame Bay. New World and FOGO are the largest islands in the bay, and FUNK I, 60 km E of Fogo, is one of Newfoundland's primary bird sanctuaries.   P.C. SMITH

Notre-Dame Church, Place d'Armes, Montréal, built as a parish church, 1823-29, by the congregation of St-Sulpice, is the earliest surviving example of a Gothic revival church in Canada. This daring and innovative design on a scale then unequalled in North America was by James O'Donnell, an Irish architect who had immigrated to New York. It was carried out in the face of strong criticism from the architecturally conservative Abbé Jérôme DEMERS of Québec City, who decried the "protestantism" of its Gothic style and rectangular plan (without apse or transepts).   CHRISTINA CAMERON

Notre Dame de Lourdes, Man, Village, pop 628 (1986c), 627 (1981c), inc 1963, is situated on the NE slope of the Pembina Hills, 130 km SW of Winnipeg. French Canadians homesteaded in the area 1881, followed by French and Swiss immigrants 1890-91. The main settlement began under Dom Paul Benoît of the Chanoines Réguliers de l'Immaculée-Conception who surveyed the Roman Catholic mission of Notre Dame de Lourdes 1890. He returned 1891 with settlers and fellow priests, who established a church, a monastery and schools for boys and for aspirants to the priesthood. Over the next 4 years, 5 groups of settlers and priests followed, including the Chanoinesses des Cinq Plaies du Sauveur who began a convent 1895. The clerics from Notre Dame served in surrounding parishes and the Chanoinesses developed new convents. Dom Benoît left the parish 1910 and many of his companions became secular priests. The Chanoines remained at Notre Dame until 1948. Today the village is a service and commercial centre.
    D.M. LYON

Nottaway, Rivière, 776 km (via Rivière Bell to head of Rivière Mégiscane), rises in W-central Québec and flows N via Lacs Parent and Quévillon into Lac Matagami. Here it is joined by its chief headstream, Rivière Waswanipi, and then drains NW through Lac Soscumica. It empties into SE JAMES BAY at Rupert Bay where a trading post was established. Its drainage basin covers 65 800 km² and it has a mean discharge of 1130 m³/s. This powerful river's name is Indian (possibly Algonquin) in origin and has been variously translated as "the enemy" or "the river of the enemy."
    DAVID EVANS

NOVA Corporation of Alberta, with head offices in Calgary, is a Canadian energy company with 1986 sales of $2.7 billion, assets of $4.8 billion, and 7100 employees. Ownership is widely distributed with over 90% of the shares held by Canadians. Originally known as the Alberta Gas Trunk Line Company Ltd, the corporation was established in 1954 to build, own and operate Alberta's natural gas gathering and transmission facilities. In the early 1970s the corporation broadened its base, and today it is involved in natural gas transmission, resource development, petrochemicals and manufacturing. It was renamed in 1980. The Alberta gas transmission system is one of the largest and most technically advanced in the world. In addition, NOVA is the largest manufacturer and marketer of polyethylene products in Canada. The group of companies currently operating under the NOVA banner in Canada includes Husky Oil Ltd, Foothills Pipe Lines (Yukon) Ltd and Novacor Chemicals Ltd. NOVA also has energy-related enterprises in the US, Italy and elsewhere.

Nova Scotia juts out into the N Atlantic, some say like a giant lobster-shaped pier; others call it the wharf of N America; its tourist literature describes it as "Canada's ocean playground." Nothing has influenced Nova Scotia and its people more than the sea. Because the province is nowhere more than 130 km wide, no part of it is far from the sea. With its fine harbours located near major sea-lanes, it has served as a military and naval bastion in many wars. Halifax, in truth, was the warden of the north.

Today the sea retains its significance, having made Nova Scotia the big fisherman of the N Atlantic, outrivalling its nearest competitors, Newfoundland and New England. Its serrated, 7 579-km shoreline embraces the rugged headlands, tranquil harbours and ocean beaches so attractive to tourists. One of its 3809 coastal islands, SABLE ISLAND – 193 km offshore and once "the Graveyard of the Atlantic" – has rich deposits of gas and oil under the surrounding waters. Many other islands and much coastal land have been purchased by outsiders in the last decade or two. Once regarded as the boondocks, Nova Scotia is seen increasingly as a place where the good life can be lived even with a per-capita income that is below the national average. Nova Scotians generally insist that material development does no harm to the pleasant living they now enjoy.

Land and Resources

Main Regions The chief physical feature of Nova Scotia is the Atlantic Upland, which shows itself in 5 fragments, separated in places by extensive lowlands. Of these fragments, the largest is the Southern Upland, which occupies the southern and central part of the province. Starting at the rugged Atlantic coast, marked by many inlets, islands, coves and bays, it rises at the rate of 2.75 m/km to an altitude of 180-210 m in the interior. Its northern border constitutes the South Mountain. The second fragment is the North Mountain, a range of trap rock which runs parallel to the South Mountain for 190 km along the Bay of FUNDY from Cape Blomidon on Minas Basin to Brier Island. Between the 2 ranges lie the fertile valleys of the Annapolis and Cornwallis rivers, the celebrated apple-growing region of Nova Scotia. The third fragment consists of the flat-topped Cobequid Mountain, rising to 300 m and extending 120 km across Cumberland County; the fourth has its beginnings in the eastern highlands of Pictou County and extends in a long narrowing projection through Antigonish County to Cape George. The fifth fragment, on northern CAPE BRETON ISLAND, is a wild, wooded plateau, which at one point rises to a height of more than 520 m above sea level. It largely accounts for the highly scenic character of CAPE BRETON HIGHLANDS NATIONAL PARK, especially as viewed from the Cabot Trail, which runs through it. In contrast, the southern part of Cape Breton I is largely lowland.

Geology The deep drainage channels that have been cut through the uplands have exposed the roots of the mountains and laid bare rocks which are among the oldest of the Earth's crust and are representative of most of the geological time scale. Peninsular Nova Scotia consists of Paleozoic cover pierced by a granite backbone which, because it is highly resistant to change, occupies the higher elevations. The North Mountain resulted from volcanic action in Triassic times, and the Annapolis and Cornwallis valleys were carved out in the same period. Practically all the industrial minerals, including gypsum, limestone, sandstone, salt and barites, occur in rocks of the Mississippian age. The coal deposits of the province are to be found in the several groups of Pennsylvanian rocks, especially the Pictou, Stellarton and Morien groups.

Surface Only 10% (about 538 000 ha) of Nova Scotia is agricultural land. That with the greatest potential for farming is situated in the lowlands where the soils have developed on deep tills; the uplands usually have shallow, stony soils. The most extensive lowlands, and hence the best agricultural land, are to be found along the Bay of Fundy and Northumberland Str. The tremendously high tides of the Bay of Fundy have created large areas of marshland, which, by means of dikes begun in Acadian times, have been converted into valuable agricultural lands.

Originally, most of the province was covered by forest, but little of the virgin forest remains, except in the plateau of NE Cape Breton I. Because of the acid soil and the slow growing season, secondary growth has tended to be coniferous, but hardwoods continue to exist in sufficient abundance to produce a colourful display in the autumn. In swampy areas and rocky barrens, mosses, li-

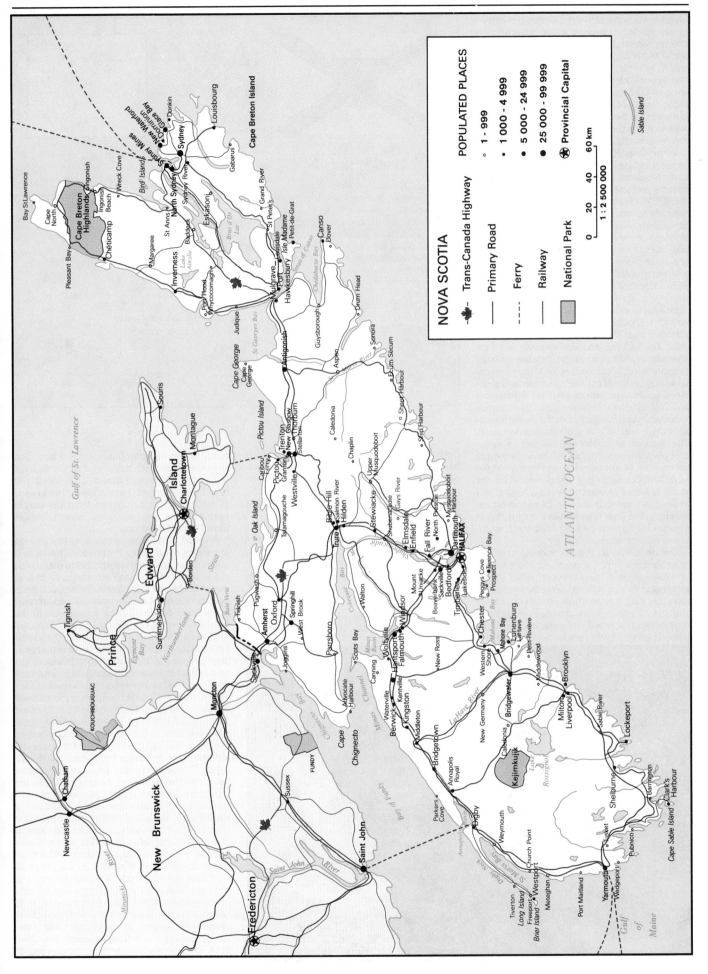

NOVA SCOTIA

POPULATED PLACES

○	1 - 999
•	1 000 - 4 999
●	5 000 - 24 999
●	25 000 - 99 999
✪	Provincial Capital

——	Trans-Canada Highway
——	Primary Road
- - -	Ferry
——	Railway
▨	National Park

0 20 40 60 km

1 : 2 500 000

Sable Island

ATLANTIC OCEAN

Gulf of St. Lawrence

Prince Edward Island

New Brunswick

Gulf of Maine

chens, ferns, scrub heath and similar growths are common. Wild flowers grow in profusion, among which the mayflower, pitcher plant, white water lily and several varieties of violets stand out for their beauty. Widely found throughout the province are herbaceous plants such as Clintonia, cranberries, blueberries and many species of goldenrod. The European cuckooflower has become common in the Annapolis Valley, while the ragwort has spread over eastern Nova Scotia.

Water Over 3000 lakes have been impounded by the irregularly high and low terrain, especially in the Southern Upland region, and hundreds of streams and small rivers have eroded their way through it. Because of the general direction of the watersheds, the rivers cannot be long, but with moderately heavy precipitation, normally no shortage of water occurs. The province's largest lake, the 930 km² BRAS D'OR, was created when the sea invaded the area between the upland and lowland areas of Cape Breton; saline and tideless, it is widely used for recreation. On the peninsula the largest lake is Lk Rossignol in the SE central area, a focus of both lumbering and recreational activities. Though short, the rivers have had considerable significance historically and economically. The Sackville and Shubenacadie, used extensively by the Indians, were important in early transportation; some, such as the Mersey, continue to play a significant role in lumber and pulpwood production; others, such as the Margaree and St Mary's, have become celebrated as salmon streams; several have afforded the means to construct hydroelectric power plants, however small. The high tides of the Bay of Fundy are a remarkable phenomenon. The bay, 77 km at its mouth, narrows to 56 km where it divides into Minas Basin and Chignecto Bay. For about 240 km the water is forced forward to reach a height over 16 m above low-tide level in its narrowest extremities. The high tides facilitate the loading of gypsum, lumber and the like by freighters, which at low tide rest on mud flats.

Climate Although systems moving eastward from the interior of the continent dominate the province's weather, they are only part of a complex process which at times makes the meteorologist's task a nightmare. These systems often react with low pressure systems coming from the S and moving northeastward along the coast, and the whole is affected by the proximity of the Labrador

Nova Scotia

Capital: Halifax
Motto: Munit Haec et Altera Vincit ("One defends and the other conquers")
Flower: Mayflower
Largest Cities: Halifax, Dartmouth, Glace Bay, New Glasgow, Amherst
Population: 873 176 (1986c); rank seventh, 3.4% of Canada; 54.0% urban; 46.0% rural; 16.5 per km² density; 5.4% increase from 1976 and 3.0% from 1981
Languages: 93.2% English; 3.5% French; 1.8% Other; 1.5% English plus 1 other language (1986)
Entered Confederation: 1 July 1867
Government: Provincial – Lieutenant-Governor, Executive Council, House of Assembly of 52 members; federal – 10 senators, 11 members of the House of Commons
Area: 55 491km², including 2650 km² of inland water; 0.06% of Canada
Elevation: Highest point – Cape Breton (532 m); lowest point – sea level
Gross Domestic Product: $10.8 billion (1986)
Farm Cash Receipts: $267.6 million (1986)
Value of Fish Landings: $424 million (1986)
Electric Power Generated: 7511 GWh (1986)
Sales Tax: 10% (1987)

Current and the Gulf Stream. Generally the water has a moderating influence upon the climate, particularly along the Atlantic coast where the average Jan temperature is about -4°C and the summer mean temperatures are in the high teens Celsius.

The influence of the sea is felt in other ways. Ice brought down by the Labrador Current leads to a late spring marked by cold winds, rain and mist. In summer, especially in June and July, the mingling of the warm Gulf Stream and the cold Labrador Current produces a great deal of sea fog, which often drifts over the coastal areas. Au-

Nova Scotian fishing village of Prospect (*photo by Jim Merrithew*).

tumns are consistently fine, clear and long. The coastal areas are both milder and wetter than the rest of the province. Yarmouth has about 160 frost-free days a year compared with 100 in parts of the interior. Rain may vary from 140 mm in coastal areas to 100 mm inland. Snowfall ranges from 200 cm to 300 cm.

Resources The natural resources of Nova Scotia are somewhat limited. Today those which sustained the early settlers remain vital to the provincial economy. The FISHERY remains most important. The province is plentifully supplied with both metallurgical and thermal COAL, and recently the latter has been given prominence in the province's overall energy strategy. The discovery of offshore OIL AND NATURAL GAS along the southern coast should provide a large boost to the economy. It appeared by 1987 that the Venture gas field off Sable I was sufficiently large and economically worthwhile to bring into production.

Conservation Natural resources are conserved in a variety of ways. The adoption in 1977 of the 200-nautical-mile (370 km) offshore fishing zone and recognition of the federal government's right to regulate the fishery has permitted it to take the action needed to restore badly depleted fishery stocks. To preserve and promote the inland salmon and trout fisheries, the provincial government provides water control, restocking of lakes and research. At Shubenacadie it maintains a wildlife park and a bird hatchery. But its major effort is directed towards protection and renewal of the forests. Part of its protection service is provided by fire towers and an aerial patrol service aimed at early detection of fires. The Dept of Lands and Forests provides seedlings for planting on crown lands and also supplies them to individuals and companies for private reforestation. It has also entered into a program with the federal government designed to improve the yield of the forests through modern management practices. But it has been unable to prevent the ravaging of large areas of the Cape Breton Highlands by the

Clark's Harbour on the western side of Cape Sable Island, NS. The island is connected to the southwestern tip of NS by a causeway (*photo by J.A. Kraulis*).

spruce budworm, in part, perhaps, because of strong public resistance to the use of chemical sprays.

People

Settlement and Immigration The French who established the first successful settlement of Europeans in the province at PORT-ROYAL in 1605 named it ACADIA, from the name assigned to the coast by VERRAZZANO. Lasting British settlement did not occur until the founding of HALIFAX in 1749 by Governor Edward CORNWALLIS who brought with him some 3000 settlers. Over the next 3 years about 2500 foreign Protestants, mostly German, arrived and were largely settled in LUNENBURG. Between 1760 and 1768 up to 8000 New Englanders, the pre-Loyalists, came as settlers, together with several hundred emigrants from northern Ireland. About 1000 Yorkshiremen who arrived between 1772 and 1774 settled at the Isthmus of Chignecto and the first Scots reached Pictou in 1773 aboard the HECTOR. The AMERICAN REVOLUTION brought about 20 000 LOYALISTS, disbanded soldiers and REFUGEES to Nova Scotia as permanent settlers. Some BLACKS came with the pre-Loyalists and Loyalists, some from Jamaica in 1796, and although many did not stay, a few hundred were left to be joined by the 2000 who arrived following the WAR OF 1812. Between 1815 and 1851 about 55 000 Scots, Irish, English and Welsh established themselves in the province, and after the expansion of the coal and steel industries – beginning in the 1890s – newcomers arrived from the British Isles and continental Europe to settle mostly in Cape Breton.

Ethnicity, Mother Tongue and Religion In 1986 the total population was 873 176, an increase of 5.4% over the previous 10 years and 3.0% over the previous 5, but a continuing decline in the percentage of the national total. About 72% of the people in 1981 were of only British and about 8% of only French descent, and a further 8% had some British or French in their background; the remainder were European, Asian, African or American Indian in origin. The mother tongue in 1986 of 93.2% was English; of 3.5%, French. Most Acadians are in Digby and Yarmouth counties on the mainland, and in Inverness and Richmond counties on Cape Breton I. Nevertheless, many Acadians have moved elsewhere, especially to Halifax, and a speedy loss of their mother tongue has often occurred.

Legislation enacted in 1981 provides for Acadian children to be taught in French wherever the numbers make it practicable. But most Acadian parents want their children to be fluent in English as well as French. In 1981, 36.9% of the population was Roman Catholic; among Protestants, United Church adherents constituted 20.2%, Anglicans 15.6%, Baptists 12.1%, Presbyterians 4.6% and Lutherans 1.5%.

Labour Force In June 1987 the total number of Nova Scotians in the labour force was 404 000, a participation rate of 59.8%; 12.9% were unemployed. Despite a reliance upon natural resources as the principal driver of the provincial economy, the service sector provides the most employment and accounts for some two-thirds of the jobs. In contrast with past experience, the percentage of unemployment in recent years has usually been only slightly above the national average and occasionally a little lower. A continuing problem of Nova Scotian labour is that wages generally lag considerably behind the Canadian average.

Urban-Rural Living As in the rest of Canada, a marked shift from rural to urban living has occurred in recent decades. From 1941 to 1961 the proportion of rural dwellers declined from 54.6% to 43.4%, with a corresponding increase in urban dwellers. But in the late 1960s the process slowed down somewhat since in 1971 rural dwellers had fallen to 42.0%, and by 1986 the process had actually reversed because rural dwellers had increased to 46.0%.

In 1986 Halifax County had over one-third of the provincial population, and the people in metropolitan Halifax, the largest urban centre in Atlantic Canada, numbered 238 162: 113 577 in the city of Halifax, 65 243 in the city of Dartmouth and 59 342 in the suburbs. The second-largest urban centre, SYDNEY and the 6 surrounding towns, GLACE BAY, New Waterford, SYDNEY MINES, Dominion, North Sydney and LOUISBOURG, had a population of about 89 280 in 1986. That centre's future is unclear because of continued uncertainties surrounding the Sydney steel plant and the closing of the heavy-water plant at Glace Bay. The third urban area, encompassing the Pictou County towns of NEW GLASGOW, Stellarton, Trenton, WESTVILLE and PICTOU, has a population of 27 048. Although its coal-mining industry has declined substantially, it has been assisted materially by a relatively new paper plant and a tire-manufacturing factory.

Economy

The per-capita income of Nova Scotians has seldom risen much above 80% of the national average. Limited natural resources and the great distance from central Canada are partly responsible, but greater blame has been attached to national transportation policies and, more especially, to the protective tariff or NATIONAL POLICY. The few provincial industries fostered by the NP have recently deteriorated and many of the early secondary industries have disappeared, unable to compete with central Canadian rivals. Nova Scotia has therefore had to rely mainly upon primary industries.

Agriculture Although the Micmac relied on hunting for their food, fishing captains in the early 16th century are believed to have cultivated

Gross Domestic Product - Nova Scotia 1986 at Factor Cost ($Millions)	
Agriculture	176.4
Forestry	45.6
Fishing	218.4
Mining	157.2
Manufacturing	1228.8
Construction	799.2
Utilities	316.8
Goods Producing	2942.4
Transportation and Communication	874.8
Wholesale and Retail Trade	1341.6
Finance, Insurance and Real Estate	1704.0
Community, Business and Personal Service	2442.0
Public Administration and Defence	1506.0
Service Producing	7868.4

vegetable gardens to feed their crews. At the same time the French were growing grain at Port-Royal and in 1609 they erected the first water-powered gristmill in N America. To secure salt for curing fish, they also built dikes along tidal marshes and later used them to begin a dikeland agriculture. The Marshlands Reclamation Commission in recent times has preserved and extended this system of dikes.

About 538 000 ha, 10% of the land, is agricultural. The largest cultivated areas are found in the Annapolis Valley and in some parts of northern Nova Scotia. But subsistence living on family farms has been common throughout wide areas of the province.

Near the coast, farming and fishing are often combined, as are farming and lumbering inland. Recent years have shown a trend towards larger, fewer farms, with a smaller total area, and a decrease in farm population.

The total value of farm cash receipts in 1986 was $267.6 million, and the annual net farm income runs in the area of $60 million derived from 16 specialized commodities.

The largest single sector is DAIRYING, which supplies fluid milk for home use as well as for dairy-product manufacturing. The production of eggs, chickens and turkeys has also thrived in recent years; indeed, dairy and poultry products bring a greater return than do the fruits, vegetables and greenhouse products for which the province is better known. Beef and hog production, another expanding sector, yields over $30 million each annually. The county fair is an important institution, and the one at Windsor, established in 1765, is the oldest of its type in N America.

Industry Nova Scotia has over 800 manufacturing plants employing about 47 000 people (12.8% of the labour force). Most of the plants are relatively small, and the great majority of them are based on primary products such as pulpwood, fruit and vegetables. Over 60 of the industries have been established since the 1960s, largely as a result of incentives provided by the provincial and federal governments.

At least half the manufactured products are destined for export, 67% to the US. Many newer industries involve investment from the US, Britain and Germany, and a few make no use of the province's natural resources. Of these, the 2 heavy-water plants at Glace Bay and the Str of Canso have recently been closed, but Michelin of Canada successfully operates tire-producing plants at Granton, Bridgewater and Waterville, making extensive use of Nova Scotian labour.

As a province abounding in recreational and cultural opportunities and possessing more historic sites than any province except Québec, Nova Scotia has become a favourite of tourists in the June-Oct season. Although the number of tourists visiting the province peaked in 1975, the gross value of the industry has grown more than 100% in the past decade. In 1985 the money expended by tourists exceeded $600 million for the first time; the total number of out-of-province visitors was over 1.1 million, down from a high of 1.37 million in 1975. About 27 000 people were employed in the tourist industry.

Although several major Canadian banks had their origin in Halifax, their head offices are now located in central Canada; only the BANK OF NOVA SCOTIA still holds its annual meetings in Halifax. Many large Canadian corporations do, however, locate their regional offices in Halifax. That more Nova Scotians work in business, trade, finance and transportation than in resource and manufacturing industries is sometimes attributed to the continuation of a historical pattern among people whose ancestors were sea traders. Office buildings, hotels and stores are more prominent than

Sydney, NS, noted since 1900 for its huge steel mill, the largest and most modern in Canada at the time of its construction (*photo by John deVisser*).

factories and two-thirds of the province's employed work in the service industries.

Mining The value of mineral commodities has increased steadily and reached over $340 million in 1986. Coal, SALT, GYPSUM and other construction materials are the principal products in an industry employing about 6300 people. By far the most important mineral is coal; the resource is estimated at 3 billion t, one-third of it estimated to be recoverable, and 925 million t being within 64 m of the surface. Nova Scotia coal has had a chequered history. The rapid increase in production following the establishment of the Whitney Syndicate and the development of the steel industry were primarily responsible for the province's prosperity in the early 20th century. After WWI conditions in the coal areas were often troubled, and in the late 1950s the market contracted greatly in the face of competition from petroleum and natural gas. Production declined from about 6.6 million t in 1950 to about 2 million in 1971. But coal has made a striking comeback; following large increases in petroleum prices by the OPEC cartel, the province has determined to reduce the dependency on foreign oil by replacing it with thermal coal. Production in 1986 amounted to over 2.5 million t worth more than $165 million. By 1986 thermal coal accounted for 71.1% of the province's electrical needs, a significant increase from 1980 when it accounted for only 23%. The near exhaustion of earlier mines in Cumberland, Pictou and Inverness counties means that practically all the coal is now mined in Cape Breton County.

Gypsum and salt, found largely in Hants and Cumberland counties, are the most valuable minerals after coal. Gypsum, quarried more extensively here than in any other province, is sent to the US for processing. Nova Scotia also has the largest barite deposits in Canada as well as large deposits of sand, gravel and other construction materials. Production difficulties during 1982 brought about the closure of a small lead-zinc mine which had recently been opened at Gay's River. New mines, though, are being developed. A tin mine near Yarmouth City began full operation in 1986 and several sites are being considered for gold mines.

The quest for energy sources has led to offshore exploration for gas and oil, especially on the Scotian Shelf in the neighbourhood of Sable I where substantial quantities of gas have been discovered. In Mar 1982 Prem John BUCHANAN signed a 42-year agreement with the federal government giving Nova Scotia the same benefits from its offshore

resources that Alberta receives from its land-based oil and gas. A crown corporation, Nova Scotia Resources Ltd, was established to take an equity position in energy development and has applied to the NEB for export licences for the natural gas and expects to produce and export to the NE United States 3.0 million cubic feet/day by 1990.

Forestry Lumbering has always been important in Nova Scotia's economy (*see* TIMBER TRADE HISTORY). In the 19th century much of the prosperity came from wooden ships and from the planking, deals and other lumber they carried overseas. Today more than 4.1 million ha, about 77% of the total area, is still forested, 70% of which is in the hands of private-sector owners. The PULP AND PAPER INDUSTRY has now outstripped the sawn-lumber industry in importance and value. Of approximately 4.2 million m³ of pulpwood harvested in 1986, only a small proportion (78 000 m³) was exported. The most common softwood is spruce. Balsam fir is used not only for pulpwood but also as the basis of a second industry – the export of Christmas trees. Lumber production annually ranges around 500 m³; in 1986

Looking up George Street, Halifax, NS, Notman Studio, c1880. Vendors are gathering for Saturday morning market at Bedford Row, just off to the left (*courtesy Public Archives of Nova Scotia*).

it was 531 078 m³. The most important commercial hardwoods are red maple, sugar maple and yellow birch. Sugar maple also forms the basis of an industry for woodlot owners, especially in the N, through the production of maple syrup and allied products.

Fisheries Nova Scotia is second only to BC in the value of its fishery, which first attracted Europeans to its shores. Salt and dried fish for export to Latin America was once the staple of the market, but quick-frozen and filleted fish altogether dominate the modern market. Since WWII, schooners with dories have given way to draggers that fish the entire year. In 1986 nearly 15 000 fishermen and about 9300 shore-based workers were participating in the industry; about 6100 fishing craft, large and small, were supplying 235 processing plants throughout the entire province.

In a highly diversified industry, inshore fishermen account for about 70% of the total. No less valuable than groundfish such as haddock and cod are molluscs and crustaceans such as scallops and lobsters. The groundfish are caught both by offshore trawlers and draggers and by inshore boats including long-liners. Lobsters are taken largely inshore by Cape Island boats; scallops by both offshore and inshore draggers; herring by seiners. In 1971 the swordfish industry ceased because of fear of MERCURY contamination.

With the agreement of other fishing nations Canada declared a 200-mile fishing limit in 1977, assuming the right to regulate most fishing banks on its continental shelf with the aim of letting the fish stocks recover from depletion by large, foreign factory ships. Although fish landings average in value about $250 million annually, the industry has been beset by problems. The offshore industry had long complained that the inshore fishermen, through a powerful lobby and a sympathetic minister, had been favoured at its expense. All the fishermen objected to over-regulation by the federal authority, especially to a recent sector management plan, which discouraged flexibility. The new 200-mile limit had attracted hundreds of newcomers with deleterious results. Forced to operate under a quota system, large fish plants and draggers with heavy overheads found it costly to operate at less than full capacity. Processors experienced difficulties because of sales by inshore fishermen to foreign

Perspective view of the Province Building from the NE, published at Halifax, NS, 1819; etching in brown ink, coloured by hand, by John Elliott Woolford (*courtesy National Archives of Canada/C-3561*).

trawlers. An additional problem was having to sell a high-cost product of sometimes poor quality during a recession.

A long-standing dispute between Canada and the US over the ownership of Georges Bank, one of the world's richest fishing areas, was settled by the World Court in 1984. Although Canada received only one-sixth of the disputed territory, it was the most valuable portion and Nova Scotia fishermen suffered much less serious harm than the New Englanders.

Transportation In early Nova Scotia the sea was the only highway, but in the late 1760s road building began. Today, about 26 000 km of highways extend to every community in the province although only 12 000 km are paved. Politics in the latter 19th century was largely railway politics; practically all the province's 1900 km of railway were built between 1854 and 1914, partly as government works and partly privately. In the last 3 decades, however, a steady decline in railway services has occurred. There are now only 710 km of mainline track being used in the province. In 1987 the only passenger trains in operation were provided by VIA from Halifax through the Annapolis Valley to Digby to Yarmouth, from Halifax to Amherst and on to Montréal, and from Halifax to Sydney. Freight services provided by the railways diminish year by year as permission is granted to discontinue operations on little-used trackage. Public transportation by road is provided by Acadian Lines and smaller bus companies, while a large part of the freight is moved by truck.

The attempt to build up a deep-water, bulk-cargo superport in the Strait of Canso has failed for the moment, but Halifax, a full day closer to Europe than any other American mainland port, continues to maintain pre-eminence in cargo handling. In the late 1960s a large container terminal was built on a 24 ha site in S Halifax. In the early 1980s a second was built at Fairview Cove in Bedford Basin at the north end of Halifax Harbour. In 1986 an additional terminal of equal size was added at Fairview Cove making Halifax the 50th largest container port in the world and the second largest in Canada.

Seagoing car ferries connect southwestern Nova Scotia with New Brunswick (via Digby and Saint John) and with New England (via Yarmouth and Bar Harbor, Maine, and via Yarmouth and Portland, Maine). In addition, car ferries run to Newfoundland (from North Sydney) and to PEI (from Caribou, near Pictou). Air Canada provides passenger and air-cargo services to major Canadian and international centres through Halifax International Airport; it also uses regional airports at Yarmouth and Sydney. Eastern Provincial Airways (EPA) acts as a regional carrier and also flies directly from Halifax to Toronto; Canadian Airlines International flies directly from Halifax to Montréal.

Energy Before 1973 the generation of electric energy was in the hands of the Nova Scotia Power Commission, a government agency established in 1919, and the Nova Scotia Light and Power Company, a private utility. In 1973 they were united in a crown corporation, the Nova Scotia Power Corp. Per-capita energy consumption in 1980 was about 87% of the national average, the smaller usage attributable in part to the relatively underdeveloped industrial base. In 1950 about 70% of the province's energy needs were met by hydroelectric power and indigenous coal. Convinced that cheap oil would continue to be available and that nuclear energy would be less expensive than that derived from coal, governments allowed a situation to develop in which, by 1978, over 70% of the electricity was produced from oil. Because of major increases in oil costs, Nova Scotia had the most expensive energy in Canada, excepting PEI.

In 1979 the Energy Planning Board was established under the new Dept of Mines and Energy to devise an energy strategy. This strategy aimed at the development of the few remaining hydroelectric opportunities; the opening of new coal mines and the expansion of existing ones so as to permit oil-fired generating plants to be phased out; and the completion on the Annapolis R in 1984 of the first tidal plant in N America, using the largest turbine ever built for hydroelectric development. This strategy has been extremely successful and by 1986 oil accounted for only 7.7% of the province's electrical energy while coal accounted for 71.7%. But the government's main concern remains with offshore gas and oil development. Exploratory drilling continues off Sable I and economically feasible production is seen to be realistic, possibly as early as 1990.

Government and Politics

Basic Structure Although some of the Nova Scotia constitution still rests on the prerogative, especially on the commissions and instructions of the pre-Confederation governor, in practice this does not differentiate it from other provinces. Legally, provincial executive power is vested in the LIEUTENANT-GOVERNOR, practically it is exercised by the Executive Council or Cabinet, which has increased in size from an 18th-century COUNCIL OF TWELVE to a high of 23 members. Beginning in 1838 the legislative power was vested in a general assembly consisting of a lieutenant-governor, legislative

Lieutenant-Governors of Nova Scotia 1867-1987	
	Term
Charles Hastings Doyle	1867-73
Joseph Howe	1873
Adams George Archibald	1873-83
Matthew Henry Richey	1883-88
Archibald Woodbury McLelan	1888-90
Malachy Bowes Daly	1890-1900
Alfred Gilpin Jones	1900-06
Duncan Cameron Fraser	1906-10
James Drummond McGregor	1910-15
David MacKeen	1915-16
MacCallum Grant	1916-25
James Robson Douglas	1925
James Cranswick Tory	1925-30
Frank Stanfield	1930-31
Walter Harold Covert	1931-37
Robert Irwin	1937-40
Frederick Francis Mathers	1940-42
Henry Ernest Kendall	1942-47
John Alexander Douglas McCurdy	1947-52
Alistair Fraser	1952-58
Edward Chester Plow	1958-63
Henry Poole MacKeen	1963-68
Victor deBedia Oland	1968-73
Clarence L. Gosse	1973-78
John Elvin Schaffner	1978-84
Alan Rockwell Abraham	1984-

Premiers of Nova Scotia 1867-1987		
	Party	*Term*
Hiram Blanchard	Liberal	1867
William Annand	Anti-Confederation	1867-75
Philip Carteret Hill	Liberal	1875-78
Simon Hugh Holmes	Conservative	1878-82
John Sparrow David Thompson	Conservative	1882
William Thomas Pipes	Liberal	1882-84
William Stevens Fielding	Liberal	1884-96
George Henry Murray	Liberal	1896-1923
Ernest Howard Armstrong	Liberal	1923-25
Edgar Nelson Rhodes	Conservative	1925-30
Gordon Sydney Harrington	Conservative	1930-33
Angus Lewis Macdonald	Liberal	1933-40
Alexander Stirling MacMillan	Liberal	1940-45
Angus Lewis Macdonald	Liberal	1945-54
Harold Joseph Connolly	Liberal	1954
Henry Davies Hicks	Liberal	1954-56
Robert Lorne Stanfield	Conservative	1956-67
George Isaac Smith	Conservative	1967-70
Gerald Augustine Regan	Liberal	1970-78
John MacLennan Buchanan	Conservative	1978-

council and legislative assembly. In 1928, however, Nova Scotia abolished its council and left Québec as the only province with a bicameral legislature until 1968 when it too abolished its Legislative Council. The Fifty-Second General Assembly elected in 1981 was unique in that for the first time all of its 52 members were chosen by single-member constituencies. Universal suffrage for males and females over 21 came into effect in 1920; the voting age was reduced to 19 in 1970 and to 18 in 1973.

The senior court, the Supreme Court of Nova Scotia, is a provincially constituted court whose judges are appointed by the federal Cabinet, although the Meech Lake agreement, if implemented, would alter the method of appointment. In the early 1960s it was divided into trial and appellate divisions; in 1987 the latter consisted of the chief justice of the Appeal Division and 6 other judges; the former of the chief justice of Nova Scotia and 11 other judges. Until 1981 the County Court, constituted and appointed in the same way, had 8 judges, but legislation in that year provided for the appointment of 2 additional judges and the naming of a chief county court judge to exercise general supervisory power. Because much of the criminal business, although not the trial of the most serious offences, is dealt with in the Provincial Court (formerly the Provincial Magistrates' Court), a completely provincial court, the number of its judges has increased substantially in recent years to a total of 25 in 1987; since 1980 one of them has exercised some supervisory powers as chief judge.

Municipal Government Local government is carried on in 3 cities, 39 towns and 24 rural municipalities. Although the last generally conform to the county boundaries, 6 counties have 2 rural municipalities each. Despite several attempts made to amalgamate or alter these units, they have remained practically untouched since 1879. The only substantive changes in the status of the units since 1923 have been the incorporation of Dartmouth as a city in 1961 and Bedford as a town in 1980; and the reversion to their rural municipalities of the towns of Port Hood, Wedgeport, Joggins and Inverness. Smaller communities may organize themselves under the Village Service Act to secure services not provided by their rural municipality. Over the past 3 or 4 decades many responsibilities of the municipalities have been shifted to the provincial government, but the latter is well aware that it lays rough hands on the municipal government only at great peril to itself.

Federal Representation As was constitutionally provided in 1867, Nova Scotia's membership in the Senate is 10, but its representation in the House of Commons has fallen from 21 in the 1870s to 11 in the 1980s, with a corresponding decrease in clout in federal politics. It has been suggested that the voters' propensity to support the old-line parties through thick and thin has harmed the province's bargaining position. It has also been argued, but no less strongly denied, that Nova Scotia's leverage would be substantially greater in a union of MARITIME PROVINCES.

Public Finance Until Confederation most government revenues came through import duties (see CUSTOMS AND EXCISE), which could readily be adjusted as circumstances warranted. After 1867 payments from Ottawa became by far the largest source. Not until the turn of the century did the province have its first million-dollar budget and coal royalties rank ahead of the federal subsidy as the chief producer of revenue. Principally because of the expanding coal and steel industry, the decade before WWI was the only period in which the provincial exchequer has been in a genuinely healthy condition since Confederation. Since 1918 the province has almost always been strapped for money and, in common with the other have-not provinces, has had to make all sorts of demands upon the milch cow at Ottawa. In the 1960s Nova Scotia was a leader in pressing upon the federal authorities the principle of full equalization.

By 1976 the province had its first billion-dollar budget. In the year ending 31 Mar 1986 expenditures had risen to $2.98 billion and revenues to $2.7 billion. Of the expenditures, 27.5% went to health, 25.4% to education, 17.8% to servicing the public debt, 10.0% to social welfare and 3.0% to municipal affairs. Of the revenues, 41.3% came in various forms from Ottawa, 22.8% from personal and corporation taxes, 23.9% from sales taxes, 3.2% from liquor sales and 1.3% from motor-vehicle revenue. Because of financial difficulties, in 1982 the sales tax was increased from 8 to 10%, the corporate tax by 2 points to 15% and the personal income tax by 4 points to 56.5% of the federal tax.

Health The Dept of Public Health administers an extensive program with its divisions of dental health, nursing service, public-health engineering, nutrition, tuberculosis, hospitals and nursing homes, child and maternal health, communicable disease control, industrial health and emergency health services. In 1959 the province entered the national hospital insurance plan and in 1968 the medical-care insurance plan. To ensure greater administrative efficiency these 2 plans were merged under the Health Services and Insurance Commission in 1973. To the free services already provided, dental care for children up to 7 was introduced in 1974 (since increased to the age of 16) and shortly afterwards prescription drugs for those 65 and over. The province's share of the cost is obtained in large measure from a 10% retail sales tax levied under the Health Services Tax and a levy imposed upon marriage, birth and death certificates. Medical research is carried on primarily by the Faculty of Medicine at DALHOUSIE UNIVERSITY, which, because it does not receive enough funding from national agencies, has established the Research and Development FOUNDATION.

Politics The first genuine political parties appeared in the election of 1836 when Tories (Conservatives) battled Reformers (Liberals), who had come into existence almost overnight under the guidance of Joseph HOWE. Until 1867 the parties contended fairly equally, but the Confederation issue upset the rough balance in favour of the anti-Confederates (Liberals). Until 1956 the Conservatives won only 3 elections and were in office only 12 of the 89 years. Since WWII, however, a

lessening in traditional voting, combined with divisions within the Liberal Party and the influence of John DIEFENBAKER and Robert STANFIELD, have combined to narrow differences in electoral strength and to make the parties genuinely competitive. It has been very difficult to supplant established Nova Scotian premiers, and W.S. FIELDING, George Murray, Angus L. MACDONALD and Stanfield maintained their political ascendency over lengthy periods. But to describe Conservative Stanfield as less liberal or more conservative than Liberals Fielding, Murray and Macdonald would be a deception, since the old-line parties pragmatically base their programs and platforms on electoral needs, not on ideology.

The traditionalism of the political culture has complicated the difficulties of third parties. In 1920 factors arising largely out of WWI permitted the Farmer-Labour group to make the best third-party showing ever – 11 members and 30.9% of the popular vote, compared to the Conservatives' 3 members and 24.7%. Since 1941 the CCF-NDP has at times elected one federal member and up to 4 provincial assemblymen. In 1945, when the Conservatives failed to elect anyone, the 2 CCF members constituted the official opposition in the Assembly. Before 1981 all the CCF-NDP victories were in the urban part of Cape Breton County, but that year the NDP leader won a seat in metropolitan Halifax, where the total party vote almost equalled that of the Liberals. That year its province-wide vote was 18.1%, the highest on record. In 1984 Prem John Buchanan won his third and most decisive victory when the Conservatives won 42 seats, the Liberals 6, the NDP 3 and the Cape Breton Labour Party 1.

Education

Administration Provincial aid to education was first provided by the "forgotten school act" of 1808, but because of the fear of direct taxation, it was not until the 1865 Act, which provided for compulsory assessment, that a free, universally operative system of common-school education came into being. Although the legislature has always refused to give legal recognition to separate schools, even before Confederation the Catholic schools in Halifax were treated as part of the public system if they followed that system's course of study and observed its regulations. Later the same recognition was granted to Catholic schools in the larger towns of Cape Breton and eastern NS. Recently, with the enlargement of Halifax's boundaries and the consolidation of schools resulting from declining enrolments, the separate system has been substantially eroded in Halifax. From 1864 to 1950 the policymaking function was vested in a council of public instruction, which was basically the provincial Cabinet; in 1950 the province got its first minister of education.

In addition to school consolidation, 2 other basic changes have been made in the public system since WWII. Following the Pottier Report, an Act of 1946 established a foundation program providing for a basic level of educational services financed partly by the provincial government and partly by municipal taxes equalized across the province. Based upon the Walker Report on Public Education Finance, an Act of 1982 provided for the reduction of the existing 85 school boards to 22, on the ground that the change would create an administrative situation in which sufficient students, funds, professional staff and specialist expertise would permit a far wider and more enriched program. Although it was left to all the municipal units to enter into this arrangement voluntarily, all but the town of Hantsport acquiesced.

Institutions The religious denominations gave

an early impetus to higher education and at one time in the 19th century Dalhousie alone of the 7 colleges was nondenominational. It has been contended that the province suffers from a surfeit of universities, but strong religious sentiment, if nothing else, has prevented consolidation. The exception has been that Pine Hill Divinity Hall, formerly a Presbyterian and later a United Church institution, became the Atlantic School of Theology in 1971, the country's first ecumenical college, in which the Roman Catholic, Anglican and United churches participate. Institutions providing regular university programs in Halifax are Dalhousie, SAINT MARY'S, MOUNT SAINT VINCENT and the UNIVERSITY OF KING'S COLLEGE; outside Halifax are ACADIA in Wolfville, ST FRANCIS XAVIER in Antigonish and UNIVERSITY COLLEGE OF CAPE BRETON at Sydney. UNIVERSITÉ SAINTE-ANNE at Church Point is the only francophone college in the province. Institutions providing specialized training in Halifax are the TECHNICAL UNIVERSITY OF NOVA SCOTIA and the NOVA SCOTIA COLLEGE OF ART AND DESIGN; in Truro are the NOVA SCOTIA AGRICULTURAL COLLEGE and the Nova Scotia Teachers' College. The Atlantic Institute of Education in Halifax was eliminated in 1982 for financial reasons. Training in the new high technology of fishing is offered at the Nova Scotia Fisheries Training Centre; technical education for mariners is provided by the NOVA SCOTIA NAUTICAL INSTITUTE and by the CANADIAN COAST GUARD College at Sydney. A program of post-secondary education for candidates for business and industry is offered by 14 regional vocational schools, 3 modern institutes of technology similar to community colleges and the apprenticeship program of the provincial Dept of Labour.

Cultural Life

Until the last few decades Nova Scotia's geographical position had kept it removed from some of the main currents of national life. But improvements in travel and the strong impact of nationwide COMMUNICATIONS have eroded some features of the traditional life-style and introduced greater modernity.

Arts In recent years especially, the Nova Scotian government has taken steps both to preserve the province's heritage and to support artistic and cultural forms and activities. In 1975 it established the Art Gallery of Nova Scotia as an agency of the province for the acquisition, preservation and exhibition of works of art, but financial considerations have so far prevented the construction of a suitable building for exhibition purposes. The next year it provided that any building reflecting the cultural, social, economic, political or architectural history of the province might be designated a Registered Historic Property. In 1978, a third Act established the Cultural Foundation to accept, raise and administer funds for the promotion and encouragement of cultural affairs.

All 3 levels of government have supported Halifax's NEPTUNE THEATRE, which has established a national reputation although it performs in inadequate quarters. Despite assistance from the CANADA COUNCIL and the province, the Atlantic Symphony Orchestra, based in Halifax but performing throughout the Atlantic provinces, collapsed for financial reasons in 1982. Since that time it has been revived on a smaller scale as Symphony Nova Scotia. Scottish culture is particularly vigorous in eastern Nova Scotia; St Francis Xavier offers courses in Celtic studies (see CELTIC LANGUAGES), while the Gaelic College at St Anns, Cape Breton, fosters piping, singing, dancing and handicrafts, and annually hosts the Gaelic Mod, a festival of Highland folk arts. Recently, art galleries and craft shops have proliferated, run by both natives and newcomers, with estimated sales approximating $20 million annually.

View of the town and fort of Annapolis Royal, NS, watercolour by J. Hamilton (*courtesy National Archives of Canada/C-2706*).

Communications The newspaper circulating widely throughout the province is the morning Halifax *Chronicle-Herald;* its afternoon edition, the *Mail-Star,* is largely limited to the Halifax area. These papers have sometimes been criticized for their blandness and the Davey Committee (1970) accused them of "lazy, uncaring journalism." The daily serving Cape Breton in particular is the *Cape Breton Post.* Four other dailies serve various regions in the province and county weeklies abound. Radio service is provided by CBC and a large number of private stations; television, by CBC and the stations of the Atlantic Television network (ATV) affiliated with CTV. Considerable production for radio and television emanates from the Halifax program unit of the CBC. CABLE TELEVISION stations transmit mainly the signal from the American networks, which is received via Bangor, Maine and Detroit, Mich (*see* NEWSPAPERS; BROADCASTING).

Preservation of the Past Through the efforts of the federal and provincial governments, the Royal Nova Scotia Historical Society, and a plethora of local heritage and historical societies the province's storied past is exhibited to the public in various ways. Standing out among the national historic parks are a restored LOUISBOURG; a replica of Champlain's Habitation Port-Royal; and the HALIFAX CITADEL. The provincial government has restored numerous old houses that are representative of earlier eras, including Uniacke House, home of Richard John UNIACKE, near Halifax; Perkins's House, home of Simeon PERKINS, at Liverpool; and "Clifton," home of Thomas Chandler HALIBURTON, at Windsor. Scores of HISTORIC SITES have been marked with plaques on the advice of the Historic Sites and Monuments Board of Canada, the Nova Scotia Historic Sites and Advisory Council, and the Royal Nova Scotia Historical Society. The Nova Scotia Museum provides displays on provincial history. The Public Archives of Nova Scotia building, opened in 1980, is unexcelled in any province and is a veritable treasure house of paintings, documents and manuscripts.

History

Discovery and Early Settlement The early inhabitants of Nova Scotia were the MICMAC, a branch of the Algonquian language group. Some evidence of their numbers and their migrations with the hunt can be gauged from shell heaps discovered in various parts of the province. With the coming of Europeans they almost invariably established better relations with the French than with the English. In recent years the Micmac have presented LAND CLAIMS similar to those of Indians in other provinces, but their bargaining power is weak because they constitute only about 0.6% of the population.

Long before John CABOT made a landfall in 1497 (probably on Cape Breton I), NORSE adventurers may have reached Nova Scotia. Scores of other explorers and fishermen plied its coasts before de MONTS and CHAMPLAIN established Port-Royal in 1605, the first agricultural settlement by Europeans on land which is now Canadian, and the beginnings of Acadia. King James I of England granted New Scotland (called Nova Scotia in its Latin charter) to Sir William ALEXANDER in 1621, and the province was endowed with an Order of Baronets and a coat of arms in 1626. Two settlements were set up by Scots 3 years later, but both were unsuccessful.

Three times in the 17th century – by Samuel Argall in 1613, Robert Sedgewick in 1654 and Sir William PHIPS in 1690 – the French settlements were captured by the English, each time to be returned. The small group of French settlers that were left after the conquest of 1613, together with 300 sent by the Company of New France in 1632 and 60 brought out by Grandfontaine in 1671, constitute the ancestors of Nova Scotia's Acadian people today. The fourth capture of Port-Royal (renamed ANNAPOLIS ROYAL) by Francis Nicholson in 1710 was to be the last, because in 1713, by the Treaty of UTRECHT, Acadia, but not Île Royale (Cape Breton I) or Île Saint-Jean (PEI), passed to British hands. Until 1749, however, it was little more than a "counterfeit suzerainty" (*see* NOVA SCOTIA, 1714-84). The founding of Halifax that year, followed by the arrival of the pre-Loyalists and later by about 20 000 Loyalists (including some 3000 blacks) and disbanded troops, marked the beginnings of British Nova Scotia. An immediate result (1784) was the formation of the new colonies of New Brunswick and Cape Breton from territory that had been part of Nova Scotia, the latter since the Treaty of PARIS, 1763.

The 19th Century Many Loyalists had been men of wealth and influence who, because of their sacrifices, expected privileged treatment. Although not unsympathetic at the outset, Gov John PARR eventually had a cooling off with them because of their unending demands for office and their frequent clashes with the pre-Loyalists. But time was on their side, for Parr's successor, Loyalist John Wentworth, used his 16 years as governor (1792-1808) to establish a Loyalist ascendancy in the higher levels of government. As a result, the Loyalists no longer needed to press their claims vigorously and, partly through intermarriage, distinct Loyalist influence disappeared within a relatively short time.

Always a strong defender of the prerogative, Wentworth became increasingly so and in the early 1800s he became embroiled with a so-called "country party," an undisciplined grouping led by William Cottnam Tonge. Eventually, Wentworth got the better of Tonge by rejecting his election as Speaker of the Assembly and dismissing him from his position as naval officer of Halifax. But despite his best efforts the Assembly gained substantial control over the disposition of road moneys, something most country assemblymen regarded as their principal *raison d'être.* Since the military governors who followed chose not to disturb these arrangements, relative political calm prevailed until the mid-1830s, in marked contrast with the situation in the Canadas.

The NAPOLEONIC WARS brought prosperity to Nova Scotia, especially to the lumbering and SHIPBUILDING industries. The War of 1812 also added to the province's well-being; indeed, more than one Halifax fortune was accumulated through PRIVATEERING in these years. But peace, accompanied by poor harvests several years in a row, brought recession in its wake, and recovery did not begin until the mid-1820s, partly promoted by William Huskisson's trade Acts of 1825. Nevertheless, a new wave of IMMIGRATION followed the war and by mid-century the newcomers totalled about 55 000. Some 2000 blacks arrived shortly after the war and in 1818-19 about 200 WELSH. But the bulk were Irish or Scottish, the former largely remaining in Halifax and the latter

Dam and mill on the Gaspereau R, White Rock Mills, NS *c*1896. Lumbering has always been important in the province's economy (*courtesy National Archives of Canada/PA-126482*).

going to Cape Breton I and the northeastern part of the peninsula. From the early part of the century, a slow but steady intellectual awakening had been making itself felt, first in trade, next in literary activity, and finally reaching its zenith in politics in the 1830s. One manifestation was the celebrated Brandy Dispute of 1830 in which almost the entire province turned upon the Council of Twelve for daring to assert a power relating to money bills which had long lain in abeyance.

The movement for RESPONSIBLE GOVERNMENT got under way in earnest in 1836 when, mainly through the efforts of Joseph Howe and his *Novascotian,* a majority of reforming assemblymen was elected to the legislature. Their struggle was against an interrelated merchant-official oligarchy, largely from Halifax, which through the Council of Twelve dominated the business, political and ecclesiastical life of the province in its own interest. The Halifax group, even more than its Upper Canadian counterpart, was a FAMILY COMPACT.

Howe was a conservative reformer, and his followers could later echo his words, that they had achieved their ends without a blow struck or a pane of glass broken. Howe's moderation is shown in his willingness to enter into an ill-starred coalition with the Tories, 1840-43, in the hope of attaining his objectives gradually. The Reformers finally achieved success when, in the election of 1847, they won 29 seats to their opponents' 22. On 9 Feb 1848 James B. Uniacke became premier with Howe acting as provincial secretary. Uniacke formed the first ministry operating under responsible government in the British Empire overseas.

Two positive accomplishments marked the next 17 years. Under the leadership of Howe, Nova Scotia entered the railway era and by 1858 the government-owned Nova Scotia Railway was operating lines from Halifax to Windsor and Truro.

Charles TUPPER took the lead in the enactment of the school Acts of 1864 and 1865, which required the opening of schools elsewhere without payment of fees and introduced the disliked compulsory assessment which would make free schools possible. Otherwise, these were years of issueless, bitterly partisan politics. Following a bitter clash between Howe and the Irish, the Catholics deserted the Liberals and sectarian politics prevailed for a short period after 1857, the only instance of its kind in Nova Scotia history.

Starting in 1865 the CONFEDERATION question left a mark on the province. Contrary to general belief, Howe did not initiate the movement against the Quebec Resolutions. Rather it began in western Nova Scotia and among the Halifax merchants on economic grounds; people relying on seaborne traffic eastward and southward did not relish setting up new links with a remote, unknown interior. To Howe it seemed obvious that colonial union should at least wait until railway communication had been established with the PROVINCE OF CANADA and monstrous that it should be effected on the basis of a resolution adopted by a 3-year-old assembly that had been elected when union was not an issue. A delegation under him could not prevent the BRITISH NORTH AMERICA ACT from being enacted, but in Sept 1867 Nova Scotia's voters returned 18 anti-Confederates out of 19 to the House of Commons and 36 out of 38 to the provincial House of Assembly (*see* REPEAL MOVEMENT). Finally, convinced that repeal was impossible, Howe negotiated and accepted "better terms" and entered the federal Cabinet in Jan 1869. Until his death in 1873 he devoted himself to preventing the "slumbering volcano" of Nova Scotia from erupting. Not until the federal election of 1874 and the entrance of 2 Nova Scotian Liberals into Alexander MACKENZIE's Cabinet did the anti-Confederates finally "accept the situation"; the stage had been set for them to become the official provincial wing of a national party. But bitterness did not die easily and as late as 1927 some Nova Scotians still flew flags at half-mast on July 1.

Obviously, Tupper had set Nova Scotia's financial needs too low in the Confederation bargain, for even with Howe's better terms the province found it difficult to maintain existing services, much less to continue the expansion of the railway system. By 1867 the branch from Truro to Pictou had been built as a government undertaking, and by 1876 the Dominion government had completed the INTERCOLONIAL RAILWAY as part of the Confederation bargain. After an increase in the province's debt allowance in 1873 the provincial government provided subsidies for building the Western Counties Railway from Annapolis to Yarmouth, the Nictaux and Atlantic from Middleton to Lunenburg, the Eastern Extension from New Glasgow to the Str of Canso, and several lines on Cape Breton I. But because of the province's straitened financial circumstances, none of them would be completed either easily or quickly. Numerous pleas for aid having been rejected or unanswered by Ottawa, Prem W.S. Fielding campaigned on the repeal of Confederation in the election of 1886 and took 29 of 38 seats. But it all came to naught when the Conservatives won 14 of Nova Scotia's 21 federal seats the following year.

The 20th Century Nonetheless, Fielding, a cautious financier, quickly established his pre-eminence in provincial politics. By 1893 he had persuaded Henry M. Whitney of Boston to embark on coal mining in Cape Breton County and soon the Whitney Syndicate had laid the foundation of a substantial coal and steel industry. George Murray succeeded Fielding in 1896 in circumstances so auspicious that he held on to the premiership for an unequalled 26 years. Greatly expanded coal royalties and an increased federal subsidy in 1907 overcame Nova Scotia's financial difficulties for the first time since Confederation and enabled Murray to complete with ease the province's last major railway, the Halifax and Southwestern from Halifax to Yarmouth, and to make the first cautious advance into the social-service state. The economy of Nova Scotia was stimulated by an increased demand for iron, steel, fish and lumber during WWI. But war's end brought recession which lasted long after recovery had begun outside the Maritimes. That Farmer-Labourites could win 11 seats in politically conservative Nova Scotia in the provincial election of 1920 indicates the depth of the malaise.

Hitherto the major demands on Ottawa had been to relieve the provincial government of its financial burden. But in the early 1920s came the realization that it was the deleterious effects of national economic policies relating to transportation and the tariff which were preventing Nova Scotia from sharing fully in the benefits of Confederation. A MARITIME RIGHTS movement which began in 1922 was quickly taken over by the Conservatives and used to overthrow a 43-year-old Liberal government in 1925. A federal royal commission headed by Sir Andrew Rae Duncan recommended more favourable freight rates and increased federal grants for the Maritimes, but failed to consider the greatest grievance, the protective tariff. Liberal Angus L. Macdonald appointed the Jones Commission to rectify the omission on his becoming premier in 1933.

Macdonald, the third of Nova Scotia's outstanding political leaders after Confederation, headed what was probably the strongest of all Nova Scotian Cabinets and conducted a highly progressive government before he entered the federal Cabinet in 1940. Again Nova Scotia enjoyed good times during WWII and Halifax became the major port for shipping munitions and other supplies to Western Europe. The Macdonald who returned to Halifax from Ottawa adopted a much more conservative stance than in prewar days. Following his death in 1954, Nova Scotia's voters conducted a mild political revolution in 1956 by returning the Conservatives for the first time since Confederation under noncrisis conditions: Robert Stanfield then became the fourth premier to establish political dominance over the province.

Since the mid-1950s economic development has been the primary concern of provincial politicians. Industrial Estates Limited (IEL), est 1957, was the chosen instrument of the Stanfield government, and its early successes led to a belief in the early 1960s that Nova Scotia might be coming into its own. But the serious losses incurred by Clairtone and Deuterium of Canada injected a note of pessimism. The same period was marked by serious difficulties in the coal and steel industries, almost the only ones of substance to be developed in the province as a result of the protective tariff. The apparently permanent collapse of the coal market led in 1967 to the establishment of the Cape Breton Development Corporation (Devco), a federal CROWN CORPORATION with provincial involvement, aimed at developing alternatives for miners as the coal industry was phased out. In 1967, to prevent the closing of Dosco's steel plant at Sydney, the Nova Scotia government took it over and operated it as a crown corporation, the Sydney Steel Corporation (Sysco); to date it has added massively to the provincial debt and its future is far from certain, although in 1987 the federal and provincial governments agreed on a massive infusion of capital to modernize the plant. In contrast, coal has made a comeback as a viable substitute for oil in energy production.

Recently, there have been 2 philosophies concerning provincial development. Ought it to be confined to industries making use of the province's natural resources? Or, despite past failures, should continued efforts be made to establish secondary industries which may be altogether unrelated to those resources? Whatever the answer, Nova Scotians are insisting more and more that their pleasant way of life should not be sacrificed to material considerations.

J. MURRAY BECK

Reading: J. Murray Beck, *The Government of Nova Scotia* (1957) and *The Evolution of Municipal Government in Nova Scotia, 1749-1973* (1973); J.B. Brebner, *New England's Outpost* (1927) and *The Neutral Yankees of Nova Scotia* (1937); D. Campbell and R.A. MacLean, *Beyond the Atlantic Roar* (1974); G.G. Campbell, *The History of Nova Scotia* (1949); R.E. George, *A Leader and a Laggard* (1970); J.F. Graham, *Fiscal Adjustment and Economic Development: A Case Study of Nova Scotia* (1963); J. Leefe and P. McCreath, *History of Early Nova Scotia* (1982); W.S. MacNutt, *The Atlantic Province* (1965); B. Moody, *The Acadians* (1981); B. Murdoch, *A History of Nova Scotia or Acadie*, 3 vols (1865, 1866, 1867); T.H. Raddall, *Halifax: Warden of the North* (1948).

Nova Scotia Agricultural College, Truro, NS, opened in 1905 to provide agricultural education and training for the Atlantic provinces. It amalgamated the School of Agriculture (fd Truro, 1885) with the School of Horticulture (fd Wolfville, 1893). The college offers technical and vocational courses, pre-professional studies in agricultural engineering and veterinary medicine, and an agricultural science degree. The college approaches agricultural studies from various directions, including an active research program, and emphasizes direct involvement with the organized industry. Graduates have occupied prominent positions in agricultural services both in Canada and abroad. In 1985-86 there were 532 full-time undergraduates enrolled.

LOIS KERNAGHAN

Nova Scotia College of Art and Design, Halifax, was established 1887. It offers instruction in fine art, crafts, art education, communication design and environmental planning. It achieved university status in 1969, and is the only degree-granting art school in Canada. Four-year programs lead to the bachelor of fine arts degree (in fine art or art education), bachelor of design (in communication design or environmental planning) or bachelor of arts (in art education). Master's degrees are offered in fine arts and art education. The college also offers diplomas in fine art and graphic design. The college is noted for its publishing ventures on source material in contemporary art. In 1978 it completed an innovative move to a campus within Halifax's restored waterfront. In 1985-86 there were 507 full-time undergraduates enrolled. LOIS KERNAGHAN

Nova Scotia Nautical Institute, institute for seamanship training fd *c* 1872. It was common in England and Canada, which followed England in marine matters, to have people called "crammers" to assist mariners to pass their examinations, following apprenticeship on board ship. The school was known as the Halifax Marine School from its start to 1 July 1951 when it passed from federal to provincial control and was renamed Nova Scotia Marine Navigation School. In 1973 it amalgamated with the Nova Scotia Marine Engineering School (est 1948). In 1974 the union became the NS Nautical Inst, with a staff of 14. The school provides courses of instruction, but the exams are conducted by the Canadian Coast Guard.

Nova Scotia Research Foundation Corporation (NSRFC), research organization established by the province as the Nova Scotia Research Foundation in 1946 in response to H.M. TORY's recommendation that a provincial board be established to co-operate with universities and the NATIONAL RESEARCH COUNCIL in seeking solutions to problems of economic development and rehabilitation. In 1975 a new Act changed the name to Nova Scotia Research Foundation Corporation as a result of its advisory role to industry. In 1981 a proposal was made to extend the corporation's role to other parts of the Maritimes, in collaboration with the NEW BRUNSWICK RESEARCH AND PRODUCTIVITY COUNCIL. The corporation supports economic development in NS and elsewhere by means of technical advice and through research conducted in 4 divisions at a laboratory in Dartmouth. NSRFC has established a world reputation for research in OCEAN technology. More recent expertise involves BIOTECHNOLOGY, COAL desulphurization, and arsenic and methane removal. Developments of NSRFC's Engineering Physics Division and Centre for Ocean Technology include underwater data-acquisition systems, rare-earth magnetic couplers and multi-pass fluid rotary unions. With DALHOUSIE UNIVERSITY and TECHNICAL UNIVERSITY OF NOVA SCOTIA the council has established the Applied Microelectronics Institute to develop microelectronic marine products. NSRFC is governed by a board of scientists and industrialists, the chairman serving as president of the corporation. Total staff is about 122 people. Two-thirds of funding comes from sales and contracts to industrial and government clients; the remainder from grants. *See also* OCEAN INDUSTRY.   MARTIN K. MCNICHOLL

Nova Scotia, 1714–84 Confirmed as British by the Treaty of UTRECHT in 1713, the peninsula of NOVA SCOTIA was neglected until 1749 – a period of "phantom rule" and "counterfeit suzerainty." Since the only English inhabitants were the garrison and a few merchants at Annapolis, and fishermen and a handful of troops at Canso, the elective assembly prescribed by the governors' commissions was impracticable. The main body of inhabitants, the ACADIANS, had been given a year to take an unqualified oath of allegiance, but although they persistently refused, they were not forced to leave; instead they flourished, increasing from nearly 2000 in 1710 to more than 12 000 by 1750.

Determined to remove the danger posed by the presence of the French at LOUISBOURG on Île Royale (Cape Breton I), Gov William Shirley of Massachusetts and New England troops, with a British naval force, captured the fortress in 1745. Much to their chagrin, it was returned to the French by the Treaty of Aix-la-Chapelle in 1748. The British government decided, however, to establish a counterpoise to Louisbourg, and in June 1749 Edward CORNWALLIS with some 2500 settlers founded HALIFAX and made it the provincial capital. Over the next few years a considerable number of "foreign Protestants," largely German, also arrived, many of whom founded LUNENBURG in 1753.

On the eve of the SEVEN YEARS' WAR Gov Charles LAWRENCE sought to remove the danger presented by the French at FT BEAUSÉJOUR and by the French missionary, Abbé Jean-Louis Le Loutre, who was promoting anti-British sentiment among Acadians and MICMAC. Beauséjour fell to Lawrence's forces in June 1755, and within the next few months, after the Acadians had rejected a final ultimatum to take the oath, he deported 6000 on his own initiative. After the war some 2000 Acadians returned and resettled in the province, many in the new township of Clare. Cape Breton and PEI were annexed to Nova Scotia after the war, but the latter was separated permanently in 1769 and the former temporarily 1784-1820.

Because New Englanders in Halifax kept insisting on the "rights of Englishmen," Lawrence, on instructions from Britain, reluctantly summoned an elective assembly which met in Halifax on 2 Oct 1758, the first in what is now Canada. To fill the lands formerly occupied by the Acadians, he also issued proclamations inviting settlers. Between 1760 and 1763 alone no fewer than 4500 New Englanders entered the province. About the same time 500 Ulstermen arrived, mostly under the auspices of the adventurer Col Alexander McNutt; they were followed in 1772 and 1773 by some 1000 Yorkshiremen who settled on the Isthmus of Chignecto and in 1773 by nearly 200 Scots who settled at PICTOU (*see* HECTOR). But it was the New Englanders who laid the enduring foundations of Nova Scotia, making it, in a very real sense, a "new New England." A population of about 8000 in 1763 increased to more than 17 000 in 1775, well over half of them New Englanders.

The Expedition against Cape Breton in Nova Scotia, 1745, by an unknown artist (courtesy National Archives of Canada C-1090).

Yet the New Englanders were unable to establish some of their customary modes of self-government. Instead of town meetings they were forced to accept the undemocratic English system of local government by courts of sessions and grand juries. These institutions remained until 1879 because the province was under the rule of a Halifax merchant-official oligarchy, which dominated the COUNCIL OF TWELVE and manipulated the Assembly to serve its own interests. For a dozen years prior to 1775 this group under the leadership of Joshua MAUGER, latterly a British MP, plundered the province, secured the recall of 3 governors and defeated the well-intentioned, but inept, attempts of Gov Francis Legge to disclose their abuses.

During the AMERICAN REVOLUTION many of the province's New Englanders undoubtedly sympathized with the Americans; certainly they were as willing to trade with Massachusetts as with the British forces. But outside strongly British Halifax, Nova Scotians showed no desire to become involved, and John Bartlet BREBNER's description of them as the "neutral Yankees of Nova Scotia" is exceedingly apt. If nothing else, their existence at scattered intervals along the edges of a narrow peninsula separated by rough terrain prevented concerted, united action on their part. Except for the short-lived, ineffectual "Eddy rebellion" at Ft Cumberland, Nova Scotia remained quiet. By 1782 LOYALISTS began to arrive, the first of a large influx, which affected the province markedly and led in 1784 to the creation of New Brunswick and Cape Breton as separate provinces.

J. MURRAY BECK

Novascotian The *Novascotian* is remembered as the newspaper of Joseph HOWE and as the embodiment of its motto, "The free constitution which guards the British press." It began under George R. Young in 1824, as the *Nova Scotian or Colonial Herald*. Howe assumed control in 1827, and thereafter the weekly reflected both the intellectual awakening of Nova Scotia and Howe's evolving political thought. A letter published in the *Novascotian* in 1835 led to his famous libel trial; upon his acquittal, he announced, "the Press of Nova Scotia is free."

By 1840 his publication was the leading provincial newspaper, with 3000 subscribers. Howe's growing political involvement forced the newspaper's sale during the 1840s. Under the Annand family, it remained the voice of liberal reform. During WWI it reached a peak circulation of 20 000, as the weekly *Nova Scotian, Nova Scotia's Farm and Home Journal*. Its support of the Union Government in 1917, however, alienated its readers and it was discontinued in the mid-1920s.   LOIS KERNAGHAN

Novel in English In its first phase, from the earliest fiction writing in Canada to WWI, the novel acquired a truly Canadian voice. But the pre-Confederation period was a time far more of development than of achievement. Novels were written and published, but few had literary merit and few could be called distinctively Canadian in their subject matter or point of view. This was to be expected. The country itself was taking shape, and with it a society and a culture for the novelist to represent, analyse and judge. Colonial uncertainty is reflected in the derivativeness and poor quality of fiction in this period; yet some novels did contribute to the establishment of a tradition, and a few achieved lasting significance.

Frances BROOKE's *History of Emily Montague* (1769) is usually described, somewhat misleadingly, as the first Canadian novel. The author lived only briefly in the colony of Québec, and much of her novel is sentimental romance of the kind common in England. Brooke does, however, give some serious attention to French-English relations, the colony's future relations with Britain and the potential threat posed by the American colonies, issues that were to be prominent in later Canadian novels. Her interest in the landscape also anticipates the continuing use of Canada as an exotic setting for fiction by British novelists (eg, Frederick Marryat and R.M. Ballantyne) and by Canadians themselves.

Of more importance to the Canadian quality of Canadian fiction was the publication, in newspapers and magazines, of sketches (sometimes loosely linked as a series) and serialized novels (*see* SHORT FICTION; LITERARY MAGAZINES); some of the early work of Susanna MOODIE and Rosanna LEPROHON appeared in these forms. Many writers continued merely to imitate British models, but there were 2 notable exceptions: Thomas MCCULLOCH and Thomas Chandler HALIBURTON.

McCulloch's "Letters of Mephibosheth Stepsure" (in the *Acadian Recorder*, 1821-23), a satirically comic depiction of his Pictou, NS, neighbours, can still delight modern readers (*see* HUMOROUS WRITING).

McCulloch's work undoubtedly influenced Haliburton, the first Canadian fiction writer to achieve an international reputation. Haliburton's "Clockmaker" sketches of 1835-36 appeared in book form as *The Clockmaker; or The Sayings and Doings of Samuel Slick, of Slickville* (1836), which was instantly popular in N America and Britain. Sam Slick remains one of the great creations of the comic imagination, and served Haliburton well as a vehicle for serious investigation of his own Nova Scotia and of the growing crudity and materialism of the US. *The Old Judge* (1849) is the best of Haliburton's many other works of fiction. Haliburton for a time rivalled Charles Dickens in popularity, and he was the one major writer of fiction to appear in the pre-Confederation period; he remains important in the Canadian literary tradition.

Two other novelists of this period retain an interest for later readers. Rosanna Leprohon's "The Manor House of De Villerai" (1859-60) and *Antoinette de Mirecourt* (1864) do not avoid sentimentality and melodrama, yet in their presentation of Québec society after the British conquest they reveal a skill and a sensitivity still not fully appreciated; and although John RICHARDSON tried his hand without success at the novel of manners, when he made use of Canadian history in *Wacousta* (1832) and its sequel *The Canadian Brothers* (1840) the results revealed a powerful (if undisciplined) imagination. Both novels are marred by sentiment and melodrama, and exhibit the pervasive influence of Sir Walter Scott on writers of historical novels (with some influence as well from the American writer James Fenimore Cooper). Despite these detractions, Richardson's ability to present violent action, and his attempt to define the developing Canadian character, ensure him at least a minor place in the history of the Canadian novel.

The nationalistic and optimistic spirit following CONFEDERATION is reflected in the increasing variety and quality of Canadian novels. Several writers achieved international popularity, if not lasting literary merit; among them were May Agnes Fleming, Basil King and Margaret Marshall Saunders, whose *Beautiful Joe* (1894), a sentimental story of a dog, is reported to have sold more than one million copies in 14 languages. James DE MILLE was also a popular writer, but in *A Strange Manuscript Found in a Copper Cylinder* (1888) he produced an unusual, disturbing and still-fascinating novel. Popular novelists of this sort may seldom have written good novels; nevertheless, they demonstrate that Canadian writers were gaining an increasing confidence that they could write for audiences outside Canada.

Historical novels were also popular and often skillfully written. Charles G.D. ROBERTS produced several, as did Gilbert PARKER, but these and other novelists were seldom able to present more than the surface of the historical periods they dealt with. William KIRBY's *The Golden Dog* (1877) does penetrate the surface in its attempt to recreate and analyse the society of NEW FRANCE before its fall. Kirby may be guilty of transforming this society to produce a unifying national myth of French-English harmony, yet his knowledge and sympathy make his novel, despite its length and frequent clumsiness, live in a way that others do not.

An increased interest in representing the regions of Canada is also characteristic of the post-Confederation novel; for example, *Anne of Green Gables* (1908) and its successors by L.M. MONTGOMERY are set in Prince Edward Island; *Duncan Polite* (1905) and others by Marian Keith (Mary Esther MacGregor) in Scottish communities in southern Ontario; *The Way of the Sea* (1903) and *Doctor Luke of the Labrador* (1904) by Norman DUNCAN and *The Harbour Master* (1913) by Theodore Goodridge Roberts are set in Newfoundland and Labrador.

The opening up of Canada's West and North was also a frequent subject. Sometimes the treatments were mainly superficial and popular, as in novels by Gilbert Parker, Agnes Laut and Robert SERVICE. More valuable work was done by Ralph Connor (C.W. GORDON) in *The Sky Pilot* (1899) and *The Foreigner* (1909), and by Nellie MCCLUNG in *Sowing Seeds in Danny* (1908). While their portraits of the developing West are not free of sentimentality and obtrusive didacticism, they do show some movement towards the realistic presentation of a sense of place, a movement even more pronounced in Martin Allerdale Grainger's *Woodsmen of the West* (1908), a good novel set in BC.

Didacticism and a moralizing tone were prominent in many novels. Two writers who made serious and important attempts to combine entertainment with intellectual substance, Agnes Maule Machar (social justice, Christianity) and Lily Dougall (religious themes), had limited artistic success for this reason. The major novels of the post-Confederation period largely overcame this difficulty, achieving moral seriousness without preaching to the reader. To various degrees and in various ways these novels also integrated historical, regional, social, intellectual and international concerns.

Francis William Grey's one novel, *The Curé of St. Philippe* (1899), is both a subtly comic novel and a shrewd analysis of education, religion, politics and French-English relations in a small Québec town of the period. Robert Barr wrote many works, including an important collection of detective fiction, *The Triumphs of Eugène Valmont*

(1906), but his most successful Canadian novel, *The Measure of the Rule* (1907), is a satiric criticism of teacher training and educational theorizing, with some attention paid to the shortcomings of Toronto society at the turn of the century.

By the beginning of the 20th century the Canadian novel had moved beyond its formative period, as is evident in the best works of that period's major novelists, Sara Jeannette DUNCAN and Stephen LEACOCK. Duncan's novels, written after her successful career as a journalist, are the product of an informed and sensitive intelligence with a wide range of serious interests. *A Daughter of Today* (1894) is, until its awkward conclusion, a compelling study of the "new Woman" and the artistic temperament. *An American Girl in London* (1891), one of her "international" novels, is a comedy dealing with the differences between American and British social customs. *Cousin Cinderella* (1908), a less lively comedy, returns to this theme and adds to it by introducing the question of where Canadians stand in this relationship. *The IMPERIALIST* (1904) is set in southern Ontario, yet international themes are again prominent, presented as they impinge upon the consciousness of a Canadian town, whose society Duncan depicts and analyses with wit and skill. Duncan resided in India for almost 30 years after 1890, and her novels set there become increasingly dark in tone, from *The Simple Adventures of a Memsahib* (1893) to later works such as *His Honour, and a Lady* (1896) and *Set in Authority* (1906), which are critical of the British establishment in India and increasingly sympathetic towards the native population and its aspirations. Duncan continued to write until the 1920s, but the quality of her work after 1910 is uneven.

Leacock began his literary career by parodying, with exuberance and an underlying note of surrealistic violence, the various forms, styles and aberrations of conventional fiction. *Literary Lapses* (1910), *Nonsense Novels* (1911) and later *Frenzied Fiction* (1918) give Leacock a well-deserved international reputation as one of the great humorists in the English language. He was to write much more in this vein, often successfully, but never again did he reach the consistently high quality of this early work. Leacock's major achievements are SUNSHINE SKETCHES OF A LITTLE TOWN (1912) and *Arcadian Adventures with the Idle Rich* (1914). In the first we find a humorous presentation of the foibles and follies of the residents of a small Ontario community, with understated satire and criticism directed at social pretension, materialism, urbanization and politics. The second book is overtly satiric, as its title suggests, but much less filled with sunshine. The idle rich and their hangers-on have no redeeming qualities, and Leacock offers no consolation to his readers poised on the brink of a world war that was to have far-reaching consequences for Canada.

DAVID JACKEL

Novel in English, WWI-1959

At the end of WWI, the self-confidence engendered by Canada's role in the war brought an upsurge of NATIONALISM which included a renewed interest in a national literature. Between 1920 and 1940, 700 works of fiction were published by Canadians. While the popular genres of mystery, adventure and romance continued to flourish, Canadian writers showed themselves to be aware of the progress made in fiction by such writers as Dreiser, Joyce and Woolf. The first important development in Canada after the war was the advent of realism, heralded in Prairie fiction. Novels recorded the life of the homesteader with increasing fidelity to experience; writers tended less and less to romanticize or

idealize either landscape or life. The prolific Arthur STRINGER bridges the earlier and later periods of the Prairie novel, stylistically as well as chronologically, with his Alberta trilogy *The Prairie Wife* (1915), *The Prairie Mother* (1920) and *The Prairie Child* (1922). Robert Stead's *Neighbours* (1922) and *The Smoking Flax* (1924) most obviously demonstrate the move toward realism, although plot lines and occasional melodramatic incidents continue the romantic trend.

With Stead's *Grain* (1926), and with the publication in 1925 of the first novels of Martha OSTENSO and Frederick Philip GROVE, realism in Prairie fiction was firmly established. Ostenso's *Wild Geese* vividly depicts the harshness of life in a homesteading community, but its central figure is the romantic villain Caleb Gare, whose lust to possess the land causes him to enslave his family and eventually destroys him. Grove followed his first novel, *Settlers of the Marsh*, with 3 more Prairie novels: *Our Daily Bread* (1928), *The Yoke of Life* (1930) and FRUITS OF THE EARTH (1933). Although his patriarchal heroes often succeed in their struggle against nature, they are inevitably brought to see that their success is ephemeral.

The strong regional consciousness of these authors characterized much Canadian fiction, as writers portrayed the impact of environment on character and on human relationships (*see* REGIONALISM IN LITERATURE). While realism was developing, the popular romantic tradition continued in Prairie fiction, presenting a more optimistic view of pioneer life, as in Laura Goodman SALVERSON's *The Viking Heart* (1923), a novel about Icelandic settlers. Frederick NIVEN, after writing several successful novels about his native Scotland, traced the historical development of the Prairies in an accurate and entertaining trilogy: *The Flying Years* (1935), *Mine Inheritance* (1940) and *The Transplanted* (1944). The romantic tradition continued with W.O. MITCHELL's WHO HAS SEEN THE WIND (1947), the story of a child growing up on the Prairies. The wind provides the central, unifying symbol of the boy's attempt to comprehend the spiritual world.

Thomas RADDALL's historical novels of Nova Scotia are among the best popular fiction. *His Majesty's Yankees* (1942) and *The Nymph and the Lamp* (1950) are lively, exciting and historically accurate. But the outstanding popular success of the period was MAZO DE LA ROCHE'S JALNA series (1927-60). Set in rural Ontario, the series continued through 16 sentimental novels characterized by lively dialogue, dramatic incidents and memorable characters. The Jalna books continue to be read throughout the world.

Meanwhile, other Ontario writers were, like their Prairie contemporaries, producing realistic fiction. Raymond KNISTER, author of some of the best and most experimental short stories of the 1920s and some of Canada's earliest modernist poetry, wrote what is possibly the first realistic novel of rural Ontario, *White Narcissus* (1929). Knister used elements of the landscape as symbols reflecting the emotions of his protagonist, whose journey from city back to farm becomes a journey of self-discovery.

With the novels of Morley CALLAGHAN, urban realism became firmly established. Callaghan's early novels, *Strange Fugitive* (1928), *It's Never Over* (1930) and *A Broken Journey* (1932), incorporate deterministic elements: characters often appear to be victims of forces beyond their control. Callaghan writes in a deceptively simple, economical style which changed very little when he turned to a more Christian outlook in his next 3 novels: SUCH IS MY BELOVED (1934), portraying a priest's loving attempt to save 2 prostitutes; *They Shall Inherit the Earth* (1935), a father-son conflict set against the backdrop of the Great Depression; and *More Joy in Heaven* (1937), the story of a reformed bank robber misunderstood by society. In these novels the saint figure stands in opposition to society, as it does in the later *The Loved and the Lost* (1951), in which Callaghan's style softens and he effectively uses myth and symbol.

The optimism following WWI disappeared with the onset of the Great Depression. Fewer novels were published and fewer read. Some novelists attempted to record the disillusionment of the time and the best fictional record of social protest is West Coast journalist Irene Baird's *Waste Heritage* (1939), a documentary novel of Vancouver and Victoria in 1938. The desperation of the time in the urban areas of eastern Canada is reflected in Callaghan's early novels and stories. Hugh GARNER's *Cabbagetown* (1950) is a later account of growing up in a Depression slum in Toronto. Sinclair ROSS's first novel, AS FOR ME AND MY HOUSE (1941), and some of his earlier short stories give the best fictional record of the Prairies of the Depression years.

With *As For Me and My House*, the atmosphere of a particular time and place and its influence on the human spirit received a newly sophisticated and imaginative treatment. In this novel of a minister and his wife trapped in a puritanical Prairie town, Ross exploits the setting and its impact on the psyche to voice such modern concerns as alienation, the failure of communication, the problem of the imagination and the search for meaning in an incomprehensible universe. The outer world mirrors the inner state. In the next decade, Ernest BUCKLER wrote *The Mountain and the Valley* (1952), set in the Annapolis Valley of Nova Scotia. Buckler's complex symbolism and sensuous, richly textured language create a pastoral world through which he voices his themes of isolation and the problem of the imagination.

Hugh MACLENNAN, the best-known Canadian novelist of the 1940s and 1950s, began writing as a post-Depression surge of nationalism swept Canada. In 1941, with the publication of *Barometer Rising*, MacLennan began chronicling the Canadian psyche. Set in 1917, with its focal point the HALIFAX EXPLOSION, this novel explores Canada's developing national spirit. MacLennan's second novel, TWO SOLITUDES (1945), deals with the English-French relations in Canada through 2 generations, from WWI to the beginning of WWII. When *The Precipice* (1948), less overtly Canadian, was less successful, MacLennan returned to his role as spokesman for the national spirit. *Each Man's Son* (1951), set in a Nova Scotia mining town, dramatizes the Calvinistic puritanism which is seen to pervade much of Canadian life. *The Watch that Ends the Night* (1959), which has received the most critical acclaim, is more expansive. The age-old love triangle is acted out in a Canadian milieu, involving an introspective man, a spiritually strong artistic woman and a larger-than-life man of action. In this work, as in his earlier novels, MacLennan excels in both description and narration, while his weaknesses are lengthy explanations and stilted dialogue.

WWII became the subject for a number of novels. Among the best are Hugh Garner's *Storm Below* (1949), a story of 6 days on a Canadian corvette; Earle BIRNEY's *Turvey* (1949), a humorous look at army life; Colin McDougall's *Execution* (1958), an appallingly realistic account of Canadian combatants on the Italian front; and David WALKER's *The Pillar* (1952), based on his experiences as a prisoner of war. Walker, who immigrated to Canada after the war, produced a variety of successful novels, many of which, including the broadly humorous *Geordie* (1950),

are set in his native Scotland. His first novel with a Canadian setting, *Where the High Winds Blow* (1960), is a well-written romance and adventure story of the opening up of the North, with an entrepreneurial hero who is equally at home in northern wilderness and southern civilization.

The immigrant experience continued to be a major theme. Joining Walker, Grove, Salverson and Niven was Henry KREISEL, the Jewish-Austrian author of *The Rich Man* (1948), the story of an immigrant to Toronto who pretends to be wealthy when he visits his family in Vienna; and the more complex *Betrayal* (1964). John Marlyn's *Under the Ribs of Death* (1957) describes the struggle for material success of a Hungarian immigrant's son. Brian MOORE, who spent 14 years in Canada before moving to the US, wrote a moving, intense novel of a Belfast spinster, *The Lonely Passion of Judith Hearne* (1955), and a perceptive and entertaining novel of an Irish immigrant in Montréal, *The Luck of Ginger Coffey* (1960). Malcolm LOWRY, the most celebrated of our temporary residents, completed *Under the Volcano* (1947) and wrote *October Ferry to Gabriola* (1970) in Canada. *Under the Volcano* is brilliant, a complex novel which uses cinematic techniques, cabalistic and theosophical symbolism, myth and unusual metaphors to tell of the last 12 hours in the life of an alcoholic.

The Jewish immigrant experience was told by a number of voices. Mordecai RICHLER's *Son of a Smaller Hero* (1955) and *The* APPRENTICESHIP OF DUDDY KRAVITZ (1959) portray the third generation of a family of Jewish immigrants in Montréal. Kravitz is a picaresque hero whose story is told in an exuberantly written social satire employing broadly humorous dialogue. Adele WISEMAN's *The Sacrifice* (1956) is the tragic story of a Jewish-Ukrainian immigrant's attempt to cope with a new world and yet to live according to his own tradition. His own tragedy is mitigated by the hope of a good future for his grandson.

While realism and regionalism became increasingly sophisticated, several fine experimental writers moved further from the traditional use of the elements of the novel to produce symbolic, lyrical, fragmented narrative. Howard O'HAGAN's *Tay John* (1939) is based on an Indian legend of a golden-haired child who emerges from the grave of a pregnant woman and is last seen disappearing into the earth. The novel begins with the legend and blends mythical with realistic narrative in an episodic structure. In the 1940s F.P. Grove turned from realism to more innovative techniques. *The* MASTER OF THE MILL (1944) is a futuristic novel dealing with the complexities of industrial society and the problems of automation. The narrative method is complex, involving flashbacks of the protagonist, a manuscript written by another character and the recollections of others. In *Consider Her Ways* (1947), Grove based his story of the ant world on scientific fact and used his ant characters to satirize humanity.

Elizabeth SMART's remarkable lyrical novel, *By Grand Central Station I Sat Down and Wept* (1945), was first published in England and received scant attention in Canada until a N American edition appeared in 1975. The novel explores the dualities of experience, especially the pain and pleasure of love, through paradoxical structures. The plot is minimal; the setting takes on the texture of imagery and becomes an adjunct to emotional expression. Sheila WATSON's *The* DOUBLE HOOK (1959) also explores the dualities of experience. Watson describes her characters as "figures in a ground from which they could not be separated." The novel is a mythical and allegorical exploration of the interconnections between good and evil, and of the redemption of a community to love. Poet A.M. KLEIN turned to fiction to tell the

story of the return of the Jews to the Promised Land. In *The Second Scroll* (1951), he presents a pattern of Jewish exile and return parallel to that in the First Scroll (the Torah) to recount the Jews' return to Israel after WWII. Like the Torah, *The Second Scroll* includes glosses, which take the form of poetry, drama, a prayer and an excerpt from a letter. The novel's central religious theme demonstrates man losing and finding God, and grapples with the problem of the existence of evil.

Ethel Wilson's 4 novels and 2 novelettes, published in less than 10 years, are among the best crafted and most subtly expressed of Canadian fictional works. Wilson's strong sense of place links her to realistic writers. Her style is marked by clarity, economy, deceptive simplicity, unobtrusive imagery and the acute observation of people. Her complex world view includes an awareness of life's ironies, of the interplay of chance and Providence. John Donne's "No man is an Iland," the epigraph to her first novel, *Hetty Dorval* (1947), is central to Wilson's view of life. SWAMP ANGEL (1954), possibly Wilson's best novel, presents in Maggie Lloyd a convincing character who leaves an impossible marriage to forge a new life for herself.

Among the novelists of note whose careers in fiction began in the 1950s and continued through the 1980s is Robertson DAVIES, who first made his mark as a dramatist and journalist. The satire central to his Samuel Marchbanks essays characterizes his Salteron trilogy, *Tempest-Tost* (1951), *Leaven of Malice* (1954) and *A Mixture of Frailties* (1958), in which snobbishness, materialism and hypocrisy are satirized.

The hero took on various guises through the 40 years of fiction writing following WWI. In accord with the shift in action from the external to the internal world, the strong, confident, at times patriarchal or even epic hero of some early novels of the period (eg, Abe Spalding of Grove's *Fruits of the Earth*) soon gave way to the more introspective, less confident protagonist (eg, Philip Bentley, the uncertain, guilt-ridden minister of Ross's *As For Me and My House*; David Canaan, the frustrated artist of Buckler's *The Mountain and the Valley*; and the intellectual George Stewart of MacLennan's *The Watch that Ends the Night*). The antihero who ruthlessly manipulates others makes an occasional appearance, as in Richler's Duddy Kravitz. Yet a further shift in the concept of the hero can be noted in Wilson's Maggie Lloyd. Self-reliant and courageous, but sensitive and loving, Maggie is the forerunner of the strong female characters created by the outstanding women writers of the 1960s and 1970s.

Some of the literary trends and techniques which began in the 1940s and 1950s came to fruition only in the 1960s and 1970s, and many of the writers continue to write some of the best-known and most highly regarded novels. Canadian novelists who began their careers in the 1960s and 1970s looked back to such writers as Ross, Grove and Wilson for examples of the possibilities for artistic response to their own particular place and time. Post-modernists have their forerunners in Watson, Smart and Lowry.

LORRAINE MCMULLEN

Novel in English, 1959-1980s

The years following 1959 marked the flowering of the novel in Canada, for in these years, as writers began to explore more fully the formal possibilities of the genre, they at last won public recognition both inside and outside Canada. Canadian novels became Book of the Month Club selections in the US; major American and British magazines published Canadian fiction; the size of press runs often increased tenfold; and translations abounded of novels by Leonard COHEN, Margaret ATWOOD, Robertson Davies and many others. At home, Canada also managed to generate commercially viable popular fiction. Much of this intensified activity was the result of the long campaign to create a literary community in Canada, a campaign that grew out of the economic and cultural nationalism of the period. Government support of the arts (see CANADA COUNCIL) played major roles in the financial and psychological development of a cultural climate that made Canadian literature blossom. New SMALL PRESSES proliferated, often established to champion experimental or noncommercial novels that would otherwise perhaps be unpublishable.

Since the novel form is usually closely tied to the social background of its time and place of production, the changes occurring during the 25 years after 1960 in Canada played their part in the changes appearing in the fiction of the period. The 1960s were years of relative plenty that seemed to free young people from worry about immediate need and allowed them to turn their attention to broader social concerns. These were the years of confrontational politics and of the challenging of accepted norms. The retrenchment in later years of conservative middle-class values in the face of economic recession was likely a predictable response to the antiestablishment, iconoclastic counterculture of the 1960s. Many of the writers of the 1970s and the 1980s, however, were "formed," intellectually and ideologically, by those earlier years. Many, such as Atwood, Timothy FINDLEY and Rudy WIEBE, saw their role as that of a conscience or even a voice for the oppressed. In 1981 Canadian writers actively participated in Amnesty International's "Writer and Human Rights" Congress in Toronto. But the oppressed to whom novelists gave a voice were not necessarily victims of external political tyranny; they often suffered more local oppression, by what could be called bourgeois values. For many Canadian novelists, such as John METCALF (General Ludd, 1980) and Michael Charters, metaphors of madness acted as the focus for attacks on the social and psychological labels which serve to control misfits who transgress the often unacknowledged norms of middle-class behaviour.

These themes were not, of course, unique to Canadian writers. Novels from Canada shared with those of other Western nations a concern for those staples of the novelistic tradition, social analysis and psychological investigation, along with a new emphasis on the role and status of women. *Bildungsroman* (stories of growing up) continued to be written, by novelists such as Clark BLAISE (*Lunar Attractions*, 1979), Keith Maillard, Alice MUNRO (*Lives of Girls and Women*, 1971) and Alden NOWLAN (*Various Persons Named Kevin O'Brien*, 1973) among others. Canadian fiction increasingly showed signs of breaking away from the conventions of realism. Reflexivity (the concern within a work to speak of the creative process itself) became prominent. This may have been a result of the increasing desire of writers – many of them academics – to deal openly with the technical aspects of their art; or it may have arisen from an increasing engagement with structuralism in linguistics, anthropology and theories of communication, including those of Harold INNIS and Marshall MCLUHAN.

While taking part in the international literary trends, the Canadian novel also revealed a continuity with its own past, with its regional roots and its tradition of treating minority groups as more than just local colour – obvious reflections of the geographic and ethnic diversity of the country. Writers who had established their reputations earlier continued to publish (eg, Hugh MacLennan, *Voices in Time*, 1980; Morley Callaghan, *A Time for Judas*, 1983). However, most important during these years was the emergence of a number of significant new voices. This phenomenon was remarkable in both its quantity and quality.

Regional writing in Canada had never been provincial, although it had tended to balance the natural novelistic attraction toward the exotic. After 1959 many Canadian writers – among them Margaret LAURENCE, David Knight, Audrey THOMAS and David GODFREY – used as settings Africa and Europe, but they did so either as analogues that enabled them to comment implicitly upon their own culture, or as the source of new perspectives that allowed them to see Canada more clearly. Writers who anchored their works in a specifically Canadian geography followed the tradition, established and continued by Prairie writers, of making the landscape both real and symbolic, both local and universal. Canadian fiction in general was spatially oriented around 2 opposing *topoi:* the city and the country. Urban novels by Juan Butler (*Cabbagetown Diary*, 1970), John Buell (*The Pyx*, 1959), Hugh Garner and others were frequently both realistic accounts of the corroding violence and alienation of the modern city and symbolic representations of the infernal "Unreal City" of T.S. Eliot's "The Waste Land."

At the other extreme were the idyllic or nostalgic descriptions of small towns and their rural environs. More often, however, these small communities became symbolic microcosms, this time of a limited and limiting society: Alice Munro's Jubilee, Robertson Davies's Deptford, Matt CO-HEN's Salem, Margaret Laurence's Manawaka, David Adams Richard's Miramichi Valley. The land – often in the form of the family farm – continued to be regarded ambivalently, as both man's essential roots and his major burden. Frequently the land was connected more to a temporal than to a spatial dimension: it was here that characters either searched for their collective or individual past or rejected its haunting authority. The Canadian wilderness also became the subject, as well as the setting, of fiction in modes ranging from the metaphoric to the ecological.

There was a similar double interpretive pull (toward the symbolic and toward the documentary) in the portrayal of minority groups in Canadian fiction. During these years, there was a greater interest in native Indian and Inuit literature, particularly in memoirs and collections of myths and folktales. Middle-class white Canadian novelists such as W.O. Mitchell, Rudy Wiebe, Wayland Drew and James HOUSTON evinced an increased respect for native culture and a desire to learn from it.

Many immigrant groups became the foci of attention of Canadian novelists: Jewish (Adele Wiseman, Jack Ludwig, Mordecai Richler), Japanese (Joy KOGAWA), Mennonite (Rudy Wiebe), West Indian (Austin CLARKE, Harold Sonny Ladoo), and so on. These novels often consisted of commentaries on social problems experienced by immigrants to Canada, frequently mixed with suggestions that the newcomers could also be seen as symbolic of the alien and the separate in each individual.

Both of these interpretations were also to be found in the gay literature of Jane RULE (*The Young in One Another's Arms*, 1977) and Scott Symons. Leonard Cohen's BEAUTIFUL LOSERS (1966) was perhaps the archetype of the challenge to sexual mores (and literary forms) of the 1960s, and with that challenge came the questioning of sexual roles in general. Although men such as Ian McLachlan and David HELWIG also wrote of these issues, feminism as an ideology tended to be the domain of female writers. Canadian writing by women about women partook of the general radicalization of the time, of the desire to right the balance, as feminist literature everywhere was attempting to do. In English Canada there was little of the more abstract Québecois interest in defining a new female discourse. Instead, an awareness of feminist issues became part of the overt themes of fiction whose aim ranged from objective documentation of the condition of women to virulent attack on the causes of repression. While remaining engaged or committed, the feminist novels of writers like Constance BERESFORD-HOWE (*The Book of Eve*, 1973), Marian ENGEL (*Bear*, 1976), Carol SHIELDS (*Small Ceremonies*, 1976), Aritha Van Herk (*Judith*, 1978) and Doris Anderson (*Two Women*, 1975) allowed for a variety of tones and styles, from the thoughtful and worried through to the angry and strident.

Given the didactic stance behind many of these novels, it is not surprising to find certain formal, as well as thematic, constants. In an attempt to redress the balance of characterization in a traditionally male literary form, feminist novelists tended either to idealize women characters or to present them as pure victims of masculine domination. Male characters, as a result, were often caricatured or else had their roles reduced to the skeletal ones usually reserved for women in novels that have men as heroes. The major themes of these novels centered on the experience of women, especially in relation to power structures (on all levels). There was an intense awareness of the relationship between bonding and bondage, ie, between a woman's need for connection with others and her equally strong need for freedom and independence, a theme that made feminist novels political in the broadest sense.

However, the concern with power and victimization was not restricted to this one context. Following the lead of Québec writers of the 1960s, English Canadian novelists too became more politicized. Some focused on specific events (the OCTOBER CRISIS of 1970) or situations (federalism versus separatism). Others – David Lewis Stein, Margaret Atwood and many more – investigated the tension between social or political structures and the individual psyche. Again the stylistic and tonal range was great – from the irony of Richard Wright to the bitter satire of Leo Simpson to the sometimes ponderous earnestness of Peter Such – as *homo canadensis* confronted the forces of corporate, consumer, industrial and technological society. Ian McLachlan and Timothy Findley included in this kind of investigation a study of the role of art in such a society and the ideological implications of its involvement or its alienation.

Many novels in Canada – those by Robert Harlow, Graeme GIBSON, Helen Weinzweig, Robert KROETSCH and Ray Smith – could be seen as part of the general literary movement that has been labelled "postmodernism," for they too exhibited an increased self-consciousness about the creative processes. This immanent concern for their reception and interpretation prevented them from being merely introverted and precious. Their self-representation in form became a means of investigating the politics of how and why we read, as well as a way of focusing on the literary materials themselves: language and narrative. This increased interest in form may be due to the number of poets who turned to writing fiction during these years: Cohen, Atwood, George Bowering, bp Nichol, Gwendolyn MAC-EWEN and Michael ONDAATJE among others. Another possibility suggests itself in the role of the university in Canadian letters during these years: many of the novelists were either professors (eg, Graham Petrie, Anthony Brennan, Tom Marshall, Robert Kroetsch, etc) or writers-in-residence. Besides increasing formal awareness and experimentation, this institutionalization also produced many academic novels, ranging from satiric cuts at the intellectual community to rather boring *romans à clef*.

Postmodernist, reflexive fiction in Canada appeared to organize itself around 2 new formal traditions: the written chronicle and the oral tale. On the one hand, there was almost an obsession with the written product of history as something fixed and fixing. Munro, Ondaatje, Kroetsch, Findley and others frequently used photographic images to signal this thematic pole. On the other hand, they looked to metaphors of music, film and tape recording to express the opposite pole, that of the storytelling process. Often other oral traditions were called upon: African (David Godfrey, in *The New Ancestors*, 1970), Indian (Rudy Wiebe, in *The Temptations of Big Bear*, 1973), and Irish (Jack HODGINS, in *The Resurrection of Joseph Bourne*, 1979). Perhaps these 2 poles reflected the legacy of Marshall McLuhan, for whom oral cultures were collective, simultaneous, auditory and oriented toward the present, while written cultures were individual, signed, linear, visual and under the control of the past. Yet even those novels positively stressing an oral tradition themselves only existed as written, individual, signed works. It was this consciousness of the oral-written tension that marked the peculiarly Canadian brand of literary postmodernism, which had as a by-product a reawakening of interest in myth and fantasy.

Contemporaneous with these self-conscious experimental novels was a more generally accessible body of popular fiction. Publishers such as MCCLELLAND AND STEWART retained their commitment to "serious" fiction, but the economic situation demanded as well that local mass-market sales (traditionally American) be somehow diverted to Canada. Just as Canadians came to realize that good comic novels and fine children's books were being produced right at home, they became aware too of the local popular fiction.

POPULAR LITERATURE is generally regarded as light entertainment and therefore as literature which confirms rather than challenges the reader's beliefs, usually by relying on more or less preformulated verbal and narrative structures. Often, following (or hoping to entice) television and movie scripts, popular novels provided information about a sector of contemporary society (such as drug dealing in William Deverell's novels). Frequently, this format was combined with the conventions of the thriller. Canadian novelists, however, also produced other forms of popular literature, from the detective story to historical fiction to soft-core pornographic melodrama, and the quality of the writing varied considerably. Forms of popular fiction were also incorporated into more serious postmodernist novels. This could be seen either as a cultural democratization of the high/low art split, or just as a source of parodic satire. Some novels used the gothic romance (Atwood's *Lady Oracle*, 1976) or the western (Kroetsch's *The Studhorse Man*, 1969), while others turned to comic books or Hollywood movies (*Beautiful Losers*).

Since 1959 Canada has been able not only to enjoy the consolidation of the renown of successful writers of earlier decades, but to continue with ease the process of forming an ever-growing literary canon. In the 1960s were firmly established the reputations of Margaret Laurence, Robertson Davies and Mordecai Richler; in the 1970s those of Alice Munro, Rudy Wiebe, Robert Kroetsch, Jack Hodgins, Timothy Findley and Margaret Atwood. The fact that such a short list as this is embarrassingly insufficient is ample testimony to the variety, richness and high quality of recent Canadian fiction.   LINDA HUTCHEON

Reading: M. Atwood, *Survival* (1972); F. Davey, *From There to Here* (1974); M. Fee and R. Cawker, *Canadian Fiction* (1976); N. Frye, *The Bush Garden* (1971); W.H. New, *Articulating West* (1972) and, ed, *Fiction in the Seventies* (Special Issue of *Canadian Literature* 92, spring 1982); G. Woodcock, ed, *The Sixties* (1969) and, ed, *The Canadian Novel in the Twentieth Century* (1975).

Novel in French Although the Québec novel was born in the turbulent days preceding the REBELLIONS OF 1837, it bore no trace of those events. Instead, it fictionalized real-life incidents (François-Réal Angers, *Les Révélations du crime ou Cambray et ses complices*, July 1837; tr *The Canadian Brigand*, 1867) or claimed kinship with Victor Hugo while borrowing heavily from the heritage of anecdotes, tales and legends (Philippe AUBERT DE GASPÉ, Jr, *L'Influence d'un livre*, 1837). With *Les Fiancés de 1812* (1844) by Joseph DOUTRE, the novel became resolutely Canadien and adventure oriented. The first part of *Une de perdue, deux de trouvées* (1849-51) by Georges Boucher de Boucherville was along these lines and led the way for the serialized novel which was developed by Henri-Émile Chevalier ("La Jolie Fille du faubourg Québec," 1854). The French authors of such serials (Alexandre Dumas, père, Eugène Sue, Frédéric Soulié) continued to be read, but the adventure story gave way to the rustic novel. *La Terre paternelle* (1846) by Patrice Lacombe had the shape of a long short story and a clear message: one must not give up the family land or leave it for the city. Pierre-Joseph-Olivier CHAUVEAU (*Charles Guérin*) fell first under the influence of Honoré de Balzac (1846) and then turned to the theme of settling the land. Antoine GÉRIN-LAJOIE developed this theme in *Jean Rivard, le défricheur* (1862; tr *Jean Rivard*, 1977) and *Jean Rivard, économiste* (1864), in which his hero, who had left college in order to homestead, established a new parish in just a few years. Rivard became a role model whose example was preached, off and on, until the middle of the 20th century. The historical novel emphasized the moral grandeur of the vanquished of 1760 (Philippe AUBERT DE GASPÉ, Sr, *Les Anciens Canadiens*, 1863; tr *Canadians of Old*, 1890), who, having fallen heroically before their opponents, nonetheless preserved their French soul, language and traditions. In *Jacques et Marie* (1865-66), Napoléon BOURASSA paid homage to the courage of the deportees of 1755 from ACADIA (lovers lose track of each other and then, after long periods of wandering, are reunited).

The best novels of the late 19th century (1866-95) are historical. Though Québecois read a great deal of Walter Scott and James Fenimore Cooper, authors such as Joseph Marmette (*François de Bienville*, 1870) and Laure Conan (the pseudonym of Félicité ANGERS) were more strongly influenced by François-Xavier GARNEAU, whose *Histoire du Canada* (tr *History of Canada*, 1860) began to appear in 1845, and by puritanical and conservative literary critic Henri-Raymond CASGRAIN. Marmette knew the historical material well but constructed his novels awkwardly, whereas Conan, the first female Québec novelist, knew better than previous writers how to develop complex characterizations (*A L'Oeuvre et à l'épreuve*, 1891, tr *The Master Motive*, 1909; *L'Oublié*, 1900). She undoubtedly owed her success to the experience she gained with *Angéline de Montbrun* (1881-82; tr 1975), considered to have been the first psychological novel written in Québec. Jules-Paul TARDIVEL moved forward in history rather than back: his nationalistic *Pour la patrie* (1895; tr 1975) was set in 1945, at a moment when French Canadians, after difficult political struggles, were finally about to win their own French and Catholic state.

At the turn of the century, rustic novels were revived, at first in rather weary form by Ernest Choquette (*Claude Paysan*, 1899; *La Terre*, 1916) but then more confidently by Damase Potvin (*Restons chez nous*, 1908). However, it was a Frenchman, Louis HÉMON, who brought the genre to full flower. Readers were deeply moved by his MARIA CHAPDELAINE (tr 1973), which appeared in a French newspaper in Paris in 1914 and then in book form in Québec in 1916. In 1921, in France, this novel began its long international career: today, it is still the best known of all Québec works. Though it is criticized for its myopic view of Québec as a land of tillers of the soil where nothing has changed or should ever change, the impressionistic realism of *Maria Chapdelaine* nonetheless forced writers to modernize their style and to observe their fellow citizens with more care. At about the same time (1918), *La Scouine* appeared discreetly – only 60 copies, privately printed. Albert Laberge divided his stark, unrelievedly sombre tale of a Québec farmer into 33 remarkably concise tableaus, all written in a style reminiscent of Émile Zola. This novel was rediscovered in 1958 and was translated as *Bitter Bread* in 1977. The rustic novel reached its culmination in 1938 with TRENTE ARPENTS (tr *Thirty Acres*, 1940) by Ringuet (pseudonym of Philippe PANNETON). Here the land, which in the 19th century had been viewed as society's salvation, no longer supported its master: these were the days of economic crisis, industrialization was occurring and rural people were being drawn to the city. Novels celebrating the cult of the soil were no longer written in Québec, except for the excellent *Le* SURVENANT (1945; tr *The Outlander*, 1950) by Germaine GUÈVREMONT, a kind of poetic revival of the genre.

The historical novel knew a similar kind of evolution into the 20th century. Robert Laroque de Roquebrune published *Les Habits rouges* (1923), a tale of the early revolutionary events of 1837, and *D'un océan à l'autre* (1924), a history of Canada's expansion westward in the days of Louis RIEL (1869-85). Alain Grandbois produced a book with a unique style, *Né à Québec...* (1933; tr *Born in Quebec*, 1964), a poetic prose account of the life of explorer Louis JOLLIET that displayed the gifts of this future poet to their best advantage. Léo-Paul DESROSIERS somewhat more prosaically recounted the early 19th-century FUR TRADE battles; his *Les Engagés du grand portage* (tr *The Making of Nicolas Montour*, 1978) was the most beautifully realized of all Québec historical novels. Even so, although Desrosiers was praised for his technique, reservations were expressed about the too neat, antithetical opposition of his characters, Nicolas Montour, the totally unscrupulous adventurer, and Louison Turenne, the flawlessly honest voyageur. This was the last of the tradition; the few historical novels that occasionally appeared thereafter were decidedly mediocre.

The historical novel had been the favoured art form of literary nationalism. Almost invariably, authors stressed the moral virtue of French Canadian and Acadian characters and the treacherous nature of Anglo-Saxon ones. Sometimes a few of the latter had redeeming qualities, or were even thoroughly good, but they rarely, if ever, triumphed over their Canadien counterparts. The rustic novels offered a more subtle version of the same approach. This accounts for the survival, well into the 20th century, of the Tardivel-style nationalistic novel. It takes a more refined form in *L'Appel de la race* (1922) by Lionel GROULX, a more poetic form in MENAUD MAÎTRE-DRAVEUR (1937; tr *Master of the River*, 1976) of Félix-Antoine SAVARD. *L'Appel de la race* is set against the background of the Franco-Ontarians' struggle for the right to French-language education: the race that thought itself superior was pitted against the race that *was* superior, both in the public drama and within the family, for the father had had the misfortune to marry an Anglophone. The original version of *Menaud maître-draveur* was a highly coloured epic in the Claudelian manner. Strangers come to the land of Maria Chapdelaine intending to seize its riches for themselves; Menaud, an old raftsman, undertakes the defence of his people, but the combat is illusory for the strangers remain invisible, a kind of gangrenous presence silently devouring an entire people. Menaud goes mad and his madness is a warning: death is on its way. And so it was, but it was only the death of a certain kind of nationalism.

The psychological novel slowly developed as characters began to escape the usual stereotypes. Its progress can be traced from *Angéline de Montbrun* to *Un Homme et son péché* (1933) by Claude-Henri GRIGNON. A great reader of Balzac, Grignon drew, in all simplicity, the portrait of an avaricious peasant. Radio and then television turned Séraphin Poudrier into a new stereotype and he became the best-known fictional character in Québec. Rex Desmarchais, who read Maurice Barrès and Paul Bourget, pushed character analysis a step further (*L'Initiatrice*, 1932; *Le Feu intérieur*, 1933), but his novels were weak and it was only when the work of French writer François Mauriac began influencing authors in the 1940s that good psychological novels began to appear. Even so, Desmarchais helped break ground that encouraged his successors to be more daring. They were able to free themselves from the narrow morality which had so hindered the development of the Québec novel and demand that their works be judged purely on aesthetic grounds. The novel of social criticism had great difficulty establishing itself, and for the same reason: only morality tales won the approval of the religious-literary institution, only conformist novels won that of the ecclesiastical-political establishment. In 1934, for example, an archbishop condemned Jean-Charles HARVEY's *Les Demi-Civilisés* (tr *Sackcloth for Banner*, 1938). The novel was poorly structured and badly written, but it had the luck to criticize hypocrisy at an opportune moment and it sold well. The great works in this field did not appear for another decade.

In 1938 the Québec novel was 100 years old. It was the expression of a people who had maintained their rural mentality despite the urbanization of the past 20 years and it had just produced its greatest examples of the 3 genres that its authors and readers collectively endorsed: the rustic novel (*Trente Arpents*, 1938), the historical novel (*Les Engagés du grand portage*, 1938) and the nationalist novel (*Menaud, maître-draveur*, 1937). WWII would stimulate the move to the cities and exposure to the outside world; the individual would escape somewhat from the supervision of the authorities; and writers from the traditional ideologies, especially nationalism, freer than in earlier days, would move further away from the traditional ideologies. The novel changed its orientation, and thus came to know the city and the individual.

RENÉ DIONNE

Novel in French, 1940-60

Some 300 narrative works (novels, personal accounts, collections of stories) were published in Québec between 1940 and 1960 – a total equal to the production of the entire preceding century and large enough to contain a respectable number of enduring works. In fiction, this 20-year period saw significant diversification of subject matter, notable improvement in technique and much greater psychological depth. The long tradition of the novel of the soil came to a beautiful end with the publication of Ger-

maine Guèvremont's *Le Survenant* and *Marie-Didace* (1945, 1947; tr together as *Monk's Reach*, 1950). These books presented the day-to-day life of the people of Chenal du Moine at the turn of the century in a serene and realistic way, free of moralizing overtones. Yet they are more properly classified with the 1930s, kindred spirits to Ringuet's *Trente Arpents* (1938), whereas Ringuet himself, after the *Héritage* stories (1946), turned his attention to city dwellers with *Fausse Monnaie* (1947) and *Le Poids du jour* (1949).

The WWII years, which followed the GREAT DEPRESSION and increasing industrialization, changed the country's social and demographic realities to produce an urban world soon reflected in the mirror of fiction. Roger LEMELIN pioneered with his vivid, satirical account of life in a working-class Québec City neighbourhood, *Au pied de la pente douce* (1944; tr *The Town Below*, 1948). His very similar *Les Plouffe* (1948; tr *The Plouffe Family*, 1950) was followed by the uneven *Fantaisies sur les péchés capitaux* (1949) and then, in an abrupt change of pace, by the extravagant adventures of *Pierre le magnifique* (1952; tr *In Quest of Splendour*, 1955).

International acclaim greeted Gabrielle ROY's great novel of urban life, *Bonheur d'occasion* (1945; tr *The Tin Flute*, 1947) in which the moving story of Florentine and her poverty-stricken family was deftly set against the backdrop of Montréal's Saint-Henri district in early 1940 and a world at war. Roy excelled in her presentation of physical and social space but she was most interested in the psychological development of the individual and her grasp of it was deep and sure. Her subsequent works displayed her talents to the full – in the semiautobiographical *La Petite Poule d'eau* (1950; tr *Where Nests the Water Hen*, 1951), *Rue Deschambault* (1955; tr *Street of Riches*, 1957), and *Alexandre Chenevert* (1954; tr *The Cashier*, 1955), her touching story of a Montréal bank clerk tortured by metaphysical anguish and physical illness, who nonetheless arrives at a certain kind of personal peace and happiness.

The novel of psychological introspection first appeared during this period. In *Ils posséderont la terre* (1941), Robert CHARBONNEAU tried to maintain the autonomy of his adolescent characters even as he wrote about their lives and destinies, thereby respecting the principle he later developed in his essay *Connaissance du personnage* (1944), one of the era's few published theories on the art of the novel. The austerity and discipline of his first novel were admirable, but its excessive detachment was not – a defect even more pronounced in his next novel, *Fontile* (1945), and not fully corrected in *Les Désirs et les jours* (1948), the last in the trilogy.

The author of the psychological novel commonly uses every technique at his command to explore the nuances of his characters. André Giroux, in *Au-delà des visages* (1948), ingeniously examined one incident from a variety of viewpoints, which allowed him to develop every facet of his protagonist's deepest spiritual being. Some writers try to compensate for limited imagination with efficiency of narrative technique but, as Giroux's second novel, *Le Gouffre a toujours soif* (1953) and his collection of short stories, *Malgré tout la joie* (1959), both show, what really matters is to touch the core of the human condition.

A similar balance between technique and depth of comprehension exists in the works of some authors who wrote well but little and enjoyed only brief celebrity in the 1950s. In Robert Elie's *La Fin des songes* (1950; tr *Farewell My Dreams*, 1955) and *Il Suffit d'un jour* (1957), the basic elements of the human drama are obsession with the meaning of life, inevitable solitude and the lack of communication between people.

In Jean Filiatrault's *Terres stériles* (1953), *Chaînes* (1955) and *Le Refuge impossible* (1957), love is just a mask for hatred in the troubled family relationships (filial, maternal, conjugal, fraternal, etc) of complex-ridden individuals. In *Les Témoins* (1954) and *Les Inutiles* (1956) by Eugène Cloutier, on the other hand, apparently gratuitous (but perhaps simply critical) fantasy replaces the agonized expression of the great problems of mankind, humanity's social maladjustment and fundamental absurdity.

Other novelists, more moralizing and deliberately abstract, had begun to write satirical tales that often verged on being essays instead. The characters in François Hertel's trilogy, *Mondes chimériques* (1940), *Anatole Laplante, curieux homme* (1944) and *Journal d'Anatole Laplante* (1947), mirror their author: free, cynical, without illusions, and garrulous, they study the trivia and important events of life with equal parts perception and irreverence. Pierre Baillargeon puts a great deal of himself, including his crisp and lively style, into the biting arguments of *Les Médisances de Claude Perrin* (1945) and *Commerce* (1947), and into the introverted but incisive protagonist of *La Neige et le feu* (1948). Jean Simard draws on his own life for the ironic sketches of *Félix, livre d'enfant pour adultes* (1947) and *Hôtel de la reine* (1949). His *Mon fils pourtant heureux* (1956) was a more introspective work, its satire darker. In *Les Sentiers de la nuit* (1959), Simard seemed more objective but in fact, under cover of a well-executed caricature of Anglo-Saxon puritanism, he symbolically attacked French Canadian JANSENISM as well, handling the most serious of subjects – God, religion, suffering and death – in a touchingly humorous way.

The most important psychological novelist is unquestionably André LANGEVIN. He led the way in incorporating the universal themes of existentialism made famous in France by Sartre, Camus and others. His trilogy of novels on the theme of man's essential solitude argues that the only possible relationship between human beings leads inevitably to despair: it consists of the evil they inflict or themselves suffer, no matter how they try to avoid it. His characters, stripped of all transcendence, grapple with meaningless suffering in a strictly contingent universe. The randomness of their lives drives them to choose between extremes: either they seek the escape of suicide, like Jean Cherteffe in *Évadé de la nuit* (1951) or, however feeble or illusory their weapons, they try to fight their fate, like Alain Dubois in *Poussière sur la ville* (1953; tr *Dust over the City*, 1955) or Pierre Dupas in *Le Temps des hommes* (1956). In the first of these novels, Langevin failed to integrate his rigid metaphysical doctrine with the flesh-and-blood story of his protagonist. The other 2 works, however, each drawing in its own way on rich resources of time and space, achieve a high degree of aesthetic success.

These books seemed to drain Langevin, for he withdrew into silence until the publication of *L'Élan d'Amérique* (1972), which was followed in 1974 by *Une Chaîne dans le parc*. Yves THÉRIAULT, on the other hand, has become more productive over the years. The novel is only part of this author's infinite variety: he has also written hundreds of scripts for radio and television and numerous popular stories and novels for adolescents. Although 6 years elapsed between his highly original stories, *Contes pour un homme seul* (1944), and his first novel, *La Fille laide* (1950), his output thereafter was abundant – and, at times, of uneven quality. Among his best works during the 1940-60 period are *Le Dompteur d'ours* (1951), *Aaron* (1954) and *Agaguk* (1958; tr 1963). Thériault has used his works to promote a wide variety of causes. The graphic presentation of man's unbridled instincts has inherent shock value: it preaches the authenticity of vigorous primitivism. The acts of sex and violent death in particular are of great value, both for the way they bring out the individuality of each character and for the role they play in the emancipation of the oppressed: all kinds of "little people" (Indians, Inuit, Jews), fighting the established structures, moral, religious, social and ethnic, that prevent their full growth as human beings. One must complement the discussion of these outstanding writers with at least a mention of some of the others who have also made their contribution to the postwar Québec novel: Jean-Jules Richard, *Neuf jours de haine* (1948); Françoise Loranger, *Mathieu* (1949); Louis Dantin, *Les Enfances de Fanny* (1951); Roger Viau, *Au milieu, la montagne* (1951); Jean Vaillancourt, *Les Canadiens errants* (1954); René Ouvrard, *La Veuve* (1955); Maurice Gagnon, *L'Échéance* (1956); and Claire France, *Les Enfants qui s'aiment* (1956; tr *Children in Love*, 1959). Pierre Gélinas wrote *Les Vivants, les morts et les autres* (1959), one of very few novels depicting the labour movement. Several novelists first appeared in this period but did not come into their own until the 1960s. Anne HÉBERT is one, notable for her *Les Chambres du bois* (1958; tr *The Silent Rooms*, 1974), a dream-novel that perhaps crosses the line into poetry, and especially for *Le Torrent* (1950; tr *The Torrent*, 1973), a collection of stories of many levels that reflects the whole spiritual adventure of the French Canadian people. Claire Martin polished her skills in a collection of elegantly biting short stories, *Avec ou sans amour* (1958), before tackling the novel with *Doux-amer* (1960), while Marie-Claire BLAIS found her voice in *La Belle Bête* (1959; tr *Mad Shadows*, 1971) and *Tête blanche* (1960; tr 1974), 2 stories of adolescent revolt played out in a dream state. Gérard BESSETTE published *La Bagarre* (1958; tr *The Brawl*, 1976), a novel of social events, and *Le Libraire* (1960; tr *Not for Every Eye*, 1963), which appeared at the perfect moment to contribute to the QUIET REVOLUTION, the "ideological exorcism" of Québec.

RÉJEAN ROBIDOUX

Novel in French, 1960-80s

During the 1960s and 1970s new developments in the Québec novel coincided with important social changes. Although it did not provide a direct reflection of reality, the novel nevertheless interacted with other current forms of discourse and in this way responded to its social environment. The arrival of a new generation of writers during the Quiet Revolution helped turn these changes into something of an event – a dramatic period of contestation and rebellion, from which the Québec novel emerged transformed.

Several writers advocated the use of popular levels of language (JOUAL) in order to portray more accurately the long-ignored realities of the working class. Initially these writers were connected with the magazine PARTI PRIS. Jacques RENAUD (*Le Cassé*, 1964) and André MAJOR (*Le Cabochon*, 1964, and *La Chair de poule*, 1965) contributed to bringing about this transformation, using popular forms of language to reflect and symbolize the degrading effects of self-contempt, colonization and social deprivation. Apart from the political implications of writing in *joual*, this new approach rapidly led to the formulation of a new kind of literary style exemplified by Jacques GODBOUT in SALUT GALARNEAU! (1967) and Victor-Lévy BEAULIEU in *Race de monde* (1969) and *La Nuitte de Malcomm Hudd* (1969). For all these writers the juxtaposition of different levels of language was a way of establishing a new linguistic identity and of setting out a new conception of Québec reality.

The same period brought the appearance of extremist characters who personified or expressed revolt, radicalism and intransigence, such as the revolutionaries in Hubert AQUIN's *Prochain épisode* (1965) and *Trou de mémoire* (1968), and Claude Jasmin's *Ethel et le terroriste* (1964). Réjean DUCHARME's character Bérénice in *l'Avalée des avalés* (1966) is a clear example of this dynamic negativism whose goal is to sweep away all existing social and cultural values. Bérénice provides the foremost expression of an impulse to deny reality, which to varying degrees motivates the characters in many of the novels of this decade. As in Ducharme's works, this rejection is personified by children and adolescents in the writing of Marie-Claire Blais (*Une saison dans la vie d'Emmanuel*, 1965, *L'Insoumise*, 1966, *Les Manuscrits de Pauline Archange*, 1968, and *David Sterne*, 1967). The values of childhood and art are often presented as a refuge from the degraded world of adults.

In many cases subversion or repudiation is expressed in parody. The novels reinterpret history and ridicule older forms of writing and obsolete values in order both to laugh at them and to advocate their opposites. In La GUERRE, YES SIR! (1968) Roch CARRIER presents a carnival-like version of the CONSCRIPTION crisis by showing farmers in the process of gleefully reversing the "civilized" values of the army and the church. In *Le Ciel de Québec* (1969) Jacques FERRON presents an absurd mock epic dealing with Québec history and French Canadian messianism, and at the same time settles his accounts with writers of the previous generation (such as Saint-Denys Garneau and Jean LE MOYNE). Irony also provides an important dimension to Blais's *Une Saison...* and *Les Manuscrits...*, in which she parodies "uplifting" literature, and the writing of Ducharme, who mocks and inverts many different styles in *La Fille de Christophe Colomb* (1969) and *L'Hiver de force* (1973).

These stories not only undermine history and contest it; they also propose a new version of it. This reinterpretation and reconstruction of history connects with the use of *joual* in that it brings the oral tradition (*see* ORAL LITERATURE) back into literature. In this way the historical novel and the novel of the land are reinterpreted in the light of a new form of awareness: the awareness of being dominated. This can be seen in the work of Antonine MAILLET and Victor-Lévy Beaulieu, among others. It is the voice of the people that is heard when Maillet recalls the Acadians' historical misfortunes and the delights of their language in a series of novels culminating in *Les Cordes de bois* (1977), *Pélagie-la-charrette* (Prix Goncourt, 1979) and *Cent ans dans les bois* (1981, republished 1982 in France as *La gribouille*). For his part, Beaulieu tells the "true saga of the Beauchemins," a grandiose and preposterous story of a working-class family transplanted from the Gaspé coast to the sleepy suburb of Montréal-Nord (or, as he writes it, Moréal-Mort). By 1985, 6 titles in the series had been published: *Race de monde* (1969), *Jos Connaissant* (1970), *Les Grands-pères* (1971), *Don Quichotte de la démanche* (1974), *Satan Belhumeur* (1981) and *Steven le Hérault* (1985).

In a similar vein to these extended series, a number of other novels were involved in transforming or contesting the novel's basic conventions. Previously Gérard Bessette, in *L'Incubation* (1965) and *Le Cycle* (1971), and André Langevin, in *L'Élan d'Amérique* (1972), had introduced new ways of telling a story along the lines of the "nouveau roman" in France. In the writing of Aquin and Beaulieu the ambiguities of the narration create some uncertainty in the story, since the plot does not evolve in the usual chronological order. For these writers, however, the ambiguities stem from the social and political alienation they are intended to reflect. For others such as Jean-Marie Poupart, in *Angoisse play* (1968), *Chère Touffe, c'est plein plein de fautes dans ta lettre d'amour* (1973) and *C'est pas donné à tout le monde d'avoir une belle mort* (1974), and Jacques BENOÎT, in *Patience et Firlipon* (1970), the interrogation and disintegration of the traditional narrative structure are more gratuitous and playful, with the narrator thinking aloud about his telling of the story. More than the theme of the writer as hero, the act of writing itself has now become a determining factor in the process of narration.

Even an early novel such as Bessette's *Le Libraire* (1960) contains statements that undermine the story's realism: it is the narrator himself who invites us to undertake a second reading by describing the room in which he is writing his diary as having dimensions ($8\frac{1}{2}'$ x 11') that are analogous to those of the sheet of paper on which he is writing ($8\frac{1}{2}''$ x 11''). To Bessette, in this example, and especially to Aquin and Beaulieu, historical references often become a metaphor for the process of writing. At its most extreme, as critic Jean Ricardou has pointed out, the writing of adventure is paralleled by the adventure of writing. In *Prochain épisode* and *Don Quichotte de la démanche* the reader witnesses a sort of short circuit between the levels of the story or, an interference between the storyteller and the story told. The autobiographical form, which is most prevalent in the Québec novel, favours this interchange between the story being narrated and the circumstance in which it is narrated. This game of cross-references, even as it destroys the traditional impression of verisimilitude, creates a new effect: that of a writer writing his story within the context of a history that is beyond his control but in which he is necessarily involved.

In an even more radical fashion, a few writers, such as Nicole BROSSARD in *Un livre* (1970), *Sold Out* (1973) and *French Kiss* (1974), have advocated "completely getting rid of the plot" and dispensing with all logic in the narrative. Here the traditional narration is replaced by a series of fragmented, often autobiographical texts arranged in symbolic order; both because of their expressive qualities and their layout, such texts tend to resemble poetic discourse more than traditional prose. This new "textuality," a blend of theory and fiction, was taken up with particular enthusiasm by the feminist writers who used it both as a trademark and as an area in which they could wage war on "patriarchal" language. Since the publication of *L'Euguélionne* (1976) by Louky Bersianik, the new women's writing has made constant gains in strength and importance. By liberating the novel from its conventional structures, this feminist contribution has brought about a new brand of writing and a new way of expressing the feminine, as is apparent, for example, in *La Mère des herbes* (1980) by Jovette Marchessault, *Lueur* (1979) by Madeleine Gagnon and *La Vie en prose* (1980) by Yolande Villemaire. Several women writers express a desire for a new language that can be reconciled with women's "otherness." In *Nous parlerons comme on écrit* (1982), France Théoret clearly shows the determination to "denaturalize" language and culture through the exercise of writing. Such an undertaking is based on a demanding literary ethic that emphasizes the modernist precept of transforming our relationship to language as a means of thoroughly transforming reality itself.

Among the older, more traditional writers, Gabrielle Roy, Anne Hébert and Yves Thériault, all of whom began their writing careers during WWII, continued publishing in the 1960s and 1970s. With *La Route d'Altamont* (1966) and *Ces enfants de ma vie* (1977), Roy presents highly personal stories that are evocative of her life in Manitoba, whereas Hébert continues her exploration of the tormented, extreme world of guilt and passion in 3 novels with historical settings, KAMOURASKA (1970), *Les Enfants du sabbat* (1975) and *Les Fous de bassan* (1982), as well as a supernatural short story entitled *Héloïse* (1980). Thériault, meanwhile, followed his existing series of Inuit and Amerindian stories with *Ashini* (1960), *Tayaout, fils d'Agaguk* (1969), *Agoak, l'héritage d'Agaguk* (1975) and *La Quête de l'ourse* (1980).

During the 1970s writers such as Claude Jasmin and André Major moved away from novels of protest to delve more deeply into introspection. Major produced a trilogy, *L'Épouvantail* (1974), *L'Épidémie* (1975) and *Les Rescapés* (1976), in which the characters observe themselves and their lives in the little world of Saint Emmanuel. The main events in the story are almost always told retrospectively, with the remoteness of hindsight, and the distance between past and present seems to condemn the characters to perpetual remembrance. The displacement between the hero's life and his acute awareness of it not only coincides with the narrative process but also confines the character to solitary dreaming. Excluded from direct action, the character is left with no immediate grasp of reality. Rather than acting, he is acted upon; rather than being shown in acting, he is shown dreaming about the things he has done. Similarly impotent characters, imprisoned in their past, appear in Hébert's *Kamouraska*, Langevin's *L'Élan d'Amérique* and Beaulieu's *Un Rêve québécois* (1972). The narrative juxtaposes a series of retrospections representing the discontinuous flow of memory in an alienated individual who has stopped evolving. Rebellion has given way to dumbfounded amazement in a character dazed by the trauma of unavoidable events. (This kind of stunned reaction is not unrelated to the moral depression affecting many writers after the imposition of the WAR MEASURES ACT in 1970.) For Jasmin too, the "cycle of violence" gave way to what the author himself called the "cycle of memories," in which he recalls the happy childhood and adolescence he spent in his family surroundings: *La Petite Patrie* (1972), *Pointe-Calumet Boogie-Woogie* (1973), *Sainte-Adèle-la-vaisselle* (1974) and *La Sablière* (1979).

Early in the 1980s it was possible to discern various tendencies indicating something of a return to established traditions in the novel. The historical novel reappeared in the series "Les Fils de la liberté" by Louis Caron: *Le Canard de bois* (1981) and *La Corne de brume* (1982). And the social chronicle was making a comeback in the form of the first volumes of the "Chroniques du Plateau Mont-Royal" by Michel TREMBLAY: *La Grosse Femme d'à côté est enceinte* (1978), *Thérèse et Pierrette à l'école des Saintes-Anges* (1980), *La Duchesse et le roturier* (1982) and *Des Nouvelles d'Edouard* (1985).   JACQUES MICHON

Reading: A. Belleau, *Le Romancier fictif* (1979); M. Lemire, ed, *Dictionnaire des oeuvres littéraire du Québec* (5 vols to date, 1980-88); G. Marcotte, *Le Roman à l'imparfait* (1976); B.Z. Shek, *Social Realism in the French-Canadian Novel* (1977); G. Tougas, *History of French Canadian Literature* (1966).

Nowlan, Alden, poet (b at Windsor, NS 25 Jan 1933; d at Fredericton, NB 27 June 1983). Largely self-educated, Nowlan was a former newspaperman whose many collections of poetry grew steadily in their power and intensity. Primary among them are *Bread, Wine and Salt* (1967, Gov Gen's Award), *Playing the Jesus Game* (1970) and *Between Tears and Laughter* (1971), all of them rich in regional sensibility and in affection for or-

dinary people but connected by Nowlan's intelligence, temperament and reading to a literary world far beyond folk culture. He was also a playwright, a story writer and, with *Various Persons Named Kevin O'Brien* (1973), a novelist; several other Nowlan books appeared posthumously. He was often at the centre of the literary community in Fredericton and Atlantic Canada generally, through the vivid example of his craftsmanship, through his work at UNB, where he became writer-in-residence in 1969, and through his individualistic personality.   DOUGLAS FETHERLING

Nowlan, George Clyde, lawyer, politician (b at Havelock, NS 14 Aug 1898; d at Ottawa 31 May 1965). A gunner in WWI, educated at Acadia and Dalhousie, he was elected an MLA for Kings County, NS, in the MARITIME RIGHTS election of 1925. Defeated in 1933, he continued to be active in the demoralized Conservative Party and captured the federal riding of Digby-Annapolis-Kings in a series of spectacular elections (1948-50). President of the PC Party (1950-54) and spokesman for Atlantic Canada, Nowlan served as minister of national revenue (1957-62) and finance (1962-63) in the DIEFENBAKER government. Never comfortable with Diefenbaker, who suspected him of treachery on the leadership question, he remained loyal to the Conservative Party until his death.   MARGARET CONRAD

Reading: Margaret Conrad, *George Nowlan: Maritime Conservative in National Politics* (1986).

Nuclear Energy is ENERGY from the nucleus of an atom. In stars such as the SUN, pairs of light atoms (mostly hydrogen) fuse together and release the radiation received on earth as SOLAR ENERGY. This NUCLEAR FUSION, the joining of the nuclei of atoms, is one form of nuclear energy. Another form is the splitting (fission) of heavy atoms such as URANIUM. Each atom of naturally occurring uranium has a very small probability of undergoing spontaneous fission at any given moment. When this happens, a pair of lighter atoms (known as fission products) are formed and 2 or 3 neutrons (subatomic particles from the original nucleus) are released. Nuclear reactions are fundamentally different from other common energy reactions. When a conventional fuel burns or when water flows through a hydroelectric generator, the atoms themselves are unaffected, although in the case of fuels they recombine chemically. Hence, the amount of matter remains the same. In nuclear reactions, the atoms themselves are altered and a tiny amount of matter is converted into energy.

To understand how the opposite processes, fusion and fission, can both release energy requires some knowledge of the "curve of binding energy" and Einstein's equation $E=mc^2$. The nuclei of all atoms consist of nucleons. A nucleon is either a proton, a subatomic particle with positive electric charge, or a neutron with a neutral charge. The mass of any nucleus is slightly less than the sum of the masses of its constituent nucleons. This difference, or "mass defect," represents the binding energy holding the nucleons together. According to Einstein's equation relating energy (E) to mass (m) through the square of the velocity of light (c), even tiny masses represent large energies: a mass of 100 kg completely converted to energy would supply all Canadian needs for one year. If the binding energy per nucleon is plotted against the number of nucleons in the nucleus, the hump-backed "curve of binding energy" is obtained. Starting at hydrogen (1 nucleon), the curve rises rapidly to oxygen (16 nucleons), then more slowly to arsenic (75 nucleons), before dropping slowly to uranium (238 nucleons). Thus, fusing 2 light nuclei into a heavier one releases some nuclear-binding energy; fissioning a very heavy nucleus

into 2 intermediate ones releases a smaller amount of energy per nucleon but involves many more nucleons.

Radioactivity Nuclear energy is also released as radioactivity, which is associated with naturally occurring radioactive minerals (eg, RADIUM ores) and with man-made radioisotopes used in medicine and industry. Most fission-product nuclei are radioactive. All radioactive nuclei are unstable and, sooner or later, will decay through the emission of subatomic particles accompanied by gamma radiation (similar to X radiation). The particle released may be an alpha particle, a particularly stable combination of 2 neutrons and 2 protons, or a beta particle (also known as an electron), which is a negatively charged subatomic particle formed when a neutron transforms into a proton. After emission the nucleus may remain radioactive, or may be stable. Just when any given radioactive nucleus will decay is unpredictable. However, in a large number of nuclei of the same kind, half will decay in a period characteristic of that kind of nucleus, its "half-life." Half the remainder will decay in a second half-life period, and so on. Consequently, only about 1/1000 of the original amount of any radioactive material will remain after 10 half-lives. GEOTHERMAL ENERGY, the heat flowing to Earth's surface from its core, results from the radioactive decay of heavy nuclei such as uranium and is therefore another form of nuclear energy.

Radioisotopes are extremely reliable sources of heat for certain applications. An isotope of plutonium (plutonium-238) formed as a by-product in nuclear fission reactors is used to power heart pacemakers and space satellites. Cobalt-60 can be used to power navigation buoys. If the radioisotope emits gamma radiation, equipment using it must incorporate shielding to protect anyone nearby. A fundamental limitation is inherent in radioactive sources: the more intense the radioactivity (hence, the greater the heat produced), the shorter the source's half-life. For instance, cobalt-60 has a half-life of 5.27 years; therefore after 5.27 years it will produce half as much heat and radiation as it did initially.

Nuclear Fission A vital contribution to the understanding of radioactivity was made by Ernest RUTHERFORD and Frederick Soddy working at McGill U in Montréal early in this century. It was they who first suggested the manner in which a nucleus of one element became a nucleus of another element, ie, by radioactive emissions. In 1904 Rutherford conjectured "that an enormous store of latent energy is resident in the atoms of the radio-elements" and that this energy could be tapped if the rate of radioactive disintegration could be controlled. While it has not been possible to control that rate, human control of nuclear fission has proved practicable. This fact, first demonstrated by Enrico Fermi in a squash court at the University of Chicago in 1942, has made this particular nuclear reaction so important.

Control of the fission process depends on the existence of a chain reaction. Naturally occurring uranium consists of 99.28% of the uranium-238 isotope, 0.71% of uranium-235 and very small amounts of other isotopes. When hit by a neutron, the nucleus of a uranium-235 atom has a high probability of fissioning; if the atom is uranium-238 the probability is very low. This induced fission process was first discovered in 1938 by the Germans Otto Hahn and Fritz Strassmann. When a uranium-235 atom fissions, it emits 2 or 3 neutrons. If one of these neutrons hits and thus causes fission in another uranium-235 atom, more neutrons are emitted, one of which could possibly cause a further fission, and so on in a chain reaction. Thus, once started, the fission process can be self-sustaining. If, on the average, exactly one

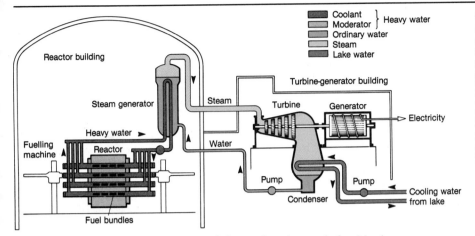

Schematic of a CANDU nuclear power system. A fuel bundle 500 mm x 100 mm, weighing 22 kg, can produce as much energy as burning 2000 barrels of oil (*courtesy Atomic Energy of Canada*).

neutron from each fission results in one other fission, the process is in equilibrium and a steady level of heat is produced. The other neutrons escape from the mass of uranium or are absorbed by materials, other than uranium-235, within the mass. This is the situation in a nuclear reactor operating at steady power.

To increase the power, some of the competitive absorbers of neutrons are removed, allowing the chain reaction to diverge until the desired power level is attained. The equilibrium production of neutrons is then restored to stabilize the power. To decrease the power or shut down the reactor, more absorbers are introduced.

However much natural uranium is heaped up, no significant fission will result, because there are not enough fissile uranium-235 atoms present to sustain a chain reaction. The few neutrons produced are absorbed by the much more abundant uranium-238 atoms and so are unavailable to cause further fission. One solution is to increase the proportion of uranium-235 atoms artificially; this is done in uranium-enrichment plants which exploit the small differences in physical properties between the 2 uranium isotopes. A more subtle solution is to divide up the uranium into small packets, each surrounded by a "moderator" which slows down the neutrons emitted from one packet of uranium before they hit the next packet. Slow neutrons cause fission in uranium-235 much more readily than faster ones. Generally, elements with light atoms are good moderators: ordinary water is not good enough to sustain a chain reaction with natural uranium; very pure graphite (carbon) is better; heavy water, a compound of deuterium and oxygen is best. Deuterium, the heavy isotope of hydrogen, is present in all naturally occurring hydrogen (about one part in 7000). Heavy water is produced by enriching the deuterium content of natural water in heavy-water plants.

A neutron absorbed by a uranium-238 atom is not lost, merely stored. The resulting compound nucleus subsequently transforms spontaneously by radioactive decay into an isotope of another element, plutonium-239. Although uranium-238 is not fissile, plutonium-239 is. Thus, uranium-238 is said to be fertile. Plutonium-239 can be used to sustain a nuclear fission reaction in the same way as uranium-235. Thorium, another naturally occurring nuclear fuel that is somewhat like uranium, consists almost entirely of the fertile isotope thorium-232, which can yield the fissile uranium-233 by absorbing a neutron. These alternative nuclear fuels and moderators can be combined to

produce heat and electricity in NUCLEAR POWER PLANTS.

History Natural nuclear reactors predated the man-made variety by about 2 billion years. At that time, nuclear chain reactions generating considerable heat occurred in several rich uranium deposits at Oklo, Gabon, W Africa. This prehistoric event, which has been deduced recently from chemical analysis of the remaining uranium, illustrates basic principles of radioactivity and fission. Since uranium-235 is radioactive, with a half-life of 0.7 billion years, natural uranium then would have contained over 5% uranium-235, a sufficiently high fissile concentration to sustain a chain reaction with ordinary water as a moderator.

The nuclear reaction presumably started when groundwater seeped into the deposits. When the chain reaction and the associated fission heat built up to a sufficient level to boil the water and expel it, the resulting lack of a moderator would have caused the reaction to shut down automatically. This cycle must have repeated itself many times, like a gigantic coffee pot percolating away over hundreds of thousands of years. Analysis shows that, despite the absence of any deliberate means of retention, the plutonium produced in these natural reactors remained trapped in the uranium deposits until it had decayed away by its own radioactivity.

Since the early work of Rutherford and Soddy, Canada has contributed significantly to the science and application of nuclear energy. In 1933 Gilbert LABINE brought into production Canada's first radium mine at Port Radium, NWT, on Great Bear Lk. Uranium, always found in association with radium, was then considered a waste product. In 1940 George LAURENCE started experiments in the National Research Council's Ottawa laboratories with uranium and a graphite moderator. Had his materials been purer, he might have achieved a chain reaction before Fermi. The Port Radium mine of ELDORADO Gold Mines Ltd was reopened in 1942 to produce uranium.

In 1943, as part of the Allied war effort, a joint Canadian-UK team, with important French participation, was established at Montréal to pursue the concept of nuclear reactors with heavy water. In the same year heavy water was first produced in Canada at the synthetic ammonia fertilizer plant of the Consolidated Mining and Smelting Corp at Trail, BC, using a Norwegian process. In 1944, C.J. MACKENZIE, who was then in charge of the Canadian program, wrote with great foresight to C.D. HOWE, who was the minister responsible for it: "In my opinion Canada has a unique opportunity to become involved in a project which is not only of the greatest immediate military importance but which may revolutionize the future world in the same degree as did the invention of the steam engine and the discovery of electricity." The Chalk River, Ont, laboratories were established in 1944,

and in 1945 the Zero Energy Experimental Pile (ZEEP), the first reactor outside the US, started up at Chalk River. In 1946, W. Bennett LEWIS, who subsequently was primarily responsible for the technical development of the Canadian CANDU reactor system, became technical director at Chalk River, replacing John Cockcroft who went on to lead the United Kingdom's program. The first radioisotopes produced in the NRX reactor at Chalk River were marketed in 1949. In 1951 the world's first cobalt radiotherapy units for the treatment of cancer, using radioactive COBALT produced in the NRX reactor, were developed by Harold Johns and others. These units were installed in the Victoria Hospital in London, Ont, and in the University Hospital in Saskatoon, Sask.

Since then Canada has exported more than 1300 units, and the associated cobalt, to more than 80 countries. These units are credited with saving 13 million person-years of life for the patients involved. In 1962 Canada's first nuclear power plant, the Nuclear Power Demonstration Plant, was opened at Rolphton, Ont. This plant demonstrated all-important principles for the CANDU design of reactor.

Future Although it has not yet been possible to control fusion, the required conditions are reasonably well established. It is known that fusing atoms of ordinary hydrogen (the reaction that occurs in the sun) would be extremely difficult. Instead the hydrogen isotopes deuterium and tritium are used in fusion experiments. The deuterium-tritium combination is believed to offer fusion more easily than deuterium-deuterium. First, the atoms of deuterium and tritium must be at very high temperatures, about 100 million °C; then, the atoms must be together long enough for fusion to occur. The time needed is least for densely packed atoms and increases as the density decreases. The minimum requirement commonly quoted for the product of density and time for fusion of deuterium and tritium is 10 atom s/cm³.

Since no structural materials can operate at the high temperatures required for the fusion reaction, other means of confining the reacting atoms had to be found. At these temperatures the atoms are ionized, ie, electrically charged, and subject to forces when they move in a magnetic field. Hence, magnetic fields can be designed to keep the hot atoms "bottled up" through magnetic confinement. In inertial confinement a small pellet of solid deuterium-tritium would be bombarded from all sides by high-energy beams of LASER light or charged particles. The intense beams would heat the pellet and, by causing shock

NRX reactor, Chalk River, Ont, June 1952 (*courtesy National Archives of Canada/PA-116481/NFB/Chris Lund*).

waves, compress it to about 1/1000 of its original volume. The increased density means that a shorter period of confinement is necessary.

Until controlled fusion has been demonstrated and a practical fusion reactor designed, it would be premature to estimate costs. Like solar energy and nuclear fission, the fuel is abundant and cheap, but the cost of the equipment needed to provide the energy in usable form will be appreciable. Long before fusion becomes an alternative to fission as an energy source, the 2 may complement each other in a hybrid system. In addition to releasing energy, the fusion reaction provides high-energy neutrons which could, through other nuclear reactions, be multiplied into many neutrons of lower energy. These, in turn, could be absorbed by fertile materials, such as uranium-238 or thorium, to produce fissile materials to fuel conventional fission reactors. For this purpose another nuclear reaction, spallation, must be regarded as an alternative to fusion. In spallation, heavy atoms (eg, lead) bombarded by light particles (eg, hydrogen nuclei) emit high-energy neutrons which can be used in the same way to provide fuel. Unlike fusion, spallation has already been demonstrated in the laboratory.

Nuclear energy offers a new energy source just when the limits of the chemical fuels, oil, natural gas and coal, are being realized. If recycled, the world's nuclear fuels are virtually inexhaustible. However, the radiation from nuclear energy, like the fire of chemical energy, has its hazards as well as its benefits.

Like fire, radiation should be respected but not feared. All life has evolved in a sea of radiation that existed from the start of time. To ensure the safety of the public and of workers, and to protect the environment, the federal government regulates the ELECTRICAL UTILITIES and the hospitals, universities and other institutions which use nuclear energy and radioisotopes. The regulations are based on internationally agreed standards; in Canada the regulatory body is the Atomic Energy Control Board. In addition, more than 10 public inquiries have been held in Canada, dealing with various aspects of the nuclear industry, from uranium PROSPECTING and MINING, through reactor safety to the disposal of nuclear HAZARDOUS WASTES. The overwhelming conclusion of these examinations has been that it is in the public interest to continue with the exploitation of nuclear energy, subject to proper regulation.

J.A.L. ROBERTSON

Nuclear Fusion is the combination of the nuclei of 2 light atoms to form a heavier one. The resulting atom has a smaller mass than the original ones; therefore, nuclear fusion is a method of transforming mass into ENERGY. This reaction produces the energy of stars such as the SUN. By weight, the fusion process yields 8 times more energy than the fission of uranium (see NUCLEAR ENERGY), and over a million times more than the burning of fossil fuels. Fusion is a very attractive energy source not only because of its high-energy yield but also because of the almost limitless abundance of its fuels and the fact that its principal by-product, helium, is inert, unlike the radioactive by-products of conventional fission reactors. Supplies of one major fuel, deuterium, a hydrogen isotope found in ordinary seawater, are virtually inexhaustible. The other major fuel, tritium, could be produced from lithium found in land deposits and seawater, which contain supplies for thousands of years. The amount of fuel in the reactor at any time is very small, so there is no hazard of uncontrolled energy release or runaway reactions. Problems of radioactivity, fuel handling, contamination and waste disposal are small compared to those associated with fission

reactors in NUCLEAR POWER PLANTS. The first manmade fusion reaction was the US thermonuclear hydrogen bomb tested in 1952. Unfortunately, the reaction has proved very difficult to contain and harness for peaceful purposes. Controlled experiments have barely reached the point where the energy released is greater than the energy put in, but if research and development proceed successfully, fusion could be an important commercial energy source early in the 21st century.

The important fusion reactions are those involving the isotopes of HYDROGEN: hydrogen (H), consisting of 1 proton and 1 electron; deuterium (D), 1 proton, 1 neutron and 1 electron; and tritium (T), 1 proton, 2 neutrons and 1 electron. The products of such reactions are helium (^{4}He), also known as an alpha particle, and energetic neutrons (n) or protons (p). Fusion reactions are difficult to achieve because the interacting nuclei each has a positive electrical charge and, therefore, strongly repel one another. Fusion can occur only if the nuclei approach each other at very high velocities, sufficient to overcome their electrostatic repulsive forces. To release energy at a practical level, using gaseous deuterium-tritium as a fuel, requires the heating of the mixture to a temperature of 100 million °C or more. Even at lower temperatures, the gas becomes ionized as the electrons become detached from the atoms. In this state, called a plasma, the separated negatively charged electrons and positively charged nuclei move freely, giving the mixture properties different from those of a normal gas. To release more energy than was supplied, it is necessary to confine the plasma to permit a sufficient number of fusion reactions to take place. In the sun the gravitational field heats and confines the hydrogen fuel, resulting in the formation of helium and other heavier elements. On Earth there are 2 classes of approach to containing and heating the plasma: magnetic confinement and inertial confinement.

Since a plasma is a very good conductor of electricity, it can be influenced by magnetic fields. In a magnetic field, the plasma particles are forced to follow spiral paths about the field line; hence, magnetic fields can confine the charged particles of the high-temperature plasma and prevent them from striking the walls of the containing vessel. Many magnetic containment schemes have been suggested and experimentally investigated. One very successful approach has been the tokamak, a closed magnetic-field device with a hollow, doughnut-shaped vessel through which magnetic fields twist to confine the plasma. The fields are produced by external magnetic-field coils and by electrical currents made to flow through the plasma. Initial heating is often achieved by passing a current through the plasma or by rapidly changing the confining magnetic field, but the required temperatures cannot be reached by such methods. Hence, auxiliary heating techniques are used, eg, neutral beam injection, whereby high-energy neutral atoms are introduced into the hot plasma where they are immediately ionized and trapped by the magnetic field, and radio-frequency heating, which uses high-frequency electromagnetic waves generated by external oscillators and introduced into the plasma where the energy is transferred to the charged particles.

In the inertial-confinement approach to fusion, a small spherical pellet containing the fuel is compressed to extremely high density. This process heats the pellet to the required temperature and causes the fuel to ignite before the compressed mass can disassemble. The interaction occurs so rapidly that the compressed pellet remains together by its own inertia. High-power, short-pulsed LASERS and ion-particle beams are the principal candidates for delivering the intense

pulses of energy required to heat the outer layers of the fuel pellet rapidly. The ensuing blow off of vaporized material creates an implosion of the fuel. For ignition of D-T fuel to occur, compression of the order of 20 times the density of lead is necessary. The hydrogen bomb uses this approach.

Intensive research is being conducted on controlled fusion energy in many countries, particularly the US, the USSR, Japan and the European Economic Community.

In Varennes, Qué, Canada has a national research facility based on a tokamak machine. The $40-million facility was financed by NRC and Hydro-Québec. The research program is being conducted by a joint utilities/university/industry team composed of Institut de recherche de l'hydro-Québec, Intitut national de la recherche scientifique, U de Montréal, MPB Technologies Inc and Canatom Inc under the management of both Atomic Energy of Canada Ltd and Hydro-Québec.   M.P. BACHYNSKI

Nuclear Power Plants generate electricity from NUCLEAR ENERGY. As in all thermal-electric generating stations (see ELECTRIC-POWER GENERATION), heat is used to boil water into steam, which turns a turbine and drives a generator, producing electricity. A conventional thermal generating station obtains heat by burning coal or other fuels; a nuclear power plant obtains heat from the fission of nuclear fuel in a nuclear reactor. There are many ways of applying the basic principles of fission to the design of actual reactors. In Canada, a unique design known as the Canada Deuterium-Uranium (CANDU) is used. Other countries employ various other designs. A number of auxiliary plants also are needed for nuclear-power generation. All current power reactors use URANIUM as fuel. Uranium is relatively abundant, being present in most rocks and soils and in the oceans. Currently ores that contain about 0.1% uranium by weight, or greater, are economic to mine. After mining and milling, the uranium is a yellow powder (yellowcake); after further chemical treatment, it becomes black (uranium dioxide).

CANDU Reactors To make fuel pellets for a CANDU reactor, the uranium dioxide is compressed, then baked at high temperatures to yield hard, insoluble, ceramic cylinders about 14 mm in diameter by 20 mm long. To make one fuel element, a 500 mm long stack of pellets is loaded into a metal tube (made of the zirconium alloy, Zircaloy), which is sealed at each end by welding. For present CANDU reactors 37 elements are assembled by further welding to form a fuel bundle, with individual elements held apart from each other. This fuel bundle is the first basic building block for the reactor. Uranium is a very concentrated energy source. A fuel bundle 500 mm long, 100 mm in diameter and weighing 22 kg could be carried in an overnight bag. When put in a CANDU reactor, it can produce as much ENERGY as burning about 400 t of coal or 2000 barrels of oil.

In the reactor, 12 bundles are placed end-to-end in a tube through which water coolant is pumped. Since the water is at nearly 300°C, it develops a pressure of about 100 atmospheres; the tubes are therefore known as pressure tubes. Each pressure tube, with its contained fuel and coolant and with end fittings to get the coolant in and out, constitutes a fuel channel, the next larger building block for a CANDU reactor. The reactor core consists of several hundred fuel channels positioned in a carefully calculated grid and passing horizontally through a tank, or calandria, containing heavy water as a moderator. Heavy water is a compound of hydrogen and oxygen, having a higher proportion of the heavy hydrogen isotope deuterium than does natural water. The presence of the heavy water and the particular arrangement of channels are essential for fission to occur in the uranium. This arrangement contributes to the safety of the reactor: if the reactor were to be seriously damaged one or both of these conditions would probably be affected and the fission process would stop automatically. This is an example of what is known as a fail-safe feature.

The coolant from the fuel channels is piped to steam generators, where the heat from the fuel is used to boil water in a secondary circuit. The resulting steam drives the turbine and turns the generator to produce electricity. The reactor coolant, now at a lower temperature, circulates back to the reactor in the closed primary circuit.

When a fuel bundle has to be replaced (after about a year and a half in the reactor), remotely controlled fuelling machines are clamped to each end of its fuel channel. Fresh fuel is pushed in from one end and the used fuel is deposited in the machine at the other end. A used fuel bundle, which looks much the same as a fresh one, retains all its wastes sealed within it. Used bundles are stored in a water-filled tank, like an extra-deep swimming pool, in a building adjacent to the reactor. The water cools the bundles and absorbs the radiation they emit. The ability to change fuel without having to shut down the reactor makes the CANDU design unique among current commercial reactors, and contributes to their exceptionally high capacity factors, ie, the electricity actually generated during some period, expressed as a percentage of what is theoretically possible.

To control the power level of the reactor, control rods are moved into or out of the reactor core. They are contained in tubes which penetrate the top of the calandria and pass between fuel channels. A reactor control system is used much as is an accelerator in controlling the speed of a car. However, unlike the car's accelerator, the control rods in the reactor can also bring things to a stop, ie, shut down the chain reaction. In addition to control rods there are 2 independent systems, each capable of shutting down the reactor quickly. These can be compared to 2 independent braking systems in a car, although the shutdown systems, unlike brakes, are neither needed nor used in normal operation. They are called upon only if some other system fails. One type consists of rods similar to control rods but capable of being inserted into the reactor core more rapidly; the other consists of perforated horizontal tubes in the calandria through which a liquid can be squirted into the heavy-water moderator. Control rods and shutdown systems both work by introducing into the reactor materials (eg, cadmium or gadolinium) that absorb neutrons strongly. Adding absorbers slows down, then stops the fission chain reaction; withdrawing them allows the reaction to start up again.

The fuel in an operating reactor (and even when discharged) is highly radioactive, ie, it emits gamma radiation similar to medical X rays. To protect the station operators, the reactor core is surrounded by heavy shielding, typically of reinforced concrete about 1 m thick. To protect the public against the possibility of radioactive releases which might occur in the event of an accident, the whole reactor and its primary coolant circuit are located within a sealed containment building, a massive concrete structure. No dwellings are allowed within a radius of about 1 km; thus any escaping radioactive material would be diluted and dispersed before reaching the public.

Other Commercial Reactors CANDU reactors are moderated and cooled by heavy water; the moderator and coolant are in separate circuits. Another general type of power reactor, known as a light-water reactor, uses ordinary or "light" water for moderator and coolant, without any separation. All the fuel is immersed in water under pres-

Ontario Hydro's nuclear generating plant on Lake Ontario, at Pickering (*photo by Jim Merrithew*).

sure, contained in a single large pressure vessel. Since light water is not a good enough moderator to sustain a fission chain reaction in natural uranium, the uranium fuel for light-water reactors has to be artificially enriched in uranium-235. The light-water reactor, first developed in the US, has 2 subtypes: the pressurized-water reactor and the boiling-water reactor. In the first, the cooling water in the pressure vessel is maintained at a high enough pressure to prevent boiling. Thus, just as in the CANDU design, steam for the turbines is produced in a secondary circuit with heat being transferred from the primary to the secondary circuit in steam generators. In the boiling-water reactor the coolant is under less pressure, so that boiling occurs. After separation from entrained water, the steam passes directly to the turbine. This procedure has the benefit of eliminating the cost and temperature drop associated with the steam generator, but the presence of radioactive coolant in the turbine makes maintenance more difficult.

Another type of power reactor, originally developed in the UK and France, uses graphite as moderator and a gas as coolant, hence the term gas-graphite reactor. The earliest of these used uranium metal contained in magnesium-alloy cans as fuel and carbon dioxide as coolant. The UK's design is called the Magnox Reactor after the particular magnesium alloy developed for the fuel cans. Graphite, being intermediate between light and heavy water as a moderator, enables natural, unenriched uranium to be used. This type is no longer competitive. In the UK it has been superseded by the advanced gas-cooled reactor which uses graphite and carbon dioxide but, by changing the fuel to uranium dioxide in stainless-steel cans, is able to take the coolant to higher temperatures. This system gives a higher thermal efficiency, ie, more electricity can be obtained from the same amount of heat. There is insufficient operating experience with advanced gas-cooled reactors to assess how well they will compete with established water-cooled reactors.

Several countries are investigating a high-temperature gas-cooled reactor that promises even higher temperatures. Here the carbon-dioxide coolant is replaced by noncorrosive gaseous helium, and the fuel consists of myriads of tiny particles of uranium carbide individually coated with graphite and embedded in a graphite block or sphere. The concept is technically attractive but, in the absence of any full-size commercial plants, the economics are largely unknown.

The USSR has developed 2 types of reactor for use in central power stations: the VVER (pressure-vessel-type water-water reactor) and the RBMK (channel-type water-graphite boiling reactor). The VVER is very similar to the US design of pressurized-water reactor; the RBMK is a unique design. It has hundreds of fuel channels generally similar to those in the CANDU, but these are in a moderator of hot graphite, not heavy water.

Fuel Recycling All currently commercial nuclear-power reactors consume only about 1% of the uranium fed to them. As long as uranium is relatively abundant and cheap, the present procedure, the "once through" fuel cycle, which involves storing the used fuel discharged from the reactor, is the simplest and most economic. Used in this way, the world's known resources of economically recoverable uranium have an energy content comparable to the world's recoverable resources of conventional oil. When the richer uranium ores have been exploited and leaner ores have to be mined, it may make economic sense to recycle the used fuel to obtain more of the energy potentially available. Recycling would involve dissolving the used fuel, removing the true wastes (about 1% of the total fuel weight) and fabricating the residues into fresh fuel for reactors. Fuel recycling is an essential component of any proposal to extract appreciably more energy from our nuclear-fuel resources.

The best-known application for fuel recycling is in the liquid-metal fast breeder reactor, a radically different design that is not yet available commercially. "Liquid-metal" refers to the coolant, usually a molten alloy of sodium and potassium. "Fast" refers to the speed of the neutrons in the reactor core. Since fast reactors do not incorporate a moderator, the neutrons are not slowed down much from their speed at birth in the fission process. "Breeder" refers to the fact that more fissile material is bred from fertile material than is consumed by fission. Often, and misleadingly, this type of reactor is said to produce more fuel than it consumes. However, the essential characteristic of this reactor type is that it consumes much less nuclear fuel (normally uranium) than current reactors. Thus the cost of the electricity produced is largely independent of the cost of the uranium.

Fuel recycling would greatly extend the world's nuclear fuel resources for 2 reasons. Since ELECTRIC UTILITIES could afford to pay a higher price for uranium, mining leaner ores would become feasible and much more uranium could be economically recovered. For any particular amount of uranium mined, a larger fraction would be consumed and converted to energy. Together, these factors mean that nuclear-fission energy, with fuel recycling, becomes a nearly inexhaustible energy source. In Canada, the same principle of largely decoupling electricity costs from fuel costs is possible in the existing and commercially proven design of CANDU reactors, by exploiting fuel recycling and switching from uranium to thorium (another naturally occurring nuclear fuel) as feed. Thus, Canada could be assured of the same indefinite supply of energy without having to introduce a new reactor type.

J.A.L. ROBERTSON

Nuclear Research Establishments The research company of ATOMIC ENERGY OF CANADA LTD (AECL) operates 2 major NUCLEAR ENERGY research centres in Canada: Chalk River Nuclear Laboratories (CRNL), established during World War II on the Ottawa R some 200 km NW of Ottawa; and Whiteshell Nuclear Research Establishment (WNRE) opened in 1963 beside WHITESHELL PROVINCIAL PARK, 105 km NE of Winnipeg, Man. Both conduct research and development on a wide variety of energy-related projects on behalf of AECL and under contract to outside companies and government bodies. At both sites reactor safety and the effects of radiation on living cells are studied. Test rigs which simulate the effects of system failures are used to ensure the correctness of safety codes and the effectiveness of safety-design features. Studies on the interaction of radiation and cells provide assurance that human safety is adequately protected by the codes and regulations.

Chalk River was the site of Canada's first large research reactor, NRX, a 10 megawatt (MW) facility which used natural uranium fuel and a deuterium moderator. Originally operated as a project of the NATIONAL RESEARCH COUNCIL, CRNL became the main laboratory of AECL, the crown corporation established in 1952 to develop peaceful uses of nuclear energy. The Allies designed NRX to be an efficient producer of plutonium-239 for nuclear weapons; however, after WWII, CRNL turned its attention to research in other fields. NRX proved to be a uniquely powerful research tool and attracted worldwide attention to Chalk River in the postwar era. A complete technology evolved around the use of NRX and its later, more powerful companion, NRU. Designers of the Canadian nuclear power system, CANDU, relied heavily upon the experience at Chalk River, not least as a training ground for engineers and technologists from private-sector companies which would become suppliers of CANDU fuel and components (see NUCLEAR POWER PLANTS). Now these reactors also produce radioisotopes used for medical diagnoses and therapy. W. Bennett LEWIS, CRNL's technical director 1946-76, left a lasting imprint on CRNL and on CANDU. Under his direction, the laboratories expanded from a wartime project of 200-300 professional and support staff to a world-class science centre, making important contributions to physics, chemistry, biology, nuclear technology and engineering. The new Tandem Accelerator Superconducting Cyclotron (TASCC) which was designed and built at CRNL will be a major Canadian facility for research in nuclear physics. Research in genetics illuminated the processes of repair in damaged living cells and shed new light on the genetic basis of susceptibility to cancer. Former Chalk

River scientists and engineers are found in universities, industry and government services across Canada and the US. Devices and techniques developed at Chalk River, such as those for cancer therapy, neutron-activation analysis and radiation measurement, are in use around the world.

The Whiteshell research centre employs about 1000 scientists, engineers and support staff. An early project at WNRE was WR-1, a 40 MW research reactor, moderated with heavy water but cooled with a special, noncorrosive organic liquid (OS-84). It could achieve temperatures of 400°C without boiling. A demonstrator small reactor, designed to be a simple nuclear energy system for heating buildings and institutions, is now operating at WNRE. This reactor will be used to heat buildings there and such reactors could also generate electricity for remote communities. In collaboration with universities and federal and provincial authorities, WNRE devotes a very large effort to evaluating the disposal of HAZARDOUS WASTES such as the radioactive by-products of nuclear-power generation. Near WNRE is the Underground Research Laboratory, a dedicated geoscience research facility used for developing technologies relevant to nuclear-fuel-waste disposal.

F.H. KRENZ AND D.K. EVANS

Nueltin Lake, 2279 km², elev 278 m, max length 144 km, is located on the border of the NWT and northeastern Manitoba, about 660 km S of the Arctic Circle. An irregularly shaped lake, it has a heavily indented shoreline and contains numerous small islands. It is fed by a number of surrounding lakes and is drained NE into Hudson Bay by the Thlewiaza R. There has long been a trading post on the lake and the area has been explored extensively since WWII – beginning with the Nueltin Lake Expedition (1947). The lake takes its name from the Chipewyan *nu-thel-tin-tu-ch*, meaning "sleeping island lake." Discovered by Samuel HEARNE (1770-72), it appears on his map as Island Lk. Aaron Arrowsmith's map of MACKENZIE's journeys (1789, 1793) shows it as Northlined Lk.

DAVID EVANS

Nugent, John Cullen, artist, educator (b at Montréal 1921). Nugent has been making steel SCULPTURE in Lumsden, Sask, for 30 years and has combined this with a teaching career at U of Regina, liturgical commissions and even a candle-making enterprise. Early in his studies at St John's (Collegeville, Minn), his attitudes were marked by left-leaning ideals stirred by Catholic theology, as reflected in his "Christian craftsman" manufacture of sacred objects for church use and decoration. More significant, however, is his steel collage sculpture. Cutting, welding and adapting prefabricated steel elements, Nugent recombines pieces into sculptures often recalling a prairie landscape metaphor or encoding a primitive agricultural symbolism. His public commissions include works for the National Capital Commission (Ottawa), the Banff Centre and the CBC Broadcast Centre, Regina.

CAROL A. PHILLIPS

Nunatak [Inuktitut, "lonely peak"], MOUNTAIN rising above large ice sheets. Nunataks were first described from Greenland but also occur in Antarctica and Canada, particularly ELLESMERE ISLAND. The term is also used for any nonglaciated area, highland or lowland, which was surrounded by GLACIER ice. Such nunataks may have been biological refugia where plants and animals survived Quaternary GLACIATION and from which they dispersed as the glaciers melted. This controversial "nunatak hypothesis" was developed to explain strange biotic distributions in Canada and Scandinavia. Quaternary nunataks have been identified in the highlands and leeside lowlands

of Baffin I and Labrador, above or beyond the Laurentide ice limit. Lowlands around Clyde Inlet (Baffin I) and Iron Strand (Labrador) have undisturbed raised beaches with FOSSILS predating the last glaciation. Mountain nunataks have heavily weathered rock surfaces with former ice limits marked by MORAINES or trimlines, below which the rocks appear freshly ice scoured. Several weathering zones, at different altitudes, indicate that the nunataks survived several glaciations. Similar weathering zones and certain plant distributions suggest that Quaternary nunataks exist around the Gulf of St Lawrence. Counter arguments attack the biological evidence and suggest that cold-based glaciers, known to perform little EROSION, may have protected the weathered surfaces during glaciation.

R.J. ROGERSON

Nunavut, meaning "our land" in Inuit dialects of the eastern Northwest Territories, is a proposal for a new territory and government to be carved from the present NWT. This would provide government responsive to the Inuit majority in the unique arctic region comprising the Keewatin and Baffin Island regions, the arctic mainland coast E from Coppermine, and the islands of the Arctic Archipelago. First proposed by Inuit as a single package in the early 1970s, and later separated into claims and Nunavut government negotiations at federal insistence, the proposal recognizes the traditional unity of this large region. Motivating the Inuit are loss of control of their way of life to a non-Inuit administration and the search for oil, gas and minerals by industry without sufficient regard for the impact on wildlife and environment. In 1982 a record voter turnout in the eastern NWT supported Nunavut 4-1 in a plebiscite. Trudeau and Mulroney governments successively pledged their support, but Nunavut has been delayed by uncertainty about hunting grounds and development opportunities for communities close to the proposed western boundary. An approximate boundary has been negotiated by Inuit with DENE and MÉTIS. It has been proposed that a Nunavut government should make Inuktitut an official language of work and law, as in Greenland; should protect non-Inuit rights and should decentralize the administration.

PETER JULL

Nursery School, as part of early childhood education, refers to group experience for 3 and 4 year olds and includes DAY CARE as well as various types of "nursery" programs. Influenced by the work of the McMillan sisters in England and their commitment to nurturing all aspects of the child's development, nursery schools in America took root in the early 20th century. Nursery-school practice today is best described as eclectic in its philosophy and is characterized in Canada, as elsewhere, by much diversity in program function, setting and sponsorship. However, the nursery school's long-standing commitment to parent involvement continues and illustrates a feature of its practice that has influenced thinking about the parent's role in the educational process. See also EDUCATION, EARLY-CHILDHOOD.

ELLEN M. REGAN

Nursing Marie Rollet Hébert [Hubou] has been credited with being the first person in what is now Canada to provide nursing care to the sick. The wife of Louis HÉBERT, a surgeon-apothecary, she arrived in Québec in 1617 and assisted her husband in caring for the sick. The first "trained nurses" to immigrate to the present site of Québec City in 1639 were members of religious orders. In fact, these nurses were not like modern nurses; they served as administrators much of the time, as doctors most of the time (making medicines and undertaking surgery), and many miracles were attributed to them. The 3 nurses were Augustinian Hospitallers whose journey was financed by the

Duchesse d'Aiguillon in France (the duchess, a niece of Cardinal Richelieu, had been stirred by the reports published in JESUIT RELATIONS in France of the needs of Jesuit missionaries in New France). In 1642, in Ville-Marie [Montréal] Jeanne MANCE established a 30-bed hospital called the HÔTEL-DIEU; she was later assisted by nursing Hospitallers of St-Joseph from la Flèche.

The Sisters of Charity of the Hôpital Général of Montréal (GREY NUNS) a noncloistered order, began their work in Québec in 1737. Although these sisters, who might be considered Canada's first PUBLIC HEALTH nurses, built a hospital and an orphanage, they concentrated their work on home visits to the sick. Their free health care was funded by philanthropic gifts, but mostly through a number of entrepreneurial activities that they undertook, eg, a brewery and a freight and cartage company.

In the 18th and 19th centuries the most common health problems in Canada were the frequent EPIDEMICS of smallpox, INFLUENZA, measles, scarlet fever, typhoid, typhus and tuberculosis. Because the nursing sisters recognized the need to segregate the sick, and because much of the population was migrant and homeless, the Grey Nuns built hospitals – one (1845) in Bytown [Ottawa]. In 1844 these women canoed to uncharted areas. In 1855 they built a hospital in the RED RIVER COLONY, and they established an orphanage and a home for the aged at Lac Ste-Anne near Ft Edmonton in 1859. Later they built substantial hospitals in Ft McMurray, Alta (1938), Ft Resolution, NWT (1939), and Ft Rae, NWT (1940).

In 1819 the 24-bed Montreal General Hospital was opened in a building on Craig Street. By 1822 it had moved to a new building and expanded to 72 beds. It was affiliated with the Montreal Medical Institution which was eventually absorbed by the medical faculty of McGill University. The early allopathic physicians tried to introduce untrained lay nurses into the hospital – an act that was unheard of in the French community, where it was believed that the sick should be nursed by sisters devoted to the service of God. The outcome was a duel (not fatal) between one of the anglophone doctors, Dr Caldwell, and a member of the legislature, Michael O'Sullivan; the result was that untrained lay nurses were hired.

In the 19th century, during the height of epidemics, the hospitals of the nursing sisters were filled to capacity, so tents and other temporary shelters had to be erected to house the sick. To alleviate some of these problems, wealthy women created benevolent societies in their communities. Assisted by municipal and provincial funds, many of these women's groups managed to construct hospitals. These hospitals were reminiscent of the institutions in England before Florence Nightingale's time – sanitary conditions were not considered important, and the care of the sick was undertaken by untrained staff who were paid in beer and shared the food and lodgings of the patients.

Other hospitals were established as moneymaking ventures by private individuals. It was in one of these hospitals, started by an entrepreneurial physician, Dr T. Mack, that the first school of nursing was established, at the General and Marine Hospital in St Catharines, Ont, in 1874.

After several unsuccessful attempts, nursing schools based on a modification of the Nightingale system were also started at the Toronto General Hospital (1881) and Montreal General Hospital (1890). Apart from a director of nursing and perhaps a supervisor-instructor, the student nurses generally comprised the entire nursing staff of the lay hospitals. Often the students were sent out to attend private cases, but their wages were usurped by the hospitals. Graduate nurses,

most of whom were not employed in these institutions, marketed their services in the community, undertaking private nursing in the homes of the more wealthy citizens.

To close the gap between the nursing care of the affluent and the poorer working people, the VICTORIAN ORDER OF NURSES (VON) was set up in 1897 by Lady ABERDEEN, the wife of the governor general. The opposition of doctors to an order of health workers who were chosen by their communities and who returned to the communities after a short training in first aid, hygiene, etc, turned this national, nonprofit organization into one that employed many professional nurses under more restricted circumstances than previously designed. In its early years, however, the VON was largely concerned with the treatment and control of communicable diseases and with child health care. To meet an acute need for hospitals, especially in western Canada, the VON built and operated some 40 hospitals, ranging in size from 6 to 40 beds. Its nurses also administered to miners during the KLONDIKE GOLD RUSH and staffed the newly built hospital in Dawson City. After 1924, when control over the last of its hospitals had been transferred to municipal authorities, the VON concentrated on visiting nursing.

Promoted by the International Council of Nurses, an organization arising out of the women's movement in the late 19th century, the Canadian nurses, led by Mary Agnes Snively, the superintendent of nurses at the Toronto General Hospital from 1884 to 1910, established a national organization in Canada and lobbied for legislation granting nurses the status of professionals. Their aims were to ensure the quality of nursing care through improved educational programs for nurses and the licensing of graduates to protect the title of nurse. In 1907 the Canadian National Association of Nurses, the precursor to the present Canadian Nurses' Association (CNA), was formed; in 1908 it joined the international body. In 1916 it founded its national monthly magazine publication, *The Canadian Nurse*.

Securing legislation for nurses was not easy. Legally, women had the same status as imbeciles and children, and many members of Parliament did not feel that women were capable of managing such worldly affairs. The schools of nursing and the hospitals were run by male doctors and administrators who did not wish to relinquish their control over the nursing programs to the professional nurses. Even after nurses' Acts had been passed in all provinces (the first in Nova Scotia in 1910) changes in the nursing curriculum were not easily introduced. The first university degree program for nurses, initiated at UBC in 1919, was for a long time the only one in Canada. In a 1932 report on nursing education across Canada, Dr G. Weir found that between 1913 and 1930 there had been a sevenfold increase in the number of hospital-nursing schools, but that these did not provide the quality of education necessary for highly competent nurses. The 220 training schools turned out a disciplined work force largely used to make hospitals attractive for patients. The money charged the patients was not paid to the student nurses for their labour but invested in expanding the physical plant. The working day of a typical nurse was between 12 and 20 hours, with one day (or one half-day) free weekly. The schools themselves were mostly primitive and cramped. In response to this situation the Canadian Nurses' Association and the Canadian RED CROSS SOCIETY (which founded the Metropolitan Demonstration School of Nursing in Windsor, Ont, in 1946) initiated a nursing education program, independent of hospital control, to prove that, if it controlled the curriculum, a school of nursing could train skilled clinical nurses in only 2 years.

Another report, issued under the auspices of the Pilot Project for the Evaluation of Schools in Canada in 1960, recommended that the CNA undertake a study of nursing education in Canada; that a national school improvement program be implemented; and that a national evaluation of nursing service programs be undertaken. Within 10 years, in all but the Atlantic provinces, nursing education was to be carried out within the educational system. In 1984 there were 142 diploma schools of nursing. While some are still located in the hospitals, most are in community colleges. All programs are conducted at the post-secondary level under provincial education requirements. The programs vary from 2 to 3 years. By 1985, 28 universities offered undergraduate degrees (BScN, BN) in nursing; 11 universities offered graduate degrees at the master's level.

Because the primary aim of the hospital schools of nursing had been to supply the institutions with cheap labour, little importance had been paid to the educational programs and none to the community's demand for private-duty nursing. The continual supply of graduates resulted in a high unemployment rate that was exacerbated by the GREAT DEPRESSION. During the 1930s very few people could afford a private nurse. The governments at the time responded by providing funds so that the sick could be sent to hospitals and graduate nurses could be hired to care for them. But high unemployment and poor wages plagued the profession until WWII, when many nurses joined the armed forces as officers. Nevertheless, many women were still attracted to nursing because it was one of the few "respectable" occupations open to them.

The military recruitment of the nurses resulted in a shortage in Canada that was filled by older women returning to the profession they had been forced to leave when they married. Because of demands of homes and families, hospital authorities could no longer require nurses to live within hospital premises and many single women also took this opportunity to move out of nurses' residences. In the community the nurses found their living costs to be higher than their salaries, and they began to demand higher wages. Married nurses also argued for shorter hours to enable them to manage their home responsibilities. Legislation had granted nurses professional status and had given them rights and some power over educational curriculum, but it had not given them the power to improve their wages or working conditions. Thus, they turned to unionization.

The first group of nurses to negotiate an employment contract in 1939 did so through a professional organization formed by a nursing sister in Québec City. In 1945 the BC nurses' professional association became the first to assist nurses in becoming unionized province wide. It was not until 20 years later that nurses in the rest of the country followed suit. In 1973 the Saskatchewan Supreme Court ruled that the professional association in that province could no longer involve itself in union activities. As a result the collective bargaining arm of the association split off and became a full-fledged nurses' union. Similar separations occurred in other provinces as well; by 1980 all of the medical nurses had 2 provincial organizations to represent their interests – a professional body and a nurses' union.

In 1981 the 3 nurses' federations (unions) in Québec joined together to form a bargaining cartel called the Fédération d'infirmières et infirmiers du Québec. That same year the nurses' unions in most provinces other than Québec joined to form the National Federation of Nurses' Unions. At the national level the nurses' interests were then represented by the union and by the professional body, the Canadian Nurses' Association.

Georgina Fane Pope, First Matron of the Canadian Army Medical Corps (*courtesy Canadian War Museum/ NMC/84-5738*).

In 1986 there were 240 000 registered nurses and 205 000 in active practice in Canada. Most of them were employed in hospitals while others worked as nurse educators or nurse practitioners. About 7% were employed in areas such as community health, public health, outpost nursing, home-care nursing and industrial nursing. Only 2% (some 5500) nurses are male.

Psychiatric Nursing The history of psychiatric nursing is separate from that of medical nursing but follows a similar pattern. The first psychiatric nurses were the French religious sisters who in 1714 established a 12-bed ward in the hospital in Québec City. The forerunners to the contemporary psychiatric nurses were employed as custodial workers in the new asylum in Brandon, Man. In 1921 regular training programs for nurses were organized in this hospital. Other training programs were soon established in the psychiatric hospitals in the other 3 western provinces.

In contrast to the medical nurses, psychiatric nurses were unionized with the rest of the public service beginning in the 1940s, but they soon felt the need for control of their own profession. The movement for professionalization of psychiatric nurses began in Saskatchewan in 1948. The BC psychiatric nurses gained recognition as recently

Canadian nursing sisters at 1st Canadian General Hospital, Étaples, France, helping to clean up after German bombing in which 3 nurses were killed, June 1918 (*courtesy National Archives of Canada/PA-3747*).

as 1968. A few years prior to this, the precursor to the Psychiatric Nurses' Association of Canada had been formed. In 1961 the *Canadian Journal of Psychiatric Nursing* succeeded an earlier publication devoted to issues in the profession.

In 1987 there were 5400 registered active psychiatric nurses in western Canada, most of whom were employed in psychiatric hospitals and homes for the mentally handicapped. A new area has opened up for psychiatric nurses in community health and a few are employed in this type of work.

Public Health In 1919 a federal department of health was founded in response to the influenza epidemic, and provincial departments of health began to replace provincial health boards. Provincial public-health nursing services were developed, beginning in Manitoba in 1916, to assist with municipal immunization and child health-protection programs. The federal health department, which was replaced in 1944 by the Department of NATIONAL HEALTH AND WELFARE, is now responsible for all federal matters relating to the promotion and preservation of health, social security, emergency health services, and for the provision of health, medical and hospital services to Indians, Inuit and the general population of the 2 territories, etc (*see* NATIVE PEOPLE, HEALTH). Since 1945, nursing positions have been established to advise the department, provide consultative services to the provinces and direct services to certain segments of the population. The Medical Services Branch of Health and Welfare also provides direct nursing services to a small segment of the population, ie, Indians, Inuit and other residents of the territories. The branch administers and staffs the outpost nursing stations and health services where registered professional nurses function as general practitioners. *See also* NURSING SISTERS.

PHYLLIS MARIE JENSEN

Reading: A. Baumgart and J. Larsen, *Canadian Nursing Faces the Future* (1988); J.M. Gibbon, *Three Centuries of Canadian Nursing* (1947).

Nursing Sisters Until the NORTH-WEST REBELLION of 1885, women who cared for the wounded worked without official military recognition. At this time, Hannah Grier Coome, mother foundress of the Sisterhood of St John the Divine in Toronto and Kate Miller, head nurse at the Winnipeg General Hospital, were requested by Lt-Col Darby Bergin, surgeon general of the Canadian Militia, to arrange for the care of the wounded in units at Moose Jaw and Saskatoon, respectively.

In the SOUTH AFRICAN WAR, women volunteering in 1899 for nursing service were sent overseas under Georgina Fane POPE to serve with the British Medical Staff Corps as nursing sisters. The third group sent in 1902 were commissioned as lieutenants in the Canadian Army Nursing Service, an integral part of the Canadian Army Medical Corps.

Between 1914 and 1918, more than 3000 nursing sisters with officer rank served in Canada, England, France, Belgium and around the Mediterranean. Nicknamed the "bluebirds" by soldiers grateful for a glimpse of their blue dresses and white veils, they received many honours and gained a high reputation for their courage and compassion. Forty-seven lost their lives while on active duty, victims of enemy attack or disease contracted from patients.

With the declaration of war in Sept 1939, hundreds of nurses rushed to enlist. By the war's end, 4480 nursing sisters had served – 3656 with the Royal Canadian Army Medical Corps, 481 with the Royal Canadian Air Force Medical Branch and 343 with the Royal Canadian Naval Medical Service. On duty overseas and in Canada, they staffed more than 100 major hospital units and cared for over 60 000 wounded Canadians and numerous casualties from other countries.

The nursing sisters during WWII received lectures on military law, map reading and security, instruction in gas warfare and casualty evacuation, training in large-scale military maneuvers. They worked in conditions ranging from canvas tents with wooden floors to established hospitals. They were torpedoed while on ships, were interned as prisoners of war in Hong Kong, and were casualties of accidents and disease. Sixty nurses served in the Korean War, and at present 469 serve in militray bases in Canada and Europe.

NANCY MILLER CHENIER

Nutchatlaht ("people of the mountain") a NOOTKA tribe on the W coast of Vancouver I, BC. They formerly consisted of independent groups, which became reduced from warfare and disease, and amalgamated as a tribe in the historical period. The tribal village is Nuchatl at the mouth of Esperanza Inlet. JOHN DEWHIRST

Nuthatch (Sittidae), family of small, tree-climbing birds with short tail, pointed bill and long, sturdy toes and claws. Of the 18 species of true nuthatches in the genus *Sitta*, 3 occur in Canada. Red-breasted nuthatch (*S. canadensis*) is found coast to coast; white-breasted nuthatch (*S. carolinensis*) has a patchy distribution in southern areas. The pygmy nuthatch (*S. pygmaea*) is restricted primarily to the southern interior of BC. They eat invertebrates and seeds and often store seeds in crevices in bark. Hard-shelled seeds are hammered open in such crevices, hence the name "nuthatch." Nuthatches excavate nest cavities in trees and may modify natural cavities with mud masonry to reduce the size of the entrance hole. They lay 4-10 eggs. The young have a very long nestling period (22-24 days). Nuthatches do not migrate but sometimes undergo massive eruptive flights. They are easily identified by their loud and characteristic calls and sometimes associate with chickadees, kinglets and other birds in mixed-species feeding flocks. JAMES N.M. SMITH

Red-breasted nuthatch (*S. canadensis*) (*artwork by Claire Tremblay*).

Nuu-Chah-Nulth ("All along the mountains") in reference to the mountains of Vancouver I, BC, which are common to all the NOOTKA tribes. This name was devised in 1978 by the (then) West Coast Tribal Council to replace "Nootka" as the ethnic name for the Nootka. "Nootka" is a European misnomer, and the Nootka traditionally had no national or collective name for themselves as a people. The new name has been widely adopted by the Nootka and by government agencies and non-Indians. JOHN DEWHIRST

O Canada!, Canada's national anthem, was approved by Parliament in 1967 and officially adopted under the National Anthem Act, 27 June 1980. The music was written by composer Calixa LAVALLÉE and the words by Judge Adolphe-Basile ROUTHIER. Several attempts had been made to compose a national song for French Canadians, including one by Sir George-Étienne CARTIER, who sang his "O Canada! mon pays! mes amours!" at the founding meeting of the ST-JEAN BAPTISTE SOCIETY in 1834. The origins of Lavallée's work, however, are not clear. He may have been invited to compose a national song for the St-Jean Baptiste celebrations in June 1880. An article in *La Presse* (Dec 1920) claimed that Routhier wrote the words first and that Lt-Gov Théodore Robitaille begged Lavallée to put them to music. Routhier's own version was that he had heard Lavallée perform the "march héroïque" and wrote all 4 verses the next night.

In any case, words and music were completed by early May 1880 as announcements were made in the press that 5000 copies would be distributed to the public. It is not known if "O Canada!" was premiered, as intended, during a mass held on the Plains of Abraham on the morning of 24 June 1880, but it was certainly performed that evening at a banquet at the skaters' pavilion at Québec City, attended by Gov Gen the marquess of Lorne. The song's popularity grew in Québec, but it was not heard in English Canada until 20 years later. It was likely sung in Toronto in 1901 for a visit of the future King George V, but in a literal translation that was not well received. The translation that gained popularity was written in 1908 by Robert Stanley Weir, Montréal-based lawyer and author (1858-1926). The words were somewhat altered after debate in Parliament in 1967. The words of the first verse in English and in French are as follows.

O Canada! Our home and native land!
True patriot love in all thy sons command.
With glowing hearts we see thee rise,
The True North strong and free!
From far and wide, O Canada, we stand on guard for thee.
God keep our land glorious and free!
O Canada, we stand on guard for thee.
O Canada, we stand on guard for thee!

Ô Canada, terre de nos aïeux,
Ton front est ceint de fleurons glorieux,
Car ton bras sait porter l'épée,
Il sait porter la croix!
Ton histoire est une épopée
Des plus brillants exploits.
Et ta valeur de foi trempée,
Protégera nos foyers et nos droits,
Protégera nos foyers et nos droits

Oak (*Quercus*), genus of trees and shrubs of the beech family (Fagaceae). Of the estimated 200 species found worldwide, 75-80 occur in N America and 10 in Canada. Canadian species grow very locally in Ontario and eastward, except Garry oak, found only in BC, and bur oak, which occurs as far W as Manitoba. Oaks are usually divided into 3 groups: red or black oaks (red, black and pin); white oaks (white, Garry and bur); and chestnut oaks (swamp white, chinquapin, dwarf cinquapin and chestnut). These beautiful trees have a fairly short trunk, a broad crown and alternate, simple, usually lobed leaves of variable shape and size. The acorns, produced in large quantities, are important to the diets of various wild animals. Oaks are generally found in areas with moderate precipitation. They flourish on hillsides where the most suitable lighting and well-drained soil are found, except swamp white oak which prefers low, wet terrain. The hard,

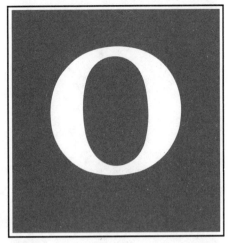

strong wood, highly valued for cabinetmaking and parquetry, is also used for casks for whisky. Known for its strength and longevity, the oak has been the national symbol of several peoples and is often referred to in literature. The generic name means "most excellent of trees."

ESTELLE LACOURSIÈRE

Oak Bay, District Municipality, pop 17 065 (1986c), 16 990 (1981c), area 1637 ha, inc 1906, is located on the SE corner of Vancouver I, adjoining the city of VICTORIA. Oak Bay is surrounded by the Pacific Ocean on the S and E and overlooks Haro Strait.

Oak Bay has developed into a high-quality residential area and retirement community, and contains no large industries. A strong British influence can be seen and heard in the many tea shops, English-styled buildings, English accents and private schools. Oak Bay is governed by a mayor and 6 aldermen, and shares some responsibility with the Capital Regional Dist. The townscape includes many fine examples of BC's grandest architectural era, including many residences designed by F.M. RATTENBURY. Oak Bay also contains the oldest continuously occupied dwelling in western Canada – Tod House, built in 1851 for John Tod, an HBC fur trader. The most famous annual event is a giant tea party held in early June. ALAN F.J. ARTIBISE

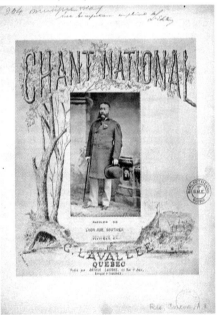

"O Canada!," the first edition (*courtesy Musée du Séminaire de Québec/photo by Pierre Soulard*).

Bur oak (*Quercus macrocarpa*), with flowers and acorn (*artwork by Claire Tremblay*).

Oak Island, one of over 300 islands in MAHONE BAY on Nova Scotia's Atlantic coast, is about 1.6 km long and 0.8 km wide. It is reputed by legend to be the site of buried treasure, the loot being attributed to various pirates, including William Kidd, Henry Morgan and Blackbeard, as well as to Inca refugees fleeing from Spanish conquistadores in S America. In 1795, 3 men discovered a depression in the ground near a huge oak tree and evidence that a block and tackle had been used there. Their digging revealed a filled-in shaft with platforms of decayed oak logs at 3 m levels. They quit digging at 9 m, but in 1804 another group reached the 30 m level before the shaft filled up with salt water. Subsequent digs uncovered tunnels connecting the "money pit" with the ocean. A dam built to solve the problem was destroyed in a storm. Vast sums of money have since been spent in excavations that have cratered the island, and 3 treasure hunters have died in an accident in 1965. Though no treasure has been found, a submarine TV camera, lowered into a cavity 60 m below the surface in 1971, produced faint images of 3 chests, a pick and a dismembered human hand. EDWARD BUTTS

Reading: W.S. Crocker, *The Oak Island Quest* (1978).

Oakes, Sir Harry, prospector, mine owner (b at Sangerville, Maine 23 Dec 1874; d near Nassau, Bahamas 8 July 1943). A graduate of Bowdoin College, Oakes abandoned medical school in 1898 to prospect in the Klondike. After working in mining camps around the world, he staked the Lakeshore and Tough-Oakes properties near Swastika, Ont, in 1911. He became immensely wealthy from the Lake Shore mine, N America's second-largest gold producer, but ill health, disappointment at not being appointed to the Senate, and rising taxes were apparently the reasons for his move to the Bahamas in 1935. There he became a member of the legislature and council and a major real-estate developer. He received a baronetcy in 1939 for his philanthropy in England. Eccentric, unpopular in Canada and exuding the manner and dress of the mining frontier, Oakes died at his home – victim of an unsolved murder. His estate in NIAGARA FALLS, Ont, forms the basis of that city's scenic parks. J. LINDSEY

Oakes Case 1986, in which David E. Oakes was accused of possession of drugs for the purpose of trafficking. The Supreme Court of Canada concluded that, even if drugs are a scourge, s8 of the Narcotic Control Act runs counter to the presumption of innocence enshrined in s11(d) of the CANADIAN CHARTER OF RIGHTS AND FREEDOMS. Section 8 states that if a person is found in possession of a drug, he is presumed to have intended to traffic in it. This constitutes a limitation of rights and freedoms which cannot be justified in a free and democratic society according to s1 of the Charter.

To meet the basic criteria of s1 of the Charter, one must prove the existence of a purpose of sufficient importance to justify the suppression of a right. The concerns must be urgent and real. Moreover the means used to achieve this objective must be reasonable and the measures must not be arbitrary, unfair or irrational. The Court in this instance ruled that s8 did not meet the criterion of a rational connection between possession and drug trafficking. This judgement is the most important to date by the Supreme Court concerning s1 of the Charter. GÉRALD-A. BEAUDOIN

Oakville, Ont, Town, pop 87 107 (1986c), 75 773 (1981c), inc 1857, located on Lk Ontario at the mouth of Sixteen Mile (Oakville) Cr, midway between Toronto and Hamilton. The site, originally inhabited by Mississauga Indians, was purchased 1827 by William Chisholm, a wealthy merchant and politician, and developed as a townsite. The name derives from the local oak-stave industry. Blessed with a good harbour, it became a shipbuilding centre as well as serving an extensive agricultural hinterland. Several buildings have been preserved from the 19th century, including decorous Georgian manses, Victorian follies, the Old Post Office Museum (1835), Thomas House (1829) and a customhouse (1855). An important component of the local economy is the FORD MOTOR CO plant which was built following WWII. A campus of Sheridan College of Applied Arts and Technology is located here. DANIEL FRANCIS

Oats (*Avena sativa*), member of the grass family (Gramineae) grown for its CEREAL grains. For commercial purposes, oats are classed as a small or coarse grain. The origin of cultivated oats cannot be traced, but the species came to Canada with settlers from Europe and was used primarily as livestock feed (it was the principal grain fed to horses) and as a staple breakfast food for humans. Oats are best suited to cool, moist climates. The plant usually reaches 1-1.5 m and requires 90-115 days to mature, depending on variety and growing conditions. Under field conditions, each seed yields 1-3 stems, each of which carries a single panicle (cluster of reproductive organs) bearing hulled seeds. At one time, oats were second only to WHEAT as a grain crop in Canada, occupying up to 6.8 million ha. Oats now occupy 1.16 million ha (1986), the reduction resulting partly from the decline in horse population and partly from the introduction of herbicides to control the closely related weed, wild oats (*A. fatua*). These herbicides affect common oats but do not interfere with crops such as wheat and barley. Canadian scientists have developed many oat varieties with improved disease and lodging resistance, earlier maturity and better yield, as well as hull-less varieties. Oats are still used primarily for livestock feed or breakfast food. M.L. KAUFMANN

Obasan, novel by Joy KOGAWA (1981), is the first novel to trace the internment and dispersal of 20 000 Japanese Canadians from the West Coast during WWII. The narrator, a schoolteacher, was a child when her family was exiled to an interior BC ghost town; after the war ended, the fractured family was again shunted, this time to southern Alberta. Kogawa explores the family's ambivalent responses to these injustices: one member becomes a civil-rights activist who assembles facts to gain redress, while an elder aunt (Obasan)

Lucius O'Brien, *Sunrise on the Saguenay*, oil on canvas, 1880 (*courtesy National Gallery of Canada/Royal Canadian Academy, Diploma Work, deposited 1880*).

fatalistically and silently accepts her sorrow. At the death of her uncle, the withdrawn narrator, who has longed to forget the past and concentrate on the future, uneasily relives her fragmented history, ultimately questioning Obasan's stoicism. That the novel is a harsh indictment of the treatment of the Japanese is clear, but Kogawa's controlled, lyrical prose prevents it from becoming mere bitter recrimination. Rather, it is a moving, powerful and truthful story of human rejection and suffering. DONNA COATES

Oblates of Mary Immaculate, founded in France in 1816. In 1841, at the invitation of Bishop BOURGET, Canada became their first foreign mission. With steady reinforcement from France and Canadian recruits, they moved up the Ottawa Valley and in 1845 into the North-West where the establishment of the Catholic Church in western Canada was largely Oblate work. Their first work was to bring Christianity to the Indians, but in the West especially this led to a large role in bringing about reconciliation between the native peoples and the European settlers and civilization; Fr Albert LACOMBE was particularly important in this area. From the time of Alexandre TACHÉ, one of the first 2 Oblates to come to the West, and later second Bishop and first Archbishop of St-Boniface, Oblates provided the first bishops for most of the dioceses of western Canada.

In 1848 they founded the College of Bytown, renamed College of Ottawa in 1861 and, by Parliament in 1866 and papal charter in 1889, UNIVERSITY OF OTTAWA. In 1965 the Oblate foundation became U Saint-Paul, federated with U of O which was reconstituted as a secular university. Since the 1920s the Canadian Oblates have also been active in foreign missions. They started in Basutoland in 1923 and have continued to be active in Africa and S America. There are now about 150 Canadian Oblates in this work. The Canadian community had been organized into 11 provinces, but consolidation has reduced the number to 8. There are now about 1000 Oblate priests and 300 brothers in Canada. JAMES HANRAHAN

Obomsawin, Alanis, singer, filmmaker (b near Lebanon, NH 31 Aug 1932). An Abenaki, raised on the Odanak reserve, Qué, and later at Trois-Rivières, she was committed at an early age to the celebration of native tradition and the preservation of its culture. In the late 1950s she began to sing professionally and to collect and write songs

on Indian and folk themes; she has since become a popular performer, native activist and philanthropist. She has made educational and documentary films and audio-visual packages, recording elders' and remote peoples' experiences of Indian life. She directed *Christmas at Moose Factory* (NFB, 1971) and directed and produced *Amisk* (1977), *Mother of Many Children* (NFB, 1977) and *Incident at Restigouche* (1984). The latter 2 were shown at U of A at the Third World Film Festival in 1985. BENNETT McCARDLE

O'Brien, Lucius Richard, painter (b at Shanty Bay, UC 15 Aug 1832; d at Toronto 13 Dec 1899). He studied art under John G. HOWARD at Upper Canada College, Toronto. Although he demonstrated youthful artistic ability, he worked as a civil engineer in Toronto until about 1872. Thereafter, as a professional artist, he was considered the country's most proficient landscapist, in both oil and watercolour. O'Brien painted widely, in Ontario and Québec, on Grand Manan and along the Atlantic seaboard and, sponsored by the CPR, in the Rockies and along the Pacific. Many of his landscapes are distinguished by a sense of light similar to that in paintings by Albert Bierstadt and the American "luminists," and by the realism similar to that in paintings by John A. FRASER and other artists associated with the Notman photographic studios. O'Brien supported the Ontario Society of Artists, helped organize the Royal Canadian Academy, serving as its first president, 1880-90, and edited *Picturesque Canada* (1882). After 1882 he painted and taught in Toronto. J. RUSSELL HARPER

Obscenity became an offence in 1663 when Sir Charles Sidley was convicted for his behaviour after a drinking orgy. He appeared naked on a balcony and threw bottles filled with his own urine down among the people in Covent Garden. This case was the basis for convicting Edmond Curl in 1727 for publishing a pornographic book, an English case that established the crime of obscene libel. The Obscene Publications Act of 1857 (England), with its definition of obscenity, was most famously applied in the *Hicklin* case (1868). In upholding an order for the destruction of a publication, Chief Justice Cockburn declared, "I think the test of obscenity is this, whether the tendency of the matter charged as obscenity is to deprave and corrupt those whose minds are open to such immoral influences, and into whose hands a publication of this sort may fall."

From its enactment in 1892, the Canadian Criminal Code has included as an offence the publication of obscene matter tending to the corruption of morals. Definition of "obscene matter" was not provided; the test applied was the *Hicklin* case.

The 1959 amendment to the code (s159.8) reads: "For the purposes of this Act, any publication a dominant characteristic of which is the undue exploitation of sex, or of sex and any one or more of the following subjects, namely, crime, horror, cruelty and violence, shall be deemed to be obscene." The "undue exploitation of sex" is determined either by "the internal necessities" of the work itself, or by "the standards of acceptance of the community," the best guide for which was provided by Mr Justice Freedman of the Manitoba Court of Appeal in the *Dominion News & Gifts* case (1963), upheld by the Supreme Court of Canada: "Those standards are not set by those of lowest taste or interest. Nor are they set exclusively by those of rigid, austere, conservative, or puritan taste and habit of mind. Something approaching a general average of community thinking and feeling has to be discovered . . . Community standards must be contemporary. Times change, and ideas change with them . . . Community standards must also be local. In other words, they must be Canadian. In applying the definition in the Criminal Code, we must determine what is obscene by Canadian standards, regardless of attitudes which may prevail elsewhere, be they more liberal or less so." In 1985 the Supreme Court of Canada, in the *Town Cinema Theatres Ltd* case, added that the "community standards" test is one of tolerance – not what Canadians think is right for themselves to see, but rather what they could not abide other Canadians seeing because it would be beyond contemporary standards of tolerance to allow them to see it. *See also* CENSORSHIP; PORNOGRAPHY.

WALTER S. TARNOPOLSKY

Observatory Since the earliest civilizations, princes and priests have maintained observatories where, by observing the sun, moon, stars and planets, astronomers could determine the passage of the months, seasons and years, and watch the skies for any changes, which they often interpreted as portents. Remains of these early observatories are found worldwide, Stonehenge being one well-known example. Early observatories were located to take advantage of their surroundings, ie, in open terrain with natural or artificial markers, and modern observatories continue to be located at carefully selected sites.

Of the observatories in use before the invention of the telescope, perhaps the most scientifically productive was that of Tycho Brahe, built 400 years ago on the island of Hveen in the Baltic Sea. Johannes Kepler used Tycho's precise sightings of the planets to establish his laws of planetary motion. The first telescopic observatory was that of Galileo (1609). The telescope consisted of tiny lenses mounted in wooden tubes. The era of big-telescope observatories began just over 200 years ago with Sir William Herschel and his metal mirrors in England. The 20th century has seen a constant growth in telescope size, number, complexity and performance.

Optical Observatory

Optical observations are made by means of light, ie, those "optical" photons to which our eyes are sensitive. Stars emit them in great abundance. Modern optical telescopes employ concave (parabolic) mirrors of low-expansion glass as the primary means of collecting photons. One or more following mirrors help form the images of celestial bodies in the focal plane of the telescope. There they are recorded photographically or by means of a modern photon detector. The aim is to extract the maximum information carried by the photons about the nature, origin and behaviour of the object from which they came. Knowledge is greatly increased if the spectrum of the object, rather than its direct image alone, can be observed.

Successful observations depend on many factors, one of which is the siting of the observatory. The best locations will have relatively few cloudy periods throughout the year, air as transparent as possible (mountain tops are preferred) and freedom from local air turbulence of thermal origin, which could blur the image by causing the photons to arrive "out of step." Stable electric power, staff living quarters and technical support facilities must be provided. The largest observatories are usually so remote and of such complexity that they must be supported at the national or international level. Astronomers from distant places take turns as users. It is commonplace for one observatory to contain several telescopes, ranging from 3 or 4 m to a few tens of centimetres in mirror diameter. A small telescope can be effective and is often preferred for certain types of observation.

The earliest observatory in N America was likely that at Louisbourg (1750-51) and a number of observatories with modest telescopes were created in Canada in the 19th century: Fredericton, 1851; Québec City, 1854; Kingston, Ont, 1856; and Montréal, 1879. An early observatory at Toronto, under government auspices, was devoted to observations of geomagnetism and, later, METEOROLOGY as well as ASTRONOMY. In those days, much effort was expended in the determination of longitude by astronomical observations, and indeed it was the opening up of the Canadian West and the need for accurate surveys and maps that led to the founding of the Dominion Observatory in Ottawa in 1905. Although its primary purpose was geodetic and included the provision and distribution of precise TIME signals, research in "physical astronomy" was not neglected. Physical astronomy, now called astrophysics, was to develop rapidly.

Within 8 years the federal government decided to build an astrophysical observatory to be furnished with a telescope which, in its time, was the largest in the world. After a careful survey, Victoria, BC, was selected as the best site in Canada, with "good seeing" and a large percentage of clear nights. The Dominion Astrophysical Observatory (DAO) began its work in 1918, specializing in observing the spectra of faint stars and measuring their radial velocities by means of the Doppler effect. The DAO has 2 large telescopes (now operated by the NATIONAL RESEARCH COUNCIL), the original (1.83 m) and a more modern, smaller one (1.22 m).

In 1933 Mrs David DUNLAP presented U of T with a 74-inch (1.88 m) telescope and in 1935 the David Dunlap Observatory was completed in nearby Richmond Hill. Two smaller telescopes have since been added, and DDO's research has recently expanded into southern skies. In 1971 a 61 cm telescope was erected by the university on Las Campanas in Chile; surprisingly, this small telescope soon became the most productive of all Canadian telescopes. In 1987 Manitoba-born Ian Shelton discovered Supernova 1987A in the Large Magellanic Cloud.

Canada's latest development in optical observatories has been the construction of the Canada-France-Hawaii Telescope (CFHT) on Mauna Kea in Hawaii. During the 1960s several groups in Canada pointed out the need for a larger and more up-to-date telescope. The federal government was sympathetic and finally decided on a joint undertaking with France and the state of Hawaii. The site, at an altitude of 4200 m (and above 40% of Earth's atmosphere), is regarded as the best in the Northern Hemisphere. A 3.6 m telescope of the most modern design (the mirror was ground and polished in Victoria) was inaugurated in Sept 1979. Canadian astronomers from all across the country compete for 45% of the CFHT telescope time; the rest is used by France and Hawaii. Recent studies have included nearby objects, such as Halley's Comet and Loki, the lava lake on Jupiter's satellite Io.

Canada, like other countries searching for a fuller understanding of the universe, has many smaller observatories from coast to coast. Most major universities maintain telescopes for instruction and research, including U de Montréal and Laval (jointly at Mégantic, Qué), U of Western Ontario (at London), York U, U of Alberta, U of Calgary, UBC and U of Victoria. Several amateur centres across Canada have their own telescopes.

DONALD A. MACRAE

Radio Observatory

Soon after the discovery of radio waves by Heinrich Hertz in 1887 came the realization that objects that emit light and heat also emit radio waves. Thomas Edison appears to have been the first to suggest the possibility of detecting radio waves from the sun and several early attempts were made. However, extraterrestial radio signals were not discovered until 1932. During an investigation of the origin of radio interference (static) Karl Jansky, an American engineer, noticed that his antenna was receiving radio noise from the direction of the centre of our GALAXY. Grote Reber built the first equipment specially designed to study long-wave radiation from celestial bodies. The first radio astronomical observations in Canada were made in 1946 by A.E. COVINGTON, working at the NRC, Ottawa. When RADAR research was curtailed at the close of WWII, Covington used surplus equipment to construct a radio telescope which he used to detect radio emissions from the sun. The NRC has continued the program of radio observations of the sun to the present day.

Both optical and radio telescopes collect energy in the form of electromagnetic radiation. They differ, however, in the frequency (wavelength) of the radiation that they can detect. Radio waves that can penetrate Earth's atmosphere have wavelengths ranging from a few millimetres to tens of metres (about 10 000 to 100 million times longer than light waves). Telescopes for observations at shorter radio wavelengths often resemble optical telescopes and normally consist of a parabolic dish, analogous to the mirror of a reflecting telescope. Telescopes for use at long wavelengths are quite different, usually consisting of large arrays of individual radio antennae.

Radio signals reaching Earth from celestial sources are exceedingly weak; therefore, radio telescopes must have large collecting areas. A more important consideration is often the telescope's resolving power, ie, its ability to reveal detail in an object's radio image. The resolving power of a telescope is directly proportional to its linear dimensions (not its collecting area) and inversely proportional to the operating wavelength. Since radio wavelengths are long, radio telescopes must have large dimensions to possess even modest resolving powers. For example, the human eye can just distinguish 2 points with an angular separation of one minute of arc. To do the same thing, a radio telescope operating at a wavelength of one metre must have a diameter of about 3 km. Since it is impractical to build single structures of such dimensions, radio scientists have devised ways of interconnecting several smaller elements (dishes or antennae) to produce a single telescope. Both single- and multi-element telescopes are used at Canadian radio observatories.

The NRC's Herzberg Institute of Astrophysics operates 2 national radio observatories: Algonquin Radio Observatory (ARO) and Dominion Radio Astrophysical Observatory (DRAO). Both sites were chosen for their freedom from man-made radio interference which can readily spoil measurement of the very weak signals from astronomical sources.

ARO, located in the central region of Ontario's ALGONQUIN PROVINCIAL PARK, began operation in 1960 with the transfer from Ottawa of the solar program, which was becoming increasingly affected by radar and radio interference. A parabolic telescope was installed to monitor solar emission continually at a wavelength of 10.7 cm. To extend the time during which the sun is under continuous observation, an identical telescope was later installed at DRAO. The dish is relatively small (1.8 m diameter), since its purpose is to collect radiation from the sun's entire disk. The intensity of the radiation at a wavelength of 10.7 cm is an effective measure of the general level of solar activity and a sudden enhancement indicates the occurrence of a solar flare. The measurements are important in studies of the relationship between solar activity and geophysical phenomena (eg, NORTHERN LIGHTS). Determination of the position of localized regions of intense solar emissions is made at noon each day, using a multi-element telescope that produces strip scans of the sun with a resolution of 1.5 minutes of arc (ie, one-twentieth of the sun's diameter) in the E-W direction. When compared with optical photographs, these scans enable the regions of enhanced emission to be identified.

Another telescope located at the ARO is a large parabolic dish (46 m in diameter) completed in 1966. This instrument has been used by many observers on a variety of programs, including studies of PLANETS, interstellar matter, external galaxies and QUASARS. These observations are limited by the accuracy of the parabolic surface to wavelengths longer than about 1 cm. It had been planned to replace the original surface with a more accurate one which would permit observations to be made at wavelengths as short as 3 mm. However, in 1987 the NRC decided not to proceed with the resurfacing but opted instead to close down operation of the 46 m telescope and acquire a 25% share of a telescope nearing completion by the UK and the Netherlands on Mauna Kea in Hawaii. This telescope, known as the James Clerk Maxwell Telescope, has a parabolic dish, 15 m in diameter, with an extremely accurate surface. This precision, combined with the altitude of the site, will enable observations to be made at wavelengths as short as 0.4 mm, thus opening up to Canadian astronomers a new, relatively unexplored, region of the electromagnetic spectrum.

DRAO, situated in a secluded valley S of Penticton, BC, opened in 1960. The first instrument, a 26 m parabolic telescope and associated receiver, was designed primarily for studies of our galaxy, a field in which Canadian optical astronomers have made significant contributions. The dish's surface is aluminum mesh, an almost perfect reflector at a wavelength of 21 cm, which is the wavelength of emission and absorption of hydrogen gas, the major constituent of interstellar space. From observations of the distribution of this gas in the galaxy and its motions, as revealed

The Canada-France-Hawaii Telescope on Mauna Kea in Hawaii is located at an elevation of 4200 m, above 40% of the Earth's atmosphere. It is regarded as the best site for an observatory in the Northern Hemisphere (*courtesy National Research Council*).

by shifts in the observed wavelength, much has been learned about our galaxy's structure and dynamics.

The telescope accepts radiation from an area of the sky about 0.5° in diameter, but the much smaller angular structures of many nebulae and other objects in our galaxy cannot be revealed by the telescope. In addition, the resolving power is inadequate for studies of even the closest external galaxies. Since construction of a parabolic telescope of sufficient size is impractical, a different instrument has been constructed, the Aperture Synthesis Telescope, which employs a technique first developed at Cambridge University. The telescope consists of four 8.5 m parabolic dishes, the outputs of which are combined. Two of the dishes are movable on an E-W track 300 m long; 2 are fixed, one 300 m E of the track and the other 300 m W. The 4 dishes observe the same region of the sky for 12 hours at each of about 120 positions of the movable dishes. When used with its spectrometer receiver, the system produces computer maps at 128 wavelengths of an area of the sky 2° in diameter, with a resolution of one minute of arc. The performance of this telescope is soon to be improved by increasing the number of dishes from 4 to 7.

For observations at a wavelength of 13.5 m, the observatory employs a telescope consisting of a large number of collecting elements or dipole antennae, laid out in a horizontal plane in the form of a "T." Each dipole is connected by cable to the centre of the array, where the signals are amplified and recorded. The crossbar of the "T" is 1.3 km long and the entire array occupies an area of 65 000 km². Its performance is approximately equivalent to that of a conventional paraboloid 750 m in diameter.

In 1967 radio astronomers and engineers from Canadian universities and the NRC pioneered the development of a powerful new technique which has dramatically increased the resolution attainable at radio wavelengths. Known as Very Long Baseline Interferometry, the technique allows signals collected with widely separated telescopes to be combined to form a single instrument. Independent, highly stable atomic clocks are used to convert the signals collected at each telescope to lower frequencies which can be recorded on magnetic tape, together with accurate time markers. The tapes are subsequently brought together and played in unison. For the initial experiments, the parabolic telescopes at Penticton and Algonquin Park were used to form a 2-element interferometer. More recently, how-

ever, a number of the world's radio telescopes have been used simultaneously to form a powerful, integrated instrument capable of producing images that reveal detail of the order of one-thousandth of one second of arc. This is 100-1000 times better than can normally be obtained with the largest optical telescopes. Thus, it is now possible to study the structure of quasars and the small cores of galaxies, to observe changes in their structure with time and to investigate details of many other radio sources. In addition, very accurate determinations of the positions of radio sources are now possible, permitting the investigation of relativistic and other effects. In geophysics the ability to measure small angular displacements can be inverted to study the motion of Earth's axis of rotation, variations in its rate of rotation, movements of its crust, etc. These and other possibilities have led to an imaginative proposal by Canadian scientists to build a Canadian Long Baseline Array, consisting of 8 radio telescopes, in a line from BC to Newfoundland, operating as a single instrument. If constructed, it would be the world's largest telescope, as large as Canada itself. However, approval for this major undertaking has not been obtained.   J.L. LOCKE

Space Observatory

Various kinds of electromagnetic radiation (ie, very low-energy infrared radiation and high-energy ultraviolet and X-ray radiation) are incapable of penetrating Earth's atmosphere and must be observed from the upper atmosphere or from space. Upper-atmosphere observations have been an ongoing part of Canada's satellite-research program since its inception, and NRC is involved in various space-oriented programs with the US and European space authorities (NASA and ESA, respectively). The most dramatic of these projects is Starlab, a joint Australia-US program to construct a 1 m telescope equipped with a camera and spectrograph, to be carried to one of NASA's proposed space platforms aboard a Space Shuttle flight in the late 1980s. The Canadian government withdrew from the program in 1984.

Occupational Diseases are disorders of health resulting from conditions related to the workplace. They are distinguished from occupational injuries, which are disorders resulting from trauma such as strains or sprains, lacerations, burns, or soft-tissue injuries such as bruises. In general, occupational disorders are related to exposures to physical, chemical or, controversially, psychological hazards; they usually develop over time and often resemble or duplicate diseases occurring in other settings. By comparison, occupational injuries are mostly the result of mechanical factors such as lifting or bending, or failures in safety measures resulting in accidents or fires. In practice, the dividing line is rather arbitrary (eg, established because of administrative convenience): certain types of injury, such as tendonitis resulting from repetitive movements, are counted as "diseases" and certain types of what would normally be considered a disease, such as acute poisoning by chemicals discovered immediately, are counted as "injuries."

Occupational diseases often develop over many months or years, depending on the intensity and circumstances of exposure. Cancer resulting from inhalation of ASBESTOS fibres, for example, generally takes at least 20 years to develop and when it does develop it is difficult or impossible to identify the exact cause in the individual patient. Occupational diseases often resemble other medical conditions; for example, LEAD poisoning duplicates the symptoms of several illnesses, and asthma resulting from sensitization to chemicals in the workplace is often attributed to exposures at home. For these reasons, most occupational diseases are often overlooked or misdiagnosed and are often much more common than is generally realized.

The importance of recognizing a disease as occupational in origin is threefold: to limit its effect on the patient; to prevent its occurrence in others; and to compensate those disabled by it. Toxic effects can often be limited if exposure ceases and treatment is started early. When a worker is recognized as having an occupational disease, others exposed to the possible cause can be protected before they, too, develop the illness. Compensation is the role of the WORKERS' COMPENSATION systems in all provinces and among employees of the federal government.

Workers' compensation is a system of mandatory insurance against injury to employees required of all employers in business and industry above a certain size. It was set up in order to avoid the necessity of frequent lawsuits between workers and employers. Occupational diseases present difficult problems for workers' compensation boards compared to the relative ease by which injuries are handled. As noted, recognition of an occupational disease is often delayed and uncertain, and may be disputed in a given case, requiring the opinion of expert consultants. Provincial boards vary in their acceptance of certain types of claims. Proving a case generally means demonstrating that the patient has the disease, was exposed on the job to a substance or to conditions known to cause it, and had no other likely cause. Virtually every board in Canada would accept any of the 29 groups of occupational diseases recognized by the International Labour Organization as being work-related, but acceptance of less well-established conditions such as suspected but not proven causes of cancer would vary among the boards. Few, if any, would accept highly speculative or unproven work-related causes of illness as the basis for a judgement. On the other hand, many boards have found it so difficult to sort out cancer due to cigarette smoking from that due to occupational exposure that they routinely disregard smoking as the most likely cause in cancer patients known to have been exposed to cancer-causing chemicals in the workplace.

Certain occupational diseases occur exclusively in certain industries or occupations; these are often given fanciful names such as *welder's flash* (an inflammation of the eye caused by ultraviolet light from welding) or *farmer's lung* (an inflammatory lung disease caused by inhalation of mold spores). Others occur in almost every industry, such as low back pain (more properly considered an injury) and noise-induced hearing loss. About half of all occupational diseases are skin disorders, followed in order by eye disorders, lung disorders, poisonings involving the body as a whole (as by lead, MERCURY or pesticides), and other conditions including disorders of the nervous system, heart and musculoskeletal system. Psychiatric and stress-related disorders are very controversial because a clear relationship to work is very difficult to prove.

The history of occupational diseases is as old as organized economic activity. Back pain resulting from strain at work is described in an Egyptian papyrus dating to at least 1600 BC. Other occupational disorders were prominently mentioned by Hippocrates in 460 BC and by Roman authors. In the Middle Ages and early Renaissance, several medical treatises were written on the hazards of mining and smelting. The modern era of occupational medicine dates from the early 1700s, when the great Italian physician Bernadino Ramazzini wrote the first comprehensive textbook in the field. Charles Thackrah wrote the first such book in English in 1831, during which time unprecedented and extensive legislation was being enacted in Britain to protect the health of workers, to control CHILD LABOUR, and to protect the public health at a time of rampant pollution and adulteration of food. These laws formed the basis for Canadian legislation before Confederation, and occupational health and workers' compensation are provincial responsibilities under the terms of the Constitution. In 1914, workers' compensation, patterned after the German system, was introduced into Canada in Ontario. In the 1920s, Dr J. Grant Cunningham founded the Industrial Health Branch in the federal government and through research, education and demonstration promoted the concepts of prevention and early recognition of occupational diseases to industry and to provincial governments. His pioneering work led to many changes and to the training of a generation of occupational health professionals who influenced the practices of Canadian industry and provincial governments. Best known of these was Dr Earnest Mastromatteo of Toronto, who has been prominent for many years in national and international affairs related to the prevention of occupational diseases.

Canada has long been a leader in research on occupational diseases, particularly occupational lung diseases. Sir William OSLER, considered by many to be the greatest and most influential physician Canada has yet produced, wrote extensively on various occupational diseases; in 1876, he wrote a paper on coal workers' pneumoconiosis (often called "black lung") that first brought him to the attention of colleagues in Montréal. Cunningham was particularly interested in silicosis among miners in Ontario. Dr Frederick BANTING, better known as one of the discoverers of insulin, made many contributions to research on silicosis and to aviation medicine.

Interest in occupational diseases in major centres of research tends to be stimulated by economically important problems in local industries. Because of its importance to Québec, studies of asbestos and its health effects have been the principal focus of research at institutions in that province. In Ontario investigators have had particular interests in the mining industry. In BC, occupational causes of asthma and disorders of the flow of air in the lungs have been a major emphasis because of an unusual and common pattern of asthmatic reaction typical of responses to western red cedar, an economically important wood.

All physicians treating adults should have some concern for occupational diseases, whether in treatment or diagnosis or for the implications of certain exposures on the health of their patients. In Canada, physicians may qualify by special training and examination to be specialists in the field of occupational medicine and to be so certified, either by the Royal College of Physicians and Surgeons of Canada if they complete a formal fellowship, or by the Canadian Board of Occupational Medicine if their preparation is otherwise. The national organization of occupational physicians is the Occupational Medical Association of Canada.

Although physicians play an important role in the diagnosis, treatment and certification for compensation due to occupational diseases, this role is shared by occupational health nurses (a specialized nursing field). The critical role of prevention is even more of a team effort, shared by physicians, nurses, safety officers, occupational hygienists (an engineering field of specialization) and several other professionals. All occupational diseases – without exception – are preventable. The obstacles to prevention are usually cost, lack of education and lack of motivation to change practices. The technical means to solve a problem are almost always available. Success in prevention ultimately rests on acceptance by the employer of one's responsibility, co-operation by the workers, teamwork by occupational health professionals, overseeing of government and education of the public.   TEE L. GUIDOTTI

Ocean The world ocean and its marginal seas cover about 71% of the Earth's surface. Its division into individual oceans and seas is largely arbitrary and has varied through the years. Historically, people referred to 5 oceans: Atlantic, Pacific, Indian, Arctic and Antarctic (or Southern). Modern convention speaks of only the first 3: the Arctic is considered a marginal sea of the Atlantic; the Southern, the southern continuation of the Atlantic, Indian and Pacific oceans. Thus, Canada can be seen to be surrounded by 2 (Atlantic, Pacific) or 3 (Atlantic, Pacific, Arctic) oceans, depending on the scheme of division used. The interplay of these ocean waters with freshwater runoff from land creates the conditions that support large biological production on Canada's continental shelves and embayments (*see* COASTAL LANDFORM; DRAINAGE BASINS). The COASTAL WATERS also affect shipping, offshore resource industries and maritime climate. OCEANOGRAPHY is the science that studies the physical, chemical, geological and biological properties of the oceans and analyses the impacts resulting from exploitation of their resources.

The average oceanic depth is nearly 4000 m; that of the marginal seas 1200 m. The continents generally extend under the ocean, forming continental shelves tens to hundreds of kilometres wide and up to 500 m deep. At their outer edge, the water depth increases rapidly to the ocean basin depths of 3000-6000 m. This region is called the continental slope. The oceans are divided into several deep basins by mid-ocean ridges where new oceanic crust is formed (*see* PLATE TECTONICS). Rising to depths of 2000 m or shallower and sometimes forming ISLANDS (eg, Iceland, the Azores), these ridges constrain the distribution of the deep waters and affect the upper-ocean circulation. Transverse ridges (eg, the shallow ridges joining Greenland to Iceland and Scotland) also separate ocean basins.

Island arcs and deep-sea trenches are formed where oceanic crust is moving under another tectonic plate. The deepest oceanic depths are found in such trenches, the greatest being over 11 000 m in the Mariana Trench, western N Pacific. Island arcs (eg, Antilles, Aleutians) frequently form the boundaries between marginal seas and the adjacent ocean. The deep basins are also interrupted by isolated seamounts rising several thousand metres from the seafloor and often forming elongated chains. Some of these volcanic structures rise above the surface and form islands (eg, Hawaiian Is).

The density of seawater is determined by its salinity and temperature, colder or more saline water being denser. In the ocean, water characteristics change with depth: the least dense water is at the surface; the most dense at the bottom. In tropical and temperate latitudes, density is largely controlled by temperature; temperature generally decreases with depth. In polar and subpolar regions, salinity plays a more important role; here cold, low-salinity surface layers overlie warmer, saltier deep layers.

In the upper few tens of metres of the ocean, the euphotic zone, one-celled planktonic organisms use sunlight to convert various nutrients (eg, inorganic carbon, nitrates, phosphates) into organic molecules through photosynthesis. By this means they multiply to form a food source for larger organisms, thus forming the basis for

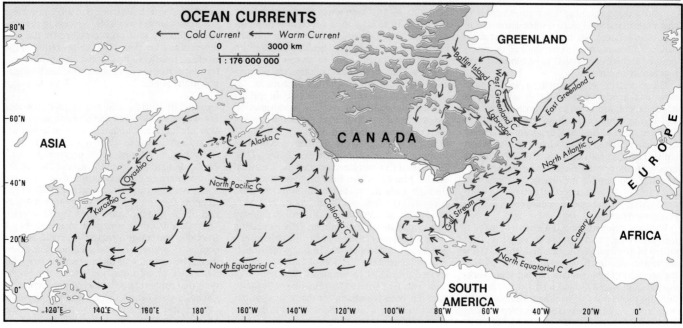

OCEAN CURRENTS
← Cold Current   ← Warm Current
0   3000 km
1 : 176 000 000

marine food chains and webs. The upper ocean usually consists of a "mixed layer" some tens of metres thick which is homogenized through wind and wave action. At the bottom of the mixed layer, the density of the water increases markedly; this region is called the seasonal pycnocline. During spring and summer, in temperate latitudes, shallow mixed layers are formed because solar radiation absorbed in the surface layers makes them warmer and less dense. Biological productivity within the mixed layer depletes the nutrients and the seasonal pycnocline inhibits the transfer of nutrients from below; hence, after an initial spring bloom, biological productivity is limited by the rate at which nutrients can be regenerated from the standing crop. In fall and winter, stronger winds and waves as well as convection caused by cooling at the surface causes the mixed layer to become denser and deeper, incorporating deeper nutrient-rich waters into the surface waters in preparation for the following spring. In subpolar regions, mixed layers deeper than 2000 m can form in late winter.

In general any mechanism which causes mixing of ocean waters contributes to an increase in biological productivity. Frontal mixing between lower salinity inshore waters and warmer offshore waters results in the injection of heat, salt and nutrients into the coastal waters. On Canada's East Coast the boundary or front between inshore and offshore waters generally lies beyond the edge of the Continental Shelf, making this an especially rich area for fishing (see GRAND BANKS). Other factors which can promote horizontal and vertical mixing include wind action and eddies spinning off major currents. Mixing between surface and bottom waters occurs more readily if the water is relatively shallow (up to 200 m). Hence, the continental shelves are more productive than open-ocean areas. Canada has a much greater area of shelf on the East Coast than on the West Coast, a fact reflected in much greater fish catches in the East.

The seasonal pycnocline changes in depth and temperature from season to season. Below it is found the main thermocline where, from depths of 200-4000 m, the water temperature falls from as high as 18°C to 2.5°C. The main thermocline arises because water from the progressively colder, denser, winter-mixed layers of higher latitudes flows equatorward below the warmer, less dense layers. The deepest waters of the main ther-

mocline are formed by winter convection in a few high-latitude locations, then spread to fill the deep basins of the world oceans. These deep waters are remarkably uniform in temperature and salinity. For example, fully 10% of the total volume of the ocean has temperatures of 0.6-1.6°C and salinities of 0.03467-0.03472.

Half of the ocean's volume occurs in 2 concentrations. The first, with temperatures of -0.8 to 2.6°C and salinities of 0.03457 to 0.03476, is formed off Antarctica (especially in the Weddell Sea). It sinks, flows eastward around Antarctica and northward to fill the deep basins of the Indian, Pacific and S Atlantic oceans. The second concentration, with temperatures of 1.7-3.0°C and salinities of 0.03487-0.03496, is formed in the Norwegian and Greenland seas and enters the Atlantic between Greenland and Iceland, and Iceland and Scotland, filling the entire N Atlantic Basin below 2000 m and continuing to flow southward in the S Atlantic, above the Antarctic water moving northward.

Only a small percentage of the total volume of these waters is affected even by an exceptionally severe winter. To change the properties of the deep waters requires periods of hundreds of years or longer; this stability is believed to have a direct effect in moderating short-term climate variations. The deep ocean also contains a vast volume of dissolved carbon dioxide (CO_2) and, by regulating the atmospheric levels of CO_2, plays an important role in determining the world's temperature (see CLIMATE CHANGE).

Early in the atomic age, nations began using the deep oceans as disposal sites for low-level nuclear wastes. It was theorized that these concentrations would be diluted by the large volumes of water and diminished by radioactive decay to levels inconsequential to health before reaching surface waters. The tracking of radioactive isotopes injected into the oceans by atmospheric nuclear testing in the 1950s and 1960s and the direct measurement of deep current velocities have forced a change in the idea of a nearly motionless deep ocean. The practice of dumping in the deep oceans is now being re-evaluated by international agencies. See also HAZARDOUS WASTES; LAW OF THE SEA.   R. ALLYN CLARKE

Ocean Current, large (100 km or more), mostly permanent, horizontal movement of water at all depths in the oceans. Currents are generated by winds, excessive cooling or evaporation at the

ocean surface (thermohaline processes) and tidal forces.

Wind-Driven Currents In the Atlantic and Pacific oceans N of the equator, the combined effects of the strong westerly winds (between 30 and 60° N) and the NE trade winds (10-20° N) cause the near-surface waters to circulate in 2 large, clockwise gyres. Wind drag on the water is the primary driving force. The rotation of the Earth then causes the net movement of the upper layer (ie, Ekman layer, from 0-100 m depth) to be to the right of the wind direction (the Coriolis effect). A convergence of water develops in the Ekman layer between the westerlies and the trade winds, creating a high-pressure area in the ocean around which water circulates clockwise. In the Atlantic this subtropical gyre includes the Gulf Stream and the North Atlantic, Canary and North Equatorial currents; in the N Pacific, the North Equatorial, Kuroshio, North Pacific and California currents.

North of the westerlies, divergences in the Ekman layers create low-pressure areas leading to counterclockwise subpolar gyres. The N Atlantic subpolar gyre includes the North Atlantic, Irminger, Greenland and Labrador currents; the N Pacific subpolar gyre, the North Pacific, Alaska and Oyashio currents. The main currents in BAFFIN BAY are partly an extension of the N Atlantic subpolar gyre.

These ocean-scale gyres are asymmetrical: currents on the western side of the oceans, the Gulf Stream and the Kuroshio, are narrow (100 km) and strong (up to 2.5 m/sec). Zonal currents (those running W to E or E to W) on the eastern sides of the oceans are broad (500-1000 km) and slow (0.2 m/sec). The intensification on the western side results from an increase in the Coriolis effect between the equator and the North Pole, caused by the Earth's spherical shape. Speeds in the major currents diminish with increasing depth, rapidly in the upper 300 m, but there are significant manifestations of the strongest currents at the ocean bottom. The Gulf Stream and the Kuroshio are each estimated to transport, at their maximum, 15×10^7 m³/sec of water. This volume is roughly 15 000 times the average flow of the St Lawrence R or enough to fill Lk Superior in about one day.

South of the equator, the prevailing winds generate anticlockwise subtropical gyres that are similar but less intense than those in the northern oceans. The southern subpolar gyres merge to form a circumpolar current around Antarctica, as there are no landmasses to break up the flow into gyres. Ocean currents vary from day to day but, averaged over a month or so, they appear as constant features.

Variability can be caused by long-period waves (100 hr), especially when the current is in contact with the continental slope. Away from the coasts, the Gulf Stream and Kuroshio exhibit large meanders in their paths that have typical periods of 75 days. The meanders may be started by internal instabilities or by encounters with submarine mountains.

Thermohaline Currents The second group of currents, those driven by thermohaline processes, are found below the wind-driven currents down to the bottom of the ocean. They are not important to high-seas commerce and are generally known only to oceanographers. Most of these deep flows are created by intense cooling of the ocean surface water in the Arctic and Antarctic. Cooling increases the density of water, causing it to sink. This new water (because it was recently at the sea surface) then moves away from the sinking region in distinct currents. High evaporation, eg, in the Mediterranean, also increases density and subsequent sinking by increasing the salinity of the water.

In the mid-ocean, alternate layers of water come from different locations. For example, in most of the N Atlantic Ocean, water at the bottom comes from the Antarctic, but N of 45° N and W of the mid-Atlantic Ridge, the bottom water comes from the Iceland Sea, through the Denmark Str between Greenland and Iceland. Above this layer is the water known as the North Atlantic Deep Water that partly originates in the Norwegian Sea and flows into the Atlantic across the ridge between Iceland and the Faroe Is. Next highest (at 1500-2000 m depth) are the intermediate waters. Labrador Sea water, renewed during severe winters in the deep water E of the pack ice off Labrador, is found in the N Atlantic (N of 45° N). This water is recognizable by its low salinity relative to the waters above and below. Mediterranean water flows out of the Str of Gibraltar and is recognized over much of the N Atlantic by its high salinity, a result of excessive evaporation in the Mediterranean Sea.

Effects Currents have 2 very important effects: they influence both FISHERIES and climate. Currents provide a means by which the deep, nutrient-rich waters are raised up to the sunlit surface layers, thus promoting biological productivity. They also transport significant quantities of heat which strongly influences climate in coastal areas. For Canadians, the most important currents are the LABRADOR CURRENT off the East Coast, and the North Pacific Current, off the West Coast. The Labrador Current gives rise to one of the world's largest fisheries on the Labrador Continental Shelf and the GRAND BANKS of Newfoundland. The North Pacific Current provides a vast reservoir of heat and water that is partly transferred to coastal BC to produce a mild climate and a large, productive forest industry. *See also* COASTAL WATERS; TIDE.
JOHN LAZIER

Ocean Falls, BC, Improvement District, is at the head of Cousins Inlet, an arm of mid-coast Dean Channel. The site was chosen for a pulp-and-paper mill in 1903 because of the power potential of a cascade flowing into the inlet. Sawmill operations commenced in 1909; Pacific Mills' pulp-and-paper mill opened in 1917. In 1972 Crown Zellerbach (Canada), owner since 1954, announced the imminent closure of the mill. In 1973, the New Democratic government bought the town and mill; the Social Credit government closed the mill in 1980 and auctioned the machinery in 1986. The extension of electricity to Bella Bella and exportation of water are projects under way. Ocean Falls, noted for its world-class swimmers (1940s-60s) and for its mean annual precipitation of 4386.8 mm, suffered a mud-ice slide in 1965 in which 7 area residents were killed.
GEORGIANA BALL

Ocean Industry The search for hydrocarbon resources in offshore areas, the driving force behind the development of the ocean industry, began in earnest in the early 1960s in the shallow waters of the Gulf of Mexico. Since then, the hunt has expanded to include the coastal waters of the North Sea, Australia, South-East Asia, India and Canada. More than 40 countries have plans for supporting such activities, creating a potential for the export of services and equipment, which has heavily influenced the development of the Canadian ocean industry.

In 1978 a federally sponsored sector task force identified 180 companies engaged in the ocean industry. Of these, 40 were core organizations depending on the market for most of their revenues. By the end of 1982 the number of companies in the field had grown by about 15%. Approximately 50% of all industry sales, including hardware (drilling rigs, SUBMERSIBLES, offshore-drilling accessories) and diving and subsea SURVEYING services, are exported.

Drilling Platforms The largest items produced in Canada for offshore work are the various platforms which support drilling equipment. Between 1978 and 1982, MIL Davie Inc (formerly Davie Shipbuilding Ltd) of Lauzon, Qué, the largest shipyard in Canada, moved strongly into this field when orders for conventional vessels dropped off in the wake of a worldwide shipping slump (*see* SHIPBUILDING). In 1983 Davie had orders for construction of 12 jack-up platforms under licence from the designer, Marathon le Tourneau Inc of Vicksburg, Miss. Most of these systems, designed to operate directly on the seafloor in relatively shallow water, were destined for the Gulf of Mexico. During the 1980s, none of the Canadian-built jack-ups had been built specifically for use in Canadian waters, although foreign-constructed rigs of the bottom-supported type were in use in the shallow, ice-free zone off SABLE ISLAND, NS. The slump in the oil industry in the late 1980s has adversely affected sales.

In 1987 Davie had no orders for platform construction. Development of bottom-supported systems capable of withstanding impact by moving SEA ICE is being studied by several Canadian organizations, including Mobil Oil Canada Ltd and Dome Petroleum Ltd.

In areas where floe ice and ICEBERGS do present dangers, such as the BEAUFORT SEA in the western Arctic and the Grand Banks off Newfoundland, the most widely employed strategy is one of avoidance rather than confrontation. Hence, mobile drilling platforms are used, either drilling ships or semisubmersible rigs (ie, platforms mounted on submerged, neutrally buoyant pontoons, which are anchored or positioned by motors over the drill site). The first Canadian-built semisubmersible was under construction in 1982 at Saint John Shipbuilding & Dry Dock Co Ltd of Saint John.

Undersea Vehicles It is in the HIGH-TECHNOLOGY field associated with exploration in the deeper waters of the world's continental shelves that Canadians are probably best known – particularly in the design and construction of manned and remote-control undersea vehicles and systems. One of the most famous Canadian submersible builders (until it went into receivership in 1978) was International Hydrodynamics Co Ltd of Vancouver, which manufactured the Hyco family of manned submarines, named after signs of the zodiac. During its best year, 1976, Hyco employed 165 people, but a surplus of submersibles on the world market, coupled with a drastic cutback in North Sea operations by a major British customer, eventually contributed to the breakup of this innovative company.

Submersibles have been around for nearly 20 years, but only since the mid-1970s have remote-control vehicles (which do not require complex and expensive life-support systems) become sophisticated enough to challenge manned craft. Remotely operated submersibles, built by International Submarine Engineering Ltd of Port Moody, BC, are being used in the Far East, the North Sea, the Middle East and other oil-producing areas.

Founded by company president James McFarlane in 1974, when the field was still in its infancy, ISE had designed and built more than 158 systems by the end of 1987, mostly for export. ISE manufactures a family of submersibles, most of which are unmanned and controlled through cables by a surface operator. New technology is conceived and developed with breathtaking speed. Early remote-control submarines were equipped with cameras for PIPELINE inspection; modern computer-controlled machines can perform more complex tasks, including oil-rig inspections and underwater shackle-ups at depths exceeding 1000 m. On-board diagnostic apparatus on the latest models enables technicians at ISE's Port Moody laboratory to monitor the internal workings of a submersible operating from a drillship as far afield as Australia.

A vehicle, designed to support drilling to even greater depths (about 2500 m, a world record), was constructed at ISE in 1983. In 1987 it was adapted for depths of 5000 m. The first in a new generation of untethered submersibles known as ARCS (autonomous remotely controlled submersible) has also been developed by ISE.

In addition to manned and remote-control self-propelled submersibles, Canadian companies also design and manufacture towed underwater devices, designed to perform tasks ranging from location of enemy submarines to identification of shipwreck sites and of geological structures capable of containing hydrocarbon deposits. A leader in this field is Fathom Oceanology Ltd of Mississauga, Ont, which has grown steadily since it was founded in 1978. Fathom's products include fish-shaped housings for detection packages and associated shipboard towing systems; drilling-rig accessories (eg, fairings for cables, pipes, drill risers) and SONAR domes for naval vessels and related marine equipment. The company's expertise extends beyond the purely mechanical side of underwater towing systems into microprocessing and electronics.

In 1986 Fathom exported about 75% of its sales, while the navies of N America and western Europe accounted for half of the company's revenues of $19.4 million. A towed system known as BATFISH, designed by the Bedford Institute of Oceanography and equipped to carry oceanographic-research instrument packages, is manufactured by Guildline Instruments Ltd of Smiths Falls, Ont.

Diving For the most delicate tasks associated with the ocean industry, divers working with their hands are still needed. Because they are exposed to enormous pressures and other potential dangers, Canadian divers earn good wages. In 1987, those working in domestic offshore oil and gas fields earned up to $60 000. Specialists willing to work elsewhere in the world earned even higher wages, a situation that raised concern over whether these highly trained people would be available to work in Canadian waters. Today, about 75% of divers working in the domestic industry are Canadian. Newfoundland is the only province that discriminates in favour of residents in its offshore industry.

Divers operating from diving bells now work at depths of more than 330 m and tests have indicated that humans can survive (though not very efficiently) at more than twice that depth. Work at even 200 m by unprotected divers was unheard of until 1968, when Phil Nuytten, president of Can-Dive Services Ltd of Vancouver and a pioneer in the development of underwater systems, along with a team of Canadian and US divers, established a commercial DIVING record to that depth.

As humans have gone deeper into the oceans, new problems have been encountered and, while technology has provided some solutions, many dangers are still only partially understood. Rapid compression to working depths was found to cause uncontrollable muscle tremors, dizziness and nausea.

Consequently, divers now spend up to 24 hours inside a hyperbaric chamber, slowly adjusting to the immense pressure. This delay in attending to an underwater problem can cost tens of thousands of dollars in oil rig downtime. Under pressure, divers sometimes complain of painful stiffness, where joints creak and pop and any movement causes discomfort. Sometimes bone necrosis (bone death) occurs under pressure, a problem whose cause is not fully understood.

Perhaps the best-known danger associated with deep diving is decompression sickness ("the bends"), which can occur if a diver ascends too quickly. On the way down, under increasing pressure, gases are dissolved in the blood. Reduced pressures during ascent cause the gases to bubble out; if this occurs too quickly, the bubbles can lodge in joints and cause severe pain, even death. Divers must ascend slowly or, as is often done with divers working in waters too cold for dallying, spend hours, days or even weeks in a surface decompression chamber which gradually reduces outside pressure on the body. Divers are paid for time in the chamber, so deep dives, even of short duration, are expensive.

Wherever possible, the dangers and associated costs are reduced by using one-atmosphere armoured diving suits that allow diver-operators to breathe air at sea-level atmospheric pressure. The suits are not cheap (they can cost about $250 000) but they offer greater safety, quicker response time and savings in breathing gas. A 2-week decompression can consume more than $100 000 worth of helium and oxygen breathing gas.

Can-Dive (formerly part of the Oceaneering International group of Houston, Texas, now an independent, Canadian-owned company) developed in 1986 an atmospheric diving suit called Newtsuit. It is an articulated suit with arms and legs, meant for walking on the ocean floor or on underwater platforms up to depths of 300 m.

The company has also been involved in the development of submersibles. The Haida, a ROV that can operate to depths of 700 m, was developed in conjunction with ISE in 1984. DEEP ROVER, which was launched in the same year, was built in Dartmouth, NS, in co-operation with Deep Ocean Technology of San Francisco. It is a one-man acrylic "bubble" known as the underwater helicopter and can operate to 1000 m. *See also* OCEAN MINING; OCEANOGRAPHY; DIVING.

CAREY FRENCH

Ocean Mining Several types of valuable MINERAL deposits are known to exist under the oceans or under other large bodies of water. Where wa-

ter is shallow, placer deposits can be recovered by large dredges (eg, tin minerals off the coasts of Java and Borneo). Where deposits lie in shallow water near the shore, dams may be built around sections of the shoreline and the areas pumped out so that shovels or scrapers can be used to excavate the material. Diamond-bearing gravels are mined in this way along the coast of southwestern Africa.

Conventional underground MINING methods may be used to follow mineral deposits extending beyond shorelines if the rock strata above the ore bodies or COAL seams are thick, strong and not porous or fractured. For example, coal is mined beneath the Atlantic Ocean near CAPE BRETON I. The seams were first found on land, and mine buildings, shaft and slope entrances were established on land. Mining by the room-and-pillar and then longwall methods has followed the seams as they dip beneath the ocean. One mine, now closed, advanced more than 8 km beyond the shoreline. Although the rock strata above the seams subside into the excavated areas after they are mined, no water has entered these mines. Mining of IRON ORE also extended 5.5 km beyond the shore at Wabana, Nfld. The empty chambers remained dry and are available for storage purposes.

Deep-ocean exploration has discovered jets and springs of hot water (to 350°C) rising from fissures and vents in ocean floors. These emissions appear to occur mainly along major ocean ridges and along fractures of the Earth's crust, such as in the Red Sea and off the BC coast. They may carry various metals and other elements in solution which, on encountering cold ocean water, precipitate as muds, layers, crusts or chimneys. Sulphides of copper, zinc, iron and other metals have been found in such deposits. These discoveries provide new information to geologists about the origin of hydrothermal mineral deposits. They may also provide future sources of economically recoverable minerals, if deposits of suitable size, grade and location are found.

The recovery of such deposits and of other mineral deposits known to lie at some depth below the ocean floor and at considerable distances from the nearest land will be difficult. Where the distance is too great to warrant driving long tunnels from shore-based shafts, it may be necessary to adapt techniques for offshore PETROLEUM recovery. The difficulties are further complicated by the need to establish national and international legal controls. The recovery of metal-bearing nodules, for example those occurring on the ocean floor in the mid-Pacific at depths of up to 5 km, is a challenge for the future. These fist-sized nodules contain manganese, copper, nickel and cobalt. Recovery will depend on the development of suitable technology and on the establishment of international agreements to regulate the work. Several multinational groups are investigating methods of recovery, including use of continuous lines of buckets, drag scrapers and suction devices. Research is also needed to develop suitable methods for processing nodules on boats or barges at sea.

T.H. PATCHING

Ocean Ranger On 15 Feb 1982, the world's largest semisubmersible drill rig, *Ocean Ranger*, capsized and sank in a fierce storm on the Grand Banks with the loss of all 84 crew members, 56 of whom were Newfoundlanders. Owned by the New Orleans-based Ocean Drilling and Exploration Co (ODECO) and under contract to Mobil Oil Canada, Ltd, the rig was working in the HIBERNIA oil field, about 315 km E of St John's. The Ocean Ranger and 2 smaller rigs drilling in the area at the time were hit by winds of 145 km per

hour and 18 m waves. The other 2 rigs, the *Sedco 706* and the *Zapata Ugland*, survived the storm.

Three inquiries, the joint Federal-Provincial Royal Commission on the Ocean Ranger Marine Disaster and 2 US studies, found that the rig sank after seawater entered its ballast control room through a broken porthole and caused an electrical malfunction in the ballast panel controlling the rig's stability. The commission concluded that the capsizing and loss of life was caused by a "chain of events which resulted from a coincidence of severe storm conditions, design inadequacy and lack of knowledgeable human intervention." Following these inquiries and based mainly on the recommendations of the royal commission, sweeping regulatory changes were made in training and safety practices and procedures offshore.

ROBERT D. PITT

Ocean Wave Energy is undoubtedly the most visible of the various forms of energy present in the world's water bodies. The sight of waves breaking on a beach or against a cliff at any of Canada's thousands of kilometres of marine or freshwater shoreline appears to give rise in many people to a desire to invent a device to harness this seemingly abundant source of energy. Extensive wave-recording programs have defined the annual average levels of ocean wave energy in deep water, just off the Continental Shelf, at about 80 kW/m (kilowatts per metre) of wave front on Canada's Atlantic coast, and at about 100 kW/m on the Pacific coast. Closer to shore, where it would be more practical to exploit this potential source of renewable energy, the annual averages are substantially lower, about 20 kW/m for both coasts. In the Great Lakes and the Arctic Ocean, levels of wave energy are even lower and, during the winter months, ice eliminates it altogether. The averages for the open-water season in the Great Lakes is about 3-5 kW/m.

Despite the relatively high averages of wave energy along the E and W coasts, commercial exploitation of this energy source has not been economically practical so far. The actual level of wave energy can vary by up to 3 orders of magnitude during any one year.

During most of the summer, the level of wave energy will be less than 5 kW/m, but during a severe winter storm the level can easily exceed 1000 kW/m. This variance makes it very difficult to design an efficient extractor capable of withstanding winter storms and equally capable of extracting energy at a much reduced level of wave activity – a difficulty which has often been underestimated. Hundreds of patents of wave-energy extractors have been claimed over the last 100 years, but none has reached the commercial development stage.

Between 1976 and 1979 Canada joined the UK, US, Ireland and Japan in the Kaimei project, a full-scale wave-energy project off the coast of Japan, under the auspices of the International Energy Agency. The study confirmed a relatively low efficiency of the energy extractor and a high price per kilowatt hour. In Canada, many other sources of renewable energy are available to produce energy at a lower price.

J. PLOEG

Reading: B. Count, ed, Power from Sea Waves (1980).

Oceanography is the science that studies the OCEANS and seas in all their aspects: the movement and composition of their WATERS; their origin; the evolution of their form; the nature, distribution and interactions of their plant and animal denizens; and their interactions with the atmosphere which affect climate and weather.

Subfields From descriptive beginnings as the geography of the sea, oceanography has matured into a quantitative and multidisciplinary science

A submarine made by International Submarine Engineering Ltd in BC (*courtesy SSC Photocentre/photo by K. Nagai*).

bringing together experts from many basic fields. The interconnectedness of marine problems demands from scientists of many disciplines a close collaboration which gives oceanographic research a special flavour. Physical oceanography combines the work of instrument makers who design sophisticated apparatus to measure or sample the corrosive and often inaccessible oceanic medium, analysts and computer specialists who interpret the data, and theoreticians who explain the observed physical properties of the ocean using the physics of rotating fluids. HYDROGRAPHY is an applied branch of physical oceanography concerned with mapping the ocean depths, calculating TIDE tables and producing navigational charts (*see* CARTOGRAPHY). Chemical oceanography studies the composition of seawater, the elements and compounds it holds in solution, their reactions with inert and living matter, and the effects of natural and man-made POLLUTION. Marine geology and geophysics study the origin of ocean basins, the spreading and shrinking of seas through geological ages, the EROSION of shorelines and the evolution of bottom sediments. Biological oceanography brings together botanists, zoologists, bacteriologists, FISHERIES experts and other biological specialists in the study of marine life and its availability to mankind. Marine ecology, an important interdisciplinary aspect of oceanography, studies marine ecosystems.

Relations to Other Fields Oceanographers share common theoretical and methodological approaches with researchers working in related areas. For example, oceanography is closely related to limnology, the study of lakes; and physical oceanography has much in common with meteorology, which studies the motion of another fluid, the atmosphere. Oceanographers can also supply important practical data to workers in other fields. For example, ocean engineering combines oceanographic knowledge with engineering techniques in the design and protection of coastal installations and offshore structures.

History in Canada The growth of oceanography in Canada, a country abutting 3 oceans (Atlantic, Pacific, Arctic) and containing large freshwater inland seas, has been continuous for almost a century. Oceanography was first applied, in Canada as elsewhere, to problems of navigation. The Canadian Tidal Survey (now Canadian Hydrographic Service) was formed in 1893. Under the leadership of its first director, William Bell DAWSON, it started its work of compiling marine charts and measuring currents and sea levels, a task which rapidly transcended its purely practical goals. Hydrography is the progenitor of physical oceanography. In the same period a board of management for fisheries and marine research was established under the Department of Naval Service. The board was superseded by the Biological Board of Canada, later the FISHERIES RESEARCH BOARD of Canada.

Although biological oceanography originated,

in part, in the practical concerns of fisheries, it received much of its life breath from the scientific interest generated by voyages of discovery in the second half of the 19th century, especially the CHALLENGER EXPEDITION (1872-76). The expedition, based in Halifax for a time, pioneered deep-sea dredging for marine organisms. During the late 19th century, marine research laboratories proliferated in Europe and the US. Two marine stations were established in Canada in 1908, at St Andrews, NB, and Nanaimo, BC, under the impetus and direction of E.E. PRINCE. These establishments, formally under the direction of the federal Department of Fisheries, were given a broad mandate to study not only fish, but also the plants, chemistry and motions of the ocean. Under the direction of the Fisheries Research Board of Canada, the Atlantic and Pacific biological stations were for decades focal points of Canadian oceanography, mapping fisheries resources and water properties, mounting deep-sea expeditions and providing expertise for Canadian participation in international bodies. On the Atlantic coast, fisheries oceanographers A.G. HUNTSMAN, W. Mackey and L. Lauzier participated in the description of local waters and in the work of the International Commission for North Atlantic Fisheries; W. Ford led Canadian participation in the study of the Gulf Stream during Operation Cabot in 1950. In the Pacific J.P. TULLY and his colleagues in Nanaimo pioneered the study of fjords and participated (with the US and Japan) in the North Pacific expeditions that mapped the ocean habitat of salmon. The waters of the ARCTIC ARCHIPELAGO were also explored; in the East, the *Calanus* expeditions (1948-79) led by M. DUNBAR of McGill U investigated Hudson Bay and its approaches; in the West, W.M. CAMERON played a leading role in the joint Canadian-US expeditions to the Beaufort Sea in the early 1950s.

Following WWII, defence research laboratories in Canada and elsewhere rapidly became interested in physical oceanographic problems, such as ocean wave forecasting and ocean acoustics. In the late 1940s and the 1950s, the need for professional oceanographers led to the foundation of graduate research and teaching institutes at the universities of British Columbia, Dalhousie and McGill. The spread of oceanographic studies to academic institutions continued in the 1960s with the formation of the Groupe interuniversitaire de recherches océanographiques du Québec (GIROQ), to which Laval, U de M and McGill contribute, and with the establishment of teaching and research laboratories at Université du Québec à Rimouski. Oceanographic studies are also offered at the universities of Victoria, Guelph and Memorial, and at Royal Roads military college on Vancouver I.

A major recent development in Canadian oceanography has been the concentration and significant expansion, through the 1960s and 1970s, of research and service operations run by the federal government through the Department of Fisheries and Oceans in 3 large institutions: the BEDFORD INSTITUTE OF OCEANOGRAPHY (BIO), Dartmouth, NS; the CANADA CENTRE FOR INLAND WATERS (CCIW), Burlington, Ont; and the Institute of Ocean Sciences (IOS), Sidney, BC. These are on a scale comparable to that of other major oceanographic research centres of the world, housing hundreds of scientists concerned with all aspects of marine science. A new laboratory, the Institut Maurice Lamontagne, opened in 1987 in Mont-Joli, Qué. A central information storage and dissemination agency (the Marine Environmental Data Service) is based in Ottawa. Fisheries laboratories in Nanaimo and St Andrews (as well as in St John's, Nfld, and Halifax, NS) have become more specialized in fish-stock management. Federal re-

search laboratories also operate Canada's oceanographic fleet, which includes a few medium-sized deep-sea vessels (eg, *Baffin, Hudson, Parizeau, Dawson, Endeavour, Tully*) and smaller vessels for hydrographic and coastal work. A research SUBMERSIBLE, the *Pisces IV*, is used for deep-visual exploration and has contributed to the description of deep-sea hot vents on Juan de Fuca ridge off Canada's West Coast. Although these ships are used mainly for coastal work, occasional long-range cruises take Canadian oceanographers to remote seas. The HUDSON 70 EXPEDITION accomplished the first complete circumnavigation of the Americas, taking a group of UBC oceanographers, led by G.L. PICKARD, on the first scientific survey of the fjords of southern Chile, and taking a team from the Bedford Institute, led by C.R. MANN, to make deep-flow measurements through Drake Passage, S of Cape Horn.

Practical problems now facing Canadian oceanography include fisheries management and the complex interactions between its scientific and socioeconomic aspects; problems of nearshore pollution and deep-ocean dumping; improved understanding of SEA-ICE conditions for purposes of navigational safety and offshore operations; exploitation of offshore petroleum and mineral resources on the Canadian continental shelves; and development of instruments for in-situ and remote sampling of the ocean to gather the information necessary to tackle the above problems. The arctic regions continue to be an area of special concern. In the early 1970s joint government and industry surveys of the Beaufort Sea paved the way for current hydrocarbon exploration. A few years later, the Eastern Arctic Marine Environmental Studies (EAMES) program gathered extensive baseline information about marine ecosystems and circulation patterns in Baffin Bay, Lancaster Sound and adjacent passages. Geophysical and oceanographic expeditions to the deep Arctic Ocean, north of the archipelago, such as the Lomonosov Ridge Experiment (LOREX, 1979) and the Canadian Expedition to Study the Alpha Ridge (CESAR, 1983), have confirmed Canada's interests in the High North (*see* ARCTIC OCEANOGRAPHY).

Canadian oceanographers also participate in the elucidation of fundamental problems of a global nature, such as the role played by the oceans in climate change (now examined in the international Geosphere-Biosphere Program) and, in particular, their capacity for holding in solution much of the carbon dioxide released by the burning of fossil fuels (the subject of the Joint Global Ocean Flux Study). A significant increase in the concentration of this gas in the atmosphere could lead to a net warming trend, a significant concern to subpolar countries. A detailed understanding of oceanic dynamics is still lacking, and oceanic weather prediction will not be achieved until a more intimate knowledge of ocean currents is attained and supported by a dense network of observation stations. This task will occupy physical oceanographers for years to come; it is in great part co-ordinated through the current World Ocean Circulation Experiment. The history of seafloor spreading and its relation to the formation of deep-sea mineral deposits is also of great interest. In Canada seafloor spreading occurs off the BC coast at the Juan de Fuca and Explorer ridges, submarine mountain chains where new ocean floor is continually being created (*see* OCEAN MINING; PLATE TECTONICS).

Of the more than 1000 oceanographers in Canada, most work for the federal or provincial governments, a few teach in universities, and an increasing number are employed by the private sector to help in offshore exploitation and nearshore engineering and pollution problems.

The Canadian Meteorological and Oceanographic Society, the principal professional society of oceanographers in Canada, gathers together mainly physical and chemical oceanographers. It publishes a quarterly journal of scientific research, *Atmosphere-Ocean,* and a newsletter of general information, and holds an annual scientific congress. Another Canadian research publication devoted mainly to fisheries science is the monthly *Canadian Journal of Fisheries and Aquatic Sciences,* published by the Scientific Information and Publications Branch of the federal Dept of Fisheries and Oceans. PAUL H. LEBLOND

Reading: K. Johnstone, *The Aquatic Explorers* (1977); P.H. LeBlond and L.A. Mysak, *Waves in the Ocean* (1978); D.A. Ross, *Introduction to Oceanography* (1982).

Oceanography, Biological, branch of OCEANOGRAPHY that studies living organisms (ie, the biota) in the sea in relation to their environments. The subject is interdisciplinary, requiring an understanding of the interactions among different marine organisms and of how the physical and chemical processes of the sea affect its living communities. The biota is generally taken to include 3 major groups of organisms: the PLANKTON (pelagic plants or animals that float or drift almost passively in the water), the nekton (swimming pelagic animals) and the benthos (seafloor organisms). Biological oceanography is often viewed as a series of food chains in the sea. Phytoplankton (planktonic plants), the primary producers, are consumed by the ZOOPLANKTON (planktonic animals) or secondary producers. Plankton-eating fish (planktivores) form the third level of production and above these are the fish-eating fish which consume the planktivores. A typical example of such a food chain would consist of diatoms (phytoplankton) eaten by copepods (zooplankton) which are consumed by herring (planktivorous nekton) which in turn are eaten by dogfish (piscivorous nekton). Such a representation is convenient but it oversimplifies actual relationships, since there are many more interconnections than are implied.

The biological oceanography of the Pacific and Atlantic regions of Canada is governed by the subarctic water lying off both coasts. The subarctic communities of these water masses are characterized by a strong seasonal progression of plankton blooms, starting in spring and ending in fall. Production of larval and juvenile fishes is generally associated with the spring bloom; migration of adult fishes takes place in spring and fall. The release of benthic larvae is also generally associated with the spring phytoplankton bloom. The eventual settlement of some benthic organisms in relatively shallow areas is an important connection in the food chain for the commercially important FISHERIES found on the GRAND BANKS and other continental shelf areas. In the Arctic Ocean a single summer pulse of plankton occurs after the break up of fast ice. This bloom, which may last for several months, supports an extensive food chain including zooplankton, fish, seals, polar bears and humans. However, the quantity of commercially available fish in the Arctic Ocean is very small compared to Canada's subarctic waters where plankton production is greater for a longer period of the year.

Recent developments in biological oceanography have included the REMOTE SENSING of biological events from space, and the remote sensing of deepwater communities from SUBMERSIBLES capable of descending to the greatest ocean depths (below 10 000 m). Satellite studies have been used to show the amount of plankton in different water masses, as determined by the chlorophyll concentration which influences the colour of the water. Deep submersible studies have recently shown the existence of biological communities which feed off energy-rich compounds that are given off at thermal vents in the seafloor (ie, deepsea INVERTEBRATES). Other new techniques include the outfitting of commercial vessels for biological monitoring; the use of large plastic bag enclosures (over 1000 t) to study the ecology of the sea; and scuba-diving techniques allowing observation of delicate forms of plankton and direct experimentation with benthic communities.

In Canada, biological oceanographic studies are performed in the Atlantic, Pacific and Arctic oceans by university departments of oceanography and government oceanographic institutes, and at a large number of federal fisheries stations. Consulting companies have taken part in biological oceanographic studies in connection with environmental planning. This last area is of growing importance since the possible dire effects of manmade POLLUTION on the oceans have become recognized in certain limited environments, eg, when oil spills occur in coastal water or when urban or industrial sewage systems discharge into the sea (*see* WATER TREATMENT). The biological oceanography of these altered environments differs with each location. *See also* MARINE ECOLOGY. T.R. PARSONS

October Crisis, the kidnapping on 5 Oct 1970 of James Cross, the British trade commissioner in Montréal, by members of the FRONT DE LIBÉRATION DU QUÉBEC. The kidnappers' demands, communicated in a series of public messages, included the freeing of a number of convicted or detained FLQ members and the broadcasting of the FLQ manifesto. The manifesto, a diatribe against established authority, was read on Radio-Canada, and on Oct 10 the Québec minister of justice offered safe passage abroad to the kidnappers in return for the liberation of their hostage; but on the same day a second FLQ cell kidnapped the Québec minister of labour and immigration, Pierre LAPORTE. On Oct 15 the Québec government requested the assistance of the Canadian Armed Forces to supplement the local police, and on Oct 16 the federal government proclaimed the existence of a state of "apprehended insurrection" under the WAR MEASURES ACT. Under the emergency regulations, the FLQ was banned, normal liberties were suspended, and arrests and detentions were authorized without charge. Over 450 persons were detained in Québec, most of whom were eventually released without the laying or hearing of charges.

On Oct 17 the body of Pierre Laporte was found in a car trunk near St Hubert airport. In early Dec 1970, the cell holding James Cross was discovered by police, and his release was negotiated in return for the provision of safe conduct to Cuba for the kidnappers and some family members. Four weeks later the second group was located and arrested, subsequently to be tried and convicted for kidnapping and murder. Emergency regulations under War Measures were replaced in Dec 1970 by similar regulations under the Public Order (Temporary Measures) Act which lapsed on 30 Apr 1971. The federal response to the kidnapping was intensely controversial. According to opinion polls, an overwhelming majority of Canadians supported the Cabinet's action, but it was criticized as excessive by Québec nationalists and by civil libertarians throughout the country. Supporters of the response claim that the disappearance of terrorism in Québec is evidence of its success, but this disappearance might equally be attributed to public distaste for political terror and to the steady growth of the democratic separatist movement in the 1970s, which led to the election of a PARTI QUÉBÉCOIS government (1976).

After the crisis the federal Cabinet gave ambiguous instructions to the RCMP Security Service, permitting dubious acts which were later condemned as illegal by the federal INQUIRY INTO CERTAIN ACTIVITIES OF THE RCMP and the Keable Commission (D'enquête sur des opérations policières en territoire Québecois) in Québec. The federal minister of justice in 1970, John TURNER, justified the use of War Measures as a means of reversing an "erosion of public will" in Québec, and Prem Robert BOURASSA similarly conceded that it was intended to rally popular support to the authorities rather than to confront an "apprehended insurrection." DENIS SMITH

Octopus, common name for all 8-armed cephalopod MOLLUSCS; it more properly refers to the largest genus in order Octopoda (over 100 species). Octopuses are also called devil fishes for the "horns" (cirri) behind their eyes, but the image of an 8-legged cat is more apt. They have large slit eyes and explore the sea bottom with catlike intelligence, pouncing on prey, eg, crabs. Canada has 2 of the world's largest octopods: the Pacific *Octopus dofleini,* a slow but typical benthic (bottom-dwelling) hunter that may exceed 80 kg; and the Atlantic *Alloposus mollis,* which floats in the PLANKTON like a 40 kg jellyfish. There are 9 smaller species. The paper-thin "shells" of the octopod *Argonauta* (paper nautilus) occasionally drift to Canadian shores from the tropics. Not true shells, they are boatlike nests secreted by the female and used by her as a brood chamber and retreat. R.K. O'DOR

Odell, Jonathan, doctor, clergyman, spy, poet, politician (b at Newark, NJ 25 Sept 1737; d at Fredericton 25 Nov 1818). He was trained in medicine but entered the Church of England ministry. He served as parish priest at Burlington, NJ, until his LOYALIST political sympathies forced him to flee to New York in 1776 during the AMERICAN REVOLUTION. There he worked for the Loyalist cause as an administrator and satiric poet-propagandist. He was also a secret go-between in the espionage activities of Benedict ARNOLD and John André. In 1784 Odell immigrated to New Brunswick, having been appointed provincial secretary as a reward for his loyalty. He was influential in NB politics. THOMAS B. VINCENT

Odjig, Daphne, artist (b at Wikwemikong IR, Manitoulin I, Ont 11 Sept 1919). Child of a Potawatomi father and English war-bride mother, she was encouraged in her early artistic expression by her grandfather and father, tombstone carvers and artists. Leaving the reserve in 1938, she migrated to BC and was ultimately elected to the BC Federation of Artists. Her work has been influenced by the growing political awareness of her people and her experiences in native communities in Manitoba during the 1960s. In 1970 she opened a gallery devoted to native art in Winnipeg and, with MORRISSEAU, JANVIER, BEARDY and others, formed a short-lived but significant association of native artists (1973). Odjig has developed a unique synthesis of western styles (cubism, surrealism) and native world view to express the universal themes of identity, family relationships and spirituality. A central motif is the curved arch enclosing her figures in lyric, rhythmic line. Her work has been exhibited in Europe, Israel and Japan. Her great mural *The Indian in Transition* (1978) graces the National Arts Centre in Ottawa, and her influence is evident in the work of many younger native artists. Odjig has received honorary degrees from 2 universities and in 1987 was made a Member of the Order of Canada. ROSAMOND M. VANDERBURGH

Odlum, Victor Wentworth, journalist, soldier, diplomat (b at Cobourg, Ont 21 Oct 1880; d at Vancouver 4 Apr 1971). He served in the South African War and WWI, and between the wars pursued a career as a journalist. He was connected with several newspapers, including the Vancouver *Daily Star*, of which he was publisher 1924-32. In the late 1930s he served on the board of the Canadian Broadcasting Corp. With the rank of maj-gen, he commanded the 2nd Canadian Division (1940-41) and was released to become high commissioner to Australia and Canada's first ambassador to China, 1943-46. An admirer of Jiang Jieshi, Odlum was out of step with events in China, although many of his proposals regarding Canada-China relations were innovative. He was ambassador to Turkey 1947-52.   BRIAN L. EVANS

O'Donoghue, Daniel John, printer, trade union leader, politician (b at Lakes of Killarney, Ire 1844; d at Toronto 16 Jan 1907). "The father of the Canadian labor movement" began his apprenticeship as a printer in Ottawa at age 13. He helped to organize the Ottawa Typographical Union, 1867, promoted the Ottawa Trades Council, and was elected vice-president of the Canadian Labor Union in 1873. He was elected to the Ontario legislature in 1874 as an independent workingman, but moved ever closer to Oliver MOWAT's Liberal government. As chairman of the legislative committee of the Toronto Trades and Labor Council, he was at the centre of labour politics in the 1880s. Joining the KNIGHTS OF LABOR in October 1882, O'Donoghue quickly emerged as the chief Canadian lieutenant, handling the delicate negotiations with French Canadian Roman Catholic bishops who had condemned the order as a "secret society." Although loyal to what he thought best for his class, he remained a Liberal partisan. Appointed a clerk in the Ontario Bureau of Industry in 1885, he was Canada's first federal fair-wages officer, 1900-07. His son John was to become Canada's first prominent labour lawyer.
                                                 G.S. KEALEY

Office Automation is a general term that includes a wide range of applications of computer, communication and information technologies in office environments. Though the process is still considered to be in its early stages, it is clear that the technology available in 1987 is much more advanced than what was on the market in the mid-1970s. Automation is in a state of flux, but the size of the market is already huge, with annual investments measured in billions of dollars. The potential market for office automation is huge: it is estimated that 85 billion pages of business documents were produced in Canada in 1981, and 140 billion in 1985.

The technology we see today had its start in the 1960s, when 3 clearly identifiable streams of development became evident. The first was computing, where the earliest applications were automated payroll and inventory-control systems. Other applications were also limited to the processing of numerical data. These systems were usually operated only by programmers in the data-processing division of the organization, who jealously guarded their computers and the power their knowledge of the computer gave them. Nevertheless, the applications of computers in organizational settings grew to include more and more kinds of data processing.

The second stream of technological development was in the area of text processing. In the mid-1970s IBM introduced a product called the MCST – Magnetic Card Selectric Typewriter. This device had a box crammed with electronic equipment. The operator would insert a specially coated card the size and shape of a standard IBM punch card into a slot on the top of the box and would type on the attached typewriter as usual.

The card served as a memory device, on which the text would be written in a code based on magnetized spots. Once it was entered, the text could be edited and played back, causing a new copy to be typed out on the attached typewriter. Compared to current word-processing systems, this one was primitive, but it worked.

While the first 2 streams were centered around the processing of information in the office, the third, COMMUNICATIONS TECHNOLOGY, focused on the movement of information from one place to another. A wide range of techniques to achieve this end were introduced, from telex and facsimile services to services using specially conditioned TELEPHONE lines and others using sophisticated satellite links between distant points (*see* SATELLITE COMMUNICATIONS). The industry today includes several types of coaxial cables, fibre optic lines, cellular telephones, and packet-switched radio and telephone links.

When the 3 technologies are incorporated into an office environment, many improvements become possible, but they are mostly improvements in the speed with which work is done rather than in the kind of work that is done. Office automation in the 1980s began a new trend – the integration of previously separate capabilities into single powerful "work stations." An automated office using the best technology commercially available in 1988 would probably have at least the following capabilities. *Communicating word-processing* abilities include spelling correction and access through a local-area network or over telephone lines to information previously stored on files at other locations, together with the ability to communicate with other stations on the net or on other nets. *Electronic messaging systems*, including any combination of text, graphics and voice, connect users to others on the same net or, through gateways, to people on different nets in other places. *Activity-management systems*, including time-management, project planning and scheduling, and electronic calendar capabilities. *Information management systems* range from straightforward storage and retrieval systems, where the user does much of the work of storing and retrieving, to sophisticated natural-language expert systems. These provide assistance for people who deal with large volumes of diverse types of rapidly changing information. *Decision-support systems* incorporate sophisticated programs on large data bases that allow the user to perform complex analyses on large data bases in a way that improves the speed and quality of decisions that are made.

Most of the capabilities mentioned above make use of 2 or 3 of the original technologies. It is this integration of the previously separate capabilities that gives the new technology its power and provides the base upon which new applications will be developed in the near future.

As we move toward the last decade in the century we are seeing major developments in several areas. The power of the computers driving most of the technology is continuing to be increased. By the late 1990s there will be chips with a billion components. Some of today's microcomputers have more information processing power than the fastest mainframes did in 1975. Innovations coming to the market in the next decade include "desktop publishing" packages, which incorporate text and graphics into coherent packages.

The Impact of Office Automation The computer is changing the office environment much like the automobile has changed the city. Effectively integrated office automation systems may result in the restructuring of entire organizations, with the emergence of new structural configurations and the elimination of departments or entire divisions. The new information technologies have led

to a large reduction in the size of the average organization's middle ranks. The new technologies may also have the potential to strengthen the power of trans-national corporations in Canada, contributing to the erosion of Canadian autonomy and displacing many people whose jobs will be automated. In most organizations office automation has been viewed as a means to computerize old procedures and to make employees more productive, rather than to make the organization more effective.

There is a rising level of fear of the new technologies and the impact they will have on job security and on the privacy of the individual (*see* COMPUTERS AND SOCIETY). There is also concern that the Canadian ECONOMY will suffer greatly if Canadian organizations do not develop and adapt to the new technologies. Whether or not Canadian industry will learn to use information technologies to their advantage in the increasingly competitive world system remains to be seen. It is safe to say, however, that the technologies will have a significant impact on the working lives of millions of Canadians in the coming decades. *See also* INFORMATION SOCIETY.   WILLIAM RICHARDS

Reading: S.R. Hiltz and M. Turoff, *The Network Nation* (1978); R. Landau, J.H. Bair and J.H. Siegman, eds, *Emerging Office Systems* (1982); H. Menzies, *Women and the Chip* (1981); P.A. Russell, *The Electronic Briefcase: The Office of the Future* (1978); J.M. Shepard, *Automation and Alienation: A Study of Office and Factory Workers* (1971); D. Tapscott, *Office Automation* (1982); G.B. Thompson, *Memo from Mercury: Information Technology Is Different* (1979); R.P. Uhlig, D.J. Farber and J.H. Bair, *The Office of the Future* (1979).

Office de la langue française (French Language Office) was created 26 Aug 1977 by the Charter of the French Language (BILL 101), thus replacing the Régie de la langue française (French Language Administration). The office is responsible for the implementation of the charter, except in the case of language in education. Its functions are to define and apply the Québec policy related to research in linguistics and terminology, and to ensure that within Québec, French becomes the language of common use in communications, in the work place and in trade and business, both in the civil service and in companies employing a minimum of 50 people. To achieve these goals, the office offers a variety of services, including advice on linguistics and workshops for secretarial and administrative personnel. It also offers grants for research in fields of study related to linguistics, and prepares French exams aimed at future members of professional associations whose French proficiency fails to meet the requirements of the charter. The office administers the *Banque de terminologie du Québec*, a computerized, bilingual dictionary comprising over 3.5 million words. Since its inception, the office has published over 100 lexicons, booklets on vocabulary and lists of terms and expressions.   GISÈLE VILLENEUVE

Official Languages, Commissioner of, is appointed to a 7-year term by Parliament under the OFFICIAL LANGUAGES ACT (beginning in 1969); a reappointment may not exceed 7 years. The commissioner, responsible for compliance with the spirit and intent of the Act in the Government of Canada and in Parliament and for ensuring equal recognition of the status of English and French as official languages (*see* LANGUAGE POLICY), has the authority to investigate complaints of violations of the Act as well as to initiate the examination of possible violations. Results of such investigations may be reported directly to the individuals or agencies involved and are outlined in some cases in special reports to Parliament. The commissioner reviews his office's activities and makes recommendations in an annual report.

Official Languages Act (1969), federal statute that declares French and English to be the official languages of Canada, and under which all federal institutions must provide their services in English or French at the customer's choice. The Act (passed following the recommendation of the Royal Commission on BILINGUALISM AND BICULTURALISM) created the office of Commissioner of Official Languages to oversee its implementation. Politically, the Act has been supported by all federal parties, but the public's understanding and acceptance of it has been mixed. In June 1987 the Conservative government introduced an amended Official Languages Act to promote official language minority rights. The new Act would also give financial assistance to provincial and municipal governments to extend services in French and English. *See also* LANGUAGE POLICY.

MAX YALDEN

Official Secrets Act, the most important statute relating to national security, is designed to prohibit and control access to and the disclosure of sensitive government information; offences cover espionage and leakage of government information. The term "official secrets" is not defined comprehensively in the legislation, but broadly, official secrets may be considered any information of an official character. It is clear that prohibited places, code words, passwords, plans, models, and articles, notes or other documents can be regarded as official secrets under the Act. There is some controversy over whether information involved must be secret (in Britain there is no such requirement). In the 1978 prosecution of the Toronto *Sun*, the judge presiding at the preliminary inquiry assumed that the information did indeed have to be secret. In one 1948 case the Québec Court of Appeal determined that the Act does not apply to information that has been published, publicized or has fallen into the public domain. By contrast, in the recent (1987) English "Spycatcher" case (involving the upholding, by the House of Lords, of an injunction banning publication of the memoirs of a former British counterintelligence agent), Lord Ackner wrote that "the cat is indeed out of the bag, but...there is all the difference in the world between tolerating importation of casual copies as opposed to mass circulation of the material."

The first Official Secrets Act was passed in England in 1889 and with minor modifications became law in Canada in 1890. In 1892 its provisions were transferred to the first Criminal Code of Canada until their repeal and replacement by the Official Secrets Act, 1939. This new Act combined into one the English Acts of 1911 and 1920. Minor changes were made in 1950, 1967 and 1970. Also, an important addition was made in 1973 in the form of a broad power to conduct wiretap investigations pursuant to executive, as opposed to judicial, authorizations.

The Mackenzie Royal Commission on Security Procedures of 1969 described the legislation as "an unwieldy statute couched in very broad and ambiguous language" and one possessing "unusual" and "extraordinarily onerous" evidentiary and procedural provisions relating to espionage cases. Successive royal commissions have criticized the broad powers of search and seizure conferred under the legislation of substantive offences, eg, leakage of classified information, created by the statute. Over 50% of the 22 Canadian prosecutions under the Official Secrets Act arose as a result of the defection of Igor GOUZENKO in 1945 and his revelations about a series of Soviet spy rings operating in Canada. Only a handful of prosecutions have occurred since 1961. Two cases involved the leakage provisions of the Act, and in both of these 1978 prosecutions, charges were

dismissed. The most recent prosecution was the so-called "Longknife" case. In it, James Morrison (code named Longknife) was charged with conspiracy to breach the provisions of the Act and passing secret information to Russian agents between 1955 and 1958. These 1983 charges were pressed after Morrison gave interviews to television and print media in 1982 respecting his RCMP intelligence work. Morrison initially challenged the validity of the 30-year old proceedings brought against him as being in violation of the CANADIAN CHARTER OF RIGHTS AND FREEDOMS' guarantee of trial within a reasonable time. His trial on the 3 charges abruptly ended with a plea of guilty to one of the charges against him. He was sentenced to 18 months in prison. The Royal Commission of INQUIRY INTO CERTAIN ACTIVITIES OF THE ROYAL CANADIAN MOUNTED POLICE (McDonald Commission) noted in 1979 that "much more is needed by way of legislative reform than the mere dismantling of the Official Secrets Act and the recognition of espionage and leakage as separate kinds of offences. The definition of these offences in the Official Secrets Act leave much to be desired...It is now time for this part of our law to be revised so that it is both clear and in tune with the values and needs of contemporary Canada." Despite these and other calls for an overhaul of the Act, it remains essentially unaltered. *See also* INTELLIGENCE AND ESPIONAGE. STANLEY A. COHEN

Offshore Mineral Rights Reference (1967) The Supreme Court of Canada, in a decision about the ownership of seabed mineral rights off BC and on the legislative jurisdiction over these rights, decided that Parliament, not the BC legislature, owned the territorial seabed adjacent to that province and enjoyed exclusive legislative jurisdiction by virtue of the CONSTITUTION ACT, 1867 (s91.1A), ie, Parliament's residuary power. Rights in the territorial sea derive from INTERNATIONAL LAW and Canada is the sovereign state recognized by international law. BC could not claim the rights of the Continental Shelf either, according to the rights under international law defined in the Geneva Convention (1958).

GÉRALD-A. BEAUDOIN

Ogden, Peter Skene, fur trader, explorer (b at Québec C 1790; d at Oregon C 27 Sept 1854). One of the most important and turbulent personalities in the N American FUR TRADE in the first half of the 19th century. Ogden spent his first years in the fur trade as a servant (1809-21) of the NORTH WEST CO.

There, he gained an unenviable reputation for violence which delayed for 2 years his appointment as chief trader by the HUDSON'S BAY CO after the merger of the 2 companies in 1821. In 1824 Ogden began a series of trapping expeditions to the Snake Country. Because it was assumed that this area S of the Columbia R would eventually go to the US, Ogden's instructions were to trap the country bare. He did this, and more, for on 6 separate expeditions he obtained a better knowledge of the puzzling geography of this region than any other explorer. Overcoming natural hazards, rival American traders and sometimes hostile Indians, Ogden discovered the Humboldt R, sighted Great Salt Lake, and on his last expedition in 1830 probably reached the lower Colorado R. From 1831 to 1844 Ogden operated in BC, at first based at Fort Simpson. Promoted chief factor in 1834, he spent 10 years commanding the New Caledonia district where for the first time he was not faced with direct competition. In 1845 he was posted back to Ft Vancouver on the lower Columbia, which the OREGON TREATY of the next year placed in the US. So the last years of Ogden's career were spent trading in an area under foreign control, where settlers and prospectors were more visible than fur traders and Indians.

GLYNDWR WILLIAMS

Ogilvie, Will, painter (b at Stutterheim, S Africa 30 Mar 1901). The first official Canadian war artist (appointed Jan 1943), he painted many of his war works under fire, for which he was awarded the OBE. In Johannesburg, Ogilvie studied with Erich Mayer. After emigrating in 1925, he studied at New York's Art Students League (1927-30) with Kimon Nicolaides, whose standard text on drawing, *The Natural Way to Draw* (1941), gave Ogilvie solid preparation for his war work. War artists Alex COLVILLE, Charles COMFORT, Lawren HARRIS and Campbell Tinning considered Ogilvie the best of the group. He loved Goya, Piero della Francesca and British war artist Paul Nash. There seem to be few traces of his enthusiasms, however, in his detailed, lovingly drawn work. His drawings in the field were spontaneous; his paintings more formal and symbolic. After the war, he taught at the Ontario College of

Will Ogilvie's fine drawing *Return of a Foot Patrol*, shows Canadian soldiers in the flooded terrain of Holland during WWII (*courtesy Canadian War Museum/CMC/NMC/ 13537*).

Art 1947-57, then as lecturer at U of T (1960-69). He is a Member of the Order of Canada.

JOAN MURRAY

Ogilvie, William, surveyor (b at Ottawa 7 Apr 1849; d at Winnipeg 13 Nov 1912). Trained as a surveyor, he worked from 1875 to 1898 in the Canadian West and North. He surveyed the Alaska-Yukon boundary at the Yukon R in 1887-88, and in 1896 the Klondike goldfields and the townsite of Dawson. As commissioner of the Yukon Territory 1898-1901, he enjoyed a reputation as the most honest and able civil servant in the territory. He was elected a fellow of the Royal Geographical Society in recognition of his pioneering northern surveys. In 1966 a mountain range north of Dawson was named in his honour.

WILLIAM R. MORRISON

Reading: W. Ogilvie, *Early Days on the Yukon* (1913).

Ogopogo, fabled aquatic monster which is said to inhabit OKANAGAN LAKE. The Salish called it "snake in the lake"; the Chinook called it "wicked one" and "great beast in the lake." Representation appeared in precontact petroglyphs. Like "Nessie," the Orm of Loch Ness, Ogopogo is variously described as having the head of a sheep or a horse and a long serpentine neck, and is reported to swim with an undulating motion; it is generally "sighted" as several humps moving rapidly through the water. The name "Ogopogo" is a palindrome from a comic English music-hall song, "Ogopogo Song." Okanagan Lake has temperamental weather conditions, which might explain the apparition, and an ill-defined lake bottom, which gives rise to speculation about long-trapped dinosaur eggs released by movements of the Earth's crust.

CAROLE H. CARPENTER

O'Grady, Standish, clergyman, farmer, poet (*fl* 1793-1841). Born in Ireland, he was educated at Trinity Coll, Dublin, and was ordained into the Church of Ireland ministry. Poverty forced him to immigrate to Lower Canada in 1836 where he settled on a farm near Sorel. He is remembered in Canada for his long narrative poem *The Emigrant*, published in Montréal in 1841, in which he describes the hardships of settlement life and expresses his profound dislike for the social, cultural and climatic environment of Canada. In his nostalgic yearnings for the "old country" and his unhappiness over hardships in the "New World," he epitomizes the main characteristics of the emigrant theme in early Canadian literature.

THOMAS B. VINCENT

O'Grady, William John, Roman Catholic priest, journalist (b in Ireland; d at Pickering, Canada W *c*18 Aug 1840). He arrived in Upper Canada in 1828 and soon began serving the Catholic congregation at York [Toronto]. Within a couple of years, however, complaints about his conduct began circulating, and in mid-1832 Bishop MACDONELL decided to transfer him to another parish. O'Grady refused to leave and launched a series of unsuccessful appeals – to Lt-Gov Sir John COLBORNE, to the Colonial Office and to the Vatican. Late in 1832, suspended from the priesthood, he founded a reform newspaper known as the *Canadian Correspondent*. He remained as editor of the paper when in Nov 1834 it merged with William Lyon MACKENZIE's *Colonial Advocate* and was renamed the *Correspondent and Advocate*. Closely associated with Mackenzie, he was a key figure in the reform movement until late 1837, when he sold his paper and moved to Pickering Twp. Mysteriously, he took no part in Mackenzie's abortive rebellion that December and appears to have lived an uneventful life until his death. A coroner's inquest ruled

that his death had been caused by a "visitation of God."

CURTIS FAHEY

O'Hagan, Howard, writer (b at Lethbridge, Alta 17 Feb 1902; d Dec 1982). O'Hagan was one of the first native-born westerners to make a mark on Canadian literature and is best known for his novel of the Rocky Mountains, *Tay John* (1939). His life is almost as noteworthy as his writing. As a youth, he worked on survey parties in the Rockies. He later studied law at McGill and, upon graduation in 1925, returned West. In his oft-quoted words, "I practised law for a month in Jasper, put one man into jail and got another out." He returned to guiding and packing through the mountains. After a stint as chief of publicity for the Central Argentine Ry, he lived in Australia, the US, England and Italy.

More than any other modern writer, O'Hagan has been the quintessential "mountain man" who knew the wilderness intimately and celebrated it through fiction. The protagonist of *Tay John* is a blonde giant, "Tête Jaune," whose legend inspired the naming of Yellowhead Pass through the Rockies. It is a fictional account, set in 1880, about a primitive half-breed outcast who becomes a myth, both worshipped and despised, before disappearing into the earth from which he had sprung. O'Hagan's short fiction is also respected. *The Woman Who Got on at Jasper Station & Other Stories* (1963) is a collection of 11 powerful short tales. *Wilderness Men* (1958), 10 biographies of western heroes, includes Grey Owl and the legendary West Coast fugitive, GUN-AN-NOOT. A more recent novel is *The School-Marm Tree* (1977). O'Hagan lived in Victoria, BC, with his wife Margaret Peterson, a noted artist.

KEN MITCHELL

Oil, Chemical and Atomic Workers International Union v Imperial Oil Limited et al In 1961 the BC Legislature prohibited trade unions from using membership fees paid under a collective agreement checkoff provision for political purposes. The OCAW challenged the statute on the grounds that only Parliament has constitutional jurisdiction to restrict a union's federal political activities. The majority of the Supreme Court of Canada rejected the union's argument and held that the legislation was within provincial jurisdiction as it concerned the control of labour relations in the province. This decision upheld a major restriction on trade-union political activity.

TIMOTHY J. CHRISTIAN

Oil and Natural Gas, *see* BITUMEN; ENERGY POLICY; PETROLEUM; PETROLEUM EXPLORATION AND PRODUCTION; PETROLEUM INDUSTRIES; PETROLEUM SUPPLY AND DEMAND.

Oil City, Alta, site of western Canada's first producing oil well, known previously as Original Discovery No 1, located in WATERTON LKS NATIONAL PK. Kutenai had used oil from seepage pools along Cameron Cr and early settlers used it to lubricate wagons. In 1878 A.P. Patrick, a Dominion surveyor, drilled a primitive well, but it was not until 1901, when Patrick, John Leeson and John Lineham (a local rancher) formed the Rocky Mountain Development Co, that drilling began in earnest. Oil was struck at 300 m in Aug of that year. Hopes for a local boom were raised, but the well was erratic and was closed in 1906 after producing 32 000 litres. A cairn in the shape of an oil rig marks the historic site of this pioneer development in Alberta's oil industry.

ERIC J. HOLMGREN

Oilseed Crops are grown primarily for the oil contained in the seeds. The oil content of small grains (eg, wheat) is only 1-2%; that of oilseeds ranges from about 20% for SOYBEANS to over 40% for SUNFLOWERS and rapeseed (CANOLA). The major world sources of edible seed oils are soybeans,

sunflowers, rapeseed, cotton and peanuts. Seed oils from FLAX (linseed) and castor beans are used for industrial purposes. Edible fats and oils are similar in molecular structure; however, fats are solid at room temperature, while oils are liquid. Fats and oils are essential nutrients, comprising about 40% of the calories in the diet of the average Canadian. Edible vegetable oils are used as salad or cooking oils, or may be solidified (by a process called hydrogenation) to make margarine and shortening. These products supplement or replace animal products (eg, butter, lard), supplies of which are inadequate to meet the needs of an increasing world population.

While there are many uses for industrial vegetable oils, total world production is only about 3% of that of edible oils. Industrial applications are based on the properties of particular fatty-acid components of these oils. For example, flaxseed oil, rich in the unsaturated fatty acid linolenic, is a drying oil and is used in protective coatings (eg, paints, varnishes). Vegetable oils are used in putty, printing inks, erasers, coating or core oils, greases, plastics, etc. The residue remaining after the oil has been extracted from oilseeds is an important source of nutrients for farm animals. Oilseed meals from soybeans, peanuts, rapeseed and flaxseed are rich in protein; mixed with other ingredients (eg, cereal grains), they provide nutritionally balanced feeds.

The major oilseeds grown in Canada are soybeans, sunflowers, canola and flax. In addition, experimental production of peanuts on a commercial scale began in 1981 in SW Ontario. Plant breeding experiments are underway at the Agriculture Canada RESEARCH STATION, Saskatoon, Sask, to develop an edible oil from mustard seed and a usable animal feed from the residue. The program involves reducing the content of 2 harmful substances, erucic acid and glucosinolate, which were formerly a problem in rapeseed oil.

Soybeans require a relatively long growing season (100-140 days) and warm temperatures; hence, Canadian production is concentrated in SW Ontario. Sunflowers will tolerate a somewhat shorter (100-120 days), cooler growing season; most Canadian production occurs in southern Manitoba. Flax and canola are adapted to the relatively short, cool growing season of the Prairie provinces and most production occurs in that area. The size of the area of adaptation and the development of varieties with improved quality have permitted canola to become the major edible oilseed crop in Canada.

Cultural practices have been developed to obtain optimum production from each crop. Soybeans and sunflowers are usually grown as row crops; flax and canola are solid seeded. The usual seeding rate for soybeans is 130 kg per hectare; sunflowers, 6 kg/ha; canola, 7 kg/ha; flax, 38 kg/ha. Small-seed crops, flax and canola, are seeded at depths of 2.5-4 cm; larger-seed crops, sunflowers and soybeans, may be seeded up to 10 cm deep if deep seeding is required to reach moist soil. Weeds are controlled by cultivation in the row crops; by crop rotation in solid-seeded crops; and by extensive use of herbicides. Diseases are controlled by using disease-resistant cultivars (commercial varieties), and by seed treatments and fungicides. Insecticides are used to control outbreaks of INSECT PESTS (*see* PESTICIDES).

In 1985-86 the average seed yields for flaxseed, canola, soybeans and sunflowers in Canada were 1270 kg/ha, 1325 kg/ha, 2455 kg/ha and 1265 kg/ha, respectively. High soybean yields can be attributed to the longer growing season and relatively favourable moisture conditions in Ontario. The other major oilseed crops are grown in a shorter, dryer season, and yields are often reduced by moisture deficiencies. From 1984 to

1986, the average annual production of flaxseed, canola, soybeans and sunflowers in Canada was 8 874 000 t, 36 075 000 t, 9 933 000 t and 770 000 t, respectively, valued at over $1 billion annually. Edible oilseed production, which began during WWII, now provides the raw material for a multimillion-dollar crushing, refining and processing industry. During the last 3 decades, Canada has changed from a major importer to a net exporter of edible oil and oilseeds.

B.R. STEFANSSON

Ojibwa The term Ojibwa (Ojibway, Chippewa) derives from Outchibou, the 17th-century name of a group living N of Sault Ste Marie, Ont. They were one of a series of closely related but distinctly named groups residing between northeastern Georgian Bay and eastern Lk Superior to whom the term Ojibwa was later extended. Those peoples who congregated near present-day Sault Ste Marie were also called Saulteurs or Saulteaux. Although groups identified as Ojibwa in 17th-century French records totalled around 4500 persons, historic population movements into new areas, combined with the later application of the label Ojibwa to some neighbouring groups, enlarged the population and the territory occupied. The Ojibwa speak a Central Algonquian language closely related to ALGONQUIN, OTTAWA, CREE and Potawatomi.

At contact, the Ojibwa subsisted by hunting, fishing and gathering, resided in conical or dome-shaped birchbark dwellings, wore animal-skin clothing and travelled by birchbark CANOE in warm weather and SNOWSHOES in winter. Politically autonomous summer villages of 150-300 persons appear to have borne totemic names. An appropriate spouse was a person categorized as a cross-cousin – the child of either the mother's brother or father's sister. Ojibwa religion was animistic, the natural world being inhabited by numerous spirits both good and evil, some of which required special treatment. Bear ceremonialism and the vision quest to obtain a guardian helper were practised. A SHAMAN cured the ill and performed SHAKING TENT rites to communicate with spirits. After about 1700, the MIDEWIWIN or Grand Medicine Society was conducted by an organized priesthood among the more westerly Ojibwa.

The European FUR TRADE profoundly affected the Ojibwa. Initially, they received French trade items for furs from Nipissing and Algonquin, but following the mid-17th-century dispersal of the HURON and neighbouring Algonquians, the Ottawa and their Ojibwa allies became middlemen to tribes farther west. The Ojibwa participated in the occasional multi-tribal FEAST OF THE DEAD at which furs and trade goods were distributed. The western expansion of the French fur trade and the establishment of the English HUDSON'S BAY COMPANY trade near James Bay and Hudson Bay drew some Ojibwa into new areas, first as temporary trader-hunters, but later as permanent residents. Between 1680 and 1800, 4 divisions of Ojibwa emerged, each representing a different adaptation to environmental and contact conditions. Those who moved S of Lk Superior into Wisconsin and Minnesota, displacing, often forcefully, the Dakota, are known as the Southwestern Chippewa. The harsher environment of the coniferous forests of northern Ontario and Manitoba was exploited by the Northern Ojibwa. After 1780 some shifted to Manitoba, Saskatchewan and N Dakota, becoming the Plains Ojibwa or Bungi. Still others, now known as Southeastern Ojibwa, moved into S-central Ontario and the lower Michigan Peninsula. Although most Ojibwa continued to live by hunting, fishing and gathering, some, particularly those in southern Ontario, adopted farming. Today, Ojibwa occupy

Dancer from the Ojibwa tribe of the Great Lakes region performing at the Odawa Native centre, Nepean, Ont (*photo by Jim Merrithew*).

reserve communities in these 4 areas.

Before 1760 most Ojibwa supported the French, but they became British allies during the American Revolution and the War of 1812. The social and economic life of all Ojibwa groups was affected by the fur trade. Aboriginal items were replaced by western materials and certain natural resources became depleted. Family-possessed fur-hunting territories emerged among northern groups. First in the SE and later in more remote areas, Ojibwa became at least nominal Christians. Most Ojibwa did not sign treaties with the government until after 1850, at which time each BAND-reserve community elected a chief and council.

From perhaps 10 000 persons at contact whose descendants are now called Ojibwa, the population grew to over 79 839 (registered) in 1986, two-thirds of whom lived in Canada. There is also a large MÉTIS population. Among and within Ojibwa communities there is considerable socioeconomic variability, depending on the ability to exploit natural resources and gain access to Canadian markets. Arts and crafts have recently been revitalized and several Ojibwa artists have gained international recognition. *See also* NATIVE PEOPLE: EASTERN WOODLANDS, and general articles under NATIVE PEOPLE.   CHARLES A. BISHOP

Reading: Handbook of North American Indians, vol 6: Subarctic, ed J. Helm (1981); vol 15: Northeast, ed B.G. Trigger (1978).

Oka, Qué, UP, pop 1532 (1986c), 1538 (1981c), is located on Lac-des-Deux-Montagnes, just W of Montréal I. Established in 1875, the village developed at a strategic position on a point of land that extends well into the lake. In 1717 the governor of New France granted the seigneury of Lac-des-Deux-Montagnes to the clergy of the Séminaire de Montréal so that they could build a mission for the Indians. In 1881 Trappist monks from France founded their famous Abbey of Notre-Dame-du-Lac. La Trappe, as it is also called, is one of the largest Trappist monasteries in the world. In 1962 the provincial government developed Parc Paul-Sauvé a few km downstream from the village, its

main attraction being its large bay, an ecological sanctuary and the Montagne du Calvaire, on whose peak the seigneurs built a pilgrimage site in 1739 for the Indians who went there every autumn before setting out on their hunt. Some 600 Indians still live at Oka.   GILLES BOILEAU

Okak, archaeological sites in northern LABRADOR that represent a microcosm of more than 5000 years of PREHISTORY. Excavations have revealed sites of 4 major cultures that occupied the area. The earliest of these is a southern-derived Indian culture called the Maritime ARCHAIC tradition. About 4000 years ago a new people, known to archaeologists as Early Paleoeskimos, arrived from the north and expanded southward at the expense of the earlier Indian peoples. These people continued to move southward along the Labrador coast and eventually populated the island of Newfoundland. They became extinct shortly after 2200 years ago but were replaced by a second group of Paleoeskimos known as Dorset Eskimo. They, in turn, apparently became extinct sometime following 1200 AD, perhaps at about the same time that the ancestors of the present-day LABRADOR INUIT arrived from the N in the Okak region. *See also* ARCHAEOLOGY.

JAMES A. TUCK

Okanagan Valley, BC, roughly 200 km long (in Canada) and 20 km wide, lies between the Columbia and Cascade mountain ranges in south-central BC. Its landscape of low hills and oblong lakes was formed by glacial activity during the Tertiary and Pleistocene eras, the final retreat of the ice (between 11 000 and 9000 years ago) leaving large deposits of gravel, silt and sand on the bottom and sides of the valley. These sediments were eroded by water and wind, resulting in large alluvial fans and deltas such as those on which VERNON, KELOWNA and PENTICTON partly stand. It is these sediments which have been colonized and used for agriculture. Spilled along the valley floor are the watery remnants of a large glacial lake, the largest of which is Okanagan Lk. Lying in a string to the E are Swan, Kalamalka and Wood lakes; to the S lie Skaha, Vaseaux and Osoyoos lakes. The whole system drains S through the Okanagan R into the COLUMBIA R.

The valley lies in the shadow of the Cascade Mts, creating a hot, sunny, dry climate. Most of the valley receives about 2000 hours of sunlight per year and 30-40 cm of precipitation. The southern valley, around Vaseaux Lk, which gets less than 30 cm of precipitation, is desertlike, with cactus, rattlesnakes and painted turtles.

The valley contains the largest concentration of population in interior BC (about 7% of the provincial total). The 3 largest centres (1986c) are Kelowna (61 213), Penticton (23 588) and Vernon (20 241). Enderby (1714) and Armstrong (2706) lie in the dairy and vegetable-growing region of the northern valley, and Okanagan Falls (1101), OLIVER (1963) and OSOYOOS (2956) lie in the dry fruit-growing area S of Penticton.

The valley was first inhabited by the Okanagan tribe of the Interior SALISH, who likely gave the valley its name, translated roughly as "place of water." There are large Indian reserves on the NW

Located between the Columbia and Cascade mountain ranges, the Okanagan Valley is one of Canada's premier fruit-growing areas. This photo was taken near Osoyoos (*photo by John deVisser*).

arm of Okanagan Lk, SW of the lake and N of Osoyoos, and others near Enderby and Kelowna. David Stuart, a Scottish fur trader in the employ of the PACIFIC FUR CO, was likely the first white person to see the valley (1811), and his cousin, John Stuart of the HBC, followed the trail (1814) through the valley that continued to be used until 1847 by fur traders, and later by miners. Missionaries built the first settlements at the head of Okanagan Lk about 1840 and near Kelowna in 1859. Some miners stayed on after a small gold rush at Cherry Creek (50 km E of Vernon), as did a few of the OVERLANDERS OF 1862. Ranching, in the northern valley, was the first viable industry.

Next to the FRASER RIVER LOWLANDS, the Okanagan Valley is the most important agricultural region in BC. The primary crop is fruit, which was first planted by Oblate missionaries near Kelowna (1862) and by Hiram "Okanagan" Smith near Penticton (about 1869). Gov Gen ABERDEEN, who owned a huge range in the northern valley, gave a strong impetus to fruit growing (1890s) by offering land for this purpose. New plantings were made around Osoyoos for soldiers returning after WWI. The pioneer orchards suffered from inadequate irrigation, winter freezes, the codling moth and an inadequate marketing system. It was not until the 1930s that irrigation turned the semidesert of sagebrush into a premier fruit-growing area. Today the valley produces 34% of Canada's apples, 100% of its apricots, 38% of its sweet & sour cherries, 31% of its peaches, 34% of its pears and 39% of its plums and prunes. The first commercial plantings of grapes were made around Kelowna (1926) and today local and coastal wineries are supported by grapes grown in the valley.

Growing numbers of tourists are attracted by the valley's scenic splendour, warm summers, freshwater beaches and numerous festivities. There are 2 large (Silver Star and Okanagan Mountain) and several smaller provincial parks in the valley. JAMES MARSH

O'Keefe, Eugene, brewer, banker (b at Bandon, Ire 10 Dec 1827; d at Toronto 1 Oct 1913). He came to Canada in 1832, was educated in Toronto schools and in 1846 became a junior accountant in the Toronto Savings Bank. On borrowed capital he founded Victoria Brewery, Toronto, in 1861, and the next year he bought Hannath and Hart Brewery, also of Toronto. By the 1890s O'Keefe was the largest brewer of lager beer in Canada, using refrigeration technology imported from the US. The company was incorporated as the O'Keefe Brewing Co Ltd in 1891. During the TEMPERANCE agitation he campaigned publicly to defend the sale of beer as an alternative to hard liquor, claiming that whisky was too cheap in Canada. Devastated by the death of his son in 1911, he sold out to a holding company under Sir Henry PELLATT, Sir William MULOCK and Charles

Miller. This company was bought by E.P. TAYLOR in 1934 and incorporated into Canadian Breweries Ltd. O'Keefe was recognized for his benefactions to the Roman Catholic Church.

ALBERT TUCKER

Okotoks, Alta, Town, pop 5214 (1986c). Okotoks meaning "Stoney Crossing" (also known as Dewdney after the lt-gov 1892-96), is believed to date to the location of an 1870s stopping house. The routing of the CPR through Calgary made Okotoks a resting point on overland connecting trails from the S, and in 1891 with the completion of the railway to Fort Macleod, Okotoks boomed as a flourishing transportation, ranching and sawmilling centre. The discovery of the oil field. W of the town in 1914 added further impetus to growth. The impact of the 1954 highway bypass was redressed in the 1960s and 1970s when Okotoks became a commuter suburb of Calgary.

FRITS PANNEKOEK

Old-Age Pension The first old-age pension (1927) was jointly financed by federal and provincial governments but administered by the latter. It paid up to $20 per month, depending on other income and assets, and was available to Canadian citizens 70 years of age and older, but only after they had passed a strict means test. In 1951 the federal government introduced the Old Age Security Act, which provided a universal pension of $40 per month paid and administered by the federal government to all Canadians, age 70 and over, without a means test. A second piece of legislation, the Old Age Assistance Act, a cost-shared program with the provinces, made a pension available to Canadians age 65 to 69, but retained the means test. By 1964 the universal pension had been raised to $75 per month, widely regarded as inadequate. The federal government then introduced the CANADA PENSION PLAN, which became effective in 1966 and which requires almost all workers and their employers to contribute to a social-insurance plan that provides a wage-related pension on retirement as well as other benefits. It also introduced the Guaranteed Income Supplement program (1966), which paid a supplement of up to $30 per month to pensioners with little or no income other than their Old Age Security pension. At the same time, the age of eligibility for Old Age Security was lowered in stages to 65. In 1975 the Old Age Security system (OAS/GIS) was supplemented by a Spouse's Allowance (SA), guaranteeing a minimum monthly income to couples where only one person receives a pension and the other is between 60 and 64 years of age.

Old age pensions became a topic of national concern from the mid-1970s until the early 1980s chiefly because of the high inflation rates and their effect on fixed incomes. A federal Green Paper (1982) identified the 2 goals of the Canadian pension system as ensuring elderly persons a minimum income (the anti-poverty objective) and maintaining a reasonable relationship between the individual's income before and following retirement (the income replacement objective). The OAS/GIS/SA programs are designed to meet the anti-poverty objective; the income replacement objective is met by the Canada/Québec Pension Plan (C/QPP), plus employer-sponsored pensions and private, individual savings. The latter have been encouraged by provisions in the tax system. Some of the most pressing issues identified in the national debate on pensions included the inadequacies of the private pension system, most notably the failure to index benefits to the cost of living; the poverty rate among the elderly and especially single, elderly women; the future cost of pensions as the number of Canadians 65 and over was predicted to increase from 2.3 mil-

lion in 1981 to an estimated 3.5 million in 2001 and peaking at 6.6 million in 2031. Recommendations to improve the public pensions (OAS/GIS/SA) and to raise the benefits of the C/QPP from 25% to 50% of average industrial wages were put forward. A proposal for a homemaker pension for those women who spend their life working in the home and are thereby excluded from any existing occupational pension was discussed. Finally, there were recommendations that more uniform and higher standards of performance be demanded of the more than 14 000 private pension plans. Despite nearly a decade of debate very little substantive change occurred. The Guaranteed Income Supplement was raised by $50 per month in 1984 and a homemaker pension was promised by 1989. In an effort to reduce its deficit, the federal government proposed in 1985 to partially de-index the Old Age Security benefit by limiting cost of living increases to amounts exceeding 3 percentage points. Organizations of senior citizens effectively lobbied Ottawa and had the proposal withdrawn. In July 1987 the OAS benefit paid to people 65 and over was $303.64 a month. The maximum GIS was $360.87 for a single pensioner or $235.03 for a married person whose spouse also received an OAS pension or a Spouse's Allowance. In March 1984 there were 2.4 million recipients of OAS, 50.03% of whom also qualified for part or all of the Guaranteed Income Supplement. There were 87 890 recipients of the Spouse's Allowance for a total cost of the OAS/GIS/SA programs of $15.7 billion. A minority of pensioners also have an employer-sponsored pension to supplement their retirement income and a growing number also qualify for a Canada or Québec Pension Plan benefit. *See also* SOCIAL SECURITY. DENNIS GUEST

Reading: Dennis Guest, *The Emergence of Social Security in Canada* (2nd ed. rev 1985); National Council on Welfare, *A Pension Primer* (1985).

Old Believers, also known as Old Ritualists, are descendants of conservative members of the Russian Orthodox Church who refused to accept a reform imposed in the mid-17th century by the patriarch Nikon. With the exception of some congregations in the US, the approximately 5 million OB in the USSR, Europe, Australia, and S and N America are not in any way affiliated with other ORTHODOX CHURCHES. Some 500 OB live in Canada, most of them in 3 congregations located in northern Alberta. A "bishop of Canada" was appointed by the Old Orthodox Church in 1908, but the composition and history of his see remain unknown. Probably the largest influx of OB immigrants occurred 1924-28 as part of the post-revolutionary wave of Russian refugees. The only remnant of this wave is the priestist congregation near Hines Creek, Alta, which built the first known OB church in the Western Hemisphere. Its membership has been declining since WWII because of dispersal of the young generation.

Two additional parishes were founded between 1973 and 1975 by OB from Siberia/Manchuria who arrived in Alberta via S America and Oregon. Their residents adhere to traditions discarded by other Orthodox Christians, including appearance and dietary rules formulated in Byzantium and medieval Russia. Each household constitutes an independent economic unit, with agriculture and forestry as its backbone. Russian is spoken at home.

The OB do not differ in dogma from the official Russian Orthodox Church. They refuse, however, to employ liturgical books printed during or after Nikon's tenure or to abandon Church Slavonic as the sole permissible liturgical language. Further differences include iconographic and ritual distinctions, such as the insistence of the OB on making the sign of the cross with 2 rather than 3 fingers, and on baptism involving a full triple immersion.   DAVID SCHEFFEL

Old Crow, YT, UP, a settlement of Loucheux Indians on the Porcupine R, is located 770 km N of Whitehorse and 112 km inside the Arctic Circle. The Loucheux settled at New Rampart House near the Alaska boundary in the 1870s when their original village around Ft Yukon was found to be on American soil. A smallpox EPIDEMIC decimated their numbers in 1911 and the survivors moved to the muskrat breeding grounds at the confluence of the Crow and Porcupine rivers. The new settlement was named for Walking Crow, a revered chief who died in the 1870s.   H. GUEST

Old Crow Basin, in northern Yukon Territory, is important for the richness of its fossil record and the discovery there of some of the oldest artifacts in Canada. During the last major glacial period (the Wisconsinan), the basin was occupied by a single large lake in which a thick layer of clay was deposited. When the glacial lake drained, about 12 000 years ago, Old Crow R cut through the clay and deeper, older layers, creating vertical bluffs more than 30 m high. Hundreds of thousands of fossils, representing many varieties of plants, invertebrates and vertebrates, were eroded from the layers beneath the lake clay. Many fossils were redeposited in and on newly formed riverbanks and bars. Among the vertebrate fossils are bones that bear the distinctive marks of breakage and cutting by people who may have killed or scavenged the animals – bones that radiocarbon dating places at 25 000-30 000 years ago. The analysis of these fossils yields a record of environmental change spanning more than 100 000 years. *See also* ARCHAEOLOGY; PREHISTORY. RICHARD E. MORLAN

Old Crow Plain, about 5000 km², elev 300 m, referred to locally as Old Crow Flats, is the northernmost part of the Porcupine Plateau in the Yukon, lying N of the Arctic Circle and 150 km S of the BEAUFORT SEA. The name honours the memory of an Indian chieftain of the Loucheux tribe. The plain is a pristine wilderness area underlain by continuous PERMAFROST and covered with a myriad of shallow lakes and ponds, some of which have an oriented rectangular shape related to prevailing wind directions and to patterned ground phenomena, eg, ice polygons and wedges.

The vegetation is of the tundra type, with outliers of the boreal spruce forest; willow thickets line the course of the Old Crow R. Geologically the plain represents the floor of the intermontane Old Crow Basin, a structural depression of Tertiary age linking the Eastern and Interior Systems of the Cordillera. The basin is bordered on the E by the Richardson Mts, on the N by the British Mts and on the W and S by the Old Crow Range. The underlying sediments include a veneer of Holocene and Pleistocene clays, silts, sands and organics, overlying a thick sequence of Tertiary, Mesozoic and Paleozoic sediments, some of which are potentially oil bearing. The basin was one of the few areas in Canada untouched by glaciation during the Pleistocene ice ages, and it served as a refuge for many ice-age animals. However, abandoned high-level shorelines indicate that the flats were inundated by proglacial lakes during the ice ages. The modern Old Crow R, which joins the Porcupine R at the Indian village of Old Crow, is a meandering stream with numerous cutoffs and a well-defined terrace system. The river bluffs have yielded an enormous quantity of mammalian bones, together with artifacts of PREHISTORY.   ALAN V. JOPLING

Oldman River, 430 km, rises near Mt Lyall in the Rockies of SW Alberta and flows S then E to

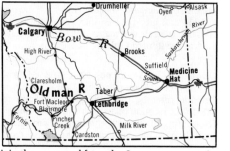

join the BOW R and form the S SASKATCHEWAN R in Alberta. The Oldman R's name may come from the Cree term for "old man's playground." It receives tributaries from the US (St Mary R) and WATERTON LAKES NATIONAL PARK. One of few major nonglacial-fed rivers in Alberta, it drains 27 500 km² of mountains, foothills and prairie. Important as a water supply for FORT MACLEOD and LETHBRIDGE, it has numerous dams and diversions for irrigation in the Lethbridge Irrigation Dist and St Mary and Milk river developments. A new $350-million dam has been proposed for the Oldman near Pincher Creek. It will supply irrigation and municipal water supplies to Lethbridge and adjacent areas of southern Alberta. The dam has aroused considerable controversy, with opponents claiming serious adverse effects on river habitat, archaeological sites and trout-fishing. Proponents view the expansion of irrigation development and increased surety of water supplies as benefits that outweigh environmental concerns.   IAN A. CAMPBELL

Olds, Alta, Town, pop 4871 (1986c), inc 1905, is situated in a transition zone between prairie grassland and partially wooded parkland 89 km N of Calgary. Just to the NE, the Lone Pine stopping house once marked the early cart trail that the McDougalls of the Morley Methodist Mission cleared along an established north-south Indian and fur-trade route in 1873. Upon construction of the Calgary-Edmonton Ry in 1891, CPR officials named a new townsite after George Olds, long-time general traffic manager. Homesteading began in the parkland environment to the north, filling in the Olds vicinity only after 1900. Ranching developed to the east, and Olds is still known for championship cattle breeding. While Olds has since WWII become a regional centre for servicing oil and natural gas exploration and production, agriculture still predominates. Olds College (fd 1913), a public college with a range of programs, specializes in agricultural courses.
    CARL BETKE

O'Leary, PEI, Village, pop 823 (1986c), situated in Prince County 59 km NW of Summerside. It came into being in 1872, when the railway was constructed. Because of transportation problems, few colonists lived inland. On the other hand, needing to limit costs, the tracks were built through the Island's heartland rather than to circumscribe it. To service the West Cape settlers, the O'Leary rail station was constructed 20 km from the coast. As the local focus of trade, merchants soon gathered around the station. Today, O'Leary remains a viable small commercial centre.
    W.S. KEIZER

O'Leary, Michael Grattan, journalist, senator (b at Gaspé, Qué 19 Feb 1889; d at Ottawa 7 Apr 1976). O'Leary joined Ottawa's Press Gallery in 1911, representing the OTTAWA JOURNAL. He was close to most Conservative Party leaders. PM Arthur MEIGHEN took him along to the 1921 Imperial Conference, and O'Leary repaid the favour by standing as Gaspé's candidate in 1925, though unsuccessfully. O'Leary also supported Liberal ministers, such as C.D. HOWE, in columns and ed-

itorials. He eventually became editor of the *Journal*, which earned a reputation for high literary standards and good reporting. In 1961 O'Leary headed the Royal Commission on Publications, and in 1962 PM John DIEFENBAKER appointed him to the Senate.   ROBERT BOTHWELL

Oliphant, Betty, ballet teacher (b at London, Eng 5 Aug 1918). A grande dame of Canadian dance and an internationally famed educator, Oliphant came to Canada in 1947, where she founded the Canadian Dance Teachers Assn, opened a school and became ballet mistress of the NATIONAL BALLET OF CANADA (1951). In 1959 she became founding principal of the NATIONAL BALLET SCHOOL, now acclaimed one of the best anywhere. As principal of the school, and as associate artistic director of the National Ballet (1969-75), and since then artistic director, Oliphant helped shape the company's style and trained dancers and teachers for Canada and the world. Her accomplishments are widely recognized. At Erik BRUHN's request she reorganized the Royal Swedish Opera Ballet School (1967). Among the honours she has received are the MOLSON PRIZE 1979 and the Diplôme d'honneur of the Canadian Conference of the Arts (1982). As well, she has been awarded the Order of Canada (Officer 1973 and Companion 1985).   PENELOPE DOOB

Oliver, BC, Village, pop 1963 (1986c), 1893 (1981c), inc 1945, is located in the OKANAGAN VALLEY, 27 km S of Penticton. It was named after Prem John OLIVER, whose Liberal government (1918-27) sponsored the Southern Okanagan Lands Project, irrigating land to be settled by soldiers returning from WWI. Some mining, cattle ranching and fruit growing had existed previously in the area. Agriculture is the most important activity today, followed by mining, logging, tourism and specialized horticultural crops, with some manufacturing and grape growing.   WILLIAM A. SLOAN

Oliver, Farquhar Robert, farmer, politician (b at Priceville, Ont 6 Mar 1904). First elected to the Ontario Legislature in 1926 as a member of the United Farmers, he was re-elected continuously until his retirement in 1967. In 1940 he entered the Liberal Cabinet of Mitchell HEPBURN as minister of public works; in 1941 he assumed responsibility for welfare as well, but resigned both portfolios in 1942 during the confusion following Hepburn's resignation as premier. Oliver apparently was offered the premiership by Hepburn, but he declined because the offer was unconfirmed by caucus. In 1943, when Harry Nixon became premier, Oliver re-entered the Cabinet; but although he held his seat in the ensuing election, the Liberal government was defeated. In 1945 and 1954 he was elected leader of the shattered party but was unable to engineer its political recovery.   STANLEY GORDON

Oliver, Frank, newspaper publisher, politician (b in Peel County, Canada W 14 Sept 1853; d at Ottawa 31 Mar 1933). He was the son of Allan Bowsfield but took his mother's maiden name. He brought the first printing press to Edmonton and in 1880 founded the Edmonton *Bulletin* which he published until 1923. He was a member of the North-West Council 1883-85 for Edmonton, and was elected to the Legislative Assembly of the North-West Territories in 1888 and 1894. He sat in the House of Commons as a Liberal under Sir Wilfrid LAURIER 1896-1917 and was minister of the interior and superintendent general of Indian affairs 1905-11. As the former, he continued the immigration policies of Sir Clifford SIFTON.   ERIC J. HOLMGREN

Oliver, John, politician, premier of BC (b at Hartington, Eng 31 July 1856; d at Victoria 17

Aug 1927). Coming to Ontario with his family in 1870, he moved to BC in 1877 and took up a farm in Delta. After serving in local politics he was elected to the BC legislature in 1900 and became leader of the opposition, but lost his seat in the 1909 election. Re-elected in the sweeping 1916 Liberal victory, he was appointed minister of agriculture and railways. On Harlan BREWSTER's death in 1918, Oliver became premier, remaining in office until his own death. Known as "Honest John," he was a plain man of considerable integrity but not an innovative politician. He governed BC through the difficult readjustments after WWI and the economic stagnation of the early 1920s. He was involved in efforts to develop fruit growing in the OKANAGAN VALLEY, to solve the problems of the financially troubled Pacific Great Eastern Ry, and to secure freight-rate concessions from the federal government. Late in his premiership, he passed some social legislation. The village of OLIVER, BC, is named for him.   ROBIN FISHER

Olympic Games The original Olympic Games developed in ancient Greece, probably from harvest festivals held at the religious centre of Olympia in the eastern Peloponnese. Religious rites in honour of Zeus were an integral feature of the celebration. From 776 BC onward the games were held once every 4-year period, called an "Olympiad." Only foot races appear to have been contested during the early years, and by the mid-5th century BC the events took 3 days of the 5-day festival. The program changed over the years, but during the period of greatest Olympic glory it included chariot and horse races, 3 distances of foot races, boxing, wrestling, *pankration* (a wide-open style of wrestling), pentathlon, a race in armour, and boys' events. A sacred truce, *ekecheiria*, was announced for a period before and after the games to assure safe travel for athletes and spectators and to stop warfare in the areas surrounding Olympia. The Olympic Games exemplified the Greek search for excellence, their love of competition and belief in the development of physical health and skill.

The initiative to revive the Olympic values of harmonizing physical, mental and spiritual development came from French aristocrat baron de Coubertin, who presided at a congress of some 12 or 13 nations at which it was resolved to hold a sports competition every 4 years, inviting all nations. The first modern Olympic Games were held, appropriately, in Athens in 1896, and the games have been held every 4 years since, except during WWI and WWII (1916, 1940, 1944). By 1908, when the games were held in London, England, they were gaining worldwide significance, and they continue to be the premier sporting event in the world. The control of the games rests with the International Olympic Committee. New members are selected by present incumbents and represent the IOC to their countries, not the reverse. The IOC has about 90 members; women were first included on it in 1981. The first Winter Olympic Games held under IOC jurisdiction were in 1928, although a 1924 winter sports competition held in Chamonix, France, was later recognized as the first Winter Olympic Games. The sports comprising the Olympics have altered since the early years. The program has expanded considerably – eg, table tennis ("ping pong") will be included in 1988 – although some sports (golf) have been eliminated. Getting new sports accepted into the program is not easy, as the IOC wishes to retain a 2-week festival. At present the Summer Games offer 23 sports and the Winter only 6.

Canadians participated in the 1900, 1904 and 1906 ("interim") Olympics, but Canada sent its first real national team – of 84 athletes – to Lon-

Opening ceremonies at the 1988 Winter Olympic Games, Calgary, 13 Feb 1988 *(Photo by Brian Gavriloff/ Edmonton Journal)*.

don in 1908. Canadians have won 37 gold medals at the Summer Olympic Games: George ORTON, steeplechase *(Paris, 1900)*; Étienne DESMARTEAU, weight throwing, George LYON, golf, Winnipeg Shamrocks, lacrosse, and a team from Galt, Ont, soccer *(St Louis, 1904)*; William Sherring, marathon *(Athens, Interim Olympics 1906)*; Robert KERR, 200 m race, Walter EWING, shooting, and National Team, lacrosse *(London, 1908)*; George GOULDING, 10 000 m walk, and George HODGSON, 400 m and 1500 m swim *(Stockholm, 1912)*; Earl Thompson, 110 m hurdles, Bert SCHNEIDER, boxing, and Winnipeg Falcons, hockey *(Antwerp, 1920)*; Percy WILLIAMS, 100 m and 200 m dashes, Ethel CATHERWOOD, high jump, and women's 4x100 m relay team *(Amsterdam, 1928)*; Duncan MCNAUGHTON, high jump, and Horace Gwynne, boxing *(Los Angeles, 1932)*; Francis AMYOT, canoeing *(Berlin, 1936)*; George GENEREUX, shooting *(Helsinki, 1952)*; Gerry OUELLETTE, shooting, and UBC Fours, rowing *(Melbourne, 1956)*; Roger Jackson and George Hungerford, rowing *(Tokyo, 1964)*; and Jim ELDER, Jim DAY and Tom GAYFORD, equestrian *(Mexico, 1968)*. In addition the EDMONTON GRADS won 4 "unofficial" championships in women's basketball (1924, 1928, 1932 and 1936) when it was an auxiliary event.

Canada had by far its most successful Olympic performance at Los Angeles in 1984, with 10 gold medals: Larry CAIN, C-1 500 m; Hugh FISHER and Alwyn MORRIS, K-2 1000 m canoeing; Linda THOM, match pistols, Lori FUNG, rhythmic gymnastics; Sylvie BERNIER, springboard diving; Anne OTTENBRITE, 200 m breaststroke, Victor DAVIS, 200 m breaststroke, Alex BAUMANN, 200 m and 400 m individual medley, swimming; National Team, 8s rowing.

In the Winter Olympics, Canadians have won 13 gold medals: Toronto Granite Club, hockey *(Chamonix, 1924)*; U of T Grads, hockey *(St Moritz, 1928)*; Winnipeg Hockey Team, hockey *(Lk Placid, 1932)*; Barbara Ann SCOTT, figure skating, and RCAF Flyers, hockey *(St Moritz, 1948)*; Edmonton Mercurys, hockey *(Oslo, 1952)*; Anne HEGGTVEIT, slalom, and Barbara WAGNER and Bob PAUL, pairs skating *(Squaw Valley, 1960)*; Vic and

John EMERY, Douglas Anakin and Peter Kirby, bobsledding *(Innsbruck, 1964)*; Nancy GREENE, giant slalom *(Grenoble, 1968)*; Kathy KREINER, giant slalom *(Innsbruck, 1976)*; and Gaëtan BOUCHER, 2 gold medals and 1 bronze in speed skating *(Sarajevo, 1984)*.

Montréal hosted the Olympic Games in Aug 1976, amid a cloud of controversy over the runaway cost of its new Olympic Stadium. Canada boycotted the 1980 Olympic Games, held in Moscow, to protest the Soviet invasion of Afghanistan. Calgary hosted the Winter Olympics in Feb 1988.   JEAN M. LEIPER

Reading: W. Bryder, *Canada at the Olympic Winter Games* (1987); Lord Killanin and John Rodda, eds, *The Olympic Games 1980* (1979); H. Roxborough, *Canada at the Olympic Games* (1975).

Ombudsman, an independent officer of the legislature who investigates complaints from the public against administrative action and, if finding the action unfair, recommends a remedy. Unlike a court, an ombudsman does not have power to annul a decision, but in most cases recommendations to the administrative authorities are accepted. If not, the matter can be reported to the legislature. The complaint procedure is much less formal and costly than a court appeal; all it involves is writing a letter to the ombudsman. Originating in Sweden (the word is Swedish for "agent" or "representative"), the office of ombudsman was adopted by Norway and New Zealand in 1962, and then spread rapidly to other countries. By 1983 there were 78 offices in 28 countries. Canada's provinces have been among the world's leaders in adopting the institution. Alberta and NB created the office in 1967, Québec in 1968 *(Protecteur du citoyen)* and Manitoba in 1969. Five other provinces followed in the 1970s, and the institution has been successfully established now in all provinces except PEI.

The first International Ombudsman Conference was held in Edmonton in 1976. The International Ombudsman Institute was established at U of Alberta in 1978, and it serves as the centre for research studies on ombudsmanship. In 1977 a committee of senior officials supported the appointment of a federal ombudsman but, although the government introduced a bill in 1978 to create the office, ombudsmanlike offices for special purposes were created instead. The first, the commissioner of OFFICIAL LANGUAGES, was created in 1969 to investigate complaints about the use of English or French by federal agencies. A second, the correctional investigator's office, was set up in 1973 for prisoners' complaints. A third office, created in 1977, is the privacy commissioner. This office receives complaints and makes recommendations regarding the protection of personal files and any refusal of access to one's own file held by the federal government. In 1982 the office of information commissioner was set up to receive complaints and make recommendations regarding refusals of public access to federal documents. If the federal government creates a general ombudsman office, these specialized offices will perhaps become subunits of it.   DONALD C. ROWAT

Reading: Donald C. Rowat, *The Ombudsman Plan* (2nd ed, 1985).

On Canadian Poetry, a fine overview of 19th- and early to mid-20th-century Canadian poetry by E.K. BROWN (Toronto, 1943; rev 1944). Brown begins with a cogent analysis of the "problem of a Canadian literature," continues by tracing the development of Canadian poetry from the late 18th century to the 1940s and closes with an evaluation of our 3 "masters" – Archibald LAMPMAN, D.C. SCOTT and E.J. PRATT. The Governor General's Award-winning *On Canadian Poetry* is largely responsible for the current general view that these poets are the major figures of the era, and that Charles G.D. ROBERTS and Bliss CARMAN are of less importance. Brown provides subtle and penetrating interpretations of individual poems and poets, as well as what Northrop FRYE has assessed as the most clearly defined context within which to study Canadian literature.   NEIL BESNER

On to Ottawa Trek In early Apr 1935, 1500 residents of federal UNEMPLOYMENT RELIEF CAMPS in BC went on strike and moved by train and truck to Vancouver. Organized by the radical Workers' Unity League and led by WUL officer Arthur "Slim" EVANS, the subsequent Vancouver sit-in grew out of an angry concern for improved conditions and benefits in the camps and the apparent reluctance of the federal government to provide work and wages programs. In Vancouver the strikers organized themselves into divisions, undertook alliances with civic, labour, ethnic and political elements, held demonstrations, and conducted interviews with government officers, among them Prem T. Dufferin PATTULLO and Mayor Gerald MCGEER. Highlights of the 2-month sojourn included occupation of the Hudson's Bay store and the city museum and library, and a May

Strikers from the unemployment relief camps en route to eastern Canada during the "On to Ottawa Trek," shown at Kamloops, BC, June 1935 (*National Archives of Canada/C-29399*).

Day parade to Stanley Park of some 20 000 strikers and supporters.

When local governments refused responsibility for the strikers' welfare, and when the men themselves began to grow restless at the apparent failure of their movement, Evans and his associates decided to take the strike to Ottawa. On June 3, over 1000 strikers began the "On to Ottawa Trek," determined to inform the nation of their cause and to lay complaints before Parliament and Prime Minister R.B. BENNETT. The strikers commandeered freight trains and made stops in Calgary, Medicine Hat, Swift Current and Moose Jaw before arriving in Regina. There the railways, supported by an edict from the prime minister, refused further access to their trains. Negotiations with the federal government resulted in the dispatch of 8 Trekkers to Ottawa to meet with Bennett, while the 2000 remaining marchers waited in the Regina Exhibition Grounds, food and shelter being supplied by townspeople and the Saskatchewan government.

The talks in Ottawa quickly broke down and the delegation returned, having decided to disband the Trek. A rally was called for July 1 to secure last-minute assistance from the townspeople. Although the Trek was dispersing, Bennett had decided to arrest its leaders. That day Regina constables and RCMP squads moved into the crowd of some 300 to arrest Evans and other speakers, thus provoking the Regina Riot. The conflict raged back and forth on Regina streets, as Trekkers assaulted police with rocks and clubs. The fracas ended by midnight, after the rioters had returned to the Exhibition Grounds. One city constable had been killed, several dozen rioters, constables and citizens had been injured, and 130 rioters had been arrested. Four days later, the provincial government assisted the marchers on their way, most returning on passenger trains to Vancouver. The repression of the Trek and Bennett's antagonism towards Evans contributed to the PM's political decline. *See also* GREAT DEPRESSION.
                                                    VICTOR HOWARD

Reading: Ronald Liversedge, *Recollections of the On to Ottawa Trek* (1973).

Ondaatje, Michael, poet, filmmaker, editor (b at Colombo, Ceylon [Sri Lanka] 12 Sept 1943). Ondaatje's work often blends or counterposes the factual and the imaginary, poetry and prose. His longer narrative works often include documentary sources, such as photographs, first-person accounts, interviews and newspaper articles. The imagery is characterized by exoticism and surreal wit, a result of the juxtaposition of real and imaginary voices and events, and of Ondaatje's experience in diverse cultures. His work is also notable for its cinematic quality – its frequent presentation of startling freeze-frame images.

Ondaatje immigrated to Canada via England in 1962, and attended U of T (BA) and Queen's (MA). His first books of poetry include *The Dainty Monsters* (1967), *The Man with Seven Toes* (1969) and *Rat Jelly* (1973). *The Collected Works of Billy the Kid,* an account of the factual and fictional life of the notorious outlaw, won the Gov Gen's Award in 1970 and has been adapted for stage and produced at Stratford, Toronto and New York. *Coming Through Slaughter* (1976) tells of real and imagined events in the life of New Orleans jazz cornetist Buddy Bolden. His collection of poems, 1963-78, *There's a Trick with a Knife I'm Learning to Do,* won a second Gov Gen's Award in 1979. *Running in the Family* (1982) tells of the often bizarre life of his parents and grandparents in colonial Ceylon. *Secular Love,* a book of poems, was published in 1984. *In the Skin of a Lion,* published in 1987, is a novel which takes place in Toronto in the 1930s.

Poet Michael Ondaatje has won the Governor General's Award for *The Collected Works of Billy the Kid* and *There's a Trick with a Knife I'm Learning to Do* (*photo by Ron Watts/First Light*).

Ondaatje's films include *Sons of Captain Poetry* (about poet bp NICHOL), *Carry on Crime and Punishment, The Clinton Special* (about Theatre Passe Muraille's Farm Show) and *Royal Canadian Hounds.* His critical work on Leonard COHEN was published in 1970, and as editor of Mongrel Broadsides he published poems by James REANEY, Margaret ATWOOD and others. He has also edited a collection about animals, *The Broken Ark: A Book of Beasts* (1971); *Personal Fictions: Stories by Munro, Wiebe, Thomas, and Blaise* (1977) and *The Long Poem Anthology* (1979). In 1971 Ondaatje began teaching at York U.   SHARON THESEN

Onderdonk, Andrew, contractor (b at New York City *c*1849; d at Oscawana, NY 21 June 1905). Trained in engineering at the Troy (New York) Institute of Technology, Onderdonk was contractor in charge of government construction of 355 km of the CANADIAN PACIFIC RY between Port Moody and Savona's Ferry on Kamloops Lake, 1880-85. To overcome the shortage of white labour, he employed about 6000 Chinese workers. He also built the section of the CPR main line from Savona's Ferry east to Craigellachie in Eagle Pass, BC. In 1895 he obtained a contract to build part of the Trent Valley Canal in eastern Ontario for the federal government.   JOHN A. EAGLE

Reading: Pierre Berton, *The Last Spike: The Great Railway 1881-1885* (1971).

One Big Union On 13 Mar 1919 delegates from most union locals in western Canada met at the Western Labour Conference in Calgary and proclaimed support for the Bolshevik and other left-wing revolutions. They decided to conduct a referendum among Canadian union members on whether to secede from the American Federation of Labor and the TRADES AND LABOR CONGRESS OF CANADA, and form a REVOLUTIONARY INDUSTRIAL UNION to be called the One Big Union. The vote, held almost entirely in the West – and during the WINNIPEG GENERAL STRIKE – showed overwhelming support, and the OBU was launched in early June. Thousands of workers joined it, including large parts of the mine, transportation and logging labour force. At its peak in 1920, the OBU had close to 50 000 members from northern Ontario to the Pacific, with other locals in eastern and central Canada and the US. The international CRAFT UNION movement fought back, aided by governments (especially federal) and employers. The counterattack was particularly effective when splits appeared among OBU leaders over policy and tactics. Although by 1923 the union was reduced to approximately 5000 members, it had set an example for later, successful INDUSTRIAL UNIONISM. In 1956 it was absorbed into the CANADIAN LABOUR CONGRESS. D.J. BERCUSON

100 Mile House, BC, Village, pop 1692 (1986c), 1925 (1981c), located in south-central BC on Highway 97, 458 km NE of Vancouver. Originally part of the territory of the Shuswap, the community began in 1862 as a stopping house on the old CARIBOO ROAD during the CARIBOO GOLD RUSH. It received its name as it was 100 miles from Mile 0 at Lillooet. Cattle ranching, still a major industry in the region, began around the same period. In 1912 the marquess of Exeter in Britain purchased a large ranch surrounding 100 Mile House. His son, Lord Martin Cecil, took up residence on the ranch in 1932 and built 100 Mile Lodge to replace the old lodge. Today the village serves a wide region where ranching, lumber, mining and tourism supply the economic base. JOHN STEWART

Oneida, the smallest of the 5 nations of the IROQUOIS Confederacy, occupied a single village near Oneida Lk in NY state for most of the historic era. They had only 3 matrilineal clans (Wolf, Bear and Turtle). Nine Oneida chiefs sat on the confederacy council. It is possible that it was an Oneida town that CHAMPLAIN attacked unsuccessfully in 1615; their town was burned by the French in 1696. Unlike most of their brethren in the confederacy, the Oneida espoused the rebel cause in the American Revolution, owing to the influence of the New England missionary Samuel Kirkland. They were subjected to American pressures to sell their NY lands, however, after the war. A sizable portion of the tribe moved to Wisconsin, and another group of 242 individuals purchased a tract of land and settled near London, Ont, in 1839. Although Methodist and Anglican when they migrated to Ontario, some have since taken up the HANDSOME LAKE RELIGION. In 1986, 2772 names were recorded on the Ontario band list as Oneidas on the Thames and 1074 are registered at the Six Nations Reserve. See also NATIVE PEOPLE: EASTERN WOODLANDS. THOMAS S. ABLER

Reading: B.G. Trigger, ed, *Handbook of North American Indians,* vol 15: *Northeast* (1978).

O'Neill, James Edward, "Tip," baseball player (b at Springfield, Canada W 25 May 1858; d at Montréal, 31 Dec 1915). He played amateur baseball in Woodstock, Ont, before beginning a 10-year major-league career in 1883. A popular idol in St Louis, Mo, where he played from 1884 to 1889 and then again in 1891, O'Neill was greeted at bat by blaring trumpets, and in 1888 his picture adorned the team's train. He holds the all-time major league season-high batting average of .492, achieved in 1887 when bases on balls were calculated as hits. His career batting average of .326 is a Canadian major league high. WILLIAM HUMBER

Onion (*Allium cepa*), biennial, herbaceous plant of the Amaryllidaceae family. It is Canada's most important CONDIMENT CROP. Onions are native to western Asia; their cultivation predates recorded history. Botanical varieties include *A. cepa solaninum* (Multiplier Onion) and *A. cepa viviparum* (Top or Tree Onion). The bulb is formed of hollow leaves, thickened into 1.5-5 mm fleshy layers which overlap near the root juncture. Bulb skins are usually yellow, white or red. Depending chiefly on variety, mature bulbs range from 6 cm to 14 cm in diameter. The pungent taste derives from sulphurous, volatile oils (eg, pyruvic acid). Onions germinate at temperatures of 9-30°C, tolerate frosts to -2.5°C and mature in 115-135 days. Insect pests include onion maggots and thrips; plant diseases, smut, downy mildew, pink root, damping-off, leaf spot, purple blotch and neck rot. Young, green bulbs and tops contain useful amounts of vitamins A and C; dehydrated onions contain protein, phosphorus and potassium. Average Canadian production in 1985 (on 3841 ha) was 147 956 t, worth $19.6 million; Ontario produced over one-half. V.W. NUTTALL

Onley, Norman Antony, "Toni," painter (b at Douglas, Isle of Man, UK 20 Nov 1928). Onley received his early art training on the Isle of Man. His family immigrated to Canada in 1948, and he worked at various occupations in Ontario, later moving to BC. He studied in Mexico, where he came under the influence of American abstract expressionism, and later moved to Vancouver. A Canada Council grant allowed him to travel to England in 1963, where he studied the great artists of the British watercolour tradition. He returned to Vancouver in 1964 and began painting sparse, formal landscapes that were so successful he was soon able to earn his livelihood exclusively from his art; in Aug 1980 he sold 800 works for $900 000. In 1985 he collaborated with George WOODCOCK to produce *The Walls of India,* the sale of which, along with the sale of Onley's original watercolours used for the illustrations and matching grants from CIDA, was to generate revenue for the Canada-India Village Aid Assn, which provides public-health services in rural Indian villages. Onley's watercolours are always done on location and are the spontaneous reaction to the landscape forms he sees. He works in broad washes, usually using a large Chinese brush. The watercolours are the basis for studio oil paintings or silk-screen prints. ROGER H. BOULET

Reading: Roger H. Boulet, *Toni Onley: A Silent Thunder* (1981).

Onondaga, geographically at the centre of the 5 IROQUOIS nations, were designated "firekeepers" of the Iroquois league, serving as moderators at councils and retaining the WAMPUM records of the confederacy. Thadodaho, the most celebrated title among the 50 confederacy chiefs, was held by an Onondaga. Despite this central position in the confederacy, they often pursued an independent policy, as in 1649 when they remained neutral while the SENECA and MOHAWK fought and defeated the HURON. The main Onondaga town served as "capital" of the Iroquois Confederacy, and as a hub of frontier diplomacy for 2 centuries. The Onondaga themselves burned their town when an army under FRONTENAC invaded their country in 1696. The village was also burned by Americans during the American Revolution, although the Onondaga had for the most part remained neutral. In population the Onondaga were the third-largest Iroquois group immigrating to lands in Canada on the Grand R in 1785. They did not increase as rapidly as other groups and in the 1970s constituted only 6% of the official band list of over 9000 for the Six Nations Reserve. By 1986 they numbered only 735. Another portion of Onondaga retain lands in their ancestral homeland, outside Syracuse, NY. See also NATIVE PEOPLE: EASTERN WOODLANDS and general articles under NATIVE PEOPLE. THOMAS S. ABLER

Reading: B.G. Trigger, ed, *Handbook of North American Indians,* vol 15: *Northeast* (1978).

Ontario is Canada's most populous, richest and second-largest province; it stretches from Middle Island in Lake Erie in the S (41°40' N) to the Manitoba-Ontario border on Hudson Bay in the N (56°51' N) and from the banks of the St Lawrence R in the E (74°20' W) to the Manitoba border in the W (95°09' W). For the most part Ontario's frontiers run through the lakes and rivers of the GREAT LAKES system, on the S, and along the Ottawa R to the E; only in the NE and NW do borders follow geographical abstractions. The name Ontario, from an Iroquoian word sometimes translated as meaning "beautiful lake" or "beautiful water," is apt, since lakes and rivers occupy one-sixth of the province's total area of just over one million km². The word was first applied in 1641 to

Ontario

Capital: Toronto
Motto: Ut Incepit Fidelis Sic Permanet ("Loyal it began, loyal it remains")
Flower: White trillium
Largest Cities: Toronto, Ottawa, Hamilton, Kitchener, St Catharines-Niagara, London, Windsor, Oshawa, Thunder Bay, Sudbury
Population: 9 101 694 (1986c); rank first, 36% of Canada; 82.1% urban; 17.9% rural; 9.9 per km² density; 5.5% increase from 1981-86; 10.1% increase from 1976-86.
Languages: 76.3% English; 4.7% French; 15% Other; 4.0% English plus one or more languages
Entered Confederation: 1 July 1867
Government: Provincial – Lieutenant-Governor, Executive Council, Legislative Assembly of 125 members; federal – 24 senators, 95 members of the House of Commons
Area: 1 068 582 km², including 177 388 km² of inland water; 10.8% of Canada
Elevation: Highest point – Timiskaming District (693 m); lowest point – Hudson Bay shore
Gross Domestic Product: $177.5 billion (1986)
Farm Cash Receipts: $5.4 billion (1986)
Electric Power Produced: 121 661 GWh (1985)
Sales Tax: 7% (1987)

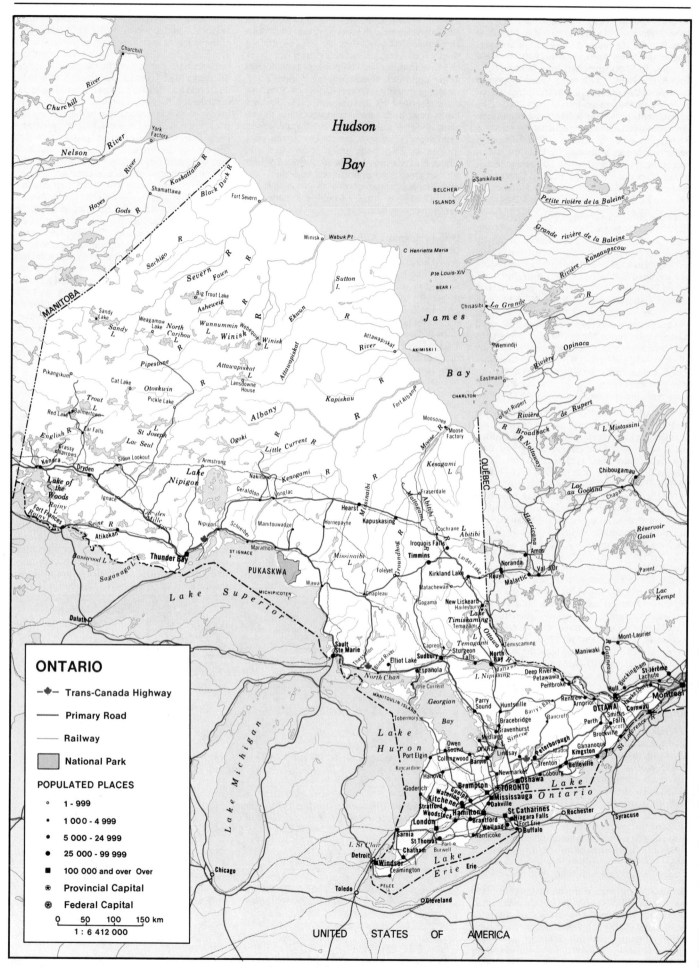

ONTARIO

- ◆ Trans-Canada Highway
- —— Primary Road
- —— Railway
- National Park

POPULATED PLACES

- ○ 1 - 999
- • 1 000 - 4 999
- • 5 000 - 24 999
- ● 25 000 - 99 999
- ■ 100 000 and over Over
- ⊛ Provincial Capital
- ⊛ Federal Capital

0   50   100   150 km

1 : 6 412 000

the easternmost of the Great Lakes, and "Old Ontario" was used to refer to the southern portion of land nearest the lake and was applied to the whole province in 1867.

Land and Resources

Ontario has the most varied landscape of any Canadian province. Two-thirds of the province lies under the Canadian SHIELD, which covers most of the N, except the Hudson Bay Lowland. From Georgian Bay in the W and near Renfrew in the E the edge of the Shield forms a triangular wedge, with its apex near Brockville on the St Lawrence R. To the E lies the eastern Ontario plain, between the Ottawa and St Lawrence rivers. To the W, from Kingston on, there are belted rolling hills and plains culminating in the flat country in extreme southwestern Ontario. The NIAGARA ESCARPMENT, traversing the area from Niagara to Tobermory and through MANITOULIN I in Georgian Bay, is the most conspicuous feature.

Ontario is often considered to be 2 distinct regions. To the S of the Shield lies southern Ontario where agriculture and most of the population are concentrated; northern Ontario, with nearly 90% of the land, contains only 10% of the population. Nevertheless, geology, climate, soil, vegetation and other factors combine to create distinct areas within this broad classification.

Geology The rocks of the Shield are among the oldest on Earth, dating from the Archaean and Proterozoic eons of the Precambrian era; the oldest sections date from 2000 million years ago; the most recent a mere 900 million. These formations contain the large mineral deposits that are so important to the economy of northern Ontario. Sedimentary limestone, shale and sandstone underlying southern Ontario are more recent, dating from the Paleozoic era, and are generally of the Ordovician, Silurian and Devonian periods. Outcrops of these rocks are rare, excepting where differential erosion of beds has exposed the Niagara Escarpment.

All of Ontario was, at one time or another, covered by glaciation. About 10 000 years ago the last ice sheet covering the province receded, resulting in the many lakes in the N and the Great Lakes along its southern and western borders. The proto-Great Lakes were considerably larger than their present descendants. As they evolved, they left behind a sand base along which many of the early roads of the province were located. The rivers that once drained them now flow through broad valleys such as the Grand R.

The effect of the ice age is still apparent. Scattered across southern Ontario are rocks left behind by the glaciers. Systems of moraines, marking the edges of stalled glaciers, traverse the province. The Oak Ridge Moraine, forming the height of land between Lake Ontario and Georgian Bay, is the most conspicuous. The Horseshoe Moraines parallel the eastern shore of Lk Huron to the base of the BRUCE PENINSULA and SE along the escarpment, then SW toward Lk Erie. Other deposits, drumlins, are especially frequent in the Peterborough region.

Surface The Canadian Shield is mostly, but not entirely, unsuitable for agriculture. The podzolic soils of northern Ontario are extremely thin and are low in fertility, although sufficient to support boreal forests. There are only a few areas, such as the clay belts in northeastern Ontario or the Rainy R area in the NW, where enough farming is possible to create the impression of an agricultural landscape. The forest cover of the N is not uniform. In the extreme N, stunted willows and black spruce struggle to grow in bogs; farther S spruce, aspen and jack pine dominate the northern Shield. Farther S again, to the E and W of Lake

Superior, the Shield is covered by a mixed forest, known as the Great Lakes-St Lawrence forest region. In the early 19th century, magnificent stands of white pine, the foundation of the central Canadian forest industry, were to be found in this region, as well as hard maples.

The grey-brown luvisolic (grey-brown podzolic) soils of southern Ontario that developed under forest vegetation from till and glacial deposits are reasonably fertile. Deltas, left behind from the Ice Age, form sand plains, especially to the N of Lk Erie.

Water Of the total surface area of 177 388 km² of water, almost half is in the Great Lakes. The ST LAWRENCE R and Great Lakes drew explorers, traders, soldiers and settlers into the heart of the continent. More recently, Ontario's abundant rivers and lakes have made possible hydroelectric power and the more obvious forms of industrialization. Ontario's water resources are fed by an abundant rainfall, and in most sections of the province by snow. Precipitation is most regular in the southern and central parts of Ontario where variations between winter and summer or spring and fall are not especially great; but winter and spring are somewhat less aqueous in northern and northwestern Ontario. The lower half of the province lies in the Great Lakes-St. Lawrence drainage basin, and the largest amounts of water flow along Ontario's southern borders: a peak monthly mean of 2390 m³/s on the NIAGARA R. Unlike the rivers that connect the Great Lakes, where there are not large variations in volume of flow from month to month, Ontario's inland rivers are subject to large increases in volume during the spring runoff when melting winter snows create an annual threat of flooding. The volume of the OTTAWA R practically triples in May to 2150 m³/s from its lowest monthly mean flow of 735 m³/s in August. An even more extreme example is the Thames R of southwestern Ontario, whose mean flow in March of 143 m³/s is over 11 times greater than its Aug mean of only 12.9 m³/s.

Climate Ontario has a wide range of climates. In the N a bitter subarctic climate prevails, with mean daily temperatures near Hudson Bay of 12° to 15°C in July and -22° to -25° in Jan. Winter temperatures are highest along the Great Lakes in southwestern Ontario and below the Niagara Escarpment, with mean daily temperatures ranging from -3°C near Windsor to -6°C near Toronto in Jan. In July the area between Chatham and Windsor is warmest (22°C). The winters are severe and stormy through much of the province. The areas receiving westerly winds off the Great Lakes are often called the "Snow Belt"; the areas S of Owen Sound, around Parry Sound and W of Sault Ste Marie, receive snowfall in excess of 250 cm. The areas around Toronto and Hamilton are in the partial rain shadow of the Niagara Escarpment and receive less than 150 cm of snow annually. Although differences in relief are not great, they have a significant impact on climate. The upland areas of Grey County, the Algonquin Park area and the Superior Highlands are notably cooler. Hudson Bay freezes over in winter and makes northern temperatures even colder. The Great Lakes, on the other hand, moderate winter temperatures.

The climate of Ontario greatly affects its agricultural patterns. Most specialized crops such as grain corn, soybeans and sugar beets are concentrated in the SW, with 2000 to 2600 growing degree days. Fruit growing is associated with (but not confined to) the Niagara Peninsula and tobacco growing is done in Norfolk County. The northern Clay Belts, with roughly 1480 to 1500 growing degree days, are suitable for a narrower range of crops, such as silage corn, hay, barley and potatoes. Frost is unusual in the S after the first week

of May but can persist into June in the N. Despite frequent bouts of rain and snow, the province's weather tends to sun. Sault Ste Marie receives roughly as much sun in July as sunny Victoria.

Ontario contains the largest amount of Class I agricultural land of any province and is abundantly endowed with rivers that can be harvested for hydroelectric power. The world's largest deposits of NICKEL and COPPER, along with lead, zinc, silver and platinum, were found in the Sudbury Basin in 1883. The largest GOLD deposits in N America were discovered near the towns of Porcupine and KIRKLAND LAKE from 1906 to 1912 (with another more recent find near Hemlo), and one of the largest uranium deposits in the world at ELLIOT LAKE in 1954. Major copper, zinc and silver deposits were discovered near Timmins in the 1960s. There is IRON ORE in the Algoma district N of Lk Superior. Southern Ontario has fewer minerals, although there is iron ore near Marmora, uranium near Bancroft and minor oil and gas deposits in southwestern Ontario. Limestone, sand and gravel are available in many parts of southern Ontario as a result of glacial deposits. Some 377 000 km² of Ontario's forest is considered to be productive, and the province ranks third in forestry-related industries.

Conservation The history of Ontario's forests has been one of depletion, sometimes from lumbering, sometimes from fires. The principle that forestland belongs to the Crown and that cutting rights are bestowed by licence rather than sale has long been recognized. Ontario has developed an extensive tree-planting program under its forest-resources service, issuing 150 million seedlings in 1985-86, and encourages the planting of "submarginal" land with trees in the hope that failed farms may at least become productive tree plantations. In addition, Ontario and the federal government cemented a 5-year $150-million agreement in 1984 to jointly fund forest renewal and fire-fighting improvement projects. Consciousness of the value of the wilderness resulted in the establishment of a provincial park system, beginning with ALGONQUIN PROVINCIAL PARK (7511 km²), established in 1893. There are now 220 provincial parks, ranging from RONDEAU PROVINCIAL PARK on Lake Erie in the S to Hudson Bay, whose Polar Bear Provincial Park, a true "wilderness" establishment, is practically inaccessible. Among national parks are GEORGIAN BAY ISLANDS NATIONAL PARK; POINT PELÉE NATIONAL PARK; PUKASKWA NATIONAL PARK; ST LAWRENCE ISLANDS NATIONAL PARK; and Bruce Peninsula National Park (announced in 1987).

The government has encouraged the establishment of local conservation authorities and has promoted various schemes for channelling and controlling waterflow. Of all provinces Ontario has the largest and most complex government structure for dealing with land use; the loss of agricultural land is a major concern, and has been the subject of political controversy and government study and planning. Areas of great natural beauty, such as the Niagara Escarpment, have attracted both environmental and political interest, and in 1984 the 2 constituencies achieved a conspicuous meeting of minds when a far-reaching plan to preserve the escarpment was announced to universal praise. Since then, 11 provincial parks have been established in the area.

Considerable energy has been expended on discovering a means of reversing the trend in the Great Lakes fishing industry. As early as the 1920s efforts were being made to restock the lakes with fish; later, attention was directed towards ridding the lakes of the plague of the LAMPREY eel, which preyed on other fish, further reducing stocks. Governments have attempted to improve water quality along the lakes, in many instances suc-

Toronto is Canada's largest city. In the foreground is Ontario Place, a multi-purpose recreational centre (*courtesy Colour Library Books*).

cessfully. This success combined with stringent regulations of both commercial and sport fishing has greatly enhanced fish stocks in the Great Lakes. Problems such as ACID RAIN (with its Canadian-American dimensions) make it difficult to predict ultimate success with any confidence; however, research conducted in Ontario has proven that certain species can survive the acid rain and in fact can perform well in lakes where water quality improves.

People

Indian settlement began in Ontario far back in prehistoric times. By the time Europeans came in the 17th century, the Indian population of the present province was divided into the nomadic Algonquian hunting tribes of the N and NW, and the Iroquoian tribes of the S, including the NEUTRAL, HURON and Erie. HURONIA was destroyed and the Huron dispersed in the IROQUOIS WARS in the 1640s; the wars also forced the abandonment (1649) of the Jesuit mission STE MARIE AMONG THE HURONS – the first European establishment in present-day Ontario.

Large-scale settlement of the province did not begin until the 1780s. There were scattered French settlements, especially around Detroit, but the first major immigration was that of the LOYALISTS, refugees from the American Revolution. The Loyalists gave the province its Anglo-Saxon character, which was reinforced by waves of immigration from the US and, during the 19th and early 20th centuries, from the British Isles. From the later 19th century there was localized immigration from Québec into eastern and northeastern Ontario, creating a French-language fringe along the province's frontiers. Although northern Ontario received some overseas immigration early in the century, it was not until after 1945 that immigration from continental Europe, the West Indies and East Asia had a discernible impact on the main populated areas of the province.

Ontario was first settled mostly by farmers, but in the mid-19th century the population was channelling into the cities until, by the time of WWI, Ontario had become predominantly urban. Despite the attraction of the US, the province has had Canada's largest population from 1867 to the present, and by a considerable margin: according to the 1986 census, Ontario had gained 476 000 people over the previous 5 years, 50% of the total national growth, bringing the population to 9 101 694.

Urban Centres Ontario is the most highly urbanized province in Canada, with 82.1% of the population found in urban centres at the time of the 1986 census. The outstanding feature of the urban pattern is the south-central conurbation around the western end of Lk Ontario – the so-called Golden Horseshoe – which includes the cities of ST CATHARINES (CMA pop 343 258), HAMILTON (CMA pop 557 029), TORONTO and OSHAWA. Nearly one-half of the population of Ontario lives in or around these 4 cities. With a population of 3 088 421 (1986), Toronto is Canada's largest city and plays a dominant role in Ontario's economy. Hamilton ranks ninth in Canada in population but third in manufacturing.

The urban centres of southwestern Ontario lie around KITCHENER-WATERLOO (pop 289 242) and LONDON (pop 275 449); both are transportation, service and manufacturing centres. WINDSOR (pop 219 733), the longtime home of the AUTOMOTIVE INDUSTRY, is geographically part of the Detroit urban complex. Apart from KINGSTON, the largest city on the eastern end of Lk Ontario, and OTTAWA, which has the largest part of its work force in the federal public service, eastern Ontario has no substantial urban concentration.

The cities of northern Ontario are strung out along the railway lines to which most of them owe their origin. NORTH BAY is still a transportation centre; SUDBURY is at the heart of Canada's largest mining district; SAULT STE MARIE is the country's second-ranked steel producer; and THUNDER BAY is a major transshipment port. With the exception of Thunder Bay on Lake Superior (108 802 inhabitants) and Windsor on the Detroit R, the other Great Lakes have no major urban centres along their Canadian shores.

The trend of habitation over time has been, and continues to be, to the suburbs: cities such as Toronto, Ottawa and Hamilton have tended to lose population as their surroundings sprout. In the Toronto area, for example, Scarborough and Mississauga show strong growth rates; however, older postwar suburbs, such as North York, virtually ceased to grow in the 1970s. Unlike their Ameri-

can counterparts, the central cores of Ontario's large cities have remained in large part residential; there are relatively few blighted areas.

Labour Force Ontario was once predominantly agricultural. Now, however, out of a labour force totalling 5.1 million in 1987 (up from 4.4 million in 1981), workers in agriculture and related occupations numbered only 155 000 on about 81 000 farms. But for those who believe that Ontario is still largely industrial, there is another surprise in store. Jobs in manufacturing (1.1 million) certainly overwhelm those in agriculture, but the growth industry of the 1960s, 1970s and 1980s is the service sector (1.64 million). The industrial work force suffered serious attrition in the recession of the early 1980s, as reflected in the drastic decline in numbers of the once-powerful steelworkers union. The most powerful, and best entrenched, unions in Ontario in the 1980s are those in the civil service or other public enterprises. Ontario now has more than 70 000 provincial civil servants, more than 500 for every member of the Legislative Assembly, as compared with 7 for every MPP in 1904. Traditionally male-dominated industries have also suffered, at least in the number of persons employed.

The labour force is divided between 2.875 million males and 2.27 million females. Those areas where men heavily outnumber women, such as agriculture and mining, are employing fewer and fewer people, while clerical and service occupations, where women tend to outnumber men, are on the rise.

The number of women is also growing in professional occupations and in management, as they now account for 47% of provincial employment in those areas. Despite having the lowest unemployment in the nation (5.8% in 1987), the problem of the 1980s, as it is throughout the country, is unemployment among the young. The level of unemployed youth, however, compares favourably with the national rate, as it has over the decades.

The "Golden Horseshoe" is the most highly urbanized area of Canada, stretching from Oshawa (top), past Toronto to Hamilton and St Catharines (*courtesy Canada Centre for Remote Sensing, Energy, Mines and Resources*).

Lieutenant-Governors of Ontario 1867-1987

	Term
Henry William Stisted	1867-68
William Pearce Howland	1868-73
John Willoughby Crawford	1873-75
Donald Alexander Macdonald	1875-80
John Beverley Robinson	1880-87
Alexander Campbell	1887-92
George Airey Kirkpatrick	1892-97
Oliver Mowat	1897-1903
William Mortimer Clark	1903-08
John Morison Gibson	1908-14
John Strathearn Hendrie	1914-19
Lionel Herbert Clarke	1919-21
Henry Cockshutt	1921-27
William Donald Ross	1927-32
Herbert Alexander Bruce	1932-37
Albert Matthews	1937-46
Ray Lawson	1946-52
Louis Orville Breithaupt	1952-57
John Keiller MacKay	1957-63
William Earl Rowe	1963-68
William Ross Macdonald	1968-74
Pauline Emily McGibbon	1974-80
John Black Aird	1980-85
Lincoln MacCauley Alexander	1985-

Language and Ethnicity Over three-quarters (76.3%) of Ontario's 9.1 million people counted English as their mother tongue in 1986. Of the remainder, 424 720 had French as their mother tongue, and 1 361 405 were grouped into "other" languages. But these figures do not tell the whole story. It is estimated that 373 460 people speak at least one of Canada's official languages plus one or more "nonofficial" languages. For instance, 254 525 people speak English and at least one more language besides French. Also, 104 550 respondents said they speak English and French. Most of the remainder claim to use English, French and one or more languages.

About 652 000 Ontarians claim French as their sole ancestry. Although the Ontario French community is still numerous and, on the whole, centered in the E and NE of the province, it appears to be slowly declining. In part this can be ascribed to ease of access for Francophones in the Ottawa area to suburbs on the Québec side of the border, so French speakers holding federal jobs can and do locate in a more concentrated French-language environment. In part the trend also reflects the decline of farming and other primary industries and the general drift to the cities.

If Ontario's citizenry of French ancestry has

Premiers of Ontario 1867-1987

	Party	Term
John Sandfield Macdonald	Liberal-Conservative	1867-71
Edward Blake	Liberal	1871-72
Oliver Mowat	Liberal	1872-96
Arthur Sturgis Hardy	Liberal	1896-99
George William Ross	Liberal	1899-1905
James Pliny Whitney	Conservative	1905-14
William Howard Hearst	Conservative	1914-19
Ernest Charles Drury	United Farmers of Ontario	1919-23
George Howard Ferguson	Conservative	1923-30
George Stewart Henry	Conservative	1930-34
Mitchell Frederick Hepburn	Liberal	1934-42
Gordon Daniel Conant	Liberal	1942-43
Harry Corwin Nixon	Liberal	1943
George Alexander Drew	Conservative	1943-48
Thomas Laird Kennedy	Conservative	1948-49
Leslie Miscampbell Frost	Conservative	1949-61
John Parmenter Robarts	Conservative	1961-71
William Grenville Davis	Conservative	1971-85
Frank Miller	Conservative	1985
David Robert Peterson	Liberal	1985-

been dwindling as a proportion of the population, so have the British (including, for this purpose, the IRISH). Once overwhelmingly so, Ontario is now just over 50% "British" (1981c). No other ethnic group, however, constitutes even 10% of the population, although the French come close. There are 487 310 Ontarians of ITALIAN descent, including 255 000 born in Italy, and 373 410 of GERMAN ancestry, 93 565 of whom were European born. The PORTUGUESE are even more recent arrivals. Only 34 000 Ontarians of Portuguese descent were actually born in Canada; the other 95 000 were born in Portugal. Immigration from the West Indies, the Indian subcontinent and East Asia has also greatly increased the population, but the largest single group of residents born outside Ontario still hails from the United Kingdom, to the tune of almost 500 000.

English is Ontario's sole official language, although in practice and to a lesser extent in principle its exclusive use has been modified. The Ontario government has gradually extended French rights in the legal and educational systems and in areas of provincial administration and has gone so far as to consider the inclusion of French as an official language. Other languages have been encouraged by a variety of programs of MULTICULTURALISM up to and including the level of university chairs in Ukrainian, Baltic and Hungarian studies, while school authorities have been experimenting with the teaching of "heritage" languages in Toronto schools. The teaching of French has increased at the elementary-school level, but relaxed educational policies have not encouraged Ontario students to persevere with a difficult and noncompulsory subject in the high schools. University study of French has also fallen off over time, a fate shared with other modern languages. The results of this confusing pattern of concern and neglect are not yet apparent.

Religion Ontario's population continues to be divided among what are traditionally its largest religious denominations. The biggest church is the Catholic Church, strong among the French, Irish and Italian communities, with nearly 3 million members (1981c). Next are the UNITED CHURCH, with 1.7 million and ANGLICANS with 1.2 million, while those Presbyterians who did not join the United Church number 517 000. The remaining larger sects include the BAPTISTS (288 465), LUTHERANS (254 180) and Greek ORTHODOX (140 610). JEWS number 148 255, while ISLAM claims 52 110 adherents and Hindus count 41 660 among their numbers. In most cases, women slightly outnumber men in organized religion. The number of people professing no religious belief (359 085 men and 259 515 women), and relatively low attendance show the dramatic change in religious affiliation since the early 20th century.

Economy

Ontario's economy began with hunting and trapping. It expanded with the arrival of the settlers and until the latter part of the 19th century remained predominantly rural and agriculturally based. By the early 20th century rail lines built across Ontario's northland opened up rich mineral resources in places such as COBALT and TIMMINS. The discovery and growth of hydroelectric power, combined with the export boom of the turn of the 20th century, stimulated great industrial expansion and the growth of cities, large and small. Ontario has been predominantly urban since 1911, and agriculture has shifted from mixed diversified grain and livestock to more specialized regional patterns serving broad urban markets – dairy products, corn to fatten livestock, vegetables, fruit and tobacco.

Ontario is a major exporter of the goods it pro-

Gross Domestic Product - Ontario 1986 at Factor Cost ($Millions)

Agriculture	3580.1
Forestry	576.6
Fishing	24.1
Mining	2444.8
Manufacturing	45 226.0
Construction	11 711.0
Utilities	4 643.1
Goods Producing Industries	68 205.7
Transportation	10 261.6
Trade (Wholesale & Retail)	20 872.5
Finance	27 692.4
Service	40 027.9
Public Administration and Defence	10 541.0
Service Producing Industries	109 395.4
Total	177 601.1

duces – such as automobiles – but the principal market for Ontario products is and always has been heavily populated central Canada. Sales to the West and the Maritimes were for the most part marginal. As with other parts of the country, the greatest expansion of recent years has been in service industries, while older, heavier industries have declined. After lagging behind the national rate of growth in overall real domestic product for most of the 1970s, Ontario has come out ahead in the mid-1980s. By 1987 the province had the lowest unemployment, the lowest per capita debt and the highest growth rate.

Agriculture Ontario has the largest amount of Canada's "best" agricultural land, just over 50% of the Canadian total of Class 1 land. Ontario ranked first in Canada in cash receipts for farm products in 1986. Most farming is done in the S, although clusters of farms on the Shield serve local dairy markets. Forage crops are the largest, but CORN, mixed grains, winter wheat and BARLEY are also grown. Ontario is therefore well able to sustain commercial hog, dairy and beef livestock farms. It ranks second to Québec in dairy farms. The latter are most numerous in the London-Woodstock region, in the Bruce Peninsula and in eastern Ontario. Only Québec ranks ahead of Ontario in milk and dairy products; total Ontario receipts in this category were $958.7 million in 1986. Despite heavy regulation at both the federal and provincial level, 4 big companies process 87% of Ontario's milk. One of the 4 is the John Labatt brewery (using the Silverwood and Sealtest brand names), which accounts for one-seventh of Canada's milk.

Ontario is first in Canada by a very wide margin in prosperous and lucrative farms – those producing $100 000 or more of products a year. There are a large number of farms at the lowest end of the scale as well, and while both the federal and provincial governments have encouraged the de-

Holland Marsh, just N of Toronto (*photo by J.A. Kraulis*).

The Inco smelter in Copper Cliff, northern Ontario. Despite recent downturns, mining is still important to the provincial economy (*photo by Karl Sommerer*).

population of submarginal farmland, this process is not complete. The lowest incomes in the province, according to the 1986 census, are to be found in counties with large amounts of marginal or submarginal land still under cultivation – along Georgian Bay, Lk Huron or in parts of eastern Ontario.

As in other jurisdictions, Ontario farmers are accustomed to selling their products through marketing boards, established as far back as the 1930s. These boards do not command universal support, even among farmers, but they are intended to introduce a degree of regularity and predictability into the marketing of agricultural products. Economic conditions during the late 1970s and 1980s stimulated protests from "survival" groups that the economic system was operating to the disadvantage of small farmers burdened by debt and high interest rates.

Industry Ontario is and always has been the leading manufacturing province in Canada. This situation was well established at the time of Confederation, and the trend since has been to place industry in a province favoured by ample transportation, abundant natural resources and accessibility to export markets in the US. Proximity to the American automotive industry, for example, encouraged the location of manufacturing plants in Ontario. The establishment of Ford, General Motors and Chrysler in Ontario in turn spun off a vast series of related industries dotted all across southern Ontario. Transportation equipment of all kinds, including aircraft and railcars, accounts for $1 out of every $5 of value-added production in industrial Ontario.

The latest available estimate (1986) establishes that Ontario produces over half the gross domestic product of manufacturing industries in Canada, or $45.2 billion. Metropolitan Toronto had half (7608) of the provincial manufacturing establishments in 1984, shipping, in that year, $42-billion worth of manufactured products. Hamilton ($8.7 billion), Windsor ($8.4 billion), St Catharines-Niagara ($4.8 billion) and London ($2.4 billion) each shipped more than $2-billion worth that same year. During the late 1970s, Ottawa, frequently seen as a staid national capital completely dependent on the largesse of the federal government, confounded its critics by emerging as Canada's equivalent of California's

Silicon Valley, a centre for HIGH TECHNOLOGY industries, producing computers and the like. Ontario accounts for almost 60% of Canada's high-tech output, but remains (like the rest of Canada) a net importer of technology.

The appearance of this new and promising venture consoled commentators in the early 1980s, when a slump in the automobile industry seemed to indicate that the industrial system was creaking at its joints, becoming obsolete in precisely those areas where Ontario's greatest strength and heaviest investment was concentrated. The concurrent weakness of an earlier generation of high-tech industries, such as the DE HAVILLAND LTD aircraft company just outside Toronto, gave pause as well. As a result, certain prominent Ontario companies became targets of official concern and well-publicized governmental rescue efforts, notably Chrysler, MASSEY-FERGUSON (now Varity Corp) and de Havilland (now owned by Boeing).

Mining The development of Ontario's mining industry is closely associated with the rise of Toronto as Ontario's and Canada's financial centre. The exploitation of minerals in northern Ontario from around 1900 made Toronto first a competitor and then a winner in its long-standing competition with Montréal. Nickel made the prosperity of the Sudbury Basin; silver, lead and zinc caused a rush to Cobalt in the early 1900s; gold helped keep the provincial (and to some extent the national) economy afloat during the 1930s. In the 1950s another great impetus was given the Ontario economy by the discovery of fabulously rich uranium deposits at Elliot Lake.

Mining is still extremely important in the provincial economy, although recent years have been less prosperous ones for the industry as downturns occurred in the international market for one major metal after another. Even so, in 1987 the value of nickel production in Ontario was $902 million; uranium, $509 million; copper, $675 million; gold, $1.03 billion; and zinc, $412 million. Shipments of iron ore in 1986 were worth more than $176 million.

Forestry In 1981 Ontario had 807 000 km² of forestland, less than half of which was available for forest farming. Almost all (87%) of it was owned by the province, meaning that forestry was carried on under licence by companies obtaining the necessary permission from the government. In 1986 production from Ontario crown lands was over 20 000 000 m³, valued at almost $600 million. Most of Ontario's pulp and paper products – in fact over 80% – are directed southward to the US for export.

Fisheries Ontario's once-prosperous fishing industry has gone into a considerable decline. Whitefish, pickerel and trout were once the principal fish produced in Ontario's Great Lakes fishery, but overfishing and deterioration in water quality, especially in Lk Erie, have taken their toll. During the 1920s, approximately 10 000 people gained their employment from Ontario's inland fishery. This has declined and the industry now makes only a modest contribution to the Ontario economy, although still an important one in northern communities. Ontario's modest commercial fishery has been hurt by POLLUTION, which also affects the tourist industry of sportfishing, especially in parts of northern Ontario. Nevertheless, sportfishing in 1985-86 was estimated to generate $700 million in total expenditures, thanks mainly to improved fish-stocking techniques.

Finance Toronto's Bay Street area is the centre of the Canadian financial system. All the principal Canadian chartered banks have their head offices in Toronto, in fact if not in name, as do many of Canada's major corporations and brokerage firms. The Toronto Stock Exchange, housed in opulent quarters, is the country's largest. First Canadian Place, chock-full of lawyers, accountants and executives, is Canada's tallest office building at 290 m. The CN TOWER, another monument to commerce, is the world's tallest, free-standing structure at 533 m. BANKING is a national business in Canada, and there is no study that shows whether Ontario as a whole secures any quantifiable benefit from the location of banks in its provincial capital beyond the *joie de vivre* that bankers and their staffs impart to their community. There is, however, a discernible architectural impact as the banks compete in raising towers to the sky – ziggurats rather than the basilicas that characterized an earlier period in Canadian banking symbolism (*see* BANK ARCHITECTURE).

Canadian banks maintained more than 2700 branches in Ontario in 1986. If numbers of branches are any indication, Ontarians tended to favour the CANADIAN IMPERIAL BANK OF COMMERCE, a bank with a long history in the province. A largish number of depositors, second only to Québec, preferred to do business with CREDIT UNIONS rather than chartered banks. Toronto is the principal clearing centre for cheques cashed in Canada, and accounts for the vast majority cashed in the province, not to mention more than half those cleared in the whole country. Toronto is, as well, the headquarters for some of Canada's largest insurance companies, with all the financial resources they bring in their train. Other cities also sport insurance headquarters: Kitchener-Waterloo has several, and London even more.

Transportation Ontario had 13 294 km of mainline railway track in 1985, and more than

Engine/auto body assembly, General Motors of Canada. Automobile manufacturing is the single most important industry in Ontario (*photo by Mike Dobel/Masterfile*).

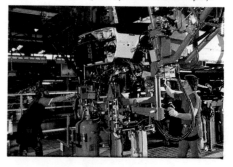

The Adam Beck No 2 powerhouse opened in 1954 at Niagara Falls, Ont (*photo by John Reeves/Masterfile*).

21 000 km of paved roads operated under the 2 senior levels of government, federal (the TRANS-CANADA HWY) and provincial. Roads reach most of the province S of the watershed between Hudson Bay and the Great Lakes; N of that line roads are few; reliable transportation is either by air or by water. Sales of motor gasoline in 1986 totalled 9.6 million m^3, propelling a very considerable motor transport industry as well as an enormous fleet of private motor vehicles.

Much debate has occurred in recent years concerning the best or most economical means of transportation. The Ontario government has supplied several answers. It has built and is still expanding a superhighway system across the southern tier of the province, stretching from Montréal to Windsor (although it is still impossible to travel all the way from Toronto to Ottawa by 4-lane highway except via Montréal). The province has also created a rail-and-road commuter service, GO (Government of Ontario) Transit to serve the Hamilton-to-Oshawa corridor along Lk Ontario, and has intervened in municipal transport through its Urban Transit Development Corp.

Ontario has a large navigable water system, the ST LAWRENCE SEAWAY, along its southern frontier. The WELLAND CANAL, an important part of the seaway channel, links Lakes Ontario and Erie. The advent of the seaway, and subsequently the practice of "containerization" of cargo unloaded at East Coast ports, have had a considerable negative impact on the structure of Ontario's water transport. The most notable casualty has been the port of Toronto, where the number of tonnes shipped and the number of employed have dropped drastically – Montréal, Saint John and Halifax being the beneficiaries.

Energy Ontario is and always has been an importer of ENERGY. The primeval forest provided sufficient fuel in pioneer times, but with urban and industrial growth Ontario's energy needs were met by COAL from the nearby pits of Ohio, Pennsylvania and West Virginia. This coal was of a higher quality than that from Nova Scotia, and cheaper to ship. Ontario does have coal deposits of its own, near James Bay, but they have so far been judged uneconomical. Oil and gas were also possibilities, and here Ontario had a slight initial advantage. The oil fields around Petrolia were first exploited in the late 1850s. Natural gas came somewhat later, and for many years Ontario

ranked first as a Canadian producer of these commodities. Production, however, is now insignificant in the overall energy picture.

Oil and gas therefore also have to be imported. For many years this meant imports from the US or through East Coast ports. This could sometimes prove precarious, when American shortages of oil and gas (and coal too) placed Ontario heating at risk. During the 1950s the federal and provincial governments made it a priority to connect Ontario with western Canadian oil and gas fields. Oil came first, followed by gas through the TRANS-CANADA PIPELINE, completed in 1958.

Technological advances during the 1880s and 1890s brought Ontario its first large and significant energy source from within the province itself: HYDROELECTRICITY. Ontario is abundantly endowed with streams, rapids and falls. First used for SAWMILLS, these falls could be put to work to generate electricity. NIAGARA FALLS, Ontario, has one of the great waterfalls of the world, as well as one of its major tourist attractions. When Niagara power was developed southern Ontario acquired a significant advantage over rival industrial areas. In 1906 most electricity in Ontario was nationalized under the aegis of the Hydro-Electric Power Commission of Ontario, now known as ONTARIO HYDRO, and its aggressive and dynamic founder, Sir Adam BECK. (There is still one private power source, Great Lakes Power.) Over the years Ontario Hydro expanded into the Ottawa R system and then the St Lawrence. Hydro also began to import power from Québec, emphasizing the limited untapped sources of power for the province. Hydro managers, however, had a strong preference for self-sufficiency.

As this realization was dawning, in the early 1950s, Ontario faced the possibility of building thermal (coal- or oil-fired) power plants (using imported fuel), or of taking a new road. It did both. Thermal plants were built in the 1950s and 1960s, raising the proportion of power generated thermally from practically none in 1960 to over one-third in 1970. At the same time, in conjunction with Atomic Energy of Canada Limited, the federal government's reactor arm, Ontario Hydro began to build nuclear power stations. The first full-scale nuclear power station, at Douglas Point, was opened in 1966, and others have followed at Pickering and Bruce. In 1986 coal (24%), water-power (30%) and nuclear power (46%) accounted for nearly all of Ontario's generated electricity, with nuclear power being the largest single producer since 1981. Sales of electricity to the US –

some $351 million in 1985 – are expected to continue at around 10% of production. More nuclear plants as well as a new coal-generating station are planned for the early 1990s, despite the controversies that have surrounded NUCLEAR ENERGY.

Government and Politics

Ontario's governmental structure is similar to that of other Canadian provinces. A LIEUTENANT-GOVERNOR, appointed by the federal government, nominally heads the administration, assisted by an executive council or Cabinet, led by a PREMIER. The Cabinet governs as long as it maintains the confidence of the Legislative Assembly or provincial parliament, a unicameral body of 130 members, elected for a maximum term of 5 years. The term can, in extraordinary circumstances, however, be extended by legislative action. All Canadian citizens over the age of 18 resident in Ontario can vote in elections. The judiciary, as in other Canadian provinces, is appointed by the province only at the lowest level – "provincial judges," formerly known as magistrates. All other levels of the judiciary are appointed by the federal government. These judges' salaries are paid by Ottawa; the other costs of the courts are borne by the province.

Local Government For many years the basic structure of LOCAL GOVERNMENT in Ontario was that provided by Robert BALDWIN's Municipal Corporations Act of 1849, which divided the southern part of the province into COUNTIES, cities, towns and villages. The growth of urban population in the 20th century began to strain the traditional jurisdictions. Rather than let the province's cities expand indefinitely into the surrounding suburbs and countryside, the provincial government looked to the creation of supermunicipalities that could operate on a regional basis and encompass a variety of jurisdictions. The first of these to be created (1 Jan 1954) was the Municipality of Metropolitan Toronto, a federation of Toronto and its suburbs carved out of the southern half of York County. In the 1960s and 1970s various "regional municipalities" on the model of Toronto were created, sometimes to the intense resentment of the local citizenry.

There are now 11 regional municipalities and 1 district municipality (Muskoka), governed by assemblies of locally elected politicians, with jurisdiction over such items as police, water supply and arterial roads. Local cities that come under them have not, however, been abolished, and they still enjoy limited powers. There are 49 cities in the province, 146 towns, 1 borough, 119 villages and 477 townships, all of which enjoy powers of local taxation based on property. There are also 8 "improvement districts" and 70 POLICE VILLAGES, entities that have no independent taxation powers. All Ontario municipalities are subject to the review of their actions by the Ontario Municipal Board, which must approve any bylaws creating debt, and which acts as the court of last resort for appeals against municipal actions.

Federal Representation Ontario has 95 members in the House of Commons (99 as of the next federal election) and 24 senators. Metropolitan Toronto and its environs have more MPs than any province outside Ontario and Québec. When judging its political "clout" it is useful to see Ontario as an assemblage of subregions that seldom vote together federally or provincially. It is difficult for any single federal politician to say that he or she "represents" Ontario in Ottawa, as Alexander Mackenzie was able to claim over 100 years ago. Mackenzie King, a Torontonian by upbringing, found it possible to constitute most of his governments from 1921 to 1930 and 1935 to 1948 with little or no representation from that city. Nevertheless, since then federal prime ministers have given adequate representation to Toronto

Toronto Parliament Buildings (*photo by J.A. Kraulis*).

and the regions of Ontario in forming their Cabinets. Third parties have enjoyed a smattering of support in various federal elections, but they have usually been a distant third in the number of MPs sent to Ottawa.

Public Finance Much of Ontario's history has been concerned with wringing what the province considered to be adequate tax resources from the federal government in Ottawa. This traditional rivalry abated considerably after 1948, when premier George DREW left for federal politics in Ottawa. Since then, while there have been tensions, co-operation and soft words have been more usual vehicles of discussion than the bellowing practised by many previous administrations.

Ontario derives large revenues from such items as the taxation of liquor and cigarettes (much higher today than in earlier times), as well as the more commonly thought of forms of revenue, such as personal and corporate income tax. Ontario's income and corporate income taxes are collected by the federal government as part of its national tax system, and the proceeds remitted to the province. In the fiscal year 1985-86 provincial gross general revenues totalled $26.06 billion, and provincial expenditures were $29.30 billion. In 1987, Ottawa and the provinces agreed on a common sales tax arrangement, extending the principle of tax-sharing.

Health In 1986 Ontario had 220 "general" and 40 "special" hospitals, and about 55 000 hospital beds, an average of 6 beds per 1000 population. In 1984 Ontario employed over 18 000 doctors, more than 66 000 nurses and an additional 100 000 people in various support functions. Provincial governmental health expenditures were $9.264 billion in 1985-86 (up from $5.9 billion in 1981). Ontario's health services, and the means by which they are supported, are similar to those in other provinces. Federal Acts in 1958 and 1966 first established hospital insurance, paid for by the general public from compulsory premiums, and then comprehensive medical care services ("medicare"). These acts are federal-provincial in nature, as is the co-operation necessary to make them work. This co-operation occasions some political pain, as in 1986 when, in the aftermath of the Canada Health Act, Ontario banned extra billing by doctors. The 2 levels of government frequently debate the amount that each should put into the system, as well as the ways in which it should be spent.

Ontario's public-health insurance system is now consolidated in the Ontario Health Insurance Plan, into which solvent citizens pay a premium and which supports, through subsidy, those unable to pay full or partial premiums.

Politics There are 3 political parties in Ontario with representation in the provincial legislature. The first two, the Progressive CONSERVATIVE PARTY ("Tories") and the LIBERAL PARTY ("Grits"), go back to before Confederation. The third party, the NEW DEMOCRATIC PARTY (NDP), grew out of the CO-OPERATIVE COMMONWEALTH FEDERATION. The Liberals were in power most of the time to 1905, and the Conservatives most of the time since.

The PC Party governed Ontario from 1943 to 1985. Part of the explanation for its success lay in the noisy and somewhat gamey government which preceded it, that of the Liberal Mitchell HEPBURN (1934-42), and in the fragmentation of the opposition vote between the Liberals and CCF-NDP. But the Conservative Party consistently found ways to appeal to widely differing groups across the province and to rely on their solid and continuing support, as with the Conservative voting bastion in eastern Ontario. It had a formidable political organization: the "Big Blue Machine," strengthened under the successive premierships of Leslie FROST (1949-61), John ROBARTS (1961-71) and William DAVIS (1971-85). Davis cautiously and gradually conceded the substance of BILINGUALISM – for example, education in the French language, or the right to a French trial anywhere in the province – without giving in on the principle. The Conservatives consistently refused to give constitutional recognition and protection to the French language or to make it an official language of the province. This permitted amelioration in practice for Francophones without rousing anti-French voters in various parts of the province – while tarring the pro-bilingual Liberals with the French-language brush. Following Davis's resignation in 1985, the new Conservative leadership under Frank MILLER opted for a platform of more small-c conservative policies, and it was the Liberal Party, under its new leader David PETERSON, that emerged as the successor to the Tory tradition of middle-of-the-road politics, winning a minority government in 1985 and ending 4 decades of Tory rule. A subsequent Conservative attempt to exploit the bilingual issue in the 1987 provincial election flopped, as Peterson's middle-of-the-road appeal enabled him to win a large majority in Sept. The essentially leaderless Conservatives were third in both popular votes

and seats, while the Liberals harvested the largest caucus in Ontario's political history.

Education

Ontario has the traditional 3-tiered educational system common to most Canadian provinces: primary, secondary and post-secondary. The system comes under strict provincial control, reflecting whatever the province and its educational advisers for the time being think is most appropriate for study by Ontario learners.

The basic system is further divided between 2 kinds of public school: public, in the strict sense, or nonsectarian; and "separate" or Roman Catholic. Each of these systems enjoys powers of taxation, and each is run by boards elected by members of the public who choose to support them through their taxes. This is the result of a compromise at the time of Confederation, when rights for Catholics in Ontario were traded off against those for Protestants in Québec. Unluckily for the Catholics, the Confederation bargain was held not to include complete financial support of separate schools. This was the cause of occasional political protest and action, most notably during the provincial election of 1934. In the 1960s the government extended its full support of elementary separate schools to grades 9 and 10, but for years it steadfastly declined to go further, even in the face of pressure from Catholic leaders. In 1984 Premier Davis startled Catholics and non-Catholics alike with a sudden announcement that his government would cover all the costs of separate school education in grades 11, 12 and 13 by 1988.

Ontario's primary system runs through grade 8; high schools then complete the education through to graduation, what was formerly called junior (grade 12) or senior (grade 13) matriculation. Grade 13, however, is gradually being phased out. The curriculum the students study has varied considerably through the years, according to the fashions current in education. The Ontario curriculum reflected the "progressive" ideas current in the 1930s and early 1940s; it showed a greater concern with structure during the 1950s and early 1960s; and it frequently dissolved into a free-form exercise appropriate to the shapeless decade of 1965 to 1975. Since then it has been lurching back to a greater concern with the basic skills, which seemed to be lacking in recent graduates from the school system.

About 5% of Ontario's students are Francophones. Although French-language schools existed in eastern and northern Ontario long before 1968, boards since then have been able to set up French schools "when numbers warrant" (*see* SEPARATE SCHOOL). The interpretation of this phrase has caused much dispute in certain parts of the province, Penetanguishene being a notable example. In 1984 the Ontario Court of Appeal ruled that every francophone (and anglophone) student in the province has a right to education in his or her mother tongue. Linguistic minorities, the court also made clear, must be guaranteed representation on school boards and a say in minority-language instruction. The government immediately moved to give effect to the court's ruling, which was based upon the Charter of Rights and Freedoms.

Beyond high school there is the post-secondary structure: 21 degree-graduating UNIVERSITIES, scattered from Ottawa to Windsor to the Lakehead; 22 colleges of applied arts and technology, or COMMUNITY COLLEGES, and 4 colleges of agricultural technology, a school of horticulture, a chiropractic college and an institute of medical technology. The post-secondary system expanded greatly during the 1960s, at a time when politicians held education in high regard as a motivator of economic growth. Later, when opinion changed to hold that education and growth were not strictly related, politicians discovered that education cost a great deal and had no obvious constituency. Cutbacks and freezes on spending followed. Education nevertheless remained a large item in the provincial budget. In 1986-87, $6.7 billion (21%) of gross provincial general expenditure was spent to keep 1.85 million primary and secondary students and 277 000 post-secondary students in school.

Cultural Life

Little now survives of indigenous art forms, although early inhabitants of Ontario left behind considerable cultural remnants, from the SERPENT MOUNDS near Peterborough to subsequent, more sophisticated examples of carving and pottery. Later settlers brought their own cultural heritage with them, derived from European models. The forms of the mid-19th century, embodied in contemporary handicrafts, still enjoy a considerable popularity and sale with tourists in quest of their heritage. Ontario artists generally follow international styles, whether literary, artistic or architectural, and their work should be, and sometimes is, judged by the best international standards. Artistic and cultural endeavour is encouraged through a variety of government subsidy programs, some federal and some provincial, such as the Ontario Arts Council (fd 1963), an independent government agency which gives grants to individuals and organizations.

Ever practical, the government points out that the arts create jobs. Every grant dollar to orchestras, the taxpayer is reminded in Arts Council literature, directly produces almost $7.00 in wages, fees and operating expenditures. There are symphony orchestras in Toronto (TORONTO SYMPHONY), Ottawa, Hamilton and Kitchener-Waterloo, as well as a major Shakespearean festival (STRATFORD FESTIVAL, fd 1953) held each year in Stratford, and the Art Gallery of Ontario and the ROYAL ONTARIO MUSEUM in Toronto.

Communications Except for Toronto, Ontario's cities support only one English-language daily paper each, and these NEWSPAPERS are almost invariably owned by newspaper chains. Toronto's newspaper life is the most lively, with 3 widely differing newspapers. Toronto is also the home for the large majority of Canada's large magazines, including *Maclean's, Canadian Business* and *Saturday Night*, and the headquarters of the larger national publishing firms, such as MC-CLELLAND & STEWART and UNIVERSITY OF TORONTO Press, are located there. The main English-language facilities of the CANADIAN BROADCASTING CORPORATION and the private CTV network are also in Toronto; besides the English-language media there are 3 French-language TV stations in Ontario, plus dozens of repeater stations and 16 radio stations, not to mention stations broadcasting in a variety of other languages. TVOntario, a public station, broadcasts in both languages. Most of Ontario is, however, not confined to domestic Canadian television. The 3 major American networks, and the Public Broadcasting System, are within viewing range, either by direct transmission or through cable TV networks. Their availability gives southern Ontario one of the largest choices of TV programming anywhere in the world.

Historic Sites Ontario has long enjoyed a vigorous HISTORIC SITE program and rare is the township lacking a plaque or cairn commemorating a notable person or event. Provincial legislation makes possible the designation of heritage building, and while not an absolute protection this has made possible the preservation of buildings of greater or lesser merit throughout the province.

The stark beauty of the landscape of northern Ontario has inspired artists and photographers, notably members of the Group of Seven such as Lawren Harris, whose *North Shore, Lake Superior* is shown (*courtesy Lawren P. Harris/National Gallery of Canada*).

Among the first historic sites to attract interest were the mid-17th-century JESUIT missions to the Hurons. Having supported research in the area since 1890, the Ontario government undertook the reconstruction of STE MARIE AMONG THE HURONS near Midland in 1964, and opened it to the public 3 years later. Picturesque forts, the legacy of a hundred years of tension along the Canadian-American border from the beginning of the American Revolution, dot the southern reaches of the province. At Kingston, FORT HENRY, whose stone walls were originally completed in the 1830s, is perhaps the best known, but Fort George and FORT ERIE on the NIAGARA HISTORIC FRONTIER, Fort Wellington (Prescott), Fort York (Toronto) and Fort Malden (AMHERSTBURG) have also been restored to their appearance at the time of the international crises and conflicts during the first part of the 19th century. The life of the province's pioneers is depicted in reconstructed townsites, including UPPER CANADA VILLAGE near Morrisburg and BLACK CREEK PIONEER VILLAGE north of Toronto; in 1973 the Ontario government began to rebuild FORT WILLIAM (at Thunder Bay), a fur-trading post established by the NORTH WEST CO in 1803. Boating enthusiasts enjoy two 19th-century canals – the RIDEAU CANAL, built from 1826 to 1832 by the Royal Engineers for the movement of troops and military supplies, and the Trent, which dates back to 1833.

History

The first immigrants to Ontario seem to have arrived during the last ice age, approximately 10 000 years ago. As the ice retreated, Ontario's paleo-Indian inhabitants moved into the northern region of the province. For many years Ontario's peoples probably lived by fishing and hunting; deer, elk, bear and beaver were to be found in the S and caribou in the N. By 1000 BC pottery had been introduced, and archaeological sites disclose a far-flung trading system, with importations from as far as the Gulf of Mexico. By 100 AD the inhabitants of the province can be identified with the Algonquian tribes (OJIBWA, CREE and ALGONQUIN found by the explorers), and with the Iroquoian tribes of the S (Iroquois, Huron, Petun, Neutral, Erie and Susquehannock).

Exploration The first Europeans known to have approached the present frontiers of Ontario were the luckless Henry HUDSON, cast adrift off the N coast, Étienne BRÛLÉ and Samuel de CHAMPLAIN, who travelled along the Ottawa R in 1613, reaching the centre of the province in 1615. Brûlé was likely the first to see Lakes Huron and Ontario. Champlain allied the French with the Huron. After the dispersal of the Huron in the late 1640s, the OTTAWA took the role of middlemen in the fur trade. The Iroquois Confederacy, located across Lakes Ontario and Erie in what is now New York state, dominated the region without significantly settling it. Despite the hostility of the Iroquois, the French continued their penetration of the Great Lakes region, utilizing both the Ottawa-French R-Lk Huron route to the W and the St Lawrence-Great Lakes path. The adventurer LA SALLE built and sailed the GRIFFON on the lakes, and the Ontario region became a vital link between the French settlements in Québec and their fur-trading posts in the Mississippi. During the 18th century the main French posts in the Great Lakes region were FORT FRONTENAC [Kingston], FORT NIAGARA, Fort Detroit and FORT MICHILIMACKINAC. France's rivals, the British, did not successfully penetrate the region until 1758-59, when they burned Fort Frontenac and captured Fort Niagara. British occupation was not secure until the Indian allies of the French were defeated after an uprising in 1763-64. The Great Lakes region also served as a base of operations for British (regular and Loyalist) forces during the American Revolution. A series of bloody campaigns and raids did not shake the British hold over their Great Lakes forts but did result in the arrival of Loyalist and Iroquois refugees displaced from the American frontier. The Treaty of PARIS (1783) divided the Great Lakes down the middle, and created the southern boundary of what is now Ontario.

Settlement The modern settlement of Ontario began with the arrival of some 6000 to 10 000 Loyalists during and after the American Revolution. After them came other Americans, attracted by cheap land; crown land was available for six-pence an acre plus survey costs and an oath of allegiance. Under the CONSTITUTIONAL ACT, 1791, the old PROVINCE OF QUEBEC was divided and UPPER CANADA created. A regular colonial government was established, with a lieutenant-governor, an elected legislative assembly, and appointed legislative and executive councils. The first lieutenant-governor was John Graves SIMCOE, an English veteran of the revolutionary war, who aimed to turn Upper Canada into a bastion of the British Crown in the heart of the continent. Simcoe only half succeeded; Upper Canada continued to mark the northern fringe of the American frontier, but by 1812 approximately 80% of the estimated 100 000 settlers in southern Ontario were of American origin. When the WAR OF 1812 broke out with the US, the attitude of parts of the province's population proved highly ambivalent, and a few Upper Canadians actually sided with and fought alongside the invaders. The British army, with assistance from Indians and local militia, succeeded in defending most of the province, repelling American invasions along the Niagara frontier in 1812 (QUEENSTON HEIGHTS) and 1813 (BEAVER DAMS and STONEY CREEK). But also in 1813, Americans thrust into SW Ontario and raided the provincial capital, York [Toronto], where the government buildings were burned. After several more bloody battles in 1814, the war drew to an end. When news of peace arrived, each side handed back what it had conquered and the boundary remained unchanged.

In the years between 1825 and 1842 the population of Upper Canada tripled to 450 000 and doubled again by 1851. Most of the immigrants came from the British Isles, roughly in the percentages of 20% English, 20% Scottish and 60% Irish. Settlement spread generally from S to N, moving away from the lakes as land along them was occupied. Accessibility to land away from the lakes depended on roads – usually of abominable quality – many of which were built by the settlers themselves. Rampant land speculation added greatly to the irregularity of early settlement patterns. Southern Ontario's fertile land was substantially occupied by the mid-1850s, by which time the form of government had changed again. In the aftermath of the REBELLIONS OF 1837, led in Upper Canada by Toronto "firebrand" William Lyon MACKENZIE, the British government brought Upper and Lower Canada together in the united PROVINCE OF CANADA. A further decade of fractious politics resulted in a measure of RESPONSIBLE GOVERNMENT in 1848-49, by which time immigration, combined with a prolific birthrate, had raised Upper Canada's population (952 004 in 1851) to about 60 000 more than its partner, LOWER CANADA. The agitation, led by George BROWN, for REP BY POP ("representation by population"), so that Upper Canada would receive additional representation in the legislature, led to the increasing paralysis of the province's political system. The crisis was finally resolved in 1864 by the formation of a joint-party regime (see GREAT COALITION) to seek a union of the British North American colonies. This CONFEDERATION was gained in 1867, and Ontario became a province of the new Dominion of Canada.

Development Ontario's economy in the 1850s was primarily agricultural, with the emphasis on wheat. Over time the balance shifted to dairy, fruit and vegetable farming, and at the same time there was a drift away from farming areas; emigration took place to the US, to the Canadian West or to the cities. Urban and industrial growth rose apace from the 1850s through the 1860s, with the development of textiles and metalworking, farm implements and machinery. Moreover, Toronto grew especially, both as a railway and

manufacturing centre and as provincial capital.

Ontario's governments thereafter took up developing the province's natural resources – lumber, mines and later hydroelectricity. Much political energy was then consumed by a lengthy series of quarrels with the federal government over patronage, waterpower and the northern BOUNDARIES of the province – a problem settled in 1889, at the expense of Manitoba, by confirming Ontario's western boundary at the LAKE OF THE WOODS. The final boundary was drawn in 1912. Under Sir Oliver MOWAT's Liberal government (1872-96), Ontario led the way in advocating provincial rights against the overriding powers of the federal government under Sir John A. MACDONALD. It also extended government services for a province now thriving on quite intensive agriculture, widening resource activities and industrial advance in Canada's richest internal market. But the Liberal regime gradually declined from the later 1890s and was at last terminated in a flurry of scandals in 1905.

Its Conservative successor, under Sir James WHITNEY (1905-14), made its mark by establishing the Hydro-Electric Power Commission of Ontario. Whitney's successor, Sir William HEARST, was turned out by a political revolution among the province's farmers, who took office with labour support in 1919 as the UNITED FARMERS OF ONTARIO. Although the UFO government curbed some of the peculiarities of its Conservative predecessor, it was politically accident prone and quickly fell victim to a revitalized Conservative Party under Howard FERGUSON (1923-30). Ferguson was a determined man, as well as an able and wily politician. He tapped Ontarians' desire to enhance the provincial revenues through the provincially owned Liquor Control Board of Ontario, which was designed to promote TEMPERANCE as well as revenue. He also defused a long-standing controversy with the province's French-language population by reintroducing official French classes in schools; and as his predecessors had done, he continued a policy of developing provincial resources, including the colonization of the Ontario northland, an enterprise with many pitfalls. Ferguson's successor, George HENRY, had to cope with the ravages of the Great Depression, not to mention the attacks of a reinvigorated provincial Liberal Party under Mitchell Hepburn. Hepburn swept Henry out of office with promises of reform and economy in 1934. Neither object was really achieved, although Hepburn did succeed in achieving the pasteurization of Ontario's milk against the cries of opposition from dairy farmers.

Hepburn battled the appearance of industrial unionism from the US and in 1937 fought and won a provincial election on the issue. His regime is principally remembered for his violent attacks on his fellow Liberal, PM Mackenzie King, and for his obstructionist attitude towards attempts to solve Canada's constitutional perplexities. Hepburn resigned in 1942, and his party was turned out of office in an election in 1943 that made the Conservatives under George Drew the government and the Socialist CCF the official opposition. Drew's government vigorously promoted immigration, especially from the British Isles, and a series of overdue reforms. Like Hepburn, Drew combatted Ottawa and its "centralizing" schemes. It was only after Drew's departure in 1948 that Premier Leslie Frost adopted a quieter and more co-operative attitude to the central government, a major reversal in Ontario's policy. Frost shared the developmental objectives of Liberal ministers in Ottawa such as C.D. HOWE, and the 2 governments co-operated on major projects such as the St Lawrence Seaway, the TransCanada PipeLine and the development of nuclear power. Frost's successors, John Robarts and

William Davis, were cast in his low-key, down-to-earth mold; both strove to minimize conflict between Conservative Ontario and the usually Liberal federal government. Through his Confederation for Tomorrow Conference in 1967, Robarts tried to work out an accommodation that would satisfy Québec and keep it in Confederation. In 1981-82 Davis strongly supported Pierre Trudeau in patriating and reforming the Canadian Constitution. David Peterson's relations with Brian Mulroney were not as smooth. A reluctant supporter of Mulroney's 1987 MEECH LAKE ACCORD, Peterson strongly opposed the federal FREE TRADE initiative with the US the same year.

Though Ontario has often been perceived by other parts of Canada as a massive "central Canada" monolith, it is in reality a conglomerate of considerably different subregions – most obviously in its far-flung, primary-resource-based northern area and its industrialized, urbanized south. Despite its overall prosperity, Ontario itself suffers from regional disparities. Peripheral areas believe that they experience discrimination at the hands of the urbanized core, particularly Metropolitan Toronto. Attempts to classify these regions (eg, the Ontario government's *Ontario Economic and Social Aspects Survey*, 1961, which outlined 10 "economic regions") have proven inadequate because of the complex factors that must be considered. Nevertheless, many of the problems that are referred to on a national level (such as rural poverty, heavy concentration of industry in a few areas, the precarious life of communities based on a single economic activity, and disparities of income and of economic growth) are clearly evident within the province itself.

Still, Ontario does have some aggregate distinctive traits: a political conservatism, seen in the longevity of its provincial regimes; a practical readiness to adapt, evinced in many applications of the power of its governments; and a keen awareness of the all-but-embracing US around its core, which has meant both strong cross-border ties and determined responses to perceived threats of American power.

ROBERT BOTHWELL AND NORMAN HILLMER

Reading: C. Armstrong, *The Politics of Federalism* (1982); Robert Bothwell, *A Short History of Ontario* (1986); G.P. de T. Glazebrook, *Life in Ontario: A Social History* (1975); D.C. MacDonald, ed, *Government and Politics of Ontario* (rev ed 1980); H.V. Nelles, *The Politics of Development* (1974); F.F. Schindeler, *Responsible Government in Ontario* (1973); J. Schull, *Ontario Since 1867*; J.D. Wood, ed, *Perspectives on Landscape and Settlement in Nineteenth Century Ontario* (1975).

Ontario, Lake, 19 000 km² (10 000 km² in Canada), drainage area 90 130 km², elev 74 m, mean depth 86 m (max 244 m), length 311 km and width 85 km. It is the smallest in surface area and most easterly of the GREAT LAKES and eighth-largest body of fresh water in N America. The lake receives most of its water supply from the other Great Lks through the NIAGARA R and discharges into the ST LAWRENCE R through the Kingston Basin at its NE end. Other tributaries are the Genesee, Oswego and Black rivers in New York state and the Trent R in Ontario.

Lk Ontario occupies a bedrock depression originally produced by stream erosion and later modified by glaciation. Several glacial lakes of varying elevation occupied the basin before the current level and outlet were established about 11 000 years ago. The present basin has an elliptical plan with an E-W orientation and a complex lake bed reflecting its underlying rock structure and the effects of glaciation. The lakeshore is typically a low bluff of rock or glacial sediment with a narrow beach. The intersection of older and higher glacial and lake deposits just E of TORONTO has produced the Scarborough Bluffs – spectacular, cathedral-

like cliffs rising as high as 100 m above the lake. Other scenic shore features include the rocky coasts and islands of the Kingston Basin and the extensive sandy beaches at HAMILTON and Toronto on the Canadian side and Mexico Bay in the US. Because Lk Ontario is deep and its winter climate is moderated by incursions of warm air from the SW, its open waters rarely freeze in winter. From Nov to May the main body is well mixed at uniform temperature. From June through Oct the lake is stratified, with a warm upper layer 10-20 m thick and a cool lower layer. Temperatures at depths below 100 m are almost always less than 5°C. The average residence time of water in Lk Ontario is 8-10 years, compared with 3 years for Lk ERIE and more than 100 years for Lk SUPERIOR.

The first European known to have visited the lake was Étienne BRÛLÉ in 1615. The name Ontario is sometimes thought to be of Iroquoian origin, meaning "beautiful lake" or "sparkling water." It was first applied to the lake by Europeans in 1641 and appears on maps of N America as early as 1656. Conflict between the English and French and their Indian allies over the local fur trade inhibited European settlement until after the English takeover in 1763. The first major group of settlers were LOYALISTS, many of whom settled on the N shore. The most vigorous campaigns of the WAR OF 1812 between the US and Great Britain were fought on or near Lk Ontario. (The vessels *Hamilton* and *Scourge*, lost in a squall during a naval engagement at that time, have been found on the lake bed near Niagara.)

Nearly one-quarter of the present population of Canada lives in southern Ontario near the lake. The "Golden Horseshoe," which encompasses the western end of the lake and includes the major cities of ST CATHARINES, Hamilton and Toronto, is the industrial heartland of the country. Urban centres on the lake E of Toronto include OSHAWA, PORT HOPE, COBOURG, BELLEVILLE and KINGSTON. The other major factors promoting vigorous settlement and growth have been the productive farmland of southern Ontario and northwestern New York state, and access to ocean shipping via the ST LAWRENCE SEAWAY and to upper Great Lake ports via the WELLAND CANAL. Smaller craft can travel the RIDEAU CANAL from Kingston to Ottawa and the TRENT CANAL between the Bay of Quinte and Georgian Bay. Unfortunately, industrial and agricultural wealth has also led to the degradation of Lk Ontario water quality by pollution. Cautious optimism prevails, however, since the lake seems to be recovering as pollutant levels are reduced.

N. RUKAVINA AND F.M. BOYCE

Ontario Agricultural College, *see* AGRICULTURAL EDUCATION; UNIVERSITY OF GUELPH.

Ontario College of Art is Canada's best known and largest art school. It was founded in 1876 by the Ontario Society of Artists with the assistance of a $1000 provincial grant. The college received a provincial charter in 1912 to teach fine art and design and opened its own building in 1921 beside the Art Gallery of Toronto (now ART GALLERY OF ONTARIO), which had donated the site. This was the first building in Canada to be used solely for art education. In 1986 the college accommodated 3210 full- and part-time students in 3 buildings in

Toronto and off-campus study centres in Florence, Italy, and New York City. Many Canadian artists and designers, including Harold TOWN, Michael SNOW, Allan Fleming, Jack BUSH, Ken DANBY and members of the GROUP OF SEVEN, have attended OCA as students or staff. In recent years, the traditional skills such as drawing and painting have been augmented by contemporary courses such as holography and photoelectric arts. *See also* ART EDUCATION.   JON McKEE

Ontario Economic Council (1968-85), est to advise the Executive Council of Ontario on ways to contribute to public awareness, discussion and understanding of socioeconomic issues of special significance to the people of Ontario. The council was composed primarily of economists and business persons and kept a small staff in Toronto. Studies examined a range of issues, including the elimination of rent controls, the possibility of user charges for social services, the establishment of a N American free-trade area (which it advocated) and the appropriate role of industrial policy and income distribution.   W.F. FORWARD

Ontario Hydro is a CROWN CORPORATION owned by the Ontario government. In 1986 it held assets of $31.4 billion (ranking 1st among companies in Canada), had sales or operating revenue of $4.9 billion (ranking 13th) and employed 32 405 people. It was the first provincially owned electric utility in Canada and is one of the largest public ELECTRIC UTILITIES in N America. Its generation and transmission system includes 68 HYDROELECTRIC, 8 fossil-fueled and 5 NUCLEAR-POWER stations (one more is under construction), along with over 130 000 km of transmission and distribution lines. The system provides power to an estimated 3 million customers in Ontario, in all areas of its 650 000 km² jurisdiction. The utility is a special statutory corporation (like a crown corporation) established by the provincial legislature in 1906. Its founding chairman was Sir Adam BECK. In 1908, just 2 years after Ontario's legislature passed the Hydro-Electric Power Commission of Ontario Act, the novice utility entered into agreements with 14 municipalities to provide power at cost. Similar agreements now link Ontario Hydro and 316 co-operating municipalities. Ontario Hydro is responsible for the generation and transmission of ELECTRIC POWER and for its sale to participating utilities. It also acts as a central supervisory body with authority to approve and control certain features of the utilities' operations. Ontario Hydro also plays a prominent role in nuclear technology, operating uranium-fueled generating stations at Bruce "A" and "B" (6400 MW), Pickering "A" and "B" (4320 MW) and Rolphton (20 MW). A 4-unit station is being constructed at Darlington (3600 MW). Nuclear technology has brought new problems and responsibilities, eg, nuclear safety, irradiated fuel management and other environmental concerns, each of which is given high priority by Ontario Hydro.

The mandate of the corporation is to provide power to its customers at the lowest feasible cost. Applications for increases in rates to meet costs are subject to examination at public hearings before the Ontario Energy Board. Ontario Hydro has also been called to account before various committees of the Ontario legislature. The corporation's board of directors consists of a chairman, a vice-chairman, a president and not more than 10 other directors.   J.R. WHITEWAY

Reading: H.V. Nelles, *The Politics of Development: Forests, Mines & Hydro-Electric Power in Ontario 1849-1941* (1974).

Ontario Northland Transportation Commission is a provincial CROWN CORPORATION

which operates a transportation and communication network throughout northeastern Ontario. Established by provincial statute in 1902 as the government-owned Temiskaming and Northern Ontario Railway, it was designed to open up resources and encourage settlement northward from the city of NORTH BAY.

Between 1903 and 1909, construction of the railway extended to a junction with the National Transcontinental Railway at the town of Cochrane, a distance of 390 km. Branch lines made possible the exploitation of mineral and timber resources and the founding of new towns such as Cobalt, Timmins and Iroquois Falls. In the 1920s the railway was extended another 300 km northward, from Cochrane to Moosonee at the southern tip of James Bay (reached 1932), and from Swastika eastward to the gold of Kirkland Lake and the copper and zinc of Rouyn-Noranda.

At the same time that lucrative gold mines were being established (Hollinger, Dome, McIntyre, Lake Shore and Teck), and forest products hauled southward, the T&NO Railway was also opening northeast Ontario to farming and settlement. It was a community railway; the first 4 decades of its history were identified with the social and cultural life of the northeast, before the advent of highways, automobiles and buses. Because of its vital regional function, the commission has been administered like a public corporation by successive Ontario governments, the Cabinet and the premier functioning as major shareholders. The beneficiaries of their partisan politics, however, have generally been small businessmen from the north, so that local political patronage has been combined with a genuine commercial approach to the operation of the commission as a vehicle of development. To reflect its expanding role for the whole of northeastern Ontario, the provincial government of Premier George DREW changed the name to Ontario Northland Transportation Commission in 1946.

Over the following 2 decades, diesel locomotives steadily replaced steam; trucks, buses, boats and Otter aircraft were purchased to extend transportation facilities, while further investments were made to gain control of electronic means for the integration of long-distance TELEPHONES and TELECOMMUNICATIONS into a separate division called Ontario Northland Communications.

In 1986 assets of the ONTC were valued at almost $233 million. Its net income was $17.8 million, more than 60% of which came from telecommunications and 33% from railway freight revenue. Passenger rail service is subsidized annually by the provincial government, which has directed the mechanical department of the ONTC at North Bay to become a servicing and manufacturing unit for GO Transit locomotives and for the Urban Transportation Development Corporation, both of which also come under ownership of the Ontario government.

ALBERT TUCKER

Reading: Albert Tucker, *Steam into Wilderness* (1978).

Ontario Provincial Police, the third-largest deployed police force in N America, with jurisdiction over all Ontario except in municipalities having their own police. This modern organization of more than 5000 men and women maintains some 200 branch and field offices, patrols all provincial highways, and maintains a Criminal Investigation Branch. The OPP, with headquarters in Toronto, was created on 13 Oct 1909, by the appointment of 51 officers from Ontario frontier police forces, government detectives, and from provincial constables in the northern part of the province. In 1974, the OPP became the first deployed police force in Canada to recruit, train, equip and assign women to perform the same duties as their male counterparts at equal remuneration. The Provincial Police academy at Brampton provides force training, and the OPP operates such specialized units as anti-rackets, intelligence, security, canine, underwater, helicopter, computer services, tactics and rescue, marine, auxiliary police, technical identification and Indian policing. Air patrols serve the remote communities of northern Ontario. Since 1964, the ranking officers of the OPP have been granted the Queen's Commission. DAHN D. HIGLEY

Reading: Dahn D. Higley, *O.P.P. The History of the Ontario Provincial Police Force* (1984).

Ontario Research Foundation (ORF) was established as an independent corporation by a provincial Act in 1928; laboratory facilities were provided at the outset. Although initially academic in outlook, ORF gradually shifted its focus and began to promote industrial development, especially of small companies, through scientific and technological innovations. ORF has developed expertise in ceramics, fuel blends, textile and knitting technology, asbestos analytical methodology, hydro metallurgy, microelectronics, SOLAR ENERGY and POLLUTION research. Its facilities were expanded substantially in 1969. The president is responsible to a board of governors appointed by the lieutenant-governor-in-council from the industrial, commercial and scientific communities.

Initial funding was provided by an endowment fund through the CANADIAN MANUFACTURERS' ASSOCIATION and by a matching provincial grant. Since 1967, annual provincial grants have been tied to foundation income. ORF receives about half of all federal funding granted to provincial research organizations. About half of exploratory research is federally funded; industrial contracts finance most applied research. In 1987 ORF served over 2000 industrial clients. A portfolio style of management prevails, with 9 business centre managers reporting to 2 division heads. Areas covered include problem solving in production and processing, testing, research and product development. Expertise in many fields and specialized equipment are available. ORF is also responsible for drawing the attention of government and industry to research opportunities that promise social and economic benefits.

MARTIN K. McNICHOLL

Ontario Schools Question, an issue regarding the use of the French language in Ontario elementary schools. It was the first major schools issue to focus on language rather than religion, as English-speaking Catholics and Protestants were both aligned against the French-speaking Catholics. English had been made a compulsory subject in Ontario schools in 1885. In 1890 regulations further required that English be the language of instruction, except where it was impracticable. In 1910, after their numbers had grown, Franco-Ontarians organized the French-Canadian Education Assn of Ontario to promote French language interests. They were opposed by the ORANGE ORDER, which demanded "English only" education, and by Irish Catholics, led by Bishop FALLON of London. In 1912 Ontario Prem James WHITNEY's Conservative government issued Regulation 17, which limited the use of French as the language of instruction and communication to the first 2 years in elementary schools. Regulation 17 was amended again in 1913 to permit French as a subject of study for one hour per day.

During WWI the Ontario schools issue escalated to a national conflict, contributing to the tensions of the 1917 CONSCRIPTION crisis and further alienating French Canadians in Québec and Ontario from PM Robert BORDEN's Conservative government. At the federal level the JUDICIAL COMMITTEE OF THE PRIVY COUNCIL decided that Regulation 17 was constitutional, because denominational school guarantees did not include language; however, it ruled that the commission appointed by the government to enforce its policy in Ottawa was unconstitutional. A political compromise came after war tensions were removed. In 1927, unable to enforce Regulation 17, Howard FERGUSON's Conservative provincial government accepted the recommendation that the use of French in each school be considered on its merits by a departmental committee. *See also* MANITOBA SCHOOLS QUESTION; NEW BRUNSWICK SCHOOL QUESTION; NORTH-WEST SCHOOLS QUESTION.

MARILYN BARBER

Ontario Science Centre is located in the Don Valley, Toronto. It was opened (1969) as one of Ontario's projects for the Canadian CENTENNIAL, funded both provincially and with a federal grant. Construction costs were approximately $23 million and an additional $7 million was spent on initial exhibit development. The full-time staff of 200, plus students, have built over 850 exhibits, of which 650 are participatory experiments in 15 disciplines.

Yearly attendance at the centre is about 1.3 million, but another 250 000 people are reached by a travelling "Science Circus." A day school teaches and gives credits to 25 senior high-school students, all talented in science, who attend for one semester. The centre publishes a small quarterly paper, *Newscience*, which is given to visitors and mailed to subscribers. Britain, the US, France, China, Japan, Malaysia and Australia have purchased exhibits and rented exhibitions from the centre. To meet this demand the centre has licensed private industry to manufacture and sell copies of its exhibits to museums and SCIENCE CENTRES around the world and in Canada. In 1987 the centre was an agency of the Ontario Ministry of Culture and Communications which provided the annual operating budget of about $12 million. J. TUZO WILSON

Ontario Veterinary College, see UNIVERSITY OF GUELPH; VETERINARY MEDICINE, EDUCATION; VETERINARY MEDICINE, HISTORY.

Ookpik [Inuktitut, "snowy" or "Arctic owl"] is the name of one of the most popular of Inuit handicrafts, a souvenir sealskin owl with large head and big eyes. The appealing figure was created at the Ft Chimo Eskimo Co-operative in Québec in 1963, and it has become a symbol by which Canadian handicrafts are identified around the world. JOHN ROBERT COLOMBO

Oonark, Jessie, "Una," artist (b in the Back R area, NWT 1906; d at Churchill, Man 2 Mar 1985). She is known for her drawings and wall hangings, and her decorative, hieratic, brilliantly coloured images come from a lifetime of cutting caribou skins and sewing them into clothing. She created a unique personal vision by combining traditional Inuit images of the SHAMAN's flight with symbols from her experience as a devout Christian. A widow with 8 children, she moved from the land to Baker Lk in 1955; 5 of her children have become recognized artists. The printmakers at the Sanavik Co-op have made many stone-cut and stencil prints from her drawings, and one of their largest and most important wall hangings was commissioned by the National Arts Centre in Ottawa. She was elected to the Royal Canadian Academy of Arts in 1975. In 1987 the Art Gallery of Ontario presented a major retrospective of her work. *See also* INUIT ART.

K.J. BUTLER

Untitled hanging (1972-75) by Jessie Oonark, who combined traditional shamanistic and Christian images in her work (*courtesy Sanavik Co-operative, Baker Lake, NWT*).

Opera was slow to take root in Canada. Once established, it blossomed sporadically before finally flourishing. One musico-dramatic forerunner of opera was Marc LESCARBOT's masque *Le Théâtre de Neptune*, played from small boats in PORT-ROYAL harbour on 14 Nov 1606. An isolated incident, this was concurrent both with the first European settlements in Canada and with the early flourishing of opera in Italy.

Operatic performances by itinerant foreign theatrical companies began in the late 18th century in Montréal, Québec City and Halifax, with light operas of English and French provenance such as Charles Dibdin's *The Padlock* of 1768 (performed in Québec City in 1783 and Montréal in 1786) or Egidio-Romualdo Duni's *Les Deux Chasseurs et la laitière* (performed in Montréal in 1789). Indigenous Canadian opera started with Louis-Joseph QUESNEL's *Colas et Colinette* (composed in 1789 (?) and performed in Montréal in 1790). At this time, operas were performed as "afterpieces" to evenings consisting of a play, in addition to a song, dance or recitation. Typically, the operas had spoken dialogue alternating with musical numbers (ie, ballad opera or opéra-comique).

From the 1790s to about 1830, the repertoire favoured Arne, Duni and Shield. The first operas performed in Toronto were John Braham and C.E. Horn's *The Devil's Bridge*, Coleman's *The Mountaineers*, and Stephen Storace's *No Song No Supper* in 1825.

Social and political considerations exert an influence on operatic production, and the improvement in means of travel affected the dissemination of opera. In the 1830s, however, political unrest and cholera epidemics seem to have caused a lull in performances. In the 1840s and 1850s opera revived, in abridged form staged by small visiting companies, and the repertoire expanded to include more demanding works by Auber, Bellini, Boïeldieu, Donizetti, Rossini and Verdi. International vocal stars, including John Braham, Jenny Lind, Henriette Sontag and Adelina Patti, visited Montréal, Québec City and Toronto to perform operatic excerpts in recital. During the second half of the 19th century, Montréal and Toronto enjoyed performances of numerous travelling US companies led by American manager-entrepreneurs and prima donnas, includ-

ing the expatriate Canadian soprano Emma AL-
BANI. By the end of the century the repertoire included Meyerbeer, Wagner, Gounod and Puccini,
though not Mozart.

The formation of resident opera associations in
Montréal and Toronto during the 1860s and
1870s – eg, the Holman English Opera Troupe –
was an important step followed, in Montréal, by
the shorter-lived Société d'opéra français (1893-
96) and the Montreal Opera Co (1910-13). The
majority of performances, however, were by foreign companies, and cities such as Montréal and
Toronto enjoyed more opera than at any other
time in their histories. After WWI, over 30 opera
associations, including amateur, student and
light-opera companies, were formed in Montréal
and about a dozen in Toronto, though most were
short-lived. Of these, the CANADIAN OPERA CO
(COC), founded 1950 as the Opera Festival Association, has been the most successful. The Théâtre
lyrique de Nouvelle-France began in 1961,
changed its name to Théâtre lyrique du Québec in
1966, and dissolved in 1970. L'Opéra du Québec,
a co-operative venture for productions in Montréal and Québec City, 1971-75, was revived as the
touring company Opéra de chambre du Québec
and l'Opéra de Montréal in 1980. The main opera
associations currently are based in Vancouver,
Calgary, Edmonton, Winnipeg, Hamilton, Toronto, Montréal and Québec City. The Vancouver, Edmonton, Manitoba and Southern Alberta
Opera Assns (Calgary) joined forces as Opera
West in 1973.

Opera has been promoted in Canada through
the CANADIAN BROADCASTING CORPORATION, BANFF
CENTRE, and various FESTIVALS and universities.
CBC broadcasts in the 1940s and 1950s on radio
and from 1953 on television helped disseminate
opera. The CBC has commissioned operas from
Healey WILLAN, John BECKWITH, Kelsey Jones, Ben
McPeek, Murray ADASKIN, Godfrey RIDOUT,
Maurice Blackburn, Raymond Pannell and
Robert Turner. Festival performances have in-
cluded the STRATFORD FESTIVAL, Guelph Spring
Festival, Vancouver International Festival, and
Festival Ottawa (until 1983).

The Metropolitan Opera appeared sporadically
in Montréal and Toronto, from 1899 to 1952,
when regular Met spring tours started to include
Toronto. These ended in 1961 owing to pro-
hibitive costs, except for the one-week visit to the
Toronto International Festival, 1984. In 1967
some of the leading opera companies in the world
– La Scala, the Royal Swedish Opera, the Vienna
State Opera – visited EXPO 67. Although the COC
no longer tours, the COC Ensemble has increased
its touring in Ontario, including a production
with Orchestra London in 1984.

Among the more prestigious of Canada's oper-
atic performers have been conductors Wilfrid PEL-
LETIER and Mario BERNARDI, singers Emma Albani,
Pauline DONALDA, Edward JOHNSON, Raoul JOBIN,
James Milligan, Victor Braun, Maureen FOR-
RESTER, Louis QUILICO, George London, Lois MAR-
SHALL, Léopold SIMONEAU, Teresa STRATAS, Jon
VICKERS, Claude Corbeil, Ermanno Mauro and Al-
lan Monk.

From the time of Quesnel's Colas et Colinette, indigenous Canadian opera has followed a sporadic
course. Nineteenth-century works include Oscar
Ferdinand Telgmann's Leo, the Royal Cadet 1889,
Calixa LAVALLÉE's 3 light operas of the 1870s and
1880s, Charles A.E. HARRISS's Torquil, 1894, and
Susie Frances Harrison's Pipandor of the late
1880s. Although Calixa Lavallée composed 4
light operas between 1865-66 and 1886, these
were neither written nor performed in Canada at
that time (Lavallée's The Widow was performed in
Hamilton in 1876). In the 20th century, more
Canadians have written operas, aided from the

1940s by the CBC. Many of the works composed
in the 1950s and 1960s were one-act operas commissioned by CBC. The trend begun by Eugène
Lapierre in the 1940s or Barbara PENTLAND in the
1950s to focus on Canadian subjects was augmented during Canada's CENTENNIAL YEAR in
1967, the most successful being Harry SOMERS's
Louis Riel, commissioned by the COC. Through
the 1960s and 1970s short operas for small orchestra were most common, by composers such
as Gabriel CHARPENTIER, Pannell, Charles Wilson,
Tibor Polgar, Violet ARCHER, Somers, Norman SY-
MONDS, Paul McIntyre, Barrie Cabena and John
Rea.

Large operas are relatively rare in recent years
owing to production costs. Exceptions are
Wilson's Heloise and Abelard (commissioned by
the COC in 1973) and Psycho Red (commissioned
by the 1978 Guelph Spring Festival), Derek
Healey's Seabird Island (commissioned by the
1977 Guelph Spring Festival), and Beckwith's
Shivaree (premiered by Comus Music Theatre,
1979). R. Murray SCHAFER's Ra (premiered by Comus Music Theatre, Toronto, 1983) is probably
the longest, most experimental musico-theatrical
work of the recent past, taking 11 hours to perform. See also MUSIC HISTORY.   GAYNOR G. JONES

Reading: Encyclopedia of Music in Canada (1981); Opera
Canada magazine.

Operation Dismantle, founded in 1977 by T.
James Stark and Peter Brown, is a nonprofit, nonpartisan organization whose goal is to bring the
pressure of international public opinion to bear
on national governments to negotiate an end to
the nuclear arms race. A principal project has
been a UN-sponsored world referendum on disarmament, which the organization believes
would be the best way to provide governments
with a sufficiently powerful mandate. Dismantle
has some 10 000 members and supporters; funding is provided by donations and membership
fees. Operation Dismantle in Canada pioneered
the idea of municipal referenda on disarmament;
the campaign led to 195 votes in municipal campaigns, with the results 76.2% in favour. In 1983,
it led a coalition to stop the testing of the cruise
missile over Canadian territory. In 1985 the case
went to the Supreme Court, which ruled that Operation Dismantle had insufficient grounds, under the CANADIAN CHARTER OF RIGHTS AND FREEDOMS,
to argue in court the merits of an injunction on
Cruise missile testing. The organization led a
campaign during the 1984 federal election to
make a nuclear freeze an election issue. See also
PEACE MOVEMENT.

Operation Morning Light, the name given to
the first phase of the search for the nuclear-pow-
ered Soviet satellite that accidentally re-entered
the Earth's atmosphere over northern Canada
early on 24 Jan 1978. Cosmos 954 had behaved
abnormally almost since being launched 18 Sept
1977; early Jan 24 the satellite experienced increasing friction as it plunged deeper into the atmosphere on its last orbit. NORAD had predicted
the time of re-entry and its Hawaiian telescopic
tracking station noted the satellite's dull red glow
as it passed towards the Queen Charlotte Is. Minutes later people in Yellowknife, NWT, noticed a
bright whitish object streaking across the sky.

Debris was sent to Edmonton and then to
Whiteshell Nuclear Research Establishment in
Pinawa, Man, for analysis and final storage. At
the peak of the search, approximately 220 people
were located at Edmonton and at Yellowknife,
which was the base of operations for helicopters
used in the search. The first charred object was
found late Jan 26 near the mouth of the Hoarfrost
R, 27 km north of Fort Reliance. Further discov-

ery of more particles increased the evidence that
they were the remains of a nuclear reactor core
that had melted or "burned up" in the upper levels of the dense atmosphere – more or less as had
been asserted by the Soviets Jan 24. It was clear
that there no longer was need to be concerned
that the core could have reached the ground to
become a hazard. Nevertheless, some larger, intensely radioactive and potentially lethal core
fragments were found on the ice over the middle
of Great Slave Lake. On Feb 23 the most intensely
radioactive piece, a flake about the size of a nickel,
was recovered.

Operation Morning Light ended Apr 20 because of spring breakup. The search area covered
an area greater than 124 000 km² and more than
4500 hours of flying time had been logged. All
inhabited areas had been searched, including the
sites of the 1978 Arctic Winter Games in Hay River and Pine Point.

The second phase of the search, July-Oct, was
done under contract from the ATOMIC ENERGY CON-
TROL BOARD. By mid-Oct, more than 4000 particles, flakes and pieces had been recovered and
more than 4700 lab analyses had been done. All
seasonally inhabited areas, as well as the whooping crane nesting area in WOOD BUFFALO NATIONAL
PARK, had been searched and cleaned. The total
cost incurred by the various Canadian departments and agencies involved in the first phase
was $12 048 239 of which $4 414 348 was included in Canada's claim to the USSR under the
1972 Convention on International Liability for
Damage Caused by Space Objects. The total cost
incurred during the second phase totalled
$1 921 904 of which $1 626 825 was included in
Canada's claim. The USSR made payment of
approximately $3 000 000.   KEN SHULTZ

Opetchesaht, a NOOTKA tribe of the Alberni Valley, Vancouver I, BC. They formerly consisted of
3 Coast Salish groups which, reduced by disease
and prolonged warfare in the historic period,
amalgamated as a tribe. Their traditional territories included Alberni Inlet, the Somass R, Sproat
Lake and Great Central Lake. In the late prehistoric and early historic period, Nootka groups invaded Alberni Inlet, pushing the Coast Salish
groups into their Alberni Valley territories. Eventually the Opetchesaht adopted the Nootka language and culture, but retained their Salish orientation to river, lake and inland environments. Elk
and deer were important for subsistence. Today
the Opetchesaht live at Ahahswinis reserve, near
Port Alberni.   JOHN DEWHIRST

Ophthalmology is the medical specialty concerned with the eyes and their relationship to the
body. An ophthalmologist (also called eye physician and surgeon, oculist, eye doctor) is a medical
doctor who has studied eye conditions and diseases for 3 to 5 years beyond medical internship
before taking examinations set by the Royal College of Physicians and Surgeons of Canada or by
the College of Physicians and Surgeons of Québec. Once qualified, an ophthalmologist becomes
part of the general medical team, not only treating
diseases and conditions of the eye but also helping
to diagnose many general medical problems, including circulatory disorders (eg, high blood
pressure and atherosclerosis), neurological disorders (eg, multiple sclerosis and stroke) and en-
docrine problems (eg, diabetes and thyroid disease). These conditions can be associated with
blurred vision and other symptoms, and it is the
ophthalmologist who often initiates not only vi-
sion-saving but also lifesaving treatments.

The modern study of the eye as a medical specialty gradually evolved during the 1800s. Henry
Howard of The Montréal Eye and Ear Institution
was likely one of the first doctors in Canada to

limit his practice to eye problems. His 1850 book, *The Anatomy, Physiology and Pathology of the Eye,* based on his 4 years of practice in Montréal, was published before the invention of the ophthalmoscope in 1851. The ophthalmoscope, a small hand-held telescope for looking through the pupil of the eye, allows doctors to see inside the eye and to examine the retina and optic nerve, which are extensions of the brain. In 1864 Toronto doctors pioneered retinal photography by connecting an ophthalmoscope to a camera to photograph the retina of a cat, a first step in photographing the inside of the living human eye and a technique that today is essential all over the world in evaluating and treating patients with eye diseases. In 1922 Dr Walter Wright pioneered the use of fascia lata (leg tissue) for repair of ptosis (droopy lids) in a manner that is still in use. The Canadian Ophthalmological Society was formed in Oct 1937, but it was not until the early 1940s that Dr Walter Wright at U of T set up the first in-Canada training program for ophthalmologists. Soon afterwards, Dr Harold Ridley, an Englishman, replaced an opacified lens (cataract) with a new clear plastic one (intraocular lens). Canadian ophthalmologists were among the pioneers to use these lenses.

As part of any complete eye examination, ophthalmologists determine vision and the refractive error for each eye, and inspect the retina, cornea, iris and lens in order to diagnose and treat disease. Ophthalmologists can reconstruct many parts of the diseased eye. The diseased cornea can be replaced by a clear donor cornea in a corneal transplant operation; a clouded lens can be replaced by a clear plastic one in a cataract extraction and lens implantation operation; and glaucoma can be treated with newer medications, laser surgery and glaucoma surgery. Retinal disease can be treated with various lasers and with scleral buckling and vitreous cutting operations. Specialists and subspecialists in all new areas of treatment practise in most major centres across Canada. Training centres at medical schools for ophthalmologists are located in Halifax, Québec City, Sherbrooke, Montréal, Ottawa, Kingston, Toronto, London, Winnipeg, Saskatoon, Edmonton and Vancouver.

Operating microscopes now allow functional magnification; tissue can be repaired with stitches finer than a human hair; and membranes more delicate than tissue paper can be cut, left, or picked clean of scar tissue. LASERS that are capable of evaporating cloudy tissues are manufactured in Canada for international use. Technical advances and clinical data about contact lens technology emanate from Canada to around the world. Techniques for surgically modifying the shape of the eye, or to reduce or eliminate the need for glasses in certain patients, are evolving and are starting to be used in Canada. Newer techniques for detection and treatment of glaucoma are also being tested in Canada, and computerized visual field testing machines are commonly used. *See also* BLINDNESS AND VISUAL IMPAIRMENT.
MICHAEL M. HENRY

Opossum, common name for about 8 genera and 65 species of omnivorous mammals comprising the family Didelphidae, one of 2 families of MARSUPIALS found outside of Australia. The N American opossum (*Didelphis virginiana*) is the only marsupial native to Canada. An easily recognized, cat-sized animal, it has a long, pointed nose, naked ears, coarse black to white fur; scaly, prehensile (grasping) tail; and a hindfoot with a clawless, opposable first toe. This species probably evolved from the very similar tropical species *D. marsupialis* during the Pleistocene (1.6 million to 10 000 years ago). Young are born in an under-

The opossum (*Didelphis virginiana*) is the only marsupial native to Canada (*artwork by Claire Tremblay*).

developed state after a gestation of less than 13 days; development is completed in a pouch on the mother's belly. Two litters of up to 13 young each may be produced annually. The opossum, poorly adapted to severe cold, reaches the northern limit of its range in Canada and is found in extreme southern Ontario and the lower Fraser Valley, BC.
C.G. VAN ZYLL DE JONG

Opting-Out originated as a device by which one or more provinces do not participate in a federal-provincial shared cost program; instead the province receives direct payment (in cash or tax room) of funds which would have been spent there. Under pressure from Québec, the Established Programs (Interim Arrangements) Act was passed in 1965, permitting opting-out of major programs, including hospital insurance, vocational training, public health and aid to the old and disabled. Only Québec opted out. Defended as an example of the ability of the federal system to respond to Québec's needs, the legislation was also attacked for allowing a measure of "special status." The Act set the stage for later developments in fiscal federalism, notably Established Programs Financing (1977). The CONSTITUTION ACT, 1982, extends the principle. In its amendment procedures it provides for some opting-out in that a province may remove itself from any amendment that derogates from its existing legislative powers, proprietary rights, "or any other rights or privileges" of its legislature or government. If an amendment transfers powers relating to education or culture, the federal government must provide "reasonable compensation" to a province which opts out. Section 33 of the Constitution Act, 1982, permits a government to opt out of some sections of the Canadian Charter of Rights and Freedoms. Parliament or a provincial legislature may declare that an Act will operate "notwithstanding" sections 2 (fundamental freedoms), and 7 to 15 (legal and equality rights) of the Charter. Such a provision can last a maximum of 5 years, but may be re-enacted.
RICHARD SIMEON

Optometry [Gk *optos,* "visible" and *metron,* "measure"], the profession of examining eyes for faults of refraction, ocular mobility and visual perception and of the treatment of abnormal conditions with correctional lenses and orthoptics. The royal charter signed by Charles I of England (1629), which conferred the responsibility for the quality of spectacles and the training of apprentices upon "The Worshipful Company of Spectacle Makers," has been continually renewed by successive monarchs to the present. The word "optometrist," however, originated in the US in the mid-19th century and has been in general and legal use since about 1880.

Optometrists were first trained through apprenticeships. Later they attended proprietary schools which provided theoretical education,

while practising optometrists provided clinical training. Neither the quality nor the quantity of the programs of such schools or of the clinical training were controlled. University programs, which included didactic, laboratory and clinical education, first became available in 1925. Recently, optometric education has been increasingly integrated with other health-science programs, particularly at the clinical training stage. In N America all programs of optometric education are accredited by the Council on Optometric Education of the American Optometric Assn.

Two Canadian universities, Montréal and Waterloo, have schools of optometry. Some 40 students graduate from U de M annually, about 60-70 from Waterloo. Both Canadian schools are accredited by the council. Entry to these programs requires a minimum of 2 years basic science education at a university. The professional programs are 4 years in length. Graduates may enter practice after graduation without serving an internship, but all Canadian provinces require that they pass a provincially administered licensing examination. Graduate education in visual science (physiological optics) to the level of the master of science degree is available at both U de M and Waterloo. In addition, Waterloo offers a doctoral program in visual science. In the late 1980s the faculties of both schools were contributing new knowledge of visual function through fundamental and clinical vision research programs.

In each province, optometry Acts or health-care legislation confer a self-governing status on the profession. Optometric associations in each province are organized to promote ethical practice and the continuing education of members, to provide for the welfare of the profession's membership and to negotiate fees with governments under the medicare legislation. Continuing education of optometrists is required by law in a majority of Canadian provinces. The Canadian Association of Optometrists, a national body, is a confederation of the 10 provincial associations.

Optometry graduates may establish their own practices, but there is a trend toward group practice. There is also a trend toward specialization in areas such as contact-lens care, low-vision care, pediatrics, geriatrics, electrodiagnosis, ultrasound diagnosis, orthoptics and visual training. Optometrists concerned with occupational health are trained to assess work environments to identify hazards to eyes and vision. They may plan, implement and administrate eye-protection programs, establish vision standards for various types of work, and assist in planning visually efficient work and recreation environments.
M.E. WOODRUFF

Oral History, accounts of the past transmitted by word of mouth. Since the beginnings of its modern form, oral history has made important contributions to the ways in which we understand and interpret the past; it has become a "subprofession" and has resulted in some valuable books. Allan Nevins of Columbia U, New York, generally considered to have started the modern oral-history movement, began his interviewing in 1948 accompanied by a graduate student who "took notes in long hand as Nevins evoked a stream of reminiscences from his subject." This method has a long history: Herodotus got information for his account of the Persian Wars in the 5th century BC by writing down what the survivors remembered. Much later, Walter Scott's interviews with the Jacobite remnants of 1745 became the basis for his Waverley novels.

In the early 1950s recording on tape came into general use in N America. The first really portable recording equipment was the Webcor tape machine, which was the size of a suitcase and weighed over 11 kg. By the 1970s the cassette recorder was small enough to be carried over the shoulder or in a pocket. Oral history in the 1980s is a child of the electronic age and, as an organized activity, popular movement or pastime, has expanded as recording equipment has grown smaller.

Although oral history includes FOLKLORE and even folk songs (*see* FOLK MUSIC), at its centre is the interview. Much of the oral history course offered at Simon Fraser U, Burnaby, BC, is devoted to study of the interview, of which there are various types. Columbia U favours recording the memoirs of important people, or what British oral historian Paul Thompson calls "the great man project." There is also the ordinary-person interview which American historian Louis Starr called "history-from-the-bottom-up"; this has proved to be immensely popular when presented in book form, as in Studs Terkel's *Working* (1974), which became a Broadway show, and Barry Broadfoot's best-selling oral history of the Great Depression in Canada, *Ten Lost Years* (1973), which was also highly successful when it was adapted for stage presentation. Interviews with ordinary people form the basis of the social and community histories favoured by Thompson, numerous local and regional ethnic projects, and such large-scale surveys as the one at Duke U (Durham, NC) on how black disenfranchisement came about in the southern US.

The ordinary-person interview, perhaps requiring more skill and empathy than does recording the memoirs of the famous, has given a human dimension previously lacking in historical accounts. It can be said that oral history has made the illiterate literate and has given the silent masses a voice. Furthermore, the experience of hundreds of interviews has shown that the average person is much more frank and forthcoming when speaking, even in the presence of a microphone and recording machine, than when writing. (This fact may be attributed to use of the telephone, which has largely replaced the pen as the instrument of social contact and communication.) Good oral history requires much more than a microphone and a willing subject: during interviews, questions must be presented deftly and fairly. If the results are to be published, the interviews need to be subjected to careful, often difficult and sophisticated editing which allows the subject's story to be told in his or her own words, with a minimum of distortion.

Canada's academic historians tend to be suspicious of oral history; they argue that people's memories are distorted by time, and that oral history is therefore frequently unreliable. They often side with British historian A.J.P. Taylor, who dismissed it contemptuously as "old men drooling about their youth." Some Canadian historians point out that oral history can be no more accurate than AUTOBIOGRAPHY, and urge that a subject's memories must be checked, whenever possible, against documentary sources. In contrast, American historians seem to be much more attuned to the electronic age and, although they may have reservations, many of them make use of interviews in their work. There are oral-history courses in many universities in the US and, in most cases, the history departments run these courses, whereas the history departments of Canadian universities tend to ignore the subject. The movement was first institutionalized in the US: the Oral History Assn (US) was formed in 1967, the British Oral History Assn in 1973 and the Canadian Oral History Assn in 1974.

Universities took the lead in the US, and their projects have been funded by private sources such as the Rockefeller Foundation (*see* "Soundings of the Sony Age" in *RF Illustrated*, 3 May 1977). In Canada the government archives and agencies are the main proponents of oral history, while the universities, with the exception of Simon Fraser, have taken little interest. The NATIONAL ARCHIVES OF CANADA, under the direction of W.I. Smith, a creative archivist, has actively assisted in oral-history projects. The CANADIAN BROADCASTING CORPORATION was the first institution to collect interviews. The NATIONAL MUSEUMS and provincial archives have continuing projects, the most remarkable of which is the BC government's Sound Heritage Series, published in Victoria since 1973.

But oral history is not the domain of institutions alone. Many individuals and amateur groups have taken up oral history as a hobby. In Canada it received a special impetus with the preparations for the Centennial of 1967: many groups, often assisted by government grants, collected and published local histories, and the trend has continued with such projects being tied to special anniversaries of towns, cities and provinces. *See also* ORAL LITERATURE.   PETER STURSBERG

Reading: Allan Anderson, *Remembering the Farm* (1977), *Salt Water, Fresh Water* (1979) and *Roughnecks and Wildcatters* (1981); Barry Broadfoot, *Six War Years 1939-1945* (1975), *The Pioneer Years 1895-1914* (1976) and *Years of Sorrow, Years of Shame* (1977); Peter Stursberg, *Diefenbaker, Leadership Gained* (1975), *Diefenbaker, Leadership Lost* (1976), *Lester Pearson and the Dream of Unity* (1978) and *Lester Pearson and the American Dilemma* (1980).

Oral Literature in English The term "oral literature" is sometimes used interchangeably with "folklore," but it usually has a broader focus. The expression is self-contradictory: literature, strictly speaking, is that which is written down; but the word is used here to emphasize the imaginative creativity and conventional structures that mark this form of discourse. Oral literature shares with written literature the use of heightened language in various genres (narrative, lyric, epic, etc), but it is set apart by being actualized only in performance and by the fact that the performer can (and sometimes is obliged to) improvise. Oral literature may be composed in performance; transmitted orally over generations, like many Scottish and Irish ballads that have been brought to Canada; or written down specifically for oral performance. The process of transmission itself (often, in recent years, to collecting folklorists and oral historians) shows that oral literature has not been replaced by the ubiquitousness of books and the electronic media. Indeed, whenever a ghost story is told around a campfire, whenever a protest song or a lullabye is sung, whenever a riddle, tongue twister, counting rhyme, shaggy-dog story or knock-knock joke is shared, or fables and proverbs told, oral literature lives in performance.

The attitudes of scholars and the literate public toward oral literature were largely shaped by the 19th-century Romantic movement. William Wordsworth, in his *Preface to Lyrical Ballads* (1798), claimed to have found in the oral discourse of unlettered rustic people the source of literary spontaneity, sincerity and integral unity. At about the same time a rise in nationalism, with its emphasis on local origins, encouraged the study of "popular antiquities" – ie, the oral tradition of history and narrative. Writers in Canada adopted the trend, transforming tales, legends, proverbs and anecdotes into written form, and sometimes incorporating tale-tellers, such as T.C. HALIBURTON's Sam Slick, into their written work. The techniques were borrowed by Susanna MOODIE, who, in ROUGHING IT IN THE BUSH (1852), tells a life history that is also a "liar's tale": a hyperbolic account of the hellish life in the new land to counter the land company's lie that Canada was a new Eden. Other examples of borrowing – of techniques or of actual tales (canoe songs, tales of encounters with the devil, etc) – appear in 19th-century Canadian written literature, and the use of dialect further emphasizes their oral underpinnings. At the end of the century the so-called Confederation poets (Mair, Roberts, Crawford, Johnson, Carman, Lampman) reworked extensively such sources as traditional ghost stories and Indian mythology.

Oral literature has been studied principally by folklorists, who emphasize its ability to act as the voice of a tradition; they collect oral literature in order to preserve something of the culture of ethnic groups facing assimilation into the mainstream. But there are problems associated with gathering and preserving such materials. The communicative act is distorted to a greater or lesser extent by recording methods (eg, gestures are lost when recording is done shorthand or on tape; even on videotapes the ambience of an occasion is lost, although the speaker is recorded both aurally and visually). More significant is the "freezing" of the oral moment into an artifact, when part of the essence of oral literature is its capacity to be changed through generations, and even from occasion to occasion, by storytellers and bards.

Folklorists in Canada, using the classification system devised by Antti Aarne (*The Types of the Folktale*, translated and enlarged by Stith Thompson, 1961), which was designed primarily for narrative, have placed most items they have collected in the broad categories of legend, joke and anecdote. Myths and *märchen* are rare, though they are found among the Indians and as archaic elements in areas of Celtic settlement or in those with close connections to French speakers (eg, New Brunswick). Legends represent the localizing of the marvellous; for example, Captain Kidd's treasure is located in many a Nova Scotia town, the devil is known to have danced at Kensington, PEI, and the burning ship of Chaleur Bay makes periodic appearances elsewhere on the coast. Political oratory and sermons have seldom been studied in Canada as oral literature.

The heroes of cycles of tall tales, yarns and anecdotes include the Wizard of Miramichi and Paul BUNYAN. Sometimes folk heroes tell whoppers about themselves, especially in front of tenderfeet from other regions. Tall tales are often used, as are the Joe MUFFERAW tales of the Ottawa Valley, to promote a locality or "prove" its superiority over others. Sometimes these yarns provide the mainstay of local radio programs, as the electronic media disseminate oral culture.

The performance of oral literature is readily experienced in the form of children's playground rhymes and songs, such as those recorded by Sharon, Lois and Bram, Raffi and others. Although the performance, once recorded, is in a fixed form, the variants in such things as skipping rhymes show that the oral tradition – typically mutable – is alive; and one seldom hears 2 identical recordings of such tall-tale songs as "The Cat Came Back." Less accessible to most Canadians is the living oral tradition of the Newfoundland Mummers' plays (*see* MUMMING). The ritual aspect of their performance is common to much of oral literature performed in its proper context.

No other extended poetic forms are found in Canada's oral literature. The lyric predominates in ballads, laments and work songs (eg, sea chanties, lumbering songs and milling songs). Whereas many of these songs are traditional ones from Europe, others embrace new themes reflecting the social and political realities of Canada (eg, Gaelic elegies, songs of emigration, satires and humorous songs). Themes from Canadian history are celebrated in ballads such as "General Wolfe." Newfoundlanders have contributed a rich treasure of sea chanties and ballads of shipwrecks, and have also produced well-known dance songs such as "I's the B'y that Builds the Boat." From Ukrainians in the West have been collected a variety of carols, wedding songs, dance ditties, cumulative songs and drinking songs. Much oral poetry is chanted rather than sung, as are children's counting rhymes and the charms, spells and alliterative rhymes collected from German speakers in Ontario.

Many songs and chants of the native peoples have been recorded, but more attention has been paid to their narratives. Two broad groups of myths involving tales of when the world was young and of the beginning of Indian ways of living may be found across the continent: stories of the great flood are related by the Cowichan in the West and the Iroquois in the East, and the discovery of fire is variously attributed to heroes such as NANABOZO of the Ojibwa and Coyote of the Salish.

This native literature, as well as that of the medieval troubadours and the Yugoslav composers of oral epic, has inspired numerous contemporary writers in N America to adopt an oral poetics. Charles Olson's idea of a "poetry of utterance" and Jack Kerouac's "spontaneous prose" have found extensions in the work of Canadian sound poets such as bp NICHOL, the Four Horsemen, Re:Sounding and Owen Sound, as they attempt to make literature from the ephemeral and improvise before audiences. As he tries to create a sacred ritual for himself and his audience, bill BISSETT's composition in performance draws heavily on Indian chants.

Writers of narrative have been as attracted to the concept of orality as the poets have. Robert KROETSCH, for example, tells liars' tales through his characters. In *The Diviners* Margaret LAURENCE provides a genealogy and history of oral narrative in Canada, from improvised Scottish heroic narratives and legends and Métis songs through novels to the new orality of modern popular ballads. Although Laurence does not use material from traditional folklore but creates anew from the formulas and conventions they employ (a practice folklorists consider "fakelore"), and although her material is neither composed in performance nor written specifically for performance, her novel, like those of other contemporary novelists, places the text in a context of performance and analyses the nature and function of its own telling.

The role of the theatre in keeping alive oral literature in Canada is exemplified by James REANEY's dramatic versions of 2 Ontario legends, the Baldoon mystery of poltergeists and the legend of the folkheroes, the DONNELLYS. In these plays Reaney uses traditional jokes, songs, stories and proverbs. The range of his creative freedom is greater than that of the traditional performer, but his materials are similar. Contemporary developments suggest that the growth of a written literature does not mean the death of an oral one, but announces change and displacement. While the oral literature of rural Canada may be fading, a new one is being created in the city, where supernatural happenings, numbskull stories and yarns continue as typographers create their genres in the workplace and science fiction groupies compose songs for their conferences. *See also* ETHNIC LITERATURE; FOLKLORE; ORAL HISTORY.

BARBARA GODARD

Reading: R. Finnegan, *Oral Poetry* (1977); Edith Fowke, *Folkore of Canada* (1976); N. Rosenberg, *Folklore and Oral History* (1978).

Oral Literature in French, including tales, songs, sayings, legends, superstitions, proverbs and other forms, is part of the heritage left by the first French settlers in N America. Transmitted orally through the centuries, these anonymous traditional forms have enjoyed an excellent environment (an immense, predominantly rural re-

gion) for their preservation and transmission. By the 19th century, Ernest GAGNON and others first felt the need to preserve them in written form, but they still circulate orally today, despite the pervasive presence of the mass media. French Canadian oral literature remains faithful to its origins although, after 3 centuries in the new land, it has evolved, adapted and acquired both autonomy and originality. Since it is not formalized in writing, oral FOLKLORE is in a state of perpetual change. Popular tales have been handed down from the earliest days of French civilization. Most of the legends deal with universal themes, but some, concerning historical events and characters, began in Québec. Innumerable different versions of songs have resulted from exchanges between immigrants from different French provinces; as with legends, the repertoire of folk songs grew in the new land to include songs about the COUREURS DE BOIS, the VOYAGEURS of the PAYS D'EN HAUT, and life in the forest.

The 19th century was still the golden age of the traditional tale, and storytellers were very popular. Crowds spontaneously formed around tramps and peddlers to hear the stories of La Grand'Margaude, La Bête à Sept-Têtes, La Canarde and L'Eau de la Fontaine de Paris, and the incredible adventures of Ti-Jean. In rural areas, people liked to organize entire evenings of storytelling. Forest life was important in preserving and spreading tales, as lumberjacks and raftsmen fought the boredom of long isolation by gathering to tell each other tales in the camps.

Although formal study of folklore in America began relatively recently, each of the major oral genres – tales, legends and songs – is the subject of study and research. Until the early 20th century, popular tales had such vitality that few felt the need to collect them. Their scientific collection and study really began in 1914 with Marius BARBEAU, an anthropologist with the NATIONAL MUSEUMS OF CANADA. Although his field was native peoples, his attention was drawn to francophone folklore by Franz BOAS, an American colleague interested in European influences on Canadian Indians. Barbeau's research was quickly extended to all Québec. Barbeau and his collaborators, Adélard Lambert, Gustave Lanctot, Édouard-Zotique MASSICOTTE and others, presented their rich find to the general public. Since that time, general interest has continued to grow. Among the major publications on the subject, the *Journal of American Folklore* contains more than 200 tales in the francophone repertoire. The most important collections are that of Father Germain Lemieux of Sudbury, *Les vieux m'ont conté* (18 vols, 1973 ff), Carmen Roy's *Contes populaires gaspésiens* (1952) and the other volumes of the *Mémoires d'homme* collection, *Contes de bûcherons* by Jean-Claude Dupont (1976) and Conrad Laforte's *Menteries drôles et merveilleuses* (1978).

After working with Barbeau, Luc Lacourcière, a teacher of Canadian literature at Université Laval, made the popular tale his preferred field of research; in 1944 he founded the Folklore Archives at Laval. Thirty years later, his inventory and analysis of several thousand tales from various sources provided him with material for the first *Catalogue raisonné du conte populaire français en Amérique*. This exceptional work will help complete the international catalogue of tales prepared by Stith Thompson on the basis of work by Antti Aarne (*Motif Index of Folk Literature*, 6 vols, 1955-58) and the catalogue developed in France by Paul Delarue and Marie-Louise Ténèze (*Le Conte populaire français*, 1957-64).

Popular tales are composed in a particular style. First, they are marvellous recitations whose sole purpose is to amuse. They often begin and end with well-known sayings. Usually the action is

not located in any particular place or time and the characters are not seen as individuals. They are animals, magical beings (kings, princes, princesses or fairies) or fantastic beings (ogres, monsters, giants) who change form, use charms, potions and talismans, and dominate the elements of nature. The tale is therefore not intended to be believed, but to be enjoyed as pure fiction. Unlike tales, legends appear to have historical bases that appeal to the listener's credulity. The site of the action is often indicated with great precision and the characters are carefully developed in space and time. In French Canada, legends have come down in a manner different from that of the tale because the 19th century has left many legends in print. The work of Aurélien Boivin, *Le Conte littéraire québécois au XIXe siècle* (1975), provides an exhaustive treatment of them. Québec writers in the 19th century used "conte" to mean legend rather than the traditional tale, although the forms have been distinct in the eyes of both modern folklorists and the original illiterate audiences. By their nature, legends lend themselves more easily to written presentation, and Canadian authors have drawn abundant material from them. Philippe AUBERT DE GASPÉ (father and son), N.H.É. Faucher de Saint-Maurice, Honoré Beaugrand, Henri-Raymond CASGRAIN and many others have used werewolves, sirens, ghosts, the legend of La CORRIVEAU or Alexis-le-Trotteur and a host of others. As Lacourcière notes, the many categories of legends include those dealing with the fantastic and the supernatural, those attempting to explain the origins and causes of natural phenomena and those more directly related to history and to real persons; and this is not a complete classification.

The third major genre in oral literature is song (*see* FOLK MUSIC). It has been said that song gives full expression to the French spirit and, consequently, that it is the richest, most vibrant and most pleasant of French Canadian traditions. The reason is perhaps that song is suited to all life's circumstances and to all ages. Religious at times, ribald at others, its themes encompass the full range of human feelings. Its form, rhythm and assonances have preserved it from the ravages of time. In a rigorous classification, more than 3000 titles of folk songs contained in Laforte's *Le Catalogue de la chanson folklorique française* (1958) reveal all the themes treated in this form of popular poetry, which is often mixed with uniquely Canadian variations.

In the many French Canadian regions, folklorists, ethnomusicologists, researchers in various disciplines and lovers of the oral traditions continue gathering this important part of French Canada's cultural heritage. The documents they produce are the subject of study and research and are preserved and scientifically treated in archives in Québec, Moncton, Ottawa, Sudbury and elsewhere.

MADELEINE BÉLAND

Orange Order, Protestant fraternal society, fd 1795 in Ireland to commemorate the victory of William of Orange at the Battle of the Boyne in 1690. During the Irish insurrection of 1798 it became the principal link between the British government and the Protestants in Ireland, with Orangemen filling the ranks of the volunteer militia and gaining control of most of the civil service. Although it remains powerful in Ulster, the order lost much of its influence in Ireland after passage of the Catholic Emancipation Act of 1829. The lodges adopted a Masonic-type ritual and organization, providing for mutual aid and organizing social events. Orangemen who migrated to Britain and the colonies found the lodges useful in their adjustment to new environments.

The Grand Lodge of British North America was

Orangemen's Parade (1984), egg tempera by D.P. Brown, juxtaposes the Orange paraders and the Roman Catholic Church (*from the collection of J.B. Aird*).

founded 1 Jan 1830 in Brockville, UC, by Ogle R. Gowan. He sought to use the lodges as a base for a political career, bringing Catholics and Orangemen together in 1836 to support the conservative cause. By 1844 the power of the Orange vote induced John A. MACDONALD to become an Orangeman. There was a schism in 1853 over the Conservatives' alliance with the French Canadian Bleus. This was healed in 1856, but henceforth the Orange vote was divided. Orangemen have been accused of bringing old world quarrels to the new, but anti-Catholicism arrived in America with the Pilgrims. In Canada during the early 1860s, George Brown's liberal *Globe* accused Orange Grand Master Ogle Gowan of selling out the Protestant cause. Indeed, the Orange Grand Lodge acted as a brake on the ultraprotestant EQUAL RIGHTS ASSOCIATIONS of the 1880s and the American-based PROTESTANT PROTECTIVE ASSOCIATIONS of the 1890s. On both sides of the Atlantic, Orangemen have kept alive Irish Protestant folklore. The anniversary of the Battle of the Boyne is the Irish Protestant counterpart of St Patrick's Day. Its celebration is still an occasion for tension in Ulster, but in Canada it is merely one of many annual celebrations. The lodges reached the peak of their importance in Canada, both politically and socially, in the last quarter of the 19th century. They remained a force until the 1950s, and still retain some influence in rural communities.

HEREWARD SENIOR

Orangeville, Ont, Town, pop 14 440 (1986c), 13 740 (1981c), located 58 km NW of Toronto in Dufferin Co. Named for Orange Lawrence, a pioneer miller, the community became a village in 1863 and a town in 1874. The Toronto, Grey & Bruce Ry arrived in the 1870s. The town is now noted for well-preserved buildings. Industries produce appliances, wire & cable, chemical products, business forms, glass and furnaces.

K.L. MORRISON

Orchestral Music Composers of orchestral music, though they often use a piano as a point of reference in the composing process, conceive their work in terms of the musical colours, timbres and textures available only in an orchestra, which is an ensemble that may vary in size from about 30 musicians to over 100.

Orchestral instruments are divided into 4 families: strings, woodwinds, brass and percussion. Orchestral music is scored by the composer so that the various instrumental parts are arranged in a particular manner. Each bar of the musical score consists of as many staves as there are instrumental parts. A standard orchestral full score indicates the instrumental parts in the following order, from top to bottom: piccolo, flutes, oboes, English horn, clarinets, bass clarinet, bassoons, double bassoon, horns, trumpets, trombones, tuba, timpani (and other percussion instruments), harp (if any), violins I, violins II, violas, solo voice(s) and chorus (if any), keyboard (if any), cellos and double bass. In concertos the solo instrument's music is usually placed immediately above the strings' music. Conductors read the full score while individual players are provided with their respective parts.

Orchestral music is composed in a variety of forms, the most common being symphony, concerto, overture, suite and tone poem, and its styles change from age to age and from composer to composer. However, many orchestral works, especially contemporary compositions, defy neat labels. Although the history of European-style music in Canada dates back to the time of the explorers, orchestral compositions by Canadians have been produced mainly in the 20th century. The 19th-century French Canadian composer Calixa LAVALLÉE wrote a number of orchestral works, including 2 suites, one of which was performed in Paris in 1874. But these manuscripts, as well as those of some of his other works, are lost, and he is remembered primarily as the composer of "O Canada." The only Canadian orchestral work to be published before 1900 was Guillaume COUTURE's *Rêverie*, published by Girod soon after its performance in Paris in 1875.

A significant problem facing Canadian composers before the turn of the century was the lack of orchestras in this country. There were few permanent orchestras before the early years of the 20th century. In 1898 a Montreal Symphony Orchestra was formed that flourished for 20 consecutive seasons. A Halifax Symphony Orchestra, formed in 1897, lasted for several seasons. Vancouver, Regina, Winnipeg, Edmonton, Saskatoon, Moose Jaw and other cities had amateur orchestras before WWI. An orchestra was formed in Toronto in 1906, becoming in 1908 the first TORONTO SYMPHONY Orchestra, which performed regularly until 1918. The oldest orchestra in Canada is the Société symphonique de Québec (1902), which changed its name in 1942 to ORCHESTRE SYMPHONIQUE DE QUÉBEC.

Ontario-born Clarence Lucas, one of the most prolific Canadian composers of orchestral music during this period, is credited with writing symphonies, symphonic poems, overtures, cantatas and several operas. Other composers of the early

20th century include Alexis Contant, C.A.E. HARRISS, Donald Heins and Rodolphe MATHIEU.

The period between the wars saw a greater number of Canadian orchestral works being composed, but they were usually short because Canadian orchestras, when they could be persuaded to perform Canadian works at all, placed them at the beginning of a program as "warm-up" pieces. Particularly notable are Claude CHAMPAGNE's *Hercule et Omphale* (1918), Ernest MACMILLAN's *Concert Overture* (1924), Healey WILLAN's *Symphony No 1 in D minor* (1936) and works by Colin McPhee and Percival PRICE. A few longer works were also composed, often as doctoral exercises.

The establishment of the CANADIAN BROADCASTING CORPORATION in 1936 and the NATIONAL FILM BOARD in 1939 provided Canadian composers with new opportunities and outlets for orchestral music. Both organizations were keen to use original Canadian music and began to commission composers to write music for radio and film. John WEINZWEIG, Louis APPLEBAUM and Eldon Rathburn were among the first of many composers to have works commissioned by these organizations. Similarly, dance companies were being established during the 1940s, and they too began to commission works by Canadian composers. Walter Kaufmann's *Visages* and Robert FLEMING's *Chapter 13* were both commissioned by the Winnipeg Ballet in 1947. In 1949, 2 important works were commissioned: Jean PAPINEAU-COUTURE's *Papotages/Tittle-Tattle* for the Ballets Ruth Sorel of Montréal, and Weinzweig's *Red Ear of Corn* for the Boris Volkoff Canadian Ballet.

The CANADIAN LEAGUE OF COMPOSERS was formed in 1951 to promote the music and advance the professional interests of Canadian composers. Its 1957 *Catalogue of Orchestral Music* listed 233 works composed by Canadians between 1918 and 1957. The league was instrumental in setting up the CANADIAN MUSIC CENTRE in 1959. A nonprofit agency for the distribution and promotion of Canadian music in Canada and abroad, the CMC provides, among other services, a lending library of Canadian music. Though most Canadian orchestral works remain unpublished, copies are available through the CMC.

The commissioning of Canadian composers was given a major boost in 1957 with the establishment of the CANADA COUNCIL, a granting agency that provides funds to cover the composing and copying costs of commissions. Of 90 orchestral works sampled for the period 1968 to 1978, two-thirds were composed on commission and most of these through the assistance of the Canada Council. Furthermore, all orchestras that receive operating grants from the council are urged to devote at least 10% of their programming to the performance of Canadian music. Provincial arts councils make funds available for the commissioning of Canadian compositions.

With well-established orchestras throughout the country and organizations and agencies existing to assist the arts in general and composers specifically, the number of works composed for orchestras increased dramatically. The CMC's 1976 *Catalogue of Canadian Music for Orchestra* together with its 1979 *Supplement* list more than 1000 works by 145 composers.

Postwar composition in Canada has best been described as eclectic. One of the most influential composers is John Weinzweig. Born in Toronto in 1913, Weinzweig is credited with bringing the 12-tone technique to Canada. Among his students at U of T were Harry SOMERS, R. Murray SCHAFER, John BECKWITH, Samuel Dolin, Murray ADASKIN, Norma BEECROFT, Harry FREEDMAN, John Fodi and John Rea, all of whom became well-respected composers. The avant-garde in Canadian orchestral music is associated with the names of composers such as Pierre MERCURE, Serge GARANT, Bruce MATHER, Gilles TREMBLAY, Robert AITKEN, Barbara PENTLAND, István Anhalt, Otto Joachim and, in particular, R. Murray Schafer. Alexander BROTT has written more performed orchestral works than any other Canadian composer, and Roger Matton, Clermont PÉPIN and André Prévost are also important.

An examination of the season brochures of 15 major Canadian orchestras in the 1980s revealed that on average 70 different works by 39 Canadian composers were programmed. The 5 most frequently performed Canadian composers were Oskar MORAWETZ, Jacques Hétu, Godfrey RIDOUT, François MOREL and Violet ARCHER. *See also* MUSIC BROADCASTING; MUSIC HISTORY; and individual entries for the Edmonton, Montréal, Québec Toronto, Vancouver and Winnipeg symphony orchestras.　　　BARBARA NOVAK

Reading: Canadian Music Centre, *1976 Catalogue of Canadian Music for Orchestra* and *Supplement* (1979); *Encyclopedia of Music in Canada* (1981); C. Ford, *Canada's Music: An Historical Survey* (1982); H. Kallmann, *A History of Music in Canada, 1534-1914* (1960); R. Markow, "The Puzzle of Orchestral Programs," *Music Magazine* (Jan/Feb 1983).

Orchestre symphonique de Montréal was founded in 1934 as the Montreal Symphony Orchestra. It was the fourth orchestra established in Montréal (the first, 1894-96 was directed by Guillaume Couture; the second, 1898-1919, by J.J. Goulet; and the third, 1927-29, by J.J. Gagnier). In 1979 the MSO became the Orchestre symphonique de Montréal (OSM). Wilfrid PELLETIER was its first artistic director, 1935-40, followed by Désiré Defauw, 1940-52. Distinguished guest conductors led the orchestra until the appointment of Igor Markevitch, 1957-61. Under Zubin Mehta, 1961-67, the orchestra embarked in 1962 on the first European tour ever undertaken by a Canadian symphony orchestra. In 1963 it moved to new quarters in Place des Arts. The OSM toured Japan in 1970 under the direction of Franz-Paul Decker, 1967-75. In 1976 it made its US debut in Carnegie Hall under Rafael Frühbeck de Burgos,

The sound quality of the highly regarded recordings of the Orchestre symphonique de Montréal under conductor Charles Dutoit has been greatly enhanced by the marvellous acoustics of the church at St-Eustache, Qué (*courtesy Charles Dutoit/Orchestre symphonique de Montréal*).

who succeeded Decker. Charles Dutoit (b in Lausanne, Switz) took over as artistic director in 1978. Markevitch instituted the annual commissioning of a Canadian composition, and since 1965 the orchestra has sponsored an annual competition; winners of the Concours OSM are featured as soloists with the orchestra in concert. First prize winners in 1987 were Jamie Parker (piano) and Josée Allard (piano). The OSM has received 3 Performing Rights Organization of Canada awards for the exceptional quality of its contemporary music programming. Its recording of Ravel and Berlioz have led some critics to call the OSM the finest French orchestra today. Under Dutoit, the OSM's recordings, made in the church of St-Eustache, have been greeted with acclaim and have won many prizes. Its album *The Planets* won the 1987 Juno Award for Best Classical Album.　　　BARBARA NOVAK

Orchestre symphonique de Québec, founded in 1902, is the oldest active Canadian orchestra. It gave its first concert (28 Nov 1902) in Tara Hall under the direction of Joseph Vézina. It won the Earl Grey Trophy in Ottawa in 1907 and in 1924 Robert Talbot took over as conductor after Vézina's death. The society had financial and recruitment difficulties 1935-42 largely because of competition from the Cercle philharmonique de Québec (inc 1936). In 1942 the 2 groups merged, taking the name of Orchestre symphonique de Québec, with Edwin Bélanger as conductor. Wilfrid PELLETIER succeeded him in 1951. He in turn was replaced by Françoys Bernier (1960) who took the orchestra touring throughout Québec and added several Canadian works to its repertory. These 2 directors brought in a number of internationally celebrated guest soloists, including Wilhelm Kempff and David Oistrakh. Bernier succeeded Pelletier as artistic director in 1966; subsequent artistic directors have been Pierre Dervaux (1968), James de Preist (1976) and Simon Streatfeild (1983). François Magnan has been director-general since 1972. The orchestra won an award from the Performing Rights Organization of Canada Ltd for having given a prominent place to contemporary works in its programs (1977-78). Among Canadian works commissioned and performed by the OSQ are *Mouvement symphonique no 1* and *no 3* as well as the *Te Deum* of Roger Matton; *Ouranos* by Serge GARANT; *Concerto for piano and orchestra* by Jacques Hétu; *Chorégraphie II* by Andre PRÉVOST and *Le Dict de l'aigle et du castor* by Gilles VIGNEAULT, Claude LÉVEILLÉE and Neil CHOTEM.　　　HÉLÈNE PLOUFFE

Orchid, perennial herbaceous plant of family Orchidaceae. The family is one of the largest among flowering plants, represented by 735 genera and 20 000 species worldwide. The genera hybridize readily. Most orchids are tropical and epiphytic (ie, grow in moss and debris on tree branches), but the 17 genera and 63 species native to Canada are terrestrial. Orchids are found throughout Canada. Some are arctic, eg, *Habenaria albida* and *H. hyperborea;* most grow in moist, wooded areas, eg, *Cypripedium,* LADY'S SLIPPER, which has large, striking flowers varying from white through yellow to pink. *Calypso bulbosa* has similar but smaller, delicate pink flowers. Some *Spiranthes* and *Habenaria* species have small, whitish, fragrant flowers in a spike. Two genera, *Eburophyton* (plant is white) and *Corallorhiza* (plant is yellow to purple), live on decaying vegetable matter. Attempts to transplant orchids from the wild usually result in the plants' death. Orchids are recognized internationally as endangered species, and trade in wild orchids is prohibited.　　　PATRICK SEYMOUR

Order-in-council, at the federal level, is an order of the GOVERNOR GENERAL by and with the

Striped coral-root orchid (*Corallorhiza striata*) (*photo by Mary W. Ferguson*).

advice and consent of the Queen's PRIVY COUNCIL for Canada. In fact, it is formulated by CABINET or a committee of Cabinet and formally approved by the governor general. Some orders simply make appointments. About a third are legislative, forming part of the law and enforceable by the courts. Most legislative orders are made under authority expressly conferred by ACT of Parliament. With the expansion of state activity in recent decades (public ownership, state regulation of industry, social security), it has become impossible for Parliament to legislate directly and in detail to meet complex and varying problems, and more and more Acts are cast in general terms and empower the governor-in-council to make regulations to carry out the intent of the legislation. Such regulations on, for example, unemployment insurance, fisheries and aeronautics, now form an enormous part of our law (*see* REGULATORY PROCESS). They are called "subordinate legislation" because they are made by the governor-in-council, subordinate to Parliament, and are subordinate to, and limited by, the Act which authorizes them. A few legislative orders are based on royal prerogative (the relatively small remainder of the SOVEREIGN's ancient law-making power) but are limited by the content of the particular prerogative which confers the power to make them (*see* ADMINISTRATIVE LAW). Provincial orders-in-council – orders of the lieutenant-governor-in-councils – are similar to federal ones.　　　EUGENE A. FORSEY

Order of Canada, centrepiece of the Canadian system of HONOURS, was instituted on 1 July 1967, the 100th anniversary of Confederation. Every Canadian is eligible for the order, which is conferred in recognition of exemplary merit and achievement in all major fields of endeavour. Appointments are made by the governor general, based on the recommendations of the Advisory Council of the Order, which meets twice a year under the chairmanship of the chief justice of Canada to consider nominations submitted by members of the public.

When it was created in 1967, there were 2 ranks, Companion and Medal of Service. There are now 3 levels of membership, in which the number of appointments is limited: Companion (not to exceed 150 at any one time) for "out-

Order of Canada, centrepiece of the Canadian system of honours, est 1 July 1967, on the 100th anniversary of Confederation. It is conferred in recognition of exemplary merit and achievement (*courtesy National Archives of Canada/4386/photo by John Evans*).

standing achievement and merit of the highest degree"; Officer (46 appointments maximum in any year) for "achievement and merit of a high degree"; and Member (92 appointments maximum in any year) for "distinguished service in or to a particular locality, group or field activity". Companions may be appointed only when a vacancy occurs. Recipients of the Officer or Member level may be upgraded. Investitures take place each spring and autumn at the governor general's official residence, Rideau Hall, Ottawa. The order's badge is in the form of a stylized snowflake of 6 points and is worn at the neck by Companions and Officers and on the left breast by Members. Recipients are entitled to have placed after their names the letters representing the category in which each is appointed: CC, OC or CM, and all may wear a small replica of the badge on street clothes. The motto on the awards is *Desiderantes meliorem patriam*, meaning "they desire a better country." CARL LOCHNAN

Order of Military Merit In 1972 the Canadian HONOURS system was extended to include the Order of Military Merit in recognition of exceptional service. All regular and reserve personnel of the ARMED FORCES are eligible. There are 3 grades of membership: Commander, Officer and Member. The number of appointments made yearly may not exceed 0.1% of the strength of the Armed Forces; of that number 6% may be made Commanders, 30% Officers and the remainder Members. The appointments are made by the governor general on recommendation by the minister of national defence. A list of members is available from the Chancellery of Canadian Orders and Decorations, Government House, Ottawa.

The badge is a blue enamelled cross patée (ie, a cross with expanding arms) with a dark blue ribbon edged in gold. The badge of Commander is worn at the neck, those of Officer and Member on the left breast. Recipients are entitled to place after their names the initials corresponding to their grades: CMM, OMM or MMM.

CARL LOCHNAN

Order of St John, formally The Most Venerable Order of the Hospital of St John of Jerusalem, is a religious military order founded in the 11th century at the time of the Crusades and named for the Church of St John the Baptist in Jerusalem where a hospital for sick pilgrims was established. (The order still maintains the hospital in Jerusalem.) The revival of the order in Britain occurred in the reign of Queen Victoria, who became head of the order in the British realm; succeeding monarchs have continued this office. The order focused on the need for care of the injured during the Industrial Revolution. In this way the St John Ambulance Assn and the St John Brigade were established, the former to teach first aid and the latter to set up a uniformed brigade of workers for the care of the injured in mines and other industries.

In 1883 the St John Ambulance Assn and the brigade began work in Canada. It has continued caring for injured people at the site of their employment or in large crowds, and also teaching first aid to the general public. During the 1960s the Order of St John was instrumental in promoting the use of mouth-to-mouth resuscitation in Canada, which is now universally accepted, along with cardio-pulmonary resuscitation, as the most effective method of saving lives. St John Ambulance has councils in each province and territory, some 25 000 volunteers, 8750 certified instructors and over 300 staff members. It trains over 400 000 Canadians each year in first aid, cardio-pulminary resuscitation and health care.

As the queen is head of the order of Canada, the governor general and all lieutenant-governors automatically become, at the time of their appointment, Knights of the Order of St John. The present knights of the order are those who have given particular service to the work of the order. Others who have rendered service may become members of the order in the ranks of serving brother or sister, officer brother or sister, or commander brother or sister. HARVEY D. HEBB

Ordre de Bon Temps ("Order of Good Cheer"), fd at PORT-ROYAL in 1606 by Samuel de CHAMPLAIN. After a disastrous winter at STE CROIX I, when many of the French settlers perished from scurvy, the colony was moved to Port-Royal in 1605.

Order of Military Merit, est 1972 and awarded to regular and reserve personnel of the Armed Forces in recognition of exceptional service (*courtesy National Archives of Canada/4389/photo by John Evans*).

Scurvy again took its toll but the following year the colony enjoyed a more pleasant winter. "We passed this winter most joyously, & fared lavishly," wrote Champlain, and in this genial atmosphere he founded the order – modelled loosely on a European order of chivalry – to maintain spirits and pass the time. Members took turns providing fresh game and, as chief steward of the day, leading a ceremonial procession to the table.

JAMES MARSH

Ordre de Jacques-Cartier (familiarly La Patente), fd 1926, a secret, hierarchically structured French Canadian society. It spread through French Canada during the 1930s but never had many more than 10 000 members, who were recruited primarily among the bourgeois elite. The society championed various religious and national causes, infiltrated scores of existing organizations and promoted public-opinion campaigns linked to morality, anticommunism, education and the French language. Its actual influence, however, remains debatable. After it officially disbanded in 1965, it unsuccessfully attempted to reconstitute itself regionally. RICHARD JONES

Ordre national du Québec (National Order of Québec) is the highest distinction conferred by the Government of Québec. Founded 20 June 1984, it seeks to pay tribute to individuals born or living in Québec who, through their high achievements and exceptional merit, inspire pride and gratitude among the people of Québec. The order's motto, "Honour to the people of Québec," reflects the democratic approach to the selection of its new members, which occurs in the following manner. First, a public notice is published in Québec's daily newspapers inviting readers to nominate candidates. Then the council, which is elected by the members of the order, makes its recommendations to the premier. After they are confirmed by decree, the premier announces the names of new members and their grade (high officer, officer or knight). They receive insignia at a ceremony held during the Semaine de la Fête nationale. GISÈLE VILLENEUVE

Oregon Treaty, 15 June 1846 between Britain and the US, describing the boundary between BNA and the US west of the Rocky (or Stony) Mts. A compromise between the American desire for a boundary with Russian Alaska at 54°40' N lat to the Columbia R mouth, the treaty set the boundary at 49° to the middle of the channel between the mainland and Vancouver I, thence through the middle of the channel and Juan de Fuca Str to the Pacific. But the "middle of the channel" could have followed either Rosario Str or Haro Str between the Str of Georgia and Juan de Fuca Str and and between them lay San Juan I which was claimed by both Britain and the US. The Americans landed troops on the island in 1859. The boundary through the strait thus remained in doubt until 1872, when it was referred to the German emperor, Wilhelm I, for arbitration. The settlement favoured the US claim, ie, Haro Str. N.L. NICHOLSON

O'Reilly, Gerald, physician (b at Ballinlough, Ire 11 Aug 1806; d at Hamilton, Canada W 26 Feb 1861). After medical studies in Dublin, Ire, and London, Eng, he immigrated in 1833 to Hamilton, where he was a prominent practitioner. In addition to his wide private practice, he served publicly as surgeon to the Hamilton jail, to the 3rd Gore Militia and to Wentworth and Halton counties. He was a founder, original shareholder and medical officer to the Canada Life Assurance Co, as well as one of the first to hold a policy. Presumably his widow collected on it at his early death, from blood poisoning, after a minor operation. CHARLES G. ROLAND

Orford String Quartet was formed in 1965 at the JEUNESSES MUSICALES DU CANADA Orford Art Centre at Mt Orford, Qué, and consisted of Andrew Dawes and Kenneth Perkins, violinists, Terence Helmer, violist, and Marcel St. Cyr, cellist. The quartet remained the same until 1980 when Denis Brott replaced St. Cyr; in 1986-87 Robert Levine replaced Helmer and was himself replaced 1 Aug 1987 by Sophie Renshaw. After its initial concert, the quartet embarked on a series of JMC Canadian tours, which in turn were followed by JMC engagements abroad. The 1967 Carnegie Hall debut brought great praise and signalled a very successful international touring career which was assisted financially by the CANADA COUNCIL and the Dept of External Affairs. Based in Toronto since 1965, and in great demand as concert performers throughout Canada, the group became U of T quartet in residence in 1968. Subsequently, its master classes, individual recitals and performances of complete cycles, such as the 16 Beethoven quartets at Walter Hall in Toronto in 1977, and repeated at Festival Ottawa, have made the Orford Quartet one of the best known and most highly regarded string quartets in the world. It has received many awards, including the valuable MOLSON PRIZE in 1976, Canadian Music Council awards in 1978 and 1986 for its performances in concert and its many recordings. Its repertoire includes virtually all of the quartet literature as well as works requiring additional performers. It has also served Canadian composers well and has encouraged many aspiring young string players. Frequently the guest performers at festivals across Canada, the "Orfords," as they are affectionately known, are also featured performers at festivals abroad. Their list of recordings, which includes the Beethoven quartets on the Delos Label (1987), is a clear indication of the breadth of their musicianship.　MABEL H. LAINE

Organ Music and Organ Building The sound of an organ was first heard in a Québec church in 1660-61, some 60 years ahead of our American neighbours. Records show that 2 organs were in use in Québec Cathedral by 1663-64. It is likely that the organ compositions used at the time were, as in most French organ literature, short and clearly divided into sections. This facilitated the French *alternatim* practice of interspersing the organ pieces with chanted passages sung by the choir. The recently discovered *Livre d'orgue de Montréal* (repr 1981), brought to Québec in 1724 by Jean Girard (1696-1765), suggests that this French tradition was an accepted and well-established part of liturgical life in New France.

The monumental English influence was Healey WILLAN who came to Canada in 1913. His renowned *Introduction, Passacaglia and Fugue* (1916) set a Canadian standard for original organ compositions and his music for church use led to an exhaustive list of practical compositions for amateur church organists, based primarily on hymn tunes. Stemming from this English tradition, a number of fine original and practical compositions have been added to the body of Canadian organ works. Notable Anglo-Canadian composers include Gerhard Wuensch, Gerald Bales, Barrie Cabena, Derek Healy, Bengt HAMBRAEUS, Gerhard Krapf and Jacobus Kloppers.

The Franco-Canadian contributions remained rooted in the French romantic tradition of César Franck, Louis Vierne and others. Significant additions to organ literature include works by Raymond DAVELUY, François MOREL, Roger MATTON, André PRÉVOST, Maurice Dela and Otto JOACHIM.

All of the early organs in 17th-century New France were small, imported from Europe, and reflected the liturgical demands of the time. This pattern of importing French-style instruments re-mained undisturbed except for one Canadian-built organ completed in 1723 by a young Montréal carpenter, Paul-Raymond Jourdain, which was apparently his first and last instrument. The English influence in organ building began in 1786 when an instrument, or at least an addition to an existing organ, was imported for St Paul's Church in Halifax. Several imported organs followed, but by 1824 the work of a French emigrant, Jean-Baptiste Jacotel, had established a Canadian tradition of organ building. The first Canadian-born builder was Joseph Casavant (1807-74) whose sons, Claver and Samuel, established CASAVANT FRÈRES LTÉE, still one of Canada's leading organ builders. Other notable 19th- and early 20th-century builders included Samuel Russell Warren, Louis Mitchel, and Napoléon Déry, whose work in Québec was to be a strong impetus for the organ revival movement in Canada.

All of the early builders relied on the traditional mechanical or tracker-action method of construction for their organs but, by the late 19th century, organs that made use of electric action in one way or another soon took over in the marketplace. From 1893 on, the Casavant brothers devoted themselves to the development of an electro-pneumatic organ design; the last tracker-action instrument built by Casavant Frères for more than 60 years was completed in 1902.

The organ reform movement, which sought to restore traditional methods of organ building (mechanical or tracker-action) and encouraged a revival of the organ's baroque sound, began in Germany shortly after WWI but did not reach Canada until mid-century. In 1959 the first new tracker-action organ, built by Rudolf von Beckerath of Germany, was installed in Montréal. Spurred by this first new revival organ, a few dedicated Québec organists formed a group in 1960 known as *Ars Organi* to further the performance of organ literature on the best examples of tracker-action organs. Largely through their efforts, Casavant Frères began building tracker-action organs again in 1963. A number of important small firms devoted to building tracker-action instruments after the ideals of the organ reform movement have emerged. Among the best known are organ builders Hellmuth Wolff, André Guibault, Guy Thérien, Karl Wilhelm, Fernand Létourneau, Gerhard Brunzema, Adrian Koppejan, and Gabriel Kney. Modelled on solid historical foundations, Canadian organ builders in the 1980s hold a reputation that rivals the best in the world.　BRUCE A. WHEATCROFT

Organized Crime has been officially defined by the Canadian police as "two or more persons consorting together on a continuing basis to participate in illegal activities, either directly or indirectly, for gain"; it has been defined by a former US organized crime boss as "just a bunch of people getting together to take all the money they can from all the suckers they can. Organized crime is a chain of command all the way from London to Canada, the US, Mexico, Italy, France, everywhere." There is much more to organized crime in Canada and the US than the Italian criminal association known as the Mafia, Cosa Nostra or Honoured Society. In N America, just about every major national or ethnic group and every segment of society has been involved in organized crime. American criminologist Dr Francis Ianni has developed a theory explaining how organized criminal activity is developed and passed on in N America from one ethnic group to another, based on the length of time the group has been in N America, the language and cultural knots that bind the group, and the degree to which the group's members have been assimilated into the prevailing society.

For a long time many scholars and academics did not believe organized crime was highly structured or capable of sophisticated operations. Their skepticism derived partly from a reaction to the Hollywood portrayal of the Mafia from the 1930s to the 1950s, typified in its treatment of Al Capone ("Scarface"), and partly from the fact that documented, scholarly studies and books on organized crime did not exist.

All this changed because of the revelations at the US Senate "Valachi" hearings in the early 1960s; because of the documentary evidence from police wiretaps and bugs in the 1970s, which allowed police to listen to Mafia leaders discussing their hierarchy and operations in both the US and Canada; and partly because of the establishment of the American Witness Protection Program, by which Mafia defectors and informers could build a new life.

Through various court cases and royal commissions and through television and newspaper exposés, the existence of a highly organized criminal network in Canada became known to the Canadian public in the late 1970s. In 1984 a joint federal-provincial committee of justice officials estimated that organized crime in Canada took in about $20 billion annually, almost $10 billion of which was from the sales of narcotics. (There is no way of estimating, however, the amount of dirty funds that are "laundered" in Canada by members of organized crime in the US and other foreign countries. *See* UNDERGROUND ECONOMY.) The committee was formed in response to a 1980 report on organized crime by the BC attorney general's office, which claimed that organized crime figures in Canada had interests in the textile industry, cheese industry, building industry, disposal industry, vending-machine companies, meat companies, home-insulation companies, autobody shops and car dealerships, among others. The joint committee calculated that the sources of organized crime revenues could be broken down as follows: PORNOGRAPHY, PROSTITUTION, bookmaking, gaming houses, illegal LOTTERIES, other GAMBLING offences, loansharking and extortion, which together brought in an estimated $567.3 million.

Other activities, such as WHITE-COLLAR CRIMES (eg, insurance and construction frauds and illegal bankruptcies), arson, bank robberies and motor vehicle thefts, raised the estimate to $10 billion; drugs accounted for the rest.

Mafia Of all the organized-crime groups operating in Canada, the Mafia is perhaps the best known. This is because the Québec crime probe report of 1976 (which was based primarily on the information gathered by the "bug" planted in the milk cooler of the Montréal mobster Paulo Violi's headquarters) revealed the structure of the Montréal Mafia and its interrelationship with and dependency on the US Mafia family of Joe Bonanno. Public knowledge of the Mafia is also the result of media attention, eg, the "Connections" series broadcast by CBC TV in the late 1970s.

Scholars do not agree on the origin of the term "Mafia," referring to the original organization in Sicily. According to the Québec Organized Crime Commission's report of 1977, it describes "a state of mind, a feeling of pride, a philosophy of life and a style of behaviour. The mark of a known and respected man, it derives from the Sicilian adjective *mafiusu*, used since the 18th century to describe magnificent or perfect people." While originally a Sicilian society, the Mafia was exported and adapted to N America by a small group of Italian immigrants. Joe Bonanno, a self-described Mafia don, describes it thus in his memoirs: "Mafia is a process, not a thing. Mafia is a form of clan co-operation to which its individual members pledge lifelong loyalty. Friendship connections, family ties, trust, loyalty, obedience – this was the 'glue' that held us together." In Sicily, and later in the US and Canada, Mafia came to refer to an organized international body of criminals of Sicilian origin, but it is now applied to the present dominant force in organized crime – the predominately Sicilian and Calabrian organized-crime groupings or "families." These families are held together by a code emphasizing respect for senior family members; by "Omerta," ie, a vow of silence about the family's activities; by the structure or hierarchy of the family; and by an initiation rite or ceremony.

Although Italian crime families (such as the old Rocco Perri gang in Hamilton) have been active in Canada since the prohibition era, they have since operated in more clearly structured and defined areas acceptable to other crime families. Many of the Canadian Mafia families immigrated in the 1940s and 1950s and went to work with older, established Mafia figures, settling in Montréal, Toronto, Hamilton and Vancouver. Though located mainly in the major cities, family members tend to gravitate to where wealth moves; thus, in the late 1970s and early 1980s, some moved westward following the movement of business to BC and Alberta.

Structure of the Mafia in Canada In Toronto until recently at least 4 major Mafia-style criminal organizations were run by Canadians of Sicilian or Calabrian origin, 2 of whom were named as members of the Mafia during the Valachi hearings. Since the murder of Paul Volpe (Nov 1983), his old organization has lost its control. The Hamilton organized-crime family, connected with the Magaddino family of Buffalo, NY, has tried to move into the vacuum caused by the deaths, murders and imprisonments of leading members of the other organizations. A third group, also active in Hamilton, is connected with the Magaddino organized-crime family in Buffalo. The most recently established of the 4 is a family known as the Siderno group, so called because many of the members are from the town of Siderno and its environs in Calabria.

In Montréal the major Mafia family is known as the Cotroni family. Led by the late Vincenzo "Vic" Cotroni (the "godfather") and his brother Frank, it constituted the first significant crime family in Canada. The Québec crime probe exposed the membership and activities of this highly structured group in a number of its reports. Established in the 1940s by Vic Cotroni, the family evolved in the 1950s into an important branch of the powerful New York City Mafia family of Joe Bonanno. It has extensive ties with Mafia families in Italy and throughout the US, as well as with the Toronto, Hamilton and Vancouver organizations.

A serious challenge to the supremacy of the Cotroni family in Québec came from the Dubois family, an indigenous French Canadian gang, comprising 9 brothers, which dominated crime in the west end of Montréal until the early 1980s.

Serious internal problems between Sicilians and Calabrians in the Montréal organization led to the violent deaths of Paulo Violi (the chief lieutenant of Vic Cotroni) and his brothers in the late 1970s. The Cotroni family has primarily been involved in illegal gambling, loansharking, drug importation (utilizing the famous French Connection), extortion, and the murder and corruption of public officials.

Other Groups Motorcycle gangs such as the Hell's Angels, the Outlaws, Satan's Choice, and the Grim Reapers have become significantly involved in organized crime. Their initiation rights have made it difficult for law enforcement officers to penetrate the groups, which have become major suppliers of illegal drugs. They have also been involved in prostitution and contract killing. It is now not unusual to find them working with other organized crime groups.

Various Chinese and Vietnamese organized-crime groups have become more prominent over the past 20 years in Vancouver and Toronto, following a wave of immigration from Hong Kong in the 1960s and 1970s. Chinese youth gangs in Toronto and Vancouver are involved in protection rackets and extortion, but the more sophisticated groups are organized by senior "Triad" members from Hong Kong to import heroin from Southeast Asia through Vancouver. The Triads are ancient Chinese organizations that have evolved into organized-crime groupings.

The organized-crime structure changes quickly in Canada, and usually exists for some years before it is detected in cities or locations; therefore, there are undoubtedly other groups that have not yet been identified.

Activities of Organized Crime Organized crime in Canada provides some illegal services which certain sectors of the general public want, eg, gambling, prostitution, loansharking and the sale of soft drugs such as hashish, marijuana, speed and cocaine. In every large Canadian city, local bookmakers are involved in organized crime through an elaborate playoff system established to protect the individual bookie from large losses. Other organized-crime activities are not so readily desired by society at large. They involve the importation and distribution of hard drugs such as heroin (many drugs of the French Connection came into the US through Montréal with local Mafia involvement), the fencing of stolen goods, and murder and extortion. Other activities that aid and abet organized crime include the ongoing corruption of public officials and the "laundering" of the proceeds of criminal activities.

One of the simplest ways to "launder" money is to use activities in which there is a constant flow of cash, eg, slot machines and gambling. If the owner of a gambling casino claims to have taken in $1 million when he has actually taken in only $100 000, to which has been added $900 000 of illegally obtained money, it is almost impossible to demonstrate that the $1 million was not procured in the normal course of business.

Corruption Without corruption, organized crime would find it very difficult to exist, and the efforts of organized crime to corrupt police, judges, politicians, lawyers, and government and civilian officials are probably more deleterious to society than any other activity in which it engages. WILLIAM I. MACADAM AND JAMES R. DUBRO

Reading: J.P. Charbonneau, *The Canadian Connection* (1976); James R. Dubro, *Mob Rule* (1985) and *King of the Mob* (1987); C. Kirby and T. Renner, *Mafia Assassin* (1986); W. Rowland, *Making Connections* (1979).

Orienteering is a sport in which participants navigate with the aid of a map and compass around a prescribed course, checking in at specified and clearly marked control points. It is done on foot, either by walking, jogging or running, and can be done individually or in groups. In organized competitions the competitor completing the course in the fastest time is the winner. Orienteering combines athletic ability and mental exercise: participants continually have to choose among possible routes between control points. It is this unique combination that has caused orienteering to be described as "the thinking man's sport."

Newspaper records show that some orienteering activities took place in Norway and Sweden in the 1890s; however, it is generally accepted that orienteering as an organized sport began in Sweden in 1919 with Major Ernst Killander the acknowledged founder. Orienteering remained essentially a Scandinavian sport until after WWII when it spread throughout Europe. First introduced in Canada in 1948, it was the mid-1960s before any significant development was seen. The Canadian Orienteering Federation (COF) was founded in 1967 and the first Canadian championship was held in 1968. In 1969 the COF was accepted as a member of the International Orienteering Federation (IOF).

The first World Orienteering Championships were held in Finland in 1966 and a Canadian team competed for the first time in 1972. World championships are held every 2 years with teams of 5 men and 5 women representing each country. Norway and Sweden, and then Finland, Denmark, Switzerland and Hungary have dominated the world championships. The best Canadian performances in the world championships have been, for men, Ted de St. Croix, Ottawa, 10th, and for women, Denise DeMonte, Hamilton, 18th, at the 1985 event in Australia. Ted de St. Croix won the Canadian Elite Men's Championship 11 consecutive years 1976-86. In Sweden each July a mammoth 5-day competition called the "O'Ringen" is held. This event, with over 25 000 competitors for each of the 5 days, is recognized as the largest single participant sport event in the world. COLIN KIRK

Orillia, Ont, City, pop 24 077 (1986c), 23 995 (1981c), inc 1867 (village), 1875 (town), 1969 (city), located at the narrows between lakes SIMCOE and Couchiching in central Ontario. The site was originally used by a band of Ojibwa led by Chief William Yellowhead. White settlement forced them to move in 1838-39 to nearby Rama. "Orillia" means riverbank in Spanish; the name was applied by Sir Peregrine MAITLAND, lieutenant-governor of UC 1818-28, who had served in Spain. Originally logging and farming were the bases of the economy; later in the 19th century Orillia developed into a summer resort area. In 1902 Orillia established the first municipally owned hydroelectric generating station in Canada, on the nearby Severn R. Orillia served as the model for "Mariposa" in humorist Stephen LEACOCK's satire on small-town Ontario life, SUNSHINE SKETCHES OF A LITTLE TOWN (1912). The manuscript of *Sunshine Sketches* and a collection of Leacock's papers are held in the summer home, at nearby Old Brewery Bay, where he wrote many of his books. DANIEL FRANCIS

Oriole, common name for members of 2 families of birds. The Old World family Oriolidae occurs from Europe through Africa and Asia to Australia. In the Western Hemisphere, the name refers to brightly coloured, black and yellow or orange birds of genus *Icterus*, family Emberizidae. Thirty species of these melodious songbirds are known, with greatest diversity found in Mexico and Central America. In most species males are larger and more brightly coloured than females. Yearling males often resemble females, perhaps reducing predation or aggression from older males. Two species breed in Canada. The orchard oriole (*I. spurius*) breeds locally in southern Ontario and recently in Manitoba. Northern orioles (*I. galbula*), common throughout southern Canada, breed in scattered trees and open woodland, weaving pendulous nests of plant fibres and hair. The female lays 4-5 greyish white eggs marked with brown or black scrawls. Northern orioles consume insects and small fruits. They winter from southern Mexico to Colombia and Venezuela. The term "northern oriole" is a recent taxonomic revision and includes the Baltimore (*I. galbula*) and Bullock's orioles (*I. bullockii*).

R.J. ROBERTSON

Orion, and Other Poems Sir Charles G.D. ROBERTS's first book, *Orion, and Other Poems*, was published by J.B. Lippincott & Co of Philadelphia in 1880, an event which is widely seen as marking the renaissance of POETRY in Canada. In a stirring and famous tribute, Archibald LAMPMAN wrote that "It seemed to me a wonderful thing that such work could be done by a Canadian....It was like a voice from some new paradise of art, calling us to be up and doing." Ironically, despite its influence, *Orion* does not contain Roberts's best work; the poems, many of them based on classical mythology, are derivative and tedious. It is only in Roberts's second book, *In Divers Tones* (1886), that poems such as "The Tantramar Revisited" and "The Potato Harvest" begin to justify Lampman's historic faith.

STEPHEN SCOBIE

Orkneymen Immigrants from the Orkney Is, off the N coast of Scotland, played a major and largely unrecognized part in the exploration and settlement of Canada's North-West in the 18th and 19th centuries. The majority came as labourers and boatmen for the HUDSON'S BAY CO until 1870, although the practice of hiring Orkneymen for their northern stores continued until the mid-20th century. Inhabitants of the Orkney Is, sometimes known as Orcadians, have been characterized as farmers who fish: they dwell on some of the most fertile land in the British Is and they are surrounded by the sea. In the 1700s, the Orkney Is emerged from centuries of isolation as a source of manpower for fishing and whaling fleets in peacetime and the Royal Navy in times of war. The HBC, always able to recognize a bargain, was soon attracted to the same recruiting ground where good men could be had for less than half the wages enjoyed by Londoners.

The first Orkneymen were brought out in the first decade of the 18th century, but the practice did not become regular until the 1730s. At the peak of their involvement with the HBC in 1800, Orkneymen comprised 80% of a labour force of almost 500. The majority of the company's men at the bay were Scots from these northern isles until 1810 when steps were taken to diversify recruitment, although Orkneymen continued to be favoured for some positions, including those of boatmen and fishermen.

Although most of the Orkneymen returned home after a few years of service in relatively menial positions, a few chose to stay on. Some rose to positions of prominence, including Joseph Isbister, governor at York Factory in the 1740s; William Tomison, a later governor at the same place and founder of Edmonton; and Sir John RAE, the Arctic explorer who discovered the fate of the Franklin Expedition. After 1810 many decided to take up land in the Red River settlement where they were joined by the country-born offspring of their unions with native women. The Orkneymen and these offspring played a pivotal role in the early history of Manitoba and the Canadian West. In their number can be found prominent historic figures such as the Hon John NORQUAY, premier of Manitoba. Descendants of the Orcadian employees of the Hudson's Bay Co can now be found in every province and territory, but the majority still live in the West and the North in the land that their ancestors first came to more than 250 years ago.

JOHN S. NICKS

Orléans Île d', 190 km², 33.3 km long by 8 km wide, is situated just downstream from QUÉBEC C in the ST LAWRENCE R. The largest island in the river after the island of Montréal, it is a relatively level plateau, 137 m at its highest point, and steep sided. It is surrounded by wide sandbanks on the N and a narrow bank on the S. The plateau is the vestige of an old eroded Appalachian surface, progressively isolated from the mainland by 2 river channels until it formed an island. The central part is wooded; the island is very fertile and drained by the Maheu, la Fleur, Dauphine and du Moulin rivers. Jacques CARTIER called it Île de Bacchus in 1535 because of the vines growing there, and rebaptized it Île d'Orléans in 1536 to honour the duc d'Orléans.

In 1636 the island was granted to 8 associates by the COMPAGNIE DE LA NOUVELLE FRANCE. It became Île Ste-Marie during the HURON settlement of 1650 to 1657. These first farmers, installed on land belonging to Éléonore de Grandmaison at the far upstream end, were massacred in 1656 by the Iroquois. Land clearing began again in 1660. The parish of Ste-Famille was founded in 1661 and the first church built in 1669 (*see* RELIGIOUS BUILDING). Jean de Lauson, seneschal of New France, fell victim to Iroquois in 1661. The island became the property of Mgr de LAVAL, first bishop of Québec, in 1668 (it had 471 inhabitants, as many as Québec). It was ceded as a fiefdom to François Berthelot in 1675, under the name of Isle de St-Laurent. The parishes of St-Pierre, St-François and St-Jean were founded in 1679. St-Paul parish became St-Laurent parish in 1698, and a precise map of the island was made in 1689 by Robert de Villeneuve.

By 1725, again under the name of Île d'Orléans, it was very prosperous. In 1759 it was used as a base for British operations against Québec and was ransacked by the troops of WOLFE and Guy CARLETON. In 1824 and 1825 a short-lived naval yard at the upstream end of the island built the *Columbus* and the *Baron Renfrew*. A seaport developed at this site and became the Ste-Pétronille parish in 1870. Île d'Orléans has been immortalized in a Felix Leclerc song, "Le tour de l'Île." Agriculture still thrives, and the island's beauty, historical buildings, handicraft and horticultural products draw many tourists.

SERGE OCCHIETTI

Ormsby, Margaret Anchoretta, historian, educator (b at Quesnel, BC 7 June 1909). Educated at UBC and Bryn Mawr, she joined the department of history at UBC in 1943 and was head of the department, 1965-74. Her research and teaching made major contributions to the knowledge of the history of her native province. Although always a "British Columbia loyalist," a major theme of her work is the relationship of the province to the larger Confederation. *British Columbia: A History* (1958; rev 1971), her most important work, displays a characteristically fine literary style which has helped to make the book popular with the general public. A member of the Historic Sites and Monuments Board of Canada (1960-68) and president of the Canadian Historical Assn (1965), she was also made a member of the Royal Society (1966).

MARGARET E. PRANG

Reading: John Norris, "Margaret Ormsby," in John Norris and Margaret Prang, eds, *Personality and History in British Columbia: Essays in Honour of Margaret Ormsby* (*B.C. Studies*, No 32, Winter 1976-77).

Ornamentals, in horticulture, are woody and herbaceous plants used primarily as amenities. Woody ornamentals are perennial (ie, persist for more than 2 years) and include trees, shrubs and vines; herbaceous ornamentals are annual, biennial or perennial (persist for one, 2 or more years) and make up the vast array of things that provide colour in flower beds and borders. In Canada, winter hardiness is very important to growers of woody ornamentals. The ability of a woody plant to survive a Canadian winter of moderate severity depends largely on the annual stage of maturity reached and the cold resistance achieved by the end of the growing season. Plants that require a long season in which to mature seldom achieve this state when grown in regions with short growing seasons.

Winter hardiness does not present the same problem with herbaceous ornamentals. Annuals do not overwinter. When the normal growing season is not long enough for them to grow and produce FLOWERS, the grower simply starts them indoors (eg, in a GREENHOUSE), and transplants them outside when the risk of frost is over. The common snapdragon, for example, is generally seeded in the greenhouse in Feb and planted outside in late May or early June. If such plants were seeded directly outdoors in May, in regions where the frost-free period is 90 days or less, they could blossom for only a few weeks before being killed by frost. Herbaceous biennials and perennials are allowed to remain in the soil all year; their winter survival is generally assured if they receive adequate snow cover to protect them from severe temperatures and prevent alternate freezing and thawing of the soil around the roots.

Generally, ornamentals are either selected forms of specific plants (ie, cultivars or commercial varieties) or hybrids between species. Because of the winter-hardiness problem, many woody ornamental cultivars and hybrids have been derived from plants indigenous to Canada and the northern US. However, plants from NW China, Manchuria, Siberia and Korea, regions with climates similar to many of our own, have provided good parent material for new hybrids, as well as making a valuable contribution on their own. Herbaceous ornamentals are also made up of cultivars and hybrids. Improvement programs involving hybridization, both within and between species, are commonplace. Hardy perennials and biennials are chiefly temperate-region plants; annuals derive mainly from South African and Californian natives.

The Canadian Ornamental Plant Foundation was chartered by the federal government in 1964 to promote selection, testing and distribution of better ornamental plant varieties. The procedures have provided breeders of new cultivars with the means of getting worthwhile new introductions into the trade and, thence, to the general public. Much research into the development of cold-hardy plants takes place at Agriculture Canada RESEARCH STATIONS across the country. Successes include a cultivar of *Alstroemeria*, a member of the amaryllis family, developed at the Saanichton Research and Plant Quarantine Station, BC; Northline (a silver maple), Autumn Blaze (a white ash), Wascana (a hybrid linden) and Baron (a box elder), all developed at the Morden Research Station, Man, for prairie use; and 2 new winter-hardy rose cultivars (Charles Albanel and Champlain), developed at the Ottawa Research Station.

R.H. KNOWLES

Oromocto, NB, Town, pop 9656 (1986c), 9064 (1981c), inc 1955, is located at the junction of the Oromocto and Saint John rivers, 22 km SE of FREDERICTON. The Malecite called the Oromocto *Wel-a-mook'-took* ("deep water") because of its good canoeing. The French had a small settlement there in the late 1600s and after 1763 New England traders used the location during their speculations on the SAINT JOHN R. About 1776 the British army built Fort Hughes to protect the new settlements, the overland route to Québec City and the rich harvest of pine masts for the Royal Navy. Prosperity continued after the arrival of the LOYALISTS after 1783. Timber remained the economic mainstay well into the 20th century with shipyards, sawmills and the business of the local

merchants supplying the hinterland settlers. The most far-reaching changes occurred in the 1950s when CFB GAGETOWN – the largest land-manoeuvres training area in the Commonwealth – was established on Oromocto's borders. When the town expanded to provide for the military influx, a comprehensive plan was adopted and Oromocto became "Canada's Model Town." Its economy has fared well, servicing and supplying the base, and the town has also attracted several nonpolluting manufacturers to its 34 ha industrial park.
DALE R. COGSWELL

Oronhyatekha ("burning cloud"), or **Peter Martin**, medical doctor (b on the Six Nations Reserve near Brantford, Canada W 10 Aug 1841; d at Savannah, Ga 3 Mar 1907). Oronhyatekha paid for his own education at the Wesleyan Academy at Wilbraham, Mass, and later at Kenyon College in Ohio. The Prince of Wales on his 1860 visit to Canada became sufficiently interested in him to invite him to study in England. Oronhyatekha spent 3 years at Oxford, and later completed his medical degree at University of Toronto, the first Canadian Indian to receive a degree from a Canadian university. In Ontario he practised at Frankford (near Belleville), Stratford, Neepanee and London. He joined, and rose rapidly to become supreme chief ranger (1881) of, the Independent Order of Foresters. For 26 years he guided the IOF's growth from a struggling bankrupt fraternal organization of 400 members, to a membership of more than 250 000, and a fund of over $11 million. Oronhyatekha wrote *History of the Independent Order of Foresters* (1894).
DONALD B. SMITH

Orr, Robert Gordon, "Bobby," hockey player (b at Parry Sound, Ont 20 Mar 1948). He was an outstanding junior player with Oshawa Generals and joined Boston Bruins in 1967 at the age of 18, winning the CALDER TROPHY. He revolutionized the role of the defenceman with his end-to-end rushes, his playmaking and his incredible scoring feats – he is the only defenceman ever to win the ART ROSS TROPHY as leading scorer, accomplishing the feat twice. He dominated the flow of play, surging forward and skating with an intensity exemplified in the photograph of him soaring through the air after scoring the Stanley Cup-winning goal.

Bobby Orr of the Boston Bruins flies through the air after scoring the winning goal in overtime in the Stanley Cup finals of 1970 (*courtesy Canapress Photo Service*).

He was voted the greatest athlete in the history of Boston, ahead of the great baseball and basketball stars. His list of awards is to date unmatched by any defenceman in NHL history: HART TROPHY 1970, 1971 and 1972; CONN SMYTHE TROPHY 1970 and 1972; and JAMES NORRIS TROPHY 8 years 1968-75. He was first-team all-star 8 consecutive years, 1967-75, and scored 270 goals and 645 assists in 953 games, adding 92 points in 74 playoff games. He suffered his first knee injury in his rookie season, and by the time he left Boston to sign a $3-million contract with Chicago Black Hawks (1976-77), he had had 6 knee operations. His legs destroyed, he played only 26 more games before retiring.
JAMES MARSH

Orser, Brian, figure skater (b at Belleville, Ont 18 Dec 1961). An outstanding free-skate performer, Orser won the world figure skating championship in 1987, the first Canadian man to win this title in 24 years. He started skating at age 6 and by 1979 was the Canadian junior champion. Orser won the senior championship in 1981, and held that title through 1988 – a record 8 consecutive wins. He began his climb to the pinnacle of the world's skaters in 1983, winning a bronze medal at the world championships. For the next 3 years, he placed second in the world championships and in the 1984 OLYMPIC GAMES, seemingly unable to break the barrier to first place; his problem usually lay with the figures portion of the competitions, but in 1987 Orser improved on his figures. In his long program, he produced a flawless and beautifully choreographed performance, with 6 triple jumps. As part of this winning feat, Orser became the first competitor in the world championships to complete 2 triple axels successfully in one program. He was appointed to the Order of Canada in 1985. BARBARA SCHRODT

Orthodox Church, also commonly known as the Eastern, Greek or Byzantine Church, a family of Christian churches historically found in eastern Europe, the Near East, Africa and Asia (*see* CHRISTIANITY). The 1981 census indicated that it served some 362 000 Canadians, although the total constituency claimed by the churches is higher. The ancient patriarchal provinces of Rome, Constantinople, Alexandria, Antioch and Jerusalem were all established by the 5th century AD, but thereafter theological, liturgical and canonical divergence, as well as political differences, came between Rome and the other provinces. The great schism of 1054 formally separated Rome (the Roman Catholic Church) from Constantinople and most of the population of the remaining 3 jurisdictions (the Orthodox Church). The issues leading to the schism, which still separate the Roman and Orthodox churches, include differences in trinitarian theology and church organization: the Orthodox churches dispute the Roman church's teachings on the Holy Spirit and the nature of authority in the church, specifically the primacy of the pope. The juridical ethos of Roman CATHOLICISM and Protestantism is perceived by the Orthodox as the central problem in Western Christian thought and institutions.

The present-day Orthodox Church includes the ancient patriarchates of Constantinople, Alexandria, Antioch and Jerusalem; the "national" Orthodox churches of Russia, Serbia, Romania, Bulgaria, Cyprus, Greece, Albania, Poland and Czechoslovakia; daughter churches of these, formed relatively recently in Europe and N America; and the autonomous churches of Sinai, Finland and Japan.

The unity of these "Byzantine" churches is theoretically found in their mutual recognition of a common faith and worship, rather than in any external authority or administrative structure. In practice, however, patriarchs of the various

branches, though independent, tend to recognize the primacy of the Ecumenical Patriarch of Constantinople. A second group, the Oriental Orthodox (non-Chalcedonian) churches, includes the Armenian, Coptic, Syrian, Ethiopian and South Indian Orthodox churches. Members of this family who do not formally subscribe to the doctrine defining the dual nature of Christ as adopted by the Council of Chalcedon (451 AD), are nevertheless within the larger Orthodox family.

Orthodox Church buildings are laid out to reveal the experience of God dwelling among men, and are patterned after the image of heaven in the Book of Revelation. The focal point is the Holy Table. An icon screen unites the sanctuary and the place of assembly. Everything which is in and of the church is considered "sacramental," ie, manifesting the mystery of salvation and integrating the faithful into the life of the Kingdom of God. Among numerous rites and acts the Holy Mysteries are central: initiation through baptism (by triple immersion) and chrismation (anointing), the Eucharistic liturgy, marriage, monastic tonsure, reconciliation, anointing of the sick or dying, holy orders and burial.

Icons (religious images) are held to be necessary spiritual witnesses to the unity of the church through time and space, making present the Kingdom of God in the persons and presence of the saints. There are daily, weekly and yearly cycles of prayer and worship. The primary focus of the church year, which begins Sept 1, is Pascha (Easter); each Lord's Day (Sunday) is seen as the extension of Pascha.

Most Orthodox Christians in Canada are affiliated with churches of the Byzantine tradition: Russian, Greek, Antiochian, Ukrainian, Byelorussian, Estonian, Bulgarian, Serbian, Macedonian and Romanian. Although an earlier attempt was made to settle Orthodox Christians in Florida, the coming of Russian missionary monks among the Aleut peoples of Alaska in 1794 marked the real advent of Orthodoxy in N America. (The first Orthodox church in Canada may have been that at Wostok, Alta, est 1898.) A diocese centered on Sitka, established 1799, expanded into other parts of N America. In 1905 it became an archdiocese with headquarters in New York, amid successive waves of immigration from Russia, Carpatho-Russia, Ukraine and Byelorussia. After the 1917 Russian Revolution, the Russian church came into conflict with the new communist government. In 1924 most Russian and associated parishes in N America declared their administrative independence, and a new metropolia, the Russian Church in America, was established. Its irregular and tense relationship with the mother church was resolved in 1970 when the Patriarch of Moscow and All Russia granted it autocephalous (self-governing) status. Now called the Orthodox Church in America, it affirmed the patriarch as its spiritual father, though remaining administratively independent. OCA's Canadian diocese serves some 20 000 adherents with 52 parishes and about 30 clergy. The Liturgy of St John Chrysostom is celebrated in Church Slavonic, Romanian, English or French. Some communities use the Julian (old style) calendar, others the Gregorian (new style) calendar. The church operates vigorous catechetical and mission programs.

Some Russian parishes chose to remain under the authority of the Patriarch of Moscow and All Russia. They are known as the Patriarchal parishes of the Russian Orthodox Church in Canada. Seventeen parishes in Alberta and Saskatchewan are served by 7 clergy, whose bishop is based in Edmonton. English has been introduced, but Church Slavonic remains the liturgical language. The remaining Russian Orthodox believers are

Church of the Russian Orthodox Synod near Holden, Alta (*photo by V. Claerhout*).

part of the Russian Orthodox Church Outside Russia, formed 1920 in Yugoslavia by refugees of the Russian Revolution. Its headquarters are in New York. Conservative and monarchist, it has broken communion with canonical churches and supported other ethnic traditionalist groups. Its Canadian Diocese is administered from Montréal, with 25 parishes and several monastic *sketes*. Church Slavonic is the customary language of worship and the Julian liturgical calendar is used.

The Greek Orthodox Archdiocese of N and S America, the major daughter church of the church of Constantinople, has 62 Canadian parishes with a Toronto-based diocese which is a member of the CANADIAN COUNCIL OF CHURCHES (CCC). Substantial Greek immigration in the 1960s and 1970s has caused the membership to rise to over 200 000, served by 48 clergy. The principal language is Greek, and the church maintains strong links with Greek culture. The Gregorian calendar has been used since 1923, although 5 "Old Calendarist" parishes in Montréal and Toronto broke with the Greek church over its adoption of the revised calendar and involvement with the World Council of Churches.

The majority of Canadian Christians with Syrian, Lebanese and Palestinian ancestry are part of the Antiochian Orthodox Christian Archdiocese of N America, daughter of the patriarchate of Antioch (Damascus, Syria). A mission established 1892 by the Russian Orthodox Church, and another established 1914 by the Antiochian patriarchate for the Syrian immigration, were its seeds. They merged in 1936, and the present name was adopted in 1969. The Antiochian church, which maintains close links with OCA, has made a concerted effort to use English, which is now the principal liturgical language. Eleven parishes are scattered from PEI to Vancouver.

The Ukrainian Orthodox Church in Canada, formerly the Ukrainian Greek Orthodox Church, comprises 278 communities with about 140 000 parishioners. These are largely descendants of immigrants from Galicia, Ukraine, who settled on the Prairies from the turn of the century to 1929, and other Ukrainians who settled in Ontario cities after WWII. In 1932 the church established St Andrew's College, which affiliated with Univer-

sity of Manitoba in 1962. St Michael's parish at Gardenton, Man, the first Ukrainian church in Canada, is the site of an annual PILGRIMAGE.

Historically, Galicia was under the Ruthenian Rite of the Roman Catholic Church. Tension developed between the Canadian community and the Catholic hierarchy over the Galicians' historic right to have married clergy and to use the vernacular language in the liturgy. Oblate priests, sent into various parishes, raised fears among Galicians that they were being "westernized." In response the Ukrainian Greek Orthodox Brotherhood was formed in 1918, and led many Ukrainian Catholics into the Orthodox Church. A Syrian Antiochian Orthodox bishop assumed spiritual responsibility and ordained 3 priests. In 1951 the election of Ilarion Ohienko as metropolitan confirmed the church's autonomy. Metropolitan Ilarion, a noted Slavic linguist, translated the Bible into Ukrainian under the sponsorship of the British and Foreign Bible Society. The church's government is by consistory, a council of laymen and clergy, which is its highest authority. The liturgy is conducted mostly in vernacular Ukrainian. Consistent with its vision of itself as the bearer of Ukrainian culture, the church supports schools and folk groups, which form an integral part of community life.

The Ukrainian Orthodox Church of America (Ecumenical Patriarchate), organized 1928, has 4 parishes in Canada. It became a metropolia in 1983. The (Holy) Ukrainian Autocephalic Orthodox Church in Exile, with 2 Canadian parishes, is a body formed 1954 by clergy and laymen who fled Ukraine following its return to the Soviet sphere in 1944. The church traces its ecclesial origins to the Orthodox Church of Poland, which in 1924 received autocephalous status.

The Bulgarian Eastern Orthodox Church (Diocese of North and South America and Australia), begun as a mission of the Holy Synod of Sofia to Bulgarian and Macedonian immigrants in N America, became a metropolia following the Second World War. Ties with the Holy Synod were broken 1947-62 as the community debated its relationship to the mother church, which was under the communist umbrella. In 1962 some Bulgarians rejoined the mother church, but others condemned that action. At first organized under the Russian Church in Exile as the Bulgarian Orthodox Church, Diocese of the US and Canada, the dissidents merged with the OCA, with a dio-

cese centered in Toledo, Ohio. The Patriarchal Church and the Russian Church in Exile each has one Bulgarian community in Canada. Complicating this situation is the Macedonian Orthodox Church, Diocese of America, Canada and Australia, administered from Toronto. Comprising Macedonians and Bulgarians, it is the result of the re-establishment of the ancient Macedonian see of Ohrid as an independent church along national lines.

Created in the 14th century, the Orthodox Church in Byelorussia has almost constantly struggled for autonomy from the patriarch at Moscow. Following the local government's 1946 alignment with Moscow, Byelorussians established churches in exile. In 1968 the diocese of the Byelorussian Autocephalic Orthodox Church based in Toronto received its first archbishop. There one church serves several missions in mid-Canada's industrial belt. A translation of the Divine Liturgy into Byelorussian has been prepared in Canada. In 1951 a Byelorussian church in Toronto became part of the canonical Byelorussian Orthodox Parishes under the jurisdiction of the Ecumenical Patriarch, who exercises his authority through the Greek archbishop of Toronto.

A similar struggle for autonomy has marked the history of the Estonian Orthodox Church, a national church since 1920. At various times it was under the Ecumenical Patriarch or the Patriarch of Moscow. When the USSR occupied Estonia in 1944, Archbishop Aleksander of Tallinn fled to Sweden and established the church in exile under the Patriarch of Constantinople. It was brought to Canada by Estonian immigrants after WWII. Parishes in Toronto, Montréal and Vancouver serve 1500 Estonians.

Serbian immigration began in the 1850s with settlements in BC. Communities on the prairies developed following the turn of the century and in the 1920s others were established around Hamilton, Ont. Initially, these were served by a Serbian Mission of the Russian Orthodox Church. With the re-establishment of the Holy Synod in Belgrade in 1921, N American churches were transferred to its jurisdiction and became the Serbian Orthodox Church in the US and Canada. Attempts to establish N America as a metropolia failed, and in 1963 the Holy Synod in Belgrade created 3 dioceses for the continent. The 17 Canadian churches are served by 12 clergymen. Church Slavonic is used and the Julian calendar observed. The Serbian Orthodox Free Diocese in the USA and Canada resulted from a schism in 1963, when the Church-National Assembly voted to retain a bishop suspended by the Holy Synod. The assembly declared its autonomy from the Yugoslavian church, arguing that it was dominated by the communist government. The Serbian communities maintain ties with several autocephalous churches, although some canonical bodies do not recognize them. There are 7 Canadian parishes.

The Romanians adopted Christianity in the 4th century, but a national church was not established until 1859; it became a Holy Synod in 1885. The first Romanian parishes in Canada were established about 1909 on the Prairies, among immigrants from the provinces of Bukovina and Transylvania. In 1930 the patriarchate established the Romanian Orthodox Missionary Episcopate in America, which became an archdiocese in 1973. Though autonomous, it maintains ties with the mother church in Bucharest. Canada's 20 parishes, located largely in the Prairie provinces, follow the Gregorian calendar and use Romanian in the liturgy. In 1951 many Romanians in N America rejected the bishop appointed by the church in Romania. The resulting schism led to the Romanian Orthodox

Bishop Ioasaph blessing the waters on White Fish Lake, Alberta, c1949 (*courtesy Monastery of All Saints of North America, Chilliwack, BC*).

Episcopate of America. Through the Ukrainian Orthodox Church of the US a bishop was consecrated, and in 1960 he placed the jurisdiction under the Russian Metropolia (later OCA). The episcopate's 13 Canadian churches in Ontario and the Prairie provinces use Romanian and English in their liturgy and follow the Gregorian calendar.

Oriental Orthodox Christians in Canada (non-Chalcedonians) are of Armenian, Coptic, Ethiopian, S Indian and Syrian origin. The Canadian diocese of the Armenian Church of N America (est 1898) is governed by an assembly of laymen and clergy who elect a primate for a 4-year term, and is a member of CCC. The church is under the patriarch of Etchmiadzin (USSR), head of the Armenian Church, and historically linked to the patriarchates at Jerusalem and Constantinople. The Armenian community in Canada was established following WWI, and in the 1950s and 1960s a second immigration largely from Turkey, Egypt, Syria, Lebanon and Iran occurred. Eight Canadian parishes now serve 50 000 Armenians. The first parishes were established in St Catharines and Hamilton, Ont, followed by those in Toronto, Montréal, Ottawa, Edmonton and Vancouver. The Liturgy of St Basil is customarily celebrated in classical Armenian. The use of unleavened bread at communion reflects the influence of a brief union with the Roman church in the 13th and 14th centuries. Though the Armenians follow the Julian calendar, they continue the ancient form of celebrating the Christ's nativity as part of the feast of Epiphany.

The Coptic Orthodox Church, Diocese of N America, was established 1961 to serve recent Egyptian immigrants, who settled principally in Montréal, Toronto, Kitchener and Ottawa. Followers of the Coptic Church of Ethiopia and the St Thomas Church of S India have joined in their liturgy. The Coptic Church traces its origin to the apostle Mark who, tradition claims, evangelized Egypt. The patriarchate of Alexandria was of great significance in the early church, ranking in importance with Rome and Jerusalem. The N American diocese functions directly under the Coptic patriarch. The Liturgy of St Basil is regularly celebrated using the ancient Coptic chant and modern Arabic with occasional English and French. The Canadian church has recently translated this liturgy. It also sponsors a quarterly publication, *Coptologia Studia Coptica Orthodoxa*, and holds membership in the CCC.

The Syrian Orthodox Church of Antioch in the US and Canada (frequently termed "Jacobite" after 6th-century organizer Jacob Baradaeus) is part of the ancient Antiochian patriarchate in Damascus. Along with the Syrian Liturgy of St James, a distinctive aspect of piety is a rigorous private prayer life. The 2 churches in Canada, in Montréal and Toronto, serve Syrians who immigrated in the 1950s.

Two additional bodies which regard themselves as Orthodox exist in Canada. The Evangelical Orthodox Church, Saskatoon Diocese, separated from an Evangelical Mennonite Brethren church and identified with similar movements in the US, initially as the New Covenant Apostolic Order. Members developed a PRESBYTERIAN form of government, adopted apostolic forms of ministry and developed liturgical worship. This movement formed the Evangelical Orthodox Church of America, a portion of which in 1987 joined the Antiochian Orthodox Church. The African Orthodox Church, of which the single Canadian parish was established in Sydney, NS, in 1921, developed as part of the movement of black self-consciousness early in the century. It accepts the teaching of the 7 ecumenical councils and conforms to standard Orthodox practice.

In addition to these, there is a small Canadian Orthodox Church movement centered at the Monastery of All Saints of North America in Chilliwack, BC. The movement, which is affiliated with the Old Calendarist Churches in Greece, has a publishing house, Synaxis Press, 2 parishes in BC and a number of small missions. It rejects the use of the Gregorian calendar for the liturgical cycle of the church and Orthodox involvement in the World Council of Churches. The movement advocates "traditionalism" and the formation of a Canadian Orthodox Church which is not bound to a specific ethnic community. Orthodox churches in Canada, while reflecting world Orthodoxy, have been affected by political activities and ethnic divisions in their regions of national origin. Some jurisdictions argue that such divisions contravene the canonical principle that the church be united, with all the faithful gathered around a common episcopate. Efforts are being made in N America to realize this principle. Although the churches in Canada continue to serve their historic constituency, the initial immigrants, they now face new generations whose linguistic and cultural formation has taken place entirely in Canada. Questions about liturgical language and practice and about the mission of the church in Canadian society form the agenda of today's church. *See also* CHRISTIANITY.
DAVID J. GOA

Reading: T. Hopko, *The Orthodox Faith* (1976); A.C. Piepkorn, *Profiles in Belief* (vol 1, 1977); T. Ware, *The Orthodox Church* (1963); Paul Yuzuk, *Greek Orthodox Church of Canada, 1918-1951* (1981).

Orton, George W., runner (b at Strathroy, Ont 10 Jan 1873; d at Meredith, NH 26 June 1958). Canada's first OLYMPIC champion, Orton was one of N America's premier track competitors in the 1890s. Regarded as the most scientific student of middle-distance running, he won the Canadian and American mile championships in 1892 and 1893. By 1900 he had accumulated 121 victories, including 15 American championships. Since Canada sent no team to the 1900 Paris Olympics, he competed for the US, winning the 2500 m steeplechase and finishing 3rd in the 400 m hurdles. He was a prolific writer on sport and running.
J. THOMAS WEST

Ortona, Battle of, 20-27 Dec 1943. As part of the general advance of Gen Montgomery's Eighth Army up the Italian Adriatic coast, Maj-Gen Christopher VOKES's 1st Canadian Division was ordered to take the medieval seaport of Ortona, perched on a high promontory and impregnable from 3 sides – flanked by sea cliffs on the N and E, and by a deep ravine on the W. Supported by their own armoured brigade, Canadian troops attacked from the S on Dec 20. Infantry from the Loyal Edmonton Reg and the Seaforth Highlanders of Canada suffered numerous casualties from the stiff resistance. After a week of fierce fighting the town was finally taken, and the remaining German forces withdrew on the night of Dec 27. One war correspondent reported that the Germans had been "staging a miniature Stalingrad in hapless Ortona." Canadian losses in taking this "unimportant" town and its environs included 1372 dead – almost 25% of all Canadians killed in the Mediterranean theatre.
DAVID EVANS

Osgoode, William, judge (b at London, Eng 1754; d there 17 Jan 1824). Educated at Christ Church, Oxford, he was admitted to Lincoln's Inn in 1779. After some years of chancery practice, he took office in 1792 as the first chief justice of Upper Canada and 2 years later took up a similar post in Lower Canada. In 1801 he returned to England and lived the rest of his life as a country gentleman. He was a man of tranquil temperament who played an important mediating role during his time in Canada. He did not leave a strong judicial legacy but drafted much of the pioneering legislation. The law courts in Toronto and Canada's best-known law school are named after him.
GRAHAM E. PARKER

Osgoode Hall, named after William OSGOODE, was built 1829-32 as the headquarters of the Law Society of Upper Canada. It was later expanded to house law courts and the Osgoode Hall Law School. As originally designed by John Ewart and W.W. Baldwin, Osgoode Hall was a modest 2½ storey brick building. In 1844 and again 1855-57 it was extensively refurbished and enlarged, first by the Toronto architect, Henry Bower Lane, and then by the local firm of Cumberland and Storm. The 1829 building became the east wing of a larger composition defined by a long central pavilion surmounted by a dome and flanked by 2 projecting wings fronted by a classical portico. Despite this gradual evolution, the building presents a unified appearance, and the design, with its classical porticos set on rusticated arcades, provides one of Canada's most important examples of a late Palladian style.
JANET WRIGHT

Oshawa, Ont, City, inc 1924, pop 123 651 (1986c), 117 519 (1981c), is located 52 km E of Toronto on Lk Ontario. Originally called Skae's Corners, its present name is an Indian term whose exact meaning is disputed, though "portage" is a common choice. In 1974 Oshawa became part of the newly formed Regional Municipality of Durham. Its initial function as a transportation centre was based on its excellent harbour, good road connections and the GRAND TRUNK RY, which in 1856 was completed from Toronto to Montréal. Manufacturing soon took precedence. Especially notable was the Oshawa Manufacturing Co, owned by Joseph Hall, who developed it into the largest producer of agricultural implements in Canada. The dominant manufacturer was to become McLaughlin Carriage Works, developer of the McLaughlin Buick automobile. In 1918 the McLaughlin Motor Car Co and the Chevrolet Motor Car Co of Canada were merged into GENERAL MOTORS of Canada Ltd with local entrepreneur Robert S. "Colonel Sam" MCLAUGHLIN as president. In the years that followed, GM became the dominant employer, but after several years of

Population: 123 651 (1986c), 117 519 (1981c); 203 543 (1986 CMA), 154 217 (1981 CMA)
Rate of increase (1981-86): (City) 5.2%; (CMA) 9.2%
Rank in Canada: Sixteenth (by CMA)
Date of Incorporation: 1924
Land Area: City 143.41 km²; CMA 894.19 km²
Elevation: 84 m
Climate: Average daily temp, July 20.3°C, Jan -5.6°C, Yearly precip 863.5 mm; Hours of sunshine 2045 per year

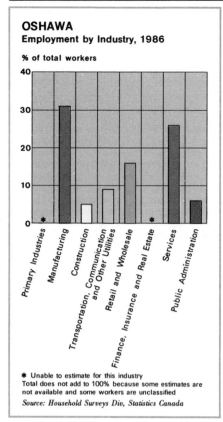

OSHAWA
Employment by Industry, 1986

% of total workers

[bar chart with y-axis from 0 to 40, showing bars for:
Primary Industries (*), Manufacturing (~31), Construction (~5), Transportation, Communication and Other Utilities (~9), Retail and Wholesale (~16), Finance, Insurance and Real Estate (*), Services (~26), Public Administration (~6)]

* Unable to estimate for this industry
Total does not add to 100% because some estimates are not available and some workers are unclassified
Source: Household Surveys Div, Statistics Canada

poor labour relations, it was the target of a major strike. GM workers certified the United Automobile Workers, an industrial union affiliated with the American-based Committee for Industrial Organization (CIO; later Congress of Industrial Organization). Much to the chagrin of Ontario's premier, Mitchell HEPBURN, who hoped the UAW would lose the strike, the union, despite the use of special police, established itself as a force in Canadian labour (*see* OSHAWA STRIKE).

Oshawa has a symphony orchestra, the Robert McLaughlin Gallery and numerous sports and recreational facilities. Parkwood, the grand estate of R.S. McLaughlin, preserves a bygone era.

Prominent Oshawans have included Michael Starr, Cabinet minister in the Diefenbaker government; Edward BROADBENT, federal leader of the New Democratic Party; and Donald JACKSON, world figure-skating champion. GERALD STORTZ

[map showing area around Toronto, Ontario, with Owen Sound, Orillia, Simcoe, Lindsay, Peterborough, Barrie, Kingston, Trenton, Belleville, Brampton, Cobourg, Waterloo, Kitchener, Toronto, Oshawa, Oakville, Lake Ontario]

Oshawa Strike, 8-23 Apr 1937, when more than 4000 workers of the huge GENERAL MOTORS plant in Oshawa, Ont, struck. Their requests were simple: an 8-hour day, better wages and working conditions, a seniority system and recognition of their union, the new United Automobile Workers. This last demand had caused the strike: the UAW was an affiliate of the recently created Committee for Industrial Organization (CIO; later Congress of Industrial Organization), which was organizing industrial workers throughout the US. Vigorously supported by Ontario Premier Mitchell HEPBURN, GM management strove to keep the CIO out of Ontario. Both the company and the premier wanted a pliant labour force – unorganized, impotent and cheap. To break the strike, Hepburn even created his own police force, known irreverently as "Hepburn's Hussars" and

"Sons-of-Mitches." Two of Hepburn's Cabinet colleagues who opposed his actions, Minister of Labour David Croll and Attorney General Arthur Roebuck, were persuaded to resign. Supported by fellow unionists, neighbours, and CCF and communist activists, but significantly not by the CIO which had little money to spare for Canada, the workers held out for 2 weeks. Eventually, GM, afraid of losing markets to its competitors, capitulated. In the Apr 23 agreement GM accepted many of the union's demands, without recognizing the union. To gain recognition, the union leadership publicly repudiated the CIO connection. Nevertheless, everyone knew it was a great CIO victory – the first major one in Canada. According to some, the strike marked the birth of INDUSTRIAL UNIONISM in Canada. IRVING ABELLA

Osler, Sir William, physician, writer, educator (b at Bond Head, Canada W 12 July 1849; d at Oxford, Eng 29 Dec 1919). His importance stems from his contributions to knowledge in a wide spectrum of clinical fields, his educational activities both in person and through his writings, his stimulation of students who later became leaders of the medical profession, his enthusiastic support of scientific libraries, and his example as a person of integrity, equanimity and sincere humanity. Osler was raised in Dundas, Canada W, and educated at U of T and McGill, where he graduated with a MD in 1872. After postgraduate training in England and Europe, he began his teaching career at McGill, lecturing in medicine and pathology, publishing extensively and building an international reputation as an astute and humane clinician. In 1884 he accepted an invitation to join the faculty of U of Pennsylvania, and 5 years later he became the first professor of medicine at Johns Hopkins U in Baltimore.

By the turn of the century, Osler was probably the best-known physician in the English-speaking world. He achieved this position with a combination of superb practice, excellent and innovative teaching, wide-ranging publication, and association with outstanding colleagues in the most advanced school of its time. His professional interests were unusually wide, but he was particularly expert in diagnosis of diseases of the heart, lungs and blood. His textbook, *The Principles and Practice of Medicine*, first published in 1892 and frequently revised, was considered authoritative for more than 30 years. His description of the inadequacy of treatment methods for most disorders was a major factor leading to the creation of the Rockefeller Institute for Medical Research in New York City.

Osler was an outgoing, vivacious man, given to practical jokes and pranks. He knew how to dispel gloom in the sickroom and how to inspire his patients with hope. He advocated changes in the medical curriculum to decrease the amount of lecturing and increase the time students spent with patients. He was one of those who formalized the methods of postgraduate training for physicians, helping to create the system being followed today. Osler married at age 42, his wife being a direct descendant of Paul Revere. One of their 2 children died at birth, the other in WWI. In 1905 the family left N America for Great Britain, where Osler became Regius professor of medicine at Oxford. The recipient of many honorary degrees, he was created a baronet in 1911. His last years were spent carrying on a busy consultant's practice, writing, teaching and building up his extensive library in the history of medicine, which eventually was bequeathed to McGill. In 1919 Osler died of pneumonia developed after a lengthy trip of consultation. His ashes rest in the Osler Library, Montréal. He is still much quoted and his life remains an exemplar for students and physicians. CHARLES G. ROLAND

Outstanding physician and educator Sir William Osler (*courtesy National Archives of Canada/C-7105*).

Osoyoos, BC, Village, pop 2956 (1986c), 2738 (1981c), inc 1946, is located on Osoyoos Lk, 60 km south of Penticton in the OKANAGAN VALLEY. *Soyoos* ("where two lakes meet") was an Okanagan Indian name. Hudson's Bay Co brigades passed here 1812-48. The British Columbia GOLD RUSHES helped open the area. A customs house was placed at the narrows in 1865. Customs collector John Carmichael Haynes, justice of the peace for Osoyoos and Kootenay districts, was a pioneer settler at Osoyoos and accumulated 8900 ha of land for a cattle and horse ranch. The first commercial orchard was established nearby in 1890. The South Okanagan Irrigation Project brought an irrigation canal to the area by 1919. Agriculture is now the largest sector and gives rise to some manufacturing; less important are cattle raising and forestry. In addition, many tourists are attracted to the area's warm lakes. Osoyoos was the site of the 1985 British Columbia Winter Games, which furthered the development of Mt Baldy, a ski area E of the village.

WILLIAM A. SLOAN

Osprey (*Pandion haliaetus*), large, cosmopolitan BIRD OF PREY characterized by a crested head and contrasting black, white and grey plumage. It feeds exclusively on fish and is commonly called fish hawk. Adaptations for fishing include nostrils that close, feet designed with sharp spicules (small spines) on the underside, and a reversible outer toe, for catching and holding quarry. Although frequently accused of feeding on sport fish, ospreys feed mainly on nongame fish found near the surface or in shallow water. Ospreys breed across Canada, building large, stick nests near or over water. Early each fall they migrate to S America. R.W. FYFE

Ostell, John, architect, surveyor (b at London, Eng 7 Aug 1813; d at Montréal 6 Apr 1892). The most important architect in Montréal between 1836 and 1859, Ostell designed the Custom House, Place Royale, the McGill arts building, the Episcopal Palace, the Grand Seminary of St-Sulpice, the Court House and the Church of St-Jacques. Appointed city surveyor in 1842, he was also the provincial surveyor in the late 1840s and early 1850s. In 1859 he gave up his practice to concentrate on lumber manufacturing. Ostell became a director of the New City Gas Company in 1850, president of the Montreal and Champlain Railroad in 1860, and helped to found the Montreal City Passenger Ry in 1861. ELLEN S. JAMES

Ostenso, Martha, novelist (b near Bergen, Norway 6 Sept 1900; d at Seattle, Wash 1963). Ostenso's family immigrated to the midwestern US in 1902, then to Brandon, Man, and later to Winnipeg, where Ostenso completed high school. Before attending U of Manitoba, she taught briefly in Hayland, Man, which she drew upon for the setting of her novel *Wild Geese* (1925). Ostenso worked briefly as a reporter, but then moved to the US in 1921. She studied the novel with the Canadian Douglas DURKIN (who had taught in Brandon and Winnipeg) at Columbia U in New York, and did social work in Brooklyn for several years before moving with Durkin to Gull Lake, Minn, in 1931. The couple married in 1944, following the death of Durkin's first wife, and retired to Seattle in 1963.

Ostenso's major achievement, *Wild Geese*, was her only novel set in Canada. A compelling romance, it realistically explores the strange unity between man and nature, and the spareness of both physical and spiritual life in a pioneering farm community. Originally titled *The Passionate Flight*, it won the lucrative first-novel prize offered by *The Pictorial Review*, the Famous Players-Lasky Corporation and Dodd, Mead & Co. It has recently come to light, however, that Durkin collaborated extensively with Ostenso on the novel, but because he had already published, it was submitted only under her name. (Ostenso had published *In a Far Land*, a volume of poetry, in 1924.) In spite of their continued co-operative efforts, none of Ostenso's subsequent dozen works of fiction, including *The Dark Dawn* (1926) and *The Mad Carews* (1927), achieved the power and insight of *Wild Geese*. DONNA COATES

Ostry, Bernard, public servant (b at Wadena, Sask 10 Jun 1927). After studying history at U of Man, Ostry launched an academic career at the universities of London and Birmingham in England. There, in collaboration with H.S. Ferns, he published *The Age of Mackenzie King: The Rise of the Leader* (1955; 2nd ed, 1976), a critical and controversial study of the former prime minister. Ostry returned to Canada in the late 1950s, working for the CBC 1960-68 as a broadcaster and subsequently as an administrator in the public affairs department. He was then a commissioner on a prime-ministerial task force regarding government information, and one of the authors of its report, *To Know and Be Known* (1969); this provided a transition for the ambitious and now well-connected Ostry to the top level of the federal government cultural bureaucracy. He was assistant undersecretary of state 1970-73; secretary general, National Museums of Canada, 1974-78; and finally deputy minister of communications 1978-80.

His strong views on the importance of the arts and the government's role in cultural life are contained in his *The Cultural Connection* (1978). In 1981, after a brief sojourn in France with his wife Sylvia OSTRY, he moved to the Ontario government, where he served in a series of deputy minister appointments before becoming head of TVOntario, the province's public television service, in 1985. NORMAN HILLMER

Ostry, Sylvia, née Knelman, economist, public servant (b at Winnipeg 3 June 1927). Ostry was educated in Winnipeg and at McGill and Cambridge. She began her career in university teaching at McGill and Oxford. In 1964 she joined the federal public service as assistant director and then director, Special Manpower Studies, Dominion Bureau of Statistics (1964-69). She was director, Economic Council of Canada (1969-72); chief statistician of Canada (1972-75); deputy minister, Consumer and Corporate Affairs (1975-78); chairman, Economic Council of Canada (1978-79). In 1980 she was appointed head, Dept of Economics and Statistics, Organization for Economic Cooperation and Development, Paris. In 1983 she returned to Ottawa as special adviser to the Privy Council Office on loan to the Inst of Research on Public Policy. Since 1985 she has been a ambassador for multinational trade negotiations, based in Ottawa. Called the "ultimate public servant," she has contributed especially in the areas of labour economics, manpower studies and productivity. She is co-author of *Labour Economics in Canada* (1979) and has also published on demography, productivity and competition policy. In Dec 1987 she was given the Outstanding Achievement Award, the highest award for federal public servants.

O'Sullivan, Shawn, boxer (b at Toronto 9 May 1962). O'Sullivan's amateur record of 94-6 is matched by few Canadian boxers. From a boxing family, he started boxing at the Cabbagetown Youth Centre under Ken Hamilton, his original mentor. As a 16-year old, he won the Canadian junior title in Whitehorse. In 1981, as a 19-year old, he defeated Cuban Olympic gold medallist Armando Martinez twice, the second time en route to winning the gold medal in the World Amateur Championships. That year he was named Canada's Athlete of the Year. In the 1984 Los Angeles Olympics, after totally dominating his earlier opponents, he lost the gold medal match to Frank Tate of the US. He turned pro immediately after, and by Sept 1987 his record stood at 16-1. However, O'Sullivan's career suffered a severe setback in Jan 1988 when he was knocked out by Luis Santana. A.J. "SANDY" YOUNG

Reading: S. Brunt, *Mean Business: The Creation of Shawn O'Sullivan* (1987).

Ottawa (or Odawa) were an Algonquian-speaking people living north of the HURON at the time of French penetration into the Upper Great Lakes. A tradition of the Ottawa, shared by the Ojibwa and Potawatomi, states that these 3 groups were once one people. The division of the Upper Great Lake Algonquians apparently took place at Michilimackinac, the meeting point of Lakes Huron and Michigan. The Ottawa, or "traders," remained near Michilimackinac, while the Potawatomi, "Those-who-make-or-keep-a-fire," moved S, up Lk Michigan. The Ojibwa, or "To-roast-till-puckered-up," went NW to Sault Ste Marie.

The farming, fishing, hunting and trading economy of the Ottawa resembled that of other Great Lakes people. The Ottawa were closely tied to their Huron neighbours and, in fact, were a vital part of the so-called "Huron Trading Empire." When HURONIA was destroyed by the IROQUOIS in the mid-17th century, the Ottawa fled west. After 2 decades they were back on MANITOULIN I, but they continued to occupy settlements elsewhere on the shores of the Great Lakes. They located their principal settlements near the French fort at Michilimackinac, though many migrated to the Detroit area when the French built a fort there in 1701. During the final struggle for northeastern N America, the Ottawa supported the French.

After the French defeat, the Ottawa, under PONTIAC of the Detroit region, organized a pan-Indian uprising against the English who threatened to encroach on Indian lands. Though unsuccessful, the uprising encouraged the British to issue the ROYAL PROCLAMATION OF 1763, which recognized the legal right of Indian tribes to claim title to the lands they occupied. The proclamation is critical to Indian land rights in Canada, and still applies today (*see* INDIAN TREATIES; LAND CLAIMS).

During the American Revolution and the War of 1812, the Ottawa (or Odawa as they prefer to be called) sided with the British, Chief Jean-Baptiste Assikinack being one of their leaders in the War of 1812. After signing treaties in the 1820s and 1830s with the Americans, many Ottawa in Michigan moved to Manitoulin I. Assikinack, who had become a Roman Catholic catechist, persuaded many of his people on the island to become Christians. Although Assikinack supported the surrender of Manitoulin I to the government of the Province of Canada in 1862, many Ottawa refused and the eastern section of the island, at Wikwemikong, remains unceded land.

Because the Ottawa tended to settle in mixed communities, it is difficult to state population figures. Many Ottawa descendants are identified as Ojibwa or Potawatomi. In 1986 there were 2311 registered Ottawa in Canada. Some 5000 lived in the US, on reservations in Michigan, Wisconsin and Oklahoma.

In the 19th century many Ottawa operated their own farms, or worked as farm labourers and lumbermen. Since 1945 a number of Ottawa have moved from Wikwemikong to Sudbury and Toronto to find employment. Daphne ODJIG, a well-known Indian artist, is the great-great-great-granddaughter of Assikinack. *See also* NATIVE PEOPLE: EASTERN WOODLANDS and general articles under NATIVE PEOPLE. DONALD B. SMITH

Reading: H.H. Peckham, *Pontiac and the Indian Uprising* (1961); B.G. Trigger, ed, *Handbook of North American Indians,* vol 15: *Northeast* (1978).

Ottawa, Ont, capital of Canada and centre of the Regional Municipality of Ottawa-Carleton, is located on the OTTAWA R on Ontario's eastern boundary with Québec, about 200 km W of Montréal.

Settlement Evidence of Algonquian settlements has been found throughout the Ottawa Valley. "Ottawa" is thought to derive from a tribe of the same name, probably from a word meaning "to trade." As the Ottawa R and its tributaries form the most direct water route between the St Lawrence and the continental interior, it was part of aboriginal trading systems and, from the 17th to 19th centuries, the chief artery of the Montréal FUR TRADE. Minor fur outposts were established in the valley before 1800, when the first permanent settlement, an agricultural community at the site of HULL, was established by New Englander Philemon WRIGHT. Itinerant lumberers were drawn by the trade in squared timber begun in 1806 by Wright. An unnamed campsite, established 1826 by Royal Engineers under Lt-Col John BY as construction base for the RIDEAU CANAL, was situated on a 30 m bluff flanking the headlocks, near Chaudière Falls and the mouths of the Rideau and Gatineau rivers. It immediately attracted contractors, labourers, and a small community of merchants, tradesmen and professionals. By 1827 a considerable town named Bytown had sprung up. In the 1830s the TIMBER TRADE to Britain became the focus of economic activity. Bytown eclipsed "Wrightsville" (later Hull) as the principal valley town. A new industry emerged in the 1850s when the power of Chaudière and Rideau falls was employed to saw logs into lumber for the American market.

Development By the 1860s, in addition to a large trade in squared timber, Ottawa contained one of the largest milling operations in the world, accompanied by huge cutting, driving and barging operations, and was connected to the GRAND TRUNK RY and American rail networks. The rail-

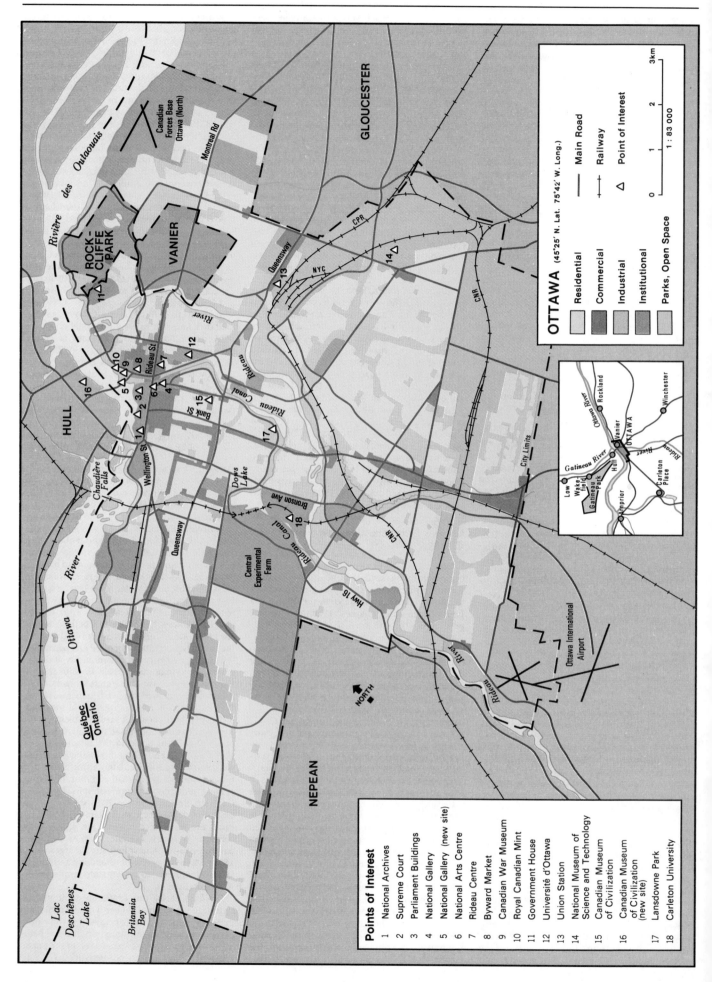

OTTAWA (45°25' N. Lat. 75°42' W. Long.)

	Residential	—— Main Road
	Commercial	╫ Railway
	Industrial	△ Point of Interest
	Institutional	
	Parks, Open Space	1 : 83 000

GLOUCESTER

Canadian Forces Base Ottawa (North)

ROCK-CLIFFE PARK

VANIER

HULL

Québec
Ontario

Rivière des Outaouais

Ottawa River

Chaudière Falls

Wellington St

Bank St

Rideau St

Rideau Canal

Rideau River

Montreal Rd

Queensway

CPR

NYC

CNR

City Limits

CNR

Central Experimental Farm

Dows Lake

Bronson Ave

Hwy 16

Queensway

Rideau Canal

Rideau River

Ottawa International Airport

Lac Deschênes Lake

Britannia Bay

NEPEAN

NORTH

Points of Interest

1 National Archives
2 Supreme Court
3 Parliament Buildings
4 National Gallery
5 National Gallery (new site)
6 National Arts Centre
7 Rideau Centre
8 Byward Market
9 Canadian War Museum
10 Royal Canadian Mint
11 Government House
12 Université d'Ottawa
13 Union Station
14 National Museum of Science and Technology
15 Canadian Museum of Civilization
16 Canadian Museum of Civilization (new site)
17 Lansdowne Park
18 Carleton University

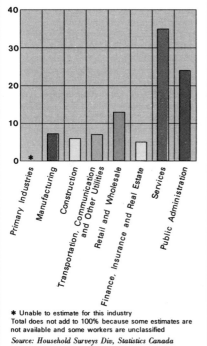

OTTAWA - HULL
Employment by Industry, 1986

% of total workers

* Unable to estimate for this industry
Total does not add to 100% because some estimates are not available and some workers are unclassified
Source: Household Surveys Div, Statistics Canada

way made Ottawa a serious candidate as permanent capital of the PROVINCE OF CANADA, but urban rivalries made any choice politically dangerous and the matter was thrust upon Queen Victoria. Colonial officials ensured her only possible choice would be Ottawa, as announced the last day of 1857. Construction of PARLIAMENT BUILDINGS began 1859, and were officially opened in 1866. In 1867 the city was made capital of the new Dominion of Canada. About 1890, the hydroelectric potential of Ottawa's rivers was exploited, the chief industrial application being in the production of pulp and paper using the inferior logs of depleted valley forests. The sawn lumber industry declined significantly in the 20th century.

By 1940, the federal government had emerged as the dominant employer. Ottawa has also developed as a centre for tourism, the city's second-largest industry. It now caters to an estimated 4 million visitors annually.

Cityscape Ottawa has an outstanding physical endowment. Rapids and falls punctuate river courses, which are protected by parks and driveways. Lower Town, E of the canal, was the first growth pole, and much of the mid-19th-century city is found here, including the restored "Mile of History" along Sussex Dr and the Byward Market. It was outstripped in the 1860s by Upper Town, which was entrenched by a government economy as the chief retail and office locus of the city. The large Central Experimental Farm, located in the SW part of the city, and a federal "greenbelt" girdling the built-up region are treasured amenities though they have been completely surrounded by suburban expansion.

Since the 1920s, much of the core area has been appropriated and redeveloped with parks (Confederation Square) or major national buildings (National Arts Centre, National Defence Building, Bank of Canada Building) by the federal authority. It also collaborated on construction of the Rideau Centre, a downtown convention, hotel and shopping complex opened in 1983. Office towers, which from the 1960s began to

overwhelm the Parliament Buildings, are the dominant feature of the downtown landscape. The NATIONAL CAPITAL COMMISSION and its predecessors have carried out much of the beautification of the city, removing rail lines and yards from the city core and preserving the scenic canal. The NCC maintains the extensive system of driveways in the city, lined with millions of tulip bulbs and other flowering plants; it operates a number of parks and in winter maintains the world's longest skating rink on the frozen Rideau Canal. City planning is conducted by the Ottawa Planning Board.

Population With 300 763 inhabitants, Ottawa is Canada's twelfth-largest city (fourth by CMA). The contours of this population have persisted for 150 years: about one-quarter French Roman Catholics, one-quarter Irish Roman Catholics, and most of the remainder Protestants of British origin. Small communities – chiefly Jewish, German and Italian – arrived at the turn of the century and now comprise about 10% of the population. An Arabic-speaking (mainly Lebanese) community has also struck roots in Ottawa, and an older Asian community has recently experienced much growth. In general, the Protestant and English community has favoured Upper Town, the Roman Catholic and French community, Lower Town. Religious institutions (churches, schools, hospitals), ethnic associations, and even political organizations have solidified this pattern. Nineteenth-century Ottawa became a focal point of Catholic and Protestant-Orange mili-

National Capital Region, Ottawa, showing the cities of Ottawa (S side) and Hull (N side) of the Ottawa R and the Gatineau Hills to the N. The Rideau R (from the S) and Gatineau R (from the N) also converge on the cities (*courtesy Canada Centre for Remote Sensing/Energy, Mines & Resources Canada*).

Population: 300 763 (1986c), 295 163 (1981cA); 819 263 (1986 CMA), 743 821 (1981A CMA)
Rate of Increase (1981-86): (City) 1.9%; (CMA) 10.1%
Rank in Canada: Fourth (by CMA)
Date of Incorporation: Town of Bytown (1st), 1847
Town of Bytown (2nd), 1850
City of Ottawa, 1855
Land Area: (City) 110.15 km²; (CMA) 5138.34 km²
Elevation: 79 m
Climate: Average daily temp, July 20.6°C, Jan -10.8°C; Yearly precip 846.2 mm; Hours of sunshine 2008.5 per year

tance, and also emerged as the capital of Franco-Ontario and the centre of conflicts over language. In the 1850s, sawmilling firms at Chaudière generated a working-class community, broadly French and Irish Catholic. The growing public service tended to diffuse into the pre-existing communities. Renewal and renovation in older areas have altered this pattern, attracting professionals to all core areas.

Economy and Labour Force Though patterns in the Ottawa work force have undergone dramatic change, "service" to a dominant industry has been a continuing motif. Original settlers serviced the needs of canal construction, the squared timber trade and agriculture. In 1861 "industrial" jobs, most associated with saw milling, comprised about 48% of the labour force. Government employment, only 10% in 1871, grew by 1971 to about one-third, including large numbers of women, while manufacturing fell to about 6%. Today, manufacturing employs about the same percentage of the labour force, while the public service sector stands at about one-quarter. Few corporate head offices have been established in the Ottawa area, with the exception of Metropolitan Life Insurance and a number of burgeoning computer firms. Aerial surveying has also developed, contracting about

40% of the world's business outside the Soviet Bloc, and a major computer chip technology industry has developed since 1970.

Transportation Rivers formed the city's original transportation corridors and were the basis of its claim to be the economic capital of central Canada: the Rideau to Kingston; the Gatineau into the Québec Laurentians; and the Ottawa E to Montréal and W to Lk Huron. However, transportation is now largely by road and rail; the city is on both transcontinental rail lines and on the Trans-Canada Highway. It has one of Canada's busiest air terminals, largely owing to its location on the Montréal-Toronto-Ottawa air triangle, and is the centre for the federal government's air fleet and a large Armed Forces base. Uplands and Rockcliffe are the airports in the Ottawa-Carleton region. Public transportation is provided by quasi-autonomous OC Transpo, based on the Ottawa-Carleton region.

Government and Politics Ottawa's jurisdictional divisions, its location in a population-poor region (shared with its sister city, Hull) and its distance from provincial capitals, coupled with the predominating economic influence of nearby Montréal, make for a complex but weak metropolitan system. In addition, the municipal regions of Ottawa (Ottawa-Carleton) and Hull (the Outaouais Regional Community), covering together about 3066 km², overlap the 4660 km² national capital region National Capital Commission, which wields considerable influence as autonomous landowner and developer of public works.

From the outset, Ottawa had a ward system sensitive to the Upper Town/Lower Town division. Administration was a council-committee system until 1908, when a council-board of control system (the mayor and 4 controllers elected at large), was adopted. In 1980, the city returned to the original pattern. Reform politics emerged in the 1970s and have changed the traditional small-business configuration at City Hall. The federal authority, though the city's largest landowner, is constitutionally exempt from city bylaws and taxes, and the extent of its responsibility to respect laws and provide grants in lieu of taxes has for more than 100 years been a chronic, controversial and unresolved issue between the Crown and the Town. Since 1841 Ottawa's Irish-French Catholic communities have mainly voted reform or Liberal; the Anglo-Protestant communities, Conservative. An NDP presence and shifting social patterns have recently altered this tendency. A complex school system is overseen by the "public" Ottawa Board of Education and the Ottawa Roman Catholic Separate School Board. The separate board traditionally educated in English and French about equally, but until 1987 its schools were publicly funded only to Grade X. The "public" system was thus responsible for most high school education in French. As well, it operated nondenominational elementary schools in French. In 1987, approval was given for a single "French" board to be carved out of the French panels of the 4 boards in the Ottawa-Carleton region. The 4 will retain their large French-immersion programs, launched about 1970 under the influence of the federal government's bilingual thrust.

Cultural Life CARLETON UNIVERSITY is located in the SW. The UNIVERSITY OF OTTAWA offers programs in both English and French and, though formally secular, embodies much of the tradition of the Oblate Order, which ran it for many years. St Paul's U is affiliated with U of O. Through Algonquin College, Ottawa is also the centre of the region's community college system.

Much of the city's cultural life and most of its facilities are dominated by the federal govern-

ment. Almost all federal cultural agencies have showcases in Ottawa, including the NATIONAL MUSEUMS, the NATIONAL GALLERY, the NATIONAL ARCHIVES and the National Library. The NATIONAL ARTS CENTRE, with its symphony orchestra and theatres in French and English, also attracts international and N American performers. The city also has a symphony orchestra and supports several theatre companies, including Ottawa Little Theatre and Great Canadian Theatre Co. The Bytown Museum operates in one of Col By's original buildings and the city operates a municipal archives and a museum. Lansdowne Park is the site of the annual Central Canada Exhibition, home of the OTTAWA ROUGH RIDERS professional football team and the amateur Junior A hockey team, the '67s. Rowing, canoeing, skiing, track and gymnastics clubs also operate in the city. Ottawa is served by at least 3 private TV networks, the CBC's French and English services and the public networks of Ontario and Québec. Its daily newspapers are *Le Droit* (French) and *The Citizen* (English). The *Herald* began as a weekly in 1983 and is now a biweekly.   JOHN TAYLOR

Reading: David B. Knight, *A Capital for Canada* (1977) and *Choosing Canada's Capital* (1977); John Taylor, *Ottawa: An Illustrated History* (1986).

Ottawa Agreements, 12 bilateral trade agreements providing for mutual tariff concessions and certain other commitments, negotiated 20 July-20 Aug 1932 at Ottawa by Britain, Canada and other COMMONWEALTH Dominions and territories. They may be seen as the culmination of a trend towards IMPERIAL PREFERENCE, which began with Canada's unilateral grant of such preferences in 1897. Among the Canadian industries that may have benefited from the agreements were wheat growing, lumbering and milling, apple growing, automobile manufacturing and the nonferrous metals industry. Canada's negotiators, anxious to gain a lot and to give a little, nevertheless promised to admit British manufactures on terms that would give them a fair chance in the Canadian market. Canada also lowered some tariffs on British goods while raising them on some non-British goods, widening the margin between ordinary and preferential rates and thereby annoying the US. Similar arrangements were made by Britain with South Africa, Australia and New Zealand. Britain promised to impose no duties on empire foodstuffs, to raise duties and to impose quotas on many non-empire foodstuffs, and to continue duty-free or low-tariff arrangements for empire manufactures, such as Canadian automobiles. Thus there were new duties on "foreign" dairy products, quotas for certain meats, and many other realignments of British and Dominion duties. The agreements succeeded in giving the Dominions a larger share of the British market, but they did not arrest the decline in Britain's share of the imperial market. The Anglo-Canadian Agreement was modified in 1937, again in 1938 and many times since 1945. Some mutual concessions still exist, and most of them can be traced to the Ottawa Agreements.

IAN M. DRUMMOND

Reading: Ian M. Drummond, *Imperial Economic Policy 1917-1939* (1974).

Ottawa Journal was founded in 1885 by A.S. Woodburn, who briefly employed J.W. DAFOE as the paper's editor. In 1886 the paper was bought by P.D. Ross, who ran it for many years as Ottawa's Conservative evening newspaper. The *Journal* merged in 1917 with E. Norman Smith's *Ottawa Free Press*, and thereafter ran a morning edition, until 1949. Ross controlled the paper until his death, also in 1949. Smith then became the paper's president, until his death in 1957. Under

Ross and Smith, M. Grattan O'LEARY dominated the *Journal's* editorial page, and he was Smith's natural successor as *Journal* president, a post he held until 1966. The *Journal* succeeded, within the limits of its finances, in maintaining a highly literate editorial page while specializing in parliamentary reporting. Although Conservative, the paper kept its partisanship within bounds, between elections.

The *Journal's* finances were never strong. O'Leary brought about the sale of the paper to FP Publications (representing a group of western newspapers including the Winnipeg *Free Press*) in 1959, while retaining editorial control. During the 1970s the *Journal* began to experience financial difficulties and considerable labour trouble. In 1980 it was sold to the THOMSON GROUP, and some months later closed down. *See also* JOURNALISM; NEWSPAPERS.   ROBERT BOTHWELL

Reading: I.N. Smith, *The Journal Men* (1974).

Ottawa River, 1271 km long, chief tributary of the ST LAWRENCE R, rises in a chain of lakes in the LAURENTIAN HIGHLANDS. It continues with Dozois Reservoir, Grand-Lac-Victoria, Lac Granet, Decelles Reservoir, Lac Simard and Lk Timiskaming, entering each slowly and discharging with a heavy rush. South from Lk Timiskaming, it grows broad and forceful, widening into marshy lakes, then constricting into turbulent rapids. At St-André-Est, the Ottawa expands to form Lac-des-Deux-Montagnes, from which it enters the St Lawrence through Rivière des Prairies and Rivière des Mille-Îles to the E, and by a channel to Lac St-Louis to the south. Tributaries from the north-side highlands are often wild and swift: DUMOINE R (129 km), Coulonge R (217 km), Gatineau R (386 km), du Lièvre R (330 km), Petite Nation R (97 km) and Rouge R (185 km). From the south, the Petawawa R (187 km) and Madawaska R (230 km) also flow through rugged terrain, but the Mississippi R (169 km), Rideau R (146 km) and South Nation R (161 km) drain gentler land. After the last glacier melted, it was the Ottawa that drained the Great Lakes until the land rose and a new channel was found via the St Lawrence. The fine clay soil of the southern valley was deposited by the Ottawa in its journey to the sea, forming a long fertile intrusion into the otherwise implacable Canadian SHIELD. From Lk Timiskaming to Montréal, the river forms the border between Ontario and Québec, but the division is more than political – to the south are rich farms and gentle hills, to the north the forests of the Laurentians.

For several hundred years, the Ottawa was the primary transportation route to the western interior. The Algonquin controlled it in early times and one group exacted tolls from a strategic base on Allumette I, where they also grew corn and tobacco. Jacques CARTIER probably saw the river from atop Mount Royal, but Étienne BRÛLÉ was likely the first European to travel it (1610). In 1613 via the Mattawa and FRENCH rivers to Georgian Bay, CHAMPLAIN travelled the route which was used to carry furs for the next 200 years. The river was a tough challenge for the voyageurs,

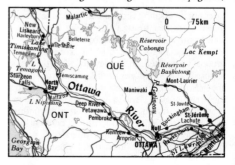

requiring 18 portages, some of the most difficult being at Long Sault, Deschênes, Lac des Chats, Chenaux, Portage-du-Fort, Chaudière Falls, Rocher Fendu, Des Joachims, La Cave and Des Érables. The French made small impact on the river valley, though they built a few posts and even drove some timber in the 1740s. L'ORIGNAL, granted in 1674, was the first seigneury in present-day Ontario but was not developed for 100 years. HAWKESBURY was founded in 1798, and there Thomas Mears built the first gristmill, sawmill and later the first steamer, the *Union*, on the Ottawa. The first paper mill in Canada was built 1803-05 at St-André-Est, and the American Philemon WRIGHT founded Wrightsville (later HULL) in 1800 with American settlers. Loyalists, led by Sir John JOHNSON, moved into the valley in 1814, and French settlers onto Petite Nation seigneury. In 1817 land along the Rideau R was granted to 1000 British veterans, and in 1825 Archibald MCNAB led a group of Scots to the mouth of the Madawaska R.

Log rafts descended the Ottawa even before it ceased to be the prime route of the fur trade after 1821. Wright showed that the route was feasible in 1807, and the British demand for pine grew until, by 1830, the valley timber trade dominated the Canadian economy. After 1850 the British demand for square timber fell, but in 1854 RECIPROCITY gained free access for Canadian lumber into the US market. The timber trade pervaded the social life of the valley. Armies of men lived in crude shanties during winter and descended on civilization with their rafts come spring. Competition among shanties and between French and Irish led to feuds and violent clashes (*see* SHINERS' WARS). After the completion of the RIDEAU CANAL (1832), Bytown (later OTTAWA) grew to be the largest lumber centre on the river. Though a few timber barons, such as E.B. EDDY and J.R. BOOTH, made fortunes, many lumbermen and Irish labourers lived in poverty and disease. The ravages of the axe swept up the river and its tributaries. By 1828 there was a sawmill at the future site of PEMBROKE; after 1850 cutting reached the Madawaska R, and by the 1870s Lk Timiskaming. Railways challenged the river by the 1850s, carrying lumber to BROCKVILLE and Ogdensburg, NY. By the 1870s rail lines reached CARLETON PLACE, RENFREW, ALMONTE and Pembroke. Steamers plied the river with goods and passengers, aided by a canal at Carillon, which permitted uninterrupted travel from Montréal to Ottawa. This river transport ceased by 1900.

Most of the valley's stands of pine had been decimated by 1910. Where land was fertile, farmers settled; elsewhere there remained a wasteland of stumps and debris vulnerable to fire. Part of the wilderness was saved from the axe when ALGONQUIN PROVINCIAL PARK was created (1893), and in 1918 Canada's first forestry research station was established at Petawawa to study the effects of logging, disease and fire. With the loss of the larger trees, most mills converted to pulp and paper, still an important industry along the river. But except for the farming area of the lower valley, the heritage of the timber trade is a depressed economy, with little industry and high unemployment. Much of the hydroelectric power gained by harnessing the Ottawa is transmitted to Toronto and elsewhere. Ottawa, which was chosen as Canada's capital in 1857, is clearly the dominant urban centre, but its prosperity is based on the federal government, not on valley resources or its riverine connections. First called the Grand Rivière des Algonquins, the river took its name from a later group of middlemen in the fur trade, the Ottawa. JAMES MARSH

Ottawa Rough Riders, football team. Ottawa has had FOOTBALL teams since the 1870s, including the Canadian Rugby Union, champions in

The river otter (*Lutra canadensis*) is found primarily along the BC coast (*artwork by Claire Tremblay*).

1898, 1900 and 1902, and the Ottawa Senators (a combination of the Rough Riders and Ottawa St Brigid's), which won the GREY CUP in 1925 and 1926. The Rough Riders returned to the Dominion final in 1939, 1940, 1948 and 1951, defeating Toronto Balmy Beach and Saskatchewan respectively in 1940 and 1951. Coach Frank Clair and quarterback Russ JACKSON, probably the greatest Canadian ever to play that position, took Ottawa to Grey Cups in 1960, 1966, 1968 and 1969, losing only to Saskatchewan in 1966. In 1973 Jack Gotta coached the Riders to another Cup victory and his successor George Brancato won the championship in 1976 and lost to Edmonton in 1981. Fred Glick was appointed head coach in 1987. Their present stadium at Lansdowne Park was opened in 1967 (and now seats 34 838) although the site has been their home since the early 1900s. DEREK DRAGER

Ottenbrite, Anne, swimmer (b at Whitby, Ont 12 May 1966). She won gold medals in the 200 m breaststroke and 4 x 100 m medley relay and silver in the 100 m breaststroke at the 1982 COMMONWEALTH GAMES in Brisbane, Australia, and a gold medal in the 100 m breaststroke and a silver in the 4 x 100 m relay at the 1983 Pan-American Games, where she was disqualified in the 200 m breaststroke for using a dolphin kick. At the 1984 Los Angeles OLYMPICS, while still a high-school student, she won a gold medal in the 200 m breaststroke, silver in the 100 m breaststroke and bronze in the 4 x 100 m relay. She has been a Member of the Order of Canada since 1984 and in 1985 was inducted into the Canadian Amateur Sports Hall of Fame. JAMES MARSH

Otter The river otter (*Lutra canadensis*) occurs throughout N America except in desert and arid tundra regions. In Canada it is scarce, except along the BC coast, where it is abundant and often wrongly identified as a SEA OTTER. The otter is a large WEASEL, males reaching 1.3 m in length and weighing 8 kg; females are slightly smaller. Its colour is dark brown, paler below. It is amphibious, its streamlined body and tail, short legs, webbed feet and dense waterproof fur equipping it to hunt in water. The otter's food is 90% fish, but crustaceans, amphibians, mammals and birds are also important. It has a lengthy mating period in late winter and spring; gestation lasts $9\frac{1}{2}$-$12\frac{1}{2}$ months. Young (1-4) are born in a nest under a rock pile or in a burrow or similar shelter. The pelage is dense with an underfur of several fine hairs per follicle, protected by long guard hairs. It is valued as a beautiful and durable fur and several thousand otters are trapped each year. Where not harassed, otters tame easily. They are abundant even in such busy harbours as Vancouver. *See also* FUR TRAPPING. IAN MCTAGGART-COWAN

Otter, Sir William Dillon, soldier (b at Clinton, Ont 3 Dec 1843; d at Toronto 6 May 1929). A veteran of the Battle at RIDGEWAY in 1866 and a

part-time soldier, Otter joined the permanent force in 1883. He commanded the Battleford column in the North-West Campaign of 1885 (*see* NORTH-WEST REBELLION) and was the first commanding officer of the Royal Canadian Regiment of Infantry in 1893. In 1899 Otter was the obvious choice to lead the first Canadian contingent in the SOUTH AFRICAN WAR. His austere professionalism was unpopular with subordinates but contributed to Canadian prestige. In 1908 he was the first Canadian-born chief of the general staff and was inspector general of the Canadian Militia 1910-12, when he retired. He commanded INTERNMENT operations during WWI. Otter was knighted in 1913 and in 1922 became the second Canadian soldier, after Sir Arthur CURRIE, to reach the rank of general. DESMOND MORTON

Reading: Desmond Morton, *Ministers and Generals* (1970) and *The Canadian General, Sir William Otter* (1974).

Ouellet, Fernand, historian, educator (b at Lac Bouchette, Qué 6 Nov 1926). After taking his doctorate from U Laval, Ouellet did specialized study in Paris, returning to teach history at Laval, then at Carleton U, the U of O and, finally, York U in Toronto. He is a member of the Royal Society of Canada and an Officer in the Order of Canada. The most important figure in the transformation of French Canadian history since WWII, Ouellet repudiated the nationalist interpretations previously dominating the field and replaced traditional methods with quantitative and scientific techniques derived from modern French scholarship. The "Ouellet Revolution" shifted Canadian historians' attentions from nation to class and from dramatic events to social and economic structures and tendencies. Especially noteworthy are his *Histoire économique et sociale du Québec, 1760-1850* (1966, tr in 1980 as *Economic and Social History of Quebec, 1760-1850*), and *Le Bas-Canada, 1791-1840* (1976, abridged and tr in 1980 as *Lower Canada, 1791-1840*). A.I. SILVER

Ouellette, Fernand, writer (b at Montréal 24 Sept 1930). He is one of the most active intellectuals of his generation. Cofounder of the journal LIBERTÉ in 1959 and a member of its editorial board, he established with Jean-Guy Pilon the Rencontre québécoise internationale des écrivains. He was a member of the commission of inquiry into the teaching of the arts in Québec 1966-68, and has been writer-in-residence or visiting professor at various universities. In addition, he has produced radio programs on cultural topics for Radio-Canada. He published poetry with Éditions de l'hexagone, notably *Ces anges de sang* (1955), *Le Soleil sous la mort* (1965), *Dans le sombre* (1967), *Ici, ailleurs, la lumière* (1977), which were collected with others in *Poésie* (1972) and *En la nuit la mer* (1981). Though metaphysical or mystical, his poetry is profoundly physical, taut, erotic, filled with flashes of insight. His quest for the absolute resembles that of the German Romantics — see *Depuis Novalis: errance et gloses* (1973) — while his rigorous demands are like those of Pierre-Jean Jouve. Also a critic and theorizer of his preferred genres, he is an excellent essayist. Shortly after the declaration of the War Measures Act in 1970 during the October Crisis, Ouellette refused the Gov Gen's Award for *Les Actes retrouvés* on poetry and poetics, power, violence and tolerance. *Écrire en notre temps* (1979) continues the same aesthetic and ethical themes. A friend of a number of painters, including Chagall, and of composer Edgard Varèse, whose biography he wrote (1966; Eng tr 1968), Ouellette is interested in the art that underlies all art. His *Journal dénoué* (prize of journal *Études françaises*, 1974) is an important intellectual biography. Three novels, *Tu regardais intensément Geneviève* (1978), *La Mort vive* (1980) and *Lucie ou Un midi en novembre* (1985) were controversial. The last won a Gov Gen's Award in 1985.   LAURENT MAILHOT

Ouellette, Gerald, marksman (b at Windsor, Ont 14 Aug 1934; d near Leamington, Ont 25 June 1975). Ouellette was introduced to shooting during his high-school cadet training. By 1952 he was a veteran of several teams that competed at Bisley, Eng. He became proficient in the small-bore rifle competition and captured the 1956 OLYMPIC gold medal with a perfect score of 600. In 1959 he was Canadian sporting rifle champion and won a Pan-American Games gold medal. He was on Canada's Olympic team in 1968. He died flying his own aircraft.   J. THOMAS WEST

Ouellette-Michalska, Madeleine, novelist, poet, essayist (b at Rivière-du-Loup 27 May 1930). She graduated from U de M (1968) and received a master's degree from U du Q à Montréal (1975). At first a teacher she became in 1976 a journalist and literary critic for *Perspectives, Châtelaine, L'Actualité* and *Le Devoir*. She also taught creative writing and journalistic criticism at the universities of Montréal and Ottawa. She contributed articles to many Québec literary reviews and the FM network of Radio-Canada broadcast her plays. She has received the Governor General's Award and the Prix Molson (from the ACADÉMIE CANADIENNE-FRAN-CAISE). She made her literary début as a short-story writer with *Dôme* (1968), and she has published a poetry collection, *Entre le souffle et l'aine* (1981), and 5 novels whose characters, especially the female ones, experience painful lives but slowly free themselves from their burdens to interrogate history itself. A theoretical essay, *L'Échappée des discours de l'oeil* (1981), shed light on all her works through its anthropological and psychoanalytical reflections on the patriarchal system, on relations between men and women, and on feminist attitudes toward writing. In her personal journal, *La Tentation de dire* (1985), the writer continues to develop the subjects close to her heart: Québec culture, the workings of the imagination, and the genetic memory of the body.   MARIE-JOSÉ DES RIVIÈRES

Ouimet, Gédéon, premier of Québec (b at Ste-Rose, Qué, 2 June 1823; d at Saint-Hilaire-de-Dorset, Qué 23 Apr 1905). Conservative premier for 19 months (Feb 1873 to Sept 1874), he was forced to resign by financial scandals. Also minister of public instruction during his premiership, he was superintendent of education for Québec 1876-95.   DANIEL LATOUCHE

Ouimet, Joseph-Alphonse, engineer, CBC president (b at Montréal 12 June 1908). Educated at U de Montréal and McGill, Ouimet worked for a firm developing television and built a prototype TV receiver in 1932. He joined the Canadian Radio Broadcasting Commission, later the CBC, in 1934 and as chief engineer from 1948 was responsible for the creation of Canadian TV broadcasting. He became general manager of the CBC in 1953 and president in 1958; under his leadership the national television service was established from coast to coast and in both languages. BROADCASTING legislation was politically contentious during this period and Ouimet resigned in 1967, after Secretary of State Judy LAMARSH criticized the CBC's "rotten management." He was chairman of the board of Telesat Canada 1969-80. Among other awards he was appointed Companion to the Order of Canada in 1969 and received the McNaughton Medal for public service in 1972.   DONALD J.C. PHILLIPSON

Ouimet, Léo-Ernest, director, producer, distributor, exhibitor (b at St-Martin, Qué 16 Mar 1877; d at Montréal 2 Mar 1972). On 1 Jan 1906, he opened the first permanent cinema in Mont-

réal, the Ouimetoscope, and a year later opened the first large cinema theatre in N America. Ouimet became one of Canada's first film distributors. To add local flavour to his programs he also made shorts, some based on his family (*Mes espérances en 1908*, 1908) and some on current affairs (*L'Affaire de la gare Windsor*, 1909 and *L'Incendie du Herald*, 1910). Clashes with the clergy over Sunday opening of cinemas forced him out of the exhibition business. He produced a feature-length drama, *Le Feu qui brûle* (1918), and organized the British Canadian Pathé News. In Hollywood he produced *Why Get Married* (1924), which virtually marked the end of his career in cinema.   PIERRE VÉRONNEAU

Overlanders of 1862, a group of some 150 settlers who travelled from Ontario to the BC interior, led by brothers Thomas and Robert McMicking of Stamford Township, Welland County, Ont. They went in groups by ship and American railway to Ft Garry [Winnipeg]. Leaving there in early June 1862, equipped with Red River carts and a few horses, they reached Ft Edmonton on July 21 and traded their carts for pack horses. With the help of Indian guides they crossed the Rockies. All but 6 survived the perilous descent of the Fraser R by raft to Ft George [Prince George]. Most went on to the Cariboo goldfields, and many, including the McMickings, had successful careers in BC. The only woman Overlander, Catherine O'Hare Schubert, took her 3 children with her and gave birth to her fourth only hours after arriving at Kamloops in Oct.   BARRY M. GOUGH

Owen, Donald, filmmaker (b at Toronto 19 Sept 1934). Owen studied anthropology at U of T and joined the NFB in 1960, where he made a few short films before directing *Nobody Waved Good-bye* (1964), a feature film dealing with teenage alienation that delineated many of the themes of Canadian cinema. *The Ernie Game* (1967) took up where *Nobody Waved Good-bye* left off, but its detached hero failed to win audience sympathies. In 1969 Owen left the NFB. His third feature, *Partners* (1976), was not successful, forcing him to concentrate on commercial TV work between projects. Recent features are *Unfinished Business* (1984) and *Turnabout* (1987).   PIERS HANDLING

Owen, Lemuel Cambridge, merchant, politician, premier of PEI (b at Charlottetown 1 Nov 1822; d there 26 Nov 1912). Successful in shipbuilding and trade, Owen, a leading colonial merchant, was postmaster general of the colony from 1860 until elected to the Assembly in 1866. As premier 1873-76, Owen supervised the end of the proprietorial landholding system – the cost of which was borne by the federal government as a result of the 1873 Confederation agreement.
                                      H.T. HOLMAN

Owen, William Fitzwilliam, naval officer, hydrographic surveyor (b at Manchester, Eng 17 Sept 1774; d at Saint John 3 Nov 1857). He is renowned for surveying E and W coasts of Africa in the 1820s. In Canada 1815-17 Capt Owen laid the foundations of scientific charting of the Great Lakes: fixing the longitudes of places from Québec to Penetanguishene; making a preliminary survey from Lake Erie to Georgian Bay to locate a naval base and describe border waters; completing the charting of Lake Ontario and the St Lawrence above Prescott. He recruited H.W. BAY-FIELD to the work and trained him. He named Owen Sound (the body of water) in 1815 for his brother Sir Edward W.C.R. Owen. On half-pay, he moved to the Owen family estate at Campobello I, NB, in 1836 and entered actively into local and provincial affairs (JP, MLA 1838-42, legislative counsellor, lay reader). The family lived as English gentry, virtually a feudal outpost against

yankee initiatives. Owen's 5 years of surveying the Saint John R and much of the Bay of Fundy ended with admiral's rank in 1847.
                                      PAUL CORNELL

Reading: E.H. Burrows, *Captain Owen of the African Survey* (1979).

Owen Sound, Ont, City, pop 19 804 (1986c), 19 883 (1981c), inc 1920, is located on an inlet at the S end of GEORGIAN BAY, at the outlet of the Sydenham and Pottawattomi rivers, 190 km NW of Toronto. A preliminary survey was made of the site in 1837 and the first building was erected in 1840. Originally named Sydenham after Lord SYDENHAM, the community was renamed 1857 in honour of William Fitzwilliam OWEN, RN, who had charted the bay in 1815. (It had been intended to name it after Owen's son, William F. Owen, but as he was still a serving officer, he could not be honoured in this way.) Owen Sound's fine harbour became a port of call for the steamers plying Georgian Bay and later a transshipment point and a shipbuilding centre. Now the seat of Grey County, it services a mixed-farming hinterland. Major employers are manufacturers of auto accessories and industrial equipment, and the printer Richardson, Bond and Wright. In the winter it is a popular skiing area. The painter Tom THOMSON grew up nearby and is honoured by the Tom Thomson Memorial Gallery.   DANIEL FRANCIS

Owl (order Strigiformes) efficient, carnivorous, nocturnal BIRD OF PREY. Owls' eerie hoots and calls at night often make them seem mysterious – even

Fifteen species of owl reside in Canada, including the barn owl shown here (*Tyto alba*), whose usual nesting place is a ledge in a barn (*photo by Stephen J. Krasemann/ DRK Photo*).

Snowy owl (*Nyctea scandiaca*) (*artwork by John Crosby*).

birds of ill-omen. Fifteen of the world's 133 species reside in Canada. In most species, the substantially smaller adult male feeds the female incubating on the nest. Incubation begins as each egg is laid and there is often an interval of 2 or more days between eggs. As it can take food away from younger nestlings, the oldest owlet is well fed even when prey populations are low. With severe famine, the parent owl may feed the smaller owlets to the larger nestmates. Owls are downy at hatching and most species remain in or near the nest until able to fly. No owl builds its own nest. Canada's best-known owl, the great horned (*Bubo virginianus*), usually appropriates the discarded nest of a red-tailed hawk. Great horned owls will also use an artificial platform or even a ledge in a barn. The latter is the usual nesting place of the common barn owl (*Tyto alba*), a species restricted to southern parts of Ontario and BC. The large, reclusive great gray owl (*Strix nebulosa*) of the boreal forest prefers a northern goshawk nest in a tamarack swamp. The crow-sized, long-eared owl (*Asio otus*) takes over nests of the common crow or black-billed magpie. The short-eared owl (*A. flammeus*), present transcontinentally, and the snowy owl (*Nyctea scandiaca*), restricted in summer to the arctic TUNDRA, both nest on the ground. The burrowing owl (*Athene cunicularia*) of the western provinces occupies badger holes underground. The barred owl (*Strix varia*) of the southern boreal forest fringe prefers a broken-off, balsam poplar trunk, and the rare spotted owl (*S. occidentalis*) of southern BC uses a large tree cavity or cliff crevice. Smaller owls, such as the northern saw-whet owl (*Aegolius acadicus*) and eastern and western screech owls (*Otus asio* and *O. kennicottii*) of the deciduous woods of southern Canada, the northern pygmy (*Glaucidium gnoma*) and flammulated owls (*O. flammeolus*) of BC, and the boreal (*Aegolius funereus*) and northern hawk owls (*Surnia ulula*) of the boreal forest, all nest in woodpeckers' holes in hollow trees.

Owls are generally beneficial. Great gray, long-eared, short-eared, boreal and saw-whet owls eat substantial numbers of mice. Great horned owl numbers rise and fall with the 10-year cycle of its favourite prey, the snowshoe hare. Great horned owls also take Norway rats, American coots and pocket gophers. Occasionally, a young great horned owl learns about poul-

try and visits a farmyard nightly. Regurgitated, well-formed pellets or casts, containing undigested bones and fur, show what owls have been eating. Two of Canada's largest owls, the great gray and great horned owls, are year-round residents, as are the barred, hawk, both screech, boreal and northern saw-whet owls, although large numbers of the last migrate through S Ontario. When hares are scarce in Saskatchewan and Alberta, great horned owls often move as far as 1500 km SE. The snowy owl, Canada's third-largest owl, visits southern Canada in winter, and some of the northern owls sometimes undergo large, eruptive flights to the S.

C. STUART HOUSTON

Oyster, common name for bivalve (hinged shell) MOLLUSCS, including true oysters (order Ostreoida) and tropical pearl oysters (order Pterioida), found chiefly in temperate and warm shallow waters. True oysters have been cultivated for centuries and are much used for food; they are the *huîtres* of French cuisine. Their shells are irregular in outline and fixed to a surface by the left (lower) valve or half-shell. They are divided according to whether young are brooded within the shell, or whether development occurs free in the PLANKTON. Incubatory oysters have no commercial significance in Canada, although a substantial fishery for the Olympic oyster (*Ostrea lurida*) existed on the West Coast until its depletion in 1930. An attempt has been made to introduce the European flat oyster (*O. edulis*) to NS. Nonincubatory oysters (eg, eastern oyster, *Crassostrea virginica*, and Pacific oyster, *C. gigas*) support significant AQUACULTURE operations on both coasts.

FRANK R. BERNARD

Oystercatcher, name given to 10 species of large SHOREBIRDS of the family Haematopodidae. Oystercatchers are either black and white or entirely black. Their orange-red bills are elongated and compressed from side to side, allowing the birds to chisel open clams and other molluscs. Two species occur in N America: American oystercatchers (*Haematopus palliatus*) breed from Long I south to Mexico (occasional visitors to Canada); American black oystercatchers (*H. bachmani*) breed from the Aleutians S to Baja,

California, where they hybridize with the American oystercatcher.

A.J. BAKER

Ozone Layer, or ozonosphere, region of the atmosphere containing the highest concentration of ozone gas (O_3). On average, it is located at an altitude of about 25 km (range 10-50 km), but is higher near the equator and lower near the poles. Maximum ozone concentration in the ozonosphere rarely exceeds a few molecules per million molecules of air; the average concentration in the entire atmosphere is even smaller. The smallest total amounts of ozone are found over the equator, the largest over the poles in winter.

The development of the ozone layer is thought to have been a significant factor permitting the evolution of life on Earth. Ozone is the main atmospheric gas that absorbs the biologically damaging part of the sun's ultraviolet radiation, known as UV-B (ultraviolet-biologically active). The small fraction that reaches the Earth's surface causes sunburn and is implicated in skin cancer, eye damage and suppression of the human immune system. UV-B radiation also reduces crop yields and affects the phytoplankton in the ocean food cycle.

Atmospheric ozone influences climate in 2 ways. First, since ozone also absorbs infrared solar radiation, it contributes to the greenhouse effect. Second, chemical processes which produce the ozone layer also heat the stratosphere, where the layer occurs. This heating, in turn, affects the temperature and radiation balance of the lower atmosphere and the Earth's surface. Ozone concentrations may increase locally, in the lower atmosphere, especially in smog, as a by-product of chemical reactions. There is also concern that the use of certain chlorofluorocarbons in aerosol spray cans, refrigerators and plastic foam products can deplete the ozone layer. This led to restrictions on the use of some of these compounds in Canada and elsewhere.

H.I. SCHIFF AND L. DOTTO

In 1985, a United Nations Environment Program meeting produced a Convention for the Protection of the Ozone Layer which was signed by more than 20 countries. A Control Protocol to control the release of chlorofluorocarbons (CFCS) was signed at a conference in Montréal in Sept 1987. Under this protocol, the signatory nations have agreed to reduce CFC usage to 50% of the 1986 production levels by the year 2000.

Environment Canada operates a network of stations for monitoring ozone at Edmonton, Toronto, Resolute, Churchill and Goose Bay. The total ozone amount and the height profile are monitored. UV-B radiation is also monitored at Toronto. Canada has developed new technology for monitoring the ozone layer; the Brewer ozone spectrophotometer is used around the world for ozone monitoring. Research on the chemistry of the ozone layer is conducted by Environment Canada (Project Stratoprobe) using high-altitude research balloons. In 1985, a phenomenon called the Antarctic ozone hole was discovered using satellite imagery. Each spring, a large hole appears over the Antarctic continent; this hole has been getting deeper each year since 1979. In the period since 1986, studies have been conducted to determine whether a possible Arctic ozone hole exists. This project, called CANOZE (Canadian ozone experiment), uses stations such as Saskatoon, Resolute and Alert to study this phenomenon. Balloon and ground-based instruments are used to measure ozone and other gases at northern locations during the spring. This work has determined that a craterlike hole appeared in the Arctic ozone map in Mar 1986, but it is not evident that it is getting deeper year by year as is the Antarctic hole.

W.F.J. EVANS

Paardeberg, Battle of, first major British success in the SOUTH AFRICAN WAR since "Black Week," 10-15 Dec 1899. Faced by a reorganized British offensive directed at their capitals, the Afrikaners made a stand at Paardeberg, a point on the Modder R some 130 km from Bloemfontein. Canada's 1st contingent fought first at Paardeberg Drift on 18 Feb 1900 where, after hours under fire in the scorching sun, they were ordered to make a suicidal assault. Their second engagement took place on Feb 27, 3 km from the Drift. The Canadians, attacking before dawn, faced withering Afrikaner rifle fire. Although the regiment was ordered to retreat, 2 companies from the Maritimes, who failed to hear or heed the order, maintained their position and returned the fire. Shortly thereafter Gen Piet Cronje and almost 4000 exhausted Afrikaners surrendered. The battle for Paardeberg cost Canada 31 men; another 92 were wounded.   CARMAN MILLER

Pacey, William Cyril Desmond, professor, literary critic (b at Dunedin, NZ 1 May 1917; d at Fredericton 4 July 1975). Educated at U of T and Cambridge he taught English at U Man (1940-44) before moving to UNB, where he remained. Though an accomplished short-story writer, Pacey was best known as a critic and scholar. He produced an anthology of Canadian stories (1947) and editions of Frederick Philip GROVE's stories (1971) and letters (1976). His criticism ranges from Frances BROOKE to Leonard COHEN, and includes books on Grove (1945) and Ethel Wilson (1968). Pacey's balanced judgements have generally endured and his close studies of individual works have been influential. His finest work is found in *Creative Writing in Canada* (1952) and *Ten Canadian Poets* (1958).   TRACY WARE

Reading: D. Pacey, *Essays in Canadian Criticism* (1969).

Pacheenaht ("people of the sea foam"), a NOOTKA Indian tribe of San Juan Harbour on the W coast of Vancouver I, BC. The Pacheenaht were once a Ditidaht group that became independent, and amalgamated with other groups to form a large tribe. Their traditional territories include San Juan Harbour, the outer coast from Bonilla Point to Point No Point, and the San Juan R valley. Once very numerous, the Pacheenaht were severely reduced by disease in the historical period. They live today in their village of Pachena, near Port Renfrew.   JOHN DEWHIRST

Paci, Frank Gilbert, writer (b at Pesaro, Italy 5 Aug 1948; immigrated to Sault Ste Marie 1952). He was educated at U of T (BA 1970, BEd 1975) and Carleton U (MA 1980) and taught school in Sault Ste Marie and Toronto. Paci is one of the first and most important Italian Canadian novelists writing in English with *The Italians* (1978), *The Father* (1984) and his most significant work, *Black Madonna* (1982). While on one level his novels deal with ethnic duality and the struggle of Italian immigrant families, on another, they also explore the process of self-discovery and the conflict of man's ultimate concerns. *See also* ITALIAN WRITING.   JOSEPH PIVATO

Pacific Ballet Theatre, BC's only professional ballet company, employs 10 dancers for a 30-week season, with regular performances in Vancouver and throughout BC. Founded by Morley Wiseman, incorporated (1970) as "Ballet Horizons," it became the Pacific Ballet Theatre (1972) when Maria Lewis became director. Renald Rabu became resident choreographer (1978), artistic director (1978), and received the Clifford E. Lee Award in Choreography (1980). The company was reorganized in 1986 to become Ballet British Columbia under the direction of Annette AV PAUL. Reid Anderson was appointed the sole artistic

director in 1987. The new company performs works by Anderson, Cranko, Butler and Forsythe and has gained a strong reputation as a neoclassical company.   GRANT STRATE

Pacific Fur Company, est 23 June 1810 and headed by New York fur dealer John Jacob Astor. Principal partners included ex-Nor'Westers Alexander McKay, Donald McKenzie and Duncan McDougall. Astor envisaged a string of fur posts and settlements across the US and planned a fort, Ft Astoria, at the mouth of the Columbia R. On 6 Sept 1810 he sent the TONQUIN from New York to the Columbia (arrived 22 Mar 1811) to inaugurate trade with Indians of the NORTHWEST COAST; in June 1811 Tonquin was taken by Indians, probably in Clayoquot Sd (Vancouver I). An overland party did not reach Astoria until Feb 1812. During the WAR OF 1812, on 25 June 1813, the partners decided to sell their supplies to their competition, the NORTH WEST COMPANY. In July they dissolved the company and on 16 Oct 1813 sold everything to the Nor'Westers; Astoria was later renamed Ft George. The arrival of HMS RACOON in Nov 1813 and the NWC's ship ISAAC TODD in Apr 1814 speeded the decline of the PFC. Astor subsequently put his energies into the American Fur Co.   BARRY M. GOUGH

Pacific Rim The term Pacific Rim has been used to refer to all those countries with coastlines bordering the Pacific Ocean. However, in recent years the term has become synonymous with the Asia Pacific region which encompasses East and Southeast Asia, South Asia, Australia, New Zealand and N America. This new terminology reflects a growing sense of regional interdependency and acknowledges the expansion of the economic and political significance of this region in the 20th century.

As a nation with a long Pacific coast Canada has always had some cultural and economic association with the Pacific Rim. Approximately 25 000 years ago, Canada's first inhabitants migrated from Asia across the BERINGIA land bridge. Beginning in the late 15th century, European explorers repeatedly (and unsuccessfully) attempted to find a sea passage through Canada which would lead them to the riches of Asia. In the 18th century, while European settlement and trade commenced on the East coast, other Europeans initiated trade with Asia from Canada's NORTHWEST COAST. From there, furs and timber were shipped to Asia in return for luxury items such as porcelain and tea.

After the completion of a transcontinental rail link in 1885, Canada was finally able to provide Britain with an alternative passage to its considerable interests in Asia. The building of this railway and the earlier Fraser R GOLD RUSH also coincided with the first significant modern immigration of

Asians to Canada. Yet while Asian immigration increased, Canada's cultural identity and economic priorities still were determined by its historic ties with Britain and its population who were mostly of European origin. However, in the post WWII period, as a result of the general process of decolonization and in accordance with an international political and economic shift away from Europe and towards the Asia Pacific region, Canada has also begun to change its cultural identification and economic priorities. Today, Canada's major trading partners are the US and Japan, while Europe has fallen to third place.

As one of the nations most dependent on trade, Canada's continued development is reliant upon success in acquiring new markets for raw materials and manufactured goods. While both the federal government and private business recognize the potential for Canadian markets in the Asia Pacific region, they also recognize that successful development must be accompanied by an improved understanding of the variety of economic, cultural and political factors which influence trading practices in this region. In response to this need Canada participates in regional associations such as the Pacific Basin Economic Council and has established federal and private organizations such as the Canadian National Committee for Pacific Economic Co-operation.

By the year 2000, there will be over 25 megacities in the world with populations of over 10 million people. Thirteen of these cities will be in Asia and only 3 in Europe and N America. It is apparent that Canada's future economic development will depend on its successful identification as a member of the Pacific Rim community of nations.

Pacific Rim National Park (est 1970) stretches for 105 km along the rugged W coast of VANCOUVER I. It comprises 3 sections: Long Beach, a 10.3 km sweep of surf-pounded sand and rock; the Broken Is Group, including more than 100 islands accessible only by boat; and the West Coast Trail, a 72 km hiking trail between Bamfield and Port Renfrew. Each unit is separate, with its own special character. The park is unique in that its boundaries extend offshore to the 10-fathom line to protect the marine environment. Heavy rains and mild temperatures year-round have produced a dense coastal rain forest of Sitka spruce, western hemlock, amabilis fir and western red cedar. The forest, framed to the W by the ocean and to the E by rugged mountains, is home for black bear, black-tailed deer, cougar, marten, otter and squirrel. Offshore the dense forest of giant kelp is home to an amazing variety of fish and invertebrates, eg, giant octopus. LILLIAN STEWART

Pacific Salmon, 7 species of fish belonging to genus *Oncorhynchus*, family Salmonidae. Two are native to Japan (*O. masou* and *O. rhodurus*); 5 to Canada, pink (*O. gorbuscha*), chum (*O. keta*), sockeye (*O. nerka*), coho (*O. kisutch*) and chinook (*O. tshawytscha*). The genus name refers to the hooked snout characteristic of most spawning males. The native range of Pacific SALMON includes the north Pacific Ocean, Bering Strait, SW Beaufort Sea and surrounding fresh waters. They occur in an estimated 1300-1500 rivers and streams in BC, notably the SKEENA R and NASS R in the N; the FRASER R in the S accounts for about 75% of the total. They have been introduced successfully to New Zealand, parts of Eurasia, the Great Lakes and S America. Pacific salmon are distinguished from other salmonids by their large number of anal fin rays (13-19). In fall, all Canadian species migrate into rivers and streams to spawn; eggs are buried in gravel. The young emerge in spring and stay in fresh water from 1 week to 3 years. Most then go to sea for 1-5 years, although some species have developed landlocked forms (eg, kokanee, a freshwater sockeye). At sea the species attains the following average adult weights: 1-3 kg, pink; 5-7 kg, chum; 3.5-7 kg, coho; 2-4 kg, sockeye; 6-18 kg, chinook (the largest recorded chinook was 56.8 kg). They return to their native stream to spawn and die. Marine adults have dark blue-black or blue-green backs, some species with black spots, and silver sides and belly. Spawning adults become colourful: golden brown (chinook), spotted brown and green (pink), purple (coho and chum) or bright red with green head (sockeye).

All Canadian species are found up the West Coast into Alaska, with pink and chum found as far N as the Mackenzie R. Pink salmon have been introduced to Lk Superior and are spreading through the Great Lakes. In Canada, chum have not been successfully introduced outside their native range. Coho were planted successfully into Lk Michigan in 1966 and have spread throughout the Great Lakes where they support an important sport fishery. Kokanee has been transplanted widely throughout Canada; populations can be found from BC (native and introduced) to Ontario. Attempts to establish chinook outside their range have been made more frequently than for any other species, but success is still questionable. Coho and chinook dominate the BC coastal sport fishery and are fished commercially by hook and line, and, to a lesser extent, by gill and seine nets. Sockeye, pink and chum are harvested primarily by commercial net fishermen. Approximately 41.8 million salmon, weighing 107.6 million kg, were harvested in 1985 in BC. Until 1985, with the signing of the Pacific Salmon Treaty between the US and Canada, the International Pacific Salmon Fisheries Commission governed the Pacific salmon fishery. The new organization, which is based in Vancouver, is the Pacific Salmon Commission. E.D. LANE

J.W. Bengough cartoon deploring the political morality during the Pacific Scandal (*courtesy National Archives of Canada/C-78604*).

"WE IN CANADA SEEM TO HAVE LOST ALL IDEA OF JUSTICE, HONOR AND INTEGRITY."—THE MAIL, 26TH SEPTEMBER.

Pacific Scandal, the result of solicitation by PM John A. MACDONALD, George-Étienne CARTIER, and Hector LANGEVIN of some $360 000 in campaign funds for the Aug 1872 general election, from promoters including Sir Hugh ALLAN. Macdonald and his Conservative colleagues needed money to fight the elections in Ontario and Québec, where a number of seats were in jeopardy. Notwithstanding his bribery of electors, Macdon-

ald did badly, his 1867 majority being substantially reduced. After the election Allan was rewarded with the contract to build the Pacific railway, on the assumption that he would divest himself of American control on his board of directors. Since Allan, unknown to Macdonald, had used American money to bribe the government, this proved difficult, and finally produced blackmail. The Liberals broke the scandal on 2 Apr 1873; a spate of damaging letters and telegrams appeared in Liberal newspapers in July. The government was stunned. It managed to weather a royal commission struck on Aug 14, but it could not survive Parliament. The Commons met on Oct 23; with the threat of new PEI votes against it, and its supporters in disarray, the Macdonald government was obliged to resign. Allan's company never did get started, and a new agreement had to wait until 1880. P.B. WAITE

Pacific Western Airlines Ltd (now Canadian Airlines International), with headquarters in Calgary, provides scheduled air transportation to passengers and cargo to over 89 destinations in 15 countries on 5 continents. With its fleet of 78 jet aircraft, the airline also provides charter services across Canada and to destinations throughout the world. PWA began in 1946 as Central British Columbia Airways Limited and grew by purchasing other airlines, including Kamloops Air Services (1950) and Skeena Air Transport (1951). In 1953 it became Pacific Western Airlines Ltd. In Mar 1987 Canadian Pacific Airlines was purchased by PWA Corp, the holding company of Pacific Western Airlines. CP Air had already acquired Nordair and Eastern Provincial Airways. The 4 airlines combined to form Canadian Airlines International. In 1986, PWA Corp had sales or operating revenues of $352 million, assets of $946 million and 2725 employees. Shares are broadly held.

Pacifism, an outlook based upon religious or humanitarian belief that condemns war and social violence as inhuman and irrational, if not absolutely and always morally wrong, and therefore demands personal nonparticipation in war or violent revolution as well as a commitment to nonviolent methods of resolving conflicts.

In Canada pacifism is rooted in 2 traditions. One is sectarian pacifism, the historic non-resistance of pacifist religious sects that have tried to remain separate from the mainstream of Canadian society. By the beginning of the 20th century the QUAKERS, MENNONITES, HUTTERITES and DOUKHOBORS had been guaranteed the right to live according to their pacifist beliefs. They received specific exemptions from military obligations, and thus their immunity became entrenched in Canadian law and custom. Sectarian pacifists have provided the largest and most consistent pacifist witness, particularly as conscientious objectors during both world wars.

The second tradition, which attracted popular support, is the liberal Protestant and humanitarian reform tradition, based upon the pacifist teachings of Jesus and belief in the irrationality of war and the brotherhood of man. The various expressions of liberal pacifism in Canada began with the progressive peace movement at the turn of the century, which emphasized international arbitration and conciliation as the best way to achieve world order. Nearly all political, church, farm, labour and women's groups had endorsed that principle before the outbreak of WWI. During the war, however, the liberal peace movement disintegrated, leaving only a few committed pacifists such as J.S. WOODSWORTH and William Ivens, renegade Methodist ministers who openly broke with their church in opposition to CONSCRIPTION. (Most anticonscription sentiment, notably in Québec, was not based upon pacifist belief.)

The postwar resurgence of liberal pacifism was fueled by both disillusionment with war and support for the LEAGUE OF NATIONS and DISARMAMENT. While Woodsworth and Agnes MACPHAIL pressed the peace issue in Parliament, and the WOMEN'S INTERNATIONAL LEAGUE FOR PEACE AND FREEDOM led a campaign to abolish cadet training and militarism in schools, an interwar PEACE MOVEMENT gained momentum. By the early 1930s it had expanded into a broad front representing various religious and political persuasions, but it was united by the Depression in the quest for socioeconomic justice as well as peace. Under Woodsworth's leadership, the CO-OPERATIVE COMMONWEALTH FEDERATION became the major political expression of this pacifist-socialist alignment. At mid-decade, however, social radicals began to abandon pacifism for the fight against fascism in Spain, and by WWII even the CCF altered its traditional neutralist foreign policy, leaving only Woodsworth in Parliament to voice the pacifist position. The movement narrowed to a few Christian pacifists, primarily United Church ministers in the Fellowship of Reconciliation, who publicly reaffirmed their pacifism in the controversial "Witness Against War" manifesto and were repudiated by their own church leaders. Although sectarian pacifists had remained aloof from the interwar peace movement, they co-operated with liberal pacifists during the war in an effort to ensure the exemption of conscientious objectors from military service.

The dawn of the atomic age increased the urgency and popular appeal of pacifism, and the ranks of the postwar peace movement swelled. Since the new "nuclear pacifists" believed it was nuclear weapons that made war unthinkable, they emphasized nuclear disarmament and the easing of tensions between the USSR and the West. The new movement was initially dominated by the leftist Canadian Peace Congress under the leadership of James ENDICOTT, but in the early 1960s the Canadian Campaign for Nuclear Disarmament and the VOICE OF WOMEN generated wider public support. In the 1980s such organizations as the CANADIAN PHYSICIANS FOR SOCIAL RESPONSIBILITY, PROJECT PLOUGHSHARES and OPERATION DISMANTLE further broadened the base of the peace movement in Canada. Both sectarian and liberal pacifists were swept up in the antinuclear campaign, which remains the focus of pacifists and other peace activists in Canada.

THOMAS P. SOCKNAT

Padlock Act (Act Respecting Communistic Propaganda), a 1937 Quebec statute empowering the attorney general to close, for one year, any building used for propagating "communism or bolshevism" (undefined). A judge could order the lock removed if the owner could prove that the building had not been so used during the preceding year. Further, the Act empowered the attorney general to confiscate and destroy any printed matter propagating communism or bolshevism. Anyone printing, publishing or distributing such material could be imprisoned for up to a year, without appeal. In 1957 the Supreme Court of Canada declared the Act unconstitutional, an invasion of the federal field of criminal law. EUGENE A. FORSEY

Page, John Percy, educator, basketball coach, politician, lieutenant-governor (b to Canadian parents at Rochester, NY 14 May 1887; d at Edmonton, Alta 2 Mar 1973). He coached the EDMONTON GRADS, the best and most respected women's basketball team in the world, throughout their 25-year history (1915-40). Page was the most important factor in their success, using simple well-executed plays and demanding disci-

Portrait of P.K. Page (1971) by Harold Town, white pencil on purple paper (*courtesy National Archives of Canada/C-100377/Harold Town*).

plined behaviour. His feeder-team system maintained the supply of talented players. When the Grads and Page retired from basketball in 1940, he entered provincial politics. He was lieutenant-governor of Alberta 1959-65. CATHY MACDONALD

Page, Patricia Kathleen, poet, prose writer, visual artist (b at Swanage, Dorset, Eng 23 Nov 1916). With her family, P.K. Page left England in 1919 and settled in Red Deer, Alta; she was educated in Calgary and Winnipeg and later studied art in Brazil and New York. In the late 1930s, she lived briefly in Saint John, NB; in the early 1940s she moved to Montréal and worked as a filing clerk and historical researcher. There she was part of the group that founded *Preview* (1942-45); her poems first appeared in periodicals and in *Unit of Five* (ed Ronald Hambleton, 1942). From 1946 to 1950 she worked as a scriptwriter at the National Film Board. She married W.A. IRWIN in 1950, and from 1953 to 1964 lived in Australia, where her husband was high commissioner, and in Brazil and Mexico, where he served as ambassador. Since 1964 she has lived in Victoria.

Her first book was *The Sun and the Moon*, an intensely romantic novel published in 1944 under the pseudonym Judith Cape (rep in 1973, with stories from the 1940s, as *The Sun and the Moon and Other Fictions*). Books of poetry include *As Ten As Twenty* (1946); *The Metal and the Flower* (1954, Gov Gen's Award); *Cry Ararat!* (1967); *Poems Selected and New* (1974); *Evening Dance of the Grey Files* (1981, including the story "Unless the Eye Catch Fire..."); and *The Glass Air* (1985, CAA Award, including 2 remarkable essays). P.K. Page is also the editor of an anthology of short poems, *To Say the Least: Canadian Poets from A to Z* (1981), and the author of a memoir, *Brazilian Journal* (1987).

In Brazil, P.K. Page began to draw and paint; this intricate and beautiful work, produced under the name P.K. Irwin, has been widely exhibited and has been reproduced in several of her books. She is an Officer of the Order of Canada.

CONSTANCE ROOKE

Paige, Brydon, professional name of Brydone James Duncan, dancer, teacher, choreographer, ballet director (b at Vancouver 13 Jan 1933). As artistic director of the Alberta Ballet from 1976 to 1987, Paige significantly raised the profile and quality of BALLET in western Canada. He was a

founding member of Les Ballets Chiriaeff and remained with the company as it evolved into LES GRANDS BALLETS CANADIENS, becoming resident choreographer and ballet master. The creator of many ballets, Paige has also been artistic director of the National Ballet of Guatemala and briefly of the National Ballet of Portugal, as well as assistant head of Banff Centre's summer dance program.

MICHAEL CRABB

Paintbrush, herbaceous plant of genus *Castilleja*, figwort family, Scrophulariaceae. Most are perennial. Common name, Indian paintbrush, is applied to several species. About 200 species occur worldwide, mostly in western N America; 23 in Canada (one an annual). In Canada paintbrushes are most common in southern BC and Alberta, decreasing eastward to Ontario. One species is found from the YT and Mackenzie Dist to the Atlantic provinces (excluding NS and PEI). Paintbrushes grow on dry or wet soils, from low grassland to alpine meadows, usually in open areas, but also in thickets and forest openings. Stems are clustered and erect, arising from a curved base. Tiny, tubular, usually greenish flowers occur in a terminal spike, and each is concealed by an enfolding, modified, floral leaf (bract). Bracts (red through orange, yellow and purple to greenish white) form the showy, terminal "brush." Flowers and bracts appear June-Aug. The fruits are cylindrical capsules containing many seeds. Few species are botanically well defined, and most are not readily distinguishable because of hybridization. Paintbrushes are somewhat parasitic on roots of other plants and cannot be transplanted from the wild.

Painters Eleven dates from 1953 when a group of artists – Jack BUSH, Oscar CAHÉN, Hortense Gordon, Thomas Hodgson, Alexandra Luke, J.W.G. MACDONALD, Ray Mead, Kazuo NAKAMURA, William RONALD, Harold TOWN and Walter Yarwood – banded together with the purpose of exhibiting abstract art in Toronto. Although by the late 1940s the AUTOMATISTES in Montréal and the abstract expressionists in New York had developed a new artistic vocabulary, Toronto in 1950 was still dominated by the GROUP OF SEVEN. The first public exhibition of abstract artists in Ontario was organized by Luke in 1952 and included 9 of the future members of Painters Eleven.

The group came together in the fall of 1953 as a result of the "Abstracts at Home" exhibition organized by Ronald at the Robert SIMPSON department store. Assembling for publicity photographs, the 7 artists represented decided to meet again at Luke's studio to discuss their common interests in abstraction. With the addition of 4 more artists to the group, Town proposed the name Painters Eleven. Bush undertook to approach his dealer about an exhibition, and the members agreed to finance group exhibitions. In Feb 1954 the first exhibition of Painters Eleven opened at the Roberts Gallery, drawing large crowds but no sales. Annual exhibitions were held at the Roberts Gallery in 1955 and 1956 and the Park Gallery in 1957 and 1958. A high point came in 1956, when Painters Eleven gained international recognition as guest exhibitors with the American Abstract Artists in New York. Exhibitions organized by regional galleries and the National Gallery of Canada circulated through Canada, 1957-61.

Painters Eleven held no single vision of the nature of abstraction. Although Macdonald had explored abstraction as early as 1934, the majority of the group (many a generation younger) became aware of it more than 10 years later, some of them through his teaching. Their sources were varied: Mead trained in England, Cahén in Europe, and Luke, Gordon, Macdonald and Ronald

travelled to the US to study with Hans Hofmann. Though the New York school provided an important example for the group, they developed their own personal painterly vocabulary and expressive forms. Initially critical response in Toronto ranged from bewilderment to hostility, but gradually, reviews became more favourable. Robert FULFORD gave important press support, and international critics such as Sir Herbert Read (Britain) and Clement Greenberg (US) praised their work. The 1958 Park Gallery exhibition was the last annual group show: Cahén died tragically in 1956; in 1957 Mead moved to Montréal and Ronald resigned from the group. In 1960 Painters Eleven voted to disband. Their goals had been achieved, commercial and public galleries exhibited their work, and they had become recognized leaders in the local art scene. The National Gallery, the AGO and the Robert McLaughlin Gallery, Oshawa, hold important collections of their work. *See also* PAINTING.

JOYCE ZEMANS

Reading: D. Burnett and M. Schiff, *Contemporary Canadian Art* (1983); J. Russell Harper, *Painting in Canada* (1977); J. Murray, *Painters Eleven Retrospect* (1979) and *The Best Contemporary Canadian Art* (1987); D. Reid, *A Concise History of Canadian Painting* (1973).

Painting The first references to Canadian subjects appeared in the decorated margins and vignettes of maps ("Mappemonde" by Pierre Desceliers) and atlases (Vallard's "Atlas," Guillaume Le Testu's "Atlas" in the mid-16th century. Made in Europe by artists who had never seen Canada but who based their pictorial work on travellers' accounts, these illustrations of the fauna, flora and human population of the newly discovered lands reflected their creators' prejudices as much as they did facts; in 1550 Desceliers placed pygmies near Hochelaga! Indian canoes, however, were frequently portrayed accurately. The map of Hochelaga in *Delle navigationi et viaggi* (1550-59) of Giovanni Battista Ramusio looked more like a utopian Renaissance city than an Iroquois village, whereas the illustrations in Champlain's accounts were reasonably accurate, such as a Huron woman grinding corn in a mortar, or a Huron hunting scene. The most remarkable document of this type is the *Histoire naturelle des Indes occidentales* (c 1685) by the Jesuit Louis Nicolas. His manuscript was illustrated by pen-and-ink drawings (the *Codex canadensis*) of the vegetation, animals and people of the New World. Certainly his versions of the fauna were inspired by the engravings in the *Historia animal-*

Frère Luc, *Assumption of the Virgin* (1671) located in the Hôtel-Dieu chapel, Québec City (*photo by John deVisser*).

ium of the great Swiss biologist Konrad Gesner, and his portraits of Indians by some poor illustrations in *Historia Canadensis, seu Novae Franciae...* by Francois du Creux. But the abundance of detail, the representation of the flora, and the naive nature of the drawings combined to make this an important work. The engravings in *Moeurs des sauvages amériquains comparées aux moeurs des premiers temps* (1724) by Joseph-François LAFITAU, although they drew heavily on the works of Théodore de Bry, also showed the extensive ethnographic knowledge of this Jesuit. The *Histoire...de la Nouvelle-France...* (1744) by Pierre-François-Xavier de CHARLEVOIX included several plates devoted to flora.

While these first images of Canada were appearing in Europe, the 17th-century French colonists in New France were importing paintings and engravings from France. Catholic missionaries used engravings and paintings to convert Indians and remind the settlers of their faith, as is suggested in the large painting *La France apportant la foi aux Indiens de la Nouvelle-France* (post-1666, Ursuline Convent, Québec), in which France is personified by Anne of Austria, teaching an Indian kneeling before her. We know that some priests (Jean Pierron and Claude CHAUCHETIÈRE) were painters themselves, but their work has been lost, except possibly for the portrait of Kateri TEKAKWITHA (*c*1681) attributed to the latter.

For the late 17th-century Jesuits, the engraving by Grégoire Huret of 1664, the *Martyre des pères jésuites...* was important enough to have a copy painted in France. Painted or engraved portraits of the Sun King (Louis XIV) made in the mother country were seen in New France; one such portrait certainly existed in the Château St-Louis, the governor's residence in Québec. Even Frère LUC, who spent 16 months in New France, must be considered an uncommitted transient, even though he left behind a fair-sized body of church paintings (*L'Assomption*, 1671, for the Hôpital-Général, Québec) and a *Portrait de Monseigneur...Laval* (1671-72). It is less certain whether paintings hung in the more modest homes; however, inventories recorded by notaries of the French regime for estate purposes included paintings and engravings which had probably been imported.

Few paintings were commissioned in the colony itself. Under the mercantile system it was more profitable to sell paintings to the colony than to support local talent (*see* MERCANTILISM). Consequently, the painter as a full-time professional was as yet rare; there were some clerics such as Hugues POMMIER and Jean GUYON; amateurs like Michel DESSAILLIANT, dit Richeterre, and Jean Berger; it is debatable whether they produced all the works attributed to them. It is just as unclear who created the ex-votos (*see* VOTIVE PAINTING) during the French regime that are now preserved in Ste-Anne-de-Beaupré, Qué. As was customary at the time, sombre, bold and highly simplified posthumous portraits, such as that of *Marguerite Bourgeoys* (1700) by Pierre LE BER, were occasionally painted, but few lifetime representations of the great men of New France were made in Canada. Portrait illustrations in books of Canadian history were, for the most part, mid-19th-century imagination.

The British Conquest (1759-60) introduced new approaches to subject matter and style. Whereas during the French regime views of Canada continued to be fantasy rather than reality, the early TOPOGRAPHIC PAINTINGS were precise, small in format and often colourful. This new group of artists were members of the British army; they were taught at the Royal Military Academy of Woolwich to make not only strategic maps but also agreeable scenes of the environ-

Thomas Davies, *Otter Creek Falls, Lake Champlain* (*c*1759), watercolour (*courtesy Royal Ontario Museum*).

ment with which they came into contact. As products of the Age of Enlightenment they looked for the "picturesque and sublime" in nature, the exotic and awe inspiring; majestic mountains and dramatic waterfalls were among their favourite subjects. The scenes were painted on the spot in watercolour and then often engraved in London – as in works by Richard Short, George HERIOT and Capt Hervey Smyth. One of the earliest and most interesting of these topographic artists was Thomas Davies, who was posted to the garrisons in Halifax, Montréal and Québec between 1757 and 1790, leaving a fine series of views, some of which were later reproduced in a travel book.

The period of stability, prosperity and expansion that followed the Conquest and the American Revolution was marked by a general desire to recreate European culture in Canada and emulate European taste. In the towns a variety of societies and clubs were founded (*see* ARTISTS' ORGANIZATIONS) where art and painting became the occasional focus of attention. French and English theatre flourished and some painters provided stage decorations. A moneyed middle class took over from the church as patron of the arts. A demand for portraits increased; the sitters were no longer only the clergy or government officials, but wealthy merchants and their families as well. Some painters were now able to make a reasonable living as portraitists and decorators. The retired French soldier, Louis Dulongpré, is supposed to have painted more than 3000 portraits between 1785 and 1815. Canadian-born artists such as François Beaucourt and François BAILLAIRGÉ studied in France and returned to Canada with a new stylistic assurance, while a few European artists came to Canada who had learned their trade well. William BERCZY had worked in Europe as a painter and architect and had exhibited with the Royal Academy in London. Soon after his arrival in Markam (near York) in 1794 he painted Joseph BRANT, Loyalist chief of the Mohawks, and in 1808 was commissioned to paint *The Woolsey Family* in Québec City, one of the masterpieces of Canadian art. That same year Robert Field arrived in Halifax where, for the next 8 years, he painted fine portraits of NS society. In contrast to the towns, rural Québec continued to be dominated by tradition, the church remained at the centre of life, and FOLK ART flourished. *Saint Louis tenant la couronne d'épines* (1777), painted by Jean-Antoine AIDE-CRÉQUY for the church of St-Louis on the Île aux COUDRES (where the patron

saint bears the features of Louis XVI), symbolized the attachment these French Canadians, turned British subjects, still felt for the French Crown.

As a result of the turmoil following the French Revolution, the Abbé Louis-Joseph Desjardins was able to bring to Québec some 200 European paintings from 1816 onwards. Some of these paintings were used to embellish churches in Lower Canada, the remainder were bought by Joseph LÉGARÉ in 1817, who then established the first art gallery open to the public in Canada. Although minor works for the most part, the Desjardins shipments introduced into Lower Canada a new range of subject matter: still lifes, historical subjects, and different approaches to landscape that had not been considered before by Québec painters.

Légaré's own paintings suggest that he was sensitive to stylistic peculiarities in his collection, which led to his greater technical freedom. As well, Légaré collected engravings which must have influenced him and his friends. He was also an art teacher, though his pupils are best remembered as portraitists, such as Antoine PLAMONDON, who studied in Paris after his apprenticeship with Légaré and was famous as a church painter (he decorated his parish church in Neuville). In 1841 Plamondon painted a series of young nuns of the Hôpital-Général, all daughters of prominent Québec merchants. Whereas Légaré's style did occasionally show boldness, Plamondon's was controlled, almost formal. Théophile HAMEL apprenticed to Plamondon, studied in Europe, and on his return to Québec became a most successful portrait painter for the next 20 years. It was often necessary for him to travel in order to receive commissions; these trips took him to Montréal, Kingston and Toronto. Meanwhile, Toronto had welcomed its own able portraitist in 1841; George Théodore BERTHON, a French-trained artist, settled in the city after a sojourn in England.

FRANÇOIS-MARC GAGNON

1840 to 1940

Before the 1840s painting in Canada was dominated by European taste and conventions. There was no dramatic change after that date, but increasingly Canadian content came to have a major influence on the form art took in the country. The most popular and prolific of the romantic painters of the Canadian scene was Cornelius KRIEGHOFF who, after 1841, recorded a variety of local scenes along the St Lawrence – some humorous, some anecdotal. Krieghoff had seen genre painting at Düsseldorf Academy and his naturally ebullient temperament transformed his

Cornelius Krieghoff, *Winter Landscape, Laval* (nd), oil on canvas (*courtesy National Gallery of Canada*).

Antoine Plamondon, *La Chasse aux tourtes* (1853), oil on canvas (*courtesy Art Gallery of Ontario/gift from The Albert H. Robson Memorial Subscription Fund, 1943*).

snapshots of everyday life into subjects of immense popular appeal. He had a lifelong interest in Indians and, as his wife was of French birth, he knew the habitant life-style intimately. It is interesting that Krieghoff's support came from English-speaking patrons in the Canadas, for the French bourgeoisie found his work a vulgar caricature of habitant life and an insult to their cultured life-style.

Parallel to Krieghoff's fascination with the everyday life he observed in Québec was a growing preoccupation with the western frontier. Swissborn Peter RINDISBACHER immigrated to the RED RIVER COLONY in 1821 as a boy of 15. He was so excited by the way of life in Ft Garry that he painted a remarkable series of watercolours of the local scene, of Indians in strange dress and buffalo on the prairies in winter. Two decades later Paul KANE made himself famous by painting this same western scenery and its native people. He had been a minor Ontario portrait painter who aspired to artistic greatness and studied in Europe. Inspired by George Catlin's American Indian portraits then displayed in London, Kane conceived a similar project of picturing Canadian natives. During a celebrated wilderness trip with fur

traders from Ontario to Ft Vancouver, 1846-48, he sketched the landscape and tribes he encountered. Subsequently, he painted 100 canvases based on these sketches and published an account of his travels. Kane inspired other artists. In 1872 Frederick VERNER made a similar sketching trip to picture Indians and buffalo. William G.R. HIND spent a season as an expedition artist with his scientist brother, Henry, exploring Labrador, then joined the 1862 OVERLANDERS, gold-seeking adventurers who travelled by land to the newly discovered BC goldfields.

Prior to Confederation, the documentary tradition had dominated Canadian painting, whether recording the frontier, high society in the garrison towns, or the scenic wonders of a new land. The remaining years of the 19th century were filled with growth and optimism, and saw industrialization, the Riel rebellions and western expansion. Yet little of this development was recorded by contemporary artists. As PHOTOGRAPHY took over the role of documenting society, Victorian artists escaped to an ideal world of the rural landscape. They established professional art societies, where they could exhibit, promote and sell their works, mostly in Montréal and Toronto.

John A. Fraser, *Laurentian Splendour* (1880), oil on canvas (*courtesy National Gallery of Canada*).

Several talented artists worked in the studios of William NOTMAN, a Montréal photographer who had achieved an international reputation for his portrait photographs by the 1860s, then went on to greater heights with landscape and genre subjects. The company had its own exhibiting space and art collection, and it rapidly became the leading, if unofficial, art school in the country. There was a camaraderie among the staff as they painted in their spare time and made sketching trips to the lakes and hills of the Eastern Townships and beyond. John FRASER, an acknowledged leader, opened a branch in Toronto and was instrumental in organizing the Ontario Society of Artists, providing space in the Notman studio for the society's first annual exhibition in 1873. Associated with him were his brother-in-law, Henry Sandham, who later opened a Notman studio in Saint John, Paris-trained Allan EDSON, and Otto Jacobi, who had enjoyed an earlier career in Germany.

The search for the Canadian landscape by Notman photographers and artists was intimately connected with the railway expansion which was opening up the new Dominion. Painters had travelled from Montréal by train in the earlier years to sketch through Québec and the Matapedia Valley. Now they broadened their vision as the transcontinental line of the Canadian Pacific edged its way across the Prairies and through the Rockies. Sir William VAN HORNE, president of the railway and himself an art collector, gave artists free passes to produce promotional pictures for the CPR. Notman sent a camera crew with the work trains to detail progress through the mountains. Fraser and other artists associated with Notman went to the West to make an oil and watercolour record of the magnificent scenery. Their paintings of the West, technically brilliant and marked by photographic realism, dominated many art exhibitions until the end of the century.

Canadian art achieved new prestige with the founding of the Royal Canadian Academy in 1880, primarily through the efforts of Governor General the marquess of LORNE and his wife Princess Louise. Lucius O'BRIEN, first president of the RCA, was swept up in this new search for the face of Canada. He visited NS and NB, then, as the railway reached the Pacific, he travelled west to paint the mountains and the Vancouver area. Some of his finest paintings, such as his majestic views of Québec or *Sunrise on the Saguenay*, introduced a glowing quality which incorporated the luminism found in contemporary American painting of the Hudson River School.

During the 1880s and 1890s Europe once again became the model for artists in Canada, and

On the Grand River at Doon (c1880), oil on canvas, by Homer Watson (*courtesy National Gallery of Canada*).

painters aspired to study in Paris academies and exhibit at the Salon. It was the conservative French and English masters, not the avant-garde, who attracted the young Canadians, men who painted heroic images in a highly finished naturalistic style. William BRYMNER and Robert HARRIS followed this path and on their return taught "in the French manner" in Montréal and Toronto. In 1883 Harris was commissioned by the federal government to paint *The Fathers of Confederation.* Paul PEEL was acclaimed in Paris and at home for his studies of bathers and children but demonstrated little Canadianism. George REID used the same monumental figure tradition in his scenes of rural Ontario, such as *Mortgaging the Homestead.*

Two young painters who derived their inspiration from their rural Canadian surroundings and who visited Europe only after they were established were Homer WATSON and Ozias LEDUC. Watson early became a celebrity when *The Pioneer Mill* was purchased for Queen Victoria's royal collection. Leduc lived in St-Hilaire, Qué, supporting himself from church decoration while painting still lifes and people and landscape close to him for his own satisfaction. Meanwhile in Paris the slick, narrative style of the Salon was increasingly attacked by innovative painters of the impressionist, Barbizon and Hague schools. Horatio WALKER was influenced by this naturalistic depiction of nature and, on his return to Canada, his paintings of rural scenes on Île d'ORLÉANS rapidly brought him acclaim in N America. In 1910 the National Gallery of Canada paid $10 000 for *Oxen Drinking.*

Maurice CULLEN and James Wilson MORRICE were among the first artists to apply the principles of French impressionism to the Canadian landscape. Cullen attracted attention in Paris before returning to spend his mature years in Québec. Criticism was harsh and sales were poor, but he exerted a tremendous influence through his teaching at the Art Assn of Montreal. Morrice, independently wealthy, lived much of his life in Paris, travelled widely, befriended Henri Matisse

The Old Ferry, Louise Basin, Quebec (c1897), oil on canvas, by Maurice Cullen, one of the first Canadian artists to apply the principles of French Impressionism to Canadian landscape (*courtesy National Gallery of Canada*).

Tom Thomson's *The Drive* (1916-17), oil on canvas, is typical of the bold, imaginative landscape painting which, after Thomson's death in 1917, dominated Canadian art (*courtesy MacDonald Stewart Art Centre/University of Guelph Coll*).

and was influenced by James Whistler. Through annual exhibitions with the Canadian Art Club in Toronto, 1907-15, Cullen, Morrice and Marc-Aurèle de Foy SUZOR-COTÉ served as models for young artists.

The face of Canadian painting changed completely when a new landscape movement emerged in Toronto in the years immediately preceding WWI. Tom THOMSON died in 1917, but the remaining painters – Frank CARMICHAEL, Lawren HARRIS, A.Y. JACKSON, Franz JOHNSTON, Arthur LISMER, J.E.H. MACDONALD and F.H. VARLEY – organized the first exhibition of the GROUP OF SEVEN in 1920. "Group" subject matter and style dominated Canadian art for the next 30 years. It was bold, imaginative painting employing strident colouring and tending to postimpressionist mannerisms. It was also an art movement which aroused bitter controversy and patriotic fervour, which caught the public interest and allowed little room for serious development of divergent art styles. The group disbanded in 1933 to make way for the broader-based Canadian Group of Painters, which included artists from across the country and encouraged figure painting and modernism as well as the landscape.

Two artists working at the same time as the Group of Seven but disregarded until the late 1930s were Emily CARR and David MILNE. They worked in semi-isolation, devoted to the area in which they had grown up and pursuing their own personal vision while struggling with financial privation and lack of recognition. Carr had visited England and France and was moved by the Fauves' vigorous strokes and strident colour. On her return she painted the dense Pacific forests, Indian villages and totems with an exultant celebration of nature and its mysteries. In contrast to Carr, who began painting with renewed vigour

after her meeting with the Seven, Milne had none of the national consciousness of the group but was concerned with individual aesthetic expression and painterly problems. He studied in New York and was represented at the famous Armory Show of 1913 which introduced modernism to America. Thereafter, in the Catskills and at various secluded rural locations in southern Ontario, he experimented with evocative shapes, tonal contrasts and unique picture planes, simplifying his technique to the bare minimum.

The Great Depression, combined with the continued hold of the Group on Canadian art, meant that many excellent painters were virtually ignored. Opportunities for exhibition were dominated by the academies and societies; collecting of new art was negligible; and institutional and public awareness was resistant or indifferent to

Frederick Horsman Varley, *Gipsy Head* (1919), oil on canvas (*courtesy National Gallery of Canada/gift of the Hon Norman Paterson, 1947*).

David Milne, *Blue Church* (1926), oil on canvas and masonite (*courtesy The McMichael Canadian Coll/Anonymous donor*).

change. Lionel LeMoine FITZGERALD painted canvases of intimacy and gentleness centered on his surroundings in Winnipeg, but Charles COMFORT's *Young Canadian*, a haunting portrait of his friend Carl SCHAEFER, best symbolized the era. In Feb 1927 an exhibition of paintings by Bertram BROOKER was held at the Arts and Letters Club in Toronto, the first exhibition of abstract art in Canada. Later that year Lawren Harris helped organize a show of abstract European art at the Art Gallery of Toronto, but it was ridiculed by critics and contemporary artists alike. Developments in Canadian painting would have to await prosperity, another world war, and a new generation of artists working in Québec.   J. RUSSELL HARPER

1940 to the Present

The years since WWII have witnessed an unprecedented expansion in the visual arts throughout Canada, evidenced in the number of professional artists, the proliferation of galleries and exhibitions, and the development of art magazines. The CANADA COUNCIL and the provincial art councils have played crucial roles in this development, as has the expansion of museums, art galleries, and alternate and artist-run spaces, and the growth of art departments in colleges and universities. In describing the character of recent painting in Canada it is essential to bear in mind 3 factors: the strength of regional identities, the increased knowledge of developments across the country and internationally, and the differing sizes of the artistic communities. These factors have combined and recombined in complex ways, producing a dynamic which has discouraged the uniformity of "a Canadian painting" and encouraged the strength of painting in Canada.

John Lyman, *Rose* (*c*1947), oil on canvas. Lyman's works reflect advanced formal concerns and a personal vision (*courtesy Montreal Museum of Fine Arts*).

The breakthrough to modern movements came in Montréal in the 1940s through efforts initiated by artists themselves. The 3 leading figures, John LYMAN, Alfred PELLAN and especially Paul-Émile BORDUAS, had different, often conflicting views, from which came an energy in ideas and a dynamic of change. Lyman returned to Montréal in 1931 after almost 24 years abroad, mostly in France. Besides the example of his own work and his advocacy of modern European art, he wrote criticism for the *Montrealer* (1936-40) and initiated the founding of the CONTEMPORARY ARTS SOCIETY in 1939. The society, open to artists who were not members of the Royal Canadian Academy, organized annual exhibitions during its 9-year existence and introduced European modernism to Canada. The founding membership comprised 26 artists, including Prudence HEWARD, Fritz BRANDTNER, Goodridge ROBERTS, Louis MUHLSTOCK, Marian SCOTT and Philip SURREY. Borduas was among only 5 French Canadian members.

A more radical source of inspiration came from Pellan, who returned to Canada in 1940 after 14 years in Paris. An artist of sparkling eclectic talent, his interpretations of cubism and surrealism were a revelation to artists in Montréal. Borduas, initially struck by Pellan's work, determined a still more radical approach related to the ideas of André Breton, the founder of surrealism. Borduas was set not simply on an imitation of French art but an original expression of spiritual revolution. He became the centre of a group of young men and women, including Fernand LEDUC, Pierre GAUVREAU, Jean-Paul RIOPELLE, Marcel BARBEAU, Françoise Sullivan and Jean-Paul MOUSSEAU. A clearly defined group by the mid-1940s, they gained the name AUTOMATISTES from an exhibition in 1947. Direct connections with French surrealism were maintained through Riopelle, the most prodigious of the young painters, who moved to Paris in 1946, and Leduc, who lived there from 1947 to 1953. The climax of the Automatiste action came with the collective signing of Borduas's 1948 manifesto, REFUS GLOBAL. Advocating personal freedom in cultural and spiritual expression, the pamphlet attacked the repressions of the government and the dominant place of the church in Québec culture and education. The document caused an uproar and led to Borduas losing his teaching post at the École du Meuble. After 5 years of personal and professional hardship, Borduas left Canada. He went to New York (1953-55), coming into contact with the work of the abstract expressionists, and then to Paris (1955-60). Both in his painting and his advocacy of cultural change, Borduas represents one of the major achievements in Canadian art.

The Automatistes split the Contemporary Arts Society. The older members could not follow their direction and Pellan led a short-lived "anti-automatiste" group, Prisme d'yeux (1948-50), with Léon Bellefleur, Jacques de TONNANCOUR and Albert DUMOUCHEL. The Automatiste movement gave way in the mid-1950s to a rigorous form of hard-edge abstraction first marked in the work of Leduc and the PLASTICIENS, a group that was formed in 1954 by the critic Rodolphe de Repentigny (who painted under the pseudonym Jauran) and 3 other painters; it first exhibited in 1955. This group, influenced by the ideas and work of Malevich and Mondrian, was soon absorbed into the Non-Figurative Artists' Assn of Montréal, which was formed in 1956 with Leduc as president, Repentigny as secretary and Guido MOLINARI as treasurer, and which included artists such as Rita LETENDRE and Jean MCEWEN. The direction somewhat hesitantly begun by the Plasticiens was rapidly developed by Leduc, Molinari

Fernand Leduc, *Fanfare* (1954), oil on wood (*courtesy Montreal Museum of Fine Arts*).

and Claude TOUSIGNANT. Leduc returned to France in 1959, and it was the work of Molinari and Tousignant, in particular, rigorously hard-edged and abstract and developed on the dynamics of colour, that led Montréal painting in the 1960s. But their concerns were not exclusive, as is evidenced by the work of Yves GAUCHER, first as a printmaker and from the mid-1960s as a painter, and Charles GAGNON, whose work has been in painting, assemblages and photography.

Toronto, in the 1940s, lacked the atmosphere of radical debate found in Montréal. There were only a few artists, such as Paraskeva CLARK, Robert "Scottie" Wilson, Albert FRANCK and Jock Macdonald (a major figure as both painter and teacher), who worked against the dominance of the Group of Seven, their followers in the Canadian Group of Painters and continued academicism. Others, such as Jack BUSH, and younger artists such as Oscar CAHÉN, Walter Yarwood, Harold TOWN and William RONALD, were by the end of the 1940s actively developing more radical solutions, looking to European and, in particular, New York painting. Alexandra Luke organized the touring Canadian Abstract Exhibition in 1952 and in 1953 Ronald initiated an exhibition at Simpsons department store called "Abstracts at Home," including his work and that of 6 other artists, Kazuo NAKAMURA, Luke, Bush, Cahén, Ray Mead and Tom Hodgson. Deciding to contin-

Fleurs d'eau (1956) by Alfred Pellan, whose interpretations of cubism and surrealism were revelations to Montréal (*courtesy Montreal Museum of Fine Arts*).

ue to exhibit together, the group expanded to include Hortense Gordon, Yarwood, Town and Macdonald, and took the name PAINTERS ELEVEN. They first exhibited together in 1954 and formally dissolved in 1960. Differing widely in approach and style, the best of the group's work was characterized by strong painterly surfaces found in Town, Ronald, Hodgson and Cahén. In 1956 the group exhibited with the American Abstract Artists in New York. Ronald, then working in New York, arranged in 1957 for the critic Clement Greenberg to visit the Toronto artists in their studios, though Town and Yarwood refused to participate. Greenberg's visit had most impact on Bush, whose work from the 1960s brought him into the ambience of American post-painterly abstraction, and who became a major influence on many younger Toronto artists.

Even as Painters Eleven was breaking up, their example was important to a strong and energetic group of young artists centered on Av Isaacs' gallery. The work of this group, reflecting a wide range of interests from dada to abstract expressionism, was characterized by powerfully expressive figurative styles and included Graham COUGHTRY, Joyce WIELAND, John Meredith, Gordon RAYNER, Dennis BURTON, Robert Markle, Nobuo Kubota, Richard Gorman and Robert Hedrick. The most original was Michael SNOW, who began his career as a painter but soon moved into a wide range of media – sculpture, photography and film.

A vital centre of activity also developed through the 1960s in London, in particular with Jack CHAMBERS, Tony URQUHART and Greg CURNOE. Chambers and Curnoe, in different ways, have given forceful definition to regionalism as a vital expression of the reality of living and working in a particular community. It was Chambers who initiated the development of the Canadian Artists Representation in 1967 to set standards in exhibition and copyright fees and to assert the professional status of artists. The community in London, if small, remains a vital and active one in sculpture, installation work and painting; among the painters special mention must be made of Paterson EWEN, who moved there from Montréal in 1968, and Ron MARTIN (since 1983 working in Toronto).

The visual arts in the Atlantic provinces developed radical directions much more slowly than in Québec and Ontario. The first artists in the region seriously to address contemporary issues were Miller BRITTAIN and Jack HUMPHREY in Saint John and, after the war, Bruno BOBAK and Molly Lamb BOBAK in Fredericton. Lawren P. Harris at Mt Allison U in Sackville was essentially alone as an abstract painter. The dominant figure in the Atlantic region since the war has been Alex COLVILLE. His painting has set a new standard for realist art, and through his teaching at Mt Allison (1946-63) he has had an important impact on the development of artists such as Christopher PRATT, Mary PRATT, Tom FORRESTALL, D.P. BROWN and Hugh MacKenzie. Since the mid-1960s the Nova Scotia College of Art and Design, with artists such as Garry Neill KENNEDY, Gerald Ferguson and Eric Cameron, has been a gathering point for radical Canadian, American and European artists.

In the West each of the major urban centres has established a distinctive character and sense of community. Vancouver has the largest concentration of artists and the longest history of interest in modern art; Jock Macdonald was working there in the 1930s and Lawren S. Harris settled there in 1940. The 2 principal artists from the 1940s, both as artists and teachers, have been B.C. BINNING and Jack SHADBOLT. Binning is best known as a draftsman and a painter of abstractions of ships and landscape. Shadbolt, deeply af-

fected by the richness of the landscape and NORTH-WEST COAST INDIAN ART, has interpreted these themes in a highly personal surrealist manner. A combination of landscape and lyrical abstraction characterizes the work of Gordon SMITH, Takao TANABE and Don Jarvis, a direction reinforced by Toni ONLEY who went to Vancouver in 1959. A more rigorous form of abstraction, important for a younger group of painters, came from Roy KIYOOKA, who moved from Regina to Vancouver in 1959. In the 1960s and 1970s Vancouver experienced the diversification of interests that occurred in Toronto and Montréal, with particular strengths in conceptual and communication art, video and performance, through the work of Iain and Ingrid BAXTER in their N.E. Thing Co (formed in 1966), and Michael Morris and Gathie FALK, whose work has encompassed performance, painting and mixed media. Mention must also be made of painters such as Alan Wood, Robert Young and Glen Howarth.

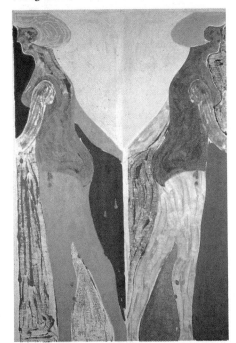

Michael Snow, *Beach-Hcaeb* (1953), oil and graphite on canvas (*courtesy The Isaacs Gallery, Toronto*).

In Regina the focus of activity in the 1950s was on a small group of artists determined to overcome their sense of isolation from the principal centres, particularly New York. The summer school at Emma Lake, founded by Augustus KENDERDINE in 1936, was extended in 1955 by Kenneth LOCHHEAD and Arthur MCKAY to include a workshop for professional artists, the first of which was led by Jack Shadbolt. Subsequently many of the leaders were Americans, the most significant being Barnett Newman (1959), Clement Greenberg (1962), Kenneth Noland (1963) and Jules Olitski (1964). In 1961 Ronald BLOORE, director of the Norman Mackenzie Art Gallery, organized the "Five Painters from Regina" exhibition with work by himself, Lochhead, McKay, Ted Godwin and Douglas Morton. Later that year this show toured Canada under the auspices of the National Gallery, giving rise to the name the REGINA FIVE.

The Emma Lake workshops also had a major effect on artists in Saskatoon, currently a tight-knit community, uniting artists of different generations and styles of work. The doyen of painting in the city is Ernest LINDNER, who has gained national attention over the past 20 years with his

precisely rendered close-ups of trees and plants and figure studies. Landscape painting, for instance that of Reta Cowley, Wynona Mulcaster and Dorothy KNOWLES, has become a major force and has encouraged the work of younger artists such as David Alexander. A sensibility to the landscape has also been a major factor in the development of abstract painting, for instance in the dissimilar work of William PEREHUDOFF and Otto ROGERS. Among younger painters, for instance Robert Christie, there is a substantial interest in colour-field abstraction. Separate from these concerns is the constructivism of Eli BORNSTEIN, founder and editor of the journal *Structurist*.

For artists in Alberta, as in Saskatchewan, the Emma Lake workshops and the BANFF CENTRE for Continuing Education have been the most significant centres for development of the visual arts. In Calgary an informal group developed around Maxwell BATES, including Ron Spickett, Marion Nicoll and Roy Kiyooka. Bates, a practising architect, painted in Calgary until 1961 (when he moved to Victoria) in an expressionist style. Subsequently, the modernist direction has been developed by artists such as Bruce O'Neil and Gerald Hushlak. A modernist landscape style is found in artists such as Ken Christopher and in various forms of image painting with John Hall, Derek Michael Besant, Ron Moppett and Gary Olson. In Edmonton the interest in formalism, developed out of the Emma Lake workshops, has made the strongest mark, not only in painting but in sculpture. The substantial group of formalist painters working there, led by Douglas HAYNES, includes Ann Clark, Robert Scott, Phil Darrah and Terrence Keller.

In Winnipeg in the 1930s the most significant artists were Fritz BRANDTNER and LeMoine Fitz-Gerald. Subsequent developments centered on University of Manitoba with artists and teachers such as George Swinton and Joe Plaskett and, from 1964, Ken Lochhead. In recent years Winnipeg, though somewhat isolated from other centres, has continued to be an active and varied community with such painters as Don Reichert, Ivan EYRE, Esther Warkov, Jack Butler, Sheila Butler and Suzanne Funnell.

Through the 1970s the place of painting at the leading edge of the visual arts was challenged critically by developments in conceptual art, installation art, sculpture, video and performance (*see* ART, CONTEMPORARY TRENDS; VIDEO ART). For many people, painting, if it survived at all, would do so as an essentially reactionary form. But painting did not come to a standstill, and in recent years activity in the field, internationally as well as in Canada, has developed rapidly, especially among younger artists. What is notable, in Toronto and Montréal in particular, is a concern with what may be called expressive abstraction and with figurative and image painting, although not to the exclusion of geometric abstraction. At a time when the outcome of these developments is impossible to predict, it is important to recognize that such terms are inexact and arbitrary; for we can describe the work of artists such as Christian Knudson, Richard Mill, Leopold Plotek, Christian Kiopini and Jocelyn Jean in Montréal as abstract and geometric, but must distinguish their concerns not only from each other but also from the approaches of, say, Toronto artists such as Ric Evans and Jaan Poldaas, Milton Jewell and Paul Sloggett. The significant factor is to recognize how the matter of painting, in each case, is addressed to the spectator – a point underlined in the work of Ron Martin, whose recent shift from an open and painterly form to a geometric colour structure is a syntactical, not a stylistic change. For many painters, such as Jacques Hurtubise in Montréal and Josef DRAPELL, Milly Ristvedt-Han-derek and Harold Feist in Ontario, the character of painting remains abstract, formal and personal. Nor is the distinction between the abstract and figurative exclusive in terms of a concern with painting itself. In the work of David Bolduc, Harold Klunder, Paul Fournier, Alex Cameron, Paul Hutner, Howard Simkins, Eric Gamble and Christopher Broadhurst, among others in Toronto and elsewhere, figurative images are woven into the abstract concerns of the activity of painting.

There can be no question of the importance for many younger painters of an explicit concern with the image as such. It has been a sweeping development, spawning terms – new image, neoexpressionism, postmodernism, postcubist representation – in an attempt to identify the manifestations of this energy. We must cope with the precise images of painters such as Tim Zuck, Doug Kirton and Lynn Donoghue in Ontario; David Thauberger in Regina; and the expressive images of painters such as Luc Beland, Michel Jolliffe, Landon Mackenzie, Lynn Hughes and David Elliot in Montréal; and Shirley Wiitasalo, Brian Burnett, John Scott and Oliver Girling among others in Toronto.

What appears now to be a situation of stylistic anarchy arises, in substantial part, from the tendency of criticism since the war to stress a historicist view of current painting. From a wider viewpoint of art in our century it is apparent that it will take many decades to comprehend all that has happened, to realize the potential of the recent past. The revival of interest, for instance, in German expressionism, and in Matisse and de Kooning, is not an aberration from a determinist thrust of progress but the outcome of successive generations of painters responding to their own time and seeking a voice within the complex of possibilities to which they are heir. Such a situation, in its very complexity, speaks not of decline, but of health.
DAVID BURNETT

Reading: D. Burnett and M. Schiff, *Contemporary Canadian Art* (1983); J. Russell Harper, *Painting in Canada* (1977); J. Murray, *The Best Contemporary Canadian Art* (1987); D. Reid, *A Concise History of Canadian Painting* (1973) and *Our Own Country Canada* (1979).

Paleoindian, a loose designation for a cluster of early cultures: the CLOVIS (Llano), Folsom and Plano, and various others of coeval and earlier age which have been proposed by archaeologists but are not fully verified. These 3 cultures are characterized by a subsistence pattern focused on big game – mammoth, big-horned bison, deer and presumably mastodon – and there is evidence of this after 10 000 BC in western N America. Llano, 9500-9000 BC, is characterized by Clovis fluted projectile points. The Folsom culture, 9000-8000 BC, is typified by the Folsom point (finer and smaller than Clovis fluted). Plano, 8000-6000 BC, extends to the early ARCHAIC cultures. All 3 overlap to some extent, depending on geographical area. Paleoindian archaeological sites are generally widespread in Canada, usually in the south, with the exception of early material from the Yukon and a late northern variant of Plano. The best-known site is DEBERT (NS). Most of these sites are mass-kill sites where the remains of butchered animals are found in direct association with Paleoindian projectile points. The Paleoindian cultures disappeared with the extinction of the large mammals upon which they depended. *See also* PREHISTORY. RENÉ R. GADACZ

Paleontology, the study of FOSSILS, gives us knowledge of past life, helps us understand the nature of ancient organisms and provides information about the composition of the biomass of past times. The organisms now living represent a stage in the succession of life forms and, according to the concept of EVOLUTION, have descended from

past life forms. It is difficult to estimate how many species now exist; the number may be in excess of 45 million. Some authorities estimate that 1.5 million living species (monerans, protistans, fungi, plants and animals) have actually been found and described. The fossil record, largely representing the past 600 million years, has been estimated to contain about 250 000 species, a low figure since new species are constantly being described. Nevertheless, the actual number of species represented in the fossil record is low (possibly as low as 5%) compared to the number of species living today, because not all organisms have an equal chance of being preserved as fossils, eg, the delicate bodies of insects. In exceptional circumstances, soft-bodied animals may be preserved, eg, the bodies of organisms very quickly buried in sediment. Canada is fortunate in having one of the most famous faunas of this type, British Columbia's Cambrian BURGESS SHALE, first discovered by C.D. Walcott (1909). The Burgess Shale fauna is of great interest to paleontologists because of the unique state of preservation and variety of organisms represented (more than 120 species of soft-bodied marine animals).

By far the greatest proportion of fossils are of animals that had hard skeletal parts. The groups most commonly represented in the fossil record are the protozoans, Archaeocyathids (now extinct), Porifera (SPONGES), Coelenterates (CORALS), Bryozoa, BRACHIOPODS, MOLLUSCS (clams, nautiloids), arthropods (TRILOBITES) and ECHINODERMS (crinoids, echinoids). Various minerals have been and are being used by animals for skeletal construction (eg, chitin, calcium carbonate, silica and calcium phosphate). Once an organism dies, its body is incorporated in the sediment and subjected to groundwaters percolating through the area. Such solutions can have dramatic effects on the buried organism. In some cases, the skeletal material is removed completely, leaving no trace of the organism. In other instances, new minerals such as silica are precipitated into pore spaces within the skeleton, thereby increasing its weight. TREE material and bones (eg, DINOSAUR bones found around Drumheller, Alta) are commonly preserved in this manner. In another common process, the entire original skeletal material is replaced by a new mineral. Other fossils occur simply as a carbon residue on the surface of rock, the carbon remaining after the more volatile materials have been removed. Fossil plants and graptolites (Paleozoic colonial animals) are commonly preserved in this manner.

The fossil record encompasses a tremendous variety of organisms, ranging from microscopic conodonts to the giants of the fossil world, the dinosaurs. Obviously, there is a need to order the organisms, placing related organisms in groups. This process of classification was initiated by Aristotle, who recognized the differences between major groups, eg, birds and insects. The classification scheme now used by all paleontologists is that proposed by the 18th-century Swedish naturalist Linnaeus. This hierarchical system divides organisms into kingdoms, phyla, classes, orders, families, genera and species. The names attached to each division are associated with a particular group of organisms; therefore, they show relationships among organisms. The most commonly used part of the system is the "binomial designation," eg, the 2-part name *Tyrannosaurus rex* implies that the species name is *rex* and that it belongs to the genus *Tyrannosaurus*. The name *Tyrannosaurus rex* should immediately convey the nature of the beast being described, in this case a large dinosaur – the "king of the terrible lizards."

The study of fossils has many important applications in a wide variety of fields. For example, the study of the fossil record can give insight

about when and in what form life first appeared on Earth. The oldest known fossils are thought to be remains of ALGAE, bacteria and possibly fungi, which have been fortuitously preserved in cherts of Precambrian age. For example, the "Fig Tree" chert from South Africa contains algae which are considered to be more than 3.2 billion years old. A famous locality in Canada, the "Gunflint" chert exposed in southern Ontario, has yielded bacteria and algae that are about 1.9 billion years old. Stromatolites, structures formed by algae, are also common in Precambrian rocks dating back to about 2.8 billion years ago. Such stromatolites are quite common in Canadian Precambrian rocks.

The fossil record can also help the paleontologist to pinpoint various important stages in the evolution of life. For example, it shows that life during Precambrian times (before 570 million years ago) was entirely soft bodied. At the beginning of Cambrian times (between 570 and 505 million years ago) organisms developed the ability to secrete hard skeletons. It is through the fossil record that it is known that the Paleozoic era was the time when INVERTEBRATE animals dominated the biomass. Similarly, the fossil record reveals the dominance of the dinosaurs during the Mesozoic era (between 245 and 66.4 million years ago) and the MAMMALS during the Cenozoic (66.4 million years ago to the present). From the fossil record, it can also be shown that groups of animals have become extinct. Charles Darwin made extensive studies of fossils in the strata of S America and used this information along with data from modern species to formulate his theory of evolution. The fossil record also permits the study of the ecology of past times by describing the environment in which an organism lived and the interrelationship of the different groups of organisms present (*see* BIOGEOGRAPHY).

Perhaps the most important use of fossils is for the relative dating of the rocks in which they occur. It was demonstrated in the 19th century that a distinct succession of fossils will be found in any given sequence of sedimentary rock layers (horizons) and that rocks of a particular age will contain particular types of fossil. This discovery led to the development of biostratigraphy, literally, the tying together of rock units on the basis of their biological content. The principle follows from Darwin's concept of evolution: life changes gradually with time, and once a species has become extinct it will not reappear. As a basic tool in deciphering the geological evolution of an area, biostratigraphy has widespread economic application, playing an integral role in the exploration for oil, gas and minerals. In Canada, many important PETROLEUM discoveries have been based on detailed biostratigraphical studies. *See also* GEOCHEMISTRY; GEOLOGY; PALYNOLOGY. BRIAN JONES

Paleontology, History in Canada The study of FOSSILS was a relatively new science when the geological exploration of Canada began. The first Canadian geologist, and the first to apply the principles of geochronology (GEOLOGICAL DATING) in Canada, was William LOGAN, a native of Montréal, trained in the geology of England and Wales. In 1842, he was appointed to make a geological survey of the United PROVINCE OF CANADA. He began in 1843 by measuring, mapping and systematically subdividing the Devonian rocks (408-360 million years old) of the Gaspé Peninsula. Within the next few years he extended his surveys to the earlier Paleozoic formations of the Eastern Townships of Québec, as well as to the non-fossil-bearing rocks of the Lk Superior region. Thanks to the progress that had been made in identifying and mapping the Paleozoic rocks (570-245 million years old) of western New York and northern New England, Logan was able to establish the

Two of the great horned *Triceratops* dinosaurs. An artistic interpretation based on fossils unearthed by paleontologists in Alberta (*courtesy Eleanor M. Kish, National Museum of Natural Sciences*).

broad correlations of the formations in the St Lawrence region. However, he did not have the time, and probably not the knowledge, to work out the details of the fossil succession. In 1856 he appointed Elkanah BILLINGS of Ottawa to be the full-time paleontologist of the GEOLOGICAL SURVEY OF CANADA (GSC).

Billings, a successful lawyer and journalist, was an enthusiastic collector and student of fossils. In the next 20 years he amassed large collections of Paleozoic fossils, which he described and assigned to their stratigraphic positions. Although concentrating on the Ottawa and St Lawrence river valleys, he extended his collecting and identifying to southwestern Ontario and NS. He was especially interested in fossil ECHINODERMS and BRACHIOPODS.

While Logan and his colleagues were working out the GEOLOGY and fossil sequence for central Canada, J.W. DAWSON was doing the same for the Maritime colonies. In the process, he began the study of FOSSIL PLANTS in Canada, describing the flora of the "Coal Measures" (Pennsylvanian or Upper Carboniferous period, 320-286 million years ago) of NS and the Devonian of Gaspé. He became the first principal of McGill and founded there the Redpath Museum, a centre for paleontological research. Fossil plants from western Canada came to his notice, and he described AMPHIBIANS and MOLLUSCS from the hollow tree stumps associated with the coal seams of NS.

Billings was succeeded (1876) as paleontologist of the GSC by J.F. WHITEAVES of Montréal, an all-round naturalist. By this time, the geological exploration of the then North-West Territories and of Manitoba was beginning with the work of G.M. DAWSON and his GSC colleagues. Their fieldwork brought to light a series of new faunas, Ordovician (505-438 million years old), Silurian (438-408 million years old) and Devonian in Manitoba; Cretaceous (144-66.4 million years old) and Tertiary (66.4-1.6 million years old) from the future Saskatchewan and Alberta. These were described by Whiteaves, who made correlations with faunas discovered in the western US. Whiteaves also began the study of fossil FISHES in Canada. His detailed accounts of the Devonian fish faunas of the Baie des Chaleurs area (Qué and NB) revealed persistent archaic groups (ostracoderms, antiarchs) contemporary with early lung-

fish and teleosts and, most exciting, a fringe-finned fish that was on the verge of becoming a limbed VERTEBRATE. Meanwhile, paleontological work was proceeding in the classic fossil fields of central and eastern Canada. The basic work on the Paleozoic faunas of Ontario, begun by Billings, was refined and expanded by W.A. PARKS of University of Toronto, and by E.M. KINDLE, M.Y. Williams and Alice E. WILSON of the GSC. The older (Mississippian or Lower Carboniferous, 360-320 million years old) floras of NB and NS were studied by G.F. Matthew of Saint John and W.A. Bell of the GSC. Their work, added to that of J.W. Dawson, established the sequence of plant life for the Paleozoic.

The Cretaceous DINOSAUR faunas of Alberta and Saskatchewan are famous. They were first revealed by G.M. Dawson in 1874, and by his successors in the 1880s. L.M. Lambe, assistant to Whiteaves, provided the early descriptions of these fossils, but it was not until Barnum Brown of the American Museum of Natural History came to Alberta with a staff of well-trained collectors (1910) that the wealth and excellence of preservation of Canadian dinosaurs came to be realized. To share in these discoveries, the GSC engaged the services of C.H. Sternberg of Kansas and his 3 sons. Their work, and especially that of the second son, C.M. STERNBERG, resulted in the assemblage, at the National Museums of Canada, of a very important dinosaur collection described by Lambe and later by Sternberg. W.A. Parks, assisted by Levi Sternberg, the youngest of the brothers, built up a fine collection of Alberta dinosaurs at the Royal Ontario Museum, and made them known to science. Fossil MAMMALS of Oligocene age (36.6-23.7 million years old) were found (1883) in the Cypress Hills, Sask, by R.G. McConnell of the GSC and described by E.D. Cope of Philadelphia. Subsequently, Lambe collected and described additional specimens, correlating them with the White River Group of S Dakota. A late Miocene mammalian fauna (23.7-5.3 million years old) was found (1929) in southern Saskatchewan by C.M. Sternberg. L.S. Russell described Paleocene mammals from Alberta and Saskatchewan, a late Eocene mammalian fauna from Saskatchewan and an early Oligocene fauna from southeastern BC. Another famous fossil occurrence in Canada is in the Middle Cambrian BURGESS SHALE in the Rocky Mts near Field, BC. This was discovered (1909) by C.D. Walcott of the Smithsonian Institution, who was a specialist in Cambrian faunas. The remarkable aspect of the Burgess Shale fauna, revealed by Walcott's 5 sea-

sons of excavation and by numerous monographs, was the presence of a rich assemblage of soft-bodied animals, remains of which would ordinarily not be preserved.

Early in the 20th century, commercial companies began drilling for PETROLEUM in the plains and foothills of Alberta. To carry out this activity intelligently, the companies required detailed stratigraphic data, which depended on knowledge of the succession and correlation of fossil faunas. A major step in this direction was provided by the work of F.H. McLearn of the GSC. He revised the Triassic (245-208 million years old), Jurassic (208-144 million years old) and Lower Cretaceous fossil molluscs of the foothills and northern plains of Alberta and those of the Queen Charlotte Is, and established correlations with similar faunas in the US, Europe and Asia. P.S. Warren of University of Alberta also made important contributions in this field, as well as with the late Paleozoic faunas of the Rocky Mts and the Subarctic. Interest in exploration for oil and gas also stimulated the study of "microfossils," mostly Foraminifera, the hard parts of which could be recovered from well cuttings. Although some pioneer observations on such fossils had been made by G.M. Dawson, modern investigation of them in western Canada was begun (1927) by J.A. Cushman of Harvard and continued by one of his students, R.T.D. Wickenden of the Geological Survey. Among more recent workers in this field have been J.H. Wall and C.R. Stelck in Alberta and W.G.E. Caldwell in Sask and Man.

A similar use has been made in Paleozoic biostratigraphy of the jawlike and toothlike microfossils known as "conodonts." In 1897 G.J. Hinde, then at University of Toronto, described conodonts from local Ordovician rocks. In recent years there has been a revival of interest in them because of their stratigraphic importance; faunas have been described from Alberta, Ontario and farther east. Other Canadian paleontologists have become recognized specialists on particular groups of fossils. W.A. Parks was noted for his numerous papers on stromatoporoids (Paleozoic colonial organisms which superficially resemble corals). Madeleine Fritz, of U of T, has contributed much to the knowledge of Paleozoic Bryozoa. G.W. Sinclair, of the GSC, specialized in the Conularida, early Paleozoic organisms possibly related to JELLYFISH. INSECTS are rare as fossils, but numerous specimens do occur in the Eocene tuffaceous shales of interior BC. These were described by S.H. Scudder of Boston and Anton Handlirsch of Vienna, Austria. Scudder also described late Paleozoic insects from NS.

Almost every university in Canada has a collection of fossils, mainly used in teaching; but for size and number of type specimens, the most important collections are those of the GSC and the National Museum of Natural Sciences in Ottawa, the Redpath Museum of McGill U in Montréal, the Royal Ontario Museum in Toronto, U of Alberta in Edmonton and the Saskatchewan Museum of Natural History in Regina.   L.S. RUSSELL

Reading: M. Zaslow, *Reading the Rocks* (1975).

Palliser, Hugh, naval officer, governor of Newfoundland (b at Kirk Deighton, Eng 26 Feb 1722/23; d at Chalfont St Giles, Eng 19 Mar 1796). He was a naval officer at the siege of Québec in 1759, and was appointed governor of Newfoundland 1764. He travelled widely within his jurisdiction policing the French fishery to confine it to the limits set by the Treaty of PARIS, 1763. Palliser's concern was for the English migratory fishery only, but his attempts to discourage settlement failed. Assisted by Moravian missionaries, he was the first official to establish relations with the LABRADOR INUIT and Indians, and he also encouraged

Captain James COOK in his hydrographic survey 1763-67.   JOHN PARSONS

Palliser, John, sportsman, explorer (b at Dublin, Ire 29 Jan 1817; d at Comeragh House, Cty Waterford, Ire 18 Aug 1887). He spent nearly 3 years (1857-60) exploring what is now western Canada as instigator and leader of the PALLISER EXPEDITION. His interest in the southern prairies and mountains of western British N America had been aroused on an 1847-48 tour of the US, when he had spent almost 11 months hunting buffalo, elk and grizzly bear in the Missouri country. On his return he wrote a popular book about his adventures, *Solitary Rambles and Adventures of a Hunter in the Prairies* (1853; new ed, 1972).

Heir to an Irish landowner and descendant of a Protestant archbishop of Cashel, he attended Trinity College, Dublin, and saw intermittent militia service 1839-63. Besides his exploration of what is now western Canada, he made 2 important journeys. One was a confidential, semiofficial mission in 1862-63 to the Caribbean and Confederate States, and the other was a voyage in 1869 with his brother Frederick in his own specially reinforced vessel, *Sampson,* to Novaya Zemlya in Russia [USSR] and the Kara Sea, exploring and hunting walrus and polar bear. Apart from visits to London (where he discussed possible railway routes with Sandford FLEMING) and to Rome, Switzerland and France, he spent the rest of his life caring for nieces and nephews, in public duties such as justice of the peace, in administering his heavily mortgaged estates, playing Bach's music and walking in the lovely Comeragh Mountains.   IRENE M. SPRY

Reading: Irene M. Spry, ed, "Introduction," *The Papers of the Palliser Expedition, 1857-1860* (1968).

Palliser Expedition (British North American Exploring Expedition), 1857-60, initiated by John PALLISER, who submitted to the Royal Geographical Society a plan to travel from RED RIVER COLONY to and through the Rocky Mts along the unsurveyed American boundary. The society expanded the project into a scientific expedition and applied for a grant of £5000 from the imperial government, which was then facing the problem of the future of the HUDSON'S BAY COMPANY's territories and badly needed information about them. To exploration of the plains south of the N Saskatchewan R and southern passes through the Rockies, the COLONIAL OFFICE added an examination of the old NORTH WEST COMPANY canoe route W from Lk Superior. Under Palliser's command, Dr James HECTOR was appointed geologist and naturalist, Eugène BOURGEAU botanical collector and John W. Sullivan secretary and astronomical observer. Magnetical observer Lt Thomas W. BLAKISTON brought his delicate instruments via Hudson Bay to join them on the prairies.

The explorers amassed astronomical, meteorological, geological and magnetic data, and described the country, its fauna and flora, its inhabitants and its "capabilities" for settlement and transportation. They concluded that to establish a "communication" entirely within British territory from Canada to Red River would be difficult and costly; access through American territory was much easier. Although some semiarid country (which is now known as "Palliser's Triangle") stretched across the American border into the prairies of modern Canada, it was surrounded by a "fertile belt" well suited for stock raising and agriculture. There were deposits of coal and other minerals. The party traversed 6 passes in the southern Rockies, some of them feasible for a railway (the CPR was later built through one of them, KICKING HORSE PASS, named by Hector), but found the mountains farther W a formidable obstacle.

The expedition's reports (published in 1859, 1860 and 1863) and its comprehensive map (1865) were for some time the major source of information about the sweep of country from Lk Superior to BC's Okanagan Valley, and are still of value today.   IRENE M. SPRY

Reading: Irene M. Spry, *The Palliser Expedition* (1963) and, ed, *The Papers of the Palliser Expedition, 1857-1860* (1968).

Palmer, Edward, lawyer, landed proprietor, land agent, politician, judge, premier of PEI (b in Charlottetown, PEI 1 Sept 1809; d there 3 Nov 1889). The son of an Irish-born attorney, he took his schooling in Charlottetown and studied law in his father's office. A Tory, he represented the capital in the legislature 1835-70. Though lacking brilliant abilities, he was a capable political strategist with great force of character, and became premier in 1859, after 10 years as party leader in the assembly. Conflicts within his party led to Palmer's replacement as premier in 1863; he resigned from the Cabinet 2 years later in opposition to union of the colonies. In 1872 he was elected as a Liberal as part of an attempt to prevent the Island from joining CONFEDERATION. When the Island joined the following year, however, Palmer began a new career, as judge of the Queens County Court. He was named provincial chief justice 1874 and held this position until his death.   IAN ROSS ROBERTSON

Palmer, Herbert James, lawyer, politician, premier of PEI (b at Charlottetown 26 Aug 1851; d there 22 Dec 1939); son of Edward PALMER. Called to the bar in 1876, appointed Queen's Counsel in 1878, Palmer was elected to the Legislative Assembly in 1900. A Liberal, he became premier in 1911 but was defeated in a by-election 7 months later. He resigned that Dec and returned to his practice.   NICOLAS J. DE JONG

Palmer, James Bardin, lawyer, politician (b at Dublin, Ire *c*1771; d at Charlottetown 3 Mar 1833). Trained as a lawyer in Ireland, Palmer immigrated to PEI in 1802. He quickly embroiled himself in politics and became a leading member of the LOYAL ELECTORS. This led in 1812 to clashes with Gov C.D. Smith, who dismissed Palmer from the courts in 1816. Palmer had to appeal to England to be reinstated as a lawyer. He served as member of the Assembly and of the executive council before 1812, but later attempts to be elected to the Assembly were unsuccessful. In a colony with little legal talent Palmer soon became the leading lawyer and he was responsible for some reforms in the legal system, but his inability to get along with all but a few of the community meant that his progressive ideas in other areas were largely disregarded.   H.T. HOLMAN

Palynology, the study of spores and pollen, has many applications in BOTANY, GEOLOGY and MEDICINE. Spores are primitive reproductive bodies of FUNGI and some plants. Pollen grains are small male reproductive bodies produced and dispersed by seed plants. Spores and pollen are small (5-100 μm), spherical or oblong structures, identifiable under a compound light microscope. Fine details of wall structure and sculpturing can be seen under the scanning electron microscope (20 000 to 40 000 magnification). The detailed structure of the wall (exine layer), and the number and arrangements of pores and furrows in the wall, are the diagnostic characters used in identification. Pollen is a key tool in reconstructing past vegetation and environments (paleoecology), because the outer wall is both extremely resistant to decay and elaborately and beautifully constructed so that identification to species or family level is possible. Pollen of many plants is discharged into the air annually (*see* POLLINATION) and falls into lakes

and bogs as a "rain" which represents the surrounding vegetation. Many forest regions in Canada produce a total pollen fallout of 30 000 to 60 000 grains per cm² annually, while tundras produce fewer than 1000.

Pollen is preserved in lake or bog sediments that accumulate each year. This preservation results in a sequence of pollen assemblages representing the succession of past vegetation. For example, Tertiary sediments 10-20 million years old, under the Mackenzie Delta, NWT, contain deposits of spores which indicate that a rich coniferous forest grew there, similar to modern forests in coastal BC and Washington. Analysis of the spore content of such rocks is used in the search for fossil fuels and the petroleum industry employs palynologists as part of this exploratory activity. Pollen analysis of sediments that have accumulated since the end of the latest GLACIATION reveal the vegetation changes and tree migrations that have produced the present vegetation of Canada.

In addition to showing the responses of vegetation to climatic change, pollen data indicate effects of human cultures such as clearing, burning and agriculture. A pollen record from a small lake near Toronto shows evidence of maize cultivation (1380 AD) in an Iroquoian village near the site, and evidence of forest clearance. The same site shows the beginning of European agriculture by the abrupt rise in frequency of ragweed pollen. Palynology is used in quality control tests of honey to identify the source plants used by bees, and it has been used in forensic science to solve crimes (eg, when pollen adhering to clothing can indicate the scene of a crime).   J.C. RITCHIE

Reading: P.D. Moore and J.A. Webb, *An Illustrated Guide to Pollen Analysis* (1978).

Pan-American Games are a multi-sport, quadrennial festival for the nations of the Western Hemisphere, conducted in a similar manner to the OLYMPIC GAMES and held one year prior to them. A comparatively recent event, the first Pan-Am Games were held at Buenos Aires (Argentina) in 1951, when 19 nations were officially represented in 18 sports. Since then they have been celebrated at Mexico City (Mexico) 1955 and 1975; Chicago (USA) 1959; Sao Paulo (Brazil) 1963; Winnipeg (Canada) 1967; Cali (Colombia) 1971; San Juan (Puerto Rico) 1981; Caracas (Venezuela) 1983; and Indianapolis (USA) 1987. Canada did not officially compete in the 1951 Games (although a small group of Canadian swimmers did give a demonstration in synchronized swimming) but has been a consistent and successful competitor ever since, with Canadian athletes providing many world-class performances in various sports. In fact, an analysis of medal winners in the 4 Pan-Am Games between 1963 and 1975 shows Canada with a total of 329, 2nd only to the US. The 5th Pan-Am Games at Winnipeg proved a fitting celebration for Centennial Year, 1967, when 2451 athletes from 29 countries participated in 29 sports. Canada's finest performance to date was in Indianapolis in 1987, with 30 gold, 57 silver and 74 bronze — an increase of 51 medals over the 1983 games in Caracas.   GERALD REDMOND

Pan-Indianism, an intertribal movement of native resistance to white domination and assimilation, is characterized primarily by political and religious expression and solidarity. Key historical figures include PONTIAC and HANDSOME LAKE. Leaders since colonial times have advocated that Indians free themselves, even if this means violence. The Peyote Cult, a reaction to Christian teachings and beliefs, originated in the southern plains area during the later 19th century and gradually symbolized the unity of Indians all over N America. Red Power is pan-Indian sentiment committed to radical political action, as in the National Congress of American Indians (NCAI, 1944) and the American Indian Movement (AIM, 1968). These rights-oriented groups believe that natives must choose between assimilation and being Indian, and that Canadian and American government obligations to Indians are binding. *See also* NATIVE PEOPLE, POLITICAL ORGANIZATION.   RENÉ R. GADACZ

Panama Canal, the interoceanic canal between Atlantic and Pacific, controlled by the US and operational since 1914. It has been useful to the Royal Canadian Navy as well as to Canada-bound commercial shipping. Prime ministers Robert Borden and Arthur Meighen argued successfully for strict enforcement of US-UK treaty obligations guaranteeing a uniform fee structure to all vessels using the canal. Any alternative, they said, would benefit ports in the northern US at the expense of Canadian ports.

Controversy erupted in the 1920s when the Panama Canal undercut Canadian railways in shipments from eastern Canada to Alberta and BC. Effective lobbying by Canadian railway interests persuaded PM Mackenzie King to maintain tariffs against commodities re-entering Canada via the Panama Canal. The canal also proved useful during the energy crisis of 1973-75 for shipments of Alberta oil to Montréal and Atlantic Canada.   GRAEME S. MOUNT

Panet Family Established in Québec City by **Jean-Claude Panet** (1719-78) in 1740, and in Montréal by his brother, **Pierre-Méru Panet** (1731-1804) in 1746, for generations the Panet family has made a remarkable contribution to Canadian legal, political, religious and above all, military life. Shortly after his arrival in Canada Jean-Claude Panet, a private in the TROUPES DE LA MARINE, became a royal notary, and later one of the 2 first Catholic judges of the Court of Common Pleas under the British regime. His son, **Bernard Claude Panet** (1753-1833) became bishop of Québec in 1825. Another son, **Jean-Antoine Panet** (1751-1815), a notary and seigneur of Bourg-Louis, became the first speaker of the Legislative Assembly of Lower Canada (1791-94; 1797-1814), member of the Legislative Council (1815), judge of the Court of Common Pleas (1794-97) and a militia officer who participated in the defeat of American arms in 1775-76. Jean-Claude Panet's grandson, Elzéar-Alexandre Panet's son, **Philippe Panet** (1791-1855), was also a lawyer, member of the Legislative Assembly (1816-20; 1830-32) and the Executive Council (1831), judge of the King's Bench and a captain of the Canadian VOLTIGEURS who fought the Americans during the War of 1812; his second son, **Louis Panet** (1794-1884), was a notary, member of the Special Council of Lower Canada (1837-41), member of the Legislative Council (1852-67), member of the Legislative Council of Québec (1867-84), a senator (1871-74) and lieutenant-colonel of the 1st Battalion of the Québec Militia (1857-69). Philip Panet's son, **Charles-Eugène Panet** (1829-98), a lawyer, senator (1875) and lt-col of the 9th Voltigeurs de Québec (1869-80) was deputy minister of Militia (1875-98). Six of his 7 sons by 3 marriages also held high military rank: Col Antoine Chartier de Lobinière Panet (1865-1926); Brig-Gen Alphonse-Eugène Panet (1867-1950); Maj-Gen Henri-Alexandre Panet (1869-1959); Col Charles Louis Panet (1870-1955); Col Arthur Hubert Panet (1877-1944); and Maj-Gen Edouard de Bellefeuille Panet (1881-1977), a distinguished military tradition which continues into the seventh generation, and which has established the Panets reputation as "Canada's Foremost Military Family."

Pierre-Méru Panet's Montréal branch of the Panet family followed a familiar pattern. Pierre-Méru Panet himself became a royal notary, judge of the Court of Common Pleas (1778-84), a member of the Executive Council in 1791 and a militia officer who fought the Americans in 1775-76. His son, **Pierre Louis Panet** (1761-1812) was also a notary, member of the Legislative Assembly (1792), member of the Executive Council (1801) and a judge of the King's Bench (1795-1812); a second son, **Bonaventure Panet** (1765-1846), was a member of the first Legislative Assembly of Lower Canada and fought in the War of 1812. Pierre-Louis Panet's son, also called **Pierre-Louis** (1800-70) became a judge of the Court of the King's Bench.

Other Panet descendants through the maternal line in the Taschereau, de Bellefeuille, MacDonald, de Lobinières and Harwood families, reinforce the Panet's distinguished record in Canadian public life.   CARMAN MILLER

Reading: J. Gouin and L. Brault, *Legacy of Honours: The Panets* (1985).

Pangman, Bastonnais, Métis buffalo hunter and leader (b at N Saskatchewan R 1778), son of fur trader Peter Pangman and a Cree mother. A skilled hunter, he helped provide buffalo meat to the colony founded by Lord SELKIRK in 1812-13. Angered by the "Pemmican Proclamation" of 1814, Pangman was active in MÉTIS raids upon the new settlement and helped negotiate for the withdrawal of the settlers from Red River in 1815. There is no evidence that he was present at the SEVEN OAKS INCIDENT (1816), and in 1818 he was acquitted of charges of arson.   HARRIET GORHAM

Pangnark, John, sculptor (b at Windy Lk, NWT 1920; d at Rankin Inlet, NWT 1980). An inland CARIBOU INUIT, Pangnark was relocated in the late 1950s to Eskimo Point, where he spent his later years carving. Represented in the *Sculpture/Inuit* exhibition of 1971 to 1973, Pangnark was one of 4 Inuit artists chosen to go to Expo 70 in Osaka, Japan. Because of his preoccupation with resolving formal concerns, often at the expense of easily recognizable subject matter, his sculpture is unlike the narrative and naturalistic work of much contemporary Inuit sculpture. His highly individualized abstractions are most appreciated by the critic who sees, outwardly at least, similarities to 20th-century abstract sculpture.   NORMAN ZEPP

Pangnirtung, NWT, Hamlet, pop 1004 (1986c), 839 (1981c), is located on the southeastern shore of Pangnirtung Fjord on the S shore of BAFFIN I's CUMBERLAND SOUND, 2330 air km NE of YELLOWKNIFE. The name derives from an Inuit word said to mean "place of the bull caribou." The area, which is near the edge of a tundra flat between the base of glaciated mountains and the sea, was first visited by John DAVIS in 1585. By 1840 it had become one of the arctic points where WHALING ships gathered most often. Some local Angmarlik Inuit

Aerial view of Pangnirtung, located on the SE shore of Baffin I, NWT (*courtesy SSC Photocentre/photo by Karl-Heinz Raach*).

became well-known whaleboat skippers. Several local Inuit provided invaluable guidance to explorers such as C.F. HALL (*c*1860). During 1882-83 Cumberland Sd was the base camp of German scientists participating in the INTERNATIONAL POLAR YEAR. By *c*1910 whaling was in decline, but interest in white fox took up the slack; the HBC built a trading post at Pangnirtung in 1921. The RCMP post was established 1925. In 1968 the local Inuit formed a co-operative to promote soapstone and whalebone carvings. Today the community is known for its artworks, particularly the world-famous woven tapestries made by local Inuit artists. It is also the access point to AUYUITTUQ NATIONAL PARK (est 1972). *See also* INUIT ART. ANNELIES POOL

Panneton, Philippe, pen name Ringuet, physician, professor, diplomat, novelist (b at Trois-Rivières, Qué 30 Apr 1895; d at Lisbon, Portugal 28 Dec 1960). Panneton was a leading figure in French Canadian literature, thanks primarily to his novel, TRENTE ARPENTS (1938), which is considered a classic of Canadian literature. Panneton was a true man of letters and combined work as a professor at U de M with a full literary life. He wrote for many periodicals, was a founding member and chairman of the Académie canadienne-française and published 7 books, including a pastiche, a collection of short stories, and 5 novels dealing with both rural and urban history (eg, *Un Monde était leur empire,* 1943; *Le Poids du jour,* 1949).

He was acclaimed in both French and English Canada for his works, but it was primarily because of *Trente Arpents* that he received awards, including that of the Province of Québec, the Académie française's Prix des Vikings, and a Gov Gen's Award. The novel, first published in Paris, concerns the transition from agrarian to urban life in Québec. It covers the 45 years from the late 19th century to the Depression, and deals with 3 generations of peasants who exhaust themselves cultivating their 30 acres (12 ha) of land. The main character, Euchariste Moisan, prospers on the land and with maturity achieves ease and fame, but in old age he meets a series of difficulties. As a result he turns over his land to his eldest son and goes into exile in New England with a son who, like several of his brothers and sisters, has left the land for the city. The land, mother and wife, is also a hard mistress. Unyielding and unchanging, she rejects the person who cannot meet her challenge. This was a new vision of rural life. Panneton's predecessors, except for Albert LABERGE and Claude-Henri GRIGNON, all presented idyllic and moralizing accounts of no artistic or literary dimension. This novel, the best to appear until the 1940s, was quickly translated into English and German, and after 1940 was published in both languages. Panneton became ambassador to Portugal in 1957.   ANTOINE SIROIS

Papineau, Louis-Joseph, lawyer, seigneur, politician (b at Montréal 7 Oct 1786; d at Montebello, Qué 25 Sept 1871), the son of Joseph Papineau, a seigneur and moderate liberal member of the Assembly. He was educated at the the Petit Séminaire de Québec and prepared himself for a career in law, which he carried on intermittently after 1810. Representative of the growing influence of the liberal professions in French Canada, he was first elected to the Assembly of LOWER CANADA in 1809, during Gov Gen Sir James CRAIG's "Reign of Terror." With his self assurance, skill as an orator and popular following, he emerged from a group of young nationalists to leadership of the PARTI CANADIEN (later PARTI PATRIOTE) and was made Speaker of the Assembly in 1815. He came to see himself as the defender of the national heritage of French Canada and led the fight for control of the political institutions of Lower Canada. Early in his career he was a moderate who admired British parliamentary institutions, but during the 1820s his views became more radical and his parliamentary strategy was obstructionist, using the Assembly's control of revenues and the civil list to combat the policies of the English commercial class, which he considered anathema to the interests of French Canada.

Papineau travelled to England in 1823 in his campaign to defeat the Union Bill of 1822, which had been introduced to circumvent his control of the Assembly. The union was rejected and this victory reinforced his desire to reform Lower Canada's political institutions, particularly the council, which was dominated by the CHÂTEAU CLIQUE. Towards 1830 Papineau stepped up his virulent attacks on the nonelective legislative council and declared himself a republican. He became an advocate of independence for Lower Canada and became increasingly critical of imperial authority. After a sweeping electoral victory in 1834, he increased his efforts to paralyse the political system; goaded by revolutionary elements of his party, he intensified his policy of boycott and political obstruction in order to force the British government to grant reforms intended to transfer power to representatives of the French Canadian nation.

Papineau and a small committee put forward their demands in the "Ninety-Two Resolutions," which demanded control of revenues by the legislature, for responsibility of the executive and for election of the council. When the demands were categorically rejected by the British in 1837 the political crisis deepened, popular feeling, inflamed by social and economic crises, was roused and Papineau began to lose control of the events he had been so instrumental in setting in motion. He addressed a rally of 4000 at ST-CHARLES, Oct 23 1837, at which the Patriotes more or less declared the independence of the Six Counties and their willingness to resort to arms if necessary. When after the defeat at St-Charles it became clear that the Patriotes would be crushed, he fled to the US and, following the failure of the second insurrection, he sailed for France in 1839.

Papineau's career, particularly his behaviour during the REBELLIONS OF 1837, has been a continuing source of controversy and conjecture. He claimed that he had taken no part in the insurrections, yet evidence shows he acted as supreme commander until the battle at ST-DENIS, from where he disappeared just before the fight was engaged. Later, many of his fellow Patriotes accused him of cowardice, though they continued to support him as the only viable leader of FRENCH CANADIAN NATIONALISM. He professed to be a liberal and republican, yet was a staunch defender of the SEIGNEURIAL SYSTEM, which had a feudal character, as the basis of French Canada's agricultural economy. He himself owned the seigneury of Petit Nation, purchased in 1817 from his father, and by all accounts demanded full measure from his habitants. He was an economic conservative, hostile to the commercial and transportation innovations that the merchants considered essential to progress in Lower Canada. Though a deist and a violent anticleric, he nevertheless feared that a weakening of the Catholic Church would play into the hands of the English-speaking Protestant enemies of French Canada.

Papineau was granted amnesty in 1844 and returned from exile to his seigneury in 1845. He profited amply from timber concessions and built himself a grand manor house at Montebello through the help of his indebted censitaires. He re-entered politics in 1848 but was at odds with the new leadership of Louis LAFONTAINE. He vehemently opposed the ACT OF UNION and advocated ANNEXATION to the US. Around him coalesced a

Louis-Joseph Papineau, from a photo in *Portraits of British Americans* (1868) by F. Taylor and William Notman (*courtesy National Archives of Canada/C-21005*).

new group of young liberal nationalists who later became the PARTI ROUGE; Papineau himself left politics in 1854. Complex and contradictory, Papineau was nevertheless the first effective political leader of his people; if he was not the "national hero" they desired, he was a fitting symbol of their discontent.   JAMES MARSH

Reading: F. Ouellet, *Louis-Joseph Papineau, A Divided Soul* (1961) and *Lower Canada, 1791-1840* (1980).

Papineau-Couture, Jean, composer, teacher, administrator (b at Montréal 12 Nov 1916), grandson of Guillaume COUTURE. After studying in Montréal and Boston, he worked at Cambridge, Mass, under Nadia Boulanger, concentrating on Stravinsky and the French Impressionist composers. He has taught at Collège Jean-de-Brébeuf, the Conservatoire de musique de Montréal and in the music faculty of U de M, where he was dean 1968-73. He has emphasized acoustics in his teaching and his students include a number of composers, eg, Jacques Hétu, François MOREL, André Prévost and Gilles TREMBLAY. Papineau-Couture has been president of several organizations, including the Académie de musique de Québec, the JEUNESSES MUSICALES DU CANADA (Montréal branch), the Canadian Music Council, the Canadian Music Centre (of which he was a founding member), the Canadian League of Composers, the Société de musique contemporaine du Québec and the Humanities Research Council of Canada. His awards include the 1962 Prix de musique Calixa-Lavallée, the Canadian Music Council Medal (1973), the Prix Denise-Pelletier (1981) and the Diplôme d'honneur from the Canadian Conference of the Arts (1986). *Psaume CL*, *Étude in B-flat Minor*, and *Pièce concertante* (Nos 1 to 5) are considered among his major works.   HÉLÈNE PLOUFFE

Reading: L. Bail Milot, *Jean Papineau-Couture* (1986).

Paquet, Louis-Adolphe, priest, theologian (b at St Nicolas, Canada E 4 Aug 1859; d at Québec C 24 Feb 1942). Professor at Laval for nearly 60 years, he was French Canada's "national theologian" who guided – some say, created – Québec's archbishops, defining the church's position on public policy and shaping the somewhat defensive "messianic nationalism" of his day. Trained in Rome during the Thomistic revival, Mgr Paquet wrote the 4-volume *Droit public de l'église* (*Public Law of the Church*) (1908-15), a standard

text in ultramontanist terms on the relations between church and state. Having grown up during the disappointing period of the NORTH-WEST REBELLION, Paquet moderated the aggressive nationalism of his predecessors BOURGET and LAFLÈCHE in a 1902 public address on the vocation of the French race in America, calling on French Canadian Catholics to guard their faith, language and soil from contamination by materialistic foreigners. He formulated the church's official position on such issues as the MANITOBA SCHOOLS QUESTION 1896, Ontario's Regulation 17 (1912) and overseas CONSCRIPTION 1917. A powerful orator, systematizer and teacher, he shaped the church leaders of his day, but his influence waned in the face of the social problems that arose during urbanization in the 1920s.   TOM SINCLAIR-FAULKNER

Parachuting, Sport, also known as skydiving. The earliest jumps were made from balloons, and the first successful parachute descent was performed in 1797 over Paris. Free-falling jumps were not possible until 1908, when the ripcord was devised, though the ripcord was not used from an airplane until 1912. Contests began in the US in 1926, and the first world championship was held in Yugoslavia in 1951. Competitors normally use light aircraft to carry them to about 3600 m, and parachutes are usually opened at about 760 m. Sport parachutists compete in 4 world championship areas: free-fall individual style maneuvres, combined with precision accuracy landing; 4- and 8-person group free-fall competition, with recreational jumping in groups of 2 to 100; "open parachute" formations, called canopy relative work; and "paraski," combining precision accuracy with giant slalom skiing.

The first parachute jump in Canada was made in 1919, when Frank Ellis descended from a Jenny aircraft over Lake Erie; the Frank Ellis Trophy commemorates this event. After WWII, clubs and competitions were organized in Canada. The oldest surviving club is the St Catharines Parachuting Club, formed in 1947. The Canadian Sport Parachuting Assn was founded in 1967. The Canadian National Parachuting Team has ranked among the top 10 countries in international competition since 1960. S.F. Wykeham-Martin became the first Canadian to win a medal in world competition, placing 2nd in individual accuracy in 1966. In 1976 Pierre Forand won the silver medal in the men's absolute overall category, missing the world championship by one-five-hundredth of a second. In 1980, Kathy Cox won the women's world accuracy championship. Canadian teams dominated parachuting in the late 1970s, winning the world overall relative-work (2 or more parachutists maneuvering together during free-fall) championships in 1977 and 1979. They placed 2nd overall in 1981, and won gold (4-way) and silver (8-way) in 1984, and silver (4-way) and bronze (8-way), in 1985. Five licences of proficiency are awarded, and competition jumping (in both 4- and 8-person teams) is also organized by the CSPA. The G.R. Masterson Trophy is the premier parachuting award in Canada.   BARBARA SCHRODT

Paradis, Suzanne, poet, novelist, essayist and literary critic (b at Québec City 27 Oct 1936). Though she had already published several poems and stories, it was only in 1962 that she decided to devote herself to writing. She remained largely unknown to the general Québec public, despite winning several prestigious literary awards (*La Malbête*, 2nd prize, Concours littéraire du Québec, 1963; *Pour les Enfants des morts: Poèmes*, Prix France-Québec, 1965; *L'Oeuvre de Pierre: Poèmes*, Prix Du Maurier, 1970). Her novel *Miss Charlie* (1979) published by Éditions Leméac finally brought her wide public attention and critical acclaim. With a scrupulous concern for stylistic detail and story structure, she chose to rewrite her earlier works. Paradis is also a critic and has contributed to several cultural periodicals.

GUY CHAMPAGNE

Paradise, Nfld, Town, pop 3346 (1986c), inc 1981, is situated inland approximately 13 km from downtown St John's. It was founded in the late 1800s as a farming and livestock area near the railway line connecting St John's to Harbour Grace. Many early settlers also travelled to Conception Bay to fish during the summer and further supplemented their income in the area's good forests, selling rinds for ships and wood for barrel making and fuel. The modern community has grown rapidly, from 191 people in 1945, mainly through the town's growth as a residential site. The major local occupation is construction but most residents commute to work in St John's.

ROBERT D. PITT

Parasitology, branch of BIOLOGY dealing with organisms (animals or, rarely, plants) which live in or on other species (hosts) from which they derive nourishment. These organisms are called parasites. Some cause disease in humans and domestic and wild animals. Several have complex and fascinating cycles of development in 2 or more hosts. This rather simplistic definition includes some viruses, bacteria and protozoa, various kinds of worms and certain INSECTS, TICKS, MITES and copepod CRUSTACEANS.

Several types of parasites occur in humans, domestic animals and wild animals in Canada, but fortunately they cause less disease than some species in warmer countries. A higher prevalence noted recently results from increased travel to, and emigration from, tropical lands. Canadian researchers have contributed to the knowledge of parasites that occur in Canada and elsewhere. For example, almost 100 years ago the Canadian W.G. MacCallum studied a malarialike parasite in the blood of birds and found a stage of development that provided a clue to a facet of development of the malaria parasite of humans. J.L. Todd, the first professor of parasitology in Canada (at McGill), studied the trypanosomes (parasitic protozoans) that cause sleeping sickness in humans in Africa and discovered the spread of relapsing fever by ticks.

Early explorers related gruesome stories of attacks by MOSQUITOES and BLACK FLIES. Bedbugs in logging camps and boarding houses caused misery. In the middle of the last century, thousands of immigrants died from typhus fever en route to or after landing in Canada. It was not then known that this dreaded disease is transmitted by lice. The significance of ENTOMOLOGY to agriculture and to human and animal health was recognized in 1884 with the appointment of James FLETCHER as the first Dominion Entomologist. In 1832 Dr. John ROLPH established a medical school where he gave instruction on malaria. As early as the 1850s Canadians were writing papers on parasites. The private veterinary college begun by Andrew SMITH in 1862 (later the Ontario Veterinary College) had lectures on parasitology from the beginning. Robert Ramsay WRIGHT at Toronto and William OSLER at McGill were studying parasites in the 1880s. Investigations increased in the early part of the 20th century. Veterinarians such as E.A. WATSON and Seymour Hadwen, associated with the Dominion Health of Animals Branch, were prominent investigators. The former studied the trypanosome that causes dourine in horses. Thanks to his work and that of colleagues, the disease was eradicated from Canada. Hadwen also established the life cycle of the warble fly of cattle.

Parasitology expanded in 1932 with the forma-

tion of the Institute of Parasitology at Macdonald College with T.W.M. CAMERON as the first director, and the creation of a Department of Veterinary Science at the Ontario Research Foundation with Hadwen as director. At the same time, E.M. Walker in zoology and D.T. Fraser in preventive medicine at U of T were encouraging research and teaching. With the appointment of Ronald Law as director of the Ontario Experimental Fur Farm, more attention was directed to parasites in wild animals. The Ontario Veterinary College, with its longtime interest in the subject, created a department of parasitology with Anthony Kingscote as head. Interest surged during the next 50 years and parasitologists were appointed to each of the larger universities. Several universities offer graduate courses leading to both master's and doctoral degrees.

For those engaged in it, research is a challenging, occasionally frustrating, and at times exciting occupation, although it may require years of patient endeavour to make a single significant discovery. The satisfaction of discovery is itself rewarding, especially when the knowledge, along with that produced by others, can be applied to benefit humans. Hadwen's contribution to an understanding of the life cycle of the warble fly of cattle was fundamental to the work in recent years to control and, in places, eradicate the pest. Watson's achievement in eradicating dourine in horses was likewise of immense practical value. Several investigators have worked on ticks and flies affecting livestock and have introduced measures to control these pests more effectively. Tick paralysis in sheep and humans in western Canada is now understood, thanks to intensive research for several years.

Commercial FISHERIES in western Canada were, at one time, adversely affected by a tapeworm, *Triaenophorus crassus*. It was shown that an intermediate stage of the worm in the whitefish developed into a mature worm when an infected fish was eaten by pike. Practical research followed to eliminate the pike and thus prevent transmission. Research by L. Margolis at the Fisheries Research Laboratory, Nanaimo, illustrates a different practical application of the study of parasites. A survey showed that parasites present in fish from different localities vary. The parasites are therefore useful biological tags indicating the origin of the fish.

For decades scientists and laymen were baffled by paralysis observed in moose in certain areas of the country. The cause was elusive until R.C. Anderson observed a species of lungworm on the membranes of the brain. Elucidation of the life cycle, essential to an understanding of the situation, revealed that the worms also occur in whitetailed deer, but they are relatively harmless. The worms' eggs are passed in the feces of deer; their larvae penetrate into various snails and undergo development in them. Moose or deer become infected when they eat vegetation to which infected snails are attached. The deer are an important part of the story, for moose paralysis occurs only in places where the ranges of moose and deer overlap. The results are especially important for the management of moose populations. *See also* WILDLIFE CONSERVATION AND MANAGEMENT.

A.M. FALLIS

Reading: G.D. Schmidt and L.S. Roberts, *Foundations of Parasitology* (1985); R.S. Desowitz, *New Guinea Tapeworms and Jewish Grandmothers* (1987).

Parc de Val-Jalbert, Qué, 5 km E of ROBERVAL on the shores of Lac SAINT-JEAN. A ghost town and a very beautiful park, Val-Jalbert since 1960 has become a major attraction in the Saguenay-Lac Saint-Jean region. The village of Val-Jalbert was born at the turn of the century, when a pulp and paper mill was built at the foot of the falls on the

Rivière Ouiatchouane (1901). The company village, very modern for its day, grew rapidly and had 1000 inhabitants by the mid-1920s. In 1927, however, Quebec Pulp and Paper Mills, the plant's final owner, closed it down and soon Val-Jalbert was deserted (1930). The Québec government bought the site in 1949 and in 1960 decided to make it a park. The abandoned village and mill, important parts of Canada's industrial and urban heritage, now draw hundreds of thousands of visitors each year.

MARC ST-HILAIRE

Parent, Étienne, journalist, lawyer, public servant, essayist (b at Beauport, LC 2 May 1802; d at Ottawa 22 Dec 1874). He was editor of *Le Canadien* 1822-25 and then became editor of the French section of *La Gazette de Québec* in 1825. While working 1825-38 as translator, legal officer and then librarian of the Assembly of Lower Canada, he revived *Le Canadien* in 1831, giving it its famous motto: "Our institutions, our language and our laws." He argued for a national existence for French Canadians, demanding "all the civil and political rights that are the prerogative of an English country." As the REBELLIONS OF 1837 approached, Louis-Joseph PAPINEAU was becoming more radical; Parent, a clearheaded pragmatist, abandoned him in 1835 and preached moderation for both parties. Denounced as a traitor by many Patriotes, he was nonetheless imprisoned by the English governor in 1838-39 for "seditious schemings." With the establishment of the PROVINCE OF CANADA in 1841, the polemicist resigned himself to fight only for the equality of "the two populations and the two countries." He was elected to the Assembly in 1841 but soon had to withdraw because of his deafness, developed in prison. Appointed clerk of the Executive Council 14 Oct 1842, he resigned from the management of *Le Canadien*, although he continued to contribute to it occasionally (1847, 1851-54). He became assistant secretary for Lower Canada in 1847 and federal undersecretary of state from 1868 to his retirement in 1872. After 1840 he was often consulted by political figures, and between 1846 and 1852 he gave 8 important lectures including 5 at the INSTITUT CANADIEN of Montréal. In these he invited his compatriots to become involved in industry and business and to study political economy; he proposed ways to improve education and ameliorate the lot of the working class; and he stressed the importance of the intellectual and spiritual, and of the priest in society. Nourished by the best American and European sources, his strong-minded originality was rooted in Canadian soil. He was called the Nestor of the Canadian press and the Victor Cousin of America.

RENÉ DIONNE

Parent, Madeleine, labour organizer (b at Montréal June 1918). Despite her conventional upbringing in a middle-class Canadian family, Parent dedicated herself to organizing the ununionized. In 1943, she joined Kent ROWLEY, who she later married, as an organizer for the United Textile Workers of America. In 1946, 6000 workers they had organized in Montréal and Valleyfield won a strike against the combined forces of the employer, Dominion Textile, the church and the state. A year later, after a 3-month trial, Parent was convicted of seditious conspiracy. In DUPLESSIS's Québec, she had to wait until 1954 for her acquittal in a new trial. Fired by the international headquarters of the UTWA in 1952 on the false charge that she was a communist, she, with Rowley, established the Canadian Textile and Chemical Union (1952) and the Confederation of Canadian Unions (1969). She led some bitter strikes in the 1970s, including the 1979 Purtex strike over surveillance of workers via closed-circuit TV.

MARGARET E. McCALLUM

Parent, Mimi, painter, engraver (b at Montréal 1924), daughter of architect Lucien Parent. While enrolled at the École des beaux-arts in Montréal, she met Alfred PELLAN, who introduced her to surrealism, a genre in which she and fellow student Jean BENOÎT are 2 of the leading contemporary practitioners. Expelled from the École des beaux-arts for lack of discipline, she proceeded to hold a solo exhibition at the National Gallery in 1947. In 1948 she signed the Prisme d'yeux manifesto on artistic freedom, and left for Paris with Benoît. She joined the surrealist movement in 1959 at an international exhibition devoted to Eros, where she was in charge of the fetishism room and did the catalogue layout. André Breton cited her 1949 work, *J'habite au choc*, in the final edition of his book, *Le Surréalisme et la peinture*. She participated in all the major surrealist demonstrations, and, during the 1960s in particular, published plates for the surrealist works of Fernando Arrabal, Joyce Mansour and José Pierre. In 1984 a major retrospective of her work, about 40 pieces done since 1970, was mounted in France and W Germany.   ANDRÉ G. BOURASSA

Parent, Simon-Napoléon, lawyer, businessman, Liberal politician, premier of Québec (b at Beauport, Canada E 12 Sept 1855; d at Montréal 7 Sept 1920). Québec City's first "modern" mayor (1894-1906), promoting city planning and economic development, Parent became provincial minister of lands and forests in 1897, and immediately encouraged the large-scale exploitation of Québec's forest and hydraulic resources. He became premier after Félix-Gabriel MARCHAND died in 1900, but was driven from office in 1905 by a combination of personal rivals and young nationalists critical of his concessions to foreign capitalists. He retired as mayor shortly afterwards but became chairman of the federal Transcontinental Railway Commission and later the Québec Streams Commission.   BERNARD L. VIGOD

Parfleche is a variety of Plains Indians container made of rawhide. The name comes from that given by the VOYAGEURS to untanned skin. It is a single piece of prepared hide that folds much like an envelope for storage of dried meat (PEMMICAN) and other food. Saddlebags, tubular headdress containers, and small pouches for personal belongings were also all made of light, durable rawhide and were often painted or decorated with QUILLWORK.   RENÉ R. GADACZ

Paris, Ont, Town, pop 7898 (1986c), 7485 (1981c), inc 1855, located 50 km W of Hamilton at the confluence of the Nith and Grand rivers. It was founded in 1829 when Hiram Capron, an American developer, founded a settlement he called Forks of the Grand to develop the local gypsum deposits, used to make plaster of Paris, from which the present name derives. Paris has always been a rural community, the centre of a farming and dairy district, but its manufacturing sector, principally textiles, furnishings and pharmaceuticals, now comprises 40% of the town's employment. The Plains Church, a unique cobblestone structure built in 1845, stands as a memorial to pioneer settlement and Penmarvian, a house built by John Penman, a textile manufacturer, remains a landmark. A downtown building marks the site where in 1876 Alexander Graham BELL received from BRANTFORD the first long-distance telephone call.   DANIEL FRANCIS

Paris (1763), Treaty of, signed 10 Feb 1763 by France, Britain and Spain after 3 years of negotiations, ended the SEVEN YEARS' WAR. Britain obtained Île Royale [Cape Breton I] and Canada, including the Great Lakes Basin and east bank of the Mississippi R, from France, and Florida from Spain. France retained fishing rights in New-foundland and the Gulf of ST LAWRENCE, acquired Saint Pierre and Miquelon as an unfortified fishing station and had her lucrative West Indian possessions, trading centres in India and slaving station in Goré (in present-day Chad) restored. In accordance with the conditional capitulation of 1760, Britain guaranteed Canadians limited freedom of worship. Provisions were made for exchange of prisoners; Canadians were given 18 months to emigrate if they wished; and government archives were preserved.

Britain had acquired a large empire and France was still able to challenge British naval supremacy, but Spain achieved none of her war aims. *See also* ROYAL PROCLAMATION OF 1763.

CORNELIUS J. JAENEN

Paris (1783), Treaty of, concluded the AMERICAN REVOLUTION. On 20 Sept 1783 Britain acknowledged American independence and recognized a boundary along the centre of the 4 northerly Great Lakes and from Lake of the Woods "due west" to the imagined location of the Mississippi's headwaters, then S along the Mississippi R. This gave the US Niagara, Detroit and Michilimackinac, and valuable lands reserved to Indians by the ROYAL PROCLAMATION OF 1763. The Americans, negotiating through the French comte de Vergennes, obtained fishing rights off Newfoundland and access to the E banks of the Mississippi; in turn they promised restitution and compensation to British LOYALISTS.

The treaty was ineffective. Britain retained its western posts until after JAY'S TREATY (1794), and denied the US free navigation of the St Lawrence. The Americans largely ignored their promises to the Loyalists, many of whom settled in Canada. Nevertheless, Britain soon resumed trade with and investment in the new republic.

CORNELIUS J. JAENEN

Parizeau, Gérard, underwriter (b at Montréal 16 Dec 1899). After graduating from the École des hautes études commerciales at U de M, Parizeau worked in the civil service from 1920 until 1925, when he became head of the francophone section of Irish & Maulson, an insurance brokerage firm. In 1925 he also founded *L'Actualité économique*,

Jacques Parizeau, finance minister in the PQ government, was an outspoken advocate of sovereignty and resigned in 1984 to protest his party's softening on the issue (*photo by Bernard Brault/Reflexion*).

the official magazine of the École des hautes études commerciales, at which Parizeau has taught since 1928. In 1938 he founded his own brokerage house and made it one of the most important in Canada. In 1961 he helped create the reinsurance brokerage house Le Blanc, Eldridge, Parizeau and was its chairman for many years. He bought in 1965 La Nationale, a Canadian reinsurance company until then a subsidiary of La Nationale of Paris. In 1972 he founded the management firm of Sodarcan, grouping under it a dozen insurance and reinsurance companies. Parizeau and his son Robert hold majority control. Another son, Jacques PARIZEAU, is a strong supporter of the Parti Québécois's commitment to separatism.   JORGE NIOSI

Parizeau, Jacques, economist, politician (b at Montréal 9 Aug 1930). One of Québec's most articulate and accomplished economists, Parizeau achieved political influence as a consultant and adviser to successive provincial governments during the 1960s, becoming a part of the small group that shaped the QUIET REVOLUTION. His advice was influential in the nationalization of HYDRO-QUÉBEC; and he played a key role in the establishment of the QUÉBEC PENSION PLAN and in the formation of the Common Front of public-sector unions. He joined the PARTI QUÉBÉCOIS in 1968 and was finance minister from 1976 until his resignation in 1984 when he repudiated René LÉVESQUE's decision to shelve the PQ's commitment to separatism. Despite his break with Lévesque, Parizeau remained personally popular in the ranks of the PQ; and when Pierre-Marc JOHNSON unexpectedly resigned the party leadership in Nov 1987, Parizeau seemed the obvious choice to succeed him.   STANLEY GORDON

Parka is a tailored garment worn by the INUIT to protect head, arms and upper body from the rigours of the arctic climate. Style varied from region to region, and parkas for women had a distinctive cut, distinguishing them from male garments. Young children rode inside the parkas, on their mothers' backs or in the hood. Fur ringed the hood or it could be tightly closed with drawstrings; both served to trap air warmed by the body inside the garment. In the past, caribou hide, often sewn in a decorative mosaic pattern, was used to make the parka. Today, materials imported from the south are most frequently used to construct the garment.   THOMAS S. ABLER

Parker, Sir Horatio Gilbert George, journalist, author, politician (b at Camden E, Canada West 23 Nov 1862; d in London, Eng 6 Sept 1932). Best known for his historical novels, which introduced French Canadians and the North-West to English literature, Gilbert Parker left Canada in the mid-1880s after teaching for several years in Ontario. He settled in England from 1890, became MP for Gravesend (1900-18), and organized British propaganda directed at the US during WWI. Widely travelled, he expressed strong support for British IMPERIALISM. His fiction set in Canada, such as *Pierre and His People* (1892) and *Carnac* (1922), contributed to the validation of Québécois culture within English Canada. His many novels consist mainly of melodramatic plots with idealistic characters in exciting or exotic settings.   TERRENCE CRAIG

Parker, John Dickerson, "Jackie," football player (b John D. Flanagan at Knoxville, Tenn 1 Jan 1932). As a youngster, Parker excelled in baseball, and reached Mississippi State on a baseball scholarship. He turned to FOOTBALL and became an outstanding quarterback. He joined the EDMONTON ESKIMOS in 1954 and helped lead the Eskimos into the GREY CUP against highly favoured Montréal. The image of Parker scooping up a fumble in the final minutes and running 90 yards to tie the score and set up the winning convert is one of the most vivid in Canadian sports history. He returned to quarterback Edmonton to another Grey Cup win in 1955 and was a receiver and halfback in the 1956 victory. During 9 years with the Eskimos (1954-62), he won the Jeff Nicklin Memorial Trophy (MVP in the West) 7 times, and was Schenley outstanding player 3 times. Parker was traded to the TORONTO ARGONAUTS after the 1962 season. He was general manager of BC LIONS 1970-75. On retirement Parker was the Canadian Football League all-time scoring leader with 750 points. As a quarterback, he successfully completed 1089 passes for 16 476 yards. He rushed for 5210 yards and gained 2308 yards on passes. He was head coach of the Edmonton Eskimos 1983-87, and in 1987 was inducted into Canada's Sports Hall of Fame.   FRANK COSENTINO

Parker, Jon Kimura, pianist (b at Burnaby, BC 25 Dec 1959). In the virtuosity and musicianship of this young Canadian pianist, critics and audiences worldwide have come to recognize a major international talent. Following his debut at age 5 with the Vancouver Youth Orchestra, Parker went on to win over 200 firsts in local, national and international competitions. His win at the 1984 Leeds International Piano Competition was the key to many prestigious recital and orchestral engagements including a Royal Command Performance for Queen Elizabeth II. His teachers included Edward Parker (his uncle), Kum-Sing Lee and Marek Jablonski in Canada, and Adele Marcus at New York's Juilliard School, where he received the Masters degree at age 21. His first major recording (1986) was of Tchaikovsky's B6 minor piano concerto and Prokofiev's Concerto No 3 for Piano, with André Previn and the Royal Philharmonic Orchestra.   BARCLAY MCMILLAN

Parkin, Sir George Robert, educator (b at Salisbury, NB 8 Feb 1846; d at London, Eng 25 June 1922). In his own words, the "wandering evangelist of Empire," Parkin was a successful teacher at NB high schools who became in the 1880s a leader of the Imperial Federation Movement, about which he wrote 3 books. He was principal of Upper Canada Coll from 1895 to 1902 when he became secretary of the Rhodes Scholarship Trust in England, where he lived until his death. He wrote in 1908 the first biography of Sir John A. MACDONALD, whom he had known, arguing that autonomous dominions could still co-operate in a reorganized British Empire. He was knighted in 1920.   DONALD J.C. PHILLIPSON

Parkin, John Burnett, architect (b at Toronto 26 June 1911; d at Los Angeles, Calif 17 Aug 1975). Parkin graduated in architecture from U of T in 1935 and worked in London, Eng, before returning to Toronto in 1937 to establish a small architectural practice. Joined in 1947 by John C. PARKIN (no relation), he created an integrated practice that included all the skills necessary for the design and supervision of the construction of major buildings. The firm offered landscape design under his partner and brother, Edmond T. Parkin, graphic and interior design, structural, electrical and mechanical engineering, and specialized experience with hospitals, schools, airports and factories. During the later 1950s and 1960s the firm was the largest in Canada and was responsible for such buildings as Union Station (Ottawa), the head office of IBM (Toronto) and, in collaboration with others, TORONTO CITY HALL and the Toronto Dominion Centre. Though still within the mainstream of modern architecture its work shows considerable variety, reflecting both the firm's size and changing international fashions. In 1970 Parkin established an associated

American practice in Los Angeles, Calif, which continues with his son John B. Parkin, Jr, as a principal.   MICHAEL MCMORDIE

Parkin, John Cresswell, architect (b to Canadian parents at Sheffield, Eng 24 Mar 1922). After graduating in architecture from U of Man and studies at Harvard under Walter Gropius, Parkin joined John B. PARKIN (no relation) in 1947. As senior partner and partner-in-charge of design, Parkin oversaw the creation of a large number of outstanding works whose style was generally rectilinear, undecorated and classical modern. John B. Parkin moved to Los Angeles in the early 1960s to found a US practice, leaving John C. Parkin as CEO of the holding corporation which owned both the Canadian and US architectural firms. In 1970 John C. Parkin established the Parkin Partnership when other partners of the John B. Parkin firm continued that practice as Neish, Owen Roland and Roy. The partnership won the competition for the design of a new National Gallery of Canada (Ottawa, 1976), though that design was not built, and also that for the additions to the Art Gallery of Ontario. Through his career, Parkin has been an energetic and influential advocate for modern design, not just in architecture but in industrial and urban design as well, and a mentor for the architects under his supervision. In 1987 a new firm, Parkin Architects Ltd, was formed and J.C. Parkin retired from active practice.
     MICHAEL MCMORDIE

Parkin, John Hamilton, aeronautical engineer (b at Toronto 27 Sept 1891; d at Ottawa 14 Nov 1981). After graduating in engineering from U of T, Parkin joined the faculty and worked during WWI on explosives production and aviation under T.R. Loudon. In 1917 he built a wind tunnel at U of T where models were tested for the Vickers flying boats, the first commercial aircraft designed in Canada, built at Montréal in the 1920s. Parkin joined the NATIONAL RESEARCH COUNCIL staff in 1929 and was director of mechanical engineering 1936-57. The Depression largely stifled the Canadian aviation industry, but Parkin wrote in that period a seminal paper on transatlantic airliners. During WWII Parkin's NRC staff provided technical support to new crown corporations building British aircraft and engines, began jet engine design in 1944, and perfected the system of keeping ice off aircraft propellors that was adopted throughout the world in 1945. Their work was completely reorganized in the postwar years to support the AVRO and DE HAVILLAND companies' design and production of aircraft. Parkin also laid the foundations of the National Aeronautical Museum (now National Aviation Museum) and wrote extensively on the early history of Canadian aviation, notably *Bell and Baldwin* (1964).
     DONALD J.C. PHILLIPSON

Parks, City Parks were originally defined (following the British example) as the private grounds of a gentleman's estate. Public parks were not an integral part of the earliest Canadian cities and towns. The city park as we know it actually entered N America in the 1830s through the "rural cemetery" movement, as burial grounds were landscaped, serving as quiet places to stroll or to have family picnics. Mt Pleasant Cemetery, Toronto, which was designed by H.A. Engelhardt in 1874, was one such area.
     The period of intense park building (1880-1914) was stimulated by an interplay of 4 factors. The first was a belief that the city dweller's increasing separation from nature caused physical, mental and moral distress. Parks were seen as healing antidotes to this urban malaise. The second factor was the rise of "CITY BEAUTIFUL" thought (a loosely integrated philosophy of urban im-

Winter, Edwards Gardens, Toronto (*photo by Bill Ivy*).

provement) which promoted beautification planning including grand civic centres and aesthetic streetscapes, as well as parks. The third motivation stressed the economic benefits of parks, and was part of the popular promotion of cities and towns called "boosterism" at the time. Parks raised the value of adjacent land and were touted in real-estate campaigns as visible proof of a prosperous community, a "wide-awake" community concerned about the welfare of its residents.
     The final factor was the creation in 1874 of Mount Royal Park in Montréal by Frederick Law Olmsted (1822-1903), the pre-eminent landscape architect of N America. Olmsted's philosophy of park design and the purpose of urban green space profoundly affected Canadian park development. He advocated a unified design based on the creation of a pastoral landscape. His approach was heavily influenced by the ideals of the English Landscape Style: rolling hills, long stretches of lawn, vistas of shrub and tree groupings, flower beds set among winding paths – a setting for family picnics, strolls and Sunday afternoon band concerts. Opened to the public in 1909, Assiniboine Park in Winnipeg, designed by the Canadian landscape architect Frederick Todd, is another prime example of this style. Olmsted asserted that this style was the most effective in combatting the ill effects of urban life. He also stressed that parks should be accessible to all social classes. Stimulated by these varied motivations, legislation concerning public parks was passed by BC in 1876, Ontario in 1883 and Manitoba in 1892.
     However, the creation of large, planned and designed parks, on the scale of Mount Royal, was not a high priority of city planning in these early years. Rather the main emphasis at the turn of the century was on establishing small urban parks, ornamental squares, or small "breathing spaces" throughout the city. Queen Square, Charlottetown, PEI, was largely landscaped by public-spirited citizens in the 1880s. Many park projects were carried out, not just by professionals, but also by small, amateur groups such as horticultural societies, newly formed improvement associations, and even boards of trade. Park expansion was more intense in smaller cities and villages, where concerned citizens, often without public funding, devoted weekends to planning and planting. Galt, Ont, was cited for its progressive, energetic parks policy – out of 567 ha of city land, 50 ha were devoted to parks and playgrounds.
     While many park promoters were concerned with beautification, others wanted to utilize parks as tools of social reform. These horticultural reformers felt strongly that cities needed space for more vigorous recreation, a place for the landless worker to dissipate dangerous energy, which unchecked, might be channelled into Bolshevism, unionism or intemperance. Tension between the aesthetic and the athletic continued up into the 1920s.
     Ultimately, parks evolved into centres of public

Public Gardens, Halifax (*photo by J.A. Kraulis*).

recreation, and more services were provided for the general public. Beacon Hill Park in Victoria, BC, by the 1930s boasted a cricket field, lawn-bowling green, race track, bandstand, zoo, boating lake, flower gardens and tree-shaded walks.

Parks also functioned as historical "scrapbooks" for a town. For example in 1898, school children planted and labelled trees in the Halifax Public Gardens honouring the war dead of various S African campaigns. In major parks, royalty planted trees commemorating their visits, and societies celebrated anniversaries by planting shrubs and trees. Fountains and statues were donated memorializing local or national events and individuals. Parks were also used as living textbooks by school children as they studied scientifically labelled plant material.

The collapse of the real-estate boom coupled with the onset of WWI left many cities unable to finance civic beautification schemes. Improvement associations disappeared as their members turned to other activities. Park building halted until after the war when memorials rekindled interest and released some civic money. By the 1920s park creation had become thoroughly bureaucratized and professionalized, with less amateur involvement in park creation and maintenance.

The Depression again slowed down major park building projects; however, the idea of public space devoted to beauty and recreation did not disappear. The 1960s saw a resurgence in park building, in part stimulated by CENTENNIAL year activities. Today parks no longer need to be justified either as tools of social reform or as "lungs of the city," rather they are regarded as expected features in the urban landscape.

EDWINNA VON BAEYER

Parks, National Canadians live in a land rich in natural beauty. The diversity of landscapes and seascapes and of the flora and fauna inhabiting them is part of a natural heritage preserved in national parks. National parks serve 2 main functions: they protect in an unchanged state areas representative of major natural ENVIRONMENTS; they encourage public appreciation of the national heritage. For millennia Canada's landscape was affected only by natural forces. Now, however, agricultural and industrial activities are alter-

ing the environment at an accelerating pace. National parks protect ecosystems from the negative impact of human activities and allow ecological processes to function, ensuring the perpetuation of naturally evolving environments. National park staff inform the public about the parks, either through first-hand experience or through educational programs designed to bring knowledge of the parks to people in their homes. Opportunities are provided for recreational activities compatible with long-term preservation of park resources. Simultaneous preservation of park environments in a natural state and encouragement of public use of the parks requires the maintenance of a delicate balance. Preserving this balance is a major task for staff, who must study and document park resources and then apply this knowledge so that human impact on park ecosystems is minimized.

Beginnings

The Canadian national parks system began in Nov 1885, when an area of approximately 26 km² on the N slope of Sulphur Mt was set aside for public use. This area, the Cave and Basin Hot Springs, was the beginning of what is now BANFF NATIONAL PARK. The hot springs were discovered in 1883 by 2 railway employees working on the construction of the first transcontinental railway through the ROCKY MOUNTAINS. Knowledge of the discovery (and its potential as a tourist attraction) spread rapidly among the railway workers, and several conflicting claims were addressed to the minister of the interior. The government chose not to grant private title to the lands; instead, it was decided that they should be preserved for the benefit of all Canadians. In 1886 a Dominion land surveyor was hired to undertake a legal survey of the Hot Springs Reserve. This work resulted in a report by the commissioner of Dominion Lands that "a large tract of country lying outside of the original reservation presented features of the greatest beauty, and was admirably adapted for a national park." A bill to establish the first national park in Canada was introduced in the House of Commons in Apr 1887. The Rocky Mountains Park Act, establishing what is now Banff National Park, was passed on 23 June 1887.

Growth and Organization

Banff became a symbol of a new respect for the land. Interest in the development of other reserves ran high among members of Parliament and CPR officials and, in the years 1887-95, 5 new mountain reserves were set aside, unavailable for "sale, settlement or squatting." These later became YOHO, KOOTENAY, GLACIER, MOUNT REVELSTOKE and WATERTON LAKES national parks. The availability of large tracts of undeveloped public lands in western Canada had facilitated establishment of the mountain national parks. Early in the 20th century action was taken to develop national parks in eastern Canada, starting with the establishment of ST LAWRENCE ISLANDS NATIONAL PARK in 1904. The world's first distinct bureau of national parks, the Dominion Parks Branch, was formed in Canada in 1911 under the authority of the Department of the Interior. J.B. HARKIN, the first commissioner, served 1911-36. During his tenure, 9 national parks were established: ELK ISLAND (1913), Mount Revelstoke (1914), POINT PELÉE (1918), Kootenay (1920), WOOD BUFFALO (1922), PRINCE ALBERT (1927), RIDING MOUNTAIN (1929), GEORGIAN BAY ISLANDS (1929) and CAPE BRETON HIGHLANDS (1936). Harkin, who emphasized protection of the natural resources of the new parks, directed the passage of the National Parks Act in 1930. Section 4 of the Act sets the guiding philosophy for the management of na-

tional parks, which "are hereby dedicated to the people of Canada, for their benefit, education and enjoyment...." This Act still provides the legislative protection for national park lands.

Further establishment of national parks was sporadic until, in 1961, John I. Nicol became director of the National and Historic Parks Branch. Under his administration, 10 new national parks were created. Nicol also oversaw the preparation of the first Parks Policy in 1964. The present Environment Canada, Parks Policy, written in 1979, also shows his influence as it emphasizes the preservation of natural ecological processes above all else. National Parks are one component of a federal system of heritage sites which includes National Historic Parks, National Historic Sites, Heritage Canals, Heritage Rivers and National Marine Parks. These comprise Environment Canada, Parks, part of the Dept of the Environment since 1979. Five regional offices administer park operations. The headquarters in Ottawa-Hull are responsible for policy development and long-range planning and research. There are now 34 national parks and national park reserves (national park reserves are areas designated to become national parks, but the final boundaries and other terms have yet to be negotiated with the province or territory in which the park area is located) in Canada, ranging from Ellesmere Island National Park Reserve 660 km from the North Pole to Point Pelee National Park at the southernmost tip of Canada's mainland; from TERRA NOVA NATIONAL PARK on the E shore of Newfoundland to SOUTH MORESBY NATIONAL PARK in the Queen Charlotte Islands, off Vancouver I. The total area of Canada's national parks (as of Dec 1987) is 182 033 km², an area as large as the Canadian Great lakes *or* 31 Prince Edward Islands *or* 3 times as large as Nova Scotia *or* larger than the 3 maritime provinces and equal to 1.8% of Canada's landmass.

Parks Policy - *To Protect for All Time*

The first national parks policy, produced in 1964, drew attention to the importance of protecting natural resources in the parks. The current policy, written in 1979, emphasizes that, in order to protect resources, natural ecological processes must be allowed to function in parks with minimal interference from man. The policy also provides a framework for the long-range planning of new parks and for the provision of quality visitor services and appropriate recreational opportunities. In 1986, a separate policy for National Marine Parks was approved. National parks are protected by federal legislation from all forms of extractive resource use such as mining, forestry, agriculture and sport hunting. Only activities consistent with the protection of park resources are allowed. Efforts are directed at maintaining the physical environment in as natural a state as possible. If this can be done by allowing natural ecological processes to function with minimal interference, the perpetuation of naturally evolving land and water environments and their associated species is assured. Under certain conditions, however, active manipulation of natural ecological processes does take place. Active manipulation is necessary if the balance of park ecosystems has been so altered by human activities that a natural environment cannot be restored through natural ecological processes, or if park visitors, facilities or neighbouring lands are threatened. If active interference becomes necessary, techniques duplicate natural processes as closely as possible.

The effective protection and management of national parks requires an intimate understanding of park resources and the ecological processes

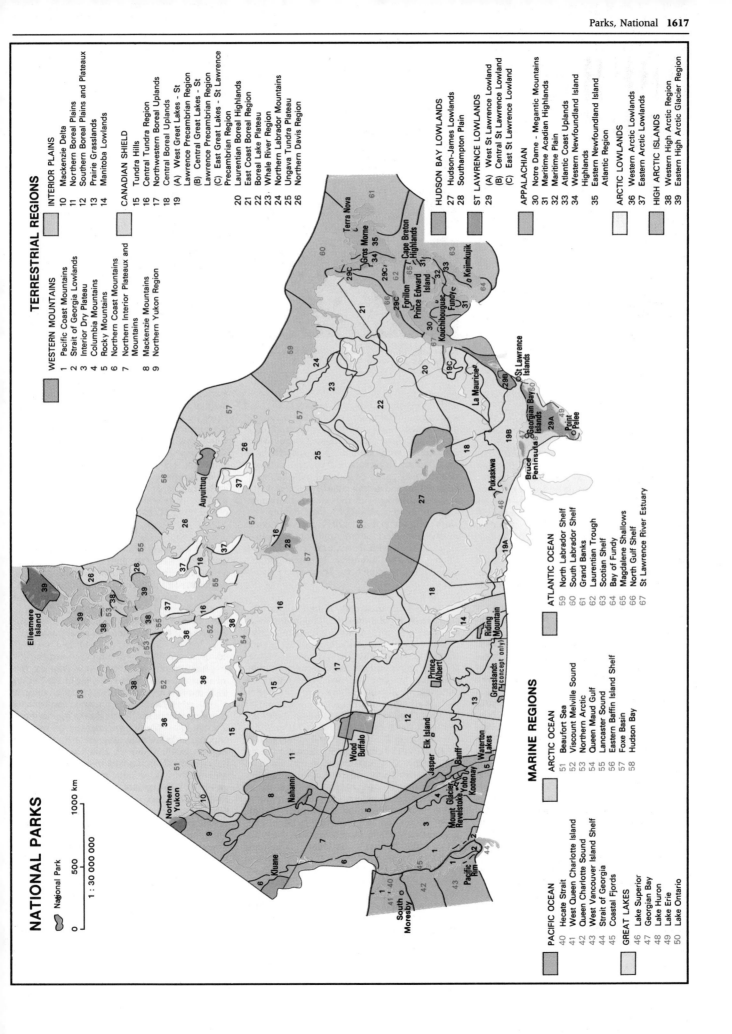

NATIONAL PARKS

⌁ National Park

0   500   1000 km

1 : 30 000 000

TERRESTRIAL REGIONS

WESTERN MOUNTAINS
1 Pacific Coast Mountains
2 Strait of Georgia Lowlands
3 Interior Dry Plateau
4 Columbia Mountains
5 Rocky Mountains
6 Northern Coast Mountains
7 Northern Interior Plateaux and Mountains
8 Mackenzie Mountains
9 Northern Yukon Region

INTERIOR PLAINS
10 Mackenzie Delta
11 Northern Boreal Plains
12 Southern Boreal Plains and Plateaux
13 Prairie Grasslands
14 Manitoba Lowlands

CANADIAN SHIELD
15 Tundra Hills
16 Central Tundra Region
17 Northwestern Boreal Uplands
18 Central Boreal Uplands
19 (A) West Great Lakes - St Lawrence Precambrian Region
(B) Central Great Lakes - St Lawrence Precambrian Region
(C) East Great Lakes - St Lawrence Precambrian Region
20 Laurentian Boreal Highlands
21 East Coast Boreal Region
22 Boreal Lake Plateau
23 Whale River Region
24 Northern Labrador Mountains
25 Ungava Tundra Plateau
26 Northern Davis Region

HUDSON BAY LOWLANDS
27 Hudson-James Lowlands
28 Southampton Plain

ST LAWRENCE LOWLANDS
29 (A) West St Lawrence Lowland
(B) Central St Lawrence Lowland
(C) East St Lawrence Lowland

APPALACHIAN
30 Notre Dame - Megantic Mountains
31 Maritime Acadian Highlands
32 Maritime Plain
33 Atlantic Coast Uplands
34 Western Newfoundland Island Highlands
35 Eastern Newfoundland Island Atlantic Region

ARCTIC LOWLANDS
36 Western Arctic Lowlands
37 Eastern Arctic Lowlands

HIGH ARCTIC ISLANDS
38 Western High Arctic Region
39 Eastern High Arctic Glacier Region

MARINE REGIONS

PACIFIC OCEAN
40 Hecate Strait
41 West Queen Charlotte Island
42 Queen Charlotte Sound
43 West Vancouver Island Shelf
44 Strait of Georgia
45 Coastal Fjords

GREAT LAKES
46 Lake Superior
47 Georgian Bay
48 Lake Huron
49 Lake Erie
50 Lake Ontario

ARCTIC OCEAN
51 Beaufort Sea
52 Viscount Melville Sound
53 Northern Arctic
54 Queen Maud Gulf
55 Lancaster Sound
56 Eastern Baffin Island Shelf
57 Foxe Basin
58 Hudson Bay

ATLANTIC OCEAN
59 North Labrador Shelf
60 South Labrador Shelf
61 Grand Banks
62 Laurentian Trough
63 Scotian Shelf
64 Bay of Fundy
65 Magdalene Shallows
66 North Gulf Shelf
67 St Lawrence River Estuary

controlling and influencing them. Enviroment Canada, Parks has developed several tools to help achieve this understanding, eg, the natural resource management process, the basic component of which is a comprehensive natural resources data base, regularly updated for all parks. This information allows a park's capabilities and limitations for visitor use to be evaluated, problems identified, and specific plans for the protection of fragile resources or features made. Zoning, another technique for managing the tension resulting from the dual goals of preservation and use, ensures that most national park lands are protected in a wild state. The system defines 5 zones into which a park's land and water areas may be classified according to their fragility and their capacity to accommodate visitors. In zone I, access is strictly limited or prohibited; zones II, III and IV provide increasing visitor facilities and allow more activities. Motorized access is prohibited in zones I and II. Zone V comprises townsites, visitor centres and park administration offices.

National parks are also protected through the environmental assessment and review process, which ensures that all the possible adverse effects of any project or activity proposed for lands or waters in national parks are identified and evaluated, and that measures are taken to reduce impacts or to cancel the project if its impacts are deemed unacceptable.

Representative Natural Areas of Canadian Significance

In the early days of park establishment, no method or set of criteria was used to designate potential park sites so as to ensure that the system of national parks would be truly representative of Canada's landscapes. Scenic vistas with potential for tourism were often chosen as locations for national parks; others were set aside to conserve unique or fragile habitats or to protect endangered species. To protect representative areas, Environment Canada, Parks developed the natural region concept. A natural region is an area containing a unique set of biological and ecological characteristics. In Canada, 68 natural regions have been identified: 39 terrestrial, 29 marine. Environment Canada, Parks plans to establish a park in each region. The park system is far from complete. Proposals for new national parks have resulted in new national parks or national park reserves on N Ellesmere I and N Yukon. In 1987 an agreement was signed with BC to establish a new national park in the South Moresby area of the Queen Charlotte Is. Also in 1987, Bruce Peninsula National Park was created in Ontario. Park proposals are in place for the Saguenay R-St Lawrence R confluence, the West Isles area, south of the Bay of Fundy, and the East Arm of Great Slave Lake.

The early emphasis was on providing recreational facilities with leisure orientation, eg, golf courses, tennis courts, ski resorts. Today the aim is to provide outdoor recreational opportunities consistent with the long-term protection of natural resources and requiring a minimum of man-made facilities.

Hiking, canoeing, cross-country skiing and snowshoeing are examples of activities considered compatible with a park setting. In all national parks, naturalists are on hand to interpret the park environment to visitors. Interpretation programs are designed not simply to lecture visitors about the park but to facilitate learning through first-hand experience. Self-guiding HERITAGE TRAILS, pamphlets and exhibits are also provided to assist enjoyment.

Beyond the park gates, naturalists work with schools, clubs and other associations, bringing

Above Lake O'Hara in Yoho National Park, BC (*courtesy Environment Canada, Parks/P. McCloskey*).

park experiences to those who may never have visited a national park. Through television and motion pictures, all Canadians have an opportunity to participate. The range of visitor activities compatible with national park objectives is great, but not all acceptable activities can be carried out in all parks. To determine the appropriate activities and the tolerable intensity of use for a particular park or site, the visitor activity management process (VAMP) is used. VAMP provides a framework for identifying those activities that will not affect the environment of a particular park. Used with the natural resource management process, it ensures long-term protection, while providing better services to visitors.

International Role

Canada's national park system is part of a global network of more than 2000 protected areas in 120 countries. As a member of the International Union for the Conservation of Nature and Natural Resources (IUCN), Environment Canada, Parks contributes to the development of internationally accepted standards and criteria for parks the world over. Environment Canada, Parks is also the primary agency responsible for fulfilling Canada's obligations under the World Heritage Convention of the United Nations Education, Scientific and Cultural Organization (UNESCO). The convention recognizes the responsibility of all nations to protect places of such unique natural and cultural value that they are considered part of the heritage of all mankind. KLUANE and NAHANNI national park reserves, L'ANSE AUX MEADOWS National Historic Park, the BURGESS SHALE of Yoho National Park and Anthony Island (South Moresby Park National Park Reserve) have been designated WORLD HERITAGE SITES. Waterton Lakes National Park, Riding Mountain National Park, Long Point (Ont) and Mont St-Hilaire (Qué) have been chosen as Biosphere Reserves under UNESCO's Man and Biosphere Programme, which recognizes outstanding examples of natural ecosystems throughout the world. *See also* ARCHAEOLOGICAL SURVEY OF CANADA; CONSERVATION; FORILLON NATIONAL PARK; FUNDY NATIONAL PARK; GRASSLANDS NATIONAL PARK; GROS MORNE NATIONAL PARK; HISTORIC SITE; JASPER NATIONAL PARK; KEJIMKUJIK NATIONAL PARK; KOUCHIBOUGUAC NATIONAL

PARK; LA MAURICIE NATIONAL PARK; PARKS, PROVINCIAL; PUKASKWA NATIONAL PARK.

LILLIAN STEWART AND MAX FINKLESTEIN

Parks, Provincial, areas of land and water, large or small, natural or man-modified, designated by any of the provincial governments for the purposes of nature protection, recreation, TOURISM, historic preservation and education. They range in character from Polar Bear Provincial Park on Hudson Bay, a 29 093 km² wilderness park visited by less than 1000 people each year, to Bronte Creek Provincial Park, a 0.01 km² recreation park near Toronto which received 308 624 visitors in 1986.

History

As in the case of national parks, provincial parks originated at the end of the 19th century as a result of growing concern among civil servants, politicians and the general public about the depletion of natural resources, the degradation of scenic places and the need for an ever-expanding and increasingly urbanized population to have opportunities for recreation in a natural setting. The first provincial park established was ALGONQUIN, now a 7653 km² provincial natural environment park about 250 km N of Toronto. The idea for such a park was conceived in 1885 by an Irish immigrant, Alexander Kirkwood. As a clerk of the Crown Lands Department he had become concerned about the destruction of the northern forests and wildlife and was impressed by the new national parks at Yellowstone in the US and BANFF in the Canadian Rockies. Kirkwood advocated the creation of a National Forest and Park called Algonkin, to "perpetuate the name of one of the greatest Indian nations that has inhabited the North American continent." His enthusiasm and the practical support of a provincial land surveyor, James Dickson, led to the appointment of a royal commission and to the investigation of 18 townships in the District of Nipissing, S of the Mattawa R and lying between the Ottawa R and Georgian Bay. In 1893 this area, Algonquin, was declared "a public park and forest reservation, fish and game preserve, health resort and pleasure ground for the benefit, advantage and enjoyment of the people of the Province." Initially the park was a remote wilderness, still subject to lumbering but afforded improved fire and wildlife protection. However, as communications improved and accommodation was provided, its recreational function gained in importance and, in the early 1900s, it became a fashionable destination for tourists wishing to canoe, fish and camp in a wilderness setting.

The next provincial park, RONDEAU, comprising a peninsula on the N coast of Lk Erie, was declared in 1894. Featuring a Carolinian FOREST of species normally found farther S, and frequented by numerous migratory birds, it was already popular with duck hunters and picnickers. Over the next 50 years, as demands for CONSERVATION and recreation areas increased, 5 other provincial parks were established in Ontario. In the granite SHIELD and Boreal Forest Zone, Quetico was created in 1913 and LAKE SUPERIOR in 1944. Along the GREAT LAKES shoreline, Long Point was designated in 1921, Presqu'ile in 1922 and Ipperwash in 1938.

Québec's first provincial parks were created contemporaneously to those in Ontario and for similar reasons. In 1894 Laurentides Provincial Park, N of Québec City, and MONT TREMBLANT Provincial Park, N of Montréal, were created to protect the forests, fish and wildlife for public benefit; however, resource exploitation continued in these areas. Other provincial parks were designated in the 1930s: Gaspésie in 1937, Mont Orford in 1938 and La Vérendrye in 1939. In the last 30 years many smaller parks have been established near cities to meet the demand for recreation in a natural setting.

British Columbia was the first western province to create provincial parks. STRATHCONA, a mountain and lake area on Vancouver I, gained park status in 1911 as a result of public support from such groups as the ALPINE CLUB OF CANADA, the BC Natural History Society and the Vancouver I Board of Trade. Attention then focused on the mountains and glaciers of eastern BC, Mt ROBSON being declared a provincial park in 1913, followed by MOUNT ASSINIBOINE and Kokanee Glacier in 1922. The province's largest park, 9698 km² Tweedsmuir, located in the Coast Range, gained park status in 1938; Wells Gray, in 1939. In more recent years many more provincial parks, including large wilderness areas and small recreational sites, have been designated near cities in the S, as well as in the N.

Provincial status and ownership of resources came later to the Prairie provinces, and so did provincial parks. While the federal government designated national parks and forest reserves in the prairies, it was only with the transfer of resources legislation in 1930 that provincial parks, often originally forest reserves, were created. Alberta passed a Provincial Parks and Protected Areas Act in 1930; 2 years later, Aspen Beach, Park Lk, Gooseberry Lk, Saskatoon I, Sylvan Lk, Lundbreck Falls, Ghost R and Hommy were declared provincial parks. The last 3 were later deleted from the park system but, after jurisdictional changes in 1951 and 1967, more and larger parks were created. By 1972 Alberta had 51 parks, totalling 567 km². Saskatchewan's first 3 provincial parks were created in 1931 from the former forest reserves of Duck Mt, Cypress Hills and Moose Mt. Manitoba likewise took over the management of forest reserves such as Turtle Mt and Spruce Woods but the province's first provincial park, WHITESHELL, was only established in 1962.

The Atlantic provinces began establishing provincial parks in the 1950s, when recreation opportunities in natural areas relatively close to cities were increasingly in demand. Parks with both a recreational and nature conservation orientation have now been established but the number and area remains relatively small. Territorial parks in YT and NWT are an even more recent innovation, primarily because most land in the territories is federally owned, recreation demand has been very limited (because of the small population and low levels of seasonal tourism); and

Milk River RCMP post at Writing-on-Stone Provincial Park, one of 61 provincial parks in Alberta (*photo by Harry Savage*).

because unspoiled wilderness is generally quite abundant.

Provincial Parks Systems Today

Today, nearly 100 years after the first provincial park was established, all provinces have provincial park systems which usually consist of provincial parks and various other land units designated for recreational and nature conservation purposes. Each provincial system is different, and new parks are being designated each year.

British Columbia, in 1986, had 330 provincial parks, 39 recreation areas, and one wilderness conservancy, totalling 47 926 km². Parks range from large, remote wilderness areas such as Tweedsmuir, to marine parks and small, recreational parks near cities. They are divided into 3 classes: class "A" comprises 291 fully protected natural or historic parks in which no commercially extractive industrial uses are permitted; discrete and regulated resource extraction is allowed in the 4 class "B" parks; the 35 class "C" parks are small, local, primarily recreational in character and, in time, will be transferred to local government jurisdiction. In 1985 the BC provincial park system received 15.9 million visitors. A major review of the system was undertaken by a Wilderness Advisory Committee in 1986.

Alberta, in 1986, had 61 provincial parks, 3 wilderness areas, 43 recreation areas and 8 ecological reserves, together encompassing 2965 km². They range in character from large, lightly used, unspoiled wilderness areas in the Rockies (eg, Siffleur), to heavily used water-based recreational parks in the more populated areas of central and eastern Alberta (eg, Sylvan Lk). In addition there are preserved areas such as bison jumps, fossil beds, native rock art and other sites of historical significance (eg, Dinosaur Provincial Park). In 1985 Alberta's provincial park system received approximately 5 million visitors.

Saskatchewan, in 1986, had a provincial park system covering 9630 km². The system includes large wilderness areas in the northern forest, smaller parks on wooded prairie hills (eg, CYPRESS HILLS), and lake-based recreational parks (eg, Lac Peltier, near Swift Current). The parks are categorized as provincial parks, (of which there are 31 covering 9081 km²), protected areas (21), recreation sites (173), historic sites (8) and regional parks (101). In 1986 Saskatchewan's provincial park system received 6.4 million visitors.

Manitoba, in 1987, had 164 provincial parks covering 10 332 km². They are categorized as natural or recreational or given a designation such as wilderness, wayside, heritage or marine. Whiteshell, E of Winnipeg, is a natural park as is Nopiming, a Saulteaux word meaning "into the wilderness." St Malo and Birds Hill, the latter 22

km N of Winnipeg, are primarily recreational. In 1986 Manitoba's provincial park system received 5.3 million visitors.

Ontario, in 1986, had 219 provincial parks encompassing 56 591 km². Additional lands designated by provincial conservation authorities and the St Lawrence and Niagara Park Commissions also serve nature conservation and recreational purposes. The park system includes wilderness areas (eg, 4758 km² Quetico), HISTORIC SITES (eg, Petroglyphs) and intensively used recreational areas (eg, Wasaga Beach on Lk Huron). The provincial parks are categorized as follows: wilderness (of which there are 8 covering 4 139 396 ha), natural environment (60-1 199 883 ha), waterway (9-221 099 ha), nature reserve, (68-53 302 ha), recreation (70-43 406 ha), and historical (4-2019 ha). Since 1983, 104 new parks have been established and 51 others have been identified for future designation. In 1986 Ontario's provincial park system received 7.5 million visitors.

Québec, in 1986, had 16 provincial parks, including 2 in the process of designation, encompassing 3948 km². The system includes large wilderness areas (eg, Mont-Tremblant – 1248 km²) and smaller areas (eg, Miguasha – 62.3 ha). Since 1977 they have been classified as conservation parks and recreation parks. In 1986 Quebec's provincial parks registered 3.1 million visitor days of use. Quebec also has 28 wildlife reserves, totalling 68 364 km² and receiving 1.1 million visitor days of use, as well as 13 tourist recreation areas, totalling 16 km², and receiving 695 436 visitor days of use.

New Brunswick, in 1986, had 48 provincial parks covering 249 km². Varying in size from 17 427 ha to .2 ha, they are classified as picnic, campground, beach, recreation, wildlife or resource parks. In 1986 they received approximately 2 million visitors.

Nova Scotia, in 1986, had 113 provincial parks, the operational ones covering 75 km², and reserve areas, 198 km². Primarily oriented to roadside, coastal and urban recreation, they are classified as campgrounds, picnic, beach or roadside rest sites. An estimated 1.6 million visitors used these parks in 1986.

Prince Edward Island, in 1987, had 34 provincial parks, encompassing 17 km². While small in number and area they include nature preserves, natural environment, recreation, beach and historic parks. In 1986 the provincial parks of Prince Edward Island received approximately 700 000 visitors.

Newfoundland, in 1987, had 76 provincial parks encompassing 236 km². The system comprises 42 camping, 15 day use and 19 natural-scenic attraction parks. In 1986, these parks had 271 612 campers and 1.5 million visitors. The provincial parks program was expanded in 1986 to include administration of 7 ecological reserves, notably SEABIRD sanctuaries, covering 34 km², and the Avalon Wilderness Reserve covering 1070 km². In addition, there are 3 provisional ecological reserves and 1 provisional wilderness reserve.

Yukon Territory, has 49 territorial campgrounds, comprising from 10 to 100 sites. Herschel Island territorial park was established in 1987, with another, Coal River Springs, planned to open in 1988.

Northwest Territories, in 1986, had some 3 dozen territorial parks covering 30 km², and more and larger ones are proposed. They are classified as natural environment recreation, outdoor recreation, community, wayside and historic parks. In addition, in 1985 there were 3 wildlife reserves covering 33 091 km², and 9 critical wildlife areas covering 140 000 km².

Administration

Provincial parks are administered by provincial government agencies, which are commonly part of departments dealing with natural resources, tourism or culture. For example, in Ontario the provincial parks branch is part of the Ministry of Natural Resources; in BC it belongs to the Ministry of Lands, Parks and Housing. Staff are located in offices in the provincial capitals, in regional offices and in the parks, where a superintendent is normally in charge, assisted by wardens and interpreters.

Most provincial agencies have developed park-system plans that guide decisions on how many parks are needed and what characteristics, size and location are appropriate. A management plan is normally prepared for each park to facilitate decisions on the protection of the park environment, on the development of facilities and the provision of services. Given the wide variation in the character and purpose of parks, many agencies classify parks (eg, as wilderness, recreation or historic) and manage them accordingly. Because parks, especially large ones, are diverse in character and purpose, they are often zoned, some areas being designated for strict nature protection and others for tourism development. The classification and zoning of a park is difficult and may require public involvement.

In trying to protect park environments, yet allow them to serve the needs of visitors, park agencies face many management problems. Few parks are now ecologically self-sufficient; hence, management is needed to deal with fires, wildlife imbalances, diseases of animals and vegetation, and human impacts. The use of parks by visitors necessitates the provision and management of accommodation, transport and recreation facilities, information and education services, and safety features. Some of the problems facing park managers in recent years include maintaining fish stocks; preventing FOREST FIRES, littering and vandalism; protecting visitors from bears; eliminating poaching; reducing crowding in popular areas; dealing with new technologies (eg, snowmobiles, hang gliders, wind surfers); and reducing accidents from risk activities (eg, mountaineering, canoeing, winter camping). In recent years, to improve planning and management, environmental protection and visitor satisfaction, park agencies have undertaken more research and have regularly consulted the public through surveys and public hearings. Increasingly, opportunities are being provided for private enterprise, public interest groups and volunteers to become involved in running parks.   JOHN S. MARSH

Parks, William Arthur, geologist, paleontologist, teacher (b at Hamilton, Ont 11 Dec 1868; d at Toronto 3 Oct 1936). A graduate of U of T (BA, 1892; PhD, 1900), he joined its staff in 1893 and became professor and head of the geology department in 1922. One of the founders and original directors of the ROYAL ONTARIO MUSEUM, he trained many students who became professional geologists and paleontologists. Parks was noted for his pioneer explorations in northern Ontario, his reports on Canadian building and ornamental stones, his studies on Paleozoic invertebrate fossils, and his discoveries and descriptions of Alberta dinosaurs. A fellow of the RSC and the Royal Soc of London, he was the author of some 80 scientific papers and (with A.P. Coleman) of *Elementary Geology, with special reference to Canada* (1922).   LORIS S. RUSSELL

Parksville, BC, Town, pop 5828 (1986c), 5216 (1981c), inc 1945, is located on the E coast of Vancouver I, 35 km NW of Nanaimo. First known as Englishman's River, Parksville was renamed

after a pioneer resident, Francis Parks. It became an important stagecoach stop when the road between Nanaimo and Alberni was completed 1886. Early settlers, chiefly English, had arrived by 1890. Parksville depends primarily on tourism; it is a popular summer resort, having fine sandy beaches and good saltwater and freshwater fishing, and numerous motels. The town is also the commercial centre for a large logging and agricultural area. The townscape of Parksville is beach oriented and includes many attractive subdivisions and tree-lined streets. Nearby geographic features include Cathedral Grove, Little Qualicum Falls Provincial Park and the Mt Arrowsmith Ski Area.   ALAN F.J. ARTIBISE

Parlby, Mary Irene, née Marryat, farm women's leader, politician (b at London, Eng 9 Jan 1868; d at Red Deer, Alta 12 July 1965). An early supporter of the UNITED FARMERS OF ALBERTA, in 1913 she helped form the first women's local. In 1916 she was elected president of the UFA's Women's Auxiliary; she transformed it into the United Farm Women of Alberta, which played a major role in fostering legislation relating to the welfare of women. In the 1921 provincial election she won the Lacombe riding for the UFA, holding it for 14 years and serving as minister without portfolio. She was the first woman to become a Cabinet minister in Alberta. She supported Acts concerning women's rights and participated in the PERSONS CASE in 1929. She was Canadian delegate to the League of Nations in 1930 and retired in 1935.   ERIC J. HOLMGREN

Parliament, strictly, according to the CONSTITUTION ACT 1982, the Queen, the HOUSE OF COMMONS and the SENATE. The Crown is represented in Canada by the GOVERNOR GENERAL. When Parliament is referred to in some formal usages, all 3 institutions are included. In common usage, however, the House of Commons alone is often equated with Parliament; this derives from a time when absolute monarchs summoned their legislature to legitimate their taxing and other measures up to a time when constitutional monarchs, with royal prerogatives "tamed" by a legislature, primarily acted only on the advice of ministers who were entitled to proffer advice only so long as they could maintain the support of the "commoners."

The bicameral nature of the Canadian Parliament was deemed a necessary inducement to bring provinces of varying size and power and with widely different regional concerns into the broader union that comprised Confederation. However necessary to the original union, the Senate, as a nonelective body, has been constantly subjected to cries for its abolition or reform, although as a committee of "sober second thought" or as a true institutional reflection of a federal Canada, it has many attractions. The House of Commons has become the more important chamber, not least because the government of the day stands or falls on its support. The practical consequence of invoking the supremacy of Parliament is the legislature's capacity to act as the great debating, if not educational, forum for the nation. This capacity, joined with the historic right to have grievances settled by the Crown before approving money in support of the Crown's activities ("control of the purse"), vests in the legislature not only the formal responsibility for approving statutes but also a continuing critical overseeing of executive actions. To this end, according to constitutional requirement, Parliament (as well as each provincial legislature) shall meet at least once a year and no more than 5 years should elapse between elections for a new legislature – only a war, invasion or insurrection can interfere with this guarantee.

A normal parliamentary session (following

rule changes in 1983) is now divided into semesters with provision for vacation adjournments. The proroguing of Parliament brings an end to a particular session and when reconvened the new session begins with a SPEECH FROM THE THRONE announcing the government's legislative program for the session. Dissolution, which marks the end of a Parliament, can occur any time within the 5-year period and is invoked by the governor general on the advice of the PRIME MINISTER. Dissolution involves an election and the formation of a new Parliament.

Protections also exist to ensure that Parliament shall not only be unconstrained in what it can debate but that the individual legislators shall enjoy complete freedom of speech. The rules of Parliament (self-prescribed) guarantee the rights of opposition parties to criticize without fear of retribution by the governing party.

The formation and operation of Parliament is dependent upon political parties; elections are fought and successful candidates find their seats in the legislature on a party basis, and it is through parties that the House and its committees conduct business. The capacity of CABINET to exert leverage on party supporters guarantees that the government's business will be piloted through the reefs of opposition. Indeed, it is the Cabinet's power, through its control of the party, that is criticized for undermining the traditional capacity of Parliament to hold government responsible through the threat of a no-confidence vote. Party discipline enables the Cabinet to counter with the threat of dissolution to force members to toe the line or place their seats at risk in an ensuing election. This shift in the balance of power puts in doubt Parliament's capacity to fulfil its traditional task of holding the executive to account. While parliamentary prerogatives are considerable, as an institution it is usually perceived as functionally inferior to the Cabinet and senior public service.   J.E. HODGETTS

Reading: C.E.S. Franks, *The Parliament of Canada* (1987).

Parliament, Library of, initially formed in 1841 by the amalgamation of the legislative libraries of Upper and Lower Canada. In 1849 the Parliament Buildings in Montréal were burned by a mob protesting the REBELLION LOSSES BILL and only 200 of the 12 000 books were saved. Re-established in Ottawa after completion of the original

Parliamentary Library, Parliament Hill, Ottawa, the only structure left after the fire of 1916 (*courtesy Environment Canada, Parks/Heritage Recording Services*).

PARLIAMENT BUILDINGS, the present building was the only structure left after the disastrous fire of 1916. The marvellous neo-Gothic structure was preserved in the new Parliament Buildings. The library's large collection of books and documents is carefully chosen to meet the demands of its parliamentary clientele. A research section provides substantial assistance to House members and parliamentary committees. The library's collections are available to other libraries through interlibrary loan. The library is considered a department for administrative purposes and the parliamentary librarian holds the rank of deputy minister.

Parliament, Opening of, may refer either to the beginning of the first session of PARLIAMENT after a general election or to the beginning of a subsequent session. All the proceedings take place in the Senate chamber and involve all 3 elements of Parliament – the CROWN, the SENATE and the HOUSE OF COMMONS. If there has been an election, on the first day of the session the Commons are summoned to the Senate, only to be told that the SPEECH FROM THE THRONE will not be read until they have selected one of their members as their spokesperson. The Commons then return to their own chamber and elect a Speaker. Later that day or on the next, the Commons, again pursuant to a summons delivered by the Gentleman Usher of the Black Rod, but now headed by their Speaker and the Sergeant at Arms bearing the mace, go up again to the Senate chamber. There the Speaker, standing at the bar of the Senate, presents himself or herself to the Queen's representative and requests that the traditional rights of the Commons be confirmed. When this has been done the Queen's representative (almost always the GOVERNOR GENERAL), reads the Speech from the Throne to the 2 Houses. The Senators are seated in their places; the Commons stand crowded behind their Speaker beyond the bar at the south end of the chamber. The prime minister is seated to the right of the throne. When the speech has been concluded the Commons are dismissed, and the Speaker leads them back to their own chamber. Once the governor general has departed the 2 Houses normally adjourn. On the next day both Houses begin working on the business of the session. If the session is not the first of a new Parliament, the Speech from the Throne can be delivered at once because a Speaker already has been chosen. JOHN B. STEWART

Reading: John B. Stewart, *The Canadian House of Commons* (1977).

Parliament Buildings, Ottawa, present one of Canada's most visually striking and historically remarkable building complexes. As first conceived, they were intended to serve a union of Upper and Lower Canada, but after CONFEDERATION had been negotiated they were available for the 4 constituent provinces. They provide space for the HOUSE OF COMMONS, SENATE, many members' offices and committee rooms. Four main elements make up the complex: Centre Block with tower, the flanking East and West Blocks, and the Library of Parliament at the rear. The complex occupies a picturesque site above the Ottawa R.

Architecturally, the Parliament Buildings represent Canada's best example of the developed picturesque Gothic revival style. Prominent are such elements from medieval architecture as pointed arches, lancet windows with tracery, pinnacles with crockets, prominent exposed buttresses, and contrasting variegated stonework set off by brick trim. The East and West Blocks (1859-65, Stent & Laver) and the Library (begun by Fuller & Jones, 1859, redesigned with wrought-iron dome in 1870, completed in 1877) represent the original mid-19th-century Gothic revival style. The Centre Block was first designed in 1859

The original Parliament Buildings (destroyed by fire in 1916) were a masterpiece of the mid-19th-century Gothic revival style. This view is from the western approach (*courtesy National Archives of Canada/PA-8338*).

by Thomas FULLER and Chilion Jones, reworked in 1863 by Fuller and Charles BAILLAIRGÉ, and in 1865 was sufficiently advanced for many departments to move up from Québec; the official opening was 6 June 1866. It was rebuilt (after a spectacular fire in 1916) by J.A. Pearson and J.O. Marchand in academic Gothic revival, more archaeologically correct but less colourful and eye-catching. Its grand central tower was originally called Victoria Tower, then, as rebuilt in 1917, Victoria Tower; in 1933 it was renamed the Peace Tower. ALAN GOWANS

Reading: National Film Board, *Stones of History: Canada's Houses of Parliament* (1967).

Parliamentary Press Gallery is a loosely knit association of about 350 journalists assigned by media organizations to cover Parliament and government. Traditionally seen as a small club of elite newspaper writers, it has expanded and become less cohesive since the admission of broadcasters in 1959 and the admission of camera and sound people in 1982. Many of its early records were destroyed in the Parliament Buildings fire in 1916, but the press gallery is known to have existed at least since Confederation, and its organization has become more structured over the years. In the 19th century its members were usually attached to a political party, and even into the 20th century Conservative and Liberal reporters sat at opposite ends of the gallery, though this pattern disappeared as newspapers detached themselves from political affiliation.

As a group, members have often been described

The current Parliament Buildings, built after the fire of 1916, are more authentically Gothic revival than their predecessors but less colourful and eye-catching (*courtesy SSC Photocentre*).

as an important instrument of political communication, but as an association the gallery has only minor influence. The executive of the association facilitates news coverage and arranges news conferences or access to information. Occasionally, it is drawn into more difficult problems, such as controversial applications for admission, the gallery's right to discipline members or its right to take a stand on public issues. A number of cases have established that although the gallery as an association has the right to deny membership, the Commons Speaker, as representative of the House, has the final authority to determine who will have access to facilities for coverage of Parliament.   CARMAN CUMMING

Reading: W.H. Kesterton, *A History of Journalism in Canada* (1967).

Parliamentary Procedure There are 5 basic principles of parliamentary procedure: first, the HOUSE OF COMMONS is master of its own proceedings; second, all discussion must be relevant to a motion and directed at a decision by the House; third, if possible, the House should not be taken by surprise (the usual required notice for debates is 48 hours); fourth, a majority of those voting, not a majority of the membership, is required to carry a motion; and fifth, the entire session and not just one sitting is used as the basic time unit for procedural purposes.

The House of Commons has adopted a large number of *standing orders* to govern its work but it is guided also by law, by the SPEAKER's rulings, and by practice. If there is no applicable Canadian rule, the House looks to the British House of Commons. All orders of the House are recorded in its minutes – the daily Votes and Proceedings and the sessional Journals – and from time to time consolidations of the standing orders are prepared for the convenience of members. The last major changes in the standing orders were made on 20 Dec 1968, 24 July 1969, 12 Dec 1975, 29 Nov 1982, 27 June 1985 and 13 Feb 1986. When points of order are being discussed members refer frequently to *Rules and Forms of the House of Commons of Canada*, by Arthur Beauchesne, and to Erskine May's *Parliamentary Practice*, a British work (1844), kept up to date by the clerks at Westminster.

The House expresses its opinions in *resolutions* and its will by *orders*. Most orders relate to its own conduct, eg, the decision that a bill be read a second (or third) time is in effect an order to the clerk to have the bill read. Most orders are particular, eg, "That Bill C-27 be now read a third time." Standing orders are those that remain in effect until altered by the House.

The House communicates by messages, addresses and bills. Messages are often sent to and received from the SENATE. The most famous address was that sent jointly with the Senate to Her Majesty in 1981 requesting the patriation of the CONSTITUTION. A *bill* is a request to the Queen that she assent to the text of the bill, making it a statute. No bill may go forward for royal assent unless it has passed the Senate and the House of Commons.

Decisions by the House are initiated by *motions,* most of which must be preceded by a printed notice, which is sent to all members in the daily Notice Paper. The decision of the majority of the members voting on a question is taken as the decision of the House. Many votes are unanimous. Recorded divisions are very formal – each member rises in his place and his vote is recorded in the minutes. The expression "on division" is often used to show there is opposition but that those opposed see no point in using time for a recorded division. Since the Speaker and 19 other members constitute a quorum, a bill may pass the

House even if the vote at every stage is only 10 Yeas and 9 Nays.

The many different kinds of business are dealt with in an exact program, the basic distinction being between items taking little time – often called routine proceedings – and the rest. Oral questions and routine proceedings take up a little more than an hour at the beginning of each sitting. Under routine proceedings, public bills are introduced and given first reading, standing COMMITTEES and special committees report to the House, written questions are answered and motions are made for concurrence mostly in committee reports. At the end of routine proceedings the House turns to the orders of the day. The second distinction is between private members' business and government business. Under the standing orders most of the House's time after routine proceedings is at the government's disposal (16 hours weekly); at best, the private members have 4 hours a week.

Private members' business comprises *motions* (for proposed orders or resolutions), *private members' bills* (to change the general law) and *private bills*, and *motions for the production of papers*. Under rules established in 1986, 20 items of private members' business, selected at random, receive priority in debate and 6 items, chosen by a committee, must come to a vote. Previous to this almost all private members' bills and motions were "talked out" with almost no prospect of being passed; now a small number receive extensive debate in the House and have a real possibility of becoming law. In contrast, all government orders go on one mixed list, Government Orders. The government House Leader may have items of government business dealt with in any priority and may have the House return to the same item day after day. Government items are never talked out, although they may be delayed by FILIBUSTER. The 5 lists, together with written questions, are printed in the *Order Paper*, which grows thicker as a session progresses. Private bills are now used mainly to incorporate certain kinds of federal companies. Private members' motions are almost always talked out. Motions for the ministers to bring forth letters, documents and reports are relatively unimportant unless the government is in a minority; if the government has no objection they carry without debate, and debated motions will be defeated if the government has a majority.

The expression *orders of the day* originated with the House at Westminster which planned its work by ordering that particular items come up on specified days, even at specified hours. After a first reading the Speaker at Ottawa still asks, "When shall the said bill be read a second time?" and after the report stage, "When shall the said bill be read a third time?" Each item is really an order, and at the end of routine proceedings the Speaker announces, "Orders of the day." An item of business taken after routine proceedings is in the form of an order, and the order may be that the motion is to be moved that a particular bill be read a second (or third) time. Orders, motions and bills are often confused in the news. Government motions are intended not to change the law, but to produce an order or resolution of the House; they parallel private members' motions. Government legislative business is composed of nonfinancial bills, Ways and Means business which results in taxation bills, and Supply business which results in appropriation bills (*see* BUDGETARY PROCESS).

The first 2 motions of the ordinary legislative process – that permission be given to introduce the bill and that the bill be read a first time – are treated as routine proceedings without debate, but perhaps with a division. The motion that the bill be read a second time is debatable, so it is moved pursuant to an order of the day. If that motion carries, one of the Table Officers "reads" the

bill. Nowadays the reading is symbolic; he simply says, "Second reading of this bill." Next the bill is sent to a committee, where it is studied closely, clause by clause, with or without amendments. It is then reported back to the House. If the bill has been to a committee other than a Committee of the Whole House, any member may move amendments to it after written notice. But if the bill has been to a Committee of the Whole House the report stage is only a formality. The last stage concerns the motion that the bill "be now read a third time and do pass." If this motion carries, the bill is sent to the Senate for passage there, or, if it has already passed there, it returns there to await royal assent. Bills introduced in the House of Commons are numbered C-1, C-2, etc, and Senate bills are numbered, S-1, S-2, etc. Royal assents, like SPEECHES FROM THE THRONE, are given in the Senate chamber.

Appropriation bills – allotting money for particular purposes – follow a similar process but normally take only a few minutes because the members have had time to examine the Crown's request (estimates) for supply in the standing committees. The standing orders set aside 25 days a year in the House as Opposition Days, to allow the Opposition to criticize the government before the House is asked to appropriate money.

Taxation bills, too, are advanced through a variation of the ordinary legislative process. The minister of finance usually announces major tax changes in a budget speech, moves a standard motion, "that this House approves in general the budgetary policy of the government," and the budget debate, limited to 6 days, then begins. Often the Official Opposition will move an amendment and a third party a subamendment. On 8 May 1974, the TRUDEAU government was defeated on a New Democratic Party subamendment to the budget motion, and on 13 Dec 1979, the CLARK government was defeated in the same way. During his speech the minister tables notices of Ways and Means motions outlining his proposed tax changes in some detail; these are intended to elicit comments on the practicality of the proposed changes from tax lawyers, accountants and others. Later, perhaps months later, he brings in his taxation bills, one for each Ways and Means motion. Taxation bills, which are considered in Committees of the Whole House, generally move slowly through the second-reading, the committee and the third-reading stages. The debate initiated by the Speech from the Throne is now limited to 8 days and attracts little attention unless the government is in a minority.

Debating takes place in the House, an unsuitable mode for some matters which are better considered in committees. In Committees of the Whole House the proceedings are far more flexible than they are in the House. Almost all nonfinancial bills are considered in committees specifically established for individual bills which disband once their work is completed.

The defeat of the government in a division does not necessarily bring its resignation or an election – it may be prepared to carry on without the lost bill, as was the PEARSON government in Feb 1968, and the House itself may not regard the defeat as demonstrating a lack of confidence. The rules provide regular opportunities for explicit nonconfidence motions by the Opposition; they can be moved as amendments to the Address-in-Reply motion, as amendments to the budget motion and as motions on 6 of the 25 Opposition Days. Even an explicit nonconfidence vote does not impose a legal obligation to resign or bring on an election, but a government that ignored such a vote would be mad. The House can force a government out of office by refusing to appropriate money.

The rules permit members to address oral questions to the CABINET daily. In Canada no written notices of the questions are required as they are in Britain; consequently, the Canadian *question period* is more timely, turbulent and, some observers claim, trivial. The daily period for oral questions is the source of much of the news from Ottawa. A minister is not required to answer any or every question candidly; indeed the House would often regard completely truthful answers as contrary to the national interest.

Sometimes the House agrees to debate a matter not included among the orders of the day. Once the notice time has elapsed any government order of the day can be activated, even if it is the last one on the list, so normally the government has no need for emergency debates. Standing Order 29 enables private members to request an emergency debate. A motion to adjourn under SO 26 is debatable but may not be moved without special permission. The member must apply to the Speaker following routine proceedings; if the application is found valid it needs the support of only 19 others. These debates generally begin after dinner (3 PM on Fridays) when the House does not usually sit. The Speaker can terminate them when they become repetitious but in practice they continue until all members who wish to speak have done so. Because of differences in size and in practices established over the years, many of the specific procedures followed in provincial legislatures differ substantially from those of the House of Commons, for example, in the recourse to committees, rules for private members' business and in practices relating to financial matters. The underlying principles, though, remain the same.

JOHN B. STEWART

Reading: John B. Stewart, *The Canadian House of Commons: Procedure and Reform* (1977); C.E.S. Franks, *The Parliament of Canada* (1987).

Parlow, Kathleen, violinist, teacher (b at Calgary 20 Sept 1890; d at Oakville, Ont 19 Aug 1963). Trained entirely outside Canada, Parlow completed her studies with Leopold Auer at St Petersburg [Leningrad] Conservatory and made her professional debut in Berlin in 1907. A brilliant soloist and recitalist, renowned for tone, technique and breadth of repertoire, she toured Europe, Russia, the US, Canada and Asia. After 1927 her career was centered on teaching and chamber-music performance. Returning permanently to Canada in 1941, she taught at the Toronto Conservatory and founded the Parlow String Quartet, which, as the best-known quartet of its day (1943-58), influenced the musical taste of audiences across the country, introducing much unfamiliar music, including works by Canadian composers.

BARCLAY McMILLAN

Parr's print, *Hunters of Old*, was selected for a 1977 Canadian postage stamp (*courtesy West Baffin Eskimo Co-operative, Cape Dorset, NWT*).

Parr, graphic artist, hunter (b on southern Baffin I 1893; d at Cape Dorset, NWT 3 Nov 1969). Parr led a traditional nomadic existence for most of his life. A serious hunting accident obliged him to settle permanently in CAPE DORSET in 1961, where he began drawing at age 68. In his short artistic career he produced over 2000 drawings and contributed 34 prints to the annual Cape Dorset print collections. Filled with animals and hunters and drawn in a distinctive, primitive style, with little regard for naturalism or perspective, Parr's naive images are powerful expressions of an old man's love for a disappearing way of life. Often considered crude and childish, his works were largely unappreciated during his lifetime. Only after his death were there major exhibitions of his work, and a posthumously published print, *Hunters of Old*, was selected for a 1977 Canadian postage stamp. *See also* INUIT ART.

INGO HESSEL

Parr, John, soldier, colonial administrator (b at Dublin, Ire 20 Dec 1725; d at Halifax 25 Nov 1791). After a lengthy career in the army, he became governor of NS in 1782. Taking up his post just before some 30 000 LOYALISTS entered the maritime colonies, he was forced to deal with their resettlement and shortly found himself caught between the pretensions of the newcomers and the claims of older settlers, a situation that endured until the end of his administration. On the whole he acquitted himself well, though he won little popularity or admiration for his efforts.

J.M. BUMSTED

Parrot, Jean-Claude, trade-union leader (b at Montréal, Qué 24 July 1936). He is the longtime leader of the militant, 23 000 member-strong, Canadian Union of Postal Workers (CUPW). As Chief Union negotiator (since 1975) and union president (since 1977) Parrot, a former postal clerk who began his Post Office career in Montréal in 1954, has led CUPW through contentious contract negotiations and long national strikes. He first received public attention in 1975 when CUPW's demand for a 71% wage increase led to a 43-day national strike. Three years later, he was jailed for 2 months when he defied back-to-work legislation. A tireless worker for his members, he has won impressive collective agreements which have included paid maternity leave for female CUPW members and wage parity for part-time workers. In Oct 1987 Parrot was again in the spotlight when inside postal workers were legislated back to work.

WILLIAM KAPLAN

Parrsboro, NS, Town, inc 1884, pop 1729 (1986c), located where the Parrsboro R meets N Minas Basin, abounds in native and pirate lore. The Micmac called this the place where Glooscap roamed, *awokun* ("portage"). By 1776 Partridge I was settled, and ferry service operated to Windsor. The population shifted to the mainland, choosing a name (1784) to honour Gov John Parr. Parrsboro prospered early, through shipbuilding and trade with the West Indies. The Saxby Gale (1869) drove the beach inland, joining Partridge I to the mainland. Today, Parrsboro is the largest town and tourist centre on this Fundy coast, with fishing and lumber boats still braving the famous tides in its harbour. Ottawa House, Sir Charles TUPPER's summer residence, is a museum depicting Parrsboro's maritime heritage. Rockhounds sleuth cliffs and beaches for abundant agate and amethyst. Nearby, prehistoric animal footprints have been discovered.

JUDITH HOEGG RYAN

Parry, Sir William Edward, rear-admiral, arctic explorer (b at Bath, Eng 19 Dec 1790; d at Bad Ems, Rhineland-Palatinate 8 July 1855), son of a famous physician. As a midshipman in the Royal Navy he saw action in the Baltic and North Sea

Sir William Parry's 1819 cabin, photographed at Winter Harbour in 1981 (*photo by Doug McLeod*).

until 1812; in N America, 1812-17. In 5 arctic expeditions, he commanded the last 4: 1818, through Baffin Bay to Ellesmere I; 1819, by way of Lancaster Sound to Melville Island, the first ships ever to cross 110° W; 1821, through Foxe Basin to Fury and Hecla Strait, a discovery; 1824, down Prince Regent Inlet, but HMS *Hecla* wrecked; 1827, from Svalbard north to 82°45' N, a record until 1876. Subsequent naval assignments were 1827, hydrographer; 1836, controller of steam navigation; 1846, superintendent of Haslar Hospital; 1854, lieutenant-governor of Greenwich Hospital. Civilian interludes were: 1830, commissioner of the Australian Agricultural Company; 1834, commissioner of the poor-law in Norfolk. He ranks among the great navigators for penetrating the Arctic Archipelago, for showing how ships can survive and men work through an arctic winter, and for achieving a furthest north unsurpassed for 50 years. He contributed much to the eventual discovery of the Northwest Passage and the North Pole.

ROBERT E. JOHNSON

Parry Channel is a sea passage running E-W through the arctic islands. Named for explorer W.E. PARRY, it begins at LANCASTER SOUND, passes through Barrow Str, leads into Viscount Melville Sound, finally reaching the BEAUFORT SEA through M'Clure Str. The permanent pack ice in M'Clure Str is an impassable obstacle to further navigation through the Parry Channel, forcing ships making the NORTHWEST PASSAGE to detour far to the S. The straight, parallel coastlines and great depths found in Parry Channel suggest it is a deep, submerged trough caused by past intense movements of the Earth. It marks the geological divide between Precambrian rocks of the Canadian SHIELD to the S and sedimentary rocks forming the arctic islands to the N.

DOUG FINLAYSON

Parry Islands, a group of high arctic islands comprising MELVILLE, BATHURST and CORNWALLIS islands, as well as a number of smaller ones. Melville is the largest of the 3 main islands and is also the highest, exceeding 1000 m in places. The islands are topographically similar since all are part of the same geosynclinal structure; each takes the form of a level plateau 600 m in elevation that ends abruptly in 300 m high cliffs along many parts of the coast. The most striking feature of the surface of Melville and Cornwallis islands is the almost complete absence of vegetation, exposing a great number and variety of patterned ground features.

DOUG FINLAYSON

Parry Sound, Ont, Town, pop 5977 (1986c), 6124 (1981c), inc 1888, located on the eastern side of GEORGIAN BAY, 225 km N of Toronto. The name honours British explorer Sir William Edward PARRY. The site was purchased in the middle of the 19th century by W.H. Beatty, a land surveyor looking for fresh timber limits. The settlement was laid out after 1867. Beatty family interests

were managed by a son, William, Jr, who treated the town as a personal fiefdom and was known as "the governor." He enforced prohibition and at one point circulated his own money – Beatty scrip. For many years logging was the major industry. As logging declined, tourism increased and now the town is the centre of the Thirty Thousand Islands vacation area. It is famous as the home of hockey legend Bobby ORR and of Festival of the Sound. DANIEL FRANCIS

Parsnip (*Pastinaca sativa*), perennial plant grown as an annual VEGETABLE crop and belonging to the Umbelliferae family. Of Eurasian origin, parsnips were brought to N America by European colonists. They have white, fleshy, sweet, slightly acrid roots. Stems, with ovate leaflets, are 40-75 cm high. Improved varieties (eg, Hollow Crown) have short tops and smooth roots, 25-30 cm long and 6-8 cm thick at the shoulders. Canada's temperate climate is well suited to parsnips, which are rich in potassium. In 1985 Canada's production was 2924 t, worth $1.388 million. Ontario produced 67% of this crop.

Parsons, Robert John, journalist, politician (b at Harbour Grace, Nfld, *c*1802; d at St John's 20 June 1883). With William Carson and other Newfoundland Liberals, he founded the weekly *Newfoundland Patriot* in 1833 and became its sole owner and editor (1840). Eloquent and occasionally outrageous in his defence of the Liberal cause, he wrote a satirical putdown of Chief Justice Henry BOULTON in 1835 who sentenced him to jail for contempt of court. This episode won Parsons esteem in Liberal circles. He was elected to the Assembly in 1843 and sat almost continually until 1878. He was a powerful influence, a forceful advocate of RESPONSIBLE GOVERNMENT in the 1850s, and in 1869 one of the leaders of the anti-Confederate campaign. GEOFF BUDDEN

Parsons, Timothy Richard, biological oceanographer (b in Sri Lanka [Ceylon] 1 Nov 1932). He received his doctorate in biochemistry at McGill and worked as a research scientist in Nanaimo, BC, for 11 years, Secretariat of UNESCO, Paris, for 2 years, and professor of oceanography, UBC, 1971 to present. His research is best known for studies on the Gulf of Alaska ecosystem and for the use of large experimental seawater enclosures to study biological effects of pollutants. He has published over 100 scientific papers and 2 well-known oceanographic texts. He was the organizer and chief scientist for the first Canadian transpacific oceanographic cruise on CNAV *Endeavour*, 1967. He was scientist-in-charge of the first successful application of commercial fertilizer to a large lake (Great Central Lake, BC) for sockeye salmon enhancement. He was elected fellow of the RSC in 1978. P.J. HARRISON

Parti bleu, political group formed in Québec about 1850 around the moderate reform beliefs of Louis-Hippolyte LAFONTAINE; the name derived from an attempt to establish an identity distinct from that of the extremist, anticlerical PARTI ROUGE. With the encouragement of the church, the "bleus" attracted much popular support. Members such as Augustin-Norbert MORIN and George-Étienne CARTIER provided the French Canadian leaders in the PROVINCE OF CANADA's government. The party was associated with English-speaking Tories and, through co-operation with Canada West's moderate reformers, provided the basis for the CONSERVATIVE PARTY.

Parti canadien, founded during the early 19th century, was a political party of middle-class French Canadian professionals and merchants, although it attracted some anglophones. Its newspaper, *Le Canadien*, was first published in Québec City 22 Nov 1806. Under the leadership of Pierre Bédard, the party was involved in agitation for ministerial responsibility and for greater power and control of political patronage by French Canadians. In Mar 1810, at the insistence of Gov CRAIG, Bédard and some *Le Canadien* staff were arrested, and thereafter Bédard's control of the party declined. After about 1815 Louis-Joseph PAPINEAU emerged as leader, and the party went on to fight against the 1822 proposal for union of the Canadas. In 1826, to reflect a growing sense of FRENCH CANADIAN NATIONALISM, the Parti canadien became the Parti PATRIOTE.

Parti national, political party fd in 1871 by Québec Liberals including Honoré MERCIER and Louis Jetté. It unsuccessfully attempted to acquire the clerical support for liberalism that the PARTI ROUGE lacked. Mercier revived it in 1885 during the uproar over Louis RIEL's execution. The Parti national, a coalition of Liberals and disenchanted Québec Conservatives using a platform based on French Canadian nationalism, won a majority in the 1886 provincial election. The Conservatives tried to stay in power, but without success. Sir Louis-Olivier TAILLON was premier for only 4 days, and was defeated in the House in Jan 1887. Mercier became premier and the party governed Québec until 1891, when the Mercier ministry was dismissed by the lt-gov for involvement in the BAIE DES CHALEURS SCANDAL. It was soundly defeated in the 1892 provincial election.

Parti pris, political and cultural magazine fd 1963 by Montréal writers André MAJOR, Paul CHAMBERLAND, Pierre Maheu, Jean-Marc Piotte and André Brochu, all in their twenties and convinced that Québec needed a revolution to produce an independent, socialist and secular state. Young activist intellectuals in QUIET REVOLUTION Québec soon began to gravitate to the magazine. During its 5 years (from Oct 1963 to the summer of 1968), *Parti pris* was simultaneously a high-quality magazine (53 issues appeared, in 39 installments); an avant-garde revolutionary centre which was active in demonstrations, the training of militants, the Club Parti pris and later the Mouvement de libération populaire; and a publishing house which put out some 20 works, most of them literary and some outstanding. The publishing house, Éditions Parti pris, continued to exist after the magazine had disappeared. The magazine allied itself with the major ideological currents of its time: Marxist-Leninism, Sartrean existentialism and Third World decolonization. It drew heavily on these ideologies to develop a virulent analysis of Québec as a colonized society whose inhabitants were economically, culturally and politically deeply alienated, dispossessed of their being along with their homeland. *Parti pris* consistently rejected "French Canada" and called "Québec" into existence. On the literary level, it was known for the JOUAL writing it published. The group put out powerful, shocking works, such as *Le Cassé* (1964; tr *Flat Broke and Beat*, 1964) by Jacques Renaud, *L'Afficheur hurle* (1965; tr *The Shouting Signpainters*, 1972) by Paul Chamberland, and an extraordinary essay, NÈGRES BLANCS D'AMÉRIQUE (1968; tr *White Niggers of America*, 1971) by Pierre VALLIÈRES. *Parti pris* was a brilliant literary generation. In the words of a contemporary, it was the Québec "Intellectual" Liberation Front. ROBERT MAJOR

Parti Québécois, Québec nationalist party, formed in 1968 through a union of 2 movements,

a SOVEREIGNTY-ASSOCIATION movement (the MSA) and the Rassemblement pour l'indépendance national (RIN). The MSA itself had been the result of an earlier fusion, for it allied itself with the forces of the Ralliement national (RN), led by the former Créditiste federal member of Parliament Gilles Grégoire. The MSA was created in 1967, when Liberal militants, following a policy conference of the Liberal Party of Québec where they had failed to win acceptance for their program entitled *Pour un Québec souverain dans une fédération canadienne* ("For a Sovereign Québec in a Canadian Federation"), decided to quit Jean Lesage's party. They were led by René LÉVESQUE, the former minister of natural resources. The RIN may have created what could be called the vocabulary of independence for Québec, but it was the PQ which made it acceptable to a good part of the Québec electorate. Nothing less than complete independence was acceptable to the RIN. After the RIN and its leader Pierre Bourgault wound up its affairs in 1968, the PQ became the hub of virtually all the nationalist movements and associations in Québec. It acquired workers, an infrastructure and a network of support, all of which grew rapidly. These supporters included the Société Saint-Jean-Baptiste and the Mouvement national des Québécois.

After suffering electoral defeats in its first 2 tries (in 1970, with 23.5% of the popular vote, it received only 7 seats; in 1973, despite a popular vote of 30.8%, it elected only 6 members), it won the election of 1976 (41% of the vote, 71 seats), defeating Robert Bourassa's Liberals, who in 1973 had elected 102 out of a total of 110 deputies. This victory was largely a result of a clever electoral maneuvre, orchestrated by Claude MORIN, by which the PQ promised to hold a referendum on sovereignty-association during the first péquiste term of office. One of the most important pieces of legislation of the PQ was BILL 101, which made French the sole official language of Québec (*see* LANGUAGE POLICY). The Agricultural Zoning Act, drawn up to protect Québec land, was complemented by Bill 125 for the management of lands. The Auto Insurance Act established state-run property damage insurance and no-fault compensation. Bill 89 introduced a new CIVIL CODE and reformed FAMILY LAW.

A unique feature of the PQ government was its attempt through *Sommets de Concertation* ("summit conferences") to establish trust among social groups. The first summit was held in Point-au-Pic in 1977, followed by one in Montebello in 1979. The conferences called together interested parties in various fields to participate in policymaking and to try to arrive at a consensus on the future development of Québec. One of the major concrete results of these summits was the creation of OSE (Opération Solidarité Economique, or Operation Economic Solidarity), a program of economic stimulus and job support.

The Referendum of 1980 The referendum which the PQ had promised during its 1976 election campaign was set for May 1980. Many public meetings followed an initial televised referendum debate in the National Assembly. Those who opposed negotiation for sovereignty-association won the referendum (60% to 40%). Nevertheless, the party was re-elected in 1981, winning 82 seats. Along with the belief in sovereignty-association, péquiste ideology was based on 2 sometimes contradictory tendencies: one insisting on consultation, the other on guiding people instead. The conflict blew the party apart in 1984 after the annual conference at which it was agreed that the PQ, once re-elected, could itself negotiate sovereignty-association. After a referendum-style consultation with the membership, Lévesque led a party which had lost the support of

Parti Québécois supporters celebrate the 1981 provincial election victory, Montréal (*photo by Jim Merrithew*).

a group of dissidents who refused to accept the results of a vote allowing the PQ temporarily to put aside the idea of sovereignty-association. Late in 1984, the PQ government was rocked by the resignation from Cabinet of a group of independentistes, including Jacques PARIZEAU. Lévesque eventually resigned as leader and was succeeded by Pierre-Marc JOHNSON. Faced with the resurrected Liberals of Robert Bourassa, the Parti Québécois was devastated in the election of Dec 1985, hanging on to a mere 24 seats. In Nov 1987, a week after the death of Lévesque, Johnson announced his resignation. The more independentiste-minded Jacques Parizeau was the leading leadership contender.

The Electoral Base of the PQ During the elections of 1970 and 1981, the Parti Québécois was supported by most people under 30, nationalists, union leaders and members of the working class in the regions of Saguenay-Lac-St-Jean and the east end of Montréal. This electoral support was built up through small discussion groups and through student organizations, but it began to shrink again in 1982-83. Illegal strikes in the public-service sector caused social unrest; the young people had become indifferent to politics in general. The péquiste government had to use legislation (Bills 68, 70 and 72 of June 1983) to force public-sector workers to accept salary rollbacks, and lost much of its union support. At the same time, the PQ was losing members because of its reduced commitment to sovereignty-association and to social-democratic legislation.

The Dilemma of the PQ Both as government and, from 1985 on, as the Opposition, the PQ has demonstrated a certain ambiguity. The party must attack the federal system from which it wishes to detach itself, while seeking to extract maximum benefit from this very system. A good example of this dilemma was the PQ's position during the federal-provincial constitutional negotiations of fall 1981 concerning the patriation of the Constitution (*see* CONSTITUTION, PATRIATION OF). Québec joined 7 other dissident provinces to oppose the intention of the Trudeau government first to bring back control of the constitution and then to make a new agreement. However, Québec found itself isolated when the other dissidents accepted a new constitutional agreement.

Québec under a Liberal government did not endorse the constitutional agreement until further concessions were made in 1987.
CLINTON ARCHIBALD

Parti rouge, also known as Parti démocratique, established about 1848 by a group of radical young francophone intellectuals who had helped found the INSTITUT CANADIEN and who were inspired by the republican ideas of Louis-Joseph PAPINEAU. Members included the DORION brothers, Louis-Victor SICOTTE, Joseph Papin and Joseph DOUTRE. In the legislature and through *L'Avenir* and *Le Pays*, the *rouges* advocated repeal of the ACT OF UNION, annexation of Canada to the US, extension of the elective principle of government to all offices, abolition of the SEIGNEURIAL SYSTEM and universal suffrage. Although their extremism moderated over time, they remained staunchly anticlerical and opposed to the ULTRAMONTANE doctrines of Mgr BOURGET, thereby ensuring the animosity of the church and limited popular support. After Confederation the Parti rouge merged with the CLEAR GRITS of Canada West to form the basis of the LIBERAL PARTY.

Partridge, Edward Alexander, farmer, farm leader, author (b at Whites' Corners [Dalston] near Barrie, Canada W 5 Nov 1862; d at Victoria 3 Aug 1931). Partridge grew up in an area where farm militancy was well established in the 1870s. He went west with brother Henry in Dec 1883 and taught school while homesteading E of Sintaluta. During the NORTH-WEST REBELLION he served in the Yorkton Company of Infantry. In the mid-1890s Partridge became active in the Patrons of Industry in the Sintaluta area. A bustling community dominated by Ontario settlers, Sintaluta became a centre for strong regional and political movements. In 1902 Sintaluta farmers charged the CPR with improperly allocating grain cars under the Manitoba Grain Act. Henry Partridge, the magistrate who judged the case, found the company guilty. This largely symbolic victory over the railway made the Partridge brothers important figures among the Saskatchewan grain growers. Early in 1905 a few neighbours sponsored a trip by Ed Partridge to investigate the operations of the Winnipeg Grain Exchange. Shocked by the speculation he found, he quickly developed a plan for a co-operative marketing program, and the Grain Growers Grain Co was organized in 1906. After a bitter struggle to join the Winnipeg Exchange in 1907, the company prospered. Partridge was its first president and he was also instrumental in starting in 1908 GRAIN GROWERS' GUIDE, the voice of Prairie farmers.

Partridge was a visionary who believed that the keys to western development were government control of the grain-marketing system to ensure reliable, inexpensive delivery of grain, and the development of the HUDSON BAY RAILWAY. He inevitably found himself in fierce struggles with politicians and other farm leaders and in 1912 he resigned from the Grain Growers' Grain Company. He realized that he was a weak administrator and was primarily responsible for selecting his successor. Shortly afterward he started the Square Deal Grain Co, but when it declined in 1913 he returned to Sintaluta.

Despite a number of personal tragedies and failing health, he re-entered the farm movement as elder spokesman for a new generation of agrarian radicals at the end of the war. He was revered by many within the Farmers' Union of Canada, a radical farm movement formed in 1921. He became once again a popular spokesman for farmers and in 1926 he published *A War on Poverty*. A strange mixture of Ruskinian socialism, Old Ontario Toryism, western utopianism and religious fervour, the book called for an independent west-

ern state, Coalsamao. It was a highly individualistic vision that attracted much interest but few converts. Plagued by despondency at times throughout his life, Partridge died, probably by suicide, in 1931.
IAN MACPHERSON

Partridge Island, or Canada's Emerald Isle, .18 km², 0.6 km long by 0.3 km wide, at the mouth of Saint John Harbour. The island is a 300-million-year-old volcanic ash deposit, now sparsely covered by birch, spruce, willow and alder. In 1791 NB's first lighthouse was built there to provide a safe passage into the harbour. This marine aid was later assisted by a signal station, harbour buoys, and finally, the world's first steam-operated fog alarm in 1859. In 1905 NB's first Marconi radio station was built there. The island is still an operational Coast Guard base. In 1800 the Royal Artillery constructed the first military works, and during the War of 1812 the island battery was the principal defensive position. The battery was manned during the FENIAN raid in 1866 and was used as a training battery until the Great War. During both world wars the Loyal Company of Artillery manned island defences, with the military station closing in 1947. There are several military fortifications above and below ground on the island today. In 1785 the Royal Charter of Saint John set aside the island for use as a quarantine station. In 1847, 14 892 Irish and English immigrants landed at Partridge I, of whom 1195 died; 600 were buried in mass graves in 1847. About 1200 immigrants are buried on the island in all. The island was also home to a small fishing community and a school house operated there 1871-1948. Partridge I has twice been designated a national historic site (fog alarm, 1925, quarantine station, 1974). The island is connected to the mainland at Negrotown Point by a rubble stone breakwater. A museum is scheduled to open in July 1988.
HAROLD E. WRIGHT

Party Financing Canadian political parties need money for election expenses (traditionally the only reason), to maintain organizational activities (accomplished more or less successfully) and to conduct research for policy purposes (a poor third). The financing of Canadian parties reflects the country's institutions. The Cabinet and parliamentary systems tend to centralize power and funds in the hands of the leadership, but the influences of FEDERALISM result in a dispersal of both among competing national and provincial governments and party structures. From Confederation until about 1897 party funds were an essential tool in overcoming the fissiparous tendencies of weak partisanship – the "loose fish" phenomenon and dominant ministerialism. Party chiefs such as John A. MACDONALD were intimately involved in fund raising and in distributing election funds to ensure the election loyalty of their followers. Inevitably they were also involved in questionable dealings with financial interests in search of concessions, contracts and favours, as exemplified by the PACIFIC SCANDAL of the 1870s and other railway scandals (*see* PATRONAGE). As partisanship crystallized, party leaders tried to disengage themselves from the raising of campaign war chests, but W.L. Mackenzie KING's entanglement in the Beauharnois Scandal of 1931 (King, who had accepted money from a promoter of a hydroelectric plant, called it his "vale of humiliation") proved that it continued to haunt them. Fund-raising specialists gradually assumed this role, freeing party leaders from immediate involvement in this necessary but messy aspect of party politics (*see* CORRUPTION; CONFLICT OF INTEREST).

Until recently, the large industrial and financial interests of Toronto and Montréal (hundreds rather than thousands of givers) provided nearly all the funds required by the Liberal and Progressive Conservative parties. Although recent reforms at the federal and provincial levels have modified this pattern, campaigns at all levels, including the municipal, depended largely on the same sources as the central party funds. Currently, multinational firms and their Canadian branches play a large role in the financing of the Canadian PARTY SYSTEM. Fund raising was traditionally the responsibility of committees in Toronto and Montréal and of various satellite groups in Hamilton, London, Winnipeg, Calgary and Vancouver, though western fund raisers have lately become more prominent because of shifts in the Canadian economy. The main fund raisers were not responsible to the formal, elected party organs and rarely held elective office. Appointed by the party leader, they were usually coopted from the legal or financial communities, or else they inherited their positions from older family members. Their usual reward when a party achieved office was appointment to the Senate or the bench. The traditional model was altered by the rise of third parties and the resurgence of provincial economic and political power after WWII. The CO-OPERATIVE COMMONWEALTH FEDERATION (CCF), the SOCIAL CREDIT movement in Alberta and Québec, and the PARTI QUÉBÉCOIS tapped new financial resources and became largely self-financing. The NEW DEMOCRATIC PARTY has relied heavily on its membership but receives substantial support from trade unions, some of them headquartered in the US. The emergence of provincial power has not lessened party dependence on business but has altered the entry point for party monies and reduced the former dependence of provincial organizations on federal ones.

As a result of the demise of the notorious UNION NATIONALE machine of Maurice DUPLESSIS and because of scandals in Ottawa and the provinces, such as the RIVARD (which involved a drug peddler) and Fidinam (an Ontario real-estate scandal) affairs, and because of the effect of the American Watergate scandal, there was a movement for the control of election expenses during the 1960s and 1970s. A Federal Advisory Committee on Election Expenses led to the ELECTION EXPENSES ACT (1974) while the Ontario Commission on the Legislature led to the establishment of the Commission on Election Contributions and Expenses. Reforms have now been adopted by 7 provinces, as well as by some municipal bodies. The role of party funds, formerly ignored, has been recognized. Control bodies have been instituted and ceilings imposed on party and candidate spending and contributions. Disclosure of the amounts and sources of income and expenses is mandatory. Incentives for individual donors have been provided in the form of graduated tax credits favouring smaller gifts. No other jurisdiction has yet followed Québec's lead in banning corporate and other organizational contributions. Subsidies in the form of reimbursements for a portion of the total permitted expenses for candidate and party spending at election time are now provided at the federal level and in a majority of provinces. The maximum permitted expenditures for parties and candidates at the federal level is adjusted according to the rise in the CONSUMER PRICE INDEX. In the 1984 federal general election 1449 candidates raised over $24.3 million from 116 653 contributors and spent almost $25.6 million, $11.1 million (43%) of which was reimbursed from the federal treasury. Total reported central registered party spending for the 1984 campaign amounted to $17.6 million, of which more than $4 million was reimbursed solely to the 3 parliamentary parties by the federal treasury. In the 1984 election year all parties raised over $44 million of which the PCs collected $21.1 million, the Liber-

als $10.6 million, and the NDs $6.5 million. These sums were more than twice the amounts raised by these parties in each of the 1979 and 1980 federal general elections. Parties are permitted a combined total of 6.5 hours broadcast time; the allocation to each party is roughly determined by the number of seats held and the size of the popular vote won by each party in the outgoing Parliament. Total spending by the parties in the 1980 campaign rose to almost $11.5 million, but the reimbursement was sharply higher, rising 25% to nearly $2.5 million because of the increase in broadcasting expenditures. The reimbursement of 50% of broadcasting time costs has now been transformed into a reimbursement of 22.5% of the total permitted costs of qualifying political parties.

Much of the mystery surrounding political funds has been eliminated, with consequent equity among political competitors, and escalation of costs has been checked. Grass-roots donations have been encouraged and the number of individual personal gifts has multiplied. Nevertheless, the 2 major parties (particularly the Liberals) still rely heavily on the corporate sector, as does Social Credit in BC. The New Democrats are still a grass-roots party but trade-union contributions and affiliation dues are important resources. Only in Québec are personal contributions a significant source of funds. Despite reforms, the financial dependence of the Canadian party system on corporations, on the trade-union elite and on the state persists. KHAYYAM Z. PALTIEL

Reading: Khayyam Z. Paltiel, *Political Party Financing in Canada* (1970); Howard R. Penniman, ed, *Canada at the Polls, 1984: A Study of the General Elections* (1988); *Report of the Advisory Committee on Election Expenses* (1966).

Party System Although Canada is often thought of as a 2-party system, it is more accurate to say that (federally) it is a multiparty system in which one party usually dominates. Nationally, since 1921, there have been representatives of at least 3 and sometimes 4 or 5 political parties in Parliament. The LIBERAL PARTY, the CONSERVATIVE PARTY and the CO-OPERATIVE COMMONWEALTH FEDERATION (and its successor the NEW DEMOCRATIC PARTY) have been represented in every Parliament since 1935. Other parties sometimes represented have included the PROGRESSIVE PARTY, the UNITED FARMERS OF ALBERTA, SOCIAL CREDIT, the BLOC POPULAIRE and the Labor Progressive Party. Indeed, more than 100 other political parties have run at least one candidate in an election. In 1987, 11 political parties were registered, ie, eligible to run candidates with the party name designated on the ballot, to receive donations and issue income-tax receipts, and to be reimbursed for certain expenses by the federal government. To be registered for a federal election, a political party must have had at least 12 members in the previous Parliament, or must nominate at least 50 candidates.

Provincially the situation is more complex. Not only have each of the Liberal, Conservative, CCF-NDP and Social Credit parties formed the governments of at least 2 provinces, but in provinces such as BC the NDP and the Social Credit are the only political parties to have formed governments in the last 30 years. Between 1936 and 1960, Québec politics was dominated by the UNION NATIONALE which was not represented in federal elections. Alberta has also been dominated by one party, as has Ontario.

Origins of Party System Despite the plethora of parties that have been formed to run candidates at the national level, only the Liberal and Conservative parties have ever had a realistic possibility of taking office. Both parties took shape in the mid-19th century. The Conservatives were formed from a Liberal-Conservative coalition; the Tories

and French-speaking *bleus* (see PARTI BLEU) in the Province of Canada allied with more liberal elements. The Liberal Party was created from a coalition of the CLEAR GRITS of Upper Canada, the anticlerical *rouges* (see PARTI ROUGE), and the reform element in the Maritimes. The 2 parties at their inception reflected religious, geographic and other differences. The Conservative Party was grounded in Toryism, ie, a belief in the importance of hierarchy or privilege in political and social life, in collectivism and in the nation as the fundamental basis of political life, but the party also absorbed tenets of "business liberalism," an important variant of liberalism. As a broad set of beliefs, liberalism is represented not only in the laissez-faire individualism of Western CONSERVATISM, but in the mild reformism of the moderates within the New Democratic Party. Liberalism asserts the paramountcy of the individual over the collectivity, and rejects the belief that individuals are fixed to predestined spots in a social hierarchy. Business liberalism identifies the state as a primary threat to individuals, and their freedom, particularly the right of individuals to behave as they please in the marketplace, but business liberals also attach great importance to the rule of law, the independence of the judiciary and the accountability of the executive to the legislature. In the 20th century, welfare liberalism, a rival variant, arose. Welfare liberals regard the concentrated power of large corporations as the chief menace to individual liberty and argue that the state has an important role to play in the redistribution of wealth.

In other competitive party systems, trade unions and co-operative movements are major sources of party funds, but historically (and currently) both the Liberals and Conservatives rely on the economic elite in Montréal and Toronto for PARTY FINANCING. In strategy, both parties discount the significance of class differences in Canada (see CLASS AND POLITICS), and have consequently found themselves in the difficult position of proclaiming a commitment to social reform while trying not to arouse the ire of their financial supporters. However, with the reforms in election financing in the 1970s this dependency has lessened, and both Liberals and Conservatives limit the size of any single contribution to avoid even the appearance that campaign contributions buy political favours.

In the 20th century, the party system in Canada was expanded by the growth of what have been described in C. Winn and J. McMenemy's *Political Parties in Canada* (1975) as movement or fragment parties, or a combination of both, the development of which was facilitated by the British parliamentary system employed in Canada. Because the focus of this system is the constituency, the election of only a few members of Parliament by a minor party still allows that party to criticize the government and initiate procedural motions in House of Commons debates. Fragment parties, ie, those established by a disenchanted ex-member of a parliamentary party have included the Nationalists, (founded by Henri BOURASSA), the Reconstruction Party (founded by H.H. STEVENS), the New Democracy Party (founded by W.D. Herridge) and Action Canada (founded by Paul HELLYER). These parties were mostly defined by the founder's ideology. Parties such as Social Credit and the Co-operative Commonwealth Federation originate in SOCIAL MOVEMENTS. A populist party, Social Credit was founded in Alberta by William ABERHART, and has been successful as a regional or provincial party but had limited success nationally. In Alberta, it was an alternative to the Conservative and Liberal parties on the federal level and the government of the United Farmers of Alberta, provincially. In Québec, where Social Credit erupted in 1962 under the leadership of Réal CAOUETTE, it exploited the hostility of rural and small-town dwellers to the economic and political establishment of the country (*see* CREDITISTES). The social democratic CCF, a federation of several groups and movements, rejected in its structure the model of the parliamentary parties to secure regular involvement of grass-roots members; this structure was modified in the CCF's transformation into the NDP.

The Progressives were a mixed movement led in Manitoba by T.A. CRERAR and the more radical Henry Wood in Alberta. They represented a dynamic interpretation of liberalism combined with some collectivist concerns; although they were short-lived as a national party, in the early 1930s some Progressive and UFA MPs helped found the CCF, and the Progressive premier of Manitoba, John BRACKEN, went on to become leader of the renamed Progressive Conservative Party.

Structure of the Party System All major Canadian political parties aim to promote objectives compatible with liberal-democratic values and hope to obtain their ends by achieving power through constitutional means within a parliamentary system of government. Canada's electoral system is based upon single-member constituencies, and a political party tries to win a majority of seats in a general election to form a government. The Conservative, Liberal and New Democratic parties maintain provincial associations under which are riding (constituency level) organizations that contest national and provincial elections. At annual or biennial meetings, the associations elect officers, adopt resolutions and organize party followers. The extra-parliamentary organizations are not tightly structured, and no party has a large dues-paying membership; active involvement by ordinary party members is minimal except at election time, though NDP supporters are on balance more committed.

The constitutions of all 3 federal parties protect bicultural and regional interests (eg, that of the Liberals provides for equal francophone and anglophone representation; the NDP selects an associate president and an associate secretary from a cultural group not represented by the president and secretary). Party constitutions authorize as well the appointment of paid officials. Despite some differences (eg, membership criteria), all 3 constitutions reinforce the authority of the national leader and seek to moderate internal dissension.

Each general election involves simultaneous elections in all of Canada's 282 (1987, 295 as of the next election) ridings, and in each constituency there may be candidates from registered political parties, as well as representatives of other parties without registered status, whose names appear on the ballot as "Independents." The first task of the constituency party is to choose its candidate; although the procedures for doing so are normally loosely established by the national political party, there is considerable autonomy accorded the local parties, and their practices vary widely. Usually the candidate is selected by a secret vote of all members resident in the constituency over the age of 14. Although membership in a constituency party of a major national party might normally run in the 200-500 range, this figure sometimes swells to 4000-5000 for nomination meetings. Because the rules for contested nominations are not clearly established and because these events normally involve the infusion into the party of large numbers of new members only weakly committed to the party as an institution, the system often produces conflict and tension.

Once the party's candidate is chosen, the local party tries to secure his or her election. The party will choose a campaign manager, rent a campaign office, and begin the process of publicizing the party and the candidate by signs and advertisements in the media. Closer to the election, it will organize door-to-door canvasses and the distribution of literature. After election day the party will quickly lapse into a loosely organized social club, guarding a desultory existence and waiting to be resurrected for the next election.

It is not easy to define the exact relationship between the various provincial parties and the national units with which they share a common name. For example, in Ontario membership between the federal and provincial parties is common, but in Québec there is no provincial Conservative Party, and membership in the federal and provincial Liberal parties is separate. BC's provincial Social Credit Party has weak ties with its federal counterpart, while in practice it has close informal ties with the federal BC Conservatives who in turn largely neglect their politically insignificant provincial counterpart. Even where party membership overlaps between federal and provincial parties, it is not uncommon for either activists or ordinary members to have strong preferences for one level or the other. In most provinces, many voters consistently choose one party at the provincial level and another in federal elections. NDP supporters tend to be more consistent in their voting patterns, but even here there is considerable movement in voting preferences between one election and the next.

The primary task of both provincial and federal parties is to choose the party leader (in effect the party's candidate for premier or prime minister) and then secure the election of a sufficient number of party supporters. Election of party leaders normally takes place after the resignation or death of the incumbent, although most parties have provisions for forcing a LEADERSHIP CONVENTION on an unwilling leader. The parties also elect a president and other executive members whose job it is to manage the party's administrative apparatus. As well as leadership conventions, most parties also hold policy conventions, usually every 2 years. There is often controversy between the MPs and participants in policy conventions as to how far the elected members are bound by the content of resolutions.

In a general election, it is the task of the national party to manage the overall national campaign. It plans the leader's tour, raises and spends money on advertising and campaign literature, and distributes money and other resources. At other times, the parties operate offices with a small but paid staff, whose responsibility it is to conduct party business and to co-ordinate the various constituency, provincial and national organizations. There is sometimes a conflict between the extra-parliamentary party and the senators and elected MPs. The latter see themselves as the top of the power pyramid and consider the volunteer and paid party workers as their agents, whereas the volunteers especially often consider themselves important political forces within the constituency, or within the provincial or national party, and view the elected MPs as their representatives. The parliamentary caucuses of the major parties have always tended to be unrepresentative of the nation as a whole, and even of their own voters. From the late 1960s until recently the Conservatives were very weak in Québec, while the Liberals suffered in western Canada. The New Democratic Party, which was very weak in Québec, was somewhat divided between its Ontario wing, which provided much of its popular vote, and the western wing which contributed the majority of elected members.

However, all 3 of the major national parties attempt to field candidates in each of the country's constituencies, and each party ensures that its national leader will be prominently displayed in every area of the country. In general, the Liberal Party has historically been supported by Catholics, urban dwellers, French Canadians, recent immigrants, the moderately well-to-do and professionals. The Conservative Party usually attracts greater support from Canadians of British origin, small town and rural dwellers, Protestants and small businessmen. The NDP usually draws strongly from Protestants, union members, urban dwellers in Ontario, rural dwellers in the West and the better educated. Although the NDP is strongly identified by the public with the trade-union movement, the party wins most of its seats in areas that are not heavily unionized and does not receive a majority of the votes cast by union households. It is too early to determine if the 1984 federal election, which saw a major Conservative victory and significant gains in Québec, will represent the beginning of a long-term change in traditional voting patterns. By 1987 some of the Conservative support in Québec had dissipated; some of it going, unprecedentedly, to the NDP.

The party system in Canada has major failings. First, too few Canadians are directly involved in political activities. Second, Canadian parties generate few important policies. Governments rely heavily on the civil service and other experts for ideas. Party policies are rarely pressed by governments until the policies have been approved by the bureaucratic elite. Finally, the party system has been only partly successful in enhancing national unity. Although the parties have struggled to maintain their status as national institutions, the Liberal Party has generally been identified with the interests of central Canada and the Conservative Party with those of western Canada. Conflict, instead of being contained and resolved within political parties, has often been exacerbated because partisan controversy and distrust have complicated already difficult economic and social questions. WILLIAM CHRISTIAN

Reading: William Christian and C. Campbell, *Political Parties and Ideologies in Canada* (1983); G.C. Perlin, *The Tory Syndrome* (1980); J. Wearing, *The L-Shaped Party: The Liberal Party of Canada 1958-1980* (1981); H. Thorburn, ed, *Party Politics in Canada* (5th ed, 1985).

Party Whip, member of a party caucus who ensures that the number of MPs in the legislature, or at committee meetings, is adequate to win a vote if one is called. The division bells in the HOUSE OF COMMONS ring until whips are satisfied that sufficient members of their own party are present. They can offer a few minor rewards, eg, trips and committee membership, but have few effective punishments and rely more on persuasion than coercion. They also arrange the order of speakers in the legislature, facilitating the Speaker's job. ROBERT J. JACKSON

Pasadena, Nfld, Town, pop 3268 (1986c), inc 1955, is situated on the shores of Deer Lake in the Humber Valley region of W Newfoundland, 25 km from the seaport and paper milling centre of Corner Brook. Founded in the early 1930s by Leonard Earle as a 10 km² mixed-farming operation, Pasadena, which means "Crown of the Valley," was named after Pasadena, California. The importance of farming lessened after Confederation in 1949 and Pasadena has evolved as a residential community with a growing light industrial and commercial base. It has 2 industrial parks and the first incubator mall in Newfoundland, called the "Venture Centre." Pasadena is also the site of a Geological Core Storage Library research facility operated by the provincial government, which has made the community a centre for mining exploration and development in W and central Nfld. ROBERT D. PITT

Passamaquoddy Bay is a small inlet near the mouth of the Bay of FUNDY. Its mouth is restricted by a chain of islands, including DEER and CAMPOBELLO, and strong tides (range 8.3 m) prevail in the region. Rich fisheries for herring and lobster occur here, and the St Andrews Marine Biological Station on its shores is an important research centre. Because of the tides and topography, several schemes for TIDAL ENERGY development have been proposed in the past. Recent international controversy relates to the passage of supertankers through Canadian waters in the region to reach a proposed refinery at Eastport, Maine.

P.C. SMITH AND R.J. CONOVER

Passchendaele (Passendale, Belgium) In 1917 the Germans began unrestricted submarine warfare, Russia crumbled under the impact of revolution and withdrew from WORLD WAR I, and part of the French army mutinied following the failure of Gen Nivelle's spring offensive. To relieve the resulting German pressure on the Allied forces, British Commander in Chief Gen Sir Douglas Haig launched an attack from the British front, which proved the most controversial of the entire war. After the British and Australian/New Zealand troops had fought weeks of grinding battle resulting in many casualties, on Oct 26 Lt-Gen Sir Arthur CURRIE's Canadian Corps attacked over terrain that resembled a quagmire. By Nov 7, having endured appalling conditions and having suffered over 15 000 dead and wounded, the Canadians seized Passchendaele and with it 5 km² of mud. Haig has been severely criticized for prolonging his attack, but the Canadians displayed high standards of leadership, staff work and training, and succeeded where all others had failed. Nine VICTORIA CROSSES were awarded to Canadians after the battle. R.H. ROY

Reading: D.G. Dancocks, *Legacy of Valour* (1986).

Passenger Pigeon (*Ectopistes migratorius*) is extinct. Also known as wild PIGEON, this largish, long-tailed species (family Columbidae) was once abundant, nesting in vast, densely populated colonies and migrating in flocks that, at times, darkened the sky for hours or even days. The habit of concentrating in great numbers proved disastrous because it facilitated mass slaughter by man. The species was gunned, netted and clubbed into oblivion. Its decline from the uncountable numbers that were one of the natural wonders of the continent became precipitous 1871-80. Because only one egg per clutch was being laid, the passenger pigeon's reproductive potential was inadequate to maintain the sadly decreased and scattered populations that remained late in the 19th century. The last known specimen taken in the wild was at Sargento, Ohio, on 24 Mar 1900. The last survivor died on 1 Sept 1914 in a zoo in Cincinnati, Ohio. In Canada, the passenger pigeon was a summer resident, nesting from the Maritimes through southern

View of Fort Erie with Migration of Wild Pigeons in Spring (1804). The concentration of the passenger pigeon led to easy slaughter and the bird's eventual obliteration (*courtesy Royal Ontario Museum*).

Québec, Ontario, Manitoba, central-eastern Saskatchewan and probably parts of Alberta. It was last recorded in Canada on 18 May 1902 at Penetanguishene, Ont. Specimens were last taken in 1898 at Lk Winnipegosis, Man, and in 1899 at Scotch Lk, NB. W. EARL GODFREY

Patent A patent may be granted in Canada to an inventor who submits an application to the Canadian Patent Office, setting out the details of the invention and the reasons why the inventor believes it to be a major step forward in the art. If successful, the patent holder is given the exclusive rights to produce the invention. Before 1987, the patent was awarded to the first and true inventor provided that the invention was useful and novel (not known or used previously in Canada, and not disclosed by publication more than 2 years prior to application). The 1987 amendments define the inventor as the first to file a novel application (not known, used or published prior to application).

At the Patent Office, the application is examined by technically qualified staff to determine whether it fully discloses the claims and meets the tests of novelty and utility. The patentee then receives the exclusive rights to use the invention for a period of 17 years (increased to 20 years by 1987 amendments). Special provisions in the case of food, drugs and atomic energy attempt to ensure that the rights are not used to the detriment of the public. The Commissioner of Patents may also take steps to ensure that the Canadian market is being properly supplied. Licences to produce patented drugs under generic names may be obtained after a period of time (increased from 3 years to 10 by 1987 amendments; *see* PHARMACEUTICAL INDUSTRY).

International patent protection is available through the Union for the Protection of Industrial Property which allows for registration of a patent in other countries of the union. Further, an inventor has one year within which to file in other union countries and thus preserve his original filing day in Canada. PETER J.M. LOWN

Patents, Copyright and Industrial Designs, Royal Commission on, sat between 1954 and 1960. Its brief was "to enquire as to whether federal legislation relating in any way to patents of invention, industrial designs, copyright and trademarks affords reasonable incentive to invention and research, to the development of literary and artistic talents, to creativeness, and to making available to the Canadian public scientific, technical, literary and artistic creations and other adaptations, applications and uses, in a manner and on terms adequately safeguarding the paramount public interest." The commission later requested that TRADEMARKS be removed from its brief. Three reports were published: *Copyright*, Aug 1957; *Industrial Designs*, June 1958; and *Patents of Invention*, Dec 1959. Chaired by J.L. ILSLEY, the commission heard from various public and private organizations and from individuals. In June 1966 the ECONOMIC COUNCIL OF CANADA examined the issues dealt with by the Ilsley Commission and, over the next 5 years, published a series of reports, including Special Study No 8, *Science, Technology and Innovation*, by A.H. Wilson, in 1968. The report emphasized the importance of innovation to industry. ADRIANA A. DAVIES

Patrick, Lester (b at Drummondville, Qué 30 Dec 1883; d at Victoria 1 June 1960), patriarch of a family which dominated the early development of HOCKEY as players and managers. Lester and his brother Frank Patrick (b at Ottawa 21 Dec 1885; d at Vancouver 29 June 1960) both starred with McGill U and played professionally with teams in Montréal and Westmount, and with the Renfrew Millionaires (at $3000 each per season). With their father's support (he was a millionaire lum-

berman) they formed the Pacific Coast Hockey League in 1911. They built arenas for all teams in the league and Lester played for Victoria, Spokane and Seattle before settling as player-coach and manager in Victoria, where the brothers built Canada's first artificial ice rink. In 1924 Lester coached and managed the Victoria Cougars to a STANLEY CUP victory, but faced with increasing competition from the expanding NATIONAL HOCKEY LEAGUE, he sold his entire roster to NHL owners. He became coach of the NHL's New York Rangers in 1926. In 1928, at age 48, he replaced his injured goaltender in a Stanley Cup match, preserving a Ranger victory, and creating one of hockey's enduring legends. He retired as coach in 1939 and as manager in 1946. Frank Patrick coached Boston and managed the Canadiens, but is best remembered for his innovations – 22 pieces of legislation in the NHL rulebook, including the blue line, were proposed by him.

Lynn Patrick, son of Lester (b at Victoria, BC 3 Feb 1912; d at St Louis, Mo 26 Jan 1980), joined the Rangers in 1934, playing left wing on a superb line with Bryan Hextall and Phil Watson. He was first team all star in 1942 and was later coach of the Rangers and Bruins and manager of St Louis Blues.

Frederick Murray "Muzz" Patrick, son of Lester (b at Victoria, BC 28 June 1916), was a superb all-round athlete, but a less adept skater than his brother. He was a defenceman with the Rangers 1937-41 and 1945-46 and their coach 1954-55 and general manager 1955-64.

The Lester Patrick Memorial Trophy is awarded annually to the person contributing most to the development of hockey in the US. JAMES MARSH

Patrick, Thomas Alfred, physician, legislator (b at Ilderton, Ont 23 Dec 1864; d at North Battleford, Sask 6 Sept 1943). After graduating from Western in 1888, Patrick practised medicine and surgery in Saltcoats, Sask, until 1894 and in Yorkton, Sask, until 1939. Elected from Yorkton to the North-West Territories Assembly in 1897, he used his slogan "No Annexation of Manitoba" on campaign buttons in 1898, and won decisive reelection on a "2-province" platform in 1902. He was the first to propose the present boundaries of Saskatchewan and Alberta. C. STUART HOUSTON

Patrick, William, clergyman, educator (b at Glasgow, Scot 8 Sept 1852; d at Kirkintilloch, Scot 28 Sept 1911). After studying theology at the Free Church Coll in Glasgow, he was ordained in 1878. He combined an active involvement in education with his pastoral duties and in 1900 was appointed principal of Winnipeg's Manitoba Coll, where he taught philosophy and New Testament courses until his untimely death. During his career in Canada, Patrick was a member of the Social Reform Council of Canada, acted on the royal commission to establish an agricultural college for Manitoba, and was also a strong and respected Presbyterian leader in the church union movement. NEIL SEMPLE

Patriotes, the name given after 1826 to the PARTI CANADIEN and to the popular movement that contributed to the REBELLIONS OF 1837-38 in Lower Canada. The primarily francophone party, led mainly by members of the liberal professions and small-scale merchants, was widely supported by farmers, day-labourers and craftsmen. Its more distinguished leaders included Louis-Joseph PAPINEAU, Jean-Olivier Chénier and Wolfred Nelson.

Though the Patriotes dominated the elected House of Assembly in LOWER CANADA, their adversaries, the merchant bourgeoisie, the aristocracy and the colonial administration, controlled the appointed Legislative Council, which held most of the power. The Patriotes demanded greater power for assembly members, including increased ministerial responsibility and eligibility for appointment to the council. Their demands, put forth in the name of democracy and the right of peoples to self-government, marked a liberal, nationalist and anticolonial ideology.

Some historians state that the Patriotes' political program included a comprehensive economic-development project for all Lower Canada, designed to benefit the majority of its inhabitants and, of course, their representatives. Others argue that, behind a liberal façade, this was really a retrograde and conservative socioeconomic goal. The Patriotes, except for those of 1838, favoured the retention of the SEIGNEURIAL SYSTEM and more readily supported agricultural than commercial interests. By blocking the economic projects of their adversaries, they delayed the development of British capitalism in the colony. But their positions were neither that clear nor that rigid. As social and economic conflict intensified during the 1830s, the party radicalized both its tactics and its goals, though not without some schisms between its moderate and extremist factions.

In 1834 the Patriotes listed their major complaints in the "Ninety-Two Resolutions" sent to the British government. Britain rejected this call for reform and settled the quarrel over subsidies through the Russell Resolutions of Mar 1837, which authorized the governor of the colony to obtain his budgetary estimates without a vote of the assembly. This decision caused many demonstrations; verbal violence soon gave way to physical violence. The Rebellions of 1837-38 were followed by the torching of Patriotes' homes, imprisonments, exiles, trials and hangings. The failure of the rebellions led to the disappearance of the Parti patriote. Some former leaders, however, returned to active politics in the united PROVINCE OF CANADA. *See also* FILS DE LA LIBERTÉ.
                                                      FERNANDE ROY

Patronage There are many kinds of patronage, eg, the appointment of judges, members of academic and artistic councils, etc. Political patronage is the dispensation of favours, eg, public office, jobs, contracts, subsidies, prestige, etc, by a patron (who controls their dispensation) to a client who cannot obtain the job, etc, by other means and who offers in return to vote for the patron's party or to provide money or manpower for electoral campaigning. The patron (eg, a politician) has access to resources which the client (eg, a businessman) could not otherwise obtain, even though the client's economic resources might exceed the patron's. The relationship between patron and client is usually selective and discretionary; the patron does not generally grant favours to all potential clients but picks and chooses among them. The client may be in direct contact with a patron who controls the resource distribution, eg, a minister may reward election organizers by appointing them as office staff, but clients and patrons may also be linked by a go-between. The patron may be an elected member or an election organizer who needs to approach a minister or the prime minister to obtain the favour for the client. The favour may also be obtained via an intermediary, eg, a civil servant or a politician obeying the orders of a patron. The resources – a job or position, information, prestige, material rewards – may be just as diverse.

Unlike patronage, CORRUPTION is deleterious conduct which gives an individual or group some private advantage thought to be contrary to public interest. Corruption may become part of patronage. For example, it is considered preferable that government contracts go to the lowest bidder; when a client uses influence to win a contract even though his bid is higher than others, it is said

that corruption has become part of political patronage. If a minister uses his expense money for personal pleasure, some people will call that corruption, even though it does not involve patronage. Some patronage practices are considered corrupt by intellectuals or journalists but not by politicians and their clients. For example, if an important position is given to a supporter of the governing party, this may be viewed by some as corrupt conduct, but politicians argue that if all applicants are equally competent it is normal to choose a friend over an adversary or stranger. Celebrated controversial examples of patronage (and corruption) include the PACIFIC SCANDAL, in the 19th century, and the Beauharnois Scandal of the late 1920s. In both cases individuals linked with political parties privately benefited from major public-works projects in a manner generally considered contrary to public interest.

Patronage is defended as a process that makes job, contract and subsidy allocation less expensive and as an antidote to the excessive bureaucratization of government, but others consider it to be a questionable use of public money. Many American observers claim that it can reinforce party unity and discipline among its members, but a good part of the Canadian intelligentsia oppose practices that they think undermine the principles of merit and equal access for all to the benefits of the state. It is difficult not to judge this as a class reaction; the disadvantaged members of society have long approved of (and still approve of) patronage when they have no other access to resources, while the intelligentsia, who have other means of obtaining what they want from the state, oppose patronage. However, as minor patronage, which favours the disadvantaged, declines, patronage favouring the middle and upper classes, eg, contracts and nominations to high positions, is increasing.

Less dramatically and more persistently, political machines have traditionally used patronage to maintain their advantage over rivals. The machines created by the Liberal and Progressive Conservative parties, by the Union Nationale in Québec and by Social Credit in BC existed in every region of Canada until 1960, but since then Parliament and several provincial legislatures have attempted to control political donations and election spending, and laws governing election practices and PARTY FINANCING have been tightened. The PUBLIC SERVICE has also become less vulnerable to patronage and corruption because the merit principle generally governs recruitment and promotion. Where civil servants are unionized, resistance to such practices is even greater. The spread of the WELFARE STATE has increased the number of political measures available to all, with a corresponding decrease in the more personalized and specialized individual relationships. The weakening of family ties and religious culture has also weakened the cultural and social bases for patronage, especially in Roman Catholic or rural areas. The increased ideological content of politics has also helped reduce patronage. Even so, patronage and corruption will never disappear; wherever competing parties have to depend on the support of friends against enemies, they will use patronage to win victory and offer rewards. Patronage remains an evocative issue in Canada at all political levels. Media coverage of the issue culminated in 1987 with Claire Hoy's popular book *Friends in High Places: Politics and Patronage in the Mulroney Government*. *See also* CONFLICT OF INTEREST.
                                                   VINCENT LEMIEUX

Patsalas, Constantin, choreographer, character dancer (b at Thessaloníki, Greece 1 Aug 1943). Trained in Germany, Patsalas joined the NATIONAL BALLET OF CANADA in 1972, becoming resident

choreographer in 1980. His ballets range widely in style from the abstract (*Rite of Spring, Nataraja*) to the romantic (*L'Île inconnue*) or even punk (*Past of the Future*), but his imaginative CHOREOGRAPHY is unified by its uncompromising stylistic faithfulness to the inspiring score, its structural integrity and its inventive exploration of dynamic contrasts in mood and movements. Patsalas left the National Ballet in Sept 1986.   PENELOPE DOOB

Patterson, Freeman Wilford, photographer (b at Long Reach, NB 25 Sept 1937). Patterson began his photographic career in 1965. An early success was his contribution of 75 colour images to *Canada: A Year of the Land* (1967). Besides freelancing, Patterson helped organize the National Assn for Photographic Art and edited its magazine, *Camera Canada*, for 10 years. Since 1973 he has devoted himself to his own photography and writing, and to teaching photography and visual design throughout Canada and the US and in Africa. Patterson's 5 books (*Photography for the Joy of It*, 1977; *Photography and the Art of Seeing*, 1979; *Photography of Natural Things*, 1982; *Namaqualand: Garden of the Gods*, 1984; and *Portraits of Earth*, 1987) provide considerable information on the technical as well as aesthetic aspects of PHOTOGRAPHY. The texts are illustrated with his own photographs, which reflect his documentary and interpretive approaches.   LOUISE ABBOTT

Patterson, Harold, football player (b at Rozel, Kan 1933). He became a star CFL player early in his 14-year career as a member of the vaunted MONTREAL ALOUETTE passing attack led by quarterback Sam Etcheverry from 1954 to 1960. In 1956 he enjoyed a season virtually unequalled in CFL history, catching 88 passes for 1914 yards in 14 games, records that lasted for 11 and 17 years. His record of 338 yards receiving was set that year and still stands, as does his record for the longest completion (109 yards, shared). He also won the scoring title and received the SCHENLEY AWARD that year. He was traded to HAMILTON TIGER-CATS in 1961, where he played on 3 Grey Cup champions. His career totals of 460 receptions, 9473 yards and 64 touchdowns place him among the finest receivers ever to play in the CFL. His class and physical grace earned him the nickname "Prince Hal."   PETER WONS

Patterson, John, meteorologist (b in Oxford County, Ont 3 Jan 1872; d at Clarkson, Ont 22 Feb 1956). Educated at U of T and Cambridge, Patterson returned to Canada in 1910 after serving in India as professor and imperial meteorologist. He designed a pilot-balloon system for studying the upper air and developed a new anemometer and a new barometer for operational use. In 1929 Patterson succeeded Sir Frederic STUPART as director of the national meteorological service, a position he held until 1946. Under his leadership, the service survived the Depression and expanded tenfold to meet wartime needs, providing meteorological services for the new TRANS-CANADA AIRLINES and for the BRITISH COMMONWEALTH AIR TRAINING PLAN and the Home War units. A fellow of the RSC, he was in 1954 the first recipient of the Patterson Medal for distinguished service to METEOROLOGY. MORLEY THOMAS

Patterson, Walter, army officer, colonial administrator (b 1735? in County Donegal, Ire; d at London, Eng 6 Sept 1798). He served briefly with the British army in America during the SEVEN YEARS' WAR and arrived in Charlottetown in Aug 1770 as the first British governor of the Island of St John (renamed Prince Edward I in 1799). His tenure (1769-87) was remarkable for land speculation and political uproar, but his outstanding legacy was the entrenchment of PEI as a separate political entity. The problems of his new charge were enormous: the total population was but a few hundred; the officers of government were inexperienced; and his administration had no reliable financial basis. Within a few years he had established a rudimentary government including a House of Assembly (1773); and in 1777 he succeeded in securing for the colony an annual grant of £3000. Land speculation proved Patterson's undoing. Through considerable political manipulation, he gained the tenuous possession of over 40 000 ha. In the words of Captain John MacDonald, an opponent, he "would have done extremely well, had he known where to stop." Dismissed in 1787, he was stripped of his property by his political adversaries and died in poverty. *See also* LAND QUESTION, PEI. HARRY BAGLOLE

Patterson, William John, premier of Saskatchewan 1935-44 (b at Grenfell, Sask 13 May 1886; d at Regina 10 June 1976). First elected to the Saskatchewan legislature in 1921, the popular, though prudent, Patterson became the first Saskatchewan-born premier when he succeeded James GARDINER in 1935. Although he inherited a formidable political machine, Patterson provided uninspiring leadership during the Depression and then WWII. The CO-OPERATIVE COMMONWEALTH FEDERATION, meanwhile, broadened its base of support by playing down government ownership in favour of government planning. In June 1944 the CCF under T.C. DOUGLAS won a decisive victory, reducing the once powerful Liberal Party to 5 seats. Patterson resigned as Liberal leader in 1946 and subsequently served as the province's lieutenant-governor 1951-58. He was the first person in the province's history to hold both posts of premier and lieutenant-governor. W.A. WAISER

Pattison, James Allen, entrepreneur (b at Saskatoon 1 Oct 1928). Pattison was raised in Vancouver. He became a used-car dealer in 1952 and in 1961 he bought a dealership, which he built into one of the largest in western Canada. In 1967 he acquired Neon Products, a national manufacturer and lessor of signs. Since then he has purchased over 50 other companies including airlines, soft-drink producers and magazine distributors. Although the recession of 1982-83 led to cutbacks and layoffs in a number of his companies, the assets of Jim Pattison Group amounted to over $700 million in 1986. A ruthlessly efficient businessman and devout Christian, Pattison's diligent management was largely credited with the success of EXPO 86. He is a Member of the Order of Canada. CHRISTOPHER G. CURTIS

Pattullo, Thomas Dufferin, politician, businessman, public servant, premier of BC (b at Woodstock, Ont 19 Jan 1873; d at Victoria 30 Mar 1956). Though best known as premier of BC during the 1930s, Pattullo had a long, varied career before that. He worked for the Woodstock *Sentinel* and in 1896 became editor of the Galt *Reformer*. His father's Liberal Party connections gained him the position of secretary to J.M. WALSH, commissioner of the Yukon Territory, in 1897. Pattullo worked in government service in Dawson City until 1902, becoming acting assistant gold commissioner. He then formed a business partnership in real estate and insurance, and for a time was a member of the Dawson City council. In 1908 he moved to Prince Rupert to open a branch office. He was alderman and mayor of the town, and in 1916 was elected to the BC Assembly, becoming minister of lands in the new Liberal government. After the Liberals' defeat in 1928, he became leader of the Opposition. Revitalizing the party, he led it to victory 1933 and became premier. Faced with the tremendous economic and social problems of the GREAT DEPRESSION, Pattullo was innovative in extending the role of government. His frustration with the limitations of provincial power led to a battle with Ottawa that resulted in a reappraisal of Canadian federalism. After an inconclusive 1941 election, he rejected a coalition with the Conservatives and was rebuffed by his own party. Defeated in 1945 in his old riding of Prince Rupert, he retired to Victoria. ROBIN FISHER

Reading: M.A. Ormsby, "T. Dufferin Pattullo and the Little New Deal," *Canadian Historical Review* 43 (1962).

Paul, Robert, figure skater (b at Toronto 2 June 1937). A specialist in pairs skating, Paul started skating with Barbara WAGNER in 1952, and in 1954 they placed 3rd in the N American championships. In 1957, over 16 days, they won the Canadian, N American and world championships and held them for the next 3 years. They won the gold medal at the 1960 Squaw Valley, Calif, Olympics, the first non-Europeans to win the pairs event. After 1960 they continued to skate together on the professional circuit. The partnership was dissolved in 1964, and Paul became a skating choreographer and coach in the US. BARBARA SCHRODT

Paula Ross Dance Company, founded in the mid-1960s, incorporated 1973, was one of the few Canadian dance groups with a clearly defined movement style and artistic point of view. Despite many difficult years of financial and organizational problems, Paula Ross created a large repertoire of work reflecting her personal vision and her commitment to social and political issues. She received the Jean A. Chalmers Award for Choreography in 1977. The company has been inactive since 1986. GRANT STRATE

Paull, Andrew, Squamish leader, organizer, lobbyist (b at Squamish, BC 6 Feb 1892; d at Vancouver 28 July 1959). Born into a prominent family in the Durieu system at Mission Reserve No 1, Burrard Inlet, Paull was educated at the reserve school and became a longshoreman. Secretary of his band, he was interpreter for the royal commission of 1913 to 1916. A member of the executive of the Allied Tribes of BC, he testified before a special joint committee in Ottawa in 1927. At home he organized bands and orchestras, athletic events, beauty contests, employment services and labour groups. In 1942 he joined the Native Brotherhood of BC, becoming its business manager, but in 1945 he broke with it and formed the North American Indian Brotherhood. In the late 1940s he testified before parliamentary committees considering Indian Act revisions, memorizing long portions of documents. E. P. PATTERSON II

Pauta Saila, sculptor (b at a hunting camp on the W coast S Baffin I, NWT Dec 1917). Technically skilful on paper or in stone, Pauta is known particularly for his "dancing bears," powerful, somewhat abstract sculptures of upright polar bears. The son of Saila, an important Inuit leader, Pauta grew up on his father's immense SW Baffin hunting territory and knows the habits of polar bears from close observation. He lives with his second wife, well-known graphic artist Pitaloosie, at Cape Dorset, and some 40 of his own drawings have been published as prints. Widely exhibited, his best-known work may be his massive *Bear*, executed in 1967 during the International Sculpture Symposium in High Park, Toronto, and now at the McMichael Collection at Kleinburg, Ont. DOROTHY HARLEY EBER

Pavelic, Myfanwy Spencer, painter (b at Victoria 27 Apr 1916). Largely self-taught, Pavelic's talent was noticed early by Emily CARR, who arranged an exhibition of her work in 1934. From 1944 to 1960 she spent much time in New York. The abstract art so prevalent there made her question her own style. However, the human figure remained her prime interest and her mature style is dominated by humanistic and meditative tendencies. In 1983 the British National Portrait Gallery accepted Pavelic's portrait of Yehudi Menuhin to hang in its permanent collection – the first Canadian-born artist so honoured. Pavelic was a founding member of the Society of Limners (1971), a Victoria group of artists named after the travelling journeymen painters of the Middle Ages. KATHLEEN LAVERTY

Pawley, Howard Russell, politician, premier of Manitoba (b at Brampton, Ont 21 Nov 1934). Raised in a Methodist home, Pawley moved to Winnipeg at age 17 and was educated at Manitoba Teachers Coll, United Coll and Manitoba Law School. First elected as MLA for Selkirk in 1969, he was re-elected in 1973, 1977 and 1981. In Premier Edward SCHREYER's New Democratic Party administration, Pawley held the portfolios of minister of municipal affairs (1969-76) and attorney general (1973-77). After the Schreyer government's defeat, Pawley served in Opposition and was elected permanent leader of the NDP of Manitoba in Nov 1979.

Pawley led his party to victory in the Nov 1981 and March 1986 elections. The most controversial action by the Pawley government during its first term was the introduction of a resolution entrenching French-language rights. Political opposition forced the government to refer the matter to the Supreme Court which ruled in June 1985 that the province would have to translate past and future laws into French as well as English. In order to achieve re-election, the Pawley government avoided controversial initiatives for the remainder of its first term, a cautious approach that was dropped during its second term. On the national scene, Pawley has become more prominent, questioning the erosion of federal power under the MEECH LAKE ACCORD and the proposed FREE TRADE agreement with the US in 1987-88. PAUL G. THOMAS

Pawnbroking People in need of quick cash loans may bring personal items, eg, clocks, musical instruments and pieces of jewellery, to a pawnbroker as collateral. If the loan is not repaid within a specified time, the pawnbroker may sell the item. Thus, pawnshops operate as lending institutions and as retail stores.

The procedure of pawning an item is similar across Canada. A pawnbroker inquires how much an individual is hoping to borrow. If the item is acceptable to the pawnbroker, a quick appraisal is done. Many pawnshops have trained gemologists on staff to appraise precious stones. The pawnbroker names the amount he is willing to lend and issues a pawn ticket to the customer. The loan is usually up to 25% of the value of the merchandise but may be as low as a few dollars. The item may be reclaimed at any time within the loan period marked on the ticket by full repayment of the loan, plus INTEREST and nominal service and storage charges. Pawnshops are, in fact, frequented by a cross section of Canadians. Part of the appeal of this avenue of acquiring ready cash is that no explanation is required regarding why the money is needed.

Because human need, greed and desperation are intrinsic to this trade, pawnbroking has had a colourful past and some murky connotations. Unscrupulous lenders were known in the past to strip desperate clients by accepting clothes, shoes, false teeth and glass eyes; to charge usurious interest rates; or to sell someone's cherished possession almost as soon as he or she had pledged it and left the shop. As well, some thieves saw pawnshops as places to dump stolen goods.

However, pawnbroking in Canada today is so well regulated that nearly all risks – both to borrowers and shoppers – as well as some of the drama have disappeared. A federal Pawnbrokers' Act was passed in 1886, and more recently various provincial laws concerning pawnbroking have come into effect. In general, the areas that are regulated include the safekeeping of objects left as collateral; the level of interest rates that may be charged; the length of time pledged items must be kept before being sold (usually one year); and requirements for municipal licensing. Local police usually monitor pawnbroking businesses by checking the pawnbrokers' daily records of transactions against lists of stolen goods.

Though pawnshop merchandise is often still a grab bag of odd items, pawnbrokers in Canada are more selective, some specializing only in precious metals. Approximately 80% of the items placed are redeemed by their owners. RUTH DANYS

Pay Television Although undertaken experimentally in Etobicoke, Ont, between 1960 and 1965, pay television as a major venture was licensed only in Mar 1982, after a decade of debate. Promoted for many years by the CABLE TELEVISION industry for its moneymaking potential, pay television had been opposed by established broadcasters who feared the competition, by telephone companies who resisted cable's proliferation of services and technological advance, and by cultural nationalists. The CANADIAN RADIO-TELEVISION AND TELECOMMUNICATIONS COMMISSION, in 1975 and again in 1978, having undertaken inquiries as to the desirability of introducing pay TV to Canada, concluded that inauguration was "premature." The CRTC believed pay TV would simply constitute another channel for American programming and would undermine the financial base of Canadian broadcasting (see BROADCASTING, RADIO AND TELEVISION; TELEVISION PROGRAMMING).

Nonetheless, under request from the federal Dept of Communications in 1979, the CRTC initiated a third inquiry, the Therrien Committee, which duly reported in 1980, recommending that a competitive industry be authorized. The Dept of Communications, with a mandate broader than the cultural objectives of the CRTC, has viewed pay TV as a means of stimulating satellite usage and furthering development in HIGH TECHNOLOGY industries. Therrien's recommendations were accepted by the government and the CRTC.

In 1982 the CRTC inaugurated a discretionary, pay-per-channel pay-television industry in the private sector. At one stroke 6 services were licensed – a national general-interest service (in English and French), 3 regional general-interest channels, a performing arts service, and a regional multilingual service. Subsequently, additional regional channels were authorized. For all but the multilingual licensee, progressively increasing time and revenue quotas were imposed to be allocated to Canadian programming. However, the CRTC chose not to regulate dealings between the pay companies and either program suppliers or exhibitors (cable companies); likewise, the retail price to the subscriber was left unregulated. In Feb 1983 the pay services became operational, utilizing SATELLITES to deliver programming to cable systems, which in turn billed subscribers about $16 per month for a single channel (see SATELLITE COMMUNICATIONS).

Controversies soon broke out anew, however. First Choice, the national, general-interest licensee, announced in Jan 1983 a joint venture with an American production company whereby $30 million in "adult" films would be produced to help meet Canadian regulatory obligations. Thousands marched and wrote letters to the CRTC in protest (see PORNOGRAPHY); the commis-

sion then requested the industry to draw up guidelines for self-regulation. In the spring of 1983 it became apparent that licensees could fulfil their programming obligations through "scaffolding," eg, by flowing through preproduction revenues from US sources and counting these as contributions for regulatory purposes.

During 1983-84 the industry faced severe shakedowns as projected subscriptions did not materialize. The arts network, C-Channel, collapsed after 17 weeks; Star Channel, the Atlantic regional licensee, eventually was shut down; the French-language regional service, TVEC, merged with First Choice which was itself refinanced and taken over by a film production/distribution company. Nonetheless, in 1984 a new round of licensing took place as "specialty" channels, which were to combine ADVERTISING and subscriber fees, were authorized for satellite delivery to cable systems. Since that time other specialty channels (all-news, religion, children's channels etc) have been licensed as well. In 1987 only 2 of the original pay licences remained, each now afforded regional monopolies: First Choice east of Manitoba and Superchannel. By packaging the movie channel with specialty services, and eliminating direct competition, the pay industry finally began to turn a profit.

Pay TV is a radical departure from historic broadcasting policy. First, the industry has no publicly owned or nonprofit oriented component; indeed, a competitive structure was immediately introduced with a view to giving market forces important play. Second, highest priority was accorded to increased diversity in production sources and viewing options, to be contrasted with the cultural and political goals heretofore dominant. Finally, with these decisions, it is apparent that communication policy is being formulated increasingly with a view to stimulating COMMUNICATIONS TECHNOLOGY and that cultural concerns respecting the nature of the programming are in decline. ROBERT E. BABE

Reading: CRTC, Committee on Extension of Service to Northern and Remote Communities [Therrien Committee], *The 1980's: A Decade of Diversity – Broadcasting, Satellites and Pay-TV* (1980); J. Meisel, "An Audible Squeak: Broadcast Regulation in Canada," in *Cultures in Collision: The Interaction of Canadian and US Television Broadcast Policy* (1984); R.B. Woodrow and K.B. Woodside, eds, *The Introduction of Pay TV in Canada* (1982); Task Force on Broadcasting Policy, *Report* (1986).

Payette, Lise, née Ouimet broadcaster, politician, writer (b at Montréal 29 Aug 1931). She started her radio career in Rouyn-Noranda, Trois-Rivières, Québec C and Montréal. After 6 years in Paris, she became enormously popular in Québec, first with her program *Place Aux Femmes,* which was broadcast every morning on Radio-Canada during the 1960s, and then on television, with a late-evening talk show called *Appelez-moi Lise.* She was elected a péquiste MNA in 1976 and was made minister of consumer affairs, co-operatives and financial institutions, as well as the delegate responsible for women's affairs. After being the focal point of the "Yvettes" controversy (she had accused the leader of the Opposition, Claude RYAN, of being married to an Yvette) during the referendum period of 1980, she withdrew from political life the following year to devote her time to writing TV screenplays, including *La bonne aventure* and *Les Dames de coeur,* both of which were huge successes. CLINTON ARCHIBALD

Pays d'en Haut [French "up country" or "upper country"] was an expression used in the FUR TRADE to refer to the area to which the VOYAGEURS travelled to trade. In the days of NEW FRANCE it referred to what is now NW Québec (except for the KING'S POSTS), most of Ontario, the area W of the

Mississippi and S of the Great Lakes and beyond to the Canadian prairies. Later usage was limited to the prairies and today *pays d'en haut* is used in Québec to refer to the NW part of the province.

PCB, abbreviation which stands for polychlorinated biphenyl. There are over 200 such substances. They are typically clear, colourless liquids that are extremely stable and chemically unreactive.

Hundreds of millions of kilograms of PCBs were manufactured over 5 decades. They were excellent fluids for use in electrical transformers and capacitors because of their stability, unreactivity, nonflammability and high boiling point. They were also used in innumerable other ways: as a base for printing inks, a flame retardant in oils, a plasticizer for resins, a cutting oil in machine shops, etc. Because of their unreactivity, a large percentage of all that has been made is still in the environment.

The manufacture of PCBs was discontinued on this continent in 1979, principally owing to an unfortunate incident in Japan where over 1000 people became ill from consumption of contaminated cooking oil. Although PCB was at the time thought to be the culprit, continued investigation has pointed to another cause. While it is thought prudent to discontinue the open uses that result in their being dispersed in the environment, discontinuing their use in transformers and capacitors may be a mistake.

Human experience with PCBs has been extensive. We have all been exposed at some level. In the past also, thousands of workers have been heavily involved with PCBs daily for long periods of time. For transformer-capacitor workers with high long-term exposure, neither significant increases in any type of cancer nor an increase in mortality overall has been noted. Nevertheless, we seem to be committed to the destruction of all existing stocks (such as in the Alberta high-temperature incineration facility at Swan Hills). W.E. HARRIS

Pea (*Pisum sativum*), annual VEGETABLE of the legume family. The species originated in central and western Asia, where wild types still exist and can be crossed with cultivated varieties. In Canada, English peas (sweet or garden peas) are used for canning and freezing; edible-podded peas (sugar, snow or chinese peas) are grown for the pod, which is tender and fibre free when harvested at an early stage, and are much less important commercially. Some cultivars (commercial varieties) are pole type, grown mainly on trellises; others are dwarf type, used primarily by the canning industry. Peas are a cool-season crop. Seed germination is good at 5-10°C; optimum growth is obtained at 15-20°C. The sugar in the grains is rapidly converted into starch when harvest time temperatures are too high. Sweet peas are harvested by machines which cut, shell and size the grains. The canning industry requires small, tender peas; tendrometers, instruments measuring grain tenderness, determine the time to harvest. Bigger grains are acceptable for freezing. ROGER BÉDARD

Pea, Field (*Pisum arvense*), hardy annual belonging to the legume family. Field peas, among the oldest of cultivated CROPS, originated in India, were carried to Europe in prehistoric times and introduced to the New World in the 1600s. The field pea, a viny climbing plant, occurs in dwarf, medium and tall types. Some cultivars (cultivated varieties) have branching stems. Leafy types have alternate leaves with 1-3 pairs of leaflets ending in one or more tendrils; semileafless and leafless types also occur. The reddish purple flowers are borne in the leaf axils, either singly or in 2 or 3 racemes (flowering structures). The cylindrical pod varies in length (2.5-12.5 cm), is yellow-green to green in colour, and contains 2-10 seeds. Field peas are planted 5-8 cm deep, in rows 30-60 cm apart, at a seeding rate of 130-220 kg/ha, depending on seed size. They require 90-160 days to mature and 40-100 cm of rainfall during the growing season. Field peas are grown in temperate regions worldwide; however, their susceptibility to PLANT DISEASES could limit further development as a field crop. Field peas are grown for their high-protein seed, used in soups, dhal, livestock feed and flour. Canada produced approximately 50 214 t of field peas in 1986 valued at $17 691 000. P. McVETTY

Peace, Order and Good Government, introductory phrase of section 91 of the CONSTITUTION ACT, 1867, generally stating the scope of the legislative jurisdiction of Parliament. In the eyes of some of the FATHERS OF CONFEDERATION, this clause was a general power enabling Parliament to enact laws on matters not specifically conferred upon the provinces, ie, on "residuary" matters. When examining a particular law to ascertain which legislature had jurisdiction, it became necessary to review the 2 lists of enumerated powers, including the provincial power to legislate in the matters of "property and civil rights in the province." In the 1920s the power of this provision was emasculated by Lord Haldane's interpretation of it as an "emergency" power, an interpretation rejected by Lord Simon in the 1946 Prohibition case. The Supreme Court of Canada has, since 1949, done much to revive the clause, particularly through such references as the ANTI-INFLATION ACT REFERENCE.

It can now be stated with some certainty that the opening words of s91 have both a residuary and an emergency function. Parliament can invoke the residuary function of the words "peace, order and good government" when the subject matter of legislation is a genuinely new matter not included within any of the enumerated heads of ss91 and 92 and is of national dimension or importance. This is somewhat of a departure from the "dimensions" doctrine of the 1960s, in which the general power was interpreted to mean federal jurisdiction over local matters that have assumed a national dimension. The emergency function can be invoked by Parliament to legislate matters which are normally under provincial jurisdiction, but which because of their perceived magnitude or nature are sufficiently critical to require a national or regional legislative response. The exercise of the emergency power by Parliament holds in suspension the normal distribution of powers set out in the Constitution Act, 1867; in these instances it is crucial that the legislation be temporary. For example, during WWI Parliament enacted the WAR MEASURES ACT, which empowered the government to make regulations on almost any subject.

The provinces have proposed reforms of the peace, order and good government clause and it is likely that consideration will be given to them. *See also* RUSSELL CASE; LABOUR CONVENTIONS REFERENCE. A.A. McLELLAN

Peace Movement Canada has a long tradition of an active and vocal peace movement. The Mennonites and Quakers, guided by a philosophy of nonviolence, have consistently spoken out against war and militarism. During the late 1950s and 1960s, concern over the dangers of atmospheric testing and the debate over the presence in Canada of nuclear weapons provided a focus for Canada's fledgling peace movement. In 1952, a Canadian chapter of the World Federalists was established, in response to a growing sense of

frustration with Cold War tensions and the failure of the UNITED NATIONS to operate as had been envisaged. In 1957 the first PUGWASH Conference of scientists was held in Pugwash, NS, and the Canadian Peace Research Institute was founded. The Canadian Peace Congress, which has close links to the Communist Party of Canada, was also active at this time.

It was also during these years that the VOICE OF WOMEN was established in Canada and began to hold an annual Mothers' Day Vigil. This was important, not only because it provided organized support for women who wished to challenge the assumptions of the day about military security and the role of women in society, but because it also laid the groundwork for a large section of the peace movement today who are seeking a broader definition of peace, as not just arms control but a complete restructuring of society and its priorities. Although far thinking, these groups were narrowly based, often labelled "left wing" and dismissed by a general public that continued to think of peace as a state of security resulting from the maintenance of military strength as a counter to Soviet bloc military forces.

By the late 1960s, the peace movement in Canada had coalesced around criticism of the VIETNAM WAR and a perceived failure on the part of Canada to distance itself from American policies. By comparison, and despite the fact that it was a period when there was a significant nuclear arms build-up by the USSR, the 1970s were relatively quiet. The atmosphere of detente had generated a certain amount of complacency. The turn of the decade witnessed growing tensions between the superpowers relating to such events as the Soviet invasion of Afghanistan; Soviet deployments of new intermediate range nuclear missiles targetted on western Europe and NATO's decision to counter this with its "two-track" policy to deploy intermediate range missiles, unless the Soviet ones were withdrawn; and the imposition of martial law in Poland. The American Strategic Defence Initiative (SDI) of early 1983 and the Soviet walk-out from arms control negotiations when NATO's intermediate range nuclear missile deployments began later in the same year further contributed to East-West tensions. These events created an alarming atmosphere for many and gave rise to a renewed peace movement in Canada and abroad.

The revitalized peace movement of the 1980s is a loose network of groups with different aims, philosophies and membership. The unifying factor is that all are deeply concerned by the threat to mankind posed by a spiralling arms race which consumes scarce resources and holds security hostage to ever increasing expenditures. The movement is more broadly based than ever before, including major urban coalitions such as the Toronto Disarmament Network, the Winnipeg Coordinating Committee on Disarmament, End the Arms Race in Vancouver, and religious groups such as PROJECT PLOUGHSHARES sponsored by the Canadian Council of Churches, organizations of physicians, scientists, educators, lawyers, veterans, artists and athletes. A myriad of local peace groups are established across the country; their membership is both rural and urban and all age groups are represented, with women playing an ever-increasing role.

Many groups come under the umbrella of the Canadian Peace Alliance (CPA). Founded in 1985, the CPA includes 350 individual and umbrella peace groups which represent 1500 other organizations with peace activities as their primary focus. The CPA has strong ties to organized labour and 20% of its members are Canadian Labour Congress affiliates.

One of the largest and most broadly based

peace groups in Canada is Project Ploughshares, sponsored by the Canadian Council of Churches. Established in 1976, it now has over 7500 individual associates from all the major churches throughout Canada. It focuses on 3 main areas: alternative security, ie, finding alternative approaches to defence policy and arms control and disarmament; militarism and underdevelopment, in particular military spending and the arms trade in the Third World and Canadian military production and exports policy. Ploughshares has also developed a national campaign of research, education and publication on the relationship of disarmament and development.

OPERATION DISMANTLE, founded in 1977, was particularly active during the late 1970s and early 1980s. Dismantle's main goal at that time was to gain support for a world referendum on disarmament. Today, with a membership of over 11 000, its main activities are lobbying, public education, co-ordinating campaigns and coalition building directed toward making Canada a nuclear weapons free zone.

In 1979 a group of Toronto physicians formed a chapter of CANADIAN PHYSICIANS FOR THE PREVENTION OF NUCLEAR WAR, linking up with an international medical network which has become a powerful force. By 1987 there were 26 chapters of CPPNW with 4200 supporters, including 10% of Canadian physicians. The membership is drawn from across Canada and includes some nurses, physiotherapists and other health care professionals. CPPNW has vigorously publicized the severe medical consequences of even a limited nuclear exchange. Psychologists, who have also organized themselves, have warned that the fear of nuclear war is having a deleterious effect on many Canadian youth. Scientists are another group of professionals who are examining more closely peace and security issues and, in particular, the relationship between science and society. Organizations such as Scientists for Peace focus on the arms race and the nuclear threat, while Pugwash and Student Pugwash look at a whole range of global issues from medical ethics and the environment to the arms race and Third World development. Veterans are another addition to the peace community. Veterans Against Nuclear Arms lobbies politicians and officials in the Departments of National Defence and External Affairs. Lawyers for Social Responsibility reflects the growing concern among middle class professionals about peace and security. The organization encourages and supports legal research on peace, war and disarmament, presents papers with a legal perspective on these issues and provides legal advice to groups and individuals working for peace.

Educators are among the most active participants in the peace movement. One of the most important developments of the 1980s has been the introduction of peace or global education into Canadian schools. Teachers are increasingly pressing school boards to add peace studies and global issues to the curricula.

New research institutes are making an important contribution to the debate on peace and security. The Canadian Institute for International Peace and Security (CIIPS) was created in June 1984 as a crown corporation. In order to ensure its independence, the level of financing and method of selection of the board of directors is set out in the Act. The purpose of the Institute is to increase knowledge and understanding of the issues related to international peace and security, from a Canadian perspective. It provides funding and information for groups wishing to promote a discussion of peace and security issues, as well as publishing its own research.

The Canadian Centre for Arms Control and Disarmament, established in 1983, is an Ottawa-based, private, nonprofit organization which is also doing extensive policy-related research on peace and security issues and disseminates this through an education and information programme. Although it covers all aspects of arms control diplomacy, the Centre tends to focus on issues where Canada is directly involved and where Canadian policy can have a direct impact on the international arms control process.

The Department of External Affairs has also played a role in encouraging the discussion of peace and security issues. The consultative group brings together, annually, approximately 50 Canadians to discuss peace and security issues under the chairmanship of the Ambassador for Disarmament. The Disarmament Fund has also been an important source of funding for groups or individuals engaged in balanced discussions, research, dissemination of information or publishing of material on the subject of arms control and disarmament.

The activities of the peace groups in Canada have undoubtedly helped to mold public opinion. Polls have shown a marked distrust of the superpowers by Canadians and a perception that the risk of nuclear war has increased in recent years. Many Canadians want their government to take a more active role in disarmament, but they are ambivalent about where Canada's duty, in the interests of security, lies. There is a great deal of discussion about alternative security, the need for international co-operation, and the peaceful resolution of disputes, but in the interim most of the groups have yet to come to terms with balancing the pressing need of disarmament with Canada's legitimate security needs. DOUGLAS ROCHE

Reading: E. Regehr and S. Rosenblum, eds, *Canada and the Nuclear Arms Race* (1983).

Peace River, Alta, Town, pop 6288 (1986c), 5907 (1981c), inc 1919, is located at the junction of the PEACE and Smoky rivers. It takes its name from nearby Peace Point, where Cree and Beaver Indians settled a territorial dispute. The strategic location at the river junction was first used as a base by Alexander MACKENZIE on his western journey (1793). Later, buffalo hides were brought by trail from Ft Edmonton and transported upstream to New Caledonia. The junction was an important ferry crossing, and the Edmonton, Dunvegan and BC Ry crossed the river in 1915. Missions were founded in 1879 and 1887, and Rev J. Gough Brick dramatically showed the area's agricultural potential by winning the world wheat championship at the Chicago Exposition (1893). By 1913 a permanent settlement was emerging on the present townsite, known up to 1916 as Peace River Crossing. Today the town is the distribution and administration centre for the area. Local tourist attractions include Peace River Museum, the remnants of Mackenzie's Fort Fork (1792-93), the grave of H.F. "Twelve Foot" Davis and nearby Queen Elizabeth Prov Park.

ERIC J. HOLMGREN

Peace River, 1923 km long, is one of the principal tributaries of the MACKENZIE R system. Formerly, the Peace was formed by the juncture of the Finlay R from the N and the Parsnip R from the south. Today the 2 rivers have been dammed near Hudson Point and have swelled to form WILLISTON LK. The Peace flows from the E arm of the lake, cuts through the Rocky Mts and is joined by the Halfway and Beatton rivers from the N and the Pine R from the S. Just E of the BC-Alberta border it is joined by the Pouce Coupé. It cuts a deep gash, up to 11 km wide, across the northern Alberta prairie. It is an ancient course; dinosaur tracks have been uncovered along its banks. At the town of PEACE RIVER, it is joined by the Smoky R and

swings abruptly N, meandering to near Ft Vermilion, where it turns E and, joined by the Wabasca R, flows into WOOD BUFFALO NATIONAL PK and pours into the Slave R, whence its waters are carried to the Mackenzie. Alexander MACKENZIE wintered in the river's upper reaches in 1793. Other traders, including Peter POND, may have preceded him; traders certainly followed and the river was a major freight route up to 1826. Five different forts, dating from 1805-06, were built at various times around the location of modern FORT ST JOHN, and Simon FRASER built a strategic post at Hudson's Hope (1805), the head of navigation. The valley of the Peace is fertile; it is the northernmost commercially important agricultural region of N America. The great Gordon M. Shrum hydroelectric power station near Hudson's Hope was built 1968-80 and at 2416 MW is the third largest in Canada; nearby Peace Canyon station generates additional power. JAMES MARSH

Peace River Lowland, a gently rolling lowland without clearly defined outer boundaries, extends E of the ROCKY MTS on both sides of the PEACE R, sloping downward to the E. Although it is often called a "lowland," the landform region is part of the high plains of western Alberta. The higher hills in the foothills E of the Rockies in northeastern BC have elevations of about 1000 m and the plain W of Lk ATHABASCA is about 300 m above sea level. Local landform features are illustrated by several flat-topped, erosional-remnant hills that rise a few hundred metres above the broad, gently sloping valleys. In contrast, the Peace R and its immediate tributaries are deeply entrenched about 200 m into the lowland in the western section causing significant land-transportation obstacles. However, to the E the steep-sided banks of the Peace R floodplain have decreased in height to about 70 m W of Ft Vermilion.

Most of the Peace R Lowland was covered by an aspen-poplar forest when the area was occupied by the BEAVER (Athapaskans) prior to European exploration and settlement in the 19th century. Spruce trees grew on the upper slopes, which were underlain by less fertile grey-wooded soils. Many of the broad valleys, particularly in the western section, had tall, prairie grass vegetation cover and were underlain by more fertile and darker-coloured soils. Agricultural settlers who moved into the region early in the 20th century tended to occupy the grassy areas where less forest had to be removed prior to cultivation.

The climate of the lowland is a little more favourable for agriculture than other parts of N-

Autumn harvest, Peace River, Alta. The Peace River Lowland is the most northerly grain-growing area of N America (*photo by V. Claerhout*).

central Alberta. Because the Rocky Mts are lower W of the region, Pacific air masses can cross over with less modification, resulting in about 38 to 45 cm of annual precipitation, more than in E-central Alberta. However, cold air masses from the NW may cover the area at any time, causing the average annual frost-free season to vary greatly from year to year and from place to place. An average frost-free season of about 110 days is recorded in the agricultural areas near the Alberta-BC boundary.

Fur traders penetrated this forest environment at the end of the 18th century and encouraged the Indians to trap for furs. Fur-trading posts opened and closed throughout the area, such as at Fort Dunvegan (1805) and FORT ST JOHN (1806). Pioneer agricultural settlers reached the area at the beginning of the 20th century as part of the general settling of the northern fringes of the prairies and parklands of the Canadian Interior Plains. Settlement accelerated after a railway reached PEACE RIVER in 1915 and extended to GRANDE PRAIRIE in 1916. These settlers found a physical environment that compared favourably with that of central Alberta, but they were hampered by lack of accessibility and distance of markets. By 1986 cultivated land in the western part of the area totalled 1 746 280 ha in Alberta and 408 183 ha in northeastern BC. Though most of the area still remains under forest cover, some of which is being used for lumber and pulpwood, its underground resources of petroleum and natural gas are being more widely explored and utilized.

J. LEWIS ROBINSON

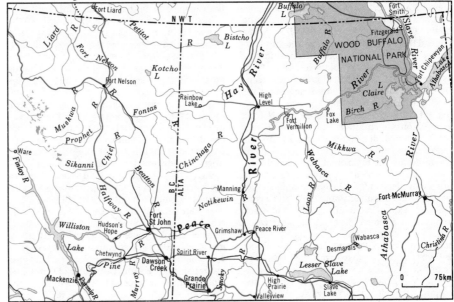

Peacekeeping, the usual term applied to UNITED NATIONS military operations. Because of L.B. PEARSON's role in the SUEZ CRISIS of 1956 and the Canadian role in the UN Emergency Force he helped create, Canadians tended to look on peacekeeping with a proprietary air. When the UN Charter was drafted in 1945 it included elaborate provisions for the maintenance of collective security. But the COLD WAR blocked every attempt to institutionalize a UN force, and the UN had to rely on improvisation. This was first evident in Apr 1948 when the UN authorized the employment of military observers in Kashmir and when it repeated this action the next month along the Arab-Israeli borders. Military observers could watch the movements of armies, supervise cease-fires and the local civilians and generally bring calm to an area. That was the theory, and it usually proved workable. Canada provided 8 officers for the UN force in Kashmir and after 1953 it sent 4 officers to the Palestine force as well as Gen E.L.M. BURNS, who took command in Feb 1954.

This type of UN peacekeeping was markedly different from that practised in the KOREAN WAR. There, because the USSR fortuitously was boycotting the Security Council when the crisis arose in late June 1950, the US was able to organize a "police action" to resist the N Korean invasion. Much more typical, even if not under the UN, was the Canadian role on the International Commissions for Supervision and Control in Vietnam, Laos and Cambodia. These commissions (usually called International Control Commissions, or ICCs) were set up by the Geneva Conference of 1954 on a "troika" model, with a communist state (Poland), a Western state (Canada) and a neutral (India).

The task was important, since the ICCs had responsibility for relocating populations, supervising elections and watching the new boundaries. The manpower commitment was relatively heavy, however, as almost 100 bilingual officers and a substantial number of External Affairs officials were required for what proved to be a notably thankless task. In Cambodia and Laos there was initially some success, but the Vietnam ICC bogged down in futility as the war there spread out of control in the 1960s.

But in 1956, when the Suez Crisis arose, Canadians eagerly seized on the opportunity for UN service. The United Nations had quickly become involved when Britain and France co-operated with Israel in an assault on Egypt. The Canadian interest was to minimize the harm done to the Western alliance by the Anglo-French aggression, and Canadian Secretary of State for External Affairs Pearson, working with UN Secretary-General Dag Hammarskjöld, produced the idea of a peacekeeping force to stabilize the situation and to permit the withdrawal of the attackers. To assist, Pearson offered a battalion of The Queen's Own Rifles. The United Nations Emergency Force (UNEF) came into being quickly, with Canada's Gen E.L.M. Burns, commander of the UN Truce Supervision Organization in Palestine, named UNEF's commander. The Egyptians, to Canada's surprise, objected to the presence of Canadians. The uniforms, the regimental name and the Canadian flags all seemed very similar to those of the British invaders and, the Egyptians argued, their people would not understand. In the end a compromise was struck: Canadian service and supply troops, vital to the success of the UN force, would replace the infantry. This experience played its part in convincing Pearson that Canada needed its own symbols; it also won him the Nobel Peace Prize.

After Suez, Canadians came to feel that peacekeeping was their métier. This was evident in July 1960 when a newly independent Congo erupted in violence. The Diefenbaker government was reluctant to participate when the UN asked for signallers and other troops, but public opinion forced the government's hand. Peacekeeping popularity had been established, and there was no hesitation in 1962 when Canada sent a small number of men to West New Guinea (Irian Jaya), or in the next year when servicemen went to Yemen for service with a UN observer mission. A much larger commitment followed in 1964 when the UN intervened to separate Greeks and Turks in Cyprus. Canadian Secretary of State for External Affairs Paul MARTIN was instrumental in creating the Cyprus UN force.

But the heyday of peacekeeping was over. Some critics were already beginning to complain that peacekeeping merely rendered situations static and did nothing to resolve them. Others worried about costs and casualties, and fretted over often unclear mandates. The death blow came in 1967 when President Nasser ordered the UNEF out of Egypt, and then ordered the Canadian force to withdraw. Another Arab-Israeli war followed. The expulsion of the Canadians amounted almost to a national humiliation, a reaction that was not eased by charges that Canadians in the ICC had been spying for the US. The idea of peacekeeping had helped to reinforce a mythos of Canada as an impartial and acceptable observer, but peacekeeping fell out of favour for a time in Canada.

By the 1980s, however, both the Trudeau and Mulroney governments seemed willing to consider new requests for troops more favourably; for Canadian service personnel, however, peacekeeping has become a chore rather than an opportunity, and the public attitude to UN service remains ill defined. *See also* MIDDLE POWER; PEACE MOVEMENT.   J.L. GRANATSTEIN

Reading: L.B. Pearson, *Mike*, vol 2 (1973); A. Taylor et al, *Peacekeeping* (1968).

Peach (*Prunus persica*, ROSE family), most widely grown of stone fruits, is native to China and was introduced to Europe 2000 years ago. Peaches are now grown in temperate zones, worldwide. They were an important crop in Ontario by the 1880s and in BC by the 1890s. Peach trees are 3-5 m tall with long, narrow, pointed leaves, single, pink flowers, and fruits (5-8 cm diameter) with light fuzz. Fuzzless peaches are called nectarines. When ripe, varieties grown for the fresh market (in Canada, 80%) have sweet, juicy flesh; those for processing (20%) have firm, almost rubbery flesh adapted to mechanical handling.

In Canada peach trees are short-lived (10-20 years), beginning to bear fruit at 2-3 years. The least cold hardy of stone fruits (injured or killed by winter temperatures below -23°C), their culture is limited to southern BC and southern Ontario. Peaches thrive where summer temperatures are high. The season extends from July to Sept; growers plant 12 or more varieties, ripening at different times. In the semiarid valleys of BC, irrigation is essential for commercial culture. In Ontario, orchards are normally cultivated until July; a cover crop is then established to absorb surplus soil nitrogen, to slow tree growth and thus aid in hardening off for winter and to hold snow to protect the roots. In BC a permanent sod cover is usually established and orchards are not cultivated. Orchards are baited in fall and trees are painted with repellants to discourage injury from animals. Peaches are susceptible to various insect pests, mites, nematodes and PLANT DISEASES. Raw peaches are high in vitamin A. In 1985, 42 204 t were produced, with a farm value of $22.0 million. 1986 production dropped to 31 269 t.
                            R.E.C. LAYNE

Peaches (*Prunus persica Botsch*) (artwork by Claire Tremblay).

Peachey, James, painter, surveyor (probably b in Eng; d in Martinique? 24 Nov 1797). He was an officer in the British army, attached to the surveyor general of Canada, Samuel HOLLAND (around 1781), and the staff assigned to settle the LOYALISTS. He was later deputy surveyor general. He is best known for his watercolour sketches of contemporary events, such as the arrival of the Loyalists along the St Lawrence R. He also illustrated *The Book of Common Prayer – translated into the Mohawk language by Joseph Brant* (1787). It is assumed he died during an epidemic in the West Indies.   JAMES MARSH

Pear (genus *Pyrus*), common name for over 20 species of fruit-bearing and ornamental trees of the ROSE family. The genus is indigenous to Europe and Asia. The European pear (*P. communis*), which produces buttery, juicy and aromatic FRUIT, is the most widely grown. In Canada, commercial pear production is limited to regions with a mild winter climate, including the OKANAGAN VALLEY, BC; southern Ontario, and NS. In other regions, hybrids of the Ussurian (*P. ussuriensis*) and European pears are grown in home gardens. Pear varieties are asexually propagated by grafting on seedling rootstocks. Bartlett, the most important variety, is marketed fresh and as canned halves and baby food. Anjou and Bosc varieties are marketed only as fresh fruit – Anjou all year with the use of controlled-atmosphere storage methods. Kieffer was once important in the canning industry but recently its use has declined. Fire blight is especially troublesome in warm, humid regions of Ontario. Pear Psylla is a sucking insect which produces a sticky ooze; a black fungal growth develops on the ooze, disfiguring the fruit. In 1985, 28 217 t of pears were produced, with a farm value of $11.8 million. 1986 production was 24 896 t.   H.A. QUAMME

Pearce, Joseph Algernon, astrophysicist (b at Brantford, Ont 7 Feb 1893). Together with J.S. PLASKETT, the first director of the Dominion Astrophysical Observatory in Victoria, BC, Pearce published the first detailed spectroscopic analysis of the structure of our Milky Way Galaxy in 1935. Using radial velocities of the very luminous hot stars visible from Victoria, they demonstrated that the sun is two-thirds out from the centre of our galaxy and rotates in 220 million years. Pearce studied radial velocities of O- and B-type stars, catalogued the observable B stars and found that 40% are double stars, and estimated the temperatures and dimensions of representative giant eclipsing double stars. Director of the Dominion Astrophysical Observatory 1940-51, Pearce was active in the International Astronomical Union, the Royal Astronomical Soc of Canada (president, 1940) and the American Astronomical Soc (vice-president, 1944-46). Elected a fellow of the Royal Soc of Canada in 1931, he was president in 1949. Pearce was a major in the Canadian forces in WWI, and is a Freemason and an enthusiastic philatelist.   K.O. WRIGHT

Pearce, William, surveyor, civil servant (b near Port Talbot, Canada W 1 Feb 1848; d at Calgary 3 Mar 1930). Pearce journeyed W as a public-land surveyor for the federal Dept of the Interior in 1874 and was promoted superintendent of mines in 1884. Responsible for resource development and land use, Pearce was particularly concerned with arid-land administration and developed the federal irrigation and grazing policies in southern Alberta. In 1904 he joined the CPR to advise the company on its vast irrigation and settlement scheme. Pearce also helped establish Canada's national parks system. DAVID H. BREEN

Pearkes, George Randolph, soldier, politician (b at Watford, Eng 26 Feb 1888; d at Victoria 30 May 1984). He immigrated to Canada in 1906, homesteaded in Alberta, and then joined the RN-WMP. He enlisted in the 2nd Canadian Mounted Rifles as a trooper in 1915 and by 1918 attained the rank of lt-col and commanded the 116th Battalion, CEF. He was wounded in action 5 times and was one of the most decorated Canadian officers. He was awarded the DSO, MC, and the Victoria Cross for bravery at PASSCHENDAELE in 1918. He remained in the army, commanding the 1st Canadian Infantry Division in the UK (1940-42) until returning to Canada as general officer commanding, Pacific Command. He resigned after a disagreement with the government over CONSCRIPTION in 1945 and entered federal politics as a Conservative, representing Nanaimo 1945-53 and later Esquimalt-Saanich. He became minister of national defence (1957-60) during a critical period when production of the AVRO ARROW aircraft was halted, the BOMARC MISSILE introduced, and the use of atomic warheads by Canada's armed forces hotly debated. Appointed lieutenant-governor of BC in 1960, he retired in 1968. R.H. ROY

Pearson, John Andrew, architect (b at Chesterfield, Eng 22 June 1867; d at Toronto 11 June 1940). Pearson, in partnership with Frank Darling, built up one of the most successful architectural practices in Canada. Trained at Sheffield, Pearson immigrated to Canada in 1888. In 1893 he was employed by Darling and Sproatt of Toronto and this firm, which became Darling and Pearson in 1893, endured until 1923. Darling and Pearson were best known for their bank designs and large office buildings designed in the grand classical manner of the École des beaux-arts. In 1916 Pearson designed with J. Omer MARCHAND the new PARLIAMENT BUILDINGS in Ottawa. JANET WRIGHT

Pearson, Lester Bowles, "Mike," statesman, politician, public servant (b at Newtonbrook, Ont 23 Apr 1897; d at Ottawa 27 Dec 1972). Pearson was Canada's foremost diplomat and formulated its basic post-WWII foreign policy. A skilled politician, he rebuilt the Liberal Party and as prime minister strove to maintain Canada's national unity. Son of a Methodist parson, Pearson spent his childhood moving from one parsonage to another before enrolling in history at U of T. With the outbreak of WWI, he enlisted in the Canadian Army Medical Corps and in 1915 was shipped to Greece to join the Allied armies fighting the Bulgarians. After 2 years of stretcher-bearing, he transferred to the Royal Flying Corps in England. His military career came to a sudden end when he was run over by a London bus and invalided home.

After taking his BA at U of T in 1919, Pearson was undecided on a career. He tried law and business, won a fellowship to Oxford, and was hired by U of T to teach history, which he combined with tennis and coaching football. Pearson also married and soon had children. Finding a profes-

**Lester Bowles Pearson
Fourteenth Prime Minister of Canada**

Birth: 23 Apr 1897, Newtonbrook, Ont
Father/Mother: Edwin/Annie Bowles
Father's Occupation: Clergyman
Education: U of Toronto; Oxford
Religious Affiliation: Methodist/United
First Occupation: Teacher
Last Private Occupation: Civil servant
Political Party: Liberal
Period(s) as PM: 22 Apr 1963 - 20 Apr 1968
Ridings: Algoma East, Ont, 1948-68
Other Ministries: External Affairs 1948-57
Marriage: 22 Aug 1925 to Maryon Moody (b 1902)
Children: 1 boy, 1 girl
Died: 27 Dec 1972 in Ottawa
Cause of Death at Age: Cancer at 75
Burial Place: Maclaren Cemetery, Wakefield, Qué
Other Information: Winner of Nobel Peace Prize, 1957.

(photo courtesy United Nations).

sor's salary insufficient, he joined the Department of External Affairs. By 1928 he had trained himself as a perceptive observer and an able writer, both useful qualities in his work. Pearson quickly attracted the attention of his deputy minister, O.D. SKELTON. In 1935 he was sent to London as first secretary in the Canadian High Commission, giving him a front-row seat as Europe drifted towards WWII. He was profoundly influenced by what he saw and thereafter attached great importance to collective defence in the face of dictatorships and aggression. In 1941 Pearson returned to Canada. He was sent to Washington as second-in-command at the Canadian Legation in 1942, where his easygoing personality and personal charm made him a great success, particularly with the press. In 1945 he was named Canadian ambassador to the US and attended the founding conference of the UNITED NATIONS at San Francisco.

In Sept 1946 Pearson was summoned home by PM KING to become deputy minister (or undersecretary) of external affairs. He continued to take a strong interest in the UN but also promoted a closer political and economic relationship between Canada and its principal allies, the US and the UK. Pearson's work culminated in Canada's joining NATO in 1949. He strongly supported a Western self-defence organization, although he hoped that its existence would persuade the USSR that aggression would be futile. By the time NATO was in place, Pearson had left the civil service for politics. In Sept 1948 he became minister of external affairs and subsequently represented Algoma East, Ont, in the House of Commons. As minister, he helped lead Canada into the Korean War as a contributor to the UN army and, in 1952, served as president

of the UN General Assembly, where he tried to find a solution to the conflict. His efforts displeased the Americans, who considered him too inclined to compromise on difficult points of principle. His greatest diplomatic achievement came in 1956, when he proposed a UN PEACE-KEEPING force as means for easing the British and French out of Egypt. His plan was implemented, and as a reward he received the Nobel Peace Prize in 1957.

By then Pearson was no longer in office. He and the ST. LAURENT government were widely blamed for not standing by Britain in 1956. The Liberals were defeated, St. Laurent resigned as leader, and at a convention in Jan 1958 Pearson defeated Paul MARTIN to become leader. The Liberals faced a minority Conservative government under John DIEFENBAKER, and in his first act as leader Pearson challenged Diefenbaker to resign and turn the government over to him. Diefenbaker ridiculed the idea and in the subsequent general election the Liberals were reduced to 49 of the 265 seats in the Commons. Pearson began the slow task of rebuilding the party. With the assistance of parliamentary debaters such as Paul Martin and J.W. PICKERSGILL and party workers such as Walter GORDON, Mitchell SHARP, and Maurice LAMONTAGNE, he re-established the Liberals as a national party and in the 1962 general election raised the party's total to 100 seats. In 1963 the Diefenbaker government collapsed over the issue of nuclear weapons and in the subsequent election the Liberals won 128 seats to form a minority government. Pearson took office 22 Apr 1963. His government was expected to be more businesslike than Diefenbaker's but proved instead to be accident-prone in aborting its first budget. Much of Parliament's time was spent in bitter partisan and personal wrangling, culminating in an interminable FLAG DEBATE of 1964. In 1965 Pearson called a general election but again failed to secure a majority. In the next year the MUNSINGER scandal erupted with even more partisan bitterness. The year 1965 marks a dividing line in his administration, as Finance Minister Walter Gordon departed and Jean MARCHAND and Pierre TRUDEAU from Québec became prominent in the Cabinet. Pearson's attempts in his first term to conciliate Québec and the other provinces with "co-operative federalism" and "bilingualism and biculturalism" were superseded by a firm federal response to provincial demands and by the Québec government's attempts to usurp federal roles in international relations. When, during his centennial visit, French President Charles de Gaulle uttered the separatist slogan "Vive le Québec libre" to a crowd in Montréal, Pearson issued an official rebuke and de Gaulle promptly went home. In Dec 1967 Pearson announced his intention to retire and in Apr 1968 a Liberal convention picked Pierre Trudeau as his successor.

For all its superficial chaos, the Pearson government left behind a notable legacy of legislation: a Canada Pension Plan, a universal medicare system, a unified armed force, a new flag and a revised transport Act. Its approach to the problem of Canada's disadvantaged regions was less thorough and its legacy, such as the Glace Bay heavy-water plant, decidedly mixed. Not all of these initiatives proved fruitful and some were costly, but they represented the high point of the Canadian WELFARE STATE that generations of social thinkers had dreamed about. In retirement Pearson worked on a study of international aid for the World Bank and on his memoirs. ROBERT BOTHWELL

Reading: R. Bothwell, *Pearson* (1978); L.B. Pearson, *Mike*, 3 vols (1972, 1973, 1975).

Pearson, Peter, film and TV director (b at Toronto 13 Mar 1938). He graduated from U of T and held various production roles at CBC TV 1961-66, including work on the celebrated THIS HOUR HAS SEVEN DAYS. He studied film in Rome, was president of the Directors' Guild of Canada, 1972, and chairman of the Council of Canadian Filmmakers, 1973. As a free-lance director and producer with the CBC and National Film Board, he has won a number of Canadian film awards (eg, for *The Best Damn Fiddler from Kaladar to Calabogie, Saul Alinsky Went to War* and the feature *Paperback Hero*), and made numerous documentaries, short subjects and commercials. In 1983 he began working for the CANADIAN FILM DEVELOPMENT CORPORATION, later called Telefilm Canada, of which he was director 1985-87.

JOHN L. KENNEDY

Peat, partially decomposed organic matter made up principally of decayed *Sphagnum* MOSS, together with other aquatic plants, grasses or sedges. Peat is formed slowly by the decay of vegetation under anaerobic (oxygen-deficient) conditions. Canada's extensive peat bogs developed since the last glaciation, about 10 000 years ago. At all stages of development peat contains about 95% water by weight. The high water content has always been the main barrier to its extensive exploitation as an energy source; however, dried peat has been one of the traditional fuels in places where bogs are of high quality and easily accessible (eg, Ireland).

Peatlands cover approximately 12% of Canada's land surface. Much of the resource is located in inaccessible northern areas but significant deposits occur in the Atlantic provinces, southern Québec and Ontario. This peat could be used for energy production, particularly in areas lacking other energy resources; however, at present, Canadian peat is recovered exclusively for horticultural purposes. Interest in peat fuel has increased recently; one study on peat-fired ELECTRIC-POWER GENERATION concluded that peat was economical, compared with oil-fired or coal-fired stations, in NB. HYDRO-QUÉBEC has studied the feasibility of peat-fired power stations and has been considering peat gasification to replace diesel generation on Île d'Anticosti. Newfoundland is developing a peat bog to determine the practicality and cost of transporting fuel peat on the island. Peat-burning tests have been conducted at a Grand Falls, Nfld, pulp and paper mill. Newfoundland is also interested in the potential of small, peat-fired generators in isolated communities. A particularly attractive option would be to produce methanol from peat-derived synthesis gas.

Perhaps one reason that peat development has been slow in Canada has been the lack of experience with the resource. In Europe, extensive research and development programs exist and the technology of harvesting and using peat is well developed. World peat resources (those over 50 cm thick) are estimated at some 145 billion t dry weight, with an energy equivalent of about 63.5 billion t of oil. The USSR has the largest reserve; Canada's reserve, second largest in the world, is about one-sixth that of the USSR. More than 6000 MW of the USSR's ELECTRIC POWER, equivalent to over 6% of Canada's electrical generation, is peat fired, and about 4.5 million t of peat are produced annually for home heating. Finland has several peat-burning power stations which produce electricity and provide steam and hot water for district heating. Ireland obtains about one-third of its electric power from 7 peat-fired generating stations, which consume about 56% of Ireland's annual peat harvest of 5 million t. The NATIONAL RESEARCH COUNCIL OF CANADA has estab-

lished a Peat Program designed to define Canada's peat resources, to develop harvesting and utilization technology, to assess and reduce environmental impacts and to develop carbon-added products.

Peat bogs differ from other types of wetlands in that they are nourished almost entirely from rainwater. Their surface is a continuous carpet of *Sphagnum* moss which supports a layer of grass and shrubs and, occasionally, trees. In Canada peat bogs may be tens of kilometres across but generally are much smaller. A peat bog is made up of layers, the top layer being living bog vegetation; the second, very young peat; the third, of varying thickness, becomes darker and denser with depth until the black colour and puttylike consistency of mature peat is encountered. Because peat occurs on the surface rather than below ground, its removal is unlikely to cause environmental problems. However, care is needed during and after harvesting to ensure that harvested bogs do not become muddy wastelands.

Because peat is 95% water, it cannot support heavy machinery; removal of as much moisture as possible is essential. A network of drainage ditches begins the process; the ditches are deepened as the bog consolidates. This stage normally takes 5-7 years and reduces the bog's water content to about 90%. After drainage, the bog is levelled to facilitate drying and mechanical handling. The final step is building a network of light railways over the bog's surface for handling and transporting the peat. The bog is then ready for decades of harvesting, typically at a rate of a few centimetres per year, as the surface dries.

ROBERT O. BOTT

Peavey, a lever for handling logs, invented in 1858 by a Maine blacksmith as a simple refinement of the earlier canthook, greatly facilitating the downriver timber drive. Each peavey carried a thumblike hook near the base of its handle. It was generally about 25 cm longer than the 100 cm canthook and its distinctive spiked tip gripped the log more securely than did the iron ferrule and jutting toe of the cant-hook.

GRAEME WYNN

Peckford, Alfred Brian, teacher, politician, premier of Newfoundland (b at Whitbourne, Nfld 27 Aug 1942). Peckford was first elected to the House of Assembly on 24 Mar 1972. In 1973 he was a special assistant to Frank MOORES; in 1974 minister of municipal affairs and housing; and in 1976 minister of mines and energy. In 1977 he asserted Newfoundland's ownership of offshore petroleum resources and regulated the conditions for exploration by oil companies. By 1978 exploration companies were using drilling permits from both the Newfoundland and federal governments. His aggressive championing of provincial rights gained widespread public support and enabled him to win his party's leadership in Mar 1979. In that year and in 1982 he won election by offering a future of prosperity based on the successful control and management of Newfoundland's resources.

His efforts to secure greater provincial control were marked by jurisdictional disputes with the federal government. In *The Past in the Present* (1983), Peckford presented his perspectives on the past mismanagement of natural resources and put forward suggestions for Newfoundland's social and economic direction. However, the prosperous future he promised did not materialize and the election of 1985 took place amid 21% unemployment. Following a stormy campaign, he was re-elected with a reduced majority. In 1987-88 he supported the federal FREE TRADE proposal in hope that it would aid Newfoundland's exports.

MELVIN BAKER

Peden, William J., "Torchy," cyclist (b at Victoria, BC 16 Apr 1906; d at Chicago, Ill 25 Jan 1980). As a youth, Peden participated in several sports and was a nationally ranked swimmer. A member of Canada's cycling team at the 1928 Amsterdam Olympics, he afterwards won several important races in Europe. He turned professional in 1929 and joined the Six-Day racing circuit, achieving acclaim in N America and Europe. A large man, he was a crowd favourite during the heyday of this unusual sport. He won 38 of 148 races between 1929 and 1948, a record that stood until 1965.

J. THOMAS WEST

Pediatrics is that branch of medicine concerned with the child, its development, care and diseases. As a specialty in Canada it originated with the development of hospitals for children. The first, the Hospital for Sick Children, was founded in Toronto in 1875 and by 1919 had established an international reputation. The Montreal Children's Hospital (at the Montreal General) was established in 1903, and the Winnipeg Children's Hospital in 1909. To these centres, in the 1920s, came eager, well-trained pediatricians such as Alan Brown (Toronto), Alton GOLDBLOOM (Montréal) and Gordon Chown (Winnipeg). As a result of the emphasis in pediatric medicine on nutrition, hygiene, and immunization against the serious infections that beset children, child mortality rates from infectious diseases dropped dramatically. The Canadian Paediatric Society was founded in 1923, to promote "the advancement of knowledge of the physiology, pathology, psychology and therapeutics of infancy and childhood." The society, which has since expanded its role, maintains close liaison with the American Academy of Pediatrics. In the 1950s some surgeons began to specialize in pediatric surgery; the Canadian Association of Paediatric Surgeons was founded in 1967 and maintains close ties with the Canadian Paediatric Society.

Internationally recognized Canadian pediatricians include Bruce Chown in Rh immunization; Robert A. Usher and Paul Swyer for the care of the newborn; Charles Scriver and F. Clark Fraser in genetics; John D. Keith and Richard D. Rowe in cardiology; and Henri J. Breault for the development of containers with safety caps for toxic medications. Other specialists are raising the standards of care and expanding research in such diverse fields as neonatal medicine, developmental pediatrics, the care of the handicapped child, intensive care for critically injured children and organ transplantation.

WILLIAM C. TAYLOR

Pedlar, a derogatory term used in the days of the FUR TRADE by HUDSON'S BAY COMPANY men to describe any trader from Québec, and later any trader from the NORTH WEST COMPANY, who "peddled" his goods to the Indians by taking them to their encampments.

JOHN ROBERT COLOMBO

Peel, Paul, figure painter (b at London, Canada W 7 Nov 1860; d at Paris, France 11 Oct 1892). He spent his formative student years learning the academic style at the Pennsylvania Academy of Fine Arts in Philadelphia, with the great American figure painter Thomas Eakins, and at the Royal Academy Schools in London and at the École des beaux-arts in Paris. His sentimental studies of children, such as *The Tired Model* (1889) and *After the Bath* (1890), followed the carefully modelled prescription of the Académie. *After the Bath* won Peel a medal at the 1890 Salon and displays his skill using light and colour. Although he was one of the first Canadian painters to portray nude figures, as in his *A Venetian Bather* (1889), these works were pale compared to those of Degas or Renoir. Works such as *Repose* (c1890) and *Good News, Toronto* (1890) show a tentative move away from academic representation and his small impressionistic sketches achieve a remarkable freshness. However, he did not live to develop his art beyond its academic sentimentalism. He died in Paris, where he had spent most of his working life, of a lung infection induced likely by overwork and exhaustion. A major retrospective of his work was held in London, Ont, in 1987.

Pegahmagabow, Francis, Anishnabe (Ojibwa) chief, Indian rights advocate, war hero (b at Shawanaga, Ont 9 Mar 1889 into the Caribou clan; d at Parry I, Ont 5 Aug 1952). A WWI hero, Pegahmagabow became a vocal advocate for Indian rights and self-determination. He was promoted lance corporal in 1915 and was awarded the military medal and 2 bars for his excellence as sniper and scout in the battles of Ypres (1915), Passchendaele (1917) and Amiens (1918). He was twice elected chief of the Parry I Ojibwa band. Throughout his life he eloquently fought with his pen against transgressions of Indian treaty rights.
FRANZ M. KOENNECKE

Peggy's Cove, NS, UP, pop 47 (1986c), 90 (1981c), located 43 km S of Halifax, on eastern St Margaret's Bay. The narrow cove probably was named after the wife of William Rodgers, an Irish immigrant to St Margaret's Bay (1770). In 1811 land was granted to 5 men who had been fishing from here since 1804. By 1827, 7 families had settled around the picturesque inlet beside the rugged granite coastline. This unique sea-splashed rock formation perpetuates Peggy's Cove as a popular tourist attraction and artists' haunt. Although the lighthouse no longer beams its fishermen home, during summer the postcard-immortalized landmark becomes Canada's only post office in a lighthouse. The Fishermen's Monument, a large mural created on a granite boulder by marine artist William de Garthe, celebrates the fishing family's relationship with their ocean.
JUDITH HOEGG RYAN

Peggy's Cove, NS, from the air (*photo by J.A. Kraulis*).

Peguis, Saulteaux chief (b near Sault Ste Marie, Ont *c*1774; d at Red River, Man 28 Sept 1864). Although a prominent leader of his own people, Peguis became famous for his role in aiding the Selkirk settlers. Upon their arrival at Red River in 1812, he defended them, showed them how to subsist from the country, and later assisted the survivors after the SEVEN OAKS INCIDENT. Peguis and his wife were baptized by Anglican missionaries in 1840 and took the names William and Victoria King, their children adopting the name of Prince. Although he remained friendly with whites, Peguis later became disillusioned because of trespassing on his reserve and violations of his 1817 treaty with Lord SELKIRK.
HUGH A. DEMPSEY

Peigan form the largest of the 3 tribes of the BLACKFOOT NATION. Their name is a corruption of the word *apiku'ni,* meaning "badly tanned robe." They were known to fur traders as the Muddy River Indians. The official spelling of the tribe's name in Canada is Peigan; in the US it is Piegan.

Of Algonquian linguistic stock, they speak the same language as the BLOOD and BLACKFOOT, with only slight dialectal variations. The Peigan once occupied a vast hunting ground which ranged along the foothills from Rocky Mountain House to Heart Butte, Montana, and extended eastward onto the plains. By the mid-19th century they had moved farther S to an area encompassing the Teton R and Marias R in Montana and the Milk R region in Alberta. They also travelled as far N as Ft Edmonton and E to the present Alberta-Saskatchewan border.

Because of the tribe's large size, the Peigan eventually divided into 2 smaller groups, the N and S Peigan, although they often travelled together and were so intermingled that a clear division was impossible. The population of the 2 groups ranged between 3000 and 5000 persons, reaching a low of 2500 after the 1837 smallpox epidemic. In 1870 the population of the S Peigan was 3240 and the N Peigan 720. The Peigan were a nomadic, buffalo-hunting tribe with complex religious and warrior societies. Their enemies included the Crow, Shoshoni, Nez Percé, DAKOTA and ASSINIBOINE tribes.

In 1855 the N and S Peigan were prominent signers of a treaty with the Americans, but by 1877 the southern group had already settled on a reservation in Montana, so only the N Peigan signed Treaty No 7 with the Canadian government. They selected a reserve near Pincher Creek, Alta. In later years the S Peigan adopted the official title of Blackfeet Indians of Montana, and the N Peigans in Canada simply called themselves Peigan. Their reserve provides some opportunities for farming and ranching, although the band has faced the common problems of integration and disruption of their social and cultural life (*see* INDIAN RESERVE). Efforts have been made to establish small industries on the reserve and many Peigan have sought employment away from the area. By 1986 the population of the reserve in Canada had grown to 2000 persons. *See also* NATIVE PEOPLE: PLAINS and general articles under NATIVE PEOPLE.
HUGH A. DEMPSEY

Reading: Hugh A. Dempsey, *Indian Tribes of Alberta* (1979).

Péladeau, Pierre, publisher (b at Outremont, Qué 11 Apr 1925). His father, Henri, won and lost several fortunes as a lumber merchant but died leaving the family in debt. Pierre studied philosophy at U de M and law at McGill. After graduating from McGill (1950), his first ventures were a number of neighborhood weeklies specializing in entertainment news. He later expanded into French-language copies of American tabloids and in 1964 founded the daily *Le Journal de Montréal,* whose circulation in 1987 was surpassed only by the *Toronto Star.* He later added *Le Journal de Québec.* In 1987 he was president and principal owner of QUÉBECOR, the major newspaper chain in Québec, which owns, in addition to dailies in Montréal, Québec and Winnipeg, 43 weeklies, 7 magazines, 8 printing plants and book-publication and film-development divisions. A new English-language daily, the *Montreal Daily News,* was to be launched in Mar 1988. Péladeau is also a director of the Caisse de dépôt et placement du Québec. He was made Member of the Order of Canada in 1987.
JORGE NIOSI

Pélagie-la-Charette (1979), by Antonine MAILLET, narrates the epic journey of the widow Pélagie LeBlanc, who in the late 1770s leads her ACADIAN people back to Grand Pré from the American South, where they had been deported in 1755. Hers is a double odyssey – the "people of the carts" are haunted by the phantom cart, the cart of death associated with Bélonie, the aging

raconteur who accompanies the pilgrims; and by the more tangible phantom ship, an English schooner taken over by Pélagie's beloved Capt Beausoleil-Broussard, also dedicated to repatriating his people. Embodying the forces of life, "Pélagie-the-Cart" survives through the many generations of squabbling storytellers nourished by her line. Interweaving Acadian legends and folklore, biblical and classical analogues, Rabelais and many other sources, Maillet articulates with humour and considerable poetry the family connection between history, the oral tradition, the imagination and literature. The novel was the first foreign work to receive France's Prix Goncourt. Philip Stratford's translation appeared in 1982.
MICHÈLE LACOMBE

Pelham, Ont, pop 12 137 (1986c), est 1970 as a Town in the Regional Municipality of Niagara, located between the Niagara Escarpment and the Welland R. Its rural-agricultural background includes the Short Hills, vineyards, orchards and sand quarries on the Fonthill Kame. It was settled in the mid-1780s by United Empire LOYALISTS, at the proposed site for a major fortress at the highest point of the Niagara Peninsula. Pioneer industrial centres were developed at St Johns and Effingham in the Short Hills. Fonthill was a crossroads settlement and has extensive former nurseries; it underwent residential expansion after WWII with middle and upper income workers commuting to Welland and St Catharines.
JOHN N. JACKSON

Pelican (Pelecanidae), family of large water birds with long, flat bills, expandable throat pouches, and 4 toes connected by a web. Six species occur worldwide; 2 in Canada. The white pelican (*Pelecanus erythrorhynchos*) nests locally in the western provinces. The brown pelican (*P. occidentalis*), a marine species of the southern US, is a casual visitor to the BC coast. Characterized by a 32-36 cm orange bill, adult white pelicans weigh 4.8-8.2 kg and have black-tipped wings, spanning 2.4-2.9 m. Flying pelicans form a line and, together, alternate between flapping and gliding flight. In flight, the head is drawn back, bill resting on the breast. White pelicans nest, colonially, on islands in remote lakes. Approximately 2200 pairs nest on Primrose Lk, Sask; most colonies contain fewer than 150 pairs. Nonbreeders frequent lakes away from breeding sites. Isolation during nest building and incubation is critical, as adults may abandon nests if disturbed. A gregarious, slow-maturing bird, the white pelican feeds from the water surface, trapping prey in the expandable lower bill and pouch. Birds often co-operate to drive prey into shallow water. Although often regarded as predators of game fish, pelicans subsist primarily on coarse fish (perch, suckers, minnows and stickleback). The belief that pelicans carry fish in the pouch is false; prey are swallowed and regurgitated to young.
PHILIP H.R. STEPNEY

Two species of pelican occur in Canada, including the white pelican (*Pelecanus erythrorhynchos*) which nests in the western provinces (*artwork by John Crosby*).

Alfred Pellan, *Self-Portrait (courtesy Alfred Pellan).*

Pellan, Alfred, painter (b at Québec City 16 May 1906). In 1923, while Pellan was still a student at Québec's École des beaux-arts (1920-25), the National Gallery of Canada purchased his painting *Corner of Old Quebec.* Pellan also won the government of Québec's first fine-arts scholarship in 1926, enabling him to study in Paris where he remained until 1940. There the colour in Pellan's still lifes and figure studies became more intense, his linear rhythms more fluid, his images more abstract. His most outstanding achievement during his Paris sojourn was winning first prize at the 1935 exposition of mural art. When he returned to Canada because of WWII he settled in Montréal. Work he brought from Paris received acclaim during exhibitions in 1940 at Québec and Montréal, but Pellan's cubist and surrealist art was considered too avant-garde and he sold little. To survive, he taught at Montréal's École des beaux-arts 1943-52. His objections to the restrictive, academic philosophy of its director, Charles Maillard, resulted in Maillard's resignation in 1945 and a more liberal atmosphere there.

In the mid-1940s Pellan began illustrating poetry books and designed costumes and sets for the theatre. During this period he developed his mature style. He was increasingly drawn to surrealism; his imagery became more erotic and his always strikingly coloured paintings larger, more complex and textured. His refusal to be affiliated with any particular school of art led to the formation in 1948 of Prisme d'yeux, a group of artists whose manifesto called for an art free of restrictive ideology.

In 1952 Pellan received an RSC grant and moved to Paris, living there until 1955, when he became the first Canadian to have a solo exhibition at the Musée national d'art moderne. On his return to Canada, numerous exhibitions and mural commissions established his reputation nationally. He is the subject of several monographs and films (eg, G. Lefebvre, *Pellan*, 1986) and the recipient of many awards and honours including the Prix Émile-Borduas (1984). As well, he is an Officer of the Ordre national du Québec (1985).

REESA GREENBERG

Reading: G. Lefebvre, *Pellan* (1973); Reesa Greenberg, *The Drawings of Alfred Pellan* (1980).

Pellatt, Sir Henry Mill, capitalist (b at Kingston, Canada W 16 Jan 1859; d at Toronto 8 Mar 1939). Pellatt was educated at Upper Canada Coll and had a distinguished athletic career before joining his father's brokerage firm. He was active in the development of hydroelectric projects at NIAGARA FALLS, Ont, and in the transmission and distribution of power in Toronto, until the provincial government created the Hydro-Electric Power Commission of Ontario and nationalized many of the private companies. He was also active in several transportation companies and in the organization of the Canadian General Electric Co. He took a keen interest in the Canadian militia. His eccentric stone mansion, Casa Loma, has become a Toronto landmark. He was created KB in 1905.

T.D. REGEHR

Pelletier, Gérard, journalist, labour and social activist, politician, diplomat (b at Victoriaville, Qué 21 June 1919). One of 8 children of a working-class family, Pelletier was educated at the Séminaire de Nicolet, Collège Mont-Laurier and the U de M. He was secretary-general of Québec's Jeunesse étudiante catholique 1939-43 and field secretary of the World Student Relief organization in Geneva, 1945-47. After touring Argentina, he returned to Montréal where he became a reporter for *Le* DEVOIR 1947-50. His reporting of the 1949 ASBESTOS STRIKE brought him the position of director of *Le Travail,* the organ of the Confédération des travailleurs catholiques du Canada. In 1961 he left to become editor of *La* PRESSE; after a prolonged strike in 1964 the owners of *La Presse* fired him for his radical editorial views. His radical ideas developed during the war when he was influenced by the French social Catholics, especially the personalist philosophy of Emmanuel Mounier and the review *Esprit.* He was inspired, with several colleagues, including Pierre Elliott TRUDEAU, to found CITÉ LIBRE. Through *Cité libre* and Radio-Canada, Pelletier and the others denounced the socially regressive and anti-democratic policies of the DUPLESSIS regime as well as the clericalism of the Québec Catholic Church. They advocated using the state and dynamic labour organizations to create a modern, democratic and pluralistic Québec society. Pelletier's SOCIAL DEMOCRACY contributed to the re-emergence of ideological pluralism in Québec during the 1950s.

With the rise of SEPARATISM in the 1960s, Pelletier, Trudeau and his longtime friend in the Catholic labour movement, Jean MARCHAND, decided to enter federal politics in 1965. Pelletier served as secretary of state for external affairs (1968-72) and minister of communications (1972-75) in the Trudeau administration. He helped formulate the federal government's response to the growing crisis in Québec/Ottawa relations. He pursued this goal as Canadian ambassador to France, 1975-81, and then became ambassador to the UN, 1981-84. In 1984 he became chairman of the board of the National Museums of Canada. He is the author of *La Crise d'Octobre* (1971), *Les Années d'impatience* (1983) and *Les Temps des choix* (1986 trans 1987 as *Years of Choice). See also* FRANCOPHONIE.

MICHAEL D. BEHIELS

Reading: Michael D. Behiels, *Prelude to Québec's Quiet Revolution* (1985); Gérard Pelletier, *Years of Impatience, 1950-60* (1984).

Pelletier, Wilfred, or Baibomsey, meaning "traveller," Odawa wise man, philosopher, author (b on Wikwemikong Reserve, Manitoulin I, Ont 16 Oct 1927). His voice is expressive of the unity of all terrestrial life with the Earth, and with his quiet eloquence he can inspire listeners of different ages and backgrounds. Especially interested in education, he believes that there are better ways of learning than traditional Western methods, and he was active in the Rochdale College experiment in alternative learning in Toronto in the late 1960s. He served as co-director of the Nishnawbe Institute, an Indian cultural and educational project, and has been involved with a network of Indian elders concerned with the application of traditional Indian wisdom to 20th-century problems.

JOHN BENNETT

Reading: Wilfred Pelletier and Ted Poole, *No Foreign Land* (1973).

Pelletier, Wilfrid, conductor, pianist, administrator (b at Montréal 20 June 1896; d at New York City, NY 9 Apr 1982). He played a major role in the formation of Québec musical life, especially in the field of lyric theatre (opera) and with young people. He studied with Mme François Héraly (piano, solfeggio, harmony), Alfred La Liberté (interpretation) and Alexis Contant (harmony, composition) in Canada, and with Charles-Marie Widor (composition) and Camille Bellaigue (lyric repertory) in Paris. He held at different times the positions of rehearsal pianist for French repertory, and assistant conductor, artistic director and regular conductor of the Metropolitan Opera of New York. His many Canadian activities include the creation of the Matinées symphoniques pour la jeunesse (1935), the Montréal Festivals (1936) and the CONSERVATOIRE DE MUSIQUE DU QUÉBEC, of which he was the founding director. He was also first artistic director of the orchestra of the Société des concerts symphoniques de Montréal (1935-40), artistic director of the Québec Symphonic Orchestra (1951-66), director of musical education for Québec's Ministry of Cultural Affairs (1961-67), a founder of the Société de musique contemporaine du Québec (1966) and national chairman of JEUNESSES MUSICALES DU CANADA (1967-69). Pelletier was awarded the medal of the Canada Council (1962) and the medal of the Canadian Music Council (1975) and made a Companion of the Order of Canada (1968).

HÉLÈNE PLOUFFE

Pelly Bay, NWT, Hamlet, pop 297 (1986c), 257 (1981c), is located on the eastern Arctic coast, 1312 air km NE of YELLOWKNIFE. The seal-dependent way of life of the Netsilingmiut Inuit of the area was untouched by the whaling and trapping periods that affected other areas of the North. Although first European contact came in 1829, it was not until 1935 that a white settler came to reside in the community (named for HBC governor Sir John Pelly). In the late 1970s a small commercial char fishery and fine ivory carving have come to supplement the hunting-trapping economy of local residents.

ANNELIES POOL

Pembroke, Ont, City, seat of Renfrew County, pop 15 223 (1986c), 14 026 (1981c), inc 1971, located on the OTTAWA R at the confluence of the Indian and Muskrat rivers, 158 km NW of Ottawa. Peter White, a retired naval petty officer who had served under Admiral Nelson and on Lk Ontario in the War of 1812, settled here 1828. The early communities, known as Campbellton and Miramichi, became Pembroke in honour of Admiralty Secretary Sidney Herbert, son of the earl of Pembroke. Long associated with the lumber trade, the city currently produces veneers, plywood, matches, boxes and office furniture. It was the site of pioneering experiments in telephones

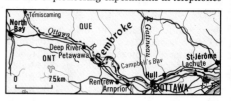

and commercial lighting. The Pembroke Lumber Kings hockey club has won numerous championships. CFB PETAWAWA is located nearby. Pembroke has a bridge link over the Ottawa R to Québec.   K.L. MORRISON

Pemmican [Cree *pimikan*, meaning "manufactured grease"], dried meat, usually BISON, pounded into coarse powder and mixed with an equal amount of melted fat, and occasionally saskatoon berries or other edibles. Cooled and sewn into bison-hide bags in 41 kg lots, pemmican could be stored and shipped with ease to provision FUR-TRADE personnel. Peter POND is credited with introducing this vital food to the trade in 1779, having obtained it from the CHIPEWYANS in the Athabasca region. Later, posts along the Red, Assiniboine and N Saskatchewan rivers were devoted to acquiring pemmican from the Plains Indians and MÉTIS. Pemmican was also made and used outside the region, eg, by the Royal Navy, which provisioned several arctic expeditions with beef pemmican made in England.   JOHN E. FOSTER

Pemmican Proclamation On 8 Jan 1814, Miles MACDONELL, the governor of Assiniboia and Lord Selkirk's agent, promulgated a proclamation forbidding the export of PEMMICAN from the colony for a year. The proclamation was meant to ensure adequate provisions for settlers expected in summer. While it applied to both the Hudson's Bay Co and the North West Co, the latter saw the document as an HBC ploy designed to deny necessary provisions to the engagés of their canoe brigades. Yet 6 months later, when Macdonell promulgated a proclamation against "running" buffalo with horses, he had the support of the NWC. It was the MÉTIS in the region of Red River who found their interests frustrated on this occasion. Both proclamations contributed to the factors that led to the SEVEN OAKS INCIDENT a year later.   JOHN E. FOSTER

Penetanguishene, Ont, Town, pop 5576 (1986c) located at the head of Penetanguishene Bay, an inlet of southern Georgian Bay. It is approximately 150 km N of Toronto by road. The earliest European visitors were Étienne BRULÉ and Samuel de CHAMPLAIN, developing links between New France and the HURON. Its strategic potential was recognized by Lt-Gov John SIMCOE in 1793 and it was developed as an Upper Lakes naval base in 1817, and had a naval and military presence until 1856. The settlement of fur traders and voyageurs (Drummond I withdrawal, 1828), commuted military pensioners from England and farm settlers from Québec (1840s) established it as a bilingual community. The reconstructed Historic Naval and Military Establishments are one of the major tourist attractions in Huronia today. The 19th-century logging industry yielded to an economy based on tourism and light industry, including fibreglass boats, auto parts and aluminum extrusions.   JOHN C. BAYFIELD

Penfield, Wilder Graves, neurosurgeon, scientist (b at Spokane, Wash 26 Jan 1891; d at Montréal 5 Apr 1976). He was founder and first director of the Montreal Neurological Inst and established the "Montreal procedure" for the surgical treatment of epilepsy.

Having obtained a BLitt from Princeton in 1913, Penfield attended Merton College, Oxford. There he was influenced by 2 great medical teachers, Sir William OSLER, who became his lifelong hero, and the eminent neurophysiologist Charles Sherrington, who introduced him to experimental investigation of the nervous system. After graduating with an MD from Johns Hopkins in 1918, he served as surgeon to the Presbyterian Hospital (affiliated with Columbia) and to the New York Neurological Inst 1921-28. His studies

in 1924 with the Madrid neurohistologist Pio del Rio-Hortega provided him with metallic staining techniques that yielded new information on the glia, the supporting cells of the nervous system. In 1928 he learned from the German surgeon Otfrid Foerster the method of excising brain scars to relieve focal epilepsy. That year he moved with his neurosurgical partner, William Vernon Cone, to work at Montréal's Royal Victoria Hospital, where they became associated with neurologist Colin K. Russel. In 1934, supported by the Rockefeller Foundation, the government of Québec, the city of Montréal and private donors, Penfield founded the Montreal Neurological Inst, which rapidly became an international centre for teaching, research and treatment related to diseases of the nervous system. He was its director until 1960.

Epilepsy became Penfield's great inspiration. His surgical studies yielded reports on brain tumours, the pial circulation, the mechanisms of headache, the localization of motor, sensory and speech functions, and the role of the hippocampus in memory mechanisms. Epilepsy arising in the temporal lobe of the brain assumed special importance because of the re-excitation of past experiences that occurred when the cortex was stimulated during surgery. Some of the modern theories of separable function of the 2 cerebral hemispheres were built upon his findings. His concept of centrencephalic seizures arising from deep midline portions of the brain had an important impact on the understanding of the relationship between the brain's structures and consciousness. Penfield's work brought him many high honours both within Canada and abroad. His scientific papers and the handbooks and monographs he wrote with associates became standard reference works on the function of the human brain.

In the last 15 years of his life Penfield enjoyed a second career as a writer of historical novels and medical biography. He devoted himself to public service, particularly in support of university education, and became first president of the Vanier Inst of the Family. He was widely known for promoting early second-language training. His writings from this period include *The Mystery of the Mind* (1975), summarizing his views on the mind/ brain problem, and *No Man Alone* (1977), an autobiography of the years 1891-1934.

Penfield's most lasting legacy was the foundation and the establishment by endowment of the Montreal Neurological Inst. This neurological hospital integrated with a brain-research complex continues to provide a centre where both basic scientists and physicians study the brain; it has served as a model for similar units throughout the world. To Penfield the brain and the nervous system represented the most important unexplored field in the whole of science. "The problem of neurology," he wrote, "is to understand man himself." Among his honours, he received the Royal Bank Award.   WILLIAM FEINDEL

Penikett, Antony David John, government leader of Yukon (b near Sussex, Eng 14 Nov 1945). Penikett's serious involvement in politics began in 1972 when he was campaign manager for Wally Firth, NDP MP for NWT. His rise in the New Democratic Party hierarchy was rapid; in 1973 he became a member of the party's federal council and during 1975-76 was executive assistant to the national leader. Election to the national party presidency followed, a post he held through 2 terms 1981-85. His success in Yukon politics was as spectacular. First elected to the legislature in 1978 as the sole New Democrat, he became leader of the Opposition in 1981 and leader of a minority government in 1985, upon defeat-

ing the incumbent Conservatives. A strong regionalist, he has been a vocal critic of the MEECH LAKE ACCORD, which he believes will prevent the achievement of provincial status for the Yukon.   STANLEY GORDON

Penner, Jacob, radical politician (b in Russia 12 Aug 1880; d at Winnipeg 28 Aug 1965). Already a Marxist when he arrived in Winnipeg in 1904, he helped found the Social-Democratic Party and was prominent in both the anti-conscription movement in 1917-18 and the WINNIPEG GENERAL STRIKE. A founder of the COMMUNIST PARTY OF CANADA, he was its western organizer for years. In 1933 he was elected to the Winnipeg City Council representing the North End, a position he would hold until his retirement in 1960. At times he was the only Communist member of any elected body in N America. His son Roland became Manitoba's attorney-general in Dec 1981.   IRVING ABELLA

Pension, lifetime payment by a government or employer in consideration of past service after individuals have retired from employment because of age or disability or because they have reached some specified age; after death this payment may be continued, at the same or a reduced level, to the individual's spouse or other survivors. The Canadian pension system has 3 tiers: the public system, the employer-sponsored system and the system to encourage private, individual savings (the last of these includes tax advantages as well). According to goals identified in a federal Green Paper, Canada's pension system is to ensure elderly persons a minimum income (the anti-poverty objective) and to maintain a reasonable relationship between an individual's income before and following retirement (the income replacement objective).

Public pension plans, which include the federal OLD-AGE PENSION (Old Age Security Programs or OAS), the Guaranteed Income Supplement (GIS), the Spouse's Allowance and the CANADA PENSION PLAN or QUÉBEC PENSION PLAN (CPP or QPP), cover all the population or virtually all the labour force. Public plans are schemes for intergenerational transfers. The pensions they provide to the retired and the elderly are financed by taxes levied largely on the younger population. Private pension plans, which cover people working for a particular employer or a group of employers, include government-employee plans. Under private plans contributions are invested to be made available (augmented) at a later period. Any element of transfer in private plans is incidental. There are over 14 500 employer-sponsored plans in Canada. Provincial governments offer to their senior citizens tax advantages and supplements to the OAS/GIS program. While public plans such as CPP/QPP cover all income groups, and the employer-sponsored groups are more restricted in coverage, other schemes such as the Registered Retirement Savings Plan are heavily skewed in favour of middle and upper income groups.

Public Pensions The first national social-security system for old-age pensions was established by German Chancellor Otto von Bismarck in 1889, although Canada was probably more influenced by the British legislation of 1908 which introduced a non-contributory, means-tested old-age pension at age 70. By 1925, most European states had enacted similar schemes. In 1935 the American Social Security Act, a pay-as-you-go system with only a relatively small fund built up to cover fluctuations in the ratio of payments to taxes, was passed.

Under Canada's first public pensions legislation, the Old Age Pension Act (1927), the federal government reimbursed provinces for 50% of the cost of pensions up to $20 per month that were paid by the provinces, after a means test, to persons aged 70 or more. In 1931 the federal share was increased to 75%, but the plan only became national in 1937 when all provinces adopted compatible legislation (*see* SOCIAL SECURITY). The level of benefits and other provisions were adjusted until 1951 when the Act was replaced by the Old Age Security Act, under which $40 monthly was paid to everyone aged 70 or over who passed a residence test. By 1963 the amount had risen to $75.00. With the introduction (1965) of the CPP and QPP, which are compulsory plans based on earnings, 91% of the labour force was covered and provision was made for the gradual reduction from 70 to 65 years of age for eligibility for OAS benefits. The CPP and QPP (phased in over 10 years) are financed by taxes levied on the employee and employer, and the resulting revenues are segregated from the general tax revenues. The revenues from these plans comprise 25% of average individual pensionable earnings; they also include survivor and disability benefits. The GIS, designed to ensure, with the OAS, a minimum socially accepted income for the aged, was also introduced in 1966. The GIS is reduced by $1 for every $2 of non-OAS income. The original maximum supplement for individuals was $40 of OAS payment per month. By 1987 it was $308.19 per month (OAS was $308.19) and was not available if non-OAS income exceeded $8807.99 (the rates are different for married couples); in either case GIS and OAS increase quarterly in proportion to cost of living increases. By Jan 1974 all 3 pensions were fully indexed to the CPI; the OAS and GIS are adjusted quarterly, the CPP and QPP annually. The Spouse's Allowance was introduced in 1975; although only a small program, it benefits women overwhelmingly.

Private Pensions Even before the 19th century, governments provided pensions for disabled veterans and for war widows. Pension plans for public servants, which replaced various ad hoc payments, were instituted in the last half of the 19th century. The GRAND TRUNK RAILWAY introduced the first private-sector employee plan in 1874, but the Labour Commission criticized the GTR for compelling its employees to pay 80% of the cost of their own benefits and for requiring them to waive their rights to any disability or death allowances, even if these resulted from company negligence. The coverage of private-sector plans established by railways and financial institutions has been expanded into other areas of the economy, but it is still partial and a matter of public concern. It has been suggested that the private plans should be made compulsory, with a transfer of pension credits between employers, or that both the level of earnings covered by the CPP and QPP and the proportion of such earnings awarded as a pension be increased. Benefits in employer pension plans are calculated by various formulas – final earnings, career average earnings and flat benefits. Under a final earnings formula, a pension is based upon the contributor's length of service and average earnings in the final years of employment, eg, 5 years or on the best average earnings over a limited period; typically, such a formula would result in a pension equal to one-sixtieth of average annual earnings just before retirement, multiplied by years of service. Career average earnings uses a similar formula. According to the flat benefits formula, the pension is calculated as a specific number of dollars for each year of service. In addition there are money-purchase plans where the benefits obtained depend on contributions over time and on the rates of return on these contributions. Although, for taxation and regulation purposes, the latter are generally considered as pension plans, they resemble

savings plans because no pension formula exists and because payments are limited to the accumulated value of contributions. An important example of individual savings plans for retirement purposes are Registered Retirement Savings Plans. Legislation providing for them was enacted in 1957, and individual contributions up to a maximum that has been altered from time to time can be deducted in calculating taxable income, so that individuals can transfer purchasing power from their working to their retirement period. Such plans are particularly important for the self-employed and, while they do encourage saving, such savings do not occur uniformly across all income classes.

Pension plans define the conditions under which pension benefits accrue to employees whose employment is terminated before retirement. Employees may be eligible, after some years of service, for deferred pensions, calculated according to their years of employment and average earnings, and payable when they reach retirement age. In other cases employees may be permitted to withdraw from pension plans and to have their individual contributions (accumulated at some specified rate of interest) returned. Because pension rights for workers who change employers could be lost, most provinces require that at a minimum pension benefit must be vested in an employee who has reached 45 years of age and worked for 10 years. In such cases the employee's pension contributions are locked in and cannot be withdrawn (subject to certain exemptions) from the plan. These provisions have helped mobile workers; but deferred pensions are related to past earnings which may be substantially below the individual's earnings at retirement. In addition, many years of employment could still slip through the safety net of these provisions, and there are proposals for earlier vesting. The CANADIAN COUNCIL ON SOCIAL DEVELOPMENT reported that of the 2.8 million (40% of the working population) persons covered by private pension plans in 1970, about 40% were employed by government or by crown corporations, so that nearly 70% of those employed by private companies were not receiving coverage. The Canadian Labour Congress estimated that of those covered, only 4-10% collect benefits because many employees quit their jobs before they can collect.

Pension Funds Employers must have sufficient funds to pay private pensions. When they were first established, benefits under private plans were often financed out of the employers' current incomes, but a guaranteed payment required that contributions be set aside each year to build up a fund adequate to cover the payment of promised pensions. Legislation now requires that private plans be funded in this way. The cost of the eventual pension earned by employment in the present depends on factors such as rates of return on investment and future earnings that can only be estimated now. Changes either in benefits or contributions might be required from time to time to meet funding standards. American legislation also requires funding for private plans, but in some European countries, eg, France, the plans are operated on a pay-as-you-go system, with only minimum reserves being kept, possibly because they are compulsory for employees in a geographical area or broad industrial sector. The pensions are guaranteed by the contributions of all workers even though the particular enterprise for which a pensioner has worked may have gone out of business. Technically, these plans, though private, resemble public plans; the compulsory contributions are similar to taxes that result in transfers.

Pensions and Inflation Problems associated with employer-sponsored plans include limited

coverage, vesting, portability, survivor's benefits and complications arising out of divorce and separation; these topics as well as the impact of inflation on pensions, were the subject of national debate in the late 1970s and 1980s. If benefits are tied to final earnings (and the importance of such provisions has increased), then the initial pensions benefit tends to be protected against inflation because earnings keep up with inflation, but its real value can be quickly eroded during retirement. With inflation of 8% over 15 years an unindexed pension for $1.00 is worth 34¢. Very few plans outside the public-sector pensions are indexed to the CPI. Funds may be invested in bonds, equities, mortgages and even real estate, but no particular real rate of return over any period of time in an uncertain world is assured. Interest rates tend to rise during inflationary periods and there have been proposals to adjust nominal pensions by the excess of interest earned over some inflation-free rate, eg, 3%. This would be an improvement over the current situation, but would not necessarily guarantee the real value of pensions. Expansion of the scope of public pensions is supported because they, with taxes based on current earnings, are protected against inflation. A potential weakness of public plans is the possible increase in the ratio of workers to pensions because of demographic changes (*see* AGING), which could increase the burden of pension taxes on workers and possibly lead to a dilution of the real value of pensions. Pension reform proposals in the mid- to late 1980s include raising CPP/QPP benefits to 50% of pensionable earnings and the introduction of pensions for homemakers.

A. ASIMAKOPULOS

Pentecostal Movement in Canada was begun by EVANGELICAL Christians who believed that the world was ripe for a spiritual revival and therefore organized prayer services. Many early Pentecostals were from HOLINESS CHURCHES and held that the faithful must be sanctified by the Holy Spirit after they had been saved. After learning that a revival had begun under W.J. Seymour in Los Angeles, some Canadian evangelicals travelled there to participate. The first report on 9 Apr 1906 emphasized the signs of the revival, especially the initial sign of speaking in other languages when the believer had been filled with the Spirit. This message of the "baptism of the Holy Spirit" was accepted first at the Hebden Mission on Queen St in Toronto. Soon ANGLICANS, MENNONITES, Roman Catholics and METHODISTS were joining those from evangelical and holiness denominations in affirming that they, like Christ's apostles on the first Christian Pentecost (Acts 2), had spoken in other, unlearned languages, as evidence of this "second blessing." In time it became accepted that "speaking in tongues" was the pre-eminent sign of the baptism of the Holy Spirit.

Hostility from home churches and the need to share their experiences led the revivalists to form an umbrella structure. The Pentecostal Missionary Union was formed 1909, initially for missionary purposes. Some leaders were reluctant to formalize the movement into an organization, either because they regarded ecclesiastical governance as man-made, or because they feared the intransigence of their old church hierarchies. By 1917 Pentecostals found that they needed to be a registered society in order to obtain building permits for churches, orphanages and schools. This fact, combined with the existence of government regulations for missionaries sent abroad and the need for doctrinal and disciplinary structure within the movement, led to the formation of a number of associations. These centered on doctrinal issues (eg, Apostolic Church of Pentecost, which rejected trinitarianism), ethnic identity (eg, German Pentecostal Church) or locale (eg, Pentecostal Assemblies of Newfoundland). The largest Pentecostal church, with a present-day membership of 134 000, received its charter in 1919 as the Pentecostal Assemblies of Canada, although for a time it was organically part of the Assemblies of God, the largest US group. In 1981 (the last year for which census figures are available) there were 300 000 active members in Canadian Pentecostal Churches. Canada's best-known Pentecostal was Ontario evangelist Aimee Semple MCPHERSON, who moved to Los Angeles and established the International Church of the Foursquare Gospel, and whose dramatic preaching style and colourful life drew much publicity. Pentecostals have also been successful in using television to propound their ideas, as *100 Huntley Street* shows. *See also* CHARISMATIC RENEWAL.

EARLE WAUGH

Penticton, BC, City, pop 23 588 (1986c), 23 181 (1981c), inc 1948, is nestled between Okanagan and Skaha lakes in S-central BC. Originally called by the Indians *Phthauntac* ("ideal meeting place") and later *Pen-tak-Tin* ("place to stay forever"), it was visited by David Stuart in 1811 and Alexander Ross in 1812. The brigade trail passed by the site 1812-48. The first orchards appeared in the 1890s; the Southern Okanagan Land Co provided irrigation in 1905. A town was formed in 1906. Transportation via rail to Okanagan Landing and stern-wheelers to Penticton had been in place since 1892. The Kettle Valley Ry linked the town to CROWSNEST PASS and HOPE by 1915. Tourism started with the opening of the Hope-Princeton highway in 1949 and increased with completion of the ROGERS PASS section in 1962. The opening of the Peach Bowl convention centre (1965) firmly established the city's year-round attractions.

The 2 largest sources of employment are the service industries and trade. Agriculture, forestry, tourism, manufacturing, mining and the retirement industry are also important. Since the 1960s Penticton has led the province in the production of mobile prefabricated houses. The wine industry is growing. Industrial and population growth, however, is leading to a substantial loss of agricultural land. A good climate, excellent beaches on 2 lakes and developing ski hills have increased tourist interest in Penticton. WILLIAM A. SLOAN

The city of Penticton, located in the southern Okanagan Valley of BC (*photo by Dennis Laing/Reflexion*).

Pentland, Barbara Lally, composer (b at Winnipeg 2 Jan 1912). One of the first Canadian composers to use avant-garde techniques, she studied at the Juilliard School of Music, New York C, and the Berkshire Music Center, Mass. Through her high-quality compositions for piano, orchestra, chamber ensemble and voice she has helped introduce 2 generations of Canadians to modern music. She taught at the Toronto Conservatory of Music from 1943 to 1949 and UBC from 1949 to 1963. Honours include a doctorate from U of Manitoba 1976 and the Diplôme d'honneur be-

stowed by the Canadian Conference of the Arts 1977. Her compositions, some of them commissioned and 17 recorded, are performed all over the world and have been featured on many radio programs, particularly by the CBC. They include *News* (1970), her reaction to violence as reported in the media; *Disasters of the Sun* (1976, text by Dorothy LIVESAY), expressing her fight against male domination; *Music of Now*, a series of 3 books that introduced young pianists to the modern sounds; and her best-known composition, *Studies in Line* (1941), a set of 4 piano pieces that reflect different kinds of linear motion.

TIMOTHY J. MCGEE

Reading: Sheila Eastman and Timothy J. McGee, *Barbara Pentland* (1983).

Pépin, Clermont, composer, pianist, professor, administrator (b at St-Georges-de-Beauce, Qué 15 May 1926). First taught composition by Claude CHAMPAGNE, Rosario Scalero and Arnold Walter, he won the 1949 Prix d'Europe as a pianist and studied composition, theory and piano in Paris. He taught at the Montréal Conservatory of Music, of which he was director 1967-72, and also at the Québec Conservatory of Music. He was VP (1966-70) and president (1981-83) of CAPAC, and national president of JEUNESSES MUSICALES DU CANADA (1969-72). His major works include *Guernica*, a symphonic poem; *Quasars*, *Symphonie No 3*; *La Messe sur le monde*, *Symphonie No 4*; *Cycle Éluard*; and a series of works called *Monade*. In 1982 he composed *Trio No 2* for violin, cello and piano (commissioned by Radio-Canada) and in 1983 completed *Implosion*, *Symphonie No 5* (commissioned by the Montréal Symphony Orchestra). He won the 1970 Prix de Musique Calixa-Lavallée and in 1980 founded Les Éditions Clermont Pépin. He is fascinated with new techniques in writing music, and all that surrounds it. He was one of the founders in 1965 of a study group about the future, the Centre d'études prospectives du Québec, of which he became president. HÉLÈNE PLOUFFE

Pepin, Jean-Luc, academic, politician (b at Drummondville, Qué 1 Nov 1924). Educated at U of Ottawa and U of Paris, Pepin later taught political science at U of O. Elected as a Liberal to the House of Commons in 1963, he held several Cabinet posts between 1965 and 1972 under PMs PEARSON and TRUDEAU. Defeated in 1972, Pepin was engaged in business 1973-75, and in 1975 became chairman of the ANTI-INFLATION BOARD. In 1977 Trudeau made him cochairman, with John ROBARTS, of a task force on CANADIAN UNITY. Returning to politics 1979-84, Pepin served as minister of transport 1980-83 and then as minister of state in the Dept of External Affairs. He later returned to U of O and is fellow in residence for the Institute for Research on Public Policy. An engaging and informal speaker, Pepin was known for his ability to tackle difficult issues, including abolition of the CROW'S NEST PASS AGREEMENT rates, which occupied him as minister of transport.

ROBERT BOTHWELL

Pepin, Marcel, labour leader (b at Montréal 28 Feb 1926). After completing an MA in industrial relations at Laval (1949) he worked for the Fédération nationale de la métallurgie. Secretary general of the Confédération des syndicats nationaux from 1961, he succeeded Jean MARCHAND as president 1965-76, promising a war on POVERTY. During his 10-year presidency the CSN became more and more radical as its leaders promoted an independent and socialist Québec. Pepin helped create the COMMON FRONT, an organization of all public- and parapublic-sector unions that invoked a general strike in 1972. Robert BOURASSA's government sent him and other union leaders to jail for

refusing to comply with back-to-work legislation. Pepin has been a member of Québec state corporations such as the Société générale de financement and the CAISSE DE DÉPÔT ET DE PLACEMENT. He was an ardent supporter of the PARTI QUÉBÉCOIS. Pepin maintained his public presence into the 1980s; in 1986 he attacked Bill 37, which proposed to outlaw strikes among government employees and that year was appointed to the publishing agency of *Le Devoir*. MICHAEL D. BEHIELS

Pepper (*Capsicum annuum*), perennial plant, cultivated as an annual and belonging to the NIGHTSHADE family. Native to tropical America, peppers were widely disseminated after Columbus's discovery of America; some botanists now claim that certain species are native to southern Asia. Some botanical varieties crossbreed naturally and many cultivars (commercial varieties) exist. Most pepper plants are well branched, 35-80 cm tall, with smooth, glossy, oblong-to-ovate leaves. They bear either erect or drooping fruits. Immature fruits of all types are green. Depending on variety, mature fruits are mostly red or yellow, and sweet or hot. Most fruits are puffy regardless of shape; all types have a central core with attached seeds. Peppers are started under glass, 8-10 weeks before transplanting, after all risk of frost is past. They require 55-80 days to mature in the field. Across Canada, common insect pests are potato aphids, flea beetles; in SW Ontario, European corn borer, pepper maggot and green peach aphid. Major plant diseases are damping-off, bacterial leaf spot, viruses and *Verticillium* wilt. Peppers, high in vitamins A and C, are eaten fresh or cooked, or used to produce condiments, pickles, sauces, etc. Varieties have been developed for Canada's different climatic regions. Commercial production is confined to the favoured climatic areas, eg, southern Ontario and BC. Canada's production in 1986 was 21 250 t, of which 16 229 t was produced in Ontario.

V.W. NUTTALL

Pepper, George Douglas, painter (b at Ottawa 25 Feb 1903; d at Toronto 1 Oct 1962). He studied under J.E.H. MACDONALD and J.W. Beatty in Toronto, and then in Paris and Italy (1924-25). He was strongly influenced by the GROUP OF SEVEN and his sense of line and rhythmic pattern produced many works in the 1920s and 1930s sympathetic to the Group's approach to Canadian landscape. Still, he forfeited none of his own originality in arrangement and perspective, as in *Totem Poles, Kitiwanga* (1930). Pepper served as an official war artist in WWII and helped illustrate many subsequent publications about the war. He painted several commissions for the Canadian government and on its behalf spent 3 months with his wife, artist Kathleen Daly, studying Inuit art in the eastern Arctic in 1960. Pepper taught at the Ontario College of Art and the Banff School of Fine Arts. He was a founding member of the Canadian Group of Painters (1933) and was elected to the Royal Canadian Academy of Arts in 1957.

ERIK J. PETERS

Pepperrell, Sir William, commander in chief of New England forces at LOUISBOURG (b at Kittery Point, Maine 27 June 1696; d there 6 July 1759). Reared in his father's counting house, the most successful in colonial Maine, trading in fish and lumber to the W Indies and England, he became a popular member of the Massachusetts Bay House of Representatives as an assemblyman and as a member of council (1727-59). He was selected to command the New England forces at the 1745 siege of Louisbourg, after a long career as a militia colonel, but his skills in business were unsuited to the military task. The capitulation of the fortress brought him a colonelcy in a newly raised regiment of foot and a baronetcy, both unique achievements, until then, for an American. His regiment formed part of the Louisbourg garrison, though he resided in Boston. Promoted maj-gen in 1755, he led his regiment in the abortive campaign against Fort Niagara. In 1757 he served briefly as acting governor of Massachusetts.

JULIAN GWYN

Percé, Qué, City, pop 4686 (1986c), 4839 (1981c), inc 1970, is located 750 km NE of Québec City on the shore of the Gulf of ST LAWRENCE. The neighbouring villages of Barachois, Bridgeville, Cap-d'Espoir and St-Pierre-de-la-Malbaie were amalgamated in 1970; the old town itself has a population of about 1500. Its magnificent location attracts many visitors from around the world. Percé takes its name from PERCÉ ROCK, which dominates the area. Dozens of species of birds flock in the thousands to Bonaventure Island Conservation Park, a few kilometres offshore. Percé's history is as old as that of NEW FRANCE. Jacques CARTIER arrived there in 1534, and European fishermen used the bay as a haven in the 16th and 17th centuries. Missionaries have served this fishing port since 1673, although the mission was destroyed in 1690 by English troops and no one lived there again until the Conquest. With the arrival of the LOYALISTS, Percé became more active. Until the end of the 19th century, the local economy depended almost exclusively on fishing, but the region then began to attract tourists and the economy is now based largely on tourism and fishing. Leading Québec and Canadian artists have made the town a centre of artistic activity.

ANTONIO LECHASSEUR

The spectacular Percé Rock is the most famous landmark on the Gaspé Peninsula and attracts visitors from around the world (*photo by Al Williams*).

Percé Rock, Qué, monolith in the GASPÉ Peninsula, 750 km E of Québec City, near its namesake, the town of PERCÉ. This island-peninsula, once attached to the shoreline, is of an impressive size: 510 m long, 100 m wide and 70 m high. Its name derives from the fact that the sea has pierced holes in its structure to form archways. According to some, there were once 4 arches, but only one large opening, 30 m wide, exists today. Enigmatic and fascinating, immortalized by artists, poets and writers, Percé Rock is one of the major tourist attractions of Québec and Canada, and is an important bird sanctuary.   ANTONIO LECHASSEUR

Perch Although perch is the common name for several distantly related species of fish, it properly refers to members of the perch family (Percidae), order Perciformes, class Osteichthyes. Perches are

Fourteen species of perch occur in Canada. The yellow perch (*Perca flavescens*), shown here, is a common sport fish (*artwork by Claire Tremblay*).

small- to medium-sized, carnivorous, bottom-dwelling, freshwater fishes usually with long, rounded, laterally compressed bodies and 2 dorsal fins. The swim bladder is usually reduced or absent; eyes are conspicuous; dorsal, anal and pelvic fins are spined. In N America, true perches were confined, originally, to the area E of the Rocky Mts, but some species have been introduced to the West.

In Canada, 14 species of true perch occur, including the yellow perch, the WALLEYE and sauger, and 11 darters (genera *Ammocrypta, Etheostoma, Percina*). Darters are very small fish, few being longer than 8 cm. They are most common in Ontario; no species are native W of the Rocky Mts. The yellow perch (*Perca flavescens*) is the one most commonly thought of as "perch." It is distinguished from other members of its warm- to cool-water community by its short, stubby, hunch-backed body; 2 dorsal fins, of which the first has spiny rays; rather large mouth; bright yellow to green eyes; and lateral pattern of 7 green to brownish, tapered bars over a bright yellow to greenish undercoat. It spawns in spring (Apr-May) in southern Canada, as late as July in the North. No nest is built, but the unique, transparent, gelatinous, accordion-folded strings of eggs are looped over vegetation. These strings can be as long as 2 m and as heavy as 1 kg, and contain an average of 23 000 eggs. The large numbers of almost transparent young are significant in the diets of other important fishes. The largest adult yellow perch are usually 20-30 cm long, weighing 170-340 g. Specimens as large as 35 cm have been taken in eastern Canada, and one taken in Québec weighed almost 2 kg. Individuals can survive to 9 years of age. This N American species has a wide native distribution in Canada, from NS (excluding Cape Breton I), across Ontario, northward through most of Manitoba, Saskatchewan and Alberta, southern BC (introduced) and N to Great Slave Lk, NWT. Both young and adults form schools of 50-200 individuals, making them attractive to anglers and commercial fishermen.

Yellow perch are regularly hosts to parasites such as yellow grub (in flesh) and blackspot (on skin), neither of which infect humans. Less frequently, perch carry the broad tapeworm, which can infect humans if raw or poorly cooked fish are eaten. In Canada, this species is classed as a sport and commercial fish. In spring, numerous larger individuals, migrating to spawning grounds, attract anglers. The white, flaky, very tasty flesh makes yellow perch a prominent commercial species in the Great Lakes. The commercial catch in Canada in 1984 was 5413 t, yielding a value of $19.3 million.   E.J. CROSSMAN

Percival, Lloyd, sport figure (b at Toronto 3 June 1913; d there 23 July 1974). A controversial and versatile entrepreneur, Percival was an all-rounder in his youth, competing successfully in many sports. His honours include Canadian junior tennis finals, Canadian bantam Golden

Gloves boxing champion, and a tour of England in 1936 with the Canadian cricket team. He also coached ice hockey and track and field. He is perhaps best remembered for his popular CBC radio Sports College, launched in 1941, which had 800 000 students registered at its peak, and his Fitness Institute, where he pioneered many testing and coaching techniques. Percival conditioned many well-known Canadian athletes, eg, golfer George Knudson. He received the Coronation Medal from Queen Elizabeth.

GERALD REDMOND

Peregrine Falcon (*Falco peregrinus*), crow-sized, long-winged BIRD OF PREY, generally acknowledged to be the swiftest bird (attaining speeds of over 320 km/h). The name, which means wandering, is well suited to this species, represented by 18 races and found breeding on every continent (except Antarctica). Adults are dark blue-grey to blue-black above with dark bars on a salmon to white breast and belly. They have either very dark cheeks or moustachelike markings on the side of the head. Immature birds have brownish plumage with darker, longitudinal stripes on the breast. Both sexes have similar plumages, although males frequently have much paler breasts. Males (tiercels) are about one-third smaller than females (falcons).

The peregrine preys almost exclusively on bird species in most parts of its range (coastal and inland cliffs). Normally, 3-5 eggs are laid on a cliff ledge in a slight depression scraped out of earth or gravel by the female. There is little or no nest. Eggs are incubated, mainly by the female, for about 33 days. The male's role is primarily to protect the territory and provide food for the female and young. When young are half grown, the female may help provide food. Young leave the nest at about 5 weeks but remain nearby and depend on parents for food until they can hunt for themselves. Shortly thereafter, the birds leave the nesting area and begin MIGRATION. The first year is very difficult for young. Band-recovery information indicates that only about 1 in 4 lives to return to the breeding grounds. Whether peregrines migrate depends on food supply and climatic conditions. The Canadian tundra peregrine (*F. peregrinus tundrius*) winters as far S as southern S America, whereas the W coast peregrine (*F. p. pealei*) is essentially nonmigratory. The third race breeding in Canada is the endangered anatum peregrine (*F. p. anatum*), which bred across Canada wherever adequate food and nesting habitat were available. These birds wintered from the southern US through Central America into northern S America. The anatum peregrine has declined to near extinction in most of the breeding range. The decline is well documented, and studies indicate that the principal cause was reproductive failure resulting from contamination by PESTICIDES (especially DDT) which cause eggshell thinning. The bird has become a symbol of the problems resulting from misuse of the ENVIRONMENT. In Canada and the US, specific conservation programs have been very successful, and many young anatum peregrines, bred in captivity, are being released in the wild annually. *See also* WILDLIFE CONSERVATION AND MANAGEMENT; ENDANGERED ANIMALS.   R.W. FYFE

Perehudoff, William, painter (b at Langham, Sask 1919). Though he has lived most of his adult life in Saskatoon, he left the Prairies as a young man to study art. He explored mural painting at the Colorado Springs Fine Art Center (1948-49), then studied with French Cubist Amédée Ozenfant in New York. Ozenfant's purism and insistence on "significant form" impressed Perehudoff deeply. The notion of stripping a painting down to its essentials is the core of his developed work

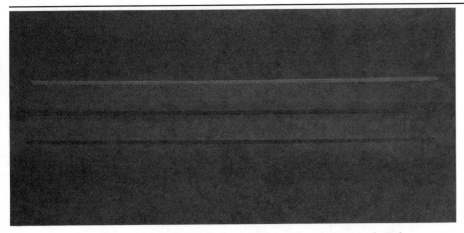

Amyot, acrylic on canvas, 1975, by William Perehudoff (*courtesy Woltjen/Udell Gallery*).

30 years later. Perehudoff's knowledge and ambition were expanded by his travels in the US and Europe in 1952. He married Dorothy KNOWLES in 1952 and they returned to western Canada, where he earned his living as a commercial artist. U Sask's summer artists' workshops at Emma Lake influenced him during the period 1957-68, notably those led by American critic Clement Greenberg (1962) and painter Kenneth Noland (1963). Their respect for his work encouraged his development of large-scale, abstract painting. Perehudoff's continuing preoccupations are with colour, surface and texture. His work has evolved through complex orchestrations of shifting, transparent bands of colour, to his most recent textured areas of intense, saturated hues. He has exhibited widely in Canada, the US and Europe, and is regarded by many as the heir to Jack BUSH as Canada's most important colour field painter.

Pérez Hernández, Juan Josef, naval officer, explorer (b *c* 1725 at Majorca, Spain; d 2 Nov 1775 off Calif). Pérez served as a pilot and marine officer in Spain's Pacific trade between Mexico and the Philippines and in the Spanish expansion into Alta California. He was curious about the unknown northern coastline and his request to explore it coincided with the Spanish government's desire for information on Russian penetration southward. In 1774 he sailed aboard the frigate *Santiago* with orders to reach at least 60°N lat. Pérez was the first European to explore the Queen Charlotte Is and to approach Nootka Sound, but unfavourable weather prevented him from landing to take formal possession for Spain. Although he reached only about 55°30' lat and left some missions unfulfilled, he collected important data that served future Spanish mariners. Pérez was second officer in the 1775 expedition commanded by Bruno de Hezeta, but he died at sea. CHRISTON I. ARCHER

Periglacial Landform, a feature resulting from the action of intense frost, often combined with the presence of PERMAFROST. Periglacial landforms are restricted to areas that experience cold but essentially nonglacial climates. The term was proposed by Walery von Lozinski in 1909 to describe frost weathering conditions in the Carpathian Mts of central Europe. Subsequently, the concept of a "periglacial zone" developed, referring to the climatic and geomorphic conditions of areas peripheral to the Pleistocene ice sheets and GLACIERS. Theoretically, this zone was a TUNDRA region extending as far S as the TREELINE. Modern usage encompasses a wide range of cold, nonglacial conditions, regardless of their proximity to glaciers in time or space. Periglacial environments exist not only in high latitudes and tundra regions but also in areas S of the treeline and in high altitude (alpine) regions of temperate latitudes.

Approximately 50% of the land surface of Canada currently experiences periglacial conditions (intense frost action, the presence of permafrost, or both). All gradations exist between environments in which frost action processes dominate and where all or a major part of the landscape is the result of such processes, and those in which frost action processes are subservient to others. Some complicating factors are the varying susceptibilities of different rock formations to frost action and the fact that there is no perfect correlation between areas of intense frost action and areas underlain by permafrost. Large areas of northern Canada have only recently emerged from the late Wisconsinan GLACIATION, and periglacial processes currently serve to modify their glacial landforms. In areas that have experienced longer histories of nonglacial conditions, eg, northern interior YT, NW BANKS ISLAND and other high-arctic islands, landscapes are more likely to be in equilibrium with current periglacial conditions. Processes unique to periglacial environments include formation of permafrost, development of thermal contraction cracks, thawing of permafrost (formation of thermokarst), and formation of wedge and injection ice. Other processes, not necessarily restricted to periglacial regions, are important because of their high magnitude or frequency in cold, nonglacial environments. These include ice segregation, seasonal frost action and various forms of instability and rapid mass movement. Nearly all frost-action processes operate in conjunction with the freezing of water.

The most distinctive periglacial landforms are those associated with permafrost. The most widespread, tundra polygons formed by thermal-contraction cracking, divide the ground surface up into polygonal nets 20-30 m in dimension. Water often penetrates the cracks to form ice wedges several metres deep and up to 1-2 m wide near the surface. In drier environments, mineral soil infills the cracks and sand wedges result. Ice-cored hills (PINGOS) are a less widespread periglacial landform. Pingos form when water moves to the freezing plane under a pressure gradient that may be hydraulic or hydrostatic in nature. Pingos are not typical of all periglacial landscapes but result from specific geomorphic and hydrologic conditions that severely limit their occurrence. Other aggradational landforms such as palsas and peat plateaus are usually associated with ice segregation rather than injection. Ground-ice slumps, thaw lakes and irregular depressions (thermokarst) resulting from the melt and erosion of ice-rich permafrost constitute a further group of related periglacial landforms.

Many periglacial phenomena result from frost wedging and the cryogenic weathering of exposed bedrock. Frost wedging is associated with the freezing and expansion of water which penetrates joints and bedding planes. The details of cryogenic weathering are still poorly understood. Coarse, angular rock debris (block fields), normally attributed to frost wedging or cryogenic weathering, occur widely over large areas above the treeline and in the arctic islands. In addition, frost-heaved bedrock blocks and extensive talus (scree) slopes are common. Angular, frost-shattered rock protuberances (tors) may stand out above the debris-covered surfaces, reflecting more resistant bedrock. These are most frequent in SEDIMENTARY ROCKS, especially in the arctic islands (eg, SOMERSET ISLAND); however, in the unglaciated interior of the YT (Klondike Plateau) tors are formed on very old and extremely resistant metamorphic rocks. Flat, erosional surfaces (cryoplanation terraces) are sometimes associated with tors but can also occur independently.

Agents of transport include frost creep, the ratchetlike movement that occurs when soil, during a freeze-thaw cycle, expands normally to the surface and settles in a more nearly vertical direction; and solifluction, the slow downslope movement of water-saturated debris. Where solifluction occurs on or above frozen ground, it is termed gelifluction. Solifluction lobes, sheets and terraces are especially well developed above the treeline and below sites of perennial snowbanks.

The small-scale relief of periglacial regions is characterized by various patterned ground phenomena. These are often related to cryoturbation, the lateral and vertical displacement of soil that accompanies seasonal or diurnal freezing and thawing. The most widespread are nonsorted circles or nets, typically 1-2 m in diameter and up to 0.5 m high. In the Mackenzie Valley, they occur over extensive areas, wherever fine-textured and poorly drained sediments exist. In Keewatin, morphologically similar forms caused by density differences in saturated sediments are termed "mud boils." A wide range of nonsorted and sorted forms of patterned ground are described from other parts of northern Canada, and no single explanation is applicable to all. *See also* PHYSIOGRAPHIC REGIONS. HUGH M. FRENCH

Reading: Hugh M. French, *The Periglacial Environment* (1976).

The distinctive polygons are the result of winter contraction cracks that have become filled with ice formed from percolating summer meltwater (*photo by Stephen J. Krasemann/DRK Photo*).

Periodical Writers Association of Canada
(PWAC) is a nonprofit organization founded in
1976 to promote the development of free lance
writers in Canada. One of its earliest achievements was the formulation of a Code of Ethics and
a contract which defines the rights and obligations of both writers and publishers. Among the
other services that PWAC offers are an annual
survey of standard fees paid by Canadian periodicals to freelancers, a bimonthly national newsletter, an annual directory of professional members,
professional development workshops and seminars and the assistance of the PWAC Grievance
Committee. The association has also produced a
best-selling guide to free lance writing entitled
Words for Sale (1979, ed by Eve Drobot and Hal
Tennant). The association, whose national office
is in Toronto, represents a membership of over
300 writers across the country.   JENIVA BERGER

Periwinkle, common name for any of the edible
intertidal SNAILS of the genus *Littorina.* Periwinkles are represented by 6 species in Canadian
coastal waters. *Littorina littorea,* the common
periwinkle, was introduced in 1850 to the East
Coast from western Europe where it is a popular
food. The northern yellow periwinkle (*L. obtusa-
ta*) is another Atlantic coast species, which is usually found associated with rockweeds. *Littorina
scutulata,* the checkered periwinkle, is a dominant
species in British Columbia's coastal intertidal region, where it nestles among BARNACLES in upper
littoral zones. Where its southern range extends
into California, *L. scutulata* is in competition with
the eroded periwinkle, *L. planaxis.* Species of *Littorina* usually occupy the upper reaches of the
rocky intertidal zones where they graze on en-
crusted algal material by means of a radula, a rib-
bonlike organ covered by many hundreds of
minute teeth. This feeding device emerges from a
snoutlike head which supports a pair of tentacles
each bearing a single eye. The littorines are a relatively advanced group of prosobranch gastropod
MOLLUSCS with separate sexes and internal fertilization. Some species release pelagic egg cases
from which larvae hatch; others brood their eggs,
giving birth to larvae or little snails.
                                    PETER V. FANKBONER

Perjury A witness in a judicial proceeding who
knowingly gives false evidence with intent to
mislead the judge or jury commits the crime of
perjury. If a person knowingly makes a false statement under oath outside a judicial proceeding, he
or she would also be guilty of an offence.
                                    VINCENT M. DEL BUONO

Perkins, Simeon, merchant, diarist (b at Nor-
wich, Conn 24 Feb 1735; d at Liverpool, NS 9
May 1812). He arrived in Liverpool in 1762 and
rapidly became the leading local merchant, dealing in fish and lumber, building sawmills and
small vessels, and developing a trade with New
England and the W Indies. During the AMERICAN
REVOLUTION he invested profitably in several Liverpool privateers. His ability, integrity and charity
resulted in a long civic career in local administrative and judicial offices. He also held high rank in
the militia. He served as MLA for Queens County
1765-99 and, although his attendance was intermittent, he was quietly effective. His diary (1766-
1812), published in 5 volumes by the CHAMPLAIN
SOCIETY, and his home, now a museum, are valuable records of a man whose career reflects NS's
economic, social and political beginnings.
                                    LOIS KERNAGHAN

Reading: C.B. Fergusson, *Early Liverpool and Its Diarist*
(1961).

Perley, Sir George Halsey, politician (b at
Lebanon, NH 12 Sept 1857; d at Ottawa 4 Jan
1938). After a Harvard education, Perley spent

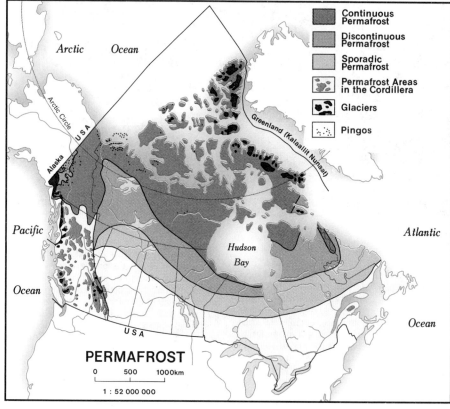

the early part of his working life carrying on his
father's business in the Ottawa lumber trade. Entering Parliament, the wealthy and socially ambitious Perley represented Argenteuil, 1904-17 and
1925-38, and served as a Cabinet minister under
PMs Borden, Meighen and Bennett. He was especially influential under Borden, who appointed
him high commissioner in London, 1914-22, and
minister of the overseas military forces of Canada,
1916-17. Here Perley consistently shielded the
Canadian Corps from the partisan personnel policies which had been standard under former defence minister Sam HUGHES.   STEPHEN HARRIS

Perley, Moses Henry, lawyer, naturalist, author (b at Maugerville, NB 31 Dec 1804; d off
Labrador coast 17 Aug 1862). An avid sportsman
and natural historian, Perley became the leading
authority on NB's resources in the mid-19th century. In 1842 he prepared a report on the
province's Indian reserves – the basis for its 1844
Indian Reserve Act. He was active in forming the
Saint John Mechanics' Institute in 1838 and the
Provincial Assn in 1844, was provincial emigrant
agent 1843-48 and in 1854 published a *Handbook...for Emigrants.* In 1846 and 1848 he prepared reports on possible railway routes. He published a report on trees (1847) and 1848-49
reports on NB's fish and the fisheries of the Gulf of
St Lawrence and Bay of Fundy. Perley collected
information used in Reciprocity Treaty (1854)
negotiations and in 1855 he became a fishery
commissioner.   W.A. SPRAY

Permafrost, ground remaining at or below 0°C
continuously for at least 2 years. It may consist of
cold, dry earth; cold, wet, saline earth; icy lenses
and masses; or ice-cemented earth or rock. Although GLACIERS fit this definition, they are a special case dealt with elsewhere. Most permafrost
includes ice cement, lenses or masses that result
from the freezing of the bulk of subsurface water.
At most surface temperatures some capillary water will be unfrozen. Saline water in soil freezes
below 0°C; hence, unfrozen permafrost occurs
below parts of the shores of the Arctic Ocean and
in cold brine pockets in the ground. If the ground

is dry, no ice will be present despite the temperature. In permafrost regions, the upper layer that
undergoes seasonal freezing and thawing is called
the active layer. Below this lies the permafrost,
the upper surface of which is called the permafrost table. Permafrost is mapped as follows:
where over 80% of the ground is underlain by
permafrost, it is continuous; 30-80%, discontinuous, with the rest being unfrozen talik; under
30%, sporadic. Taliks occur beneath water bodies
and where water flows through the ground,
keeping it warm. Permafrost is produced by a surface sub-zero winter heat flux which is greater
than the surface above-zero summer heat flux
and the annual geothermal heat flux. Its development is favoured by high latitude and altitude, by
long, cold winters and thin winter snow cover.
Cold-air drainage in mountain valleys or through
rock caves may cause pockets of permafrost in the
sporadic zone.

Permafrost underlies 20-25% of the Earth's
land area, including about 99% of Greenland,
80% of Alaska, 50% of the USSR, 40-50% of Canada and 20% of China. The greatest thicknesses in
Canada are over 1000 m at high elevations in
parts of Baffin and Ellesmere islands, ranging
down to 60-90 m at the southern limit of the continuous permafrost zone. Active layer thicknesses
range from under 10 cm in Ellesmere to 15 m at
high altitudes in the mountains of SW Alberta on
the outer margin of continuous permafrost. The
coldest ground temperatures in permafrost
worldwide are to be found on ELLESMERE I (about
-15°C). The permafrost in Canada developed
largely after the last GLACIATION, and its distribution adjusts to small climate changes. Thus the
continuous permafrost zone extended to S of Fort
Norman in the mid-19th century. A 4°C warming
of the winter air temperature resulted in the migration of its southern boundary nearly to Inuvik.
Since 1940, a 2°C cooling in the mean winter
temperature has resulted in the boundary moving
southwards to Arctic Red R. Similar changes can
be demonstrated in alpine areas and in Alaska,
northern USSR, etc.

The ice in permafrost may be interstitial or segregated, and is concentrated in the few metres immediately below the permafrost table. Water tends to move through the pores to the freezing plane, resulting in ice contents as high as 1600% by weight of the mineral matter in some silts and peats in low-lying areas, eg, the Mackenzie Delta. The segregated ice may be in isolated masses, in distinct lenses parallel to the surface or in wedges tapering downwards. Distinctive landforms are associated with permafrost (*see* PERIGLACIAL LANDFORM). The ice wedges form a polygonal pattern and are the result of winter contraction cracks that have become infilled with ice from percolating summer meltwater. In dry areas, sand may fill in the cracks, forming sand wedges within the permafrost table. On steep slopes, high ice content may permit unconsolidated deposits to move slowly downslope as rock glaciers. In taliks, the freezing of water may cause the localized growth of PINGOS, ice-cored mounds up to 100 m high. Localized ice segregation in wet lowlands can form mounds domed up by small lenses of ice (palsas). Seasonal freezing in the active layer can cause the turning up of stones, heaving of the ground, and sorting of coarse and fine rock material. These seasonal changes also cause physical weathering of the bedrock and can reduce mudstones to silts, eg, along the Dempster Hwy in Rat Pass, NWT. The sorting processes can form patterned ground in only 5 years. Thawing of the permafrost often results in subsidence where ice was present and also in the formation of thaw lakes or hummocky terrain. This terrain, called thermokarst, can be induced by human activities.

The presence of ice and the consequences of an alteration in the thermal regime make economic development of permafrost terrain difficult. All materials, except gravels or clean sand, heave or become unstable during seasonal freezing and thawing. Normal agriculture is impossible over permafrost because of subsidence, while heated structures must be separated from the frozen ground by adequate insulation. Paved roads or runways increase summer heating and require a suitable insulating subgrade. Even a slight alteration of the vegetation cover may cause thermokarst subsidence. Artificial refrigeration of the ground is too expensive for all except special cases, which is why the Alaska oil PIPELINE is placed on supports in permafrost areas. Water supplies are difficult to obtain except where natural springs or deep lakes occur. Sewage disposal is a major problem. Construction of dams for HYDROELECTRICITY requires special techniques, as do mining and drilling for oil and gas. The elasticity of ice reduces the effectiveness of explosive charges. Ice-rich ore is more difficult to process because it must be thawed. Drilling without disturbing the environment is practically impossible in Canada. STUART A. HARRIS

Reading: R.J.E. Brown, *Permafrost in Canada* (1970); G.H. Johnston, *Permafrost Engineering Design and Construction* (1981); A.L. Washburn, *Geocryology* (1979).

Permanent Joint Board on Defence, a Canadian-American advisory body established Ogdensburg, NY, 18 Aug 1940, by PM Mackenzie King and US Pres F.D. Roosevelt. This meeting, which took place at Roosevelt's suggestion in a period of crisis in WORLD WAR II, inaugurated an era of intimate military ties. The PJBD first met 26 Aug 1940, and had its greatest influence from then until Dec 1941, when the US entered the war. Consisting of 2 national sections, each composed of a chairman (usually a civilian) and representatives of the armed forces and foreign service, the board studies joint defence problems and offers recommendations to the respective governments. Although now only one of a number of agencies for Canadian-American military co-operation, it continues as an arena for frank and informal exchange of views and information.
NORMAN HILLMER

Perrault, Pierre, film director, poet (b at Montréal 29 June 1927). After working for Radio-Canada, he codirected the series "Au pays de Neufve-France" and then made a début in film at the NFB with Michel BRAULT in *Pour la suite du monde* (1963), a classic of direct cinema. Still with the NFB, he directed *Le Règne du jour* (1966) and *Les Voitures d'eau* (1968), which form a trilogy with the 1963 film. He then turned to 2 controversial issues, Québec separatism (*Un Pays sans bon sens* 1970) and the fate of the Acadians (*L'Acadie, l'Acadie* 1971). These were followed by series on the Abitibi region: *Un Royaume vous attend* (1975), *Le Retour à la terre* (1976), *Gens d'Abitibi* (1980), *C'était un québecois en Bretagne, madame* (1977); and American Indians: *Le Goût de la farine* (1976), *Le Pays de la terre sans arbre ou le Mouchouânipi* (1980). In 1982 his film about hunting (*La Bête lumineuse*) had an enormous emotional impact on Québec audiences. He then chose Saint-Malo, France, birthplace of Jacques CARTIER, as the setting for *Les Voiles bas et en travers* (1983) and his next film *La grande Allure* (1985) relived the voyage of Cartier to America. A major director of realist cinema, Perrault is a master of words and a skilful interpreter of the human soul. He was awarded an honorary doctorate by Laval in 1986. PIERRE VÉRONNEAU

Perreault, Jean-Pierre, modern dancer, choreographer, scenographer (b at Montréal 16 Feb 1947). He started dance training at 17 in Montréal with Jeanne Renaud and Peter Boneham, continuing his studies in Europe and New York City. In 1971 he became co-artistic director of Le GROUPE DE LA PLACE ROYALE, Ottawa. His creative explorations with Le Groupe were nontraditional and often controversial. He attempted to break the barriers between the arts by using dancers as singers and musicians to produce an integrated work of art. Still closely associated with the company, he resigned the co-directorship in 1980 to work as an independent choreographer and teacher. He founded his own company, Fondation Jean-Pierre Perreault in Montréal 1983. Successful productions include *Highway 86* (commissioned by Expo 86) and *Nuit* (1986).
JILLIAN M. OFFICER

Perry, Aylesworth Bowen, police officer (b at Violet, Ont 21 Aug 1860; d at Ottawa 14 Feb 1956). As commissioner of the NWMP, Perry transformed the police from a romantic frontier force into a modern national police force. A member of the first class at RMC, Kingston, Ont, Perry joined the police as an inspector in 1882, served with the Alberta Field Force during the NORTHWEST REBELLION in 1885, and was placed in command of the police in the Yukon in 1899. As commissioner 1900-23, Perry modernized the force's equipment and methods. During WWI, departures to serve overseas weakened the force, and the creation of provincial police forces in Alberta and Saskatchewan reduced its responsibilities. The future of the force was in doubt, but it proved its usefulness in controlling postwar unrest, and Perry was made responsible for reorganizing the force as the ROYAL CANADIAN MOUNTED POLICE.
A.B. McCULLOUGH

Persaud, Trivedi Vidhya Nandan, anatomist (b at Pt Mourant, Guyana 19 Feb 1940). Educated at Rostock, E Ger (MD 1965, DSc 1974), and U of W Indies, Kingston, Jamaica (PhD 1970), Persaud has received international acclaim for his research in embryology, teratology and pathology. He was editor of the *West Indian Medical Journal*, 1970-73, and president of the Canadian Assn of Anatomists, 1981-83. Author of several medical books, notably *Basic Concepts in Teratology* and *Early History of Human Anatomy*, he also has edited *Advances in the Study of Birth Defects* (7 vols). He has published more than 130 scientific papers. He was elected a fellow of the Royal College of Pathologists (London) and of the Royal College of Physicians (Ireland) in 1984. KEITH L. MOORE

Person, Clayton Oscar, scientist, educator (b at Regina 16 May 1922). Educated at Saskatoon, Alberta and overseas, Person has worked at U Man, U of A and UBC. He is recognized internationally as an authority on the genetics of host-parasite relations. His writings have made a major contribution to the development of a rigorous theoretical basis for our understanding of how the genetic structure of parasitic populations interacts with that of their host populations. His theoretical methods have been applied widely in the practical management of parasitic diseases in agriculture and forestry. In 1971 he was elected a fellow of the RSC; in 1981 he was awarded the BC Science Council's gold medal and was elected fellow of the American Phytopathological Soc; in 1982 he received the RSC's Flavelle Medal and the Genetics Soc of Canada's Award of Excellence. He was made a Member of the Order of Canada in 1986. A.J.F. GRIFFITHS

Persons Case In 1928, the SUPREME COURT OF CANADA unanimously decided women were not "persons" who could hold public office as Canadian senators. The terms of the CONSTITUTION ACT, 1867, and the historical incapacity of women to hold office under common law barred the suit of Henrietta Muir EDWARDS and her companion Alberta suffragettes. In 1929 the British Privy Council reversed the decision and called the exclusion of women from public office "a relic of days more barbarous than ours." The Governor General's Persons Award, for work on behalf of Canadian women, is named for the case.

DAVID A. CRUICKSHANK

Perth, Ont, Town, seat of Lanark County, inc 1850 (village), 1854 (town), pop 5673 (1986c), 5655 (1981c), located on the Tay R, 83 km SW of Ottawa. It was laid out 1816 as a backwoods military settlement intended to provide experienced militiamen for the defence of the inland water route linking the Ottawa R and Lk Ontario. Perth was joined to the RIDEAU CANAL by a separate canal, putting the settlement in touch with the flow of commerce through this "backdoor" to Upper Canada. Among the earliest settlers were several hundred from Perth, Scotland, and so the village received its name. Cheese making has always been an important local industry. In 1893 a local cheese weighing 9900 kg and measuring 1.8 m high and 8.56 m around was sent to the Chicago world's fair. Perth has an economy based

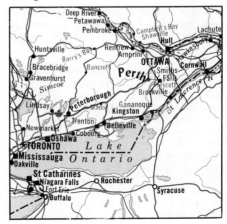

on light industry and in the summer hosts many vacationers who are attracted to the surrounding lake country. Many beautifully preserved 19th-century buildings remain, eg, the neoclassical Lanark County Courthouse (1843) and the Hotel Imperial, built before 1850 and still in use.

DANIEL FRANCIS

Pesticide Substances used to control pests include insecticides (for control of insects), fungicides (for disease-causing fungi), herbicides (for weeds), rodenticides (for rodents), avicides (for birds), piscicides (for fish) and nematicides (for nematodes). Insecticides, fungicides and herbicides are the most widely used. More than 400 pesticides are now registered for use in Canada; they are formulated as liquids, dusts, wettable powders, aerosols and granules.

Pesticides include a wide range of synthetic and natural substances. Relatively few pesticides existed before WWII: insecticides were primarily salts of arsenic, or fluorine or plant-derived products such as nicotine, pyrethrum and rotenone; fungicides were primarily based on mercury, copper or sulphur; herbicides included petroleum oils, sulphuric acid, some arsenites and salt. After WWII, many synthetic compounds became available, the first of these being DDT for insect control, the phenoxy herbicides (eg, 2-4-D) for weed control, and captan and a series of dithiocarbamates for control of fungal diseases of plants.

Toxicology Pesticides now available differ widely in their toxicity to different forms of life. The term LD_{50}, used to indicate lethal toxicity, refers to the dosage of the pesticide (expressed as milligrams per kilogram of body weight) required to kill 50% of a test population. The RAT is the most common mammal used for determining LD_{50} values but the MOUSE and the RABBIT are also usually tested. Modern pesticides are tested for a wide variety of toxic effects before they may be used. These tests include those for carcinogenicity (tumor formation), teratogenicity (birth defects) and mutagenicity (genetic damage). Other tests include studies on the environmental fate of the chemicals and effects on wildlife and other nontarget organisms. Many pesticides are selective in their toxicity, being highly toxic to some organisms and much less so to others. Within a class of compounds, however, toxicity varies widely, from 10 or fewer milligrams per kilogram to several thousand mg/kg.

The nature of the toxicity of pesticides differs between different classes of substances. In general, insecticides are more toxic to warm-blooded animals than herbicides or fungicides, but some of the older fungicides, such as mercury and the arsenite herbicides, are also highly toxic to mammals and birds. Many insecticides act on the nervous system of insects and, although less toxic to warm-blooded animals, act on the nervous system of these organisms as well. Some newer classes of insecticides have been developed that act on processes found in insects but not in mammals, eg, compounds that interfere with the molting process in insects or that affect hardening of the cuticle.

With the exception of mercury, most of the fungicides are not very toxic to warm-blooded animals because they are toxic to systems in fungi that are quite different from those found in mammals and birds. This is true also of most herbicides. Over time, target species develop resistance to specific pesticides and dosages have to be increased or new pesticides developed. New pesticides now under development will likely be of biological origins. Through genetic engineering, it has been possible to produce plants which synthesize their own insecticides and are thus protected from insects.

Registration and Use Because pesticides are toxic, their use is carefully controlled and, in Canada, pesticides may be sold only after they have been registered by Agriculture Canada. The registration process is comprehensive and includes a review of the toxicology of the product, a demonstration that the product is effective for the pest for which it is intended, and the nature of the treatment needed to control the problem. The registration process permits a pesticide to be registered only for specific uses, which are detailed on the label that accompanies the pesticide when it is sold.

One or more of the many pesticides available are used on practically every CROP grown in Canada and the use, particularly of herbicides, is increasing rapidly each year. Insecticides are also used widely to control insects around the home and for control of MOSQUITOES, BLACK FLIES and pests on livestock. Fungicides are used extensively in building materials, paint and disinfectants, and for the treatment of timbers (eg, railway ties, telephone posts) to prevent decay.

Problems Although pesticides have been widely adopted by Canadians for pest control, a number of concerns have been raised. In the 1950s and early 1960s, a number of environmental problems were found to be related to the extensive use of pesticides. These problems included contamination of water with resulting fish kill; reproductive effects in birds (eg, the PEREGRINE FALCON); and direct toxicity to birds and other non-target animals in areas where large-scale spraying operations were carried out. Other concerns have focused on the presence of toxic contaminants (such as the dioxins) in some types of pesticides. Research identified the problem pesticides and these have been restricted in use or banned. More recently, concern has been expressed that pesticides may cause long-term health effects in man and there is controversy about whether or not they should be used. There is little evidence that the pesticides now in use are likely to cause significant health effects when used properly and each is extensively tested for long-term effects before it is registered. Prudence dictates, however, that all pesticides be used with caution and that care be taken to avoid overexposure. *See also* PARASITE; PLANT DISEASE.

F.L. McEWEN

Reading: F.L. McEwen and G.R. Stephenson, *The Use and Significance of Pesticides in the Environment* (1979).

Petawawa, Canadian Forces Base Occupying 30 770 ha along the Ottawa and Petawawa rivers, 166 km NW of Ottawa, it was created (1905) as an eastern Ontario summer-training militia camp. Built astride historic fur-trading routes, it had roles in both world wars as a major military staging and training base, especially for the artillery and engineers, and as an internment centre. During the GREAT DEPRESSION there were relief camps here. After 1945 it became a permanent regular military-unit establishment. Designated "Camp Petawawa" in 1951, it underwent substantial military expansion and urban growth. Renamed CFB Petawawa 1966, the base has a total population of 3586. Its annual budget of over $100 million makes it economically important to nearby PEMBROKE and surrounding areas. At present it is the home of the elite Airborne Unit, the Special Service Force. R.G. HAYCOCK

Peterborough, Ont, City, inc 1905, seat of Peterborough County, situated on the Otonabee R, about 40 km N of Lake Ontario and 110 km NE of Toronto. With a population of 61 049 (1986c), 60 620 (1981c), it is the largest city on the Trent-Severn Waterway and the regional centre for the KAWARTHA LAKES cottage country.

The locks on the Trent-Severn waterway at Peterborough are the highest lift-locks in the world (*photo by Kim Patrick O'Leary*).

Settlement and Development Peterborough was named in 1826 for Peter ROBINSON, who directed the settlement of a large number of Irish immigrants in the area. Its history has been tied to the waterways and forests, and to its proximity to Toronto. The site, at one end of the long portage to Lk Chemung, was well travelled by the Mississauga Indians and their forebears, and was visited by Samuel de CHAMPLAIN 1615. Under European settlement, Peterborough quickly emerged as the administrative centre for the region N of Rice Lk, particularly with the Robinson settlement and the creation of the Colborne Dist in 1842. It was incorporated as a town 1850. The development of Red Fife WHEAT in the area was an important contribution to Canada's agriculture, but timber was the main source of wealth for more than half a century.

By the 1870s Peterborough was Ontario's principal timber producer, shipping over 100 million board ft to American wholesalers annually. The subsequent development of hydroelectricity along the Trent system (before Niagara Falls), together with generous municipal bonuses and concessions, attracted large manufacturers, including Edison Electric (later Canadian General Electric) and Quaker Oats. Associated with the city have been literary figures such as Catharine Parr TRAILL, Robertson DAVIES and Margaret LAURENCE; the capitalists Sir Joseph FLAVELLE and George A. COX; and Lester B. PEARSON, who attended school here.

Cityscape Peterborough features the rolling hills of a major drumlin field. Its 19th-century prosperity shows in 2 impressive blocks of pre-Confederation buildings, which include locally quarried stone buildings from the 1830s and several stately residences. The engineering marvels of the world's highest lift lock, the Centennial Fountain, and the architecturally acclaimed TRENT U reflect continuing change. By contrast, the nearby petroglyphs and SERPENT MOUNDS date back at least a thousand years.

Population Peterborough's population doubled every 2 decades before WWI thanks to the lumber economy and manufacturing, and the 1904 annexation of Ashburnham (pop 2000e), as the city grew from 4611 (1871c) to 18 360 (1911c). The modest growth since then has been more rapid than elsewhere in eastern Ontario (except Ottawa) because of manufacturing expansion. The city's unique quality is its demographic averageness – by religion, occupation and ethnicity – making it a bellwether riding provincially and federally and a favourite site for consumer market testing.

Economy and Transportation In addition to manufacturing, the economic impact of educational institutions, insurance companies, shopping plazas and tourist attractions has been strong in the past decade. Mixed agriculture remains a

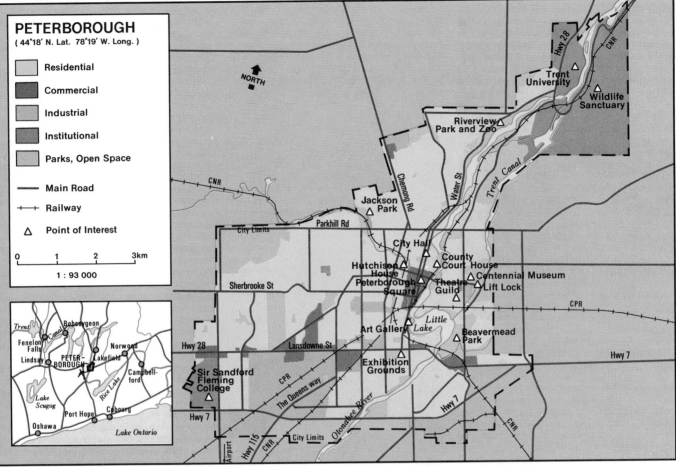

PETERBOROUGH
(44°18′ N. Lat. 78°19′ W. Long.)

- Residential
- Commercial
- Industrial
- Institutional
- Parks, Open Space

—— Main Road
+—+—+ Railway
△ Point of Interest

0   1   2   3km

1 : 93 000

feature of the area. Peterborough is on the Trans-Canada Hwy and has convenient access to Hwy 401. Until recently, it was well served by railways, starting with the Grand Trunk Ry and the CPR's first main line from Toronto to Montréal.

Government and Politics The city's municipal history has been marked by fiscal restraint since the railway failures of the 1850s. For 80 years after 1861 a Town Trust Commission managed its finances. Peterborough has usually favoured a ward system and has resisted provincial efforts to abandon the township/county system for regional government.

Cultural Life The city's vigorous cultural life features a symphony orchestra, a theatre guild and professional companies, public and private art galleries, and the Centennial Museum. It has a winter carnival (Snowfest) and summer arts and water festival (Festival of Lights). Home of the Peterborough canoe, it has won national titles in junior hockey (Petes), lacrosse and synchronized swimming. The city hosted the 1980 Ontario Summer Games.   ELWOOD JONES

Reading: R. Borg, ed, Peterborough, Land of Shining Waters (1967); A.O.C. Cole, ed, Illustrated Historical Atlas of Peterborough County 1825-1875 (1975).

Peters, Arthur, lawyer, premier of PEI (b at Charlottetown 29 Aug 1854; d there 29 Jan 1908), brother of Frederick PETERS. Called to the PEI Bar in 1878, Peters was first elected to the Assembly in 1890 as a Liberal. Appointed attorney general in 1900, he became premier 29 Dec 1901 and died holding office. He is remembered as a stout defender of fair terms for PEI within CONFEDERATION.   PETER E. RIDER

Peters, Frederick, lawyer, premier of PEI (b at Charlottetown 8 Apr 1852; d at Prince Rupert, BC 29 July 1919). A brother of Arthur PETERS, Frederick was elected to the assembly in 1890 as a Liber-

al and became premier 22 Apr 1891, serving until resigning on 27 Oct 1897. He retained his seat until 1899 although he moved to Victoria, BC, in 1897. He practised law there until 1911 when he was appointed city solicitor, and after 1916 city clerk, of Prince Rupert. During his premiership the 2 legislative chambers were merged into a single assembly.   PETER E. RIDER

Peters, Thomas, black community leader (b c1738; d at Freetown, Sierra Leone, 25 June 1792). During the American Revolution, Britain promised freedom and equality to rebel-owned slaves who joined the LOYALIST cause. Among the thousands to respond, Peters joined the Black Pioneers and gained the rank of sergeant. Following the British defeat, some 3500 black Loyalists were transported to Nova Scotia and New Brunswick. When, through disorganization and discrimination, these promises of equality remained unfulfilled, Peters was selected to present the black case before the Crown. He travelled to London in 1790 with petitions outlining the blacks' grievances, including denial of the vote, trial by jury and equitable land grants. In London Peters met the Sierra Leone Co, whose colony for freed slaves in West Africa was seeking black settlers. He returned to N America with a government-financed scheme offering free land and independence in Sierra Leone. In Jan 1792 almost 1200 blacks sailed from Halifax to Africa, where they founded Freetown. Meanwhile, administrative reforms turned Lt John Clarkson, the official agent for the migration, into a colonial governor with an appointed white council. Peters led an opposition movement against the new system, but died of "the fever" before achieving concrete results. Surviving members of the migration went on to develop Freetown as a commercial and political capital, where their descendants are still known as

"Nova Scotians" and Thomas Peters is remembered as a courageous pioneer and leader.
JAMES W. ST.G. WALKER

Peterson, Charles W., agrarian editor, printer, NWT civil servant, farmer, businessman (b at Copenhagen, Den 28 June 1868; d at Calgary, 4 Feb 1944). Peterson homesteaded in Manitoba in 1887 before becoming deputy commissioner of agriculture for the North-West Territories, where he drafted the agricultural legislation inherited by Alberta and Saskatchewan. In 1905, with Malcolm Geddes, he founded the *Farm and Ranch Review* in Calgary. From 1906 to 1912 he served the CPR as general manager of immigration and colonization and later superintendent of irrigation. During WWI he was secretary of the National Service Board and deputy fuel controller for Canada. He then returned to his first love – the *Review* – though he was also partner in a large farming concern. Author of the excellent period piece, *Wake Up Canada!* (1919), *The Fruits of the Earth* (1928), *Wheat – The Riddle of Markets* (1930), numerous economic tracts and scores of well-crafted editorials, he stressed the pre-eminence of agriculture in life. As agriculture lay in ruins at Depression-end, Peterson was distraught, and his abiding conservative business ethic was shattered. His pronouncements had become more strident, his solutions more radical.
DAVID C. JONES

Peterson, David Robert, lawyer, businessman, premier of Ontario (b at Toronto 28 Dec 1943). He was raised in London, Ont, received a BA (1964) from UWO and LLB (1967) from U of T. He joined the family electronics firm in 1969, won the London Centre riding in 1975 and was elected Liberal leader in 1982. In the 2 May 1985 election, his Liberals upset the Progressive Conservatives under Prem Frank MILLER, leading to the end of 42 years of PC rule in Ontario. After his

Ontario Premier David Peterson, whose minority government ended 42 years of Conservative rule in Ontario in 1986 (*photo by Jim Merrithew*).

party finished first in popular vote, though second to the PCs in number of seats, he signed an accord with the New Democratic Party which established a Liberal minority government. In return for a guarantee of 2 years, the accord pledged the new government to implement legislation and procedural reforms endorsed by both parties. After assuming office on 26 June 1986, Peterson moved quickly on issues such as environmental protection, health care and francophone rights. On the national scene, he endorsed the MEECH LAKE ACCORD and emerged as a leader in ensuring a provincial role in the FREE TRADE discussions. He subsequently opposed the agreement reached in Oct 1987. Peterson was returned to office with an overwhelming majority in the election of 10 Sept 1987.   PHILIP DEWAN

Peterson, Leonard Byron, playwright (b at Regina 15 Mar 1917). This prairie Norseman who has lived in Toronto since the outbreak of WWII is unquestionably Canada's most prolific playwright, with well over 1000 radio and TV original scripts and adaptations to his credit, as well as a number of stage plays. His first CBC radio play was produced in 1939, and *They're All Afraid,* a controversial "Stage 44" production, brought fame to him and producer Andrew AL-LAN, winning the top award at the Columbus, Ohio, American Broadcasting Festival, as did his *Joe Katona* in 1961. His innovativeness and versatility in form and social concern as well as his humanism in content are illustrated by such plays as *Burlap Bags* (1946), a precursor of Absurd Theatre, *The Great Hunger* (1960), an Inuit play, *Women in the Attic* (1971) and *The Eye of the Storm* (1985), a tragicomedy about the frailty of civil rights. A cultural activist, Peterson spearheaded the formation of ACTRA and cofounded Playwrights Co-op in 1972.

ROTA HERZBERG LISTER

Peterson, Oscar Emmanuel, jazz pianist (b at Montréal 15 Aug 1925). Peterson began his career after studies with Lou Hooper and Paul de Marky. He was a radio performer heard locally in Montréal on CKAC by the time he was 15, and nationally on the CBC by 20. He played with Johnny Holmes's dance band and at the Alberta

Lounge in 1948-49 with his own trio before making a remarkable US debut in Sept 1949 at Carnegie Hall, New York. He then pursued his career internationally but maintained his home in Canada: in Montréal until 1958, thereafter in Toronto. Peterson has recorded over 90 albums under his own name in the US and Germany and made many as accompanist to Lester Young, Louis Armstrong, Coleman Hawkins and others. He has been host for TV series in London (BBC), Vancouver (CTV) and Toronto (CBC).

Peterson's extravagantly skilful piano technique has drawn both praise and criticism. Full-blown and joyous, his approach to jazz, without offering innovation, is in the mainstream 1940s tradition of which he has become the outstanding proponent, working in trio and solo contexts. He has composed several jazz themes, as well as the extended *Canadiana Suite* (1963) and *African Suite* (1979), and the score for the Canadian film *The Silent Partner* (1977). Winner of many popularity and critics' polls, Peterson received Grammy awards in 1975, 1979 and 1980, a Juno in 1987. He became a member of the Juno Awards Hall of Fame in 1978 and an Officer in the Order of Canada in 1973 (promoted to Companion 1985). He became adjunct professor of music at York U in 1985.   MARK MILLER

The internationally acclaimed jazz pianist Oscar Peterson in his home studio (*courtesy Canapress Photo Service*).

Petitclair, Pierre, dramatist (b 12 Oct 1813 at St-Augustin de Portneuf, Qué; d at Pointe-au-Pot, Labrador 15 Aug 1860). He is author of the first play published by a native French Canadian, apart from dramatized political dialogues, *Griphon, ou la vengeance d'un valet* (1837). This work was never performed, but his 2 other extant plays were staged in Québec C with considerable success: *La Donation* (1842), a 2-act play visibly influenced by melodrama, and *Une partie de campagne,* first performed in 1857 and published posthumously (1865). The latter play is a satirical depiction of the dangers of aping English ways, and is the first stage text to make use of rural Québecois speech.   L.E. DOUCETTE

Petrie, Robert Methven, astronomer (b at St Andrews, Scot 15 May 1906; d at Victoria 8 Apr 1966). Brought to Canada by his parents in 1911, Petrie became interested in astronomy at high school and was encouraged by J.S. PLAS-KETT. After studying at UBC and Michigan, he joined the Dominion Astrophysical Observatory, Victoria, in 1935, when Plaskett retired, and stayed there (except while in the RCN during WWII) for the rest of his life, becoming director in 1951 and the last Dominion Astronomer in 1964. His studies of spectroscopic binaries and the motions and distances of hot B-type stars won international acclaim. When he died, he was planning the construction of a very large Canadian telescope. He was the first Canadian astronomer to become a VP of the International Astronomical Union (1958-64).   A.H. BATTEN

Petro-Canada, a federal CROWN CORPORATION given a broad legislative mandate to expedite PETROLEUM EXPLORATION and development in Canada, to acquire imported oil supplies, and to engage in a broad program of energy research and development. PM Pierre Trudeau announced Petro-Canada's creation in Dec 1973, legislation was introduced in 1974 and passed in 1975. The company's sole shareholder is the Crown and its officers report to the minister of energy, mines and resources. Established with an initial appropriation of $1.5 billion in equity and debt capital, Petro-Canada expanded rapidly during its first 6 years of operation, acquiring the Canadian assets of 4 foreign-owned multinationals. By 1986 the company had estimated assets of $8 billion, making it one of the largest petroleum corporations in Canada. Although it was nearly turned over to the private sector by the Conservative government of Joe CLARK in 1979, the company remains an agent of the national government and has performed a number of functions as an instrument of public policy, eg, investing in higher-risk energy ventures such as frontier exploration and oil-sands development, and has been used by the government to gauge the turbulent international market. Nationally the company has 7740 employees and is headquartered in Calgary. *See also* ENERGY POLICY.   LARRY R. PRATT

Petrochemical Industry, which produces chemicals using OIL AND NATURAL GAS as major raw materials, occupies an important position in Canada's MANUFACTURING and consuming sectors. Oil and natural gas are composed primarily of hydrocarbons. Most petrochemicals contain hydrogen or carbon or both. Petrochemicals can be converted into thousands of industrial and consumer products, including PLASTICS, paints, RUBBER, fertilizers, detergents, dyes, TEXTILES and solvents. The industry consists of 2 major divisions. The primary petrochemical industry produces basic CHEMICALS, such as ethylene, from oil or gas. The secondary industries convert the basic petrochemicals into materials that may be directly used by other industries.

Canada's standard of living is dependent to a significant degree on domestic petrochemical production. The availability of economic petrochemicals allows the domestic production of numerous items that could be more costly if imported. The Canadian industry was growing more rapidly than its counterparts in Europe, Japan and the US, which are the dominant world producers, but investment in the mid-to-late 1980s has dropped significantly. FOREIGN INVESTMENT is attracted to Canada because abundant energy resources can be profitably upgraded to supply growing world needs.

Many compounds now considered petrochemicals were formerly made from wood and COAL. By the late 19th century, a wood-based industry made methanol, acetic acid and other products. In 1904 an industry began in SHAWINIGAN, Qué, making acetylene and related chemicals from coke and limestone. Following WWI, Shawinigan Chemicals expanded to make vinyl resins, now an integral part of the petrochemical industry. Canadian research played a key role in the development of this important class of plastics and adhesives. The discovery of oil in Lambton County, Ont, in 1857 eventually led to a petrochemical industry that replaced the one established on acetylene. Within 7 years, 27 small oil refineries were established in Petrolia, Ont. Abraham GESNER, one of Canada's industrial pioneers, was responsible for major technological breakthroughs in refining oil. Early efforts were aimed at producing lamp and stove oil, but as automobile use grew, refineries were adapted to produce

TRANSPORTATION fuel. The new refinery processes also produced hydrocarbon mixtures suitable for petrochemical raw material (feedstock) but these were little exploited before WWII.

The outbreak of WWII made Canada an important petrochemical producer for the Allied war effort. POLYMER CORPORATION LTD (now Polysar) was established by the federal government in 1942 at Sarnia, Ont, to make synthetic butadienestyrene rubber.

St Clair Processing Corp Ltd (a subsidiary of Imperial Oil Ltd) and Dow Chemical of Canada Ltd built plants nearby to make the petrochemicals for the synthetic rubber process.

Also in 1942, Alberta Nitrogen Products began production of ammonia from natural gas at Calgary, Alta. These efforts spawned the modern Canadian industry.

The Modern Industry

After the war, the industry grew to supply the increasing demand for synthetic consumer products. The first industry-owned chemical plant based on oil was built at Sarnia by Dow in 1942, to produce polystyrene, a widely used plastic. Manufacture of many other chemical products soon developed at Sarnia including antifreeze, polyethylene, solvents and detergent materials. Montréal also grew as a petrochemical centre, especially after 1957, when Union Carbide Canada Ltd launched ethylene chemicals and polyethylene operations. The industry in Sarnia and Montréal still relies heavily on feedstocks from oil-refining plants. Meanwhile a gas-based industry was developing in Alberta. Canadian Industries Ltd established the first Canadian polyethylene plant near Edmonton in 1953, using ethane extracted from natural gas by Imperial Oil. The ethane-based industry remains the cornerstone of Alberta's petrochemical production, but the oil-based counterpart has grown since its beginning in 1953.

Location of Plants Today, most petrochemical plants are located near oil-producing and oil-refining centres or near natural-gas sources and transmission pipelines. They are concentrated in Ontario, Québec and Alberta, but plants are also present in most other provinces. Petrochemical plants are costly, some requiring more than $500 million to build. The gross investment of Canadian petrochemical plants totalled nearly $8.3 billion in 1986.

Ownership Many multinational petrochemical companies have established Canadian subsidiary companies and operations. These tend to be dominated by foreign shareholders, although Canadians also hold equity in some of the subsidiaries. Some major petrochemical companies, such as Novacor Chemicals and Polysar, are controlled by Canadian shareholders. Joint ventures between foreign-controlled and Canadian-controlled companies are important to the industry in Sarnia and Montréal. Canadian investment is increasing, though the industry is still dominated by foreign ownership.

Economic Status Annual sales of petrochemicals exceeded $4 billion in Canada in 1986, about 40% of the value of all chemical shipments. The sales volume represents under 2% of all manufacturing sales and less than 1% of the Gross Domestic Product. The industry grew rapidly until the early 1980s when it found itself overbuilt for the worldwide economic downturn. Since then, there has been a downscaling and restructuring of operations.

Nearly 59% of petrochemical production was consumed domestically in 1986. Although the amount exported has been increasing over the last 10 years, there have been negative trade balances in the 1970s and more recently in 1984 and

Imperial Oil Leduc No 1 Well, Leduc Oil Field, the day the well blew, 13 Feb 1947 (*courtesy Provincial Archives of Alberta/H. Pollard Coll*).

1986. Estimates show that for 1987 there will again be more petrochemicals imported than exported.

Over half of all exports go the the US. Other large markets include Japan and other Pacific nations, Europe and S America. Imports, mainly chemicals for which the Canadian market is too small to warrant domestic production on an economic scale, come mostly from the US.

Costs In 1986 the industry consumed about 5% of Canada's oil product and some 25% of gas. Purchases of energy and feedstocks are the largest operating costs of a petrochemical plant, typically 50%. Other major costs are related to equipment and maintenance services.

Work Force The industry employs nearly 14 000 persons in jobs ranging from equipment operators to research scientists. Wages and salaries are higher than for other manufacturing sectors. Productivity per worker is high because of the large investment in equipment. Plants normally operate 24 hours a day so that equipment can run continuously. The largest union in the industry is the Energy and Chemical Workers Union, although a significant number of workers are nonunionized.

Technology Petrochemical technology employs high pressures and temperatures, requiring sophisticated ENGINEERING and equipment in order to use energy efficiently. Most modern technology has been developed at great expense in laboratories run by multinational firms and located outside Canada.

However, Canadian research efforts have resulted in notable discoveries, such as DuPont Canada's development of linear-low-density polyethylene (a plastic resin) at Kingston and Sarnia in the 1960s. This product is becoming the preferred material for flexible packaging. Funds spent on petrochemical research in Canada are small compared with other industrialized nations, averaging less than 2% of industry sales. Most of these funds are generated by industry.

Government Control The pricing of oil and gas is critical to the international competitiveness of the

industry. It has advocated a market responsive regime for oil and natural gas pricing in Canada. The availability of feedstocks at market-related prices in combination with world-scale modern plants provide the Canadian industry with an excellent competitive base. Export of certain primary petrochemicals requires approval by the National Energy Board; otherwise normal trade regulations apply.

Environmental Status The industry has made great strides in controlling unwanted emissions; compared with other resource industries, its emissions are low per unit of output. Emissions are generally gaseous and can arise from production processes, handling and storage. Provincial regulations establish maximum emission levels that are complied with by the use of well-designed and well-maintained equipment. The industry does not generate large volumes of contaminated water.

Associations Although there is no petrochemical industry association in Canada, companies are members of the Canadian Chemical Producers' Assn (Ottawa), which represents most large industrial chemical manufacturers. The Chemical Institute of Canada (Ottawa) and its affiliate, the Canadian Society for Chemical Engineering, are important bodies for professional development. Trade publications include *Corpus Chemical Report*, *Canadian Oil Register* and *Nickles Daily Oil*, all published by Southam Communications Ltd; *Process Industries Canada*, published by AIS Communications; and *Oilweek*, published by Maclean Hunter Ltd. MICHAEL LAUZON

Petroleum Since its first commercial exploitation in the 1850s, petroleum has become the major ENERGY source of Canada and the industrial world. Petroleum is the mixture of complex hydrogen and carbon compounds, known as hydrocarbons, found in the Earth's crust. Most of these compounds are the FOSSIL remains of prehistoric forests and seabeds and can be thought of as fossilized BIOMASS. If fossil hydrocarbons are very high in carbon content and in solid form, they are classified as COAL. Petroleum, however, can occur in a solid or viscous-liquid form, known as BITUMEN, or in liquid and gaseous forms, crude oil and natural gas, respectively. The main hydrocarbon groups in petroleum are paraffins, naphthenes and aromatics, with minor amounts of oxygen, nitrogen and sulphur compounds. Except for rare deposits of exceptionally pure natural gas or crude oil, most petroleum requires processing to make it useful.

Although petroleum is occasionally found seeping out of surface rocks, most is recovered by drilling deep wells. Crude oil, the unrefined liquid found in underground reservoirs, can vary in appearance from a thin, colourless liquid composed primarily of naphtha, to a heavy, black, gummy substance with a high asphalt content. These forms require relatively complex processing. Most oil is intermediate between these extremes and can be industrially refined and distilled into a wide range of combustible fuels, PETROCHEMICAL feedstocks and lubricants.

Natural gas, a colourless, odourless, combustible mixture of methane, ethane, butane and propane, is often found associated with crude-oil deposits, as well as in separate commercial deposits or "fields." Much of the natural gas found in the foothills of the Rocky Mts in Alberta contains a significant proportion of hydrogen sulphide and is called "sour" gas. This poisonous, colourless, foul-smelling, corrosive gas necessitates extra precaution in drilling, and the hydrogen sulphide must be removed to make the natural gas suitable for domestic or industrial use. The removal yields elemental SULPHUR.

Bitumen, also known as asphalt or tar, is a dark brown-to-black mixture of oil, asphaltine and resin, which has lost its more volatile compounds through evaporation and oxidation. When found mixed with sedimentary particles, as in the vast Athabasca oil-sand deposits in Alberta, it is called tar sand or oil sand. Complex processing is required to produce usable oil from bitumen.

Most oil or gas does not form within the reservoir in which it is found. It migrates, often over great distances, from a "source rock," a sediment rich in organic matter, to the petroleum reservoir, usually a porous SEDIMENTARY ROCK. Oil can be generated from any organic material, eg, fish, marine plants, terrestrial plants and animals. A primary source of organic material is marine ALGAE. These minute, one-celled organisms form the bulk of plant life in the world's oceans. They are ideally situated for preservation in deep oceans because of their planktonic (ie, free-floating) existence. When they die, algae sink to the seafloor where they are buried within silts and clays. Since burrowing organisms are not present, the algal material builds up to form an appreciable part (1-2%) of the total sediment. Bacterial action releases oxygen from this material, further concentrating the hydrogen and carbon molecules required to produce petroleum.

Petroleum formation can begin almost as soon as the organic-laden silt becomes buried. Carbon-14 datings of such silts in the Gulf of Mexico have yielded ages of as little as 500 years. Conversely, investigations of certain types of oil fields have shown oil and gas accumulating millions of years after the deposition of the source rock. Alberta's LEDUC oil field is found in carbonate rocks of Devonian age, deposited 350 million years ago, yet the formation of oil in Devonian source rocks did not occur until they were buried to a sufficient depth in the Cretaceous period, more than 250 million years later.

Major Canadian Basins A sedimentary basin is a large downwarp of the Earth's crust in which sediment (weathered rock debris and chemical precipitates) has accumulated. Oil and gas accumulations are always found in, or associated with, sedimentary basins. Canada possesses 40 basins, covering 47% of the land surface and continental slopes, that are capable of containing hydrocarbons. Only a few of these basins, situated on land, now actually produce oil or gas. Canada's greatest potential for future sources of hydrocarbons lies offshore in the Arctic and off the East Coast. The major producing basin in Canada is the Western Canada Sedimentary Basin, situated beneath Alberta, northeastern BC, southern Saskatchewan, SW Manitoba and the western NWT. It extends from the Arctic Ocean southeastwards across the N American continent to the Gulf of Mexico. It is a virtual textbook of natural history, recording the geological, environmental and biological events that have occurred on the N American continent over the last 600 million years. The Canadian part of the basin covers 1 815 000 km².

Other major Canadian sedimentary basins include the Hudson Bay Basin (970 000 km²), beneath Hudson Bay; the Mackenzie and Banks basins, beneath the BEAUFORT SEA (131 000 km²); the Canadian Arctic Basin, covering most of the arctic islands but excluding Baffin I (1 721 000 km²); the Baffin Bay and Labrador Sea shelves, off the East Coast (780 000 km²); the SCOTIAN SHELF and the GRAND BANKS, south of Nova Scotia and Newfoundland (900 000 km²); and the Anticosti and Maritimes basins in the Gulf of St Lawrence (340 000 km²). Programs by private industry and government are under way to discover and exploit the vast resources in the Beaufort Sea, the arctic islands, the Scotian Shelf and the East Coast off Labrador and Newfoundland.

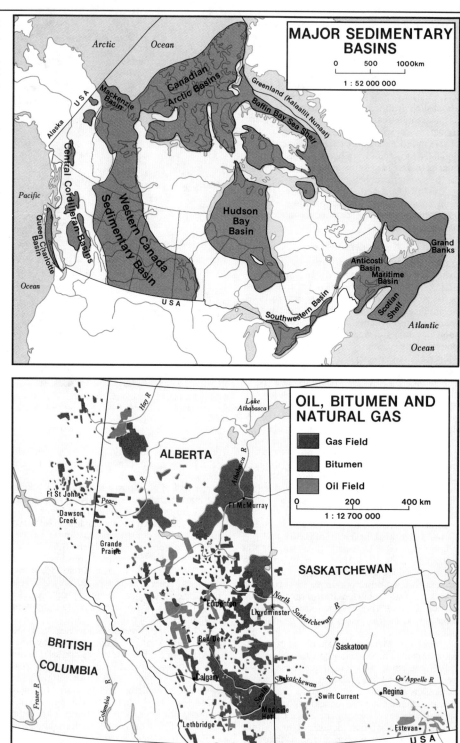

MAJOR SEDIMENTARY BASINS

0   500   1000km

1 : 52 000 000

OIL, BITUMEN AND NATURAL GAS

- Gas Field
- Bitumen
- Oil Field

0   200   400 km

1 : 12 700 000

Oil and Gas Production Oil was first discovered in SW Ontario in 1857. Early explorers used the presence of oil seeps on the surface to locate their targets. In Alberta, Canada's largest oil-producing province, gas was discovered in MEDICINE HAT in 1904 and oil at TURNER VALLEY in 1910. Major discoveries in western Canada were sporadic until after WWII, when renewed activity led to the discovery of the LEDUC oil field in 1947. Since then the industry has played a major role in Canada's development. Some of Canada's major petroleum deposits include the Cretaceous Pembina oil field, the Devonian Bonnie Glen, Leduc, Norman Wells, Redwater and Wizard Lake oil fields, the Cretaceous Athabasca oil sands, the Cretaceous Suffield gas field and the Cretaceous and Triassic Deep Basin gas fields, all in Alberta. As of Dec 1985, Canada had produced 1.9 billion m³ of oil

and 57.5 exajoules of gas, or 72% of known recoverable oil reserves in Canada (estimated at 2.6 billion m³) and 38% of total known gas reserves (estimated at 153.5 exajoules).

Ownership and Development To regulate and control the exploration and development of petroleum resources in Canada, the disposition of all oil and gas rights is controlled by various levels of government. The federal Dept of ENERGY, MINES AND RESOURCES is responsible for all federal crown acreage, which is primarily situated N of the 60th parallel and in offshore waters. Each provincial government also has a separate energy RESOURCES ministry to regulate all provincial crown acreage. The federal Dept of Indian Affairs and Northern Development acts on behalf of status Indians for all reservation land. Each government department periodically posts land sales in parts of the area for which it is responsible. The rights to explore and develop oil and gas on leases or licences are purchased by sealed bid in an open auction. The highest bidder purchases the exclusive rights to lease the land for a given period (usually 3-10 years) during which time it is allowed to explore for oil and gas in an approved manner.

If petroleum is discovered, the lease owner can apply to develop and exploit the accumulation. Regulatory bodies (eg, the Energy Resources Conservation Board in Alberta) ensure that any petroleum accumulation discovered is removed from the ground in such a way as to reclaim the maximum possible amount of oil. If no petroleum is discovered, the lease is allowed to expire, and rights to oil and gas revert to the Crown.

The federal government also maintains the right to establish exploration agreements on federal crown lands without public notice if it feels that it is in the public interest (eg, in expensive frontier exploration) or that there is a need to act quickly. Freehold lands are lands in which the mineral and surface rights were granted to individuals or large companies (eg, the HUDSON'S BAY COMPANY). In the late 19th century, large tracts of freehold land were distributed to pioneers in western Canada and to the CANADIAN PACIFIC RAILWAY. The oil and gas rights to freehold lands can be bought and sold privately by the individual or company, but the province or federal government regulates their exploitation.

Government Regulations The petroleum industry plays an important role in the energy sector of the Canadian economy. Because Canada only produces part of the oil necessary to meet its consumption requirements, large amounts must be imported. Price and supply fluctuations of imported oil affect the stability of the Canadian economy. One step taken to reduce this dependence on foreign oil was a comprehensive package of legislation, the National Energy Program, announced by the Liberal federal government in 1980. The NEP established a price structure and revenue-sharing agreement and was intended to ensure petroleum-industry stability and to redistribute the costs of petroleum consumption throughout Canada. It also established incentives to conserve energy, to increase Canadian ownership of the petroleum industry, expand exploration in Canadian frontier areas and to develop alternatives to oil consumption. The intended outcome of the program was to establish eventual total energy self-sufficiency in Canada. Ottawa, the provinces and the petroleum industry were engaged in heated, sometimes acrimonious, debate over the NEP. After the federal election of 1984, in which the Conservatives replaced the Liberals in government, most of the NEP's policies were gradually eliminated. The price of oil and natural gas was to move in concert with the world prices and more exports were allowed. The effectiveness of this move was blurred, however, by the 50% drop in world oil prices in 1986. Energy investments were cancelled across the country and the western economy was once again battered. The oil industry's prospects have improved since, caused by modest rebounds in world oil prices and by the industry's expectation that the free trade agreement with the US negotiated in late 1987 would do much to stabilize continental energy development. GORDON COPE

Petroleum Exploration and Production There is a saying in the petroleum industry that "oil is found in the minds of men." Even with the most sophisticated scientific techniques, finding hidden petroleum deposits involves a large measure of creative interpretation. Until a hole is drilled, the existence of oil or gas is theoretical; "dry" holes are common even in established pro-

duction areas. Once the resource is found, its value also depends on the "minds of men": exploration and production are expensive endeavours, worthwhile only when society needs the oil or gas badly enough to pay for it. The existence of buried petroleum had been known for many centuries, but people did not start drilling for oil until the middle of the 19th century. At that time a shortage of whale oil coincided with the invention of techniques for refining "rock oil" into lamp oil (*see* Abraham GESNER). Since then, demand for oil and gas has periodically surged and slumped, and so have prices and exploration activity.

Geology and Geophysics The Earth's surface often provides the field geologist with clues to what lies below. The hints may be obvious: seepages of oil and gas, or outcroppings of SEDIMENTARY ROCK or FOSSILS exposed in a tilted layer of rock on a mountain. That layer of rock might once have been the flat bottom of an ancient sea which, through millions of years and constant movements of the Earth's crust, was folded, tilted and exposed (*see* PLATE TECTONICS). The clue is important: accumulations of oil and gas are often found in rock strata that are folded or tilted to some degree. However, the rocks that may contain traps for reservoirs of oil and gas are often thousands of metres below the surface, sometimes covered by a fairly horizontal plain. Aerial photographs and topographical maps can be useful in determining the underground landscape, and the science of geophysics can be even more helpful in mapping the depths beneath the surface.

Geophysics studies physical properties of rocks (eg, magnetism, resistivity, radioactivity). The geophysicist's tools include a magnetometer and a gravimeter, which are used to identify rock types. Both instruments were developed in the 1800s and have continually been improved since that time. Deeply buried sedimentary rocks are often very dense and contain high concentrations of IRON and other materials detectable by a magnetometer. Differences in the pull of gravity of various rocks, measured by the gravimeter, can also help identify the locations of certain rock types beneath the surface.

Another geophysical tool, the seismograph, can virtually compose pictures of underground rock formations. The seismograph works on the principle of sound-wave transmission. As sound waves travel downwards through layers of different types of rocks, they are reflected back to the surface. Differences in wave intensity and travel time provide information about the different types and structures of rocks through which the waves travel. At the surface, the sound waves are recorded by geophones, sensitive recording devices connected to computer equipment. Computers produce the "pictures," ie, seismographs in which the geophysicist can "see" the structural composition of the rocks far below.

Drilling The only way to prove what lies in buried rocks is to drill a well. Even with modern GEOLOGY and geophysical techniques, drilling remains risky. An exploratory or "wildcat" well in an area that has not been drilled before faces high odds against success: perhaps one of 7 or even 10 exploratory wells finds commercial accumulations of oil or gas. To be commercially viable, a well must be able to produce enough oil or gas to justify the costs of drilling and placing it on production. In wildcat areas the first exploratory wells are often drilled as tests; they are not expected to yield oil or gas. Such wells, however, produce valuable information about the nature of the rocks and their oil and gas potential. In frontier areas, such as the BEAUFORT SEA or off Canada's East Coast, a series of widely separated exploratory wells is needed to determine the potential of a particular area. If exploratory wells establish the

presence of producible quantities of oil or gas, "development" wells are drilled to define the size and extent of the field. In development drilling the odds for success are higher: perhaps 6 or 7 successful wells for every 10 drilled. But the element of risk is still present: there may not be enough oil or gas to be commercially attractive; or the technology required to produce oil or gas may be too expensive.

The exploration industry in Canada has gone through "booms and busts," ups and downs that have little to do with the amount of oil or gas left to be found. The level of exploration activity is determined largely by the balance between supply and demand. For example, the NORMAN WELLS oil field in the NWT was first discovered in 1920, but it was then considered too remote to be of interest to southern Canada. A modest amount of oil was refined there to meet regional demands. It was not until the mid-1970s that decreasing supplies and increasing oil values made large-scale development at Norman Wells worthwhile. Technology also can have an impact on exploration activity. For example, extensive exploitation of the large volumes of heavy oil in the LLOYDMINSTER area was dependent on the development of enhanced recovery techniques.

There is a certain romantic air about drilling, perhaps a result of the risk, or of the movies and TV programs that show burly men wrestling with heavy equipment, gushers blowing in and wells blowing out. In today's drilling industry, however, the emphasis is on sophisticated technology. Skills are more important than brawn. Blowouts have almost been eliminated by improvements in drilling equipment and knowledge.

In the early years of Canada's petroleum industry, wells were not drilled but were punched with cable tools. On a cable tool rig, a heavy bit with a chiselled edge was suspended on a line of rope or wire cable. The hole was made through the constant raising, lowering and pounding of the bit into the earth. By the late 1920s, most operations used rotary drilling equipment, which was more efficient, drilling deeper and faster.

Today, drilling is accomplished by a bit at the end of lengths of steel pipe. Each piece of pipe is about 9 m long and is added, a length at a time, by threading onto the next piece of pipe. The bit, drill collars (which add weight to the bit) and lengths of pipe are called the drilling "string." The whole string is turned by a rotating platform, the rotary table. The revolving bit cuts and grinds through rock formations, lubricated and cooled by drilling fluid, commonly called drilling "mud," a mixture of water or oil, clay and chemicals. A deep-rated drilling rig, which might be used to drill holes 5000 m deep, is composed of much heavier, larger and stronger equipment than one used to drill shallow wells (eg, 1000 m deep). For offshore drilling, rigs generally are permanently mounted on barges or platforms so that they can be towed from well site to well site. Some offshore drilling rigs are mounted on specially designed ships which move under their own power.

Drilling operators constantly monitor the progress of a well so that decisions about completion or abandonment can be made quickly. Throughout the drilling operation, the rock cuttings are examined for traces of hydrocarbons. If the well is judged a dry hole, it will be plugged with cement and abandoned. However, if the tests show promise, the well will be "completed." The first step in completion is the installation of production casing, tubular steel pipe that is cemented in place down the length of the well bore. After this process, the drilling rig is usually removed from the well and a truck-mounted service rig is moved into place. In fracturing, or fracing, materials are pumped down the well under high pressure to prop open cracks in the reservoir rock so that the oil or gas can move more freely through the formation. Formations that years ago might have been considered capable of only minimal production now achieve good production rates through completion practices that, with better prices for oil and gas, are worth implementing.

Production Years ago, reservoirs were often damaged and depleted early because of poor production practices. Natural gas, often produced along with crude oil, was ignited and flared away. Today, as crude oil and natural gas, their products and by-products become more valuable, optimizing recovery has become more important.

Natural gas generally flows to the surface through its own pressure; thus, a natural-gas wellhead is usually composed of only a series of chokes and valves to control flow. The wellhead structure is called a "Christmas tree." Crude oil, which typically contains some natural gas or solution gases, is sometimes produced through its natural pressure, but most crude oil wells in Canada require some method of lifting the oil to the surface. Pumping equipment is known by various names including "pump jack," "horsehead pump" and walking beam. Only about 25% of the oil would be recovered from a typical reservoir by natural means or primary recovery techniques. Enhanced-recovery techniques permit production of more oil from many reservoirs. The most common enhanced-recovery method, water injection, involves injecting water into the oil-bearing formation; the water forces the oil toward the producing well bore. Such techniques can result in recovery rates that exceed 80% of the oil in place.

Transportation In a country as large as Canada, the transportation of oil and gas from areas of supply to areas of demand is a very important aspect of the petroleum industry. In western Canada's oil and gas producing provinces, long trains of tank cars are a common sight. They carry everything from asphalt (produced from heavier crude oils and used for paving roads) to propane, butane and other liquid and gaseous products of crude oil and natural gas. Many of these tank cars are headed east, to industrial centres where the petroleum products and by-products are used in a great variety of MANUFACTURING processes (*see* CHEMICAL INDUSTRIES). Before the 1950s, railway and truck transport were the only methods of transporting oil and gas across Canada, but since then PIPELINES have carried most of Canada's oil and gas production to areas of consumption. Just as the construction of railways was essential to the early development of Canada, pipelines became an integral part of Canada's industrial growth midway through the 20th century.

Refining Gasoline, diesel fuel and jet fuel are the most obvious petroleum products, but the list of manufactured products includes everything from insecticides to shampoo and plastic. The processes that result in these products are often complex, but all are based on separating crude oil's various components into useful by-products, which can be in solid, liquid or gaseous forms.

Refining begins with "boiling" crude oil past its evaporation point. In a process called distillation, the various components are vapourized and separately condensed according to their boiling points into basic hydrocarbon streams. Gasoline, kerosene, jet fuel and diesel fuel are produced from middle distillates; greases, lubricating oils, waxes and asphalt are produced from residues. Some products must be blended and improved with chemical additives in secondary refining processes to produce finished products with desired characteristics. Refineries may also produce heating fuels, heavy industrial fuels and feedstocks for the PETROCHEMICAL INDUSTRY.

Dome Petroleum drilling activities in the Beaufort Sea (*courtesy Canapress Photo Service*).

Regulation The marketing of crude oil, natural gas, their products and by-products is complex. Various regulations, both federal and provincial, govern all aspects of production and sales. Although the provinces have jurisdiction over the oil and gas produced within their boundaries, the federal government has the ultimate jurisdiction over oil and gas pricing, transmission and sales, both domestic and export. The federal and provincial governments share the revenues of producing companies through taxes and royalties. The right to revenue sharing and regulation has been a topic of dispute among federal and provincial governments (*see* ENERGY POLICY), as has the question of who actually owns the oil and gas, particularly in offshore waters. The NATIONAL ENERGY BOARD, which set prices before deregulation, now regulates interprovincial movements of oil and gas and export allocations of gas and electricity. ANNE MCNAMARA

Petroleum Industries find, develop, transport, process and market petroleum. They transform BITUMEN, OIL AND NATURAL GAS from raw resources extracted from the ground into useful products such as gasoline, kerosene, heating fuel, plastics and fertilizers. As petroleum has become the critical ENERGY resource of this century, governments have become more and more intimately involved in the operations of the petroleum industries. Compared to other industries, most sectors of the petroleum business are very capital intensive (ie, they require a high proportion of machinery and equipment relative to their labour force) and typically involve higher financial risks. The profitability and level of activity in the industries vary enormously, depending on PETROLEUM SUPPLY AND DEMAND, and they are often termed "boom-and-bust" businesses. A small number of large, vertically integrated companies engage in all activities, from initial PETROLEUM EXPLORATION AND PRODUCTION to the final retail sale of petroleum products. Most of the Canadian integrated companies are subsidiaries of multinational oil companies based in the US, the UK and the Netherlands, although the federal crown corporation PETRO-CANADA, created by Parliament in 1975, now rivals the size and scope of the foreign-controlled "majors." There also are more than 600 smaller companies that have specialized in one or more sectors; most of these "independents" are Canadian owned.

The Canadian petroleum industry began in Ontario in 1857, when James Miller WILLIAMS found oil in a well in Enniskillen Township, near the town later named Oil Springs. The well, known as Williams No 1, set off an oil-exploration boom that established southwestern Ontario as a significant oil-production area during the late 19th century. About 18 small refineries were built to convert the oil into buggy-wheel grease and kerosene lamp fuel, which were the major uses of oil until the spread of the automobile in the early 20th century. The oil and products were transported by wagons, railways, barges and leaky, wooden PIPELINES; most retail sales were made by general stores. Hundreds of drillers, producers, shippers, refiners and retailers competed in a boom-and-bust atmosphere until 1880, when several refiners merged to form IMPERIAL OIL. In 1898 John D. Rockefeller's Standard Oil Trust acquired control of Imperial Oil for $350 000, and Imperial remained a subsidiary of Standard Oil of New Jersey when the trust was split up by American authorities in 1911. Standard of New Jersey, later renamed Exxon, is still the world's largest oil company and still owns 69% of Imperial.

In 1914, when the Royal Navy was worried about the security of its oil supplies, the Canadian government decided to issue crown oil leases only to Canadian- and UK-controlled companies. Imperial Oil circumvented this regulation by acquiring freehold leases from private mineral owners (mainly the CANADIAN PACIFIC RAILWAY and the HUDSON'S BAY COMPANY) in western Canada and by setting up a subsidiary with majority Canadian ownership to exploit oil on crown leases. As a result, Imperial became a major developer of oil discoveries at Turner Valley, Alta, in 1910 and at NORMAN WELLS, NWT, in 1920. UK-based companies, eg, Royal Dutch Shell and Anglo-Persian Oil (later renamed British Petroleum), expanded their interests in Canada after 1914.

In 1946 domestic wells supplied only 10% of Canadian oil consumption. Canadian companies, eg, Canadian Oil (under the White Rose brand), McColl-Frontenac, British-American, Royalite and Home Oil, reached significant size in the first half of this century mainly as refiners and marketers of oil imported from the US. Then, on 13 Feb 1947, Imperial Oil discovered the major oil field at LEDUC, Alta, beginning the modern era of western Canadian oil production. A takeover spree by foreign companies in the 1950s and 1960s left virtually all of Canada's integrated oil companies controlled by multinational majors. By the early 1970s over half of the Canadian oil business (whether measured by assets, revenues or retail sales) belonged to units of the 7 biggest multinationals, the "seven sisters": Exxon, Royal Dutch Shell, British Petroleum, Mobil, Texaco, Gulf and Standard Oil of California. In 1973 foreign-controlled companies took in about 90% of petroleum revenues in Canada (*see* FOREIGN INVESTMENT).

Since the 1950s foreign ownership had been a growing concern of economic nationalists, consumer groups, socialists, some Canadian oilmen and independent fuel retailers. In 1959, after 2 ROYAL COMMISSIONS urged greater government control of the petroleum industries, Parliament created the NATIONAL ENERGY BOARD to oversee and regulate imports, exports, pipelines and other interprovincial oil and gas activities in Canada (although the NEB did not actually set pipeline tariffs until 1978). Provincial authorities, eg, the Alberta Energy Resources Conservation Board, also regulated the petroleum industries. But the federal government only acted to restrict foreign ownership after Oct 1973, when the Arab oil embargo set off a quadrupling of world oil prices.

The FOREIGN INVESTMENT REVIEW ACT of 1974 and the establishment of PETRO-CANADA in 1975 marked the first efforts to curb the domination of the multinationals, but these were not the first instances of government participation in the petroleum industry. During WWII the government operated a crown company called Wartime Oils and joined the US in building a pipeline from Norman Wells to the West Coast. In 1967 the government established PanArctic Oils Ltd to explore for oil and gas in the arctic islands. It was a joint venture, Ottawa owning 45% and private companies 55%. The provinces also were active in the petroleum business: Alberta Gas Trunk Line Co (now NOVA CORPORATION) was set up by the Alberta government in 1955 to organize gas-gathering pipelines in the province; the equity was then sold to Canadian investors. Another Alberta oil and gas entity, the ALBERTA ENERGY COMPANY, was formed in 1975; 50% of the equity was sold to the public and 50% retained by the Alberta government. Provincial oil corporations also have been established by BC, Sask, Man, Ont, Qué, NS and Nfld. However, Petro-Canada is the only one to become fully integrated: its coast-to-coast operations now include research and development, exploration and production, pipelines, refineries and retail outlets.

In 1986 the federal oil company had 7740 employees, $8.1 billion in assets and $5.2 billion in revenues. Its reported asset value was slightly larger than that of Imperial Oil, although Imperial had almost twice as many workers and twice as much revenue. Petro-Canada grew mainly by buying assets from Atlantic Richfield (US controlled, 1976), Pacific Petroleums (US, 1978), Petrofina (Belgian, 1981), BP Canada (UK, 1982) and Gulf Canada Ltd (US, 1985).

The foreign-owned multinationals have made substantial contributions to the Canadian petroleum industries. Except for a few brief periods (eg, the mid-19th century, 1969-74 and again in 1983) Canada has imported more oil than it has exported. The world resource base, tanker fleets and marketing expertise of the multinationals delivered most of these imports relatively cheaply and efficiently. The majors provided much of the training in management and technical skills that allowed Canadians to operate their own companies, including Petro-Canada, and to sell their expertise abroad.

The giant companies' financial strength enabled them to carry on long-term, expensive PETROLEUM RESEARCH AND DEVELOPMENT projects, including the oil-sands processing, offshore and arctic oil exploration, enhanced oil recovery, sour-gas processing, oil and gas transportation, refinery technologies and computer systems. These companies still account for a large proportion of petroleum R&D spending. The multinationals provided much of the financing for projects (eg, oil-sands plants, pipelines, refineries) that might have been too big and too risky for Canadian capital markets.

Whatever the merits of the multinationals' prominence, the structure of the petroleum industries was altered fundamentally when world oil prices quadrupled in 1973-74 and again when they nearly tripled in 1979. The first concern each time was to ensure adequate oil supplies for Canada, and government-to-government deals undermined the trading power of the oil majors. Government attention then shifted quickly to the enormous new revenues created by higher prices. From 1973 to 1985, the federal government controlled oil and gas prices in Canada, generally maintaining them at levels well below the equivalent world oil price. Taxes and royalties diverted 60% of oil revenues to federal and provincial treasuries and to programs designed to cushion consumers from the full impact of world prices. After bitter debate in 1974-75 between the federal and Alberta governments, the federal oil policy remained intact, but a much different policy was adopted for natural gas. Historically low gas prices were allowed to rise rapidly, and less than 40% of gas revenues were funnelled to taxes and royalties.

At the same time, tax provisions allowed investors to get substantial write-offs for investment in oil and gas drilling. The combination of high prices, big profit potential and generous tax

Alberta's refineries produce gasoline, diesel and aviation fuels; a refinery near Edmonton is shown here (*courtesy Petroleum Resources Communication Foundation*).

breaks set off a huge gas-exploration boom in western Canada in the late 1970s. Canadian companies (eg, DOME PETROLEUM, Nova, Sulpetro) soared to prominence. Meanwhile the majors were saddled with their many less-profitable oil investments and were effectively barred from new corporate acquisitions by the Foreign Investment Review Act.

The second major reshaping of the petroleum industries came in Oct 1980, when the federal Liberal government announced a sweeping National Energy Program (NEP). The policy further increased the federal taxation of petroleum revenues and took away the tax write-offs that had encouraged drilling in the 1970s. Instead, a Petroleum Incentive Program (PIP) paid grants to petroleum drillers depending on their Canadian-ownership level and on the location of the wells. The highest PIP grants, up to 80% of actual spending, went for wells drilled in frontier areas by companies more than 75% Canadian owned; there would be no PIP grants at all for companies less than 50% Canadian owned drilling in the provinces. The NEP was substantially modified in 1981 and 1982 after harsh criticism from the petroleum-producing provinces in western Canada and from the petroleum industries. The NEP, combined with the 15% drop in world oil price 1982-83, led to a sharp decline in petroleum activity in western Canada and to the cancellation or postponement of several proposed MEGA-PROJECTS in the Alberta oil sands. However, exploration activity continued in frontier areas such as the BEAUFORT SEA, the arctic islands and the East Coast offshore from Newfoundland and Nova Scotia.

The NEP also encouraged Canadian companies to acquire the Canadian operations of foreign oil companies. Amid slumping world oil prices and a general economic recession, the debt-financed takeovers caused financial crises for many of the Canadian oil companies. Nonetheless, Canadian-controlled companies, including Petro-Canada, increased their share of petroleum revenues from 13% in 1977 to 19% in 1980, 28% in 1983 and 48% in 1986. In late 1984, the Conservative government dismantled the NEP and began deregulating oil and gas prices.

The petroleum industries employ around 200 000 people in Canada, of whom about half are engaged in marketing, which includes heating-fuel deliveries and the operation of retail gasoline outlets. Most integrated companies have their head offices in Toronto and base their marketing operations there. Of those employed in exploration and production, equipment manufacturing and in associated service industries, most have their headquarters in CALGARY, although the exploration activities now extend to the farthest extremities of Canada. Refinery operations are scattered across Canada, but the main refining centres are EDMONTON, SARNIA and MONTRÉAL.

Petroleum transportation is mainly by pipeline companies based in Calgary, Vancouver and Toronto.

In 1986, according to the federal Petroleum Monitoring Agency, the Canadian petroleum industries made capital expenditures of $7.4 billion in Canada and another $0.4 billion abroad. The industries had total revenues of $43.3 billion and reported losses of $2.6 billion. The companies paid out $2.5 billion in dividends to shareholders. From 1976 to 1985 the petroleum companies accounted for between one-fifth and one-third of all profits reported by Canadian nonfinancial corporations. *See also* ENERGY POLICY.   ROBERT D. BOTT

Reading: Carl E. Beigie et al, *The Canadian Oil Industry in Context* (1981); David Crane, *Controlling Interest: The Canadian Oil and Gas Stakes* (1982); Peter Foster, *The Blue-Eyed Sheiks: The Canadian Oil Establishment* (1980).

Petroleum Research and Development Research has always been the backbone of the petroleum industry. Bringing crude oil, BITUMEN or natural gas to the surface presents major technological problems and, once recovered, there is little use for the RESOURCE in its raw state. When the industry was first established in Canada in the 1850s in the region of Oil Springs, southwestern Ontario, its main product was asphalt. Soon after, a Nova Scotia physician-geologist, Abraham GESNER, developed a technique for producing kerosene, a high-quality illuminating oil, initially from coal and later from petroleum. This development laid the groundwork for the petroleum-refining industry. Technology for drilling and production of crude oil was developed in the oil fields around Petrolia and Oil Springs, Ont, in the latter half of the 19th century. Notable early developments were spring-pole percussion drilling and a jerker-rod pumping system still in use in southern Ontario fields. The expertise of the Petrolia drillers was used abroad in the development of oil fields in Java, Galicia, Germany and Hungary. In 1884 a German chemist, Herman Frasch, was hired by IMPERIAL OIL to study petroleum-refining problems. He developed a process for the removal of SULPHUR from kerosene that solved the odour problems of Canadian kerosene and enabled it to compete with products made from low-sulphur Pennsylvania crude. This development initiated the use of CHEMISTRY in improving the quality of petroleum products.

The first Canadian petroleum-related laboratory was established by the federal government in Ottawa in 1910 as the Fuels Testing Station of the Dept of Mines, now the Energy Research Laboratories of the Dept of ENERGY, MINES AND RESOURCES. In 1921 the Alberta government established the forerunner of the ALBERTA RESEARCH COUNCIL, a body that has been intimately involved in petroleum, COAL and bitumen research. The first industrial research laboratory was established by Imperial Oil in Sarnia, Ont, in 1924, when R.K. Stratford was hired as a research chemist and later appointed director of the technical and research department. This laboratory is currently the largest petroleum research centre in Canada. In 1949 Imperial Oil formed a production research division in Calgary, now the research department of Esso Resources Canada Ltd. Imperial also initiated geophysical and geological research and development in exploration technology in the early 1950s; most major exploration companies now maintain programs in applied research in earth science. Syncrude Canada, originally Cities Service Athabasca Ltd, set up its research operations in Edmonton, Alta, in 1958 to support its proposed oil-sands mining and upgrading plant. Shell Canada Ltd established a research centre in Oakville, Ont, in 1962, and in Calgary, Alta, in 1982. Gulf Canada Ltd opened laboratories in

Sheridan Park, Ont, in 1964. PETRO-CANADA initiated research operations in Calgary soon after its formation in 1975. In 1985 Petro-Canada took over Gulf's Sheridan Park research facilities. NOVA-Husky Research Corp was established in 1987 to carry out research. The GEOLOGICAL SURVEY OF CANADA conducts geological and geophysical research at the Institute of Sedimentary and Petroleum Geology in Calgary and at the BEDFORD INSTITUTE OF OCEANOGRAPHY in Dartmouth, NS. In addition to these government and industry operations, substantial research into petroleum recovery is carried out in centres associated with the universities of Alberta and Calgary, notably the Petroleum Recovery Institute and the Computer Modelling Group. In Canada, in 1982, there were about 1500 people involved in petroleum research and development; since then, in the wake of low world oil prices, the figure has declined.

Much of the research carried out in these laboratories is associated with the solution of problems directly related to Canadian conditions, although the solutions have often been applied worldwide. Manufacture of high-quality lubricants from Canadian crudes, which may contain waxy components, sulphur and other impurities, has resulted in the development of extraction, dewaxing and hydrotreating processes now used in many countries. Sulphur-asphalt paving mixtures and fuels and lubricants designed to operate under harsh, winter conditions are other examples of Canadian-developed products. Since Canada has extensive deposits of heavy crude and oil sands in Alberta and Saskatchewan, many laboratories are involved in researching methods of the recovery and upgrading of bitumen to produce high-quality synthetic crudes. In the 1970s and 1980s the increase in world crude prices, accompanied by the decline in production of conventional oil and gas in Canada, led to an increase in research studies aimed at CONSERVATION and efficient use of natural resources. As well as methods to increase recovery of hydrocarbons from conventional oil fields, research has resulted in such developments as fuel-saving lubricants, high-efficiency fuel oil and natural-gas burners, and the use of alcohol fuels to extend gasoline supplies. New techniques, such as the building of artificial islands and ice-resistant drilling platforms, have been developed for hydrocarbon exploration in Canada's northern and offshore frontier areas (*see* OCEAN INDUSTRIES). Another significant area of research is in reservoir engineering, which uses computer modelling and other techniques to determine why oil accumulates in the way it does. The rapidly changing conditions in the petroleum industry and the incentives to achieve self-sufficiency ensure that R&D will remain an important part of the petroleum industry (*see* INDUSTRIAL RESEARCH AND DEVELOPMENT).

J.L. TIEDJE

Petroleum Supply and Demand Petroleum demand reflects ENERGY use in society and is usually forecast by projecting recent trends in economic growth, energy consumption, petroleum technology and prices. The supply of petroleum available to meet those demands depends on 2 factors: reserves in the ground and the productivity of those reserves. The total in-place reserves of crude oil, natural gas or BITUMEN are less important than the recoverable reserves. "Proved" reserves are the estimated quantities that analysis of geological and engineering data demonstrates, with reasonable certainty, to be economically recoverable from known reservoirs, under existing economic and operating conditions. They increase as new discoveries are made, concurrently decreasing as they are exploited. "Unproved" reserves are estimated quantities that might be eco-

nomically recoverable from known deposits but with a lower degree of certainty. A less certain category is "speculative" reserves, which are not yet discovered but which general geological and engineering judgement suggests might eventually be found or might become economically recoverable. The sum of proved, unproved and speculative reserves is termed "future potential recovery" and, when added to cumulative production, results in estimates of "ultimate potential recovery." "Productivity" is the estimate of the maximum practical rate at which oil or gas can be produced, having regard to existing proved reserves and facilities, the rate at which proved reserves will grow and new facilities will be installed, and economic, political and other factors.

Oil reserves are classified as "conventional" if the oil is produced through well bores by ordinary production methods. "Synthetic" oil results, for example, from upgrading bitumen or from COAL LIQUEFACTION. Production of conventional Canadian oil has exceeded the rate of additions to proved reserves since the early 1970s. Consequently, proved reserves have declined to some 800 million m³. Some 2100 million m³ have been produced to date indicating an initial proved reserve of some 2900 million m³. This is about one-quarter of the 10-14 billion m³ that most authorities consider to be Canada's ultimate potential recovery. Canadian synthetic oil currently comes from bitumen recovered from the Alberta oil sands. Some authorities restrict proved reserves of synthetic oil to production that is recoverable during the reasonable producing life of existing facilities. Other estimates include all volumes of synthetic oil recoverable from oil sands considered economically attractive for development. Thus, synthetic-oil proved reserves estimates range from some 230 to 3900 million m³. The ultimate potential recovery of synthetic oil is difficult to speculate about because huge deposits exist although only a small fraction is being developed. Ultimate potential recovery will depend on future technology and the economics of recovering and upgrading bitumen to synthetic oil. Estimates currently range from 1 billion m³ to 40 billion m³.

In Canada growth in proved reserves of natural gas has for many years exceeded the rate of production, but the current very large N American gas surplus has reduced drilling for gas and reversed that trend for the years 1983-86. Proved reserves are currently some 2400 billion m³ and, when coupled with production to date, indicate initial proved reserves of some 4000 billion m³. Estimates of ultimate potential recovery for natural gas in Canada range from some 12 to 15 trillion m³. For both natural gas and conventional oil, a major portion of Canada's future potential recovery is expected from frontier regions, such as the BEAUFORT SEA and the eastern Continental Shelf. Most proved reserves are in the Western Canada Sedimentary Basin, the source of current production.

Canada's total productivity of conventional and synthetic oil has declined over the past decade to some 220 000 m³ per day. The collapse of oil prices during 1986 from $30 US to $10 and back to $18 has created much uncertainty, although prices are expected to rise in the 1990s. Productivity is thus expected to decline during the late 1980s, then return to almost current levels by the mid-1990s. Natural-gas production has increased somewhat over the past decade but is much lower than existing productivity, which, in turn, is expected to grow in future.

Canadian per-capita demands for oil and natural gas have been among the highest in the world (*see* ENERGY IN SOCIETY). This rate partly results from Canada's severe climate, but also from its

high standard of living and the relatively low energy prices that prevailed until the 1970s. Canadian requirements for oil products, which include conventional and synthetic oil and condensate (a gas by-product and oil substitute), increased steadily through most of the early 1970s but recently declined as a result of CONSERVATION measures, slower economic growth and higher petroleum prices. The decline is expected to continue during the next decade with demand dropping from a current level of some 250 000 m³/day to about 230 000 m³/day by the mid-1990s. Demand for natural gas over the same period has generally increased, but lower oil prices and the resulting competition will likely eliminate growth through the late 1980s. Most authorities expect the price advantage for gas to be restored and forecast a substantial growth in future, from 160 million m³/day to 200 million m³/day by the mid-1990s.

Domestic sources have supplied most of Canada's oil and natural gas, although Canada was a net importer of oil from about 1975 to 1983. Net exports now amount to about 10% of total production. All gas requirements have been met with Canadian production. Most of Canada's oil exports are heavy oil, for which there is not sufficient Canadian refinery capacity or markets located near sources of supply. Total oil productivity is expected to decline to less than Canadian demand within a few years and remain there throughout the next decade. The shortfall, which would have to be made up by imports, could range from 50 000 to 100 000 m³/day by 1995. Gas productivity is expected to continue to exceed demand, leaving a surplus for possible export. Imports and exports of oil and natural gas are a function of Canadian demand, available productivity and government ENERGY POLICY. Oil imports have come predominantly from Venezuela and Saudi Arabia, and natural-gas surpluses have been exported to the US.

G.J. DeSORCY

Petun ("Tobacco") were an Iroquoian-speaking people, closely related to the HURON, who lived in the region of COLLINGWOOD, Ont, in the early to mid-16th century. The name Petun was applied to these people by the French, and refers to the fact that they were particularly noted for cultivating tobacco. At the time of European contact, the Petun occupied from 8 to 10 villages located below the Niagara Escarpment along the SW margin of Georgian Bay. Their precontact population is uncertain but appears to have numbered several thousand.

The Petun differed little from the Huron, who lived one day's journey to the NE. It appears from historical accounts and archaeology that the Petun were of relatively recent origin, having been formed in late prehistoric times by a union of groups of Iroquoian-speakers moving west from HURONIA and other Iroquoian groups from the areas that are now Toronto or Hamilton. They maintained trading relationships with the NEUTRAL and Huron, and with the Algonquian-speaking OTTAWA and Nipissing. They were destroyed or dispersed along with the Huron by the IROQUOIS in 1649. The surviving Petun joined with the refugee Huron and made extensive journeys through the midwestern US. They eventually settled in the 1850s in Oklahoma, where descendants of both groups now reside under the name *Wyandot*, a form of the original Huron name for themselves.

The Petun are historically recorded as consisting of 2 tribes, the Wolves and the Deer, each comprising one principal village and several lesser villages or hamlets. The villages were palisaded, occupied year-round and contained numerous LONGHOUSES. The population subsisted by cultivating corn, beans and SQUASH, as well as by hunting and fishing. The Petun are one of the lesser known native groups, partly because they were not numerous, but primarily because they were overshadowed in 17th-century European attention by the larger and politically more important Huron Confederacy. *See also* NATIVE PEOPLE: EASTERN WOODLANDS and general articles under NATIVE PEOPLE.   PETER G. RAMSDEN

Reading: B.G. Trigger, The Children of Aataentsic: A History of the Huron People to 1660 (1976) and, ed, Handbook of North American Indians, vol 15: Northeast (1978).

Pewter, essentially an alloy of the same metals as bronze (copper and tin), was probably discovered during the Bronze Age. From the early 17th century until the mid-19th century, pewter was a favourite metal for domestic flatware (spoons, forks) and small serving, pouring, eating and drinking vessels. In pure form, pewter is a mixture of about 80% tin and 20% copper. In N America, raw tin was not readily available and pewterers depended on scrap for their metal. Such scrap pewter, melted and recast into new objects, was commonly adulterated or "bulked-up" with lead, by as much as one-third for non-wearing objects (eg, organ pipes, candle molds).

Since pewter is a soft metal, objects in daily use had a short lifespan, estimated at 5 years. Two-piece manufactured bronze molds were commercially available for casting common vessels, and pewterers formed their own molds for others. In Canada a few older religious orders in Québec, notably the Congrégation de Notre Dame, still use pewter and own several spoon and plate molds used for periodic recasting.

Both French and English pewter was in common use during the French regime, and many spoons and segments of porringers, bowls and plates have been excavated at early habitation sites from Louisbourg to Montréal. Although there is no documentary evidence of commercial pewtering during this period, examples of unmarked pewter have been found which were undoubtedly local castings or recastings. Later inhabitants of NEW FRANCE and early British North America appear to have used imported pewter almost exclusively. Marked and identifiably Canadian pewter does not appear until the early 19th century and then was limited to Montréal and Québec. Present evidence indicates that pewtering in Canada never developed as a major craft industry, possibly because, by the 1830s, pewter was being replaced as a tableware by inexpensive imported English ceramics and steelware.

Few Canadian pewterers have been identified from markings on pewterwares. Chief among them was Thomas Menut of Montréal, who produced primarily spoons and forks punched with a large "T.M." and a beaver motif. His working dates appear to have been from 1810 to 1820, extending into the 1850s. He was succeeded by his son Jean-Baptiste Menut, who is listed as a Montréal pewterer in 1857-58, and again in 1868. Jean-Baptiste Menut used the mark of a spread-winged angel, flanked by his initials "I.M." A few Montréal and Québec silversmiths also appear to have been part-time pewterers. Some existing pieces are known with small "Montréal" punch-marks, identical to those used on the silver of the Arnoldis, Robert Cruikshank, Salomon Marion and Paul Morand. None of this "Montréal"-stamped pewter has corresponding marker's stamps. David Smellie of Québec City, operating from 1780 to 1827, is also known to have made a small quantity of pewter. Britannia ware, a hard pewter manufactured by spinning in molds and finishing on lathes, is not known to have been produced in Canada.   D.B. WEBSTER

Phalarope (family Scolopacidae), sandpiperlike SHOREBIRD, highly specialized for aquatic life. Phalaropes' legs are flattened laterally and toes have lobed flaps on sides and small webs at bases. Phalaropes swim jerkily, in tight circles, picking at food (aquatic invertebrates and larval fishes) stirred up by the small currents they create. They are often seen far out at sea. Females do the courting and after egg laying usually abandon their mates, leaving them to incubate eggs and care for young. Three species occur in Canada. Red phalarope (*Phalaropus fulicaria*) has circumpolar range. It usually breeds in small colonies near coastal freshwater pools; in Canada, from western Hudson Bay to northern Ellesmere I. Nests are cup-shaped depressions, often concealed by grasses domed over the 4 eggs (greenish buff with dark brown markings). This species may winter on the Indian Ocean. Wilson's phalarope (*P. tricolor*), the largest species, wades and walks more frequently than the other 2, and has reduced lobes and webs on its toes. Found only in N America, it breeds mainly in the prairies and locally in Ontario and Québec, often nesting with black terns. The nest, a scrape near shallow water, is lined with grass by the male. Wilson's phalaropes winter mainly in Argentina. The red-necked phalarope (*P. lobatus*), the smallest phalarope, breeds in the low Arctic of the New and Old worlds. In Canada, it nests from Labrador to the southern YT. It migrates mainly along the coast and winters in seas of the Southern Hemisphere.   S.D. MACDONALD

Pharmaceutical Industry The first pharmaceutical company in Canada was established in Toronto in 1879 by E.B. Shuttleworth. The first foreign-owned subsidiary was started in Windsor by Parke, Davis and Co in 1887. Branch-plant operations were primarily set up to take advantage of provisions in the Canadian tariff laws designed to protect domestic manufacturers from foreign competition. In order to undercut a competitor's price a company would establish a manufacturing facility in Canada. These branch plants usually confined their activities to secondary manufacturing (combining the active and inactive ingredients into their final form) and sales.

In the 1940s the Canadian industry underwent a dramatic transformation. As potent new drugs were rapidly developed and marketed, the location of pharmaceutical preparation shifted from the drugstore to the factory where sophisticated technological processes were employed. Economies of scale became possible in the manufacture of these drugs and production was centralized in a few locations. Unable to compete on the scale demanded by the new technology, small domestic companies fell under foreign control. By the time Merck Sharp and Dohme acquired Charles E. Frosst in 1965, the only Canadian-owned company of any consequence was Connaught Laboratories.

Companies engaged in the manufacture of pharmaceuticals fall into three types: subsidiaries of foreign multinational companies; generic companies which manufacture drugs that are ineligible for patents, drugs for which patents have expired and patented drugs for which they have obtained compulsory licences; and biological companies such as Connaught Laboratories in Toronto and the INSTITUT ARMAND-FRAPPIER in Montréal which produce products such as vaccines, insulins and blood by-products.

The Pharmaceutical Manufacturers Assn of Canada, founded in 1914, represents 64 companies, 58 of which are subsidiaries of foreign multinationals. Canadian-owned generic companies formed the Canadian Drug Manufacturers Assn in 1963, which now has 21 members.

The Canadian pharmaceutical market, estimated at $2.3 billion in 1986, is the world's ninth largest, representing about 2% of global pharmaceutical sales. While Canadian-owned companies have experienced a resurgence since 1969 when the Patent Act was amended, foreign subsidiaries still dominate. In 1980 this group accounted for over 84% of the value of shipments. The largest company in Canada is American Home Products with 1986 sales of $168.2 million. The next 18, in value of sales, are also foreign owned. Novopharm with $49.9 million in 1986 sales is the largest Canadian-owned company.

Total employment in the pharmaceutical industry was 15 184 in 1984. Foreign-controlled companies accounted for greater than 80% of the total. Ontario-based companies employed 8658 while companies in Québec had 6122 employees. Profits have traditionally been much higher than those in other industries. In the decade ending in 1984, profits before taxes, on capital employed, were 25.7% for pharmaceutical manufacturers compared to 11.3% for all Canadian industries. Profit levels in Canada are generally higher than in other well-developed countries.

Patents In Canada only the process by which a drug is made can be patented, not the product itself. Nearly all Canadian pharmaceutical patents are owned by foreign companies. The company holding the patent on a drug generally has a monopoly on its sale for the life of the patent. In order to encourage competition and thereby reduce prices, since 1923 the Patent Act has allowed compulsory licensing to manufacture. Under this provision companies could apply for permission to manufacture a drug before its patent expired. The company would pay the patent holder a royalty. Little use was made of this provision. Companies were reluctant to apply for these licences because of the high cost involved in setting up and operating a manufacturing facility to supply just the Canadian market.

In the 1960s, 3 federal reports identified patent protection as a key factor in inhibiting competition and leading to drug prices in Canada being among the highest in the world. The Harley Commission recommended that the Patent Act be amended to allow compulsory licensing to import drugs still under patent. The federal government acted, and in 1969 passed Bill C-102.

Being able to import ingredients rather than manufacture them in Canada allowed companies to bypass the high costs of producing fine chemicals. Subsequent to the passage of the amendment 306 compulsory licences have been granted as of 31 Jan 1985 on 70 drugs. Firms receiving these licences are called generic companies and the products they market are referred to as generic drugs. In return for receiving a licence, a generic company pays the patent holder a royalty of 4% of the sale price of their products.

The multinational companies strongly objected to the introduction of Bill C-102 and lobbied vigorously against it. After the bill passed they challenged it in the courts repeatedly, although unsuccessfully. They argued that compulsory licensing deprived them of the ability to recoup their investment in researching and marketing a new drug. Without being able to recover their investment, they predicted that companies would be reluctant to invest in manufacturing and research in Canada. Finally, they maintained that a royalty of 4% was far too low.

As a consequence of this continuous criticism of compulsory licensing in 1984 the federal government appointed economist Harry Eastman to head an inquiry into the pharmaceutical industry. Eastman's 1985 report concluded that compulsory licensing had stimulated competition and as a result Canadians saved at least $211 million on pharmaceutical costs in 1983. Eastman also found that since 1969 growth in the pharmaceutical industry had been more buoyant in Canada than in the US where compulsory licensing did not exist. Eastman further concluded that the introduction of compulsory licensing to import had caused no major change in investment in research. Eastman did recommend that companies introducing a drug be given a 4-year exclusivity period before a compulsory licence could be issued against that drug. He also recommended that the royalty rate be increased to 14% or more, depending on how much research the company undertook in Canada. Patent life in Canada was historically 17 years from the date of application for patent. In late 1987, after a year-long parliamentary battle, the federal government succeeded in passing Bill C-22 amending the Patent Act. The new legislation gives companies up to 10 years of protection from compulsory licensing for all drugs marketed after June 1986. In return for the increased patent protection, the PMAC member companies promised to invest an additional $1.4 billion in R&D by 1995 and to create 3000 new jobs. The legislation was opposed by the CD-MA and many consumer and senior citizen groups, including the CONSUMERS' ASSOCIATION OF CANADA. They claimed that the Patented Medicine Prices Review Board created by Bill C-22 to control drug prices would be ineffective and that drug costs could rise by over $300 million by 1995. In addition, some provinces felt that their drug plans might be endangered if there were large cost increases. There were also concerns expressed about the continued viability of some generic drug companies.

Research Drugs are often given credit for many of the significant positive changes in health that have been observed over the past century. It is undoubtedly true that INSULIN, discovered at the U of T in 1921, revolutionized the treatment of diabetes. Other developments such as the polio vaccine and antibiotics have saved many lives and reduced the suffering of millions. However, the decline in mortality from infectious diseases such as rheumatic fever and tuberculosis started long before the era of modern drugs. Most of the increase in lifespan can be traced to a sharp decrease in the infant mortality rate which largely resulted from improved living and nutritional standards.

Worldwide, the pharmaceutical industry spends billions of dollars annually on research. Drug companies do develop treatments for rare diseases, but since the companies operate on the profit motive most of their research expenditures go into developing products that serve large markets and have the potential for substantial sales. It is currently estimated to cost $50 to $100 million to research and market a new drug. About 25 new drugs are marketed annually in Canada. Ten to 15% of these represent a significant therapeutic gain over existing products; 25 to 30% a modest therapeutic gain; and 55 to 65% little or no therapeutic gain.

The pharmaceutical industry is intensive in research in comparison to other sectors of Canadian manufacturing history. Research spending is less than half that would be expected based on Canada's share of the world pharmaceutical market. The multinational companies argue that compulsory licensing is to blame, while Eastman pointed out that multinational firms tend to concentrate research spending in their home countries. Research can be divided into 3 categories: basic, clinical and process. Basic research includes the search to discover new biological processes, the synthesis of chemical compounds and testing in animals. Once the basic research has been completed the company submits a Preclinical New Drug Submission containing all known data on

the substance to the Health Protection Branch (HPB) of Health and Welfare Canada. If this submission is approved the company proceeds to the clinical research stage which is the determination of the safety and therapeutic effectiveness of the drug in humans. This phase of research, usually conducted in hospitals, is governed by a protocol giving a detailed description of the proposed tests. About 70% of research spending goes into this phase. Canada has a comparative advantage over many other countries in clinical research because of a highly skilled medical establishment and hospitals with excellent facilities.

At the conclusion of clinical testing a New Drug Submission (NDS) is sent to the HPB with complete information on the new drug. Approval of the NDS results in the company receiving a Notice of Compliance (NOC) allowing the drug to be sold in Canada. The NOC is accompanied by a Product Monograph which summarizes all the information about the drug and is available to health professionals to guide them in their use of the new drug. Prior to 1967 drugs were not required to have a Product Monograph.

The final type of research, process research, involves looking for ways to reduce the costs of drug production or of improving the quality of the product. Fifteen percent of the research dollar is spent here.

After a new drug is marketed the company is required to notify the HPB of all new and unusual occurrences with the product, until the HPB decides that enough is known about the drug. In addition the HPB operates the Drug Adverse Reaction Program. However, reporting to this program is voluntary and it is believed that only 1% of all adverse reactions are documented.

Government Activity The federal government had no power to limit the sale of drugs until the 1939 amendment to the Food and Drugs Act. That amendment gave the government the authority to control the sale of any drug likely to be injurious to health. In 1951 it became mandatory for companies to submit safety data to the Food and Drug Directorate (now the HPB) prior to marketing a new drug. This change was provoked by the realization that Canada was being used as a proving ground for foreign manufacturers to test-market their new drugs.

The Canadian laws were changed again in 1963, following the experience with thalidomide. Pregnant women who took this drug gave birth to babies with congenital malformations of the limbs. About 115 such children were born in Canada. Besides strengthening safety standards, the 1963 amendments required manufacturers to submit information showing that their products were effective for the conditions recommended. Neither the 1951 nor the 1963 changes were made retroactive and the HPB estimates that about 450 prescription drugs still available are either worthless or lack real medical benefits.

In 1971 the HPB established the Drug Quality Assessment Program involving drug analysis; inspection of manufacturers' plants; efficacy tests and assessment of manufacturers' claims; and an information system to advise pharmacists, doctors and the public of test results.

Although the Food and Drugs Act prohibits false advertising, the HPB makes only informal spot checks on drug advertisements. Products can only be promoted for those conditions for which they have been proved to be safe and useful. However, the HPB has no control over how doctors actually use drugs.

Provincial governments have all instituted programs to cover the costs of drugs. BC, Manitoba and Saskatchewan have universal coverage. The other provinces provide drugs at low or reduced cost to senior citizens and those on welfare. Thir-

ty-three percent of Canadians are covered under these programs with an additional 50% belonging to private insurance plans.

Provincial governments attempt to limit the cost of their programs by permitting pharmacists to product select; that is, to dispense a lower price generic drug in place of a more costly brand name one. Provincial formularies list those drugs where this practice is allowed. Some provinces encourage product selection by limiting the reimbursement to the pharmacist to the cost of the lowest priced version of the drug.

Promotion Advertising in medical journals is regulated by the Pharmaceutical Advertising Advisory Board, established in 1976. Representatives from the pharmaceutical industry and medical, pharmacists' and consumer associations sit on this board and there is an adviser from the HPB. Its effectiveness has been questioned especially since the only sanction for violating the board's guidelines is either modifying or withdrawing the ad in question.   JOEL LEXCHIN

Pharmacy, the act or practice of preparing, preserving, compounding and dispensing drugs. Louis HÉBERT, one of the first settlers of New France, was a pharmacist from Paris. From the time he settled in Québec (1617) until 1750, when the first medical legislation by Intendant François BIGOT was promulgated, there was little regulation of the health professions in New France. For the next 120 years, efforts to obtain more specific and effective legislation for the control of drug distribution were integrated into medical regulations and were largely ineffectual. A number of pharmacists' organizations were formed in both Upper and Lower Canada during this time in an attempt to establish pharmacy legally as a profession. These groups were short lived; there was no permanent national organization of Canadian pharmacy until the Canadian Pharmaceutical Assn was founded in 1907.

Until Confederation, 1867, efforts by pharmacy organizations to obtain appropriate regulation by federal legislation were unsuccessful. With the creation of the provinces of Québec and Ontario, pharmacy Acts were passed (in 1870 and 1871, respectively) granting self-government to the profession. These Acts served as models for the rest of Canada; each province has now passed similar legislation to regulate the practice of the profession within its borders. Under this legislation, the professional association issues the licences to practise and supervises its members.

Nevertheless, significant differences exist from province to province. Registration in any one province qualifies a pharmacist to practise also in the Yukon and the NWT, but not in other provinces, because the requirements of each province must be met separately. In response to this situation, the Pharmacy Examining Board of Canada was formed in 1963 under federal statute to establish academic qualifications acceptable to participating provincial licensing bodies.

Pharmacists no longer learn their profession through an apprenticeship system. All provinces require pharmacists to obtain a baccalaureate degree in pharmacy for licensure. Faculties of pharmacy are located at Dalhousie, Université de Montréal, Laval, U of T, U of Manitoba, Memorial U, U of Saskatchewan, U of Alberta and UBC. Courses in basic biological and physical sciences are a required prerequisite to professional pharmacy courses and the program of studies that includes supervised practical experience. Research has become important in the pharmacy colleges because advances in drug therapy arise primarily from work carried out in industry and the universities. All Canadian faculties of pharmacy provide graduate work at the master's and doctoral level for students seeking careers in teaching, research, industry, hospital pharmacy and other specialized areas.

About a third of Canadian pharmacies are large establishments (frequently part of chain stores and franchise operations), selling a variety of merchandise in addition to providing prescriptions and health needs.

The professional practice of pharmacy has changed dramatically over the years. Pharmacists now dispense a vast array of complex, potent and specific medicinal agents (the federal government has enacted regulations dealing with the quality, safety and efficacy of therapeutic agents, and specifying the terms under which certain potent and addictive drugs must be handled). The preparation of these pharmaceuticals requires special techniques of formulation and analysis that are available more efficiently and economically in the elaborately equipped laboratories of industry; therefore, most of the pharmaceuticals dispensed today are obtained by the pharmacist in the finished form. The pharmacist's role has changed from that of compounder to that of a supervisor of drug regimens and a consultant to the other health professions and to the public on drug usage. This transition was initially developed in hospitals, where it is now well established. More recently, this concept of clinical pharmacy has been extended to ambulatory patients. The community pharmacist has frequent contact with patients receiving medication and is thus able to protect against drug interactions, toxicities, side effects, allergic reactions and other untoward responses. Most pharmacies today maintain a patient-record system, usually computerized, to help the pharmacist follow the progress of drug treatment.

MERVYN J. HUSTON

The ring-necked pheasant (*Phasianus colchicus*) is found mainly in milder areas, notably S Ontario and BC (*photo by Wayne Lankinen/DRK Photo*).

Pheasant (Phasianidae), family of birds, with plumage ranging from metallic blue, green and burnished copper to cryptic patterns of browns, greys and black. Coloured wattles (fleshy protuberances) or vivid, bare skin adorn the head, and the tail may be highly modified for display, most notably in the peafowl (genus *Pavo*). The family is related to the families of fowls which include GROUSE, turkeys, QUAILS and the red junglefowl (*Gallus gallus*), presumed ancestor of all domestic POULTRY. Pheasants are henlike in form, some with sharp spurs on their longish, strong legs. Many species may be bred in captivity; wide-scale introductions outside their native habitats (Asia and Japan) have occurred. Hence, some species may survive although destruction of their habitats threatens extinction. Of the 48 pheasant species, at least 16 are endangered. In Canada, the introduced ring-necked pheasant (*Phasianus colchicus*) is a permanent resident. It is most successful in milder areas, notably southern Ontario and BC. *See also* GAME BIRDS. S.D. MACDONALD

Philately, *see* STAMP COLLECTING.

Philipps, Richard, governor of Nova Scotia 1717-49 (b in Pembrokeshire, Wales *c*1661; d at London, Eng 14 Oct 1750). Although he spent little time in NS (1720-22, 1729-31), his dealings with the Acadians in 1730 had a strong effect on subsequent events. Ceded by France in 1713, the province was populated by a French-speaking people who refused to take the normal oath of allegiance, and it was barely held by a tattered garrison at ANNAPOLIS ROYAL. Sent out to demonstrate British authority but powerless to force the issue, Philipps administered a modified oath and apparently promised verbally that the Acadians would not have to bear arms against France. Other officers had made a similar concession but Philipps was the governor; fortified with the memory of his word, the Acadians maintained a general neutrality for 25 years. Their success, however, contributed to their unpreparedness when they faced Gov Charles LAWRENCE's ultimatum in 1755 and were subsequently deported (*see* ACADIA).

Philipps went home for good in 1731. British authorities remained inattentive to Nova Scotia until the late 1740s; and the practical governor, his counsels largely unheeded, spent his last years living on his allowances in London.

MAXWELL SUTHERLAND

Phillips, Robin, director, actor (b Haslemere, Surrey, Eng 28 Feb 1942). Trained at the Bristol Old Vic, his acting career includes 2 seasons at the Chichester Festival, appearance in the BBC TV series *The Forsythe Saga* and the film lead in *David Copperfield*. In 1982 he starred in *The Dresser* at the Vancouver Playhouse. He attracted attention as a director in 1970 staging *Abelard and Heloise* in London and on Broadway. Directorial assignments for Chichester and the Royal Shakespeare Co led to artistic directorship of Greenwich's Co Theatre (1973-75) and Canada's STRATFORD FESTIVAL (1975-80). Despite initial nationalistic protest, his Canadian tenure achieved financial success due to his own 35 productions, the creation of a Young Company and the importation of international stars. Following a storm-filled departure, Phillips filmed Timothy Findley's *The Wars* (1981) and ran London Ontario's Grand Theatre for one unhappy season (1983-84). He returned triumphantly to Stratford in 1986-87, directing *Cymbeline* and *The School for Scandal* on the main stage and becoming head of the Young Company. DAVID GARDNER

Phillips, Walter Joseph, artist (b at Barton-upon-Humber, Eng 25 Oct 1884; d at Victoria 5 July 1963). Phillips's early art training was undertaken in opposition to his father's wishes. He immigrated to Winnipeg in 1913, where he was appointed art master at St John's Technical High School. There he learned etching from a colleague, Cyril Barraud, and printed on the school's press. As a means of introducing colour to his prints he began experimenting with the Japanese method of woodblock printing, producing his first complete print in 1917. Not only a fine technician, Phillips was an acute observer of his environment. His images of western Canada were widely distributed and collected. He also published a number of print portfolios and illustrated several books. In 1943 he moved to Banff, where he taught and painted in watercolour.

JUDY GOUIN

Phillips, William Eric, financier, industrialist (b at Toronto 3 Jan 1893; d at Palm Beach, Fla 26 Dec 1964). In Europe at the outbreak of WWI, Eric Phillips joined the British army, winning both the DSO and the Military Cross, and becoming lieutenant-colonel. After the war he served in

Poland before leaving the army in 1920. He married the daughter of R.S. MCLAUGHLIN and established his own company, W.E. Phillips Ltd, in Oshawa, Ont, in 1922. In 1940 C.D. HOWE recruited him to head Research Enterprises Ltd, making optical glass, range finders, binoculars and radar components. Between 1940 and 1946 Research Enterprises sold $220-million worth of equipment. At the end of WWII, Phillips joined E.P. TAYLOR in ARGUS CORP, becoming chairman of this investment firm. In 1945 he was appointed chairman of the board of governors of U of T and became known for strong and decisive management of the business and financial affairs of the university. ROBERT BOTHWELL

Philosophy, originally the love of wisdom in all its forms, both practical and theoretical. Sometimes a philosopher is thought of as a sage, a person of insight and good judgement, who shows equanimity in adversity. An individual may have a philosophy of life – a general view of the world, a life plan and a set of policies to guide action. Similarly, there may be a philosophy for any sphere of thought or activity – a basic theory and policies for it.

But over the centuries philosophy evolved into a special, technical discipline, comprising at its core: (1) *logic,* which studies principles for correct reasoning and inference; (2) *epistemology* (theory of knowledge), concerned with standards for reasonable belief and the attainment of truth; (3) *metaphysics,* the study of being as such and related notions such as existence, appearance and reality; the most basic or general categories of thought (eg, "thing," "property," "possibility," "time"); and principles of general order (eg, determinism: every event has a cause); (4) *ethics* (including social and political philosophy), which deals with values and the good, right and wrong action, obligations and rights, justice and ideal social and political arrangements. In addition, there are many "philosophies of such and such," in which the logical, epistemic, metaphysical and ethical problems of a field (science, religion, art, history, education, etc) are studied. Finally, a number of philosophers study the history of philosophy, interpreting, explaining, comparing and criticizing previous philosophical work.

Before WWII there were few philosophers in Canada, and they were separated by geography and sometimes language; and they most often worked in or under the influence of a denominational religious institution; and many of them devoted themselves mainly to teaching, historical scholarship, or the development of the thought of a particular "school" (eg, Thomism, objective idealism). Nevertheless, there were significant philosophies in Canada in this period.

After 1950 Canada's growing wealth, a population boom and a new interest in culture and education led to significant change. (The Massey Royal Commission on NATIONAL DEVELOPMENT IN THE ARTS, LETTERS AND SCIENCES, the CANADA COUNCIL and the Parent Royal Commission of Inquiry on Education in Québec, appointed 1961, were important milestones.) With the rapid growth of universities, the number of philosophers grew and they became increasingly professional and secular. They often devoted themselves to esoteric technical problems, made no pretence of being sages and had little communication with the public. But changes in communications and travel, the founding of professional institutions (eg, the Canadian Philosophical Association, 1957; the journals *Dialogue,* 1962, and *The Canadian Journal of Philosophy,* 1971) and personal encounters at conferences, eg, LEARNED SOCIETIES, helped to develop a professional community. Relative harmony and some fruitful interaction between the 2 linguistic groups have been created by the existence of a bilingual journal, the CPA policies of passive bilingualism and rotation of offices between Francophones and Anglophones, and the growing common interest in secular philosophy. Three recent trends suggest a rapprochement between professional interests and those of the public: a revival of political philosophy; an interest in both normative and applied ethics (eg, MEDICAL ETHICS); and the development of Québecois and CANADIAN STUDIES. JOHN T. STEVENSON

Philosophy Before 1950

French Canada In New France, as elsewhere in the New World, the teaching of philosophy was initially the responsibility of the church. Philosophy was taught regularly from 1665 at the Jesuit College in Québec, which, like such colleges in France, followed the dictates of the Jesuit teaching philosophy as set out in the *Ratio Studiorum.* In 2 years the college's few students took a course in logic consisting of the second book of Aristotle's *Organon, On Interpretation,* and the first 2 books of *The Prior Analytics.* The entirely Aristotelian physics program included the 8 books of the *Physics, On the Heavens,* and the first book of *On Coming to Be and Passing Away.* Metaphysics was also Aristotelian and the ethics course followed *The Nicomachean Ethics.* As often as possible, professors made reference to medieval philosopher St Thomas Aquinas (c 1224-74). In the hierarchy of the liberal arts in the Middle Ages, philosophy was the servant of theology (*ancilla theologiae*). Until 1759 the same was true in Québec, where philosophy appeared in the program as a basic prerequisite to theology for students aspiring to the priesthood.

Interrupted by the British military conquest, the teaching of philosophy was resumed in 1770 in 5 colleges. This new start led to the 1835 publication of the first Canadian philosophy textbook, the *Institutiones philosophicae ad usum studiosae juventutis,* by Abbé Jérôme DEMERS of the SÉMINAIRE DE QUÉBEC. Professors, by then more numerous and mostly of Canadian origin, based their teaching on Charles Rollin's *Traité des études* (rev ed 1845), according to which the purpose of philosophy was to establish a moral structure and to forearm youth against unbelief. Unbelief was seen to stem from the Protestant Reformation, the writings of French philosopher René Descartes (1596-1650), Denis Diderot's *Encyclopédie* (1751-80) and the impact of the American and French revolutions (1775 and 1789) in a province where from 1764 printed material was becoming more widely available. The teaching of philosophy was therefore a controversial activity, and new ideas and new objections to those ideas appeared: the origin of ideas and of certainty, immortality of the soul and the existence of God, ATHEISM, the origins of political power and the highest form of government. After Descartes and the Enlightenment, one had either to accept or to oppose the rules of reason.

It was this challenge that lay at the root of a philosophical controversy (1833-34) centered on the French philosopher Félicité de Lamennais (1782-1854) and the publication of Abbé Demers's textbooks. At issue were the establishment of certainty against Cartesian doubt in the teaching of logic, refutation of the Enlightenment's atheism in metaphysics and moral philosophy, and the affirmation that political power came from God, not from the sovereignty of the people.

Limited to objection and refutation until around 1840, the teaching of philosophy was subsequently characterized by a quest for affirmative philosophical theses, and by a frantic search for an authority and for a "Catholic philosophy" that found its ultimate expression in Pope Leo XIII's encyclical, *Aeterni Patris* (1879), on the restoration of Christian philosophy. It was in this context that Thomism appeared, so long to be considered synonymous with French Canadian philosophy. By 1879 the philosophy of St Thomas Aquinas had provided solutions to the basic, traditional problems in the teaching of philosophy. Certainty was henceforth the product of reason based on faith and no longer troubled by doubt. In ethics the hierarchy of purposes justified God's priority over man, the spiritual over the temporal and church over state, thus providing the philosophical basis of the ULTRAMONTANISM that dominated French Canadian society.

Thereafter the teaching of philosophy was rigidly standardized by means of a single baccalaureate examination at the end of the classical course in all colleges, and a single philosophy textbook was used in all colleges. The philosophical uniformity of this instruction by manual was disrupted at the beginning of the century by the "social question." Industrialization (capital, labour, strikes) and urbanization confronted the Thomist world with new problems (*see* SOCIAL DOCTRINE) and often justified the preparation and adoption of new manuals.

Philosophy took new strides after 1920 when it was introduced into the universities. A faculty of philosophy was founded 1921 at U de Montréal; Dominican monk Ceslas-Marie Forest was dean there, 1926-52. In Québec City, the École supérieure de philosophie (fd 1926) of U Laval became a faculty in 1935, and the Belgian Charles DE KONINCK was director, 1939-56. The early development of the teaching of philosophy in the universities drew support from the general expansion of the universities and the increasing importance of philosophical studies in Rome and Louvain.

Its real development occurred, however, following another papal pronouncement, *Deus Scientiarum* (1931), which favoured science as the bastion of faith and resulted in a reorganization of faculties of philosophy. At Laval the faculty had an equally Aristotelian and Thomist approach, as may be seen from professors' publications and the subjects of theses and articles in *Laval théologique et philosophique* (1945-). In Montréal, Latin was abandoned as the language of instruction in 1936, and day courses established in 1942 doubled in number by 1948. Theses incorporated a Thomist approach until around 1948, whereas the history of philosophy was predominant as the faculty was becoming more secularized.

French Canadian studies in medieval history and philosophy were probably the most important international contributions made in those fields until around 1950. The exceptional contribution made by Franciscans was belittled and in 1927 even became the subject of a heated debate in Thomist circles between the future Cardinal VILLENEUVE and the great Franciscan medievalist, Father Ephrem Longpré. In Ottawa in 1930 the Dominicans founded the Institute of Mediaeval Studies, which moved to Montréal in 1943. It was affiliated with U de Montréal. There was much philosophical activity and discussion after 1930 with the publications of de Koninck, Hermas Bastien, Fathers Louis-Marie Régis, Louis Lachance, Patrice Robert, Julien Péghaire and Arcade Monette, and the organization of philosophical societies such as La Société de philosophie de Montréal (fd 1924) and the extremely formal Académie canadienne Saint Thomas d'Aquin (1930-45).

After 1930 a new generation that included Étienne Gilson (in Toronto) and Jacques Maritain took over from the old guard and moved into the editorial ranks of new journals and of the *Journées thomistes* (1935 and 1936) organized for the young generation. Between the 1929 crash and the 1948 REFUS GLOBAL, Maritain, the catalyst in philosophical debates (with de Koninck) and ideological controversies (over Pétainism), became an important source of inspiration before the arrival of Emmanuel Mounier, Christian and atheistic existentialism, and phenomenology.
YVAN LAMONDE

English Canada Philosophy took root in English Canada with the founding of the first universities in Nova Scotia and what is now Ontario. (By 1860 Canada, with a population less than 2 million, had 12 universities.) Most philosophers teaching at these universities came from Britain, especially Scotland. They were trained primarily as clergymen, but philosophy comprised a large part of their education. It soon became apparent to these newcomers to Canada that the practice of teaching the Scottish sermon was not suited to the rapidly diversifying student population. Because of ever-present hardships, many students from rural backgrounds were beginning to suspect claims made about God as saviour and protector. The students would then have to be persuaded through reason and sound argument that moral behaviour was preferable to amoral behaviour; that the individual had a place in this new wild land; that nature could be productive and still be protected; that advanced scientific and evolutionary theories could take their place alongside theology and the idea of God; that religion could make sense in the face of natural disasters; and that in a town with many religious factions, a clergyman could give a sermon that offended no one and offered meaning and purpose to tired and harassed parishioners. The philosophers who faced these formidable tasks adjusted to the demands of the environment and tirelessly undertook to educate the future clergy, teachers, circuit preachers and civil servants of Canada.

On the surface, Canada's culture is a conglomerate of differing actions and attitudes towards events and institutions. The philosophers saw that a single set of meanings (interpretations) for these events and institutions could not easily be imposed upon groups of people spread far apart, without considerable force and pressure to conform to this particular "way of thinking." People had immigrated for many reasons, often to escape from rigid and uniform ideas. If freedom of thought was to have meaning, another basis of Canadian culture had to be established. And so the philosophers looked to "reason."

Through reason we assign meanings to events and defend ourselves from encroachment on meanings around which we structure our lives. Canadian philosophers were not alone in their concern with the nature and uses of reason, but their interpretations gave a distinctive base for a unifying cultural identity. A kind of philosophical federalism was being developed.

Three basic themes concerned the first philosophers in English Canada: the philosophical basis of religion, the idea of nature, and the philosophical examination of political ideas and systems. In the late 19th and early 20th centuries some scholars, such as John WATSON at Queen's U published on all 3 themes. George BLEWETT, U of Toronto, concerned himself with the idea of nature and its relation to God. However, philosophy in Canada was not confined to these themes. Richard Maurice BUCKE, a psychiatrist in London, Ont, wrote about evolutionary spirituality. John Macdonald, U of Alberta, published on the philosophy of education. Herbert Leslie STEWART at Dalhousie had interests ranging from CALVINISM to the work of German philosopher Nietzsche. Rupert LODGE, a Plato scholar at U of Manitoba, tackled questions about ethics, business and education.

The seeds of respect, tolerance and a commitment to explore all sides of a problem before suggesting solutions were truly being sown by Canadian philosophers such as Lodge. He believed that there may never be a right answer to a question and that any problem exists in a context. Although his writings seem biased towards idealism and the importance of preserving valued ideas, not just progressing materially at any price, he still presented the viewpoints of the pragmatist and the realist on any problem he approached in his later books. At U of T, George BRETT emphasized the importance of history in understanding man's nature and spearheaded the "Toronto school of intellectual history," which dominated philosophy there until the late 1950s. John Irving, U of T, turned that historical vision upon the first 100 years of philosophy in Canada and published the first assessment of "Canadian" philosophy. He also wrote on science, values and the SOCIAL CREDIT movement in Alberta.

The need to come to grips with religious claims and the advance of science was pressing. Industrialism, increased control over nature, and continued progress in the creation and distribution of wealth seemed to have given humans many powers previously associated with God. The geographical circumstances and the diverse population of Canada worked against the likelihood of there being an established church (*see* ANGLICANISM), which might provide interpretations of the rapid changes. Catholic philosophers sought solutions in the writings of Aquinas. The establishment in Toronto of the Institute of Mediaeval Studies (1929; papal charter 1939, when it became the Pontifical Institute of Mediaeval Studies) was testimony to the devotion and scholarship of these pioneers in Catholic thought. (Another separate Institute of Mediaeval Studies was founded by the Dominicans in Ottawa, 1930.)

For Protestants there was no clear strategy. The first philosophy book written in English Canada was *Elements of Natural Theology* (1850) by James BEAVEN. Wishing to connect religion with scientific developments, Beaven focused on law, order and structure in the universe as evidence of a rational being, or God; because the laws of the universe work together, the universe is intelligible as a whole. If "God" is what we mean by the source of intelligibility, argued Beaven, then the close relation between man and God remains intact. Major works of philosophy and religion were published by Watson, an acknowledged expert on German philosopher Immanuel Kant. In *Outline of Philosophy* (1908) and *The Interpretation of Religious Experience* (1910-12), Watson examined thoroughly the historical arguments for and against God's existence, and he proposed a metaphysical system to explain existence that drew correlations between reason, God, and a concept from idealism, developed by German philosopher G.W.F. Hegel, called the "Absolute." In "The Invisible Church," a chapter in *The Interpretation of Religious Experience*, Watson anticipated the uniquely Canadian UNITED CHURCH and foresaw its ultimate integration into Canadian life as a social agency of rational morality. He published 8 books and over 200 articles, and his sophisticated work was well known in the US and Britain.

At McGill U, John Clark MURRAY, in *A Handbook of Psychology* (1885) and *An Introduction to Ethics* (1891), pursued metaphysical problems to give both man's increasing power and God's will places in the rational explication of what exists. Murray spent many hours giving public lectures and writing newspaper articles about the plight of the working class, and he was energetic and fearless as Canada's earliest philosophical feminist. Murray was not Canada's only public philosopher: both Stewart and Irving later became lecturers on CBC Radio. At U of T George Paxton YOUNG, who wrote occasional pieces on metaphysics, ethics and mathematics and openly challenged the doctrines of his church, had a devoted following because of his classroom teaching.

The relation between God and man was highlighted by Dalhousie U's William LYALL in *Intellect, the Emotions, and the Moral Nature* (1855). Man is a part of nature, argued Lyall, and to violate nature is indirectly to violate man. Blewett, a farm boy from southern Ontario, wrote *The Study of Nature and the Vision of God* (1907) and *The Christian View of the World* (1912), concluding even then that the environment was in danger from man's waste and neglect. Blewett also believed reason to be the basis of all possible experience and all freedom, and he argued that a notion of a community of rational spirits was more fundamental than one of individual beings. The idea of community as the key to survival was becoming well entrenched in a developing, but still mainly rural, Canadian society.

Two distinctive features of Canadian society as a political entity are its many-faceted pluralism in language, culture, religion, geography, educational theory and values; and a strong commitment to tradition among its diverse communities. The French and Scots brought with them centuries-old patterns of social organization. LOYALISTS came firmly committed to old ways, having rejected new political experiments in the US. Philosophers interested in political theory had to find ways to create a conceptual basis for politics while surrounded by distinct and occasionally warring factions. Once again they focused on reason as a mediator and discovery tool.

Watson's *The State in Peace and War* (1919) emphasized the need to see progress in a historical context. New social orders could not be invented willy-nilly. People progress from experience to experience, and reason must interpret the present in relation to the past. Mistakes would be inevitable in the gradual move from theoretical to real equality. Watson was undoubtedly conservative. Brett was equally reserved; in *The Government of Man* (1913) he emphasized the need for historical understanding of problems more than the need for solutions. Still, neither philosopher believed that the state was rational and beyond challenge.

Murray faced the Industrial Revolution and concomitant social disruptions directly. In 1887 he completed *The Industrial Kingdom of God* (published posthumously, 1981), in which he openly discussed Karl Marx and Henry George, communal planning, strikes and the advantages and disadvantages of capitalism. Its Victorian prose did not hide its radical elements, a fact that may have had something to do with its remaining in manuscript form for almost 100 years. Murray believed that rational assessment of existing institutions would lead to positive change.

If political philosophy in Canada leaned to the left, it did so with reserve. The philosophers believed that men would be changed, not by rational assault but by rational exchange. It would be a slow, arduous task to create the just society, but along the way society would be more stable, less violent, less prone to fall prey to radical innovations and quick solutions. Government, if not always loved, needed at least to be understood. Dissension would be inevitable, but the dismantling of creditable institutions as an alternative would result in much more stress and disruption. The role of reason, as interpreter and key to compromise, was critical to Canada's philosophers; what they envisaged was much like the Canada we know today: orderly and reticent, but an international example of the value of discussion, tolerance and democracy. The philosophers in English and French Canada were scholars first. But a thorough examination of their works reveals as much about the national character of Canadians and Canadian culture as about the eternal questions of philosophy. ELIZABETH A. TROTT

Historical Scholarship

A major subdiscipline of philosophy in Canada for many years was and remains historical scholarship in philosophy. This includes discovering and editing texts written by philosophers of the past, writing expository and explanatory commentaries on them and discussing them in an evaluative, critical or even polemical way. Why might historical work of this sort be more important for philosophy than for another discipline, such as physics? A variety of answers have been given. For some, philosophy is concerned with enduring questions, the answers to which can best be sought in a timeless "dialogue" with great thinkers, past or present. For others a perennial philosophy, as good for today as for yesterday, has already been created; we can only understand, refine, interpret and apply it to our own time. According to both views, philosophy is only accidentally historical; it is essentially universal and timeless. The contrary view claims that time, place and circumstance do make a difference for the correctness of philosophical questions posed, answers given and standards of evaluation used. Some believe there are patterns of growth, development and progress in philosophy, others do not; but both agree that philosophy varies with historical context. In spite of these and other differences, there is a consensus that some knowledge of the classical texts is important in philosophical education and that scholarly work on them is a worthy enterprise.

In Canada the emphasis on this type of scholarship has been accentuated by religious, political and institutional circumstances. As late as the 1960s, many philosophers, both anglophone and francophone, worked in institutions with some religious affiliation. They conducted their work in an ideologically sensitive atmosphere, and there were often expectations about how the enterprise would be conducted. The study of the history of philosophy provided an acceptable way of introducing a cosmopolitan element into the climate of opinion.

At U of T, a widely shared belief in the importance of a historical approach to the humanities, and a teaching program that reflected that conviction, led to the development of the so-called "Toronto school of intellectual history." George Brett was one of its dominant figures. His own work was historical and frequently interdisciplinary. His main contribution, *A History of Psychology* (3 vols, 1912-21), presented the philosophical theories of mind that served as the historical context for the later development of scientific PSYCHOLOGY. Subsequent department heads Fulton H. Anderson and Thomas A. GOUDGE continued, in many respects, the tradition of the "school." In the 1980s attempts were being made to renew it through a new generation of promising scholars. Much good work in the history of philosophy has come from inheritors of this tradition. It includes work in classical Greek philosophy by G.M.A. Grube, John Rist, David Gallop, T.M. Robinson and Reginald Allen (*see* CLASSICS); on figures of the 16th, 17th and 18th centuries by Brett, Anderson, Robert McRae, D.P. Dryer, David Savan, C.B. Macpherson and David Gauthier; and on the 19th century by Emil Fackenheim, Kenneth Schmitz and John Robson. The work done by these and other academics has had considerable influence both in Canada and abroad.

An influence at least as great has stemmed from another Toronto institution. The (Pontifical) Institute of Mediaeval Studies was a Canadian development in the revival of medieval philosophy following the papal encyclical *Aeterni Patris*. The influence of French philosopher Étienne Gilson was keenly felt in the institute, and with it came an emphasis on careful editing and study of original texts, an effort to understand them in their proper contexts, and an interest in both their classical antecedents and their early modern descendants. Anton Pegis, Joseph Owens and Armand Maurer have been important figures in the institute's research and teaching.

In Québec, important academic figures working in this Catholic tradition were Louis Lachance, Charles de Koninck, Benoît Lacroix and Vianney Décarie. Although the influence of the church tended to restrict study of heterodox or progressive doctrines, there was an interest among younger thinkers in French philosophers such as Maurice Blondel, Henri Bergson, Emmanuel Mounier, Gabriel Marcel and especially Jacques Maritain. By the 1960s the search for alternative ideological models intensified, and there was a growing interest in Nietzsche, Freud, Marx and such 20th-century movements as existentialism and phenomenology. Students of philosophy applied lessons from these new models in "radical" periodicals such as PARTI PRIS and LIBERTÉ. Gradually the diversification of interests was followed by increasingly sound scholarship. Good work was done in the more traditional areas by such scholars as Yvon Lafrance, Léonce Paquet and Luc Brisson, and some excellent work by, among others, Olivier Réboul on Kant, François Duchesneau on Leibniz and Guy Lafrance on Rousseau, Bergson and Durkheim. The higher standards are reflected in the pages of *Philosophiques* (1974-), the official periodical of the Société de philosophie du Québec.

In English Canada there has been a relative decline since the late 1960s in the influence of Toronto institutions. Scholarship has become so widespread – and so diversified in its authors, subjects and institutional affiliations – that it is almost invidious to single out examples. In any case, one need not turn now to Toronto (or to Montréal's Raymond Klibansky, Alastair McKinnon or Charles Taylor) to find notable historical scholarship: one can find it in Calgary, Guelph, Waterloo, Peterborough, London or Fredericton. And the works studied range, in origin, from ancient Greece and India to the modern Germanys and France and, in subject matter, from the intricacies of late medieval logic to the global sweep of Hegel's system. It may be more useful to note other recent trends.

First, Canadian scholars participate extensively in international networks in which the results of individual studies are exchanged and evaluated. Second, there is the development of important international publishing projects centered in Canada, often involving several institutions, eg, publication of the collected papers of Bertrand Russell, from material in the Russell Archives at McMaster U, Hamilton; interdisciplinary projects in Toronto, one to produce an edition of the work of John Stuart Mill and another the writings of Erasmus; and an edition of C.S. Peirce's work involving U of Waterloo. Third, there is the introduction of computer technology to facilitate the production of research instruments, eg, Alastair McKinnon's Kierkegaard concordance, the concordance of the Gerhard edition of Leibniz's work being produced under the direction of Robert McRae, and the Bibliography of Philosophy in Canada Project, 1790-1976.

Finally, there is an expanding interest in philosophy as practised in Canada. Francophone philosophers have taken the lead, as is demonstrated in the pioneering work of Roland Houde, the solid historical work of Yvan Lamonde and the important writing of Maurice Lagueux on the impact of Marxist thought on Québecois ideology during the 1960s. Similar historical self-examination has excited less interest in anglophone Canada, but valuable contributions have been made by pioneer John Irving, historians Carl Berger and Brian McKillop, and philosophers Leslie Armour and Elizabeth Trott.

JOHN T. STEVENSON AND THOMAS MATHIEN

Ethics, Social and Political Philosophy

English Canada In English Canadian philosophy since 1950 a strong point has been the study of values, including ethics (what, if anything, makes an action right or wrong?), social and political philosophy (what principles should be used to assess social groups and political institutions?), and philosophy of law (what standards are inherent in law, and what is their relation to moral rules?). Some of this work arises from reflection on important figures in the history of ethics, especially on the work of Hobbes, Hume, Kant, Hegel and Marx. Such work has often led to original insights into major normative issues. Nevertheless, most work in this period has been more problem centered than historical. The predominant approach has been in the English "analytical" tradition, rather than in the manner of current European philosophy. The main work here can be conveniently divided into 3 areas: metaethics, theoretical ethics and politics, and applied philosophy.

Metaethics, the most abstract of these, received the greatest attention through the 1960s. The primary concern was with the meaning and meaningfulness of moral claims, eg, as explored in Francis Sparshott's *Enquiry into Goodness and Related Concepts* (1958). A further issue has been the relation between self-interest and morality, with some, such as Gauthier in *Morals by Agreement* (1986), arguing that self-interest grounds morality, but most, like Kai Nielsen, rejecting this claim and the view of morality implicit in it. A major focus has been what David Braybrooke labels "the ethopolitical intersection," where the philosophy of history and the social sciences intersects social and political philosophy. Outstanding work has been done by Braybrooke, Donald Brown, Charles TAYLOR, Jonathan Bennett and Gerald Cohen in differentiating scientific and normative accounts of human behaviour; for the normative approach they have developed criteria for rational and moral action. Debate continues in metaethics on the most fundamental questions, in particular over the extent to which definitive standards can be provided to resolve moral, political and legal disputes (*see*, for example, E.J. Bond's *Reason and Value*, 1983).

At the second level, theory construction, Canadian philosophers have been active. Much of their theorizing has been piecemeal, concentrating on testing rival theories on central aspects of the moral life, eg, interpersonal relations, emotions, punishment, rights, and legal and moral obligations. There have also been larger-scale efforts defending the main theories in contention: utilitarianism, individual rights and Marxism. These theories supply different answers to the question of whether the demands of justice are essentially negative (leave others alone) or are also positive (those in easy circumstances must help those in need). Since the mid-1970s there has been increasing polarization in political philosophy towards Marxist collectivism (eg, Kai Nielsen's *Equality and Liberty* (1985) or libertarian individualism; (eg, David Gauthier's *Morals By Agreement*

(1985); defenders of the status quo have been less vocal, perhaps having turned their attention to the third area.

This is the area of applied philosophy. Up to the mid-1970s most philosophers were concerned with metaethics and theory construction. They wrote principally for other philosophers and had little contact with academics in other disciplines or with the general public. But now most philosophy departments offer courses in biomedical ethics, business and professional ethics, and moral, political and legal problems. There has been increasing contact with nonphilosophers working in related areas in jointly taught courses, interdisciplinary meetings, and the establishment of institutes (such as the Westminster Institute for Ethics and Human Values in London, Ont) and societies (such as the Canadian Section for Philosophy of Law) to study leading moral issues.

Philosophers increasingly have brought their theoretical insights to bear on practical problems such as native rights, discrimination against women, moral education, nuclear energy and war. A fine example is Wayne Sumner's utilitarian *Abortion and Moral Theory* (1981). Philosophers have also been turning their attention to specifically Canadian problems, as evidenced in the 1979 discussions of CONFEDERATION and SOVEREIGNTY-ASSOCIATION.

The 1982 Constitution with its CANADIAN CHARTER OF RIGHTS AND FREEDOMS has also received philosophical attention, both from legally minded philosophers and philosophically minded lawyers. Such attention to Canadian problems may come to differentiate Canadian work in political and legal philosophy from work done elsewhere; eg, recent debate about the nature and importance of collective or group rights, including linguistic, religious, aboriginal, etc. Two recent anthologies in theoretical and applied ethics are Stanley French's *Philosophers Look at Canadian Confederation* (1979) and Wesley Cragg's *Contemporary Moral Issues* (2nd ed, 1987).

Although the emphasis on applying philosophy has grown in recent years, always implicit in specific applications are normative theories and metaethical positions. Philosophers are adept at making these implicit views explicit and providing searching criticisms of them. But this means that philosophers are inevitably led back to fundamental questions about the status and justification of moral, political, social and legal rules. Finally, while Canadian philosophers will likely make increasingly important contributions to public discussions of moral issues, it has to be said that they have not thus far become well known outside university philosophy departments. Two leading exceptions here are Charles Taylor and George GRANT. Both have raised issues of technological change, and both have been quite critical of the moral presuppositions of modern industrial society. Taylor has drawn his inspiration from 18th- and 19th-century European philosophers, especially Hegel. Grant has found his roots in ancient philosophy and in Christian thought. Both, but Grant in particular, have attracted significant followings beyond professional philosophical circles.

MICHAEL McDONALD

French Canada During the 1950s in French Canada, work in the field of ethics and social and political philosophy continued to be based essentially on the Aristotelian-Thomist tradition and to respect the social doctrine of the Roman Catholic Church. University and college courses in ethics and social philosophy conveyed the principles of Christian morality and the church's social doctrine as expressed in papal encyclicals. There was still only limited interest in political philosophy and the philosophy of law, these subjects generally being included in the teaching of social philosophy. Although little philosophical research was published, there were exceptions, such as Louis Lachance's studies of justice and law in the writings of Aristotle and Aquinas.

The end of the decade marked a new era. Pluralism entered the scene as the scholastic and systematic tradition declined, and the new generation of philosophers pursued the history of thought and comparisons between various schools of philosophy and value systems. Philosophy echoed the QUIET REVOLUTION: Marxist and existentialist values became vehicles for changes in the content of, and general approach to, philosophical research and teaching. Some sociopolitical philosophers probed the structures and values of Québec society and conducted research on cultural issues, power structures and ideologies. Important works in this area included Fernand Dumont's *Le Pouvoir dans la société canadienne-française* (1966); *Le Lieu de l'homme* (1968); and *La Vigile du Québec, octobre 1970: l'impasse?* (1974). During this period an ideology research group, led by Claude Savary, was founded.

In the 1970s, publications on social and political philosophy increased in number and became more diversified. Personal essays and popular publications included the works of thinkers involved in social and political issues in Québec, such as Jacques Grand'Maison's *Une société en quête d'éthique* (1977), *Un nouveau contrat social* (1980) and the essay by Michel Morin and Claude Bertrand, *Le Territoire imaginaire de la culture* (1979). The more academic essays deal mainly with forms of political power; they include the works of Joseph Pestieau and, in *La Confédération canadienne* (1979), the reflections of a group of philosophers. Maurice Lagueux's *Le Marxisme des années soixante* (1982) won the Governor General's Award for nonfiction.

Studies devoted to the sociopolitical ideas of the major philosophers are more common and include the works of Olivier Reboul on Kant, Leo-Paul Bordeleau on Blondel, Jean-Guy Meunier on Marx, Guy Lafrance on Bergson, Durkheim and Rousseau, and Jean Roy on Hobbes. The philosophy of history, a subject of growing interest, is dealt with by Roberto Miguelez in *Sujet et histoire* (1974). The philosophy of law, a relatively new field, is the subject of Georges Legault's *La Structure performative du langage juridique* (1977).

Ethics and social and political philosophy have also been discussed at conferences on political issues or on the relationship between philosophy and law.

Interest in interdisciplinary studies has recently grown, particularly in those relating to economics, law and the social sciences. Similarly, studies on cultural issues are coming to the fore, particularly since the founding of the Institut québécois de recherche sur la culture. This interest appears to be a feature of the new philosophy of French Canada, and clearly indicates closer links between philosophical activities and society at large. GUY LAFRANCE

Logic, Epistemology, Philosophy of Science

English Canada Logic is studied as formal deductive science (part of mathematics, including computer applications) and as a tool for investigating problems in the structure of reasoning (valid argument, semantics, hypothetical reasoning); and as that part of philosophy dealing with exact analysis of difficult concepts. In the last 3 decades philosophers in English Canada have made contributions to logic in both these areas. Bas Van Fraassen has developed a formal semantics for logic; William Harper, a probability semantics and a theory of preference and utility; Hans Herzberger, a theory of preference ordering;

and Alasdair Urquhart, a semantics for relevance logics. Urquhart has also proved the very significant result that relevance logics are undecidable. Brian Chellas has dealt with modal logics, William Rozeboom with problems in philosophical semantics. Van Fraassen and Charles Morgan have done studies of probability semantics; Anil Gupta and Herzberger have investigated the semantics of truth and paradoxes; John Woods has written on relevance and on paradoxes.

Epistemology (theory of knowledge) studies the nature and extent of human knowing. It relates to psychology, cognitive science and the arts. Work in philosophy of psychology has been done by Ausonio Marras, Patricia and Paul Churchland, Roland Puccetti and by Zenon Pylyshyn, director (1983) of the Centre for Cognitive Science at U of Western Ontario. William Demopoulos has been working in the important cognitive science field of learnability theory. An accessible work combining epistemological and other philosophical concerns is A.H. Johnson's *Experiential Realism* (1973).

An important branch of epistemology is investigation of scientific knowledge to try to determine its theoretical structure and its place in human culture. Philosophers in Canada have made important contributions in the philosophy of biology, including work on evolutionary theory by Thomas Goudge, Michael Ruse and Paul Thompson; philosophy of physics, especially of quantum mechanics, involving work in logical interpretation of the theory (Jeffrey Bub and William Demopoulos), the modal interpretation (Van Fraassen), and other aspects of quantum theory (Clifford Hooker, Edwin Levy and Leslie Ballentine). Other philosophers of physics include Mario Bunge, whose work ranges from technical philosophy of physics to science policy; Roger Angel (relativity physics); and Robin Giles (empirical treatment of thermodynamics). Some philosophers have begun to develop theories of science based on its history. Canadians have been active contributors in this venture, and they include Robert E. Butts (Whewell, Kant, historical methodology), Robert McRae (Leibniz), William Shea (Galileo), John Nicholas (Kuhnian anomalies), Jagdish Hattiangadi, James Brown and Andrew Lugg (methodology, evolutionary epistemology, the distinction between pseudoscience and science); Ian Hacking (probability theory); and James Brown whose book *The Rational and the Social* (1988) develops a theory of rationality based on the history of science. Others are working on philosophy of the social sciences. They include Charles Taylor, who wrote *The Explanation of Behaviour* (1964); David Braybrooke (general problems), Frank Cunningham (objectivity) and Jonathan Bennett (rationality). William Dray writes on philosophy of history, and co-edited *Substance and Form in History* (1981). Kathleen Okruhlik and Alison Wylie are undertaking a 3-year study of feminist criticisms of science. Alex Michalos has studied the entrenchment of values in society, Brian Cupples, problems in the logic of explanation. Fred Wilson has been developing a comprehensive empiricist philosophy of science, as in his *Explanation, Causation and Deduction* (1985).

A basic problem in 20th-century philosophy is that of the status of those things science postulates as existing: electrons, quarks and other objects unobservable by normal means. Scientific realism is the view that such objects exist; but realism is a disputed theory.

Three major Canadian contributions to the debate are Ian Hacking's *Representing and Intervening* (1983), Van Fraassen's *The Scientific Image* (1980) and Paul Churchland's *Scientific Realism and the Plasticity of Mind* (1979). A notable re-

thinking of the issue can be found in Ian Hacking's *Representing and Intervening* (1983).

Canada supports work in logic, epistemology and philosophy of science in many ways. International prominence in a major scientific and scholarly field is not easy to obtain, but in recent years Canada has achieved that presence at a level of excellence. ROBERT E. BUTTS

French Canada Between 1950 and 1960 in French Canada, the teaching of philosophy at the university level continued to be dominated by neoscholasticism. Researchers involved in other areas, including Hugues Leblanc and Roland Houde, pursued their careers in the US. From 1960 to 1970 Thomism progressively disappeared and the universities recruited a few specialists, such as Michel Ambacher and Jerzy Wojciechowski, who favoured research dealing with contemporary themes. Visits by francophone universities by thinkers such as Paul Ricoeur, Georges Canguilhem, Jean-Blaise Grize and Alan Montefiore, and the growing influence of European epistemologists such as Gaston Bachelard and Jean Piaget and analytical philosophers such as J.L. Austin, resulted in the emergence of new problematics and led some students to complete their training in Europe. After 1970 there were more exchanges with European researchers and a growing interest in Anglo-American problematics. At the same time a number of young researchers, trained in the philosophy of science and in epistemology and logic, secured university positions and provided growing support for specialized research.

Works on logic and the history of logic include those of Yvon Gauthier, Serge Robert, Daniel Vanderveken, Louis Valcke, Jaromir Danek and François Lepage; and on the philosophy of language, those of Gilles Lane, Jean-Paul Brodeur, Jacques Poulain, Ghyslain Charron, Jean-Guy Meunier, Claude Panaccio and Guy Bouchard. The most notable research in the combined field of logic and philosophy of language is being conducted in formal semantics and the theory of acts of language.

The common element linking general epistemology researchers, such as Jean Theau, François Duchesneau, Maurice Gagnon, Normand Lacharité, Robert Nadeau and Serge Robert, lies in analysis of the formation and transformation processes of science. It is striking that, in the various projects undertaken in this field, the purely structural analysis of scientific theories is replaced by consideration of the historical development of the disciplines.

The philosophy of mathematics is probed in the research of Charles Castonguay and Gauthier. Works by R. Bernier, Paul Pirlot, Camille Limoges and Duchesneau deal with the current problematics of the philosophy of biology in relation to the historical transformation of concepts and theories. Contemporary physical theories preoccupy Gauthier and Georges Hélal. The basics of physics and mathematics figure prominently in Gauthier's original research, under the label of "constructivism." Constructivism is an analysis of the constructive dimension in the language of scientific theories, and thus contrasts with realism, which suggests that theories describe a reality independent of the constructing linguistic agent.

The vast social-science field is being investigated by Maurice Lagueux, Roberto Miguelez and Nadeau in history; Charron and J.N. Kaufmann in psychology; Fernand Dumont, Lagueux and Kaufmann in economics; Georges Legault and Brodeur respectively in law and criminology; and Fernand Dumont, Panaccio, Kaufmann, Meunier, Claude Savary and Josiane Ayoub in ideological theory. F. DUCHESNEAU AND R. NADEAU

Metaphysics and Philosophy of Religion

Metaphysics includes the study of claims about what is ultimately real and important. Philosophy of religion is concerned with religious views of reality and with the evaluation and understanding of religious practice. Philosophers of religion and metaphysicians have faced 2 difficult challenges since 1950: acceptance of the sciences, especially physics, as the basic model of knowledge, and the preoccupation of philosophers with the theory of meaning. The study of reality is not the domain of any one science, and it has frequently been suggested that propositions about "reality" are too vague to be capable of scientific verification and are therefore possibly meaningless. Metaphysicians have been accused of twisting language into unintelligible shapes, and the major religions have been accused of endorsing those world views science cannot substantiate and which at times clash with "scientific" world views. Despite vigorous attacks on religious belief (eg, by Kai Nielsen in *Scepticism,* 1973), the tendency in Canada has been to seek ways in which the disputes can be resolved and through which such religious belief can be saved and made intelligible. The results may be divided into 7 groups.

First, F.W. Waters in *The Way In and the Way Out* (1967) and Alastair McKinnon in *Falsification and Belief* (1970) suggest similarities between science and religion: both involve fallible and limited attempts to apply fundamental principles. But these principles are not themselves uncertain. Thus, McKinnon argues, the scientist, committed to the principle that the world has an order, and the Christian, committed to belief in God, must try to show that experience and life become intelligible through reasonable application of the principle concerned. Donald Wiebe's *Religion and Truth* (1981) is a plea for taking religious knowledge seriously – indeed for creating an appropriate science out of that knowledge. He concedes that religious truth is very complex, but he believes that truth and falsity should be the most central concern of scholars in the field. He strongly deplores the tendency of scholars in religion to describe beliefs without evaluating them.

Secondly, there have been attempts to revivify parts of the idealist philosophy dominant in English Canada until WWII. "Idealism" has had many meanings, but the Canadian idealists' central tenet was that all reality formed a unified, rational whole. They suggested that science and religion were not antithetical but were part of a larger rational system and that there was a natural order to human affairs. These concerns were complicated by developments in science (such as quantum physics) which suggested chance elements in reality; by a growing gap between scientists' and religious believers' characterizations of the world; and by theories that suggested that meanings (interpretations) were arbitrary. In response, Lionel Rubinoff, in *Collingwood and the Reform of Metaphysics* (1970), argued in support of British philosopher R.G. Collingwood that our world views, scientific and otherwise, must be seen in the context of the presuppositions with which humans approach the world. Metaphysical systems and religious world views can be seen as intelligible if they are taken to be accounts of the way the human mind is able to see the world at different times. Science also reflects this historical process. In the course of history, these changing views begin to reveal a pattern, which Rubinoff called the "transcendental structure of reality," ie, a structure that appears through but ultimately leads beyond the immediacies of human experience. Part of the science-religion-metaphysics controversy has had to do with theories of logic, meaning and truth that were tailored

to scientific knowledge. In *The Rational and the Real* (1962), *The Concept of Truth* (1969) and *Logic and Reality* (1972), Leslie Armour argued that these notions of logic, truth and meaning are specialized subforms of more embracing notions. The more embracing notions make possible many traditional metaphysical and religious ideas.

A third group, including Thomas Goudge and Charles de Koninck, has sought to build within the structure of science. Goudge's *The Ascent of Life* (Governor General's Award, 1961) makes few explicit claims about metaphysics or religion, but meticulously examines parts of biological theory and exposes a number of points at which conceptual possibilities remain open. De Koninck, in *The Hollow Universe* (1960), insists that the scientific world view is an abstract and hollow shell that must be filled by concrete experience in order to make sense. A.H. Johnson, in a series of books including *Whitehead's Theory of Reality* (rev ed 1962), reflects British philosopher Alfred North Whitehead's attempt to move from the scientific world picture to a more embracing structure by showing where the scientific structure needed metaphysical support. Johnson's theories, expounded chiefly in *Experiential Realism* (1973), continue his attempt to achieve an ultimate theory of reality through an adequate understanding of experience.

A fourth group, drawing inspiration from St Thomas Aquinas, searches for demarcation lines between science and theology and for a way to understand religion as rational. Louis-Marie Régis describes in *Epistemology* (1959) his view of the forms and limitations of science. Joseph Owens, in *An Interpretation of Existence* (1968), defends Aquinas's notion that being is capable of a measure of general characterization and that it is both active and intelligible. In *L'Éducation à la liberté* (1978; tr *Education for Freedom*, 1982) Jean-Louis Allard offers an account, which follows the philosophy of Jacques Maritain, of the way fundamental principles become intelligible through the ordering of one's life. Reactions against details of this philosophy include André Dagenais's *Vingt-quatre défauts thomistes* (1964) and *Le Dieu nouveau* (1974). Gregory Baum's *Man Becoming* (1970) and *Religion and Alienation* (1975) represent another kind of critique of the Thomist tradition. Baum has been influenced by liberation theology and by Karl Rahner and others who want to make the Catholic tradition more responsive to social needs and to provide a basis for constructive criticism of church government. Baum has also become strongly interested in the relation between theology and social economics and his ideas have had an impact on the economic positions taken in Canada by the Catholic bishops. A distinct development of the Thomistic tradition are the works of Bernard Lonergan and his successors. This work includes not only discussions of metaphysics, religion and the theory of knowledge, but the application of the results in diverse fields of endeavour.

A fifth group is that of the many English-speaking philosophers who have worked within "analytic" philosophy, a tradition much influenced by Austrian Ludwig Wittgenstein and the British Bertrand Russell, G.E. Moore, Gilbert Ryle and J.L. Austin. Kai Nielsen uses this philosophy to question the foundations of religion and metaphysics. Alistair M. Macleod developed in *Paul Tillich* (1973) a strong negative critique of attempts to answer what Tillich called *the* question of being. Macleod urges that Tillich is confused in thinking there is one central "mystery of being," but stops short of arguing that no metaphysical or religious world views can ever be justified.

Despite the frequent hostility of the analytic tradition to metaphysics and religion, many Ca-

nadian analytic philosophers have sought to find room for religious expression. In his *Survival and Disembodied Existence* (1970), Terence Penelhum questions the meaningfulness of some religious beliefs, but his *Rationality and Religion* (1971) leaves possibilities for religious discourse. Donald Evans, after close association with the new analytic philosophy during which he wrote *The Logic of Self-Involvement* (1963), developed his defence of religious experience in *Struggle and Fulfillment* (1979) and *Faith, Authenticity and Morality* (1979). Pierre Lucier, in *Empirisme logique et langage religieux* (1976), assesses the strengths and impact of the analytic movement.

Frequently, analytic philosophers have used language analysis to sustain essentially "humanistic" positions against claims of "determinists" in psychology and history who have believed that free human action is unintelligible or impossible. A branch of philosophy known as "action theory" is concerned with analysis of the language with which human actions are described. Donald Brown, in *Action* (1968), carefully analysed such language and suggested that we cannot easily convert talk about human action into talk about events figuring naturally in the sciences. Similarly, William Dray argues in *Laws and Explanation in History* (1957) that explanations of human history cannot be reduced to the form of scientific laws.

Sixth, German phenomenologists and French existentialists had a substantial influence in Canada. Emil Fackenheim shows these influences in *Metaphysics and Historicity* (1961) along with those of Hegel and of 19th-century German philosophy in general. The most extensive work in this genre in French Canada is *Existant et acte d'être* (1977-80) by Benoit Pruche, who also draws heavily on Aquinas and Aristotle.

Concern with the idea of the self and the attempt to build a philosophical anthropology (ie, a theory of the nature of man) are strong in works such as those of Jacques Croteau, whose *L'Homme: sujet ou objet* (1981) develops ideas from European phenomenology against a background influenced by Aquinas and Maritain. In *La Genèse du concept du soi* (1980) René l'Ecuyer ties experimental psychology to ideas from a diverse group of philosophers, raising many issues that concerned the existentialists. In *The Art of Art Works* (1982) Cyril Welch applies other aspects of that tradition to our understanding of art and of the ways in which that understanding transforms reality. Existentialism and phenomenology have been criticized as well, eg, by F. Temple Kingston in *French Existentialism* (1961).

Finally, there has been a return to the rationalist metaphysics best represented by 17th- and 18th-century philosophers such as Leibniz and Spinoza. This movement, generally using modern logical and analytic techniques, has been led by John Leslie and Helier J. Robinson. The rationalists had urged that one must start with questions about what is logically possible rather than what seems to exist. They were guided by the principles that everything has an explanation and that whatever does not exist fails to do so because it is prevented from existing by something else. Leslie's *Value and Existence* (1979) argues for the reintroduction of principles of value into these discussions. In *Renascent Rationalism* (1975), which is also an attempt to make experience intelligible, Robinson admits that we cannot tell whether or not a god outside the world exists, but he believes that we can tell, for instance, that a god exists in some sense within the world. In somewhat the same vein, Hugo Meynell's *The Intelligible Universe, a Cosmological Argument* (1982) seeks to revive an argument form largely abandoned since Kant. Meynell makes use of ideas drawn from the Jesuit philosopher Bernard

Lonergan and argues that the intelligibility of the world provides the basis for God's existence.

LESLIE ARMOUR AND KEVIN SULLIVAN

Conclusion

Philosophers ask universal questions, but do philosophical answers have national characteristics? The question whether there is, could be, or should be a Canadian (or Québecois or western) philosophy is a vexed one. The following main positions in the debate can be distinguished. (1) The notion of a "Canadian philosophy" (or any other local one) is an absurdity. For philosophy, by definition, transcends the local and particular; it is transhistorical and transcultural. (2) There could be a Canadian philosophy, as there is German or American philosophy, but no such development, more or less unified, more or less distinctive, has taken place in Canada. (3) There could develop a Canadian philosophy, but such a development would be evil, for it would reflect the prejudices, oppressions and divisiveness of nationalism, when the world's survival and individual freedoms depend on the development of a cosmopolitan outlook. (4) A philosophy is a set of ultimate presuppositions (categories, principles and values) for imposing "meaning" (interpretation, explanation and significance) on experience. Philosophy is a key element in, and is as variable as, culture itself. Insofar as there is a Canadian (or Québecois) culture, there is some sort of Canadian (or Québecois) philosophy. This view may be combined either with the view that different presuppositions are incommensurable and cannot themselves be judged as true or false, good or bad, or with the view that presuppositions can be judged not only "internally" as appropriate to, or well integrated in, a culture, but also "externally" as good, correct, true, etc. (5) Philosophies are ideologies that reflect the economic base and class divisions of a society; they are usually a form of "false consciousness" that serves the ruling class as an instrument of oppression. Insofar as Canada (or a region) has a distinctive economy and class structure, it will have a distinctive philosophy. Such a philosophy should be exposed and replaced by a "scientific" (eg, Marxist) analysis. (6) The intellectual historian can discern philosophical interests, themes, trends and schools that arise in the development of a country or region, and can correlate these both with international developments and with the exigencies of the local situation. Partial explanation of philosophical change can be given in terms of these factors "external" to philosophy, but evaluation of the truth and acceptability of philosophical claims depends upon objective, transcultural standards. That is, the history of philosophy in Canada – and it may have had a distinctive development – is one thing, but the evaluation of it as correct or good is quite another.

One should distinguish questions of (a) possibility, (b) fact or actuality, (c) desirability or acceptability. Whether a national or regional philosophy is possible depends on one's definition of "philosophy." The bad faith or inconsistency to be avoided here is to admit the possibility of, for example, American philosophy and to deny the possibility of Canadian (or Québecois) philosophy. Matters of fact depend upon careful historical inquiry which, on this question in Canada, is still in its infancy. Questions of desirability or acceptability depend upon extended and rational philosophical debate. It may well be that it is easier to argue in favour of national or regional particularity in social and political principles or policies – for here circumstances do alter cases – than to arrange for such diversity in logical, epistemic and metaphysical matters. JOHN T. STEVENSON

Reading: L. Armour and E. Trott, *The Faces of Reason* (1981); C. Berger, *Science, God and Nature in Victorian Canada* (1983); D. Braybrook, "The Philosophical Scene in Canada," *Canadian Forum* 53, 636 (Jan 1974); R. Cook, *The Regenerators* (1985); *Dialogue* XXV, 1 (Spring 1986, issue mainly devoted to philosophy in Canada); T.A. Goudge, "Philosophical Literature, 1910-1960" and "Philosophical Literature, 1960-1973," in C. Klinck, ed, *Literary History of Canada*, (vols 2 and 3, respectively, (rev ed 1976); R. Houde, *Histoire et philosophie au Québec* (1979); J.A. Irving and A.H. Johnson, "Philosophical Literature 1910-1964," in C. Klinck, ed, *Literary History of Canada*, vol 1 (1965); M. Lagueux, *Le Marxisme des années soixante* (1982); Y. Lamonde, *Historiographie de la philosophie au Québec 1853-1970* (1972) and *La Philosophie et son enseignement au Québec (1665-1920)* (1980); A.B. McKillop, *A Disciplined Intelligence* (1979).

Phips, Sir William, adventurer, colonial governor (b near Kennebec, Maine 2 Feb 1650/51; d at London, Eng 18 Feb 1694/95). Knighted for recovering a sunken treasure ship off Haiti in 1686-87, Phips captured and plundered PORT-ROYAL 19 May 1690 and later that year brought 32 ships and over 2000 militiamen before QUÉBEC. His summons to surrender elicited Gov FRONTENAC's response that he had no answer "save from the mouths of my cannon." The attack was haphazard and disastrous and Phips made sail for Boston. Despite his defeat, he was named first royal governor of Massachusetts in 1692. He was summoned to England in 1694 to answer charges of maladministration but died before the investigation was completed. JAMES MARSH

Phlox (Polemoniaceae), family of flowering plants ranging from leafless annual herbs to small TREES and vines. Most species occur in N America, particularly in the western desert and in dry, cold regions. About 300 species are known worldwide. The genus *Phlox* is the best-known member of the family; 11 species occur in Canada. Wild blue phlox (*P. divaricata*), found in eastern Canadian open woodlands, blooms in May. In western Canada, *P. hoodii* (moss phlox) and *P. diffusa* (spreading phlox) form mats of colour ranging from white to bright mauve and pink in open prairie grassland and in foothill regions of the Rockies, Apr-June. Tall, vibrantly coloured summer-flowering phlox, derived from eastern N American *P. paniculata*, one of the most popular garden perennials in Canada, is often used for island beds or as border plants. Many flower colours are available and most produce a sweet fragrance during the July-Sept flowering period. Sweet William, a traditional garden plant, developed from *P. maculata* (native from Québec to Virginia) and is a popular cut flower.

ROY L. TAYLOR

Photography The invention of photography was not a sudden discovery but the result of an evolution of knowledge in chemistry and optics. Investigations into the light sensitivity of silver salts carried out in Germany by Johann Heinrich Schultze in 1727, and the Renaissance use of a *camera obscura* as a tool to render perspective accurately, developed the components necessary for photography. The actual creation of a photographic image required the receptive mind of the 19th-century world, radically changed by the innovations of the Industrial Revolution. In 1839, 2 photographic processes were announced. In France, Louis Jacques Mandé Daguerre, assisted by the research of Nicephore Niepce, succeeded in securing a unique image on a silver-plated copper plate; the daguerreotype was referred to as "a mirror with a memory." At the same time in England, William Henry Fox Talbot developed a negative/positive process on paper; the negative was identified as a "calotype," the positive, as a "salted paper print." Both processes had distinct

At Hochelaga, *c*1860-65, albumen. Albumen prints had the potential of unlimited copies, yet retained admirable detail (*courtesy National Archives of Canada/PA-126623/ photo by Alex Henderson*).

characteristics: the daguerreotype delineated each subject in minute detail; there was optical democracy. But the salted paper print emphasized broad masses and soft focus. Contact printing through a paper negative obscured detail and definition.

Through the 19th-century press network and individual couriers, the daguerreotype and the calotype became known around the world, although initially the daguerreotype enjoyed greater success since it was not restricted by patent except in England. News of the remarkable discoveries reached the Canadian public in the spring of 1839. The *Quebec Gazette*, the Toronto *Patriot* and the *Halifax Colonial Pearl* reported on the daguerreotype and on Talbot's "new art of sun painting." Itinerant daguerreotypists set up studios in suitable hotel rooms or stores with skylights and produced likenesses of their clients, or "patients" as they were sometimes called. The task was arduous: long exposure times, bad weather, erratic temperatures and difficult working conditions contributed to the low success rate of the early photographers. Few identified images have survived. Records in Canadian journals identify 2 Americans, Halsey and Sadd, who set up studios in Montréal and Québec late in 1840 and a Mrs Fletcher in Montréal in 1841, probably the first woman photographer in Canada. Thomas Coffin Doane was one of the few successful daguerreotypists in Montréal. He visited Newfoundland in 1843 with his partner William Valentine and secured some portraits, but he is best known for his daguerreotypes of Lord ELGIN

Clergyman, early photograph by Seth Park (*courtesy National Archives of Canada/C-55366*).

The colourful Breakneck Steps, on Little Champlain St, were one of Québec City's most popular photographic scenes. Stereo albumen print, c1870, by Ellisson & Co (*courtesy National Gallery of Canada*).

and family and of Louis-Joseph PAPINEAU. He also received an honourable mention award at the Paris Exhibition of 1855, along with Eli J. Palmer. In Toronto, where Palmer worked, several studios flourished for short periods of time, but their output is now lost. However, from 1847 until about 1870 Palmer produced daguerreotypes and the popular *cartes de visite*, small photographic images glued to stiff cardboard and used as calling cards or bound in photo albums for future generations.

The original *carte de visite* was popularized in France by André Adolphe Disdéri, who photographed Napoleon III in 1859 and mass-produced the image on small cards. Prominent leaders and the rising middle class rushed to portrait studios. Duplication was greatly improved by the introduction of the wet collodion process, developed by an Englishman, F. Scott Archer, in 1851. The procedure gave a clear negative on glass and, by contact printing, a finely delineated positive, the albumen print. Like Talbot's process, it had the potential of unlimited copies, yet it retained an admirable clarity of detail. The wet collodion process improved speed and reproduction, but by modern standards it was difficult. The operator had to coat the plate, then expose and develop it before the emulsion had dried and lost sensitivity. Nevertheless, in the 19th century it facilitated photographic activity. In 1851 Lovell's *Canadian Directory* cited only 11 daguerreotypists; by 1865 the *Canada Classified Directory* listed more than 360 photographers.

The most famous was William NOTMAN, who exercised his influence in Halifax, Saint John, Montréal, Ottawa, Toronto and in the US. In 1858 he documented the construction of the Victoria Bridge in Montréal, the longest tubular bridge in the world at the time. Conscious of history and the importance of the ceremony, in 1860 he recorded the royal visit of the Prince of Wales to inaugurate the bridge and was appointed photographer to the Queen. With a growing reputation, he was able to attract an extensive clientele and his business expanded. By the 1870s Notman, his sons, and a large staff turned out 14 000 negatives each year. Notman also excelled in composite photographs, where each image was made from several individual pictures, cut out, pasted onto a painting and rephotographed. An ambitious montage of the Skating Carnival in 1869 was made from about 300 single photos.

Pioneering the use of the magnesium flare in Canada, he also recreated many elaborate indigenous scenes in his Montréal studios. At the same time in Québec City, the studio of Ellison and Co produced elegant portraits notable for their simplicity, directness and power. They dispensed with extravagent studio backdrops but used conventional props such as columns and drapery to distinguish the setting. Their oeuvre included portraits, *cartes de visite* and cabinet cards of Québec dignitaries. Cabinet cards were a larger version of the *cartes de visite* and were collected with enthusiasm from 1868 until WWI. Albums of views and stereographs were also popular in the 19th century. Stereos were the 19th century equivalent of the television. "No home without a stereoscope" was the claim of the London Stereoscopic Co, and images from around the world graced the drawing rooms of the middle class. The apparatus for the production of a stereographic image was a camera with 2 lenses separated by the same distance as human eyes. It produced 2 nearly identical images which, when looked at through a stereo-viewer, gave the impression of the third dimension.

As in the albums of mounted photographs, landscapes and architectural subjects were frequently portrayed in stereographs. One of the first photographers to publish a series of mounted photos was Samuel McLaughlin who, in 1858-60, produced *The Photographic Portfolio*, views of Québec and the surrounding area. His best-known image is *The Ice Boat*, a scene on the St Lawrence framed by the Québec Citadel. In 1861 he became the official government photographer, commissioned to photograph the construction of the Parliament Buildings. In keeping with the grandeur of the project, McLaughlin used mammoth plates, sometimes as large as 27" x 36". Despite the unwieldy wet collodion process, he succeeded in producing 24 negatives of various sizes in 1861. Another photographer, Alexander HENDERSON, is distinguished for his work published in *Canadian Views and Studies, Photographed from Nature*, a series of albums which appeared in the mid-1860s. His photographs are characterized by a sense of space particular to the Canadian landscape and a sense of time and season.

Initial photographic activity was restricted to the settlements in Upper and Lower Canada. In the 1850s the westward trek began, stimulated by the discovery of gold in BC, by an effort to protect isolated communities from American expansion, and by government interest in trade and commerce. The efforts of 19th-century photographers to record the land and overcome the difficulties of an unfriendly environment were heroic and stubborn. One of the first was Humphrey Lloyd HIME,

who accompanied the government Assiniboine and Saskatchewan Exploring Expedition to survey the West for future settlement and exploration. His photographs of prairie topography, published in *The London Illustrated News*, are stark in their simplicity and economical in their vision. In 1871 Benjamin Baltzly, a Notman employee, accompanied the Geological Survey of Canada party led by Alfred Selwyn to determine a route for the extension of the CPR, thereby encouraging British Columbia to join Confederation.

With the opening of BC, the pioneering spirit of some photographers took hold and was fired by the gold rush of the 1850s and 1860s – prime photographic material. Charles Gentile accumulated historically important photos of the Leech River gold flurry in 1864. The Englishman Frederick DALLY photographed the Cariboo goldfields and Barkerville, a boom town. According to newspaper reports, he did "wonderful face work" – presumably portraits. Another Englishman, George Robinson Fardon, documented Vancouver I; his photographs and his panoramic views of Victoria, composed of several small prints carefully matched to give the impression of a panorama, were exhibited at the International Exhibition in London in 1862. Francis G. Claudet, son of the celebrated French daguerreotypist Antoine Claudet, arrived in 1859 as chief assayer for BC. He produced at least 2 albums of photographic views, though authorship of some images is disputed. Photographers often bought or accumulated photos and published them under their own name, thereby making the task of identification difficult. Some of the plates taken by Dally were eventually acquired by Richard and Hannah MAYNARD, 2 of the most successful photographers in BC. In 1862 Hannah Maynard established a portrait studio in Victoria; Richard Maynard learned the trade from her and was responsible for a number of views of the province in the 1870s and 1880s.

By the late 1870s the mass-produced gelatine dry plate was in common use and photographers no longer suffered the trials of preparing their own plates on the spot. Dry plates became standard material on government survey expeditions, including a British expedition to reach the North Pole. Through blinding snowstorms this team managed to travel to the farthest point ever reached by an expedition, and 2 members, Thomas Mitchell and George White, secured more than 100 plates, at least one at -45°C.

With technical improvements, instantaneous photography became possible. Previous attempts to photograph events in motion were extremely difficult, given the bulky equipment, imperfect lenses and slow exposure speeds. But 2 extant views are remarkable for their instantaneity: a photograph taken by James Inglis at Thomas d'Arcy MCGEE's funeral procession in Montréal in 1868, and an anonymous photograph taken at the Feu de joie in front of the Parliament buildings the same year. In 1885 Capt James Peters photographed the North-West Rebellion; using a camera equipped with a magazine to facilitate changing plates after each exposure, Peters managed to get some pictures during the battle.

In 1888 George Eastman invented the hand camera and Kodak became an immediate success. The camera was loaded with film capable of 100 exposures. Once the film had been exposed, the camera with the film still inside was returned to Kodak. The film was removed, processed, positive prints made, a new roll of film put into the camera, and the whole thing returned to the sender. "You press the button, we do the rest" was a believable slogan. As the number of amateur photographers increased rapidly, photo clubs were formed which in turn produced some distinguished photographers. The Toronto Amateur Photographic Assn was organized in 1888 and, as the Toronto Camera Club, began to hold exhibitions by 1891. In 1905 Sidney Carter, an associate member of Photo Secession, founded the Toronto Studio Club, designed after England's Linked Ring, which for one year espoused the virtues of the overtly manipulated image.

Photography had been criticized as a mechanical medium which ignored the intervention of the photographer. In an effort to give visual evidence of the nonmechanical hand of man, many advocates of the manipulated image appeared. Simultaneously, there were the champions of the straight, unretouched image as a true manifestation of the medium. The dichotomy between pictorialism or manipulated image and purism or straight photography echoed the difference between the calotype and daguerreotype.

Diverse processes were used by pictorialist photographers to achieve their objectives: gum bichromate, cyanotype and bromoil transfer all allowed the gesture of the brush stroke to show as the emulsion was applied to a paper support. In a less obvious manner, without resorting to alternative processes, photographers also used soft focus lenses or threw the image out of focus to obtain tone and an ethereal atmosphere rather than finely delineated details. In the first decades of the 20th century, Harold Mortimer-Lamb, a British engineer who had a close association with Carter and the Toronto Camera Club, and John VANDERPANT, a Dutchman who settled in Vancouver, produced romantic soft-focus portraits and concentrated on the effects of light and shadow, mass and tone. By the 1930s, Vanderpant's style was changing and he began to investigate the potential of straight photography. He exhibited widely in international salons and achieved recognition from photographers in the US. In 1926 Vanderpant and Mortimer-Lamb opened a gallery together, featuring a studio, art and antique galleries. The association was short-lived, but the gallery continued and occasionally served as a showcase for members of the Group of Seven.

In 1934 the National Gallery of Canada inaugurated the first annual Canadian International Salon of Photographic Art, this event marked the beginning of its involvement with the medium. Until the outset of WWII the gallery organized travelling exhibits. The Canadian Government Motion Picture Bureau had a still-photo division shortly after WWI, a tradition continued by its successor, the NATIONAL FILM BOARD, founded in 1939. Initially, this sector was set up to provide visual material for various government departments, and it later expanded into a photo bank for newspapers and journals across the country. An active editorial group supplied weekly photo stories to Canadian and foreign publications.

With the government's recognition of the value of documentary photography, photojournalism flourished in Canada. William James and Arthur Goss were both active before 1914 and produced significant collections. One of the first sustained efforts to document military events occurred during WWI. The Canadian War Records Office was established in 1916 by Max AITKEN (Lord Beaverbrook). One of its tasks was to secure photographs from the front in order to obtain a permanent and vivid impression of what was happening. The Englishman William Ivor Castle was appointed official Canadian photographer and went to France in 1916; he made a 2-year tour of Canada and the US with some of the first photographs to be widely circulated. Photos of men scrambling over the top of the trenches were acclaimed as accurate portrayals of men at war. In fact, it appears they were taken during combat training or staged far from the front line and later

An early daguerreotype (c 1850). This early technique was cumbersome but it created images of great depth and beauty (*courtesy National Archives of Canada/C-88068*).

cropped to eliminate any unwarlike paraphernalia. Other more instantaneous photos were taken at major battles involving Canadians from 1917 until the end of the war by William Rider-Rider, another Englishman appointed by the War Records Office.

The rise of the picture magazine also provided an outlet for photojournalists. The *Montreal Standard* and the Winnipeg *New World* were the first to commission the photo essay in the 1940s. A *Montreal Standard* photographer, Henri Paul, a Frenchman living in Montréal, was well known for his coverage of the THÉÂTRE DU NOUVEAU MONDE; he was one of the first photographers in Canada to use the 35 mm camera, well suited to the needs of reportage. *Weekend* took over from the *Montréal Standard* in the 1950s and became a national magazine in competition with the Toronto *Star Weekly*. Between them they hired photographers Kryn TACONIS, John Reeves, John deVisser, Lutz Dille, Michel LAMBETH, Walter CURTIN, Chris Lund, John Max and Yousuf KARSH. Karsh, a well-known and popular portrait photographer, established a studio in Ottawa in 1932; using dramatic studio lighting and classical poses, he photographed many contemporary leaders and celebrities.

A dramatic increase in photographic activity occurred in the late 1960s. The National Film Board began a publishing program and established a photo gallery in Ottawa. It collected work from contemporary Canadian photographers, organized travelling exhibitions and prepared support material such as catalogues and slide-tape shows. In 1985 the Canadian Museum of Contemporary Photography was established to carry on the mandate of the Film Board photo collection and exhibition program but its affiliation shifted from the board to the NATIONAL GALLERY of Canada. In 1967 James Borcoman, curator of photography at the National Gallery, began an international photo collection, particularly of historical works. The NATIONAL ARCHIVES OF CANADA houses a collection of Canadian documentary photographs from the mid-19th century to the present. These 3 government institutions attempt to provide an overview of national and international photographic representation, without overlap or competition.

Photography has yet to be accepted by galleries and museums as equal to other art forms. Only

the National Gallery and the Winnipeg Art Gallery employ full-time curators of photography and are accorded funds for the acquisition of photos. Individual exhibitions arranged by guest curators, however, have been well received by the public in many cities. Since 1973 the CANADA COUNCIL has provided program and operating funds to several artist-run spaces specializing in photography; grants are also made available to individual photographers and to galleries for particular exhibitions.

In 1967 a group of photographers began the monthly bilingual magazine *Foto Canada*, which was printed in gravure and reflected a high standard of photography in Canada. Unfortunately, financial support for the magazine waned after a year and it ceased publication. Since the 1970s magazines have exhibited various attitudes towards the medium; *Impressions* and *Impulse* present contemporary, sometimes offbeat photographic work. The Montréal magazine *OVO* promotes photography as a means of communication and social change. *Photo Communiqué*, published since 1979, attempts to provide an information exchange among members of the photographic community and a critical analysis of historical and contemporary work. *Camera Canada*, published by the National Association for Photographic Art, shows conventional, popular images. While monographs and catalogues have been put out by various museums and galleries, photographic books have not benefited as much from the support of a publisher devoted to the medium as in the US. Among the publications, *Canada: A Year of the Land* (1969) and *Between Friends* (1976), both published by the National Film Board, *The Banff Purchase* (1979) and *Contemporary Canadian Photography* (1984) attracted public attention.

Among photographers who rose to prominence in the last 20 years are Nina Raginsky, who gained recognition for her straightforward and subtly hand-tinted portraits of West Coast individuals; Gabor SZILASI, for his portraits and interiors of rural Québec; Tom GIBSON and Charles GAGNON, painters who took up a camera and walked the streets; Lynne Cohen, who photographed interiors which reflect contemporary taste; Freeman PATTERSON, who found romance in the landscape of the East; Robert Minden, who documented Doukhobors and Japanese Canadians in the West; and Orest Semchishen, who recorded the western landscape and vernacular architecture. Others who have made a contribution to photography are Geoffrey James, Robert Bourdeau, David McMillan, Sam TATA, Raymonde April, Clara Gutsche, Michel Campeau, Susan McEachern, David Miller, Evergone, Sorel Cohen, Douglas Curran, David Hlynsky, Thaddeus Holownia, Michael Mitchell, Henri Robideau, Sandra Senchuk and Richard Baillargeon.

The West and the East in Canada have their differences, which relate to the light, the lay of the land and the different tempos in the various cities. Vancouver photographers rely on diffused light from Pacific waters; the inhabitants of the Rockies focus on the anomalies between breathtaking landscape and contemporary living. The prairie terrain serves as a minimal backdrop for western towns and specific industrial forms. Toronto takes its impetus from the US and splays out in all directions. Photographers from Québec respect the political dimension and record urban and rural phenomena with the eye of a sociologist. The Maritimes provide source material for introspection through isolation. Photography in Canada is now open ended, waiting for experimentation and open minds. KATHERINE TWEEDIE

Reading: A. Birrel, *Benjamin Baltzly: 1871* (1978); *Cana-*

dian Perspectives: A National Conference of Canadian Photography (1979); R. Greenhill and A. Birrell, Canadian Photography 1839-1920 (1979); R. Huyda, Camera in the Interior: 1858, H.L. Hime, Photographer (1975); M. Langford, M. Hanna and P. Bessureault, Contemporary Canadian Photography: From the Collection of the National Film Board (1984).

Physical Education, a branch of the educational curricula of every province in Canada, which originated with a variety of forms of activity and concepts such as drill, calisthenics, gymnastics, physical training and physical culture. The modern term, "physical education," denotes a subject area of deliberate or systematic physical training undertaken in the classroom or during regular school hours, rather than an all-encompassing concept which might include all forms of games and interscholastic or extracurricular sport undertaken within educational institutions.

Because EDUCATION is under provincial jurisdiction, the history of physical education varies from province to province. Those involved in education in central Canada were responsible for early leadership and initiative in the area, particularly the first chief superintendent (minister) of education in Ontario, Egerton RYERSON. After frequent trips to Europe in the 1840s to study various educational systems, Ryerson attempted to infuse new, practical subjects such as music, art and physical education into the existing curricula of schools in Canada West.

Education in the mid-19th century was grounded in the classics (Latin, Greek) and directed mainly at the sons of well-to-do families who attended PRIVATE SCHOOLS and secondary or "grammar" institutions. Ryerson sought to rebuild the educational pyramid from its base, the elementary or "common" schools.

In Europe physical training was entrenched in institutional systems of exercise, such as the Ling system in Sweden, the Danish system and the German gymnastics or "Turnverein" societies, but Canada had no such tradition. When in 1852 Ryerson published a series of articles on "Physical Training in Schools" in his administrative mouthpiece, The Journal of Education for Upper Canada, (complete with woodcut diagrams), he was effectively advocating the inclusion of physical training into the schools. Prior to 1880, only 17% of Ontario's teachers received some form of pedagogical preparation and only the Toronto Normal School, the province's main teacher-training centre, could boast any facility for teaching physical training of any kind. However, the Normal School's first instructor of physical training, Col Henry Goodwin, a retired drill instructor, probably taught only army drill and calisthenic exercises to the few prospective teachers who did enrol. The only physical training manual available for teachers from the education office was a military drill manual.

Ryerson's advocacy of some form of physical training and the militaristic threats of the American Civil War during the 1860s resulted in the entrenchment of drill and rigid calisthenics as forms of physical education in schools. During the last third of the 19th century, the French Catholic and English Protestant schools in Québec followed the military drill precedent with some apparatus gymnastics introduced to Montréal schools through Mr Frederick Barnjum, the proprietor of a Montréal gymnasium and McGill's first physical education instructor. The idea of training and disciplining the body through military drill was also adopted in the Maritimes, where military instructors were hired to teach physical education classes. In the western provinces, which were being settled in the late 19th century, drill and calisthenics were the only forms of physical training employed by interested

BALANCING BAR.   INCLINED BOARD.

TRIANGLE.   BACKBOARD.

The introduction of physical exercise into public schools in the 19th century was intended to train the physical as well as the moral faculties of children. Different activities were prescribed for boys and girls, who were perceived to have different abilities. From a Toronto Dept of Public Instruction book, 1857 (courtesy Ontario Institute for Studies in Education, Library).

teachers or school boards; nowhere in Canada were play, games or sports accepted as legitimate aspects of the curriculum.

By the turn of the century, with the movement in many provinces toward compulsory public education and mandatory systems of teacher training, curricula (at least in theory) became more standardized. Of great importance in this regard were the development and widespread availability of teaching manuals which provided, in effect, written guidelines for lesson plans in many subject areas. In physical education, teaching manuals contained sections on physical education instructional material. In addition, early textbooks, eg, Blackie's Sound Bodies for Boys and Girls in New Brunswick and Houghton's Physical Culture in Ontario, both published in the late 1880s, offered lesson plans for teachers in drill, calisthenics and gymnastics. Ministerial reports on numbers of students in each subject area reflected dramatic increases in the number of students taking physical training, concomitant with the availability of these manuals and textbooks.

The first national program of physical education, the Strathcona Trust, was implemented in 1909 in elementary and secondary schools through a joint venture among provincial departments of education and the federal departments of militia. Sir Frederick W. BORDEN, the minister of militia, persuaded Canadian railway magnate and philanthropist Sir Donald SMITH (Lord Strathcona) to donate $500 000 to be used for the initiation and sponsoring of national programs of physical training and military drill in Canadian schools. The principal sum was invested, and the accrued interest financed the program. The Strathcona Trust sponsored 3 syllabuses or manuals that were widely used in Canadian schools; it systematized physical education as a regular subject of instruction and it encouraged teacher training in physical education. Departments of education, however, relied totally upon the trust and offered very little substantive or financial incentive to promote physical education further. Because the system was militarily based, it did not evolve in concert with American and European

trends in physical education, which were directed at the inclusion of play, games and sport to complement the systematic training of the body.

Female educators, led by McGill University's physical director Ethel Mary Cartwright, were vociferous in their opposition to the militaristic nature of the Strathcona Trust and its advocated "physical jerks," which ran contrary to the child's natural inclination toward play. Women teachers of physical education were first taught at the Margaret Eaton School of Physical Culture (originally the Margaret Eaton School of Literature and Expression) in Toronto and at the McGill School of Physical Education; they received diplomas by taking courses in anatomy, physiology, hygiene, first aid and sports instruction.

Although the last Strathcona Trust syllabus, published in 1933, included a full section on play and games, the actual teaching of classes remained rigid, formal and discipline-oriented. Dr Arthur Stanley Lamb, the director of physical education at McGill University and the proclaimed "father" of physical education in Canada, fought the Strathcona Trust system at every opportunity. Lamb sought to instil a new form of physical education by creating a national physical education professional association in 1933: the Canadian Physical Education Association, renamed, in 1947, the Canadian Association for Health, Physical Education and Recreation. Combined with the first university degree programs in physical education in Canada – U of T (1940), McGill (1945), UBC and Queen's (1946), and Western Ontario (1947) – the Canadian Association worked to inculcate sports and games in the curriculum, to teach students through physical education instead of disciplining them by it, and to make physical education a recognized, significant part of the curriculum. (In the 1920s and 1930s some universities required all students to take a minimum number of hours of physical training classes or to participate in the intramurals or intercollegiate athletics.) In the latter regard, the National Physical Fitness Act, passed by the federal government in 1943, was an important catalyst in promoting teacher training in physical education at universities across Canada. Under the Act $250 000 was offered to each province on a grant-matching basis, to encourage the development of physical education.

Modern concepts of physical education have achieved considerable recognition in a short period. Supported by a sport-conscious public, by media attention to physical fitness and by programs such as PARTICIPaction, physical education is firmly established in all levels of education from primary grades to university degree programs. See also SPORTS HISTORY.   DON MORROW

Reading: F. Cosentino, A History of Physical Education in Canada (1971); M.L. Van Vliet, ed, Physical Education In Canada (1965).

Physical Geography is that branch of GEOGRAPHY concerned with describing and analysing the distribution of physical elements of the environment; interpreting environmental systems located at or near a boundary between atmosphere, lithosphere (rigid part of the Earth's crust), biosphere or hydrosphere (the Earth's water); and determining the resilience of such systems to human activities at or near the Earth's surface. In Britain and France, GEOMORPHOLOGY is a subfield of physical geography. In N America, it is frequently a branch of GEOLOGY. Both traditions are found in Canadian universities.

The roots of physical geography in Canada lie in scientific exploration. In the 17th and early 18th centuries, explorers provided descriptions of local and regional physical geographies, but the first substantial contribution was that of David THOMPSON. He carefully surveyed the terrain, made regular meteorological and astronomical observations and discussed the hydrology and ecology, in addition to assessing the resource potential and cultural and settlement characteristics of the Canadian West. Thompson's map of western Canada (1814) was a milestone in the development of physical geography in Canada (*see* CARTOGRAPHY). The FRANKLIN expeditions of 1819-22 and 1825-27 included John RICHARDSON, whose geological and physiographic interpretation of the Mackenzie R valley and the Arctic coast was the first in a long tradition of northern physiographic studies.

Establishment of the GEOLOGICAL SURVEY OF CANADA (GSC) in 1842 marked a further stage. The PALLISER EXPEDITION (1857-60), sponsored by the Royal Geographical Society, and the Hind-Dawson expeditions (1857-58), supported by the Government of Canada, generated information on climatic, vegetation, geological and landform contrasts in the Canadian West. Henry Y. HIND documented the overwhelming influence of GLACIATION on Canada. In this period Somerville's *Physical Geography*, the first book to be so titled, appeared in England (1848) and Herschel made the first reference to physical geography in the *Encyclopaedia Britannica* (1853). Much of the information generated by scientific exploration in Canada was incorporated into European physical geography. During the 1860s the Meteorological Service of Canada was organized; in 1870 the responsibilities of the GSC were extended to the western interior. Sensitive descriptions of the physical environment of Canada ensued and meteorological networks were extended through western and northern Canada. By 1894 John MACOUN had discussed the FORESTS of Canada and their distribution and, in 1914, some of the first integrated SOIL survey work in Canada was organized by the Ontario Agricultural College at Guelph. Regular reports on FLOODS were published by the Department of the Interior, Dominion Water Power Branch, from the 1890s.

In 1915 the first Canadian university-level course in physical geography was established in the department of geology and mineralogy at UBC. A course in meteorology and climatology was added in 1920. In 1921, E. Miller, the first geography-trained geography instructor in Canada, was appointed to the Faculty of Social Science at U de Montréal to teach physical and human geography. In 1922, the name of the department was changed to geology and geography. Later in the 1920s and the 1930s, extended visits by J. Brunhes and R. Blanchard from France made Montréal the Canadian centre of academic geography. In 1935 Griffith TAYLOR became founding head of the first full department of geography in Canada, at U of T.

By 1950 general courses in physical geography were offered at UBC, Laval, McGill, McMaster, U de Montréal, U of T and U of Western Ontario, but a change in the degree of emphasis on physical geography within geography departments had taken place. This change derived primarily from the increasing dominance in Canadian geography departments of US-trained academic geographers, who came from a SOCIAL SCIENCE tradition. By 1985 there were 33 university geography departments in Canada, of which 18 had more than 15 faculty members.

Applications The federal government departments in which most physical geographers have found employment provide an indication of the range of applications of physical geography: Atmospheric Environment Service; Division of Building Research, National Research Council; GSC, Energy, Mines and Resources; Indian Affairs and Northern Development; Inland Waters Directorate and Lands Directorate, Environment Canada. Educational, private consulting and provincial governmental agencies are also major employers of physical geographers. Physical geographic expertise may be applied to problems associated with PERMAFROST, snow, GLACIERS, mountain environments, urban climates, SOLAR ENERGY, CLIMATE CHANGE, LANDSLIDE and flood hazards, terrain analysis and environmental planning. The range of technologies employed to acquire and manipulate data include REMOTE SENSING, infrared and satellite photography, computers (analysis), etc.

Institutions and Journals The International Geographical Union (IGU) is one of 18 member unions of an International Council of Scientific Unions (ICSU). Canada is one of 90 member nations of the IGU. During the 1984-88 term, the union has 6 commissions, 8 working groups and 3 study groups concerning physical geography. Within Canada, the Canadian Assn of Geographers (CAG), the Québec Assn of Geographers, the Royal Canadian Geographical Soc, the Québec Geographical Soc and the Canadian Committee for Geography of the IGU form the national foci for most geographers. Physical geographers are also involved in the Canadian Geoscience Council (as representatives of CAG), the Canadian Meteorologic and Oceanographic Soc, the Canadian Quaternary Assn, the Québec Quaternary Assn and the Geological Assn of Canada, among others.

The scientific journals in which most Canadian physical geography research is published include *The Canadian Geographer, Canadian Geographic, Canadian Journal of Earth Science, Géographie physique et quaternaire, Atmosphere-Ocean, Cahiers de géographie de Québec, Revue de géographie de Montréal, Albertan Geographer* and *Ontario Geography.* The *Operational Geographer*, sponsored by the Canadian Assn of Geographers, attracts contributions on applied aspects of the work of physical geographers. OLAV SLAYMAKER

Physics is the study of matter and radiation, the space-time continuum that contains them, and the forces to which they are subject. Physics may be experimental, observing the behaviour of matter and radiation under various conditions, using increasingly sophisticated instruments; or it may be theoretical, using mathematical tools to construct models, to formulate laws governing observed behaviour and to indicate (on the basis of these models and laws) promising avenues for further experimentation. The terms macroscopic and microscopic (or, more accurately, submicroscopic), and "classical" and "modern," refer to aspects of physics characterized by different scales in the phenomena studied. Macroscopic or classical physics deals with matter in bulk, as solids, liquids or gases. The closely interrelated fields of mechanics (based on Newton's laws of motion), heat (ie, thermometry and calorimetry), thermodynamics, classical electricity and magnetism (based on discoveries by Coulomb, Ampere, Faraday and Maxwell), and some aspects of statistical physics, lie in the domain of classical physics. Submicroscopic or modern physics studies the detailed structure of matter: atoms, molecules, electrons, nuclei, nucleons and various so-called "elementary particles," many of which are unstable and very short-lived.

The transition from classical to modern physics involved recognition of the existence in nature of a number of fundamental constants, which have since been measured with ever greater precision. Thus the speed of light in a vacuum is now known to 0.004 parts per million (c = 299 792 458 m/s). Other fundamental constants, such as e (the charge of an electron), m (its mass), M (the proton mass) and h (Planck's constant), have all been measured to a precision of a few parts per million. In classical physics, radiation (eg, visible light, radio waves) is treated as continuous waves characterized by a wavelength and a frequency. Modern physics introduced the concept of discrete bundles of energy, called quanta, associated with the waves and, shortly thereafter, discovered that under certain conditions the subatomic units of matter exhibit a wavelike behaviour. To deal with this behaviour a new mode of mathematical description, known now as quantum mechanics, has been developed.

Finally, the pair of terms basic and applied represents an arbitrary division of physics into 2 broad areas, between which the boundary shifts continually. Michael Faraday's basic studies of the relation between electricity and magnetism have led to the applied field of ELECTRICAL ENGINEERING. The basic studies in nuclear physics by Ernest RUTHERFORD at McGill at the turn of the century eventually resulted in CANDU nuclear power reactors. Basic studies in SPECTROSCOPY, such as those of Canada's Nobel laureate Gerhard HERZBERG, underlie lasers, atomic clocks, and the NATIONAL RESEARCH COUNCIL OF CANADA's daily TIME signal on CBC Radio. GEORGE M. VOLKOFF

History in Canada

The history of physics in Canada involves the development of undergraduate and graduate studies and research in universities, research in government institutions and in private industry.

Universities The first professors of natural philosophy (physics combined with MATHEMATICS) were appointed at Dalhousie University in 1838 and at King's College (later University of Toronto) in 1843. Professorships were established at Dalhousie (1879), Toronto (1887) and McGill (1890). The professors were occupied primarily by teaching, doing little original research; however, the European discoveries of the 1890s (X rays, radioactivity, electrons, etc) inspired Canadian professors to become active in the development of their subject. Especially prominent were Ernest Rutherford (McGill) and J.C. MCLENNAN (U of T). Establishment of graduate programs with research followed. Until after WWI, U of T and McGill were the only Canadian universities granting PhDs in physics. However, especially after WWII, many universities set up comprehensive graduate study and research programs. Between 1974 and 1985, 1075 PhDs in physics were awarded by 28 universities (about 31% at U of T).

The early slow growth of physics research was largely the result of financial difficulties. Establishment in 1916 of the National Research Council of Canada promoted the development of SCIENCE through scholarships for graduate students and apparatus grants to professors. Financial assistance from federal and provincial government sources increased, especially after WWII. In 1980 the NATURAL SCIENCES AND ENGINEERING RESEARCH COUNCIL (est 1978) took the place of NRC as the main federal granting agency.

Dalhousie can probably lay claim to the first meaningful research by a physics professor. J.G. MACGREGOR was appointed in 1879 and, during the next 20 years, published some 50 papers and memoirs. H.L. Bronson, department head from 1910 to 1956, inspired many students, including G.H. Henderson (radioactivity, pleochroic halos) and W.J. Archibald (theoretical physics), to take up careers in physics.

McGill got off to an excellent start with H.L. Callendar and E. Rutherford as Macdonald professors of physics. Important discoveries in radioactivity and nuclear physics were made by

Rutherford and numerous assistants, some of whom (eg, H.M. TORY, J.A. Gray, H.L. Bronson, R.W. BOYLE) played vital roles in the development of science in other parts of the country. Nuclear physics at McGill culminated in 1949 in establishment of the Radiation Laboratory with the first cyclotron in Canada. This development was due chiefly to J.S. FOSTER, world-renowned for his work on the Stark effect. The Radiation Laboratory was headed by R.E. Bell for many years and J.M. Robson, a nuclear physicist, was head of the physics dept. In the 1920s, L.V. King did outstanding work in mathematical physics. D.A. KEYS and A.S. Eve initiated early work on geophysics and, somewhat later, J.S. Marshall, on atmospheric physics. McGill was the first Canadian university to develop a theoretical physics group and has produced numerous theorists with international reputations.

J.C. McLennan was director of the physics laboratory at U of T from 1906 to 1932. His first researches were on atmospheric conductivity and cathode rays, but he shifted to atomic spectroscopy with the advent of the Bohr atom in 1912. Optics and spectroscopy have continued to be one of the main interests of the department with M.F. Crawford, H.L. Welsh, Elizabeth J. Allin and, since 1965, B.P. STOICHEFF as leader of a large laser group. In the 1920s McLennan, G.M. SHRUM and others built a helium liquefier, the first in N America, for work on metals and solidified gases at low temperatures; this type of work is still actively pursued. During this early period, E.F. BURTON supervised research in colloid physics and, in the late 1930s, he and his students built the first high-resolution electron microscope in N America. In the late 1920s L. Gilchrist began work in geophysics which later, under J. Tuzo WILSON, became one of the largest research groups in the department. In the 1960s a program in atmospheric physics was inaugurated. Extensive work was begun in high-energy particle physics in the early 1960s with K.G. McNeill and A.E. LITHERLAND, and in medical biophysics with H.E. JOHNS. Until the 1960s, theoretical physics was chiefly the concern of the department of applied mathematics which included J.L. Synge and L. Infeld. However, with the appointment of J. Van Kranendonk in 1958, a strong theoretical section, embracing most of the branches of modern physics, was set up in the physics department.

UBC and McMaster, founded around the turn of the century, demonstrated a remarkable rise in scientific productivity in the 1940s. At UBC the change resulted from the appointment of G.M. Shrum (head 1938-61) and others (including G.M. Volkoff, M. Bloom, R.D. Russell and J.B. Warren) which made possible a broad spectrum of teaching and research in many branches of physics. In the 1970s, UBC became the site of TRI-UMF (Tri-University Meson Facility), one of the most important nuclear facilities in Canada. McMaster became an important centre of Canadian science following appointment of H.G. THODE in 1939. His work on mass spectroscopy and isotope abundances led to intensive work on various aspects of nuclear physics by M.W. Johns, H.E. Duckworth, B.N. Brockhouse and others. In 1957 a research reactor was set up, the first university reactor in the Commonwealth, followed in the 1970s by a particle-accelerator laboratory with extensive facilities. McMaster has achieved prominence in other research fields; eg, spectroscopy (A.B. McLay), solid state physics, biophysics and theoretical physics (M.H. Preston, J. Carbotte). Research is interdisciplinary (eg, in the Institute for Materials Research with J.A. Morrison as director).

R.W. Boyle became professor of physics at University of Alberta in 1912 and began extensive research in ultrasonics. Somewhat later, S. Smith and R.J. Lang began important work in optics and spectroscopy. Research has gradually broadened to include geophysics (J.A. Jacobs) and solid state, nuclear, medical and theoretical physics (A.B. Bhatia, W. ISRAEL).

At U Laval, Italian physicist F. Rasetti began a new era in physics teaching and research (1939-47). Rasetti was followed by his friend E. Persico (1947-50) and J.L. KERWIN, P. Marmet, A. Boivin and others. Main areas of research are optics, atomic and molecular physics, nuclear and theoretical physics. Like Laval, Université de Montréal has greatly increased its contributions to Canadian physics in the last 30 years. The 2 main areas of research are nuclear and plasma physics and associated theory, developed by P. Demers, P. Lorrain and others.

The department at Manitoba was begun by F. Allen who made applications of physics to physiology. After WWII, active work on nuclear physics was begun by R.W. Pringle and expanded rapidly by B.G. Hogg and others. More recently, A.H. Morrish has instituted important work on magnetic materials. The department at Saskatchewan developed during the long headship (1924-56) of E.L. Harrington. Upper atmospheric research, begun by B.W. Currie in 1932, led to the present Institute of Space and Atmospheric Studies with an international reputation. In the period 1935-45, Gerhard Herzberg worked on atomic and molecular structures. In the 1950s the department gained renown with its betatron in photonuclear physics and radiation therapy, including development of a cobalt-60 unit by H.E. Johns and others. Plasma physics is also an important field of study. The younger western universities, Victoria, Simon Fraser and Calgary, have rapidly developing physics departments.

Queen's University, Kingston, and University of Western Ontario have made notable contributions to physics. Research and graduate work at Queen's was initiated by A.L. Clark in the 1920s. Nuclear physics research was begun by J.A. Gray and continued with B.W. Sargent, A.T. Stewart and others. Other fields of research are optics (initiated early by J.K. Robertson), microwave spectroscopy and solid state physics. At UWO rapid development of research began in the 1940s with a RADAR program. The work begun by R.C. Dearle, G.A. Woonton and others was continued by P.A. Forsyth, culminating in the Centre for Radio Science (1967), which studies problems in atmospheric and ionospheric physics. Nuclear research has made considerable progress, especially in the scattering of positrons (J.W. McGowan). The University of Waterloo was established in the late 1950s. The physics department immediately embarked on a program of research in experimental and theoretical solid state physics, with connected areas in laser physics and MICROWAVE spectroscopy. Geophysics and biophysics are also studied. York University has a Centre of Research for Experimental Space Sciences (CRESS) with R.W. Nicholls as director. The universities of Ottawa, Windsor, Guelph and Carleton (with its particle physics program initiated by E.P. Hincks) have promising futures. Concordia, L'École Polytechnique de Montréal and the Universities of Sherbrooke, New Brunswick, St Francis Xavier and Memorial conduct advanced studies in physics.

Physics staff members and graduates played an important role in both world wars. In WWI J.C. McLennan became director of experimental research for the British Admiralty and also organized production of helium from Canadian natural-gas wells; R.W. Boyle conducted ultrasonic experiments in the Admiralty antisubmarine division. In WWII university staffs were in danger of being completely depleted by requests for assistance from NRC and other government and national defence organizations. In addition, several universities gave concentrated courses in physics and electronics to enlisted personnel destined to operate radar and signal devices in army, navy and air force.

Federal Research The NRC has played a major role in physics research. In 1928, NRC established laboratories in Ottawa including a Division of Physics with R.W. Boyle as director. The division expanded very rapidly after the outbreak of WWII; areas of study important to the war effort included nuclear physics, submarine detection and minesweeping devices, aerial photography and range finders. To implement results in optics and radar, Research Enterprises Ltd was set up as a CROWN CORPORATION. A large part of the physics staff dispersed at the end of the war; however, things began to improve with the appointment in 1948 of Herzberg and introduction in 1949 of a program of postdoctoral assistants with one- or 2-year terms. Applied physics became a separate division (1955), under L.E. Howlett. The spectroscopy section of the pure physics division rapidly attained world renown with the work of Herzberg, A.E. Douglas, D.A. Ramsay, T. Oka and others. In the 1970s the spectroscopy section was incorporated with ASTRONOMY and astrophysics in the Herzberg Institute of Astrophysics. The solid state section under D.K.C. MacDonald (1951-63) also attained renown. After establishment of the Herzberg Institute, the divisions of physics and applied physics were reunited. Sections of this division include electric and time standards, high-energy physics and solid state science.

In 1942 a British-Canadian atomic energy project, under NRC administration, was begun in Montréal, leading to the building of NRX, a heavy-water uranium research reactor, which began operation in 1947 at Chalk River, Ont. In 1952 administration of the project was transferred to ATOMIC ENERGY OF CANADA LTD. In 1957 a much larger reactor, NRU, came into operation, and an MP Tandem Van de Graaf accelerator was installed. The aim of this program was to develop research reactors for nuclear experimentation and NUCLEAR-POWER reactors for generation of electricity. W.B. LEWIS was in charge of research. Many Canadian physicists have been involved in the project, including G.C. Laurence, B.W. Sargent, J.M. Robson (neutron decay), R.E. Bell, B.N. Brockhouse (neutron scattering), E.P. Hincks (cosmic rays) and A.E. Litherland.

Provincial Research Physics-related research is carried out by many of the 8 provincial research organizations, the oldest being the ALBERTA RESEARCH COUNCIL (est 1921). The hydroelectric corporations of most provinces have research facilities relating to ELECTRIC-POWER GENERATION and transmission, the largest of these being that of HYDRO-QUÉBEC.

Industrial Research Compared with other industrialized nations, Canada shows a rather low level of INDUSTRIAL RESEARCH AND DEVELOPMENT. Many of the better industrial laboratories doing physics-related research have been set up as Canadian subsidiaries of American companies. For example, the Radio Corporation of America maintained for many years the RCA Canadian Research and Development Laboratories Ltd (under M.B. Bachynski from 1958); in 1976 a large part of its work was taken over by MPB Technologies Inc, with Bachynski as president and director. The Xerox Research Centre of Canada Ltd is a recent example of an American firm locating a part of its research in Canada. Bell-Northern Research Ltd (with D.A. Chisholm as chairman and president since 1977) is doing excellent work.

H.L. WELSH

Subfields

Physics has been divided into various subdisciplines unified by the basic laws of mechanics and quantum mechanics, thermodynamics, etc.

Theoretical Physics Physics proceeds by the constant interplay between experimentation and the conceptual interpretation of the results. Until late in the 19th century the 2 often went hand in hand; early 19th-century physicists often engaged in both activities. With the development of increasingly sophisticated techniques of experimentation on the one hand and of mathematical analysis on the other, and with a rapid acceleration of the acquisition of knowledge in the 20th century, specialization became more general and theoretical physics, which was leading a revolution in the conceptual structure of physics and exploiting its power, emerged as a more or less distinct discipline. The division of physicists into the categories "theoretical" and "experimental" has now become almost universal. A distinction should, however, be made between "theoretical physics" and "mathematical physics," the former being preoccupied with concepts and models of the physical world and the latter with development of mathematical technique and rigorous analysis per se. (Thus, Michael Faraday a century and a half ago, though completely unversed in mathematics, made fundamental changes in physical thought whose importance is reflected in contemporary physics.)

The modern revolution in physics stems from 3 major developments of the late 19th and early 20th centuries. The first of these was the generalization from the science of thermodynamics, by Rudolf Clausius (1822-88) and J. Willard Gibbs (1839-1903) to a general statistical theory which was to become one of the cornerstones of modern physics. The next involved the formulation of the general theory of relativity by Albert Einstein in 1917. This theory laid the basis for the first scientific COSMOLOGY by integrating gravity, the principal motor of the cosmos, into the very structure of space and time. The third was the development of an integrated and coherent quantum theory arising out of the work of Max Planck, Einstein, Louis de Broglie, Niels Bohr, Erwin Schrödinger and Werner Heisenberg among others. An elegant general formulation of this theory, as well as its adaptation to the requirements of relativity, were accomplished by P.A.M. Dirac. Quantum theory permits understanding of the subatomic structure of matter.

The 20th-century developments began in Europe, primarily in Germany and Great Britain. The American continent, with its emphasis on technology and an empirical tradition, contributed only modestly. The rise of European fascism caused a mass emigration from Europe to the US and refugees (eg, Einstein, Fermi, Wigner, Bethe) propelled American physics, in the space of a generation, into a position of world leadership in theoretical physics.

In Canada, where the empirical tradition had been firmly established by Rutherford and others, theoretical physics was almost nonexistent until after WWII and even then most often found its first home in departments of mathematics. Only at U of T had Leopold Infeld, a refugee from Poland, working in a new department founded by the Irish theorist J.L. Synge, laid the groundwork for a new school. The enhanced prestige of theoretical physics resulting from its dramatic contributions to the winning of the war created the conditions for the rapid expansion of theoretical physics in the universities. By 1957 a theoretical physics division was created within the Canadian Assn of Physicists. The balance between theoretical and experimental physics is now much the same as in the US, and internationally recognized work is being done by Canadian theorists in all domains. At the same time, graduates of major Canadian schools, such as McGill, are prominent in leading American universities.   P.R. WALLACE

Upper Atmosphere and Space Physics deals with the physical behaviour of matter in regions beginning about 60 km from Earth's surface and extending to the far reaches of the solar system. In such regions a near vacuum exists. Most of the material present is in the plasma state, ie, the electrons are separated from the parent atoms and thus produce an "electrified fluid," which is easily influenced by electric and magnetic forces. Near Earth, streams of charged particles from the SUN distort Earth's magnetic field to form a vast region called the magnetosphere, within which complex interactions take place between the electrons, ions and electric and magnetic fields. A visible result of these processes is the NORTHERN LIGHTS.

The first explorers in northern Canadian waters recognized that frequent gross compass errors were the result of magnetic disturbances that were somehow linked to the Northern Lights. The first organized attack on the problem was made by expeditions from Europe during the first INTERNATIONAL POLAR YEAR (1882-83). By the time of the Second International Polar Year (1932-33), Canadian groups were able to participate in the study of auroral phenomena. Following WWII there appeared new spectroscopic instruments of sufficient sensitivity to permit analysis of the rapidly changing auroral luminosities, and new radio and radar devices that permitted direct study of auroral ionization. By that time, it had become apparent that radio communications in northern Canada were adversely affected by ionospheric disturbances. Finally, during the International Geophysical Year (1957-58), Canadian scientists came to the forefront of this area of research. In 1957 a research rocket range was established at Churchill, Man, initially under US sponsorship. It has provided the stimulus for the development of a Canadian "family" of research rockets, the Black Brants. Such rockets can place an instrument directly in the region of interest, albeit for only a few minutes. Satellites make it possible to take continuous measurements over weeks or years.

Stimulated by Canadian radio studies of the ionosphere, a joint US-Canada program led to 4 Canadian-made scientific satellites: Alouette 1 in 1962, Alouette 2, 1965; ISIS 1, 1969; ISIS 2, 1971. These satellites provided a wealth of new information about the structure of the ionosphere, the precipitation of energetic charged particles into the high-latitude atmosphere, the global distribution of auroras and phenomena of the magnetosphere. Today, Canadian scientists are active in several international co-operative programs making use of satellites, the US Space Shuttle and interplanetary space probes. The Canadian program focuses on tracing the energy flow from the solar particle stream through many intermediate processes to heating of the atmosphere. For such global studies international co-operation is mandatory.   P.A. FORSYTH

Earth Physics studies the solid Earth and its atmosphere and oceans. Although LAND, sea and air are often studied in isolation by separate disciplines (geophysics, OCEANOGRAPHY, METEOROLOGY), modern investigations are often intensely multidisciplinary. The physics of the solid Earth encompasses both academic and applied aspects. The questions of how and of what was Earth formed and what physical and chemical processes control its evolution remain at the forefront of current research. Perhaps the most important scientific advance in the past century of geophysical inquiry has been the dramatic verification of the hypothesis of continental drift, achieved since 1965. This PLATE TECTONICS theory received support from the geophysical methods of seismology and geomagnetism (*see* GEOLOGY). These methods are also employed, with considerable practical success, in exploring the near-surface crustal region of Earth for economically important deposits of PETROLEUM and base metals. Electrical methods, many of which have been developed in Canadian laboratories, have proven to be particularly suited to the discovery of MINERAL deposits. These methods include electromagnetic induction, induced polarization and direct current resistivity measurements. Other geophysical techniques that are of major industrial significance include both seismic reflection and refraction SURVEYING, and also potential field methods based on the analyses of minute variations in Earth's gravitational and magnetic fields. In all these areas Canada has played a leading role in developing and implementing the new methodology.

The atmospheric sciences, often considered together under meteorology, are also characterized by a multifaceted collection of applied and fundamental concerns, including questions regarding the detailed processes through which precipitation (rain, hail and snow) is formed; the potential negative effects of increases in carbon levels in the atmosphere; the sensitivity of the atmosphere to small changes in insolation and to changes in stratospheric concentrations of ozone and the oxides of nitrogen; and the assessment of air quality, especially relating to the problem of ACID RAIN. Considerable recent progress has also been made in understanding the planetary-scale hydrodynamics of the atmosphere, through the use of detailed mathematical models implemented on the largest digital computers available. Practical by-products of this fundamental research include the numerical weather prediction models routinely employed to make twice-daily forecasts. Canada's Atmospheric Environment Service has played a leading role in developing and improving such models.

The science of oceanography has many similarities to both solid Earth geophysics and meteorology. Physical oceanographers study the waves and currents of all spatial and temporal scales that characterize the motions of the sea in the major ocean basins. Chemical oceanographers study the composition of the sea and, more recently, have begun to employ measurements of trace-element concentrations to reveal the patterns of oceanic circulation. Biological oceanographers are concerned with the life systems that the oceans sustain. The necessity for acquiring improved understanding of the oceans has been made particularly clear by recent and unsuccessful United Nations attempts to formulate a LAW OF THE SEA that would control exploitation of the mineral wealth of the ocean floors. This economic incentive and that provided by large-scale offshore programs of drilling for subsurface deposits of hydrocarbons have enhanced traditional concerns about the sea as a source of food.   W.R. PELTIER

Optics The Greek word *optikes* originally meant the study of the eye and vision. Today, optics encompasses the whole spectrum of electromagnetic waves, radio waves, microwaves, infrared, visible light, ultraviolet, X rays and gamma rays. Classical optics dealt mainly with lenses, mirrors, gratings and instruments made with them. Such artifacts can be designed and analysed using the classical (ie, geometrical and wave) theories of light. The main proponents of geometrical theory were Johannes Kepler (German astronomer) and Sir Isaac Newton (English physicist and mathematician). This theory assumes that a light source emits light rays, which propagate rectilinearly in a homogeneous medium. When the medium changes, the rays are reflected, refracted or both. Pinhole cameras and shadows of objects cast by light beams demonstrate the truth of this theory. The main proponent of wave theory was Christian Huygens (Dutch scientist). It assumes that a light source emits waves that travel out in spheres; at any moment, every point on a wavefront acts as a new secondary source emitting new wavelets. The optical phenomena of interference, diffraction and polarization can be studied by this theory. Optics has always been an extremely important component in spectroscopy, which has played a vital role in the study of atoms and molecules. In Canada, Gerhard Herzberg won a Nobel Prize (1971) for his work in molecular spectroscopy.

Optics was revitalized and revolutionized by the invention of the maser and LASER by Charles Townes (American physicist), N.G. Basov and A.M. Prokhorov (Soviet physicists), winners of the 1964 Nobel Prize for physics for their work in this field. The first laser was built by Theodore Maiman (American physicist) in 1960. The main types of lasers are (according to the lasing materials used) solid, liquid, dye, gas and semiconductor. Extreme high-intensity pulses can be produced by transversally excited atmospheric carbon dioxide (TEA-CO_2) lasers. The Canadian Defence Research Establishment, Valcartier, Qué, was among the important pioneers and inventors of TEA-CO_2 lasers. Canada has a few laser-manufacturing companies, including internationally renowned Lumonics Inc.

Among the latest developments in optics is fibre optics. Optical waves can propagate inside optically transparent fibres by total internal reflection. The diameters of the fibres may be a few micrometres (single mode) to a few hundred micrometres (multimode). Because of their high frequencies, optical waves in the visible and near infrared regimes can carry far more information than electrical currents in metal wires. Canada is one of the leaders in fibre optics. Much research is done at the Communications Research Centre. Commercially, Bell-Northern Research and Canada Wire and Cable are the leading Canadian companies. The world's first fibre-optic, cable-television, digital super trunk system was installed in London, Ont. Some other early Canadian systems were installed at Dept of National Defence headquarters, Ottawa (1976), downtown Montréal (1977), Toronto (1978) and Vancouver (1979). Two recent and very advanced systems were the Calgary-Cheadle (Alta) and the Elie-St Eustache (Man) projects.   JOHN W.Y. LIT

Atomic and Molecular Physics is concerned with understanding the physical nature of atoms and molecules and with observing and understanding processes involving a small number of atoms and molecules, which may or may not be electrically charged. The emphasis on the small number of particles distinguishes atomic and molecular physics from solid state physics, statistical mechanics and thermodynamics, and plasma physics. The subject has diffuse borders with many branches of physics, CHEMISTRY and astrophysics. The ultimate aim of atomic and molecular physics is to establish the physical laws that govern observed atomic and molecular processes. At present, it is generally believed that all known phenomena are compatible with the laws of quantum mechanics and quantum electrodynamics. While many elegant verifications of these laws have been obtained for simple physical systems, the quantitative application to more complex systems is limited by mathematical and computational difficulties.

The term electronics was first used to describe the branch of physics that evolved from the discovery of the electron by English physicist J.J. Thomson in 1897. The subject then involved the determination of the fundamental properties of individual electrons (eg, charge, mass, magnetic moment) and the properties of free electrons in vacuum tubes. Today the term has a wider connotation, embracing the study, design and application of devices (eg, electronic tubes, transistors, integrated circuits) the operation of which depends largely on the characteristics and behaviour of electrons. Electronics plays a key role in COMMUNICATIONS and computers.

Spectroscopy is concerned with the interaction between matter and radiation. Historically the subject started in the visible region of the spectrum and was primarily concerned with the emission and absorption spectra of atoms. Today the subject embraces the complete electromagnetic spectrum and is concerned with atoms, molecules and charged species in the gas, liquid and solid phases. The emission or absorption of radiation by a system accompanies a transition between 2 energy levels or quantum states of the system and gives information on the nature of these quantum states (*see* CHEMISTRY SUBDISCIPLINES). The spectrum of a substance is probably its most characteristic single property; this fact underlies the widespread use of various forms of spectroscopy in both qualitative and quantitative analysis.   D.A. RAMSAY

Nuclear and Particle Physics The atomic nucleus is a small, dense object containing nearly the entire mass of the atom. The existence of the nucleus was demonstrated by E. Rutherford in 1911, but an understanding of its composition came only with English physicist James Chadwick's discovery of the neutron in 1932. The existence of the neutron provided the key to understanding the nucleus as a composite body, formed of neutrons and protons. The neutrons and protons (referred to as nucleons) are bound in the tiny nuclear volume by a force that is very strong (ie, much stronger than the energies involved in binding atoms to form a molecule) and of very short range. The most important manifestations of nuclear energy are found in the processes of NUCLEAR FUSION and fission, in which a fraction of the internal nuclear energy is transformed into kinetic energy, which ultimately appears as heat (*see* NUCLEAR-POWER PLANTS). A chemical element has a characteristic number of nuclear protons but nature permits a certain latitude in the number of neutrons that may bind to the protons, under the influence of the strong force. The differing neutron numbers give rise to what are known as isotopes. Several isotopes of a chemical element may be absolutely stable, but the remainder manifest an instability called radioactive decay. Some radioisotopes occur naturally in the heavy elements and many more have been produced artificially. Many radioisotopes are valuable in medicine and industry.

A nucleus may have a number of distinct excited states, differing from one another by discrete amounts of internal nuclear energy. Such states undergo radioactive transformation under the perturbing effects of internal electromagnetic interactions or the very feeble, but significant, weak interaction. These excitations and transformations have been much studied as a means of understanding the complexities of the strong nuclear force. Although the structure of a nucleus is explicable in terms of just 2 particles, scores of other subatomic particles have been observed, studied and classified. These particles are grouped in 3 families: baryons, mesons and leptons. The lepton family is characterized by its insensitivity to the strong interaction; the most notable attribute of the baryon and meson families is their affinity for the strong interaction. Baryons and mesons appear to have an important internal structure of their own: the baryon family is believed to be formed of different combinations of 3 fundamental constituents, known as u, d and s quarks; the meson family is formed by the binding of 2 constituents, a quark and an antiquark. The quarks are thought to be permanently confined or bound and hence unobservable as free particles. The quark hypothesis received strong support in 1974 and 1977 with the discoveries of massive long-lived mesons, known as psi and upsilon mesons, formed by the binding of heavy quarks, called c and b, with their respective antiquarks. A very important concept in particle physics is the unified theory of weak and electromagnetic interactions. According to this theory the weak interaction is associated with particles about 100 times more massive than the proton. These particles are expected to be observed in the large electron-positron and proton-antiproton colliding beam machines now in operation or construction in Europe and the US.   D.G. STAIRS

Condensed Matter Physics studies the fundamental, microscopic properties of matter in the solid and liquid phases, and their technological uses. Condensed matter physics is an outgrowth of solid state physics that blossomed in the post WWII period. Most research was done on crystalline materials, in which the atoms are in ordered positions, especially semiconductors. The discovery of the transistor revolutionized electronics. It is now at the heart of modern communications and SPACE TECHNOLOGY, computers, commercial electronic devices and microelectronics. Solid state physics evolved into condensed matter physics in the 1970s in Canada. There is strong affinity between the properties of liquids and solids, and between techniques used to investigate them. There are similarities between the disordered (amorphous or glassy) materials and liquids. There is a parallel between superfluids, which flow without friction, and superconductors, in which electrical currents flow without losses, at low temperature. These co-operative phenomena, which implicate all particles in unison, have applications in computers, electric-power transmission and public transport (superconducting motors and levitation). Liquid-crystals (eg, watch displays) have properties of both the liquid and solid.

Condensed matter physics calls on a host of experimental techniques such as microwave, optical, X ray, magnetic resonance, neutron and electron spectroscopies, thermal, acoustic, magnetic and electrical probing. It is also strongly dependent on theoretical techniques such as quantum mechanics and statistical physics. It is a broad and diversified field that blends into most other fields of physics and chemistry, biology, engineering and medicine. The Canadian effort in condensed matter is quite substantial, and Canada played a leading role in development and use of neutrons and positrons to probe condensed matter. There is now considerable interest in using unusual but promising materials, such as layered solids (eg, graphite) and polymer conductors, in batteries, organic conductors and ceramic superconductors (Nobel prize, 1987). The conversion of light to electricity and the storage of energy (eg, solar heat, hydrogen) in materials are of practical interest. The electron tunneling microscope (Nobel prize, 1986), which allows one to see individual atoms on solid surfaces, has great potential use in materials science.   LAURENT G. CARON

Plasma Physics American chemist Irving Langmuir was the first to make systematic studies on electrical properties of ionized gases or plasmas. Atoms or molecules in a gas become ionized when bombarded by energetic particles or when irradiated by short-wavelength electromagnetic waves. In general, a plasma contains equal amounts of positive and negative charges and maintains electric neutrality. An ionized gas is appropriately called a plasma if there are a sufficiently large number of electron-positive ion pairs in a characteristic sphere (Debye sphere) and the space occupied by the gas is much larger than the Debye length. A plasma is a good electric conductor because of the presence of highly mobile free electrons. In a fully ionized plasma, electric conductivity rapidly increases with the temperature, but is practically independent of the density of the plasma electrons.

Plasmas can be found in such engineering devices as glow discharge tubes, mercury vapour rectifiers, fluorescent lamps and gas lasers. Plasmas in these devices are initiated and maintained by electrical discharge through neutral gases. Ionization, however, is maintained by plasma electrons themselves, which can acquire a temperature of several thousand degrees. Tube walls, usually glass, do not melt since gases are extremely rarefied.

Plasmas can be found in nature. LIGHTNING is caused by an electric discharge or breakdown among clouds or between clouds and Earth. Air, being a good electric insulator otherwise, becomes a plasma and provides conduction paths for electric currents. Auroras, another example of a natural plasma, occur when Earth's upper atmosphere becomes ionized when exposed to solar radiation. More importantly, stars and nebulae are all in the plasma state with energy released through the nuclear fusion process.

A plasma greatly modifies the nature of electromagnetic waves. For example, shortwave radio, out-of-sight communication is possible because of wave reflection by the ionospheric plasma. Self-generation of plasma waves (instability) is largely the result of intrinsic temperature difference between an energetic plasma and its environment. A plasma tends to establish thermal equilibrium through thermal and particle diffusion which can be greatly enhanced by plasma instabilities, and often jeopardizes plasma confinement in nuclear-fusion devices. However, plasma instabilities have also been utilized as various microwave sources. A. HIROSE

Societies

The Canadian Assn of Physicists, the national society of Canadian physicists, has a membership of over 1800 individuals and 30 corporations. CAP was founded in 1945 and incorporated in 1951. It publishes a bimonthly bulletin, *Physics in Canada*, and holds an annual 3-day congress for discussion of current research. Since 1945, the Canadian Assn of Physicists Medal has been awarded annually for distinguished achievement in physics and, since 1970, the Herzberg Medal for outstanding achievement by a physicist not more than 38 years of age. From time to time, CAP produces special reports on the state of physics in Canada. Canada's national physics journal is the *Canadian Journal of Physics*. Many physicists are members of the Association canadienne-française pour l'avancement des sciences. ACFAS was established in 1923 for the advancement of science in Québec and in French-speaking communities of N America. With a membership of over 2500, ACFAS holds an annual congress attended by 2000 researchers and students, who gather to hear approximately 1000 scientific papers.

Most Canadian physicists are also active members of the many scientific societies in physics and astronomy that form the American Institute of Physics (AIP). Canadian physicists have taken an active part in international organizations, eg, the

International Council of Scientific Unions and the International Union of Pure and Applied Physics, which promotes international co-operation in physics, and international agreements on the use of symbols, units, nomenclature and standards. Scientific exchanges have permitted collaboration of many groups in nuclear and particle physics research, making use of the costly accelerators at national laboratories in Europe, the US and Canada (AECL and TRIUMF).

Canadian physicists have been honoured by both national and international bodies. Physicists who have served as presidents of the ROYAL SOCIETY OF CANADA include G. Herzberg, H.E. Duckworth, J.T. Wilson, J.L. Kerwin and R.E. Bell. In the past decade, a number of Canadian physicists have been made fellows of the Royal Society (of London), including Z.S. Basinski, R.E. Bell, B.N. Brockhouse, A.E. Douglas, G. Herzberg, W.B. Lewis, A.E. Litherland, M.H.L. Pryce, D.A. Ramsay, B.P. Stoicheff, H.L. Welsh and J.T. Wilson.

BORIS P. STOICHEFF

Physiographic Regions Physiography originally meant "the study of natural phenomena," but later usage limited its application to PHYSICAL GEOGRAPHY in particular and, more recently, to landforms alone. The latter usage makes the word redundant, as GEOMORPHOLOGY is the universally accepted term for the study of landforms; nevertheless, in many works about physiographic regions, only landforms are considered. Physiographic regionalization is here defined as the process by which regions with relatively homogeneous physical geography are delimited. The 4 elements, land, air, water and vegetation, in distinctive combinations, define the physiographic regions of Canada. Geologic structure (*see* GEOLOGICAL REGIONS), relief attributes of land, the distribution of continuous PERMAFROST (a measure of broad-scale atmospheric and hydrologic effects) and the position of the TREELINE (a significant vegetation boundary) are the criteria used in the following physiographic regionalization. Combinations of these generate the major physiographic regions of Canada: Arctic Lands, Cordillera, Interior Plains, Hudson Bay Lowland, Canadian Shield Forest Lands, St Lawrence Lowlands and Appalachia. These regions have broadly homogeneous physical geographic characteristics, and differences between them are visible from a jet travelling at 10 000 m altitude or from satellite images (*see* REMOTE SENSING). Areas quoted for these regions are the land areas and do not include adjacent continental shelves or bodies of ocean water within Canada's territorial limits. Certain parts of Canada may be properly classed in 2 regions (eg, arctic portion of the Canadian Shield). OLAV SLAYMAKER

Arctic Lands

The Canadian Arctic Lands lie N of the treeline and cover 2.6 million km², or 26% of the country (including the Arctic Coastal Plains, the Innuitian Region, Arctic Lowlands and part of the Canadian SHIELD). Except on the Canadian Shield, where much bare ROCK is exposed, the mainland TUNDRA is a closed mat with up to 900 species of vascular plants. The richness of tundra vegetation decreases towards the Pole. The islands S of Parry Channel (the official name for the body of water whose parts are called Viscount Melville Sound, Barrow Str, Lancaster Sound and M'Clure Str) are rock and moss surfaces; the Queen Elizabeth Is are a desert of mainly bare rock and soil with patch vegetation on moist sites. Freshwater lakes and rivers are ice-free June-Oct in the S, July-Aug in the N; they are ice-covered for the rest of the year. Slightly more than half the precipitation falls as snow which, in a treeless zone, is greatly affected

Rock outcrops on the Manitoba tundra (*photo by Barry Griffiths/Network*).

by wind. Snow is moved over the surface, drifted into hollows and becomes hard packed, with wave and ripple forms related to prevailing wind directions. The NW and the High Arctic are dry with annual precipitation averaging 10 cm. The central Arctic receives 20-30 cm; S Baffin and N Québec, up to 50 cm.

Several thousand years of cold CLIMATE have created a condition of perennially frozen ground (permafrost), in which GROUNDWATER occurs as ice in crystals, lenses and layers up to tens of metres thick. In some areas, rock may be frozen but it contains no ice. Permafrost may be tens of metres thick in the S increasing to more than 500 m in the NW islands. Each summer the top, active layer may melt down from a few centimetres to a metre or more. Associated with permafrost is the formation of patterned ground (surface circles, ovals, polygons and stripes). Tundra polygons, a tortoise-shell pattern of cracks up to 30 m apart with ice wedges below the cracks, cover many thousands of square kilometres. Other distinctive PERIGLACIAL LANDFORMS are PINGOS, over 1500 of which have been counted near the Mackenzie Delta.

Land surfaces owe their character, in part, to the underlying GEOLOGY. The mainland E of Great Bear and Great Slave lakes, the Ungava Peninsula and most of Baffin I are part of the Canadian Shield. These ancient rocks have been much changed through GEOLOGICAL HISTORY and have been glaciated to form an upright saucer with the centre flooded by Hudson Bay. The eastern rim, extending from Labrador N along Baffin I and into Ellesmere I, is a mountainous zone with elevations 1500 m and higher in the N, and a fjorded coast. This zone possesses GLACIERS covering about 5% of the Arctic's surface. The zone between the Shield and the Western Cordillera is a Paleozoic plain (570-245 million years old) gently sloping from 500 m elevation downwards to the Arctic Ocean. The islands are mostly of SEDIMENTARY ROCKS which form plains, uplands and hills. The rock layers are mainly flat-lying in the S but have been folded, then eroded, in the ARCTIC ARCHIPELAGO. Surface elevations rise from near sea level in the NW to approach the high mountain rim in the E. The many channels among the ISLANDS may be caused by faulting, or may be fault-controlled and further deepened by riverine EROSION and GLACIATION. JOHN K. STAGER

Cordillera

This region is part of the MOUNTAIN system that extends the length of the Pacific Coast of N and S America. The Canadian part of the Cordillera is about 800 km wide, and extends northwestward from 49° N for over 2000 km to the Alaska border at 141° W. Most of the Cordillera lies within BC and YT, but it also extends into southwestern Alberta and NWT. The total area covered by this physiographic region is 1.6 million km² (16% of Canada). The Cordillera includes plateaus, val-

Rolling prairie near the proposed Grasslands National Park, Sask (*photo by Brian Milne/First Light*).

leys and plains as well as rugged mountains. The most continuous mountain chains form high rims along the SW and SE sides of a belt of varied terrain. The Eastern system consists of sedimentary rocks that have been tilted, faulted and folded. The Interior system's mountain ranges and dissected plateaus are underlain by folded sedimentary and volcanic strata, by metamorphic rocks and numerous, small IGNEOUS intrusions. In the Western system, the Coast Mts consist of a mass of interlocking igneous intrusions and metamorphic rocks, but the outermost mountains are geologically similar to the Interior system.

The oldest recognizable feature of the Cordilleran landscape is the gently rolling upland of its interior plateaus. This ancient surface was sculpted by erosion many millions of years ago. Since then, it has been uplifted, partly buried by lava flows, dissected by river erosion and modified by glaciers. The most widespread landforms and surface deposits of the Cordillera date from the glaciations of the past million years. South of 61° N, only the highest mountain peaks projected above the Cordilleran ice sheet. Farther north, extensive parts of the YT and the NWT were too dry for glacier formation, although very cold. In the glaciated areas landforms such as cirques and U-shaped valleys are common in the mountains and along the edges of higher plateaus. Features such as striations, DRUMLINS, ESKERS and till plains are widespread on plateaus and plains. Valleys and lowlands commonly contain thick silts and clays that were deposited in ice-dammed lakes during glacier melting, and sands and gravels that were deposited by meltwater streams.

During the 12 000 years of postglacial time, rivers have formed terraces, alluvial fans, floodplains and deltas (*see* RIVER LANDFORM). Valley sides have been modified by rockfalls, debris flows, LANDSLIDES, soil creep and snow AVALANCHES. Periglacial landforms are present above treeline. In the south, permafrost exists beneath only the highest, windswept ridge crests, but northward it becomes lower and, in the central and northern YT, occurs at all elevations. Volcanic activity has occurred sporadically at scat-

Shield country near Goose Bay, Labrador (*photo by Freeman Patterson/Masterfile*).

tered locations in the western and interior systems up to the present. Some eruptions occurred during glaciation. The youngest lava flows and cinder cones are only a few hundred years old; these eruptions are described in Indian legends.

The Cordillera encompasses a great variety of climates because of its great latitudinal extent, its location between the Pacific Ocean and the continental interior, and its rugged terrain. Several significant effects of climate are visible in the natural landscape. Heavy rain and snow on the Coast Mts give rise to luxuriant forests and maintain extensive snowfields and glaciers at relatively low elevations. The altitudinal treeline and the snowline rise eastward as snowfall decreases, and descend northward as temperature declines. Differences in climate caused by elevation in any particular area are reflected by altitudinal vegetation zones. The highest of these is the alpine tundra. In the semiarid valleys of the Interior system, the lowest vegetation zone is grassland.

The Cordillera as a whole is distinguished by its mountainous and irregular topography, and its great variety of climates, soils and vegetation. Many aspects of its physiography, including steep slopes, natural hazards and severe climate, restrict land use by humans. Other features, such as FORESTS, grasslands, lakes and rivers, and varied scenery, are natural RESOURCES. *See also* KARST LANDFORM.   J.M. RYDER

Interior Plains

The Canadian Interior Plains extend from the 49th parallel to the Arctic Ocean, between the Canadian Shield and the Cordillera. They cover 1.8 million km², or 18% of Canada's land surface. The regional topography is largely determined by flat-lying sedimentary rocks. An uneven surface of SAND AND GRAVEL, deposited by rivers flowing from the Rocky Mts, was superimposed on this sedimentary substratum. Deposition was followed by periods of erosion associated with uneven uplift which resulted in the carving of the surface into isolated uplands. In addition to these erosional remnants, the relatively uniform slope of the southern portion of the region is broken into 3 levels by the Manitoba Escarpment and the Missouri Coteau. The Manitoba Plain lies below the Manitoba Escarpment at elevations under 400 m. It is the lowest and flattest of 3 PRAIRIE steps. The underlying Paleozoic rocks (570-245 million years old) are covered by a mantle of glacial drift, overlain in most areas by glacial lake silts and clays. The Saskatchewan Plain, the dip slope of the Manitoba Escarpment, is covered almost entirely by glacial deposits, largely hummocky MORAINE, with lesser amounts of large, flat areas of former glacial lakes, which are lower and smoother than the Alberta Plain to the W. Surface elevations range from 460 to 790 m, reaching 915 m in hillier areas. West of the Missouri Coteau is a gradual slope upwards to the foothills of the Rocky Mts. This third step, the Alberta Plain, has a bolder, more varied relief. Hummocky moraine is once again a dominant component of the landscape. More striking are the BADLANDS, formed from the severe dissection of soft, underlying rocks in the more arid region. The Alberta Plateau, N of the Athabasca R, is virtually a continuation of the plain to the S. It is a ring of plateaus with summits from 760 to 970 m, separated by the wide valleys of the Peace, Fort Nelson and Hay rivers. North of the Peace R, the plateau surface forms a disconnected escarpment overlooking the Great Slave Plain. Widespread distribution of glacial lake deposits is the most striking feature in the plateau area; till plains and hummocky moraines are also common. The northern Interior Plains, composed largely of peat-covered till plains below 300 m in elevation, stretch from

the Alberta Plateau to the Arctic Ocean.

The Interior Plains are characterized by grassland vegetation (prairie) under semiarid climatic conditions in the S. This grassland gives way to a parkbelt region, to the N and E, under slightly cooler temperatures and higher precipitation. As this trend continues northward, a coniferous forest predominates. Finally, through the northern extension of the Interior Plains, forest gives way to treeless tundra.   D.F. ACTON

Hudson Bay Lowland

This land area of 320 000 km² (3.5% of Canada's land surface) is only 40% of a sedimentary basin in the middle of the Canadian Shield, 60% of which lies beneath HUDSON BAY and JAMES BAY. Apart from the Sutton Ridges in the NE of the lowland, the bedrock terrain is completely masked by a mantle of glacial and marine sediments associated with the advance and retreat of ice during the last glaciation. The inland edge of the lowland (about 180 m high) coincides approximately with the highest level of marine inundation which followed the disappearance of glacial ice from Hudson Bay about 7500 years ago. In the western part of the lowland, landform subdivisions tend to parallel the Shield edge and coast. Nearer the Shield are found streamlined hills of glacial till, which were formed beneath ice moving SW from Hudson Bay towards Manitoba. These have not been totally masked by younger marine deposits and, thus, give the surface a corrugated appearance. Closer to the coast, where the marine mantle is thicker, vast level plains with thick PEAT accumulations and innumerable ponds are typical. These plains contrast with terrain in a wide zone (50-80 km) inland of the coast. There, scores of parallel, gravel beach ridges were thrown up by storm waves during the last 5000-6000 years, as sea level fell in response to rapid uplift of Earth's crust. This zone is characterized by dry, forested, low ridges separated by boggy depressions. At the coast the almost level offshore zone is exposed at low tide as marshy and muddy flats, often strewn with glacial boulders (*see* SWAMP, MARSH AND BOG). At present, sea level is still falling at approximately 60 cm/100 years, continually exposing more of the offshore zone. In the eastern lowland, flooding by marine waters was immediately followed by readvance of the ice sheet margin approximately along longitude 86-87° W. This caused the molding of the marine deposits into more prominent, streamlined hills.

I.A. BROOKES

Canadian Shield Forest Lands

The Shield proper (area 4.6 million km²) covers 46% of Canada's land surface (including freshwater lakes and arctic islands). If the Arctic Shield is excluded, this remains the largest physiographic region in Canada, comprising 32% of the land surface. It is a vast, saucer-shaped region: the rim on its S, E and NE sides like that of a soup plate; the centre a sedimentary rock basin, the southern fringe of which underlies the Hudson Bay Lowland. The Shield is composed of crystalline Precambrian rocks formed during several phases of mountain building between 3.5 and 1 billion years ago. In the last billion years it has remained a relatively stable bulwark, unaffected by the PLATE TECTONIC movements which have impinged on it to form the mountainous fringe of Canada. The stability of the Shield has allowed denudation to level its surface, giving it characteristic level or undulating skylines. The southeastern and eastern borders have been uplifted in the relatively recent geological past as a result of tectonic movements associated with the opening of the Atlantic Ocean. Glacial erosion had little effect, except along the eastern rim.

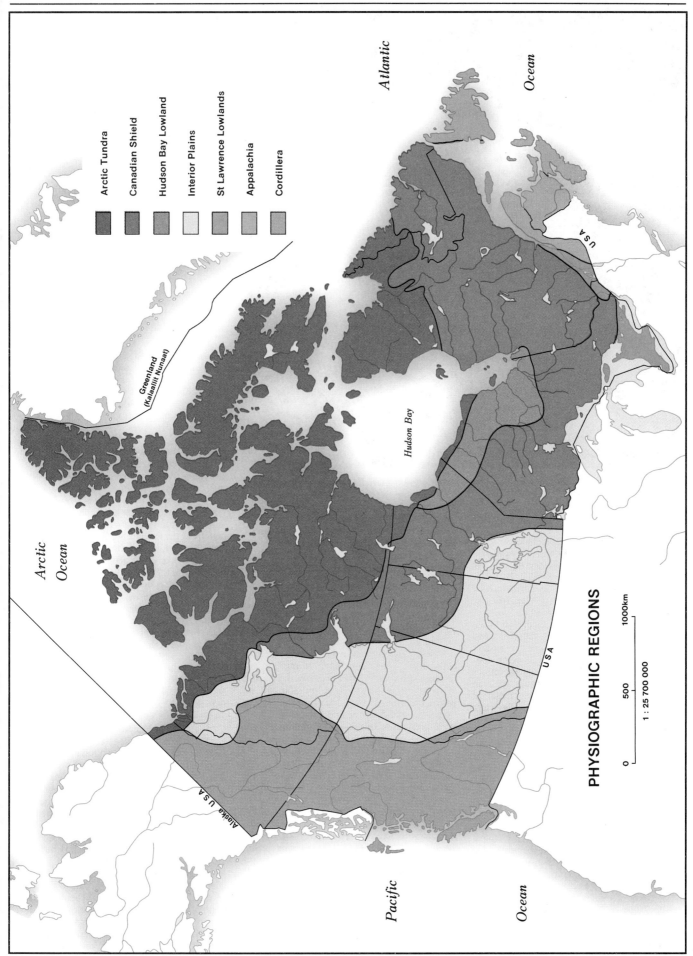

Atlantic

Ocean

USA

Greenland
(Kalaallit Nunaat)

Hudson Bay

Arctic
Ocean

USA

Alaska U.S.A

Pacific

Ocean

Arctic Tundra

Canadian Shield

Hudson Bay Lowland

Interior Plains

St Lawrence Lowlands

Appalachia

Cordillera

PHYSIOGRAPHIC REGIONS

1 : 25 700 000

0   500   1000km

Peaks near Elaho Valley, BC. The Canadian Cordillera extends from the US border NW for over 2000 km (*courtesy Colour Library Books*).

Approximately half of the Shield is classified as upland. Extending from NW Québec through N Ontario, Manitoba and Saskatchewan to NW Keewatin and E Mackenzie districts, NWT, this terrain (200-500 m elevation) is upland only by virtue of its elevation above the Hudson Bay Lowland and the Interior Plains which border it. Bedrock relief of only 50-60 m has been smoothed by a thin mantle of glacial till and sediment deposited in glacial lakes. The eastern Shield is dominated by plateaus between Hudson Bay and the Gulf of St Lawrence. Elevations increase from 300 m near the coasts to 900 m in central Labrador-Nouveau Québec. Relief of 150-300 m is caused by incision of valleys into the higher terrain. At several places over the Shield, uplands and plateaus are broken by belts of hills, in which relief increases because of differential erosion of linear geological structures formed in former mountain belts. Examples are the Labrador and Port Arthur hills. The high, rugged terrain along the E and SE rim of the Shield is classified as highland. In Baffin I and northern Labrador it stands at 800-1500 m and possesses rolling plateau surfaces which are deeply dissected by glacial troughs, giving a fjordlike aspect to these coasts. Highlands N of St Lawrence R stand at 500-900 m with isolated summits at 1000-1200 m in terrain which is more dissected, with few plateaus.

The 2 extensive shield zones, E and W of Hudson Bay, were the centres of ice sheet outflow during the last glaciation (from 100 000 to 6000 years ago). The central parts of these zones show unorganized terrain mantled with till and also pocked with irregular, shallow lake basins.

Around these, glacial scouring of the bedrock is more obvious, with occasional ice-molded till hills and many eskers marking the courses of subglacial rivers, and large moraines marking pauses in retreat of the ice front across the Shield. The periphery of these 2 core areas is marked by more level terrain which was flooded by lakes and seas during ice retreat. I.A. BROOKES

St Lawrence Lowlands

The Lowlands (180 000 km², 1.8% of Canada's land surface) lie between the Shield to the N and the Appalachian Region to the E and SE, and are broken into 3 subregions.

West St Lawrence Lowland This subregion lies between the Shield and Lakes Huron, Erie and Ontario. The West St Lawrence Lowland consists of a limestone plain (elevation 200-250 m) which is separated by a broad, shale lowland from a broader dolomite and limestone plateau, W of Lk Ontario. This plateau is bounded by the NIAGARA ESCARPMENT. From the escarpment the plateau slopes gently SW to Lakes Huron and Erie (elevation 173 m). Glaciation has mantled this subregion with several layers of glacial till, the youngest forming extensive, undulating till plains, often enclosing rolling drumlin fields. Prominent moraines on the western plateau and north of Lake Ontario mark temporary pauses in the retreat of glacial lobes, between 14 500 and 12 500 years ago. Level clay and sand plains, which were deposited in glacial lakes, fringe present lakes.

Central St Lawrence Lowland This subregion has undulating topography, developed on sedimentary rocks beneath the lowland, which is largely masked by glacial and marine deposits. The 7 Monteregian Hills (eg, Mont Royal), which are aligned approximately W-E between the Shield W of Montréal and the Appalachians,

stand at 200-400 m. Along the Shield and Appalachian fringes of the lowland, sandy terraces (elevation up to 200 m) were deposited in the CHAMPLAIN SEA which flooded the newly deglaciated lowland approximately 12 500 years ago. These have been eroded by postglacial streams to form more broken terrain. The low, gently hummocky, Drummondville moraine trends southwest from near Québec City to near the Vermont border.

East St Lawrence Lowland This is a subregion which widens from the lower St Lawrence estuary into the Gulf of St Lawrence and narrows again to the NE at the Str of Belle Isle. There are small, isolated low plateaus and plains along the N shore of the Gulf of St Lawrence, eg, Mingan Is; a coastal plain at less than 100 m in NW Newfoundland; and a larger, undulating plateau at 100-200 m with a central spine at 300 m on Anticosti I. These fragments have a smooth terrain influenced by flat or gently dipping sedimentary bedrock. Surface conditions may be barren and dry, or boggy, depending on surface slope and the influence of coastal winds.

I.A. BROOKES

Appalachian Region

The Appalachian Region (360 000 km², about 2% of Canada's land surface) lies between the St Lawrence Lowlands to the NW and the Atlantic Continental Shelf to the E and SE. Like other mountain regions, its terrain is a mosaic of uplands and lowlands, the characters, boundaries and shapes of which reflect the complexity of rocks and structures inherited from tectonic movements between 480 and 280 million years ago. Since then, denudation has removed several kilometres of rock, revealing once deeply buried structures. At the same time, regional uplift has maintained smooth-topped uplands and highlands on stronger rocks, while weaker rocks have been fashioned into lowlands and plains. Highlands and mountains are disposed in a Z-shaped belt, from the Québec border with Vermont and New Hampshire, northeastwards to Gaspésie, then southwestwards across NB, and continuing NE north of the Bay of Fundy to Cape Breton I. Thence, broken by Cabot Str, the belt continues along the high, western spine of Newfoundland. These highlands reach over 1200 m in central Gaspésie (Mt Jacques Cartier, 1268 m). In western Newfoundland and northeastern NB summits stand at 600-800 m; elsewhere in the region, this highland belt is flanked by uplands at 300-600 m in Québec, northwestern NB, southern and eastern Newfoundland, and southern NS. Except in southern NS, the uplands share with the highlands smoothly undulating skylines and deeply cut valleys.

In eastern NB, PEI, Îles de la Madeleine, northern NS and the triangular Newfoundland Central Lowland, weak rocks have allowed the development of plains and lowlands. In Newfoundland and southern NS, terrain strongly resembles that of the Shield, with extensive, glacially smoothed bedrock plains, patchily covered with bouldery till and dotted with irregular lakes. In the rest of the region, even highland and mountain zones show only locally severe glacial erosion, particularly in valleys crossing the "grain" of the terrain. Glacial deposits are thicker there and, although mostly sandy and infertile, locally they may be good soil parent materials. With deglaciation, between 14 000 and 10 000 years ago, crustal uplift was sufficiently great to exceed sea-level rise in the central and northern zones of the Appalachian Region, so that a coastal fringe exhibits raised marine terraces which often provide pockets of arable land. In the S, bordering the

Atlantic Ocean, sea-level rise has exceeded uplift along this submerging coast with rocky headlands and irregular bays. Sea level continues to rise at up to 30 cm/100 years.   I.A. BROOKES

Reading: J.B. Bird, *The Natural Landscapes of Canada* (1978).

Piano Manufacturing The piano is a keyboard instrument which produces sound by means of strings, stretched over a soundboard, which vibrate when struck by a hammer. The decisive invention is generally attributed to Bartolomeo Cristofori about 1709. The piano has developed from a softer-sounding, delicate, wood-framed instrument to one which is sonorous and sturdily constructed, the frame reinforced with cast iron and steel. The shape of the piano has evolved from earlier square or rectangular designs to the contemporary horizontal, wing-shaped grands, and the uprights.

By the late 18th century, pianos were imported from Europe for sale in Canada. This was a costly practice, and often the instrument's sensitive mechanism suffered during transit. As the demand for pianos increased during the early 19th century, a few skilled British and German immigrant craftsmen began to build pianos in the workshops where they also carried out the business of piano tuning and repair. From these small beginnings in Québec City, Montréal and Toronto grew a major domestic and export industry, which flourished especially from the 1880s to the 1920s. At some point during this period there existed close to 100 companies or craftsmen involved in the manufacture of pianos or their accessory parts. Firms such as HEINTZMAN AND CO LTD, R.S. Williams, Mason & Risch, Karn, Lesage, Gerhard Heintzman, Martin-Orme, Mendelssohn, Rainer, Weber, Nordheimer, Bell, Pratte, Sherlock-Manning, to name but a few, provided excellent quality, prize-winning pianos at reasonable costs. Except for a few firms, the industry was centered in southern Ontario and the Montréal region but pianos were readily available through retailers across the country.

Many factors brought about the decline of the piano manufacturing industry, notably the increasing popularity of alternative forms of home entertainment, such as the phonograph and the radio, and the effects of the GREAT DEPRESSION. As the economy stabilized in the 1930s and 1940s, renewed interest in piano purchasing was served by 7 surviving companies (Lesage, Quidoz, and Willis in Québec, Sherlock-Manning, Heintzman, and Mason & Risch in Ontario, and Edmund in BC). The advent of television and sophisticated home sound systems, the introduction of cheaper, mass-produced Japanese pianos, and the durability of existing Canadian pianos, however, caused a decrease in sales and the closure of more firms. In 1984, 3 manufacturers remained in Canada but by 1987 they had all ceased operation. Sherlock-Manning closed in 1987 but reopened in 1988 under new ownership. *See also* MUSICAL INSTRUMENTS.   FLORENCE HAYES

Picard, Gérard, labour leader, (b at Stratford-Centre, Qué 27 May 1907). After completing a law degree at Laval, he was a journalist for *L'Événement* and *L'Action catholique* in Québec C during the early 1930s. Secretary-treasurer, then secretary general of the Confédération des travailleurs catholiques du Canada, he succeeded Alfred CHARPENTIER as president in 1946. Under his leadership the CTCC became more militant, as in several bitter and prolonged postwar strikes, including the 1949 ASBESTOS STRIKE and the violent 1952-53 strike of Louiseville textile workers that almost precipitated a province-wide general

strike. During the 1950s the CTCC devoted itself to democratizing the workplace through co-management, profit sharing and co-ownership, and it was one of the few organizations to oppose the policies and practices of the Union Nationale government of Maurice DUPLESSIS. In 1961 the CTCC became the Confédération des syndicats nationaux. Picard encouraged union activists to partake in political action. In 1959 he joined the Québec wing of the CCF, and in 1961 helped found the New Democratic Party, becoming its first associate president. In the mid-1960s he was appointed to the Canadian Council of Industrial Relations.   MICHAEL D. BEHIELS

Pichon, Thomas, alias Thomas Tyrell, colonial official, spy, author (b at Vire, France 30 Mar 1700; d at St Helier, Jersey 22 Nov 1781). Seeking advancement after an unrewarding career in Europe, Pichon arrived at LOUISBOURG in 1751 as the governor's secretary and at FT BEAUSÉJOUR in 1753 as chief stores clerk. Enticed by financial promises, he began spying for the neighbouring British garrison at Ft Lawrence. He passed along information, encouraged Acadian neutrality, discouraged French defence schemes, and generally facilitated the British capture of Beauséjour in 1755. He moved on to Halifax and then London, and in 1760 published a reliable but uneven history of Cape Breton. Although condemned for ambition, avarice, treason and moral dissipation, Pichon remains an intriguing figure in early Canadian history.   LOIS KERNAGHAN

Pickard, George Lawson, oceanographer, educator (b at Cardiff, Wales 5 July 1913). Following military service with the RAF during WWII, Pickard came to Canada in 1947. He was professor of physics at UBC 1947-79 and director of the Institute of Oceanography there 1958-79. He began the studies of water properties and circulation that have provided much of our understanding of the OCEANOGRAPHY of BC's fjords and estuaries. His expertise in fjord studies later took him to study in Chile and NZ. As a teacher and administrator, Pickard was influential in the development of marine sciences in western Canada; his textbooks on physical oceanography have received worldwide circulation.   P.H. LeBLOND

Pickerel, common name for 3 closely related, carnivorous, soft-rayed, freshwater fishes in the PIKE family (Esocidae). In parts of Canada, the name is applied, erroneously, to the WALLEYE. The name is derived from an English diminutive of pike. Pickerel occur naturally only in eastern N America. The group consists of 2 species: *Esox niger,* chain pickerel; *E. americanus,* divisible into 2 forms, redfin pickerel, which grows to 35 cm, and the slightly smaller grass pickerel. In Canada, one or more species occur in limited portions of the territory from southern NS to Ontario, inhabiting smaller, warm waters (eg, ponds, small streams, bays of lakes). Only the chain pickerel, growing to about 50 cm long and 1.4 kg, is of any consequence as a sport fish.   E.J. CROSSMAN

Pickersgill, John Whitney, public servant, politician, historian (b at Wycombe, Ont 23 June 1905). "Clear it with Jack" was the Ottawa watchword through the KING and ST. LAURENT eras, a testimony to Pickersgill's extraordinary influence. He was raised on a poor Manitoba farm and secured a good education at U Man and Oxford thanks to his great abilities – and an extraordinary mother. He taught history at Wesley College, Winnipeg, 1929-37, and then joined the Dept of External Affairs. Quickly shifted to the PMO, Pickersgill assisted King and St. Laurent on virtually all aspects of policy and politics. In 1952 he became clerk of the Privy Council and the next year secretary of state. He held 2 portfolios in the

PEARSON government and was appointed president of the Canadian Transport Commission when he left politics in 1967. Pickersgill's historical studies of the King-St. Laurent years are of importance.   J.L. GRANATSTEIN

Reading: J.L. Granatstein, *The Ottawa Men* (1982); J.W. Pickersgill, *My Years with Louis St. Laurent* (1975) and *The Road Back* (1986).

Pictographs and Petroglyphs, prehistoric paintings executed with the finger in red ochre (pictographs), and carvings (petroglyphs) incised, abraded or ground by means of stone tools upon cliff walls, boulders and flat bedrock surfaces. They have been discovered throughout Canada. "Rock art" constitutes Canada's oldest and most widespread form of artistic expression, and is part of a worldwide genre of prehistoric art which includes the cave paintings of Spain and France. No foolproof method for the precise dating of rock art has been discovered, other than speculative association with stratified, relatively datable archaeological remains. While the tradition of rock art was no doubt brought into Canada by the earliest Indians some 25 000 years ago, it is most unlikely that examples of antiquity will ever be found.

Rock art in much of Canada is linked with shamanism, a widespread religious tradition in which the SHAMAN's major tasks are healing and prophesy, along with the vision quest; and with the search for "helping" spirits. Several broad regions of rock-art "style areas" have been distinguished. The petroglyph sites in KEJIMKUJIK NATIONAL PARK in NS reveal a unique, small-scale and fine-line style that has been attributed to the MICMAC. The Canadian SHIELD, extending from the St Maurice R in Québec to N Saskatchewan, has many pictograph sites, while petroglyphs are confined to the S. The Peterborough petroglyph site in southern Ontario has several hundred images of humans, animals, birds, snakes, turtles and boats.

Here, as at many sites in the Shield, there are no pictorial boundaries such as frames or groundlines. Nor is there any evidence of a deliberate grouping of images. Aesthetic order is in accord with nature, and images are often integrated with the numerous hollows, crevices and seams of the rock itself. Pictograph sites are less extensive in scale and contain fewer image clusters. Although sites at Bon Echo Provincial Park in southern Ontario and at Lake Superior Provincial Park near Wawa, Ont, are well known, the majority of pictograph discoveries have been made in Quetico Park and at Lake of the Woods in northwestern Ontario.

Despite the lack of rock surfaces on the prairies, petroglyphs and pictographs are an important prehistoric art form of southern Saskatchewan and Alberta. Many pictographs have been found on isolated boulders and rocky outcrops along the foothills near Calgary, and there is an extensive series of small-scale petroglyphs incised on the sandstone bluffs of the MILK R in southern Alberta. They depict typical prairie Indian subject matter, mythological motifs such as THUNDERBIRD and shaman figures, and sometimes give evidence of European contact: horses, men bearing shields and guns, battle scenes with camp circles dotted with tipis, and a wheeled cart.

Some of the most intriguing images of Canadian rock art are painted on cliffs in interior BC. Those near Keremeos are probably abstractions of the spirits the shaman encountered in his visions. The BC coast has several petroglyph sites, though the few pictograph sites are probably more recent. Stylistically, West Coast rock art is unique in Canada, often showing form and subject-matter linkages with the later historic art of the 19th century.

Indian petroglyphs near Peterborough, Ont (*photo by John deVisser*).

Outstanding sites are located primarily on Vancouver I – Nanaimo Petroglyph Park and Sproat Lake – but sites have been discovered as far N as Prince Rupert and along the Nass and Skeena R system.

Only 2 rock-art sites have been discovered in the Canadian Arctic. At Qajartalik on a rocky outcrop in the Joy Bay region, Ungava, for example, a clustering of 44 human faces has been attributed to the prehistoric DORSET CULTURE.

Pictographs and petroglyphs in Canada were mentioned by explorers, travellers, and settlers in the late 18th and early 19th centuries. But significant records and studies appeared only after 1850, initially by American scholars. The first to illustrate and interpret pictographs from the point of view of the Indians themselves was Henry Rowe Schoolcraft, US Indian agent stationed at Sault Ste Marie, Mich, in the early 19th century. He described the pictographs at Agawa Bay near Wawa, Ont, and wrote on the practice and meaning of pictography among Algonquian speakers of N America in a 6-volume publication dated 1851-57.

The work of Col Garrick Mallery for the Smithsonian Inst, however, was primarily responsible for stimulating scholarly and popular interest in rock art. His still definitive survey, *Picture-Writing of the American Indians* (1893), includes descriptions and drawings of several Canadian sites in Nova Scotia, Ontario, Saskatchewan and BC. In 1887 and 1888, eg, Mallery visited and first recorded some of the extensive Kejimkujik petroglyphs in Nova Scotia.

Discoveries and accounts of rock art by Canadian authors appeared sporadically in the 1890s and more abundantly in the early decades of the 20th century. In BC, James A. TEIT reported on pictographs of interior BC (1896-1930) and in Ontario, one of Canada's pioneer archaeologists, David BOYLE, did most of the early rock art recording in that province, notably the first description and illustration in 1896 of the pictographs at Lake Mazinaw.

In these early years, too, Harlan I. Smith, archaeologist with the National Museum, wrote many of the earliest accounts of petroglyph sites along the BC coast (1906-1936), following upon initial discoveries on Vancouver I by the American anthropologist Franz BOAS (1891). While rock art research abated considerably across Canada between 1930 and the early 1950s, BC remained a focus of activity. Between 1936 and 1942, for example, Francis J. Barrow surveyed and reported (1942) on south coastal sites and the Norwegian archaeologist and rock art authority, Gutorm Gjessing, published 2 major studies of BC rock art (1952, 1958) after a cross-Canada survey undertaken in 1946-47. In 1949 BC novelist and author Edward Meade began recording coastal petroglyph sites from Alaska to as far south as Puget Sound, the results of which appeared in 1971. Starting in 1960, the same territory was

thoroughly covered by Beth and Ray Hill, whose lavishly illustrated book (1974) did much to attract public interest in BC rock art. On the BC interior, apiarist John Corner continued Teit's research. Corner's exhaustive search for pictograph sites resulted in a popular illustrated survey (1968), which remains a key publication for the region.

The 1960s were particularly rich years for rock art investigation in Canada, culminating with the foundation of the Canadian Rock Art Research Association (CRARA) in 1969. This national association of specialists devoted to research, public education and preservation of pictograph and petroglyph sites in Canada was instrumental in fostering public awareness and increased scholarly interest across the country through its biannual conferences and newsletters (1970-). Selwyn Dewdney (1909-79) was elected first senior associate in recognition of his long-standing contribution to rock art recording in the Canadian Shield and to public education. A commercial artist and art therapist, Dewdney had begun recording pictographs and petroglyphs for the Royal Ontario Museum in 1957. Aiming for a continuance of Boyle's pioneering work, Kenneth E. Kidd, then curator of ethnology, had sought funding for the systematic documentation of Ontario's rock art sites. With initial support of the Quetico Foundation, Dewdney was selected for the task of locating and recording new as well as forgotten sites in the rugged Shield. From 1957 to his death in 1979, Dewdney discovered and traced hundreds of sites throughout Ontario and westward to Manitoba, Saskatchewan and Alberta. The book co-authored by Dewdney and Kidd (1962, rev 1967) has stimulated enormous public interest in rock art of the Canadian Shield.

By the late 1960s, the scientific study of pictographs and petroglyphs had become widespread across Canada. More accurate systems of photographic as well as other means of recording have been applied and experiments have been undertaken, chiefly by scientists of the Canadian Conservation Institute, for the dating and preservation of unprotected rock art sites. In the 1970s and continuing into the 1980s, new sites have continued to be discovered by an entire new generation of investigators and research has tended recently to focus on the interpretation of both the function and meaning of rock art in the context of native culture and on the relationship of pictographs and petroglyphs to other forms of native visual expression.

JOAN M. VASTOKAS

Reading: John Corner, *Pictographs in the Interior of British Columbia* (1968); Selwyn Dewdney and Kenneth E. Kidd, *Indian Rock Paintings of the Great Lakes* (1962, rev 1967); Beth and Ray Hill, *Indian Petroglyphs of the Pacific Northwest* (1974); Edward Meade, *Indian Rock Carvings of the Pacific Northwest* (1974); Joan M. and Romas Vastokas, *Sacred Art of the Algonkians: A Study of the Peterborough Petroglyphs* (1973).

Picton, Ont, Town, pop 4235 (1986c), 4361 (1981c), inc 1837, seat of Prince Edward County, a peninsula of rolling farmland and sand beaches which juts out into Lk Ontario about 160 km E of Toronto. Located on an arm of the Bay of Quinte, Picton developed as a harbour and distribution centre for the surrounding countryside. It was originally settled by LOYALISTS in the 1780s and was first named Hallowell. During the 1820s the introduction of steamboats made the harbour more accessible to lake traffic. An adjacent village called Picton was laid out, and the 2 were amalgamated as Picton in 1837. Sir Thomas Picton was a British officer who died at the Battle of Waterloo. For 2 years, 1833-35, Sir John A. MACDONALD practised law here. Picton has remained a small lake port and service centre for an agricultural hinterland.

DANIEL FRANCIS

In the 17th century Pictou was an active port, shipping timber to Great Britain (*by permission of the British Library*).

Pictou, NS, Town, pop 4413 (1986c), 4628 (1981c), inc 1878, shire town of Pictou County is located on Pictou harbour adjacent to Northumberland Str and the Gulf of St Lawrence. The traditional centre of Scottish settlement in the Maritimes, it was first occupied by Micmac. Visited by French fur traders and missionaries, and later the site of a land grant to the Philadelphia Co (1762), its settlement followed the arrival of nearly 200 highland SCOTS on the HECTOR in 1773. By the early 19th century, it was an active and free port, shipping timber to Great Britain. Sawmills, foundries, tanneries, biscuit making and flour milling supported the export trade. Shipbuilding brought further prosperity. Scottish-styled stone houses and commercial buildings are still prominent on Water Street. Pictou Academy, founded by Thomas MCCULLOCH signalled the end of Anglican-dominated education in NS. J.W. DAWSON, McGill's first principal, was an academy graduate. Late 19th-century growth focused on port functions connecting northern NS to PEI, the Magdalen Is and Cape Breton I, but Pictou's isolated location eventually brought decline. Nearby towns were better situated to develop the county's coal and iron-ore resources. Railways and highways bypassed the town. Today, Pictou benefits from an administrative role, some marine industries and tourism based on its rich Scottish heritage.

L.D. MCCANN

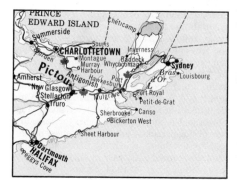

Pidgeon, George Campbell, Presbyterian and United Church minister (b at Grand-Cascapédia, Qué 2 Mar 1872; d at Toronto 15 June 1971). After being ordained (1894) and earning his DD from Presbyterian Coll, Montréal, Pidgeon served churches in Montréal, Streetsville, Ont, and Toronto. He taught practical theology at Westminster Hall, Vancouver (1909-15), then served Bloor St United Church, Toronto, from 1915 until his retirement in 1948. From 1949 until 1960 he wrote a religious column for the Toronto *Telegram*. Pidgeon led the Presbyterian Church into the union of 1925 and was unanimously elected the first moderator of the UNITED CHURCH OF CANADA. During his long and distinguished career, he was a staunch supporter of temperance and home mission work and helped promote the World Alliance of Reformed Churches, the Canadian Council of Churches and the World Council of Churches. He was chief spokesman of the United Church and was its embodiment to the country and to the Christian community. NEIL SEMPLE

Pidgeon, Lloyd Montgomery, chemist (b at Markham, Ont 3 Dec 1903). After studies at McGill under Otto MAASS (1927-29) and at Oxford (1929-31), Pidgeon joined the NATIONAL RESEARCH COUNCIL in Ottawa, initially working on electrochemical problems. During this period he developed his well-known process for the production of magnesium metal of high purity (*see* METALLURGY). Because of the demand for magnesium during WWII, 6 magnesium plants were built throughout N America. In Canada, his discovery led to the formation of Dominion Magnesium Ltd, which he joined in 1941 as director of research. In 1943 Pidgeon was appointed professor and head of the dept of metallurgical engineering at U of T. There he built a strong graduate school in metallurgy of worldwide reputation. Although he was a chemist by background, his appreciation of the physics of metals led to the growth of physical metallurgy within his department. Under Pidgeon's leadership, the department expanded into materials science in 1965, thus catalyzing creation of a Materials Research Interdisciplinary Group within the Faculty of Applied Science and Engineering. J.M. TOGURI

Pierce, Lorne Albert, publisher, editor, writer (b at Delta, Ont 3 Aug 1890; d at Toronto 27 Nov 1961). Editor in chief of RYERSON PRESS 1922-60, Pierce championed Canadian writers and writing for over 40 years. He attended Queen's; Victoria College, Toronto; Union Theological Seminary, NY; NY University; and United Theological College, Montréal. He was ordained a Methodist minister in 1916. Pastoral work, in Ottawa and elsewhere, and wartime army service preceded his association with Ryerson Press in 1920, briefly as literary adviser, then as editor. Pierce typified the enthusiastic nationalism of English Canada in the 1920s: he launched the important Ryerson Chapbook poetry series, the pioneering Makers of Canadian Literature volumes of criticism, and the textbook series, The Ryerson Books of Prose and Verse.

Pierce's own writings include studies of William KIRBY and Marjorie Pickthall, a critique and an anthology of Canadian literature, and editions of the poetry of Pickthall and Bliss CARMAN. In 1926 he established the Lorne Pierce Medal of the RSC for literary achievement and in 1927 the Edith and Lorne Pierce Collection of Canadian Literature at Queen's. He was prominent in the Canadian Authors' Assn, the Canadian Bibliographical Soc, the Canadian Writers' Foundation, the ROYAL ONTARIO MUSEUM and the Art Gallery of Toronto (ART GALLERY OF ONTARIO). In 1940 Pierce was a founder of what became the Canadian Hearing Society, a by-product of his own deafness. SANDRA CAMPBELL

Reading: C.H. Dickinson, *Lorne Pierce* (1965).

Pigeon (Columbidae), large family (300 species) of birds, many of which are called doves, distributed throughout temperate and tropical areas worldwide. Species vary from sparrow size to that of a female turkey. Many are plainly attired but some Old World, tropical species are strikingly coloured in green, red, orange or purple. All are characterized by a plump body with short neck, small head and short, slender bill with a fleshy, naked area at its base. All drink by immersing the bill and sucking up water. Vocalizations are mostly cooing sounds. Six species are known in Canada. The mourning dove (*Zenaida macroura*) inhabits both open woods and groves and farmland

transcontinentally, extending to northern Manitoba and Saskatchewan, but it is restricted to the extreme southernmost parts on both coasts. Band-tailed pigeon (*Columba fasciata*) prefers open woods, edges and openings in southwestern BC. Wild populations of rock dove (*C. livia*), a widely domesticated Eurasian species, are common in cities, towns and farmland across Canada. The PASSENGER PIGEON (*Ectopistes migratorius*) is now extinct. All but rock dove are migratory, however, some mourning doves winter in southern Canada. W. EARL GODFREY

Pika, common name for smallest members of order LAGOMORPHA, which also includes RABBITS and HARES. Pikas are like guinea pigs in size and shape, have relatively short legs, no external tail and almost circular, prominent, external ears. They are distributed discontinuously along the W coast of N America and throughout Asia and European Russia. They are known by various names including cony and rock rabbit, the latter referring to the fact that N American and some Asian pikas occur only in rocky habitats. Two species are known in Canada; 18 worldwide. Rocky Mountain pika (*Ochotona princeps*) is found throughout the Rocky Mts in BC and Alberta. Collared pika (*O. collaris*) is found in northern BC and throughout YT and Alaska. Pikas are versatile feeders, eating most plants in their habitat. As they do not hibernate, pikas gather cuttings of preferred plants, cure them in sheltered, sunny places, and store them among rocks for winter use. Pikas are diurnal and both Canadian species are colonial. Within a colony, individuals tend to occupy exclusive home ranges but during breeding season, male and female ranges overlap. Breeding generally occurs twice, in spring and summer; 2-6 offspring are born per litter. Although of no direct economic value to man, pikas are an important source of food for many furbearing mammals.

M.L. WESTON

Pike, common name for the group of 5 species of predaceous freshwater fish with elongated snouts, sharp teeth, cylindrical bodies and forked tails, belonging to family Esocidae, order Salmoniformes, class Osteichthyes. Northern pike (*Esox lucius*) is circumpolar in distribution; amur pike (*E. reicherti*) is native to Siberia and China; MUSKELLUNGE (*E. masquinongy*) and PICKEREL (*E. niger* and *E. americanus*) are confined to N America. Pikes are lie-in-wait predators, rushing on prey from cover, capturing it sideways, then returning to cover to turn the victim around and swallow it head first. The northern pike is the fish most commonly thought of as "pike." It is a large, soft-rayed fish with an oval body and a large, flattened head with duck-billed snout, well armed with large teeth. The single dorsal fin and the anal and caudal (tail) fins are close together. The northern pike is distinguished by a pattern of horizontal rows of bean-shaped, yellow spots on a green to brown background, 4-6 pores on the underside of each lower jaw, and the presence of scales over the whole of the cheeks and half of the gill covers. Pike spawn in early spring (Apr-May); adults often move towards spawning grounds under the ice. No nest is built; no parental care is provided. Adults eat other fishes almost exclusively. Reproductive capability is achieved at 2-4 years of age. Specimens are known to exceed 24 years of age, 1-1.5 m in length and 14-20 kg in weight. The N American angler record fish, caught in 1940, was 133.3 cm long and weighed 20.92 kg. The record for Canada, caught in Saskatchewan in 1954, weighed 19.39 kg. The northern pike occurs throughout Canada, except in the Maritimes, Gaspé, most arctic coastal areas and all but the

Northern pike (*Esox lucius*), which inhabits warm to cool lakes and rivers, is a commercial as well as a sport fish (*artwork by Claire Tremblay*).

NE corner of BC. This species inhabits warm to cool lakes, rivers and large ponds, usually in association with aquatic vegetation. The northern pike is subject to cancerous lymphosarcoma and to a disease called red sore. Pike carry parasites known as yellow grub (in the flesh) and blackspot (on the skin) which cannot infect humans and are killed when the pike are properly cooked. In certain locations, pike carry the broad tapeworm, which can be transferred to humans. Northern pike is a commercial fish as well as a sport fish. It ranks fourth, by weight, of fish taken annually in Saskatchewan. In 1984, the total Canadian commercial harvest was 3233 t, with a value to fishermen of $2.4 million. E.J. CROSSMAN

Pilgrimage, journey to a sacred place for religious or spiritual purposes. There are several sites in Canada which attract many Canadian and foreign pilgrims. Foremost are the CATHOLIC shrines of Québec, the oldest being the church of STE-ANNE-DE-BEAUPRÉ, some 30 km NE of Québec City. During construction of the first shrine on this site in 1658, the miraculous cure of a workman was reported. Other cures followed, and the shrine soon became renowned for miracles. Pilgrims and patrons came, among them Anne of Austria, mother of Louis XIV of France. Today the stone basilica attracts over 250 000 pilgrims per year. The principal gathering is on the feast of Ste Anne (July 26). A more recent shrine which now enjoys great popularity is St Joseph's Oratory on Mount Royal, Montréal. The pious Brother ANDRÉ, a member of the Order of the Holy Cross and a devotee of St Joseph, built the first small chapel to the saint in 1904. A stone crypt was added in 1917. A basilica with a capacity of 5000, begun in 1922, now stands on the site. The annual number of pilgrims today exceeds 3 million, with the largest gatherings on May 10 and Labour Day.

Ste-Anne-de-Beaupré and St Joseph's Oratory attract pilgrims because of their fame as sites of miracles. The SAINTS of these shrines are now popularly believed to be effective intercessors, taking the pilgrim's message to God. The long racks of crutches and canes, braces and corsets discarded by pilgrims are seen to bear testimony to the many healing miracles that have occurred. For those who do not seek a miracle, the shrines offer objects of devotion for prayers.

The basilica of Cap-de-la-Madeleine at Trois-Rivières is another important Catholic shrine in Québec. The First Plenary Council of Québec declared the church a shrine of national pilgrimage in 1909. In 1964 the church at the shrine was given the status of minor basilica.

Another shrine to Ste Anne at LAC STE ANNE, Alta, attracts large numbers of native Indians from across Canada to a pilgrimage of several days, culminating on July 26, the saint's day. Healing is an important feature of this pilgrimage as well.

The shrine of STE MARIE AMONG THE HURONS near

Midland, Ont, reflects another aspect of the history of Catholic interactions with the native people. Six of N America's 8 martyred saints (killed between 1642 and 1649) were missionaries here.

Religious and ethnic communities have developed and supported their own pilgrimage centres. The Polish population visits the Grotto of Our Lady of Lourdes at Skaro, Alta, for the Vesper of the feast of the Assumption of the Holy Virgin (Aug 15). The first Ukrainian church in Canada, at Gardenton, Man, is the site of an annual pilgrimage for that community.

Canadians also travel outside Canada to centres sacred to the various religions. Thousands of Muslims (*see* ISLAM) annually make the *hajj* (pilgrimage) to Mecca and Medina in Saudi Arabia, places made holy through their importance in the life of the prophet Muhammad. Christians make pilgrimages to Rome, Canterbury, Lourdes, Fatima and many other shrines. Muslims, Christians and JEWS all journey to Jerusalem for their devotions. HINDUS and BUDDHISTS visit the many shrines of India. Through their journeys the faithful renew connections with the global centres of their religions.

Pilgrimage was formerly a difficult, dangerous austerity from which the pilgrim could not be sure of returning. Although today the sacred journey may appear to resemble a package tour more than a spiritual exercise, it is still an important feature of popular religion. In an uncertain and sorrow-laden world, there is magnetism in places where the divine is believed to manifest itself in a living, active, miraculous form to heal the sick and ease the burden of the faithful.   ALAN MORINIS

Reading: P. Boglioni and B. Lacroix, eds, *Les Pèlerinages au Québec* (1981).

Pilon, Jean-Guy, writer (b at Saint-Polycarpe, Qué 12 Nov 1930). He studied at the Valleyfield seminary (1943-48) and the Coll Bourget in Rigaud (BA 1951); he received his LLL (1954) from U de Montréal. At first a producer for Radio-Canada talk shows, he was named (1970) head of cultural programming, a position he occupied until 1985 when he returned to production. Co-founder of the magazine *Liberté* (1959), he has published a narrative and 8 poetry collections, for which he has received the Prix David (poetry, 1956), the Prix Louise-Labé and the Prix France-Canada (1969), the Gov Gen's Award (1970) for his retrospective *Comme eau retenu*, plus the Prix Athanse-David (1984) for his work as a whole. From his early poems, in *La fiancée du matin* (1953) to "Dix phrases pour Jérusalem," which was published in *Estuaire* (1977), he has evolved from poetry of largely romantic inspiration to a much simpler and more concise writing style combining a strong sentiment of love with an awareness of nature. He was elected fellow of the RSC in 1967 and was made Officer of the Order of Canada in 1987.   ROGER CHAMBERLAND

Pilot, Robert Wakeham, painter (b at St John's 9 Oct 1898; d at Montréal 17 Dec 1967), stepson of painter Maurice CULLEN. Pilot's best pictures are moody views of the St Lawrence R, such as *Quebec from Levis,* and seascapes of NS and NB. Pilot is also widely recognized as the painter of snow-covered Rockies that contributed to the prevailing view of Canada as a country of blue and white peaks with pink and purple shadows. He studied in Paris (1920-22), then returned to work with William BRYMNER, Edmond DYONNET, and Cullen in Montréal. His later oils, sketches and murals had a stiff literal quality, but his work was well received. He was elected associate of the Royal Canadian Academy of Arts in 1925, and was president 1952-54.   ANNE MCDOUGALL

Pimlott, Douglas Humphreys, conservationist, wildlife biologist, ecologist, environmentalist

(b at Quyon, Qué 4 Jan 1920; d at Richmond Hill, Ont 31 July 1978). A founder of the modern environmental movement in Canada, Pimlott advocated the conservation of wolves as predators with a rightful place in nature. He eliminated the wolf bounty in Ontario and launched conservation programs in Europe where only a few wolves remained. He was also one of the first spokesmen in the 1970s for protecting the northern Canadian environment. Pimlott directed a number of Canadian environmental organizations, founded the Canada-US Environmental Council and chaired an international wolf specialist group. He taught at U of T and published many professional articles and books, including *The Ecology of the Timber Wolf in Algonquin Park* (repr 1978), and coauthored *Oil Under the Ice* (1976).   MONTE HUMMEL

Pinawa, Man, Local Government District, pop 2078 (1986c), 2011 (1981c) is located 120 km NE of Winnipeg on the Winnipeg R at the mouth of the Lee R (Pinawa Chan). Pinawa derives its name from a Cree term meaning "quiet waters." Old Pinawa was first developed in 1903 when the Winnipeg Electric Street Railway Co began construction of a hydroelectric generating plant at the site. Electricity was produced there from 1906 until 1951. The LGD was established in 1960 when the federal crown corporation, Atomic Energy Canada Ltd, decided to build its WHITESHELL NUCLEAR RESEARCH ESTABLISHMENT just downstream from a new townsite at Pinawa which would house its employees. AECL initially owned most of the housing and infrastructure, is still the town's major employer and remains the principal source of town revenues.
    JOHN SELWOOD

Pincher Creek, Alta, Town, pop 3800 (1986c), inc 1906. Pincher Creek was established in 1878 as a police post and farm on Pincher's Creek. In the 1880s several police retired there to ranch. In the heart of the large ranch leases it served as the commercial centre for the Walrond, Roodee and Alberta ranches. In 1882 the townsite was laid out by C. Kettles; the first store was constructed in 1883 and the town itself incorporated in 1906. T. Lebel and Co, based in the town, became the largest merchandising concern in southern Alberta. In the early 1900s wheat farming and in the 1940s gas processing became critical additions to the economic base.   FRITS PANNEKOEK

Pine (genus *Pinus*), evergreen CONIFERS for which the Pinaceae family is named. The 80-90 species

---

Jack pine (*Pinus banksiana*), with male flowers (left) and cones (*artwork by Claire Tremblay*).

occur in the Northern Hemisphere; 9 in Canada. Most are trees but some are shrubs. Long, needle-like leaves are found in clusters of 2-8 (rarely one) on dwarf shoots. Seed cones are woody, often with sharp spines on scales. Each scale bears 2, usually winged, seeds, maturing the year after POLLINATION. Most are either "soft" pines with 5 needles per shoot or "hard" pines with 2-3 per shoot. The most familiar soft pines are western white pine (*P. monticola*) of BC, and eastern white pine (*P. strobus*), east of Manitoba. Others include limber pine (*P. flexilis*) and whitebark pine (*P. albicaulis*) of the western mountains. Hard pines include ponderosa pine (*P. ponderosa*) and lodgepole pine (*P. contorta*) in the West, jack pine (*P. banksiana*) in the boreal forest, red pine (*P. resinosa*) and pitch pine (*P. rigida*) in the East. Eastern white pine provides a very valuable softwood which was exported from New France as early as 1700, as well as being used in the colony for construction and shipbuilding. As a group, pines are still the most common Canadian conifers and yield lumber, pulp and paper. *See also* FORESTRY; TIMBER TRADE HISTORY; VEGETATION REGIONS.   JOHN N. OWENS

Pine Pass, elev 874 m, crosses the continental divide NW-SE in northeastern BC. The Pine R rises southwest of the pass then flows NW to meet the Peace R, near Fort St John. The most northerly and lowest of the 6 highway passes through the ROCKY MTS, it was known by whites as early as 1806, when one of Simon FRASER's men deserted and travelled this way. Joseph Hunter "rediscovered" the pass in 1877 as a possible CPR route. Hart Hwy crosses it, linking Prince George and Dawson Creek.   GLEN BOLES

Pine Point, NWT, Town, pop 1558 (1986c), 1861 (1981c), inc 1974, is located 10 km inland from the S shore of GREAT SLAVE LK, 190 air km S of YELLOWKNIFE. The discovery of lead-zinc deposits near this mining town were closely related to the KLONDIKE GOLD RUSH. In 1898 prospectors, heading overland to the Yukon, met a party of DENE who had musket bullets and fish weights, fashioned from local metal. Originally the metal deposits were considered uneconomic because they lacked silver. But in the early 1920s the deposits began to be considered for their lead-zinc content alone. Further exploration took place in 1948 and Pine Point Mines, owned by Cominco Ltd, was formed in 1951. Production started in 1965, but by the mid-1980s depressed prices caused economic difficulties for the mine. Cominco shut down operations in summer 1987, although it continued to mill until the following spring. The population of the community is expected to drop to 20-50 people by the 1989.   ANNELIES POOL

Pingo, ice-cored hill typically conical in shape, growing and persisting only in PERMAFROST. "Pingo" is of Inuit origin and was first used by the botanist A.E. PORSILD (1938) to describe the ice-cored hills typical of the Mackenzie Delta. Subsequently, the term has been widely adopted elsewhere in Canada and in Alaska and Greenland. In the USSR the equivalent is *bulganniakh,* of Yakut origin. Pingos range from a few metres to several tens of metres in height. The greatest concentration (about 1450) and some of the largest in the world occur in the Tuktoyaktuk area of the Mackenzie Delta. Two of the best known are Ibyuk, 50 m high and about 1000 years old, and Aklisuktuk ("the one that is growing"), first sketched by the explorer John RICHARDSON in 1848. Other concentrations occur in the interior of the YT, along the western coastal plains of the northern YT and Alaska, and on BANKS ISLAND. Pingos grow through the freezing of water which moves under a pressure gradient to the site of the

Pingo on Tuktoyaktuk Peninsula, NWT. The pingo's unique shape is caused by the force of freezing water (*photo by Fred Bruemmer*).

pingo. If water moves from a distant, elevated source, the pingo is a hydraulic-system pingo (eg, open-system pingos of Alaska, the YT and Greenland). If water moves under hydrostatic pressure resulting from local permafrost aggradation, then the pingo is a hydrostatic-system pingo (eg, closed-system pingos of the Mackenzie Delta and Banks I). The latter type typically forms in recently drained lake basins or drainage channels. Field studies by J.R. Mackay in the Mackenzie Delta indicate that pore water expulsion and the accumulation of subpingo water lenses can lead to rapid pingo growth (0.1-0.5 m/year), especially in the initial stages.   HUGH M. FRENCH

Pinky Schooner, ancient type of vessel adapted to a primitive sloop or schooner rig in the British N American colonies and widely used in the Maritime provinces until the early 1900s. Often less than 14 m long, they were cheap to build and ideally suited for fishing. The distinctive upward sweep of the bulwarks protected the outside rudder and gave shelter to the man at the tiller – an obvious advantage to the exposed head of most colonial ships. "Pinks" were popular in NS for mackerel jigging and were used in the WAR OF 1812 as privateers. Today the pink is still occasionally seen as a cruising yacht. The origin of the name is unknown.   JAMES MARSH

Pinsent, Gordon Edward, actor, writer (b at Grand Falls, Nfld 12 July 1930). Diversely talented, he began his successful career as an actor in Winnipeg where he joined John HIRSCH's Theatre 77. He appeared in many stage roles in Winnipeg, Toronto and at the STRATFORD FESTIVAL, and performed on radio and TV, including the title role in the notable CBC TV series *Quentin Durgens MP* (1966-69). Newfoundland settings and characters are important in his writings. Pinsent, who is responsible for many of his own best roles, wrote the screen play and the musical version of *The Rowdyman* (film released 1972), playing the charming and irresponsible character in both. *The Rowdyman* was published as a novel in 1973 and was followed by *John and the Missus* in 1974. He also adapted the latter for the stage, playing the leading role at NEPTUNE THEATRE in Halifax. He wrote the screenplay for *John and the Missus* (film released in 1986) and won the Genie Award as best actor for his portrayal of the title character. His other Canadian film appearances include *Who Has Seen the Wind, Silence of the North* and *Klondike Fever*. He received a Genie Award as Best Supporting Actor for *Klondike Fever* (1980) and was named best actor for *The Rowdyman*. He created and appeared in the CBC series *A Gift to*

Last, for which he received an ACTRA Award in 1979.   JAMES DeFELICE

Pioneer Life As each new area of Canada was opened to European settlement, pioneers faced the difficult task of building homes and communities from the ground up. Pioneer life revolved around providing the basic necessities of existence in a northern wilderness – food, shelter, fuel and clothing – and adapting familiar institutions (churches, schools, local government, and the web of social manners and customs) to new conditions. Some pioneer settlers brought personal belongings, including furniture, kitchen utensils, books and ornaments; some settled on land prepared by COLONIZATION COMPANIES or within reach of villages or towns. For most, however, and especially before roads, canals and railways provided communication and transportation of goods, pioneering on all Canada's frontiers meant isolation, deprivation and hardship, success being measured by sheer survival. Yet, usually within a few years, primitive pioneering was followed by relative comfort, and the prospect of security and even prosperity for one's children. Thus, persistence, optimism, thrift, resourcefulness and the acceptance of unremitting hard work became character traits valued by succeeding generations long after pioneer conditions had passed.

Pioneer houses varied with local building materials and the newcomers' origins and means, but all had to be designed to withstand Canada's long, cold winters. A settler's first house was typically a one-room structure made of logs, fieldstone, spruce poles or prairie sod (*see* LOG HOUSES; SOD HOUSES). Frame or brick houses with partitions, second storeys, glass windows and shingled roofs signalled the end of pioneering, as the original dwelling became a stable. Furniture was often homemade, eg, the chair made from a barrel described by Catharine Parr TRAILL in *The Female Emigrant's Guide* (1854). Also homemade were the cloth for blankets and clothing; carpets to cover unplaned wood floors; pails and children's toys. The mending of boots, harness and tinware might await an itinerant tradesman. Providing fuel for the huge fireplaces, usually the dwelling's only source of heat, was a constant chore; timber, although plentiful in many areas, had to be felled, trimmed, cut into lengths and carried home.

Pioneer diet depended on local produce and was generally nourishing but monotonous. Diaries and travellers' accounts (*see* EXPLORATION AND TRAVEL LITERATURE) tell of pork served 3 times a day, month in and month out, varied only by coarsely ground meal cakes, stewed dried apples or preserved small fruits and berries, and potatoes and other root vegetables. But game, fish and wildfowl were abundant in most places, and home gardens, dairy cattle and domestic fowl soon led to a more rounded and appetizing menu.

The characteristic CO-OPERATIVE principle that found expression in community work parties ("bees"), whether for house building, barn raising, clearing fields or making quilts, was reflected in local organization as well as in relations between the sexes. A church might serve Presbyterians in the morning and Methodists at night; a school district would speedily be formed, with the teacher being paid by local assessment and "boarded around" in the community. Settlers worked together to build roads, to attract tradesmen and small industry, and generally to promote the prosperity of their district.

Although pioneers on fur-trading, lumbering, mining and ranching frontiers were usually single men, women joined in the settlement of NEW

FRANCE in the 17th and 18th centuries, of the MARITIMES and UPPER CANADA from 1760 to 1860, and throughout the prairie HOMESTEADING era, 1870-1914. Women's work was essential to the comfort and long-term success of a farm operation, and Canadian immigration and the DOMINION LANDS POLICY encouraged family life as a guarantee of social stability and a larger population. Pioneer women worked tirelessly for their family's material and cultural betterment, and although they suffered loneliness and hardship, their courage and strength gave them a place of respect in Canadian life.   SUSAN JACKEL

Reading: E.C. Guillet, *Pioneer Days in Upper Canada* (1933); J.G. MacGregor, *North-West of Sixteen* (1958); A.Y. Morris, *Gentle Pioneers* (1966); L. Rasmussen et al, comp, *A Harvest Yet to Reap* (1976); Catharine Parr Traill, *The Backwoods of Canada* (1936).

Pipeline In the late 1940s, sufficient reserves of oil and natural gas were developed in Alberta to justify their transportation to markets in the East and the US. Since pipelines are the most economical method of transporting liquids and gases, the Canadian pipeline system grew rapidly. This system is currently the second longest in the world (242 000 km), ranking after the US (2 080 000 km) and tied with the USSR (242 000 km). Alberta has the most developed system with 105 850 km, followed by Ontario with 52 690 km, Saskatchewan with 43 120 km, BC with 24 570 km, Manitoba with 8380 km and Québec with 6060 km. In total, 200 100 km carry gas and 42 300 km carry oil and liquid products.

Structure of the System A simple pipeline is a long length of pipe with pumps, valves and control devices for conveying liquids or gases. A pipeline network consists of gathering systems, main trunk lines and distribution systems. These parts are analogous to the roots, trunk and branches of a tree. The gathering system transports a mixture of oil, gas and sometimes water from the production wells to collection points such as a gas processing plant or a treating facility where the water is removed and the oil and gas are separated. Most of the gathering lines are located in the West.

The trunk or main pipelines move oil or gas at high pressures over long distances through large diameter pipes from the collection points to the market centres. Energy to overcome friction is supplied by pump or compressor stations spaced at approximately 100 km intervals. As markets expand, the capacity of the trunk lines is increased by installing parallel lines (loops) or adding more pumps or compressors. The location and construction starting dates of the major trunk lines are shown on the map. Although the initial construction is complete in 2 to 3 years, additional construction may continue for decades as the capacity of the line is increased to meet market demands.

In the case of oil, trunk lines supply the refineries which, in turn, distribute the products to the retailer by truck or product pipelines. Product pipelines move more than one product at a time. This is done by pumping batches of each commodity, say gasoline and diesel fuel, one after the other. Most product lines are located near population centres in the East, although the Cochin line crosses much of the country (Edmonton to Sarnia via the US).

Natural gas is withdrawn from the trunk line and delivered to the consumer via the distribution system. This part of the network is the longest of the 3 systems. The total length of the distribution systems is about equally divided between eastern and western Canada. Typically, the pipes in this system are of small diameter and are operated at low pressure.

Regulations and Politics The first Pipe Line Act

Major Pipelines

Oil Pipelines

Name	Start of Construction
Portland/Montréal	1941
Interprovincial	1950
Lakehead	1950
Trans-Mountain	1951
Rangeland	1956
Peace River	1957
Norman Wells	1984

Gas Pipelines

Consumers'	pre-1890
TransCanada	1955
Nova	1956
West Coast	1956
Alberta Natural Gas	1960
Foothills	1980
T Q and M	1981

Product Pipelines

TransNorthern	1952
Alberta Products Pipeline	1970
Cochin	1977

Province	Liquids	Gas	Total
Alberta	24 256	81 595	105 850
BC	2 484	22 081	24 570
Sask	8 078	35 040	43 120
Man	2 157	6 227	8 380
Ont	3 593	49 093	52 690
Qué	594	5 463	6 060
Canada	42 273	200 085	242 360
USSR	78 000	165 000	242 000
US	276 000	1 803 000	2 079 000

was passed in 1949. In 1959 the federal government established the National Energy Board which has the authority to regulate pipelines crossing provincial or international borders. The primary function of this body is to issue export permits and set pipeline tariffs. In addition the NEB considers allied issues such as petroleum reserve estimates, costs, environmental factors and engineering and safety practices. Occasionally a commission is appointed to examine a particular issue, as was the case for the MACKENZIE VALLEY PIPELINE where environmental and land claims posed difficult problems.

Pipeline construction has been politically controversial with debate raging about many major lines. Intense controversy surrounded the TRANS-CANADA PIPELINE (*see* PIPELINE DEBATE) and the Mackenzie Valley pipeline, which was never built. However, the construction of the NORMAN WELLS pipeline, which follows the MacKenzie R for 520 km, was completed with little objection. Once the political issues are resolved, the design, construction and operation of all portions of the pipeline system are subject to governmental regulations. All pipelines must conform to accepted engineering, environmental and safety standards of federal as well as provincial jurisdictions.

Pipeline Technology Most pipelines are constructed of steel, although plastic and aluminum are sometimes used in natural-gas distribution networks. Steel pipelines are formed by welding short (20 m) sections of pipe together. After the welds are x-rayed, the pipe is wrapped with a protective coating and then buried. All pipelines, regardless of type, are inspected and pressure tested before being used. Small diameter plastic lines are commonly "plowed in" instead of being laid in a trench. The plastic pipe is unreeled from a large spool through a special plow which is pulled by a large tractor. This method is quick and causes very little surface disturbance. The usual depth of burial is about 1.5 m for large pipes and slightly less for small pipes, although the Interprovincial crosses the Strait of Mackinac at water depths exceeding 70 m. Canada is the world leader in winter pipeline construction, having developed unique trenching machines for permafrost and muskeg. Canadian pipeline companies are designing and constructing pipelines in the USSR, China and Southeast Asia.

Pipelines are operated every day of the year. Increasingly, the operation of the pipelines is directed by a computer from a remote control room. This technology allows the pressure, flow and energy consumption throughout the line to be monitored continuously. The computer can do leak detection calculations quickly and initiate remedial action such as closing emergency valves, shutting off pumps and alerting repair crews. As a

Pipeline being laid across the Chalk R, near Petawawa, Ont, by TransCanada Pipelines (*photo by Jim Merrithew*).

further precaution, periodic tests are made to assure the safe operation of lines. Occasionally wax and foreign material are removed from oil lines by "pigging." A pig is a bristle-covered cylinder which is pushed through the pipeline by the fluid pressure moving the wax in front of it. The term pig is derived from the squeal made as the bristles rub against the pipe wall. "Smart pigs" are equipped with sensors and recorders so that the inside of the line can be inspected for corrosion and weak spots.

Future Technology No major breakthroughs are expected in land-based pipelines; however, technology is evolving to accommodate the increasing amount of heavy oil being produced. These technologies include heated lines, piping of heavy oils diluted with a light oil and pumping an emulsion of heavy oil and chemically treated water. The Canadian climate imposes 2 serious problems for off-shore underwater piping systems: pack ice and icebergs. In the high arctic islands, pipelines must be trenched completely through the pack ice before being laid on the ocean floor. Large-scale tests are now under way to develop this technology. Off the East Coast, icebergs gouge the ocean floor to a depth of 50 m when they approach the shoreline. Since these gouges are deeper than pipelines can currently be buried, new technologies are being developed to overcome this problem.   J.T. RYAN

Pipeline Debate, 8 May-6 June 1956, one of the most famous confrontations in Canadian parliamentary history. Liberal Minister of Trade and Commerce C.D. HOWE decided that a PIPELINE to carry natural gas from Alberta to central Canada was a national necessity. Howe argued that it must run entirely in Canada and deliver to Canadian consumers. The project required very large sums of capital and specialized products and expertise. In 1954 Howe assembled a private syndicate of Canadian and American businessmen to give effect to TRANSCANADA PIPELINES, a corporate shell incorporated in 1951; a temporary predominance of the Americans in the syndicate raised charges that the pipeline was a sellout to American interests. After many vicissitudes, a bill to authorize the pipeline and provide a loan for part of its construction was introduced in May 1956. Social Credit supported it, but the CCF and the Progressive Conservatives attacked the bill from

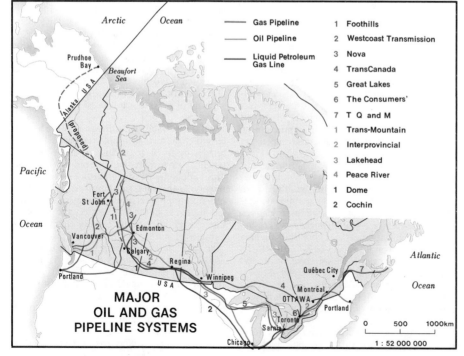

MAJOR OIL AND GAS PIPELINE SYSTEMS

| Gas Pipeline | | Oil Pipeline | | Liquid Petroleum Gas Line |

1 Foothills
2 Westcoast Transmission
3 Nova
4 TransCanada
5 Great Lakes
6 The Consumers'
7 T Q and M
1 Trans-Mountain
2 Interprovincial
3 Lakehead
4 Peace River
1 Dome
2 Cochin

0   500   1000km

1 : 52 000 000

every angle. The CCF preferred public ownership; the Conservatives objected to what they saw as American control. But these substantive concerns were overshadowed by the procedural issue of CLOSURE, by which the Liberals placed a strict time limit on debate. As they and the Opposition knew, laying the pipe had to begin by early June or nothing could be done until the next year. The government charged obstruction and the Opposition charged dictatorship, but the bill passed. A 3700 km pipeline was completed from Burstall, Sask, to Montréal by Oct 1958, and TransCanada became a principally Canadian-owned company. The debate, however, discredited Howe and the Liberals, and contributed to their defeat in the 1957 general election. ROBERT BOTHWELL

Pipes, William Thomas, lawyer, politician, premier of NS (b at Amherst, NS 15 Apr 1850; d at Boston, Mass 7 Oct 1909). Pipes, a leading figure in the NS Liberal Party, held various Cabinet posts and was premier between 1882 and 1884. During the provincial election of 1886 he created consternation within party circles, referring to Premier FIELDING's secession from the Confederation campaign as "the putrid carcass of repeal." In part his opposition reflected his attachment to the industrial development of his home town of Amherst. At his death, Pipes was a director of Amherst Boot and Shoe Manufacturing Co, a large shareholder in the Rhodes Curry Co, director and secretary of the Nova Scotia Lumber Co and attorney general of the province. COLIN D. HOWELL

Pipit, common name for some birds of the family Motacillidae, which also includes wagtails. The family, comprising 54 species, occurs worldwide except on some oceanic islands. Only 3 species occur regularly in Canada: yellow wagtail (*Motacilla flava*), water pipit (*Anthus spinoletta*) and Sprague's pipit (*A. spragueii*). These small passerines (perching birds) range in length from 12 to 22 cm. Plumage varies from black, grey or brown, to olive or yellow and may be plain or streaked. Outer tail feathers are often white. The bill tends to be long, slender and pointed. Legs and toes are often long; the hind toe is elongated in most species. These birds are mainly terrestrial and habitually "wag" their tails when on the ground. They feed primarily on insects, spiders and small molluscs. They are gregarious, particularly out of breeding season. The nest is a cuplike, sometimes domed, structure built on the ground, in rock cavities, walls or trees. Parents share incubation of the 2-7 speckled eggs and feeding of young. Pipits and wagtails have simple, repetitive songs, often delivered in flight, sometimes very high above the ground. HENRI OUELLET

Piracy, seizure and robbery of craft at sea or in the air, has played only a slight role in Canada's history. In 1612 Peter EASTON, an English pirate, embarked on a series of raids on English, French and Portuguese fishing fleets in Newfoundland harbours from Trinity Bay to Ferryland; he inflicted little injury but caused an estimated £20 400 damage. Much of Canada's piracy centers on tales of buried booty. A fabulous treasure ascribed to William Kidd (hanged in 1701) is reputed to be buried on OAK I, off Nova Scotia's S shore. More certain is the June 1720 attack on Trepassey, Nfld, by Bartholomew ROBERTS, the most successful corsair of piracy's Golden Age. Roberts captured 22 merchant ships and 4 vessels, and sank a few fishing boats. Proceeding to the Grand Banks, he captured 6 French vessels. Roberts, who during his 4-year career captured 400 ships, was apprehended in 1722 by ships of the Royal Navy off West Africa.

Halifax has been the site of 2 piracy trials. In 1809 Edward and Margaret Jordan and a sailor named Kelly were tried for seizing the *Three Sisters*, previously owned by Jordan, and for murdering a number of the crew. The vessel's master, John Stairs, threw himself overboard on a hatch cover upon which he floated 4 hours before being picked up by an American fisherman. Margaret and Kelly were acquitted, but Edward Jordan was found guilty of murder and piracy and was hanged on 23 Nov 1809. His tarred and chained corpse was gibbeted at the entrance to Halifax Harbour.

In 1843 Capt George Fielding and his son sought passage home to England from Peru. Sailing from Valparaiso on the barque *Saladin*, Fielding successfully persuaded some crew members to seize the vessel and murder 6 shipmates. Under Fielding's command the *Saladin*, with a valuable cargo of guano, copper and silver, a chest of dollars and several money letters, set course for Newfoundland. So terrified of Fielding were his fellow conspirators that they threw him and his son into the sea. The *Saladin* went aground near Country Harbour, NS. The crew members were charged with piracy, a charge that was later changed to murder. Two were acquitted because they had not taken part in the murders and were deemed by the court to have been unwilling partners in the death of the Fieldings. The other 4 were hanged 30 July 1844 on a knoll where Victoria General Hospital now stands.

In more recent years Canada has experienced a limited number of incidents of hijacking or sky piracy. On 29 Nov 1974 Naim Djemal hijacked an aircraft over Saskatchewan, assaulted a stewardess and ordered the pilot to fly to Cyprus. Upon landing for fuel in Saskatoon, Djemal handed a knife to the captain, and then walked off the aircraft and was subsequently arrested, tried and found guilty. JOHN G. LEEFE

Pitcher Plant, common name for family (Sarraceniaceae) of insectivorous perennial plants. The family is restricted to N and S America. It occurs chiefly in eastern N America where 9 native species of genus *Sarracenia* occur. The pitcher (ascidium) is a modified leaf. Lined with downward-pointing bristles, it prevents insects attracted by nectar from escaping. These insects drown in water in the bottom of the tube and are decomposed by bacterial action or by an enzyme. The plant assimilates some of the nutrients; however, the many micro-organisms inhabiting the bottom of the ascidium probably benefit most. The purple pitcher plant (*S. purpurea*), the only species native to Canada, grows in bogs from Newfoundland to Saskatchewan. Its rot-resistant leaves are purple veined or completely green. This plant flowers May-June, producing a solitary, drooping, purple flower. Newfoundland adopted it as

its provincial floral EMBLEM in 1954. The plants grow from seeds; seedlings may be transplanted in a garden, terrarium or any very humid, acidic location. Pitcher plants belonging to different families occur in Asia (Nepenthaceae) and SW Australia (Cephalotaceae). *See also* CARNIVOROUS PLANTS. CÉLINE ARSENEAULT

Pitfield, Peter Michael, civil servant, senator (b at Montréal 18 June 1937), son of financier Ward C. Pitfield and brother of current financier Ward Pitfield of Dominion Securities Pitfield. Although he came to Ottawa in 1959 to work for Conservative Davie FULTON, Pitfield became closely identified with Pierre TRUDEAU and the Liberals after 1968 and became Canada's most prominent and sometimes controversial civil servant. In 1975 he became clerk of the Privy Council and secretary to Cabinet and profoundly influenced the policies and processes of government. PM Joe CLARK dismissed Pitfield, but he was reinstated when Trudeau returned in 1980. Though he chose to sit as an independent, his appointment to the Senate in 1982 was accompanied by widespread accusations of favouritism. JOHN ENGLISH

Pitseolak, Peter, photographer, artist, writer (b on Nottingham I, NWT Nov 1902; d at Cape Dorset, NWT 30 Sept 1973). A camp leader, he recognized early that traditional INUIT life was disappearing and strove to record its passing, writing diaries, notes and manuscripts, drawing Inuit customs and legends, and photographing the life around him. He took his first photograph in the 1930s for a white man who was afraid to approach a polar bear; and in the early 1940s, while living in Cape Dorset working for fur traders, he acquired a camera from a Catholic missionary. With help from his wife Aggeok, he developed his first pictures in a hunting igloo, using as a safelight a 3-battery flashlight covered with red cloth. He photographed over a 20-year period, and after his death more than 1500 negatives, images increasingly valued as an insider's record of the final moments of Inuit camp life, were purchased from

Peter Pitseolak, an Inuk camp leader, recognized the passing of traditional Inuit life and strove to record it in photographs, writing and art (*courtesy McCord Museum/McGill University*).

The insectivorous pitcher plant (*Sarracenia purpurea*) is found in bogs from Newfoundland to Saskatchewan and is the provincial floral emblem of Newfoundland (*photo by Bill Ivy*).

his widow for the National Museums of Canada. A fine artist, he is credited too with Cape Dorset's earliest contemporary works on paper: watercolour drawings executed in 1939 for John N.S. Buchan, later 2nd Baron Tweedsmuir, at the time a fur trader with the Hudson's Bay Co. Shortly before his death, Pitseolak put down in Inuit syllabics the story of his early life (published in 1975 as *People from Our Side*, with oral biography by D. Eber) and an account of near disaster among the ice floes (published in 1977 as *Peter Pitseolak's Escape from Death*, D. Eber, ed). *See also* INUIT ART; INUIT PRINTMAKING.

DOROTHY HARLEY EBER

Reading: D. Bellman, ed, *Peter Pitseolak (1902-1973)* (1980).

Pitseolak Ashoona, graphic artist (b on Nottingham I, NWT *c* 1904; d at Cape Dorset, NWT 28 May 1983). She is known for lively prints and drawings showing "the things we did long ago before there were many white men" and for imaginative renderings of spirits and monsters. She began working in the late 1950s after James HOUSTON started PRINTMAKING experiments at Cape Dorset. She created several thousand drawings reflecting her love and intimate knowledge of traditional INUIT life. Talent ran in her family. She was married in 1922 to Ashoona, a capable hunter who died young, and their sons Kumwartok QAQAQ and KIUGAK Ashoona and daughter Napadive Pootoogook also became artists. Highly articulate, she told her story in the illustrated oral biography *Pitseolak: Pictures out of My Life* (from recorded interviews by D. Eber, 1971), which became an NFB animated documentary. She was elected a member of the Royal Canadian Academy of Arts in 1974. *See also* INUIT ART.

DOROTHY HARLEY EBER

Pitt Meadows, BC, district municipality, pop 8004 (1986c), primarily an agricultural area located in the lower Fraser Valley E of Vancouver, BC, on the N side of the Fraser R at its junction with the Pitt R. The municipality takes its name from the Pitt R and Pitt Lk which were possibly named after British Prime Minister William Pitt. Katzic Indians, the original inhabitants, today make their living largely as commercial fishermen and live on 5 reserves in the district. Originally known as Bonson's landing, settlement in the area began in the 1870s. The municipality was first incorporated in 1874 and included Maple Ridge to the E, but was separately incorporated in 1914. Settlers were mostly Anglo Saxon until after 1910 when many French Canadians and Japanese arrived. A large group of Dutch farmers reclaimed much of the low-lying land in Pitt Meadows after WWII.

JOHN STEWART

Place des Arts, Montréal's major performing-arts complex, consists of 3 halls. Salle Wilfrid-Pelletier, originally named Grande Salle when it opened in 1963, is the largest, with a seating capacity of about 3000. Designed by Montréal architects Affleck, Desbarats, Dimakopoulos, Lebensold, Sise, the structure is made of reinforced concrete and the roof of steel. It is the home for the ORCHESTRE SYMPHONIQUE DE MONTREAL, and the Opéra du Québec and Les GRANDS BALLETS CANADIENS have performed there. Édifice des Théâtres, comprising 2 halls, one built on top of the other, was opened in 1967. The upper Théâtre Maisonneuve accommodates about 1300, and the lower Théâtre Port-Royal about 750. This part of the complex was designed by Montréal architects David, Barott, Boulva, Dufresne and opened in time to showcase EXPO 67 events. In 1978 the Théâtre du Café de la Place, with a seating capacity of about 130, was opened for intimate theatrical performances. Many international stars of music, theatre and dance have appeared at Place des Arts, including Maria Callas, Vladimir Horowitz, Jean-Pierre Rampal and Miles Davis.

FREDERICK A. HALL

Place-names To many Canadians the name CANADA reveals strength, generates pride and reflects much of this land's rugged character and its resourceful people. Happily, the name is derived from the land itself, for Jacques CARTIER in 1535 noted that the Huron and Iroquois applied the designation "*kanata*," meaning a cluster of dwellings, to the present site of Québec City. The name clearly impressed Cartier, for "Canada" appears in the Saguenay and Gaspé regions on the various maps compiled shortly after his historic voyages. For a number of years the name Québec ("narrow passage" in the Algonquian languages) was assigned to the French territory from the Gulf of St Lawrence to the Ohio River and the British adopted "Province of Quebec" as the name of British lands or territories in present-day Ontario and Québec, 1763-91. By 1791 the name Canada was restored to the area of present southern Québec (Lower Canada) and southern Ontario (Upper Canada); from 1841-67, these divisions, united as the Province of Canada, were known as Canada East and Canada West. In the 1860s numerous patriotic and clever suggestions were made to identify the new country being created from the union of the provinces of Canada, NS and NB; a designation with substantial heritage was assigned to the "one Dominion under the name of Canada."

Besides Québec, 3 other provinces and one territory have names of native origin. Ontario is often reported to mean "handsome lake," but such a vague description is not really in keeping with native naming. Dr Henry SCADDING suggested in 1862 that Ontario is more likely derived from the name used by the Seneca Indians for themselves, *Entouhonorons* ("the people"), with the present spelling of the lake's name appearing on mid-17th-century maps. Manitoba, first given to the lake, is said to be derived from the roaring noise ("strait of the spirit") at the narrows of Lake Manitoba. Saskatchewan comes from the Cree for "swift flowing river." Yukon means "great river" in Kutchin and was first noted (as "Youcon") by John Bell (1799-1868) in 1846.

Newfoundland may be the oldest European name in continuous literary and cartographic use, dating from a letter of 1502. Nova Scotia could have come down in history as simply New Scotland, but the form in the Latin text of Sir William ALEXANDER's grant of 1621 was preserved as a distinctive name. New Brunswick was chosen in 1784 to honour King George III (1760-1820), who was descended from the House of Brunswick. Canada's smallest province was known as "Isle de Saint Jean" to the French, and then St John's Island 1759-98, when its present name – Prince Edward Island (for the Duke of Kent then in command of troops in Halifax) – was chosen to reduce the confusion among various places called St John's and Saint John. Unfortunately, neither St John's, Nfld (possibly named on 24 June 1497), nor Saint John in NB (named by royal charter in 1785 after the river discovered by de MONTS and CHAMPLAIN on 24 June 1604) has deemed it wise to effect a change to resolve toponymic confusion. British Columbia dates from 1858 when Queen VICTORIA selected it over New Caledonia. The Columbia R had been named in 1792 by the American explorer, Robert Gray, for his ship. The word "British" was added to distinguish the province from the S American country, Colombia. Queen Victoria's son-in-law, the marquess of LORNE, suggested Alberta in 1882 for a district of the then North-West Territories in honour of his wife, Princess Louise Caroline Alberta. LAKE LOUISE was also named for her.

The names that are, on the whole, truly unique to Canada are those applied by the original peoples of Canada who spoke a multitude of tongues, from Cree and Micmac in the E to Blackfoot and Haida in the W and to Chipewyan and Inuktitut in the N. Most of their names describe an outstanding physical characteristic of each feature; others reflect a significant incident or relate to some activity. Some denote Indian bands or tribes, often as they were known in a language of a neighbour, friend or foe. So rarely was a personal name applied that such names in the official records, eg, Muskoka and Donnacona, are probably company titles or designations given by white settlers. In many instances meanings of names are unreliable, and frequently the language source is uncertain. Well-known names relating to physical characteristics include Niagara ("thunder of waters"), Restigouche ("fine river"), Gaspé ("end place"), Nepisiguit ("rough waters"), Mississauga ("large outlet"), Saguenay (probably, "water flows out"), Nipissing ("little body of water," in contrast to the Great Lakes), Chicoutimi ("end of deep water"), Timiskaming ("deep water"), Caughnawaga ("rapids"), Athabasca ("where there are reeds"), Kamloops ("meeting of the waters"), Keewatin ("north wind"), Minnedosa ("swift water") and Winnipeg ("murky water"). Names associated with occupancy or the tribes themselves include Ottawa ("traders"), Toronto ("meeting place"), Kitimat ("people of the snow"), Kootenay ("water people"), Penticton ("always place," ie, permanently settled), Nanaimo ("big strong people") and Assiniboine ("cook by placing hot stones in water"). Names such as Iroquois Falls, Sioux Lookout, Stony Plain, Cree Lake, Algonquin Park, Lake Erie, Indian River and Eskimo Point reflect communal names. Kelowna means "grizzly bear," Aklavik, "place of bear" and Tuktoyaktuk, "reindeer that looks like caribou." Inuvik," place of man," was assigned in 1958 to the new town set up to replace Aklavik. Saskatoon was named for a wild berry found in abundance by the first settlers in 1882. Some of Canada's most interesting and evocative names are really translations of the aboriginal designations of the present places or associative features, eg, Medicine Hat, Moose Jaw, Yellowknife, Peace River, Qu'Appelle River, Swift Current, Thunder Bay, Battle River, Red Deer, Crowsnest Pass and Grand-Mère. A trend towards recognizing native names is apparent. In 1980, for example, Fort-Chimo, Qué, became Kuujjuaq, and in 1987 Frobisher Bay was changed to Iqaluit.

Virtually every province has a city, town or village named after Queen Victoria. The most widely known, Victoria, BC, was given in 1843 to the Hudson's Bay Company fort. In 1882 the marquess of Lorne gave the Queen's Latin title, Regina, to the capital of what was then the North-West Territories, replacing the Indian Wascana and its English derivative, Pile O'Bones. Victoria's consort is recalled in Prince Albert. Royalty is reflected in names such as Queen Elizabeth Foreland adjacent to Baffin Island, for Elizabeth I, to Queen Elizabeth Islands in the Arctic Archipelago, for Elizabeth II. Annapolis Royal was named in 1710 for Queen Anne, replacing PORT-ROYAL, established in the area in 1605 by de Monts and Champlain. George III was honoured in Georgetown (PEI), Kingston, Prince George and Lancaster Township (Ont); his wife, Charlotte, in the adjoining Charlottenburgh Township; and their children, beginning with the duke of Cornwall, in adjacent townships. Charlottetown was named for Queen Charlotte. Fredericton was named for their son in 1785. The city of Guelph was named by John Galt in 1827 for the British royal family. In 1906 the name of Prince Rupert was chosen after a national competition was sponsored by the Grand Trunk Pacific Ry. The last major island in the Canadian Arctic was discovered in 1948, and named for the newly born Prince Charles. Non-British royalty honoured include King Christian of Denmark in the name of an island in the Arctic, Prince Gustaf Adolf of Sweden in a sea in the Arctic Ocean, and King Louis XIV of France in LOUISBOURG.

Many of the same reasons (respect, allegiance, hope for continued financial support) for using royalty names applied to the practice of honouring political leaders, government officials and military commanders, eg, Richelieu River (duc de Richelieu, 1585-1642), Île d'Orléans (duc d'Orléans, son of François Ier) and Churchill River (duke of Marlborough, 1650-1722). Churchill Falls in Labrador was named for Winston Churchill. Perhaps regrettably, Hamilton River, named in the early 1800s for Sir Charles Hamilton, was changed to Churchill River by provincial legislation; now 2 major Canadian river systems have the same name.

Among British political leaders, the duke of Wellington, the earl of Chatham (William Pitt), the earl of Halifax (George Montagu Dunk) and the earl of Beaconsfield (Benjamin Disraeli), have been honoured several times. Brandon derives its name from Brandon House, a Hudson's Bay Company post established in 1793 and named for the duke of Brandon, a company shareholder.

There has been a trend away from honouring foreign leaders, one of the last being John F. Kennedy, whose name was assigned in 1964 to a mountain in the Yukon. Great military leaders, eg, Montcalm and Wolfe, had their names applied to a number of places; Robert MONCKTON was honoured in the name Moncton (efforts to respell it in the 1920s were sharply rejected); Jeffery AMHERST, the victor at Louisbourg, in Amherst (NS), and Amherstburg (Ont); Isaac BROCK, the hero of the War of 1812, in Brockville; Garnet WOLSELEY, leader of the RED RIVER EXPEDITION in 1870, in Wolseley (Sask); and Horatio Herbert Kitchener, after whose death at sea in 1916 Berlin (the centre of German immigration in southwestern Ontario) was renamed Kitchener. Among exploration promoters honoured were Sir Felix Booth, a London distiller, in the name, Boothia Peninsula, and Axel Heiberg and Amund and Ellef Ringnes, patrons of SVERDRUP's expedition at the turn of this century, in the names of islands adjacent to Ellesmere Island.

Cabot Strait, Mont Jacques-Cartier, Baffin Bay, Davis Strait, Frobisher Bay, Hudson Bay, James Bay, Juan de Fuca Strait (BC) and Vancouver Island recall the early explorers, although in Juan de FUCA's case the voyage may be apocryphal. Labrador and Bras d'Or Lake can be traced to John Cabot's contemporary, the Portuguese explorer, João Alvares FAGUNDES. Some of those who first mapped and described the interior of the country are remembered in Lake Champlain (Samuel de Champlain), Mackenzie River (Alexander MACKENZIE), Fraser River (Simon FRASER), Thompson River (David THOMPSON) and Dawson and Dawson Creek (George M. DAWSON).

Prominent Canadian political leaders, statesmen, industrialists and scientists have often been honoured. Numerous features commemorate John A. Macdonald, Wilfrid Laurier, Robert Borden and Mackenzie King. In recent years the names Mount Louis St. Laurent and Mount Lester Pearson have been given to mountains in BC's Premier Range, and Lake Diefenbaker has been assigned to a huge reservoir on the South Saskatchewan River. The earl of Dalhousie, Sir

Guy Carleton and Sir John Sherbrooke are among governors general honoured; since Confederation, numerous places and features have been named for their successors, from the earl of Dufferin and Earl Grey to Roland Michener. The official naming of Mount Michener in 1979 with Michener present was a rare event in Canada's toponymic history. Georges P. Vanier is remembered in many features and places.

Personal names of local developers, community founders and settlement promoters have provided an extensive source for Canadian names. Hamilton was named for George Hamilton (1787-1835), Timmins for Noah TIMMINS, Lloydminster for Rev (later Bishop) George Lloyd (1861-1940), Joliette for Barthélemy Joliette (1787-1850) and Lethbridge for William Lethbridge (1824-1901). Forenames as well as surnames have been used for place-names, eg, Peterborough (Peter Robinson), Belleville (Arabella Wentworth Gore) and Orangeville (Orange Lawrence) in Ontario, Melville (Charles Melville Hays) in Saskatchewan, Raymond (Raymond Knight) in Alberta and Rossland (Ross Thompson) in BC. At one time the assigning of personal names was done quite liberally, eg, Kirkland Lake was named in 1907 after a secretary in the Ontario Department of Mines. In recent years the approval of personal names has been stringently controlled by the names authorities in all the provinces and territories.

A distinctive characteristic of Canada's toponymy, especially in Québec, is the profusion of saints' names; the 1978 Québec gazetteer records over 2200 of them. Many of the hagionyms not only recall specific saints but were also the forenames of certain community founders, missionaries and priests. They include St-Hyacinthe, for Hyacinthe Delorme who purchased the seigneury there in 1753, St-Lambert, for Raphael Lambert Closse, a 17th-century merchant in the Montréal area, St-Jean-sur-Richelieu, for Jean Phélypeaux, a French minister of marine, and Ste-Thérèse, for Thérèse de Blainville. Others across Canada include St Albert (Alta) for Fr Albert LACOMBE; St Thomas for Thomas TALBOT, who developed a large part of southwestern Ontario; St Marys (Ont) for Mary Strachan Jones, daughter of Bishop John STRACHAN; and St Catharines (Ont) for Catharine Hamilton, the mother of Hamilton's founder. Religious naming extends to the Île Jésus, Maniwaki ("place of Mary") (Qué), Trinity Bay (Nfld), Conception Bay (Nfld) and Bay of Gods Mercy (NWT).

From the Avalon Peninsula in the E to New Westminster on the W, Canada's linguistic mosaic preponderantly reflects Anglo-Celtic influences. Calgary traces its roots to the Isle of Mull in Scotland; Edmonton to the suburbs of London. Ontario has a multitude of Anglo-Celtic names, eg, Renfrew, Pembroke, Sudbury, Windsor, Woodstock, Dublin, Listowel, Stratford, Brampton; as does Québec, eg, Hull, Windsor, Thetford-Mines, Thurso, Armagh, Bedford, Buckingham; and the Atlantic provinces, eg, Truro, Windsor, Perth-Andover, Newcastle, Kensington. Evidence of the French as the first Europeans to occupy large parts of Canada is not only revealed in Québec, where 80% of the names are of French origin, but in every one of the provinces and territories – Rideau River, Point Pelée, Lake Superior and Sault Ste Marie in Ontario, Portage la Prairie (Man), Lac la Ronge (Sask), Lac La Biche (Alta), Cariboo (BC), Liard River (BC, Yukon, NWT), Bay of Fundy (NB, NS), Minas Basin (NS), Cape Breton (NS); and in Newfoundland, Port aux Basques, Notre Dame Bay, Strait of Belle Isle. Montréal is generally thought to be a variant of Jacques Cartier's "Mont Roiall," although there may have been an Italian influence in the choice

of the name. Names transferred from other countries include Dresden and New Hamburg (Germany), Gimli (Iceland), Delhi and Lucknow (India), Zurich (Switzerland), Florence (Italy), Brussels (Belgium), Warsaw (Poland), Odessa (Ukraine), Moscow (Russia), Ladysmith (South Africa), Corunna (Spain). The personal names of settlers and early postmasters from European countries provide a fascinating array of community names from languages other than English and French, but few of them are widely known beyond their own immediate regions.

Several of Canada's names reflect classical origins, eg, Acadia given by VERRAZANO in 1524 to suggest a land of rustic peace, Avalon Peninsula assigned by Sir George CALVERT in the early 1600s, Sarnia given by Sir John COLBORNE in 1839 for the Roman name of Guernsey, and Athens named in 1888 to replace the prosaic Farmersville, but perhaps the commonest type of name in Canada is descriptive, either of physical characteristics or of fauna, flora or minerals. Examples are Percé, Trois-Rivières, Rivière-du-Loup, Glace Bay, Midland, North Bay, Sturgeon Falls, Broadview, Grande Prairie, Cobalt, Asbestos, Petrolia, Val-d'Or, Gypsumville, Coppermine River, Whitehorse (referring to rapids in the Yukon River resembling a horse's mane) and Old Man on His Back Plateau, Rivière Qui-Mène-du-Train, Pinchgut Tickle, Cape Gargantua and Giants Castle. Newfoundland's share of unusual names include Joe Batt's Arm, Come By Chance, Little Seldom, Happy Valley, Pick Eyes, Bareneed, Hearts Delight, Bay d'Espoir (meaning "hope" but pronounced "despair") and Lushes Bight. Ecum Secum is in NS and Peekaboo Corner is in NB. In Québec there is Saint-Louis-du-Ha!Ha!, the expression "ha ha" implying "dead end" or "one way." Punkeydoodles Corners near Kitchener, Ont, presumably derives from a mispronunciation of Yankee Doodle. Flin Flon is derived from a character in the novel *The Sunless City* – Josiah Flintabbatey Flonatin. Saskatchewan has Eyebrow and Elbow; Alberta, Hairy Hill and Pincher Creek; BC has Kleena Kleene, Bella Bella, Horsefly. Snafu Creek in the Yukon recalls an indelicate WWII expression assigned by army engineers who also baptized Tarfu Creek; Sons of the Clergy Islands, Old Lady's Ghost Creek and Man Drowned Himself Lake are all in the NWT. Some names have resulted from a single incident or unusual circumstance. Lachine, Qué, dates from 1688 when LA SALLE failed to reach China. In NB, when land grants across a lake in 1784 were considered as impossible to attain as the perfection ascribed to Utopia, the lake was appropriately named Lake Utopia. Kicking Horse Pass in the Rockies was named for an 1858 incident when James HECTOR was kicked by one of his packhorses. Lindsay, Ont, was named for an assistant surveyor who died after being accidentally shot while doing a street survey there in 1834.

In 1905 the adjoining places of Keewatin, Norman and Rat Portage provided initial letters for Kenora. Arvida, now part of the city of Jonquière, Qué, was bestowed in honour of Arthur Vining Davis, an official of the Aluminum Company of Canada. Noranda, Qué, was derived from "North Canada," the name of the mining company established there in 1922. In Saskatchewan, Robert Kerr, a CPR traffic manager, is remembered in Kerrobert. Castlegar, BC, is derived from Castle Gardens, a former immigration centre in New York; the community's railway station reminded the namer of the New York structure. National and international literary figures have been commemorated in a number of place-names, from Shakespeare and Haliburton in Ontario to Carlyle and Lampman in Saskatchewan. In the Yukon, Stephen Leacock and Robert Service have been memorialized in the names of mountains. Gravenhurst, Bracebridge and Nokomis are derived from literary characters or places.

The problem of duplication of names, eg, Trout River, Wolf Lake and Mud Lake, has frequently bothered map users. Although some efforts have been made to change some of the more common names and to discourage the use of such names in the future, arbitrary substitution by authorities has usually not been successful, especially when local people have been ignored in the process. The best-known example was the change of Castle Mountain to Mount Eisenhower in 1946. During the following 30 years, several efforts were made to reverse this decision. Late in 1979, the federal and Alberta authorities agreed to restore Castle Mountain, and assigned the name Eisenhower Peak to its most prominent summit. Attempts to change names considered by authorities to be repugnant have usually not been supported locally. In 1826 there was an effort to replace Pugwash (NS) with Waterford, but the former, of Micmac origin, was retained. In Ontario the residents of Swastika have resisted attempts to change their name, given in 1906 as a reflection of a good luck charm. Residents of Strassburg, Sask, and Berlin, Ont, were given little choice in being assigned the new names: Strasbourg and Kitchener. In 1986 the Ontario Legislature replaced the name of Stalin Township with Hansen Township, for "man-in-motion" Rick HANSEN. In recent years, Galt, Hespeler and Preston have had the common name Cambridge, Ont, superimposed, and Fort William and Port Arthur have been amalgamated to form Thunder Bay. The derivation or meanings of some names in Canada are disputed, eg, Barrie (Ont), The Pas (Man) and Mount Robson (BC), and in many cases the records are not clear.

Almost every place-name has a single correct form, but several are commonly misspelled. St Catharines (Ont) is frequently written St Catherines, Edmundston (NB) is often written Edmunston and Athabasca River (Alta) is sometimes spelled Athabaska River. Some names of features crossing provincial or international boundaries have more than one spelling. One often sees Temiskaming, but this is not one of the 3 official forms of the name; the country in Québec is Témiscamingue, the town in Qué is Témiscaming, the district in Ont is Timiskaming. The Kootenay River in BC becomes Kootenai River in the US. Hyphens are used in all populated place-names of Qué with 2 or more words of French origin, thus Ste-Marthe-du-Cap-de-la-Madeleine, although names with initial articles do not have hypens, eg, La Décharge, Le Grand-Village. Hyphens are not used in Québec names of non-French origin, eg, Campbell's Bay, Ayer's Cliff.

There are no fixed rules for name pronunciation. Some names like Toronto and Calgary seem to allow for more than one suitable pronunciation. Others often receive pronunciations not used by the people who live there, eg, Newfoundland, Elginburg (Ont), Gleichen (Alta) and Maugerville (NB). Some names receive different pronunciations where they occur in different locations, eg, Dalhousie (NB, Ont) and Souris (PEI, Man).

While most of Canada's 350 000 official names will endure unchanged, a number will undoubtedly be modified by political and cultural pressures, and by geographical reality and local usage. Many geographical features are still unnamed, at least officially. The official names records expand at the rate of about 25 000 new names a year so that by the end of the century there may be nearly a million names on record. *See also* CANADIAN PERMANENT COMMITTEE ON GEOGRAPHICAL NAMES; MINERAL NAMING. ALAN RAYBURN

Reading: G.P.V. and H.B. Akrigg, *1001 British Columbia Place Names* (1973); R. Coutts, *Yukon Places and Names* (1980); P. Ham, *Place Names of Manitoba* (1980); W.B. Hamilton, *The MacMillan Book of Canadian Place Names* (1983); N. and H. Mika, *Places in Ontario*, 3 vols (1977-83); Alan Rayburn, *Geographical Names of Prince Edward Island* (1973) and *Geographical Names of New Brunswick* (1975); E.R. Seary, *Place Names of the Avalon Peninsula of the Island of Newfoundland* (1971); E.T. Russell, *What's in a Name: The Story Behind Saskatchewan Place Names* (1980); J.T. Walbran, *British Columbia Coast Names, 1592-1906: Their Origin and History* (1909, repr 1977).

Place Royale In July 1608, Samuel de CHAMPLAIN put up a building at the foot of Cap Diamant on the shore of the St Lawrence R, thereby creating the colonial post of QUÉBEC. Other buildings joined it, to establish the village of the lower town. In 1624 Champlain had his quarters rebuilt and for more than 50 years the place was a busy centre of activity. A raging fire of 5 Aug 1682 reduced the public square to a pile of cinders, but it was rebuilt. In 1686 Intendant Jean Bochard de Champigny had a bronze bust of Louis XIV erected in the public square, which then took the name of Place Royale. Two years later a chapel was build on the exact site of Champlain's first and second habitations. Place Royale continued to be a business centre until 1759, when war and bombardments once again turned it to rubble.

Witness to several important chapters in our history, major archaeological digs on the site have revealed an ancient Amerindian habitation, vestiges of Champlain's second habitation, and walls and thousands of objects which have made it possible to recreate the activity of former ages. These studies have also aided in the reconstruction of the old districts. Place Royale is today a major cultural attraction the significance of which has helped to place Québec City on UNESCO's selective list of world heritage sites. *See also* ARCHAEOLOGY IN QUÉBEC. NORMAN CLERMONT

Place Ville Marie, Montréal (architects I.M. Pei, with Ray AFFLECK, 1958-65), was developed as an entire city block by CN Real Estate. It was a phased development. The first to be constructed (1958-63) was the cruciform (cross-shaped) 45-storey tower, commonly called the Royal Bank Building; its grand plaza and lower office buildings, designed by internationally famous US architect I.M. Pei, helped to set new standards for architecture in Canada in the 1960s. It confirmed for Montréal the importance of the below-ground pedestrian walkway system (which had its origins in CN's Central Station). Phase II, consisting of 3 smaller structures, dates 1963-65. Shops, restaurants and cinemas are located below the plaza, and are reached by generous square wells providing daylight as well as access. The tower's smooth aluminum and glass surface and crisp unadorned geometric form demonstrate Pei's adherence to the mainstream of 20th-century modern design. MICHAEL McMORDIE

Placentia, Nfld, Town, pop 2016 (1986c), 2204 (1981c), inc 1945, is located on PLACENTIA BAY on the W coast of the AVALON PENINSULA. The site, called *Plaisance* by the French, was a BASQUE fishing station in the late 1500s. The name may derive from Plasencia, a town in Salamanca, Spain. After the French claimed Newfoundland in 1624, Plaisance became the first official French colony on the island. It remained the French capital of Newfoundland, guarding French fishing activities, until the Treaty of UTRECHT, 1713. It was defended by a number of forts and was the base for French raids on English settlements on the Avalon Pen in 1696, 1705 and 1709. After the Treaty of Utrecht, 1713, Placentia became a British stronghold and further fortifications were erected until the garrison was withdrawn in 1811. With its wide beaches and strategic location, Placentia grew as an important fishing and trading centre in the 1800s; but it later became heavily dependent upon employment at the nearby Argentia Naval Base, built 1940-41. Since the phase-down of the base in 1969 and 1974, employment has depended on the fishery and tourism attracted by the town's historic buildings and Castle Hill National Historic Pk (since 1968). JANET E.M. PITT AND ROBERT D. PITT

Placentia Bay, from the French *plaisance*, is a large, deep bay formed by Newfoundland's Burin Pen to the W, and the SW AVALON PENINSULA to the E. From Ferryland Head in the W and CAPE ST MARY'S 90 km E, the bay runs 125 km to its head, the Isthmus of Avalon. Ringed with coves and harbours, the bay has 2 extensive islands, Merasheen and Long, formerly populated, which divide the bay into channels to the N. Once utilized by Dorset Eskimo and the BEOTHUK, the fine fishing grounds were probably first frequented by BASQUES and French in the 1500s; by the 1660s French fishermen occupied the bay, as modern place-names still attest. After the Treaty of UTRECHT, 1713, when the French settlements were ceded to Britain, English use and settlement slowly followed in Placentia B. Today the principal settlements are in the Burin-MARYSTOWN area and in the vicinity of PLACENTIA and ARGENTIA, once the location of a major US military facility and now the terminus of a CN Marine ferry service to NS. Fishing, shipbuilding and services are now the main employers, though there was once a large oil refinery at COME BY CHANCE. ROBERT D. PITT

Plains of Abraham, Battle of the, 13 Sept 1759, during the SEVEN YEARS' WAR, fought upstream from Québec on a tract of land that is thought to have been named after Abraham Martin, to whom it was granted 1635-45. A powerful British force under Maj-Gen James WOLFE and Vice-Adm Charles Saunders was sent up the St Lawrence to capture Québec. The French, commanded by Lt-Gen the marquis de MONTCALM, at first held the British at bay. Having sailed upstream past the city on Sept 5 and 6, Wolfe's army landed without opposition on Sept 13, climbing the cliffs a few km above Québec. Montcalm's communications with his source of supplies were threatened; he felt obliged to accept battle and impulsively attacked without waiting to collect all his forces. The armies actually on the field seem to have been about numerically equal – some 4500 each – but the British were all regulars, whereas many of the French were ill-trained militia. The French attack was broken by British infantry fire, and the French retired in disorder. Both Wolfe and Montcalm were mortally wounded. The French field army retreated up the St Lawrence by a circuitous route that night. Québec surrendered on Sept 18. A French attack early in 1760 failed to recover the city, and later in the year the British captured Montréal and NEW FRANCE fell. C.P. STACEY

A View of the Taking of Quebec, September 13, 1759, published by Laurie & Whittle, 1759. The engraving shows the British scaling the cliff at the undefended cove (*courtesy National Archives of Canada/C-1078*).

Plamondon, Antoine, painter (b at Ancienne-Lorette, Qué 29 Feb 1804; d at Neuville, Qué 4 Sept 1895). After a 6-year apprenticeship with Joseph LÉGARÉ, Plamondon left for Europe in 1826. He studied in Paris under J.B. Paulin Guérin, official painter to King Charles X. Returning to Québec in 1830, he specialized in portraits of the bourgeoisie and copies of religious works. In 1838 the Literary and Historical Soc of Québec awarded him a medal for his portrait *Zacharie Vincent, le dernier des Hurons,* which was bought by Lord DURHAM, and the following year he exhibited in the House of Assembly his famous Stations of the Cross intended for Notre-Dame de Montréal. In 1841 he painted 3 remarkable portraits of nuns, including *Soeur Saint-Alphonse.* He taught drawing in various educational institutions and counted Théophile HAMEL among his disciples. A fervent polemicist, Plamondon frequently wrote to the newspapers to argue his pictorial ideas and attack his rivals. In 1851, a year after winning a first prize with his *Chasse aux tourtes* at the Exposition de Québec, he moved his studio to Neuville, about 30 km upstream from Québec. There he continued painting until the 1880s, turning out a stream of religious paintings of uneven quality and portraits copied from photographs. His long career was crowned in 1880 when he was named founding VP of the Royal Canadian Academy of the Arts.   JOHN R. PORTER

Antoine Plamondon, *Self-Portrait* (1882) (*courtesy Musée du Séminaire de Québec/Pierre Soulard*).

Plamondon, Joseph-Marcel-Rodolphe, tenor, teacher (b at Montréal 18 Jan 1876; d there 28 Jan 1940). After cello and voice training in Montréal and early success as a church soloist, Rodolphe Plamondon continued his musical education in France. Prior to WWI he appeared frequently in opera roles. However, his reputation rests primarily on his proficiency as a concert and oratorio soloist, which kept him in constant demand with Europe's leading choirs and orchestras until the late 1920s. Plamondon's concerts often included music by Canadian composers. In 1925 and 1926 he made several recordings of French songs. Plamondon's singing tours brought him to Canada only rarely, but he returned to Montréal permanently in 1928 and taught there until his death. BARCLAY MCMILLAN

Plamondon, Luc, songwriter (b at Saint-Raymond-de-Portneuf, Qué 2 Mar 1942). He studied piano, pedagogy and letters and then, in 1970, wrote his first song, "Dans ma Camaro," interpreted by Steve Fiset. Monique LEYRAC made him

famous by singing several of his texts and he has written for Renée Claude, Robert Charlebois, Julien Clerc and others. He also composed Diane Dufresne's greatest triumphs (music by François Cousineau). He went to Paris (1976) at the invitation of Michel Berger, where he composed the rock opera *Starmania*; several of its songs have become immensely popular. His skill at adapting style and language to the particular singer has made him much in demand. A defender of author's rights, he founded (1981) the Société professionelle des auteurs et compositeurs du Québec.   HÉLÈNE PLOUFFE

Planet and Satellite A planet is a nonluminous body that revolves in an orbit about a STAR; a satellite is a body that revolves about a planet. In our own solar system, these "worlds" range from Jupiter, nearly 145 000 km in diameter, to small lumps of rock less than 1 km across. Our knowledge of the physical and chemical nature of planets and satellites has increased very rapidly since the launching of the first interplanetary spacecraft in the early 1960s.

The diameter of a world is a significant value because, given the same densities, the surface gravity will vary roughly with the diameter. A diameter of 350 km is the approximate dividing line between the larger, near-spherical bodies and the smaller objects of irregular shape. Another important parameter is the average distance of the world from the SUN, as this distance controls the basic chemistry and conditions on the body's surface. Since the energy received from the sun falls off as the inverse square of the distance, the worlds in the outer part of the solar system are much colder and have retained more lightweight elements (eg, hydrogen, helium, carbon, nitrogen, oxygen) than have inner worlds. A high surface gravity also helps retain light gases; thus, large quantities of these elements and their compounds are found in the 4 largest planets, all of which are in the outer solar system.

These 4 planets probably have relatively small solid cores of ice and rock, but the gaseous atmospheres of cloud belts extend for thousands of kilometres and effectively prevent us from glimpsing any solid surface. At least 3 of the 4 have ring systems composed of countless, small (metre-sized) solid particles of stony material combined with ice. These particles revolve about the planet and tend to form discrete, narrow ringlets, apparently constrained by the dynamic action of certain bodies that are very much larger than the normal ring particles. These bodies have been called "shepherds." The 4 planets of the inner solar system (Mercury, Venus, Earth, Mars) are very different from the large outer worlds, being significantly small with higher concentrations of heavier elements. Although described as terrestrial (ie, Earth-like) they are also very different from one another. Above a solid surface, their atmospheres range from effectively none, for Mercury, transparent with some clouds for Mars and Earth, to opaque clouds of carbon dioxide, sulphuric acid and chlorine compounds on Venus, where surface detail is mapped by radar or by a spacecraft landed on a furnace-like (400-500°C) terrain.

In the gap between the inner and the outer solar system move many minor planets, called asteroids. By 1987 over 3500 asteroids had been identified with well-determined orbits and had been given official reference numbers. Of these more than 2900 have been named. With a few exceptions, worlds smaller than 4000 km in diameter have no appreciable atmospheres as their surface gravities are too small to hold gas molecules for more than a few thousand years.

The commonest features on the solid surfaces (as demonstrated primarily by photographs transmitted by spacecraft) are craters of widely differing sizes. The observational evidence points to space impacts in the early eons of the solar system as the origin for most of these craters, but some outstanding examples, including features on Earth, Mars and Io, have been produced by volcanic action. Sulphur volcanoes are active on Io and currently active volcanic areas on Venus and Europa have been tentatively identified. A common constituent of many of the worlds in the outer solar system is ice of various compositions and Europa seems to be completely covered by ice, possibly to a depth of 10 or more kilometres in certain areas.

Several centuries of tradition have given us names from Greek-Roman mythology for the planets and satellites themselves (*see* table) except for the satellites of Uranus. This planet was first actually "discovered," an achievement of the English astronomer William Herschel in 1781. The currently known satellites of Uranus are now 15 in number, thanks to the records of Voyager 2 made in January 1986, and in this case all 15 have been named after fictitious characters in the writings of Shakespeare and Alexander Pope.

Standard cartography and nomenclature for the solid surfaces of recently explored worlds have proceeded rapidly, with consultation among the world's nations organized by the International Astronomical Union. As of 1987 over 4100 topographic names had been approved on 26 different extraterrestrial worlds. After craters, the most frequently named features have been valleys, mountains, canyons, ridges and plains. Some 40 Latin terms are used to define the vari-

---

Planets and Satellites of the Solar System

Diameters (km)	*Names	Average Surface Gravity (Earth = 1)
150 000-40 000	JUPITER, SATURN, URANUS, NEPTUNE	1.5
15 000-6000	EARTH, VENUS, MARS	0.75
6000-4000	Ganymede(J), Titan(S), MERCURY, Callisto (J)	0.20
4000-2000	Io(J), Triton(N), Moon(E), Europa(J), PLUTO	0.12
2000-1000	Oberon(U), Titania(U), Rhea(S), Iapetus(S), Ariel(U), Dione(S), Umbriel(U), Tethys(S), Ceres(A), Charon(P)	0.025
1000-350	Pallas(A), Vesta(A), Enceladus(S), Miranda(U), Nereid(N), Mimas(s), Chiron(A)	0.010
350-100	Hyperion(S), Juno(A), Pheobe(S), Amalthea(J), Janus(S), Himalia(J), Epimetheus(S)	0.006
100-25	Thebe(J), Elara(J), Metis(J), Pasiphae(J), Atlas(S), Carme(J), Sinope(J)	0.0010
25-1	Telesto(S), Calypso(S), Phobos(M), Eros(A), Adrastea(J), Lysithea(J), Ananke(J), Deimos(M), Leda(J), Icarus(A)	0.0005

* The planets and satellites have been listed together in order of their diameters. Planets are identified by giving the name in capital letters only, satellites by the use of both small letters and capitals. The capital letters in brackets indicate the planet to which each satellite belongs, according to the following code: (E) Earth, (M) Mars, (J) Jupiter, (S) Saturn, (U) Uranus, (N) Neptune, (P) Pluto. An asteroid (minor planet) is identified by (A).

ous categories of features. The Working Group for Planetary System Nomenclature has endeavoured to bequeath to the future some international elements of Earth's cultural heritage in the names we use on other worlds. Over the years, the names of deceased scholars and scientists have been placed on the Moon and Mars. Now we have outstanding individuals in the humanities (Beethoven, Shakespeare, Raphael) on Mercury; feminine names (Eve, Cleopatra, Pavlova, Nightingale) on Venus; and deities of fire and volcanoes (Ra, Pele, Surt, Amaterasu) on Io. Name sources for other worlds include terrestrial place names and many of the familiar legends and mythologies of the world. On Mars we have small craters called Hope, Chinook, Chapais and Nain, taken from towns in BC, Alberta, Québec and Newfoundland, respectively.   PETER M. MILLMAN

Plankton [Gk *planktos*, "drifting"] plants and animals, phytoplankton and zooplankton, respectively, that float freely or drift with currents in oceans, freshwater ponds and LAKES. At present, phytoplankton is considered to include members of 3 kingdoms (Monera, Protista, PLANT); zooplankton contains members of 2 kingdoms (Protista, ANIMAL). Unattached and having weak powers of independent movement, plankton contrast with organisms that are benthic (attached to or living in bottom sediments) or nektonic (active swimming). They are usually microscopic, although some zooplankton (eg, JELLYFISH) may be several metres long. Planktonic food chains are the basis of the aquatic ecosystem. At the lowest level are phytoplankton, primary producers able to use SOLAR ENERGY, carbon dioxide and water to photosynthesize organic matter. Smaller zooplankton, feeding on phytoplankton, represent the second, "grazing" trophic level (herbivores). Larger zooplankton, feeding on the smaller zooplankton, represent the third trophic level (predators or carnivores).

Plant, member of a large and diverse group of organisms sharing certain common features, but difficult to separate absolutely from all other living things (*see* BIOLOGY). Two characteristics stand out because of the sharp contrast with ANIMALS. Plants are primarily autotrophs (self-feeders), using light energy from the sun to synthesize organic molecules from inorganic precursors (photosynthesis). They are stationary organisms and obtain their energy while fixed in one place. These properties are reflected in the structure of a typical land plant which is organized into 2 basic systems, shoot and root. The shoot system (stem and leaves) grows upward into the light and is the site of photosynthesis; the root system penetrates the soil, anchors the plant and absorbs necessary water and minerals. Both systems are potentially unlimited in growth, thus providing for the immobile plant a means of adjustment to the environment. This open-ended growth pattern results from the functioning of regions of continued growth (meristems) at the tip of each shoot and root. Meristems originate in early embryonic development. The fertilized egg (zygote) develops into many cells which, like those of the animal embryo, begin to specialize for a function in the adult body. Two groups of cells remain unspecialized or embryonic (ie, capable of continued cell division). These become the first shoot and root apical meristems. The shoot apical meristem initiates stem tissues, produces outgrowths that develop into leaves and initiates primordia of lateral branches just above the leaf axil (junction of leaf and stem). With suitable stimulation, the shoot apical meristem may be transformed to give rise to a flower, inflorescence or cone, thus relinquishing its capacity for unlimited growth. The root apical meristem initiates root tissues and a

Leaf section of sugar maple (*Acer saccharum*), showing the epidermis ("skin"), the inner food-producing cells (mesophyll), a food-and-water-carrying vascular bundle ("vein"), and a pore (stoma) whose size is controlled by the surrounding guard cells (*courtesy National Museums of Canada/National Museum of Natural Sciences/artwork by Marcel Jomphe*).

protective covering over itself (root cap). It forms no appendages comparable to leaves or branches; branch roots arise internally, emerging some distance behind the root tip.

Cell Structure

A plant's immobility is readily understood when its cells are examined. Unlike animal cells, each plant cell is enclosed in a boxlike wall, the main structural component of which is cellulose. Furthermore, the walls of adjacent cells are held together by a cementing substance (but intercellular spaces occur frequently, especially where several cells meet at their edges). All plant cells have a relatively thin, outer primary wall, capable of extension during cell growth. Certain supporting and conducting cells have an inner, often relatively thick secondary wall which is incapable of growth. The secondary wall does not cover the primary wall completely but is interrupted by small pits or by more extensive gaps. Clearly, nerve and muscle tissues, the bases of animal motility, could not be constructed of such cells. The meristems continually add new, functionally active cells at the growing tips, apparently accomplishing the result achieved in animals by cell turnover. Thus, there is a steady replacement of leaves as the shoot grows and of absorbing root hairs near the root tip.

Inside the cell wall, the protoplasmic contents are bounded by a differentially permeable membrane, like that surrounding the animal cell.

Section through the stem and a leaf of cord moss (*Funaria hydrometrica*) (*courtesy National Museums of Canada/National Museum of Natural Sciences/artwork by Marcel Jomphe*).

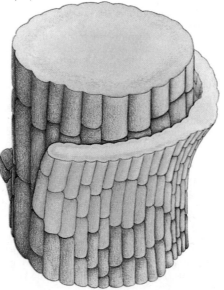

Plants lack an organized nervous system but have plasmodesmata connecting almost all living cells. These are fine strands of protoplasm (bounded by membrane) that extend through the primary wall and provide cell-to-cell continuity. When a secondary wall is present, plasmodesmata are restricted to the pits. The cytoplasm (generalized cell protoplasm) contains a nucleus and several organelles of diverse structure and function. Conspicuous among these are plastids, which in photosynthetic tissues contain chlorophyll and are known as chloroplasts. A further, distinctive characteristic of plant cells is the presence of fluid-filled vacuoles bounded by a membrane similar to the cell membrane. Small and often numerous in immature cells, they enlarge and fuse during cell growth so that a single, central vacuole, sometimes traversed by cytoplasmic strands, occupies most of a mature cell.

Types of Cells

Plant cells have many different forms, but those encountered in vascular plants fall into a few classes.

Parenchyma cells are roughly equidimensional in shape, have only thin primary walls and carry on most of the plant's metabolic activities (eg, photosynthesis, storage).

Collenchyma cells also retain active protoplasmic contents, but are elongated with thickened primary walls, often unevenly distributed around the cell's circumference. They combine support with flexibility.

Sclerenchyma cells have thick secondary walls and provide rigid support. When mature they are usually dead, containing no protoplasmic contents. Elongated sclerenchyma cells are called fibres, and more nearly equidimensional ones are sclereids.

Conducting cells of the xylem (water-transporting tissue) are tracheids and vessel cells. Both are dead at maturity and have secondary walls (either a continuous wall with pits or in the form of rings, spirals or a network). Tracheids are elongate and spindle shaped. Water passes between them through pits or other gaps in the secondary wall. Vessel cells vary from elongate to barrel shaped and are superimposed one above the other to form vessels. The end walls of a vessel cell are perforated, leaving no barrier to water flow within the limits of a vessel.

Sieve elements are conducting cells of the phloem (tissue that transports organic solutes). Unlike xylem elements, these are living cells, but the protoplasm has undergone substantial alteration (usually including loss of nucleus). In flowering plants, sieve elements are superimposed to form sieve tubes and are connected by plates through which enlarged intercellular connections extend.

Epidermal cells form a surface barrier against water loss. They resemble parenchyma but the outer wall is often thickened and impregnated with cutin. A layer of cutin, the cuticle, is also deposited on the outer surface. Certain epidermal cells are modified in shape and function as guard cells for the stomata (minute openings on leaf or stem surfaces). Others may form unicellular or multicellular outgrowths (hairs or trichomes).

Cork cells are dead when mature, have walls modified by deposition of suberin and reduce water loss.

Tissues and Organs

The diverse cells of the plant body are organized into tissues, some relatively homogeneous, others more complex. On the basis of structure and function, tissues may be grouped into 3 systems: vascular (conducting) system; dermal (protective) system; and fundamental (metabolic) system. These systems occur, in somewhat different configurations, in each major plant organ (root, stem and leaf).

In the root, the vascular system consists usually of a central core of xylem, with radiating ridges, and phloem, located in troughs between the ridges. Around the phloem is a layer of parenchyma (pericycle) in which branch roots originate. Surrounding the pericycle is the endodermis, cells of which have a band of suberized material in the transverse and radial walls that restricts the passage of materials into or out of the vascular system. Tissues inside the endodermis are sometimes referred to as the stele. The fundamental system is represented by the parenchymatous cortex and sometimes by a core (pith) in the centre of the xylem. The cortex is bounded by the epidermis. In a zone just behind the root's growing region, certain epidermal cells extend outward in projections (root hairs) which are extremely important in absorption from the soil. The root cuticle is usually very thin, particularly in the absorbing region.

In the stem of SEED PLANTS the vascular system consists of interconnected bundles of xylem and phloem, the phloem outside the xylem. These bundles are continuous with the vascular supply of the leaves, and one or more diverge into each leaf at the level of its node (point of attachment to stem).

In dicotyledons (plants with 2 embryo leaves), the bundles form a ring around a central pith; in monocotyledons (plants with one embryo leaf), they are scattered throughout the centre of the stem, embedded in fundamental tissue. The cortex is often photosynthetic. The stem is bounded by an epidermis with stomata.

In the leaf, the petiole (stalk that supports leaf) contains one or several vascular leaf traces embedded in fundamental tissue, which often includes collenchyma. In the blade (lamina) the vascular system is subdivided into a network of veins and veinlets serving all parts of the photosynthetic tissue. The fundamental system (mesophyll) is composed of chloroplast-containing parenchyma with extensive intercellular spaces. Often one or 2 layers of columnar cells, the palisade layer, occur just below the upper epidermis and above the more open, spongy mesophyll. Stomata are usually more numerous in the lower epidermis. The veins traversing the mesophyll are surrounded by a compact layer of parenchyma, the bundle sheath, often associated with substantial amounts of collenchyma (sclerenchyma in larger veins).

Secondary Growth

Although an entire plant body can be formed by the shoot and root apical meristems, a substantial supplement is often provided by additional or secondary meristems, especially in TREES and shrubs. The vascular cambium and cork cambium contribute additional tissues to the vascular and dermal systems, respectively, a further example of cell replacement by addition. The vascular cambium is a layer of meristem situated between the xylem and phloem. By longitudinal division of its cells parallel to the surface of the stem or root, it forms secondary xylem or wood to the inside and secondary phloem to the outside. In trees and shrubs this activity may continue for years. Wood is one of Canada's major natural resources. In herbaceous plants cambial activity is greatly restricted, or absent (in most monocotyledons). Even without a cambium, plants such as palms and tree ferns can build up a massive body and maintain a long life span. The continued expansion of the vascular system

internally cannot be long contained by the epidermis, the rupture of which would have serious consequences if the dermal system were incapable of replacement.

However, the cork cambium, located near the surface, produces a periderm (bark) composed largely of suberized cork cells which restrict water loss. Lenticels, which perforate the periderm with loose, spongy parenchyma, accomplish aeration. These openings are not controlled but may be sealed by development of cork and reopened by further production of spongy tissues.
T.A. STEEVES

Reading: W.A. Jensen and F.B. Salisbury, *Botany: An Ecological Approach* (1972).

Plant Breeding is the process of modifying plant species to suit human needs or preferences. The underlying principles were not well understood until the present century. Discovery of the laws of GENETICS and subsequent developments in that science greatly increased our understanding of the plant breeding process, which involves modifying plant populations by changing the frequencies of genes controlling various traits. Continuing advances in GENETIC ENGINEERING may have considerable impact on plant breeding in future.

Methods

Most plant breeding programs include creation of new genotypes (genetic combinations) and selection, testing and evaluation of some of the new combinations. Although the basic steps are the same, details of the programs vary considerably with the longevity of the species, its primary mode of reproduction and the genetic structure of the varieties that are released for commercial production.

Self-fertilized Species include wheats, oats, barley, flax, tobacco, tomatoes, peas and peanuts. These species usually have "perfect" flowers, ie, the pollen produced in a flower pollinates the stigma located in the same flower. Self-fertilization leads to high levels of inbreeding. Commercial cultivars (cultivated varieties) are normally highly inbred, pure-breeding lines.

To produce new genotypes in self-fertilizing species, it is necessary to force hybridization between plants from different cultivars. Hybridization is usually accomplished by manually removing the anthers from the flowers of the designated female parent and subsequently transferring mature pollen from the designated male parent. The resulting hybrid seed carries genetic information for characteristics of both parents.

Hybridization is usually followed by 6-8 generations of self-fertilization, which produces several thousand different but genetically pure plants, ie, plants which will breed true to type. New genotypes must be tested in various locations for several years and evaluated for characteristics relating to productivity, processing quality, storability and exportability. Of thousands of new genotypes evaluated in each cross, only one or 2 may come to be considered potential cultivars.

In cereal and forage crops, potential cultivars must then undergo extensive evaluation for approximately 3 years before they can be licensed for commercial production in Canada. Many crosses will fail to produce any genotypes with sufficient merit for licensing.

Cross-fertilized Species include rye, bromegrass, timothy, alfalfa and clover. Commercial cultivars usually are mixtures of several to many genotypes. New genotypes may occur naturally as the result of cross-fertilization among different genotypes within a commercial cultivar or

among genotypes from different cultivars grown in mixtures. Single plants are evaluated on the basis of their own performance, that of clones produced from them, or that of progeny produced by cross-fertilization or forced self-fertilization. Selected plants may be combined to form a new cultivar, either by mixing their seed and allowing the new cultivar to maintain itself by cross-fertilization or by mixing seed from the parents each time a new planting is required. The latter method can be used only if some form of vegetative propagation is available to maintain the parents as a seed source.

Asexually Reproducing Species Some annual species and many perennials can be reproduced asexually from vegetative tissue, such as stems, modified stems (rhizomes, tubers, corms and bulbs), leaves or roots, and, in some species, by apomictic seed production (ie, independent of fertilization).

In those species that also reproduce sexually, genetic variation can be generated through hybridization. In species in which seed production is difficult to achieve, new genotypes may occur naturally as "sports" (spontaneous mutations) or may be created by using mutagenic agents (eg, radiation or chemical mutagens). Selection of new genotypes in an asexually reproduced species is similar to that in other species, except that any superior genotype can be cloned and tested in its original state in a great number of different environments.

Hybrid Cultivars Commercial cultivars of maize (Indian corn) and many garden vegetables and flowers consist of highly uniform plants produced by crossing 2 inbred lines. This practice is economically feasible only when the cost of seed is small, relative to the value of the crop, or where the cost of producing hybrid seed can be minimized by using a system of genetic male sterility and fertility restoration. Hybrid seed usually results in more rigorous plants than those produced by inbred lines.

Backcrossing is used to transfer one or a few desirable genes from a donor parent to an otherwise acceptable recipient parent. It requires repeated crossing of new hybrids to the recurrent parent and selection for the desired gene from the donor parent. In cereal grains, resistance to rust and other obligate parasites has been achieved and maintained primarily through the use of backcrossing.

Applications

Plant breeding has been used to improve productivity, quality and disease resistance of most agricultural crops. Severe epidemics of rust and other fungal plant diseases have become infrequent because breeders and pathologists have succeeded in incorporating genetic resistance into new cultivars. The "pasta" quality of durum wheat has been modified to meet changing requirements of export markets and the baking quality of wheat has been altered to make it better suited to continuous-flow baking methods. Similarly, enzyme concentrations in barley have been increased to meet the needs of newer brewing techniques.

Plant breeding has played a major role in altering crop species (eg, maize, sunflowers, soybeans) so they can be grown over a wider area in Canada. The development of rapeseed as a significant export commodity stands as a major accomplishment of Canadian plant breeders, working with chemists, pathologists and agronomists (*see* CANOLA). Hardiness and persistence of many perennial forages have been improved through breeding, creeping-rooted alfalfa being one important example. In addition, efforts to reduce the alkaloid content of reed canary grass, the coumarin content of white and yellow sweet clover, and the levels of bloat-causing agents in alfalfa have all been successful. Plant breeding has also been used to reduce seed shattering in reed canary grass and to incorporate disease resistance into several perennial forages.

In HORTICULTURE, plant breeding has been used effectively to improve productivity and quality of fruits (eg, strawberries, apples) and vegetables. Dwarf cherry trees were developed by plant breeding and the science has made it possible to combine the desirable fruit characteristics of European cultivars with the hardiness of native Canadian species of raspberry and grape. Winter hardiness and adaptation to a short growing season are important characteristics of ornamentals as well as fruits. Significant improvements in these characteristics have been achieved in flowering crabapples, poplars, lilacs, roses, junipers and willows.

Plant breeding techniques have been used to improve the cooking and chipping quality of potatoes and to develop cultivars that are better adapted to short growing seasons. Improvements in the quality and maturity of sweet corn have made this species a part of home gardens throughout the country. Hybrids have been developed in crops such as tomatoes and cucumbers to provide more vigorous plants for home and commercial growers.

Institutions

Early plant breeding was carried out by individuals as a hobby associated with farming or horticulture. Now, however, most plant breeding is carried out by private or government institutions. In 1886 the federal government established the Dominion Experimental Farms Service, which soon became active in breeding cereal crops. The Experimental Farms Service eventually became the Research Branch of Agriculture Canada, which has RESEARCH STATIONS in all provinces. Agriculture Canada has active plant breeding programs in cereal crops, oilseeds, forages, tobacco, vegetables, flowers, fruits and ornamental shrubs. The federal government also has breeding programs for various shelterbelt and commercial tree species.

Plant breeding is carried out in the departments or colleges of agriculture of many Canadian universities, by several farmer co-operatives and by many seed companies. The Canadian Agricultural Services Co-ordinating Committee overseas is a network of committees which play co-ordinating and regulatory roles in the development and licensing of new cultivars. Expert committees on grain breeding, grain diseases and grain quality evaluate and recommend for licensing candidate cultivars of cereals, oilseeds and legume crops. A similar system of evaluation and approval exists for forage crops and certain horticultural crops.

R.J. BAKER

Reading: N.W. Simmonds, *Principles of Crop Improvement* (1979).

Plant Classification Popular classification usually divides living beings into PLANTS and ANIMALS and, sometimes, microbes. Scientific classification long followed a similar system, with 2 principal kingdoms: the animal order and the vegetable order. Plants and plantlike organisms (eg, fungi, algae) were those lacking complex sensory organs and organs of locomotion, and capable either of making their own food from inorganic elements or of absorbing it directly from the surrounding environment. This system is outdated; biologists now generally divide living beings into 5 kingdoms: Monera, Protista, FUNGI, Plantae and Animalia. These kingdoms are themselves organized into super kingdoms: Prokaryota and

Eukaryota. Prokaryotes are single-celled organisms lacking membrane-bound organelles (Monera); eukaryotes are composed of cells with membrane-bound nuclei (the other 4 kingdoms). Thus, true plants are multicellular and eukaryotic, contain pigments responsible for fixing light energy, have rigid cell walls and reproduce sexually.

There are probably some 600 000 species of plants and plantlike organisms, and a classification system is needed to give order to this diversity. Specialists in classification of living beings (systematists or taxonomists) have developed a hierarchical system to classify organisms in increasingly generalized groupings, according to common characteristics. The super kingdom is the most general grouping and is divided into increasingly narrow categories down to the species level. Species may be subdivided into subspecies, varieties and forms. The sugar maple is thus classified as follows: super kingdom - Eukaryota; kingdom - Plantae; division - Anthophyta; class - Magnoliopsida; subclass - Rosidae; order - Sapindales; family - Aceraceae; genus - *Acer*; species - *Acer saccharum* Marsh.

The name of a species is always a binomial, giving the name of the genus (here, *Acer*) and a specific epithet (*saccharum*). The species designation is followed by the name, usually abbreviated, of the first person to name the species in question: for sugar maple, the American botanist Humphrey Marshall (1722-1801). Plant names obey a set of rules (eg, that scientific names be in Latin) which make up the International Code of Botanical Nomenclature. The classification of living beings is not fixed; it is modified and improved through research. Modern classification depends on data from CHEMISTRY, BIOCHEMISTRY, cytology, PALEONTOLOGY, MOLECULAR BIOLOGY, embryology, etc, as well as on traditional morphological and anatomical details, and attempts to build a system that reflects the evolutionary history and relationships of plants. *See also* entries under individual species; ALGAE; BLUE-GREEN ALGAE; BIOTECHNOLOGY; BOTANY; CLUB MOSSES; MOSS; MUSHROOMS AND PUFFBALLS; LIVERWORTS; VEGETATION REGIONS. PIERRE MORISSET

Reading: Lyman Benson, *Plant Classification* (1979); H.J. Scoggan, *The Flora of Canada*, 4 vols (1978).

Plant Disease can decrease the economic, aesthetic and biological value of all kinds of plants. Plant pathology (phytopathology) is the study of the nature, causes, prevention and socioeconomic aspects of plant diseases. Plant diseases are recognized by symptoms such as necrosis (death of cells or tissues), chlorosis (yellowing), wilting (shoot and leaf drooping), rot, dwarfing, tumefaction (formation of gall or localized swelling), bronzing, damping-off (plant toppling), etc. Plant diseases are separated into nonparasitic (noninfectious, nontransmissible) and parasitic (infectious) diseases.

Nonparasitic diseases are caused by improper environmental conditions such as deficiencies and excesses of nutrients, biological toxicants, adverse soil and weather conditions, and pollutants. Deficiencies of mineral nutrients (nitrogen, phosphorus, potassium, boron, calcium, copper, iron, magnesium, manganese, molybdenum, sulphur and zinc) can induce some diseases in all kinds of crops. Diseases caused by pollutants can also be found. Air pollutants from combustion include sulphur dioxide and fluorides; those from photochemical reactions include complex nitrates and ozone. In addition, some toxic chemicals occur naturally.

Most plant diseases are caused by parasitic FUNGI, bacteria, mycoplasma, spiroplasma, viruses, viroids, nematodes and protozoa. In addition,

some plants (eg, dodders, MISTLETOES) can parasitize other green plants.

Fungi are microscopic or macroscopic threadlike organisms which lack the photosynthetic pigment, chlorophyll, and which bear reproductive structures (usually spores). Thousands of fungi cause approximately 100 000 diseases in green plants including rusts, smuts, powdery mildews and ergot of cereals; blights of potatoes and tomatoes; scab of apples; heart rots of trees; downy mildew of tobacco, damping-off of seedlings, etc.

Bacteria, Mycoplasma and Spiroplasma are simple cells which lack chlorophyll and which usually reproduce by cell division. Mycoplasma can be considered as simple forms of bacteria which lack cell walls. Spiroplasma are mycoplasmalike cells with a spiral structure. In nature, mycoplasma and spiroplasma are essentially dependent upon leafhoppers for their dispersal. In some cases, bacteria can be disseminated by insects but may also be dispersed by splashing rain, wind, contact, etc. A few hundred species of bacteria attack plants.

Viruses and Viroids represent the simplest form of parasitic entities. Viruses are made up of proteins and nucleic acids; viroids, of unprotected ribonucleic acids. They are considered molecular parasites, using host components for the replication (ie, multiplication) of their infectious nucleic acids. A few hundred plant viruses cause diseases known as tobacco, cucumber or tomato mosaics, potato leafroll, raspberry ringspot, tulip flower breaking, barley yellow dwarf, etc. Several viroids cause diseases such as potato spindle tuber, cucumber pale fruit, hop and chrysanthemum stunt, etc. Viroids and some viruses are transmitted by contact. Many viruses are disseminated in nature by arthropod vectors (eg, APHIDS, leafhoppers, THRIPS, white flies, mealy bugs, MITES); some are also transmitted by nematodes and soil-borne fungi.

Nematodes (eg, eelworms) are nonsegmented INVERTEBRATE animals. Most plant-parasitic nematodes cause root galls, rots and lesions and can severely retard root growth. Some nematodes feed on plants with their stylets (spears). Nematodes produce eggs and larvae which undergo several molts before becoming plant-pathogenic adults. Nematodes are also troublesome because they can act as very efficient vectors of 2 groups of plant viruses.

Protozoa are primitive forms of microscopic animals. A few species have been associated with some plant diseases.

Control

Because of the economic losses (billions of dollars worldwide each year) resulting from plant diseases, control measures are commonly used. Exclusion is prevention of the entry of a pathogen into an area by plant quarantines, certification programs, voluntary or mandatory inspection and pathogen-free production of plant material. Eradication is accomplished by removal of the pathogen hosts, by crop rotation and by heat or chemical treatment of the soil harbouring the pathogen. Protection methods depend primarily on chemical PESTICIDES such as fungicides, bactericides, nematicides, fumigants and insecticides (against insect vectors). However, some plant pathogens (eg, viruses and viroids) cannot be chemically suppressed because these agents multiply so intimately with the plant cells. Some cultural practices (eg, early and shallow seeding, fertilization) can also protect the plants against the disease-causing agents or conditions. Genetic manipulation is the best overall control method, when stable resistance or tolerance genes are easily found and incorporated into the plant's hereditary material. Many agronomically important crops have resistance or tolerance genes against several fungal and viral diseases. Biological control measures and integrated pest-management approaches represent promising avenues in the search for effective and safe control of plant diseases. These methods involve using natural predators against the disease-causing organism (*see* INSECT, BENEFICIAL).

Research in Canada

Because of the importance of FORESTRY operations and the AGRICULTURE AND FOOD system to Canada's economy, control of plant diseases has been a major focus of research (*see* AGRICULTURAL RESEARCH AND DEVELOPMENT). Forest stands and extensive hectarages seeded to a single crop, because they are both monoculture systems, are particularly vulnerable to damage from disease pathogens. The cost of such losses, however, is difficult to estimate. For example, in a 2-year study completed by Agriculture Canada's London Research Centre, crop losses caused by insects, disease and weeds in potato, rutabaga and onion crops were 64%, 88% and 100%, respectively. Cost of such losses, based on 1985 farm value of these crops, would have been $168.9 million, $13.1 million and $19.6 million. Research into the eradication or control of plant diseases takes place in federal and provincial government laboratories, university faculties or colleges of agriculture and forestry and some private companies. Because many horticultural plants begin as transplants from US nurseries, the possibility of introducing disease-causing organisms in these plants presents special problems.
ALAIN ASSELIN

Reading: G.N. Agrios, *Plant Pathology* (1980).

Plante, Jacques, hockey goaltender (b near Mont Carmel, Qué 17 Jan 1929; d at Geneva, Switz 26 Feb 1986). He began playing goal for a factory team in Shawinigan and played junior for Québec Citadels before turning professional with Montreal Royals at age 22. He played several games with MONTREAL CANADIENS during the 1953 playoffs and the final 17 games of the regular 1953-54 season, becoming Montréal's regular goalie 1954-55. He was the first goalie to win the VEZINA TROPHY 5 straight seasons (1955-56 to

Jacques Plante, known for his roving and his pioneering use of a face mask (*courtesy National Archives of Canada/C-29951*).

1959-60), and after an off-year in which he was injured, he won the Vezina again in 1961-62, as well as the HART TROPHY (most valuable player). He was traded to New York Rangers in 1963 after bouts of asthma had gained him a reputation for being undependable, but retired after less than 2 seasons. He returned to the NHL with St Louis 1968-70, sharing the Vezina with Glenn HALL in 1968-69 and, playing perhaps his best hockey ever, with Toronto 1970-73 and briefly with Boston in 1973. He finished his playing career with Edmonton Oilers (WHA) 1974-75 and coached Québec Nordiques 1973-74.

Plante played goal with superb technical ability and with drama and flair. He was famous in the sport for roving beyond his net, and after being struck in the face with a puck 1 Nov 1959 he was the first goalie to wear a protective mask regularly. In 17 NHL seasons, Plante played 837 regular season and 112 playoff games and compiled a 2.37 regular season and 2.16 playoff goals-against average, with 82 regular season and 14 playoff shutouts. He lived in Switzerland from 1975 to the time of his death.
JAMES MARSH

Planter, a term which usually designated, from the 1600s to the 1800s, an independent fisherman who owned his own "fishing," room or "plantation," on the coast of Newfoundland, and perhaps several large, inshore fishing boats. He employed other fishermen and might act as a local merchant or as middleman for a larger firm. Usually a permanent resident of Newfoundland, or LIVEYER, he might, like the BYE-BOAT keeper, frequently return to Britain or retire there (*see* FISHERIES HISTORY). In more recent times, applied to the Labrador fishery, the term was nearly synonymous with stationer.
ROBERT D. PITT

Planters The Treaty of UTRECHT in 1713 marked the British defeat of the French. During the troubled years until 1755 in ACADIA, the colony of Nova Scotia under British rule, the French settlers who refused to give allegiance were expelled under the direction of Gov Charles LAWRENCE. To settle the vacant lands, particularly along the shores of the Bay of Fundy, Lawrence offered New Englanders free lands and passage. In 1760 about 1800 people, mostly Connecticut and Rhode Island farmers, took up their prearranged grants, to become Planters, an Elizabethan name for those who "planted" colonies. Several vessels had brought settlers and their movables to Cornwallis and Horton and Falmouth Townships in extensive King's County. Each grantee received 500 acres of diversified lands, including a section in the Town Plot, where a blockhouse for defence and spaces for a school and for the first minister were located.

The terms of settlement promised religious freedom, except to Roman Catholics, but the Church of England initially had advantages and gave leadership for schooling youths. Most of the settlers were Congregationalists.

Though used to governing through town meetings, for several years the Planters were denied local rule, retained by the governor and council at Halifax. An assembly allowed county and township representatives to gather at the capital, but local officers were chosen at Halifax. The new settlers, occupied with immediate needs, accepted this. Most of them stayed and bettered themselves, many becoming leaders.
JAMES D. DAVISON

Plants, Native Uses Over a thousand plant species were used traditionally by Indian and Inuit peoples. These species, ranging from ALGAE to CONIFERS and flowering PLANTS, provided food, medicine and materials, and played an important role in native language, ritual and mythology.

Many species remain important in today's native cultures. The study of direct interrelationships between humans and plants is called ethnobotany. In Canada systematic ethnobotanical studies have been few, but with contributions from researchers in various disciplines, much has been learned. The roles of plants in traditional cultures are summarized below.

Food Plants Cultivation of food crops was practised by native Canadians, before the arrival of Europeans, only in southern Ontario and the St Lawrence Valley. Crops included the "three sisters" – corn, beans and squash – as well as sunflowers, tobacco and, possibly, Jerusalem artichoke. Over 500 species of wild plants provided foods for native peoples in Canada. Some of these foods are similar to those eaten today: root and green vegetables, fruits, nuts, seeds and MUSHROOMS. Others, eg, some types of LICHENS, marine algae and inner bark tissues of some trees, are not normally part of the modern diet. Plants were also used as sweeteners, flavourings and beverages. Many wild plants provided more than one type of food. Today, maple syrup, wild rice and many wild fruits are enjoyed by native and non-native Canadians.

Medicinal Plants Plants were an important component of native medicine. Curing of disease and maintenance of health were usually carried out by herbal specialists. Although administering herbal medicines was sometimes associated with ritual and "magic," and in many cultures herbal curing and magical curing were virtually inseparable, the specialists were not necessarily shamans who invoked supernatural powers in healing. Sometimes, special curative and spiritual organizations existed, eg, the Ojibwa MIDEWIWIN (grand medicine society) in which initiates passed through stages, eventually learning the ritual and herbalism for curing disease.

More than 500 plants were used in native medicine. These were administered as herbal teas, preparations to be chewed and swallowed, poultices, or inhaled vapours, although a variety of more exotic modes of application (eg, pouring a concoction in the patient's ear) were also used. Any part of a plant, alone or in combination with other HERBS, could be prescribed.

Although native herbal cures have been alternately rejected as superstition or embraced as cure-alls, an objective assessment by medical authorities indicates that treatments of certain ailments (eg, wounds, skin sores, gastrointestinal disorders, coughs, colds, fevers and rheumatism) were rational and effective. In many cases, pharmacological constituents of plants can be correlated with the native application. A famous example is the curing of CARTIER'S men of scurvy (winter 1535-36). They were treated by natives of Hochelaga with a conifer tea of high vitamin C content (probably eastern white cedar). For other plants, the "ritual" or "magical" element may be more important, an example being the use of spiny or thorny plants as protective agents to ward off "spirits" associated with illness and death. This approach was probably effective for psychosomatic ailments, and it may have improved the outlook of patients with organic complaints as well. Native practitioners were skilled in selection, preparation and dosage of herbal medicines. The reader is cautioned that many plant species used as medicines are highly poisonous and should not be used except under qualified supervision.

Utility Plants Various plant materials, from several hundred different species, were used by Canadian native peoples. Woods were of prime importance as fuels, and as major components of utilitarian items: buildings, dugout canoes, boxes, totem poles and implements (eg, paddles, dig-

Examples of Some Pharmacologically Valid Native Medicines

Plant	Use/ Preparation	Native group	Medicinal principle
balsam fir	colds/inhale vapours	many groups	monoterpenes— nasal stimulants
cascara	constipation/ tea from bark	western groups	anthracenes— cathartics
gold-thread	mouth sores/ tea from roots	Iroquois & others	alkaloid— antibacterial
kinni-kinnick	kidney ailments/tea from branches	Okanagan	glycoside & other compounds— diuretic
red oak	diarrhea/tea from bark	Maliseet	tannins— astringents
poplar	back pain/ tea from roots	Ojibwa	salicin— analgesic

ging sticks, spear shafts, bows, arrows, snowshoe frames, etc). Sheets of bark, especially birch, were made into containers and canoes. Bark was also used to cover roofs and line storage pits. Fibrous tissues from stems, roots, bark and leaves served for twine, rope and weaving materials for baskets, mats and clothing. Tree resin was used as glue and waterproofing. Plants provided dyes and pigments, scents, absorbent materials, abrasives, linings and wrappings, insect repellents, toys and recreational items, and personal adornment.

Conclusion Plants have provided varied and abundant resources for native peoples for thousands of years. A vast traditional knowledge of plant foods, medicines and materials has enabled Indian and Inuit peoples to thrive in Canada's diverse environments. Many plants they depended on have been adopted into our modern life-style. Others have potential as nutritional supplements, future food resources, and sources of new pharmaceuticals and other useful compounds.

NANCY J. TURNER, J.T. ARNASON, R.J. HEBDA AND T. JOHNS

Reading: A.F. Szczawinski and Nancy J. Turner, *Edible Wild Plants of Canada*, vols 2-4 (1978-80).

Plaskett, John Stanley, astronomer (b at Hickson, UC 17 Nov 1865; d at Esquimalt, BC 17 Oct 1941). Born on a farm, Plaskett joined the Edison Co in Schenectady, NY, and Sherbrooke, Qué. Foreman of the workshop in the dept of physics at U of T in 1890, he enrolled as a student in 1895 and graduated in 1899. In 1903 Plaskett joined the astronomical branch of the Dept of the Interior, Ottawa, helping to design and construct instruments for the new Dominion Observatory there. He observed a solar eclipse in 1905 and did important work on radial velocities of stars. His proposal for a large telescope was approved and the 72-inch (1.8 m) telescope (then the world's largest) was completed in 1918 at Victoria, BC. Plaskett became the first director there, retiring in 1935. He worked on spectroscopic binaries (a massive one that he discovered still bears his name) and together with J.A. PEARCE published the first detailed analysis of the structure of the Milky Way Galaxy (1935). They demonstrated that the sun is two-thirds out from the centre of our galaxy and rotates once in 220 million years. In 1984 Minor Planet No 2905 was named Plaskett in honour of J.S. Plaskett and his son H.H. Plaskett, also an astronomer. A.H. BATTEN

Plasticiens, Les In the mid-1950s, following the excitement generated by the AUTOMATISTES, many Québec artists felt a need to return to a more controlled and ordered style of PAINTING. This sentiment was noticeable in the recent work of Fernand LEDUC, a loyal follower of Paul-Émile BORDUAS and automatism from the beginning.

Leduc now felt that automatism had unconsciously held on to a dated concept of pictorial space by maintaining the dichotomy of object and background. A new pictorial movement was launched with the 1955 publication of the *Manifeste des plasticiens*. Drafted by critic and painter Rodolphe de Repentigny (who signed his paintings with the pseudonym Jauran) and countersigned by Louis Belzile, Jean-Paul Jérôme and Fernand Toupin, it was quite different from the REFUS GLOBAL, which had appeared in 1948. The group had worked out their ideas in 1954 and held an exhibition in Feb 1955. The *Manifeste des plasticiens* encouraged young Québec artists to follow the example of the pioneers of abstract art, in particular that of Mondrian. The Plasticiens preferred a strict use of 2-dimensional space in their paintings. In 1956, Guido MOLINARI (Noirs et Blancs) and Claude TOUSIGNANT (Monochromes) proposed even more radical departures: 2-dimensional surfaces, reversible spaces and the series concept. The Plasticien movement remained a force in the Québec art community; artists such as Yves GAUCHER, Jacques Hurtubise and Charles GAGNON were influenced by it. Only with the rise of postmodernism at the end of the 1960s did the Plasticien movement give way to a new avant-garde in the Québec art world.

FRANÇOIS-MARC GAGNON

Reading: D. Burnett and M. Schiff, *Contemporary Canadian Art* (1983); J. Russell Harper, *Painting in Canada* (1977); D. Reid, *A Concise History of Canadian Painting* (1973).

Plastics-Processing Industry Plastics are based on giant molecules (polymers) which have a structure so ordered that they can be shaped at elevated temperatures and pressures, ie, these long-chain polymers exhibit "plastic flow" when heated. They are often modified with other materials (eg, plasticizers, fillers, stabilizers) before being processed in the molten state. Certain "thermosetting" polymers are subject to irrevocable chemical changes (curing or cross-linking) so that once shaped they are infusible. The "thermoplastic" types (notably polyethylene, polyvinyl chloride, polypropylene, polystyrene) can be recycled because they do not lose their ability to flow when remelted.

The forming of plastics into film, pipe, bottles and a myriad of molded shapes is estimated to involve approximately 72 000 (1985) people in Canada. Shipments by plastic fabricators totalled $4 billion in 1986. Some of the major processors include Leco Inc, Toronto; Union Carbide Canada Ltd, Toronto; and Canadian General-Tower Ltd, Cambridge, Ont. The industry is the third-largest employer in the manufacturing sector and was estimated in 1985 to have generated $8.2 billion in GDP. This manufacturing activity has defied easy classification because the output (from bathtubs to wire and cable insulation) is more often than not an integral part of another industrial operation. Where the plastic part is a component of a larger assembly (eg, automobiles, TV sets), the same blurring of industrial categories occurs. Many producers of durable goods operate plastics-processing equipment on their own premises. In contrast to the manufacture of the resins, usually undertaken by multinationals strong in polymer technology, the fabricating of plastics products is often guided by entrepreneurs. The most successful of these are generally members of the Society of Plastics Engineers (SPE) and the Society of Plastics Industry (SPI).

The equipment, whether the property of over 1400 small and medium-sized independent establishments or "captive" to a particular assembly line, has increased in sophistication and size over the last century. In 1881 a Toronto cabinetmaker began laminating cellulose nitrate (ie, celluloid)

sheet onto piano and organ keyboards. The advent of phenolformaldehyde polymers in 1909-1910 (products in which Lawrence Redmond, had a pioneering role) paved the way for compression-molding presses.

Not until thermoplastic cellulose acetate, initially a material employed for coatings and fibres, was recognized as an excellent molding compound, did processors accept the injection-molding machine. The injection system entails melting the polymer and forcing the molten material under high pressure into closed-mold cavities. In 1931 French Ivory Products of Toronto, making cellulose acetate caps for toothpaste tubes, operated the first injection-molding machine in N America. The molding of cellulosics had limited application but, in the next 30 years, processors learned to work with new materials: nylon, polyvinylchloride, polystyrene, polyethylene and polypropylene came out of the laboratory before 1960. Today a mold is designed to exploit the particular properties of a wide range of thermoplastics. Cost is of major importance; therefore, most injection-molded products are formed from so-called "commodity" resins (eg, ethylene, styrene, propylene, vinyl chloride). For certain high-performance parts requiring toughness, special electrical properties, or resistance to elevated temperatures or similar "hostile" environments, the molder is likely to choose one of several engineering resins (eg, nylon, polyphenylene oxide, polycarbonate, acetals, terephthalates).

Polyethylene is the most ubiquitous of thermoplastics; in 1986 Canadian consumption of the various grades exceeded 691 000 t. Polyethylene is popular because it can be extruded through a shaping die to form a thin film. Film products such as milk pouches, bread bags, grocery sacks and garbage bags have transformed the flexible packaging industry. Vinyl films have a place in meat packaging and household wraps; polypropylene film is displacing paper and cellulose film for many types of overwraps.

The weathering characteristics of polyvinyl chloride have made it a popular material for other extrusions as well. Vinyl pipe is gaining ascendancy over metal, asbestos, clay and concrete for water and sewer lines, electrical conduits and ducts. Vinyl competes with aluminum and wood for house siding. Vinyl extruded "profiles" make excellent sashes and thermal breaks for windows. Other plastics vie for a part of the pipe market. Most homes are now equipped with drain, waste and vent pipes extruded from a styrenic compound. Industrial effluent pipe is normally extruded from polyethylene. Farmland is often reclaimed with the help of polyethylene (or polypropylene) corrugated drain tubing. Either extrusion or injection molding is a necessary step in another plastics process, in which a parison (round hollow tube) is formed for subsequent blow molding. The parison is put between 2 halves of a mold and expanded with air pressure into a blown part. Bottles, drums and other hollow containers are made economically by this process. Polyethylene bottles are favoured for packaging detergents, bleaches and a wide range of other products. Vinyl bottles most often hold hair shampoos. *See also* CHEMICAL INDUSTRIES.

CHARLES LAW

Plate Tectonics is the theory describing motions of Earth's crust and part of the underlying mantle. It states that large fractures divide the Earth's brittle surface layer into a few large and many smaller rigid plates, and that forces in the hot, deformable interior very slowly move these plates about relative to one another. These movements are considered the principal cause of geological change. Over GEOLOGICAL HISTORY they have opened and closed OCEAN basins, raised MOUNTAINS, facilitated accumulation of MINERAL and petroleum deposits, and influenced EVOLUTION and CLIMATE CHANGE. Friction between plates prevents steady motion and stores energy that is intermittently released in sudden movements, causing EARTHQUAKES. Most VOLCANOES erupt close to plate boundaries.

Past Theories Early scientists assumed that the Earth's major features were fixed. The discovery of the Americas showed that the opposite coasts of the Atlantic or, more precisely, the edges of the continental shelves have similar shapes and seem once to have fitted together. At that time the Earth was believed to be only about 6000 years old; therefore, it was thought that any separation must have occurred as the result of cataclysmic events at the time of creation.

During the 19th century, geologists argued that to provide time for the great thicknesses of SEDIMENTARY ROCK to have accumulated, the Earth must be older than 6000 years, perhaps hundreds of millions of years old. Conversely, physicists argued that the Earth was losing heat to space and that, since no adequate sources of internal energy were known, it must be cooling. They pointed out that, even if the Earth had been red-hot when formed, it would have cooled to its present temperature in a few tens of millions of years at most. They also held that the ensuing contraction would have squeezed the surface and uplifted mountains. In 1896 the discovery of radioactivity led to the realization that radioactive elements are widespread in common rocks and provide a heat source for the Earth. It also permitted development of methods to determine the Earth's age (about 4.6 billion years). In 1908 the American geologist Frank B. Taylor proposed that the continents are slowly moving about and that their collisions give rise to mountains. Almost immediately Alfred Wegener, a German meteorologist, proposed that 200 million years ago a single supercontinent, Pangea, had broken apart and that since then the continents had been moving separately through the ocean floors like ships. Opponents rightly objected that he had not provided a cause or enough supporting evidence. At a large conference held in 1926, authorities strongly rejected Wegener's ideas. A few supporters held out in areas where evidence for drift was strongest, eg, the Alps and S Africa. In the latter, A.L. du Toit proposed that Pangea had broken into Gondwanaland in the S and Laurasia in the N before fragmenting into existing continents. Plate tectonics is a modified version of the theory of continental drift. The essential difference is that the latter theory assumed that each continent was propelled separately through stationary ocean floors. According to plate tectonics, continents do not form individual plates but are incorporated with sections of ocean floor in larger, moving plates constituting the surface of the Earth.

Seismology and Earth's Interior In the early 20th century too little was known about the ocean floors and the planet's interior to allow the development of any clear idea of how the Earth behaved. Nothing has done more to increase knowledge about and understanding of the planet than the study of seismology (*see* GEOLOGY). Earthquakes were familiar but little understood until, in the late 19th century, the Emperor of Japan invited John Milne from England to study them. Milne and his contemporaries produced the first satisfactory seismographs, the first worldwide network for reporting earthquakes and a theory to explain earthquake waves. Seismographic studies revealed the general pattern of the Earth's internal structure. Visualized as a boiled egg, Earth's shell is a cool, brittle crust of the visible rocks; the white, a far thicker mantle of denser rocks, white-hot and deformable, but solid; the

yolk, a core rich in liquid iron. The existence of a readily deformable layer at a depth of a few tens of kilometres beneath the surface is well illustrated by the depression of north-central N America beneath the load of GLACIERS during the recent ICE AGES and the uplift of the land since the ice sheets melted (*see* GLACIATION). This uplift has left beaches raised by hundreds of metres around the shores of the Great Lakes and Hudson Bay. If the surface can move up and down through hundreds of metres, the interior must be deformable and it follows that, if the surface layer is ruptured, the pieces may move horizontally. Improvement in recording of earthquakes enabled the French Rothés, father and son, and the Americans B. Gutenberg and C.F. Richter to show that most earthquakes follow the principal mountains and island areas around the Pacific Ocean and the Himalayan and Alpine ranges across Eurasia.

Ocean Floors The collection of information about the ocean floors began in the mid-19th century, when Commodore M.F. Maury, US Navy, made soundings across the Atlantic Ocean. These soundings revealed that the central part is much shallower than the rest. The CHALLENGER EXPEDITION (1872-76) showed this centre to be part of a great ridge along the axis of the ocean. Later expeditions found shallow mid-ocean areas in other oceans and located deep trenches off some continental coasts and on the convex side of island arcs. In the 1920s the Canadian geologist R.A. Daly advocated a mobile Earth and in 1930, in England, A. Holmes suggested that radioactive heating causes convection currents to rise within the Earth beneath the mid-ocean ridges, uplifting them and spreading out in either direction to descend beneath mountain ranges. Unfortunately, until instruments were developed to permit detailed study, too little firm evidence was available at that time to permit acceptance of these ideas.

Starting with the echo sounder in the 1930s, the period during and since WWII has seen rapid development of instruments for studying the ocean floors. In 1956 M. Ewing and B.C. Heezen of Columbia U, using data much of which they had collected, noticed that the axial belt of earthquakes coincided with the crest of known mid-ocean ridges. Observing the continuity of the earthquake belts, they speculated that the ridges were also continuous. By 1960 they had proved this. They also established the existence of the Earth's greatest mountain system, winding its way for 60 000 km down the axis of the Atlantic Ocean, around S Africa to the middle of the Indian Ocean, whence one branch follows the Gulf of Aden into the Red Sea and another passes S of Australia and New Zealand to cross the Pacific and join the San Andreas Fault at the head of the Gulf of California. The ridge rises to form islands such as Iceland, the Azores and Easter I.

Great Faults Californian oceanographers observed that the crest of the ridge was offset, as much as hundreds of kilometres, by fracture zones which resembled faults, but appeared to end abruptly. Similar, smaller fractures were soon found in other ridges, notably in the equatorial Atlantic. These mysterious submarine features added fuel to arguments about huge faults recognized on land, eg, in 1924 by C.H. Stockwell alongside Great Slave Lk. In 1946 geologists in Scotland and New Zealand proposed that huge faults with offsets over 100 km crossed those countries, beginning and ending in the sea. In 1953 California geologists proposed an even greater offset along the San Andreas Fault which began in the Gulf of California and ended in the Pacific off Cape Mendocino. These discoveries posed a problem for believers in a rigid Earth, because they could not explain such large offsets or how such large faults could be terminated.

Rock Magnetism That some pieces of rock, usually of an iron ore (magnetite), are naturally magnetized was known to the ancients and led to the invention of the mariner's compass. Early in this century it was shown that many rocks are weakly magnetized and retain their direction of magnetism permanently. It was supposed that they had acquired direction when formed, but the first investigations proved puzzling and only slowly were 3 causes of irregularity discovered. First, the North GEOMAGNETIC POLE has moved a few hundred kilometres across northern Canada since it was discovered 150 years ago. It is now agreed that the magnetic poles and field are slowly moving about the geographical poles of rotation. Thus, to determine the former latitude (relative to the geomagnetic pole) of any place, many measurements must be made upon a series of nearly contemporaneous lava flows or strata, and the average taken. Secondly, the Earth's magnetic field varies in strength and periodically dies away to zero, before starting up in the reverse direction. This results in a reversal of the poles so that the north pole becomes a south pole and vice versa. Fortunately, each reversal is complete and no intermediate positions occur. Reversals occur at irregular intervals varying from a few thousand to millions of years; many reversals have been dated. Third, some rocks have been altered or do not hold their original magnetization; these produce irregular results.

Plate Tectonic Theory By the mid-1950s these problems were understood and reliable magnetic directions were available from rocks of different ages from different parts of the world. These data revealed a fourth cause for changes in the direction of magnetization in rocks. At a symposium held in Tasmania in 1956, it was established that on any continent the apparent magnetic latitude changes systematically with increasing age of the rocks. This alteration strongly suggested that steady continental motions had occurred and that these motions agreed with the evidence from geology and the fit of the continents across the Atlantic. The symposium inaugurated a change of opinion which, over the next 2 decades, converted most earth scientists to a belief in continental movement, although a precise mechanism had still to be found. In 1960 H.H. Hess elaborated on Holmes's idea of convection currents. He suggested that such a current is rising beneath the mid-ocean ridge crossing the Pacific Ocean, and that it splits the crest apart creating fresh ocean floor, while the ocean floors on either side are carried away to sink beneath the mountain and island areas along the Pacific coasts. In 1963 Canadians L.W. Morley and A. Larochelle first showed that long lines of magnetic anomalies in the Atlantic form parallel stripes situated symmetrically along both sides of the ridge crests. They realized that magnetic stripes were caused by natural reversals in the Earth's magnetic field. Their ideas seemed so strange that 2 reputable journals rejected their paper; however, later that year, F. Vine and D.H. Matthews made similar observations in the Indian Ocean which they also interpreted as the result of reversals in the Earth's field.

Their paper was ignored until, 2 years later, a plot of earthquake locations was superimposed on a magnetic map of the N American Pacific coast which R.G. Mason of England had made. This superimposition showed that linear magnetic anomalies could be interpreted to show the existence of 3 small, spreading ridges off BC, forming an extension to the main mid-ocean ridge system and connected to it by the San Andreas Fault. Hence, the spreading of the ridge system controls motions on the faults. When Vine saw the results, he pointed out that the time scale of reversals established in California could be used to date reversals on the ocean floor off BC. Hence, the date of commencement and rate of spreading of the ridges off BC had been established. Their behaviour determined the date of the start of motion and rate and direction of movement in the San Andreas Fault with which the ridges connect off Cape Mendocino, Calif.

This result was quickly accepted and applied by Vine and scientists at Columbia University and in California to interpret magnetic anomalies and date the ocean floors. The oldest part is near the Mariana Arc in the western Pacific where the floor is a little under 200 million years old. Clearly, the oceans are being constantly renewed. In contrast, the continents contain small areas of rocks as much as 3800 million years old. This discovery also led to an explanation of the behaviour of great faults and their relation to spreading ridges. For example, in the equatorial Atlantic, the mid-ocean ridge does not follow the same curved shape as the adjacent coasts of Brazil and Africa, but is broken into a series of steps. It seems that, as soon as continents separate, the ridge breaks up into alternating segments of 2 kinds. Spreading segments form at right angles to the direction of separation of the continents and new lava flows up along them. They are joined by shearing segments (ie, transform faults) parallel to the motion of the continents.

When these large faults were first discovered, it was assumed that they would extend for great distances, but actually they stop abruptly. In 1965 J. Tuzo WILSON pointed out that, because of the formation of new crust, the surface area of the Earth in such localities is increasing; hence, the laws of ordinary geometry cease to apply and faults are of a special type called transform. These faults extend, are active and produce earthquakes only between spreading segments; they stop abruptly at either end. The direction of motion on transform faults is the reverse of that in faults occurring in regions of unchanging surface area. These discoveries showed that Earth's surface is divided into rigid segments, changing shape only at boundaries; hence, the name "plate tectonics" was coined. Evidence from magnetism, seafloor spreading and faulting has made it difficult not to accept the theory. Because the Earth is not believed to be changing appreciably in size, the spreading of the mid-ocean ridges with its accompanying growth of new ocean floors must be balanced by a return somewhere of older crust into the interior. This occurs especially off the coasts surrounding the Pacific Ocean, where the ocean plates are bent down beneath the overriding continental plates producing deep trenches – except where rapid sedimentation from adjacent coasts fill the trenches. K. Wadati and H. Benioff showed that most large earthquakes occur beneath circum-Pacific island arcs and mountains. The patterns traced by the foci of numerous earthquakes form parts of vertical cones that reach the surface in the trenches and extend to depths of 700 km. They mark the zones of contact between the overlapping plates. The disturbance caused by the sinking plates produces melting and lava rises to form the arcs of volcanic islands.

F.C. Frank explained the conical zones and circular surface trenches and arcs by pointing out that, if part of the surface of a sphere is pushed inwards, the depression tends to be circular (as when one pinches a soft tennis ball). This theory holds in East Asia where the crustal layer forming the Pacific plate is advancing over the underlying mantle and sinking under the continental Eurasian plate, which is stagnant relative to the interior. The theory fails where S America is advancing over the interior and over the stationary Nazca plate, which is not free to move but is forced down following the outline of the continental coast. The trenches follow the coast and the zone of deeper earthquakes is irregular.

Continents are less dense than ocean floors and, like a granitic scum, cannot readily be overridden. Where 2 continental blocks (eg, India and the rest of Eurasia) have met, closing a former ocean that lay between them, the collision piles up mountains and plateaus. It appears that, from time to time, such collisions halt or change the direction and motion of plates.

Present System of Plates The surface of the Earth is now broken into 6 or 7 major plates: the African, Antarctic and Eurasian plates each contain one continent; the Pacific plate none; the Indian and American plates 2 each, but some separate the N and S American plates. There are many smaller plates. All plates grow by the formation of new oceanic crust along mid-ocean ridges. They slide past one another along transform faults and they overlap and absorb crust beneath island areas and growing mountains. The pattern is slowly, but ceaselessly, changing. Most changes are gradual, but occasional reorganization takes place. No parts of the Atlantic or Indian oceans are more than 180 million years old; the Red Sea and Gulf of Aden are about 10 million years old; the East African rift valleys are younger still and are only beginning to open. This progression of age and width suggests a cycle of growth in oceans but, since the Earth is most unlikely to be expanding, it must be complemented by a progression of shrinking oceans. Coasts of the Pacific Ocean and Mediterranean Sea are overriding their respective basins and, in the Himalayan region, India has closed the Tethys Sea and collided with the rest of Eurasia. These reductions represent the later stages of what K. Burke and W. Kidd have called the Wilson cycle of ocean history.

In 1930 H. Cloos drew attention to the associations of faults, earthquakes and volcanoes along the Rhine and East African rift valleys. Volcanism and domal uplift are greatest at triple points, eg, in Ethiopia where the Red Sea, Gulf of Aden and rift valleys meet, and at Sinai where the Red Sea and Gulfs of Aden and Aqaba meet. The Red Sea appears to join these 2 places. In Africa there are many domed uplifts with volcanoes, called hotspots, and the rift valleys appear to join some of them. This fact suggests that oceans start to form where rifts have connected a succession of volcanic hot-spots (or uplifts) and that these fractures spread to form widening oceans. Hot-spots form on continents and in oceans. Some, like the island of Hawaii, are isolated, as are some on continents; others, like Iceland, the Azores, St Paul Rocks and Tristan da Cunha, lie along mid-ocean ridges. Both types have associated trails of extinct and progressively aging volcanic islands or submarine ridges: in the first case, a single trail; in the second, a double trail, which, in the case of Tristan, forms the Walvis and Rio Grande ridges. At the shoreward ends of these 2 ridges, volcanic rocks 130 million years old crop out on the coasts of Africa and S America. This evidence supports the views that, at that date, a single volcanic hotspot formed in Gondwanaland, linked by rift valleys to other hot-spots. These hot-spots and rifts, which determined the Atlantic Ocean, have remained active. Hot-spots may represent the tops of columns of heated rock rising through the mantle to carry off the Earth's surplus heat.

Earlier Cycles of Ocean and Mountain Building The present oceans mark only the last part of a cycle that began when Pangea broke apart; however, there is no marked change in the types of rocks observed before and after that 200-million-year-old event, although the Earth's age is great and radioactive heating continuous. Thus, it is likely that the supercontinent of Pangea existed only briefly, and that oceans had opened and closed in many places and at many times earlier. Paleomagnetism and geology indicate that this has been happening regularly since near the start of Proterozoic time (2500 million years ago). Rocks older than that, from Archean time, are different; therefore, the Earth's behaviour must have been different. The Himalayan and Ural mountains are thought to be uplifts formed where continents collided. If the 2 sides of the Atlantic are reassembled, it is evident that the Scandinavian, Scottish, Appalachian and Moroccan mountains once formed part of a single chain which came together to close a proto-Atlantic 400 million years ago, then 200 million years later broke up to help form the present Atlantic. In that case, it may be that not hot-spots but the concentration of radioactive elements in the mountain belts caused the oceans to form.

Consequences of Tectonic Movement The evidence that continents have often collided and separated has provided an explanation for the transfer of living forms that evolved on one continent to another continent, and shows that all continents are in effect mosaics of many fragments. The movement of continents has also affected climates and caused periodic ice ages. In some configurations of continents, ocean currents flow between the warm equatorial regions and the cold polar regions, distributing heat and giving rise to equitable climates. If one continent becomes isolated, with currents flowing around and not towards it (eg, modern Antarctica), that continent loses much heat, the world's climates are uneven and an ice age results.

Vast deposits of copper ores have been worked on Cyprus for thousands of years and the surrounding rocks have recently been shown to be typical of those formed on ocean floors. Beginning in 1977, great hot springs or jets of extremely hot water rich in minerals were observed along the crests of some spreading mid-ocean ridges. These jets are surrounded by mineral deposits, which they precipitated on emerging. It is now believed that many ore deposits were formed in the oceans and later uplifted, and that these juvenile waters from the interior are a major factor in creating ore bodies and in modifying ocean GEOCHEMISTRY (*see* OCEAN MINING). In 1987 the suggestion, which H.W. Menard raised in 1960, was revived: that oceanic ridges penetrate beneath the continental crust. Considering the angles of collision between mid-ocean ridges and drifting continents improved the theory. Where at right angles, rifts such as the Gulf of Aden formed. Where oblique, shallow coastal faults such at those in California (San Andreas) and BC form, the overridden ridge uplifted the southwestern US. With parallel collisions, as in older mountains of Pacific and Atlantic Canada, overridden hot welts pushed folds and thrusts inland until the welts cooled and subsided before disturbing the Canadian Shield.   J. Tuzo WILSON

Reading: J. Tuzo Wilson, *Continents Adrift and Continents Aground* (1976); P.J. Wyllie, *The Way the Earth Works* (1976).

Platinum (Pt), heavy, greyish white metallic element that melts at 1769°C. It occurs with the other platinum group metals: palladium, iridium, rhodium, osmium and ruthenium. Platinum does not easily enter into chemical combination with other elements and is soluble only in hot aqua regia (mixture of nitric and hydrochloric acids). The usual natural form is native platinum, in which platinum is alloyed with small amounts of other platinum metals, appreciable amounts of iron and, often, copper, nickel or silver. It is usually found in small grains and scales, and occasionally in irregular masses and large nuggets. Initially platinum was recovered from placer deposits, but it has become possible to recover it from platinum-bearing ultrabasic rocks. Platinum is a rare, precious metal, valued at up to $1000 per troy ounce. Modern knowledge of the metal dates from the 16th century when it was discovered in S America by Spaniards who named it *platina* ("little silver"). South Africa and the Soviet Union are the main suppliers, with Canada 3rd, producing about 6% of world supplies in the 1980s – most of it drawn from masses of nickel-copper ores from the Sudbury Basin. 1986 production was 8793 g. Platinum is intrinsically valuable and is used in jewellery, but its greatest use is in catalytic converters controlling emissions from automobile exhausts and in rhenium catalysts used to break down crude oil. Platinum's inertness makes it the choice metal for pacemaker electrodes placed in the human heart. Much of the world's platinum is hoarded in bank vaults.

Palladium, lightest of platinum-group metals, has the lowest melting point of the group (1552°C). Palladium is more reactive chemically than other platinum metals and is, therefore, known in more compound mineral forms than any other platinum-group metal. In the nickel-copper ore bodies of the Sudbury Basin, palladium forms about 45% of the platinum-group metals. In the USSR it forms about 65% and in the Merensky Reef of S Africa about 26%. Palladium is used as a component in brazing alloys. It gives colour and hardness to white gold used in jewellery. Palladium and palladium-rich alloys are widely used for electrical contacts, especially those that must operate at low voltages, eg, telephone switching relays.   S.A. HAMILTON

Plattsburgh, Battle of In Sept 1814, Sir George PREVOST led a combined army-navy invasion of upper New York State. His plan called for his 11 000 troops, including many experienced veterans of European battles against Napoleon, to capture the town of Plattsburgh, NY, defended by only 4000 men, while the British Lk Champlain fleet under Capt George Downie destroyed its American counterpart under Commodore Thomas Macdonough. Goaded by Prevost's constant urgings into a premature attack upon the US ships' strong defensive line in Plattsburgh Bay, Downie lost his life and his squadron before the indecisive Prevost mounted an attack on the land defences. News of the naval setback convinced Prevost, against the advice of his major-generals, to call off the offensive and to move back up the Richelieu R to the safety of Lower Canada before the Americans could cut off his retreat. The entire campaign, its conception, planning and particularly its prosecution and abandonment, tarnished Prevost's reputation and probably contributed to his deteriorating health and premature death in Jan 1816 at the age of 48.   CARL A. CHRISTIE

Plaunt, Alan Butterworth, organizer, broadcaster, journalist (b at Ottawa 25 Mar 1904; d there 12 Sept 1941). Born of a wealthy lumbering family, he devoted his life to national unity, public broadcasting, economic reform and pacifism. As cofounder, with Graham SPRY, of the Canadian Radio League in 1930, Plaunt was instrumental in mobilizing popular and political support for public broadcasting. He was a leading force in the league until his appointment to the original board of governors of the CBC (1936-40). As a member of the LEAGUE FOR SOCIAL RECONSTRUCTION, he helped draft the Regina Manifesto. He founded the New Canada Movement in 1933 and, as co-proprietor with Spry of the *Farmers' Sun* (1932-35), used the paper to advance the movement's causes, namely a "new deal" for rural peoples. In the late 1930s he helped organize the Neutrality League to promote pacifism and political neutrality for Canada.   ROBERT E. BABE

Plaut, W. Gunther, rabbi, author (b at Münster, Germany 1 Nov 1912). He left Germany, where he was raised and educated, to escape the Nazis before WWII. He immigrated to the US and studied to become a Reform rabbi at the Hebrew Union College in Cincinnati, Ohio (ordained 1939). He was Jewish chaplain in the American forces 1943-46, and has held reform pulpits at Chicago, St Paul, Minn, and Toronto's Holy Blossom Temple (1961-77), where he became senior scholar in residence in 1978. His most important scholarly works include *The Rise of Reform Judaism* (1963), *The Growth of Reform Judaism* (1965) and *The Torah: A Modern Commentary* (1981); the latter, a 17-year project, supports the school of modern biblical scholarship. Hence, he has parted company with traditional Talmudists, placing himself firmly within the secular Jewish camp. Rabbi Plaut writes a weekly column for the *Canadian Jewish News* and writes frequently for the *Globe and Mail*. Although many orthodox Jews do not accept his religious views, he has still managed to earn himself the position of chief spokesman of the Canadian Jewish community. He has turned to fiction late in life in "an attempt to reach as many people as possible." He published his first collection of short stories, *Hanging Threads*, in 1978 and in 1986 he published *The Letter*, a novel about the Holocaust.   SHARON DRACHE

Playing-Card Money The administration of New France counted on the arrival of cash from France in order to pay civil servants, suppliers, soldiers and clerks. There was confusion if the ship did not arrive until the end of the season, and even more if it did not come at all. In 1685 Intendant Demeulle invented a type of paper money with the purpose of meeting the expenses. He printed various face values on playing cards and affixed his seal to them. When the king's ship arrived, he redeemed this "card money" in cash. This system was brought to an end after 1686, but it was necessary to return to it during the period 1689-1719. In 1714, card money to a value of 2 million livres was in circulation, some cards being worth as much as 100 livres. The King later returned to using card money in 1729 because the merchants themselves demanded it, this time using white cards without colours, which were cut or had their corners removed according to a fixed table. The whole card was worth 24 livres (which was the highest sum in card money); with the corners cut off, it was worth 12 livres; etc. In the 18th century card money was not the most important form

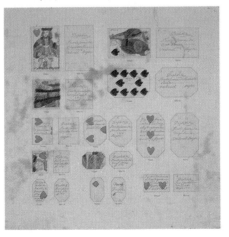

Playing card money used in New France in 1714, illustration by Henri Beau. This unique form of money was first used in 1685 to meet expenses (*courtesy National Archives of Canada/C-17059*).

of paper money. There was the *certificat* (certificate), a certified sum given to the supplier by the storekeeper. The *ordonnance*, a promissory note, was signed by the intendant on a printed form, and like cards and certificates, was redeemable by a *lettre de change* (bill of exchange) on the Naval Treasury. Finally, there was the *lettre de change*, or *traite*, used between private citizens to avoid a cash transfer, which the state also used, particularly to redeem paper money. After the Conquest Canadians still held some 16 million livres in paper money, of which only 3.8% was in card money.

Playwrights Union of Canada, The, the national association and voice of Canada's playwrights, is the successor to the Playwrights Co-op founded in 1972 by playwrights in Toronto. The Co-op was founded to promote the works of Canadian playwrights. By 1973 the Co-op had published over 60 scripts in an inexpensive mimeograph format and by 1982 the number of playscripts widely circulated to theatres and schools had grown to over 500. In 1979 the Co-op was reincorporated as Playwrights Canada and became the Playwrights Union of Canada in 1984 after a merger with the Guild of Canadian Playwrights. Besides maintaining more than 400 titles in print in playscript and paperback formats, published under the imprint Playwrights Canada, PUC organizes national and provincial reading tours for its more than 300 members and functions as a resource centre for Canadian plays and playwrights.   ANTON WAGNER

Plea Bargaining is a form of negotiation between a person charged with an offence and a crown prosecutor. The accused person usually negotiates through his counsel. Plea bargaining can take several forms. For example, an accused charged with several offences may agree to plead guilty to some of these offences while the Crown agrees to withdraw the remaining charges. It may also take the form of an accused pleading guilty in exchange for the Crown recommending to the court a lesser sentence than the accused might otherwise risk receiving. As well, the Crown and the accused often negotiate over the facts upon which a guilty plea will be entered. In some cases, the Crown will agree not to allege an aggravating fact, which is nonessential to the admission of guilt, in return for the accused agreeing to plead guilty. For example, the accused might agree to plead guilty to the robbery of a bank if the Crown accepts the accused's version that while committing the robbery the handgun he was carrying was unloaded rather than loaded. Obviously, a concession of this nature by the Crown does not affect the validity of the guilty plea but could result in a lesser sentence.

Plea bargaining usually takes place before the actual trial, in which case, if an agreement is reached, the witnesses (upon whom the Crown was relying to prove its case) are spared the necessity of having to attend court. One of the major motivations causing the Crown to become involved in plea bargaining is its desire to save civilian witnesses the inconvenience and, in some cases (especially for victims), the trauma of having to testify at a criminal trial.

Plea negotiations may also take place during the course of a trial; for instance, when unexpected evidence arises at trial and greatly increases the risk to either the Crown or the defence of not securing a conviction or acquittal, respectively. Also, negotiations concerning the disposition of a case may even arise in the appeal context; for example, where the Crown appeals and the defence cross-appeals, both sides may agree, if it is mutually satisfactory, to abandon their respective appeals.

Plea bargaining has essentially 2 main purposes. The first is to increase certainty. The Criminal Code generally allows judges, for most crimes, a wide discretion concerning the imposition of sentences. Consequently, it is often difficult for the Crown or the defence to assess exactly what sentence will be imposed. Similarly, the outcome of a trial, whether before a judge or a judge and jury, can sometimes be difficult to predict. Thus, either the Crown or the defence may be willing to make certain sacrifices in order to obtain greater certainty and to insure that their most important objective is achieved.

Secondly, plea bargaining is also entered into in order to save valuable court time and, more importantly, to save the expense and inconvenience of a criminal trial. It is a fact of life in the Canadian criminal justice system that the Crown will usually be more disposed to consider plea negotiations when it is involved in a lengthy and complicated prosecution that requires a significant expenditure of funds to obtain the evidence or witnesses required by the Crown to prove its case.

Although in a sense plea bargaining may take the determination of a case out of the court's hands (for instance when the Crown decides to accept a guilty plea to some of the charges and withdraw the remainder), it is subject to limitations. For example, although the Crown may recommend a specific sentence to the court, the imposition of sentence is ultimately the court's responsibility, and the court may reject the Crown's recommendation where it feels that recommendation is inappropriate. Moreover, it has been held by various appellate courts in Canada that the Crown is divisible; in other words, the Crown can occasionally on appeal change its position despite a previous agreement made by the prosecutor in the court below, but such a change is only allowed where the Crown can demonstrate good reason for taking a different position. It is important to realize that the judge hearing the case is never a party to this agreement nor is he involved in the plea negotiations. Thus there is always the danger that the judge might not adopt the position taken by counsel as a result of the plea negotiations.

Finally, when plea negotiations do not result in an agreement or where the circumstances of a particular case make it inappropriate for counsel to engage in plea bargaining, then the accused will either take the case to trial or simply plead guilty without any understanding having been reached with the Crown concerning the process of sentencing. A. PRINGLE

Plessis, Joseph-Octave, archbishop of Québec (b at Montréal 3 Mar 1763; d at Québec City 4 Dec 1825). After his ordination in 1786, Plessis served as secretary to 3 bishops and as parish priest at Québec. Chosen coadjutor in 1797, he became bishop in 1806, and in 1819 was named first archbishop of Québec by Rome though never recognized as such by the British government. A small, corpulent man, Plessis was ambitious, methodical and a realist with a flair for diplomacy. He cooperated with the British colonial authorities in civil matters while resisting their efforts to weaken and dominate the church. He urged Canadians to support the British during the War of 1812, and in 1817 he was appointed to the Legislative Council of Lower Canada. He opposed a plan for state-controlled education but encouraged the establishment of Catholic primary education in the parishes. Plessis maintained the church's position in the struggle for the social leadership of Lower Canada between the British colonial government and a rising Canadian bourgeoisie. Though his clergy were too few to meet all the pastoral needs in the parishes, Plessis deliberately channelled a significant number of young ecclesiastics into classical and clerical education, a policy which eventually halted the persistent decline in clerical recruitment. Largely through Plessis's efforts, the Roman Catholic diocese of Québec, then including all the BNA colonies except Newfoundland, was divided into a number of administrative units, still the basis of today's diocesan organization. JAMES H. LAMBERT

Pleure pas, Germaine (1965), by Claude Jasmin, one of the most accessible and poetic contributions to "the joual debate" in the French Canadian novel, narrates the journey of Gilles Bédard and his family from Montréal to Gaspé. Escaping from drink and debt, hunting the rapist who killed his daughter, and visiting his wife's parents, Gilles is caught between the desire for revenge and his innate capacity for love. He is freed by a case of mistaken identity in a dénouement that blends New Testament imagery with political engagement. Reflecting Gilles's point of view, the narrative is structured around the names of rest-stops on the journey of discovery, using JOUAL to communicate the complex predicament of a simple man. The title, a line from Roger LEMELIN's *Au pied de la pente douce* (1944), associates the novel with earlier experiments with joual. MICHÈLE LACOMBE

Plouffe, Les (1948), a novel by Roger LEMELIN in which the author's expansive comic gift offers an insider's view of Québec's working-class Lower Town district. Spanning WWII, the saga of the Plouffe family presents unforgettable characters within a social-realist tradition – the sensitive Ovide, wavering between religion and romance; the prankish Guillaume, a local sports hero; Cécile, a sour spinster; and many others. The imbroglios of Ovide's ambitious journalist friend Denis Boucher, the protagonist of Lemelin's first novel, lead to trouble for all in a community faced with censorship, conscription and militant Catholic trade unions. Populated by streetcar conductors, newspaper typographers, meddlesome priests and nosy neighbours, Lemelin's fiction gently satirizes and celebrates a blend of American and Catholic influences in local popular culture. Translated as *The Plouffe Family* (1950), the story was made into French and English CBC television series in the 1950s and a film by Gilles CARLE, released in 1981. MICHÈLE LACOMBE

Plover, common name for family (Charadriidae) of SHOREBIRDS with 2 subfamilies: Charadriinae, including true plovers and surfbirds; and Vanellinae, including lapwings. Of the 63 species occurring worldwide, 10 are found in Canada. These include the northern lapwing (*Vanellus vanellus*), an occasional visitor to eastern Canada. Killdeer, semipalmated, black-bellied and lesser golden plovers (*Charadrius vociferus, C. semipalmatus, Pluvialis squatarola, P. dominica,* respectively) are the most widely distributed species in Canada. Common ringed plovers (*C. hiaticula*) breed in NE arctic Canada; piping plovers (*C. melodus*) from SE central Alberta to Manitoba, in the Maritimes and, until recently, Ontario; and mountain plovers (*C. montanus*) in SE Alberta and probably SW Saskatchewan. Plovers have plump bodies, short necks and short bills, which are expanded near the tip. Although none are brightly coloured, many have strongly marked plumage patterns of black, white and brown that are conspicuous in flight. Because invertebrate prey are located visually, plovers have relatively large eyes and good eyesight. True plovers are characterized by tapering wings. Many species have one or more breast bands; most have melodious calls. Lapwings are much larger than true plovers and are recognizable by their broad, rounded wings. Some have feather crests or wattles of skin on the face and spurs on the wings, features that are important in courtship displays and territory defence. Most plovers are gregarious outside the breeding season, gathering in flocks of several hundreds to thousands. They fly strongly and migrate from coastal, winter feeding areas on bays and estuaries, N to breeding sites in remote arctic regions. Nests are a shallow scrape in the ground with little or no lining. Usually 4 eggs are laid (range 2-4). Chicks are down-covered on hatching and leave the nest soon after they are dry. Normally, parents share incubation (21-30 days) and guarding of chicks. All plovers use elaborate distraction displays, such as the "broken wing" display, to lure predators away from eggs or young. A.J. BAKER

Plum, common name for certain members of genus *Prunus* of the ROSE family, which produce a smooth-skinned, elliptical, heart-shaped, oblong, ovate or round FRUIT with a flat seed. About 18 plum species are horticulturally important, including the European plum (*P. domestica*), which probably originated in the Caspian Sea area; Japanese plum (*P. salicina*), of Chinese origin; cherry plum (*P. ceracifera*), native to SE Europe or SW Asia; and *P. nigra* and *P. americana*, of Canadian and American origin respectively. In N America, plum growing began towards the end of the 18th century. European plums were first brought to the Maritimes by French colonists; Japanese plums were introduced to N America around 1870; and domestication of native species began around 1850. European and Japanese plums are hardy only in milder areas of Canada and are grown commercially in BC, Ontario and NS. The native species lack size and quality but hardy hybrids have been developed that have excellent fruit quality and are relatively winter hardy. Most plums produced in Canada are for the fresh market. The main varieties are Bluefre, Bradshaw, Burbank, Early Golden, Italian, Peach, Shiro and Stanley. Common INSECT PESTS are red mite, curculio, scale, aphid, maggot and lesser peach tree borer. The main diseases are brown rot, black knot and leaf spot. In 1985, 5485 t of plums and prunes were produced in Canada, with a farm value of $3.9 million; 1986 production was 5133 t. G. TEHRANI

Plummer, Arthur Christopher Orme, actor (b at Toronto 13 Dec 1929), great-grandson of PM Sir John ABBOTT and a stylish international star who divides his time between the US, Britain and Canada. He apprenticed with the Montréal Repertory Theatre and made his professional debut in 1948 with Ottawa's Stage Society, performing over 100 roles with its successor, the Canadian Repertory Theatre. Performances in Bermuda led to a US tour of *Nina* (1953) and Broadway recognition in *The Starcross Story* (1954), *The Lark* (1955) and as Marc Antony in the American Shakespeare Festival's 1955 inaugural season. Other notable New York City engagements include the musical *Cyrano* (1973), for which he won a "Tony" Award, Iago in *Othello* (1981) and *Macbeth* (1988). In 1961 he appeared at Stratford-upon-Avon, Eng, as Richard III while alternating in London as Henry II in *Becket* and continued his British career at the National Theatre. At Canada's STRATFORD FESTIVAL he has played Henry V, Hamlet, Aguecheek, Mercutio, Leontes and Macbeth, as well as other roles. Among his many movies are *Stage Struck* (1957), *The Sound of Music* (1965), *Oedipus the King* (1967), *Waterloo* (1970), *The Man Who Would Be King* (1975), *The Silent Partner* (1978), *Murder By Decree* (1979), for which he won a Genie Award,

Somewhere in Time (1980) and *The Boy in Blue* (1986). His work on television includes *Little Moon of Alban* (1958) and *Hamlet at Elsinore* (BBC 1965), both nominated for Emmy Awards, *The Money Changers* (Emmy Award 1977), *Riel* (CBC 1979) and *Spearfield's Daughter* (1986). He is Companion of the Order of Canada.

DAVID GARDNER

Pocket Gopher (Geomyidae), family of medium-sized, solitary, nonhibernating, subterranean RODENTS. About 31 species occur in N and Central America, 2 in Canada. The northern pocket gopher (*Thomomys talpoides*) lives in southern Manitoba, Saskatchewan and Alberta, and in southcentral BC. The larger plains pocket gopher (*Geomys bursarius*) barely extends into Canada via the Red River valley, Man. Pocket gophers have a round body, small eyes, short ears and tail, and large, curved claws on the forefeet for digging. Their short fur is grey to brown and can lie in any direction. They carry food or nesting materials in fur-lined, external cheek pouches, which they empty with their forefeet. The mouth closes behind ever-growing, gnawing teeth, enabling the rodent to harvest underground vegetation and to excavate networks of tunnels in prairies and mountain meadows without ingesting earth. The fan-shaped mounds they raise are burrow exits, and are usually closed with round, earthen plugs. Each year 1-2 litters of 2-11 young are raised in deep tunnels. Pocket gophers damage crops but also aerate soils and bring nutrients to the surface.

J. MARY TAYLOR

Pocket Mouse, small, jumping RODENT of the N American family Heteromyidae. The 75 species of Heteromyidae are adapted to desert and semidesert environments. Three live in Canada: olive-backed and Great Basin pocket mice (*Perognathus fasciatus*, *P. parvus*, respectively) and Ord's KANGAROO RAT. Pocket mice occur in the dry western plains and the basin between the Rocky Mts and the BC coastal range. They are greyish above with white underparts. Pocket mice have large hindlimbs and smaller front limbs, all 4 used in jumping. The tail, almost as long as the head and body together, serves as a prop, particularly when the animal feeds in its characteristic sitting position. Food is carried to the burrow in external, fur-lined cheek "pockets." Stored food enables pocket mice to survive winter, alternating between dormant and feeding periods. Insects and plants complement the primarily granivorous diet. Pocket mice can survive long periods without water and are nocturnal. Mating occurs in Apr; the gestation period is 3-4 weeks; 2 litters are produced, each averaging 4-5 young. The relatively scarce olive-backed pocket mouse, the smallest rodent in Canada, measures about 12.5 cm. Except for killing weeds, it has little economic value. The much larger and more common Great Basin pocket mouse causes considerable damage to cereal crops.

JEAN FERRON

Podborski, Steve, alpine skier (b at Toronto 25 July 1957). On skis at age 2, he began racing at 10 and joined the Canadian alpine ski team in 1973. His international downhill racing performances as a key member of the "Crazy Canucks" improved steadily, despite a serious knee injury in 1976, up to his first World Cup win in 1979 (at Morzine, France). In 1980 his Olympic bronze medal in the downhill provided one of only 2 Canadian medals. In 1982 he won 3 consecutive World Cup downhills, skiing with extreme technical skill, particularly on the tough icy courses he preferred. His strength, skill and daring were particularly apparent in the 3rd victory, where his winning speed of 166 km/h was the fastest ever recorded at Kitzbühel, Austria. In 1982 he com-

In 1982 skier Steve Podborski became the first non-European to win the World Cup downhill championship (*courtesy Canapress Photo Service*).

bined 3 more wins with consistent top placings to become the first non-European winner of the World Cup downhill championship title. Upon winning the Canadian Downhill Championships in 1983 and 1984, he retired from skiing to enter the business world. During 10 years of international racing he won 8 World Cup races to become the most successful Canadian male skier to date. He was made an Officer of the Order of Canada in 1982.

MURRAY SHAW

Poems for All the Annettes Al PURDY was a late starter at poetry, and most of his early work is derivative and negligible; it was in *Poems for All the Annettes* (1962) that the mature poet's voice was first heard, ranging from the "Cambrian trilobite" to "Uncle Fred on Côte des Neiges" in those vast associate leaps of time which were to become his trademark. In "Postscript" Purdy writes, "I say the stanza ends, but it never does" – and that open-ended sense of form has vitalized all his writing. A later edition of the book (1968) added some new poems (including "At the Quinte Hotel") and gave early evidence of Purdy's passion for revision (Uncle Fred reappeared as Uncle John). The sweep and exuberance of Purdy's work have informed Canadian poetry ever since.

STEPHEN SCOBIE

Poetry in English Addressing the poets of the classical, European tradition in *Quebec Hill* (1797), J. MacKay asks: "Ye who, in stanzas, celebrate the Po,/Or teach the Tyber in your strains to flow,/How would you toil for numbers to proclaim/The liquid grandeur of St. Lawrence' Stream?" Besides pointing to a major concern of pre-Confederation poetry – the representation in European verse forms of the Canadian physical and social landscapes – MacKay's question anticipates similar concerns in much later Canadian poetry, suggesting the continuity that exists through poetry written in Canada from the earliest to the most recent times.

It is convenient to divide pre-Confederation poetry, somewhat arbitrarily but justifiably, into two chronological categories: poetry written before 1825 and that written between 1825 and 1867. Before 1825 the verse written in what would become Canada (primarily in Lower Canada, Nova Scotia and New Brunswick) was largely dominated by neoclassical models. Among the

major influences on the poetry of this period were the heroic couplets of English poets Alexander Pope and Oliver Goldsmith and the blank verse of James Thomson's *The Seasons* (1726-46), a poem with evident application to a land with Canada's seasonal variations. Whereas the relatively fluid and continuous form of blank verse seems to have been a fitting vehicle for such subjects as the sublime spectacle of Niagara Falls and the "liquid grandeur" of the St Lawrence, the rational order of the heroic couplet was a formalistic means by which the early poets affirmed and reflected a sense of governance in their environment and in themselves. After 1825 the influence of romanticism (which had been present in Canada earlier, just as neoclassicism would continue to be felt later) came increasingly to be evident in Canadian poetry. The result was that from the 1820s writers turned to such poets as Byron, Wordsworth, Shelley and Thomas Moore for their models. Frequently employed forms now were *ottava rima* (for satire), the Spenserian stanza (for framing picturesque scenes and momentary insights) and the sonnet. Also in evidence after 1825 were the romantic narrative and the "dramatic poem" (Adam Kidd, "Preface," *The Huron Chief and Other Poems*, 1830), genres that were appropriate to the depiction of emotionally and spiritually complex issues, conflicts and quests. By 1864 there was enough Canadian verse in various forms to enable Edward Hartley Dewart (although ignoring material from before 1825) to produce *Selections from Canadian Poets* (1864) – the first anthology of Canadian poetry in English and the only one before Confederation. The anthology's division into poems "Sacred and Reflective," "Descriptive and National" and "Miscellaneous" (a category that includes pieces entitled "Heroes," "Childhood," "Twilight," "Taapookaa – A Huron Legend," "Glimpses of Highland Superstitions" and "The Beech-Nut Gatherer") indicates the emphasis and content of pre-Confederation poetry.

Practically all the verse of this period was written by amateur poets, men and women who did not attempt to make their living as writers but wrote to occupy "a few leisure hours" (Thomas Cary, "Preface," *Abram's Plains*, 1789). Like Cary, these amateurs usually produced only one poem of note that they published in a newspaper, as a pamphlet or in a slim volume with "Other Poems." Yet the recreational products of these amateurs were not merely belletristic amusements written to beguile the time between sermons, mess dinners, harvests, household duties and other employments; the early poets aimed to describe the aesthetic and economic attractions of Canada, to chronicle the achievements of their colonial society, to warn their readers of life's moral pitfalls, and to express the spiritual and cultural aspirations of sensitive people in a new land. All these things are attempted in what is probably the most important treatment of pioneer life (in Nova Scotia) from the early period: *The Rising Village* by Oliver GOLDSMITH (grand-nephew of the Irish author of the more famous *The Deserted Village*, 1770). The publication history of *The Rising Village* – as a pamphlet in 1825 in England, in excerpts that year in *The Canadian Review* (Montréal) and finally with "Other Poems" in 1834 in Saint John – also runs the gamut of available possibilities. Throughout the pre-Confederation period there were poets such as Jacob Bailey, Charles HEAVYSEGE and Charles SANGSTER, whose poetic output would fill several substantial volumes and might have permitted them to make a living by writing poetry if the population had been larger.

As in the case of prose, the Maritimes – where many LOYALISTS had settled – were the centre of poetic activity prior to 1825. Long before the Loyalist influx, John Hayman had celebrated Newfoundland as a settlers' paradise in *Quodlibets* (1628); and in the pre-Loyalist period Henry ALLINE wrote his accomplished *Hymns and Spiritual Songs* (2 vols, 1782-86). With the Loyalists and their descendants, such as Bailey (author of several Hudibrastic satires), Jonathan ODELL and Joseph Stansbury (whose *Loyal Verses...* appeared posthumously in 1860), Joseph HOWE and Goldsmith, came the flowering of early pre-Confederation poetry. This took the form of a body of work that treats of both the present and future of the Maritimes and the present and past in the US.

Not all poetic activity before 1825 occurred in the Maritimes: in 1690 Henry KELSEY had written a versified description of the prairies and in 1825 James Lynn Alexander published a dramatic narrative, *The Wonders of the West*, centered on Niagara Falls. Between these years the poems of Cary, MacKay, John Hood Burwell (*Talbot Road*, 1818) and numerous others attest to the existence of poetic activity in what is now Québec and Ontario, as do 2 later poems by John RICHARDSON, *Tecumseh* (1828) and *Kensington Gardens* (1830).

An important node of activity around 1825 was Montréal, the home of several flourishing newspapers and periodicals (*see* LITERARY MAGAZINES). A number of poems and volumes were published there in the 1820s, including the suggestively similar Byronic imitations of Levi Adams (*Jean Baptiste*, 1825) and George Longmore (*The Charivari*, 1826), which remain interesting for their satire, depictions of life in Canada and poetic accomplishment. Adam Kidd's *The Huron Chief* is among the more adroit of the Montréal publications, but the work of William Hawley, Margaret Blennerhasset and Ariel Bowman will also repay the sympathetic reading (demanded by all pre-Confederation poetry) that is attentive to its combination of imported form and local subject. With the founding of the *Literary Garland* (1838-51), the longest-running pre-Confederation periodical, Montréal's position as a literary centre was consolidated. In the *Garland* appeared the work of such poets as Rosanna (Mullins) LEPROHON. And from Montréal publishers in the late 1830s and 1840s came such works as Standish O'GRADY's *The Emigrant* (1841), with its frank descriptions of the Canadian environment.

Although numerous volumes of interest, including the *Sonnets* (1855) and *Jephthah's Daughter* (1865) of Charles Heavysege and *Canadian Ballads* (1858) of Thomas D'Arcy MCGEE, were published in Montréal in the 1850s and 1860s, other centres, particularly Toronto in Canada West, were publishing their share of poetry. Charles Sangster, who had published *The St. Lawrence and the Saguenay and Other Poems* in New York in 1856, saw his *Hesperus* (1860) published in both Montréal and his native Kingston; Alexander MCLACHLAN had his works, including *The Emigrant and Other Poems* (1861), published in Toronto, and William KIRBY's *The U.E.: A Tale of Upper Canada* (1859) was printed in Niagara-on-the-Lake. The long, narrative poems of Heavysege, Sangster, McLachlan and Kirby have been subjected to closer critical scrutiny than most pre-Confederation poems, probably because the grandeur of their design does much to compensate for their unevenness of execution.

Several poetic productions of the pre-Confederation period did not appear in print until after 1867, when the natural self-examination of the new nation prompted the publication of Howe's *Poems and Ballads* (which included *Acadia*), Kirby's *Canadian Idylls* and Leprohon's *Poetical Works*, volumes belonging, in form and approach, to an earlier era. That era produced a quantity of poetry which, though only sporadically distin-

guished by real talent and too frequently characterized by acquiescent imitativeness, cannot be dismissed as devoid of interest for later readers or of significance for Canadian culture.

D.M.R. BENTLEY

Poetry in English, 1867-1918

The honour of publishing the first volume of verse in the newly confederated Canada belongs to Charles MAIR, whose *Dreamland and Other Poems* appeared in 1868. Negligible as verse, the volume gained interest when Mair escaped after being captured by Louis RIEL during the RED RIVER disturbances of 1869-70. His *Tecumseh: A Drama* followed in 1886, and although its blank verse is pedestrian and untheatrical, Mair's attempt to interpret Canadian subject matter in a traditionally heroic manner gives the play a certain power.

Far more promising, though notoriously uneven, is the work of Isabella Valancy CRAWFORD, whose *Old Spookses' Pass, Malcolm's Katie, and Other Poems* was published at her own expense in 1884. She lived a lonely, frustrated life in Peterborough and Toronto, with few literary contacts, but at its best her poetry is remarkable for presenting the Canadian landscapes with an almost Blakean visionary power, often containing diction and imagery derived (not altogether accurately) from Indian life and tradition. "Malcolm's Katie," a long and somewhat melodramatic narrative poem of love and deception set against a background of logging and pioneering, is remembered for passages of vivid scenic description, whereas shorter poems, especially "The Camp of Souls," "Said the Canoe" and "The Dark Stag" employ seasonal and elemental imagery with colourful intensity.

The "Confederation Poets," so called because they were born within a decade of Confederation, were in no way a cohesive group. They did, however, lay firm foundations for a tradition of Canadian poetry – a tradition, moreover, that attracted attention beyond the boundaries of Canada. Their early work was naturally imitative (following British and, to a lesser extent, American models), but they gradually developed a modestly distinctive native style. Charles G.D. ROBERTS, who later became well known for his animal stories, set an example with *Orion and Other Poems* (1880). This volume displays considerable technical skill; it concerns itself, however, with "alien matters in distant regions." His next book, *In Divers Tones* (1886), makes more conspicuous use of Canadian subjects, and contains the well-known "Tantramar Revisited," whereas *Songs of the Common Day* (1893) includes a series of descriptive sonnets that evoke the landscapes of his native New Brunswick. Unfortunately, his later poetry, written mainly in the US and Europe, only fitfully maintains the promise of his earlier work.

His cousin and fellow Maritimer, Bliss CARMAN, became known as much for his personality as for his poetry. He is the most lyrical of the group, and his more characteristic poems envelop a simple, romantic story or theme in a wealth of evocative, though vague, imagery. His collaboration with American poet Richard Hovey in *Songs from Vagabondia* (1894) and its sequels gave him a reputation for wandering Bohemianism. The title poem of his first volume, *Low Tide at Grand Pré* (1893), is probably his best.

The other members of the group were products of Ontario. Archibald LAMPMAN was inspired to devote himself to poetry after reading Roberts's *Orion*. He spent his short working life as a postal clerk in Ottawa, and his poems are for the most part close-packed melancholy meditations on natural objects, emphasizing the calm of country life in contrast to the restlessness of city living.

Limited in range, they are nonetheless remarkable for descriptive precision and emotional restraint. Although characterized by a skilful control of rhythm and sound, they tend to display a sameness of thought. Best known are "Heat" from *Among the Millet* (1888) and the nightmarish "City of the End of Things" from *Alcyone* (1899).

Duncan Campbell SCOTT, who did much to popularize Lampman's poems after his early death, worked as a civil servant in the Dept of Indian Affairs and derived much of the inspiration for his poetry from official trips into northern Ontario. He communicates a vivid sense of the northern landscape, and in poems such as "The Onondaga Madonna" in *Labor and the Angel* (1898) and "The Forsaken" in *New World Lyrics* (1905) he writes poignantly about the decline of the Indian way of life. "The Height of Land," in *Lundy's Lane* (1916), a meditation on human culture and the mystery of life in a symbolically appropriate setting, is a central poem which brings together Scott's major poetic and philosophical preoccupations. Also loosely associated with the Confederation Poets was Wilfred CAMPBELL, who proved most successful when writing about the "lake region" of western Ontario.

The generation of Canadian poets that began to publish at the turn of the century was more varied in approach but noticeably less distinguished. Pauline JOHNSON, daughter of a Mohawk father and an English mother, achieved popularity as a poet and reciter; her poems about Indian life and legend possess a facile charm but little permanent value. William Henry DRUMMOND became extremely popular on the publication of *The Habitant and Other French-Canadian Poems* (1897), but the dialect he employed, though considered amusing in its time, now reads as unpleasantly condescending. Robert SERVICE aimed at verse rather than poetry, and celebrated the worlds of trapping, ranching and the KLONDIKE GOLD RUSH. Volumes such as *Songs of a Sourdough* (1907, containing "The Shooting of Dan McGrew," for which Service is best known) and *Rhymes of a Rolling Stone* (1912) were popular for their strong stories and emphatic rhythms. Francis Sherman and Marjorie Pickthall both wrote poems that combine technical competence with an eloquent lyricism but which lack originality and depth. They are minor figures who could offer little more than a civilized conventionality. These poets failed to match the work of their immediate predecessors, and the achievement of the Confederation Poets remained unchallenged until the emergence of E.J. Pratt after WWI.

W.J. KEITH

Poetry in English, 1918-60

The first rather tentative experiments in 20th-century poetic technique began in 1914. The earliest evidence of this activity came from the pen of poet and popular novelist Arthur STRINGER, who that year presented his free-verse collection *Open Water*. A truly consistent expression of modernist principles did not occur, however, until a configuration of circumstance and career brought F.R. SCOTT, A.J.M SMITH and Leon Edel to McGill University. In 1925 Smith and his associates (who later included A.M. KLEIN and Leo KENNEDY) launched the *McGill Daily Literary Supplement* (1924-25; followed by the *McGill Fortnightly Review*, 1925-27), in which they published poems in the modern manner and articles on contemporary trends. At the same time the CANADIAN FORUM (est 1920 in Toronto), with a wider cultural focus, promoted debate on current art and the quality of Canadian criticism. It featured a series of articles and statements by young writers and critics comparing the old poetry with the new, thus claiming the attention of the informed reader and laying the groundwork for a vigorous Canadian criticism. Felix Walter, E.J. PRATT and Dorothy LIVESAY, to name only a few, were part of this debate.

The early 1930s were not a good time for the new poetry. The GREAT DEPRESSION dampened creative activity in some poets and drove others into political action. The better-known, older and more conservative poets continued to publish, but the new movements, with the exception of Kennedy's *The Shrouding* (1933), were still not accepted. In 1936 the situation changed with the appearance of the first serious offering of the new poetry in a pioneer anthology called *New Provinces*. Its publication had been orchestrated – with difficulty – by Scott, who had assembled poems by Pratt and Robert Finch of Toronto with those of Smith, Kennedy, Klein and himself. A bold and forward-reaching introduction by Smith was set aside as too provocative, and was replaced by the moderate tones of Scott's tiny "Preface." The anthology sold very few copies. That year also, W.E. Collin, a professor of French at University of Western Ontario, published *The White Savannahs*, the first collection of criticism of contemporary poetry from the modernist point of view. It admirably complemented *New Provinces*. The modernist credo – rejecting past poetic practice, discarding the norms of punctuation, typographical conventions and traditional verse forms and cultivating new subject matter, which drew on the modern city with its variousness, its social ills, its machinery, its politics, its intellectual predisposition for the new in art, its ironies, tensions and structural complexities, and its new vocabulary – pointed in a fresh direction. But the gestures of 1936 were not exclusively modernist. That year the CANADIAN AUTHORS ASSOCIATION established *Canadian Poetry Magazine*, which soon became identified with a more traditional poetic line. The CAA, in which Pratt took a strong hand, stood adamantly for a more conventional approach to poetry.

When WWII broke out, Canadian poetry appeared to be firmly set in 2 camps, the modern and the traditional, although the conservative group was much more successful in reaching its audience and in finding publishers for its work. The war seemed to provide a new impetus for poetry, chiefly in the surge of activity involving little magazines, which had suffered during the economically troubled 1930s. In 1941 *Contemporary Verse*, a periodical of eclectic taste edited by Alan Crawley, began to publish in British Columbia. In Montréal in 1942 F.R. Scott joined forces with newly arrived Patrick Anderson to launch a group publication called *Preview* (1942-45), which was intended to keep the writing of a poetry workshop before its readers.

Within a few months a newer generation of writers with a more realistic bent and a stronger political tone gave notice of itself in Montréal with a mimeographed little magazine called *First Statement* (1942-45). This group, headed by John SUTHERLAND, included Irving LAYTON and Louis DUDEK, and its poetry would be characterized by stronger social concern and a more direct sense of urban experience. In *First Statement* were published articles and reviews on literature in which the issue of national identity in Canadian writing found voice. Out of this group and its periodical there developed a modest series of books published under the First Statement imprint and featuring the early work of Layton, Anderson, Raymond SOUSTER and Miriam WADDINGTON. The group also published the important anthology of this generation, *Other Canadians* (1947). The SMALL PRESS movement in Canada was truly established, and now helped to focus attention on, and to pull together, the work of solitary spirits who

had been writing modernist poetry. Dorothy Livesay, Raymond Knister, R.G. EVERSON and W.W.E. Ross had made their mark as early as the 1920s and 1930s, but the real momentum for modern poetry would be supplied by the little magazines (*see* LITERARY MAGAZINES) and small presses, and the collective action that they were able to generate. *First Statement* did not function only as a vehicle for the work of a group of like-minded writers. It was as much a little magazine in the classical sense, an outlet for new critical thinking on Canadian writing and a centre for activity destined to supply the motive force for a little press. It would later provide the energy to fuel the pivotal little magazine *cum* literary periodical, NORTHERN REVIEW (1945-56). (*See* LITERARY PERIODICALS.)

The years of WWII, when writers were traumatized by mass slaughter and the destruction of much that was prized by civilization, also witnessed an unusual burgeoning of Canadian poetry. In 1942 Ralph GUSTAFSON scored an international coup with his *Anthology of Canadian Poetry*, which carried English Canadian poets to a large readership under the prestigious imprint of Penguin Books. Gustafson's selection included writing not only by poets who had by now become familiar (Scott, Klein, Smith, Kennedy, Pratt and Finch), but also by the relatively unknown Livesay, P.K. PAGE and Earle BIRNEY. In 1943 Gustafson was guest editor of No 113 of Harold Vinal's quarterly *Voices*, in which the new names to appear were Anderson, Layton and Souster. A "pattern of notice" had begun to develop, as a result of which modern Canadian poetry was being recognized in its own right through being featured in a number of significant international magazines. *Poetry: A Magazine of Verse* (Chicago) had featured a "Canadian Number" in Apr 1941. It bore the mark of the cautious taste of E.K. BROWN, who in 1936 had initiated the annual review of Canadian writing under the "Letters in Canada" section of UNIVERSITY OF TORONTO QUARTERLY; his selection for *Poetry* reached back to Duncan Campbell Scott and forward to Livesay, F.R. Scott, Finch, Kennedy and Anne Marriott. The issue also featured Brown's essay, "The Development of Poetry in Canada, 1880-1940," which foreshadowed in its scope and approach his important study, *On Canadian Poetry* (1943). This book complemented, almost as opportunely as *The White Savannahs* had done with *New Provinces* in 1936, the Canada-US publication of A.J.M. Smith's milestone anthology, *The Book of Canadian Poetry* (1943). Smith's book is distinguished by his high critical standards and by a controversial introduction that segregated the Canadian moderns into "The Native Tradition" and "The Cosmopolitan Tradition." Smith's classification anticipated a split in Canadian poetry which occurred in the second half of the 20th century between a poetry deriving from the large framework of ideas, structures and literary influences of Britain as the mother country, and a poetry written in the language of Canadians, based on an outlook and experience peculiar to this country, and showing a N American sensibility.

At the end of the war, *Preview* merged with *First Statement* to form NORTHERN REVIEW, under the editorship of John Sutherland. But the modernists soon began to draw apart. The critical quarrel between the "cosmopolitans" and the "natives" grew sharper. The late 1940s and early 1950s were grim years for Canadian poetry. Publishers other than The RYERSON PRESS were painfully modest in their efforts, nor were the poetry magazines doing much. FIDDLEHEAD was active in Fredericton, *Northern Review* and the *Canadian Forum* in central Canada, *Contemporary Verse* in Vancouver, while *Canadian Poetry Magazine* functioned na-

tionally. But the mood was one of disillusionment, even of failure. It was as if the momentum of the war years had spent itself completely.

The renewal began in 1952 with the appearance of a new mimeographed poetry magazine, CONTACT (1952-54). It was the brainchild of Raymond Souster of Toronto, who had aligned himself during the 1940s with *First Statement;* he had served his own little-magazine apprenticeship by editing *Direction* (1943-46) from an RCAF base in the Maritimes and by producing 6 issues of *Enterprise* in Toronto in 1948. Prompted by a desire to challenge the conservative drift that had become apparent in Sutherland's thinking, Souster, egged on and joined by Dudek and Layton, launched *Contact*. The new direction taken in Canada was similar to a shift towards the new poetry taking place in Europe and the US in the second half of the century. The 1950s also saw the emergence of the ideas of Marshall MCLUHAN, who coedited the magazine *Explorations* (1953-59), and the establishment of Northrop FRYE as a major critic and literary theorist.

Frye's work had a major effect on certain young Canadian poets. In 1949 *The Red Heart*, a collection of poems written by James REANEY, a student of Frye, won the Governor General's Award and marked the beginning of the "mythopoeic school" in Canadian poetry. This movement included others influenced by Frye, such as Jay MACPHERSON, Eli MANDEL, D.G. JONES and later Margaret ATWOOD.

Contemporaneously, and through the effort of *Contact*, there appeared Contact Press (1952-1967), which became an important publisher of Canadian poetry. Created in order to give young poets a chance to publish, despite seeming indifference on the part of commercial publishers, Contact Press produced the work of Dudek, Layton and Souster, and gave a start to many of the poets who went on to create the poetry of the 1960s and the 1970s. Atwood, George Bowering, Al Purdy, Alden Nowlan, Mandel and Phyllis Webb, Gwendolyn MacEwan, John Newlove, Frank Davey and Ron Everson all published under its imprint. The press also kept in touch, through the translations of Gael Turnbull and Jean Beaupré, with the contemporary poets of French Canada.

As the 1950s progressed the poetry scene began to change rapidly once again. In 1954 Fred COGSWELL began to publish a series of chapbooks called Fiddlehead Poetry Books, which featured Purdy and Nowlan, among others. In 1956 TAMARACK REVIEW was established by Robert Weaver. Dudek launched the McGill Poetry Series, in which the first books of Leonard COHEN and Daryl Hine appeared. Canadian poetry was becoming diverse, and with the help of a general popularization of the arts, poetry was on the verge of finding a broad audience. In this it was helped by the sudden popularity of coffeehouses, the marriage of jazz to poetry, the new vogue for public readings and the effects of McLuhan's message which confirmed the importance of the reading as a happening and supported the idea of the concrete in poetic self-expression. The poet had "gone public," and no one succeeded better at projecting a popular persona than Irving Layton, who boldly and outrageously carried poetry to its Canadian audience. In 1959 Layton, who had hammered at the insensitivity of the public and had been misunderstood and neglected by the critics, broke through with his collection *A Red Carpet for the Sun* to win the Governor General's Award. A new phase had begun. MICHAEL GNAROWSKI

Poetry in English, 1960-1980s

A Red Carpet for the Sun marks both an end and

a beginning: it established Layton as a major poet and marked the ascendancy of second-generation modernism in Canada. The Layton of *Red Carpet* is an interesting mixture: essentially traditional in form, yet popular in content and often aggressively colloquial in speech. The attitude to poetry he championed, along with his Contact Press colleagues Louis Dudek and Raymond Souster, triumphed in the years to come, but although he continued to publish voluminously his influence has proved slight beyond winning poets the right to use all aspects of language. The important advances or transformations in art tend to be formal, and Layton is essentially conservative in form. Far more important for the possibilities it presented, in Canada as well as in the US, was *The New American Poetry, 1945-1960,* edited by Donald Allen; it affected the writing of at least one generation of Canadian poets, bringing up to date the open forms promoted by William Carlos Williams after Ezra Pound. Here the contemporary N American voice clearly challenged the traditional British one; if, as some critics argue, Canadian poets only shifted from one colonial master to another, at least the accent now belonged to their own continent.

The early 1960s saw the emergence of many new poets. One of the most important was Al PURDY, an older poet who had been steadily learning his craft throughout the 1950s. With *Poems for All the Annettes* (1962) he achieved a unique personal voice which contained the lessons of modernism, yet was determinedly Canadian, even regional (central Ontario, United Empire Loyalist, mid-20th century). In *The Cariboo Horses,* which won the Governor General's Award in 1965, Purdy consolidated his poetic: here was a colloquial, quizzical, wide-ranging and engaging bumbler who somehow articulated the Canadian presence as never before. Although not as popular as Leonard Cohen, whose *The SPICE BOX OF EARTH* appeared in 1961, Purdy became a more important model to younger poets, for his laconic, open-ended, mytho-colloquial yarns suggested formal possibilities previously barely recognized in Canada. Purdy's second Gov Gen's Award, for *The Collected Poems of Al Purdy* in 1986, confirmed his continuing centrality.

Meanwhile, excellent young poets began to publish during the early 1960s: Margaret AT-WOOD, John Robert COLOMBO, Gwendolyn MACEWEN and Joe ROSENBLATT in Toronto; George BOWERING, Frank DAVEY, Lionel Kearns, Daphne MARLATT, John NEWLOVE and Fred WAH on the West Coast; Alden NOWLAN on the East Coast. At-wood and MacEwen, the first of a growing number of fine female poets, neatly divided the literary terrain between them: the former was restrained, ironic and modernist; the latter exuberant, mythic, passionate and romantically postmodernist in sensibility. Bowering, Davey, Kearns, Marlatt and Wah were associated with the poetry newsletter *Tish* and with the new poetics championed in *The New American Poetry* by such writers as Robert Creeley, Robert Duncan, Denise Levertov, Charles Olson and Jack Spicer. The *Tish* group was more cohesive than most associations of writers. This had both advantages and disadvantages. The *Tish* poets gave each other support and criticism, but they also generated a certain paranoia: they felt they were ignored while poets in the rest of Canada felt ignored by them. These feelings did not dissipate until the mid-1970s.

It seems obvious, in retrospect, that what happened in Vancouver in the early 1960s has deeply influenced Canadian poetry. Although not part of the *Tish* group, writers as different as John Newlove, Gerry Gilbert and bill BISSETT were also writing there; bp NICHOL came from Vancouver, although he has done most of his writing in To-

ronto; Pat LANE went there with Barry McKinnon later in the decade; UBC began its creative-writing program; and a number of poets of different persuasions found positions at Simon Fraser. Vancouver became and remained a hotbed of poetic activity. Older poets, too, were excited by all this energy: Earle Birney's *Selected Poems 1940-1966* revealed, in its revisions and typography, how taken he was by the formal concepts of the New American poets, as did Dorothy Livesay's first new collection in over a decade, *The Unquiet Bed* (1967). In Edmonton, Eli Mandel, earlier identified with the "Frye school," won the Governor General's Award for *An Idiot Joy* (1967), a book announcing a new directness in his poetic speech that later books would push even further.

Some later critics argued that the lessons taught by Olson and the others were a form of American imperialism, but this was to miss the point. As Marlatt put it: what these poets taught about language and "composition by field" was "one of those crucial developments one has to come to terms with in some way. And to ignore it or try to divide it off as simply a regional American phenomenon" would be absurd. Moreover the charge that Canadian writing incorporating these lessons would somehow prove not fully Canadian was simply "ridiculous." Indeed, one of the basic tenets of the new poetics was that poetry must be rooted in the place of its imagining. Purdy taught the same lesson, for no matter how far he travelled, his language and perceptions were rooted in the harsh Loyalist "Country North of Belleville," to which he always returned.

Alongside the influence of "composition by field" poetics, such eastern US poets as Robert Lowell and Sylvia Plath, as well as older Canadians such as F.R. Scott, Birney, Livesay and Ralph Gustafson, also made an impression on younger writers. Essentially modernist, they did not have the profound impact of *The New American Poetry* and certain contemporary European influences, yet they demonstrated that a contemporary Canadian poetry was possible. Then in 1965 Phyllis WEBB published *Naked Poems,* reinventing the long poem in Canada along the lines of contemporary poetics. Its impact has continued to be felt; its suites of brief lyrics present with exquisite craft the same lessons concerning language and seriality of composition as the American works. Transformed into something new, rich and strange, the long poem emerged as perhaps the most important poetic genre in Canada in the 1960s, 1970s and 1980s, as Robert Kroetsch, himself the author of one of the most innovative long poems, *Field Notes,* has argued.

If there are important outside influences on contemporary writing, there was also a renewed Canadian nationalism associated with the Centennial of 1967, which asserted itself in the appearance of a number of small presses dedicated to the publication of the new writing. Whereas Contact Press had stood almost alone in the 1950s (with Fred Cogswell's Fiddlehead Books), by the late 1960s there were the HOUSE OF ANANSI and Coach House Press in Toronto, Oberon Press in Ottawa and Talonbooks in Vancouver. Since that time, other little presses have arisen throughout the country and often fallen. Without their industry and commitment to the new Canadian poetry, much of the excitement and discovery of recent years would never have occurred. In one of its final acts, Contact Press published *New Wave Canada* (1966), edited by Raymond Souster. Of the 17 poets represented there, at least 8 – Daphne Buckle (Marlatt), Victor Coleman, Gerry Gilbert, Robert Hogg, David MCFADDEN, bp Nichol, Michael ONDAATJE and Fred Wah – have been influential innovators; David Cull, David Dawson, E. Lakshmi Gill and George JONAS have all contin-

ued to write and publish; which leaves only 4 who have given up poetry. Shortly after the publication of *New Wave Canada,* the triumph of the young poets was certain. In 1966 Margaret Atwood's first full-length collection, *The Circle Game,* won the Governor General's Award. By 1968 Nelson Ball, Wayne Clifford, Dennis Lee, Tom Marshall, bissett, Coleman, Hogg, Lane, McFadden, Marlatt, Nichol, Ondaatje, Rosenblatt and Wah had all published first books, most with small presses.

In 1970 the Governor General's Awards confirmed the place of the new writing in Canadian culture: all 3 awards for writing in English went to experimental works. In prose and poetry, Michael Ondaatje won for his long collage poem, *The Collected Works of Billy the Kid,* while bp Nichol won for 4 books, including a box of minimalist visual poems, *Still Water,* and an anthology of "concrete poetry," *The Cosmic Chef.* All these books were published by small presses. Although visual "concrete poetry" had appeared in the work of bissett, Nichol and others in the early 1960s, *The Cosmic Chef* clearly signalled its importance as an experimental form to a wide range of writers. Bissett and Nichol had also begun to experiment with "performance" or "sound" poetry, chants and chantlike structures, ways of breaking down intellectual meaning in order to involve audiences with more basic emotional connections to the poet's voice. In 1970 Nichol, Steve McCaffery, Paul Dutton and Rafael Barreto-Rivera formed The Four Horsemen, Canada's first sound-poetry ensemble. During the 1970s other ensembles formed and performed across Canada – the Cold Mountain Group in Montréal, Owen Sound in Ontario, Re:Sounding in Alberta – as did many solo performers. Other forms of experimentation include various kinds of "found poetry" and "homolinguistic translation" – the translation of texts in a language into new texts in the same language by a variety of methods. What these experimental forms share is a fascination with potentialities of language.

While the newer poets were making their presence felt, many older writers continued to work with undiminished, even renewed, vigour. In 1972 Livesay published her *Collected Poems: The Two Seasons.* In 1974 Gustafson won the Governor General's Award for *Fire on Stone.* One feature differentiating the contemporary period from earlier ones is that the younger writers do not feel the need utterly to displace the old. Instead a very broad range of writing continues to appear. This breadth is signalled not only by continued output by, and recognition of, older and more traditional writers, but by the variety of approaches taken by new poets. For example, in 1973 alone, first books appeared by John Thompson, a learned, highly symbolic poet; Tom WAYMAN, a post-Purdy narrative poet; and Christopher DEWDNEY, a complex and stringent explorer of language-centered poetics.

In the 1970s, there was a resurgence of REGIONALISM, a shift away from Toronto as the centre of culture. The West Coast, protected by the mountains from both the harsh climate and the cultural assumptions of the rest of Canada, had always been a place unto itself. But now the Prairies asserted their identity, especially as the import of the poetry of Robert KROETSCH and Andy SUKNASKI made itself felt. Purdy's influence was important here, for his narrative line and colloquial speech provided a means for Prairie poets to tell their own stories (a method that has recently degenerated into a standard "Prairie-anecdotal" form that is too often banal and prosaic). As poets appeared in the Prairie West so did regional publishing houses: NeWest Press in Edmonton, Thistledown Press in Saskatoon, Turnstone Press in

Winnipeg, Longspoon Press in Edmonton, and, more recently, rdc press in Red Deer. In Montréal, which had been active in the 1940s and 1950s, a number of poets, including Richard Sommer, Artie Gold, Ken Norris and Stephen Morrissey, many of them associated with Véhicule Press, created new excitement. In the Atlantic provinces, many young writers appeared to bolster the Fredericton group centered on the late Alden Nowlan and *Fiddlehead* magazine. Most of these poets are not known nationally, since they have been published by presses unable to promote their books across the country (*see* AUTHORS AND THEIR MILIEU). One major exception is Don Domanski, whose visionary poems are published by Anansi.

In the early 1980s, many of the new poets and presses of the early years of the period appeared to be as well established as they could hope to be. The differences between now and then are many, however, and include funding by the Canada Council and various provincial arts councils, which have provided generous support for writers and presses. Although exciting new poets continue to appear, eg, Pamela Banting, Dionne Brand, Roo Borson, David Donnell, Diana Hartog, Colin Morton, Erin Mouré, Gerry Shikatani, Sharon THESEN and Lola Lemire Tostevin, they are not making quite the great steps into new poetics which the generation of the 1960s made; instead they are building on and extending the poetic innovations of that earlier period. In one area, however, new and radical writing is very strong; feminist poetry and poetics have become a major source of poetic power, especially since the groundbreaking Vancouver Women and Words/ Les Femmes et Les Mots conference of 1983. The ongoing poem by bp Nichol, *The Martyrology* (by 1987 he had published 6 books and was working on Books 7 and 8) is an important long poem, and a wide variety of poems in extended forms have appeared; two of them, Stephen Scobie's *McAlmon's Chinese Opera* (1980) and Fred Wah's *Waiting for Saskatchewan* (1985), won Gov Gen's Awards. Many small presses, seen originally as antiestablishment, have become entrenched and necessary parts of our culture. Coach House Press, for example, which began by publishing only new and experimental authors, published D.G. Jones's Governor General's Award-winning *Under the Thunder the Flowers Light Up the Earth* (1977) and Phyllis Webb's extraordinary return after more than 10 years' silence, *Wilson's Bowl* (1980). In the mid-1980s poetry of every kind was healthy all across Canada. If perhaps too many mediocre poets were being published, that was a small price to pay for an active and lively culture. Poetry is still the one form of literature where, finally, the language is served most selflessly. While it remains in good health, the prospects for Canadian culture as a whole are good. DOUGLAS BARBOUR

Reading: E.K. Brown, *On Canadian Poetry* (rev ed 1944); Frank Davey, *From Here to There* (1974) and *Surviving the Paraphrase* (1983); Louis Dudek and Michael Gnarowski, eds, *The Making of Modern Poetry in Canada* (1967); Carl F. Klinck, ed, *Literary History of Canada* (2nd ed, 1976); Robert Kroetsch, *Essays* (1983); Eli Mandel, *The Family Romance* (1986); Tom Marshall, *Harsh and Lovely Land* (1979); William Toye, ed, *The Oxford Companion to Canadian Literature* (1983); George Woodcock, ed, *Colony and Confederation* (1974) and *Poets and Critics* (1974).

Poetry in French Satirical and epigrammatic verse in French appeared in 18th-century Québec NEWSPAPERS, but only 2 poets writing before 1820, both Frenchmen, deserve mention. Joseph Quesnel (1746-1809), captured at sea off Halifax in 1779, later settled near Montréal and wrote songs, poems and plays. Joseph Mermet (1775-1828?), sent to Canada with DE MEURON troops to help repel the American invasion of 1812, wrote dozens of poems, including a description of Niagara Falls and an account of the French Canadian victory at the Battle of CHÂTEAUGUAY (1813).

The first volume of verse (1830) published by a French Canadian contained didactic poems by Michel Bibaud (1782-1857), among them satires on avarice, envy, laziness and ignorance. By that time the new "classical colleges" were producing young men with political aspirations and literary interests. The French romantic poets Lamartine and Hugo were being read and imitated by the future historian François-Xavier GARNEAU and Québec's future premier, Pierre-Joseph-Olivier CHAUVEAU. Before 1850, however, poetry was primarily a political weapon or an elegant diversion, and poems were printed only in newspapers and magazines.

After 1850 poets became more numerous, and can be grouped in 3 "generations." The first, born in the 1820s, includes Joseph Lenoir, author of exotic oriental fantasies and of skilful verse translations of Burns, Longfellow and Goethe; Louis-Joseph-Cyprien Fiset, who wrote long narrative poems on Canadian historical subjects or on the emigration crisis (*see* FRANCO-AMERICANS); and the most competent versifier of this group, Octave CRÉMAZIE, who, before his self-imposed exile for bankruptcy in 1862, became the unofficial bard of French Canada with his poems on international topics (Crimean War, unification of Italy), the glories of the French regime in Canada and the obligations of the living to the dead.

But Lenoir died prematurely, Crémazie left Canada and Fiset abandoned poetry for law. A new generation of poets, born during the 1830s and associated with the literary movement of 1860, succeeded them. Alfred Garneau (1836-1904), self-effacing son of the historian, left some 60 poems attesting to his sensitivity and his wide knowledge of French poetry. Léon-Pamphile Le May, librarian of the Legislative Assembly of Québec, published almost a dozen collections of poems, including a verse translation of Longfellow's EVANGELINE. Le May's best-known volume, *Les Gouttelettes* (1904), consisted entirely of the new sonnet form, although his themes – religion, friendship, patriotism, the beauties of rural nature – remained those of his youth, and linked the 1860 movement with regionalism in early 20th-century Québec. The most important poet of this generation was Louis FRÉCHETTE, author of Québec's first volume of lyric poetry (*Mes loisirs*, 1863) and of the most important collection of narrative poems published in 19th-century Québec (*La Légende d'un peuple*, 1887). He was also the first Québec poet to be honoured by the French Academy (1880), and the first to publish a collected edition (3 vols, 1908) of his own verse.

After Confederation took Parliament to Ottawa in 1867, the 1860 literary movement in Québec City languished until 1875, when a new generation of poets, born about 1850, began to publish. Nérée Beauchemin (1850-1931), an obscure country doctor in Yamachiche, wrote tastefully of the joys of rural life in poems that were not collected until 1897. William Chapman (1850-1917) was a youthful admirer of Fréchette, but later turned against his idol, denouncing him as a plagiarist. Chapman's most successful collections were those he published in France early in the 20th century (*Les Aspirations*, 1904; *Les Rayons du nord*, 1909), which depicted a colourful Canadian northland peopled by VOYAGEURS, trappers and lumberjacks. The most original of this last generation of romantic poets was Eudore Évanturel, whose one slim volume, *Premières poésies* (1878), was attacked by the enemies of its prefacer, Joseph Marmette; Évanturel, discouraged, never returned to his whimsical accounts of flirtations and his witty personifications of the Canadian seasons.

Between 1830 and 1895, some 50 Québec poets published about 100 collections of verse. Their work was frequently inspired by the French romantics, but, unlike their models, 19th-century Québec poets neglected the themes of passionate love, individualism or pantheism, preferring patriotic, social, historical or religious subjects. Yet their experiments with versification were varied: in their youth Fréchette and Le May attempted dozens of verse forms. Gradually sonnets and 6-line stanzas became the accepted lyric forms, whereas alexandrine (12-syllable) rhyming couplets were used in narrative poems. The period 1830-95 was thus one of poetic apprenticeship. There were no great poets and no outstanding works, but there was considerable imitation, adaptation and experimentation. A poetic tradition was being created, a reading public being formed. DAVID M. HAYNE

Poetry in French, 1896-1930

The École littéraire de Montréal (fd in 1895) concentrated on purifying the French language and seeking out new forms of literary expression. The movement, which survived into the 1930s, lived through a period marked by the emergence of rural poetry (the "terroir" school) and the "art for art's sake" (Parnassian) movement.

The École's first 5 years culminated in the publication of its first collection, *Les Soirées du Château de Ramezay* (1900), followed by Émile NELLIGAN's *Poésies* in 1904. Nelligan, the youngest member of the group, created a remarkable collection of poetic works over a 3-year period (1896-99). Strongly influenced by Paul Verlaine, Charles Baudelaire, Georges Rodenbach, Maurice Rollinat, Edgar Allen Poe, José de Heredia and Leconte de Lisle, he had a gift for imagery and music, successfully mastered the sonnet and the rondeau, and plunged with determination into the depths of his troubled soul to create a sad, delirious and sometimes hallucinatory poetry. His "Romance du vin" and "Vaisseau d'or" describe his destiny as an artist and bear witness to his marvellous mastery of verse.

After 1900, the symbolist dream crumbled. The École sought to evoke "the soul of the people," in the words of Charles GILL, whose *Cap Eternité* (1919), the fragments of a Dantesque fresco, reflects the trends of that period. Some poets, among them Louis-Joseph Doucet, Lionel Léveillé, Hector Demers and Albert Ferland (author of *Le Canada chanté*) devoted themselves to nationalist poetry. The review *Le Terroir* lasted scarcely a year, and its 10 issues were published in book form in 1910.

Some members of the École concentrated on poetry with a philosophical bent: Jean Charbonneau (*Les Blessures*, 1912); Alphonse Beauregard (*Les Forces*, 1912; *Les Alternances*, 1921); and Jean-Aubert Loranger (*Les Atmosphères*, 1920; *Poèmes*, 1922), the last enriching his meditation on man with oriental and unanimist influences. The school's third collection, *Les Soirées de l'école littéraire de Montréal* (1925), contained the works of 10 poets. Around 1930 the École disbanded, but a few collections were still published: Charbonneau's *La Flamme ardente* (1928), Gonzalve Desaulniers' *Les Bois qui chantent* (1930) and Joseph Melançon's *Avec ma vie* (1931).

The rural theme continued to develop. The fields, rivers, forests and villages of this poetry carried an often nostalgic tune, echoing the early settlers' songs. This tradition was a carry-over from the previous century. The young poets of Crémazie's era, strongly attached to the homeland, suddenly found themselves at the dawn of the

20th century. The rural theme became the leitmotif of all Blanche Lamontagne-Beauregard's poetry, her second collection, *Par nos champs et nos rives* (1917), being a striking example. Rural poetry is found in the works of Alphonse Désilets (pseudonym, Jacquelin), eg, *Heures poétiques* (1910), *Mon pays, mes amours* (1913) and *Dans la brise du terroir* (1922). Jules Tremblay, an intimist poet, took up rural poetry in *Arômes du terroir* (1918), his fourth collection. Émile Coderre (pseudonym Jean Narrache) created a sort of dialectic poetry in *Quand j'parl'tout seul* (1933), but the best rural poets were without doubt Nérée Beauchemin and Alfred DESROCHERS. Beauchemin wrote 2 collections evocative of Canadian history and life in Trois-Rivières: *Les Floraisons matinales* (1897) and *Patrie intime* (1928). DesRochers is noted for his startling vision of reality and his mastery of sonnet, rondeau, madrigal, chanson, acrostic, ode and elegy. The life of early settlers, vigorous thought and masterly art dominate DesRochers's *L'Offrande aux vierges folles* (1928) and *À l'ombre de l'Orford* (1929). With its powerful epic flavour, his poem "Hymne au vent du nord" is a landmark in the history of rural poetry.

The "art for art's sake" movement began in Québec in 1895 with the exotic sonnets of Arthur de Bussières. Although Alfred Garneau, Émile Nelligan, Jules Tremblay, Guy Delahaye, René Chopin and Marcel Dugas all practised symbolism, they also occasionally indulged in Parnassian art. The best representative of art for art's sake in Québec was lawyer Paul MORIN. Sonorous vocabulary, striking imagery and exotic landscapes are all found in his *Paon d'émail* (1911) and *Poèmes de cendre et d'or* (1922). The short-lived review, *Le NIGOG* (1918), launched a Parnassian movement which rapidly faded when it ceased publication.

At the beginning of the century, there emerged many poets who had little or no attachment to any particular school. An example is Louis Dantin (pseudonym Eugène Seers), the author of philosophical poetry and a literary critic, but above all, the person who revealed Nelligan's poetry to Montréalers in 1902. Also worthy of mention is the paralytic poet, Albert Lozeau, whose nostalgic landscape is found throughout his collections, *L'Âme solitaire* (1907) and *Le Miroir des jours* (1912); and Antonio Desjardins, author of *Crépuscules* (1924). Most important is Robert Choquette, whose first 3 collections, *À travers les vents* (1925), *Metropolitan Museum* (1931) and *Poésies nouvelles* (1933), are permeated by a visionary force and probe the destiny of modern man.

Between 1895 and 1930 Québec poetry dealt with a wide range of experiences. Beginning with the romantic tradition, it soon evolved toward symbolist poetry, later the "terroir" movement, and lastly the Parnassian school. Having turned away from traditional forms, it moved slowly toward free verse. PAUL WYCZYNSKI

Poetry in French, 1930-1970

In poetry, as in other matters, change was often resisted in Québec: Clément Marchand (*Les Soirs rouges*, 1947) and Alphonse Piché (*Remous*, 1947) attempted new themes while adhering to traditional forms. Simone Routier (*Les Tentations*, 1934) adopted free verse but without any other advance. The mercurial François Hertel (*Axes et parallaxes*, 1941), a Jesuit and for over a decade a leading cultural figure, did much to encourage a climate of change; yet his intellectual poems failed to acknowledge the realities of Québec's future. The real vanguard in poetry at this time consisted of 4 rather isolated poets: Hector de Saint-Denys GARNEAU, Anne HÉBERT, Rina LASNIER and Alain GRANDBOIS.

Garneau published only one collection in his lifetime, *Regards et jeux dans l'espace* (1937). A second collection, *Les Solitudes*, appeared posthumously in his *Poésies complètes* (1949). Living in seclusion, Garneau devoted himself to poetry and to an increasingly difficult spiritual journey. His poems, written in rigorously controlled free verse, have a magical quality, expressing anguish and joy with equal simplicity and beauty.

In Hébert's *Les Songes en équilibre* (1942) the poet becomes a priest-magician with a social function. Hébert's psychological explorations reached the collective unconscious in *Le Tombeau des rois* (1953), in poetry pared to the bone. In the second half of *Poèmes* (1960) she entered a new phase, addressing Québec (or humankind) with epic generosity of line and spirit.

Beginning with *Images et proses* (1941), Lasnier wrote principally on religious themes. Though her early work is too intellectual to be of lasting interest, in *Escales* (1950), *Présence de l'absence* (1956) and later volumes her poetry is an impassioned plunge into contradictions wherein darkness and light come to coexist. Other women poets of this period include Medjé Vézina (*Chaque heure a son visage*, 1934), Jovette Bernier (*Les Masques déchirés*, 1932), Cécile Chabot (*Vitrail*, 1939) and Jeannine Bélanger (*Le Visage dans la roche*, 1941).

Grandbois became the most influential of the new poets, but his influence was primarily among the younger poets who came to dominate the 1960s. *Les Îles de la nuit* (1944) was a breath of fresh air, treating the poet's obsessive world travels, and conveying a sense of the cosmic and of human fraternity, as well as an unconstrained eroticism. The poems were fragmented and often surrealistic, yet thoroughly accomplished, as were the volumes that followed: *Rivages de l'homme* (1948) and *L'Étoile pourpre* (1957).

During the "Dark Years" of the rule of Premier Maurice DUPLESSIS (1944-59), an important minority of poets chose surrealistic modes of expression. Most had ties with the visual arts or jazz. REFUS GLOBAL (1948), a revolutionary cultural manifesto by painter Paul-Émile BORDUAS, included poems by Claude Gauvreau (*Brochuges*, 1957), whose work consisted of strangely meaningful nonsense words. Roland GIGUÈRE was an accomplished painter, engraver and typographer as well as a major poet. His poems, brought together in *L'Âge de la parole* (1965), are in revolt against anything that might suppress or sterilize life. Gilles Hénault sought "signs" in the remote past, among native peoples and in the collective unconscious as encountered in dreams. His 3 volumes of poetry are collected in *Signaux pour les voyants* (1972). Other poets whose writings touched upon surrealism include Yves Préfontaine (*Boréal*, 1957), an editor of LIBERTÉ; Marie-Claire BLAIS (*Pays voilés*, 1963), better known for her novels; and Claude Péloquin (*Jéricho*, 1963). Foremost was jazz musician Paul-Marie LAPOINTE, whose "automatiste" method of writing (*see* AUTOMATISTES) was akin to jazz improvisation. Only his first volume, *La Vierge incendiée* (1948), is truly surrealistic, but it contains the basic themes of all his poetry — justice for mankind, sexual freedom and the liberating power of love — expressed through repetition and inventory, and with great musicality. In later works, brought together in *Le Réel absolu* (1971), individual rebellion becomes collective revolution.

Though a gradual shift was taking place toward politicized poetry, many poets continued to write within their personal worlds. Éloi de Grandmont (*Plaisirs*, 1953) wrote charming verses celebrating the pleasures of love. Sylvain Garneau (*Les Trouble-fête*, 1952) lived in an adolescent dreamworld, pure yet disturbing, before killing himself

in his early twenties. Gilles Constantineau (*Simples Poèmes et ballades*, 1960) portrayed an intimate world illuminated with striking perceptions and happiness. Luc Perrier (*Du temps que j'aime*, 1963) precisely evoked the strange poetry of daily existence. At the opposite extreme, Suzanne Paradis (*Pour les enfants des morts*, 1964) poured out her ardent will to live, affirming a powerful feminine mystique and expanding it to affect all areas of life.

The publication in 1958 of *La Poésie et nous*, consisting of essays by Hénault, Préfontaine, Michel Van Schendel, Jacques BRAULT and Wilfrid Lemoine, signalled the development of indigenous poetic theories. During the 1940s the magazines, *La Nouvelle Relève* and *Gants du ciel*, had helped introduce the ideas of the French avant-garde. By the 1960s it was clear that the ideas most relevant to Québec were those emerging within the province itself. The magazines *Liberté* and PARTI PRIS fostered a vigorous exchange of literary and political thinking. Publishing houses were equally important, especially les Éditions de l'hexagone (fd in 1953).

During the 1960s Québec experienced a sudden growth in collective self-awareness and political ferment (*see* QUIET REVOLUTION). FRENCH CANADIAN NATIONALISM and the arts began to seem inseparable, justifying and stimulating each other. Although much nationalist writing was little more than propaganda, a surprising amount achieved the highest poetic quality, as did Brault's *Mémoire* (1965). Brault, like Paul-Marie Lapointe and many others of the period, belonged to the Hexagon movement, which consisted of essentially nationalist poets. At the centre of the movement, and principal force behind les Éditions de l'hexagone, was the energetic and charismatic Gaston MIRON. After *Deux Sangs* (1953), which he published with Olivier Marchand, Miron refused to collect his own poems until 1970, though he was a gifted poet and performer.

The theme of the land was a constant in the poetry of the 1960s, which gradually pulled away from the pan-Canadian perspective offered in Pierre Trottier's *Le Combat contre Tristan* (1951). The St Lawrence R became a national symbol. Pierre Perrault celebrated its islands in *Toutes isles* (1963), and Gatien Lapointe's effusive poetry reached its highest expression in *J'appartiens à la terre/Ode au Saint-Laurent* (1963). Van Schendel's *Poèmes de l'Amérique* (1958) was a reaction to the violence of modern America, but his *Variations sur la pierre* (1964) conveyed a sense of being reborn in Québec. Nationalist themes entered the powerful writing of Fernand OUELLETTE in *Le Soleil sous la mort* (1965), a title suggestive of national regeneration. That idea is made explicit in Andrée Maillet's *Le Chant de l'Iroquoise* (1967). In addition, although Paul CHAMBERLAND's *Genèses* (1962) may suggest a solitary spiritual struggle, that struggle is made concrete and collective in his *Terre Québec* (1964), a work of unfailing intensity and originality.

Language, affecting both the form and the content of Québec poetry, was the most important nationalist theme of all. Whether as JOUAL or as a "legitimate" dialect of French, Québec French was long a source of humiliation. As that humiliation was confessed, probed and held up for redress, the language gradually became a national birthright; for poets, *le parler québécois* became a vivid mode of expression as well as a symbol both of the nation and of the very enterprise of poetry. Fernand Dumont published a group of poems entitled *Peuple sans parole* (*Liberté*, 1965), and Yves Préfontaine published *Pays sans parole* (1967). Language dominated the poems of the future PARTI QUÉBÉCOIS culture minister, Gérald Godin (*Les Cantouques*, 1966). Most famous is Michèle

Lalonde's *Speak White* (1974), a bitterly ironic poem first recited in 1968.

By the end of the 1960s the nationalist, populist phase of Québec poetry was coming to an end, though Lalonde carried it to the extreme in *Défense et illustration de la langue québécoise* (1979). Poets like Luc Racine (*Les Dormeurs*, 1966) and Raoul Duguay (*Ruts*, 1966) began to argue for more concern with pure writing and less with messages. As though it had proven its worth after a decade or more of activism on a common front, poetry now could afford to turn inward, to adapt to individual interests in the mundane or the metaphysical.　　　　　　　　ROD WILLMOT

Poetry in French, 1970-80s

This period is marked by a shattering of the ideological, nationalist and humanist unity that permeated the poetry of the 1960s. Although the break is not complete, the young generation of poets turned away from the "poésie du pays" movement exemplified by Gaston Miron's *L'Homme rapaillé* (1970) and adopted surrealism and its Québec variant, automatism. The works of Paul-Marie Lapointe, Claude Gauvreau, Roland Giguère and Gilles Hénault, all born between 1920 and 1930 and affiliated with surrealism, have been republished and widely read. The new poetry is not a simple extension of this trend, but reflects a mentality. It is the radical rebuttal of all social and cultural institutions and the values associated with them, and is critical of the dogmatic unity inherent in "la belle poésie."

The avant-garde finds its most coherent expression in the poetry of the group associated with *Les Herbes rouges*. Inspired more by the theories of the French avant-garde than by those of the American counterculture found in poets like Denis Vanier and Lucien Francoeur, the journal *Les Herbes rouges* is in fact a publishing house which has issued 100 or so brochures over a 10-year period. The influence of Nicole Brossard figures prominently in its publications. Two of her collections, *Suite logique* and *Le Centre blanc* (1970), set the tone for the decade: disjointed syntax, preoccupation with the irrational (desire, the body, loss of the senses, madness) in a reflective and critical manner. Roger Des Roches and André Roy follow the trend set by *Les Herbes rouges*, while François Charron tends to depart from it through the use of parody and a return to lyricism.

The poetry of this period generally rebels against the previously dominant telluric and cosmic-inspired lyricism, an exception being the mystical-çosmic utopia created by Paul Chamberland in *Demain les dieux naîtront* (1974). Elsewhere, private life and the urban world are dominant. This poetry of everyday existence is expressed in the work of Michel Beaulieu, particularly in *Variables* (1973) and in *Anecdotes* (1977), which uses analytical language to convey modern man's drift through his body, desires and memory. For Juan Garcia and Alexis Lefrançois, private life becomes the focal point for the metaphysical experience of experimentation and purification; the concisely expressed individualism of Gilbert Langevin (*Mon refuge est un volcan*, 1978) is a scathing denunciation of modern society. By contrast, Michel Garneau and Pierre Morency affirm the "torrential" and "amorous" energy of the individual. Finally, 2 poets of the Hexagone generation, Jacques Brault, in *L'endessous l'admirable* and *Poèmes des quatre côtés* (1975), and Fernand Ouellette in *Ici, ailleurs, la lumière* (1977), undertake an inner journey and react against the more superficial aspects of the modern world.

The major poetic movement of the latter part of the decade is linked to the modernism of *Les Herbes rouges*. Inspired by Brossard's reflection on the imaginary, this new movement places great importance on feminist concerns. Madeleine Gagnon's *Pour les femmes et tous les autres* (1974), Brossard's *La Partie pour le tout* (1975) and France Théorêt's *Bloody Mary* (1977) are the first examples of "feminist writing" to challenge patriarchal symbolism and develop fiction documenting the history and experiences of women. This trend appears to be leading poetry toward less revolutionary forms and to a fusion with other literary genres, particularly narrative writing and the essay, examples being the works of Yolande Villemaire and Suzanne Jacob. At the end of the decade, there was evidence of a "new imagination" and a "new readability" embodied in *Les Passions du samedi* (1979) by André Roy, the neo-lyricist writing of François Charron, the transparency of Philippe Haeck and, at another level, that of Marie Uguay. The resounding success of *Estuaire* (a journal published since 1976), publishing houses like Éditions du Noroît, poet Gatien Lapointe's Écrits des forges, and the production of works at Éditions de l'hexagone all attest to the continuity and diversity of Québec poetry in the early 1980s. Two new works of note are François Charron's *La Vie n'a pas de sens* (1985) and Normand de Bellefeuille's *Catégoriques* (1986).

　　　　　　　　PIERRE NEPVEU

Reading: Réginald Hamel et al, *Dictionnaire pratique des auteurs québécois* (1976); M. Lemire, ed, *Dictionnaire des oeuvres littéraires du Québec*, 5 vols (1980-88); L. Mailhot and Pierre Nepveu, eds, *La Poésie québécoise* (1981).

Point Pelée National Park (est 1918) is located at the tip of Point Pelee, a long peninsula jutting abruptly into LK ERIE, the southernmost tip of Canada's mainland. It is on the same latitude as Rome and northern California and its climate is somewhat warmer than in the rest of Canada; many species found in the park are typical of southern areas. The park sits atop a deposit of sand up to 70 m thick left by glacial meltwaters on a submerged limestone ridge. Over the centuries a thin but rich soil has formed, supporting a lush deciduous forest of such exotic species as shagbark hickory, sassafras and hackberry, one of Canada's few remaining stands of Carolinean forest. A boardwalk gives access to the marshlands comprising much of the park. REPTILES and AMPHIBIANS abound and several species rare elsewhere in Canada, such as the fox snake and spotted turtle, thrive; it is the home of eastern Canada's only lizard, the five-lined skink. Point Pelée is best known as Canada's finest BIRD WATCHING spot. Located on the crossroads of 2 major MIGRATION flyways, over 100 species can sometimes be seen in a day. Over 300 species have been recorded in the park. The spit was named by French ex-

plorers, who called it Pointe Pelée, meaning "bald point" for its lack of vegetation. Lobbying by naturalists and by duck hunters led to formation of the park in 1918, though it was still dotted with cottages and, by 1939, 2 hotels. Only 2 cottages remain, but the fragile vegetation which keeps the point from washing away is threatened by visitors. Point Pelée is a day-use park, permitting hiking, swimming and bird watching.　　LILLIAN STEWART

Poirier, Anne Claire, film director, producer (b at St-Hyacinthe, Qué 6 June 1932). She joined the NFB in 1960, eventually going into film direction, which had been essentially a male preserve. Her first full-length film, *De mère en fille* (1968), dealt with the physical and emotional experience of pregnancy. In 1973 Poirier produced the "En tant que femmes" series which offered female film producers their first organized platform for expression. In this series, Poirier directed *Les Filles du roy* (1974) and *Le Temps de l'avant* (1975), the latter a sensitive study of the abortion issue. She then produced the powerful *Mourir à tue-tête* (1979), a film about rape. *La Quarantaine* (1982) deals with the critical fifth decade of a person's life.

　　　　　　　　PIERRE VÉRONNEAU

Poison Ivy (*Toxicodendron*), small genus of woody perennial plants of cashew family (Anacardiaceae), closely related to and sometimes classified with the SUMACS (genus *Rhus*). The name most commonly refers to *T. rydbergii*, found from southern BC to the Atlantic provinces but also refers to *T. radicans* subspecies *radicans*, occurring in southern NS and *T. radicans* subspecies *negundo*, in southern Ontario. The plants spread by underground stems. Most are small shrubs (0.5-1 m tall); others are vinelike plants, 15 m or longer, supported by aerial roots. Shrubby forms are sometimes called poison oak. Leaves have 3 leaflets, shiny, somewhat concave, entire or coarsely toothed or lobed. Greenish yellow berries turn white and remain on plants all winter. They are found in various habitats (eg, sandy or gravelly soils, dunes, talus slopes) but generally prefer calcareous places. Dermatitis can develop on contact with any plant part throughout the year (especially spring and summer), even from smoke from fires containing it. Skin blisters develop, exuding liquid if broken. Washing with strong soap helps; juice of jewel weed (*Impatiens capensis*) is also supposed to be effective. *See also* PLANTS, NATIVE USES; POISONOUS PLANTS.　　　　　　　　J.M. GILLETT

Poison ivy (*Toxicodendron*). The resin from crushed leaves or stems causes an extremely irritating skin rash (*artwork by Claire Tremblay*).

Point Pelée National Park occupies a 17 km peninsula jutting into Lk Erie. It is Canada's finest bird-watching site – over 100 species have been sighted on one day (*courtesy Environment Canada, Parks*).

Skunk cabbage leaves not only smell terribly when crushed, they also contain toxic oxalic acid (*photo by Dan Schneider*).

Poisonous Plants Most major groups of PLANTS contain species that can produce toxic reactions ranging from discomfort, through organ damage, to death. Poisons may be assimilated by being eaten, inhaled, or absorbed through the skin. Nontoxic plants and plant products may cause simple physical damage followed by infection. Toxic reactions are caused by compounds that may be produced by plants or absorbed from soil. Alkaloids (bitter-tasting, semialkaline substances containing nitrogen) occur throughout plants in soluble organic acid salts. Polypeptides and amines are organic substances containing nitrogen. Glycosides are compounds that break down to form sugars and toxic aglycones. Oxalates occur as soluble or insoluble salts. Insoluble calcium salts are irritants that are deposited in kidneys. Resins or resinoids irritate muscle tissue. Phytotoxins or toxalbumins (protein molecules acting as enzymes) break down natural proteins, causing ammonia accumulation and protein deficiency. Many plants take up minerals (eg, copper, selenium, lead, molybdenum, nitrates or nitrites) from soils in sufficient quantities to cause poisoning.

Allergies Many people are sensitive to plant substances. Airborne material (eg, FUNGI spores, soil ALGAE, pollen grains, etc) causes hayfever. Pollen, the most serious problem, is seasonal. Early flowering trees cause reactions in spring. A midsummer peak is caused primarily by GRASS species. In autumn, a peak is caused by herba-

Jack-in-the-pulpit (here in fruit) contains oxalic acid, which penetrates mouth tissues causing a burning sensation (*photo by Dan Schneider*).

Principal Poisonous Plants of Canada (fungi and algae excluded)

Common Name	Scientific Name	Distribution	Notes
almond (bitter)	*Prunus amygdalus dulcis*	cultivated, ornamental	seeds rich in glycosides; inedible
almond (sweet)	*Prunus amygdalus amara*	cultivated	seeds edible
apricot	*Prunus armenica*	cultivated	seeds rich in glycosides; inedible
black cherry	*Prunus serotina*	Ont to NS	glycosides in leaves and fruit stones
bracken fern	*Pteridium aquilinum*	southern Canada	toxic to cattle and horses
buttercup	*Ranunculus*	45 species in Canada	plant acrid in taste, or even toxic
castor bean or castor oil plant	*Ricinus communis*	ornamental	all parts, especially seeds, poisonous to children
chokecherry	*Prunus virginiana* var *melanocarpa* var *virginiana*	BC and Alta eastern provinces	all have high levels of cyanogenetic glycosides (cause cyanide poisoning)
columbine	*Aquilegia*	throughout Canada	flowers toxic to humans
Daphne	*Daphne mezereum*	ornamental shrub	all parts, especially berries, poisonous to children
death camas	*Zygadenus elegans* *Z. venenosus*	across Canada BC, Alta and Sask	steroid alkaloids responsible for death of sheep
dogbane	*Apocynum*	southern Canada to YT	milky juice toxic
dumbcane	*Dieffenbachia maculata*	ornamental house plant	oxalate crystals can cause tongue swelling and block breathing
false azalea	*Menziesia ferruginea*	western mountains	
false hellebore	*Veratrum viride*	alpine	poisonous to grazing animals
foxglove	*Digitalis purpurea*	weed escaped from gardens in BC and eastern Canada	medicinal plant once; overdose very dangerous as contains cardiac or steroid glycosides
groundsel	*Senecio jacobaea*	weed	causes Pictou disease of cattle in NS
horsetail	*Equisetum*, especially *Equisetum arvense*	throughout Canada	toxic to cattle and horses
ivy	*Hedera helix*	ornamental	leaves poisonous
Jack-in-the-pulpit	*Arisaema triphyllum*	eastern Canadian wet woods	irritation, swelling about mouth; contains oxalates
larkspurs	*Delphinium*	3 species in West, some cultivated species	toxic to man or animals
lily of the valley	*Convallaria majalis*	cultivated and garden escapes	all parts poisonous, especially underground stem; contain glycosides
locoweeds	*Oxytropis* and *Astragalus*	arctic, alpine and prairie	poisonous to animals
lupines	*Lupus*	28 species, most southern Sask to BC	untreated seeds poisonous to livestock
milkweed	*Asclepias*	over 12 species: 2 from BC to Man, others from Man to Nfld	milky latex poisonous to livestock; fortunately unpalatable
monkshood or aconite	*Aconitum columbianum* *A. nagellus*	BC cultivated	toxic to man or animals
mustard family (eg, horseradish, broccoli, turnip, etc)	*Cruciferae* family	cultivated or woody	contain varying quantities of mustard oil; if grazed in quantity can poison cattle, sheep, swine
nightshade	*Solanum*	across Canada	poisonous alkaloids in many species
oleander	*Nerium oleander*	ornamental pot plant	contains cardiac glycosides; all parts extremely toxic to humans or livestock
peach	*Prunus persica*	cultivated	pits and tree parts rich in glycosides
pin cherry	*Prunus pensylvanica*	southern Canada	bright red, acid fruit recognized by 2 small glands at base of leaf blade
poinsettia	*Euphorbia pulcherrima*	sold as pot plant	especially dangerous to children
poison hemlock	*Conium maculatum*	roadsides, fields, ditches	cattle poison
poison ivy	*Toxicodendron rydbergii* *T. radicans*	BC to Atlantic provinces eastern provinces	causes dermatitis
poison sumac	*Rhus vernix*	eastern provinces	causes dermatitis
poppy	*Papaver*	mostly gardens	hallucinogenic; opium poppy unlawful to grow
precatory or jequirity bean	*Abrus precatorius*	seeds imported from tropics as beads by tourists	importation illegal; made into necklaces; chewing one bean can be fatal
rhubarb	*Rheum*	cultivated, occasionally escapes	blade of leaf can be fatal; stalk safe; contains oxalates
Saint-John's-wort	*Hypericum perforatum*	weedy in eastern Canada and BC	causes photosensitivity in livestock
sheep laurel or sheepkill	*Kalmia angustifolia*	woods or bogs Lab to central Ont	leaves eaten in spring when other grazing scarce; can poison animals
snow-on-the-mountain	*Euphorbia marginata*	garden subject; occasionally weed	especially poisonous to children
spurges	*Euphorbia*	all weedy	milky sap can cause blisters
trapper's tea	*Ledum glandulosum*	BC to Alta	twigs, leaves and flowers toxic
water hemlock	*Cicuta maculata*, *C. bulbifera*	wet habitats throughout southern Canada	dahlialike root very poisonous to cattle; death within hours
water parsnip	*Sium suave*	wet places	cattle poison
white snakeroot	*Eupatorium rugosum*	eastern Canadian woodlands	causes trembles in livestock
wild lettuce	*Lactuca scariola*	weed	early growth harmful to grazing animals
yew	*Taxus brevifolia* *T. canadensis* *T. cuspidata*	BC southern Man to Nfld ornamental	foliage, bark or seeds toxic to man or animals

Bittersweet nightshade poisons livestock with solanine. The berries contain less toxin than the rest of the plant (*photo by Dan Schneider*).

ceous plants, chiefly spiny-pollened ragweed (3 species of genus *Ambrosia*) in Canada. The Atlantic provinces, BC, Saskatchewan, northern Ontario, Québec and Manitoba are relatively free of ragweed. Allergies rarely kill.

Dermatitis Several plants (eg, POISON IVY, poison sumac and primrose) cause skin irritation (redness, itching or blisters). Cultivated *Cyclamen* (primrose family) also causes reactions in some people, the severity depending on degree of contact and individual susceptibility. Contact with stinging nettle (*Urtica*), woodnettle (*Laportea*) and stem hairs of some species of Avens (*Geum*) can cause temporary discomfort.

Internal Poisoning Poisoning cannot occur unless plants, or parts of them, are consumed. Peo-

---

The destroying angel mushroom claims the most victims. About half of the persons who eat it die (*photo by Dan Schneider*).

ple can avoid them, but animals left to graze native range may eat them. Internal poisoning depends upon type and quantity of plant eaten, the condition and age of person or animal and other factors.

Mechanical Injury While not poisonous, certain plants cause physical injury followed by secondary infection. Hawthorn (*Crataegus*), rose (*Rosa*) and blackberry (*Rubus*) have prominent thorns. The West Coast Devil's-club (*Oplopanax horridus*) is spiny throughout and forms thickets. Barbs of grasses such as wild barley (*Hordeum*), brome grass (*Bromus*), wild rye (*Agropyron*) and needle-grass (*Stipa*) can stick in the throat of an animal. Cocklebur (*Xanthium*) has prickly fruits. Mullein (*Verbascum*), crimson and rabbit-foot clovers (*Trifolium*) can form hair balls in the stomach. *See also* individual species entries.

J.M. GILLETT

Reading: John M. Kingsbury, *Poisonous Plants of the US and Canada* (1964).

Pokemouche, NB, UP, pop 362 (1986c), 341 (1981c), in rural area of Inkerman, is located 15 km S of CARAQUET, close to the centre of the Acadian Pen (S of CHALEUR BAY). The marshy lagoon at the mouth of the Pokemouche R prevents port development, but Pokemouche was important in land and river communications. Two MICMAC village sites, 3 campsites and 3 portages were in this area. The first European settlers were ACADIAN refugees arriving in 1797. English ex-soldiers and many Irish settlers followed after 1800, but French influence is now dominant. The lumber industry that flourished after 1825 declined around 1860, and the labour force is now mostly employed in farming or in service industries. The nearby airport, opened 1978, has improved communications.

SHEILA ANDREW

Polanyi, John Charles, chemist, professor (b at Berlin, Ger 23 Jan 1929), son of scientist and philosopher Michael Polanyi. He is widely recognized and honoured for his brilliant research on the dynamics of chemical reactions, his views on science policy and his dedication to achieving a rational approach to nuclear disarmament. He was educated in Manchester, Eng, where his family had settled after leaving Germany in 1934. Following postdoctoral research at NRC and Princeton, he was appointed lecturer at University of Toronto in 1956 and professor of chemistry in 1962. Development of his discovery in 1958 of the emission of infrared radiation from newly

John Polanyi (left) receiving his Nobel Prize for Chemistry from King Carl Gustaf of Sweden, 10 Dec 1986 (*photo by Rolf Hamilton ©Pressens Bild*).

formed molecules has led to new levels of understanding of the nature of chemical transformations. In 1986 he was co-winner of the Nobel Prize for Chemistry, for his work on infrared chemiluminescence.

D.J. LE ROY

Polar Bear (*Ursus maritimus*), large, white BEAR with long, narrow head and very small ears. Polar bears inhabit ice and coastlines of arctic seas, mostly in Canada, but also in Alaska, USSR, Norway's Svalbard I and Greenland. In Canada, polar bears are found in coastal regions of both territories and in Manitoba, Ontario and arctic Québec. The James Bay region is the southern limit of their range. Unlike most other bears, polar bears remain active during winter, hunting and travelling on sea ice. They eat mainly seals, hunted by waiting beside a breathing hole in the ice. In summer, the breakup often forces them to live on land,

---

The polar bear (*Ursus maritimus*) inhabits the ice and coastlines of the Canadian Arctic as far south as James Bay (*photo by Fred Bruemmer*).

where they eat various foods, including waterfowl, berries, marine vegetation and even smaller polar bears. Females become fertile every second year. In late fall, the pregnant female builds a den in a large snowdrift, where cubs are born. The family stays there until Mar, when a move to sea ice occurs and the mother begins hunting. Twins are the rule (range 1-3). Cubs stay with the mother for over a year. Polar bears breed in spring with embryo implantation delayed until fall; hence, cubs are extremely small (about 1 kg) at birth. Adult males, however, can weigh 650 kg; females, 350 kg. BRIAN KNUDSEN

Poles In 1795 Russia, Prussia and Austria partitioned the territories of Poland. The assimilation of Polish territories, as well as religious persecution and a poor economy, inspired the emigration of the Poles. The majority of the first Polish newcomers to Canada did not arrive directly from Poland. The first Polish immigrant arrived in Canada in 1752. Two other Poles reportedly in Canada in 1776 were August F. Globenski, an army surgeon of the Hesse-Haynau regiment, and Leveright Pinze, a surgeon of the auxiliary forces from Brunswick. Karol Blaskowitz, a captain-cartographer of the British army, arrived in 1802 and Aleksander E. Kierzkowski, an engineer who became politically active in the St-Hyacinthe riding in 1867, arrived in 1841. Among the Swiss regiments that fought at Fort Barrie in 1812, there were about a dozen Poles from former Napoleonic legions. Sir Casimir GZOWSKI, a prominent civil engineer, railway builder and social activist, arrived from the US in 1842. Izaak Helmuth, from Warsaw, Poland, came via England and was one of the founders of U of Western Ontario.

Migration The major periods of Polish immigration to Canada were 1858-94 (1000), 1895-1913 (119 600), 1920-39 (55 500), 1946-56 (62 000) and 1957-82 (42 000). The first 2 waves included many family groups from villages and small towns of Austrian-occupied territory. Hardworking, religious peasants, many received land grants from the government or bought lots in Manitoba, Saskatchewan and Alberta where they built farms. Others worked on railway construction or in the coal mines. The second generation very often moved to larger settlements or towns, where they opened small businesses.

The immigrants of 1920 to 1939 arrived from an already independent Poland and settled (at least until 1931) primarily on the Prairies. Until 1945 Winnipeg had the largest Polish community. The first wave of immigrants after 1945 (over 50% of whom settled in Ontario) consisted largely of former soldiers of the Polish armed forces who had fought in Western Europe, former inmates of Nazi concentration or forced-labour camps and political REFUGEES from communist Poland. From 1957 to 1981, immigrants again arrived directly from Poland. The latest wave 1981-86 (about 28 000) was motivated by the deep economic and political crisis in Poland; 50% settled in Ontario, about 9000 in the Toronto area.

Settlement Patterns With the exception of one homogeneous group from German-occupied territory, which arrived in 1858 and settled in Renfrew County [Ont], the Polish newcomers frequently homesteaded (eg, in Manitoba around Springfield, St Clement's, Brokenhead, Lac du Bonnet, Whitemouth, Gimli, Bifrost, Glenella, Rosedale, McCreary and Dauphin) close to already established Ukrainian farmers, who were often from neighbouring villages in Poland. A widespread movement of immigrants to larger centres started in the 1930s. There are

222 260 Poles living in Canada (1986e). The largest Polish communities are, in descending order, in Toronto, Winnipeg, Montréal, Edmonton, Hamilton, Vancouver and St Catharines. Lesser concentrations live in Calgary, Ottawa, Kitchener, London, Sudbury, Regina, Saskatoon, Thunder Bay, Windsor and Oshawa. Eighty-eight percent of the Poles in Canada live in urban areas.

Economic Life The first Polish immigrants helped settle the prairies of Manitoba, Saskatchewan and Alberta, and made up a large percentage of the labour force in mines, in the forest industry and in public works. The second generation and the post-WWII immigrants were more financially secure, with professional experience and technical qualifications. They opened their own enterprises, occupied executive positions in industry, and were prominent in social and health services and in higher education.

Social and Community Life The majority of Poles are Roman Catholic, but there are also Lutherans and United Church members. A separate Polish Catholic Church, which is not affiliated with the Roman Catholic Church, has parishes in various cities (*see* CATHOLICISM). Parishes formed the first organizational units, providing a framework for community and social life. Lay organizations appeared in towns only shortly before WWI.

The 1930s marked the appearance of social clubs that helped maintain Polish customs and traditions, as did the Polish government through its consulates. Polish credit unions were created across Canada. The first, the St Stanislaus Credit Union, was organized in Toronto; it is now the largest financial institution of its kind in N America, with capital assets of $119 million in 1987 and 22 000 members. In the mid-1950s women formed a self-contained and independent organization (the Federation of Polish Women in Canada), which was concerned with cultural and political issues. Various folk groups or dance ensembles surfaced at different times and in different communities.

The Catholic Church has played a very important role in the life of the Polish nation, especially in difficult times. For many immigrants in the past it provided the sole contact with their native country and its culture. The priests were advisers, defenders, spokesmen, religious leaders and community leaders. Catholics in Polish communities still observe the customs of Christmas, Lent, Holy Week and Easter.

The first Polish newspaper, which appeared in Winnipeg in 1904, was short-lived. The second attempt, *Gazeta Katolicka* (*Catholic Gazette*), was founded in Winnipeg in 1908. The Polish press in Canada today is very active and includes several different publications, some of them running up to 10 000 copies.

Polish writers and poets include Louis DUDEK, W. Iwaniuk, B. Czaykowski, Florian Smieja, J. Ihnatowicz, A. Busza and the late Zofia Bohdanowicz and Danuta Bienkowska. Artists include Mary Schneider, Krystyne Sadkowska, E. Koniuszy, S. Katski, E. Chruscicki, T. Jaworska, G. Staron, M. Ciechomska, B. Michalowska, H. Hoenigan, J. Lubojanska, J. Kolaer and G. Denisiuk.

Education The first 2 phases of Polish immigration included numerous illiterate peasants, but later immigrants were generally well educated. The children were sent to public schools, but a network of part-time Polish-language schools was also established. Most of the latter are affiliated with the Polish Teachers Federation.

Ethnic identification is fully realized only within groups directly connected with Polish organizations or parishes. The Polish Congress encompasses some 160 independent organizations whose membership varies from a few dozen to a few thousand people. According to the 1986 census, Polish was the mother tongue of 123 120 Canadians.

Politics Until 1980 the majority of Poles voted Liberal in federal elections. Candidates of Polish origin have always been supported by their ethnic constituents. Stanley Haidasz, born in Toronto of Polish parents, was the first Polish Liberal MP. He later became minister for multiculturalism in the Trudeau government and the first Polish representative in the Senate. There were 3 ministers of Polish origin in the Saskatchewan NDP government until its defeat in 1982. A small group of Polish communists had been quite active during the GREAT DEPRESSION, especially in Winnipeg, Timmins, Sudbury, Hamilton, Toronto and Montréal. Their paper, *Kronika Tygodniowa* (*A Weekly Chronicle*), still appears in Toronto in small runs.

Group Identification The feeling of unity among Polish Canadians has been expressed primarily in support of the Polish nation. Political and financial support for Poland was strong during WWII, when Poland was under German occupation, and later when the communist government attempted to suppress the church. An extensive "Help for Poland" program established in Canada after Oct 1956 has recently been revived. Contact with the motherland remains vivid through Polish-organized travel tours, family visits and language courses for the young. National pride was reinforced by the election of Pope John Paul II, the choice of Czeslaw Milosz in 1980 for the Nobel Prize for Literature and the selection of Lech Walesa in 1983 for the Nobel Peace Prize.

The Polish Canadian Research Institute, established in 1956, conducts studies on Poles in Canada. It has an extensive library and archives and publishes its research (over 17 volumes have appeared in English so far). The institute co-operates with associate scientific centres both in Canada and Poland, provides scholarships and assistance to young researchers and organizes lectures. The Polish Scientific Institute, headquartered in Montréal, provides information on Poland's history and Polish ethnic groups abroad. In addition, 3 foundations have been established to assist Polish schools and cultural life.

BENEDYKT HEYDENKORN

Reading: Benedykt Heydenkorn, *The Organizational Structure of the Polish Canadian Community* (1979) and ed, *A Community in Transition* (1985) and with R. Kogler, *The Structure of the Polish Ethnic Grays* (1988); R.K. Kogler, *The Polish Community in Canada* (1979); W.B. Makowski, *History and Integration of Poles in Canada* (1967); H. Radecki and Benedykt Heydenkorn, *A Member of a Distinguished Family: The Polish Group in Canada* (1976); V. Turek, *Poles in Manitoba* (1976); L.K. Zubkowski, *The Poles in Canada* (1968).

Police The primary function of police is to preserve order (sometimes referred to as "keeping the peace") between people within a community. Ideas about what this order is may be widely shared within a community or they may be imposed by a dominant group.

Type of Police When the authority under which police operate is public, eg, a municipality, public POLICING exists; when the authority is private, eg, a large corporation, it is called private policing (also referred to as private security to avoid confusion with the public police). Public policing is usually carried out by a full-time police force, but sales staff and apartment superintendents are frequently required to engage in private policing as part of their jobs. In 1986, according to Statistics Canada, there were 54 604 public police and some 50 000 specialized private police. About 66% of private police, referred to as "in-house security," work directly for the authorities on whose behalf they police. The remainder, "contract security," act for companies who provide security services for hire.

History and Development Prior to the 19th century, public policing was the responsibility of the ordinary citizenry and private policing was the norm. The Industrial Revolution disrupted the traditional police structures, leaving a gap that government filled in the early 19th century by developing the modern public police. This "new police" model was also adopted in Canada. Canadian municipal policing was modelled primarily on the London Metropolitan Police, whereas the NORTH-WEST MOUNTED POLICE (now the ROYAL CANADIAN MOUNTED POLICE) was modelled on the more militaristic Royal Irish Constabulary. Even in Québec, where the French influence is of obvious importance, public police are organized on the British model. There are signs that the organization of policing may be reverting to its earlier forms. The public police are relying less frequently on their own resources and are increasingly involving the public directly in policing through community-based programs such as "block parents" (which encourages parent participation in making their neighbourhoods safer for their children) and "neighbourhood watch." In some cases, public police forces and governments have hired private police agencies to do a variety of tasks, including patrolling, which they had previously undertaken themselves. In addition, corporations have become increasingly active in providing their own police, eg, to maintain order in areas such as commercial shopping malls.

Methods Policing operates by fostering voluntary compliance with the desired order, by forcibly insisting on it, or both. As physical force is the ultimate coercive resource available to police, the instruments of force they most commonly use (eg, the billy club and the handgun) have come to symbolize the police. However, police in Canada usually rely on voluntary compliance, and when they do rely on force it may only be as an implicit or overt threat of force. Another central feature of police work is intelligence gathering. This function has shaped the organization of the police. For example, the traditional grid system of patrol was developed to extend the net of police surveillance as widely as possible.

Police surveillance is constantly frustrated by the institutions of PRIVACY, which restrict where and how the police may seek information. For example, public police on patrol are largely limited to public places. Therefore they must routinely patrol public streets, although crimes usually occur in private places. Private police, as agents of the owners of private property, usually have greater routine access to private property.

Many of the changes in the structure of public policing are a result of attempts by police to deal with the restriction of the institutions of privacy. For example, 2-way radios, telephones and automobiles are used in an attempt to provide a quick response to members of the public. These devices take advantage of the citizen access to private places. Similarly the recent use by the public police of "team policing," in which a team of police officers remains in an area and works together to police it, is largely a strategy to improve policing intelligence.

The tension between privacy and police intelligence is an essential feature of policing. It creates pressures on police to circumvent legal and social restrictions on their power. This tension is greatest for political police, such as Canada's CANADIAN SECURITY INTELLIGENCE SERVICE, who can seldom use evidence of wrongdoing to legitimize intrusions into privacy.

Sources of Police Powers Police powers derive from the power resources at the disposal of the authorities on whose behalf they act. Where the authority is the STATE this capacity is ultimately physical force, because access to such force is an essential characteristic of state power. Where the authority is private, the resources to which police have access vary considerably. In educational communities, for example, they include sanctions such as the denial of library privileges and the withholding of educational certificates. Similarly, in economic communities the sanctions will tend to be economic in character, eg, loss of pay or credit privileges. In private policing the threat of physical force may underlie other sanctions because the private police may be able to draw on the assistance of the public police. In addition, they may be able to act themselves as agents of government, eg, by exercising citizen powers of arrest or by acting as special constables, a status that is used to extend some police powers to a few private police.

Safeguards The law (both the general law, especially the Canadian CRIMINAL CODE, and provincial Police Acts) limits police power by defining the circumstances in which the police may act. These limits may be overridden by legislation giving the police "special powers" in particular circumstances. The most extraordinary example in Canada is the WAR MEASURES ACT, invoked during the 1970 OCTOBER CRISIS in Québec.

Authorities to whom police are responsible may restrict the police in other ways. The public police are bound by departmental regulations. Private police may also be bound by internal regulations, such as the terms of management-labour agreements.

All restrictions on police power are characterized by the fact that they limit the extent to which the police can legitimately intrude upon the privacy of others; the institutions of privacy thus help determine police boundaries.

Police Deviance and Accountability When police disregard the restrictions placed on their exercise of power they expose themselves to possible sanctions. Traditional legal sanctions have not been effective in controlling police deviance because of the problems of securing evidence that will stand up in a court (in the case of criminal charges) and because of the costs involved (where civil remedies are pursued). Thus the sanctions most often used against police misconduct are internal disciplinary procedures, but the use of such remedies has raised accusations of "cover up" and has resulted in considerable political pressure to establish independent bodies to hear complaints against the public police. Although such boards have been established in a few jurisdictions, they rely on the public police to undertake investigations and have been criticized for lack of independence.

In addition, several commissions of inquiry have been established by governments over the last decade to investigate allegations of public police misconduct (*see* INQUIRY INTO CERTAIN ACTIVITIES OF THE RCMP). While these inquiries have led to few criminal charges being laid against the police, they have resulted in significant changes in the way complaints against the police are handled and in internal disciplinary procedures.

In many cases the news media have initially reported the allegations and lobbied for an inquiry. The press, however, while acting as an important watchdog over the public police, has until recently been less attentive to abuses on the part of private police.

Comparative Jurisdictions of Public Police Forces Under the Constitution, responsibility for public policing is primarily a provincial matter. In exercising this responsibility, the provinces, through provincial Police Acts, have followed the British tradition and delegated the responsibility for public policing to municipalities when they are large enough to take it on. Nonetheless, provinces exercise considerable control over policing by paying part of the cost of municipal policing and by penalizing municipalities that fail to maintain standards. In most provinces this supervision is undertaken by a police commission established to avoid at least the appearance of direct governmental control over the public police. In addition, at the municipal level many towns and cities have established police boards to oversee the operation of the public police. Most municipal police forces, however, are governed directly by municipal councils or their committees.

The provinces not only provide provincial police for those areas that fall outside municipal jurisdiction but also support and co-ordinating services such as police training, criminal intelligence and forensic facilities.

Although the federal government does not have primary constitutional responsibility for policing, the federal police force, the RCMP, headquartered in Ottawa, is the largest single police force in the country and operates at both the municipal and provincial level in all provinces – except Ontario and Québec – and in the Yukon and the NWT. RCMP involvement in policing at the provincial and municipal levels arises because the RCMP contracts to provide policing services to the provinces and municipal jurisdictions. In addition to acting as a contract agency for policing in Canada, the RCMP provides services to all Canadian public police forces. The 2 most important services are the Canadian Police Information Centre, which provides information on such matters as criminal records, and the Canadian Police College, which provides advanced police training.

Apart from federal, provincial and municipal police, governments in Canada authorize other forms of police with legal powers which, while limited to specific areas or specific groups of people, or both, are not unlike those of the public police. The Harbour Police, Military Police and Railway Police are examples. *See also* INTELLIGENCE AND ESPIONAGE.

C.D. SHEARING AND P.C. STENNING

Reading: R. Ericson, *Reproducing Order: A Study of Police Patrol Work* (1982); W. and N. Kelly, *Policing in Canada* (1976); W. McGrath and M. Mitchell, eds, *The Police Function in Canada* (1981).

Police Village The police village system of local government in Ontario predates Confederation. The original purpose was to establish a local body in a hamlet ("village") to maintain public order (hence "police") within a rural township municipality. The legislation to establish new police villages was repealed in 1965 and only 70 remain. Each police village was created by a bylaw of the particular county council. As the population and associated demand for services increased, many police villages changed their status to incorporated municipal villages and towns.

Policing The police in Canada are an armed paramilitary force charged with the general responsibility of social control. The ROYAL CANADIAN MOUNTED POLICE, federal descendants of the North-West Mounted Police, exist and operate under federal statute and contract their services to 8 provinces (only Ontario and Québec have their own provincial police forces while in Newfoundland the Royal Newfoundland Constabulary police St John's, and in NB there is a highway traffic enforcement force); other Canadian police forces are governed by provincial legislation. Police-science texts characteristically refer to the police functions of preventing crime, crime detecting and the apprehending of offenders, keeping order and protecting life and property – all of which may be summarized as order maintenance and law enforcement. The latter is the most publicized and romanticized of police activity. The police are expected to control disruptive social deviance, especially violations of formal law, but maintaining social order involves other activities as well, including the monitoring of deviant actions not explicitly illegal, surveillance and crowd control. By responding to deviance, intervening and pressing charges on behalf of the public or by ignoring offences, the police participate in the definition of social norms or moral standards, as exemplified by their selective enforcement of PORNOGRAPHY violations. The police enjoy considerable discretionary power in Canada that can be used by the political authorities on whom the police depend for financial support (see INQUIRY INTO CERTAIN ACTIVITIES OF THE RCMP). For example, between the wars police were often used in strikebreaking. Their intervention in the WINNIPEG GENERAL STRIKE in 1919 probably saved the RCMP from contemplated disbandment. Intelligence gathering, or security, a traditional responsibility of the RCMP, has been transferred to a federal intelligence agency (see CANADIAN SECURITY INTELLIGENCE SERVICE; INTELLIGENCE AND ESPIONAGE).

Traffic or civic bylaw enforcement and general order maintenance comprise the bulk of police work, 20-30% of which is directly related to crime control. The remainder is devoted to random patrol, traffic control and clerical work. Motor patrol (either one or 2 persons) is the major police activity. The Metropolitan Toronto Police Force has 2-person patrol units; foot patrol is common on only a small number of downtown city beats. Detective and CRIMINAL INVESTIGATION by specialized personnel is also important, although most legal violations are handled by uniformed officers. Police intervene in domestic crises and conduct searches for missing persons. These activities, difficult to measure and evaluate, are not highly regarded by the police, who define their role in relation to crime control and evaluate their efficiency and justify their budgets on the basis of crime-related policing.

Several cities, such as Vancouver, Calgary and Halifax, have decentralized their police service in an attempt to make them more responsive to community needs, reorganizing them into team and zone policing, respectively. In both systems 12-50 men working under a staff sergeant will be assigned for several years to neighbourhoods or sub areas of a city. Calgary describes zone policing as an attempt to encourage better relations between police and citizens and to enlist community help in solving problems.

All police forces in Canada are public agencies, responsible to either one or all municipal, provincial and national civil authorities. Most large Canadian cities maintain local municipal police forces (in BC several municipal forces as well as the RCMP are under contract). Through the late 1970s the numbers of police in Canada increased proportionately more rapidly than the total population, reflecting the effects of urbanization and the elaborate demands on police for services ranging from law enforcement to emergency health care and traffic control. In 1962 there were 1.7 police employees per 1000 population, including 1.5 sworn police officers. By 1977 the figures had risen to 2.8 and 2.3, respectively. The largest proportion was in Québec, with 3.0 per 1000 in 1977, and in the territories, 5.5 per 1000 in the Yukon and 5.3 in the NWT. In 1962 there were 27 744 police officers in Canada; in 1985 there were 53 464, an increase of 96.8%, and in 1986, 54 604. The greatest growth was in the QUÉ-BEC PROVINCIAL POLICE, from 1562 in 1962 to 4 248 in 1985, or 172.0% as contrasted to 109.5% growth in the RCMP and 113.1% increase in the ONTARIO PROVINCIAL POLICE. Policing cost each Canadian $28 in 1971 and $40 in 1976 (in 1971 dollars). The largest municipal force is the Metropolitan Toronto Police, followed by the Montréal Urban Community Police Force. In 1986 the former employed 5222 sworn police officers. Calgary employed 1136 police employees in 1986, including 319 civilians. Toronto and Calgary expenditures for police in 1977 totalled, respectively, $156.7 million and $31.9 million. By 1986 Calgary police expenditures had risen to $63.6 million. Police salaries in major Canadian cities and for the Royal Canadian Mounted Police are similar; Montréal, Toronto and Vancouver establish the standards against which other police associations bargain. By 1986, a first-class constable, with 4 years' experience, in major Canadian cities received over $35 000. In 1981 the RCMP agreed to a salary for recruits of $20 650; after 4 years constables received a maximum salary of $27 400. All Canadian police forces, except the RCMP, which is not unionized, use COLLECTIVE BARGAINING. Only in NS, NB, Manitoba, Saskatchewan and BC can police legally strike.

Recruitment and Training There is no standard training for Canadian police, although major regional training centres exist in the Maritimes, Québec, Ontario and BC. Training standards vary; a formal period of basic recruit training lasts only an average of 12 weeks. The national Canadian Police College in Ottawa, managed by the RCMP, offers courses in specialized areas, eg, police management for selected police officers from across Canada. The RCMP offers 22 weeks of basic training at the Regina depot. Recruit selection also varies, although high-school diplomas are generally preferred and sometimes compulsory. A very small number of university graduates, comprising from 0 to 12% of a police force, are recruited to serve as career police officers, but for a senior officer position no formal education beyond grade 10 or 11 is required. Because police forces have tended to recruit persons primarily from the working class, white, male population, police forces are not broadly representative of the experiences and attitudes of the Canadian population. In the past decade broadly based recruitment has been emphasized in an attempt to develop police forces more responsive to the population and more capable of investigating or discerning WHITE-COLLAR CRIME, eg, computer fraud. Training is aimed more at prevention than reactive enforcement. Public pressure for a more publicly representative force has increased, particularly in Toronto, with its concentration of immigrants, and there has also been an attempt to recruit members of minority groups. The RCMP has recruited and trained native Indian police in the western provinces, but they have been given "special" constable status only, limiting their responsibilities to specific tasks. The RCMP also employs "specials" for responsibilities such as airport security. However, although Canadian police forces have been under pressure to recruit more women and better educated persons, male high-school graduates still comprise the bulk of recruits. For example, in 1977 women comprised only 1.7% of sworn police personnel in Canada, compared to 2.7% in the US and 7.3% in Britain. By 1986 women constituted 4.1% of Canadian police officers.   DENNIS FORCESE

Political Campaign, an organized effort to secure the nomination and ELECTION of those seeking government office. In a system of representative democracy, electoral campaigns are the primary means by which parties (see PARTY SYSTEM) and candidates communicate and by which voters are informed of a party's or candidate's views. In Canada, political campaigns take place at the federal, provincial and municipal levels of government (see LOCAL ELECTIONS). Federal campaign practices are regulated by the Canada Elections Act (see ELECTION EXPENSES ACT; ELECTORAL SYSTEMS). At the provincial and municipal levels, campaign practices are regulated by analogous provincial legislation.

The conduct of political campaigns in Canada has evolved gradually as a result of nearly 2 centuries of experience, as well as the adaptation of British (and, to a considerable extent, American) practices to the needs of a parliamentary federation with 2 official languages, a severe climate and a relatively small population spread over half a continent. Technological developments, such as television and air transport, and socioeconomic changes have dramatically influenced the evolution of campaign practices in recent years. Federal and provincial campaigns are quite similar. Municipal campaigns do not usually involve parties, but in other ways they resemble federal and provincial campaigns.

Early History of Campaigns Because representative institutions were established in the British N American colonies of Lower Canada, Upper Canada, Nova Scotia and New Brunswick before the end of the 18th century, political campaigns in Canada have a long history. Early campaigns preceded the establishment of organized political parties and were therefore largely a series of individual efforts in the constituencies. Until RESPONSIBLE GOVERNMENT was established in the middle of the 19th century, the governor of each colony, as the appointed representative of the Crown, frequently intervened in electoral campaigns to ensure the election of members who would co-operate with him and who would make the necessary funds available to his administration.

Once responsible government was achieved, recognized government and opposition leaders sat in the legislature and attempted to co-ordinate the campaigns of their respective followers to elect as many of them as possible. With Confederation in 1867, campaigns had to be extended over a vast geographical area, but the general election campaigns of 1867, 1872 and 1874 were conducted in a highly decentralized manner and largely followed the rules and practices that the various provinces had inherited from pre-Confederation days.

The most striking difference between these early campaigns and their modern counterparts was that early campaigns did not culminate in a single polling day. Elections were spread over several weeks, with different constituencies voting on different days. This enabled the government to schedule the polling in its safest ridings at an early date to create a bandwagon effect that might persuade voters in more doubtful ridings to support the government candidates. Opposition strongholds would be left to the last so as not to discourage supporters of the government. Party leaders and other notables often were candidates in more than one constituency so as to be sure of retaining a seat. Within each constituency, voting might extend over 2 days. Voting was by a show of hands rather than by secret ballot, and bribery and intimidation were therefore a common and more or less accepted aspect of campaigns. The small size of the electorates facilitated a more personal approach to campaigning than is possible today. Skilful politicians such as Sir John A. MACDONALD knew most of their supporters by name. In the federal election of 1867 an average of fewer than 1500 votes was cast in each constituency.

The federal election campaign of 1878 was in some respects the first modern campaign. Virtually all candidates represented one of the 2 recognized parties, LIBERAL or CONSERVATIVE. The parties were clearly differentiated on issues of policy that were extensively discussed during the campaign, and the Conservative victory could be regarded as a mandate to implement that party's policies of tariff protection and rapid completion of the transcontinental railway. Virtually all constituencies voted on the same day and a secret ballot was used for the first time. This was also the first election in which candidates were required to appoint an official agent and to file a statement of their campaign expenditures. The most important procedures followed by future campaigns were largely established in 1878.

Strategies, Issues and Leaders Modern electoral campaigns are carefully planned and co-ordinated efforts requiring lengthy preparation and centralized control. The leader of a political party appoints a campaign committee with a campaign director reporting to the leader. Specific persons are responsible for various aspects of the campaign, eg, fund raising, advertising, travel arrangements, relations with the media and the measurement of PUBLIC OPINION. In the Liberal Party it is customary to run a virtually separate campaign in Québec with its own autonomous organization reporting directly to the national leader. Until the mid 1980s in the Conservative Party and the NEW DEMOCRATIC PARTY, the campaign in Québec was merely a part of the overall national effort; this changed for the Conservatives as a result of their large majority in Québec in the 1984 federal election. Planning is somewhat easier for the party that controls the government because the PRIME MINISTER normally determines the date of the election. The election date will be selected to maximize the effectiveness of the governing party's campaign and will thus be influenced by economic conditions, by the government's popularity and the progress of its legislative program through PARLIAMENT. However, this important advantage is lost when an election is precipitated by the loss of a vote of confidence in the HOUSE OF COMMONS. In such cases (eg, the federal elections of 1926, 1963 and 1980) the governing party loses this advantage. Since an election must be held every 5 years, a prime minister can lose this advantage as well by letting Parliament run its time, as in 1896 and 1935.

Political campaign strategies must take into account the fact that Canadians display widely varying degrees of affiliation with particular political parties. Each party seeks to mobilize its own supporters, to secure the votes of those who are leaning in its direction, and to persuade as many as possible of the uncommitted. Governing parties emphasize their accomplishments in office and announce initiatives designed to attract uncommitted voters. Opposition parties attack the government's record and make promises to do better if elected. The issues in election campaigns emerge out of the interaction between government and Opposition. However, not all campaigns have been characterized by well-defined issues. Partly for this reason, and partly because Canadian parties are not sharply differentiated by ideology, campaigns emphasize the personal characteristics and presumed capabilities of the party leaders. Campaign strategies are designed to acquaint voters with the leaders and to convince voters of their attractiveness; they may or may not include overt attacks on the leaders of other parties.

General election campaigns that appear to have been dominated by particular issues include those of 1878 (*see* NATIONAL POLICY), 1891 (commercial RECIPROCITY with the US), 1896 (MANITOBA SCHOOLS QUESTION), 1911 (reciprocity again), 1917 (CONSCRIPTION), 1926 (the constitutional

powers of the governor general, *see* KING-BYNG AFFAIR), 1957 (the government's imposition of CLOSURE during the PIPELINE DEBATE), 1963 (nuclear weapons), 1974 (WAGE AND PRICE CONTROLS) and 1980 (ENERGY POLICY). Most of these issues were promoted and emphasized by the Opposition, more than by the government, and most of the campaigns listed ended with the defeat of the governing party. In the majority of campaigns in which the opposition parties failed to generate a dominating major issue, the governing party was reelected. The governing party usually prefers to emphasize its competence and overall record rather than a specific issue.

Virtually all campaigns have emphasized leadership, a fact sometimes deplored by those who would prefer a more intellectual and rational approach to politics. This is not a new phenomenon, as former slogans attest: "The Old Man, The Old Flag, and The Old Party" (used for Macdonald's last campaign in 1891), "Let Laurier Finish His Work" (1908), "King or Chaos" (1935) and "It's Time for a Diefenbaker Government" (1957). The leader referred to in the slogan won in each case.

In early campaigns the ability of the leaders and their "image" to influence the voters was largely indirect and was dependent on the persuasive powers of local candidates and of newspapers that supported the leader. As a result of modern transportation and communication, party leaders are better known to the voters. Macdonald and his Liberal opponents, Alexander MACKENZIE and Edward BLAKE, campaigned only in southern Ontario. Sir Wilfrid LAURIER, in 1917, was the first party leader to visit the western provinces during a campaign. W.L. Mackenzie KING failed to visit Québec, his party's major stronghold, during his successful campaign in 1921. Today, leaders of national parties are expected to campaign in every province, and planning the leader's itinerary during the 2 months of the campaign is a major activity of the campaign committee. Up to and including John DIEFENBAKER, party leaders relied mainly on the railways for their travel arrangements, but today they use specially chartered aircraft. At each stop on the tour the leaders promise new policies of particular interest to the locality.

Media, Advertising and Polls Electronic communications have made it possible for voters to hear and see party leaders without leaving their homes. Nationwide radio broadcasts by party leaders were first used in the campaign of 1930 and television was first employed in the campaign of 1957. In each case an opposition leader who was particularly effective in employing the new medium won the election.

Television tends to keep voters at home in the evening and has made it impossible, as well as unnecessary, to attract large numbers of them to political meetings. Party leaders still address large rallies in the hockey arenas and auditoriums of the major cities, but nowadays such events are attended mainly by reporters, television cameramen and persons directly involved in the party's local campaign. Those in the latter category are often brought to the rally by chartered bus to ensure that empty seats will not be seen by voters viewing the event on television.

Political advertising is now an essential feature of any campaign. Modern advertising techniques were first applied to political campaigns before WWII. Today, advertising agencies help shape the campaign strategies of the parties, and advertising experts such as Dalton CAMP and Keith DAVEY have served as influential advisers to Canadian politicians. Slogans, leaflets, posters, lapel buttons and other paraphernalia, as well as newspaper advertisements and the tapes and films made available to the electronic media, seek to create the desired "image" of the party, its leaders and its

Pierre Trudeau campaigning at Edmonton City Hall during "Trudeaumania" of the 1968 election (*courtesy Provincial Archives of Alberta/Edmonton Journal Coll*).

policies. In recent campaigns, about one-half of all advertising expenditure has been devoted to television.

Modern campaigning has also been affected by the development of scientific techniques for sampling and measuring public opinion. The periodic measurements of party standings by independent polling organizations are reported in the media and may affect the timing of elections and create a bandwagon effect during the campaign, similar to the effect of nonsimultaneous voting prior to 1878. The parties themselves employ pollsters (whose findings are normally not published) to identify areas of strength and weakness and to discover the voters' attitudes towards leaders, candidates, issues, policies and events.

Campaigning in the Constituencies Television, air transport and modern techniques of measuring and manipulating public opinion have all tended to increase the importance of centralized organization in a national or provincial campaign. Nonetheless a strong local campaign at the constituency level, co-ordinated with the central campaign, is still necessary for electoral success.

Local campaigns are primarily the responsibility of the candidate, the official agent and the campaign manager. The main objectives are to introduce the candidate to as many voters as possible, to identify the voters who are likely to support the candidate and to ensure that those voters actually vote. The first objective is accomplished mainly by having the candidate visit voters in their homes, although in industrial and mining centres it is also customary to visit the factories and mines where many voters are employed. Community associations in middle-class neighbourhoods often sponsor debates among the local candidates, but it is widely believed that only voters who have already made up their minds attend them.

Identifying the committed vote was easy in the stable rural communities and small towns of Macdonald's and Laurier's Canada. Among the heterogeneous and mobile populations of modern metropolitan centres it can only be accomplished by an army of canvassers who attempt to visit each household at least once during the campaign. On election day the same persons will check periodically to ensure that friendly voters have actually voted, and may provide transportation to the polling place as an inducement.

Local campaigns, now generally honest and fair, were not always so. In rural areas it was once common to bribe voters with food, alcoholic beverages and money. In the larger cities, particularly in Montréal before the QUIET REVOLUTION, there were many instances of impersonating voters, placing fictitious names on the voters' lists, stealing ballots and intimidating the other party's volunteers by the threat or use of violence. Stricter regulation of campaigns and a more affluent and sophisticated electorate have brought about the virtual disappearance of such practices. However, the manipulation of the electorate through advertising and the frequency with which campaign promises are ignored after the election continue to raise questions about the quality of the democratic process. GARTH STEVENSON

Political Culture refers to the collective opinions, attitudes and values of individuals about POLITICS. There are 2 traditional approaches to the study of political culture. The "individualistic" approach examines the values and attitudes of individuals, frequently through the use of surveys. Because political culture cannot be directly measured, respondents are asked questions designed to illuminate their views about political culture. Unfortunately, there is always the possibility that the questions asked do not adequately represent the feelings of the population and may not properly measure the concepts being tested.

The "institutional" approach involves the analysis of documents to discern the collective behaviour of political institutions. This approach has been applied in 3 different ways. First, academics attempt to describe a political culture by observing and analysing political behaviour as reflected by a constitution and by legislation and the structure of government. Second, the geographic, demographic and socioeconomic features of a society are analysed; and third, the historical underpinnings which have determined a political system are sometimes examined. The systems approach has resulted in 2 popular theories of political culture. According to the first, Canada's political culture is based on tensions between its 2 founding cultural groups, French and English. According to the second, the members of the 2 founding cultures and the later immigrants from other cultures have combined to produce a new and distinct political culture.

Canada's political culture can usefully be described as "layered," although the layers are not easily demarcated. The first layer of political values encompasses Canadians' belief in the parliamentary and democratic system of government. This includes a belief that the majority rules in the political decision-making process. (That this belief is not unconditional is reflected in federalist structures, BILINGUALISM and the CANADIAN CHARTER OF RIGHTS AND FREEDOMS.) The recognized legitimate role for competing interests in Canadian society is qualified by the view that the majority will prevail when a compromise solution cannot be found. Also, according to the principle of majority rule, any political decision can be changed once the majority has altered its own position. A belief in parliamentary democracy also suggests support for political equality, eg, support for the notion of "one person, one vote." The last feature of parliamentary democracies, popular sovereignty, is expressed in regular elections and the involvement of citizens in the political process.

Under the first layer lies a uniquely Canadian political culture which transcends provincial boundaries. For example, Canadians are committed voters, but at the same time they do not participate widely in the political process (see POLITICAL PARTICIPATION). It has been suggested that this "spectator-participant" characteristic reveals a unique feature of the Canadian political culture. As well, research indicates that Canadians strongly support political authority and widely accept the role of elites in leadership. Unlike Americans, Canadians often prefer to rely on government intervention (eg, through public ownership) rather than the private sector to solve economic problems (see PUBLIC OWNERSHIP; CROWN CORPORATION).

Another feature of Canadian political culture is

Canada's "approach and avoidance" relationship with the US (see CANADIAN-AMERICAN RELATIONS). Despite the fact that the US is Canada's greatest trading partner, and a country with which Canadians share a large number of common interests, many Canadians have been frustrated by the way in which their culture (especially in English Canada) and their businesses have been dominated by American interests. As a consequence, Canadians have attempted to regulate this relationship by creating a number of government institutions designed to promote Canadian culture (see CULTURAL POLICY) or to restrict the flow of FOREIGN INVESTMENT into Canada. These contradictory sentiments toward the US have occasionally helped to unite Canadians and at the same time have helped the development of their political and popular culture.

The third layer of political culture contains attitudes which are uniquely Canadian but which, at the same time, distinguish one Canadian from another. There may be several different belief systems in this category, including one involving French-English differences and another, more difficult to define, based on notions of economic development and geographical diversity. This latter belief system is known as REGIONALISM.

The political cultures of English- and French-speaking Canada are different because the 2 communities have experienced different patterns of development and different educational systems, religion and language. For example, it has been observed that French-speaking Québeckers tend to look toward Québec City for direction whereas English-speaking Canadians within Québec are more likely to expect Ottawa to solve their problems. Moreover, it is apparent that symbols such as the Canadian flag and the monarchy are much less popular among French-speaking Québeckers than among English speakers.

Finally, Canadians living in different regions vary markedly in the degree to which they trust politicians and government and perceive government as being responsive to their needs. What is clear, however, is that in certain parts of Canada, eg, western Canada and Québec, a sense of alienation from the federal government is long-standing and deeply rooted. DAVID ZUSSMAN

Political Economy is the study of the relationship between POLITICS and ECONOMICS. Economists study the workings of the economic system, while political scientists study the workings of political systems, the nature of government and the STATE, the functioning of political parties and the participation of citizens in decision making. To political economists, the notion that a phenomenon can be "purely political" or "purely economic" is wrongheaded. For example, it is difficult to analyse the role of the corporation in the economy without understanding the political system in which it functions. Political science and economics must also be studied together to understand how income and wealth are distributed, how economic priorities are established, etc. A political economist examines the cultural, constitutional and political context within which economic developments occur, but also analyses the nature of the productive system in a given society and the social relationships that interact with it. Political economy as a discipline predates the separate study of economics and POLITICAL SCIENCE. Today the special area of study of political economists is the meeting point of the 2 newer disciplines.

Most Canadian scholars in the field agree that the pre-eminent Canadian political economist was Harold INNIS. He studied the FUR TRADE, the building of the railways, the relationship between the extraction of staple products and the nature of the Canadian state, and theorized about the interaction between the means of communications and

systems of government. Contemporary Canadian political economists have built on the work of Innis. They have concentrated on the relationship of the Canadian economy and the Canadian state with the economies and states of other more powerful countries, principally Britain and the US, but have also examined subjects such as the formation of the bourgeoisie and working class, the "national question" in Québec, industrialization and natural resources. J. LAXER

Political History is the study of the processes, activities and institutions of GOVERNMENTS, the influences on them and the individuals involved with them. Political historians traditionally examined and documented the deeds of monarchs and prime ministers, of politicians and parties, of governments and related institutions. More recently, however, political historians and political scientists have been preoccupied with broader questions linked to the exercise of power within society, such as the attempts of interest groups to determine policies, the circulation of ideas and ideologies and their influence in the political arena, and the impact of increasing intervention by governments in society (see POLITICAL SCIENCE). While biography has remained important for understanding and explaining our political history, it has been supplemented by examinations of nearly every facet of Canadian political life. In the process our perception of Canada's political evolution has had to be adjusted to encompass such things as the views of working people, the role of women in society, the impact of social and political reform movements, etc. The horizons of political history have been broadened forcibly in the historians' effort to understand and explain the practice of power within Canadian society. Thus Canadian political history no more than begins with the study of politicians and parties.

The modern political historian attempts to find and follow the various threads of Canadian life — economic, social and cultural – that have affected Canadian politics through time and bear on the historian's understanding of political events. Certain issues have been of perennial concern to Canadian politicians and are of current interest to historians. For example, Canada is a vast, resource-rich but lightly populated land which, especially after the mid-19th century, invited politicians to build platforms around programs of national economic expansion. For Sir John A. MACDONALD and Sir Wilfrid LAURIER, this meant industrializing central and eastern Canada through PROTECTIONISM, while colonizing the West by railway construction and massive IMMIGRATION. For John DIEFENBAKER, economic expansion signified support for the opening of Canada's NORTH.

Political parties have long used economic themes as a means of uniting Canadians. CONFEDERATION, for instance, was promoted as, among other things, a solution to BRITISH NORTH AMERICA'S economic woes. But economic questions have often bitterly divided Canadians. For example, policies of "national" development, such as the protective tariff, could be presented to the people as good for everyone, not merely for the manufacturer who was being offered a more or less captive market. But the tariff was also denounced by opposing parties as bad for everyone outside the industrialized communities of central Canada. Railways were necessary to open up the nation and to further trade, but questions as to how many, whether they should be privately or publicly owned, and what the state's railway policy should be have divided Canadians and influenced political decisions (see RAILWAY HISTORY). The many potentially divisive economic issues have been at the heart of most federal-provincial disputes (see FEDERAL-PROVINCIAL RELATIONS). A large and diverse territory also fostered the growth of regional economies whose interests have been exceedingly difficult to harmonize (see REGIONAL ECONOMICS). The exploitation of natural resources was promoted as certain to enrich the entire country, but when it has come time to divide up the profits, national unity has always been sorely taxed. It is scarcely surprising that Canadian economic and political unity has obsessed federal politicians. Federal parties, to gain power, have had to build coalitions of classes and regional interest groups whose goals are often contradictory. Moreover, provincial governments have seen themselves as more attuned to local and regional interests and have thus often been obliged to defend those interests against federal intrusion.

Other influences on political development, and therefore of interest to political historians, include RELIGION, once the primary factor affecting the citizen's vote. Issues such as the denominational schools questions (see CATHOLICISM; SEPARATE SCHOOLS) and TEMPERANCE have often been the subject of acrimonious political debate. As education came to be seen as a necessity, politicians at all levels had to elaborate policies to reform traditional institutions, revamp curricula, train teachers, and increase funding and access to educational institutions. INDUSTRIALIZATION made it necessary to protect workers and improve working conditions, and governments had to intervene increasingly in disputes between workers and employers. The spectre of UNEMPLOYMENT made it necessary to define policies that would not only alleviate misery but would support workers' buying power for economic reasons. URBANIZATION changed the needs of Canada's population. Citizens' health became an important question, and governments began to assume an active role in improving medical and hospital care and facilitating access to it. Some debates have centered on housing, URBAN AND REGIONAL PLANNING, municipal and regional organization, child care, WOMEN IN THE LABOUR FORCE, consumer protection and CRIME. Lobbies and interest groups have developed to promote specific policies.

POPULATION characteristics have also greatly influenced Canadian politics. The existence of a French-speaking minority constituting about 30% of Canada's population, largely concentrated within Québec, has had special implications for the debate on Canadian unity. Indeed, many French Canadian spokesmen have perceived the interests of their society as being clearly different from the interests of Canada as a whole. For them, Canadian unity has meant assimilation and the destruction of the foundations of French Canadian culture (see FRENCH CANADIAN NATIONALISM). On the other hand, the "two nations" (*deux nations*) debate, with roots in the mid-19th century (see DURHAM REPORT) and one of the most controversial themes in Canadian politics during the 1960s and 1970s, has tended to becloud the cultural heterogeneity of English-speaking Canada. Politicians have usually found it easier to unite French Canada than English Canada around a cause. Indeed, outside of war, there has been no issue powerful enough to unite a large majority of English-speaking Canadians. Regional, provincial, social and ethnic differences have proven to be stronger, in most cases, than a common LANGUAGE that for many has not even been the mother tongue (see ETHNIC LANGUAGES).

It is impossible to study Canadian political history without recognizing the great strength of Canada's economic and social links with Britain and later with the US (see COMMONWEALTH; CANADIAN-AMERICAN RELATIONS). As long as most Canadians were of British origin, ties with the mother country, notably in wartime, remained close. But as Canadians whose bonds with Britain were dis-

tant or nonexistent became a majority, Canada came increasingly to define itself by reference to its N American setting. The influences of such events as the American abrogation of RECIPROCITY in 1866 and the AMERICAN CIVIL WAR have been great. Economic links with the US became much more important in the 20th century; the tariff debate and the question of reciprocity have to a certain extent given way since the 1960s to problems associated with FOREIGN INVESTMENT and foreign control of Canadian INDUSTRY. Canada's cultural independence has been at issue as well. In the 1920s Canadians were already reading American magazines, listening to American radio and watching American movies. Later their leisure hours included more and more American television. Canadian university students were often taught by American professors, but after the early 1980s indigenous Canadian political history studies and HISTORIOGRAPHY were again on a firm footing, with a greater breadth of vision and variety of approaches than ever before.

For broad surveys of Canadian political history, see NEW FRANCE; ACADIA; PROVINCE OF QUEBEC; UPPER CANADA; LOWER CANADA; PROVINCE OF CANADA; ATLANTIC PROVINCES; MARITIME PROVINCES; PRAIRIE WEST; and separate articles on each province and territory, as well as entries on FUR TRADE; FISHERIES HISTORY; AGRICULTURE HISTORY; and HISTORY SINCE CONFEDERATION. The many articles dealing wholly or in part with political themes include CONQUEST; LOYALISTS; RESPONSIBLE GOVERNMENT; REPRESENTATIVE GOVERNMENT; REPEAL MOVEMENT; PACIFIC SCANDAL; NATIONAL POLICY; URBAN REFORM; WOMEN'S SUFFRAGE; GREAT DEPRESSION; EXTERNAL RELATIONS and others. Canada's involvement in a number of domestic conflicts and international wars has been determined and directed largely at the political level, and these conflicts have affected other political events; see SEVEN YEARS' WAR; WAR OF 1812; REBELLIONS OF 1837; RED RIVER REBELLION; NORTH-WEST REBELLION; SOUTH AFRICAN WAR; WORLD WAR I; WORLD WAR II; and KOREAN WAR. There are, as well, numerous other areas of concern which can affect the understanding of Canadian political history, eg, CONSTITUTIONAL HISTORY; INTELLECTUAL HISTORY; SOCIAL HISTORY; and WORKING-CLASS HISTORY.

RICHARD JONES AND MICHAEL BEHIELS

Reading: J.M. Beck, *Pendulum of Power* (1968); R. Cook with J. Saywell and J. Ricker, *Canada* (1964); R.M. Dawson, *The Government of Canada* (6th ed, 1987); Paul Fox, *Politics: Canada*, 4th ed (1977); J.L. Granatstein and P. Stevens, eds, *A Reader's Guide to Canadian History 2: Confederation to the Present* (1982); E. McInnis, *Canada: A Political and Social History* (rev ed 1982). W.L. Morton, *The Kingdom of Canada* (1963), and ed, The Canadian Centenary Series; D.A. Muise, ed, *A Reader's Guide to Canadian History 1: Beginnings to Confederation* (1982).

Political Participation may describe any voluntary act to influence elections or public policy (see PRESSURE GROUP). It may be as simple as casting a ballot or it may mean running for office; it may be intended to influence the broad outlines of policy, or it may be very specific, eg, seeking benefits for an individual (see PATRONAGE). It may even be illegal (see CONFLICT OF INTEREST; CORRUPTION). Paying taxes would not usually be regarded as political participation, but refusing to do so can be a political act. Striking over wages or working conditions, while usually voluntary, is not considered a form of political participation, although some strikes are explicitly political, eg, the widespread protest, 14 Oct 1976, against the Anti-Inflation Board measures. Certain political issues, such as FREE TRADE with the US, may result in increased participation in different parts of the country in the processes that influence public policy.

The frequency of political participation depends on several factors. About 90% of Canadians eligible to vote have done so at least once. In national

ELECTIONS, turnout is typically just over 75% of those registered (considerably higher than in the US, where it is about 55%); turnout in provincial elections is usually slightly lower, although the opposite is true in Québec and some other provinces (see ELECTORAL BEHAVIOUR). Municipal turnout is usually the lowest of all. In both provincial and national elections, turnout has increased gradually since 1945. Participation falls off sharply for more difficult activities during POLITICAL CAMPAIGNS. According to sample surveys, about one person in 5 tries to persuade a friend to vote for a particular party or individual, and about one in 6 attends a rally or meeting, and displays a lawn sign or bumper sticker. Between 5% and 10% of the population canvass, help to mail campaign literature, make campaign-related telephone calls, or act as election-day drivers or scrutineers. Fewer than one in 20 give money to a party or a candidate (see PARTY FINANCING) or belong to a party. Fewer still run for office or engage in illegal political activities.

Costs of political participation for individuals are usually more psychological than monetary, although some political acts obviously cost money. Political participation usually requires social and bureaucratic skills, a mastery of language and an ability to process information, and is therefore most powerfully influenced by levels of education. Other differences in political involvement, such as those between occupation or income groups, partly reflect such differences in levels of education, although these differences can be offset by experience. For example, whatever their education, older citizens are more active than younger ones. Skills developed through nonpolitical experiences, eg, in the BUREAUCRACY or voluntary associations, are often useful to political participation. Women, who were enfranchised for national elections in 1918 and who have traditionally been excluded from those social roles that encourage political learning, are politically less active than men; however, as they have accumulated political experience, women have sometimes moved into roles formerly reserved for males. Sex differences in political activity count for less among the younger age groups and the more highly educated.

The benefits of political activity are as important a determinant of its frequency as are the costs. For example, people are more likely to vote and engage in other campaign activities when a race is close than when it is one-sided. Some occupation groups are more affected by government decisions than others and so are more likely to act politically whatever the cost of the act. PUBLIC SERVICE employees, whose incomes depend on political decisions, vote at a significantly higher rate than other citizens, although legally they cannot participate in certain other political actions. Farmers, whose incomes are greatly affected by government price and supply management decisions, are much more active than other groups with similar income and education levels.

Levels of political activity vary greatly across provinces, partly reflecting the competitiveness of the PARTY SYSTEM. Alberta, with its one-sided national and provincial elections, has the lowest electoral turnout in Canada. PEI and NS have the highest turnouts. In Québec, participation is greater in the highly competitive provincial elections than in federal ones, which before 1984 were typically one-sided. In rural Saskatchewan, democratically managed co-operatives are major producers and consumers; members acquire skills that are transferred to politics, and this involvement, combined with the competitiveness of the province's party system, raises participation in Saskatchewan politics to levels far exceeding those of Alberta.

Some political actions generate social benefits

for the individual, regardless of their effects on policy or on the outcome of an election. Canvassing and committee-room work, because they provide opportunities to meet people, are popular among those who particularly enjoy the company of others. Donating money requires few social skills; displaying a lawn sign or bumper sticker requires neither money nor highly developed social skills, but does require sufficient commitment to a party or a candidate to withstand possible criticism from neighbours. Survey evidence suggests that the overlap between different kinds of action is weak. A person is more likely to engage in the same action in both provincial and federal elections than to engage in more than one action within either type of election.

Some observers argue that the present participation level of Canadians is sufficient. Survey evidence suggests that low-level participants care and know little about politics and often have a weak grip on democratic values. Other observers argue that participation is valuable in itself and ought to be encouraged, and that participation is the best teacher of democratic values; the relatively weak democratic commitment of those who do not participate is largely a consequence of their exclusion from political life, even if that exclusion is self-willed.

Any attempt to increase participation should either increase the benefits or reduce the costs of political action. Increased benefits might include changes in electoral law or in tax rules. The ineffectiveness of individual votes and campaign efforts in one-sided constituencies could be averted by a shift to an electoral formula of proportional representation, although other, undesirable consequences might result. Allowing tax credits for contributors to parties or candidates can transform a cost of participation into a benefit, which is precisely what has occurred in national elections and in many provinces in recent years. Individuals now contribute more money to Canadian parties than ever before. Increases in education levels, however, have not produced corresponding increases in participation, in spite of the positive association at any time between educational attainment and participation. The principal agents for reducing the cost of participation in campaigns must be political parties themselves, eg, by more active recruitment of volunteers. According to survey evidence, many more citizens are willing to work in campaigns than are asked. But the increased importance of electronic mass media in campaigns indicates that parties are substituting capital for labour rather than the reverse. Legislation to restrict party access to media might force the parties to seek voluntary assistance but might also infringe upon other political freedoms. Perhaps the most effective means of encouraging participation in campaigns and other political arenas lies in the democratization of activities that are not commonly regarded as political.

RICHARD JOHNSTON

Political Protest is the kind of political activity, eg, demonstrations, strikes and even VIOLENCE, usually but not always undertaken by those who lack access to the resources of organized PRESSURE GROUPS, or by those whose values conflict sharply with those of the dominant ELITE. Sometimes a protest centres around a specific issue or set of issues; at other times it is concerned primarily with the general grievances of such groups as ethnic or linguistic minorities, farmers, women or youth. Political protests may arise from any sector of society, and they reflect either left-wing or right-wing ideology.

When protest movements resort to extraparliamentary means of expression, the STATE usually responds with repression, with some form of

The Day of Protest (against wage controls, 14 Oct 1976), Toronto (*courtesy National Archives of Canada/PA-126362/ Mike Emre*).

symbolic accommodation, or a mixture of both. Where the leadership of a protest movement is itself middle class, accommodation is often facilitated by some form of co-optation of the leadership into the political process. In such cases, the protest movement itself tends to become institutionalized as a new organized interest group which participates, however uneasily, in the process. Sometimes such movements themselves evolve into political parties organized around their particular protest issue or issues, become contestants in the electoral and parliamentary processes, and more or less abide by the established rules of the game. At other times, protest movements are met by repression and become violent, resorting to TERRORISM or civil insurrection. Some movements have tried to steer a middle course between violence and co-optation by carrying out peaceful civil disobedience.

Protest movements in Canada, which were concerned particularly with the economic grievances of farmers and workers, erupted in the early part of this century. Farmers adopted various tactics to bring their grievances to the attention of the Canadian state, culminating in farmers' protest parties which won office in Ontario, Alberta and Manitoba, and became briefly the second-largest party in the House of Commons after the 1921 federal election. Once in office, however, the farmers' parties behaved very much like the previous Conservative or Liberal governments.

The protests of workers in 1919 against low wages, poor working conditions and the refusal of employers to recognize unions resulted in the WINNIPEG GENERAL STRIKE. The government responded with repression. Another important protest movement early in the century was the WOMEN'S SUFFRAGE movement which engaged in widespread agitation. The grant of adult female suffrage in federal elections (1918) resulted in a decline of this early feminist movement, which had concentrated its energies on the issue of the vote.

The GREAT DEPRESSION of the 1930s, with the consequent misery of unemployment and economic collapse, sparked many protest movements, several of which, radical or socialist in nature, challenged the dominant values of private enterprise. The CO-OPERATIVE COMMONWEALTH FEDERATION was founded to give political direction to many of these movements, while the COMMUNIST PARTY OF CANADA offered a yet more radical form of expression. Police repression against radical protest, especially strikes, and marches and demonstrations of the unemployed, such as the ON TO OTTAWA TREK of 1935 (which resulted in a bloody riot in Regina), were common. There were also populist right-wing protest movements, grounded in the ideology of FASCISM, in the 1930s, especially in Québec (*see also* KU KLUX KLAN).

During WWII there was a widespread and popular protest movement in Québec against the imposition of CONSCRIPTION by the federal government. This movement, which led to the formation of a political party, the BLOC POPULAIRE, encountered a certain amount of repression, but was sufficiently popular to force the federal government to delay imposing conscription until 1944.

During the 1960s, political protest became a familiar part of the political process (*see* HIPPIES; NEW LEFT). Antiwar demonstrations against nuclear weapons and the Vietnam war; student and youth protests; feminist movements; protests against racial discrimination; protests by community associations against urban redevelopment schemes; and protests against attacks on the environment imparted a new and more clamorous tone to Canadian politics. Perhaps the most serious protest movement of this decade was the movement for independence in Québec, which assumed several forms. The FRONT DE LIBÉRATION DU QUÉBEC, a violent and revolutionary wing, used bombings and terrorism. In October 1970 the kidnapping of a British diplomat and the kidnapping and later murder of Québec Cabinet minister Pierre LAPORTE led to the imposition of the WAR MEASURES ACT. With the virtual disappearance of the violent separatist movement, a moderate, constitutional wing devoted to independence for Québec grew stronger around the PARTI QUÉBÉCOIS, which came to provincial office in 1976 (*see* SOVEREIGNTY-ASSOCIATION), an instance of a protest movement that was sufficiently respectable and institutionalized to become the government of a province.

The WOMEN'S MOVEMENT remains an important protest movement in Canada. Women's groups, although diverse, have become a permanent source of protest and pressure on a wide spectrum of issues. Environmental and ecological groups (*see* GREENPEACE) have also continued to exercise pressure over issues such as ACID RAIN and the dangers of nuclear power and industrial POLLUTION. Native groups have become increasingly vocal. In the early 1980s the antinuclear peace movement mobilized large numbers of protesters across Canada, especially against the testing in Canada of the American Cruise missile. More traditional sources of protest have also continued: labour unions mounted the largest demonstration on Parliament Hill in Canadian history in 1982 to protest against high INTEREST rates and UNEMPLOYMENT; farmers have mounted protests against farm foreclosures and against changes in the CROW'S NEST PASS AGREEMENT (*see* NATIONAL FARMERS UNION).

Another feature of protest movements in the late 1970s and 1980s has been the emergence of widespread right-wing and populist (*see* POPULISM) protests. Protest campaigns against bilingualism and metrification, the movement for western SEPARATISM and the movement against ABORTION (eg, the Pro-Life Campaign) have all shown that protest movements are no monopoly of the political left.

Protest movements are now a normal part of

the political process, frustration breeds violence, which in turn brings on repression. In other cases, protests have been successful enough to win wide acceptance and have been met with accommodation. The dangers of co-optation for relatively successful protest groups are considerable; in such cases the protest group leadership is integrated into the normal political relationships between government and interest groups, and the original protest may tend to fade away. The dangers of electoral success for protest movements that evolve into protest parties is that the original cause may itself become a victim of success, as the cause becomes submerged in the day-to-day electoral politics of political parties. REG WHITAKER

Political Science has been defined as the systematic study of government processes by the application of scientific methods to political events, but this rather narrow definition has been questioned by those who believe that power and its organization in human relations is the subject matter of political science, and that power is a phenomenon that may be studied in forms of human association other than the state. Toward the middle of the 20th century, a narrower interpretation of power – that it leads to control over processes through which public decisions are made – gained popularity, although it is important to distinguish political from other kinds of decisions, eg, those in corporations. Another fundamental starting point for political analysis is the study of how scarce resources are allocated among competing groups of persons, how support is acquired and maintained for human projects. Politics exists because people do not always agree about what the community should be doing, or about how things should be done; politics is about the rules that are agreed upon for resolving conflict and about how these rules are accepted, even by those who disagree with the decisions made. It can also be about the breakdown of these rules and about revolutionary changes in political organization.

Political science is the systematic development of our knowledge and understanding of politics. Before the 20th century, what we now call political science tended to be philosophy, political history or the study of constitutional law – the latter 2 involving the description of political institutions. These 3 areas continue as aspects of modern political science, but they have evolved together into a separate, specialized, academic discipline.

Political philosophy is primarily concerned with the study of political ideas, eg, the place and order of values, the meaning of terms such as "right," "justice" and "freedom" often in the context of their times. Written political philosophy originated with the Greeks (philosophy meaning "love of wisdom," and politics, which referred to the activity of the city). Socrates, Plato and Aristotle were primarily interested in the nature of justice.

Plato applied philosophy to the question of what is best, or what ought to be done in politics. Aristotle, comparing and classifying different forms of government, asked as well: "How does politics actually work?" Plato's question led to the tradition of political philosophy or political theory, and political philosophers are still concerned with political values. Aristotle's question led to the tradition of the scientific or empirical investigation of politics, which is concerned first of all with facts and with how to draw useful conclusions from factual observations about how political institutions actually function.

If philosophy began with the Greeks, medieval and more modern notions of law derive from the Romans and the more ancient Hebrew tradition of a covenant. In 1159, in *Policratus*, John of Salisbury compared the physiology of the body to that of the state; in *Summa Theologica*, the 13th-century theologian and philosopher Thomas Aquinas described man as naturally political and the state as a natural institution. Aquinas assumed that the universe was inherently orderly, and that in law and politics, like everything else, the world moved from imperfection to perfection. Machiavelli, in the early 16th century, is often credited as the first modern political theorist; his credo was "For how we live is so far removed from how we ought to live, that he who abandons what is done for what ought to be done will rather learn to bring about his own ruin than his preservation." Hobbes, Locke and Rousseau, Montesquieu, Burke, Mill and Hegel among others all contributed to the literature of political philosophy. Marx, originally a follower of Hegel, decried philosophers for merely interpreting the world and not trying to change it, and claimed that he had taken a scientific approach to the world. By the end of the 19th century, it is often said that ideology had replaced political philosophy.

Contemporary political science owes its development to the 19th and early 20th centuries' enthusiasm for the SOCIAL SCIENCES, which was stimulated by the rapid growth of the natural sciences. The major change characterizing the growth of political science as a field of study is an emphasis on analysis. Instead of simply describing the formal rules and procedures involved in political institutions, eg, how a bill travels through Parliament to enactment, modern political science is equally interested in analysing the processes involved, how people actually behave.

Political Science in Canada In Canada political science is also an academic discipline. Departments of political science, or political studies, exist in some 45 universities, as well as in community colleges. Canadian political scientists are engaged in extensive research on the various aspects of politics and publish their findings in books, specialized academic journals, research reports and other forms of scholarly communication. Political science at Canadian universities dates to the late 19th century; originally it was strongly connected to constitutional law and to economics. The latter connection is somewhat distinctively Canadian, reflecting perhaps Canada's status as a developing nation with a strong concern with economic questions. At University of Toronto, which dominated political science until the mid-20th century, political scientists were colleagues of economists in a department of political economy. The first professional association, established permanently in 1929-30, was the Canadian Political Science Association, a joint venture with economists. Its official journal, another joint venture, the CANADIAN JOURNAL OF ECONOMICS AND POLITICAL SCIENCE, existed until 1967, when separate associations and separate journals were created.

Although Queen's, McGill, Dalhousie and later the universities of Saskatchewan and BC also taught political science, until after WWII academic departments were very small, faculty were poorly paid and political science (along with the social sciences in general) had little prestige. As late as 1950, there were only 30 political scientists in all Canadian universities. The 1940s, however, witnessed a coming-of-age of Canadian political science. The publication of major books by R. McGregor DAWSON, J.A. Corry, Alexander Brady and H.McD. Clokie indicated that indigenous Canadian scholarship in political science concerned with the study of Canadian political institutions was now possible, separate from economics or constitutional law.

In the 1960s, Canadian universities underwent a dramatic expansion. New universities sprang up and older institutions expanded their faculties and their offerings. Political science, gaining in prestige along with the other social sciences, shared in this rapid growth.

By the early 1970s, there were about 30 times more political scientists teaching at Canadian universities than there had been in 1950; according to a survey of the Canadian Political Science Association, in 1979 there were 687 political scientists with permanent teaching positions in 45 universities. Sixteen percent of these were located in Québec, and 14% were in French-language or bilingual departments. This does not include the political scientists who became public servants, politicians, journalists, lobbyists, consultants, researchers and advisers to various organizations, or high-school or community-college teachers.

During the 1960s, English Canadian political science was strongly influenced by American political science. Because the relatively small departments and small graduate programs of the 1950s had not produced a sufficient number of graduates to fill all the new positions created by expansion, Canadian universities turned to the relatively better-developed American political-science departments and a large number of American political scientists were recruited throughout the 1960s.

By the end of the 1960s, nearly 50% of faculty members in political-science departments in Canada were non-Canadian by birth. The influence of American schools, American concepts and models and American authors and journals was very strong at a crucial period in the development of Canadian political science.

At the same time the so-called "behavioural revolution," an attempt (originating in the US) to make political science as scientific as possible, gained precedence. Value judgements were to be excluded. Political facts that could be given numerical values and could be systematically analysed were called "hard data." For example, with voting, representative samples of electorates are drawn up, questionnaires administered and sophisticated statistical techniques applied to the results. Not all aspects of politics, however, are as easily quantified, nor is there any real basis for a science of politics exactly comparable to the hard sciences.

Political scientists are themselves part of what they study and not detached observers. Within the discipline, during the 1960s, a major controversy concerned with the limits of this behavioural revolution erupted. Some political scientists claimed that the scientific study of politics alone was legitimate; others argued for the continuation of more traditional ways of looking at politics, claiming that political facts could not be separated entirely from political values. This conflict has now moderated considerably. Behaviourism is generally accepted as a legitimate but not exclusive part of the study of politics. Political science in Canada is varied and pluralist in its approaches.

During the 1960s and 1970s, French-speaking political scientists were influenced by different forces. In Québec social sciences were relatively underdeveloped and very much in the shadow of religious influence before the 1960s. The first political-science faculty in Québec was created at Laval in 1954, followed by a major expansion throughout Québec universities in the 1960s. However, American political science did not influence the development of the discipline in Québec as strongly as it did in English Canada. New positions in political science faculties were filled primarily by Québecois, but most of their graduate training was in France. European influences on political science were much more marked in Québec than in English Canada. Marxism was one such influence, and there was a greater emphasis on ideas and on political ideology. Another major difference in Québec was that the growth of Québec political science coincided with the QUIET REVOLUTION. As a result of the rapid rise of Québec nationalism and the debate over the constitutional future of Québec in (or out of) Canada, political science enjoyed a more central position than it held in English Canada. Political scientists became major participants in public debates and Québec political scientists are consequently more engaged politically than their English Canadian counterparts.

There is both autonomy and collaboration in the relations between the English- and French-speaking political-science communities. The Canadian Political Science Assn had about 1200 members in 1988. A separate francophone association was established in the early 1960s (first called the Société canadienne de science politique, but since 1978 known as the Société québécoise de science politique). The *Canadian Journal of Political Science/Revue canadienne de science politique* is a bilingual journal with editors and contributors drawn from both communities. A separate French-language journal, *Politique*, is also published by the Société québécoise. The Société holds separate annual meetings, although many francophone political scientists hold joint membership in the Canadian Political Science Assn and participate in its meetings as well.

Fields of Study There are a number of fields of study within the discipline of political science. Political theory is either about the explicit study of values (sometimes still called political philosophy) or about the methodology of political inquiry. The latter is concerned with more technical questions, such as the construction of hypotheses, deductive and inductive logic, and the use of statistical tests. Political theory in this sense is a much more specialized field than political philosophy, which sometimes spills over into debates over democracy, liberalism, conservatism, socialism or federalism. Sometimes public debates invoke the concepts developed by political philosophers – as in the debate over independence for Québec or the Canadian Constitution – although rarely in a form that political philosophers would recognize.

A second subfield is comparative politics, which compares political forms, institutions, values and processes in different countries. This is a vast field, encompassing a considerable amount of detailed information about many countries. Comparative politics has also evolved more specialized branches, eg, area studies, which focus on particular groups of nations and geographic regions such as Latin America, Africa, the Soviet Union. Political developments are concerned with the problems of developing nations. In political-science departments in Canadian universities, the study of Canadian politics not surprisingly forms a distinct subfield in itself, as does Québec politics in Québec universities. Within this field provincial and municipal politics are also studied. International relations focuses on the interrelationship of states, diplomacy, foreign and defence politics, war and international organization. Yet another subfield is PUBLIC ADMINISTRATION, primarily the study of BUREAUCRACY. Public policy focuses attention on the process of policy formation.

An important subfield of growing importance to Canadian political science is POLITICAL ECONOMY, which is both a subfield of study and an approach to politics in itself. It attempts systematically to relate economic, social and political factors together, partly a reflection of the older Canadian connection between economic history and the study of politics, but also a reflection of the influence of Marxist analysis and of a recent

trend to more interdisciplinary research, wherein politics is linked with economics, sociology and history in particular.

At annual meetings of the Canadian Political Science Association and the Société québécoise de science politique, scholarly papers are presented from all the subfields. The *Canadian Journal of Political Science/Revue canadienne de science politique* and *Politique* publish articles from all of them as well. There are also more specialized journals, such as *Canadian Public Administration, Canadian Public Policy, International Journal, Studies in Political Economy, Canadian Journal of African Studies, Recherches sociographiques.* Canadian and Québec political scientists publish in journals edited abroad. Canadian political science is well respected internationally in a number of fields, particularly in the area of political theory.

REGINALD WHITAKER

Politics broadly refers to any or all conflicts among human beings over the allocation of power, wealth or prestige, when interests are pursued by means other than the use of physical violence. According to a more optimistic view, politics is an essential means by which collective goals can be achieved through peaceful co-operation. Narrowly the term describes activities associated with GOVERNMENT and the STATE. The state serves the purpose of managing conflicts and imposing solutions that are binding on all individuals and groups subject to its authority. To be viable, a state must enjoy unchallenged authority over a particular territory and population.

There are many schools of thought in POLITICAL SCIENCE concerning the role of the state. David Easton, a Canadian-born political scientist of international renown, has defined the role of the state as "the authoritative allocation of values." Marxists, however, interpret politics as class conflict and consider the state the institution that reflects and expresses the common interests of the dominant SOCIAL CLASS. Pluralists define politics as competition among organized groups and interests, the state being the neutral referee that imposes generally acceptable solutions. Other observers view politics as the conflict among ELITES who manipulate the masses as a means of pursuing their own ends.

Politics have existed in Canada for thousands of years, although political authority among the native peoples before the arrival of Europeans differed significantly from that which exists in a modern state. In the narrower sense politics probably began under the French regime and certainly no later than the latter part of the 18th century, when elected legislatures were established in Upper Canada, Lower Canada, Nova Scotia and New Brunswick.

Politics in the Canadian state usually include activities associated with the federal, provincial and municipal levels of government, as well as the relations among these 3 levels of government. Political activities among these levels of government involve legislative, executive and judicial institutions, the administrative departments and agencies of government, and political parties and interest groups.

A large proportion of the events reported and commented upon by the news media involve politics (*see* POLITICS AND THE MEDIA). Most Canadians can identify the PRIME MINISTER, the PREMIER of their own province and other leading participants in the political process, and the vast majority of adult Canadians participate in politics by voting in elections. The academic study of politics is called political science but other subjects, eg, history, geography and sociology, also involve the study of politics.

The term "politics" is sometimes associated in

people's minds with the cynical manipulation of PUBLIC OPINION, the trading of favours for political support, and the enrichment of politicians and their friends at the expense of society (*see* CORRUPTION). While such activities no doubt exist, they make up only a small part of the substance of politics.
GARTH STEVENSON

Reading: R.M. Dawson, *The Government of Canada* (6th ed, 1987); P. Fox, *Politics: Canada* (5th ed, 1982); R. Van Loon and P.M. Whittington, *The Canadian Political System* (3rd ed, 1981).

Politics and the Media Much of what Canadians know about their political leaders, party politics or public policy comes from the media – especially television, radio and newspapers – the primary information link between the Canadian population and the political sphere. The media try to explain the government's goals and policies, helping to mobilize and reinforce public support necessary for effective political action, but they also focus attention on controversial policies, expose corruption and hold politicians accountable to public opinion. In reporting on politics, the media help select the issues that are to receive public attention and help shape the public agenda.

The free flow of a meaningful account of political events and issues is necessary for the public's understanding of politics, the formation of PUBLIC OPINION and the public's participation in the political process. The freedom of the media from political interference; the vitality of the media and the way they conduct their political functions; the way freedom of the media is reconciled with the pressures of the commercial system that finance media institutions; and the openness of the government in providing information all influence the health and vigour of Canadian democracy.

During the 19th century, there were bitter struggles between newspaper editors and political authorities. In 1835 the Joseph HOWE libel trial in Halifax established important precedents about the right of the press to criticize the authorities (*see* LAW AND THE PRESS; NEWSPAPERS). In the 20th century the Supreme Court of Canada has supported press freedom in a number of cases. In the 1938 ALBERTA PRESS ACT REFERENCE the Supreme Court ruled that attempts by the Social Credit government in Alberta to curb press criticism were unconstitutional; in Québec, the PADLOCK ACT was used as an instrument of CENSORSHIP for 20 years until it was ruled unconstitutional in 1957. Censorship was also practised in WWI and WWII and during the OCTOBER CRISIS in 1970.

There are restraints on the flow of information about government in every society. Canada's parliamentary process tends to be secretive compared to the congressional system in the US. The public's "right to know" is often sacrificed to the penchant of the government to conduct business away from the glare of publicity. In 1982 Parliament partly corrected this situation with the enactment of the Access to Information Act (*see* FREEDOM OF INFORMATION). In 1982 Canada's new Constitution – in the CANADIAN CHARTER OF RIGHTS AND FREEDOMS – provided guarantees for freedom of expression, including freedom of the press and other media of communications. The charter guaranteed formal recognition to a tradition of press freedom that evolved, despite occasional serious setbacks, over 150 years.

Economics and Free Press While Canada's media are part of the machinery of POLITICS, they are generally operated for profit. (The major exception is the CANADIAN BROADCASTING CORPORATION). Daily newspapers and privately owned broadcast operations have been among the most profitable business enterprises in Canada. The pursuit of profits, however, has led to the growth of newspaper chains and the virtual disappearance of newspaper competition. Of Canada's nearly 100 newspaper cities, in 1987 only 10 have more than one daily. Of the 110 dailies, half are owned by 2 companies, SOUTHAM Newspapers Inc and THOMSON Newspapers, which sell 6 out of 10 English papers produced each day; one Québec chain, Québecor, controls nearly half of the French-language circulation. In broadcasting, there is also much concentration of ownership. Some companies own daily newspapers and broadcast stations in the same cities. The Royal Commission on Newspapers (Kent Commission) reported in 1981 that the extensive concentration of newspaper ownership that exists in Canada was "entirely unacceptable" for a democratic society: "too much power is put in too few hands and it is power without accountability." The commission called for federal government intervention to curb the power of chains and make the operation of newspapers more democratic and responsible. Critics charged that the proposals would increase the potential for political interference in news operations (*see* MEDIA OWNERSHIP) and the recommendations were not acted upon.

Changing Role of Media in Politics Canada's press became deeply involved in politics around 1820 when the economies of the British N American colonies could support a competitive newspaper system through advertising, subscriptions and print jobs. By focusing attention on politics, newspapers helped to politicize the population and mobilized public support for democratic institutions, especially RESPONSIBLE GOVERNMENT. In the latter part of the 19th century, press and politics were so entwined that Canada's leading journalists were often politicians. At the CHARLOTTETOWN CONFERENCE of 1864, which led to Confederation, 23 of the 98 delegates were journalists (*see* JOURNALISM). Furthermore, newspapers helped spur the growth of political parties, while political patronage helped finance newspapers. In the early 1900s technological changes in newspaper production and the changing interest of advertisers led to a new relationship between press and politics. Newspaper competition declined and there was less party attachment. The introduction of radio in the 1920s and television in the 1950s revolutionized the mass communications industries. By 1986 almost half of Canada's 9.3 million households had 2 or more television sets and there were almost as many radios as people. Canadians, who spend 6 hours watching television for every hour of newspaper reading, regard television as the most important and reliable news medium. Television has become the great battleground for public opinion in the struggle for political power. However, the transmission of political electoral information tends to be dictated by the medium, ie, television may have helped expose more Canadians to politics than ever before, but it has done so at the cost of oversimplifying complex issues. Election campaigns are increasingly run for the news media and there is much less concern with convincing live audiences on the hustings. Political leaders crisscross the country to provide television filming opportunities in the right places, and great emphasis is placed on the "images" portrayed by the party leaders in formal television debates. Party campaign strategies are aimed at effective use of media. Public opinion surveys are used to help parties decide the acceptable image and to determine party platforms (*see* POLITICAL CAMPAIGN).

Media and Nationhood It is often said that Canada's mass media – especially electronic communication – help build Canada's national identity without erasing the multiple cultural and linguistic dimensions of society. It is for this reason that Canadian governments have played a dynamic role in shaping the broadcast media. Canada has

been a world leader in the application and development of new COMMUNICATIONS TECHNOLOGY. It is possible, however, that technology has not helped to bridge major communication gaps in Canada's heterogeneous society. For example, the French and English media provide very different accounts of Canadian political developments. The French media generally support Québec nationalism; the English media are closely tied to the American media and broadcast enormous amounts of American TELEVISION PROGRAMMING. This and other evidence indicates that in some ways Canada's media have in fact been principal agents of denationalization and have not necessarily contributed in major ways to a national identity.   ARTHUR SIEGEL

Reading: F. Peers, *The Public Eye: Television and the Politics of Canadian Broadcasting, 1952-1968* (1979); P. Rutherford, *The Making of the Canadian Media* (1978); Arthur Siegel, *Politics and the Media in Canada* (1983); B. Singer, ed, *Communications in Canadian Society* (2nd ed 1983); W.C. Soderlund et al, *Media and Elections in Canada* (1984).

Pollock, Sharon, playwright, actor, director (b Mary Sharon Chalmers at Fredericton 19 Apr 1936). She grew up in Québec's Eastern Townships, and attended UNB. Her first attempt to write, *A Compulsory Option*, won the 1971 Alberta Playwriting Competition. Subsequently, she taught playwriting at U of A, ran the Playwrights' Colony at the Banff Centre, and was playwright-in-residence at Calgary's Alberta Theatre Projects. In 1984 she became the first female artistic director of a major theatre in western Canada, at Theatre Calgary. Pollock also has written 6 plays for children, several television and radio scripts, and award-winning dramas. She received the 1980 "Nellie" ACTRA award for Best Radio Drama (*Sweet Land of Liberty*); the 1981 Golden Sheaf Award for the television film *The Person's Case*; and the 1982 Gov Gen's Award for *Blood Relations*, about Lizzie Borden, the acquitted axe murderer. Her major works – *Walsh* (1974), *The Komagatu Maru Incident* (1978) and *One Tiger to a Hill* (1981) – which have been produced in every major theatre centre in Canada, have earned her a reputation as a playwright of conscience. More recent works – *Generations* (1981), *Blood Relations* and *Doc* (1984, Gov Gen's Award) – are less concerned with social issues and more with domestic conflict. *Doc* is loosely based on Pollock's own family background; like her other plays, it is brutally honest, and painfully telling. Her play *Whiskey Six Cadenza* was shortlisted for (but did not win) the 1987 Gov Gen's Awards, and in Jan 1988 she was awarded the Canada-Australia Literary Prize.   DONNA COATES

Pollution was viewed initially as the unsightly mess or visible environmental damage resulting from careless disposal of various materials. Most commonly, pollution was seen as the dirty scum on rivers or lakes, or the grey and yellow smog in the skies over cities. These relatively obvious problems (confirmed by dead fish floating on waters or irritation of eyes and throats on particularly smoggy days) were considered local concerns which would be cleaned up by reducing emissions from sewer pipes and smokestacks, thus giving the environment time to absorb and purify materials. Dilution was considered the solution.

Scientific research increasingly has shown that pollution also includes odourless and colourless chemicals that remain in soil, air and water long after the materials they were used in have disappeared. Pollution now also includes chemicals that were not carelessly dumped but were gradually sprayed on farmland as fertilizers and PESTICIDES, others from inside pressurized spray cans, and others plastered on walls and ceilings as as-

The wastes produced by mines and mills often create abstract designs when viewed from above. These tailings are close to the copper smelting centre of Rouyn-Noranda (*photo by J.A. Kraulis*).

bestos fireproofing. Problems caused by these pollutants can take over 20 years to develop, as exemplified by the fatal lung disease asbestosis, caused by exposure to asbestos dust. Problems are now known to be widespread. ACID RAIN that kills fish in Ontario lakes comes largely from AIR POLLUTION emitted by smokestacks hundreds of kilometres away in Ohio. Snow falling in the Canadian Arctic includes chemicals from Japan. Scientists have also discovered that some chemicals which are not harmful alone bond with other chemicals to create new and dangerous pollutants.

Pollution is now recognized to include more than just substances. It can take the form of excessive NOISE, causing damage to hearing; heat discharged as hot water from power plants, destroying aquatic life; electronic transmissions (eg, microwaves, X rays), damaging human tissue. Scientists are still unsure how much exposure to many modern pollutants is dangerous to humans and other living matter. In some cases, no exposure may be the only safe exposure. Our ENVIRONMENT now appears as a garbage dump filling up to overflow with invisible additives. In a strict sense, pollution can be defined as the release of any material or energy that may cause immediate or long-term harmful effects to the natural environment. On this basis, very little can be used or thrown away without consideration of its long-term effects. Thus, pollution involves all products and processes that we use except those proven not to be harmful.

Pollution arises largely from the sheer volume of throwaway material created to meet the needs of the Earth's rapidly expanding population. Much of the world is already at the limit of unconsidered and uncontrolled growth of both products and their effects as pollutants. In one day the average Canadian citizen discards about 2.5 kg of solid garbage. Almost 7000 L of fresh water are needed per Canadian per day. This average person throws away more than 10 000 bottles and 17 500 cans during a lifetime. Residents of Toronto discard a total of 87 000 t of plastic per year in municipal garbage (*see* WASTE DISPOSAL).

To meet the demands of consumer society growth in the 1950s, many new and unnatural chemicals were developed for use in manufacture of food and drugs, etc. More than 60 000 chemical compounds are now used commercially in Canada; another 1000 are developed annually. About 15 000 drug products are sold in Canada; over 1500 flavourings, many of them synthetic, are permitted in foods (*see* FOOD ADDITIVES). Many synthetic chemicals do not decompose through natural biological processes (eg, the action of sunlight, heat and cold, bacteria). They slowly leak out into the environment, contributing to the steady accumulation of potential pollutants in land, air, water, vegetation and our bodies.

The pesticide DDT provided an early example

of the danger of bioaccumulation. Millions of kilograms of DDT were used to kill insects in N America, until scientists discovered that the chemical was accumulating in insect-eating birds. The pesticide accumulated to the point of damaging the birds' eggs; thus, for example, the PEREGRINE FALCON came close to extinction. DDT was banned in Canada by 1971, but its chemical components are still found in soil and water.

Pollution is now analysed in laboratories and evaluated medically for its cancer-causing potential, its longevity (often hundreds of years) and its volumes (usually microscopic). The scientific danger level of "one part per million," roughly equal to a drop of pollution in a barrel of water, has entered common parlance. Many chemicals that Canadians have accepted, tasted, worked with and relied on since the 1950s are now known to be "toxic" or deadly in low doses over large periods of time.

The 1970s was a period of awakening to the reality of the costly effects of pollution resulting from industrial by-products. This recognition was based on scientific investigations and frightening, sometimes painful, experience. For example, in northern Ontario hundreds of residents along the English-Wabigoon river system lost their jobs as commercial fishermen, as well as their community stability and their expectation of a long and healthy life because of invisible, poisonous MERCURY in the fish (see GRASSY NARROWS). The mercury was dumped as waste material by a local paper mill before 1970, but will remain a danger in the water and fish for another century. At Port Hope, Ont, thousands of tonnes of slightly radioactive wastes, dumped years earlier, were removed from beneath houses, schools and stores to lessen the danger of cancer developing among citizens. In Toronto, public clinics are held to test the blood of residents of some neighbourhoods for low levels of LEAD dust from nearby factories, which could lead to nervous disorders and learning disabilities.

Pollution poisoning is increasingly becoming a risk and a concern to Canadians, especially in urban areas. When most of the chemicals were developed, research on their long-term impacts was minimal. Through ignorance or greed, many industries long ignored the obvious pollution they were creating by dumping wastes into the public environment. As the SCIENCE COUNCIL OF CANADA pointed out in its scathing 1977 report "Policies and Poisons," governments were for too long ill-equipped to measure pollution and too hampered by red tape and political compromise to tackle polluters. Heightened public awareness of pollution dangers and public pressure on governments and industries are changing these attitudes. Public opinion surveys show that environmentalism and pollution fighting are now consistently important concerns of Canadians. Pollution is no longer perceived as a simple choice between halting pollution or shutting down the polluting factory. Jobs are created by cleaning up and protecting the environment. Waste materials can be recycled instead of dumped, thus saving companies' money. The cost of cleaning up and preventing pollution is far less than that of repairing environmental and health damage, or losing an environmental resource forever.

Science and citizens are working in 2 directions: in laboratories, studying new and existing chemicals for subtle but long-lasting consequences for the environment; and in legislation, writing new laws to ensure proper cleanup of existing problems and prevention of new ones (see ENVIRONMENTAL LAW). Prevention accomplishes far more in the long run than belated reaction. More money is required for scientific research and technologies to reduce pollution and pro-

mote recycling. Producers and consumers will pay more for safer, less wasteful products, but these measures will reduce long-term economic and social impacts. Pollution problems are very wide ranging.

Water Pollution Polluted water can destroy valuable commercial and sports FISHERIES, make vital supplies of drinking water unfit for human and animal consumption and damage a recreational and aesthetic resource of unmeasurable value to all Canadians (see WATER POLLUTION; WATER TREATMENT). Sewage wastes exceed millions of gallons per day for most Canadian cities; by itself this flow would vastly exceed the capacity of local rivers or lakes for dilution and neutralization. The algae choke out other vegetation on lake and river bottoms, often causing bad odours and tastes and creating a breeding ground for disease-bearing bacteria. In the 1960s Lk ERIE became clogged and its beaches strewn with foul algae; a huge portion of this shallow lake became effectively "dead." Complex pollutants such as dissolved and suspended metal particles (eg, arsenic, lead, cadmium) and chemicals (ranging from oils to acids) washed into the waters with city grit and dirt pose greater problems. Many of these invisible particles are toxic to aquatic life and, when they accumulate in water and fish, can be harmful to humans consuming either. In 1981 Canadian scientists discovered, for the first time, very small amounts of one of the most deadly man-made chemicals, DIOXIN 2, 3, 7, 8-TCDD, in the Great Lakes. Dioxin is a by-product of agricultural chemical production and the degradation of industrial wastes. As little as a droplet of the pure chemical is deadly in thousands of litres of water. Researchers are only beginning to consider the problems which would be involved in the protection and purification of Great Lakes water for human consumption if dioxin concentrations increased. The ultimate solution will require expensive barriers to stop leaks from chemical dumps, and bans on chemical products containing components which degrade into dioxin. Some such products are disappearing from use in industry, homes and farms, but more research is needed to identify all sources.

Land Pollution Industrial and urban waste dumping, poor agricultural practices and mineral exploitation all produce pollutants that reduce or destroy the ability of soil to sustain healthy plant life. Many of these pollutants are ultimately transferred to water bodies, but en route they can sterilize, poison and erode the soil. Millions of tonnes of industrial chemicals, in liquid form, and commercial and residential garbage, particularly in a semisolid form, are disposed of annually in open pits, giant holes and artificial mountains across Canada (see SOLID WASTES; WASTE DISPOSAL). Even with daily efforts to cover the garbage with layers of dirt, these "sanitary landfills" cause aesthetic problems, odours and health risks. The gradual disintegration and decomposition of garbage also releases potentially dangerous chemical pollutants into surface and underground water supplies. Carefully designed dumps can reduce seepage, but many municipalities lack conveniently situated disposal sites.

Incineration of garbage can substantially reduce the volume to be buried, but adds its own risks of air pollution. Recycling and reduction of unnecessary packaging can significantly reduce the volume of garbage before incineration or landfill disposal. Disposable plastic packaging, for example, comprises 36% of plastic materials produced for society. At present, almost one third of commercial-residential garbage is paper; 20% glass and metal; 17% food wastes. Recycling and source reduction are becoming important industries as people realize that pollution is best prevented by reducing the use of source materials.

Other sources of land pollution include poor AGRICULTURAL SOIL PRACTICES and logging, which expose the bare topsoil to wind and water EROSION, or excessive use of chemical fertilizers and pesticides, which gradually accumulate in soil and reduce crop growth or make crops unsafe for human consumption. Polluted soil which lacks vital minerals and micro-organisms to hold it together is also more subject to erosion. Erosion can lead to enormous accumulations of silt in rivers and streams, blocking the flow of water and making it unsuitable for aquatic life.

Industrial liquid wastes of highly toxic composition are another critical source of pollution in Canada (see HAZARDOUS WASTES). In Ontario an estimated 35-70 million L of the total 350 million L of liquid industrial wastes produced annually are considered hazardous. At present, there are almost no fully safe sites and systems operating in Canada to handle these wastes. These liquids pose high risks of long-lasting pollution of underground and surface water supplies if they leak out of garbage dumps where they are often discarded. Most of these liquids can be first reduced in volume by filtering out useful chemicals for reuse, then neutralized by adding other chemicals, or destroyed in specially built high-temperature furnaces. Finally, they can be converted into permanently solid wastes that will not leak or decompose when buried in special sites.

Air Pollution is the accumulation in the atmosphere of substances that can endanger health or otherwise damage materials or living matter. Air includes a wide range of substances produced by natural and man-made sources; most of these substances have not accumulated to obviously harmful levels. The major source of these pollutants is the burning of carbon-based fuels (eg, coal, oil, natural gas), which produces invisible potential pollutants. These can cause local, regional and worldwide pollution problems, either as individual chemicals or in combination. Smog, for example, is a combination of nitrogen oxides, hydrocarbons and carbon monoxide, which, under the action of sunlight and water, are blended together into pollutants such as ozone, which irritates human lung tissue and damages vegetation; aldehydes, which irritate human eyes and skin; and acids, which damage human tissue and buildings. A week-long smog in London, England, in 1952 caused more than 4000 deaths and prompted enactment of new limits on the burning of coal in city factories and homes. On a global scale, carbon monoxide resulting from combustion converts to carbon dioxide and permanently accumulates in the Earth's upper atmosphere, reducing the atmosphere's ability to block out cancer-causing rays from the sun.

In Canada, particulate or gritty air pollution has been reduced by installation of filters on smokestacks and by better-tuned automobiles. But automobiles, fossil-fueled power plants, factories and mineral smelters all produce other air pollutants which can reach levels threatening to human health when local weather conditions allow them to accumulate. These local episodes require industry to reduce operations until weather improves, ie, until the local smog is diluted by fresh winds. Even when local conditions appear clean and safe, regional accumulations of pollutants can pose other problems. Acid rain, for example, is caused by the accumulation of nitrogen and sulphur oxides, which blow long distances, gradually changing to nitric and sulphuric acids in the moist air and falling as acid rain.

In Canada, controls have been introduced on most major types of air pollution. Technologies are being developed to reduce fossil-fuel emissions further but, over a longer period, a significant reduction in consumption of these fuels is necessary. The problem of air pollution will ultimately be solved by development of less-polluting energy sources, not by pollution controls.

The pollution outlook for Canadians for the next 20 years is murky. Despite the vast size of the country, most people live in cities, where pollution problems are concentrated. Ultimate solutions to pollution require major changes in what we produce, use and throw away. Pressures for these changes will increase and the costs of changes will be more readily shared when people realize that everyone shares the risks.

ROSS HOWARD

Reading: Donald Chant, ed, *Pollution Probe* (1970); Ross Howard, *Poisons in Public: Case Studies of Environmental Pollution in Canada* (1980).

Pollution Probe Foundation Pollution Probe was established in 1969 to provide education and advice on ways to restore and preserve the Canadian environment. It became the Pollution Probe Foundation (a registered charity) in 1971, and has successfully addressed a wide range of environmental issues, including ACID RAIN, PESTICIDE abuse, FOOD ADDITIVES, industrial-waste reduction and recycling, WATER POLLUTION, toxic chemicals and energy CONSERVATION. The foundation also operates Ecology House, an urban demonstration of energy and resource conservation in downtown Toronto, and publishes *Probe Post: Canada's Environmental Magazine.* The organization is governed by a 25-member board of directors. Financial support comes from individuals, corporations, charitable foundations, sale of publications and services and a Canada-wide membership.

COLIN F.W. ISAACS

Polo is a game that originated in Persia, and over the centuries spread throughout Asia. It was discovered in the mountainous areas of northern India by British army officers during the 19th century and was organized in its modern form. It is now played chiefly in ranching areas and in countries where the traditions of wealthy horsemen prevail. An international handicap system gives each player a rating for purposes of competition.

Polo was first played in Canada in 1878 by British garrison officers stationed in Halifax. The game was more widely played in western Canada, however, and by 1889 weekly matches were organized in Victoria between garrison teams and British naval officers. Alberta was a centre of polo activity, with the NORTH-WEST MOUNTED POLICE providing much of the initiative for organization. Clubs were formed in Calgary and High River in the 1890s, and by the turn of the century in Toronto and Montréal. The first national Canadian polo tournament was held in Toronto in 1903. In 1905, the High River team won both the Canadian and American championships. Between the world wars, Vancouver, Victoria and Kamloops, BC, and Calgary were strongholds of polo in the West, and Montréal the leading city in the East. But after WWII, the sport almost died out entirely. In the early 1950s it was revived in Vancouver, Victoria and Calgary; and in the 1960s clubs in southern Alberta banded together to form the Calgary Polo Club, now the strongest polo organization in Canada. Competition in the West is usually with teams from the US. In Toronto, the most popular form is arena, or indoor, polo.

BARBARA SCHRODT

Polymer Corporation, a federal CROWN CORPORATION established in 1942 to produce artificial rubber to substitute for overseas supply cut off by WWII. A factory was established at Sarnia, Ont, where, using German patents from an American

licensee, Polymer produced 5000 tons of artificial rubber from oil every month. The product was used in everything from tires to airplane parts, and much of it was sold to the US as part of the common war effort. The company was adjudged a roaring success, more efficient than its American counterparts and a national asset. C.D. HOWE, under whose Dept of Munitions and Supply the company fell, decided to keep Polymer going as a crown corporation after the war. It was a highly profitable enterprise, and he was not convinced that any buyer would pay a proper price or keep it going. Polymer therefore survived the war, reporting through Howe and his successors to Parliament until in 1971 it was sold to the CANADA DEVELOPMENT CORPORATION. The corporation was renamed Polysar in 1976.   ROBERT BOTHWELL

Pond, Peter, fur trader (b at Milford, Conn 18 Jan 1739/40; d there 1807). In 1775, with proverbial Yankee shrewdness, Pond moved from the area SW of the Great Lakes, where he had been trading for most of the previous decade, to focus on what is now the Canadian West, which proved a much richer territory. In 1778 fellow traders chose him to take goods from the lower Saskatchewan R into the Athabasca country, which they had heard of from the Indians. He accomplished the difficult journey, wintering on the Athabasca R and doing an extremely good trade. In 1779 he received one share in the partnership that brought together the trading interests of Benjamin FROBISHER and Simon MCTAVISH. He returned to the Athabasca country in 1783-84, and again from 1785 to 1788 as a partner in the NWC. Alexander MACKENZIE was his second-in-command during the winter of 1787-88 and was greatly influenced by Pond's conception of the region's geography. Having been implicated in the murder of 2 competitors, Pond left the FUR TRADE under a cloud. He went back to the US, probably to his birthplace. The map of the North-West that he drew in 1784-85, based on his own exploration and Indian reports, is the earliest to depict what is now called the Mackenzie Basin. He subsequently prepared other versions of the map and wrote an account of his early adventures, a work which radiates the energy and enormous confidence that drove him.   JANE E. GRAHAM

Pondweed, common name for members of the family Potamogetonaceae [Gk *potamos,* "river"], which consists of the genus *Potamogeton.* Formerly, pondweeds were classified as family Zosteraceae, along with several other genera, eg, *Ruppia* (ditch-grass), *Zannichellia* (horned pondweed) and *Zostera* (eelgrass or grass-wrack). All these have representatives in Canada and are now generally regarded as distinct families. Pondweeds grow submerged in fresh or, occasionally, brackish water. The genus *Zostera* is a true marine aquatic and, in Canada, *Z. marina* is widely distributed on both the E and W coasts. *Potamogeton* species are perennial, herbaceous plants anchored in the mud at the bottom of shallow lakes and ponds by underground stems (rhizomes). The leaves, varying considerably in shape, are arranged alternately and all may be submerged or some may float. The flowers are small, often borne in elongated clusters that may be submerged, allowing for POLLINATION by water, or emergent from the water for wind pollination. Pondweeds are widely distributed, but a majority of the approximately 100 species occur in the N temperate region. About 30 species occur in Canada, several extending into arctic areas.

Ponoka, Alta, Town, pop 5473 (1986c), is located approximately 100 km S of Edmonton in rolling, rich parkbelt land. It was incorporated as a village in 1900 and as a town in 1904. The

Methodists established a mission to the Stoney Indians at the nearby Samson Reserve in the late 1870s. Limited European settlement began in the early 1880s. There was some activity in this area during the NORTH-WEST REBELLION when Indians looted the Hudson's Bay Co store at the Battle River Crossing. Afterwards, the store was temporarily fortified to secure the Edmonton-Calgary Trail. With the construction of the Edmonton-Calgary Railway (CPR) in 1891 the area grew in popularity as a mixed farming area and Ponoka grew as a service centre. In 1911 the province established a psychiatric hospital just N of the town. Ponoka has continued as a service centre and the hospital remains an important element in its economy.   D.G. WETHERELL

Pontbriand, Henri-Marie Dubreil de, sixth bishop of Québec (b at Vannes, France Jan 1708; d at Montréal 8 June 1760). Educated by the Jesuits and Sulpicians, appointed bishop of Québec in 1740, Pontbriand arrived in Aug 1741, determined to remedy the abuses of episcopal absenteeism. He visited the religious institutions, parishes, missions and reserves of his vast diocese 1741-44 and again 1749-52. After the fall of Québec in 1759 he urged conciliation with Gen James MURRAY. He died before Montréal capitulated, leaving New France without a spiritual leader in her darkest hour.   CORNELIUS J. JAENEN

Pontiac, chief of the OTTAWA (b 1720?; d at Cahokia [Ill] 20 Apr 1769). He may have served with the French and Indian forces that defeated Maj-Gen Edward Braddock at FORT DUQUESNE (1755). He later was able to organize Indians discontented with the English regime, arranging a series of secret meetings among the SENECA and other groups. In spring 1763 he ignited hostilities, leading an alliance of OTTAWA, HURON, Potawatomis and OJIBWA against Ft Detroit and killing or taking captive a contingent of 46 English soldiers at Pt Pelée. Detroit was held under siege, and the uprising spread throughout the PAYS D'EN HAUT, as Michilimackinac, Ft Sandoské, Ft St-Joseph, Ft Miami and others fell to the widening alliance. On July 29 at Bloody Run, Pontiac's forces routed an encampment of 260 reinforcements heading for Detroit. Pontiac's direct control was limited to the warriors around Detroit, but even that group disintegrated as the Potawatomis and Huron left, and even the Ottawa deserted to winter hunting grounds. A series of peace treaties was signed in July 1765, with the prestigious Pontiac a key signatory. He insisted that the Indians were not surrendering their land by making peace. Those still hostile to the English turned against him, expelling him from his own village. He led a wandering life until murdered by a Peoria assassin.   JAMES MARSH

Pope, Georgina Fane, military nurse (b at Charlottetown 1862; d there 6 June 1938), daughter of W.H. POPE, sister of Sir Joseph POPE. A graduate of the Bellevue Hospital School of Nursing in New York, she served in various administrative positions at hospitals in the US until she volunteered for nursing service in 1899 with British forces in the SOUTH AFRICAN WAR. She headed the first small group of nurses (4 in total) and sailed with the volunteers leaving Québec in Oct. After more than a year of enduring the extreme physical and emotional hardships of caring for the wounded, she returned to Canada only to go back to South Africa in 1902 to serve the continuing guerilla warfare. This third small contingent under her leadership was officially the Canadian Army Nursing Service, an integral part of the Canadian Army Medical Corps. Her contribution was recognized in 1903 when she became the first

Canadian to receive the Royal Red Cross for conspicuous service in the field. After demobilization she served briefly in the reserve force and in 1906 was appointed to the permanent forces in Halifax, within 2 years becoming the first Matron of the Canadian Army Medical Corps. During WWI she served at Canadian stationary hospitals in both the UK and France. Invalided home she lived in retirement until her death.

NANCY MILLER CHENIER

Pope, James Colledge, entrepreneur, landed proprietor, land agent, politician, premier of PEI (b at Bedeque, PEI 11 June 1826; d at Summerside, PEI 18 May 1885). Second son in a family prominent in PEI business and politics (he was the younger brother of W.H. POPE), he participated in several types of business and was PEI's third-largest shipowner of the 19th century. He entered politics as a Tory in 1857, and served as premier 3 times: 1865-67 (Conservative), 1870-72 (coalition) and Apr-Sept 1873 (Conservative). As premier he called upon troops to quell TENANT LEAGUE disturbances in 1865, negotiated purchase of the Cunard estate in 1866, commenced construction of a railway in 1871, and led the Island into Confederation on 1 July 1873. He was elected one of PEI's first 6 federal MPs. He was minister of marine and fisheries in John A. MACDONALD's government 1878-82. Burdened with illness and anxiety arising out of business losses, he died in greatly reduced circumstances.

IAN ROSS ROBERTSON

Pope, Sir Joseph, public servant, EXTERNAL AFFAIRS (b Charlottetown, PEI 16 Aug in 1854; d Ottawa 2 Dec 1926), son of W.H. POPE, brother of Georgina POPE. After early experience in PEI government and banking, he came to Ottawa in 1878 as private secretary to his uncle, James Colledge POPE. He served as secretary to Sir John A. Macdonald, 1882-91, and wrote his biography (2 vols, 1894). He was under-secretary of state, 1896-1909, responsible for the conduct of Canada's early relations with foreign states. He persuaded the government of Sir Wilfrid Laurier to establish a department, 1909, to assemble documents, draft correspondence, provide advice and conduct negotiations regarding Canada's external relations; he was first permanent head of the Dept of External Affairs 1909-25. He assisted in resolution of many bilateral issues with the US, including the ALASKA BOUNDARY DISPUTE. Unsympathetic to the advances in Canada's status externally, Pope was nonetheless a loyal and competent public servant, a respected adviser to prime ministers from Macdonald to King. D.M.L. FARR

Reading: Maurice Pope, ed, *Public Servant, The Memoirs of Sir Joseph Pope* (1960).

Pope, Maurice Arthur, engineer, army officer, diplomat (b at Rivière du Loup, Qué 9 Aug 1889; d at Ottawa 20 Sept 1978). Son of Sir Joseph POPE and grandson of Sir Henri T. Taschereau, he was a strong nationalist who believed that Canadians must respect the traditions of both founding peoples. He joined the Royal Canadian Engineers in 1915 and served overseas in the CANADIAN EXPEDITIONARY FORCE. Remaining in the army, he became vice-chief of the General Staff (1941), senior Canadian Army member of the PERMANENT JOINT BOARD ON DEFENCE (1942), chairman of the Canadian Joint Staff Mission, Washington (1942-44), and military staff officer to PM Mackenzie KING. He was ambassador to Belgium (1950-53) and Spain (1953-56). His memoirs, *Soldiers and Politicians,* were published in 1962. STEPHEN HARRIS

Pope, William Henry, lawyer, journalist, politician, judge (b at Bedeque, PEI 29 May 1825; d at St Eleanors, PEI 7 Oct 1879). Born into a family important in the economic and public life of PEI, he became a lawyer after study in London. Like many other Island lawyers, he served as a land agent, and in 1854 made his name from a controversial real-estate transaction in which he and 3 associates made more than £10 000 at the expense of his employer. He was editor of the colony's leading Tory newspaper, the *Islander,* 1859-72. Elected to the Assembly in 1863, he enthusiastically supported union of the British colonies in N America. His position being unpopular, he left the Cabinet in 1866 and did not contest subsequent elections. As the colony's most tenacious advocate of CONFEDERATION, however, he continued to promote the Island's union with Canada. When this was accomplished in 1873 under the leadership of his younger brother, James Colledge POPE, the government of Sir John A. Macdonald appointed him judge of the Prince County Court.

IAN ROSS ROBERTSON

Poplar, short-lived, deciduous, hardwood tree of genus *Populus* of the willow family, widely distributed in the N temperate zone. The genus includes ASPENS and cottonwoods. In N America, they grow from the TREELINE to northern Mexico. Forty species occur worldwide; 5 are native to Canada. Aspen (*P. tremuloides*) and balsam poplar (*P. balsamifera*) occur across Canada. Hybrids and introduced poplars, such as white or silver-leaved poplar (*P. alba*) and black poplar (*P. nigra*), are planted as ORNAMENTALS and windbreaks. Leaves are simple, alternate, roundish and toothed. Bark of young trees is smooth, yellowish green, becoming grayish green to brownish and furrowed. Male and female flowers are clustered in drooping catkins on separate trees.

Wind-pollinated flowers appear before leaves; seed matures as leaves develop. Seeds are tipped with long, silky down (cotton) for wind distribution. The widespread, shallow root system facilitates regeneration by "suckers" on cutover and burned land. Abundant suckers allow single trees to produce copses of clones with identical characteristics (eg, early leafing or late retention of autumn colour). Rapid growth makes poplars useful for reclamation. In ideal conditions, pulpwood is produced in 10 years, small sawlogs in 15 and veneer stock in 20. Infertile hybrids that produce no "cotton" have been cloned for ornamental plantings. Natural hybridization is common and causes difficulty in defining species.

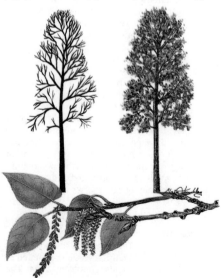

Balsam poplar (*Populus balsamifera*), with male flowers (right) and fruits (left) (*artwork by Claire Tremblay*).

Popular Literature in English, writing which has shown wide and continued acceptance, measured by sales, frequent imitation, adaptation to other cultural forms and general commercial success. The word "popular" is meant as a synonym for "successful," not as an antonym for "serious." Certain books are carefully tailored by authors and publishers to capture the attention of a wide range of potential readers.

In Canada, whether published in paperback or cloth editions or both, trade or general books are considered to have had satisfactory sales if they have sold 1500 copies (poetry, play), 3000 (first novel) or 7000 (political commentary); at double these figures the publisher may have a BEST-SELLER. Arguably the best-selling Canadian author of all time is Arthur HAILEY, many of whose novels, such as *Hotel* (1965) and *Airport* (1968), have sold millions of copies each. Popular, nonfiction authors such as Pierre BERTON, Farley MOWAT and Peter C. NEWMAN, who write serious books of particular interest to Canadians, enjoy hardcover sales of 75 000-150 000 copies per title. As substantial as such figures may seem, they pale in comparison with the sales record of *Coles Notes.* This series of study aids in monograph form (over 400 titles since 1947) has sold more than 40 million copies worldwide.

Reference Books A number of notable, single-volume sources of Canadian information are revised and updated at intervals. The Government of Canada has compiled, irregularly since 1867, its official statistical record called *Canada Year Book.* Commercial publishing houses have brought out 2 volumes with some overlap in coverage: *Canadian Almanac & Directory* (since 1847) and *The Corpus Almanac of Canada* (since 1966; in 2 volumes since 1981). A useful Canada-and-the-world compendium is *The Canadian World Almanac and Book of Facts* which was to appear annually after 1987. More compact is *Quick Canadian Facts,* over one million copies of which have been sold since 1946. Other annual tomes are *Canadian Who's Who* (1910-), with some 8000 biographies of prominent living Canadians, and *Canadian Books in Print* (issued since 1967), which lists about 24 000 Canadian books (over 10% of which are new each year). A specialized, single-volume reference work is *The Oxford Companion to Canadian Literature* (1983), general editor William Toye.

Cookbooks Books of recipes traditionally sell well, although this was not true of *The Cook Not Mad; or Rational Cookery* (1831), the first Canadian cookbook (or at least "Canadianized," for it reprints American recipes with some "Canadian content"), which was not reprinted until 1972. Probably more copies of *Canadian Cook Book* have been sold than have those of any Canadian competitor. It was originally compiled by Nellie Lyle Pattison in 1923 and has been frequently revised and enlarged. Large sales have been reported for more recent titles: *The Laura Secord Canadian Cook Book* (1966); Elizabeth Baird's *Classic Canadian Cooking* (1974); and numerous collections by Mme Jehane BENOÎT, particularly *Enjoying the Art of Canadian Cooking* (1974) and *New and Complete Encyclopedia of Cooking* (1978). The regional cookbook, such as Edna Staebler's *Food that Really Schmecks* (1968), is a staple in the fast-changing world of contemporary cuisine.

Romantic Fiction Romantic novels are usually published only in mass-market, paperback editions. What such novels may lack in depth and sophistication, they more than make up in their strong appeal to a devoted N American readership that seems to be predominantly female. The field of romantic fiction is less interesting for literary than for social, psychological and commercial reasons. The world's largest publisher of romantic fiction is HARLEQUIN Books, founded in Winnipeg in 1949 and located in Toronto since the 1960s. Having found a market for reprints of romantic novels, the company discovered the successful formula of commissioning the novels, 65 000 words in length; it now issues about a dozen each month. Many are set in hospital wards or gothic castles. A Harlequin romance invariably has a happy ending.

At least 3 Canadian women authors have found success writing commercial romantic fiction. Novelists such as Joy Carroll, Joy Fielding and Charlotte Vale Allen have been called, by literary columnist Beverley Slopen, "paperback princesses," because their works, perhaps modelled on those of American popular novelist Jacqueline Susann, have sold many thousands of copies apiece. But the country's most prolific author of romantic and other popular fiction is a man: between 1962 and 1978, under various pseudonyms, W.E. Dan Ross wrote 342 novels.

Mysteries Common to stories of intrigue and espionage, detective novels and thrillers, is the notion that a mystery is about to be revealed. In the past, Canadian addicts of mystery fiction have not required that their mysteries be Canadian in locale or character. The earliest Canadian work in this genre was probably James DE MILLE's *The Cryptogram* (1871), which followed by 3 years the English writer Wilkie Collins's *The Moonstone,* which it resembles. Two turn-of-the-century writers with Canadian connections, Grant Allen and Robert Barr, enjoyed large Anglo-American readerships. Allen's *An African Millionaire* (1897) and especially Barr's *The Triumphs of Eugène Valmont* (1906) – with a French detective not unlike the later Hercule Poirot – are important in the history of world detective fiction.

Three residents of the US who were born in Canada – Hulbert Footner, Frank L. Packard and Arthur STRINGER – also contributed to the genre. The first detective in Canadian fiction, November Joe, "detective of the woods," was created by Englishman H. Hesketh Prichard in *November Joe* (1936). Although they lived in California for many years, Margaret Millar (who was born in Canada) and her husband Ross Macdonald (who was raised here) wrote many novels, some with Canadian characters and settings.

Howard ENGEL, in the series that begins with *The Suicide Murders* (1981), has created what many regard as the first truly Canadian private investigator in fiction: Benny Cooperman, who is something of a *schnook,* works in the small city of Grantham (modelled on St Catharines, Ont). Eric WRIGHT's fictional Detective Inspector Charlie Salter of the Metropolitan Toronto Police Dept made his debut in *The Night The Gods Smiled* (1983). Other writers who have contributed notable novels to the genre are Hugh GARNER (*The Sin Sniper,* 1970), Ian Adams, David Gurr, Shaun Herron, Donald MacKenzie, Larry Morse, Philippe van Rjndt, Sara Woods and L.B. Right. Michael Richardson edited *Maddened by Mystery: A Casebook of Canadian Detective Fiction* (1982), which includes 13 stories, a historical introduction and a list of over 100 Canadian fictional sleuths.

Of related interest is The Bootmakers of Toronto, fd 1970 as the Canadian counterpart to Britain's Baker Street Irregulars to study the Sherlock Holmes "canon." The Arthur Conan Doyle Collection of the Metropolitan Toronto Library was opened in 1971 and has the world's largest public collection of books relating to Doyle's detective.

Fantastic Fiction Unreflective people who are content with their value systems and unenthusiastic about scientific research and technological development are unlikely to place a premium on fantastic fiction, ie, fantasy fiction, weird fiction and SCIENCE FICTION, which emphasizes the impact on man and society of imaginative, supernatural and innovative values, respectively.

Such reasoning has been used to explain Canadians' lack of awareness of their own fantastic tradition. The relative weakness of the periodical and BOOK PUBLISHING industry has meant the importation rather than the creation of mass-market genre fiction. Nevertheless, well over 1000 books in the fantastic vein have been written by Canadians or have been set in Canada by foreign authors. Two landmark novels are James De Mille's *A Strange Manuscript Found in a Copper Cylinder* (1888), an adventure set in a polar world of inverted values, and Frederick Philip GROVE's *Consider Her Ways* (1947), a satiric fantasy about sentient ants who maintain that their society is superior to man's.

A celebrated contributor to the so-called golden age of science fiction, A.E. Van Vogt, was born in Manitoba and wrote over 600 000 words of fantastic fiction (including his classic novel about a persecuted mutant, *Slan,* 1946) before settling in California. The distinguished anthologist of speculative literature, Judith Merril, reversed the migration and settled in Canada. Her donation of 5000 books and periodicals to the Toronto Public Library in 1970 formed the nucleus of The Spaced Out Library, which was created under the direction of former chief librarian Harry Campbell. In 1987, with holdings totalling 35 146 items, this was the world's largest public collection of such literature.

Two contemporary novelists command particular attention. Phyllis GOTLIEB, in her stories and especially in such novels as *Sunburst* (1964), writes with sympathy about humans and aliens in societies in which ESP is a fact. Richard ROHMER, in a series of near-future thrillers beginning with *Ultimatum* (1973), has found a wide readership for descriptions of disasters extrapolated from present social unrest.

Distinctive Canadian contributions to the fantastic genres include novels set in the Arctic, notably *Sick Heart River* (1941) by John BUCHAN (Baron Tweedsmuir) and *The Time Before This* (1962) by Nicholas Monsarrat (a South African novelist who spent several years in Canada); and novels concerned with Québec nationalism, such as Jules-Paul TARDIVEL's *Pour la patrie* (1895, tr *For My Country,* 1975) and William Weintraub's *The Underdogs* (1979). Brian MOORE has written science fiction (*Catholics,* 1972), fantasy fiction (*The Great Victorian Collection,* 1975) and weird fiction (*The Mangan Inheritance,* 1979). Hugh MACLENNAN's *Voices in Time* (1980) is a remarkable, near-future story deeply rooted in contemporary social and spiritual problems. Two best-selling and award-winning novels are *Neuromancer* (1984), a Cyberpunk adventure by William Gibson, and *The Handmaid's Tale* (1985) a dystopian feminist work by Margaret Atwood.

Authors who write exclusively in the field of the fantastic in Canada include Michael G. Coney, Terence M. Green, Crawford Kilian, Donald Kingsbury, Edward Llewellyn, Spider Robinson, Charles R. Saunders and Andrew Weiner.

Authors of outstanding fantastic novels for younger readers (*see* CHILDREN'S LITERATURE) include Pierre Berton, Monique Corriveau, Christie Harris, Monica HUGHES, Suzanne Martel, Ruth Nichols and Mordecai RICHLER. The standard anthology is *Other Canadas* (1979), edited by John Robert COLOMBO, which includes a short bibliography and a critical commentary. A work of related interest is *The Dictionary of Imaginary Places* (2nd ed, 1987) by Alberto Manguel and Gianni Guadalupi. JOHN ROBERT COLOMBO

Popular Literature in French, an urban phenomenon born in the industrialization of the turn of the 20th century, includes many types of writing: adventure and historical NOVELS, detective and spy stories, romantic novels, even "morally uplifting" literature (lives of saints, apologias, or the *Journal* of Gérard Raymond). In 1923 publisher Édouard Garand decided to fight the success of the American "dime novel" in Québec by bringing out a collection of his own. The series, called "Le Roman canadien," published monthly novels by, among others, Jean Féron, Ubald Paquin and Alexandre Huot that glorified patriotism and conservative ideology. A craze for weekly 32-page serials was born in 1941 with the series *Les Aventures policières d'Albert Brien, détective national des Canadiens français.* In 1948 Imprimerie Judiciaire alone published 8 series. Between 1947 and 1966, Pierre Saurel (pseudonym of Pierre Daigneault) published, through that same company, 934 *Aventures étranges de l'agent IXE-13, l'as des espions canadiens.* The sentimental novel did not pay off as handsomely. From 1940 to 1960, *Les plus belles histoires d'amour,* with its sermons on the virtues of marriage, family, suffering and submission, was practically the only series aimed at women. Today, although Canadian HARLEQUIN romances are popular, foreign multinationals control the market in this genre. The 250 000 photo-romances bought every month in Québec are also foreign, usually Italian, in origin. Television, the growing popularity of the paperback and foreign book dumping have all combined to kill off local production. The specialized collections of detective stories are at their last gasp. Writers known for this genre include Pierre Saurel, "Le Munchot," Claude JASMIN and Chrystine Brouillet.

Fantasy and Science Fiction In 19th-century Québec newspapers and magazines, short stories mixed the natural with the supernatural, never setting them in opposition to each other – the main criterion of fantasy. Fantasy, itself more than a genre, is woven right into a story, and today Jacques FERRON, Anne HÉBERT, Jacques BENOÎT and Michel TREMBLAY all add elements of fantasy to works otherwise not fantastic. Science fiction was flourishing in English-speaking countries long before it developed in Québec. Despite a few series – *IXE-13* for one – and the occasional publication of a novel, it took the QUIET REVOLUTION and the new emphasis on science to boost science fiction. Some authors (eg, Louky Bersianik, François Barcelo, Claire de Lamirande, Roger de Roches) use the genre as a pretext for speculation or social criticism; others (eg, Jean Tétreau, Emmanuel Cocke) play at it as dilettantes.

Authors who devote themselves to science fiction or fantasy (Esther Rochon, Elisabeth Vonarburg, Jean-Pierre April, Michel Bélil, Daniel Sernine and René Beaulieu) appeared with, or after, the magazines *Requiem* (fd 1974, renamed *Solaris* 1979), which organized writing workshops, a story competition and an annual convention, "Boréal"; and *Imagine...,* publishing only science fiction. There are also 2 specialized collections: "Nuits d'encre" (fantasy), published by Desclez, and "Chroniques du futur," from Le Préambule. There is an effort underway to make Québec science fiction regularly available, as it was with the Volpek (Yves THÉRIAULT) and Unipax (Maurice Gagnon) series published by Lidec in the 1960s.

Comic Strips Unlike the other forms of popular literature, comic strips appeared in Québec at the same time as they did elsewhere. Raoul Barré first published "Pour un dîner de Noël" in 1902 in *La Presse.* That paper fought with *La Patrie* for control of the market. "Le Père Ladébauche" by *La Presse* editorial cartoonist Albéric Bourgeois was one of the few strips to withstand the syndicates which, after 1910, began providing the world's newspapers with their daily comics. "Onésime," by Albert Chartier, first appeared in 1944 in the *Bulletin des agriculteurs,* and his "Séraphin illustré" (an adaptation of C.H. GRIGNON's *Un homme et son péché*) followed, 1951-70; "Ti-Prince," a sequel to "Séraphin," began in *Bonnes soirées* in 1955. Apart from these, the Québec comic strip, until the end of the Quiet Revolution, consisted of *Histoire en images* (1919-36), published by the ST-JEAN-BAPTISTE SOCIETY, and the Fides comics for schoolchildren (1944-65, *François, Claire, Hérauts*). These moralizing strips were usually foreign in origin. With few exceptions, daily papers would not give space to Québec comics.

The comic-strip boom coincided with the student and counterculture explosion of the late 1960s. The Chiendent group (1968), led by Claude Haeffely and André Montpetit, encouraged the creation of strips, and *Le Magazine Maclean* and *Perspectives* published the first ones. Pierre Dupras, *Québec-Presse* cartoonist, published a few collections in 1970 and 1971. Some short-lived magazines burst on the scene; for example *BD, L'Hydrocéphale Illustré, L'Écran.* Robert Lavaill and Léandre Bergeron had a smash hit with their *Histoire du Québec.* In 1972 the publishing house L'Hydrocéphale Entêté started the co-operative Les Petits Dessins, which in 1974 turned out 6 daily strips for the newspaper *Le Jour.* It did not last long. In 1973 *La Presse* ran 2 Québec comic strips daily: "Les Microbes" by Michel Tassé and "Rodolphe" by Bernèche.

Québec comic strips then divided into 2 main tendencies. The information bulletin and publishing house, BDK, and *Prisme* and *Baloune* magazines (the latter the heir to *Mainmise*) encourage experiments outside the usual rigid commercial format. *Croc* magazine has published humorous comic strips since 1979 and, in 1982, put out books by Réal Godbout and Jacques Hurtubise but discontinued its magazine *Titanic* after a few issues. *Cocktail* (1981-82) ran classic as well as Québec strips. The young publishing house Ovale has marketed the adventures of characters such as Humphrey Beauregard and Ray Gliss.

But commercial publishers are also looking for new readers. Some of them (Mondia, Mirabel, Ovale, Ville Marie) want to take over part of the market, which is now 95% foreign controlled. Since 1973, books based on children's programs (*Capitaine Bonhomme, Bobino et Bobinette*) have been flooding the market. *La Presse* cartoonist Jean-Pierre Girerd has tried comic strips (*On a volé la Coupe Stanley*) with little success. In 1981 Henri Desclez, who had been editor in chief of *Tintin* magazine and later worked for Éditions Héritage (which published "Nic et Pic" by Serge Wilson and Claude Poirier; "Monsieur Petitbois" by Bastien) produced a series of comics, the first volume being *Atlantic City* by Cedric Loth and Pierre Montour. Nevertheless, it is difficult and expensive for Québec publishers to succeed. *See also* LITERATURE IN FRENCH.   BENOÎT MELANÇON

Reading: A. Amprimoz, "French Language Science Fiction and Fantasy," in *A Bibliography of Canadian Science Fiction and Fantasy* (1979); "La bande dessinée kébécoise" in *La Barre du jour,* nos 46-49 (winter 1975); V.-L. Beaulieu, *Manuel de la petite littérature du Québec* (1974).

Popular Music Attempting to succeed in the "big time" while trying to maintain an indigenous cultural identity has placed many Canadian popular singers and musicians at cross-purposes. Living directly in the shadow and glare of the US, the world's most imposing entertainment machine, has defined this condition. Canadians often believed they had to "sound American" in order to "make it," and, owing to Canada's proximity to the US, many have assimilated popular American

styles. However, in recent years Americans have embraced a number of singers whose styles are identifiably Canadian. Canadian Francophones face a double bind; maintaining a viable career is dependent upon reflecting regional realities, thus virtually eliminating American acceptance.

In the first half of the century, Canada's wide open spaces and sparse population made the nation's popular music (often COUNTRY AND WESTERN MUSIC) regional in character. Radio was the only existing link, but listeners living near the US border often preferred American broadcasts of that country's popular bands and orchestras. It was probably Guy LOMBARDO and His Royal Canadians, originally from London, Ont, who put Canada on the musical map – but only because of the orchestra's name, as there was nothing inherently Canadian about his mellifluous dance style.

The advent of Canadian television in 1952 spurred the modest beginnings of a national "star system," basically a string of smooth, if somewhat bland, singers who emulated American crooners. Among the most prominent were Wally Koster; Giselle McKenzie; vivacious blonde JULIETTE ("our pet"); Robert GOULET, who went on to Broadway and movies; Tommy AMBROSE and Alan Blythe, who became successful television producers on both sides of the border; Don Messer's Jubilee, a young Anne Murray, Lucille Starr who had a big hit with "The French Song"; and country singer Tommy HUNTER, who 25 years later was more popular than ever and whose TV series was the only non-US country music production to be aired in N America. Canada's first and foremost JAZZ superstar was the one and only Oscar PETERSON. Heading into the 1990s, he is still in a class by himself.

The rock 'n' roll era that began in 1955 brought 3 Canadian harmony groups into prominence: the Four Lads, who counted the innocuous "Standing on the Corner" among their dozen US "Top 40" hit records; the Diamonds, with 15 hits, including "Little Darlin'," a "whiteified" adaptation of the popular black "do-wop" street-corner style, and the Crew-Cuts. All 4 have now been inducted into the Juno Hall of Fame.

The first Canadian pop superstar was Ottawa's teenage sensation Paul ANKA. Son of a Lebanese restaurant owner, he knocked on doors in Los Angeles and New York for 3 years before he struck gold in 1957 with "Diana," a ditty about an older babysitter. He was 16. He differed from other greasy-haired teen stars because he wrote his own songs and aimed to be accepted in the same circles as Frank Sinatra (for whom he wrote "My Way" in 1968). With over 40 American hits, more than 400 of his songs recorded, records in French, Italian and German, royalties in the millions from songs, commercials and theme music (including "The Tonight Show"), and regular performances at the Las Vegas-Atlantic City showcases, he has succeeded in his goal. Anka still retains his Canadian citizenship. Indeed, career longevity – and the ability to avoid the pitfalls of fame – has become a major characteristic of numerous Canadian pop stars.

Canadian singers, songwriters and musicians played a major role in the FOLK MUSIC boom of the early 1960s and its subsequent "folk-rock" hybrid. IAN & SYLVIA's "Four Strong Winds" was one of the most performed songs of the folk movements and, in its cool yet impassioned way, the first lyric to explore the Canadian temperament, borne of wide open spaces. The duo was also the first to introduce 2 songs, "Early Morning Rain" and "For Lovin' Me," by Gordon LIGHTFOOT. Lightfoot's understated lyric style, delivered in clipped southern Ontario tones, has since graced over a dozen best-selling albums and 6 hit songs. "The Canadian Railroad Trilogy" superbly por-

trayed the nation's growing pains while "Wreck of The *Edmund Fitzgerald,*" about an ill-fated ore ship, was the only piece of authentic history to find massive radio airplay in 1976. Lightfoot has performed with the same musicians for many years and retains a loyal international following.

While Lightfoot has continued living in Canada, others fled what they termed deaf ears: Zal Yanovsky became a driving force behind the "good-time" band The Lovin' Spoonful; Denny Doherty harmonized with the millions-selling Mamas and the Papas; Andy Kim wrote the 8-million-selling "bubble gum" classic "Sugar Sugar" and sold 3 million copies of "Rock Me Gently" internationally; and David CLAYTON-THOMAS became lead singer of Blood, Sweat and Tears.

The most influential singer-songwriters were Joni MITCHELL and Neil YOUNG, who became integral parts of the Los Angeles music scene. Mitchell reflected the Canadian qualities of tolerance and acceptance in "Both Sides Now," which has been recorded by hundreds of singers. Her collection of albums (including *Court and Spark, Blue*) are lyrically and musically idiosyncratic. Young, formerly of folk-rocking Buffalo Springfield and counterculture favourites Crosby, Stills, Nash and Young, has claimed his stake with desultory songs about loss of innocence and alienation, and cynicisms about America. His style is best summed up by album titles *Everybody Knows This Is Nowhere* and *Rust Never Sleeps.*

No other group reflected such devotion to N American roots, regions and traditions as The BAND. The 4 southern Ontarians and their Arkansas drummer forged their solidly eclectic style over 10 years barnstorming the continent with rockabilly singer Ronnie HAWKINS who settled in Canada in 1959. As if that was not enough they went on to become Bob Dylan's back-up band on his highly controversial Electric Tour of 1966-67. Their first 2 albums, issued in 1968-69, came as a breath of fresh air in the hectic "blow-your-mind" rock scene of the time. Their finely crafted, intelligent songs were filled with a plethora of characters. Their music was pure Americana: rock 'n' roll, country, rhythm & blues, folk and church music. Clearly The Band's upbringing – close to the US, yet tempered by Canadian distance – was the major factor in the remarkable quality of their music. After 7 acclaimed albums, they performed a gala farewell concert in 1976, resulting in *The Last Waltz,* regarded as the best pop film ever. Robbie Robertson, leader of the Band, returned to rock in late 1987 with a self-titled LP that was so good it immediately re-established him as one of the best rock songwriters.

The lack of support by Canadian radio, resulting in the painful fact that Canadians had to achieve success abroad to gain respect at home, prompted the CANADIAN RADIO-TELEVISION AND TELECOMMUNICATIONS COMMISSION into adopting regulations requiring AM radio stations to play at least 30% of records that were in some way Canadian. Although the US was still the barometer of success, the CRTC rulings did provide a solid national base for many singers and bands.

Anne MURRAY was the first star of the CRTC era. Her 1970 multimillion-selling "Snowbird" set forth a clean, clear, crisp style that has made her the most popular female "middle-of-the-road" singer since then. She has had over 2 dozen hits, sold millions of albums, won Grammy awards in both pop and country categories.

The 1970s and 1980s marked the coming of age of Canadian rock groups, most fitting the popular formula of lightning and thunder combined with indefatigable touring. The GUESS WHO were the pioneers; among their 14 hit discs was 1970s "American Woman," which jeered at the Vietnam War and American racial tensions. Bach-man-Turner Overdrive followed with a more basic, "blue-collar" view of life. The STAMPEDERS' jaunty "Sweet City Woman" became number one internationally. The most popular group over the past 10 years was RUSH, whose high-pitched excursions into cosmic mythology ("New World Man") and space-age life-styles have sold over 15 million albums worldwide. LOVERBOY emerged in 1980 with textbook examples of how to blend popular rock components into a commercially effective, but hardly original, style. Other international successes were achieved by April Wine, who travelled more kilometres across Canada than any other group; Glass Tiger which in 1986 reached international prominence with their debut album *The Thin Red Line*. The LP, with the writing and production help of Jim Vallance, won the Junos for best LP and single in 1985-86. Other mainstream rocker outfits included Europe-based Saga, Triumph, Streetheart and CHILLIWACK. Many of the above acts capitalized on the popular 1980s "video clip" phenomenon that set their sounds to televised images and from the movement was born Canada's video channel Much Music and its Québec equivalent Musique Plus. Special mention must be made of the ever-surprising West Coast scene, led by BTO, Loverboy, Payolas/Rock and Hyde, Doug and the Slugs, Headpins, Chilliwack, DOA and many more but especially by Bryan ADAMS, who along with his writing partner Jim Vallance wrote and sold more albums than any group in Canada. Adams was the first Canadian recording artist to sell over a million LPs in Canada (*Reckless*). He has received many Juno awards. His live shows play to sold out concerts around the world. Now 5 LPs into a career, Adams looks to be maintaining his status for many years to come.

The name of Juno and Grammy winner David FOSTER should not go unnoticed as well. Originally from Victoria, Foster has been writing, producing and arranging hits for countless artists on both sides of the border since 1975. While he continues to be based in Los Angeles, he is always coming home to work. One of the greatest gatherings of Canadian talent took place as a direct result of Foster's Canadian roots. In Mar 1985, with the help of Adams, Vallance, and Vancouver managers Bruce Allen and Lou Blair, he helped gather 55 Canadian artists to record "Tears Are Not Enough" under the group title Northern Lights to raise funds for African Famine Relief. (To date $2.5 million has been raised and distributed.)

Western talents with wonderful futures ahead of them are K.D. Lang and Colin James, 54-40, the Grapes of Wrath, Paul Janz along with producers Bruce Fairbairne and Bob Rock. Every year the list of talent grows, eg, Platinum Blonde, Luba, Tom Cochrane and Red Rider, Jane Siberry, Kim Mitchell, Gino Vanelli, Haywire, Liona Boyd, Parachute Club, Honeymoon Suite, the indescribable Skinny Puppy, Blue Rodeo, Northern Pikes, Barney Bentall, The Nylons, Corey HART. Canada's international star is surely on the rise!

Despite the recent glut of rock groups, Canada's most individualistic voices remain singer-songwriters. Bruce COCKBURN grew from introspective folksinger of the early 1970s to embrace rock, jazz and reggae styles, painting pastoral scenes as well as sociopolitical statements. Murray MCLAUCHLAN delivered good-natured, workingman's folk-rock. Dan Hill sold 4 million copies of his excruciatingly sensitive "Sometimes When We Touch" in 1977. Poet Leonard COHEN set his disquietingly romantic works to song ("Suzanne," "Bird On A Wire"), selling over a million albums internationally yet, strangely, few in N America. American expatriate classic rock 'n' roller Michel Pagliaro was the only Canadian to earn "gold" singles in both English and French. Kate and Anna McGar-

rigle garnered an international following for songs, in both languages, that embrace traditional folk, gospel, ragtime and pop ("Heart Like A Wheel," "The Work Song").

Québec's Popular Music reflects its people's struggle for survival amid Anglo-American culture, as well as the struggle to be competitive with American styles and market appeal.

Cultural and political struggles were best defined by the "chansonniers" of the 1950s and 1960s, who sang poetry to the accompaniment of music in the folk and European music hall traditions. Leading the way was Félix LECLERC, whose plaintive emotional style was recognized first in France in 1951. He blended pithy statements of Québecois sentiment with pointed reflections of cultural and political alienation, survival, exploitation and the "boss." His songs remain evergreen and today Québec's popular music awards bear his first name. His success also cleared the way for Raymond Lévesque (with "Quand les hommes vivront d'amour," 1956) and, towards the turn of the decade, for a new wave of chansonniers reflecting the transition from a Québec

Group photo of Northern Lights Feb 1986. Most of Canada's popular music stars participated in the benefit recording "Tears are Not Enough" for African famine relief, including David Foster, Bryan Adams, Anne Murray, Gordon Lightfoot, Burton Cummings, Joni Mitchell, Neil Young and others (*photo by Dimo Safari*).

society dominated by Duplessis and the Catholic church to the QUIET REVOLUTION of the 1960s asserting Québec's identity.

The most influential artist of the early 1960s was Gilles VIGNEAULT from Natashquan, whose people's traditions, pride and worries were conveyed in lively, almost theatrical songs. Vigneault's passionate "Mon Pays" became Québec's anthem for the late 1960s; his more banal "Gens du pays" accompanied the Parti Québécois' rise to power in the 1970s.

Others to emerge were Claude LÉVEILLÉE, a sophisticated singer-pianist whose "Pianos mécaniques" was recorded by France's Edith Piaf; the subtle, soft-spoken Claude Gauthier; fiery Pauline JULIEN, Vigneault's leading interpreter, whose passion was often matched with vitriol; Jean-Pierre Ferland, a romantic whose *Jaune* was the first double-album ever released by a Canadian; Monique LEYRAC, Georges Dor and Clémence Desrochers, who blended song with monologue. This wave of singer-songwriters was accompanied by the rise of the "boîtes à chanson" ("song boxes"), frequented by students, artists, intellectuals and some future politicians.

However, a totally different form of music was making its impact on the population at large. The explosion of the Québec record industry, spurred by the Beatlemania phenomenon, was largely founded on translated versions of Anglo-American hits; this success, in turn, provoked rock and pop original material. The tabloid press covered such local stars as Pierre Lalonde, Donald Lautrec, Michel Louvain, Michèle Richard, Johnny Farrago, Renée Martel, Renée CLAUDE, Tony

Roman (the province's most flamboyant producer), and child-singer René Simard, who a decade later appeared with younger sister Nathalie, both selling over half a million albums. By far the most talented stars of this regional pop were Ginette Reno, whose best-selling albums (300 000) included *Je ne suis qu'une chanson* (1982), and Michel Pagliaro, a master of classic rock and pop styles, who created the rollicking anthem "J'entends frapper" ("I Hear Knocking").

The gap between intellectuals and populists was bridged in 1968 by Robert CHARLEBOIS, then an "enfant terrible" because of his raucous use of JOUAL, Québec's street slang rife with anglicisms.

Charlebois' success spurred a mini-explosion in the homegrown RECORDING INDUSTRY, resulting in a wave of rock bands of all descriptions. Beau Dommage parlayed clean harmonies and pop music clichés with picturesque breezy postcard greetings from Québec. Their debut album sold over 200 000 copies, a record for any Canadian group in its native market.

Other popular groups included Ville Emard Blues Band, an 18-member "musical cooperative" (composed mainly of accompanists of the stars) that offered differing musical excursions and spurred offshoots, such as progressive-rockers Contraction (the only group to issue French and English versions of the same album) and Toubabou's Afro-Québec rock. The first and longest-lasting group was Offenbach, specializing in a rough-hewn blues-rock sound ("Câline de blues"). Two members of this group eventually formed Corbeau.

Since 1985 Québec pop music has begun to rebuild, led by single artists and groups such as The Box, Tchukon, Véronique Belliveau, performance artist Michael Lemieux, Céline Dion, Martine St. Clair and Nuance (the first francophone artist to be nominated for the Juno "Single-of-the-Year"). Lastly, because the list goes on and on, Men Without Hats (Grammy nominees) broke through with the single and LP *Pop Goes The World*. TERRY DAVID MULLIGAN, TOM HARRISON AND JUAN RODRIGUEZ

Reading: M. Melhuish, *Heart of Gold* (1984); Juan Rodriguez, *Profiles in Canadian Music* (1985); R. Yorke, *Axes, Chops & Hot Licks* (1971).

Population The settlement of Canada by Europeans resulted from the agricultural and Industrial Revolution in western Europe and the subsequent expansion of European population that began during the 17th century. The French were among the early explorers of the New World and their establishment of NEW FRANCE was primarily the consequence of their political and military concerns, the search for natural wealth and the Roman Catholic Church's interest in converting the native people. Environmental conditions were harsh and the survival of early settlements depended to a great extent on the continuing flow of traders, soldiers, priests and administrators from France. In 1666 the population of New France was just 3215. As was typical of early settlements, most of the inhabitants were single and male, but increasing numbers of settlers arriving from France ultimately established a population capable of sustaining itself through natural increase. During the next 100 years, birthrates ranged from 50-65 births per 1000 population and produced a sufficient excess of births over deaths for the population to reach 70 000 at about the time that the British had won political control from the French at the end of the SEVEN YEARS' WAR. Rapid population growth continued and the non-French population increased dramatically under the impetus of the migration of British Empire LOYALISTS from the American colonies after the Revolution and increasing IMMIGRATION from Eu-

Population of Canada and Components of Change: Canada, 1851-1986

(Source: Employment and Immigration Canada, *1980 Immigration Statistics;* and Statistics Canada, Vital Statistics annual reports, 1977 to 1987)

Decade	Population Total: (End of Decade)	Natural Increase: Births/Deaths (000s)	Net Immigration (000s)
-1851	2 436 297	–	–
1851-1861	3 229 633	641	152
1861-1871	3 689 257	651	-191
1871-1881	4 324 810	723	- 87
1881-1891	4 833 239	714	-206
1891-1901	5 371 315	718	-180
1901-1911	7 206 643	1 120	716
1911-1921	8 787 949	1 230	351
1921-1931	10 376 786	1 360	229
1931-1941	11 506 655	1 222	- 92
1941-1951	14 009 429[1]	1 972	169
1951-1961	18 238 247	3 148	1 081
1961-1971	21 568 311	2 703	724
1971-1981	24 343 180	1 920	855
1981-1986	25 354 064	–	–

[1] Includes Newfoundland

rope. By 1867 the population was about 3.3 million.

Population growth was alternately stimulated and depressed by recurring fluctuations in economic conditions and immigration. The economy was depressed at Confederation and EMIGRATION consistently exceeded immigration during the last 4 decades of the 19th century. Population would have declined had it not been for the high levels of fertility that still characterized the popu-

lation towards the end of the century. Crude birthrates varied between 45 and 36 births per 1000 population, while death rates declined moderately from 21 to 18 deaths per 1000 during this period.

At the turn of the century, with both fertility and mortality rates declining, high natural increase combined with the heavy immigration of the early 1900s to boost the average annual rate of growth for the country to a high of 3%. Unsettled times followed WWI, culminating in the GREAT DEPRESSION of the 1930s. By 1941 growth rates had declined to 1%, but the long-term decline in fertility was interrupted by the approach of WWII and a period of increasing political and economic activity. During the postwar period, both immigration and birthrates were greatly stimulated by the unexpectedly high level of economic development. Canada's average annual rate of growth reached 2.8% during the BABY BOOM of the late 1940s and the 1950s. By the beginning of the 1960s, a weakening economy and continuing social change brought an end to the unprecedented postwar growth; the consistent decline in birthrates was relatively unaffected by fluctuations in the economy. During the early 1960s, immigration was encouraged by changes in IMMIGRATION POLICY. Longstanding restrictions based on racial and ethnic origins were removed and selection criteria were introduced based on education, occupational skills and LABOUR-FORCE needs, but despite this the average annual growth rate by 1966 had declined to 1.7%. During the 1970s it declined further to 1.3%. Notwithstand-

Selected Measures[1] of Mortality and Fertility: Canada, 1921-1985

(Source: Statistics Canada, Vital Statistics, Annual Reports, 1977 to 1985)

Year	Crude Death Rate	Infant Mortality Rate	Crude Birth Rate	Gross Reproduction Rate
1921	10.6	88.1	29.3	1.712
1931	10.1	84.7	23.2	1.555
1941	10.0	59.7	22.4	1.377
1946	9.4	46.7	27.2	1.640
1951	9.0	38.5	27.2	1.701
1956	8.2	31.9	28.0	1.874
1961	7.7	27.2	26.1	1.868
1966	7.5	23.1	19.4	1.369
1971	7.3	17.5	16.8	1.060
1976	7.3	13.5	15.7	0.887
1981	7.0	9.6	15.3	0.829
1985	7.2	7.9	14.8	0.811

[1] Selected measures of mortality and fertility:
Crude Death Rate: The number of deaths per 1000 population in a given year.
Infant Mortality Rate: The number of deaths to infants under 1 year of age per 1000 live births in a given year.
Crude Birth Rate: The number of live births per 1000 population in a given year.
Gross Reproduction Rate: The average number of daughters that would be born to a woman during her lifetime if she passed through her child-bearing years conforming to the age-specific fertility rates of a given year.

ing worsening national and global economics, the same numbers of immigrants (1.4 million) arrived between 1971 and 1981 as between 1961 and 1971 (only slightly less than the numbers that had arrived during the decade of the baby boom). In 1978 Canada introduced annual global ceilings on admissible numbers of immigrants to achieve better control over the continuing influx of immigrants. These ceilings are now established after consultations with provincial governments.

Canada is one of the 3 main immigrant-receiving nations in the world; its ratio of immigrants to population during the latter half of the 1971-81 decade was one of the highest. From 1976 to 1981, immigration varied between 149 429 and 86 313, averaging about 122 000 annually. In spite of continuing high levels of unemployment in 1982, Canada publicly committed itself to maintaining immigration ceilings of between 135 000 and 145 000 for the 3-year planning period ending in 1984, and raising them in subsequent years as a means of partially offsetting the effects of a declining rate of population growth. However, between 1980 and 1985, immigration declined from 143 133 to 84 273, while pressures to admit increasing numbers of refugees remained high.

Natural Increase and not immigration, however, has been the major factor in the nation's growth for more than 100 years. Since 1871 Canada's population increased by almost 22 million, about 80% of which can be attributed to an excess of births over deaths. As birthrates were declining during this period, the positive contribution by natural increase largely reflected the improvement in the general quality of life and concomitant decline in the death rate. With an annual rate of natural increase below 1.0% since 1971, Canada is characteristic of industrialized and urbanized populations that have experienced the demographic transition from high to low levels of vital rates. While considerably below the global average of 1.7%, the estimated rate of 0.8% for 1985 is about the same as that for the US and Australia, but significantly above those for the western and northern European countries, some of which have already experienced negative rates of natural increase, eg, West Germany and Denmark.

Mortality levels have been declining since the

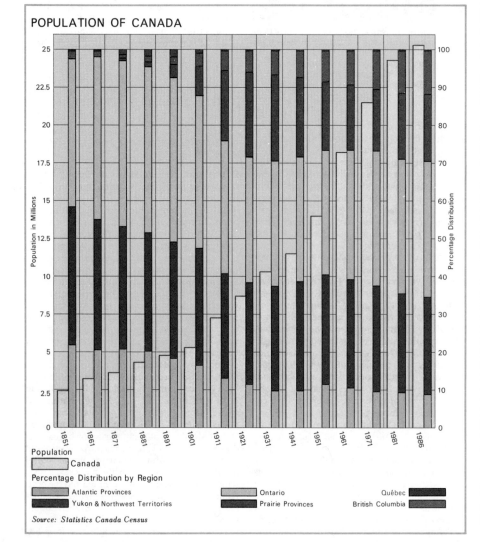

POPULATION OF CANADA

Population
☐ Canada

Percentage Distribution by Region
Atlantic Provinces / Ontario / Québec / Yukon & Northwest Territories / Prairie Provinces / British Columbia

Source: Statistics Canada Census

Selected Population Characteristics:
Canada, 1901-1986
(Source: Statistics Canada, 1971 and 1986
Censuses of Canada; and Dominion Bureau
of Statistics, Censuses of Canada, 1901 to 1961)

Year	Males per 100 Females	Average (Median) Age	Percent under 15 Years	Percent 65 Years and over	Percent Population Foreign-born
1901	105	22.7	34.6	5.0	13.0
1911	113	23.8	33.1	4.5	22.0
1921	106	23.9	34.5	4.7	22.3
1931	107	24.7	31.7	5.5	22.2
1941	105	27.0	27.8	6.7	17.5
1951	102	27.8	30.4	7.7	14.7
1961	102	26.5	34.0	7.6	15.6
1971	100	26.4	29.5	8.1	15.3
1981	98	29.6	22.5	9.8	16.1
1986	97	31.6	21.3	10.7	na*

*na: data not available in 1988.

latter part of the 18th century, but the decline has been more pronounced since 1867. The major gains in life expectancy have been attributed more to improved nutritional levels, personal hygiene and better housing than to medical science or improved medical services. The gradual elimination of infectious and parasitic diseases as major causes of death has significantly increased life expectancy for Canadians. The most dramatic improvements have resulted from reductions in infant mortality rather than gains for the older population, and women have benefited more from these improvements than have men. In 1931 the number of years a person could expect to live at birth under prevailing mortality conditions was 60.0 for males and 62.1 for females. By 1985 life expectancies had reached 72.9 and 79.8 years respectively, reflecting gains of 20% and 27% for males and females respectively. Life expectancy in Canada is very similar to that in the US, but is still exceeded by most of the Scandinavian countries, eg, Norway, Sweden and Iceland which continue to enjoy the highest reported life expectancies of any country circa 1981. The expectation of moderate increases in life expectancies are reflected in projections to 1996 of 75 and 82 years for males and females respectively.

Improvements in living conditions and in the STANDARD OF LIVING have drastically altered the health concerns and medical-care problems of Canadians. The current major causes of death are the degenerative diseases (cancer, cardiovascular diseases), caused by stress and deteriorating environmental conditions. During the 1980s, cardiovascular and heart diseases accounted for almost 33% of all deaths; cancer 25% and infant deaths for only 1.5% (1985).

Fertility Before the 19th century, fertility levels in N America were as high, or higher, than present levels in many of the world's lesser developed countries. As Canada developed and living conditions improved, birthrates declined steadily from their early levels of around 50 births per 1000 population. By the 1920s the crude rate had dropped below 30 and during the 1930s had reached a low of 20 births per 1000 population (1937). WWII revived the economy and reversed the declining trend in birthrates; they reached record highs during the baby boom, of 28.9 in 1947 and again in 1954 before resuming the long-term historical decline beginning in the 1960s. By 1985, Canada's birthrate reached an all-time low of 14.8 births per 1000 population. There is little evidence to indicate that fertility rates will return to replacement levels in Canada during the 1980s.

The significance of declining birthrates for future population growth is more evident in the gross reproduction rate (GRR), which reveals how many female children women may expect to have on the average if they live through their reproductive years experiencing the age-specific fertility rates of a given year. The GRR for Canadian females had dropped from a rate of 1.7 in 1921 to a low of 1.3 in 1937, before increasing to 1.9 during the latter half of the 1950s at the end of the baby-boom years. The rate again dropped sharply and after 1971 the GRR fell below the replacement level reaching 0.98 in 1972. By 1985 the rate had reached 0.81 and women were even less likely than before to produce enough daughters to replace themselves during their lifetime. Continuation of such low fertility levels for an indefinite period would eventually lead to an actual decline in Canada's population, provided there was no significant revival of immigration.

Historically, Canada's birthrates have remained somewhat higher than those of the US, with almost identical patterns of change. N American birthrates have tended to be somewhat higher than those reported for northern and western European countries, but slightly below the average for countries of eastern Europe. In contrast, birthrates for most of the lesser developed regions of the world have been more than twice that of Canada's.

Population Characteristics Relatively greater numbers of young adult men than women immigrated to Canada in the early years. Following the heavy immigration during the first decade of the 20th century, the census of 1911 reported 113 males for every 100 females living in Canada. Since 1921 the ratio of males to females has gradually declined for the country as a whole, reaching parity shortly after the 1971 census. The AGING of the population, with longer life expectancies for females, and the increasing proportion of women among arriving immigrants have continued to erode the sex ratio. In 1981 the sex ratio had reached 98. Five years later, the 1986 census reported only 97 males for every 100 females.

A relative excess of males can still be found in the more rural populations and in the West and North. Alberta's sex ratio as recently as 1986 was 104 to 100, in favour of males. It was much higher in the Yukon and the Northwest Territories where the number of males per 100 females was 110. In contrast, relatively more women can be found in the larger urban centres where they have been attracted by greater employment opportunities. This trend was already noticeable in 1961 when the sex ratio had declined in 7 of the 11 metropolitan areas. The ratio of males per 100 females varies significantly by age group and between rural and urban areas. Sex ratios at birth are consistently about 106 in favour of males, but the relative number of males compared to females gradually declines with increasing age. For the population over 75 years, there were only 60 males per 100 females in 1986 and for those over 85 years, females outnumbered males more than 2 to 1. As recently as 1981, no age group under 80 in the rural population had a sex ratio less than 100, while for urban populations only the age group under 20 years still had more men than women.

Age Composition Canada's population has gradually aged as the importance of immigration has waned and birthrates have declined. By 1951 the average (median) age had increased to 27.8 years before the unprecedented birthrates of the 1950s lowered the median age to 25.6 years in 1966. Between 1976 and 1986, however, the median age of the population increased from 27.8 to 31.6 years. The relative size of the young dependent population (those under 15 years of age) regained its 1901 level of 34% in 1961, before dropping sharply to 21.3% in 1986. During the same period, the percentage of Canada's population 65 years of age and over more than doubled, to 10.7%. Canada's population has shifted from an "early mature" status in 1881, when 4.1% of the population was 65 and over, to, since 1979, an "aged" population, signifying that the proportion of the population that was 65 years of age and over exceeded the 8% criterion established by the UN. As the baby boom generation ages and if levels of fertility remain low, the relative numbers of the latter group will continue to show significant increases.

While the relative size of the young, dependent population was quite similar to that in the US and the northern and western European countries, the proportions of those aged 65 and over for most European countries continues to be somewhat higher, ranging from 14% in Denmark, Norway, France and the UK, to 16% in Sweden. By contrast, the least economically developed countries in the world continue to be characterized by proportions of their populations under 15 years of age and over 65 years close to 50% and 2% respectively.

Native and Foreign-Born Population Variations in immigration and the natural increase of the native-born population have altered the relative size and importance of the native-born and for-

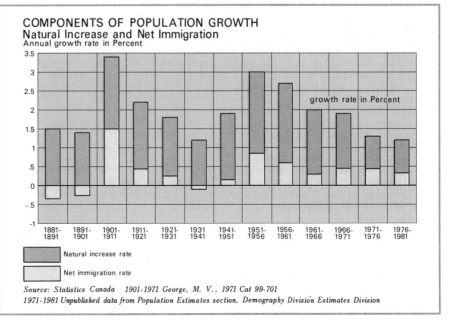

COMPONENTS OF POPULATION GROWTH
Natural Increase and Net Immigration
Annual growth rate in Percent

Source: Statistics Canada   1901-1971 George, M. V., 1971 Cat 99-701
1971-1981 Unpublished data from Population Estimates section, Demography Division Estimates Division

eign-born populations over the years. When colonization by the French first began, the native-born were the native Indians and Inuit, and the foreign-born were the European explorers, traders, military and government personnel, priests, missionaries and settlers. The native Indian population was hard pressed to survive in the face of the European encroachment and by mid-20th century their numbers were estimated to be fewer than they had been when New France was first established. During the interim period, the native-born population was greatly augmented by the children of the European immigrants and tended to grow more rapidly through natural increase than the foreign-born population did through immigration. Because the native Indian population had great difficulty in maintaining their numbers, their long-term survival was seriously threatened. It was not until the 1930s that they began to show consistent increases and by 1971 the combined populations of native Indians and Inuit reached 313 000. During the decade of the 1970s, their population increased by 32%, bringing it to 413 000 by 1981. Accurate enumerations of the native Indian and Inuit populations are still difficult to obtain. Political factors are becoming of equal or greater importance than their general social and physical isolation have been in preventing complete and accurate enumerations in the past. However, there is little question that given their high fertility and general improvement in living conditions, this particular native-born population, unlike the native-born Canadians of European descent, will continue to experience strong growth from natural increase.

Just before Confederation, the foreign-born population accounted for 21% of Canada's total. Emigration during the late 1800s reduced the proportion to 13% in 1901, but the heavy immigration of the early 1900s boosted their relative size to 22% between 1921 and 1931. The native-born population grew more rapidly during the Depression and early war years, but heavy postwar immigration reinforced the numbers of foreign-born in Canada. While birthrates declined after the postwar baby boom, immigration continued to add to the foreign-born population, raising its relative size from 14.7% in 1951 to 16.1% in 1981.

The countries of origin of Canada's foreign born have both established and altered the cultural nature of Canadian society. Its bicultural nature is a consequence of the early settlement by the French and the subsequent acquisition of military and political control by the British, after which most immigrants came from the British Isles, the US and Europe. Between 1881 and 1891, the proportion of immigrants originating in the UK varied between 21% and 37%, while those from the US varied between 46% and 76%. In 1871, 84% of the foreign-born had been born in the UK. As the character of immigration has shifted, particularly after WWII, the proportion dropped to 36% (1971) as immigration from other European countries, notably Germany and Italy, increased.

The main birthplace of those born outside Canada is still Europe, but the proportion born in Europe decreased from 80% in 1971 to 67% in 1981. At the same time, those born in the US declined from 9% to 8%. Reflecting the significant changes in Canada's immigration sources in recent decades, Asian-born immigrants more than tripled in numbers to about 543 000 between 1971 and 1981, increasing their proportion of the foreign born from 5% to 14%. Those born in Latin America and the Caribbean increased from 3% to 7%, while those born in other countries increased from just under 3% to 4% in 1981. Regardless of the future levels of immigration to Canada, world

conditions will continue to maintain pressure for immigration from non-European sources. Canada's population, particularly in its more highly urbanized areas, can be expected to increase in its ethnic and cultural diversity as it responds to these pressures in the future. It is estimated that Canada reached a population of 25 million on 1 Jan 1984. On 3 June 1986, Canada's population was enumerated to be 25 354 064, an increase of 4.2% over the 1981 census total.

WARREN E. KALBACH

Reading: Warren E. Kalbach and W.W. McVey Jr, *Demographic Bases of Canadian Society* (1979).

Population Genetics, area of GENETICS that studies the distribution of genes (the units of genetic inheritance) and genotypes (the genetic complement at one or more loci), and the mechanisms determining genetic variability within a population. A population is a group of individuals among whom marriages potentially can occur; thus, French Canadians, Japanese Canadians and American Indian tribes constitute populations. Large populations are usually subdivided into smaller groups constituting geographic, religious or ethnic units. In addition to contributing to our understanding of EVOLUTION, population genetics theory can be applied to evaluating the long-term consequences of genetic screening programs and GENETIC COUNSELLING. Genetic variability is determined by the forces of evolution: mutation, natural selection, random genetic drift and migration.

Mutation is a spontaneous or induced alteration in the information encoded in a cell's genetic material. When a chromosome replicates itself many kinds of errors can occur: substitution, addition, deletion or transposition of DNA nucleotides. Mutation is the ultimate source of genetic variation, although most newly arising mutations when made homozygous (the situation arising when each parent provides identical alleles, ie, alternate forms of a gene at a locus on a particular chromosome) are harmful in normal environments. The harmful allele is kept at a very low frequency by a balance between recurrent mutation and loss by selection. Increased mutation rates, caused by radiation or chemical mutagens, may have serious long-term consequences for a population.

Natural Selection An individual's "fitness" is his or her ability to survive to maturity and to reproduce. Should an environmental change favour the survival and reproduction of an individual carrying a rare allele (perhaps a new mutation), then that individual will contribute more offspring to the next generation. Over time, the frequency of that particular allele will increase in the population. This process is the principle of natural selection. One way that alleles can be maintained in a population at intermediate frequencies — a polymorphism — is by selection for heterozygotes (individuals carrying 2 different alleles at the same locus on the chromosome pair).

The structure of a population interacts with the forces of evolution to determine the distribution of genotypes within it. Included in the effects of population structure are deviations from random mating resulting from, for example, marriages among relatives or subdivision of the population into smaller groups. The effect of inbreeding is to increase the chance that the offspring inherit 2 identical copies of a particular gene that was present in a common ancestor. Thus, inbreeding increases the chance of appearance of a rare recessive trait if it is present in the population.

Random Genetic Drift and Migration Chance genetic fluctuations, called random genetic drift, result in dispersion of gene frequencies of small, genetic isolates as time goes on. The effect is greater the smaller the population size. Migration among

subpopulations counteracts the genetic differentiation caused by genetic drift. Genetic isolates are usually founded by a small number of ancestors and thus some alleles will be lost by chance while others are retained. If a founder happens to be a carrier of an otherwise rare allele and has many descendants, the allele — be it harmful or not — may reach an appreciable frequency as a result of genetic drift. Endogamous populations that have apparently elevated frequencies of one or more recessive GENETIC DISEASES have been studied in various regions of the world. For example, hereditary tyrosinemia, an inborn error of metabolism, has been studied in French Canadians in Québec. It is important to recognize that, while a particular inherited disorder may be elevated in frequency, other inherited disorders may be relatively less common and many will be absent.

One component of human genetic variation is expressed as a hereditary disorder of genetic susceptibility to a disease induced by environmental agents. In BC it has been estimated that approximately 6% of individuals will suffer during their lifetime from a disability or handicap caused by a single gene disorder, chromosomal aberration, other congenital malformation or multifactorial disorder. Ethnic variability in genetic disease has been documented. Thalassemia (often fatal anemia associated with enlargement of the liver and alteration in bones and skin) is relatively more frequent, and cystic fibrosis is relatively less frequent in Mediterranean peoples compared to other Caucasian populations. Tay-Sachs disease, phenylketonuria and albinism are inborn errors of metabolism that are infrequently encountered. Tay-Sachs disease is relatively more common and phenylketonuria less common in the Ashkenazi Jewish population. Albinism is relatively more frequent in some American Indian groups.

The total amount of genetic variation in humans is not known exactly but it must be large. Surveys of genetic variation of DNA, enzymes and blood-group markers suggest that all human beings — with the exception of identical siblings — are genetically unique. Furthermore, most human genetic diversity occurs among individuals comprising a "racial" group (the visible variations that have typically been used to define "race" make up a rather small proportion). Anthropologists have attempted to establish the affinities between populations by analysing differences in gene frequencies. N American native groups can be clustered on the basis of genetic distances. The patterns of genetic similarity correlate to varying degrees with linguistic and cultural relationships. However, there is still controversy over the evolutionary interpretation of genetic similarities and differences among groups of descendants of the aboriginal populations. KENNETH MORGAN

Populism now ordinarily refers to political movements and ideas based on a strong faith in the ability of ordinary people to act together politically, despite potentially serious class, racial, regional or religious cleavages. Populist movements generally support DECENTRALIZATION of economic and political power, believing that such power should be spread among individuals or among regional and local governments. Politicians may be described as populists, although their party may not be a populist movement. René LÉVESQUE, former leader of the PARTI QUÉBÉCOIS, former mayor of Toronto John Sewell, and former PM John DIEFENBAKER have all been labelled populists. "Populists" were originally supporters of the Peoples' Party in the US, which enjoyed considerable electoral success during the agrarian revolt of the 1890s. In Canada populist parties developed during the depression after WWI, when farm organizations entered federal and provincial politics. The PROGRESSIVE PARTY (1920) under T.A. CRERAR, a Manitoba leader, became the second-largest party in the House of Commons after the 1921 election but refused to form the Opposition. The populist UNITED FARMERS OF ALBERTA (UFA), under Henry Wise WOOD, and the UNITED FARMERS OF MANITOBA (UFM) formed governments in their respective provinces.

North American agrarian populist movements have traditionally polarized into left and right; in Canada the divergent CO-OPERATIVE COMMONWEALTH FEDERATION (CCF) and SOCIAL CREDIT were both formed during the 1930s. Left-wing populists usually attempted to organize an explicit farm-labour alliance. They criticized corporate capitalism, the railways, mining companies, manufacturing trusts and financial institutions. They demanded that government generate countervailing power by nationalization if necessary, and undertake extensive welfare-state reforms. Left-wing populism typically emerged as an extension of co-operative societies and frequently had strong links to congregationally based Protestant sects. Right-wing populists typically attacked both the power of banks to limit the money supply and raise the price of credit, and "big government." They were less interested in democracy and more authoritarian, and their religious ties were often with evangelical Christianity.

Social Credit, founded by William ABERHART, a charismatic radio evangelist, inherited agrarian group support from the UFA, which had allied itself with the socialist CCF. Aberhart expounded the British theory that the GREAT DEPRESSION could be cured by providing people with an appropriate increase in purchasing power: social credit. In 1935 Aberhart became premier of Alberta. In 1962 Social Credit elected 26 MPs in Québec under Réal CAOUETTE, but no strong national consensus emerged. The CCF, in its Regina Manifesto, committed itself to public ownership of industry, and to government planning. In the 1940s it enjoyed widespread national support. The Liberal government adopted CCF programs supporting the expansion of the welfare state and the maintenance of full employment. In Saskatchewan, under T.C. DOUGLAS, the CCF came to power (1944) and pioneered many social-insurance programs that later became national and launched numerous CROWN CORPORATIONS in new industries. After allying with the Canadian Labour Congress in 1961, the CCF was renamed the NEW DEMOCRATIC PARTY.

The popularity of populist movements has varied directly with the level of effort ordinary people make in realizing political reforms. When high, such movements flourish; when low, they wilt. Also, the administrative competence of many populist governments has been poor, because pure populist movements have lacked access to an administrative elite. The administratively competent (such as the CCF in Saskatchewan) were hybrid alliances of a populist movement with a cadre of professional administrators. In search of a more stable existence, leaders of populist movements may transform them into political parties representing well-organized interest groups. Social Credit in Alberta achieved such a relationship with the major oil companies that invested heavily in the province following oil discoveries at Leduc in 1947; the CCF did likewise with organized labour after 1961. Ultimately the importance of populism is to insist that "democracy matters": that people can play a far more active role in government than the passive one of choosing among alternative rulers at infrequent elections. JOHN RICHARDS

Porcupine Of the world's 23 species, only the N American porcupine (*Erethizon dorsatum*) occurs

The North American porcupine is Canada's second-largest rodent (*artwork by Claire Tremblay*).

in Canada, throughout mainland forests and thickets. Canada's second-largest RODENT (up to 18 kg and 103 cm long, including a 30 cm tail) has a stout, black-and-white body bearing 30 000 sharp, slightly barbed quills (up to 8 cm long) on upperparts and tail. When cornered, a porcupine erects its quills and lashes its tail. Quills are easily dislodged from the porcupine's skin, but cannot be thrown. Mammal predators (eg, fishers, wolverines) avoid them by flipping the porcupine over to attack unprotected underparts. Slow-moving porcupines are vulnerable to automobiles and fires. One young is born 7 months after fall mating. It soon walks and climbs, is weaned within 10 days, and leaves its mother by fall. Porcupines are usually nocturnal and do not hibernate. Usually solitary, they sometimes share good dens or feeding areas. They eat bark, buds, and the leaves and twigs of trees and other plants. Food, cut by 4 chisel-shaped incisors, is ground by 16 ridged cheek-teeth. Some trees are damaged but extensive harm to forests is rare. Porcupines gnaw tools and other salty objects, wooden buildings and may damage corn or alfalfa.
DONALD A. SMITH

Porkeater [French, *mangeur de lard*], in the parlance of the FUR TRADE, was a derogatory term for a VOYAGEUR hired by the NORTH WEST COMPANY who made only the short run between Montréal and GRAND PORTAGE (and not into the North-West) and whose staple diet was pork, unlike the WINTERER, or *homme du nord*, who made do with fish and PEMMICAN. Later it came to refer to any voyageur who was a newcomer to the North-West.
JOHN ROBERT COLOMBO

Pornography For most of Western cultural history, pornography has been defined loosely as "material depicting erotic behaviour and intended to cause sexual excitement." The word derives from the Greek *pornographos*, meaning "the writing of prostitutes." Sexually explicit materials have likely circulated in one form or another – sketches, photos, poetry, novels, lantern slides – since the mid-19th century in Canada. In the last half of the 20th century the industry aimed at the distribution and sale of pornography has experienced a remarkable boom. In 1972, 8 so-called "girlie" magazines were available on Canadian newsstands; by 1982, 32 such magazines were marketed. In this same decade in N America, the pornography industry in magazine, film and video form grew

from a $5 million to an estimated $7-billion-a-year enterprise. The rapid growth in COMMUNICATIONS TECHNOLOGY has helped create new vehicles for pornography. The development of video technology, in particular, has made it possible for consumers of pornography to circumvent public venues (eg, commercial movie theatres) and to lease video tapes and equipment for home use. Images depicting graphic sex have proliferated in advertising and rock video.

The traditional definition of pornography generally embraced all erotic materials and graphic depictions of sex. The definitions of these matters changed in a community over time and have been used to ban materials that have later been deemed acceptable. Recently, concern has grown as mainstream pornography has become more aggressive and preoccupied with coercion and violence in conjunction with sexuality. There are currently several different approaches to defining pornography. One argues that a clear definition of pornography is not possible, that what is considered pornographic is a matter of taste and that one person's erotica is another person's pornography. From another perspective, *Playboy* is considered to be on one end of a continuum while child pornography, bestiality and sex fused with violence are on the other end; the difference between the materials and hence of their deleterious effects is considered a matter of degree. According to this view it is meaningless to lump an advertisement for designer jeans in the same category as sadomasochistic depictions. A third perspective, held by most feminists, defines pornography as the images of overt domination and coercion of women. According to this view images in which women are consistently depicted as victims encourage or at least condone actual violence against women.

The first organized Canadian protest on these grounds occurred in 1977 in Toronto, when a group of women protested against the film *Snuff*, which purported to show the actual murder of a woman. In 1982 in BC a group of Vancouver women (Women Against Pornography) mounted a determined protest campaign when Red Hot Video, a chain that leased "hard-core" videos, gang-rape tapes and other violent pornography, opened 15 new outlets in 3 months. In 1983 numerous women across Canada angrily opposed the plans of a Canadian pay-television network to broadcast programs developed by Playboy. The proliferation of pornography has prompted the founding of at least one national group, the Canadian Coalition Against Media Pornography.

While more recently the demands for legislation directed against pornography have focused on the premise that pornography is linked to sexual crimes, Canadian obscenity legislation was originally framed on the assumption that pornography corrupts morals. Section 159 of the Criminal Code provides that it is an offence to distribute materials "a dominant characteristic of which is the undue exploitation of sex, or of sex and any one of the following subjects, namely crime, horror, cruelty and violence." It has been argued that under this provision Canadian courts have paid more attention to sexually explicit materials than to the more threatening violent materials that critics see as dangerous to the mental health and physical safety of women. As a result, the Liberal government commissioned (1983-84) a study – the so-called Fraser Committee – to study this and other related issues and, in addition, introduced a Bill in the House of Commons (1984) which, among other things, redefined obscenity in such a way as to avoid the existing linkage between sex and violence, thus allowing violent or degrading materials, in themselves, to be regarded as obscene. The change in the federal government in Sept 1984 and anticipation of the Fraser Report late in 1984 has stalled actions on the bill.

In 1987, the PC federal government established its legal strategy by tabling Bill C54 which sought to replace the offence of OBSCENITY with the offence of pornography; "undue exploitation" was removed from the law; and pornography was defined as the possession or distribution of depictions of sexual acts, most of which were described in the language of degradation and pain. However, included in the list of proscribed depictions were other kinds of activities such as oral and anal intercourse, and lactation and menstruation in a sexual context. The breadth of the law sparked intense debate and criticism and, as of early 1988, representatives of the Dept of Justice were accepting suggestions for changes.

The discussion of pornography and how to regulate it in a democracy invariably raises difficult questions. Those who demand legislation to eradicate pornography make the point that the objectification of women for commercial purposes is attitudinally harmful to society, but it is very difficult under this premise to distinguish the various degrees of objectification, and therefore degrees of harm. A second, and critical, problem is that the abolition of pornography is a form of CENSORSHIP, which must be balanced against the constitutionally protected rights of free expression. From the feminist perspective, these individual rights of free expression must be balanced against the human rights of those they believe are victimized by pornography, as well as the societal effects of such victimization. SUSAN COLE

Porsild, Alf Erling, botanist, northern explorer (b at Copenhagen, Denmark 17 Jan 1901; d at Vienna, Austria 13 Nov 1977). Assistant botanist 1922-25 at the Danish Biological Station, Greenland, he was hired (with his brother Robert) by the Canadian government in 1926 to investigate reindeer grazing in arctic Canada and Alaska. In 1936 he was appointed acting chief botanist of the National Museum of Canada. He served as Canadian consul to Greenland 1940-43. Returning to the National Museum, he was chief botanist 1946-67. He was the author of over 100 publications and his botanical collections included about 80 new species. W.J. CODY

Port Alberni, BC, City, pop 18 241 (1986c), 19 892 (1981c), inc 1912, amalgamated with Alberni 1967, is located on central VANCOUVER I, 195 km N of Victoria, at the head of Alberni Inlet, a deep inlet that almost divides the island from the west. The Alberni inlet was named after Don Pedro Alberni, the Spanish officer in command of the Nootka garrison in 1791 during the Spanish occupation. HBC employees led by Adam Horne started fur trading with the region's Indians, the Coast SALISH and NOOTKA 1850-59. The English shipping firm Anderson and Co erected a sawmill 1860 in Port Alberni as the inlet offered easy access. Pioneers came to the area to farm and mine and many eventually turned to logging.

Lumbering has always been Port Alberni's most important industry. It has the largest forestry complex on the island and one of the largest in the world, and also benefits from the manufacture and servicing of forestry-related equipment. The lumber industry has helped make Port Alberni the third-largest port by volume in BC. Fishing and mining are important.

Port Alberni has a marina in the heart of the city, 2 golf courses, the Echo Centre (library, museum, pool and meeting complex), the Rollin Art Centre and the J.V. Clyne Bird Sanctuary. Della Falls are within hiking distance. In the area are Mt Arrowsmith and 2 large freshwater lakes, Sproat and Great Central. ALAN F.J. ARTIBISE

Port Alberni, located at the head of a deep inlet on Vancouver I (*courtesy Colour Library Books*).

Port au Choix, Nfld, Town, pop 1291 (1986c), 1311 (1981c), inc 1966, is located on the W side of the Great Northern Pen. Its name derives from the Basque *Portuichoa,* "little harbour." Two major archaeological sites have been investigated at Port au Choix. The first, excavated during the 1950s, is a large site of DORSET Eskimo culture dating between about 200 and 600 AD. It consists of a group of rectangular winter house remains and outdoor hearths suggesting year-round use. The many tools, weapons, ornaments and other objects were used to define "Newfoundland Dorset Culture," now thought to represent a variant of the more general Middle Dorset period in Newfoundland and Labrador. The second Port au Choix site was a large cemetery from which the Maritime ARCHAIC tradition was defined. The tools, weapons, religious and other objects discovered, along with more than 100 skeletal remains, indicate a people whose way of life was attuned to the coastal resources of Newfoundland between 2000 and 1200 BC. Port au Choix is the location of a national historic park commemorating aboriginal occupations of the site. In recorded history, Port au Choix was a major BASQUE fishing station in the 1500s and an important French station on the FRENCH SHORE from the 18th to the late 19th century, when the site was settled by Newfoundland and English fishermen who vigorously asserted their right to settlement on this disputed coast. The town is a fish-processing and fish-collecting centre that serves as a regional services centre. JANET E.M. PITT, ROBERT D. PITT AND JAMES A. TUCK

Reading: James A. Tuck, *Ancient People of Port au Choix* (1976).

Port au Port Peninsula is a roughly triangular peninsula with 130 km of rocky coastline but no harbours, joined to SW Newfoundland W of STEPHENVILLE. It was named *Ophor portu,* "port of rest," by the BASQUES. An eroded highland with hills to the S and sloping lowlands on the N side, the once heavily forested peninsula is bounded by Port au Port Bay, the Gulf of ST LAWRENCE and St George's Bay, and terminates in Cape St George in the S and fingerlike Long Point 50 km N. Scattered settlement occurred around the peninsula's shores by the mid-1800s, though it continued as part of the FRENCH SHORE until 1904. The population represents a more varied ethnic and linguistic mix than is commonly found in Newfoundland, with the highest proportion of French-speaking settlement on the island (15%). Since 1971 the peninsula has been designated insular Newfoundland's only bilingual district. The economy has been based on fishing, woodcutting and limestone mining (c1900-60) at Aguathuna. From 1940 to 1966, many people in the peninsula's more than 20 small communities were employed at the US military base in Stephenville. JANET E.M. PITT

Port Colborne, Ont, City, pop 18 281 (1986c), 19 225 (1981c), inc 1966, located on Lk ERIE at

the S port of entry to the WELLAND CANAL. The settlement was founded 1833 with the construction of the canal, and changed as the waterway was enlarged. The largest lock on the canal is located here; at 421 m it is one of the longest in the world. The town also benefited from its location on the Welland Ry, and the Buffalo and Lake Huron (now CN) Ry. Industries associated with the canal include servicing, flour mills, repair and breakup of vessels, lake fishing, marinas and limestone quarrying. The city has an important nickel refinery. The harbour is man-made, and some intensive agriculture occupies reclaimed marshland.   JOHN N. JACKSON

Port Coquitlam, BC, City, pop 29 115 (1986c), 27 535 (1981c), inc 1913, is located on the Pitt and Fraser rivers, 27 km E of VANCOUVER, of which it is a satellite. It is bounded on the N and W by the Dist of Coquitlam. The name is from the Coquitlam (meaning "small red salmon") Indians who originally settled at the mouth of the Coquitlam R, known for its abundant fish. The Canadian Pacific Ry end of rail was at PORT MOODY to the W; an industrial area around the CPR's Pacific Coast Terminal became the city of Port Coquitlam. WWI cut short the hope of extensive trade after the opening of the Panama Canal. Prior to and during WWII, most of the work force was employed in railways, but after WWII, metal, rubber and iron-casting industries, TUNGSTEN refining, boat building and nearby gravel operations were established and the population grew to 3200 in 1951, 8100 in 1961 and 19 500 by 1971. The city has encouraged industrial and commercial development in recent years, devoting 125 ha to industrial use, with a further 120 ha held in reserve. Much land in the surrounding district is devoted to dairy, poultry and fruit farming.
                        ALAN F.J. ARTIBISE

Port Dover, Ont, Town, inc 1954, located on Lk ERIE at the mouth of the Lynn R, 60 km from Hamilton. A Neutral village was originally on the site. Jesuit priests François DOLLIER DE CASSON and René de Galinée landed here 1669 and claimed the land around Lk Erie for French King Louis XIV. In 1804 a gristmill was built and a small hamlet developed, named after Dover, Eng. This was destroyed by invading American troops during the WAR OF 1812, but the village recovered and developed as an agricultural centre and lake port. Blessed with a good harbour, it was home port to a large commercial fishing fleet. In 1974 it was amalgamated with several other communities to create the city of NANTICOKE.   DANIEL FRANCIS

Port Edward, BC, Village, pop 704 (1986c), located near PRINCE RUPERT on BC's northern mainland coast 350 km N of Vancouver, at the mouth of the Skeena R. The townsite was laid out in 1908 during the railway construction boom prior to WWI. Speculators hoped the new community would become the railway terminus but that honour fell to nearby Prince Rupert. The village was named Port Edward after King Edward VII. The first fish cannery had been built there as early as 1889 and eventually the village became a major fish canning centre. After WWII the village declined and the canneries gradually closed, with the last shutting down in 1983. The 1889 cannery complex has been designated a heritage site.
                        JOHN STEWART

Port Hardy, BC, District Municipality, pop 5389 (1986c), 5075 (1981c), area 3965 ha, inc 1966, is located on the NE coast of Vancouver I, 390 km by road N of Nanaimo. Its harbour is the largest and most sheltered on the north island. The economy is based on the nearby Island Copper Mine, logging, fishing and a cannery. Tourism has become a growing industry since completion of the Island

Hwy and ferry service to Prince Rupert in the late 1970s.   ALAN F.J. ARTIBISE

Port Hawkesbury, NS, Town, pop 3869 (1986c), inc 1889, is located on the eastern side of the Strait of Canso. The town gained Canadawide recognition in the 1960s as the planned showcase for large-scale industrial development. Federal and provincial funds were intended to transform and modernize the Canso area. The ice-free and deep-water facilities were ideal and had attracted French, New England and other fishing interests centuries earlier. Some farming and a local forest industry supported the livelihood of the dominant Scottish population. As an early 19th-century ferry terminus and later a railway centre, the town suffered the loss of these activities from the building of the Canso Causeway in the mid-1950s at nearby Port Hastings. A pulp mill was built in 1960 at nearby Point Tupper relieving unemployment. Subsequent construction of an oil refinery created a boom-town atmosphere but planned economic diversification failed to materialize, and today the refinery stands silent.
                        L.D. McCANN

Port Hood, NS, UP, pop 710 (1986c), 701 (1981c), is located on NORTHUMBERLAND STR on Cape Breton I, 30 km SW of Inverness. It was named *Ragweamkek* ("sandbar") by the Micmac, Juste-au-Corps by the French and Port Barrington before 1775, when Samuel Hood, later a viscount, was honoured. The French built vessels here for their Newfoundland trade and quarried stone for LOUISBOURG and forts in the French West Indies. Early French settlers reported coal deposits, but these have been mined with disappointing results. The area prospered 1850-71 with the fishery, but declined following the expiration of a treaty with the US. Federal government programs in the 1960s have helped the industry redevelop.   JANICE MILTON

Port Hope, Ont, Town, pop 10 281 (1986c), 9992 (1981c), inc 1834, located on Lk Ontario at mouth of the Ganaraska R, 60 km E of Toronto. The site originally was an Indian village named Cochingomink. It was a fur-trade post from 1778, and was named for a time Smith's Creek after Peter Smith, a trader. In 1817 citizens chose the name Port Hope, for Col Henry Hope, former lt-gov. Long a manufacturing and regional commercial centre, its main street is one of the best preserved from late 19th-century Ontario. It is now a centre for uranium refining and the manufacture of machinery, tools, plastics and rubber. Trinity College School, fd 1865, is one of the oldest private schools for boys in Canada.
                        K.L. MORRISON

Port Moody, BC, City, pop 15 754 (1986c), 14 917 (1981c), inc 1913, lies at the head of Burrard Inlet, 20 km E of Vancouver. Port Moody's foreshore contains abundant evidence of pre-European occupation by the Coast Salishan peoples. It was named in 1859 after Richard Clement MOODY, who came to BC as a colonel with the Royal Engineers. The townsite originally constituted crown grants to 2 sappers of the Royal Engineers. A land boom began when the first steel arrived for construction of the CPR on 12 Mar 1883. In 1879 Port Moody had been officially named western terminus of the CPR. The first passenger train to reach the Pacific from Montréal arrived 4 July 1886, marking the first transcontinental crossing of a passenger train.

Port Moody was the link to the Far East silk trade and many of the famous square riggers were early visitors. From the early days to about 1950 lumbering was the main industry; in recent years, however, it has declined. Other industries operating in the city include a major oil refinery, a steel-

The arrival of the first regular passenger train at Port Moody, noon, 4 July 1886 (*courtesy Canadian Pacific Corporate Archives*).

pipe mill, furniture, electronics and chemical plants, a winery and a house-trailer factory. The most significant recent development (1960s) has been the advent of deep-sea dockage, equipped with highly automated bulk-loading facilities.

Coal, fertilizer, ore and woodchips are exported through these facilities. Large oceangoing ships are able to reach Port Moody via Vancouver Harbour.

Port Refuge is a small bay on the S coast of Grinnell Pen, DEVON I, in the high Arctic. It was named by Sir Edward Belcher in 1853, when it provided shelter from moving ice to his expedition in search of Sir John FRANKLIN. Archaeology has shown that this bay has been occupied sporadically over the past 4000 years. Four distinct Paleoeskimo occupations between about 2000 BC and 1000 AD have been recognized, as well as a THULE-culture Inuit occupation of about 1200-1400 AD. Prehistoric hunters were attracted to this area by the presence of an offshore polynia, where currents maintained open water for most or all of the year and which supported a concentration of sea mammals. The area is of interest to ARCHAEOLOGY since most of the prehistoric occupations of the High Arctic islands are represented at sites on the beach that surround Port Refuge. *See also* PREHISTORY.   ROBERT McGHEE

Port-Royal (near ANNAPOLIS ROYAL, NS), est in summer 1605 on the N shore of the Annapolis Basin near the mouth of the Annapolis R by a French colonizing expedition led by Pierre du Gua de MONTS and Samuel de CHAMPLAIN. De Monts hoped that the site would prove more congenial than the ST CROIX RIVER where his men had spent a disastrous winter in 1604-05. The *habitation* consisted of buildings grouped around a central courtyard. The garden became the first European experimental seed plot in N America. During the winter of 1606-07 Champlain organized the ORDRE DE BON TEMPS, the first social club in N America, and it was here that the first theatre event in Canadian history took place in 1606 – Marc LESCARBOT's *Le Théâtre de Neptune en la Nouvelle-France*. Hopes for a prosperous colony were disappointed, however, and the site was abandoned in the summer of 1607.

The colony was re-established in 1610 by one of the original colonists, BIENCOURT DE POUTRINCOURT, but the *habitation* was destroyed 3 years later by English freebooter Samuel Argall. In 1628 Sir William Alexander, eldest son of Sir William Alexander, Earl of Stirling, established a Scottish colony there, but in 1632 following the Treaty of Saint-Germain-en-Laye, the French repossessed the area. Although the buildings were rudimentary, Port-Royal remained the earliest European settlement of any permanence in N America N of St Augustine, Florida. The first dikes were built on the marshes before mid-century and the concentration of troops and administration around the fort was the only compact village in ACADIA. The farmers lived in relative poverty, compared to elsewhere in Acadia, though they

Champlain's drawing of the habitation of Port-Royal, from *Les Voyages*, 1613 (*courtesy National Library of Canada/Rare Book Division*).

developed small orchards and were able to provide cattle, sheep and wheat for export to the fortress of LOUISBOURG. When retaken by the English in 1654, Port-Royal had a population of about 200; at the time of the CONQUEST (1759-60) it was about 350. In 1938-39 the federal government reconstructed the *habitation* and in 1940 created Port-Royal Habitation National Historic Park. *See also* HISTORIC SITE. ROBERT ALLEN

Portage, a way by land around an interruption in a water route. Until the early 19th century most inhabitants of what is now Canada travelled mainly by water. Alexander MACKENZIE and Simon FRASER demonstrated that it is possible, by portaging 100 times, to canoe from the St Lawrence to the Arctic or Pacific oceans.

The first trails around waterfalls and rapids were often made by moose. Then Indians used the same paths, carrying their marvellously light birchbark CANOES. The organized FUR TRADE required the transport of heavy goods. VOYAGEURS were expected to hoist 2 packs (*pièces*), each weighing about 41 kg. The first was slung on the back with a TUMPLINE across the forehead and the second was placed on top. It was fatiguing work, usually done at a slow jog to reduce the strain on the back. On a long portage, the voyageurs would dump loads at *poses* every kilometre or so and go back for more loads. Two or 4 voyageurs would combine to carry the North or Montréal canoes, and when heavy YORK BOATS came into widespread use in the 1820s, portages were often equipped with rollers.

Paul Kane's *White Mud Portage, Winnipeg River* (*c*1851-56), shows an Indian brigade portaging rapids on the Winnipeg R (*courtesy National Gallery of Canada*).

Packhorses were used on the trail to Ft Assiniboine and across the Athabasca Pass. Oxcarts were needed for the heavier freight on PORTAGE LA LOCHE and at Ft Smith. In eastern Canada, canals and roads improved and supplemented water routes. At Niagara and between Montréal and the Richelieu R, early "portage railways" were a partial answer to transport needs (*see* RAILWAY HISTORY). The GRAND TRUNK RAILWAY in the 1850s and the CANADIAN PACIFIC RAILWAY in the 1880s marked the shift to continuous land transport across southern Canada. C.S. MACKINNON

Portage La Loche (Methye Portage), in present-day northern Saskatchewan, was the longest PORTAGE (20 km) in the regular FUR TRADE, traversing the height of land between the Hudson Bay watershed and the Arctic watershed. It lies between Lac La Loche (the top of the CHURCHILL R system) on the SE and the CLEARWATER R (which flows into the Athabasca R) on the NW. *Methy(e)* is Cree for burbot (*see* COD); after long use, this name was gradually supplanted by the French term for the same fish, *loche* (or *lotte*). Peter POND explored this traditional Indian route in 1778, and soon NOR'WESTERS were portaging canoes and outfits into the rich Athabasca area. The system was later reorganized by the HUDSON'S BAY COMPANY: in 1823 the Athabasca brigade left its YORK BOATS at the NW end of the portage, carried the fur packs across and embarked in other boats which were waiting for them at the SE end. In 1826 the more distant Mackenzie R brigade simply exchanged furs for supplies with the La Loche brigade coming from the SE. In the early years local Indians were hired to help portage the heavy loads. By the 1850s, packhorses and ox-carts had come into use, and over 100 tonnes could be portaged annually. After 1886, this route was displaced by the ATHABASCA LANDING TRAIL, which had been developing since 1875. C.S. MACKINNON

Portage la Prairie, Man, City, pop 7233 (1986c), 13 086 (1981c), inc 1907, situated 85 km W of WINNIPEG, is an important regional service centre for the flat but highly fertile soils of the surrounding Portage Plains. Fort La Reine was built in the vicinity by LA VÉRENDRYE in 1738, but voyageurs gave the locality its name. After 1794 both the NWC and HBC maintained trading posts at the portage, but permanent white settlement began only after 1851, when the Reverend Cockran established a mission there. In 1867-68 the still tiny settlement became the capital of Thomas Spence's short-lived "colony" of Manitobah. After the Pacific Railway reached there in 1880, the population grew rapidly, and the town was incorporated. Since then, Portage la Prairie has weath-

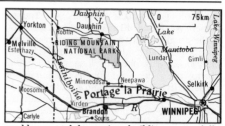

ered boom and depression, building successfully on its accessibility and exceptional agricultural resource base to become one of the most prosperous communities in Manitoba.

Food-processing industries are a mainstay of the economy. Along with handling the district's traditional grain and field crops, Portage la Prairie industries now process such diverse products as mushrooms, soups and frozen foods. There are also large cold-storage facilities, as well as the Manitoba Research Council's Food Products Development Centre. Location on the TRANS-CANADA HWY and the CPR and CNR main lines has attracted a variety of nonfood-related businesses to the city's modern industrial park. Important government-operated facilities include the Canadian Forces Base nearby. H. JOHN SELWOOD

Porter, John Arthur, sociologist (b at Vancouver 12 Nov 1921; d at Ottawa 15 June 1979). Regarded by many as Canada's leading sociologist, he published his most important work, *The* VERTICAL MOSAIC, in 1965. Porter's chief concerns were equality of opportunity and the exercise of power by bureaucratic, economic and political elites in Canada. He had a profound influence on students, some of whom have become leading social scientists and carry on his work. A graduate of London School of Economics, Porter spent most of his scholarly career at Carleton U where he was teacher, department chairman, dean and academic vice-president. Porter was also visiting professor at Harvard and U of T. Shortly before his death he put together what he regarded as his 10 most significant essays in a volume entitled *The Measure of Canadian Society: Education, Equality, and Opportunity* (1979). FRANK G. VALLEE

Ports and Harbours Harbour administration in Canada is the responsibility of the federal Dept of Transport. Small-craft harbour facilities used exclusively for the fishing industry and recreational boating are generally the responsibility of the Dept of Fisheries and Oceans. Some marinas are the responsibility of the Dept of Indian Affairs and Northern Development, or the provinces, municipalities or private owners.

There are 3 categories of FERRY terminals: international and interprovincial terminals under departmental jurisdiction, and private ferry terminals. All commercial cargo-handling harbours fall into the following categories:

Ports Canada Ports Ports Canada is a federal CROWN CORPORATION reporting to Parliament through the minister of transport. The Canada Ports Corporation Act, proclaimed 24 Feb 1983, changed the name of the organization from National Harbours Board to Ports Canada (officially the Canada Ports Corporation), and established the corporation's responsibility for promoting domestic and international trade through Canadian ports. The 15 ports administered under this Act are generally large, multipurpose ports which provide a full range of competitively priced ships' services, berthage facilities and cargo handling and protection. Nine other large ports are operated semi-autonomously by harbour commissions under the supervision of the Canadian Marine Transportation Administration (CMTA).

Half of Canada's waterborne trade passes

Aerial photograph of Prince Rupert harbour. As the terminus for the Grand Trunk Pacific Ry, it was hoped that the port would rival Vancouver. Recent facilities have been built to handle coal and wheat (*courtesy Prince Rupert Port Corporation*).

through Ports Canada ports, making them vital links in the overall TRANSPORTATION system. These ports frequently act as landlords, leasing property and facilities to the private sector, including stevedoring firms, shipping companies and terminal operators. Ports Canada personnel direct navigation within the harbour limits, administer and collect tariffs and manage property. Ports Canada also provides police and security forces for the protection of cargo and personnel and operates specialized facilities, such as GRAIN ELEVATORS, terminal facilities and in-port railway systems.

The new Act gives the board powers to establish local port corporations at any of the Ports Canada ports which meet the criteria of national and regional significance, local interest and financial viability. Local corporations have their own boards of directors and manage and operate their ports with a high degree of autonomy. Ports Canada is responsible only for ensuring that they meet federal government transportation objectives and make optimum use of resources. Ports Canada ports with local port corporation status are St John's, Nfld; Halifax, NS; the city of Québec, Montréal; Vancouver and Prince Rupert, BC. Noncorporate ports are Saint John and Belledune, NB; Chicoutimi, Sept-Îles and Trois-Rivières, Qué; Prescott and Port Colborne, Ont; and Churchill, Man. Ports Canada in 1986 handled 161 million t of cargo (50% of the total waterborne traffic in Canada, 63% of international cargo and 71% of grain exports).

Harbour Commissions handle approximately 29% of Canadian cargo (93 million t). They operate semi-autonomously in 9 ports in Canada. Seven harbour commissions have been incorporated under the 1964 Harbour Commissions Act at Thunder Bay, Windsor and Oshawa in Ont, as well as Fraser R (New Westminster), North Fraser, Nanaimo and Port Alberni in BC. Harbour commissions with separate statutes are located in Toronto and Hamilton, Ont. To a large extent the control and management of the harbour are placed in the hands of local commissioners. Harbour Commissions are not agents of the Crown but operate as quasi-commercial bodies. They are

responsible for day-to-day administration, planning, construction, operation and maintenance of port facilities, infrastructure and services.

Public Harbours and Port Facilities are administered through the Harbours and Ports Directorate of the CANADIAN COAST GUARD, under the authority of the Public Harbours and Ports Facilities Act proclaimed on 24 Feb 1983. These commercial transportation ports are found in approximately 341 locations across Canada, extending from Long Pond Manuels, Nfld, in the E, to Port Clements, BC, in the W; and from Pelee Island, Ont, in the S, to Tuktoyaktuk in the Arctic. There are 101 public ports on the West Coast of Canada, 34 in the Arctic, 33 on the Great Lakes, 60 on the St Lawrence, and 96 on the East Coast and Newfoundland. Public ports serve approximately 85 communities on the East, West and arctic coasts that have neither rail nor road access, providing a lifeline for Canada's isolated communities. Canada's public ports handle about 21% (67.3 million t) of Canada's waterborne tonnage. Of this total tonnage, 64% was international and 46% was domestic. Major commodities handled include salt, petroleum products, gasoline, newsprint and dry bulk commodities such as ores, sand and grain.

Public ports tend to serve a local and regional clientele. For example, about 500 000 t of zinc concentrates are shipped to Europe from Dalhousie, NB, annually. The product is moved by rail from the mine, which is only 200 km away. An extreme example of local customers is found at the port of Goderich, Ont, where the salt mine shaft is located on the wharf. Expansion of this port, completed in 1987, allowed it to handle 3 million t of salt per year.

Public ports are managed directly by Transport Canada, which ensures that the public port system contributes to a safe, efficient and equitable marine transportation system. Transport Canada does not itself operate port facilities; all cargo activities are undertaken through arrangement with the private sector. Management of the port varies by local operational requirements. Full-time area and port managers are available in a small number of the most active locations. Fees of Office appointees, known as wharfingers and harbourmasters, are used at other sites, where traffic volumes are inadequate to support a full-time port manager.

Portugal Cove, Nfld, Town, pop 2497 (1986c), inc 1977, is located in a small, steep-sided cove on

the NE shore of Conception Bay approximately 15 km from St John's. Portugal Cove, which appears on maps by 1630, was probably named for the Portuguese fishermen who occupied the cove seasonally in the 1600s while the English and French dominated St John's and other major fishing sites on the Avalon Pen. Originally settled by fishermen from Devon and Jersey, Portugal Cove was one of the English settlements captured by Pierre Le Moyne d'IBERVILLE on his 1696-97 expedition during the Anglo-French struggles for control of Newfoundland. Portugal Cove at that time numbered 3 inhabitants; but the population grew to 651 by 1857 and 1026 by 1911. Portugal Cove, which was connected to St John's in 1811 by one of the earliest major roads in Newfoundland, became a provincial transportation route to nearby Bell I after iron-ore mining began there in the 1890s. In their heyday these mines provided a major source of employment for Portugal Cove residents, most of whom now commute to St John's to work. Portugal Cove continues to be the ferry terminus to Bell I and is the site of a poultry co-op and a fish plant.   ROBERT D. PITT

Portuguese explorers were among the first Europeans to see Canadian soil. It is believed that Diogo de Teive (1452), João Vaz Corte-Real (1470), João FERNANDES and Pedro de Barcelos (1493) touched on the eastern coast of Canada, and conclusive evidence exists about explorations by Miguel and Gaspar CORTE-REAL, who were lost in Newfoundland waters in 1501 and 1502, respectively. That Portuguese subsequently fished for cod on the GRAND BANKS is attested to by numerous place-names. Labrador, likely from the Portuguese *lavrador* ("small landowner or farmer") indicates that the Portuguese knew of this territory. During 5 centuries of intermittent contact, however, only a handful of Portuguese fishermen settled on the Atlantic coast. The Portuguese in New France were descended from a few families founded by immigrants of 1668 and later.

From a trickle in the 1940s (some 200) Portuguese immigration to Canada increased rapidly after 1953. Immigrants arrived from the Azores (comprising 70% of Portuguese immigration to Canada) and Madeira archipelagoes and from continental Portugal. Many of the 1950s arrivals were recruited to work in rural and isolated locations in Canada, but soon established themselves in the larger cities. Between 1951 and 1957, 8115 persons immigrated; between 1958 and 1962, 16 731; between 1963 and 1967, 32 473; between 1968 and 1973, 54 199; and in 1984, 869. Portuguese immigrated for the same reasons many other nationalities immigrated – economic opportunity, underemployment at home and a desire to escape political oppression. By 1986 the number of Portuguese in Canada was estimated at 199 595.

Migration and Settlement Portuguese is the mother tongue for 153 985 Portuguese Canadians (1986 census). Most Portuguese Canadians reside in Ontario (70%), followed by Québec (15%), BC (8.5%) and the Prairie provinces (7.5%). They usually live in urban centres. Thirty-eight percent of the population of Canada who report Portuguese as the mother tongue live in Toronto, primarily in city-core areas, a residential pattern evident also in Montréal. The centre with the highest percentage of Portuguese relative to the total urban population is CAMBRIDGE, Ont. Winnipeg and Vancouver also have settlements of several thousand Portuguese. The only rural concentrations of Portuguese (fruit farmers) are in the southernmost Okanagan Valley of BC.

Social and Cultural Life For the first generation

of Portuguese, community cultural life was largely bound up with popular entertainments, eg, soccer matches, dances, picnics and music. Recreational activities were sponsored by clubs with Portuguese regional affiliations, or with particular parish congregations or Portuguese political parties. Today, Portuguese formal culture and language is taught in after-hours schools and in various schools and universities across Canada where numbers permit.

Many of the first generation prefer to attend social activities in Portuguese, but this is not true for their Canadian-educated children. Economic advances followed urbanization. Most of the labourers first worked in Canada as farmhands or railway labourers. When they transferred to the cities, they sought out janitorial, construction and factory work. Women were employed as cleaners or as textile or food-processing workers. During the 1960s, increasing numbers of families opened variety and clothing stores, fish shops, bakeries and restaurants. The minority with secondary education often became realtors, travel agents, or driving-school instructors, or provided other services for the community members. By the 1970s a second, Canadian-trained generation included high-school teachers, lawyers, social workers, engineers and civil servants. Many more entered semiskilled and skilled trades.

Most Portuguese are Roman Catholics, but recently some have converted to other Christian denominations, eg, Pentecostal, Baptist and Seventh Day Adventist.

Group Maintenance The first generation of Portuguese are concerned to maintain their *Portuguesismo*, "Portugueseness" – but regional loyalties to the Portuguese area of origin are equally compelling. At the local level emphasis on individual and family economic advances, heightened by class distinctions based on education and ways of life, induces rivalries which serve as a barrier to community-wide co-operation. Among the second generation, intermarriage with a non-Portuguese spouse occurs occasionally. Several Portuguese newspapers have been published in Toronto, Montréal, Winnipeg and Vancouver.

DAVID HIGGS AND GRACE M. ANDERSON

Reading: Grace M. Anderson and David Higgs, *A Future to Inherit: The Portuguese Communities of Canada* (1976).

Post, Sandra, golfer (b in Oakville, Ont 4 June 1948). She became Canada's first female professional golfer in 1968 and won the Ladies Professional Golf Assn Championship at Sutton, Mass, during her rookie year. She won 8 official LPGA events 1968-83 and $746 714 in prize money – more than any Canadian professional, male or female, had ever won. Post's finest year came in 1979, when she won $178 750 and 3 tournaments for second place on the LPGA money list. That year she won the LOU MARSH TROPHY as Canada's athlete of the year. She had won the Canadian junior girls championship 1964-66, and when she decided to turn professional, she moved to Florida, where she could practise year-round. That determination, coupled with her success, eventually encouraged more Canadian women to try professional golf. By 1984, 7 women in addition to Post held LPGA tour playing cards. That year she decided to retire from the professional golf tour. LORNE RUBENSTEIN

Postage Stamps The first adhesive postage stamps were issued in Great Britain on 6 May 1840 as part of the innovative postage scheme proposed by Sir Rowland Hill in 1837. Prepayment of postage by the use of stamps was a practice quickly adopted by many countries. The provinces of Canada followed the lead of Britain beginning with the Province of Canada, NS and

The Three-Penny Beaver, designed by Sandford Fleming, was Canada's first postage stamp (*courtesy Canada Post Corporation*).

NB (1851), Nfld (1857), BC (1860) and PEI (1861). With Confederation, all of the provinces ceased to issue their own stamps and used the Dominion of Canada general issue. Newfoundland continued to issue its own postage stamps until it too joined the Confederation (1949).

Design of Stamps Canada's first stamp was the Three-Penny Beaver designed by Sandford FLEMING. It was issued 23 Apr 1851, and was the world's first pictorial stamp. Stamps prior to this depicted either the head of the ruler or some other official device. Until the post WWII period most Canadian stamps were designed by staff artists of the various security printers under contract to the Post Office. In the 1950s, however, more emphasis was placed on design, and the policy of inviting designs from individual artists was begun. Since 1969, stamps have been chosen on the advice of a Stamp Advisory Committee made up of competent people from the visual arts, printing and philately. The present committee is headed by the chairman of the board of the CANADA POST CORPORATION. Subjects and design proposals are examined by the Stamp Advisory Committee and a stamp program is recommended to the minister responsible for the Canada Post Corporation.

Stamp Printing Stamps have a monetary value and are produced only by security printers under very strict control. The production methods must be difficult to duplicate in order to prevent forgery. Almost all Canadian stamps issued before 1967 were printed by an engraving process. In this process the design is engraved in actual size in reverse on a block of steel called the master die. During this process various prints are made to show progress; these trial prints are called "die proofs." When a die proof is approved by Canada Post, the die is hardened and impressions of the design are transferred to a hardened steel roller. The impressions are then rolled into a steel plate, curved to fit modern rotary presses. A recent modification of this process involves the transfer of the plate impressions to a plastic sheet which is then used to produce an electrolytically deposited duplicate used for printing. In the late 1960s the techniques of multicoloured offset lithography were sufficiently developed to use this process in stamp production. Since then Canadian stamps have been unrestricted in their use of colour, giving stamp designers far greater flexibility than when confined to the one-colour or 2-colour process. Several kinds of paper have been used including laid, wove and coated varieties. During recent years the sheets of stamps have been overprinted with a transparent ink that when exposed to ultra violet radiation fluoresces. This process assists in the process of mechanical sorting of various classes of mail. The use of these printing methods and papers has given Canada unusual variety and beauty in stamps.

Usage Canadian postage stamps are used strictly for postage purposes. Some countries, notably Britain, have their stamps inscribed "postage and revenue," thus validating them for both postal and excise use. In Canada special stamps are made available for excise purposes by both federal and provincial governments. *See also* STAMP COLLECTING. K. ROWE

Postal Strikes, CUPW Since 1965 the Canadian Union of Postal Workers (previously Canadian Postal Employees Assn) has been involved in approximately 18 major disputes over several complex issues. The " big strike" of July 1965 was one of the largest Canadian "wildcat" strikes and the largest involving government employees; it played an important role in gaining collective bargaining rights for civil servants. The 1968 strike and the 1970 rotating 24-hour walkouts were mainly the result of wage grievances; the latter secured an increase above the Trudeau government's guidelines. Strikes in the 1970s centered on wages and the threats posed by automation. Demands included legal guarantees of job security and maintenance of existing job classifications, as well as firm controls over the use of casual and part-time employees. In 1974 and 1975 CUPW, under Joe DAVIDSON, undertook long, bitter strikes which turned public opinion against it. In 1976 and 1977 postal service was disrupted by a series of illegal regional strikes: the union claimed that changes were being made without the promised consultation. A national strike in 1978 met with back-to-work legislation: union president Jean-Claude PARROT was jailed for refusing to comply, and relations became strained between the union and the CANADIAN LABOUR CONGRESS. There was a strike-free settlement in 1980, but in June 1981 workers struck over demands which included one for 17 weeks' paid maternity leave. CUPW became the first federal civil service bargaining unit to win this concession.

On 16 Oct 1981 the post office became a CROWN CORPORATION, something CUPW had been urging in the hope that it would streamline negotiations by placing the union under the Canada Labour Code. The corporation inherited a bitter legacy of mistrust, and although negotiations brought a new agreement without a strike in 1985, strikes shut down the system again in 1987.

C.D. CHORNIAWY

Postal System, a network of postal facilities serving people in all parts of Canada, of transportation services linking post offices, and thousands of people dedicated to transmitting mail. It is a service used for personal, social and commercial purposes. Co-operation between postal systems transcends political differences and makes it possible to exchange mail almost anywhere in the world. About 8 billion pieces of mail are handled by Canada's more than 8500 postal facilities each year.

Post Offices The Gateway postal plant near the international airport in Mississauga, Ont, covers 10 ha under one roof and is one of 30 mechanized postal plants in Canada. In addition to these large, mechanized sortation plants there are about 400 staff post offices in urban communities large enough to warrant a letter-carrier service and about 2000 semi-staff post offices in smaller communities. Nearly 3500 revenue post offices serve villages and rural areas; traditionally, their postmasters and assistants are paid from postal revenues. Seasonal post offices are set up to accommodate people during the busy vacation season in certain areas.

Postal stations are an extension of the main post office and provide the basic services. Sub-post offices are found in stores and businesses for the convenience of the public. In these the owner of the business acts as the postmaster and provides a postal clerk as necessary. In rural areas of a certain density a rural delivery service is provided. In some cases group mail boxes may be set up at convenient points where customers can pick up their mail. Lock boxes are also provided in urban locations. Mail may be sent to a specific address or by general delivery to a post office to be picked up by the addressee.

Postal History Early commerce required a means of exchanging information as well as goods and services. The growth of empires required a speedy and reliable system for issuing orders and receiving and responding to reports. Using a system of relay posts, ancient Egypt was able to send messages quickly over long distances. The Romans, with fast horses and good roads, were able to assure next-day delivery up to 280 km by post. The next great improvement came with the development of steam vehicles in the 19th century. The railways carried mail over 800 km in a day. In the 20th century, aircraft carry mail thousands of kilometres a day, and recently with electronic facsimile transmittal by satellite, mail has been sent around the world in only a few hours. The modern postal system began in England with the introduction of the adhesive POSTAGE STAMP by Rowland Hill in 1837. Hill also devised the uniform postage-rate schedules based on weight, rather than size, and made the prepayment of postage both possible and practical. The British government adopted Hill's system in May 1840 and its use quickly became worldwide.

Significant Developments in Canada When the French arrived in N America in the 16th century, messages were carried among the native people by swift and trusted messengers. The French adopted the practice of using canoes between settlements along the St Lawrence R. In 1735 a road was opened between Québec and Montréal and a special messenger was appointed to carry official dispatches. He also carried messages for a fee. At intervals along the route "Post Houses" with a "Maître de poste" were set up to receive messages and fees and to provide conveyance to the next post. In 1753 Benjamin Franklin was appointed deputy postmaster general for the British colonies. In 1755 Franklin organized the first regular monthly mail packet service between Falmouth, Eng, and New York and opened the first official post office in Canada in Halifax, NS, to link Halifax with the Atlantic colonies and the packet service to England. A post office for local and outgoing mail had been started by Benjamin Leigh in Halifax in Apr 1754.

After the Treaty of Paris in 1763, Franklin established a post office in Québec City with subsidiaries in Montréal and Trois-Rivières. A Scottish immigrant, Hugh Finlay, became postmaster. A monthly courier service by way of Lk Champlain connected Montréal with New York and the Atlantic packet service. In 1774 Franklin was dismissed because of his sympathy with the American revolutionary cause, and Finlay became deputy postmaster general for the northern colonies. By 1775 the mails were being seriously disrupted by the revolutionaries, and because of the threat to the couriers' lives Finlay stopped the inland service. Peace returned in 1783 and on 7 July 1784 Hugh Finlay became the deputy postmaster general for Canada. The revolution brought a major immigration of LOYALISTS to Canada and a demand for improved postal services. Early in 1784 Finlay hired a courier, Pierre Durand, to pioneer a Canadian route to Halifax from Québec City through 1000 km of forest. The round trip with the mail took 15 weeks.

The Quebec Royal Mail, Canada East, 1848 (*courtesy National Archives of Canada/C-40269*).

By 1851 there were deputy postmasters general in NS, NB and the Province of Canada, but the British government still administered the postal system. The provincial deputies were convinced that they could operate the system more efficiently and petitioned Queen Victoria for a transfer of authority. The queen's approval was gazetted on 22 Feb 1851 and became effective 5 Apr 1851. From then until Confederation, the provinces co-operated in providing the mail service required, with W.H. Griffin, secretary in charge, reporting to the Honourable James Morris, postmaster general of the Province of Canada. The new decentralized, co-operative arrangement lived up to the expectation of its advocates. Rates were reduced and volumes doubled in the first year of provincial co-operation.

By 1850 sail had largely given way to steam as a reliable way to move the mail over Canada's major water routes. During the navigation season mail steamers regularly carried mail from Kingston to Montréal, and from Montréal to Québec. In 1852 these services were put on an interconnecting schedule and extended to the head of Lake Ontario to speed up the mail from Canada West. By 1865 there were mail steam boats on the Upper Lakes connecting Parry Sound, Collingwood, Sault Ste Marie and Fort William with the US Postal Service. A weekly steamer service also brought mail from Québec to the Gaspé and the ports around the Gulf of St Lawrence.

Toronto Postmaster W.M. McLean closes the inaugural ceremonies of Post Office "all-up" service by loading the last bag, Toronto, 1940s. Canada was the first country in the world to introduce domestic "all-up" services (*courtesy National Archives of Canada/PA-143523*).

In 1860 the postal department decided to establish its own Atlantic service from Montréal to Liverpool, Eng. The year 1861 was disastrous. The *Canadian* struck ice and foundered off Newfoundland on June 4, and the *North Briton* went down on the Perroquet Rocks in the Gulf of St Lawrence on Nov 5. New rules made the service safer, more reliable and less costly, and by 1890 Canada had scheduled Ocean Mail services to Britain and Europe from Montréal and Halifax, to the W Indies from St John, and to China and Japan from Vancouver, A direct line to Australia calling at Honolulu and Fiji was established in 1893. In 1899 the Canadian Development Co took over the mail service from the North-West Mounted Police and began a semi-weekly boat service between Atlin and Bennett, and between Bennett and Dawson during the navigation season in the Yukon. Postal clerks began sorting and distributing the mail en route on the Niagara-to-London [Ont] run in 1854. By 1857 there were specially equipped cars called railway post offices, and the railway mail service had reduced the delivery time for a letter from Québec City to Windsor [Ont] from about 10 days to a dependable 49 hours. By 1863 the trial period for the travelling post offices was over and an order-in-council established the standards for their use on the Grand Trunk Railway 12 Aug 1863.

The post office was one of the first federal-government departments formed after Confederation and took over the postal service on 1 Apr 1868. As the Canadian Pacific Ry stretched across the prairies in the 1880s a railway post office, addressed "End of the Line," moved with it, bringing banking, money-order and mail-order facilities to the settlers. On 28 June 1886 another railway mail car left Montréal and arrived in Port Moody, BC, on July 4. It began a national mail service which for 80 years was the envy of the world. Free letter-carrier delivery service was introduced in Montréal on 1 Oct 1874. Free rural mail delivery began between Hamilton and Ancaster, Ont, on 10 Oct 1908. Captain Brian Peck flew the first official Canadian air mail from Montréal to Toronto 24 June 1918. Two weeks later, Katherine Stinson became Canada's first woman air-mail pilot when she flew 259 authorized letters from Calgary to Edmonton. Prepaid, stamped air mail was flown between Haileybury, Ont, and Rouyn, Qué, 21 Sept 1924, reducing mail time between these remote northern mining towns from weeks to a few hours.

On 4 Oct 1927 the first contract air-mail service commenced between Lac du Bonnet, Bissett and Wadhope in Manitoba. The post office also began an experimental air service (1927) to meet the ocean liners at Rimouski and fly the mail to Québec, Montréal and Ottawa. This service continued until 1939. In Jan 1929, famed bush pilot Punch Dickins, with engineer L. Parmenter, F. Lundy of Western Canada Airways and post office inspector T.J. Reilly, flew mail to Ft McMurray, Fort Resolution and Aklavik. In Dec 1929 air mail between Ft McMurray and Aklavik linked the NWT with the postal system and established a postal service 480 km within the Arctic Circle. An air-mail contract helped finance TRANS-CANADA AIR-LINES in 1937. On 1 Mar 1939 a daily air-mail service between Montréal and Vancouver began. It was extended to the Maritimes in Jan 1940. On 1 July 1948 Canada became the first country in the world to introduce domestic "all-up" service. First-class mail was carried by air at regular postage rates.

Technological Change In the 19th century steamboats and trains made it possible to carry more mail quickly over long distances, at the same time sorting it en route, thus eliminating some of the dead time and post-office handling.

Mechanization of the postal transportation system brought a tremendous improvement in speed and reliability. In the 1920s the introduction of conveyor belts, elevators and gravity-feed systems greatly reduced the time and labour required to move mail within the post offices. An Alberta mail man, J.A. Lapierre, built a snow machine to deliver mail between St Paul and St Lina, Alta, in the winter of 1923. He replaced the front wheels of a Model T Ford with skis. The front wheels were then connected in tandem with the rear wheels and a double-length set of chains went on over each pair of wheels. The enclosed cab used heat from the radiator, and the machine looked not unlike an early snowmobile. It worked so well it was used as a taxi to dances and meetings when the roads were otherwise impassable.

The introduction of the all-up air-mail service, the improvement in paved roads and TRUCKING services and a railway strike in 1950 brought about the rapid decline of the railway mail service and shifted its sortation load back into the post offices. Air mail also increased the public's expectations of the postal service. People now anticipated delivery at the speed of the airplane.

Distribution systems became more complicated as the nation grew and became urbanized and as the composition of the mail changed. Then, in the mid-1960s, the annual examinations on distribution skills and rules and regulations were dropped, and the speed and efficiency of the manual memory sortation declined. To meet this problem the simplified alphabetic sortation, used at Christmas, was extended. It required less training, but more people, overtaxing crowded facilities and equipment. The obvious need was to mechanize the sortation process itself.

The Post Office Dept first sought to simplify and streamline existing work methods and make the best of existing facilities through work simplification, measurement and standardization. This led to mechanizing the steps of the sortation process. A British-designed mechanical segregating, facing and cancelling machine called Sefacan was introduced in Winnipeg, and a sortation machine from Holland, called the Transorma, was installed in Peterborough in the 1950s. The early machines were noisy and inefficient. The Post Office Dept then commissioned Dr Maurice Levy, an electronics scientist, to design and supervise the building of a new, electronic, computer-controlled, automatic mail sortation system for Canada. A hand-made model sorter was tested at postal headquarters, Ottawa, in 1953. It worked, and a prototype coding and sortation machine, capable of processing all of the mail then generated by the City of Ottawa, was built by Canadian manufacturers and assembled in the Langevin Building, Ottawa, in 1956. It could process mail at a rate of 30 000 letters per hour, with a missort factor of less than 1 letter in 10 000. Visitors from around the world who came to the Universal Postal Union Congress in 1957 were impressed, but a change of government brought about the closing of Dr Levy's laboratory. Further development was contracted to Canadair, Montréal, which was unable to complete the work, and eventually the equipment was sold for scrap. In 1970 Canada Post chose a proven Belgian coding system and letter-sorting machine, and Japanese-designed, high-speed culler-facer-canceller and optical character reader equipment. Canada now has the most mechanized and potentially efficient postal system in the world.

The Postal Process When a person deposits a letter in the red mailbox on the corner, the box is cleared at a scheduled time and the letter is taken by truck to the main post office where parcels, large envelopes and metered mail are separated out and the rest is sent to be cancelled. Mail ad-

dressed to the community in which it was posted is sorted by street names into letter-carrier routes or sent to postal stations for the letter carriers, who sort it by street and house number for delivery. The letter carrier takes about 16 kg at a time in his bag. The rest is taken by truck to relay boxes at convenient places along the letter carrier's route. Large parcels are delivered by drivers. Mail addressed to places outside the community is sorted, packaged and sent to the country, city or distribution centre for that address. There it is sorted again and put into boxes to be picked up, turned over to the letter carriers or rural mail couriers for delivery to the addressee.

Starting in Ottawa in 1972, the post office installed equipment to mechanize the sortation process. The system is based on a 6-character postal code which forms the last line of every address. This postal code is made up of alphabet letters and numbers, arranged in the order ANA NAN. The first group, ANA, represents a geographic area; the second group, NAN, is a local code that may identify a street, an apartment building or a group of rural post offices. Mail brought into a letter processing plant (LPP) is unloaded, dropped onto a conveyor and taken to a bag shake-out machine. There it is shaken out and taken by a conveyor to a culling station where oversize, undersize and nonacceptable articles are removed to be sorted manually. The mail then goes to a culler-facer-canceller (CFC) where it is culled again if it does not meet machine standards of size and thickness. The machine then faces up the remainder and the stamp is located by a photoelectric cell that triggers its cancellation. Letters are then stacked in coded trays and sent to a temporary storing system from which a computer dispatches them to the next step according to a scheduling program.

The next step may be an optical character reader (OCR), which locates and reads typed or printed codes and applies a coloured-bar code that actuates a letter-sorting machine (LSM). As many as 20 000 letters an hour can be sorted into the LSM's destination bins. Addresses that cannot be identified by the OCR are rejected and sent to the group desk suite (GDS) where the code is read by an operator who keys the coloured-bar code onto the letter by hand. Uncoded or indecipherable coded letters are rejected at the GDS and sent to manual sorters. Both the OCR and the GDS take care of the primary sortation of the mail and add the bar codes for the final sortation by the LSM. Mail that does not meet the standards, or does not bear the code legibly printed, has to be separated out of the main flow. Large envelopes or magazines, called flats, are sent to flat-sorting machines (FSM) for processing. Small parcels and small objects such as hotel keys also have their own sorting system. An operator indicates their postal code to a computer, which directs them to a mechanism that sorts them according to their destination. Standard mail, parcels, large envelopes or manually sorted mail come together in a consolidation area where mail for a particular destination is assembled and packaged for transport by conveyor or fork lift to the dispatching dock. Local mail goes out to the postal stations by shuttle trucks for delivery. Forward mail goes by truck to other post offices or to the air-mail facility (AMF) for shipment to other cities or countries.

The Universal Postal Union, an international organization, facilitates the exchange of mail between nations. It is a forum in which countries can discuss and work out problems that interfere with the free flow of mail among them. It originated in Berne, Switzerland, in 1874, and Canada became a member in 1878. The Universal Postal Union is a specialized agency of the United Nations, made up of 168 member countries comprising a single postal territory. Freedom of transit for postal items is guaranteed throughout the union territory. Canada is also a member of the Postal Union of the Americas and Spain (PUAS) in which it has played an active role.

Canada Post Corporation Canada Post became the Canada Post Corporation on 16 Oct 1981. Deputy Postmaster General J.C. Corkery was replaced by President R. Michael Warren, reporting to a board of directors chaired by Judge R.J. Marin. The assistant deputies were replaced by executive vice-presidents and vice-presidents, and the CROWN CORPORATION was reorganized along divisional lines. COLLECTIVE BARGAINING is, under the rules of the Canada Labour Code, administered by the Canada Labour Relations Board and the federal Dept of Labour. Canada Post Corporation had some 61 000 regular full-time and part-time employees in 1986. Over 90% were members of its 26 bargaining units, represented by 7 unions, the largest of which was the CANADIAN UNION OF POSTAL WORKERS representing about 23 000 inside mail-processing and counter staff; and the Letter Carriers' Union of Canada, with about 20 000 truck drivers and letter carriers; the Canadian Postmasters and Assistants Assn, representing 9300 rural postmasters and assistants; the Assn of Postal Officials of Canada, representing more than 3500 postal operations supervisors; the Public Service Alliance of Canada, representing about 5700 maintenance and administrative staff; the Professional Institute of the Public Service of Canada, with about 250 computer specialists, engineers and other professionals; the International Brotherhood of Electrical Workers, representing about 70 electrical and electronic workers.

Canada Post Corporation is in competition with a number of forces. Its survival depends on the restoration of a speedy and reliable postal service. Its future lies in co-operative ventures such as Priority Post, with links to the International Express Mail network; Telepost, with links to CNCP Telecommunications; and Intelpost, with links to Teleglobe Canada and the world. More information about the postal system can be obtained from the National Postal Museum in Ottawa and from the Corporate Communications Branch of the Canada Post Corporation.   H. GRIFFIN

Reading: W. Boggs, *The Postage Stamps and Postal History of Canada* (1974); Canada Post, *Postal Service Down the Centuries* (1974); S.M. McDonald, *The Posts in Canada to 1776* (1975); D. Stewart-Patterson, *Post Mortem: Why Canada's Mail Won't Move* (1987).

Potash refers to potassium compounds and potassium-bearing materials, the most common being potassium chloride (KCl). Potassium is one of 14 elements essential to plant life and, with nitrogen and phosphorus, makes up mixed fertilizers. About 94% of world potash consumption is in fertilizers, with small amounts used in manufacturing soaps, glass, ceramics, chemical dyes, drugs, synthetic rubber and explosives. The term potash comes from the pioneer practice of extracting potassium fertilizer (K_2CO_3) by leaching wood ashes and evaporating the solution in large iron pots. As early as 1767, potash from wood ashes was exported from Canada, and exports of potash and pearl ash (potash and lime) reached 43 958 barrels in 1865. There were 519 asheries in operation in 1871. The industry declined in the late 19th century when large-scale production of potash from MINERAL salts was established in Germany. In 1943 potash was discovered in Saskatchewan in the process of drilling for oil. Active exploration began in 1951 and by 1958 the Potash Company of America began MINING from a flat-lying bed 1 km underground. In June 1962, International Minerals and Chemicals Corp (Canada) Ltd completed a mine shaft to a depth of

1030 m near ESTERHAZY, Sask, now the world's largest potash mine. In 1964 Kalium Chemicals Ltd opened the world's first potash solution mine near Regina, at a depth of 1585 m. By 1970, 9 mines were in operation in Saskatchewan, with a total capacity of 6.8 million t K_2O equivalent. Potash sales were unable to keep up with this growth rate: less than 3.5 million t were sold in 1969. By January 1970 prorationing of production to market demand was introduced by the Saskatchewan government to stabilize the price. These regulations were in force until demand caught up to supply. From 1977 to 1979 the Saskatchewan government bought 4 mines and created the Potash Corp of Saskatchewan (PCS) to run them. By 1986, PCS accounted for over 40% of provincial capacity. In 1987, a weak market situation prompted US potash producers to launch an antidumping petition against potash imports from Canada. The ensuing investigation resulted in charges by the US government that Canadian potash had been sold in the US at less than fair market value. The investigation was suspended in Jan 1988 when Canadian potash exporters agreed to maintain "fair" prices.

Western Canada's potash deposits occur in the prairie evaporite formation underlying a broad, northwesterly trending belt extending across and beyond south-central Saskatchewan. Reserves recoverable by conventional underground mining are estimated at a minimum of 14 billion t; those available for solution mining may be 3 times as large. Significant reserves occur in formations of the Windsor group in NB (about 400 million t), where 2 mines came into production in 1983 and 1985. Their annual capacity is 1.1 million t. Canada and the USSR each produce about 25% of the world's potash. The USSR uses most of its own; Canada contributes over 40% of world trade. By 1987 total capacity reached 10.8 million t. Canada developed from an importer of potash in 1961 to a producer of 7.0 million t valued at $579 million in 1986. Exports contributed over $800 million to Canada's BALANCE OF PAYMENTS in 1986.　　G.S. BARRY AND W.E. KOEPKE

Potato (*Solanum tuberosum*), herbaceous annual of the NIGHTSHADE family, which produces tubers at the end of underground stems. Potatoes are an important vegetable crop, with total production slightly greater than wheat. The principal cultivars (commercial varieties) grown in Canada for table stock and processing are Superior (early), Norchip (mid-season), Kennebec (main crop) and Russet Burbank (late). Tubers are about 80% water; the remainder contains useful amounts of minerals, vitamins B_1 and C, carbohydrate and protein. Eight hundred grams of potatoes and one egg will supply the daily protein requirements of a 70 kg human. A cool-season plant, the potato originated in the Andes and is now grown in temperate regions worldwide. Taken to Spain by conquistadores in about 1500 AD, it remained a botanical curiosity for some 200 years before being recognized as a useful food source. Potato cultivation spread slowly across western Europe and, thence, to Britain and N America. The greatest production and highest yields occur in eastern Europe and the USSR, where much of the crop is used to produce starch, alcohol and animal feed. In Canada the greatest production is still in the eastern provinces. The crop is produced by planting seed pieces, whole tubers or portions of larger tubers. Total Canadian production in 1986 was 2.85 million t, grown on about 114 000 ha: Nfld, 200 ha; PEI, 28 400 ha; NS, 1600 ha; NB 20 600 ha; Qué, 19 800 ha; Ont, 13 100 ha; Man, 16 600 ha; Sask, 1000 ha; Alta, 9100 ha; and BC, 3200 ha. Crop value varies from year to year and in 1985 was $237 million. Exports of seed and table

stock, mostly from PEI and NB, total about $67 million. Half that amount was imported from the US in 1986.　　G. ROWBERRY

Potato Wart Disease is a fungal disease of potato sprouts, eyes and stolons; also called potato canker. The disease is primarily a kitchen garden disease; it is spread through the distribution of contaminated soil and potatoes, animal droppings when infected potatoes are used in feed, digging implements, boots and shoes, etc. In this sense it is a social disease largely transmitted by humans. The disease was first reported in N America in Newfoundland in 1909 by Dominion Botanist H. Güssow. The disease, however, remains in Newfoundland; about 94% of outports contain pockets of infested soil. In 1912, Ottawa forbade the movement of Newfoundland soil and produce into Canada. This quarantine is still in effect, and ground transport leaving Newfoundland is washed and checked. The causal fungus is a single-celled organism called *Synchytrium endobioticum*, a lowly fungus (Phycomycete) with a complicated life history. On rotting, cankers caused by infection release spores which, returned to the soil, can live for 40 years. As chemical control is extremely difficult, resistant varieties of potato are bred to control the disease.
MICHAEL C. HAMPSON

Potlatch, a highly regulated event historically common to most Northwest Coast Indian groups (*see* NATIVE PEOPLE: NORTHWEST COAST). The potlatch, from the Chinook word Patshatl, validated status, rank and established claims to names, powers and privileges. Wealth in the form of utilitarian goods such as blankets, carved cedar boxes, food and fish or canoes, and prestige items such as slaves and COPPERS were accumulated to be bestowed on others or even destroyed with great ceremony. Potlatches were held to celebrate initiation, to mourn the dead, or to mark the investiture of chiefs in a continuing series of often competitive exchanges between CLANS, lineages and rival groups. A great potlatch could be many years in the making, might last for several days, and would involve fasting, spirit dances, theatrical demonstrations and distribution of gifts. An intolerant federal government banned the potlatch from 1884 to 1951, ostensibly because of native treatment of property. The last major potlatch, that of Daniel Cranmer, a KWAKIUTL from Alert Bay, was held in 1921. However, the goods were confiscated by Indian agents. By the time the ban was repealed in 1951 serious damage had been caused to tribal identities and social stratification. Potlatches are again held today, but they are not the large affairs they were in the past.
RENÉ R. GADACZ

Potlatch dance, Carcross, YT, date unknown (*courtesy National Archives of Canada/C-48241/E.J. Hamacher*).

Potts, Jerry, or *Ky-yo-kosi*, meaning "Bear Child," scout, guide, interpreter (b at Ft McKenzie, US 1840; d at Fort Macleod, Alta 14 July 1896). Of Blood Indian and Scots parentage, he became famous among the BLACKFOOT as a great warrior and hunter. Hired by NWMP Commissioner G.A. FRENCH, Potts led the police to the notorious whisky post Ft Whoop-up. He also di-

rected them to an island in the OLDMAN R where they constructed FORT MACLEOD. Hero to the Blackfoot Confederacy and a special constable in the NWMP, Potts educated each group about the other and ensured friendly relations. His influence with the Blackfoot helped to get Treaty No 7 signed and to assure that his people remained neutral during the NORTH-WEST REBELLION of 1885.
D. BRUCE SEALEY

Reading: D. Bruce Sealey, *Jerry Potts* (1980).

Potvin, Damase, journalist, writer (b at Bagotville, Qué 16 Oct 1879; d at Québec C 9 June 1964). After studies at the Petit Séminaire de Chicoutimi in 1903, Potvin entered the novitiate of the White Fathers of Africa in Algiers. He returned to Chicoutimi in 1905 and began his long career in journalism as founder and editor of *Le Travailleur*. Over the next few years he worked for several newspapers as well as publishing an agricultural novel, *Restons chez nous*! (1908). In 1910 he became parliamentary correspondent for *L'Événement*, was made head of Associated Press in Québec in 1912 and head of the Québec Press Gallery in 1915, as well as publishing a political novel, *Le "Membre"* (1916). He founded the Société des arts, sciences et lettres de Québec with some friends, among them Alonzo Cinq-Mars, and in 1918 helped found *Le Terroir*, the society's journal, in which he published some 500 articles and reviews. A second rural novel, *L'Appel de la terre* appeared in 1919. Moving from *L'Evenement* to *Le Soleil* in 1920, he left the latter in 1925 for *La Presse*, and continued to write for it into the 1960s. During his long career he appeared in more than 150 national and foreign periodicals and published 36 books. In 1945 he joined the Québec Dept of Public Instruction. His many honours and distinctions included the Prix David in 1938. He perfected the format of the agricultural novel and deeply influenced authors of this kind of book.　　AURÉLIEN BOIVIN

Potvin, Denis Charles, hockey player (b at Ottawa 29 Oct 1953). After a junior career with the Ottawa 67s, Potvin was the first player chosen in the 1973 NHL draft. He earned the CALDER TROPHY as a New York Islander rookie in 1974 and went on to become a great playmaking defenceman and leader of the Islander team that won the STANLEY CUP 4 times (1979-83). He was awarded the JAMES NORRIS MEMORIAL TROPHY in 1976, 1978 and 1979.　　DEREK DRAGER

Potvin, Gilles, music encyclopedist, producer, critic (b at Montréal 23 Oct 1923). With Helmut KALLMANN and Kenneth WINTERS he was coeditor of the *Encyclopedia of Music in Canada*, responsible in particular for the text of the French-language version. After musical studies in Montréal, Potvin began a long career with the CBC in 1948. Appointed head of music production of the corporation's International Service in 1966, he led his department to remarkable success in record production. During most of his career he has been a part-time impresario and a music journalist.
BARCLAY McMILLAN

Pouce Coupe, BC, village, pop 813 (1986c), inc 1932, is located 6 km SE of Dawson Creek on the highway and railway between there and Edmonton. It is named after a Sekani trapper who had lost a thumb in a gun accident; it means "thumb cut off." Pouce Coupe Prairie was one of the first areas settled in the PEACE RIVER Block when the area was opened for homesteading in 1912. Government offices, a Red Cross Hospital and a creamery were located in the village that served the mixed-farming area. When the railway was completed in 1931 a large number of farmers from Saskatchewan and Alberta migrated to the Block during the Depression.　　MARIE ELLIOTT

Poultry Farming Poultry are domesticated birds kept for their meat or eggs. Common varieties in Canada are chickens (*Gallus gallus* or *G. domestica,* family Phasianidae), turkeys (*Meleagris gallopavo,* family Phasianidae), ducks (*Anas-platyrhynchos, Cairina moschata,* family Anatidae) and geese (genus *Anser,* family Anatidae). In 1986 there were over 371 million hens and chickens on farms across Canada: Ont had 133.5 million; Qué, 106.5 million; BC, 38.9 million; Alta, 34.0 million; Man, 18.1 million; NS, 13.6 million; Sask, 11.4 million; NB, 10.4 million; Nfld, 4.9 million; PEI, 0.7 million. In the same year, there were over 17 million turkeys: Ont had 6.9 million; Qué, 4.5 million; Alta, 1.3 million; Man, 1.2 million; BC, 1.6 million; Sask, 718 000; NS, 513 000; NB, 323 000; and PEI, 1 000; As well, ducks and geese were grown across Canada. In 1986 Canadian per capita consumption averaged 17.9 dozen eggs (12.2 kg), 21.8 kg of chicken and 4.2 kg of turkey, ducks and geese. Sale of poultry and eggs contributed over $1.4 billion to Canada's 1986 total farm-cash receipts.

Foundation breeders have developed hybrid strains of chickens for commercial egg and meat production; to a lesser degree, the same has been done for turkey meat production; little breeding work has been done on WATERFOWL. Foundation breeders must keep pure bloodlines for crossing; however, most purebreds are kept as a hobby by poultry fanciers or exhibition breeders' men. The only world-class foundation breeding companies in Canada are Shaver Poultry Breeding Farms Ltd, Cambridge, Ont, and Hybrid Turkeys Ltd, Kitchener, Ont. However, nearly all foundation breeders worldwide sell parent stock to franchised hatcheries in Canada which, in turn, supply commercial stock to poultry producers.

Chickens The basic egg-producing breeds are White Leghorn and Rhode Island Red. The commercial layer is white feathered and weighs about 1.8 kg. Most lay white-shelled eggs, but brown-shelled egg layers are gaining in general popularity and efficiency of production. Laying chickens produce 265-280 eggs during the 13-14 months they are in lay. They are expected to produce one dozen eggs for every 1.64 kg of feed. White Plymouth Rock females are used in crosses with other breeds (eg, Cornish, New Hampshire) to produce meat-type birds sold as broilers or roasters. The commercial bird is white feathered, fast growing, vigorous and well fleshed. Chicken broilers are generally slaughtered when 47 days old, at a liveweight of 1.77 kg. They require 888 g of feed to produce 1 kg liveweight. The Shaver chicken, developed in Canada, is used for both egg and meat production. Other popular stocks include Dekalb (egg), Hyline (egg or meat), Hubbard (meat), Arbor Acres (meat), Ross (egg or meat) and Babcock (egg).

Turkeys Most commercial turkeys are white feathered, vigorous, fast growing and plump. Turkey broilers are slaughtered at 13-14 weeks, when they weigh 4.44 kg (females) or 6.50 kg (males). They require 1.06 kg of feed to produce 1 kg liveweight. Tonnage turkeys are slaughtered at 21 weeks when they weigh at least 1.10 kg. They require 1.30 kg of feed to produce 1 kg liveweight. The Broad Breasted Bronze and the White Holland turkeys were used to develop the modern varieties Hybrid (in Canada) and Nicholas (US).

Ducks and Geese Purebreds and crosses are the sources of commercial stock. The White Pekin is the most popular meat duck; the Rouen, Aylesbury and Muscovy are used to a limited extent. A few Indian Runner and Khaki Campbell are kept for egg production. The 3 most popular breeds of geese are Embden, Chinese and Toulouse.

Poultry farms may be classed as producers of eggs, chicken meat, turkey, waterfowl or game

and exotic birds. Production of eggs, chicken meat and turkey is regulated federally (Agricultural Products Marketing Act) and provincially (AGRICULTURAL MARKETING BOARDS). Federal agencies allocate production quotas to the provinces, remove market surpluses and regulate import and export of products. Provincial boards allocate production quotas to producers, set prices, advertise the product and deduct board levies from producers for operating costs. The general strategy is to ensure that each province is self-sufficient. Waterfowl and the relatively new GAME BIRD and exotic bird production have little control and few statistics are available. JOHN P. WALKER

Poundmaker, Cree chief (b in central Saskatchewan *c*1842; d at Blackfoot Crossing, Alta 4 July 1886). Although he was the son of a Stoney, his mother's brother, Big Child, was a leading chief of the Eagle Hills Cree. In 1873 Poundmaker became influential when he was adopted by CROWFOOT, head chief of the Blackfoot. In 1876 he opposed Treaty No 6, but finally accepted it and 2 years later was recognized as a chief. During the NORTH-WEST REBELLION of 1885, Poundmaker's followers ransacked the abandoned village of Battleford and placed the fort under siege. A short time later, Col W.D. OTTER led a military force to "punish" the Indians, but when they attacked Poundmaker's camp near CUT KNIFE HILL they were forced to retire under heavy fire. Although Poundmaker had not taken part in the fight, he did prevent the warriors from pursuing the retreating army. At his subsequent trial for treason-felony, Poundmaker protested his innocence but was sentenced to 3 years in prison. After serving only a year he was released, broken in spirit and health, and died a few weeks later while visiting his foster father on the Blackfoot Reserve. HUGH A. DEMPSEY

Poussière sur la ville (1953), a novel by André LANGEVIN, dramatizes, with the simple structural elegance of Greek tragedy and the complex tone and perspective of modern existentialist literature, the failure of a marriage. The setting of Macklin, an industrial town modelled after Thetford-Mines, Qué, and dominated by dreary winter weather, grey asbestos dust and garish neon lights, encloses the narrator's despair and inability to communicate, pitted as he is against repressive community standards. A city boy, Dr Alain Dubois recalls his unlikely marriage to the passionate Madeleine; his ambivalence about her affair with Richard Hétu, broken up by the parish priests; and finally her suicide, reinforcing his decision to remain in Macklin to practise medicine – an act of compassion and revenge. Awarded the Prix du Cercle du livre de France, the novel was translated by John Latrobe and Robert Gottlieb as *Dust over the City* (1955). MICHÈLE LACOMBE

Poverty One of the fundamental problems in estimating the number of poor people is agreeing on a definition of poverty. How badly nourished, housed and clothed, how much insecurity and stress, and how much withdrawal and powerlessness must people suffer before they are considered or feel poor? It is one task to describe the conditions of poverty, but establishing an objective measure is more difficult. The 2 distinct and opposing methods ("absolute" and "relative") used to establish the basic level of income that defines poverty are evidence that the definition and measurement of poverty is an exercise in values and politics, ie, society's beliefs about poverty and its causes largely determine the way poverty is defined and measured. The absolute approach is based on the belief that poor people only require the absolute necessities of life, eg, substandard housing and the bare essentials of food and

clothing, and that these can be objectively established. This view stems from the belief that poverty is an individual's own doing and should not be rewarded or encouraged by the provision of adequate levels of social assistance. Although the absolute approach and the income levels or poverty lines resulting from it are not used in practice for measuring poverty in Canada, the levels of income provided by provincial and municipal authorities for welfare recipients ensure only absolute (ie, substandard) levels of living.

In the relative approach, the absolute notion that poverty can be objectively defined without reference to prevailing community standards is rejected. A poor Canadian household exists in the context of a highly interrelated, well-to-do Canadian community; therefore the economic, social and political functioning of that household is relevant. Two well-known national measures based on the relative approach are those developed by the national, nonprofit social organization, the CANADIAN COUNCIL ON SOCIAL DEVELOPMENT (CCSD), and the special Senate committee on poverty. The CCSD poverty line is based on average Canadian family income, and a family is defined as poor if its income is less than 50% of average family income. Adjustments are then made for family size. The poverty line established by the Senate is similar although it uses post-tax (disposable) income. The calculation of the line is more complex, but the final effect is to produce a poverty line set at about 56% of the level of average Canadian family income.

If either the CCSD or Senate lines (and not those of STATISTICS CANADA) are used as indicators of the poverty rate, there has been no decline in poverty since 1969, which also suggests (correctly) that the relative distribution of income in Canada has remained unchanged. The CCSD and Senate lines do not adjust the poverty line for rural-urban residency, taking the view that there is no significant difference between rural and urban areas in the cost of purchasing the necessities for a basic standard of living.

The leading relative standard, however, is that employed by Statistics Canada. Canada is one of the few countries to take an annual survey of the poor, and the Statistics Canada approach has become by common usage the "official" measure of poverty, although it has never been accorded this status formally. For its annual survey, Statistics Canada begins with an income line based on the actual share of income that an average Canadian family devotes to food, clothing and shelter purchases (thus the amount of income allotted to poor families is related to the expenditure standards of the community), and then adds 20% to this share. Any family that must spend more than this share of its income on food, clothing and shelter, has so little discretionary income left that it lives in "straitened circumstances." As the living standard of the average Canadian household has risen over time, so has the poverty line, in order to maintain a relationship with living standards. Statistics Canada adjusts its income line for family size, and according to whether the household is located in an urban or rural setting. The poverty line for rural households is about 25% lower than that for urban households. StatsCanada refrains from calling its income measures poverty lines, preferring to label them "low-income cut offs."

The actual calculation of the number of people who are poor is conducted each spring through a questionnaire survey covering a representative sample of some 40 000 Canadian households (excluding native households on reserves). Among the many questions asked in the survey is the total amount of income received in the previous year. Income is defined to include wages, interest payments, government TRANSFER PAYMENTS, pension income and some income in "kind" such as free room and board given to farm workers. The family is defined as all people sharing a dwelling and related by blood or marriage.

After the income data is collected for the sample, and projections made for the Canadian population as a whole, family and individual incomes are ranked according to whether they fall above or below the poverty lines. Statistics Canada publishes the results of its income survey in such a way that it is possible to determine how many individuals and families are poor, as well as the characteristics of these households.

A major shortcoming of this type of poverty survey is that it produces a "snapshot" of poor households for that year only. In preceding or succeeding years, it is not known whether the same or different households registered poverty incomes. This is a serious omission because it is almost certainly the length of time that a person or household suffers such an income that leads to poverty conditions. In the annual survey, no distinction is made between the university student with a temporary low income, and the single-parent mother or disabled person who has been living on a poverty income for years with little prospect of escaping. Nonetheless, this survey does provide much information on how many and which types of people suffer from poverty.

The method chosen to define poverty will determine how many Canadian households are officially considered poor in any one year. Statistics Canada, in its annual report on low incomes, has estimated that 851 000 families (12.3%) and 982 000 unattached individuals (34.3%) have low incomes in Canada (1986). Female-headed single-parent families comprise 32% of poor families; indeed, this type of family with dependent children faces a 44% chance of being poor. The aged comprise 34% of the total of poor unattached individuals; elderly females face a 46% chance of being poor. Data for native people and the disabled are not systematically collected, but the consensus among experts is that these groups face above-average chances of being poor. Among low-income families in Canada it is important to note that 56% are headed by a person in the labour force. These families are frequently referred to as the "working poor" because they rely primarily on employment earnings, not public assistance, for their income. The other 44% of all poor families ("welfare poor") rely primarily on some form of public assistance for support.

As measured by Statistics Canada, the rate of family poverty declined from 21% in 1969 to 12% in 1986. However, since about 1973, the family rate has stabilized around the 12-13% level. The most likely cause for this arrested decline is the prolonged economic slump in virtually all Western industrialized economies. The resulting UNEMPLOYMENT has made it difficult for an increasing number of families to earn adequate incomes. Among unattached individuals, the decline in poverty has not been so marked. It fell from 43% (1969) to almost 34% (1986). Most of the decline has taken place in recent years, primarily as a result of gradual improvements in government-funded income retirement programs. Since a large fraction of unattached individuals are aged, improvements in programs such as the CANADA (or QUÉBEC) PENSION PLAN, OLD-AGE PENSION, Guaranteed Income Supplement, Spouses' Allowance and some provincial income supplement programs have helped more elderly to escape complete poverty.

There have been noticeable shifts since 1969 in the composition of poor households. For example, poverty is less regionally concentrated. In 1969 a family in the Atlantic provinces had almost 3 times the chance of being poor as a family

in Ontario, but by 1986 the poverty rate for families in Ontario was 9%, and for those in the Atlantic provinces 16%. Regarding the elderly in 1969, families headed by a person 65 years of age or older constituted 30% of all poor families, but by 1986 this had dropped to 11%. On the other hand, female-headed families constituted 18% of all poor families in 1969, but 35% by 1986. The shift in the composition of poverty among families has been so dramatic that poverty is less strongly associated with old age than with being female.

Poverty has also been "urbanized," ie, in 1969 just over 50% of all poor families were rural dwellers, but by 1986 this share has declined to 19%. In the largest cities (500 000 population or more), the proportion of poor families increased from 16% (1969) to 44% (1986).

Official measures of poverty in Canada date only to the 1960s, when poverty became a public issue. Much of the concern was generated by the appalling living conditions under which many of Canada's native people and elderly lived, and by large regional income disparities. This sudden "discovery" of poverty contradicted the vision of affluence prevailing in the post-WWII era. In 1964 the US launched its "war against poverty" and Canada began a more quiet campaign of study and legislation in an effort to understand better the causes of and remedies for poverty. In 1965 the federal PRIVY COUNCIL OFFICE established a group of specialists to study and encourage greater federal-provincial co-operation in combatting poverty. In the same year the COMPANY OF YOUNG CANADIANS (CYC) was created to help coordinate and stimulate local self-help efforts to overcome poverty. Although the CYC was later disbanded, it was a precursor of federal government programs such as Opportunities for Youth (OFY), the Local Initiatives Program (LIP) and Canada Works which attempted to provide employment and reduce poverty through local initiative efforts.

In 1968 Statistics Canada released a study on the incomes of Canadians that became the basis for defining and measuring low incomes in Canada. In the same year, the ECONOMIC COUNCIL OF CANADA (ECC) shocked the nation by using this new low-income measure to estimate the extent of poverty in Canada. It concluded that 27% of the Canadian population lived in poverty. In 1968, partly because of these findings, the influential special Senate committee on poverty, chaired by David CROLL, began its cross-country hearings and investigations. Its widely publicized report, released in 1971, reiterated much of what had been revealed in the ECC's report and proposed a guaranteed annual income program to eliminate poverty in Canada. Another influential commission created during this period, headed by Claude Castonguay, also released its report following a massive examination of social security in Québec. This commission also advocated (among many recommendations concerning health care, income security, employment and social services) a guaranteed annual income. The concern with poverty during the 1960s, particularly its disturbing presence among affluence, also led to several significant new pieces of antipoverty legislation. Negotiations between the provinces and the federal government, which began in 1964, resulted in the introduction of the Canada and Québec pension plans, which were based on the recognition that the private pension system did not provide adequate coverage to low-income retired workers and their families. In conjunction with these new pension plans, the Guaranteed Income Supplement Program, which assured all low-income aged a basic income support level, was implemented. The Canada Assistance Plan (CAP)

was also introduced in 1966. A comprehensive social-assistance program, it replaced the many piecemeal cost-shared programs that the federal and provincial governments had begun entering into as far back as 1927. As well as providing a major source of funds for the disabled, blind and unemployed, the CAP assisted other low-income persons, including the working poor. Also brought into federal cost sharing under CAP were a wide range of SOCIAL SERVICES, including DAY CARE, family counselling, visiting homemaker and CHILD WELFARE services. Exponents of CAP claimed it would allow for the expenditure of funds to the needy who could not secure sufficient aid, ie, it was a promise to use public funds to prevent, and not just respond, to poverty. In practice, however, CAP maintained the earlier tradition of only responding to poverty.

Another innovation in social service provision was the implementation in 1968 of the Medical Care Act (Medicare), which provided free access to a basic level of health care for all Canadians (*see* HEALTH POLICY).

During the 1970s and early 1980s, most legislative activity either represented slight improvements to, or cutbacks in, earlier legislated programs. The UNEMPLOYMENT INSURANCE Act was amended in 1971 to provide more extensive coverage to the unemployed as well as to the sick. The Child Tax Credit of 1978 extended federal benefits to families with children in a manner that was most beneficial to low-income families. Several provinces instituted income-tested payments to the aged, while Saskatchewan, Manitoba and Québec introduced programs that provided assistance to the families of the working poor. But the comprehensive federal-provincial review of Canada's social-security system conducted in the mid-1970s failed in its central purpose to establish a guaranteed annual income, and the 1980s have been marked by budget cuts on income provision and social services directed towards the poor.

The concern and legislation of the 1960s also raised the question of why there were so many poor people in a country as rich as Canada. In the prevailing ethos, poverty is perceived and treated as an individual, not a social problem, ie, individuals who are poor have themselves to blame. Therefore, it is not a country's total wealth that is relevant, but how that country distributes its wealth. A society can distribute its wealth under the laissez-faire or free-enterprise economic system, according to which people are presumed to get out of the marketplace what they put in, ie, those that put in very little or nothing get little or nothing back, and those that work at home for their lifetimes also receive nothing directly. Theoretically a society can also distribute its wealth through a collective or socialist system under which the fruits of economic production are distributed according to need. The economic and income distribution system in Canada has evolved and is still evolving from the precepts of 19th-century capitalism, although government involvement in the income distribution process ensures that those in need and those without economic means do receive some assistance. Thus the Canadian system is generally described as mixed. Most wealth is distributed through a market-based economic system, under which ownership of resources and well-paying jobs are the keys to an adequate share of the country's economic benefits. Those who are unable to find a decent place within this market system – women, the elderly, disabled persons, those with poor skills and native people – must rely on some combination of assistance from family, social organizations and government, but because individuals are held responsible for their inability to benefit from the economic system, the amount of aid is generally small and extended begrudgingly.

The plight of women and the relationship of women with the labour force have a unique history. Historically, it was accepted that women belonged in the home, where they received no direct income for their labour. If the male breadwinner leaves the household or dies, there is little provision under the Canadian legal and economic system for the woman, and she is particularly vulnerable if there are young children in her care. Divorced, separated and widowed women thus become prime candidates for poverty. On the other hand, WOMEN IN THE LABOUR FORCE are discriminated against in the labour market. On average women earn about 60% of the income of the average male worker because women have not had access to the same type of training and advancement opportunities as men; they are placed in lower-paying, lower-skilled jobs, and they frequently receive less pay than men for jobs that are identical. Consequently, women working in the labour force are not ensured of a life out of poverty, particularly if they are single parents.

Low-income households can be subclassified as either welfare poor or working poor. The former tend to be people who cannot produce, or who are believed to be incapable of producing at a level high enough to make them attractive as employees. Single-parent mothers, who are not necessarily expected to take employment while they are caring for their young children, are a large group in this category, as are native people, although in their case the reasons for their situation are complicated by the long history of PREJUDICE AND DISCRIMINATION they have suffered at the hands of Canada's non-native population.

The welfare poor depend for most of their assistance on CAP. To rely almost exclusively on the social assistance benefits provided by provincially administered plans (plus federal family allowances and child tax credits, where applicable) guarantees a poverty income. Averaging across Canada, provincial social assistance (welfare) rates provide 60% of official poverty-line income.

The working poor includes itinerant workers who are always on the margin of the labour force. They are frequently the last hired and the first laid off, but even when they are employed they work for low wages and poor benefits, are seldom able to accumulate savings, and rarely qualify for benefits such as sickness insurance, health and dental plans, private pensions and paid vacations. Their life is marked by extreme economic insecurity. The fact that about 50% of the working poor actually work year-round should put to rest the time-worn belief that people can always work their way out of poverty, but the persistence of this belief has led to a situation in Canada where the social security system provides very little comprehensive assistance to the working poor while they are working, even though they are earning poverty incomes. DAVID P. ROSS

Reading: David P. Ross, *The Canadian Fact Book on Poverty, 1983* (1983).

Powell, Ray Edwin, "Rep," business executive (b at Table Grove, Ill 7 Dec 1887; d at Montréal 9 Nov 1973). Educated at U of Ill, Powell served in the US army during WWI. He then joined Alcoa, the Aluminum Co of America, and in 1928 came to Canada, becoming a VP of ALCAN (Aluminium Co of Canada), a subsidiary of Aluminium Ltd. From 1937 to 1957, Powell was Alcan's president, overseeing an extraordinary expansion in the company's business. Because ALUMINUM was a vital war material, Powell was able to use loans from the British, American and Australian governments and tax arrangements with the government of Canada to expand his company's facili-

ties along the Saguenay R. Between 1937 and 1944, Alcan's assets increased 500%. Alcan expanded again in the early 1950s, establishing a power development and smelter at KITIMAT, BC. Under Powell, Alcan moved from being an American subsidiary to becoming an independent Canadian company. ROBERT BOTHWELL

Powell, William Dummer, chief justice of Upper Canada (b at Boston, Mass 1755; d at Toronto 6 Sept 1834). Powell went to England with his family in 1776; he revisited Boston only after the AMERICAN REVOLUTION, in a vain attempt to claim his father's confiscated estates. Called to the English Bar, in 1779 he moved to Montréal to practise law. A spokesman for Loyalists' dissatisfaction with the QUEBEC ACT, he lobbied unsuccessfully for an elected assembly and wrote the report that induced Guy CARLETON, Baron Dorchester, to set up 4 new administrative districts in what was soon to become Upper Canada. In 1789 he was appointed the first judge of the Court of Common Pleas for the district of Hesse, with headquarters at Detroit. In 1794 he became a judge of the Upper Canadian Court of King's Bench and in 1807 a member of the Executive Council. An able lawyer and a conscientious administrator, he rose to become in 1816 Speaker of the Legislative Council and chief justice, the first permanent resident of the province to hold that office. His most controversial case was the trial of Robert GOURLAY. He retired in 1825. S.R. MEALING

Powell River, BC, District Municipality, pop 12 440 (1986c), 13 423 (1981c), area 410 ha, inc 1955, is located on the E side of the Strait of GEORGIA, 140 km NE of Vancouver. It is bounded on the E by the Smith Mt Range, Powell Lk and Haslam Lk, and enjoys a mild climate year-round, moderated by the warm current of the strait. Named for Israel Wood Powell, BC Indian superintendent in the 1880s, the original settlement was a pulp and paper-milling centre. The region's economy is based on forest industries, in particular the pulp and paper operations of MACMILLAN BLOEDEL LTD, the largest source of employment. The climate and scenery make Powell River and its hinterland an attractive summer resort area. Saltwater and freshwater fishing and boating are important activities. Inauguration in 1965 of an automobile ferry from Comox, on Vancouver I, has boosted tourism. ALAN F.J. ARTIBISE

Power, Charles Gavan, "Chubby," lawyer, politician (b at Sillery, Qué 18 Jan 1888; d at Québec C 30 May 1968). Power was seriously wounded in WWI and won the Military Cross for gallantry. He denounced military "brass hats" ever after. He was MP for Québec S (his father's seat) 1917-55, when he went to the Senate. The popular MP was brought into Mackenzie KING's government – despite the PM's legitimate doubts about Power's temperance – on the advice of Ernest LAPOINTE. Power was minister of pensions and national health 1935-39, and postmaster general 1939-40, but his greatest contribution came as minister of national defence for air, 1940-44, when he fought to promote the interests of RCAF personnel serving under British command and to create Canadian squadrons in NW Europe. Blunt and emotional, he opposed CONSCRIPTION for service abroad and therefore resigned from the Cabinet in 1944. His memoir, *A Party Politician* (1966), is among the best of those written by a Canadian politician. NORMAN HILLMER

Power Corporation of Canada, controlled by Paul DESMARAIS, is a large diversified company engaged in communications, financial services, pulp, paper and packaging. Through its subsidiary, Gesca Ltée, Power publishes 4 daily newspapers in Québec, including *La Presse*. In ad-

dition, Gesca has 2 separate book-publishing operations; it also has TV and radio stations in Ontario and Québec. Its financial services include controlling interest in the Great-West Lifeco Inc, Montreal Trustco Inc, the Investors Group Inc and Pargesa Holding S.A. The company's pulp, paper and packaging interests are held in Consolidated-Bathurst Inc, a major Canadian pulp and paper firm. Power Corp's assets in 1986 exceeded $1.3 billion, with revenues amounting to $153 million. PETER S. ANDERSON

Reading: D. Greber, *Rising to Power: Paul Desmarais & Power Corporation* (1987).

Powwow, a traditional Indian celebration, in the same category as religious ceremonies, festivals, dances, rodeos and athletic contests, at which Indians and Inuit participate throughout N America. RENÉ R. GADACZ

Prairie French explorers had no precise word for the large N American grasslands, but the term *prairie* [Fr, "meadow"] implied that it was an open, grass-covered, treeless landscape. The Canadian prairies occupy the southern parts of Alberta, Saskatchewan and Manitoba and comprise a nearly semicircular arc resting on the 49th parallel and extending through Calgary, Edmonton, North Battleford, Yorkton and Winnipeg. The region is the northern extremity of a vast grassland region extending almost to the Gulf of Mexico. Prairie, often considered a featureless flatland, actually contains great diversity: from broad plains to rolling hills and plateaus, often dissected by beautiful valleys and escarpments. While GRASSES dominate the natural vegetation, prairie flowers such as violets, daisies, crocus and goldenrod add to its beauty. The prairie is also the natural habitat of PRAIRIE DOG, BISON, COYOTES, grasshoppers, gophers, prairie chickens, songbirds, deer and antelope. Extremes of CLIMATE typify the prairies: cold winters, hot summers, a wet season followed by a period of DROUGHT or very dry conditions. The severity of drought increases with distance from the forest margins. Periods of above and below average conditions are common and tend to be cyclical. The highly fertile prairie soils induced settlers from Europe, eastern Canada and the US to move into the region to farm and ranch in the latter part of the 19th century. Native prairie grasses have been largely replaced by another grass, WHEAT, the major component of western Canadian agriculture. In Canada, the word prairie is also used to refer to the 3 provinces of Manitoba, Saskatchewan and Alberta (*see* PRAIRIE WEST). *See also* GRASSLANDS NATIONAL PARK; PHYSIOGRAPHIC REGIONS. D.F. ACTON

Prairie Dog, highly gregarious, diurnal, terrestrial SQUIRREL that lives in colonies or "towns." It is very vocal and one call, a bark, prompted its generic name *Cynomys* [Lat, "dog mouse"] and its common name. Prairie dogs have receded in distribution as a result of deliberate exterminations because, although they aid soil by their excavations, they compete with domestic livestock for green plants. Of 4 species, only black-tailed prairie dog (*Cynomys ludovicianus*) extends into Canada (near Val Marie, Sask). It is pinkish-brown above, whitish below, with short ears and short, black-tipped tail. Adults weigh 1-1.5 kg. Prairie dogs remain close to elevated bare mounds that surround the mouths of their burrows, using them for vantage points. Their habit of sitting upright has given them the name "picket pin." One litter (4-5 young) is born each spring in a nesting chamber 4-5 m below the surface. Deep chambers are also used during extreme winter conditions. Prairie dogs do not hibernate, but use body fat accumulated in autumn when food is scarce. J. MARY TAYLOR

Prairie Dry Belt Disaster Situated in southeastern Alberta and southwestern Saskatchewan, the prairie dry belt was originally intended as a ranching preserve. Under insistent pressure from promoters and settlers, and blessed by dry farming "experts," the region was unwisely opened for HOMESTEADING by the Dominion. After the 1908-12 land rush, the dry belt yielded freakish, mammoth harvests in 1915 and 1916. Then DROUGHT struck with fury. In the worst-hit subregions, mostly in Alberta, not a crop of consequence was reaped until 1927. Combined with other postwar farm ills, these troubles spelled calamity.

Five major investigations were commissioned, but to little avail. Between 1921 and 1926, 138 townships in southern Alberta, comprising nearly 3.2 million acres (1.3 million ha), lost at least 55% of their population; by 1926 80% of the Tilley-East country was permanently evacuated. Farm abandonments in Alberta and the SE in the twenties exceeded those of the Great Depression. Fleeing settlers moved west, north and mostly south to the US whence most had come. In Alberta, which bore the brunt, the catastrophe stimulated the election of the UNITED FARMERS OF ALBERTA in 1921, new dry-farming techniques, more irrigation, large school divisions, county government, the "special areas" and a revolutionary arrangement between creditors and debtors – the Debt Adjustment Act.

For the dubious southeast, the 1930s was merely a bitter sequel. In the end, the great blunder of settlement ruined thousands, precipitated a spate of ghost towns, and nearly bankrupted Alberta.   DAVID C. JONES

Prairie Farm Rehabilitation Administration This agency was established by the federal government in 1935 in the midst of a prolonged and disastrous DROUGHT to deal with the problems of soil EROSION (and related SOIL-CONSERVATION problems) and lack of water resources for agricultural development. Emergency programs instituted to deal with the devastating drought included on-farm dugouts for the conservation of water for livestock, strip farming to prevent extensive soil drifting, seeding of abandoned land for community pastures, and extensive tree-planting projects to protect against wind-induced soil erosion. The PFRA's soil-conservation role was transferred to another agency in 1946, but work in the area of water development continued. The PFRA has been heavily involved in large-scale water development and conservation programs, including the St Mary River Irrigation Project, the Bow River Irrigation Project and the South Saskatchewan River Irrigation Project. There are few prairie communities which have not benefited from its activities. Today the agency is involved in the operation of 4 programs: Rural Water Development, Community Pastures, Tree Nurseries and Engineering Services.   J.C. GILSON

Reading: James Gray, *Men Against the Desert* (1967).

Prairie West, the "western interior" of Canada, bounded roughly by Lk Superior and the Rocky Mts, the 49th parallel of latitude and the low Arctic. It was peopled in 5 great eras: the migration from Asia, probably 20-40 000 years ago, produced a native population of 20-50 000 by about 1640; several thousand European and Canadian fur traders followed by several hundred British immigrants, between 1640 and 1840, created dozens of small outposts and a few European-style settlements, the largest being the RED RIVER COLONY; the third wave, 1840s-90s, consisted chiefly of Canadians of British heritage; the fourth and by far the largest was drawn from many nations and occurred 1897-1929, with a

hiatus 1914-22 associated with WWI; and the fifth, drawn from other Canadian provinces and from around the world, commenced in the late 1940s and has continued with fluctuations to the present. Throughout the last century, the region has also steadily lost residents, as a result of migration to other parts of Canada and the world.

The first immigrants moved between resource zones according to the dictates of the season, the fortunes of the hunt, and diplomatic relations with neighbouring groups. In the 18th century they utilized European trade goods such as axes and knives, and were affected by some European innovations, particularly the gun and the horse, but they remained in control of their domestic economies and diplomatic alliances. Native autonomy was lost in the 19th century, partly through population pressure from eastern N America and partly because of the destruction of the single, crucial element in the plains economy – the buffalo (*see* BISON; BUFFALO HUNT). Seven INDIAN TREATIES were negotiated in the 1870s between the Canadian government and the natives of the western interior, exchanging native sovereignty over the land for government promises of economic assistance, education and the creation of reserves for native people. Thus, in a few short decades, prairie natives became wards of the state.

From the European perspective, the early history of the western interior was the story of FUR-TRADE competition. The English HUDSON'S BAY COMPANY, fd 1670, traded from posts on Hudson Bay until competition forced it to establish inland houses in the 1770s. The French and later the NORTH WEST COMPANY, with Montréal as headquarters, created an extensive network of posts that was pushed into the Prairie West by the LA VÉRENDRYES in the 1730s, and extended by Peter POND in the 1770s and Alexander MACKENZIE, 1789-93. Deadly competition finally forced the merger of the HBC and the NWC in 1821. The restructured HBC ruled the fur trade and the region for another 5 decades.

Some traders established liaisons with native women. Their offspring, whether French-speaking (Métis) or English-speaking ("mixed bloods" or country born), were sufficiently numerous by the early 19th century to constitute the largest group in the Red River Colony and an important component of fur-company operations. They led the defence of local interests against incoming speculators when outside interest in the region quickened in the 1840s-60s. Canada eventually secured sovereignty over RUPERT'S LAND, but only after the 1869-70 RED RIVER REBELLION led by Louis RIEL resulted in significant revisions to the terms allowing the region's entry into CONFEDERATION.

Because of the federal government's great powers and because of PM J.A. Macdonald's decision to retain control of western lands, the policy framework for development was created in Ottawa. Decisions taken between 1870 and 1874 on the dispatch of the North-West Mounted Police, the square survey (*see* DOMINION LANDS POLICY; SURVEYING), the policy on HOMESTEADING and immigration recruitment activities remained cornerstones of prairie history for 2 generations. Crucial decisions on tariff policy and the CANADIAN PACIFIC RAILWAY followed, 1879-80. The region was to become an agricultural hinterland, built upon international IMMIGRATION and the family farm, and integrated with a growing manufacturing sector in central Canada. The failure of the 1885 NORTHWEST REBELLION and the passage of the Manitoba Schools Act and other language legislation in 1890 made plain that the defining elements of prairie society were henceforth to be Protestant, English speaking, and British. The creation of Saskatchewan and Alberta in 1905 (*see* AUTONOMY

BILLS) seemed to demonstrate that the British tradition of peaceful evolution from colony to self-governing state had been fulfilled.

New forces at work in the Prairie West around 1900 made complacency inappropriate. Social leaders were troubled by the arrival of hundreds of thousands of non-British immigrants who placed great strains upon prairie institutions during the next few decades. The newcomers, on the other hand, relinquished much of their traditional culture as they helped to build the new West. Scandinavians and Germans assimilated quickly; MENNONITES, JEWS and UKRAINIANS sought to retain more of their cultural heritage, and eventually helped to create a multicultural definition of Canada; HUTTERITES remained isolated from the larger community; and some other religious groups – notably a few DOUKHOBORS and Mennonites – preferred to leave the region rather than accommodate to its norms. By the 1950s the Prairies were far closer to a British Canadian model than to that of any other culture.

Political institutions, too, underwent severe testing in the early 20th century. A wide gap between the wealthy and the poor produced real tension. In cities such as Winnipeg and Calgary, luxurious homes in segregated residential areas, exclusive clubs, colleges and social events, and the concentration of political and economic power in the hands of a few were signs that a ruling class was evolving. By contrast, the squalor of slum areas such as Winnipeg's North End, some frontier construction camps, and resource towns such as Lovettville and Cadomin, Alta, suggested that a class struggle was in the making. The intensity of labour-management conflicts, especially in Winnipeg (*see* WINNIPEG GENERAL STRIKE) and the Alberta coal towns, should be seen in this context.

A full-scale class struggle did not develop in the early 20th century for 3 reasons. The first was the relative openness of the agricultural frontier: the availability of homesteads undercut the militancy of many camp and mine workers by offering a ready alternative, a modest living and hope for the future. At this early stage, the future of agriculture was too uncertain to permit the existence of firm class identities among farmers. Second was the development of a professional middle class: the teachers, doctors, social workers and journalists belonged neither to the business elite nor to the working class, and simultaneously tempered the crudeness of the economic decision makers while offering aid and hope to the workers. The third factor working against class formation was the GREAT DEPRESSION. So devastating was the combination of drought, international trade crisis, commodity price declines and the disappearance of local investment that prairie society went into prolonged stasis. Ethnic hostility, serious in the late 1920s (*see* KU KLUX KLAN), dissipated in the face of this more serious crisis. Political expressions of anger were channelled into either the moderate CO-OPERATIVE COMMONWEALTH FEDERATION or Alberta's variant of the SOCIAL CREDIT movement. The Prairie West entered WWII poorer and more united than at any time since 1900.

After 1940 a remarkable shift in prairie fortunes occurred. Wealth flowed into the region as OIL and POTASH, as well as URANIUM and other minerals, diversified an economy that had once relied on WHEAT. Improvements in agriculture, which ranged from larger equipment to fertilizers, herbicides and new plant strains, increased productivity, reduced the size of the work force and hastened the departure of farm children to urban centres; prairie farms in 1986 numbered half the 1941 total. Accompanying the economic gains was a significant change in material culture. Television, cars, airplanes and universities brought the Prairie West closer to a growing global cultur-

At the elbow of the North Saskatchewan R, Sept 1871. The Red River Cart was the primary means of transporting goods among the Métis traders of the Prairie West (*courtesy National Archives of Canada/PA-138573/photo by Charles Horetzky*).

al consensus. Social issues within the region increasingly resembled those in other nations: the indigenous peoples' renaissance, an international political and cultural phenomenon, was an important development; the growing gulf between fundamentalists and modernists in the Christian churches was part of an international trend; and political debates about the fate of the region, as in other nations, were grounded upon local perceptions of MULTINATIONAL CORPORATIONS and the global balance of power. Similarly, social change assumed an international cast: the remarkable changes in the family that accompanied widespread birth control, higher employment rates for women, higher divorce rates and increases in life span were evident in the Prairie West and around the N Atlantic world. Prairie art also became international: though rooted firmly, even self-consciously, in local images, prairie artists, novelists and performers in theatre and dance found their context, their standards and their audience in an international rather than a local or regional community. The Prairie West, 1940s-80s, became a neighbourhood of the N Atlantic industrial capitalist world. GERALD FRIESEN

Reading: Gerald Friesen, *Prairie Road* (1984); J.A. Lower, *Western Canada* (1983).

Pratley, Gerald Arthur (b at London, Eng 3 Sept 1923). A noted film critic and commentator, he is the founder-director of the Ontario Film Institute, established in 1968, an organization with a mandate to preserve, catalogue, publish and exhibit world cinema. He came to Canada in 1946 and 2 years later became the CBC's first film critic. During this time he was active with the Toronto Film Society, the Toronto and District Film Council, the A-G-E Film Society. From 1970-75 he was the director of the Stratford International Film Festival, and from 1969-76 the chairman of the International Jury of the Canadian Film Awards. He has published extensively in a number of international journals and written books on the cinema. One of the first defenders of a strong, indigenous cinema for Canada, he has tirelessly worked in the cultural arena to make this a possibility. In 1984 Pratley was made a Member of the Order of Canada. PIERS HANDLING

Pratt, Edwin John, poet, professor, critic (b at Western Bay, Nfld 4 Feb 1882; d at Toronto 26 Apr 1964). Son of a Methodist minister, Pratt grew up in a succession of Newfoundland outports, completing his schooling at the Methodist Coll, St John's. After teaching for 2 years he became a candidate for the Methodist ministry in 1904, serving a 3-year probation before entering Victoria Coll, U of T, where he studied theology and psychology. Ordained in 1913, Pratt never served as a regular minister, teaching psy-

chology at U of T before being appointed to the department of English at Victoria Coll in 1920, where he taught until retirement in 1953.

Pratt began publishing poetry in 1914, but made no notable impression until *Newfoundland Verse* (1923). Thereafter in a dozen volumes of varied poetry, from *The Witches' Brew* and *Titans* in 1926 to *Collected Poems* in 1958, he established himself as the foremost Canadian poet of the first half of the century. Recipient of many honours, he was elected to the Royal Soc of Canada in 1930, and was awarded its Lorne Pierce Medal for poetry in 1940. Books of his poetry won Governor General's Awards in 1937, 1940 and 1952. In 1946 he was made a CMG by King George VI. From 1936 to 1943 he was editor of *The Canadian Poetry Magazine*.

Pratt's poetry frequently reflects his Newfoundland background, though specific references to it appear in relatively few poems, mostly in *Newfoundland Verse*. But the sea and maritime life are central to many of his poems, both short (eg, "Erosion," "Sea-Gulls," "Silences") and long, such as *The Cachalot* (1926), describing duels between a whale and its foes, a giant squid and a whaling ship and crew; *The Roosevelt and the Antinoe* (1930), recounting the heroic rescue of the crew of a sinking freighter in a winter hurricane; *The Titanic* (1935), an ironic retelling of a well-known marine tragedy; and *Behind the Log* (1947), the dramatic story of the N Atlantic convoys during WWII. Themes from science and technology also appear frequently in his work, and during the 1930s his poems manifested much concern with contemporary economic and social problems; *The Fable of the Goats* (1937) was an antiwar poem written on the eve of WWII. In *Brébeuf and His Brethren* (1940) and *Towards the Last Spike* (1952), Pratt turned to specifically Canadian, historical, heroic themes, in the former recounting with accuracy and vivid depiction the martyrdoms of the Jesuit missionaries to HURONIA in the 17th century, and in the latter giving a dramatic account of the building of the CPR.

Poet E.J. Pratt, *c* 1930 (*courtesy David Pitt*).

Pratt presents a generally realistic, unsentimental view of life, often tinctured with humour and irony. The qualities he most values and celebrates are courage, self-sacrifice, loyalty and defiance of oppressors. A major poet, he is, nevertheless, an isolated figure, belonging to no school or movement and directly influencing few other poets of his time. DAVID G. PITT

Reading: Sandra Djwa, *E.J. Pratt: The Evolutionary Vision* (1974); David G. Pitt, *E.J. Pratt: The Truant Years 1882-1927* (1984) and *E.J. Pratt: The Master Years 1927-1964* (1987); E.J. Pratt, *Collected Poems*, ed N. Frye (1958); John Sutherland, *The Poetry of E.J. Pratt: A New Interpretation* (1956); Milton Wilson, *E.J. Pratt* (1969).

Memorial Window (1982), original signed screenprint by Christopher Pratt (*courtesy Mira Godard Gallery/Christopher Pratt*).

Pratt, John Christopher, painter, printmaker (b at St John's 9 Dec 1935). He was encouraged by his wife Mary PRATT to study at the Glasgow School of Art (1957-59) and at Mount Allison (1959-61), where he worked with Alex COLVILLE. He then taught at Memorial before deciding to paint full-time in 1963. He is well known for his realistic and curiously intense studies with typically eastern Canadian settings, purged of all extraneous detail. He focuses on realistic images drawn from recollection (many of his memories evoke physical environments). Through Pratt's eyes, Newfoundland resembles another country; it is a stark land of sharp contrasts. His architectural studies are equally trim and lacking in sentimentality. All his work projects a mood of aloneness and stark, austere beauty, the simple facts of life.

Pratt's figure subjects suggest the same hauntingly remote but sturdy reality. Sometimes their shy sensualism can be disturbing in the midst of Pratt's focus on a quiet existence. Along with Colville he is one of the greatest classicists of contemporary Canadian PAINTING. A major retrospective of the artist's work toured Canada in 1986. JOAN MURRAY

Pratt, Mary, née West, painter (b at Fredericton 15 Mar 1935). For subject matter Mary Pratt uses things found in the kitchen of her home at St Mary's Bay, Nfld: baked apples or cod fillets on tin foil, eviscerated chickens on a Coca-Cola box, 2 lunch pails. Some of her earlier paintings have a whimsical mood; some of her later ones, ambitious figure works in a large format, such as a moose carcass hanging in a service station, are more sombre. But her kitchen imagery is what has established her reputation. Pratt paints with care. Her training has been long in the making. She took her first colour lessons from her mother, Katherine E. MacMurray. Then she studied at Mount Allison (1953-56) with Alex COLVILLE, Lawren Phillips HARRIS, and drawing master Ted Pulford, graduating in 1961. Often she works

Many of the subjects in Mary Pratt's paintings are things found in the kitchen home, such as *Christmas Turkey* (1980), oil on board (*courtesy Robert McLaughlin Gallery, Oshawa*).

from slides, a recent tendency in international art which relates her to American photo-realists such as Richard Estes, Chuck Close and Ben Schonzeit. But unlike their work, her domestic images recall old masters like Chardin. She illustrated the book *Across the Table: An Indulgent Look at Food in Canada* (1985), by Cynthia Wine. She is married to painter Christopher PRATT.

JOAN MURRAY

Pre-Dorset Culture, 2000-500 BC, represents the first occupation of arctic N America by Paleoeskimos. These people, probably related biologically and culturally to the INUIT, seem to have crossed Bering Strait from Siberia shortly before 2000 BC and then spread rapidly across arctic Canada and Greenland. Lacking much of the technology that allowed the more recent Inuit to adapt to arctic conditions, they nevertheless developed a successful way of life based on the hunting of seals and other small sea mammals, caribou, muskoxen and small game. They lived in temporary settlements of tents and perhaps snowhouses. Their tools and weapons had remarkably small cutting edges chipped from stone, which has led archaeologists to refer to Pre-Dorset and the related Denbigh Flint Complex in Alaska as the "Arctic Small Tool tradition." Pre-Dorset developed into DORSET CULTURE *c* 500 BC. *See also* PREHISTORY. ROBERT McGHEE

Prehistory The first human occupants of Canada arrived during the last ICE AGE, which began about 80 000 years ago and ended about 12 000 years ago. During much of this period almost all of Canada was covered by several hundred metres of glacial ice. The amount of water locked in the continental GLACIERS caused world sea levels to drop by over 100 m, creating land bridges in areas now covered by shallow seas. One such land bridge occupied what is now the Bering Sea, joining Siberia and Alaska by a flat plain over 1000 km wide (*see* BERINGIA). Across this plain moved large herbivores such as caribou, muskoxen, bison, horse and mammoth, and at some time during the ice age these animals were followed by human hunters who had adapted their way of life to the cold climates of northern latitudes.

There is continuing argument regarding the time of the first immigration to the New World. It was long thought that humans could not have reached the American continents until the end of the ice age, that prior to the last major ice advance, 25 000 to 15 000 years ago, human cultures in the Old World had developed neither technologies capable of living in the cold arctic conditions of NE Asia nor watercraft capable of crossing the open water of a flooded Bering Strait. Recent research indicates, however, that man had reached Australia across a wide stretch of open sea by at least 30 000 years ago, and that as

long as 200 000 years ago the Paleolithic (Old Stone Age) occupants of Europe were living under extremely cold environmental conditions and may have had watercraft capable of crossing the Strait of Gibraltar. It is theoretically possible, therefore, that humans could have reached N America from NE Siberia at any time during the past 100 000 years.

Paleoindian Period During the past few decades, several New World archaeological sites have been claimed to date to the period of the last ice age. The earliest widespread occupation that is universally accepted by archaeologists, however, begins only 12 000 years ago. Much of Alaska and the Yukon Territory remained unglaciated throughout the ice age, probably because of a dry climate and insufficient snowfall (*see* NUNATAK). Joined to Siberia by the Beringian Plain, and separated from the rest of N America by glaciers, these regions, called Beringia, were essentially part of Asia. The environment was a cold TUNDRA, although spruce forests were present at least during interstadial or nonglacial periods, and supported a wide range of animals. Archaeological finds along the OLD CROW BASIN in the northern Yukon have been claimed to indicate the presence of Paleolithic hunting populations in the period 25 000 to 30 000 years ago; however, all these objects have been found in redeposited sediments, many of them may have been manufactured by agencies other than man (such as carnivore chewing or ice movement), and the age of the few definitely man-made artifacts has been questioned.

The archaeological site of the earliest accepted occupation by man is BLUEFISH CAVES in N Yukon. Here, in 3 small caves overlooking a wide basin, have been found a few chipped stone artifacts in layers of sediment containing the bones of extinct FOSSIL ANIMALS, which radiocarbon dating indicates have an age of at least 10 000 to 13 000, and possibly 15 000 to 18 000 years ago (*see* GEOLOGICAL DATING; GEOLOGICAL HISTORY; PALEONTOLOGY). The artifacts include types similar to those of the late Paleolithic of NE Asia, and probably represent an expansion of Asian hunting peoples across Beringia and Alaska into northwestern Canada. We do not know whether people similar to those who occupied the Bluefish Caves expanded farther into N America. A relatively narrow ice-free corridor may have existed between the Cordilleran glaciers of the western mountains and the Laurentide ice sheet extending from the Canadian SHIELD, or such a corridor may have opened only after the glaciers began to melt and retreat about 15 000 years ago (*see* GLACIATION). No early sites have been found along the route of this corridor in the western NWT and Alberta, but by 12 000 years ago some groups had penetrated to the area of the western US and had developed a way of life adapted to hunting the large herbivores that grazed the grasslands and ice-edge tundras of the period.

By about 11 000 years ago some of these PALEOINDIANS, as they are known to archaeologists, began to move northward into Canada as the southern margin of the continental glaciers retreated. Environmental zones similar to those found today in arctic and subarctic Canada shifted northward as well. In many regions the ice front was marked by huge meltwater lakes (eg, Lk AGASSIZ), their outlets dammed by the glaciers to the N, surrounded by land supporting tundra vegetation grazed on by caribou, muskoxen and other herbivores. To the S of this narrow band of tundra were spruce forests and grasslands, and the Paleoindians probably followed the northern edge of these zones as they moved across Canada. Paleoindian sites are radiocarbon dated to around 10 500 years ago in areas as far separated as central Nova

Scotia and northern BC. The largest sites yet found in Canada are concentrated in southern Ontario, where they are clustered along the southern shore of Lk Algonquin, the forerunner of the present Lk Huron and Georgian Bay (*see* GREAT LAKES). By about 10 000 years ago Paleoindians had probably occupied at least the southern portions of all provinces except Newfoundland. Most sites are limited to scatters of chipped stone artifacts, among them spearpoints with a distinctive channel or "flute" removed from either side of the base to allow mounting in a split haft. Such "fluted points" are characteristic of early Paleoindian technologies from Canada to southern South America, and serve to define the first widespread occupation of the New World about 9 000 to 12 000 years ago.

Because very little organic material is preserved on archaeological sites of this period, it is difficult to reconstruct the way of life that the Paleoindians followed. In the dry western regions of the US, where sites are better preserved, they appear to have concentrated on hunting large herbivores, including bison and mammoths. In Canada we can only speculate that Paleoindians preyed on the caribou herds of the E and the bison herds of the northern plains, as well as fishing and hunting small game. Coastlines were well below present sea level, so any evidence of Paleoindian use of coastal resources has been destroyed by the later rise in sea level.

While the Paleoindians occupied southern Canada, the continental glaciers melted rapidly and disappeared by about 7000 years ago. A warmer climate than the present existed until about 4000 years ago, and the environments of the country diversified as coniferous forest, deciduous woodland, grassland and tundra vegetation became established in suitable zones. The ways of life of the Paleoindians occupying these environmental zones became diversified as they, and later immigrants from Siberia, adapted to the conditions and resources of local regions. The development over time of the various cultures of prehistoric native peoples is therefore best described on a regional basis.

West Coast There is little evidence that the classic "fluted point" Paleoindian cultures penetrated the coastal regions of BC and the earliest occupants of the area appear to have been related to other cultural traditions. About 9000 to 5000 years ago the southern regions were occupied by people of the Old Cordilleran tradition, whose sites are marked by crude pebble tools made by knocking a few flakes from heavy beach cobbles and by more finely made lanceolate projectile points or knives chipped from stone. No organic material is preserved on these sites, but their locations suggest that these people were adapted primarily to interior and riverine resources, gradually making greater use of marine resources.

The northern and central coast was occupied by people of the early Coast Microblade tradition who also used pebble tools but lacked lanceolate points. Microblades are small razorlike tools of flint or obsidian made by a specialized technique developed in the Old World and were widely used during this period in Alaska and NW Canada. It is suggested that these people entered BC from the N and that they were related to Alaskan groups who may have crossed the Bering land bridge shortly before it disappeared.

It is unclear how either of these 2 groups were related to those who occupied the West Coast after 5000 years ago, but it seems likely that both contributed to the ancestry of the later occupants. At about 5000 years ago a major change occurred in coastal occupation. Whereas earlier sites were all relatively small, indicating brief occupations by small groups of people, large shell middens characterize most of the more recent sites. Stabilization of sea levels probably resulted in increased salmon stocks, which in turn allowed people to store more food and live a more sedentary life in coastal villages that were occupied for years or generations. Animal bones and bone tools have been preserved in the shell middens and artifacts of wood or plant fibre in occasional waterlogged deposits, allowing archaeologists to reconstruct a more complete picture of the way of life of these people than of earlier occupants of the region.

Artifacts recovered from the earliest sites indicate an efficient adaptation to the coastal environment. Barbed harpoons for taking sea mammals, fish hooks, weights for fish nets, ground slate knives and weapon points, and woodworking tools that could have been used for the construction of boats occur on coastal sites of the period. Waterlogged sites have produced examples of basketry, netting, woven fabrics and wooden boxes similar to those known from the historic period. By about 3500 years ago there is evidence that this adaptation was beginning to lead to the development of the sophisticated societies known from the historic NORTHWEST COAST. Burials that show differential treatment in the number of grave goods for members of the community, as well as the appearance in some regions of artificial skull deformation, suggest the existence of the ranked societies with which these practices were later associated. The high incidence of broken bones and skulls among male burials, coincidentally with the appearance of decorated clubs of stone or whalebone, suggests the development of a pattern of warfare. Social organizations based on status and wealth may also account for the appearance at this time of numerous art objects, personal ornaments such as beads, labrets and earspools, and exotic goods indicating widespread trade networks to the interior and the south. In the Strait of Georgia region, the Locarno Beach (3500-2500 years ago) and the Marpole (2500-1500 years ago) phases are seen as a local cultural climax, producing evidence of a richer culture than that which existed in the area in more recent times (*see* INDIAN ART).

A similar situation appears to have characterized most coastal regions during the past 1500 years. This interpretation is based on the decline of the sculpted stone artwork that characterized the preceding period, perhaps indicating only a change from art in stone to art in wood and woven fabrics, which are poorly preserved archaeologically but were highly developed by the historic occupants of the region. This period produces the first definite evidence for occupation of the large plank-house villages characteristic of the historic period, and of major earthworks and defensive sites indicating an increase in warfare. Stone pipes mark the introduction of TOBACCO, the only agricultural crop grown in the area in prehistoric times. Building on the adaptational base developed over the previous 3000 years, the people of the past 1500 years developed the various tribal traditions and ways of life of the historic Northwest Coast Indians (*see* NATIVE PEOPLE).

Intermontane Region The valleys and plateaus of interior BC are characterized by diverse environments, ranging from boreal forests through grasslands to almost desert conditions. The prehistoric cultures of the area were correspondingly diverse and this variety, combined with the lack of sufficient archaeological research in the region, results in an unclear picture of the prehistory of the area.

Finds of Paleoindian projectile points and other artifacts indicate that the earliest occupants of the area came from the plains, adapting their grassland bison-hunting way of life to the pursuit of

bison, wapiti and caribou in the intermontane valleys. Little is known of these people, but the skeleton of one man who died in a mudslide near Kamloops is radiocarbon dated to about 8250 years ago and is thus the earliest well-dated human skeleton known from Canada. Analysis of the composition of the bones indicates that this man lived primarily on land animals rather than on the salmon of the Thompson R. Between 8000 and 3000 years ago the area appears to have been occupied by various groups who manufactured and used microblades and who are thought to have been related to the microblade-using peoples of the N coast or of the Yukon interior. The riverine location of many microblade sites suggests that these groups were developing adaptations based on the salmon resources of interior rivers, but little else is known.

A major change in the occupation of the region began about 3000 years ago, with the introduction of semisubterranean pit houses from the Columbia Plateau to the south. Pit house villages grew larger through time, indicating a more efficient economy and an increasingly sedentary way of life. As in the coastal areas to the W, the appearance of exotic trade goods (shells), stone sculpture and differential burial patterns is interpreted as evidence of more complex societies in which ranking was based on wealth and display. Over the past 3000 years cultural influences from the West Coast, the plains and the Columbia Plateau combined to form the cultures of the various interior people of BC.

Plains and Prairies The northern plains and prairies of central Canada, like no other region of N America, provided an environment in which the Paleoindians of 10 000 years ago were able to continue their way of life with relatively little alteration until the time of European contact. As the large herbivores of the ice age became extinct in the early postglacial period, these people transferred their pursuit to the various species of now-extinct bison that occupied the grasslands. Although heavily dependent on bison, Paleoindians and their later descendants must also have been hunters of smaller game and gatherers of plant foods where available. They almost certainly developed techniques of communal hunting involving ambush or the driving of bison to hunters armed with spears and darts thrown with throwing boards. ARCHAEOLOGY knows these people primarily through the chipped flint spearpoints that they used. By about 9000 years ago their fluted projectile points had been replaced by lanceolate or stemmed varieties characteristic of the late Palaeoindian Plano tradition. Between approximately 9000 and 7000 years ago the Plano people developed a widespread and apparently efficient bison-hunting adaptation across the northern plains, and by at least 7000 years ago caribou hunters using spearpoints obviously related to those of the Plano tradition had pushed northward to the Barren Lands between Great Bear Lake and Hudson Bay.

The following 2 millennia, between approximately 7000 and 5000 years ago, are poorly known on the northern plains. This period saw the climax of the postglacial warm period or altithermal, and it is suggested that heat and drought reduced the carrying capacity of the grasslands so that the area was occupied by fewer bison and consequently by fewer bison hunters. Sites around the fringes of the plains, and some sites in the plains area itself, show continuing occupation, and the development of spearpoints with notches for hafting. Such points are characteristic of the following Middle Prehistoric period (approximately 5000 to 2000 years ago), during which various groups developed more efficient communal bison-hunting techniques, including

the use of pounds and jumps over which the bison were driven.

The past 2000 years saw the introduction to the plains area of various influences emanating from the eastern woodlands and from the Mississippi and Missouri valley peoples to the S. During the early first millennium AD small chipped stone arrow points began to replace the spearpoints of earlier times, and the introduction of the bow must have increased hunting efficiency. Pottery cooking vessels and containers, of types similar to those in use to the E and S, were used. Burial mounds were constructed in some regions, especially in southern Manitoba, and exotic trade goods indicate contacts with the farming people of the Missouri Valley. Although most of the northern plains was beyond the limit of prehistoric agriculture, relatively small-scale farming was attempted in the more southerly regions.

The westward push of European settlement in the 18th century caused a rapid acceleration of change in prehistoric plains life, as tribes from the eastern woodlands began to move westward onto the grasslands. Horses, which had gradually spread northward from the Spanish settlements in the American SW, reached the Canadian plains about 1730, causing a revolution in aboriginal techniques of hunting, travelling and warfare. For the next 150 years, until the disappearance of the bison in the late 19th century, the Canadian plains and prairies saw the development of a way of life that must have been dramatically richer, more nomadic and more varied than that of earlier occupants of the area.

Eastern Woodlands Early Paleoindian hunters using fluted spear points had occupied southern Ontario, and probably the St Lawrence Valley, by at least 10 000 years ago. With the draining of the large ice-edge lakes and seas of the region, the extinction of the ice-age fauna, and the establishment of coniferous forests, the environments of these regions changed dramatically during the following 2 millennia. The next occupation of the region was by late Paleoindians using artifacts similar to those of the Plano tradition, which developed on the plains to the W. The best evidence for Plano occupation comes from the northern shores of Lks Superior and Huron, but Plano-related sites are known from the upper St Lawrence Valley and as far E as the Gaspé Peninsula. These eastern Plano people of some 9000 to 7000 years ago were probably big-game hunters who were heavily dependent on caribou, the predominant herbivore in the subarctic forests of the period.

The following millennia, with warmer climates and the establishment of deciduous forests, saw the development of ARCHAIC cultures. The Archaic label is applied to cultures throughout eastern N America which show adaptations to the utilization of local animal, fish and plant resources, and which are consequently much more varied than the widespread but relatively uniform Paleoindian cultures that preceded them. These adaptations probably allowed increases in the populations of many areas, and greater social complexity is suggested by complex burial practices and the existence of long-distance trade. The Archaic stage is also marked archaeologically by the development of new items of technology: stemmed and notched spear points and knives, bone harpoons, ground stone weapon points and woodworking tools (gouges, axes), and in some areas tools and ornaments made from native COPPER.

The Canadian Shield area of central and northern Québec and Ontario was occupied at this time by groups belonging to the Shield Archaic culture. They apparently developed about 7000 years ago out of northern Plano cultures such as those which occupied the Barren Grounds west of Hudson Bay or those known from northwestern

A lanceolate-triangular stone point, a small-stemmed point and a stemmed point from the Klo-kut site, Old Crow, YT (*courtesy National Museums of Canada/Canadian Museum of Civilization/K75-946*).

Ontario. Since the acid forest soils of the region have destroyed all organic remains, we know relatively little of their way of life. From the locations of their camps, however, they were probably generalized hunters heavily dependent on caribou and fish. Although pottery and other elements were introduced from the S over the past 3000 years, marking the Woodland period of local prehistory, it seems likely that the Archaic way of life remained relatively unchanged and was much like that of the Algonquian peoples of this area at the time of European contact and the beginning of the FUR TRADE.

The deciduous forest areas to the S supported denser populations than the spruce forests to the N and saw the development, about 6000 years ago, of the Laurentian Archaic, probably from earlier Archaic cultures of the area. These people were generalized hunters and gatherers of the relatively abundant animal and plant resources of the region. Exotic materials, such as copper and marine shells, most often found as grave goods in an elaborate burial ceremonial, indicate extensive trade contacts to the S, E and W.

The appearance of pottery, introduced from areas S of the Great Lakes between 3000 and 2500 years ago, is used archaeologically to mark the beginning of the Woodland period. As in the regions to the N, the initial Woodland period probably saw few changes in the general way of life of local peoples. During the following centuries, however, there is evidence of continuing and expanding influence from the S, including an elaborate mortuary complex involving mound burial, which appears to have been transferred, or at least copied, from the Adena and Hopewell cultures of the Ohio Valley. The most important introduction was agriculture, based on crops that had been developed in Mexico and Central America several millennia previously, and which had gradually spread northward as they were adapted to cooler climatic conditions.

The first crop to appear was maize, which began to be cultivated in southern Ontario about 1500 years ago and was a major supplement to a hunting and gathering economy. The early maize farmers occupied relatively permanent

villages of multifamily wood and bark houses, often fortified with palisades as protection from the warfare that appears to have intensified with the introduction of agriculture. By 1350 AD beans and squash were added to local agriculture, providing a nutritionally balanced diet that led to a decrease in the importance of hunting and gathering of wild foods (*see* PALYNOLOGY; PLANTS, NATIVE USES). At the time of European contact this agricultural life-style was characteristic of the Iroquoian peoples who occupied the region from southwestern Ontario to the middle St Lawrence Valley. It is the only region of Canada in which prehistoric agriculture was established as the local economic base, and was the area of greatest aboriginal population density. The late prehistoric Iroquoians lived in villages composed of large multifamily LONGHOUSES, with some of the larger communities containing more than 2000 people. Wide-ranging social, trade and political connections spanned their area of occupation, as a complement to the warfare which occupied much of their attention. These patterns intensified with the appearance of Europeans and European trade goods during the 17th century, and eventually led to the destruction of the Canadian Iroquoians during the mid-17th century at the hands of their Iroquois neighbours to the south of Lk Ontario.

East Coast Paleoindians had occupied the Maritime provinces by at least 10 000 years ago, but evidence of their presence is slight as sea levels were much lower than at present and only traces of interior camps can be found above present sea level. The same problem restricts our knowledge of early Archaic sites, although we can probably assume that there was continuous occupation throughout this period as there was in the Eastern Woodlands area to the west. The best evidence of early Archaic occupation is found in the Strait of Belle Isle area of Labrador, where initial occupation occurred before 8000 years ago and is marked by chipped stone artifacts suggesting a late Paleoindian/Archaic transition. The coastal location of these early Archaic sites suggests a

Artist's recreation of a prehistoric mastadon hunt. Human hunters first came to N America in pursuit of large mammals. Painting by Lewis Parker (*courtesy National Museums of Canada and Lewis Parker*).

maritime adaptation, an interpretation reinforced by the 7500-year-old burial mound at L'ANSE AMOUR BURIAL SITE in which was found a toggling harpoon, a walrus tusk and an artifact of walrus ivory. The term Maritime Archaic is applied to these people and their descendants.

Coastal hunting and fishing allowed Maritime Archaic people to expand to far northern Labrador by 6000 years ago, and to Newfoundland by about 5000 years ago. For the following 2000 years they were the primary occupants of these areas, developing a distinctive maritime way of life with barbed harpoons, fishing gear, ground-slate weapons and ground-stone woodworking tools. They also elaborated a mortuary complex in which large cemeteries were used over considerable lengths of time, the burials accompanied by large numbers of grave goods and heavily sprinkled with red ochre. Cemeteries of this type are found in the Maritime provinces and New England. Similarities in burial traditions, artifacts and the physical type of the skeletons suggest relationships to the contemporaneous Laurentian Archaic of the Eastern Woodlands, and it seems likely that Laurentian people occupied some regions of the Maritime provinces.

Between 4000 and 2500 years ago the Maritime Archaic people were displaced from most of coastal Labrador by a southward expansion of Paleoeskimos from the Arctic, and by other Archaic groups moving eastward from the Shield area and the St Lawrence Valley. The Dorset Paleoeskimos also occupied Newfoundland for about a millennium, beginning about 2500 years ago. With the withdrawal of the Paleoeskimos from Newfoundland and all but northern Labrador about 1500 years ago, these areas were reoccupied by Indians who were probably ancestral to the Labrador Naskapi and Newfoundland BEOTHUK. We do not know whether these were the descendants of earlier Maritime Archaic people, or of other groups that moved to the area at a later time.

In the Maritime provinces to the south of the Gulf of St Lawrence the past 2500 years saw the introduction of ceramics from the S and the W. The possible extent of other cultural influences is suggested by the 2300-year-old Augustine burial mound in New Brunswick, which duplicates the Adena burial ceremonialism of the Ohio Valley and includes artifacts imported from that region.

Early in this period local groups apparently began to develop a more sedentary way of life, as shell middens began to accumulate in some coastal regions. Evidence from these sites indicates a generalized hunting and fishing way of life, utilizing both coastal and interior resources. This life-style was characteristic of Atlantic Canada at European contact, and the sites dating to the past 2000 years almost certainly represent those of the ancestral MICMAC and MALISEET peoples.

Western Subarctic The forest and forest-tundra area between Hudson Bay and Alaska is, archaeologically, one of the least-explored regions of Canada. Although the far NW of the region has produced evidence of extremely early human occupation, later developments are only vaguely known.

In the area to the W of the Mackenzie R there is thought to be evidence of 2 distinct early postglacial occupations dating between 11 000 and 7000 years ago. One is by groups related to the Paleoindians of more southerly regions, and marked by lanceolate spearpoints. Probably the earliest Paleoindians to occupy the area used fluted points, since a few such artifacts are known from Alaska and the Yukon Territory; however, these finds have not been dated earlier than the fluted point sites to the south, so it is still uncertain whether they represent the original movement of Paleoindians to the S or a subsequent return movement northward. Somewhat more recent occupations are marked by spearpoints which relate either to the late Paleoindian Plano tradition of the northern Plains, or to the Old Cordilleran tradition of BC and the western US. The second major occupation is by groups related to the Paleoarctic tradition of Alaska, a people whose microblade technology is derived from eastern Asia and who are thought to have crossed the Bering Land Bridge.

It is unclear how these early occupations relate to those of the Northern Archaic, which was present in the area from about 6000 to at least 2000 years ago. This culture is characterized by notched spearpoints and other elements of apparent southern origin, but at least the early sites of the period also produce microblades, and microblades may have been in use in some regions until close to the end of this period. Neither is it known how the Northern Archaic relates to the ancestry of the Athapaskan-speaking peoples who occupied interior NW Canada. Definite ancestral Athapaskan sites can be traced for only about the past 1500 years in this area. This may represent an intrusion of Athapaskans from elsewhere, or continous development out of the Northern Archaic of earlier times.

The earliest occupation of the region between Mackenzie R and Hudson Bay was by Plano-tradition people who moved into the Barren Grounds from the S shortly before 7000 years ago. Notched spearpoints and other types of stone tools from at least 6000 years ago led to the definition of the Shield Archaic tradition. It seems that the Shield Archaic developed locally out of Plano culture, rather than representing an intrusion of people from the S, and there was little change in the way of life followed by local groups. The Barren Grounds continued to be occupied by Shield Archaic Indians until about 3500 years ago when, perhaps in response to climatic cooling that caused the treeline to shift southward, the region was taken over by Paleoeskimos from the Arctic coast (*see* CLIMATE CHANGE). This occupation lasted for less than 1000 years, when Indians using various forms of lanceolate and stemmed spearpoints, and later arrow points, reoccupied the territory. The origin of these Indian groups is not clear, but they probably moved into the Barren Grounds from the S and W, and may have arrived at various times between 2500 and 1000 years ago. At least the more recent of these prehistoric groups were ancestral to the Athapaskan-speaking occupants of the historic period, who led a caribou-hunting way of life not greatly different from that of the Plano and Shield Archaic peoples of much earlier times.

Arctic The coasts and islands of arctic Canada were first occupied about 4000 years ago by groups known as Paleoeskimos. Their technology and way of life differed considerably from those of known American Indian groups and more closely resembled those of eastern Siberian peoples. Although there is disagreement among archaeologists on the question of Paleoeskimo origins, it seems likely that the Paleoeskimos crossed Bering Strait from Siberia, either by boat or on the sea ice, shortly before 4000 years ago, and rapidly spread eastward across the unoccupied tundra regions of Alaska, Canada and Greenland. These early occupants seem to have preferred areas where they could live largely on caribou and muskoxen, but were also capable of harpooning seals and in some areas adapted to a maritime way of life. Early Paleoeskimo technology, based on tiny chipped flint tools including microblades, was much less efficient than that of the historic INUIT occupants of the region. There is no evidence that they used boats, dogsleds, oil lamps or domed snowhouses, as they lived through most or all of the year in skin tents heated with fires of bones and scarce wood. Nevertheless, between 4000 and 3000 years ago they occupied most arctic regions and had expanded southwards across the Barren Grounds and down the Labrador coast, displacing Indian occupants.

After about 2500 years ago the Paleoeskimo way of life had developed to the extent that it is given a new label, the DORSET culture. There is slight evidence that the Dorset people used kayaks and had dogs for hunting if not for pulling sledges; soapstone lamps and pots appear, as well as semipermanent winter houses banked with turf for insulation. Dorset sites are larger than those of their predecessors, suggesting more permanent occupation by larger groups, and in some regions it is apparent that the Dorset people were efficient hunters of sea mammals as large as walrus and beluga. A striking art form was developed in the form of small carvings in wood and ivory (*see* INUIT ART). It was the Dorset people who, around 2500 years ago, moved southward to Newfoundland and occupied the island for about 1000 years.

The Dorset occupation of arctic Canada was brought to an end between 1000 and 500 years ago, with the movement into the area of THULE culture Inuit from Alaska. Over the preceding 3000 years the ancestors of the Inuit, who were probably descended from Alaskan Paleoeskimos, had developed very efficient sea-mammal hunting techniques involving harpoon float and drag equipment, kayaks and large, open skin boats from which they could hunt whales. The Thule movement across the Arctic, during a relatively warm climatic period when there was probably a decrease in sea ice and an increase in whale populations, occurred rapidly. Travelling by skin boat and dogsled, by 1200 AD they had established an essentially Alaskan way of life over much of arctic Canada and displaced the Dorset people from most regions. In Greenland and probably in the eastern Canadian Arctic they soon came into contact with the Norse who had arrived in Greenland about 980 AD. Norse artifacts have been recovered from several Thule sites.

The Thule way of life, characterized by summer open-water hunting and the storage of food for use during winter occupation of permanent stone and turf winter houses, became more difficult after 1200 AD as the arctic climate cooled, culminating in the Little Ice Age of 1600 to 1850 AD. During this period many elements of their way of life had to be changed, and the Thule people either abandoned portions of the Arctic or rapidly adapted to the new conditions. It was during this late prehistoric period that much of the culture of the historic Inuit was developed. ROBERT McGHEE

Reading: Knut R. Fladmark, *British Columbia Prehistory* (1986); J. Jennings, *Prehistory of North America* (1968) and, ed, *Ancient Native Americans* (1978); Robert McGhee, *Canadian Arctic Prehistory* (1978); J.A. Tuck, *Newfoundland and Labrador Prehistory* (1976); J.V. Wright, *Six Chapters of Canada's Prehistory* (1976), *Ontario Prehistory* (1972) and *Quebec Prehistory* (1979).

Prejudice and Discrimination Prejudice usually refers to an unsubstantiated negative prejudgement of individuals or groups because of their ETHNICITY, race or religion (*see* RACISM). Discrimination is the exclusion of individuals or groups from full participation in society because of their ethnicity, race or religion. Prejudice (an attitude) and discrimination (behaviour) are usually linked, but they are distinct phenomena. In a vicious circle, prejudice frequently leads to discriminatory behaviour while discrimination reinforces or creates social and economic inequalities which then reinforce prejudices.

Prejudice arose early in the contact between native peoples and the European colonizers who came to N America in the 17th and 18th centuries. The European view of native peoples was complex and ambivalent, ranging from seeing them as "noble savages" to soulless barbarians. While there were significant differences in French-native and British-native relations in pre-Confederation Canada, in both cases the economic interests of the FUR TRADE helped to cement a tolerable working relationship between the colonizers and the native peoples until large-scale settlement led to a deterioration in relations, as Indians became an impediment rather than an aid to economic development. As a result of European settlement during the 1700s and 1800s, of the British CONQUEST in 1759-60 and of the geographical isolation of Indians, NATIVE-WHITE RELATIONS gradually became less important than the relations between the colonizing powers. The economic, political, social and religious co-operation and rivalries between British and French settlers shaped much of Canada's development from the 1750s to the present. Prejudice and discrimination existed on both sides. Because the 2 groups shared a technologically based Western culture, the nature of their relationship and the kinds of prejudice and discrimination that characterized it were considerably different from those that characterized Indian-white relations.

By far the largest group of non-British, non-French and non-natives in Canada at the time of Confederation, 1867, were the GERMANS, who had little trouble being accepted in Canadian society. Their arrival had been within the context of British colonial policy; they were seen as energetic and conservative, and they were isolated and scattered.

BLACKS, however, encountered significant prejudice in the pre-Confederation era. Although there were many opponents to it, SLAVERY existed in New France and British N America. By the 1860s, the 40 000 blacks in Canada included descendants of black slaves in New France, black Loyalists, Jamaican Maroons, black American refugees from the WAR OF 1812, and black fugitives who came to Upper Canada to escape slavery.

Many white Canadians opposed slavery on moral grounds and assisted refugees from the US, but many others feared the influx of black settlers, seeing them as backward, ignorant, immoral, criminal and an economic threat. Blacks were treated primarily as a source of cheap labour. Following the final abolition of slavery throughout the British Empire in 1833, blacks were victims of fewer legal barriers, but nonetheless faced a great deal of social prejudice.

The numbers of people of other than British, French or native origin remained small until the end of the 19th century, when large numbers of immigrants arrived in Canada, settling primarily in the West. Most English-speaking Canadians saw this non-British and non-French immigration primarily as a way of speeding Canada's economic development. Others, however, worried about the social impact of non-British immigration and labour, feared economic competition and opposed an open-door IMMIGRATION POLICY. French Canada opposed it on the grounds that such a policy would further erode the status of French Canada within Confederation. Most English-speaking Canadians shared prejudices concerning the comparative desirability of immigrant groups. During the late 19th and early 20th centuries, the belief in progress and white superiority was taken for granted throughout the Western world. Bolstered by pseudo-scientific ideas of race, derived primarily from SOCIAL DARWINISM, English-speaking Canadians believed that the Anglo-Saxon peoples and British principles of government were the apex of biological EVOLUTION and that Canada's greatness depended on its Anglo-Saxon heritage (*see* IMPERIALISM). Their assessment of a group's desirability, therefore, varied almost directly with the degree to which its members conformed to British culture and physical type. British and American immigrants were regarded as the most desirable, followed by northern and western Europeans, central and eastern Europeans and then by JEWS and southern Europeans. Close to the bottom of the pecking order were the pacifist religious sects, the German-speaking HUTTERITES and MENNONITES and the Russian-speaking DOUKHOBORS, who were invariably lumped together by public officials and the general public. Their social separatism made their assimilation problematic, their thrift and industry made them strong economic competitors, and their pacifism raised doubts about their commitment to Canada. Last were the blacks and the Asian immigrants – the CHINESE, JAPANESE and SOUTH ASIANS – who were considered inferior and unassimilable. Chinese immigration was curbed by a "head tax" and was stopped altogether by the Chinese Immigration Act of 1923. A "gentlemen's agreement" was arrived at with Japan in 1907, restricting the number of Japanese immigrants. Orders-in-council banned immigration from India in 1907. Blacks were informally denied entry from 1910. The government also introduced restrictive immigration laws in 1906, 1910 and 1919 to control European immigration.

Between 1896 and WWII, French Canadian nationalists charged that large-scale immigration (particularly since little of it was French speaking) was a British Canadian plot to undermine the status of French Canada. Immigration was not as significant a public issue in Québec as it was in Ontario and the West because so few immigrants settled there. However, by 1914 the Jewish community of Montréal was the victim of strong anti-Semitism, much of it stemming from the religious bias of FRENCH CANADIAN NATIONALISM. Jews were depicted as exploiters, as threats to Christian morality and civilization, and as symbols of the evils of internationalism, liberalism, bolshevism, materialism and urban life. Public controversies involving both the French and British in Montréal emerged over the Jews' place in the denominationally based school system and over Sunday-closing legislation. Antagonism to Jews was ex-

Head tax certificate of Ma Ton Hang. Measures such as the head tax were used to limit Asian immigration (*courtesy Chinese Canadian National Council*).

pressed in occasional cemetery desecrations and street fights. The French Canadian hostility to Jewish immigration was paralleled by the hostility of ultra-Protestants in English-speaking Canada to Catholic immigrants from Europe, who were regarded as subservient tools of Rome and potential political allies of the French Canadian Catholics.

The ethnic stereotypes of turn-of-the-century Canada emphasized the peasant origins of central, eastern and southern Europeans and Asians, depicting them as poor, illiterate, diseased, morally lax, politically corrupt and religiously deficient. The alleged predilection of central and southern Europeans for drink, violence and crime, and of the Chinese for drugs, gambling and white women were powerful and popular images with the dominant society. Opprobrious ethnic slurs were widely used in the pre-1950s era.

Prior to WWII, extensive patterns of social, economic and political discrimination against non-Anglo-Saxons developed throughout Canada. Northern and western Europeans encountered relatively little discrimination compared to Jews and those from central and southern Europe, while nonwhites, especially in BC, suffered a pervasive pattern of discrimination that affected almost every aspect of their lives. Discrimination was one of the factors that led to the transference of the ethnic "pecking order" of immigration policy to a VERTICAL MOSAIC of occupations and incomes – the British on top and so on down to the Chinese and blacks who occupied the most menial jobs. Non-British and non-French groups had very little economic power, and they did not even begin to make any significant inroads into the middle echelons of politics, education or the PUBLIC SERVICE until after WWII (*see* ELITES).

The most widespread legalized pattern of discrimination occurred against Asians in BC, where anti-Asian sentiment was endemic from the 1850s to the 1950s. Asians were regarded as alien, inferior and unassimilable. Organized labour claimed that Asians took jobs from whites and lowered living standards for all workers because they were willing to work for less money than white workers. Asians were excluded from most unions, and as a matter of policy employers paid Asian workers less than others.

Because of discriminatory legislation and social practices in BC, Chinese, Japanese and South Asians could not vote, practise law or pharmacy, be elected to public office, serve on juries or work in public works, education or the civil service. Public opinion on Asian immigration was expressed on several occasions in violent anti-Chinese and anti-Asian riots, the most serious being in Vancouver in 1887 and 1907. Various attempts were also made by anti-Asian groups to exclude Asians from public schools, to restrict the sale of land to Asians and to limit severely the number of

licences issued to Japanese fishermen. In 1892 and 1907 smaller scale anti-Chinese riots occurred in Alberta; and Québec, Nova Scotia and Saskatchewan passed legislation prohibiting white women from working in restaurants, laundries and any other business owned by Chinese or Japanese.

Blacks also faced a widespread pattern of discrimination in housing, employment and access to public services during the late 19th century and early to mid-20th century. They had difficulty being served in hotels and restaurants, and in being admitted to theatres and swimming pools, and were on occasion forced into segregated schools, particularly in Nova Scotia and Ontario where they were most concentrated. The discrimination against blacks occasionally erupted into violence. In both world wars, armed forces units were reluctant to accept blacks, Chinese, Japanese and South Asians, although some from each group did eventually serve.

The levels of prejudice and discrimination against nonwhite minorities only reached comparable levels for white immigrants during the periods of intense NATIONALISM generated by war. During WWI, Germans and immigrants from the Austro-Hungarian Empire were victims of intense prejudice and persecution. "Enemy aliens" were dismissed from their jobs. Some were placed under police surveillance or in INTERNMENT CAMPS. Their language schools and many of their churches were closed; their newspapers were first censored and then gradually suppressed; and during the war, rioting soldiers and civilians attacked the premises of German clubs and German-owned businesses. Loyalty and cultural and linguistic uniformity were assumed to be synonymous, and Prairie provincial governments abolished bilingual schools and classes. The UNION GOVERNMENT disenfranchised "enemy aliens" who had become Canadian citizens after March 1902.

Opposition to the pacifist religious sects also intensified during the war, eventually leading to the 1919 order-in-council (rescinded during the 1920s) that specifically barred the entry of members of these groups into the country. From 1919 to 1953, Doukhobors in BC were denied the right to vote and this prohibition was extended to the federal level from 1934 to 1955. The return of WWI veterans and the postwar economic depression brought hostility toward these pacifist sects to a peak and contributed to antiradical "nativism," ie, the conviction that immigrant political radicals posed a threat to Canadian national life. Slavic immigrants were no longer perceived as "stolid peasants," but as dangerous revolutionaries. The connection between immigrants and radicalism in the public's mind was strengthened by the WINNIPEG GENERAL STRIKE. One of the measures passed by the federal government to end the strike was a bill providing for the deportation of foreign-born Canadian citizens under certain circumstances. Veterans and radical Slavic workers clashed in violent labour incidents across western Canada in 1919 as veterans asserted what they saw as their priority right to jobs.

By the early 1920s, central, southern and eastern European immigrants were officially classified among the "nonpreferred" and restricted categories of immigrants. In the mid-1920s, however, in response to public pressure, the federal government loosened restrictions on immigration from Europe as a way of promoting economic development. The federal government allowed the railways to import more than 185 000 central and eastern Europeans and Mennonites as farmers, farm labourers and domestics during the late 1920s. The new wave of immigration reawakened prejudices. Organizations such as the KU KLUX KLAN (KKK), the Native Sons of

Canada and the ORANGE ORDER criticized the new immigrants as a threat to Canada's "Anglo-Saxon" character. Several of the organizations, particularly the KKK, also opposed Catholic immigrants. The Klan began organizing in Montréal, Ontario, BC and Manitoba in the early 1920s, and its membership in Saskatchewan in the late 1920s reached 20 000. The Klan organized boycotts of Catholic businessmen, intimidated politicians who seemed sympathetic to French or Catholic interests, opposed federal immigration policy, opposed Catholic schools and the alleged Catholic influence in public schools, and tried to prevent interracial and Catholic-Protestant marriages. The Klan was sufficiently powerful in Saskatchewan to contribute to the defeat of the Liberals in the 1929 provincial election.

Because Anglo-Saxon workers demanded, and often received, priority in obtaining and keeping jobs, a large number of non-Anglo-Saxons were forced onto relief during the GREAT DEPRESSION. Central and eastern Europeans suffered covert discrimination in the administration of relief, while Chinese were victims of open discrimination in relief administration in BC and Alberta. The federal government, in the Immigration Act, provided for deportation of non-Canadian citizens on relief. Government officials took advantage of the law to reduce their relief rolls.

A vicious circle of prejudice and discrimination became further entrenched during the 1930s. The discrimination that non-Anglo-Saxons encountered led them to support radical political movements, eg, communism (see COMMUNIST PARTY) and FASCISM, and this reinforced discrimination against them. Between 1930 and 1935, Prime Minister R.B. BENNETT used deportation as a way of thwarting support for the communists. In labour conflicts in western Canada and Ontario during the Depression, a predominantly non-Anglo-Saxon work force was frequently pitted against an Anglo-Canadian management that attempted to destroy labour solidarity and discredit the strikers by stressing their foreign origins.

During the 1930s, patterns of social discrimination against Jews (eg, informal residential restrictions, quotas in university professional schools and exclusion from elite social clubs, beaches and holiday resorts in Montréal, Toronto and Winnipeg) were extended by fascist groups into a vicious and virulent anti-Semitism, which also influenced immigration policy. Canada closed its doors to Jewish immigrants at the time when they desperately needed refuge from Nazi persecution in Europe.

During WWII Germans, Italians, and members of pacifist sects encountered hostility. Popular prejudice against the Doukhobors, strong in rural BC during the 1920s and 1930s, was reinforced by wartime attitudes. In 1942 the Alberta government passed a law banning all land sales to Hutterites for the duration of the war; from 1947 to 1972 it legislated restrictions on the amount of land Hutterite colonies could own and on the areas of the province in which they could expand.

Hostility toward Japanese Canadians both before and during the war, was sustained, widespread and intense, especially in BC. Waves of anti-Japanese feeling, each of several months duration, swept BC in 1937-38, 1940 and 1941-42. The assault by Japan's navy on Pearl Harbour ignited the most violent hostility towards Japanese Canadians. Following a federal government order of 24 Feb 1942 that all Japanese must evacuate the Pacific coast area, some 22 000 Japanese Canadians were relocated to the interior of BC and to other provinces, where they continued to encounter racial prejudice. The government sold their property to preclude their return at the end of the war. Towards the end of the war

the government also encouraged the Japanese to seek voluntary deportation to Japan, and after the war it proceeded with these deportation plans. Intense pressure from civil-rights groups finally led to the dropping of the deportation orders (1947), to a partial compensation for property losses, and an end to the restrictions that prevented Japanese from returning to the coast (1949).

Nevertheless a number of developments during and after the war undermined certain prejudices against various minority groups. Groups such as the Chinese and UKRAINIANS won a new respectability through their support for the war effort. The involvement of all levels of society in wartime industries undermined social barriers, and revulsion against Hitler and Nazism also eventually extended to a reaction against Hitler's concept of a superior race and against public expressions of anti-Semitism.

Canada's signing of the UNITED NATIONS charter in 1944 and the Universal Declaration of Human Rights in 1948 brought Canada's discriminatory policies into glaring focus. Following intense lobbying by Asian groups and an increasingly sympathetic white public, Asians were finally given the vote (South Asians and Chinese in 1947, Japanese in 1949) and the ban on Chinese and South Asians was repealed, although only wives and children of Canadian citizens were eligible for immigration.

The immigration that began after 1945 was still biased in favour of Europeans, although the government allowed a small quota of immigrants from India, Pakistan and Ceylon (1951). The post-WWII immigrants were better accepted, partly because a large proportion were educated and skilled. Probably the most important factor in accounting for a new tolerance towards immigrants in the 1950s and 1960s (exemplified and encouraged by the passage of provincial HUMAN RIGHTS bills and codes, the passage of the federal CANADIAN BILL OF RIGHTS (1960), and the establishment of both provincial and federal human rights commissions) was the undermining of the intellectual assumptions and social respectability of Anglo-Saxon racism. This resulted from a revulsion against Hitler's racism, the decline of the UK as a world power, and the growth of the American civil-rights movement, among other factors. The prosperity of the 1950s and 1960s facilitated the upward socioeconomic mobility of second- and third-generation non-Anglo-Saxons and helped weaken the fairly rigid relationship between class and ethnicity.

The postwar acceptance of immigrants in Montréal (the destination of most immigrants settling in Québec) was complicated by their tendency to choose English rather than French as the language of instruction for their children, and strong political pressure was brought to bear to force immigrants to send their children to French-speaking schools (see LANGUAGE POLICY).

International pressures for ethnic tolerance and human rights and the continuing need for skilled workers at a time when immigration from Europe was declining led in 1962 and 1967 to the introduction of new immigration regulations that allowed significant numbers of nonwhites from the Third World, particularly from Hong Kong, India and the West Indies, to enter Canada (see CANADA-THIRD WORLD RELATIONS). The influx during the 1970s reawakened latent fears and hostilities toward nonwhite immigrants. The negative sentiments reached a crescendo during the 1975 national debate on the federal governments's Green Paper on Immigration. The group now singled out frequently for racist attention are immigrants of South Asian origin who have come to Canada not only from India, Pakistan and Bangladesh, but from East Africa, the West Indies

and other parts of the world. Between 1974 and 1977, South Asian immigrants in various Canadian cities were victims of vandalism and assaults. Hostility toward South Asians, in particular Sikhs, surged again in the mid-1980s as a result of the violent activities of a tiny group of Sikh extremists who were trying to promote the cause of an independent Sikh state in the Punjab. West Indian immigrants in Toronto and Montréal have complained of job and housing discrimination and of police harassment. In 1986 and 1987, there was also a public backlash against the growing number of immigrants who arrived in Canada claiming refugee status. While Tamils fleeing civil war in Sri Lanka and many Central and South Americans fleeing repressive right-wing regimes had strong reasons to seek political refuge, some Canadians felt immigration laws were lax, and that undesirable immigrants were flooding the country masquerading as political refugees.

Sociological studies reveal that the relation between the ethnic hierarchy, which has such a long history in Canada's immigration policy, and the class system, is still a reality in Canada, although the ethnic pecking order has been removed from Canadian immigration policy and is more difficult to maintain in the class system because of changing attitudes and because discrimination in jobs and housing has been made illegal by human-rights legislation.

The attitudes toward native peoples in the 19th and 20th centuries parallel in many ways those toward immigrants and other ethnic groups. The treatment of native peoples was always conditioned however by a special status resulting from their aboriginal status and by a special legal status embodied in treaties and the Indian Act which "protected" Indians from white society and fostered a paternalistic approach by governments which has not yet entirely ended. The pre-confederation notion of native peoples as either noble savages, military allies or essential partners in the fur trade was gradually supplanted by the view of Indians as backward stumbling blocks to progress. Governments isolated them on reserves and in conjunction with the major Christian denominations, attempted to eradicate their native culture through the introduction of European agriculture and education and Christianity. The dominant Anglo-Canadian view in the late 19th and early 20th century toward the native peoples was that they were at the bottom end of the ladder of biological and social evolution.

As with the new immigrants, it was thought that their languages and cultures must be eradicated and they would have to be assimilated to a new and superior way of life. The Protestant missions to the native peoples, Chinese, Jews and Ukrainians in Canada, as well as abroad, were all motivated by the same underlying belief in the superiority of the British-Canadian Protestant way of life. The prevailing belief in the inevitable assimilation of immigrants was paralleled by a belief in either the inevitable assimilation, or extinction of the native peoples. To the consternation of Indian agents and missionaries, Indians were occasionally encouraged to display their native culture for visiting dignitaries or at local fairs, but these displays were viewed as quaint remnants of the past rather than as an integral part of the developing Canadian society. Ironically, during WWI, the government, in order to increase enlistments began to encourage the warrior ethic among Canada's native peoples which it had been trying for decades to suppress. But this encouragement ended quickly at war's end as the federal authorities expected the Indian veterans to return to the same inferior legal, political, social and economic status that they had before the war. Like most non-white immigrants, the Indians could not vote, were relegated to the bottom rungs of the economic order, were socially stigmatized and encountered a good deal of prejudice and discrimination in their dealings with whites. As with early central and eastern Europeans, perceptions of poverty and alcohol abuse came to play dominant roles in attitudes toward native peoples.

Throughout the interwar period, the native peoples ceased to be major points of public debate. Their powerlessness, lack of economic competition and geographic isolation contributed to their absence from public attention. Unlike the Asians and blacks who were largely excluded from coming to Canada during this period, native peoples could obviously not be targeted by racists for exclusion from the country. Their status as original peoples protected them from some of the intense nativism which faced other non-white groups.

The post-WWII period led to new developments in white-native relations which paralleled some of the changing attitudes toward immigrants and non-British and non-French ethnic groups. Native peoples gradually became more educated and better organized, and a number of native spokesmen began to challenge their second-class status. In 1960 the Diefenbaker government ended the discriminatory measure which prevented Indians from voting federally. The public became more sensitive to native values, and culture. The assimilation programs which had previously attempted to eliminate immigrant and native culture came into disrepute and government programs began to promote pride of ancestry, social and economic advancement, and language and cultural retention for both immigrant minorities and native peoples. One turning point was the strong opposition to the federal government's White Paper of 1969 which proposed to terminate the Indians' special status. In response to this opposition, the federal government disavowed its assimilationist goal.

As they increasingly moved into urban centres in the post-1950 era, native peoples still encountered a good deal of prejudice and discrimination in housing, restaurants and other public facilities, but they had recourse to redress through human rights legislation. Governments professed a desire for new approaches in dealing with native peoples, and the protracted discussions over land claims and a new constitutional status for the native peoples in the 1970s and 1980s were accompanied by a good deal of public support for modest native claims. Native peoples, like many non-British and non-French ethnic groups (particularly non-white "visible minorities") still encounter a good deal of prejudice and discrimination, but it is diminished from the past. Though fewer people demonstrate outright prejudice, both immigrant and native minorities still suffer psychologically and socially from the effects of prejudice and discrimination. HOWARD PALMER

Premier, the chief minister of a provincial government. Because of the shared framework of CABINET government, the office of provincial premier is similar to that held by Canada's PRIME MINISTER. The policy direction and management of the provincial governments is visibly dominated by their premiers. Though this capability has been eroded by the increased scope of provincial government activity, premiers remain in every sense the "first" ministers.

The constitutional powers of the LIEUTENANT-GOVERNORS as the representatives of the Crown for the provinces are ordinarily exercised solely on the advice of the premier. Other provincial Cabinet members therefore owe their appointments to the premier and may be removed or shuffled be-

tween ministries at the premier's discretion. Party or other sociopolitical interests may determine the choice of Cabinet colleagues, but the specific composition of the Cabinet is decided by the premier. He may hold a government portfolio of his own, as well as the title of President of the Executive Council. The growth in staff support for the premiership in the form of policy and public relations advisers has directly added to the commanding position of the office itself. The appointments of deputy ministers as the administrative heads of government departments and those of the heads of government corporations are also generally subject to the premier's approval.

The premier shapes the conduct and decisions of Cabinet and speaks for the government, regardless of the departmental responsibilities of other ministers. Although a provincial general election is not called without some Cabinet discussion, a lieutenant-governor will dissolve a Legislative Assembly only on the advice of the premier.

In addition to his authority as head of government, a premier possesses an additional source of power as the head of the governing political party. His selection as party leader through the trials of a party LEADERSHIP CONVENTION is the first step on the road to premiership. This confirms a personal power base within the party that is unrivalled by any other party member. Since the image of party leader is a prime determinant of voting behaviour, leadership status is further enhanced by the electoral victory that propels a party into government office. Successive victories add to this source of power.

The growth in the importance of FEDERAL-PROVINCIAL RELATIONS in the making of Canadian public policy has also enhanced the personal status of the premiers. Federal-provincial and interprovincial meetings of first ministers on a broad range of policy issues made such premiers as Brian PECKFORD of Newfoundland, Joe GHIZ of PEI and Don GETTY of Alberta known to more people outside than within their own provinces.

It should be emphasized that the sources of authority and prestige establish only the potential for strong political leadership in the office of premier. The realization of this potential will in large part depend on the propensity and ability of each premier to utilize the power of his office.

NORMAN J. RUFF

Prent, Mark George, sculptor (b at Lodz, Poland 23 Dec 1947, Canadian citizen 1948). Prent works with plastics such as polyster resin, fibreglass and found objects and occasionally bronze. His works are extremely realistic and frequently feature motion or sound. His subjects are mostly human figures treated in an exaggerated manner (eg, a male nude figure, mouth open as if screaming, encased in a block of ice set upright in a freezer) and are seldom attractive in the superficial sense. Sometimes there is a certain ironic humour in his work. He has often worked on a large scale, creating 3-dimensional, extremely detailed, room-sized environments. Prent's subject matter is considered disturbing by many and a great deal of controversy surrounds it. In exhibitions of his work in 1970 and 1972, The Isaacs Gallery in Toronto was charged "with displaying disgusting objects," contrary to the Criminal Code of Canada. Both charges were dismissed. Prent is the recipient of a number of awards including the Ludwig Vogelstein Foundation Fellowship (1985) and now lives in Vermont.

AVROM ISAACS

Prerogative Powers, defined as "the residue of discretionary or arbitrary authority which at any given time is legally left in the hands of the CROWN." Originating in common law from prac-

tices developed through centuries, the sovereign delegates them to the GOVERNOR GENERAL on advice from the federal Cabinet, and to the lieutenant-governors through the governor-in-council. They include appointment and dismissal of the prime minister, and the summoning, proroguing and dissolving of Parliament in accordance with ministerial advice, parliamentary practice and constitutional remedies for unusual emergencies, such as electoral deadlock or a premier's death. FRANK MacKINNON

Presbyterian and Reformed Churches All Christian churches of the "Reformed" tradition derive from the 16th-century Protestant Reformation and from CALVINISM. They function through a system of presbyterian or representative elected courts, rising from the congregational session to presbytery to synod, and for the Presbyterian Church in Canada to the annual General Assembly. Although French Calvinists (HUGUENOTS) shared in the early FUR TRADE, non-Catholics were generally barred from New France until the British CONQUEST. Early Scottish and other settlers brought Presbyterianism to the Maritimes and central Canada in the late 18th century. Attempts by Scottish, Irish and American churches to organize congregations in the colonies and efforts to found an indigenous Canadian Presbyterian church all failed, but by the early 19th century branches of the Church of Scotland and its smaller "Secessionist" offshoots had been established. Their complex relations, caused by disagreements about church-state connections, were further confused in 1844 when some colonial members of the C of S started "Free" churches in sympathy with the Free Church Disruption in Scotland, which also stemmed from church-state disputes.

In 1860 and 1861, respectively, the Secession and Free churches in the Maritimes and in central Canada formed 2 regional unions. In 1875 these and the remnants of the C of S combined to form the Presbyterian Church in Canada, which the 1891 census showed to be the Dominion's largest Protestant denomination. Before WWI the new church expanded rapidly in the West and added missions in China, Korea, Taiwan and India to older ones in the Caribbean and New Hebrides. These foreign missions included large medical and educational operations that employed hundreds of Canadians. In that same period Canadian Presbyterians, both lay and clergy, actively supported the ideals of the SOCIAL GOSPEL movement in crusades for moral and political purity, TEMPERANCE and social justice.

By the opening of the 20th century the combination of nationalism, a co-operative climate in religion, and the expansionist spirit of the major Canadian Protestant denominations led the Presbyterian Church to seek union with other Protestant bodies in a single Canadian church. This movement was opposed by a Presbyterian minority, and when the UNITED CHURCH OF CANADA was formed in 1925 about one-third of all Presbyterians (chiefly in Montréal and Southern Ontario) refused to join. Those who continued as Presbyterians lost most of their educational and charitable institutions and home and foreign missions. Since 1925, the total of members and adherents (proportionately wealthier and better educated than the national average) has remained almost constant at about 700 000 (1981c, latest figures available), making the Presbyterian Church the fourth-largest denomination in Canada.

Because of the corporate structure of Presbyterianism, individual leadership is not especially evident in church life, but the church has numbered among its members such well-known Canadians as the vocal nationalist G.M. GRANT, principal of Queen's U, 1877-1902; PM Mackenzie KING; novelist Charles W. GORDON (Ralph Connor); George BROWN, publisher of *The Globe;* Canada's first woman senator, Cairine WILSON; Thomas MCCULLOCH, pioneer NS educator; and Ontario's long-time premier, Oliver MOWAT. The Presbyterian Church in Canada retains its Calvinist and Scottish heritage in its organization and church life, emphasizing the central role of preaching and scripture reading, and severe simplicity in worship and church decor. Nevertheless, it has abandoned harsher elements in Calvinist theology and practice, such as double predestination and rigid sabbatarianism (sabbath observance). Although linked historically most closely to Scotland, the Presbyterian Church contains ethnic congregations of French and Swiss, Hungarians, Koreans and Chinese. It maintains active connection with such co-operative Christian bodies as the World Council of Churches, the World Alliance of Reformed Churches, and the Canadian Council of Churches.

In Canada the Reformed tradition is also represented by Dutch Calvinists. LOYALIST members of the colonial Dutch Reformed Church were absorbed by Presbyterian groups after the WAR OF 1812, but a later schism in the DRC (Reformed Church in America after 1867) produced the Christian Reformed Church (headquarters in Grand Rapids, Mich), which established several mission congregations in the Canadian West before 1920. In the 15 years following WWII, when nearly 150 000 Dutch migrated to Canada, Canadian CRC membership increased by more than 30 000 to reach 62 000 in 1961, and new congregations were formed in Ontario and BC. There are also 4 smaller Dutch Calvinist bodies – the Protestant Reformed Church, the Canadian Reformed Churches, the Free Reformed Churches of N America, and the Netherlands Reformed Congregations – all dating from the 1950s and from the same wave of Dutch immigration. Older members of these ethnic churches preserved their Dutch heritage through their religion, but Canadian-born members accommodate more easily to Canadian life-styles.   JOHN S. MOIR

Reading: John S. Moir, *Enduring Witness* , 2nd ed (1987).

Prescott, Ont, Town, pop 4583 (1986c), 4670 (1981c), inc 1834, located 18 km E of Brockville on the St Lawrence R. The site was strategically located at the head of navigation above the former St Lawrence rapids. The French built Fort de Lévis nearby in 1760, and the town was founded in 1810 by LOYALISTS under Major Edward Jessup, and named for Governor-in-Chief Robert PRESCOTT. Ft Wellington was built here during the WAR OF 1812 and used as the base for an attack on Ogdensburg, NY. The blockhouse (1838) has been restored and made part of Fort Wellington National Historic Pk. The stone windmill (1822), which served as a makeshift fort for rebels during the bloody Battle of the Windmill, has been preserved nearby. The town produces colour televisions, paper containers, clothing, electronic components and plastic pipe. The weekly newspaper is the *Prescott Journal.*   K.L. MORRISON

Prescott, Robert, soldier, colonial administrator (b in Lancashire, Eng *c* 1726; d at Rose Green, W Sussex, Eng 21 Dec 1815). He joined the British army in 1745 and saw service during the SEVEN YEARS' WAR at Louisbourg in 1758. He was appointed aide-de-camp to General Jeffery AMHERST in 1759 and took part in the advance on Montréal the following year. He later served in the AMERICAN REVOLUTION in the W Indies. Briefly governor of Martinique (1794-95), Prescott was appointed governor-in-chief of the Canadas, NB and NS and commander of forces in British N America in 1796.

He assumed office in Apr 1797. Although governor-in-chief until 1807, he spent only 3 years in Canada. Prescott was noted for stubbornness and irascibility, but he was not without skill. His decisive and judicious manner, however, was not enough to help him resolve the difficulties he faced in LOWER CANADA, especially those related to land affairs. He was recalled in 1799.   DAVID EVANS

Press Gallery, *see* PARLIAMENTARY PRESS GALLERY.

Presse, La Montréal NEWSPAPER started in 1884 by William-Edmond Blumhart and other conservatives in opposition to *Le Monde,* edited by Hector LANGEVIN, and its support for John A. MACDONALD. Under the ownership of Trefflé Berthiaume its editorial orientation became liberal, 1899-1904, but with the Berthiaume-Du Tremblay family, 1906-55, it was generally conservative. Paul DESMARAIS bought the paper in 1965. Since 1958 its editors have been liberal-oriented: Jean-Louis Gagnon (1958-61), Gérard PELLETIER (1961-64), Roger Champoux (1965-69), Jean-Paul Desbiens (1969-72), Roger LEMELIN (1972-80) and Roger D. Landry (1980-). Daily circulation was 14 000 in 1896, 64 000 in 1900, 121 085 in 1913, 147 074 in 1940, 285 787 in 1962, and 213 605 in 1986 (321 468 on Saturday). Its content has always been diversified, with excellent coverage of both national and international news. In the early 1980s the weekly supplement *Plus* included reports from the Third World. The influence of *La Presse* is growing in intellectual and business circles, especially since Michel Roy became the main editorialist in 1982.

ANDRÉ DONNEUR AND ONNIG BEYLERIAN

Pressure Group, also known as interest group or lobby, is an organization formed by like-minded people who seek to influence PUBLIC POLICY to promote their own interest. Pressure groups exist in all modern pluralist democracies and have sprung up on all sides: some to defend consumers, others to defend producers, others push for broad policies such as protection of the environment. The proliferation of some pressure groups is so extensive, their size so large and their organization so sophisticated that they virtually constitute another arm of government. Examples of powerful pressure groups are the industry-financed CANADIAN TAX FOUNDATION, the commercial banks, the Canadian Federation of Agriculture, the CANADIAN MEDICAL ASSOCIATION, the automobile, steel, rubber, chemical and energy industries, which act alone or through their trade associations, eg, the Business Council on National Issues (an association of chief executive officers of large Canadian corporations formed in 1977 to co-ordinate business participation in the policy-making process), the CHAMBER OF COMMERCE and the CANADIAN MANUFACTURERS' ASSOCIATION. The Institute of Association Executives, which in Ottawa alone has 318 members, constitutes a virtual lobby of lobbyists. Other pressure groups, such as Executive Consultants Ltd and Government Policy Consultants Inc, comprise former politicians.

Lobbying by pressure groups can take the form of a mass-media campaign or paid advertisements which oppose or support a particular policy, informal meetings with senior bureaucrats, or the presentation of a brief to a parliamentary committee. Lobbying in Canada, however, has been described as "keeping things pleasant, dull and controlled" and is usually characterized by private, informal meetings with influential advisers and Cabinet ministers. The closeness of these lobbyists to the politicians and bureaucrats sometimes results in charges of CONFLICT OF INTEREST.

Some pressure groups are much more powerful and more successful than others. Successful pressure groups are almost always well financed, cohe-

sive and stable, and their leaders, many of whom are former politicians, tend to represent causes favourably regarded by politicians and civil servants. In other words, they facilitate the process by which leaders of the ruling party and senior bureaucrats work out their policy arrangements with the business community, the professions and other organized interests in society. They usually maintain permanent offices near the capital and their leaders frequent important clubs and associations. The less successful groups are generally poorly financed, are led by people remote from the elite groups and advocate causes not generally favoured by the leading political parties. They are often organized around a single issue, or appear suddenly on the scene to protest a particular policy proposal. Others soldier on for years, defending small or lost causes. The losers simply lack the means to succeed. Unlike the elite leaders, they cannot command the ear of Cabinet ministers at will or project an air of legitimacy. While well-financed pressure groups establish personal contact within the government, contact leading journalists and conduct slick media campaigns or even submit legal arguments relating to the drafting of legislation, less effective groups must resort to a more episodic, guerrilla-type campaign. The latter tend to use more noisy, flamboyant techniques, such as demonstrations with slogans, signs and contrived "media opportunities."

Because legislative decision making in Canada is highly centralized and party discipline is strong, the rivalries between legislators cannot be easily exploited. However, the same monopoly of power that allows the Cabinet to ignore pressure groups' demands also allows it to respond to them. The development of legislation usually follows a certain sequence. First, the need for policy change is perceived, then the policy proposal is developed, frequently with interest-group representatives, and circulated within government, eg, the PRIME MINISTER'S OFFICE and CENTRAL AGENCIES. It is then sometimes sent to the media, to experts and occasionally to provincial governments, before it is circulated to more government departments. At this point the policy may also be reviewed by pressure groups. Before amendments or new statutes are introduced into Parliament the proposal is reviewed by a COMMITTEE, whose opinions are confirmed or modified by Cabinet; the bill is drafted by the Department of Justice, considered by another Cabinet committee, confirmed by Cabinet and signed by the prime minister. But to be effective, legislation must be implemented, for which purpose public servants enjoy great discretion and power. Furthermore the impact of legislation is often determined by the interpretation of the courts. Because the legislative process, particularly policy initiative, is controlled in practice by the BUREAUCRACY, interest groups often express their opinions or provide information to public servants as well as to Cabinet. But interest groups can also exert their influence on parliamentary committees, whose suggestions regarding modifications of a bill are often confirmed by Cabinet; on the Senate, which can wield influence through the powerful Banking Committee; and on backbenchers, who may someday become Cabinet members, although it is generally acknowledged that once a bill has reached Parliament it is more difficult to influence the government's intentions.

Despite the conclusions of the Royal Commission on CORPORATE CONCENTRATION that farm, labour and other interest-group organizations are successful in affecting government policy, many such groups are excluded from any effective role by the ability of powerful, recognized interests and bureaucrats to inhibit organizational efforts of groups that do not share accepted attitudes. If a group's representatives do not enjoy confidential intimacy with senior civil servants and Cabinet ministers, they resort to other tactics to excite the attention of the government, but tactics such as protest rallies underline their marginal political status. Among experienced lobbyists such tactics, although they are becoming more common, are considered illegitimate. Consumer, environmental and labour groups are also less successful, not only because they are socially and ideologically further from government but because they are trying to facilitate, not prevent, change.

Pressure groups are growing in importance in Canada for several reasons. As Parliament and provincial legislatures decline in influence with the weakening of political parties, power tends to shift to interest groups. Election campaigns are becoming ever more costly, and parties rely more on contributions from interests. A growing Americanization of Canada has resulted in the development of sophisticated techniques of lobbying and public relations, especially with the large multinational corporations. Increasing disputes between federal and provincial governments have aided the attempts of powerful interests to play off one level of government against another. Groups with strong regional interests, eg, the western oil and gas industry, or the secondary manufacturing industries of Ontario, have successfully mobilized their provincial governments in their cause against the federal government and the other regions of Canada. It is when pressure groups do not pursue the same goals that the big battles are waged. The petroleum-pricing issue of the 1970s and early 1980s pitted the oil industry and the governments of producer provinces against the manufacturing industries in central Canada and the Ontario government (*see* NATIONAL ENERGY POLICY). In general, big business has been successful when it is united. For example, it succeeded in preventing an effective strengthening of the Combines Investigation Act, which the Trudeau government had pledged to reform when it came into office. Also it prevented reform of the TAXATION system, despite the recommendations of the Carter Commission. In 1987, the organized multinational pharmaceutical industry succeeded in inducing the Mulroney government to end the compulsory licensing of pharmaceuticals, thereby permitting these firms to enjoy a monopoly on the production of their new drugs for 10 years. This may lead to substantial price increases; but it is defended as a means of attracting investment to Canada. Generally, pressure groups in Canada have reinforced the status quo, but then for the most part they are the status quo. *See also* LOBBYING.   HUGH G. THORBURN

Preston, Isabella, plant hybridist, horticulturist, writer, civil servant (b at Lancaster, Eng 4 Sept 1881; d at Georgetown, Ont 31 Jan 1965). Immigrating to Ontario in 1912, Preston entered the Ontario Agricultural Coll in 1913, but soon gave up formal studies to conduct practical work under the supervision of Prof J.W. Crow. By 1916 she had not only become the first professional woman hybridist in Canada, but had vaulted into the front ranks of plant hybridizers when a judicious cross produced the acclaimed "George C. Creelman" lily. She joined the Central Experimental Farm's (Ottawa) Horticultural Division under W.T. Macoun in 1920, at a time of great horticultural activity. From then until she retired in 1946, Preston originated nearly 200 hybrids (roses, lilacs, Siberian iris, Rosybloom crabapples and lilies). Her lily hybrids alone guaranteed her horticultural fame, although awards and recognition came to nearly every breeding program she attempted. She wrote numerous, wide-ranging horticultural ar-

ticles as well as the first book on lily cultivation in Canada.   EDWINNA VON BAEYER

Prévost, André, composer, teacher (b at Hawkesbury, Ont 30 Jul 1934). He studied at the Conservatoire de musique in Montréal, the Conservatoire de Paris with Olivier Messiaen, the École normale de musique and electronic music at the ORTF. He won the Prix d'Europe for composition (1963). His symphony *Fantasmes* won him the award of the Amis de l'art foundation (1963) and the MSO award (1964). *Terre des hommes,* a work composed after the poem by Michèle Lalonde, was created for the opening of Expo 67. Several of his pieces have been choreographed: *Sonate* for violin and piano, *Sonate no 1* for cello and piano, *Diallèle, Evanescence, Fantasmes, Quatuor à cordes no 2* and *Chorégraphie 1*. Since 1964 he has taught at U de Montréal. He is an Officer of the Order of Canada.   HÉLÈNE PLOUFFE

Portrait of Sir George Prevost attributed to Robert Field, Halifax, *c*1808-11 (*courtesy McCord Museum, McGill University, Montréal*).

Prevost, Sir George, soldier, administrator, governor-in-chief of Canada (b in New Jersey 19 May 1767; d at London, Eng 5 Jan 1816). Prevost was a captain of foot in the British army by 1784. In the Napoleonic Wars he saw service primarily in the West Indies as commander on St Vincent (1794-96), lieutenant-governor of St Lucia (1798-1802) and governor of Dominica (1802-05). He was appointed in 1808 lieutenant-governor of Nova Scotia. Prevost became governor-in-chief of British N America and commander of British forces in N America in 1811, taking over in July 1912. He was a suitable choice to take over the administration of Québec, given his ability to speak French, and demonstrated talents in colonial administration. As commander of the British forces during the WAR OF 1812, Prevost was held responsible for the failure to take Plattsburgh, NY, in 1814, which resulted in his recall to England in 1815. He died before an inquiry could be held.   DAVID EVANS

Price, Frank Percival, carillonneur, campanologist, composer (b at Toronto 7 Oct 1901). The first non-European graduate of the renowned Beiaardschool for carillonneurs in Mechelen, Belgium, Price became Canada's first Dominion carillonneur when the instrument he helped design for the Peace Tower of the Parliament Buildings in Ottawa was installed in 1927. Devoted to bells and their music, he became an international

authority on campanology, initiating reforms and innovations in design and performance practice. From 1939 to 1972 he taught at U of Michigan, Ann Arbor, where he was also university carillonneur. A brilliant recitalist, Price has played carillons the world over. He is a prolific composer and arranger, and has contributed many hundreds of works to his instrument's repertoire.
          BARCLAY McMILLAN

Price, Sir William, lumber merchant, manufacturer (b at Talca, Chile 30 Aug 1867; d at Kenogami, Qué 2 Oct 1924). The grandson of William PRICE, young Price was educated at private schools in Québec and England before entering the family firm, Price Bros and Company, in 1886. In 1889 he became president, managing-director and owner. Rejuvenating the then tottering company, he used its huge timber limits and capital resources to move into the developing paper industry. Price bought the pulp mill at Jonquière, using its pulp to produce cardboard and then paper. As he concentrated on supplying the American newsprint market, his Kenogami-Jonquière establishment became the largest Canadian producer of newsprint and revived the economic fortunes of the Saguenay. Price was a Conservative MP for Québec W 1908-11. Associated with many Québec business enterprises, he was a strong imperialist and raised 2 companies for the SOUTH AFRICAN WAR. He was accidentally killed while inspecting his timber limits at Kenogami.   CHRISTOPHER G. CURTIS

Price, William, entrepreneur (b at Hornsey, Eng 17 Sept 1789; d at Québec C 14 Mar 1867). An enterprising lumber and timber merchant, William Price, "the father of the Saguenay," developed a business empire that extended throughout the Saguenay, St Lawrence and Ottawa river areas. At age 14 Price became an employee of Chistopher Idle, a prominent London businessman. Six years later he was sent to the Québec branch of the British firm as a clerk, becoming manager of the office in 1815. In 1820 he became a partner in Montréal, Québec and London. The William Price Company at Québec specialized in exporting timber. Price reinvested profits from this trade, which by 1833 had grown to over 100 shiploads per year, in sawmills, timber limits and financing lumber and timber operations and eventually bought out his partners, forming William Price and Sons in 1855. At his death the company continued under the management of his sons. *See also* TIMBER TRADE HISTORY.
          CHRISTOPHER G. CURTIS

Prime Minister, the chief minister and effective head of the executive in a parliamentary system, normally the leader of the majority party in the HOUSE OF COMMONS. If there is no majority, the PM is the leader of that party most likely to win support from other parties in the House. In Canada the title is usually reserved for the head of the federal government while the term PREMIER is normally (but not always) used to designate the head of the executive branch of a provincial government. Formally, a PM is appointed by the GOVERNOR GENERAL who has little discretion in the matter, except in a crisis such as the death of the incumbent PM. Although the position and responsibilities of office are not defined in any statute or constitutional document, the PM has always been the most powerful figure in Canadian politics. He controls the party, speaks for it, and after appointment to office has at his disposal a large number of PATRONAGE appointments with which to reward party faithful. The PM appoints and dismisses all members of CABINET and allocates their responsibilities. As chairman of Cabinet, he controls the agenda and discussions at

W.L. Mackenzie King with his dog at Kingsmere, Qué. King was the longest-serving PM in Canadian history (*courtesy National Archives of Canada/C-55540*).

Prime Ministers of Canada 1867-1987		
	Party	Dates of Administration
Sir John A. Macdonald	C[1]	1 Jul 1867 – 5 Nov 1873
Alexander Mackenzie	L[2]	7 Nov 1873 – 9 Oct 1878
Sir John A. Macdonald	C	17 Oct 1878 – 6 Jun 1891
Sir John J.C. Abbott	C	16 Jun 1891 – 24 Nov 1892
Sir John Sparrow Thompson	C	5 Dec 1892 – 12 Dec 1894
Sir Mackenzie Bowell	C	21 Dec 1894 – 27 Apr 1896
Sir Charles Tupper	C	1 May 1896 – 8 Jul 1896
Sir Wilfrid Laurier	L	11 Jul 1896 – 6 Oct 1911
Sir Robert Laird Borden	C	10 Oct 1911 – 12 Oct 1917
Sir Robert Laird Borden	U[3]	12 Oct 1917 – 10 Jul 1920
Arthur Meighen	U	10 Jul 1920 – 29 Dec 1921
W.L. Mackenzie King	L	29 Dec 1921 – 28 Jun 1926
Arthur Meighen	C	29 Jun 1926 – 25 Sep 1926
W.L. Mackenzie King	L	25 Sep 1926 – 6 Aug 1930
Richard Bedford Bennett	C	7 Aug 1930 – 23 Oct 1935
W.L. Mackenzie King	L	23 Oct 1935 – 15 Nov 1948
Louis St. Laurent	L	15 Nov 1948 – 21 Jun 1957
John G. Diefenbaker	C	21 Jun 1957 – 22 Apr 1963
Lester Bowles Pearson	L	22 Apr 1963 – 20 Apr 1968
Pierre Elliott Trudeau	L	20 Apr 1968 – 4 Jun 1979
Charles Joseph Clark	C	4 Jun 1979 – 3 Mar 1980
Pierre Elliott Trudeau	L	3 Mar 1980 – 30 Jun 1984
John Napier Turner	L	30 Jun 1984 – 17 Sep 1984
Martin Brian Mulroney	C	17 Sep 1984 –

[1] Conservative [2] Liberal [3] Unionist

meetings. He appoints the members of Cabinet committees and is chairman of the Priorities and Planning Committee. Because of these factors and the convention of party solidarity, the PM has great influence over the activities and agenda of PARLIAMENT. He also enjoys a special relationship with the CROWN, as he is the only person who can advise the governor general to dissolve Parliament and call an election. In recent years the PM has chosen a personal staff to advise him on policy. This enables him to have a direct influence on policy discussions and committee decisions, making it highly unlikely that any policy proposal not meeting his approval will be put into effect.

Political reality, various conventions and the CONSTITUTION do limit the power of the PM. He must always be wary of offending the various regions of the country and must be able to conciliate competing factions within the party and the Cabinet and throughout Canada. He must also be able to delegate authority without losing control. This requires rare qualities and few prime ministers, if any, have been generously endowed with all of them. The prime minister's official residence is located at 24 SUSSEX DRIVE, Ottawa.

W.A. MATHESON

Reading: W.A. Matheson, *The Prime Minister and the Cabinet* (1976); R.M. Punnett, *The Prime Minister in Canadian Government and Politics* (1977).

Prime Minister's Office (PMO), a central agency that came into its own in the late 1960s. It differs from its counterparts in that it is staffed with temporary political appointees rather than full-time, career civil servants and has no statutory base, its budget being a component of the estimates for the PRIVY COUNCIL OFFICE. The PRIME MINISTER determines the PMO's organization and role; its functions derive from his political responsibilities as leader of his party rather than as head of government, though in practice the division between these responsibilities is not clear, thereby providing opportunities for the PMO to trespass on the more purely administrative preserves of other CENTRAL AGENCIES. It is responsible for press and public relations, the PM's large correspondence, his speaking engagements, etc; it advises on candidates for appointment to the numerous order-in-council appointees, eg, directorships on

CROWN CORPORATIONS, members of regulatory commissions, on which the PM's recommendation is essential and decisive; it maintains contact with the party's officials outside the legislature and with the party caucus in the legislature; it generally serves as a listening post and a "gatekeeper" determining which matters will be brought to the PM's attention and ensuring that the political dimensions of public policies are not overlooked by the permanent bureaucracy. There is potential for overlap and competition with the Privy Council Office. The expansion of the personnel and functions of the PMO under PM Pierre TRUDEAU was a clear reflection of the increasingly dominant role of the PM, as both head of government and head of party.

This trend was perpetuated when Brian MULRONEY became prime minister. The inherent tension between the political party-oriented role and the policy advisory functions of his PMO staff has given rise to contradictory conclusions that either the PMO is weak and failing to provide direction or else is too strong and trespassing on the turf of other central agencies – most notably the PCO.

J.E. HODGETTS

Reading: C. Campbell and G. Szablowski, *The Superbureaucrats: Structure and Behaviour in Central Agencies* (1979); B.G. Doern and P. Aucoin, eds, *The Structures of Policy-Making in Canada* (1971).

Prince, Edward Ernest, fisheries biologist (b at Leeds, Eng 23 May 1858; d 10 Oct 1936). Educated at St Andrews, Cambridge and Edinburgh universities, Prince was a disciple of W.C. McIntosh of St Andrews, a leading fishery scientist. In 1893 he was appointed commissioner of fisheries. He immediately advocated a marine scientific station for Canada through the RSC, of which he became a fellow, and through the British Assn for the Advancement of Science meeting in Toronto in 1897. When Parliament appropriated $7000 for establishment of the station in 1898, Prince became director and chairman of its board of management. In 1912 this became the Biological Board of Canada and in 1937 the FISHERIES RESEARCH BOARD – a unique and successful Canadian experiment in the administration of research by a body with a majority of university scientists working with representatives of government and industry. Prince was chairman until 1921.

A.W.H. NEEDLER

Prince, Richard Edmund, sculptor (b at Comox, BC 6 Apr 1947). Prince has been making

conceptual sculpture since his studies at UBC (1971). He has developed a provocative style that intentionally forces the viewer's participation either physically or visually in a sequence of causes and effects. His early work centered on trying to depict forces, such as gravity, that have been largely ignored in Western art. The sculptures are well-executed models that use found objects encased in a box. They create, with a touch of humour, a miniature environment that implies levels of meaning. Recent solo exhibitions include shows at the Hamilton Art Gallery (1984) and at the Charles H. Scott Gallery in Vancouver (1985).

KATHLEEN LAVERTY

Prince Albert, Sask, City, pop 33 686 (1986c), 31 380 (1981c), inc 1904, is located on the south shore of the NORTH SASKATCHEWAN R near the geographical centre of the province some 140 km N of Saskatoon. It is a service centre for agriculture, forestry, gold and uranium mining and the gateway to northern Saskatchewan. The city is governed by a mayor and 8 aldermen. A provincial agency, the Local Government Board, oversees municipal financing.

Named for Queen Victoria's consort, Prince Albert was founded 1866 as a Presbyterian mission. Its character changed dramatically with the selection of a route through the valley of the N Saskatchewan for the Transcontinental Railway. Prince Albert grew rapidly, but the boom collapsed when the CPR adopted a more southerly route.

After the turn of the century Prince Albert embarked on a scheme to harness nearby La Colle Falls, in the confident expectation that inexpensive electric power would obviously attract industry. These dreams were never to be realized, however, and the project brought Prince Albert to the verge of bankruptcy.

For 4 decades the city marked time, but resource development and the growth of tourism at nearby Prince Albert National Park since 1945 have revived its economy. Some of the richest deposits of gold and uranium in N America have been identified to the N and numerous mining companies are now using Prince Albert as a supply and service base.

The majority of the population is native born, and nearly half is British in origin. People of French, Ukrainian and German ancestry form sizable groups as well. The largest religious denominations are Roman Catholic, United Church, Anglican, Lutheran and Presbyterian.

The Prince Albert Pulp Co, owned by Weyerhaeuser Canada Inc, is the city's largest employer. At peak production its mill employs 450; another 500 are engaged in timber harvesting operations. A paper mill plant employing 215, which will be the second largest in Canada, opens in 1989. Prince Albert is also a well-known centre in western Canada for its penal institutions. A federal maximum security penitentiary, a men's correctional jail, a women's correctional jail and a young offenders institution harbour over 700 prisoners. Prince Albert is served by one scheduled airline, 2 charter airlines, branches of the CPR and CNR, 28 transport companies and one bus line. The city is served by 2 English-language

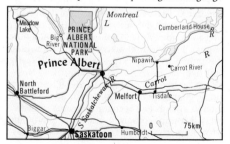

TV stations, an AM and FM radio station, a weekly newspaper and a daily newspaper, the Prince Albert *Daily Herald.* Three prime ministers have represented Prince Albert in the House of Commons: Wilfrid LAURIER, Mackenzie KING and John DIEFENBAKER. J. WILLIAM BRENNAN

Reading: G.W.D. Abrams, *Prince Albert: The First Century, 1866-1966* (1966).

Prince Albert National Park (est 1927) is located 200 km N of Saskatoon and covers 3874 km². It is characterized by boreal forests, prairie grasslands and clear lakes. Eskers, drumlins, glacial lakes, moraines, meltwater channels and other glacial features mark the land. The cabin and grave of Grey Owl (Archibald BELANEY) are located in the park beside Ajawaan Lk, where he spent the last 7 years of his life. The park is rich in the wildlife he fought to protect. Elk, moose and deer browse in the trembling aspen forests; wolves and caribou roam the forests of jack pine, larch and balsam fir; badger and a herd of 20 bison inhabit the prairie meadows and fescue grasslands. Park waterways harbour beaver, the animal most closely associated with Grey Owl. Over 195 bird species have been seen; white pelicans and double-crested cormorants nest on an island in the park. Commercial facilities and accommodation are available in nearby Waskesiu, Sask. LILLIAN STEWART

Prince Charles Island, 9521 km², 130 km long and 100 km wide, is the largest island in FOXE BASIN, W of BAFFIN I. It is an outcrop of a coast of postglacial marine deposition, and exhibits the characteristics of this kind of topography, having monotonously straight, flat coasts with a shallow offshore zone. The shore consists of wide mud flats, littered with boulders and crossed by occasional watercourses, and passes imperceptibly to the inland tundra marshes. The maximum elevation is only 73 m; local relief generally is in the order of 10 m or less. The island was discovered by a 1948 RCAF aerial survey.

DOUG FINLAYSON

Prince Edward Island, Canada's seventh and smallest province, is affectionately referred to by its people as "the Island." Known to its earliest settlers, the MICMAC, as *Abegweit* ("cradle in the waves"), the province has other names that highlight aspects of its history and character: the "Garden of the Gulf," the "Million-Acre Farm," the "Cradle of Confederation" or, less eloquently, "Spud Island." Situated in the Gulf of St Lawrence and separated from NS and NB by the shallow Northumberland Strait, the Island has a crescent shape and extends for 224 km, with a width ranging from 4 to 60 km. The Island makes up only 0.1% of Canada's total land area, and although the population is only 0.5% of the Canadian total, it is the most concentrated in the country, with over 22 persons per square kilometre. In spite of its high density the Island is the most rural province in the nation as only 38.1% of the population is classed as urban. The Island's deep red soil has always been its most striking feature and important resource and together with the sea has been the mainstay of the population since the early 18th century. The Island was described by Jacques CARTIER in 1534 as "the fairest land that may possibly be seen." The 15 km of water between the Island and the Canadian mainland has helped develop and maintain a strong sense of distinctiveness in the province, which continues to cherish its rural past while it faces the unsettling challenges of the 20th century.

Although designed to reflect its reliance on Great Britain, the province's crest – 3 small oak trees beneath the shelter of a larger oak – and its

Prince Edward Island

Capital: Charlottetown
Motto: Parva Sub Ingenti ("The small under the protection of the great")
Flower: Lady's slipper
Largest urban centres: Charlottetown, Summerside
Population: 126 646 (1986c); rank tenth, 0.5% of Canada; 38.1% urban; 61.9% rural; 22.4 per km² density; 3.4% increase from 1981-86; 7.1% increase from 1976-86
Languages: 93.6% English; 4.1% French; 1.1% Other; 1.2% English plus one or more languages
Entered Confederation: 1 July 1873
Government: Provincial – Lieutenant-Governor, Executive Council, Legislative Assembly of 32 members; federal – 4 senators, 4 members of the House of Commons
Area: 5660 km²; 0.1% of Canada
Elevation: Highest point – Queens County (142m); lowest point – sea level
Gross Domestic Product: $1.365 billion (1986)
Farm Cash Receipts: $189.9 million (1986)
Value of Fish Landings: $51.9 million (1986)
Electric Power Produced: 2 GWh (1985)
Sales Tax: 10% (1987)

motto – *parva sub ingenti* ("the small under the protection of the great") – also aptly describe the position of the province within the Canadian Confederation.

Land and Resources

Geology Prince Edward Island's insular status is of relatively recent origin in geological terms. An enormous sedimentary basin underlying the present Gulf of St Lawrence was laid down by freshwater streams that drained ancient highlands. The surface geology of the Island is of more dramatic origin. The ice ages left an imprint on the land, especially during the late Pleistocene period between 75 000 and 15 000 years ago. When the last glaciers receded, uncovering what is now PEI, glacial debris and the marks of glacial scouring were left on the exposed land, which began gradually to assume its present character. Because of lower ocean beds and land

depressed by the glaciers' weight, the Island was connected to the mainland by a low plain covering much of the present Northumberland Strait. As ocean levels rose with the melting of the glaciers, and as the land rebounded, the crescent shape of the Island emerged about 5000 years ago.

Surface The present land surface of the Island ranges from nearly level in the W, to hilly in the central region and to gently rolling hills in the E. The highest elevation is 142 m in central Queens County. The Island's predominant reddish brown sandy and clay soils are occasionally broken by outcroppings of sedimentary rock, most commonly a red-coloured sandstone or mudstone. The heavy concentrations of iron oxides

Sea view, PEI, showing the Island's distinctive and fertile red soil (*photo by Freeman Patterson/Masterfile*).

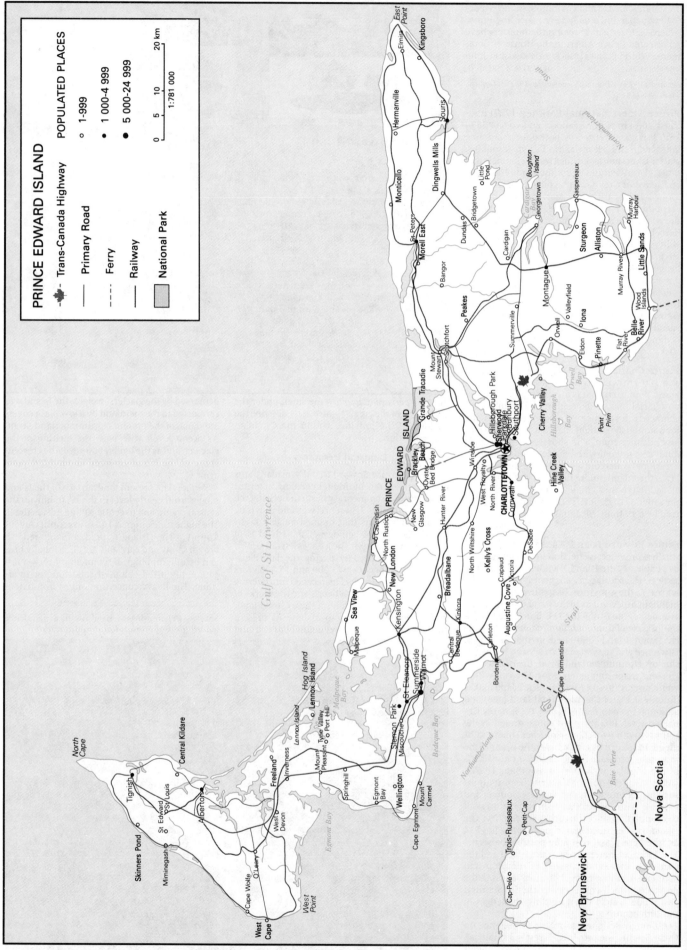

PRINCE EDWARD ISLAND

- ⚜ -- Trans-Canada Highway
- —— Primary Road
- ---- Ferry
- —— Railway
- ▨ National Park

POPULATED PLACES
- ○ 1-999
- ● 1 000-4 999
- ⬤ 5 000-24 999

20 km

0 5 10

1:781 000

Gulf of St Lawrence

East Point
Elmira
Kingsboro
Hermanville
Souris
Monticello
Dingwells Mills
Little Pond
Bridgetown
St Peters
Morell East
Dundas
Cardigan
Boughton Island
Gaspereaux
Georgetown
Bangor
Murray Harbour
Peakes
Sturgeon
Alliston
Little Sands
Scotchfort
Summerville
Montague
Murray River
Wood Islands
Mount Stewart
Valleyfield
Iona
Belle River
Grande Tracadie
Orwell
Eldon
Flat River
Pinette
Hillsborough Park
Sherwood
Parkdale
Bunbury
Point Prim
Southport
Cherry Valley
Hillsborough Bay
Brackley Beach
Winsloe
Oyster Bed Bridge
CHARLOTTETOWN
Cornwall
Hine Creek Valley
Cavendish
North Rustico
New Glasgow
Hunter River
West Royalty
North River
PRINCE EDWARD ISLAND
New London
North Wiltshire
Kelly's Cross
DeSable
Sea View
Kensington
Breadalbane
Crapaud
Victoria
Kinkora
Augustine Cove
Malpeque
Central Bedeque
Carleton
Borden
Cape Tormentine
St Eleanors
Summerside
Wilmot
Bedeque Bay
Cape Traverse
Malpeque Bay
Northumberland
Strait
Hog Island
Lennox Island
Lennox Island
Sherson Park
Miscouche
Trois-Ruisseaux
Petit-Cap
North Cape
Central Kildare
Tyne Valley
Port Hill
Inverness
Mount Pleasant
Springhill
Egmont Bay
Wellington
Mount Carmel
Freeland
Egmont Bay
Cape Egmont
Baie Verte
Tignish
St Edward
St Louis
West Devon
Alberton
O'Leary
Cap-Pelé
Skinners Pond
Mimminegash
Cape Wolfe
West Cape
West Point
New Brunswick
Nova Scotia
Northumberland

Cavendish Beach, PEI (*photo by Richard Vroom*).

in the rock and soil give the land its distinctive reddish brown hue.

The coastline is deeply indented by tidal inlets. The N shore of the Island, facing the Gulf of St Lawrence, features extensive sand-dune formations. These shifting sands pose problems for fishermen by clogging harbour entrances, but they provide a haven for summer tourists. The shoreline of the Island generally alternates between headlands of steep sandstone bluffs and extensive sandy beaches. Many of the Island's harbours have been created by dredging tidal runs and are usable only by vessels of shallow draught, such as inshore fishing boats. A few natural harbours, such as those of Summerside, Charlottetown, Georgetown and Souris, provide access and shelter for larger vessels.

Because the Island has only small ponds, few significant rivers and generally low elevation, waterpower has not been developed. In the last century numerous gristmills and sawmills used the limited hydropower available, but few survive today. Lacking hydroelectric capability, the Island has been forced to rely on fossil fuels to generate power and on electrical power transmitted from NB via submarine cable.

Little is left of the original forests of the Island; 3 centuries of clearing for agriculture and ship-building, as well as fire and disease, have radically transformed them. Only 100 years ago the upland areas of the province were forested with beech, yellow birch, maple, oak and white pine. Today, most of the woodlands have deteriorated into a mixture of spruce, balsam fir and red maple, which cover over 241 000 ha of the province.

Climate The Island climate is moderate. Winters are long but relatively mild; springs are late and cool. Summers are cool and marked by prevailing SW breezes. Average mean temperatures are approximately -7°C in Jan and Feb and 18°C in July. The Island is relatively free of fog year-round, unlike neighbouring provinces. Annual precipitation averages 112 cm, ensuring adequate groundwater supply. The waters of both the Gulf of St Lawrence and Northumberland Strait are warmer in summer than the coastal waters of NS and NB, although in winter ice covers both the strait and the gulf, and ICEBREAKERS are needed to keep shipping lanes open. Drift ice is often found in Island waters as late as the latter part of May, causing difficulty for fishermen and slowing the arrival of spring.

Resources The 2 major resources of the Island are the soil and the sea. Mineral resources have not been discovered in commercial quantities although trace deposits of coal, uranium, vanadium and other minerals exist. Since 1940, drilling has revealed the existence of natural gas beneath the seabed off the NE part of the province, but no commercially exploitable finds have been made. Mining to date has been restricted to open-pit removal of sand and gravel, but the latter is of low quality and in insufficient quantities to meet even local demand.

Agriculture, based on the rich soil and temperate climate of the province, is the most important primary resource industry. Most Island soils are coarse-textured sandy loams with a very low stone content. In general the soil is moderately acidic and it is common practice periodically to add lime to the soil to reduce the acidity. Close to 50% of the Island's land has been identified as being highly productive and upwards of 90% of the entire province is potentially farming land. Although the area actually in agricultural production has dropped in recent years, some land is still being cleared, especially for high value crops such as potatoes and tobacco. Fishing, especially for lobster and cod, is the second important resource industry of the Island. A supplementary shellfish fishery includes scallops, oysters, clams and lately mussels.

Forestry is relatively undeveloped on the Island, because of the depleted state of the woodlands and lack of effective management of the remaining resource. There have, however, been some attempts to improve the quality of the forest cover. Since 1945, through exploiting the appeal of PEI's unspoiled landscape and sandy beaches, tourism has emerged as a major industry. It has not been an unmixed blessing; often it has brought inappropriate and random development, dependence on low seasonal wages and loss of land to off-Island owners.

Conservation Conservation has become a major concern of government and of public interest groups in the province. Overcropping, extensive mechanization, reliance on chemical fertilizers and removal of hedgerows had led to considerable wind and water erosion of some of the Island's best land. It is estimated, for example, that up to 5 t of soil per ha can be eroded from an unprotected, plowed field in one year. This soil erosion has also led to heavy siltation of the creek and river systems, turning many streams, navigable in the last century, into shallow and unusable creeks. Another major concern has been the purchase of large tracts of land by non-residents for recreation or development and by vertically integrated business for farming. Both problems led to the establishment of a Royal Commission on Land Use and Ownership and to the subsequent creation of a Provincial Land Use Commission, which regulates zoning, ownership and development questions. Groups such as the PEI Nature Trust have attempted to bring public attention to many of PEI's imperilled natural areas, but most of the land is privately owned and is vulnerable to inappropriate development, misuse or unwitting neglect.

People Prince Edward Island is the most culturally homogeneous province of Canada. The population is overwhelmingly British in origin, with roughly 12% of Acadian descent. Small communities of Dutch, Lebanese and Micmac also exist. The Micmac can trace their ancestry to Indian tribes that inhabited the Island as far back as 8000 to 10 000 years ago, although the Micmac, a branch of the Algonquians, actually came to the Island within the last 2000 years. Although left only with small parcels of land of poor quality and suffering from disease and high unemployment, the Micmac population has remained relatively steady. The majority of the Acadian population can be traced to several hundred Acadians who escaped deportation at the time of the British occupation of the Island following the fall of LOUISBOURG in 1758. Today the group numbers approximately 15 000, and there are large numbers of this population sharing common surnames. ENGLISH, SCOTS and IRISH arrived in the late 18th and early 19th centuries and by 1861 the population had grown to just over 80 000. Thereafter growth slowed and after 1891 natural increase was unable to keep up with the number of Islanders leaving, especially for New England. Most of the other ethnic groups in the population are the result of immigration in the last 40 years. The 1950s and 1960s were periods of slow population growth as Islanders continued to leave the province in search of economic opportunities elsewhere. The last decade has seen a small balance of in-migration, and this, combined with natural increase, has allowed growth to the 1986 level of 126 646. Within this population, however, the percentage of those over 65 years of age has steadily increased and the government has indicated some concern about this shift in demography.

Urban Centres CHARLOTTETOWN, the capital city, is the largest urban centre of the province, with a population of 15 776 in 1986. Growth in the capital region has been most notable in the suburbs, and if the populations of the smaller communities bordering Charlottetown were included the population was 53 868 (1986c). Charlottetown is the only incorporated city in the province and is the seat of most government offices, the provincial university and the Confederation Centre theatre and art gallery. At one time the city was a major port, but in recent years the number of vessels entering has declined significantly, although efforts by several agencies have resulted in regular visits by summer cruise liners. In 1984 the federal Department of Veterans Affairs was moved to the city, resulting in an increase in federal government employees in the area.

The next largest urban centre is SUMMERSIDE (8020, 1986c) in the western part of the Island, which with its surrounding communities houses 15 614 people. Summerside's principal economic bases are agricultural service industries, government offices and the nearby Canadian Forces

Base. Other population centres in Prince County include Kensington (1105), Alberton (1103) and Tignish (960). In King's County, Montague (1994), Souris (1379) and Georgetown (729) are the major towns. Like other parts of Canada, PEI has seen a shift from rural to urban population and many smaller villages have declined in size.

Labour Force In 1987 the labour force of Prince Edward Island numbered 60 000, but unemployment is a chronic problem with the rate rarely falling below 10% in recent years. Wage rates and per capita income for Islanders are near the lowest in Canada and personal income is only 74% of the national average. Transportation difficulties, lack of natural resources, and high energy costs make the outlook for the expansion of the provincial labour force remote, despite the development plans of both provincial and federal governments.

Language and Ethnicity The overwhelming majority of the Island's population reported English as their mother tongue in 1986. Although approximately 12% of the Island's population is of Acadian descent, only 4.1% of the total population reported French as their mother tongue. Attempts are being made to preserve and expand the use of French. One of the 5 regional school districts is French, and the St Thomas Aquinas Society, an influential cultural group, actively promotes Acadian language and culture. The native language of most of the Highland Scots who came to the Island in the 18th and 19th centuries has fared less well. Gaelic is virtually extinct because of school systems that rewarded English speakers.

According to the 1981 census, 77% of the Island's population is British, primarily Highland Scots, followed by Irish, English and Lowland Scots. Acadians constitute about 12% of the population, and those listed as British *and* French constitute a further 5%. Dutch, Lebanese, Scandinavian and native Indian represent 2%; a small but vigorous Micmac population of 440 is concentrated at Lennox I on the N shore and at Scotchfort on the Hillsborough R.

Religion There are almost equal numbers of Protestants and Catholics in PEI. The United Church is the largest Protestant group, followed by the Presbyterian, Anglican and Baptist churches. Small but rapidly growing evangelical groups are also active, and there is a tiny Jewish community. Until recently religion has played an important role in Island life. Bitter struggles over religion and education were not resolved until the era of Confederation.

Economy

The economic history of PEI has been dominated by geography. In the 18th and 19th centuries its insularity was a benefit. Produce and manufactured goods had to travel only short distances before they could be loaded aboard cheap water transportation and the forests of the Island provided the resources for SHIPBUILDING, which became a major industry in the mid-1800s. The prosperity of the Island was further reinforced by the RECIPROCITY Treaty of 1854 that led to increased export of agricultural products to the US. At the time of Confederation trade links were well established along the Atlantic seaboard and with the United Kingdom. However, the shift of focus after 1873 towards central Canada and western expansion, together with changes in technology, left the Island – which had been a relatively strong economic partner in Confederation – in a weakened condition that has persisted to this day. PEI was ill equipped for the industrial age. It lacked coal and water resources essential to industrial

Gathering Irish Moss at Tignish on Prince Edward Island's northern tip (*photo by Richard Vroom*).

development, and the cost and availability of transportation proved to be a difficulty that has not been completely overcome. Industries on the Island were soon crushed by larger and more efficient plants in central Canada, but at the same time the NATIONAL POLICY provided no protection or markets for the Island's natural products. The change in technology was most strongly felt in the shipbuilding industry. As the wooden sailing ship was replaced by steam vessels constructed of iron and steel, the entire industry died, having neither the raw materials nor the capital to make such a fundamental shift. One activity in which the Island did provide a successful lead was in fox farming. Beginning in 1890 with the work of industry pioneers Charles Dalton and Robert Oulton, the province became the centre of a lucrative silver fox pelt industry. Fox breeding became very widespread, with many Island farmers supplementing their limited income from traditional agriculture in this way. By the late 1930s new technology, changing fashions and the great depression caused a rapid decline in the industry. Few fox farms survived into the postwar period. Although there was more of a stagnation in the economy than an absolute decline, by the early 1950s the per-capita income in PEI was just over 50% of the national level and the outlook for the future was bleak.

Gross Domestic Product - Prince Edward Island 1985 at Factor Cost ($millions)	
Agriculture	128.3
Forestry	0
Fishing and Trapping	30.0
Mining	1.4
Manufacturing	98.3
Construction	77.8
Utilities	25.9
Goods Producing Industries	360.4
Transportation	92.8
Wholesale and Retail Trade	158.3
Finance	140.6
Services	288.0
Public Administration and Defence	323.5
Service Producing Industries	1003.2
Total	1365

The post-WWII development of what amounted to a new National Policy has had the most profound impact on the Island. Income support programs, human-services programs and new federal-provincial fiscal policy have dramatically altered the Islanders' way of life. Attempts to alleviate regional disparities by using forced economic growth have caused a social revolution. Certainly personal income levels have risen substantially, and markedly better health and educational facilities have been established. The Federal-Provincial Comprehensive Development Plan, begun in 1969, has been central to much of this development. This new period of development through government intervention has not been an unmixed blessing. Increasing dependence has been the principal cost. By 1981 federal spending amounted to 67% of the gross domestic product of PEI. If the provincial government's funding is included, by 1981 total government spending amounted to 87% of the gross domestic product. At the same time, the number of persons engaged in primary industries has declined sharply and the number of government and related jobs increased. Facing a heavy burden of fixed costs to support social programs and the new infrastructure, it is unlikely that the province will be able to undertake significant initiatives. The outlook in the private sector is not encouraging. For example, per-capita investment in the province, as a percentage of the Canadian average, dropped from 70% in 1971 to 58% in 1985. If the province is to develop a secure and less dependent economic future, clearly some new directions must be sought. Obviously a solution to the transport and energy problems is essential, together with a fresh look at ways of utilizing the primary resources of the province.

Agriculture In the last 30 years there have been major changes in agriculture on Prince Edward Island. As late as 1951 over 90% of all farms on PEI had horses for a total of 21 000 animals. Today, workhorses are rarely seen, and fields used to produce the huge amount of forage for these animals have been turned to other uses. The number of farms has dropped from 10 137 in 1951 to 2833 in 1986. At the same time the area in farms has been reduced by 39% although in recent years the area used as cropland and pasture has remained stable. The size of the average farm has increased from 44 ha in 1951 to 96 ha in 1986, but owing to heavy investment in equipment needed on larger farms the margin of profit for Island farmers has been reduced from approximately 50% to 25%; thus a producer has to sell twice as much to have the same net income. Total farm cash receipts in 1986 were $189.9 million. Of this total the largest single crop was POTATOES, which earned over $63 million. Potatoes flourish in the soil and climate conditions found in Prince Edward Island. Over 25 000 ha are planted annually and the average yield is about 25 t per ha. Three-quarters of this yield is high-grade seed potatoes that are exported to more than 15 countries. Table stock is either sold fresh in eastern Canada and the US or processed into french fries and other potato products. There are about 1000 dairy farms in the province with a total of 22 000 dairy cattle, which produced 100 million litres of milk for the first time in 1986. Eighty percent of this is processed into milk products, such as evaporated milk, most of which are exported. In 1986 the cash receipts from dairy products totalled over $30 million. Cattle are also raised for beef. Although recent fluctuation in beef prices has resulted in uneven production, Island farmers sent about 30 000 cattle to slaughter per year between 1978 and 1986, and in 1986 the receipts from cattle and calves amounted to $32 million. Almost as important is the production of hogs, which are raised on a commercial scale by about 250 farmers. TOBACCO has been produced on Prince Edward Island since 1959. Despite being a crop sensitive to unpredictable weather and faced with high energy costs and high labour requirements, tobacco has been successful, with the 1986 crop, for example, exceeding 2500 t and selling for over $10 million.

The provincial and federal governments have put in place a large number of programs to halt the exodus of farmers from the land and to increase farm incomes, and they have met with some degree of success, but the high cost of entering the industry remains a problem. Both levels of government are active in agricultural research and Agriculture Canada maintains a large research facility in Charlottetown. The Atlantic Veterinary College on the campus of University of Prince Edward Island has a significant impact on both animal and aquatic research that will be of benefit to the fishing industry.

Industry Tourism, construction, primary-resource-related manufacturing and services are the major industries of PEI. Of these TOURISM has grown most in the last 2 decades, although growth has stopped and in 1983 the number of tourist parties was lower than in any of the preceding 6 years. The Island still attracts more than 600 000 tourists annually and in 1985 this group spent over $58 million. Since the 1960s the government has been deeply involved in the promotion of industry and in the construction and operation of attractions and accommodations. Attempts have been made to divert tourists from the central part of the Island, which is dominated by Prince Edward Island National Park, to eastern and western parts of the province, which have benefited less from the tourist dollar. A major problem is the shortness of the season, which consists of only 8 to 10 weeks in July and August. Government has been promoting attractions and activity in other seasons, and the recent openings of new hotel and convention complexes are part of the attempt to promote year-round tourism. The major attraction remains the fine warm sandy beaches along the 1760 km of shoreline. Golf, deep-sea fishing and horse racing are among the sports available for tourists. In the last decade government and private developers have established a number of "heritage" attractions, including sites operated by the Prince Edward Island Museum and Heritage Foundation.

Manufacturing in the province is dominated by fish- and farm-product processing. This area grew rapidly until 1979, but since then has declined as expansion in product lines has not offset the closure of some major plants. In 1986 some 2000 were employed and the dollar value of goods shipped in that year was $300 million. One of the development strategies explored by the government in the Comprehensive Development Plan was the establishment of manufacturing plants in industrial parks, but many of the attempts to introduce non-food-related manufacturing have failed. The last 2 decades have seen increased employment in the service sector and both the federal and provincial governments are major employers with over 7000 persons on government payrolls in 1986.

Forestry Although forestry was a principal industry in the 1800s, it has since declined dramatically. About 37% of the province is covered by woodland, 99% of which is privately owned. Most of the best timber was harvested in the 19th century and over 80 000 ha have regenerated in inferior species of little commercial value. Today, forests are being reconsidered as a source of both fuel and lumber for provincial use. Many Island homes are now being heated at least in part by wood fuel, and the number will likely increase as costs of fuel oil and electricity continue to rise.

Lieutenant-Governors of Prince Edward Island 1873-1987	
	Term
W.C.F. Robinson	1873-78
Robert Hodgson	1878-79
Thomas H. Haviland	1879-84
Andrew A. Macdonald	1884-89
Jedediah S. Carvell	1889-94
George W. Howlan	1894-99
P.A. McIntyre	1899-1904
D.A. MacKinnon	1904-10
Benjamin Rogers	1910-15
Augustine C. Macdonald	1915-19
Murdock Mackinnon	1919-24
Frank R. Heartz	1924-30
Charles Dalton	1930-33
G. Des Brisay Deblois	1933-39
Bradford Lepage	1939-45
Joseph A. Bernard	1945-50
T. William L. Prowse	1950-58
F.W. Hyndman	1958-63
William J. MacDonald	1963-69
J. George MacKay	1969-74
Gordon L. Bennett	1974-80
Joseph A. Doiron	1980-85
Lloyd McPhail	1985-

Fisheries In 1985 there were just over 3200 fishermen and helpers in the province. Almost all of the 2500 vessels used were small inshore boats, most of which were employed in the lobster fishery. The fishery also provided seasonal employment in processing plants for up to 2000 workers. Fish landings in 1985 had a value of $51.9 million, but when processing, outfitting and vessel construction are included, the contribution to the provincial economy was estimated to exceed $100 million. Lobster is by far the most valuable species, with 1985 landings of 6700 t, having a value of $33.5 million. Other shellfish, including scallops and the famous Malpeque oysters, added a further $7 million to the industry. The shellfish industry was shut down in late 1987 until a toxin, domoic acid, was identified and restricted after 100 people became ill and at least 2 died after eating poisoned molluscs from PEI. Fishing for the giant bluefin tuna has become an important attraction for sportfishermen from around the world, but the species is also fished commercially. Groundfish such as cod, hake, flounder and redfish and pelagic species such as herring and mack-

Premiers of Prince Edward Island 1873-1988		
	Party	*Term*
J.C. Pope	Conservative	1873
L.C. Owen	Conservative	1873-76
L.H. Davies	Liberal	1876-79
W.W. Sullivan	Conservative	1879-89
N. McLeod	Conservative	1889-91
F. Peters	Liberal	1891-97
A.B. Warburton	Liberal	1897-98
D. Farquharson	Liberal	1898-1901
A. Peters	Liberal	1901-08
F.L. Haszard	Liberal	1908-11
H. James Palmer	Liberal	1911
John A. Mathieson	Conservative	1911-17
Aubin A. Arsenault	Conservative	1917-19
J.H. Bell	Liberal	1919-23
James D. Stewart	Conservative	1923-27
Albert C. Saunders	Liberal	1927-30
Walter M. Lea	Liberal	1930-31
James D. Stewart	Conservative	1931-33
William J.P. MacMillan	Conservative	1933-35
Walter M. Lea	Liberal	1935-36
Thane A. Campbell	Liberal	1936-43
J. Walter Jones	Liberal	1943-53
Alexander W. Matheson	Liberal	1953-59
Walter R. Shaw	Conservative	1959-66
Alexander B. Campbell	Liberal	1966-78
W. Bennett Campbell	Liberal	1978-79
J. Angus McLean	Conservative	1979-81
James M. Lee	Conservative	1981-86
Joseph A. Ghiz	Liberal	1986-

erel are also caught in the Island's waters, accounting for a value of $8.4 million in 1985. An important industry in the western part of the Island is the harvesting of IRISH MOSS, a marine plant that, when processed, yields carrageenin, an emulsifying and stabilizing agent used in many food products.

Transportation Transportation to and from the Island by sea is currently handled by 2 ferry systems. CN operates a year-round service from Borden, PEI, to Cape Tormentine, NB, for passengers, motor vehicles and railcars; icebreaking ferries are used in winter. Northumberland Ferries, a private company heavily subsidized by the federal government, operates between Wood Islands, PEI, and Caribou, NS, from April to November, closing when ice and weather become severe. The province is also connected to major Canadian centres by daily air routes operated by both Canadian Airlines International and Air Canada. There has been recurring interest in a fixed crossing to the mainland. A popular proposal in the late 19th century was for a tunnel under Northumberland Strait. As recently as the late 1960s, work was actually begun on a causeway but was abandoned in favour of the negotiation of the Comprehensive Development Plan. In 1987, renewed proposals for constructing a fixed link in the form of a bridge or tunnel came forward from the federal government and private developers. Jan 1988 saw a plebiscite held on the question by the provincial government of Prem Joe Ghiz. In this controversial vote 59% voted in favour, and 41% were opposed to the idea of a fixed link to the mainland. In recent years the deterioration of the province's railway system has been a cause for concern. As operation of branch lines has become less economical, CN has drastically reduced services. Opposition to these cutbacks has been strong, especially from farmers who market their produce via the rail system. The road network within the province has been substantially improved and now almost all primary and secondary routes are paved, which has greatly increased the use of road transportation in the shipping of primary and manufactured products.

Energy Energy costs are one of the most serious problems facing PEI. Electrical energy is the most expensive in Canada. All power is either generated in oil-fixed thermal plants or is imported via submarine cable from NB. Since there is no potential for large-scale hydroelectrical development, alternative energy sources such as wind, solar and wood-fired generators are being investigated. As yet, none of these alternatives has been proved to have the required capacity, despite successful small-scale applications. The reduction of energy costs is certain to be a major topic of future interprovincial and federal-provincial negotiation.

Government and Politics

Government and politics are closer to the people in PEI than in any other province. Its 126 646 people have a full range of federal, provincial and municipal institutions. As a result, constituencies are small, politicians familiar, and a sense of informality pervades the political process. The basic structures of provincial government are similar to those of other provinces, but there are important distinctions arising from the size and political history of the province. Government was established in PEI by order-in-council in 1769, but it was not until the post-Confederation period that the modern structure and practice of government emerged. There is a lieutenant-governor appointed by the governor general for a 5-year term. The Executive Coun-

This pencil and ink drawing by Robert Harris illustrates events on election day in Charlottetown in the late 19th century (*courtesy Confederation Centre Art Gallery and Museum*).

cil, or Cabinet, usually consists of 10 members responsible for single or multiple departments and is headed by the premier. The Legislative Assembly has 32 representatives, with one councillor and one assemblyman drawn from each of 16 electoral districts. Charlottetown elects 4 members and Summerside 2. Most of the constituencies are rural and small, some having barely 2000 voters. The judicial system consists of the Supreme Court, which has Estates, Family and Trial divisions and which sits on Appeals *en banco*, Provincial Courts and the Small Claims Court. There are no county courts in the province.

Local Government There are 3 levels of municipal government in the province: city, town and community. Charlottetown (inc 1855) is the only city, governed by a mayor and councillors, elected for 2-year terms. The 8 towns are Parkdale, Alberton, Borden, Georgetown, Kensington, Montague, Souris and Summerside, the largest and oldest. In 1987 there were 77 incorporated communities. The towns are governed by mayors and councillors and the communities by elected commissioners.

Federal Representation The Island is represented by 4 members of Parliament, elected from the ridings of Egmont, Malpeque, Hillsborough and Cardigan, and 4 senators. When PEI entered Confederation in 1873 it was entitled to 6 members, but declining population relative to the rest of Canada reduced this figure to 5 in 1892 and 4 in 1904, and by 1911 it was entitled to only 3 members. After vigorous protests, the BNA Act was amended in 1915, stating that no province should have fewer members of Parliament than senators. Thus, PEI was guaranteed its current 4 seats.

Public Finance Total provincial expenditures as of 31 Mar 1988 were $532 million. The largest expenditure was for health, social services and hospitals at $180.3 million and education was next at $123.8 million. Transportation and public works both exceeded $43 million each. Debt charges amounted to $73 million. In the same year, provincial revenues amounted to $522 million, 49% of which came from the federal

government, $156 million in direct equalization payments. The dependence of the Island on federal funding is underlined by the fact that expenditures by the federal government, including payments to individuals, were more than one and one-half times the provincial budget.

Health The Island is reasonably well served by hospital and health facilities, especially since the introduction of a provincial health-care plan in the late 1960s, providing nonpremium medical and hospital services. The largest hospital is the Queen Elizabeth Hospital in Charlottetown. There are 8 smaller hospitals in the province, with a total bed capacity for all Island hospitals in 1985 of 690. In 1985 there were 167 practising physicians in the province, a ratio of 1.31 physicians per 1000 people. As in other provinces, health-care costs have risen sharply. For example, the cost of physicians' services rose from about $4.3 million in 1974 to $15.2 million in 1985, a cost per-capita rise from $37 to over $119. Hospital costs rose in similar fashion from $102 per capita in 1974 to $379 per capita in 1985.

Politics The emergence of fairly stable political parties in PEI was a product of the 1870s. From that time to the present the Liberal and Conservative parties have dominated the electoral scene. Although a provincial NDP organization exists, and although the CCF/NDP has run candidates in both provincial and federal elections since the 1940s, no third-party candidate has ever come close to gaining a seat in the legislature. When PEI entered Confederation it had a bicameral legislature, an upper house or council elected by property owners, and an assembly elected by universal male suffrage. As provinces moved in the late 19th century to abolish upper houses, a unique compromise emerged in PEI. A single Legislative Assembly was created in 1893, but for each constituency there was one candidate designated a councillor and one an assemblyman. Property owners elected the councillor and all males the assemblyman. Persons holding property in more than one riding could vote in each riding, a system that led to all manner of obvious abuses. This property qualification was maintained until 1963, and the practice of electing a councillor and an assemblyman from each district continues to the present. The franchise was extended to women in 1922. Because the population is almost equally split between Ro-

man Catholics and Protestants a practice developed of ensuring that opposing candidates in provincial elections faced a coreligionist, but in recent years this tradition has weakened. Owing to the small size of constituencies and the nearly even division of political allegiances, elections tend to be decided by narrow margins. Each vote is important, and candidates stay in touch with their constituents, especially when patronage is to be distributed. The introduction of the secret ballot in 1913 reduced the impact of patronage but by no means eliminated it. Political issues have tended to be relatively low key. Governments more often change because the party in power has grown tired and it "is time to give the other guys a chance." Politics has become relatively more sophisticated in the past decade; television advertising and the emergence of "image" as an important factor have affected PEI as they have other provinces.

Education

The educational system of PEI has undergone revolutionary changes in the last decade. The public school system originated in the Free Education Act of 1852, which authorized the establishment of autonomous school districts based on local communities. Each of the 475 districts was entitled to a one-room school, usually offering grades one through 10. The school districts were governed by local boards, who collected taxes, hired teachers and organized volunteer services. Along with the church and the general store, schools became focal points in each community. This system served the Island well in the 19th and early 20th centuries, but began to show serious deficiencies by the 1920s and 1930s. Inadequate facilities, lack of opportunities to study beyond grade 10 (except for a fortunate few who could attend high school in Charlottetown) and poorly paid, underqualified teachers all began to reach public attention. By 1956 per-capita expenditures for elementary and secondary education were the lowest in Canada – $92 compared with the $279 Canadian average – and by the 1960s the local schools, while providing an essential focus of community life, had fallen far behind Canadian educational norms.

The Comprehensive Development Plan provided the vehicle and the rationale for transforming the Island educational system. Beginning in 1970 the many small school districts were replaced by 5 regional boards, and the process of closing schools and building new, consolidated institutions began. In 1971 there were 245 schools; by 1985 that number had declined to 69. New regulations requiring university degrees for teachers were introduced, and teachers' salaries rose from an average of $5724 in 1971 to $31 806 by 1985. The facilities and opportunities available to Island students improved immeasurably as a result of the consolidation process. Yet much of the interaction of home and school and the cohesiveness of local communities has been lost. In 1985-86 there were just over 25 000 children enrolled in the public school system. Expenditure on education has increased almost as dramatically as the number of schools has dropped, rising from $30.6 million in 1974 to $124 million in 1985.

Higher education in PEI began with the creation of Prince of Wales College (1834) and St Dunstan's University (1855). These 2 institutions remained small and separated along religious lines. In 1969 a single new university, the University of Prince Edward Island, was founded. This university, established as another phase of the development plan, offers undergraduate programs in arts, science, education and busi-

A Meeting of the School Trustees (c1885), oil on canvas, by Robert Harris, Prince Edward Island's best-known artist. The paper on the desk is inscribed "Roll/Pine Creek School/Kate Henderson/Teachers" *(courtesy National Gallery of Canada)*.

ness administration and a degree in veterinary medicine. In 1985-86, a total of 2549 full-time and part-time students were enrolled. Holland College, created in 1969, is responsible for a wide range of vocational and occupational training programs at several locations throughout the province.

Cultural Life

The rich cultural heritage of Prince Edward Island developed as an integral part of the community partially because of the relative isolation of the province. Even within the province there was little communication between the Acadian communities in the western part of the Island and the predominantly Scots communities in the SE. Although the French language and Acadian culture have been strengthened in recent years, the Gaelic language has all but disappeared. Because of threats to the cultural life of the province many groups have emerged in recent years supporting aspects of the Island's cultural heritage. The provincial government's Department of Community and Cultural Affairs assists these groups and funds a wide variety of activities. The PEI Museum and Heritage Foundation, for example, not only administers historic sites but is also active in collecting and interpreting material culture. The PEI Council of the Arts also assists and encourages local cultural development. Both Holland College and UPEI are vital contributors to the contemporary cultural life of the Island.

Arts The Confederation Centre of the Arts was built as a memorial to the FATHERS OF CONFEDERATION in 1964 to mark the 100th anniversary of the CHARLOTTETOWN CONFERENCE. The centre is a major arts complex with theatres, an art gallery and a public library. The gallery has a fine collection of Canadian Art and features a large collection of the works of Robert HARRIS, a portraitist of the late 19th and early 20th century whose most notable work is the group portrait of the Fathers of Confederation. The theatre is home to the CHARLOTTETOWN SUMMER FESTIVAL, a showcase of Canadian musical theatre. Recent years have seen the growth of community theatre productions across the province. Summer stock theatres operate in the communities of Victoria and Georgetown. At present there is an active artistic community on the Island and in addition to the Confederation Centre Gallery there are several other private and public galleries. While the province has been the home or birthplace of a large number of popular or academic writers, none is so well known as Lucy Maud MONTGOMERY, author of ANNE OF GREEN GABLES. Most of Montgomery's stories are set on the Island and

each year thousands of visitors come to the Island to see places mentioned in her books or associated with her life.

Communications PEI is served by an English-language CBC radio station and by English- and French-language CBC television. The CTV television network also covers the Island but is not produced locally. Two private radio stations broadcast in Charlottetown and one operates in Summerside. Cable television systems operate in all Island population centres, offering a wide range of programs, mostly of US origin. There are 3 daily newspapers published in the province: the *Guardian* (morning) and the *Evening Patriot* (evening) in Charlottetown and the *Journal-Pioneer* in Summerside. The liveliest newspapers are the weekly *Eastern Graphic* published in Montague and the *West Prince Graphic* published in Alberton. *La Voix acadienne* is a French-language weekly produced in Summerside.

Historic Sites Of PEI's many important historic sites, the best known is Province House, the location of the Charlottetown Conference of 1864. Government House, the residence of the lieutenant-governor, is a fine early 19th-century building, which has been carefully refurbished. Other sites include Green Gables, the L.M. Montgomery home at Cavendish, and heritage sites operated by the Museum and Heritage Foundation at Port Hill, Basin Head and Orwell Corner. A visitor can appreciate much of the Island's architectural heritage by simply walking in the older areas of Charlottetown or Summerside, or by driving along the country roads. Many fine examples of both rural and urban buildings from the last century are still intact and functional.

History

The first inhabitants of Prince Edward Island were the precursors of the Micmac. These native people may have occupied sites on PEI as much as 10 000 years ago by crossing the low plain now covered by Northumberland Strait. Occupation since that time has most likely been continuous, although there are some indications that there may have been seasonal migrations to hunt and fish on the Island as well. The Micmac have inhabited the area for the last 2000 years.

Exploration The first European to record seeing the Island was Jacques Cartier, who landed at several spots on the N shore during his explorations of the gulf in the summer of 1534. Although there was to be no permanent settlement for almost 200 years, the harbours and bays were known to French and BASQUE fishermen, but no trace of their visits has survived.

Settlement French settlement of the Island (then known as as Île St-Jean) began in the 1720s with the colony being a dependency of Île Royale, although a small garrison was stationed near what is now Charlottetown. Settlement was slow with the population in 1748 reaching just over 700. However, with increasing British pressure on the Acadian inhabitants of Nova Scotia culminating in the decision to expel them in 1755, the population of the Island was significantly increased. Some 5000 settlers were on the Island at the fall of LOUISBOURG in 1758 but the British quickly forced all but a few hundred to leave, even though the colony was not ceded to them until the Treaty of PARIS (1763).

Under the British administration the name of the Island was anglicized to the Island of Saint John. This was the first of the new possessions to benefit from a plan to survey all of the territory in N America. Surveyor General Samuel HOLLAND was able to provide detailed plans of the Island by 1765. He had divided it into 67 townships of 20 000 acres each. Almost all of these were grant-

ed as the result of a lottery held in 1767 to military officers and others to whom the British government owed favours. With the exception of small areas surrounding the land allotted for towns, there was no crown land. The proprietors were required to settle their lands to fulfil the terms of their grants, but few made an effort to do so. As a result the Island had vast areas of undeveloped land, yet those who wished to open up farms often had to pay steep rents or purchase fees. Some proprietors refused to sell land at all and settlers found that they had no more security of tenure than they formerly had as tenants in England or Scotland. Further, the costs of the administration of the Island were to be borne by a tax paid by the proprietors on the land they held. This was often impossible to collect, and efforts made by the local government to enforce the terms of the grants were usually overruled by the British government under the influence of the landowners, most of whom never set foot in the colony. The LAND QUESTION was the dominating political concern from 1767 until Confederation. Confrontation between the agents of the proprietors and the tenants frequently led to violence, and attempts to change the system were blocked in England. During the 1840s the government was able to buy out some of the landowners and make the land available for purchase by the tenants, but funds available for this purpose were quickly exhausted.

In spite of these difficulties the population grew from just over 4000 in 1798 to 62 000 around 1850. Although there was an influx of LOYALISTS after the American Revolution the majority of the newcomers were from the British Isles. Several large groups were brought from Scotland in the late 1700s and early 1800s by landowners such as Captain John MacDonald and Lord SELKIRK, and by 1850 the Irish represented a sizable proportion of the recent immigrants.

Colonial Government After 1758 the Island had been governed as part of Nova Scotia, but in 1769, following representations made by the proprietors, a separate administration was set up complete with governor, lieutenant-governor, Council and Assembly. In 1799 the name of the colony was changed by the Assembly to Prince Edward Island to honour a son of King George III stationed with the army in Halifax at the time. With rapid growth in the second quarter of the 19th century, demands came for more effective control over the affairs of the colony by the elected Assembly. Although the concept of representative government had been accepted since 1773 the administration was still dominated by the appointed Executive Council. In 1851 RESPONSIBLE GOVERNMENT was granted to the colony and the first elected administration under George COLES took office. The period was not a politically stable one, however, for in the next 22 years a total of 12 governments were in office. The land question continued and, in addition, matters such as assistance to religious schools divided the population.

Confederation The Charlottetown Conference of 1864, the first in a series of meetings leading to Confederation, was held in the colony, and it marked the beginning of a period of political change that would leave a deep imprint. The meeting had been called to discuss maritime union, but when visiting representatives from Canada began to promote a larger union the original proposal failed to capture the imagination of Islanders. When the other British North American colonies joined in the new federation in 1867, few people in PEI regretted not being part of the union. The aloofness of the Islanders, however, could not last for long. A massive debt incurred by the Islanders in building a railway running from one end of the colony to the other, combined with

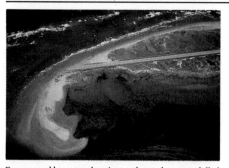

Encouraged by a stray hurricane, the sea has remodelled the western tip of Rustico I, part of the normally hospitable beachland of Prince Edward Island National Park (*photo by J.A. Kraulis*).

pressures from the British government and Canadian promises, pushed the Island into Confederation in 1873. The enticements held out by the Canadians included an absorption of the colony's debt, year-round communication with the mainland, and the provision of funds with which the colony could buy out the proprietors and end the land question. Although few Islanders displayed much enthusiasm, most accepted the union as a marriage of necessity.

Post-Confederation The post-Confederation period brought severe blows to the Island's economy and population as new technology, the National Policy and other forces combined to reduce the Island's prosperity. Although the province reached a population level of 109 000 in 1891, the lure of employment in western and central Canada and in the US led to a drain on the population, which had slipped to 88 000 by the time of the GREAT DEPRESSION. Dominion-provincial relations dominated the political sphere as the Island sought to increase its subsidy from Ottawa, retain the level of political representation it had enjoyed at Confederation, and finally establish the continuous communication with the mainland that had been promised in 1873. Throughout the first half of the 20th century the economy of the province was stable, with only slight changes in both farming and fishing, with the notable exception of the fox-farming industry between 1890 and 1939. By the mid-1960s, however, the situation had changed considerably. The number of farmers and fishermen had dropped and the economy, which had lagged behind that of the rest of Canada, was in serious trouble. The 20th century has forced Islanders to give up more and more of their cherished independence, but it has also brought with it better lives for almost all Islanders, at least in material terms. Education, health and social support programs, higher incomes and greater mobility have had a price, but it is one that most Islanders have been willing to pay. Though Islanders might still regard the rest of the world as being "from away," they are also securely a part of Canada. S. ANDREW ROBB AND H.T. HOLMAN

Reading: J.M. Bumstead, *Land, Settlement and Politics on Eighteenth Century Prince Edward Island* (1987).

Prince Edward Island National Park (est 1937, 18 km²) is a narrow strip of coastline stretching over 40 km along the N shore of PEI. The park is a fragile seascape of red sandstone cliffs and sweeping beaches, backed by shifting sand dunes held together by the delicate roots of slender grasses. Inland are forests of spruce and birch inhabited by raccoon, skunk, red fox, muskrat and mink. Saltwater marshes and inland ponds are havens for migrating SHOREBIRDS. Many species, eg, great blue heron and the rare piping plover, nest here. The area was inhabited over 5000 years ago by the "shellfish people." More

recently, Micmac spent their summers on the coast. Europeans first arrived in the 15th century. About 200 years later settlement occurred and farming and shipbuilding gained importance. Green Gables, the house that inspired Lucy Maud MONTGOMERY's classic novel, *Anne of Green Gables,* is preserved in the park. LILLIAN STEWART

Prince George, BC, City, pop 67 621 (1986c), 67 559 (1981c), inc 1915, is the third largest population centre in the province. It is situated in the geographical centre of BC at the junction of the NECHAKO and FRASER rivers, 784 km N of VANCOUVER by road. The aboriginal inhabitants, the Carrier Dene people, aided Alexander MACKENZIE on his journey to the Pacific coast in 1793. The region was called NEW CALEDONIA by Simon FRASER when the North West Co began fur trading there in 1805. Fraser established Fort George trading post, named after George III of England, at the confluence of the Nechako and Fraser rivers in 1807. From 1814 until the 1860s Cariboo gold rush, Fort George was on the Brigade route from Stuart Lk in the N to the forts in the S. It remained outside the area settled during the gold rush though the main party of the OVERLANDERS led by R.B. McMicking passed the fort in 1862 on their way down the Fraser to the goldfields. Fort George closed in 1915. Settlement in the region was negligible until the land boom (1908-14) during construction of the Grand Trunk Pacific Ry (now part of CNR). For several years 3 neighbouring townsites vied for dominance, with the railway townsite eventually winning out. The town's name was changed to Prince George after a referendum held during the first civic election (1915), this time for a former duke of Kent, who died in an air crash in 1942. Growth of the city was slow until after WWII when a booming forest industry brought prosperity and rapid growth to the region with many newcomers from the prairies. Between 1961 and 1981 Prince George grew from a rough mill town to the major manufacturing, supply and government and education centre for N-central BC. By 1986 the city had 15 sawmills, 2 single pulpmills and 1 twinned pulpmill, one of the largest in the world. Other industries include wood products, pulpmill chemicals, a refinery and a brewery.

Prince George has large railway yards and locomotive repair shops to service grain, coal and lumber trains to the coast. It is the divisional headquarters on the Tete Jaune Cache/Prince Rupert CNR line and the northern terminus for passenger service on the BC Ry, formerly the Pacific Great Eastern Ry (PGE). From 1952-58, it was the northern terminus for the PGE, until the line was extended to Dawson Creek, then Fort Nelson. The city is a major highway junction and the airport is served by Canadian Airlines International.

The city has a large, modern library, regional college, art gallery, regional museum, symphony orchestra and amateur theatre. It is a centre for sportfishing, moose hunting and cross-country skiing. JOHN STEWART AND KENT SEDGWICK

Prince of Wales Island, 33 338 km², eighth-largest island in the ARCTIC ARCHIPELAGO. Composed almost entirely of sedimentary bedrock formations, its northern part is hilly, reaching up to 415 m; the rest is gently undulating. The vegetation is sparse polar desert and semidesert, but well-vegetated broad valleys occur, especially in

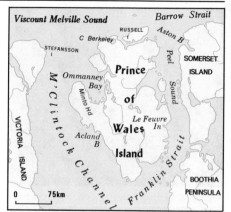

the E. Muskoxen are common, mainly in the NE. Peary caribou are also common, especially in the N. The shores of the island were explored during the FRANKLIN SEARCH expeditions in 1851 under Capt T.H. Austin and in 1852 under William KENNEDY. S.C. ZOLTAI

Prince of Wales Strait is situated in the ARCTIC ARCHIPELAGO between the uplands of western VICTORIA I and the E coast of BANKS I. About 275 km long and generally about 20 km wide, its depths reach 160 m at the southern end and become progressively shallower towards the northern entrance. The NE-SW orientation prevents prevailing winds from driving heavy pack ice down the strait, which is primarily covered with locally formed ice that breaks up more readily, leaving a reasonably clear channel. Linking Viscount Melville Sound and Amundsen Gulf, the strait is one of 4 possible routes in the NORTHWEST PASSAGE and was first surveyed by a land party led by MCCLURE in 1850, though it was not navigated until the RCMP patrol of Sgt LARSEN in 1944. It has since become the preferred route of large vessels making the passage. DOUG FINLAYSON

Prince of Wales Trophy is awarded annually to the team finishing first in the Prince of Wales Conference of the NATIONAL HOCKEY LEAGUE. It was donated by the Prince of Wales (later King Edward VIII) to the NHL in 1924. From 1927-28 to 1937-38 it was presented to the first-place team of the American Division, and from 1938-39 to 1967-68 to the team finishing first in the NHL overall. It became a divisional trophy again after expansion in 1967-68, going at first to the East Division and now to the Prince of Wales Conference. JAMES MARSH

Prince of Wales's Fort (Churchill) In 1686 HUDSON'S BAY COMPANY men sailed into the CHURCHILL R, but it was not until 1717 that James Knight built a permanent post there, about 11 km from the mouth, which was called Churchill River, Churchill or Churchill Factory until 1719, when the name was changed to Prince of Wales's Fort. The company was interested not only in furs, but also in establishing a whaling industry. Fear of a sea attack by the French led the HBC to construct a stone fort that would command the entrance to Churchill R. By Aug 1731 tradesmen had picketed the fort, which was 91.4 m square, on Eskimo Point. The walls of the original ramparts were completed in 1739, and the following year HBC Gov Richard Norton moved to the new site. Work on the fort appears to have been practically continuous until 1771. In Aug 1782, 3 French ships and about 300 men, under command of the comte de Lapérouse, arrived at the mouth of the

Prince of Wales's Fort, later called Ft Prince of Wales, was first established in 1717. Restoration work was begun 1934-35 and the fort is now a tourist attraction (*courtesy Hudson's Bay Company Archives/R.V. Oleson*).

Churchill R. The fort was easily captured; its masonry was poor and Samuel HEARNE, governor of the fort, had insufficient men to operate its 42 guns. Hearne and the men were taken prisoner. Before sailing, Lapérouse spiked the cannon and blew up the buildings. The company ship arrived the following year and Hearne re-established the fur-trading post about 7-8 km upriver. He called it both Churchill Factory and Prince of Wales Factory. Ft Prince of Wales was left until 1934-35 when the Canadian government had the cannon dug up and remounted and the walls repaired. Today the partially restored fort is one of the main tourist attractions in CHURCHILL, Man. *See also* HISTORIC SITE.   SHIRLEE ANNE SMITH

Prince Patrick Island, 15 848 km², is the farthest W of Canada's Arctic QUEEN ELIZABETH IS. Topographically, it is a low-elevation, dissected plateau that rises gently from an exceptionally low coast to a maximum elevation in the SE of only 200 m. It lies within the Sverdrup Basin geological structure and consists of thick beds of Upper Devonian deposits, dipping at a shallow angle to the SW. During the Tertiary, the island was uplifted and faulting occurred. The area is still seismically active, and tectonic movement along the faults appears at surface as fissures and small scarps. A thin strip of sand and gravel deposits of nonglacial origin was laid down along the island's Arctic Ocean coastline during the early Pleistocene. The island was named for Prince Arthur William Patrick, duke of Connaught, governor general 1911-16.
                                      DOUG FINLAYSON

Prince Rupert, BC, City, pop 15 755 (1986c), 16 197 (1981c), inc 1910, is situated on Kaien I, at the mouth of the SKEENA R in the Coast Mtn Range of BC, 1520 km by road NW of Vancouver (720 km by air) and 730 km W of Prince George. Kaien I was once the meeting place of the TSIMSHIAN and HAIDA and the city has preserved numerous relics of its native past. The western terminus of the Yellowhead Hwy and, as a seaport, a link between the US, Vancouver and Alaska, it is the industrial, commercial and institutional centre for BC's NORTHWEST COAST.

Prince Rupert (named for the first HBC governor) was envisioned in the early 1900s as the western terminus of the GRAND TRUNK PACIFIC RY and as a rival of Vancouver as Canada's Pacific outlet, but the hoped-for boom never materialized. The fishing industry became important to the city's economy after WWI. During WWII the port became a shipbuilding centre and was used

by the American army as a transportation base for men and materials to Alaska, the Pacific Is and the Far East. New interest in the coalfields of northeastern BC and strategies to speed up grain movement to the Prairies' Pacific Rim markets have affected the city and led to the construction of the Prince Rupert Grain Terminal, funded largely (80%) by the government of Alberta. The new terminal, located on Ridley I, 7 km S of Prince Rupert began operations in March 1985 and will be able to handle up to 7 million t of grain per year. In addition, Prince Rupert is the most important fish-landing port on the N coast, and the terminus of the BC and Alaska ferry systems. *See also* PORTS AND HARBOURS.
                                      ALAN F.J. ARTIBISE

Reading: P. Bowman, *Prince Rupert* (1973); R.G. Large, *Prince Rupert: Gateway to Alaska* (1960).

Princess Sheila According to popular accounts, Sheila Na Geira Pike was an Irish princess captured and married by a naval-officer-turned-pirate, Gilbert Pike, in the early 17th century. Her adventurous husband established a homestead in Carbonear, Conception Bay, where Pikes today recount tales of their beautiful, proud and aristocratic ancestor. Throughout Newfoundland, she is sometimes associated with various weather conditions such as Sheila's Brush.
                                      CAROLE H. CARPENTER

Princeton, BC, Town, pop 2910 (1986c), 3051 (1981c), inc 1951, is located at the junction of the Tulameen and Similkameen rivers, 114 km W of Penticton. Originally known as Vermilion or Red Earth Forks, it was also called Similkameen and Allisons, after the first pioneer, John Fall Allison. It became a stop on the pack trail from Fort Colvile to Fort Hope after the OREGON TREATY. Allison established a ranch there in 1859 and lived there until 1900, discovering coal and copper in the area. James DOUGLAS had a townsite laid out 1860 and named it in honour of a visit to British N America by the Prince of Wales (later Edward VII). The region boasts a long mining history, starting with the Rock Creek gold rush in the 1860s, which brought many placer miners to the creeks. The much larger strike (1885-90) saw up to 8000 men working at Granite Creek, including many Chinese. Copper was mined 1878-1957 and coal 1898-1950. A key event was the arrival of the Great Northern and Canadian Pacific railways, which opened the Coquihalla-Kettle Valley route to Vancouver. The nearby Nickel Plate Mine at Hedley also benefited the town. The opening of the Hope-Princeton highway, of which Princeton is at the E end, in 1949 helped to offset mine closures, and a brewery that had been est in 1903 shut down in 1961. The Princeton area is rich in copper, gold and other metals as well as large copper properties and coal and low-grade iron ore. Tourism and agriculture supplement mining, and logging has been carried on from earliest times; numerous smaller mills were merged into one large mill in 1976.
                                      WILLIAM A. SLOAN

Principall Navigations, Voyages and Discoveries of the English Nation, The, written by Richard Hakluyt (c1552-1616). A passionate enthusiast of trade and colonization, convinced that English navigators "excelled all ... peoples of

the earth," Hakluyt participated personally in launching the Virginia Company of 1606, encouraged the search for the NORTHWEST PASSAGE and was an adviser to the EAST INDIA CO. Through his lectures, his connections with people in high public office and his extensive publications he was enormously influential in stimulating and popularizing the overseas ventures of Elizabethan and early Jacobean England. Though he published accounts of the voyages of other peoples, his most important work was *The Principall Navigations, Voyages and Discoveries of the English Nation*, which first appeared in one volume in 1589 and then in an enlarged 3-volume edition a decade later. Hakluyt's publication of the discoveries of the Cabots and their successors established English claims to large parts of N America and the Arctic. Hakluyt is commemorated by the Hakluyt Society, founded in the mid-19th century, which continues his work of publishing accounts of explorations and voyages.
                                      G.A. ROTHROCK

Print Industry The process of producing multiple copies or reproductions is traditionally associated with a printing press but may also describe photographic or electrostatic copier processes of duplication. In the 20th century the print medium has become but one part of a complex and rapidly changing COMMUNICATIONS process. Within its own area, printing is allied with the graphic arts industry, which involves preparation, actual press work and finishing procedures.

Prior to the printing process of putting impressions on paper, foil, plastic or cloth, there are pre-press procedures such as design, artwork, layout, creation of type or graphics, film and platemaking, and press makeready. In the past all these processes were done by hand or camera. Today, type is set by microcomputer phototypesetters and can be produced in negative or positive film as an automatic process. It can be stored and retrieved from magnetic tape or discs, and manipulated into any form. Pagination systems can combine halftone or line graphics, type and page layout in a single process. Little handwork is done after the creation of the written script or the artist's finished work. The newer equipment can combine these elements into a page, produce a printing plate automatically, and send the information by wire or SATELLITE to any distant point. The GLOBE AND MAIL national edition is transmitted by satellite to locations across Canada, where it is printed and distributed. CABLE TELEVISION connections and videotex as a means of transmitting information are augmenting or replacing print in many areas (*see* TELIDON).

There are 4 major printing processes: the letterpress, or relief printing method, in which printing areas are raised above nonprinting areas and the impression is made directly from the inked raised surface to the substrate or paper; the planographic, or offset, lithographic system, in which the image and nonimage areas lie on the same plane but are distinguished by application of the principle that grease and water do not mix; the intaglio or gravure system, by which the image is engraved into the cylindrical or flat plate surface, then inked and printed onto the substrate; the screen-printing or serigraphy process, in which ink is pushed through a screen to the substrate. In recent years, other methods of producing multiple copies from one master have been developed: flexography, a raised image system using rubber plates and aniline inks; electrostatic printing, either in a photocopier or through a fine screen; and jet ink printing, in which tiny globules of ink are jetted on to the substrate, often prompted by a computer or magnetic tape. Laser beam printing is now commercially successful, and electro-erosion printing is a strong probability for the future.

Beyond the press are the bindery or finishing procedures, many of them in-line with the press as a continuing operation. These steps could include folding, stitching and trimming on computerized cutters or cutting equipment on-press; or they may involve punching, perforating for tear-away, fan folding as in business forms, collating many signatures, round-cornering, adding carbon sheets, laminating and embossing.

History Wooden handpresses (flatbed or "common" presses) imported from the US or Great Britain introduced printing to eastern Canada in the 1750s and were replaced only in the 1830s in large centres by the iron Washington handpress. The first known press was established in Halifax by Bartholomew Green, Jr, of Boston in 1751; his partner, John Bushell, launched the first Canadian newspaper, the *Halifax Gazette*, in 1752. Following the outbreak of the American Revolution, in 1775, a large number of skilled LOYALIST printers arrived from New England, and by the mid-1780s there were presses in Saint John and Charlottetown. In Québec City the 2 most important printing pioneers were William Brown and Thomas Gilmore, who founded the *Quebec Gazette* in 1764. In addition to the newspaper, the printing shop produced calendars, order forms and eventually pamphlets and books. Fleury Mesplet, who had learned the printing trade in France, brought the first press to Montréal in 1776. Initially, he produced religious works, but in 1778 began publishing the *Montreal Gazette (Gazette du commerce et littéraire)*. After John Graves SIMCOE was appointed lieutenant-governor of Upper Canada in 1791, he convinced Louis Roy, a French Canadian, to establish his press in Newark [Niagara-on-the-Lake], the capital of the province. Although Roy's stay was brief, he started the province's first paper, the *Upper Canada Gazette*, in 1793. Because there was little commerce in Canada, printers relied heavily on newspaper subscriptions, government patronage (the printing of proclamations and laws) and the church (the countless tracts that arose from the religious controversies of the era).

It was missionary zeal that prompted the introduction of printing to the West. In 1841 Methodist pastor James EVANS compiled a system of syllabic signs for the Cree language. When he was unable to get financing for a printing press, he cut molds in wood, melted the lead linings of old tea boxes into characters, constructed a handpress and, using ink made of soot, printed his book on birchbark. Commercial printing in the RED RIVER COLONY began in 1859 when William Buckingham and William Coldwell began publishing the *Nor'Wester*. Printing in BC originated with the founding of the *Victoria Gazette* in 1858. Its presses also printed various government proclamations. In 1878 Patrick Laurie founded the *Saskatchewan Herald*, in Battleford, and in 1880 Frank OLIVER took a press by oxcart from Winnipeg to Edmonton and began publication of the *Edmonton Bulletin*. The first press arrived in Dawson, YT, in 1897 to print the *Caribou Sun*.

Until the 1830s, printers in Canada looked to the US or Great Britain for their presses and ink, type and paper supplies. The cylinder press, for example, developed in the US in the 1830s, was adopted during the next decade by large circulation NEWSPAPERS in Canada. George BROWN bought the first such press in Canada West for his *Globe* in Aug 1844. Paper was first made in the Toronto area from rags in 1826 by Eastwood and Skinner, and Alexander Buntin is credited with introducing the groundwood process to N America in his Valleyfield mill in the 1860s (*see* PULP AND

Printing and Allied Industries, 1985

Province	Establishments	Shipment ($)
Newfoundland	33	32 600 000
PEI	14	11 000 000
NS	105	115 550 000
NB	74	69 000 000
Québec	1378	2 540 000 000
Ontario	2340	5 050 000 000
Manitoba	205	334 000 000
Saskatchewan	169	161 150 000
Alberta	453	562 000 000
BC	599	650 000 000

PAPER INDUSTRY). The Montreal Type Foundry (MTF) opened in the 1830s and, until it closed 40 years later, was among the earliest producers of type in Canada and a supplier of both imported and domestic presses. In 1887 the Toronto Type Foundry (TTF) was established, an indication that the centre of the printing industry had moved from Montréal to Toronto, and by 1898 had branches across the country from Halifax to Vancouver. The TTF used American matrices exclusively, and it was only in 1967 that Carl DAIR created Cartier, the first Canadian-designed type face (*see* GRAPHIC ART AND DESIGN). Of the few manufacturers of printing presses in Canada, none were as commercially successful or long lived as Westman and Baker of Toronto. Producing Gordon presses (invented by the American G.P. Gordon in 1858) from 1874 to 1922, the business also manufactured a wide variety of printers' and bookbinders' equipment which was distributed nationwide.

Two models of Linotype machine were built in Canada, the first manufactured by the Linotype Co in Montréal in 1891 and the second by the Canadian-American Linotype Co Ltd of Toronto after it acquired the Montréal firm. Both models were exported to Australia, S America and S Africa in competition with Mergenthaler Linotype of the US.

As print shops proliferated between 1810 and 1830, printers' societies or unions were formed in Québec City, Montréal, Hamilton and Toronto. In 1832, for example, a group of 24 journeymen printers set up the York Typographical Society to fight for better conditions; the union failed after bitter struggles, but was revived in 1844 and, as the Toronto Typographical Union, is today the oldest trade union in Canada. At first these unions represented workers who set type, ran letterpresses, or did hand bindery, but as new equipment was introduced and typesetting and presswork became increasingly mechanized, the unions began to represent specific crafts, so that by the late 19th century there were unions of pressmen, compositors, stereotypers, mailers and bookbinders.

By 1900 they had created federations such as the Toronto Allied Printing Trades Council in the larger cities. In 1892 John Bayne MACLEAN founded the *Canadian Printer and Publisher* as a monthly magazine, designed as the official organ of the Canadian Press Assn.

The final 3 decades of the 19th century saw a great number of technological changes in printing in Canada. W.A. Leggo and G.E. DESBARATS of Montréal are credited with having invented the halftone process of graphic reproduction in 1871 and, although others have also claimed this honour, there is no doubt that these Canadians played an important role in its development. In 1873 the weekly *Grip* was founded and became the first paper to make its own engravings. Its production manager, Samuel Moore, left the company in 1882 to found Moore Business Forms to make and sell the carbon flipover Paragon Sales book. In 1905 *Grip* made the first 4-colour plates

in Canada, and thereafter consumer MAGAZINES saw a greater use of colour in both advertising and illustrations.

Contemporary Developments Commercial printing, publishing and printer-publishing have enjoyed an unspectacular but steady growth in the years following WWII. In the industry that Statistics Canada calls Print, Publishing & Allied Industries (which includes platemaking, typesetting and trade bindery companies), the number of establishments grew from 3650 in 1970 to 5280 in 1984. The number of employees increased from 84 041 to 114 047, with wages and salaries of $2.76 billion. Selling value of shipments swelled from $1.5 billion to $8.66 billion, expected to be $10.59 billion in 1986. At the same time, many "instant printing" shops have opened, and industries not related to printing have established in-plant printing and finishing plants, now a substantial part of the print supply business. Consequently the number of commercial printing plants has shown little increase, slowed to some extent by amalgamations and acquisitions by larger companies and the development of institutional and government printing plants.

Since the invention of personal computers and their widespread use, a massive change has taken place in the production of printed documents. Desktop or electronic publishing is now achieved by these PCs with the added use of electronic page makeup systems and laser printers which can produce camera-ready text and artwork or offset plates ready for printing. Multicolour work can now be done by a scanner which does the colour separations on film, processes the film and then sends the separations directly to an electronic platemaker.

Canada makes a great deal of paper, much of it in the form of newsprint exported to the US and the Caribbean, but it also imports many fine papers. Most ink used in Canadian printing, publishing and package houses, including in-plant shops, is made in Canada. Two companies, one in Québec and one in Ontario, design and manufacture business forms, presses and decollators. An Ontario company creates and manufactures folding, inserting, high-speed imprinting and paper-cutting machines. Nearly all this production is exported mainly to Europe, Asia and the US. A small computer invented in Toronto will convert non-computer cutters and guillotines to automated computer operation. A domestic market has been created, but exports will account for the majority of business. Some labelling equipment is also manufactured in Canada. In 1974 Mitel Corporation was established in Kanata, Ont, to invent and distribute microelectronic devices for electronic communications, and was the first to develop complete in-house publishing using laser (Xerox 9700). The Mitel systems have been adopted worldwide and are used by many American manufacturers in the production of communications systems.

Imported printing inks in 1986 were worth $22 615 000 and 95.1% of it ($21 509 000) came from the US. Graphic arts imports in that year from all countries were $39 597.9 million and the US maintained its position as Canada's largest supplier, with values of $30 520 million or 77.1%. Imports by category were machinery & equipment, $708.1 million; paper and paper products, $942.8 million; printed matter, $1466.5 million; plastic film and sheet, $478.0 million; and miscellaneous, $292.6 million, all in Canadian dollars. *See also* ALMANACS; BOOK PUBLISHING; PRINTMAKING.   WILLIAM FORBES

Reading: Canadian Printer and Publisher (May 1967); L.B. Duff, *Journey of the Printing Press across Canada* (1937); A. Fauteux, *The Introduction of Printing into Canada* (1930); J.N. Field et al, eds, *Graphic Arts Manual* (1980); J. Gibson and L. Lewis, eds, *Sticks and Stones: Some Aspects of Canadian Printing History* (1980); H.P. Gundy, *Early Printers and Printing in the Canadas* (1964); Dept of Regional Industrial Expansion, *A Study of the Canadian Commercial Printing Industry* (1987); V. Strauss, *The Printing Industry* (1967); M. Tremaine, *Early Printing in Canada* (1934).

Printmaking, which encompasses the production of images by any one of the numerous processes of intaglio, relief, planographic and screenprinting techniques, has a long and complex history in Canada. Both the evolution of printmaking techniques and artistic innovation on the N American continent play major roles in this history, but the records of these developments are scattered, rare and often nonexistent.

There seems to have been little demand for printed images in New France, and what was needed for educational or religious purposes was invariably imported from Europe. Certainly no examples remain of any Canadian-produced prints from the French regime in Canada up to 1760. The earliest printmaking coincided with British attempts to conquer Canada in the mid-1750s and was closely related to the printed word. In 1751 a printing press was established at Halifax, but it was a flatbed type, imported from Britain or the American colonies and was incapable of printing images other than small vignette woodcuts used for advertising or announcements. With the end of the SEVEN YEARS' WAR in 1763 England sought to colonize its newly won territories by encouraging skilled tradesmen to emigrate from Europe and America. Among these immigrants were some from southern Germany who had the knowledge and ability to make prints. The result was the appearance of a woodcut *View of Halifax* in the *Nova Scotia Calender* of 1777 published by an Alsatian émigré to Halifax, Anthon Henrich. He published similar and more elaborate woodcuts in succeeding decades in both English- and German-language versions of his calendar, as did another German émigré, Christopher Sauer (or Sower), whose prints were issued in New Brunswick calendars published in Saint John from 1786 onwards. Unfortunately, this early woodcut tradition did not outlast the 18th century, since it was only a sideline to the more serious venture of book and ALMANAC publications.

Instead, artistic impetus and public approbation for the art of printmaking grew in the region of Québec City, the centre of the British Empire in the northern half of the continent. Here British officers and officials were headquartered, and lively interest in the arts, expressed primarily in watercolour sketching, was maintained (*see* TOPOGRAPHIC PAINTING). Many military artists (most notably Thomas Davies, Edward Walsh and George Fisher) brought topographic sketches back to England to be engraved and published prior to the WAR OF 1812, but there were also a few experiments in etching and engraving carried out by officers while stationed in Canada. James PEACHEY, a member of the surveyor general's staff, executed a small copperplate etching of the MONTMORENCY FALLS in 1779, of which only the plate still exists. George HERIOT, deputy postmaster general of British N America, a prolific artist and author of several English publications illustrated with his own works relating to Canada, also experimented with etching. Heriot was associated with Samuel and John Neilson, the publishers of the *Quebec Magazine*, in which one of Heriot's etched and aquatinted views appeared in 1792. The Neilsons made the first serious attempt to establish professional printmaking in Canada in that year by importing a rolling or intaglio press and hiring the German émigré printer J.G. Hochstetter to produce a series of

views, portraits and allegorical prints for their publications in the early 1790s. The Neilson press was probably responsible for a number of single-sheet broadsides and other prints that appeared during this decade, but by the turn of the century such productions had virtually ceased. For the next decade, no work in professional printmaking seems to have taken place, evidently because Canada had neither the population nor the prosperity to support such activity before the War of 1812. Newfound wealth brought about by a war economy, a rising tide of immigration, and an enriched national fabric derived from the conflict with the US all combined to allow artistic developments to flourish in the second decade of the 19th century. In the interim, various professional and amateur artists were experimenting with printmaking for their private amusement or satisfaction, including William BERCZY, Elizabeth SIMCOE and Judge Alexander Croke, an Admiralty court official in Halifax, all of whom made Canadian-inspired etchings that have survived to the present day.

The next phase of professional printmaking occurred in Halifax where Robert Field, an English-born artist resident since 1808, executed and published an etching copied from his full-length oil portrait of Lt-Gov Sir John Sherbrooke in 1816. The print was probably produced on an intaglio press owned by Charles W. Torbett, a local printer specializing in books and maps, who also executed portrait prints, club certificates and book illustrations. His press was probably the one on which a set of 4 coloured aquatint etchings showing views of public buildings in Halifax was printed in 1819 by John Elliott Woolford, official draftsman to Lord Dalhousie, Sherbrooke's successor.

Though Halifax after 1815 was the new centre for printmaking developments, tentative renewals of the art were occurring in Lower Canada. A few prints were published between 1815 and 1820 by isolated firms specializing in jewellery or metalware engraving, but not until the mid-1820s did professional printers establish themselves. In Québec, the arrival from Scotland of the Smillie family in 1821, and James Smillie Jr's subsequent development as a printmaker resulted in patronage from the local military and colonial elite, while Montréal by 1829 saw the beginning of the long career in printmaking and publishing of Adolphus Bourne. Although he was apparently never an active printer himself, Bourne worked in conjunction with a number of artists and engravers, including William S. Leney, Robert A. Sproule, Charles Crehen and John Murray, in producing over 50 separately issued prints (etchings, engravings and lithographs) before Confederation.

Amateur work in printmaking by military artists continued and was stimulated by the decision of the British government in 1807 to purchase the rights to Aloys Senefelders's lithographic process for use in its official establishments throughout the empire. By 1824 Québec City had a press, and lithographic prints of both a public and private nature were widely produced and diffused by the 1830s. Lithography represented a great advance for would-be printmakers because it was easy to operate the press and to copy images. Lithography would become the dominant type of printmaking in Canada from the 1840s onwards, but it was not introduced professionally until 1831, when Samuel O. Tazewell, an English-born printer who had immigrated to Kingston, built himself a press and sought out local varieties of limestone for use in his operations. Tazewell, after producing an image of the Chaudière bridges in Ottawa in Jan 1832, moved to York [Toronto] in hopes of be-

coming the province's official printer. There he produced several single-sheet prints for sale and worked in conjunction with the artists George D'Almaine and Henry Bonnycastle until his hopes for official patronage were dashed in the politics of the day. In 1835 he retired to St Catharines to resume his former occupation as a watch and clock repairman, and apparently never printed again.

Other printers, including Bourne, Hugh Greene and George Matthews of Montréal, and Napoleon Aubin of Québec City, rapidly followed Tazewell's example in printing and publishing lithographic views and portraits in the late 1830s and 1840s. Matthews worked with the artist James Duncan to produce a set of 6 lithographed views of Montréal in 1843, following Bourne's format of a set of engraved views published 13 years earlier, while Aubin published prints of local politicians and celebrities, St-Jean-Baptiste Society dinners and a portrait of Bishop LAVAL.

In the Maritimes the proximity of the great printmaking centre of Boston had a strong influence on local development. As artists such as William Eagar and Mary G. Hall took their work to Boston to be lithographed in the mid-1830s, interest in printmaking withered, not to be revived until the late 1850s. The same was not true of Toronto, which in the 1840s saw a rapid expansion in the field. The most prominent enthusiast was Scottish-born Hugh Scobie, who set up business in 1838. Working with several artists, including John Gillespie, John HOWARD and Sandford FLEMING, and in partnership with John Balfour from 1846 to 1850, Scobie published a number of beautiful and well-received prints until his early death in 1853. Another pioneer was John Ellis, an English printer who opened a shop in 1843, publishing lithographic views until his retirement in 1868 (*see* PRINT INDUSTRY).

By the 1850s many large printing companies had been established in Toronto, Montréal, Québec City, Ottawa and elsewhere. Technological developments such as the steam-driven rotary press, colour lithography and wood engraving stimulated the demand, production and market for prints to prodigious levels, but the quality of these prints was generally inferior. Thus, an artist like Cornelius KRIEGHOFF, in seeking a printer who could reproduce his pictures, turned first to a firm in Munich, and then in New York, to carry out the work. Paul KANE found the Toronto firm of Fuller & Benecke (or Bencke) able to produce a remarkably beautiful multiple colour woodblock print of his *Death of Big Snake*. Kane did not repeat this exciting achievement and the firm soon failed, a victim of economic circumstances and the trend towards the industrialization of printing techniques.

Canadian artists were becoming increasingly frustrated with their role in printmaking in the 1860s and 1870s, as commercial concerns, technological innovations and the advent of photography reduced them to the status of craftsmen, especially in the larger centres of Montréal and Toronto. At the same time, they were becoming more conscious of their place within Canadian society. Native-born artists were also learning from immigrants about a new attitude towards printmaking that had developed in Great Britain and France. Known as the "Etching Revival," the movement was espoused by artists such as Alphonse Legros and the American James Whistler. These men began to treat the print, not as a method of reproducing images created in other mediums or solely as an illustration, but as a work of art unto itself, of which the artist was not only the designer but also the maker of the plate, the printer and the publisher. This radical new direction also involved the concept of limited editions of prints, each numbered and signed by the artist and able to stand on its own merit. As these ideas spread and artists elsewhere, including in Canada, took them up, a dichotomy arose between the fine-art print and the reproductive or commercial print that remains even today.

Early Canadian manifestations of the movement occurred among Canadian artists studying abroad. Among the first was Elizabeth Armstrong Forbes, who studied with the Art Students League in New York before going on to London, Munich and Brittany, where she began etching at Pont Aven in 1882. Her example influenced such artists as Charles Henry White, who studied with Whistler in England, and Clarence GAGNON, who went to Paris in 1904 and in the next 5 years developed an international reputation as an etcher/artist. Regrettably, none of these artists had much influence in their native country; Forbes and White both remained abroad, while Gagnon abandoned etching upon his return to Canada in 1909, although he gained a considerable reputation as a painter.

In Canada a number of events occurred that also gave an impetus to fine-art printmaking. The publication of *Picturesque Canada* in 1882, which featured the work of a number of American artists as well as employing several Canadians, including J. Henry Sandham, Lucius O'BRIEN and John A. FRASER, had a twofold effect: it demonstrated the potential of the print medium as a means of displaying the beauty of the Canadian landscape; and it evoked a conscious desire among Canadian artists to train themselves in the skills of fine-art printmaking. The relative neglect of the print medium by the Royal Canadian Academy and the Ontario Society of Artists also had an effect. As the ideas of the "Etching Revival" spread, it was inevitable that its influence would be felt in Canada, particularly in Toronto, where the Assn of Canadian Etchers was formed in 1885. The association was made up of several British émigré artists, including Arthur Cox, William Cruikshank and Thomas Mower Martin, as well as the younger Canadian artists William W. Alexander, Henry S. Howland and William J. Thomson. As an organization, they sponsored an exhibition of their work and of earlier European masters; it failed because of financial problems and public indifference but set the example for the development of similar artists' groups in Toronto. In 1886 the Toronto Art Students' League, loosely based on similar American and English artists' societies, was formed with the purpose of meeting once a week for life study and composition classes. The league lasted until 1904, and included printmakers William J. Thomson, John Cotton, later known for his exquisite aquatints, W.W. Alexander, Alfred H. Howard and William D. Blatchly, as well as artist/illustrators John D. Kelly, Charles M. Manly, R. Weir Crouch, Charles W. JEFFERYS and Fred Brigden. The league provided a congenial atmosphere for artistic endeavour, and was a training ground for younger artists and a means by which international artistic trends could be diffused within the Canadian art community. Many members were commercial artists with F. Brigden Ltd and Grip Ltd, where their skills were translated into graphic design, and several of them eventually left Canada to work elsewhere: David F. Thomson and Norman Price pursued successful commercial careers in the US, as did C.W. Jefferys and David MILNE, who, however, later returned; Milne's drypoint engravings constituted an outstanding body of work, some of the finest printmaking ever produced in Canada. Arthur C. Goode and A.A. Martin went to England and founded the Carlton Studio, which was

to develop into that country's dominant commercial art studio.

The Toronto Art Students' League had several offshoots, notably the Mahlstick Club, 1899-1903, and the Little Billee Sketch Club, 1898-99. Its most important successor, however, was the Graphic Arts Club, founded in 1904 by Jefferys, Manly, Brigden, Kelly, Robert Holmes, Thomas G. Greene, John W. Beatty, who would later become a teacher at the ONTARIO COLLEGE OF ART, and Albert H. Robson, art director at Grip Ltd, which would later employ Tom THOMSON, J.E.H. MACDONALD and other GROUP OF SEVEN artists. In 1924, on the occasion of its first public exhibition, the Graphic Arts Club renamed itself the Canadian Society of Graphic Art, a name formally incorporated in 1933. This organization became the primary artists' group in Canada by the 1940s, with a nationwide membership that included Ivor Lewis, Eric Aldwinckle, Miller BRITTAIN, Carl SCHAEFER, Nicholas Hornyansky and H. Eric Bergman (*see* ARTISTS' ORGANIZATIONS).

Toronto continued to be the centre for fine-art printmaking in the first 2 decades of the 20th century, owing mainly to the effort of William Thomson to gain wider public acceptance for the medium. He found a powerful friend in Sir Edmund WALKER, whose influence resulted in the pivotal loan exhibition of prints and drawings at the Art Gallery of Toronto in 1912, with an accompanying catalogue. Further annual exhibitions at the gallery from 1914 to 1917, and the decision of other art bodies, notably the Art Assn of Montreal, the Ontario Society of Artists and the Royal Canadian Academy, to recognize printmaking as a legitimate art form on its own, contributed to the foundation in 1916 of the Society of Canadian Painter-Etchers/Engravers. This society, with Thomson as its first president, drew artists from across the country, including Herbert Raine of Montréal, Henry Ivan Neilson of Québec, who was to form and become the first president of the Québec Society of Artists in 1920, and Walter J. Phillips of Winnipeg.

Developments in printmaking in western Canada deserve much closer examination than they have so far received. Although numerous artists recorded views of the West throughout the 19th century, prints based on their work were generally published elsewhere. Little is known of the early developments in printmaking, but by 1882, a steam cylinder and a chromolithographic press had been established in the *British Colonist* office in Victoria. The Montréal firm of Bishop Printing and Engraving Co established an office in Winnipeg in 1883, and was soon followed by other eastern firms such as Brigdens. By 1900 there were several commercial firms of printers in business across the West.

Serious developments in printmaking, however, only occurred with the arrival in Winnipeg just prior to WWI of the English-born artists Cyril J. Barraud, Hubert V. Fanshaw and Walter PHILLIPS, and of German-born H. Eric Bergman. Cyril Barraud taught Phillips etching and sold him a press before returning to England in 1915 and becoming a war artist. In 1919, as part of the Canadian War Memorials Exhibition, Barraud, in conjunction with Caroline Armington, Gerard De Witt and Gyrth Russell, published a series of drypoints and etchings of Canadian battle scenes. During and after the war Phillips and Bergman began developing national reputations for their work in etching and wood engraving, and both joined the Society of Canadian Painter-Etchers/Engravers. Phillips also began experimenting with colour woodblock printing, a medium in which he became internationally recognized by the late 1920s. In 1925 Phillips, Bergman and the Scottish-born Alexander Mus-

grove formed the Manitoba Society of Artists, which also included the Canadian-born Lionel LeMoine FITZGERALD, better known for his paintings than his delicate etchings and drypoints.

By the 1940s printmaking was firmly established as a fine-art medium in Canada. Many printmakers were able to live comfortably from the sale of their work, while others had taken up prestigious positions as teachers in the field. Among the latter were the painter Edwin HOLGATE, also reputed for his woodcuts, who was an instructor at the École des beaux-arts in Montréal; Frederick Haines, who became the principal of the Ontario College of Art in 1932; and Ernest LINDNER, an Austrian-born émigré who came to Canada in 1926 and in 1935 became an instructor at the Saskatoon Technical College where he experimented in linoleum and linocut printing. Lindner was a forerunner of developments to come, as etching and wood engraving gave way to other print processes in the 1930s and 1940s.

Colour screenprinting (or serigraphy) was introduced into Canada in the 1920s by the Toronto commercial firm of Sampson-Matthews, and gradually gained acceptance as a fine-art medium in the hands of artists such as Leonard Brooks. Lithography also enjoyed a renaissance in the 1940s after falling into disfavour at the end of the 19th century. Together with linocuts, lithography and screenprinting would come to dominate post-WWII developments. They were peculiarly suited to the next generation of Canadian artist/printmakers, who continued the traditions of their predecessors in absorbing international trends and ideas and adapting them to the Canadian art scene. JIM BURANT

Contemporary Printmaking

Printmaking in Canada received wider public acclaim in the mid-1950s following an international rediscovery of the artistic and aesthetic challenges of prints. National and international print exhibitions flourished and Canadian prints won recognition in prestigious international shows. Modern prints differ from earlier ones in their style and subject matter, larger scale, use of more colour, combination of several techniques, and photographic processes.

Contemporary developments occurred first, and were most pronounced, in Montréal, already a centre for printmaking and teaching. Artist and teacher Albert DUMOUCHEL inspired print artists Peter Daglish, Richard Lacroix, Robert Savoie, Serge TOUSIGNANT, Vera Frenkel, Pierre Ayot, Ghitta CAISERMAN-ROTH, Janine Leroux-Guillaume and Roland GIGUÈRE. The painter Yves GAUCHER pursued printmaking intensively after studying with Dumouchel. From 1960 to 1964 Gaucher created only prints, experimenting with uninked or minimally inked, heavily embossed intaglio prints. In the late 1950s Toronto painter Harold TOWN devoted his energies to lithography, creating exceptional "single autographic prints," unique accretions of various printing techniques, including stencil, linocut and overprinting. In the 1950s and 1960s Jack NICHOLS's black-and-white lithographs impressed the public and critics with a disciplined, yet modern, approach and their forceful images disclosing humanity's anguish and melancholy. Other early, innovative artists include Moe Reinblatt, Gilbert Marion, Walter Bachinski, James Boyd, Tobie STEINHOUSE, Aba BAYEFSKY, Richard Gorman and David Partridge. Image makers first and foremost, these influential artists were uninhibited about experimenting with new approaches, materials, printing procedures or uses of paper, setting the stage for creative explorations of traditional techniques.

Niagara Falls, 1939, Frederic Waistfall Jopling, mixed process print (*courtesy National Archives of Canada/C-43968*).

The sincere interest in prints in Québec and Ontario was evidenced by the national print societies, whose membership came largely from eastern Canada. The societies provided printmakers with professional standards, a congenial artistic climate and exhibition opportunities. The Canadian Society of Graphic Art and the Society of Canadian Painter-Etchers/Engravers amalgamated in 1976, forming the Print and Drawing Council of Canada. Toronto's Ontario College of Art played a significant role in educating successive generations of printmakers.

Printmaking was not well established in western Canada. Although Gordon SMITH set up lithographic and silkscreen facilities at the Vancouver School of Art in the mid-1940s and, with Orville Fisher, Bruno BOBAK and Alistair BELL, created prints in the late 1950s, the art community was small. Victoria's early print artists include Herbert Siebner and Pat Martin BATES. Known internationally, Bates has set an example for younger artists seeking to further their reputation through international, open-juried exhibitions; like Gaucher, she has experimented with uninked surfaces, which developed into perforated *estampille* prints. Calgary's Maxwell BATES and John Snow became self-taught pioneers in lithography after rescuing 2 discarded presses in 1953; Bates's figurative prints are expressive, Snow's lyrical. Through John K. Esler's teaching and artistic efforts, printmaking blossomed in Calgary, which became a major print centre. Serigraphy was introduced to Edmonton in 1948 by George Weber. Presses were unavailable in Saskatchewan before 1965, although Eli BORNSTEIN brought serigraphy to Saskatoon in 1955.

The renewed interest in prints was manifested through the growth of print exhibitions, commercial galleries specializing in prints, university printmaking facilities, graphic workshops and a lessening of prejudices toward innovations like collagraphy, serigraphy and mixed techniques. The relative ease of shipping prints allows printmakers to participate in exhibitions throughout the world. Canadian print societies, public art galleries and educational institutions organize shows exclusively for prints. Unique exhibition opportunities have been provided by the Canadian Printmakers' Showcase and the Burnaby Print show (both now defunct), annual shows such as Graphex and Concours d'estampe et de dessin québecois, or the biennial exhibitions of the Print and Drawing Council of Canada.

The first commercial galleries specializing in print, Agnes Lefort (1950) and Galerie 1640 (1961), opened in Montréal. In Toronto, Dorothy Cameron, who opened her gallery in 1959, organized an important print exhibition in 1965 to demonstrate that the best contemporary Canadian printmaking compares with the best printmaking anywhere. Toronto's Gallery Pascal opened in l963.

Canadian university print departments are now among the leaders in the world and have greatly stimulated printmaking in Canada. As enrolment increased and as fine-arts departments were developed in the 1960s, printmaking equipment was acquired and technically competent and aesthetically aware instructors were hired. Print workshops emerged to relieve the high cost of equipment and to provide a stimulating and creative environment for print artists. These shops may offer equipment rental, collaboration with a professional printer and publication of print editions. Although Roland Giguère founded Éditions Erta in 1949, publishing deluxe editions that included prints, the first contemporary workshops in Montréal were L'Atelier libre de recherches graphiques (1964) and La Guilde graphique (1966), founded by Richard Lacroix. Montréal's GRAFF, established by Pierre Ayot in 1966, is active with working printmakers, demonstrations for school children, print courses for adults and an annual auction. The Grand Western Canadian Screen Shop was founded in Winnipeg in 1968 by Bill Lobchuk; many artists now working across Canada began there.

In 1976 Rudolf Bikkers founded Editions Canada in London as a publisher where artists worked closely with the printers throughout the production process. Ontario's major printshops are Open Studio (1970) and Sword Street Press (1978). At Open Studio artists may print their own images or work with a professional printer, but Sword Street Press offers only the latter option. Open Studio has attracted and influenced artists and printers from all of Canada. Other workshops are located in St Michael's, Nfld; Québec City, Trois-Rivières and Val-David, Qué; and in Halifax, Winnipeg, Calgary, Edmonton and Vancouver.

Contemporary Print Artists have been very successful in international competitions and are often better known abroad than in Canada. David BLACKWOOD's subject matter is rooted in his Newfoundland birthplace. His large etchings of fishermen, sealers and their families depict human relationships and humanity's battle with the elements. Technically traditional, Blackwood's etchings are credited with attracting many collectors to purchase prints. Jo Manning renders nature in a contemporary manner in her linear black-and-white etchings. Ed Bartram's colour viscosity etchings of the boldly textured rocks of Ontario's Precambrian Shield area are a continuation of earlier Canadian landscape interpretations, intimately linking content and process.

During the 1960s it was common for several techniques to be used in a single print, as may be seen in the abstracted landscapes by Roslyn Swartzman and Anne Meredith Barry who combine embossing or collagraphy in etchings or serigraphs. Serigraphy, the youngest of the traditional techniques, has gained popularity, its clear-cut shapes and flat colours being most appropriate for works of the pop, op, hard-edge or minimal art styles. Prints by Harry Kiyooka, Tony Tascona and Rita LETENDRE are examples of such uses. Although pop art never had a large Canadian following, artists associated with GRAFF, especially Ayot, use serigraphy for their witty pop prints. Works by Winnipeg's Bill Lobchuk, Don Proch and E.J. Howorth incorporate the prairie landscape tradition into flat, partially drawn, partially photographic images. Images by Maritimer Jim Hansen, relying on line and incorporating handwritten words, are first drawn on acetate, then photomechanically transferred to screens.

Painters Gordon Smith and Toni ONLEY have used prints, particularly serigraphs, to bring their art to a larger audience. Both have explored nonobjective or abstract subject matter but are artistically strongest in their personal depictions of West Coast landscapes. Newfoundlander Christopher PRATT's high realist works use subject matter from everyday life: crisp clapboard houses, quiet interiors or harmonious seascapes. In Pratt's serigraphs, superimposed layers of colour achieve subtle chromatic and textural effects. Ann McCall and Lauréat Marois have also created outstanding realistic serigraphs.

Photography has long been used in commercial screenprint processes. During the 1970s, especially, artists such as Michel Leclair began to explore photographic techniques creatively. The founder of Open Studio, Richard Sewell, incorporates serigraphy, lithography, photography and even 3-dimensional imagery in his highly original prints; Judy Gouin uses her own landscape photographs, often incorporating unusual vantage points and reflections, as the basis for her prints. Ottawa artist Leslie Reid uses photoserigraphy and photolithography for her monochromatic naturalistic works.

Serge Tousignant, who worked with Dumouchel, pursues formal explorations of space and favours serigraphy and photomechanical processes. Walter Jule and Lyndal Osborne of University of Alberta, using different imagery and techniques, explore the possibilities of mixed media in their art and teaching. Unlike many technically excellent print artists, Jule is able to join technique and content without rendering his imagery subservient to his technical virtuosity. Carl Heywood, principally known for his lithographs and serigraphs incorporating a variety of photographic techniques, depicts his subject matter realistically but incorporates symbolic references.

Lithography became the most popular technique in the 1970s. Such artists as Don Holman, Bob Evermon, Charles Ringness and Edward Porter came to Canada from successful American lithographic workshops. Teaching in Halifax, Porter has contributed to contemporary awareness of lithography, as have Maritime artists Frank Lapointe and Roger Savage. Printmakers Jack Cowin and Charles Ringness work in Saskatchewan, Ringness making serigraphs or lithographs on which he applies drawing and collage. John Will combines many separate realistic images in a larger one, and frequently includes clever words or sentences. Evermon often presents his nonobjective lithographs, with their beautiful, coloured transparent washes, as diptychs. Otis Tamasauskas has mastered the subtleties and forcefulness of both lithography and intaglio, and his abstract compositions cover the complete surface of the paper.

Never exclusively a printmaker, Jennifer Dickson has had a significant influence on the visual arts through her art and her teaching. With Irene Whittome, she was a pioneer of photographic techniques in etching, and continues to combine these methods with serigraphy, embossing or painting.

Relief printing, the oldest print technique, has not experienced the same revival as other techniques; nevertheless, relief artists such as Pierre-Léon Tétreault, René Derouin and Noboru Sawai excel. Tétreault's more recent print work is in wood, both relief and engraving, but he is also known for the offset lithographs that he produced at Gaston Petits's workshop in Japan in the mid-1970s. A student of Japanese techniques, Derouin blends the oriental with the occidental and produces highly stylized, richly coloured contemporary images, some of conventional size, others very large. Primarily an etcher, Sawai intriguingly contrasts the firm linear qualities of occidental copper etching with the softly coloured, oriental-style woodcut. The 2 cultures also figure in his unique subject matter: engraved images which are based on paintings by European old masters are contrasted with woodcuts depicting oriental erotic encounters.

Printmakers are conscious of their paper, ensuring that the paper's texture is appropriate for the image and that the composition is correctly placed on the sheet. Some artists, however, have become interested in other aspects of paper. Helmut Becker makes his own printing paper; Paul Lussier makes multiples out of paper; and Betty Davison, reconstituting rag paper into pulp, creates cast paper prints, which are then hand coloured.

Some printmakers, like other artists, are experimenting with new technology (see ART, CONTEMPORARY TRENDS). Artists not primarily known as print artists have also contributed to printmaking. By exploring the print medium, either independently or with a professional printer, these artists have achieved more exposure for their own works and for prints. Contemporary Canadian prints do not exhibit a national style or subject matter, though in both temperament and preoccupation distinct regional characteristics may be discerned (see PAINTING). In general, however, printmaking in Canada is the product of an individual artist's creativity and aesthetics. *See also* INUIT PRINTMAKING. BENTE ROED COCHRAN

Reading: Patricia Ainslie, *Images of the Land: Canadian Block Prints, 1919-1945* (1986); M. Allodi, *Printmaking in Canada* (1980); J. Russell Harper, *Early Painters and Engravers in Canada* (1970).

Prior, Edward Gawler, mining engineer, businessman, premier of BC (b at Dallaghgill, Eng 21 May 1853; d at Victoria 12 Dec 1920). In 1873 Prior immigrated to Vancouver I, BC, and worked for a mining company in Nanaimo. Appointed inspector of mines in 1877, he returned to business in 1883, becoming manager of E.G. Prior, the leading hardware and machinery business in BC. Elected an MP, he lost his seat in 1900 because of violations of the Electoral Act. Returning to provincial politics he became minister of mines in 1901 and premier in 1902. Dismissed in 1903 following a charge of conflict of interest, he remained an MLA until his defeat in 1904. Appointed lieutenant-governor in 1919, he died in office. SYDNEY W. JACKMAN

Reading: Sydney W. Jackman, *Portraits of the Premiers* (1969).

Prism, West Coast Canadian rock group formed in Vancouver by producer Bruce Fairbairn. The group – consisting of singer Ron Tabak, lead guitarist Lindsay Mitchell, rhythm guitarist Allan Harlow, drummer Rocket Norton and John Hall on keyboards – had several hit singles and albums in Canada beginning with their self-titled debut album. The release of the follow up album, *See Forever Eyes*, in 1978 coincided with a minor breakthrough for the group in the US. A powerful third album featuring the single "Armageddon" recorded with the Vancouver Symphony Orchestra proved to be the career highpoint for the band. Tabak was replaced with singer Henry Small in 1981; however the move was unsuccessful and the original band soon broke up. JOHN GEIGER

Prison, as a term meaning a place in which people are kept in captivity, covers a variety of institutions in Canada. Jails, increasingly called detention or remand centres, are used to incarcerate persons awaiting trial or those sentenced for short terms. Traditionally the responsibility of municipalities or counties in most provinces, they are now part of the correctional system that also includes reformatories (correctional centres) for those sentenced to less than 2 years. Sentences of 2 years and over are served in federal peniten-

tiaries that are part of the Correctional Services of Canada, administered through the federal ministry of the solicitor general. The division is based only on length of sentence. Constitutionally, criminal law is federal, but offences are listed not only in the Canadian Criminal Code and other federal statutes but also in numerous provincial statutes (see CRIME). Offences arising from federal statutes may be served in provincial institutions and vice versa.

Institutions for juveniles, commonly called training schools, are under provincial jurisdiction. A new Young Offenders Act received royal assent in July 1982 and was, in part, proclaimed in 1983. This Act applies to persons, from age 12 (the new age of criminal responsibility) to age 17 inclusive, charged with offences arising from federal statutes. By 1986 most provinces, though critical of the Act, had taken some action, either passing new Acts or modifying old ones. Differences still exist among the provinces.

Historical Developments In the early 1800s, prisons were essentially jails attached to courthouses. They were used for holding debtors for the civil process and to a lesser extent for holding accused persons awaiting trial. The first large prison, opened in Kingston, Upper Canada (June 1835) was designated to serve Upper and Lower Canada by the Act of Union in 1840. By 1867, Saint John, NB, and Halifax, NS, also had penitentiaries and in 1880 Dorchester penitentiary was built in the Maritimes. The penitentiaries of St Vincent de Paul, Qué (1873), Stony Mountain, Man (1874), New Westminster, BC (1878), and Prince Albert, Sask (1911) completed the chain of fortress-like prisons across Canada. In 1930 another opened in Collins Bay, Ont.

The development of provincial prison systems depended on the size and growth of populations, as well as on resources. Sentencing patterns also varied provincially, influenced by the number and kinds of available institutions. By 1986 there were about 30 000 prisoners in Canada on any given day, almost 13 000 of whom served sentences in federal penitentiaries. Admissions over one year are much higher and amounted to more than 150 000 sentenced prisoners. After remaining fairly stable in the 1970s the number of prisoners began to grow again in the early 1980s, despite the increase in other sentencing options, eg, PROBATION, community service orders, restitution and fines.

The debate about prisons as institutions of punishment began with their inception. Prisons originated partly because it was no longer possible to banish offenders, and partly as a result of public abhorrence of the infliction of bodily pain and the exposure of offenders to public ridicule and shame, although stigma remains one of the essential elements not only of conviction and punishment but even of official accusation. Penitentiaries (meant to lead the offender to penitence through isolation, silence and religious instruction) and reform institutions (meant to reform deficiencies in the character of criminals) reflected the values of their society. Work followed penitence as the major condition for salvation, but it was the work regime, often involving meaningless tasks and submission to rules, that was important. An emphasis on training and education to "upgrade" the social position of offenders came next, followed by focus on rehabilitation and treatment and in the 1970s emphasis on due process – prisoners' rights and administrative fairness. Because almost all offenders are eventually released, it is highly questionable whether the expenditure of about $45 000 annually per inmate makes much sense. It is now generally conceded that prisons exist because we do not know what else to do. Various groups, including the Quakers,

who were instrumental in trying to make prisons places of humanitarian reform, have demanded their abolition.

Programs Kingston penitentiary, opened with great hopes of solving the problem of crime and criminals, was plagued by dissension, corruption and inhumanity from the beginning. The first major investigation, the Brown Report (1849), is full of cases like that of Peter Charboneau, a 10- or 11-year-old child lashed 57 times in 8 1/2 months for offences including staring, winking and laughing. Although there have been major changes in the handling of prisoners as well as in the administration of the institutions, the problems and the reports continued. The last major one, the MacGuigan Report (1977), was conducted by the Sub-Committee on the Penitentiary System in Canada of the Standing Committee on Justice and Legal Affairs.

A diversity of more than 200 institutions, generally classified as maximum, medium and minimum according to their security measures, as well as work camps and Community Release Centres now exist. Programs are still modelled on the traditional beliefs in penitence (moral improvement), education, work and rehabilitation, but life in most prisons is essentially characterized by making time pass. Riots and hostage taking, although widely publicized, are remarkably rare events considering the tensions created by a rigidly controlled environment.

Relationship to Community Although generally isolated from the community, prisons depend on it for even a semblance of purpose and proper functioning. A network of interest groups with a variety of programs inside and outside the institutions has grown up around prisons, eg, the John Howard and Elizabeth Fry societies, halfway houses, prison visitors and self-help groups. Citizens in general, however, tend to know little and seem to care less about who is in prison, what happens there and what happens to people after they leave. JOHANN W. MOHR

Prisoners of War (POWs), those captured by the enemy while fighting in the military, a byproduct of relatively sophisticated warfare. In primitive fighting, prisoners were rarely taken, the vanquished being tortured (often ritualistically) or killed. The concept of permanent enslavement of a defeated enemy developed, and from that the idea of ransom in the case of the rich or powerful. These options were practised by the indigenous inhabitants of N America, and all, except ritualistic torture, by the early European settlers. By the end of the 18th century, however, most communities had accepted the principle of simply quarantining prisoners, either by confining them or paroling them in some fashion. Such were the usual practices in the Anglo-French wars, the AMERICAN REVOLUTION and the WAR OF 1812.

International rules to govern the treatment of POWs were first formulated at Geneva in 1864 and were refined at The Hague in 1899 as part of a broader codification of the rules of war. Canadians taken prisoner during the SOUTH AFRICAN WAR had little need of these rules, since the Afrikaners, fighting a guerrilla campaign for most of the war, had no facilities for holding prisoners. After being relieved of their weapons, equipment and supplies, prisoners were usually released.

The Hague Convention was revised in 1907, and the 2818 men of the CANADIAN EXPEDITIONARY FORCE taken prisoner during WORLD WAR I, as well as the 2005 German POWs held in Canada, were treated in accordance with the revisions. But in Europe there were many complaints that the spirit of the convention was not observed. In 1929 a Geneva Convention relating specifically to the

Group of German, Italian and Japanese prisoners of war in prison camp, Sherbrooke, Qué. Some 34 000 German, Italian and Japanese POWs were imprisoned in Canada at the end of WWII (*courtesy Canapress Photo Service*).

Treatment of Prisoners of War was negotiated through the LEAGUE OF NATIONS. Prisoners were to be treated humanely, subject to the need to secure them. A prisoner need only give his captors his name, rank and number; he might be required to work but must not be assigned to work with direct military implications.

In WORLD WAR II about 8000 Canadians became German POWs and were generally treated in accordance with the Geneva Convention. Two glaring exceptions were the execution of some participants in a mass escape attempt from *Stalag Luft* III in Mar 1944 and the manacling of British and Canadian prisoners in Oct 1942 as a reprisal for the temporary tying up of German prisoners taken at DIEPPE and in a minor British commando raid. The British retaliated by shackling some of their prisoners and asked the Canadians to do likewise. Canada acquiesced and some Germans were handcuffed until the British and Canadian governments decided in Dec 1942 that retaliation was counterproductive. The Germans continued shackling until Nov 1943, but long before that most of the prisoners were only manacled while on parade.

Among the 30 000 German and Italian POWs held in Canada during the war, Luftwaffe Oberleutnant Franz von Werra distinguished himself as "the one that got away," escaping from a train near Prescott, Ont, the night of 23-24 Jan 1941, crossing into the US, and subsequently returning to Germany. He was later killed in action. Others escaped but did not succeed in recrossing the Atlantic; one, at least, got to Mexico. Several POWs were murdered by their fellow prisoners for not conforming to Hitlerian standards of conduct.

Thirty-two Canadians were taken POW during the KOREAN WAR and treated harshly, neither N Korea nor the People's Republic of China being signatories to the revised Geneva Convention of 1949. Efforts were made to "brainwash" them in attempts to alter their political perceptions; none died in captivity. Canadian soldiers were briefly used to guard POWs after a rising of N Korean and Chinese POWs in a UN prison camp on KOJE-DO in May 1952. *See also* INTERNMENT.

BRERETON GREENHOUS

Reading: D.G. Dancocks, *In Enemy Hands* (1983); J. Melady, *Escape from Canada!* (1981); K. Burt and J. Leasor, *The One That Got Away* (1956).

Privacy In a primarily rural society, such as 19th-century Canada, privacy was basically a territorial concept. Today, privacy tends to be defined not only territorially but as the right of individuals to determine when, how and to what extent information about themselves is to be communicated to others. When Canadians refer to "invasion of privacy," they may include electronic camera surveillance and unapproved computer record-linking of personal information. It is

the marriage of data files and the computer that poses the greatest threat to privacy (*see* COMPUTERS AND SOCIETY). Government intervention has primarily been directed at giving individuals access to personal information held by government. However, the same legislation also gives to third parties in certain situations the right of access to personal information about other people, and creates exemptions allowing individual access to some personal information.

Federal legislation regarding privacy includes the 1982 Privacy Act (which supplanted and reinforced provisions regarding privacy in the Canadian Human Rights Act of 1977) and the 1974 Protection of Privacy Act, which allows wiretaps under certain conditions.

Québec in 1984 proclaimed a privacy and access to information law and Ontario and Manitoba are likely to implement such legislation by 1988. BC in 1968, Manitoba in 1970, and Saskatchewan in 1974 have passed enabling legislation recognizing legal causes of action for invasion of privacy, but these laws have been described as "unused and unusable."

The Québec Charter of Rights (but not the CANADIAN CHARTER OF RIGHTS AND FREEDOMS) also contains a right to privacy clause. In 1981 the joint committee on the Constitution defeated an amendment that would have provided for "freedom from unreasonable interference with privacy, family, home, and correspondence."

Personal privacy is protected under other federal and provincial statutes as well. For example, the federal Statistics Act prohibits disclosure of personal statistical information, and Ontario's fair credit-reporting legislation allows access to personal credit records and provides some rights to correct inaccurate information. Another level of privacy protection is provided by the courts, which hear cases argued on grounds such as trespass and theft, but there is no recognizable legal right to sue on the grounds of privacy invasion. The federal government recently passed proposals for amendments to the CRIMINAL CODE to protect individuals against the misappropriation and misuse of personal information stored on computers.

Canadians became aware of extensive violations of privacy through the controversy surrounding the use of SOCIAL INSURANCE NUMBERS (SIN) and the federal Commission of INQUIRY INTO CERTAIN ACTIVITIES OF THE RCMP (McDonald Commission). SIN was developed as a administrative registration number for social-security programs. The use of social insurance numbers, however, both in the public and private sectors, has now become a means of identifying individuals. SIN is used, for example, to register PEI babies as well as some amateur hockey teams. This has raised concerns about the potential abuse of SIN as a means of linking together much personal information stored in files and computer banks. No direct parliamentary action has been taken to restrict SIN usage but individuals are no longer required to divulge their SIN to cash Canada Savings Bonds coupons. The Oct 1986 alleged theft of some 16 million Canadian tax records containing SIN identifiers from the Toronto Revenue Canada office served to remind Canadians how vulnerable key information can be. The McDonald Commission learned that the RCMP had enjoyed unauthorized access to personal information about thousands of Canadians and had opened files on 800 000 Canadians. The Commission also learned of RCMP infringements on personal privacy through the use of wiretapping, break and entry, and mail openings. No Mounties were brought to trial on such charges. In 1984 the Canadian Security Intelligence Service Act gave security agents very broad powers of privacy

invasion. Agents' actions are subject to limited scrutiny, primarily behind closed doors.

The vulnerability of Canadians to invasion of privacy was also made evident in 1983, when the public learned that Revenue Canada claimed many sweeping powers of access to personal information, and demanded unrestricted access to certain municipal financial data banks. That incident was followed in 1984 by 2 Supreme Court decisions (*James Richardson & Sons Limited* v *The Minister of National Revenue*, 1984, SCR 614; and *Hunter Southam Inc*, 1984, 14CCC [3d] 97 SCC) limiting the extent of the powers officials had under the Income Tax Act. As well, the Privacy Commissioner and privacy advocates have been calling attention to the growing use of computer matching of personal data to, among other matters, check for fraud, to locate debtors and to trace suspected criminals.

Governments and law enforcement officials are not the only violators of personal information. In the early 1980s the Ontario Commission of Inquiry into the Confidentiality of Health Information (Krever Commission) learned that certain insurance representatives were impersonating medical officers to obtain medical information about claimants.

The greatest threat to personal privacy lies in the growing reliance on information machines with their immense and quick capacity for record-linking and transmitting data. With the advent of electronic banking, shopping and mails, information about an individual's employment and financial and health status and personal habits can be easily recorded and traded.

Problems arise when the computers storing personal information can be surreptitiously entered by third parties and when the terminal containing the information is not located in Canada (for example, medical insurance information about many Canadians is stored in Boston).

Unlike some European countries, Canada has no legislation to restrict and protect the access to and distribution of personal information on Canadians held in computers abroad.

A House of Commons Justice Committee report (31 March 1987) recommended reviewing and extending the 1982 Privacy Act to trans-border data situations, and to the federally regulated private sector. As well, the report made recommendations to audit and include matters such as electronic monitoring of the workplace, drug testing and polygraph testing in new privacy legislation should the Canadian government adopt a broader privacy protection package.

Canadians are increasingly aware of how delicate is their personal control over information about themselves. In a 1984 Gallup of 1071 adults, 68% said they did not believe there was any real privacy in Canada, because the government could learn anything it wanted to learn about any individual. There is a growing sensitivity to how we collect, report and use personal information and nothing highlights this better than the confidentiality treatment accorded diagnosed AIDS victims and individual carriers of the AIDS virus. KEN RUBIN

Private Presses are dedicated to the art of fine printing and, as the name implies, are usually operated by individuals who normally perform or oversee all aspects of production: selecting the text, designing, typesetting, illustrating, printing (on fine handmade papers) and binding the book. More often than not, the book becomes an art object in itself. This production in limited editions (it can go from one copy to a few hundred copies, often numbered and signed by the author and the artist) is intended for the book lover.

The concept of private presses originated in Eu-

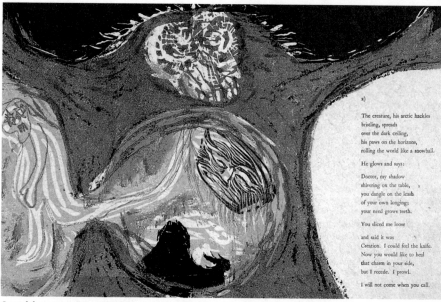

The creature, his arctic hackles
bristling, spreads
over the dark ceiling,
his paws on the horizons,
rolling the world like a snowball.

He glows and says:

Doctor, my shadow
shivering on the table,
you dangle on the leash
of your own longing;
your need grows teeth.

You sliced me loose

and said it was
Creation. I could feel the knife.
Now you would like to heal
that chasm in your side,
but I recede. I prowl.

I will not come when you call.

One of the great rarities in modern Canadian literature is Margaret Atwood's *Speeches for Doctor Frankenstein*, designed and printed by Charles Pachter in 1966. Only 15 copies were made, from linen and cotton, and the illustrations were printed in various combinations from blocks of wood and linoleum, silk screens and certain found objects (*courtesy of the artist and Bruce Peel Special Coll Library/U of Alberta*).

rope at the end of the 19th century. In England, William Morris founded the Kelmscott Press in 1891. He dreamed of recreating the art of the *incunabula* – a tradition of fine-book printing prevailing before 1500 – and conceived new types, commissioned hand-made papers with his own imprints, and used parchment for his most precious productions. The emphasis, however, was on the use of types and page design. He gave birth to a tradition which was to influence English Canadian and American hand printers for years. In France, bibliophiles were more interested in lavishly illustrated books. In 1875 Manet produced 8 lithographs to illustrate Mallarmé's translation of Edgar Allan Poe's "The Raven," the text occupying another 8 pages. A new tradition was born, that of the "livre d'artiste," a concept that has permeated French Canada's private presses, the emphasis there being on PRINTMAKING rather than fine printing. Few exceptions are to be found, although the situation is slowly changing in English Canada where Charles PACHTER (who studied in Paris) has produced some magnificent albums, the twelfth of which, *The Journals of Susanna Moodie* (1980), comprises 30 poems by Margaret ATWOOD and 30 serigraphs by Pachter. A few Ontario artists have taken that route, including Brender à Brandis of Brandstead Press (Carlisle, Ont), Elizabeth Forrest of Greyn Forest Press (Toronto) and Soren Madsen of Mad-Ren Press (Toronto), whose books are fine examples of well-balanced, imaginative book design. For most of their books both Pachter and Madsen have created their own handmade papers.

Research on the history of private presses in Canada has only begun, and knowledge is still fairly fragmented. Claudette Hould, in *Répertoire des livres d'artistes au Québec, 1900-1980*, has catalogued 249 titles from private presses in Québec, 195 of them published between 1970 and 1980. Marilyn Rueter (in David B. Kotin and Marilyn Rueter, *Reader, Lover of Books, Lover of Heaven*) and Maureen Bradbury (in *News From the Rare Book Room* 17 and 18, U of A) have indexed hundreds of titles from some 50 publishers, most of which appeared after 1960.

The 1950s, however, had marked a turning point, with the founding in Montréal of Éditions Erta (1949) by Roland GIGUÈRE, poet and printmaker, and in Thornhill, Ont, Gus Rueter's Village Press (1957). They were the first hand printers who themselves executed all aspects of book production. Others, like J. Kemp Waldie of Golden Dog Press (Toronto) and Louis Carrier (Montréal), had, in the early 1930s, published under their imprints good examples of fine printed books, but these were usually printed commercially.

Private printing in Canada is flourishing. The foundation of the Guild of Hand Printers (Toronto, 1959) and publications in their *Wrongfount* series have been instrumental in stimulating private printers' production of well-wrought books. Similarly, the Alcuin Society (Richmond, BC, fd 1965) brings finely printed books to its membership and provides them with the periodical *Amphora*, devoted to the art of fine printing. Many private-press proprietors have contributed to the publications of both these societies, eg, Wil Hudson (Vancouver), Gus Rueter, W. Craig Ferguson of Basement Cage Press (Kingston), John Robert COLOMBO of Hawkshead Press (Kitchener and Toronto) and Purple Partridge Press (Kitchener and Toronto), William Rueter of Aliquando Press (Toronto), Roger Asham (Toronto and Tillsonburg) and Peter Dorn of Heinrich Heine (Don Mills and Kingston), to name but a few.

In Québec the driving force came from the artistic milieu, and many contributors were printmakers who commissioned master hand printers, such as Pierre Guillaume, for their typography. Among some 75 private presses, a handful have produced half the books indexed to date: Éditions Erta, Éditions de la guilde graphique, Éditions Graffofones, Michel Nantel, Éditions du songe, Arts global and, more recently, Éditions du Noroît.

In addition to their excellence in design, private presses, like little magazines, often publish first editions of poems and prose by major Canadian writers (*see also* SMALL PRESSES).

JEAN-MARCEL DUCIAUME

Private School Fee-supported educational institutions at the primary and secondary level not under direct government control have existed in Canada from the earliest years of white settlement to the present day. Until the 1830s, most schooling was private. Today, although the private schools' proportion of total enrolment is very small (5%), their appeal to Canadian society con-

tinues to give them significance.

During the first centuries of settlement, EDUCATION was still considered the responsibility of the family and the church (*see* EDUCATION, HISTORY OF). Local clerics or parents taught some children to read and write. Other children attended schools founded by enterprising individuals as private ventures, and yet others remained illiterate. A handful of grammar schools and denominational institutions also existed. A COLLÈGE CLASSIQUE, or academic SECONDARY SCHOOL for boys, was founded by the Jesuits in Québec City in 1635. King's College School, also restricted to boys, was begun by an Anglican missionary cleric in Nova Scotia in 1789.

The movement away from a reliance on private education began in the early 19th century with the growing recognition that all children, not just a select few, should receive some formal education. The governments of British N America began assisting some existing schools and created new ones, mainly at the elementary level.

The emergence of free public educational systems did not, however, spell the demise of all private schooling. By the terms of the CONSTITUTION ACT, 1867, education was placed under provincial control with the intention that patterns of schooling officially recognized prior to Confederation should remain in place. Québec, Ontario, and later Saskatchewan and Alberta accepted Catholic and nondenominational Protestant schools (under certain conditions) within their provincial systems. Manitoba did so originally but in 1890 defied legal rulings to join the Maritime provinces and BC in supporting a single nondenominational public system (*see* MANITOBA SCHOOLS QUESTION).

The private schooling that remained differed among the provinces. All Catholic schools in the Maritimes, in Manitoba after 1890, and in BC, were in effect still private. So were all schools, in whatever province, that were affiliated with other religious denominations. Ontario's acceptance of Catholic schools into its public system originally included only those at the elementary level, but has now been extended through grade 13. Moreover, Catholic classical colleges, still the principal form of secondary education in Québec, retained their private status even while becoming provincially subsidized. Not surprisingly, when the first federal statistics on private education were compiled in the 1920s, it was determined that the proportion of children in school who were being educated privately varied from about 10% in Québec to 3-5% in provinces where Catholic schools were excluded from public systems to 1-2% in the remaining provinces.

As well as retaining a religious function, private education continued to play a role in class differentiation. Early tuition-free public systems centered on the elementary level, which meant that families desiring more advanced schooling for their offspring had to be able to afford a private institution or the fees of a public secondary school. The identification of private education with socioeconomic status was reinforced by developments in Great Britain, where during the second half of the 19th century the middle and upper classes had opted almost exclusively to retain their traditional commitment to private education, treating the emerging state system as a visibly inferior alternative serving only families unable to afford anything better. Numerous boys' and girls' schools in the Maritimes, Ontario and Québec, many of them established as Anglican or other Protestant denominational institutions, began consciously to identify with their British counterparts and to take on a distinct class character. Toronto's UPPER CANADA COLLEGE, for instance, began terming itself "the Eton of Canada." Additional schools on the British model also

Upper Canada College, Toronto, in the 1890s. UCC is still the private school most often cited as preserving the social and economic elite of Canada (*courtesy National Archives of Canada/RD353*).

appeared, both in eastern Canada and in BC. There, a massive influx of British middle-class settlers, who arrived during the halcyon years of Canadian immigration preceding WWI, provided both the organizational impetus and the clientele to sustain several dozen new schools adhering to the principles and practices of British private education. It has been primarily the existence of schools in this British tradition that has prompted such general assessments of Canadian private education as that by John PORTER in *The Vertical Mosaic:* "The acquisition of social skills and the opportunities to make the right contacts can be important reasons for the higher middle classes to send their children to private schools."

Several important shifts in private education occurred in the decades following WWII. Increasing prosperity and a general mood of egalitarianism encouraged governments to upgrade public systems. Some private schools found it difficult, even impossible, to compete with higher teacher salaries, updated curricula and improved physical facilities, particularly in the sciences. Others fought back. Private schools in the British tradition abandoned the self-appellation "private," with its implication of exclusivity and private profit, in favour of "independent," which was thought to suggest most of the schools' nonprofit status and their independence from government control. The Roman Catholic Church undertook a major fund-raising campaign to improve and expand private schools under its control.

The recovery of private education was facilitated by the appearance of a new dynamic. Of the immigrant groups entering postwar Canada, DUTCH Calvinists most keenly felt that existing public systems did not serve their special needs and so established their own "Christian" schools. Concentrated in areas of Dutch settlement in Ontario, Alberta and BC, Christian schools have been characterized by a very strong moral and religious base. In addition, the widespread dissatisfaction of the 1960s and early 1970s brought a proliferation of alternative schools focusing on the uniqueness of the individual child; however, most of them soon disappeared or became part of public systems (*see* EDUCATION, ALTERNATE). From the 1950s onward, both new and older private

schools began lobbying their provincial governments for financial assistance to allow them to compete more equitably with public systems. Success eventually came in Alberta, Québec, BC and Manitoba, and in Saskatchewan at the secondary level. In these provinces private schools meeting designated standards of personnel, curriculum and facilities receive an annual per capita grant out of public monies. In contrast, Québec's classical colleges were integrated into the province's public system in the late 1960s.

The growing conservatism which has characterized the 1970s and 1980s across N America has had its effect on private education. Enrolments have risen steadily from 2.5% of all children in school in 1970-71 to 4.1% in 1980-81 and an estimated 4.6% in 1986-87. Ironically the importance of provincial funding to this growth is questionable, for proportions have risen as much in Ontario (2.1% in 1970-71 to 3.6% by 1986-87) where schools receive no assistance, as they have in Alberta and BC, where schools do receive assistance (1.3% to 2.8% and 3.9% to 6.5%). Rather, it would seem, the search for more traditional values and disillusionment with the public system have turned many families both toward existing private schools and toward a new, second variety of Christian school. Generally small independent entities, affiliated with local evangelical churches, these Christian schools have proliferated largely as a result of the development in the US of self-directed, highly religious curriculum packages, the best known being Accelerated Christian Education, which can be purchased individually as pupils enrol.

Private schools have appealed and will continue to appeal to a minority of Canadians who are convinced that their children's special needs outweigh the benefits accorded by participation in the common socialization experience that is public education. A few private schools offer training in such specialized areas as dance and remedial education at a more intensive level than is generally available in the public system. Adherents to a variety of denominations believe that education must be more firmly based in morality and in religious belief than is possible within a single public system that serves pupils of all faiths and backgrounds. Of the 800 or more private schools existing across Canada, about 33% are Catholic, 33% Calvinist or evangelical Christian and perhaps 200 are affiliated with other denominations.

As well, the tendency of many private schools, particularly the 50 or more schools in the British tradition, to focus on traditional academic subjects leading to university entrance, appeals to many families, including recent immigrants who want to ensure their children's integration into Canadian society. Even at Upper Canada College, the private school most often cited as maintaining the generational continuity of Canada's social and economic elite, many of the pupils enrolled come from families who arrived in Canada since WWII. More generally, the appeal of private education may simply be that because access is restricted by fees, by academic entrance examinations or some combination of factors, the desire to partake increases on the assumption that the product being offered must almost by definition be superior to that freely available.

JEAN BARMAN

Privateering, government licensing of private vessels to wage war against enemies of the state. In Canada this commenced with Samuel Argall's attack in 1613 on PORT-ROYAL, Acadia. English privateers, operating out of harbours in New England and Newfoundland, included the KIRKE brothers who captured Québec in 1629. French privateers operated out of Port-Royal, LOUISBOURG and many isolated harbours, and included Pierre Le Moyne d'IBERVILLE, who in 1696-97 captured and burned St John's and terrorized several coastal communities in Newfoundland. From 1756 to 1815 British privateers sailed from Halifax, Liverpool, Shelburne, Annapolis Royal, St Andrews and Saint John, cruising as far S as Venezuela. Britain's embroilment in numerous wars presented no shortage of conflicts in which privateersmen could become involved.

A cruise began when merchants invested risk capital. Usually a merchant vessel was converted, although infrequently a ship was specially built. A privateering licence (letter of marque) was acquired from the governor and the vessel was fitted out appropriately. Privateersmen received no salary, but rather signed aboard in the hope of sharing prize money. Although most came home, many were buried abroad or consigned to the ocean in canvas sacks with cannonballs at their feet. A captured vessel and its cargo were sent before the Court of Vice Admiralty in Halifax and, if judged to have been legally taken, were sold at public auction. During the WAR OF 1812 the *Liverpool Packet* sent some 50 vessels before the court. The judge and court officials received commissions, and further proceeds were shared among each vessel's owners, its captain and crew, and the "informer" (as the captor was termed).

Privateering from Canadian ports ceased in 1815 with the Treaty of GHENT, although it was not ended by international convention until the Declaration of Paris in 1856. Privateering was more than an economic activity, for it provided a means of defence and offence managed at the local level, much like the Canadian militia.

JOHN G. LEEFE

Reading: John G. Leefe, *The Atlantic Privateers* (1978).

Privy Council, common name for the Queen's Privy Council of Canada, established under the Constitution Act, 1867, to advise the Crown. Privy councillors are appointed for life by the governor general on the prime minister's recommendation, and include the chief justice of the Supreme Court, provincial premiers, former and present federal CABINET ministers, and speakers of the House of Commons and Senate. The Cabinet, which has no statutory basis, acts formally as the Privy Council through ORDERS-IN-COUNCIL issued in the name of the governor-in-council.

J.E. HODGETTS

Privy Council chamber in the East Block of the Parliament Buildings, Ottawa (*photo by Jim Merrithew*).

Privy Council Office (PCO), prime minister's government department headed by the clerk designated (since 1940) secretary to the CABINET. Perhaps the most important and certainly the most senior of the CENTRAL AGENCIES of government, the PCO's pre-Confederation roots can be traced to the position of the clerk of the executive council of the Province of Canada; under the CONSTITUTION ACT, 1867, the PCO was only responsible for preparing and registering ORDERS-IN-COUNCIL. In fact no specific statutory basis for most of its functions exists; the bulk of its activities are conducted pursuant to the unwritten, conventional authority of the PRIME MINISTER and the Cabinet. It can be said that the PCO is the prime minister's administrative agency, with the clerk of the PCO essentially serving as his permanent deputy minister.

From 1940 on, the PCO has provided the secretarial functions not only for the full Cabinet but for the numerous Cabinet committees created in response to the mounting burdens on the political executive. It co-ordinates the activities of Cabinet and Cabinet committees and acts as a liaison with government agencies and departments on Cabinet matters; it examines, edits and registers statutory regulations and arranges for their publication, and it traditionally advises the prime minister on those senior appointments in the public service not under the purview of the Public Service Commission. It has also exercised independent political initiatives, eg, in 1978 it was revealed that the PCO had initiated RCMP scrutiny of PARTI QUÉBÉCOIS financing (*see* INQUIRY INTO CERTAIN ACTIVITIES OF THE RCMP).

In 1974 Parliament created the Federal-Provincial Relations Office, which assumed some of the responsibilities previously under the PCO. During the administrations of PMs Pierre TRUDEAU and Brian MULRONEY the PCO was criticized by those who objected to the growing power of the executive. *See also* PRIME MINISTER'S OFFICE.

J.E. HODGETTS

Reading: C. Campbell and G.J. Szablowski, *The Superbureaucrats* (1979); J.L. Granatstein, *The Ottawa Men* (1982).

Prix de musique Calixa-Lavallée, created in 1959 and awarded annually by the Saint-Jean-Baptiste Society of Montréal to a Québécois whose musical activities "have served or serve the highest interests of the Québec nation, whether in Québec or abroad." Its recipients are given a cash prize ($1500 as of 1986) and a medal inscribed "bene merenti de patria." The prize is not necessarily handed out in the year for which it has been awarded (the year used in the following list): 1959, Léopold Simoneau and Pierrette Alarie; 1960, Jacques Beaudry; 1961, Françoise Aubut; 1962, Jean Papineau-Couture; 1963, Gilles Lefebvre; 1964, Victor Bouchard and Renée Morisset; 1965, Louis Quilico; 1966, Gilles Vigneault; 1967, Joseph Rouleau; 1968, Gilles Tremblay; 1969, Roger Matton; 1970, Clermont Pépin; 1971, Colette Boky; 1972, Claire Gagnier;

1973, Gaston Germain; 1974, Pauline Julien; 1975, Félix Leclerc; 1976, Jean Carignan; 1977, Lionel Daunais; 1978, Monique Leyrac; 1979, Serge Garant; 1980, no award made; 1981, Kenneth Gilbert; 1982, Marie-Thérèse Paquin; 1983, Gilles Potvin; 1984, 1985, Maryvonne Kendergi; 1986, no award made; 1987 Yvonne Hubert.

HÉLÈNE PLOUFFE

Prix du Québec In 1922, Athanase David, then secretary of the Province of Québec, created 2 prizes to recognize and encourage the work of Québec writers and scientists. The David Prize was created for literature and the Scientific Prize for research. The Québec government increased the number of prizes to 5 in 1977, and added a sixth in 1980, to represent better the diversity of cultural, social and scientific life in the province. The 6 Prix du Québec are awarded in the fall of each year to Canadian citizens who live or have lived in Québec. The prizes cannot be awarded posthumously, nor can they be shared. Each laureate receives $15 000, a parchment and a silver medal, created exclusively by a Québec artist. The names and categories of current prizes are Athanase-David, for literature; Marie-Victorin, for natural sciences; Léon-Gérin, for social sciences; Paul-Émile-Borduas, for visual arts; Denise-Pelletier, for theatrical arts; and Albert-Tessier, for cinema.

GISÈLE VILLENEUVE

Pro Pelle Cutem [Lat, "a skin for a skin"], the official motto of the HUDSON'S BAY COMPANY, was adopted soon after the company received its charter in 1670. Both the origin and the interpretation of the motto have been much debated. It may be an adaptation of *pellem pro pelle* (Job 2:4, usually translated "skin for skin") or of *pro cute pellem* (Juvenal, *Satires* 10.192, "a hide in place of a skin"). The motto is often taken to mean "[animal] skins obtained at the cost of [human] skin."

Probation and Parole Probation, in law, is a correctional method under which a convicted offender is given a suspended sentence and released under supervision, rather than being sentenced to PRISON terms. It has come to be recognized as a judicial device for providing another chance for first offenders. The theory of probation derives from a long-standing tradition in Anglo-American courts to suspend judgement in certain cases. In practice it originated with John Augustus, a Boston shoemaker, who through his interest in the TEMPERANCE cause agreed to supervise the behaviour of an offender in lieu of a prison term. By the time he died Augustus had made himself responsible for nearly 2000 offenders.

In Canada, probation is an exclusively provincial jurisdiction. Probation services, which exist in all provinces, are responsible for preparing presentencing reports that focus on the accused's background. The reports may suggest that the offender make restitution to the victim and may identify specific skills that the accused possesses that could be incorporated into a community service order. The report may also recommend that the offender be required to take treatment for alcohol or drug problems or to accept a psychiatric referral (*see* JUVENILE DELINQUENCY). Although authorities concerned with the legal and sociological aspects of law enforcement agree that probation is more effective and less expensive for the rehabilitation of most offenders than institutional confinement, relatively few countries adhere to the principles on which its success depends: careful selection of suitable cases, suspension of sentence for offenders selected for probation, supervision by trained personnel, release of the probationer at the end of the specified time contingent on satisfactory behaviour or revocation of probation if the contrary is true.

As a judicial process probation is a function of the court. Parole, however (derived from the Fr, *parole d'honneur*, "word of honour," meaning particularly the pledge of a prisoner of war not to try to escape or bear arms, in return for conditional freedom), is an executive process, a function of an administrative body or board. The National Parole Board, under the authority of the solicitor general of Canada, reviews parole requests made by inmates of federal penitentiaries and provincial prisons if there is no provincial board (provincial boards in Québec, Ontario and BC handle parole requests from prison inmates in their provinces). During the first one-sixth of a sentence no consideration is given to parole; for the period of one-sixth to one-third of a sentence the individual is eligible for day parole consideration; for the period one-third to two-thirds consideration may be given to full parole; and for two-thirds to expiry most individuals are released on mandatory supervision.

Before CAPITAL PUNISHMENT was abolished, those serving a life sentence could be considered for release after serving 7 years, but in July 1976 the law changed to provide mandatory life imprisonment for first- and second-degree murder. Those convicted of first-degree murder are ordinarily ineligible for parole until 25 years have been served, although there is a possibility of judicial review after 15 years. For those convicted of second-degree murder the judge must determine how many years must be served before the individuals can be considered for parole; to be eligible for parole an individual must have served more than 10 but not more than 25 years. The main criteria for deciding whether parole will be granted are the plans for the post-liberation period, the severity and frequency of the inmate's delinquent behaviour and his character. Supervision of parolees is entrusted to federal or provincial correctional services, or to private-sector agencies, eg, John Howard Society, Salvation Army, Native Counselling, Elizabeth Fry Society, or to individuals, eg, a police officer, an elder in an Indian band or a volunteer. Offenders may receive full parole or be granted day parole for a specific period of time. Halfway houses are available as an intermediate step between prison and freedom.

A number of Exchange of Service Agreements exist between the federal government and the provinces providing for respective correctional services to house individuals who would normally be serving time in federal or provincial correctional centres. Transfers may be made from either the province to the federal authority or vice versa. In addition, Canada has 24 international agreements providing for the exchange of prisoners.

GUY LEMIRE

Procedural Law, legal rules governing the process for settlement of disputes (criminal and civil). In contrast, SUBSTANTIVE LAW sets out the rights and obligations of members of society. Procedural and substantive law are complementary. Procedural law brings substantive law to life and enables rights and duties to be enforced and defended. Because procedural law qualifies substantive law it is sometimes referred to as "adjectival" law.

K.G. MCSHANE

Prochain Épisode is Hubert AQUIN's first novel (1965). Its nameless narrator, like the author, turns his adventures into a spy thriller in order to pass the time while he is detained in the psychiatric ward of a Montréal prison, pending trial for an unspecified revolutionary crime. The psychological thriller develops into a suspenseful confession with suicidal overtones as the individual quest for revolution fails: confronted with H. de Heutz, his enemy and double, in a Swiss chateau, the narrator cannot bring himself to kill this man, a fellow art-lover. The beautiful and elusive K stalks through the novel, possibly a double agent, certainly an allegorical symbol for the protagonist's long-lost love, the Québec nation. Acclaimed by both critics and radicals during the QUIET REVOLUTION, *Prochain Épisode* is a densely allusive, poetic text, containing a self-referential postmodern theory of art and language. It was translated by Penny Williams in 1967.

MICHÈLE LACOMBE

Proclamation of 1763, *see* ROYAL PROCLAMATION OF 1763.

Proctor, Henry, army officer (d at Bath, Eng 31 Oct 1822). Proctor entered the British army on 5 Apr 1781 and was serving in Canada with the 41st Regiment when war with the US broke out in 1812. As commander of the western front, he led a force of regulars and Indians to victory over Gen Winchester at Au Raisin R Jan 1813. Reversals in May and July forced a retreat, however, and in Oct 1813 Proctor was defeated by Gen Harrison at MORAVIANTOWN. Proctor was court-martialled and suspended for 6 months without pay. Maj-Gen Henry Proctor is often confused with the younger Henry Adolphus Procter (1787-1859) who served in Canada during the War of 1812 as a major in the 82nd Regiment and later rose to the rank of lt-gen.

CARL A. CHRISTIE

Progressive Conservative Party, *see* CONSERVATIVE PARTY.

Progressive Party was formed in 1920 when Ontario and prairie farmers on the Canadian Council of Agriculture united with dissident Liberals led by Thomas CRERAR, who resigned from the federal Cabinet in 1919 opposing high tariffs. In Nov 1918 the CCA had proposed a "New National Policy" of free trade, nationalization (particularly of railways) and direct democracy. Under Crerar the Progressive Party permanently broke the 2-party pattern of federal politics in the 1921 election: it won 65 seats in the West, Ontario and NB, and was the second-largest party in Parliament. However, it was unable to act cohesively when facing the new minority Liberal government. Many party members were former Liberals who wanted only to shift their old party to free trade. Others wanted a more radical party. Although public support dropped in the 1925 and 1926 elections, agrarian revolt and the Progressive Party had transformed Canadian politics. The more radical members joined the CO-OPERATIVE COMMONWEALTH FEDERATION in 1932 and others linked with the CONSERVATIVE PARTY in 1942.

PETER A. RUSSELL

Prohibition was an attempt to forbid by law the selling and drinking of intoxicating beverages. It was enacted in Prince Edward Island in 1901 and in the remaining provinces, the Yukon, and Newfoundland during the First World War. The Canadian government controlled the making and trading of liquor and in Mar 1918 it stopped, for the duration of the war, its manufacture and importation into provinces where purchase was illegal. The zenith of prohibitionist success in Canada was reached in the early 1920s when imports from the outside were again cut off by provincial plebiscites.

Though seen as a patriotic duty and a sacrifice to help win the war, prohibition was also the culmination of generations of effort by TEMPERANCE workers to close the bars and taverns, which were the sources of much drunkenness and misery in an age before social welfare existed. The main temperance organizations were the Dominion Alliance for the Total Suppression of the Liquore Traffic and the WOMAN'S CHRISTIAN TEMPERANCE UNION, whose organ was the *Canadian White*

CITIZENS AWAKE AND ACT

The serious nature of the campaign for Prohibition is illustrated in this cartoon from an early 20th-century prohibitionist newspaper, the *Pioneer*.

Ribbon Tidings. Various legislative successes occurred in the nineteenth century such as the passage of the Dunkin Act in the United Province of Canada in 1864, which allowed any county or municipality to prohibit the retail sale of liquor by majority vote; in 1878 this "local option " was extended to the whole Dominion under the Canada Temperance Act, or Scott Act. By 1898 the temperance forces were strong enough to force a national plebiscite on the issue, but the government of Sir Wilfrid Laurier felt the majority of 13 687 in favour of prohibition was not large enough to warrant passing a law, especially since Québec had voted overwhelmingly against. Much of the country was already "dry" under local option, however, before the war, and provincial prohibition was not a radical break with the past. The fight against "demon rum" was connected to other reforms of the time, such as the WOMEN'S SUFFRAGE movement, and it was motivated in part by SOCIAL GOSPEL sentiments.

The provincial temperance Acts varied, but in general they closed legal drinking establishments and forbade the sale of alcohol for beverage purposes and its possession and consumption except in a private dwelling; in some provinces native wines were exempt. Alcohol could be purchased through government dispensaries for industrial, scientific, mechanical, artistic, sacramental and medicinal uses. Distillers and brewers and others properly licensed could sell outside the province.

Although enforcement was difficult, drunkenness and associated crimes declined significantly. However, illicit stills and home-brewed "moonshine" proliferated. Much inferior booze hit the streets, but good liquor was readily available since its manufacture was permitted after the war. Bootlegging (the illegal sale of alcohol as a beverage) rose dramatically, as did the number of unlawful drinking places known as "speakeasies" or "blind pigs." One way to drink legally was to be "ill," for doctors could give prescriptions to be filled at drugstores. Scandalous abuse of this system resulted, with veritable epidemics and long line-ups occurring during the Christmas holiday season.

A dramatic aspect of the prohibition era was rum running. By constitutional amendment, the US was under even stricter prohibition than was Canada from 1920 to 1933: the manufacture, sale, and transportation of all beer, wines, and spirits were forbidden there. Liquor legally produced in or imported into Canada was exported legally under Canadian law to its "dry" neighbour. SMUGGLING, often accompanied by violence, erupted in border areas and along the coastlines. Cartoons showed leaky maps of Canada with Uncle Sam attempting to stem the alcoholic tide.

Prohibition was too short-lived for real success. Opponents maintained that it violated British tra-

ditions of individual liberty and that settling the matter by referendum or plebiscite was an aberration from Canadian parliamentary practice. Québec rejected it as early as 1919 and became known as the "sinkhole" of N America, but tourists flocked to "historic old Québec" and the provincial government reaped huge profits from the sale of booze. In 1920 BC voted "wet" and by the following year some alcoholic beverages were legally sold there and in the Yukon through government stores. Manitoba inaugurated a system of government sale and control in 1923, followed by Alberta and Saskatchewan in 1924, Newfoundland in 1925, Ontario and New Brunswick in 1927, and Nova Scotia in 1930. The last bastion, Prince Edward Island, finally gave up "the noble experiment" in 1948, though pockets of dryness under local option still exist throughout the land.

GERALD HALLOWELL

Project Ploughshares, an organization launched in 1976 to research militarism and underdevelopment. Its founding principle is that international development cannot progress unless deep cuts in world arms spending occur and the spread of militarism in the Third World is halted. Research, education and advocacy programs involving such issues as nuclear modernization plans, the crisis in deterrence and alternatives to Canada's nuclear involvement are now supported. A research and documentation centre in Waterloo, Ont, contains extensive files on economic, disarmament, military and political issues, as well as a database that documents the activities of some 2000 arms contracts. The central publication is the quarterly *Ploughshares Monitor* and a working paper series approaches issues in greater depth. Ploughshares groups in 45 Canadian centres initiate local activities, carry out educational events, conduct training workshops, etc. The organization is sponsored by the Canadian Council of Churches and is supported by a number of ecumenical and educational organizations. *See also* PEACE MOVEMENT.

Promyshlennik, Russian (chiefly Cossack) free-lance exploiter of natural resources, notably furs. Like the COUREURS DE BOIS, *promyshlenniki* had a sure instinct for rivers, forests and terrain. They travelled in bands, sharing resources and profits. Pathfinders of the Russian empire, they were active in the fur trade on the NORTHWEST COAST from the 18th until the early 19th century. They were forerunners of the Russian American Fur Co (chartered 1799).

BARRY M. GOUGH

Pronghorn (*Antilocapra americana*), small, trim ungulate, the last surviving species of a once abundant and diverse subfamily (Antilocaprinae) of American ruminants. Although sometimes called pronghorn antelope, it is not a true antelope. The species reflects the harsh predator regimes under which the American ungulates evolved, for no mammal is more fleet of foot. The extinct American cheetah probably helped shape the pronghorn, as did the erratic prairie environment with its grass fires, blizzards, droughts and floods. These factors resulted in a highly social, short-lived species, which possesses a large brain, indicative of adaptability and learning. Sexes move together and readily travel hundreds of kilometres to avoid bad winter conditions or vacate burned-over areas. Its very high reproductive rate permits rapid restoration of losses from catastrophic kills by blizzards, drowning or fire. Like other plains ungulates, pronghorns have strongly patterned coats. Males and females are similar in size and appearance. When bucks shed horn sheaths after mating season, they assume female form and become difficult for predators to detect. In mating season, bucks are territorial in

Pronghorn (*Antilocapra americana*), last surviving species of a once-abundant subfamily of American ruminants. It is extremely fleet of foot (*photo by Stephen J. Krasemann/DRK Photo*).

some populations, harem herders in others. Pronghorns are unusual because males shed the horn sheath annually, unlike bovids in which the sheath is permanent. In 1900, they were near extinction, but the CONSERVATION and management of pronghorns has been successful. Rigorous protection and reintroduction have made them common in the western US. SW Saskatchewan and SE Alberta are the northern fringe of the pronghorns' distribution. VALERIUS GEIST

Property Law The popular notion of property as something owned encourages the conception of property rights as absolute and indefeasible, but property in the legal sense is more accurately regarded as the aggregate of legal rights of individuals with respect to objects and obligations owed to them by others and guaranteed and protected by government. Ownership of property is classified as "private" (property owned by an individual or individuals) or "public" (property owned by some form of government unit).

Property law is also classified under COMMON LAW, as real or personal. Real property (or realty) is land, any buildings on that land, any mineral rights under the land, and anything that is attached to the land or buildings that can be considered permanently attached. Personal property (sometimes known as "chattels") includes any property that is not real property. The dichotomy between real and personal property derives from early English law, under which property was considered "real" if the courts could restore to the dispossessed owner the thing itself rather than simply awarding damages as compensation for its loss.

Origin and Development of Canadian Property Law Property law, for all common law provinces, originated in England. The laws were established at various times, eg, in Nova Scotia and (including what later became) New Brunswick in 1758, PEI in 1763, Upper Canada [Ontario] in 1792, Newfoundland in 1832, BC in 1858 and the North-West [later the 3 Prairie provinces] in 1870. The Constitution Act, 1867, allocated legislative power over property and civil rights to the provinces. Thus general property law, including succession law and matrimonial property law (*see* FAMILY LAW), may only be enacted by the provincial legislatures. However, certain kinds of property (eg, bills of exchange and promissory notes, patents, copyrights and interest for the use of money) are within federal legislative competence. Parliament may incidentally affect property rights through legislation regulating interprovincial or international trade and commerce,

through its power of taxation and through its power of expropriation for federal purposes. Nevertheless, general property law is the preserve of the provincial legislatures.

The development of property law has generally been gradual and unspectacular. In the latter part of the 19th century, Canadian provinces and territories enacted statutes that permitted married women to hold property separate from their husbands. Prior to this time, on marriage a woman's personal property was vested in her husband. Separate property for a married woman permitted the matrimonial home to be held in joint tenancy and during the 20th century this has become popular.

In the 19th century, the succession law of real property became the same as that for personal property. The rule of primogeniture, ie, inheritance by the eldest son, gave way, where there was no will, to a sharing of land among the spouse and children in the same way that personal property could be shared. In 1910 Alberta and Saskatchewan, following the example of New Zealand, became the first provinces to enact legislation restricting the power to leave property by will (respectively, the Act Respecting the Rights of Married Women in the Estate of their Deceased Husbands and the Act to Amend the Devolution of Estates Act). Gradually, all the common-law provinces enacted legislation, called testators' family maintenance or dependants' relief legislation, that empowered a judge to set aside a will if the maker of the will had failed to provide adequate maintenance for a spouse or other dependants.

In 1975, in the MURDOCH CASE, the Supreme Court of Canada held that an Alberta rancher's wife whose marriage had broken down was not entitled to a share in the ranch, which was registered in the husband's name, even though she had worked hard to make the ranch a success. The patent unfairness of the law, graphically illustrated by this case, resulted in a profound change in matrimonial property laws throughout the common-law provinces in the 10 years following the decision. Provincial legislation now permits a judge to order a division of property after a marriage has broken down to achieve fairness between spouses no matter who owns the assets. There has also been a corresponding response by the courts, and property law concepts have been modified to achieve fairer results. In the *Rathwell* case, the Supreme Court of Canada, in order to prevent unjust enrichment by the title-holding husband, resorted to the constructive trust as a remedial device to prevent such unjust enrichment occurring from the contributions made to the acquisition of assets by the wife. In *Pettkus v Becker*, the same concepts leading to an equal division of assets were applied between an unmarried man and woman who had been living together for approximately 20 years, where the contribution of the woman enabled the man to acquire assets.

The property laws of the common-law provinces are generally similar, but one area in which the real property law does differ is in the system of recording the ownership of land. In the Atlantic provinces and in southern Ontario, there is a deed registration system and in the 4 western provinces and in northern Ontario there is a land titles or Torrens system. Under the deed registration system, individuals establish ownership to land derivatively through their predecessors in title. Theoretically, to establish ownership they should trace the title to the original grant of the land from the Crown. In southern Ontario, it is necessary now to show a good root of title dating back 40 years. Under the land-titles system or Torrens system, named after Sir

Robert Richard Torrens who developed the system in South Australia, the state registers all lands within its jurisdiction by listing who owns them and who has claims against them. Under this system, prospective purchasers need only be concerned with who the register says is the owner and not with whether there is a good root of title. The Council of Maritime Premiers has created an agency to develop and implement a unified land registration system to replace the existing deed registration system. In northern Ontario and parts of southern Ontario a modified Torrens system has been adopted modelled on that in western Canada.

Types of Property reflect the economic and social aspects of society. INDUSTRIALIZATION introduced new forms of property rights in factories and machines. The growth of joint-stock companies, the forerunners of modern corporations, created new property rights in the form of bonds and shares. Recently the nature of property rights has been transformed by the tendency of modern governments to draw in revenue and power and to pour forth money, benefits, services, contracts, franchises and licences. This government largesse may replace the traditional forms of wealth and new rules will be required to protect individuals from arbitrary government action. It has been suggested that property should no longer be defined solely as the right to exclude all others from the use or benefit of something, but should also comprehend the right not to be excluded from the use or benefit of the achievements of the whole society.

Property and the Charter of Rights Although the Canadian Charter of Rights and Freedoms does not expressly provide for the protection of property rights, property rights are created and are therefore protected by common law and by statute law, although both can be changed by legislation. Any constitutional guarantee should recognize that property is a social institution that must be constantly remolded. A great jurist has warned that an absolute right of property would result in the dissolution of society. The importance of this warning can perhaps be best illustrated by considering a person who buys a gun. The property rights that this person acquires in the gun cannot extend to permission to use the gun in any way. Similarly, landowners should not be permitted to pollute the air and water because this would lessen the enjoyment and property values of adjacent owners and because of the moral obligation to pass on to succeeding generations a habitable planet. Property rights may therefore be modified to respond to new threats to the environment. There is no preordained harmony between private rights and public welfare; society will always face the dilemma of how to combine efficient use of resources with effective regulation in the interests of all society.

Property Law in Quebec

In the widest sense, the law of property in Quebec comprises the principles regulating the ways in which all kinds of property may be disposed of and acquired, ie, all the mechanisms and transactions by which property circulates. In a narrower sense, Quebec property law is concerned with defining what constitutes property. In fact, anything with a financial value (ie, anything that constitutes wealth) can be defined as property, and such a definition would embrace any right assessable in monetary terms and not merely rights in things ("real rights") or indeed those things themselves. Traditionally, however, property law is limited to the realm of real rights in intangible or corporeal things.

Quebec property law is firmly rooted in the

French CIVIL LAW tradition and derives, therefore, from Roman law. Anglo-American common law has had little influence on its institutions (except for the mechanism of the TRUST and a number of security devices). Quebec law, like French law, has historically attached the greatest importance to land and rights in land as objects of wealth. Indeed, feudal landholding (the SEIGNEURIAL SYSTEM) was only abolished in Quebec in 1854, a necessary reform before the civil law itself could be codified in a modern form (1866). Land in Quebec, whether once held in seigneurial tenure under the French regime or granted by the Crown (since 1763), is now in all cases held by individuals in a "free" tenure, ie, it is held as independently of the Crown as absolutely as possible.

The Quebec Civil Code contains the fundamental principles of property law applicable to private persons. Since 1866 it has been supplemented by much ancillary legislation regulating new forms of property (such as hydraulic power) and controlling the use of property in view of contemporary concerns (such as environmental hazards and cultural heritage). The code nonetheless enshrines 2 fundamental tenets of Quebec property law: the right of private property (private ownership of lands and goods) and, as a corollary, the free circulation of such property. The code itself regulates private property in this sense, whereas statutory legislation regulates Crown or public and municipal property to which special rules apply.

More technically, Quebec civil law views all types of property either as "immovable" (land and its appurtenances, and all rights in land) or as "movable" (physically movable objects as well as claims for money and performances under contracts and obligations in general). This distinction is the thread that runs throughout Quebec law and it is the basis for many of the different legal technicalities attached to various properties. For example, rights of all kinds in land are subject to official recording in the land titles registration system, whereas rights in movable property are not.

Rights in things (technically "real rights") can be divided into 3 broad categories. Individuals may have either a right of ownership, ie, the right in their own property; a right in the thing belonging to another, ie, a right less than ownership but nonetheless composed of some of the prerogatives associated with ownership; or a right in the form of claim by a creditor to seize and sell a debtor's property to satisfy an unpaid debt.

Ownership, the most complete real right, is the right of using, enjoying and disposing of things in the most absolute manner provided no use is made thereof contrary to law or regulation. Ownership is an "exclusive" or individual right and, as a concept, is unitary. Thus, the law discourages 2 or more persons from owning the same property jointly (with certain notable exceptions such as of condominiums and aspects of property relations between married persons). Nor does the civil law admit the distinction, known to the common law, of legal and equitable ownership, eg, property shared between a trustee and a beneficiary of a trust. And, because ownership is viewed as exclusive and individual, the general policy of the law is that rights less than ownership vested in other persons are normally limited in time so that the full integrity of the prerogatives attaching to ownership itself is preserved.

The rights in the second category – rights in things of which someone else is the owner – carry some of the prerogatives of ownership but are less complete than the right of ownership. The right of "usufruct" is the right of possessing, using and enjoying the property (movable or immovable) of another, subject to the obligation of restoring the property (or sometimes its equivalent in money) at the end of the period of enjoyment. This scheme (or variations thereof) is often encountered in the context of estate planning. "Emphyteusis" is the right, under a long-term lease of land belonging to another, whereby the lessee agrees to make improvements in return for the right to enjoy the land as owner for the period specified. It is used principally in connection with large urban development projects. "Real servitudes" are rights of various kinds linking 2 lands whereby one land (or landowner) is subject to specified obligations or services in favour of the other, such as rights of view or of passage or the obligation not to build a wall above a certain height.

In the third category of rights, a creditor may have a right over the property of his debtor enabling him to seize and sell the property, under the authority of the court, if the debtor is unable to pay his debt. The property subject to seizure by the creditor may previously have been transferred into the possession of the creditor or may have remained in the possession of the debtor. These various security devices in Quebec are known either as privileges, ie, rights attaching to the movable or immovable property of the debtor that have been created by law to secure a wide and varied list of creditors' claims; or as "hypothec," the right of the creditor to seize and sell the immovable property (land, buildings) of his debtor made liable to secure the debt by contract. The hypothec is the civil law equivalent of the MORTGAGE in common-law Canada.

It is not certain in Quebec law to what extent it may be open to private persons to create, under the principle of freedom of contract, real rights or rights of property other than those already laid down in the civil code or in ancillary legislation. The most commonly used property rights are now provided for in these sources.

GORDON BALE AND JOHN E.C. BRIERLEY

Prospecting Exploration for new MINERAL RESOURCES began with the first use of metal (COPPER) about 7000 years ago. In N America indigenous peoples used native copper before the arrival of Europeans in at least 2 areas: the southern shore of Lk Superior and the mouth of the COPPERMINE R, NWT. The first organized mineral exploration by Europeans in what is now Canada was led by Martin FROBISHER in his 3 expeditions to Baffin I (1576, 1577 and 1578). Although his first expedition was directed primarily to finding a NORTHWEST PASSAGE to Asia, the much larger, privately financed, programs of 1577 and 1578 were largely prompted by the hope of finding gold ore. The program was a failure and the supposed gold ore brought back seems to have been schist or gneiss containing sparkling mica. The next recorded prospecting venture, near the present harbour of St John's, Nfld, was instigated by Sir Humphrey GILBERT. In 1583 Gilbert brought out a Saxon miner, named Daniel, who prospected the shores and reported silver. No commercial deposits of any mineral were found, however, and both Gilbert and Daniel were lost on the return voyage.

There is little evidence of prospecting in the early French settlements of eastern Canada (see DIAMONDS OF CANADA) and not much by the employees of the Hudson's Bay Co. The exception was Samuel HEARNE, employed by the HBC at Prince of Wales's Fort near the present port of Churchill, Man, who undertook a cross-country expedition to find the source of the native copper used by members of a northern Indian tribe. In 1771, after 2 unsuccessful attempts, Hearne reached the source of the copper on the banks of the Coppermine R near the Arctic Ocean. Apart from these expeditions, there was little deliberate search for metals in Canada from 1600 to 1800, except for a general alertness for mineral deposits shown by traders and trappers in their wilderness travels, especially through the Precambrian SHIELD. LEAD was found near the Ottawa R and on the E shore of Lk Timiskaming. The first discovery of copper to reach commercial production was at Bruce Mines on the N shore of Lk Huron; production began in 1847-48. SILVER was found at SILVER ISLET, on the N shore of Lk Superior, in 1868. The copper-nickel deposits of Sudbury were discovered by chance, in the early 1880s, as a result of railway construction in the area.

The founding of the GEOLOGICAL SURVEY OF CANADA (1842) and of the geological departments of the Ontario Bureau of Mines (1891) and the Québec Department of Colonization and Mines (1898) encouraged prospecting in these provinces. The Porcupine area, first noted as favourable for GOLD mineralization by W.A. PARKS in his report to the Ontario Dept of Mines (about 1900), became the scene of a GOLD RUSH in 1909. In 1903 silver was discovered at Cobalt, Ont, and in the following 2 decades the area became the world's largest silver producer. In the meantime, prospecting had progressed from the West Coast into the valleys and mountains of BC. Placer gold first attracted prospectors N from earlier gold rushes in the western US in the mid-19th century. In 1896 discovery in the YT of placer gold on the Klondike R and its tributaries led to the most extensive gold rush in Canadian history (see KLONDIKE GOLD RUSH). In BC, prospecting for lead, silver and copper followed that for gold. Several base-metal mines were active by the end of the 19th century, including the Sullivan Mine near the Slocan R, which is still one of the largest producers of lead and silver.

During this period, prospecting, aided by the GSC, was carried on in the Eastern Townships of Québec, S of the St Lawrence R. Placer gold had been found in the area earlier but had reached only limited production. By the end of the 19th century, interest had extended to copper and, later, to ASBESTOS. In northern Québec, copper was first noted in the Chibougamau area in 1870, but it was 25 years before this discovery resulted in widespread prospecting. The turn of the century also saw vigorous prospecting for gold in eastern NS that resulted in the establishment of many small-scale producers. By 1920, prospecting was active in some parts of all provinces (except PEI) and, since the end of WWII, has occupied a significant part of Canadian expenditures on natural RESOURCES.

Aids to Prospecting

Geology Until after WWII, prospecting in Canada and elsewhere depended essentially on the use of the pick and shovel, guided by some knowledge of GEOLOGY. Prospectors chose areas for exploration aided by geological maps prepared and distributed by the GSC and by geological departments in the various provinces. Mineral deposits in Canada occur in 3 main areas: the mountainous belt of BC and the YT affected by the Cordilleran folding from 230 to 50 million years ago; the Precambrian Shield, extending from the Labrador Coast W to northern Saskatchewan and N to the Arctic coast, which has rocks and periods of folding and intrusion dating from over 3 billion to 570 million years ago; and southeastern Qué, NB, NS and Nfld, all of which were affected by the Appalachian folding of 470-320 million years ago. Each area has its own mineral characteristics and prospecting targets.

Geophysics Since 1946 there has been an increasing use of geophysical techniques (see PHYSICS). This trend has coincided with an increased proportion of MINING exploration conducted by companies and syndicates, as compared with that by individuals or small groups of prospectors. The first application of geophysics was the design and use of the dip needle and its successor, the magnetometer. The latter instrument, first developed in Sweden in the latter part of the 19th century, measures the relative magnetic attraction of different parts of the Earth's surface (*see* GEOMAGNETIC POLE). Magnetite (magnetic iron oxide) gives the strongest magnetic pull of any mineral, but sulphide-nickel ore also has above-average magnetic intensity and, under soil or rock covering, presents a suitable target for the magnetometer. In Canada, Thomas Edison, the American inventor, was the first recorded user of the magnetometer on nickel. Near Sudbury, Ont, shortly after WWI, he noted a strong magnetic anomaly between 2 known copper-nickel deposits on the projection of the same geological contact, but in an area covered by a thick layer of gravel. The shaft sunk on the indicated location did not go deep enough and it was not until some years later that deeper investigations proved the existence of the ore body that had given the magnetic indication. The magnetometer was also used before WWI in areas known to have IRON formations in Ontario and Québec. Its use became widespread in the 1930s, both for the direct indication of magnetic ores and in tracing geological contacts under surface covering.

In Canada, in the late 1920s, geophysics was also applied to prospecting in the measurement of earth voltages. It was discovered that naturally occurring weak electric currents flow between rock formations having different electrical charges. These electric currents are stronger in the vicinity of metallic sulphide bodies and produce a measurable voltage or self-potential which can be detected through shallow soil cover. The use of electrical measurements then moved to the introduction of artificial currents into the ground by one set of current electrodes and the measurement of the subsequent voltage variations in the ground by a second set of measuring electrodes. The resistivity method, as it is called, measures the degree of resistance the ground has to current flow. Metallic minerals in the earth aid current flow and have low resistance, whereas barren rocks have high resistance.

A further development was the indirect energization of the ground by a primary alternating current using a powerful transmitting coil. Around natural conductors, such as metallic orebodies, a secondary electrical field is produced by the primary electrical field. These electromagnetic fields can be detected by a receiving coil much like a radio receives a station signal from a remote transmitter. The variation in the signal strength is an indication of conductive differences in the underlying ground and rock composition. Using the electromagnetic method, conductive metallic mineral concentration can be detected through thick earth and rock cover.

These developments took place prior to WWII, but it was not until the 1950s when advances in electronics and instrumentation made the electromagnetic method a major and successful tool for prospecting for hidden orebodies. At this time, both magnetic and electromagnetic equipment were installed in fixed-wing aircraft and used in systematic air surveys, thus increasing production and ground coverage. As the electronic equipment for these airborne systems became smaller and lighter and navigation systems improved, they could be installed in helicopters for use in rugged terrain, particularly BC and the Yukon.

Airborne geophysical methods cannot define the location of a conductor or magnetic body with sufficient accuracy to allow direct testing by

drilling. Normally, when an anomaly is noted by airborne techniques and selected for investigation, a ground party is sent in to prospect the area by conventional methods and to confirm, by ground geophysical techniques, the airborne indications. The first discovery in Canada of an ore body by means of airborne electromagnetic methods was the one that became the Heath-Steele Mine, NB, in 1952. From 1950 to 1959, 19 of a total of 59 discoveries resulted initially from indications collected by airborne geophysical methods. The most important such discovery took place in 1963, and became the Kidd Creek Mine, N of Timmins, Ont, one of the richest base metal mines in the world.

In the late 1950s, as a result of advances in electronic measuring techniques, the resistivity technique was further developed. Up to this time, discrete metallic mineral particles within rock that were not electrically connected, could not be detected using conventional electrical methods. From laboratory experiments, however, it had been shown that metallic mineral particles disseminated throughout a rock, if energized electrically, become charged particles for short periods and as a whole, act like a capacitor or condenser to store electricity. Over a period of time, these charges dissipate into the ground. By measuring the voltage of the ground at 2 different very low current frequencies, this capacitive effect could be calculated. The induced polarization measurement, as it is called, can also be made by energizing the ground and then turning the current off very quickly and measuring the decay time of the voltage. Certain types of base and precious metal orebodies, such as the porphyry copper/molybdenum ore deposits of the Highland Valley of BC, are associated with disseminated metallic minerals. The application of the induced polarization method was a major breakthrough in the detection of such orebodies hidden by overlying earth or rock. More recently, this method has been instrumental in assisting in the discovery of gold deposits. Gold is not directly detectable by geophysical methods but is commonly associated with disseminated metallic minerals.

With the growing interest in URANIUM following WWII, instruments to measure radioactivity, such as the Geiger counter or scintillometer, became important prospecting aids. Many discoveries, especially in the Athabasca area of Saskatchewan, have resulted from tracing trains of radioactive boulders, plucked from their source by GLACIERS in the Pleistocene ICE AGE and distributed in a rough line in the direction of the ice movement. Measurement of the radioactivity of waters of lakes overlying radioactive deposits has also led to discoveries. Radioactive measuring techniques have become increasingly accurate

Northern Ontario prospectors' camp, c1900 (courtesy Ontario Northland Transportation Comm).

and sensitive. The use of radioactive measurements from aircraft is now routine and the GSC, in collaboration with some provincial surveys, has carried out such surveys in a reconnaissance fashion over the Precambrian Shield.

D.R. DERRY AND IAN S. THOMPSON

Reading: M. Zaslow, *Reading the Rocks* (1975).

Prostitution is generally defined as the practice of providing sexual services for money, but because it requires a buyer and a seller it can more appropriately be defined as the practice of exchanging money for sexual services. Heterosexual prostitution (men as buyers and women as sellers) is most common; homosexual prostitution between men exists on a smaller scale.

The buying and selling of sex has been organized through street prostitution, brothels and call-girl operations. Throughout the 1800s, prostitution in Canada was organized around brothels. The houses were grouped together, often sharing their neighbourhood with taverns in the poorer parts of town. In Ottawa and Québec City the brothel districts were in the "lower towns"; in Saint John, Halifax, and in Kingston, Ont, they were near the docks; Montréal and Toronto each had a couple of districts. The brothels in Saint John and Halifax provided gambling in addition to sex and alcohol, and were known to be some of the most financially successful houses in the first half of the 19th century.

In the mid-1840s, as the first wave of settlers moved west, the sexual exploitation of Indian women by white men became commonplace. The North-West Mounted Police reported that Indians brought their wives and daughters to the river flats below Lethbridge, Alta, for the purpose of prostitution, and in 1886 the traffic in Indian women became a national scandal involving employees of the Indian affairs department.

In 1880 the federal government decided to regulate against the prostitution of Indian women and "An Act to Amend and Consolidate the Laws Respecting Indians" was introduced. The Act prohibited keepers of bawdy houses from allowing Indian women to work as prostitutes on their premises. Four years later the Act was amended to state specifically that keepers of "tents and wigwams," as well as houses, fell within the bawdy house provisions. This was done to ensure that native Canadians could be convicted of being brothel keepers.

With the development of the transcontinental railways, there was a mass migration westward at the turn of the century. Unlike the earlier settlers of the West who had been mainly farm families, these migrants were mostly single men, either bachelors or husbands who had temporarily left their wives and families at home. This mass migration of single men upset the normal male-female ratio and created an environment in which prostitution flourished.

Brothels were established within convenient distance of the railway stations and unless they or their inmates came to the attention of social or moral reformers, who then exerted pressure on the authorities, little was done to close them. The authorities were inclined to feel that prostitution had to be tolerated because it could not be eradicated. On occasions when the NWMP did take action, it was usually for reasons other than a mere violation of the prostitution laws. Such reasons included arguments that prostitution was having a damaging effect on the Indians or on the railway construction projects, or evidence that brothel inmates were involved in other criminal activities. Local police across the Prairies followed the NWMP policy and prosecuted brothel owners and inmates only when something worse than "illicit sex" was brought to their attention.

It was the parishioners and clergy of the Anglo-Saxon Protestant churches who took the least tolerant view of the existence of brothels. In some instances they mounted crusades to wipe out the traffic in women; in others they demanded that the women be driven out of town. Most often, however, since the brothels were regarded more as adjuncts to the liquor trade than as evils in themselves, the attention of the crusaders was directed toward combatting the evils of alcohol.

Public pressure to do something about prostitution was not always directed at the police or the politicians. On some occasions it was directed at the municipal authorities. Evidence suggests that this tactic may have been more successful, for between 1851 and 1881 many municipalities passed bylaws suppressing houses of prostitution, prostitutes, inmates and frequenters.

From 1890 on, legal repression made it more difficult to operate brothels, and streetwalking became a much more common type of prostitution. Prostitutes became dependent on middlemen, especially pimps. Brothels (sometimes organized as massage parlours) and call-girl operations (often disguised as escort services) still exist today, but street prostitution is the most visible form of prostitution and receives the most attention. Yet it has been estimated that only a small proportion of the prostitute population is engaged in street prostitution (estimates range from 10% to 33%). A significant number of the prostitutes who work the streets and other public places are juveniles; about 50% of these are young men engaged in homosexual prostitution.

Legislation and Enforcement Prostitution itself has never been a crime in Canada. However, various activities associated with it, eg, street solicitation, the operation of bawdy houses, procuring, and living off the avails of prostitution, have been and still are illegal. The earliest legislation grew out of general vagrancy statutes that were designed to remove indigents and other undesirables from the streets. Lower Canada (Québec) enacted a comprehensive statute dealing with prostitution in 1839. Police were authorized to apprehend "all common prostitutes or night walkers wandering in the fields, public places or highways, not giving a satisfactory account of themselves." Persons "in the habit of frequenting houses of ill-fame" could also be arrested if they failed to give a satisfactory account of themselves. In 1858 this legislation was extended to the United Province of Canada.

In 1867 Parliament passed an Act Respecting Vagrants that condemned all vagrants and disorderly persons to a maximum of 2 months in prison, a fine of $50, or both. Vagrants were defined as including all common prostitutes wandering in the streets and persons in the habit of frequenting bawdy houses who could not give a satisfactory account of themselves; all keepers of bawdy houses; and all persons who lived off the avails of prostitution. Only women were charged as prostitutes under this Act, and prostitution remained a status offence (one in which specific offensive behaviour is not a prerequisite for detention) until 1972 when the vagrancy law was repealed in response to a recommendation by the Royal Commission on the STATUS OF WOMEN IN CANADA, and because of pressure from women's groups and civil liberties groups. It was replaced by a soliciting law: "Every person who solicits any person in a public place for the purpose of prostitution is guilty of an offence punishable on summary conviction." The words "every person" were intended to prohibit both males and females from soliciting, but courts of appeal differed about whether a male could be a prostitute and about whether a client could be charged with soliciting. In 1978 the BC court held that a male could be a

prostitute but that a client could not be charged with soliciting; in the same year the Ontario court held that a male could not be a prostitute (because dictionary meanings of prostitutes only dealt with females) but that a customer could be charged with soliciting. In 1978 the Supreme Court of Canada held that "soliciting" means conduct that is "pressing or persistent," and it later stated that "pressing and persistent" means repeated soliciting of the same person. According to the same judgement, a car is not a public place.

Subsequent growth in the visibility of street prostitution in middle-class residential neighbourhoods reopened the debate regarding prostitution legislation. The debate focused on the validity of the municipal bylaws (enacted in Montréal, Calgary, Vancouver, Niagara Falls and Halifax) and on proposals to amend the soliciting section of the Criminal Code. The first issue was resolved in 1983 when the Supreme Court of Canada (in *Westendorp* v *The Queen*) found the Calgary bylaw to be invalid and ULTRA VIRES of the city of Calgary. The debate over the amendments, however, is still raging.

Representatives of the police, citizens' groups and municipal governments lobbied the federal government to strengthen the soliciting section of the Criminal Code so that it will apply both to customer and prostitute; to redefine "public place"; and, most importantly, to reword the legislation so that soliciting need be neither pressing nor persistent to constitute an offence. Women's groups and civil-liberties groups, as well as groups organized around the rights of prostitutes, opposed this amendment on the grounds that it would so expand the soliciting section that it would amount to a return to the old vagrancy law. These groups pressured the federal government to remove both the soliciting and the bawdy house sections from the Criminal Code on the grounds that they cause more social harm than they prevent.

In 1983 an amendment to the Criminal Code provided that both male and female persons could be charged as prostitutes, but this amendment did not deal with the cloudy issue of the prosecution of clients nor did it resolve the public debate. Somewhat later in 1983, a proposal to amend the soliciting section of the Criminal Code was tabled in the House of Commons. It was worded to ensure that the offence can apply to anyone who solicits, whether this be a prospective customer or prostitute, and to include within the definition of a "public place" a motor vehicle in or on a public place. The actual legislation passed into law 2 years later in Dec 1985 was much more sweeping. It states that police can arrest anyone who is disrupting pedestrian or vehicular traffic or communicating or attempting to communicate with anybody to sell or purchase sex in a public place, which includes a motor vehicle. The offence carries fines of up to $2000 or 6 months in jail. Since this new legislation makes any communication for the sake of prostitution in a public place illegal it overcomes the restrictions placed on police as a result of the 1978 Supreme Court of Canada ruling that soliciting must be pressing or persistent before charges could be laid under the Criminal Code.

The coming into force of the new legislation did not serve to still the public debate. It has generated criticism from lawyers, prostitutes, civil rights groups and feminists and is being challenged on several grounds, including its legality under the freedom of expression section of the CANADIAN CHARTER OF RIGHTS AND FREEDOMS. The latter has been successfully challenged in some provinces and upheld in others. Until dealt with by the Supreme Court of Canada, however, its constitutionality remains unresolved. In the

meantime, enforcement strategies continue to focus on the selling and not the buying of sex – data compiled by some municipalities shows that there are still more prostitutes than customers being arrested and charged – and it has yet to be determined whether the new soliciting law will reduce the visibility of street prostitution. A comprehensive review of the impact of the soliciting section is to be undertaken by parliamentary committee in 1988, 3 years after the coming into force of the Act.

Community attitudes have always governed the approach taken to prostitution. Parliamentarians have been pressured to amend the laws, municipalities have been encouraged to enact bylaws, and from time to time police have been pressed by public sentiment to enforce the laws against prostitution by closing brothels and arresting streetwalkers. Suppression has usually been spasmodic and ineffective; once brothels were closed or prostitutes driven from the streets, the public would turn its attention elsewhere, the brothels would reopen, the prostitutes would return and law enforcement officers would permit prostitution to exist until another public protest.

Three main approaches have been taken historically toward prostitution in Canada – regulation, prohibition and rehabilitation. Proponents of regulation believed that prostitution resulted from the different sexual needs of men and women. They felt that prostitution should be recognized as a necessary social evil and regulated to contain its worst side effects, eg, the spread of SEXUALLY TRANSMITTED DISEASE and the traffic in women. Proponents of prohibition believed that prostitution should be eradicated, and wanted criminal law to serve as a tool to root out all forms of prostitution activities. Those in favour of the third approach believed that individual prostitutes should be rehabilitated. Feminists, social reformers and government officials all vigorously debated which approach was preferable, and each approach was tried in some form or other. All of these legislative schemes, either as provided in law or as enforced, were interlaced with class, race and, most significantly, sex discrimination. They were doomed to failure because they did not address the major causes of prostitution, which are deeply rooted in social inequality, in a long-time double standard of sexual morality as applied to men and women, and in the general inability of society to satisfy the sexual needs of men and women.

In recent years a fourth approach has been taken toward prostitution, that of abolition. Abolitionists consider prostitution to be a personal choice and hence a private matter between consenting adults. Their aim is to eradicate the objective conditions that lead people into it and to ensure that those profiteering from the prostitution of others are penalized. They want activities between prostitute and customer decriminalized, arguing that this is the best way to prosecute profiteers.   FRANCIS M. SHAVER

Reading: F. Finnegan, *Poverty and Prostitution* (1979); James H. Gray, *Red Lights on the Prairies* (1971); J. James et al, *The Politics of Prostitution* (1977); E. McLeod, *Women Working: Prostitution Now* (1982); R. Symanski, *The Immoral Landscape* (1981).

Protectionism, government policies that shield domestic production (and producers) from foreign competition. For example, a Canadian tariff of 15% on an automobile that costs $5000 in a foreign country means that a tax (CUSTOMS duty) of $750 will be levied on the car when it is imported to Canada. The Canadian price will be $5750, and Canadian producers of similar vehicles who can operate profitably at a price of $5750, but not $5000, will be able to compete with imports in the

Canadian market. Producers dependent on protection cannot normally export, since their costs are above world prices, and they therefore depend almost entirely on the home market. (The effect of the 1965 CANADA-US AUTOMOTIVE PRODUCTS AGREEMENT is that automobiles produced in Canada can be exported to the US, although the price in Canada is higher.)

Economic analysis shows that economic losses from a tariff exceed its benefits. Theoretically, a tariff is wasteful because it leads to a substitution of higher-cost home production for lower-cost imports; if tariffs were repealed, manpower and capital in protected industries would shift to other employments, at home or abroad, and everyone, in their role as consumers, would gain from lower prices. Owners having to change the employment of their resources would suffer losses: landowners and shareholders in the contracting industries would lose more as owners than they would gain as consumers; specialized workers in the contracting industries would probably face retraining or lower-paying jobs; and others would bear the "transitional" costs of reorganizing their economic lives. Probably the many net winners would each gain a relatively small amount, while the relatively few net losers would suffer fairly heavy losses. Nevertheless, in principle it should be possible for a government to compensate losers and still produce a net social "profit" by repealing tariffs.

The debate about protectionism has revolved around attempts to find an intellectually respectable rebuttal to the economic argument, but none has been found. Public discussion of protectionism would be better if its proponents would argue that, although it involves economic costs, these are outweighed by noneconomic benefits. The intriguing question is why virtually all governments have passed laws known to reduce their citizens' economic well-being.

Protectionist policies may confer benefits that cannot be bought in the marketplace, such as increased military security, a larger population and more diversified production, and a heightened sense of national identity. These vague contentions cannot be definitively refuted, but they seem not to fit the Canadian situation. The defence argument is largely irrelevant in countries of small populations. Belief in the virtues of size and diversification, although given no credence by economists, seems widely shared by politicians. Voters may view size and diversification as matters of national pride, in which case the "diversification" argument merges with the "national identity" argument. In Canada, arguments for protectionism are generally not supported by residents in 8 provinces who observe that the tariff diversifies production mainly in Ontario and Québec.

A second explanation may be that political dynamics almost ensure protectionist policies. Politicians are likely to support tariffs where the "protectionist" vote is concentrated, and ignore tariffs or pay lip service to "free trade" elsewhere. Even voters who would gain by repeal may vote against it in compassion for those "vested interests" whose lives would be disrupted. But this explanation is not fully satisfying. Practical techniques exist for compensating the losers from a change in government policies, so that the "compassion" argument loses force; and the "vote-getting" argument begs the question of why a political party could not promise both to raise the standard of living by phasing out tariffs and to adopt policies to ease the transition. A third possible explanation for protectionism suggests some deep psychological or biological "imperative" compelling people to favour domestic producers and protect production in the "home territory."

Although the British North American colonies had relied upon relatively low tariffs on specific commodities for government revenues, the first coherent Canadian system of protection was established well after Confederation. Sir John A. MACDONALD won the 1878 general election largely on the strength of the NATIONAL POLICY, a policy of ECONOMIC NATIONALISM designed to protect Canadian businesses against competition from lower-cost US firms. Since that time, although the 1911 general election was contested over the question of FREE TRADE with the US (*see* RECIPROCITY), protectionism in some form has always been part of Canada's international economic relations.

After WWII Canada signed a GENERAL AGREEMENT ON TARIFFS AND TRADE (GATT) that obligated member nations to reduce tariffs and other barriers to trade by multilateral negotiations. GATT has been effective in reducing tariff rates, but not in reducing "nontariff barriers." Indeed, the decline of tariffs has been accompanied by a growth of other barriers: import quotas; threats of quotas or other measures that induce foreigners to accept "voluntary export restraints" when shipping specific goods to Canada; administrative protection, by which customs officers restrict or impede the entry of imports; and many other policies ranging from exchange controls to health and safety regulations.

Canada can perhaps claim to have pioneered another form of protection: "content" provisions, which make it easier for firms to import when they produce in Canada a certain proportion of the content of the goods they sell. Content provisions have been applied to automobile firms since 1926 and are also used in the broadcasting industry.

Since WWII, several tariff substitutes have been adopted by Canadian provinces in a pronounced movement to "provincial protectionism." Marketing boards have been established to raise the incomes of certain farmers (notably milk, egg and poultry producers) by restricting provincial production, and by persuading the national government to apply tariffs to imports from abroad and "production quotas" to all provinces. Provincial governments also favour provincial producers in letting government contracts by accepting "domestic" bids even if they are higher than bids from other provinces. Recently some provinces have required firms bidding for contracts to abide by "provincial-content" rules, and some have required that particular industries give priority in hiring to applicants who reside (or perhaps were born) in the province.

The phenomenon of provincial protectionism, and the suspicion that there would also be municipal protectionism if it were feasible to restrict trade between cities – as it was in the Middle Ages when local protectionism flourished – suggests that protectionism is not simply a matter of national economic diversification or national identity. *See also* FOREIGN INVESTMENT; FREE TRADE; INTERNATIONAL TRADE.   JOHN H. DALES

Reading: John H. Dales, *The Protective Tariff in Canada's Development* (1966); Economic Council of Canada, *Looking Outward* (1975).

Protestantism is the religious tradition of Western CHRISTIANITY that rejects the authority of the pope of Rome. Protestantism originated in the Reformation of the 16th century in Christian Europe, and Protestants have been said to share 3 basic convictions: 1) the Bible is the ultimate authority in matters of religious truth; 2) human beings are saved only by God's "grace" (ie, unearned gift); and 3) all Christians are priests, ie, are able to intercede with God on behalf of others and themselves, able to bear witness, able to confess their sins and be forgiven.

When a carefully engineered Catholic majority voted down certain reforms at the Diet of Speyer in Germany in 1529, the defeated minority earned the name "Protestant," derived from the Latin phrase meaning "to testify in favour of something." The rejection of Roman Catholic teaching and practice quickly became focused on rejection of the authority of the pope, often referred to as the "Anti-Christ" by Protestants. Repudiation of the papacy has been the only common characteristic of all Protestants at all times.

It has been said that Western civilization has been shaped decisively by the other 3 convictions of Protestantism. For example, the veneration of the Bible fostered literacy and popular education. The experience of God's gracious gift paradoxically moved Protestants to insist upon a stern standard of morality, and to work hard (the so-called "Protestant Ethic" described by sociologist Max Weber). The "priesthood of all believers" led to modern democracy, and to worldly activity that ironically favoured the growth of secularism (ie, a standpoint independent of the sacred). While scholars are seriously divided over the validity of these claims, most Protestants have been happy to assert them.

In fact, Protestant practice has often obscured the 3 disputed characteristics. If Protestants unite around the authority of the Bible, they frequently interpret it differently and usually give emphasis to different parts of it. Protestants have been known to speak of God's grace, but to act as if everything depended upon their own human effort. And respect for the ordained ministry of word, sacraments, and pastoral care has undermined the priesthood of all believers.

In contrast to the Catholics (*see* CATHOLICISM), Protestants generally celebrate only 2 sacraments (baptism and the Lord's supper) and they emphasize preaching, singing and relative informality in their services of Sunday worship. The high points of their religious calendar are Christmas, Easter and Pentecost (feast of the descent of the Holy Spirit and the founding of the Church). Only in some instances do Protestants (notably Anglicans) include bishops among their clergy, whose ranks usually include women, although not in large numbers. Lay people generally play significant roles in the life of the local congregation, which remains the basic and most characteristic unit of Protestant churches.

The early French explorers brought Protestant chaplains with them to Canada, and their violent disputes with Catholic chaplains established a pattern that recurred in the religious history of Canada. By 1659, however, it was clear that Protestants would not be tolerated in New France. Then the British CONQUEST shifted ascendancy to the Protestants and, until about the time of WWII, Protestants exercised hegemony over the culture and institutions of English-speaking Canada. That Protestant hegemony was finally dissipated by the presence of immigrants from Europe, many of whom were Catholics, Jews and Orthodox Christians, and by the secularizing of Canada. Today Protestants constitute 39% of the Canadian population, and about two-thirds of those Protestants are members of the UNITED CHURCH OF CANADA and the Anglican Church of Canada (*see* ANGLICANISM).

Protestantism took a distinctive form in Canadian history. In continental Europe, Lutherans played a large part, but not in English-speaking Canada. In Britain, the Anglican Church was the established church, but in Canada Anglicans never achieved dominance. In the US, there were many Protestant denominations, but in English-speaking Canada church unions occurred more readily and a few dominations rose to pre-eminence. Until the 20th century, with its non-

Protestant immigration and secularization, Canadian Protestants had relatively little to *protest*.

We have seen that historians dispute what the heritage of Protestantism is. Today many wonder what its future will be. Protestants marry non-Protestants with increasing freedom and regularity; Canadian society is increasingly secularized; and religious life itself is more private that it once was. With the new attention that Canadian Catholics are paying to the study of the Bible, to the experience of God's grace in the CHARISMATIC RENEWAL, and to the importance of lay ministry and vocations, the 3 alleged convictions of Protestantism seem less distinctively Protestant. On the Protestant side, the affection and respect which many have shown for some recent popes encourage speculation that the only consistent anchor of Protestantism may be working itself loose.

TOM SINCLAIR-FAULKNER

Proulx, Maurice, priest, filmmaker (b at St-Pierre-de-Montmagny, Qué 13 Apr 1902). Born into a farming family, he entered Séminaire de Québec in 1924 and was ordained in 1928. Though trained in agronomy after his ordination, Proulx developed an interest in filmmaking and used it to record the colonization of the Abitibi and other regions of Québec in the 1930s. His most famous film, the feature-length *En pays neuf* (1934-37), offers an extraordinary testament to the settlement of the Abitibi area, but he also made 36 other films for the provincial government and for industry between 1934 and 1961, mostly on agriculture, tourism and religion. He retired in 1966. His films were acquired for preservation by the Québec government in 1977.

PETER MORRIS

Provancher, Léon, priest, naturalist (b in the parish of Bécancour, Qué 10 Mar 1820; d at Cap-Rouge, Qué 23 Mar 1892). While still simply a country priest, Provancher came to the attention of scholars and the public when he published *Flore Canadienne* (1862) and launched a magazine, *Le Naturaliste canadien* (1868). After taking up residence in the small village of Cap-Rouge in 1872, Provancher devoted his remaining years to natural history. His *Petite Faune Entomologique du Canada*, describing over 1000 new insect species, principally Hymenoptera, made him known to naturalists around the world. A prolific author, his works included *Traité Élémentaire de Botanique* (1858), *Le Verger canadien* (1862), *Histoire du Canada* and *De Québec à Jérusalem* (1884). In 1888 he founded *La Semaine religieuse de Québec*. His brooding temperament, virulent polemics and strict ultramontane convictions made Provancher stand out among the intellectuals of Québec. A true scholar, but without a following, he left a rich legacy of contributions to science.

RAYMOND DUCHESNE

Provencher, Joseph-Norbert, Roman Catholic priest, bishop of St-Boniface (b at Nicolet, PQ 12 Feb 1787; d at St-Boniface, Man 7 June 1853). Ordained a priest in 1811 he was sent to the troubled RED RIVER COLONY in 1818 to build its first Catholic church and to help introduce some stability into a community the bulk of whose people, Scots, Irish and Métis, were Catholic. A modest but strict and uncompromising man with a strong suspicion of Protestantism, he sought to strengthen Catholicism in the North-West by undertaking several important tasks: the education of the young, the conversion of the Indians and the encouragement of Catholic emigration, a policy continued by his successors. Appointed a bishop and apostolic vicar of the North-West in 1820, his authority was extended to the Pacific coast in 1835; and in 1847 he became the first bishop of St-Boniface.

STANLEY GORDON

Provigo Inc, with head offices in Montréal, is a holding company involved in the wholesale and retail distribution of foodstuffs, tobacco, drugs and general merchandise. Provigo began operations in Québec in 1961 and has since expanded to Ontario, the West and the Maritimes, and in Québec its Dellixo Inc now ranks as the province's largest supplier to the food services industry. In late 1987, through a wholly owned subsidiary, it acquired most of the Class A and B shares of Consumers Distributing Co Ltd. Through its subsidiaries it is also active in the US. As of Jan 1987, it had annual sales or operating revenue of $5.3 billion (ranking 10th in Canada), assets of $971 million (ranking 90th) and 12 000 employees. Its major shareholders are Unigesco Inc (20.05%), the CAISSE DE DÉPÔT ET PLACEMENT DU QUÉBEC (10.5%), Sobey Stores Ltd (19%) and Unigesco (20%).

D.C. SAWYER

Province, The, independent Vancouver daily, founded 1898. Average paid circulation in 1986 was 175 262 Mon-Fri, 223 301 Sunday. The newspaper was launched in 1894 in Victoria, BC, as a weekly, called *The Province*, by Hewitt BOSTOCK and his associates. In 1898 the Klondike Gold Rush started business booming in Vancouver and it was decided to transfer the operation there. The first issue of *The Vancouver Daily Province* came out on 26 Mar 1898. Bostock soon bought out the interests of his associates and took into partnership Walter C. Nichol. When Bostock became involved in politics, Nichol became sole owner and, in 1923, the Southam organization acquired the paper from him. In 1952 the name was changed to *The Vancouver Province* and in 1956 yet again to *The Province*. *The Province* moved out of the evening field in 1957 and in 1983 went to a tabloid format. Readership is people 18-34, women working outside the home and 2-income households.

JEAN O'CLERY

Province House (rear), Halifax, NS. Built 1811-18, it is the finest example of Palladian architecture in Canada (*courtesy Environment Canada, Parks/Heritage Recording Services*).

Province House, Halifax, built between 1811 and 1818 to house Parliament, the courts and the public service of NS, is a sophisticated example of the influence of the Palladian style on Canadian architecture. Each floor of the building is clearly set off, and the central vertical part of the main facade is emphasized by 6 Ionic columns supporting a large triangular pediment decorated with coats of arms. In the lateral sections, 2 pilasters also support small pediments. The placement of the decorative elements, the openings, the pilasters and the columns show a rare attention to harmony and symmetry. Tradition has it that John Merrick designed the building, but the name of Richard Scott is also frequently mentioned. Province House is the most noteworthy example of Palladian architecture in Canada.

NATHALIE CLERK

Province of Canada, 1841-67. This union of the former provinces of UPPER CANADA and LOWER CANADA stemmed from the DURHAM REPORT of

An anonymous lithograph depicting London, Canada West, *c*1850 (*courtesy National Archives of Canada/C-40810*).

1839, after an imperial mission to investigate REBELLIONS OF 1837 in both Canadas. Lord DURHAM proposed a united province to develop a common commercial system, and particularly to complete canals on the St Lawrence. No less important, a combined Canada would have an overall English-speaking majority, thereby controlling the divisive forces Durham saw in largely French LC, and making it safe to grant the RESPONSIBLE GOVERNMENT he also advocated. Britain agreed to union, though not to the principle of responsible government. In 1840 the British Parliament passed the ACT OF UNION, which went into force 10 Feb 1841, establishing a single government and legislature. But whereas Durham advocated basing representation on population, counting on British immigration steadily to increase an existing Anglo-Canadian majority, the Act of Union provided equal representation for each of the Canadas in the new parliament, even though British UC then had a considerably smaller population: some 480 000, compared to 670 000 in LC, of whom about 510 000 were French Canadians. The French element would thus be underrepresented, and safely submerged from the start. Yet the device of equal representation had an unforeseen result. The old Canadas, each with its separate history, society and culture, virtually remained equal, distinct sections inside one political framework. They were now Canada West and Canada East geographically, but even the names Upper and Lower Canada survived in popular and some official use. The Union Act had embedded dualism in the very constitution, resulting in dual parties, double ministries and sectional politics.

As the Union began, French Canadians well realized its purpose was to submerge them. But a rising liberal leader, Louis LAFONTAINE, saw the advantage of an alliance with Canada W Reformers to seek responsible government. French Canadians would then share in ruling the United Province, maintaining themselves as a people, while co-operating with Anglo-Canadian allies. Hence LaFontaine readily responded to overtures from leading Canada W Reformers Francis HINCKS and Robert BALDWIN. Hincks, a Toronto journalist and shrewd strategist, was already backing Baldwin's campaign for responsible rule, centered on the British principle of responsible government. Its adoption in Canada would mean that governments would depend on elected parliamentary majorities. Baldwin and LaFontaine built up a powerful Reform alliance behind this principle. In Sept 1842 they won admission to the government, essentially compelling Gov Gen Sir Charles BAGOT to reconstruct his ministry because of the weight of parliamentary support behind them. On 26 Nov 1843 they and other party colleagues resigned, claiming they could not take responsibility for appointments by a new governor, METCALFE, that they had not advised. But in a succeeding Tory-Conservative ministry, William DRAPER,

Parliaments of the Province of Canada 1841-1867

Parliament	Session	Opening	Prorogation	Dissolution	Election Held
1st	1st	June 14, 1841	Sept 18, 1841		1841-Apr
Apr 8, 1841	2nd	Sept 8, 1841	Oct 12, 1842	Sept 23, 1844	
Sept 23, 1844	3rd	Sept 28, 1843	Dec 9, 1843		
2nd	1st	Nov 28, 1844	Mar 29, 1845		1844-Oct
Nov 12, 1844	2nd	Mar 20, 1846	June 9, 1846	Dec 6, 1847	
Dec 6, 1847	3rd	June 2, 1847	July 28, 1847		
3rd	1st	Feb 25, 1848	Mar 23, 1848		1847-8 Dec Jan
Jan 24, 1851	2nd	Jan 18, 1849	May 30, 1849	Nov 5 1851	
Nov 6, 1851	3rd	May 14, 1850	Aug 10, 1850		
	4th	May 20, 1851	Aug 30, 1851		Nov 6, 1851
4th	1st	Aug 19, 1852	Nov 10, 1852*		1851-Dec
Dec 24, 1851		Feb 14, 1853	June 14, 1853	June 22, 1854	
June 23, 1854	2nd	June 13, 1854	June 22, 1854		
5th	1st	Sept 5, 1854**	Dec 18, 1854		
		Feb 23, 1855	May 30, 1855		1854-Aug
Aug 10, 1854	2nd	Feb 15, 1856	June 1, 1856	Nov 28, 1857	
Nov 28, 1857	3rd	Feb 26, 1857	June 10, 1857		
6th	1st	Feb 25, 1858	Aug 16, 1858***		1857-Dec 3rd Week
Jan 13, 1858	2nd	Jan 29, 1859	May 4, 1859	June 10, 1861	
June 10, 1861	3rd	Feb 28, 1860	May 19, 1860		
	4th	Mar 16, 1861	May 18, 1861		
7th	1st	Mar 20, 1862	June 9, 1862	May 15, 1863	1861-July
July 15, 1861	2nd	Feb 12, 1863	May 12, 1863		
May 16, 1863					
8th	1st	Aug 13, 1863	Oct 15, 1863		
July 3, 1863	2nd	Feb 19, 1864	June 30, 1864		1863-June
	3rd	Jan 19, 1865	Mar 18, 1865	July 1, 1867	
June 30, 1867	4th	Aug 8, 1865	Sept 18, 1865		
	5th	June 8, 1866	Aug 15, 1866		

* Parliament adjourned Nov 10; it was not prorogued. The session continued Feb 14.
** Parliament adjourned Dec 18; it was not prorogued. The session continued Feb 23.
*** Double Shuffle, July 29, Aug 4. Brown-Dorion

Table compiled by D.H. Brown

acting virtually as a party premier, freely managed patronage himself to help stay in power. In fact, he held on until May 1847, thus furthering responsible government in practice even before its full acceptance.

A shift in imperial policy finally brought full acceptance. In 1846, Britain's repeal of the CORN LAWS signalled a movement towards FREE TRADE, ending a centuries-old pattern of imperial trade controls and protective duties. It no longer saw much need to withhold internal self-government from its more politically advanced colonies. Lord ELGIN came to Canada as governor general in 1847, instructed to implement responsible rule. Early in 1848, after Reformers swept elections in both Canadas, Henry Sherwood's Tory-Conservative ministry resigned, and Elgin at once called on Reformers to form a government. Responsible rule was plainly confirmed when in March an all-Reform Cabinet took office under LaFontaine as premier (he had the larger following) with Baldwin as co-premier. There was still a severe testing to come. Trade was at a low ebb, the newly completed St Lawrence canals half used. Tory English merchants of Montréal blamed the problem on the loss of imperial tariff protection, although world depression spreading since 1847 was a deeper cause. In the thriving earlier 1840s, moreover, expanding farm and lumber frontiers, canal building, and rising towns had readily absorbed a surge in British immigration; but now, when times were hard and frontier expansion was halting against the margins of the rugged Shield, a new tide of Irish immigrants poured in – destitute and typhus-infected, fleeing famine in their homeland. Amid these strains, the Reform ministry brought in the 1849 REBELLION LOSSES BILL.

Meant to compensate damages suffered in the LC Rebellion of 1837-38 (Upper Canadians had already settled their claims), the bill seemed vital social justice to French Canadians – proof also that responsible government could work for them. Canada East's British Tories, however, saw it as a blatant rewarding of rebels. The Reform-dominated legislature, meeting in Montréal, passed the bill over heated protests; but Tory-Conservatives still looked to a British governor to refuse his assent. Elgin did not: the measure had been recommended by a responsible ministry with support of the parliamentary majority. All the strains in Montréal burst forth in the MONTRÉAL RIOTS. Yet Elgin and his ministers rode out the storm, which subsided after a few wild days in Apr. Then in Oct the ANNEXATION manifesto appeared in the city, urging union with the US. It proved only a bitter, passing gesture. Most French Canadians saw colonial self-rule to be working; eastern Tories drew back; while in Canada West, apart from a few radicals, Reformers and Conservatives held firm to British connections. Responsible government survived its first test.

By 1850, depression had given way to an era of rapidly expanding world trade. Grain and timber production rose. The St Lawrence canals were bustling; Montréal merchants soon forgot annexationism. And with increasing British and American capital available, Canadian entrepreneurs took eagerly to railway building. Tracks linked Montréal to ice-free Portland, Maine, on the Atlantic, and Toronto to the Upper Great Lakes at Collingwood. A line from Niagara Falls to Windsor, via Hamilton, tied in with rails to New York at one end and Chicago at the other, and soon extended to Toronto as well. Above all, the GRAND TRUNK, incorporated 1852, built a transprovincial route connecting the lower St Lawrence by way of Québec, Montréal and Toronto to Sarnia, Ont. This first great railway boom subsided after 1857 in another world depression. The Grand Trunk in particular, overpromoted and extravagantly built, was left deep in debt, blighted with political deals and scandals. Nevertheless, rail lines had re-

made Canada, breaking inland winter isolation, vastly improving long-range transport, and focusing development on major towns. Railway-connected factory industries grew, notably in Montréal, Toronto and Hamilton, which rapidly advanced in urban size, wealth and complexity.

The 1854 RECIPROCITY Treaty with the US stimulated growth by giving Canadian grain and lumber free access to American markets. It also tied Canada far more closely to the American economy; the US Congress decision in 1865 not to renew reciprocity would thus spur Canadian efforts to seek economic integration with other BNA provinces. Yet the fifties also brought a Canadian protective tariff, promoted by the very rise in provincial industry. In 1858 and 1859 duties were raised enough to shelter manufactures effectively, though this was "incidental" protection – incidental to needs for revenue made pressing by the heavy public debt incurred from lavish railway grants. Duties were lowered again in 1866. Still, the tariff of 1858-59 was a foretaste of the later high-tariff NATIONAL POLICY, and signified the increasingly close ties between government and business in an era of advancing capitalism.

Meanwhile, since the early 1850s, other factors had been steadily disrupting the union's political life. Around 1850, left-wing Reform elements had emerged, the PARTI ROUGE in Canada E, the CLEAR GRITS in Canada W, advocating fully elective democracy and an American-style written constitution. In 1851 Baldwin and LaFontaine gave up combating radicalism in their own ranks and left politics. Their chief lieutenants, Francis Hincks and Augustin Morin, took over the ministry, which at first looked more secure as radical ardour waned in an atmosphere of widespread enthusiasm for railway promotion. But soon freshly divisive issues loomed, chiefly concerning public education and church-and-state relations. Predominantly Protestant Canada W widely believed in nondenominational public schools and rejected state-connected and state-supported religion. Largely Catholic Canada E, where mainstream French Liberals had made increasing links with the Catholic hierarchy, widely upheld denominational schools and church-state ties. More specifically, French Canadian votes backed bills in Parliament to enlarge the rights of state-aided Catholic schools in Canada W. Many Upper Canadians came to feel that their own interests were being thwarted by unchecked French Catholic power. Moreover, the census of 1851-52 revealed that the western section now had the greater population, and so was underrepresented, while paying the larger share of taxes. The strenuous editor of the powerful Toronto Globe, George BROWN, entered the Legislative Assembly as a Reform independent to battle for "justice" for Canada W. In 1853 he proposed representation by population to give the western section its full weight in seats. His initial attempt got nowhere; but it began a sharpening sectional struggle over REP BY POP: sought by Upper Canadians to overcome "French domination," fought by French Canadians to prevent their being submerged in the Union anew.

On 22 June 1854 the Hincks-Morin ministry fell. The old Reform alliance had crumbled under sectional strains. In its stead, a new ruling Liberal-Conservative COALITION appeared, which combined the moderate Liberals of Hincks and Morin with Tory-Conservative forces, among whom a Canada W politician from Kingston, John A. MACDONALD, was rapidly gaining stature. This broad coalition managed to abolish both the old CLERGY RESERVES and the SEIGNEURIAL SYSTEM. Brownites, Clear Grits and Rouges, left in the cold, called the Conservative-oriented combination "unprincipled." Actually, it rested on essential agreement

Ministries of the Province of Canada
1841-1867

Date	Name of Ministry	Comments
	REPRESENTATIVE GOVERNMENT	
1841 Feb 13	Draper-	1) William Draper, AG, UC
1842 Sept 15	Ogden	Charles Ogden, AG, LC
1842 Sept 16	Baldwin-	2) Robert Baldwin, AG, UC
1843 Nov 27	LaFontaine	Louis-Hippolyte LaFontaine, AG, LC
1843 Dec 12	Draper-	3) See 1 for Draper. Denis Benja-
1846 Jan 17	Viger	min Viger, pres of Council
1846 Jan 18	Draper-	4) See 1 for Draper. Denis-Benja-
1847 May 28	Papineau	min Papineau, commiss of crown lands
1847 May 29	Sherwood-	5) Henry Sherwood, AG, UC.
1848 Mar 10	Daly	Dominick Daly, prov sec
	RESPONSIBLE GOVERNMENT	
1848 Mar 10	LaFontaine-	6) See 2. Baldwin resigned June
1851 Oct 27	Baldwin	30; LaFontaine, Sept 26
1851 Oct 28	Hincks-	7) Francis Hincks, prov insp gen.
1854 Sept 10	Morin	Augustin Norbert Morin, prov sec
1854 Sept 11	MacNab-	8) Allan MacNab, pres of the
1855 Jan 26	Morin	council and min of agricul-ture, UC. See 7 for Morin
1855 Jan 27	MacNab-	9) Étienne-Paschal Taché, re-
1856 May 23	Taché	ceiver general. See 8 for MacNab
1856 May 24	Taché-	10) John A. Macdonald, AG, UC.
1857 Nov 25	Macdonald	See 9 for Taché
1857 Nov 26	Macdonald-	11) George-Étienne Cartier, AG,
1858 July 29	Cartier	LC. See 10 for Macdonald
1858 Aug 2	Brown-	12) George Brown, no office.
1858 Aug 4	Dorion	Antoine-Aimé Dorion, com-miss of crown lands. Double Shuffle
1858 Aug 6	Cartier-	13) See 10 and 11 for Cartier and
1863 May 23	Macdonald	Macdonald
1862 May 24	Macdonald-	14) John Sandfield Macdonald,
1863 May 15	Sicotte	AG, UC. Louis-Victor Sicotte, AG, LC
1863 May 16	Macdonald-	15) See 14 for Macdonald, 12 for
1864 Mar 29	Dorion	Dorion, who was AG, LC in this administration
1864 Mar 30	Taché-	16) See 9 for Taché, who was the
1864 June 14	Macdonald	titular head of this administra-tion; 10 for Macdonald
1864 Aug 7	Belleau-	17) On Taché's death he was suc-
1867 June 30	Macdonald	ceeded by Narcisse-Fortunat Belleau, receiver general

Abbrev: AG, Attorney General; LC, Lower Canada; UC, Upper Canada.

Table compiled by D.H. Brown

between the major parties: on railway and business development, maintenance of the Union, and defence of the French Canadian place within it. Furthermore, the coalition shortly came under the command of another outstanding Canadian partnership: that of John A. Macdonald, easygoing but brilliantly resourceful, and George-Étienne CARTIER, a formidable party manager and Montréal Grand Trunk lawyer. Under them, the CONSERVATIVE PARTY of the future gradually took shape. On the other side, Brown and the Clear Grits, earlier adversaries, moved together. On 8 Jan 1857 a party convention at Toronto hailed a rebirth of UC Reform, as Brownites, Grits and some returning moderate Liberals adopted a platform calling for rep by pop, nonsectarian education and acquisition of RUPERT'S LAND, which had lately attracted attention both from Toronto's businessmen, keen to expand their city's trade domain westward, and from agrarians eager for new land frontiers. The resulting Brownite-Grit party powerfully consolidated Canada W sectionalism, while its stress on farmers' rights and its hostility to big railway interests and expensive government also had a long political future.

There followed an incessant struggle between Macdonald-Cartier conservatism and Brownite liberalism, loosely allied with the limited Rouge eastern group under A.A. DORION. In Aug 1858 a Brown-Dorion government lasted just 2 days (*see* DOUBLE SHUFFLE). The returning Conservatives now took up BNA federal union to answer Canada's troubles, urged on by Alexander GALT, a leading Montréal financier, who joined the ministry. Yet the other provinces proved uninterested, and general federation was soon laid aside. In Nov 1859 at another Reform convention, Brown moved his Grits behind a dual federation of the Canadas (already suggested by Dorion), which as quickly failed in Parliament. While both sides had now adopted the federal principle as a way out of sectional disruption, neither was actually ready for it, and rows over rep by pop returned.

In May 1862, the Macdonald-Cartier forces were defeated on a costly Militia Bill, a response to border tensions roused by the AMERICAN CIVIL WAR. A moderate Reformer, Sandfield MACDONALD, tried to keep the union running by double majority, requiring majorities for government measures from both halves of the province. Sandfield's principle failed, though he hung on until early 1864, when John A. Macdonald returned, to be defeated in 3 months. Elections and government shifts had achieved nothing in the equal balance of sectional forces. By June 1864, with the United Province plainly deadlocked, Brown made a crucial offer to back a government willing to remake the Union. Negotiations between Macdonald, Cartier, Galt and Brown led quickly to an agreement to seek general federation and include the North-West, or a federation of the Canadas if that failed. The first aim did not fail. Brown and 2 Liberal colleagues joined the ministry, and the GREAT COALITION took up the federation cause with the other BNA colonies. The outcome was the scheme for CONFEDERATION and the BRITISH NORTH AMERICA ACT of 1867.

Throughout the shaping of the confederation plan Canadian representatives had played commanding roles, especially John A. Macdonald. When it went into force on 1 July 1867, the day of the old Canadian union was over, scarcely mourned amid bright aspirations for the future. Before the union ended, its Parliament endorsed the federal scheme with both English and French majorities in 1865, and in 1866 drafted constitutions for the successor provinces of Québec and Ontario. The United Province had gone through much and achieved much. But its final achievement lay in Confederation itself.

J.M.S. CARELESS

Reading: J.M.S. Careless, *The Union of the Canadas* (1967) and *Brown of the Globe* (1959); D.G. Creighton, *John A. Macdonald: the Young Politician* (1952); W.L. Morton, *The Critical Years* (1964).

Province of Quebec, 1763-91 At the end of the SEVEN YEARS' WAR, Great Britain organized the territories that were confirmed as its possessions by the Treaty of PARIS, 1763. By the ROYAL PROCLAMATION OF 1763, the Province of Quebec was created out of the inhabited portion of NEW FRANCE, taking the shape of a quadrilateral on each side of the St Lawrence R and stretching from Lk Nipissing and the 45th parallel to the Saint John R and Ile d'Anticosti. These boundaries were modified by the QUEBEC ACT (1774) to include the fishing zone off Labrador and the Lower North Shore and the FUR-TRADE area between the Ohio and Mississippi rivers and the Great Lakes. The Treaty of PARIS, 1783, pushed the boundary farther N. The "old province of Quebec," to use historian A.L. Burt's expression, ceased to exist when it was divided into 2 separate colonies, LOWER CANADA and UPPER CANADA, after the CONSTITUTIONAL ACT of 1791.

Since many of the province's inhabitants were, or had been, employed by fur-trade companies and merchants, their geographic universe was not limited to these official boundaries; it stretched westward to include the PAYS D'EN HAUT and the North-West, the source of the colony's main export. The fur trade had been virtually destroyed during the war and then hobbled first by PONTIAC's revolt and later by the restrictions imposed by British authorities. It took nearly a decade to revive the trade, but the traders eventually occupied the previous French territory. Then, following the example set by Peter POND, they explored and exploited new areas. By 1789, when Alexander MACKENZIE descended the Mackenzie R to the Arctic Ocean, the entire North-West, from Lk Superior to the Rockies, had been linked to the Province of Quebec through the activities of the VOYAGEURS and fur traders. During the period 1763-91 Montréal merchants drained off most of the furs from the SW. Competition from New York and Albany was gradually eliminated by the 1768 decision to return to the colonies the regulation of the fur trade and by the 1774 annexation of the Ohio territory to the province. That region had ties with Montréal even after the 1783 treaty, since Britain retained the posts S of the Great Lakes until 1796 (*see* JAY'S TREATY).

Although the fur trade was vital for the province and its commerce with Britain, it was not the main domestic economic activity. Agriculture, especially the growing and preparation of wheat products, occupied the largest number of people and supplied the local market. Surpluses increasingly allowed food to be exported to the W Indies and Britain. Industrial production at the artisan level supplied domestic needs and the smaller needs of the fur trade.

The domestic market should not be underestimated: as a result of a high birth rate the population more than doubled, from nearly 70 000 in 1775 to nearly 144 000 in 1784 and over 161 000 in 1790. Migration played little part in this growth. About 3000 people left the St Lawrence Valley after the CONQUEST, and the expected British immigration did not take place. The number of "old subjects" was very small – some 500 in 1766 and perhaps 2000 in 1780. Their number grew significantly only after the AMERICAN REVOLUTION, when LOYALISTS arrived in significant numbers – the 1784 census listed some 25 000. The Loyalists settled mainly in the SW part of the province, which later became Upper Canada [Ontario].

The British, many of whom were merchants and officials, had influence and position out of proportion to their numbers. The governors, James MURRAY, Guy CARLETON and Frederick HALDIMAND, were responsible for the province; they and their entourages (which often, in fact, included Francophones) therefore held social as well as political power. The merchants, with the advantage of credit in London, soon controlled commercial relations with the mother country. At first supported by the military authorities and helped by francophone voyageurs, they acquired in less than 2 decades the lion's share of the fur trade. They established the NORTH WEST COMPANY, which took an increasingly larger share of the trade and was, by 1790, the most powerful fur-trade organization in the Province of Quebec.

The administrators and merchants often failed to see eye to eye. The merchants even managed to have Murray, the first governor, recalled. The dispute with Murray centered on the application of British law and the creation of an Assembly, as provided for in the Proclamation of 1763. The merchants felt that these institutions were essential to the anglicizing of the colony and the protection of British interests. They perceived and defined these interests as those of Britons resident in the colony. But both Murray and Carleton defined British interests as the interests of the British Crown, and they therefore felt that their main task was to avoid any threat to the Crown's possession of the colony. Given the style of government adopted during the period of military occupation (1760-63), the lack of British immigration and the growing unrest in the Thirteen Colonies, the governor had no choice but to try to win over the majority of the population. Major portions of the Proclamation were set aside and "new subjects" were appointed to official positions.

In 1774 Carleton, who was determined to preserve a military base of operations in N America, obtained the passage of the Quebec Act. It fell far short of pleasing the merchants, who wanted an Assembly, even though it strengthened their monopoly on the fur trade to the south. The governor hoped the Act would win the support of the francophone elite. Murray had already gained the collaboration of the Roman Catholic clergy (*see* CATHOLICISM). The death of Bishop Henri-Marie Dubreil de PONTBRIAND in 1760 had left the church without a bishop to run its affairs and ordain new priests; moreover, funds were desperately short and war-destroyed buildings had to be replaced. Murray therefore made himself the champion of the church and was instrumental in bringing about the 1766 consecration in France of Jean-Olivier Briand as the new bishop of Québec. The Quebec Act allowed the free practice of the Catholic faith, re-established the COUTUME DE PARIS in civil matters and restored property rights to the church and SEIGNEURS. A council was created and the abolition of the Test Oath allowed Catholics to enter public office. But these conciliatory measures failed to have the desired effect. The habitants showed little enthusiasm for British interests, especially during the American invasion of 1775-76. Nevertheless, for various reasons, they also failed to side with the revolutionaries. And so Carleton's strategy had partial success: the province remained British.

The sociopolitical structure created by the Quebec Act failed to survive the consequences of war. It was upset by the arrival of the Loyalists, and this increase in British population greatly strengthened the merchants' position and intensified their conflict with the governor. The British authorities asked Carleton (now Lord Dorchester) to suggest a solution to the problem. In order to satisfy, at least partially, the merchants and the Loyalists without angering the Francophones, in 1791 London produced a revised Quebec Act and a new constitution, which included the creation of a House of Assembly. The new provinces of Lower and Upper Canada were created, with Lower Canada retaining many of the institutional forms of the Province of Quebec.

The 30 years following the Conquest are of major importance to the understanding of Canadian history. The economic structure of the St Lawrence Valley remained almost unchanged: 2 economies coexisted, one commercial and oriented towards the mother country, the other agricultural and artisanal, and oriented toward the local market. These 30 years were marked on one hand by the intention, explicitly expressed in 1763, to anglicize the colony, and on the other hand by the need to come to terms with changing circumstances on the N American continent. During those 30 years, 2 ethnic groups came together, anticipating many of the points of contact, co-operation and tension that characterized much of subsequent Canadian history. By 1791 the process of anglicization proposed in 1763 was no longer practicable, and the francophone culture would survive. GRATIEN ALLAIRE

Reading: H. Neatby, *Quebec* (1966); F. Ouellet, *Economic and Social History of Québec, 1760-1850* (tr 1980).

Provincial Floral Emblems

Floral emblems are generally selected from among the flora of the country, nation, state, territory or province that they are meant to represent. Tradition dictates that the plant selected be popular and commonly found throughout the region. Floral emblems

Floral Emblems of Canada		
Canada	sugar maple *Acer saccharum*	1867
Alberta	prickly or wild rose *Rosa acicularis*	1930
BC	Pacific dogwood *Cornus nuttallii*	1956
PEI	showy lady's slipper *Cypripedium reginae* replaced by	1947
	pink lady's slipper *C. acaule*	1965
Manitoba	prairie crocus or crocus anemone *Anemone patens*	1906
NB	purple violet *Viola cucullata*	1936
NS	mayflower *Epigaea repens*	1901
Ontario	white trillium *Trillium grandiflorum*	1937
Québec	Madonna lily *Lilium candidum*	1963
Saskatchewan	western red or prairie lily *Lilium philadelphicum*	1941
Newfoundland	pitcher plant *Sarracenia purpurea*	1954
NWT	mountain avens *Dryas integrifolia*	1957
YT	fireweed *Epilobium angustifolium*	1957

may thus differ from coats of arms or flags, since the latter are more symbolic in nature (*see* HERALDRY). For historical reasons, however, a non-indigenous plant or one linked to the founding nation, an industry or a particular landscape may be chosen. The entire plant or only the flower may be represented. The latter is a true floral emblem. The emblem may also be the leaves or branches of a tree. Some countries have both a floral and a tree emblem. Some emblems are adopted officially or legally, others are unofficially recognized by the people for historic, religious or other reasons.

The accompanying table lists the floral emblems of Canada and its provinces and territories, along with the dates adopted (by Act of the provincial or territorial legislature). Because they are known by various common names, French and English, the scientific names, given in italics, are most accurate. *See also* EMBLEMS OF CANADA; EMBLEMS, PROVINCIAL AND TERRITORIAL.

CÉLINE ARSENEAULT

Provincial Government

Under Canada's federal system, the powers of government are shared between the federal government and 10 provincial governments. The provincial governments are primarily responsible for public schooling, health and social services, highways and LOCAL GOVERNMENT (through municipalities), but overlapping and, at times, conflicting regional and national interests have stretched provincial concerns across virtually every area of Canadian public policy. Each province is free to determine levels of provincial public services, and each provincial government has been true to its regional economic and cultural interests in its own fashion. Generalizations about provincial activities such as "province building" or "policy convergence" therefore do not always stand up to close scrutiny, and it is easier to cite the exceptions than to frame universal rules. The CONSTITUTION ACT, 1867, which outlined the DISTRIBUTION OF POWERS between the provinces and the central government established a federal union in Canada (*see* FEDERALISM), but not a perfect or ideal federal state. Preoccupied with nation building, the FATHERS OF CONFEDERATION designed the original constitutional arrangements with a bias toward

a strong central government. The powers of the federal government to disallow provincial statutes within one year of their passage (*see* DISALLOWANCE); to appoint provincial lieutenant-governors; to declare provincial works to be for the general advantage of Canada or 2 or more provinces; to appoint judges of superior, district and county courts (*see* JUDICIARY); and to enjoy broad lawmaking powers all confirm the intended junior status of provincial governments. However, the evolution of Canadian society, despite the centralizing swings occasioned by the 2 world wars and the economic depression of the 1930s, has long eroded this early sense of provincial subordination. Although not all contemporary provincial governments have been as assertive as those of Québec or Alberta, most claim a more equal partnership with Ottawa.

CONFEDERATION was predicated on a primary role for the central government in the promotion of an economic union and in the stimulation of national economic expansion through the development of transportation links (railways, harbours and canals) and other forms of public-policy support (*see* RAILWAY HISTORY) but by the 1880s the momentum behind nation building had slowed and was soon overtaken by the assertion of provincially based political and economic attachments. Other elements that helped enhance the status of provincial governments included the political leadership of such provincial spokesmen as Oliver MOWAT, Honoré MERCIER and William FIELDING; PM LAURIER's more sympathetic attitude towards the provinces; the development, in various provinces, of resource-based economic interests (*see* RESOURCE RIGHTS); and the emergence of a provincial bias in the decisions of the JUDICIAL COMMITTEE OF THE PRIVY COUNCIL on the distribution of powers. The provincial governments always played some role in their own regional economic development through public investment in transportation and the growth of their public education systems; the expansion of these activities and the later growth of social welfare, health and hospital programs have changed the original conception of the functions and the jurisdictions of provincial governments.

Legislative Power Under the Constitution Act, 1867 (s92), the powers of the provincial legislatures were carefully circumscribed. The legislatures were granted specific jurisdiction in 16 subject areas. In s91 powers were granted to Parliament in 29 areas, but these powers were intended for "greater Certainty" in the application of Parliament's more comprehensive (and controversial) residual power to make laws for the PEACE, ORDER AND GOOD GOVERNMENT of Canada in relation to all matters not assigned exclusively to the provinces. The scope of provincial legislative power was broadly defined in the final subsection of their grant of powers as "generally all matters of a merely local or private Nature in the Province." Other enumerated areas include property and civil rights, the management and sale of provincially owned public lands, hospitals, municipal institutions, local works and undertakings, the incorporation of companies with provincial objectives, the solemnization of marriage and the administration of justice. Provincially established courts enforce both civil and CRIMINAL LAW. Under s93, education is an exclusive provincial responsibility, subject to certain qualifications. Under s95 agriculture and immigration are matters of concurrent jurisdiction but with federal paramountcy, ie, if there is conflicting legislation, the federal government prevails. The control of public lands and provincial ownership of natural resources has proved to be of particular importance; however, the most significant interpretations of the Constitution regarding provincial rights have been in the area of property and civil rights. These interpretations have protected provincial jurisdiction against encroachment and have provided specific support for the provincial government regulation of labour relations, marketing and business contracts.

Provincial taxing powers are limited to direct TAXATION within the province, ie, personal and corporate income taxes, consumer taxes and certain property taxes. From their jurisdiction over the management and sale of public lands, timber and ownership of natural resources, the provinces derive authority for the principal source of nontax revenues. According to a 1982 constitutional amendment (92A), the provinces were granted an unrestricted taxing power ("any mode or system") in the natural-resource field. This amendment, which clarified and expanded provincial legislative and taxing powers over nonrenewable resources, forestry resources and electrical energy, was designed to resolve the constitutional difficulties posed by revenue raising that strayed into the indirect tax field. Although the federal government still retains the power to disallow a provincial statute, it has not done so since 1943. Any federal Cabinet that contemplated using disallowance today would encounter significant political difficulties. A LIEUTENANT-GOVERNOR's power to reserve a bill passed by a provincial legislature for action by the governor general can similarly be regarded as a relic of an earlier age of intergovernmental relations. The last reservation, which occurred in Saskatchewan in 1961, went against an 80-year-old understanding that this power would only be exercised on instructions from the governor general, and the bill was subsequently approved.

Between 1867 and 1987 there have been only 6 constitutional amendments directly affecting the powers of all provincial legislatures. The amendments of 1940, 1951 and 1964 transferred powers to Parliament with the agreement of the provinces; those of 1930, 1931 and 1982 expanded provincial powers. The 1940 amendment of s91 (ss 2A) secured exclusive federal government jurisdiction for a national UNEMPLOYMENT INSURANCE scheme. In 1951 the addition of s94A permitted national OLD-AGE PENSIONS with concurrent jurisdiction under provincial paramountcy. This section was further broadened to include supplementary benefits in 1964 to provide for the introduction of the CANADA PENSION PLAN. Québec was the only province to OPT OUT of this agreement. The Constitution Act, 1930, under which natural-resource powers were transferred to the western provinces, was the first constitutional amendment to increase the jurisdiction of a province. In the following year, the STATUTE OF WESTMINSTER gave powers to both provincial and central governments to repeal British colonial statutes. Despite concerted provincial demands for an expansion of their jurisdictions during the constitutional reform conferences of the late 1960s and 1970s, the Constitution Act, 1982, made only one direct change in provincial jurisdiction – the addition of s92A.

Provincial Government Activities Levels of government expenditure only partly reflect the range of provincial government activity, but they do underscore the role the provinces play in the provision of public goods and services and in the making of transfer payments to individuals. Since 1926, total government expenditures for all governments has risen from 16% to 48% of the gross domestic product (GDP) in the mid-1980s. In this time, provincial government expenditures (excluding intergovernmental transfers) have risen from 3% to nearly 15% of GDP and those of their municipalities from 7% to 8%. Government ex-

penditures, including federal government spending for income-security payments and regional assistance programs, are of special significance for the less prosperous of the Atlantic provinces. Their provincial government expenditures as a proportion of provincial gross domestic products are double those of the other 6 provinces.

Provincial expenditures are primarily in the fields of hospital and medical care, education, income maintenance and other social services. The participation of all provincial governments in federal-provincial, shared-cost arrangements for hospital insurance and medicare (*see* HEALTH POLICY) has helped ensure nationwide standards of service, despite some differences in their modes of financing and program coverage. In contrast, the retention of a high degree of provincial autonomy in the provision of elementary and secondary education and the accommodation of religious and linguistic cleavages has resulted in a variation in SCHOOL SYSTEMS.

Over 50% of total provincial government revenues are derived from personal income taxes, general sales taxes, natural-resource revenues and returns from their investments. The relative importance of these sources varies for each province because of differing taxation policies as well as the wide variations in their economic bases. As of 1987 Alberta was the only province that did not levy a general retail sales tax. In the Atlantic provinces at least 25% of revenue is derived from EQUALIZATION PAYMENTS from the federal government. Since 1962 the joint occupancy of the income-tax fields by both the federal and provincial governments has been governed by a series of 5-year fiscal and tax-collection arrangements. Under the current 1982-87 agreement, the federal government collects personal income taxes for 9 provinces (excluding Québec) and corporation income taxes for 7 provinces (excluding Alberta, Ontario and Québec).

The growth of provincial activities has not only been marked by a full exploitation of their direct tax and other revenue-raising powers, but also by federal government encouragement and financial assistance. Federal conditional shared-cost programs in social assistance and other areas of provincial jurisdiction, plus unconditional grants in the form of equalization payments, have all contributed to the expansion and maintenance of provincial public services. Since 1977 the federal Established Programs Financing arrangements have resulted in a greater degree of provincial autonomy through the substitution of more unconditional fiscal transfers and cash payments for the medicare, hospital insurance and post-secondary education grant programs. Expenditure on social services may account for the largest proportion of provincial government spending, but it is only one dimension of a far wider range of government intervention. Regulatory activity and programs for economic development conducted by a variety of provincial government agencies and CROWN CORPORATIONS play an equally important role in provincial life. Workers' compensation, labour relations, agricultural marketing, energy and public utilities are all, for example, regulated by provincial agencies. All provinces have publicly owned development corporations or other agencies which provide assistance, loans and other incentives for the expansion and diversification of their economies, and often compete with each other, with varying degrees of success. Other provincial crown corporations, particularly those responsible for the generation of electrical power, are also important in provincial economics. Both ONTARIO HYDRO and HYDRO-QUÉBEC, for example, have assets of more than $30 billion and sales of over $4.7 billion. The rapid growth in the number of provincial crown corporations has

been one of the most striking aspects of the recent expansion of provincial activities. Nearly 50% of the more than 200 such corporations were established during the 1970s.

Government Institutions Distinctive patterns of economic and social development have produced wide variations in provincial political life and provincial PARTY SYSTEMS, but all provincial government institutions and the political conventions that shape their operation are closely modelled after the British parliamentary tradition and the practice of Cabinet government, and reflect the principles of RESPONSIBLE GOVERNMENT. The Crown is represented through the office of lieutenant-governor. Provincial public policymaking and administration is controlled by an executive council, ie, a Cabinet, comprising ministers of the Crown and headed by a PREMIER. A provincial legislature is defined, for lawmaking purposes, as being composed of the lieutenant-governor and the provincial Legislative Assembly in the same way that the central Parliament is composed of the Crown, SENATE and HOUSE OF COMMONS. In ordinary usage, however, the term legislature refers only to the Assembly. Four provinces originally had a bicameral legislature made up of an elected Assembly and an appointed Legislative Council: Québec (1867-1968), New Brunswick (1867-92), Nova Scotia (1867-1928) and Manitoba (1870-76). PEI also had a bicameral legislature but with an elected council which was absorbed into the lower chamber in 1893. Today, all have a unicameral system composed of a single elected chamber. Appointments to Cabinet are ordinarily made from members of the political party that holds the majority of seats in the Legislative Assembly. The further requirement that the premier and Cabinet maintain the support of the majority in the legislature is a principle of responsible government that had been formally acknowledged in 1848 by the colonial antecedents of the 4 original provinces.

Office of the Lieutenant-Governor Provincial government is carried out in the name of the Crown; the lieutenant-governor of the province acts as the Crown's representative in all areas of provincial jurisdiction and in the exercise of any related prerogative powers. The lieutenant-governors appoint and may dismiss the provincial premiers and the members of their Cabinets. They summon, prorogue and dissolve the provincial legislatures and assent to provincial legislation in the name of the Crown. The lieutenant-governors still retain a power to withhold or reserve a bill for consideration of the central government. The latter power is presumed dormant, if not entirely unexercisable. In practice the lieutenant-governor's constitutional responsibilities are circumscribed by the conventions of responsible government and conducted on the advice of the premier and Cabinet. The discretionary powers enabling a lieutenant-governor to act alone in the appointment or dismissal of a premier or the dissolution of the provincial Legislative Assembly remain potentially important, however, should there be any uncertainty about who commands the support of the majority in the Assembly. If a premier or Cabinet acted in a way that was unquestionably contrary to constitutional conventions, the office of lieutenant-governor might also be used to protect those fundamental principles.

The lieutenant-governors are appointed by the federal Cabinet on the advice of the prime minister, with little participation from the provincial governments in the selection process. Their salaries are fixed and are paid by Parliament and before 1892 they were regarded as federal officers. The Judicial Committee of the Privy Council ended any suggestion of subordinate status for the lieutenant-governors – and by extension for the provincial legislatures – when it held the appointment to be an act of the Crown and the office to be as much the representative of the Crown for all the purposes of provincial government as the office of governor general was for Canada.

Premiers and Cabinets Provincial premiers ordinarily hold the position of President of the Executive Council, and enjoy the same pre-eminent status as head of their provincial governments as the PRIME MINISTER holds in relation to his CABINET colleagues. Virtually all Cabinets have assignments for such policy areas as health, education, labour and manpower, social services, energy, environment, natural resources (forests, lands or mines), economic development, agriculture, highways and transportation, tourism and recreation, justice (ATTORNEY GENERAL), finance, municipal affairs and consumer protection. The Atlantic provinces and Québec have specific fisheries portfolios. Others, such as the minister for the status of women in Québec, the minister for francophone affairs in Ontario, the minister of rural development in Saskatchewan, and the minister for northern affairs in Manitoba, express the particular policy commitments of a province. Both Ontario and Québec have also experimented with horizontal portfolios that combine responsibilities for policy development and co-ordination in broadly defined areas (eg, social development and resources development) under a single minister. In 9 provinces there is a specific assignment of responsibilities for intergovernmental relations – in some instances a position held by the premier. In 1987 the average size of the provincial Cabinets was 20 members – the largest being Québec with 28, the smallest being PEI with 11.

Since 1960 the increasing size of the provincial Cabinets and attention to improved policy planning and co-ordination has spawned the growth of Cabinet COMMITTEE systems. These typically include a central policy or management board/planning and priorities committee, and a treasury board (for financial, personnel, and general government management policy). This development has in turn given rise to the introduction of provincial Cabinet secretariats which provide administrative and professional assistance.

Legislatures The provincial Legislative Assemblies (known as the House of Assembly in Nova Scotia and Newfoundland and the National Assembly in Québec) are significant institutional expressions of the central values of Canadian democracy. As in other parliaments, the making of provincial law requires that the government's legislative proposals (bills) move through the formal state of first reading, second reading and detailed review in committee stage, and a final third reading before receiving assent by the lieutenant-governor. The BUDGETARY PROCESS also requires that the legislature annually approve the funds required for government programs and that expenditures are to be only for those purposes authorized by the Legislative Assembly. In practice there is rarely room for independent action by the legislature in the lawmaking process. The party loyalty of individual members of the Assembly, the power of the party leadership to maintain discipline, and the government's control of the timetable of the Assembly ensure that the work of the Legislative Assembly is determined by the premier and Cabinet. With the modern emphasis on executive government, the lawmaking powers of the Cabinet and of its individual ministers is considerable. The weight of government business undermines the backbencher's right to sponsor private members' bills, and few such bills advance beyond second reading and even fewer become law. The general rule that only the government may initiate spending and taxing proposals is

strictly interpreted to curtail such initiatives. MINORITY GOVERNMENTS, such as the 1985 Liberal government in Ontario, are rare in the provinces, and one-party dominance of the Assembly has historically been far commoner. The Conservative Party of Ontario enjoyed the longest period of uninterrupted government office (from 1943 to 1985), and the Conservatives captured over 90% of the seats in the Alberta legislature in the 3 successive general elections of 1975, 1979 and 1982. In NB, however, Frank McKenna's Liberals captured all seats in the Legislature.

Despite the power of the government within the Legislative Assembly, the debates on the various stages of a bill, question period and the other scheduled opportunities for debates on public policy, together with the other work of the members in representing and servicing their constituents, help ensure some measure of accountable government. The premier and members of the Cabinet are generally challenged, in the Assembly, to answer for their direction and management of provincial affairs, and the reporting of the proceedings through the media exposes the government to public scrutiny. All provinces, save for PEI, publish a HANSARD report of their debates and proceedings and both Saskatchewan and Québec have instituted full television coverage.

In 1987 the provincial legislatures varied in size from 32 members in PEI to 122 in Québec and 125 in Ontario. Newfoundland and Nova Scotia both had 52 seats; BC, 69; Manitoba, 57; New Brunswick, 58; Saskatchewan, 64; and Alberta, 83 seats. Two members are elected from each provincial riding in PEI, and until the next general election BC will continue to have a number of dual-member electoral districts. All other provinces have single-member ridings.

Judged by the number of days spent sitting in debate, the provincial legislatures are less active than the House of Commons. Over the past 20 years, however, their sessions have increased in length and are generally more productive in their legislative output than their counterpart in Ottawa. Most meet for 75 or more days per year and the average number of public statutes passed by the Legislative Assemblies regularly far exceeds that passed by the House of Commons. This may in part reflect the more crowded agendas of provincial governments but is also attributable to the smaller-sized legislature and to greater Cabinet control. All provincial legislatures have a standing-committee system and at times use ad hoc special or select committees to investigate particular areas of public policy. The Québec National Assembly has particularly strong committees, but elsewhere the roles and resources of committees are more limited than in Ottawa. In 1986 the total remuneration (salary and tax-free allowances) of ordinary private members of the legislatures varied from $23-33 000 in PEI, Saskatchewan and Alberta, to $36-43 000 in Manitoba, Newfoundland, Nova Scotia, New Brunswick and BC, and over $48 000 in Ontario and Québec.

The growth in the scope and quality of provincial government activities has been accompanied by a considerable increase in the numbers of provincial government employees who provide the managerial, clerical and manual skills required for the provision of provincial services. In September 1986 the total number of provincial departmental employees reached 325 680; a further 158 000 were employed in provincial government enterprises and 181 536 others in boards, commissions, agencies and institutions. Combined with the employees of municipalities, hospital and school boards, they comprise 75% of the total number of public employees in Canada. In recent years, the measures taken by provincial

governments to restrain the growth of their expenditures have centered in large part on the containment of salary and wages expenditure through contracting out, privatization and the reduction of the size of their public services.

NORMAN J. RUFF

Prowse, Daniel Woodley, judge, publicist, historian (b at Port de Grave, Nfld 12 Sept 1834; d at St John's 27 Jan 1914). Educated in St John's and Liverpool, Eng, Prowse was called to the Newfoundland Bar in 1859. He practised law and served as a member of the Legislative Assembly between 1861 and 1869, when he was appointed a judge of the Circuit Court and later of the Central District Court. An experienced if sometimes eccentric justice and an indefatigable publicist of Newfoundland, he was a prolific journalist in local, American and British journals and wrote *Manual for Magistrates in Newfoundland* (1877), *Newfoundland Guide Book* (1905) and *A History of Newfoundland* (1895), still the most comprehensive general history of the Island and the first to be written "from the English, Colonial, and Foreign Records."

G.M. STORY

Prus, Victor Marius, architect (b at Minsk Mazowiecki, Poland 24 Apr 1917). Educated at Warsaw Technical U (1939), he served with the Polish forces in the Middle East and with the RAF during WWII. He studied at U of Liverpool and practised in London, immigrating to Canada in 1952. After research with Buckminster Fuller at Princeton he set up practice. With his wife Maria Fisz Prus and various associates he has designed outstanding buildings that are characterized by an appropriate "ambience" – in his view the "ultimate objective" in architecture. His principal works include Rockland Shopping Centre (Massey Medal), Savoie Apartment Bldg and Palais de Congrés in Montréal; RCAF Memorial, Trenton; Grand Théâtre and Conservatory of Music in Québec City; and Canada/France Astronomical Observatory in Hawaii.

NORBERT SCHOENAUER

Pryce, Maurice Henry Lecorney, research physicist, professor (b at Croydon, Eng 24 Jan 1913). Following a BA at Cambridge and a PhD (1937) at Princeton, he lectured in mathematics at Cambridge for 2 years and served a year as reader in theoretical physics in Liverpool. Three years of wartime research in RADAR at the Admiralty Signal Establishment preceded his first sojourn in Canada in 1944-45 as a member of the secret joint Canadian-UK-US Atomic Energy Project in Montréal. He came to Canada for permanent residence in 1968 after having occupied a number of distinguished positions at Oxford (1946-54), Bristol U (1954-64) and U of Southern California 1964-68. Pryce was appointed professor of physics at UBC in 1968. On retirement in 1978 he was made first an honorary professor and then professor emeritus. He is the author of over 75 publications on a wide variety of topics in theoretical physics and astronomy. In 1951 Pryce was elected a fellow of the Royal Society in London. Currently he is serving as a member of the Technical Advisory Committee to Atomic Energy of Canada Ltd on the Nuclear Fuel Waste Management Program.

GEORGE M. VOLKOFF

Psychiatry is the branch of medicine concerned with disorders of the mind (or mental illnesses) and a broad range of other disturbed behaviours, including behavioural and emotional reactions to physical disease, life stresses and personal crises; personality problems; and difficulties with coping, adjustments and achievement.

Psychiatrists are physicians, and in Canada they need to have passed the fellowship examination of the Royal College of Physicians and Surgeons of Canada, or, in Québec, to have obtained the specialist's certificate of the Professional Corporation of Physicians. The examination is preceded by a clinical internship and 4 years of postgraduate training in a recognized training centre. The program seeks to ensure that graduate psychiatrists are capable of independent diagnosis and management of the entire range of psychiatric disorders, are skilled in emergency psychiatry and competent in other long- and short-term psychotherapy as well as the biological therapies. All postgraduate trainees must register with a university and plan their programs in collaboration with the director of the residency program. Of the 4 years of training, 3 must be spent in intensive learning that provides basic clinical experience and theoretical instruction. There must also be at least 2 years of weekly supervision in long-term psychotherapy.

The areas of skill and knowledge which must be covered in basic psychiatric training in Canada include basic patterns of disease; historical trends in psychiatry; normal and abnormal psychosexual development; contributions of biological, psychological and sociocultural sciences; child and adolescent psychiatry; mental retardation; genetics; theories of personality and psychopathology; psychiatric assessment; psychiatric emergencies; psychosomatic medicine; psychosocial reactions to disease; psychiatric syndromes; treatment methods (eg, psychopharmacology, behaviour therapy, psychotherapies, social therapies); community psychiatry; forensic psychiatry; alcoholism and other addictions; psychiatric research and research methods.

Each Canadian medical school now offers postgraduate training programs in psychiatry, and in 1986, 567 psychiatrists were enrolled throughout Canada.

Psychiatry, in common with other mental-health professions, specializes in psychotherapy. In psychotherapy (often confused with psychoanalysis) a professionally trained person establishes a clinical relationship with a patient for the purpose of modifying symptoms, changing behaviour or promoting personality growth. There are many kinds of psychotherapy which differ in their emphasis upon restructuring attitudes, changing emotional responsiveness or modifying behaviour directly (supportive and re-educative psychotherapies are also used to deal with behavioural problems not classified as mental illness, such as vocational, school or marriage problems). Psychoanalysis, a term coined by Freud to characterize his system of free association, dream interpretation of resistance, and transference, is not widely practised in Canada, where few psychiatrists are trained in its methods. Biological treatments, eg, drugs and electroconvulsive therapy, supplement psychotherapeutic approaches to treatment by psychiatrists.

Psychiatric Disorders The overall knowledge about mental illness is greater than usually assumed, although specific measures for diagnosis have not yet been found. In an examination of a patient, the psychiatrist enquires into the personal, medical and family history of the patient and into the history of the complaint; notes the patient's behaviour, speech, mood, perceptions; observes the stream, form and content of thought; and tests memory, awareness of time, place and person, and abstract thinking. Throughout the world the *International Classification of Disease* is used to classify mental disorders (the usually affective disorders).

Organic psychoses are diseases associated with impaired brain tissue function, and are characterized by loss of memory, disorientation, and behaviour changes associated with later life. Most are due to degenerative diseases, eg, Alzheimer's disease. Arteriosclerosis (hardening of the arteries)

causes only a small proportion of dementias. Between 5% and 10% of those over 65 years of age may develop dementia.

Schizophrenia, often a lifetime disease, is characterized by impaired thinking, delusions and hallucinations, limited emotional response, lack of drive and poor judgement, but not, contrary to popular opinion, a "split personality." Many believe that this disorder is to some extent inherited, that it is influenced considerably by social environment, and that biochemical brain disturbances are involved. Drug treatment has markedly improved the outlook for patients.

Depression Affective disorders include bipolar (mania and depression) and unipolar (only depression) depressions. While 10% of the population may suffer from some symptoms of depression, only 0.2% suffer a major affective disorder at any one time. Depressions are episodic, rather than chronic. Bipolar depression, (which includes manic phases) generally begins in the 20s and 30s and affects men and women equally; unipolar disorders, which appear mainly in the 50s and 60s, are more frequent in women. SUICIDE is a considerable risk among severely depressed patients, 15% of whom may die. Treatments include antidepressant drugs, electroconvulsive treatment and lithium carbonate.

Neuroses (anxiety, mild depression, insomnia, loss of appetite, fatigue, irritability, poor concentration and hypochondriasis) are common short-lived disorders and are treated by family doctors with psychotherapy and drugs. Some disorders require consultation with specialists.

Personality Disorders are disorders that are characterized by permanent and limited patterns of behaviour, ineffective functioning and difficulty with interpersonal relationships.

Hospital Services By the 1940s most persons with major mental illnesses were being treated in mental hospitals remote from their communities and other health services. In the early 1950s, 75% of mental-hospital patients had been hospitalized for more than 5 years and were more likely to leave the hospital by dying. Few services were available outside the mental hospitals.

The advent of effective drug treatment for mental illnesses helped patients in hospitals re-enter the community and reduced the need for both long- and short-term hospitalization. Effective drugs for psychiatric treatment were introduced around 1953 and are now widely used in the medical treatment of mental illness by family physicians as well as psychiatrists. There are now 51 psychiatric hospitals in Canada (annual cost of services: over $1 billion), with 34 000 staff. There are about 35 000 patients admitted each year, half of whom remain for less than 1 month. In some provinces over one-third of mental-hospital admissions are involuntary. The use of mental-hospital beds (for patients staying in hospital less than 1 year) ranges from 1 bed per 32 000 population in Nova Scotia to less than 1 per 189 000 population in Saskatchewan.

The rate of "long-stay" (over 1 year) patients in mental hospitals peaked in the 1950s at 286 per 100 000 population, most of whom were elderly or brain damaged. Ontario now has 16 long-stay patients per 100 000 (under age 65). The number of new patients requiring long-term hospitalization is decreasing each year.

Substantial numbers of those still remaining in mental hospitals could be appropriately treated in out-patient, day-treatment and residential settings. Studies of the needs of patients currently hospitalized in BC, Ontario and NB have repeatedly shown that 40-60% need not remain in hospital for treatment, but adequate services and accommodation for these patients in the community do not exist.

In some cities – Victoria, Calgary, Regina, Saskatoon, St Catharines, Windsor and Sherbrooke – mental hospitals are not greatly used. Seriously ill patients, as well as less disturbed patients, are treated in general hospital psychiatric units close to their communities. These are "psychiatric oases" in which psychiatrists based in general hospitals treat most of the patients requiring hospitalization. There are currently more admissions to general hospital psychiatric units than to mental hospitals. The number of general hospital psychiatric units grew from 45 in 1958 to 190 in 1985.

In comparison with other countries, Canada has a relatively high ratio of general hospital psychiatric beds; in 1985 there were 25 general hospital psychiatric beds per 100 000 population, ranging from 19 per 100 000 in NB to 36 per 100 000 in PEI.

Provincial HEALTH POLICY as well as the needs of patients determine the kinds of services provided. The marked regional variation in the use of mental hospitals and general hospital psychiatric units across Canada results mainly from differences in the way services are organized, rather than from clinical differences in patients.

Personnel There are some 2700 psychiatrists in Canada; 73% of them are engaged in some private practice. About 33% completed their medical training outside Canada. The majority of psychiatrists work in the metropolitan centres, while 7% practise in communities with a population of under 50 000.

Some 80% of psychiatrists are men, but this is changing, as 44% of psychiatrists in training are now women. The majority practise general psychiatry, but there is some subspecialization into child psychiatry, geriatric psychiatry, forensic psychiatry, liaison psychiatry, behaviour therapy, family therapy, sexual counselling, psychoanalysis and research. Private psychiatrists render services comprising 3.8% of medicare costs. On the average, full-time psychiatrists spend 29 hours a week (82% of their clinical time) in psychotherapy and continuing care; the remaining 18% of their time is spent in office consultations and hospital visits.

The case load of psychiatrists varies greatly, depending not only on the amount and type of psychotherapy practised, but on the length of treatment. In some Canadian centres, 50% of psychiatrists' time is taken up with long-term patients who comprise one-eighth of the case load. The average private psychiatrist in some provinces sees 250 patients a year.

Within the Canadian health-care system, family physicians, psychiatrists in private practice, community mental-health clinics, psychiatric units in general hospitals and public mental hospitals provide treatment for mental illness. Most patients with mental disorders can be treated by family doctors, without any consultation with a psychiatrist.

During any year, about 10% of adults may see a family physician for psychiatric problems; another 2% may consult a private psychiatrist or mental-health clinic. At least another 10% of the population annually seek help from church, social or psychological services for personal problems or other crises. Between the ages of 18 and 24, over one-third of the population are expected to consult a psychiatrist.

There has been a large-scale increase in the number of psychiatrists in private practice and in the provision of psychotherapy by family physicians. In 1985 the ratio of hours by private psychiatrists varied regionally from 62 to 1118 hours per 1000 Canadians. During 1984-85, 5.4% ($226 million) of Canadian medicare fee-for-service expenditures were for psychotherapy and counselling services by physicians. Some 45% of these services were provided by family physicians. Between 1972 and 1985, the number of psychotherapy and counselling services by family physicians increased from 57 to 140 per 1000 Canadians, and these psychotherapy services now account for 7.7% of the costs of visits to family physician.

Canadian Contributions to Psychiatry Canada has contributed significantly to the field of psychiatry. Canadian mental-health services have been fostered by unique medicare and hospital insurance programs which provide comprehensive universal medical coverage for mental illness. The 1964 Royal Commission on Health Services stated that medicare should not discriminate in coverage for the diagnosis and treatment of psychiatric conditions. Therefore, there is no restriction on the extent or duration of psychiatric treatment by family physicians or by psychiatrists.

Saskatchewan has been an international leader in changing psychiatric services. In this province, psychiatric services are no longer based in mental hospitals, but in regional general hospital psychiatric units. Comprehensive community care systems enable patients to complete treatment near their homes, and they also promote follow-up and continuity of care. Canada has also been a leader in the development of general hospital psychiatric units and in the development of day and night hospitals. The concept of partial hospitalization for persons not requiring 24-hour hospital care, but requiring daily contact, supervision or medication, originated in Montréal.

The Canadian Mental Health Association's 1963 publication *More for the Mind* emphasized the need for a number of changes: integration of mental-health services within general health services; regionalization; decentralization of psychiatric services from the provincial government to regional agencies; and co-ordination of psychiatric services for patients through all phases of their illness. These basic principles are reflected in the goals advocated in every subsequent review of psychiatric services in Canada.

Major contributions were made to the development of psychiatry by D.E. Cameron (a leader in psychiatric research in Canada who was instrumental in promoting the development of day hospitals); F.C.R. Chalke (first editor of the *Canadian Psychiatric Association Journal*); G.B. CHISHOLM (former director-general of medical services of the Canadian Army in WWII and first director-general of the World Health Organization); C.B. Farrar (founder of the first Canadian postgraduate training program in Canada, former head of the department of psychiatry at U of T and editor of the *American Journal of Psychiatry* for 34 years); C.M. HINCKS (founder of the Canadian National Committee for Mental Hygiene, which is now the Canadian Mental Health Association, and director of both the Canadian and US committees for Mental Hygiene in the 1930s); R.O. Jones (initiated the first university-based training program for psychiatry); D.C. Meyers (founder of the first general hospital psychiatric unit in Canada in 1906); and A.B. Stokes (former chairman of the department of psychiatry at U of T who helped in the development of the Clarke Institute of Psychiatry). Textbooks on psychiatry by Canadians include the 1980 publication *A Method of Psychiatry*, and the 1981 publications *Précis pratique en psychiatrie* and *Psychiatrie clinique: approche contemporaire*.

Problems and Prospects Despite the advances made by psychiatry, there is still much dissatisfaction with psychiatric services. Nearly every province, in reviewing its mental-health services

since the late 1970s, has found that the goals described by the Canadian Mental Health Association 20 years ago have not been met. Unfortunately, adequate treatment as early and as continuously as possible, and with as little dislocation and as much social re-establishment as possible, is not yet available. The increase of psychiatric staff, facilities and programs is offset by an expanding demand for additional psychiatric services. Increasingly, many psychiatrists have changed their role, spending less time as consultants to other physicians and assuming more responsibility for the primary care of patients with mental illness, particularly those persons with "relative" as opposed to "absolute" need, ie, persons with neuroses and adjustment reactions that are less disabling, for whom working or social capacity is maintained and for whom psychotherapy or social treatment could be provided by family physicians or by individuals in specialized nonmedical mental health disciplines. However, the psychiatric treatment and social support of patients with long-term schizophrenic and major depressive disorders is still inadequate. *See also* MENTAL HEALTH. ALEX RICHMAN

Reading: J.S. Tyhurst et al, *More for the Mind* (1963); J. Marshall, *Madness: An Indictment of the Mental Health Care System in Ontario* (1982).

Psychology [Gk, *psyche* "spirit" and *logos* "study"], literally "the study of the spirit or soul." The term seems to have been used for the first time by Melanchthon in the 16th century. Originally, the subject was part of PHILOSOPHY and its roots can be traced to antiquity. Sir Francis Galton (1822-1911), a half cousin of Charles Darwin, is generally acknowledged as the founder of individual psychology as a branch of science, but whether it should be classified as a biological or social science was a contentious issue among scholars until 1960, after which time it was increasingly described as a behavioural science, ie, the science of the behaviour of organisms. It is considered a science because it seems to constitute, by means of the scientific method, a body of organized knowledge, the purpose of which is to describe, explain, predict and in some cases influence behaviour. "Behaviour" includes conduct and internal processes (thoughts, emotional reactions, feelings, etc), that may be inferred from external actions.

Psychology is an applied science because it attempts to solve concrete problems. Because it is so inclusive, it encompasses many specialities. These include experimental psychology, characterized by laboratory experiments in the investigation of areas such as sensation and perception, learning and memory; physiological psychology, the study of the physical basis of behaviour, particularly how the brain and the rest of the nervous system (which is affected by a wide variety of factors, eg, heredity, diet, drugs, etc) function in activities perceived as characteristic of man and other animals; developmental psychology, the study of factors influencing the development of behaviour from infancy to old age (see GERONTOLOGY); social psychology, which studies the relations between the group and the individual; clinical psychology, which is concerned primarily with the diagnosis and treatment of emotional disorders; counselling psychology, which, although similar to clinical psychology, is primarily concerned with helping emotionally balanced individuals having difficulty deciding vocational and educational goals, etc; educational psychology, concerned with behavioural problems in school; industrial psychology, the study of human factors in industry and organization; personality psychology, the study of personality traits; and cognitive psychology, the study of the higher mental processes, eg, processes of perception,

language, intelligence, imagery and creativity.

It is generally believed that psychology belongs to the family of behavioural sciences which includes SOCIOLOGY, ANTHROPOLOGY, etc, but in its research and application it maintains close ties with BIOLOGY and the health sciences.

Psychology in Canada The development of psychology in Canada paralleled that in Europe and the US. Courses were taught during the first half of the 19th century in moral and mental philosophy. Thomas MCCULLOCH apparently taught the first psychology course in eastern Canada in 1838 at Dalhousie University, but the field did not really grow until the last half of the 19th century. In 1855, William LYALL, who taught in Halifax, wrote the first basic psychology text to be published in Canada.

In 1879 Wundt opened the first psychology laboratory in Leipzig, and psychology distinguished itself from philosophy and became a science. Ten years later one of Wundt's students, James Mark Baldwin, who taught in Toronto, founded the first psychology laboratory in Canada. In the 1920s, independent departments of psychology began to appear: one at McGill, directed by W.D. Tait, and one at Toronto, led by E.A. Bott. After 1940, other departments of psychology began to separate from philosophy and take on independent stature. The same process occurred somewhat later in western Canada. J.M. McEachran, who in 1909 became professor of philosophy at U of Alberta, may be called the first psychologist in a western university. After that, teaching and research in psychology developed in the other universities, but once again it was not until the 1940s that the psychology departments became autonomous and were truly separated from philosophy.

Although psychology in the francophone universities followed a similar path, it was the result of different influences. The anglophone universities based their view of man on a mixture of Scottish realism and British idealism, but the francophone universities were dominated by Catholic Thomist philosophy. Of the first francophone psychology departments, one was founded in 1941 in Ottawa by R.H. Shevenel and the other in 1942 in Montréal by N. Mailloux. These departments retained a Roman Catholic orientation for some time and stressed clinical and applied research. Basic research began to develop at the end of the 1950s and is today as well developed as that of the anglophone universities. Psychology has developed very rapidly in Canada in the last 2 decades and departments of psychology now exist in most Canadian universities.

Psychology and Its Applications Parallel with its development as an academic discipline, psychology, since the beginning of the 20th century and especially since the 1950s, has grown dramatically as an applied science. At the beginning of the century, A. Binet in France developed the first intelligence test. The development in the US of tests to select soldiers during WWI established psychology's credibility as a science with practical applications. Today, psychology is applied in every field of human activity.

Contrary to widespread belief, psychologists do not work exclusively with people suffering from mental illness or from serious problems of adaptation. Generally, psychologists apply their knowledge to solve or prevent behavioural, cognitive and affective problems. For example, some psychologists concentrate on the design of control panels for sophisticated equipment to ensure machines are well adapted to the characteristics of their users; some are concerned with problems of adaptation in school, the work place, etc, and, with the people involved, try to establish organizational structures and ways of interaction that will facilitate study or work; others try to alter behaviours and life-styles that cause or accompany the development of psychosomatic problems, eg, ulcers and allergies.

Scientific and Professional Associations Like many other disciplines in Canada, psychology owes much of its development and vitality to various scientific and professional associations. In Canada the most influential, the Canadian Psychological Association, was established in 1939 to bring Canadian psychologists together, a role previously filled by the American Psychological Association, founded in 1892 as a continental organization. The imminence of a war in which Canada was likely to be involved much sooner than the US sparked the establishment of the Canadian organization. During WWII, the CPA was instrumental in legitimizing psychology as an applied science. In 1941 the NATIONAL RESEARCH COUNCIL was the first federal organization to give a research grant in psychology for one of a long series of projects undertaken by the CPA. With its annual conference, its various study committees, its political lobbying and its 3 publications, *The Canadian Journal of Psychology, The Canadian Journal of Behavioural Science* and *Canadian Psychology,* the CPA is still the most important of all national organizations of psychologists.

Provincial associations, however, also play an important role. Under the Canadian Constitution the provinces are responsible for the standards of accreditation and practice in the professions. One or more associations exist in each province. The 2 oldest, the BC Psychological Association, established 1938, and the Association de psychologie du Québec, established 1944 and since transformed into the Corporation professionnelle des psychologues du Québec, each publishes one or more scientific or professional journals.

LUC GRANGER

Ptarmigan are distinguished from other members of the GROUSE subfamily by their all-white wings. Like other grouse, they are well adapted to cold environments, eg, nostrils are hidden by feathers, body feathers have a long, downy aftershaft that increases insulation, and toes are feathered. Ptarmigan are the only birds with snow-white winter plumage. Summer plumage is mottled brown. Willow ptarmigan (*Lagopus lagopus*) and rock ptarmigan (*L. mutus*) are the only grouse native to both Old and New Worlds. Willow ptarmigan has circumpolar distribution. In Canada, it occupies higher western mountain elevations and tundra habitats as far N as Melville I. Rock ptarmigan, the most northern grouse, prefer habitats higher and drier than those of willow ptarmigan. Both are strong fliers but rock ptarmigan are more migratory, moving from high latitudes to escape the dark arctic winter. White-tailed ptarmigan (*L. leucurus*), the smallest grouse, lacks the black tail common to the other 2. It is found only in N America, occupying windswept upper slopes of the western mountains year-round. Its high-pitched, cackling scream contrasts with guttural calls of the others. All ptarmigan nest on the ground, laying 6-10 cryptically marked eggs. Incubation is by females; males frequently abandon their territories at this time. Male willow ptarmigan usually remain and may assist in raising chicks, a trait not found in most grouse. Ptarmigan are important GAME BIRDS. *See also* ANIMALS IN WINTER.

S.D. MACDONALD

Public Administration has no generally accepted definition. The scope of the subject is so great and so debatable that it is easier to explain than define. Public administration is both a field of study, or a discipline, and a field of practice, or an occupation. There is much disagreement about whether the study of public administration can properly be called a discipline, largely because it is often viewed as a subfield of 2 other disciplines — POLITICAL SCIENCE and administrative science (or administration).

In Canada the study of public administration has evolved primarily as a subfield of political science. Knowledge of the machinery of government and of the political and legal environment in which public administrators work is essential to understanding the political system. Also, public administrators play an important role by providing policy advice to elected politicians and by active involvement in the making, enforcement and adjudication of laws and regulations. As a subfield of administrative science, public administration is part of the generic process of administration. The broad field of administration is divided into public, business, hospital, educational and other forms of administration. The similarities between these forms of administration are considered to be greater than their differences. There is, however, increasing recognition of public administration as a separate field of study, which is reflected in the creation within universities of schools of public administration which take a policy-management approach combining elements of the 2 earlier approaches with an examination of PUBLIC POLICY. Public administration is taught as an interdisciplinary subject by political scientists, economists, sociologists and others.

No single date or event clearly marks the beginning of the study of public administration in Canada. The multivolume work CANADA AND ITS PROVINCES (1913-17) by A. Shortt and A.G. Doughty covered the practice of public administration, and several books written by R. MacGregor DAWSON between 1919 and 1933 made an enduring contribution to the field. The first degree program in public administration was established at Dalhousie U by Luther Richter and R.A. Mackay in 1936. Carleton College (now Carleton U) had its first graduates in 1946, and in 1952 founded its School of Public Administration. There are now schools or faculties of public administration at Dalhousie, UQAM, U of Ottawa, Carleton, Queen's, Scarborough Coll (U of T), York, Brock, U of Manitoba and U of Winnipeg (combined), U of Regina, U of Alberta and U of Victoria. Beginning in the early 1950s, significant contributions to the literature on Canadian public administration were made by such prominent scholars as Roch Bolduc, J.E. HODGETTS, J.R. Mallory, D.C. Rowat and Malcolm Taylor.

Public administration is a relatively new but vigorous and important field of study. The increasing number of people who study it are — or would like to be — employed by a federal, provincial or municipal government. Even public employees who are trained in law, engineering, medicine, etc, often study public administration to help them understand and perform management tasks. Job opportunities exist in regular government departments and in government agencies, boards and commissions. If the scope of public administration is broadly defined, it also includes such occupational categories as hospital and educational administration. Among the many fields of work in public administration are the broad areas of personnel management, financial management, regulation and policy analysis. The major institution or society in the field of public administration is the Institute of Public Administration of Canada, a national organization and a learned society of public employees from all levels of government and university teachers. It sponsors seminars, conferences and publications, including the journal *Canadian Public Administration*.

KENNETH KERNAGHAN

Reading: Kenneth Kernaghan and D. Siegel, eds, *Public Administration in Canada: A Text* (1987).

Public Archives of Canada, *see* NATIONAL ARCHIVES OF CANADA.

Public Art is commissioned for a specific public space by an individual or a group. Parks, government buildings, banks, schools, churches, hotels, stations, head offices and restaurants are some of the settings for displaying immobile works, with the composition, dimensions and proportions blending into and gaining meaning from the surroundings. The theme of the particular artwork may relate to the function of the building or environment it enhances. Public art is often produced for celebrations or propaganda, commemorative and educational purposes. The decorative function may be coupled with a political, social or religious message that represents the ideology of the group or individual who commissioned it.

Among native people in N America many tribes produced an elaborate public art, particularly in the form of wood carvings. This art served both a social and ritual function (*see* INDIAN ART; INUIT ART; NORTHWEST COAST INDIAN ART).

During the French regime the most common form of public art was SCULPTURE. Paintings, mostly imported, were small and adaptable to different settings, and only Frère LUC designed paintings that blended with the architecture of the retables. In 1686 Intendant Bochart de Champigny had the bronze bust of Louis XIV erected in Place Royale, Québec City. Intersections were decorated with statues of saints in niches of corner buildings, and these ornaments helped to identify particular streets. Monumental sculptures, mostly carved in wood, graced the facades of churches, such as Ste-Famille (Île d'Orléans) or Cap-Santé (Portneuf), and the retables on the main altar were rich in gilded statues, bas-reliefs and paintings. One of the most beautiful examples, executed by Pierre-Noël LEVASSEUR and members of his workshop, is found in the Ursulines' Chapel in Québec City. In the 18th and 19th centuries sculptors expanded into the field of naval sculpture and made the names of Québec and Maritime shipyards and shipowners known throughout the Atlantic world. The tradition of religious and naval sculpture was maintained during the 19th century by members of the BAILLAIRGÉ family in Québec and by the workshops of QUÉVILLON and his competitors in the Montréal region.

These early examples were tied to French cultural traditions and marked the presence of a royal and Catholic power. Changes brought about as a result of the Conquest were mainly iconographic. The new political power was less demonstrative, and GOVERNMENT BUILDINGS were surmounted by British arms. The major example of this change in political power is a stone column dominating the city of Montréal, constructed in 1808 to celebrate Admiral Nelson's victory at Trafalgar (1805). In 1828 a stone obelisk was dedicated in Québec City to the memory of Generals Montcalm and Wolfe. It became the first of similar austere MONUMENTS in Canada commemorating valour in death.

The flourishing economy, growing population and arrival of itinerant immigrant artists in the colony led to a proliferation of public artworks. In the 19th century, ephemerals were popular, works such as triumphal arches, allegorical chariots and posters (*see* PAINTING). Artists Louis Dulongpré, Joseph LÉGARÉ and, later, Alfred PELLAN all produced theatre sets.

Mural painting was inspired originally by foreign artists, chiefly from Italy and Germany. The earliest documented example of a painted décor, designed as a whole and created on site in collaboration with the architect, were the columns and vault of Notre-Dame in Montréal in the years following 1828. In 1844, reflecting a growing secularization in art in Canada, Andrew Morris produced the allegories of Commerce and Agriculture for Montréal's legislative building. In Europe the Nazarenes and pre-Raphaelites encouraged public art, an influence absorbed by the Canadian Catholic clergy during their frequent trips abroad. Immigrant artists such as Lamprecht at St Romuald Church, the Mulleir brothers at Gésu in Montréal and Luigi Cappello in the Montréal region left evidence of their ability to create an entire iconographic program in proportion to the ARCHITECTURE for which it was designed. In sculpture, Italian artists introduced to Canada a taste for elaborate funeral stelae and monuments, often decorated in relief bronze or figures in the round. The Montréal firm of Carli and Petrucci was a leader in the eastern Canadian market at the end of the 19th century.

Gradually, Canadian artists took over the market for mural painting as major programs for commemorative monuments encouraged the development of their careers. A rich iconographic decoration was planned for the façade of the Québec legislative building, though work was delayed until 1890, when Louis-Philippe HÉBERT produced sculptures of Frontenac, Elgin, Salabery, Wolfe, Montcalm, Lévis and the groups *Halte dans la forêt* and *Pêche au nigog*. Napoléon BOURASSA, who completed his training in Italy and France, was the pioneer Canadian muralist, the architect and decorator of Notre-Dame-de-Lourdes in 1883 and founder of a studio where Hébert and many mural painters were trained. The decoration by 5 young artists of the Sacré-Coeur Chapel in Notre-Dame in Montréal marked the domination by Canadian artists of mural art. Charles HUOT and Ozias LEDUC continued well into the 20th century to develop Canadian themes directly related to the setting. With political evolution came a greater awareness of history, and local historical societies, historians and genealogists multiplied. The number of historical figures and events that had to be marked increased rapidly and fathers of the new Canadian nation such as George-Étienne Cartier and John A. Macdonald were celebrated in many monuments (*see* Robert HARRIS). In Toronto in 1899 George A. REID designed a series for the lobby of the new City Hall depicting the establishment of settlements in Upper Canada. Although this project was not completed, he left several important murals in Toronto, among them those of the Earlscourt Library and the auditorium of Jarvis Collegiate Institute. Like most mural artists in Canada at that time, Reid did not use the fresco technique, but mounted the painted canvas on the wall. In Europe and the US, at the turn of the century, vast construction projects featuring sculpture monuments, murals, mosaics and stained-glass windows were popular. In 1898 the Toronto Guild of Civic Art was established and, after 1895, the Royal Canadian Academy of Arts sometimes devoted a room during its annual expositions to mural painting.

As a relatively peaceful country, Canada had few war memorials. The WAR OF 1812 was commemorated by a heroic statue of Isaac BROCK placed atop a tall classical column at Queenston Heights, Ont. The SOUTH AFRICAN WAR was commemorated by George W. Hill in Montréal (Lord Strathcona Memorial) and W.S. Allward in Toronto. After 1918, and again after 1945, private donations and public funds provided considerable revenues for artisan-founders and sculptors. Cities and public buildings were decorated with commemorative plaques, busts, standing figures, or even depictions of soldiers in combat, generally surmounted by an allegory of Victory, such as the

eloquent monument in Confederation Square in Ottawa. Fountains and monuments celebrating historical or contemporary figures provided subjects for beautiful works by artists such as E.O. Hahn, Alfred LALIBERTÉ and Elizabeth WYN WOOD. The architect/sculptor John M. LYLE integrated many allegorical reliefs based on Canadian iconography into his buildings.

The industrial growth that Canada experienced during WWI resulted in the construction of numerous public buildings by the private sector (head offices, hotels, banks), many of which included murals. Some artists used this technique only sporadically (Charles COMFORT, Arthur LISMER), but others such as Gustav Hahn, Guido Nincheri or Frederick Challener made it the focal point of their career. In 1923 and 1924 the RCA organized 2 competitions in mural art. In 1924 a group of 10 artists was commissioned to decorate St Anne's Church in Toronto.

This trend toward decorating large surfaces was encouraged by the art schools and a number of striking works were produced before and after the Depression, though, unlike the US, Canada had no public art projects to provide work for artists. Among the rare examples of these years was the construction and decoration of the Chalet du Mont-Royal, noteworthy for the effort to renew an historical iconography based on facts, rather than myths.

The applied art professions evolved slowly in Canada. The main development came after 1960, and glazing, ceramics, weaving and glassmaking are now represented in public art. Many auditoria, exhibition centres, university campuses and airports are integrating the arts with architecture in new ways. Weavers such as Mariette Rousseau-Vermette and Micheline BEAUCHEMIN, respectively, made stage curtains for the Place des Arts in Montréal and the National Arts Centre in Ottawa. Jordi Bonet produced ceramic and bronze murals and doors for many theatres and public places, and encircled the main hall of the Grand Théâtre in Québec City with a relief that was as controversial as it was inspired.

EXPO 67 in Montréal, the sad fate of "Corridart" during the 1976 Olympic Games, and the construction and enlarging of the Montréal and Toronto subway systems all provided occasions for the production of public artworks. Collaborations between architects, engineers and artists helped integrate light and movement in these settings, illustrating the new relationships between man and his environment. Public art, however, is often seen as mere decoration. The federal government, paralysed in its role as commissioning or buying agent by its elaborate administrative committees, has lost sight of the relationships between art and public space. In this respect the commissions for the major airports and acquisitions for the national capital are nothing but a very sad apogee. One example of a successful collaboration between public art and architecture, in breadth, scope and sensitivity, is the work of sculptor Anne KAHANE at the Canadian Embassy at Islamabad, Pakistan.

In an effort to revitalize, support and sometimes disguise urban space, a "city walls" campaign was begun by many communities in the early 1970s. Supported by private business and government assistance projects, these murals were of uneven quality and were intended only as ephemera. The art form of installations seldom invades public space. Unfortunately, their short lifespan does not allow them to make an impact, although they can be seen as the most critical and stimulating contemporary production – questioning the meaning of the concept of public art.

The concept of public art is often limited to an invitation to decorate a building just prior to its opening. A few provinces legislate that part of the

budget for the construction of public buildings is to be assigned to the integration of works of art, and architects and artists co-operate from the start of the project. The dominant concept in large corporations is all too often that of commissioning a well-known artist to produce a "decorative" work that will impress visitors as soon as they enter the vestibule, and perhaps also the boardroom. Even if architects give all their attention to the treatment of space, it is up to the artists, in co-operation with them, to provide the elements that, fused with the architecture, help users identify with the space. LAURIER LACROIX

Public Debt Governments finance their expenditures by taxing and borrowing. They sometimes raise money from the public or from institutions by selling securities, eg, bonds. The accumulated total of all such government liability is called the "public debt." The interest and principal on the portion of public debt held by nonresidents must usually be paid in foreign currencies, which must be earned and which represent debits on Canada's BALANCE OF PAYMENTS. Long-term debt, eg, that due in 10 years or more, is usually in the form of bonds; short-term debt indicates a maturity date of less than 5 years. Direct obligations comprise securities issued by government itself; contingent obligations comprise securities issued by government corporations, eg, funds for corporations such as the CNR and Ontario Hydro are raised by bonds issued by them and guaranteed by the respective governments.

In 1867 Canada's debt was $94 million and it grew slowly until 1915. WWI pushed the figure to $2.4 billion, it rose to $5 billion during the Great Depression and to $18 billion by the end of WWII. From 1977 to 1986 the net federal debt in the public accounts increased from $37.8 to $233.4 billion. As a proportion of Gross Domestic Product (GDP) the "debt ratio" grew from 19.7% to 50.6% between 1977 and 1986. This "net debt" is the difference between gross debt (unmatured government bonds, bills, notes and other liabilities) and certain recorded financial assets of the federal government, eg, cash, investments and loans. Basically, changes in net debt equal budgetary deficits or surpluses, and the federal government's total net debt at any time therefore equals its accumulated overall deficit since Confederation. The federal government's debt can also be measured as the difference between its liabilities to other sectors of the economy and its financial assets (claims on those sectors); net federal liabilities measured in this way equalled only $186 billion (1986), compared to $233.4 billion on the public accounts basis. The difference of $47 billion was "owed" to the federal government by itself. On the same basis, the debt of provincial and local governments in 1982 was about $23 billion, most of which will finance capital expenditures expected to benefit future generations who will bear much capital outlay cost in debt service charges.

However, although the public debt has increased as a proportion of GDP, it is about the same size as it was in the 1930s and smaller than in the mid-1940s because of the financing of the war effort. In 1986 net federal debt (public accounts basis) was 50.6% of GDP compared to 50.6% in 1932 and 106.6% in 1947, and inflation has lessened the real value of the outstanding debt (by over $6 billion in 1980), although this is not reflected in government accounting. Nevertheless the management of the federal debt, an important aspect of MONETARY POLICY, has become more difficult in recent years, mainly because the average life of government debt instruments has shortened so that the government constantly has to roll over its debt through campaigns, the issuing of new treasury bills, etc. Although, for all governments to-

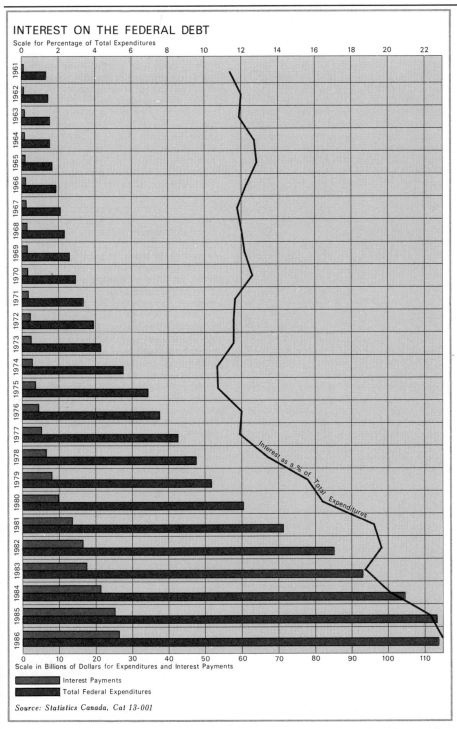

INTEREST ON THE FEDERAL DEBT

Scale for Percentage of Total Expenditures
0 2 4 6 8 10 12 14 16 18 20 22

Interest as a % of Total Expenditures

0 10 20 30 40 50 60 70 80 90 100 110
Scale in Billions of Dollars for Expenditures and Interest Payments

Interest Payments

Total Federal Expenditures

Source: Statistics Canada, Cat 13-001

In the 1970s, 79% of the increase in public expenditure was attributable to transfers and only 21% to expenditures on goods and services, and by 1985 transfer expenditures accounted for over 52% of all government spending.

The relative prices of the goods and services that government purchases must also be taken into account. In real terms, the relative expansion of government spending as a proportion of GDP from 1947 to 1985 was 56%, not 70%. Since 1970 the proportion of real goods and services produced in the economy that is used by the government sector in the course of its activities has actually declined by about 10%. In contrast, transfer payments in real terms have increased slightly during this period, largely owing to a significant liberalization of the family allowance and unemployment insurance.

Fifty percent of the postwar increase in government expenditure is accounted for by expenditures on health, education and welfare. Since 1970 government expenditures on education actually declined in relation to GDP, but in the 1960s public-health spending rose substantially, largely in substitution for private expenditures, however, since total health expenditures in relation to GDP changed relatively little. In the 1970s only expenditures on social welfare, mainly in the form of large cash-transfer programs, continued to expand significantly until the end of the decade.

Provincial and local governments are responsible for almost all educational and health expenditure. Over the postwar period the federal government expenditures accounted for only 9% of the total growth in government expenditures, compared to 86% for the provincial-local sector (including hospitals). The remaining 5% is accounted for by the CANADA PENSION PLAN and the separate, but closely related, QUÉBEC PENSION PLAN. In 1985 the federal government was responsible for only 42% of total government expenditures (excluding intergovernmental transfers) – a proportion that has changed little since the mid-1960s.

The decline in federal defence spending freed resources that financed the expanding provincial-local health and education sectors. At the same time, programs such as OLD AGE PENSION, FAMILY ALLOWANCES and UNEMPLOYMENT INSURANCE, which were financed by a considerable increase in taxes, in the end appear to have redistributed income among Canadians only slightly because so many of the taxes were paid by the same broad groups that received the transfers. *See also* PUBLIC FINANCE.   R.M. BIRD

Public Finance, both a name for government finance – the way governments secure and manage their revenues – and the name of a branch of ECONOMICS that studies the public sector of the economy. Government finances its expenditures through TAXATION, the borrowing of funds by the public sector (*see* PUBLIC DEBT) and the printing of money (*see* MONETARY POLICY). This article is concerned with the pattern and role of government expenditures.

The relative importance of government expenditures in the Canadian economy has risen almost continuously over the past 50 years, from 10% of the Gross Domestic Product (GDP) in the late 1920s to 47.3% of GDP in 1982 and 48.2% in 1985. This rise has reflected a gradual trend which was interrupted by WWII when government expenditures reached a peak of 45% of GDP, largely because of the war effort. Of the 1985 percentage, 45.3% can be accounted for by federal government expenditures, 38.2% by provincial governments and 16.4% by local governments.

gether, real public debt has been retired since 1979, freeing resources for other purposes, constant activity in the financial markets has created concern that private borrowers will be crowded out. Also, because of shorter maturities of government debt, debt service charges are more vulnerable to interest rate variations. The average rate of interest on unmatured debt rose from 7.5% in 1977 to 10.7% in 1986; consequently interest on the public debt charges rose to $26.4 billion by 1986, or about 23% of total federal expenditures, compared to only 11% in 1977, exacerbating the federal deficit problem. From one viewpoint, the substantial part of the deficit attributable to the higher debt charges induced by INFLATION and the resulting high interest rates is simply a transfer to compensate bondholders for the loss in the real value of their bonds, but their loss is government gain, roughly offsetting the higher debt costs.

From another viewpoint, deficits do not reflect high inflation-related interest rates, but rather cause both inflation and high interest rates.
R.M. BIRD

Public Expenditure refers to government spending. From an average of 23% of Gross Domestic Product (GDP), 1947-51, total government expenditure rose to 48.2% of GDP, in 1985. Over the 1947-85 period as a whole, total government expenditures as measured in the national accounts (a comprehensive series of statistics) rose 96% faster than GDP to its peak in 1985. For many economic purposes, however, the total size of government expenditures is less significant than its components. The division between transfer expenditures, which shift private income from one person to another, and exhaustive expenditures, which use goods and services for government activities proper, is particularly important.

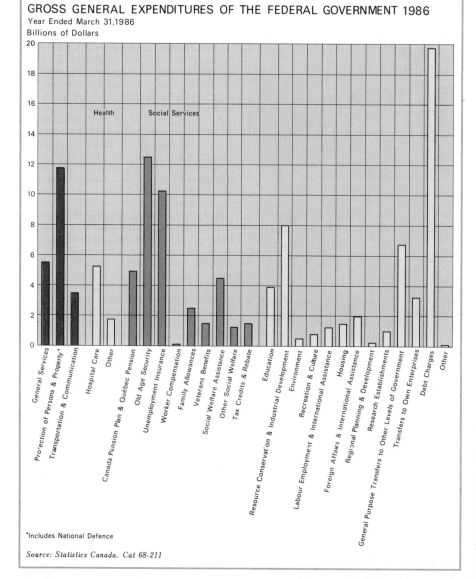

GROSS GENERAL EXPENDITURES OF THE FEDERAL GOVERNMENT 1986
Year Ended March 31, 1986
Billions of Dollars

*Includes National Defence

Source: Statistics Canada, Cat 68-211

Total government expenditures are of 2 fundamentally different types – those on goods and services, and those on TRANSFER PAYMENTS. Government expenditures on goods and services represent the diversion of productive resources from the private sector to governments (only these expenditures are included in the GDP), while transfer payments financed by taxes represent the shift of purchasing power from one group of individuals to another. Upper level governments also transfer some of their revenues to lower levels to assist them in meeting their financial responsibilities (*see* INTERGOVERNMENTAL FINANCE).

In 1982 expenditures by all levels of government on goods and services was 24.7% of GDP (a figure similar to that of 1970 but somewhat higher than the early postwar figure of 14%) of which the federal government was responsible for only 5.7 percentage points, the remainder being divided roughly equally between provinces and municipal governments, and largely comprising expenditures for education and health. Government expenditure on transfers (about 20% of GDP) accounted during the 1970s for roughly 80% of the growth in government expenditures. In 1970 only 13% of GDP comprised transfer payments; in 1985 the proportion was over 20%. This rapid growth resulted primarily from the expansion of FAMILY ALLOWANCE and UNEMPLOYMENT INSURANCE payments.

Rationale for Government Expenditures In mixed economies such as Canada's, the private sector is generally viewed as the "engine of growth" and is left to undertake those activities for which its profit-oriented behaviour is theoretically suited. The public sector is made responsible for tasks the value of which it is felt should not be judged solely on the basis of whether they will generate profit. Economists usually identify 5 different components which comprise the rationale for public-sector intervention into the markets of the economy, but the rationale for public expenditures is not always economic in nature.

Provision of Public Goods The goods produced and sold by the private sector are called "private goods" (eg, food, clothing, shelter). "Public goods" by their very nature (eg, defence, general government, justice, external affairs, police protection, penal services, communications) provide services to many or all households simultaneously. These goods could not be provided by markets, so they must be provided collectively. Some are provided by the federal government, others by provincial or local governments.

Externalities Another phenomenon, closely related to public goods, occurs when activities undertaken by consumers or producers generate significant benefits, or "externalities," to those other than themselves. Although the undertaking of such activities could be left to private markets,

those undertaking them would lack the incentive to purchase the amounts that would be warranted by the social benefit generated by their consumption or production. For example, the benefit to an individual of purchasing an inoculation against a communicable disease would be significantly less than the benefit to society as a whole; the individual benefits from his or her own safety from the disease, while others in society benefit from the reduction in the risk that the person will spread the disease. Similarly, research activities or manpower training by firms can generate benefits (knowledge, a trained work force) that benefit firms other than those bearing the cost. Individuals or firms acting out of self-interest would not have an incentive to acquire the socially desirable amount or might not procure it at all, which is one reason children are forced by regulation to obtain immunization before they can go to school.

Governments encourage the production and consumption of goods generating externalities in 2 ways. On the one hand, the private sector may be left to undertake these activities while being encouraged by subsidies (or tax concessions) to involve itself more fully than it would otherwise choose to do. For example, financial assistance is provided to encourage INDUSTRIAL RESEARCH AND DEVELOPMENT, manpower training and regional development. On the other hand, the government may simply assume responsibility for the provision of such goods, for example, certain health services and education at all levels. There is some dispute over whether the public provision of such goods is always appropriate.

Natural Monopolies Some goods, eg, those provided by UTILITIES and by the transportation or communications industries, can be provided more cheaply by one or a few large firms rather than by several competing small firms. However, if the private sector were allotted sole responsibility for the provision of these goods according to the criterion of profitability, prices could be set too high and outputs too low, because no effective competition would exist to induce firms to provide services to consumers at the lowest possible price. In response to these "natural monopolies," governments may create public or CROWN CORPORATIONS, eg, Air Canada, the CBC and the CNR (*see* PUBLIC OWNERSHIP). Alternatively, they may choose to leave the enterprises in private hands but regulate the prices they may charge. (*see* ECONOMIC REGULATION).

Income Redistribution Governments also transfer incomes among persons, partly because the distribution of income would be far more unequal if it were determined solely by the operation of markets in the private sector. Income is redistributed partly through the tax structure, especially the progressive income tax, and partly through transfers to low-income earners. These transfers can include welfare schemes operated by provincial and local governments (but financed 50% by the federal government under the Canada Assistance Plan; *see* PROVINCIAL GOVERNMENT), family-allowance payments by the federal government, and income-related pension payments by federal and provincial governments; but they can also include transfers that incidentally redistribute income, having been designed primarily for other reasons.

Social Insurance Some transfer payments are designed to supplement an individual's income at times of abnormally low earnings or abnormally high expenditures and therefore act as a sort of insurance. Unemployment insurance represents income transfers made by the federal government to persons temporarily out of work; WORKERS' COMPENSATION payments are made by provincial governments to those who have ceased working because of injury incurred on the job; public PENSION payments, including the universal payments by the federal government to all persons over the age of 65 and payments made by the federal government to the retired and disabled under the contributory CANADA PENSION PLAN or QUÉBEC PENSION PLAN, are transfers to persons who have lost income because of retirement. These pension payments are partly related to past earnings and contributions and are made to contributors and to their surviving dependents. The federal government also makes transfers to war veterans. Another type of social insurance covers medical care and hospitalization; payments to cover both are made on behalf of all residents and are financed jointly by the federal and provincial governments. Governments also operate various forms of insurance in the agricultural sector to assist farmers whose incomes have fallen temporarily due to market conditions.

The CONSTITUTION ACT, 1867, outlines the expenditure responsibilities of the federal and provincial governments. Generally, expenditures for services which are national in scope (eg, defence, trade and commerce, external affairs, the money and banking system, criminal law, penitentiaries, postal service, fisheries, unemployment insurance, and a number of lesser matters which tend to affect residents in more than one province) are designated as federal responsibilities, while those primarily affecting residents within a province are allocated to the provinces. In turn the provinces themselves delegate certain responsibilities of a purely local nature to the municipalities within their jurisdiction.

The provincial governments' most significant spending responsibilities are health, education and welfare (see PROVINCIAL GOVERNMENT). The provinces administer the system of hospitals and health care; provide primary, secondary and post-secondary education; and administer social programs, including the welfare and social services provided under the Canada Assistance Plan, a program jointly financed by the federal and provincial governments. Provinces are also responsible for natural resources within their boundaries, the administration of justice, property and civil rights, local works and transportation, municipalities and other matters of a purely provincial or local nature.

The provinces tend to delegate to the municipalities responsibility for providing local services such as garbage pickup, fire and police protection, water and sewage, maintenance of local streets and recreational facilities. The municipalities also help in the local administration of provincial programs such as primary and secondary education, welfare assistance and hospitals (see LOCAL GOVERNMENT).

Finally, there are areas, such as agriculture and immigration, in which both the federal and provincial governments may exercise concurrent power. One other important area of joint responsibility is that of OLD AGE PENSIONS. A constitutional amendment in 1951 permitted the federal government to enact old age pension legislation, provided it did not affect the operation of provincial old-age pension legislation.

All of these designated responsibilities of the federal and provincial governments give rise to government expenditures. The largest categories are social services, education and health, which together comprise almost 50% of total government expenditures. The majority of social service expenditures are made by the federal government, of which old age security and unemployment-insurance transfer payments comprise over 50%. Sizable amounts are also accounted for by the Canada Pension Plan, family allowances and the Canada Assistance Plan.

Much of the provincial and local government social-service expenditures result from welfare programs jointly funded by federal and provincial governments under the Canada Assistance Plan. Education is a major responsibility of the provincial and local governments; they finance all primary, secondary and post-secondary education, although the latter has been partly financed by federal-provincial transfers. Again, health expenditures are the responsibility of the provincial government, but the financing of medical and hospital insurance is assisted by federal government transfers. The federal government is also responsible for large interest payments on the national debt, which makes up 23.2% of federal expenditure (see PUBLIC DEBT). Provincial and local governments also spend a considerable amount (11.4% of expenditures in 1986) on interest payments on their debt. *See also* PUBLIC EXPENDITURE.

ROBIN W. BOADWAY

Reading: R.M. Bird, *The Growth of Government Spending in Canada* (1970); Canadian Tax Foundation, *The National Finances*, Annual.

Public Health is concerned with the overall physical and MENTAL HEALTH of the community. Interest in public health was fostered by the poor health standards that prevailed in the overcrowded cities of the Industrial Revolution. In the 19th and early 20th centuries, public health was concerned with quarantine measures and emphasized improved sanitation and vaccination campaigns that were initiated in an attempt to control major infectious DISEASES. Today, public health is concerned with education, counselling about living habits, some infectious disease control, the safeguarding of the well-being of children and, through government health insurance and HOSPITAL grants, the provision of medical care.

Canada followed Great Britain's lead in public health reform during the 19th and early 20th centuries. Reformers agitated for environmental solutions to the high mortality rate which particularly afflicted children. Sanitation campaigns to clean up housing and streets were under way in the major eastern Canadian cities by the late 19th century. Water and milk supplies were also sanitized; after the turn of the century pasteurized milk was introduced into Toronto and Montréal in an effort to curtail the spread of bovine tuberculosis, a major cause of crippling in children. School (and to some extent preschool) children were immunized against acute diseases such as smallpox and diphtheria or were monitored for more chronic afflictions such as tuberculosis and eye infections. Although hospital beds were available, care of the sick took place mostly at home.

Under the CONSTITUTION ACT, 1867, jurisdiction over health was roughly divided between the federal and provincial governments. The Dominion was given jurisdiction over border quarantine and the provinces were given responsibility for hospitals. The jurisdictional authority of municipalities varied in scope from province to province and even from city to city. All 3 levels of government initiated new tasks in health reform, the nature of which was often decided by the personal interests of the officials in charge. For example, the federal government assumed control of the leper lazaretto in New Brunswick in 1880, largely in response to agitation by the federal deputy minister of agriculture. In 1896 responsibilities under the Constitution Act were renegotiated, but although the great majority of previously unmentioned functions were placed under the jurisdiction of the provinces, health provisions in Canada remained haphazard for some years to come.

The first great attempt at administrative reform was spurred by the post-WWI Spanish flu EPIDEMIC

Cover illustration depicting the fight against smallpox in Montréal, 1876, with Mayor Hingston as St George slaying the dragon (*courtesy National Archives of Canada/C-64647*).

of 1918-19, which killed some 50 000 Canadians (*see* INFLUENZA). Conscious of a need to rebuild its population, especially should there be a return to hostilities, governments were also gravely concerned about SEXUALLY TRANSMITTED DISEASES, which caused sterility and produced defective offspring, and about "feeblemindedness," which prevented those born from being of service to their country.

Like many other nations at this time, Canada established its first federal department of health in 1919. The new department was created to take charge of all the old federal health functions, largely to do with quarantine and standards for food and drugs, and to co-operate with the provinces and with voluntary organizations in campaigns against venereal disease (VD), tuberculosis and "feeblemindedness," and to promote child welfare. It funded a chain of VD clinics across the country and began a public education program about child care. Tuberculosis and "feeblemindedness" were mainly handled by the provinces and voluntary organizations. In 1928 the Department of Health became the Department of Pensions and National Health; it provided, in particular, health services for war veterans.

The GREAT DEPRESSION caused a crisis in Canada's health system. The demands on all levels of government exceeded the resources available. Furthermore, the voluntary organizations and the medical profession, which traditionally provided some free services, were equally hard-pressed. Canadian governments were faced with an impoverished population that needed more health care but could not pay for it. Because the federal government reduced the funds available for health care, the onus fell on the provinces, municipalities and voluntary organizations to take up the slack. Some regions of Canada fared better than others; Québec could rely on the ministrations of its religious communities, Ontario negotiated a system of care with its doctors, and Saskatchewan introduced a clinic program. By 1939 the federal government was forced to increase its own activities in the field of health.

WWII brought about a revival of the campaigning spirit regarding health. In 1941 PM Mackenzie King summoned a Dominion-Provincial Conference to discuss the Rowell-Sirois royal commission's recommendations regarding public health, and a health-insurance plan. The actual proposal for a nationwide system of health insurance foundered, however, at the Dominion-Provincial Conference of 1945-46, partly because of opposition from the provinces and from the

Wetaskiwin baby clinic, 1928 (*courtesy Provincial Archives of Alberta/A6604*).

medical profession and partly because wartime prosperity had helped Canadians forget depression and want. Instead, the federal government turned its attention towards the provision of health through welfare (*see* HEALTH POLICY; WELFARE STATE). The federal health department (which in 1944 had changed again to the Department of National Health and Welfare), now turned its concern to the standard of living rather than the standard of health. The provinces were expected to assume responsibility for initiatives in medical care in aid of which the federal government established a series of health grants.

In 1968 Canada embarked upon a federal cost-sharing program that allowed all Canadians in all provinces to take part in a national health-insurance scheme, an indication that medical care would be provided through subsidized private medical practice rather than through public clinics and that the era of public health, as understood at the time of its great triumphs, had ended. Public health is now concerned primarily with the health of individual members of the public. Education and immunization campaigns still exist, but many environmental battles have been won.

With the exception of current concern regarding AIDS, serious infectious disease has largely been conquered in Canadian society. New challenges have arisen in the fields of genetic and deteriorative diseases but these offer much smaller scope for sweeping health reform. Medical treatment and medical research offer the best hope for solutions to these diseases and efforts of government and of the voluntary organizations have shifted in that direction. However, there is still need to ensure that expensive medical treatment and research are utilized in a cost-efficient manner. The much-publicized skyrocketing health costs of the 1970s and 1980s have moved public health in the direction of community health. Now a recognized field of instruction in medical and nursing schools alike, community health is an attempt to combine the medical, social and behavioral sciences to provide the best of medical science tempered by an assessment of society's real needs. These curative measures are supported by campaigns aimed at undermining the social causes of ill health, such as ALCOHOLISM, drug abuse, SMOKING and inadequate exercise (*see* FITNESS; DRUG USE, NON-MEDICAL).

In its move towards community health, Canada is following a worldwide trend towards more economic and productive use of the fruits of medical science.   JANICE DICKIN McGINNIS

Public Interest Advocacy Centre, founded in 1976, is a nonprofit, "public interest" law firm, with offices in Ottawa and Toronto. The centre provides legal services and counsel to consumer, low income, handicapped, native and other such groups intervening in regulatory cases involving such matters as the quality and price of telephone service and electricity and gas rates. The centre has also been involved in environmental and hu-

man rights test cases across Canada. Advocacy training and publications on matters of public policy are other activities of the centre and its sister organization, the Public Interest Research Centre. The centre is also the model for the British Columbia Public Interest Advocacy Centre, formed in 1981, which is based in Vancouver and carries out a similar range of activities. The centre has been sustained by grants from the federal Department of Consumer and Corporate Affairs, the Donner Canadian Foundation, the British Columbia Law Foundation, costs awarded by tribunals in a number of regulatory cases and donations from corporations, law firms and individuals.

Public Opinion, a term popularized by Jacques Necker, Louis XVI's finance minister, who wrote that public opinion influenced the behaviour of investors on the Parisian financial markets. In England Jeremy Bentham insisted that public opinion was a significant force for the social control of misrule and an important basis of democracy. In ancient societies, only among the Greeks did public opinion develop any potency. Public opinion in Europe was frequently considered the weapon of the middle class. Tocqueville, observing the role of public opinion in the US in 1835, wrote, "the majority raises formidable barriers around the liberty of opinion" and "I am not the more disposed to pass beneath a yoke because it is held out to me by the arms of a million of men."

There is no accepted definition of public opinion, although it is now part of daily vocabulary, especially that of politicians and journalists. It is generally defined as a collection of individual opinions on an issue of public interest. It does not necessarily refer to values or beliefs because opinions are more unstable and less focused. Attitude and opinion are frequently used interchangeably, but attitude is conventionally regarded as a more fundamental generalized predisposition, while opinion is a specific manifestation of underlying attitudes. When an event occurs, people form, discuss and then modify or strengthen their attitudes and public opinion is the result. Opinion is often characterized by direction, intensity, breadth and depth.

Long before systematic measures of opinion developed, it was noted that public opinion appeared to equal more than the sum of individual opinions, which led scholars observing crowd behaviour to speculate on the existence of a group mind, although the concept, at least in social science, was discarded for lack of empirical evidence. Some 20th-century social scientists postulate that the relation of individual opinions to each other results in a form of organization. Despite the lack of research on the internal structure of public opinion, some public-relations practitioners see their task as that of transforming individual attitudes into a collectivity that can exert influence. The biggest users of public-opinion research are business and industry. Newspapers, magazines, broadcasters and political parties also use polls to gather opinions.

Measuring Public Opinion Public opinion is measured by questionnaires. The population under study is quite large, so a sampling, taken to represent the entire population, is generally used. This is the public-opinion poll, and its validity depends on the quality of the questions and of the sample taken. Efforts to measure public opinion began in the early 19th century. Some American newspapers, in an attempt to calculate the outcome of an upcoming election, asked their readers to send in their straw votes, which the paper then compiled and published. The practice became widespread during the early 20th century, especially as a result of the activities of the *Literary*

Digest, which carried out national polls from 1910 to 1936. The election of 1936, however, was a disaster for this kind of poll. Despite a massive sample of 2.4 million mailed-in ballots, the *Digest* underestimated the election of Franklin Roosevelt by 19.3%, largely because the poll ignored a significant section of the electorate. However, newcomers to the field, notably George Gallup, accurately predicted the results. In Canada the first Gallup polls appeared in the early 1940s and now occur monthly. They are conducted by the Canadian Institute of Public Opinion. Each month the CIPO surveys the opinions of about 1000 Canadians. Gallup polls use statistical inference, estimating the attributes of an entire population from one sample. Many questions are asked and they vary from poll to poll. Gallup does ask the same questions at intervals over several years, allowing the evolution of public opinion to be traced. On the other hand, as a general rule the relatively large number of respondents unable to express an opinion clearly are presumed to have the same preferences as those that can. The presentation of results can also be misleading. A national sample used to measure voting intentions must appropriately represent demographic categories of age, sex, rural or urban residence, occupation, income, education and religious or ethnic affiliation. Like most national-opinion surveys, Gallup polls use a combination of the quota-stratified method, which involves choosing characteristics of the population to be sampled, determination of the proportion of the population with such characteristics, and the assignment of quotas to interviewers; and the area-probability method, which involves choosing characteristics of a population to be studied, dividing the country into "areal" units, eg, counties, rural municipalities, cities, etc, arbitrarily dividing these units into area segments, selecting a certain number of dwelling units in each segment and selecting the adults (or eligible voters) to be interviewed.

The Gallup organization claims a 4% margin of error for final election results. However, this polling error, expressed as an unweighted percentage-point average (obtained by dividing total percentage-point error by the number of categories of parties), does not reflect polling competence; eg, in 1957 the average error was 3.5%, but the forecast error was 53%, or about 1 million votes. Even when, in 1962, the average polling error was only 1.5%, the disparity between the error expressed in actual votes (446 000) and the leading party's plurality of 8000 votes was very large. Between 1945 and 1974, in 11 federal elections, the CIPO accurately predicted the percentages of votes cast for party categories in only 7 of 44 instances, and in the case of the 2 major parties the institute grossly overestimated Liberal strength in 1957 and 1965. In recent provincial elections, polling sponsored by newspapers and conducted by private organizations has increased dramatically. In many cases the polls attempt to forecast proportional vote distributions and not actual constituency outcomes. Usually a random provincial sample is consulted through telephone interviews. Some of these studies, eg, those of the Centre de recherches sur l'opinion publique, conducted during the 1970 and 1973 Québec elections, succeeded in predicting election trends only in a general manner.

Many politicians and observers have claimed that polling strongly influences the opinions it seeks to measure. It has been suggested that polls can cause voters to change their minds in order to be on the winning side, that weaker parties benefit as a result of an underdog effect, and that polls discourage voting by many who feel the results are foregone. There is no clear evidence to substantiate any of these theories, although corporate leaders, media executives, politicians and civil servants are often powerfully influenced themselves by survey results. The literature on voting behaviour indicates that the psychology of voting is very complex and includes many determinants. Generally, citizens in democracies appear to tolerate polling errors or the use or misuse of polls by the media. After the 1970 Québec elections, evidence suggested that certain newspapers had flagrantly misrepresented pre-election survey results. In response 9 Montréal polling organizations, to forestall an outright ban on certain polling activities such as exists in BC, recommended an elaborate set of rules to control media presentation of results. Federally, the Barbeau Committee on Election Expenses recommended no poll results be published during any pre-election period. A private member's bill to the same effect was tabled in the House of Commons in 1970, but no such proposals have been passed.

In fact, Canadian political parties have used polls with increasing frequency, as have Canadian government agencies, royal commissions, task forces and other policy-oriented groups. The Liberal, Progressive Conservative and New Democratic parties all regularly commission surveys for their private use. Well-known pollsters in Canada include Allan Gregg, of Decima, Michael Adams and Martin Goldfarb. New techniques of motivational and mass-attitude analysis are deployed at national, provincial and constituency levels. These surveys are conducted not only by conventional polling specialists but by sociologists and social psychologists as well. The newer survey methods are costly, which may affect competition between parties. The motivation behind the polling, for some politicians, also suggests a preoccupation with image projection, a tendency for party leaders to dominate in elections and consequently in decision making, and a tendency to negotiate or bargain with voters, rather than persuade them. However, researchers claim that some leaders have always sought to follow or manipulate public opinion and always will, and also point to many cases where minority viewpoints have ultimately become the prevailing opinions of the public. For obvious reasons, some politicians view published pre-election surveys with scorn, as reflected in Mr Diefenbaker's famous comment, "Every morning when I take my little dog, Happy, for a walk, I watch with great interest what he does to the poles." ANDRÉ BLAIS

Public Ownership, government provision of goods and services; the commercial or business activities of the STATE. Although the boundaries between the public and private sectors have been blurred by governments' expanding role in the economy, public ownership generally refers to enterprises, wholly or partially government owned, which sell goods and services at a price according to use. According to this definition, government-owned railways, airlines, and utilities are examples of public ownership, but hospitals, highways and public schools are not. In Canada the latter are provided by the state but are financed primarily by general government revenues, not by fees paid by individuals in relation to the quantities of goods or services produced. Such a definition, though not absolute, does distinguish public ownership from private ownership and other sorts of state activity.

Although many Canadians probably believe private enterprise dominates their economy, public ownership is important at all 3 levels of Canadian government. For example, in 1987 the federal government owned AIR CANADA, Canada's largest airline; CANADIAN NATIONAL RAILWAYS; the CANADIAN BROADCASTING CORPORATION and PETRO-CANADA; as well as coal and uranium mines and

financial institutions. Provincial public ownership is very diverse. Not only are most provinces involved in the generation and transmission of electricity (see UTILITIES), the retail sale of liquor and the provision of financial services to farmers and small businesses; but telephone service in the Prairie provinces, railways in BC, Alberta and Ontario, steel mills in Québec and NS, automobile insurance in several provinces, and energy companies in most provinces are also publicly owned. Public ownership is also important in Canadian municipalities where it may include the provision of urban transportation, water, electricity and, in a few cases, notably Edmonton, telephone service. Although the election of NEW DEMOCRATIC PARTY provincial governments has led to greater public ownership, Canadian governments do not resort to it out of political ideology. Public ownership, which generally supplements private enterprise and the market, is used to promote economic growth through the provision of economic infrastructure, to achieve federal and provincial control over certain firms and industries, to maintain employment and to promote national security. Private enterprise has not always been willing or able to provide important goods and services in such a large, sparsely populated country. The threatening presence of the US, the need to extend important services over vast distances, and regional and cultural forces have played a large role in determining the use of public ownership.

However, public ownership has not been uncontroversial in Canada. Public ownership of hydro in several provinces, the nationalization of automobile insurance in BC and Manitoba, and the creation and growth of Petro-Canada are a few of the government actions that evoked conflict about government's role in the economy. The effectiveness of Canada's burgeoning public-enterprise sector has been seriously questioned. Some interests now argue that public ownership has been too widely extended in Canada, a common prescription being the "privatization" (return to private ownership) of a number of publicly owned firms. Since 1984, the federal Progressive Conservative government of Brian Mulroney has pursued an active privatization program. Several crown firms, including Canadair and de Havilland, have been sold to private investors, the latter to Boeing Aircraft of Seattle in a controversial sale. Petro-Canada, Air Canada and the CNR have also been named as possible candidates for sale to private interests. Privatization also proceeds apace in the provinces. In late 1987, the Social Credit government of BC provoked an intense debate when it released a blueprint for the privatization of many government firms and services. Public ownership also has many supporters and defenders. It remains an important policy instrument for Canadian governments of diverse persuasions.

Public ownership in Canada has been achieved in several ways. Occasionally governments have created new firms, or less frequently they have acquired or nationalized private ones. The NATIONALIZATION of industries such as potash in Saskatchewan, asbestos in Québec and hydroelectric power in Ontario has been very controversial. However, the owners of firms that have been nationalized normally received financial compensation. Public ownership is generally administered through a CROWN CORPORATION, but a publicly owned industry need not be in corporate form. Government departments may also administer state-owned businesses. Recently, governments have employed "mixed" corporations that involve, in varying degrees, public and private ownership within a single firm. The ALBERTA ENERGY COMPANY, a firm owned jointly by the Alberta

government and many individual Canadian investors, is a good example of a mixed enterprise. But the political and economic effectiveness of such enterprises remains undetermined. But concern is often expressed about whether such firms can reconcile in their decision making the sometimes conflicting imperatives of public-policy goals and the pursuit of profit. ALLAN TUPPER

Public Policy generally denotes both the general purpose of government action and the views on the best or preferred means of carrying it out; more specifically it refers to government actions designed to achieve one or more objectives. "Policy" can have at least 2 distinct meanings: it can refer both to how something is done (rules and procedures), which may be called administrative policy, or to what is being done, eg, substantive programs. Studies of public policy often employ both meanings. In order to make various actions more coherent, governments usually formulate major priorities that form the basis of general policies, eg, social, economic and foreign policy, which in turn encompass more particular sectoral policies, eg, trade, police, health care, agriculture. AGRICULTURAL POLICY can therefore be described as a sectoral policy created to meet particular agricultural objectives that are based on more general policies, eg, ECONOMIC POLICY.

Many measures or means are often necessary to implement policy, and these are frequently controversial because they involve coercion or the threat of a penalty if they are not followed. In every instance, the measures involve resources (levied, borrowed or purchased, produced and consumed, accumulated, distributed, loaned or sold) and rules (bans, obligations, authorizations, permissions, rights and privileges to do or not to do something). Government policymaking is nominally a response both to problems and opportunities. Policies (both ends and means) are also controversial because they are influenced by the general ideologies of the major political parties, the struggle for political power and the interests of PRESSURE GROUPS. Policies already in effect are also subject to change when the problems they are intended to solve persist or when new problems arise or are added to them. Government policies reflect changes in society but they also produce them. Initially government policies were designed to guarantee the physical safety of the population and to maintain peace. With the increasing production of goods and the growth of trade, governments intervened to regulate the so-called market economy and to facilitate more production by providing infrastructures such as railways, roads, canals, aqueducts, ports and warehouses. In response to urbanization and the consequent transformation of society, governments developed EDUCATION and HEALTH POLICIES and launched vast land-development operations. After WWII, particularly as part of their social-welfare policy, they have intervened in the stabilization of production and services, in health insurance, and in INCOME DISTRIBUTION.

The federal government has jurisdiction over a number of sectors, sometimes exclusively, eg, EXTERNAL RELATIONS, DEFENCE POLICY, currency, weights and measures, and patents, and sometimes in co-operation with provincial governments, eg, scientific research and agriculture (see DISTRIBUTION OF POWERS). Other policy areas generally fall under local or regional jurisdiction. For example, education, highways and local public works are primarily the responsibility of provincial governments. Provincial governments also intervene in a large number of other sectors, including electrical-energy production, mining and forestry development, health-care services and police.

Government activities are financed essentially

through taxes, a generalized obligatory deduction with no compensation other than the benefits derived from certain government policies. Taxes, which are the compulsory price for these benefits, are not negotiated with individual taxpayers but are the result of government decisions formulated within the framework of FISCAL POLICY – one of the most important and controversial policies of any government. In Canada, government policies result from many conflicting points of view, not all of which have an equal opportunity of being implemented.

Policy Studies Studies of public policy can be characterized as historical, descriptive, legal and normative. In addition, most political scientists use a case-study format and are concerned with the merits of a policy, with suggesting solutions to public-policy problems, and with influencing the policy under study. As a result of efforts to classify policies, distinctions have been made between the substance of policies, the institutions making them, the people whom they are meant to affect, periods of time in which they have been followed, the ideology and values they reflect, the extent of their support and the level of government responsible for their implementation. *See also* CULTURAL POLICY; ENERGY POLICY; FISHERIES POLICY; INDUSTRIAL STRATEGY; LABOUR POLICY; LANGUAGE POLICY; MONETARY POLICY; MUSEUM POLICY; NATIONAL POLICY.

ANDRÉ BERNARD

Public Relations consists of communications initiatives intended to influence favourably attitudes toward a corporation, public body or public figure, in order to promote acceptance of values pertaining to products, policies or concepts of the group or individual. Public relations is widely practised by modern business and governments in Canada.

Public Relations Activities and Techniques Any communications strategy aimed at influencing an organization and its products, an individual or a concept involves public relations. While some ADVERTISING is a component of public relations, advertising and public-relations functions are usually regarded as separate disciplines.

Early steps in any public-relations campaign are to identify the "public" to whom a message is directed and to devise a strategy to ensure the credibility of the message. The strategy should also establish objectives relative to the various publics and define means to reach these groups. Activities might include community relations, which could provide support for charities or corporate positioning; consumer relations, involving strategies to improve a company's competitive position in the marketplace; government liaison, which may involve LOBBYING public officials and taking steps to win public support; and media relations, for the purpose of gaining increased awareness through publicity.

Public Relations Credibility The credibility of public relations has occasionally been affected adversely by conscious efforts of some individuals to engage in "public-relations exercises" in an effort to obscure facts or even mislead public opinion. Responsible public relations, however, is concerned with communicating factual information, with full disclosure of sources and open discussion of all aspects of controversial issues.

History of Canadian Public Relations The contemporary public-relations business can be traced back to advertising, business writing and press-agents' activities in the late 19th century. One of the earliest examples of public relations in Canada – the trans-Atlantic campaign of the Liberal government of Sir Wilfrid Laurier to attract immigrants to the West – actually pre-dates the emergence of recognized PR activity, although it employed tactics which still form the basis of much

public-relations practice. More than 2 million newcomers found their way to Canada between 1896 and 1911, attracted by a massive publicity campaign and grants of free land. The campaign, orchestrated by Minister of the Interior Clifford Sifton, saw lecturers tour fall fairs in the US, backed up by thousands of pamphlets and ads in 7000 American newspapers. Six hundred US editors (in an early version of the modern "media tour") were given free trips to Canada, as were British MPs. Agents scoured Britain, Germany and other European countries to publicize the "golden fields" of the West and to lure to Canada city workers and the "peasants in sheepskin coats" whom Sifton proclaimed were the "good quality" settlers needed to fill the Canadian North-West. While public relations was unknown in a commercial sense at the time, Sifton's campaign stands as a model in communications, targeted to specific audiences, and it probably represents the greatest and most successful public-relations campaign in Canadian history.

Since WWII the growth of public relations has mirrored the growth of the Canadian economy. The field sees its greatest growth in the future, as private corporations and public institutions find themselves under increasing scrutiny from a skeptical public.

In 1948 the Canadian Public Relations society was formed in Montréal and the Public Relations Assn of Ontario in Toronto. The groups merged in 1953 as the Canadian Public Relations Society (CPRS), which was incorporated by federal charter on 17 Apr 1957. By the mid-1960s the growth of public relations in Canada as a para-profession led CPRS to introduce a voluntary accreditation program in 1969. Successful applicants are designated APR (Accredited, Public Relations), which indicates that a practitioner has worked full-time in public relations for at least 5 years, has completed a 3-part examination, and has agreed to abide by the society's Code of Professional Standards. By the late 1980s there were more than 500 APRs and a total of more than 1500 CPRS members in Canada.

Other major associations serving public-relations practitioners in Canada are the International Assn of Business Communicators (IABC), the Health Care Public Relations Assn of Canada

---

Poster from Sifton's "Last Best West" campaign, which brought hundreds of thousands of settlers to the prairies from 1896 to WWI (*courtesy National Archives of Canada*).

(HCPRA), the Canadian Assn of Communicators in Education (CACE) and the Public Affairs Assn (PAA).

Careers in Public Relations Communications skills, particularly good writing ability, are essential for success in the public-relations field. Formal education in public relations is relatively new in Canada, with established programs at Laval U, McGill, U of Calgary, Mount Saint Vincent U, Mount Royal College in Calgary, Grant MacEwan College in Edmonton, Algonquin College in Ottawa, Durham College in Oshawa, Humber, Seneca and Centennial College in Toronto.

The lack of formal entry procedures in the past meant that many public-relations practitioners began their careers in other fields, especially journalism, or in finance, technology, teaching or medicine. Public relations requires an understanding of print and broadcast media, the graphic arts and advertising techniques.

According to industry surveys conducted by the Canadian industry newsletter, *PR Strategies*, in 1986 and 1987, Canadian public-relations practitioners regard themselves as professionals and over 60% favour compulsory licencing.

Public relations falls in the middle range of economic reward in the communications field; more than journalists and sometimes less than their counterparts in advertising. Public-relations practitioners may be employed with not-for-profit, professional associations, government, corporations, or on the staff of a public-relations consulting firm.   DAVID G. NORMAN

Reading: W.B. Herbert and J.R.G. Jenkins, eds, *Perspectives on Public Relations in Canada* (1984).

Public School refers to state-controlled, tax-supported and (generally) nonsectarian schools which are funded by provincial and local taxes (although federal funds, transferred through provincial governments, may be directed into public schools in special cases). Provincial political authority alone determines their aims and controls their curriculum, textbooks and standards, and authorizes who may serve in them as teachers and administrators. (Although local SCHOOL BOARDS construct and manage public schools, they do so within powers delegated by provincial governments.) SEPARATE SCHOOLS and tax-supported denominational schools are a special kind of public school for citizens of either Catholic or Protestant faith, although usually of the former. There are some jurisdictions where public schools are sectarian; in Saskatchewan, eg, public schools can be either Protestant or Roman Catholic, the "separate schools" being the schools of the smaller group. Children are required by law to attend school for a minimum of 10 years from the age of 6, although they may be excused from attendance at a public school if they receive other, equivalent education.

Public Service, also known as the civil service, is the public BUREAUCRACY comprising, in Canada, departmental organizations that support the political executive in the development, implementation and enforcement of government policies. It includes some 50 departmental organizations (and more than 200 000 employees) normally established by Acts of Parliament designating the positions of minister, the political head and the senior official or deputy head, and outlining the powers, duties and functions of the organization. Nondepartmental organizations – CROWN CORPORATIONS, REGULATORY COMMISSIONS AND ADMINISTRATIVE TRIBUNALS – are also part of the public service. They are designed to perform certain functions of government that are deemed to require varying degrees of independence from the political control of ministers and the administrative controls applied to the public service. They are agents of the Crown and report to Parliament through a minister.

By convention, the prime minister selects ministers and assigns to them statutory responsibilities, although their formal appointment is made by the governor general. The Cabinet theoretically directs the public service in its application and enforcement of current policies and the development of new ones, and is responsible to the legislature for the administration of it. Cabinet committees and the PRIME MINISTER'S OFFICE have in recent years been used to counter independent policy making within the public service, but the Cabinet secretariat, the PRIVY COUNCIL OFFICE (PCO), is itself part of the bureaucracy. The effectiveness of the budgetary process designed to control bureaucratic financial expenditures is also questionable, because the Treasury Board Secretariat (TBS) is part of the bureaucracy as well.

Cabinet is supported in the co-ordination of government policies and in the direction and management of the public service by central agencies, by departments such as finance, justice and external affairs, which have traditionally been major central policy departments, and by policy secretariats such as the ministries of state for economic development and social development, which co-ordinate departmental activities in these policy sectors. Particular government policies and programs are developed and implemented by a large number of program departments, eg, agriculture, national health and welfare, national defence, labour and transport. There is also a small group of departments, such as public works and national revenue, that provide common administrative services for other government departments.

The rights and responsibilities of public servants are outlined in statutes such as the Public Service Employment Act, the Canadian Human Rights Act, the Public Service Staff Relations Act and the regulations and directives passed under the authority of these Acts. Appointment to the public service and subsequent career advancement are based on the merit principle, which, although not defined in legislation, is generally considered to be "the selection of the most qualified candidates competing for a position based on their relative knowledge, experience and abilities, without discrimination or favouritism." It is administered through the merit system, which includes the regulations, policies, procedures and directives related to the recruitment, hiring and promotion of public servants and which has been adapted to changing circumstances. For example, after the OFFICIAL LANGUAGES ACT (1969) was passed, bilingualism became an element of merit in the staffing of positions. Moreover, efforts to increase the participation of individuals from underrepresented or disadvantaged groups, eg, women, Francophones, native peoples and handicapped persons, have involved special recruitment and staffing measures. Equal opportunity programs have been directed at removing discriminatory practices in recruitment and promotion and affirmative programs have attempted to increase the participation of individuals from these groups directly.

The convention of political neutrality in the public service is maintained by the principle of appointment on the basis of merit rather than on political affiliation. The traditional separation of politics and administration and of the anonymity of public servants theoretically meant public servants could remain neutral in supporting the government in power, but in recent years the recognition that politics, policy and administration are interrelated has modified the convention. As part of their jobs, public servants are involved actively in developing policy and are often expected to explain these policies to the public on their minister's behalf.

Political rights of public servants are restricted to voting and other forms of passive participation, eg, attending political meetings and contributing funds to political parties. They are legally forbidden to criticize government policy publicly or to disclose confidential information. Public servants wishing to seek a nomination and contest an election for national or provincial office must apply for a leave of absence without pay, which may be denied if it conflicts with job responsibilities, but they are allowed to take an active part in elections at the municipal level.

COLLECTIVE BARGAINING in the public service provides the majority of its employees (not those in managerial or confidential capacities, or members of the RCMP or armed forces) the right to belong to public-service unions and to participate in a process of joint determination of salary and compensation benefits. The employer, represented by Treasury Board, retains the right to determine the classification of positions, standards of discipline and other conditions of employment. The Public Service Staff Relations Board, which administers the Public Service Staff Relations Act, determines bargaining units and agents, hears complaints of unfair practices and is generally responsible for the administration of collective bargaining legislation that falls under the Act. It reports to Parliament through a minister, the president of the PCO, who does not sit on the Treasury Board. Bargaining is between Treasury Board and its representatives and certified bargaining agents representing employees. Dispute settlement options include binding arbitration and conciliation, which sometimes allow the right to strike. Collective bargaining, like other rights of public servants, is granted by Parliament and may be changed or withdrawn by that same authority; parliamentary action to legislate striking public servants back to work or to impose wage controls may modify collective bargaining processes.

Responsibility for personnel management is divided between departmental organizations, Treasury Board and the PUBLIC SERVICE COMMISSION. Public servants are employees of their department and the public service as a whole. The Treasury Board has overall responsibility for personnel management policies and represents the employer in collective bargaining, but the Public Service Commission, under the Public Service Employment Act (1967), establishes staffing criteria for departments and assists them in training and development. It exercises full authority for appointments to senior executive positions except at the deputy-minister level. It hears appeals on appointments, investigates allegations of discrimination, decides on cases of political partisanship and audits staffing actions of departments. Established to rid the public service of political patronage, it has remained an independent central staffing agency dedicated to guarding the merit principle.

Provincial Variations The basic structure and organization of provincial public services are similar to that of the federal government; in recent years provincial public-service activities in areas such as social services, education and resource development have grown significantly. The recruitment of a large number of skilled employees has led to the reform of personnel management practices and the development of professional public services. The role of provincial public-service commissions in staffing and training employees varies widely. Collective bargaining systems have also been introduced at the provincial level but again there are variations in the rights accorded employees in each province. In some provinces, public servants do not have the right to strike. AUDREY D. DOERR

Public Service Commission The Civil Service Commission (CSC) was established in 1908 under the Civil Service Amendment Act, which introduced the principle of merit as established by competition. The Civil Service Act of 1962 preserved the independence of the CSC and the Public Service Employment Act of 1967 reaffirmed the merit principle and changed the name of the CSC to Public Service Commission. The powers and duties of the PSC are to appoint qualified persons, to hear appeals against staffing actions, to make decisions on allegations of political partisanship, and to investigate allegations of discrimination. The commission reports directly to Parliament, though the president of the Privy Council usually represents the commission in the House. *See also* PUBLIC SERVICE.

Public-Service Unions The public sector is one of the most highly unionized in Canada. Approximately 80% of those public-sector employees eligible for collective bargaining are covered by collective agreements, compared with only 25% in the private sector. Most municipal employees belong to the 330 000-member CANADIAN UNION OF PUBLIC EMPLOYEES (CUPE), and have bargaining rights similar to those in the private sector. However, since the early 1980s a number of provincial governments moved to restrict these rights. Health-care workers in some provinces are denied the right to strike. Provincial employees, largely represented by affiliates of the 275 000-member National Union of Provincial Government Employees are covered by more restrictive legislation. Most school, health-care and social-service employees bargain with a variety of boards and agencies that primarily administer provincial-government monies. New Brunswick public-sector unions bargain directly with the province. In Québec a coalition of militant public-sector unions representing members of the CONFEDERATION OF NATIONAL TRADE UNIONS, the Québec Federation of Labour and the Québec Teachers' Corporation bargains directly with the province.

Most federal government employees belong to the 180 000-member Public Service Alliance of Canada, and have had bargaining rights since passage of the 1967 Public Service Staff Relations Act. This Act, however, severely limits the provisions that unions may negotiate. The smaller Canadian Union of Postal Workers (25 000 members) is considered the most militant (*see* POSTAL STRIKES, CUPW) and has bargained such breakthroughs as paid maternity leave, premium pay for weekend work and the right to bargain on technological change.

All of these public-sector unions have evolved from docile employee associations into genuine trade unions. All except the CNTU and the QTC are affiliated with the CANADIAN LABOUR CONGRESS, where public-service employees now make up more than half the membership. Professional unions in the public sector – eg, nurses, teachers, academics, engineers – have largely remained independent. But even these groups have recently become militant and have frequently struck.

Great expansion occurred in public-sector programs and services from 1965 to 1975, and a tremendous upsurge in union membership allowed many federal and provincial government employees to obtain limited bargaining rights. After 1975, limited economic growth resulted in cutbacks in many government programs. Bargaining rights were curtailed by wage-control legislation and limitations on the right to strike. Employees designated "essential" were prohibited from striking, and others were subjected to special legislation to terminate their legal strikes. The result was a sharp increase in public-sector strikes. Several union leaders were jailed during this period for defying back-to-work legislation. In recent years it has become increasingly difficult for unions to defend their members. Up to 1982, public-employee unions faced a choice: to revert to being benevolent associations, playing the limited role that they had prior to the advent of collective bargaining, or to become militant political organizations in order to win back the bargaining rights they enjoyed in the 1965-75 period. By 1987 repressive legislation and huge services cutbacks forced public-sector unions to take the militant route, eg, the Operation SOLIDARITY strikes in BC in the autumn of 1983 and the Newfoundland public-sector strikes of 1986. GILBERT LEVINE

Public Works Canada (PWC) has been the builder and custodian of the federal government's real property assets since before Confederation. Created in 1841, PWC is one of the nation's oldest federal departments. It functions as the government's realty manager, real-estate agent, caretaker, engineering and marine consultant, designer, architect and builder. It constructs and maintains buildings and facilities as diverse as remote nursing stations, downtown office complexes, small craft harbours and scenic highways. Public Works is responsible for negotiating and administering grants in lieu of property taxes to municipalities in which federally owned properties are located. In 1985 PWC launched a major program to dispose of surplus lands and buildings. The department also administers all expropriation activities of the federal government and is responsible for the Canada Mortgage and Housing Corporation and the NATIONAL CAPITAL COMMISSION. The department's net expenditure for 1985-86 was $1.2 billion.

Publications, Royal Commission on, est Sept 1960 to examine the impact of foreign publications in Canada on domestic periodicals, with particular emphasis on questions of competition and national identity. It is also known as the O'Leary Commission for its chairman, Grattan O'LEARY. The commission's recommendation that the deduction from income tax of advertising expenditures aimed at the Canadian market but appearing in a foreign publication be eliminated became law 16 years later, when Bill C-58, the so-called "Time-Reader's Digest Act," was proclaimed despite the aggressive lobbying campaign of *Time* magazine in particular against the proposed legislation. RICHARD STURSBERG

Pubnico, NS, UP, pop 223 (1986c), 173 (1981c), is located 30 km SE of YARMOUTH, at the head of Pubnico Harbour. Several communities around the harbour share the name, from Lower East to Lower West Pubnico, and their populations total about 2600. The name evolved through many variations of the Indian word *pogomkoup* ("land from which the trees have been removed to fit it for cultivation"). Philippe D'Entremont founded Pubnico on a grant from his friend Charles de LA TOUR in 1651 or 1653. In 1755 the ACADIANS were expelled from NS, but many later made their way back. Today the D'Entremont surname survives in a large part of Pubnico's population. Shipbuilding was for some time a major industry in this area, acting as a support for trade in nearby Yarmouth. Both E and W Pubnico depend economically on fishing and farming, the region being famous for its lobsters during the winter season. Several small boatbuilding yards produce the famous Cape Sable Island fishing boat. JEAN PETERSON

Pudlo Pudlat, graphic artist (b at Kamadjuak Camp, Baffin I, NWT 4 Feb 1916). One of the

Inuk artist Pudlo incorporates modern technology, as in his *Aeroplane (courtesy West Baffin Eskimo Co-operative, Cape Dorset, NWT).*

most original contemporary Inuit artists, Pudlo began drawing in the early 1960s after he had moved to CAPE DORSET, NWT, leaving a semi-nomadic life of seasonal hunting and fishing behind him. His preferred medium is a combination of acrylic wash and coloured pencils. In contrast with most of his contemporaries, Pudlo has included in his imagery icons of the modern technology that has brought such profound changes to the Canadian North. In his work, airplanes, helicopters and telephone poles enter into strange interactions with the arctic landscape and its animals. A muskox rider lassoing an airplane or a loon steering a motorboat are examples of his juxtapositions. In many ways Pudlo's work symbolizes the paradoxes of the encounter between 2 cultures. *See also* INUIT ART. MARIA MUEHLEN

Puffin, common name for 3 species of medium-sized SEABIRDS of the AUK family. Most commonly, the name refers to the Atlantic puffin (*Fratercula arctica*), about 33 cm long, with a distinctive triangular bill, red with a bluish grey base. Puffins are highly colonial in breeding season, usually nesting in burrows in grassy slopes or flattish ground, sometimes in rock crevices and boulder skree. They first breed when 4-5 years old, a pair normally remaining together for entire breeding life. The single, white egg is incubated by both parents for about 42 days. The chick is fed small fish for 6-7 weeks. Both adults and immatures winter offshore, but where they spend the 7-8 months before returning to the colony is poorly known. Atlantic puffins breed along both coasts and on many islands of the North Atlantic. Their North American breeding range centers on the Newfoundland and Labrador coasts. The North American breeding population is estimated at about 365 000 pairs; almost 62% nest on 4 islands in Witless Bay, SE Nfld. Populations in the Gulf of St Lawrence-New England states area and in the NE Atlantic have declined considerably since 1900, probably because of human persecution, variation in food availability, and oil pollution.

The tufted puffin (*Lunda cirrhata*) is found in the Bering Sea and N Pacific Ocean (*photo by Lyn Hancock*).

Horned (*F. corniculata*) and tufted puffins (*Lunda cirrhata*) occur in the Bering Sea and N Pacific Ocean. Both breed in coastal colonies from eastern Siberia and NW Alaska S to the Aleutian Is and SE Alaska. Tufted puffins also breed in BC, Washington, Oregon and California.

D.N. NETTLESHIP

Pugsley, William, lawyer, politician, premier and lieutenant-governor of NB (b at Sussex, NB 27 Sept 1850; d at Toronto 3 Mar 1925). A prominent political figure in NB in the early part of the 20th century, Pugsley was a tough politician who employed patronage blatantly to win support for the Liberal cause. He served as Speaker of the House, solicitor general and attorney general before becoming premier in 1907. He resigned after a few months to enter the federal Cabinet as minister of public works. Following a term as lieutenant-governor, 1917-23, he was appointed commissioner of the settlement of war claims in Ottawa, a position he held until his death.

ARTHUR T. DOYLE

Pugwash, NS, UP, pop 768 (1986c), 648 (1981c), is located 65 km NW of TRURO, at the mouth of the Pugwash R. It takes its name from the Micmac *Pagwechk* ("shallow water" or "shoal"). Cyrus EATON, multimillionaire industrialist and humanitarian, opened his summer home here for a "Thinkers' Conference" where statesmen, philosophers and businessmen could discuss issues of world concern. These successful international meetings, known as "Pugwash Conferences," have since been held around the world, and Pugwash is internationally known as "the Global Village." Famous as well is its annual Gathering of the Clans and its Fisherman's Regatta; many of its street signs are bilingual – English and Gaelic. Shipbuilding and fishing were major industries in the 19th century, but they declined with the advent of the steamship and railway. A vast salt mine, opened 1957, is a major employer. Today, Pugwash also supports a commercial fishery, as well as numerous businesses and artisans.

JANICE MILTON

Pukaskwa National Park (est 1971, 1888 km²) is bracketed on the W by the coastline of Lk Superior, an impressive stretch of massive headlands and boulder beaches, in SHIELD country, an ancient plateau of granite and gneiss riddled with lakes and dissected by tumbling rivers. In this wilderness roam moose, black bear, woodland caribou, wolves and smaller species adapted to the northern forest of black spruce, jack pine and white birch. The "Pukaskwa Pits" are evidence of early habitation by OJIBWA Indians. The purpose of these carefully arranged boulders remains a mystery. In the 17th century European explorers came, soon to be followed by fur traders and the logging industry. Today, Pukaskwa challenges the modern explorer to paddle its turbulent spring rivers and hike the rugged hills. Commercial accommodation is available in nearby Marathon, Ont. LILLIAN STEWART

Pulp and Paper Industry comprises manufacturing enterprises that convert cellulose fibre into a wide variety of pulps, papers and paperboards. About 95% of their fibre comes from wood from Canadian FORESTS, the balance from wastepaper and a very small quantity of linen and cotton rags. Wood is reduced to fibre by mechanical means or by cooking in chemicals. The fibres are then mixed with water, adhering to one another as the water is removed by pressure and heat. This is the fundamental principle of papermaking, discovered by the Chinese nearly 2000 years ago and brought to Spain by the Moors, probably during the 12th century.

Papermaking today is a large, capital-intensive

Great Lakes Paper Mill, Thunder Bay, Ont (*courtesy Colour Library Books*).

industry, characterized by high-speed machines and complex systems of control for manufacturing to close tolerances thousands of products vital to education, communications, marketing, packaging, construction, etc. Canada today ranks second to the US in pulp and paper manufacture, and first in pulp and paper exports. It has about 140 pulp, pulp and paper, and paper mills, every province except PEI having at least one.

Pulp and paper production in the mid- to late 1980s has been valued at some $14 billion annually and has accounted for about 3% of the Gross Domestic Product. Exports of around $11 billion have comprised about 9% of total Canadian exports. The industry is the largest of Canada's manufacturing industries, with about 85 000 workers in mills and offices, some $2.8 billion paid in wages and salaries and some $6 billion in value added by manufacture. Furthermore the industry makes a net contribution to Canada's BALANCE OF PAYMENTS of some $8 billion, larger than that of any other Canadian industry.

The first Canadian paper mill was completed in 1805 at St Andrews [Qué], by 2 entrepreneurs from New England. It produced printing, writing and wrapping papers for sale mostly in the growing markets of Montréal and Québec City. Sites chosen for early mills were on rivers or streams, which provided water necessary for papermaking processes and waterpower to run machinery. Waterways also provided a convenient means of transporting raw materials (rags) to the mill and finished goods to markets. Throughout the 19th century, pulp and paper was largely a domestic industry, serving the gradually increasing needs of Canadians. As literacy spread and commercial and industrial activity quickened, the need for cultural and packaging papers grew. Many new mills were established along the Great Lakes-St Lawrence system and its tributaries and in the Maritimes. For many centuries the traditional source of cellulose fibre for paper manufacture

had been cotton and linen rags. The full potential of a Canadian pulp and paper industry based on a vast forest resource began to be realized only after the discovery of how to make paper from wood (around 1840). Alexander Buntin is credited with inaugurating Canada's groundwood mill at Valleyfield, Qué. Groundwood, prepared by grinding the wood, is used primarily for inexpensive papers, such as newspaper. The exact date for Buntin's mill is not known, but he had 2 grinders imported from Germany in operation by 1869. The first chemical wood-pulp mill in N America was built by Angus & Logan at Windsor Mills, Qué, in 1864. It was erected under the supervision of John Thomson, a Scot who had conducted experiments in Saint John, NB. Chemical pulp is prepared from wood chips boiled under pressure with chemicals – Thomson used soda – to leave mostly cellulose fibre. The wood pulp is washed, bleached, blended and then poured over a wire screen, leaving a fine layer of fibre. Wood pulp then gradually displaced rag pulp for most uses, and the era of modern papermaking began.

Two developments, both occurring within a relatively short period, moved Canada onto the world papermaking stage. The first, in the 1890s and early 1900s, was the prohibition of exports of pulpwood from crown lands, applied by provincial governments. The second was the removal of the US tariff on newsprint in 1913. These actions stimulated large investments in Canadian pulp and papermaking for foreign markets and set the industry on the course it has followed ever since. By the end of WWI, Canada had already become the world's largest exporter of pulp and paper.

Each subsequent decade of the industry's history has had its particular flavour. Rapid growth took place in the 1920s, especially in northwestern Ontario and the St-Maurice Valley, Ottawa Valley and Lac Saint-Jean regions of Québec. Mills were sited in northern locations that offered hydroelectric power potential as well as spruce stands. Establishment of a mill frequently necessitated development of a townsite such as KENORA, Ont (*see* RESOURCE TOWNS). Expansion was followed by the worldwide depression of the 1930s,

when some companies went bankrupt and most others were in very serious financial straits. WWII brought a return to higher levels of activity and even some expansion as European wood-pulp supplies that had formerly served the US market became unavailable. The postwar economic boom arrived in the late 1940s, continuing almost uninterrupted through to the late 1950s. Pulp and paper companies, by now fully restored to financial health, refurbished their manufacturing operations, steadily raised shipments and exports and, for a number of years, ran at maximum capacity.

With the 1960s came the greatest surge of expansion in the industry since the 1920s. It occurred everywhere, but the pacesetter was BC. Canadian and foreign interests, spurred by provincial governments eager for new industrial investment, scrambled to participate as large areas of public forestland were made available. Sixteen new mills opened between 1965 and 1970, mostly for the production of bleached kraft pulp for world markets.

The 1970s were a turbulent period for the industry, marked by greatly intensified competition in international markets, periods of worldwide overcapacity, a deep recession in mid-decade, large changes in currency exchange rates, rapidly rising inflation throughout the industrial world and a decline in the competitiveness of the Canadian economy as a whole. Nevertheless, as the decade ended, devaluation of the Canadian dollar had helped restore the competitive strength of the pulp and paper industry, and large programs of mill modernization were under way in every region.

The early 1980s brought other abrupt changes: a deep recession and sharp cutbacks in pulp and paper production. This was followed by economic recovery, a sustained period of moderate growth in major markets in the middle and later years of the decade, and the prospect of substantial future growth in worldwide use of pulp and paper. This prospect was accompanied by the knowledge that the Canadian industry would continue to face intense competition in all its traditional markets. In quantity, Canada's pulp and paper shipments now total about 23 million t: about 40% is newsprint, of which Canada has been the world's largest producer for over 50 years; about 37% is wood pulp, for further processing into paper and paperboard; 23% is a wide variety of packaging papers and boards, book and writing papers, tissue and sanitary papers and building papers and boards.

Some 79% of Canadian production is exported; 21% is used in Canada. The largest export market has for many years been the US, which now absorbs about 52%. Western Europe takes about 12%; Japan some 5%; all other world markets together about 10%. Nearly 87% of exports consists of newsprint and wood pulp, which have entered the major world markets duty free for many years.

Historically, other papers and paperboards have encountered tariffs around the world and, partly for this reason, have been manufactured largely for use within Canada. Although this situation is now changing, as a result of successive rounds of multilateral tariff reductions negotiated through the GATT, newsprint and wood pulp remain the export staples of the Canadian industry, with various grades of printing papers other than newsprint increasing rapidly.

The pulp and paper industry uses about 90 million m³ of wood annually: over 90% is SPRUCE, FIR, PINE and other softwoods; the balance is hardwoods. Over the past 20 years the most significant development in the industry's fibre requirements has been the tremendous increase in the use of

Pulp logs in the river at the Great Lakes Forest Products Ltd plant at Dryden, Ont (*photo by Jim Merrithew*).

wood chips, reject lumber and other wood residues from sawmills. Such residues now account for more than half of all wood used in Canadian pulp and paper mills, as compared with around 10% in the early 1960s. This development has meant a more efficient use of the forest resource and has stimulated greater integration of pulp and paper and lumber manufacture.

Québec accounts for the largest share of total production, about 35%; Ontario about 25%; BC about 22%; and the Atlantic and Prairie provinces together have some 18%. Most mills are located in communities near the forests from which they draw their chief raw material; some that purchase pulp for conversion into finished products or use mostly wastepaper have been built in the large metropolitan areas. About 70% of Canada's pulp and paper is manufactured by companies that are controlled in Canada; some 23% comes from companies controlled in the US; and 7%, from companies controlled elsewhere. Canadian ownership is largely via the private sector. There has been some public-sector ownership by provincial governments or their agencies in Québec, Manitoba and Saskatchewan, but this amount represents only some 10-15% of the industry's total manufacturing capacity. The major Canadian companies are ABITIBI-PRICE INC, British Columbia Forest Products Ltd, Canadian Forest Products Ltd, CIP Inc, Consolidated-Bathurst Inc, DOMTAR Pulp & Paper Products Group, Great Lakes Forest Products Ltd, Kruger Inc, MACMILLAN BLOEDEL LTD and Repap Enterprises Inc.

The pulp and paper industries of Canada and the other large producing regions of the world (eg, the US, Europe, Japan) have traditionally shared information on technological development. Hence, the major advances in wood harvesting, pulping and papermaking during the 20th century have tended to result from research work in several countries. Canada has participated fully in these developments and has had a very important role in some of them, such as the chemical-recovery system used in alkaline pulping, which stimulated the growth of the kraft pulp industry all over the world; improved pulp-bleaching techniques, which opened new markets for many papers and paperboards; and twin-wire forming, one of the most significant developments in the papermaking process since the invention of the Fourdrinier machine in the first decade of the 19th century (*see* CHEMICAL ENGINEERING). Scientific research is carried out by a number of Canadian pulp and paper manufacturers and the industry also carries on co-operative research through the Pulp and Paper Research Institute of Canada and the Forest Engineering Research Institute of Canada, both situated in Pointe-Claire, Qué. The industry makes large capital expenditures on air and water POLLUTION abatement; in recent years, $100-150 million annually. Mill effluent losses have been reduced substantially: suspended solids per tonne of production have

dropped by 90%; biochemical oxygen demand, by 72%.   GORDON MINNES

Pulse Crops are members of the legume family, seeds or plant parts of which are edible. Pulses have taproots with the potential to form symbiotic associations with nitrogen-fixing *Rhizobium* bacteria. The fruit is a pod containing one to several seeds, which are high in carbohydrate, protein and, in some instances, oil. Pulses are primarily warm-season annuals, requiring 40-100 cm of precipitation annually. Of the pulses of economic importance, chickpeas and SOYBEANS originated in China; common BEANS and lima beans in Central and S America; cowpeas, LENTILS, mung beans and PEAS in India; and FABA BEANS and mung beans in central Asia. Throughout the world, soybeans are the most important pulse crop grown. Canada produces significant quantities of common beans, faba beans, lentils, peas and soybeans.   P. McVETTY

Pump Drill, used prehistorically and historically by the INUIT, the Indians of the American southwest and the IROQUOIS, may have come into N America from northern Asia, where it is also quite common. This drill consisted of a crossarm with a hole, through which a shaft was run. Cords were tied to the top of the shaft and to the 2 ends of the crossarm. When the crossarm was pushed down, the shaft rotated, helped along by the cords. As the rotating shaft did not spin fast enough to rewind the cords, a flywheel attached to the shaft served to rewind the cord and keep the shaft spinning continuously, first in one direction, then in the other. A cap mounted on top of the shaft enabled the user to increase the downward pressure of the drill.   RENÉ R. GADACZ

Pumpkin, common name for SQUASH with large, orange fruits. In N America the term most commonly refers to those fruits of *Cucurbita pepo* that are picked after the rind has hardened but before the first frost. In Europe, the word is used for various squashes, eg, *C. maxima*. Pumpkins have little economic importance in Canada and the US, being used mainly for making pies and for jack-o'-lanterns during Halloween.   ROGER BÉDARD

Purcell, Gillis Philip, journalist (b at Brandon, Man 25 Nov 1904; d at Toronto 16 Nov 1987), educated at U of Manitoba and U of Toronto. He was general manager of CANADIAN PRESS from 1945 to 1969, having been No 2 man for 13 years before that. During his tenure CP emerged as one of the world's leading news services. He set up such services as photography and broadcasting and a service in French. One of his major responsibilities was the development of war coverage. Purcell served briefly as press officer for the 1st Div, Canadian Army, and later as public-relations officer with the 1st Canadian Corps overseas, where he lost his left leg during maneuvres. He was an Officer of the Order of Canada and a member of the Canadian News Hall of Fame.   BRUCE LEVETT

Purcell, Jack, badminton player (b at Guelph, Ont 24 Dec 1903). He was famous as a lanky, lithe athlete with a wide repertoire of badminton strokes and tremendous court presence. In the 1920s he won numerous Ontario titles and was Canadian singles champion in 1929 and 1930 before turning professional in 1932. Professional play was of the barnstorming, challenge variety. After defeating top professionals from Canada, England and the US, he was acclaimed in 1933 the professional champion of the world, retaining his title until retirement in the early 1940s. Canadian sportswriters chose Purcell in 1950 as one of the outstanding Canadian athletes of the half century.   JOHN J. JACKSON

Purcell, James, architect (*fl* St John's 1841-58). Purcell arrived in ST JOHN'S from Cork, Ire, in 1841 to superintend the building of the Roman Catholic cathedral and departed 1858 following his bankruptcy. Apparently the principal architect in the capital at the time, he designed for both the Catholics (St Bonaventure's College 1858) and the Anglicans (Christ Church at Quidi Vidi 1842; a rejected design for the Anglican cathedral 1842). His most significant work is the Colonial Building, constructed in the classical revival style 1847-50.   SHANE O'DEA

Purcell Mountains, one of the interior ranges of BC located between the Rocky Mountain Trench to the E, Kootenay Lake to the W, the Trans-Canada Highway to the N and extending beyond the US-Canadian border to the S. The Purcells are generally 300 to 600 m lower than the Rockies, but contain more than 50 peaks between 3353 and 3408 m. Its mountains are composed mainly of SEDIMENTARY rocks, including argillites, sandstones and limestones. Of great interest to mountain climbers are the numerous granitic intrusions, such as the Bugaboos, the Leaning Towers and the St Mary Batholith. The Purcells expose the oldest rock to be found on the N American continent, except those in the Grand Canyon. The highest peak in the range is Mt Farnham at 3457 m. The Purcell Wilderness Conservancy covers many of the headwaters of the rivers draining the central Purcells. Fry and Carney Creeks on the W side are a recreational reserve. The St Mary's Alpine Lakes Park and the Bugaboos are Class A provincial parks.   MARGIE JAMIESON

Purcell String Quartet The Vancouver-based PSQ was founded in 1969 by 4 Vancouver Symphony Orchestra principals, Norman Nelson and Raymond Ovens (violins), Simon Streatfeild (viola) and Ian Hampton (cello). The ensemble was joined in 1969 by Philippe Etter (viola) and in 1979 by Sydney Humphreys and Bryan King (violins). The quartet has toured, broadcast and recorded extensively in Canada. International appearances have included London, New York and San Francisco as well as Japan. In 1987, its 18th season, it toured Cuba, Florida and Mexico. The PSQ was quartet-in-residence at Simon Fraser U (1972-82). It has commissioned or given premiere performances of numerous Canadian works. Marc Destrubé replaced Humphreys in 1987.   MAX WYMAN

Purdy, Alfred Wellington, (b at Wooler, Ont 30 Dec 1918). Al Purdy is one of a group of important Canadian poets – Milton ACORN, Alden NOWLAN and Patrick LANE are others – who have little formal education and whose roots are in Canada's working-class culture. He was brought up in Trenton, Ont, educated at Albert Coll, Belleville, but did not attend university. During the Depression, he rode the rods to Vancouver and worked there for several years at a number of manual occupations.

In WWII he served in the RCAF, and after the war – until the late 1950s – he worked as a casual labourer in Ontario. Eventually, he settled in Ameliasburgh, the small Loyalist community celebrated in his poems. By the early 1960s Purdy was able to support himself by free-lance writing, poetry reading and periods as writer-in-residence at various colleges. He has been a restless traveller throughout Canada (including the High Arctic) and around the world, and all these journeyings have been reflected in his writing.

Like other writers who live by their craft, Purdy has worked in a variety of genres: radio and TV plays, book reviewing, travel writing, magazine features. He has edited anthologies, particularly of younger poets, and also a collection of essays entitled *The New Romans* (1968), which revealed his deep Canadian nationalism. But it is poetry, written and read, that is Purdy's essential mode. He has written it since he was 13, and by 1982 had published 25 volumes. The evolution of his verse shows an interesting progression from the conservatively traditional lyrics of his first collection, *The Enchanted Echo* (1944), to the open, colloquial and contemporary style of his later years, which began to emerge in his fourth collection, *The Crafte So Longe to Lerne* (1959).

Important factors in Purdy's poetic liberation from his early dependence on moribund romantic models were the humour and the anger he began to introduce, a characteristic style and form with relaxed, loping lines and a gruff, garrulous and engaging poetic persona. Purdy was at the heart of the 1960s movements that set Canadian poets wandering the country, reading their poems to large audiences. There is no doubt that this experience helped him to develop a poetry more closely related to oral speech patterns than his 1940s apprentice poems. The influence of readings on his work is one aspect of the close contact between experience and writing in Purdy's work. He has been described as a "versifying journalist," and some of his books have in fact been poetic accounts of journeys, such as *North of Summer* (1967), based on a trip to the Arctic, and *Hiroshima Poems* (1972), on a visit to Japan. Many of the poems such books contain were written during the journeys, as if entries in a diary. In them the interval between experience and creation is brief, which leads to an unevenness of tone, though the best of Purdy's travel poems are superb examples of their kind.

Purdy travels in time as well as in space. His poems reveal the generalist erudition that is acquired by a self-taught man with a passion for reading, and he has sought especially to bring into poetry a sense of Canada's past, of the rapid pattern of change that has made much of Canada acquire the quality of age in so brief a history. Few Canadian poets have evoked our past as effectively as Purdy in poems like "The Runner," "The Country North of Belleville," "My Grandfather's Country," "The Battlefield of Batoche" and the long verse cycle for radio that he wrote about the Loyalist heritage, *In Search of Owen Roblin* (1974).

Among the most successful of Purdy's many volumes are *Poems for All the Annettes* (1962), *The Cariboo Horses* (1965), which won him the Gov Gen's Award, *Sex & Death* (1973), which won him the A.J.M. Smith Award, *The Stone Bird* (1981), and *Pilim's Blood* (1984). There are 2 important selections of his verse, *Being Alive* (1978) and *Bursting into Song* (1982), which between them contain all his memorable poems except those in *The Stone Bird. Collected Poems, 1956-1986* (1986) received a Gov Gen's Award. Purdy's oral presentation of his poems, essential for a full understanding of his work, is preserved in the CBC recording, *Al Purdy's Ontario.* GEORGE WOODCOCK

Reading: George Bowering, *Al Purdy* (1970).

Purple Martin (*Progne subis*), largest (14.4-14.9 cm) and most urbanized of Canadian SWALLOWS, is the northernmost representative of an otherwise tropical New World genus. Martins extend into NB, S Ontario and adjacent Québec, the southern prairies (NW to Peace R) and southwestern BC (from which they may now be gone). They are migratory and formerly nested in tree cavities, but now largely in nesting box colonies around human settlements. Males are dark, glossy purplish black with blackish wings and tail; females and young, dark blue and grey. Martins feed on flying insects and generally forage higher than other swallows. A.J. ERSKINE

Pursh, Frederick, botanist (b Friedrich Traugott Pursch in Grossenhain, Saxony 4 Feb 1774; d at Montréal 11 July 1820). At age 25 Pursh left Dresden to try his luck in the New World. After working in the Baltimore and Philadelphia gardens, he became the collector for the rich naturalist Benjamin Smith Barton. On behalf of Barton and several other wealthy botanists, Pursh explored the eastern US from North Carolina to Vermont 1806-11. He also examined the specimens brought back by explorers Lewis and Clark. Pursh went to England with his notes and collections and found there the support and resources that allowed him to publish his main work, the *Flora Americae Septentrionalis* (1814). Despite major errors, it was an important contribution to knowledge of N American flora. Having for a while hoped to join Lord SELKIRK's Red R expedition, Pursh settled in Montréal to prepare a flora of Canada. In 1818 he explored ANTICOSTI I but his specimens were destroyed in a fire the following winter. Discouraged and reduced to poverty, he died at age 46. RAYMOND DUCHESNE

Purvis, Arthur Blaikie, industrialist (b at London, Eng 31 Mar 1890; d at Prestwick, Scot 14 Aug 1941). At the age of 20 Purvis joined Nobel's Explosives Co of Glasgow, which became part of Imperial Chemical Industries of London. It was as an employee of ICI that Purvis was sent to Canada to be president and managing director of Canadian Industries Ltd, one of Canada's most technologically advanced companies. A liberal-minded employer, with broad views on social and economic questions, he was appointed chairman of the National Employment Commission (1936-38) by PM Mackenzie KING, but the 2 clashed over the commission's recommendation that the federal government should bear all relief costs and responsibility for the unemployed. In WWII the British government (not the Canadian) made Purvis head of the British Supply Council in charge of British purchases in N America. Purvis reconciled himself with King but quarrelled repeatedly with Lord Beaverbrook [Max AITKEN], the British minister of aircraft production. Purvis was killed in an air crash. ROBERT BOTHWELL

Put-In-Bay, site of a battle fought between British and American naval forces on 10 Sept 1813 during the WAR OF 1812, in the SW portion of Lake Erie. Both fleets were newly built of green lumber, and both experienced technical problems. The American ships were superior to the British in tonnage, weight and broadsides, and number of seamen; the bold American commander, Oliver Hazard Perry, made effective tactical use of his advantages. After determined and gallant resistance by Robert Barclay of the Royal Navy, the British fleet was forced to surrender. The Americans controlled Lake Erie for the rest of the war. But the British were still able to provision their posts on the upper lakes by creating a new route via York [Toronto], Lake Simcoe, Georgian Bay and Lake Huron. ROBERT S. ALLEN

Putnam, Donald Fulton, geographer, educator (b at Lower Onslow, NS 15 Aug 1903; d at Toronto 23 Feb 1977). Although his early training was in agriculture and soils, he was invited by Griffith TAYLOR, founder of the Dept of Geography at U of T, to join the department in 1938. His outstanding contribution with co-author Lyman Chapman was *The Physiography of Southern Ontario* (1951), the first published account of the glacial landforms of the region. Putnam was head of the department at U of T 1953-63 and was awarded the Massey Medal in 1969. MARIE SANDERSON

Puttee, Arthur, printer, editor (b at Folkestone, Eng 25 Aug 1868; d at Winnipeg 21 Oct 1957). Puttee was Manitoba's first Labour MP, as member for Winnipeg 1900-04. He had immigrated to N America in 1888, settling in Winnipeg 3 years later, where he was especially influential as publisher 1899-1918 of *The Voice*. In this labour weekly, Puttee popularized his reforming ideas, emphasizing the links between "labourism" in Canada and the philosophy of labour representation in Britain. However, political opponents charged that behind him lurked unnamed "revolutionists" and "assassins," accusations that led to his defeat in the 1904 general election. Puttee was an advanced Liberal, not a socialist, and won his seat in 1900 only after soliciting important Liberal support and promising Winnipeg electors that he would not vote down war credits for South Africa. Himself a critic of alleged "Industrial Workers of the World methods" during WWI, Puttee was replaced by younger and more radical leaders and played no major part in the 1919 WINNIPEG GENERAL STRIKE, whose seed he had nonetheless helped sow. ALLEN SEAGER

Pyrite, *see* GOLD; IRON ORE.

Qaqaq Ashoona (also known as Kaka), sculptor (b 19 Aug 1928). Elder son of Inuk artist PITSEOLAK ASHOONA, Qaqaq is a central figure in this remarkable creative family. A reserved man with traditional values, Qaqaq has for most of his life chosen not to reside in the modern settlement of CAPE DORSET, NWT, preferring instead to maintain a year-round camp nearby on the land. He began his artistic career at about age 18, and his sculpture is acclaimed for the sense of monumentality and strength he imparts to animal and human subjects alike. *See also* INUIT ART.

MARIE ROUTLEDGE

Qitdlarssuaq, Inuk leader (b at Cape Searle, NWT; d near Cape Herschel, NWT 1875). He led an epic migration from Baffin I to northern Greenland. A powerful *angakkuq* (SHAMAN) he was so respected that more than 50 Inuit followed him far into unknown territory as he escaped vengeance for murder. The journey took many years and he navigated, it is said, partly by spiritual flights, leaving his body and examining the terrain ahead. After spending several years with the Polar Eskimos, to whom they introduced the kayak, the bow and arrow and the fish spear, Qitdlarssuaq and his followers set out for their homeland, but the old leader died along the way. The survivors returned to Greenland, where their descendants still live, and where the story has become important in local tradition.

JOHN BENNETT

Quadra Island, 269 km², is situated at the N end of the Str of GEORGIA between VANCOUVER I and mainland BC, opposite CAMPBELL RIVER. The forested island, about 35 km long, forms the E side of Discovery Passage, a narrow, treacherous ship channel leading N out of the strait. Four small communities are dotted around its coast. It was named after 18th-century Spanish naval explorer BODEGA Y QUADRA.

DANIEL FRANCIS

Quail, name most commonly applied to an Old World species, *Coturnix coturnix*, of chickenlike birds, which migrate seasonally in vast flocks and have long been an important human food source, eg, for the Israelites in the wilderness. New World quail are the only members of the PHEASANT subfamily native to N America. New World quail are not migratory. Some are adapted to desert habitats and can survive indefinitely without water if succulent food is available. In Canada, 3 species are found: California quail (*Callipepla californicus*) and mountain quail (*Oreortyx pictus*) in the mildest parts of southern BC; northern bobwhite (*Colinus virginianus*) in southern Ontario and introduced elsewhere. The northern bobwhite is the best-known species and, in the US, is the most widely hunted GAME BIRD. Unlike the other 2, it lacks an ornamental crest.

S.D. MacDONALD

Quakers (properly The Religious Society of Friends), a body of Christians that arose out of the religious ferment of mid-17th century Puritan England. Founder George Fox (1624-91) was the son of a Leicestershire weaver. The popular name, "Quakers," may have arisen from Fox's admonition to his followers: "Tremble at the Word of the Lord." Persecuted at home, many Quakers immigrated to the N American colonies. In the late 17th century, Quaker "Publishers of Truth" visited Newfoundland, but it was not until the mid-18th century that Quaker whalers from Nantucket established permanent settlements in Nova Scotia. In the 19th century more Quakers settled in what is now southern Ontario, where they established meetinghouses and schools. By 1860 there were over 7300 Quakers in Canada, mostly in Canada W. The number then declined to about 1000, a strength that has been maintained to this day, mainly through new members.

Throughout the 19th century, Quakers were a religious community identified by a distinctive faith and form of worship, and by special marriage customs, dress, forms of speech and "testimonies" against SLAVERY, CAPITAL PUNISHMENT and war. In the 20th century, Quakers in Canada have been active in the Christian antiwar movement (*see* PACIFISM; PEACE MOVEMENT) and in opposition to capital punishment. This witness has been carried out principally by the Canadian Friends Service Committee, Toronto. Today, Quaker groups are found in many Canadian cities, parts of a worldwide Society of Friends.

DAVID L. NEWLANDS

Reading: Arthur G. Dorland, *A History of the Society of Friends (Quakers) in Canada* (1927).

Qualicum Beach, BC, Town, pop 3410 (1986c), inc 5 May 1942, is located on the E coast of Vancouver I, 48 km N of Nanaimo. The name Qualicum is an Indian word meaning "where the dog salmon run." The town has long been a major resort area owing to its fine sandy beaches and mild climate. The town is also known for its good sportfishing and sweeping view of Georgia Str and its islands. Nearby are the 2 fine provincial parks of Englishman R and Little Qualicum Falls. The climate and recreational advantages have also made it a retirement centre.

JOHN STEWART

Qu'Appelle River, 430 km long, rises in Lk DIEFENBAKER and meanders generally E across southern Saskatchewan, joining the ASSINIBOINE R just E of the Manitoba border. The broad, tranquil river valley is rich agricultural land, and is famous for the berries that grow on the moist, north-facing slopes. At Ft Qu'Appelle the river widens into a chain of pleasant lakes bordered by parks. The charming name comes from a Cree legend. A young man heard someone call his name as he crossed one of the valley lakes. He replied "Who calls?" (*Qu'appelle*), but only his echo answered. He realized later it was his bride-to-be, calling him at the instant of her death.

JAMES MARSH

The Qu'Appelle River valley is rich agricultural land famous for the berries that grow along the river's north-facing slopes (*photo by Richard Vroom*).

Quarrying Industry Commercial production of natural stone is an important industry in all provinces. The value of all stone quarried in 1984 was nearly $335 million, representing a total production volume of over 71 million t. Stone is taken from a large open excavation or pit by cutting, digging or blasting, depending on the method best suited to each deposit. Quarried stone is handled with mechanical equipment appropriate to the operation, eg, draglines, loaders, conveyors, forklifts and trucks. Often quarries are owned and operated by companies associated with the CONSTRUCTION INDUSTRIES.

The principal types of stone quarried in Canada are LIMESTONE, granite, sandstone and marble. Limestone accounts for 75% of the total volume both in tonnage and value. Granite accounts for over 20% of the annual total. By comparison, output of marble and sandstone is relatively small. Limestone quarries are widely distributed in Canada and economics usually dictate that sources nearest the largest markets become volume producers on the largest scale. Québec produces nearly half of Canada's annual quarry production; Ontario accounts for over a third; the balance comes mainly from British Columbia.

Nearly all of the stone produced is crushed and used by the construction industries for concrete and asphalt aggregates, as a stabilizing base material in road building, for rubble and riprap used for fill and embankment reinforcement, as railway ballast, as roofing granules, and as chips for stucco and terrazzo. Other industries consume about 8% of annual quarry production. The CHEMICAL INDUSTRIES use crushed limestone in the neutralizing of acids; in the extraction of aluminum oxide from bauxite; in the manufacture of soda ash, calcium carbide, calcium nitrate and carbon dioxide; in PHARMACEUTICALS; in the manufacture of dyes, rayons, paper, sugar and GLASS; and in WATER TREATMENT. Limestone is used in METALLURGY as a fluxing material to cleanse impurities from molten metal. Pulverized limestone is used extensively by industry as a filler and extender for CEMENT and as a whiting used in CERAMICS, PLASTICS, floor coverings, insecticides, paper, wood putty, paints and other commodities. Limestone is used in the manufacture of fertilizer and has other agricultural applications. About 2% of all stone quarried in Canada is used as dimension stone or ornamental building stone. Most prominent are the granites of Québec and the limestones of Ontario, Québec and Manitoba. Perhaps the best known of the latter is Manitoba Tyndall Stone, an attractively mottled dolomitic limestone quarried near Winnipeg.

In 1986 the value of stone exported from Canada was about $15 million. By comparison, total imports in 1986 were about $52.2 million. The quarrying industry is directly influenced by the construction industry: a decline in the latter causes reduced demand for building materials. In addition, stricter environmental controls could limit or even close many quarries, particularly those near larger urban centres, where dust and noise create objections and where extensive rehabilitation of spent pits may be required.

I.B. BICKELL

Quasar, extraterrestrial object which emits radiation over a wide spectral range. Although the name is a contraction of "quasi-stellar radio source," these objects also radiate light, X rays and even gamma rays. The term "QSO" (quasi-stellar object) refers to objects with many quasar-like properties but no detectable radio emission. No quasar is visible with the unaided eye. Even on photographs made with large telescopes, they look very much like faint STARS; hence, quasars were not recognized as distinct entities until the early 1960s and it is still not clear what they really are. Examination of their colours and spectra has demonstrated that quasars are not stars. Most emit a larger proportion of their light in the ultraviolet and blue part of the spectrum than do stars. The Doppler shifts shown in the light spectra of quasars show that they are receding at very great velocities. These velocities imply very great distances: quasars are probably the most distant objects known. Because quasars are 100-1000 times as luminous as GALAXIES, they can be observed at much greater distances and provide a means of studying the large-scale structure and dynamics of the universe.

A few of the brightest quasars are surrounded by faint emitting regions which have spectra resembling those of galaxies. It is therefore reasonable to infer that a quasar is a type of galactic nucleus, an inference which becomes more plausible if combined with the fact that many galaxies, including our own, have compact nuclei which, in some cases, are brighter than the rest of the galaxy.

The recognition of quasars as a distinct class of objects arose from attempts to identify optically extraterrestrial radio sources whose positions had been accurately measured using radio interferometers. Subsequent quasar observations have shown radio-wave intensity variations from month to month. Similar but not identical intensity changes have been observed in their light emissions. The occurrence of such rapid changes implies that quasars (or at least their emitting regions) are much smaller than galaxies, although they are many times more luminous.

Canadian scientists made the first direct measurements of the angular sizes of quasars using the 46 m Algonquin radio telescope and the 25 m radio telescope near Penticton, BC, to form a long-baseline interferometer. Such radio measurements, combined with distance measurements inferred from optical spectra, indicate that quasars have energies far exceeding those of any other objects. Measurements repeated over several years have shown distinct structural changes in a number of quasars. These quasars appear to consist of 2 or more regions, moving apart at speeds considerably faster than the speed of light. Such speeds are in contravention of well-established physical laws. This paradox is one of the most important unsolved problems in ASTRONOMY or PHYSICS. *See also* OBSERVATORY.　　JOHN GALT

Quastel, Judah Hirsch, professor of neurochemistry (b at Sheffield, Eng 2 Oct 1899). Quastel is a founder of modern neurochemistry. During 1927-28, he put forward the active-centre hypothesis of enzyme action, leading to his discovery of the principle of competitive inhibition of an enzyme by a substrate analogue. He pioneered the use of suspensions of *E. coli* for systematic biochemical studies of the living cell and coined the term "phenylketonuria" in studies of mental defect. His contributions to the study of membrane transport processes include the original demonstration of the necessity of sodium ion in the active, energy-assisted process. A professor at UBC from 1966-83 and professor emeritus since then, he has received the RSC Flavelle Medal and the Gairdner Foundation International Award (1974), and is a Companion of the Order of Canada. He has published more than 370 scientific papers and several books.
　　　　　　　　　　　　SHAN-CHING SUNG

Québec, Canada's largest province, is partly detached from the rest of Canada by Hudson Bay and faces both Europe and the heart of N America. Representing 15.5% of the surface area of Canada, the province occupies some 1.5 million km², an area 3 times the size of France and 7 times

that of Great Britain. A distance of 1700 km separates towns in the Gaspé region of the province's eastern extremity from Ville-Marie in the NE. Québec has common borders with Ontario, New Brunswick and Newfoundland although Québec still disputes the exact location of the Labrador boundary (*see* LABRADOR BOUNDARY DISPUTE). Québec continues to refuse to recognize the boundary established by the British Privy Council in 1927, though it was recognized in the CONSTITUTION ACT, 1982. Québec also neighbours on 4 American states: Maine, New Hampshire, Vermont and New York. The word "Québec" comes from an Algonquian word meaning "where the river narrows." It first appeared on a map in 1601 to designate the present site of Québec City. Until the ROYAL PROCLAMATION OF 1763, the word was used only for the city, but it now applies to the entire province.

Québec is more than a province; it is the national territory and home of over 90% of Canadians of French origin. It is the only predominantly French-speaking territory in N America (apart from the islands of SAINT-PIERRE AND MIQUELON) and has one of the largest francophone communities outside France. Forming a culturally distinct society within the Canadian community, francophone Quebeckers consider themselves one of Canada's 2 founding peoples. Their language, traditions, culture and institutions set Québec apart from all other provinces.

Land and Resources

Québec is composed of 3 major geological regions. The Canadian SHIELD, covering 80% of the province, is a vast plateau with many lakes, rivers and forested areas, extending over all of northern Québec. To the S lies the ST LAWRENCE R valley and lowlands, where 90% of the population is concentrated. This is the most fertile and developed region. Finally, on the S bank of the St Lawrence, between Québec City and Lk Champlain and extending the full length of the Gaspé Peninsula, lies the Appalachian region, part of a very old mountain chain, extending from Newfoundland down to Alabama.

Geology and Relief The St Lawrence Lowlands region was the first settled by French colonists. Its location on the St Lawrence R permitted easy travel and the land was arable. Wedged between the Appalachians and the Shield, this land is composed of a series of broad terraces sloping gently toward the river. With an average elevation of 150 m, the area has fertile soil and a pleasant environment. On the other hand, only about 5% of the Shield is arable land, most of which is located in the lower section, known as the Laurentides or LAURENTIAN HIGHLANDS. The Laurentides cover half of southern Québec N of the St Lawrence. The southern extension of the Laurentides is dotted with villages that have become summer and winter resort areas. The third area, the Appalachian region, consists of a succession of small mountain formations intersected by arable plateaus and plains. The EASTERN TOWNSHIPS, the meeting point of the US and Québec, are the heart of this region and the area in which the first LOYALIST immigrants settled after their flight from the US. Overall, Québec has a fairly even elevation, half of the province lying between 300 and 600 m and only 7% above 600 m. Mt d'Iberville, in the Torngat Mts in northern Québec, is the highest point at 1652 m. In southern Québec, Mt Jacques Cartier in the Gaspé region rises to 1248 m.

During the Quaternary period, the entire province was covered with glaciers. Their gradual retreat began some 15 000 years ago in the Appalachians. This retreat was accompanied by the formation of a vast inland sea, the Champlain

Sea, which covered a large portion of Québec between what are today Québec City and Montréal. This deglaciation was partly responsible for the worn and rounded relief that characterizes Québec, as well as for the many lakes that dot the province.

Flora and Fauna Québec flora have had a relatively short time to evolve. The glaciers, which did not disappear until fairly recently, were followed by a cold climatic period. Consequently, present vegetation was born essentially from the northward movement of vegetation originally found along the US border. Climate has thus been the determining factor for the province's vegetation (*see* VEGETATION REGIONS). Generally, as one moves N, the variety, size and number of plant species decline. N of the 56th parallel, the arctic tundra is characterized by a lack of forest covering. Here are lichens and mosses, as well as peat bogs broken up by rocky outcroppings. This desolate landscape is the habitat of certain animal species that are particularly well adapted to the northern climate – the polar bear, fox and arctic hare.

The taiga, the transition zone between the arctic tundra and the boreal forest to the S, covers hundreds of square kilometres between the 52nd and 56th parallels. Although this is an essentially nonforested zone, trees are found in more sheltered areas. These are most often spruce and fir mixed with dwarf shrubs and trees. Here lichens form a carpet, soaking up water at night and crackling in the heat of the day. Herds of caribou, which move N over several hundred kilometres to calve, form the largest group of cervidae in Québec. The George R herd alone numbers approximately 600 000. The boreal forest covers a large part of the Canadian Shield. Despite being heavily forested, this area is largely unpopulated and has not been extensively exploited. Fir and spruce survive, along with tamarack and pine. Lakes and rivers are numerous and abound with trout and other fish.

Dominating the Ottawa Valley, St Lawrence Lowlands, Appalachians and Lac Saint-Jean areas, the temperate forest is composed essentially of maple, ash, beech and oak. This forest is the primary source of Québec's forestry industry and the source of its spectacular autumn colour. The temperate forest is also the habitat for large herds of deer, Ile d'ANTICOSTI alone accounting for some 60 000 head. Large herds of moose are concentrated in the Laurentide region and in the heart of the Chics-Chocs mountains in the interior of the Gaspé Peninsula. Coyotes, wolves, mink and even a few lynx also inhabit this region.

Since the St Lawrence provides a route to the interior, a number of sea mammals have become permanent or seasonal inhabitants of Québec waters, eg, several hundred beluga whales in the estuary, as well as seals, killer whales and humpback whales. There are about 105 species of freshwater fish, and about another one dozen which live in salt water but spawn in fresh water. These include salmon and smelt. Pike, all types of trout, yellow perch and black bass are found throughout the area.

Québec has some 350 species of birds, only 5-7% of which winter in the province. Birds of prey such as the merlin, kestrel and great horned owl all winter in Québec and inhabit the boreal forest. A little farther S live red-tailed hawks, gyrfalcons and several migratory birds such as the herring gull and the Lapland longspur pass through the S on their migrations. Populated areas contain the greatest variety of birds, such as crows, starlings, finches and swallows. In the summer months, the waters are inhabited by Canada geese and snow geese. Their southward migration signals the advent of winter.

Waterways The St Lawrence R is undoubtedly

Baie-St-Paul, a typical Québec community on the St Lawrence R (*photo by Karl Sommerer*).

Québec's most important geographical feature. Flowing at an average rate of 10 100 m³/s, it ranks with the great rivers of the world. These lakes and rivers, purportedly more than one million in number, represent an area larger than half of France. Québec's waterways can be divided into 3 major watersheds, the St Lawrence R, estuary and gulf being the largest. Its main tributaries to the S are the RICHELIEU, Yamaska, CHAUDIÈRE and Mata-pédia, and in the N the ST-MAURICE, SAGUENAY, MAN-ICOUAGAN and OTTAWA. Major hydroelectric projects have created large reservoirs such as the one in the Manicouagan R (1942 km²) and the Gouin Reservoir (1570 km²) on the St-Maurice. Major lakes in the St Lawrence area include the EAU CLAIRE (1383 km²) and SAINT-JEAN (1002 km²), which lies at the end of the Saguenay R in the heart of a major settlement which Quebeckers affectionately call the "Kingdom of the Sague-nay." More than any other Canadian province, Québec owes its development to its rivers, particularly the St Lawrence, which has been celebrat-ed by poets and songwriters and is part of Qué-bec's collective consciousness. The St Lawrence is Québec's central nervous system, the main transit way for its exports and imports. Although big and magnificent the St Lawrence has always present-ed serious problems to navigation. Between Qué-bec City and Montréal the fairway is tortuous and often quite narrow. To reach the Great Lakes, canals had to be built, and it is only recently with the opening of the ST LAWRENCE SEAWAY in 1954 that the river has realized its full potential. But periodically this direct link between the Great Lakes and the Atlantic has not benefited Mont-réal, which can no longer claim to be Canada's entry point to the world.

Most of the largest rivers in Québec flow into the JAMES BAY and HUDSON BAY basin. This area contains so many lakes that from the air it is hard to tell whether land or water predominates. Since 1973 the area's vast potential, particularly around the Nottaway, Rupert and Eastmain riv-ers, has been harnessed as part of the largest hy-droelectric project in Canada, under the authority of the James Bay Development Corporation. The first phase of the JAMES BAY PROJECT alone will add over 10 billion kW to Hydro-Québec's produc-tion. The third watershed is UNGAVA BAY, whose major rivers are the KOKSOAK and the Caniapias-

cau. Here lies the Nouveau-Québec Crater, a lake 3.3 km in diameter which was created by a mete-orite and has no tributaries or draining rivers.

Climate Québec's CLIMATE is severe and irregu-lar. Because of the province's relatively moderate relief, continental air masses circulate freely. Nei-ther the Canadian Shield nor the Appalachians is a large enough natural obstacle to block these air currents. Peripheral marine currents can also have an effect on temperatures. The cold Labra-dor Current, which moves southward and disap-pears near Newfoundland, causes cool East Coast summers. The Gulf Stream, moving northward along the East Coast, has virtually no effect on Québec's winter climate. In winter the prevailing winds blow from the interior towards the ocean, cancelling out any possible effects of this warm current. In summer, however, ocean winds often bring humid heat waves. Another feature of Qué-bec's climate is the frequent stormy meetings of cold, dry air masses from the N and W with warm, tropical air from the Gulf of Mexico. In winter the meetings of these fronts cause a great deal of snow to fall over the entire province. In summer, hu-midity and heavy rainfalls take the place of snow.

Quebeckers like to claim that spring and au-tumn do not exist. Summers lengthen in the S, where most of the population resides. In the plain of Montréal, summer light and a higher number of frost-free days create an environment that is not only more favourable to agriculture but also quite enjoyable. With its blazing colours, autumn is often the most breathtaking season around Québec City and Montréal, along the Richelieu,

and in Mauricie and the Eastern Townships. Win-ter, however, is the season that has most influ-enced Québec society. It has taken 4 centuries to tame and conquer it. Today, it is no longer syn-onymous with hardship and isolation but has be-come a season with its good points as well: skiing, skating and skidooing. Also, without winter there would be no HOCKEY, which Quebeckers consider their national sport.

Resources Although abundant natural re-sources gave Québec an early comparative ad-vantage in raw material extraction, this advan-tage has not produced balanced economic development. Distant markets, the small percent-age of francophone managers in extraction com-panies, and a lack of economic planning have meant that natural resources are extracted in Québec but processed outside the province. The province in 1986 nevertheless produced more than 80% of Canada's ASBESTOS, 28% of its GOLD, 37% of its IRON ORE and 100% of both its TITANIUM and COLUMBIUM.

Québec's subsoil contains a number of other industrial minerals such as PEAT, limestone, silica, granite and mica. With the exception of peat, however, these products have been mined only to meet the primary needs of local markets. Al-though Québec is not mining uranium at the mo-ment, it is believed to have great potential in this area. In building materials such as stone, cement, sand and lime, the Québec construction industry is largely self-sufficient. In 1985 these products were worth $436 million.

Environmental Protection Like all societies, Québec produces a considerable amount of solid wastes which, when introduced into the ecosys-tem, become pollutants. To these solid wastes must be added toxic liquid wastes from factories, mines and farms. Since 1977, open-air dumps have been banned and must be replaced by un-derground waste-disposal sites. A toxic material recycling centre has been constructed recently N of Montréal.

ACID RAIN, which threatens almost all of Qué-bec's lakes and forests, is the most worrisome air-pollution phenomenon. Many groups and associ-ations are fighting to protect the environment and have successfully urged the Dept of the Environ-ment to impose strict regulations on water and air pollution. Huge de-pollution programs are under way, notably for the rivers around Montréal, and in the Gulf of St Lawrence.

Population and Society

France took a long time to establish its roots on the shores of the St Lawrence. There were scarce-

View of Montréal from the St Lawrence R (*photo by Ken-non Cooke/Valan*).

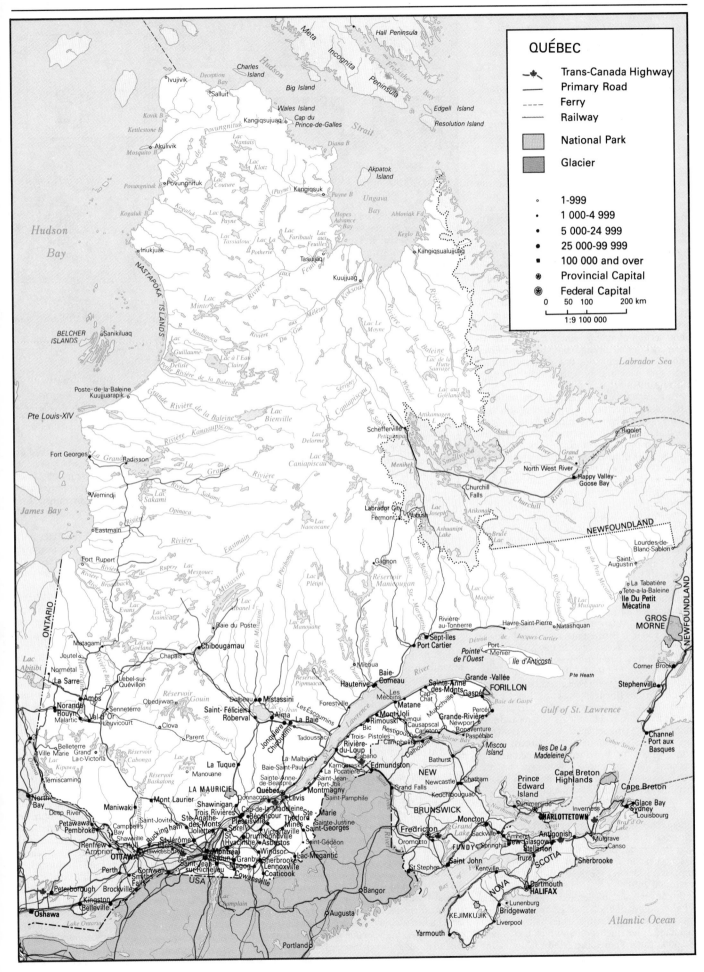

QUÉBEC

Trans-Canada Highway
Primary Road
Ferry
Railway

National Park

Glacier

○ 1–999
· 1 000–4 999
• 5 000–24 999
● 25 000–99 999
■ 100 000 and over
⊛ Provincial Capital
◉ Federal Capital

0   50   100   200 km

1:9 100 000

ly 100 inhabitants in 1627 and only 3418 by 1666. The period between 1608 and 1760 witnessed the arrival of only 10 000 immigrants in all: 3500 soldiers, 1100 women, 1000 prisoners, 3900 volunteers and 500 free men.

Three centuries later, these 10 000 colonists had grown to approximately 10 million people, of which half still live in Québec and the rest in New England and in some areas of Canada, especially in Ontario. The unique Québec culture results solely from the perseverance of these first colonists, for after 1760 there was virtually no French immigration.

Land Settlement Québec's land was settled in a unique fashion, in the rows, or rangs, of the SEIGNEURIAL SYSTEM. This method had enormous impact not only on the distribution of the HABITANTS, but also on their social organization. The colonists built their farm buildings along the rivers, which were the only thoroughfares navigable by canoe in summer and by sled in winter. Each colonist's land was therefore necessarily very narrow (200 to 250 m wide) but 2000 to 2500 m long. The same pattern was repeated behind the first row – some municipalities had over 10 rows. The system had a number of advantages: co-operation for defence, the relative ease of plowing a short section of road in winter, and the encouragement of sociability and community initiatives. People helped each other, and when it was time to marry off daughters or sons, people looked to their neighbours first.

Thus, each row became an individual social entity, obliging each person to share but also to be relatively independent because of the scattered population. With time, certain habitants developed their own areas of expertise; schools were created and businesses opened. They gathered in villages built around their church. Only the Eastern Townships, which were originally colonized by Loyalist immigrants, were not settled in this manner.

Population Growth and Distribution Under the French regime, Québec's population grew very slowly. More than 50 years after the founding of QUÉBEC CITY, it had grown to only 2500, compared to a population of 80 000 in the American colonies. By 1760 Québec's population had reached only 65 000. Because of a very high birthrate, one of the highest in the world (65 per 1000 inhabitants), the population increased very quickly. By 1791 Lower Canada had a population of over 160 000. By this time, however, the major change was the presence of 20 000 Anglophones (12.5% of total population), some of whom had been forced to flee the US during the American Revolution. They were welcomed by British authorities who wished, among other things, to anglicize their new colony. These new arrivals joined with a rising tide of SCOTS, ENGLISH and IRISH immigrants. Many settled in Montréal and Québec City, or SE of Montréal in the Eastern Townships, where they benefited from generous concessions and organized themselves on the TOWNSHIP system. For a time, Montréal even had a majority of anglophone inhabitants.

By 1871 Québec's population had reached 1.2 million, 20% of whom claimed to be of British origin. This increase had been mainly owing to a birthrate that was much higher than anywhere else in Canada. Despite this, the proportion of Quebeckers in Canada had already begun to drop, from 43% in 1866 to 30% in 1926. Today, it is around 26%.

At the time of Confederation, 1867, only 20% of the population of Québec lived in cities, chiefly in Montréal, which then had 90 000 inhabitants, and Québec City, which had almost 60 000. These figures increased rapidly as the province became industrialized. In 1901, 36% of

Québec

Capital: Québec City
Motto: Je me souviens ("I remember")
Flower: Fleur-de-lis (Madonna lily)
Largest Cities: Montréal, Québec City, Laval, Sherbrooke, Verdun, Hull, Trois-Rivières
Population: 6 532 461 (1986c); rank second, 25.8% of Canada; 77.9% urban, 22.1% rural; 4.8 per km² density; 1.5% increase from 1981-86; 4.8% increase from 1976-86
Languages: 81.9% French; 8.9% English; 6.1% Other; 3.1% English plus one or more languages
Entered Confederation: 1 July 1867
Government: Provincial – Lieutenant-Governor, Executive Council, National Assembly of 122 members; Federal – 24 senators, 75 members of the House of Commons
Area: 1 540 680 km², including 183 889 km² of inland water; 15.51% of Canada
Elevation: Highest point – Mont d'Iberville (1652 m); lowest point – Gulf of St Lawrence shore
Gross Domestic Product: $102.8 billion (1986)
Farm Cash Receipts: $3.2 billion (1986)
Value of Fish Landings: $85.9 million (1986)
Electric Power Produced: 136 727 GWh (1985)
Sales Tax: 9% (1987)

the population lived in cities, and by 1921 the figure had grown to 52%. Montréal continued to grow and in 1930 had almost one million inhabitants. Over 30% of all Quebeckers (half of Québec's urban population) lived on the island of Montréal. Today, almost 80% of the population may be considered urban, giving Québec the second-largest urban population after Ontario (82%). Only 3% of the entire population live on farms.

With 60% of Québec's total population, the region of MONTRÉAL is by far the most populated area of Québec. It is followed by the Québec City region with 16%. Less than 5% of the population is found in the 8 other regions (Lower St Lawrence, Saguenay-Lac Saint-Jean, TROIS-RIVIÈRES, Estrie, the Outaouais, the Northwest and the North Shore).

Since 1950, and even more rapidly since 1960, Quebec's birthrate has been decreasing steadily, stabilizing in the late 1970s and now standing around 13.4 per 1000 inhabitants, a rate now lower than that in the rest of Canada. Considering the systematic emigration that has taken place since the 1970s, this low growth rate raises a number of worrisome issues principally concerning the aging of the population. By 1981 Montréal was no longer Canada's largest city, having lost that position to Toronto.

Labour Force In 1986, 5% of Québec's labour force was concentrated in the primary sector (compared to 12% in 1961), 28% in the secondary sector (35% in 1961) and 67% in the tertiary sector (54% in 1961).

Québec's very high UNEMPLOYMENT rate has not dropped below 8% since 1975. It increased steadily, reaching 10% in 1980 and 14% at the low point of the economic recession in 1982-83. Since then unemployment has slowly returned to the 10% level by 1987. Certain regions such as Abitibi-Témiscamingue, the Lower St Lawrence and Mauricie are especially hard hit, with rates 20% higher than the Québec average. The very rapid increase in the active work force, from 1.9 million to 3.2 million between 1963 and 1987, is the main reason for higher unemployment. Be-

tween 1977 and 1986, 50 000 new jobs were created annually, resulting in the recent reduction of the unemployment rate.

Although Québec continues to be marked by major regional disparities in favour of Montréal, opportunities have equalized somewhat since 1971. This process has resulted more from a reduction in Montréal's advantages rather than from any noticeable improvement in the situation of the regions.

Language and Ethnic Groups Québec is the only region in N America where French is the language of the majority. In 1986, 81.9% of Québec's inhabitants claimed French as their mother tongue. Approximately 11% of Quebeckers are of British origin, a percentage which has steadily declined from the mid-19th century when the British represented 25% of the total Québec population. About 6% of Quebeckers have neither English nor French as the mother tongue. However, since the vast majority of this group have made English their language of usage, it is generally estimated that about 16% of Québec's population is English speaking. Traditionally, eastern Europeans and ITALIANS were the most important ethnic groups. Since 1960 they have been joined by PORTUGUESE, Haitians, GREEKS and various SOUTHEAST ASIAN groups which have all contributed in giving Québec a more multicultural atmosphere, particularly in Montréal where the majority of immigrants have settled.

This assimilation of over 85% of new arrivals to Québec into the anglophone group, coupled with the rapid decline in the birthrate of francophone families, has led every Québec government since 1969 to pass legislation guaranteeing the survival and growth of the French language in Québec. Since the adoption of BILL 101 in 1977, French has been the sole official language of Québec. Despite their opposition to this legislation, anglophone Quebeckers benefit from a complete school system, including 3 universities, a number of newspapers, radio and television stations, hospitals and many kinds of cultural institutions, making them the best-served ethnic minority in Canada. Recognizing the important role of ethnic groups in Québec society, the government renamed its Dept of Immigration the Dept of Immigration and Cultural Communities.

Religion Statistics on church attendance aside, religion has always occupied a special place in Québec society. Although Quebeckers have long since stopped defining themselves as a Catholic society, religion and language helped them stay together as a group after the Conquest of 1760 and throughout the entire English colonial regime. For a long time, the parish was Québec's major social structure and the clergy one of the principal local elites through its control over educational and health-related structures.

Roman CATHOLICISM has the largest number of adherents among Quebeckers (87%), followed by the Anglican Church (3%), the United Church (3%), Judaism (2%) and the Greek Orthodox Church (1%). Analysis by ethnic group provides some interesting results: although 97% of Quebeckers of French origin officially claim to be Catholics, only 88% of Catholics are of French origin. This reveals the existence of sizable Catholic communities other than the French, chiefly among Quebeckers of Irish, Italian and German origin.

Social Institutions It is essentially language and culture that distinguish Québec's society from any other. These distinctions led to the creation of social institutions that have made Québec a distinct society within the Canadian community. Québec's legal and judicial system occupies an important place among these institutions. Québec is governed by the CIVIL CODE, developed from the old French laws, rather than from English COMMON LAW. Consequently, relationships between individuals, societies and groups are based on principles different from those in the rest of Canada.

Québec's distinctiveness in this respect is evident in the way its social services are integrated, combining medical and social assistance with a network that provides services for children, the sick, the aged and anyone who has a particular need. This network is the responsibility of a government department, and comprises some 800 establishments, including 227 hospital centres and 102 local community-service centres. Québec's social-benefits program, established in 1965, differs from those in the rest of Canada. An agency of the Québec government sets and collects premiums and administers benefits. Also established in 1965, the CAISSE DE DÉPÔT ET PLACEMENT administers funds received from depositors such as the Régie des rentes, the Régie de l'assurance-automobile and the Commission de la santé et de la sécurité au travail. With a 1986 net income of $3 billion and assets worth $25 billion, the caisse has become one of the major economic powers in Québec and Canada.

The existence of a charter of human rights and a consumer protection Act (both the most comprehensive in Canada), a legal-aid and small-claims-court system, a well-established network of day-care centres, a unique automobile insurance system and a distinct income-security and family-allowance system all show the autonomous nature of Québec society.

Economy

Québec has a highly industrialized and relatively diversified economy. With an immense territory abounding in natural resources and located near developed and inhabited regions, and with a young and well-trained labour force, Québec has an economy that has not yet reached its full potential. The problems assailing it since WWII have not yet been solved and tend to mask the progress that has been made. These problems include its outdated industrial structure, stubborn regional disparities, the lack of co-operation among the various sectors of the economy and the small degree of control that francophone Quebeckers exert over the main levers of their own economic development.

A number of these problems have historical roots. Although New France's small population was scattered over a large area and received little attention from France, it was able to maximize its resources and make the most of the land. The FUR TRADE was the basis of the colony's economy. In fact the desire to control this trade was at the root of the Franco-British rivalry to dominate the colonization of N America. However, the enormously profitable and risky fur trade was never the settlers' only economic activity. Contrary to the popular image of colonists as COUREURS DE BOIS, 80% of settlers lived permanently on their farms; hence their name "habitants." By 1750 it was clear that New France had chosen to become a colony of settlers. Montréal, Trois-Rivières and Québec City already had fairly large populations. Fishing was profitable and there were enough mills and bakeries to produce a surplus for export. In 1743 the FORGES SAINT-MAURICE produced 175 000 kg of iron, and there were already some shipyards in operation.

The British takeover was both beneficial and catastrophic for the Québec economy – beneficial because everything had to be reconstructed after the ravages of war. Agricultural production resumed; increased demand stimulated forest exploitation; and fishing, iron-ore mining and fur trading all expanded considerably because of an injection of new capital and the opening of new markets.

Between 1800 and 1815, a new economy was being established in Québec, one from which, for all practical purposes, French Canadians were excluded. At that time a primitive economic system requiring only the support of a few financiers and abundant manpower was replaced by a system that heralded an industrial revolution. Large landowners and adventurer merchants began to dwindle in number, to be succeeded by a generation of great entrepreneurs, who were dynamic, decisive and eager to free themselves of the restrictions imposed by outmoded political and legal structures.

Although the period between 1820 and 1880 was the golden age of the Québec economy, it was deceptively so. Montréal was Québec's economic centre. It was here that large transportation projects were planned. The canal system, completed in 1848, enabled ships to go all the way to the Great Lakes without taking the Ottawa R route. By 1860, 3000 km of railway had already been built across the various British colonies. Forest exploitation and shipyards profited from the European and Anglo-American wars. Agriculture became an industry. From 1880, however, Québec became a victim of its own success. The NATIONAL POLICY inaugurated in 1879 established a true Canadian common market, a powerful foil to the American market to the S. Sheltered by these protectionist barriers, new markets developed in the West and the country's manufacturing industry moved toward Ontario, which by 1900 was the centre of 51% of Canadian manufacturing production, as compared to Québec's 32%.

By 1860 Québec already had a viable industrial sector, notably in the textile, shoe, railway, food, clothing and wood sectors. At the turn of the century, natural resources provided new possibilities but also required foreign capital, American and British for the most part, to develop the new resources of hydroelectricity, pulp and paper mills and metals industries (aluminum principally).

Gross Domestic Products - Québec 1986 at Factor Cost ($Millions)	
Agriculture	2 088
Forestry	643
Fishing	41
Mining	974
Manufacturing	22 858
Construction	6 915
Utilities	4 649
Goods Producing Industries	36 169
Transportation	7 066
Wholesale and Retail Trade	12 890
Finance	16 083
Services	23 967
Public Administration and Defence	6 620
Service Producing Industries	66 627
Total	$102 796

Foreign investment and control became the rule of the day, and it was only after 1960 that a succession of Québec governments began to play an active role in the economic development process. By nationalizing private electricity companies in 1962, establishing many CROWN-CORPORATIONS and showing a genuine willingness to support small and medium enterprises, the backbone of the Québec economy, all Québec governments since 1960 have aimed at the dual goal of a more Québec-controlled economy and a more dynamic Québec economy.

Agriculture Québec's share of total Canadian agricultural production has averaged 13% since 1978. Owing to its geographical position, Québec has only 6.8 million ha of arable land, of which just 2.4 million ha had been improved by 1986. Speculation and urban growth reduced this area significantly between 1971 and 1978 until the government began protecting agricultural land. The family nature and small size of most farms has constituted a serious obstacle to the efficiency of production.

Since the late 1970s, agriculture has revived and has produced promising results. The Agricultural Land Protection Act, passed in 1978, now protects Québec's best farmland. Harvest insurance and stabilization insurance plans, as well as a considerable increase in allocations to various assistance programs, have resulted in a 63% rise in total farm cash receipts since 1979. The Québec government has succeeded in increasing the province's self-sufficiency in food, by giving top priority to grain cultivation, horticulture and beef production. Success in these areas has been impressive: receipts from wheat, barley and oats have risen from $16.6 million in 1979 to $55 million in 1986, vegetables from $53 million to $103.5 million and beef production from $236 million to $295 million. This success combined

Aerial view of farmland near Granby, Qué, displaying the familiar "rangs" that date back to the French regime (*courtesy SSC Photocentre/photo by Michel Gagné*).

Soulard House near Neuville is over 250 years old (*photo by Jim Merrithew*).

with Canada's largest dairy products industry bodes well for the future of Québec agriculture.

Industry The Québec manufacturing sector comprises over 10 000 plants, 30% of the Canadian total. In 1986 these plants shipped a total value of $60.7 billion worth of products, 24% of the Canadian total, as compared to 53% for Ontario and 8% for BC. Today, this sector employs over 620 000 people, 31% of whom are women.

Five groups of industries form the core of Québec's manufacturing sector and account for 65% of plants and over 50% of manufacturing jobs: clothing and textiles (20%), food and beverages (9%), paper and related products (14.5%), metal products (11%) and wood products (10%). Seventy percent of Québec's plants are located in the Montréal region.

Forests With its 500 000 km² of forests, Québec has the third-largest area of forestland in Canada after Ontario and BC. Over 90% of this land is provincially owned. About 300 000 km² are accessible productive forests, three-quarters of this being located in the Saguenay-Lac Saint-Jean, Abitibi and North Shore regions where it has always constituted the backbone of regional economic development.

Québec harvests around 35 million m³ of wood each year, more than 90% of it conifer, and has an annual production potential of over 40 million m³. Cut wood is used for lumber (60%) and pulp manufacturing (40%). Since 1978 a vast REFORESTATION program has been under way and over 32 million saplings are planted annually.

The PULP AND PAPER INDUSTRY is one of the most important in Québec, which is among the 10 leading producers in the world and the second-largest exporter of newsprint in Canada. With its 53 plants, this sector employs close to 20 000 workers, who produce about 35% of Canada's pulp and paper. Timber, wood pulp and newsprint together comprise 20% of Québec exports, accounting for $4 billion in 1986. One-third of these forest-based exports go to the US.

Since the early 1970s, the lumber industry has been particularly active. In 1986 it produced 10.7 million m³ of wood. Exports, which in 1960 totalled barely 5% of that of pulp and paper, had reached 40% by 1980. In 1985 there were 365 sawmills and workshops with more than 15 000 employees.

Fishing With only 6700 full-time fishermen and catches valued at around $68 million in 1985, the maritime fishery contributes relatively little to Québec's employment and gross domestic product, although in certain regions, notably in the GASPÉ Peninsula, it plays a significant role. Between 1970 and 1976, the volume of catches decreased dramatically from 125 000 to 37 000 t.

Improved resource management and the extension of Canadian jurisdiction to 322 km has since helped increase this figure to 90 000 t, but

Québec still landed only 6.0% of the total catch of all the maritime provinces. Of the Québec catch, 63% were groundfish, 7% ocean fish and 30% various molluscs and crustaceans. Despite the increase in jurisdiction 92% of Québec's fleet of 2900 boats are inshore vessels less than 15 m long.

Since 1978 Québec has implemented a plan to upgrade fishing. This plan is focusing upon the upgrading and upsizing of the fleet and a quota system on landings to ensure a stable supply.

Domestic consumption is not very high. Quebeckers do not eat much fish, and there is a corresponding lack of local production in many areas. Cod, snow crab and ocean perch, the main fish caught in Québec, represent about 75% of the total catch.

Energy Québec in the 1970s embarked on a program designed to reduce the province's reliance on petroleum products. This program entailed massive development of hydroelectric energy sources, focused primarily on the James Bay area (*see* JAMES BAY AND NORTHERN QUÉBEC AGREEMENT). The La Grande project alone is now producing over 10 000 MW on its own. Québec is now the largest producer of electricity in Canada with a net generation in 1986 of 24 475 MW. Another 1000 MW will be coming on-stream in 1989 and there is additional potential for another 15 000 MW to be developed. A large portion of this electricity is exported to users in Ontario, New Brunswick and the northeast US. The abundance of electricity has resulted in a reduction in petroleum usage.

Petroleum now accounts for only 46% of all energy used in the province in 1986, down from 74% in 1970. Almost all of this was used for transportation. Electricity has increased to 39% from 19% in 1970. Natural gas consumption also increased during this period from 4% to 13% while coal has dropped from 3% to 1%.

Montréal and Service Activities Fewer than one dozen N American cities are larger than metropolitan Montréal. Unlike other cities of comparable size, however, Montréal is much closer to its hinterland, which includes the rest of the province, part of the Maritime provinces

Manic 2 Dam, on the Manicouagan R. More than 25% of Québec's energy comes from hydroelectric developments on the province's great rivers (*photo by J.A. Kraulis*).

and part of the New England states. Montréal has the infrastructure appropriate to a major financial metropolis – a stock exchange – and is the headquarters of 4 chartered banks and 3 major Canadian trust and life-insurance companies. In 1987, 175 000 people were employed in the financial sector, which has enjoyed an annual rate of growth of 9% since 1971. The metropolitan region is the location of 70% of Québec's manufacturing research firms and 90% of its research personnel. Montréal has developed particularly in the space and aeronautics industry (Pratt and Whitney, Canadair, Spar Aerospace, CAE Electronics), telecommunications (Northern Telecom, Marconi), energy (Hydro-Québec) and transportation (Bombardier, Deutz Diesel). The head offices of over 1000 companies are located in Montréal and employ some 100 000 persons. About 100 of these head offices belong to firms with over 1000 employees. Consulting engineering firms are particularly important to Québec's economy.

Three of the world's major corporations are Québec owned, and Québec alone employs 16 000 of the 26 000 Canadian workers in this sector – more than W Germany, Australia, France or Sweden. A number of large construction projects such as EXPO 67, the 1976 OLYMPIC GAMES, Mirabel Airport and Montréal's subway system enabled Montréal's consulting engineering firms to grow to nearly 250 in total. In 1986 Québec firms took in a total of $800 million in fees; a substantial amount came from outside Québec, particularly from the Middle East and from African and Latin American countries.

First with BILL 22, then with Bill 101, recent Québec governments have shown a desire to emphasize the French nature of the city and to accelerate the promotion both of the French language and of francophone managers. The city's cosmopolitan character, its intense cultural and artistic life, its reputation for good food and the quality of life all contribute to Montréal's great appeal.

Transportation Montréal is one of the hubs of the Canadian and American transportation networks, thanks to the St Lawrence Seaway and the head offices of Air Canada, Canadian National and many transportation companies, including over 50% of the Canadian aeronautics and space industry.

South Québec is well equipped for automobile transportation, having 58 000 km of roads, including 2300 km of super highway and just under 3 million licensed vehicles in 1985. There are about 2500 trucking firms, employing about 40 000 workers, and sharing about $2 billion in annual revenue. The industry's main problems are long distances, often troublesome regulations, a lack of capital and excessive operating costs. A plan to help this sector has been in effect since 1982.

Despite the fact that Montréal was the base from which Canada's epic CANADIAN PACIFIC RAILWAY was constructed, the railway network is less developed in Québec than in other parts of the country, resulting mainly from the concentration of the population in a small area.

In international shipping, Québec's 33 ports handled about 32 million t of cargo in 1985. Major ports are SEPT-ÎLES/Port Cartier, Montréal, Québec City and Baie-Comeau. Paradoxically, while the opening of the St Lawrence Seaway contributed to the rapid development of North Shore ports, it also helped establish Ontario ports of entry on the Great Lakes for Canada's international trade. With the seaway, the port of Montréal lost its privileged position. It now handles only 6% of freight passing through Canadian ports, as compared to Vancouver's 11%.

Québec has 3 international airports: Dorval, Mirabel and Québec City. The small increase in air traffic has delayed plans to develop Mirabel, which was to have been Québec's main airport and one of the major airports in Canada. The 2 Montréal airports handle 15% of Canadian passengers, compared to Toronto's 30%. Fourteen percent of all air freight passes through Montréal and 38% through Toronto. In 1985, 85% of the 8 million passengers who used Québec's airports passed through Dorval and Mirabel. The other large airports are those of Québec City (7%) and Sept-Îles (2%).

Government and Politics

Initially a French colony, Québec was later administered directly by British authorities. In 1841 it became part of a legislative union, and in 1867 a member of the Canadian federation. In 1982 Québec did not sign Canada's repatriated constitution although it signed an accord in 1987 to enter into Canada's constitutional agreement (*see* MEECH LAKE ACCORD). The evolution of Québec's institutions has thus not been marked by any legal discontinuity.

Central Political Institutions Québec, like all constitutional regimes of British tradition, has no rigid division of legislative and executive functions among its various agencies. Its political system is based on co-operation rather than on a separation of powers. The Assemblée nationale, formerly known as the Legislative Assembly, represents Québec citizens directly and is composed of one member from each of the province's 122 ridings. Each riding has about 34 000 voters. The Assemblée nationale passes laws in areas over which Québec has jurisdiction. The LIEUTENANT-GOVERNOR is the Queen's representative in Québec. Although his role is purely symbolic, in certain extreme cases he or she may be called upon to settle an issue. As the sovereign's direct and personal representative, the lieutenant-governor ensures the continuity of government. Although technically a federal public servant, the lieutenant-governor's actions are in fact governed by the directives of Québec's Conseil executif, also called the Conseil des ministres, which is composed of the premier ministre (PREMIER) and his ministers. It is the Conseil executif that decides on the general orientation of government action. It expresses its will through draft bills and *décrets*. The 25 or so Cabinet ministers are appointed by the premier and are bound by the principle of ministerial solidarity.

Since the 1970s, major reforms have transformed the operations of these central bodies. The Assemblée nationale's rules of procedure were modernized and adapted to Québec's circumstances: a total of 18 parliamentary standing committees have been established and debates are now televised. The Conseil executif is operating more and more with the assistance of departmental standing committees, each headed by a minister of state. A priorities committee provides better planning; and a treasury board, headed by a minister, is responsible for formulating and implementing the government's financial policies.

Legal Institutions Québec's judicial system has 2 levels: lower-court powers are shared by a number of courts, but there is only one Court of Appeal. Québec courts interpret and apply Québec law, and a large part of federal law. The federal Parliament has not fully exercised its constitutional right to create courts in order to ensure that its laws are implemented. The lower-court hierarchy has 7 components: 1) Justices of the peace have jurisdiction in criminal matters such as minor crimes, infractions of federal and provincial laws and of certain municipal regulations. 2) Municipal courts may be created by town councils to decide how municipal regulations should be implemented. They are presided over by judges appointed by the Québec government. 3) Juvenile courts are presided over by up to 42 judges appointed by the Québec government and have jurisdiction in certain civil and criminal matters involving juveniles. 4) Courts of Sessions of the Peace are presided over by up to 64 judges who deal mainly with criminal matters in urban areas. 5) The Provincial Court is composed of up to 149 judges and its jurisdiction extends throughout Québec in less important civil matters and for municipal and school taxation issues. 6) The Superior Court has up to 107 judges appointed by the federal government and acts as a common-law trial court. 7) The Court of Appeal is composed of 22 judges who are also appointed by the federal government.

Municipal Institutions Under the CONSTITUTION ACT, 1982, the Québec government has authority to organize and administer its municipal institutions. Québec has 1571 municipalities, of which 2 are cities, 255 are towns, 439 are villages, 439 are parishes, 116 are townships, 449 have no designation, 9 are Cree or Naskapi villages and 12 are northern villages. All fall under the Municipal Code and the Towns and Cities Act. Some of the larger municipalities, such as Québec C and Montréal, also have their own charters specifying their status. Québec has 2 urban communities, Montréal and Québec C, and one regional community, the Outaouais; all 3 have jurisdiction over their assessment, development, public transportation, taxation and public safety provisions.

Since 1978 Québec's municipalities have been extremely active. Municipal tax reforms for the first time granted a large degree of financial autonomy and a more solid tax base to the municipalities. The Agricultural Land Protection Act has saved large areas of land from urban expansion and obliged municipalities to plan their development more carefully. Finally, regional county municipalities have been established to pool certain community services outside the larger urban centres.

Public Finance The Québec government derives its revenue from 2 sources: taxes levied under Acts passed by the Assemblée nationale, and transfer payments received from the federal government in accordance with fiscal arrangements and agreements on established programs. In 1985-86 the Québec government's revenues totalled $24.1 billion, of which $10.6 billion (44%) came from income and corporate taxes, $5.3 billion (22%) from various taxes on consumer goods (tobacco, retail sales, fuel), $1.1 billion (5%) from copyrights, permits and fines, and $680 million (3%) from transfers from crown corporations. Transfer payments from the federal government were $6.5 billion (27%).

In 1987-88 expenditures roughly totalled $30 billion, distributed roughly as follows: social services $12.1 billion, education and culture $8.7 billion, government $5.8 billion, and resources, industries and transportation $3.4 billion.

Intergovernmental Relations Québec has 75 representatives in the federal House of Commons and 24 members in the Senate. The federal and Québec authorities co-ordinate their activities, not without difficulty, through about 100 joint committees and a number of federal-provincial conferences. It is in international relations, however, that Québec has distinguished itself. In 1871 Québec opened 2 offices abroad and, in 1882, a trade officer was appointed to France. Closed shortly after, these "foreign" offices received a new lease on life in 1961 when the first Department of Intergovernmental Affairs was created. Québec delegations have been established in the US, France, Italy, Belgium, Venezuela, Great Britain and elsewhere. Co-operative agreements link Québec to a number of countries, particularly France. Québec is also a member of the Agence de co-opération culturelle et technique, which is composed of the major francophone countries.

Politics Since 1960 Québec politics have been characterized by change and affirmation. The election of Premier Jean LESAGE's Liberal government in June 1960 set in motion what is commonly known as the QUIET REVOLUTION. The principal manifestations of this revolution were increased government intervention, cleaner political ethics and an affirmation of a distinct political personality for Québec. The UNION NATIONALE's return to power in 1966 under Premier Daniel JOHNSON accelerated the movement to create a true national Québec state. Between 1970 and 1976, the Liberal Party under Premier Robert BOURASSA consolidated some of the gains made during the Quiet Revolution and gave the province new direction in health insurance and legal reform, and in economic development by making the decision to harness the hydroelectric potential of the rivers that empty into James Bay.

The election of a PARTI QUÉBÉCOIS government in Nov 1976 brought to the fore the most significant issue in Québec society – the province's relations with the rest of Canada. Firmly convinced that Québec had to be considered as a separate society, the government of Premier René LÉVESQUE proposed to Quebeckers a new contract of association with the rest of Canada. Known as SOVEREIGNTY-ASSOCIATION, this proposal called for political equality between Québec and Canada as well as a close economic, trade and military association between both communities.

In the referendum of 20 May 1980, 60% of the voters rejected this proposal, although within the francophone community itself the split was closer to 50-50. Most citizens preferred the federal prime minister's solemn promise of renewed FEDERALISM. However, in face of the threat that this renewal posed for the autonomy and distinct nature of Québec, Quebeckers re-elected the Parti Québécois in April 1981. Subsequently the Québec government, supported by the official opposition in the Assemblée nationale, opposed the federal government's proposed CANADIAN CHARTER OF RIGHTS AND FREEDOMS and constitutional amending formula and did not sign the constitution upon repatriation in 1982. The defeat of the PQ in the provincial election of 1985 returned the Liberals and Robert Bourassa to power. Bourassa continued with his policy of economic development, supporting a free trade initiative with the US, and bargained hard for Québec's inclusion in the constitution, an effort rewarded by the tentative agreement of the federal and all 10 provincial governments, reached in Meech Lake.

Education

Beginning in the mid-17th century, primary schools in the major cities of New France – Québec City, Montréal and TROIS-RIVIÈRES – were run by male and female religious orders. Secondary education began with the establishment of the Collège de Québec in 1635, which from 1680 on also offered a number of more advanced courses, notably in law, mathematics and surveying. After the arrival of the Loyalists and British immigrants, a complete English-language school system, from nursery school to university, was established and financed by government in the same way and according to the same criteria as the French-language system.

Major Reforms Until the mid-1960s, the French-language education system was highly decentralized, with local school boards responsible for day-to-day operations and the Roman Catholic Church dominating those state bodies that decided on programs and curricula. The Parent Commission on Education changed this situation. In 1960 the Québec government made education its priority – a priority that arose from the need to increase the public's general level of education and to produce highly qualified manpower. This educational reform had 5 principal goals: 1) Universal access to secondary education

through the establishment of regional school boards and a network of high schools. 2) Creation of COLLÈGES D'ENSEIGNEMENT GÉNÉRAUX ET PROFESSIONNELS (CEGEPs), the intermediate level between secondary school and university that provides broader access to post-secondary studies while preparing students for university by offering advanced job-related technical training. 3) Creation of the UNIVERSITÉ DU QUÉBEC system, which offers university training in all regions of Québec. 4) Establishment of the Department of Education, which has become the ultimate authority on education issues. 5) Use of active teaching techniques focused on students and their needs, on promotion by subject and on decompartmentalization. An initial evaluation in the mid-1970s revealed that while the major objectives of accessibility, democratization and modernization had been met, a number of grey areas still remained. Some of these included improvement in the quality of education, special attention to certain disadvantaged groups and greater parent participation in school management. These areas are now the new priorities.

Administration The Québec primary- and secondary-school system is based on a mixture of linguistic and religious criteria. The 29 Protestant school boards and the 201 Catholic boards and the 4 nondenominational boards control 2547 schools. There are 267 private schools. All schools are French-language except for 105 that are bilingual and 348 that are English-language. The CEGEP system includes 40 francophone and 4 anglophone colleges, one of which administers 3 campuses. These colleges are in fact corporations and are managed by boards of directors.

The university system comprises 7 universities, 3 of which are English-language institutions. The Université du Québec, the largest institution, has full-scale campuses at Montréal, Chicoutimi, Hull and Rouyn-Noranda and 5 affiliated research institutions.

In 1986, 1.14 million students were enrolled in Québec's primary and secondary schools, a decline of 6% from 1980. In that same year, however, 164 017 students were registered in colleges, an increase of 22%. The universities had over 113 000 full-time and 115 000 part-time students. The primary, secondary and college systems are financed entirely by the provincial government, which also finances up to 75% of the costs of private schools. The elementary, secondary and college systems are financed almost entirely by the provincial government, which also financed 50% of private schools in 1984-85. In 1986-87, the provincial government contribution to all levels of education reached $8.1 billion, of which $1.3 billion went to university education.

Cultural Life

Culture is one of the most dynamic elements in Québec society. It is chiefly through its culture, which has now reached maturity, that Québec has been able to stand as a distinct society both in Canada and throughout N America. Today, Québec exports its culture, as Québec LITERATURE IN FRENCH is studied in a number of countries. Québec's painters and sculptors are known worldwide and its TV is recognized as one of the best.

Rural and folk traditions were so dominant until 1950 that no one could have expected the cultural explosion of the 1960s. In the 1950s, however, artists and intellectuals began to show their dissatisfaction with the monolithic society that was characterized by an obsession with survival and the status quo. After 1960 the old beliefs began to crumble. Naturally, Québec artists found themselves in the forefront of this movement to define a new identity. The term "Québécois" be-

gan to replace "French Canadian" and confirmed this new cultural surge. Following the flood of change that occurred in the 1960s, the 1970s were years of consolidation marked by the emergence of various groups – women, regional communities, cultural minorities. The creation of the Ministry of Cultural Affairs (1961) helped give institutional foundation to this cultural development. Today, with a budget of over $200 million, Québec is a leader in governmental support of cultural endeavours.

The Arts Québec, particularly Montréal, is a very productive centre for theatre. Montréal has 10 established companies with their own premises, traditions and government grants, as well as about another 100 relatively active and truly innovative troupes.

All the other major Québec cities also have permanent or semiprofessional groups that have developed original theatre productions independently of Montréal. In the summer, over 50 troupes present plays in Québec's major resort areas, and occasionally foreign troupes from New York, Paris or Brussels appear in Québec theatre.

Québec has one symphony orchestra in Québec City and another in Montréal (see ORCHESTRE SYMPHONIQUE DE MONTRÉAL). In addition to these 2 pillars of Québec's musical world, there are the Société de musique contemporaine du Québec, the McGill Chamber Orchestra, the Ladies' Morning Club, the Montréal Opera, and various conservatories, music schools and medieval music ensembles.

Montréal has a privileged role in the FILM industry as the commercial meeting place of American and European films. It is therefore not uncommon to see the most recent American, French, Italian and Japanese films playing simultaneously. In addition to repertory theatres, Montréal has some 200 commercial cinemas. The annual Montréal Film Festival, long known as one of the premiere festivals for new films worldwide, reinforces Montréal's status in the film world. As well, as many as 30 full-length features of various types are produced locally each year. Notable Québec directors include Gilles CARLE and the late Claude JUTRA.

Poetry, the novel and the essay are particularly well-developed genres in Québec's publishing industry. Songwriters and singers, such as Gilles VIGNEAULT, Félix Leclerc, Robert CHARLEBOIS, Pauline JULIEN, the operatic bass Louis QUILICO and pianist Louis LORTIE are recognized well beyond Québec's borders. Dance, mime, sculpture, singing and crafts are also forms of cultural expression in which Quebeckers excel.

Communications In 1987 Québec had 175 television stations, compared to Ontario's 140. French-language stations include Radio-Canada, Radio-Québec and TVA, while on the English-language side there are the CBC, CTV and American stations. In addition, there are 176 cable networks reaching about 60% of the market, and 51 AM and 26 FM radio stations and hundreds of rebroadcasters across the province. Québec has 10 French-language and 2 English-language daily newspapers, 185 weeklies, over 150 periodicals and 15 ethnic publications.

Heritage Since the mid-1960s, interest in preserving and developing Québec's cultural heritage has increased considerably. The Ministry of Cultural Affairs and local historical societies have been the prime movers in this area. In Québec City, major archaeological projects have revitalized a number of sites, including Place Royale, which is a genuine recreation of an architectural ensemble that dates from the French regime, and the QUÉBEC CITADEL. In Montréal, Vieux Montréal (Old Montréal) is a city within a city. More than 300 archaeological sites have been documented

Rooftops of Place Royale, Québec City, a partial reconstruction of the old city at the end of the French regime (*photo by Barry Griffiths/Network*).

throughout the province. This search for the sources of Québec culture is part of Quebeckers' desire to understand and establish their roots more firmly in N America.

History

Although explorers in the 16th century had found many large Iroquois villages in the lower St Lawrence Valley (eg, STADACONA, HOCHELAGA), these settlements had vanished by the time the first colonists arrived in the 17th century. About 4000 MONTAGNAIS-NASKAPI lived along the N shore of the St Lawrence, and the first permanent contacts were established with these people and a firm alliance established by Samuel de CHAMPLAIN with the HURON. Farther N, the Cree had very little contact with the first settlers.

French Colonization Jacques CARTIER landed in Gaspé on 14 July 1534, where he officially took possession of the land in the name of the king of France. The following year, he returned and went as far as Stadacona [Québec C] and Hochelaga [Montréal]. However, the first settlement was not established until Champlain established the village of Québec in 1608. The colony's beginnings were hampered by France's lack of interest in a permanent colony of settlers. By 1628 the colony still had only 76 settlers, all in Québec, which was little more than a trading post. By 1640 the population had grown to 300, and it was not until the end of the IROQUOIS WARS that NEW FRANCE could truly be said to exist. By 1666 the population had reached 3418.

From the outset, the colony's social organization was different from that of the mother country. The divisions among social classes were much less rigid. The seigneurs had privileges, of course, but these were not inherited; like the settlers, they were merchants, farmers and soldiers. From 1686, wars with the English colonies increased but were interrupted by relatively long periods of peace. These recurring conflicts against an enemy superior in numbers seriously hindered the colony's development. Peace came in 1713 with the Treaty of UTRECHT, but New France was cut off from Acadia, Newfoundland and the lands around Hudson Bay. After scarcely one generation of peace, war with England resumed. It was an uneven battle between 65 000 French settlers,

backed by an indifferent French government, and some one million English colonists supported by the Royal Navy. In 1759 a British expeditionary force took Québec City, and the following year Montréal. The end of the era of New France broke the colony's natural development, particularly since most of the political and commercial leaders returned to France.

British Colonization and Confederation In order to secure the co-operation of its new subjects, the first English governors allowed the French to keep their language and religion, although they excluded Catholics from administrative positions. The QUEBEC ACT (1774), which attempted largely to reinstate the former boundaries of New France (to the great annoyance of the American colonies), effectively reinforced the power of the seigneurs and the clergy, who became convenient allies for the aristocratic British governors, who rejected the demands of the new English merchants for an elected assembly.

In order to satisfy recent Loyalist immigrants, the CONSTITUTIONAL ACT, 1791, divided the colony into 2 provinces, UPPER and LOWER CANADA, each administered by a governor, a legislative council and a legislative assembly. The British merchants in Montréal had a difficult time accepting the fact that they were to be isolated in a province with a French-speaking majority. Political battles multiplied, and in 1837 Louis-Joseph PAPINEAU, Jean-Olivier Chénier and Wolfred Nelson led a revolt. Poorly led and lacking arms, the PATRIOTES were crushed by the British authorities, who restored peace at the price of political repression (*see* REBELLIONS OF 1837).

In the still-famous DURHAM REPORT, Lord Durham advocated the creation of an English majority by massive immigration and through the anglicization of French Canadians in areas where they were a minority. Thus, section 41 of the ACT OF UNION stated that English would be the only language of the new united PROVINCE OF CANADA and that Canada East [Québec], with a much larger population than Canada West [Ontario], would have the same number of elected representatives and would have to repay a large share of Canada West's debt.

The economic crisis that forced 40 000 French Canadians to immigrate to the US between 1840 and 1850 (*see* FRANCO-AMERICANS) and the continuing political crisis stemming from inadequate political structures raised the issue of the survival of the French Canadians who, for the first time in their history, had no political recourse of their own. When English Canadian political leaders proposed the idea of a federal pact to break the impasse, French Canadian opinion was divided. Those following the lead of George-Étienne CARTIER accepted the federal solution because it gave Québec control over language, religion and civil law, which were considered to be the foundations of French Canada. A mixture of more liberal and progressive elements favoured a looser federation, where provincial rights would be more explicit and guaranteed, so as to counter the status of inferiority that the new Constitution would impose on Québec. Lastly a third, much smaller, group proposed outright independence for Québec. With the militant support of the clergy and English-speaking commercial elites from Montréal, the federal proposal won out (though with some difficulty, and without any consultation with the people, as the proposal's opponents had demanded). On 1 July 1867 Québec, a former French and British colony, became a Canadian province.

Modern Québec At the time of Confederation, 1867, Québec was a poor province, particularly ill equipped to step into the Industrial Revolution. Cities were small and few – Montréal (90 000 in-

habitants), Québec City (58 000), Trois-Rivières (6000) and Sorel (4700). Farming was at subsistence level and most companies were small. Larger manufacturing companies were located only in Montréal and were owned almost exclusively by Anglophones. The resources of the new Government of Québec were sorely limited: 60% of its $1.5-million budget came from the federal government, which also had tight control over provincial legislation because of its authority to appoint the lieutenant-governor and to disallow certain provincial laws (*see* DISALLOWANCE). The only avenue of intervention that remained was to colonize distant regions. Thus the Gaspé Peninsula, the Lac Saint-Jean region and the Laurentides were opened up to settlers. Despite this movement, between 1850 and 1900, 500 000 Quebeckers left for the US, while thousands of others moved on to the western provinces where they formed a few small francophone settlements (*see* FRENCH IN THE WEST).

Culturally and intellectually, this is one of the saddest periods in Quebec's history. The provincial government was unable to handle the new responsibilities of a modern state (education, health, colonization), and the federal government was preoccupied with Ontario's industrial development and with opening up the West. As a result, the church took charge of the educational and health needs of Quebeckers. Uninterested in questioning the established authorities and the excesses of industrialization, and wary of new ideas, the Québec church was more concerned with maintaining its privileged position than with helping Quebeckers enter the 20th century. It extolled the virtues of rural life, cautioned against the evils of the city and the dangers of education, and preached the need to accept one's lot in life.

The surge in the American economy around 1896 also gave impetus to the development of Québec's economy. Between 1900 and 1910 manufacturing production volume increased by 76%. By the time a second industrial revolution took hold in 1920, Québec was in a very good position to follow the movement. This time it was electricity and nonferrous metals such as copper, aluminum and nickel that propelled the changes. Industries that exploited Québec's natural resources replaced light industry. External markets, good lines of communication and large sources of capital were more important than the domestic market or qualified manpower.

Between 1920 and 1940, the face of Québec changed. Whereas in 1920 agriculture still accounted for 37% of Québec production, compared to 38% for manufacturing and 15% for forestry, by 1941 manufacturing accounted for 64%, mining for 10% and agriculture for 10%. This accelerated industrialization caused classic transformations to take place in Québec society – urbanization, a higher standard of living and a better-educated population. It was English and then American capital that stimulated this economic surge. In addition, the priority given to the export of natural resources obscured the fact that the archaic manufacturing sector was still founded on labour-intensive but relatively unproductive industries such as textiles and shoes.

In politics, this period was marked by the long reign of the Liberal Party, which remained in power from 1897 with Premier F.G. MARCHAND until the fall of Adélard GODBOUT's government in 1936. For much of this same period, the federal Liberals were also in power in Ottawa. It was the time of "red in Québec, red in Ottawa" and of a tacit alliance between businessmen and politicians. The former suggested projects, the latter granted railway subsidies, authorized road building and passed special legislation, handing out patronage and favours of all kinds. The Conservative Party, so powerful in Québec in the 19th century, was but a shadow of its former self after the CONSCRIPTION crisis of 1917.

The GREAT DEPRESSION in the 1930s challenged both this course of development and the primacy of the Liberal Party. The economic crisis was accompanied by a moral crisis; for the first time, individuals and groups condemned the political, cultural and economic inferiority to which they believed French Canadians had been subjected by Confederation and by Canadian business. There was talk of social renewal, NATIONALIZATION and economic change aimed at reappropriating natural resources. In 1936 Maurice DUPLESSIS and the new UNION NATIONALE Party won the election by taking 76 of the 90 seats. Swept into power by a desire for change, Duplessis hastened to direct his action toward an increased conservatism that represented the disparate interests of a number of groups – traditional elites, foreign capitalists, rural people and the Catholic hierarchy. Temporarily removed from power in 1939, he returned in 1944. He died in 1959 and his party was defeated in the 1960 elections.

During its long reign, the Duplessis regime faced 2 major problems: the federal government's desire to centralize all major economic, social and cultural authority in Ottawa and the difficulties engendered by the new economic order established in 1945. Duplessis was somewhat successful in blocking Ottawa's centralist aims by establishing a corporate income tax in 1947 and a personal income tax in 1953 and by refusing certain federal programs in areas under provincial jurisdiction. He was less successful, however, in the social and economic spheres. By refusing federal subsidies, Duplessis protected the autonomy of the Québec political system but also deprived it of precious resources. Even today, historians disagree on the causes of this marked backwardness in Québec society between 1945 and 1960. Would it have been better to overlook Québec's distinct social and cultural character and to allow the federal government to organize its development? Was the conservatism of the Union Nationale the consequence of federal centralism?

Opposition to the Duplessis government came particularly from intellectual, academic and union groups. The new generation of university graduates were beginning to question the traditional elites. They condemned the government's absence from major areas of concern. Teachers questioned the clergy's hold on the education system. Magazines such as CITÉ LIBRE, and one newspaper in particular, Le DEVOIR, spearheaded the socioeconomic opposition. The deaths of Maurice Duplessis and his successor Paul SAUVÉ, a few months later, made it easier for the Liberals to come to power on 22 June 1960. This election was to change the course of Québec and of Canadian history. It was the beginning of the Quiet Revolution.

The New Québec This period, neither revolutionary nor quiet, was marked from the outset by the new government's will to build a modern administration capable of countering all the backward influences that had assailed Québec for a century. This desire to act on all fronts made the period from 1960 to 1966 appear extremely frenetic. Public finances were reorganized and control measures instituted. The Parent Commission of Inquiry completely overhauled the educational system. The Société générale de financement was formed to take care of weaknesses in the private sector, and the Conseil d'expansion économique (Economic Development Council) was established to lay the foundation for an economic plan. Four new departments were created, including those dealing with education and cultural affairs.

For the first time, trade unionism penetrated the public service. In 1962, following an election fought on this theme, the government nationalized private electricity companies. Between 1945 and 1963, Québec's budget grew from $96 million to $851 million. Economic expansion was so great between 1961 and 1966 that the unemployment rate dropped from 9.2% to 4.7%. Increasing control exerted by the Québec government began to cause more serious conflicts with the federal government. In October 1961 Premier Lesage inaugurated the Maison du Québec (Québec House) in Paris and signed co-operation agreements with France. Since then, Québec has established 16 delegations on 3 continents. Ottawa became concerned about Québec's desire to act autonomously on the international scene, even though this action was limited to sectors which, according to the constitution, were under provincial jurisdiction. Numerous conflicts ensued between the 2 governments after 1960, as a result of the dissatisfaction with federal-provincial tax agreements, which were considered to be unfavourable to Québec.

Between 1960 and 1965, the federal government, anxious to show Quebeckers that the federal system could accommodate a renewed Québec, made a number of compromises with the Québec government by transferring part of the tax base to the province.

While negotiating these special agreements, Ottawa created the Royal Commission on BILINGUALISM AND BICULTURALISM. In its preliminary report in 1965, the commissioners concluded that Canada was in the throes of a serious crisis, one which, they said, could be resolved only when Quebeckers were convinced that they could exist both individually and collectively in equality and mutual respect with the rest of the country. The Union Nationale's return to power after the 1966 election marked the beginning of a fundamental realignment of Québec's political forces. Re-elected with a majority of seats, but only 41% of the popular vote compared to the Liberal's 47%, the Union Nationale, this time led by Daniel Johnson, was forced to continue in the tradition of the great reforms of the Quiet Revolution. Already on shaky ground with its more conservative electorate, the party lost its leader in Sept 1968. Jean-Jacques BERTRAND took over as leader and as Québec's premier, but his leadership was contested within party ranks. The government was accused of fence-sitting, of being neither sufficiently nationalist nor federalist. The Québec Liberal Party, led by Robert Bourassa, was clearly federalist and in 1967 rejected the sovereignty-association proposal submitted by René Lévesque. Lévesque left the party and founded the Mouvement souveraineté-association which, in the autumn of 1968, joined with one of the small existing separatist parties to become the Parti Québécois. Soon afterwards the Rassemblement pour l'indépendance nationale, the major separatist group, chose to fold and join the Parti Québécois. Between 1967 and 1970, Canadian political representatives joined in an important round of constitutional negotiations. At the Victoria Conference in the summer of 1971, an agreement in principle was reached on an amending formula and on the inclusion of a charter of rights in the new constitution. In the end, Québec's new Liberal government, elected the previous spring, withdrew its support because the Victoria agreement provided for no transfer of legislative powers between the 2 levels of government – a priority for Québec since 1965.

In October 1970 the government had to face a major political and social crisis when, after a campaign of terrorist bombings, the FRONT DE LIBÉRATION DU QUÉBEC (FLQ) kidnapped a British diplomat, James Cross, and a Québec minister, Pierre LAPORTE, who was later killed by his abductors. The federal government proclaimed the WAR MEASURES ACT, which provided for the suspension of civil liberties. Hundreds of Quebeckers were held for questioning and then released, but no charges were laid. Subsequent inquiries (McDonald Commission, Cliche Commission) revealed that the Royal Canadian Mounted Police were conducting burglaries and other illegal activities at the time.

Aided by the improving American economy, Robert Bourassa's Liberal government (which had been elected in 1970) was easily able to surmount these difficulties and was re-elected in October 1973. The Parti Québécois, which in the 1970 election had received 24% of the popular vote but only 7 seats (6% of the total), this time obtained 30% of the popular vote, though only 6 seats. Despite this imbalance in the electoral system, the PQ was still the official Opposition.

From 1973, the energy crisis, rampant inflation and increased unemployment created a new and more difficult situation for the government, which also had to face militant trade unions and many strikes in public services. Events such as the campaign by the Association des gens de l'air du Québec to use French in Québec air space, and the stir caused by the implementation of Bill 22, which gave priority to the French language, only aggravated the political climate.

On 15 November 1976 the Parti Québécois swept to victory and immediately undertook or completed some major reforms: automobile insurance, the charter of the French language, control of the financing of political parties, agricultural zoning, and dental insurance for children. During the government's first mandate, Québec's economic situation improved, as shown by the creation of 65 000 new jobs annually between 1977 and 1980. The PQ government suffered a major defeat, however, in the 1980 referendum. In the meantime the Liberal Party, headed since 1978 by Claude RYAN, former editor of Le Devoir, completely revamped its political thinking and practices. Financed directly by contributions from its supporters, open to ideas and to participation, and proposing a new federalism, the Liberals appeared about to win the next election. Nevertheless the Québec electorate accepted on good faith the PQ's promise to shelve its sovereignty-association proposal, and on 13 April 1981 the party handily won re-election. The economic downturn was responsible for sagging public support for the PQ. This, combined with the fact that Lévesque's late 1984 announcement that the next provincial election would not be fought on the issue of Québec sovereignty encountered resistance among PQ members, led to the resignation of several Cabinet ministers. However, at a Jan 1985 party convention, the majority of delegates supported Lévesque even though it was quite clear his leadership was over. Lévesque resigned shortly afterward with Pierre-Marc Johnson, son of former premier Daniel Johnson, succeeding Lévesque as premier. The election in late 1985 ended a decade of PQ rule and returned the Liberals, again under the leadership of Robert Bourassa, to power. The air of co-operation between Bourassa and PM Mulroney led to renewed constitutional talks and a tentative agreement in 1987 to an amendment to the Constitution Act (1982) that included Québec as a signatory to the Constitution. The friendliness between the 2 governments was also certainly instrumental in Mulroney's FREE TRADE initiative with the US, for it would surely have not gotten off the ground without support from Québec. It seems Québec has now finally become the full partner in Canada it was always supposed to be.

DANIEL LATOUCHE

Quebec Act (An Act for making more effective Provision for the Government of the Province of Quebec in North America) was a British statute which received royal assent 22 June 1774 and became effective 1 May 1775. The Act enlarged the boundaries of the PROVINCE OF QUEBEC to include Labrador, Île d'Anticosti and Îles de la Madeleine on the E, and the Indian territory S of the Great Lakes between the Mississippi and Ohio rivers on the W. The colony was to be governed by a governor and 17 to 23 appointed councillors; an elected assembly was not provided. Religious freedom was guaranteed for the colony's Roman Catholic majority, and a simplified Test Oath, which omitted references to religion, enabled them to enter public office conscientiously (*see* CATHOLICISM). The Act established French civil law and British criminal law and provided for continued use of the SEIGNEURIAL SYSTEM.

The Quebec Act was framed largely by Gov Sir Guy CARLETON, although not all of his policies were incorporated into it. The Quebec Act has been interpreted in a number of ways. Some felt it was an attempt to rectify some of the problems created by the ROYAL PROCLAMATION OF 1763, which dramatically reduced the size of NEW FRANCE, provided an untouchable Indian territory out of the vast western interior and promised an elected assembly. Others felt it was an attempt to deal more fairly with the colony's French Catholics, perhaps with a view to ensuring their loyalty in the event of troubles with the American colonies, and it effectively guaranteed the survival of the *ancien régime* society in N America. Territorial expansion was a recognition of Montréal's role in the continental economy, and the Act returned to the Québec economy its traditional links with the fisheries and interior FUR TRADE.

American settlers were enraged when Québec acquired the Indian territory, which they perceived to be theirs by right; they considered the Quebec Act one of the "Intolerable Acts" which contributed to the outbreak of the AMERICAN REVOLUTION. Anglophone members of Québec's population, although pleased with the territorial expansion, were dissatisfied that an elected assembly was not provided for.

The Quebec Act became less effective when LOYALISTS began arriving in the colony after 1783. It was eventually replaced by the CONSTITUTIONAL ACT, 1791, which created UPPER CANADA and LOWER CANADA.   NANCY BROWN FOULDS

Reading: Hilda Neatby, *The Quebec Act* (1972).

Québec Bridge Disasters Construction on the Québec Bridge, 11 km above QUÉBEC CITY, officially began in 1900. On 29 Aug 1907, when the bridge was nearly finished, the southern cantilever span twisted and fell 46 m into the St Lawrence R. Seventy-five workmen, many of them Caughnawaga Indians, were killed in Canada's worst bridge DISASTER. An inquiry established that the accident had been caused by faulty design and inadequate engineering supervision. Work was resumed, but on 11 Sept 1916 a new centre span being hoisted into position fell into the river, killing 13 men. The bridge was completed in 1917 and the Prince of Wales (later Edward VIII) officially opened it 22 Aug 1919. *See also* BRIDGES.   HUGH A. HALLIDAY

Québec Citadel, a military FORTIFICATION built 1820-31 in Québec City. According to a number of 19th-century authors including Charles Dickens, the Citadel, which crowns a 100 m escarpment named Cap-Diamant, made Québec the "Gibraltar of N America." It was built when Québec was Canada's main port, and its purpose was

The Québec Citadel was built by the British in the early 19th century to protect the city from attack from the St Lawrence below (*photo by J.A. Kraulis*).

to protect the city from attack from the St Lawrence R below and from the Plains of Abraham to the W. It could also serve as a last refuge for the garrison if the city was captured by an enterprising enemy. The Citadel replaced or incorporated defence works built during the French regime, eg, the western rampart (still in existence opposite the National Assembly). After the CONQUEST, 1759-60, the British considered this rampart inadequate; by the early 19th century, they completed construction of the present ramparts, encircling the Upper Town cliff and also built the 4 MARTELLO TOWERS on the Plains of Abraham. Designed by British engineers on a classical model, the Citadel was somewhat anachronistic, given the recent evolution of European military architecture. It was begun in 1820 and completed in 1831. The garrison provided most of the labour. Although the Citadel was designed as an arms, munitions and supplies depot as well as a barracks, only part of the 1000-man garrison was lodged there. Soldiers were also billeted in Artillery Park and in the Jesuit Barracks (the site of the present city hall).

After the mid-19th century, improvements in weaponry, particularly the introduction in 1856 of more precise and longer-range rifled artillery, led the British military authorities to modify their defence system substantially. Military fortifications were then located farther from the city centre. During the AMERICAN CIVIL WAR the threat of an American invasion encouraged the military to construct 3 forts between 1865 and 1871 on the heights of Pointe-Lévis across the river from Québec. None of these structures was ever subject to assault (other than by tourists).

The British military departed Québec in 1871. The Citadel served as headquarters for one of the artillery schools of the Canadian Army and became the headquarters of the Royal 22nd Regiment during WWI. Lord DUFFERIN was the first governor general to make the Citadel a vice-regal residence and persuaded local politicians to save the old French walks from destruction.
                              YVON DESLOGES

Reading: André Charbonneau, Yvon Desloges and Marc Lafrance, *Québec: The Fortified City* (1982).

Québec City, Qué, City, capital of the province of QUÉBEC, is located on the N shore of the ST

LAWRENCE R where it meets the Rivière St-Charles. Here the St Lawrence narrows to a width of just over 1 km and navigation is made difficult by a group of islands, the largest of which is the Île d'ORLÉANS. Cap-Diamant, a promontory with an elevation of 98 m, dominates the site and was used effectively as a fortification, earning Québec City the name "Gibraltar of N America." The town successfully repulsed assaults by Sir William PHIPS in 1690 and by a large American force in 1775-76. The name "Québec" is probably derived from an Algonquian word meaning "narrowing of the river."

Settlement For several thousand years prior to the arrival of the Europeans, the site of Québec was occupied by Indian hunters and fishermen. In 1535 Jacques CARTIER discovered a fairly large Iroquoian village, STADACONA, whose 1000 or so inhabitants lived from fishing, hunting and the cultivation of corn. Some time between 1543 and 1608, when Samuel de CHAMPLAIN arrived at the site, the Stadaconans had disappeared and been replaced by the occasional nomadic Algonquians, likely MONTAGNAIS-NASKAPI. Cartier wintered near Stadacona in 1535-36 and returned in 1541-42, spending a difficult winter at Cap-Rouge, a few kilometres upriver, before heading home with barrels of worthless minerals (*see* DIAMONDS OF CANADA). ROBERVAL spent the following winter at Cap-Rouge, but failure of these early expeditions diminished French interest in the area, and a permanent settlement was not established until 1608 when Champlain founded a trading post. The post was captured by the KIRKE brothers in 1629 but was restored to the French by the Treaty of ST GERMAIN in 1632.

Development Québec's strategic location on the St Lawrence R determined the nature of its development. In the age of sail, it held a dominant position as a port of entry and exit for oceangoing vessels. It quickly became the transfer port for domestic and foreign trade (especially furs and timber) and the arrival and departure point for travellers and immigrants to N America. From the

Population: 164 580 (1986c) 165 968 (1981cA);
     603 267 (1986CMA) 583 820 (1981ACMA)
Rate of Increase (1981-86): (City) -.8%; CMA 3.5%
Rank in Canada: Eighth (by CMA)
Date of Incorporation: 1833
Land Area: 88.86 km²; CMA 3150.27 km²
Elevation: Citadel 98 m; Parc des Champs de bataille
Climate: Average daily temp, July 19.1°C, Jan -12.1°C;
     Yearly precip 1174 mm; Hours of sunshine 1851.7 per
     year

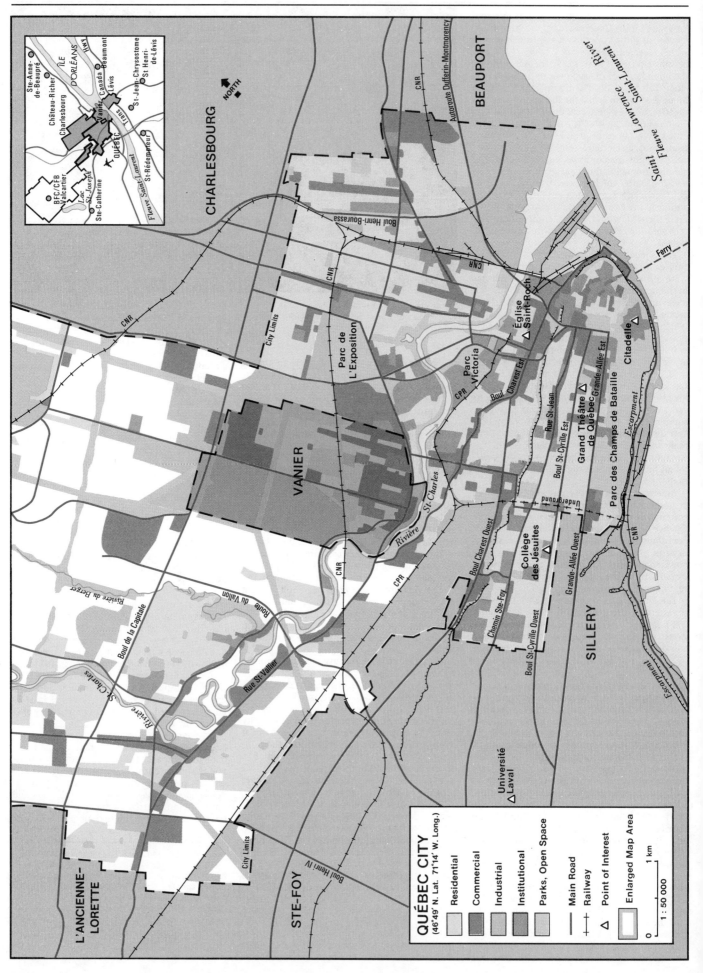

CHARLESBOURG

BEAUPORT

NORTH

Saint Lawrence River

Fleuve Saint-Laurent

Ferry

ÎLE D'ORLÉANS

Ste-Anne-de-Beaupré
Château-Richer
Charlesbourg
Beaumont
St-Jean-Chrysostome
St-Henri-de-Lévis
Lévis
Vanier
Trans-Canada Hwy
Québec
St-Rédempteur
BFC/CFB Valcartier
Lac St-Joseph
Ste-Catherine
Fleuve Saint-Laurent

CNR

Boul Henri-Bourassa

Autoroute Dufferin-Montmorency

Parc de L'Exposition

CPR

Parc Victoria

Église Saint-Roch △

Boul Charest Est

Citadelle △

VANIER

City Limits

Rivière St-Charles

Grand Théâtre de Québec △

Grande-Allée Est

Parc des Champs de Bataille

Escarpment

Rue St-Jean

Boul St-Cyrille Est

Underground

Grande-Allée Ouest

CNR

Collège des Jésuites △

Boul Charest Ouest

Chemin Ste-Foy

Boul St-Cyrille Ouest

SILLERY

Rivière du Berger

Boul de la Capitale

Route du Vallon

Rivière St-Charles

Rue St-Vallier

Université Laval △

Escarpment

L'ANCIENNE-LORETTE

STE-FOY

Boul Henri IV

City Limits

CNR

CPR

QUÉBEC CITY
(46°49′ N. Lat. 71°14′ W. Long.)

	Residential
	Commercial
	Industrial
	Institutional
	Parks, Open Space
—	Main Road
+++	Railway
△	Point of Interest
	Enlarged Map Area

1 km

0

1 : 50 000

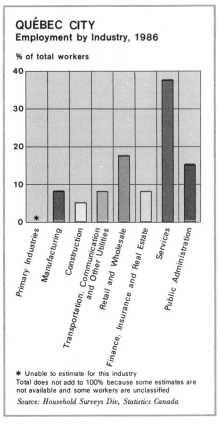

QUÉBEC CITY
Employment by Industry, 1986

% of total workers

[Bar chart with y-axis values 0, 10, 20, 30, 40 and x-axis categories: Primary Industries (marked with asterisk), Manufacturing, Construction, Transportation, Communication and Other Utilities, Retail and Wholesale, Finance, Insurance and Real Estate, Services, Public Administration]

✱ Unable to estimate for this industry
Total does not add to 100% because some estimates are not available and some workers are unclassified.

Source: Household Surveys Div, Statistics Canada

beginning, its location made Québec a political, administrative and military centre.

The long delay in establishing a rail link to the city, the technological developments in oceangoing vessels enabling them to bypass the city and sail directly to MONTRÉAL, and finally the shift of population and the economy westward, tended to reduce Québec's importance in the mid-19th century. Despite repeated efforts, the city was unable to maintain its earlier position as a focus of economic production and trade, and it gradually became a provincial and regional administrative centre. However, over the past quarter century, the considerable growth of the provincial government has accelerated the growth of the city and its suburbs and has given added emphasis to the relative importance of its administrative function. The city has also continued to develop as a centre for TOURISM.

Cityscape In the 17th century, the inhabitants of Québec first occupied the narrow strip of land between the promontory and the port (Lower Town) and then the promontory itself, following in the wake of the religious institutions and colonial administration that occupied Upper Town. This expansion was strongly influenced by the construction of and improvements to the town's FORTIFICATIONS, which were established mainly in the Upper Town but also along the banks of the river (*see* QUÉBEC CITADEL). The fortifications and military barracks occupied a considerable area and restricted the establishment of a residential civilian population, which was already limited by the development of religious institutions (the Bishop's Palace, the cathedral, the seminary, colleges and convents, the HÔTEL-DIEU and the Château St-Louis). Lower Town was for many years the residential and commercial centre. Both parts form the core of the old city, which is still well preserved and has been partially reconstructed as part of the Place Royale project.

At the end of the French regime, Lower Town stretched along the port toward the Intendant's Palace, to the N of the promontory. During the 19th century, the town broke out of its fortified confines and stretched westwards on the promontory, along the shores of the Rivière St-Charles and to the foot of the N face of the promontory. These new parts of town were often built hastily and of wood, and fell victim to a number of major fires (St-Roch, 1845; St-Sauveur, 1866, 1870 and 1889; St-Jean-Baptiste, 1845, 1876 and 1881). The result was major reconstruction and improved protective infrastructures (water supply, fire-fighting services, etc).

Growth to the W and N of the city has been even more substantial in the 20th century, particularly since the 1950s. The small parishes in outlying areas grew quickly as both residential and commercial suburbs: Sillery, Sainte-Foy, Charlesbourg, Cap-Rouge, Ancienne Lorette, etc. Although the downtown area was quite radically transformed with the appearance of private and governmental buildings and a few major hotels, the historic character of the old city has been largely preserved and the modern buildings blend quite well with the characteristic landscape of Québec City: the promontory, fortifications, Château Frontenac, Parliament Buildings, Rivière St-Charles, the Port and the Québec Bridge.

Population Although Québec was the capital of the French empire in N America in the days of NEW FRANCE, for many years it was little more than a large village. In 1608 it had 28 inhabitants and by the time of the CONQUEST in 1759-60 its population only slightly exceeded 8000. Growth was rapid in the first half of the 19th century and by 1861 it numbered nearly 60 000 inhabitants. The growth resulted from the economic expansion associated mainly with the TIMBER TRADE and the important political and administrative activities

---

An aerial view of Québec City (*courtesy Colour Library Books*).

centered in the city. Québec was also both the entry and transit port for the substantial annual influx of immigrants heading towards Upper Canada and the rest of N America. In some years the city's population doubled during the summer, causing many attendant problems such as EPIDEMICS and drunkenness.

As a result of the gradual but significant slowdown in the timber trade and SHIPBUILDING in the second half of the 19th century, the population of Québec remained relatively stable until the early 20th century. In fact, the Lower and Upper Town experienced a decline as people moved to the new areas, particularly St-Roch. The overall population increase in a 40-year period, 1861-1901, was only 14.7% (60 000 to 68 840). Besides experiencing unfavourable economic conditions, the old city lacked residential space; only with the amalgamation of small outlying municipalities did its population begin to grow at the beginning of the 20th century. Metropolitan Québec nevertheless grew more rapidly from the 1950s until the end of the 1970s. In the early 1980s this growth again slowed, partly as a result of stabilization of growth in the province overall. The population is now 164 580 (1986c; CMA, 603 267). Metropolitan Québec includes, among its largest municipalities, Charlesbourg (pop 68 996), Sainte-Foy (pop 69 615), Beauport (pop 62 869), Lévis (pop 18 310) and Loretteville (pop 14 335).

Prior to the Conquest, Québec's population had been French. But in the early 19th century this changed with the influx of British immigrants. In 1851 the city's population was 41% British and other groups, a figure that rose to 51% in 1861. This high proportion dropped rapidly as immigration to Québec stopped and as many British immigrants moved to other parts of Canada and to the US. By 1871 the percentage of non-

Bird's-Eye View of Countryside Around Quebec City (1664), looking eastward. The Beaupré shore is to the left, the Île d'Orleans centre, the S shore between Pointe-Lévis and Berthier to the right, and Québec City in the foreground (*courtesy Bibliothèque Nationale, Paris*).

Francophones had dropped to 31.5%, by 1921 to 10%, and by 1981 to 4%, both for the city itself and for the metropolitan area. Thus, the city has regained its essentially French character, which continues to this day.

Economy, Transportation and Labour Force The early economy of Québec was directly dependent upon its activities as a transit port for basic products exported to Europe (furs, cereals and lumber) and for imported manufactured products. The considerable expansion of this trade enabled Québec to maintain a relatively competitive position with Montréal as the major trading centre of the province until the mid-19th century. At that time, the commercial position of Québec was seriously affected by the decline in the timber trade and the shift from raw timber to lumber, the development of railway networks that bypassed Québec (the GRAND TRUNK RY OF CANADA passed on the S shore opposite the city), the weakness of Québec's hinterland, the dredging of the St Lawrence between Québec and Montréal, the expansion of economic relations with the US, and the impact of technological change on trade and transportation. Montréal rapidly acquired a dominant position in the second half of the 19th century in trade and finance, transportation and industry.

Québec's middle class, which was already declining in numbers, attempted to maintain its position but failed. It struggled to attract the transcontinental railways, such as the Quebec, Montreal, Ottawa and Occident Ry (which in 1879 was the first railway to reach the city), the National Transcontinental Ry and the Canadian Northern, and to have them adopt the port of Québec as their ocean terminal. Efforts were also made to have the 2 shores of the river connected by a bridge. Begun in 1900, the Québec Bridge is still the largest cantilevered bridge in the world, but experienced serious construction difficulties in 1907 and 1916 (*see* QUÉBEC BRIDGE DISASTERS). The bridge actually helped promote the circula-

tion of products to ports farther east. A second bridge, the Pierre Laporte, was built in 1970. It is a suspension bridge, several hundred metres longer than the earlier one.

In the middle of the 19th century, the city of Québec went through an industrial revolution, particularly in the FOOTWEAR INDUSTRY, which gradually became the largest source of employment for the region. However, the city was unable to maintain growth in its manufacturing sector and the footwear industry declined in the 1920s. Even though various other concerns appeared and disappeared and offered employment to a significant number of people, they did not manage to diversify the city's industrial base. These enterprises included shipbuilding, breweries, textiles and clothing, pulp and paper and, more recently, the Ultramar refinery. Most jobs in Québec are concentrated in public administration, defence and the service sector, as well as trade and transportation; only around 10% of jobs are in manufacturing. Québec benefits from its status as the provincial capital and the regional administrative and services centre. It also attracts large numbers of tourists.

Government and Politics From 1765 to 1833 and from 1835 to 1840, the city was administered by a commission of justices of the peace appointed by the governor and composed largely of landowners, French Canadian professionals and British merchants. The commission was responsible for ensuring that the orders of the legislature of LOWER CANADA were respected. Following pressure from the local population, Québec received its first municipal charter in 1833. This lasted until 1835 and a second was issued in 1840. These charters established an elected municipal council with the power to adopt regulations in their area of jurisdiction. From 1833 to 1856 and 1870 to 1908 the mayor was elected by the reeves and councillors, and then directly by citizens (property owners and tenants) by secret ballot from 1856 to 1870 and after 1908. The number of reeves, councillors and districts changed on many occasions as a result of amal-

gamations, in particular those of St-Sauveur (1889), St-Malo (1908), Limoilou (1909), Montcalm (1913), Notre-Dame-des-Anges (1924), Les Saules (1969), Duberger (1970), Neufchatel (1971) and Charlesbourg Ouest (1973). Currently, 21 councillors are elected by universal suffrage. Since 1970 the urban community of Québec has included 26 municipalities on the N shore, and it is responsible for public security, building regulations, property evaluation and industrial and tourist promotion.

The role played by Québec as a "national" capital until 1841 (and subsequently 1851 to 1855 and 1859 to 1865 during the Union period) and as a provincial capital since 1867 has given it a special relationship with national, provincial and municipal politicians – so much so, in fact, that with the exception of a few businessmen prior to 1870, most Québec mayors have also been involved in political careers at higher levels before, after and even during their mandates. One of the most famous mayors of Québec City, Simon-Napoléon PARENT (1894-1906), was also premier of Québec 1900-05.

Cultural Life The city of Québec remains the major centre of French culture and the seat of the only francophone government in N America. In addition to conserving these traditions, it has managed to maintain a greater cultural homogeneity than Montréal, the other major pole of French culture.

Its teaching institutions include the SÉMINAIRE DE QUÉBEC (1663) and UNIVERSITÉ LAVAL (1852). Until 1920 the latter was the only francophone university in Québec; its satellite campus in Montréal, founded in 1876, became the U de Montréal (1920). This situation often produced acrimony within the ranks of the clergy and in Québec political circles. Long located in the old city, from the 1950s on the university gradually moved to the suburbs.

The historical character of Québec is reflected in the architecture of the old city, which has been the subject of major restorations and has become the site of exceptional museums. In 1985 this

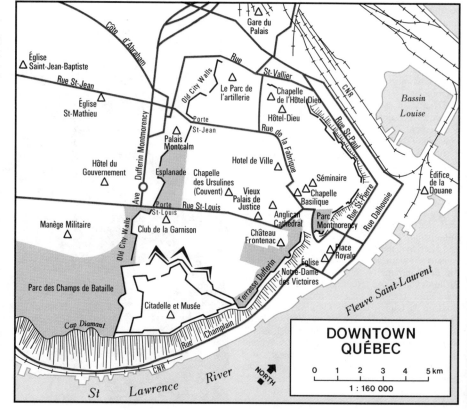

DOWNTOWN QUÉBEC

0   1   2   3   4   5 km

1 : 160 000

part of the city was recognized as a UNITED NATIONS WORLD HERITAGE SITE. The municipal, provincial and federal governments have combined their efforts to restore PLACE ROYALE, Artillery Park and the fortifications (Citadel, walls, gates, S shore forts), the Old Port, the Voûtes du Palais, the Musée du Séminaire, a number of private religious museums, and the Musée de la Civilisation. The MUSÉE DU QUÉBEC (1934) contains collections of ancient and modern works and is part of a large urban park, the Plains of Abraham, or Parc des Champs de Bataille (1908), which commemorates the battle leading to the fall of the city in 1759 and ultimately of New France to the British army a year later. There is also a zoological garden in Charlesbourg, N of the city, an aquarium near the Pont de Québec, and the Grand Théâtre de Québec (1971), home of the ORCHESTRE SYMPHONIQUE DE QUÉBEC.

A number of downhill and cross-country ski centres, including Mont Sainte-Anne and Lac Beauport, are located within a few minutes of the city. After having excellent minor hockey league teams for many years, Québec finally entered the realm of major league hockey with the QUEBEC NORDIQUES (1972), who have been members of the NHL since 1979. The city is also host to an international peewee hockey tournament.

Tourists and residents are attracted by a number of popular events: the Québec Carnival (since 1954), the Summer Festival each July, and a number of major anniversaries, including the 300th in 1908, the 375th in 1983 and the 450th anniversary of Cartier's arrival (1984).

Of Québec's many literary figures, mention should be made of Roger LEMELIN, whose novels depict the working-class districts of the city. Three TV stations serve the city, one of which is English, and there are a number of radio stations and 2 daily newspapers, *Le Soleil* and the *Journal de Québec*. MARC VALLIÈRES

Québec Conference, 10-27 Oct 1864. At the earlier CHARLOTTETOWN CONFERENCE, representatives from the 3 Maritime colonies and the PROVINCE OF CANADA had agreed on a scheme for the federation of BRITISH NORTH AMERICA. On Oct 10, 33 delegates, including 2 from Newfoundland, met in Québec City to formulate a detailed plan for union. The Maritime delegates were drawn from government; Canada was represented by its Cabinet, which set the agenda, proposed the resolutions and dominated the conference. Canadian PM Sir E.P. TACHÉ acted as chairman. Voting was by colony; Canada was given 2 votes. The greatest controversy was over the composition of PARLIAMENT: only PEI disagreed that members of the HOUSE OF COMMONS should be elected on the basis of representation by population, but the distribution of seats in the SENATE led to a prolonged dispute. The financial arrangements proposed by Alexander T. GALT also precipitated considerable discussion. The distribution of powers between federal and provincial governments was settled with comparative ease and followed the outline suggested by John A. MACDONALD and Oliver MOWAT. The delegates completed their work and adjourned Oct 27. Their conclusions were embodied in 72 resolutions, which became the focus of the CONFEDERATION debates. Although the Québec Resolutions were formally adopted only by the Province of Canada, they formed the basis of the BRITISH NORTH AMERICA ACT, which created Canada. P.A. BUCKNER

Quebec Nordiques, hockey team. An original World Hockey Assn franchise (1972), the Nordiques won the WHA championship in 1977, and 2 of their stars, Marc Tardif and Réal Cloutier, won the last 4 WHA scoring titles (1976-79). In 1977 the Carling O'Keefe Brewery became full

owners for approximately $2 million. Under the leadership of President Marcel Aubut, the Nordiques were part of the WHA-NHL merger of 1979. They play in the 15 434-seat Colisée as members of the Adams Division and have established an intense rivalry with the MONTREAL CANADIENS. The Nordiques were the first team to sign defected players from Czechoslovakia – star brothers Peter, Anton and Marian Stastny. In 1982 they eliminated the Canadiens and the Boston Bruins en route to the Prince of Wales conference final. In 1986, led by Peter Stastny and high-scoring winger Michel Goulet, the Nordiques won their first regular season division championship. DEREK DRAGER

Quebec, North Shore and Labrador Railway links the towns of Labrador City, Wabush and Schefferville to the port of SEPT-ÎLES. The contract for the 573 km of main track was awarded Sept 1950 and work was completed, through very difficult terrain and under harsh climatic conditions, in Feb 1954. Iron ore is hauled from Labrador City and Wabush throughout the year. In a typical year, the track is subjected to some 14.5 billion tonnes of traffic per km – a challenge to maintenance, along with some 2500 culverts and 7 bridges. Construction of the railway necessitated one of the greatest airlifts in the history of civil aviation. JAMES MARSH

The Quebec, North Shore and Labrador Railway was built in the early 1950s to transport iron ore to the port of Sept-Îles (*courtesy Iron Ore Company of Canada*).

Québec Pension Plan (QPP), established in 1966, is the counterpart for the Québec labour force of the CANADA PENSION PLAN. The plan has the same rate of contributions, maximum pensionable earnings, retirement pensions and annual escalation of benefits, but the QPP flat-rate components of disability and surviving spouses' benefits are higher. The QPP allows women to exclude from the formula used to calculate pensions the periods during which they were at home in charge of a child under 7 years of age. Women in this category would be eligible for higher pensions under the QPP than under the CPP. QPP funds are deposited with the CAISSE DE DÉPÔT ET PLACEMENT DU QUÉBEC. In 1986 its total assets of more than $25 billion, of which approximately $13.5 billion are QPP funds, were invested in bonds (60%), shares and convertible securities (26%), mortgages (6%), short-term investments (5.4%) and real estate (1.4%). A. ASIMAKOPULOS

Québec Provincial Police In 1838 Lord DURHAM established a municipal police force for Montréal and Québec, and a rural force with jurisdiction over the rest of the province. Its structure was reorganized in 1938 by Maurice Duplessis, who at the time was both premier and solicitor general of the province. The force was renamed the Sûreté provinciale du Québec, and permanent provincial police stations were created in each of the 9 judiciary districts of the province. In 1961, the administrative structure of the force was redefined by a law passed by the newly elect-

ed Liberal Party of Jean Lesage, and in 1968 its name was shortened to Sûreté du Québec. With 107 stations across the province, the Sûreté maintains law and order as well as public safety. It enforces Québec and specific federal laws, eg, the Criminal Code and narcotics laws. It also assists municipal police forces. GISÈLE VILLENEUVE

Quebec Referendum, called by the PARTI QUÉBÉCOIS (PQ) government on 20 May 1980 to ask the people of Québec for a mandate to negotiate, on an equal footing, a new agreement with the rest of Canada, thus honouring the promise it had made in 1976 to hold a REFERENDUM before making any radical change in Québec's status. The concept of SOVEREIGNTY-ASSOCIATION was rejected by about 60% of voters, although it is estimated about 50% of the Francophones supported it. The PQ leadership maintained that sovereignty remained the only viable option for Québec and would someday win majority support. The federalist side, organized into one group as required by the law governing the referendum, was led by Claude RYAN. PM TRUDEAU, in an official statement near the end of the referendum campaign, persuaded a number of the Québecois that a rejection of the *péquiste* option would lead to negotiations for a new Canadian FEDERALISM. The intense negotiations between the federal government and the provinces began after the referendum but broke down when all 10 provinces rejected the proposals made by the federal team, although later many of the provinces (not Québec) agreed to them. Despite its defeat in the referendum, the *péquiste* government won re-election in 1981 with a marked increase (9%) in the popular vote. The situation evolved following the election of the federal Conservatives in 1984 and the return to power of Québec Liberals in 1985. An agreement was reached in June 1987 by which Québec is recognized to be "a distinct society"; however, approval must be given by Parliament and the provincial assemblies. *See also* MEECH LAKE ACCORD. R. HUDON

Quebec Seminary, *see* SÉMINAIRE DE QUÉBEC.

Québec Shoe Workers' Strike, properly a lockout, 27 Oct-10 Dec 1900, the first direct intervention in a labour conflict by Québec Catholic clergy and the first step toward the creation of Catholic unions (*see* CONFEDERATION OF NATIONAL TRADE UNIONS). Unionized boot and shoe workers had grown too militant to suit Québec manufacturers, who closed their factories, planning to keep them shut until the workers quit their unions. But the 4000 workers directly affected resisted. Finally the conflict was submitted by mutual consent to the arbitration of Archbishop Bégin. His decision, pronounced 14 Jan 1901, recognized the workers' right of association, but insisted that passages in the union constitutions that contravened the principles of "honest and just ends" and "means consistent with the standards of morality, honesty and justice" be revised by an ecclesiastical committee. The committee modified the overly radical passages to conform to the SOCIAL DOCTRINE of the church and recommended that a chaplain attend all union meetings. JACQUES ROUILLARD

Québec Since Confederation Confederation opened the way to a permanent settlement of a political problem that Canada had faced for several decades – the existence of a French Canadian nation in what had now become, through immigration, a predominantly English-speaking country. The solution that had begun to take shape with the Act of Union (*see* PROVINCE OF CANADA) took on its definitive form with CONFEDERATION in 1867, and there would be few challenges to it in the century that followed. Confederation confirmed French Canadians as a minority but gave them in return – in addition to bilingualism in federal institutions – provincial status for their heartland, the former LOWER CANADA. They were a majority in Québec, the new province, securely in control of their own cultural and social development. But this political reorganization was only one of the fundamental changes that Québec society was undergoing at the time.

The Late 19th Century For a long time, writers concerned with Québec's development characterized it as a traditional society, largely closed to the changes occurring elsewhere in N America, and described Québec as a peasant society, emphasizing its stability, arguing that at bottom its characteristics changed little between the 18th and mid-20th centuries. In the 1960s, however, new historical research began to show that Québec was a much more complex society, constantly evolving and with phases of apparent stability between periods of rapid transformation. Québec participated in the major developments that characterized the Atlantic world between 1815 and 1930: large-scale population movements and increasing industrialization and urbanization, in which respects the second half of the 19th century was a pivotal period.

This can be seen first by looking at developments in demography. The ethnic composition of Québec's population changed significantly over the 19th century. Heavy immigration from the British Isles occurred between 1815 and 1860; in 1867 a quarter of Québec's 1.2 million people traced their roots to the British Isles (mostly to Ireland) while three-quarters were of French origin. Around 1870, however, this large wave of immigration ended.

Meanwhile, French Canadians were also increasing rapidly in number because of their high birth rate. In Québec's older rural areas they soon became too numerous and farmers' children had to look for jobs elsewhere. A French Canadian who wanted to be a farmer had to go to a distant colonization zone in Québec where the soil was typically poor and living conditions were difficult. The colonist was isolated and the deficiencies of his marginal farm forced him to work in the forest as a lumberjack to make ends meet. Few rural Quebeckers were attracted by the new colonization regions, and most, regarding even the long hours of factory work as preferable to the life of a colonist, went to urban areas instead.

The textile mills of New England needed cheap and plentiful labour, which they found in the Québec countryside. In the late 19th century immigration to the US became a mass movement (*see* FRANCO-AMERICANS); it is estimated that between 1850 and 1930, almost a million French Canadians left Québec for American destinations. The rural population surplus also stimulated the emergence of industries in Québec itself. This was one of numerous reasons for the growth of industry in Québec, others being the expansion of the Canadian domestic market, railway construction, and the Canadian government's economic policies – especially the protective tariff of 1879 (*see* NATIONAL POLICY).

Industrialization in Québec during this period occurred in two stages. The first, in the mid-19th century, was concentrated primarily in Montréal. That city's industrial structure was also strengthened in the second stage, in the 1880s, but during this period industry grew in many small and middle-sized cities and towns as well, especially Québec City and the urban centres of the Eastern Townships.

Industrialization in Québec was based mainly on light manufacturing, employing plentiful, underpaid labour and producing goods for immediate consumption, such as shoes, textiles and food.

There was also some heavy industry, linked mostly to the transportation sector and concentrated in Montréal.

Industrialization increased the process of urbanization, and by the end of the 19th century a third of all Quebeckers lived in cities and towns. The most significant urban and industrial growth took place in Montréal, where half of Québec's industrial production was concentrated and almost a quarter of all Quebeckers lived in 1901.

Nevertheless the majority of Québec's population was still in rural areas, where subsistence was beginning to yield to more commercial forms of agriculture. The farmers were weaned from their traditional attachment to grain cultivation and started to concentrate on dairy farming and the production of more specialized, market-oriented commodities. This change took place slowly, and its pace varied widely from region to region.

As a result of the period's economic growth, a new bourgeoisie emerged. Unlike the bourgeoisie of the previous period, whose interests were purely commercial, this class also invested in transportation, the financial sector and industrial corporations. It was drawn overwhelmingly from the English and Scottish groups, and was concentrated in Montréal, Canada's leading economic centre. It controlled the major economic institutions that operated Canada-wide, such as the powerful BANK OF MONTREAL (fd 1817). French Canadians were almost completely absent from the upper level of the bourgeoisie. At the same time, however, there arose a class of French-speaking businessmen with a much more local or regional economic base. They actively exercised a share of political power in Québec and established specifically French-speaking institutions, eg, banks, business periodicals and chambers of commerce.

Industrialization also led to the formation of a working class. In Montréal, Québec City and the smaller industrial centres, Quebeckers who had left farms to become workers lived under difficult conditions: low wages, long working hours, poor housing conditions, a high death rate and widespread seasonal unemployment. French Canadian workers had the fewest skills and had to be satisfied with the lowest-paying jobs. This was especially true of women, whose numbers were increasing in the textile, clothing, shoe and tobacco industries. The growing importance of the working class was confirmed by the rise of the labour movement in the 1880s and 1890s (*see* WORKING-CLASS HISTORY). The trade union movement quickly became dominated by 2 American organizations, the KNIGHTS OF LABOR and the American Federation of Labor, which established affiliates in Canada. During this period, only a small proportion of Québec's workers – primarily the most highly skilled ones – belonged to these unions.

This period was marked politically by the domination of the Conservative Party which, except for brief intervals, held power in both Ottawa and Québec. After the death of George-Étienne CARTIER in 1873, the party was gradually eroded by quarrels between its ULTRAMONTANE and moderate wings. Between 1867 and 1897 Québec had 10 premiers: 8 Conservatives, including P.J.O. CHAUVEAU (1867-73) and J.A. CHAPLEAU (1879-82), and 2 Liberals, one of whom was Honoré MERCIER (1887-91).

The Roman Catholic Church (*see* CATHOLICISM) was a powerful social force. It controlled the public education system, and through its network of parishes and religious associations it exercised tight control over people's morals. The rapid numerical growth of the clergy and religious communities, starting in the mid-19th century, was evidence of the church's vitality and its power in society. Nevertheless the church was not ubiqui-

tous and all-powerful. Despite its success in the social and cultural spheres, it was less effective in the political and economic realms. The clergy did not have the power to stop industrialization or immigration to the US. And although the clergy did try to dominate Québec's politicians, to the point of supporting the formation of a Catholic party in 1871, it was unable to control government institutions. Many priests were openly hostile to the Liberal Party, but the Liberals, under federal leader Wilfrid LAURIER and provincial leader Honoré Mercier, followed a strategy of softening their radicalism and increased their support among the population.

Although rural life was still a major feature of late 19th-century Québec, the province's social and economic development was parallel to that of other parts of N America that were becoming industrialized. There were still significant differences of language and culture between Québec and the rest of the continent. In addition, French Canadians were not masters of Québec's economic development; they occupied a secondary economic position and were much more likely to be workers than employers.

1896-1930 In the first 30 years of the 20th century, Québec experienced strong economic growth and the pace of the changes that had marked the previous period quickened. Industrialization and urbanization continued: by WWI half the population lived in cities and towns, and this proportion grew to 60% by 1931.

To an increasing extent, Montréal was Québec's metropolis, and in 1931 Greater Montréal accounted for 35% of the province's population. The city's industrial growth was remarkable: new industries developed while some old ones substantially increased production to meet the demand caused by Canada's rapid economic growth. Through its railway systems, large banks and many commercial and industrial corporations, Montréal became the metropolitan centre for the development of western Canada. Canadian wheat was exported to Europe from its harbour. It remained Canada's leading industrial centre and accounted for two-thirds of the value of Québec's manufacturing production.

At the same time the Québec countryside was being changed by a new kind of industrialization based on the exploitation of natural resources. Industries linked to hydroelectric and forest resources (pulp and paper, aluminum, chemicals) developed quickly in former colonization zones, such as the St Maurice Valley and the Saguenay-Lac Saint-Jean region. Immigration to the US slowed, although it remained substantial until the 1930s.

As concentration in the industrial and banking sectors increased early in the century, economic power increasingly became centralized in the hands of a few Montréal capitalists, almost all of them English Canadian; the French Canadian bourgeoisie was reduced to a marginal position and increasingly limited to local institutions and traditional sectors. However, it maintained a strong political presence, especially at the provincial level.

But the vast majority of French Canadians could choose only farming or factory work. The situation of Québec farmers improved as the trend towards specialization and market orientation continued up to WWI. In the 1920s Québec farmers tended to come out of their traditional isolation and join together in associations and co-operatives (*see* UNITED FARMERS OF QUÉBEC; CO-OPERATIVE MOVEMENT).

In the cities and towns, French Canadian workers had to compete with a new wave of immigrants who came increasingly from continental Europe. The largest ethnic group that was neither French nor British consisted of eastern European Jews, and Italians were a distant second. In the second half of the 19th century, the proportion of French Canadians in Québec's population had increased from 75% to 80%, and it remained at this level through the early part of the 20th century. The proportion represented by the British group, however, declined to 15% by 1931, while people of neither French nor British origin accounted for almost 6%. At the same time, ethnic diversity was a phenomenon that was increasingly limited to Montréal Island, where people of French origin represented approximately 60% of the population.

As they had in the late 19th century, French Canadian politicians and businessmen strongly supported Québec's industrial development. The provincial Liberal Party, in power from 1897 to 1936, was solidly behind big business and the entry of American capital in the new resource-based industries. Premiers F.G. MARCHAND (1897-1900), S.N. PARENT (1900-05), Lomer GOUIN (1905-20) and L.A. TASCHEREAU (1920-36) all pursued programs of modernization. However, a group of intellectuals and members of the liberal professions, led in turn by Henri BOURASSA and Abbé Lionel GROULX and calling themselves nationalists, reacted by trying to resist rapid industrialization, and especially the sale of natural resources to foreigners. The nationalists' opposition to large-scale industrialization received considerable support from the Catholic clergy, which was alarmed at the massive rural exodus and the rapid urbanization of the population. However, the clergy was not rejecting outright a process over which it had no control; instead, it developed a new strategy of establishing organizations to make it possible to dominate the new economic and social order from within. For example, the clergy promoted the establishment of Catholic unions, which were especially active in Québec's smaller industrial towns. However, these new unions largely failed to take root in Montréal, and, despite clerical support, only a quarter of all unionized workers in Québec belonged to Catholic unions in the late 1920s, the great majority remaining with the big US-based international unions.

Throughout the period, 2 opposing conceptions of Québec society confronted each other. The first, which can be called the liberal ideology, was upheld by businessmen and most politicians. Emphasizing economic growth and the idea of progress, it placed a high value on the individual and free enterprise. Its representatives believed that the well-being of the nation would flow from the individual progress of its members, and that economic growth was the only road Québec could take. Since they took the position that individual progress would lead to collective progress, they also believed that better education was the path to an improved economic situation. At the same time, they favoured modernizing Québec's economic and social structures.

Opposed to the liberal ideology was the deeply traditionalist clerical-nationalist ideology, which suggested that the French Canadian collectivity would achieve national well-being by withdrawing into itself and returning to rural life and traditional French Canadian and Catholic values. Upheld by nationalist intellectuals and many clergymen, this ideology was opposed to almost everything foreign. It was forcefully expressed in a number of publications and in sermons and speeches. It was much more explicit and more fully articulated than was the liberal ideology, and hence historians and sociologists long maintained that it was Québec's dominant ideology. However, the real situation was much more complex. Despite the resistance of clerical-nationalist

Former French President Charles de Gaulle saluting a crowd in Montréal 24 July 1967. De Gaulle stirred nationalist sentiment in Québec and widespread controversy across Canada (*courtesy Canapress Photo Service*).

ideologues, industrialization continued and increasing numbers of Quebeckers left their farms to live in cities and towns. A return to traditional rural society was a dream that did not come true.

Socialist ideological currents were very important in Europe at the time, but they occupied only a marginal position in Québec. Some representatives of the labour movement became involved in politics through the Parti ouvrier, but they were closer in their thinking to the British Labour Party than to European socialists.

The rise of Québec nationalism, moreover, posed the question of Québec's place in Confederation. While Laurier was prime minister, French Canadians felt that they held some power. In fact, they witnessed the reduction of their educational and linguistic rights throughout various parts of the country, despite the vigorous battles fought by the nationalists. The nationalists' real political setback, however, the election of a Conservative government to Ottawa in 1911 – and especially the CONSCRIPTION crisis of 1917 – served to highlight the isolation of Québec, which henceforth bound its fortunes to those of the Liberal Party.

1930-45 The GREAT DEPRESSION of the 1930s appeared to be a partial vindication of the clergy and the nationalist intellectuals who had long been predicting that the liberal model of society would fail. The area of Québec most seriously affected was Montréal. Because Montréal was Canada's leading port, it suffered substantial unemployment when international trade and Canadian exports collapsed. In addition, its industries were hurt as a result of decreased domestic consumption. Montréal teemed with tens of thousands of unemployed people living on public assistance.

All over Canada, traditional solutions based largely on private charity proved inadequate to cope with the Depression. Governments had to intervene. Provincial governments were overwhelmed and appealed to Ottawa, which participated financially in assisting the unemployed. This intervention by the federal government in social policy led to a rethinking of Canadian federalism in the form of the Rowell-Sirois Commission. It also marked the beginning of a long process of centralization favouring the federal government, which had a considerable impact on Québec. WWII, during which Ottawa intervened extensively in economic management, played a determining role in this respect. During the Depression and the war, the idea of more systematic government intervention, based on Keynesian economic policies, was gradually accepted. In a federal system such as Canada's, however, such a development raised a fundamental question: which level of government should be in charge of

the regulatory instruments that were established? In general, English Canadians believed that this was properly the responsibility of the federal government, which should provide for equality of opportunity from coast to coast. By contrast, most French-speaking political thinkers and politicians in Québec were opposed to concentrating power in Ottawa's hands in this way, on the grounds that it threatened the autonomy that French Canadians had gained through the existence of a provincial government over which they had majority control. The question seemed especially complicated in Québec's case because most Québec representatives in Ottawa, the Liberals who were in power 1935-57, supported federal centralization. During the war the federal government could impose its own solution, but once the war was over the issue reappeared, as vexatious as ever. As a result, the recent history of Québec – and of Canada as a whole – has been marked by federal-provincial struggles.

In the economic disorder brought about by the Depression, there were many challenges to the prevailing political and social system. Although communist and socialist groups grew substantially in Canada during the 1930s, they had little success in recruiting French Canadians, among whom left-wing traditions were very weak. In Québec, only immigrants and English-speaking intellectuals in Montréal were attracted to these groups. Among French Canadians, nationalist and traditionalist movements enjoyed new popularity instead, and new groups emphasizing nationalism and corporatism (such as ACTION LIBERALE NATIONALE and, later, BLOC POPULAIRE) had considerable success at the ballot box.

Their success was short-lived, however, as the ideological effervescence of the 1930s was calmed by the war. In Québec the war was synonymous with a return to prosperity and full employment. Quebeckers actually profited from the war – although they were reluctant to pay the price for their new prosperity. Thousands of French Canadians joined the Canadian Army to fight in Europe, but in its culture and operation the Canadian Army was a profoundly anglophone institution and held little attraction for French-speaking Quebeckers. Nationalist leaders portrayed the war as something foreign that did not concern French Canadians, so that intense resistance to Canadian military participation in Europe, and especially to conscription, developed in Québec. In 1942 Ottawa held a Canada-wide plebiscite on the question of conscription. An overwhelming majority of Quebeckers voted against compulsory military service, whereas a majority of English Canadians in the other provinces voted in favour of it; a deep national cleavage ensued.

The war also had highly significant long-term social consequences, which manifested themselves both concretely and in attitudes. Quebeckers who served in Europe came into contact with different cultures and ways of life. Thousands of women worked in factories as part of the war production system, and even though many returned to traditional family life after the war, this exposure had long-term effects. But the impact of the war was probably felt most strongly by rural Quebeckers. They were increasingly integrated into the industrial capitalist economy, as many of them left the countryside to work in factories while others introduced changes that made their farms much more productive. Meanwhile, war propaganda, the increasing availability of radio and improved communications all tended to bring rural Quebeckers into the broad current of modernization that had been felt in Québec for several decades but had not reached all parts of the province in equal measure.

The Duplessis Era, 1945-60 After the war Québec entered another period of rapid economic growth. This was conspicuous in the natural resource sector, where it was stimulated by American demand. Its most spectacular manifestation was the opening up of the North Shore of the St Lawrence and the far north of the province, Nouveau Québec, to mining development. But growth was also visible in the manufacturing and service sectors. Québec underwent a new wave of urbanization, its standard of living improved substantially, and Quebeckers had greater access to the consumer society. Rural exodus speeded up and by 1960 farmers were a small minority of Québec's economically active population.

Québec's population grew substantially. The number of births increased and remained at a high level until the early 1960s. Immigration, which had almost stopped in the 1930s and during the war, resumed. The many newcomers came from the British Isles as before, but also – and in greater numbers – from southern Europe, especially Italy. Montréal became even more cosmopolitan, and by 1961 Italian Quebeckers constituted the largest ethnic group of neither French nor British origin.

Economic growth also had significant social effects. It brought about the rise of a new middle class made up of highly skilled workers, executives, managers and teachers. This group increasingly favoured a modernization of the social and political structures of Québec, in which traditionalism and social control by the church played too large a role. The gap between socioeconomic reality and the needs of the population on the one hand, and the traditionalism that characterized Québec's institutions and structures on the other, was increasingly evident.

Throughout the postwar period the Québec government was dominated by the UNION NATIONALE Party under Maurice DUPLESSIS. Maintained in power by Québec's most traditional elements, political corruption and an outdated electoral map, Duplessis ran a conservative, narrow-minded government with no overall vision of society. While the need for a wide range of reforms was ever more strongly felt, the Union Nationale effectively delayed them.

The Duplessis government used Québec nationalism to justify its policies. Its nationalism was traditionalist and conservative, emphasizing the classic themes of religion, language and the rural character of French Canada. It resisted the federal government in the name of provincial autonomy. At the same time, the federal government represented a new and reform-oriented brand of liberalism which attracted many young French Canadian intellectuals, who described this period as the era of the "Great Darkness." Moreover, the federal government was led by a French Canadian, Louis ST. LAURENT, who had strong backing from the Québec electorate. Thus, much of that electorate simultaneously supported 2 first ministers of opposing orientations.

The Duplessis period was especially difficult for the trade union movement, which came into conflict with the anti-union policies of the government. A number of strikes, especially the ASBESTOS STRIKE of 1949, had wide repercussions. There were also changes within the unions themselves: the Catholic unions became more secular and radical (*see* CONFEDERATION OF NATIONAL TRADE UNIONS; UNION CENTRALS, QUÉBEC), and the merger of the 2 American trade union congresses, the American Federation of Labor and the Congress of Industrial Organizations (*see* AFL-CIO), led to a similar reorganization among Québec affiliates.

The Quiet Revolution and After Some of Québec society's institutions – especially the educational system, the social services and the administrative arm of the provincial government – were increasingly ill suited to the postwar world. When Duplessis died in 1959, it was the signal for the start of a new era, known as the QUIET REVOLUTION, which lasted roughly from 1960 to 1966. The political and ideological heritage of the Duplessis era was liquidated with a speed that indicated how little it corresponded to contemporary socioeconomic realities. The provincial Liberal Party, led by Jean LESAGE (1960-66), proceeded to modernize government institutions, the school system and social services. This direction was followed, though less spectacularly, by subsequent governments: the Union Nationale of Daniel JOHNSON (1966-68) and Jean-Jacques BERTRAND (1968-70), the Liberal Party of Robert BOURASSA (1970-76, 1985-) and the PARTI QUÉBÉCOIS of René LÉVESQUE and Pierre-Marc JOHNSON (1976-85). Québec society also broke with a much longer historical tradition by becoming declericalized: religious observance declined, the clergy decreased in numbers and the church lost its former hold on social services and, more generally, on people's attitudes.

But the 1960s and 1970s also evidenced the persistence of long-term trends in the development of Québec society. The effects of industrialization, urbanization and the growth of the service sector, all of which had been in process for a long time, were then fully felt. Other trends continued: a rising standard of living, the emergence of a new middle class and new elites, and a higher level of education.

While postwar prosperity brought benefits to Francophones, it also made them see much more clearly the extent of ethnic discrimination. In the workplace, French Canadians were limited to subordinate jobs, while in Montréal department stores and the public arena in general their language held second place to English.

A new form of nationalism emerged. Unlike Duplessis's nationalism, it was essentially reformist and demanded a change in Québec's position in Confederation. This new nationalism manifested itself in a number of different tendencies. There were the Liberals, who favoured autonomy for Québec but remained federalists; the independence movement, which grew in size and credibility during the 1960s; and the socialists, working within a newly strong trade union movement and in intellectual circles, who wanted to go beyond reformism.

Major struggles for power took place in Québec in the 1960s and 1970s between old and new elites and between Francophones and Anglophones. Especially noteworthy were battles over language, the economy and politics.

The struggle on the language front was aimed at having French, the language of the majority, fully recognized as Québec's primary language. One major objective was to integrate Quebeckers of neither French nor British origin into the French-speaking majority, and this engagement was fought on the battleground of the language of education. The goal of making Québec French was achieved in stages, and at each stage it encountered resistance from non-francophone groups. In the late 1960s the language struggle was fought in the streets, but it later found its way into Québec's National Assembly and, more generally, into the forum of public debate. Three language laws were passed by 3 different provincial governments between 1969 and 1977. Step by step, these pieces of legislation increased the pressure in favour of French, widened its recognition as Québec's official language and made its use compulsory. The third of these laws, known as BILL 101 or the Charter of the French Language, went well beyond the educational field. It was aimed not only at bringing more children into French schools but also at making all of Québec society French, and dealt with corporations, professional services, public signs, etc. By 1980 French was spoken and recognized everywhere in the province. The Anglophones, nevertheless, retained their own institutions as is guaranteed by the constitution.

Another struggle was over the question of economic power. One government objective was to introduce changes into the workplace so that French Canadians would have better jobs and career opportunities in the private sector. Another goal was to support and assist French Canadian businessmen and the companies they owned so that they would grow and gain a larger share of the market. A third aim was to have large Canadian and international corporations which operated in the province take Québec's specific needs increasingly into account. And a final objective was to make the Québec government a major partner with private enterprise in Québec's economic development. In the 1960s and 1970s French Canadians made considerable economic progress. The growth of new French Canadian financial groups was significant, as was the increasing intervention of the Québec government in the economy through such publicly owned corporations as HYDRO-QUÉBEC and the CAISSE DE DÉPÔT ET PLACEMENT. These successes, however, were counterbalanced by the weakening of Québec's economic position as the country's economic centre of gravity moved westward. Toronto replaced Montréal as Canada's metropolis and many companies moved their head offices or manufacturing operations to Ontario.

The third struggle was over political power within Canada. Throughout the 1960s and 1970s there were continuing attempts to increase Québec's influence in Confederation and to revamp the division of powers between the 2 levels of government. The Québec government's goal was to stem the tide of federal centralization and to make itself the government with primary responsibility for French Canadians. The debate over the Constitution was clearly one of the major themes of the 1960s and 1970s. It was marked by provocative statements and battles over protocol and appearance, and also by discussions, negotiations and federal-provincial conferences. Québec's firm self-assertion during the Quiet Revolution was followed by a period of federal resistance to the provinces' desire to increase their autonomy; the new federal stance became explicit when P.E. TRUDEAU came to power in Ottawa in 1968.

This long political conflict even had some violent episodes with the Front de libération du Québec and the OCTOBER CRISIS of 1970. It was nevertheless fought through the legal democratic system. It mobilized much of Québec's energy for 2 decades and culminated in 2 defeats for Québec: advocates of independence were the losers in the 1980 QUÉBEC REFERENDUM, and the adoption of the new Canadian Constitution in 1982 represented a defeat for those who supported a stronger Québec within Confederation. The political struggle led only to increased federal centralization and the confirmation of Québec's minority status in Confederation. In 1987 the MEECH LAKE ACCORD indicated a will to ease the tension and permitted Québec to accept fully the CONSTITUTION ACT, 1982.

In fact, however, the position of Québec with respect to the federal government appeared to be improving. Under Trudeau (1968-79 and 1980-84) there were more Québécois than ever before in Cabinet, and federal institutions adopted a far more pronounced bilingual stance. But these circumstances depended on the influence of Québec representatives in the Liberal Party, and in the 1980s the number of Francophones in administrative posts remained low – particularly at the senior levels.

In addition, there were conflicts internal to French Canadian society. The growing strength of the trade-union movement during the 1960s led in the next decade to serious confrontations between the major union federations and the provincial government. At the same time there were profound tensions within the new French Canadian middle class, which had grown up gradually in the postwar period and occupied centre stage during the 1960s and 1970s. There was relative unanimity during the Quiet Revolution, but afterwards deep divisions appeared – politically, with the polarization between the Liberal Party and the Parti Québécois, and socially, with the tensions between trade union leaders and provincial government administrators.

Although the province enjoyed a higher standard of living, serious inequalities continued to characterize Québec society. There were regional inequalities, as Montréal flourished while other regions remained underdeveloped, and social inequalities, as Québec's unemployment rate was substantially higher than the Canadian average and many of its citizens lived in poverty. Awareness of these problems was much greater in the 1960s and 1970s, and demands for a change in the situation were increasingly heard.

The Turning Point of the 1980s The period of upheavals and rapid transformations which had characterized Québec since the start of the Quiet Revolution ended in the early 1980s. The recession of 1981-82, the most serious since the 1930s, put an abrupt halt to expansion, and recovery has been slow. Buying power, which had steadily increased since the end of the war, now decreased instead. Unemployment and welfare rolls both rose steeply. Faced with ever-greater deficits, the Lévesque government had to make drastic budget cuts and considerable reductions in salaries paid to public and para-public-sector employees. The crisis caused even the basic direction of the last 2 decades to be thrown into question: there was a trend away from the WELFARE STATE toward privatization and deregulation. This reorientation began under the *péquistes* and gained momentum when the Liberals again took power.

Politically speaking, the referendum of 1980 and the patriation of the Canadian Constitution sounded the death knell of the independentist movement. The Parti Québécois, racked with internal dissent, had to redefine its program. The departure of PM Trudeau, in 1984, and that of Premier Lévesque, in 1985, marked the end of an era. Pierre-Marc Johnson did not manage to win the confidence of the electorate during his few months as premier, and in 1985 had to hand over power to Robert Bourassa's Liberals. Johnson himself resigned his leadership in Nov 1987, shortly after Lévesque's death.

Thus the 1980s saw the gains of the Quiet Revolution thrown in doubt once again. Even the linguistic question, which had seemed settled, resurfaced in 1986. This situation shows once again that Québec's evolution is not a linear affair; it consists of steps forward and back, of pauses as well as growth.

And so, despite its unique cultural nature, Québec society is like all others – complex and tension-ridden. As the 1980 referendum (among other events) shows, Québecois always have been and still are far from unanimous in their interpretation of Québec's past, its goals and its politics.   PAUL-ANDRÉ LINTEAU

Quebecair, with headquarters in Dorval, Qué, is a regional airline that began in 1946 as the Rimouski Aviation Syndicate. This company became Rimouski Airlines in 1947, merged with Gulf Aviation to create Quebecair in 1953, and acquired Matane Air Service, Northern Wings

A stream meanders through the rainforest vegetation of South Moresby I in the Queen Charlottes. The area is biologically unique, containing some vegetation that is also found only in Japan or Ireland (*photo by Paul Bailey*).

(now Regionair) and Northern Wings Helicopters in 1965. Quebecair now operates scheduled passenger flights in Québec, western Labrador and Ontario, and offers domestic and international group charters. The company has about 900 employees. Its major shareholder was the Québec government, which assumed control in 1981. The airline did not fare well and in 1986 was sold to Nordair-Metro, after losing the government $80 million 1981-86. Soon after, Nordair was sold to CP Air, itself soon taken over by PWA and now operating under the name Canadian Airlines International.   DEBORAH C. SAWYER

Quebecor Inc, controlled by Pierre PÉLADEAU, publishes 2 French-language morning tabloids, *Le Journal de Montréal* and *Le Journal de Québec*. Its interests in English-language newspapers include the *Winnipeg Sun* and *Winnipeg Magazine*. Other interests include *Filles d'aujourd'hui* and *Vivre*, trade magazines, *Messageries dynamiques*, one of the largest publications distribution networks in Québec, *Trans-Canada*, a distributor of records and cassettes serving mainly the Québec market; and it is a shareholder in Premier Choix/First Choice PAY TELEVISION in Québec. In 1985 Quebecor made a number of acquisitions, including a Québec City publisher and a second American company. In 1987 it purchased Donohue Inc, a major forest-products company, putting Quebecor among the leading producers of newsprint. The company's assets in 1987 included 38 regional weeklies, 6 weekly magazines, 3 dailies, 3 book publishers and 16 printing plants. In March 1988 Péladeau announced the launching of the *Montreal Daily News*, an English-language daily to be produced with British publisher Robert Maxwell.
      PETER S. ANDERSON

Queen Charlotte Islands, named for the wife of King George III, lie off the N coast of BC. They include about 150 islands in a scimitar-shaped archipelago 250 km long. Graham and Moresby islands comprise the bulk of the 9033 km² area. Separated by 45-130 km of open water (HECATE STR) from the mainland islands, the Charlottes are among the most isolated islands in Canada. Also unique is the absence of a continental shelf off the steep western ramparts of Moresby I.

Archaeological evidence indicates human occupation of the Charlottes for at least 6000 to 8000 years. Juan PÉREZ was the first European to sight the islands (1774). They were visited by James COOK in 1778 and named by Capt George Dixon in

1787. At that time the HAIDA nation populated the islands and probably numbered 6000 to 8000. European diseases drastically lowered the Haida to about 588 individuals in 1915, the most dramatic drop for any tribe recorded in the province. The present population of all peoples on the Charlottes is about 5700. Until recently, most people were loggers, fishermen or miners in the towns of Masset, Port Clements, Skidegate, Queen Charlotte, Sandspit and Tasu. Today geologists, biologists and recreationists come to study and enjoy the rugged mountain scenery (peaks up to 1200 m) along the western backbone of the islands, spectacular fjords, seabird and sea lion colonies, dark giant Sitka spruce and cedar forests, and remnants of decaying Haida TOTEM POLES.

Recently, geologists have documented that the Charlottes were formed by the movement of huge plates under the Pacific Ocean from the region of the South Pacific to their present location. Biologists have determined that, unlike most of Canada, much of the Charlottes escaped glaciation. This, coupled with the islands' isolation, has resulted in the Charlottes becoming a biologically unique area in Canada. There are numerous plants here that are found either only on the Charlottes or in distant lands such as Japan or Ireland. All the native land mammals and 3 kinds of birds are subspecifically unique, with the black bear being the largest in N America. The absence of some predators has permitted the Charlottes to

become the home of almost half a million pairs of nesting seabirds.

The old Haida village of Ninstints, on Skungwai I, has been made a UNITED NATIONS WORLD HERITAGE SITE. Its spectacular totem poles are now being protected from the elements as part of a collection of world treasures. All these natural features are attracting tourists in swelling numbers. Naikoon Provincial Park, with its vast beaches and bogs, attracts hikers. The S Moresby area, with its outstanding totem poles, marine life, hot springs, forests and mountain scenery, is unrivalled in Canada as a place to explore by water.

BRISTOL FOSTER

Queen Elizabeth Islands, NWT, group of islands in the Canadian ARCTIC ARCHIPELAGO lying N of a great bathometric trench composed of (E to W) LANCASTER SD, Barrow Str, Viscount Melville Sd and M'Clure Str. The islands form a triangle at the northern tip of Canada, with ELLESMERE I at the apex and DEVON, CORNWALLIS, BATHURST, MELVILLE and PRINCE PATRICK across the base. The islands are further grouped as the Parry Islands (Prince Patrick, Melville, MACKENZIE KING, Borden, Bathurst and Lougheed) and the Sverdrup Islands (ELLEF RINGNES, AMUND RINGNES, AXEL HEIBERG, CORNWALL and Meighen). The total area of land in the group (about 425 000 km²) is roughly equivalent to one of the Prairie provinces. About one-fifth of the land is covered with land ICE, with the largest mass on Ellesmere and concentrations on Devon and Axel Heiberg. Ice caps and glaciers cover a greater area than elsewhere in the North, owing to the cooler, shorter summers and the widespread uplands.

The islands consist of Cambrian to Upper Devonian rocks formed during the late Silurian period (*see* GEOLOGICAL HISTORY) and again in the late Devonian. As a result of intense folding and erosion the islands are characterized by folding mountains. In the eastern islands (Ellesmere, Axel Heiberg and Devon) remnants of the folds rise over 2000 m – the highest point in eastern N America lies in northern Ellesmere. Elsewhere the land is lower, much of it formed of horizontally embedded sediments, or peneplains. Spectacular cliffs rise above Lancaster Sd on Devon I. Melville I is largely formed of an erosion platform of folded rocks, although the Raglan Range in the NW approaches 915 m. The islands along the NW margin generally lie below the 150 m contour.

The occupation of the Queen Elizabeth Is by the Inuit is fairly recent. Their European discovery may be attributed to William BAFFIN (1616). However, they were not rediscovered until 1818, when John Ross confirmed their existence. In 1819 Parry sailed to Melville I, naming Devon, Cornwallis, Bathurst and Byam Martin. The exploration of the islands at the turn of the century in effect completed the geographical discovery of N America. From 1898 to 1902 a Norwegian expedition led by Otto SVERDRUP surveyed the N coast of Devon, S and W coasts of Ellesmere, Axel Heiberg, King Christian and the Ringnes islands. In 1916-17 Vilhjalmur STEFANSSON found Brock, Borden and Meighen islands. The islands remain remote and, except for weather and research stations, uninhabited. It is known that there is oil and gas in the area, primarily in the Sverdrup Basin. The islands were named in 1953 for Queen Elizabeth II.   JAMES MARSH

Reading: M. Zaslow, ed, *A Century of Canada's Arctic Islands* (1981).

Queen Elizabeth Way, connecting Toronto with Niagara Falls and Fort Erie, Ont, was Canada's first 4-lane, controlled-access superhighway. Using the latest concepts in streamlined design, the highway was built to overcome local traffic

bottlenecks and to open the province to US motorists entering via the Peace Bridge at Fort Erie. Construction began in the early 1930s on the Toronto-Burlington section, first called the Middle Road. The highway was officially opened by Queen Elizabeth, queen consort of King George VI, at St Catharines, 7 June 1939. Four lanes of pavement were completed to Fort Erie in 1956.

ROBERT M. STAMP

Queen's Counsel (QC), title conferred on lawyers by the CROWN; also King's Council (KC) when the sovereign is a king. Originally awarded to those considered worthy to argue cases for the Crown, in many provinces it has lost its distinction, being awarded to most practitioners of generally 10 years or more standing who conform politically to the government in office. The title can be conferred by either the provinces or the federal government. Duties no longer attach to the rank, which entitles holders to seniority within the profession and to wear a silk BARRISTER gown.   K.G. McSHANE

Queen's Plate, a stakes race for thoroughbred horses, was first run at the Carleton Race Track, Toronto, on 27 June 1860. It received royal assent by Queen Victoria in 1859. In 1918 and 1919, to retain its perpetuity during WWI, the 59th and 60th runnings were staged as features of a Red Cross Horse Show in Toronto, the only racing held those 2 years. Thus, it is the oldest uninterrupted stakes race on the continent. (The Kentucky Derby's inaugural was held in 1875.)

Politicians lobbied to hold the race in their constituencies in the early years. It was raced in Ontario at Toronto, Guelph, St Catharines, Whitby, Kingston, Barrie, Woodstock, Picton, London, Hamilton and Ottawa before it settled permanently, with the Queen's approval, in Toronto in 1883. In its early years the race's atmosphere resembled that of a country-fair meet. Two or 3 heats, or trials, were run to select a winner. It was claimed that the race attracted a "rowdy" crowd, and there were charges of fixed races.

The race was called the Queen's Plate until 1902, the year after Victoria's death, when it became the King's Plate (after Edward VII). It reverted to the former name upon the ascension of Elizabeth II in 1952. George VI (with his queen consort Elizabeth) was the first reigning monarch to attend the race, at Woodbine racetrack, Toronto, in 1939. Elizabeth II and Prince Philip attended the 100th running in 1959. The race was confined to Ontario-bred horses until 1944, when it

Queen Mother congratulating jockey Gordon Moses at the 1981 running of the Queen's Plate (*photo courtesy Michael Burns Photography Ltd*).

was opened to 3-year-olds foaled in Canada. The race's distance varied from a mile (1.6 km) to 2 miles until 1957, when it was fixed at a mile and a quarter. At that distance, the race record is 2:02, set in 1960 by E.P. TAYLOR's Victoria Park. The renowned NORTHERN DANCER, a Kentucky Derby and Preakness winner, and the world's leading sire in 1982, won in 2:02:1 in 1964.

Plate winners earn a gift of 50 guineas from the monarch. But the little purple bag of coins contains not guineas but sovereigns. Minting of guineas was discontinued by George III, whose forebear, George I, instituted the royal gift of 50 guineas for thoroughbred race winners, a tradition that remains today.

Queen's Quarterly, fd 1893 at Queen's U, largely on the initiative of Queen's president, G.M. GRANT, is the oldest of Canadian scholarly journals. At first, contributors were chosen mainly from the Queen's faculty, but in 1928 it became open to national and even international contributors. It also began to publish fiction and poetry. In the 1930s the stories of F.P. GROVE appeared in its pages, and the *Quarterly* launched Sinclair ROSS as a writer. Its real flowering began in the 1950s during the brief editorship of Malcolm ROSS, who actively sought to bring the *Quarterly* into contact with the current growth in Canadian writing. Since that time the work of many of Canada's best writers has appeared in its pages, including that of fiction writers Rudy WIEBE, Sheila WATSON, W.P. KINSELLA, Hugh HOOD and John METCALF, and that of poets Margaret ATWOOD, Irving LAYTON, Al PURDY, George BOWERING, John GLASSCO, F.R. SCOTT, A.J.M. SMITH and Tom WAYMAN. The *Quarterly* has continued to publish scholarly articles in many disciplines and has maintained an extensive section of book reviews.   GEORGE WOODCOCK

Queen's University, Kingston, Ont, was founded 1841. Queen's today is a nondenominational and coeducational university with students from all parts of Canada, the US and some 60 other countries. Nine out of 10 Queen's students live away from home; thus, most "live Queen's" 24 hours a day. This commitment no doubt contributes to the strong loyalty of graduates and students – the famous Queen's spirit.

Queen's has 13 faculties and schools ranging in age from the original Faculty of Arts and Science (est 1842) to the School of Industrial Relations (1983). The affiliated Queen's Theological College prepares students for the UNITED CHURCH ministry. Queen's is also a major research university in almost every aspect of health sciences, engineering, basic sciences, humanities and social sciences. It has centres and institutes devoted to transportation, resource development and intergovernmental relations. It is the home of the government- and industry-supported Canadian Microelectronics Corporation. Facilities on campus include one of Canada's finest university libraries. Queen's Archives houses one of the most notable and widely used nongovernmental collections of Canadian historical materials in the country.

Queen's roots run deep in the history and life of Canada. It is located in one of Canada's historic cities, and modern buildings blend with old limestone buildings to provide a distinctive campus. "Cha Gheill" (a Gaelic battle cry which is part of the school song), freshmen tams and tartans, and a small theological college are the only apparent reminders of Queen's College, established by the PRESBYTERIAN Church of Canada in association with the Church of Scotland "on the old Ontario strand" in 1841. On Oct 16 of that year Queen's received a royal charter from Queen Victoria, for whom the new college was named. Classes began on 7 Mar 1842 in a rented building with 2 profes-

Enrolment: Queen's University, 1985-86
(Source: Statistics Canada)

Full-time Undergrad	Full-time Graduate	Part-time Undergrad	Part-time Graduate
9 579	1 780*	3 269	517

* Includes medical interns and residents

sors and 10 students. It was intended primarily as a college to train young men for the ministry, but denominational ties progressively diminished. In 1912 Parliament, by amending the charter, completed the separation of church and university. Thus the college became Queen's University at Kingston, an independent institution controlled primarily by its graduates who, through the years, have conscientiously honoured their convocation pledge "to maintain a generous loyalty to the university."

Queenston, Ont, a quiet residential village in the town of NIAGARA-ON-THE-LAKE. Founded at the N end of the Niagara portage in the 1780s, and named for the Queen's Rangers stationed there, the village prospered on trade and a ferry crossing to Lewiston, NY – an important route of pioneer immigration. The house in which Laura SECORD overheard American troops planning to attack has been restored as a pioneer museum. Brock's Monument (1854) commemorates the British victory over American invaders at the Queenston Heights (1812); beneath it lies the tomb of Gen Sir Isaac BROCK. To the S are the 2 massive Sir Adam Beck generating stations. *See also* MONUMENT; NIAGARA HISTORIC FRONTIER. JOHN N. JACKSON

Queenston Heights, Battle of Before dawn on 13 Oct 1812, the New York state militia launched an invasion across the treacherous currents of the Niagara River at QUEENSTON, UC. Discovering a hidden path to the top of the escarpment, the Americans were able to seize a redan from which a gun had been hampering the flow of reinforcements across the river and gain control of the battle. Maj-Gen Isaac BROCK, commanding British and Canadian forces, personally led a charge to regain the position, losing his life in the unsuccessful attempt. After Brock's aide-de-camp, Lt-Col John Macdonell, was mortally wounded in a similar vain assault, Maj-Gen Roger Hale Sheaffe, arriving from Fort George with reinforcements, ascended the heights out of sight of the Americans. Attacking from the rear, Sheaffe trapped the enemy between his army and the cliff. When the smoke had cleared, almost 1000 Americans were taken prisoner while the victors lost only 28 killed and 77 wounded – regular, militia and Indian. Unfortunately, one of the losses was irreplaceable – the much-admired Isaac Brock. The victory, following hard on Brock's bloodless capture of Detroit, did much to raise the morale of the inhabitants of Upper Canada and convince them that they could resist conquest by their larger neighbour to the south. *See also* WAR OF 1812.
CARL A. CHRISTIE

Quesnel, BC, City, pop 8358 (1986c), 8240 (1981c), inc 1928, is located at the junction of the Quesnel and Fraser rivers in central BC, 625 km NE of Vancouver. It takes its name from the river and lake (to the SE) named by explorer Simon FRASER after NWC clerk Jules Maurice Quesnel, his companion on his 1808 journey of discovery down the Fraser R. Settlement began in 1860 when the area became the best access into the Cariboo goldfields. For many years Quesnel was a steamboat terminus which served to and from the goldrush town of BARKERVILLE to the E. The log HBC store, built in 1866, is still standing today. Farm settlement increased before WWI, and the Pacific Great Eastern Ry, now called the BCR,

reached Quesnel in 1918, opening up the region's rich forest reserves. Forestry, mining and agriculture (mostly ranching) are the major industries today, with some oil and gas exploration. Quesnel is the gateway to Barkerville Historic Park and Bowron Lake Provincial Park.
JOHN R. STEWART

Quesnel, Louis-Joseph-Marie, merchant, composer, poet, playwright (b at Saint-Malo, France 15 Nov 1746; d at Montréal 3 July 1809). Canada's first opera composer arrived here quite by chance. While captain of a French vessel carrying munitions to the Americans in 1779, Quesnel was captured by the British and taken to Québec where Governor HALDIMAND granted him a safe conduct. He set up a fur-trading and wine-import business at Boucherville, near Montréal. Missing the sophisticated entertainments of France, Quesnel began to write and compose. Many poems and several plays survive intact, but from his musical remnants only the opera *Colas et Colinette,* first performed in Montréal in 1790, can be restored. Using the surviving vocal and second-violin parts, composer Godfrey RIDOUT reconstructed the opera in 1963. The charming period piece has been published, performed and recorded.
BARCLAY McMILLAN

Quévillon, Louis-Amable, woodworker, sculptor, architect (b at St-Vincent-de-Paul [Laval, Qué] 14 Oct 1749; d there 11 Mar 1823). He began his career as a woodworker in St-Vincent-de-Paul in the early 1770s. Working mainly in the Montréal region, he was hired by about 40 parishes to do carvings and to decorate their churches with gilding, silvering and marbling. At the turn of the century he penetrated the market around Québec C where he worked in various churches. Throughout his career Quévillon trained apprentices, and his studio, which employed 14 sculptors, companion sculptors and apprentices in 1818, produced a great number of works, many of which have been lost to fire. An altarpiece remains in the church at Verchères and some of his church furniture is found in museums in Québec, Montréal and Ottawa. *See also* SCULPTURE; RELIGIOUS BUILDING. NICOLE CLOUTIER

Quiet Revolution (Révolution tranquille) was a period of rapid change experienced in Québec from 1960 to 1966. The vivid, yet paradoxical, description of the period was first used by an anonymous writer in the *Globe and Mail.* Although Québec was a highly industrialized, urban and relatively outward-looking society in 1960, the UNION NATIONALE Party, in power since 1944, seemed increasingly anachronistic as it held tenaciously to a conservative ideology and relentlessly defended outdated traditional values. In the election of 22 June 1960 the Liberals broke the hold of the Union Nationale, taking 51 seats and 51.5% of the popular vote as compared to the latter's 43 seats and 46.6% of the vote. Under Jean LESAGE the Québec Liberal Party had developed a coherent, wide-ranging reform platform. The main issue of the election was indicated by the Liberal slogan, "It's time for a change."

In 2 years the Lesage government managed to carry out or plan many reforms. Everything came under scrutiny, everything was discussed; a new age of open debate began. The government attacked political patronage and changed the electoral map to provide better representation for urban areas. To reduce the size of secret electoral funds, it limited authorized expenditures during election periods. It also lowered the voting age from 21 to 18. Lesage attempted to put the public purse in order by promoting a dynamic provincial budget and by raising loans. From 1960-61 to 1966-67, the budget grew from $745 million to

$2.1 billion. The spectacular development of government institutions and the vastly increased role of the state in the province's economic, social and cultural life unleashed forces that would have major consequences.

The pressures exerted by the BABY BOOM generation, which had now reached adolescence, created a dramatic situation and pushed Québec's weak educational system to the breaking point. The government introduced new legislation on education and established a commission of inquiry on education, which was chaired by Mgr Alphonse-Marie Parent. The resulting Parent Report tackled the entire system. In recommending the creation of a department of education, it questioned the role of the Catholic Church, which controlled the public Catholic school system. The church resisted recommended changes, but without success. The Parent Report contributed significantly to creating a unified, democratic, modern school system accessible to the entire population.

The desire to modernize was also evident in the social sphere. Upon taking power, the government decided to participate in the federal-provincial hospital-insurance program. In 1964 it introduced 3 major pieces of legislation: an extensive revision of the labour code; Bill 16, which abolished a married woman's judicial handicap by which her legal status was that of a minor; and a pension plan.

The government's most spectacular accomplishment in economics was the nationalization of private electricity companies, an idea that was promoted in 1962 by René LÉVESQUE, minister of natural resources. The government decided to go to the electorate on this issue, and on 14 Nov 1962 the Liberals won again, with 56.6% of the vote and 63 seats. The many objectives of nationalization included standardizing rates across the province, co-ordinating investments in this key sector, integrating the system, encouraging industrialization, guaranteeing economic benefits for the Québec economy through a buy-Québec policy, and making the sector more French in nature. HYDRO-QUÉBEC not only met most of these objectives but became a symbol of success and a source of pride for Quebeckers. Another major success was the creation in 1965 of the CAISSE DE DÉPÔT ET PLACEMENT DU QUÉBEC. The caisse was made responsible for administering the assets of the QUÉBEC PENSION PLAN, which rapidly grew to several billion dollars.

The *maîtres chez nous* ("masters in our own house") philosophy that permeated the government and its reforms was bound to have an influence on FEDERAL-PROVINCIAL RELATIONS. The Lesage government demanded a review of federal policy and won a major victory following a stormy first ministers' conference in 1964. Lesage forced the federal government to accept Québec's withdrawal from several cost-sharing programs and to compensate Québec fiscally. The issue of special status arose when Québec was the only province to win acceptance of the right to withdraw. It was perhaps to calm the anxieties of English Canada and to show his good will that in 1964 Lesage agreed to the proposal for repatriating and amending the constitution by a method known as the Fulton-Favreau formula. However, because of the extreme reactions of various nationalist groups within the province, Lesage had to withdraw his support and to dissociate himself from the other 10 governments that had accepted the formula.

The Québec government also sought to stake out international rights. In 1961 it opened the Maisons du Québec in Paris, London and New York. However, when Québec signalled its intention to sign cultural and educational agreements with France, Ottawa intervened, asserting that there could be only one interlocutor with foreign countries.

These federal-provincial quarrels raised the question of the place of Québec and French Canadians in Confederation. In 1965, for instance, the Royal Commission on BILINGUALISM AND BICULTURALISM noted that "Canada, without being fully conscious of the fact, is passing through the greatest crisis in its history. The source of the crisis lies in the Province of Quebec." FRENCH CANADIAN NATIONALISM, which was becoming more and more Québecois in nature, was exacerbated by this crisis. The number of separatist groups increased; some of them adopted more extreme positions and the FRONT DE LIBÉRATION DU QUÉBEC began to indulge in TERRORISM.

At the same time, other Francophones worried about this growth of nationalism. Among them were Jean MARCHAND, Gérard PELLETIER and Pierre Elliott TRUDEAU, who joined the federal Liberal Party and were elected to Parliament in 1965.

When the Québec Liberals again faced the electorate in 1966 they were confident of re-election. But the Union Nationale had renewed its image and attracted dissatisfied individuals among conservatives, nationalists and those who had voted CRÉDITISTE in the federal election. The party still had a solid base in the rural areas that were left largely untouched by the Quiet Revolution. On June 5 the Union Nationale won 56 seats against the Liberals' 50. However, the Liberals obtained 47% of the popular vote whereas the Unionistes, led by Daniel JOHNSON, obtained only 41%.

The Quiet Revolution has been the major reference point used by all Québec governments who have held power since the Liberal defeat in 1966, a fact which illustrates the importance of this episode in Québec's history.   RENÉ DUROCHER

Reading: R. Jones, *Community in Crisis* (1972); S.M. Trofimenkoff, *The Dream of Nation* (1983).

Quilico, Louis, baritone, teacher (b at Montréal 14 Jan 1925). Quilico studied in Rome (1947-48), returning to Montréal to study (1948-52) with Lina Pizzolongo whom he soon married. He completed his studies (1952-55) at Mannes College in New York. His professional stage debut (1954) in Canada was with the Opera Guild of Montréal and though he won the Metropolitan Opera Auditions of the Air, his New York debut in 1955 was with the New York City Opera. His first official appearance with the Metropolitan Opera did not take place until 1973. During his long and respected operatic career Quilico sang in major roles with most of the important operatic companies throughout Europe and N America. As a teacher at U of T since 1970, Quilico helped to develop several important young singers, including his son **Gino Quilico,** who has performed with his father in Canada and the US. They appeared together Nov 1987 in the Met's production of Massenet's *Manon.* Louis Quilico was awarded the 1965 Prix de musique Calixa-Lavallée and the 1985 Canadian Music Council Award; in 1975 he was made Companion of the Order of Canada.   MABEL H. LAINE

Quill & Quire is a magazine of the Canadian book trade. It is read chiefly by publishers, booksellers, librarians, writers and educators. Founded by the Seccombe family in 1935, it was a monthly magazine serving stationers and booksellers. By 1971, the year in which the magazine was purchased by Michael de Pencier, president of Key Publishers, it had shifted its emphasis to the book trade alone.

Since 1972 the magazine has grown in size and scope. Its regular features include a book-review section, spring and fall publishers' announcements, author profiles, industry statistics, and in-depth features on magazine and BOOK PUBLISHING, government policy, BOOKSELLING and librarianship. Its paid circulation is 8000. A bi-monthly supplement, *Books for Young People,* addresses the developments in children's literature. Twice annually, *Quill & Quire* issues the *Canadian Publishers Directory,* and in the fall it produces *Books for Everybody,* a gift catalogue for distribution to consumers.   SUSAN WALKER

Quill Lakes, comprising 2 connected lakes, Big Quill and Little Quill, totalling *c* 500 km², elev 152 m, are located 150 km N of REGINA and 152 km E of SASKATOON. Both lakes are fed by numerous small streams, creeks and lakes, and they drain in a southeasterly direction, via the meandering Whitesand R, eventually emptying into the ASSINIBOINE R. The lakes are shallow, and very salty owing to the mineral-laden streamflow into them. The resulting salt flats are a noticeable feature of the shoreline and restrict vegetation in the area to the hardiest shrubs. The lakes are named for the many feathers (quills) shed by the migrating birds that stop over here. The nearby Slovenian village of Quill Lake (est 1905) is on the CNR line.   DAVID EVANS

Quillwork included decorated buckskin clothing, birchbark boxes, CALUMETS, knife sheaths, MEDICINE BUNDLES, PARFLECHES, drums, TIPI covers and MOCCASINS. Widespread in aboriginal N America and highly developed among the Plains tribes, porcupine quill embroidery was done by women. Among the Cheyenne the club of robe quillers was a women's association.

There were 4 ways of using dyed porcupine quills – sewing, weaving, wrapping and pushing into tiny bark perforations – though sewing was the most common method. Quills were moistened to make them pliable and flattened by drawing them between the teeth or over the thumbnail. Thin strips of sinew were used as thread. Among older western Cree articles, quills woven with sinew strands without a hide background and then attached to the item were almost always of angular geometric design. After European contact quills were replaced by glass trade beads, and geometric designs were replaced by human and animal figures and floral designs.

RENÉ R. GADACZ

Eastern Ojibwa or Ottawa pouch made from tanned skin and decorated with porcupine quillwork, sewn with sinew (*courtesy National Museums of Canada/Canadian Museum of Civilization*).

Quilt, bedcover consisting of 2 layers of cloth separated by a soft substance (eg, unwoven cotton or wool). To keep the filling from shifting, the 3 layers are tacked together, ie, tied with pieces of yarn or sewn, usually in a pattern, by running seams through all the layers. This tacking process is called "quilting." This method of providing warm bedcovers has been used in Europe and northern Asia for centuries, and quilts were first made in Canada in the late 18th century when settlers from the British Isles and the US began to arrive.

Warm bedding was very important in Canada because of the severe winters. Because of the scarcity of cloth, scraps of worn clothing and blankets were used to make the first patchwork quilts. Hence, despite a strong influence from British and American traditions, a distinctive Canadian quilt developed, the patchwork woolen quilt made in both simple and elaborate patterns. The designs were strong and simple, making use of diamonds, triangles, rectangles and squares.

The women of the 19th century lived in a world in which the seasons and cycles of life dominated their lives, and the themes of the quilts reflect this fact. Although bedding was a daily chore, most women took the trouble to make their quilts aesthetically pleasing. Women of artistic sensibilities found such creativity stimulating, and it was one of the few ways in which they could express themselves. By the late 19th century, pattern books were circulated and, except in isolated communities, people began to follow patterns fashionable at the time. In contrast to Europe where descriptive names varied little, there was an exuberance in the naming of quilts in Canada. Many names reflect rural humour: Old Maid's Ramble, Toad in the Puddle, Swallow on the Path, Duck's Foot in the Mud, Corn and Beans, Hole in the Barn Door.

By 1930 the tradition of making quilts as part of a daily routine had come to an end, except in a few rural areas. Around the middle of the 20th century there was a revival of interest in making quilts for use as decorative bedspreads rather than as utilitarian bedcovers. These large quilts, made of springy materials, look quite different from the old ones. Women interested in maintaining the tradition of quilt making have formed quilting guilds in urban areas.   RUTH MCKENDRY

Reading: Ruth McKendry, *Quilts and Other Bed Coverings in the Canadian Tradition* (1979).

Quimper, Manuel, naval officer, explorer (*fl* 1790). At the outbreak of the NOOTKA SOUND CONTROVERSY, Quimper and 6 other young naval lieutenants were transferred from Europe to bolster Spain's Pacific strength. In 1790 he commanded the captured British vessel *Princess Royal* during the expedition to reoccupy Nootka Sound. In June Quimper was ordered to explore and trade in Juan de Fuca Str. Quimper visited Chief WICKANANISH at Clayoquot Sound and then explored harbours and bays around present-day Victoria. Later he crossed the strait to explore Puerto Nuñez Gaona (Neah Bay), which became the second Spanish post on the Northwest Coast. In 1791 Quimper sailed the *Princess Royal* to Hawaii and the Philippines to return the vessel to its British owners.   CHRISTON I. ARCHER

Quispamsis, NB, Town, inc 1982, pop 7185 (1986c), located 16 km NE of Saint John, immediately N of Fairvale, was incorporated as a village in 1966. The name is derived from the Maliseet word for "little lake," probably for Ritchie's Lake, and was assigned by the European and North American Ry in 1857 when that line was being built through the area. Prior to that it was known successively as Wetmore's, Gondola Point and Lakefield. This essentially rural area was primarily a summer community until the mid-1960s; since then the population of the town has increased by 460% as it developed as a dormitory community of Saint John. Only 17% of the work force is employed in the town. It is the site of Stoneycroft, the old "Twelve Mile House," built around 1800 and now a provincial historic site.

BURTON GLENDENNING

R v Coffin In the summer of 1953 the bodies of 3 American hunters were found in a Gaspé forest. Wilbert Coffin, a local prospector, was charged with and convicted of the murder of one of them, Richard Lindsay. Almost from the beginning, the case was controversial; it was charged that Coffin had not received a fair trial and that the Québec government had applied pressure on police and crown prosecutors to obtain an immediate conviction because of concern over possible loss of American tourist trade. Largely because of public concern, the federal Cabinet ordered a special reference to the SUPREME COURT OF CANADA, which upheld Coffin's conviction. He was hanged on 10 Feb 1956.

Notwithstanding the Supreme Court's ruling, the controversy did not diminish and various books continued to claim that Coffin was innocent and had been the victim of unprofessional conduct by police and prosecutors. The Québec government appointed a royal commission in 1964 (Brossard Committee) to investigate the accusations. The commission's report concluded that there was no evidence of wrongdoing on the part of the prosecutors or police officers and that Coffin had received a fair trial.

To lawyers the Coffin case is an important decision on evidence dealing with rules relating to hearsay evidence, leading questions and contradiction of one's own witness, but the Coffin case is important as well in any debate over CAPITAL PUNISHMENT, in which it is inevitably cited in support of the argument for abolition.   A. PRINGLE

R v Olson In the summer of 1982, Clifford Robert Olson was arrested for the murder of 11 children. He entered guilty pleas to the charges of murder, but it was later revealed that the attorney general of BC had agreed to a proposal by Olson that $100 000 be held in trust for Olson's wife and infant son in return for Olson's help in finding 6 missing bodies and providing information on 4 bodies already discovered. Reports of the deal sparked bitter controversy across the country over the ethics of a criminal benefiting from his crimes and over police payment for information. The debate raised questions about the propriety of deals made with any criminal, including payment for information and withdrawal of charges in return for information or evidence. It has been argued that such inducements could lead to the creation of "professional witnesses" who are involved in crimes and yet benefit from them. Although the SUPREME COURT OF CANADA held in *R v Palmer and Palmer* (1979) that payment for evidence was legal, there has been a growing demand for attorneys general to establish ethical guidelines for such payment. In the context of CIVIL LAW, the payment to Olson's wife and son was challenged by the families of Olson's victims, who argued that they were entitled to compensation for the deaths of their children. Justice Trainor of the British Columbia Supreme Court decided that the families of the victims were entitled to claim against the money paid in trust to Olson's wife and son, but this decision was reversed by the BC Court of Appeal, and a later application for Leave to Appeal to the Supreme Court of Canada was dismissed.   RICHARD A. STROPPEL

R v Truscott In 1959, 14-year-old Steven Truscott was convicted in adult court of the murder of 12-year-old Lynn Harper. Few cases in Canadian legal history have created so much controversy. In the book *The Trial of Steven Truscott* (1966), Isabel LeBourdais strongly asserted that Truscott was innocent. Citing inconsistencies in the evidence and what she believed was questionable medical testimony, LeBourdais suggested that the evidence did not support a conviction and that the emotions surrounding the case precluded the

possibility that Truscott could receive a fair trial. Because of public interest in the case, in 1967 Parliament took the unusual step of referring the case to the SUPREME COURT OF CANADA for a further review. The court upheld the conviction, but nevertheless the controversy surrounding the case remains. After serving 10 years of a life sentence, Truscott was released on parole, still asserting his innocence. The case sparked discussion of the law governing juvenile offenders, of CAPITAL PUNISHMENT and of methods of presenting evidence to a jury.   A. PRINGLE

Rabbit, common name for some MAMMALS of order Lagomorpha. The young, born in fur-lined nests, are naked, blind and helpless in contrast to the well-developed young of HARES. Gestation lasts 26-30 days, with 2-7 young per litter and usually 3-4 litters per year. Young are nursed for 16-22 days and leave the nest after about 2 weeks. Family units are often formed, lasting up to 7 weeks. Females frequently mate within 2-3 days after the birth of a litter, while still nursing. Fe-

The eastern cottontail (*Sylvilagus floridanus*) is found in southern Ont, Québec and Manitoba and was introduced to BC (*artwork by Claire Tremblay*).

male rabbits are usually larger than males. In Canada, both native rabbits belong to genus *Sylvilagus*. The eastern cottontail (*S. floridanus*), found in southern Ont, Qué and Man (introduced to BC), is small (average weight 1.2 kg) and active at dawn, dusk and night. Nuttall's cottontail (*S. nuttalli*) is found in parts of BC, Alta and Sask. This smaller, paler version of eastern cottontail inhabits arid sagebrush areas. Both species form important links in the food chain and are often hunted for food and sport by man. The common or Old World rabbit (*Oryctolagus cuniculus*), the ancestor of our domestic rabbit, has proved valuable in many ways, eg, for food, for laboratory research and as pets. Some local, wild populations exist in various parts of the country, but these are largely released domesticated rabbits rather than true Old World rabbits.   M.L. WESTON

Rabbit Farming in Canada is not the highly organized, market-oriented industry typified by the poultry, hog or beef sectors. Originally, N American rabbit production was developed to supply felt-hat manufacturers; meat production was secondary. With the changing population base after WWII, the demand for rabbit meat has been increasing in Canada. Rabbit farms may specialize in meat production, fancier or breeding stock production or research animal production. Statistics Canada does not record rabbit meat production; volume varies because of the volatile nature of the industry and the influence of large foreign imports. Estimated annual consumption in Canada is 50 g per capita (in France, 5 kg). Fanciers or hobbyists account for a measurable amount of production and tend to remain in production regardless of financial returns. Production of rabbits for research establishments is conducted under contract and is the most profitable aspect of rabbit raising. Some provinces provide inspection services to maintain and certify standards of health for these rabbits. Farm size varies, but the average commercial production unit has 100-150 does. New Zealand White is the most popular breed, followed by the Californian breed. Some attempts are made to capitalize on the body size of Flemish Giant; however, this breed generally has low reproduction performance.

Rabbits produce low-fat meat and have the best meat-to-bone ratio of any meat-producing animals except turkeys. The high labour input of rabbit-meat production, coupled with unsteady markets, allows only a small profit margin, even for efficient producers. Marketing is a serious industry problem. Large chain stores insist on a constant flow of product, a demand difficult to meet because of the high summer, low winter production. Limited killing facilities for rabbits often force long haulage of live animals for processing and encourage farm-gate marketing, which further disrupts supply. The future for rabbit-meat production is promising because rabbits consume a high forage diet and do not compete with humans for food. Furthermore, on a given amount of alfalfa, a doe can produce almost 5 times as much meat per body weight as a beef cow. The industry will have to improve technology to reduce labour costs, develop effective disease-control measures, regulate supply and improve the quality of the hide for effective use.

JOHN R. HUNT

Rabbit Starvation Hunting and gathering people were never immune to starvation prior to their involvement in state welfare systems. Among most subarctic and arctic hunting peoples, such as the MONTAGNAIS-NASKAPI of Labrador and Québec, the KUTCHIN of the Northwest and the COPPER INUIT, starvation was fairly common. In times of hardship, when game such as caribou, moose or bear was unobtainable, much greater reliance was put on smaller animals, eg, rabbits, hares. Rabbits in particular offer very lean meat, and "rabbit starvation" refers to the almost total lack of fat in such a diet. At the end of a long winter, when even larger game animals were lean, the same fate might occur. An individual could ingest many pounds of meat at frequent intervals but derive little nutrition.

RENÉ R. GADACZ

Rabinowitch, David, sculptor (b at Toronto 6 Mar 1943). Like his twin brother Royden RABINOWITCH, he first came to national attention as a member of the artistic community in London, Ont, around Greg CURNOE, celebrated in the National Gallery of Canada's exhibition, *The Heart of London* (1968). He has since produced one of the most challenging bodies of work in contemporary SCULPTURE. He shares minimalism's interest in exploring the demands made by sculpture within the space and time of its interaction with the viewer. His "Romanesque" sculptures, constructions of flat steel masses whose horizontal extension is counterpointed by vertical holes bored through each mass, present themselves as fields of perception in which the appearance of the sculpture depends on the position of the perceiver. A series of independent appearances follow one another as the viewer moves around the sculpture. It is as if the world dissolves into an irreconcilable, if related, succession of unique appearances. The possibility of unity is known because all the material facts of the sculpture are always present, but it is a product of intellect or desire, not of experience. Rabinowitch moved to New York in 1972 and has taught at Yale U 1974-75 and at Düsseldorf 1984.

ROALD NASGAARD

Rabinowitch, Royden, sculptor (b at Toronto 6 Mar 1943). One of Canada's truly original contributors to modern SCULPTURE, he began his career in London, Ont, during the 1960s (as did his twin brother David RABINOWITCH) and moved to New York in the 1970s. He has exhibited widely, especially in Europe. Although Rabinowitch's early work showed characteristics of minimalism, his sculpture is also a critique of it – as it is of most other nonfigurative sculpture (which he contends has been based on assumptions about

space that are too mechanical, abstract and visual). Typical of his style is the group of works titled "Handed, Limited and Numbered Manifolds" – low, ground-hugging constructions, each composed of a single polygonal steel plate bent to form a series of angled planes (the manifold), on top of which, aligned with the edges, are other steel plates (the limits) on the right or left, depending on whether the individual sculptures are left- or right-handed. Although purely abstract, the sculptures evince the principal properties of the human body that apply to its orientation in space.

ROALD NASGAARD

Raccoon (*Procyon lotor*), the only Canadian member of the Procyonidae (a primarily tropical New World family of carnivores). Raccoons are distinguished by their black facial mask and ringed tail, and vary from almost black to light brown. They weigh 5-12 kg (maximum 22-26 kg). Raccoons are found in northern Alta, southern BC and Sask, central Man and Ont, southern Qué and the Maritimes. Raccoons have a nest only when nursing young. Breeding begins at one year. Usually 3 kits are born, in Mar-May after 63-65 days gestation. Young become independent in autumn. Raccoons are omnivorous, and they manipulate but do not wash their food. They have sensitive hands used in foraging, eg, in capturing crayfish, etc. They may foul their nest when adult. They are agile climbers and strong but reluctant swimmers. Raccoons can whistle, shriek, chatter, click their teeth, snarl, growl and make other sounds. They coexist with man in urban areas and, with sufficient food, will remain active all winter. Young raccoons make good pets but become independent and antisocial when mature. Their pelts were used to make overcoats. Their flesh is edible when the scent glands are removed.

C.S. CHURCHER

The raccoon (*Procyon lotor*) has sensitive hands which are used for foraging (*artwork by Claire Tremblay*).

Racism The disagreement among scholars over the meaning of "race" does not extend to its derivative, racism; there is virtual agreement that racism refers to the doctrine that some races are innately superior or inferior to others. Because racism indiscriminately includes groupings such as religious sects, linguistic groups and cultural groups under its concept of "race" it can be regarded as a virulent form of ethnocentrism (the belief that one's own ethnic group is superior to others). Racism is based upon the assumption that organic, genetically transmitted differences between human groups are intrinsically related to the presence or absence of certain social, psychological or cultural traits of that group. It is also predicated on the false assumption that human beings are naturally and permanently composed of separate, pure races (eg, mongoloid, caucasoid), and that the physical, mental and cultural qualities of each group are determined by its supposed genetic constitution.

Individual racism is a belief by one individual

about another person's "racial" inferiority. Institutional racism exists when the political, economic and social institutions of a society operate to the detriment of a specific individual or group in a society because of their alleged genetic make-up. Cultural racism is the expression of the superiority of a socially defined race's culture over that of another race. Racism does not derive from the fact that races or groups of individuals in a society are different but from the social meaning attributed to these differences by society. It is not a study of race or of the present inequality of certain groups in society, but it is an assertion that inequality is absolute and unconditional.

Racism as we know it originated in the 16th and 17th centuries with the spread of capitalism and later SOCIAL DARWINISM. Racism is also a formal doctrine whose contemporary intellectual notions are derived from the 1853 *Essai sur l'inégalité des races humaines* by Joseph Arthur, comte de Gobineau. In the 20th century this doctrine was promoted by H.S. Chamberlain, the English-born German publicist. Racism in Canada from 1800 to 1945 was reflected in restrictive IMMIGRATION POLICIES and practices regarding nonwhite immigrants, particularly the CHINESE, BLACKS and JEWS, and by the treatment of native peoples. Today certain groups, eg, the KU KLUX KLAN and the Western Guard, promulgate racist beliefs in various parts of the country.

Over the past 25 years the federal and provincial governments have implemented legislation to combat racism, eg, by the creation of human-rights commissions and the positions of ombudsman and commissioner of official languages. *See also* ANTI-SEMITISM; PREJUDICE AND DISCRIMINATION.

J.S. FRIDERES

Reading: H.D. Hughes and E. Kallen, *The Anatomy of Racism: Canadian Dimensions* (1974).

Racoon, 26-gun British sloop of war sent to seize Astoria, the American PACIFIC FUR COMPANY post at the Columbia R mouth, and to establish an outpost there during the WAR OF 1812. When the vessel, under Capt William Black, arrived 30 Nov 1813, Astoria had already been purchased by Nor'Westers led by John George McTavish. On Dec 13 Black, following his original orders from the British government, nevertheless claimed the country for King George III, naming the post Ft George. The Treaty of GHENT provided for a return to the *status quo ante bellum*; since Black had claimed the territory as a conquest of war, Astoria was returned to the US. The voyage of the *Racoon* constituted official government support for Canadian FUR-TRADE interests and initiated co-operation between fur traders and the Royal Navy on the NORTHWEST COAST.

J.W. SHELEST

Racquetball, one of the newest and most popular sports in N America today, is played indoors on a 4-wall court 20 ft (6 m) wide, 40 ft (12 m) long and 20 ft high. The 2 1/2-in (6.35 cm) rubber ball must be returned to the front wall before it bounces twice, and floor, ceiling and walls are in play. Only 50 000 people played in 1970, whereas it was claimed that there were nearly 3 million participants by the mid-1970s. The game probably derived from paddleball, invented in the 1930s and transformed by a Connecticut squash professional into "paddle-racquets," in which a short-handled, gut-string racquet is used. The first National Paddle Racquets Tournament (1968) attracted the attention of media and businessmen, and within a year the International Racquetball Assn was formed.

The Canadian Racquetball Assn was incorporated in 1971, and considerable growth has occurred, particularly in the western provinces. Edmonton has been described as "North America's

Racquetball City" and U of A has hosted many championships. Private clubs now exist in several cities, as do racquetball facilities in colleges and YMCAs. Two landmarks in 1976-77 were a grant for racquetball from Sport Canada, and grants-in-aid to 2 racquetballers from the federal government. Some Canadian players, such as Wayne Bowes and Lindsay Myers, have competed with success in the US, where there is a lucrative professional circuit. During the 1980s, however, the racquetball boom has abated somewhat as the rival sport of SQUASH RACQUETS has experienced a revival.   GERALD REDMOND

Radar (*ra*dio *d*etection *a*nd *r*anging), a device that obtains information about an object of interest (eg, distance, position) by emitting an electronic signal and observing the echo returned from the object. The key elements of radar systems are the transmitter, the receiver and the data-processing unit. Radars use radio-frequency transmissions, first described theoretically by J.C. Maxwell in 1864. Radio waves are part of the electromagnetic spectrum, as is visible light. H.R. Hertz provided practical demonstration of Maxwell's theory and, in 1888, actually performed radio-wave-reflection experiments. In 1900 Nikola Tesla suggested that moving targets should be observable through radio-frequency shifts (predicted by C.J. Doppler in 1842 for waves in general). The first patent for a rudimentary radar was issued in Germany in 1904. It required the threat of WWII to motivate real progress. In 1934 Robert Watson-Watt proposed to the British government the principle of aircraft detection by ground-based pulsed radar. By spring 1935 an experimental system had proved successful, leading to construction of the British Home Chain. Five stations facing Europe were operational in 1938. The system is credited with making the decisive difference in the Battle of BRITAIN.

Development of radar exploded during WWII, aided by high-level technical exchange agreements among the Allies. Scientists at the NATIONAL RESEARCH COUNCIL OF CANADA participated, and A.E. COVINGTON in 1946 used surplus radar research equipment to construct Canada's first radio telescope (*see* OBSERVATORY). The range and sensitivity of radars were constantly improved and smaller units were built for shipborne and airborne use. In 1935 radars worked at wavelengths of 25 m; by 1940, at 10 cm, thus initiating microwave radar. The critical development was that of the cavity magnetron by John T. Randal and Henry A. Boot of Birmingham U (1939-41). The device was capable of generating microwave pulses at up to 500 kW and permitted construction of small but, for the time, very accurate radars. Development of radar by the Allies was considered classified information during WWII. Therefore, wavelengths received code names, still recognized today: L-band (25 cm), S-band (10 cm), C-band (5 cm), X-band (3 cm) and K-band (1 cm). Shorter waves are used by "millimetre radars."

Operation Radar devices emit energy within a beam shaped by the radiating antenna. The beam-limited radiated energy propagates in range at the speed of light. When it strikes an object, a small fraction of the energy is reflected back, to be received by the radar. The echo arrives at a time delay after transmission; delays are usually very short (for terrestrial radars) and are measured in microseconds. Since the speed of light is known, each microsecond (0.000001 second) of delay corresponds to 150 m in range. The ranging pulse must be short and powerful to detect reliably several small, closely spaced objects, such as aircraft in formation. These properties are speci-

Air-defence technician operating a radar set (*Canadian Forces photo/WO Vic Johnson*).

fied by the range resolution (usually given in metres) and the sensitivity (usually given in m²); both factors are "better" for smaller numbers. A good radar may be described as "high resolution" because it is able to separate targets only a few metres apart.

Types of Radars Today there are many radar systems, from the speed-measuring units used by police forces (costing a few thousand dollars each) to Magellan (costing approximately $350 million). Magellan, approved by NASA in 1983, is expected to yield a radar map of Venus, based on a SATELLITE system, in 1990. Military applications, especially surveillance, targeting, guidance, navigation and EARLY WARNING, are the most important uses. Canada and the US continue to co-operate in the area of ballistic missile defence. For example, BMEWS (Ballistic Missile Early Warning System) has major radar electronics and antennae sited in Canada's North, yet the system's data-processing centre is an underground control centre in Colorado, which has access to the information from many other systems, including AWACS (Airborne Warning and Control System).

In the civilian area, the most important application is in air-traffic control. Ship navigation and maritime vessel traffic-management radars are essential for safe operations on Canada's waterways. Other applications include weather and storm-centre tracking, atmospheric sounding and radar ASTRONOMY.

Radar Remote Sensing Since 1976 Canada has developed a world-recognized reputation in certain radar techniques, taking a lead in the application of radar to the observation and monitoring of vast areas (*see* REMOTE SENSING). In addition to routine mapping of ice in the Arctic and North Atlantic by airborne radar, Canada benefited from the US Seasat, an experimental satellite (July-Oct 1978) that carried the first imaging radar into Earth orbit. This was an L-band, high-resolution system, capable of sweeping out a continuous image 100 km wide. The instrument was a synthetic-aperture radar (SAR), the operating principles of which are closely related to holography. The data could be processed optically from the image. Canada developed the first digital processor for such data; MacDonald, Dettwiler and Associates of Vancouver published the first image in Nov 1978. This technology continues to set the world standard. Airborne and spaceborne SAR radar technologies are areas of active development in Canada and promise to contribute to RESOURCE MANAGEMENT. The Canada Centre for Remote Sensing has developed airborne X- and C-band SARs, and the STAR 1 and 2 radars operated by Intera of Calgary are the best civilian imaging radars in the world, used to monitor Canada's Arctic ice, map cloud-covered tropical regions,

such as Indonesia, and for many other applications. *See also* SONAR.   R.K. RANEY

Raddall, Thomas Head, historical novelist (b at Hythe, Eng 13 Nov 1903). Raddall was brought up as a boy to Nova Scotia, the province about which he was to write in a score of books, fictional and nonfictional. In an age of public appetite for magazine fiction, Raddall first made his name as a short-story writer; his debut collection, *The Pied Piper of Dipper Creek and Other Tales* (1939), won him his first Gov Gen's Award (1943). But larger renown awaited him as a historical novelist, particularly with *His Majesty's Yankees* (1942) and *The Governor's Lady* (1960). Yet his most highly regarded book was not historical and drew on his own experiences as a Sable Island radio operator after WWI: *The Nymph and the Lamp* (1950). His history, *Halifax, Warden of the North* (1948, Gov Gen's Award), has remained the most popular of his nonfictional books. His autobiography, *In My Time* (1976), reflects the agonizingly slow development of Canadian literary life since the 1920s. In 1986 a collection of stories originally published in magazines between 1928 and 1955 was brought out under the title *The Dreamers*.
                                       DOUG FETHERLING

Radio Broadcasting, *see* BROADCASTING.

Radio Drama, English-Language The production of radio dramas in Canada began in 1925 when the Canadian National Railways Radio Dept began broadcasting plays. The national broadcasting networks, CNR, CRBC and CBC, have been in the forefront of radio-drama production and experiment, and have provided audiences and training for many Canadian theatre professionals.

The radio play shares the usual dramatic qualities of drama on the stage and in films and television, with this primary difference: the absence of the traditional visual resources of drama. Reliance on sound alone to communicate has forced the creators of radio drama to refine the available sound techniques: voice, music, sound effects and the control and mixing of sounds. Canadian radio drama has been in the vanguard of these developments, achieving flexibility in the representation of scenes and scene transitions, original music and depiction of character.

The first regular drama series in Canada was the CNR Drama Dept's "CNRV Players," produced from Vancouver by Jack Gillmore 1927-32. The productions included Shakespeare, adaptations from American and European plays and from fiction, and some original Vancouver dramas. The first national series of Canadian radio plays was the "Romance of Canada," 24 plays based on Canadian history, written by Merrill DENISON and produced in 1931-32 in CN Radio's Montréal studios. Tyrone GUTHRIE directed the first 14 plays, and Rupert Caplan and Esmie Moonie produced the second season. Another pioneer radio-drama series, the "CKUA Players," was produced by Sheila Marryat throughout the 1930s from CKUA, the station of U of Alberta, over a network of western stations.

The CN Radio network was nationalized in 1932 and became the Canadian Radio Broadcasting Commission (*see* BROADCASTING, RADIO AND TELEVISION). In 3 years, from Nov 1933, the CRBC increased the number of weekly English national-network radio-drama series to 17, under its program director Ernest BUSHNELL. Rupert Caplan's "Radio Theatre Guild" was the best-known national drama series, including original Canadian, American and European plays. Popular too were Don Henshaw's "Forgotten Footsteps" and the serial "Youngbloods of Beaver Bend." In Nov 1936 the CRBC was reorganized as the CANADIAN BROADCASTING CORPORATION. Its first supervisor of drama, Rupert Lucas, continued the development of drama offerings: Shakespeare and the classics, adaptations from fiction, documentaries and original radio plays. He established regional weekly drama series in Winnipeg, Toronto, Montréal and Vancouver. With the beginning of WWII the CBC Drama Dept series became important instruments of war education and publicity, and the project of centralizing prestige radio drama was begun.

With the appointment of Andrew ALLAN in 1943 as national drama supervisor, the golden age of Canadian radio drama began, with productions of original Canadian plays challenging the previous domination of theatre by British and American professionals. In Jan 1944 Allan introduced a new national play-anthology series, the weekly "Stage" series from Toronto. With its balanced mix of ambitious original Canadian plays and the best of the classical and modern American and European dramas, "Stage" attracted large national audiences. It became in effect our national professional theatre, setting the pace for the regional CBC drama series, completed by the Halifax series in 1947.

That same year another CBC national drama series was established in Toronto, "CBC Wednesday Night," which included international plays and some original Canadian dramas. Four senior drama producers shared its direction: Andrew Allan, Rupert Caplan, Esse W. LJUNGH and J. Frank Willis.

This CBC network of major national and regional drama series was the primary showcase for the best of Canadian and world drama, as well as a training ground for many Canadian theatre professionals. Among the well-known writers for the national series were Fletcher Markle, Len Peterson, Joseph SCHULL, Mac Shoub, Lister SINCLAIR, Gerald Noxon, Alan King, Mavor MOORE, Hugh Kemp and W.O. MITCHELL. In the period 1944 to 1961 an estimated 6000 plays were produced in over 100 CBC series across the country; more than half of them were Canadian originals.

CBC television, with its own drama series, arrived in 1952, and began to wean audiences away from radio drama (*see* TELEVISION DRAMA). The growth of the legitimate stage in the 1950s in Canada had a similar effect, especially the STRATFORD FESTIVAL, which many CBC drama professionals helped to establish. The pace of CBC drama production did not slacken, however, until the mid-1960s. The second-generation CBC producers, notably John REEVES and Gerald Newman, began new experiments in radio-drama forms and techniques. "Stage" and "Wednesday (later "Tuesday) Night" continued well into the 1970s, and radio-drama production from all regions has continued to the present.

Things have come full circle in the 1980s. Audiences in Canada and the US are rediscovering "talking radio," the radio of ideas and of drama. The CBC now produces an increasing number of drama series. "Stereo Theatre," "Vanishing Point" and "Morningside Drama" are series reminiscent of "Wednesday Night," while the flagship series of original Canadian plays is "Sunday Matinee."

Few of the more than 3000 original Canadian radio plays have been published, though they represent the largest single group of Canadian dramas. The official script archives of CBC radio plays is the Centre for Broadcasting Studies, Concordia U, Montréal. Many sound versions of the broadcasts are at the Sound and Moving Image Division, National Archives of Canada, Ottawa. Specialized script collections exist, notably at U of Calgary, McMaster, and the Manuscript Division, NAC. *See also* RADIO PROGRAMMING. HOWARD FINK

Reading: A. Allan, *A Self Portrait* (1974); Howard Fink, *Canadian National Theatre on the Air, 1925-61, CBC-CRBC-CNR Radio Drama in English: A Descriptive Bibliography and Union List* (1983), *National Theatre on the Air Vol II: CBC Radio Drama 1962-85* (1988) and "North American Radio Drama," in *Radio Drama,* ed, P. Lewis (1981); Fink and J. Jackson, eds, *All the Bright Company: Radio Drama Produced by Andrew Allen* (1987); N. Alice Frick, *Image in the Mind: CBC Radio Drama 1944 to 1954* (1987).

Radio Drama, French-Language Radio drama in Québec is of 2 kinds, *radioromans* (serials or "soap operas") and *radiothéâtre* (radio plays).

The radio serial took its form from the theatre and its structure and length from the novel. When radio came to Québec, THEATRE was still considered somewhat heretical and novels frivolous if not outrightly immoral. Moreover the French Canadian press had not published many indigenous serialized novels. The immediate success of the first broadcast serial, Alfred Rousseau's "L'Auberge des chercheurs d'or" (CKAC, Jan 1935-June 1938), inspired other writers and commissions. In 1937 Edouard Baudry launched "Rue principale" on CKAC, which ran for 22 years. Fall 1938, when 4 series went simultaneously on air, marked the beginning of the golden age, which lasted more than 20 years and created in Québec a phenomenon that was as much sociocultural as literary.

Between 1939 and 1960 there were 10-15 serials a day on Québec airwaves, averaging 3 hours daily, excluding comedy skits (more than 100) and episodic and historical dramas (120 and over 90, respectively). The accumulated repertoire of 71 radio serials equalled 260 000 typed pages, or several hundred printed volumes and almost 13 000 hours of programming. Some 30 Québec writers were involved in varying degrees with this radio genre 1935-65, including Paul Gury, responsible for 15 years of "Rue principale" and all 14 years of "Vies de femmes"; Aliette Brisset-Thibaudet, who for 11 years wrote the weekly half-hour "Ceux qu'on aime"; and Claude-Henri GRIGNON, who for 23 years supplied the daily half hour of "Un Homme et son péché." Though there were some translations or adaptations of American soap operas, more than 75% of the serials were original Québec works, most of them by young authors. Some, such as Roger LEMELIN's "La Famille Plouffe" or Grignon's "Un Homme et son péché," had been preceded by published novels, which had been used as springboards for entirely new situations.

Three stations in particular, CKAC, CBF and CKVL, broadcast radio serials at prime time to hundreds of thousands of listeners. The daily scheduling of these serials, usually 15 minutes long, created a ritual of tuning in. The serial genre is limited in scope and remained stable over the years, a mixture of popular novels and romances. The tone was usually melodramatic, sometimes comic, occasionally lighthearted. The topics were rooted in the realist tradition and reflected Québec family mores. Jeered at by intellectuals, the genre was exploited until it was threadbare. Some serials, however, deserve inclusion in literary history, especially those of Robert CHOQUETTE ("Le Curé de village," "La Pension Velder," "Métropole") and of Henri DEYGLUN ("Les Secrets du docteur Morhange"). Television killed radio serials (*see* TELEVISION DRAMA). Their numbers began to decline in the late 1950s, and gradually they disappeared from Québec airwaves. There was a fleeting revival on CKVL in 1974, and in 1984 CHRC attempted to revive the genre again with *La Minute de vérité*. It lasted a few months, Sept to Dec, but was not renewed.

Radio plays were not as popular in Québec as radio serials, but they played an important role in Québec cultural life. Chronologically, plays preceded the serials, since CKAC created the first program, "Le Théâtre de J.O. Lambert," in Nov 1933. Radio plays took over from stage theatre, which had been hard hit by the Depression. In 35 years, 80 anthology series were broadcast on Québec AM stations and had provided a living for writers and actors. The genre increasingly detached itself from written theatrical tradition to exploit the different possibilities of the microphone. At first, authors adapted novels, short stories and works from repertory theatre ("Le Théâtre N.G. Valiquette," "Le Théâtre lux français," "L'Atelier"), a custom used throughout the history of radio plays, especially on CBF. Public radio broadcast 26 foreign-play series, including "Radio-Théâtre" (1939-40), "Le Théâtre classique français" (1940), "Théâtre" by Radio-Collège (1941-50), "Sur toutes les scènes du monde" (1953-70), "Théâtre populaire" (1950) and "Petit Théâtre" (1966-67). In addition, there were 10 programs, such as "Le Radiothéâtre de Radio-Canada," which presented both adaptations and original Québec plays. Many great works of international theatre, from the classics to the avant-garde, were mounted by talented producers. These adaptations were the first efforts of young authors such as Marcel DUBÉ, Louis Pelland, Hubert AQUIN and Yves THÉRIAULT.

These original Québec radio dramas were a small part of the total amount of material broadcast, but they played an essential cultural role. They were a training ground for many young French Canadian playwrights and helped form a body of Québec theatrical works. More than 1500 radio plays may be listed, the work of more than 200 authors. Each week, for 20 years, at least one original Québec play was broadcast. In the 1950s up to 4 new works were aired each week. From 1930 to 1970, 44 original Québec series were presented on the province's AM stations. CKAC's first series was "Le Théâtre de chez nous," which was broadcast 1938-47 and in which Henri Letondal played a major part. Robert Choquette was the first important author to present a series of theatrical radio works (CRCM, 1934). CBF put its first Québec theatrical series on the air in 1944 ("Entrée des artistes"), followed by such programs as "L'Equipe aux quatre vents," "Les Voix du pays," and "Le Théâtre des nouveautés." The most important program, because of its experimental nature, was "Les Nouveautés dramatiques," produced by Guy BEAULNE 1950-62, which launched many authors. Among the 58 who worked on it were Yves Thériault, Marcel Dubé, Louis-Georges Carrier, Marcel Cabay, François Moreau, Jacques GODBOUT, Jacques LANGUIRAND, Félix LECLERC and Robert Gadouas. More than 320 plays were presented in this series.

A wide variety of Québec plays were produced for radio, ranging from psychological to street theatre, via character comedies, social satire, melodrama and surrealism. Different types were given priority, depending on the era and the station, but they were almost always indigenous plays, raising Québec problems, using Québec language and destined for a Québec audience. It was definitely popular theatre, as the names of some of the series clearly show.

During the 1960s, plays like serials deserted the AM airwaves. Since then drama has been found almost exclusively on television. The only remaining bastion of radio drama is the FM network of Radio-Canada, with its "Théâtre de lundi." GÉRARD LAURENCE

Reading: R. Legris, *Robert Choquette: romancier et dramaturge de la radio-télévision* (1977); Legris and P. Pagé, "Le Théâtre à la radio et à la télévision au Québec," in *Archives des lettres canadiennes,* vol 5 , *Le Théâtre canadien-français* (1976).

Radio Programming Radio has proven an extremely flexible medium. The technology of BROADCASTING enabled the radio producer to reach much larger audiences than was usually possible for the journalist. The reliance on sound alone liberated radio producers from many of the constraints that have restricted their counterparts in visual media. The costs of production are much lower. The expectations of the audience are not so demanding. The radio producer can experiment with an array of program types to activate the listener's imagination or engage his mind. Consequently, radio has played many roles in society to meet the changing needs of the public.

Over the past 60 years, radio programming has gone through 3 distinct stages. Radio shifted from being a novelty to becoming a mass medium between 1920 and 1940. During the 1920s, the small, low-power Canadian stations filled their abbreviated schedules with all manner of cheap, live productions: music, comedy, drama, education, preaching, news or poetry or story reading, nearly all of which were amateurish. Audiences preferred the more polished products of American radio and at the end of the decade, 80% of the programs listened to were American. In 1929, 2 stations in Montréal and Toronto became affiliates of American networks.

The solution seemed to lie in the organization of Canadian networks. The pioneers were commercial enterprises intent on self-promotion. Canadian National Railways Radio Dept began broadcasting plays in 1925 and by 1930 was offering a few hours a week of high-quality French and English programming on its own and independent stations across the country: symphony, chamber and folk music; original drama and operas; children's tales; grain price reports and even health talks. There were national broadcasts sponsored by Imperial Oil and Canadian Pacific Railway. What killed these initiatives was the arrival in 1932 of public broadcasting, to which the government granted a monopoly of network broadcasting. The Canadian Radio Broadcasting Commission created the initial national service which was much expanded after 1936 by the new CANADIAN BROADCASTING CORPORATION. Indeed, the CBC organized separate French- and English-language networks using its own stations and private affiliates.

By the end of the 1930s listeners could already enjoy a wide range of programs. Much American material was available because of the widespread use of recorded popular music and transcribed programs, because of the service of a few Canadian affiliates of American networks, and because of the CBC itself, which offered popular, sponsored American programs in the evening hours. American daytime soap operas, such as "Ma Perkins" and "Big Sister," and evening comedy shows, such as "Amos 'n' Andy" and "Fibber McGee & Molly," were enormously popular. Private radio broadcast much live programming in the form of big-band music from hotels, adult and children's drama, and talk or commentary shows. The CBC carried more and more national programs: hockey broadcasts, variety shows such as "The Happy Gang" from Toronto, dance-band programs such as Mart Kenny's group from Vancouver, the farm family drama "The Craigs," and round tables and forums. Even so, public radio was still too novel to attract large and devoted audiences, except in Québec where the appeal of its French-language programming was enormous.

The war years changed the situation. Suddenly a vital instrument of propaganda, the CBC developed a balanced schedule of programs to inform, inspire and entertain the mass audience as well as more select publics. The first initiative was the creation of a special news department, which

1947 "Citizens' Forum" broadcast. The talk show was one of the best-known CBC radio programs (*courtesy National Archives of Canada/MISA/CBC Coll/12658*).

supplied eager listeners with bulletins and reports on the war effort abroad and at home. News was supplemented with talks and education: the famous "Citizens' Forum" and FARM RADIO FORUM, war-related miniseries such as "Let's Face the Facts" and "Arsenal of Democracy," and the French network's "Radio-Collège." Much effort was put into developing musical programming, such as "Les Joyeux Troubadors," "Victory Parade," and feature variety broadcasts studded with American stars for the assorted Victory Loan drives. The CBC's most memorable achievements, however, were in the field of radio drama. Many series were linked to the war, such as the "Theatre of Freedom," "Fighting Navy," "L for Lanky" and "Soldier's Wife" (a soap opera sponsored by the Wartime Prices and Trade Board!). In a different vein was the "Stage" series of radio plays, many of them written by Canadian playwrights, begun by Andrew ALLAN in 1944 for discriminating listeners. In order to carry the wealth of Canadian and American entertainment, the CBC launched a second, evening-only network in English Canada, the "Dominion," to supplement the full-day "Trans-Canada" network.

The success of the war years had inaugurated the golden age of Canadian radio. Radio news and views were able to attract a huge cross-section of listeners, much to the chagrin of NEWSPAPERS and MAGAZINES. Programs such as "Les Idées en marche" probed topics which ranged from child discipline to price control, and from the St Lawrence Seaway to Canada's international policies. CBC broadcasts of serious music and opera made the networks renowned as great sponsors of high culture. The many plays of producers such as Allan, Esse W. LJUNGH, Rupert Caplan and J. Frank Willis made the CBC a national theatre for English Canada. In 1947 the CBC began its grand experiment in highbrow radio, "CBC Wednesday Night": 3 noncommercial hours under the general direction of Harry BOYLE which offered opera, musicals, classical and original plays, even documentaries, and won enormous fame among intellectual and artistic communities in Canada.

The networks, of course, were able to capture much larger audiences for their regular coverage of Canadian sports, notably hockey, which bolstered one of the few pan-Canadian sources of identity in the country. In French Canada the CBC produced some extraordinarily popular forms of light entertainment: serial drama (*see* RADIO DRAMA, FRENCH-LANGUAGE), eg, "Un homme et son péché" (which sometimes won an 80% share of the listening audience), programs specializing in the FOLK MUSIC and FOLK DANCE of Québec, eg, "Soirée à Québec," and talent shows, eg, "Nos futures étoiles." Even in English Canada the CBC had some very popular variety and comedy shows, notably "The Happy Gang" and "The Wayne and Shuster Show." There were also specialized programs for minority audiences: the schools, the regions, women ("Lettre à une cana-

dienne"), children ("Maggie Muggins"), farmers ("Le Choc des idées") and the religious-minded ("National Sunday Evening Hour"). Between 1945 and 1955 the CBC was a central institution serving and nurturing many aspects of the country's culture.

Yet the CBC was only one among a number of sources of radio programming. A survey of one broadcast week in Apr 1949 showed that the radio scene boasted a range of different styles of programming because of the mix of CBC-owned outlets, privately owned network affiliates and 36 independents. The amount of British material broadcast was minuscule. Canadian-originated programs might be dominant throughout the broadcast day on the public outlets and in the evening hours on all but the independent stations; but Canadian listeners could enjoy American records and programs at any time, especially on private stations, making the US the single most important source of programming in English Canada. The top shows in the ratings were usually American. What was called "local live" programming – news, sports, entertainment, religion and talks – persisted, notably on the independent stations where over one-third of evening air time was devoted to such offerings. Yet imported popular music had become the most common program ingredient, except on CBC's French network which still devoted much air time to "serious" music. The CBC's own stations supplied a varied and Canadian brand of programming, notable for the number of sustaining (noncommercial) shows, which explained why the corporation was perceived as a Canadian version of the British Broadcasting Corporation. But the programming of the major private stations, even the CBC affiliates, was designed on the American model to attract large audiences and more advertising revenue. In English Canada then, radio was bringing listeners into closer contact with the cultural mainstream of the US.

The arrival of Canadian television in 1952 spelled disaster for radio's golden age. As Canadian families acquired television sets, evening radio lost money, listeners and eventually programs. Variety stars Johnny WAYNE and Frank SHUSTER, Don MESSER and his Islanders, and others shifted to television. The popular American hits had been taken off the air by the end of the decade. The radio play series was retired. The CBC officially recognized the change in radio's significance by closing down the Dominion network in 1962.

If radio had lost family and evening audiences, it swiftly regained stature as the companion of the individual. Assisting that renaissance was the spread of transistor radios and car radios which enabled consumers to listen when they pleased and in solitude. Private radio made the transition with ease, actually increasing its ad revenue by two-thirds during the 1950s. Programs as such disappeared in the new radio format, which emphasized the continual playing of recorded music interspersed with newscasts and commercials and which was hosted by disc jockeys who changed every few hours. The exceptions were broadcasts of sporting events and the new "open line" or phone-in programs, both legacies of the tradition of live radio. More and more stations came to specialize in a particular brand of music: "middle-of-the-road," "easy listening," "rock" and eventually "country." This kind of formula programming succeeded on the rising FM stations as well. The Canadian Radio-television Commission did promulgate various regulations to ensure a minimum of Canadian content on AM and to differentiate programming on FM. American music remained the staple because it was so obviously popular with listeners, even in French

CBC's "As It Happens," with hosts Barbara Frum and Alan Maitland, c1976 (*courtesy National Archives of Canada/MISA/CBC Coll/14595*).

Canada where regulations were necessary to protect the broadcast of francophone songs threatened by stations giving too much air time to American rock. As early as 1967 private stations had captured over three-quarters of the radio audience. The listening peaks were now in the early morning and in the late afternoon.

The CBC was much slower to adapt to the times. Up to the late 1960s its schedule continued to look old-fashioned, filled with short, distinct programs. First in English Canada, and eventually in Québec, audience levels plummeted, suggesting that the network was irrelevant to the needs of listeners. Finally, after 1971, the CBC scrapped the old daytime program format and added 7 hours a day of morning and late afternoon information programs. New talk and discussion shows, eg, "As It Happens," "Aux 20 heures," "This Country in the Morning," "Présent à l'écoute," were launched on the AM networks. Revamped programs in popular music, arts, drama and criticism remained, especially in the evening hours. Likewise the CBC established its FM stereo network to offer listeners a chance to indulge their taste for high culture, particularly classical music and sophisticated learning. These changes were complemented by the elimination of all advertising in 1975.

The renaissance of CBC programming almost doubled the audience share of the network's own stations in English Canada between 1967 and 1977. "This Country in the Morning" (later "Morningside") and "As It Happens" won substantial numbers of fans. CBC radio gained a N American reputation as a showcase of excellence. Nonetheless, the revival did not seriously challenge the dominance of private radio in French or English Canada, where the CBC's own stations won about 10% of the audiences in both French and English Canada in 1987.

Little has changed in recent years. The growing popularity of FM radio (which by 1988 had an audience share of over 40%), the increased availability of American signals via cable, the timid experiment of an "all-news" FM service, and the re-emergence of radio networking, may alter the shape of the radio scene in time. At present, however, radio remains the grand music box (even CBC radio, where 20% of AM broadcasting and 70% of FM broadcasting is devoted to music), dispensing a range of sounds to serve a variety of different tastes. *See also* EDUCATIONAL BROADCASTING; MUSIC BROADCASTING.

PAUL RUTHERFORD

Reading: B. McNeil and M. Wolfe, *Signing On: The Birth of Radio in Canada* (1982); A.E. Powley, *Broadcasting from the Front* (1975); S. Stewart, *A Pictorial History of Radio in Canada* (1975).

Radish (*Raphanus sativus*), hardy annual or biennial vegetable belonging to the Cruciferae family. Roots are mostly rounded with a red exterior and white, acrid flesh. Originating in Eurasia, radishes were prized by the Egyptians and Greeks. Commercial varieties now include Red Prince, Champion, French Breakfast and White Icicle. Radishes are a cool-season, fast-germinating crop. Outdoors, they require 25-35 days from seeding to table; winter types, 50-60 days. Radishes tolerate light frosts and are seeded 1 cm deep as soon as soils are workable in spring; precision seeders provide accurate spacing for commercial crops. With skilful management and cool, moist soils, seeding every 10-14 days provides radishes from Apr to Sept (early Nov in SW Ont). Growth checks by heat or drought result in inedible, hot, tough roots. Flea beetles, cabbage-root maggots and damping-off require control. Appreciated for their crisp texture and mild, tangy flavour, radishes are high in potassium and a good source of vitamins A and C. Production figures for Canada in 1985 were 5167 t (on 582 ha), worth $3.45 million. These figures include Qué, 2230 t (on 350 ha), worth $1.25 million; Ont, 2172 t (on 192 ha), worth $1.62 million; and BC, 765 t (on 40 ha), worth $582 000. V.W. NUTTALL

Radisson, Pierre-Esprit, explorer, fur trader (b in France 1636; d at London, Eng June 1710). This shrewd opportunist was valued for his knowledge of Indian life and N American geography. He followed his half sister to Trois-Rivières in 1651 and observed the IROQUOIS as their adopted captive 1652-53 and with the Jesuit mission to the Onondaga 1657-58. In 1659 he was taken on an unlicensed fur-trading expedition to Lks Superior and Michigan by his sister's husband, Médard Chouart DES GROSEILLIERS. In the lands beyond they found a "great store of beaver" and heard of "the Bay of the North Sea" that gave direct access to the region. After the governor of New France punished them for this expedition, the partners went to Boston to arrange a voyage to Hudson Bay. In 1665 they sailed to England, where their plan of bypassing the St Lawrence R to reach the interior fur-producing region found backers. The NONSUCH's voyage 1668-69 proved that the plan was practical and profitable. After the HUDSON'S BAY CO was incorporated in 1670, Radisson established its Nelson R post and served as guide, translator and adviser.

Their "dissatisfaction" with the company and a generous offer from the French secretary of state, Jean-Baptiste Colbert, led the brothers-in-law to desert to France in 1674. With a wife in England, Radisson was never fully trusted. As Canada's governor would not employ him, Radisson was a French navy midshipman 1677-79. In 1682 the COMPAGNIE DU NORD engaged him to challenge the English traders in Hudson Bay. Radisson destroyed rival posts and established Ft Bourbon on the Nelson R. When the governor of Canada taxed their furs and released a ship they had captured, the brothers-in-law sought restitution in France. They failed because Colbert, their patron, was dead. Radisson returned to England in 1684, and despite the losses he had caused, the HBC reemployed him, hoping to profit by "his great Experience & dexterity." He had his nephew surrender Ft Bourbon and its contents to the company. Radisson was chief director of trade at Ft Nelson 1685-87. With a price on his head in Canada, he retired with his family to Westminster [London], Eng, where he completed the narrative of his voyages. *See also* FUR TRADE. PETER N. MOOGK

Radium (Ra), rare, radioactive metal found in naturally occurring URANIUM (about 1 part radium to 3 million parts uranium). It was discovered in 1898 by Pierre and Marie Curie and G. Bémont who chemically treated pitchblende, a uranium ore obtained as a by-product from a silver mine in Bohemia. Most of the world's radium has come from the Shinkolobwe mine, in what is now Zaire (beginning 1921), and the Port Radium mine in the NWT (beginning 1933). The high-grade pitchblende concentrates were treated at radium refineries at Oolen, Belgium, and PORT HOPE, Ont, respectively. Both mines closed in the late 1930s but were reopened in the early 1940s as sources of uranium. Radium was recovered as a by-product of uranium at the Port Hope refinery until 1953. The most important use for radium has been to destroy cancer cells. Radium compounds, sealed in tubes or needles, were implanted in patients at cancer sites. Radium has also been employed industrially, eg, in luminous paint used in watches and instruments. However, there is now little demand for radium as radioisotopes such as COBALT-60 can be processed more cheaply and are more effective in most applications. R.M. WILLIAMS

Rae, John, trader, explorer (b in Orkney Is 30 Sept 1813; d at London, Eng 22 July 1893). An expert boatman, swimmer and climber, Rae qualified as a surgeon in 1833, entered the HBC and was posted to Moose Factory. In 1846-47 he explored the coast W from Fury and Hecla Str to Boothia Isthmus, and in 1848 he accompanied Sir John RICHARDSON on a search for Sir John FRANKLIN. In 1851, with the same purpose, he searched the western, southern and eastern shores of VICTORIA I; much was original discovery. From an 1853-54 exploration, he brought back the first authentic tidings of the Franklin disaster (*see* FRANKLIN SEARCH). In 1860 Rae was employed to carry out the land part of a survey for a projected telegraph line from Great Britain to N America by way of the Faeroes, Iceland and Greenland. In 1864, for a similar purpose, he carried out a survey from Winnipeg to the Rocky Mts. He spent his later life in London. Rae was supremely gifted in arctic survival, living off the country in comparative comfort and security. But he lacked a proclivity for self-advertisement, and his modesty permitted Vilhjalmur STEFANSSON to appropriate the honours owing to him. L.H. NEATBY

Rae-Edzo, NWT, Hamlet, pop 1378 (1986c); 1878 (1981c), is located near the N arm of GREAT SLAVE LK, 106 km NW of Yellowknife. It comprises the traditional Dogrib DENE community of Rae and the government settlement of Edzo. Today the largest Dene community in the NWT, Rae was originally a trading post, established 1790. The area had been the traditional hunting grounds for the Dogrib for centuries. Edzo, about 24 km from Rae, was constructed by the government 1965 as an alternative site to Rae, which offered poor drainage. However, most of the Dogrib preferred to remain at the original site and today still pursue hunting and trapping from there. Edzo has a small cluster of houses occupied mainly by NWT government employees. ANNELIES POOL

Raft Once the spring timber drive reached the main rivers, the timber was assembled into rafts for transportation to the shipping port. On the Ottawa, Saint John and Miramichi rivers, rafts comprised several "cribs" or "joints," each about 20 sticks secured in an ingenious 2-layer wooden frame. On the St Lawrence, "drams," larger frames secured with withes (sapling "ropes"), were used. Both types varied greatly in size. On the Saint John, rafts of 12-140 joints came downriver in the 1830s, but the largest were on the St Lawrence and probably contained 2000-2500 t of timber. GRAEME WYNN

Raginsky, Nina, photographer (b at Montréal 14 Apr 1941). Educated at Rutgers, Raginsky turned to photography seriously in 1964. She worked first in black and white but later began to sepia-tone and hand-colour her prints. She has also created oil paintings based on photographs. Between 1972 and 1981, Raginsky was an instructor at the Emily Carr College of Art, formerly Vancouver School of Art. Her work has appeared in solo and group exhibitions in Canada and the US and in various magazines and books, including those of the National Film Board's *Image* series, *Canada: A Year of the Land* and *Between Friends*. She is best known for her frontal, full-figure portraits, particularly of eccentric or whimsical personalities. In 1985 she was made an Officer of the Order of Canada.   LOUISE ABBOTT

Ragweed, annual or perennial plant of genus *Ambrosia*, family Compositae or Asteraceae. Fifteen species are native to N America; 3 occur across Canada: common ragweed (*A. artemisiifolia*), perennial ragweed (*A. coronopifolia*) and giant ragweed (*A. trifida*). Ragweed pollen is the most prevalent cause of hay fever in Canada, and common ragweed can also cause dermatitis. Common ragweed, the most abundant, is an erect, hairy-stemmed, coarse, annual herbaceous plant, 5-200 cm high, usually with deeply divided, dark green leaves. Greenish, male flowers with obvious yellow stamens are borne in clusters along an erect stalk. One-seeded fruits (achenes) occur singly or in clusters, and are found at bases of upper leaves. It is an abundant weed in cultivated fields, open disturbed areas and along roadsides, especially in southern Ontario and Québec.
PAUL B. CAVERS

The sora rail (*Porzana carolina*) breeds in almost every province (*artwork by Claire Tremblay*).

Rail, common name for some members of the rail family (Rallidae) of birds which also includes COOTS and GALLINULES. About 132 species occur worldwide; 44 are confined to islands or archipelagos; 13 are extinct. Many of the flightless forms may have evolved on isolated islands. In N America, rails are generally tawny coloured, or with grey-brown stripes or bars. They are hen-shaped and secretive, rarely seen but often heard. Rails probe soft mud for snails, clams, crustaceans, insects and small frogs and pick plant material. They fly hesitantly, with legs dangling, and quickly drop back into the marsh where their strong legs and long toes serve them well.

In Canada, the sora (*Porzana carolina*) and yellow rails (*Coturnicops noveboracensis*) breed in almost every province. Virginia rails (*Rallus limicola*) have a westward breeding range similar to that of yellow rails but do not occur as far N, except in Alberta. They also nest in southern British Columbia. King (*R. elegans*) and clapper rails (*R. longirostris*) occur, rarely, in southeastern Canada. Nests are woven baskets of marsh plants, sometimes roofed with plant stalks. Clutches contain 5-12 buff eggs.   E. KUYT

Railway History The development of steam-powered railways in the 19th century revolutionized TRANSPORTATION in Canada and was integral to the very act of nation building.

The railway fever which began in the 1850s continued into the 1860s. William Armstrong captured this enthusiasm in his painting of Prince Arthur turning the first sod for the Toronto Grey and Bruce Ry at Weston, Ont, in 1869 (*courtesy National Archives of Canada/C-21861*).

Mining railways, used to carry ore and coal from pitheads to water, were introduced to England early in the 17th century – the motive power being provided by horses. A primitive railway of this type may have been used as early as the 1720s to haul quarried stone at the fortress of LOUISBOURG. An incline railway of cable cars, powered by a winch driven by a steam engine, was used in the 1820s to hoist stone during the building of the QUÉBEC CITADEL. Another railway was used during the building of the RIDEAU CANAL to carry stone from the quarry at Hog's Back [Ottawa].

Steam locomotion, together with the low rolling friction of iron-flanged wheels on iron rails, enabled George Stephenson (the first of the great railway engineers) to design and superintend the building of the Liverpool and Manchester Railway (1830), which began the railway age in England. By 1841 there were some 2100 km of rail in the British Isles and by 1844 the frenetic promotion of railways aptly called "The Mania" was under way. Many of the lasting characteristics of the railway were established in this early stage: steam locomotion, the standard gauge (1.435 m) and the rolled-edge rail (bellying out on the underside for strength).

Early Railways Railway fever came a little later to British N America, which had a small population and much of its capital tied up in the expansion of its CANALS AND INLAND WATERWAYS. Nevertheless, it did not take long for politicians and entrepreneurs to realize the potential benefits. The Province of Canada (1841) was an enormous country. Its roads were poor and its waterways were frozen for up to 5 months per year. The first true railway built in Canada was the CHAMPLAIN AND SAINT LAWRENCE RAILROAD from La Prairie on the St Lawrence R to St Johns on the Richelieu R (St-Jean-sur-Richelieu). Backed by John MOLSON and other Montréal merchants, the line opened officially 21 July 1836. Built as a "portage" between Montréal and Lk Champlain, in practice the railway carried little freight. The first railway in the Maritimes was the ALBION MINES RAILWAY, built to carry coal from Albion Mines some 9.5 km to the loading pier at Dunbar Pt (near Pictou, NS), opened 19 Sept 1839. The MONTREAL AND LACHINE RAILROAD (1847) was another short (12 km) line built to supplement water transportation.

More ambitious was the ST LAWRENCE AND ATLANTIC RAILROAD, promoted initially by John A. Poor of Portland, Maine, and Canadian entrepreneur Alexander Tilloch GALT. The dual purpose of the line was to provide Montréal with a year-round ocean outlet and Portland with a hinterland. Promotion of the railway set a pattern often repeated later. In the initial enthusiasm, Montréalers subscribed £100 000 but paid up only 10% of that amount. Galt raised another £53 000 in England and mortgaged his land

company to get the project moving. But it was the GUARANTEE ACT, 1849, sponsored in the Canadian legislature by Galt's friend Francis HINCKS, that ensured the railway's completion (1853). The Act guaranteed interest of not more than 6% on half the bonds of a railway longer than 75 miles (120 km). A similar collaboration lay behind the GREAT WESTERN RAILWAY, which began construction in Oct 1849 and was completed from Niagara Falls to Windsor, Canada W, in Jan 1854. In this case Conservative politician and businessman Allan MACNAB arranged for partners in Canada and the United States, persuaded the legislature to proffer a loan of £200 000, and profited mightily himself.

The most ambitious pre-Confederation railway project in Canada was the GRAND TRUNK RAILWAY – a bold attempt by Montréal to capture the hinterland of Canada West and traffic from American states in the Great Lakes region. The GTR aroused great anticipation, but Canadians had neither the money nor the technicians to build it. The success of Hincks and other promoters in raising money for the GTR and other railway projects was largely due to their determination and the seemingly unbounded enthusiasm of British investors for railways. By the time it was completed from Sarnia to Montréal in 1860, the GTR was £800 000 in debt to the British banks of Baring Bros and Glyn Mills. Edward WATKIN, sent out by head office to reorganize the railway, declared the GTR "an organized mess – I might say a sink of iniquity." In 1862 the Grand Trunk Arrangements Act put an end to the annual government handouts to the GTR by injecting new capital. The contempt and hostility with which the GTR began to be viewed by the public matched in intensity the early enthusiasm for its potential.

The financial difficulties experienced by all early railways forced massive public expenditures in the form of cash grants, guaranteed interest, land grants, rebates and rights-of-way. In return, the railways contributed to general economic developments, and the indirect benefits for business and employment were clearly large. Unlike canals, railways extended into new territories and pushed the agricultural and timber frontiers westward and northward. The effect of railways on emerging urban centres was crucial and dramatic. Toronto's dominant position in S-central Ontario was clearly established by its rail connections. It benefited from its connections with the Great Western and its central place on the GTR (neither of which it had done much to help build) and tapped the northern hinterland via the Ontario, Simcoe and Huron Railway (completed to Collingwood, Georgian Bay, in 1855, with a branch line to Belle Ewart on the S shore of Lake Simcoe), Toronto, Grey and Bruce Railway (completed to Owen Sound, Georgian Bay, in 1873), and Toronto and Nipissing Railway (extended to Lk Simcoe 1877). In sparsely populated and nonindustrial areas such as Newfoundland,

Chinese village opposite Keefers, BC, during the building of the CPR, 1885 (*courtesy Vancouver City Archives*).

railways were built for the same reasons and attended by the same problems as were those in central Canada, and have tended to diminish in size and importance over time. The development of a Newfoundland Railway system, which was taken over by the CNR in 1923, was a case in point. In 1919 the CPR was earning $16 000 per mile while the Newfoundland system was earning $1500.

The railways played an integral role in the process of industrialization, tying together and opening up new markets while, at the same time, themselves creating a demand for fuel, iron and steel, LOCOMOTIVES AND ROLLING STOCK. The pioneer wood-burning locomotives had huge appetites, and "wooding-up" stations were required at regular intervals along the line. The first locomotive built in Canada, in 1853, was made by James Good of Toronto (the *Toronto No 2* of the Ontario, Simcoe and Huron). Entrepreneurial talents invested in the manufacture of almost everything that went into the operation of the railway, and consequently railways had a positive effect on levels of employment. Some small towns became in fact railway service and maintenance centres, with the bulk of the population dependent on the railway shops; eg, the Cobourg Car Works employed 300 workers in 1881. The railway also had a decisive impact on the physical characteristics of Canadian cities, since the tracks, the yards and the stations became central urban features, around which industries and hotels were built in ways that made the railway a central feature of the urban landscape. The railway greatly stimulated ENGINEERING, particularly with the demand for BRIDGES and TUNNELS. Canadians contributed a few inventions, notably the first successful braking system (W.A. Robinson, 1868) and the rotary snowplough (J.W. Elliott, 1869; developed further by O. Jull), which made possible safe, regular travel in Canadian winters. The great Canadian railway engineer Sir Sandford FLEMING devised his famous zone system of time to overcome the confusion of clocks varying from community to community along the rail routes.

The Transcontinentals The second phase of railway building in Canada came with CONFEDERATION, 1867. As one historian has put it, "Bonds of steel as well as of sentiment were needed to hold the new Confederation together. Without railways there would be and could be no Canada." In fact, the building of the INTERCOLONIAL RAILWAY was a condition written into the Constitution Act, 1867. Because political considerations often overrode economic realities (eg, in the circuitous routes the Intercolonial and other railways took to avoid American territory) and because of the grand scale of the new nation, government assistance was crucial. The Intercolonial was owned and operated by the federal government and was largely financed with British loans backed by imperial guarantees. Despite the badgering of commissioners determined to make political advantage, Sandford Fleming built the Intercolonial to the highest standards and completed it by 1876.

In 1871 BC was lured into Confederation with the promise of a transcontinental railway within 10 years. The proposed line – 1600 km longer than the first US transcontinental – represented an enormous expenditure for a nation of only 3.5 million people. Two syndicates vied for the contract, and it was secretly promised to Sir Hugh ALLAN in return for financial support for the Conservatives during the closely contested 1872 election. The subsequent revelation that Allan was largely backed by American promoters and that he had sunk $350 000 into the Conservative campaign brought down the government (*see* PACIFIC SCANDAL). The contract with the CANADIAN PACIFIC RAILWAY Co, headed by George STEPHEN,

The rotary snowplow was used by railway companies across N America (*courtesy CP Rail Corporate Archives*).

was signed 21 Oct 1880. Macdonald's controversial decision in favour of an expensive all-Canadian route seemed to be vindicated during the NORTH-WEST REBELLION; how would the American government have reacted to Canadian troops moving across American territory? The "Last Spike" was driven 7 Nov 1885 and the first passenger train left Montréal June 1886, arriving in Port Moody, BC, July 4. Completion of the railway was one of the great engineering feats of the day and owed much to the indefatigable supervision of William VAN HORNE and the determination of Macdonald.

Though ostensibly a private enterprise, the CPR was generously endowed by the federal government with cash ($25 million), land grants (25 million acres), tax concessions, rights-of-way, and a 20-year prohibition on construction of competing lines on the prairies that might provide feeder lines to US railways. Whether or not the country received adequate compensation for this largesse has been hotly debated ever since. However, the CPR was built in advance of a market and by a very expensive route through the Shield of northern Ontario. It had a profound effect on the settlement of the PRAIRIE WEST, and new cities, from Winnipeg to Vancouver, virtually owed their lives to the artery. Other western towns were strung out along the railway like beads on a string.

The flood of immigrants to the Prairie West after 1900 and the dramatic increase in agriculture

Dramatic bluff on the Kaslo & Slocan Railway, 1900. The railway line hauled ore from Sandon to Kaslo on Kootenay Lake. Many passengers disembarked and followed the train around the bluff (*courtesy City of Vancouver Archives/CVA2-99*).

soon proved the CPR inadequate, and a third phase of railway expansion began. Numerous branches sprouted in the West, of which the most notable was the CANADIAN NORTHERN RAILWAY, owned by the 2 bold entrepreneurs Donald MANN and William MACKENZIE. The Canadian Northern grew by leasing and absorbing other lines; constructed new links to Regina, Saskatoon, Prince Albert and Edmonton, and pushed on through the YELLOWHEAD PASS. It was linked to the East, with its main eastern terminus at Montréal, and also operated mileage in eastern Québec and the Maritimes. Though sometimes portrayed as rapacious promoters, Mackenzie and Mann built their railway to serve western needs that were not being met by the CPR, and they invested most of their own fortunes in the enterprise. Nevertheless, the railway received public assistance of one-quarter billion dollars, most of it in the form of provincial and federal bond guarantees.

Meanwhile, the formerly aloof Grand Trunk was finally roused, under the leadership of Charles M. HAYS, to take part in western railway expansion, enthusiastically encouraged by PM LAURIER. Mutual jealousies precluded logical cooperation between the GTR and Canadian Northern, and the federal government itself undertook to build a line from Winnipeg to Moncton (the National Transcontinental Railway) and to lease it to the GTR on completion. The GTR's subsidiary, the GRAND TRUNK PACIFIC, undertook to build the more profitable line westward from Winnipeg. The NTR was built through the empty expanse of northern Québec and Ontario in hopes of encouraging development there; begun in 1905, it was completed in 1913 at a cost of $160 million. The GTP began construction in 1906 and was completed in 1914 through the Yellowhead Pass and along the spectacular SKEENA R valley to PRINCE RUPERT, BC.

The ill-planned proliferation of railways (about half of the track now in operation was built between 1890 and 1914) proved disastrous. Rumours of outrageous patronage in the building of the NTR were later confirmed. The Canadian Northern and GTP were constantly begging aid from the public purse. WWI delivered the knock-out blow – ending immigration and stifling the flow of British capital. In confusion and frustration PM Robert BORDEN called a royal commission, headed by Sir Henry Drayton and British financier W.M. Acworth, which recommended (May 1917) "immediate nationalization of all railways of Canada except for American lines and the CPR . . . that the Intercolonial . . . National Transcontinental, the old Grand Trunk, the Grand Trunk Pacific and the Canadian Northern be brought together into one system, to be owned by the people of Canada." The name CANADIAN NATIONAL RAILWAYS was authorized for this conglomeration in 1918, but organization was not completed for 5 years.

The period after formation of the CNR was essentially one of consolidation, although several lines were pushed into northern frontiers. The HUDSON BAY RAILWAY, beginning at a line built by Mackenzie and Mann to The Pas in 1906, was finally opened to traffic in 1929. The Pacific Great Eastern began pushing uncertainly into the interior of BC in 1912. It was completed from Squamish to Quesnel by 1921, but only reached Prince George and Dawson Creek in the 1950s. Northern Alberta Railways (owned jointly by CNR and CPR) ran lines from Edmonton N to Grande Prairie and to Dawson Creek by 1931. Perhaps the most successful of these ventures was the ONTARIO NORTHLAND Railway, which reached James Bay in 1932. Owned by the Ontario government, the railway led directly to a fantastic mining boom in the Timmins-Porcupine area as well as to the emergence of the giant PULP AND PAPER INDUSTRY. The QUEBEC, NORTH SHORE AND LABRADOR RAILWAY, completed in 1954, provided access to the massive iron-ore deposits of the deep interior of Québec and Labrador. The Great Slave Railway was opened in 1965 between Roma, Alta, and Hay River, NWT.

Did the railways achieve the ends expected of them? Did they repay the large infusions of public money? A final accounting can likely never be done, particulary in trying to judge the satisfaction of nationalistic and long-term economic goals. Regulation of the railways (now the responsibility of the CANADIAN TRANSPORT COMMISSION) and freight-rate agreements (notably the CROW'S NEST PASS AGREEMENT) have been highly controversial, and very different views have been taken by western farmers and the railway companies on these issues (*see* TRANSPORTATION REGULATION). At the same time, the railwaymen – from Fleming and Van Horne to Allan, Mann, Mackenzie, Stephen and Lord SHAUGHNESSY – have been among the most prominent figures in Canadian history, evoking by turns admiration for their outstanding engineering feats and contempt for their perceived bleeding of the public purse. The building of the transcontinentals perhaps provided for Canada the closest approximation of a heroic age.   JAMES MARSH

Reading: Pierre Berton, *The National Dream* (1969) and *The Last Spike* (1971); A.W. Currie, *The Grand Trunk Railway of Canada* (1957); W.K. Lamb, *History of the Canadian Pacific Railway* (1977); R.F. Legget, *Railways of Canada* (1973); T.D. Regehr, *The Canadian Northern Railway* (1976); G.R. Stevens, *History of the Canadian National Railways* (1973); A. Tucker, *Steam Into Wilderness* (1978).

Railway Safety Each year in Canada there are thousands of railway accidents. Most are minor and cause little damage and only a slight delay to the train. Some, however, result in injury, loss of life and substantial property damage. In 1985 there were 3264 "accidents" reported. Perhaps one-third were classified as "train" accidents; the rest were "normal industrial accidents." Train accidents resulted in 126 deaths and 475 injuries. Most of the fatalities were occupants of automobiles involved in grade-crossing accidents; 7 were railway employees; none were passengers. Most of the injuries involved railway employees. Although there are individual years which do not fit the trend, the number of accidents, deaths and injuries has declined since 1960, in spite of a vast increase in freight traffic.

One of the most famous railway accidents in recent years was the 1979 "Mississauga Derailment" (*see* DISASTERS). There were no injuries, but the accident involved leaking chlorine cars and forced the evacuation of 250 000 nearby residents. This, and a rash of similar accidents, served to focus public attention on railway safety, especially the problems of handling DANGEROUS GOODS in urban areas. The ensuing Commission of Inquiry conducted by Mr Justice Samuel Grange made a number of sweeping recommendations regarding equipment design and inspection and train-operation procedures, especially for trains handling dangerous cargo such as poisonous or explosive gas. Many of these recommendations were subsequently imposed on the railways by the Transport Commission.

The other major accident was a head-on collision between a freight and passenger train at Hinton, Alta, in Feb 1986. Twenty-three people were killed, 71 hospitalized and $30 million worth of property damage done. This accident and a number of much less serious incidents again led to the appointment of a commission of inquiry, under Mr Justice René Paul Foisy. Mr Foisy found that the specific cause of the accident was the failure of

the freight train to obey a stop signal. In more general terms, however, he was concerned that inadequate priority was placed on safety by many groups within the railway sector, including government. Many of the recommendations of the inquiry, especially those regarding crew rest and hours of work, were subsequently adopted by the CTC. The accident has also given impetus to the investigation of some form of Automatic Train Control, which may be able to prevent such accidents in the future. While such standards have an impact on the possibility of derailments, collisions and other types of accidents, nearly 20% of all railway accidents, and most of the deaths, are at grade crossings, where driver behaviour plays an important factor. A complete but expensive solution for this type of accident is grade separation (overpass or underpass). There is an ongoing federal-provincial program to install signals and barriers at busy crossings.   CHARLES SCHWIER

Railway Station Rail service began in Canada in 1836 with the opening of the CHAMPLAIN AND SAINT LAWRENCE RAILROAD east of Montréal. The new TRANSPORTATION system required a new building type: stations to accommodate the passengers and freight that it carried. No information has survived on stations for the first Canadian RAILWAYS, if indeed there were stations; the earliest ones known are the "road stations" built between 1855 and 1857 for the GRAND TRUNK RAILWAY's line from Montréal to Toronto and Sarnia. Most, such as the station at St Marys Junction, were small rectangular one-storey stone buildings with broad-eaved gabled roofs and round-arched windows and doors; those at Kingston and Belleville had a second storey within a mansard roof. The designer may have been Grand Trunk chief engineer A.M. Ross or Thomas S. SCOTT, the future federal chief architect who served for a time as architect to the railway. A number of the early Grand Trunk stations were of frame construction, as were those built in 1867 for the INTERCOLONIAL RAILWAY's route from Truro to New Glasgow, NS, and likely designed by Sir Sandford FLEMING. The 5 shingled "way stations" on this route combined passenger and freight facilities and had a separate long platform.

The CANADIAN PACIFIC RAILWAY used a number of station types and designers for its transcontinental route. Several stations, such as the one at Peterborough, Ont (Thomas Charles Sorby, 1883), were built of brick, with the passenger waiting room separate from the freight shed and the stationmaster's quarters located above the waiting room. This arrangement became the basis for standard plans subsequently adopted by the CPR and other lines and continued well into the present century. In several early western CPR stations the passenger and freight facilities were joined by a covered platform. The Vancouver station (Paul Marmette, 1886, frame construction) followed this plan, as did stations at Calgary (1893, in stone) and Banff, Alta (1889, log con-

Domed rotunda of the CNR station in Winnipeg, 1911, in the fashionable beaux-arts style (*courtesy CN*).

struction), both designed by Edward Colonna.

Urban stations, many of them terminals, were much larger than stations along the line and were designed in the fashionable architectural styles of the time. Toronto's second Union Station (E.P. Hannaford, 1871-73) was an Italianate design with 3 tall mansard-roofed towers; the Intercolonial's North Street Terminal in Halifax (Dept of Public Works, 1874-77) displayed a fine Second Empire design; and the CPR's Windsor Station in Montréal (Bruce Price, 1888-89) was in the Richardsonian Romanesque style. All featured large train sheds of utilitarian iron or steel construction located behind the passenger building.

Many stations were designed in the years before WWI, and 20th-century designs generally continued the styles developed in earlier years. The station at Smith, Alta, built in 1914 for the Edmonton, Dunvegan and British Columbia Railway, has a low freight shed alongside a gabled 2-storey passenger wing similar to CPR stations of a generation earlier, and is typical of smaller stations built by most lines. Many railways had a series of standard designs that were repeated in various locations, particularly on the Prairies. The Union Station in Winnipeg (Warren and Wetmore, 1911) and Toronto's third UNION STATION (Ross and Macdonald, Hugh G. JONES and John M. LYLE, 1915-20) continued the practice of using fashionable "high" styles for urban stations, in both instances beaux-arts classicism. The Toronto station is notable for its grand concourse and its effective use of levels to separate functions. Modernism was first applied to station design with the erection of the CANADIAN NATIONAL RAILWAYS' Central Station in Montréal (John Schofield, 1938-43). The deceptively simple brick structure also became the core of an extensive commercial development, which culminated in the PLACE VILLE MARIE office complex (I.M. Pei and Associates, 1956-65). After 1960, many railway stations were demolished. The numerous line abandonments and the elimination of passenger service from many surviving lines, combined with the need to renew aging building stock, brought about a wave of station removal. The few new stations built generally used simple contemporary design, as in the CN stations at Dorval, Qué, and Kingston, Ont. In other communities, stations were removed and replaced with small shelters (eg, CP Rail at Arnprior, Ont, 1981). Public interest in the preservation of unusual railway stations has resulted in a number being reused as museums (eg, High River, Alta), as community facilities (eg, Theodore, Sask) and others as integrated transportation facilities (eg, Regina, Vancouver). The former Ottawa station is now a conference centre. The railways are beginning to co-operate with communities wishing to retain unused stations, although removal of stations continues at a rapid pace.   HAROLD D. KALMAN

Railway station, Churchill, Man (*courtesy Provincial Archives of Manitoba*).

Railways, Contemporary In the 4 decades following WWII, Canada's 2 major railways became major conglomerates, among the largest companies in Canada. In 1986 railway activity accounted for 22% of CP's $15.0 billion revenues (but contributed 79% of total net income). CP's net railway assets were $3.5 billion of a total of $12.8 billion. CN had revenues of $4.7 billion in 1986, 89% earned from railway operations. Of CN's half-billion dollar assets, 50% are railway related. Between them, CP and CN account for 82% of the Canadian railway business. The balance is handled by 30 regional and short-line carriers. In addition, both CP and CN have subsidiary railways in the US, own major trucking operations and have considerable other investments.

In general terms, the railway network is much the same in the 1980s as it was in the 1940s, although many independent railways have become part of the CP or CN systems. Total length in 1985 was 95 670 km, compared to 90 221 km in 1945. Many thousand km of low-density branch lines have been retired, but there has also been considerable new-line construction, particularly in northern Québec, Alberta and BC. During the 1950s and 1960s a number of major resource railways were completed. The Pacific Great Eastern (now the BRITISH COLUMBIA RAILWAY) has had a construction program extending over several decades to serve mining and timber areas in northern BC. The Great Slave Lake Railway was built by CN to serve mining and timber areas in northern Alberta and the NWT. The QUEBEC, NORTH SHORE AND LABRADOR RAILWAY was completed in 1954 to haul iron ore from the Knob Lk region near the Qué/Labrador boundary to Sept-Iles, Qué, on the N shore of the St Lawrence R. The mid-1980s has seen the establishment of short-line railways to operate former parts of the CN and CP systems.

Passenger Transportation The post-WWII era saw a contraction in the railway share of passenger transportation as the AUTOMOBILE and airplane became dominant (*see* AVIATION). In 1945 the railways carried 55.4 million passengers (including commuters), accounting for 20% of their revenue. Ten years later passengers had fallen to 27.2 million, accounting for less than 10% of revenue, in spite of both major railways having invested in new fleets of passenger equipment. In 1985 some 23 million passengers were carried. This decrease, coupled with inflation, led to losses on almost all passenger-train runs.

This decline was one of the problems addressed by the MacPherson Royal Commission 1959-61. Noting the advantages of the automobile and airplane, the commission recommended that uneconomic passenger trains be discontinued, with provision of a subsidy during a transitional period. This recommendation was adopted in the 1967 National Transportation Act, which provided for a federal subsidy of 80% of the losses sustained by passenger trains retained in the public interest. Even with this provision, during the 1960s and 1970s many of Canada's passenger trains were withdrawn and the number of stations served was gradually reduced as many trains became express or semiexpress. Over this period the railways, especially CN, undertook various initiatives, such as the Red-White-and-Blue discount fares introduced in the 1960s, to improve passenger service, but with limited success. Although there was some resurgence of passenger traffic, the subsidies grew.

In 1977, at a time when annual passenger subsidies had increased to more than $200 million, a new step was taken with the formation of VIA RAIL CANADA INC, a crown corporation which assumed responsibility for most passenger trains, operating them under contract with the federal government. VIA Rail owns only the trains and employs only some of the staff. The remainder of its services it purchases from the railways at cost. VIA Rail has introduced service improvements and new equipment such as the LRC (Light Rapid Comfortable) train. In 1986 there were over 5.7 million passengers; the cost to government, however, was $12.7 million. Although traffic had increased, the number of cities served was reduced in 1981 as 20% of VIA Rail's runs were cut. A number of these trains were restored in early 1985. Most of Canada's railway passenger service is provided in the densely populated Québec-Windsor corridor. Coast-to-coast service is provided with 2 daily Montréal-Maritime trains, a daily train between Montréal, Toronto, Calgary and Vancouver, and a Winnipeg-Edmonton-Vancouver train. A few regional services are also provided. By 1986, passenger volumes had fallen to 6.3 million and government funding had risen to 10% of VIA's cost. In the mid-1980s, VIA entered into a period of modernization, constructing its own new maintenance facilities in Halifax, Montréal, Toronto, Winnipeg and Vancouver. By late 1987, most of the train crews and other operating and maintenance staff had been transferred from CN and CP to VIA. In 1987, VIA also took delivery of the first of its 50 new 3000-hp locomotives, and announced plans for a multi-million-dollar modernization program for 190 of its 30-year-old long-distance rail cars. GO Transit, an agency of the Ontario government, began running commuter trains in the Toronto area in 1967, using CN and CP tracks. A similar arrangement started in Montréal in 1984.

Freight Transportation Freight, especially bulk commodities, has become the dominant railway service. Freight ton-kilometres increased from 92.5 billion in 1945 to 239.1 billion in 1986. The principal commodities which account for this increase are iron ore (via 2 new railways, the Quebec, North Shore and Labrador and the Québec Cartier in northern Québec) and coal, sulphur and potash (in western Canada). Other major freight commodities include grain, forest products, chemicals, petroleum, and automobiles and automobile parts. Among them, they account for more than 75% of total Canadian freight shipments. High-value, manufactured goods traffic has not grown as fast as bulk traffic, but, contrary to popular belief, the railways have not lost all of this traffic to trucks (*see* TRUCKING INDUSTRY). With the advent of intermodal services – containers and piggyback – there was a resurgence of manufactured goods traffic on the railways from the early 1970s to the mid-1980s.

The railways have withdrawn from the "small package" freight market, leaving it to their trucking or express subsidiaries. Many rail shipments are multiple carload lots, much of it in unit trains. For the most part, freight stations in smaller cities have been closed and low-density branch-lines abandoned. A number of uneconomic branch lines have been retained in the public interest. Losses on these lines are paid for from federal funds. In 1985 such payments amounted to $176 million, most of which was for grain-dependent lines. In areas still served by rail, orders are placed with regional carload centres rather than with a local agent.

Substantive changes have occurred in the regulation of freight movements. As a result of the MacPherson Royal Commission recommendations in 1961, railway freight rates were deregulated in the National Transportation Act of 1967. Rather than seeking the permission of the CANADIAN TRANSPORT COMMISSION to alter freight rates, the railways were now free to set rates as competition dictates and have only to publish increases 30 days in advance. Protection for other carriers

A VIA Rail turbo near Port Hope, Ont (*courtesy SSC Photocentre*).

from predatory pricing by the railways was provided by a minimum rate set at variable cost. In addition, section 23 of the Act stipulates the disallowance of any rate that is "not in the public interest." This 1967 regulatory philosophy came after a long period of freight-rate complaints set off by a postwar cycle of inflation, railway wage increases and freight-rate increases. This cycle made freight rates one of the political issues in the late 1950s, culminating in a federal government rollback of rates and payment of a general subsidy in the summer of 1959.

After deregulation, freight rates did not increase substantially until the inflation and fuel crisis of the mid-1970s. Even then, freight-rate increases did not keep pace with general price levels. With the exception of the Crow grain rates and a brief flurry of activity during the start of the inflationary period of the 1970s, railway freight rates have ceased to be the issue they once were (*see* CROW'S NEST PASS AGREEMENT).

In 1985, the new Conservative government introduced significant changes in railway regulation in a White Paper entitled "Freedom to Move." These changes were embodied in a new National Transportation Act, 1987, which replaced the CANADIAN TRANSPORT COMMISSION (CTC) with a National Transportation Agency and transferred some of the CTC's powers to other agencies. In general, the new legislation expands the emphasis on intramodal competition and explicitly recognizes the role that transportation plays in regional economic development. One of the more controversial provisions of the new regulatory environment is the competitive line rate, which will have the effect of lowering the freight rates for many shippers with a corresponding reduction in railway revenues.

Modernization The period since WWII has been a time of modernization and technical change for the railways. The most visible of the early steps to modernization was the conversion from steam to diesel-electric power. While there already existed an electrified line in Montréal, nearly all of the railways' 4400 locomotives in 1945 were steam engines, although many were oil rather than coal fired. Conversion to diesel-electric began in the late 1940s. In 1950, 91% of Canadian trains were pulled by steam engines; by 1960, steam engines accounted for only 1.4%.

The diesel engine was less expensive to operate, and more powerful and flexible. In the 1980s the bulk of the locomotive fleet was made up of 3000-hp units which could go 800 to 1000 km without servicing. Larger trains with multiple locomotives could be operated. Firemen were no longer required, and the need to change or service steam locomotives every 150 to 200 km was eliminated. Both these developments created labour difficulties in the 1950s and led to a decreased importance of many small towns which had been railway division points. The typical freight train of the 1980s may have over 100 cars pulled by 3 or

4 locomotives, with a 4-man crew, running non-stop between major terminals.

There have also been changes in freight cars. The 40-foot boxcar, long the standard of the industry and capable of carrying 40 to 50 tons, has been replaced by larger cars and special purpose cars. In the 1980s much of the bulk freight is handled in 100-ton (91 t) cars. The railways have an increasing number of unit trains which were dedicated to specific services and move directly from shipper to consignee without intermediate classification. Between 1945 and 1980 such innovations allowed the railways to increase the amount of freight carried while reducing the number of employees required by 32%, and to offer freight rates which have increased far below inflation rates.

Other, less visible, technological changes adopted by the railways since the 1940s include the use of Centralized Traffic Control, microwaves and radios for train control, modern metallurgy and continuous welded rails, automated rail-laying machinery, automatic car identification and the application of computers in all aspects of the railway business.

CHARLES SCHWIER

Reading: H.J. Darling, *The Politics of Freight Rates* (1980); W.G. Scott, *Canadian Railway Freight Pricing: Historical and Current Perspectives* (1984); Western Transportation Advisory Council, *Special Newsletters*, 1987.

Railways, Track and Yards Railway track is the assembly of the 5 basic components, rail, ties, fastenings, ballasts and subgrade, over which trains run. Rails are rolled steel lengths bolted or welded together to form the running surface for trains. The tie, usually wood or concrete, is the transverse member of the railway track structure to which the rails are fastened; it provides proper gauge and transmits the stresses through the ballast. Fastenings for wooden ties are spikes driven into the tie through holes in the metal plate on which the rail rests; the head of the spike grips the rail base; for concrete ties the rail rests on a polymer pad and can be secured by various patented clip systems. Ballast is selected rock material placed on the roadbed to hold the track in place. The subgrade, usually good quality soil, further distributes the track loading into the ground to provide a stable base.

A turnout or switch is the device used to divert trains from one track to another. Trackage can be divided into 2 categories: line and yards. The line is the running portion of the railway. A yard is a system of tracks for making up trains, sorting and storing cars, maintaining rolling stock and other activities. At major terminals, large classification yards are used to facilitate the sorting of freight cars. Often a hump is located at one end of the classification yard and freight cars are rolled down by gravity to various tracks to make up trains.

The objective in railway design is to select the route that will give the most economical combination of construction costs and operating expenses. There are 2 basic restraints to train performance: curvature and gradient. Curvature limits speed and leads to high maintenance costs for track and rolling stock. Gradient increases the requirements for locomotive horsepower and leads to an increase in fuel consumption and braking. Single-track routes are also a major limiting factor in performance because of the delays that occur unless trains moving in opposite directions meet at their designated passing tracks with perfect timing.

Railway traffic control is provided by means of a signal system. The basic element in most railway signal systems is the block, a length of track to which entrance is governed by signal indicators,

Aerial view of the CN Symington yards in Winnipeg, Man (*courtesy SSC Photocentre*).

usually coloured lights. In the Automatic Block Signal system (ABS), block signals are activated by the presence of a train in the block, or the position of track turnouts (switches). Though ABS provides collision protection, it does not provide a means of authorizing train movements – a severe limitation for a single-track or even a double-track railway with trains of varying speeds. This problem can be overcome by Centralized Traffic Control (CTC), by means of which a dispatcher at a central control panel can actuate all power-equipped turnouts for a certain segment of track. Thus the dispatcher can control the routing of trains either meeting or overtaking. The dispatcher can also monitor track-mounted detection devices for hot wheel bearings, dragging equipment, broken wheels and shifted loads. Computer-aided dispatching can be used on congested lines. One of the innovations in some other countries is in-cab signalling. By means of coded track circuits the status of track-side signals is continually displayed in the locomotive cab. An extension of in-cab signalling is the Automatic Train Control system (ATCS). With ATCS, the locomotive automatically responds to reduced speed requirements or is automatically stopped if the engineer does not respond. A further refinement of ATCS is an on-board control unit that computes the train's braking distance and controls the train's speed to maintain a safe braking distance between trains.

JEFFERY YOUNG

Rain is liquid precipitation – precipitation being liquid and solid WATER that condenses in and falls from the atmosphere. A typical raindrop is about 2 mm in diameter (range, 0.5-5 mm). Almost all rain-producing CLOUDS are formed as a result of upward motion of air charged with water vapour. Such motion produces cooling and subsequent condensation into water droplets and ICE crystals. Normally the crystals melt before reaching the ground. In Canada rain is usually an event of the warm season. Rainfall is sometimes classified according to the process responsible for the initial lifting of the air. Cyclonic rainfall occurs when moist air converges and lifts in low-pressure (cyclone) areas. This process accounts for much of Canada's rainfall. Central US lows, entering Canada somewhere between Manitoba and Québec, are of major environmental significance because they pass through the industrial heartland of the US and frequently bring ACID RAIN. Frontal rainfall results from the lifting of warm air on one side of a frontal surface (zone separating air masses of dissimilar characteristics) over colder, denser air on the other side. Convective rainfall, caused by warmer air rising in colder surroundings, is sometimes associated with thunderstorms. Orographic rainfall, however, occurs when moist air is lifted over mountains.

For synoptic purposes, rain is classified as slight if it falls at a rate less than 0.5 mm/h; moderate if the rate is 0.5-4 mm/h; heavy if the rate is greater than 4 mm/h. The heaviest rainfall in Canada oc-

curs along the BC coast, where annual precipitation can exceed 2500 mm. Canada's one-day record rainfall of 489 mm fell at Ucluelet on Vancouver I (6 Oct 1967). The second zone of high rainfall is the Maritimes. Average annual precipitation in parts of NS and Newfoundland exceeds 1500 mm. Occurrences of heavy rainfall in other parts of Canada are frequently associated with the extratropical phase of hurricanes: HURRICANE HAZEL dumped over 18 cm of rainfall in less than 24 hours in parts of southern Ontario (15-16 Oct 1954). Arctic regions receive the least rainfall, followed by the southern prairies and the deep valley systems of interior BC. But even in these areas, isolated very heavy rains are not uncommon. For example, 17.8 mm fell in 5 minutes in Winnipeg (14 July 1968). The benefits of rainfall are considerable. Rain is a major vehicle through which Canada's freshwater resources are renewed. In many parts of the country, especially in the prairies, crop yield is closely related to the amount and timing of rainfall during the growing season. But very heavy rainfall can cause flash FLOODS and washouts.

L.C. NKEMDIRIM

Rainbow, coloured arc that occurs when sunlight shines onto falling raindrops and is refracted, then reflected back towards the observer. In this process, each drop acts as a tiny prism, splitting the SUN's rays (according to wavelength) into their component colours. One of the reflected bundle of rays is much more intense than the rest and emerges at an angle of 42° to the direction of incoming sunlight. The strong reflections from each drop of similar size reinforce each other and a visible image of the sun's spectrum appears as an arc (ie, a primary rainbow). Occasionally, sunlight and rainfall may be intense enough to produce a second, fainter rainbow above or beyond the first. The secondary rainbow results from 2 internal reflections of light in raindrops and occurs at an angle of 50° (compared to the one internal reflection and 42° angle of primary rainbows). As rainbow formation requires that the sun be visible in some part of the sky while RAIN is falling in another, rainbows are seldom seen during extensive frontal-type rains but are restricted to THUNDERSTORMS and light showers. Because of the angle requirement, they are also more likely to be observed during or just after late afternoon showers. Rarely, the light of the full moon may be bright enough to produce a rainbow arc from a night shower.   J. MAYBANK

Rainbow, a light cruiser serving in the Royal Navy from 1891 until 1910, when the Canadian government purchased the ship for the new Royal Canadian Navy. After its arrival at Esquimalt, BC, 7 Nov 1910, its duties included training and fisheries patrol. In July 1914 its appearance persuaded the KOMAGATA MARU to leave Vancouver harbour. From Aug 1914, when powerful German cruisers briefly appeared in the NE Pacific, until early 1917, *Rainbow* performed defensive patrols. It was sold for scrap in 1920.   ROGER SARTY

Rainmaking Rainfall is vitally important to mankind and many techniques have been used to induce it. In ancient times, bonfires were built to appease the gods. In Napoleonic Europe, cannons were fired during cloudy weather. North American Indians performed elaborate dances. Unfortunately, it is unlikely that any such techniques had more than psychological value. Scientific rainmaking or rainfall enhancement began in 1946 when American scientists Vincent Schaefer and Bernard Vonnegut discovered, in independent studies, that it was possible to cause supercooled cloud droplets (those below 0°C) to freeze into ice crystals by introducing dry ice (solid carbon dioxide, with a temperature of -72°C) or silver iodide crystals into cloud.

In natural rain formation, cloud droplets develop as water vapour ascends, and rapidly reach equilibrium at a diameter of 5-20μ. Ultimately a million or more such droplets are needed to produce an average raindrop. Although these cloud droplets can combine and grow by collision, this is an unusual and inefficient process in temperate latitude clouds. Instead a highly efficient process involving ice crystals and supercooled water droplets is the dominant process by which rain is formed in Canada.

By freezing cloud droplets directly (through the injection of dry ice pellets), it is possible to induce ice-crystal growth, eventually leading to rainfall. Silver iodide operates in a more subtle fashion. Its molecular crystalline dimensions are very similar to those of an ice crystal. Consequently, when silver-iodide particles contact supercooled cloud droplets, they cause the water molecules to align themselves like ice molecules and the droplet freezes.

In Canada modern rainmaking began in 1948 with a federal government experiment that used dry ice dispersed into clouds to stimulate rainfall. Under appropriate conditions, rainfall did result. However, the classic question with all rainmaking activities is, what would have happened if man had not intervened? The results of this project were questioned since a randomly selected control population of unseeded clouds was not available for comparison with the population of seeded clouds. Nonetheless, in spite of scientific uncertainties, the 1950s saw a blossoming of rainmaking activities on the prairies for agricultural purposes, and in eastern Canada for forestry and hydroelectric power. Silver iodide was the seeding agent, dispersed variously from ground-based and airborne generators. These operations were not designed as scientific experiments, and later analyses were inconclusive; when compared with precipitation averages, small increases and small decreases in precipitation were found.

In 1959 one of the first of a series of international statistical rainmaking experiments was mounted by the federal government in NE Ontario and NW Québec. The outcome of this 4-year experiment on large-scale storm systems was an overall 2.5% decrease in rainfall. This decrease was not statistically significant and could have been the result of chance. However, an operational rainmaking project in the Lac SAINT-JEAN area, Qué, was perceived by residents as having been very successful – so successful, in fact, that "Operation Umbrella" was mounted and mothers petitioned the Québec government for vitamins for their children because of lack of sunshine. In 1965 the Québec minister of natural resources ordered all rainmaking activities in the province to cease.

Rainmaking declined throughout Canada during the 1960s and 1970s, although some projects continued sporadically in Nfld, Ont and Alta. By the mid-1970s revolutionary advances in techniques to observe cloud and precipitation particles from aircraft resulted in a federal 4-year single cumuliform cloud-seeding experiment in NW Ontario and the NWT. While the sample of clouds seeded was small, strong evidence was found for the possibility of initiating a precipitation process if the cloud did not dissipate in the 20 minutes following seeding. Clouds in NW Ontario were found to be short-lived and not susceptible to seeding; clouds in the NWT were long-lived and reacted positively. Rainmaking research conducted in Alberta during the 1980s has provided strong additional evidence that both dry ice and silver iodide can be used to initiate an ice crystal growth process in non-precipitating clouds.

Similar results have been found in other countries. However, the international scientific community is still cautious about whether rainmaking works. There is not a good general answer: the success of rainmaking probably depends on a variety of geographical and meteorological parameters that science has yet to delineate.

A.J. CHISHOLM

Rainy Lake, 932 km² (741 km² in Canada), elev 338 m, is located in rough woodlands astride the Ont-Minn border, 240 km W of Lk Superior. It discharges into the Rainy R, which flows W along the border to LK OF THE WOODS. Originally inhabited by Cree and Assiniboine, the lake was first visited by Jacques de Noyon in 1688. The explorer Pierre LA VÉRENDRYE ordered a post built at the western end in 1731. The lake was located on the well-travelled FUR-TRADE ROUTE to the northwest. Later, logging and the pulp-and-paper industry were important. FORT FRANCES, the lake's main settlement, is located at a waterfall where the river leaves the lake.

DANIEL FRANCIS

Rainy River Burial Mounds, archaeological sites on the Canadian bank of the Rainy R, were built by the Laurel and Blackduck peoples between the early Christian era and the early historic period. Most of them are low, broad structures, but one, at the Long Sault Rapids, is 34 m in diameter and 7 m high. Both within the mounds and in pits below are clusters of human bones and, occasionally, rich assortments of grave furniture. Clay pots filled with food for the departing spirits were placed in the grave; shell, bone and copper beads were scattered across the graves; and the whole was then sprinkled with red ochre. In the historic period, although articles of European manufacture replace many native artifacts, the burial pattern remains ancient and aboriginal. *See also* PREHISTORY.

W.A. KENYON

Ralston, James Layton, lawyer, politician (b at Amherst, NS 27 Sept 1881; d at Montréal 21 May 1948). A WWI battalion commander with a reputation for bravery and competence, Ralston was twice minister of national defence, 1926-30 and 1940-44. Intense, scrupulously honest, and an able representative of the political interests of the Maritime provinces, he was a stalwart in PM Mackenzie KING's WWII Cabinet, serving briefly as minister of finance, 1939-40, before becoming defence minister. Depite a tendency to become mired in administrative detail, he was a fine judge of generalship and a devoted defender of Canada's fighting men. King forced Ralston's resignation in 1944 because of his outspoken support of overseas CONSCRIPTION.

NORMAN HILLMER

Ramezay, Claude de, officer, acting governor of NEW FRANCE (b at La Gesse, France 15 June 1659; d at Québec C 31 July 1724). An officer in the TROUPES DE LA MARINE, he arrived in Canada in 1685. He served as governor of Trois-Rivières 1690-99, as commander of the Canadian troops 1699-1704, and as governor of Montréal 1704-24 (except for the period 1714-16 when he was acting governor of the colony during VAUDREUIL's absence). During much of this time he was also involved in the FUR TRADE and lumber business. The magnificent Château de Ramezay, which he built in 1705-06, still stands in Montréal.

MARY McDOUGALL MAUDE

Ramezay, Jean-Baptiste-Nicolas-Roch de, officer (b at Montréal 4 Sept 1708; d at Blaye, France 7 May 1777), son of Claude de RAMEZAY. He rose through the ranks of the TROUPES DE LA MARINE in New France, serving in the West and in Acadia, until becoming in 1758 king's lieutenant at Québec C, the senior military post in the town under the governor. In Sept 1759, operating under instructions from Governor VAUDREUIL given the night of MONTCALM's defeat on the PLAINS OF ABRAHAM, petitioned by the townspeople, and advised by a council of war, he negotiated terms for the capitulation of the town. These were signed by the British on Sept 18 and he surrendered Québec C to them the next day.

MARY McDOUGALL MAUDE

Ramsay, Donald Allan, physicist (b at London, Eng 11 July 1922). Educated at Cambridge U, Ramsay joined the National Research Council (NRC) in 1947. Since 1975, he has headed the spectroscopy section of NRC's Herzberg Institute of Astrophysics. Ramsay's research has advanced knowledge of the spectra of molecules, free radicals and molecular ions in the microwave, infrared, visible, ultraviolet and vacuum ultraviolet regions. The basic knowledge obtained has many applications in chemistry, physics and astrophysics, and provides a rigorous base for testing theoretical calculations. Over the years, he has been visiting professor at universities and scientific institutes worldwide. In 1975-76 he was named vice-president of the Academy of Sciences, Royal Society of Canada, and from 1976-79 honorary treasurer of that society. He is a Fellow of the Royal Society of Canada, the Royal Society of London, the American Physical Society and the Chemical Institute of Canada.

Ranching History Ranching developed where physical and climatic features combined to provide sufficient natural grassland for livestock – primarily BEEF CATTLE but also sheep – to graze relatively independently year-round. It began in the BC interior in the late 1850s, and was encouraged by markets created by the gold rushes. Livestock was brought in from the western US to the mild, sheltered Cariboo and Chilcotin areas and the Thompson and Nicola river valleys. Ranching expanded quickly into other British Columbia valleys, the Rocky Mt foothills and eventually into the CYPRESS HILLS and semiarid plains of southeastern Alberta and southwestern Saskatchewan.

Still a centre of the contemporary beef cattle industry, the heartland of the old ranching frontier was the foothill country of southwestern Alberta, where the sheltered, well-watered valleys and the chinook winds which bare the hills of winter snow combine to make it one of the continent's preferred stock-raising areas. After 1874 the North-West Mounted Police provided the 2 essentials of an incipient range-cattle industry: a small local market and security for open grazing. The police were soon joined by Joseph MacFarland, an Irish-American frontiersman, and George Emerson, an ex-Hudson's Bay man, who drove in small herds from Montana. At the same time in the Bow R valley W of Ft Calgary, George and John McDOUGALL established a herd near their mission at Morleyville [Morley, Alta]. Numerous policemen joined the ranching fraternity when their terms of enlistment expired, thus forming a distinctive core about which the industry developed and helping to define its emerging social character. The British-Canadian orientation of the ranching frontier was reinforced by the arrival of Englishmen attracted by the great publicity accorded in Britain to N American cattle ranching. They typically described themselves as "gentlemen" and came generally from the landed classes, with sufficient capital to establish their own ranches.

Access to distant markets was assured when the CANADIAN PACIFIC RAILWAY reached the prairies in the early 1880s, and interest in ranching grew dramatically. Led by Montréal capitalist and stock breeder Sen Matthew COCHRANE, Canadian businessmen vied to obtain the grazing leases provided through the DOMINION LANDS POLICY. The lure of being able to ship cheaply grown western beef to the rapidly expanding British market and cashing in on the "beef bonanza" led Cochrane

Fall roundup: lead man John Thompson herding cattle back to ranches, Alberta, Oct 1975 (*courtesy National Archives of Canada/PA-142584/photo by Ted Grant*).

and others to organize the great cattle companies that soon dominated the Canadian range: the Cochrane, Bar U, Oxley and Walrond ranches in Alberta, the '76, Hitchcock and Matador ranches in Saskatchewan, and the Douglas Lake, Gang and Empire Valley ranches in BC.

The railway, however, also brought the threat of general settlement, especially in Saskatchewan and Alberta, and an accompanying grid of barbed wire fences. Ranchers were determined to keep the "sodbusters" out and settlers were equally bent on penetrating the grazing leases. Finally the government yielded to the overwhelming demand for open settlement: in 1892 the ranchers received 4 years' notice that all old leases restricting HOMESTEAD entry would be cancelled. But the powerful cattle compact argued that the ranching regions were too dry for cereal agriculture. Recognizing that the upper hand was with those who controlled the water supply, cattlemen persuaded Ottawa to protect the cattle industry by setting aside major springs, rivers and creek fronts as public stock-watering reserves. Most choice sites thus became inaccessible to settlement, and the ranchers' hegemony continued.

After the election of Wilfrid Laurier's Liberals (1896), the cattlemen faced a government committed to unrestricted settlement. Convinced that dryland agricultural techniques were surmounting the obstacle of moisture deficiency, the Liberals began to auction off the elaborate system of stock-watering reservations. The spirited defence of the ranchers' cause by stock growers' associations, and strong beef markets, only slowed the decline of the industry. Soon in full retreat before the rush of homesteaders who settled on even the most marginal lands in southern Alberta and Saskatchewan, the faltering cattle kingdom was dealt the ultimate blow by nature. Whereas homesteaders had enjoyed years of above-average rainfall, the winter of 1906-07 was without the accustomed chinook, bringing stock losses in the thousands for many large-scale ranchers.

The passing of the great cattle companies in Alberta and Saskatchewan brought a new generation of local ranchers, including A.E. CROSS of the A7 and George LANE of the Bar U, to prominence. At the same time the predominantly American origin of most dryland settlers, and heavy WWI enlistments and casualties sustained by the British-Canadian population, combined to change profoundly the social character of the ranch country. Nonetheless, during the war ranchers' fortunes began to improve: their political party had returned to power in Ottawa, beef prices were buoyant and the return of a dry cycle caused settlement in the region to ebb. A decade later the ebb became a flood and the out-migration of thousands of drought-driven refugees in the 1930s brought grudging recognition that the cattlemen had pioneered, and would carry on, an enterprise especially suited to semiarid environments. *See also* ANIMAL AGRICULTURE.

DAVID H. BREEN

Reading: David H. Breen, *The Canadian Prairie West and the Ranching Frontier 1874-1924* (1983); E. Gould, *Ranching* (1978); D.C. McGowan, *Grassland Settlers* (1975).

Rand, Ivan Cleveland, judge, labour and international arbitrator, educator (b at Moncton, NB 27 Apr 1884; d at London, Ont 2 Jan 1969). He achieved prominence in labour relations for his development, in the 1945 WINDSOR STRIKE, of the RAND FORMULA for dealing with closed union shops; in international affairs for his leading role in the UN Special Committee on Palestine (1947); as a jurist for his uncompromising civil-libertarian and natural-rights orientation on the Supreme Court of Canada (1943-59); and as educator as inaugural dean of Western's Faculty of Law (1959-64). The frugal, principled, eloquent and often brusque son of a Baptist railway mechanic, Rand was committed to judicial activism in pursuit of social justice, a commitment encouraged at Harvard under mentor Louis D. Brandeis, and in a frontier litigation practice at Medicine Hat, Alta (1913-20). After working as a lawyer in Moncton (1920-24) and a brief foray into politics as Liberal attorney general of NB (1924-25), Rand was corporate counsel to Canadian National Rys (1926-43). He was elevated to the Supreme Court by the Mackenzie KING government, and his judicial profile later led to his appointment to various royal commissions.

G. BLAINE BAKER

Rand Formula, a form of union security whereby an employer deducts a portion of the salaries of all employees within a bargaining unit, union members or not, to go to the union as union dues ("checkoff"). It was named for a decision handed down 29 Jan 1946 by Mr Justice Ivan RAND of the Supreme Court of Canada while he was arbitrating the WINDSOR STRIKE (12 Sept-20 Dec 1945). The original formula was based on the assumption that the union is essential for all workers and must be responsible for them. Two interrelated provisions following from this assumption guaranteed the union the financial means to carry out its programs, and established the financial penalties for employees and unions engaging in work stoppages or illegal strikes. For employees, these sanctions could consist of daily fines and loss of seniority; for the union, the suspension of union dues. Collective agreements have spread a modified Rand Formula throughout Canada, and some provinces have given it legal force. *See also* LABOUR RELATIONS.

GÉRARD DION

Randazzo, Peter, dancer, choreographer (b at Brooklyn, NY 2 Jan 1943). He joined the Martha Graham company in 1962 and went on to create roles in several of her works. In 1968 he left to co-found TORONTO DANCE THEATRE with Patricia BEATTY and David EARLE. The most prolific choreographer of the TDT triumvirate, Randazzo has observed close movement ties with his great teacher. His style, distinctively sharp, angular and staccato, is best seen in his dramatic earlier works. Later choreographies have revealed a darkly comic side and relied more on pure movement for their impact. In 1986, the TDT played his *Rewind* during a week-long engagement in Toronto's Premiere Dance Theatre, and in 1987 the TDT's show Mystery, Mayhem & Mozart included his *L'assassin menacé*, a piece of choreography based on a Magritte painting, which is described as a TDT classic.

GRAHAM JACKSON

Random Island, 235 km², runs 40 km E-W and 14 km N-S, and is situated in a deep western indentation of TRINITY BAY, Nfld. Its name may come from the Old English *randon*, "disorderly," referring to the sea. The heavily forested island is separated from the mainland by Smith Sd to the N, Northwest Arm and Random Sd to the SE. Dominated by Baker's Peak, 166 m, on its NE tip, Random I has massive beds of red shale and limestone on the NW side that supported brick factories at Elliot's Cove and Snooks Harbour from the late 1800s. The 9 communities that now ring the island were founded in the mid-1800s by fishermen. Today the island is connected to insular Newfoundland by the Hefferton Causeway.

JANET E.M. PITT

Rankin, Alexander, timber merchant, politician (b in parish of Mearns, Scot 31 Dec 1788; d at Liverpool, Eng 3 Apr 1852). Rankin became a clerk in the firm of Pollok, Gilmour and Co, Glasgow merchants who traded with the Baltic ports. He was sent to New Brunswick in 1812 and opened the company's first branch in British N America at Gretna Green [Douglastown]. The company shipped timber to Britain, sold supplies to shipbuilders and lumbermen and thus became a bitter rival of Joseph CUNARD, whose firm was established at Chatham, NB. A deeply religious man, Rankin was noted for his charitable work and his hard and ruthless business practices. He entered politics in 1827 and continued to represent Northumberland County in the House of Assembly until his death. He was a member of the executive council from 1847.

WILLIAM A. SPRAY

Rankin, Harry, civic politician, lawyer, journalist (b at Vancouver 8 May 1920). For 30 years Rankin has been an outstanding advocate and leader of the citizens' movement for reform in Vancouver. After serving in WWII, he completed a law degree at UBC, where he became a socialist and consequently was almost refused admission to the bar in 1950. Rankin earned a reputation as an articulate defender of the underprivileged, specializing in labour law, criminal and civil liberties cases. He was elected to Vancouver City Council in 1966 and joined other groups in 1968 to form a union-based left-wing coalition, the

Committee of Progressive Electors. As COPE's only alderman and in a weekly newspaper column, Rankin challenged pro-development politicians and focused attention on neglected social issues throughout the 1970s. In civic elections he regularly topped the polls as an aldermanic candidate but lost as a mayoralty candidate in 1986. ANDREA B. SMITH

Rankin, Robert, timber merchant, shipowner (b in parish of Mearns, Scot 31 May 1801; d in Cheshire, Eng 3 June 1870). Rankin served in the office of Pollok, Gilmour and Co of Glasgow and in 1818 was selected to go out to the firm's Miramichi, NB, branch where he won recognition as a shrewd bargainer and advocate of the establishment of further branches, including one at Saint John. Under him, by 1838, the company operated 130 ships in the timber trade and employed 15 000 men in its sawmills. That year he bought out Allan Gilmour and reconstructed the firm, moving its head office from Glasgow to Liverpool, Eng, its name now being Rankin and Gilmour. He was the leading figure in the Anglo-Canadian timber and shipping trade of his time.

DAVID S. MACMILLAN

Rankin Inlet, NWT, Hamlet, pop 1374 (1986c), 1109 (1981c), is located on the W coast of HUDSON BAY, 1150 km E of Yellowknife. Named after Rankin Inlet (discovered by John Rankin), on which it sits, the community was established as a mining centre in 1955 by North Rankin Nickel Mines. In 1956 a 250-ton concentrator was built on the mine property and production of nickel concentrates began in 1957. When the mine closed in 1962, the mostly Inuit residents suffered a serious setback. Today the economy has recovered with a fishery and an Inuit craft industry. It is also a key government, transportation and communications centre. ANNELIES POOL

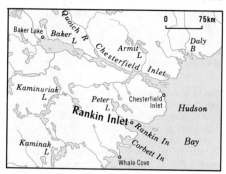

Rape Until it was amended in 1982 the Criminal Code contained the offence of rape. The offence required proof that a man had sexual intercourse with a woman other than his wife, without the woman's consent. It was punishable by up to life imprisonment.

The offence of rape, perhaps more than any other offence, demonstrated the tensions arising in CRIMINAL LAW from conflicting principles: the presumption of innocence (and thus, the requirement that the Crown prove all of the elements of the offence beyond a reasonable doubt) and the need to protect potential victims and to punish offenders. The emotional and traumatic nature of the trial (which might include cross-examination of the complainant about her prior sexual conduct with the accused and others), aggravated by the feelings of shame and degradation suffered by a rape victim, may have contributed to the fact that rape was an underreported crime. Sometimes the accused was a "friend" or relative, which led to the imposition of even greater pressure upon the complainant.

With the passing of Bill C-127, Parliament has abolished the offence of rape, replacing it with the offences of sexual assault. There are 3 categories of such assault: basic sexual assault, ie, sexual touching or sexual intercourse without consent, punishable by up to 10 years imprisonment; sexual assault with a weapon or threatened violence, punishable by up to 14 years in prison; and aggravated sexual assault, in which the victim is wounded or disfigured, punishable by up to life imprisonment. The distinction between men and women, in that only men could commit rape, has been abolished, since sexual assault is a crime which either sex can commit; spousal immunity has been ended, ie, sexual conduct between spouses must now be consensual; proof of vaginal penetration by the penis is no longer a requirement, and so failing to report the crime within a matter of hours (and certainly a day) will no longer be fatal to the Crown's case because of insufficient evidence as it previously might have been; and the doctrine of recent complaint has been abolished so that failure to complain at the first reasonable opportunity will no longer lead to a comment to the jury that may harm the complainant's credibility. MARGARET A. SOMERVILLE

Rapeseed, *see* CANOLA.

Raphael, William, painter (b in W Prussia 1833; d at Montréal 15 Mar 1914). A graduate of the Berlin School of Art, Raphael came to Canada in 1860, bringing academic status, as well as striking apricot colours, to his genre painting of the Montréal harbour and market life. The elegance and precision of his townspeople waiting by the docks is also found in his portraits in the Parliament Bldgs (Ottawa). He painted wild winter storms and wolves, and was included in *Picturesque Canada* (1882). By 1904 he was giving drawing and painting classes in Montréal and was appointed a member of the Conseil des arts et manufactures. ANNE McDOUGALL

Rapson, William Howard, chemical engineer, professor, consultant (b at Toronto 15 Sept 1912). After 12 years of research at the Canadian International Paper Co, Hawkesbury, Ont, he returned to U of T where he had received his doctorate in chemical engineering in 1941. In addition to teaching, research and administration at the university, he became consultant on the manufacture and application of chemicals for the pulp-and-paper industry. From his research came new methods of bleaching woodpulp which enabled pine wood to be used for strong, white paper for the first time and gave Canada important advantages in export trade. He also invented processes for the manufacturing industry. In recent years he turned his attention to the amelioration of water pollution by woodpulp mills. A fellow of the RSC and honorary fellow, and former president (1986) of the Chemical Institute of Canada, he has been honoured in Canada and abroad. In 1986 he received the Canada Council's Isaak Walton Killam Memorial Prize in Engineering.

MORRIS WAYMAN

Rasminsky, Louis, banker (b at Montréal 1 Feb 1908). Rasminsky played a major role in creating the post-WWII international monetary system. He attended U of T and London School of Economics, specializing in the study of money. In 1930 he joined the Economic and Financial Section of the League of Nations in Geneva, Switz, and by 1939 had established a high reputation. In 1940 he became a member of the Foreign Exchange Control Board, Ottawa, organizing its research and statistics section, and by 1942 was alternate chairman. Much of his time was devoted to producing a "Canadian plan" for an international monetary system. In meetings before and during the conference at Bretton Woods, NH, in 1944, Rasminsky's plan was thoroughly studied and partially accepted. After WWII Rasminsky rose through the BANK OF CANADA hierarchy to become governor in 1961. He headed the bank for 11 years, carefully shepherding MONETARY POLICY through difficult times. He was chairman of the board of governors of the International Development Research Inst 1973-78. J.L. GRANATSTEIN

Reading: J.L. Granatstein, *The Ottawa Men* (1982).

Rat, common name for certain mammals of order RODENTIA. Three species occur in Canada, the bushy-tailed wood rat (*Neotoma cinerea*) of the Cricetidae family being the only native. The Eurasian black rat and brown or Norway rat (*Rattus rattus, R. norvegicus,* respectively), of the Muridae family, were introduced to N America by man. The bushy-tailed wood rat, which may grow to 50 cm long, has a long, hairy tail and long, soft fur. It inhabits the CORDILLERA of western N America from the YT to New Mexico. It is solitary and nocturnal, feeds chiefly on vegetation, and scavenges around cottages. In Canada, it produces one litter annually (averaging 3-4 young). Black and brown rats have short, straight-haired coats and scaly, hairless tails. The brown rat is the larger, growing to 68 cm. Both species inhabit populated areas, black rats being found only along the BC coast, brown rats, in almost every inhabited region of Canada. These species are gregarious. The black rat, an excellent climber, inhabits lofts and roofs of houses or farm buildings. Brown rats mainly burrow. Both are prolific, reproducing throughout the year, mainly spring through autumn. The brown rat produces 3-12 (usually 5) litters annually, each averaging 9 young. These omnivorous rats eat food produced by humans, transmit disease and may even attack sleeping humans. They damage homes, transmission wires and drains. JEAN FERRON

Rat Control in Alberta, administered and coordinated by the Alberta Department of Agriculture, was established in 1950 to keep Alberta free of Norway rats (*see* RAT) which were introduced to the E coast of N America in 1775 and spread westward. They entered Saskatchewan about 1919 and moved NW at about 24 km per year. They were first reported on a farm on the eastern Alta border in 1950, and 30 rat infestations had been confirmed along 180 km of Alta's eastern border by fall 1951. The Agricultural Pest Act of Alberta (1942) authorized the minister of agriculture to designate as a pest any animal likely to destroy crops or livestock, and declared that landowners and municipalities must destroy and prevent the establishment of designated pests, and a buffer control zone was set up along the Sask border from Montana to Cold Lake. Municipal pest control officers (PCOs), supported by a public education program and a rat-poisoning program undertaken by a private firm in 1952-53, destroyed all rat infestations found. In 1954 the Department of Agriculture agreed to pay 50% of the salary and expenses of full-time PCOs for each municipality along the eastern border; by 1975 it was paying 100%. The cost of the rat control program rose from $50 000 in 1969-70 to $220 000 in 1986-87, but the latter includes expenditures for rabies control. Natural barriers, eg, Cypress Hills to the S, Rocky Mts to the W and boreal forest to the N, have halted rat migration into Alberta. Infestations rose to 637 between 1956 and 1959 but then dropped 1960 to 1980, when they varied from 36 to 216. In Alberta it is unlawful for anyone, except research institutions with the appropriate permits, to import, possess or transport live rats, even white laboratory rats. J. BOURNE

Rattenbury, Francis Mawson, architect (b at Leeds, Eng 11 Oct 1867; d at Bournemouth, Eng 28 Mar 1935). As a young architect, he left England for BC (1892) where he won the competition to design Victoria's Legislature Buildings. He won other government contracts to design various BC courthouses and designed homes for numerous wealthy clients. During the KLONDIKE GOLD RUSH he established 2 companies to carry men and supplies to the goldfields, but both had failed by 1899 and he returned to architecture. As architect for the Bank of Montreal he designed banks in Rossland, Nelson and New Westminster, and as house architect for the CPR he designed Victoria's Empress HOTEL. One of his last works in BC was the Crystal Garden in Victoria. Rattenbury's abilities as an architect have been questioned; he was known more for his grand schemes than the aesthetics of his architecture. His reputation fell after he left his wife and appeared publicly with his mistress, Alma Victoria Clarke Dolling Pakenham. They left Victoria for England about 1930; their life together soon disintegrated, and in 1935 Alma and her young lover, George Stoner, were charged with Rattenbury's murder. After being acquitted Alma committed suicide. Stoner was sentenced to life imprisonment but was later released.

DAVID R. ELLIOTT

Three species of rattlesnake are native to Canada, including the massasauga rattlesnake (*Sistrurus catenatus*) (*photo by Mary W. Ferguson*).

Rattlesnake, common name for 31 species of venomous viperid snakes in the genera *Crotalus* and *Sistrurus,* found from southern Canada to S America. Characteristic features include a broad, triangular head with movable fangs, a stout body and a "rattle" made up of unmolted, modified scales, each of which once capped the tip of the tail. The buzzing sound produced by rapidly vibrating the tail is believed to act as a defensive warning to intruders. Rattlesnakes are pit vipers, ie, have a heat-sensing pit on either side of the face. Three species are native to Canada: the western rattlesnake occurs in arid grasslands of Saskatchewan, Alberta and BC; the timber rattlesnake (probably extirpated in Canada) and massasauga rattlesnake are restricted to southern Ontario. Rattlesnakes often hibernate communally in rocky outcrops. Mating occurs in late summer; fertilization takes place the following spring. In early fall 5-10 live young are born. Females reproduce only every 2-3 years. Diet consists mainly of rodents, other small mammals and birds. The venom used to kill prey is a mixture of neurotoxins and hemotoxins (affecting nerve and blood tissues, respectively) delivered through the fangs. Rattlesnakes rarely strike humans, unless provoked or accidentally stepped on. The bite can cause painful swelling, muscular paralysis and tissue destruction, and may result in death. Less than 2% of all snakebites in N America are fatal if given medical attention. The incidence of snakebite in Canada is low.

J. MALCOLM MACARTNEY

Raudot, Antoine-Denis, intendant of New France, 1705-10 (b 1679; d at Versailles, France 28 July 1737). He had begun a career in the min-

istry of marine when he and his father Jacques RAUDOT were jointly appointed INTENDANT. Intelligent and rational in approach, Antoine-Denis devoted his energies to the colony's economy, depressed because of a glut of beaver on the European market. He wanted to improve the economic base by developing agriculture, fishing and lumbering. His most imaginative proposal, outlined in a lengthy 1706 memoir, was to establish a new city on Cape Breton I to act as an entrepôt for the French Empire, which by its location would ease the transportation problems between France and her colonies. Unable to achieve any such solution because of the ongoing WAR OF THE SPANISH SUCCESSION and because of his father's feud with Governor VAUDREUIL, he requested a recall and went on to a successful career in France.

MARY McDOUGALL MAUDE

Raudot, Jacques, intendant of NEW FRANCE, 1705-11 (b 1638; d at Paris, France 20 Feb 1728). He was related to the powerful Pontchartrain family and had had a distinguished legal career when he and his son Antoine-Denis RAUDOT were jointly appointed to the intendancy (with only Jacques salaried). Leaving finance largely to his son, Raudot concentrated his attention on the administration of justice and public order, attempting to bring in reforms of the seigneurial and judicial systems, education, agriculture and the militia. Though sociable and cultured, he had an emotional nature and was quick to take affront. He had a low opinion of Canadians in general and resented Governor VAUDREUIL's pre-eminent position. The last years of his term he spent unproductively feuding with the governor.

MARY McDOUGALL MAUDE

Raven, black bird with a purplish lustre, belonging, like the CROW, to genus *Corvus.* Ravens are similar to crows in appearance but larger, with heavier bills. Throat feathers are pointed and elongated. Ravens are scavengers and inhabit mountainous and wild hill country and seacoasts in both forested and unforested regions. The common raven (*C. corax*), a fierce and crafty bird, is found in both the Old and New Worlds. It is the only raven native to Canada and breeds from the high arctic islands (Prince Patrick I, southern Ellesmere I) across to Nfld, but is absent from central Alta, SW Man and central and southern Sask. The only other N American raven, the chihuahuan raven (*C. cryptoleucus*), is restricted to the southwestern US and Mexico. Ravens nest, in single pairs, on cliff ledges and in cavities, sometimes in trees. Evidence suggests that pairs mate for life. Ravens are majestic fliers and aerobatic displays seem to be involved in their courtship rituals. Their long lives, uncanny intelligence and fearlessness have given them a unique place in native mythology. LORRAINE G. D'AGINCOURT

Raven Symbolism The Indians of the Northwest Coast had numerous origin myths which explained, for example, how daylight began or why summer and winter alternate. The principal character in many of these myths is a powerful trickster, Raven, who is known to different tribes under various names. On the northern part of the coast, Raven was the most popular crest figure. In the south he was valued as a guardian spirit. Possessors of this spirit are fine hunters who enjoy special ease in killing game. Raven combined the characteristics of good and evil, and for his mischief he was turned black forever. The HAIDA, TLINGIT and TSIMSHIAN had moieties they called Raven.

RENÉ R. GADACZ

Rawson, Donald Strathearn, limnologist (b at Claremont, Ont 19 May 1905; d at Saskatoon 16 Feb 1961). His doctoral dissertation (U of T, 1929) on the bottom fauna of Lk Simcoe was a

model for ecological limnology for 20 years. His studies of Great Slave and Athabasca lakes opened those lakes to rational exploitation. He pioneered the study of Rocky Mountain lakes and was active on the prairies and Canadian Shield. His definition of the influence of lake basin on lake productivity is the basis of the widely used "morphoedaphic index" to estimate potential fish yield. He joined the faculty of U of Sask in 1928 and became head of biology in 1949.

J.R. NURSALL

Ray, fish with cartilaginous skeleton, closely related to sharks and belonging to order Rajiformes, subclass Elasmobranchii. The order includes sawfishes, guitarfishes, sting rays, electric rays, mantas and skates. Rays occur widely in world oceans, with some also inhabiting tropical or subtropical estuaries. Skates of genus *Raja* are the most common batoid fishes in temperate and cool seas of higher latitudes. There are about 400 species of batoids, some 100 of which are skates of genus *Raja.* In Canada, there are 17 species of batoid fishes in Atlantic waters, 8 in Pacific waters. Skates of genus *Raja* are the most common, comprising 13 species in Atlantic and 6 in Pacific waters. Electric and sting rays also occur occasionally off both coasts. Rays are flattened dorsoventrally, the body appearing disclike. The pectoral fins are attached to the side of the head. The mouth, nostrils and 5 pairs of gill slits are located on the white lower surface. A pair of spiracles occurs on the upper surface behind the eyes. The skin may be smooth or variously covered with short spines. The tail is usually elongate and whiplike. Species vary greatly in size, from a disc width of about 30 cm in small forms up to 6 m and 1300 kg for the mantas. Rays swim by an undulating motion of the pectoral fins or by a winglike flapping of the whole fin. Most rays feed primarily on bottom organisms, which they crush with their specialized grinding teeth. Skates are oviparous, depositing each large egg in a horny capsule, but most other rays bear living young. Rays are of little commercial importance. Skates are processed and marketed for food in Europe but in Canada they are a by-catch used mainly for fish meal and only occasionally eaten.

W.B. SCOTT

Ray, Carl, Cree artist, author (b at Sandy Lk, Ont 18 Jan 1943; d at Sioux Lookout, Ont 26 Sept 1978). After his schooling he became a trapper, logger and gold miner. He contracted tuberculosis and continued his painting as therapy. A superb draughtsman, Ray was capable of painting in several different styles and media. His work stands out in the flat 2-dimensional Anishnabe (Ojibwa) school for the implied third dimension he gave each creature and for the graceful curves and original compositions. His influence is evident in the work of many Anishnabe artists today. Universally admired, he was, with Norval MORRISSEAU, one of the first native Ontario artists to defy tribal taboos and depict the sacred legends. Ray was commissioned to work on the Indians of Canada Pavilion at EXPO 67. Editor of *Kitiwin,* the Sandy Lk newspaper, he was coauthor and illustrator of *The Sacred Legends of the Sandy Lake Cree* (1971).

MARY E. SOUTHCOTT

Reading: Mary E. Southcott, The Sound of the Drum: The Sacred Art of the Anishnabe (1984).

Raymond, Claude, baseball player (b at St-Jean-sur-Richelieu, Qué 7 May 1937). He played 17 seasons of professional baseball, 12 of them in the majors. "Frenchy," as his teammates called him, went to the MONTREAL EXPOS on 19 Aug 1969 when they bought his contract from the Atlanta Braves. His best season was 1970, with 23 saves. He also played for the Milwaukee Braves, for the

Houston Astros in the National League and a few games for the Chicago White Sox in the American League. In 1966 he took part in the major league all-star game. In Jan 1972 he retired, becoming a radio and TV baseball commentator. YVON DORE

Raymond, Louis-Marcel, botanist, man of letters (b at St-Jean, Qué 2 Dec 1915; d at Montréal 23 Aug 1972). He was a disciple and co-worker of Brother MARIE-VICTORIN at the Jardin Botanique in Montréal, and the literary quality of his scientific writing made it enjoyable to people outside the scientific community. Educated at U de M, he worked at the Jardin Botanique from 1943 until his retirement in 1970 at age 54. He wrote at least 240 scientific works and another 500 literary articles. His *Esquisse phytogéographique du Québec* (1950) is the only provincial phytogeographical study and was for 25 years the principal work on the subject. His treatises on the *Cypraceae* (the sedge family) of different countries are basic reference works. For the last 2 years of his life he worked on a botanical history of Canada. Raymond was interested in reintroducing poetry into theatre, and his *Le Jeu retrouvé* (1943) is a panorama of French history between the world wars. BERNARD BOIVIN

Rayner, Gordon, painter (b at Toronto 14 June 1935). Renowned for his manipulation of painting materials, Rayner has been called "the carpenter" of contemporary Canadian art. He learned his craft from his father, a landscape painter, and worked in various commercial art firms, including Wookey, Bush and Winter with Jack BUSH. An exhibition of William RONALD'S work at Toronto's Hart House turned his attention to abstraction. Rayner's early 1960s work, with its juxtaposed materials, experiments in canvas shape and sense of humour, reflects the neo-dada mood then prevalent in Toronto. In time he became a sumptuous painter of Canadian landscape, especially the area around Magnetawan, Ont. His cityscapes reflect his home on Toronto's Spadina Ave. Rayner's work boldly ricochets from one concern to another, even within the same PAINTING, though his inventions are united by his broad touch and spectacular sense of colour. JOAN MURRAY

Razilly, Isaac de, naval captain, knight of Malta, colonizer and lieutenant-general in Acadia (b at Château d'Oiseaumelle, Touraine, France 1587; d at La Hève, Acadia 1636). In 1626, after naval service in various parts of the world, Razilly wrote an influential memorandum to Cardinal Richelieu on French sea power and the need for the expansion of French colonies in N America. In 1632 he was selected to lead an expedition to re-establish the colony of ACADIA after 3 years of Scottish occupation. With his headquarters at La Hève and an establishment of some 300 soldiers and colonists, Razilly worked effectively to consolidate the French hold on Acadia until his unexpected death in 1635. JOHN G. REID

Razorbill (*Alca torda*), medium-sized (about 42 cm long) member of the AUK family. Head, neck and upperparts are black, with a narrow white line extending from the base of the laterally flattened bill to the eye; underparts are entirely white. Razorbills breed in loose groups on sheltered sites in rock crevices or under rock slabs and boulders. They first breed at 4-5 years. The one egg produced is incubated for 34-39 days. The chick is fed small fish by the parents for about 18 days and then leaves the colony for the sea, accompanied by one parent (the male), which cares for the chick for several weeks. Razorbills winter offshore. They breed along both coasts of the N Atlantic; in N America, mainly in small colonies throughout Atlantic Canada with most of the

population centered in southern Labrador. The northernmost colony in Canada is in Digges Sd at the eastern entrance to Hudson Bay and there may be small groups off southeastern Baffin I. The total world breeding population, estimated at about 700 000 pairs, is one of the smallest of any auk. Recently, substantial reduction in numbers has occurred throughout its range, probably because of mortality from oil spills, and in eastern Canada, by hunting as well. D.N. NETTLESHIP

Razutis, Al, filmmaker, videographer, holographer, professor (b at Bamberg, W Germany 28 Apr 1946). Razutis moved to Vancouver from the US in 1968. His interest in the garish and vivid imagery of popular media, his desire to produce strong sensations through his art and his willingness to deal with political issues tie him more closely to American West Coast filmmakers than to other Vancouver film artists, such as David RIMMER. A brilliant technician, Razutis was one of the first experimental filmmakers in Canada to use the optical printer and the video synthesizer. Razutis's films are collected in 2 large series: *Amerika* (1972-83), a study of the effects of "a media-excessive culture," and *Visual Essays: Origins of Film* (1973-82), which comprises a number of "essays" that attempt to reconstruct the vision of "cinematic creation occurring in the minds of cinema's 'primitives'." R. BRUCE ELDER

Reach For The Top (RFTT) Based on a successful US television program called G.E. College Bowl, the idea for a Canadian version was brought to CBC Canada by producer Richard St John and sold to CBC Vancouver in 1961. The first program of RFTT was broadcast that year and was hosted by West Coast free-lance broadcaster Terry Garner. The next year the program was picked up by CBC Edmonton and gradually spread across the country. By 1966, 23 stations in all 10 provinces were carrying it, with approximately 600 schools taking part. That year the first of the national playoffs was broadcast with Winnipeg quizmaster Bill Guest as host. Lorne Jenkin High in Barrhead, Alta, which offered a one-semester credit course based on the program, became the series' most successful competitors. The school represented Alberta in the national playoffs for 6 of the last 10 years of the program's life, winning the national finals twice.

Although initially a ratings winner, RFTT always generated controversy. Its proponents maintained that the program gave positive exposure to students who were academically proficient; but its opponents, such as Winnipeg writer Heather Robertson, suggested that "'Reach for the Top' continues to ram home the most deadly kind of memory work." By 1983, CBC surveys indicated that RFTT had lost its teenage audience. Only 12% of the audience was 18 or under while more than half was 55 and over. When steps were instituted to cancel the program the CBC received 800 letters and petitions of protest, representing about 4000 people. After MP Bud Cullen rose in the House to urge the CBC to save this "all-Canadian young people's show," the program was reprieved, but only temporarily. CBC dropped RFTT in 1985. A French version of the program, "Genies en Herbe," continues on Radio-Canada and the winners annually engage in worldwide competitions. COLIN MacLEAN

Read, John Erskine, lawyer, judge (b at Halifax 5 July 1888; d at Toronto 23 Dec 1973). A Dalhousie professor (and dean) of law in the 1920s, Read was present during the formative years of the Dept of External Affairs, which he served as legal adviser 1928-46, and the International Court of Justice at The Hague, where he was a judge 1946-58. In External Affairs, Read acted for

Canada in disputes such as the I'M ALONE case, seizing opportunities to extend Canada's legal independence, and rose to be deputy undersecretary of state. An expert in constitutional and international law, progressive in his views, he wrote *The Origins and Nature of the Law* (1955) and *The Rule of Law on the International Plane* (1961). NORMAN HILLMER

Read, Kenneth John, alpine skier (b at Ann Arbor, Mich 6 Nov 1955). He was raised in Calgary and began skiing at 3 and competing at 8. First selected to the World Cup Team in 1974, he opened the 1975 season with a victory in the downhill at Val d'Isère, France, the first World Cup win by a Canadian male. With 4 further World Cup victories, he was a key member of the "Crazy Canucks" downhill team which took the European press by storm in the late 1970s. He won 5 consecutive Canadian national championships 1975-1980 (the 1977 race was cancelled). He was co-winner of the 1978 Lou Marsh Trophy as Canada's outstanding athlete. After retirement in 1983 he has become a television commentator on skiing, an author (*White Circus*, 1987) and the first Canadian representative on the IOC Athlete's Committee. He was VP of the Canadian Olympic Assn, director of the Calgary Olympic Development Assn and spokesman for the 1988 Olympic Coin Program. MURRAY SHAW

Real Estate can refer to land itself (real property), including what grows or is built on the land; ownership of real property; and the real-estate business, ie, brokers, agents, builders, developers, property managers, mortgage lenders, investors, consultants and appraisers who work in the real-estate industry.

Real estate is commonly classified as residential (eg, houses, condominiums, duplexes), rural (eg, farms and ranches), commercial (income-generating, eg, shopping centres, apartments, office or industrial buildings) or institutional (eg, churches, schools, hospitals or airports). Land without improvements is regarded as residential, rural, commercial or institutional according to its intended use. Real estate is characterized by immobility, by durability (the availability of services or income over a long period) and by uniqueness (no 2 properties are identical), as well as by a special body of laws and legal institutions. Real-estate values tend to fluctuate, increasing during periods of (and in regions experiencing) rapid economic growth and remaining stable or declining during periods of (and in regions experiencing) slow economic growth. The durability of real estate contributes to the price fluctuations. For example, a small change in the rents of an apartment building may have a significant impact on its value if the new rent will be received for many years to come. Values may also fluctuate as a result of the slow adjustment of supply to a change in demand, and they are sometimes magnified through speculation (demand or supply arising from expectations of further price changes). Improvements to one property generally affect the value of another, and transaction costs are high (commissions, legal and appraisal fees, financing, surveying and registration costs). For residential properties the commission alone often amounts to 6% or 7% of the selling price.

It is common for vendors to use a real-estate agent to assist with the sale. The property is then generally listed for sale with a real-estate company (listing agent) which handles marketing, advertising, open houses, placement of signs, etc. The listing agent often co-operates with other real-estate companies, through a multiple-listing service, whereby a member firm may list properties to be sold by other members, as well as sell properties listed by others. The firm finding a purchaser becomes the selling agent. Both listing and selling agents are agents of the vendor, who pays the commission when the property changes hands. Normally, no commission is payable if the deal does not close. If more than one company is involved in the transaction, the commission is shared among them, often equally, but unequal splits are also common. The companies in turn share with the sales people involved. It is common for the actual transfer and registration, as well as all legal documents, to be handled by a lawyer. The term "deal pending" refers to a property being sold with one or more conditions of the sale yet to be satisfied, eg, a mortgage to be arranged. The comparatively high value of real estate would put it beyond the reach of most people were it not for mortgages. The security of real estate enables financial institutions to lend a substantial portion of the value of the property, making ownership possible with a limited amount of owner equity (nonmortgaged portion of value). This, however, also makes real-estate values dependent on mortgage rates, which then become another source of price fluctuations.

Ownership rights originally extended from the centre of the earth to the sky, but are now generally limited to surface rights only. In Canada, subsurface rights, particularly mineral rights, are usually reserved by the Crown, even where the real estate is privately owned. Air rights are also held by the Crown. In addition, government also retains the right to tax, expropriate, escheat (inherit in the absence of heirs) and regulate (through land-use and zoning laws, building, health and fire codes, or rent controls). Property title in many provinces is registered in the local land-titles office and provides proof of ownership. Real estate can be owned individually or collectively, by corporations, co-operatives, partnerships, syndicates, etc (see PROPERTY LAW).

Real estate is formally referred to by its legal description, eg, in cities, towns and hamlets by lot, block and plan. Condominiums (high-rise, row house or office) are described by unit number and condominium plan. In rural areas land is normally referred to by sections, townships, ranges and meridians.

Housing starts are an important economic indicator, and construction expenditures play a major role in the economy. The annual total of housing and housing-related expenditures generally amounts to close to 20% of GDP. In 1985 the total value of all mortgage loans outstanding in Canada was $183.5 billion; the total value of new mortgage loans placed was $30 billion; and the total value of all building permits issued in that year (which conveys approximately the value of additions to the stock of buildings and other improvements, but not the value of land upon which they are being built) amounted to $19.5 billion. The estimated total amount of property tax collected in 1986 was $16.8 billion, compared to $78.4 billion for income tax.

The total value of all real-estate sales processed through the Multiple Listing Service (MLS) systems in Canada during 1986 exceeded $29.1 billion. There were in excess of 300 000 total transactions by some 70 000 members of the Canadian Real Estate Association. Valuation of real property for a variety of purposes is performed by accredited appraisers. The national association of professional real-estate appraisers, the Appraisal Institute of Canada, was formed in 1938, and in 1987 had about 6000 members. Valuation (assessment) for property tax purposes is performed by assessors. A number of universities (eg, UBC, Laval) offer degree programs in real estate and urban and land economics. There are also a number of journals devoted to real estate.

CHRISTIAN T.L. JANSSEN

Reading: M. A. Goldberg and P. Chinloy, *Urban Land Economics* (1984).

Real Wages are estimates of money or nominal wages that have been adjusted to take into account their effective purchasing power or command over goods and services. The actual calculation of real-wage estimates involves dividing an estimate of money income (hourly, weekly or annual wages) by an index of consumer prices for the region being considered. The CONSUMER PRICE INDEX is a weighted sum of the percentage change in the price of commodities commonly bought by households compared to a particular base year.

From 1870 to 1950 real hourly wages of wage earners increased by over 346% – an annual average rate of 1.9%. The change did not occur at a constant rate: variations between periods are caused by cyclical factors that influence the demand of businesses for labour and the price level faced by consumers. Over the longer run, however, the fundamental determinant of the growth rate of real wages is the productivity of labour, which itself is determined by the skills of the labour force, CAPITAL FORMATION by business, and technological change. Canadian weekly money and real wages experienced an increase of 370.3% from 1961 to 1981. This change largely reflected a high rate of INFLATION, particularly during the late 1960s and throughout the 1970s. In the period 1981-85, however, there was no growth in real wages, in part reflecting both the slowdown in productivity growth and the generally sluggish economic conditions.

Estimates of national real wages can be somewhat misleading as a measure of individual economic well-being. The tendency toward a diminishing work week must be taken into account. In 1870 the standard work week in goods producing industries was 64.0 hours; by 1967 it was down to 40.8 hours and in mid-1987 the average work week was 38.8 hours. This decline in the length of the work week means that the change in hourly real wages tends to overestimate the growth of weekly real incomes. UNEMPLOYMENT is also neglected. Even though real wages rose during the Great Depression, high levels of unemployment meant that expected real incomes (real wages weighted by the probability of employment) probably declined significantly. Finally, in the Canadian context an emphasis on national real wages also conceals differences in real wage levels and trends between regions. M.B. PERCY

Reaney, James Crerar, poet, playwright, children's writer, professor, literary critic (b at Easthope, near Stratford, Ont 1 Sept 1926). Reaney has been engaged in an energetic program of "rousing the faculties" by holding up the shaping mirror of literary forms to life in Canada, particularly in southwestern Ontario. His first book, *The Red Heart* (1949), won the first of his 3 Gov Gen's awards, the other 2 going to *A Suit of Nettles* (1958) and a joint award to *Twelve Letters to a Small Town* (1962) and *The Killdeer and Other Plays* (1962). Reaney's poetry, collected in *Poems* (1972), has earned him a reputation as an erudite poet at once deriving structures from metaphor, mythology and a cosmopolitan literary tradition while deeply rooted in a regional sense of place. His latest book of poetry was *Imprecautions* (1984).

In 1960 Reaney moved from Winnipeg, where he had been teaching English at U Man, to London, Ont, to join Western's English department. In a shift of emphasis from poetry to the public and communal form of drama, he followed up *The Killdeer* with *Colours in the Dark* (1969), *Listen to the Wind* (1972), *Masks of Childhood* (1972) and plays for children. *Take the Big Picture*, juvenile fiction, was published in 1986. In such plays as

Wacousta, The Canadian Brothers and his landmark trilogy The Donnellys, Reaney has combined archival research, poetry, elements of romance and melodrama, mime and myth to tell the central stories and legends of Ontario.

CATHERINE ROSS

Rebellion Losses Bill, modelled on Upper Canadian legislation, was introduced by Louis LAFONTAINE in Feb 1849 to compensate Lower Canadians whose property had been damaged during the Rebellions of 1837-38 (totalling approximately £100 000). It was similar to legislation for Upper Canada and was based upon a claims report approved in principle in 1846. LaFontaine saw the bill as a symbolic means to heal the wounds of the rebellion and buttress French Canadian claims to equality and power in the Canadas by testing the strength of responsible government. Consequently the growing influence of Louis-Joseph PAPINEAU could be stemmed. The Tories saw the bill as a sign of French domination of the union and their own loss of power; they criticized it as payment for disloyalty. (In fact, because it was difficult in any given instance to determine which side in the conflict had caused the damage, some rebels, as well as those who remained loyal to the government, were compensated for losses; only those convicted or exiled were excluded.) Over heated Tory opposition, the legislation was passed by a majority of Reformers in both sections; the Tories then demanded that Gov Gen Lord ELGIN refuse assent. Despite his misgivings, Elgin understood the meaning of local responsibility and signed the bill into law 25 April 1849. He was attacked by an English-speaking mob in Montréal and the Parliament buildings were burned (see MONTRÉAL RIOTS). The Montréal merchants, feeling the effects of an economic depression, advocated ANNEXATION to the US. However, Elgin was supported by the British government, and the concept of RESPONSIBLE GOVERNMENT was confirmed. DAVID MILLS

Rebellions of 1837 took place in both Upper and Lower Canada. In LOWER CANADA the rebellion was in large part an expression of a resurgent FRENCH CANADIAN NATIONALISM. The French Canadian majority constituted the overwhelming majority in the locally elected Assembly established by the Canada or CONSTITUTIONAL ACT, 1791.

Following the WAR OF 1812, the Assembly was dominated by the representatives of the French Canadian middle class, who, under the leadership of a new professional elite, developed a national consciousness and sought to wrest power from the Roman Catholic Church, in areas such as education, and from the anglophone merchant class which was expanding its economic base because of the rapid growth in the timber trade. The nationalists, led by Louis-Joseph PAPINEAU, who was elected Speaker of the Assembly in 1815, first organized the PARTI CANADIEN and then the Patriote Party after 1826. They demanded the right to determine how all of the revenues raised within the colony were spent, challenged the authority of the appointed upper house or Legislative Council, and sought control over the provincial civil service, including the advisory body to the governor, the Executive Council. During the 1820s, these demands were vigorously resisted by Gov Gen the earl of Dalhousie, but after a select committee of the British House of Commons reported unfavourably on his activities in 1828, the British Colonial Office embarked upon a new policy of conciliating the Lower Canadian Assembly and replaced Dalhousie with a series of more conciliatory governors: Sir James KEMPT 1828-30, Lord AYLMER 1830-35 and Lord GOSFORD 1835-38. Yet despite their efforts, the situation in Lower Canada gradually deteriorated.

The early 1830s was a period of widespread economic distress, fueled by a rapidly worsening agricultural crisis which brought many French Canadian habitants to the verge of starvation. At the same time, the province also saw a rapid increase in emigration from the British Isles, which gave the British minority close to a numerical majority in the urban centres of Montréal and Québec. The immigrants brought with them the dreaded CHOLERA which killed many thousands of French Canadians and fed the growing xenophobia of the French Canadian majority. A series of incidents, such as the shooting deaths of 3 French Canadians by British troops during an electoral riot in 1832, increased tensions between the majority and the minority and led to increased polarization. The Patriote Party, shorn of its moderate wing and of most anglophone support, became more extreme in its demands, which it embodied in 92 Resolutions adopted by the Assembly in 1834.

The Assembly refused to vote any supplies, with the result that the civil service went unpaid, all public works ground to a halt and the government was virtually paralyzed. The British minority reacted by forming constitutional associations and appealing to the British government to resist the pretensions of the Assembly. Since neither the Patriote Party nor the British Party was a monolithic entity there was more to Lower Canadian politics than "two nations warring in the bosom of a single state," as Lord DURHAM described the problem in 1838, but as the extremists on both sides drifted toward violence, the ethnic division became more pronounced. In Mar 1837 the British government reluctantly pushed through the British Parliament the 10 Russell Resolutions rejecting all the major demands of the PATRIOTES and gave Lord Gosford the power to take money from the provincial treasury to pay the officials in the colony. The Patriotes organized a boycott of British goods, held mass protest rallies across the colony and began seriously to prepare for an armed insurrection, although there were deep divisions among the Patriote leadership over this strategy and the moderates agreed to it in the belief that the British government would back down if faced by the prospect of an uprising.

The Patriotes had fatally underestimated the resolve of the British government, which had already begun to despatch troops to Lower Canada from throughout the empire and which began to turn a blind eye to the rifle clubs organized by the British minority. In Montréal the militant Patriotes established the FILS DE LA LIBERTÉ and on Nov 6 there was a skirmish between the latter and the DORIC CLUB, which represented the militant Anglophones. Meanwhile British authority in the countryside rapidly deteriorated as French Canadians began to practise widespread civil disobedience. On 16 Nov 1837 the government sought to forestall the rebellion by arresting the Patriote leaders, who took refuge in the countryside. On Nov 23 the government forces under Col Charles Gore suffered a minor defeat in the first major engagement of the rebellion, at St-Denis (*see* ST-DENIS, BATTLE OF), but the ill-organized, poorly equipped and badly led Patriotes were crushed by a force of British regulars under Col Charles Wetherall 2 days later at St-Charles (*see* ST-CHARLES, BATTLE OF), despite the desperate courage displayed by the rebels. On Nov 30 Gore returned to St-Denis, but the town surrendered without a struggle and the soldiers sacked it, leaving 50 homes blazing. On Dec 14 the British commander in chief, Sir John COLBORNE, captured St-Eustache (*see* ST-EUSTACHE, BATTLE OF), after fierce resistance from the habitants under Jean-Olivier CHÉNIER's leadership, and the first rebellion collapsed. There was widespread looting and burning of French

Lower Canada proclamation charging Louis-Joseph Papineau with high treason (*courtesy National Archives of Canada/C-54741*).

Canadian settlements by the British volunteers. Papineau and a number of the Patriote leaders fled to the US. Several hundred insurgents were wounded or killed, many more were captured, and the Constitution was suspended. Lord Durham, sent out as governor general and special commissioner, issued an amnesty for most of the prisoners and tried to restore harmony, but when his measures were inadequately supported by the home government, he resigned.

With the encouragement of American sympathizers who had organized themselves into HUNTERS' LODGES, the rebels had been preparing for a second rebellion, which broke out immediately upon Durham's departure in early Nov 1838. Led by Dr Robert Nelson and Dr Cyrille Côté, the rebels hoped to be able to cut communications between Montréal and the S shore of the St Lawrence and thus set off a mass uprising of the habitants. They were poorly organized and supplied and were defeated at Napierville and Odelltown. One group of rebels was captured at Caughnawaga by the Iroquois, who were allied with the British. The Patriotes defeated a small British force at Beauharnois on Nov 9 but then scattered as a larger force approached. Within a week the second outbreak had been put down, almost entirely by the actions of the volunteers, who rampaged across the country, leaving a trail of devastation. The makeshift prisons were filled with suspects and 108 men were convicted by court-martials. Rumours of risings and invasions from the US continued, but there was no substance to them and even Papineau left for exile in Paris. Of the 99 condemned to death, only 12 went to the gallows, while 58 were transported to Australia. In total the 6 battles of both campaigns left 325 dead, 27 of them soldiers and the rest rebels, while 13 men were executed (one by the rebels), one was murdered, one committed suicide and 2 prisoners were shot.

By comparison the UPPER CANADA rebellion was a more limited affair. There was growing discontent with the network of officials, erroneously described as the FAMILY COMPACT, who dominated

the administration of the government and controlled the distribution of patronage throughout the province. Popular opposition developed over land-granting policies, particularly the setting aside of large blocks of land as CLERGY RESERVES, the education policies of the government and its economic priorities, and the general favouritism shown to the Church of England and its supporters and to recent emigrants from Britain. This discontent was strongest among the American-born settlers who had migrated prior to the War of 1812 – the so-called late loyalists – and their descendants, nonconformist in their religious views and somewhat republican in their political sympathies, who were denied political rights during the struggle over the ALIEN QUESTION in the 1820s. Although the settlers of American origin constituted a declining proportion of the population as British immigrants flooded into Upper Canada in the early 1830s, the oligarchic form of government which had been established by the CONSTITUTIONAL ACT of 1791 came increasingly under attack, and the nascent Reform Party won control of the Assembly in 1828 and again in 1834. Lt-Gov Sir Francis Bond HEAD was sent to the colony to appease the reform majority in the Assembly, but he succeeded only in precipitating a rebellion. He assisted the conservatives in winning the election of 1836, in which Marshall Spring BIDWELL, who had been Speaker of the Assembly and the real head of the reform movement, and many of the moderate reformers, such as Robert BALDWIN, were defeated. The more extreme elements in the Reform Party began to mobilize under the leadership of William Lyon MACKENZIE.

Mackenzie at first sought only to exert pressure on the government by organizing a network of political unions and a boycott of imported goods and by entering into a working relationship with the reformers of Lower Canada. At least until the late summer of 1837, he did not decide to turn from extra-parliamentary protest to rebellion. But during 1837 political unrest grew more serious because of a crisis in the international economy which spread to Upper Canada and uneven crop yields which led to food shortages. When Head sent all the troops in the colony to Lower Canada, Mackenzie persuaded the radicals on Nov 16 to issue a draft constitution for Upper Canada, modelled on that of the US, and to attempt to seize control of the government in early Dec. Something close to 1000 men gathered at Montgomery's tavern in Toronto over the 4 days of Mackenzie's rebellion between Dec 5-8. They came largely from the Home District north of Toronto and represented a cross section of the agrarian community from which Mackenzie had always drawn the bulk of his support, with a disproportionate number of settlers of American origin and of members of the dissenting sects. On Dec 5 some 500-700 rebels bearing rifles, staves and pitchforks marched S on Yonge St to meet a smaller force of about 200-250 volunteers and militia. They ran into a picket of about 20 loyalists who opened fire and then fled. The front rank of the rebels returned the fire and then dropped to the ground. In the poor early evening light the rebel force thought the men in the front had been killed and they turned and ran. In total only 3 men, 2 rebels and one loyalist lost their lives during the initial stages of the rebellion. On Dec 8 a force of 1000-1500 loyalists marched to Montgomery's tavern and dispersed the remaining rebels. A second unco-ordinated outbreak took place a few days later near Brantford, where 500 men gathered under the leadership of Charles DUNCOMBE, but they too were easily dispersed by volunteers under the command of Sir Allan MACNAB. Mackenzie and Duncombe escaped to the US. With the support of those Americans who wished

Patriote insurgents at Beauharnois, Lower Canada, watercolour by Mrs E. Ellice (*courtesy National Archives of Canada/C-13392*).

to liberate Canada from British rule, Mackenzie took control of Navy Island and proclaimed a republic of Upper Canada, but he was forced to withdraw on Jan 14 after Canadian volunteers burned the rebel supply ship CAROLINE. During 1838 the rebels continued to organize expeditions across the border, including major raids at Pelée I in Lk Erie in Feb, where a substantial American force was driven back after a severe fight, at Short Hills on June 30, and at Prescott (*see* WINDMILL, BATTLE OF) in mid-Nov and Windsor in early Dec. These raids, though poorly organized and easily crushed, kept the border in a constant state of turmoil and brought Britain and the US to the verge of war. Moreover, the rebellion and the raids played into the hands of the ultra-Tory faction in Upper Canada who were placed in a temporary ascendancy. Although only 2 of the original rebels, Samuel LOUNT and Peter MATTHEWS, were executed, many reformers, including Bidwell, fearing reprisals, fled to the US and the conflicts along the border led to many more executions, deaths and deportations than the original, somewhat pathetic uprising.

The causes and consequences of both rebellions remain controversial. Some writers point to the inherent weaknesses of the 1791 constitutional arrangements, which gave the elected assemblies the power to thwart the executive but not to control it, and blame the British government for failing to respond adequately to the legitimate grievances of the colonists. But this interpretation ignores the sincere effort which was made after 1828 to conciliate the reformers in both colonies, downplays the ethnic division in Lower Canada and overlooks the fact that the majority of colonists did not support the rebellion in Upper Canada. In Lower Canada the rebellion was precipitated by the economic and social tensions of the 1830s, but the underlying cause was the conflict between the French Canadian majority, which demanded that all power be centralized in the popularly elected Assembly, which it controlled, and the British minority, which was no less determined to resist French Canadian domination. The Patriote leadership to some extent drifted into rebellion, which it was ill equipped to win, and many moderate French

Canadians opposed the use of force, including the hierarchy of the Roman Catholic Church, which benefited from the defeat of the anticlerical Patriote leadership. But the revolt had widespread support among the French Canadian population and Papineau and his lieutenants earned a lasting place in the hearts of French Canadian nationalists. In Upper Canada there is a continuing debate over who was responsible for the rebellion and the degree of popular support it commanded among the people. Among more radical historians there is considerable sympathy for the rebels and a feeling that they represented the authentic voice of the majority, at least of the colonial working classes. But the majority view is that the uprising had limited support and was largely a historical accident precipitated by the inexcusable partisanship of Head and the rash behaviour of that most unlikely of Canadian heroes, Mackenzie. Few historians see any necessary connection between the 2 outbreaks, though without the Lower Canadian rebellion the Upper Canadian revolt would probably not have taken place.

The impact of the rebellions is equally disputable. The influence of the radicals in both colonies was undermined and more moderate leaders, Louis-Hippolyte LAFONTAINE in Lower Canada and Robert Baldwin in Upper Canada, reconstructed the reform movement. The rebellions led directly to the appointment of Lord Durham and the Durham Report, which recommended that the Canadas be united into one colony, as the British minority, particularly the merchant class, had long demanded, and the introduction of what became known as RESPONSIBLE GOVERNMENT. The ACT OF UNION was passed in 1840 and the United PROVINCE OF CANADA came into being in 1841; the details of responsible government were gradually worked out between 1841 and 1848. Whether the rebel leaders should be given paternity for these measures, both of which they opposed, remains controversial. In an earlier period, most writers insisted that without the rebellions change would have come slowly, if at all. The more recent trend is to dismiss the rebellions as unnecessary since Britain was moving towards gradual reform. But without some form of wider union, it is doubtful whether any British government could have gone further in the direction of devolution in Lower Canada, and it is even more doubtful whether any form of union could have been forced on the French Canadians without widespread resistance. In this sense, the rebellion in Lower Canada did break the impasse that had been reached in the mid-1830s. It is more difficult to find any redeeming purpose for the rebellion in Upper Canada, although by discrediting extremists on both sides of the political spectrum it did assist in the rise to power of moderates who focused on the campaign for responsible government and were thus prepared to make a success of the union. Yet there can be no doubt that even among conservative historians who see the rebellions as unnecessary bloodletting, which complicated and probably delayed the transition to greater self-government, there remains considerable sympathy for the attempts of the rebels to establish a more popular system of government, and the status of Mackenzie and Papineau as Canadian heroes, like that of another ill-fated rebel, Louis Riel, seems secure.   P.A. BUCKNER

Reading: P.A. Buckner, *The Transition to Responsible Government: British Policy in British North America 1815-1850* (1985); G. Craig, *Upper Canada* (1963); Jacques Monet, *The Last Cannon Shot* (1967); Desmond Morton, *Rebellions in Canada* (1979); F. Ouellet, *Social and Economic History of Québec* (tr 1980) and *Lower Canada 1791-1840: Social Change and Nationalism* (1980); Colin Read, *The Rising in Western Upper Canada* (1980); Read and Ronald J. Stagg, *The Rebellion of 1837 in Upper Canada* (1985);

Elinor Kyte Senior, *Redcoats and Patriotes: The Rebellions in Lower Canada 1837-38* (1985).

Recession, technically, 2 or more successive quarters of declines in real Gross Domestic Product, calculated by adjusting for price changes. For example, if GDP increases by 12% and the price level by 8%, real GDP has risen by 4%. Recessions are caused by a decline in one or more of the components of aggregate demand for goods and services – consumer expenditure, business-investment expenditure, government expenditure or exports. Investment expenditure is the most volatile component. In a recession the demand for the products of most businesses declines, causing a fall in sales, production and employment. Recessions can usually be halted by expansionary monetary policy, which involves increasing the money supply, thus reducing interest rates and making credit easier to obtain, or by expansionary FISCAL POLICY, which involves increased government expenditure. One reason for the reduced severity of recessions after WWII is the effect of built-in stabilizers (mechanisms that automatically increase government expenditure in downturns and reduce it in upturns), eg, unemployment insurance. A depression is a severe recession.   W.C. RIDDELL

Reciprocity, a mutual reduction of duties charged on goods exchanged between Canada and the US. The movement toward reciprocity began 1846-50 in Canada West and the Maritime colonies, particularly New Brunswick. Its earliest major advocate in Upper Canada was William Merritt. British diplomats negotiated in Washington without success before 1852, when a dispute developed over the rights of American fishermen in British coastal waters in N America. Both governments became anxious for a comprehensive settlement to dispose of the reciprocity and the fisheries issues. The Reciprocity Treaty was finally signed by BNA Gov Gen Lord ELGIN and US Secretary of State William Marcy, 6 June 1854. It was accepted by the US Congress in Aug. The treaty's principal provisions were the admission of American fishermen to the Atlantic coastal fisheries of BNA, a similar privilege to British N American fishermen in US coastal waters N of 36° N lat, and the establishment of FREE TRADE in a considerable list of natural products. Trade between the US and the colonies increased sharply after 1854, although other factors such as the Canadian railway boom and the effects of the AMERICAN CIVIL WAR (1861-65) were largely responsible.

At first the treaty was popular in both countries, but owing to a combination of political and economic factors it became unpopular in the US. Abrogated by the US, it ceased to be operative on 17 Mar 1866. Canadians continued to desire renewal, and John A. MACDONALD, George BROWN, Charles TUPPER and others made pilgrimages to Washington without success. A notable disappointment was Macdonald's failure to have a large measure of reciprocity included in the 1871 Treaty of WASHINGTON. In the 1880s an extensive free-trade arrangement, called "commercial union" or "unrestricted reciprocity," was advocated by Erastus WIMAN, Richard CARTWRIGHT and others, but protectionist and pro-British sentiments brought about the rejection of these proposals during the 1891 general election. The last major attempt at reciprocity was negotiated in 1911 by the Liberal government of Sir Wilfrid LAURIER. This Reciprocity Agreement, to be implemented by concurrent legislation, provided for free trade in natural products and the reduction of duties on a variety of other products. The agreement was accepted by the US Congress but repudiated by Canadians, who ousted the Liberals in the general election of 21 Sept 1911. After 1911 reciprocity played a less prominent part in CANADI-AN-AMERICAN RELATIONS. In 1935 the Mackenzie KING administration negotiated a trade agreement which was much less sweeping in its removal of trade barriers than that of 1854. In 1938 a new and more comprehensive trade agreement was signed, granting Canada additional concessions as well as those in the 1935 agreement. The 1938 agreement was suspended in 1948 after participation of both countries in the GENERAL AGREEMENT ON TARIFFS AND TRADE (GATT).   D.C. MASTERS

Reading: J.B. Brebner, *North Atlantic Triangle* (1945); D.C. Masters, *The Reciprocity Treaty of 1854* (2nd ed, 1963).

Récollets, a reformed branch of the Franciscan family, came to France at the end of the 16th century. The main objective of the Récollets was to observe more strictly the Rule of St Francis, and like other semiautonomous branches, they came under the minister general of the Franciscans. The Récollets came to New France in 1615 and were present at various times in Acadia, Newfoundland and Québec. Missionaries and preachers, they were known for their simple and austere life; however, in 1763 British authorities forbade them to receive novices, and thus the order disappeared in 1848 when the last Canadian Récollet died in Montréal. Récollets returned to Trois-Rivières, Qué, in 1888 but they were united in 1897 with other branches to form the order known today as the Friars Minor (or Franciscans).

MICHEL THÉRIAULT

Reconstruction, the process of readjustment to a peacetime economy following WWII. Many believed the end of the war would mean a return to the economic depression of the 1930s, with falling production and widespread unemployment. When the Mackenzie KING government established a Dept of Reconstruction in 1944, however, it turned the department over to C.D. HOWE, one of the most optimistic men in the Cabinet. Howe believed there would be a shortage of goods at war's end rather than a surplus, and he concentrated on reconversion of factories to civilian and consumer production, while stimulating the construction industry to make up for losses since the onset of the Great Depression. Howe's program was very successful; government regulations were largely abolished and Canada was returned to a free-enterprise economy. *See also* WORLD WAR II; HISTORY SINCE CONFEDERATION.

ROBERT BOTHWELL

Recording Industry Sound recordings were first manufactured in Canada in 1900 by the Berliner Gramophone Co in Montréal, from masters recorded by the company's European and US companies. Berliner's first Canadian recording artist was French Canadian baritone Joseph Saucier. Before 1960 nearly all records sold in Canada were of non-Canadian performers; however, a steady growth in the production and sale of records by Canadians resulted from the worldwide boom in the record industry as popular music became a major cultural force in the late 1960s. This trend was augmented by a radio broadcast ruling implemented in 1970 by the CRTC (now the CANADIAN RADIO-TELEVISION AND TELECOMMUNICATIONS COMMISSION) which required that AM broadcasters play a minimum of 30% Canadian material in a week. To qualify as "Can con" (Canadian Content), a recording must be Canadian in 2 of the 4 following criteria: music, artist, production or lyrics (known as the MAPL code). While there were many attempts to start Canadian-owned record companies during the 1960s, few survived prior to the implementation of the "Can con" rulings.

Retail sales of records in Canada in 1986 were valued at approximately $600 million. Canadian-owned companies accounted for about 10% of those sales. The other 90% of the market was held by a handful of multinational companies, but only 10% of their releases were Canadian, while 50% of the recordings released by Canadian-owned firms were "Can con." Because of the limited size of the domestic market, Canadian companies depend on foreign income for a significant portion of their earnings. In general, inadequate investment capital, rapidly escalating costs owing to new technology, home taping, poor marketing skills and the lack of a viable independent distribution network in Canada are the primary causes for the market imbalance and the slow pace at which the market share for independents is increasing. Figures compiled for 1986 indicate that the recording industry accounts for roughly 15 000 employees in Canada, with 65% in retail, 5% in distribution and 30% in production (including the creative artists – composers, songwriters and performers). Because of a tariff imposed on the physical form (disc, tape or compact disc), the manufacturing of foreign-originated works is largely done in Canada. The creative work itself is not taxed, in conformity with international agreements.

In 1986, 86% of the recordings sold in Canada were in the "popular" music category – pop, rock and middle-of-the-road. In descending order the remaining sales were in classical, country/folk, children's and jazz recordings. Examples of internationally known Canadian performers are RUSH, Bryan ADAMS and Glass Tiger (in the rock idiom); Anne MURRAY, Gordon LIGHTFOOT, Bruce COCKBURN and René Simard (in the middle-of-the-road genres); Maureen FORRESTER, Glenn GOULD, Ofra HARNOY, Liona BOYD, Louis LORTIE, Louis QUILICO, Jon VICKERS and Anton KUERTI (in the classical field); Oscar PETERSON, Hagood HARDY and the Boss Brass (in jazz); and chansonniers Pauline JULIEN and Félix LECLERC.

The Canadian Broadcasting Corporation has played an important role in recording Canadian classical artists and compositions. The first album was issued in 1945, but it was not until the early 1970s, when it became clear that the CBC's listeners were anxious to hear more of the performances that were available on radio and TV, that they offered records for sale to the public. Within 10 years, the Canadian Broadcasting Corporation has become the largest manufacturer and distributor of Canadian classical recordings.

In Canada, the performer is paid in the form of royalties on records sold. Publishers and composers are paid from "mechanical" royalties, a fixed fee paid for each record manufactured. Mechanical royalties are collected on behalf of artists and publishers by the Canadian Mechanical Reproduction Rights Agency (CMRRA) and the Société du droit de reproduction des auteurs, compositeurs et éditeurs du Canada (SODRAC). Performance royalties are paid to composers and publishers for the use of the music for public broadcast purposes, such as radio or television broadcasts.

Performance royalties are collected and disbursed by 2 associations in Canada: the Composers, Authors and Publishers Association of Canada (CAPAC) and the Performing Rights Organization of Canada (PROCan). The entire payment scheme is dictated by the Copyright Act of Canada and by negotiated agreements between rights holders and record companies.

Trade associations are active in the recording industry. The multinationals are represented by the Canadian Recording Industry Assn (CRIA); the independent sector by the Canadian Independent Record Production Assn (CIRPA) and the Association du disque et de l'industrie du spectacle québécois (ADISQ); and publishers by the Canadian Music Publishers Assn (CMPA). These associations deal with industry-wide issues, including responding to home taping, which drains estimated millions from the industry each year; encouraging private-sector investment; creating a viable government cultural and economic policy; and understanding and adapting to new technologies such as compact disc (CD), digital audiotape (DAT), music videos, and all the new forms of distribution by fibre optics cable and direct satellite to home systems.

The JUNO AWARDS (est 1964) are the awards presented annually by the Canadian Academy of Recording Arts and Sciences (CARAS). There are a variety of categories in the fields of performance, production and composition, and awards are made on the basis of record sales over a specific period. ADISQ introduced its own awards in 1979 called the Felix Awards. *See also* CHAMBER MUSIC; COUNTRY AND WESTERN MUSIC; FOLK MUSIC; JAZZ; MUSIC PUBLISHING; ORCHESTRAL MUSIC; POPULAR MUSIC.   CANADIAN INDEPENDENT RECORD PRODUCTION ASSOCIATION

Reading: Encyclopedia of Music in Canada (1981); E.B. Moogk, *Roll Back the Years/En remontant les annees* (1975).

Recycling Canadians generate about 2-2.5 kg of garbage per person per day, of which about 50-60% is household garbage. In 1984 disposal costs averaged about $40 per person per year. With an effective recycling program, half of household refuse could be recycled as useful resources. There is a major move into community recycling programs – over 50% of Ontario's population received curbside collection of recyclables during the late 1980s – as well as increased interest in "energy from waste" for a variety of materials.

Recycling can be accomplished centrally, after collection, or at source (eg, in the household). Post-collection separation is rarely economically feasible, involving as it does mixing materials and then transporting them to an expensive plant to be separated into components again. Most existing central plants shred the garbage and separate glass and tinplate, a low value ($0-20/t) ferrous metal composing 5% by weight of garbage (ie, tin cans). The remaining garbage is burned to produce steam or heat, which may be sold at widely varying values ($0-30/t of garbage burned). Ash can be sold as aggregate for concrete in some areas of the country. Capital and operating costs for a recycling plant would be about $50-60/t of garbage processed. These costs would be offset by disposal cost savings of $4-35/t, depending upon location.

Separation at source requires an education program and commitments by householders not to mix garbage, as they currently do in most communities. It also requires a system of local depots for recycled material or separate pickups from households. Organic materials, however, can be recycled fairly simply during summer through composting for garden use.

Markets and prices for recycled materials fluctuate locally and internationally. For example, prices for recycled paper vary from $0-180/t, depending on type, quality, cleanness and demand. Paper, including cardboard, is consistently the largest component of domestic garbage (30-40%) and much of it could be recycled if separated at source. "Deinking" plants remove ink and allow a high-quality recycled product to be produced. An effective paper recycling system would reduce the amount of the garbage available for production of steam heat.

High energy savings can be made by recycling metals instead of processing new metals: 74% for steel, up to 95% for aluminum. Most ferrous material in household garbage is tin cans and of reduced value because the tin coating must be removed for uses of the high-quality steel. Almost all aluminum in garbage comes from beverage containers. Aluminum is very valuable (approximately $1200/t). Canada lost an estimated 24 000 t of copper and 50 000 t of aluminum in garbage in 1976. At 1987 prices the value of waste aluminum alone would have been nearly $60 million.

Where legislation requires refunds on all beverage containers (soft drinks, beer, wine, liquor, etc), recycling of bottles and glass is very effective. In 1986 in Alberta, 85% of liquor and wine bottles were returned, almost 50% of cans, 95% of plastic and 75% of nonrefillable glass soft-drink bottles. Refillable beverage bottles cost 10-15 cents each and can be used 20-30 times. If beer bottles are used 12 times, savings are over 50%. Cans cost as much to produce but can be used only once.

Clean crushed glass can be used profitably to reduce energy and material costs in making new glass. Unacceptable contaminants include metals, aluminum foil, dirt, window glass and mixed colours of glass. Plastics comprise almost 5% of domestic garbage and are difficult to recycle if different kinds are mixed together. If unmixed, the recycled plastic can cost only one-third as much as virgin polymer. Alberta recycles about 1000 t of polyester per year from 2 litre plastic soft-drink bottles. Canadians dispose of about one tire per capita per year, totalling 25 million used tires per year. Tire rubber can be processed cryogenically (ie, using extreme cold) to produce rubber crumb for rubberized asphalt for roads, or can be recycled into new tires.

Lubricating oil is a major disposal problem. During engine operation, about 20% of engine oil is burned. The remainder is drained when the oil is changed. At least half of the drained oil could be collected for rerefining to marketable-grade lubricating oil. The price of used oil in Alberta in 1985 reached 13-17 cents per litre but has since fallen almost to nothing because of the fall in world oil prices. Tests show no significant differences between new and recycled oil.

Recycling can save energy, reduce direct POLLUTION caused by WASTE DISPOSAL and indirect pollution from processing of virgin materials; can conserve resources, reduce SOLID WASTE disposal costs (a complete system would mean about a 25% reduction in volume of garbage), create new employment and increase community pride and environmental awareness.   DIXON THOMPSON

Red Bay, Nfld, Community, pop 334 (1986c), 316 (1981c), inc 1973, is located on the Str of Belle Isle, off Labrador's S coast. Named for its prominent red cliffs, it was one of 2 major BASQUE whaling stations established in the 1540s. After research into Spanish documents and archaeological finds on Saddle I and under water, Red Bay was designated a historical site 1978-79. A sunken whaler, *San Juan,* one of the oldest-known and best-preserved shipwrecks of the post-medieval period, yielded information about some of the estimated 2000 men who caught and processed whales at Red Bay at the peak of the fishery. Several other sunken ships have since been discovered in the area. The community, settled by Newfoundland fishermen from CONCEPTION BAY by the early 1800s, originally alternated between winter and summer sites, but now occupies the former summer harbour year-round. Red Bay was the site of the first co-operative store in Labrador, the second such venture in the colony.
JANET E.M. PITT AND ROBERT D. PITT

Reading: Selma Barkham, "The Basques: Filling a Gap in Our History Between Jacques Cartier and Champlain," *Canadian Geographical Journal* 96 (Feb-Mar 1978).

Red Carpet for the Sun, A Published in 1958, *A Red Carpet for the Sun* marked the beginning of Irving LAYTON's long association with McClelland and Stewart; it is also the only one of Layton's books to have won the Gov Gen's Award. It includes poems reprinted from 12 previous collections and contains much of the best work, not only of Layton's early years but also of his whole career: "The Birth of Tragedy," "The Cold Green Element" and "Berry Picking." It also contains a typically robust Layton foreword, in which he castigates other poets as "insufferable blabbermouths" and proclaims his own "impeccable ear for rhythm." As capable of genius as he is of utter triviality, Layton remains among the most rewarding and infuriating of Canadian poets.
STEPHEN SCOBIE

Red Cross Society The International Committee of the Red Cross is an independent institution recognized by international law (in Oct 1986 the organization changed its official title to the International Red Cross and Red Crescent Movement). There are Red Crescent societies in 145 countries. The League of Red Cross Societies (est 1919) co-ordinates relief to disaster areas. The world Red Cross movement was founded in Geneva, Switz, by Henri Dunant, who had organized help for the wounded at the Battle of Solferino (1859). A book he wrote about the carnage he witnessed stirred a worldwide sensation. His work resulted in the signing of the Geneva Convention (1864), which provided for the neutrality of medical personnel in war and humane treatment of the wounded. He shared the first Nobel Peace Prize in 1901. The famous red cross symbol (the reverse of the Swiss flag) was adopted to identify and guarantee the safety of relief workers.

The founder of the Red Cross movement in Canada was George Sterling Ryerson. He accompanied the militia force sent to quell the NORTH-WEST REBELLION in 1885 and used a makeshift red cross to protect his horse-drawn ambulance. This flag (now in the Metropolitan Toronto Library) was flown during the Battle of BATOCHE, 9-12 May 1885. In 1896 Ryerson organized a Canadian branch (Toronto) of the British Red Cross Society which raised money for the relief of combatants in the SPANISH-AMERICAN WAR in 1898 and in 1899 distributed medical supplies during the SOUTH AFRICAN WAR.

In 1909 the federal government passed the Canadian Red Cross Society Act, which established the society as a corporate body. During WWI the society raised $35 million in relief, shipped supplies overseas, maintained 5 hospitals in England and one in France, and provided recreation huts and ambulance convoys. After the war, outpost hospitals were set up in isolated areas and in 1927 the International Committee recognized the CRC as an independent national society. During WWII the society contributed volunteer services and $125 million in goods and money, followed in later years by veterans' services and overseas services for orphaned children and refugees.

The Canadian Red Cross supervises a number of programs, including the Blood Transfusion Service (est 1947), which accepts blood from over one million donors each year. The Water Safety Service trains instructors who implement the program in all parts of Canada. Volunteers provide transportation and recreational facilities for veterans, hospital outpatients, the aged and the disabled, and contribute articles of clothing for victims of disaster. The CRC is made up of 10 provincial divisions and 608 branches, with headquarters in Toronto.

Red Crow, Blood chief (b at Belly R, Alta *c* 1830; d near Stand Off, Alta 28 Aug 1900). Head chief of the BLOOD tribe, Red Crow was one of the prominent leaders whose support was required for the peaceful settlement of the West. Born of a long line of chiefs, he became a noted warrior before succeeding to the chieftainship of his branch of the BLACKFOOT nation in 1870. He greeted the NORTH-WEST MOUNTED POLICE as friends when they came west in 1874 and, because of his trust in them, 3 years later he signed Treaty No 7. When he settled on his reserve (the largest in Canada), he pursued self-sufficiency for his people, introducing ranching and stressing the importance of education. At the same time, he remained a strong proponent of native customs and religion.
HUGH A. DEMPSEY

Reading: Hugh A. Dempsey, *Red Crow, Warrior Chief* (1980).

Red Deer, Alta, City, pop 54 425 (1986c), 46 393 (1981c), inc 1913, is located on the RED DEER R, 150 km S of Edmonton. The Cree applied the name "Elk" to the river, but Scottish settlers appear to have confused elk with the red deer of their homeland. The original settlement began 1882 where the old Calgary-Edmonton Trail crossed the Red Deer R. During the Riel Rebellion (1885) the Canadian militia constructed Fort Normandeau at this site. The post was then used by the NWMP until 1893. In 1891 the settlement moved 7 km downstream to a site on the newly constructed Calgary-Edmonton Ry (now part of the CPR). Around the turn of the century, the community experienced a surge of growth as a huge number of settlers flooded into the area to take up homesteads.

Red Deer developed primarily as an agricultural service and distribution centre, an activity enhanced by its location midway between Calgary and Edmonton, in the centre of a very fertile mixed-farming district. It became a major divisional point of the CPR in 1907, and in 1911 the Alberta Central and Canadian Northern railways entered the town. The provincial institution for the care of the mentally handicapped, currently known as the Michener Centre, established 1922, has had a great impact on the community. After WWII, with the discovery of significant oil and natural-gas fields in the area, Red Deer entered a prolonged boom. In the late 1950s it may have been the fastest-growing city in Canada.

The petroleum service industry became an increasingly important part of Red Deer's economy. After a lull in growth in the early 1970s, another boom accompanied the construction of world-scale petrochemical plants E of the city at Joffre and Prentiss. Red Deer is a modern city with excellent recreational and cultural facilities, a college, a large regional health-care centre, and extensive convention and exhibition facilities. It is also the centre of the parkland district of central Alberta. Attractions include the award-winning city hall (1964), ST MARY'S CHURCH (1968), Red Deer and District Museum and Archives (1978), Fort Normandeau Interpretive Centre (1985) and Kerry Wood Nature Centre (1986).
MICHAEL DAWE

Reading: G.C. Parker, *Proud Beginnings: A Pictorial History of Red Deer* (1981); K. Wood, *A Corner of Canada* (1966).

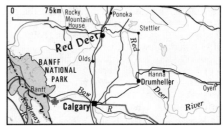

Red Deer River, 740 km, is glacier fed by streams from Mt Drummond and Cyclone Mt in the Rockies of Banff National Park, Alberta. It flows E then S to join the S SASKATCHEWAN R just inside Saskatchewan. Its 44 500 km² basin includes mountains, foothills and semiarid prairies; recognized white-water courses occur on its wilder upper reaches. On its lower portion, 300 km are lined by famous scenic BADLANDS containing dinosaur fossils, examples of which may be seen in the TYRRELL MUSEUM OF PALAEONTOLOGY (DRUMHELLER, Alta) and DINOSAUR PROVINCIAL PARK, a UNESCO World Heritage Site. The city of RED DEER is a major industrial (petrochemicals) user of water, along with irrigation and water-diversion schemes.   IAN A. CAMPBELL

Red Ensign (often "Canadian Red Ensign"), the recognized flag of Canada until 1965 when it was replaced by the maple leaf design. Based on the ensign flown by British merchant ships, the Canadian Red Ensign is a red flag with a Union Jack in the upper corner next to the staff and the Canadian coat of arms in the fly. The Red Ensign, bearing the appropriate coats of arms, is now the official flag of Ontario and Manitoba. *See also* EMBLEMS OF CANADA; FLAG.   JOHN ROBERT COLOMBO

Red Lake, Ont, Twp, Kenora District, pop 2166 (1986c), 2125 (1981c), is located in northwestern Ontario on the shore of Red Lake, 571 km NW of Thunder Bay. Originally the site of a Hudson's Bay Co fur-trading post, Red Lake's modern fortunes have been tied to gold mining. Survey work in the area was first carried out by the Geological Survey of Canada in 1883, but no mineral discoveries were recorded until 1897. Even then, the remoteness of the region prevented serious mining activity until 1925 when claims registered by Ray and Lorne Howey touched off a major gold rush. Over a thousand prospectors flooded into the area, and at the peak of the boom in the 1930s and 1940s there were 12 producing mines. As gold mining stagnated during the next 3 decades and the number of mines in the region was reduced to a handful, Red Lake's prospects dimmed. The 1980s brought renewed activity, however, as by mid-decade both Campbell Red Lake and Arthur W. White (formerly Dickenson) mines were setting record production levels.   MATT BRAY

Red River, 877 km long (to the head of the Sheyenne R), rises in Lk Traverse on the Minn-S Dak border, as the Bois de Sioux R, joins the Otter Tail R and flows directly N past Fargo and Grand Forks, crossing the Canadian border between Pembina, N Dak, and EMERSON, Man. It receives its major tributary, the ASSINIBOINE, at the "forks" in WINNIPEG and enters Lk Winnipeg through a labyrinth of channels. As the last glacier receded, the river actually flowed S; today, it flows N across a flat plain, rich in topsoil left by the glacial Lake AGASSIZ. Though in time of drought (eg, 1934) the river can virtually dry up, a late spring thaw after heavy snow can cause it to spill over its shallow banks onto the plain, with disastrous effect. The flooding threat is made worse because the river flows S to N, meaning the upper reaches thaw before the lower river.

The river was discovered (1734) by the LA VÉRENDRYE expedition; a French post, Ft Maurepas, was built on the delta that year and Ft Rouge (1738) at the forks. Retired voyageurs and their Métis offspring settled along the river, but systematic farming only began with the SELKIRK colonists (1812). The river was the heart of the RED RIVER COLONY; farms were laid in narrow strips along the riverbanks for irrigation and easy transport. By 1831 enough wheat was being

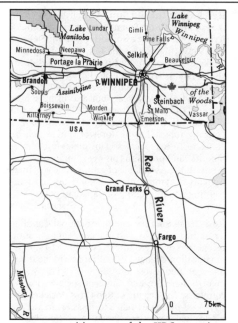

grown to provision part of the HBC operation. The MENNONITES (1870s) were the first to farm the prairie, away from the river. Key settlements on the river were Upper and Lower Ft Garry (*see* FORT GARRY, LOWER; FORT GARRY, UPPER), Selkirk and, after 1865, the growing town of Winnipeg. The N-S flow of the river encouraged commerce with the US, but this attraction lessened with the arrival of the railway from Canada. Works to prevent flooding began as early as 1844, but the major project began after the devastating flood of 1950; it drove 100 000 people from their homes and inundated 15 000 farm buildings and businesses. The Red River Floodway, a wide channel 47 km long, diverts floodwaters around Winnipeg. The river's name is a translation of the French Rivière Rouge (about 1740), which in turn is a translation of the Cree *Miscousipi*, "red water river." The river takes its red colour from the clay deep in its trench.   JAMES MARSH

Red River Cart Likely originating in both French and Scottish traditions, the Red River cart was constructed entirely of wood and was tied together with leather. It was easily repaired and was wonderfully adapted to prairie conditions; its 2 high, deeply dished wheels made it stable, and it could be drawn through mud and marsh. Wood and leather produced an ear-piercing squeal audible for kilometres. The cart was buoyant and could be floated across streams, yet it was strong enough to carry loads as heavy as 450 kg. Two shafts attached to the axle were strapped to a pony or ox. The Red River cart was first used by the MÉTIS to bring meat from the buffalo hunt and later in farm work. By the 1850s organized brigades of carts were making the 885 km journey from Ft

---

A group of Métis carters, camped with their Red River carts on the trail to St Paul, Minn, 1858 (*courtesy Minnesota Historical Society/405*).

Garry to St Paul, Minn, and by the 1860s some 600 carts were making 2 round trips annually, carrying some 270-360 kg each. The most important long-distance cart road was the Carlton Trail from FT GARRY to FT ELLICE and FT CARLTON (on the N Saskatchewan R) and on to Ft Edmonton. For several years into the 1860s about 300 carts made one trip per season from the RED RIVER COLONY, carrying trade goods and furs. The carts were gradually replaced by the steamboat and ultimately the railway.   JAMES MARSH

Red River Colony, settlement on the Red and Assiniboine rivers in what is now Manitoba and N Dakota, fd 1812 by the earl of SELKIRK. From 1801 Selkirk had sought British support for settlement in the region occupied by the HUDSON'S BAY COMPANY, but not until he and his family had gained control of the company in 1810 did his scheme become practical. In 1811 the company granted Selkirk some 300 000 km² in the Winnipeg Basin, which he called ASSINIBOIA. Under Miles MACDONELL, Selkirk's choice as governor, an advance party was sent from Scotland to Hudson Bay in July 1811, and finally arrived on the Red R on 29 Aug 1812. A second group joined them in Oct. Macdonell established his base near the junction of the Red and Assiniboine rivers (now downtown WINNIPEG) with a subsidiary centre 130 km S at Pembina (N Dak).

The settlers had difficulty becoming self-sufficient, and only the assistance of resident NORTH WEST COMPANY traders and local freemen enabled them to survive. Naturally bellicose and fearing that new settlers would strip the area of food supplies, Macdonell attempted to monopolize the region's provision trade through the PEMMICAN PROCLAMATION of 8 Jan 1814, by which he prohibited the export of provisions from the region. This threat to the NWC's transcontinental transportation system which took provisions, especially PEMMICAN, from the area to supply its canoe brigades, led the NOR'WESTERS and their MÉTIS allies to retaliate. In early 1815 the Nor'Westers seduced many colonists back to Canada by promising better land. Macdonell was arrested, the remaining inhabitants withdrew, and the settlement was burned. Later that year the colony was reoccupied under Colin Robertson, and Robert SEMPLE replaced Macdonell as governor. Continual complaint with the NWC led in 1816 to the SEVEN OAKS INCIDENT, after which the Nor'Westers again evacuated the colony. Meanwhile, Selkirk had recruited new settlers among the DE MEURONS, discharged mercenary soldiers, and was leading this group to Red River when he learned of Seven Oaks. On Aug 13 he seized the NWC's FORT WILLIAM, which lay on his route, and on 10 Jan 1817 sent a force to retake Ft Douglas. When Selkirk finally arrived that July, he distributed land and restored the settlers' confidence, promising them schools and clergymen. Roman Catholic priests arrived in 1818, but not until 1820 did a Protestant missionary come, and he was Anglican rather than Gaelic-speaking Presbyterian, a source of grievance to the Scots settlers for years.

After 1817 the environment became the major threat to the infant colony. Locusts devastated the crops in 1818 and 1819, and the greatest known flood of the Red R virtually destroyed the settlement in 1826. After Selkirk's death in 1820 his executors administered the colony, and sought to reduce expenses by ending settlers' subsidies and refusing to recruit new European immigrants. Population growth came largely through the retirement of fur traders and their native families to the colony, encouraged after 1821 by the newly amalgamated HBC's draconian reduction of the number of its employees. On 4 May 1836 Assini-

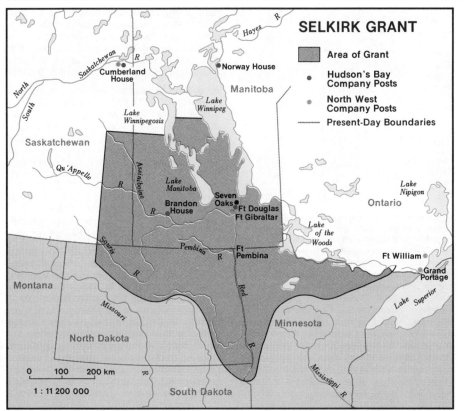

SELKIRK GRANT

Area of Grant

● Hudson's Bay
   Company Posts

● North West
   Company Posts

—— Present-Day Boundaries

0   100   200 km

1 : 11 200 000

boia was transferred to the HBC by Selkirk's family and administrative confusion ended.

Population grew slowly but steadily, composed largely of Métis (French-speaking Roman Catholics) and "mixed-bloods" or "country-born" (English-speaking Protestants), the former slightly more numerous than the latter. Despite continual conflicts over language, religion and class, a promising multiracial society was developing. The roots of its problems were economic, because of the colony's isolation. The HBC attempted to control commerce, although its limitations were made clear by the HBC's prosecution in 1849 of Pierre-Guillaume Sayer for illicit fur trading (*see* SAYER TRIAL): the outcome was, in effect, free trade for the Métis. Perhaps equally critical was the inability of the colony to provide suitable employment for an increasingly literate population, leading the younger generation to become extremely restive. When in the wake of CONFEDERATION (and without consultation with the colony's inhabitants or guarantees of their rights) arrangements were made to transfer the colony and RUPERT'S LAND to Canada, the stage was set for the RED RIVER REBELLION. The colony was reluctantly admitted to Canada as the province of Manitoba, its boundaries limited to the existing areas of settlement N of 49° lat.   J.M. BUMSTED

Reading: W.L. Morton, *Manitoba* (2nd ed, 1967).

Red River Expedition, the military force sent to Manitoba after the transfer of the Hudson's Bay Co territory to Canada in 1870. Under Col Garnet WOLSELEY were 400 British regulars and 800 Ontario and Québec militiamen. The government tried to give the impression it was not a punitive expedition against Louis RIEL's provisional government, but the militiamen wanted to avenge the execution of Thomas SCOTT. The expedition left Toronto May 1870 and reached Fort Garry on Aug 24. They found the fort deserted for Riel had fled at their approach. The British quickly returned to Ontario, leaving the militia to garrison the community. Militia harassment of Métis exacerbated already intense feelings and assaults and at least one death resulted.   BOB BEAL

Red River Rebellion (also known as Red River Resistance), a movement of national self-determination by the MÉTIS of the RED RIVER COLONY in what is now Manitoba, 1869-70. The settlement was after 1836 administered by the HUDSON'S BAY COMPANY and populated mainly by people of mixed European and Indian blood. Slightly over half were francophone (Métis), slightly under half anglophone ("country-born"). The inhabitants were continually in conflict with the HBC, particularly over trading privileges. By the 1850s the company's rule was under attack from Britain, Canada and the US, and by the 1860s it had agreed to surrender its monopoly over the North-West, including the settlement. Arrangements were negotiated to transfer sovereignty to Canada. During the lengthy bargaining period, Canadian and American settlers moved in, and their pretensions led the mixed bloods to fear for

Painting by F.A. Hopkins showing the *Red River Expedition* (1870) (*courtesy National Archives of Canada/C-2775*).

the preservation of their land rights and culture. Neither the British nor the Canadian government made serious efforts to assuage these fears, negotiating the transfer of RUPERT'S LAND as if no population existed there.

Mixed-blood concerns were exacerbated by Canadian attempts to resurvey the settlement in defiance of existing occupancy, and by the appointment of Canadian annexationist William MCDOUGALL as the territory's first lieutenant-governor. In late 1869 Louis RIEL emerged as the Métis spokesman. He recognized that his people must work with the more reticent anglophone mixed-bloods to satisfy their grievances. While local HBC officials maintained a studied neutrality, Métis opposition late in 1869 caused the Canadian government to refuse to take over the territory on 1 Dec 1869 as had been agreed. This encouraged Riel's insurgents, who had already prevented McDougall from entering the settlement; they seized Upper Ft Garry and fought against supporters of Canada. Representatives of the settlers were summoned to an elected convention, which in Dec proclaimed a provisional government, soon headed by Riel. In Jan 1870 Riel gained the support of most of the country-born in a second convention, which agreed to form a representative provisional government to negotiate with Canada the terms of entry into CONFEDERATION.

Armed conflict persisted over the winter, but Riel seemed in control until he made the colossal blunder of court-martialling and executing a prisoner, Ontario Orangeman Thomas SCOTT. Although the Canadian authorities were still willing to deal with Riel, they later seized upon the Scott case as a reason for refusing to grant an unconditional amnesty.

The legislative assembly of the provisional government organized the territory of ASSINIBOIA in Mar 1870 and enacted a law code in Apr. Although the Canadian government recognized the "rights" of the people of Red River in negotiations in Ottawa that spring, the victory was limited. A new province called Manitoba was created by the MANITOBA ACT, its territory severely limited to the old boundaries of the settlement, whereas the vast North-West remained firmly in Canadian hands. Even within Manitoba, public lands were controlled by the federal government. Mixed-blood land titles were guaranteed and 607 000 ha were reserved for the children of mixed-blood families, but these arrangements were mismanaged by subsequent federal governments. The Métis nation did not flourish after 1870 in Manitoba. There was no amnesty for Louis Riel and his lieutenants, who fled just before the arrival of

British and Canadian troops in Aug 1870. Although the insurrection had ostensibly won its major objectives – a distinct province with land and cultural rights guaranteed – the victory was hollow. The Métis soon found themselves so disadvantaged in Manitoba that they moved farther W, where they would again attempt to assert their nationality under Riel in the NORTH-WEST REBELLION of 1885. J.M. BUMSTED

Reading: W.L. Morton, "Introduction," *Alexander Begg's Red River Journal* (1956); G.F.G. Stanley, *The Birth of Western Canada* (1936).

Red Tory, popular term describing Canadian Conservatives who favoured an interventionist state and feared the increasing influence of the US upon Canada. To Gad Horowitz, Canada's SOCIALISM developed from the conservative ideology of the LOYALISTS, who rejected liberal individualism and believed in an organic state where each part bore responsibility for the welfare of the whole. George GRANT, a self-described "red Tory," believed he was part of a tradition essential to the distinctiveness of Canada in N America. Conservative interventionism is now more easily explained by political needs than by philosophy. "Red Tory" is used to refer loosely to the left wing of the CONSERVATIVE PARTY. JOHN ENGLISH

Redcliff, Alta, pop 3834 (1986c), 3876 (1981c), inc 1912, is located 7 km NW of Medicine Hat and named for the outcroppings of red shale occurring along the banks of the nearby S Saskatchewan R. Although a modest coal mine and brickworks existed in the area in the 1880s, the community really began in 1907 with the construction of the Redcliff Brick Co plant. In that year the townsite was surveyed, a water system was installed, and brick cottages and associated buildings were erected. By 1912 the town referred to in early promotional materials as the "smokeless Pittsburgh" had attracted more than 3000 people to work in the numerous industries lured by a plentiful supply of natural gas. At that time 3 major brick plants were operating, as well as the Dominion Glass Co, an ironworks and a truck-manufacturing plant. Unfortunately, however, the boom ended with WWI, when all but a few businesses permanently closed. Although most of the original industries no longer operate in Redcliff, the Dominion Glass Co (now Domglas Inc), still manufactures glass containers, I-XL Industries Ltd continues to manufacture clay bricks. MARK RASMUSSEN

Redistribution describes both the allocation of seats in the HOUSE OF COMMONS to the several provinces and the procedure for drawing specific constituency boundaries within that provincial allocation (*see* ELECTORAL SYSTEMS; ELECTIONS). Each revision of the allocation has attempted to construct a system that will reasonably reconcile a number of very different interests and principles. The allocation of 282 seats in the House of Commons for the 1984 election was reached by the application of a procedure set out in the Representation Act (1974). This introduced an extremely complicated formula which allowed for a different basis of allocation for "large provinces" (those with a population of more than 2.5 million), "small provinces" (with populations of under 1.5 million) and "intermediate provinces" (with populations between 1.5 and 2.5 million). The basic quotient was to be derived from the population of Québec, which was given an initial allocation of 75 seats, to be increased by 4 seats following each decennial census. It very quickly became clear that this would increase the size of the House to unacceptable limits in a relatively short time. Parliament therefore suspended further reassignment under the 1974 formula. New

Allocation of Seats in the House of Commons		
	number of seats	
Province	a	b
Ontario	95	99
Québec	75	75
Nova Scotia	11	11
New Brunswick	10	10
Manitoba	14	14
British Columbia	28	32
Prince Edward Island	4	4
Saskatchewan	14	14
Alberta	21	26
Newfoundland	7	7
Northwest Territories	2	2
Yukon	1	1
Total	282	295

a–number of seats under the Representation Act (1974)
b–number of seats under the 1985 formula after the application of the senatorial and grandfather clauses

legislation, the Representation Act (1985), which came into effect in Mar 1986, has greatly simplified the process. Starting from the present House of 282 members, 2 seats are set aside for the Northwest Territories and 1 for the Yukon. The total population of the 10 provinces is then divided by 279 to arrive at a quotient, which, when divided into the population of each province as reported at the previous decennial census, provides its basic allocation. If the division produces a remainder of more than 0.5, the number of seats is rounded up to the next whole number. This first allocation is then adjusted by applying what are referred to as the "senatorial and grandfather clauses." The senatorial clause, in effect since 1915, guarantees that no province will have fewer seats in the House of Commons than it has in the Senate. The new grandfather clause provides that at future redistributions no province will be allocated fewer seats than it had when the Representation Act (1985) was passed.

The actual drawing of individual constituency boundaries within a provincial allocation is governed by the Electoral Boundaries Readjustment Act (1964), which not only provided for a long-overdue redistribution of federal constituencies but entrusted responsibility for redistribution to a set of independent provincial boundary commissions. In each province the commission is chaired by a judge, designated by the chief justice of the province, and 2 other members, not elected members of any legislature, appointed by the Speaker of the House of Commons. Previously this task had been undertaken by Parliament with mixed results, including overt gerrymandering (the deliberate manipulation of constituency boundaries to give the maximum partisan advantage to one party).

Under the 1964 Act, new boundary commissions are set up after each decennial census, in a process now bound up with the regular reallocation of seats to the provinces. The principle of redistribution in the 1964 legislation was population. The total population of a province was divided by its allocation of seats to produce its provincial electoral quota. The commissions were then to proceed on the basis that "the population of each electoral district in the province...shall correspond as nearly as may be to the electoral quota of the province." Although a commission could depart from a strict application of this rule where necessary, no commission could propose an electoral district in which the population departed from the provincial electoral quota by more than 25% either way. The interpretation and application of these principles have produced long and bitter debates. Members of Parliament may object to, but may not overrule, commission proposals. The timing of a redistribution is such

that more than 3 years can elapse (as was the case in the 1984 federal election) from the publication of the census, through the allocation of seats to the provinces and the setting up of the commission, to the final proclamation of the new boundaries. TERENCE H. QUALTER

Reed, George Robert, football player (b in Mississippi 2 Oct 1939). Reed was a slashing, determined fullback with the SASKATCHEWAN ROUGHRIDERS 1962-75. He set 44 Canadian Football League records, including 16 116 yards gained, 137 touchdowns, 11 seasons of over 1000 yards, and 300 passes caught for 2772 yards. A CFL all-star 9 times and Schenley outstanding player in 1965, he was also president of the CFL Players' Assn. He began the George Reed Foundation for the Handicapped and his contributions as a citizen of Saskatchewan were recognized by the province in 1973. FRANK COSENTINO

Reeves, Hubert, astrophysicist (b at Montréal 13 July 1932). He studied at College Jean-de-Brébeuf, U de M, McGill U and Cornell U, where he received a doctorate in nuclear astrophysics. Returning to Canada, he taught physics at U de M while acting as a scientific adviser to NASA. Since 1966 he has lived in Paris where he is research director of the Conseil national de recherche scientifique (CNRS), and works at the Saclay Centre d'études nucléaires and the Paris Institut d'astrophysiques. He won international scientific attention with his writings, the last 2 of which have been best-sellers: *Patience dans l'azur* (1981 tr *Atoms of Silence*, 1984) and *Poussières d'étoiles* (1984). FRANÇOISE CÔTÉ

Reeves, John, judge (b probably at London, Eng *c*1752/53; d there 7 Aug 1829). He studied at Oxford and was called to the bar in 1779. In 1791 he became "chief judge" of a new temporary court of civil jurisdiction instituted to correct a defect that had been revealed in Newfoundland's existing judicial system. In this capacity he was in Newfoundland from 10 Sept to 1 Nov 1791. In 1792 he became "chief justice" of another temporary court, "the supreme court of judicature of the island of Newfoundland," and again visited his jurisdiction. In 1793, on the basis of his advice, permanent judicial reforms were legislated for Newfoundland. In the same year Reeves published his *History of the Government of the Island of Newfoundland*. This pitted local residents against English West Country merchants involved in the Newfoundland trade, a theme to which later historians would frequently return. Though transient, Reeves's connection with Newfoundland was nevertheless influential, both judicially and intellectually. PETER NEARY

Referendum, the referring of a political question to an electorate for direct decision by general vote. Deriving from the Latin, *ad referendum*, meaning that which must be taken back or that which must be submitted to an assembly, its roots lie in ancient Rome where the vote of the plebes ("plebiscite") invested the emperor with his position. Referendum and plebiscite are often used interchangeably.

Referendums do not easily fit in with the traditions of British parliamentary practice and are inherently polarizing, even impassioning, processes and thus are risky undertakings for political parties. However, for many observers a referendum is a useful and inherently democratic device that provides a precise answer from the population to a specific measure. Referendums have taken place since the 15th century in Switzerland. In France and other European countries the practice was used in the 18th century but did not spread widely until the second half of the 20th century. In Australia they are used for constitutional amendments, and some of the American states and municipal legislatures use them for policy and constitutional issues.

As the Canadian experience demonstrates, referendums may be constitutional or simply legislative, or they may have a nonlegislative function of arbitration. They may have binding power on the government or be merely consultative in nature and may be initiated either by the government or by the people. The latter take place at the local or regional rather than national level. In Canada, the federal government has held only 2 referendums: a legislative one, in 1898, on prohibition and an arbitrative one, in 1942, on CONSCRIPTION. In neither case were they binding. The latter, called a plebiscite, was more dramatic than the former. The Liberal government of Mackenzie KING asked Canadians if they were in favour of releasing the government from any obligations arising out of past commitments restricting the methods of raising men for military service. Over 60% of the voters replied yes; the others, no. In Québec, however, about 72-73% voted no – virtually the entire francophone population. In the other provinces, the no vote was about 30%.

In 1948, 2 important constitutional referendums in Newfoundland were held on the issue of union with Canada. The first failed to give an absolute majority to any of the 3 options: confederation with Canada, responsible government as it existed in 1933, or COMMISSION OF GOVERNMENT for 5 years. But a second vote, held a month later on July 2, resulted in a slim majority (52.3%) for confederation. The QUÉBEC REFERENDUM (constitutional) of 20 May 1980 was the most recent in Canada. In it, 60% of the voters refused to give the Parti Québécois government a mandate to negotiate SOVEREIGNTY-ASSOCIATION.

All the provinces, with the exception of New Brunswick, have held nonconstitutional referendums, including dealing with the prohibition of liquor and related problems; switching to daylight-saving time; votes for women; public health; ownership of electric companies; and grain marketing. In Jan 1988 a referendum was held in PEI to determine if PEI should have a fixed link to the mainland. The outcome was 59% to 41% in favour. Four provinces – British Columbia, Alberta, Saskatchewan and Manitoba – have enacted statutes making public initiative possible. These statutes were enacted at the time of WWI. The Manitoba statute, enacted in 1916, was challenged in the courts and finally declared to be ultra vires by the Judicial Committee of the Privy Council in 1919.

In the other provinces, there was no provision for public initiative. Provincial referendums in Canada are traditionally consultative or advisory in nature, although some have been considered binding on the part of the governments that have called them. VINCENT LEMIEUX

Reforestation, the re-establishment of a FOREST where an earlier one existed. Afforestation means starting a forest where there was none. Reforestation (or regeneration) may occur naturally over time or may result from the artificial introduction of seeds or plants. Natural regeneration will nearly always take place eventually; artificial reforestation reduces the time required, improves the spacing of seedlings, controls the species mix and allows the establishment of faster-growing, healthier seedlings from genetically improved seed orchards.

During the first three-quarters of the 20th century in Canada, too much logged or burned forest was left to regenerate naturally; the result was that a great deal of land was unsatisfactorily reforested. As awareness of this problem grew, more efforts were directed to artificial reforestation.

This process begins with collection and storage of seed. Seed may be sown directly, but more commonly seedlings grown in nurseries are planted in spring or fall. Seedlings grow better when planted near the area in which the seed originated. The site may be prepared for planting by burning off unwanted debris or by scarification (stirring up of surface soil). Most seedlings planted in Canada are native species, but occasionally "exotics" or new species are tried. M.F. PAINTER

Reform Movement in Upper Canada The rapid development of UPPER CANADA after the WAR OF 1812 produced social and economic tensions which were translated into politics through such issues as the expulsion of Robert GOURLAY, the ALIEN QUESTION, the Anglican monopoly of the CLERGY RESERVES and education, and TORY domination of patronage. A varied group, calling itself the Reform movement and including the BALDWINS, the BIDWELLS, William Lyon MACKENZIE, John ROLPH and Egerton RYERSON, presented opposition to the dominant FAMILY COMPACT. By 1828 the Reformers formed a majority in the assembly, but their program was blocked in the Tory-dominated councils.

During the early 1830s the Reform movement split. Moderates, led by Robert BALDWIN, were committed to the British constitution, the imperial connection and the concept of a stable, hierarchical society; they simply wanted to enlarge the ruling elite through the introduction of RESPONSIBLE GOVERNMENT. Radical reformers increasingly demanded the application of republican principles to create a social and economic democracy modelled on the US; they also sought greater colonial independence. Mackenzie led a third, extreme faction.

In 1836 Baldwin entered the executive council but Lt-Gov Sir Francis Bond HEAD refused to accept responsible government. The administration resigned and the moderates were squeezed out of the political process. Mackenzie's group, devastated in the subsequent election, became more revolutionary but was crushed in the REBELLIONS OF 1837. The moderates, led by Baldwin and Francis Hincks, re-emerged as a potent political force in the United PROVINCE OF CANADA, and the nonrevolutionary radicals sank into oblivion.
DAVID MILLS

Reform Party of Canada, western-based political party that grew out of a coalition of discontented western interest groups. Originally the coalition began in 1986 as an attempt to voice western concerns at the national level. In May 1987, the Reform Association of Canada voted to "support a broadly based party to voice Western economic and constitutional concerns." The association began a fund-raising and membership drive that culminated in a founding convention of the Reform Party in Oct 1987. The convention assessed its policy formulation process and elected the Reform Party's first leader, Preston Manning, son of former Alberta Socred premier E.C. MANNING. As of 1987, the party planned to run a full slate of candidates in the West in the next federal general election.

Refugees, those who flee their home countries to escape persecution or danger. Canada is a country of immigrants – a country, most Canadians believe, with a long tradition of welcoming refugees and dissidents from all over the world. This, at least, has been part of the Canadian mythology. The first great wave of immigrants to arrive in Canada, the United Empire LOYALISTS, is widely regarded as Canada's first refugee contingent. But as Gerald Dirks points out in *Canada's Refugee Policy*, most were not refugees but were British settlers who preferred their old flag to the new American one. Among them were some legitimate refugees, mostly QUAKERS, MENNONITES and other noncon-

formists who, fearing persecution by the new American government, fled northwards. Before 1860 thousands of fugitive American slaves arrived in Canada, and the public recognition given Canada as the final stop on the UNDERGROUND RAILROAD reaffirmed to many that this country was indeed a sanctuary for the oppressed and the enslaved. An estimated 30 000 BLACKS came to Canada. It was perhaps not much of a haven, because as soon as they could (after the Emancipation Proclamation and the end of the AMERICAN CIVIL WAR) most of these ex-slaves returned home.

Over the next generation, 2 groups of refugees, Mennonites and DOUKHOBORS, arrived from Russia. Both found life under the tsars intolerable and were anxious to leave. The Canadian government, desperately searching for immigrants – especially agriculturalists – to settle the West, was just as anxious to have them. Indeed, until the 1930s Great Depression, almost any immigrants except blacks and Asians could come to Canada. Among the millions who arrived were obviously numbers of refugees, but no special arrangements were made for them.

A major test of Canada as a refuge for the oppressed occurred in the 1930s as German JEWS begged for admission to any country. Many nations suffering far worse economic distress than Canada were nonetheless much more receptive. While Canada grudgingly accepted some 4000 of these refugees, the US welcomed 240 000, Britain 85 000, China 25 000, Argentina and Brazil over 25 000 each, and Mexico and Colombia received some 40 000 between them. But xenophobia and ANTI-SEMITISM permeated Canada, and there was little public support for, and much opposition to, the admission of refugees.

This attitude did not change until after WWII. With Europe full of "displaced persons" (a newly minted term to describe an old phenomenon, the refugee), Canada became much more receptive, largely because of a booming economy and a desperate need for manpower. Hundreds of thousands of DPs came to Canada, their journeys often subsidized by the Canadian government. Indeed, Canada now began to play an increasingly active role in the UNITED NATIONS refugee organization.

In 1956 Canada was put to the test again; this time however, it did not fail. Within months of the Hungarian uprising against the Soviets, the government succumbed to much domestic pressure, especially from ethnic and religious groups, and announced that it would accept a large number of HUNGARIAN refugees. Almost 37 000 arrived. The Canadian government was pleased; not only did these refugees bring some badly needed skills, but they provided the Western world with a not-to-be-missed opportunity of embarrassing the USSR. In 1968, 11 000 CZECHS, following the Soviet invasion of their country, settled in Canada. Most were highly skilled and rapidly integrated into Canadian society. In 1972 Canada accepted 7000 highly trained and educated Ugandan Asians who were fleeing the notorious regime of Idi Amin. Like the Czechs they quickly began making important contributions to Canada.

A more controversial group of refugees were the American war resisters ("draft dodgers"), who fled across the border to escape service in the VIETNAM WAR. Though some returned home after the war, many took up new lives in Canada. Most controversial of all, however, were the Chilean and other LATIN AMERICAN refugees forced out of Chile by the Sept 1973 overthrow of Salvador Allende's Marxist government. Fearing that most of these political refugees were too left-wing, and not wishing to alienate either the American or new Chilean rulers, the Canadian government took only a small number. This is in sharp contrast to Canada's humanitarian behaviour during the Vietnamese "boat-people" crisis of the late 1970s. Touched by the plight of the hundreds of thousands who escaped the communist regime by taking to the high seas in leaking, unsafe boats, many Canadians offered to sponsor their journey to Canada, and the government admitted some 70 000 refugees.

A 1978 amendment to the Immigration Act made it possible for the first time for refugees to apply for admission as immigrants. Refugees had previously been permitted into Canada only by special orders-in-council. Their future admission would now depend less on Canada's political and economic vagaries. Although the government has not determined its precise definition of a refugee, Canada has agreed to accept the comprehensive definition of the United Nations High Commissioner on Refugees (UNHCR). The Immigration Act (1976) refers to a refugee as one who "by reason of a well-founded fear of persecution for reasons of race, religion, nationality, membership in a particular social group or political opinion" is outside his own country and cannot, or fears to, return there.

In 1986 as a recognition of its generous policies Canada was awarded the coveted Nansen medal by the UNHCR. Ironically, within a year, because of a public outcry against the admission of increasing numbers of refugees – Sri Lankans [Ceylon], East Indians and especially Central Americans – and concerned over abuses of the system by bogus claimants, the Canadian government introduced tough legislation to restrict the flow of refugees into the country. *See also* IMMIGRATION.

IRVING ABELLA

Refus global, a manifesto written by painter Paul-Émile BORDUAS, poet Claude GAUVREAU, Bruno Cormier (later a psychoanalyst), dancer Françoise Sullivan and painter Fernand LEDUC; signed by the 15 members of the AUTOMATISTES; and published (400 copies) in Montréal on 9 Aug 1948. Borduas wrote the main essay, from which the manifesto's title was taken, and 2 other texts. *Refus global* not only challenged the traditional values of Québec society but proposed the "refusal" of any ideology that hampered creative spontaneity. The manifesto referred to the strong need for liberation and "resplendent anarchy," and depicted the coming of a new hope. That was enough to cause the authorities to have Borduas removed from his post at the École du meuble, where he had been teaching since 1937. The press echoed the government and largely condemned the manifesto. *Refus global* had far more than artistic impact in Québec; it served as a benchmark for the emergence of a new pluralism in the province.

FRANÇOIS-MARC GAGNON

Regan, Gerald Augustine, lawyer, politician, premier of NS (b at Windsor, NS 13 Feb 1928). He was elected MP in 1963 and leader of the Nova Scotia Liberal Party in 1965. His vigorous tactics did much to undermine the George Smith Conservative government and secure a Liberal minority government in 1970, followed by a solid victory in 1974. As premier, he espoused such undertakings as a new steel complex at Gabarus, industrialization and a superport at the Strait of Canso, harnessing the tides of the Bay of FUNDY, and development of the offshore oil and gas resources. Before any came to fruition, his government was defeated by John BUCHANAN's Conservatives in 1978, mainly because of the large increase in domestic energy costs resulting from more expensive foreign oil. Re-elected to the House of Commons in 1980, he has served as minister of labour and minister of state for international trade. Since suffering personal defeat in the election of 1984, he has followed private business pursuits.

J. MURRAY BECK

Regiment, a body of troops composed of squadrons, batteries or companies, and often divided into battalions for military operations. A single-battalion regiment numbers 300-1000.

In Canada the meaning of the term "regiment" is complex. Infantry regiments are administrative parent organizations that raise one or more battalions for service. Armoured regiments are normally battalion-sized units, though they may have both regular and reserve force components and administrative elements. The artillery organizes its batteries into regiments, but it also traditionally calls the entire artillery branch a regiment. Engineer and communication regiments are also battalion sized. Armoured and infantry regiments are the centre of collective pride for their members and maintain close "family" relationships. For artillery and others, the branch rather than the individual regiment is the traditional family focus. In Canadian practice, a regiment's "life-time" is the number of unbroken years of existence, though disbanded units (and their customs and battle honours) can be perpetuated by others with a proven connection. Armoured and infantry regimental precedence is determined largely by this seniority.

In Europe, prior to the 16th century, the basic organization raised for battle was the company. Companies came to be grouped into regiments under a single superior officer for recruiting, training and administration. Regiments soon developed their own insignia and customs, and became the focus of esprit de corps. In battle array such groupings were called battalions, and this term then often was used interchangeably with regiment. Later, Revolutionary France structured each of its regiments permanently into 3 battalions, a common, but never universal practice.

French settlers in Canada very early formed a militia (*see* ARMED FORCES), organized into companies from each parish. These companies worked together in battalions as the need arose. The first regiment to serve in Canada was the CARIGNAN-SALIÈRES REGIMENT, which arrived in 1665, but almost all its troops returned to France after 3 years. Until the SEVEN YEARS' WAR the militia and the regular infantry serving in the colony, TROUPES DE LA MARINE, were responsible for defence. Only in 1755, on the eve of war, did the French regular army return when battalions from 8 regiments arrived at Louisbourg and Québec. That war also brought to Canada the British regular army, which had previously garrisoned Nova Scotia and Newfoundland. After the CONQUEST the British retained and built upon the French militia organization, adding their own military heritage. When the Americans marched against Québec in 1775, the garrison consisted only of 2 weak British regular battalions, 2 composite battalions of militia and the Royal Highland Emigrants. This last, eventually 2 battalions, was a British unit raised locally for full-time service in N America. It was the first of a number of colonial regular or "fencible" regiments. The AMERICAN REVOLUTION resulted in the resettlement of members of American LOYALIST regiments in Upper Canada and New Brunswick. Such units as Butler's Rangers, settled at Niagara, provided veteran leaders for the militia in later years. As Britain's difficulties with Revolutionary France grew, the authorities again made use of fencible regiments. From 1793 to 1802 the Royal Nova Scotia Regiment, the Royal Canadian Volunteers and the Queen's Rangers were on full-time service in Nova Scotia, Lower Canada and Upper Canada respectively.

The WAR OF 1812 was fought, on the British side, by regular regiments, some fencible units and the militia. By this time the militia of Upper and Lower Canada was organized into regiments based upon counties, with one or more from each coun-

ty as population allowed. It was impractical to call out all the inhabitants of an area for lengthy periods. Instead, in Lower Canada portions of the militia were embodied into service battalions, whereas in Upper Canada only the "flank companies" (a term for the 2 elite companies in a regular 10-company battalion) were trained and equipped. The Battalion of Incorporated Militia, which figured prominently in several battles, was really a Canadian full-time regiment made up of volunteers from such flank companies.

The Canadian regimental system changed substantially with the MILITIA ACTS of 1846 and 1855. The "lifetime" of many of Canada's oldest present-day regiments officially begins with volunteer units created then. A few semiofficial units already in existence gained official status. For instance, the York Dragoons, since 1822 part of the West York Regiment of Militia, were gazetted in 1847 as the 1st Toronto Independent Troop of Cavalry, and eventually became The Governor General's Horse Guards. The Royal Regiment of Canadian Artillery traces its continuous existence from field batteries formed 1855. Initially the volunteer cavalry and infantry were organized only as troops and companies. However, threats of war with the US and invasion by the FENIANS in the 1860s demonstrated the need for larger units. The 1st Battalion, Volunteer Militia Rifles of Canada, was formed 1859 and is today The Canadian Grenadier Guards. By Confederation most of the force was consolidated into such numbered battalions. The Canadian system was extended to the Maritimes in the Militia Act of 1868 and absorbed volunteer regiments already in existence there.

The regular Canadian army came later. The first permanent units, schools of gunnery formed 1871, still exist as batteries in the Royal Canadian Horse Artillery. Three companies of the Infantry School Corps, established 1883, were the beginnings of The Royal Canadian Regiment. The Cavalry School Corps, also begun in 1883, was the nucleus for The Royal Canadian Dragoons. During the SOUTH AFRICAN WAR The Royal Canadian Regiment formed 2 new battalions. The 2nd Battalion went overseas and the 3rd relieved British troops at Halifax. Both were disbanded after the war. Several battalions of Canadian Mounted Rifles were raised for war service and also were disbanded upon their return. Donald SMITH, Lord Strathcona, privately raised Strathcona's Horse for South Africa. This was later perpetuated in the permanent force as Lord Strathcona's Horse (Royal Canadians).

In 1900 all militia infantry battalions were renamed as regiments, although most retained only one battalion. The organization created for WWI was very different. The CANADIAN EXPEDITIONARY FORCE was composed of new numbered infantry battalions, artillery batteries and other arms and services. Militia regiments served only as recruiting bases, and in many cases a regiment raised more than one overseas battalion. There were a few exceptions, eg, Princess Patricia's Canadian Light Infantry, which was formed primarily from British ex-soldiers settled in Canada; it fought for a year in the British army before joining the Canadian Corps in France. Other units remained outside the Corps. The Canadian Cavalry Brigade, composed of The Royal Canadian Dragoons, Lord Strathcona's Horse (Royal Canadians), the Fort Garry Horse and the Royal Canadian Horse Artillery, served throughout the war with the British army. (The Royal Newfoundland Regiment also fought with the British since Newfoundland was not part of Canada.) After the war Canada disbanded the CEF units, but decided that existing regiments would perpetuate wartime battalions with which they were most closely associated in order to preserve their battle honours. At the same time, names replaced numbers in regimental titles. Two new regiments joined the permanent force: PPCLI and the Royal 22nd Regiment ("Vandoos"), the latter a French-speaking unit that had served with distinction as a CEF battalion. Later, reserve force reorganization converted several regiments from one role to another. Six infantry regiments became "tank," and others became "machine gun," previously a separate corps. Cavalry generally converted to "armoured" (tank or armoured car) regiments.

In WWII the army mobilized the Active Service Force from existing regiments. Individual units fought from HONG KONG to NW Europe. Artillery batteries, until then brigaded for tactical purposes, were combined permanently into regiments. A unique Canadian-American unit, the First Special Service Force, was formed, organized along American regimental patterns.

The regular force greatly expanded in the 1950s for the KOREAN WAR and NATO service. Additional infantry battalions formed a new regiment, The Canadian Guards, and regular components of 2 existing reserve regiments, The Queen's Own Rifles of Canada and The Black Watch (Royal Highland Regiment) of Canada. Other reserve regiments such as The Loyal Edmonton Regiment (4th Battalion, Princess Patricia's Canadian Light Infantry) became reserve battalions of the remaining regular infantry regiments. New artillery regiments and a signal regiment were raised. Two reserve armoured regiments, the 8th Canadian Hussars (Princess Louise's) and The Fort Garry Horse, also raised regular components. Tight defence budgets and reduced manpower in the 1960s led to a smaller army in the unified Canadian Armed Forces. The Canadian Guards disappeared, as did the regular components of some other units. In order to broaden francophone representation in the forces, 2 new regular regiments were formed, the 12e Régiment blindé du Canada and the 5e Régiment d'artillerie légère du Canada. The Canadian Airborne Regiment was also created.

The following armoured and infantry regiments, in order of precedence, were active on the order of battle in 1987. An asterisk (*) indicates both regular and reserve components, listed separately. *Regular Armour:* The Royal Canadian Dragoons; Lord Strathcona's Horse (Royal Canadians); *8th Canadian Hussars (Princess Louise's); *12e Régiment blindé du Canada. *Militia Armour:* The Governor General's Horse Guards; *8th Canadian Hussars (Princess Louise's) (Militia); The Elgin Regiment; The Ontario Regiment; The Queen's York Rangers (1st American Regiment); The Sherbrooke Hussars; *12e Régiment blindé du Canada (Milice); 1st Hussars; The Prince Edward Island Regiment; The Royal Canadian Hussars (Montreal); The British Columbia Regiment (Duke of Connaught's Own); The South Alberta Light Horse; The Saskatchewan Dragoons; The King's Own Calgary Regiment; The British Columbia Dragoons; The Fort Garry Horse; Le Régiment de Hull; The Windsor Regiment. *Regular Infantry:* *The Royal Canadian Regiment; Princess Patricia's Canadian Light Infantry; *Royal 22e Régiment; Canadian Airborne Regiment. *Militia Infantry:* Governor General's Foot Guards; The Canadian Grenadier Guards; The Queen's Own Rifles of Canada; The Black Watch (Royal Highland Regiment) of Canada; Les Voltigeurs de Québec; The Royal Regiment of Canada; The Royal Hamilton Light Infantry (Wentworth Regiment); The Princess of Wales' Own Regiment; The Hastings and Prince Edward Regiment; The Lincoln and Welland Regiment; *The Royal Canadian Regiment; The Highland Fusiliers of Canada; The Grey and Simcoe Foresters; The Lorne Scots (Peel, Dufferin and Halton Regiment); The

Brockville Rifles; The Lanark and Renfrew Scottish Regiment; Stormont, Dundas and Glengarry Highlanders; Les Fusiliers du St-Laurent; Le Régiment de la Chaudière; *Royal 22e Régiment; Les Fusiliers Mont-Royal; The Princess Louise Fusiliers; The Royal New Brunswick Regiment; The West Nova Scotia Regiment; The Nova Scotia Highlanders; Le Régiment de Maisonneuve; The Cameron Highlanders of Ottawa; The Royal Winnipeg Rifles; The Essex and Kent Scottish; 48th Highlanders of Canada; Le Régiment du Saguenay; The Algonquin Regiment; The Argyll and Sutherland Highlanders of Canada (Princess Louise's); The Lake Superior Scottish Regiment; The North Saskatchewan Regiment; The Royal Regina Rifles; The Rocky Mountain Rangers; The Loyal Edmonton Regiment (4th Battalion, Princess Patricia's Canadian Light Infantry); The Queen's Own Cameron Highlanders of Canada; The Royal Westminster Regiment; The Calgary Highlanders; Les Fusiliers de Sherbrooke; The Seaforth Highlanders of Canada; The Canadian Scottish Regiment (Princess Mary's); The Royal Montreal Regiment; The Irish Regiment of Canada; The Toronto Scottish Regiment; The Royal Newfoundland Regiment.

M.V. BEZEAU AND O.A. COOKE

Reading: Canada, Army Headquarters, Historical Section, *The Regiments and Corps of the Canadian Army* (1964); George F.G. Stanley, *Canada's Soldiers* (1954).

Regina, Sask, capital and commercial and financial centre of the province, is situated 160 km N of the US border. The city is set in a wide, level alluvial plain.

Settlement Regina, named for Queen Victoria – mother-in-law of then Gov Gen the marquess of Lorne – was founded in 1882 and made capital of the North-West Territories in 1883. The town was a creature of the CPR, which determined the location of the townsite, near the meandering Pile O' Bones (Wascana) Cr, and influenced Regina's street layout and land-use patterns.

Development Regina grew slowly at first, reaching a population of 2250 by 1901, but thereafter its fortunes improved dramatically. Named provincial capital when Saskatchewan was formed in 1905, Regina grew quickly, and by 1911 numbered over 30 000 inhabitants. The boom mentality of the period survived the destruction wrought by a 1912 tornado, but an economic depression in 1913 and the outbreak of WWI temporarily halted the city's growth. Economic conditions remained unsettled after the war, and Regina continued to mark time. Not until the mid-1920s did prosperity return, as the population leaped from 34 400 to 53 200 in the decade, but then a decade of drought and depression reduced life in Saskatchewan to bare subsistence. When better times returned for the province's farmers after 1939, Regina's economy began to revive as well. Since WWII the city has experienced steady, though unspectacular, growth, with the primary spurt in the 1950s, when the population grew by 57%.

Cityscape Reginans have transformed the cheerless prairie into a city of shaded parks and streets. Wascana Centre, surrounding man-made

Population: 175 064 (1986c), 186 521 (1986 CMA); 162 986 (1981cA), 173 226 (1981 ACMA)
Rate of Increase (1981-86): City 7.4%; CMA 7.7%
Rank in Canada: Eighteenth (by CMA)
Date of Incorporation: 1903
Land Area: City 110.06 km² (CMA); CMA 3421.58 km²
Elevation: 577 m
Climate: Average daily temp, July 18.9°C, Jan -17.9°C; Yearly precip 402.9 mm rainfall; Hours of sunshine 2331.2 per year

Aerial view of Regina. The Legislative Building and man-made Wascana Lk are in the foreground (*courtesy Colour Library Books*).

Wascana Lk, is a unique 920 ha area in the heart of Regina, within which may be found the stately Legislative Building (1912) and other provincial government offices, UNIVERSITY OF REGINA, the Museum of Natural History and the Saskatchewan Centre of the Arts. Interest in town planning dates from 1913 when Thomas Mawson was engaged to prepare a plan for Regina; completed in 1921, it was never implemented. The city's first town-planning bylaw, passed 1927, established 6 land-use zones.

Population Regina's population has more than doubled since WWII, in part through immigration from outside the province, but more from a general population shift from farm to city within Saskatchewan. The majority of citizens are native-born and nearly half are British in origin. People of German, Ukrainian and Scandinavian ancestry form large groups as well, and during the last 2 decades many native people have come to the city. The largest religious denominations are

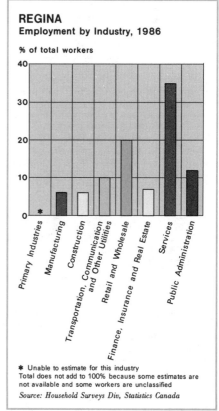

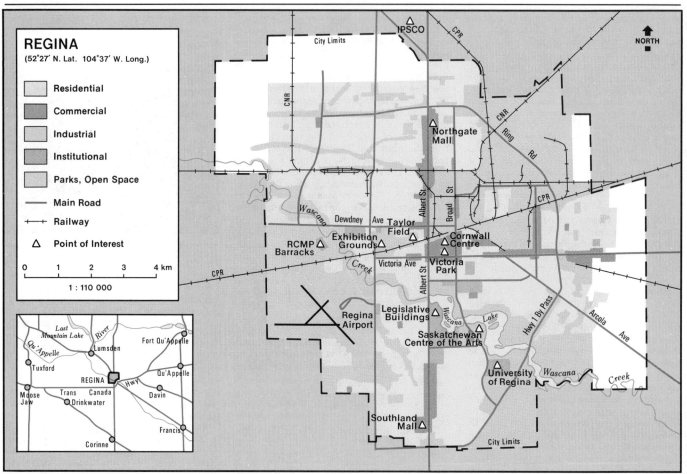

Roman Catholic, United Church, Lutheran, Anglican and Greek Orthodox.

Economy and Labour Force Regina is surrounded by a rich wheat-growing plain on which its economy is largely dependent. The city is the most important retail, distribution and service centre in southern Saskatchewan. Within a 40 km radius, Regina serves a retail trade population of 185 000 (1986), and within a 240 km radius a wholesale trade population of 500 000. The headquarters of the SASKATCHEWAN WHEAT POOL, the world's largest grain-handling co-operative, is located here.

The provincial government continues to be a major factor in the urban economy. The number of government and crown corporation employees has grown steadily since 1945, and they have been accommodated in new high-rise office buildings that have dramatically altered the city's skyline. The most significant federal government presence is the RCMP, whose training facilities have been located in Regina since 1885. In recent decades Regina has also diversified its economy, the principal new developments being in cement, paper products and steel fabricating. In 1984 Regina and area accounted for 40% of the total value of manufacturing activity in Saskatchewan.

Transportation Regina is located on the TRANS-CANADA HWY, on the main line of the CPR and on a branch line of the CNR. Three airlines and 2 bus lines serve the city.

Government and Politics Regina is governed by an elected mayor and 10 aldermen, each of the latter representing a specific "division" or ward. The ward system, first introduced in 1906, was abolished in 1914. It appeared again 1934, only to be abandoned 2 years later. The present wards were established 1973. The powers of city council are set out in The Urban Municipality Act, and a provincial agency, the Local Government Board,

oversees municipal financing. Public and separate (Roman Catholic) school boards administer Regina's 3 tax-supported elementary and high-school systems.

Cultural Life Regina's educational facilities include University of Regina, the Wascana Institute of Applied Arts and Sciences and the Regina Plains Community College. The Regina Symphony Orchestra is one of the city's most distinguished cultural institutions. The Norman Mackenzie and the Dunlop art galleries have substantial permanent collections and feature many travelling exhibitions. The Globe Theatre has gained a national reputation for its professional theatre productions. Regina is served by 2 English-language and one French-language TV stations, 8 radio stations and one daily newspaper, the *Leader-Post*. The pride of the city, and indeed of the whole province, is the SASKATCHEWAN ROUGHRIDERS, a Canadian Football League team that plays at Taylor Field.   J. WILLIAM BRENNAN

Reading: E.H. Dale, ed, Regina: Regional Isolation and Innovative Development (1980); E.G. Drake, Regina: The Queen City (1955).

Regina Five, the name given to the artists in the 1961 National Gallery of Canada's circulating exhibition "Five Painters from Regina," presented the work of Kenneth LOCHHEAD, Arthur MCKAY, Douglas Morton, Ted Godwin and Ronald BLOORE. These young painters (b 1925-33) from Ontario and the Prairies had studied in Canadian and foreign centres before moving to Regina. Along with painter Roy KIYOOKA and architect Clifford Wiens, they shared a common professional commitment and became a small but active artistic community in Regina.

Since 1958 Bloore, as director of the Norman Mackenzie Art Gallery, brought national and international exhibitions to Regina; in 1961, to coincide with a Canadian Museums Association

meeting, he organized the "May Show" that became the basis for the exhibition that Richard Simmins of the National Gallery arranged to travel across Canada. The bold, nonfigurative paintings (often employing a central or all-over image) in this exhibition represented a new direction in abstract painting in Canada and reflected theoretical considerations comparable to contemporary New York directions.

Several factors contributed to this burst of mature creative expression in a previously isolated cultural centre. Primarily there was the Regina College at U of Sask and its faculty. In 1955 its director, Lochhead, with fellow faculty member McKay, initiated the Emma Lake Artists Workshop, a series of professional workshops held for 2 weeks each year in Aug. In early years, visitors included Joe Plaskett, Jack SHADBOLT and Will Barnet. For future members of the Regina Five, the 1959 visit of American artist Barnett Newman provided a catalyst. Three years later American critic Clement Greenberg had a significant impact on a number of western artists, including Lochhead. In the next decade 3 of the Five left Regina to pursue their careers as painters and teachers. *See also* PAINTING.   JOYCE ZEMANS

Regina Manifesto, *see* CO-OPERATIVE COMMONWEALTH FEDERATION.

Regina Riot, *see* ON TO OTTAWA TREK.

Regional Development Planning is undertaken by governments with the aim of improving the well-being of people in areas where there is concern about present and future living conditions. Economic conditions normally receive the greatest attention, but economic problems (such as high rates of unemployment, low income levels or lack of investment opportunities) are closely associated with a broad range of physical and social problems. These include substandard health and housing conditions, inadequacies in physical infrastructure (eg, water supplies, waste disposal, transport facilities), environmental pollution, and deficiencies in educational, recreational and social services. A planned program of regional development normally attempts to treat these problems comprehensively.

Canada has a long history of development programs of many kinds, the most notable being the system of income transfers among the provinces that followed from the Rowell-Sirois report of 1940. Yet the federal government did not adopt an integrated approach to the problem of regional disparities until 1969, when the Dept of Regional Economic Expansion (DREE) was established. DREE's chief purpose was to help create employment opportunities, but 2 levels of need were recognized. The first related to "designated regions" where unemployment was high but the infrastructure for development was already in place; here, grants were provided to firms willing to invest in new or expanded manufacturing plants. The second were "special areas" where infrastructure was not available, and social facilities and services were lacking as well. For these areas, DREE adopted comprehensive programs that included the development of industrial parks, vocational training, the construction of new housing, the provision of a wide range of health and social services, and the creation of jobs, which could be in service industries or in manufacturing. Both types of programs were funded and administered as federal-provincial partnerships, although the federal government bore a larger proportion of costs in the poorer provinces.

Beginning in 1973, in response to criticisms that the regional development programs were too much under central control, the provincial governments were given more autonomy over the design and implementation of projects supported by DREE. Then, in 1982, most of DREE's programs were moved to a Dept of Regional Industrial Expansion (DRIE) in the Ministry of Trade and Commerce. A new Ministry of Economic and Regional Development was created at this time to co-ordinate federal government actions to generate beneficial regional impacts. With the national economy performing badly, it came to be argued that regional development could not be effective unless well-thought-out development strategies had first been formulated at the national and provincial levels. If regions were left to compete with one another for limited opportunities, it was feared that Canada would fail to develop an international comparative advantage in such emerging fields as communication electronics or northern transport equipment.

In 1987 the federal government effected several significant changes in regional development policy. Firstly, a new Ministry of Industry, Science and Technology was created to formulate national development policy, particularly in the context of making Canada more competitive internationally. This new ministry is an amalgam of the former Ministry of Science and Technology and DRIE and, to some extent, replaces the functions of the Ministry of Economic and Regional Development which was disbanded in 1984. Secondly, 3 regional development agencies were created. One, the Department of Western Diversification, is designed to be a planning agency and a conduit for funds to assist in the diversification of western Canada's economy. Another, the Atlantic Canada Opportunities Agency, is designed to plan and deliver projects and programs to improve welfare and expand the economy of the Atlantic Region. A third agency, the Federal Northern Ontario Development Agency (Fednor), is designed to plan and fund economic expansion and employment creation, including the tourism

sector, in northern Ontario. It is possible that additional agencies will be created; eg, there has been discussion of a similar agency for the northern Territories of Canada. The creation of these new agencies indicates a trend toward creating larger regions for developmental programming in Canada – 2 of the new agencies are multi-provincial in composition. In all cases, the emphasis is on strengthening large-scale regional economies by concentrating on areas of potential comparative advantage. These swings in federal government policy reflect a fundamental disagreement about the proper approach to regional development in Canada. For their part, provincial governments have shown little enthusiasm for the idea of national strategies or plans. In general, provincial governments have seen regional development planning as their responsiblity, on the grounds that they are closer to the problem areas than any national agency and have a better understanding of regional needs and priorities. Certainly the various provincial governments have instituted a wide variety of development programs of their own over the years, and are likely to continue to do so. DOUGLAS WEBSTER

Reading: Economic Council of Canada, *Living Together: A Study of Regional Disparities* (1977); R. Matthews, *The Creation of Regional Dependency* (1983); P. Phillips, *Regional Disparities* (rev ed 1983); D.J. Savoie, *Regional Economic Development: Canada's Search for Solutions* (1986); C. Weaver and T.I. Gunton, "From Drought Assistance to Mega-Projects: Fifty Years of Regional Theory and Policy in Canada," *Canadian Journal of Regional Science* 5 (spring 1982); D. Webster, "Developmental Planning: State of the Art and Prescription," in W.T. Perks and I.M. Robinson, eds, *Urban and Regional Planning in a Federal State: The Canadian Experience* (1979).

Regional Economics, a subject concerned with understanding and explaining the geographic configuration of the economy, particularly regarding industrial location, regional development, urbanization, migration, land use, etc. The first major works devoted to theories of location for economic activity appeared, chiefly in Germany, at the turn of the century. As a field of study, regional economics has flourished in most industrialized nations, including Canada; it has much in common with economic geography and the new field of regional science in its emphasis upon both economic principles and the role of spatial relationships. Courses on it are offered by most Canadian universities.

The Distribution of Economic Activity in Canada Economic activity in Canada is highly localized. Ontario has, since 1910, regularly accounted for about 40% of the national total of income and production, although the percentage declined slightly during the 1970s. Ontario's gross domestic product (GDP) in 1986 was $177.6 billion, roughly comparable to Sweden's. Ontario accounts for over 50% of Canadian manufacturing, economic activity being highly concentrated in southern Ontario from Windsor to Oshawa. Corporations headquartered there, chiefly in Toronto, controlled over 50% of Canadian production in 1977 and over 50% of the assets of Canada's major financial institutions.

Québec's economy, with a GDP of $102.8 billion (1986), has since 1910 accounted for about 23% of Canada's income and production, but its share of the national total has been declining since the 1970s. The Montréal region accounts for about 45% of Québec's income and production, making it Canada's second major business centre. Corporations headquartered there controlled about 25% of Canada's production and close to 35% of the assets of Canada's major financial institutions. The 1170 km corridor from Windsor, Ont, to Québec City has sometimes been referred

to as the economic heartland of Canada, representing, during the 1980s, over 55% of Canada's population, generating over 60% of its income and production, and accounting for over 70% of its manufacturing employment.

Manitoba, Saskatchewan, Alberta and BC, with a combined GDP of about $151 billion, accounted in 1985 for roughly 32% of Canada's GDP. BC's domestic income and product have been increasing since 1910 and Alberta's energy-based economy grew dramatically in the 1970s, but has stabilized since. Vancouver and, to a lesser extent, Calgary are becoming important corporate and financial centres, although they do not yet rival Montréal and Toronto. Since the Great Depression, Manitoba's and Saskatchewan's shares of national income have decreased steadily; Manitoba's gradually, Saskatchewan's erratically, reflecting the volatility of its wheat-based economy. The position of Winnipeg as the traditional manufacturing and service centre of the Prairies is now challenged by Edmonton and Calgary. Newfoundland, NS, NB and PEI generated a combined GDP of $25.8 billion in 1986, accounting for about 6% of the national total. The economies of NS, NB and PEI have declined steadily over the last century. They represented 5% of the national GDP in 1985, compared to 16.2% in 1890. The decline (which has slowed significantly in recent decades) is often blamed on the NATIONAL POLICY following Confederation and technological changes in shipbuilding. The growth of personal income in the Atlantic provinces has generally followed the national average since 1961.

Regional Income Disparities The continuing disparity between the Atlantic region and the more affluent parts of the nation, particularly Ontario and BC, remains Canada's principal regional economic problem. During the 1980s, personal income per inhabitant in Ontario, Alberta and BC was about 35% higher than in Newfoundland, 33% higher than in NB and PEI and less than 30% higher than in NB and NS. Per capita income in Québec has also remained systematically below the national average. However, per capita income in Québec was 31% below that of Ontario in 1961, but only 15% below in 1986. The improvement can be attributed partly to efforts begun in Québec in the early 1960s to raise the educational level of its population (traditionally among the lowest in Canada). With the dramatic decline in birthrates and increasing number of women workers, the proportion of the population in the LABOUR FORCE (and of working age) has risen substantially. On the other hand, the encouragement of French language and culture in Québec has probably had an economic cost, reflected in the decline of Montréal as a business centre. Income disparities between the Prairie provinces and the rest of Canada are reflected in alternate patterns of divergence and convergence and severe fluctuations in per capita income, the result of dependence upon primary production (wheat, oil, natural gas, potash) and levels of demand, which are often determined by uncontrollable natural and international factors. Saskatchewan's relative per capita income changes erratically, 59% of the national average in 1941, 107% in 1951, 71% in 1961 and 92% in 1986. In Manitoba, where there is a stronger manufacturing base, per capita income, since 1956, has tended to remain below the national average. During a brief period in the late 1970s and early 1980s, Alberta ranked above Ontario and BC in having a per capita income above the national average. In the mid-1980s Ontario ranked first, followed by Alberta and BC.

Following the international oil crisis of 1973-74, corporate and other business income from oil production increased sharply. Most of this "windfall" income was generated in Alberta. The income generated in one region may flow to another in the form of federal government transfer payments, eg, EQUALIZATION PAYMENTS, unemployment benefits, or in interest, dividends and profits accruing to investors outside the region (see INTERGOVERNMENTAL FINANCE). The outflow from Alberta to other regions of Canada (1982-83) was about $8 billion. From the mid-1970s the federal government and energy-producing provinces (especially Alberta) were in conflict over the right to regulate, tax and redistribute energy profits. The surge of revenues from energy production upset the traditional regional balance in which Ontario was the senior "have" province and chief contributor to federal transfer schemes. However, as oil prices began to fall during the early 1980s, Alberta's oil-based economy equally began to decline, although its per capita income has remained above the national average.

The economic history of the West amply demonstrated the fragility of resource-based prosperity. Alberta's recent experience is a prime example. The recent relative deline of BC's per capita income from its traditionally very high levels must equally be traced to its high dependance on the forestry sector.

Causes of Regional Income Disparity Differences in income per person between regions may exist at any time because of variations in employment, wage rates, investment income or income from government transfer schemes. In Canada, where about 70% of personal income is derived from wages and from other labour income, employment and wage rates are by far the most important factors.

The uneven distribution of jobs in Canada is measured by variations in the portion of each province's employed population, which is based on the proportion of the population of working age (15-64 years old), the percentage of the working-age population in the labour force and the unemployment rate. The proportion of the population of working age has traditionally been lower in Atlantic Canada than elsewhere, partly as a result of EMIGRATION; labour-force participation rates have also remained low while unemployment rates have remained high. Fifty-three percent of Newfoundland's labour force was employed in 1986, compared to 72% of Alberta's, which accounts for a major portion of the disparity in per capita income.

Regional differences in wage rates may result from differences in labour productivity and in industrial structure. The traditionally high level of per capita income in BC largely reflects high wages. However, because of influences such as unionization, labour mobility, social legislation and the growth in public-service employment, a national trend towards wage equalization exists. Wage rates in Québec and Ontario, for instance, were roughly equivalent during the late 1980s. Many economists maintain that high wages may actually reduce employment opportunities in regions where they are not warranted by labour productivity. The regional disparities of employment and wages can be partly attributed to comparative advantages of location. The first areas to develop, because of natural or historical advantages, will often continue growing as the necessary markets, institutions and infrastructures are created. The St Lawrence Valley was developed because of its unique transportation advantage and agricultural potential. By building canals, roads and other infrastructures, settlers enhanced this initial natural advantage so that even before Confederation the combined populations of Québec and Ontario were already considerably larger than that of the Maritimes.

Canada's internal market is small by world

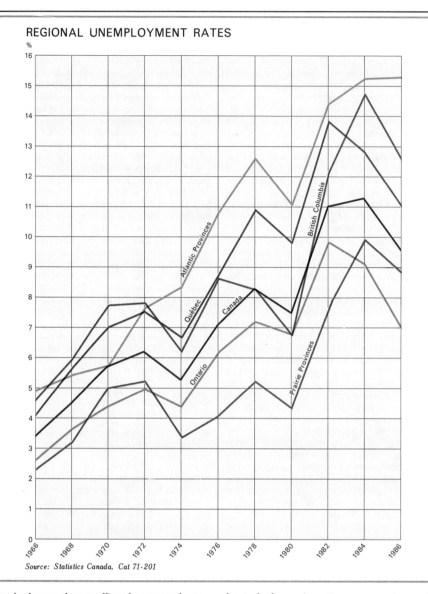

REGIONAL UNEMPLOYMENT RATES

Source: Statistics Canada, Cat 71-201

standards; one plant or office often serves the entire country. The centre of that market is clearly situated in southern Ontario and southwestern Québec. Industries in the Maritimes and the Prairie provinces were poorly located for serving the Canadian market. Modern industry and offices often require services, skills and infrastructures only found in large cities, and Atlantic Canada possesses no large urban metropolis of international calibre. Halifax cannot compare, as a business and financial centre, to Winnipeg, Calgary or Edmonton. The lack of waterways on the Prairies confounds the difficulty of reaching major markets and constitutes a special handicap to industrial development.

The position of the US as Canada's chief trading partner and source of foreign investment since WWI has benefited some regions more than others. Southern Ontario benefits not only from its access to the Great Lakes but also by its proximity to the major industrial zones of the American Midwest, of which it has in many ways become an extension – the development of an automobile industry in Windsor, across the river from Detroit, is perhaps the most obvious example. American investment is heavily concentrated in Ontario, and Toronto is the centre for US-controlled head offices. The integration of Canada into the N American economy has undoubtedly increased the isolation of Atlantic Canada, whose economic links with the UK were traditionally stronger than

those of other regions. In more recent years the growth of the PACIFIC RIM economies (Japan, China, California) has significantly benefited BC and, to some extent, Alberta.

The human element is the most elusive in regional development. Migration, for example, has a decisive impact on the quality of human resources in a region. Low-income regions in Canada are often locked into a cycle of decline because the most dynamic and educated people of working age emigrate.

The resources of British Columbia and Alberta help account for their growth. BC's high wages and productivity are the result partially of its forest resources, but also of its advantageous location and skilled labour force and Vancouver's role as an emerging industrial and business centre. The Atlantic provinces are handicapped not only by the lack of competitive, high-quality, natural resources, but by disadvantages of location and a history of decline. Natural-resource exploitation alone, however, rarely constitutes a sufficient basis for sustained economic growth. In Canada, as elsewhere, industrial and office-location patterns have had more lasting impact in determining the emergence and persistence of regional income disparities.

Regional Economic Policies Since Confederation Canadian economic policy has been influenced by regional considerations. National policies have important repercussions, intentional and

Personal Income Per Capita, by Province, 1936-1986
(Relative to the National Average; Canada = 100)
(Source: Statistics Canada, Provincial Economic Accounts)

Province	1936	1941	1946	1951	1956	1961	1966	1971	1976	1982	Excluding transfer income* (1982)	1986	Excluding transfer income* (1986)
Newfoundland	–	–	–	48.2	53.5	58.2	59.9	63.6	68.5	64.0	52.5	67.3	55.5
PEI	55.6	46.9	58.2	54.4	58.7	58.8	60.1	63.7	68.6	71.0	62.9	70.9	63.1
Nova Scotia	79.6	77.1	85.9	69.1	71.9	77.5	74.8	77.4	78.8	79.1	74.8	81.2	77.1
New Brunswick	67.4	63.9	75.2	67.0	65.9	67.8	68.9	72.2	75.6	71.1	65.3	75.1	68.3
Québec	92.1	86.6	81.5	83.9	86.1	90.1	89.0	88.8	93.0	94.5	91.3	94.2	91.4
Ontario	125.5	129.4	115.7	118.3	117.8	118.3	116.9	117.0	109.0	107.0	109.6	110.9	115.3
Manitoba	92.4	92.8	102.9	100.8	96.9	94.3	91.9	94.0	93.7	89.5	89.3	92.8	93.1
Saskatchewan	58.0	59.3	96.1	107.1	93.5	70.8	92.9	80.3	99.6	91.0	90.0	92.3	87.9
Alberta	76.3	80.0	107.8	111.0	104.6	100.0	100.0	98.9	102.6	111.6	115.4	104.6	104.9
British Columbia	131.9	120.9	114.9	119.2	121.1	114.9	115.9	109.0	109.1	111.3	113.5	99.4	98.6
Yukon & NWT	–	–	–	86.7	129.8	96.6	80.7	86.8	91.9	102.9	108.4	105.7	108.9

* Transfer income (excluded in the last column) comprises items such as unemployment benefits, family allowances and other social-welfare related payments.

unintentional, at the regional level, often creating tensions between the provinces and the federal government and between the individual provinces themselves. In recent years regional policies specifically directed at low-income areas have been developed.

Canada's protective tariff structure, a legacy of John A. MACDONALD's National Policy, designed to encourage Canadian industrialization, primarily benefited the manufacturing areas of Québec and Ontario, providing them with a captive market. Canada's tariff policies continue to grieve Atlantic Canada and the West, where consumers feel they are subsidizing the protected industries of central Canada and stifling the development of their own regions. On the other hand, Québec and Ontario have financed and continue to subsidize Canada's elaborate transport network linking the less accessible regions to major markets. The Maritime Freight Act (1927) provides for subsidies to reduce freight rates for rail shipments moving from points E of Lévis, Qué, to the rest of Canada. The subsidy has since been raised and extended to commercial trucking. Freight rates on grain shipments out of the Prairies were kept artificially low from the turn of the century by the CROW'S NEST PASS AGREEMENT (modified in 1984) and Prairie wheat farmers are assisted in the transport and marketing of their output by multiple subsidy schemes and by the Winnipeg-based CANADIAN WHEAT BOARD.

With Canada's long tradition of state enterprise, subsidies and regulation, the effect of state intervention, including fiscal and monetary policy, immigration and procurement, is difficult to evaluate. Federal ENERGY POLICY, for example, has become controversial. Before the 1972-74 oil crisis, energy policy favoured the oil-producing provinces because of the so-called Borden Line (1961), which divided Canada into 2 oil-marketing zones at the Ontario/Québec border. West of the line no imported oil could be refined or sold; foreign oil and its by-products were limited to the market east of it. The then more expensive western oil was ensured a captive market, including Ontario, but the expansion of the Montréal-based (and more easterly based) oil-refining and petrochemical industry was hampered by artificial limitation of its market at the Québec and Ontario borders. From 1973 until the mid-1980s, the national energy policy has tended to favour oil-consuming provinces by keeping internal oil prices below international levels and by redistributing a significant portion of western oil royalties. Late in 1984, the Mulroney government indicated it intended to allow domestic oil prices to match world prices.

Canada's comparatively generous system of TRANSFER-PAYMENT programs, comprising transfers both to other governments and to individuals

(unemployment benefits, family allowances, pensions), accounted for about 50% of the federal budget during the mid-1980s. Income differences would appear much greater if transfer income to individuals was excluded from personal income calculations. Newfoundland's income per person in 1986, for example, would fall from 67.3% to 56.5% of the national average. Without transfer payments, the level of regional income disparity in 1986 would be about the same as it was in 1961, implying that the improvement in Atlantic Canada's income position may be more the result of money transfers than of real improvement in the region's economy. Specific programs to encourage the development of low-income areas were established in 1962 under an Area Development Agency. In 1969 it was replaced by the Department of Regional Economic Expansion (DREE), which in 1982 was integrated into the Department of Regional Industrial Expansion (DRIE). Following a partial merger with the Department of Industry, Trade and Commerce, in 1987, DRIE was in turn in the process of being dismantled as the Mulroney government announced the creation of new regionally based agencies, the Dept of Western Diversification and the Atlantic Canada Opportunities Agency, which in part would inherit the responsibilities of the old federal departments. With the demise of DREE (1969-82) and of DRIE (1982-88), Canada seems, for the moment, to have rejected the idea of a single federal department to oversee regional development policies. DREE, during its brief existence, administered a Regional Development Incentives Act, which provided grants, special depreciation allowances and loans to encourage the location of firms in designated areas. DREE also entered into General Development Agreements with the provinces, which included infrastructure programs, mineral exploration, industrial restructuring incentives, rural development schemes, etc. The Cape Breton Development Corporation is an example of the type of undertaking in which DREE has participated. Regional policies have clearly benefited smaller regions, especially in the more depressed zones of Atlantic Canada. On the other hand, it is by no means certain, considering the scale of DREE's intervention (1.2% of the federal budget) and the effects of other national policies, that area-directed regional policies have profoundly altered the pattern of regional development in Canada.

Regional problems and policies similar to those on the national level may be found within almost every province. For example, within Ontario, disparities in per capita income and employment levels between the industrialized south and the less developed north are as distinctive as they are between provinces. In Québec, per capita income and employment levels in the Abitibi and Gaspé

regions have remained considerably below those of the greater Montréal regions. In NS the Halifax and Cape Breton regions are, respectively, fairly prosperous and economically depressed; in the western provinces and in Québec a clear difference exists between the richer urbanized southern regions and the sparsely populated northern areas. Most provinces have developed their own regional policies and objectives, often independently of the federal government; eg, Québec has established location subsidies, infrastructure investments, preferred loans, etc. MARIO POLÈSE

Reading: W.J. Coffey and Mario Polèse, *Still Living Together: Recent Trends and Future Directions in Canadian Regional Development* (1987); Economic Council of Canada, *Living Together: A Study of Regional Disparities* (1977); H. Lithwick, *Regional Economic Policy: The Canadian Experience* (rev ed 1983).

Regional Government is a structure created by the provinces, in particular Ontario, Québec and British Columbia, under which municipalities are regrouped under a regional administration. Regional governments have been created by the superimposition of a geographically larger level of government over existing municipalities to make certain municipal functions more economical and establish a tax base sufficient to enhance local services or create new ones. In Alberta there are 29 single-tier rural regional governments called counties which, since 1950, have been created through the consolidation of municipal districts with their respective school divisions. The most comprehensive reform occurred in Ontario, which in 1969 began to replace COUNTY governments (in place since 1849) with a system of 11 larger regional municipalities, which were assigned extensive responsibilities for land-use planning, water and sewerage, solid waste disposal, policing, transportation, social services and public health. The regions include CITIES, suburbs and rural TOWNSHIPS at the lower level. Regional councils comprise delegates from the lower-tier municipalities. Similar reforms took place in Québec for the regional communities centered on Montréal, Hull and Québec City. In BC a 2-tier system of 29 regional districts covering the province and focusing upon urban centres was created by statute in 1965, although the districts came into existence only at the minister's discretion. Few local boundaries were changed. The Greater Vancouver Regional District, the most developed region, is a type of METROPOLITAN GOVERNMENT. In 1967 it took over long-standing regional agencies providing water, sewerage and drainage services, later adding responsibilities such as regional parks, hospital financing and labour relations. JAMES LIGHTBODY

Reading: C.R. Tindal, *Structural Changes in Local Government: Government for Urban Regions* (1977).

Regionalism may refer to the distinctive local character of different parts of the world or to a people's perception of and identification with such places. The concept is rarely applied, for example, to differences between parts of a city or to those between continents or countries. Rather, it is usually used as an intermediate scale. In Canada the term has acquired a particular vogue as a result of many recent tensions between national and more local economic, institutional and emotional attachments. Generally the phrase "Canadian regionalism" refers broadly to the vitality of regional differences within Canada.

That regionalism is an inescapable component of society, economy and politics in Canada is hardly surprising; a national organization was imposed over a vast territory and scattered different peoples little more than 100 years ago. The nature of Canadian settlement and the spatial structure of the Canadian economy have ensured the persistence of a complex regional texture alongside the increasingly standardized late 20th-century technology, the functionally integrated economy and the national sentiments that are also part of Canadian life.

Canadian settlement developed within confined spaces characteristically bounded on the N by inhospitable land, and to the S by the US, between which are the discontinuous patches of land capable of supporting more than a handful of people. European settlers arrived early in the 17th century when a few fishermen were left behind in rockbound Newfoundland harbours. Simultaneously, a few French settlers occupied the marshlands of the Bay of Fundy, and more began to farm the narrow borders of cultivable land along the St Lawrence R. Much later, Irish, Scots and English, propelled by Highland clearances, Irish famine or the technological and demographic changes of early 19th-century industrialization, filled up the Ontario peninsula and the fishing harbours, the lumber camps and the meagre agricultural patches of Atlantic Canada (see IMMIGRATION). The descendants of all these settlers soon faced a common predicament. The patches of settlement were small, their agricultural possibilities circumscribed, and as numbers multiplied in still rural preindustrial societies, there was soon a shortage of land. The pioneer fringe ran into rock. Until the end of the 19th century, there was no western safety valve, only the granitic Canadian SHIELD and other already settled patches of British America. The surplus young faced the choice of striking N into rock and spruce or S into the US. In Atlantic Canada, Québec and Ontario, most went S where they were absorbed into a larger America; N of the border, local societies that now exported people bypassed the mixing effects of the migrations they had launched. Only when the CANADIAN PACIFIC RAILWAY reached Winnipeg in 1881 did Canada really acquire a West, but one that would be cut off to French Canadians by the Protestant outburst over Louis RIEL and by the collapse in Manitoba of French educational and linguistic guarantees. Although Ontario would be better represented there, the Canadian Prairie was settled over a short generation before WWI by migrants from eastern Canada, emigrants directly from the British Isles and from the northern fringe of the late 19th- and early 20th-century peasant migration to America from central Europe, and with a wave of American settlement moving northward along the eastern flank of the Rockies. In BC the mix was different again; much less of continental Europe, a good deal of Ontario, something of Atlantic Canada and, on the Pacific Ocean, elements from the Orient.

This was how the patches of arable land between an implacable North and the US were settled. There was no continuous, expansive Canadian experience with the land. Settlement proceeded in patches. One patch would fill up, then people would emigrate, S more often than N because the US was more inviting than the Shield. Until the last century, there was no settlers' West. The next Canadian patch was inaccessible or occupied, and when a West finally did open, the eastern settlements would be partially represented and much diluted there. The process of Canadian settlement had imparted striking discontinuities. Canada did not expand westward from an Atlantic beginning. Different patches were settled at different times by people of different backgrounds who depended on different technologies and economies.

This pattern of settlement sharply differentiated the Canadian experience from the American. There the land was perceived as a garden as readily as wilderness, and it attracted far more settlers and focused European dreams. There eastern

seaboard beginnings could migrate westward to desert margins over 3000 km inland that were the first major environmental obstacle to an expanding agrarian civilization. There the West was a lure for 300 years. As different streams from the initial settlements along the colonial seaboard, augmented by newcomers from Europe, moved westward, different ways met and substantially merged. As it gathered momentum in the late 18th and early 19th centuries the American occupation of an essentially welcoming land had the capacity to mold different peoples into a relatively homogeneous culture as it spread them over an astonishing area. But in Canada, where all of this was checked by the physical limits of settlements, the country's underlying population structure was disjointed and discontinuous.

The spatial structure of the Canadian economy also worked to strengthen Canadian regionalism. In the late 19th century an industrial technology with the capacity to integrate the bulky products of a large area within a single market was superimposed on the patches of Canadian settlement. Such spatial integration could create metropolitan centres where there were clear economies of agglomeration and distribution, and extensive resource and market hinterlands. Railways and factories would impose this economic structure on Canada; the only issues were at what scale and in what direction. The decision to create a Canadian market was implicit in Confederation and explicit in the NATIONAL POLICY that followed it. Protected by tariffs from the US, the metropolitan centre (see INDUSTRIAL STRATEGY) stabilized in the St Lawrence-Great Lakes lowland where most of the market was located and where there was optimal overall access to the hinterlands to the E and W. The rest of the country would consume the manufactures of the core, and would supply it with some raw materials. This structure could be intensified by public or private policy, eg, by changing freight rates, but given the pattern of Canadian settlement at Confederation and the character of industrial economy, it followed in all essentials from the decision to create a Canadian market. Canadian settlements achieved a considerable functional economic integration; most secondary industry and associated financial institutions were concentrated in Montréal or around the western end of Lk Ontario, resource-based primary industries were scattered across the land, and core and periphery were linked by growing commercial and financial networks.

Economically, such integration encouraged sharp regional specialization, reflected, for example, in the Prairie wheat economy. Emotionally, it laid the basis for strikingly different regional perceptions of Canada. Those at the core tended to feel expansive about the country on which their economy relied and over which their institutions exerted much influence, although French Canadians, who worked in the factories but did not own them, would have no entrepreneurial enthusiasm for a transcontinental country and a good deal of cultural suspicion of it. But for most English speakers in the core a British Canada from sea to sea, which would reinforce their traditions as it expanded their markets, seemed authentic and just. On the other hand, those on the peripheries would be suspicious of the core, their suspicion stemming from a sense that local circumstances were controlled from afar, and from the conviction that by being forced "to sell cheap and buy dear" they were subsidizing central Canada and absorbing the cost of Confederation. What was a National Policy in central Canada could easily be interpreted by the Maritimes as Upper Canadian imperialism, and in the West as the manipulation of James and Bay streets. From a Prairie or Mar-

itime vantage point, the "Big Interests" and "Special Privilege" lived in central Canada.

The pattern of Canadian settlement and the tensions between core and periphery inherent in a national economy are sufficient to account for a strikingly regional Canada, but factors such as distance, the varied physical geography of a vast land and, in many parts of Canada, the considerable, growing presence of native peoples, also contributed. Canadian regionalism has not always expressed itself in the same fashion, however. Since Confederation regional feelings have been associated with local settlements, with substantial parts of provinces (eg, Cape Breton I), with provinces, and with such amorphous, poorly defined territories as the Maritimes, central Canada and the West. Among these, the provinces are now the primary exponents of the country's fragmented structure. Settlements that once provided definition and defence for traditional ways have been overridden by modern transportation and communications, while the state has assumed a growing symbolic and practical importance. In this situation, the Canadian province, with its constitutionally defined power, tends to replace both the local settlements that no longer define Canadian life and the broader but amorphous regions that have no clear political definition. It is this simplified and thereby politically more powerful regionalism that increasingly confronts the concept and the sentiment of Canada.

The consolidation of regional sentiment in the provinces occurred while governments were assuming a larger role in Canadian life and while the evolution of the Canadian economy was changing the significance of some of the terms of the BRITISH NORTH AMERICA ACT (now CONSTITUTION ACT, 1867). Provincial governments have played a growing role in the economy, and the provinces a growing role in Canadian feeling. Many activities that were once organized at different regional levels are now organized provincially. Simultaneously, federal power has increased as Ottawa has expanded its services and its economic presence. The result of this growth of provincial and federal governments is an increasingly polarized debate between national and more regional conceptions of Canada that is also a debate between 2 levels of government. The political consolidation of regionalism in provincial governments is felt across the country, but is probably most obvious in Québec. The culture of a French-speaking, Roman Catholic people was once defended by the local community, by a variety of nationalistic societies, and above all by the Roman Catholic Church. For some, the clearest defence of culture was a rural life and a high birthrate, and from this perspective the provincial government could do little more than encourage colonization. In recent years government has assumed the defence of culture; many French-speaking Québecois have concentrated on increasing the political power of the Québec government. The protection of the French language, a central element of the regional variety of Canada, has become an essentially political issue dependent on different conceptions of federal and provincial responsibility. The economy is an even more pervasive source of federal-provincial conflict. The location of oil and coal fields and the growing economic importance of the Pacific basin have challenged economic assumptions held by Canadians for almost 100 years. Core and peripheries seem to have come unstuck and in a country like Canada it takes only the possibility of this change to raise the ghosts of 100 years of spatial tension. For some provinces it seems their turn has come – as long as the natural momentum of different circumstances is left to run its course. But if federal political power resides in the core, and if the Constitution Act leaves ample opportunity for federal influence on resource policy, then the economic advantages of the peripheries can be compromised by the protective instincts of the core, which accounts for the aggressiveness of western provinces and Newfoundland over resource control. As long as the federal government is elected in central Canada, as it is likely to be, a conflict over the spatial economy is immediately translated into a conflict between different levels of government.

Canadian regionalism is now most vigorously promoted by provincial politicians and is most stridently expressed in federal-provincial debate, but underneath this rhetoric lies the far more subtle regional texture of Canadian life. It is expressed in the distinctive landscapes of farm, village and city, across the breadth of Canada. It is expressed in different accents and different memories of different pasts. It is expressed in the ways of life associated with different resource-based economies in different physical settings. It is expressed in the relationships of towns to different hinterlands and to different positions in the urban system. And it is expressed most sensitively throughout Canadian painting and literature. *See also* FEDERALISM. R. COLE HARRIS

Regionalism in Literature Geographer R. Cole Harris describes the inhabited part of Canada as "an island archipelago spread over 4000 east-west miles.... Different islands were settled at different times within different technologies and economies by people from different backgrounds." Throughout Canada's history this concept has been a powerful alternative to the idea of a homogeneous nation spreading from sea to sea. To the writer, Northrop FRYE argues, the concept is essential: "What affects the writer's imagination...is an environment rather than a nation.... Regionalism and literary maturity seem to grow together."

But in 1943, E.K. BROWN suggested in *On Canadian Poetry* that REGIONALISM threatened the growth of a Canadian literature, "because it stresses the superficial and peculiar at the expense, at least, if not to the exclusion, of the fundamental and universal." The main achievement of Canadian literature before WWII was finding the vocabulary, and some sense of appropriate forms, to articulate authentically a new place. Given the power of the imperial language and its literary tradition, the accomplishment was great but in itself could only be "superficial." Those early writers, committed to naming the details of a new world, inevitably emphasized a local area. T.C. HALIBURTON, our first humorist, was regional in his recording of the dialects and folkways of pre-Confederation Nova Scotia; Charles G.D. ROBERTS depicted the New Brunswick landscape, particularly in *Songs of the Common Day* (1893); D.C. SCOTT evoked several northern settings in his narratives of Indian life. The popular romance, which dominated Canadian fiction until 1920, encouraged the more sentimental side of regionalism, with quaint peculiarities of mannerism or costume to provide relief from the didacticism and melodrama. Gilbert PARKER's historical romances are unusual in suggesting a connection between setting and character. Ralph Connor (C.W. GORDON) animated his best-selling, fictionalized sermons with the local colour of Glengarry and the Canadian West.

Regional literature in the more precise sense is tied to the conventions of realism because it attempts to distinguish accurately the features of a clearly definable region, either rural or closely linked to the land. In its fullest achievement such regional literature, as the works of Thomas Hardy and William Faulkner show, is not synonymous

with surface detail and pedestrian style but with profound exploration of the shaping influence of particular regions on individual lives.

Anticipated by D.C. Scott's connected short stories *In The Village of Viger* (1896), by Sara Jeannette DUNCAN's finely detailed picture of Brantford in *The* IMPERIALIST (1904), and by Stephen LEACOCK's humorous insights in SUNSHINE SKETCHES OF A LITTLE TOWN (1912), literary regionalism firmly established itself in Canada in the 1920s, particularly in Frederick Philip GROVE's suite of essays, *Over Prairie Trails* (1922), and his novels *Settlers of the Marsh* (1925) and FRUITS OF THE EARTH (1933). Other western writers more inclined to the romance, such as Martha OSTENSO, Robert STEAD and Frederick NIVEN, contribute to an identification of literary regionalism and the Prairies in this period. In LITERATURE IN FRENCH, the interest in *le terroir*, associated with the École littéraire de Montréal in the late 19th century, continued strongly into the 1930s; comparison of Louis HÉMON's MARIA CHAPDELAINE (1916) with TRENTE ARPENTS (1938) by Ringuet (Philippe PANNETON) shows the same shift from sentimentalism to realism that took place in LITERATURE IN ENGLISH.

Until 1940, however, even Grove's frequently ponderous prose and the nostalgia implicit in *le terroir* justify Brown's view of the inherent weakness of regionalism. But Sinclair ROSS's AS FOR ME AND MY HOUSE (1941) demonstrated that Canadian literature could be intensely concerned with regional landscape and social structure, and that it could also be challenging in its shrewd use of form and language. Certainly much of the most interesting Canadian fiction of the next 15 years is confidently regional: Emily CARR's KLEE WYCK (1941), W.O. MITCHELL's WHO HAS SEEN THE WIND (1947), Hugh MACLENNAN's *Each Man's Son* (1951), Ernest BUCKLER's *The Mountain and the Valley* (1952), Ethel WILSON's *Hetty Dorval* (1947) and SWAMP ANGEL (1954), and Charles BRUCE's *The Channel Shore* (1954). More recently Margaret LAURENCE's Manawaka, Alice MUNRO's Jubilee and, in drama, James REANEY's SouWestO have become favourite places in Canadian literature. Except for Edward McCourt's *The Canadian West in Fiction* (1949; rev 1970), sustained critical comment on literary regionalism did not appear until the early 1970s when a proliferation of studies and anthologies began to change the direction of Canadian studies. The concurrent decentralization of political power in the 1970s was reflected in various stimuli to the growth and awareness of regional literatures: the development of provincial arts councils or departments of cultural affairs, the creation of academic courses and centres for regional studies, the organization of many conferences with regional emphases, and the appearance of dozens of LITERARY PERIODICALS with pronounced regional loyalties.

A fantastic, or burlesque, or even anti-regional regionalism emerged as a significant extension of regional fiction, especially in the works of such writers as Sheila WATSON, Robert KROETSCH and Jack HODGINS. Meanwhile, many regional SMALL PRESSES, from Breakwater in St John's, Nfld, to Oolichan in Lantzville, BC, appeared to promote the growth of regional poetry, in which the connection between region and realism continues to be strong. Al PURDY's fusing of artifacts, stories and voices of particular regions has been extremely influential. Canadian regional poets, as various as Alden NOWLAN, Don Gutteridge, Andrew SUKNASKI, Glen Sorestad and Peter Trower, find inspiration in Purdy's casual combining of historical processes and the immediately local.

In the 1980s writers and critics have developed a different approach to region, one that is conceptually broader (embracing ideas of culture, wealth and class) and theoretically more focused

(incorporating the sciences of perception, cognition, anthropology and rhetoric). Regional presses expanded ambitiously, from poetry to chapbooks to fiction and nonfiction, consolidating their regional interests. A connection to place and land remains important, but the multitude of historical, economic, ethnic and linguistic regions which comprise Harris's archipelago are shifting or destroying the boundaries of the traditional regions (Atlantic, Québec, Ontario, Prairies, British Columbia, North), which have too simplistically shaped the understanding of Canada's literary regionalism. LAURIE RICOU

Régis, Louis-Marie, priest, Thomist philosopher (b at Hébertville, Qué 8 Dec 1903). Régis is one of the most productive Catholic philosophers in Canada and one of the few whose work is well known in both languages. He was educated chiefly at Dominican colleges in St-Hyacinthe, Qué; Hainault, Belgium; and Ottawa; though he also studied briefly at Oxford, Cologne and Paris. He has taught in Montréal and Ottawa. Of his some 60 books and articles, the best known are *St. Thomas and Epistemology* (1946) and *Epistemology* (1959). The latter, widely used in Catholic colleges and universities, emphasizes and theorizes about the importance of scientific knowledge. LESLIE ARMOUR

Regulatory Process All levels of government in Canada are involved in regulation. Because many activities in Canada are regulated (eg, airline routes, the types and prices of service provided by telecommunications companies, the number of taxicabs in a municipality and how much they may charge), regulatory systems must be tailored to particular needs. However, certain standard models of regulatory agencies have been widely adopted. In the 1980s there was growing concern over regulatory reform, partly in the form of "deregulation" (though not as thoroughly as in the US) and in proposals and actions that have led to more, or expanded, regulation.

Regulatory Agencies There are 3 main types of regulatory agency: self-governing bodies, which regulate the conduct of their own members; independent government agencies and boards; and regular line departments headed directly by ministers, which regulate specified industries and activities. Familiar examples of self-governing bodies include the professions, eg, law, medicine and accounting, which are empowered by provincial legislatures to determine their own requirements for admission and to discipline members who do not adhere to prescribed standards of professional conduct.

With self-governing bodies, regulators are drawn from the professions themselves. Government regulatory agency members, on the other hand, are appointed by government. Called commissions (eg, Public Service Commission), boards (eg, NS Board of Public Utility Commissioners) or tribunals (eg, Ontario Commercial Registration Appeal Tribunal), these agencies derive their authority from the legislature, and no regulatory agency has any more authority than that expressly delegated to it by the legislature.

An occupational safety branch of a provincial Department of Labour that decides and enforces employment safety standards is an example of a departmental regulatory agency. Certain agencies may appear more independent than they really are; eg, the FOREIGN INVESTMENT REVIEW AGENCY (FIRA) assessed the benefits of foreign investments but in reality only advised the federal Cabinet, which made the actual decisions. In many fields of public policy (eg, energy, communications) often all 3 types of regulatory agency are in existence.

If the members of an agency are appointed for

fixed terms with tenure (unlike other civil servants who may be reassigned at any time) and if the agency has a separate and distinct existence outside of any government department, then it is an independent regulatory agency. A typical agency of this type is the CANADIAN RADIO-TELE-VISION AND TELECOMMUNICATIONS COMMISSION (CRTC), which regulates the Canadian broadcasting system and the federal telecommunications carriers. It has its own staff and and is completely separate from the federal Dept of Communications. Although these types of agencies are created by the legislatures and are answerable to them and rely on them for operating funds, they are still, when compared to a branch of a government department, relatively independent. Independence, however, is rarely absolute, in that the Cabinet or a particular minister (or both) may often issue directives to a board and has the power to appoint regulators and approve their budgets.

Policy Formulation and Implementation Independent regulatory agencies characteristically operate in an open manner, though the degree of openness varies greatly. Their procedures are designed to allow for some degree of public participation. In a typical proceeding a company will apply either for an increase in the rates it charges customers or for a licence for some procedure. Notice of this application will appear in the government's official gazette and possibly in local newspapers so that interested persons may attend a public hearing to state their support or disapproval of the applications. The agency then renders a decision. Such procedures may be appropriate for specific decisions but may not be suitable for determining broader policy issues. Here a somewhat different procedure is often used. Notice is given of a proposed new policy rule and interested persons are invited to comment. There may be an informal public hearing.

Regulators will often discover that they must fill a policy gap. When legislatures create regulatory agencies, they often leave it to the regulator to develop rules that give specific meaning to broad legislative standards. For example, a regulator may be instructed to issue licences for commercial trucking operations where "public necessity and convenience" indicate that licences should be issued. Another regulator may issue airline routes "in the public interest" or allow only "just and reasonable" rates to be charged to telecommunications consumers, phrases so vague that regulators will feel obliged to outline precisely the applicable criteria, which in effect means they are making policy and exercising considerable discretionary power. Theoretically, in the Canadian system of government, only elected officials make major policy decisions because they alone are politically accountable and may be voted out of office for unpopular policies. But the broad statutory language employed not only allows but in practice requires regulators who are appointed to determine major policies about, eg, trucking and air transportation and telecommunications. Consequently, it is often suggested that the Cabinet be given authority to issue binding policy directives to the independent regulatory agencies. Indeed, in the case of some agencies, this power already exists. This provision often creates dual standards of political accountability that are not always wholly compatible, since one provision ensures greater political accountability through elected ministers whereas the other seeks to provide opportunities for direct public participation in policymaking.

Evaluation of Regulatory Process Professional self-regulation is usually in the best interests of a profession but not necessarily of the public. Self-regulating bodies need to be continually scruti-

nized both by the public and by legislatures. The major need in departmental regulation is for increased access, for the public and elected legislators, to precise information. Unless the public has access to information, it cannot hold regulators accountable. Where regulation is by way of an independent agency, it is essential that opportunities for public participation exist and are acted upon; otherwise such agencies tend to be influenced by the industries they are supposed to regulate. The ultimate evaluation of regulatory agencies is not only based on the process used but is also dependent upon the often – indeed usually – conflicting underlying values that govern the purposes that regulation in particular sectors is supposed to serve. H.N. JANISCH

Reading: G.B. Doern, ed, *The Regulatory Process in Canada* (1978).

Reichmann Family, real-estate developers. The 3 brothers, Albert, Paul and Ralph were born in Austria where their parents had moved in 1928 and after further moves to France, Spain and Morocco, they arrived in Canada in 1956. They started their business career in Montréal, where they bought Olympia Floor and Wall Tile. In the 1950s they moved into real estate and in 1969 incorporated Olympia & York, a private enterprise entirely controlled by the family. In 1962 they moved into office-tower development. Their real-estate company started operations in the US in 1976 and is now reportedly the largest private real-estate company in the world, with holdings held directly and indirectly in about 30 N American cities. In 1980 they bought English Property Corp, one of the largest British developers, and also bought a 50.1% interest in Brinco Ltd. In 1981 they paid $502 million for Abitibi-Price Inc, the world's largest newspaper producer and in 1985 acquired the majority interest in GULF CANADA RESOURCES, in the second-largest takeover in Canadian history. Olympia & York also has investments in Royal Trust and several other large Canadian companies. A much publicized take-over struggle with a British conglomerate, Allied Lyons PLC, for control of Hiram Walker-Gooderham & Worts ended up with the brothers becoming the largest shareholder of Allied Lyons. In 1987 the Reichmanns unveiled plans for a massive development in Miami and a $6.5-billion project in London, Eng. JORGE NIOSI

Reid, Daphne Kate, actress (b at London, Eng 4 Nov 1930). She studied at the Royal Conservatory of Music, Toronto, and trained with Uta Hagen, New York. She first appeared at Hart House Theatre and made her professional debut with Muskoka's Straw Hat Players. By 1962 this warm and vulnerable performer had starred in London, Eng, at the STRATFORD FESTIVAL and in New York, and since then she has divided her time between the US and Canada. She has been nominated for an Emmy Award as Queen Victoria (*Disraeli* 1963) and 2 "Tonys" (*Dylan* 1964 and *Slapstick Tragedy* 1966). In 1984-85, she starred as Linda Loman opposite Dustin Hoffman in the Broadway revival of *Death of a Salesman*. Honours in Canada include ACTRA and Dora Mavor Moore Awards in 1980 and 1981. Some Stratford Festival roles have been Juliet's nurse (1960), Lady Macbeth (1962), Chekhov's Mme Ranevskaya (1965) and Fonsia in *The Gin Game* (1980). She has played also at Stratford, Conn (1969, 1974), the SHAW FESTIVAL (1976) and the NATIONAL ARTS CENTRE (1983). In addition to frequent TV appearances ("Phillip Marlowe," "The Execution of Raymond Graham"), she has been in a number of feature films, including *The Andromeda Strain, A Delicate Balance, Atlantic City* and *Captive Hearts*. DAVID GARDNER

Reid, Escott Meredith, diplomat (b at Campbellford, Ont 21 Jan 1905). A graduate of U of T and Oxford, Reid concentrated on Canadian foreign policy and neutrality after he became national secretary of the Canadian Institute of International Affairs in 1932. In 1938 he joined the Dept of External Affairs; he served in Washington (1939-41, 1944-45), in Ottawa where he helped shape air transport policy, and in San Francisco and London where he worked on the creation of the UN. Lester PEARSON's chief aide, 1946-49, Reid was instrumental in devising the idea of a collective security alliance of Western democracies, which culminated in NATO. Thereafter, his career led to New Delhi and Bonn, to the International Bank for Reconstruction and Development, and to Glendon College, York U, as first principal. Reid's own important writings on politics and diplomacy include *Time of Fear and Hope* (1977), *Envoy to Nehru* (1981) and *Hungary and Suez, 1956: A View from New Delhi* (1987). J.L. GRANATSTEIN

Reid, George Agnew, painter (b at Wingham, Canada W 25 July 1860; d at Toronto 23 Aug 1947). Reid brought Parisian Academy precision to emotional genre paintings of his own Ontario country people. Trained at the Central Ontario School of Art, Toronto (1879), the Pennsylvania Academy (1883), and the Julian and Colarossi academies, Paris, and the Prado, Madrid (1888-89), Reid turned from portraiture to genre, as in *The Foreclosure of the Mortgage* (1893), making his name with these successful narrative pictures. He was elected to the Royal Canadian Academy of Arts in 1889, and was principal of the Central Ontario School of Art and Design (later Ontario Coll of Art) 1912-18. He also did murals and private and public commissions, including Toronto City Hall. ANNE MCDOUGALL

George Agnew Reid, *The Call to Dinner* (1887), oil on canvas. Reid turned from portraiture and made his name in genre painting (*courtesy McMaster U Coll*).

Reid, Richard Gavin, farmer, politician, premier of Alberta 1934-35 (b at Aberdeenshire, Scot 17 Jan 1879; d at Edmonton 17 Oct 1980). Reid served in the British Royal Army Medical Corps in the SOUTH AFRICAN WAR 1900-02 and sought his fortune in Canada in 1903. Following interludes of lumbering in Ontario and farming near Winnipeg, Reid moved to a homestead S of Mannville, Alta. One of the successful UNITED FARMERS OF ALBERTA candidates in the 1921 provincial election, Reid held several portfolios over the next 13 years. When Premier John E. BROWNLEE resigned in 1934, Reid was selected as his successor and sworn in as premier, president of the Executive Council and provincial secretary on 10 July 1934. Despite bringing in innovative debt adjustment legislation, Reid and his government were placed in an impossible political position facing, on the one hand, UFA executive preference for the new Co-operative Commonwealth Federation and, on the other hand, the strong appeal to farmers of William ABERHART's Social Credit proposals. The UFA government was swept from office in the 1935 election. Reid set himself up briefly as a commission agent, then served on the Canadian government's mobilization board during WWII, and finally acted for many years as librarian for Canadian Utilities in Edmonton. CARL BETKE

Reid, Sir Robert Gillespie, bridge and railway builder, financier (b at Coupar Angus, Scot 1842; d at Montréal 3 June 1908). He worked briefly in Australia as a contractor and then came to Canada (1871). His fame in Canada as a bridge builder comes from his construction of the Lachine bridge across the St Lawrence R at Montréal, the bridge at Sault Ste Marie and the international bridge over the Niagara R (with Casimir GZOWSKI 1870-73). Reid became involved in the building of the CPR and constructed difficult sections of the line along the N shore of Lk Superior. In 1890 he contracted to build railways for the Newfoundland government. Within 6 years, Reid's line had crossed the Island, and thereafter he developed telegraphs, steamships and natural resources. Reid, and later his sons, controlled communication and transportation systems on the Island through Reid-Newfoundland Co until the Nfld government took over in 1923. DAVID EVANS

Reid, William Ronald, Bill, sculptor (b at Vancouver 12 Jan 1920). An internationally recognized HAIDA artist, Reid is frequently credited with the revival and innovative resurgence of Northwest Coast Indian arts in the contemporary world. Son of a Haida mother and a Scots-American father, Reid was a teenager before he knew of his native heritage. Later in life, while a CBC broadcaster, he studied jewellery and engraving at Ryerson, Toronto (1948), and began investigating the arts of the Haida in 1951. Furthering these studies, he went to the Central School of Art and Design in London, Eng (1968). Returning to Vancouver, he became involved with the creation of a monumental sculpture for UBC, *Haida Village*, eventually becoming a recognized leading authority on Haida art and life. Accomplished in many media, Reid carves in silver, gold, wood and argillite and casts in bronze. He has issued several editions of serigraphs and has illustrated and collaborated on many books, including *The Raven Steals the Light* (1984). Among his major works are the 4.5-ton cedar sculpture *Raven and the First Humans* in UBC's Museum of Anthropology (1980); a bronze killer whale sculpture, *The Chief of the Undersea World*, for the Vancouver Aquarium (1984); and a canoe commissioned for Expo 86 (1986). He was awarded an honorary doctorate from UBC in 1976 and the Molson Prize in 1977. Reid is an eloquent and outspoken proponent of native rights in Canada and has been especially active in the battle to preserve the national and cultural history of S Moresby in the Queen Charlotte Is. CAROL SHEEHAN

Reindeer, see CARIBOU.

Reindeer Lake, 6650 km², elev 337 m, max length 233 km, located on the border between

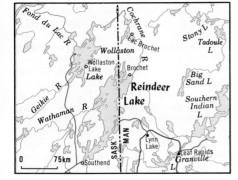

northeastern Saskatchewan and northwestern Manitoba, is the second-largest lake in Saskatchewan and ninth largest in Canada. It has a heavily indented shoreline and contains numerous small islands. On its E shore is the community of Kinoosao, at its N end Brochet, Man, and at its S end, Southend, Sask. It drains mainly to the S, via the Reindeer R and a controlled weir, to the CHURCHILL R and thence E to Hudson Bay. Fishing is an important industry in the area, and sportfishermen are drawn by its clear and deep waters. The name of the lake appears to be a translation of the Algonquian name. DAVID EVANS

Reisman, Sol Simon, public servant (b at Montréal 19 June 1919). Reisman was educated at McGill U and London School of Economics. He joined the Canadian Dept of Labour in 1946 and shortly thereafter moved to the Finance Dept, then the nerve centre of the federal government. Reisman specialized in trade policy, as a member of Canada's delegation to the first GATT talks and as an assistant director of research for the Royal Commission on CANADA'S ECONOMIC PROSPECTS (Gordon Commission). He was promoted to the new post of deputy minister of industry in 1965; he subsequently served as secretary of the Treasury Board (1968-70) and deputy minister of finance (1970-74). He was Canada's principal negotiator for the Autopact of 1965 (*see* CANADA-US AUTOMOTIVE PRODUCTS AGREEMENT), a role for which his forceful personality and ingenious disposition was ideal. After a spell as an Ottawa lobbyist, he was chosen by the Mulroney government to head Canada's negotiating team in the FREE TRADE negotiations with the US in 1985. After 16 months of often fractious negotiation, an agreement was finally signed by PM Mulroney and Pres Reagan in Jan 1988 and awaited ratification in the 2 countries. ROBERT BOTHWELL

Reitman, Ivan, film producer, director (b at Komarno, Czech 27 Oct 1946). His family fled their native country in 1950, later immigrating to Toronto. While attending McMaster U (majoring in music), he became involved with theatre and film, and after attending a summer course at the National Film Board made 2 short films, one of which he sold to the CBC and 20th Century Fox. In 1969 he produced a 16 mm soft-core sex feature, *Columbus of Sex*, and entered the world of the exploitation movie, where he thrived. Two B-budget horror movies with a touch of humour, *Cannibal Girls* (1973) and *Shivers* (1975, directed by David CRONENBERG), were highly successful on the world market and paved the way for *National Lampoon's Animal House* (1978) and *Meatballs* (1979), huge trend-setting hits which earned hundreds of millions and introduced such performers as John Belushi and Bill Murray to avid, teenaged movie audiences. Now based in Los Angeles, Reitman sealed his reputation as a producer of commercial gold-mines with *Stripes* (1981) and, especially, with *Ghostbusters* (1984), which grossed $310 million and became the biggest moneymaking comedy ever. Reitman's successes have had an enormous impact on the kinds of movies made in Hollywood in the 1980s, and he is regarded there with almost superstitious awe despite the relative failure of his $40-million romantic comedy *Legal Eagles* (1986).
WILLIAM BEARD

Relève, La, monthly magazine fd 1934 in Montréal by Paul Beaulieu, Robert CHARBONNEAU, Jean Le Moyne and Claude Hurtubise. The magazine published 103 issues before its demise in 1948, the first 48 as *La Relève* and the rest as *La Nouvelle Relève*. Major Québec contributors included Le Moyne, Robert Élie, Roger Duhamel and Saint-Denys GARNEAU, and later Guy Frégault, Berthelot

Brunet and others; among the major French ones were Daniel-Rops, Jacques Maritain, Emmanuel Mounier and Georges Bernanos. The original objective was to establish an "independent, national and Catholic" group to work towards correcting the sad lack of art, literature and philosophy in the country. The main themes were the economic crisis of the 1930s, perceived as a crisis of civilization; revolution, ie, the transformation of society in accordance with a Mounier-inspired "personalist" and communal belief system (*see* CITÉ LIBRE); CATHOLICISM, the best way to establish a new social consensus modelled on the Christian Middle Ages; art and literature as a means of spiritual development; marriage and the family, values badly needed in a chaotic world. The magazine explored these subjects with great openness of spirit – something that set it apart from other nationalist and traditionalist publications. However, edited by young bourgeois Montréalers with no financial worries, it was also highly idealistic: its articles frequently posed general questions about contemporary civilization but ignored the real problems then facing Québec society. It had little social, economic or political impact, but it did make a significant contribution to the world of ideas. *See also* LITERARY PERIODICALS IN FRENCH.
JACQUES PELLETIER

Religion [Lat *religio*, "respect for what is sacred"] may be defined as the relationship between human beings and their transcendent source of value. In practice it may involve various forms of communication with a higher power, such as prayers, rituals at critical stages in life, meditation or "possession" by spiritual agencies. Religions, though differing greatly in detail, usually share most of the following characteristics: a sense of the holy or the sacred (often manifested in the form of gods, or a personal God); a system of beliefs; a community of believers or participants; ritual (which may include standard forms of invocation, sacraments or rites of initiation); and a moral code.

In Canada the principal religion is CHRISTIANITY, to which 90% of the population claims adherence. Before European settlement the native peoples practised a wide variety of religions (*see* NATIVE PEOPLE, RELIGION). Many native individuals and groups were converted to Christianity through missionary work that began in New France, but in recent years there has been a revival of native religions in a number of regions. During the 19th century, and boosted particularly by 20th-century immigration, numerous other traditions have come to Canada. By the 1980s JUDAISM, BUDDHISM, SIKHISM, HINDUISM, ISLAM and the BAHA'I FAITH were well represented. The various traditions can be contrasted according to whether their sense of the sacred is focused on historic events (Judaism, Christianity, Islam, Sikhism and the Baha'i Faith) or on the natural cycle and rhythms of life (Hinduism, Taoism and, to some extent, Buddhism). But such contrasts overlook the fact that similar phenomena are found across traditions.

In the academic study of religion, Christians have generally been among the leaders, and therefore Christian usages and definitions of the descriptive vocabulary of religious studies tend to dominate discussions of the subject, as do Christian views of what constitutes religion. In N America this tendency has been influenced most strongly by Protestant Christianity. The Protestant Reformation of the 16th century marked a reaction initiated against priestly religion by scholars such as Martin Luther (*see* LUTHERANS) and John Calvin (*see* CALVINISM), who studied the Bible in its original languages of Hebrew and Greek, rather than in Latin translation. Following

St Paul, Luther stressed what God does for humanity through Christ, rather than how human beings prove themselves for God, with the result that faith (trust in God's action), rather than ritual (human routines), became the touchstone of what Protestants regarded as true religion. The preachers, rather than the priests, became the leaders in Protestantism, basing the Christian message on the prophetic tradition of the Hebrew Bible and summarizing it in set creeds. Consequently, to most N Americans religion has come to mean a system of beliefs. Since Christians are theists (believers in a personal god), their central belief has been in God as creator, redeemer and judge of the world.

In recent centuries, partly under the impact of the prophetic emphasis on personal faith and social justice, Christians and Jews influenced by the PHILOSOPHY of Immanuel Kant have emphasized the moral life as the key to true religion. Consequently, a full account of religion in our culture typically refers to moral codes, as well as cultic practices and creedal affirmations, as equally necessary components of any organized religion.

The contrast between the cultural compromises of different churches and "true religion" (considered as true faith, moral probity or purified ritual) means that, in the case of Christianity and other major religious movements such as Buddhism, one has to distinguish between the cultural forms associated with a religious tradition and its "critical edge"; this is usually derived from its otherworldly perspective, or from contrasting the ideal life portrayed in its scriptures with the historical practices of different congregations. Allowing for both aspects, one may then see religion as the present interplay between past and future: ie, between traditional faith and ultimate hope in the life of individuals and communities. For instance, Christianity includes a range of practices, organizations and expectations of a life where God's will is fully realized (defined by many as heaven); Buddhism includes the ordinary customs of the monks and laity with respect to life in this world (*samsara*), and the expectation of ultimate bliss (*nirvana*). One reason that traditional religion is thought to be contradicted by secular culture is that the secular outlook makes no allowance for any ultimate hope resting on expectations not bound by historical circumstance. As religion loses its hold on its sacred reference it seems to lose its reason for being.

Christian views have tended to dominate discussions of religion, but in the academic study of the subject the impact of the SOCIAL SCIENCES has led to a more functional approach to the data. As anthropologists have made us more familiar with so-called primal traditions, including those of native N American peoples, scholars of religion have had to reconsider emphases and choice of categories. For instance, where a culture is shaped without a codified scripture (such as the Bible) and without official creeds, the meaning of different rituals is typically carried by myths relayed orally from generation to generation. Scholars have tended to fasten on cosmogonic myths (myths of creation) as the religiously significant ones. However, the most significant myths may remain concealed from researchers: the SHAMANS or tribal seers and medicine men who perform the rituals often keep secret their most sacred traditions, which relate the ways of the group's ancestors to the ordeals of tribal life. Analysis of such traditions uses the contrast between the religious and the secular, since the sacred is equally secular ("this-worldly") in these traditions. By "sacred" is meant whatever is of foundational value in a given society, its point of reference for bringing order out of chaos. Through myth and ritual the symbolic system of values is often tied to specific

events and places, so that within any given group we find sacred mountains, sacred trees and rivers, sacred plants, etc.

The functional approach to religion can be used also in analysing the literary religious traditions that rely on written scriptures. For instance, the importance of Mt Zion or Jerusalem in Judaism, Rome in CATHOLICISM, and the river Jordan in revivalist Protestant sects indicates the importance of sacred places and times in Judaeo-Christian culture, as does the close association of Christmas and Easter with winter and spring festivals. One consequence of the use of social-science methodology in the study of religion is that a given people's profession of faith is now much less likely to be taken at face value than it was when its leaders controlled the study of religion. (For instance, the hierarchical structure of the Catholic and major Protestant churches, with its identification of God as Heavenly Father, may be viewed by some as a set of myths and rituals serving to reinforce male supremacy, rather than as a response to divine revelation.)

At the same time, a functional approach teaches us to look beyond the confines of formally organized religious groups for the full picture of religion. In modern Canada, a complete analysis would look to rituals associated with Hockey Night in Canada and the Grey Cup, as well as with the Hebrew Bible, when the discussion turns to our foundational values. Among our sacred places, in popular imagination, may be the North, as the horizon of our sense of identity, and the St Lawrence R, as the locus of early European settlements. In this connection it is worthy of note that the parliamentary system, as contrasted with the American presidential and congressional system, so far has not fostered a nationalistic civil religion in Canada such as the one sociologist Robert Bellah has identified in the US. Quasi-religious creeds, codes and cults exist in such contemporary movements as MARXISM and feminism (*see* WOMEN'S MOVEMENT), as these develop articulated traditions and criticize the compromises of present culture in the name of some ultimate hope. Only an assumption that religion necessarily means belief in God or supernaturalism prevents us from including such movements under the heading "religion."

As various Asian traditions have been introduced to N America through IMMIGRATION, one indirect consequence has been the development of NEW RELIGIOUS MOVEMENTS. Some of these are actually ancient but are newly transplanted and are attractive to Westerners disaffected with the secularism of Judaism and Christianity (eg, Hare Krishna, which has its roots in Hinduism). Other groups represent a fusion of Christian and Asian motifs (eg, the Unification Church, which combines Christian with Korean ideas). Still others (eg, Scientology) are the invention of individuals who gain a following by using traditional philosophies to meet secular aspirations. So far, these movements are known to us mostly through the functional analyses of social scientists or the apologetic claims of converts. While traditional, organized religious practice may seem to be on the decline, fascination with the occult and esoteric rituals seems to be on the rise in N America. This suggests to some scholars that some form of religious behaviour is typical of all human societies, even when formal religion is repudiated.

Religion as a mode of human behaviour often reflects an awareness of human weaknesses. Much religious imagery is based on the projection of human fears concerning death and social decay onto the symbols of ultimate power. In the name of religion, wars have been started, minorities persecuted and social inequalities such as

apartheid perpetuated. At the same time, religion as a response to the deepest spiritual values in the universe has been the motive for major reform movements in history. Spiritual and moral leaders such as Gotama Buddha, Jesus, Confucius, Socrates, Muhammad and Mahatma Gandhi have directly or indirectly inspired the abolition of slavery and the caste system, and the alleviation of ignorance and disease. One way to account for the paradox is to contrast extrinsic and intrinsic motivations in religion, following psychologist Gordon Allport. Extrinsic motivation involves the use of religious institutions for other purposes, social or economic. Intrinsic motivation involves living by such commands as those to love strangers and to seek justice for widows and orphans. By and large, the priestly caste views religion positively. The prophetic traditions view religion with suspicion.

Finally, it is useful to distinguish among magic, science and religion. Magic uses formulas supposed to effect changes willed by manipulative individuals. Science uses formulas or laws to explain general physical processes. Religion reflects ancestral wisdom and a spirituality which brings one to terms with one's personal destiny. In so-called primal societies, such distinctions are less frequently made. With the increasing complexity of, and emphasis on specialization in, the industrial world, the significance of such distinctions is beginning to be recognized. As it is, many critics have come to accept that science and religion need not conflict and that magical practices can be found in all cultural modes, including religion.

PETER SLATER

Religious Studies

English Canada Important in the early history of many Canadian universities and colleges, religion has continued to make a contribution, especially in seminaries. Seminaries were established to teach ministers and full-time church workers the particular doctrines of their denomination. Christianity was seen as the one true religion, and the denominational formulation of Christian doctrine was regarded as authoritative. Seminaries with their residences were frequently attached to universities, and their degrees were usually given the status of university degrees. A few general religion courses, eg, in biblical literature or church history, were offered for the arts and science faculties by seminary staff; all other teaching was confessional. Many university faculty suspected seminary staff of clericalism, anti-intellectualism and proselytism. Whether these concerns were justified or not, seminaries and theology departments were far more interested in the Judaeo-Christian tradition than in religion in general.

In the 1960s a distinction was made between confessional and academic studies of religion. This provided the philosophical prerequisite for new departments of religious studies established at McMaster U, Sir George Williams U [Concordia] and UBC, located in faculties of arts and science without denominational ties. An academic approach was taken to religious studies as an intellectual discipline.

The Canadian Society for the Study of Religion (CSSR) was established 1965 to supplement 3 existing societies: Canadian Society of Biblical Studies, Canadian Society of Church History and Canadian Theological Society. The academically oriented CSSR was the first society connected with religion to join the LEARNED SOCIETIES and to adopt bilingualism. In 1970 the 4 societies formed the Canadian Corporation for Studies in Religion/ Corporation canadienne des sciences religieuses. In 1971 CCSR began publication of *SR: Studies in*

Religious Affiliation: Percentage of Total Population
(Source: derived from Statistics Canada, 1981 census)

| | Christian: | | | | | | | | No |
	Catholic	Protestant*	Orthodox	Jewish	Islamic	Hindu	Sikh	Buddhist	Religion
Canada	47.3	41.2	1.5	1.2	0.4	0.3	0.3	0.2	7.3
BC	19.3	54.7	0.9	0.5	0.5	0.3	1.5	0.4	20.5
Alta	27.7	56.0	2.2	0.5	0.8	0.3	0.3	0.3	11.5
Sask	32.4	58.3	2.4	0.2	0.1	0.1	**	0.1	6.2
Man	31.5	56.6	2.1	1.5	0.2	0.2	0.2	0.2	7.3
Ont	35.6	51.8	2.0	1.7	0.6	0.5	0.2	0.2	7.1
Qué	88.2	6.4	1.2	1.6	0.2	0.1	**	0.2	2.1
NB	53.9	42.9	0.1	0.1	**	0.1	**	**	2.8
NS	37.0	58.0	0.3	0.2	0.1	0.1	**	0.1	4.0
PEI	46.6	50.5	**	0.1	0.1	0.1	**	**	2.6
Nfld	36.3	62.6	**	**	**	0.1	**	**	1.0
NWT	40.3	52.0	0.4	**	**	**	**	**	6.4
YT	24.2	53.3	0.1	0.1	**	**	0.2	0.3	19.5

* Includes Anglicans
** Below 0.05% of region's population
NB: Data not available from 1986 census at time of printing

St Gabriel Street Scotch Church, rue Saint-Gabriel, Montréal, c1885, watercolour by A.W. Holdstock (courtesy National Archives of Canada/C-40117).

Religion/Sciences religieuses, which succeeded the *Canadian Journal of Theology.* CCSR also publishes various series of books.

Most universities and many colleges offer religious studies programs treating the major world religions, and sacred languages such as Hebrew and Sanskrit. Opportunities for graduate work have developed in many provinces. Graduates become university and college instructors, or teachers in high-school social studies and world religions classes. Although most offerings still emphasize biblical studies and Christian thought, there is a serious effort to present all world religions. This is especially important, given the pluralistic nature of contemporary Canadian society.

Wilfred Cantwell Smith (b 1916) stands out in the academic study of religion in Canada. A Presbyterian minister and an Islamic specialist, in 1951 he organized McGill U Institute of Islamic Studies to foster academic, interreligious dialogue. In 1964 Smith became Director of Harvard U's Centre for the Study of World Religions. Returning to Canada in 1973, he developed a religious studies department at Dalhousie U. Smith has emphasized the cumulative history and the personal faith experience of each religion. His books, known worldwide, include *The Meaning and End of Religion* (1963), *Belief and History* (1977), *Towards a World Theology* (1981) and *On Understanding Islam* (1984). Traditional Christian theology's assumption that it has a monopoly on divine grace and salvation is, in Smith's view, morally wrong and must give way to thinking which allows that God is active in other traditions as well.

French Canada In French Canada, the academic study of religion was long totally identified with the study of theology as practised in seminaries for the formation of clergy. However, various phenomena and events of the QUIET REVOLUTION era (1960-66) helped break that monopoly and speed the introduction of a new tradition in religious study. This new approach to the religious phenomenon had been known in Europe for a century, mainly under the German name *Religionswissenschaft.* In Québec it takes a number of names: human sciences of religion, sciences of religion, religious sciences, religiology. The *Guide to Religious Sciences in Canada* (1972) listed 13 university-level institutions (including U de Moncton, Laurentian U and U of Ottawa) teaching theology or religious sciences in French Canada. Nine of them concentrate largely or exclusively on theology.

French Canadian scholars participate in the activities of the CCSR and have also founded a section within the Association canadienne française pour l'avancement des sciences (a francophone counterpart to the learned societies) called "Sciences of Religion," which holds a conference each May.

Francophone theologians belong to the Société canadienne de théologie, of which most members are from Québec. In 1944 the francophone exegetes formed the Association catholique des études bibliques au Canada, which holds an annual conference. ACEBAC did a translation of the New Testament in 1953; in 1982 it was reissued, with commentaries, by Bellarmin in Montréal.

French-language Canadian journals devoted to the scientific study of religion include *Sciences religieuses* and the *Cahiers du centre de recherche en sciences de la religion* of Laval. Francophone theologians publish in magazines such as *Science et esprit, Laval théologique et philosophique, Église et théologie* and *Sciences pastorales. Cahiers éthicologiques* follows research being done in ethics by the religious sciences department at U du Québec à Rimouski.

The importance of the Christian tradition in the formation of Québec society and its growing religious pluralism augur well for the development of theology and the science of religion. *See also* BIBLE SCHOOLS; SUNDAY SCHOOLS.

HAROLD COWARD AND ROLAND CHAGNON

Reading: R. Bibby, *Fragmented Gods: The Poverty and Potential of Religion in Canada* (1987).

Religious Building Canadian religious architecture began with the arrival of the first missionaries to New France. The Récollets and Jesuits, who arrived in 1615 and 1625, respectively, built mission chapels, sometimes using Indian construction techniques. They later replaced these buildings with more solid timber structures. Early in the 17th century, religious orders also built chapels and small churches for the colony's settlers. Like mission chapels, the construction of these buildings was simple and basic, initially of wood and later of stone.

Later in the 17th century, under Jesuit influence and with the arrival of more artisans and builders trained in France, certain traditional features of religious architecture were used to construct churches in Québec City and Montréal. These were built in the shape of a Latin cross, with steeples where the nave and transept met. The Jesuit church in Québec City (1666, destroyed 1807) was a striking example of this classical French monumental architecture. The first bishop of Québec City, François de LAVAL, was instrumental in spreading this style to small villages by encouraging and supervising the construction of many stone churches adapted and simplified from French architectural models.

During the first half of the 18th century, the king's engineer, Gaspard-Joseph CHAUSSEGROS DE LÉRY prepared all plans for a second cathedral in Québec City and designed a new façade for the parish church in Montréal. Small rural churches built by local people when new parishes were es-

tablished illustrate the originality and quality of the general architectural tradition of French Canada. Physically and symbolically the parish church was the community's most important building. Until the early 19th century, 3 models were used to construct these churches: the Jesuit Latin cross design; the Récollet plan, consisting of a broad nave with a narrower semicircular apse; and the even simpler MAILLOU plan, consisting of a nave ending with a semicircular apse. With its fieldstone walls and arched openings, the Saint-François church (1734-36) on Île d'ORLÉANS, built according to the Récollet plan, is representative of these small parish churches with very plain exteriors. However, the rich ornamentation (*see* SCULPTURE) inside many of these churches contrasts sharply with their austere exteriors. The superlative quality of this ornamentation can be seen in the interior of the Ursuline Convent chapel in Québec City, carved by Noël and Pierre-Noël LEVASSEUR (1734-39).

The arrival and establishment of a new, mainly Anglican and British, society brought major developments to Canadian architecture after 1750. In various parts of eastern Canada, churches were built in a Palladian style which was closely associated with the Anglicans and had been popular in England since the beginning of the 18th century. Features of the Palladian style include symmetry, order and a restrained classical vocabulary. St Paul's in Halifax (1750) was the first Anglican church in Canada and was modelled on the Marybone Chapel (1721-22) in London, designed by the Palladian architect James Gibbs. Similarly, Québec City's Holy Trinity Cathedral (1800-04) drew its inspiration from Gibbs. These new buildings, as well as the arrival of skilled workers from England or the US, helped spread

St Paul's Church, Halifax, NS (courtesy Environment Canada, Parks/Heritage Recording Services).

the Palladian style and its variants, particularly in Québec and the Atlantic colonies. Many little wooden churches of various denominations in NS and NB incorporated Palladian elements, notably the wide pediment gracing the façade, the venetian window in the apse, the vaulted openings and the classical ornamentation around the main door.

LOYALIST immigrants arriving in the late 18th century introduced a new type of church to the Atlantic provinces, used particularly by the Congregationalists. Primarily a meeting place, this type of wooden building (eg, Barrington's Meeting House in NS) is designed like a 2-storey private home where part of the floor is removed to provide a high room with a gallery for sermons and prayer meetings.

The Palladian style did not affect traditional religious architecture in Québec until the 1820s and even then its greatest influence was on exterior ornamentation. The architect François BAILLAIRGÉ was most successful in integrating the decorative aspect of the new Palladian architectural style into Québec churches. Through his *Précis d'architecture* (1828), Abbé Jérome DEMERS was also instrumental in spreading new ideas among a generation of builders. At the beginning of the 19th century, with the encouragement of Abbé Conefroy, the Récollet, Jesuit and Maillou plans were abandoned in favour of a Latin-cross plan, evoking the 17-century Jesuit Latin-cross plan. From the 1820s until the 1860s interest in classical architecture shifted from the Renaissance era to more ancient times, thereby giving certain features of church façades (columns, pillars, entablature) new importance. This neoclassical period was exemplified in Québec between 1830 and 1840 by the work of the architect Thomas Baillairgé. In certain cases the influence of Greek architecture was expressed simply through decorative details on the church's façade. On other occasions, however, the church design was modelled on a Greek temple, an example being St Andrew's Church (1831) in Niagara-on-the-Lake.

The construction of the NOTRE-DAME CHURCH in Montréal (1823-29) marks an important moment in Canadian architectural history. For almost the next century, the Gothic revival style was closely associated with religious architecture for all denominations throughout Canada. This was not immediately accepted, particularly in eastern Canada where it had to coexist with a well-established classical tradition. Yet Gothic revival began to flourish in the 1840s, when there was a trend toward realism and archaeological authenticity particularly suited to religious architecture.

The Ecclesiologists, a group of English theologians who from 1839 promoted a renewal of religious architecture, encouraged builders of Anglican churches to return to the plan of medieval Catholic churches, based on a nave flanked by aisles, surmounted by galleries and facing the chancel. From then on, the chancel became a focal point. Each component of the interior plan was henceforth expressed on the exterior of the building. Toronto's St James's Cathedral (1849-53), Fredericton's CHRIST CHURCH CATHEDRAL (1846-53) and St John the Baptist Cathedral (1848-80) in St John's, are examples of this desire to follow medieval models.

It was not as easy for the Gothic revival style to become established in Québec as in other regions because there the classical tradition was already closely associated with Catholic architecture. Thus, in reaction to the construction of the Anglican Christ Church Cathedral (1857-59) in Montréal, a Gothic revival building, Mgr Ignace BOURGET had the St-Jacques Cathedral (1875-85)

Interior of the Cathedral Marie Reine du Monde, Montréal (*photo © Hartill Art Associates, London, Ont*).

built on the model of St Peter's in Rome. Bourget, who in this way sought to dissociate the Catholic faith from the Gothic revival style, opened the way for an intense interest in Neobaroque architecture between 1870 and 1880.

The Gothic revival style's evolution toward High Victorian Gothic was most powerfully expressed in Ontario in the work of Henry Langley, who built Anglican, Methodist, Baptist and Catholic churches for over 40 years. Just as this style began to wane in eastern Canada, it became popular in the West. The side tower, wide roof and massive proportions of St Paul's Cathedral (1895, Regina), and the vertical proportions and ornamentation of St John-the-Divine Cathedral (1912, Victoria), are characteristic of the Gothic revival style.

At the same time, small churches were also incorporating some striking features of the Gothic revival style. This "Carpenter's Gothic" (when done in wood) style is found in such eastern Canadian churches as St John's Anglican (about 1840) in Lunenburg, NS, and the United Church in MALPÈQUE, PEI (about 1870). In Ontario, one group of small churches uses contrasting coloured bricks to accentuate the picturesque aspects of certain Gothic revival details, particularly around the windows. The Crown Hill United Church (about 1880) exemplifies this trend. In Ontario, Manitoba and Saskatchewan other simply constructed small churches retained only the Gothic revival arched windows and central tower added to the façade. Examples of this are St Clement Anglican (1860-61) in Selkirk, Man, and St James Anglican (about 1909) in Star City, Sask. In the extreme west, many wooden mission churches made picturesque use of certain Gothic revival details. The façade of the Holy Cross mission church (about 1905) in Skookumchuk, BC, has many such features, and the one in Fort Good Hope in the NWT (1864-82) contrasts a fairly conventional exterior with a richly decorated interior.

Between 1880 and 1890, some architects abandoned the Gothic revival for a new architectural mode popular in the US. They built large churches whose rustic masonry and wide, rounded openings expressed the Romanesque revival influence. The Metropolitan United Church (1890-91) in Victoria is an example. Also at this

time, a number of architects adopted an auditorium layout, particularly for Methodist and Presbyterian churches. Generally speaking, the plans of 19th-century Catholic and Anglican churches were similar in that they were rectangular, with the altar in the centre of the sanctuary. The interior of Anglican churches was usually plainer than that of Catholic churches. Methodist and Presbyterian churches were also very sparsely decorated but had the pulpit as the focal point. Other religious groups, such as the Congregationalists, Unitarians, Seventh-Day Adventists and Baptists, also constructed very simple meeting places.

In the last quarter of the 19th century, a number of immigrant groups from Scandinavia and Russia settled in the West, bringing their architectural traditions with them. The Ukrainian immigrants who settled in Manitoba and Saskatchewan constructed churches reminiscent of the Byzantine style, with their cruciform plan, barrel-vaulted nave, dome-shaped belltowers and coloured interior ornamentation.

At the beginning of the 20th century, under the influence of the École des beaux-arts in Paris, architects moved away from the 19th-century emphasis on the picturesque, historical models and stylistic details, and gave more thought to layout, composition, proportions and overall organization. Church plans began to be designed on a system of axes; with new emphasis on the nave. Using the composition principles of the École des beaux-arts, churches continued to be built in the Gothic revival, Classical, baroque or Romanesque styles – eg, the Catholic cathedral in St-Boniface, Man (1908), was built in the Romanesque tradition, and the one in GRAVELBOURG, Sask (1919), reveals the neobaroque influence. The influence of the École des beaux-arts marked the end of the era when architects turned to the past for inspiration and models. Nineteenth- and early 20th-century churches, because of their size and symbolic importance for each community, best illustrate the contribution of these important architectural currents.   NATHALIE CLERK

Modern Religious Building

Churches and temples built in Canada during the post-WWII period occupy an important place in Canadian religious architecture. In urban areas, where population increased the most, more churches were built than in all previous periods combined. Most of these new churches were built in suburbs and reflect the character of their neighbourhoods, with their widely dispersed population and small-scale buildings. The number of parishioners was often small and the budget restricted. Because most worshippers had to drive to church, parking lots became essential. These physical problems reduced the importance of the church in the cityscape and left an ambiguous image of this type of building. A more fundamental problem arose from the redefining of churches.

Precious Blood Church, St-Boniface, Man, designed to resemble an Indian tipi (*photo by Henry Kalen*).

Anglican church at Iqaluit, NWT, built to resemble an igloo (*photo by Karl-Heinz Raach*).

Though architects and their clients recognized the need to renew religious architecture, they were uncertain of what form the change should take. Their uncertainty was compounded by the debate over the role of religion in the modern world. Following fiery debates held in Europe between the 2 wars, various Canadian cities (Toronto 1956, 1961, and Vancouver, 1960) hosted seminars on church construction. Was a church to be a house of God or a house of man? Should it be a shelter for the faithful to pray and hear the word of God? Is it a refuge for meditation, or should it be more a part of everyday life? The interior arrangement was affected as well by the redefining of liturgical functions. The locations of the baptistry, the altar and other liturgical places were influenced by the symbolism enshrouding them. Though construction of churches (some of which are also community centres) attests to the continuing evolution of liturgy and religious conception, many modern churches have limited architectural interest, and from 1970 on very few churches were being built.

While theologians tried to define the nature and role of the church, architects were trying to renew the design of the church and convince their clients of the need for these changes. Until WWII it was accepted that churches were built in one of the historical styles. This usually meant Gothic revival in English Canada and one of the classical styles in Québec. However, in the mid-1930s new forms began to appear in church architecture just as in secular architecture.

St James's Anglican Church (1935), Vancouver, by London architect Adrian G. Scott, appears to mark the beginning of the modern movement on the Pacific coast. The Greek-cross plan and the barrel vaults of this concrete church give a Byzantine effect to the interior, but the extreme starkness highlights the geometry of the forms. On the outside, the rectilinear recesses of the portal and the large, smooth, stuccoed surfaces of the geometric masses indicate the influence of functionalist architecture, and the prismatic forms of the upper parts are reminiscent of art deco. Scott's associates were Sharp and Thompson, local architects who built Vancouver's Crown United Church during the same period. The narrow windows capped with mitre arches, such as those of St James's, are a compromise between the pointed arch of Gothic architecture and the geometrical forms of the international style. The cubic mass of the church and its stucco covering are further evidence of the entrenchment of the modern style in BC.

During the same period, religious architecture in Québec was influenced by Dom Bellot, a French Benedictine monk who came to Canada for the first time in 1934. He came again in 1936 to design the cupola and the interior of St Joseph's Oratory in Montréal, a monumental church begun during WWI in the style of the Beaux-Arts tradition. Inspired by medieval architecture, Dom

Bellot had devised a structural system of polygonal arches for reinforced concrete and parabolic arches for brick. As early as 1935-36, examples of both types were built: St-Jacques, of concrete, in Montréal (Gaston Gagnier) and Ste-Thérèse-de-Lisieux, of brick, in Beauport (Adrien Dufresne). They marked the beginning of a 20-year trend that gave Québec a distinctive, if only moderately modern style in religious architecture.

After 1950, the difference between churches in Québec and those elsewhere in Canada began to fade. Two styles in particular grew in popularity. In the first category are churches with horizontal roofs or very slight slopes, such as the small Anglican church in Montréal, St Cuthbert's (1946-47), by Fred Lasserre. The churches in the second category have very steeply sloped roofs and low lateral walls. Many of these have a laminated wood structure. In both styles the structure determines both the exterior shape and the interior space. This rationalism, particularly stark in churches of the first category, was criticized for not inspiring uplifting feelings in the congregation. To solve the problem, one device was to give the slopes of the roof an excurved profile in order to increase the effect of ascension, as in Westminster Presbyterian Church (Salter and Allison) in Barrie, Ont. Another device was the piercing of the ridge of the roof, sometimes along its entire length, in order to provide the interior with a skylight, as in Scarborough's West Ellesmere United Church (Eberhard ZEIDLER). Some churches, for example, St-Raphaël in Jonquière (St-Gelais and Tremblay) and Notre-Dame-des-Champs in Repentigny (D'Astous and Pothier), combine the 2 devices.

At the beginning of the 1960s, it became more common in Catholic churches to replace the longitudinal plan by the central plan. The resolution of the Vatican Council to encourage the participation of the congregation in the mass popularized this plan, which created a close relationship between the congregation and the altar. These churches, some of which are the most expressive of all postwar religious architecture, are in general low, with a single roof over the choir and the nave. Examples of this architecture can be found across the country; for example, St-Jean-Baptiste-de-la-Salle, Montréal (Lemay and Leclerc), St John Brébeuf, Winnipeg (Libling, Michener and Associates) and ST MARY'S in Red Deer, Alta (Douglas CARDINAL). There are also several Manitoba churches by Étienne GABOURY in this category (*see* ARCHITECTURE).

It must be noted that during the 1960s a number of architects attempted to renew the styles of churches of the oriental rites, though continuing to respect their architectural traditions. Most examples are to be found in Ukrainian churches, such as Holy Family in Winnipeg and St Michael's in Tyndall, Man (Radoslav Zuk). The cupolas which give the traditional churches their distinctive silhouette are recalled in the elegant geometric shapes which at the same time respect the nature of the wood or concrete of which they are built. Another example of this is Montréal's Greek Orthodox Cathedral (Affleck, Desbarats, Dimakopoulos, Lebensold, Sise), which respects the Byzantine tradition with its concrete cupola set on a rectangular nave plan.

CLAUDE BERGERON

Reading: Claude Bergeron, *L'Architecture des églises du Québec, 1940-1985* (1987); N. Tardif-Painchaud, *Dom Bellot et l'architecture religieuse au Québec* (1978).

Religious Festivals Each major religion practised in Canada has, in addition to its own system of beliefs, a way of marking the passage of time and commemorating sacred events. Two main measures are used to establish years and their internal division: the solar cycle (including the

length of days, of the seasons and of entire years) and the lunar cycle (linked especially to the definition of months).

Hinduism Hindu tradition boasts a plethora of festivals dated according to several luni-solar calendar systems. The proper date for a given festival involves complicated calculations resolving the cycles of the sun and the moon. The 4-day New Year festival, *Divali*, falls in Oct/Nov. Krishna, a popular Hindu diety, is honoured in the carnival atmosphere surrounding the festival of *Holi*, in Mar. Lord Rama is honoured at the spring equinox, *Rama-navami*, Mar/Apr, and the goddesses Sarasvati and Lalita are worshipped along with family ancestors at the autumnal equinox, Sept/Oct. Two nativities are celebrated in Aug/Sept, in the Hindu month of *Bhadrapada*, those of Lord Ganesha and Lord Krishna. A *puga* (worship service) is conducted with appropriate *mantras* (prayers) to the deity whose feast day it is. Specific elements of local Indian folk tradition animate the occasion.

Buddhism Buddhist festivals commemorate the historical Buddha, the founders of particular Buddhist movements, and Buddhist teachings as embodied in the cycle of nature. Canada's Japanese community follows the Jodo Shinshu school of Buddhism. Their dating system places the birth of the Buddha on Apr 8, which is celebrated as *Wesak*, or *Hanamatsuri* (Flower Festival); his enlightenment, upon which the core of Buddhist teaching is based, is celebrated on Dec 8 as *Bodhi* day; and Feb 15, *Nirvana* or *Parinirvana* day, celebrates his death which, tradition suggests, occurred in Nepal in 486 BC. The Jodo Shinshu movement was founded by Shinran Shonin (1173-1262). Festivals commemorate his birth on May 21 and his death on Jan 16. At the spring and fall equinoxes most Buddhists celebrate Devotion day. These focus on the Buddha's teaching, called the 6 perfections, which lead to a balanced life like the universe at the equinox. The greatest festival among Japanese Buddhists is O-Bon (July/Aug). Devotees visit cemeteries and perform various rites to commemorate their family ancestors.

The Theravada tradition of Buddhism common among SOUTHEAST ASIANS is marked by 2 major festivals. *Vaisakha*, the full-moon festival in May, commemorates the birth, enlightenment and death of the Buddha; *Vas* (Lent), the period of monastic enclosure beginning in July, is preceded by a festival and culminates in a grander Lent-end festival in Oct. In addition, Theravada Buddhists celebrate *Dharma-chakka*, a day commemorating Buddha's proclamation of his "gospel," on the full moon in July. *Dharma-vijaya* celebrates the missionary work carried out by Indian Emperor Asoka which spread the faith to Sri Lanka.

Sikhism Sikh festivals are rooted in the historical development of the faith. They include the birth and martyrdom of the key gurus (teachers): Guru Nanak's and Guru Gobind Singh's birthdays, and Guru Arjun Dev's and Guru Tegh Bahadur's martyrdom. A major festival marks the founding of the Sikh brotherhood, the *Khalsa*, on April 13.

Judaism The Jewish festival year begins with the carnival celebration at the feast of *Purim*, 14 of Adar (falling in Feb/Mar). It commemorates the biblical account of Esther and her role in rescuing the Jewish community from Persian oppression. *Pesach* (Passover, or the Feast of Freedom) focuses on the freeing of the Jews from exile in Egypt. It lasts 8 days beginning on the 15 of Nisan (Mar/Apr), and is celebrated largely through a ritual meal in the home. In May/June, 6-7 of Sivan, *Shavuoth* (Feast of Weeks or Pentecost) commemorates God's giving of the Torah to Moses on

Mt Sinai. *Rosh Hashanah* (New Year) falls in Sept/ Oct. Preparation involves 10 days of penance followed by a 2-day celebration. *Yom Kippur* (Day of Atonement) is the holiest of all festivals except *Shabbat*. It involves a day of rigorous fasting and collective penitential prayers. Five days later an ancient harvest festival is combined with a commemoration of the Israelites' 40-year sojourn in the wilderness prior to settlement in Palestine. *Sukkot* (Feast of Tabernacles, or Booths) lasts 8 days, falling in Sept/Oct. The final reading of a cycle in the Jewish Scripture is marked by *Simchat Torah*, Sept/Oct, accompanied by expressions of delight in the revelation embodied in the Hebrew Bible.

Hanukkah, an 8-day Dec festival of lights, commemorates the struggle for liberty under the Maccabees against the Syrian-Greek rulers of Palestine in 168 BC. Technically a minor feast, it has become prominent in N America because of its proximity to Christmas. The greatest of Jewish festivals is *Shabbat* (Sabbath, or Saturday), the final day of the week, when the Creator's rest from his labours is celebrated.

Christianity The festivals of Christian traditions follow 2 calendars, the Julian, devised in 46 BC by Julius Caesar, and the Gregorian, a reformed calendar introduced by Pope Gregory XIII in 1582. A portion of the ORTHODOX CHURCH and Eastern Rite Catholic Church continues to follow the Julian calendar, which runs approximately 13 days behind the Gregorian. Christmas, which in the Gregorian calendar falls on Dec 25, celebrates the birth of Jesus Christ, after a 4-week preparation period called Advent. Epiphany (Jan 6) commemorates Jesus' baptism and, for some, the visitation of the Magi after the nativity. Easter, which is the greatest feast in Christianity, is a series of rituals marking the suffering, death and resurrection of Christ. It is dated following the Jewish lunar calendar as the first Sunday after the full moon following the spring equinox (Mar/ Apr). Lent, a 40-day period of penitential preparation, begins with Ash Wednesday and culminates on Palm Sunday a week before Easter Sunday.

Ascension day, a major feast 40 days after Easter, marks Christ's last earthly appearance and is named for his ascension to God the Father. The cycle of feasts following Easter is closed with Pentecost Sunday 50 days after Easter when, tradition teaches, the Holy Spirit descended upon the disciples and the church was formed.

Many Protestant churches celebrate a founder's day, eg, Reformation Sunday (closest to Oct 31), commemorating Martin Luther's formal protest in 1517 against Roman Catholic practice and belief.

Islam The Islamic year is lunar, and 11 days shorter than the solar year. Muslims celebrate the Great Festival or Feast of Sacrifice, *'Id al-Adha*, at the end of the annual pilgrimage to Mecca. It consists of several rites focusing on the sacrifice of a consecrated animal at Mina, near Mecca. The founding of the city of Mecca and the devotion to monotheism of Abraham and his son Ishmael are commemorated.

The little festival, *Id-al-fitr* (festival of fast-breaking) ends the 28-day fast of *Ramadan*, the ninth month. It begins with the appearance of the new moon. The followers of Shi'ite Islam have an additional festival called after the first Islamic month, *Muharram*, in which it occurs. A passion play commemorates the martyrdom of Husain, the son of Ali and grandson of the Prophet Muhammad. This occurred on the 10th of Muharram, 61 AD (10 Oct 680 AD) when he died in a battle with the Damascus caliphs. *See also* HINDUISM; BUDDHISM; SIKHISM; JUDAISM; CHRISTIANITY; ISLAM.   DAVID J. GOA

Religious Music may be said to have begun in Canada with the arrival of the first settlers, but the indigenous peoples used music in a religious context prior to the 16th century. The first Christian service of which we have a record was a mass sung at Brest (Bonne Espérance Harbour) in Labrador on 14 June 1534. Missionaries in the early 17th century soon found that the Indians' love of music could be a powerful factor in their conversion to CHRISTIANITY. They were easily taught the simpler forms of church music. In 1610 the converts sang the *Te Deum* at the baptism of the Micmac chief Membertou and his tribe at PORT-ROYAL. The so-called "Huron Carol" is a relic of these times – a French Christmas tune wedded to Huron words. There is some doubt about both dates and authenticity, but the first religious composition to have been written in Canada may well have been the prose from the *Office de la Sainte Famille*, attributed to Charles-Amador Martin, which dates from about 1700. The JESUIT RELATIONS contain many references to church music, both choral and instrumental. It is known that there was an organ in the Jesuit Chapel in Québec City by 1661.

There is a disappointing lack of references for the first half of the 18th century, although there are collections of polyphonic music in libraries in both Montréal and Québec City dating from this period. By 1775 the picture becomes clearer. English-speaking settlers had brought the Church of England and Protestant observances with them, choirs had been established (eg, St Paul's Church, Halifax, in the 1760s), and churches in a few towns had organs (eg, Montréal, Québec City, at both the Roman Catholic and Anglican cathedrals, and Halifax). There are references to a continuing tradition of sung high masses and vespers in the Roman Catholic Church, while the Church of England and other congregations relied more on the singing of psalms (metrical versions, almost certainly), hymns and, occasionally, anthems (*see also* ANGLICANISM; CATHOLICISM).

The early years of the 19th century saw a growth of choral activity in the East and a gradual spread westward across the country. The popularity of the singing school movement gave an impetus to this development. Trained church musicians appeared on the scene. Most importantly, these years saw the start of what was to be, by the latter years of the century, a flood of publications devoted to church music. *Le Graduel romain* was published in Québec in 1800, Stephen Humbert's *Union Harmony* appeared in Saint John in 1801, Mark Burnham's *The Colonial Harmonist* in Port Hope [Ont], in 1832, and, in Toronto, William Warren of St James's Cathedral published *A Selection of Psalms and Hymns* (music edition in 1835). The greater availability of published materials encouraged the formation of choirs in smaller centres and facilitated the introduction of a repertoire based on a European heritage, particularly in the Church of England (to become the Anglican Church of Canada in 1955). There was a vested choir at Holy Trinity Cathedral in Québec City in 1804, though Toronto had to wait until 1868 for its first choir to appear in surplices. This was at the Church of the Holy Trinity. Anglican choirs at this time led their congregations in the singing of metrical psalms and hymns and often sang, as anthems, adaptations from the works of the great composers (eg, Handel, Haydn and Mozart, Beethoven and Rossini). The appearance of *Canadian Church Psalmody* in 1845 paved the way for the use of Anglican chant for the psalms.

Roman Catholic Church music in the 19th century also reflected a European heritage. Though factual evidence is hard to discover, some choirs did sing music by Haydn, Beethoven, Rossini and Gounod. Music by Canadian composers J.C.

Brauneis, Jr, and Antoine DESSANE was also available, though this may not have been known outside of Québec. The motu proprio on sacred music, issued by Pope Pius X in 1903, ordered a return to the renaissance ideals of unaccompanied polyphonic music and restored the pre-eminence of Gregorian chant. In Catholic churches around the world this order made for a glorious period of good music, reverently sung.

A parallel development in the early years of the 20th century had an immense effect in the Anglican Church. Cheap editions of liturgical music by the great masters of the Tudor and Jacobean period in England facilitated a return to simple, uncluttered music and fostered a similar style of composition. However, the music of Stainer, Barnby, Gounod, Spohr, Simper and Maunder still had a stranglehold, especially in smaller towns and churches.

Meanwhile, the Protestant churches had been moving slowly towards a form of worship in which music, both congregational and choral, could take a larger part. BAPTIST, METHODIST and CONGREGATIONAL churches had always allowed the organ, and eventually PRESBYTERIAN churches welcomed its inclusion in their service. Even quite small churches acquired instruments and formed choirs, and began to undertake the singing of an anthem. Large churches gave their choirs visibility and gowned them and finally began to spend money on them; often there would be a paid quartet of professional singers, who not only led the choir but also sang solos. This type of organization also spread to Anglican churches. Better choirs, in addition to leading Sunday services, now undertook to perform oratorios, or extracts from them, in almost concertlike circumstances. The first oratorio performance in a Canadian church is known to have been given in 1769 in St Paul's Church, Halifax, though we do not know what was sung. In the Protestant churches a mixed choir was the norm, often with a junior choir of children of both sexes. All-male choirs of men and boys were common in larger Roman Catholic and Anglican churches.

By the mid-20th century, in the Roman Catholic Church, choirs were occasionally all-male but more often mixed, were sometimes vested but mostly unvested in rear galleries, sang a repertoire spiced with Palestrina, but based more often on 18th- or 19th-century settings, and used plainsong with varying degrees of success. These choirs were almost never paid, and frequently the posts of organist and choirmaster were divided. In the Anglican Church, choirs were either mixed or all-male (the latter showing a decline in numbers from 1950 onwards), were almost always vested, and sat in choir stalls in a chancel area. The repertoire was largely English in origin but drawn from a wide range of periods. Some members of the choir might be paid, and the organist-choirmaster was often well trained. The typical Protestant church would have a senior mixed choir and a junior choir. It was always visible, often sitting in curved stalls behind the minister, and was gowned. Its repertoire is hard to characterize but would have a leaning towards 19th- and early 20th-century English music, with some American and Canadian compositions. The qualifications of the choir director and organist could vary greatly with the affluence of the church. Organs were often large.

Developments in the 1960s and 1970s changed the pattern of religious music in Canada. Vatican Council II of 1962-65, while specifically recommending the continuing use of Gregorian chant, was taken by many Roman Catholic clergy as giving them "carte blanche" to do away with Latin, Gregorian chant and polyphony in one clean sweep. The use of vernacular texts, and a new spirit of liturgical experimentation, led to a "popular" style of church music. "Song leaders," armed with microphones, are now the arbiters of sacred music, though there are some pockets of resistance.

In the Anglican Church, change has not been so widespread or so sudden. Many clergy, however, have copied the Roman Catholic reforms and, fortified with new texts as alternatives to the Book of Common Prayer, have seen congregational participation as the only goal of church music. This trend has resulted in some parishes in so-called "folk masses," hymns in "pop" style, and the downgrading of choirs and organs. In some areas change has been minimal, and in other churches sympathetic pastors and musicians have compromised so as to make effective use of the vast heritage of church music.

Modern change is harder to describe in the Presbyterian and United churches. Traditionally, these denominations relied less on forms and texts from a missal or prayer book, so the shift to contemporary texts has not been a potent force. Nevertheless, styles of acceptable church music have changed in response to movements in the Roman Catholic, Anglican and Evangelical churches.

The LUTHERAN Church has been active in Canada since the 18th century. As its members have come from a wide variety of countries, there has been a lack of tradition in the form of service. The US is the major source for hymnbooks, service music and anthems. Choirs are active, almost exclusively amateur, and church musicians have generally been trained in the US.

Music plays a central role in the SALVATION ARMY's ministry, particularly hymn singing with or without band accompaniment. Choirs are formed both to lead services and to give concerts.

"Gospel" music has an important teaching and persuasive role in Evangelical churches (see EVANGELICAL AND FUNDAMENTALIST MOVEMENTS). A soloist is normally featured, with choir and an instrumental group providing a back-up. The fact that televised services are an integral element in this ministry has some effect on the styles of presentation.

Jewish religious music in Canada is divided between traditional chants, some of great antiquity, sung by the cantor, and more modern music (often late 19th-century in style) sung by choir or congregation, or both. Canadian cantors have studied with older European-trained cantors or have trained in the US. Music is seen as a vital part of synagogue worship, in both Orthodox and Reform traditions, though only Reform synagogues admit the use of the organ.

Other Christian denominations that have strong musical traditions, both based on European practice, are the various MENNONITE churches and the Greek Orthodox Church.

All denominations have produced composers of church music. The name of Healey WILLAN stands out. English-trained, he wrote mostly for the Anglican Church in a wide variety of forms but his music has been sung in Roman Catholic, United, Presbyterian and Lutheran churches and has been used in both England and the US. Earlier musicians wrote for the church, particularly in Québec for the Roman Catholic Church, but it is doubtful that their works are much heard these days. Other composers include W.H. Anderson, Alfred Whitehead, Bernard Naylor, Keith Bissell, Ben Steinberg and Srul Irving Glick.

Publication of religious music in Canada, while in no way equalling the volume in the US, has continued, though the British legacy of many of the churches with choirs means that much music is imported. Waterloo Music Company, Frederick Harris Music Co Ltd and Gordon V.

Thompson Ltd are particularly active in English-language music. Most of the major denominations have their own Canadian hymnbooks (see HYMNS). Many of the larger churches in Canada have issued recordings of their choirs, thus enabling them to reach a wider audience. Several organizations exist to assist choirs and choirmasters to achieve better standards, particularly the various provincial choral federations, the Royal School of Church Music, and the Royal Canadian College of Organists.   GILES BRYANT

Reading: Encyclopedia of Music in Canada (1981); H. Kallmann, *A History of Music in Canada, 1834-1914* (1960).

Remembrance Day, honouring the war dead, is a legal holiday observed throughout Canada on Nov 11. It commemorates the armistice that ended WWI at 11:00 AM of that day in 1918. Originally called Armistice Day – as it continues to be known in Newfoundland – it was merged with Thanksgiving Day from 1923 to 1931, when it was renamed Remembrance Day and its observation reverted to Nov 11. The symbol of this day is the poppy of Flanders, replicas of which are distributed by the ROYAL CANADIAN LEGION. Characteristic of Remembrance Day are patriotic and memorial ceremonies on steps of cenotaphs and other war monuments in Canada and throughout the Commonwealth.   JOHN ROBERT COLOMBO

Remittance Man, a term once widely used, especially in the West before WWI, for an immigrant living in Canada on funds remitted by his family in England, usually to ensure that he would not return home and become a source of embarrassment.   JOHN ROBERT COLOMBO

Remote Sensing means "sensing" at a distance or, more specifically, deriving data or information about Earth's surface or the atmosphere by observing reflected or emitted electromagnetic radiation. The oldest remote-sensing instrument is the photographic camera, which has a long history of use in making observations of Earth from aircraft and, more recently, spacecraft. The earliest recorded air photo in Canada was taken of the HALIFAX CITADEL, from a balloon at an altitude of about 1450 feet (442 m), by Captain H. Esdale, Royal Engineers, in Aug 1883. Aerial photography and air-photo interpretation were developed during WWI for military intelligence and after the war were applied to mapping. The first Canadian air-mapping photograph was taken in 1923. By 1963, 97% of the country had been photographed in black and white.

Since the 1960s, colour aerial photography has been used extensively for forestry and land-use mapping and planning. The first photograph from space was taken from the NASA Gemini III spacecraft in 1965. Since then, space photography has been acquired on Gemini, Apollo, Skylab and shuttle missions. The electromagnetic spectrum extends in a continuum from microwave wavelengths of 0.1-100 cm through infrared, visible, ultraviolet and X-ray to gamma-ray wavelengths (measured in billionths of a metre). Photographic film can be used to sense only a small part of this spectrum, ie, mainly the visible region. Remote-sensing instruments use the much larger nonvisible portions of the spectrum as well; this technology has enormously improved man's ability to observe, measure and manage the world's resources and environment.

Instruments Photographic films sensitive to the infrared spectral region (0.7-0.9 μm) responsive to living flora were developed during WWII for camouflage detection. Infrared photography is now regularly used for measuring plant vigour and detecting stress caused by disease or lack of moisture and for terrain mapping. Photographic film is not sensitive to wavelengths beyond the

near infrared region; thus, nonphotographic sensors must be used. The infrared line scanner detects radiation in the thermal infrared band (3-14 μm) and produces an image in which the brightness of an object in the scene is related to the temperature of the object. This technique is used from aircraft to measure heat loss through the roof of buildings caused by poor insulation, to trace effluents from power plants and sewers into rivers and lakes, to detect incipient forest fires and to locate water supplies by detecting where underground streams empty into the ocean. It is used from spacecraft to map temperature distribution in water bodies. Laser-based sensing systems have been developed in Canada to measure and map water depth in clear coastal waters, as well as to make terrain profiles for topographic mapping and tree height assessment.

The camera and the infrared scanner have a serious shortcoming as remote-sensing instruments: they cannot see through clouds. RADAR, which operates in the microwave region of the spectrum, can provide all-weather, night-and-day remote-sensing information. For earth surveying, SLAR (Side-Looking Airborne Radar) and SAR (Synthetic Aperture Radar) are used. SAR produces radar images of high resolution by using special processing techniques. As a result of the need for all-weather monitoring of ice in Canada's Arctic in support of the oil industry, Canadian industry developed an efficient, compact, solid-state airborne SAR which has become the world standard. It is a major source of export revenue to Canada in the remote-sensing field and is also the radar most suitable for use on SATELLITES.

The first satellite designed specifically for remote-sensing purposes was ERTS 1 (later named Landsat 1), launched 23 July 1972. It was followed by Landsat 2 in Jan 1975 and Landsat 3 in Mar 1978. Landsat 4 and 5, which carry a unique new sensor, were launched in July 1982 and Mar 1984, respectively. These satellites travel in a polar orbit and carry instruments which sense the energy reflected from a 180 km wide swath underneath the satellite path. They provide complete coverage of Earth every 16-18 days. Data is transmitted from the satellite to ground stations, where they are recorded on magnetic tape for conversion to image (photographic) form or for computer analysis. Technology developed in Canada is being used in most ground stations now operating around the world.

In Canada, data from these satellites have been received, recorded and distributed to users from a station at Prince Albert, Sask, since 1972. A second station, designed for the reception of SPOT (Système probatoire d'observation de la Terre) data, went into production in mid-1986 at Gatineau, Qué. The information has been used for purposes as diverse as mapping of snow and ice distribution, geological structures, wetlands of importance for waterfowl habitat, forest clear-cut and burns, revising topographic maps, making studies of EROSION, assessing the effect of engineering projects on aquatic vegetation, measuring the vigour and acreage of crops, and determining present land use and changes.

Seasat was a short-lived satellite (June-Oct 1978) that carried 5 sensors for use in measuring oceanographic parameters (eg, ocean-surface temperature, surface wind speed and direction, wave height). This satellite was of particular interest to Canada because one of the 5 sensors was a SAR, which demonstrated the usefulness of spaceborne radars in measuring ice distribution in the Canadian Arctic as an aid to shipping and offshore exploration.

Weather satellites (eg, the NOAA, TIROS and NIMBUS series) carry instruments primarily for use in METEOROLOGY but have also produced use-

Landsat image of the Canada-US border, showing the difference in land-use practices in Alberta, top (rangeland) and Montana (intensive farming) (*courtesy Canada Centre for Remote Sensing, EMR Canada*).

ful information of ice distribution and water-surface temperature as well as details on drought and crop conditions for the Canadian Wheat Board. The NIMBUS-7 satellite carries an instrument that is used primarily for measuring sedimentation and chlorophyll levels in water. SPOT is a French satellite launched in Feb 1986. It carries 2 pointable instruments which operate in 2 modes – a high resolution (10 m) panchromatic band for use in mapping, and a 20 m resolution multispectral solid-state sensor operating in the green, red and near infrared to yield a colour-infrared type image. SPOT can also provide stereoscopic representations for topographic mapping. Canada's SPOT receiving stations provide image data for Canada and the US.

A number of nations and agencies are now planning a new generation of remote-sensing satellites for launch until 2000. These vehicles will carry sensors with improved performance, including more and different spectral bands, including radars – leading to all-weather sensing capabilities.

Data Analysis The power of remote sensing as a means of providing information for resource management and environmental monitoring is greatly enhanced by the use of computer techniques. All higher resolution satellite and specialized airborne images are created using computers. The images may be in the form of photographs or in a machine-readable format. Canada first began research in the area of digital image processing of satellite data for resource studies in 1973.

Research by the federal government resulted in sophisticated Canadian image analysis technology which was then transferred to industry. Since then, Canada has exported 35 systems for every one imported – some 25% of the total world market is held by Canadian industry. Canada continues to do research in ARTIFICIAL INTELLIGENCE and computer vision for remote sensing image interpretation. Images can be processed by computer to overlay a map or another image accurately, thereby permitting the updating of maps and the detecting of changes such as those caused by forest depletion or engineering projects (eg, MEGAPROJECTS). Another computer technique allows "themes," such as water, crops, summer fallow or forest-fire burns, to be identified and displayed cartographically, and the area of each theme to be computed. This technique is being used in Canada for computing potato acreages and forest-fire burn areas. Using still another technique, images are processed to make features of interest easier to identify visually. For example, variations representing different rangeland conditions are accentuated to assist in range management. An optically based system has

been developed in Canada by industry to project images in photographic transparency format onto maps to identify areas of change, or to map features of interest using traditional photo-interpretation techniques. The system, used to update Canada's 1:250 000 topographic maps, has been exported to more than a dozen countries in the past 2 years.

The Canadian remote-sensing industry's sales and employment have been growing at a compounded rate of approximately 30% per year since 1974 to stand at about 1600 employees with total activity approaching $160 million annually in mid-1987. *See also* CARTOGRAPHY.

E.A. GODBY AND R.A. RYERSON

Renaud, Jacques, novelist, poet (b at Montréal 10 Nov 1943). Associated in the 1960s with the radical journal PARTI PRIS, Renaud also worked as a journalist and television researcher for Radio-Canada. Active in the Réseau de résistance, an underground independentist group that preceded the FRONT DE LIBÉRATION DU QUÉBEC, Renaud is best known as the author of the novella *Le Cassé* (1964, *Broke City*, 1984), a violent story replete with fractured and anglicized "*joual,*" considered the best fictional work produced by the publishing house of *Parti pris.* A 2nd edition of *Le Cassé* (1977) added several short stories and the "Journal du Cassé," dealing with the impact of and controversies surrounding that publication. *En d'autres paysages* (1970) is a novel that attempts to wed realism and fantasy, and points to his later interests in esotericism and orientalism, evident in *Le Fond pur de l'errance irradie* (1975) and *Le Cycle du scorpion* (1979), *La Colombe et la brisue éternité* and *Clandestine(s) ou la tradition du couchant* (1980) – the latter mixing occultism with political violence.

B.-Z. SHEK

Renfrew, Ont, Town, pop 8314 (1986c), 8283 (1981c), inc 1895, located on the Bonnechere R, 100 km W of Ottawa. The first settlers were timber squatters; Scottish settlers followed, the most prominent being John Lorne McDougall, the first store owner and later a member of Parliament, whose mill (1855) is now a museum. About 1848 the site received its present name, for Renfrew, Scotland, ancestral home of the Stuarts. In 1850 Sir Francis Hincks offered free water sites to those who would build mills, and a boom followed. The town was first prominent for lumber, butter making and textiles. Now it produces magnesium and aluminum products, clothing, telecommunications, office equipment, high-frequency cable, tape and aerospace products. Financed by wealthy contractor and industrialist, Ambrose J. O'Brien, the famed Renfrew Millionaires ruled hockey for several years in the early 20th century.

K.L. MORRISON

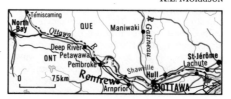

Renfrew, George Richard, furrier, businessman (b at Québec C 9 Feb 1830; d at Shipley, Eng 4 Sept 1897). After his father died in 1834 in Québec during a cholera epidemic, Renfrew was brought up in Montréal by an aunt and uncle. He apprenticed to his uncle's firm, John Henderson Furriers, which he eventually inherited. The firm's name changed to G.R. Renfrew Furriers and, based in Québec, Montréal and Toronto, it acquired a great reputation for quality furs in Canada and Europe. Renfrew became a director of a number of Québec institutions, including the Quebec Bank. After his death, his sons and a

cousin, John Holt, inherited the company which eventually became known as Holt Renfrew & Co.

H.R. STOKER

Rennie, Man, UP, pop 100 (1986c), 98 (1981c), is located 110 km E of Winnipeg, at the western boundary of the 2735 km² WHITESHELL PROVINCIAL PARK, of which it is the headquarters. Named after the British engineering family that designed and built the London Bridge, Rennie became a coal and water station for CPR locomotives 1880, and later housed construction shops and a station for the Grand Trunk Pacific. In 1884 the area was incorporated into Manitoba. Whiteshell Forest Reserve was created 1931, and ranger headquarters were established at Rennie 1941. Rennie is adjacent to the Alfred Hole Goose Sanctuary, a breeding and staging site for giant Canada geese, a species once thought to be extinct.

D.M. LYON

Rep by Pop ("representation by population"), demanded by citizens of Canada West to replace equal representation of the 2 Canadas in the PROVINCE OF CANADA after 1850, when Canada West gained a growing population lead over the largely French-speaking eastern section. Urged by George BROWN from 1853 on, it led to sectional breakdown by 1864; the ultimate remedy was federal government within CONFEDERATION.

J.M.S. CARELESS

Repeal Movement In 1867 many Nova Scotians were reluctant to endorse CONFEDERATION. In the elections of Sept 1867 anti-Confederates captured 36 of 38 seats in the local legislature, and 18 of 19 seats in the Dominion Parliament. Opposition to Confederation was based on the conviction that Nova Scotia was a maritime community with a natural affinity to Britain and historical ties with New England. Confederation meant a reorientation of its commercial life towards the interior of the continent, an unattractive prospect for those whose prosperity was based upon international commerce and the sailing ship. Britain was unwilling to allow Nova Scotia to secede, however, and when Joseph HOWE accepted the inevitable, agreeing to enter Sir John A. MACDONALD'S government in return for an increased provincial subsidy in 1869, the anti-Confederate protest collapsed.

In 1886 the secession movement re-emerged, led by Liberal premier William S. FIELDING. Campaigning on the issue of repeal and stressing the need for increased subsidies to the province, Fielding's party won 29 of 38 seats in the provincial elections that year. The bulk of support for secession came from those areas most closely tied to the traditional maritime economy and the international shipping trades. Opposition to repeal was strongest in those parts of the province which were beginning to industrialize, particularly in coal-mining areas and towns along the INTERCOLONIAL RAILWAY, which linked Nova Scotia to the continental interior. This second repeal movement quickly collapsed when the Conservative Party won 14 of 21 seats in Nova Scotia during the federal election of Feb 1887.

COLIN D. HOWELL

Repentigny, Marie-Jeanne-Madeleine Legardeur de, dite de Sainte Agathe (1698-1739), remembered because of the "lamp which is never extinguished," a lamp burning at the foot of the statue of Notre-Dame du Grand Pouvoir in the Ursuline convent in Québec City. Madeleine entered the convent after the death of her soldier fiancé, according to official accounts, but legendary tradition remembers her as having an Indian lover, who was killed by a sentry when she tried to help him escape from imprisonment. After entering the convent, she had difficulty in maintaining her vocation but succeeded through prayer to the Virgin Mary. In gratitude, a legacy ensured that the lamp would burn at the foot of the statue in perpetuity. NANCY SCHMITZ

Reppen, John Richard, Jack, artist, painter (b at Toronto 17 July 1933; d there 2 June 1964). Studying design at the Ontario Coll of Art in the evening, he was a free-lance cartoonist for the Toronto *Star* 1952-64 and art director for the Prudential Insurance Co, Toronto, 1952-62. From 1959 he devoted himself to his painting, exhibiting regularly in solo and group shows, and created several murals on commission. Travel – to Mexico (1961, 1963) and northern France (1962) – was an important source of Reppen's imagery. His best works have a strong feeling for surface and texture, with an almost relief quality, being often built on a matrix of gesso, with collage elements and incised surfaces. JOYCE ZEMANS

Representative Government, a system of government possessing an elected assembly (government elected, in part at least, by the people). In colonies settled by the English, it was long recognized that, although the Crown might institute governments, the inhabitants could be legislated for and taxed only by a legislature in which they were represented, or by the British Parliament itself. In conquered colonies the Crown might legislate as it pleased; however, once colonies were promised or granted an assembly, that privilege could be taken away only by Parliament. The manner in which the Canadian provinces and territories received representative assemblies differed markedly, as did the powers of those assemblies. In Nova Scotia, the governors' commissions after 1719 looked to the establishment of an assembly, and the first elective assembly in what is now Canada met on 2 Oct 1758 in Halifax. Because of the difficulty of communications, the Crown granted PEI a separate government in 1769 and an elective assembly in 1773. In 1784, following the influx of LOYALISTS, New Brunswick was separated from Nova Scotia and given representative institutions. In 1832, after considerable debate in Britain, the governor of Newfoundland was instructed to summon an assembly.

Elsewhere today's representative institutions rest on statutes. The conquered colony of Canada was promised an assembly, but the British Parliament passed the QUEBEC ACT of 1774, establishing rule by governor and council. Hence the Crown lost its power to legislate for the province. A second British statute, the CONSTITUTIONAL ACT of 1791, created Upper and Lower Canada, each with an assembly; a third, the ACT OF UNION of 1840 (proclaimed 1841), reunited the 2 Canadas and established their Parliament; and a fourth, the BRITISH NORTH AMERICA ACT of 1867, created Québec and Ontario and laid the foundation of their present assemblies. The colony of Vancouver's I possessed an assembly, 1856-58, but the present form of legislature in BC stems from that of the elective assembly constituted under British authority before Confederation; it was first elected in 1871.

In 1870 the Canadian Parliament created Manitoba out of former HBC lands, granting it representative institutions. When the validity of the MANITOBA ACT was questioned, the British Parliament the following year empowered the Canadian Parliament to create provinces out of the same lands. The old North-West Territories received a fully elective assembly in 1886 by federal statute (*see* NORTH-WEST TERRITORIES ACT), before the creation of the provinces of Alberta and Saskatchewan with the usual elective assemblies, again by federal statute, in 1905 (*see* AUTONOMY BILLS). Parliament established the Yukon in 1898 and made its territorial council fully elective in 1908; the NWT Council, constituted in 1905, became partly

elective in 1951 and fully elective in 1974. If history is a guide, these territorial councils are the forerunners of provincial assemblies. The conversion of representative into responsible government occurred over varying periods of time as circumstances permitted or dictated in a particular province (*see* RESPONSIBLE GOVERNMENT). See also PROVINCIAL GOVERNMENT. J. MURRAY BECK

Reptile, class of VERTEBRATE animals derived from AMPHIBIANS and ancestral to birds and mammals. Reptiles are primarily tetrapod (4-legged), but with legs lost in snakes and some lizards. Epidermal scales cover the outside skin, providing protection from injury and drying. Dermal scales (in underlayer of skin) are best developed in turtles, fusing to each other and to the ribs dorsally to form the shell. Crocodilians, tuatara and some lizards also have dermal scales. Epidermal scales are modified to form the horns of the horned lizard and the rattles of rattlesnakes. Modern reptiles are mainly relatively small, active forms. The largest, the marine leatherback turtle, may weigh up to 680 kg. Reptiles have lungs, not gills. Some turtles can supplement their oxygen supply through pharyngeal breathing to stay underwater for extended periods. The reptile heart is 3-chambered, except in crocodilians, which have a 4-chambered heart. Skin glands are almost entirely missing, but many reptiles excrete a foul musk for protection, or more pleasantly scented secretions for sexual attraction. One group of lizards and several groups of snakes have labial poison glands in the upper jaw.

The key to reptile success in invading the land was the amniote egg with a protective shell and embryonic membranes. The shell is permeable, so it must have some environmental moisture, but it is much more resistant to desiccation than the amphibian egg. Eggs are usually buried in loose soil or sand, or deposited in rotting vegetation. Tuatarans, crocodilians and turtles lay eggs. Many lizards and snakes do also, but many evolutionary lines hold the eggs within the mother, and the young are born after hatching. Like amphibians, reptiles are ectothermic, ie, have a relatively low metabolic rate and depend largely on external heat to attain the temperature at which they function best. Most reptiles maintain preferred temperatures by alternately basking and seeking shelter. Although reptiles are most abundant in the tropics, turtles, snakes and lizards are fairly successful in temperate climates. By hibernating in cold months they avoid having to eat just to maintain their body temperature and can use proportionally more food energy for growth and reproduction.

Although reptiles are not as diverse as in the Mesozoic (245-66.4 million years ago), the dominant modern group, the squamata, is very successful. There are 3307 species of lizards, 135 of amphisbaenians and 2267 of snakes. Turtles (222 species), crocodilians (22) and tuatara (1) are less diverse. Lizards, snakes and turtles have worldwide distribution in both tropical and temperate areas. Crocodilians are largely tropical although they invade the fringes of the temperate zone.

In Canada 42 species are native: 12 turtles, 5 lizards and 25 snakes. Southwestern Ontario and grassland valleys of southern BC have most species. No reptiles occur on the tundra and few species in the boreal forest. All are postglacial immigrants. The common garter snake, the most northerly ranging species, reaches Fort Smith, NWT, and the southern coast of James Bay. Reptiles are not economically important in Canada, except as predators, such as the rodent-consuming snakes. Turtles are trapped and sold as food, mainly in the East, most apparently going to US markets. Garter snakes are collected, particularly

in Manitoba, for sale to universities for laboratory dissection. Fatal bites from rattlesnakes are rare and Canada's 3 restricted species do not represent a hazard to people or livestock. F.R. COOK

Reading: F.R. Cook, *An Introduction to Canadian Amphibians and Reptiles* (1984).

Research, Provincial Organizations All provinces except Newfoundland and PEI have provincial research organizations functioning to promote economic development through the application of modern TECHNOLOGY to regional INDUSTRY. The first to be established was what is now the ALBERTA RESEARCH COUNCIL (1921); the latest, the CENTRE DE RECHERCHE INDUSTRIELLE DU QUÉBEC (1969). Most are CROWN CORPORATIONS, but the MANITOBA RESEARCH COUNCIL operates essentially as a government branch and the BRITISH COLUMBIA RESEARCH COUNCIL is an independent, nonprofit society. The organizations co-operate with other agencies in federal programs. The NOVA SCOTIA RESEARCH FOUNDATION CORPORATION and NEW BRUNSWICK RESEARCH AND PRODUCTIVITY COUNCIL may be expanded to serve the entire Atlantic region. The organizations fulfil their mandates by a combination of free advice to small business, advice to government, and contracted, nonprofit short-term research and longer-term investigations. Emphasis varies according to provincial needs and the activities of other provincial agencies. All have achieved expertise in fields appropriate to regional resources, varying from textiles by the ONTARIO RESEARCH FOUNDATION to uranium by the SASKATCHEWAN RESEARCH COUNCIL. Although a number of economists criticize the emphasis on small business, most agree that the provincial research organizations play a vital role in helping Canadian industry keep pace with technological developments. MARTIN K. McNICHOLL

Research Stations, Agricultural For more than a century, agricultural research has been among the major scientific research and development activities in Canada. For the whole of this time, the federal government has been the dominant force in agrifood research and development. The principal medium was and is a network of federal agriculture department (Agriculture Canada) research establishments that came to cover all provinces and various soil and climate regions.

Most of Agriculture Canada's research activity is concentrated in 2 branches. The Food Production and Inspection Branch conducts animal disease research programs at 2 major institutes (at Ottawa and Lethbridge) and 4 smaller laboratories throughout the country. But the major research thrust lies in the Research Branch, which by 1988 operated some 46 research establishments of varying size, sophistication and mandate, serving the complex and economically important agrifood industry. Of the Research Branch staff of 3450, some 900 are professional scientists.

The Research Branch originated with the Experimental Farm Station Act passed 2 June 1886. Under the authority of the Act, 5 experimental farms were established, including the Central Experimental Farm at Ottawa. The other 4 were located at Nappan, NS; Brandon, Man; Indian Head, Sask (then North-West Territories); and Agassiz, BC. All 5 of the original stations continue to flourish. The early experimental farms concentrated on improving livestock, dairy products, field crops, fruits and vegetables, fertilizers and seeds and on controlling plant diseases, insect pests and weeds.

William SAUNDERS, a practical scientist from London, Ontario, was the founder and first director of what was called the Dominion Experimental Farms system. The organization evolved into the Research Branch, which celebrated its 100th anniversary in 1986. In the early days, under Saunders's direction, one of the marked successes was the development of MARQUIS WHEAT, which helped western Canada become one of the great wheat-growing regions of the world. Marquis was largely the work of Saunders's son, Charles, who became the first Dominion Cerealist in 1903 in the agriculture department. Marquis arose from the collaborative work of Charles Saunders with the Brandon, Indian Head and Agassiz experimental farms. The result was a spring-sown wheat that set an enviable quality standard. Marquis became available in 1909. By 1920, it accounted for 90% of western Canada's nearly 7 million ha of land sown to spring wheat.

Marquis has long since been superseded by superior varieties. In the modern era, the bulk of the Canadian bread wheat crop arose from varieties developed by plant breeder Barrie Campbell and his colleagues at Agriculture Canada's Winnipeg Research Station. In 1987, one of these varieties, Neepawa, formally supplanted the famous Marquis. Campbell-bred varieties have been the dominant bread wheat in prairie acreage since 1966 and reached a record 89% share in 1987, the year before Canada's pre-eminent wheat breeder retired from Agriculture Canada. At retirement Dr Campbell had produced 9 varieties, several of which were central to the prosperity of Canada's huge export-oriented prairie wheat economy.

The durable Neepawa was licensed in 1969 and was still widely grown 2 decades later along with such subsequent and important Campbell varieties as Columbus and Katepwa. The other Campbell varieties are Pembina, Canthatch, Manitou, Napayo, Benito and Roblin, in order of their arrival through the years.

Although Agriculture Canada is paying increasing research attention to food processing, most activity is still centered on primary agriculture, ie, the growing of crops and the raising of livestock. In this context, breeding of commercial crop varieties such as wheat continues to have great importance.

Annually, Research Branch scientists develop 30 to 35 new varieties of oilseeds, grains, fruits, vegetables and forages for animals for use by the Canadian farmer and for the benefit of the food-processing industry which depends on the farm community for its raw product. New ornamentals are also developed.

Over the last generation, the rapeseed variant, CANOLA, has emerged in Canada as a major source of vegetable oil for margarines, shortenings, salad dressings and cooking. Variety development and the associated background scientific work, much of it conducted by Agriculture Canada scientists such as Keith DOWNEY of the Saskatoon Research Station, made the creation of this new prairie-based industry possible. Such canola varieties as Westar and Tobin, developed by the Saskatoon station, came to dominate the industry. In response to a 6-year science-based petitioning process, the US Food and Drug Administration declared Canadian canola safe for human consumption in the US in 1985, opening up that vast market to the Canadian oil.

Protection of crops from insects, disease and weed competition remains a long-standing Research Branch priority. As well, scientists deal with soil and water conservation, improved crop-management systems and techniques, preservation and storage of foodstuffs, improvement in milk and meat production and prevention of animal disease. Much research work is aimed at increasing the safety and quality of food and reducing the cost of food production. Many scientists seek ways to reduce the farm community's dependence on PESTICIDES, often criticized because of cost, health and environmental concerns.

In the modern era, several research stations have become deeply involved in BIOTECHNOLOGY, involving in part the manipulation of genes in the laboratory. Such research is destined to have major impacts on the breeding of superior plants and trees (for fruits), protecting crops from insects and disease, improving the performance of farm animals and developing new food products and manufacturing processes. Canola is the economic crop most technically amenable to such GENETIC ENGINEERING and it is here where breeding breakthroughs are soon expected, as in the building in of disease resistance in new varieties. Biotechnology applications are an important component of the work of the St-Hyacinthe Food Research Centre in Québec near Montréal, formally opened in 1987. Animal biotechnology work at Agriculture Canada is concentrated largely at the Animal Research Centre operations in the Ottawa area.

Agriculture Canada emphasizes the preservation of genetic material for possible future use in the breeding of new crop varieties. The principal focus for this work is a unit of the Plant Research Centre in Ottawa which protects genetic material principally through the storage of seeds from grain and other crops. The agency has some 82 000 seed samples, half of which are oats and barley species, wild and cultivated.

To further protect genetic diversity, the Smithfield Experimental Farm in Ontario has been designated as a national repository for the storage of horticultural genetic material. Some 1000 varieties of apple trees, other fruits, flowers, shrubs and a few vegetable plants will be preserved as growing matter to ensure their genes do not disappear when varieties carrying them are no longer commercially grown.

The tax-supported Agriculture Canada research establishments tend to focus on long-term projects deemed to be in the public interest. This approach provides some assurance that research important to the agrifood industry and the country is done. At the same time, Agriculture Canada depends on the private sector, universities, provincial governments and other institutions to help carry the rest of the research load. The federal research stations, therefore, place a heavy emphasis on collaboration with other research players to achieve mutual goals.

For administrative purposes the Agriculture Canada Research Branch is grouped into 3 regions – Eastern, Central and Western. Each region is under the control of a director general, who reports to the assistant deputy minister in charge of the branch as a whole. All 4 of these officials are based at Research Branch headquarters in Ottawa. The Eastern Region covers research establishments in the Atlantic provinces, Québec and Ontario outside the Ottawa area (which comprises the Central Region). The 4 western provinces comprise the Western Region.

The 6 establishments of the Central Region are called "centres," which denote institutions with a focus on national rather than regional demands, as in the case of the Animal Research Centre and the Plant Research Centre. Both these institutions are in the Central Region along with other centres covering land and soils, engineering and statistics, food processing and biosystematics.

All told, there are 8 establishments classified as centres throughout the country. Twenty-six others are classified as "stations," which tend to focus their research, although not exclusively so, on the needs of the regions in which they are located. Reporting to the directors of these stations are "experimental farms" and "substations."

In the Eastern Region, centres are located at St-Hyacinthe, Qué, and London, Ont, the latter focusing on the chemical side of agricultural operations, including pesticide research and the de-

velopment of biological controls. Stations are located at St John's; Charlottetown; Fredericton; Kentville, NS; Lennoxville, St-Jean-sur-Richelieu and Ste-Foy, Qué; and Vineland, Delhi and Harrow in Ont. Experimental farms are located at Buctouche, NB; Nappan, NS; La Pocatière, Normandin, L'Assomption and St-David, Qué; Kapuskasing, Thunder Bay, Woodslee and Smithfield, Ont.

Western Region stations are located at Winnipeg, Brandon and Morden, Man; Regina, Saskatoon, Swift Current and Melfort, Sask; Lethbridge, Beaverlodge and Lacombe, Alta; Summerland, Vancouver, Kamloops and Agassiz, BC. Experimental farms are located at Scott and Indian Head, Sask; Fort Vermilion, Alta; and Prince George, BC.

Of all the Agriculture Canada research establishments, the best-known is the Central Experimental Farm at Ottawa, one of the 5 original 19th-century institutions from which the whole system sprang. Most of the operations of the 6 research centres of the Central Region are located on the central farm, a 500 ha tract within the urban confines of the national capital. The national headquarters of both the Research Branch and the agriculture department as a whole are on the historic farm.   KENNETH R. CLARK

Reserve Force of Canada comprises part-time members of the ARMED FORCES whose role is to augment and support the Regular Force. Compulsory universal military service for early settlers eventually became part-time, volunteer soldiering. This reserve ("militia") tradition remained the dominant feature of Canadian military service, despite the evolution of a regular permanent land force; not until the 1950s did the regular components outnumber the reserves. The Royal Naval Canadian Volunteer Reserve was formed 1914, although there had been naval companies in colonial militias long before. The Canadian Air Force, est 1920, was almost entirely an air militia until the 1924 formation of the Royal Canadian Air Force, which had its own reserve component from the beginning.

The present Reserve Force is made up of 4 parts: the Primary Reserve, the Supplementary List, the Cadet Instructors List and the Canadian Rangers. The Primary Reserve is divided into the Naval Reserve, the Militia, the Air Reserve and Communication Reserve; all are composed of volunteers who train evenings, on weekends or at short camps. The Supplementary List consists of those who have left the Regular Force or Primary Reserve but are still available if needed. Officers on the Cadet Instructors List supervise, administer and train CADETS. The Canadian Rangers, whose special contribution is expert local knowledge, are reservists in sparsely settled areas. The 1987 White Paper on Defence proposed an extensive reorganization and upgrading of the reserves.
                    NORMAN HILLMER AND O.A. COOKE

Reservoir, surface water – a pond or LAKE created by building a dam or river at the outlet end of a lake or reservoir to store WATER. Reservoir water may be used for both off-stream (consumptive) uses such as irrigation, municipal and industrial; and in-stream, (nonconsumptive) uses such as power, recreational developments, FLOOD control and wildlife habitat improvement. Reservoirs may be used to improve the holding capacity of an existing lake or to create new reservoirs on rivers, creeks or coulees. Reservoirs, as discussed here, do not include any type of subsurface reservoir structure that stores water, gas or oil.

Reservoirs are usually classified by 3 basic physical characteristics: maximum depth, flooded area and the volume of water stored at their full surface level. Large reservoirs may have several

Principal Reservoirs in Canada

Reservoir	River	Province	Total Storage Capacity*	Year Operational
Lk St Lawrence	St Lawrence	Ont	808	1958
CrossLk-CedarLk	Saskatchewan	Man	9 643	1965
Williston Lk	Peace	BC	70 309	1968
Manicouagan	Manicouagan	Qué	141 851	1968
Diefenbaker Lk	S Saskatchewan	Sask	9 400	1968
Mactaquac Lk	Saint John	NB	913	1968
Abraham Lk	N Saskatchewan	Alta	1 768	1972
Kinbasket Lk	Columbia	BC	24 670	1972
Wreck Cove	Wreck Cove	NS	126	1978
Hinds Lk	Humber	Nfld	305	1980

* In millions of cubic metres

target levels, each level planned to ensure a usable amount of water at a certain time of year. For instance, in addition to its normal or full supply level (FSL), a reservoir may have a conservation storage level (ie, the desirable level for a flood-control reservoir at the start of each flooding period), a flood storage level (the maximum desirable level that is permitted for reservoir safety during floods), a dead storage level (the level below which water may not be withdrawn for consumptive uses) and various other target levels established to meet such needs as summer recreational use, irrigation use and hydropower withdrawals throughout the year.

Before construction, reservoir sites are subjected to detailed studies to determine their ability to meet the needs of potential users and to assess the overall benefits that can be derived from the project. Studies are usually carried out on a monthly basis, using a 50- or 60-year period of estimated or recorded historical streamflow to evaluate the project's performance under DROUGHT and flood conditions that have actually happened in past years. The results are used to determine if the proposed reservoir would adequately serve its potential users if we experience the types of drought that occurred in the past. Thus, a reservoir used for municipal purposes will be designed to have no shortages because the users, people in cities, will not tolerate periods without water. When uses are such that shortages, although they may be inconvenient, will not cause severe economic hardship, reservoirs are often designed to allow for an acceptable percentage of shortages in critically dry years. This permits more efficient use to be made of the available water resources. Two or more reservoirs are often used to maximize the supply potential of a DRAINAGE BASIN. The potential improvement that might be achieved by adding one or more reservoirs to an existing system may be evaluated by doing similar detailed hydrologic studies on both reservoirs.

Water evaporates from the surface of reservoirs when they are not covered by ICE. These losses, net evaporation, may be estimated by subtracting measured or estimated precipitation from estimated evaporation. The volume of reservoir losses caused by net evaporation is then calculated by multiplying net evaporation by the reservoir's surface area. When hydrologic studies indicate that the addition of further storage capacity will not significantly increase the yield of the reservoir either because the additional water stored would evaporate before being used or because all available water has been developed, the project is at its optimum storage capacity and further storage increases would be wasted.

Reservoirs have spillways to divert excess water during above-normal periods. The spillway's capacity is based both on the economic loss and on the potential danger to human life that might occur if the dam fails. When the potential exists for downstream loss of life, extensive property damage or both, spillways are usually designed to carry the largest flood that may be expected to

occur at that site. After construction, reservoirs are operated to co-ordinate consumptive, recreational and power uses with downstream releases to maintain predetermined levels of minimum flow, thus establishing monthly reservoir levels, regulated discharge and diversions.

Several changes occur to the environment adjacent to a reservoir. The newly created lake provides an additional recreational area, but the pre-existing river is destroyed and the area at the river's edge that used to provide shelter to animals and birds is lost. The river downstream from the reservoir usually has lower peaks and higher low flows because of the moderating effect of the reservoirs during floods and because of additional water released during dry periods. Colder water is released from the reservoir and fish must either adjust to the new environment or emigrate. However, there is often an increase in volume and diversity of the fish stocked in the reservoir itself, resulting in a net gain to the fishery. The overall water quality in the reservoir and downstream tends to improve because the reservoir acts as a mixing bowl, averaging out normal seasonal fluctuations. The clarity of downstream water also improves as the river's sediment load is trapped by the reservoir. This process may have an adverse effect on the channel below the reservoir as the river's streambed erodes. Similarly, at the upstream end of the reservoir, the capacity of the inlet channel is decreased by sedimentation.

DIEFENBAKER LAKE is a good example of a multi-use reservoir. After 100 years of proposals and plans the project was approved in 1958. On 25 May 1959 an inaugural ceremony marked the start of construction on the project's main dam, GARDINER DAM on the S Saskatchewan R. This dam, and the Coteau Creek generating station, designed to develop hydroelectric power at the damsite, were completed in 1967. A second dam was built on the Qu'Appelle R to keep water from escaping down that stream. In the spring of 1968 Diefenbaker Lake filled to operating capacity and the first power was generated. In 1970, the reservoir filled to its full capacity for the first time.

At its full supply level the dam controls a reservoir that stores a total of 9.4 billion m³, but only 4 billion m³ of this is live capacity. The remaining 5.4 billion m³ is dead storage, and this 5.4 billion m³ cannot be used for power or to release water downstream. The maximum depth of water at the dam is 58 m and the reservoir created by Gardiner Dam is 225 km long with a shoreline of 760 km. The spillway is 161 m wide and can pass, at its peak capacity, 400 000 cubic m of water. In an average year over 200 000 acre feet of water is lost to evaporation from the lake's surface area of 43 000 hectares.

Some 16 000 hectares are now (1986) irrigated with Diefenbaker Lake water and it is estimated that, by the year 2030, 115 000 hectares will be irrigated. The Coteau Creek generating station develops an average of 775 million kWh each year, and the downstream hydropower stations in the basin benefit directly from the flow regulation of Diefenbaker Lake. For instance, the Squaw Rapids Plant on the Saskatchewan R near Nipawin, Sask, is now able to generate 40% of its power in the winter (double the previous amount) owing directly to improved outflow from Diefenbaker Lake. Water from the lake is also used to supply 3 potash mines, 8 communities and a series of recreational and wildlife projects using water diverted from the lake.

The lake itself has become a water-based resort area, creating a major recreational lake in a traditionally dry area of Saskatchewan, and waters from this lake are annually diverted into the Qu'Appelle R system to augment the municipal water supplies of Moose Jaw and Regina and to

improve the quality and quantity of water in the basin.   R.B. GODWIN

Reading: B. Henderson-Sellers, *Reservoirs* (1979).

Resolute, NWT, Settlement, pop 184 (1986c), 168 (1981c), is located on the S coast of CORNWALLIS I, 1561 air km NE of Yellowknife. It was named for a ship which wintered here in 1850, but its development began in 1947 with the construction of a joint US-Canadian HIGH ARCTIC WEATHER STATION. In 1955, Inuit families from other areas were relocated to the area to take advantage of the island's game resources. These included Idlouk, whose camp is pictured on one of the Canadian $2 bills.   ANNELIES POOL

Resource Management usually refers to the responsibility of governments to ensure that natural resources under their jurisdiction are used wisely or conserved. "Wise use" excludes unnecessary waste and, in the case of renewable resources, implies that their use will be constrained to provide a sustained use in the future. Where the use of a resource conflicts with other natural resources, eg, where FORESTRY operations interfere with the spawning of salmon, sound resource management implies that policies will recognize the desirability of multiple uses and place restraints on single purpose uses that are detrimental to other resource values. Sometimes governments decide to preserve natural resources from all consumptive uses. Ecological reserves maintaining lands indefinitely in their natural state are one method of preserving such resources.

The use of a natural resource often raises conflicts among individuals and groups with special interests in the resource. Conflicts may arise among industrial users of FORESTS, MINERALS and FISH; the recreation industry, which depends on lakes, streams and forests; and naturalists who advocate wilderness preservation and conservation of wildlife. Such clashes may occur at levels ranging from the broad scale (industry versus wilderness) to conflicts between industries (dams versus forestry), between recreation users (snowmobilers versus hikers) or between naturalists and their objects of study (eg, when too much disturbance interferes with nesting). Native peoples whose aboriginal rights have not yet been recognized claim natural-RESOURCE RIGHTS based on their historic relationship with the land.

These conflicts and others require careful management strategies by governments. In Canada government ownership of natural resources provides the foundation for management strategies and policies. The 4 original provinces in Confederation retained ownership and control of their natural resources. British Columbia and Prince Edward Island also retained ownership of natural resources on joining the union. When Manitoba, Alberta and Saskatchewan were formed, natural-resource ownership was retained by the federal government, in part to provide revenues to support colonization and the construction of the transcontinental railway. In 1930 a constitutional amendment transferred ownership and control of what remained of the publicly owned natural resources from the federal government to the Alberta, Saskatchewan and Manitoba governments. Hence, in Canada publicly owned natural resources now belong to the provinces, although jurisdiction over migratory birds and fish is largely federal. In the NORTH, the natural resources in the YT and the NWT remain under the control of the federal government. Conflicting claims of the federal and provincial governments to resources in the offshore regions have been settled in favour of the federal government by a March 1984 decision of the Supreme Court of Canada. In many regions of Canada, both onshore and offshore, native peoples have unsettled aboriginal claims.

In the earlier years provincial governments followed policies that permitted outright alienation of farm and urban lands and even of forest and wildlands. More recently, particularly in western Canada and the North, government policy has been to grant only limited tenures of forest and mineral lands. Thus, governments function as landlords of forestry and oil companies and, to a lesser extent, of mining companies. Consequently, provincial and federal natural-resource management in these cases is dual in nature; a government acts as an owner/landlord and as a regulator of resource use.

As owner/landlord, a provincial government may become a joint developer with industry. In this capacity, the government's management policies may be to stimulate investment and jobs (as in the NE coal development in BC), to maximize rents and royalties (eg, of publicly owned oil and gas resources), to maintain a sustained yield (eg, in forests and FISHERIES) or to influence the structure of industry participation (eg, the "Canadianization" of the PETROLEUM INDUSTRY).

As regulator, a government controls natural-RESOURCE USE through statutes authorizing resource management by various departments, branches and agencies. In Canada constitutional powers are divided between the national and provincial governments by the CONSTITUTION ACT, 1982. Provincial legislatures are authorized to enact laws for the management and sale of natural resources and for the regulation of primary production; the Parliament of Canada is given legislative power to regulate coastal and inland fisheries and interprovincial and export trade in natural-resource commodities. Each level of government may tax natural-resource revenues. Consequently, while a province may adopt and enforce resource management policies, these policies must be consistent with national policies adopted by Parliament. These overlapping powers and responsibilities lead to conflicts between the provincial and national governments over such matters as markets, pricing and sharing of natural-resource revenues, and may sometimes hamper broad-scale management. Intergovernmental conflicts are further complicated in urban areas, where municipal governments may own the land. In the past, natural-resource statutes created a variety of single resource management entities, designating a separate department or branch for each individual resource, eg, the federal fisheries department, a provincial mines and minerals department, a provincial forest service or a provincial wildlife branch. Government departments in the natural-resources sector now usually have broader mandates and require policies that recognize the multiple demands on resources. Integrating strategies such as regional resource planning and multiple-use task forces are used more frequently in an effort to accomplish more co-ordinated resource management, and environmental impact assessments and public hearings on resource uses and projects are now common.

These trends in government are largely a consequence of the emergence of professional natural-resource planners and managers. With specific education and training in natural-resource management programs, these professionals are widely employed in industry, government and consulting firms. New statutory requirements for formal assessment and review of development projects that may impose adverse impacts on the ENVIRONMENT contribute to a climate in which wise natural-resource use is no longer taken for granted. Concerns about the finite nature of resources, about the possibility of irreversible harm to the environment and about gaining economic

efficiency and optimum benefit from the use of resources will place ever higher demands upon these professionals.

While much attention has been paid to multiple-use and social cost/benefit questions, much more could be accomplished if certain inherent features of natural-resources management are recognized and if research strategies can be more specifically directed to management priorities. Resource management is now characterized by high degrees of uncertainty about causes and effects, about mitigative measures and about the costs and benefits of different means of resolving resource use conflicts. For example, ACID RAIN is widely recognized as a major threat to the global environment, but great difficulty is experienced in getting experts and political leaders to agree on mitigative and remedial programs, even between neighbouring countries like Canada and the US. These uncertainties call for research priorities that focus on key unknowns, and management strategies that are designed to provide more adaptive and flexible means of coping with the future. The importance of natural resources in the economy and life of Canadians is so great that better resource management practices should be a matter of national priority.   ANDREW R. THOMPSON

Resource Rights Natural-resource development has played a major role in Canada's economy and continues to be a focus of national concerns. While these concerns have centered on ENERGY POLICY during the past decade, water resource management may be the issue of the 1990s. Other resource sectors such as fishing, forestry and mining also present difficult policy choices as Canadians face the issues of conservation, environmental protection, unemployment, and the maintaining of markets in a competitive world.

The right to develop resources (or to choose not to develop them) is, in the first instance, a right of ownership. Under the common law of Canada, the basic rule is that the ownership of land carries with it the right to harvest renewable resources, such as crops, trees, fish and wildlife, and also the right to extract nonrenewable resources such as coal, minerals and oil. Originally, governments in Canada gave individuals ownership of this type when crown land grants were made to settlers and developers, but new policies emerged around the turn of the century whereby governments gave only restricted ownership rights to resource developers. Mining leases and limited cutting rights began to replace outright grants of mineral and forestlands. In the case of agricultural lands, homesteaders of crown grants were not granted rights to minerals such as coal, oil and gas under their land. The government claimed ownership of minerals and gave only restricted development rights (by means of leases) to companies conducting exploration for minerals such as petroleum and natural gas. In western Canada today, provincial governments are by far the largest owners of undeveloped natural-resource rights; as well, they are the landlords of the oil, mineral and forest companies that enjoy exploration and development rights. In northern Canada and in the offshore regions, the federal government enjoys such ownership.

Under the CONSTITUTION ACT, 1867, the original provinces of Confederation retained ownership of crown lands and resources within their boundaries. When BC and PEI joined Confederation in 1871 and 1873, respectively, they too retained ownership of natural resources. But when the Prairie provinces were created (Manitoba in 1870, Alberta and Saskatchewan in 1905) a new and controversial policy emerged. In these provinces, ownership of natural resources was re-

tained by the federal government to provide funds for colonization and railway building. Not until 1930, after a sometimes bitter political struggle, were natural-resource rights transferred by the federal government to the Prairie provinces. By this time, most of the agricultural lands had been transferred into private ownership; but because the federal government had reserved mineral rights when disposing of land in the prairies and had granted restricted tenures, the provincial governments inherited a rich treasure house of resource rights under the 1930 transfer. It is as a consequence of these rights that Alberta grants oil and gas leases and receives oil and gas royalties; that Manitoba can develop vast hydroelectric power resources to sell in the US; and that Saskatchewan controls uranium and potash reserves of worldwide significance.

The mineral and petroleum resources of northern Canada and the offshore regions of the East and West coasts remain under the ownership and control of the federal government and provide a huge potential for development. The federal government has also passed legislation that provides for the issuing of exploration rights and production licences, under which developers must meet expenditure commitments and pay royalties when commercial production begins. The Canada Oil and Gas Act, 1980-81-82, established a federal regime for petroleum resources that was intended to increase Canadian ownership in petroleum companies and to ensure Canadian benefits in terms of jobs and the procurement of goods and services. With the change of government, in 1985 this statute was replaced by the Canada Petroleum Resources Act, with less emphasis on these "Canadianization" issues and greater certainty in the terms and conditions of exploration and development.

Ownership is not the only determinant of resource rights. Just as the owner of a business is subject to federal, provincial and municipal legislation setting out how the business must operate, so companies that acquire resource rights from the federal and provincial governments are subject to legislated requirements, eg, laws to protect the environment, laws providing for employee safety, or taxation laws. Obviously, resource rights acquired by an owner often clash with these legislated requirements. In a BC case, the court held that restrictions placed on operations in a provincial park were so severe as to amount to expropriation of mining rights that had been granted before the park was established. In result, the holder of the mining rights was entitled to compensation.

The classic Canadian example of conflict between resource ownership rights and restrictive legislation occurred in the 1970s when federal legislation (the Petroleum Administration Act) was perceived by the western provinces as an unconstitutional interference with provincial resource ownership rights. In particular, federal threats to establish unilaterally the wellhead prices for petroleum and natural gas, and new federal taxes levied on these resources, were seen as direct interference with the rights claimed by these provinces to sell their resources on such terms as they saw fit and to receive royalties at rates they would determine. These conflicts were temporarily resolved by agreement between the federal and provincial governments during the constitutional debates of 1981. A new section of the CONSTITUTION ACT, 1982, purports to clarify the extent to which provinces may manage their resources, giving them exclusive power to make laws dealing with the development, conservation and management of nonrenewable resources and forestry resources, and to regulate the rate of primary production from these resources. Parliament has paramount jurisdiction to regulate interprovincial and export trade in natural resources, and both levels of government are given full powers of taxation.

There are other areas of conflict over the ownership and control of natural resources in Canada. The conflict between the US and Canada over alleged discrimination against foreign investors under Canada's National Energy Program (1980) has been eliminated by the Canada Petroleum Resources Act. The claims by the US lumber industry that Canadian lumber competes unfairly in US markets because of alleged subsidies given to the Canadian industry by the federal and provincial governments have recently been resolved (see SOFTWOOD LUMBER DISPUTE). The FREE TRADE agreement (1988) between Canada and the US expressly includes energy resources and may lead to more effective bilateral trade in natural resource products generally; it may, however, also increase friction between federal and provincial governments regarding energy. Boundary disputes between Canada and the US affect fisheries and petroleum development in offshore waters on the East and West coasts and in the projection seawards of the Alaska-Yukon boundary.

Within Canada, native people have land claims to natural resources made pursuant both to treaties and to aboriginal LAND CLAIMS in nontreaty areas. In the northern territories, claims to regional self-government are accompanied by claims to ownership rights over northern natural resources. In the offshore regions, a long-standing dispute between the federal government and the coastal provinces concerning ownership and jurisdiction has been resolved in favour of the federal government in a decision of the Supreme Court of Canada concerning conflicting Newfoundland and federal claims to the Hibernia oil field (see HIBERNIA CASE).

Issues involving resource rights also surface from time to time in relation to such matters as the regulation of fishing, the protection of the environment, the control of the air waves and the management of watersheds. A recent report cites the need for an interjurisdictional agreement covering the Mackenzie R drainage basin before developments such as hydroelectric dams in Alberta and BC are allowed to proceed.

Canada is a large country with bountiful natural resources. Its size and its federal system of government (see FEDERALISM) explain why natural resources play such an important role in the Canadian economy and why government policies are so significant and so likely to be contentious. In these circumstances, it is a continuing national challenge to manage natural resources co-operatively and wisely. ANDREW R. THOMPSON

Resource Towns, or "new towns," are the small isolated communities built around resource-based industries and transportation – mining towns, mill towns, railway towns, fishing villages, etc. Examples include GRAND FALLS, Nfld (pulp and paper); GLACE BAY, NS (coal); Black's Harbour, NB (fish packing); Murdochville, Qué (asbestos); Copper Cliff, Ont (nickel); Snow Lake, Man (copper, zinc); Drayton Valley, Alta (oil); and KITIMAT, BC (aluminum). These communities are very common in Canada; eg, about 1 million Canadians live in some 1000 resource communities across Canada.

Resource development has long been recognized as a significant factor in shaping patterns of Canadian development. It has been argued that all Canadian urban growth ultimately depends on the production of staple products. Resource towns have been important agencies in this process of staple exploitation. Government involvement in the exploitation of natural resources dur-

ing recent decades has helped improve the quality of life in these towns, which are the most unstable and precarious of Canadian communities, and will remain so unless a more comprehensive approach to their planning is adopted.

In some respects Canadian resource towns resemble similar towns throughout the world, ie, towns based on the extraction or processing of resources such as minerals, forest products and hydroelectric power. Characteristically the resource town is an adjunct of an industrial enterprise, lacking control over its own economic development. The economic base is controlled by outside corporations or governments who determine the nature and extent of the extractive or processing activity and thereby determine the size of the local work force and the degree of local prosperity or growth. Because raw materials are usually shipped elsewhere, often outside Canada, for processing, most resource towns are excluded from the ultimate economic benefits derived from the resources. Boom and bust fluctuations depend on the vagaries of the international market for resources, or upon government or corporate decisions, and not on local initiative. Recurring fluctuations generate feelings of insecurity and impermanence in the community, feelings accentuated in mining towns by the knowledge that the resource base will eventually be exhausted.

Resource towns are also characterized by the simplified occupational structure inherent to them. The middle class is relatively weak and usually includes only a small group of managers, merchants and professionals who are oriented, as far as careers are concerned, to organizations outside the town. Workers often migrate between resource towns in search of employment. Several factors discourage the development of a diversified economy which would generate a more heterogeneous work force. Isolation from major markets, relatively high wages paid by resource industries, and high development costs combine to prevent the influx of secondary industry. One result is that the male-female ratio in resource towns is usually slanted heavily in favour of men, since there are fewer employment opportunities for women. Another result is that most (but not all) resource towns remain small; only a few are over 10 000 in population. Therefore, they share many of the features of any small town, regardless of its economic base. A final common characteristic is physical appearance. Although recently built resource towns tend to resemble the new suburbs of large cities, older towns are generally unattractive, ramshackle communities with a townscape dominated by a mine or mill.

While Canadian resource towns have a great deal in common both with each other and with towns in other countries, it is possible to delineate several distinctive characteristics. One basic distinction involves the origins of the population. The industrial population of many of the resource towns of the Atlantic provinces and Québec is drawn from the surrounding fishing, lumbering and agricultural population. In sharp contrast, the work force and management of the resource towns of Ontario and western Canada are drawn from populations remote from the town or from outside the country. "New towns" created in largely uninhabited areas have no physical or cultural rural connections.

A second major distinction is based on the decision-making process involved in creating and maintaining the community. Some towns are the products of decisions made by a single company or a government; others represent the outcome of a number of decisions made by a number of companies or by the residents of the community itself. The 2 types of towns which result are service and supply towns (eg, SUDBURY, Ont), which some-

times begin as boom towns, and company towns (eg, TÉMISCAMING, Qué), which are generally small, static communities closely attached to one industry's operation.

The physical appearance of resource towns depends, as does function, on who is responsible for planning and building the town. Chronologically the shaping of the towns has reflected the approach to URBAN AND REGIONAL PLANNING that has been current in Canada at specific periods. Three generations of resource towns have been built since Confederation: 1867-1920, privately built towns, eg, COBALT, Ont; 1920-39, holistically built towns, eg, KAPUSKASING, Ont; and since 1945, comprehensively planned, third-generation towns, eg, Kitimat, BC.

The modernization of some of the larger service centres and the designs of some of the new towns dramatically illustrate the advances made in resource-town building since the first-generation towns appeared in the 19th century. But regardless of the sophistication of recent planning concepts, the basic problems facing resource towns remain unresolved. Many have a limited lifetime, and prospects for activity and growth beyond the initial function seldom materialize. In some cases the resources simply run out; or perhaps market conditions change, or an international corporation moves its operation to another country. Mines or plants close and the town eventually dies (eg, PINE POINT, NWT; SCHEFFERVILLE, Qué). Hundreds of Canadian communities have disappeared in this way. In other cases the industrial plants become obsolete. But in both cases the future remains uncertain and fluctuations between boom and bust plague attempts for orderly, long-term development. See also COMPANY TOWN.
ALAN F.J. ARTIBISE AND G.A. STELTER

Reading: R.T. Bowles, ed, *Little Communities and Big Industries* (1982); Rex Lucas, *Minetown, Milltown, Railtown* (1971); I.M. Robinson, *New Industrial Towns on Canada's Resource Frontier* (1962); Alan F.J. Artibise and Gilbert A. Stelter, *Canada's Urban Past* (1981).

Resource Use Since prehistoric times, the inhabitants of what is now Canada used vegetation and animals for food, clothing and shelter. They fashioned implements and ornaments from MINERALS and, after the arrival of Europeans, used furs for trading. The FISHERIES were the first resource to be systematically exploited by Europeans. As early as the 16th century, BASQUES from France and Spain pursued WHALES in the Gulf of St Lawrence. Early in the 16th century, European fishermen took COD on the GRAND BANKS. Early resource exploitation, like exploration, was peripheral to attempts to find a NORTHWEST PASSAGE to the Orient. During his voyage into the Gulf of St Lawrence in 1534, Jacques CARTIER traded furs with the Micmac. By the late 1500s, French fishermen who sailed annually to the Grand Banks conducted a lucrative trade in furs. The FUR TRADE helped stimulate colonization as short-term monopolies on the St Lawrence fur trade were granted in return for promises to settle colonists there. From the arrival of Samuel de CHAMPLAIN to the days of Jean TALON, the colony in New France depended almost exclusively on the fur trade. The establishment of a trading post at the Indian village of Stadacona (later QUÉBEC CITY) provided a base for the trade, which eventually extended into the continental interior. This settlement, together with Tadoussac, Trois-Rivières and later Montréal, became the object of regular visits from Indians bearing furs.

The first organized attempt at processing resources came with the arrival in 1665 of the Intendant Jean Talon, who established various "manufactories" that used agricultural products to satisfy the settlers' needs and launch revenue-producing export industries. Large numbers of farm animals were introduced to New France. Wool from sheep and hides from cattle provided clothing and shoes. Talon encouraged the growing of hemp, barley and hops and the production of tar. Wood and tar were used for SHIPBUILDING in a yard on the banks of the St-Charles R. Hemp was used to make rigging for sails. With the hops and barley, beer was made in the "King's brewery" located near the shipyard. Surplus agricultural products, fish, wood and beer were exported to the West Indies on locally built ships. Talon also recognized that COPPER, LEAD, iron and COAL were potential sources of wealth for the colony. There was considerable PROSPECTING activity, but these efforts failed to discover minerals that could be exploited with the limited MINING technology of the time.

The impetus for exploitation of most resources was lost after Talon departed. Even the fur trade became more difficult as fur reserves were depleted and the French were forced to travel to Indian villages to trade. The departure of men for the woods (COUREURS DE BOIS) depleted the agricultural labour force and farming declined. Processing of minerals was stopped in 1704 when Louis XIV ordered the colonies not to compete with industries in France. This edict limited colonial economic activity to sending raw materials back to France and was a harbinger of the "further processing" issue, a principal concern in the 20th-century exploitation of Canada's resources. Thus, early in the 18th century, furs again became the principal economic resource of New France. Following the British Conquest (1760), the trade flourished until the middle of the 19th century and declined rapidly thereafter.

The exploitation of Canada's MINERAL RESOURCES began before the arrival of Europeans. The Inuit and Indians used and traded copper implements (see COPPER INUIT; PREHISTORY). In 1604 an exploration party under Champlain found native copper at Cap d'Or, NS. IRON ORE was one of the first minerals mined in Canada. Around 1670, deposits were found in swampy areas near Trois-Rivières. By the 1740s, Canada's first ironworks, the FORGES ST-MAURICE at Trois-Rivières, was turning out top-quality cast-iron stoves, pots, kettles, bullets and cannon for settlers and the military. Samuel HEARNE journeyed N in search of copper. He was to be disappointed, despite being the first white man to reach the Arctic Ocean overland. In 1770 Jesuit fathers experimented with native copper found at Point Mamainse on the N shore of Lk Superior. However, copper mining in Canada began with the discovery that led to the establishment of the Bruce Mine in the Algoma district of Ontario.

Although reports of SILVER deposits dated back to the voyages of Cartier, the first accurate account was that of Pierre, Chevalier de TROYES, a French military commander who recorded finding a silver-bearing vein of ore on the eastern shore of Lk Timiskaming in 1686. The first commercial deposit was discovered in 1868 at SILVER ISLET, a tiny rock island in Lk Superior, about 30 km E of Thunder Bay. The first discovery of GOLD in Canada, in the sands of the Fraser R (1857), led to the CARIBOO GOLD RUSH (1862). Further discoveries were made in Nova Scotia and Ontario. The KLONDIKE GOLD RUSH began in 1897. Gold rushes had a profound effect on the development of BC, and on the opening of the Yukon and North-West Territories to settlement.

Much of the exploration of western Canada was the result of the quest for beaver pelts. The railway later opened the mineral riches of the West to exploitation. Railways also brought pioneer farmers who began to reap the rich agricultural potential (see AGRICULTURE HISTORY). The explorers had opened up the vast reaches of the

West and North and later scientists and surveyors (particularly from the GEOLOGICAL SURVEY OF CANADA) would gather useful details of terrain and resources. The old fur-trading posts of the Hudson's Bay Co and North West Co were quickly transformed into settlements.   MAURICE CUTLER

Resources are those aspects of the natural environment that humans value and from which we produce goods and services. This definition demonstrates that, although natural resources originate in the natural environment, they are in a very real sense "created" by humans. Human values and abilities determine which parts of the environment societies use and benefit from. Resource and environmental systems are highly interconnected and both continually change in character. Change is usually accelerated by human use. Because of the interconnections, impacts beyond the particular resource being used are common. In fact, use of some resources may preclude use of others. Human decisions, as well as natural processes, cause resources to change over time (see BIOGEOGRAPHY). These changes may decrease or increase resource supply and may be rapid or slow.

Resources may be classified according to various criteria, including both information and availability, and the temporal, spatial and ownership characteristics.

Information and Availability Three general classes of resources (potential, conditional and current) are distinguished on the basis of information known about them and their availability. A potential resource is one which is only thought to exist (ie, positive information is still lacking); a conditional resource is known to exist but its availability for use depends upon a number of conditions; a current resource has met all conditions and is in use and yielding benefits. Progression of a resource from potential to current status occurs as information about it increases and as preproduction conditions are met. This transformation may take a long time and, until it is complete, few benefits flow to society. For example, initial information from geological and geophysical SURVEYING may indicate that a particular area has mineral potential. More information may suggest that a deposit exists, and further elaborate and expensive exploration may confirm the deposit. A potential resource has become a conditional one. Additional information is needed to determine the extent and quality of the deposit; then other specific conditions must be met before production can begin.

The first condition is that suitable TECHNOLOGY is available to produce and process the mineral in marketable form. Next, a decision must be made as to whether production is economically feasible, ie, whether economic benefits outweigh costs sufficiently to warrant financial risks. At this stage, production, processing and transport costs are assessed in relation to the expected market price. Political and legal conditions must also be met. These arise from nonmarket concerns and the relative importance different governments place upon them.

Recent concerns have included environmental degradation, health hazards and financial returns to governments (see SOCIAL IMPACT ASSESSMENT). If these conditions are fulfilled, production may commence, thus creating a current resource. The process is reversible. The resource will revert from current to conditional status if preproduction conditions change sufficiently to make use no longer feasible.

Temporal Characteristics Resources that regenerate in short periods of time (eg, months, years, decades) or that are characterized by repeated occurrence are classed as renewable. WATER, plants

and animals are generally considered renewable resources; their regenerative capabilities are measured in months for water supply, years for animal stocks and decades for FOREST stands. These varied time periods pose different management problems for users.

Furthermore, the regenerative capacity of some renewable resources can be partially or completely removed by changes in habitat (eg, fish, as the result of WATER POLLUTION), harvesting to the point of extinction (eg, overhunting of game species) or habitat destruction resulting from poor harvesting techniques (eg, erosion caused by the overcutting of a forest).

Most renewable ENERGY resources rely upon atmospheric processes that occur repeatedly but are subject to cycles and periodical changes; thus, the potential for regeneration is not always met. Solar radiation, for example, is "renewable" in the sense that, except at very high latitudes, the sun rises and sets daily, but direct solar radiation is available only intermittently, between night and day and between cloudy and clear periods. Similarly, wind blows only intermittently. Thus, although these 2 resources occur repeatedly and are thus attractive as potential energy sources, they pose management problems (see SOLAR ENERGY; WIND ENERGY).

The great advantage of renewable resources is that they can yield continual benefits if managed properly, a process requiring a high degree of knowledge of life cycles, controlled harvesting and habitat protection. For example, once an oceanic fish stock is discovered, data must be obtained about its size and life cycle and the distance over which it moves, although the information-gathering process is difficult and time consuming. Such information is necessary because fish are mobile and are regarded as common property, and therefore catch limits are needed to ensure the stock's ability to reproduce itself. Establishment of some limits requires detailed information on population dynamics, movement patterns and habitat characteristics. Poor management can convert a renewable resource to nonrenewable status, or can necessitate intensive rehabilitation efforts.

Nonrenewable resources are those that cannot be regenerated in a human life span. Minerals are the best example of this class, but there are others. Land, for example, is not used consumptively as minerals are, but on balance the land area of Canada is not likely to be increased, except for possible reclamation of wetlands. SOIL is also nonrenewable in that it forms slowly and some uses are consumptive (eg, when it is removed to make way for buildings or transportation facilities). When managed well, soil can sustain biomass production for long periods.

Spatial Characteristics The 2 spatial aspects of resources which influence their use are mobility and concentration. Mobile resources include air, water and wildlife. Control over the use and management of mobile resources is complicated because they may move widely and be subject to many influences. They may cross jurisdictional boundaries (eg, national or provincial borders) or move into areas of no specific jurisdiction (eg, the OCEANS). Concentrated resources such as minerals and RIVERS occupy relatively confined spaces in comparison with dispersed resources such as forests and agricultural land. The degree of concentration sometimes determines whether a resource moves from conditional to current status because the costs of use increase according to wider dispersion.

Ownership Characteristics Some resources are privately owned by individuals or firms (eg, farmland); others are owned by governments, and rights to their use are allocated by licence, permit, etc (eg, forests, minerals and water). Others, which are usually called common property resources, are not owned at all (eg, fish and atmospheric elements). Common property resources attract users, each of whom tries to maximize benefits from them; consequently, they may quickly become degraded or even exhausted. This class of resource raises special management problems. Access to common resources through private property may also be contentious.

Provincial Resource Profiles

According to the Canada Land Inventory, the total land with high capability for agriculture in Canada is 20.5 million ha, of which Sask has 33.4%, Alta 22.5%, Ont 21.3%, Man 13.1% and Qué 2.3%.

For recreation, the percentages are Qué 29.3%, Ont 23.6%, BC 20.2%, Nfld 10%, Sask 2.7%, Man 3.0% and Alta 2.7%. Of the allowable cut of timber (276 million m³ for Canada), BC has 36.0%, Ont 23.8%, Qué 14.8% and Alta 10.2%.

British Columbia has rich and varied resources. Most notable are the coniferous forests of the coast and central interior, the dispersed base-metal deposits and the coal and natural-gas resources of the E and NE. The PEACE and COLUMBIA rivers have been developed for HYDROELECTRICITY and considerable potential remains, particularly in the north (eg, LIARD and STIKINE rivers). Other major rivers (eg, FRASER, SKEENA) and many smaller streams are the spawning grounds of SALMON which, with herring, groundfish and crustaceans, support a large FISHING industry.

Mountainous landforms and an extensive coastline provide habitats suitable for a variety of wildlife and considerable opportunity for outdoor recreation of many kinds. High-quality agricultural land is limited to the SW corner of the province and in valley locations in the interior.

Yukon and the Northwest Territories, covering almost 40% of Canada (and constituting most of Canada's North), have a harsh winter climate and short summers, resulting in limited plant growth. The eastern parts contain TUNDRA; some of the mountains are permanently ice covered. South of the treeline, particularly in the Yukon and in the Mackenzie River Basin, extensive areas are covered with forests of low productivity. Despite limiting environmental conditions, the territories support large populations of terrestrial and marine wildlife.

Wildlife stocks are important sources of food and FUR for the native populations. Many special areas of unique environmental character afford valuable recreational and scientific opportunities. Much of the resource base (especially in minerals) is classed as potential or, at best, conditional. Base-metal resources have been developed in western sections and geological conditions suggest considerable potential. Most attention, however, is being given to exploration for PETROLEUM in the Mackenzie Delta, Beaufort Sea and the northwestern arctic islands.

Alberta consists mainly of 2 major geological areas, the Western Sedimentary Basin and the Rocky Mts. Large resources of fossil fuels (coal, oil and gas) exist beneath the surface of the former, while substantial areas of high-quality agricultural land cover the surface in the southern half of the province. Aridity limits agricultural productivity in the SE. The Rocky Mts contain large coal resources, the headwaters of many rivers and spectacular mountain and lake scenery, offering dramatic opportunities for outdoor recreation. Forested areas across central Alberta provide a modest forest resource.

Alberta's resources of conventional oil (low-viscosity oil that flows to the surface in its natural condition) have been heavily used and production is declining. There are also very large deposits of heavy oil (ie, oil too viscous to come to the surface without special production techniques) and, in the tar sands, BITUMEN. These expensive "conditional" oil resources are in production to some extent, but large-scale development depends on economic and technological factors. Collectively, these energy resources make Alberta the fossil-fuel storehouse of Canada.

Saskatchewan The natural-resource base of Saskatchewan consists of the largest area of high-quality agricultural land in Canada, extensive and productive wildlife habitat (particularly for WATERFOWL), major deposits of potash and uranium, and significant supplies of petroleum and coal. Saskatchewan is Canada's primary wheat-growing area and a major producer of other grains and field CROPS.

Boreal and mixed forest areas provide a modest forest resource. After 1962 Saskatchewan became the world's largest exporter and second-largest producer of potash. Large uranium resources in northern areas make the province the second-largest producer in Canada, while in the S strip-mined lignite coal is used extensively for thermal-power generation. Saskatchewan shares with Alberta a portion of the Lloydminster heavy and conventional oil fields.

Manitoba has a mixed resource base, including a variety of metallic minerals, hydroelectric power potential, and a significant area of good quality agricultural land. Nickel is the major mineral produced, with copper, lead, zinc and precious metals mined locally in significant quantities. Some northward-flowing rivers have already been developed for hydroelectricity (eg, NELSON R); others have large potential for development (eg, CHURCHILL R). Manitoba's current production of oil is small, but a promising hydrocarbon area has been identified along the southern border. The fish stocks of Lakes Winnipeg and Manitoba, significant areas of wildlife habitat and locally important forest resources all add to the variety of Manitoba's resource base.

Ontario is the largest market for resource-based goods and services in Canada. However, with the important exception of fossil fuels, the province's own renewable and nonrenewable resources are large. The province ranks third, after Saskatchewan and Alberta, in area suitable for agriculture; however, southern Ontario alone has over 50% of Canada's Class 1 agricultural land, which, coupled with favourable climate, provides a resource base for productive and varied crops and livestock. In central and northern Ontario the forest cover contributes almost 25% of the national allowable cut and supports a major forest-product industry. Many of the more accessible forested areas and numerous lakes and streams afford extensive opportunities for outdoor recreation.

The outstanding water resources of the GREAT LAKES and the ST LAWRENCE R offer major transportation routes, sources of hydroelectricity and recreational opportunities. Ontario lacks significant amounts of conventional fossil fuels and is only moderately endowed with industrial minerals (except SALT); however, northern Ontario is a storehouse of other minerals. The province leads Canada in production of nickel, uranium, zinc, gold and silver, and is second to BC in production of copper.

Québec has the greatest developed and potential hydroelectric resources in Canada. Many rivers running off the Canadian SHIELD into the ST LAWRENCE LOWLANDS and JAMES BAY have been harnessed to provide a large renewable source of energy, which helps compensate for the lack of fossil fuels.

The St Lawrence R affords an important transportation route. Extensive areas of fresh water (in lakes and rivers) offer considerable opportunity for both outdoor recreation and wildlife habitat. Good quality agricultural soils are limited, but Québec ranks third (after BC and Ontario) in the productivity of its extensive forested area. Important mineral resources include asbestos (the production of which is only exceeded by that of the USSR), iron, gold and some base metals.

The Atlantic Provinces Even with the relatively large size of Newfoundland, the Atlantic provinces collectively cover a land area that is less than any of the remaining 6 provinces. Much of the area is made up of islands and peninsulas, which give easy access to the FISH and CRUSTACEAN RESOURCES of the Gulf of St Lawrence and the Continental Shelf of the western Atlantic, the location of Canada's largest fishing industry (see COASTAL WATERS; FISHERIES; OCEAN INDUSTRIES). Other important renewable resources include forests (particularly in NB and Nfld), relatively small areas of productive land (eg, PEI, the Annapolis Valley of NS) and hydroelectric resources, particularly in Labrador and in the Bay of Fundy (see TIDAL ENERGY). The extensive coastlines provide many opportunities for seasonal outdoor recreation. The mineral-resource base may be divided into onshore and offshore. Onshore there is a large base-metal resource in northern NB, iron in Nfld and GYPSUM and salt in NS. The only significant onshore fossil-fuel resources are coal deposits in Nova Scotia's Cape Breton area. Offshore, the Continental Shelf has a significant potential for oil (particularly off Nfld) and gas (off NS).

Opportunities and Challenges

The economic development of Canada has been based to a great extent upon a large and varied endowment of resources, the availability of

---

Mineral Production 1986
(Percentage of National Total)
(Source: Dept of Energy, Mines and Resources, Ottawa, 1986)

	Nfld	PEI	NS	NB	Qué	Ont	Man	Sask	Alta	BC	YT	NWT
Lead	–	–	–	25.2	–	2.2	T	–	–	34.0	12.1	26.5
Zinc	0.6	–	–	15.7	4.0	28.9	5.5	0.3	–	13.0	5.2	26.8
Copper	–	–	–	0.9	8.7	37.6	9.0	0.5	–	43.3	–	–
Iron	53.8	–	–	–	36.8	9.4	–	–	–	–	–	–
Nickel	–	–	–	–	–	75.8	24.2	–	–	–	–	–
Gold	–	–	–	T	28.2	44.5	2.1	–	–	8.4	3.8	12.9
Silver	–	–	–	16.5	4.1	35.8	2.8	0.3	–	33.2	5.4	1.9
Asbestos	7.0	–	–	–	80.5	–	–	–	–	12.5	–	–
Potash (est)	–	–	–	5.0	–	–	–	95.0	–	–	–	–
Sulphur	–	–	–	–	–	–	–	T	95.7	4.3	–	–
Uranium	–	–	–	–	–	40.4	–	59.6	–	–	–	–
Coal	–	–	5.0	0.8	–	–	–	14.3	43.2	36.7	–	–
Oil	–	–	–	–	–	T	1.0	13.6	81.2	12.4	–	1.8
Natural Gas	–	–	–	–	–	0.7	–	2.8	87.7	8.4	–	0.4

Note: T denotes a production percentage of less than 0.5%

foreign capital and access to export markets (*see* FOREIGN INVESTMENT). When compared with other countries, both the magnitude and variety of resources available remain a major national advantage. Large stocks of many wildlife species and major freshwater and marine fish populations exist. Canada is second to the USSR in the volume of standing softwood timber and the area of land suitable for agriculture is extensive. Similarly, the volume of water is greater than in most countries. Because of Canada's vast landmass and the variety of geological conditions, many and varied mineral deposits await discovery. In addition, many areas with special environmental characteristics offer opportunities for a variety of outdoor recreational, educational and scientific activities. All of these resources, with the important exception of minerals, are renewable.

Some emerging challenges must be addressed if Canada is to continue to benefit from this large and varied resource base. First, heavy use has been made of the most accessible and highest-quality resources. For example, the best agricultural lands have been cultivated for many decades; the best timber has been harvested; the most accessible oil fields have passed their peak output. Consequently, attention must be directed to maintaining productivity of the land, replacing harvested trees and finding other supplies of oil (*see* SOIL CONSERVATION). For renewable resources, this process will require significant improvements in the knowledge of the processes that control plant growth so that an intensive-regenerative style of RESOURCE MANAGEMENT will replace extensive extraction. For nonrenewable resources, active exploration programs must be maintained and new technologies developed. Such technologies are required to increase the efficiency of resource extraction and use, and for work in areas that are relatively inaccessible with hostile, but often sensitive, environments (*see* NORTH).

A second challenge is an increasing competition among resource uses, resulting from population growth and a widening variety of potential uses, particularly near urban centres. For example, a tract of forestland may have logging potential or mining capability, or may be suitable for a park or WILDLIFE PRESERVE. Similarly, an area of Class 1 agricultural land near an urban centre could be used for agriculture, as the site of an airport or for a housing development. Conflicts about uses of resource complexes are growing and, if full benefits are to be derived, ways must be found to resolve such conflicts quickly and fairly. In particular, risk to human welfare and environmental quality must be assessed thoroughly and levels established in which the costs are both acceptable and realistic.

Third, if resources are to continue to contribute substantially to Canadian economic development, they must be able to compete in world markets. Access to these markets depends on price, quality and reliability of supply. Thus, some aspects of export marketing, such as a transportation infrastructure, must be provided at high efficiency. But perhaps of greatest importance is the need for a balance between competitiveness, on the one hand, and the maintenance of a high income level, social services and environmental quality on the other. J.D. CHAPMAN

Responsible Government, loosely used to mean a government responsible to the people, as popular rule is naturally conceived to be. Properly, however, as used by those who gained it in Canada, it meant a government responsible to the representatives of the people, ie, an executive or Cabinet collectively dependent on the votes of a majority in the elected legislature. This key principle of responsibility, whereby a government

needed the confidence of Parliament, originated in established British practice. But its transfer to British N America gave the colonists control of their domestic affairs, since a governor would simply follow the advice (ie, policies) of responsible colonial ministers, except in imperial matters. This control was enlarged by degrees, so that Canadians through governments based on elected parliaments gradually acquired command of their own political concerns, thereby achieving national self-direction without revolution.

The idea of responsible government was taken up in the 1830s in BNA largely by loyal admirers of the British model, who sought it both to remedy discontent with unyielding local oligarchies and to keep the provinces securely, though freely, within the Empire. Radicals such as William Lyon MACKENZIE and Louis-Joseph PAPINEAU preferred American elective patterns, but Joseph HOWE in Nova Scotia and Robert BALDWIN in Upper Canada showed far better comprehension − better even than Lord DURHAM, an influential advocate of responsible government − since they realized that an organized party system was vital. Howe in Nova Scotia, and Baldwin and Louis LAFONTAINE in the PROVINCE OF CANADA, built up strong, moderate Reform parties to gain responsible government, and by 1848 saw it fully operating, accepted by a Liberal, imperial Britain. It then was granted to other eastern colonies: PEI in 1851, NB in 1854 and Nfld last, in 1855, and as western provinces emerged in CONFEDERATION they too obtained it. J.M.S. CARELESS

Restigouche, Qué, IR, pop 896 (1986c), 1091 (1981c), is located in the GASPÉ Peninsula at the mouth of the RESTIGOUCHE R (spelled Ristigouche in Qué). A bridge links it to CAMPBELLTON, NB. Before the Europeans arrived, the Gaspé and present-day northeastern NB belonged to the MICMAC, an Algonquian family of hunters and fishers. The name originated with the Micmac *Lustagooch*, perhaps meaning "good river." In the 1750s the ACADIANS began to settle the area and, on 8 July 1760, Restigouche was the site of the last battle between the French and British during the SEVEN YEARS' WAR (*see* RESTIGOUCHE, BATTLE OF). The French lost 3 ships during that battle to the superior military tactics of the British. After colonization by whites, the Micmac territory gradually diminished to the size of the present reserve. A mission dedicated to St Anne was built in 1745 and served by the Capuchin order. One member, Father Pacifique, produced the Gospels and a dictionary in the Micmac language. Parks Canada is developing an interpretation centre for the Battle of Restigouche. ANTONIO LECHASSEUR

Restigouche, Battle of After the fall of Québec in 1759, an urgent appeal was sent to France for 4000 troops and food supplies. Not until Apr 19 did 5 merchant ships and a frigate leave Bordeaux with 400 troops and some supplies. The frigate and 2 of the merchant ships reached the St Lawrence on May 15 only to find that a strong British fleet was already upriver. The commander, François Chenard Giraudais, sought refuge up the Restigouche; he set up gun batteries on the riverbanks and a boom across it, and there they were caught by Capt John Byron with a 70-gun ship and 2 frigates. The heavy British guns knocked out the shore batteries but not before the French gunners severely damaged the British ships in an artillery duel that raged all day. Eventually, when 2 of the French ships could no longer fight or float, they were set afire and their crews and the troops slipped away. W.J. ECCLES

Restigouche River, 200 km long, rises in the highlands of northwestern New Brunswick as the Little Main Restigouche R. Fed by its tributaries

Kedgwick, Patapédia and Matapédia flowing S from Gaspé, and Upsalquitch flowing N from central NB, it flows northeasterly towards the towns of RESTIGOUCHE and CAMPBELLTON where it broadens into a wide estuary. At DALHOUSIE it empties into Chaleur Bay on the Gulf of ST LAWRENCE. From the confluence with the Patapédia to Chaleur Bay, the river forms the boundary between NB and Québec. Together with its tributaries, the Restigouche drains a large area of northern NB and Gaspé, a land of timber resources and great scenic grandeur. The name derives from the Micmac word *Lustagooch*, likely meaning "good river." The river is famous for its run of ATLANTIC SALMON. JAMES MARSH

Resurrection of Joseph Bourne, The, or A Word or Two on Those Port Annie Miracles, (Toronto, 1979), Gov Gen's Award (1980), by Jack HODGINS, is a richly inventive, life-affirming tall tale which takes place in the fictional, rain-drenched mill town of Port Annie on the NW tip of Vancouver I, a little community which keeps sliding into the ocean. Hodgins's protagonist, Joseph Bourne, once a world-renowned poet and healer, has become a bitter, reclusive derelict who wishes to live anonymously, but he is resurrected by a beautiful sea nymph who is washed ashore by a tidal wave. She restores Bourne's healing powers so that he works his magic of unselfish love on the large cast of comic and eccentric characters. Hodgins's energetic style and fertile imagination adroitly combine the ordinary with the wondrous. DONNA COATES

Retail Trade, sales of goods or services to consumers for personal or household use. Consumer spending through the retail trade accounts for 60% of the Gross Domestic Product of Canada and employs over one million people. Statistics Canada recognizes some 185 000 retail outlets in Canada, primarily shops, car dealers, supermarkets and department stores, but the number does not include street vendors, farmers' markets, roadside stands or the growing UNDERGROUND ECONOMY. There is also a great variety in the methods by which the selling takes place: over the counter, by vending machines, door-to-door or telephone canvassing, mail order and others. In 1986 Canadian retail sales totalled $140 billion, with Alta (at $6001), Ont (at $5817) and Nova Scotia (at $5427) the leading per capita spenders. Ontario remained the largest market (38.1%); Qué (24.7%) and BC (11.1%) followed.

There are 2 broad categories of retail-trade organization: retail chains, which operate 4 or more stores in the same kind of business under the same ownership, and independent retailers operating 1 to 3 stores. By Statistics Canada definition, all department stores are chains, and chains dominate variety stores (87.2% of national sales in 1986), family shoe stores (74.6%), and general merchandise stores (75.5%). Over 95% of national sales by garages, used car dealers, motor vehicle dealers and florists are made by independent retailers. There is, however, an increasing proportion of independent retailers operating under franchises. These franchising arrangements allow the independents to gain the economies of scale in buying and marketing power that have traditionally been the strength of the chains. Some of the largest corporations in Canada are retail chains. For example, Sears Canada, Loblaw, Steinberg, Hudson's Bay and Safeway Canada were among the top 30 corporations (1986 sales). Together, these corporations generated some $25 billion in sales and employed some 167 000 people.

By 1983 it was estimated that the 1100 chains in the country controlled about 29 000 stores accounting for over 40% of all retail sales. The largest chains (100 or more stores) account for almost one half of the chain stores in the country, and for 54.9% of the chain store sales. Most of the largest chain organizations are headquartered in either Toronto or Montréal.

Department Stores are huge emporiums selling a wide variety of goods. The T. EATON CO of Toronto (fd 1869) was one of the first stores anywhere to offer a wide variety of goods on a large scale, and along with Simpsons it initiated mail-order sales in Canada. Statistics Canada distinguishes major ("traditional") department stores from junior department stores, the latter selling the same wide range of goods as major department stores, but are popularly described as discount operations. The junior department category does not include all discount operations. Of the 308 major department stores in Canada in 1987, 185 (60%) are in the 10 largest metropolitan areas. Traditional department stores in the 1980s are experiencing a loss in market share to discount operations who offer lower prices and more flexible financing for such items as furniture and appliances, and to specialty retailers who offer better quality service. The HUDSON'S BAY CO, with its subsidiaries Fields, Zellers, Marshall Wells and Simpsons, had over $5 billion in sales (1986), employed 40 000 and ranked twelfth among Canadian corporations. The HBC, Sears Canada ($3.9 billion in sales) and The T. Eaton Co (sales not available) have a combined traditional department store market share of about 75%. The first *hypermarché*, or superstore (over 3500 m²) opened in Montréal in 1973. Since then the Canadian Superstore and Safeway's Food for Less operations have begun to penetrate the Canadian suburban retail landscape.

Direct Selling the majority of which take place through personal selling (32.5% of direct sales in 1985), mail order (24.9%), home delivery (23.5%) and sales from manufacturing premises (13.7%). Cosmetics and personal care items account for 22.5% of personnel selling channels, while books and encyclopedia sales (30.9%) and magazines (23%) are the leading products sold through mail order. Newspapers (47.4%) are the dominant items sold via home delivery, while dairy products (44.3%) are still important. In 1985 there were 662 vending-machine firms with 148 982 machines in factories, institutions, offices, hotels and restaurants. Sales amounted to $367 million, of which 29.6% was cigarettes, 22.2% coffee, and 20.7% soft drinks.

Retail Prices are used to calculate changes in the cost of living. The CONSUMER PRICE INDEX (CPI) measures percentage change over time in the cost of purchasing a constant or equivalent "basket" of goods and services typical of a particular group of private households – both families and individuals – living in cities of 30 000 or more in a specific period. Food, housing, household operation, household furnishings and equipment, clothing, transportation, health and personal care, recreation and similar activities, tobacco and alcohol are included in the index. The index is usually stated in relative terms, 1981 being equal to 100. The index has doubled in the past 10 years (from 62.9 in 1976 to 132.4 in 1986).

Shopping Centres Retail trade in Canada is increasingly taking place in planned shopping centres. A shopping centre is a group of retail stores and consumer service outlets (usually 5 or more) which are operated separately but occupy a single property and are managed by a single firm. These centres range in size from neighborhood centres and newly emerging "strip malls" (5-15 stores) to community centres (16-30 stores) to regional centres (more than 30 stores). It has been estimated that shopping centres account for some 40% of all retail sales in Canada. Although there is a

Dry-goods section of a south-side store in Edmonton, 1917 (*courtesy Provincial Archives of Alberta/A4998*).

greater number of neighbourhood and community shopping centres in Canada (987 centres or 89%), the regional centres have created the greatest impact on the urban landscape. WEST EDMONTON MALL, with some 800 stores and a gross leasable area (GLA) of some 483 000 m², represents Canada's entry into the "megamall" category. This mall, the largest in the world in 1988, also represents the extreme example of a trend towards mixing retailing and recreational activities in a controlled indoor environment. About one-quarter of the GLA is hotel or recreation and entertainment use. Shopping centres have been the main agents in the decentralization of retailing activities to the Canadian suburbs. A retailer in a shopping centre must learn new management skills and conform to the behaviour of retailers in the centres. The growth of shopping centres has had and will continue to have a direct impact on small independent businesses that are unable to compete or thrive within them (*see* SMALL BUSINESS). Shopping centres have also affected the variety of choice by excluding many of the smaller retail establishments.

Not all planned shopping centres are in suburban locations. Most Canadian cities have one or more major planned shopping centres, usually a mix of office and retail uses, in their downtown areas, PLACE VILLE MARIE in Montreal and EATON CENTRE in Toronto being early developments of this type. Shopping centres across Canada resemble one another because of the concentration of developers involved in their construction, and the dominance by major national chains. An estimated 34 development firms control 454 shopping centres in Canada and over 60% of the retail floor area. National chains may account for an estimated 75 to 90% of tenants in large shopping centres.

Retail Employment Retailing in Canada is a major source of employment, although retail positions are generally poorly paid. Despite the general strength of the labour movement in Canada, attempts to organize retail workers in any systematic way have been quite unsuccessful. This is partly because of the nature of retail jobs, which do not require highly developed skills, and because of the transience of retail employees. But it is also a consequence of efforts by major Canadian retailers to discourage UNIONS. With the shift to self-service and open stores, the role of retail employees has generally been reduced to taking orders. Major retailers are currently implementing new systems to increase labour productivity, including centralized "cash-points" and computer applications throughout store operations.

The retail employment pool is one of the most fickle. Students, younger women and older people move in and out of the retail trade in response to economic needs in general and to seasonal needs, eg, extra money for Christmas. Often neither time nor resources are available to develop a trained selling staff. Other jobs in retailing include

buying and merchandising, store operations (especially those related to operation and maintenance of the physical plant), personnel management, accounting, and control of operations.

Despite the trend toward bigness, retailing is still an area where individuals can gain a foothold in business. It has been a traditional means by which many immigrants have established themselves. The retail store often provides employment for the family while simultaneously serving specific markets. These establishments will always be important because of their flexibility and their ability to respond to particular market opportunities. They will always offer substantial competition to the larger, more sophisticated, types of retailers.

Retail Merchandising Practices and Regulation Choosing a product assortment and displaying it, establishing a price level, developing a promotional program and creating a store "image" are 4 aspects of merchandising. Regulation of retail trade not only protects the consumer from unfair merchandising practices, discriminatory prices, and unfair and misleading promotion and advertising, but also encourages competition among retail firms (*see* COMPETITION POLICY). The federal Combines Investigation Act theoretically regulates agreements, eg, mergers, among competitors, and restrains trade among retailers. Under the Act misleading price advertising is illegal. The Act is administered by the Dept of Consumer and Corporate Affairs, which is responsible for problems arising from misleading advertising and hazardous products, and for packaging and labelling. The department, along with similar provincial agencies, develops and distributes materials designed to help consumers become more informed shoppers. Individual provinces have also passed consumer protection laws regarding selling practices. Two of the most comprehensive Acts concerning retailing are found in BC and Québec. The Deceptive Trade Practices Act in BC lists 18 deceptive practices and is designed to curtail the "sharp" practices of sellers; the Québec legislation passed in 1971 includes provisions aimed at preventing advertising directed toward children and gives consumers the right to inspect and obtain credit records. The general principle of *caveat vendor* ("seller beware") holds in Canada, ensuring that retailers are cautious in the development of specific merchandising activities.

Development Retail trade in Canada developed along relatively specialized product lines, replacing the trading posts or general stores which had characterized retailing until the turn of this century. Single-line stores, particularly in population centres, developed for specific product groups such as drugs, food and hardware. Other areas were and still are to some degree served by mail order. In the last 20 years stores of all types have begun to practise mass merchandising in a movement toward high-volume, low-margin operations. Supermarkets began to sell, along with food items, a range of products including automotive supplies, clothing, hardware and pharmaceutical items. Department stores began to sell automotive accessories and repairs, "health foods" and services such as banking, insurance and travel. Discount operations in Canada offered a wide range of products – in contrast to those in the US which offered only narrow lines – and also expanded service operations. The control of the market by a limited number of firms is increasing. In general merchandise, the HBC controls about 11% of the market. In department-store sales, the HBC (with its subsidiary Zeller's), T. Eaton Co and Sears Canada Inc have a combined market share of more than 75%. The same concentration exists in food retailing. The 5 dominant food chains – Loblaws, Dominion, Canada Safeway,

Steinberg's and A & P – control about 60% of the market.

Retail trade is subject to fluctuations and change. In both the general merchandise and food areas, new competition appears to be coming from specialty stores. While the appearance of superstores has created massive units offering a variety of food and nonfood items, independents are gaining a foothold by acquiring conventional supermarkets and developing product mixes that cater to fragmented and specialized local markets. Television and telephone shopping is now a reality in Canada, and catalogue shopping has made inroads in the upscale markets. Canadian developers and retailers are also active in the US; 5 of the major Canadian development companies directly and indirectly own about 6 million m² of retail properties in the US (this amounts to just under 1% of total US retail space). Canadian developers are exporting expertise in shopping centre development and renovation. Sunday and evening shopping are making inroads in most provinces. This change complements the increasing blending of shopping and leisure activities, a mix that has retailing experts wondering how these activities really complement each other. The rapid growth in the variety and sophistication of consumer demand is affecting retail change, as are shifts in population and even tourism. Patterns of consumption vary across Canada; in provinces such as Alberta and BC, where population and income increased in the 1970s and early 1980s, more money became available for retail purchases, and even though recent trends have resulted in overbuilding of retail space new developments and renovations persist. Patterns vary also according to age and the number of children; younger people tend to be more receptive to new products and new forms of retailing. Within Canada expenditures are influenced by ethnic diversity and even by the weather. *See also* WHOLESALE TRADE.   RONALD SAVITT AND DENNIS JOHNSON

Revelstoke, BC, City, pop 8279 (1986c), 5544 (1981c), inc 1899 and reincorporated 1981 when the city boundaries were extended to include Big Eddy district, South Revelstoke and Arrow Heights. It is situated on the COLUMBIA R between the Selkirk and Monashee mountains, 415 km by road W of Calgary, Alta, and on the Trans-Canada Hwy at the western entrance to ROGERS PASS and Mt Revelstoke and Glacier national parks. The area was first settled in the mid-1800s and by the 1870s was known as "Big Eddy" and "Second Crossing" (of the Columbia R). The original townsite, laid out in 1880, was named Farwell after a surveyor. In 1886 the new CPR station just to the W was named Revelstoke after Lord Revelstoke, whose British bank had invested in the CPR. Mining and the railway spurred the community's growth. In 1899 Revelstoke became the mountain divisional centre for the CPR, and for many years it was the western entrance to the old Big Bend Hwy along the Columbia R through the Selkirk Mts. Today the CPR remains an important employer, along with mining, forestry and tourism. Revelstoke Dam, the highest concrete dam in Canada, is located 5 km N.

JOHN R. STEWART

Revenue Canada Until WWI the federal government financed its operations from indirect taxes, customs duties and excise taxes. Direct TAXATION was introduced in 1916 through an excess business-profits tax and in 1917 by income tax. The Dept of National Revenue was established 1927 to assess and collect duties and taxes, control the international movement of persons and goods, provide Canadian industry with protection under the customs law, and administer the statutes of other government departments and

agencies where they concern the international movement of persons and goods. The department has 2 sections: Taxation, and Customs and Excise, which has 3 branches.

Revolutionary Industrial Unionism, or syndicalism, a broad international movement dedicated to organizing all workers into single, unified labour organizations designed to overthrow the capitalist system by means of industrial actions, including the general strike. In contrast with more orthodox socialism, communism or social democracy, the movement sought to establish direct workers' control over economic and political life through unions and workers' councils. Its best expression in Canada was the ONE BIG UNION (1919-56), a coalition of INDUSTRIAL WORKERS OF THE WORLD sympathizers, socialists and trade unionists. Unlike the American-based IWW and the WORKERS UNITY LEAGUE (1929-36), which had direct or "fraternal" ties with the Communist International in Moscow, the OBU was a wholly indigenous Canadian organization.

Although preaching the general strike as a means to destroy capitalism, and fiercely denouncing the flaws of the parliamentary system, the movement did not completely eschew political action in the Canadian context. R.B. RUSSELL, OBU general secretary, W.A. Pritchard from Vancouver and others, stood for Parliament in 1921. John Angus McDonald was elected to Parliament for the OBU miners in northern Ontario in 1920; Phillip Martin Christophers was elected for the Alberta legislature for the OBU miners of the Crowsnest Pass in 1921.

In general, revolutionary unionism in Canada reflected an eclectic reading of syndicalist and socialist theory, as was appropriate to the diverse traditions and complex needs of its constituency. Canadian revolutionary unionism, in contrast to its British, German and even American counterparts, failed to make significant inroads into mass production industries (in theory its main targets). But until the 1930s it had solid backing in the forest and mining sectors, an influence long felt in such unions as the Mine, Mill and Smelter Workers and the International Woodworkers of America. It also attracted support from groups who felt estranged from the political-economic establishment on the one hand and the established labour movement on the other: non-English-speaking immigrants, farm workers, the unemployed. Finally, within the context of the OBU, revolutionary unionism briefly embraced skilled crafts workers, especially in 1919 in British Columbia and Manitoba.

Briefly after WWI it seemed that revolutionary unionism would seriously challenge or even destroy traditional patterns of industrial relations and union organization in Canada. War difficulties, including the bitter debate over CONSCRIPTION, induced a deep cleavage between eastern and western union leaders. The militant BC Federation of Labour had crossed swords continually with the majority ("eastern") bloc of the TRADES AND LABOR CONGRESS. When Albert "Ginger" GOODWIN, leader of the 1917 Trail strike, was shot and killed by a Dominion Police constable in July 1918, a one-day general strike was organized in Vancouver, and the BCFL leadership spearheaded the Western Labour Conference that advocated secession from the TLC in March 1919. The Dominion government only offered workers a royal commission, in April, to investigate the "causes of industrial unrest." Many western unionists simply boycotted the proceedings. The OBU was still organizing when the workers that its leaders claimed to represent rose independently: a one big union from below unleashed by the Canadian labour revolt in May and June of 1919.

Government, employers and international union leaders collaborated in the ensuing repression. After the failure of the WINNIPEG GENERAL STRIKE the OBU's chance for a takeover in the labour movement had passed. Workers in federally controlled industries such as the Alberta coal mines of District 18 were coerced out of the OBU, and a challenge against discrimination by Canadian National Railways of Winnipeg's OBU shopcraft workers failed in the Privy Council case of *Young v CNR* in 1927.

During the 1920s, many of the IWW's and OBU's former sympathizers drifted into the COMMUNIST PARTY OF CANADA or the "Left Wing" in the TLC unions. Best known was J.B. MCLACHLAN from Glace Bay, NS, who was jailed for his efforts in the CAPE BRETON STRIKE. This experience contributed to the zeal with which McLachlan, Harvey Murphy, Tom McEwen, Annie BULLER and countless other Canadian radicals engaged in the last attempt to build a "revolutionary union central" in Canada during the 1930s: the Workers Unity League. The WUL had originated in the minds of the Toronto-based leadership of the Communist Party, but it evolved into a genuine workers' unity league, especially during 1932-34 when the party's leadership was incarcerated in Kingston Penitentiary. In 1933 a bona fide delegate convention saw significant revisions to the League's constitution; the independent-minded J.B. McLachlan served as president of the League.

The WUL, like the IWW and the OBU, failed to build a stable membership of more than a fraction of TLC affiliates, but it mobilized over 50 000 workers in strikes; 50% of all strikes and strikers in Canada in 1933-34. The WUL's penetration of southern Ontario's factory belt in those years was a new departure in the history of revolutionary unionism in Canada, and a signal of a force in Canadian industrial life that gained major momentum in 1937. The WUL's high point was 1934 when its militants led no less than 109 strikes. Many Canadians remember the accompanying violence: 3 coal miners killed at Estevan in 1931; alleged sabotage in the Crowsnest Pass in 1932; army machine-gun carriers in Stratford in 1933; brass knuckles and machine guns on the Vancouver docks in 1935. The WUL fought for immediate demands, such as the "work and wages" sought by the 1935 ON TO OTTAWA trekkers. Its practical politics were not very revolutionary. An entire slate of WUL supporters was elected to town council in Blairmore, Alta, in 1933; they spruced up the main street and dubbed it Tim Buck boulevard.

Revolutionary industrial unionism in N America did not really die during the Depression; rather, its advocates were co-opted into the orthodox political left or into the pragmatic CIO (Committee for Industrial Organization/Congress of Industrial Organizations). Most WUL militants merged with the US-based CIO unions in 1936. Fate was not kind to the revolutionary unionists in Canada, but the situation can be favourably contrasted with that in Europe, the movement's birthplace, where by 1940 their comrades in France, Italy, Germany, Spain and the USSR were behind the barbed wire of the dictators. The "revolutionary" side of the movement proved a chimaera. Its practical side was an effective program for labour, by which "we mean all those who by useful work of hand or brain, feed, clothe or shelter; or contribute towards the health, comfort and education of the human race" (OBU General Executive Board, Vancouver Bulletin No 1). *See also* WORKING-CLASS HISTORY.

ALLEN SEAGER

Reading: D. Bercuson, *Fools and Wise Men* (1978); A. R. McCormack, *Reformers, Rebels and Revolutionaries* (1977).

Revue d'histoire de l'Amérique française, La was founded in 1947 by Lionel GROULX, professor of history at U de Montréal. At first the RHAF was devoted to the history of French colonization in America – not just the history of French Canada, but also French efforts at colonization in the US, the Caribbean and S America. The development of the RHAF cannot be separated from the evolution of francophone historiography in Québec. It was started at the same time as the history departments of the only 2 Québec francophone universities of the day, U de M and U Laval. It quickly became the favoured vehicle for communications among francophone specialists in Canadian and Québec history. It is now the major review devoted to Québec history (though it also accepts some articles on other topics). The RHAF is published quarterly by the Institut d'histoire de l'Amérique française, which selects the members of its editorial committee. JEAN-CLAUDE ROBERT

Rexton, NB, Village, pop 926 (1986c), 928 (1981c), inc 1966, is located in southeastern NB, at the mouth of the Richibucto R. At the close of the American Revolution, several LOYALIST refugees received land grants here, in an area where Acadian families were already located. From 1790 the Richibucto R attained new importance with the establishment of milling operations supplied by the abundant white pine along its bank. By the 1820s a substantial SHIPBUILDING business had evolved under the leadership of John Jardine. In 1842 the shipbuilding partnership of Holderness and Chalton founded Rexton, then called Kingston, after its namesake in England. Today, its principal economic activities remain a blend of farming and fishing for the local population. Rexton is the birthplace of Andrew Bonar LAW, who became prime minister of Great Britain. His father's farm on the banks of the Richibucto is now a historic attraction. ROGER P. NASON

Reynolds, Leslie Alan, sculptor (b at Edmonton 16 May 1947). Like many contemporary sculptors, Alan Reynolds works in a "constructivist" idiom. His initial work in wood was encouraged in 1973 by American sculptor Michael Steiner, whose influence suited Reynolds's personal vision. In the mid-1970s Reynolds worked with large blocks of laminated wood that resembled walls. Later in the decade he exploited arrangements of flat sheets, often in complex, tablelike configurations. He turned to welded steel early in the 1980s, partly because of the structural limitations of wood. He adapted his vision to the new material with surprising speed and was soon producing sculptures of cylinder and tub shapes with attached lips and rims fused into the surfaces. As a result, the works inclined towards the expressive devices of functional pottery and traditional sculptural modelling. His art has had a considerable influence on younger sculptors in Edmonton. His show "New Steel Sculptures" of works 1985-86 was held in Calgary in 1986. TERRY FENTON

Rhineland, Battle of the, 8 Feb-10 Mar 1945, fought by FIRST CANADIAN ARMY (with XXX British Corps under command) and Ninth US Army while forcing back the Germans to the Rhine R. For the Canadians it involved attacking over inundated ground in the first phase (Operation *Veritable,* Feb 8-21) and through the Hochwald forest in the second (Operation *Blockbuster,* Feb 22-Mar 10) against stubborn opposition as the Germans defended German soil. Throughout the month poor weather robbed the Allies of much of their accustomed tactical air support, while mud frequently immobilized their armoured forces. Nevertheless, the W bank of the Rhine was cleared as far S as Düsseldorf in some of the bitterest fighting of WWII. Allied casualties totalled nearly 23 000, the Canadians losing 5300. The Germans lost approximately 90 000 men, of whom some 52 000 were taken prisoner. By 23 Mar 1945 the Allies were on the Rhine from Strasbourg, France, to Nijmegen, Netherlands. *See also* WORLD WAR II. BRERETON GREENHOUS

Reading: C.P. Stacey, *The Victory Campaign* (1960).

Rhinoceros Party, founded (1963) by a group of humorists led by Montréal doctor Jacques FERRON to poke fun at federal election campaigns. First fielding candidates for 1964 by-elections, it has participated in every subsequent general election. Eighty-nine candidates (across Canada) represented the party in the federal election of 1984; it received 99 207 votes, 0.790% of the total votes cast. In May 1985, shortly after the death of Ferron, the party was officially dissolved. ANDRÉ BERNARD

Rhodes, Edgar Nelson, lawyer, politician, premier of NS (b at Amherst, NS 5 Jan 1877; d at Ottawa 15 Mar 1942). A distinguished politician, he began his career as a lawyer in Amherst in 1902. While serving as the federal Conservative member for Cumberland 1908-21, he became Speaker in 1917 and a member of the Privy Council in 1921. He then moved to provincial politics, sitting as the Liberal-Conservative member for Hants County and occupying the offices of premier and provincial secretary from 1925 to 1930. His tenure was brief but is remembered for decisive legislative action. Rhodes resigned to become federal minister of fisheries under R.B. BENNETT and the member for Richmond-W Cape Breton. He held the finance portfolio 1932-35 and was then named to the Senate. LOIS KERNAGHAN

Rhodes Scholarships Under the terms of the will of Cecil Rhodes, Canadians became eligible to hold Rhodes scholarships in colleges of Oxford U. Since 1904 nearly 900 scholars have been appointed by provincial selection committees answering to the Rhodes trustees in Britain. Candidates usually apply in the autumn of the year before they expect to attain a first degree; so equipped scholars nowadays are enabled to proceed to the Oxford BA in any final honour school after 2 years in residence. A substantial number of Canadians now read for advanced degrees (eg, BCL, DPhil, MPhil, MLitt). Candidates must be unmarried and between 19 and 25 years of age. No limitation is ordinarily placed on any field of study in which a scholar may be interested. Qualities of character and leadership, in addition to academic distinction, are regarded as prerequisites. Canadian provinces choose 11 scholars annually (2 each from Ontario and Québec; PEI was discontinued from 1926), and women have been eligible since 1977. Some notable scholars from Canada have included Gov Gen Roland MICHENER and federal Liberal leader John TURNER. JAMES A. GIBSON

Rhododendron [Gk, "red tree"], a large genus (700 species) of the heath family (Ericaceae) found in the Northern Hemisphere; 4 species are native to Canada. The genus contains both rhododendrons, usually evergreen, and azaleas, which are deciduous. Rhododendrons range from creeping shrubs to medium-sized trees, with saucerlike to bell-shaped flowers (white, pink, red, mauve, purple, yellow to orange). Rhododendrons possess a wide range of leaf types, all simple, often leathery, and frequently covered with soft hairs (indumentum) or scales. Larger-leaved species frequently exhibit very tight enrolling of leaves during freezing weather, an adaptation that prevents water loss. Indian azalea

(single- and double-flowered), derived from *R. simsii,* is sold as a pot plant at Christmas. Many variously coloured outdoor hybrids have been produced. Species and hybrids are significant ORNAMENTALS in Canadian gardens, particularly in milder coastal regions. Most rhododendrons are propagated by cuttings. ROY L. TAYLOR

Rhubarb (genus *Rheum*), common name for about 50 species of cool-season herbaceous perennial plants belonging to the BUCKWHEAT family and originating in central Asia. Common rhubarb (*R. rhabarbarum* or *R. rhaponticum*) was probably the first to be cultivated, initially as a source of purgative drugs from the powdered root. It was established as a food plant in Europe in the mid-18th century and now grows throughout Canada. Considerable hybridization has occurred to produce the present commercial cultivars. Leaves are poisonous; the edible portion is the elongated petiole (leafstalk), which may be harvested for immediate use or for processing (canning, freezing, pie filling). Dormant plants may be dug in early winter for "forcing" in heated, darkened buildings, where the delicate petioles are produced. Forced rhubarb is grown commercially in Ontario. ARTHUR LOUGHTON

Richard, Henri, hockey player (b at Montréal 29 Feb 1936). The younger brother of "Rocket" RICHARD, he played with the Montreal Canadiens 1955-75. The nickname "Pocket Rocket," which he thoroughly disliked, compared him to his famous brother at the start of his career, but gradually he earned his own reputation, becoming one of the best all-round players in the NHL. His name has been inscribed on the Stanley Cup 11 times, more than any other player. In 1256 games, he totalled 1046 points (358 goals, 688 assists); in addition to 49 goals and 80 assists in 180 playoff games. He retired at the end of the 1974-75 season. YVON DORE

Richard, Joseph-Henri-Maurice, "Rocket," hockey player (b at Montréal 4 Aug 1921). He was seriously injured in his last 2 years of amateur hockey and his first year (1942-43) with the MONTREAL CANADIENS, but collected 32 goals in his first full season. In 1944-45 he scored 50 goals in 50 games – long hockey's most celebrated record. Richard's fierce competitiveness and scoring heroics made him the most exciting player of his generation and a national hero among Québecois. He led the league in goals 5 times and won the HART TROPHY in 1947, but the scoring title eluded him. He excelled above all under pressure; in playoffs he scored 3 goals in a game 7 times, 4 goals in a game twice, and in 1944 all 5 goals in a

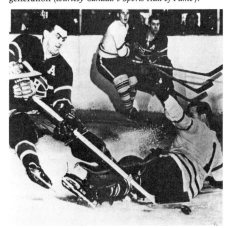

Maurice "Rocket" Richard in one of his typical assaults on the opposition goal. He was the greatest scorer of his generation (*courtesy Canada's Sports Hall of Fame*).

5-1 triumph over Toronto. He scored 18 playoff game-winning goals, still a record. Richard possessed a short temper and seldom refused a challenge or left an attack unanswered. In March 1955 he struck Boston Bruin player Hal Laycoe with his stick and attacked a linesman who intervened. His suspension for the rest of the year by NHL president Clarence CAMPBELL was considered an outrage by Montréal fans. Campbell was attacked at the Montréal Forum on St Patrick's Day and the violence spilled into the streets in the worst sports riot in Canadian history. It was indicative of the passionate devotion Richard inspired. His career ended in 1960 after he suffered a severed achilles tendon. His 544 goals in regular-season play was an NHL record on his retirement and in 1987 still ranked him seventh in NHL history; his 82 goals in Stanley Cup play remained a record until broken by Mike Bossy in 1986.

JAMES MARSH

Richard, René, artist, painter (b at Chaux-de-Ronds, Switz 1 Dec 1895; d at Baie-St-Paul, Qué 31 Mar 1982). His family immigrated to Canada and settled in Cold Lake, Alta. He became a trapper to earn enough money to carry out his great dream of becoming an artist. In Jan 1927 he left for Paris where he studied at La Grande Chaumière and became the protégé of painter Clarence GAGNON. He then did his apprenticeship at the Académie Colarossi. He returned to Canada in 1930 and visited Baie-St-Paul several times, at the recommendation of Gagnon, before settling there in 1942. The Musée du Québec held 2 major retrospectives of his work in 1967 and 1978 and, after his death, U Laval and the city of Montréal honoured him with 2 exhibitions.

MICHEL CHAMPAGNE

Richards, Charles Dow, lawyer, politician, premier of NB 1931-33 (b at Southampton, York County, NB 12 June 1879; d at Fredericton 15 Sept 1956). Initially a schoolteacher, Richards was admitted to the bar at age 33. Before becoming premier and attorney general in 1931 he was Conservative house leader in the provincial Assembly and then minister of lands and mines under J.B.M. BAXTER. His 2-year administration, in the depths of the Great Depression, instituted public bidding on crown land and fishing rights. He was appointed to the Supreme Court in 1933 and was chief justice from 1948 to 1955. He is best remembered not so much as a politician but as a dignified, scholarly lawyer and distinguished judge.

ARTHUR T. DOYLE

Richardson, Arthur Herbert Lindesay, policeman, soldier (b at Southport, Eng 1872; d at Liverpool, Eng 15 Dec 1932). Richardson served in the NWMP 1894 to 1907. In 1900 he was given leave to fight in the S African War in a Canadian regiment, Lord Strathcona's Horse. Richardson's unit was attacked by a superior force of Afrikaners at Wolve Spruit in the Transvaal on 5 July 1900 and, although ordered to withdraw, Richardson rode back under heavy crossfire to pick up a wounded comrade and bring him to safety. He was awarded the VICTORIA CROSS for this courageous feat, the first member of a Canadian military force to receive the coveted decoration.

S.W. HORRALL

Richardson, Ernie, curler (b at Stoughton, Sask 1931). He gained world acclaim as skip of the famous Richardson Rink, probably the best known in Canadian curling history. In 1959 at Québec this family group of 2 brothers (Ernie and Garnet) and 2 cousins (Arnold and Wes), all Richardsons, became the youngest team to win the Brier. Noted for aggressive, take-out play, they went on to win 4 Briers in 5 years, 4 Scotch Cups for the world championship, and numerous other champi-

onships and titles. Ernie Richardson has also written several books on curling.

GERALD REDMOND

Richardson, Hugh, lawyer, judge, chief justice of NWT (b at London, Eng 31 July 1826; d at Ottawa 15 July 1913). Called to the bar of Upper Canada in 1847, Richardson practised at Woodstock until 1872, serving as crown attorney for Oxford County 1856-62. From 1872 to 1876 he was chief clerk of the Dept of Justice at Ottawa, and was subsequently named stipendiary magistrate in the NWT, a member of the Territorial Executive Council, 1876-87, and legal adviser to the lieutenant-governor. As stipendiary magistrate, he presided at the trial of Louis RIEL and others arrested in connection with the NORTH-WEST REBELLION of 1885, a gravely important responsibility for which, according to some authorities, he was inadequately qualified. His conduct of the trial, while arguably fair, was unimaginative and in some respects uninformed, and remains one of the controversial aspects of a contentious event. From 1887 to 1903 he served as chief justice of the NWT Supreme Court, and in 1897-98 as administrator of the government.

D.H. BROWN

Richardson, James, grain merchant (b at Aughnacloy, County Tyrone, Ire 1819; d probably at Kingston 1892). Richardson immigrated to Canada in 1823 and was raised by an aunt in Kingston. A successful tailor by 1844, his acceptance of produce as payment led him into the commodities business. By 1857 Richardson was a grain merchant, with an interest in coal, mica, feldspar, phosphates and other minerals. In 1867 his firm built its first company-owned ship and in 1882 its first grain elevator.

Richardson developed an early interest in western Canadian wheat and in 1883 received from Manitoba the first prairie wheat sold in Europe. In 1912 he founded the great wheat firm James Richardson and Sons, Ltd. It was reorganized and diversified after his death by his sons George and Henry and remains the property of his descendants (*see* J.A. RICHARDSON, SR, and J.A. RICHARDSON, JR). Although the firm quickly became a major prairie institution centred in Winnipeg, it retained its head office in Kingston, Ont, until 1923, when its executive office moved to Winnipeg. Richardson's firm, the largest grain firm in the British Commonwealth, has played a major role in the development of prairie Canada.

DONALD SWAINSON

Richardson, James Armstrong, Sr, merchant, financier (b at Kingston, Ont 21 Aug 1885; d at Winnipeg 27 June 1939). Educated at Queen's, in 1906 Richardson entered the family firm of James Richardson and Sons Ltd, grain exporters, becoming VP in 1912 and president in 1919. In 1926 he established Western Canada Airways in Winnipeg. Richardson was a director of many companies, including the CPR, the Canadian Bank of Commerce, International Nickel, the Great-West Life Assurance Co, National Trust and Canadian Vickers and was also president and member of the Winnipeg Grain Exchange and several Canadian and American boards of trade.

JORGE NIOSI

Richardson, James Armstrong, Jr, grain merchant, politician (b at Winnipeg 28 Mar 1922), son of James A. RICHARDSON, SR. After studying at Queen's and serving in the RCAF as a Liberator Bomber pilot patrolling the N Atlantic, Richardson joined the family firm of James Richardson and Sons Ltd in 1945 and was chairman and executive officer 1966-68. He was elected Liberal MP for Winnipeg S in June 1968 and appointed minister without portfolio in July. Minister of supply and services 1969-72, he was re-elected in

the 1972 general election and was appointed minister of national defence. He resigned from Cabinet in 1976, over the government's language policy, and sat as an Independent 1978-79, when he returned to the family firm and became a director.

JORGE NIOSI

Richardson, John, soldier, writer (b at Queenston, Upper Canada 4 Oct 1796; d at New York 12 May 1852). Richardson's most enduring work, WACOUSTA; OR, THE PROPHECY (1832) is set at the time of PONTIAC's uprising and relates a complex story of betrayal, disguise and slaughter. Reginald Morton, the renegade Scot turned Indian leader, Wacousta, comes to represent the author's perception of the terror and savagery lurking in the Canadian wilderness. The smoother villain, Colonel De Haldimar, demonstrates how much repression, hypocrisy and cold-blooded evil is possible within the civilized garrison. As a youth, Richardson had fought in the WAR OF 1812 alongside TECUMSEH. His attempts to pursue successfully a career first as a soldier and then as a Canadian writer and journalist came to nothing. Except for his incomplete history, *The War of 1812* (1842), his other works remain of slight value. Departing from Canada about 1849, he sought a literary career in New York where he died impoverished. *Wacousta*, however, remains in print in an abridged version. Adapted for the stage in its own day, it was also dramatized by James REANEY.

DENNIS DUFFY

Richardson, Sir John, arctic explorer, naturalist (b at Dumfries, Scot 5 Nov 1787; d at "Lancrigg," Eng 5 June 1865). After qualifying as a member of the Royal College of Surgeons in 1807, Richardson enlisted in the Royal Navy. He was retired on half pay in 1815, and he studied mineralogy under Robert Jameson, professor of natural history, U of Edinburgh, and obtained his MD in 1816.

He joined both overland Franklin expeditions (1819-22 and 1825-27) as surgeon and naturalist, and commanded a search party looking for Sir John FRANKLIN (1848-49). Richardson's 1851 book on his own arctic searching expedition contains a summary of his previous work on the physical geography of present northwestern Canada as well as a geological map. His reputation as an accomplished naturalist rests largely on his contributions to the *Flora Boreali-Americana* and the 4-volume *Fauna Boreali-Americana*. Richardson presented what probably was the first geology course in British N America to Franklin's officers at Great Bear Lk in the winter of 1825-26. *See also* FRANKLIN SEARCH.

W.O. KUPSCH

Richelieu, Rivière, or Richelieu River, almost 130 km long, flows from Lake Champlain in the US northward to the St Lawrence R near Lac St-Pierre. Located in the southern part of Québec, the river is often referred to in 2 parts – the Upper and Lower Richelieu ("le Haut et Bas Richelieu"). The southern portion of the river, the Upper Richelieu, is bordered by the cities and towns of ST-JEAN-SUR-RICHELIEU, IBERVILLE, Chambly, Beloeil and Mont St-Hilaire. A set of rapids extends from Saint-Jean to CHAMBLY. From there the Lower Richelieu continues its course through smaller, albeit perhaps more picturesque communities such as St-Charles-sur-Richelieu, St-Denis and St-Ours. The Lower Richelieu then extends to the mouth or junction of the river with the St Lawrence at the city of SOREL.

The Richelieu River has played a prominent role in the historical development of Québec. Originally inhabited by Iroquois, Huron and Algonquin, Samuel de CHAMPLAIN navigated its waters shortly after his arrival in 1608. Throughout the French regime the Richelieu, named after Cardinal Richelieu, was of great military importance. The French established numerous forts along it, including Isle-aux-Noix (Fort Lennox), Fort St-Jean, Fort Ste-Thérèse, Fort St-Louis (Fort Chambly) and Fort de Richelieu (Sorel). Owing to the fertile nature of the land and its defences, French Canadian farmers settled here. Following the British Conquest, 1759-60, and the American Revolution, British military and LOYALIST settlers joined the area's local populations. Benedict ARNOLD's invasion of British N America included the capture of British forts along its route. Several uprisings of the REBELLIONS OF 1837-38, including the battles at ST-DENIS and ST-CHARLES, took place along its shores.

The Richelieu was of significant economic importance in the 19th century. In 1843, the Chambly Canal was completed, bypassing the rapids and making the river transport of such products as wood, pulp, hay and coal from the US to Montréal more direct. Consequently the regional centres of Sorel and St-Jean grew and were incorporated as towns in the 1850s. The construction of railway lines from the US to Montréal in this same period, however, contributed to the eventual decline of the river's traffic. The economic influence of the region thus changed from commerce to industry in the later 19th and 20th centuries. The Richelieu R valley nonetheless retains some importance as an agricultural base, yielding some of the province's finest produce, as well as maintaining a military and industrial presence. A division of Environment Canada, Parks Québec region deals solely with the Richelieu R valley and conducts archaeological excavations at FORT CHAMBLY and Fort Lennox, and supervises the operations of the Chambly Canal.   KATHLEEN LORD

Richler, Mordecai, writer (b at Montréal 27 Jan 1931). One of Canada's foremost novelists, a controversial and prolific journalist, and an occasional scriptwriter, Richler was educated at Sir George Williams Coll, Montréal. After a 2-year stay in Paris and Spain (1951-52), he took up residence in England in 1954, returning to live in Montréal in 1972. Richler securely established himself as an accomplished novelist with the publication of *The* APPRENTICESHIP OF DUDDY KRAVITZ (1959). A scintillating portrait of a young Montréal-Jewish entrepreneur, the novel is characterized by an energizing authorial ambivalence and a contrast between the comic and the pathetic, by rich dramatic scenes, by a lively narrative pace, and by a comprehensive depiction of the protagonist as Montréaler, Jew and individual. Richler's earlier novels, *The Acrobats* (1954), *Son of a Smaller Hero* (1955) and *A Choice of Enemies* (1957), are essentially apprenticeship pieces portraying young, intense protagonists absorbed with finding proper values in a corrupt world.

Richler's considerable talent for the comic is displayed in *The Incomparable Atuk* (1963), a zany piece on Canadian nationalism, and in *Cocksure* (1968), a comical-satirical account of the difficulty of adhering to traditional values in a world gone mad. *St. Urbain's Horseman* (1971) and *Joshua Then and Now* (1980) are ambitiously conceived novels that incorporate and go beyond the settings, characters and concerns of the preceding novels. *St. Urbain's Horseman* examines the personal, professional and ethnic experiences of a 37-year-old man subjected to intense, contradictory feelings, who, Richler has stated, is "closer to me than anybody else." *Joshua Then and Now* employs a complex pattern of flashbacks to explore the possessive nature of the past, the ironical inversions caused by the passage of time, and the sad aspects of mutability. *Jacob Two-Two Meets the Hooded Fang* (1975) and *Jacob Two-Two and the*

Novelist Mordecai Richler has received the Gov Gen's Award twice (*photo by Martha Kaplan*).

Dinosaur (1987), 2 racy, hilarious children's novels, tell of the difficulties experienced by the young child in an adult world.

Richler has published over 300 journalistic pieces in a wide range of publications in Canada, the US and Britain. He published selections in *Hunting Tigers Under Glass* (1968), *The Street* (1969), *Shovelling Trouble* (1972), *Notes on an Endangered Species* (1974) and *Home Sweet Home: My Canadian Album* (1984). His periodic ventures into scriptwriting, which he approaches with less fervour than his journalism, have produced such scripts as *Life at the Top* (1965), *The Apprenticeship of Duddy Kravitz* (1974), *Fun with Dick and Jane* (1977), and *Joshua Then and Now* (1985). His many awards include 2 Gov Gen's Awards (1968, 1971), a Screenwriters Guild of America Award (1974) and a Ruth Schwartz Children's Book Award (1976).   VICTOR RAMRAJ

Richmond, BC, District Municipality, pop 108 492 (1986c), 96 154 (1981c), area 16 807 ha, inc as a township 1879, is located adjacent to and S of VANCOUVER and W of NEW WESTMINSTER. It comprises 2 large islands, Lulu I and Sea I, and several smaller ones in the delta of the FRASER R. The 2 main islands are protected by 64 km of dikes skirting the 3 arms of the Fraser R. Richmond is governed by a mayor and 8 aldermen.

History The area's first inhabitants were Coast SALISH, though they mainly visited the islands on fishing trips. In 1861 Col R.C. MOODY, in surveying southern BC and selecting townsites on the Fraser R, named Sea I and Lulu I, the latter after an American actress called Lulu Street. Hugh McRoberts became the first settler in 1862, purchasing 648 ha on Sea I. He called his farm Richmond View after his former home in Australia – perhaps the origin of the present name. A slow but steady migration of farmers to the islands began and by 1879 the area had 30 families. During this period the port of Steveston developed to take advantage of salmon at the mouth of the Fraser R. At one time it boasted 49 canneries. The first bridge connecting Richmond with the mainland was built 1889 and by 1902 a railway link existed. With improved connections over the years, Richmond has become primarily a residential area

within Greater Vancouver. Vancouver International Airport was built on Sea I in 1931. The JAPANESE have played an important role, especially in the fishing and canning industry. Today there are more than 2000 Japanese in Richmond, and Steveston is one of the largest Canadian centres of Japanese culture.

Economy In its early years, Richmond's agriculture and fishing made it Vancouver's "bread basket." Two large fish-processing plants in Steveston and Richmond's rich alluvial farmlands continue to be productive, but the district has become increasingly residential. Today the largest employer is the international airport. Proximity to the US along Hwy 99 has also made tourism important.

Townscape The most popular landmark in Richmond is the Minoru Chapel, built 1890 and restored 1968 as a historic site to commemorate the official "twinning" of Richmond and Pierrefonds, Québec. The Steveston Salmon Festival is held on July 1.   ALAN F.J. ARTIBISE

Reading: B. Richards, *Exploring Richmond* (1979); L.J. Ross, *Richmond: Child of the Fraser* (1979).

Richmond and Lennox, Charles Lennox, 4th Duke of, soldier, administrator, governor-in-chief of British N America 1818-19 (b in Eng 9 Sept 1764; d near Richmond, UC 28 Aug 1819). After an undistinguished career in the British army, he sat as an MP in the British House of Commons 1790-1806 until he inherited the dukedom of Richmond. After serving as lord lieutenant of Ireland 1807-13, he was appointed governor-in-chief of British N America in 1818. The year after his arrival in Canada, Richmond set out on a tour of the area's internal communications and defences. Bitten by his pet fox, he developed rabies and died suddenly.   DAVID EVANS

Ricker, William Edwin, fishery and aquatic biologist (b at Waterdown, Ont 11 Aug 1908). Ricker is widely recognized as Canada's foremost fishery scientist. Through his work with the Fisheries Research Board of Canada and the Pacific Biological Station in Nanaimo, BC, he has achieved world acclaim for original contributions in the study of fish population dynamics and many other aspects of biological research fundamental to fisheries management. Educated at U of T, he joined the FRB and then was professor of zoology at Indiana U 1939-50 before returning to the FRB. During his career, Ricker authored over 200 publications. He is best known for *Computation and Interpretation of Biological Statistics of Fish Populations* (1975) and for his development of new concepts of the relationship between parent fish stock size and the number of resulting progeny: *Stock and Recruitment* (1954). Both publications have been widely used in the management of national and international fisheries important to Canada and both won him awards from the North American Wildlife Soc. He is noted as a limnologist for his theories on lake circulation and in the field of entomology as a world authority on Plecoptera, or stoneflies. Self-taught in Russian, he has done much to create an awareness of Soviet fishery science in the Western world through translations and by publishing a *Russian-English Dictionary* for students of fisheries and aquatic biology (1973). Ricker was elected fellow of the RSC 1956 and has received many awards and medals as well as 2 honorary degrees. In 1986 he was named Member of the Order of Canada.   K.S. KETCHEN

Ricketts, Thomas, soldier, pharmacist (b at Middle Arm, White Bay, Nfld 15 Apr 1901; d at St John's 10 Feb 1967). Ricketts enlisted in Sept 1916, left for Europe early in 1917, and was wounded late that year. He was awarded the VIC-

TORIA CROSS for braving heavy machine-gun fire and helping to outflank a German battery near Ledegem, Belgium, on 14 Oct 1918, the youngest winner of the award in the British army and the only recipient from the Newfoundland Regiment. After his return to Newfoundland in Feb 1919, he became a pharmacist. He received a state funeral 13 Feb 1967. RALPH DALE

Riddell, Walter Alexander, scholar, public servant (b at Stratford, Ont 5 Aug 1881; d in Algonquin Park, Ont 27 July 1963). He served as deputy minister of labour in Ontario before joining the International Labour Organization in Geneva in 1920. In 1925 he became Canadian advisory officer at the League of Nations. A strong believer in collective security, he acted without instructions in 1935 in proposing oil sanctions against Italy, which had invaded Ethiopia. Repudiated by PM KING's government in this "Riddell incident," he was subsequently posted to Washington and New Zealand. He became professor of international relations at U of T and published a memoir, *World Security by Conference,* and books on international relations. ROBERT BOTHWELL

Rideau Canal, 200 km long, links the Ottawa R at Ottawa with Lk Ontario at Kingston. Conceived as the major component of an alternative route for military purposes between Montréal and Kingston, the canal was first proposed as the War of 1812 drew to its close. Construction started (1826) to the design, and under the direction, of Lt-Col John BY. About 50 dams were necessary to control the water levels at rapids on the Rideau and Cataraqui rivers. The 47 locks in use raise vessels 83 m from the Ottawa R to the portage channel at Newboro, whence vessels descend 54 m to Lk Ontario at Kingston. The canal was built in virgin forest, all work being done by hand, and caused great hardship to its Irish labourers, many of whom died of malaria. Finished in 1832 after 5 summer working seasons, with up to 2000 men being employed by the Royal Engineers and appointed contractors, the canal ranks among the greatest early civil- engineering works of N America. By located his headquarters at the junction of the Ottawa and Rideau rivers, and started a small settlement, first named Bytown in his honour but

Pleasure boats tied up on the Rideau Canal, Ottawa. The Parliament Buildings are visible in the distance (*photo by Jim Merrithew*).

renamed Ottawa in 1855. Although it carried freight and passengers in small steamboats for a century, the Rideau Canal was never economically viable, and is now used entirely by pleasure craft. Its stone walls, ponds and bridges have preserved a quiet beauty along its course through the city of Ottawa, and in the wintertime it provides one of the world's most famous skating rinks. Its 150th anniversary of service was celebrated during the summer of 1982.   R.F. LEGGET

Rideau Hall, located in Ottawa, is the residence of the GOVERNOR GENERAL. The original stone house was built in 1838 by Thomas MacKay, contractor on the Rideau Canal, on his 100 acre estate overlooking the Ottawa and Rideau rivers. MacKay designed the house himself, in the style of a Regency villa. In 1864 the MacKay estate was leased to be used as the temporary residence for the governor general and the villa was enlarged by 3 or 4 times, 1865-68, during the residency of Lord Monck. The house was finally purchased by the government in 1868 for $82 000, and a conservatory and iron gates were added.

Rideau Hall, the governor general's residence, shown in 1880 (*courtesy National Archives of Canada/C-3884*).

Rideau Lakes, 65 km², elev 123 m, mean depth 12.3 m, is a commonly used collective name for 3 lakes: Big Rideau, Upper Rideau and Lower Rideau. They are located near the height of land on the RIDEAU CANAL system between Kingston and Ottawa in eastern Ontario. Their natural drainage is to the NE, by way of the Rideau R through the town of SMITHS FALLS.

Located on the Frontenac axis of the Canadian SHIELD, the lakes are studded with islands and their surrounding shores are rocky. They are used almost entirely for recreational activities such as boating and cottaging; their common sport fish are largemouth and smallmouth bass, northern pike, lake trout and yellow perch. The waterway through these lakes was originally an Indian canoe route. The intent of making it navigable for larger craft was strategic. Col BY built the canal 1826-32, primarily to provide access from Montréal to Kingston for troops and supplies, along a route that would be free of risk from American attack. The name of the lakes is derived from a waterfall at the mouth of the Rideau R that early French explorers named for its resemblance to a curtain. FREDERICK M. HELLEINER

Reading: K.M. Wells, *Cruising the Rideau Waterway* (1965).

Rideout, Patricia Irene, contralto (b at Saint John 16 Mar 1931). An opera singer, concert soloist and recitalist, Rideout has performed extensively across Canada. The interpreter of many roles from the standard repertoire, among them Suzuki in *Madama Butterfly,* Bianca in Britten's

The Rape of Lucretia and Mercedes in *Carmen,* she has also participated in the premieres of several operas by Canadian composers. Performances in major choral works with most of Canada's leading orchestras and choral societies have won her much acclaim. She is a fine and committed performer of contemporary music and has introduced N American and European audiences to many new Canadian works, including Bruce MATHER's *Madrigals III,* written for her. Several of these performances of new music have been recorded. BARCLAY McMILLAN

Ridgeway, Battle of, 2 June 1866. This engagement was fought between Canadian volunteers, led by militia officer Lt-Col Alfred Booker, and FENIAN Civil War veterans, commanded by Lt-Col John O'Neill, who crossed the river from Buffalo on the night of May 31 with about 800 men. On hearing that 2 columns were sent against him, one from Hamilton and one from Toronto, O'Neill marched to meet the Hamilton column, about 900 men under Booker. O'Neill took up a position about 5 km from the railway station at Ridgeway where Booker's men detrained and marched N. The forces met early on June 2. Fenian mounted scouts were mistaken for cavalry, and Booker threw his forces into confusion by ordering them to form a square. Perceiving his opponents' difficulties, O'Neill drove them from the field with a bayonet charge. The Canadians lost 10 killed and 38 wounded, and Fenian losses, though there are no records, were less.

HEREWARD SENIOR

Riding Mountain National Park (est 1929, 2970 km²) is located 272 km NW of Winnipeg, perched almost 500 m above the PRAIRIE on the Manitoba Escarpment. The park is a rolling landscape of mixed forests and grasslands dotted with lakes, streams and bogs. In many ways, the park is a blend of Canada's North, West and East with elements of the boreal forest, prairie and mixed deciduous woods present. Within its varied habitats, 233 species of birds, 60 kinds of mammals and at least 10 species of reptiles and amphibians thrive. Bison, elk, moose, wolf, beaver, black bear and white-tailed deer are the park's largest denizens. Cree and Assiniboine first entered the park area, which they favoured for hunting, 1200 years ago. By 1800 the highland was surrounded by fur-trading posts. Later, local settlers used the park's resources for timber, cattle grazing, hunting and recreation. Riding Mountain provides facilities for camping and over 300 km of hiking and riding trails. LILLIAN STEWART

Ridout, Godfrey, composer, teacher, writer, conductor (b at Toronto 6 May 1918; d there 24 Nov 1984). A student of Ettore Mazzoleni, Weldon Kilburn and J. Healey WILLAN, Ridout began teaching at the Toronto Conservatory of Music in 1940. At the Faculty of Music, U of T, from 1948 until his retirement in 1982, he guided some of Canada's best-known musicians. He was music director (1949-58) of the Eaton Operatic Soc in Toronto and long associated with the Toronto Gilbert & Sullivan Soc. His compositions, ranging from chamber music and symphonic pieces to scores for radio drama and film, are professional and tuneful. His interest in Healey Willan, the English Edwardian composers and in church music was shown in his works for voice and orchestra. MABEL H. LAINE

Riel, Louis, Métis leader, founder of Manitoba, central figure in the NORTH-WEST REBELLION (b at Red River Settlement [Man] 22 Oct 1844; d at Regina 16 Nov 1885). Riel was educated at St-Boniface and studied for the priesthood at the Collège de Montréal. In 1865 he studied law with Rodolphe Laflamme, and he is believed to have worked briefly in Chicago, Ill, and St Paul, Minn, returning to St-Boniface in 1868.

In 1869, the federal government, anticipating the transfer of Red River and the North-West from the HBC to Canadian jurisdiction, appointed William MCDOUGALL as lieutenant-governor of the new territory and sent survey crews to Red River. The Métis, fearful of the implications of the transfer, wary of the aggressive Anglo-Protestant immigrants from Ontario, and still suffering economically from the grasshopper plague of 1867-68, organized a "National Committee" of which Riel was secretary. Riel's education and his father's history marked him out as an obvious leader. The committee halted the surveys and prevented McDougall from entering Red River. On Nov 2 Ft Garry was seized, HBC officials offering no resistance. The committee then invited the people of Red River, both English and French speaking, to send delegates to Ft Garry. While they were discussing a "List of Rights" prepared by Riel, a group of Canadians, led by John Christian SCHULTZ and John Stoughton DENNIS, organized an armed resistance. Meanwhile, the federal government postponed the transfer, planned for Dec 1, and Dennis and McDougall returned to Canada. When Schultz and his men surrendered to Riel, he imprisoned them in Ft Garry, issued a "Declaration of the People of Rupert's Land and the Northwest," and on Dec 23 became head of the "provisional government" of Red River. The Canadian government sent special commissioners "of goodwill" to Red River: Abbé J.B. Thibault, Col Charles de Salaberry and Donald A. SMITH, chief representative of the HBC in Canada. Smith persuaded Riel to summon a general meeting, at which it was decided to hold a convention of 40 representatives of the settlement, equally divided between English and French speakers. Its first meeting was Jan 26. The delegates debated a new "List of Rights" and endorsed Riel's provisional government. The Canadian prisoners taken in Dec were released (some had escaped earlier) and plans were made to send 3 delegates to Ottawa to negotiate the entry of Red River into CONFEDERATION.

Meanwhile a force of some of the Canadians who had escaped, mustered by Schultz and surveyor Thomas SCOTT and led by Canadian militia officer Charles BOULTON, gathered at Portage la Prairie, hoping to enlist support in the Scottish parishes of Red River. The appearance of this armed force alarmed the Métis who promptly rounded them up and imprisoned them again in Ft Garry. The Métis convened a court-martial at which Boulton was condemned to death. Smith intervened, however, and the sentence was remitted. But, at a court-martial presided over by Riel's associate, Ambroise Lépine, the obstreperous Scott was sentenced to death. This time Smith's appeals were rejected and Scott was executed by firing squad on 4 Mar 1870.

Bishop A.A. TACHÉ of St-Boniface, summoned from the 1870 Ecumenical Council in Rome, reached Red River 4 days after Scott's death, bringing a copy of the federal proclamation of amnesty which he believed included any actions up to that date. Taché persuaded Riel's council to free all prisoners and send the delegates to Ottawa. Despite opposition from the Orange Lodges of Ontario, of which Thomas Scott had been a member, Riel's delegates obtained an agreement, embodied in the MANITOBA ACT passed 12 May 1870, and the transfer was set for July 15. In addition, the federal government agreed to a land grant of 1 400 000 acres (566 580 ha) for the Métis and to bilingual services for the new province. Other than verbal assurances, there was no specific mention of the amnesty, however.

To reassure Ontario and support the adminis-

Even after a century, Métis leader Louis Riel's execution excites political debate, especially in Québec and Manitoba (*courtesy Provincial Archives of Manitoba/N5730*).

tration of the new lieutenant-governor A.G. ARCHIBALD, the federal government sent a military force to Red River under Col Garnet WOLSELEY in the summer of 1870. Though the RED RIVER EXPEDITION was supposed to be "a mission of peace," Riel had reason to fear its arrival and fled to the US. Later he returned quietly to his home at St-Vital and, when the province was threatened with a FENIAN raid from the US in the autumn of 1871, offered a force of Métis cavalry to Archibald.

In Ontario, however, Riel was widely denounced as Thomas Scott's "murderer" and a reward of $5000 was offered for his arrest. In Québec he was regarded as a hero, a defender of the Roman Catholic faith and French culture in Manitoba. Anxious to avoid a political confrontation with the 2 principal provinces of Canada, Sir John A. MACDONALD tried to persuade Riel to remain in voluntary exile in the US, even providing him with funds. But, encouraged by his friends, Riel entered federal politics. Successful in a by-election in 1873 and in the general election of 1874, Riel went to Ottawa and signed the register but was expelled from the House on a motion introduced by the Ontario Orange leader Mackenzie BOWELL. Although re-elected, Riel did not attempt to take his seat again. Meanwhile Ambroise Lépine was arrested, tried and condemned to death for the "murder" of Thomas Scott. Subsequently, his sentence was commuted to 2 years' imprisonment and loss of political rights. In Feb 1875 the federal government finally adopted a motion granting amnesty to Riel and Lépine, conditional on 5 years' banishment from "Her Majesty's dominions."

Shortly after, Riel suffered a nervous breakdown and was admitted to hospital at Longue Pointe (Montréal) as "Louis R. David," and later transferred to the mental asylum at Beauport, Qué, as "Louis La Rochelle." Always introspective by nature and strongly religious, Riel became obsessed with the idea that his was a religious mission – to establish a new N American Catholicism with Bishop BOURGET of Montréal as Pope of the New World. Released in Jan 1878, he spent some time in Keeseville, NY, and then set out for the Upper Missouri region of Montana territory where he engaged in trade, joined the Republican Party, became an American citizen, and married a Métis, Marguerite Monet, *dit* Bellehumeur. In

1883 he became a schoolteacher at St Peter's mission on the Sun R and in June 1884 was asked by a group of Canadian Métis to help them obtain their legal rights in the Saskatchewan valley.

Early in July Riel and his family reached BATOCHE, the main centre of Métis settlement in Saskatchewan. He conducted a peaceful agitation, speaking throughout the district and preparing a petition. Sent to Ottawa in Dec, Riel's petition was acknowledged and the federal government promised to appoint a commission to investigate and report on western problems.

Early in 1885, however, Riel encountered opposition in Saskatchewan because of his unorthodox religious views, old memories of Thomas Scott's execution, and his reiteration of his personal claims against the federal government (which he estimated at $35 000) which suggested self-interest as the motive behind his political activity. His exasperation mounted and he began to contemplate direct action. But 1885 was not 1870 when Wolseley had taken several months to lead a military force to Ft Garry. By 1885 the North-West Mounted Police had been established and a railway to the West almost completed. Nevertheless, convinced that God was directing him, and seeing himself as the "Prophet of the New World," on March 19 Riel seized the parish church at Batoche, armed his men, formed a provisional government and demanded the surrender of Ft Carlton. The ensuing fighting lasted scarcely 2 months before Riel surrendered (*see* NORTH-WEST REBELLION).

On 6 July 1885, a formal charge of treason was laid against him and on 20 July his trial began at Regina. His counsel proposed to defend him on the grounds of insanity, but Riel repudiated that defence and, in the face of damning statements by his cousin, Charles Nolin, who had opposed him in 1870 and deserted him in 1885, the jury found him guilty. However, they recommended clemency. The verdict was appealed to the Court of Queen's Bench of Manitoba and to the Judicial Committee of the Privy Council. Both appeals were dismissed, but public pressure, particularly from Québec, delayed execution pending an examination of Riel's mental state. The 3 examining physicians found Riel excitable, but only one considered him insane. Owing to questionable excisions, the official version of the report did not reveal any difference of opinion and the federal Cabinet decided in favour of hanging. Riel was executed at Regina 16 Nov 1885. His body was sent to St-Boniface and interred in the cemetery in front of the cathedral.

Politically and philosophically, Riel's execution has had a lasting effect on Canadian history. In the West, the immediate result was to depress the lot of the Métis. In central Canada, FRENCH CANADIAN NATIONALISM was strengthened and Honoré MERCIER came to power in Québec in 1886. In the longer term Québec voters moved from their traditional support of the Conservative Party to the Liberal Party led by Wilfrid LAURIER. Even after a century, Riel and his fate excite political debate, particularly in Québec and Manitoba. Riel's execution has remained a contentious issue even today and demands have been made for a retroactive pardon. *See also* RED RIVER REBELLION.

GEORGE F.G. STANLEY

Reading: P. Charlebois, *The Life of Louis Riel* (1975); W.M. Davidson, *Louis Riel* (1955); T.E. Flanagan, *Louis "David" Riel: Prophet of the New World* (1979) and *Riel and the Rebellion, 1885 Reconsidered* (1983); George F.G. Stanley et al, eds, *Les Éditions complètes de Louis Riel/The Collected Works of Louis Riel* (5 vols, 1985); J.K. Howard, *Strange Empire* (1952); George F.G. Stanley, *Louis Riel* (1963).

Rigler, Frank Harold, biologist (b at London, Eng 9 June 1928; d at Montréal 26 June 1982).

Educated at U of T, in 1957 he returned from post-doctoral study in England to the zoology department there.

A world authority in aquatic biology, Rigler directed an important Canadian contribution to the International Biological Program, a study of Char Lk in the High Arctic. In 1976 he moved to McGill's biology dept as chairman and professor. Rigler believed that good science required sound philosophy and taught its importance to a generation of students. He was alarmed by environmental degradation, and his advocacy of a more applicable ecology crystallized a long tradition in Canadian freshwater research that stresses practical theory based on observation rather than precepts; his later work on eutrophication control is an example. In his honour the Society of Canadian Limnologists instituted the F.H. Rigler Memorial Lectures in 1984.   ROBERT PETERS

Riley, Gordon Arthur, oceanographer (b at Webb City, Mo 11 June 1911; d at Halifax 7 Oct 1985). A pioneer of quantitative biological oceanography, Riley became director of Dalhousie's Institute of Oceanography (later dept of oceanography) in 1965 and a fellow of the RSC. Originally an embryologist, he began graduate work at Yale in 1934 and then, influenced by the ecologist G.E. Hutchinson, switched to limnology. His work at sea, based at Yale and Woods Hole Oceanographic Institution, began in 1937. Riley used experimental methods and statistics to determine the causes of biological processes in the sea. In the 1940s he began to use differential equations, beginning quantitative modelling in biological oceanography. Later he worked on regional oceanography, transport and mixing, and particles in seawater, showing the same originality that had characterized his earlier work. At Dalhousie, Riley built a school of oceanography whose graduates work throughout N America.
                    ERIC L. MILLS

Rimmer, David, filmmaker, photographer (b at Vancouver 20 Jan 1942). His experimental film works (primarily 1968-75) are generally held to exemplify a distinctive West Coast tradition distinguishable from the Toronto school, but, although definable differences do generally distinguish experimental filmmakers on the West Coast of the US from those in New York, the evidence is against making such distinctions in Canada. Many of Rimmer's films (*Surfacing on the Thames* 1970, *Seashore* 1971, *Watching for the Queen* 1973) are no less austere, have no more surface polish and are no more contemplative than the films of Torontonians Michael SNOW and Joyce WIELAND, and most are produced using rudimentary rather than advanced technologies. Rimmer's experimental films are painstakingly careful examinations of how film constructs the illusions of movement, depth, continuity and audience presence at the situation depicted. In 1979 Rimmer released *Al Neil,* an innovative performance documentary, and has continued to work in that form since. However, since 1980 he has made several film experimental films: *Narrows Inlet* (1980), a delicate study of the sea and landscape near Vancouver, *Bricolage* (1984), *As Seen on TV* (sic) (1986) and *Along the Road to Altamira* (1986).   R. BRUCE ELDER

Rimouski, Qué, City, pop 29 672 (1986c), 29 120 (1981c), inc 1869, is located on the S

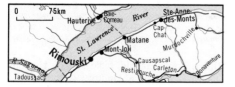

shore of the ST LAWRENCE R, 300 km NE of Québec City. Greater Rimouski, with 46 210 (1986c) inhabitants, is the most populous area of eastern Québec. The charming city is built on 3 levels, in the shape of an amphitheatre. A seigneury was granted here in 1688, but it was not settled until 1696. In the 18th century, agriculture and seasonal fishing were the only occupations, but the area experienced some growth when Québec City merchants, including William Price, began to develop the forest resources and built several sawmills.

The parish of St-Germain was established 1829; a courthouse was added 1857 and a bishop's seat in 1867. The arrival of the railway made the town a centre for expansion into the GASPÉ and Matapédia. Its economy was based on the forest industry and services such as trade, teaching and government and church administration. After a terrible fire in 1950, the town experienced more rapid growth. It became the regional capital when several federal and provincial government departments opened offices to serve the Lower St Lawrence and the Gaspé. Today the economy is based largely on long-standing activities: schools, a university, and health and social services. The town is now a major centre for oceanographic research.   ANTONIO LECHASSEUR

Rindisbacher, Peter, painter (b at Eggiwil, Upper Emmenthal, Switz 12 Apr 1806; d at St Louis, Mo 13 Aug 1834). Allegedly a Swiss army drummer boy, Rindisbacher immigrated with his family to the RED RIVER COLONY in 1821. He painted views of the HBC forts along the route from York Factory to the colony, leaving the only visual record of them, and the earliest pictorial record of the country W of the Great Lakes. He spent 5 years in the colony, contributing to family support by selling paintings of prairie and Indian life to HBC officers. Some of these, described as "taken by a gentleman on the spot," in 1823 and 1824, were lithographed and published in London, Eng, in 1824 and 1825. In 1826, repeated hardships finally drove the family to the US. Rindisbacher died at age 28, just as he was gaining success as a portrait artist.   JAMES MARSH

A War Party at Fort Douglas, watercolour by Peter Rindisbacher (*courtesy Royal Ontario Museum*).

Ringette is a skating sport played on ice using a straight stick and a hollow rubber ring. Played with 6 players on the ice at one time, ringette is a skilful game which emphasizes team play and has no intentional body contact. There are over 50 000 players currently participating at recreational and competitive levels in Canada. Players are required to pass the ring to a teammate across each (hockey) blueline, and are required to play in a specific area on the ice, eg, forwards from their net to the defensive "free play" and the centre anywhere except in the goaltender's crease. The "free play" line is parallel to the blueline touching the point on each of the 2 free pass (face-off) circles closest to each blue line. The game begins with a "free pass," the object of the game being to outscore the opponent. Opportunities for participation range from house leagues, to competition in the Canadian ringette championships, originally held in Winnipeg in 1979. Originally conceived in North Bay, Ont, in 1963 by Sam Jacks, ringette is now played in Canada, Finland, Sweden, France, W Germany and the US. The International Ringette Association was recently formed, world championships are planned and ringette is included in the Canada Winter Games.
                    WES CLARK

Ringwood, Gwendolyn, née Pharis, playwright (b at Anatone, Wash 13 Aug 1910; d near Williams Lake, BC 24 May 1984). Ringwood was western Canada's regional dramatist par excellence. Her prairie tragedy, *Still Stands the House* (first performed June 1938, publ 1939), is one of the most frequently anthologized and performed Canadian plays. A pioneer of western community theatre, she began her career as secretary to the U of A extension director of drama, and wrote and produced her first stage play, *The Dragons of Kent,* in 1935 when she was registrar of the new Banff School of Fine Arts [BANFF CENTRE]. She polished her playwriting skills at U of N Carolina drama department, where she wrote numerous folk plays, culminating in *Dark Harvest.* She received the Gov Gen's Award for outstanding service to Canadian drama (1941), and published the first volume of collected plays in 1982 by a Canadian dramatist. The Gwen Pharis Ringwood Civic Theatre (1971), Williams Lake, BC, is named for her.
                    ROTA HERZBERG LISTER

Autriche, by Jean-Paul Riopelle, the most internationally acclaimed Canadian painter of the 20th century. After WWII, Riopelle's paintings were characterized by improvisation and "raw gestures" (*courtesy Montréal Museum of Fine Arts*).

Riopelle, Jean-Paul, painter, sculptor (b at Montréal 7 Oct 1923). An original member of the AUTOMATISTES, he is the most internationally acclaimed Canadian painter of the 20th century. While a student of Paul-Émile BORDUAS at the École du meuble, Riopelle met with other artists to discuss surrealism, political radicalism and psychoanalysis. In 1946 Riopelle exhibited in Montréal along with Borduas and several others, marking the inception of the Automatistes on Canadian soil and the first show in Canada by a group of Canadian abstract painters. Under the influence of surrealism, with its emphasis on the "liberation of the human spirit," Riopelle moved from figurative painting to the gestural abstractions for which he is now famous. After WWII, against the growing standardization and depersonalization of industrial capitalism, Riopelle's paintings were characterized by personal improvisation and "raw" gestures that attested to the uniquely human process by which they were made. To increase the spontaneity of his art, he used several experimental techniques: supple gestural brushstrokes (1946-49); the controlled drip technique of squeezing paint directly from the tube onto the canvas (c 1950); and, in the early 1950s, the use of the palette knife to create mosaiclike surfaces of paint – a hallmark of his later style.

Riopelle went to Paris shortly after WWII, participated in the Automatiste exhibition at the Galerie du Luxembourg, and signed the surrealist manifesto *Ruptures inaugurales.* International recognition came quickly. He was singled out by critic Michel Tapié and surrealist leader André Breton. In 1948 Riopelle returned briefly to Montréal where he signed the manifesto REFUS GLOBAL, the cover of which featured one of his ink drawings. After returning to Paris in 1948, Riopelle increasingly gained recognition. A high point of this fame came in 1962 when Riopelle was given the UNESCO Award for cumulative achievement. He was honoured in 1963 with a retrospective exhibition at the Art Gallery of Ontario.   DAVID L. CRAVEN

Reading: David L. Craven and Richard Leslie, "The Automatic Paintings of Jean-Paul Riopelle," *Artscanada* 240/241 (1981); Marcel Paquet, *Jean-Paul Riopelle* (1987).

Riot Under the Criminal Code (s64), an unlawful assembly is created when 3 or more persons, with intent to carry out any common purpose, assemble in such a manner or conduct themselves in such a fashion as to cause persons in the neighbourhood of the assembly to fear, on reasonable grounds, that the persons assembled or others reacting to the assembly will disturb the peace tumultuously. A riot is defined (s65) as an unlawful assembly that has in fact begun to disturb the peace tumultuously. The term "riot" is often used to describe the behaviour of people who are intending to use collective violence to achieve some unlawful aim. Technically, however, the term riot can include street parades, boisterous parties and demonstrations that have been held to be unlawful assemblies. If there is evidence that the peace has been disturbed tumultuously, these activities fall within the definition of a riot. Everyone who takes part in a riot is guilty of an indictable offence and liable to imprisonment for 2 years.

Where a riot involving 12 or more people is in progress, a justice, mayor, sheriff or deputy sheriff is authorized to order the rioters to disperse in the name of the queen. Failure to disperse within 30 minutes, or hindering or obstructing the person who is making the proclamation (that is, "reading the Riot Act") is yet another offence, with punishment of up to life imprisonment. The proclamation has been used a number of times in Canadian history, for example, in Montréal in 1832 when a riot ensued during a by-election and in Winnipeg during the WINNIPEG GENERAL STRIKE of 1919.

Many social scientists agree that collective violence of the sort labelled "riot" (or "insurrection") can be conceived of as a collective act of resistance to established authority and perceived injustice (eg, the MONTRÉAL RIOTS of 1849 in which outraged Tories attacked Lord Elgin and set fire to the Parliament Buildings), but others argue that the notion of "riot" is not a legitimate concept but an ideological one used by those in power to denigrate resistance to their authority.

Within the legal system, the term "riot" has a much broader meaning and is not necessarily linked to a notion of resistance to authority or perceived injustice. *See also* VIOLENCE, POLITICAL.
                                          C.D. SHEARING

Ritchie, Albert Edgar, diplomat (b at Andover, NB 20 Dec 1916). A Rhodes scholar who worked for the British government and United Nations in the 1940s, Ritchie was a member of the Depart-

ment of External Affairs, 1944-46, 1948-80. His expertise was economics, his judgement and integrity impeccable. He was assistant undersecretary, 1959-64, and deputy undersecretary, 1964-66, before serving in the department's 2 top posts: as ambassador to Washington 1966-69 and as undersecretary 1970-74. A Companion of the Order of Canada, he was ambassador to Ireland 1976-82, after which he retired from public life.
                                          ANNE HILLMER

Ritchie, Charles Stewart Almon, diplomat, author (b at Halifax 23 Sept 1906). Ritchie joined the Dept of External Affairs in 1934, rising to assistant (later deputy) undersecretary, 1950-54. Restless in Ottawa, he escaped to Germany as ambassador 1954-58, and subsequently held the top posts in Canada's diplomatic service – ambassador to the United Nations 1958-62, to the United States 1962-66, to NATO and the EEC 1966-67, and high commissioner to the UK 1967-71. Ritchie had grown up wanting to be an author, and he kept diaries from an early age. Four volumes have been published since his retirement: *The Siren Years* (1974; Gov Gen's Award), *An Appetite for Life* (1977), *Diplomatic Passport* (1981) and *Storm Signals* (1983). The diaries, like the man, are cool, elegant and cynical about human nature but generous to individuals. *My Grandfather's House* (1987) is a memoir of his youth.
                                          NORMAN HILLMER

Ritchie, Eliza, educator, feminist (b at Halifax 20 May 1856; d there 5 Sept 1933). Ritchie graduated from Dalhousie in 1887 and 2 years later obtained her PhD from Cornell, probably the first Canadian woman to secure a doctorate. After further study at Leipzig, Germany, and Oxford she taught at Wellesley College, Mass. In 1901 she returned to teach philosophy at Dalhousie. A strong suffragist, she quickly joined sisters Mary and Ella in leadership positions in the Victoria School of Fine Art, the VON and the local Council of Women. With Agnes DENNIS and Edith ARCHIBALD she dominated the feminist movement in Halifax until the end of World War I. She showed tact in working with other women, was noted for the clarity of her writing style, and displayed a commitment to a Maritime region. Her appointment to the Dalhousie board of governors in 1919 was hailed as another first in Canada. Her publications include *The Problem of Personality* (1889) and *Songs of the Maritimes* (1931).
                                          ERNEST R. FORBES

Ritchie, Octavia Grace, married name England, physician, educator (b at Montréal 16 Jan 1868; d there 1 Feb 1948). Though a brilliant student, she was at first refused admission to McGill, but Principal Sir J.W. DAWSON relented when Donald A. SMITH provided $50 000 for women's education there. In 1888, as the first female valedictorian at McGill, she boldly but unsuccessfully demanded admission to the Faculty of Medicine. Having then entered Kingston Women's Medical Coll, she later transferred to and graduated from Bishop's, becoming the first woman to receive a medical degree in Québec (1891). Following study abroad she was appointed assistant gynecologist at Western Hospital, Montréal, and demonstrator in anatomy at Bishop's. She remained in practice and continued to be active in local, national and international groups promoting humanitarian causes and women's rights.
                                          MARGARET GILLETT

Reading: Margaret Gillett, *We Walked Very Warily: a History of Women at McGill* (1981).

Ritchie, Roland A., lawyer, judge (b at Halifax 19 June 1910), brother of diplomat Charles RITCHIE. Called to the NS Bar in 1934, Ritchie served overseas during WWII following which he returned to Halifax and established a reputation as a leading maritime counsel and part-time lecturer at Dalhousie Law School. In 1959 PM John Diefenbaker appointed Ritchie to the Supreme Court of Canada where he remained a puisne judge and briefly served as acting chief justice in 1982, the first Nova Scotian to occupy the post. Ritchie is best known for a series of puzzling and somewhat conflicting decisions he wrote regarding the applicability of certain provisions of the CANADIAN BILL OF RIGHTS to the INDIAN ACT, including the DRYBONES CASE and the LAVELL CASE. Ritchie retired from the court on 31 Oct 1984 and was made Companion of the Order of Canada in 1985.　　　　　　　　WILLIAM KAPLAN

Ritter, Erika, writer, playwright, essayist, broadcaster (b at Regina 26 Apr 1948). Ritter has achieved national stature for dramatizing the struggles of young Canadian women to achieve significant lives and careers. Her 2 outstanding successes, *The Splits* (1978) and *Automatic Pilot* (1980), brought her international recognition and production. Other plays, eg, *A Visitor from Charleston* (produced 1974, publ 1975), "The Girl I Left Behind Me" (1976, produced 1977), "Moving Pictures" (1976), *Winter 1671* (1979) and "The Passing Scene" (1982), have had amateur and professional productions from Montréal to Edmonton, as well as radio presentations. Her other publications include *Urban Scrawl* (1984) and *Ritter in Residence* (1987), 2 full-length collections of essays and short stories published in *Saturday Night, Chatelaine, Canadian Fiction Magazine* and *The Fiddlehead*. She has been the host of the CBC radio daily 2-hour information and music program "Day Shift" (1985-87).
　　　　　　　　ROTA HERZBERG LISTER

Rivard, Lucien, convicted drug smuggler (b at Montréal? 1915?). An underworld figure of no great consequence, he was arrested in Montréal in 1965 on narcotics charges filed by US authorities. While fighting extradition, he escaped from jail after obtaining a garden hose "to flood the skating rink" on a spring evening with the temperature above freezing. Allegedly, Rivard used the hose to climb the wall and was at large for 4 months. During that time, charges of bribery connected with the escape created a scandal for the federal Liberal government. A royal commission looked into the "Rivard affair" and criticized Minister of Justice Guy FAVREAU, who resigned. Rivard was extradited to the US. Convicted of smuggling narcotics, he was sentenced to 20 years in prison. He served 9 years, and was then deported back to Canada.　　BILL CAMERON

River, a course of WATER, usually growing in volume between its source and its terminus in an OCEAN, a LAKE or another river. A stream or riverlet is smaller but the volumes involved are not closely defined.

Most rivers have continuous although variable flow, but some may have no flow in very dry or very cold seasons. Streams, especially in drier and colder regions, are more prone to no-flow periods and many are intermittent. Rivers and streams with large GROUNDWATER inflow are usually less variable in flow than those dependent on surface runoff. Running water has been dominant in the shaping of the Earth's landforms, but in most of Canada the impact of GLACIATION has been major and running water is only slowly changing the glaciated landforms.

The many features that make rivers different from one another can be grouped in the following categories: hydrologic regime, ICE regime, major geomorphological setting and dominant channel processes, channel materials and stability and channel dimensions. Almost all Canadian rivers

View south of the Upper Lillooet Valley, with the braided band of the Lillooet R (*courtesy Colour Library Books*).

are characterized by variable runoff that may be modified by extensive natural storage in lakes and muskeg. Similarly, most Canadian rivers are affected by ice during winter, except on the BC coast.

Most rivers and streams in Canada occupy well-defined channels that they have developed since the last ICE AGE (within the last 6000-14 000 years for most areas). Several regions have experienced extensive glacial rebound, which has affected the present course of major rivers. Some are "misfit" in large spillway channels that were formed by glacial meltwaters. Rapids and WATERFALLS separating stretches of marshes and lakes occur where rock formations resistant to erosion are present, especially in SHIELD and CORDILLERAN regions (*see* PHYSIOGRAPHIC REGIONS). They are less common in areas of deep drift deposits and softer rock, as in the Interior Plains, where channels are more regular in gradient. Some rivers with heavy sediment loads are locally braided and many divide into distributary channels in DELTAS.

The rivers originating in Canada discharge approximately 98 000 m³/s (cubic metres per second) of flow to the ocean, ie, about 8% of world river discharge. The ST LAWRENCE and MACKENZIE rivers, each with approximately 10 000 m³/s, rank 16th and 17th among world rivers, 2nd and 3rd in N America. The Amazon is over 20 times as large as our largest river and the Mississippi is about 75% larger. The St Lawrence and Mackenzie rivers are approximately equal in annual flow, and arguments about which is larger depend upon semantic differences, such as where in the St Lawrence estuary the water becomes brackish, and if the Peel and other tributaries of the Mackenzie Delta, entering below where the main

channel divides, should be counted. The Mackenzie Basin is wholly Canadian and is 3.5 times as large as the Canadian portion of the St Lawrence Basin (*see* DRAINAGE BASINS). The Mackenzie (to the head of the Finlay R in BC) is the longest river in Canada (4241 km), followed by the St Lawrence (3058 km), Nelson (2575 km), Churchill (1609 km) and Fraser (1368 km). Tributaries such as the Saskatchewan (1939 km), Peace (1923 km), Ottawa (1271 km), Athabasca (1231 km) and Liard (1115 km) are also very long.

Almost 75% of Canada is drained northward to the Arctic Ocean, Hudson Bay and Hudson Str. According to data of the early 1970s, this northward drainage involved almost half (47.9%) of the total flow of Canada's rivers. Drainage to the Pacific (10.2% of the area) accounted for almost one quarter of the flow (23.5%); drainage to the Atlantic (15.2% of the area), for over one quarter (28.5%). A very small area is drained southward in the Missouri-Mississippi Basin. More recent measurements show that the earlier estimates for northern and Pacific regions and for Canada as a whole were too conservative, and that northern values especially might be increased substantially (possibly as much as 20% for some basins). Upward revisions might be expected as better, longer-term data become available. Canada has abundant freshwater supplies and, although regional shortages will be experienced, national shortages are unlikely.

Most of the rivers and streams of Canada have snowmelt regime patterns of flow. Winter snows, subject to very little evapotranspiration loss, provide the peak flows on melting in Mar-Apr in southern lowlands and in May-June, extending into July in higher mountain and northern areas. Summer RAINS are greater than winter snowfall in most regions, but much of the rain is lost to evap-

Principal Rivers of Canada and Their Basins

Drainage basin and river	Drainage area (km²)	Length (km)	Mean discharge (m³/s)
Pacific Ocean			
Columbia	155 000	2 000	2 800
Fraser	233 000	1 370	3 620
Nass	20 700	380	892
Skeena	54 900	579	1 760
Stikine	49 200	539	1 080
Yukon	800 000	3 185	2 300
Other	228 000		11 100
Arctic Ocean			
Back	107 000	974	612
Mackenzie	1 787 000	4 241	9 910
Other	1 663 000		5 890
Hudson Bay			
Albany	134 000	982	1 420
Arnaud	49 500	377	654
Attawapiskat	50 200	748	626
Aux Feuilles	42 500	480	575
Churchill	298 000	1 609	1 270
Eastmain	46 400	756	909
George	41 700	564	881
Grande rivière de la Baleine	42 700	724	665
Harricana	29 300	533	473
Hayes	108 000	483	694
Kazan	71 500	732	566
Koksoak	133 000	874	2 420
La Grande Rivière	97 600	893	1 720
Moose	108 000	547*	1 440
Nelson	1 132 000	2 574*	2 370
Nottaway	65 800	776	1 130
Petite rivière à la Baleine	31 900	380	581
Rupert	43 300	763	878
Severn	101 000	982	722
Thelon	142 000	904	804
Winisk	67 300	475	694
Other	1 173 000		8 950
Atlantic Ocean			
Aux Outardes	19 100	499	399
Churchill	79 800	856	1 620
Manicouagan	45 000	560*	852
Moisie	19 200	410	490
Natashquan	16 100	410	422
Petit Mécatina	19 600	547	524
Saguenay	88 000	698	1 760
Saint John	55 400	673	1 100
St Lawrence	1 026 000	3 058	10 100
St-Maurice	43 300	563	731
Other	624 000		15 400
Summary			
Arctic Ocean	3 557 000		16 400
Atlantic Ocean	2 036 000		33 400
Gulf of Mexico	29 500		25
Hudson Bay	4 010 000		30 900
Pacific Ocean	1 085 000		21 200
	10 730 000		105 000

*These figures differ from those given in the separate river entries owing to disparities involved in ascertaining overall length

otranspiration in summer and streamflow response is smaller (*see* CLIMATE). Some rivers at lower elevations in Pacific coastal areas have rainfall-based peaks of flow in midwinter. Glacier meltwater flows peak in midsummer but this pattern is not dominant for most of the larger mountain rivers. Natural storage in groundwater aquifers, lakes and marshes results in reduced peaks and more equable flow.

Artificial storage behind dams has contributed to major regime modification (*see* RESERVOIR). Much of the storage change is for HYDROELECTRIC power production and winter flow enhancement is widely present. Storage for peaking power purposes may result in low flows at night and on weekends and major surges in flow during periods of peak demand. Such flow modification, as on the Kananaskis R, Alta, may conflict greatly with recreation, WILDLIFE CONSERVATION and other objectives. Storage for irrigation purposes is usu-

ally for mid- to late-summer periods when natural flow is declining.

The larger Canadian rivers have some natural lag in flow because of the size of their basins and the distances travelled by streamflow to downstream stations. Most have been modified in regime and sometimes volume by artificial storage and diversion. Interbasin transfers, largely for hydroelectric power and irrigation, and growing diversions for urban, industrial and other uses have affected the flow of many rivers; some of the greatest impacts have been from the discharge of pollutants (*see* POLLUTION). Natural processes contributing dissolved and suspended materials to rivers and streams have always resulted in striking regional and seasonal differences in water quality. Canadian Shield rivers tend to be low in sediment, dissolved solids, calcium carbonate and turbidity; PRAIRIE rivers are high in each.

Man has added, directly and indirectly, to these substances, and chemical, physical and biological changes in water bodies have been apparent in many areas. Rivers and streams have been used as convenient means of WASTE DISPOSAL. The capacity of some water bodies to assimilate waste has been widely and carelessly exceeded. Most industrial, municipal, agricultural and mining waste disposal can be controlled at the source (*see* WATER TREATMENT). Nonpoint pollution such as that from the atmosphere (eg, ACID RAIN), storm sewers and ill-defined sources is more difficult to control. Good progress is being made in treatment of some wastes but the development of new chemical compounds is rapid; fortunately public awareness of new hazards is growing. *See also* separate entries on rivers.

A.H. LAYCOCK

Reading: Hugh MacLennan, *Rivers of Canada* (1974).

River Landform, feature resulting from the movement of WATER on the Earth's surface. In a geological context, flowing water is the most important external process shaping the Earth's surface. RIVER landforms may be depositional, eg, floodplains, river terraces, alluvial fans and DELTAS; or erosional, eg, the valleys, canyons and sculptured BADLANDS that provide some of Canada's most impressive scenery. River processes are especially important in regions ranging through semiarid, subhumid, humid, to very wet, but even in arid regions rare cloudbursts may accomplish a significant amount of geomorphic work.

In the classic era of GEOMORPHOLOGY, which employed an intuitive approach to research and ended around 1950, fluvial (river) landforms were studied in the context of W.M. Davis's cycle of EROSION. The cycle concept is a simplistic but pedagogically effective way of looking at landscape development in a humid, temperate CLIMATE where river action dominates landscape sculpture (eg, southern Canada). Davis's theory states that, after initial uplift of a landmass, the landscape passes sequentially through the stages of youth, maturity and old age. Youth is characterized by V-shaped valleys and irregular gradients; maturity by long valley slopes, meandering streams and floodplain development; old age by sluggish streams, broad floodplains, oxbow LAKES and low hills called monadnocks. Such a landscape is shaped essentially through a combination of fluvial and slope-forming processes, leading eventually to the formation of a flat erosion surface or peneplain, close to sea level. Peneplanation may be followed by uplift, resulting in the initiation of a new cycle of erosion. Uplift before the cycle is completed leads to stream rejuvenation, entrenchment and stepped erosion levels. Valley morphology commonly reflects the controlling influence of bedrock GEOLOGY. Other important models in fluvial geo-

Aerial view of the Pembina River Valley at Evansburg, Alta, in winter (*courtesy SSC Photocentre, photo by Doug Curran*).

morphology have been proposed by Walther Penck (Germany) and L.C. King (South Africa). King's model emphasizes the role of pediment formation and pediplanation in semiarid climates. Modern research is exploring new conceptual approaches in the interpretation of fluvial landforms.

Fluvial activity has played a dominant role in shaping large segments of the Canadian landscape. The scenario is complex because most regions shaped by rivers now also bear the imprint of Quaternary GLACIATION. Many of the magnificent valleys that now dissect the CORDILLERA were formed by stream rejuvenation and entrenchment during uplift in the Tertiary period (66.4-1.6 million years ago), eg, the Fraser, Thompson and Okanagan valleys in the Fraser-Nechako Plateau, BC. Some Cordilleran river valleys were also partly infilled with glacial/glaciofluvial detritus during the ICE AGES (1.6 million – 10 000 years ago), but subsequent postglacial downcutting has left a series of high-level river terraces, eg, Bow R, Alta. Terracing of valley fills is also common in central and eastern Canada.

The flattish PRAIRIES were formed by the long-continued deposition of rock waste eroded from the Cordillera by easterly flowing streams (with some contribution from glacial deposition). The modern streams that traverse the prairies (eg, Saskatchewan) are shallowly entrenched in youthful/early mature valleys to a maximum depth of several hundred metres. In some dry parts of Alberta the incision of streams into Cretaceous sediments (144-66.4 million years old) has created a badlands topography, as at Drumheller.

Most of the Canadian SHIELD had been bevelled by erosion/planation surfaces long before the advent of the Quaternary ice ages. The preglacial drainage patterns were deranged during the ice ages and valleys were buried under glacial drift, leaving a legacy of lakes. Some of the buried valleys are now being re-excavated by modern stream action. In central Canada, before the onset of the ice ages, the lowland area now occupied by the Great Lakes was drained by normal river systems. The present Great Lakes owe their origin to glaciation. Where Lk Erie now drains into Lk Ontario via the Niagara R, waters flow over an ESCARPMENT of Silurian rocks (438-408 million years old) giving rise to Niagara Falls and the downstream gorge. Farther E the waters drain from Lk Ontario into the St Lawrence R, where, in the picturesque THOUSAND ISLANDS stretch, the headward-cutting river has scoured an irregular Precambrian rock plain (an erosion surface over 600 million years old).

With its extensive coastline and many rivers and lakes, Canada has its share of deltaic landforms, eg, the deltas of the Mackenzie, Fraser and Red rivers (Lk Winnipeg).

Modern quantitative geomorphology considers fluvial landforms in an open-systems context.

The fundamental unit, the DRAINAGE BASIN, is considered an open system with inputs (eg, rainfall, solar energy), throughputs and outputs (river flow, sediment) of energy and matter. The morphology of landforms within the basin develops as a process-response or internal adjustment to the varying inputs and outputs. This conceptual approach also involves the idea of systems equilibrium: if inputs and outputs remain appreciably constant, the morphology of the landscape should assume a time-independent form in which the ridges (of more resistant rock/structure) downwaste at the same rate as the river valleys. Drainage-network analysis, first introduced by the American R.E. Horton in 1945, is part of quantitative fluvial geomorphology. Networks can be considered under such headings as pattern (eg, dendritic, rectangular) and composition, the latter involving a study of the mathematical relationships between stream orders, lengths, numbers, gradients and valley slopes. The modern approach to fluvial systems, including landforms, emphasizes stream hydrology; hydraulic geometry of stream development; stream patterns (straight, meandering and braided); ice regimes; river mechanics and fluid turbulence; processes of erosion, transportation and deposition (scour-and-fill); bed-form development; and rates of basin denudation (sediment yields). In the field of applied geomorphology, quantitative criteria for the aesthetic comparison of riverscapes have also been devised for environmental impact assessment in connection with river development projects. Interpretation of the wide range of fluvial forms is important for the identification of desirable crossing locations for highways, pipelines and railways and for the prediction of bank stability and ice-jam locations. Finally, fluvial geomorphology has important implications for the exploration of placer deposits, and for water-management studies, flood control and river-basin management in general. *See also* PHYSIO-GRAPHIC REGIONS.   ALAN V. JOPLING

Rivers, Man, Town, pop 1157 (1986c), 1107 (1981c), inc 1910 (village), 1913 (town), developed as a railway and military centre, 235 km W of Winnipeg. Agricultural settlement began in the 1870s. The townsite was established in 1907 as a terminal point on the Grand Trunk Pacific Ry. The early economy was built on the rail shops, roundhouse, and local services. In 1940, the town scrambled to accommodate an influx of military personnel when a British Commonwealth Air Training Plan navigation school was established nearby. After WWII, this base became a tri-service air training centre, with up to 3000 military and 250 civilian personnel, compensating for diminished railway activity at Rivers. The base closed in 1971. Public incentives were offered to support an industrial and urban-adaptation training centre for native people, but most of the manufacturers attracted to the site subsequently left or failed financially. The federal government sold the property in 1984, leaving Rivers as a locally oriented agricultural trading centre with some recreational activity at nearby Lake Wahtopanah.   D. M. LYON

Riverview, NB, Town, pop 15 638 (1986c), 14 097 (1981c), inc 1973, is situated on the Petitcodiac R opposite MONCTON. Formed by the amalgamation of the villages of Bridgedale, Gunningsville and Riverview Heights with the town of Coverdale, it is the product of the post-WWII growth of Moncton, to which it has been connected by bridge since the 1870s. Riverview is the largest municipality in Albert County, an area known for its gypsum and oil-shale resources and as the site of FUNDY NATIONAL PARK. Although boasting an industrial park, Riverview is mainly

residential and the bulk of the populace finds employment in Moncton.   DEAN JOBB

Rivière-du-Loup, Qué, City, pop 13 321 (1986c), 13 459 (1981c), inc 1874 under the name Fraserville, is located 200 km E of Québec City on the ST LAWRENCE R. Built at the mouth of the river of the same name, it sits on land that belonged to the former seigneuries of Rivière-du-Loup, de Verbois and du Parc, awarded in 1673 to Charles Aubert de La Chesnaye, the richest trader in New France. Rivière-du-Loup's development owes much to its location at the entrance to the Temiscouata Valley and portage. In 1783 the British administration built a military route through the town to facilitate communications with the other English colonies. Rivière-du-Loup became a major railway centre in the last 40 years of the 19th century, a terminal of the GRAND TRUNK RY (1860) and a departure point for the INTERCOLONIAL (1870) and the Temiscouata Ry (1887-88). The forestry, pulp and lumber, and tourist industries have been major factors in its economic development, especially after closure of the railway repair shops. The city still benefits from seasonal seaway links with the N Shore. Today, it has become a service-industry town, with emphasis on commerce, teaching and public administration. A paper mill employs several hundred people.   ANTONIO LECHASSEUR

Roads and Highways To a greater extent than most countries, Canada depends for its social, economic and political life on efficient communication and transportation.

History Canada's first highways were the rivers and lakes used by the native people, travelling by canoe in summer and following the frozen streams in winter. The water network was so practical that the explorers, settlers and soldiers followed the example of the Indians. There was negligible road development before the beginning of the 19th century, and the first graded road in Canada, built (1606) by Samuel de Champlain, was a 16 km military road from PORT-ROYAL to Digby Cape [NS]. By 1734 Québec City and Montréal were linked by a road and a carriage could be driven the 267 km in 4½ days. In the early days of NEW FRANCE, roads and bridges were the responsibility of a crown-appointed chief inspector, a system retained by the British until 1832. Roads were divided into 3 classes: main roads, 7.2 m wide; connecting roads to farms, 5.4 m wide; back roads, built on orders of the seigneurs (*see* SEIGNEURIAL SYSTEM).

Early roads in British North America were built out of military necessity, eg, the 60 km Yonge Street from York to Lk Simcoe (1796) blazed by the Queen's Rangers, commanded by Col John Graves SIMCOE, and Dundas Street from York to London, safely inland from Lk Erie. The concern of the state for roads set an early pattern. As early as 1801, the NB Assembly made regular grants for road construction.

In 1793 an Act of the first Parliament of Upper Canada placed all roads under the supervision of overseers, called pathmasters, and required settlers to work 3 to 12 days each year on the roads. An appropriation for roads was made in 1804, a munificent £1000, doubled 12 years later. These early roads complemented rather than replaced water transport. Mostly little more than cleared paths, a few were planked or "corduroy" (made of logs laid side by side). Nevertheless, they provided valuable inland transportation (especially in winter), reduced costs and opened up new areas to settlement.

Travel by road in early Canada was difficult and often hazardous. The roads were so bad that most people preferred horseback or walking rather than vehicular transportation. Settlers' vehicles

Between Kingston and York, watercolour by James Cockburn (*courtesy National Archives of Canada/C-12632*).

were usually homemade and crude, wheels were cut from the round trunks of huge oak trees. Later came the Conestoga wagons for carrying heavy loads (some were 9 m long, drawn by 6-horse teams) and then 4-wheeled buckboards. The elite of the new cities and towns of Lower Canada had the calèche (open carriages) and the wealthy of Upper Canada and the Maritimes drove buggies. The stagecoach era began at the start of the 19th century and lasted more than 50 years. With it, in 1805, came the toll road and the turnpike trusts. Some of the turnpike companies controlled greater or lesser stretches of road, and the countryside was a network of toll roads for more than a century.

On some roads even a traveller on foot was charged a penny. In recent years some provincial governments have revived the idea to help finance costly projects, such as the Laurentien Autoroute north of Montréal. Some international crossings also charge tolls. At the peak of the stagecoach era, regular services for passengers and mail were being run between all major cities and towns and into the US. But travel was still an adventure in clumsy, uncomfortable vehicles, ranging from open wagons to ungainly carriages hung on leather springs. In winter they were mounted on runners and some carried wood stoves for warmth. The stagecoach era waned with the coming of the RAILWAYS, and as the network of rails spread roads were used only for local travel. Trunk roads deteriorated as maintenance expenditures were cut. With vast investments in railways, there was virtually no road building.

BC's first road, from Esquimalt to Victoria, was built (1854) by sailors of the Royal Navy. Four years later gold was discovered at Hope and hordes of prospectors poured through the Fraser and Thompson river valleys all the way to the Cariboo. A road was needed to serve the boom towns that had sprung up. Royal Engineers and private contractors, recruiting out-of-luck miners as their work force, drove the CARIBOO ROAD through in 3 years at a cost of $2 million. It was one of the wonders of its age, blasted out of mountainsides, crossing gorges on suspension bridges and hanging over precipices on timbered trestles.

Road development came more slowly to the Prairies. There was little need for roads at first; the early pioneers used Indian trails, and over these rumbled the RED RIVER CARTS and the settlers' covered wagons – "prairie schooners." Crossings at rivers were provided by fords or ferries. Most of the development of the Prairies took place through the railway, with roads providing local transportation.

The road system in the North-West Territories, which included present-day Alberta and Saskatchewan, was administered from Regina from the early 1880s until the provinces were formed in 1905. The development of natural resources spurred road construction, first in Manitoba and later in the newer provinces.

Transportation development of the North received great impetus from the building of the ALASKA HIGHWAY during WWII. Like early roads it was built for military reasons, but it provided an economic link between the YT and the Peace R country. The 614 km Mackenzie Highway began as a winter road in 1938 and was completed to Hay River on the shore of Great Slave Lk after WWII and to Yellowknife in 1961. The cost-sharing Roads to Resources Program, unveiled by the Diefenbaker government in 1958, was designed to exploit the resources of the North, and the volume of traffic has increased yearly as supplies, machinery and mining equipment are moved north and minerals, fish and furs south (*see* TRANSPORTATION IN THE NORTH). However, all provinces participated in the program. In some, particularly the Atlantic Provinces, the funds were spent on tourist development, eg, upgrading and paving Cape Breton's Cabot Trail. In 8 years, $145 million was spent on 6400 km of new "roads with a future," the Government of Canada sharing 50% of the cost.

Automobile The modern highway system dates from the introduction of the internal-combustion engine some 20 years after Confederation. In 1898 John Moodie of Hamilton brought a one-cylinder Winton "horseless carriage" from the US and 6 years later Canada's AUTOMOTIVE INDUSTRY was born – a Ford assembly plant in Windsor, Ont. In 1907 there were 2131 cars registered in Canada, and by the outbreak of WWI there were more than 50 000. Some efforts were made to improve inadequate roads and streets. In 1915 Ontario completed the construction, begun 5 years earlier, of a concrete highway from Toronto to Hamilton, the first in that province and one of the longest intercity concrete roads in the world. Canada's first provincial Dept of Highways had been created by Québec (1914). Two years later Ontario, which had had a provincial instructor in charge of roadmaking attached to the Dept of Agriculture since 1896, formed its separate highways department.

Through the 1920s cars became cheaper and their numbers multiplied; registration of motor vehicles increased from 408 790 to nearly 1.62 million by the end of the decade. Good roads associations, national and provincial, led the crusade for improved road travel, and expenditures on roads by all governments tripled. By 1930 the annual outlay was $94 million. Methods and technology for building roads improved as horse-drawn scrapers and graders gave way to steam power for shovels and rollers. However, road building in most provinces ceased and maintenance was reduced during the Great Depression and WWII as men and materials were urgently needed in the war effort. The few good paved roads that had been built were almost completely destroyed by heavy wartime traffic, particularly in industrial areas. The "Last Spike" of the Canadian Pacific Railway was driven in 1885, but 61 years passed before a motor vehicle was driven

Icefields Parkway, Banff National Park, Alberta (*photo by Bill Brooks/Masterfile*).

across Canada. Brigadier R.A. Macfarlane and Kenneth MacGillivray made the journey (1946) in 9 days from Louisbourg, Cape Breton, to Victoria, BC. This was 4 years before the TRANS-CANADA HIGHWAY was started.

Post-WWII Development Burgeoning road development in Canada and around the world left virtually no facet of economic or social life unchanged. With increasing efficiency and improving technology, road builders constructed highways and streets to accommodate automotive traffic. Expenditures soared from $103.5 million (1946) to $1.5 billion (1966) and to $4.5 billion (1986). Between 1946 and 1966 the number of motor vehicles increased from 1.6 million to 7 million; by 1985 there were 14.7 million. In 1946 there was 28 982 km of paved rural highways and some 10 000 km of paved urban roads and streets. By 1966, this total had risen to 148 987 km, nearly two-thirds of which were rural highways. By 1985 the total amount, paved and unpaved, was 841 411 km. These changes left a deep imprint on the Canadian landscape, ripping through the wilderness and transforming the urban environment with expressways, interchanges, and suburban sprawl, with ribbonlike development along the highways. Rural life was also transformed, as trucks delivered necessities; livestock, fruit, vegetables and other agricultural products were quickly conveyed to market (*see* TRUCKING INDUSTRY).

Engineering Early traffic laws were very simple, concerned mostly with the marking of roads in winter by evergreen branches set in the snow. Later, sleigh bells on harnesses were used to warn of approaching vehicles when visibility was poor. Canada made 2 early notable contributions to N American road transportation. Highway numbering was introduced (1920) in Manitoba, replacing the identifying coloured bands painted on telephone poles.

In Ontario an engineer experimented (1930) with dotted white lines down the centre of a road. Within 3 years they had become standard throughout the continent. Traffic engineers, experienced in planning and electronics, were eagerly sought by municipalities in the 1940s and 1950s to help untangle the traffic snarls. In 1956 the Canadian Good Roads Assn established a Council on Uniform Traffic Control Devices and 3 years later published the first manual of standard signs, signals and pavement markings. The asso-

ciation also launched a program of scholarships to help overcome the shortage of engineers qualified to use new techniques such as photogrammetry and computer programming. Postgraduate studies began in Canada as the University of Alberta offered the first degree in road engineering (1956).

Jurisdiction Under the CONSTITUTION ACT, 1867, the provinces were given almost complete responsibility for the building of roads. The federal government did not become involved until 1919 when the Canada Highways Act provided $20 million toward the cost of improving and building roads over a 5-year period. In 1985-86 the federal contribution was $235.6 million, less than 5% of a total road expenditure of $5.3 billion. In 1985-86 the provinces paid $5.2 billion, part of which came from municipalities. Revenues from users – provincial motor-fuel taxes, the federal excise tax on gasoline, vehicle and driver licence fees, street-parking revenue and fines – were never enough to cover expenditures. Large sums came from consolidated revenue with the logic that efficient highway transportation benefited the entire economy. Alberta was the first province to levy a gasoline tax (1922) of 2 cents a gallon.

In addition to its earlier large financial contributions to the Trans-Canada Highway and the Roads to Resources Program, the federal government is responsible for roads in the Yukon, NWT and national parks; and makes grants through the Department of Regional Economic Expansion and other projects.

Street systems in cities, towns and villages are the responsibility of the municipalities, though sometimes subsidized by the provinces. In the peak years of urban freeway development, the high costs frequently brought provincial and municipal governments together in cost-sharing agreements. Each year many kilometres of new roads are added to the highway system. The escalating costs of equipment, materials and manpower for replacement, repairs and maintenance of older roads mean higher budgets.

Canadians prize their mobility and, not content to store their cars in the winter as their grandfathers did, they demand all-weather roads. The cost of snow removal therefore adds millions of dollars to maintenance budgets. Canadians are among the most mobile people on Earth. In 1986 the odometers of their more than 14 million vehicles, including 11 million cars, 3 million trucks ("for hire" transporters and corporate fleets) and 53 000 buses, ran up more than 160 billion km of road travel. C.W. GILCHRIST

Roads and Transportation Association of Canada (RTAC) Founded (1914) as the Canadian Good Roads Assn, later incorporated by Act of Parliament, the association has had a strong influence on highway development and technology. One example is the TRANS-CANADA HIGHWAY, the culmination of many years of campaigning. In 1970 the name was changed to Roads and Transportation Assn because of its increasing involvement in other transportation modes. The association's members include the federal, all provincial and many municipal governments, carriers and suppliers of transportation goods and services, planners, builders and the academic community. CGRA organized Canada's first national conference (1955) on road safety, from which came the Canada Safety Council. In 1956 it established the Council on Uniform Traffic Control Devices and 3 years later published a manual of standard signs, signals and pavement markings. In 1963 it published a Manual of Geometric Design Standards for Canadian Roads and Streets. In 1987-88 RTAC was supporting 18 research or development projects, several conferences and 25 technical and 5 news publications. Since 1952 it has awarded almost $400 000 in scholarships for postgraduate studies in transportation sciences. A technical information resource centre maintains computer links with international data banks.

C.W. GILCHRIST

Robarts, John Parmenter, politician, premier of Ontario 1961-71 (b at Banff, Alta 11 Jan 1917; d at Toronto 18 Oct 1982). He moved to London, Ont, in 1931 and graduated from U of Western Ontario in 1939. After naval service in WWII, during which he was mentioned in dispatches, he completed law studies at Osgoode Hall. Returning to London, he was elected an alderman in 1950 and a Conservative MPP in 1951. He entered the Cabinet in 1958 and was appointed minister of education in 1959; on 8 Nov 1961 he was sworn in as premier. A staunch advocate of individual freedom, he also defended provincial rights from centralist initiatives of the federal government and Canada from separatist threats in Québec. He was thus placed in the middle of Canadian constitutional struggles. In 1967 he chaired the Confederation of Tomorrow Conference. On his retirement in 1971, he joined a number of boards of large corporations, served as chancellor of UWO and later of York U, chaired a royal commission on Metropolitan Toronto (1975-76) and cochaired with J.L. PEPIN the Task Force on CANADIAN UNITY (1977-79). In 1981 he suffered a series of strokes while travelling in the US. After a lengthy program of rehabilitation, he took his own life on 18 Oct 1982.

ALLAN K. MCDOUGALL

Reading: Allan K. McDougall, *John P. Robarts: His Life and Government* (1986); Jonathan Manthorpe, *The Power & the Tories* (1974).

Robb, Frank Morse, inventor, designer, business executive (b at Belleville, Ont 28 Jan 1902). After studying at McGill, Morse Robb set out in 1926 to develop a church organ with modest demands on space and upkeep. The following year he demonstrated a trial Wave Organ in Belleville, a trailblazing electronic instrument featuring 12 rotating shafts, one for each note in the chromatic scale, on which were mounted discs edged in the shape of photographed soundwaves. Patents were obtained in 1928 and later improvements were applied, including experiments with a touch-sensitive keyboard. At least 16 Robb Wave Organs were built, among them a 2-manual, 32-pedal note organ in 1934. Demonstrations were given at department stores and at a 1936 Toronto concert, and musicians and critics were warm in their praise. Attempts to fund commercial production failed, however, and the discouraged inventor gave up the project in 1938. He joined his brother's mechanical packing company in Montréal and invented devices for the packing of guns, later becoming VP of the company. He has won acclaim also as a designer of sterling silver articles. *See also* ELECTROACOUSTIC MUSIC.

HELMUT KALLMANN

Robbery is one of the earliest and most serious felonies and was once punishable by death. Robbery is a serious, indictable offence under the Canadian CRIMINAL CODE (s302), punishable by life imprisonment. Basically robbery consists of 2 elements: the theft or extortion of property, and the use of a weapon, violence or threats of violence. In order to constitute robbery, however, rather than the separate offences of theft and assault, these elements must be linked; either the element of violence must be used for the purpose of taking the victim's property, or the 2 elements must be proximate in time. Although neither physical harm to the victim nor actual use of a weapon is essential to the crime, these factors might be con-

sidered when imposing sentences. *See also* BURGLARY.

LEE PAIKIN

Robbins, John Everett, educator, diplomat (b at Hampton, Ont 9 Oct 1903). He taught school in Saskatchewan for 3 years before entering U of Man. He later gained a PhD from U of Ottawa. He served in the Educational Division, Dominion Bureau of Statistics, Ottawa 1930-52, becoming director in 1936. In 1952 he was appointed editor in chief of the new *Encyclopedia Canadiana* (1957), a 10-volume work whose publication he supervised. In 1960 he went to Brandon U as its president and in 1969 was appointed Canada's first ambassador to the Vatican. Robbins was active in founding and directing a number of national cultural and educational societies, such as the Canadian Assn for Adult Education, Canadian Library Assn, the Social Science and Humanities Research Councils and the Canadian Writers' Foundation.

D.M.L. FARR

Reading: J.A.B. McLeish, *A Canadian For All Seasons, the John E. Robbins Story* (1978).

Robert, Guy, writer, teacher, critic, publisher, poet (b at Ste-Agathe-des-Monts, Qué 7 Nov 1933). After studies at U de M and U de Paris he was among the first to teach the literature of art in Qué. Starting in the 1960s, he threw himself wholeheartedly into the QUIET REVOLUTION. He taught and gave conferences in various institutions in Qué, Ont, France and Venezuela. He founded the Montreal Museum of Contemporary Art (1964) and ran the international exhibition of modern sculpture at Expo 67. He is author of some 50 works and many articles, introductions, radio broadcasts and art films. He has published books on artists Pellan, Lemieux, Riopelle, Borduas and others, as well as poetry collections such as *Québec se meurt* (1969) and *Textures* (1976), studies such as *Poésie québécoise actuelle* (1970) and *Aspects de la littérature québécoise* (1970) and essays of aesthetic appreciation. Winner of the Grand prix littéraire de Montréal in 1976, he was a member of the FEDERAL CULTURAL POLICY REVIEW COMMITTEE.

MICHEL CHAMPAGNE

Roberts, Bartholomew, pirate (b in Pembrokeshire, Wales *c*1682; d 10 Feb 1722). Called "the Puritan pirate" because he forbade excessive immoral conduct on board his ships, he is believed to have captured more than 400 vessels. Having appeared off the coast of NS in June 1720, he made for Trepassey, Nfld, where in a predawn raid with a single ship he captured 22 vessels. He sacked the town and then sailed N along the shore, preying on shipping and settlements and recruiting men for his crew. After he quit Canadian waters he made for the African coast. He was killed in an engagement with a British ship off Cape Lopez; most of his surviving crewmen were executed or sentenced to slavery. His death marked the end of the "golden age" of PIRACY.

EDWARD BUTTS

Roberts, Sir Charles George Douglas, poet, animal-story writer (b at Douglas, NB 10 Jan 1860; d at Toronto 26 Nov 1943). As author of *Orion and Other Poems* (1880) Roberts inspired Bliss CARMAN (his cousin), Archibald LAMPMAN and D.C. SCOTT and became a prominent member of the so-called "poets of Confederation." At his death he was regarded as Canada's leading man of letters. The son of a clergyman, he was brought up in New Brunswick, near the Tantramar Marsh and in Fredericton. He attended UNB (1876-79), and then worked as a schoolteacher at Chatham and Fredericton (1879-83), as editor of *The Week* (1883-84) and as professor at King's College, Windsor, NS (1885-95).

His finest poetry was produced in these early years, appearing in *In Divers Tones* (1886) and

Songs of the Common Day (1893), and he was elected fellow of the Royal Society of Canada (1890). Financial pressure forced him to turn his main attention to fiction. Then, in 1897, he moved to New York and subsequently lived apart from his wife and family. He wrote a number of novels and historical romances, but his most successful prose genre was the animal story, in which he drew upon his early experience in the wilds of the Maritimes. He published over a dozen such volumes between *Earth's Enigmas* (1896) and *Eyes of the Wilderness* (1933). In 1907 he left for Europe, where he continued to write, though interrupted by service in WWI. His return to Canada in 1925 led to a renewed production of verse with *The Vagrant of Time* (1927) and *The Iceberg and Other Poems* (1934). Roberts was a popular figure at this time. He lectured throughout Canada and in 1935 was knighted.

Roberts is remembered for creating in the animal story, along with Ernest Thompson SETON, the one native Canadian art form. His early descriptive and meditative poetry ("Tantramar Revisited," "The Potato Harvest," "The Sower") recreates his Maritimes years with vivid sensitivity. Although he never fulfilled his early poetic promise, he laid a foundation for future achievements in Canadian verse.

W.J. KEITH

Reading: J.C. Adams, *Sir Charles God Damn: The Life of Sir Charles G.D. Roberts* (1986); W.J. Keith, ed, *Charles G.D. Roberts: Selected Poetry and Critical Prose* (1974); C.G.D. Roberts, *The Last Barrier, and Other Stories* (1958) and *King of Beasts, and Other Stories* (1967).

Roberts, William Goodridge, painter (b at Barbados, W Indies 24 Sept 1904; d at Montréal 28 Jan 1974), nephew of Sir C.G.D. ROBERTS. He trained at Montréal's École des beaux-arts 1923-25 and New York's Art Students League 1926-28, beginning a lifelong commitment to modernism. The first resident artist at Queen's U (1933-36), he then moved to Montréal, joining John LYMAN's Eastern Group and, in 1939, becoming a founding member of the CONTEMPORARY ARTS SOCIETY. He taught at the School of Art and Design 1930-49, except for service as a war artist 1943-45. By the early 1950s, he had national prominence through his participation in numerous Canadian and international exhibitions, and in 1952 was one of 4 artists in Canada's first official participation at the Venice Biennale. He became the first artist-in-residence at UNB in 1959. In 1969 he was given a retrospective exhibition by the National Gallery of Canada, then unusual for a living artist. Roberts was the first Canadian painter to treat landscape, the figure and still life with equal emphasis. Because of his empathy for his subjects, the power of his painting rests in the ambiguity between the real and the painted.

SANDRA PAIKOWSKY

Goodridge Roberts, *Reclining Nude* (1961), oil on masonite (*courtesy Beaverbrook Art Gallery/Gift of Mrs. Goodridge Roberts*).

Robertson, Bruce Richard, swimmer (b at Vancouver 27 Apr 1953). A specialist in the butterfly stroke, Robertson established himself as a world-class swimmer at the 1972 Munich Olympics, where he won the silver medal in the 100 m butterfly and swam on the 3rd-place Canadian 4 x 100 m medley relay team. His greatest achievement was winning the 100 m butterfly race at the World Aquatic Games in Belgrade (1973) – the first world championship swimming performance by a Canadian in over 60 years. Robertson also swam on the 3rd place 4 x 100 m medley relay team there. At the 1974 Commonwealth Games in New Zealand he won 2 gold, 2 silver and 2 bronze medals. In 1973 he was named male athlete of the year.

BARBARA SCHRODT

Robertson, James, Presbyterian minister (b at Dull, Scot 24 Apr 1839; d at Toronto 4 Jan 1902). Robertson emigrated to Woodstock, Canada W, in 1855 and after teaching school entered U of T, serving in its militia company at the Battle of RIDGEWAY (1866). Following theological studies at Princeton Seminary, he became a minister in rural Ontario in 1869. In 1874 he moved to Winnipeg and in 1881 was appointed superintendent of Presbyterian mission work in the North-West. Under Robertson, "the Presbyterian bishop," 4 congregations grew to 141, in addition to 226 missions serving 1130 points.   JOHN S. MOIR

Robertson, James Wilson, dairyman, educator (b at Dunlop, Scot 2 Nov 1857; d at Ottawa 20 Mar 1930). Robertson farmed in Ontario from 1875 to 1886, when he became professor of dairying at the Ontario Agricultural Coll. As the Dominion government's dairy commissioner 1890-1904, he was influential in developing the cheese industry, especially in eastern regions unable to produce wheat as cheaply as the new prairie farms. He became the first principal of the Macdonald Coll of Agriculture, affiliated with McGill, in 1905 and was chairman of the influential Royal Commission on Technical Education (1909-13). Robertson's later career is obscure. Although honoured for his cheese work with the CMG in 1905, he lost the Macdonald principalship in 1910. Except for postwar work in 1919 on food supplies for Europe, he held no university or governmental appointments after 1913.

DONALD J.C. PHILLIPSON

Robertson, John Ross, newspaper publisher, philanthropist (b at Toronto 28 Dec 1841; d there 31 May 1918). He was the son of a Scottish-born merchant. After attending Toronto's Upper Canada College, where he published a student paper, he founded the evening *Telegram*, which became the voice of working-class, conservative, Orange Toronto. Known as "the old lady of Melinda Street," it was the bitter rival of the Liberal *Toronto Star*. Robertson was a Tory maverick whose keen interest in local history led him to compile and publish the several volumes of *Landmarks of Toronto and Canada*. His own notable collection of Canadiana was left to the Toronto Public Library. Toronto's Hospital for Sick Children also benefited enormously from his wealth. The *Telegram* was continued by his heirs until sold in the 1930s. It ceased publication in 1971.

Reading: R. Poulton, *The Paper Tyrant* (1971).

Robertson, Norman Alexander, public servant, diplomat (b at Vancouver 4 Mar 1904; d at Ottawa 16 July 1968). Well educated at UBC, Oxford and the Brookings Inst, he joined the Dept of External Affairs in 1929. He drew the attention of PM KING and O.D. SKELTON when he worked out trade policies during the Depression, and in 1941 became undersecretary. Aided by Lester PEARSON and Hume WRONG, Robertson directed Canadian diplomacy during WWII along new and untried paths – with great success. His postwar service saw 2 terms as high commissioner in London (1946-49, 1952-57), where he dealt with financial problems and the SUEZ CRISIS, one year (1957-58) in Washington as ambassador, and a second term as undersecretary (1958-64), where his deeply held antinuclear convictions reinforced those of Howard Green, his minister, and helped bring about the collapse of the DIEFENBAKER government in 1963. In his last years he was a professor at Carleton.   J.L. GRANATSTEIN

Reading: J.L. Granatstein, *A Man of Influence* (1981).

Robertson, Robert Gordon, public servant (b in Davidson, Sask 19 May 1917). Gordon Robertson was educated at U of Sask, Oxford and U of T before joining the Dept of External Affairs in 1941. He worked in the Prime Minister's Office and subsequently as a member of the Cabinet secretariat before becoming deputy minister of northern affairs and national resources (1953-63). Promoted clerk of the Privy Council and Cabinet secretary (1963-75), Robertson was admired for his mental clarity and his efficiency; he was the most influential public servant of his day. He was secretary to the Cabinet for federal-provincial relations 1975-79, and participated in the constitutional review. After his retirement, he became president of the newly formed Institute for Research on Public Policy in Ottawa where since 1984 he has been fellow-in-residence. The Institute published his *Northern Provinces: A Mistaken Ideal* (1986).   ROBERT BOTHWELL

Robertson, Sarah Margaret Armour, painter (b at Montréal 16 June 1891; d there 6 Dec 1948). She was a member of the group of women painters who studied with William BRYMNER, Maurice CULLEN and Randolph Hewton, and she joined the Beaver Hall Hill group and later the Canadian Group of Painters. She painted landscape (the Laurentians and lower St Lawrence) and went on summer sketching trips with Prudence HEWARD and A.Y. JACKSON. She had a blithe personal vision, different from GROUP OF SEVEN patterns. Her choice of subject was often the convent spires or old Martello Towers of Montréal. In the mid-1920s her style hardened into tightly controlled composition, perhaps influenced by Lawren HARRIS, but by the 1930s she had found confidence and spontaneity in works such as *Coronation* (1937) and *Village Isle of Orleans* (1939).   ANNE McDOUGALL

Roberval, Qué, City, pop 11 448 (1986c), 11 429 (1981c), inc 1976, located on the SW shore of Lac SAINT-JEAN is the county seat for Lac St-Jean Ouest (1892) and headquarters for the judicial district of Roberval (1912). Named for France's lieutenant-general in Canada in the 16th century, Roberval was founded in 1855 and grew rapidly after 1888 when the Québec-Lac Saint-Jean railway company (amalgamated into the CNR in 1917) decided to make the town its Saint-Jean terminal. A navigation centre for the lake and an internationally renowned summer resort until the early 20th century, Roberval also had a few sawmills. The Ursulines built their provincial convent here in 1882. A hospital was added in 1918. Since then, Roberval has been the service centre of the area and since 1955 has yearly hosted the prestigious swim, the International Crossing of Lac Saint-Jean.   MARC ST-HILAIRE

Roberval, Jean-François de La Rocque, Sieur de, French lieutenant-general in Canada (b in France *c* 1500; d in Paris 1560). A courtier of noble descent, he received a royal commission as lieutenant-general of Canada 1541, despite being a Protestant convert. He was set in command over explorer Jacques CARTIER, who had already made 2 expeditions to Canada and who sailed again that May.

Roberval, delayed by shortage of funds and equipment, set out Apr 1542. By that time Cartier had decided to abandon his settlement at Charlesbourg-Royal [Cap-Rouge, Qué]. The 2 expeditions met in the harbour of St John's, Nfld, going in opposite directions. Roberval, with a party of around 200, reoccupied Cartier's settlement. The ensuing winter was disastrous, the colonists' morale being undermined by climate, disease and internal disputes. After some weeks exploring in the direction of HOCHELAGA [Montréal] during the summer of 1543, the surviving colonists abandoned the colony and returned to France. The expedition's failure ended any immediate prospect of colonization of Canada and brought Roberval financial ruin. He was killed with other Protestants in a Paris street affray at the start of the French Wars of Religion.   JOHN G. REID

Reading: H.P. Biggar, ed, *A Collection of Documents Relating to Jacques Cartier and the Sieur de Roberval* (1930); Marcel Trudel, *Histoire de la Nouvelle-France: Les vaines tentatives, 1524-1603* (1963).

Robichaud, Louis Joseph, lawyer, politician, premier of NB 1960-70, senator (b at St-Antoine, NB 21 Oct 1925). Educated at Sacré Coeur U and Laval, he practised law and was elected MLA for Kent County in 1952. Elected leader of the NB Liberal Party in 1958, he led it to victory over Hugh J. FLEMMING, 1960, and served as attorney general, 1960-65, and minister of youth, 1968. The first Acadian elected premier of NB (1960), he introduced far-reaching social reforms through the centralizing Programme of Equal Opportunity. His Liberal government modernized liquor laws, abolished the Hospital Premium Tax, passed an Official Languages Act, established U de Moncton, increased Acadian administrative influence, and encouraged the mining and forest industries. In 1970 the Liberals were defeated by Richard HATFIELD and Robichaud resigned as party leader and MLA in 1971 to become chairman of the Canadian section of the INTERNATIONAL JOINT COMMISSSION. In 1973 he was appointed to the Senate, where he continued to support bilingualism and national unity.

DELLA M.M. STANLEY

Robie, Simon Bradstreet, lawyer, politician, judge (b at Marblehead, Mass 1790; d at Halifax 3 Jan 1858). A Loyalist who moved from being a liberal to an extreme conservative, he was admitted to the bar in the early 1790s and elected to the assembly in 1799, where he generally joined William Cottnam TONGE and the "country party" in resisting authoritarian governor Sir John Wentworth. Appointed solicitor general in 1815 and elected assembly speaker in 1817, he earned the distaste of governor Lord Dalhousie, who described him as "an ill-tempered crab, deeply tinctured in Yankee principles." Following his appointment as councillor and master of the rolls in the mid-1820s, he continued to be liberal in his support of Presbyterian Pictou Academy, but politically he became more and more conservative, and more and more fearful of anything savouring of democracy. Blamed for the "abominable, heart-breaking, pocket-picking system" of the Chancery Court, he resigned as master of the rolls in 1834. Appointed president of the legislative council in 1838, he invariably followed Tory lines, especially in the protection of vested rights. Even after the Reformers' electoral victory in 1847, he sought, through the legislative council, to prevent the institutionalization of responsible government. Having failed, he resigned as councillor in 1848 and abandoned politics.

J. MURRAY BECK

Robin, American (*Turdus migratorius*), largest and best-known member of THRUSH family in Canada. It is widely distributed in Canada, the northern limit of its range being the treeline. It is migratory in most parts but may winter or attempt to winter in southern parts of most provinces. The American robin is a graceful, primarily terrestrial bird with a black head, black and white streaks on the throat, grey back, blackish tail and wings, reddish orange breast, and white abdomen. Sexes differ little in size (22-28 cm long). Males are more brightly coloured than females. Young have the same general appearance as adults but, like all thrushes, are heavily marked with conspicuous dark spots on underparts. The American robin is a good singer. It has adapted to humans in inhabited areas and is relatively tame; in remote areas, it avoids them. Nests are usually built a few metres from the ground in trees or bushes. The nest is a large structure of grass, twigs and small stems, crudely assembled around a cup of mud lined with finer grasses. The female incubates 4 bluish green eggs for 12-13 days; the male assists with feeding the young. Robins frequently have 2 broods in southern parts of Canadian range. They feed extensively on insects, insect larvae and earthworms but also consume fruits and berries in season and are considered pests in many areas. Robins have many natural enemies, eg, birds, snakes, predatory mammals (eg, domestic cats). The term robin also applies to several other thrushes not closely related to the American robin and to birds of other families.

HENRI OUELLET

Robinson, Clifford William, lawyer, businessman, premier of NB 1907-08 (b at Moncton, NB 1 Sept 1866; d at Montréal 27 July 1944). In 1897 Robinson was elected mayor of Moncton and a member of the provincial Assembly. After serving as Speaker of the House and provincial secretary he became premier in 1907. A year later his government was defeated. He served as minister without portfolio and minister of lands and mines in the provincial Liberal government from 1917 until 1924, when he was appointed to the Senate.

ARTHUR T. DOYLE

Robinson, Sir John Beverley, lawyer, politician, judge (b at Berthier, LC 26 July 1791; d at Toronto 31 Jan 1863). He was enrolled at the school of John STRACHAN and made a lifelong friend of the Tory Anglican cleric. Appointed acting attorney general in 1813, he became solicitor general after the war and left for England to finish his legal studies. When he returned, he was reappointed attorney general. In 1820 Robinson was elected to the Assembly; he was government spokesman until 1828. As a member of the FAMILY COMPACT, he was a staunch defender of the imperial connection, an established Church of England and a social hierarchy headed by a chosen elite. He incurred the wrath of reformers and opponents, such as Robert GOURLAY, whom he prosecuted, and he played a leading role in depriving American settlers of their property and political rights, defining them as "aliens." Nevertheless, Robinson promoted economic development and had an outstanding judicial career. He was appointed chief justice in 1829, Speaker of the Legislative Council and president of the Executive Council. After the trials of the Upper Canadian rebels, he had Samuel LOUNT and Peter MATTHEWS executed. Critical of Lord DURHAM's report, Robinson favoured union of all British N America. He had little political influence after 1841 because he was a judge and a Compact Tory. He was

knighted and then became a baronet (1854). After an outstanding judicial career, ill health forced him to retire from the bench in 1863.

DAVID MILLS

Robinson, Laurence Clark, Larry, hockey player (b at Winchester, Ont 2 June 1951). He was a first-round selection for the MONTREAL CANADIENS in the 1971 NHL draft and, after a year and a half in the American Hockey League, was called up to play on the Canadiens' 1973 STANLEY CUP winning team. The tall redhead became the anchor of a great defence corps, leading Montreal to 5 more Cups, 4 between 1976 and 1979 and a fifth in 1985-86. He has won the JAMES NORRIS MEMORIAL TROPHY (1977, 1980), the CONN SMYTHE TROPHY (1978) and 3 NHL all-star awards.

DEREK DRAGER

Robinson, Michael, artist (b at Timmins, Ont 27 Mar 1948). A self-taught artist with a lyrical and surreal style, Robinson is noted for his ink drawings and etchings. His concerns are the conservation of natural resources and revitalization of native cultural values. He is also a glassblower of considerable merit, having graduated from Sheridan College School of Design (Mississauga, Ont), and has received many awards at national and international exhibitions since 1970. He operates Two Rivers Studio in Keene, Ont.

MARY E. SOUTHCOTT

Robinson, Peter, merchant, developer, immigration superintendent (b in NB 1785; d at Toronto 8 July 1838). Until 1822 he was active in the development of Yonge St in the Newmarket and Holland Landing area. Linked with his brother, John Beverley ROBINSON, in the FAMILY COMPACT, he served in the Upper Canadian assembly (1817-24) and, as commissioner of crown lands, on the legislative and executive councils (1827-36). Robinson is best remembered as the founder of PETERBOROUGH, Ont, which took its name from him. He supervised 2 settlements of southern IRISH immigrants assisted by the Colonial Office, one based at Shipman's Mills [ALMONTE, Ont] in 1823, the other at Scott's Mills [Peterborough] in 1825. As commissioner of crown lands he employed land agents across the province. From 1829 to 1833, his agents, under the local authority of Sir John COLBORNE, assisted indigent immigrants to settle in townships in the Peterborough area, in Nottawasaga Bay, and in Adelaide and Warwick townships, W of London, Ont.

WENDY CAMERON

Roblin, Man, Town, pop 1011 (1986c), 1953 (1981c), inc 1913 (village), 1963 (town), is situated on Goose Lake 400 km NW of Winnipeg near the Man-Sask border. Cattle ranchers and grain farmers began settlement in the 1880s. CNR surveyors chose the townsite and lots were auctioned after the arrival of the first train from Dauphin, Man, in 1903. Initially called Goose Lake, the community was renamed after Man Prem Sir Rodmond Palen Roblin. Lumbering and dairy products were added to the early economy. In the 1920s, local farmers built one of Manitoba's first co-operative grain elevators, sparking an active co-operative movement in Roblin. Modest growth occurred until WWII when demand increased for lumber and pulp products from nearby Duck Mtn and other reserves. Today, Roblin's economic base includes services, tourism and processing of wood and agricultural products.

D. M. LYON

Roblin, Dufferin, businessman, politician, premier of Manitoba 1958-67 (b at Winnipeg 17 June 1917). After attending U Man and U of Chicago and wartime service in the RCAF, "Duff" Roblin first won election to the Manitoba legisla-

ture in 1949, as an Independent Conservative, for the riding of Winnipeg S. Grandson of Sir Rodmond P. ROBLIN, the province's vigorously partisan premier 1900-15, he challenged the avowedly nonpartisan government of Douglas CAMPBELL, and after extricating the Conservatives from the government coalition in 1951, won the party leadership in 1954 and defeated the Campbell government in 1958. The Roblin administration was one of the most active in Manitoba history, upgrading highways, creating provincial parks, building the Greater Winnipeg Floodway (derided at the time as "Duff's Ditch"), modernizing hospitals and welfare agencies, consolidating schools and expanding post-secondary facilities, restoring the use of French in education and initiating a shared-services program for private schools, promoting urban renewal, co-ordinating Winnipeg's municipalities with a metropolitan structure, launching northern power and mining projects, and establishing numerous agencies to assist private economic development. On this record, his government won re-election in 1959, 1962 and 1966. In Nov 1967 Roblin resigned as premier to contest the federal leadership of the PC Party, but lost to Robert STANFIELD. In the 1968 federal election he was defeated in Winnipeg S Centre, a casualty of "Trudeaumania." After a term as executive with Canadian Pacific Investments, he established a security firm in Winnipeg. In 1978 he was appointed to the Senate where he served on committees considering constitutional and Senate reform. On the latter, he proposed that the Senate be elected. In Sept 1984, Roblin was appointed to the MULRONEY Cabinet as government house leader in the Senate. He held this position until his voluntary resignation 30 June 1986. Roblin is significant as an exponent of classic conservatism, in the John A. MACDONALD tradition, advocating an active government role in social reform.

THOMAS PETERSON

Roblin, Sir Rodmond Palen, businessman, premier of Manitoba 1900-15 (b at Sophiasburg, Canada W 15 Feb 1853; d at Hot Springs, Ark 16 Feb 1937). Roblin, of Dutch Loyalist stock, completed his education at Albert Coll, Belleville, Ont. When he arrived in Winnipeg in late May 1877, he turned his hand to various business endeavours in Carman and in Winnipeg and to local politics. On his second attempt, he won election as an Independent MLA in 1888. The paramount issue of the day was the "monopoly clause" of the CPR charter that gave the railway a stranglehold on western transportation. Roblin, as a strong provincial rights advocate, gave his full support to the GREENWAY government's struggle to overturn the monopoly, but he was hostile to Greenway's scheme for bringing the Northern Pacific Ry into Manitoba without rate control and to his government's failure to forward the plan for a railway to Hudson Bay. With the sudden death of John NORQUAY, the Conservative leader, in July 1889, Roblin's prominent and effective opposition to Greenway's railway policy made him a popular choice as the new Conservative chief. In the dramatic session of 1890, Roblin denounced Greenway's repudiation of his government's recent guarantees to the Catholic minority not to disturb the language and school laws of the province. But Greenway weathered the storm and retained power for the rest of the decade.

After 10 years in and out of politics, Roblin succeeded Hugh John MACDONALD as premier in 1900. He assumed the portfolio of railways himself and made a startling agreement with the Canadian Northern whereby the railway completed an alternative route to the Lakehead and vested control of rates in the provincial government. Roblin always considered this his greatest achievement. Under Roblin the province bought out the Bell Telephone Co, created a successful government telephone system, and established the first effective public utilities commission in the nation. His attempt to institute a publicly owned system of grain elevators, in response to farmers' demands, was a disastrous failure, but his government did introduce a workmen's compensation law as well as corporation taxes.

The Roblin "machine," as it was called, played an important role in the federal RECIPROCITY election of 1911 that turned out the LAURIER Liberals. With Robert BORDEN's Conservatives in Ottawa, the boundaries of Manitoba were finally extended and the premier became Sir Rodmond, a not unconnected series of events.

While Roblin was not directly implicated in the scandal surrounding the building of the new legislature that brought down his government in 1915, he shared in the political odium and resigned to return to business.   J.E. REA

Reading: H.R. Ross, *Thirty-Five Years in the Limelight: Sir Rodmond P. Roblin and his Times* (1936); W.L. Morton, *Manitoba: A History* (1957, 2nd ed 1967); James A. Jackson, *The Centennial History of Manitoba* (1970).

Robotics

The word "robot," was first used by the Czechoslovak writer Karel Capek in 1920 in a play entitled *R.U.R. (Rossum's Universal Robots)*. In that play the mechanical automaton created by Rossum and his son to serve mankind went out of control with disastrous consequences. Modern industrial robots are much more helpful creations, responding tirelessly to sets of programmed instructions. The patent for the first industrial robot was granted in 1957 to English inventor Cyril Walter Kenward. In N America, Joseph Engelberger, for many years associated with Unimation, Inc, is widely regarded as the father of robotics. One of the first industrial robots to be placed in full operation anywhere in N America is reported to have been in a candy factory in Kitchener, Ont, *c*1961-64. By the end of 1985 the total number of industrial robots installed in Canada had risen to more than 1000. Approximately 63% of these are in major automotive firms, and each year since 1976 over 90% of robot installations in Canada have been located in Ontario. In spite of this substantial growth, the number of robots per manufacturing industry worker in Canada is reported to be less than in other industrial countries, and is declining relatively.

A widely used definition for a robot is "a reprogrammable, multifunctional manipulator designed to move material, parts, tools or specialized devices, through variable programmed motions for the performance of a variety of tasks." Canadian robotics research in universities, industry and government laboratories is highly regarded, although the groups and workers are often regarded as rather thinly spread. The world took notice in 1981, when the Shuttle Remote Manipulator System known as the CANADARM unfolded from the cargo bay of the space shuttle *Columbia*. New and more advanced forms are now being developed for the Mobile Servicing System (MSS), to be built by Canada as a contribution to the US Space Station, which will be constructed by the 1990s.

Research and development in robotics is in progress at many Canadian universities, the National Research Council and industrial companies. Areas of investigation include machine vision and other sensors, man-machine communication, manipulation, locomotion, actuators and industrial applications. The latter includes remotely operated undersea vehicles and "telerobotics," an appropriate term for manipulators or robots operated at a distance. The Canadian Institute for Applied Research (CIAR) provides

Robotic welding, General Motors of Canada. The automotive industry was one of the earliest to use robotics (*photo by Mike Dobel/Masterfile*).

special funds to support research and development in selected disciplines in Canadian universities. In many instances robots form part of a larger system and as such are frequently closely linked to the general subject of industrial automation. As a result, there are a number of instances in which environmental and application constraints will cause automation systems developed to appear quite different from the typical industrial robot of today. For example, a number of countries have investigated the possible use of robots in mines. By means of remote control, sensing and communications techniques the operator will, in the future, be able to direct all essential operations in greater comfort and safety from a cabin or control room environment.

Government financial support for robotics R&D in Canadian universities is provided to universities through the Natural Sciences and Engineering Research Council (NSERC), and to industrial companies through the Industrial Research Assistance Program (IRAP) of the National Research Council, or the Industrial Regional Development Program (IRDP) administered by the Federal Department of Regional Industrial Expansion (DRIE).

J. SCRIMGEOUR

Robson, John

journalist, politician, premier of BC 1889-92 (b at Perth, UC 14 or 15 Mar 1824; d at London, Eng 29 June 1892). Coming to BC in 1859, Robson established the New Westminster *British Columbian* in 1861. In 1869 he moved to Victoria and became editor of the *Daily British Colonist*, a position he held until becoming paymaster for CPR surveyors in 1875. Robson was an eloquent advocate of representative and RESPONSIBLE GOVERNMENT and of CONFEDERATION, joining his rival Amor DE COSMOS in the "Confederation League" in 1868. He served on the New Westminster Council (1863-67), in the Legislative Council of BC, and in the Legislative Assembly (1871-73, 1882-92). In 1883 he became provincial secretary and minister of finance and agriculture in the Cabinet of William SMITHE and, after the death of A.E.B. DAVIE in 1889, headed the government. His administration was noted for giving bonuses to railways, attempting to check undue exploitation of natural resources, redistributing legislative seats and promoting immigration. He died in office after injuring a finger in a carriage door and developing blood poisoning.

PATRICIA E. ROY

Robson, Mount

elev 3954 m, the highest mountain in the Canadian ROCKY MTS, is located 72 km NW of Jasper townsite, 10 km SW of the Continental Divide. There is much speculation about its name, but it was probably named originally after Colin Robertson, an officer of the HBC post at St Marys in the Peace R country. Its heavily glaciated northern slopes drop steeply to Berg Lk. A high escarpment of the S side falls off 2969 m to Kinney Lk. The highly prized first ascent was

claimed earlier, but the first complete ascent was made July 1913 by guide Conrad KAIN and W.W. FOSTER and A.H. MACCARTHY. Foster and Mac-Carthy both later climbed Mt LOGAN. The mountain is now climbed by several very challenging routes.   GLEN BOLES

Rockslide

a type of LANDSLIDE common on high, steep rock slopes, which occurs when a mass of rock moves quickly downslope. When the mass moves through the air, the movement is a rockfall. If the upper part of the mass initially rotates outwards, the movement is better described as toppling. Subsidence, downward movements of rock into closed depressions in the ground, may result from the collapse of natural underground openings called caves and is typical of KARST LANDFORMS. Sliding describes the motion of a mass that remains undeformed except along its base. In slides, a rupture surface separates the displaced mass of rock from the rock over which it moves. Numerous small falls from a cliff of hard rock produce a talus or scree, an accumulation of loosely packed rock fragments sloping outward from the cliff. Such a landform is sometimes popularly called a rockslide. This entry, however, concentrates on slope movements in rock.

Rock-slope movements occur in mountainous regions or where erosion or excavation has exposed the rock. They are known throughout the Canadian CORDILLERA and along rocky coastlines and in deeply cut river valleys in eastern Canada. Rockslides also occur in artificial excavations, in cuts for roads or excavations for mines and quarries. Movements can vary in size from the fall of a single block less than 1 m³ to slides of whole mountainsides involving many millions of cubic metres. Larger slides may travel kilometres in a few minutes; the FRANK SLIDE lasted about 100 seconds and transported some boulders 2 km. Such high velocities have caused catastrophic rockslides to be called rock AVALANCHES by analogy with the rapid downslope movements of snow AVALANCHES.

Natural weaknesses often control the shape and location of rockslides. Sedimentary rocks, such as those at Frank and at Brazeau Lk, have surfaces of weakness separating the layers of sediment (or beds) from which the rocks were formed. If the sedimentary rocks are later compressed and folded into mountain chains, the beds are tilted to steep angles. Valleys eroded through the mountains by rivers or glaciers may expose a surface of weakness sloping into the valley, and a typical Rocky Mt rockslide can then take place. COAL MINING at the base of Turtle Mt may also have contributed to the Frank Slide. A contemporary official report commented that, although destructive landslides were common in the Alps, they were very uncommon in the Canadian Rockies. This comment suggests that there may have been an artificial cause for the slide.

Recent research has mapped the debris of hundreds of rockslides, comparable in size to the Frank Slide, throughout the Cordillera. These prehistoric slides and those at Brazeau Lk, Hope and Rubble Creek clearly have natural causes.

Some Historic Rockslides in Canada			
Site	*Date*	*Volume (m³)*	*Damage*
Rubble Creek, BC	1855?	25 million	unknown
Frank, NWT [Alta]	29 Apr 1903	30 million	70 fatalities; half a town destroyed
Brazeau Lk, Alta	July 1933	5 million	telephone line damaged
Hope, BC	9 Jan 1965	47 million	4 fatalities; road buried

Processes that destroy cohesion or bonding across potential rupture surfaces can trigger rock-slope movements. For example, water infiltrating the rock mass may freeze and expand, lengthening natural cracks along the growing rupture surface. At Hope, shaking caused by an EARTHQUAKE may have triggered the slide. Rupture may have occurred at Rubble Creek when debris or freezing obstructed the large springs that at present flow from the scarp of the slide. In limestones, like those at Frank, karst processes are often active in dissolving rock along bedding planes, effectively removing the natural glue holding the rock mass together. A number of different processes may contribute to a single rock-slope movement.

Large rockslides rarely occur without such precursors as cracking of the ground at the crown of the slide, or bulging of the ground surface above the toe of the rupture surface. Surveying systems have been designed to monitor slopes so that work in any excavations around the gradually accelerating, displaced rock mass may continue until slope failure approaches. Movements can be reduced by decreasing gravitational forces disturbing the rock mass through off-loading the head of the slide or by draining water from it. Resistance to movement can be increased by loading the foot of the slide or by artificially reinforcing the rupture surface. Modern engineering practice can eliminate loss of life and movable property from rock-slope movements. D.M. CRUDEN

Rockwood, Man, Rural Municipality, pop 6923 (1986c), 6332 (1981c), area 1156 km², located N of Winnipeg; it includes the communities of Stony Mountain, Grosse Isle, Argyle, Balmoral, Gunton and Komarno. Stonewall and Teulon are separate corporate entities. Stony Mountain was a haven from RED RIVER floodwaters for early traders and later for Red River Colonists. Homesteading began in the 1860s; during the 1870s settlers included Ontarians, Americans, Red River colonists and British immigrants. Scandinavians settled at Norris Lk and Teulon; Ukrainians at Komarno. Mixed farming was the main activity, but several brickyards and quarries were established and crushed limestone from Stonewall quarries became a major industry. Agriculture also remains prominent today, and industries include a rocket plant near Stonewall and a federal fish hatchery/research station close to Balmoral. A federal prison has been at Stony Mountain since 1874. D.M. LYON

Rocky Mountain House, Alta, Town, pop 5182 (1986c), 5126 (1981c), inc 1939. Located on the N Saskatchewan R 80 km W of Red Deer, near the site of the North West Co's fur trade post of that name, it was built in 1799 to develop trade with the Kootenay and was the base from which David THOMPSON crossed the Rockies in 1807. From 1821 the Hudson's Bay Co operated Rocky Mountain House intermittently but abandoned it as unprofitable in 1875. Thirty years later, settlers began arriving mainly from central Canada, the US Midwest and the UK. Coal deposits at Nordegg, 85 km to the W, attracted 2 railways through Rocky Mountain House in 1912 and 1914. Oil, lumber, mixed farming, tourism and big-game hunting support a growing population. DOUGLAS BABCOCK

Rocky Mountain House National Historic Park, near ROCKY MOUNTAIN HOUSE, Alta, a HISTORIC SITE commemorating a series of FUR-TRADE posts built 1799-1864 by the NWC and the HBC near the junction of the Saskatchewan and Clearwater rivers. The posts were established to form a link between the eastern supply routes and the Pacific Slope fur trade, and it was intended that they would promote trading relations with the KOOTENAY of eastern BC. The posts were in the territory of the BLACKFOOT Confederacy, which opposed trade with the Kootenay, so they failed in their intended purpose. Instead, Rocky Mountain House became the centre for sporadic trade with the Blackfoot. Despite HBC attempts to close the post, Blackfoot pressure kept it in operation until 1875. Little remains except 2 restored chimneys from the last establishment. The site is being developed by Parks Canada, which maintains a small interpretation centre there. C.J. TAYLOR

Rocky Mountain Trench is a great valley extending 1400 km NW through BC from Montana to the Liard Plain just S of the Yukon Territory. Its floor is 3-20 km wide and 600-1000 m in elevation. The trench is mainly demarcated by the wall-like slopes of major mountain ranges – the ROCKY MTS on the E and the COLUMBIA, Omineca and CASSIAR mountains on the W. The northern half of the trench is very straight and trends more northerly than the southern half, which is slightly sinuous to arcuate. Prior to construction of hydroelectric dams in eastern BC and NW Montana, 7 major rivers occupied different parts of the trench. Now all but the Fraser and Kechika empty into reservoirs (eg, WILLISTON LK) covering large areas of the valley floor. The trench is bordered along much of its length by faults and is an ancient zone of crustal weakness, perhaps a former continental margin. Its present form is a product of faulting and of erosion and deposition by rivers and glaciers during the Cenozoic period.

The southern trench is an important transportation and communication corridor and a popular tourist and recreation area. Mining, forestry and agriculture are important sources of employment. Numerous towns and settlements dot the area, the largest being CRANBROOK, KIMBERLEY and GOLDEN. Archaeological surveys have shown that Indians have inhabited the trench for thousands of years. The first NWC explorers and trappers came into the region in the late 18th century, followed by settlers of European stock. The discovery of placer gold in the Kootenay Valley in 1864, the completion of the CPR main line (1885) and the opening of the Sullivan Mine at Kimberley (1910) helped spur population growth in the southern trench, as have recent economic diversification and improvements in the road system. The northern trench remains largely undeveloped and sparsely inhabited. JOHN J. CLAGUE

Rocky Mountains, the Canadian segment of N America's largest mountain system, are widely known for their vistas of spacious subalpine valleys and rugged, exposed rock faces. They extend 1200 km from the American borders of BC and Alberta to the LIARD R Basin, flanked on the W by a distinct trench and on the E by rolling foothills. The Canadian Rockies of song, film, painting and postcard, however, are in the main ranges, near the rail and highway routes through 2 mountain passes. These and other passes mark the southern boundary between BC and Alberta and mark the continental divide, where Pacific watersheds back onto Atlantic and arctic sources.

The human record in the Canadian Rockies is less than 4000 years old. Kootenai and Shuswap long travelled the southern passes to hunt on the prairies. European explorers approached by northern routes; Alexander MACKENZIE, the first (1973) to cross the Rockies, used the Peace R. On the same route, Simon FRASER established the first rocky mountain trading post at Hudson's Hope (1805). KICKING HORSE PASS was chosen in 1882 for the CPR link between the Prairies and coastal BC. Castlelike mountain resorts built on the rail line at BANFF (1888) and LAKE LOUISE, Alta, have become all-season recreation centres for BANFF NATIONAL PARK's many alpine attractions, which attract over 3 million visitors annually. Development of the YELLOWHEAD PASS area, SW of Edmonton, followed the same pattern, adding railway lines (1911, 1915), JASPER NATIONAL PARK (est 1907), the town of JASPER (1913) and a resort hotel. Four adjoining national parks (Banff, Jasper, Kootenay and Yoho) form the largest body of mountain parkland in the world. Throughout this area the Rockies form NW-trending waves of sedimentary rock uppiled by vast thrust faults in the Tertiary age (less than 66.4 million years ago) and eroded by glaciers, remnants of which remain. Magnificent mountain forms, commonly higher than 3050 m, include castellate, matterhorn, sawtooth and dipping strata peaks. The highest is Mt ROBSON, BC.

To the S, in the CROWSNEST PASS area of the border ranges, a CPR railway line built in 1898 opened Rocky Mt coal and minerals to underground mine development. Open-pit mines near SPARWOOD and Elkford, BC, have greatly expanded the area's coal production since the 1960s. The southern Alberta foothills of the Rockies has been a cattle RANCHING centre since the 1870s. Natural-gas drilling has progressed into foothill country in recent decades.

N of the Kakwa R, the Rockies are entirely in BC. They subside to modest heights (maximum 2542 m), with rounded, often timbered summits and little evidence of glaciation. The forest industry followed highway (1952) and railway (1958) construction NE from PRINCE GEORGE. Open-pit coal mines at Quintette and Bullmoose mountains in the BC foothills started in 1983. The higher Muskwa Ranges, N of the Peace R, are penetrated by the ALASKA HWY, but remain little developed. PETER GRANT

Reading: B. Gadd, *Handbook of the Canadian Rockies* (1986).

Roddick, Sir Thomas George, surgeon, medical administrator, politician (b at Harbour Grace, Nfld 31 July 1846; d at Montréal 20 Feb 1923). A McGill medical graduate, he introduced Joseph Lister's antiseptic system to Montréal in 1877, a system that greatly reduced infections after surgery. He was the first chief surgeon of the Royal Victoria Hospital in Montréal, professor of surgery and dean of medicine of McGill. His greatest achievement came in 1912 with the creation of the Medical Council of Canada which provided a system of common examinations throughout the provinces for those seeking a licence to practise medicine. This followed 18 years of patient and tireless effort, including 8 years as an MP (1896-1904). In recognition of this and other services, he was knighted in 1914. EDWARD BENSLEY

Rodentia, largest and most common order of mammals, including 34 families, 354 genera and 1685 species. In Canada, 68 of the 151 species of terrestrial mammals are rodents (including representatives of 10 families). They are characterized by having upper and lower incisors specialized for gnawing. These grow continuously from living pulp. Because the front surface, composed of enamel, is harder than the rear surface, the latter wears faster, creating a chisellike edge. As there are no canines, a large gap occurs between the incisors and the 2-5 cheek teeth. When the cheek teeth are in use, the incisors do not meet, and vice versa. Hence the jaw can crush food in a backward and forward, as well as a sideways motion. The hairy lips close in the gap behind the incisors, permitting some rodents to gnaw or excavate without filling the mouth with debris. Rodents are primarily herbivorous, eating parts of trees, grasses and herbaceous plants. Some (eg, red SQUIRRELS) are omnivorous, also eating animal matter, eg, insects. Rodents range in size from 10 g (olive-backed pocket mouse) to 35 kg (BEAVER).

Their broad spectrum of evolutionary adaptations allows rodents to occupy diverse habitats. Aquatic rodents (eg, beaver) have feet webbed for swimming. Saltatorial rodents (eg, jumping mice) have hindlimbs and tails elongated for rapid movement in open habitats. Fossorial or digging rodents (eg, pocket gophers) have forepaws modified for tunnelling in soil. Arboreal rodents, eg, squirrels, have hooked claws adapted to climbing. Gliding rodents, eg, flying squirrels, have a skin fold between forelimbs and hindlimbs that allows them to glide rapidly between trees. The behaviour patterns of rodents are equally diverse. Some species (eg, deer mice) are nocturnal, some (eg, most squirrels) are diurnal, and some (eg, LEMMINGS, VOLES) are active night and day. Some form large colonies (eg, black-tailed prairie dogs); others are solitary (eg, red squirrels). Some (eg, beavers) are monogamous; others (eg, Richardson's ground squirrels) are polygamous. To cope with the Canadian winter, many rodents (including chipmunks, ground squirrels, marmots, jumping mice) hibernate; others (eg, beavers, voles) remain active throughout the year. Reproductive behaviour depends largely on size. Small species tend to mature quickly, breed several times through the year, produce large litters, and live less than one year. Larger rodents show the opposite trends and generally live longer than one year.

Humans derive direct benefit from fur-bearing rodents (eg, beavers, which also check stream erosion by their dams) and from domesticated RATS and mice used for biological research. Indirect benefit is obtained from species that serve as food for game and fur mammals. However, rodents also compete with man for resources. Some, eg, meadow voles, may injure or kill shrubs and trees by girdling (chewing a ring around the bark). Some, especially the introduced brown rat and house mouse, may consume standing or stored grain crops. Rodents may also be carriers of human diseases, eg, bubonic plague, tularemia and scrub typhus. *See also* individual species entries. R. BOONSTRA

Reading: P.W. Hanney, *Rodents: Their Lives and Habits* (1975).

Rodeo means roundup, or the gathering of livestock (usually cattle or horses) to be counted, inspected and branded; as a sport it refers to the public spectacle in which the dynamic elements of a roundup are presented as a cowboy competition: bronc riding, bull riding, steer wrestling, calf and steer roping (with more recent additions such as barrel racing, chuckwagon racing and wild-cow milking), as seen in such annual events as the CALGARY STAMPEDE. The name originates in the Spanish verb *rodear,* "to go around," or the Latin verb *rotare,* "to turn." Currently drawing spectators to cowboy contests coast to coast, rodeo is generally associated with life "in the West," the first major official Canadian rodeo being assembled 2 Sept 1912, as "The Last and Best Great West Frontier Days Celebration," at Calgary. Rodeo in N America owes its origin to a variety of historical traditions and entertainment forms. In the 16th century, *vaqueros,* Mexican herdsmen, used *la reata* (rope), clothed themselves in *chaperajos* (leggings) and tended hardy Spanish cattle from the backs of wiry N African riding stock. The 1847 diaries of travelling Irish military captain Mayne Reid provide perhaps the earliest rodeo documentation of *vaqueros* roping and throwing steers in the streets of Santa Fe, New Mexico Territory. These fiesta antics, transposed to cattle-driving communities such as Cheyenne (Wyoming Territory), Pecos City (Texas) and the pre-1900 ranches of what later became Alberta, fostered rodeo in its purest form.

In the Canadian West, broncobusting was considered sport at the Military Colonization Company ranch, and rope-throwing competitions

St Albert Rainmaker Rodeo 17 June 1974 (*courtesy Provincial Archives of Alberta/Edmonton Journal Coll/ J1335/2*).

were commonplace at the Fort Macleod Agricultural Fair in the 1880s. At the Walrond corral, John Ware is credited with some of the earliest exhibits of steer wrestling in 1892. The first Canadian rodeo was held in Raymond, Alta, in 1903. But it was not until the American show-business phenomenon of the "Wild West Show" came to Canada in the early 1900s that spectators paid to see cowboy stunts. Former American cowpuncher Guy Weadick is responsible for promoting Wild West Shows in Canada, and in 1908 took his idea for an annual frontier day celebration, "pioneer reunion" and cowboy competition for world championship titles to Calgary. With help from local politicians and businessmen, Weadick amassed over $100 000 for the first Calgary Stampede in 1912. It was a 6-day pageant and rodeo attracting more than 40 000 spectators a day, as well as legendary cowboys of the day – including some of Pancho Villa's bandits – in pursuit of $20 000 in prizes and world titles. WWI stalled the momentum of rodeo competition, but the Victory Stampede at Calgary (1919) revived cowboy contests in Canada permanently. Rodeo became an annual international event at Calgary in 1923 combined with an exhibition.

Rodeo's popularity sparked the growth of rodeo organizations in the 1930s, first with the Rodeo Assn of America (which represented primarily rodeo managers). In 1936, at an RAA rodeo in the Boston Gardens, Canadian and American cowboys broke the stranglehold that circuit managers had on rodeo purses when they staged a boycott; rodeo's first strike by professional cowboys succeeded in winning for competitors a greater percentage of the gate and precipitated the formation of the Professional Rodeo Cowboys' Assn in the US and the Canadian Rodeo Cowboys' Assn, founded 1944.

Despite periodic incursions to rearrange rodeo competition along team-sport lines, the basic premise of individual human strength and precision against animal and clock has remained. Bull riding, pitting a rider's balance and stability against a one-ton Brahma bull's instinct to remove the cowboy from its back, officially entered rodeo competition in 1921. Saddle-bronc riding dates back to a time when the livelihood of some working cowboys was broncobusting. Bareback riding began as a sideshow in rodeo, when younger cowboys earned mount money in exhibition rides aboard particularly ornery unbroken horses; the 1950s saw bareback riding gain the legitimacy of the other 2 riding events. Calf roping is one rodeo event still practised on the ranch, but in the artificial setting of the rodeo arena it reaches near perfection; when a barrier in front of a

horse and rider is released by a bolting calf, the contestant runs down the calf, throws it to the ground and ties any 3 feet; fastest time wins. The other timed rodeo event, steer wrestling (originally known as bulldogging), moved from the Wild West Shows to the first rodeos as a cowboy's test of strength in bringing down a running steer by leaping from a moving horse, locking onto the steer's horns and twisting it to the ground; in the earliest rodeos, the bulldogger had to finish the maneuvre by taking the steer's lower lip in his own teeth. While world-championship titles in early rodeo were usually awarded to the winners of year-end competitions, such as the Pendleton Roundup in Oregon, the Cheyenne Frontier Days in Wyoming or the Calgary Stampede in Alberta, championships are currently determined by a cowboy's prize-money accumulation at season's end; that is, at the National Finals Rodeo in Oklahoma City or the Canadian Finals Rodeo in Edmonton. Among Canadians who have achieved international success as world champions in rodeo are Pete Knight (Crossfield, Alta), 4-time saddle bronc champ between 1932 and 1936; Nate Waldrum (Strathmore, Alta), bareback champ in 1933; Carl Olson (Calgary, Alta), saddle bronc champ in 1947; Marty Wood (Bowness, Alta), saddle bronc champ in 1958, 1964 and 1966; Winston Bruce (Calgary, Alta), saddle bronc champ in 1961; Kenny McLean (Okanagan Falls, BC), saddle bronc champ in 1962; Mel Hyland (Surrey, BC), saddle bronc champ in 1972; Jim Gladstone (Cardston, Alta), calf roping champ in 1977; and Cody Snyder (Redcliff, Alta), first Canadian to win the world bullriding championship in 1983. TED BARRIS

Reading: Ted Barris, *Rodeo Cowboys: The Last Heroes* (1981); B. Berry, *Let 'Er Buck! The Rodeo* (1971); C. Eamer and T. Jones, *The Canadian Rodeo Book* (1982); D.K. Hall, *Rodeo* (1976); B. St. John, *On Down the Road* (1977).

Rogers, Albert Bowman, railway surveyor, engineer (b at Orleans, Mass 28 May 1829; d at Waterville, Mass 4 May 1889). Discoverer and Explorer of KICKING HORSE PASS and discoverer of ROGERS PASS through the Rocky and Selkirk mountain ranges in BC, he surveyed the route along which the CPR line was built through these passes in the 1880s. Rogers was a graduate of Yale U and did location work for the Chicago, Milwaukee and St Paul Railroad. He was hired in 1881 to do the mountain location work for the CPR. After completing his work in Canada, he did further work as a locating engineer for the Great Northern Railroad. Suffering a serious injury in 1887, he eventually died of cancer. T.D. REGEHR

Rogers, Edward Samuel, inventor, broadcasting pioneer (b at Toronto 21 June 1900; d there 6 May 1939). Son of a wealthy businessman, Rogers was obsessed with radio from childhood. At 13 he won a prize for the best amateur-built radio in Ontario, and in 1921 was the only Canadian to win an American competition for low-power broadcasts across the Atlantic. His alternating-current radio tube, perfected in 1925, revolutionized the home radio-receiver industry throughout the world. Before Rogers, home receivers had to run on direct current from rechargeable acid-filled batteries: the 25- or 60-cycle hum of alternating-current mains electricity was often louder than radio signals. Rogers's amplifying tube eliminated this problem, making mains-powered home radios practical for the first time. With his father, he founded the Rogers Majestic manufacturing company and established several broadcasting companies, including station 9RB (later CFRB, Toronto) named for the "Rogers Batteryless" system. His son **Edward Samuel** (b at Toronto 27 May 1933) heads ROGERS TELECOMMUNICATIONS LIMITED.

DONALD J.C. PHILLIPSON

Rogers, Norman McLeod, scholar, politician (b at Amherst, NS 25 July 1894; d at Newtonville, Ont 10 June 1940). Educated at Acadia and Oxford, Rogers interrupted his studies to serve in WWI. He was professor of history at Acadia, 1922-27, private secretary to PM KING, 1927-29. Although a professor of political science at Queen's, 1929-35, Rogers kept his connections with King, authoring a campaign biography, *Mackenzie King* (1935). Elected to Parliament for Kingston, Ont, in 1935, he became minister of labour and the leading progressive liberal in the Cabinet. Appointed minister of national defence in 1939, he died the next year in a plane crash.
ROBERT BOTHWELL

Rogers, Otto Donald, painter, sculptor (b at Kerrobert, Sask 19 Nov 1935). One of Canada's foremost contemporary practitioners of colour-field painting and constructivist steel sculpture, Rogers was encouraged to pursue an artistic career by Wynona Mulcaster while attending Saskatoon Teachers' Coll (1952-53). He attended U of Wisconsin (1953-59). Since 1959 he has taught at U Sask, serving as chairman of the art department 1973-77. In 1960 Rogers adopted the BAHA'I FAITH. Since then he has lectured and written extensively on this religion, emphasizing its importance to his art. While recognizing the spiritual element in his art, some critics claim that the prairie environment is equally important in his work.
NORMAN ZEPP

Rogers, Robert, author, army officer (b at Methuen, Mass 8 Nov 1731; d at London, Eng 18 May 1795). A versatile frontiersman, Rogers ably led colonial Rangers during King George's War (1744-48; *see* WAR OF THE AUSTRIAN SUCCESSION) and the SEVEN YEARS' WAR, but he had a knack for getting into trouble through prodigal spending habits, drinking and gambling. He was tried by court-martial but acquitted at Montréal in 1768 for alleged treason and overspending. During the AMERICAN REVOLUTION, Rogers raised and commanded the LOYALIST Queen's (later King's) Rangers. His most significant achievements are literary. While in London in 1765 he published his wartime *Journals,* and *A Concise Account of North America. Ponteach, or, The Savages of America,* a critical portrayal of British colonists' exploitation of Indians, was published in London in 1766.
ROTA HERZBERG LISTER

Reading: J.R. Cuneo, *Robert Rogers of the Rangers* (1959).

Rogers, Stan, singer, songwriter (b at Hamilton, Ont 29 Nov 1949; d in a fire on an Air Canada plane in the Cincinnati, Ohio, airport 2 June 1983). By the time of his death at the age of 33, Rogers had established himself as one of Canada's most talented singer-songwriters. His genre was folk music with a distinctive Canadian flavour. He recorded 6 albums during his short career: *Fogarty's Cove, Turnaround, Between the Breaks, Northwest Passage* and 2 – *From Fresh Water* and *For the Family* – that were released posthumously. Gifted with a fine, resonant voice, Rogers wrote songs with beautiful melodies and sensitive, richly poetic lyrics. Many of his songs deal with Canada's history and all display a deep empathy for the lives of ordinary people, from NS fishermen to merchant seamen on the Great Lakes. Not a few of them, eg, "Barrett's Privateers," "Make and Break Harbour," "The Mary Ellen Carter," "Northwest Passage" and others, seem destined to stand as classics.
CURTIS FAHEY

Rogers Pass, elev 1323 m, in BC's Selkirk Mts, was named for A.B. ROGERS, hired by the CANADIAN PACIFIC RY to find a route through this range. Rogers found the pass from the W via the S fork of the Illecillewaet R 28 May 1881. The following

Avalanche sheds, Rogers Pass, BC (*photo by J.A. Kraulis/ Masterfile*).

year, on July 24, Rogers again reached the pass, this time from the E to satisfy his employers that the Selkirks could be breached by the pass. During the summer of 1885 the railway was constructed over the pass at great expense. Over 6.4 km of snowsheds (31) were built to protect trains, trackage and workmen from AVALANCHES (the area receives up to 15 m of snow each winter). The CPR soon after built Glacier House, a world-renowned hostelry just W of the pass. After much damage and loss of life from avalanches, the 8 km Connaught Tunnel was pushed through below the pass (1916). A 14.66 km tunnel is now being constructed by the CPR beneath the pass to cut down track grades for westbound trains. It is slated for completion Dec 1988. The all-weather TRANS-CANADA HWY opened over the pass 1962. An extensive avalanche safety program is carried out in the pass area.
GLEN BOLES

Rogers Telecommunications Limited, controlled by the Edward S. ROGERS family, is one of the world's largest CABLE-TELEVISION holding companies, with subsidiary interests in radio broadcasting and entertainment services. Rogers Communications Inc, controlled by RTL, operates several cable-television systems in Canada (1 417 861 subscribers in 1986) and the US (547 241) and in Canada and the US provides a variety of services including special programming, interactive television, and PAY-TELEVISION services. Its principal Canadian operations are located in Vancouver, Victoria, Calgary, Toronto and southern Ontario. RTL's other holdings include CFTR-AM and CHFI-FM in Toronto and stations in Sarnia and Leamington, Ont, and CFMT-TV also in Toronto. In 1986 Rogers gained control of Cantel Inc, Canada's only national cellular telephone company. Total assets for Rogers Communications were $1.1 billion in 1986, with revenues of $411 million.
PETER S. ANDERSON

Rohmer, Richard, maj-gen (retired), lawyer, writer (b at Hamilton, Ont 24 Jan 1924). The official honours bestowed upon Rohmer, including DFC (1945), QC (1961), LLD (U of Windsor, 1975) and CMM (1979), attest to the public contributions he has made as a fighter pilot with the RCAF (1942-45), as chairman of the Royal Commission on Publishing (Ont, 1970-72) and as

counsel, principally in transportation, land use and municipal law. Originator of the concept of the "Mid-Canada Corridor" and the U of Canada North, he presented these ideas concerning the development of the North in *The Green North: Mid-Canada* (1970) and expanded on them in *The Arctic Imperative* (1973). Other publications include 10 works of fiction, of which the first, *Ultimatum* (1973), that year's best-selling novel, is typical in being a tract for the times played out against a backdrop of technical data. In 1986 he published *Rommell and Patton* and *Starmageddon.* He is chancellor of U of Windsor.
MARYLYNN SCOTT

Roller Skating is a sport with a wide range of recreational and competitive aspects. Artistic competition is closely related to ICE SKATING and includes figures, freestyle, pairs and dance events. Speed skating includes both individual and relay races. Roller hockey started as roller polo in the 1880s and is now played with a ball or puck; ball hockey is organized as an international roller sport. The use of plastic urethane wheels and sealed precision bearings, both adapted from skateboards, produced a skate that gives a smooth ride on outdoor surfaces and stimulated the roller-skating boom of the 1970s.

The roller skate was developed in Holland in the 18th century, with wooden spools attached to strips of wood. Today's 4-wheel arrangement was satisfactorily produced in 1863. Roller-skating facilities were built in the 1880s in Toronto and Montréal. In 1884, skating started in Chatham, Ont, which within a year had become one of the foremost roller-skating centres in the world. Speed skater George Berry, of Chatham, became the Canadian roller-skating champion in 1884 and in the next year won the N American championship and was acclaimed world champion. WWI signalled the end of competitive skating, but a revival in the 1930s stimulated events such as the 5-day roller-skating derby held at the CANADIAN NATIONAL EXHIBITION in 1940. The Canadian Roller Skating Assn was formed in 1961 and became the Canadian Federation of Amateur Roller Skaters in 1973. Canada sent a team to the World Artistic Roller Skating Championships for the first time in 1976, placing 5th among 19 countries. In 1979, these championships were held in Montréal. The CFARS organizes national championships in figures, freestyle and overall categories, at 3 levels for boys and girls and 6 for men and women. In the 1987 Pan-American Games, at which roller skating was introduced, the Canadian team won a bronze medal in the dance event.
BARBARA SCHRODT

Rolph, John, barrister, physician, politician, educator (b at Thornbury, Eng 4 Mar 1793; d at Mitchell, Ont 19 Oct 1870). Educated in England, he practised law and medicine in Upper Canada from 1821, operating medical schools in 1824-25 in St Thomas and from 1832 in York [Toronto]. By 1828 he shared leadership of the REFORM MOVEMENT with M.S. BIDWELL and the BALDWINS. A secretive, 11th-hour supporter of William Lyon MACKENZIE's ill-fated REBELLION OF 1837, he fled to Rochester, NY. He returned in 1843 to reopen his medical school, which soon flourished. An ineffectual member of the Hincks-Morin ministry, 1851-54, he severely disappointed his ultra-reform (CLEAR GRIT) supporters. Thereafter, he concentrated on running his school. By eloquently defending American settlers' rights and opposing special privileges for the Church of England, Rolph contributed greatly to the rising popularity of the constitutional reform movement before 1837 and did more than anyone before the 1860s to provide first-class medical training in the province.
DAVID R. KEANE

Romaine, Rivière, 496 km long with a 14 349 km² basin, rises (elev 760 m) in the Québec-Labrador lacustrine plateau, 45 km SW of the CHURCHILL R, and forms part of the Québec-Labrador boundary N of the 52nd parallel. Near its head, it crosses Lac Brûlé. The Montagnais frequently used it in their annual migrations to the Labrador coast, for there are only 15 km of lakes and portages before it joins the Churchill Basin. The river's last 35 km flow through a vast postglacial delta, on the shores of which sits Havre-Saint-Pierre (pop 3344, 1986c), terminus of Hwy 138 and of the 40 km railway that joins Québec Iron and Titanium on Lac Allard with the coast. Hydro-Québec sees great hydroelectric power potential on this river. "Romaine" is a French deformation of the Montagnais word *uramen,* which means "red ochre." JEAN-MARIE DUBOIS

Roman, Stephen Boleslav, mine executive (b at Velky Ruskov, Slovakia 17 Apr 1921). Roman immigrated to Canada in 1937, working as a farm labourer before joining the Canadian Army in 1942. Discharged in 1943, he became interested in the stock market, organized several natural-resources ventures, and in 1953 acquired an interest in a uranium prospect that formed the basis of Denison Mines Ltd. As president and later chairman of Denison, Roman expanded and diversified his firm and was periodically involved in controversies on nuclear politics and FOREIGN INVESTMENT. An outspoken advocate of private enterprise, Roman sued PM TRUDEAU and Energy Minister J.J. Greene because Ottawa tried to block the sale of Denison shares to an American-controlled firm. Roman was twice unsuccessful as a federal PC candidate. With Eugen Loebl he wrote *The Responsible Society* (1977). He was made Officer of the Order of Canada in 1987.
J. LINDSEY

Roman Catholic Church, *see* CATHOLICISM.

Romanians In 1878 Romanian independence from the Ottoman Empire was recognized. Many Romanians were living in provinces (Transylvania and Bukovina) then part of the Austro-Hungarian Empire, and it was from these provinces, particularly the latter, that many Romanians immigrated to Canada, although they had been preceded by individual priests from Bucharest sent to the early settlements of Canada. They were motivated by a wish to escape living under a foreign government, a desire to own land, and general economic conditions. Most of the early immigrants were peasants and by 1895 they were arriving by the thousands. By 1914 there were 8301 Romanians in Canada; in 1921 the number was 13 470, though these figures are tentative since many emigrated from regions which were not part of Romania until 1918, and others came from Hungary, Austria and Russia.

Early settlements were founded at Regina, Limerick, Dysart, Kayville, Flintoft and Canora (Sask); Inglis (Man); and Boian (Alta). Because French has traditionally been the second language of Romania, many Romanians were attracted to Québec where they established themselves in Montréal. Between 1921 and 1929, many new immigrants arrived to join relatives and friends, so by 1931 there were some 29 000 Romanian Canadians. After WWII a significant number of Romanians immigrated to Canada, mainly professionals who settled in cities. Preliminary estimates from the 1986 census indicate that there are 18 745 people of Romanian origin in Canada.

Most Romanians belong to the Romanian ORTHODOX CHURCH (the first such church in N America was the Church of St Nicholas, built in Regina in 1901). Many parishes are attached to a youth group which is a branch of American Romanian Orthodox youth. Mutual benefit and cultural organizations have existed at some time in most communities, many being part of an American organization – the Union and League of Romanian Societies of America. Two Romanian-language newspapers are published in Canada: *Ecouri Romanesti (Romanian Echoes)* and *Curantul Romanesc (The Romanian Voice).* Lively homeland religious and social events center around rural churches. Ethnic consciousness has decreased considerably among descendants of the early immigrants, accelerated by the high educational level and wide dispersal of the post-WWII immigrants. Fewer than 30% of Romanian Canadians now speak Romanian.
G. JAMES PATTERSON

Reading: G. James Patterson, *The Romanians of Saskatchewan* (1977).

Romanoff, Ivan, conductor, violinist (b at Toronto 8 Mar 1914). Known for his Ukrainian-music CBC series, he formed the Ivan Romanoff Orchestra and Chorus in Toronto for radio work in 1953, after having spent 20 years as a classical violinist. Romanoff's radio series ("Songs of My People," "Continental Holiday," etc) continued until 1976.
MARK MILLER

Romanow, Roy John, politician (b 1939). Very successful as a Saskatchewan politician, Romanow has risen despite his penchant for keeping even the most mundane items of his career secret. Reluctant to reveal his age or birthplace, Romanow was educated at U of Saskatchewan where he received his BA and LLB. He was elected as an NDP member for Saskatoon-Riversdale in 1967 and was an unsuccessful candidate for the party leadership in 1970. Romanow became provincial secretary (1971-72) and attorney general in the Allan BLAKENEY government in 1971. In 1979 he added the portfolio of intergovernmental affairs and played a major role in the federal-provincial negotiations that preceded the patriation of the constitution. Romanow's close relationships with both Jean Chrétien and Ontario attorney general Roy McMurtry were instrumental in working out the final package. Although defeated in the provincial election of 1982, Romanow was re-elected in 1986. He succeeded Blakeney as NDP leader in Nov 1987.
J. L. GRANATSTEIN

Ronald, William, né Smith, painter (b at Stratford, Ont 13 Aug 1926). Ronald's abstract expressionism influenced an era in Canadian art; he was the catalyst who organized PAINTERS ELEVEN, the first abstract PAINTING group in Ontario, in 1953. His gift lies in his work's spontaneity, dynamism and energy and in his natural talent for handling paint. After studies at the Ontario Coll of Art with Jock MACDONALD, Ronald went to New York in 1952 where he briefly attended Hans Hofmann's School. In the mid-1950s, after travelling frequently between Toronto and New York, he moved to New York. He was influenced by the fragmentary, explosive painting of Willem de Kooning, but by contrast created large central images with a background horizon line, painted in a savage technique. In 1957 he had his first exhibition in the Samuel Kootz Gallery with whom he remained until 1963. In the mid-1960s he returned to Canada. Because of a 1967 mural commission at the NATIONAL ARTS CENTRE in Ottawa, Ronald's style evolved into a more hard-edged format prophetic of the 1970s in Canadian art. Through the years he has maintained his interest in automatic painting using a vocabulary of symbols, often central images, that interest him. He has also had a career as a broadcaster; he was host for the CBC radio program *As it Happens* (1969-72) and of a TV variety show about the

Pierre Elliott Trudeau (1982) by William Ronald, from his prime minister series (*courtesy of the artist/photo by Jim Chalmers*).

arts, *The Umbrella* (1966-67). His recent work includes a series of abstract paintings of the prime ministers.
JOAN MURRAY

Roncarelli v Duplessis In 1946, Maurice DUPLESSIS, then premier and attorney general of Qué, caused the Liquor Commission chairman to revoke the liquor licence of Frank Roncarelli, a Montréal restaurant owner, so ruining the restaurant. Roncarelli was innocent of all misconduct, but the authorities thought him troublesome because he (legitimately) provided bail for many JEHOVAH'S WITNESSES charged (groundlessly, as the Supreme Court later held) with supposed offences resulting from the distribution of religious pamphlets attacking Roman Catholicism (*see* SAUMUR V CITY OF QUÉBEC). The Supreme Court (1959) held that the premier had committed a civil wrong and ordered him personally to pay damages.
STEPHEN A. SCOTT

Rondeau Provincial Park (est 1894, 48 km²) provides environmental protection and recreation on one of 3 peninsulas jutting S into Lk ERIE. It lies 120 km E of Windsor and 115 km SW of London. The peninsula was formed in late geological time by currents in Glacial Lk Erie that converged and deposited sediment that accumulated in a succession of sandbars. The processes continue and the cuspate sandspit is continually changing in size and shape. It has been colonized successively by grasses, oaks and white pines and, finally, by some shade-tolerant species (eg, sugar maple, American beech). In addition, plants such as tulip and sassafras, normally occurring much farther S, are found, as are some 125 herbaceous plants considered rare in Ontario (eg, species normally associated with tall-grass prairie). Eighteen species of orchids flourish in Rondeau. Over 30 mammal species have been observed in the park and amphibians and reptiles (eg, turtles, toads, fox snakes) are well represented. Rondeau is renowned for bird life: 323 species have been recorded; 124 have nested in the park and 80% of all species found in Ontario have been seen here, including the rare prothonotary warbler.

The NEUTRAL exploited the area's fish, game and

plant resources. The English recognized the timber and harbour potential, bought the land and, in 1795, declared it Ordnance Land, reserved for government purposes. Thereafter, it was used for naval purposes, exploited for timber, waterfowl, fur bearers and fish and, in the late 1800s, developed for hotels and tourism. In 1894 it became Ontario's third provincial park.   JOHN S. MARSH

Ronning, Chester Alvin, diplomat (b at Fancheng [Xiangfan], China 13 Dec 1894; d at Camrose, Alta 31 Dec 1984). He spent his early years in China and in northern Alberta. He served in the Royal Flying Corps (1918), but upon completion of courses at U of A and U of Minn, he returned to China as a teacher (1922-27) until being named principal of Camrose Lutheran College. While principal (1927-42), he was an MLA (1932) in the UNITED FARMERS OF ALBERTA government and was active in the CO-OPERATIVE COMMONWEALTH FEDERATION. After leading an RCAF intelligence unit (1942-45), Ronning entered the Dept of External Affairs, serving in China (1945-51), in Ottawa (1951-54), as ambassador in Norway (1954-57), as high commissioner in India (1957-64), and also as a member of the conference on Korea in Geneva (1954) and on Laos (1961-62). He undertook special missions to Hanoi (1965 and 1966) to attempt to mediate during the Vietnam War. Ronning was an untiring advocate of the recognition of the People's Republic of China and of its admission to the UNITED NATIONS. His knowledge of China and his friendship with such Asian leaders as Zhou Enlai made him an invaluable go-between.   BRIAN L. EVANS

Rooke, Leon, short-story writer, novelist, playwright (b at Roanoke Rapids, NC 11 Sept 1934). He was educated at the U of NC in Chapel Hill (1955-58, 1961-62) and was drafted into the US Army infantry which he served in Alaska 1958-60. Rooke has been writer-in-residence at 2 US colleges and has taught creative writing at U of Vic, where he took up permanent residence in 1969. An energetic and prolific storyteller, Rooke's writing is characterized by inventive language, experimental form, and an extreme range of offbeat characters with distinctive voices. He has written a number of plays for radio and stage, including the published works *Krokodile* (1973) and *Sword/Play* (1974), and has produced 8 collections of short stories, including *Sing Me No Love Songs I'll Say You No Prayers: Selected Stories* (1984). With John Metcalf he edited *The New Press Anthology* I (1984) and II (1985). It is his novels, however, which have received the most critical acclaim. *Fat Woman* (1980) was short-listed for the Gov Gen's Award, whereas *Shakespeare's Dog* won for 1983. Rooke received the Canada-Australia Literary Prize in 1981.
                                                        DONNA COATES

Roper, Edward, painter, illustrator, amateur naturalist (b in Kent, Eng 1854; d 1891). He made several visits to N America and spent several months in BC in 1887 and the Yukon around 1890 making careful pencil and watercolour sketches of fauna and flora and collecting specimens. He exhibited paintings of western Canada in England and published an account of his travels in *By Track and Trail through Canada* (1891). His series of lithographs of Muskoka is perhaps the earliest visual record of this area as a vacation district. He was elected a fellow of the Royal Geographical Society.   JAMES MARSH

Rose, common name for members of genus *Rosa* of the rose family (Rosaceae). This large family, comprising more than 100 genera and 2000-3000 species, includes plants as diverse as strawberries, almonds and pears. The genus *Rosa* comprises over 100 species of erect, climbing or

The prickly rose (*Rosa acicularis*) is the largest and most widespread wild rose in Canada; it is Alberta's provincial floral emblem (*photo by Al Williams*).

trailing shrubs, plus cultivars. About 14 species are native to Canada, and many introduced species have become established. The prickly rose (*R. acicularis*), the largest and most widespread wild rose in Canada, is found from Québec to BC and S to Virginia and New Mexico. This 1-1.5 m high shrub forms thick bushes that spring from underground shoots. It grows mainly in open, sunny areas. Its stems have slender spines and, in June, bear usually a single, delicately scented, pale or dark pink flower, 5 cm in diameter. The edible rose hips, which make excellent jams and jellies, are also enjoyed by birds. Since 1930 the prickly rose has been the PROVINCIAL FLORAL EMBLEM of Alberta, where it grows abundantly. It is easily grown in sandy soil. Cultivated roses have been popular ORNAMENTALS since ancient times. Most ornamental roses are hybrids of Old World species.   CÉLINE ARSENEAULT

Rose, Cultivated Roses have been cultivated from very early times, but little is known of their origin. The hybrid tea rose, the most popular of modern garden roses, was introduced worldwide in 1867. Today, roses are classified as hybrid tea (large flowered), floribunda (cluster flowered), grandiflora (large-cluster flowered), miniature, shrub, climbing and rambling types; however, these classifications are being changed because of recent introductions of different flowering types. In Canada rose breeding has concentrated primarily on developing hardy roses with better flowers for colder areas (eg, the prairies); however, except in SW coastal BC, most roses still require winter protection. Three early rose breeders were prairie nurserymen.

In recent years, Agriculture Canada's research stations in Ottawa and Morden, Man, have introduced a number of excellent garden roses, some closely resembling the popular hybrid teas and floribundas. Roses will grow in most well-drained soils but prefer a fertile loam in an open location with at least 6 hours of sunlight. They flower from early summer to late fall, depending on climate. All roses require a low-nitrogen, balanced fertilizer during the early growing season and frequent watering. Some shrub roses form

large, colourful seed heads (hips) and their leaves may turn red in fall. Common garden pests, frequent on most roses, can be controlled chemically. Black spot and mildew diseases are difficult to control; selecting resistant varieties helps avoid these problems.

Statistics are unavailable on the value of roses to the Canadian greenhouse and nursery industries. However, in 1985, almost 81 million roses were produced for sale as cut flowers in Canada. A further, undetermined number were imported from the US and Europe.

Rose, Fred, union organizer, politician (b Fred Rosenberg at Lublin, Poland 7 Dec 1907; d at Warsaw, Poland 16 Mar 1983). Rose moved with his parents to Montréal. In the 1930s, as a member of the Young Communist League, he organized unions of unemployed and unskilled workers. He was arrested in 1929 and again in 1931 at a meeting of the unemployed, and was convicted and sentenced to a year for sedition. In the 1943 by-election in Montréal-Cartier he was elected to the House of Commons as a Labour Progressive. He was re-elected in 1945, the only MP elected as a communist in Canadian history. In 1946 he was arrested in the first Cold War spy trials and sentenced to 6 years in the penitentiary for communicating official secrets to a foreign power.
                                                        MERRILY WEISBORD

Rose, Sir John, politician, banker, diplomat (b at Turriff, Scot, 2 Aug 1820; d at Langwell Forest, Scot 24 Aug 1888). He immigrated to Canada in 1836 and became a prominent corporation lawyer in Montréal. Elected to the Legislative Assembly of the PROVINCE OF CANADA in 1857, he was appointed solicitor general for Canada E in the Macdonald-Cartier administration. Chief commissioner of public works 1859-61, he resigned and sat as a private member and as a spokesman for the Protestant minority of Canada E 1861-67. Considered John A. MACDONALD's closest friend, he was minister of finance 1867-69 and responsible for the Dominion's first banking legislation. He moved to London as an investment banker in 1869 and served as a quasi-official representative of the Canadian government in England. He undertook the preliminary negotiations with the US that led to the Treaty of WASHINGTON, 1871, and was involved in setting up the original CPR syndicate in 1880. A well-known figure in English society and a financial adviser to the Prince of Wales, he was created baronet in 1872.
                                                        D.M.L. FARR

Rosenberg, Stuart, rabbi, author (b at New York C 5 July 1922). Educated at Columbia U, MA (1948), PhD (1953), and the Jewish Theological Seminary, rabbi (1945), MHL (1949), DD (1971), Rosenberg came to Canada in 1956. He has had 2 pulpits: Beth Tzedec (1956-73) and Beth Torah (1982-). He was appointed honorary fellow for life at the Jewish Theological Seminary (1976) and from 1975 to 1978 was visiting professor at the Toronto School of Theology and in 1981 visiting lecturer at San Diego State U. He has published 18 books, including *The Jewish Community of Canada* (2 vols, 1971), *Bridge to Brotherhood – Judaism's Dialogue with Christianity* (1961), *The Search for Jewish Identity in America* (1965), *Christians and Jews: The Eternal Bond* (1984) and *The Christian Problem: A Jewish View* (1986).
                                                        SHARON DRACHE

Rosenblatt, Joseph, poet, artist, editor (b at Toronto 26 Dec 1933). Raised and educated in Toronto, Rosenblatt dropped out of school to pursue a number of blue-collar jobs. He is author of 14 books of poetry, including *The LSD Leacock* (1963), *Winter of the Luna Moth* (1968), *Bumblebee Dithyramb* (1972) and *Virgins and Vampires*

(1975). His highly complex poetic persona is often multilayered or disguised in animal or organic metaphor. In 1976 he won the Gov Gen's Award for his collected poems (1960-76), *Top Soil*. After this he made 2 stylistic departures, the first resulting in a book of sonnets, *The Sleeping Lady* (1980) and the second, *Brides of the Stream* (1983), a fish poem and concerted attempt to pass from poetry to prose. *Brides of the Stream*, more than any previous collection, expresses Rosenblatt's proletarian and Jewish roots. Rosenblatt's *Selected Poems: Poetry Hotel* (1985) won the 1986 BC Poetry Prize and his autobiographical prose memoir, *Escape from the Glue Factory* (1985) was a Writers' Choice Selection in 1986. As an artist, Rosenblatt has created phantasmagoric drawings of the animal kingdom. He has published one art book, *Dr Anaconda's Solar Fun Club* (1978) and his limited-edition 30-drawing portfolio, *Snake Oil* (1978), contains many satirical references to the Canadian literary community. He was editor of the literary quarterly *Jewish Dialog* (1968-83) and president of the League of Canadian Poets (1983-85). Rosenblatt is one of Canada's true originals whose warmth and wry sense of humour permeate both his poetry and drawings.

SHARON DRACHE

Rosenfeld, Fanny, "Bobbie," track and field athlete, sportswriter (b in Russia 28 Dec 1905; d at Toronto 14 Nov 1969). Canada's woman athlete of the half century, she entered international athletics in 1928, the year women were first admitted to the Olympic Games. She held Canadian records in the running and standing broad jump and in the discus; at the 1928 Amsterdam Olympics she took the silver medal in the 100 m dash and was lead runner for the women's 4 x 100 relay team that won in a record time of 48.2 sec. Rosenfeld was also joint holder of the 11-sec, 100-yard world record. She was elected to Canada's Sports Hall of Fame in 1949 and was voted Canada's female athlete of the first half of the century in 1950. A plaque in her memory was unveiled in her hometown of Barrie, Ont, 13 June 1987.

TED BARRIS

Rosetown, Sask, Town, pop 2663 (1986c), inc 1911, is located 115 km SW of Saskatoon. It is a focal point for the major transportation routes of the region and is the dominant trade, service and governmental centre for a considerable area tributary to it. The town's initial development and continued prosperity have been dependent on both its role as a transportation hub and its location within some of the most productive wheat land on the Canadian prairies. Settlement commenced in 1904 and large-scale grain farming commenced as soon as the CNR line was routed through the district in 1908.

DON HERPERGER

Ross, Alexander, fur trader, author (b in Morayshire, Scot 9 May 1783; d at Red River [Man] 23 Oct 1856). Immigrating to Canada as an adult, he taught school for a few years. In 1810 he joined the Pacific Fur Co as a clerk serving variously at Ft Astoria, Ft Okanagan, Ft George and Ft Nez Percés for the NWC and then the HBC. He retired to Red River in 1825 where he became sheriff of Assiniboia, commander of the volunteer Corps, captain of the police, magistrate, commissioner and court examiner. He wrote several fur-trade classics: *Adventures on the Columbia River* (1849), *The Fur Hunters of the Far West* (1855) and *The Red River Settlement* (1856). He was married to an Okanagan Indian "princess," and several of their children played important roles in Manitoba's history. In his last book, Ross saw Red River as a civilized island in a barbarous wilderness, but despaired as to its future and that of its mixed-blood inhabitants.

FRITS PANNEKOEK

Ross, Sir George William, politician, premier of Ontario 1899-1905 (b near Nairn, Ont 18 Sept 1841; d at Toronto 7 Mar 1914). After some years as a teacher, school inspector and journalist, Ross was elected to the House of Commons as a Liberal for W Middlesex. On his defeat in the federal election of 1883, he joined Sir Oliver MOWAT's Ontario Cabinet as minister of education. Ross rationalized and improved the public school system, while grappling with bitter public controversies over language and religion in Roman Catholic separate schools and over the financing of the provincial university at Toronto and the denominational colleges. He succeeded Arthur Sturgis HARDY in the premiership in 1899, but his government was defeated in 1905. After leading the Opposition for 2 years, he accepted appointment to the Senate where he was Liberal leader from 1910 until his death. A noted orator, Ross also published books and pamphlets, including the autobiographical *Getting Into Parliament and After* (1913).

WENDY CAMERON

Ross, James, capitalist (b at Cromarty, Scot 1848; d at Montréal 20 Mar 1913). A professional engineer, Ross was associated with the construction of numerous railways and was manager of construction of the mountain division on the main line of the CPR. In the 1890s, he and other promoters undertook reorganization, electrification and expansion of the street railways in Toronto and Montréal, and subsequently in other cities in Canada, the US, the UK, Mexico, S America and the Caribbean. In 1901 he undertook a major and controversial reorganization of the Dominion Coal Co and the Dominion Iron and Steel Co. He was a patron of several art societies and donated substantial sums to various hospitals. He became an avid yachtsman, and his yacht *Glencairn* won several racing trophies.

T.D. REGEHR

Ross, Sir James Clark, naval officer, polar discoverer (b at London, Eng 15 Apr 1800; d at Aylesbury, Eng 13 Apr 1862). Ross gained his first arctic experience at age 18, serving with his uncle Sir John ROSS in a search for a NORTHWEST PASSAGE from Baffin Bay to Bering Str. He accompanied William Edward PARRY as an officer in 1819, 1821 and 1824, and as second-in-command of Parry's expedition to reach the N Pole in 1827. Ross was by this time the most experienced officer in arctic matters, an authority on magnetism and a good naturalist and taxidermist. He was on half pay when his uncle invited him to accompany his privately funded expedition to attempt the NW Passage in 1829. During the winter of 1829-30 he made a series of land expeditions on sleds which proved that Boothia was a peninsula. He crossed what is now called James Ross Str to Victory Pt and reached King William I. On 1 June 1831 he discovered the NORTH MAGNETIC POLE, set up the British flag and erected a cairn; the location was established at 70°05'17" N lat and 96°46'45" W long. He was later engaged to conduct a magnetic survey of the British Isles and in 1839 commanded an Antarctic expedition, spending 3 years studying magnetism and adding to the geographical knowledge of the region. In 1848 he commanded the first expedition in the search for Sir John FRANKLIN. He discovered and surveyed Peel Sd but found no trace of the missing explorer. He was made a rear-admiral in 1856.

JAMES MARSH

Ross, James Hamilton, rancher, politician, commissioner of the Yukon T, MP, senator (b at London, Canada W 12 May 1856; d at Victoria 14 Dec 1932). A popular and diplomatic representative and administrator, Ross consistently advocated increased popular participation in government in the North-West and Yukon territories. In the 1870s Ross moved with his family to Manitoba and by the early 1880s he had established a ranch near Moose Jaw in the Assiniboia District. He won election to the North-West Council in 1883 and served on that body for the next 5 years. Beginning in 1888, he was elected to several terms in the North-West Assembly, where he served in the positions of private member, as Speaker (1891-94), member of the executive committee (1895-97) and as treasurer and commissioner of public works (1897-1901). He played a key role in the campaign for responsible government for the territories.

Appointed commissioner of the Yukon T in 1901, Ross's previous experience proved invaluable as he reorganized the Yukon civil service and sponsored a wide variety of legislation. In Dec 1902, he was elected first MP for the Yukon, despite having had a paralytic stroke which left him unable to campaign. He was appointed to the Senate in 1904.

H. GUEST

Ross, James Sinclair, writer (b at Shellbrook, Sask 22 Jan 1908). Ross is one of Canada's most respected writers, in particular for his acclaimed novel, AS FOR ME AND MY HOUSE. Shortly after Ross was born, his family separated, and "Jimmy" was raised by his mother. He left school at 16 to join the Royal Bank of Canada as a clerk at Abbey, Sask. Banking became his lifelong career. He wrote in his spare time, and in 1934 his first story, "No Other Way," was published in London, Eng. Like most of Ross's fiction, it is set on the Canadian prairies. There ensued a productive period of storywriting for small Canadian magazines. The best-known stories, "The Painted Door," "A Field of Wheat" and "The Lamp at Noon," have been much anthologized. Several were later collected as *The Lamp at Noon and Other Stories* (1968). Their well-crafted structures and precise images have brought many readers to appreciate Ross's work. In them, he presented a theme that remained a preoccupation: intellectual isolation. Ross was little known to the Canadian or international public until his first novel, *As For Me and My House,* was published in New York in 1941. It was immediately hailed as superior, with its insight into the barren existence of Horizon, Sask. Often perceived as a gloomy portrait of rather miserable people, the book had surprising moments of humour and satire. The theme of triumph over the stultifying effects of small-town life and the Depression is its greatest strength and what differentiates it from *Main Street*, the Sinclair Lewis novel with which it is often compared. Its psychological penetration guarantees its place in modern Canadian literature.

Ross's next 2 novels, *The Well* (1958) and *Whir of Gold* (1970), failed to make much critical impact. His novella called *Sawbones Memorial* (1974), however, is a technical tour de force, relying more on dramatic than narrative technique. It consists of a series of dialogues and interior monologues in which the history of the town and most of its inhabitants is powerfully recreated. Upon retirement from the Royal Bank in 1968, Ross moved to Greece and then to Spain. Ill health prompted his return to Canada in 1980.

KEN MITCHELL

Ross, Sir John, naval officer and explorer (b at Balsarroch, Scot 24 June 1777; d London, Eng 30 Aug 1856). Entering naval service at the age of 9, and wounded during the Napoleonic Wars, Ross had been at sea for 30 years when in 1817 he was ordered by the Admiralty to command an expedition to explore Baffin Bay. From 1829 to 1833 he commanded a second expedition in the Lancaster Sd-Somerset I region. For 4 winters his ship, *Victory*, was ice-bound off the coast of Boothia Pen (and in 1831 his nephew and second-in-command, James Clark ROSS, located the North Magnetic Pole on the peninsula's W coast). Released by the ice in 1833, the ship returned to England, where Ross was knighted. In 1850 he commanded *Felix* in an unsuccessful search for the lost expedition of Sir John FRANKLIN. *See also* FRANKLIN SEARCH.   KENNETH S. COATES

Ross, John Jones, physician, politician, premier of Québec 1884-87 (b at Ste-Anne-de-la-Pérade, Lower Canada 16 Aug 1833; d there 4 May 1901). A rather dull and uninspiring man, Ross was premier 23 Jan 1884 to 25 Jan 1887. His Conservative government refused to take a position on the Louis RIEL affair, leading to its defeat late in 1886 by the new PARTI NATIONAL of Honoré MERCIER. In an attempt to keep the Conservatives in power, Ross resigned in favour of L.O. TAILLON; defeated in the House, Taillon resigned and Mercier became premier. PM John A. MACDONALD rewarded Ross with an appointment to the Senate.   DANIEL LATOUCHE

Ross, Malcolm, humanist, educator (b at Fredericton 2 Jan 1911). As editor of the New Canadian Library series, Ross gave Canadian readers the benefit of the enthusiasm and discrimination that made him an outstanding teacher at universities from Manitoba to Trinity, Queen's and Dalhousie. His books and articles began with work on the 17th century (*Milton's Royalism* 1943, 1970); he moved to universal issues (*Poetry and Dogma* 1954, 1969) and to critical assessment and anthologies of Canadian writings (*Our Sense of Identity* 1954, *The Arts in Canada* 1958 and *The Impossible Sum of Our Traditions* 1986). As officer and policymaker on the Canada Council, the Royal Society of Canada, and the Humanities Assn of Canada, he has been a beneficent force in Canadian culture.   ELIZABETH WATERSTON

Ross Farm, at New Ross, NS, 28 km N of Chester, dates from 1816, when Capt William Ross led 172 disbanded soldiers into the NS interior to establish an agricultural settlement. Focusing on the family dwelling called Rosebank Cottage, Ross Farm consisted of tillage, pasture and woodland, and remained the home of the Ross family until 1970, when the New Ross Dist Museum Soc and NS Museum undertook its development as a living museum of NS's agricultural heritage. Today, ploughs pulled by oxen, and grain harvested by sickle and scythe, illustrate the last century's farm technology and the significance of NS's role in the development of Canadian agriculture. Local crafts such as barrel making and woodworking are demonstrated. Period buildings include a blacksmith's shop, cooperage, stave mill and 100-year-old schoolhouse.   DEBRA McNABB

Ross Rifle During the SOUTH AFRICAN WAR, Canada requested that Great Britain supply the Canadian force with the British Lee-Enfield rifle but Britain refused. Since no manufacturer could be persuaded to establish a Canadian production facility, Canada would have to produce its own. Sir Charles Ross, a British aristocrat and inventor, offered to build a plant in Canada. He developed a 5-clip rifle model for the Canadian militia trials during August 1901 and this rifle became the Mark 1 Ross rifle which began production in 1903. In Mar 1903 the Canadian government signed a contract with Ross for 12 000 rifles to be supplied by the end of 1903.

Sir Sam HUGHES, the future minister of militia and member of the 1901 militia committee, was a supporter of the Ross rifle. The Mark 1 Ross rifle was not delivered until 1905 and 1000 units were supplied to the RNWMP but various problems plagued this model of rifle and it was eventually recalled in 1906. Changes were made to the production model until 1910 when the various models of the Mark 2 were produced. Great Britain at

that time was strongly urging Canada to adopt the Lee-Enfield rifle for its armed forces so as to have consistency within the Empire regarding weaponry, and because Canada refused to halt production of the Ross rifle, strains developed over imperial defence. The Mark 2 rifle was adopted by the Canadian armed forces in 1911, and in that year work was begun on the Mark 3, although few were produced before 1914. In the first years of WWI the Ross rifle received a bad reputation. It was seen as unsuitable for the "trench-and-charge" tactics employed during that war because of its weight, 9 lbs 14 ozs (*c* 4.5 kg), its overall length, $60\frac{1}{2}$ inches (*c* 1.5 m) with bayonet fixed, and the continual jamming problem plus the occasional "blowback." The cause of the jamming was eventually corrected but came too late for the rifle to maintain its use. In the summer of 1916 the rifle was withdrawn from service and by mid-Sept Canadian troops had been rearmed with the British-made Lee-Enfield. The Canadian government expropriated the Ross Rifle Co in March 1917 after paying Ross $2 million. The total production of the Ross rifle was approximately 420 000 with 342 040 units being purchased by the British. During WWII, the Mark 3 Ross rifle was given to the Royal Canadian Navy, the Veteran's Guard of Canada, coastal units, training depôts, the British Home Guard and the Soviets.   GLENN B. FOULDS

Ross River, YT, pop 352 (1986c), located at the confluence of the Ross and Pelly rivers, and on the Canol Road at the halfway point on the Campbell Hwy, is 360 km by road NE of Whitehorse. Tom Smith established a trading post there in 1902-03 but soon sold it to Poole Field and Clement Lewis, 2 traders from the Nahanni district of the NWT. As a number of natives had followed them and settled in the vicinity, the new owners called the site "Nahanni House." Subsequent owners, including the Whitehorse firm of Taylor and Drury, reverted to the original name of Ross River. In 1843, Robert Campbell named the river after Donald Ross, a chief factor of the Hudson's Bay Co. The settlement has a landing strip and is a service centre for travellers on the Campbell Hwy. H. GUEST

Rossiter, Roger James, biochemist, neurological scientist (b at Glenelg, Australia 24 July 1913; d at Helsinki, Finland 21 Feb 1976). Rossiter pioneered studies of the nervous system's chemical composition and was prominent in the development of biochemistry in Canada. Educated in Australia and at Oxford, he trained as a medical scientist under Sir Rudolph Peters. During WWII Rossiter conducted army research on malaria and burn injuries and studied malnutrition in repatriated prisoners of war. He immigrated to London, Ont, in 1947 as head of Western's department of biochemistry, where he later became dean of graduate studies and vice-president. Rossiter established an active research group which rapidly acquired an international reputation for studies on brain biochemistry. Over the years his work led to elucidation of lipid components in the nerve myelin sheath and processes involved in formation or degradation of these key structural elements in relation to development or to degenerative diseases of the nervous system.
                                    W.C. McMURRAY

Rossland, BC, City, pop 3472 (1986c), 3967 (1981c), inc 1897, is located 7 km SW of TRAIL at the base of Red Mt. Copper-gold mines were discovered on Red Mt 1887 by Joe Bourgeois and Joe Moris. The city was named after Ross Thompson, an early settler, and was changed from Thompson to Rossland in 1894 by postal authorities. It had 8000 inhabitants by 1897, and was connected by rail with Trail, site of a large smelter.

Mining boomed until 1916, then continued sporadically until 1930. In the 1960s MOLYBDENUM mining was opened on Red Mt; it continues intermittently. The city functions mainly as a service centre for mining and as a place of residence for Cominco employees in Trail. The development of skiing facilities at Red Mt is the most promising means for expanding the local economy.
                                  WILLIAM A. SLOAN

Rothstein, Aser, physiologist (b at Vancouver 29 Apr 1918). He has contributed enormously to the fields of cellular physiology and toxicology. A graduate of UBC, he obtained his PhD at U of Rochester, NY, in 1943. He performed pioneering experiments introducing the use of radioisotopes in the biological sciences. Rothstein's research has been mainly related to the transport of substances across biological membranes. His contributions include the identification of the protein responsible for anion transport in red blood cells. He was president of the Soc for General Physiologists and chairman of the Cell Physiology Commission for UNESCO. He was director of the Research Institute of the Hospital for Sick Children (Toronto) from 1972 to 1986. SERGIO GRINSTEIN

Roubaud, Pierre-Joseph-Antoine, Jesuit priest and missionary, spy, forger (b at Avignon, France 28 May 1724; d at Paris, France in or after 1789). Sent to the New France mission to the Abenakis of St-François-de-Sales (Odanak) in 1756, he accompanied the warriors in the campaigns of the SEVEN YEARS' WAR. He feared he would be blamed for failing to rally the Abenakis in the spring of 1760 and offered the British information in return for protection. Gen James MURRAY welcomed him and, impressed by his erudition, sent him to London as a Canadian informer. He became a Protestant, married and advocated that the Canadians be deprived of priests to force their conversion. Having lost favour through a change of government in 1765, Roubaud tried various trades and was often in debtors' prison. Most officials despised him, but they used him to spy on embassies and particularly on Canadians visiting London to argue for their rights. He betrayed his confidant Pierre Du Calvet and, to make money, even published forged letters by MONTCALM, predicting the loss of Canada and the rebellion of the Thirteen Colonies. He insisted he had a right to a share of the Jesuit estates, and backed Jeffery AMHERST, who claimed their property for his part in the Conquest. Sick and disillusioned, Roubaud retired to the Séminaire de Saint-Sulpice in Paris in 1768. AUGUSTE VACHON

Rouges, *see* PARTI ROUGE.

Rough Trade, an internationally popular Toronto-based rock group, was founded in 1974 by vocalist Carole Pope (1982 Juno Award, Top Female Vocalist) and guitarist/keyboardist Kevan Staples. Rough Trade was best known for songs "All Touch" and "High School Confidential." The group disbanded after a last performance at the Montréal Spectrum 31 Jan 1986. JOHN GEIGER

Roughing It in The Bush: or, Forest Life in Canada, by Susanna MOODIE (London, 1852; Toronto, 1871), is Moodie's best-known book and has been variously described as a novel, a romance, a diary and a history. Its subject, less elusive than its form, is Moodie's experience as an immigrant who settled with her husband near Peterborough, Canada West. Unlike the account by her sister, Catharine Parr TRAILL, of the settler's experience, Moodie's opens with a grim warning to prospective immigrants that Canada is not the Eden it is widely promoted to be in England, and that the settler's lot is a harsh one. Moodie's tone is more sombre than her sister's, but her descriptions of place and character are more imaginative, alloying the documentary with the fictional; and the personality she presents is more complex. Moodie's character inspired Margaret Atwood's fine book of poems, *The* JOURNALS OF SUSANNA MOODIE (1970).   NEIL BESNER

Rouleau, Alfred, (b at Sherbrooke, Qué 19 Aug 1915; d at Montréal 19 Oct 1985). At first an agent for the Laurentian Mutual Insurance Co, Rouleau was sent to the Montréal office. In 1948 he was asked to become first and founding general manager of Assurance-vie Desjardins by Mouvement Desjardins. He quickly made this institution one of the most dynamic and important life assurance companies in Québec and, concerned about the future of francophone minorities, saw that the company established offices in francophone communities in other provinces. Under his direction as president (1972-81), Mouvement Desjardins became one of the mainstays of economic life in Québec. Through his involvement with the CAISSES POPULAIRES, Rouleau took an active interest in the Québec, Canadian and international CO-OPERATIVE MOVEMENT and played a leading role in the preparation of laws better suited to the modern needs of co-operative institutions. He was invited to hold a number of prestigious and strategic positions, such as director of the Caisse de dépôt et de placement and of the Bank of Canada, and the Conseil de la coopération du Québec (1976) bestowed on him the Ordre du mérite co-opératif. The universities of Sherbrooke, Laval and Montréal awarded him honorary doctorates.   MARTHE LEGAULT

Rouleau, Joseph, bass (b at Matane, Qué 28 Feb 1929). He first studied in Montréal then in Milan, Italy. After singing with the Opéra national du Québec and the Opéra minute de Montréal, he appeared with the Opera Guild of Montréal (1956) and, then with Covent Garden in London. His association with that opera house lasted 25 years. In 1960 he sang with Joan Sutherland in Bellini's *La Sonnambula*, which led to his appearance with the soprano at the Opéra de Paris and in an Australian tour. He has sung in S America, S Africa and Israel and has toured the USSR 3 times. In Canada he created the role of Mgr Taché in Harry SOMERS's opera, *Louis Riel*, with the Canadian Opera Company (1967) and has frequently appeared with the major orchestras. He was elected president of the Mouvement d'action pour l'art lyrique du Québec (1977), whose pressure led to the creation of the Opéra de Montréal. In 1984 he made his debut at the Metropolitan Opera in New York, where he had great success in 1976 with Massenet's *Marie-Magdeleine* (playing Judas). Thanks to his well-developed theatrical sense and his great vocal flexibility, he has won international repute. He received the Prix de musique Calixa-Lavallée (1967) and was made an Officer of the Order of Canada (1977).   HÉLÈNE PLOUFFE

Round Table Movement, an organization devoted to the study of British Empire problems and the promotion of imperial unity, fd 1909 in London, Eng. Branches were quickly established in Canada, Africa, Australia and New Zealand and for the next 10 years the movement played an important role in imperial affairs. Its primary concerns were to involve the Dominions in defence and foreign policy decision making so that they would be able more readily to assert their nationhood, and to ensure the greater strength and continued unity of the British Empire. Its efforts to achieve imperial federation failed, partly because leading Canadian members, Arthur Glazebrook, Joseph FLAVELLE, John WILLISON, George WRONG and Vincent MASSEY, did not favour imperial union. The movement helped, however, to publicize the ideal of a COMMONWEALTH of free "British" nations.   JOHN KENDLE

Rounthwaite, Dick & Hadley Architects & Engineers, architectural firm founded by F.H. MARANI in 1919. In its early days the practice designed a wide range of private residences in Ontario and Québec; independent schools, including St Andrew's College, Aurora, Ont; the Lower School, Ridley College, St Catharines, Ont; and Prince of Wales College, Charlottetown. Joined in partnership by R.S. Morris in 1930, Marani & Morris designed the North American Life Building at the St George Street Medical Arts Building, Toronto, and the new Bank of Canada Head Office in Ottawa. After war service, the partnership was expanded to include M.F. Allan and later R.A. Dick.

During the postwar period Marani Morris & Allan, as the firm became known, designed numerous well-known insurance buildings, notably Manufacturers Life, Crown Life and Confederation Life in Toronto; Metropolitan Life in Ottawa; and Great-West Life in Winnipeg; banks, including the Bank of Canada in Ottawa, and the Royal Bank of Canada in Toronto; and public buildings, including Metropolitan Toronto Court House, and the military component of the Canadian Embassy, Washington, DC. In 1958, Morris was awarded the Royal Gold Medal for Architecture, bringing international recognition to the firm. He was only the second Canadian to be so honoured.

In 1964 the partnership merged with C.F.T. Rounthwaite (co-recipient of the Massey Foundation Gold Medal for the design of the STRATFORD FESTIVAL Theatre in 1958) to form the firm of Marani Rounthwaite & Dick. In 1972 the practice was entrusted with the extension of the head office of the Bank of Canada in Ottawa in a joint venture with Arthur ERICKSON. Following Marani's death, and upon G.R. Hadley joining the partnership, the firm's name was changed to Rounthwaite, Dick & Hadley. Recent projects include the new head office of Metropolitan Life and the Metropolitan Centre, Bank of Canada support centre (all in Ottawa), and Mutual Life in Waterloo.

Rousseau, Albert, painter, printmaker, animator (b at St-Etienne-de-Lauzon, Qué 17 Oct 1890; d 18 Mar 1982). A prolific artist whose reputation grew during the 1970s along with that of his friend René RICHARD, he studied at the Ecole des beaux-arts and soon saw his artistic ambitions curbed by the depression of the 1930s. He had to give his family's needs priority, working in a hostelry until 1965, meanwhile arranging to continue to paint regularly with such friends as Marc-Aurèle FORTIN and to show his works in Québec and Montréal. In 1956 he built a studio where his colleagues came to paint. He taught at various Québec institutions 1964-67, and his painting was stimulated by frequent trips to both the Canadian and American Atlantic seashores. In 1964 he organized a first rural exhibition near his studio, and since 1971 these exhibitions have become the annual festival of the Moulin des arts de St-Etienne, which Rousseau saved from demolition and transformed into an arts studio that draws some 200 artists and thousands of admirers each season.   GUY ROBERT

Rousseau, Jacques, botanist, ethnobiologist, ethnohistorian (b at St-Lambert, Qué 5 Oct 1905; d at Lac Ouareau, Qué 4 Aug 1970). Explorer of the Québec-Labrador peninsula and of remote regions of Québec, skilled in many natural and "human" sciences, and possessed of an encyclopedic knowledge, he produced close to 550 publications. He was founder and first secretary (1930-

46) of L'Association canadienne-française pour l'avancement des sciences. He received his doctorate in science from U de M, and later became a director of its Botanical Institute (1944-56). Because of his interdisciplinary competence, he was the first director of the Human History Division of the National Museums of Canada (1956-59). His written work (observation notes, diary, reviews, articles), including numerous articles on the "Amerindiens" — a concept now in use in ethnological writings — demonstrate rare observational skills and original views. His writings reveal a breadth of scientific knowledge and are masterpieces of interdisciplinary writing, though his innovating talents were not fully recognized in his lifetime. His co-edition, with Guy Béthune, of Pehr KALM's 1749 *Voyage* was completed by Pierre Morisset and published in 1977.
                    MARC-ADÉLARD TREMBLAY

Roussil, Robert, sculptor (b at Montréal 1925). He studied fine arts with the Association artistique of Montréal, and from 1958 to 1978 lived in Tourettes-sur-Loup, France. In 1952 he suggested the idea of international sculpture symposia in Vienna. Thus, in the early 1960s, he participated in international sculpture symposia, such as those in Yugoslavia and Montréal. Roussil's sculptures, both gigantic and miniature, express a fundamental and consistent theme: life regenerating in joy, sensuality, eroticism and love; and his principal subjects are man and bird. He uses the intrinsic structural qualities of his materials (iron, cast-iron, gold, copper, stone, clay, wood) to produce works ranging from representational allusion to abstraction (*Couple réuni*, limestone, no date). In 1983 he won a law suit against the city of Montréal for destroying 4 of his sculptures. His work is characterized by slender forms and solid mass, curved edges and conical surfaces, holes and rings. He now lives near Nice, France.
                    LOUISE BEAUDRY

Routhier, Sir Adolphe-Basile, lawyer, magistrate, man of letters, orator, professor, administrator (b at St-Placide, LC 8 May 1839; d at Saint-Irénée-les-Bains, Qué 27 June 1920). He studied law at U Laval and was admitted to the bar in 1861. He became a justice of the Superior Court (first in Saguenay district and then in Québec), and in 1904 was named chief justice of the Superior Court. Author of the French words to the Canadian national anthem, "O Canada," he also penned a great many literary works with emphasis on art, law, religion, nationalism and travel. He was the general president of the St-Jean-Baptiste Society and a founding member and president of the Royal Society of Canada.
                    HÉLÈNE PLOUFFE

Roux, Jean-Louis, theatre director, writer, actor (b at Montréal 18 May 1923). A doctor's son, Roux completed his classical studies at Collège Sainte-Marie and then enrolled in medicine at U de M (1943-46). In 1942 when Ludmilla Pitoëff was invited to mount a production with the Compagnons de Saint-Laurent, *L'Échange*, Roux played a major role. He played again in 1946 with Jean GASCON in *Phèdre* and *Le Pain dur*, when Pitoëff came again to Montréal from New York with her theatre company (including Yul Brunner). That year, war being over, Roux received a study bursary and decided to give up medicine and study theatre in Paris for 3 years.

Returning from abroad, in 1950 Roux joined Éloi GRAMMONT to establish the Théâtre d'essai, which gave place to the THÉÂTRE DU NOUVEAU MONDE (July 1951); they produced Grammont's *Un fils à tuer* (1949) and Roux's *Rose Latulippe* (Feb 1951). After the production of *Un fils à tuer* in Montréal, Roux had gone back for a while to Paris to work as a professional actor (1949-50). He played later in the TNM's first production (9 Oct 1951), *L'Avare*, along with Grammont, Gascon, Georges Groulx, Guy Hoffmann, Ginette Letondal, Denise Pelletier and others who would remain Roux's close associates for many years, during which time he produced approximately 40 of the TNM's productions and occupied the positions of secretary general (1953-63) and artistic director (1966-81). Roux wrote and produced the play *Bois-Brûlés* (1967) and translated some of the plays performed by the TNM, and has written radio and TV scripts for Radio-Canada. He has played several famous TV roles, including a part in *Septième nord* and *Les Plouffe*, and a few roles in motion picures, such as Jean Beaudien's *Cordélia*, Fernando Arrabol's *L'Empereur du Pérou* and Tony Richardson's *Hotel New Hampshire*. He served as president of the Société des auteurs, as administrative secretary and later president of the Centre canadien du théâtre, and was on the executive committee of the Institut international du théâtre. His honours include the Victor-Morin award in 1969 and the MOLSON PRIZE in 1977. In 1981 Roux was director general of the National Theatre School (1981-87). He was made a Companion of the Order of Canada in 1987.

ANDRÉ G. BOURASSA

Rouyn-Noranda, Qué, City, pop 26 189 (1986c), 25 991 (1981c), is the largest centre in the Abitibi-Témiscaming region and its administrative capital. The city was formed from the amalgamation of 2 municipalities in 1986, both of which were established after the discovery of COPPER and GOLD deposits at the Noranda mine in the mid-1920s. Noranda, pop 8870 (1986c), 8767 (1981c), was created by NORANDA MINES LTD in 1926. The town limits were those of the company's mining properties on the W shore of Lac Osisko. At the time, Noranda was considered a model northern mining town. For many years, it was completely controlled and administered by Noranda Mines, formed in 1922 to exploit one of the richest copper and gold deposits ever found in Canada. The name "Noranda" is a combination of the words "North" and "Canada." Today's vast mining empire, Noranda Mines Ltd, grew from the mine which operated 1927-66. The smelting plant is one of the largest in Québec and 8 mines are still in operation nearby.

Rouyn, pop 17 319 (1986c), 17 224 (1981c), is located just S of Noranda on the shore of Lac Osisko. It became a town in 1927 and a city in 1948. Its name honours Jean-Baptiste de Rouyn, a captain in Montcalm's Royal-Rousillon regiment in New France. Rouyn was originally a large mining village inhabited by a mixture of prospectors, miners, adventurers and merchants drawn by the gold rush that erupted in 1922 after discovery of the Noranda mine deposits. Rouyn is still a lively city.

BENOÎT-BEAUDRY GOURD

Rowan, William, ornithologist (b at Basle, Switz 29 July 1891; d at Edmonton 30 June 1957). After biological studies at University Coll, London, Eng, he became lecturer in zoology at U Man in 1919 and contributed to ornithological works in Manitoba and Ontario, participating in founding the Natural History Soc of Manitoba. He moved to Edmonton in 1920, founding the U of A dept of zoology, which he headed until retirement in 1956. Though active in naturalist and sportsmen groups, he was best known for his scientific research. Rowan's experiments on the influence of photoperiod on bird hormones, determining the timing of migration, are widely cited as a milestone in ornithological history and resulted in his being presented with the RSC's Flavelle Medal. His banding studies were also extensive. Later he turned his attention to cyclic population fluctuations in birds and mammals. His artistic prowess was exemplified by several exhibits in Canada and England, and by the selection of his crane drawing for a postage stamp. His assistant, Robert Lister (d Jan 1988), portrayed Rowan's eccentric genius in a book based on his diaries, *The Birds and Birders of Beaverhills Lake* (1979).

MARTIN K. MCNICHOLL

Reading: W. Rowan, *The Riddle of Migration* (1931).

Rowand, John, fur trader (b at Montréal 1787?; d at Fort Pitt, Rupert's Land 30 May 1854). In 1803, shortly after joining the NORTH WEST CO (NWC) as an apprentice clerk, Rowand was posted to Ft Augustus (later moved and renamed FORT EDMONTON). He spent the rest of his life there, first as a NWC partner 1820, after 1821 as a HBC chief trader, and after 1823 as chief factor in charge of the Saskatchewan District. He held this position until his death almost 30 years later. George SIMPSON, HBC governor, considered the physically short and lame Rowand, "one of the most pushing bustling Men in the Service...warm hearted and friendly in an extraordinary degree." Known as "Iron Shirt" or "Big Mountain" by the Indians, Rowand's fairness, bravery and business acumen made him the single most influential white man on the Saskatchewan plains of his time.

FRITS PANNEKOEK

Rowe, John Stanley, botanist, ecologist (b at Hardisty, Alta 11 June 1918). Educated at U of A, Nebraska and U Man, Rowe worked as a forest labourer and schoolteacher in BC and then as a research officer on the prairies with the federal Department of Forestry from 1948 to 1967, when he became professor of plant ecology at U of Sask. In his work on the ecology of boreal forest, tundra and peatlands, Rowe insisted on broad long-term conceptual approaches to resource questions, an approach reflected in his many scientific and popular articles. His 1959 treatise (rev 1972), *Forest Regions of Canada,* is a key source for foresters, biologists and land managers. An active participant in the International Biological Program and on the Canadian Forestry Advisory Council, he received the Canadian Forestry Achievement Award in 1972.

MARTIN K. MCNICHOLL

Rowell, Newton Wesley, lawyer, politician, churchman (b at Arva, Ont 1 Nov 1867; d at Toronto 22 Nov 1941). After articling in a London, Ont law firm, Rowell was called to the bar in 1891 and soon became a leading member of the Toronto legal profession, and of the Liberal Party and the Methodist Church. Leader of the Liberal opposition and MLA for N Oxford (1911-17) in the Ontario legislature his party became committed to PROHIBITION, and a platform more focused on urban issues, but made few gains from the WHITNEY Conservative government. During WWI Rowell, an early crusader for CONSCRIPTION, joined the UNION GOVERNMENT as president of the privy council (1917-20). He chaired the war committee of the Cabinet and at the end of the war was the first federal minister of health. The postwar Liberal Party had no place for Rowell, whose association with conscription, advocacy of a program of social insurance and of a positive role in external relations made him anathema in Québec and to some English Canadians who abhorred "the politics of uplift." As one of the Canadian delegates, Rowell took a prominent part in the first assembly of the LEAGUE OF NATIONS and subsequently helped to found and develop the work of the LEAGUE OF NATIONS SOCIETY and the CANADIAN INSTITUTE OF INTERNATIONAL AFFAIRS. He was president of the Toronto General Trust Corp (1925-34) and the leading layman in the formation of the UNITED CHURCH OF CANADA. Rowell appeared before the JUDICIAL COMMITTEE OF THE PRIVY COUNCIL in several important constitutional cases, including the PERSONS CASE, representing the women appellants. In 1936 he was appointed chief justice of Ontario and in 1937 chairman of the Royal Commission on DOMINION-PROVINCIAL RELATIONS (Rowell-Sirois), but in 1938 ill health forced his resignation from both.

MARGARET E. PRANG

Rowing is a sport of propelling boats or specially designed racing shells with oars on water. Shells are usually classified for either sculling (2 oars, or sculls, one in each hand) or rowing (one oar, held by both hands). Sculling shells include the single, double and quadruple, used by 1, 2 and 4 people respectively. Rowing shells include the pair (with or without coxswain), 4s (with or without coxswain) and an 8 (with coxswain).

Racing shells are lightweight, slender but strong craft with hulls less than 3 mm thick and commonly made of mahogany, cedar, fiberglass or carbon fibre; their frames are made of lightweight hardwood. Shells are equipped with sliding seats and with "shoes" attached firmly to the frame that allow the seated rower to slide forward into a powerful crouch position at the start of the stroke, place the oar in the water and then push off the foot supports, extending the legs and pulling on the oar(s) with the arms and back. This power phase of the rowing motion is very similar to the action of a weightlifter who squats to pick up a heavy weight. Oars vary in length, weight and blade design, according to their use for rowing or sculling, the strength and size of the rower, and individual preference. The shafts are hollow for lightness and the oar is balanced so as to be light in the hands of the rower.

Rowing as a sport began at least as far back as 450 BC. There are artistic and written representations linking the sport to many ancient civilizations, including the Greeks, Romans, Egyptians and Japanese. England, however, was the birthplace of modern rowing equipment and regattas as we know them today. Perhaps the oldest sculling race was instituted on the Thames R in 1715 by the Irish comedian Doggett; one can find references to regattas on the Thames by the 1770s. The sport was introduced to Canada gradually as Englishmen immigrated to the N American colonies in the early 19th century. One of the earliest recorded regattas in Canada occurred 10 Aug 1816 in St John's harbour, Nfld. The ST JOHN'S REGATTA, perhaps the oldest continuous sporting event in N America, commenced in 1818 at Quidi Vidi Lk and is still rowed in fixed-slide, 6-man boats that are considerably heavier and slower than the swift racing shells used today in national and international competitions. In the 1820s, the rowing clubs of Halifax, comprising mainly garrison and naval personnel, dominated maritime regattas.

In the 1840s, rowing clubs and regattas appeared in the Upper Canada communities of Toronto, Brockville, Monkton and Cobourg. By this time Canadian oarsmen were competing increasingly against British and American oarsmen in regattas in Halifax, Toronto, Boston, Philadelphia, Chicago and other centres. To the end of the 19th century, and into the 20th, many Canadian scullers and crews gained international fame, in both amateur and professional races. In the later

1860s, George Brown, a fisherman of Herring Cove, NS, raced successfully against the best scullers in Canada, the US and Britain. In the 1870s and 1880s, Toronto sculler Edward (Ned) HANLAN won Canadian, American and English titles, including 7 all-comers matches that were the equivalent of world championships. He has been Canada's most acclaimed oarsman and was widely hailed as Canada's first national sporting hero.

Four oarsmen from Saint John, NB (Price, Ross, Hutton, Fulton), won Canada's first world championship on 7 July 1867 in Paris, France, and were afterwards called the "Paris Four." Other Canadian greats include Bob Pearce, the Australian winner of the 1932 Olympics single sculls, who became a Canadian titleholder in 1933; Jake Gaudaur, of Orillia, Ont, world titlist in 1896; and Toronto scullers Lou Scholes and Joe WRIGHT, Sr. The Vancouver Rowing Club has had a long and glorious tradition, commencing in 1888. Different crews of one of the club's world-class coaches, Frank Read, figured in numerous international victories between 1954 and 1960, including COMMONWEALTH and PAN-AMERICAN GAMES gold medals and 3 Olympic medals, one gold and 2 silver. The 1956 Olympic gold-medal four of Don Arnold, Walter d'Hondt, Lorne Loomer and Archie MacKinnon, all UBC students, achieved probably the largest victory margin of any crew in the modern games. The 1964 Olympic gold-medal pair, from the UBC-Vancouver Rowing Club, of Roger Jackson and George Hungerford was coached by 2 disciples of Read – Glen Mervin, from the 1960 Olympic silver-medal 8, and David Gillanders, who assisted Read for many years. In the last decade, much of Canada's international success has come from junior and senior women's crews at world championships and the 1976 Olympics. Tricia Smith, Betty Craig and Susan Antoft have each won silver medals in world championships 1978-81, as well as many other international awards. Women's rowing was first introduced to the Olympics in 1976 in Montréal. In 1979 at Moscow, a junior women's crew, coached by Rudy Wieler, won Canada's first gold medal in world championship eights by beating the USSR and E Germany.

Canada's best performance ever occurred at the Los Angeles Olympic Games, where 6 medals were won.

For the first time in Canadian Olympic history the men's 8-oared crew, coached by Neil Campbell, won the gold medal in a classic stroke-for-stroke duel with the US crew. Olympic silver medals were won in both the women's coxed 4 and by the pair without coxswain rowed by Tricia Smith and Betty Craig. Bronze medals were won by Robert Mills in the men's single, by the men's quadruple sculls, and by the women's double sculls of Danielle and Silken Laumen. In 1985 Canada's quadruple sculls of Doug Hamilton, Paul Douma, Bob Mills and Mel Laforme, coached by Jack Nicholson, won Canada's first world championship sculling event, beating a strong E German crew. In the rowing events at the 1987 Pan-American Games, Canadians won 4 gold, 4 silver and 4 bronze medals.

Whereas the Olympic Rowing Basin in Montréal and the courses at St Catharines, Ont, and Burnaby Lake, BC, are rated as international-class courses, Canadian clubs from Vancouver I to Newfoundland row on rivers, lakes, ocean inlets and any type of water. The premier regatta in N America is the Royal Canadian Henley Regatta at St Catharines (named for the famous British regatta, and in which Canadian men's and women's teams have competed), 100 years old in 1982. Each year there is also a national champi-

Men's heavy eights rowing team with gold medals won at the 1984 Los Angeles Olympics (*courtesy Athlete Information Bureau/Service Information-Athlètes*).

onship for schoolboys. In 1880 the Canadian Assn for Amateur Oarsmen was created, one of the earliest sports governing bodies in Canada. Made up of clubs from across Canada, the association is responsible for the rules governing Canadian rowing. Since 1974, it has staged national championships for men, women, lightweights, youths and Masters. The association has its offices at the National Sport and Recreation Center in Vanier, Ont, and is served by full-time professional technical and administrative personnel.

ROGER JACKSON

Reading: J. A. Carver, *The Vancouver Rowing Club* (nd); R. S. Hunter, *Rowing in Canada Since 1848* (1933); P. King, *Art and a Century of Canadian Rowing* (1981).

Rowley, Robert Kent, (b at Montréal 25 Oct 1917; d at Toronto 5 Feb 1978). Rowley became a union leader at age 17, and after spending $2\frac{1}{2}$ years in jail (1940-42) for opposing military registration, he became Canadian director for the United Textile Workers of America (AFL affil) and received a 6-month jail term for initiating an allegedly illegal strike at Valleyfield, Qué, in 1946. In 1952 Rowley and his future wife, Madeleine PARENT, were fired by the UTWA for their alleged but in fact nonexistent ties with communism. Angry with American interference in Canadian sections of international unions, they began to organize all-Canadian unions and worked particularly hard to organize unorganized workers in small plants. Rowley was instrumental in establishing the CONFEDERATION OF CANADIAN UNIONS in 1968 and became its secretary-treasurer. Though the CCU remained small, its critique of American unionism contributed to a spate of breakaway movements in the 1970s and 1980s.

ALVIN FINKEL

Rowsell, Harry Cecil, veterinarian, animal-care specialist (b at Toronto 29 May 1921). After serving in the Royal Canadian Navy 1941-45, he became a veterinarian (U of T, 1949) and later conducted several years of research on cardiovascular diseases and thrombosis as part of a McMaster-Ontario Veterinary Coll team. He was the first chairman of veterinary pathology at the Western Coll of Veterinary Medicine, U of Sask 1965-68, and first executive secretary of the Canadian Council of Animal Care 1968.

Rowsell has a strong national and international reputation in the care of domestic, wild and laboratory animals and birds of all types, but in particular in experimental animal care. His efforts have resulted in dramatic improvements in the treatment of experimental animals in Canada and abroad. *See also* VETERINARY MEDICINE.

R.G. THOMSON

Roy, Camille, priest, professor, literary critic (b at Berthier-en-Bas, Qué 22 Oct 1870; d at Québec City 24 June 1943). Though largely outmoded to-

day, Roy's work was representative of his generation. After studies at Laval and the Sorbonne, Roy taught philosophy and then rhetoric at the Petit Séminaire de Québec 1894-1918 and French literature at Laval 1896-1927. Preoccupied with the survival of the French language in Canada, he helped found the Société du parler français (1902), pioneered the teaching of French Canadian literature at Laval (1902) and published the first *Manuel d'histoire de la littérature canadienne-française* (21 editions, 1907-62). His critical articles, which appeared in magazines 1902-33 and have been collected in 10 volumes, encouraged pastoral novels and reflected a classical ideal, though one open to romanticism. Tutor in the Petit Séminaire de Québec 1918-23, founder of the École normale supérieure (1920), rector of Laval (1924-27, 1929, 1932-38), dean of the Faculté des lettres (1939-43), both in print and at conferences he argued for development of a national educational system oriented towards social action. Received into the RSC 1904, he won the Prix David 1924 (*À l'ombre des érables*) and the gold medal of the Académie française 1925.

LUCIE ROBERT

Roy, Fabien, politician (b at St-Prosper, Qué 17 Apr 1928). He was elected the Ralliement créditiste MNA for Beauce in 1970, and was re-elected in 1973 under the Parti créditiste banner and in 1976 under that of the Parti national populaire, which he had founded the previous year with former Liberal minister Jérôme Choquette. He was largely responsible for the party's acceptance of nationalist and progressive ideas. In Apr 1979 he was chosen interim leader of the federal Social Credit Party. He was elected as this party's MP for Beauce in 1979, but was defeated in 1980, thereafter working for several economic development organizations in the Beauce region.

DANIEL LATOUCHE

Roy, Gabrielle, writer (b at St-Boniface, Man 22 Mar 1909; d at Québec City 13 July 1983). Winner of the Gov Gen's Award (1947, 1957, 1977) and of many other literary distinctions in Canada and abroad (Lorne Pierce Medal 1947; Prix Duvernay 1956; Prix David 1971), Roy was one of the most important Canadian writers of the postwar period.

The youngest of 8 children of a francophone family in St-Boniface, Roy lived in Manitoba until 1937. She was profoundly influenced by the prairie landscape and by the cosmopolitan world of the immigrants who settled in western Canada in the early 20th century. Her studies completed, she taught school for 12 years, first in isolated villages and then in St-Boniface, where she also did some theatre with the Cercle Molière. In the summer of 1937, she taught in northern Manitoba and after that went to Europe. It was during the 2 years that she spent in France and England that she began to write.

The approaching war forced her to return to Canada in 1939. She chose to live in Montréal, where she became a free-lance journalist and began writing *Bonheur d'occasion*. Published in 1945, this novel, which describes working-class life in the early war period, won the Prix Fémina in Paris and the Literary Guild of America Award in New York. Translated into more than 15 languages (*The Tin Flute* in English), it brought Roy literary fame. In 1947 she was the first woman to be admitted to the RSC. She married Dr Marcel Carbotte that same year.

During a subsequent stay in France, she wrote a second book based on her memories of the Canadian West. *La Petite Poule d'eau* (1950) was later magnificently illustrated by painter Jean-Paul LEMIEUX. Upon returning to Canada, Roy settled in Québec City. She continued to write about the

Gabrielle Roy, one of the most important Canadian writers of the postwar period, was made famous by her novel *The Tin Flute* (*courtesy City of Toronto Archives, The Globe and Mail Coll*).

solitude of modern man (*Alexandre Chenevert*, 1954), the obsessive preoccupations of the artist (*La Montagne secrète*, 1961, inspired by the life of painter René Richard), the conflict between the values of progress and those of tradition (*La Rivière sans repos*, 1970), the poetry of nature (*Cet été qui chantait*, 1972), immigration and travel (*Un Jardin au bout du monde*, 1975; *De quoi t'ennuies-tu, Eveline?* 1982), and particularly about her own youth (*Rue Deschambault*, 1955; *La Route d'Altamont*, 1966; *Ces enfants de ma vie*, 1977). Roy also published stories for children (*Ma vache Bossie*, 1976; *Courte-Queue*, 1979) and a volume of articles and essays (*Fragiles lumières de la terre*, 1978).

Written in a simple, uncluttered style, the works of Roy today have a vast public, both in Canada (where almost all her books have been translated into English) and abroad. The central theme of her work is that of humanity in pain and solitude, but redeemed by the love implicit in creation and by hope for a world in which all men are reconciled. *See also* LITERATURE IN FRENCH.

FRANÇOIS RICARD

Reading: G. Roy, *Enchantment and Anguish: An Autobiography* (1987).

Roy, Philippe, physician, diplomat (b at St-François, Qué 1 Feb 1868; d at Ottawa 10 Dec 1948). Educated at Laval, Roy practised medicine in Québec C, and after 1897 in and around Edmonton, where he worked to promote the interests of the FRENCH IN THE WEST. He was a senator 1906-11 and then a pioneer in Canada's foreign service: commissioner general at Paris, France, 1911-28; and the first envoy extraordinary and minister plenipotentiary in Paris, 1928-38. As commissioner general, with a princely 1911 salary of $8000 plus $5000 expenses, Roy advanced Canadian commercial interests. As minister, he had full diplomatic privileges, the second Canadian (after Vincent MASSEY in Washington) to have such status. NORMAN HILLMER

Roy-Audy, Jean-Baptiste, painter (b at Québec C 15 Nov 1778; d at Trois-Rivières *c*1848). Basically self-taught, he began his career as a painter of signs, vehicles and coats of arms in 1809, after working as a joiner, furniture maker and coach builder. He is particularly renowned as a portraitist, working mainly around Québec,

though his work is found as far away as Montréal. The Musée du Québec and Montréal's Musée des beaux-arts have collections of his works.

MICHEL CAUCHON

Royal Alexandra Theatre, completed in 1907 at a cost of $750 000, is one of the few surviving large professional theatres found in numerous Canadian cities at the turn of the century. It was designed by John LYLE in 1906 for a group of prominent businessmen headed by Cawthra Mulock. In 1963 the theatre was purchased by the Toronto entrepreneur "Honest Ed" MIRVISH and restored to its Edwardian beauty at a cost of $500 000.

With a seating capacity of 1497, the Royal Alex is noted for its large proscenium stage, excellent acoustics, and intimacy between performers and audience. Although the theatre has staged a few Canadian works, including John WEINZWEIG's ballet *Red Ear of Corn*, the revues *My Fur Lady* and *Spring Thaw*, John GRAY's *Billy Bishop Goes to War* and Linda Griffiths's *Maggie and Pierre*, the theatre for most of its history has been a touring house for drama, musicals, opera and dance, particularly from Britain and the US. In 1986 David Mirvish became executive producer and initiated a policy of coproducing with major Canadian national arts organizations such as the Canadian Opera Company, the Stratford and Shaw festivals and regional theatres such as the Manitoba Theatre Centre and Citadel Theatre. ANTON WAGNER

Royal Astronomical Society of Canada began in 1868 when 8 amateur astronomers founded an astronomical club in Toronto. An expanded group obtained a charter in 1890, and the name "The Royal Astronomical Society of Canada" was adopted in 1903 with Edward VII's permission. As membership increased, the meetings were moved from the homes of individual members to U of T, and in 1906 a branch was formed in Ottawa. There are now nearly 3000 members and 20 centres of the RASC located across Canada.

Astronomy has a special appeal for many people, from children to hobbyists to professional scientists. The observational and educational work of amateur astronomy is of tremendous value to the science of astronomy. Some members take part in regular observations of variable stars and other phenomena, whereas others develop special skills in astrophotography. Many RASC centres have built their own observatories for these purposes. Members of the RASC receive 3 publications: the *Observer's Handbook*, which is an annual guide to the night sky; the *Journal*, which contains articles of general interest to educators, amateurs and professional astronomers; and the *National Newsletter*, which appears with each issue of the *Journal* and contains RASC activities and articles. Most RASC centres have programs of public education, including special star nights when hundreds of people have an opportunity to look through telescopes, many for their first time. The national headquarters, located in Toronto, contains an excellent collection of books, periodicals, slides and films, which may be borrowed by members.

Royal Bank Award for Canadian Achievement honours a Canadian citizen or person living in Canada "whose outstanding accomplishment makes an important contribution to human welfare and the common good." The award was established in CENTENNIAL YEAR, 1967, and consists of $100 000 and a gold medal. The selection committee is composed of 7 distinguished Canadians and is independent of the ROYAL BANK.

Recipients of the award include Wilder PENFIELD, C.J. MACKENZIE, Cardinal Paul Emile LÉGER, Morley CALLAGHAN, Arthur ERICKSON, R. Keith

Royal Bank Plaza, Toronto (*courtesy Webb Zerafa Menkes Housden Partnership/photo by Derek Griffiths*).

DOWNEY and Baldur STEFANSSON, Northrop FRYE, Georges-Henri LÉVESQUE, Hugh MACLENNAN, and David SUZUKI. Recipients in 1987 were Gweneth LLOYD and Arnold SPOHR.

Royal Bank of Canada, with head offices in Montréal, is the largest Canadian chartered bank. It started around 1864-69 as the Merchants Bank of Halifax, and its present name was adopted in 1901. The bank established its first branch outside Canada in Bermuda in 1882, and between 1903 and 1925 grew by absorbing other banks, including several in the Caribbean. Today the bank provides a full range of financial services. It has long been a pioneer in home mortgages and holds over $12.5 billion in mortgages.

The first bank to install computers, it has over 95% of all customer accounts on-line. It was also the first bank to expand services to the Arctic. It operates 1496 branches and is the sixth-largest bank in N America in assets and deposits (1986). In 1982 it acquired Canadian Acceptance Corp. As of Oct 1986, it had $8.9 billion in interest income, assets of $99.6 billion and 38 186 employees. The shares are widely held.

DEBORAH C. SAWYER

Royal Canadian Academy of Arts (RCA) is the oldest national organization of professional Canadian artists and was founded in 1880 through collaboration by the Ontario Society of Artists and the Art Assn of Montreal under the active patronage of Gov Gen the marquess of Lorne and his wife HRH the Princess Louise. Among the 26 charter members were the nation's most accomplished painters, sculptors, architects and designers. These included Lucius R. O'BRIEN (1st president), noted for his luminous, majestic landscapes, such as *Sunrise on the Saguenay*, W.G. Storm, architect of Toronto's Osgoode Hall and St James Cathedral, and Napoléon BOURASSA, acclaimed for his ecclesiastical murals such as those in the Notre-Dame Church, Montréal. The fundamental aim of the RCA was to foster the development of the visual arts, and its initial resolution was the founding of the NATIONAL GALLERY in Ottawa through the creation of a diploma collection, in which each member was required to deposit a work upon election. While the adoption by Parliament in 1913 of the Act to Incorporate the

National Gallery formally severed ties between the RCA and the NG, diploma works continued to be deposited until 1976. Another precedent was the establishment of classes in life drawing, not then available through existing courses in art instruction, in Ottawa, Montréal, Toronto, and later in Hamilton, Winnipeg and Halifax.

Until a decade and a half ago, when a maturing art scene offered many alternate display opportunities, the RCA's greatest contribution to developing Canadian art was through its annual open juried exhibitions.

Considered the senior showcase for artists, they provided a consistent venue which regularly saw the work of gifted newcomers hung beside the best in the country. From the young painter Homer WATSON in 1880, through members of the Group of Seven in the 1920s, to graphic designer Allan Fleming and architect Arthur ERICKSON in the late 1960s, to note the emergence of major talent in these exhibitions is to trace the history of Canadian art.

Since 1970, under the succeeding presidencies of architect John C. PARKIN, filmmaker Christopher Chapman and architect Gene Kinoshita, the RCA has widened its constituency to embrace potentially all visual arts disciplines, including photography, fibre arts, ceramics, costume and stage design. With the opening of a national headquarters, with permanent exhibition space and a resource centre at Academy House, Toronto, in Oct 1987, the organization meets its original mandate with a revitalized membership and on a contemporary footing. REBECCA SISLER

Royal Canadian Legion originated in several small associations of ex-soldiers that banded together throughout Canada during WWI. The first national organization, the Great War Veterans Association, was established Apr 1917 and by 1919 was the largest such group in Canada. By the mid-1920s, internal problems, a decline in membership and the emergence of rival associations brought the movement near collapse. In 1925 Field Marshal Earl Haig, founder of the British Empire Service League, visited Canada and encouraged all Canadian veterans to unite in one organization.

In 1926 the GWVA and other groups amalgamated to form the Canadian Legion of the BESL. The new Legion grew steadily during the 1930s and expanded rapidly during and immediately after WWII. It concentrated on the re-establishment of veterans, advising them on pensions and other benefits available from the federal government. In 1960 the organization was renamed the Royal Canadian Legion.

The Legion continues to serve veterans by bringing their concerns to the attention of the government. The association's primary aim since 1915 has been service to the veteran and his dependants, although it now engages in many public and community service activities, helping to remind Canadians of those who have served their country in war. Each province is organized as a command, and in 1987 the Legion, with headquarters in Ottawa, had several hundred branches in Canada with over 591 000 members. *See also* WAR VETERANS. GLENN T. WRIGHT

Reading: C. Bowering, *Service* (1960).

Royal Canadian Mint, see MINTING.

Royal Canadian Mounted Police, with an establishment of more than 20 000, the national force that provides policing in all provinces and territories except Ontario and Québec. The RCMP maintains 8 crime detection laboratories, the Canadian Police Information centre in Ottawa and the Canadian Police College in Regina. There is a large marine section with a fleet of patrol boats and an aviation section with a variety of airplanes and helicopters. Liaison officers are posted in 27 foreign capitals. This large, sophisticated force had small, temporary beginnings. In the late 1860s when Canada was negotiating the acquisition of RUPERT'S LAND, the government faced the problem of how to administer these vast territories peacefully. The Hudson's Bay Co had ruled for almost 2 centuries without serious friction between fur traders and the native population. There were few fur traders and their livelihood depended on economic co-operation with the natives. The company made no effort to govern the native population.

The Canadian takeover meant the imposition of a government that would systematically interfere with native customs for the first time. Thousands of settlers would arrive to occupy the lands where Cree and Blackfoot hunted buffalo without restraint. At worst, the tensions generated by this process might erupt into the kind of warfare experienced in the American West. Apart from the cost in lives on both sides, the Canadian government could not contemplate the expense of a major Indian war, which might easily bankrupt the country. The Canadian government also feared that violence in the new territories might provide American expansionists with an excuse to move in.

Canada in the 1870s, like most other jurisdictions whose legal systems were based on English common law, had few police forces. The larger cities had primitive local constabularies; small towns and the countryside had no police at all. In these areas the burden of maintaining public order fell upon the courts, backed up in emergencies by the military.

The British government had some experience with centralized police forces in India and Ireland, however, and the forces there were unquestionably effective. Prime Minister Sir John A. MACDONALD therefore adopted the Royal Irish Constabulary as the model for Canada. The police for the North-West Territories were to be a temporary organization. They would maintain order through the difficult early years of settlement, then, having served their purpose, they would disappear. In 1869 William MCDOUGALL, sent out as first Canadian lieutenant-governor of the North-West Territories, carried instructions to organize a police force under Capt D.R. Cameron. Half the men of the force were to be local Métis. These plans had to be shelved when the RED RIVER REBELLION of 1869-70 led to the creation of the province of Manitoba, since, under the BRITISH NORTH AMERICA ACT, law enforcement was a provincial responsibility.

Not until 1873, when Ottawa created an administrative structure for the remainder of the territories, was the idea of a police force revived. Parliament passed an Act in May establishing a force, and 150 recruits were sent that Aug W to winter at Ft Garry; the following spring another 150 joined them. The new police force, which gradually acquired the name NORTH-WEST MOUNTED POLICE, was organized along the lines of a cavalry regiment and was armed with pistols, carbines and a few small artillery pieces. Several reports on the state of affairs in the North-West Territories had stressed the symbolic significance of the traditional British army uniform for the Indians. A scarlet tunic and blue trousers were thus adopted. The commanding officer was given the title "Commissioner." There was an assistant commissioner and 2 officer ranks, superintendent and inspector; noncommissioned ranks were staff sergeant, sergeant, corporal and constable. The commissioned officers were given judicial powers as justices of the peace. Lt-Col George Arthur FRENCH, commander of the Permanent Force gunnery school at Kingston, Ont, was the first commissioner.

On 8 July 1874 the 300 mounted police left Dufferin, Man, and marched W. Their destination was present-day southern Alberta, where whisky traders from Montana were known to be operating among the Blackfoot. The previous June there had been a serious incident in the Cypress Hills at a whisky trader's post in which several Assiniboine were massacred by whites. After a gruelling march of more than 2 months the force arrived to find that most of the traders had fled. The Blackfoot almost immediately tested the intentions of the police by reporting the activities of some of the remaining whisky traders. The immediate arrest and conviction of the traders pleased Chief CROWFOOT and laid the foundation for good relations with the police. Asst Commissioner James F. MACLEOD with 150 men established a permanent post at FT MACLEOD. Part of the remaining half of the force had been sent to Ft Edmonton and the rest under the commissioner returned E to Ft Ellice (near St-Lazare, Man), which had been designated as headquarters.

The following summer FT CALGARY on the Bow R and FT WALSH in the Cypress Hills were established. In 1876 another major post was set up at Battleford. The network of posts and patrols thus began, and was extended year by year until it covered all of the territories.

For a decade and a half the NWMP concentrated on establishing close relations with the Indians. The police helped prepare the Indians for treaty negotiations and mediated conflicts with the few settlers. Their success is indicated by the signing of treaties covering most of the southern prairies in 1876 and 1877 (*see* INDIAN TREATIES), by the fact that they rarely resorted to armed force before 1885 and by the small number of Indians who participated in the NORTH-WEST REBELLION that year. Growing unrest in the early 1880s because of the disappearance of the buffalo and crop failures in the Saskatchewan Valley led to an increase to 500 men in 1882. But this did not keep pace with the force's growing responsibilities. CPR construction had drawn the police into a limited role in southern BC as well as the prairies. The police were particularly concerned with the situation in the Saskatchewan Valley and warned Ottawa that serious trouble was certain unless grievances there were addressed. The warnings were ignored and the rebellion took its tragic course. Belatedly the government increased the NWMP to 1000 men and appointed a new commissioner, Lawrence W. HERCHMER, to modernize the force.

Herchmer improved training and introduced a more systematic approach to crime prevention, thus preparing the police to cope with the large increase in settlement after 1885. As memories of the rebellion faded, criticisms began. In Parliament the Opposition reminded the government that the NWMP had been intended to disappear when the threat of frontier unrest passed. The NWMP's demise seemed certain with the election of Wilfrid Laurier's Liberals in 1896; their election platform had called specifically for the dismantling of the NWMP.

In power the Liberals quickly discovered intense opposition in the West to their plan. The highly publicized murder of Sgt C.C. Colebrook by ALMIGHTY VOICE in 1895 and the manhunt that went on for more than a year raised renewed fears of a general Indian uprising.

By the mid-1890s, too, the NWMP had begun moving north. Rumours of gold discoveries in the Yukon prompted the government to send Insp Charles CONSTANTINE to report on the situation in that remote region. His recommendations led to the stationing of 20 police in the Yukon in 1895.

This small group was barely adequate to cope with the full-scale gold rush that developed when news of large discoveries reached the outside world in 1896. By 1899 there were 250 mounted police stationed in the Yukon. Their presence ensured that the KLONDIKE GOLD RUSH would be the most orderly in history. Strict enforcement of the regulations prevented many deaths from starvation and exposure by unprepared prospectors.

By 1900 the gold rush was over and the police turned their attention to other parts of the North. In 1903 the first mounted police post north of the Arctic Circle was established at Ft McPherson. Later the same year the NWMP began collecting customs duties from whalers at Herschel I in the Beaufort Sea. At the same time a detachment under Supt J.D. Moodie established a post at Cape Fullerton on the western shore of Hudson Bay. The police presence in the Arctic grew steadily from these beginnings, especially after the schooner *St. Roch* began to be used as a floating detachment among the Arctic islands in the 1920s.

The permanence of the mounted police was tacitly accepted by all parties by the early 20th century. When Alberta and Saskatchewan were created in 1905, the RNWMP (the "Royal" added 1904 in recognition of distinguished service by many NWMP men in the SOUTH AFRICAN WAR) was, in effect, rented to the new provinces. Agreements were signed under which the NWMP acted as provincial police.

This arrangement worked well until WWI. The war created severe shortages of manpower and brought new security and intelligence duties to the police. When Alberta and Saskatchewan decided to adopt PROHIBITION in 1917, Commissioner A. Bowen PERRY, who believed the new liquor laws were unenforceable, cancelled the contracts. Alberta and Saskatchewan maintained their own provincial police forces for the next decade and a half.

When the end of hostilities in 1918 reduced the need for security work, the future of the mounted police was very uncertain. Late in 1918 President of the Privy Council N.W. ROWELL toured western Canada to seek opinion about what to do with the RNWMP. In May 1919 he reported to Cabinet that the police could either be absorbed into the army or expanded into a national police force. The government chose the latter course. In Nov 1919 legislation was passed merging the RNWMP with the DOMINION POLICE, a federal force established in 1868 to guard government buildings and enforce federal statutes. When the legislation took effect 1 Feb 1920, the name became Royal Canadian Mounted Police, and headquarters were moved to Ottawa from Regina. In the 1920s the force's principal activities were enforcement of narcotics laws and security and intelligence work. The latter reflected widespread public fear of subversion that had been fueled by the Russian Revolution in 1917 and the WINNIPEG GENERAL STRIKE of 1919. In 1928 Saskatchewan renegotiated its provincial policing agreement with the RCMP, thus beginning a return to more normal police duties for the force.

In Aug 1931 Maj-Gen Sir James H. MACBRIEN became commissioner. The 7 years of his leadership of the force was a period of rapid change. The size of the RCMP nearly doubled in this period, from 1350 to 2350 men, as the force took over provincial policing in Alta, Man, NB, NS and PEI and took over the Preventive Service of the National Revenue Department. Before MacBrien died in office in 1938, he had established a policy of sending several members of the force to universities each year for advanced training, had opened the first forensic laboratory in Regina and had organized the aviation section. An RCMP Reserve

was established in 1937 in the expectation that war was coming and would make heavy demands on the force. When WWII began the RCMP had comprehensive plans for the protection of strategic installations, and in fact no acts of sabotage were recorded. Nazi sympathizers were rounded up for INTERNMENT. Despite suspicions about Russian espionage, however, the RCMP was as surprised as most Canadians by the revelations of Igor GOUZENKO in 1945.

The heightened international tensions of the COLD WAR era, which the Gouzenko case inaugurated, ensured that security and intelligence work would continue to be a major preoccupation for the mounted police. These activities attracted almost no public attention until the mid-1960s, when Vancouver postal clerk George Victor Spencer was discovered to have been collecting information for the USSR. The tacit agreement among politicians that security matters were not subjects of open debate was shattered when John Diefenbaker's Conservative Opposition attacked the Pearson government for mishandling the case.

In retaliation the Liberals revealed details of a scandal involving a German woman named Gerda Munsinger, whose ties to some Conservative Cabinet ministers and Russian espionage agents had apparently been ignored by the previous Diefenbaker government. A Royal Commission on Security was appointed in 1966 as a result of these cases and reported in 1968. The commission's recommendation that a civilian intelligence agency replace the RCMP was rejected by the new prime minister, Pierre Trudeau.

By 1969 the rise of separatism in Québec had produced a major shift in security and intelligence operations from foreign threats to a perceived threat within the country. The OCTOBER CRISIS of 1970 with the kidnapping of James Cross and the murder of Pierre LAPORTE added enormous impetus to undercover antiseparatist operations in Québec.

The RCMP was subsequently discovered to have engaged in such illegal activities as burning a barn and stealing a membership list of the Parti Québécois. These revelations raised fundamental questions about the place of the police in the state. Are there situations in which the police can break the law? Who is ultimately answerable if they do? To help answer these questions the Royal Commission of INQUIRY INTO CERTAIN ACTIVITIES OF THE RCMP was appointed under Mr Justice David McDonald. The commission again recommended re-

North-West Mounted Police lancers at Ft Walsh [Sask], 1878 (*courtesy National Archives of Canada/C-18046A*).

moving intelligence operations from the RCMP to a civilian agency. Legislation creating such an agency, the CANADIAN SECURITY INTELLIGENCE SERVICE, was proclaimed on 1 July 1984. However, problems with the ill-defined nature of CSIS plagued its first 3 years and in late 1987 the Conservative government announced that its mandate would be changed.

The postwar period also saw a continued expansion of the RCMP's role as a provincial force. In 1950 they assumed responsibility for provincial policing in Newfoundland and absorbed the BC provincial police. In 1959 the most serious conflict over the split federal-provincial jurisdiction of the force took place. A loggers' strike in Newfoundland led the superintendent in charge of the RCMP there to ask the provincial attorney general to request 50 reinforcements from Ottawa. Justice Minister E. Davie FULTON refused and Commissioner L.H. Nicholson resigned in protest. The question of which level of government controls the RCMP in a given set of circumstances remains vague. It has been a source of tension between the federal and provincial governments, leading on a number of occasions to threats by the latter to cancel their RCMP contracts and establish provincial police.

Since 1945, 3 areas of criminal investigation have occupied a large and growing portion of the force's time: ORGANIZED CRIME, narcotics and commercial FRAUD. The first 2 were closely linked, and from the late 1940s onward there was growing evidence that illegal drug traffic was controlled by Canadian branches of American crime syndicates

The RCMP Musical Ride originated in early riding drills (*photo by J.A. Kraulis*).

or "families." In 1961 the RCMP established national crime intelligence units across the country to gather information on organized crime and to improve co-operation with other police forces. Similarly, growing numbers of securities frauds and phony bankruptcies led the RCMP to establish commercial fraud sections, with specially trained personnel, beginning in 1966.

Since 1886 all basic training of RCMP recruits has been carried out at Depot Division in Regina. Today the course is 6 months in length and includes a variety of subjects from basic criminal law to driving and shooting. Depot Division also gives courses for fisheries enforcement officers, correctional services personnel, native special constables and tribal police. Since 1974 women have been recruited into the force and undergo the same training as male constables. Upon graduation the female constable is assigned duties on the same basis as her male counterpart. Female members of the force are as likely to be found in remote northern communities or on highway patrols as on desk jobs.

From the earliest years of its existence the mounted police have attracted the attention of writers. Hundreds of novels, stories and films, mostly by British and American authors, have appeared over the last century, creating a vivid popular image of the mounted police as fearless and infallible.

The Canadian government realized the usefulness of this image as early as the 1880s. The scarlet-coated policeman began to appear on Canadian immigration pamphlets and shortly after that on tourist advertisements. The police themselves have always recognized the value of good public relations. Early riding drills developed quickly into public exhibitions of horsemanship set to music. Thus the origins of the famous musical ride can be traced back to the 1870s. Although mounted training once required of all recruits has long since disappeared, the musical ride remains an enormously popular public attraction in Canada and elsewhere. The symbolic importance of the "mounties" may help to explain why they have retained their popularity in spite of adverse publicity in recent years. R.C. MACLEOD

Reading: Nora and William Kelly, *The Royal Canadian Mounted Police* (1973); R.C. Macleod, *The North-West Mounted Police and Law Enforcement* (1976); William R. Morrison, *Showing the Flag: The Mounted Police and Canadian Sovereignty in the North, 1894-1925* (1985); Keith Walden, *Visions of Order: The Canadian Mounties in Symbol and Myth* (1982).

Royal Commissions, once described by a member of Parliament as costly travelling minstrel shows, are a form of official inquiry into matters of public concern. They descend from the British monarch's prerogative power to order investigations, said by some to have been exercised first by King William I when he commanded the preparation of the Domesday Book, though the Commission on Enclosures initiated by Henry VIII in 1517 is a more likely prototype of contemporary royal commissions.

Closely related to the royal commissions and often hard to distinguish from them are several other kinds of public inquiry, eg, commissions of inquiry, TASK FORCES, and investigations established by departments and other agencies under statutory powers of the Inquiries Act, first passed by Parliament in 1868.

At the federal level royal commissions, task forces and commissions of inquiry are appointed by ORDER-IN-COUNCIL under Part I of the Inquiries Act, while departmental investigations are launched under Part II, but the distinction makes little difference in the functioning of these bodies since they all enjoy the power conferred by the Act to conduct investigations by subpoenaing witnesses, taking evidence under oath, requisitioning documents and hiring expert staff. Royal commissions have the added lustre of being created under the imprint of the Great Seal of Canada, while departmental investigations may stem from any one of at least 87 federal statutes that confer powers of inquiry with or without reference to the Inquiries Act. Aside from these minor distinctions, royal commissions are no more regal than other kinds of inquiries.

Despite their unexceptionality, however, an air of superiority still clings to royal commissions. The public takes them more seriously than other sorts of investigations, and governments tend to reinforce the myth by preferring to appoint royal commissions to examine the gravest matters of concern, eg, FEDERAL-PROVINCIAL RELATIONS, health services, BILINGUALISM AND BICULTURALISM, CORPORATE CONCENTRATION, financial management and accountability, government organization, TAXATION, energy, and ECONOMIC UNION AND DEVELOPMENT PROSPECTS FOR CANADA.

Task forces, on the other hand, have generally been regarded as more prosaic work crews composed of knowledgeable practitioners rather than eminent luminaries. Often appointed by government departments, they have been assigned to examine such practical matters as PRIVACY and computers, IMMIGRATION procedures, retirement income policy, labour market development, FISHERIES POLICY, and sports. However, while it would be tempting to conclude that task forces, departmental investigations and nonroyal commissions are used to probe particular, well-focused problems while royal commissions are devoted to more sweeping national issues, this simple dividing line cannot always be drawn. Some task forces have dealt with broad and important Canadian issues such as housing and urban development, government information, and the structure and foreign ownership of Canadian industry. At the same time royal commissions have sometimes been used to tackle specific issues like disasters (both public and personal), ranging from the burning down of the Parliament Buildings and riots in Halifax to judicial and ministerial indiscretions. In fact there is little rhyme or reason to the appellations of investigations because they have frequently been appointed haphazardly and their titles applied rather indiscriminately. The Pepin-Robarts inquiry into national unity called itself a task force when it might well have been a royal commission.

The McDonald INQUIRY INTO CERTAIN ACTIVITIES OF THE ROYAL CANADIAN MOUNTED POLICE had the dimensions of a royal commission. The probe into the loss of the drill rig Ocean Ranger was changed from a commission into a royal commission. In view of this confusion it is not surprising that the Law Reform Commission has recommended that the term "royal commission" be abandoned altogether.

Since Confederation there have been close to 450 federal commissions of inquiry with and without the royal title, more than 1500 departmental investigations, and an undetermined number of task forces. As stated earlier, royal commissions tend to be used either to secure advice upon some important and troublesome general problem or to investigate a specific contentious incident, but critics allege that royal commissions are often established to give a besieged government an excuse to do nothing while a protracted investigation cools the public's temper. Hence the frequency of royal commissions varies from decade to decade; a greater number are usually created during times of crisis, growth and adjustment.

The cost of having several such acts of national introspection operating simultaneously is not inconsiderable. Though the number of actual commissioners employed in any given inquiry may not be great, ranging from one to the 13 on the (Donald) Macdonald investigation into development prospects, the inclination in recent years to hire a proliferation of high-paid legal counsel and massive research staffs over long periods of time has cost the public a great deal. The most extensive and expensive royal commission until 1982 was the McDonald inquiry into the RCMP which ran for 4 years and cost $10 million. The royal commission on economic union and development prospects may well establish a new record with its $21.8-million budget. However, it was also given a 3-year deadline within which to report, indicating that governments are less willing to pay indefinitely for royal commissions.

On balance, royal commissions and other forms of inquiry probably do more good than harm. At least they are necessary from time to time to flush out misfeasance and malfeasance and to examine matters of major public concern. Some royal commissions have produced significant reports, eg, the Rowell-Sirois report on federal-provincial financial relations, Massey on the arts, and Laurendeau-Dunton on bilingualism and biculturalism furnished the documentation for continuing public debate and for some policy-making.

Each province has its own Inquiries Act under which it conducts investigations similar to Ottawa's. Although it is difficult to draw comparisons, because even less academic study has been devoted to provincial bodies than to federal, it appears that the provinces have not tended to use royal commissions as often as Ottawa. Québec conducted 91 commissions and committees of inquiry from Confederation to 1972 while Ontario appointed 177 royal commissions and commissions of inquiry between 1867 and 1978. The most popular subject for investigation in the 10 provinces has been education. From 1787 to 1978 there were 367 inquiries into education, of which 127 were royal commissions.

Various alternatives to royal commissions and other forms of inquiry have been discussed recurrently, including the increased use of legislative committees and white papers, which are simply studies and proposals put out tentatively by government departments for public discussion prior to possible action. But legislatures and the House of Commons do not have sufficient time and objectivity to examine many issues; and while the Senate may have the time, the public would probably not accept its views upon a controversial matter as readily as it would receive the opinions of a royal commission headed by a judge or another prominent figure. *See also* BANKING AND FINANCE, ROYAL COMMISSION ON; BROADCASTING, ROYAL COMMISSION ON; CANADA'S ECONOMIC PROSPECTS, ROYAL COMMISSION ON; CONSTITUTIONAL PROBLEMS, ROYAL COMMISSION OF INQUIRY ON; DOMINION-PROVINCIAL RELATIONS, ROYAL COMMISSION ON; ENERGY, ROYAL COMMISSION ON; GOVERNMENT ORGANIZATION, ROYAL COMMISSION ON; NATIONAL DEVELOPMENT IN THE ARTS, LETTERS AND SCIENCES, ROYAL COMMISSION ON; NON-MEDICAL USE OF DRUGS, ROYAL COMMISSION ON THE; PATENTS, COPYRIGHT AND INDUSTRIAL DESIGNS, ROYAL COMMISSION ON; PUBLICATIONS, ROYAL COMMISSION ON; STATUS OF WOMEN IN CANADA, ROYAL COMMISSION ON THE; TAXATION, ROYAL COMMISSION ON; TRANSPORTATION, ROYAL COMMISSION ON; WAR CRIMES, ROYAL COMMISSION ON. PAUL FOX

Royal Conservatory of Music of Toronto (until 1947, known as Toronto Conservatory of Music) offers preparatory and professional instruction, administers a nationwide system of practical and theoretical examinations, and operates an annual summer school, featuring a wide range of courses and workshops for teachers. The RCMT has had a significant influence on Canadian music through its recital series, publications and special projects. The conservatory was founded by Edward Fisher in 1886, and in the following year opened with 200 students and 50 teachers. By 1892 it was organized into 2 departments: the Academic Dept catered to young students and amateurs; the Collegiate Dept offered professional training to teachers and performers. In this period conservatories prepared students for examinations conducted by the universities. Originally associated with University of Trinity College, TCM affiliated with U of T in 1896.

Under the energetic leadership of Augustus VOGT (principal, 1913-26), the conservatory established a national network of examination centres. By 1921 U of T had assumed control of the conservatory and, after absorbing all rival schools (with the exception of the Hambourg Conservatory), enjoyed a position of pre-eminence by the late 1920s. Ernest MACMILLAN (principal, 1926-42) added prestige through annual performances of the TCM choir and revised the examination curricula by incorporating more rigorous requirements in aural skills and theory. In 1944 the Frederick Harris music publishing company was donated to the university, with profits to be used for conservatory scholarships and bursaries.

A modern phase of professional training commenced when diploma programs were offered in a new Senior School (1946). Activities within its opera division eventually led to formation of the CANADIAN OPERA COMPANY. Returned servicemen and students from all parts of Canada participated in these new opportunities for advanced study; concurrrently, the university initiated a degree in school music. Sir Ernest MacMillan, Ettore Mazzoleni and Arnold WALTER were prominent in these postwar developments, which produced a new generation of Canadian performers, composers and teachers.

The conservatory has survived several administrative reorganizations and, even with the recent growth of music in universities, has successfully made major accommodations in its teaching operations. In 1987 it had a teaching staff of 9778 students and conducted 81 000 examinations across Canada. J. PAUL GREEN

Royal Flying Corps, formed 13 Apr 1912 to fulfill a perceived need, common before WORLD WAR I in European countries, to participate in the expanding field of AVIATION. It comprised a military wing, a naval wing (later the ROYAL NAVAL AIR SERVICE) and a flying school; duties included reconnaissance, bombing, observation for the artillery, co-operation with the infantry in attacking enemy positions, supply drops and observation for the Royal Navy. When WWI began, Canada did not have its own air force and, until the RFC established training camps in Canada in Jan 1917, the only way for a Canadian to become a war pilot was to enlist in the regular forces and try to transfer to the air service, or to travel at his own expense to England and attempt to enlist directly. It is impossible to determine the exact number of Canadians who joined the RFC, but it is estimated that over 20 000 Canadians had joined the British flying services by the end of WWI. Many of these became pilots, among them the Canadian "aces" Lt-Col W.A. BISHOP, Lt-Col R. COLLISHAW, Lt-Col W.G. BARKER, Maj D.R. MACLAREN and others. The RFC joined with the RNAS to become the Royal Air Force on 1 Apr 1918. GLENN B. FOULDS

Reading: S.F. Wise, *Canadian Airmen and the First World War* (1980).

Royal Military College of Canada, Kingston, Ont, was founded in 1874; since the 1970s RMC

has offered bilingual instruction. The college opened 1 June 1876 with 18 cadets, staffed by British military officers and one Canadian civilian. Queen Victoria conferred the title "Royal" in 1878. The first class graduated on 2 July 1880. Before WWI most ex-cadets took up civilian professions, especially engineering, and 4 graduates received commissions annually in the British army. After 1919 RMC was staffed by Canadians, the first Canadian commandant being Maj-Gen Sir Archibald Macdonnell. Graduates were required to serve in either the active forces of the Crown or the Canadian Militia. The RMC engineering course was recognized as a qualification to practise the profession; certain Canadian universities and provincial law societies accepted RMC graduates to take degrees or diplomas in a final year. Many former cadets held high military rank during WWII. RMC closed in 1942 but was reopened in 1948 as one of the tri-service Canadian Service Colleges (CSC). From 1954 the Regular Officers Training Plan (ROTP) required all CSC graduates to take a regular commission, but a small Reserve Entry was re-established in 1961. From 1959 RMC granted degrees, and graduate courses were added in 1964. Women students were first admitted in 1979. RMC is now administered as part of the Canadian MILITARY AND STAFF COLLEGES under the Dept of NATIONAL DEFENCE.
RICHARD A. PRESTON

Enrolment: Royal Military College of Canada, 1985-86 (Source: Statistics Canada)			
Full-time Undergrad	*Full-time Graduate*	*Part-time Undergrad*	*Part-time Graduate*
722	33	64	32

Royal Naval Air Service The naval wing of Britain's ROYAL FLYING CORPS became the RNAS on 23 June 1914. In WWI it was far more than the envisaged auxiliary force for the navy, being responsible at various times for the air defence of Britain and the support of land operations in Flanders, Gallipoli (Gelibolu, Turkey), parts of the Middle East, and E Africa. It pioneered strategic bombing but was not prominent in naval operations until 1918, when it played a major part in the war against German U-BOATS. Together with the RFC it became part of the Royal Air Force on 1 Apr 1918. Prominent among the 936 Canadians known to have served in the RNAS were R.H. "Red" Mulock, later a pioneer of Canadian civil aviation, Lloyd S. Breadner, Robert LECKIE, and W.A. CURTIS. W.A.B. DOUGLAS

Royal Newfoundland Constabulary is the only major police force in Canada not to equip its members with firearms for patrol duties. The withdrawal of British troops from Newfoundland in 1870 forced the Island's authorities to replace the system of local constables with a more efficient police force. In 1871 Thomas Foley was appointed inspector of police with instructions to organize a centralized force modelled upon the Royal Irish Constabulary. The result was the Newfoundland Constabulary (prefix "Royal" granted in 1979) which eventually established itself throughout Newfoundland and along the Labrador coast. In 1935 it was replaced in Labrador and parts of Newfoundland with the Newfoundland Rangers, and was restricted to the city of St John's in 1950 when the RCMP took over provincial police duties. Its jurisdiction expanded again to greater St John's in 1982-83, Labrador City in 1984, and Corner Brook in 1986. Its strength in 1986 was 400. S.W. HORRALL

Royal Ontario Museum in Toronto is Canada's largest museum and one of the largest in N Amer-

ica. The ROM was established by an Act of the Ontario Legislature in 1912. The original building, now the west wing, was officially opened in 1914 by the duke of Connaught, governor general of Canada. In 1933, 2 new sections were opened, an east wing facing Queen's Park and centre block connecting the 2 wings to form an H-shaped main building with north and south courtyards. In the next few decades, 2 independent buildings were added to the museum complex as a result of generous donations: the Sigmund Samuel Building housing the Canadiana collections, a few blocks S of the main building, and the McLaughlin Planetarium, adjoining the main building. In 1987 the George R. Gardner Museum of Ceramic Art, opposite the main ROM building, merged operations with the ROM and became the fourth building.

In 1978 a $55-million renovation and expansion project was initiated when work began on the complete renovation of the main building and construction of a 9-floor curatorial centre building in the south courtyard. Construction of the 6-floor terrace gallery building in the north courtyard began in 1980.

The 2 new buildings are linked to the main building by skylighted atria, so that a harmonious integration of the old and the new is achieved. The renovated and expanded main building reopened to the public in 1982.

Collections When it opened in 1914, the ROM was an amalgamation of 5 separate museums, each with its own director. In 1955 the 5 museums were reorganized into 3 divisions (art and archaeology, geology and mineralogy, and zoology and palaeontology), all reporting to one director. The collections are now the responsibility of 10 science departments (Botany, Entomology, Ichthyology and Herpetology, Invertebrate Palaeontology, Invertebrate Zoology, Mammalogy, Mineralogy, Geology, Ornithology and Vertebrate Palaeontology) and 9 art and archaeology departments (Canadian Decorative Arts, Egyptian, Ethnology, European, Far Eastern, Greek and Roman, New World Archaeology, Textile and West Asian). Many of the collections, or individual items within them, are of world significance. The science departments are rich in type specimens, the scientifically accepted specimen from which a new species or mineral has been described.

The Chinese collections are internationally known, particularly the bronzes, oracle bones and tomb figurines, which comprise the largest aggregation outside China. The Greek and Roman collections are the largest and most representative in Canada. The museum holds the only comprehensive Canadian collection of Egyptian material and the largest textile and costume collections in Canada. A large percentage of the museum's 6 million artifacts and specimens form research collections available to visiting scholars from around the world. In addition, these materials are loaned to cultural and educational institutions for study and public display.

Gallery Displays, Exhibitions and Public Programs Over 1 million people visit the museum annually. New galleries and exhibit areas are continually being developed and, when they are all in place, the exhibit space will total 21 620 m². Displays are also housed in the Sigmund Samuel Building, the McLaughlin Planetarium and the R. Gardner Museum of Ceramic Art. Galleries in the new museum are organized in 8 clusters: New World Archaeology, Ethnology, Europe/Canada, East Asia, Earth Science, Astrocentre, Life Sciences and Mediterranean World. In these clusters, each display is related to the next, and all form part of an integrated whole to facilitate orientation and comprehension. In addition, there is a theme gallery called Mankind Discovering, a hands-on Discovery Gallery and several areas for rotating exhibits. The Garfield Weston Exhibition Hall is designed for travelling exhibitions of international significance, including those organized by the museum. The museum offers many public programs: lectures and films, demonstrations, concerts, dramatic performances, special events and the identification of specimens and artifacts for the public. The Members' Volunteer Committee conducts a variety of programs, including public tours of the galleries, walking tours of the city, bus tours of Ontario and world tours to all parts of the globe, led by expert museum staff.

Through travelling exhibits, a "museumobile," a speaker's bureau and resource boxes, school cases and other programs for schools, the Outreach Dept provides museum experiences to more than 800 000 people each year in hundreds of different communities in Ontario and across Canada. In addition, the teaching staff in the Dept of Education Services gives lessons in the galleries to over 125 000 students during an average year.

Research The work of the curatorial staff in the field and in sophisticated laboratories of the curatorial centre provides the solid academic base for all public activities of the museum. Archaeology departments conduct field excavations in many parts of the world; eg, in Belize, Egypt, the Middle East and Canada (*see* ARCHAEOLOGY; MEDITERRANEAN ARCHAEOLOGY).

The science departments provide consultations to a variety of international, national and provincial agencies. Several members of the curatorial staff are world authorities in their fields, and members in the science departments have been recognized by having newly discovered animals or minerals named in their honour. An impressive number of general interest and scholarly publications produced each year by the ROM record and share the results of museum research with both the academic community and the general reader. DAVID A. YOUNG

Royal Prerogative of Mercy The federal Cabinet has the power to pardon anyone who has been convicted of a criminal offence. The pardon can be free or conditional. The effect of a free pardon is that the person is deemed never to have committed the offence for which they were convicted. The SOLICITOR GENERAL of Canada has the responsibility for receiving requests for pardons for criminal offences. VINCENT M. DEL BUONO

Royal Proclamation of 1763 was issued by King George III to establish a basis of government administration in the N American territories formally ceded by France to Britain in the Treaty of PARIS, 1763, following the SEVEN YEARS' WAR. It established the constitutional framework for the negotiation of Indian treaties with the aboriginal inhabitants of large sections of Canada. As such, it has been labelled an "Indian Magna Carta" or an "Indian Bill of Rights."

The document is referred to in s25 of the CONSTITUTION ACT, 1982. This provision details that there is nothing in Canada's Charter of Rights and Freedoms to diminish the rights and freedoms that are recognized as those of aboriginal peoples by the Royal Proclamation.

King George's Proclamation became a key legal instrument for the establishment of colonial governments in the PROVINCE OF QUEBEC, E Florida, W Florida and Grenada. It also defined the legal status of a large area in the N American interior as a vast Indian reserve. The eastern boundary of this territory, which explicitly excluded the colony of Québec and the lands of the Hudson's Bay Co, was set along the heights of the Appalachian mountain range. The western border was not specifically described. These special provisions to acknowledge and protect some rights of the native peoples in the N American interior were made in recognition of the fighting power they collectively represented.

By holding out to Indians the promise of a degree of security as the sole authorized inhabitants of the larger part of their ancestral lands, the British government was endeavouring to stabilize the western frontier of the old crown colonies along the Atlantic seaboard. The decision to formalize this limited but important recognition of native rights was hastened by news that a number of Indians following Ottawa Chief PONTIAC had successfully demonstrated their defiance of crown rule over their lands by briefly seizing several British military posts recently captured from the French. Knowledge of this act only seemed to underline for imperial authorities the self-interested wisdom of affording to native groups, many of whom had recently fought the British as allies of the French, a degree of protection from the landgrabbing expansionism of frontiersmen along the western borders of the Thirteen Colonies. The implications of doing otherwise, and of thereby incurring an enormous expense for the maintenance of law and order in the N American interior, were unthinkable to the parsimonious officials responsible for the strategic defence of the British empire.

King George reserved the western lands to the "several nations or tribes of Indians" that were under his "protection" as their exclusive "hunting grounds." As sovereign of this territory, however, the king claimed ultimate "Dominion" over the entire region. He further prohibited any private person from directly buying the interest of native groups in their ancestral soil. This exclusive right of purchase he rather reserved for himself and his heirs alone. As detailed in the Proclamation, he set out a procedure whereby an Indian group, if they freely chose, could sell their land rights to properly authorized representatives of the British monarch. This could only take place at some public meeting called especially for the purpose. It was thus that the constitutional basis was established for the future negotiation of Indian treaties in British N America. The Royal Proclamation thereby established the British Crown as the essential central agent in the transfer of Indian lands to colonial settlers.

Although it proved virtually impossible for imperial authorities to check the western boundaries of the Thirteen Colonies at the Royal Proclamation line, repeated efforts were made to hold back the pressure of colonial settlement from the larger part of those lands reserved to the Indians. Outrage against this imperial policy in the Thirteen Colonies was one of the factors responsible for the outbreak of the American Revolution in 1776. The first systematic attempts to enforce consistently the treaty-making provisions of the Royal Proclamation took place in the regions north of the Great Lakes which became designated as Upper Canada in 1791. The treaty-making procedures that evolved in this colony were later largely exported to the territories purchased in 1870 by the new Dominion from the Hudson's Bay Co.

Although these regions had been specifically designated in 1763 as outside the jurisdictional framework put in place by the Royal Proclamation, Canadian government officials recognized that the native peoples of the newly annexed territory had the same rights to their unceded ancestral lands as Indians in the UC area prior to the negotiation of treaties. Hence a basis of land tenure was established throughout most of the prairie provinces and northern Ontario, where 7 numbered treaties were negotiated in the 1870s, on the basic principles outlined in the Royal Proclamation of 1763.

The Royal Proclamation tends to come under close scrutiny whenever there is cause to examine the legal character of aboriginal land title. In the St Catharine's Milling case, for example, which became in 1889 the vehicle for the settling of a constitutional dispute between the governments of Ontario and the young Dominion, lawyers for the former argued that the Royal Proclamation was of no force in the legal elaboration of Indian rights. In handing down the opinion of 3 of 7 Canadian Supreme Court judges in 1973, however, Mr Justice Emmett HALL expressed quite a different view of the Proclamation. Responding to a case involving the territorial rights of the Nisgha nation, he found that the basic principles of the Royal Proclamation were generally applicable in British Columbia, where most of the land remains uncovered by Indian treaties. If Mr Justice Hall's view is technically correct, the implications of this are that aboriginal land rights are legally enforceable over other large areas of the country such as the Yukon, the eastern Arctic, parts of Québec and the Maritime provinces. In these regions the treaty-making provisions of the Royal Proclamation have never been implemented.

It remains to be seen, therefore, whether the principles of the Royal Proclamation have constitutional application to all of Canada or only to parts of the country. Another question to be faced is whether the Proclamation is itself the source of aboriginal land rights, or whether it merely acknowledges and confirms pre-existing rights. The inclusion of reference to King George's statement in the Canadian Constitution Act, 1982, assures that the interpretation of his words will remain for a long time to come an important topic of attempts to clarify the precise character of aboriginal rights in Canadian law. *See also* ABORIGINAL RIGHTS; INDIAN TREATIES; LAND CLAIMS; and various entries under NATIVE PEOPLE. ANTHONY J. HALL

Royal Society of Canada, the senior national organization of distinguished Canadian scholars in the arts and sciences. Its aim is the advancement of learning and research in Canada. Founded in 1882 under the auspices of the Gov Gen the marquess of Lorne, it comprised some 80 French- and English-speaking members (fellows) prominent in fields from geology to literature. In time, other LEARNED SOCIETIES emerged for specific disciplines; but the "mother society" that brought together the whole range of scholarly interests kept to the fore, and election by its membership as a fellow has remained a prized professional honour. With other interested parties, the Royal Society pressed successfully over the years for the creation of the NATIONAL ARCHIVES OF CANADA, NATIONAL MUSEUMS, the NATIONAL GALLERY, the NATIONAL RESEARCH COUNCIL for the sciences, the Historic Sites and Monuments Board and the NATIONAL LIBRARY. Today the society upholds standards of excellence through its medals and prizes for achievements in literature (both French and English), history, chemistry, biology and much more. It holds annual conferences and organizes interdisciplinary regional, national and international symposia on current topics of importance, the results of which are often published, as are the *Transactions* of its annual meetings. The organization now operates in 3 large units: L'Academie des lettres et des sciences humaines, the Academy of Humanities and Social Sciences, and the Academy of Science. All 3 meet jointly part of the time, as well as separately, thus maintaining the Royal Society's basic purpose of uniting the widespread specialized interests of Canada's scholarly community. J.M.S. CARELESS

King George VI and Queen Elizabeth with PM Mackenzie King, on the steps of the Parliament Buildings in Ottawa, Oct 1939. It was the first visit of a reigning monarch to Canada (*courtesy Canapress Photo Service*).

Royal Tours in what is now Canada began when Albert Edward, Prince of Wales (later Edward VII) officially visited British North America in 1860. During a 2-month tour of Newfoundland, the Maritimes and Canada, highlighted by the opening of Montréal's Victoria Bridge and the laying of the cornerstone for Ottawa's Parliament Buildings, the prince was honoured as a visible symbol of monarchy and empire. The next major royal tour was that of the duke and duchess of Cornwall and York (later George V and Queen Mary) in 1901. This was the first transcontinental tour, and demonstrated the "steel of empire" significance of the CPR. The popular Edward, Prince of Wales (later Edward VIII), made official tours of Canada in 1919 and 1927 in addition to private visits to his Alberta ranch. In May and June 1939 King George VI and Queen Elizabeth made the first visit of a reigning monarch to Canada. The extensive tour was planned to solidify Canadian support for Britain on the eve of WWII and it succeeded admirably as ecstatic crowds poured forth pro-British sentiments. Princess Elizabeth made her first royal visit to Canada in 1951. The Queen's symbolical associations have been less popular in Québec, where at one time French Pres Charles de Gaulle was given what amounted to a royal welcome in Québec City. PM John TURNER's request that Queen Elizabeth delay her visit to avoid the political campaigning of the summer of 1984 caused a mild controversy. During her reign as Elizabeth II royal visits became fairly frequent, thus losing some of the mystique they had once possessed. ROBERT M. STAMP

Royal Trustco Ltd, with head offices in Ottawa, is a Canadian holding company incorporated in 1978 to become the parent of the Royal Trust group of companies. It carries on trust, financial, real-estate and deposit services in 134 branches in Canada, the US and overseas.

In 1986 it had sales or operating revenue of $2.4 billion, assets of $19.5 billion (ranking 10th among banks and financial institutions in Canada) and 14 835 employees (internationally). DEBORAH C. SAWYER

Royal William, the first Canadian ship to cross the Atlantic entirely under steam power. It was built by Messrs Black and Campbell and launched on 27 Apr 1831 by Lord and Lady Aylmer at Québec. The steam engines were made and installed in Montréal. It made several trips between Québec and the Atlantic colonies in 1831, but was quarantined because of the cholera epidemic in 1832 and the owners lost some £16 000 on the venture. It left Pictou on 18 Aug 1833 with 7 passengers and a load of coal and arrived at Gravesend after a 25-day passage. The *Royal William* was eventually sold to the Spanish navy. JAMES MARSH

Royal Winnipeg Ballet is the second-oldest ballet company in N America and the oldest surviving company in Canada. The RWB had its origins as a ballet club, organized in 1938 by 2 immigrant English dance teachers, Gweneth LLOYD and Betty FARRALLY, who had moved to Canada at the invitation of friends. The club made its first public appearance in June 1939 as part of a pageant planned for a visit to the city by King George VI and Queen Elizabeth. The group was not seen by the royal party but danced 2 brief ballets on prairie themes, *Grain* and *Kilowatt Magic,* both choreographed by Lloyd.

The club became the Winnipeg Ballet in 1941 and operated semiprofessionally, making occasional tours out of town, until turning professional in 1949. In 1953 it became the first company in the British Commonwealth to be granted a royal charter (London's Sadler's Wells company did not become the Royal Ballet until 1956), but it almost collapsed in 1954 as the result of a disastrous fire in which the company's entire stock of costumes, original music, choreographic scores and sets was destroyed. Following the fire, the company was directed by a succession of individuals until being taken over in 1958 by Arnold SPOHR, a former principal dancer and choreographer with the company and architect of its rise to international success in the 1960s and 1970s. Spohr built a compact touring ensemble dancing a widely diverse repertoire, performing everything with what became characterized as a "prairie freshness."

The company's first resident choreographer was Brian MACDONALD, and it was on his works of the late 1960s that the company's first major successes, in the US and Europe, chiefly rested. However, Spohr was tireless in searching out new choreographic talent, and along with the work of Macdonald and Norbert VESAK, he showcased the work of such internationally acclaimed choreographers as Oscar Araiz, John Neumeier (who gave the company its first full-length work, his highly original version of *Nutcracker),* Vicente Nebrada and Dutch choreographers Hans van Manen, Jiri Kylian and Rudi van Dantzig.

In the 1980s Spohr introduced more full-evening works in the classical style – van Dantzig's *Romeo and Juliet,* Peter Wright's *Giselle* and Galina Yordanova's *Swan Lake* – as showcases for the exceptional talents of the company's first international star, Evelyn HART, who took the women's solo gold medal at the Varna International Ballet Competition (1980). In 1982 Spohr's "courage, determination, organizational skills and singular artistic taste" earned him one of the highest accolades of N American dance, the *Dancemagazine* award.

In 1986 Spohr announced his retirement, effective June 1988, and in late 1987 principal dancer Henny Jurriëns, formerly assistant to Dutch National Ballet director van Dantzig, was named as Spohr's successor as artistic director of the RWB. The company spends approximately 20 weeks a year on tour and early in 1988 made a 7-week tour of the Orient. The RWB is a member of the Canadian Assn of Professional Dance Organizations. MAX WYMAN

Rubber Products Industry consists of establishments primarily engaged in manufacturing rubber tires, tubing, hose, belting, washers and gaskets, weather stripping, tapes, etc. The 100 large and small rubber manufacturers in Canada share annual sales of more than $2.5 billion. The industry directly employs 20 000 people; tens of thousands of additional jobs exist among suppliers and marketers of rubber products, and in the TRANSPORTATION and service sectors. In 1986 the industry had an investment of nearly $1.6 billion in plants and equipment.

The first European to record rubber in action was Christopher Columbus. While exploring Haiti in 1492, he noticed native boys playing with a ball that bounced. Upon investigation, Columbus found that it was made from the milky-white sap (latex) of a certain type of tree. When exposed to air, the sap darkened, hardened and could be bounced.

No real effort was made to use rubber commercially until the 1760s when experimenters in France found it could be dissolved by turpentine and ether. Seventy years later in Scotland, Charles Macintosh began waterproofing garments. Around the same time the English chemist Joseph Priestley found that the substance would rub out pencil marks, hence the name "rubber." Thomas Hancock, an English coachmaker, discovered that rubber could be shredded and pressed into a soft, pliable block. In 1839 the American inventor Charles Goodyear discovered vulcanization, a process by which the rubber compound is cured at high temperatures, using sulphur.

Although various rubber-yielding trees were discovered growing wild in Central and S America, the best source was the Brazilian rubber tree, *Hevea brasiliensis.* Seedlings were smuggled from Brazil in 1876 and brought to England. Ultimately plantations were set up in Malaya and other southeast Asian countries, allowing control of the quality of supply of raw natural rubber.

Production of tires in Canada began in 1895, although the first Canadian production of rubber articles probably began at Dominion Rubber (later Uniroyal Ltd) in 1854. By the late 1980s the Canadian tire industry was threatened by falling profit margins and foreign competition. In 1987-88, 2 plants, operated by Goodyear Canada Inc in Toronto and Firestone Canada Inc in Hamilton, were forced to shut down and industry spokesmen predicted more closures if the bilateral FREE TRADE agreement with the US eliminated the Canadian producers' 10.2% tariff advantage. Five manufacturers, all multinationals, currently operate 9 factories in Canada and employ some 12 000 workers. The average plant in 1985 produced 13 500 passenger and truck tires per day. Sales in 1986 numbered 22 million tires, although sales have been decreasing since the introduction of longer lasting tires. In 1986 the industry exported $418-million worth of passenger tires to many countries around the world and imported $142-million worth.

During WWII Japanese occupation of the natural-rubber-producing countries of Asia created a critical situation. The rubber industry, working closely with the federal government, pushed forward a crash program to produce synthetic rubber. The program eventually resulted in the formation of POLYMER CORP (now Polysar Ltd), Sarnia, Ont, one of the world's foremost manufacturers of "raw" synthetic rubbers. Today, about two-thirds of the rubber used in Canadian industry is synthetic.

Although automobile tires are its single most important product, rubber has many other uses. Even in the automotive market, rubber is used for much more than just tires: there are over 200 rubber items in the average car, including wiper blades, engine mounts, door and window weather stripping, fan belts, radiator hose, foot pedals, etc. The industry produces many other rubber products for the agriculture, FOOTWEAR, TEXTILE and CONSTRUCTION INDUSTRIES. The industry is concerned in developing energy-saving products, eg, radial passenger tires that wear longer and reduce gas consumption by about 10% over conventional tires. Most of the industry is represented by the Rubber Assn of Canada.　　APRIL J. MacDOUGALL

Rubenstein, Louis, figure skater (b at Montréal 23 Sept 1861; d there 3 Jan 1931). One of Canada's finest all-round athletes, Rubenstein was Canadian figure-skating champion 1883-89. In 1890 in St Petersburg, Russia, he won the unofficial world championship, displaying a mastery of figures and free skating. President of the Int Skating Union of America 1907-09, Rubenstein was also active in the administration of several sports. He was an accomplished bowler and cyclist, president of the Canadian Wheelmen's Assn for 18 years, and president of the Montréal Amateur Athletic Assn 1913-15. Rubenstein was a partner in the family firm of silver platers and manufacturers, and was a Montréal alderman 1914-31.
　　BARBARA SCHRODT

Rubeš, Jan, bass, actor, director (b at Volyně, Czech 6 June 1920). He graduated from the Prague Conservatory of Music in 1945 and became the youngest basso at the Prague Opera House. He played leading roles at the opera house in Pilsen, and in 1948 he was selected to represent Czechoslovakia at the International Music Festival in Geneva where he was awarded first prize. Rubeš decided to expand his musical possibilities and immigrated to Canada 31 Dec 1948. He has been very influential in the development of opera in Canada and has had a long association with the CANADIAN OPERA CO, singing numerous roles, including Mephisto in *Faust*, Boris in *Boris Godunov* and Schigolch in *Lulu* and has also served as director of touring and program development. In 1958 Rubeš appeared with Joan Sutherland as Leporello in *Don Giovanni* at the Vancouver Festival. He translated and has played many times the comic intermezzo, *Il Maestro di Cappella* by Domenico Cimarosa. In 1975 he directed *The Fool* by Harry SOMERS and Richard Strauss's *Adriane Auf Naxos* at the Stratford Festival's Third Stage. For 10 years, Rubeš was the singing narrator of the radio program "Songs of My People" and was writer and host 1975-83 of TVOntario's "Guess What?" He has turned to acting in recent years and has been highly acclaimed for his roles in the television productions "The Day My Grandad Died" (1977) and "Charlie Grant's War" (1984) and the films *Witness* (1985) and *One Magic Christmas* (1985).　　JAMES DeFELICE

Rugby is an amateur game played by 2 sides of 15 players who carry, kick and pass (forward passes are not permitted) an oval-shaped ball. Players score points by touching the ball over the opponents' goal line (a try) or by kicking it over the crossbar (a goal). Ball-carrying and running games have existed since before the Middle Ages and the story that William Webb Ellis invented the modern game at Rugby School in England, hence the name rugby football, has been largely refuted. Rugby football was distinguished from association football (SOCCER) in 1863 and the sport's controlling body, the Rugby Football Union, was formed in England in 1871. British settlers, garrison troops and members of the Royal Navy probably introduced the game to Canada from 1823 onwards and fostered its development in many parts of the country, especially in Halifax, Toronto, Montréal and, later in the 19th century, Vancouver, which, owing to its favourable climate and strong British tradition, became the game's stronghold. F. Barlow Cumberland and Fred A. Bethune first codified rules for rugby football in Canada in 1864 at Trinity College, Toronto, and the first Canadian game of rugby took

Rugby was introduced to Canada around 1823 by British garrison troops and members of the Royal Navy (*photo by Ted Grant/Masterfile*).

place in 1865 in Montréal when English regiment officers and civilians, mainly from McGill U, engaged in competition. Clubs across Canada were established after this and organized contests ensued: Montreal FC (1868), Halifax FC (1870), Winnipeg FC (1879) and Vancouver RFC (1889) are notable examples. In 1874 Harvard and McGill universities played the first international rugby match in N America, and thenceforth N American varieties of rugby began to evolve. Separation between the English and N American types of football occurred in 1882 with the formation of the Canadian Rugby Football Union; the English code of rugby in Canada fell under the control of individual provincial rugby unions which took administrative directives for many years from the RFU in England before eventually operating under the Rugby Union of Canada from 1929 to 1939 when it was curtailed by WWII. It re-formed in 1965 and was renamed the Canadian Rugby Union in 1967.

While British immigrants and military personnel initially fostered rugby's development, touring teams to and from Canada also helped to promote the game by demonstrating its international appeal. A Canadian team first toured the British Isles in 1902, and since that time representative teams have visited Japan, England, Wales, Ireland, Argentina and Australia. Overseas national teams visiting Canada have included Japan, England, Australia, the British Lions, New Zealand, Fiji, Wales and Italy. Provincial, club and schoolboy teams have competed against overseas opponents since 1908 when a BC representative side lost 2 games against the New Zealand All-Blacks in California. Most tours in this category have taken place after 1960 when the Rugby Tours Committee was formed. BC remains the stronghold of rugby in Canada, although the game is played in all 10 provinces. The Carling Cup, emblematic of the national championship, was first won by BC in 1958, and although dormant between 1959 and 1966, the championship was retained by the BC team until Ontario won its first championship in 1971.

Rugby has continued its development throughout the 1970s and 1980s. A junior interprovincial championship was inaugurated in 1976, and in 1982 the concept of a national junior team was realized. Canada was successful in its first game at this level, defeating a side representing Japan. Further games have been played against Welsh schools (1983, 1986) and England Colts (1985), with the Canadian side overcoming a powerful Welsh team in the 1986 Vancouver contest. A more significant development in the game of rugby has been the increasing participation of women. There are now more than 30 women's clubs across the country, and a western Canadian women's championship has been held annually since 1983. The first Canadian women's team played an international against the US in late 1987.

These developments, along with improved coaching, via the CRU's coaching program which is linked with the National Coaching Certification Program, have greatly influenced rugby's popularity in Canada, and recognition of Canada's vigorous promotion of the game was apparent in 1987 when the national senior team participated in the inaugural Rugby World Cup held in Australia and New Zealand.　　DAVE BROWN

Rugs and Rug Making A hooked rug is made by pulling loops of yarn or rag strips up through a loosely woven foundation cloth, usually burlap, using a tool like a crochet hook. Eventually, these loops of different kinds of material in a variety of colours create a design – pictorial, floral or geometric – which covers the whole foundation and forms a sturdy mat. In the mid-19th century when hooked rugs were first made, floor covering was a luxury in Canada. The wealthy might have an imported oriental rug or perhaps could afford commercial loom-woven carpeting. Others might make (or have made) a *catalogne* rug, consisting of a weft of rag strips woven on a widely spaced warp of cotton string. The hooked rug solved the problem of covering cold floors cheaply and was the final stage in the recycling of handme-down clothing.

Very little 19th-century everyday clothing is left in Canada: cloth was too precious to waste and much of it ended up in QUILTS or on the floor (*see* CLOTHING). It is probable that rug hooking developed independently and simultaneously in several centres: Québec, the Maritimes and New England. Hooked rugs were made in much greater numbers in the eastern half of the continent than in the western half since, by the time the Canadian West was settled, store-bought floor coverings had become available.

The most immediately recognizable of Canadian rugs are those from the Grenfell missions in Newfoundland and Labrador. Grenfell rugs have been made since 1913 when Dr Wilfred GRENFELL industrialized the local mat-making activities. Standard patterns (eg, dogsleds, flights of geese, polar bears) were reproduced on burlap, and then the rugs were hooked by local women. The rugs were sold widely through churches to raise money for medical missions. Grenfell mats, which are still produced today using chemically dyed synthetic fabrics in place of the original natural fibres and vegetable dyes, have always been extremely finely hooked and look almost like needlepoint. Browns and greens predominate in the early rugs, which contained much burlap yarn, as well as underwear and stockings collected on the mainland and donated to the missions. The fine workmanship of the rugs of Cheticamp, NS, is also legendary. The Cheticamp rug industry was established by Lillian Burke at the instigation of Mrs Alexander Graham Bell, who was impressed with the possibility of establishing a homecraft industry in Cape Breton.

Unlike quilts, which are often treasured within a family and passed from one generation to the next, old hooked rugs are usually orphans whose family history has been lost. It is rare to find a very old rug whose maker is known. However, one famous rug hooker was Emily CARR, who made rugs to supplement the income she earned from her boardinghouse. Many rugs designed by the artist Georges-Édouard Tremblay can be identified. As part of the Québec CRAFT revival, these rugs were copied in his Pointe-au-Pic studio from Tremblay's landscape paintings by local women working under his direction; the rugs were often hooked from heavy cotton yarn and featured a wide black edging around a snow scene.

In 1868 Edwards Sands Frost, a Maine tin peddler, devised a series of zinc cutouts that allowed him to mass-produce stencilled patterns on burlap for rug hooking (an early version of paint by number). Other companies also entered the market. By the mid-1890s Garrett's of New Glasgow, NS, was producing *Bluenose* rug patterns. In 1894 Wells and Richardson of Montréal published patterns in its *Diamond Dye Rug Books* ("Do not sell your rags to the travelling rag-gatherer; save them and work them up into handsome and useful Rugs and Mats"). By 1905 Eaton's was advertising *Monarch* hooked rug patterns in its catalogue, and in the early years of the century Hambly and Wilson of Toronto also produced patterns on burlap.

Pattern rugs are still made today, but the most impressive rugs have always been those devised by women from their own materials and visions. Many old Canadian hooked rugs are surprisingly eloquent. They speak of economy, individuality and utility. Women incorporated into these rugs generations of clothing and memory-laden cloth – the very fabric of their lives.   MAX ALLEN

Rule, Jane Vance, writer (b at Plainfield, NJ 28 Mar 1931). Educated at Mills College, Calif, and University College, London, Eng, Rule moved to Vancouver in 1956. She was assistant director at International House, University of British Columbia (1958-59) and lectured in English and creative writing at UBC (1959-76). In 1976 she moved to Galiano I, BC. Rule is an acute observer of social and emotional relationships, homosexual and heterosexual, and writes about them with refreshing candour. Her novels include *Desert of the Heart* (1964), *This Is Not for You* (1970), *The Young in One Another's Arms* (1977) and *Contract with the World* (1980). She has also written short stories (*Themes for Diverse Instruments*, 1975; *Outlander*, 1981), many essays and a study of lesbian writers, *Lesbian Images* (1975). Her most recent books are a prose collection entitled *A Hot-Eyed Moderate* (1984), *Inland Passage and Other Stories* (1985) and a novel, *Memory Board* (1987).
JEAN WILSON

Rule of Law, an underlying constitutional principle requiring government to be conducted according to law and making all public officers answerable for their acts in the ordinary courts (*see* ADMINISTRATIVE LAW). The principle was perhaps first formally enunciated by Bracton (1250), a judge and early writer on English law, who declared, "The King himself however ought not to be under man, but under God and under the law, for the law makes him king." The term was coined by the English legal scholar Dicey, in his *Introduction to the Study of the Law of the Constitution* (1885).   STEPHEN A. SCOTT

Rumilly, Robert, nationalist historian (b in Martinique 1897; d at Montréal 8 Mar 1983). In an amazing series of 42 volumes, Rumilly set forth the history of Québec from 1867 to the present. Despite a lack of professional training (he never backed up his evidence with footnotes), he was the first French Canadian writer to block out the history of his native province and thus deserves the gratitude of the writers who have followed in his path and relied heavily on his work. In his writing, he used the concept of "race" to explain the relations between Francophones and Anglophones, and as well he explored the effects of industrialization on his people. Rumilly believed that Québec was destined to be the centre of Catholicism and French civilization in N America. In his essentially conservative and even rightwing outlook, he was an eloquent spokesman in the 1950s for the traditional nationalist current which found its political expression in the Union Nationale regime headed by Maurice Duplessis.
JOSEPH LEVITT

Rundle, Robert Terrill, Methodist missionary and circuit clergyman (b at Mylor, Eng, 11 June 1811; d at Garstang, Eng, 4 Feb 1896). Sent as a Methodist missionary to the Saskatchewan country in 1840, he arrived at Fort Edmonton on 18 Oct 1840. Although it remained his headquarters until 1848, he spent several winters at Lesser Slave Lake Fort and Fort Assiniboine, and a few springs and summers at Rocky Mountain House and Gull Lake. Twice, in 1841 and 1847, he went south, deep into Blackfoot country. In 1844 he went past the first ranges of the Rockies, where he saw the mountain that today bears his name. He became a master of the Cree language, having learned CREE SYLLABICS devised by James EVANS; his journals record the adjustments made to the syllabary in the early years. Rundle was less than successful at establishing permanent missions. Only in 1848 was Pigeon Lake started by his follower, Benjamin Sinclair. After his return to England, Rundle served at various circuits until his retirement. *See also* MISSIONS AND MISSIONARIES.
FRITS PANNEKOEK

Rupert, Rivière de, 763 km long to the head of Lac Témiscamie, in which it rises and follows a twisted course through a series of lakes and across a flat coastal plain to discharge into southeastern JAMES B. Cree have inhabited its banks for centuries. English navigator Henry HUDSON wintered at the mouth in 1610-11. In 1668 the ship NONSUCH made its historic voyage to the spot that led to the creation of the Hudson's Bay Co and the beginning of the fur trade in Hudson Bay. The company's first post was built at the river's mouth and for many years it was a main artery of the trade, carrying traders and Indians between the coast and the fur-rich interior. Rupert House, an Indian settlement, is still located near the site of the original post. Prince Rupert was the first governor of the HBC.   DANIEL FRANCIS

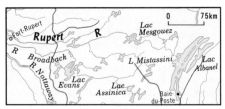

Rupert's Land On 2 May 1670 Charles II of England granted to the HUDSON'S BAY COMPANY a large portion of N America, named Rupert's Land in honour of Prince Rupert, the king's cousin and the company's first governor. This grant comprised the entire HUDSON BAY drainage system, which in modern geographical terms included northern Québec and Ontario N of the Laurentian watershed, all of Manitoba, most of Saskatchewan, southern Alberta and a portion of the NWT. The company was to have a monopoly and complete control of the territory. The HBC first established FUR-TRADE posts around James and Hudson bays. In 1774 Samuel HEARNE established the first western inland post at CUMBERLAND HOUSE [Sask]. By 1870 there were 97 posts within the territory. HBC fur traders were responsible for many early travels, explorations and cartography in Rupert's Land.

By the 1850s the Canadian movement to annex Rupert's Land was gaining momentum, and provision was made in the BRITISH NORTH AMERICA ACT for its admission into Canada. On 19 Nov 1869 the company signed and sealed the deed of transfer surrendering its chartered territory to the Crown and the governments of Great Britain and Canada set the date of transfer for 1 Dec 1869. Owing to the RED RIVER REBELLION, the date of transfer did not become effective until 15 July 1870. In exchange for Rupert's Land, the HBC re-

Hunters, Rupert House, 1868. By 1870 there were 97 Hudson's Bay Co posts in Rupert's Land carrying on the fur trade (*courtesy Archives of Ontario/S2011*).

ceived £300 000, certain land around its posts, and eventually some 2.8 million ha of farmland in what are today the Prairie provinces.
SHIRLEE ANNE SMITH

Rural Society, English Canada In Canada, rural society has been shaped by geographic and cultural diversity and by population mobility. Canada was settled in a series of westward movements, which created dispersed rural communities differentiated by their dependence on primary production (agriculture, FORESTRY, fishing or MINING), ethnic mix and time of settlement. ACADIAN communities in the Atlantic region are 150 years older than settlements in Alberta; landholding divisions in Lower Canada (*see* SEIGNEURIAL SYSTEM) are distinct from the "quarter sections" of the prairies. Wars, depressions, technological advancement and URBANIZATION have all affected established communities. Thus, in contemporary rural society, local and regional diversity is strong. However, when compared to urban society, rural society retains a firm sense of solidarity and difference.

Canadian rural society has been influenced by 4 consecutive phases of population mobility: rural settlement, labour migrations, depopulation and return migration. Early mobility was usually westward and towards the frontier. Labour migrations were also westward, eg, the movements of workers who manned the threshing crews on western grain farms in the early part of this century (*see* HARVEST EXCURSIONS). The third and longest phase, rural out-migration, began at the beginning of the century and persisted until the 1970s.

People, mainly rural youth, left farms, villages and towns to seek jobs, education and a better way of life in Canada's growing urban centres. The fourth phase saw a return flow of people from urban to rural areas in the 1970s, a movement that created large-scale commuting between rural areas and large cities.

Role of Technology and Urbanization Technological change has profoundly affected the composition of rural society. Mechanization in the primary industries has led to constant rationalization of production, with reduced need for manual labour and increased demand for technically skilled operators. Farming has become a business and farmers are referred to as "producers," a term that reflects their specialized production orientation. Farm size increases have accompanied technological change and caused many to leave the land. Farm amalgamation and loss of families have caused economic viability problems for local service centres. Small towns and villages have also suffered from technological change because modern equipment and materials tend to be pro-

Manitoba farm. The most enduring institution of rural society is the family farm (*photo by Bob Anderson/Masterfile*).

duced and distributed from cities and processing of foodstuffs now takes place in major cities.

The values of rural society have been profoundly influenced by urbanization. Agricultural fundamentalism – the inherent belief in the virtue of working the land to provide for self and family – developed into a form of "agrarianism," extolling the value of country life while combining the ethics of hard work and frugality to produce a food surplus. Urbanization has brought many benefits to rural society, such as automobiles, electrification, the "party line" and modern homes. It has also introduced some new values, which often conflicted with those of small-town life. Many small towns have continued to have 2 communities, the established and the poor. Rural society has tolerated diversity but, in so doing, has often ignored the poor.

Urbanization is particularly evident in the rural-urban fringe. A backflow of migrants from the city to surrounding rural areas has caused many changes, including conflicts with locals over "rights to farm," on the one hand, and community expansion on the other. Curiously the value conflicts are often the reverse of what might be expected: many ex-urbanites hold firm conservationist principles, whereas locals often favour progress and development.

Rural Institutions The traditional rural institutions of church, school and family have been affected not only by technology and urbanization but also by internal rationalization. Although the rural church, which was ubiquitous in rural Canadian settlements by 1900, has declined in numbers and significance, it still plays an important role in family life and continues to draw many of its ministers from farm and countryside. The rural church tends to be more fundamental in doctrine and social in function than its urban counterpart (*see* EVANGELICAL AND FUNDAMENTALIST MOVEMENTS). In recent years, many new variations of CHRISTIANITY have been established in rural areas.

Rural education changed rapidly in the 20th century. The basic shifts in attendance, curriculum and location, particularly from the local schoolhouse to the central facility, have had a profound effect on rural society. The shift provided standard educational opportunities, and central schooling also helped prepare rural youth for out-migration by detaching youngsters from their local environment.

The most enduring institution of rural society is the farm family, a unit of socioeconomic organization that has persisted from pioneer settlement (*see* PIONEER LIFE) to the modern era of industrial farming. Although the number of farm families has shrunk consistently, the essential feature of the unit has remained intact: family control over land, labour and capital. In order to finance large modern farms, families can incorporate and share the benefits of limited liability and increased access to capital (*see* FARM LAW). Farm families have, in the 1980s, been subject to considerable stress resulting from the cost-price squeeze, high debt load and high interest rates. The rural family has survived the trend of decline in the extended family and has adapted to new household formations. Rural families are smaller than they were but still have a preponderance of males, and the ethics of mutual aid, co-operation, hard work over long hours and community involvement still characterize rural family life (*see* CO-OPERATIVE MOVEMENT).

Contemporary Issues Two emergent trends illustrate the changing social relations of contemporary rural society. Women have become more active in the formal labour force and are an accepted part of the decision-making process in many rural economies. Roles and responsibilities in the rural household have changed. A demand for DAY CARE, rural transportation, more and better human services and job opportunities for women reflect a changing work ethic and an acceptance of occupational pluralism. Rural women are dealing with stress in the family, are capable of rapid occupational mobility and are adept at acquiring new skills. They are also forming new organizations to voice their opinions and needs.

The second contemporary feature is the AGING of the rural population. Demographically, rural Canada is already a mature society, but the growing number of seniors is a newfound strength in rural society. Many seniors are active, join volunteer services; more often can pay for their own needs and bring vitality as well as wisdom to rural communities. Inevitably, they also have special needs (eg, medical care), the servicing of which will form the core of social policy in rural areas in the latter part of the 20th century.   TONY FULLER

Reading: G.D. Hodge and M.A. Qadeer, *Towns and Villages in Canada* (1983); G. Schramm, ed, *Regional Poverty and Change* (1976); M.A. Tremblay and W.J. Anderson, eds, *Rural Canada in Transition* (1970).

Rural Society, Québec Québec has often been identified with rural life, an identification based more on myth than fact. In 1890 Québec, like On-

tario, was 90% rural, but by 1931 the majority of Québec's population was urban and by 1956 less than half the rural population worked in agriculture. In 1962 barely 4.2% of the province's work force was employed in agriculture, the smallest percentage of any Canadian province.

The view of Québec as a backward, rural society originated primarily with Québecois themselves, rather than with others outside the society. After the mid-19th century, a form of NATIONALISM developed in Québec which insisted that the best way to preserve the heritage of language and faith was to develop a strong, well-integrated rural society. Since the city was viewed as the stronghold of the English and of Protestants, the French Canadian who went there risked the loss of both language and faith. In the countryside, according to this ideology, Québecois could control their economic and cultural future and, above all, their existence as a people. This analysis by Abbé GROULX and others led to the conviction that the future of Québec was both agricultural and rural. The ruralist ideology persisted until the end of the 1950s and until the mid-1960s in the case of the agricultural associations (eg, the Union catholique des cultivateurs (UCC) and agricultural CO-OPERATIVES). It disappeared only when the proportion of the work force engaged in agriculture dropped below 10% and more than 75% of the total population was urban. The QUIET REVOLUTION and then the PARTI QUÉBÉCOIS gave rise to a new nationalism which defined Québec as an urban, industrial society (which might even become the first post-industrial society).

Whatever the definition provided by outsiders and by its own leaders, rural Québec (agricultural and nonagricultural) has changed a great deal since the early 20th century. Until the end of the 1930s, Québec agriculture was overwhelmingly subsistence farming. Production was diversified so that farmers could feed their own families. Production techniques were rudimentary and were passed on from generation to generation. After 1910 Québec agriculture discovered the DAIRY INDUSTRY and almost every farm had its herd, the milk being sold to butter and cheese factories and the whey being used in the production of pork. However, dairy and pork production were not considered specializations but rather sidelines which brought in cash, used to buy goods which could not be produced on the farm. There were certain exceptions to this situation (notably in the Montréal plain area), but generally speaking, subsistence farming prevailed until WWII (*see* AGRICULTURE HISTORY).

During the war, the demand for pork and eggs was so great that the normal rules of supply and demand practically ceased to operate: farmers could sell everything they produced at excellent prices. For the first time, they became specialists who earned substantial incomes. But the situation was short-lived and normal market forces prevailed again after the war. Those farmers who had used their wartime earnings to modernize were able to face postwar competition and thrive. Most, however, had purchased consumer goods and had no capital to compete successfully in increasingly mechanized agricultural production. To maintain the standard of living to which they had become accustomed, farmers abandoned agriculture, either moving into the city or working in the forests, where demand for labour was high. Thus, in less than 15 years, more than three-quarters of all farms were abandoned, the farmhouse itself often being moved into a village. At the same time, agricultural production rose dramatically. Those who continued farming did so more effectively than ever and transformed their farms into modern agricultural enterprises. In 1986 Québec's agricultural production was being carried out on about 41 450 farms, often worth around $250 000 each.

Farming organizations underwent a similar transformation. The UCC, which had been primarily an educational organization, became the Union des producteurs agricoles (UPA), bringing together farmers in specialized unions and setting up production offices. Small milk co-operatives united to produce giant co-operatives (Granby being the largest) which entered international markets. The federated co-operative developed control of successive stages of production, distribution and marketing (ie, vertical integration), especially in the area of animal production. Active integration also occurred among private companies.

The nonagricultural rural world has also been transformed. Traditionally, it consisted of craftsmen or day labourers who were few in number (10% of the rural population) and had very little influence. Since 1956 the proliferation of professional forestry workers and the increase in transportation activities and small factories has caused the nonagricultural proportion of the rural population to skyrocket to 90%. Formerly homogenous and virtually egalitarian (only day workers formed a kind of proletariat), Québec's rural social hierarchy is much more complex today. At the top are civil servants and those in the quasi-public sector (eg, teachers, social workers, inspectors) with steady, high incomes. These are followed by farmers and small businessmen, then by labourers with fairly stable employment and, finally, by people on welfare, many of whom are former farmers or lumberjacks. Labourers and those on welfare constitute by far the largest group and live in relative POVERTY. This endemic poverty has contradictory effects on the school population: while it results in a high number of dropouts after primary or during secondary school, those who do not drop out work harder at the CEGEP (COLLEGE D'ENSEIGNEMENT GÉNÉRAL ET PROFESSIONNEL, ie, senior matriculation) level than their urban counterparts. The dropout's future is limited to work in the forest or the rural day-labour force, and rural poverty is thereby perpetuated.

The most profound rural transformation has been rural urbanization. Most of the functions previously carried out locally have been transferred to small cities which have become regional capitals. Some primary and all secondary schools, major stores, credit institutions, recreational facilities and medical and social services are now located in urban centres. The youngest members of the rural population are in daily contact with the city; the oldest visit at least once a week, more often 2 or 3 times. This physical contact is reinforced by the daily intrusion of the city through the mass media, especially television. In sociological terms, the life-style of rural people closely resembles that of city dwellers. The only significant difference is that the ruralist lives in a less densely populated region, where rural culture is barely a memory, if not folklore. *See also* CHILDHOOD, HISTORY OF; FAMILY; FRENCH CANADIAN NATIONALISM; QUÉBEC SOCIETY; INTELLECTUAL HISTORY. GÉRALD FORTIN

Rush, rock band formed in Toronto area 1974, has received popular and critical acclaim with a series of innovative and complex albums, including *Moving Pictures* (1981). In 1980 and 1981 Rush led readers' polls in British rock-trade publications. Geddy Lee, Alex Lifeson and Neil Peart continue their success with platinum record sales and sold-out concert tours. *Power Windows* (1985) was their 11th album. JOHN GEIGER

Rush (Juncaceae), family of herbaceous plants consisting of 8 genera and about 300 species. They are essentially temperate, and are usually found in wet habitats. Six genera with about 10 species occur only in the Southern Hemisphere. The 2 largest genera, the common rush, *Juncus* (225 species), and the wood rush, *Luzula* (80 species), are widely distributed throughout the Northern Hemisphere, though not entirely restricted to it. They are represented in Canada by about 50 and 15 species, respectively, and are found all across the country, including the High Arctic. Most rushes are grasslike, often with sheathing basal leaves, which are sometimes reduced to the sheaths alone. The flowers are small and rather drab. The family is geologically old, dating from the Cretaceous (144-66.4 million years ago). The rushes (or reeds) of the Bible are not rushes at all but *Cyperus papyrus,* a member of the SEDGE family. *See also* GRASSES.

Rush-Bagot Agreement, finalized Apr 1817. US Secretary of State James Monroe proposed to British Foreign Secretary Lord Castlereagh in 1816 that the 2 countries should agree to limit naval armaments to one ship each, on Lks Ontario and Champlain, and 2 each on the Upper Lakes. Thus, in 1817, notes were exchanged between Acting Secretary of State Richard Rush and Sir Charles Bagot, British minister in Washington. Since naval disarmament of the lakes was virtually complete after 1817, the Rush-Bagot Agreement is considered to have ended the British-US naval race and is frequently cited as the diplomatic origin of the friendly international border. In fact, only naval power on the lakes was affected, for the US and Britain continued to build land FORTIFICATIONS along the border for the next half century. D.N. SPRAGUE

Russell, Man, Town, pop 1669 (1986c), 1660 (1981c), inc 1907 (village), 1913 (town), is an agricultural service centre 350 km NW of Winnipeg near the Man-Sask border. Homesteading began in the area in the late 1870s. Russell was founded in 1881 by Charles Arkoll Boulton and became a regional shipping point with the arrival of the Manitoba and North Western Railway in 1886. The CNR followed in 1908 with a roundhouse. Dr Barnardo, controversial British philanthropist, established an industrial training farm SW of Russell (1887-89). One of many Barnardo facilities for destitute British children, the centre trained several hundred boys for work on prairie farms before it closed in 1906 (*see* IMMIGRANT CHILDREN). Known as the Banner County since 1893, contemporary Russell has several agriculture-related industries and services for a market area of grain, oilseed and cattle farms, including the $30-million CSP Foods oilseed crushing plant. Key hunting, fishing and wetland resources are nearby, including Asessippi Provincial Park and the Shellmouth Dam reservoir. D. M. LYON

Russell, Andy, writer, conservationist (b near Lethbridge, Alta 8 Dec 1915). He was a high-school dropout, who trapped for a living in the Depression and then went to work for bighorn-sheep guide Bert Riggall. Russell's intimate knowledge of the wilderness led him to write about it, and he sold his first major article to *Outdoor Life* in 1945. Award-winning books include *Grizzly Country* (1967), *Horns in the High Country* (1973), *Adventures with Wild Animals* (1977) and his autobiographical *Memoirs of a Mountain Man* (1984). In 1987 he published *The Life of a River,* western stories and anecdotes with ecological overtones in their opposition to the Oldman R dam. He produced *Grizzly Country* and 2 other feature-length films for international lecture tours, contributing significantly to the understanding of these solitude-loving animals. He received the Crandall Award for Conservation in 1977. JOHN PATRICK GILLESE

Russell, Benjamin, jurist, author (b at Dartmouth, NS 10 Jan 1849; d at Halifax 21 Sept 1935). An accomplished and versatile jurist, Russell quickly distinguished himself after being called to the NS Bar in 1872. In addition to maintaining a successful practice at Halifax, he reported the debates in the Assembly (1869-83), acted as official reporter and unofficial legal adviser to the Legislative Council (1884-96) and was official reporter of the NS Supreme Court (1875-95). From 1883 he was a lecturer in law at Dalhousie U and thereafter wrote or edited numerous important legal works, including an *Autobiography* (1932). Created KC in 1890, in 1904 he was appointed a puisne judge of the NS Supreme Court, where he served until his death. D. H. BROWN

Russell, Edward, Ted, teacher, magistrate, politician, writer (b at Coley's Point, Nfld 27 June 1904; d at St John's 16 Oct 1977). Russell's writings, combining philosophical wisdom and ingenious wit, drew on his experiences in rural Newfoundland: as a teacher, as a magistrate after the Depression and as a director of co-operatives before Confederation. In 1949 he joined the first provincial Cabinet under J.R. SMALLWOOD, but resigned in 1951 following a disagreement over economic policy. His stories were broadcast on CBC radio 1953-62 as "The Chronicles of Uncle Mose." He wrote and read approximately 600 six-minute scripts as well as 8 radio plays – all centered on the fictitious outport Pigeon Inlet. Many of the stories have been published in *The Chronicles of Uncle Mose* (1975), *Tales from Pigeon Inlet* (1977) and in *The Best of Ted Russell, Number 1* (1982). Also in print is his best-known radio play *The Holdin' Ground* (1972) and a biography by Elizabeth Russell Miller, *The Life & Times of Ted Russell* (1981). ELIZABETH RUSSELL MILLER

Russell, John Alonzo, architect, educator (b at Hinsdale, NH 28 Oct 1907; d at Winnipeg 28 Dec 1966). A prominent figure in the arts in Winnipeg, he came to U of Man in 1928 with degrees in architecture from Massachusetts Institute of Technology. He became director of U of Man School of Architecture in 1946 and dean of the Faculty of Architecture in 1963. His involvement with the lively arts as director and designer included design of sets and costumes for the Winnipeg (later ROYAL WINNIPEG) Ballet and Little Theatre Group (predecessor to Manitoba Theatre Centre). WILLIAM P. THOMPSON

Russell, Loris Shano, paleontologist, (b at Brooklyn, NY 21 Apr 1904). Raised in Alberta, he was director of the Royal Ontario Museum of Palaeontology from 1946 until 1950, when he joined the National Museums of Canada (chief, Zoology Section, 1950-56; director, Natural History, 1956-63; and acting director, Human History 1958-63). He was then appointed chief biologist at ROM and professor of geology at U of T. During WWII he served in Canada and Europe with the Royal Canadian Corps of Signals, and afterward with the Canadian Militia, retiring with the rank of major. Russell's discoveries concerning dinosaurs and early mammals have been particularly important; he was the first to suggest that dinosaurs might have been warm blooded. He has also made original and fundamental contributions to the history of lighting and of material culture in 19th-century N America, and has published over 100 scientific papers, many popular articles and several books, including *A Heritage of Light* (1968) and *Handy Things to Have Around the House* (1979). He retired in 1971, but has continued his fieldwork in western Canada and his research in the evolution of mammals. *See also* DINOSAUR HUNTING IN WESTERN CANADA. WILLIAM E. SWINTON

Russell, Robert Boyd, labour politician (b at Glasgow, Scot 1888; d at Winnipeg 9 Sept 1964). Russell was the most prominent personality associated with the 1919 WINNIPEG GENERAL STRIKE. Subsequently charged with seditious conspiracy, he was convicted and sentenced to a 2-year prison term, the harshest treatment meted out to any accused. Russell was on the strike committee as an officer of the International Assn of Machinists, but as leading spokesman for the ONE BIG UNION in Winnipeg, his presence helped convince authorities that the strike was a tentative revolution. The Socialist Party and the OBU tried but failed to return him to Parliament for Winnipeg N in Dec 1921. Ironically, votes cast for the Communist Party candidate, Jacob Penner, helped ensure defeat of the country's most notorious "Bolshevik." Russell's long and stormy career in the labour movement lasted over 50 years. In 1956 the last remnants of the OBU joined the newly organized Canadian Labour Congress. Russell continued as executive secretary of the Winnipeg District Council until ill health forced him to retire in 1962. Long after he ceased to be a "threat," Russell was showered with honours and accolades by the CLC, Manitoba Prem Duff ROBLIN and others.
ALLEN SEAGER

Russian Civil War, Canadian Intervention in With the collapse of the Russian Empire in 1917, Germany and Austria had been able to transfer many of their troops from the Eastern to the Western Front, increasing pressure on the hard-pressed Allied forces in Belgium and France.

The Allies accordingly undertook to support anticommunist White Russian forces if they would, once back in power, resume war on the Eastern Front against Germany and Austria, a strategy warmly supported by those in London and Paris, in any case, to see the eradication of Bolshevism from Russia. Acceding to pressure from London, the Canadian government dispatched almost 6000 soldiers to join various Allied units in Russia in mid-1918. Although some Canadians died in vicious fighting in northern Russia and in the skies over the Black Sea, most, especially those in Siberia, returned without seeing action. PM Robert Borden recognized that Canada had committed both a political and a military blunder. Canada was henceforth more wary of accepting without its own scrutiny the recommendations of other nations to enter into foreign commitments.
ROY MACLAREN

Member of the Canadian Expeditionary Force and local inhabitants with wagons of firewood, Siberia, *c*Jan-May 1919 (*courtesy National Archives of Canada/C-91751*).

Russians are the largest single linguistic group among the Slavic nations and the dominant nationality in the USSR, comprising about 50% of the total population of 268 million. Preliminary estimates from the 1986 census indicated only 32 080 Canadians of Russian descent.

Except for the relatively concentrated and unified DOUKHOBORS (numbering up to about 30 000), the members of this aging, rapidly assimilating ethnic group tend to be scattered throughout the country. However, their contribution to the arts, sciences and professions in Canada has been far greater than their numbers would indicate.

Migration and Settlement The first Russians in Canada were fur hunters, who operated among the Queen Charlotte Is and along the coast farther south in the 1790s, and several officers on detached service with the British navy, who were based at Halifax 1793-96.

Russians settled in Alaska in the 18th century, but Russian aspirations were curtailed by the 1824 and 1825 conventions with the US and Great Britain, which restricted Russian America to the present Canada-Alaska boundary. Official restrictions have usually hindered emigration from Russia. Most early immigrants to Canada from Russia arrived in groups, through special arrangement.

Between 1874 and 1880, nearly 8000 German MENNONITE colonists from southern Russia settled in Saskatchewan, and in 1899, 7500 Doukhobors settled in Canada, aided in Russia by Tolstoy and in Canada by Professor James MAVOR and Clifford SIFTON, then minister of the interior. Beginning in the 1890s, several thousand Russian JEWS emigrated, seeking relief from ghetto life and the pogroms of western Russia. Small Russian communities were established in Montréal, Toronto, Windsor, Timmins, Winnipeg, Vancouver and Victoria.

Most of the early immigrants were peasants who found work in various industries. After WWI many of the one million Russians (the majority of them agricultural and industrial labourers) fleeing the effects of the Russian Revolution sought admission to Canada, but few were successful. Many Russian intellectuals, on the other hand, preferred to settle in Europe. Men willing to work as farm labourers, loggers and miners were preferred immigrants in Canada, but those who managed to establish themselves in their own professions did outstanding work in many fields. Leonid I. Strakhovsky (1898-1963) pioneered Slavic studies at U of T. Boris P. Babkin (1877-1950) resumed his career in gastroenterology at Dalhousie and McGill universities. Nicholas, Vladimir, Alexis and George IGNATIEFF, the 4 sons of Count Paul Ignatieff, the last minister of education under Tsar Nicholas II, made important contributions to engineering and government. Some Russians joined the Canadian MACKENZIE-PAPINEAU BATTALION which fought on the Republican side during the Spanish Civil War.

The Great Depression and WWII virtually halted immigration of all nationalities, but between 1948 and 1953 a significant number of Russians immigrated to Canada, including some who had originally left Russia and settled in Europe and some who found themselves in Germany after the war either because they opposed Stalin or because they had been sent there as forced labour. Both groups were generally young, well educated, urban oriented and aware of their Russian heritage.

After 1953 Russian immigration declined severely (in the early 1970s the average per year from all of the Soviet Union was only 230), although the Soviet government began at that time to allow the emigration of some Jews. By the late 1980s, about 1500 Soviet Jewish immigrants had been admitted to Canada.

BC has the largest population of Russian origin, largely because of Doukhobor settlement; next are Ontario, Alberta and Saskatchewan.

Social and Cultural Life Although Russian Canadians claim affiliation with a diversity of churches (in order of numbers: the United Church of Canada, Russian Orthodox Church, Roman Catholic), the ORTHODOX CHURCH is still the

St Mary Russian Greek Orthodox Church, north of Willingdon, Alta (*photo by Harry Savage*).

traditional centre for the most vocal and active of those claiming Russian origin or descent.

There are some 40 Russian Orthodox parishes in Canada; half belong to the Russian Orthodox Church Abroad and the remainder to the Orthodox Church in America, which includes in its membership many non-Russian churches which also follow the Byzantine rite. One of the oldest Russian Canadian parishes is that of the Church of Saints Peter and Paul (an Orthodox Church of America member) founded in Montréal in 1907.

Within the Russian community a broad spectrum of political organizations have been formed. During the 1930s, some Russian Canadians were drawn to the Russian Farmer-Worker Clubs. Closed by government order in 1939, they gave rise to the Federation of Russian Canadians (FRK) in 1942.

The FRK organized some 15 branches in various Canadian cities and published the newspaper *Vestnik* (*Herald*), still the only Russian newspaper in Canada. In 1944 the FRK had about 4000 members; by 1949, after the spy trials resulting from the revelations of Igor GOUZENKO membership dropped to 22 709 and by the late 1980s to less than 800.

The most active Russian organization in Toronto is the Russian Cultural Society (est 1950). Anticommunist in orientation, it publishes a journal *Russkoe slovo v Kanade* (*Russian Word in Canada*), and operates a centre for social and cultural activities. A small Literary Circle (1949), a Drama Circle, and the "Sovremennik" Publishing Association (1960) which publishes the literary journal, *Sovremennik* (*Contemporary*), are also active.

Education Although Russian immigrants have eagerly entered their offspring in Canadian schools, some older immigrants have favoured the establishment of schools by church groups (the 2 largest are in Montréal and Toronto) and clubs for after-hours instruction in Russian language and culture.

National Minorities The immigration of Russians has been less than that of some of the minority peoples of the Soviet Union. Soviet UKRAINIANS emigrating as displaced persons after 1945 have joined earlier immigrants from Austria and Poland to make up Canada's third most numerous ethnic element. The BYELORUSSIANS in Canada, chiefly from pre-WWII eastern Poland, and their descendants are now thought to number about 60 000. There are also smaller numbers of ESTONIANS, LATVIANS, LITHUANIANS, ARMENIANS and Jews.   RICHARD A. PIERCE

Rutabaga (*Brassica napus*, Napobrassica Group), herbaceous biennial vegetable belonging to the Cruciferae family and grown as a ROOT CROP in all provinces. Rutabaga has many other names, eg, *chou de Siam* in French and Swede turnip in English. The rutabaga originated in northern Europe and was introduced to N America around 1805. Related to the TURNIP, rutabagas differ in the root (round, elongated), flesh (thick, yellow) and foliage (broad, smooth, down covered). Cultivars (commercial varieties) include Laurentian and one of its offshoots, the York, which is immune to most strains of clubroot.   HUGUES LeBLANC

Rutherford, Alexander Cameron, lawyer, politician, premier of Alberta 1905-10 (b near Osgoode, Carleton County, Canada W 2 Feb 1857; d at Edmonton 11 June 1941). Educated in Ontario's public schools, at Woodstock College and McGill U (BA, BCL 1881), he articled at Ottawa and was called to the Ontario Bar in 1885. He practised at Kemptville (near Ottawa) until 1895 when he moved to S Edmonton, Dist of Alberta. In 1905 he became the first premier, treasurer and minister of education of the newly created province of Alberta. His administration promoted public education, a public telephone system and railway expansion. Though leader of a powerful Liberal majority in the legislature, he was forced to resign in 1910 over allegations of incompetence and personal interest in his government's agreement to insure the bonds of the Alberta and Great Waterways Ry. Although found innocent of personal interest, a disillusioned Rutherford became increasingly identified with the Conservative Party. Following his defeat in the 1913 provincial election he returned to his Edmonton law practice. He served as chancellor of U of A 1927-41. His fine library of Canadiana now belongs to the university's Rutherford Library.
                                    DOUGLAS BABCOCK

Rutherford, Ernest, Baron Rutherford of Nelson, physicist (b at Nelson, NZ 30 Aug 1871; d at Cambridge, Eng 19 Oct 1937). Although not a Canadian citizen, Rutherford made some of his most fundamental discoveries at McGill and is considered the greatest experimental physicist of the century. He graduated from Canterbury College, Christchurch, in 1895, winning the 1851 Exhibition Scholarship, and went to Cambridge to work in the Cavendish Laboratory under J.J. Thomson.

When he came to McGill in 1898 as Macdonald Professor of Physics, Rutherford had begun studying radioactivity at Cambridge and his work at the Macdonald Physics Building, then one of the best equipped laboratories anywhere, was subsidized by William MACDONALD himself. Rutherford's main contribution was his elaboration in 1902 of the disintegration theory of the atom, a theory that completely transformed the understanding of radioactivity. The results of his work at McGill are synthesized in *Radio-Activity* (1904, rev 1905). At McGill Rutherford was assisted by future Nobel Prize winner Frederick Soddy who coauthored the revolutionary papers on radioactivity. In 1904 Rutherford received the Rumford Medal of the Royal Soc of London given to the author of the most important discovery of the preceding 2 years. He complained about his isolation from the great scientific centres of Europe, however, and in 1907 accepted a post at Manchester. One year later he won the Nobel Prize in chemistry for his work at McGill. In 1911

Ernest Rutherford, considered the greatest experimental physicist of the 20th century, had a profound influence on Canadian science during his tenure at McGill U (*courtesy National Archives of Canada/C-18230*).

Rutherford made another fundamental discovery: the nucleus of the atom. In 1919 he succeeded Thomson as head of the Cavendish Laboratory, attracting students from all over the world, including many young Canadians. Knighted in 1914 and created baron in 1931, Rutherford kept in touch with his former students and colleagues in Canada; McGill named its physics laboratories after him.   YVES GINGRAS

Rutherford, John Gunion, veterinarian, administrator (b at Mountain Cross, Scot 25 Dec 1857; d at Ottawa 24 July 1923). A graduate of the Ontario Veterinary College 1879, he practised in Woodstock, Ont, and in the US and Mexico, and settled in Portage la Prairie, Man, 1884. He became veterinary inspector of Manitoba in 1887 and was an MLA 1892-96 and MP 1897-1900. He was appointed chief inspector of Canada (later veterinary director general) 1902 and Dominion livestock commissioner 1906. Rutherford's greatest contribution was in upgrading the veterinary profession and its associations. He was president of the American Veterinary Medical Assn 1908-09 and was instrumental in raising the standards of education at OVC and having it taken over by U of T and the Ontario government.
                                    R.G. THOMSON

Ryan, Claude, journalist, politician (b at Montréal 26 Jan 1925). He ran *Le* DEVOIR 1964-78 and strongly influenced public debate during the QUIET REVOLUTION in Québec. Ryan was national secretary of Action catholique 1945-62 and chaired the Ministry of Education's adult-education study committee 1962-63. Admired for his careful analyses and clear positions, he helped make *Le Devoir* one of the most respected and influential newspapers in Canada. In 1978 he was chosen to succeed Robert BOURASSA as leader of the Québec Liberal Party and entered the National Assembly the next year as the member for Argenteuil. He campaigned actively for the *Non* side against Prem René LÉVESQUE in the referendum on Québec SOVEREIGNTY-ASSOCIATION, but his participation was eclipsed by that of PM TRUDEAU. His party was defeated in the 1981 election and, despite the

democratic reforms and intellectual revival that he brought to the Liberal Party, his leadership was seriously questioned and he resigned in the fall of 1982. However he has remained an MNA, and following the Liberal victory in 1985 he was named minister of education in the Bourassa government.   DANIEL LATOUCHE

Ryan, Norman, "Red," bandit (b at Toronto July 1895, d at Sarnia, Ont 25 May 1936). Nicknamed "Canada's Jesse James," Ryan committed numerous robberies in Ontario, Québec and the US, deserted the Canadian Army in WWI, and once made a spectacular escape from Kingston Penitentiary. In 1923 he was captured by American police, deported to Canada and sentenced to life imprisonment. He became a model prisoner, impressing officials with his exemplary behaviour. His story attracted journalists who wrote vivid tales of his criminal career and sympathetic accounts of his apparent rehabilitation. Supported by such persons as PM R.B. Bennett and MP Agnes MCPHAIL, Ryan was paroled in July 1935. For 10 months he presented himself publicly as an honest spokesman for prison reform, while secretly re-establishing underworld contacts. He was killed in a shoot-out with police after an attempted robbery.   EDWARD BUTTS

Ryan, Thomas F., businessman, sports promoter (b 1872; d 1961). He introduced the first 10-pin BOWLING alley in Canada and attracted many prominent businessmen and professionals to his downtown Toronto facility. To meet complaints that the heavy ball was causing arm strain among his genteel clientele, Ryan introduced a smaller ball for a game called duckpin and had his father whittle down 5 pins to match. He invented a new scoring system and introduced his game either in 1908 or 1909. He later added the finishing touch – the rubber collar still familiar around the belly of the pin. Ryan neglected to patent his invention and saw no financial gain from it, except in his own alley.   JAMES MARSH

Rye, common name for members of the genus *Secale* of the grass family (Gramineae); grown as a cereal grain. Both annual and perennial forms exist, but only one species, *S. cereale*, is of economic importance, ranking seventh among the world's major food and feed crops. Winter rye, sown in early fall, is far more common than spring rye. Rye probably originated in Asia Minor and spread throughout Europe as a contaminant of WHEAT, which it resembles. It was brought to N America by European immigrants. Additional introductions were made by government agencies in programs to provide cultivars adapted to Canadian conditions. Rye grain is borne on a terminal spike 10-15 cm long. The alternately arranged spikelets produce 2 or 3 kernels. Kernels are generally greenish blue in colour but can range from light tan to dark brown, depending on the cultivar. In N America, rye is used primarily as an animal feed.

The fungus disease "ergot" (*Claviceps purpurea*) is its most serious plant disease, and caution should be exercised when feeding ergoty rye. Canadian production averaged 236 500 t annually (1984-86): 66% was exported (chiefly to Japan, the US and Norway); 30% fed to livestock; 13% used by the DISTILLING INDUSTRY; and 3% used as food (bread and breakfast foods). Rye is the hardiest of all cereal crops and is important in areas subject to cold and drought, eg, drier regions of Alta and Sask, where it has been used to control soil erosion.   D.S. McBEAN

Ryerson, Adolphus Egerton, Methodist minister, educator (b in Charlotteville Twp, Norfolk County, UC 24 Mar 1803; d at Toronto 18 Feb 1882). A leading figure in 19th-century Ontario education and politics, Ryerson was born into a prominent Anglican, Loyalist family, but was converted and ordained in 1827 in the Methodist Episcopal Church. He helped found and edited the *Christian Guardian* (1829), founded Upper Canada Academy (1836) and became first principal of Victoria College (1841).

He first came into prominence in 1826 when he spearheaded an attack on the assumptions and prerogatives of the Church of England, which claimed to be the official church of the colony and exclusive beneficiary of the CLERGY RESERVES. Ryerson emerged as the leading Methodist spokesman and a major figure in the Reform cause. He used the press to promote Methodism and continued as an influential political adviser for the rest of his life. He was president of the Methodist Church of Canada 1874-78.

During the Rebellions of 1837, Ryerson was in England but used his influence to oppose William Lyon MACKENZIE's radical philosophy and violent methods. During the 1840s he continued his active role in politics and, much to the anger of his Reform allies and many Methodists, supported Gov Charles METCALFE against Robert BALDWIN and LAFONTAINE in 1844. He appeared to have joined the Tories whom he had opposed for nearly 20 years.

In 1844 he was appointed superintendent of education for Canada W, continuing in this office until retiring in 1876. He believed that education should be universal and compulsory, and that it had to be religious and moral if it was to improve the individual and help society progress. Culminating in the School Act of 1871, Ontario gained a first-rate primary and secondary school system based on these principles. Ryerson also promoted denominational universities as the pinnacle of the educational process. During his long career, he wrote numerous pamphlets and texts, as well as several works on the history of the province and an important autobiography.

Ryerson based his long and active public career on a consistent, yet often misunderstood, political outlook. He blended a staunch loyalty to British-Canadian institutions and a conservative mistrust of radicalism with a liberal optimism in mankind, adding a deep and abiding religious commitment. He trusted that through religion and education man could fashion his own improvement and the natural, gradual evolution of society. During his early career, when politics in Upper Canada were

Egerton Ryerson, Methodist minister and strong-willed advocate of universal and compulsory education (*courtesy Archives of Ontario*).

polarized by Tory and Reform controversy, Ryerson was condemned for not belonging neatly to either camp. However, he fitted naturally into the moderate, Liberal-Conservative alliance that predominated after the mid-1850s and in fact helped create its ideological framework through the educational system he fostered. Arrogant and strong willed, he never backed away from controversy, combining strong administrative talents, tireless energy, an anti-partisan spirit and a keen sense of what was best for his province.   NEIL SEMPLE

Reading: Neil McDonald and Alf Chaiton, eds, *Egerton Ryerson and His Times* (1978); Egerton Ryerson, *The Story of My Life*, ed, J.G. Hodgins (1883); C.B. Sissons, *Egerton Ryerson* (1937-47).

Ryerson, Stanley Bréhaut, historian, COMMUNIST PARTY OF CANADA leader (b at Toronto 12 Mar 1911). After attending Upper Canada Coll and U of T he studied at the Sorbonne, Paris (1931-34), where he encountered European communist politics. He was a member of the Central Committee of the Communist Party of Canada 1935-69 and Québec provincial secretary 1936-40. He moved to Toronto in 1943 as the new Labour Progressive Party's education director and managing editor of its *National Affairs Monthly.*

During the difficult Cold War years 1949-54, Ryerson was party organizational secretary. In 1959 he took responsibility for the Toronto edition of *World Marxist Review,* and became chairman of the Marxist Studies Centre, Toronto; he was editor of *Marxist Quarterly* 1961-69. Ryerson's "people's history" – *The Founding of Canada: Beginnings to 1815* (1960) and *Unequal Union: Confederation and the Roots of Conflict in the Canadas, 1815-1873* (1968) – is still widely read. A pioneering aspect of Ryerson's scholarship from the late 1930s has been his contribution to the Québec/Canada national debate.

The entry of Warsaw Pact tanks into Czechoslovakia in 1968 precipitated Ryerson's departure from the party; he resigned in 1971. He joined the history department of UQAM in 1970 and throughout the 1970s was an important resource to a new generation of Québec and Canadian Marxist scholars.   GREGORY S. KEALEY

Ryerson Polytechnical Institute, Toronto, Ont, was founded 16 Sept 1948 as Ryerson Institute of Technology. The institute is situated on historic St James Square, where the Toronto Normal School was established in 1852 by Egerton RYERSON, chief superintendent of education for Upper Canada. In 1941 teacher education was shifted to another site to make room for a Royal Canadian Air Force training centre. From 1945 to 1948, the buildings served the Training and Reestablishment Institute, which offered trades training to returning war veterans. Ryerson Institute of Technology began offering 2-year, trades-oriented programs, but by the early 1950s, it had developed 3-year diploma programs with a significant academic component.

The 1963 Ryerson Act created the autonomous Ryerson Polytechnical Institute, with its own board of governors. The Act was amended in 1971 to empower Ryerson to grant degrees in addition to its diplomas. Today, as a member of the Council of Ontario Universities, Ryerson offers 32 career-oriented programs through its Faculties of Arts, Applied Arts, Business, Community Services and Technology. The majority of these programs lead to bachelor of applied arts, bachelor of technology or bachelor of business management degrees.

The program range includes applied computer science, architecture, journalism, radio and television arts, business administration, fashion design, theatre arts, aerospace engineering, chemical engineering and social work. In 1985-86 there

were 7639 full-time and 10 885 part-time students at the institute.   B. BEATON

Ryerson Press, The, was founded as a publishing company in 1829 by the Methodist Church in Toronto. Called the Methodist Book Room, it issued denominational publications and general books until William Briggs took over as book steward in 1879. Briggs developed a coherent policy of using revenue from the sale of foreign (agency) books to publish Canadian writers such as Charles G.D. ROBERTS, Wilfred CAMPBELL and Catharine Parr TRAILL. The name Ryerson Press was adopted 1919 in honour of its illustrious first editor, Egerton RYERSON. Lorne PIERCE assumed editorial control in 1920. He built up a profitable line of school texts and encouraged the careers of promising writers such as F.P. GROVE, Earle BIRNEY and Louis DUDEK. The sale of the press by the United Church of Canada to the American company McGraw-Hill in 1970 caused consternation among those believing Canadian ownership essential to an independent BOOK PUBLISHING industry.   JAMES MARSH

Ryga, George, playwright, novelist (b at Deep Cr, Alta 27 July 1932; d at Summerland, BC 18 Nov 1987). Raised in a Ukrainian farm community in northern Alberta, Ryga received little formal education but nevertheless established himself as a prominent Canadian writer. He was catapulted to fame with THE ECSTASY OF RITA JOE AND OTHER PLAYS (1970), a depiction of the plight of Indians as they struggle to come to terms with a society that incites them to rebellion while blanketing them with bureaucratic indifference. His other plays and 3 novels, *Hungry Hills* (1963), *Ballad of a Stonepicker* (1966) and *In the Shadow of the Vulture* (1985), also explored the problems of self-doubt, alienation and personal unfulfilment. While stridently critical of society, Ryga's writings are not without humour. His other works include *Captives of the Faceless Drummer* (1972), *Night Desk* (1976), *Seven Hours to Sundown* (1977), *Beyond the Crimson Morning* (1979) and *Two Plays: Paracelsus and Prometheus* (1982).   DAVID EVANS

Ryland, Herman Witsius, officeholder (b at Warwick or at Northampton, Eng 1759(?); d at Beauport, LC 20 July 1838). He arrived in Lower Canada in 1793 as civil secretary under Lord DORCHESTER and was secretary to Dorchester's successors until 1813. In 1796 he became clerk of the executive council, a post of consequence. Anti-Catholic and anti-democratic, he opposed the growing power of the Assembly and of the nationalist PARTI CANADIEN. For nationalists he symbolized British imperial domination through his accumulation of offices and political influence. He was sent to England by Sir James CRAIG in 1810 to promote repressive policies, but he largely failed. Appointed to the Legislative Council that year, he made it the scene of his political activity. Unlike many colleagues, Ryland was scrupulously honest in office and left a modest estate. His tenacious opposition to Canadian nationalism stemmed from reasoned political conservatism, and immediate self-interest.   H. LAMBERT

Ryswick, Treaty of, concluded 20 July-30 Oct 1697 between England, the Netherlands, Spain and the Holy Roman Empire on the one side and by France on the other, ending the War of the Grand Alliance (King William's War) and recognizing William III as king of England. The agreement between England and France provided for restoration of all territorial conquests (principally HUDSON'S BAY COMPANY posts seized by Pierre le Moyne d'IBERVILLE between 1686 and 1697) and the establishment of a commission to determine the status of 3 disputed forts in the Hudson Bay region.   STUART R.J. SUTHERLAND

Saanich Peninsula, BC, forms part of the Nanaimo Lowlands, along VANCOUVER I's E coast. It extends from SIDNEY in the N to VICTORIA in the S, is 20 km long and averages 4 km in width; 90% of its perimeter is fronted by sea. The dominant geographical features are Mt Newton and Saanich Inlet. Elevations in the area range from sea level to just over 305 m (Mt Newton), but generally the peninsula is of relatively low relief, rare for the rugged BC coastline. Land on the peninsula is arable and the climate is the mildest in Canada. These qualities, necessary for agriculture, also encourage residential development, and Saanich residents face an almost inevitable urban and suburban encroachment as Metropolitan Victoria grows. Agricultural activity is declining, and land that was formerly forest, pasture or cultivated field is being given over to residential and commercial uses. Besides Sidney and Victoria, the peninsula is organized into 3 other municipalities – Saanich, Central Saanich and North Saanich.

The first inhabitants of Saanich were Indians of the Coast Salish tribe. It is estimated there were about 2000 natives in the area in 1850, most of whom lived at "Sanitch" at Cordova Bay. The name Saanich comes from an Indian word meaning "good" or "fertile" soil. In 1852 Sir James DOUGLAS bought a large section of Saanich from the Indians. In 1858 the land was surveyed and marked into 40 ha allotments; in 1859 the electoral district of Saanich was created. The arrival of the railway gave Saanich a great boost.

During the past several decades agricultural activity on the peninsula has been declining, owing to rising land values and taxes, quarantine restrictions and competition from mainland and California producers. Nevertheless, many full-time and part-time farms show sufficient annual profit to justify their operation. Industrial activity is limited and localized, the most important industries being transportation and tourism. Three ferry terminals on the peninsula provide transportation links to mainland BC and Washington state.

ALAN F.J. ARTIBISE

Sabine, Sir Edward, soldier, scientist (b at Dublin, Ire 14 Oct 1788; d at Richmond, Eng 26 June 1883). He fought along the St Lawrence R in Upper and Lower Canada in 1813-14, and then, within the army, went on to a distinguished career in science. In 1819-20 he made geophysical contributions to PARRY's arctic expedition on the *Hecla*. In 1828 he became one of 3 scientific advisers to the Admiralty and, working through that body as well as through the Royal Soc and the Royal Artillery, promoted international geomagnetic studies, particularly magnetic observations in Canada. The Toronto magnetic observatory owed its survival in part to his representations. He persistently sought global interrelations between different geophysical phenomena. He was president of the Royal Soc of London 1861-71 and of the British Association for the Advancement of Science in 1852. TREVOR H. LEVERE

Sable Island, NS, is the only emergent part of the outer Continental Shelf of eastern N America, situated 300 km ESE of Halifax. Shaped like an open crescent, 38 km long and 1.5 km wide at its widest point, it narrows at both ends to W and E Spits, which continue offshore as shallow submerged bars. It stands on broad Sable I Bank of the SCOTIAN SHELF and consists of 2 parallel sand-dune ridges separated by a discontinuous, linear depression. The northern dune ridge is the bulkier, rising to 26 m; the narrower southern ridge rises to 12 m. Sable I has been evolving as a barrier island during the past several thousand years of postglacial time as sea level has slowly risen over the Continental Shelf. Southerly storm waves have driven sands from the seabed onto the S

shore. Currents related to the Gulf Stream cause a NE drift of beach material along this shore, slowly extending the island in that direction. Along the northern shore, the Belle Isle Current shifts sand more slowly southwestwards. The dune ridges were built by winds behind the northern and southern beaches, but are eroded by linear blowouts during intense northwesterly winter storms. A comparison of charts of the island made over the last 200 years shows that the northern and southern ridges were broken in the 1760s, and that after closure in the early 19th century, the central depression was occupied by a lake that has progressively shrunk in size as a result of drifting sand and plant colonization. Lk Wallace, 5.5 km long, is the present shallow remnant of this lake in the western part of the island. The dunes are stabilized by marram grass or low shrub cover, except for extensive blowout areas in the E and W.

Never permanently settled, Sable I has, however, seen temporary occupation by shipwrecked sailors, transported convicts, pirates and wreckers. The first recorded shipwreck was of one of Sir Humphrey GILBERT's ships in 1583. In 1598 the marquis de La Roche landed 40 convict settlers on the island. Only 12 survived to be rescued in 1603. Manned lighthouses were established in 1873 but have been automated since the 1960s. Canadian government weather- and navigation-station personnel comprise the only inhabitants, but visits are made by maintenance personnel, ecologists and geologists. Exploratory drilling for oil and gas was undertaken here in the mid-1970s but has since been concentrated offshore.

Natural fauna include terrestrial insects, freshwater aquatic life in Lk Wallace, birds and seals. Birds are mainly common sea and beach birds such as gulls and sandpipers, but the Ipswich sparrow is unique to the island. Gray and harbour seals are present in the thousands, the gray being a permanent resident, the harbour seal a summer visitor. Numerous SABLE ISLAND HORSES still roam the island. The island's name derives from its sandy composition, being named *Isola della rena* on the first map of New France (about 1550) by Jacopo Gastaldi. I.A. BROOKES

Reading: H.L. Cameron "The Shifting Sands of Sable Island," *The Geographical Review* 60 (1965).

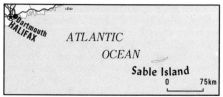

Sable Island Horses, often referred to as ponies, are not really small; stallions weigh 270-360 kg and stand about 14 hands (140 cm) at the withers (shoulders). Mares are a little smaller, averaging about 40 kg less. The HORSES, named for the island they inhabit, exhibit great variability in form and colour, but their most obvious, common characteristics are the stallions' long, flowing manes and tails. They most closely resemble the Spanish barb, a small, tough horse that originated in N Africa, and the Acadian horse, the common working horse of the Atlantic provinces from 17th to 19th centuries. The population organizes itself into family herds of 5-6 horses (stallion, one or more mares and their young). Most foals are born May-June and remain in the family herd for about 2 years. When young males leave, they run with other males in loose bachelor herds until they can attract mares and establish their own family herd. The horse population on the island varies between 150 and 400, averaging around 250. Even without human interference, population fluctuates radically, with periods of growth followed by die-offs of up to 200 horses in one winter. The animals that die are heavily parasited or are usually older horses with worn teeth that

Sable Island horses, named for the island they inhabit, closely resemble the Spanish barb and the Acadian horse, a common working horse in the early Atlantic provinces (*photo by John deVisser*).

are unable to gather sufficient nourishment throughout the winter. Attempts to feed starving horses have failed but, even if they had succeeded, would only have postponed the deaths until the following winter.

It is often stated that the ancestors of Sable Island horses were survivors of some of the hundreds of ships that have been wrecked there. However, most evidence indicates that they were introduced purposely by a Boston merchant, in the middle of the 18th century, along with cattle, hogs and sheep in the course of an unsuccessful attempt to start a farming settlement. At the beginning of the 19th century, a series of lifesaving stations was established on SABLE ISLAND to aid crews of ships wrecked there and the horses were used for riding and as draught animals. The lifesaving establishment continued until the middle of this century and several attempts were made in this period to improve the quality of the wild horses by introductions of new breeding stock. Surplus horses were rounded up periodically and sent to the mainland for sale. Since 1947, no horses have been exported from the island and they are now protected by the Department of Transport, which administers the island. The Sable Island herd is not unique in eastern N America: similar feral horse populations occupy the French island of Miquelon, south of Newfoundland; Bird Shoal and Shackleford Bank, off North Carolina; and Chincoteague I, Virginia.
A.R. LOCK

Reading: Barbara Christie, *The Horses of Sable Island* (1980).

Sackville, NB, Town, pop 5470 (1986c), 5654 (1981c), inc 1903, situated 50 km SE of Moncton on Tantramar R, near the NS border. Best known as the home of MOUNT ALLISON U (fd 1839), Sackville overlooks the wide expanse of the Tantramar Marshes, which inspired the poetry of its most famous son, Sir Charles G.D. ROBERTS. The area was first settled in the 1670s by the ACADIANS, who built dikes to reclaim its rich farmland from the sea. After the Expulsion of 1755, these lands were taken up by immigrants from New England and Yorkshire, Eng. By the mid-19th century, Sackville was a thriving port, with local shipbuilders supplying the sailing vessels needed to send farm produce and lumber to markets in Britain and the W Indies. Construction of the INTERCOLONIAL RY through the town (1870) bolstered its position as a commercial centre. With the end of the age of sail in the Maritimes after 1900, the port closed and commerce declined. A large stove foundry, established in the mid-1800s, is still in operation, and together with the university employs most of the local work force. Sackville is a town of fine old homes and tree-shaded streets, dominated by the red sandstone buildings of the university.
DEAN JOBB

Sadlermiut Inuit (or Sallirmiut) were the inhabitants of 3 islands in Hudson Bay: SOUTHAMPTON (Salliq), Coats and Walrus. The original Sadlermiut were annihilated by disease in 1902-03. Their origins, population, development of culture and cause of their decline (from some 200 to 58), prior to their demise, are unknown. The present-day Sadlermiut came mostly from Aivilik (Repulse Bay) and Baffin I and are not directly related to the earlier group. Fragmentary excavations and the notes found in journals of explorers

and whalers have excited considerable curiosity, as Sadlermiut, in appearance, behaviour, language and material culture, seem to have been significantly different from the relatively homogeneous peoples of the W coast of Hudson Bay. Three hypotheses have been suggested to account for this: that Sadlermiut were direct descendants of DORSET Eskimos, who preceded the bearers of THULE culture in the area; that they were Thule Inuit whose culture developed idiosyncratically because it was isolated from the mainland Thule culture; and that they were carriers of Thule culture who were both isolated from the mainland and in contact with Dorset people, so that they and their culture derive from both roots, through intermarriage and cultural borrowing. This last hypothesis would account for the mixture of Dorset and Thule traits that characterize the archaeological remains of the Sadlermiut.

The Sadlermiut were isolated from the mainland Inuit; they lived for most of the year in stone and sod houses, and hunted seal, walrus, whales, polar bear and caribou, supplemented with fish and birds. Though they were in contact with whalers between 1860 and 1903, they were not as involved in whaling and trapping as the mainland Inuit. *See also* NATIVE PEOPLE: ARCTIC.
JEAN L. BRIGGS

Safdie, Moshe, architect (b at Haifa, Israel 14 July 1938). Educated at McGill, Safdie had the unique opportunity of building his student thesis as Habitat for EXPO 67 in Montréal. This work was carried on from his Montréal practice, begun in 1964. Other designs have been for Jerusalem, Mexico City, Singapore, Tehran, Puerto Rico and other US sites. His most important recent Canadian projects include the new National Gallery of Canada, Ottawa, the Musée national de Civilisation, Québec, and renovations to the Musée des beaux-arts de Montréal. Safdie has written extensively on his work, has taught at McGill and in Israel, and from 1978 to 1984 was director of the urban design program at Harvard, where he continues as professor. Prefabricated cellular multi-unit housing is a concern of Safdie's, from Habitat to lighter and more economical later versions. All create diverse, irregular, informal groupings by the sensitive arrangement of repeated units. The images created recall medieval hill towns of Europe and the densely packed traditional cities of N Africa and the Middle East. The large public buildings use extensive glazed areas to make the interiors visible and inviting to those outside.
MICHAEL McMORDIE

Safety Standards, documents or codes which describe characteristics or usage for products, materials and services, are intended to protect citizens from the hazards of technology. A safety standard may specify how to test a hockey helmet for resistance to blows, or how to design an electric coffee pot that does not present the danger of electrocution. Several thousand standards are currently in use in Canada. Standards are published by sector and government organizations specializing in this field and are grouped in the National Standards System, co-ordinated by the Standards Council of Canada. The work of standardization begins when public hazards are recognized and involves field and laboratory studies. Standards are written up by experts, who volunteer their time to standards-writing organizations. Standards prepared, published and revised in this fashion are known as consensus standards; their final acceptance depends on substantial agreement among the experts.

Unless made obligatory by law, standards are applied voluntarily by those concerned. Laws making standards mandatory often refer to specific consensus safety standards, rather than specifying

detailed technical requirements. Safety standards relating to a specific subject may be collected into volumes, called codes, which are usually drawn up in a way that would allow governments to adopt them for legal use. Several codes have gained wide recognition in Canada, notably the National Fire Code, the National Building Code, the Canadian Electrical Code, the Boiler Code, the Canadian Welding Code and the Code for Hospital Operating Room Safety. The National Labour Code also includes safety legislation.

The National Fire Code sets out the requirements for safe maintenance of buildings after their occupation. Drawing heavily on American and, to a lesser extent, on Canadian standards, this code establishes standards for fire prevention, fire fighting and life safety in buildings in use. The National Building Code is essentially a set of minimum regulations for the safety of buildings with reference to public health, fire protection and structural sufficiency (*see* BUILDING CODES AND REGULATIONS). Complementing the National Fire Code, it establishes standards for fire safety during construction of new buildings or reconstruction of old ones. The code also sets out specifications for the use, occupancy and design of buildings. Provincial and territorial governments exercise jurisdiction over fire and construction safety in Canada and each has adopted, wholly or in part, the 2 national codes.

Electricity posed great danger of electrocution when it first came into public use. Over the years a collection of Canadian electrical safety standards has been assembled into what is now known as the Canadian Electrical Code, a completely Canadian product acclaimed in many parts of the world. Published by the Canadian Standards Association (CSA), the code is consulted by engineers and inspectors responsible for electrical installation in all buildings and engineering structures. Each province requires that all electrical appliances sold within it comply with the code's specifications and bear a mark certifying this compliance.

One of the earliest matters to receive attention in the field of safety standards was the control of boilers and other pressure vessels. When they were first used in steam engines for the propulsion of boats early in the 19th century, pressure vessels often exploded. Today the Boiler Code, published by the Canadian Standards Association, promotes the safe use of such vessels. Relying heavily on the American Boiler Code (first issued in 1914), it presents information for the design of pressure vessels and requirements for their construction, testing and regular inspection.

Establishment of standards in the medical field is fairly recent. With new developments in medicine the medical and engineering professions began to work closely together to develop standards, eg, for metallic surgical implants. In co-operation with representatives of industry and medicine, CSA published a Code for Prevention of Explosions or Electric Shock in Hospital Operating Rooms. This code, which specifies safety features in operating theatres (especially safety from danger of explosions caused by anaesthetics), is widely used across Canada. Certain requirements in the medical field are of international interest. For example, steel bottles containing compressed gases needed by hospitals must be safe and readily connectable to other hospital equipment; the screw couplings on these containers are a matter of lively international study. The federal government, through the Health Protection Branch of Health and Welfare Canada, plays an active role legislating standards in the medical field. It regulates medical devices (eg, cardiac pacemakers, contraceptive devices). A product cannot be sold until it is approved by the federal government.

Safety standards often bear an international flavour, as in the transportation field. Many standards used in Canada originated in other countries or with international organizations, eg, the International Organization for Standardization and the International Electrotechnical Commission, in both of which the Standards Council of Canada is actively involved. Most international marine safety standards are developed by the Inter-Governmental Maritime Consultative Organization of the United Nations. Canada is represented on this organization by marine and fire research experts. Documents resulting from this work are used as guidelines by the federal government, which legislates all aspects of international transportation. The International Civil Aviation Organization, with headquarters in Montréal, performs similar functions in the field of aviation. Nationally, transportation is administered by the federal government, with some areas delegated to provinces and territories. The Motor Vehicle Safety Act, Motor Vehicle Tire Safety Act, National Transportation Act, Railway Act, Canada Shipping Act and Aeronautics Act govern most federal transportation issues. The Acts are exhaustive and specify everything from requirements for automobile windshields and mirrors to aircraft speed limits. R.L. HENNESSY

Sagebrush (genus *Artemisia*), bitter, aromatic plant or shrub of the family Compositae or Aster-

Sagebrush (*Artemisia vulgaris*) (*artwork by Claire Tremblay*).

aceae. They include annual, biennial and perennial plants. More than 100 species are known, chiefly from arid regions of the Northern Hemisphere. Fifteen species are native to Canada; 7 others are introduced (2 European, 4 Eurasian and one from Aleutian Is). The greatest variety of native sagebrushes occurs in the western mountains, where species that range from Alaska to California and Colorado are found. Several species range across the prairies and 2 species are transcontinental in Canada. Sagebrushes grow on dry plains, hills and rocky slopes. Flower clusters, aggregations of heads that are usually loose and nodding and sometimes spikelike, appear in summer and autumn. Each head is a disc of few or many tubular florets. Fruit is small, hard and dry. Many sagebrushes are highly variable, and hybridization occurs freely. The genus includes wormwoods and tarragon. The common name derives from the characteristic, sagelike odour, and the genus is named for the Persian Queen of Caria, Artemisia. *See also* PLANTS, NATIVE USES.

Saguenay Provincial Park includes strips of land (288 km²) on either side of the SAGUENAY R, from Baie des Ha! Ha!, near Chicoutimi, to the confluence with the St Lawrence at TADOUSSAC. The Laurentide plateau lies southward; the Valin massif, dissected by the Ste Marguerite R valley, northward. Impressive sand dunes and beaches are found at Tadoussac. Climate and vegetation vary with altitude, the lower areas being dominated by maple and yellow birch; the plateau, by white birch and fir. The marine fauna is especially noteworthy, including 238 INVERTEBRATE species and 54 fish species (notably salmon). In the 19th century, the pine forests were exploited, some settlement and farming occurred, and tourism developed. Today the park is divided into preservation, ambience and service zones. The park and adjacent villages provide camping and hotel accommodation and opportunities for hiking, picnicking, boating, whale watching and, in winter, skiing. JOHN S. MARSH

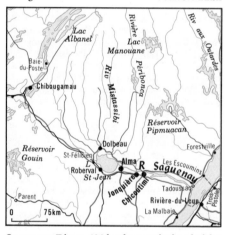

Saguenay River, 698 km long to the head of the Péribonca R, issues from Lac SAINT-JEAN in the LAURENTIAN HIGHLANDS of Québec. It has a DRAINAGE BASIN of 88 100 km² and a mean discharge of 1760 m³/s. It discharges from the lake through 2 channels, which join some 10 km from the lake near ALMA. The majesty, power and stark beauty of the river are legendary. From CHICOUTIMI to the ST LAWRENCE R the river flows through a deep gash in the Precambrian rock, 1500 m wide and 600 m deep in places, with cliffs rising 500 m above the river. The lower Saguenay is a FJORD gouged by the glaciers of the last ice age, 10 000 years ago. As the ice receded, the sea invaded; tidewaters still surge as far as Chicoutimi, rising and falling as much as 6 m at the equinox. Near Chicoutimi the fresh, warm waters of the tributaries float in lay-

Cargo on the Saguenay. Flowing through a deep gash in the Shield, the river is tidal as far as Chicoutimi (*photo by Anne Gordon/Reflexion*).

ers over the cold, salty brine beneath. The deep Saguenay waters are the breeding grounds of the BELUGA WHALE and the shallower waters near the confluence with the St Lawrence are rich in capelin and shrimp, attracting porpoise, finback, humpback, pilot and even blue whales. The dramatic scenery of the river, particularly the formidable Cap Trinité (518 m) – on which was built a huge statue of the Virgin Mary in 1881 – and Cap Éternité (549 m) at the mouth of Rivière Éternité, has drawn tourists since the 1850s.

The Saguenay was once the corridor of a trading network extending beyond the height of land to Lac MISTASSINI and beyond to JAMES BAY. TADOUSSAC, at the confluence with the St Lawrence, was a meeting point of the Algonquian peoples of the SHIELD and the Iroquoians of the St Lawrence Valley. Jacques CARTIER visited the river mouth in 1535 and eagerly gathered tales of a rich "Kingdom of Saguenay" in the river's watershed. The "kingdom" was fantasy, and the journey upriver was not made until Jesuit missionary Jacques Dequen went as far as present-day Chicoutimi in 1647; Father ALBANEL reached Lac Saint-Jean in 1671-72. Pierre Chauvin established the first trading post in Canada at Tadoussac in 1600, and the river remained an avenue for the fur trade and later the timber trade into the 19th century. Agricultural settlement began in 1838 with the founding of La Baie. Industrialization began with the building of a sawmill at Chicoutimi in 1842; the Chicoutimi pulp mills were opened in 1898.

The great power of the river and its tributaries has made the Saguenay Valley one of the industrial centres of Québec. The first power station was opened in 1925 at Isle Maligne (336 000 kW). The huge dam at Shipshaw (717 000 kW) was built during WWII to feed the gigantic ALUMINUM smelter at Arvida (now JONQUIÈRE). Generating stations at Chute-à-Caron (180 000 MW) on the Saguenay and at Chute à La Savanne (187 000 MW), Chute des Passes (742 000 MW) and Chute du Diable (187 000 MW) on the Péribonca R also supply pulp and paper mills at Chicoutimi, Jonquière and LA BAIE. SAGUENAY PROVINCIAL PARK preserves land on either side of the river, from near Chicoutimi to Tadoussac. JAMES MARSH

Sailing Ships Canada's early history occurred during the great age of sail, when sailors "under canvas" crossed the Atlantic in expeditions of trade, colonization and exploration. By the mid-19th century Canada had become a major seafaring nation. Canada's ports were crowded with sailing vessels, shipbuilding yards flourished, and Canadian ships sailed every major ocean and visited every major port doing the world's business. In Canada's age of sail (1800-75) over 4000 ships, each exceeding 500 tons burthen, were built in Canada. In 1878 Canadian-registered ships numbered 7196 and totalled 1 333 015 tons. Among the nations, Canada stood fourth in seagoing tonnage. What accounts for this phenomenal Canadian contribution of "tall ships"? Canada had an abundance of good timber – tamarack, spruce and especially pine – near shipyards, which were established in secure harbours and river mouths. Canada also possessed good ship designers and shipwrights, and Canadian builders were able to sell their vessels to US, British, Norwegian and other seaborne traders. Canadian vessels were given the highest quality rating – 14 years A 1 – by the marine insurer Lloyd's of London.

Canadian ships were built at numerous locations. The first lumber carrier, the *Columbus,* 3690 tons, was built at Île d'Orléans in 1824. The 2459-ton W.D. LAWRENCE, launched at Maitland, NS, in 1874, was the largest wooden full-rigger built in Canada. Other famous ships of this period include the MARCO POLO, launched at Saint John in 1851, which made her name trading to Australia during the gold rush; the square-rigger *Canada,* 2138 tons, launched at Kingsport, NS, in 1891, which ended her worldwide trading career in 1926; and the square-rigger *City of Toronto,* built on the Great Lakes. Canadian ports constructed a variety of smaller commercial craft. Victoria, eg, built sealing vessels; ports on the St Lawrence built one- or 2-masted traders; Atlantic yards built whalers, sealers, and fishing and trading schooners such as the BLUENOSE; York and Mackinaw built boats for specific needs determined by geography.

Canada also built naval ships. The 3-decker HMS *St Lawrence,* launched at Kingston in 1814, displaced 2304 tons and carried 112 guns and 1000 men. HMCS *Venture,* built in NS in 1937, was a 3-masted schooner for officer training. At important centres from Halifax to the lower Great Lakes, smaller naval vessels were built, maintaining shipbuilding traditions dating from Talon's shipyards in Québec and La Salle's GRIFFON, launched on the Great Lakes in 1679, and the British brig *Ontario,* launched at Oswego in 1755.

Canada's age of sail came to an end gradually with the introduction of steam propulsion and iron hulls, masts and yards. Paddle steamers came first to the St Lawrence in 1809, to the Great Lakes in 1817, and to the Pacific coast in 1835 (*see* STEAMBOATS AND PADDLE WHEELERS). In 1833 the Québec-built ROYAL WILLIAM became the first merchant ship to cross the Atlantic primarily under steam. Canada's shipbuilding industry made the transition to steam and iron, but the 200-year age of Canadian ships under canvas was rapidly coming to an end, and with it came the nostalgia of an age when Canada was known for its great sailing ships. *See also* SHIPBUILDING AND SHIP REPAIR; YORK BOAT.   BARRY GOUGH

Reading: T.E. Appleton, *Usque Ad Mare: A History of the Canadian Coast Guard and Marine Services* (1968); C.A. Armour and T. Lackey, *Sailing Ships of the Maritimes* (1975); L.R. Fischer and E.W. Sager, *Merchant Shipping and Economic Development in Atlantic Canada* (1982).

Ste-Agathe-des-Monts, Qué, Town, pop 5254 (1986c), 5641 (1981c), inc 1915, is located in the Rivière Nord Valley on the shore of magnificent Lac des Sables. Called the "Metropolis of the Laurentides," it is the region's oldest tourist centre. The peak of Mont Ste-Agathe, accessible by chair lift, offers a panoramic view of the lake and surrounding mountains. From 1849 to 1861, 27 families colonized the area, followed by 35 others from 1861 to 1865. In the 19th century, Ste-Agathe had only a few sawmills, but the construction of the Montreal and Occidental Ry in 1892 (replaced by the CPR in 1900) encouraged tourism and the development of the hotels that have become the region's economic mainstay. Today, most employment is in commerce, the ser-

vice sector and hotels. Resortgoers triple the local population.   CLAUDINE PIERRE-DESCHÊNES

St Albans Raid, one of several incidents heightening tensions between Great Britain and the US during the AMERICAN CIVIL WAR. On 19 Oct 1865 a party of Confederate agents based in Canada raided the town of St Albans, Vt. After looting the banks they fled back to Canada, where 13 were arrested and held for extradition. Their release on a technicality by a Montréal police magistrate aroused consternation on both sides of the border. Incidents such as this helped to create tension along the border which led in the British colonies to a climate of fear conducive to CONFEDERATION.
                                 ERNEST R. FORBES

St Albert, Alta, City, pop 36 710 (1986c), 31 996 (1981c), inc 1977, is located along the NW city boundary of EDMONTON. Founded 1861 by Father Albert LACOMBE as an Oblate mission, it was named by Bishop A. Taché after Lacombe's patron saint. The log chapel was built on the high ground N of the Sturgeon R. A second, large church was built in 1870 and served as a cathedral. The mission was a refuge for some 700 MÉTIS and Indians during a devastating smallpox epidemic in 1870. The mission later became Oblate headquarters and the bishop's residence.

St Albert grew into a city providing services for the extensive farming area N of Edmonton, and recently population has increased greatly as the city has become a dormitory for the adjacent capital. St Albert has preserved much of its missionary past. The mission buildings still stand, and the original log church was restored and opened in 1983 as an historic site. The chapel's holdings were removed in 1979 and are now housed in the Musée Heritage Museum. The bishop's residence has also been restored, and the tombs of Father Lacombe and Bishop Vital GRANDIN lie in the crypt of the modern church. The city has resisted the political encroachment of its growing neighbour.
                                  ERIC J. HOLMGREN

St-André-Est, Qué, Village, pop 1351 (1986c), 1293 (1981c), inc 1958. Lying mostly on the E bank of the Rivière du Nord several km from its junction with the OTTAWA R, this small town (formerly St-André d'Argenteuil) received Scottish settlers around 1800. A plaque marks the site of the first paper mill in Canada (completed by New England immigrants in 1805). One of Québec's most powerful hydroelectric stations was built *c*1960 on the Long Sault rapids at nearby Carillon. Sir John ABBOTT, Canada's first native-born prime minister, was born here.   GILLES BOILEAU

St Andrews, Man, Rural Municipality, pop 8755 (1986c), 7990 (1981c), inc 1880, area 70 523 ha, stretches from a boundary 8 km N of Winnipeg to Winnipeg Beach and Netley Marsh at the southern tip of Lk Winnipeg, and includes Lockport, Petersfield, Clandeboye and several resort communities on the W shore of Lk Winnipeg. Selkirk, Winnipeg Beach and Dunnottar are separate corporate entities. The Saulteaux settled in the Netley Cr area 1795. Red R colonists and HBC employees followed in the early 1800s, as did Anglican and Presbyterian ministers who founded some of western Canada's earliest churches and schools. Lower FORT GARRY (1830s) was a HBC provision and retail centre, a military garrison and industrial complex. By the early 1900s, German, Ukrainian and Polish homesteaders moved into the RM, Winnipeg Beach became a resort community (1903) and the St Andrews Locks opened to facilitate navigation over rapids on the Red R (1910). The RM is one focus of preservation/conservation activities by the federal and provincial governments. St Andrews Airport N of Winnipeg, a satellite of Winnipeg Inter-

national, is one of the busiest facilities of its kind in Canada.   D.M. LYON

St Andrews, NB, Town, pop 1612 (1986c), 1760 (1981c), inc 1903, is located at the mouth of the ST CROIX R in the SW corner of NB. Its earliest occupation was likely by the Passamaquoddy who had seasonal hunting camps here. By the 1760s a few New England settlers had established themselves here. However, it was not until the closing months of the AMERICAN REVOLUTION that a major influx of LOYALIST civilian refugees gave the site a new status. With the arrival of the Penobscot Assn, as they were called, in Oct 1783, the town of St Andrews was formally laid out. For nearly 50 years it remained a principal shipping port for the lucrative trade with the West Indies, but by 1850 economic stagnation hit the area. In the late 1800s, St Andrews was rediscovered by the developing tourist traffic from New England and central Canada. Commonly referred to as St Andrews-By-The-Sea, it remains today a popular N American tourist attraction for its historic architecture, scenic harbour and outstanding Algonquin Hotel.   ROGER P. NASON

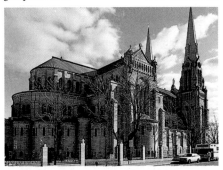

Basilica of Ste-Anne-de-Beaupré, which dates from 1926 (*photo © Hartill Art Associates, London, Ont*).

Ste-Anne-de-Beaupré, Qué, Town, pop 3162 (1986c), 3292 (1981c), inc 1855, located on the N shore of the St Lawrence R 35 km E of QUÉBEC CITY, is known worldwide for its shrine, a PILGRIMAGE site attracting over one million visitors yearly. In 1658 Étienne Lessard, one of the first settlers, ceded some land for the construction of the first wooden chapel dedicated to Ste-Anne, who was especially venerated in NEW FRANCE. Built too close to the river, it was damaged by the tides and rebuilt in 1661 at the foot of the slope. It was replaced by a stone church in 1676. Enlarged several times, the church welcomed thousands of pilgrims during almost 2 centuries. It was demolished in 1872 and replaced by the first basilica, which was destroyed by fire in 1922. The present Roman-style basilica dates from 1926. Its treasures include sacred 18th-century vases engraved by, among others, François Ranvoyzé and Laurent Amyot and a large collection of ex-votos (*see* VOTIVE PAINTING). The north chapel, built in 1878, holds several works saved from the demolition of the old church, including the steeple which had been rebuilt in 1788. The altars were designed by Charles Vézina 1702-28; the crucifix and wooden chandeliers were sculpted by François-Noël LEVASSEUR in 1779; the pulpit, put into place in 1807, shows the talents of François BAILLAIRGÉ. L'Historial, the sanctuary museum, has 17th-and 18th-century religious paintings, including 2 attributed to Frère LUC.
                            CLAUDINE PIERRE-DESCHÊNES

St Anns, NS, UP, pop 22 (1981c), is located on the E side of the Cape Breton Highlands on St Anns harbour, 34 km W of SYDNEY. The French established a fort and fishing base here in 1609. When they left Cape Breton after the fall of LOUIS-

BOURG in 1758, industrious Scots, under the leadership of Rev Norman MCLEOD, settled here. A large shipbuilding industry was established, but sharply declined when McLeod and his followers immigrated to New Zealand in the mid-1800s. Fishing, farming and, later, a plaster quarry supported the remaining residents. The only Gaelic college outside of Britain was founded at St Anns in 1938. Students may learn Gaelic language, music, dance and customs. Traditional Scottish crafts and handwoven tartans are made here. The college is home to the annual Gaelic Mod and to the Giant Angus McAskill Highland Pioneers Museum. Visitors may find personal effects of the famous giant Angus MCASKILL and other pioneers.
HEATHER MACDONALD

St Anthony, Nfld, Town, pop 3182 (1986c), 3107 (1981c), inc 1945, is located near the top of the Great Northern Pen. Originally called St-Antoine, it was a French fishing station settled by Newfoundlanders in the mid-1800s. With a superb natural harbour, St Anthony is at the crossroads of shipping and fishing routes serving the Str of Belle Isle and the Labrador coast. Dr Wilfred GRENFELL, on behalf of the Royal National Mission to Deep Sea Fishermen, in 1900 chose St Anthony as the site for a small hospital that would later become the headquarters of the International Grenfell Assn, founded by Grenfell in 1912. St Anthony's history since 1900 has been dominated by the work of the mission, the centre of a far-reaching medical and social-services network serving a large area of northern Newfoundland, Québec and Labrador. Other sources of employment have included a radar base (built 1951), a series of fish plants (beginning in 1944) and an airport built in 1957 and replaced in 1983.
JANET E.M. PITT AND ROBERT D. PITT

Reading: Sir Wilfred T. Grenfell, *A Labrador Doctor* (1948).

St-Benoît-du-Lac, Qué, a Benedictine abbey of the Congregation of St-Pierre de Solesme (France), est 1914, is located on the shores of Lac Memphrémagog, 40 km SW of SHERBROOKE. The monks are the sole inhabitants (66, 1986c) of this place, which has an area of 2.27 km² and no municipal structure. The present abbey, a lovely piece of architecture in pink granite, was designed by Dom Paul Bellot, a Benedictine monk who arrived in Canada in 1937. This famous architect of religious buildings also created the dome of St Joseph's Oratory in Montréal. His remains lie in the abbey cemetery. The monks spend their time in prayer, meditation, study, Gregorian chant, manual labour and agriculture. They make and sell cheeses under the names Ermite and St-Benoît. A hostelry welcomes people who wish to make a religious retreat.
CLAUDINE PIERRE-DESCHÊNES

St-Boniface, Man, former city and historic French community, now within the jurisdiction of the metropolitan government of the city of WINNIPEG (est 1972), is located on the banks of the Red and Seine rivers in eastern Winnipeg. With St Vital, its population totals 96 013 (1986). Together they form one of 6 community committee areas in the Unicity government. Four councillors represent St-Boniface-St Vital on Winnipeg City Council.

History Fur traders and European mercenaries hired by Lord Selkirk to protect his fledgling RED RIVER COLONY were among the area's first settlers. With the founding of a Roman Catholic mission (1818), St-Boniface began its role in Canadian religious, political and cultural history – as mother parish for many French settlements in western Canada; as the birthplace of Louis RIEL and fellow Métis who struggled to obtain favourable terms

for Manitoba's entry into Confederation; and as a focus of resistance to controversial 1890 legislation to alter Manitoba's school system and abolish French as an official language in the province. Early educational, cultural and social-service institutions were started by religious orders, including the Sisters of Charity of Montréal (Grey Nuns) who arrived in 1844. The Collège Universitaire de St Boniface, a founding college of University of Manitoba, and St-Boniface General Hospital grew from these institutions. The early economy was oriented to agriculture. Union Stockyards, developed 1912-13, became the largest livestock exchange in Canada and focal point for a meat-packing and -processing industry. By the early 1900s, numerous light and heavy industries were established. St-Boniface was incorporated as a town 1883 and a city 1908. As one of the larger French communities outside Québec, it has often been a centre of struggles to preserve French language and identity within Manitoba.

Economy St-Boniface is a residential and retail/industrial community. Despite difficult economic conditions and decline of the meat-packing industry in recent years, it still has a wide range of light and heavy industries, retail outlets and services. The CNR's Symington Yard is one of the most modern car-sorting switchyards in N America. The community has its own school division.

Townscape Early church buildings have dominated the landscape of old St-Boniface. St-Boniface Basilica was rebuilt following a disastrous fire in 1968. The Provincial House of the Grey Nuns, built 1846-47, is now a museum. Older sections of St-Boniface have been the subject of urban revitalization programs. Community cultural organizations include French-language radio and TV stations; *La Liberté,* a weekly newspaper; the Centre culturel franco-manitobain, an arts centre; the annual winter Festival du Voyageur; and performing arts groups such as Le Cercle Molière and Les Danseurs de la Rivière Rouge.
D.M. LYON

Reading: R.C. Wilson, ed, *Saint-Boniface, Manitoba, Canada 1818-1968* (1967).

St Catharines, Ont, City, pop 123 455 (1986c), 124 018 (1981c), inc 1876, former seat of Lincoln County, centre for the Regional Municipality of Niagara since 1970, lies S of Toronto across Lk Ontario (111 km by road), 19 km from the international boundary. Its hinterland is the eastern section of the Niagara Peninsula, and the city contains 40.8% of the population in the St Catharines-Niagara CMA (123 455 out of 343 258; 1986c). Located near the NIAGARA ESCARPMENT and in the Niagara fruit belt, its urban character has been influenced strongly by the backcloth of the WELLAND CANAL.

Settlement When the area was settled by LOYALISTS in the early 1780s, an agricultural centre emerged, known variously as Shipman's Corners or The Twelve. It was named St Catharines after the wife of Robert Hamilton (whose son George founded nearby Hamilton), a merchant at QUEENSTON on the Niagara portage, who constructed a storehouse on Twelve Mile Cr and deeded land for the first (Anglican) church, now St Georges.

Development The Welland Canal (1829) and an associated raceway (1830) introduced mills, shipyards and metal and machinery manufacture. Mineral springs with medicinal properties made St Catharines famous as a spa. The town was served by the Great Western and Welland railways. With power from the locks, the NIAGARA R and De Cew Falls, manufacturing evolved from concentration on domestic goods and the carriage trade to automobile production and accessories, wineries, canning factories and paper companies. Leading entrepreneurs have included William

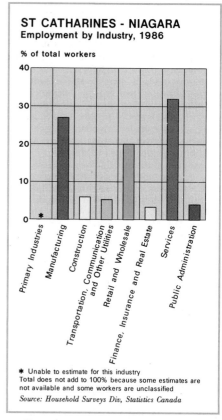

ST CATHARINES - NIAGARA
Employment by Industry, 1986

% of total workers

* Unable to estimate for this industry
Total does not add to 100% because some estimates are not available and some workers are unclassified
Source: Household Surveys Div, Statistics Canada

Hamilton MERRITT, MP, merchant and founder of the Welland Canal; Dr William Chase, the mineral springs; Hiram S. Leavenworth, publisher; W.B. Burgoyne, founder of the St Catharines *Standard;* Louis SHICKLUNA, ship manufacturer; and Dr Theophilus Mack, founder of the General and Marine Hospital and Canada's first school of nursing (1874).

Cityscape Three nodes exist: downtown, where a major E-W road crossed Twelve Mile Cr (the Welland Canal); Port Dalhousie, the northern entrance to the canal; and Merritton where the canal was crossed by the Great Western Ry. The downtown, ennobled by a curving main street with a near-continuous façade of 19th-century buildings, contains numerous "T" junctions and a radial system of former Indian roads. Because of the canal valley, growth moved N from this area, and later suburban expansion has extended the city from the escarpment to Lk Ontario and into the Niagara fruit belt. Manufacturing is dispersed along present and former canals, and along railway and highway locations. Though the downtown has attracted new office complexes, its retail capability is now secondary to the PEN Regional Centre; numerous other plazas, neighbourhood centres and strip commercial development also offer substantial competition. Open space includes the escarpment, lake beaches, river-canal valleys and city parks.

Population The city shows a broad ethnic mix; primarily of British origin (65%), but with substantial Italian (8%), French (5%) and German (5%) components. Religious affiliation is about 57% Protestant and 34% Roman Catholic (CMA, 53% and 39%).

Economy and Labour Force Manufacturing (1984) included 147 establishments with 12 100 employees, $388 million in wages and salaries, and shipments valued at $2.4 billion with a value added of $1.1 billion. Four establishments employ two-thirds of this labour force, with GENERAL MOTORS being the largest (9676 workers in 1987). In spite of new companies and the expansion of some older ones, total employment in manufac-

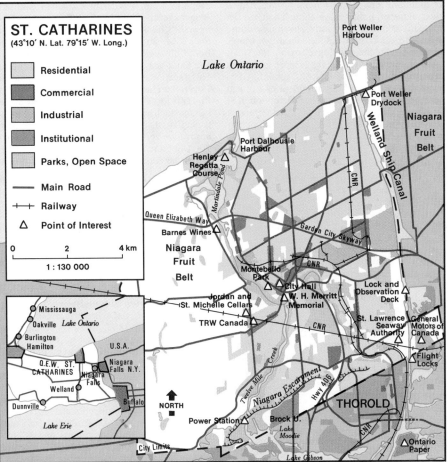

ST. CATHARINES
(43°10′ N. Lat. 79°15′ W. Long.)

- Residential
- Commercial
- Industrial
- Institutional
- Parks, Open Space
- Main Road
- Railway
- △ Point of Interest

0   2   4 km

1 : 130 000

turing has declined. Expanding service industries include the commercial and government sectors.

Transportation St Catharines is a district transportation centre, on the main land routes between southwestern Ontario and the American border. It features the Welland Canal with wharfage; main-line passenger and freight railway services; the QUEEN ELIZABETH WAY highway and Hwy 406; Niagara District Airport, with a 1524 m runway (but no passenger service); interurban routes; and limousine services to Toronto and Buffalo airports.

Government and Politics One of 12 municipalities in the Regional Municipality of Niagara, St Catharines is governed by a mayor elected at large and 12 aldermen from 6 wards. Its parks and libraries, a historical museum and municipal planning are city responsibilities. A downtown association fosters business improvement. Public and separate school boards are elected at large.

Cultural Life Educational and cultural facilities include a Crippled Children's Centre, the Niagara College of Applied Arts and Technology and BROCK U; live theatre, a symphony, art gallery and historical museum; a daily newspaper; radio and cable TV stations; and folk arts and grape and wine festivals. There is a full range of indoor and outdoor sports, highlighted by the Royal Cana-

Population: 123 455 (1986c), 124 018 (1981c); 343 258 (1986 CMA), 342 645 (1981 ACMA)
Rate of Increase 1981-86: (City) -0.5%; CMA 0.2 %; 1976-86 (City) 0.1 % (CMA) 13.7%
Rank in Canada: Tenth (by CMA)
Date of Incorporation: City 1876
Land Area: 94.43 km²; CMA 1399.80 km²
Elevation: 99 m
Climate: Average daily temp, July 21.2°C, Jan -4.7°C; Yearly precip, rain 752.1 mm, snow 158.6 mm; hours of sunshine 1939.2 per year

dian Henley Regatta, which has been held at Port Dalhousie since 1903. JOHN N. JACKSON

Reading: John N. Jackson, *St Catharines, Ontario* (1976).

St-Charles, Battle of On the morning of 25 Nov 1837, 2 days after Francis GORE's defeat at the Battle of ST-DENIS and the retreat to Sorel, the troops of Col Wetherall (about 350 men) left St-Hilaire and marched on the camp at St-Charles; Manoir Debartzch and its surrounding entrenchments, S of the village. The camp was at that time defended by some 100 men of the parish of St-Charles and others. As they approached, the soldiers exchanged gunfire with small groups of combatants. Wetherall deployed his men some distance from the fortifications, then ordered them to charge. The fight was violent and unequal (the defenders by then numbered no more than 60 or 80), caused several deaths, especially among the PATRIOTES, who could not prevent their barricades and the manor both being taken. While retracing their steps to Montréal via Chambly, the troops had a skirmish on Nov 28 (Pointe-Olivier, St-Mathies), but the defeat of the patriotes at St-Charles had potentially given the army complete control of the Richelieu region. *See also* REBELLIONS OF 1837. JEAN-PAUL BERNARD

Saint-Charles, Joseph, painter (b at Montréal 9 June 1868; d there 26 Oct 1956). After studying under Abbé Chabert in Montréal he left for Paris, enrolling in the École des beaux-arts in 1885. He also studied under Benjamin Constant, Jules Lefebvre and Jean-Paul Laurens, and spent some time at Rome's École des beaux-arts. He returned to Canada to devote himself to teaching and to art, and around 1890 he executed 3 large canvases for the Sacré Coeur chapel of Notre-Dame in Montréal. In 1906 he painted *La Présentation de la Vierge au Temple* for the chapel of the Grand Séminaire de Montréal. His career as a teacher of design began

with the Conseil des arts et manufactures, continued at U de M and then at Montréal's École des beaux-arts. From 1942 Saint-Charles was the most famous portraitist of his day. Through his studio passed the leading politicians, businessmen and indeed the most beautiful women of contemporary Québec society. MICHEL CHAMPAGNE

St-Charles-sur-Richelieu, Qué, Village, pop 346 (1986c), 401 (1981c), inc 1924, is located on the Rivière RICHELIEU, NW of SAINT-HYACINTHE. It was built on land belonging to the St-Charles seigneury (granted 1698). In the early 19th century, the village flourished from trade associated with river transportation. It played an important role in the REBELLIONS OF 1837: the Assembly of the Six Counties was formed there on October 23 (*see* ST-CHARLES, BATTLE OF). Like many places in the Lower Richelieu region, Saint-Charles experienced a decline in the second half of the 19th century. Towards the end of the century, one of the village's activities was the transportation of oats to New York City for use as feed for tramway horses. In the 20th century, bypassed by the major rail and road systems, it is dominated by the dairy industry. SYLVIE TASCHEREAU

St Clair, Lake, 1114 km², elev 175 m, 6 m deep, the smallest of the GREAT LAKES, is bordered by the province of Ontario to the E and the state of Michigan to the W. Almost circular in shape, it has a length of 42 km and maximum width of 38 km. Sulpician missionaries Dollier de Casson and Bréhant de Galinée traversed the lake in 1670. In 1679 LA SALLE, becalmed in the lake on the feast day of Ste-Claire, christened the lake (and river) in her honour.

Lk St Clair is connected to Lk HURON by the ST CLAIR R and is drained into Lk ERIE by the DETROIT R. Its most important Canadian tributary is the Thames R. The farmlands surrounding the lake are among the most productive in N America. The cities of WINDSOR, Ont, and Detroit, Mich, are located at the SW end of the lake. As part of the ST LAWRENCE SEAWAY, Lk St Clair and the river serve as a major transport route for commercial shipping vessels. Because of the many industries and large population in the area, pollutants have markedly influenced the quality of the lake's water. Its once-prosperous commercial fisheries are closed because of toxic contaminants in the fish. However, the lake remains an important recreational facility and has the largest concentration of boats and harbours of any of the Great Lks. MARIE SANDERSON

St Clair River, 64 km long, flows in a southerly direction, connecting Lk HURON in the N with Lk ST CLAIR in the S, and forms the international boundary between Canada and the US. Its northern portion has an average width of 0.8 km and depth of 8-18 m. In the S a delta called the St Clair Flats has formed, creating many channels and islands. The French were the first to explore and name the St Clair R. SARNIA is the most important centre, deriving its industrial base from large petroleum refineries and petrochemical plants. These industries reported 11 chemical spills in 1985 and the discovery of a toxic "blob" on the river's bottom resulted in a $16 000 fine to Dow Chemical Canada Inc. The river is now monitored by Ontario's ministry of the environment. The banks of the St Clair are also home to many cottagers. MARIE SANDERSON

St Croix River, 121 km long, rises in the Chiputneticook Lks and flows SE to Passamaquoddy Bay, forming part of the border between NB and Maine. It was discovered (1604) by the French, and de MONTS built the first settlement in Acadia on Île Sainte-Croix (now St Croix I) near the river's mouth. The site was chosen for its central position, good anchorage and ease of defence. However, the winter was cruel; there was no fresh water or firewood on the island. Of the 80 colonists, 36 died of SCURVY. The next summer the houses were dismantled and moved to PORT-ROYAL, a more salubrious spot across the Bay of FUNDY. The river was to serve as part of the boundary between British territory and the US, but its location was in dispute until an excavation found the remains of de Monts's camp and conclusively identified the river (1797). JAMES MARSH

St-Denis, Qué, Village, pop 949 (1986c), 861 (1981c), inc 1903, is located on the Rivière RICHELIEU, 30 km N of ST-HYACINTHE. It took its name from the St-Denis seigneury, granted in 1694 to Louis de Gannes, Sieur de Falaise, and named in honour of his wife, Barbe Denis. In the early 19th century, St-Denis was a major centre for grain shipments to Québec City. It also had business dealings with Montréal and was the fastest-developing centre in the lower Richelieu region. It was home to Canada's largest hat-making industry as well as to several craft and pottery workshops. During the REBELLIONS OF 1837 it became a centre for the PATRIOTES who fought against and forced the retreat of Col Gore's troops. In retaliation, the village was burned (*see* ST-DENIS, BATTLE OF). The development of the railway and the automobile caused St-Denis to decline as a commercial centre and become the centre of a thriving dairy industry. SYLVIE TASCHEREAU

St-Denis, Battle of In mid-Nov 1837 the government of Lower Canada decided to send out the army against the PATRIOTES and issued orders for the arrest of their leaders. In Richelieu County the patriotes, led by Thomas Storrow Brown of Montréal, seized the manor of Seigneur Pierre Debartzch and surrounded it with fortifications, while in St-Denis they organized around Dr Wolfred NELSON. Two army detachments came from Montréal to attack St-Charles, the one led by Col Wetherall taking the south route via Chambly and the other led by Lt-Col Francis GORE taking the northern route through Sorel. Gore's troops, having marched through the night in dreadful weather conditions, arrived at St-Denis on the morning of Nov 23 and attacked the rebels, who had dug themselves in at the far end of the village where the St-Germain house and Dr Nelson's distillery were to be found. The walls of the St-Germain house withstood the artillery attack and its occupants were well placed to fire from its windows on the exposed troops. Gore had to sound the retreat at about 3:00 in the afternoon when reinforcements for the besieged patriotes were beginning to flock to neighbouring villages and threatened to cut him off from Sorel. *See also* REBELLIONS OF 1837. JEAN-PAUL BERNARD

St Elias, Mount, elev 5489 m, the second-highest mountain in Canada, a boundary peak between Alaska and the YT, is located in the St Elias Range, 43 km SW of Mt LOGAN. First sighted in 1747 by a member of Vitus BERING's Russian expedition, its name derived from nearby Cape St Elias, named by the Bering Expedition. In May 1778 Capt James COOK attached an elevation of 5517 m, astonishingly close to that officially accepted today. The first successful ascent was made by a large Italian party led by the duke of Abruzzi in July 1897. GLEN BOLES

St Elmo's Fire, blue or reddish glow accompanying an electrical discharge from a pointed conducting object in an intense electric field. Caused by collision ionization and recombination of air molecules, it is similar to the light from a neon sign. In the vicinity of THUNDERSTORMS, it has been seen at night on the masts and rigging of ships, aircraft propellers, flagpoles and church steeples, and even on cattle horns or the hands and heads

of mountaineers. While remaining attached to the conductor, it may move along it and can last for many minutes. Frequently a hissing or fizzing sound is heard. There is speculation that Moses observed it in the burning bush on Mt Sinai; Shakespeare refers to it in *The Tempest;* and it was reported by early explorers of Canada. Sailors viewed it as a sign of the imminent end of bad weather. The name St Elmo is a corruption of St Erasmus, the patron saint of Mediterranean sailors. English sailors call it the corposant or cormazant, from Span or Ital *corpo santo,* "holy body" or "saint's body." E.P. LOZOWSKI

St-Eustache, Qué, Town, pop 32 226 (1986c), 29 716 (1981c), inc 1835, is located at the junction of the Rivière du Chêne and the Rivière des Mille-Îles, 30 km W of MONTRÉAL. The village was born when the owner of the seigneury of Rivière du Chêne gave the mill enough land in 1770 to build a church. The village is now an important residential suburban town. The main signs of local and regional history are the mill in the centre of town and the parish church (built, respectively, 1762 and 1780). This village was the site of a fierce battle during the REBELLIONS OF 1837 as Chenier and the PATRIOTES barricaded themselves in the church, priest's house and convent. Nearly 100 Patriotes were killed and the British troops put the village to the torch. An important regional centre, with half of its territory farmland, St-Eustache has doubled its population every decade since 1951. GILLES BOILEAU

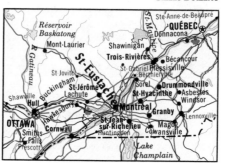

St-Eustache, Battle of, 14 Dec 1837. After destroying the PATRIOTE camp after the Battle of ST-CHARLES (25 Nov 1837), the army could prepare its attack on patriote camps to the north, those at St-Benoît and St-Eustache in the County of Deux-Montagnes. The expedition was mounted in style and in force: led in person by Sir John COLBOURNE, commander of the British army in N America, it numbered 1200 regular soldiers (including a regiment of 600 from the Québec garrison), an artillery with a dozen or so cannons and more than 200 volunteers from Montréal and St-Eustache itself. The rebels' morale had suffered badly from the news of the defeat at the Battle of St-Charles and the influential William Henry Scott soon concluded that the resistance had no further chance of success. But Jean-Olivier CHÉNIER managed to prevent the troops' demobilization and took command of the men who were dug into positions in the church, the presbytery, the convent and neighbouring houses. Colbourne's victory was decisive. Nearly 100 rebels were killed, including Chénier, and even more were taken prisoner. The next day the army took St-Benoît, where the camp was in complete disorder. The village was burned to the ground. *See also* REBELLIONS OF 1837. JEAN-PAUL BERNARD

St-Félicien, Qué, Town, pop 9324 (1986c), 9058 (1981c), inc 1976, is located at the mouth of the Rivière Chamouchouane on the W shore of Lac SAINT-JEAN. Founded in 1865, the colony St-Félicien soon became a prosperous agricultural parish. Agriculture and lumber dominated its

economy until WWII. The Canadian Northern Railway reached here in 1917. The town profited from the Chibougamau-Chapais mining boom of the 1950s, since nearly all the copper extracted from Chibougamau and Chapais (280 km NW of Lac Saint-Jean) left the region via St-Félicien. This transportation was at first by road (opened in 1949), then by railway to Chibougamau (1959). In 1960 local citizens founded the Zoo St-Félicien, which has become a major attraction in the Saguenay - Lac Saint-Jean region because of its innovative zoological approach (nature paths). The Donohue Co established a pulp and paper factory here in 1978. MARC ST-HILAIRE

Ste-Foy, Battle of, fought during the SEVEN YEARS' WAR on the road to Ste-Foy, a village 8 km W of Québec. In late Apr 1760 François de LÉVIS and his French force of 5000 engaged 3900 British troops under Col James MURRAY outside the city walls, soundly defeating them. Lévis then laid siege to the town while awaiting reinforcements from France. However, British ships arrived first. Lévis was forced to raise his siege and retreat to Montréal. W.J. ECCLES

St Francis Xavier University was founded in 1853 in Arichat, Cape Breton, and moved to Antigonish, NS, in 1855. Although founder Bishop Colin MacKinnon wished to provide higher education facilities for the Roman Catholic Highlanders in eastern Nova Scotia, non-Catholic students and faculty have been part of the university almost since its inception. Full university powers were conferred in 1866. In 1883 a girls' school and academy was founded, later to become Mount St Bernard College. Through its affiliation with St FX, degrees were granted in 1897 to 4 women, and thus it became the first coeducational Catholic institution in N America to grant such degrees. St FX also initiated the first engineering school in NS in 1899.

Well known for its efforts to serve the community, St FX established the Dept of Extension in 1928. This was headed by Moses COADY, who preached a philosophy of self-help. The extension activities were augmented in 1959 with the establishment of the Coady International Institute, which attracts students from around the world seeking to learn the techniques of the ANTIGONISH MOVEMENT. St FX offers a full range of undergraduate degrees and some graduate programs. Enrolment in 1985-86 was 2483 full-time undergraduate and 57 full-time graduate students. R.A. MacLEAN

St-François, Rivière, 280 km long, drainage basin 10 630 km², is located in southern Québec. Named in 1635 in honour of François de Lauson, eldest son of the fourth governor of New France, it was called *Alsiganteku,* "river where people no longer live," by the ABENAKI. From Lac St-François, 48 km NW of Lac MÉGANTIC, the river flows in a SW direction via Lac Aylmer toward LENNOXVILLE and SHERBROOKE, where it branches NW and flows into Lac St-Pierre, 19 km NE of SOREL. The river rises in the forested Appalachian region and, joined by the Rivière Magog at Sherbrooke, reaches the ST LAWRENCE LOWLANDS in the agricultural region N of DRUMMONDVILLE. Sherbrooke and Richmond are affected by its spring floods. As early as 1690, the river was used by the Abenaki and the French for attacks on the British in New Hampshire.

JEAN-MARIE DUBOIS AND PIERRE MAILHOT

St-Georges, Qué, Town, pop 22 214 (1986c) including St-Georges-Ouest, St-Georges-Est Paroisse and Aubert-Gallion, inc 1907, metropolis of the Beauce region, is located SE of Québec City on the CHAUDIÈRE R at its junction with the Famine R. Its first inhabitants, the ABENAKI, called it *sartigan,* "the shady river." This same name was given to the dam built upstream in 1967 to protect the town from spring flooding by the Chaudière. (Designed to hold back ice, it was the first dam of its type in Canada.) The first colonists came during the French regime to settle on seigneuries ceded to Thérèse Aubert de Lalonde Gayon (Aubert-Gallion) and Gabriel Aubin de L'Isle (Aubin-de l'Isle). The American invasion of 1775 led to British regular troops occupying the Beauce and to the presence of many English families in Sartigan. In 1807 a German named George Pozer bought the seigneury, settled there with 189 compatriots, and gave his name to the area. Population increased with the opening of the Kennebec route, linking the Beauce with New England in 1830. The town's main economic activities are forestry related. CLAUDINE PIERRE-DESCHÊNES

Saint-Germain, Treaty of, (1632), concluded 29 Mar 1632 at Saint-Germain-en-Laye, France, between Great Britain and France. The agreement restored Québec and those territories in the St Lawrence region which had been captured in 1628-29 by the British, to Louis XIII. It also provided for the return of various prize ships and their cargoes, or their financial value, and for Guillaume De Caen – representative of the United Company – to receive a large payment for merchandise that had been seized after Champlain's surrender of Québec in 1629. In consequence of the treaty, the following summer Québec was returned to the United Company and Port Royal to the Company of New France. JOSEPH RYAN

St Hubert Mission, located some 16 km SW of Whitewood, Sask, originated from the settlement of a group of titled French and Belgian nobility that apparently sought to escape from adverse changes undermining their way of life in Europe and to transplant the Old World traditions of French *noblesse oblige.* In the mid-1880s the representative of a wealthy Frenchman bought land in the area and commenced farming operations. His home, called LA ROLANDERIE, was named after the estate of his employer in France and became synonymous with the name of the district until about 1890 when a church was built and the parish of St Hubert was founded. The "French Counts," as they were known locally, arrived in the years before the turn of the century. They initiated a series of optimistic but ill-conceived, and ultimately unsuccessful, business and farming ventures which included sheep ranching, the cultivation of sugar beets and the operation of a cheese factory. As each enterprise closed down, its director closed his château and left. La Rolanderie was shut down in 1893 or 1894. The "French Counts" left behind stories of their extravagant life-style, hunts and gay social life. But they also left behind a well-endowed parish, and St Hubert retained its unique character as a French-speaking, Catholic community. GARTH PUGH

St-Hyacinthe, Qué, City, pop 38 603 (1986c), 38 246 (1981c), inc 1857, is situated in the St Lawrence R plain on the Yamaska R, about 45 km E of Montréal. From the beginning, St-Hyacinthe has been a commercial and service centre for a thriving agricultural region, known for its impressive religious and educational institutions.

History The history of St-Hyacinthe began with the granting in 1748 of a seigneury which was purchased in 1753 by Hyacinthe Delorme. In 1795 the present site, farther upstream than the original settlement, became the seigneury's focal point because of the potential for hydropower of an abrupt drop in the riverhead. A village quickly developed as a market and communications centre, serving the needs of the immediate region and of the other parishes that later appeared farther upstream. A

college for boys was founded in 1811; a convent for girls in 1816; a hospital in 1840. In 1848 a railway was opened to Longueuil, across from Montréal. The next year the line reached Richmond, then SHERBROOKE and Portland to the E and LÉVIS to the N, opposite QUÉBEC. But industrial development was slower than anticipated. Manufacturing did not become dominant until the 1870-1900 period, when St-Hyacinthe became one of Québec's main textile-production centres. In 1831 the village had some 1100 inhabitants. By 1851 the population had reached 3113; 4% were of British origin, the highest such percentage ever recorded. With a population of 9210 in 1900, St-Hyacinthe was one of Québec's 6 most populous smaller centres. Development in the 20th century was slower.

Economy Still the centre for one of Québec's thriving agricultural regions, St-Hyacinthe is well situated on rail and road networks. Although Montréal is far enough away to prevent St-Hyacinthe from becoming a suburb, its economic competition is considerable. A diversified industry, however, now has a stabilizing effect.

Cityscape St-Hyacinthe is relatively flat, like the level country surrounding it. A lower town, site of the first buildings, follows the low edge of a meandering curve of the Yamaska R. The public buildings – churches, educational institutions and so on – are noteworthy, as are the parks and green spaces and some magnificent homes built at the turn of the century. Regional market gardeners still bring their produce to market in the "lower town." In the SW are the School of Veterinary Medicine, associated with U de M, and the Institute of Agricultural Technology. JEAN-PAUL BERNARD

Saint-Jean, Lac, Qué, 1350 km², elev 98 m, 63 m deep, is located in S-central Québec, 170 km N of the St Lawrence R, into which it flows via the SAGUENAY R. The lake is the centre of a shallow glacial pan and is fed by dozens of little rivers, the most important being (W to E) the Chamouchouane, the Mistassini and the Péribonca to the N and the des Aulnaies, Métabetchouane and the Ouiatchouane to the S. It is lined by various towns, among them ALMA, DOLBEAU, MISTASSINI, ROBERVAL and ST-FÉLICIEN.

Called Piékouagami ("flat lake") by Indians, the lake was named after the patron saint of Jean Dequen, a Jesuit missionary and the first European to reach its shores (1647). Local Indians (Kakouchak and Mistassini) began trading with the Europeans at TADOUSSAC in the 16th century. Later, Lac Saint-Jean was made part of the King's Domain (1674), land reserved for trapping and farmed out to interested parties; a first trading post was built at Métabetchouane in 1676. The FUR TRADE dominated the region's economy until the 19th century, when colonization started in the Saguenay (1838) and then in the Lac Saint-Jean region (1849). Settlement was intense until the early 20th century, with settlers recruited from Québec, the US and even Europe. The economy was mainly based on agriculture and forestry until WWII. Co-operative dairy farming and cattle raising are still very important activities.

Industrial development began with 19th-century sawmills, continued with pulp mills (the first, at Val-Jalbert, opened in 1902), paper mills (after 1925) and aluminum plants (1943), and was greatly encouraged by the construction of hydro stations at Alma (1925) and on the Péribonca R (1954-60). Lac Saint-Jean also has a flourishing summer resort industry. Ever since the railway reached Roberval (1888), sportfishing (landlocked salmon and walleyed pike) have drawn thousands of enthusiasts yearly, along with vacationers who enjoy the lake's beaches. A major swimming event, the International Crossing of Lac Saint-Jean between Péribonka and Roberval,

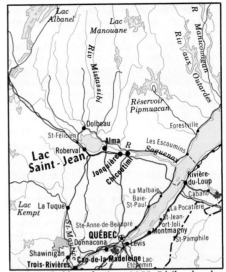

has been held yearly since 1955. Péribonka also houses the Musée Louis-Hémon, commemorating the trip made to Lac Saint-Jean by the author of MARIA CHAPDELAINE. MARC ST-HILAIRE

St-Jean-Baptiste Society (Société Saint-Jean-Baptiste), French Canadian patriotic association fd 24 June 1834 by journalist Ludger Duvernay, who wanted to stimulate a nationalist spirit among his compatriots and encourage them to defend their linguistic and cultural heritage. Gradually, branches were established throughout Québec and in francophone communities elsewhere in N America. Placed under the patronage of St John the Baptist, the society has always organized special activities, originally with religious overtones, for June 24 (the saint's day), a legal holiday in Québec since 1922. The society distributes prizes for artistic and literary merit, and since the 1920s has sponsored annual parades on June 24 with themes such as "Homage to the Patriotes of 1837." It has engaged in various financial activities and has produced numerous briefs and resolutions on subjects of nationalist, linguistic and constitutional interest to Francophones. Early in the 20th century the society gave both monetary and moral support to Francophones in Ontario, where bilingual education had been abolished. Its attention later shifted away from francophone minorities outside Québec, and in the 1960s it became principally concerned with Québec nationalism. Since the 1960s, the society's activities have become largely secularized. RICHARD JONES

St-Jean-sur-Richelieu, Qué, Town, pop 34 745 (1986c), 35 640 (1981c), inc 1858, is located on the shores of the Upper RICHELIEU R, some 40 km SE of MONTRÉAL. Across the river is the smaller, adjoining site of Iberville, long known as St-Jean, and popularly, as St-Jean d'Iberville.

St-Jean originated as one of a series of forts along the Richelieu during the French regime. After the American Revolution, numerous LOYALISTS joined the local families. Through the 19th century, St-Jean became increasingly French Canadian and Catholic. Politically, it was a Liberal stronghold; one of its inhabitants, Félix-Gabriel MARCHAND, became premier of Québec in 1897. Railways and canals were introduced early in the region to accommodate a thriving commercial trade between Canada and the US and to avert the cumbersome rapids just below St-Jean. In 1836 the first railway line in Canada, the CHAMPLAIN AND ST LAWRENCE RAILROAD, connected St-Jean and La Prairie. The Chambly Canal was finished around 1844. Owing to the success of rival railway interests and a failure to achieve industrial growth, however, the town declined in the latter 19th century.

In the 20th century, several large industries (notably American multinationals) were attracted by generous incentives and the CN and CP rail routes. The decline of secondary manufacturing over the last decade or so, however, has contributed to increasing unemployment in the region. St-Jean has experienced physical growth in recent years. Tall buildings have begun to dot an otherwise flat landscape. The original town, "Vieux Saint-Jean," is experiencing a cultural rejuvenation. KATHLEEN LORD

Reading: A.H. Moore, *The Valley of the Richelieu: An Historical Study* (1929).

St-Jérôme, Qué, City, pop 23 316 (1986c), 25 123 (1981c), inc 1881, is located on the Rivière du Nord, 40 km NW of MONTRÉAL. From the 1834 creation of the first parish to its 1881 elevation to the status of town, the village of St-Jérôme lived primarily on forestry and agriculture. From 1882 on, the Rolland Co ran one of the oldest paper mills in Canada here. A regional metropolis situated where the Rivière du Nord leaves the Laurentians, St-Jérôme dominates the entire Lower Laurentians. The bishopric, courthouse and CEGEP give the town an administrative function as well as industrial and commercial ones. Its parish priest 1868-91 was the legendary Antoine LABELLE, the determined apostle of colonization whose efforts led to the creation of several dozen Laurentian parishes and the development of the huge territory between St-Jérôme and Mont-Laurier. GILLES BOILEAU

Saint John, NB, City, largest city in New Brunswick, is located at the mouth of the SAINT JOHN R on the Bay of FUNDY.

Settlement Saint John's earliest known inhabitants were the Micmac and later the Maliseet. Samuel de CHAMPLAIN arrived at Saint John harbour on 24 June 1604 – the feast of St John the Baptist – and gave the river its name. No permanent settlement was attempted until 1630 when Charles de LA TOUR constructed a fort (Ft La Tour) at the site of present-day Saint John. In 1701 the newly appointed French governor of ACADIA, Jacques-François de Brouillan, destroyed the fort and consolidated his forces across the bay at Port-Royal. Not until the 1730s did Acadians from other parts of the Bay of Fundy begin resettling along the river. By 1749 ownership of the territory surrounding Saint John was in dispute between England and France, and in the ensuing struggle the Acadian deportations were carried out from the mid-1750s to the early 1760s. The old French fort was rebuilt by the English in 1758 and renamed Ft Frederick, but it was destroyed in 1775 by the Americans. Finally, in 1778, the English erected Ft Howe on a hill above Portland Point.

The beginnings of permanent English settlement occurred in the 1760s with the arrival from

Population: 76 381 (1986c), 80 515 (1981c A); 121 265 (1986 CMA); 121 012 (1981ACMA)

Rate of Increase (1981-86): City -5.1%; CMA 0.2%

Rank in Canada: Twenty-sixth (by CMA)

Date of Incorporation: 1785

Land Area: City 322.88 km² CMA 2904.80 km²

Elevation: 109 m (highest point Ben Lomond Mt 237 m)

Climate: Average daily temp, July 16.7°C, Jan -6.7°C; Yearly precip 1336.6 mm; Hours of sunshine 1865.3 per year

Boston of James Simonds and James White, each of whom established dwellings at the foot of present-day Fort Howe Hill. These pre-Loyalist 18th-century merchants traded with the Indians and the garrison, and formed ties with the British at Halifax. In 1783 this harbour community greatly expanded when LOYALISTS settled on the E side of the harbour in Parr Town, on the W side in Carleton, and on the N side in Portland. In 1785 Carleton and Parr Town were incorporated, taking the name Saint John – the first incorporated city in what is now Canada. NEW BRUNSWICK was made a separate province in 1784 and Saint John served briefly as the provincial capital before the capital was moved upriver to FREDERICTON.

Development The city's early economy emerged through the TIMBER TRADE, trading and SHIPBUILDING. Quickly growing in prominence as a port, Saint John's lumberyards supplied square timber, and later sawn lumber, to Great Britain and the West Indies; its shipyards produced vessels (as early as 1770) which transported the forestry products and also became export commodities themselves. Many of the city's shipbuilders and ships, such as the MARCO POLO, became famous. Equally significant, the waterfront produced the city's largest labour union, which by 1911 affiliated with the International Longshoremen's Assn.

From the 1820s through the 1840s thousands of immigrants – SCOTS and especially IRISH – altered the city's ethnic and religious composition. By 1849 tensions between Protestants and Catholics resulted in riot and loss of life. During this mid-century period, the city's economy of "wood, wind and sail" was challenged from the outside by the newer technology of steam and iron. In addition, it was visited by a host of economic woes. From 1860 to 1880 Saint John began to be deeply affected by the end of the protected British market for colonial timber, the slackening in demand for wooden ships and a general decrease in trade. These conditions were worsened by an international depression that was under way by early 1874 and by a disastrous fire in 1877 that left the city's business district, most of its waterfront and much of its residential area in ashes. To these calamities were added the adverse consequences of Confederation (1867), as the arrival of the INTERCOLONIAL RY (1876) brought Saint John's manufacturers into competition with those from central Canada, to the long-term disadvantage of Saint John.

Population The city's demographic profile reflected these political and economic shocks. Although in 1871 Saint John remained the largest urban cluster in the Atlantic region, as early as the 1860s population growth had begun to stagnate. During the 1870s and 1880s, local newspapers succinctly captioned the process of out-migration to the "Boston States" as "the exodus." Only in 1901 did there appear to be a modest reversal, an improvement due in part to an influx from the Saint John R communities into the city and the

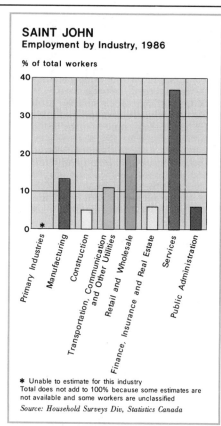

SAINT JOHN
Employment by Industry, 1986

% of total workers

* Unable to estimate for this industry
Total does not add to 100% because some estimates are not available and some workers are unclassified
Source: Household Surveys Div, Statistics Canada

revitalization of the world economy after the mid-1890s. By this time western Canadian wheat fields were poised to replace New Brunswick's forests as a primary export hinterland of the port. Throughout the 1880s Saint John's civic and business leaders had lobbied Ottawa to secure a niche for their city in the emerging Canadian system of cities. To this end, they invested substantially in the modernization of the waterfront and convinced the CPR to establish a terminus at the port in 1889. The adjacent town of Portland became part of the expanding city that same year. Thus, by 1900 Saint John's leaders were beginning to find a role within Canada by depending on water-based transport, to which had been added the railway. Saint John's newly constructed grain elevators became the "winter spout" for Canada's wheat. The traffic generated by the outbreak of WWI contributed to this new prosperity. After the war, however, a severe economic decline continued through the Great Depression.

Government Following WWII Saint John, a city containing some of the oldest and worst housing in N America, embarked on a process of urban

Saint John harbour, around 1900. The city's early economy emerged through the timber trade and shipping (*courtesy Provincial Archives of New Brunswick*).

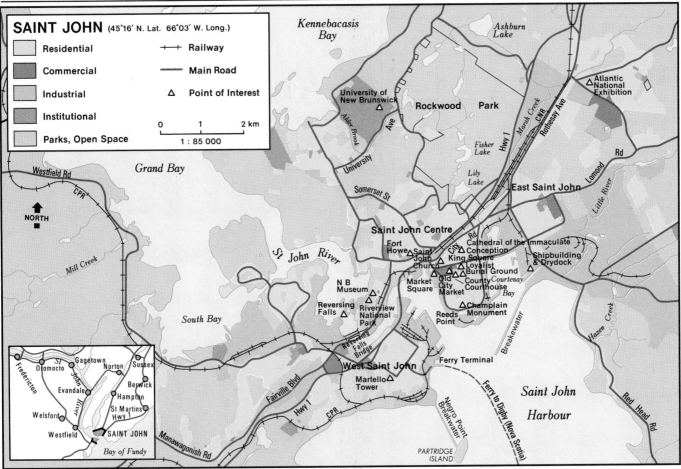

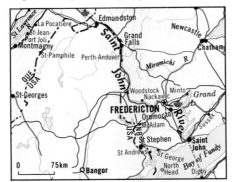

renewal. Efforts to modernize the city's street-scape were accompanied by changes in its admin-istration. With the exception of the period from 1912 to the mid-1930s, when Saint John was ad-ministered by a commission government, the city's municipal structure for most of its history consisted of a mayor and council. In 1963 the city adopted a council-manager form of government, wherein authority and political responsibility continued to rest with mayor and council, but administrative responsibility was centralized through a manager appointed by council. In 1967 the city expanded to include the city of Lancaster, the parish of Lancaster and part of the parish of Simonds. Greater access from within the city to outlying areas was achieved in the 1970s with the construction of a substantial throughway system incorporating a new Harbour Bridge.

Economy Since WWII Saint John's economic profile has maintained an emphasis on its tradi-tional industries through freight diversification at the port, revitalization of the shipbuilding indus-try, and expansion of the pulp and paper mills. In Dec 1987 Saint John was awarded a major con-tract for the construction of 6 naval patrol frigates. The development of the tourist industry is recent, encouraged by the construction of facilities for the 1985 Canada Summer Games, downtown and at the expanding Saint John campus of UNB.

Cityscape The cityscape is largely dominated by the harbour and the river. The well-known Re-versing Falls are located about 1 km from the cen-tre of town. At high tide the ocean waters surge upstream through a narrow chasm, reversing the rush of river water through the gorge at low tide. The 1980s has witnessed a major city-centre re-newal pivoting on Market Square, where a sec-tion of waterfront has been preserved and embel-lished to include indoor and outdoor malls, a trade and convention centre, and a new hotel. This development has proceeded with the emerg-

ing utilization of a few late Victorian edifices providing some examples of gentrification. City-wide enthusiasm for the enhancement of Saint John's cultural life was demonstrated in the suc-cessful Bi-Capitol Project to secure a theatre facil-ity – an acquisition at once recalling the city's rich 19th-century theatre history and its present-day rejuvenation. Thus, Saint John welcomes its third century by celebrating its past and anticipating its future through preservation and renewal of its ar-chitectural heritage and expansion of its recre-ational and educational facilities.

ELIZABETH W. MCGAHAN

Reading: D.G. Bell, *Early Loyalist Saint John* (1983); J. Fingard, *Jack in Port* (1982); Elizabeth W. McGahan, *The Port of Saint John* (vol 1, 1982).

Saint John River, 673 km long, rises in north-ern Maine and flows NE into the forests of Madawaska County to EDMUNDSTON, where it is joined by the Madawaska R and turns SE, form-ing much of the border between Maine and NB. Its DRAINAGE BASIN covers 55 400 km², of which some 20 000 km² is in the US, and it has a mean discharge of 1100 m³/s. It receives its chief tribu-tary, the Tobique R, and swings eastward south of

WOODSTOCK. Called *Oo-lahs-took*, "goodly river," by the MALISEET who lived along its banks, it is generally tranquil, except for cataracts at GRAND FALLS (25 m) and Beechwood (18 m), both of which have been harnessed for hydroelectric power. The river flows E past FREDERICTON and OROMOCTO, gradually widening and trending southward through a beautiful valley. On the lower course, numerous long, low islands have been formed by silt and molded by the current. Near the city of SAINT JOHN the river enters Long Reach, a narrow lake, and receives the Kennebe-casis R from the NE. At Saint John the powerful Bay of FUNDY tides throw the river back through a narrow gorge, called Reversing Falls. De MONTS and CHAMPLAIN anchored in Saint John harbour and named the river 24 June 1604, the feast day of St John. LA TOUR built a fort at the river's mouth 1630, but it was not until the LOYALISTS arrived in 1783 that significant settlement came to the val-ley. In the early 19th century, timber was driven from Madawaska, over Grand Falls, to Saint John, which became one of the most prosperous ports in British N America. JAMES MARSH

St John's, capital and largest city of Newfound-land, is located on the eastern side of the AVALON PENINSULA of SE Newfoundland. Its landlocked harbour is approached through a long, narrow channel and is protected by the high hills on which the city is built. The origin of the name St John's is not known, but its use appears on a Por-tuguese map by Rienel (1516-20) as "Rio de San Johem" and later, in a 1527 letter by the English seaman John Rut, as the "Haven of St John's." According to popular folklore, however, the city takes its name from the feast of Saint John the Baptist and the discovery of Newfoundland for England on 24 June 1497 by the Italian discover-er Giovanni Caboto (John CABOT).

Settlement The harbour was frequented by Eu-

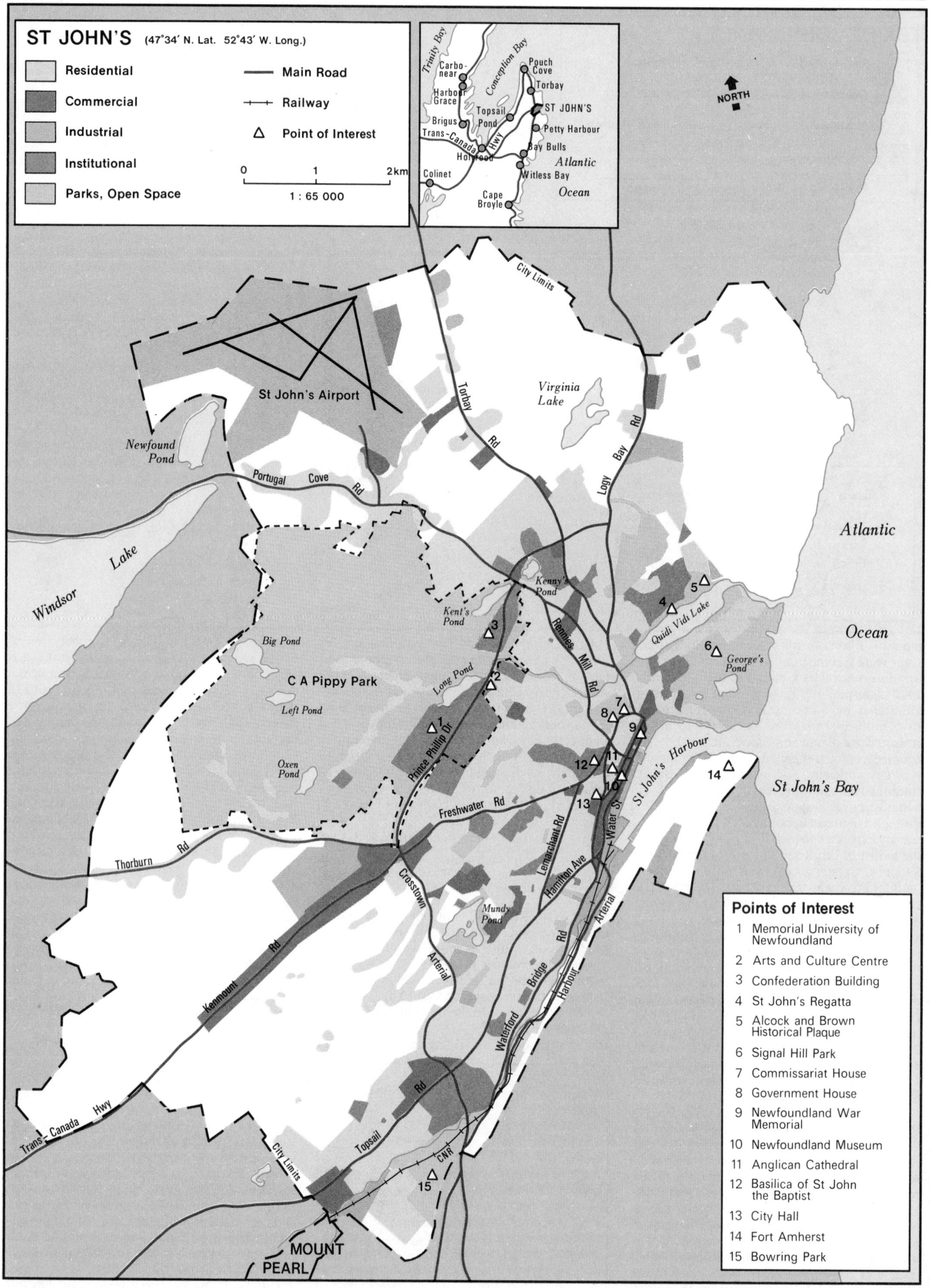
ST JOHN'S (47°34′ N. Lat. 52°43′ W. Long.)
Residential
Commercial
Industrial
Institutional
Parks, Open Space
Main Road
Railway
Point of Interest
0 1 2km
1 : 65 000
Trinity Bay
Conception Bay
Carbonear
Harbour Grace
Brigus
Topsail Pond
Trans-Canada Hwy
Holyrood
Colinet
Pouch Cove
Torbay
ST JOHN'S
Petty Harbour
Bay Bulls
Witless Bay
Cape Broyle
Atlantic Ocean
NORTH
City Limits
St John's Airport
Newfound Pond
Virginia Lake
Torbay Rd
Logy Bay Rd
Portugal Cove Rd
Windsor Lake
Kenny's Pond
Kent's Pond
Quidi Vidi Lake
George's Pond
Big Pond
C A Pippy Park
Left Pond
Long Pond
Oxen Pond
Rennies Mill Rd
Prince Phillip Dr
Freshwater Rd
Thorburn Rd
St John's Harbour
St John's Bay
Water St
Lemarchant Rd
Hamilton Ave
Crosstown Arterial
Mundy Pond
Kenmount Rd
Waterford Bridge Rd
Harbour Arterial
Topsail Rd
Trans-Canada Hwy
CNR
MOUNT PEARL
Points of Interest
1 Memorial University of Newfoundland
2 Arts and Culture Centre
3 Confederation Building
4 St John's Regatta
5 Alcock and Brown Historical Plaque
6 Signal Hill Park
7 Commissariat House
8 Government House
9 Newfoundland War Memorial
10 Newfoundland Museum
11 Anglican Cathedral
12 Basilica of St John the Baptist
13 City Hall
14 Fort Amherst
15 Bowring Park

Population: 96 216 (1986c), 96 455 (1981c A);
        161 901 (1986 CMA); 154 835 (1981 CMA)

Rate of Increase (1981-86): City -0.2%; CMA 4.6%

Rank in Canada: Nineteenth (by CMA)

Date of Incorporation: 1888

Land Area: City 101.59 km²; CMA 1129.99 km²

Elevation: 140 m (Torbay weather station)

Climate: Average daily temp, July 15.5°C, Jan -3.9°C;
        Yearly precip 1513.6 mm; Hours of sunshine
        1497.4 per year

ropean fishermen by the early 1500s, and by 1583, when Sir Humphrey GILBERT arrived in St John's to declare Newfoundland officially an English colony, settlement had developed on the central and eastern sections of the N side of the harbour. In 1832 St John's became the seat of government when Newfoundland was granted a colonial legislature by England; in 1888 it received its own municipal council.

Development Its strategic geographical location at the centre of the English migratory fishery on the Grand Banks made St John's a rendezvous for European fishermen and, after 1700, the natural focus for imperial administration and defence on the Island. As the cod fishery grew during the 18th century, St John's changed from a fishing town into a growing commercial centre for Newfoundland's increasing resident population. Although destroyed by fires in 1816, 1817, 1819, 1846 and 1892, St John's was rebuilt each time in a haphazard manner, with building regulations being stringently enforced only in the business district near the harbour. After 1870 small manufacturing industries were established in the capital. A dry dock was opened at the port 1882, and in 1897 the city became the headquarters for the trans-island railway which had been completed across Newfoundland by Canadian railway entrepreneur Robert Reid. After 1900 an improved coastal boat service to the outports further enhanced the pre-eminence of St John's.

Poor world markets for Newfoundland fish following WWI led St John's into a recession which was further worsened by the GREAT DEPRESSION. Prosperity returned during WWII with the arrival in Jan 1941 of the US armed forces to build Ft Pepperell and other military facilities in the capital. The resultant construction boom continued after 1946 with the building of new suburbs and the large infusion of federal funds after Confederation (1949). St John's became more dependent after 1949 on public-sector employment; at the same time it lost its traditional role as the fish-export centre of Newfoundland with the withdrawal from the salt-fish trade of major city mercantile firms, which chose to concentrate on a growing wholesale consumer trade.

The port of St John's has thus been transformed from an import-export centre into an import-service centre, as much of the port's revenue is now generated from supplying and repairing the local and international fishing fleet. The city has excellent air and road connections with both the rest of the province and the Canadian mainland. Close proximity to oil discoveries on the Grand Banks now holds the potential for the city's substantial economic and physical development.

Cityscape Until 1964, when the federal government completed a 915 m wharf along the N side of the harbour, the major feature of the St John's landscape in the harbour-front business district was the numerous private finger piers that jutted out from the merchants' warehouses on the S side of Water St. The city's streets ran in an E-W direction and parallel to the harbour. Before Confederation the streets were narrow and winding, reflecting the city's system of land tenure. With much of the land in the main commercial-resi-

dential area owned by British absentee landlords, the government was financially unable, following the 1846 and 1892 fires, to acquire land to create straight, wide streets in a gridiron pattern. After the creation of the St John's Housing Corp in 1944, new planned suburbs were built in the valleys W, N and NE of the principal settlement. Industry was spread throughout the adjacent harbour area. Since the 1960s, new suburban industrial parks have been created to accommodate existing industry and the further economic activity to be generated by offshore oil development.

Early St John's architecture in the 16th and 17th centuries was in the tilt, or log-cabin, form. Before the 1846 fire the Georgian style of the hip or cottage roof predominated among the $2\frac{1}{2}$-storey frame buildings. This style was then gradually replaced by the Gothic revival and the more significant International Second Empire, which was especially dominant after the 1892 fire. Notable 19th-century buildings include the colonial building (classic revival), the Roman Catholic basilica (Romanesque), and the Anglican cathedral (Gothic revival), designed by the English architect Gilbert Scott. Since the mid-1960s the city's skyline has been gradually undergoing change as several new hotels, bank and office buildings have been completed; for example, the 278-room Radisson Plaza Hotel opened in late 1987.

Population St John's experienced slow growth until the Napoleonic Wars, when substantial Irish Roman Catholic immigration increased the population from 3742 residents (1796) to 10 018 (1815). After 1832 natural increase and the migration of outport residents to the capital combined to produce steady growth and a compact, ethnically homogeneous community of Irish and British stock. Though Roman Catholics ceased to form a majority of the city's population after 1911, their influence in the social, cultural and political life of St John's was well entrenched. The steady population increase had produced serious social problems of public health, housing and un-

An overview of the port of St John's, looking NE, with Signal Hill in the background (*courtesy St John's Port Corporation*).

employment that were only partly relieved by immigration to the northeast US and Canada. The city's population doubled 1946-71 as large numbers of people came to St John's to participate in new employment opportunities in the civil-service and service sectors. Between 1971 and 1981 St John's experienced a decline, as many residents moved to Mount Pearl and other new suburbs outside city boundaries. More recently, however, the city has begun to show positive population growth. St John's population is still predominantly Anglo-Saxon and Irish.

Economy The entry after 1949 of cheaper Canadian manufactured goods into Newfoundland caused the city's industries to collapse and thereby reduced the volume of commercial activity at the port. The completion of a paved highway across the Island (1965) enabled mainland distributors to bypass St John's and use CORNER BROOK and CHANNEL-PORT AUX BASQUES to send their goods to Island centres. The growth since 1949 of a large civil service supported by the federal, provincial and municipal governments has been the key to the expansion of the city's labour force and to the stability of its economy, which supports a sizable retail, service and business sector.

Government and Politics The city was governed by the colonial government until 1888, when it received a limited form of self-rule with authority over the water supply, streets, sewers, parks, the fire brigade and building regulations. The city was governed by different councils or commissions composed of government-appointed members and elected officials until 1916, when a fully elective form of municipal council was settled on. In 1921 a comprehensive bill, drafted by the commissioners who had administered the city 1914-16, was passed by the legislature. This 1921 Act and its subsequent amendments by the legislature are the basis of today's St John's city government. In 1969 the number of elected councillors was increased from 6 to 8, and in 1981 a partial ward system was adopted, giving St John's 4 councillors elected at large and 4 elected on the basis of a ward system. There is no regional government in the St John's metropolitan area, but the city council does have representation on the St John's Metropolitan Area Board, a provincially appointed and subsidized board (est 1963) which is responsible for municipal supervision and services in revenue-weak communities on the outskirts of St John's.

Cultural Life St John's has most of Newfoundland's social, educational and religious institutions. The Benevolent Irish Society and the Convent of the Order of Presentation Sisters date from 1806 and 1833, respectively. Until the province undertook a rural high-school building program in the 1950s, the city's denominational high schools provided educational instruction for outport residents. The city is also the site of MEMORIAL UNIVERSITY, the College of Trades and Technology,

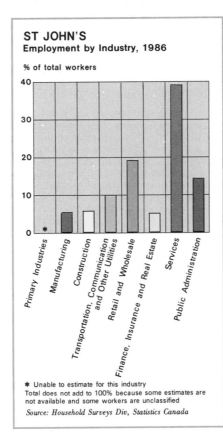

ST JOHN'S
Employment by Industry, 1986

% of total workers

*   Unable to estimate for this industry
Total does not add to 100% because some estimates are not available and some workers are unclassified
Source: Household Surveys Div, Statistics Canada

and the College of Fisheries, Navigation, Marine Engineering and Electronics. Also found here are the Newfoundland Museum, the Arts and Culture Centre, and the Signal Hill National Pk, which contains Cabot Tower, conceived in 1897 to commemorate the 400th anniversary of Newfoundland's discovery and Queen Victoria's Diamond Jubilee. Opened 1900, the tower was the site the following year for Guglielmo Marconi to receive the first transatlantic wireless message. In 1919 the city was the start of the first transatlantic nonstop airplane flight, when Sir John Alcock and Arthur Brown flew to Ireland.

St John's has one large newspaper, 2 TV stations and several radio stations. The city has a long tradition in sports; the annual ST JOHN'S REGATTA, now held on the first Wednesday in Aug, dates from about 1818 and is the oldest continuous sporting event in N America. St John's was the site of the 1977 Canada Summer Games, which left the city with improved sporting facilities. Since 1978 the city has celebrated June 24 as a civic holiday in honour of Newfoundland's discovery in 1497. From May to October 1988 the city celebrated 100 years of municipal government with a grand soirée.   MELVIN BAKER

Reading: Melvin Baker, *Aspects of Nineteenth Century St. John's Municipal History* (1982); P. Copes, *St. John's and Newfoundland: An Economic Survey* (1961); G.A. Nader, *Cities of Canada,* 2 vols (1975-76); S.J.R. Noel, *Politics in Newfoundland* (1971); Shane O'Dea, *The Domestic Architecture of St. John's* (1974); Paul O'Neill, *The Story of St. John's, Newfoundland,* 2 vols (1975-76); J.R. Smallwood, ed, *The Book of Newfoundland,* 6 vols (1937-75); R.E. Pearson, *Atlas of St. John's, Newfoundland* (1969).

St John's Regatta, believed to be the oldest continuing sporting event in N America, is a ROWING race over a 2.6 km course in long, fixed-seat shells carrying 6 oarsmen. The regatta originated in sailing and rowing races in St John's harbour in the early 19th century, but the first formal race may have taken place 22 Sept 1818 on Quidi Vidi Lk, which lies just N of the harbour and Signal Hill. Another race was recorded in 1828 or 1829. The Prince of Wales, later Edward VII, visited in 1860 and offered £100 to the winner. Times improved in the late 19th century, and in 1901 a crew from Outer Cove set a record time, 9 min, 13 sec, that was not broken until 1981 (the crew have been elected to the Canadian Sports Hall of Fame). After a suspension during WWI, the regatta resumed in 1918 and has continued since. A lively carnival is held during the regatta, often overshadowing the rowing. The regatta is run by a committee which has the authority to determine if conditions are right for the races and then to declare a commercial and bank holiday – a privilege which is perhaps unique.   JAMES MARSH

St Joseph Island lies at the E entrance of the St Marys R in the North Channel connecting Lks HURON and SUPERIOR, about 30 km SE of Sault Ste Marie, Ont. It was first settled briefly after the destruction of Huronia in 1649 by fugitive Huron and their Jesuit missionaries, who named it. In 1796 the British army built Fort St Joseph on the SW corner of the island, at the time the most westerly military post in Canada. It became a rendezvous for traders and Indians, and though it was destroyed in the WAR OF 1812 its remains are visible and have been preserved as a national historic park. Agricultural settlement occurred late in the 19th century. Today the island is a tourist and farming centre. A bridge connects the island to the mainland across St Joseph Channel, a principal navigation route.   DANIEL FRANCIS

St. Laurent, Louis Stephen, lawyer, politician, prime minister (b at Compton, Qué 1 Feb 1882; d at Québec City 25 July 1973). Born into a poor family, St. Laurent was fluently bilingual,

Louis Stephen St. Laurent
Twelfth Prime Minister of Canada

Birth: 1 Feb 1882, Compton, Qué
Father/Mother: Jean/Ann Broderick
Father's Occupation: Merchant
Education: Université Laval
Religious Affiliation: Roman Catholic
First Occupation: Lawyer
Last Private Occupation: Professor of law
Political Party: Liberal
Period as PM: 15 Nov 1948 - 21 June 1957
Ridings: Québec East, Qué, 1942-58
Other Ministries: Justice 1941-46; External Affairs 1946-48
Marriage: 19 May 1908 to Jeanne Renault (1886-1966)
Children: 2 boys, 3 girls
Died: 25 July 1973 in Québec
Cause of Death at Age: Heart failure at 91
Burial Place: Cemetery of St Thomas Aquinas, Compton, Qué
Other Information: Promoted Canadian membership in NATO

(photo courtesy National Archives of Canada/Bill and Jean Newton, Ottawa).

became a prominent lawyer and, in 1914, a law professor at Laval. During the 1920s and 1930s he was a successful corporation lawyer and served as batonnier of the Québec Bar and president of the Canadian Bar Assn (1930-32). In 1937-40 he was a counsel to the Rowell-Sirois Royal Commission on DOMINION-PROVINCIAL RELATIONS. In Dec 1941 St. Laurent was approached by PM Mackenzie KING to become minister of justice. He had no political experience but felt it was his duty to accept, and in Feb 1942 he was elected to the House of Commons representing Québec E. Alone among Liberal ministers from Québec, he was not pledged to oppose CONSCRIPTION and supported King in 1944 when he imposed it for overseas service. King was grateful and, impressed with St. Laurent's logical mind, made him secretary of state for external affairs in 1946. St. Laurent represented Canada at international conferences and the UN. He promoted Canadian membership in NATO, believing that Canada must help resist Communist expansion.

As King's chosen successor, a selection ratified by a Liberal convention, St. Laurent became prime minister on 15 Nov 1948. He headed a Cabinet of exceptional competence, including Lester PEARSON in external affairs, C.D. HOWE in trade and

commerce, Douglas Abbott in finance and Brooke CLAXTON in national defence. Old-age pensions were extended; hospital insurance was enacted; equalization payments among the provinces were approved; and Newfoundland formally joined Canada. Abroad, Canada garrisoned troops in Europe under NATO and sent forces to fight for the UN in Korea. St. Laurent's grandfatherly appearance and his government's record caused the Liberals to be re-elected in 1949 and 1953 with overwhelming majorities. In 1954 a successful round-the-world trip seemed to tire St. Laurent; thereafter, observers noticed that he seemed removed from events around him. During his last year in office the Liberals suffered reversals in public opinion, partly as a result of the PIPELINE DEBATE in 1956. In June 1957 St. Laurent's government was defeated by John DIEFENBAKER's PCs, and in Jan 1958 he retired from public life, returning to his law practice in Québec. St. Laurent was much admired for his decisiveness, patriotism and sharp mind, and was held in great personal affection by those who worked with him.   ROBERT BOTHWELL

Reading: D.C. Thompson, *Louis St. Laurent* (1967).

St Lawrence, Gulf of, a large (250 000 km²), roughly triangular inland sea receiving on average 10 100 m³/s of fresh water from the ST LAWRENCE R at its NW apex, is connected to the Atlantic by the Str of Belle Isle at the NE and CABOT STR at the SE corners. The deep Laurentian Channel extends from the St Lawrence estuary near TADOUSSAC, Qué, through the Cabot Str to the edge of the Continental Shelf. To the S lie the Îles de la MADELEINE and PRINCE EDWARD ISLAND, with the extensive Magdalen Shallows in between. N of the channel is Île d'ANTICOSTI. Additional sources of fresh water include the SAGUENAY R and other N shore rivers, plus smaller amounts from NB and Newfoundland. Much of the runoff is entrained in the Gaspé Current, flowing along the S shore of the estuary, out onto the Magdalen Shallows and eventually around the northern tip of CAPE BRETON I to form the Nova Scotian Current. The physical and biological effects of this fresh water are detectable as far away as the Gulf of Maine. Newfoundland Shelf water enters the gulf on the eastern side of Cabot Str, drifts NE along the W coast of Newfoundland and, coupled with a westerly drift along the N shore, completes a large counterclockwise gyre in the surface circulation. Deep inflow of Atlantic water through Cabot Str compensates for the net outflow of surface waters. Winter cooling and contributions from the Labrador Shelf via Belle Isle Str result in significant ice cover (and associated navigational hazards) in the gulf for at least 3 months each winter. Economically the gulf, with the St Lawrence River and ST LAWRENCE SEAWAY, forms a transportation corridor to the heartland of industrial N America, carries away its waste products, and still yields about one-quarter of Canadian fish landings, both by weight and by value.

Before European contact, the gulf was frequented by nomadic Indian tribes, such as the MICMAC, who came seasonally to fish. The N shore was inhabited by INUIT, whose fierce opposition long prevented safe harbour. Jacques CARTIER explored the gulf in 1534, but was likely preceded in the area by BASQUE fishermen.   P.C. SMITH AND R.J. CONOVER

St Lawrence and Atlantic Railroad, the world's first international railway, began service and was completed and inaugurated on 18 July 1853. The purpose of the railway was to provide Montréal, Sherbrooke and other Québec towns with access to an ice-free Atlantic port. The original plan was to build the line to Boston, but promoters in Portland, Maine, succeeded in persuading Canadians that their city was preferable. Construction of the broad-gauge railway began in 1846, but was beset by financial troubles. The section from Longueuil, Qué, to the Richelieu R was completed in Nov 1847 and the Canadian and American sections were joined in 1853 at Island Pond, Vermont. A ferry boat connected Montréal to the railhead at Longueuil. Upon completion the Canadian section was sold, and the American section leased, to the GRAND TRUNK RAILWAY. *See also* RAILWAY HISTORY. JAMES MARSH

St Lawrence Hall, built in 1850, was designed as a multipurpose building containing shops and a farmers' market on the ground level and a number of elegant meeting rooms and reception halls on the upper floors. For many years it was the centre of cultural and political life in Toronto, hosting many balls, receptions, concerts and lectures. John A. MACDONALD, George BROWN and the world renowned soprano Jenny Lind all appeared here. Designed by William THOMAS of Toronto, the architecture reflected the influence of the Renaissance style, with its raised portico over an arcaded base, but reinterpreted in a distinctly Victorian manner. Its richly carved ornamentation, picturesque skyline, and the eclectic incorporation of a French mansard roof were typical of contemporary architectural tastes. By the 1870s more modern theatres, concert halls and ballrooms had been built and St Lawrence Hall fell into decline. In 1967 it was extensively restored. JANET WRIGHT

St Lawrence Islands National Park (4 km²), est 1904, Canada's smallest national PARK comprises 19 granite islands and 85 islets scattered from Brockville to Kingston, Ont. The park islands are the summit of ancient hills of the Frontenac Axis, a strip of Precambrian granite connecting the Canadian SHIELD with the Adirondack Mts in New York State. After the retreat of glaciers, the hills were flooded by the newly formed St Lawrence R, resulting in the THOUSAND ISLANDS riverscape. From barren, lichen-covered rock to lush, deciduous woodlands, the park's islands support varied plant and animal life. Many species are typical of regions far to the S and occur nowhere else in Canada. Indians hunted and fished in the area. Explorers, fur traders and missionaries passed this way, but the scant soils did not attract settlers until the late 1770s, when LOYALISTS took up land. During the War of 1812 the area was a vital military route. Later it became a haven for boaters and cottagers. In 1904, as more islands became cottage sites, the government decided to set some aside as a national park. A campground is situated at Mallorytown Landing. LILLIAN STEWART

St Lawrence Lowland, 46 000 km² (5000 km² in the US), is a plain along the ST LAWRENCE R between Québec City in the E and Brockville, Ont, in the W, including the Ottawa R valley W to Renfrew, Ont. It is 450 km long W to E and 1000 km wide in the W half, narrowing to 35 km at Québec; an arm extends 130 km S into the Lake CHAMPLAIN valley. Altitudes range from 15 m above sea level along the St Lawrence R NE of Montréal to 150 m along the borders with the Laurentian Mts to the N, the Adirondacks to the S and the gradual transitions to the Appalachians in the SE and the Precambrian SHIELD of Ontario in the W. Tributaries of the St Lawrence that drain the lowland from the S are the Châteauguay, RICHELIEU, Yamaska, St-François, Nicolet, Bécancour and CHAUDIÈRE rivers, and from the N, L'Assomption, Maskinonge, ST-MAURICE, Batiscan and Ste-Anne rivers. Tributaries of the OTTAWA R crossing the lowland are the S Nation, Rideau, Mississippi, Madawaska and Bonnechere rivers.

The large-scale topographic features are the result of subaerial weathering and erosion by rivers, during the last 100 million years, of the nearly flat-lying early Paleozoic sedimentary rocks of the lowland. The rocks from oldest (lowest) to youngest (uppermost) are sandstone, dolomite and limestone and shale, from 520 to 480 million years old. These sediments are in a basin surrounded by older, more resistant crystalline rocks. Below the sedimentary rocks is an ancient surface of moderate relief that was eroded on the older (1000-million-year) Precambrian rocks.

The lowland is dominated by the Monteregian Hills, a series of isolated mountains in a belt about 20 km wide extending E from Montréal to the Appalachians. They are, from W to E, Mts Royal (231 m), St-Bruno (213 m), St-Hilaire (404 m), St-Gregoire (229 m), Rougemont (366 m), Yamaska (411 m), Shefford (518 m) and Brome (548 m). All are erosional remnants of igneous intrusions of early Cretaceous age (144-97.5 million years ago). Whether any volcanoes existed above the intrusions is unknown because no direct evidence remains. Igneous dikes and sills radiate from the Monteregian Hills, and some support terraces around the mountains, and form parts of the Lachine Rapids in the St Lawrence R. Hills of Precambrian crystalline rocks project through the sedimentary rocks of the lowland 30-50 km W of Montréal at the Oka Hills (260 m), Rigaud Mtn (213 m) and a hill near St-André-Est (137 m). An estimated 800-1200 m of rock has been eroded from the lowland in the last 100 million years. The N boundary is an eroded fault-line scarp in many places. The lowland is part of a rift valley originating in Cretaceous times, and is a region of high EARTHQUAKE probability where major damage can be expected; during historical times about 10 major earthquakes have occurred in each century.

The details of the lowland's present landscape are the result of the last continental glaciation, followed by marine submergence, emergence and, finally, river erosion and deposition. Evidence of early glaciation has been obliterated by later ones, but deposits exposed in valleys near Lac St-Pierre indicate that an early interval of weathering and deposition of river gravels was followed by at least 2 episodes of glaciation. These were separated by the St-Pierre nonglacial interval during which peat and lake sediments accumulated. This interval lasted from about 70 000 to possibly 34 000 years ago. The last major glacial advance covered the region prior to 18 000 years ago. This ice sheet eventually retreated with minor readvances, intermittently uncovering the S and SW parts of the lowlands, which then were inundated by proglacial lakes. Residual glacier ice obstructing the St Lawrence Valley near Québec disintegrated 13 000 years ago and the sea flooded the region, forming a body of water known as the Champlain Sea. From 13 000 to 10 000 years ago the St Lawrence Lowland rose rapidly (as much as 20 m/century) in response to the disappearance of the ice mass. The highest relict strand lines of the Champlain Sea are now 230 m above sea level on the N side of the lowlands and 75 m lower on the S side. The sea withdrew 9500 years ago and for a short time a lake with a surface at 40 m (present elevation) occupied the central part of the basin. It drained when the St Lawrence R eroded its channel past Québec deeper, and the present course of the river became established around 6500 years ago.

Much of the St Lawrence Lowland is underlain by clay deposited in the Champlain Sea. It is as thick as 60 m along the N side near the former glacier-margin source and becomes progressively thinner until it virtually disappears. When subjected to excessive water percolation from rain or snowmelt, the clay becomes unstable and often subsides in earth-flow landslides, which have caused much loss of life and property. The W and S parts of the lowland are underlain by glacial deposits (till) rather than marine clay. Wave action has removed the silt and clay from the till, leaving behind sand and gravel, so that beach deposits are common on the hills in this region. Around the margins of the lowland are numerous sand and gravel beaches, spits and bars representing former water levels. Fossils are abundant in Champlain Sea deposits, including foraminifera, molluscs and vertebrates such as seals and whales, and indicate that these waters were similar to those of the present Labrador coast and Gulf of St Lawrence.

In the lower, central part of the lowland, areas of sand N and E of Montréal are remnants of former deltas of the Ottawa and St Lawrence rivers. Low terraces covered by river sands occur in the E part of the lowland. Some of the sand has been formed into dunes; locally these have elongated sharp crests as high as 18 m and are called "*crêtes de coq.*" The aeolian sand is stabilized by vegetation. Along the Ottawa and St Lawrence rivers from Ottawa to Lac St-Pierre are troughlike abandoned river channels as wide as 2 km, with banks as high as 10 m. On the plain E of Montréal, roughly parallel to the St Lawrence, are ridges of bouldery sand 1.5-4.5 m high and 30 m wide, which appear to be material transported and pushed up by floating river ice during the river's early stages. The ridges have provided excellent building sites and road locations, and many rural communities are built on them. Much of the lowland is good agricultural land. Its clay has been used for brick and tile manufacture, and the sand and gravel deposits are exploited for road metal and construction material. The rocks of the lowland have been quarried for building stone, silica, cement, lime, crushed stone and concrete aggregate and for making brick and tile. The lowland was occupied by Iroquoian-speaking people at the time of its discovery by Jacques CARTIER in 1535. The farmlands were settled in the pattern of narrow strips fronting on the river, characteristic of the SEIGNEURIAL SYSTEM. Industry began near Trois-Rivières where bog iron was exploited in 1737. The St Lawrence Lowland now cradles the largest part of the population of Québec. *See also* ESCARPMENT. J.A. ELSON

St Lawrence River, grand river and estuary, which together with the GREAT LAKES forms a hydrographic system that penetrates 3790 km into N America. The river proper, about 1197 km long, issues from Lk Ontario, flows NE past Montréal and Québec City to the Gulf of ST LAWRENCE, from about 44° N lat near Kingston to about 50° N lat near Sept-Îles. The river's DRAINAGE BASIN covers some 1 million km², of which 505 000 km² is in the US, and its mean discharge of almost 10 100 m³/s is the largest in Canada. Its greatest tributary, the OTTAWA R, drains some 140 000 km², the SAGUENAY R about 88 000 km², the MANICOUAGAN R about 45 000 km², the ST-MAURICE R some 43 300 km² and the RICHELIEU R about 22 000 km². In geological terms, the St Lawrence is a young river, whose bed is a deep gash in the Earth's crust exposed some 10 000 years ago as the glaciers receded.

The route of the explorers and main axis of NEW FRANCE, the river figured prominently in Canada's early history, and it remains the focus of settlement for much of the province of Québec. It is still the most important commercial waterway in Canada, as well as a source of electric power and natural beauty. The St Lawrence forms much of the southwestern outline of the Canadian SHIELD, which encroaches the river at QUÉBEC CITY. At Cap-Tourmente, 40 km below Québec, the LAURENTIANS rise 579 m above the river and follow its

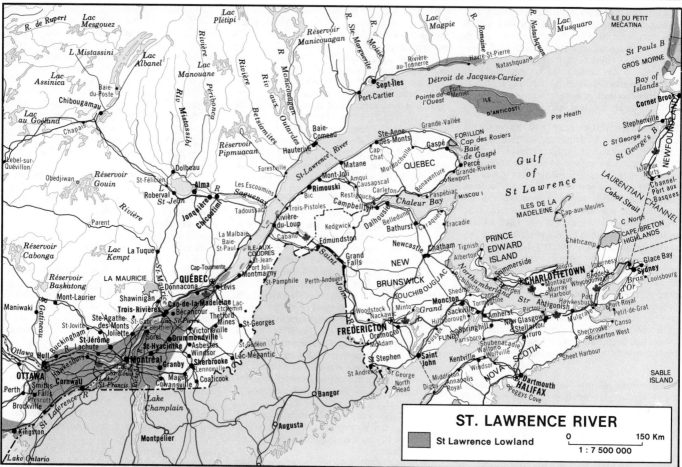

ST. LAWRENCE RIVER

St Lawrence Lowland

0   150 Km

1 : 7 500 000

course past Les Eboulements (770 m), where they begin to retreat inland, to the Saguenay. The S bank is generally lower, although the Appalachians approach the river at Matane and, continuing eastward, form the tableland of GASPÉ.

Course The westerly limit of the river itself has been set at Everett Pt, Lk Ontario. The section from KINGSTON to MONTRÉAL is called the International Rapids, as sudden drops in the riverbed create a series of rapids (this portion was flooded in the 1960s, forming Lk St Lawrence). The river begins as an extended arm of Lk Ontario, choked with numerous islands, beginning with Wolfe I and including the THOUSAND ISLANDS near Gananoque, Ont. It trends NE past Brockville, Prescott and Morrisburg to Cornwall, where it broadens to form Lake St Francis. The Beauharnois Canal now carries shipping safely past the former rapids of Lachine and Les Cèdres to another widening of the river, Lac St-Louis, SW of Montréal. The Ottawa joins the mainstream through channels to Lac St-Louis and over a NE route via Lac des Deux Montagnes, Rivière des Mille-Îles and Rivière des Prairies.The land between the various channels at the confluence forms the archipelago on which the city of Montréal is built. The port of Montréal has been developed since the 19th century by dredging and canals.

From Montréal to TROIS-RIVIÈRES, the river is generally calm and unaffected by tides. A number of long, narrow islands continue to divide the mainstream and a large cluster, similar to the group at Lk Ontario, lies at the mouth of the Richelieu R at Sorel. The river broadens into Lac St-Pierre, some 15 km wide, and narrows again at Trois-Rivières, at the mouth of the St-Maurice R. From here to Québec, the freshwater flow becomes reversible with the tides. The river constricts at Québec where a promontory commands

the entire upper course. The military value of the site was appreciated long before European settlement began. Past Québec the river divides to encircle Île d'ORLÉANS and steadily widens to 15 km at Cap-Tourmente, almost 25 km at Île-aux-COUDRES. The water becomes brackish and tides are high. Near the mouth of the Saguenay R, the riverbed drops dramatically from 25 m to 350 m, forming a drowned valley in the lower estuary. The freshwater flow mingles with cold arctic saltwater. The town of TADOUSSAC sits on a terrace of sand and clay at the confluence, but the rugged Precambrian N shore is sparsely settled. The S shore of the estuary, which forms a great curve towards Gaspé, is more open towards its hinterland, and major roads, including the TRANS-CANADA HIGHWAY, head inland from Rivière-du-Loup, Trois-Pistoles, Rimouski and Matane.

At Pointe-des-Monts, about 70 km E of Baie-Comeau and the mouth of the Manicouagan R, the N shore turns dramatically NNE for about 100 km to SEPT-ÎLES, near the mouth of the MOISIE R. The river doubles in width to over 100 km, forming a deep, broad submarine valley, in which strong currents pour in from the gulf along the N shore and sweep counterclockwise back to the E. The saline water of the estuary discourages ice, and the port of Sept-Îles is open year-round, despite its northerly location. According to the ROYAL PROCLAMATION OF 1763, a line from the mouth of Rivière St-Jean on the N shore past the W tip of Île d'ANTICOSTI to Cap des Rosiers on Gaspé marks the end of the river and the beginning of the gulf.

River Life Over the course of the river, the vegetation varies from deciduous, mixed and coniferous forest to taiga. There are sandbank grasses in the freshwater course, and seaweed and other saltwater plants in the middle and maritime estuary. Fish include smelt, sturgeon and herring. Beluga whales inhabit the lower course, on

which walrus was once also abundant. Massive flocks of migratory birds use the sandbanks or river reefs as seasonal stops, including most of the world's greater snow geese, which nest in the tidal marshes at Cap-Tourmente.

Sedentary Indian groups – likely Iroquoian – were settled at the present sites of Québec [STADACONA] and Montréal [HOCHELAGA] at the time of Jacques CARTIER's first explorations in the area in 1535. They had inexplicably disappeared by the time CHAMPLAIN founded Québec in 1608, possibly dispersed by the nomadic Montagnais, Etchemin and Algonquin, with whom the French established a lucrative trading alliance. Jacques Cartier had discovered the river in 1535, with the help of Indian guides who took him past Anticosti, which he had believed was a peninsula. He built 2 transient camps near Stadacona in 1535 and 1541, but it was not until 1608 that the French foothold was secure.

The St Lawrence R provides almost the only riverine entrance to the heart of the continent, and French explorers and traders used it to establish a colonial empire that stretched beyond Lk Superior. By 1760 most of the riverbank from Québec to Montréal was patterned with the long, narrow strips of the SEIGNEURIAL SYSTEM, with the seigneury of Beaupré marking the eastern limit of settlement. The river system was suited to the carriage of buoyant softwood logs, and in the 19th century the river became the main artery of the TIMBER TRADE. Montréal and Québec C grew into major commercial centres, as wheat and flour from UPPER CANADA were carried down the river. Under the leadership of the NORTH WEST CO, the fur traders pushed the "Empire of the St Lawrence" all the way to the basin of the Mackenzie R. Donald CREIGHTON and others have argued that the E-W axis of the St Lawrence, which provided a counterpoise to the N-S affinity offered by much

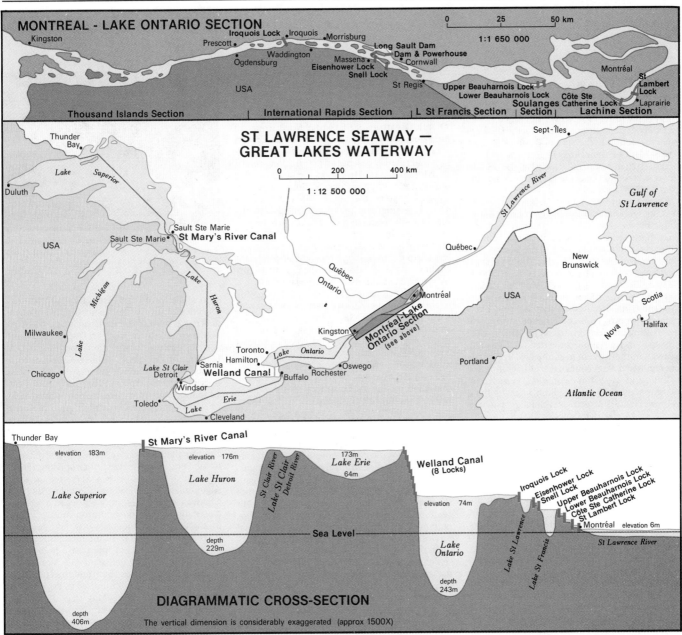

MONTREAL - LAKE ONTARIO SECTION

ST LAWRENCE SEAWAY — GREAT LAKES WATERWAY

DIAGRAMMATIC CROSS-SECTION
The vertical dimension is considerably exaggerated (approx 1500X)

of the continent's geography, helped make possible the future nation of Canada. Today, with the development of the ST LAWRENCE SEAWAY, the river links a vast area of Canada and the US with the rest of the world. It is still, as Cartier called it, "the great river of Canada." *See also* ST LAWRENCE LOWLAND.   JAMES MARSH

St Lawrence Seaway (Great Lakes Waterway) is the system of locks, canals and channels linking the Great Lakes and the St Lawrence R with the Atlantic Ocean. The construction of progressively larger canals along the St Lawrence R began as early as 1783. By 1900, a complete network of shallow draft canals allowed uninterrupted navigation from Lk Superior to Montréal. Between 1912 and 1932, the WELLAND CANAL was rebuilt, but the US was reluctant to enter a larger scheme, that is, to rebuild the Montréal-Lk Ontario channels. A threat by the Canadian government in 1951 to build a seaway entirely within Canadian territory resulted in a final agreement in 1954. Construction began that year on the Montréal-Lk Ontario section. This was opened to commercial traffic 20 Apr 1959 with the official opening 26 June 1959, attended by PM John Diefenbaker, Pres Dwight D. Eisenhower and Queen Elizabeth

II. The waterway, some 3790 km long from Anticosti I to the head of Lk Superior, now permitted vessels of up to 222.5 m long, 23.2 m wide and a maximum draft of 7.9 m to sail from Montréal to Duluth, Minn, on Lk Superior. The St Lawrence Seaway Authority, a federal crown corporation, was established by Act of Parliament in 1954 to construct, operate and maintain the Canadian portion of the waterway between Montréal and Lk Erie, including 5 of the 7 locks between Montréal and Lk Ontario and the Welland Canal between Lk Ontario and Lk Erie. The St Lawrence Seaway Development Corp was similarly formed by the US government to operate the 2 locks near Massena, NY. The 4 US locks on the St Mary's R are operated by the US Corps of Engineers and a smaller lock (18.3 m), too small for most commercial vessels, on the Canadian side of the St Mary's R is operated by Environment Canada, Parks.

Construction of the Seaway was a monumental engineering and construction feat. The Montréal-Lk Ontario section, which is often thought of as the whole Seaway, naturally divides into 4 sectors. The Lachine section includes the 33 km South Shore Canal, with the St Lambert and Côte

Ste Catherine locks bypassing the Lachine Rapids. The 2 locks provide a total lift of 13.7 m to the level of Lk St Louis. The Soulanges section includes the 2 Beauharnois locks which provide a total lift of 25 m to overcome the Beauharnois hydroelectric power dam. A further channel of 25.6 km leads westward to Lk St Francis. The Lk St Francis section stretches from the Beauharnois Canal to a point just east of Cornwall, Ont. The fourth section, the Wily-Dondero Ship Canal, which includes the US-owned Snell and Eisenhower locks near Massena, NY, allows ships to bypass the Moses/Saunders powerhouse. These 2 locks provide a lift of some 26 m to the level of Lk St Lawrence. At the W end of this lake the Iroquois lock, located at Iroquois, Ont, and adjacent to the Iroquois control dam, provides for control of the level of Lk St Lawrence relative to that of Lk Ontario. Together, all these locks between Lk Ontario and Montréal lift a westbound vessel about 65 m. West of Iroquois additional dredging was required to complete the St Lawrence Seaway to Lk Ontario. In addition to the primary works required to create the Seaway, ancillary works such as major bridge and tunnel construction were carried out in Montréal,

Beauharnois, Cornwall and Massena. In addition, the creation of Lk St Lawrence necessitated the relocation of highways and railways, as well as several small communities and parts of the towns of Iroquois and Morrisburg. In all over 500 dwellings and 6500 people were relocated to the newly created towns of Ingleside and Long Sault.

Between Lk Ontario and Lk Erie, the Welland Canal circumvents Niagara Falls. Its 8 locks lift a westbound vessel 99.4 m over a distance of 42.5 km. Between Lk Erie and Lk Huron, the US deepened the Detroit R, the St Clair R and Lk St Clair. The St Mary's R Canal links Lk Huron and Lk Superior. Each of its 4 parallel locks, on the US side, lifts a westbound vessel the required 6.5 m to bypass the St Mary's Falls.

The expenditure of public funds on the Seaway was not without opposition. The construction of the Seaway was considered by the railways and E coast ports to be unfair subsidized competition. Shippers, although in favour of the Seaway, opposed implementation of tolls. The original St Lawrence section of the Seaway cost Canada $330 million and the US $130 million. Canada has paid a further $300 million to improve the Welland Canal. Repayment of capital debt, interest and operating costs could not be covered under existing financial arrangements, and in 1977 a change in legislation converted the Canadian Seaway Authority debt to equity held by Canada but required that revenues cover all operating and maintenance costs; this change has been successful. An additional $600 million spent by the 2 countries for hydroelectric development has been recovered by electricity sales.

The Seaway has a major economic impact on Canada and the US. It provides economical freight rates for bulk commodities and makes an important contribution to the basic industries of both countries. The Seaway made possible the exploitation of the vast IRON ORE deposits of Québec and Labrador, and turned Canada from an importer to an exporter of iron ore. In 1986, 37.6 million t of cargo moved through the St Lawrence section of the Seaway, in contrast with the annual average of about 11 million t moved in the 1950s. Of the volume of cargo moving through the Seaway in 1986, 44% was grain, about 21% was iron ore, 22% was other bulk cargo and another 11% was general cargo or finished goods (most imported iron and steel products). Coal moving to Ontario steel mills and ELECTRIC-POWER GENERATING stations was important cargo on the Welland Canal (*see* LAKE CARRIERS).   GORDON C. SHAW

Saint-Léonard, NB, Town, inc 1920, pop 1512 (1986c), named in honour of an early settler, Leonard Coombes. In the late 18th century, Acadians settled this area along the Saint John R, midway between Grand Falls and Edmundston, but it was not until near the mid-19th century that a large number of settlers arrived. Agriculture was supplemented by forestry, but in recent years farming has disappeared and all mills have closed; now, many of the inhabitants work in the pulp mill in Edmundston and the food-processing plant in Grand Falls. The Madawaska Weavers produce their well-known textiles here in both a central location and as a cottage industry. The town is a border crossing point directly across the river from Van Buren, Maine, and is the site of a regional airport.   BURTON GLENDENNING

Saint-Marcoux, Micheline Coulombe, née Coulombe, composer, teacher (b at Notre-Dame-de-la-Doré, Qué 9 Aug 1938; d at Montréal 2 Feb 1985). Her teachers included Claude CHAMPAGNE, Clermont PÉPIN and Pierre Schaeffer. A cofounder of the Groupe international de musique électroacoustique de Paris (1969) and of the Montréal percussion ensemble Polycousmie (1971), she

played a role in contemporary music. *Regards* (1978), a synthesis of her research, reveals a desire to rediscover sound in its pure state: live instrumentation is combined with recorded sequences without amplification. The work is characterized by the importance of the spatial parameter, as is *Moments* (1977), which is true musical theatre.   HÉLÈNE PLOUFFE

St Margaret's Bay, 70 km², is a small inlet of the Atlantic Ocean on the SE coast of Nova Scotia, 40 km W of HALIFAX. It is a favourite summer resort area, noted especially for its relatively warm surface water, sandy beaches and ideal sailing conditions for small craft. The region also hosts a sizable tourist trade. Peggy's Cove, for instance, a tiny fishing village on the eastern side of the bay, is said to be the most photographed spot in the province. The name stems from a name bestowed on the area by CHAMPLAIN: Le Port Sainte-Marguerite. In the early days smugglers were frequent visitors to the bay, selling contraband goods, including oil and fish. However, the primary industry was and remains fishing. In the late 1960s and early 1970s St Margaret's Bay was used by marine scientists from the BEDFORD INSTITUTE OF OCEANOGRAPHY in Dartmouth, NS, as a field laboratory for studying the physical and biological processes underlying the productivity of COASTAL WATERS. Among the scientists' conclusions were that the observed counterclockwise circulation in the bay helps flush the bay waters every 10 to 30 days and that wind mixing in the surface layers controls primary-production efficiency.   P.C. SMITH

Ste-Marie, Qué, Town, pop 9536 (1986c), 8937 (1981c), inc 1855, is located on the Rivière CHAUDIÈRE. Situated on lowlands suitable for agriculture, Ste-Marie is one of the oldest settlements in the Beauce region. Built on part of the seigneury given in 1736 to Thomas-Jacques Taschereau, it was inhabited by colonists from the Beaupré shore and from Île d'ORLÉANS. During the 19th century, Ste-Marie retained its agricultural importance, but progressively became a regional service centre as the construction of the Quebec Central railway sparked the development and settlement of its hinterland. From 1880 to 1940 the wood industry was a major part of its economy. The city now has prosperous industries in the food sector and in metalworking.

CLAUDINE PIERRE-DESCHÊNES

Sainte-Marie, Buffy, folksinger, songwriter (b at Piapot Reserve, Sask 20 Feb 1941). Orphaned by Cree parents, she was raised in the US by a part Micmac family, and in the early 1960s she became an important figure in New York folk music. Since her emergence internationally as a bold social commentator and idiosyncratic singer, she has often returned to Canada for festivals, concerts and broadcasts. Her most popular songs include "Until It's Time for You To Go" and the protest song, "The Universal Soldier." Other songs concern the native peoples' experience in N America. In Oct 1987 she performed at a benefit concert in Calgary to help support the land claims of the Lubicon band of Alberta.   MARK MILLER

Ste Marie Among the Hurons Roman Catholic mission work among the HURON, begun in 1615 by the Recollets, was renewed in 1634 by the Jesuits with the arrival of 3 priests led by Superior Jean de BRÉBEUF and assisted by 5 domestics. In 1638 Jérôme LALEMANT arrived as the new superior; by 1639 there were 13 fathers active

Ste Marie Among the Hurons, Ont, located on the Wye R, east of Midland, is a reconstruction of Ontario's first European community (*photo by Odesse*).

among the Huron and PETUN. Lalemant planned an agriculturally self-sufficient, fortified missionary centre, centrally located in HURONIA, with easy access to the canoe route to Québec. It was to serve as a retreat for the priests and ultimately to become the nucleus of a Huron Christian community. Construction began in 1639, 5 km SE of present-day MIDLAND, Ont. The structure, dedicated to the Virgin Mary, was named Sainte Marie, or Notre Dame de la Conception. At its busiest in 1648 it housed 19 priests, 4 lay brothers, 23 donnés, 4 boys, 7 domestics and 8 soldiers. By the late 1640s, besides their missions to the Huron (St Joseph), the Jesuits at Ste Marie also had missions to the Petun (Les Apôtres), the Nipissing (St Esprit), the OJIBWA and OTTAWA (St Pierre) and some Algonquian bands along Georgian Bay (St Charles). In 1648 the Iroquois began a series of devastating attacks on the Huron and a year later on the Petun (*see* IROQUOIS WARS). Five Jesuit fathers who worked out of the mission lost their lives: Antoine Daniel (4 July 1648), Brébeuf (16 Mar 1649), Gabriel Lalemant (17 Mar 1649), Charles Garnier (7 Dec 1649) and Noël Chabanel (8 Dec 1649); all were canonized by Pope Pius XI on 29 June 1930. On 15 May 1649 the mission was withdrawn, and Ste Marie was burned by its occupants lest it fall into Iroquois hands and suffer desecration. A new Ste Marie was built and occupied for one year on Christian I in Lake Huron. With further defeats of the Huron and Petun, and following a severe winter famine, the mission was removed to Québec on 10 June 1650.

Exploratory excavations at Ste Marie were conducted as early as 1855 by Father Felix Martin, s.j. Serious archaeological work began in June 1941, directed by K.E. Kidd for the Royal Ontario Museum and the Jesuit order. Because of budgetary constraints the work ended in 1943, but it had resulted in the excavation and meticulous documentation of most of the mission's central section. Excavation was completed 1947-51 by Wilfrid Jury, then curator of the Museum of Indian Archaeology at U of Western Ontario. In 1964 reconstruction began under Dr Jury for the Ontario government.

The reconstruction has drawn considerable scholarly criticism because Jury's archaeology, and therefore his justification for the reconstruction, have not been made public, and because Kidd's work was ignored. Nevertheless the workmanship and lively interpretive program make Ste Marie an excellent educational and tourist facility. The attached museum begins with an outline of conditions in 17th-century France and proceeds to trace the historical development of Québec, the mission at Ste Marie and life among

the Huron. The site is enhanced by a good research library and archaeological laboratory. Although not part of the Ste Marie complex, the adjacent Martyr's Shrine, built 1926 and operated by the Jesuits, attracts PILGRIMS and evokes the spirituality that motivated the founding of Ste Marie. *See also* CHRISTIAN RELIGIOUS COMMUNITIES; SAINTS. C.E. HEIDENREICH

Saint-Martin, Albert Frédéric, educator, social activist, militant socialist (b at Montréal 1 Oct 1865; d there 9 Feb 1947). He was a leading Québec socialist, anti-conscriptionist and anti-clerical who headed the Socialist, then the Social-Democratic Party of Canada (French Canadian section), a union and civil rights supporter, and was secretary-archivist of the Parti ouvrier (1904-06). A stenographer-translator-clerk for the Montréal Superior Court from 1898, he ran unsuccessfully as workers' candidate provincially (1905) and as a socialist federally (1908). He was an indefatigable worker in socialist and labour causes, establishing teaching leagues, workers' clubs, libraries, a farming collective and grocery store, printing and housing co-operatives, unemployed committees, l'Université ouvrière in 1925 (closed by the state in 1933), and the Spartakus movement. He taught political economy at Montréal's Labour College (1920-22) and also lectured on women's rights, socialism and esperanto. He was a forceful publicist and orator, 2 provocative works being *T'as Menti* (1920) and *Sandwiches à la "shouashe"* (1933). He achieved the right to conduct May 1 Labour Day parades. F.J.K. GRIEZIC

St Mary's Bay, on the S coast of Newfoundland's AVALON PENINSULA between PLACENTIA B and Trepassey B, runs 65 km NE to Colinet Harbour from its mouth between St Shotts and Point Lance, 32 km NW. The bay branches into long harbours and inlets towards its head, with deep indentations cut into its eastern shore. Great Colinet I, 8 km long, is situated at the centre of the bay. Though the climate is better at the head, the 2 principal settlements, Branch and St Vincent's, are towards the bay's mouth, nearer the fine Atlantic fishing grounds. The bay was a traditional French fishing ground until the Treaty of UTRECHT 1713, after which the coasts were gradually settled by English and Irish. With good forests in the N, the bay saw logging operations in addition to the fishery and some fur trapping. Today the primary occupation of the sparsely populated bay is still fishing. ROBERT D. PITT

St Mary's Church, RED DEER, Alta (designed by Douglas CARDINAL, completed in 1968), the first building to bring Cardinal wide attention, established themes that have continued through his subsequent work. On a bare suburban site, the church creates a dominating presence by its size, flowing forms and the height of the upward sweeping walls. The interior explains the unfamiliar shape; the entrance wall spirals inward past a circular baptistery to shield a broad, shadowed sanctuary under the downward billowing concrete vault. Two concrete cylinders descend from the vault to shed natural light on the altar and tabernacle areas. The church is a demanding building, the forms unexpected but evocative of things ancient and deep-rooted, both incongruous and appropriate. MICHAEL MCMORDIE

St Marys River, one of the largest rivers in Nova Scotia, flows into the Atlantic Ocean at a point 190 km E of HALIFAX. It offers excellent opportunities for SPORTFISHING, especially for ATLANTIC SALMON and a char, locally called "sea trout." Salmon, in particular, are noted for their heavy runs in spring and early summer. Early French fur traders gave the river its name and in 1655 established a post at Fort Sainte Marie, where the town

of Sherbrooke now stands. In addition to the fishing industry, the river is used to transport quantities of pulpwood downstream from Sherbrooke. P.C. SMITH

St Marys River (Ont) connects Lake SUPERIOR to lake HURON and forms part of the US/Canada border. It is *c* 100 km long and drops 7 m through the *sault* ("rapids") which give the Canadian and US cities of SAULT STE MARIE their names. The obvious strategic value of the river was well known to the native people before Étienne BRÛLÉ travelled the river in 1622. The falls were shown on Champlain's 1632 map and the Jesuit mission of Ste Marie was founded on the river in 1641. The NORTH WEST CO established a post at the site in 1783 and in 1798 built the first canal around the rapids. Today there are 4 locks on the American side, operated by the US Corps of Engineers, and a smaller lock on the Canadian side. The locks and the river carry more traffic than any other canal system in the world, despite being frozen for up to 5 months of the year. JAMES MARSH

Saint Mary's University, Halifax, was chartered in 1841 to provide higher learning to young Catholic men. Founder Rev Edmund Burke, later vicar apostolic of Nova Scotia, worked tirelessly but with limited resources to maintain the college. In 1852 the NS Assembly confirmed its legal status in perpetuity, but St Mary's existed precariously for the next half century. In 1913 the Irish Christian Brothers assumed responsibility for the college, directing its affairs until 1940 when they were succeeded by the Society of Jesus (Jesuits). In 1970 the province transferred responsibility for the university from the Archdiocese of Halifax to an independent and lay board of governors. Saint Mary's is now a coeducational institution offering undergraduate programs in arts, science and commerce; preprofessional programs in engineering, medicine, law, dentistry and architecture; and theology, and graduate study in education, business administration, astronomy, history, philosophy, psychology and Atlantic Canada Studies. COLIN D. HOWELL

Enrolment: Saint Mary's University, 1985-86
(Source: Statistics Canada)

Full-time Undergrad	Full-time Graduate	Part-time Undergrad	Part-time Graduate
3213	102	1075	272

St-Maurice, Rivière, 560 km long, rises upstream from the GOUIN RÉSERVOIR, 200 km W of Lac SAINT-JEAN, Québec. It drains a basin of 43 300 km². After its confluence with the Manouane R, it feeds the Blanc Reservoir and then takes in the Vermillon, Trenche, Croche, Mattawin and Mékinac rivers. It forms a delta at its outlet into the St Lawrence R, at TROIS-RIVIÈRES—CAP-DE-LA-MADELEINE. The upper St-Maurice flows through a steeply banked valley marked by glacial erosion. Its angular course is controlled by faults in the Precambrian rocks. Its bed is bordered with alluvial terraces and, downstream from LA TUQUE, cuts through transversal moraines and marine clays. The lower St-Maurice begins at the exit from the Laurentides, at Grandes-Piles. With a rate of discharge of 730 m³/s, it runs through ancient sediments and, in places, through the sedimentary rocks of the St Lawrence platform. It is harnessed at Grand-Mère, Shawinigan Falls and La Gabelle.

The river was a route of human penetration. Several paleo-Indian sites, dating from the 2nd to 17th centuries, have been discovered. In 1535 Jacques CARTIER called it Rivière de Fouez. The delta's 3 channels occasioned the name of the city of Trois-Rivières, founded in 1634 by La Violette to promote the fur trade. The name St-Maurice

came in 1668, from the given name of Maurice Poulin de La Fontaine. The iron ore of the marshes of the lower St-Maurice area was exploited at the historic site of Vieilles-Forges and in other foundries from the 1730s until 1908 (*see* FORGES ST-MAURICE). The upper St-Maurice was explored in 1828. Hydroelectric energy and floating log booms made possible the establishment, 1890-1900, of pulp and paper mills and chemical industries in Grand-Mère and SHAWINIGAN. On the upper St-Maurice, the Attikamek live in the villages of Manouane, Weymontachingue and Obedjiwan. SERGE OCCHIETTI

St Paul, Alta, Town, pop 5030 (1986c), inc 1937, county seat for County of St Paul, is located on the N shore of Upper Therien Lk, 202 km NE of Edmonton. In 1895 Oblate Father Albert LACOMBE successfully appealed for reservation of 2 townships near the Saddle Lake Indian Reserve for MÉTIS SETTLEMENT. Meagre agricultural success and trapping barely sustained St Paul des Métis. The town developed only after the reserve was opened to general settlement in 1909. The French-speaking Québecers, Ukrainians and others who arrived did without a railway connection until volunteers completed the CNR line from nearby Spedden in 1920. Considerable soil variation made mixed farming (especially beef cattle and grain) popular, and the town contains several agricultural processing plants. Native, French and Ukrainian cultural organizations reflect St Paul's traditions, and special educational facilities include the Alberta Vocational Centre, Lakeland College and the neighbouring Blue Quills Indian College. CARL BETKE

St Peters, PEI, Village, pop 265 (1986c), 335 (1981c), 53 km NE of Charlottetown, is located at the head of St Peters Bay. The picturesque village was named after the comte de St-Pierre, who in 1720 was granted control over the Island by French authorities. As in the past, the economy of the surrounding area is dependent upon fishing and farming. St Peters's importance declined after the demise of the shipbuilding industry in the late 19th century. W.S. KEIZER

St Peter's, NS, UP, pop 711 (1986c), 669 (1981c), is situated between St Peter's Inlet and St Peter's Bay on the S shore of Cape Breton I. Nicolas Denys established a fortified fishing and trading post here in 1650. It was also used to supply LOUISBOURG with wood. After the fall of the fortress in 1758, LOYALISTS settled here among the remaining French. Farming and fishing were the major activities until 1869, when St Peter's Canal was opened. St Peter's then became important to sailing ships using the 0.8 km long canal as the safest and most efficient route between the Cape Breton interior and the Atlantic Ocean. Today, St Peter's is a quiet village with a few tourist attractions, including a national historic park and a historic blacksmith shop. The canal is now used mainly by pleasure craft. HEATHER MACDONALD

Saint-Pierre and Miquelon, French islands in the Gulf of ST LAWRENCE, 20 km SW of Burin Peninsula, Newfoundland. Miquelon (215 km²) was once 2 islands. In the mid-1700s, an isthmus formed to Langlade in the S from sand collecting in the wrecks that had foundered on the reefs and sandbars between the islands. The treacherous waters between Langlade and Saint-Pierre were up to 1900 called Gueule d'Enfer –"the Mouth of Hell." Since 1816 alone, 674 shipwrecks have been recorded. About 5600 of the total population of 6200 live on the smaller island of Saint-Pierre, where the capital town of the same name is located.

The islands were likely discovered (about 1520) by Portuguese navigator FAGUNDES, and

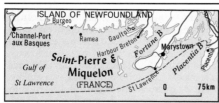

were claimed formally for France by Jacques CARTIER 14 years later. They were originally settled by 30 BASQUE and Norman fishermen in 1604, but were uninhabited in 1713 when Britain claimed them under the terms of the Treaty of UTRECHT. The claim was relinquished under the Treaty of PARIS, 1763, and France resettled the islands with 350 Acadians who had been deported to France. Britain attacked and captured the islands during the AMERICAN REVOLUTION and again in 1793. France resumed control permanently with the Treaty of Ghent, 1814, resettling the islands with French refugees and some 700 Newfoundlanders.

The rocky islands are barren, except for scrubby yews and junipers, a thin volcanic soil, and dirt removed from ships' ballast. However, the islands have provided France with a station near the richest fishing grounds in N America. By 1866, 4000 French fishermen were coming annually from St Malo, France, to fish in a fleet of 200 schooners. The fleet was devastated in 1904, when France lost its rights to the FRENCH SHORE. During Prohibition, Saint-Pierre was a storage base for Canadian liquor companies and a centre of illegal trade to the US. Today, France is determined to maintain its presence on the islands and spends some $25 million there annually; the per capita aid paid to the islands is the highest in the world. Fishing is still important, as trawlers haul 20 000 tonnes of cod a year from the gulf alone. A serious dispute has arisen between France and Canada, as Canada extended its exclusive fishing zone to 15 km (1964) and then to 220 km (1977). France retaliated with a 220 km claim of its own. The 2 claims, obviously in conflict, had not been settled by the late 1980s.   JAMES MARSH

St-Quentin, NB, Village, pop 2264 (1986c), 2334 (1981c), inc 1966, located in northern NB in the highlands between the Restigouche and MIRAMICHI rivers and tributaries of the SAINT JOHN R. Originally called Five Fingers, for a local brook, it was renamed Anderson Siding in 1910 and changed to St-Quentin in 1919 after the WWI battle in France. Early settlers followed the railway construction, established potato farms, sawmills and forest-related industries that still predominate. There are 5 shingle and hardwood mills. A major fire destroyed much of the village in 1919. The population is predominately French speaking. A multidisciplinary high school, community college and public library serve the surrounding district. The village is the entrance to Mt Carleton Campground and Resource Park in an area noted for fishing and hunting.   BURTON GLENDENNING

St. Roch, wooden schooner powered by sails and an auxiliary engine, launched in N Vancouver in Apr 1928 for ROYAL CANADIAN MOUNTED POLICE operations in the Arctic. Under the command of Sgt Henry A. LARSEN, it sailed 23 June 1940 from Vancouver to traverse the NORTHWEST PASSAGE. Taking a treacherous southerly route through the arctic islands, it was trapped in the ice for 2 winters and did not reach Halifax until 11 Oct 1942. It was the second vessel, after Roald AMUNDSEN's *Gjoa*, to traverse the Northwest Passage, and the first to make the voyage W to E. The *St. Roch* returned to Vancouver by a more northerly route, through LANCASTER SOUND and Barrow Str, in only 86 days (22 July-16 Oct 1944). This voyage made it the first vessel to negotiate the passage both ways. The ex-

ploits of the *St. Roch* strengthened Canadian ARCTIC SOVEREIGNTY. In 1950 the *St. Roch* made a southern voyage and thus became the first ship to circumnavigate N America. It was purchased by the city of Vancouver in 1954 and permanently berthed at the Maritime Museum. The federal government declared the *St. Roch* a national HISTORIC SITE in 1962.   ROGER SARTY

Ste-Scholastique, Qué. Made a parish in 1834, the village of Ste-Scholastique ceased to exist when land was expropriated in 1969 for the construction of Mirabel Airport. It then became part of the new city of MIRABEL. This former agricultural village in the NW area of the plain of Montréal was the chief town of the judicial district of Terrebonne 1857-1924. Several famous trials were held in its courthouse. A few km S of the village on the Belle R, 4 windmills long dominated communal life; one, the old Sulpician manor built in 1802, still recalls that historic age. When it merged with Mirabel, the village had some 900 inhabitants. Thereafter its life was completely changed by the enormous airport.   G. BOILEAU

St Stephen, NB, Town, pop 5032 (1986c), 5120 (1981c), is located on the ST CROIX R in southwestern NB. The site was first occupied during the AMERICAN REVOLUTION by a small band of enterprising settlers in search of timber resources for a mill operation. In 1784 they were joined by elements of the Port Matoon Assn, a group composed mainly of disbanded soldiers from the American conflict. Endowed with excellent facilities for prosecuting the timber trade, St Stephen rapidly developed into a prosperous shipping and shipbuilding centre on the Bay of FUNDY for much of the 19th century. Industrial expansion in the latter half of that century saw the rise of a cotton mill in nearby Milltown, soap and axe factories, and Ganong Bros Ltd, still an international candy manufacturer. In 1973 St Stephen was amalgamated with nearby Milltown to form St Stephen-Milltown; the incorporated name of St Stephen has been used since 1975.   ROGER P. NASON

St Thomas, Ont, City, seat of Elgin County, pop 28 851 (1986c), 28 165 (1981c), inc 1881, located in SW Ontario, 29 km S of London. In 1803 Thomas TALBOT began to place settlers on a large tract of land he owned N of Lk Erie. St Thomas, est *c*1810, was the capital of the settlement and was named for the eccentric founder of the backwoods colony, who governed it for 50 years. Originally an agricultural centre, it became an important railway town at the turn of the century; by 1911 it was on 7 different rail lines. Today it has an economy marked by diversified light industry. In 1824 the first medical school in what is now Ontario was established there by Charles DUNCOMBE and John Rolph. Nicknamed "The Garden City," it has public parks well known for their brilliant floral displays.   DANIEL FRANCIS

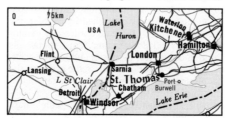

Saint Thomas University, Fredericton, NB, evolved from the Roman Catholic school system in the province and more directly from Saint Michael's Academy in Chatham. Although this school, opened in Chatham in 1860 by Bishop Rogers, lasted only until 1880, it left behind physical and intellectual structures and a community desire for a local college. However, despite exten-

sive efforts on the part of successive bishops and the clergy, it was not until 1910 that the Basilian Fathers opened Saint Thomas College, a high school and junior college. This order relinquished administration to the Diocese of Chatham in 1923. The college obtained degree-granting status in 1934 and ceased to teach high school in 1961. In 1960 the name was changed to Saint Thomas University and in 1964 it moved to Fredericton to occupy a portion of the campus of the UNIVERSITY OF NEW BRUNSWICK and to share some of the same facilities. The university grants undergraduate degrees in arts and social work and has an active program of native studies for indigenous peoples.   BURTON GLENDENNING

Saint-Vallier, Jean-Baptiste de La Croix de Chevrières de, second bishop of Québec, founder of the Hôpital Général at Québec (b at Grenoble, France 14 Nov 1653; d at Québec City 26 Dec 1727). Saint-Vallier was bishop of Québec 1688-1727. He impressed the clergy with his zeal and endless activity, but his arrival 31 July 1688 was followed by 16 years of crisis as the autocratic bishop sought to combat drunkenness, immodest dress, blasphemy, dancing, immorality and profiteering, while encouraging family devotions, church attendance and payment of tithes. He promoted missions in Acadia, Louisiana and Illinois. In a short time, however, he fell out with Governor FRONTENAC (over the performance of *Tartuffe*), with the military, cathedral chapter, Recollets, Jesuits and almost the entire diocese. In return, his adversaries denounced his writings, *Catechism* (1702) and *Ritual* (1703), as heretical, and little effort was made to gain his release when he was captured and imprisoned in England. The harsh internment for 5 years, from July 1704 to 1709, illness and his ascetic behaviour destroyed his health. He returned to Québec Aug 1713, gave up his palace to live in the Hôpital Général and donated his fortune to the poor, selling even his shoes and bed. Despite his faults, Saint-Vallier was a pious man and he undoubtedly contributed to the consolidation of the early Catholic church in America.   CORNELIUS J. JAENEN

St-Vincent de Paul, Society of, Catholic organization dedicated to works of charity. It was founded in 1833 by Frederic Ozanam, a 20-year old Sorbonne student in Paris. Ozanam and 6 other students formed the society in response to taunts that Christianity had outlived its usefulness, especially to the poor. The students put themselves under the patronage of St Vincent de Paul, who had called attention to social problems 200 years before, and set themselves to bringing assistance to the poor. The conference grew to more than 200 members in the first year and soon spread to the provinces of France and to Rome (1842), England (1844), Germany (1846) and throughout Europe. Dr Joseph Painchaud joined the conference in Paris and on returning home to Québec in 1846 founded the Notre-Dame Conference. Conferences were organized in Montréal (1848), Toronto (1850) and throughout British N America.

The efforts of the Vincentians have been focused on the parish level, although some conferences are formed for specific purposes or places, such as jails, schools or homes for the aged. Its main objectives are to encourage "the practice of Christian living," to visit, help and bring comfort to the poor and infirm. Today, the society functions in 120 countries, with a membership of 800 000. In Canada there are some 950 conferences with about 9000 members.

Saints The first N Americans to be canonized (29 June 1930) in the Catholic Church were the 5 Jesuits killed by Iroquois in inter-tribal warfare in Huronia in the 1640s: Jean de BRÉBEUF, Noël Chabanel, Antoine Daniel, Charles Garnier and Gabriel Lalemant. Isaac JOGUES, also a Jesuit missionary, and René Goupil and Jean de La Lande, donnés working for the Jesuits, lost their lives on missions to the Mohawk. All were pronounced martyrs (though they were not put to death for their religious beliefs) and their collective feast day is Oct 18. The first candidate for sainthood born in Canada was Marie-Marguerite d'YOUVILLE (1701-71, beatified 3 May 1959), founder of the GREY NUNS.

During the papacy of John Paul II, who somewhat simplified the canonization process, 8 more Canadians have been canonized or beatified: Marguerite BOURGEOYS (1620-1700, canonized 31 Oct 1982), founder of the Congrégation de Notre-Dame; Brother ANDRÉ, né Alfred Bessette (1845-1937, beatified 23 May 1982) of the Congrégation de la Ste Croix, who was instrumental in the building of St Joseph's Oratory in Montréal; Bishop François de Montmorency LAVAL of Québec City (1623-1708, beatified 22 June 1980), the first Canadian bishop; Mother MARIE DE L'INCARNATION, née Marie Guyart, (1599-1672, beatified 22 June 1980), the first Ursuline superior in Canada; Mother MARIE-ROSE, née Eulalie Durocher (1811-49, beatified 23 May 1982), founder of the Soeurs de saints noms de Jésus et de Marie; Kateri TEKAKWITHA (1656-80, beatified 22 June 1980), the first Indian candidate for sainthood; Mother Marie-Léonie, née Alodie-Virginie Paradis (1840-1912), founder of the Petites Soeurs de la Ste-Famille and the first to be beatified on Canadian soil (during the papal visit of Sept 1984); and Bishop Louis-Zéphirin Moreau of St-Hyacinthe, Qué (1824-1901, beatified 10 May 1987).

Canonization is often a lengthy process. It begins only after death and after there is popular urging that a person be declared a saint. Such popular pressure, for example, presently exists for Georges-Philéas VANIER (1888-1967), a former governor general of Canada. The next step in the process is taken by a local bishop, who formally initiates the cause and appoints someone to see to it that testimony concerning the candidate's life and holiness is carefully and exhaustively compiled. The goal is to prove that the person lived a life of heroic virtue or died a martyr's death, and a case both for and against is prepared, presented and judged. If the result is favourable, "the cause is introduced in Rome," that is, the evidence is evaluated by the Sacred Congregation for the Causes of Saints, who may then declare the candidate to be "Venerable."

At least one posthumous miracle attributable to the candidate's intercession, or a general reputation for miracles, must then be proved before the Sacred Congregation in order for the next step, beatification, to take place. The requirement is, in fact, 2 miracles but the Sacred Congregation may waive one of them. The beatification ceremony declares the candidate to be in heaven, bestows the title "Blessed" and authorizes public veneration of him in the country or countries where he lived. Canonization and the title of "Saint" comes after 2 more miracles have been verified (and again one may be waived); a canonized saint may be publicly venerated anywhere in the world.

By the mid-1980s causes had been introduced in Rome for 10 others, of whom one, Bishop Vital Justin GRANDIN of St Albert (1829-1902) has been declared venerable. Also from the Edmonton area was Brother Anthony Kowalczyk OMI (1866-1947); from The Pas, Man, Bishop Ovide Charlebois (1862-1933), apostolic vicar of Keewatin. From Montréal were those of Mother Émilie Gamelin (1800-51), founder of the Soeurs de la Providence; Jeanne MANCE (1606-73), a driving force in the founding of Ville-Marie; and Mother Marie-Anne, (née Marie-Esther Sureau,

dit Blondin) (1809-90) of the Soeurs de Sainte-Anne. From St-Hyacinthe, Qué, was the cause of Élisabeth Bergeron (1851-1936) of the Soeurs de St-Joseph and Bishop Louis Zépherin Moreau of St-Hyacinthe (1823-1901), and from Trois-Rivières, Father Frédéric Janssoone, OMI (1836-1916). Father Alfred Pampalon, CSsR (1867-96) was from Ste-Anne-de-Beaupré, Qué; and from Québec City is that of Mother Marie-Catherine de St-Augustin, née Catherine de Longpré (1633-68) of the Augustines de la Miséricorde de Jésus.

The act of formally declaring a person to be a saint is not limited to Catholicism; the Orthodox Churches also have canonized saints, although none of them are from Canada. There are, however, some Russian Orthodox saints from Alaska canonized by the Orthodox Church of America; these include Herman of Alaska (1760-1837) and a native, Peter the Aleut (d 1816).

JOHN RASMUSSEN

Saison dans la vie d'Emmanuel, Une (1965), by Marie-Claire BLAIS, is a darkly lyrical vision of Québec, an act of revolt distinguished by its black humour. Employing multiple viewpoints and blurring reality with nightmare, Blais narrates events surrounding the winter birth of Emmanuel, sixteenth child of a peasant family. The perspective of his indomitable grandmother Antoinette frames the novel, itself dominated by the autobiographical manuscripts of Emmanuel's brother Jean Le Maigre, an adolescent friar and tubercular genius. The lives and deaths of Emmanuel's siblings, like the themes of incest and corrupt monastic life, constitute an allegory of insularity and ignorance as well as a literal response to cold and hunger. Acclaimed by American critic Edmund Wilson in his preface to Derek Coltman's translation, *A Season in the Life of Emmanuel* (1966), the novel won numerous prizes at home and abroad, and has been translated into a dozen languages. MICHÈLE LACOMBE

Salaberry, Charles-Michel d'Irumberry de, soldier (b at Beauport, Qué 19 Nov 1778; d at Chambly, Lower Canada 27 Feb 1829). A protégé of the duke of Kent, he was commissioned in the British army in 1794, and served in Ireland, the W Indies and the Low Countries during the Napoleonic Wars. Returning to Lower Canada in 1810, he became aide-de-camp to Maj-Gen de Rottenburg. Promoted in the militia 1812, he raised and commanded a troop of Canadien VOLTIGEURS during the WAR OF 1812, repelling an American force and in 1813 turning back another numerically superior American advance on Montréal at the Battle of CHÂTEAUGUAY. Salaberry was retired on half pay in 1815 and was made a Companion of the Bath 2 years later. In 1818 he was appointed to the legislative council of Lower Canada. DAVID EVANS

Salamander, common name for most members of the tailed AMPHIBIA (order Caudata). About 340 species are known worldwide; 19 are native to Canada. Salamanders are found mainly in the temperate regions of the Northern Hemisphere but also occur southward to northern Africa, Iran and northern Burma and to northern S America. In Canada, salamanders occur from the Maritimes to BC and N to central Labrador and northern BC; none have been recorded from the Island of Newfoundland. Salamander species vary in size, from 3.9 cm to 180 cm. One of the largest salamanders in Canada is the 43 cm aquatic mud puppy (*Necturus maculosus*), the smallest is the 5-9 cm four-toed salamander (*Hemidactylium scutatum*). A Chinese giant salamander lived in captivity 52 years and certain species of newts 30 years; however, the life span of some of the smaller species may vary from one to a few years.

Most salamanders resemble LIZARDS and are sometimes erroneously referred to as lizards. However, salamanders lack scales and claws and have moist, glandular skin; true lizards (class Reptilia) have claws and a dry, scaly, cornified skin. All adult salamanders found in Canada have 4 legs; 3 species in southeastern US have front legs only. Hence, salamanders differ from the limbless, tropical caecilians of the amphibian order Gymnophiona. Salamanders have tails, and teeth in both jaws; thus, they differ from the third group of amphibians, the FROGS, which lack tails and lower teeth. Salamanders can pick up vibrations but are unable to hear. They are generally voiceless, although some utter faint squeaks. Salamanders have 2 nostrils connected to the mouth, eyes often with movable lids, a mouth with fine teeth, a tongue often protrusible, a skeleton largely bony, a 3-chambered heart with 2 auricles and one ventricle, and body temperature dependent on environment. They breathe by gills, lungs, mouth lining and skin, sometimes in combination, sometimes separately. Fertilization may be external or internal (internal in all Canadian species). When internal, the male deposits jellylike capsules of sperm; the female picks them up in the lips of the cloaca (chamber through which eggs pass). The eggs are fertilized as they are expelled. All Canadian species lay eggs, the number laid and incubation period varying with each species. Some species deposit eggs in fresh water in a jellylike mass attached to vegetation (mole salamanders); others, under stones in moist places along brooks (dusky salamanders); others use damp, rotted logs (redback salamanders). Some species of mole salamanders go to ponds, ditches and lakes in early spring to lay eggs, while stream and woodland species may not deposit until summer. Water-hatching young breathe through gills and may retain these for several years before transforming into adults. Land-hatching young resemble adults.

The species of salamanders found along streams and brooks are known as stream salamanders; those around springs and spring-fed brooklets, as spring salamanders; those in wooded areas, as woodland salamanders. The mole salamanders are so-called because they burrow under logs or into the earth. The mud puppy spends its entire life in water. Larvae and, usually, adult red-spotted newts live in water, but in most parts of their range after the young grow legs they leave the water and spend a year or more on land. At this stage, they are referred to as efts.

All salamanders are carnivorous: larger ones consume earthworms and adults and larvae of many insects; smaller species eat small insects, insect larvae and various small invertebrates. Larvae eat tadpoles, smaller salamander larvae and aquatic invertebrates. Salamanders are probably beneficial to forestry and agriculture as they consume injurious INSECT PESTS. Fishes, frogs, snakes, turtles, birds and mammals are natural predators. When caught, many salamanders are able to break off their tails. The tail continues to twitch for a short time, allowing the salamander to escape as the pursuer is decoyed into seizing the tail. Salamanders are able to regenerate the tail, but the regenerated part is usually shorter than the original. Most species have mildly poisonous glands in the skin that can cause irritation to some animals; newts, particularly the western species, have strong secretions.

Since they are unable to survive heavy freezing and must burrow in the earth or under leaf litter where frost does not penetrate, terrestrial species hibernate during colder months. Most aquatic species are probably active year round. Most nonaquatic salamanders are active at night, usually during wet or damp periods; dry air and warm

Salamanders in Canada

Common Name	Scientific Name	Range
yellow spotted salamander	*Ambystoma maculatum*	western Ont to PEI
Jefferson salamander	*A. jeffersonianum*	SW Ont
smallmouth salamander	*A. texanum*	extreme SW Ont
tiger salamander	*A. tigrinum*	southern BC, Man, Sask, Alta, SW Ont
long-toed salamander	*A. macrodactylum*	BC
northwestern salamander	*A. gracile*	western BC
blue-spotted salamander	*A. laterale*	eastern Canada
dusky salamander	*Desmognathus fuscus*	southern Qué and NB
two-lined salamander	*Eurycea bislineata*	Ont, Qué, Lab and NB
four-toed salamander	*Hemidactylium scutatum*	Ont to NS
spring salamander	*Gyrinophilus porphyriticus*	southern Qué
eastern newt	*Notophthalmus viridescens*	Ont to PEI
roughskin newt	*Taricha granulosus*	BC
mud puppy	*Necturus maculosus*	Qué, Ont, Man
eastern redback salamander	*Plethodon cinereus*	Ont to PEI
western redback salamander	*P. vehiculum*	southern BC
Eschscholtz's salamander	*Ensatina eschscholtzi*	southern BC
clouded salamander	*Aneides ferreus*	Vancouver I, BC
Pacific giant salamander	*Dicamptodon ensatus*	southwestern BC

sun would quickly dehydrate them. During the spring breeding season, mole salamanders may be found moving at night across highways to ditches and ponds, where they can be observed with the aid of a flashlight. If sticks or rocks are gently turned over along or in a rocky brook or around a spring, stream salamanders and spring salamanders may often be discovered. If moss is carefully removed from rotted logs and stumps, woodland salamanders can be found in moist, wooded areas during the day. A certain number of salamanders are collected each year by scientific institutions for research and by individuals for terrarium pets. Mud puppies are taken for use in university and high-school biology courses; their capture is regulated in Manitoba. At present, no comprehensive law exists in Canada to protect salamanders; however, as they consume insect pests, protection would be justified.

S.W. GORHAM

Salish, Coastal, *see* BELLA COOLA; NORTHERN GEORGIA STRAIT COAST SALISH; CENTRAL COAST SALISH.

Salish, Interior Lillooet, Shuswap, Thompson (now Atlakyapamulc) and Okanagan are the 4 native Indian groups in the interior of BC (although Okanagan territory extends into Washington state) who speak languages belonging to the Interior Salish division of the Salishan language family. Lillooet are divided into 2 main groups, linguistically, culturally and geographically: Upper or Fraser River Lillooet, mainly in the vicinity of the town of LILLOOET on the Fraser R; and Lower or Mt Currie Lillooet, mainly around the community of Mt Currie in the Pemberton Valley. Use of the word "Lillooet" is confusing, as the term actually applies to the Mt Currie people only, who call themselves *LEEL'-wat-OOL'* ("the real, original Lillooet"). The Fraser River Lillooet people refer to themselves as *STLA'-tlei-mu-wh;*

they and the Mt Currie people speak slightly different dialects of the same language, known in English as "Lillooet." A third group of Lillooet is marginally recognized: the Lakes Lillooet who live in the vicinity of Seton and Anderson lakes, situated midway between Upper and Lower Lillooet territory.

The Lillooet belong to the Plateau culture area, although the Lower Lillooet were strongly influenced by adjacent Northwest Coast cultures. There are 3348 Lillooet living on INDIAN RESERVES ranging from Skookumchuck and Mt Currie to Anderson Lk and Seton Lk and from Lillooet, Bridge River and Fountain up the Fraser R as far as Pavilion (which was a Shuswap village until the early 1900s).

Just N of the town of Lillooet is the largest late 20th-century Indian fishery on the Fraser R. Every summer, hundreds of Indian people gather to dip-net sockeye salmon from the turbulent waters. The fish are filleted and hung on covered racks to dry in the warm winds. Indians throughout BC and Washington state travel to Lillooet to barter for this delicacy.

The term "Shuswap" is an anglicization of the native word these people call themselves. The Shuswap are the northernmost Interior Salish group of the Plateau culture area. Formerly their territory was vast, extending from the Rocky Mts in the E to the Fraser R in the W, and ranging from Williams Lk in the N to Armstrong in the S. Shuswap villages are located near the numerous lakes in their territory and in the valleys of the N and S Thompson rivers and their tributaries, as well as along the Fraser R. Today there are 5110 Shuswap Indians living on Indian reserves throughout this large area.

Although the Thompson refer to themselves by the native term *in-thla-CAP'-mu-wh* (sometimes spelled "Ntlakapamux"), they have come to be known as Thompson, after the name of the river that flows through their territory. They are divided into 2 main groups: Lower Thompson, extending along the Fraser R canyon from just S of Lytton to an area just S of Spuzzum; and Upper Thompson, consisting of 4 subgroups in an area extending from Lytton and up the Fraser R to about 20 km below Lillooet, and including the Thompson R drainage system from its mouth upriver to Ashcroft, and the Nicola R drainage, including a large area around Merritt. Originally the Merritt and Nicola rivers area had been occupied by the NICOLA-SIMILKAMEEN Athapaskan, but by the late 1800s Thompson and Okanagan had taken over their territory. Today there are 3994 Thompson living on Indian reserves throughout this territory, but centered mostly in Lytton and Merritt.

The Interior Salish living in the OKANAGAN VALLEY and along the Similkameen R are known as Okanagan, although they form part of a larger group now known as "Okanagan-Colville" by some linguists and anthropologists. Okanagan-Colville territory occupies 72 500 km² in S-central BC (70%) and NE Washington state (30%).

The native term *in-seel-ick-CHEEN* refers to all those people who speak the Okanagan-Colville language. In BC this language is known in English as "Okanagan," and in Washington state it is most often called "Colville." There are 7 dialect divisions of the Okanagan-Colville language, of which 3 are (or were, in the case of "Lakes") in BC. "Northern Okanagan" refers to the dialect spoken by Indians living in the vicinity of Okanagan Lk and along the Okanagan R drainage system, and "Similkameen Okanagan" refers to the dialect spoken by Indians living along the Similkameen R (territory formerly occupied by the Nicola-Similkameen Athapaskans).

The "Lakes" dialect was formerly spoken by those Indians living along the Upper and Lower

Arrow Lks, but by about 1870 these people had moved S across the border and were later allotted land on the Colville Indian Reservation. In 1986 there were 2137 Okanagan living on Indian reserves near Vernon, Westbank, Penticton, Keremeos and Oliver.

Interior Salish Culture Lillooet, Shuswap, Thomson and Okanagan subsistence was based on a combination of fishing, hunting and gathering of plant foods. The quest for food was regimented by an annual cycle that took groups of people to various localities, the choice of which was determined by the availability of resources.

During the winter months Interior Salish lived in villages consisting of clustered semisubterranean dwellings known as pit houses. Here they existed on the provisions they had prepared and preserved at other times of the year. These pit houses were constructed in circular holes dug about 2 m deep and about 8 m in diameter. The rafters forming the conical roof of each pit house were thickly insulated with earth and grass to protect the people inside from the cold. Sometimes rectangular or conical tule-mat lodges were used as winter homes by the Interior Salish, but such dwellings were most often used during warmer months.

The basic political unit of Interior Salish society, the village, was governed communally. Within each village there was a number of leaders or chiefs known for their proficiency in such skills as fishing, hunting, war or oratory. However, all adult males had the same rights and responsibilities and took part in decision making. Men and women had clearly defined roles: men hunted, fished and manufactured tools from bone, wood and stone; women prepared food, wove baskets and mats, tanned animal hides for clothes, and looked after small children.

As preparation for adulthood, each child underwent a "vision quest" by training alone in the mountains to receive a guardian spirit power. Such spirit power guided and protected initiates throughout their lives and gave them special skills or supernatural strength or vision. Some guardian spirits were more powerful than others, bestowing upon the receiver the ability, for example, to heal the sick. Every year, through special songs and dances during winter ceremonials, the relationship with guardian spirits was renewed.

Contact with Non-Indians The first contact that Interior Salish had with Europeans occurred in 1793 when Alexander MACKENZIE made his overland journey to the Pacific and met groups of Shuswap near the northernmost extremities of their territory. In 1808, when Simon FRASER descended the river later named after him, he encountered Shuswap, Lillooet and Thompson. The first encounter of Okanagan-speaking Indians in BC with Europeans took place in 1811 in the Arrow Lks area, when David THOMPSON, an explorer for the North West Co, was searching for new supplies of furs.

Beginning in the 1870s, Interior Salish lands were surveyed, Indian reserves were established, and the LAND CLAIMS dispute (which continues to the present time) began. Out of the struggle for recognition of Indian rights there emerged several prominent Interior Salish leaders, notably Chief Michelle of the Thompson, Chief Chillihitza of the Okanagan, Chief David of the Shuswap and, most recently, Chief George Manuel, also a Shuswap. *See also* general articles under NATIVE PEOPLE. DOROTHY KENNEDY AND RANDY BOUCHARD

Reading: C. Hill-Tout, *The Salish People,* 4 vols (1978); V.F. Ray, *Cultural Relations in the Plateau of Northwestern America* (1939).

Salmo, BC, Village, pop 1014 (1986c), 1169 (1981c), inc 1946, is located on the Salmo R at its junction with Erie Cr, 40 km S of Nelson and 40 km E of Trail. Known as Salmon River before the Grand Coulee Dam cut off salmon migration, it lay on the route of the first prospectors to the Nelson area 1862-87. By 1897 a number of mines were operating in the area, and lumbering developed as an associated industry. Since 1972 several mines, accounting for most of the town's production, have shut down, as well as a forest-products operation. Completion of the Creston-Salmo Hwy link in 1963 opened some potential for Salmo as a service centre.

WILLIAM A. SLOAN

Salmon, family of fish, Salmonidae [Lat *salire,* "to leap"], with soft fin rays, short dorsal fin, adipose (fatty) fin, and teeth in the jaws. The family includes salmon, TROUT and CHAR of the subfamily Salmoninae, the GRAYLINGS of the subfamily Thymallinae and the WHITEFISHES of the subfamily Coregoninae. Salmonids are native to north temperate and subarctic waters. However, because of their tremendous sport-fishing appeal, they have been introduced to all continents except Antarctica. Five genera of Salmoninae are recognized. Two are Eurasian, *Brachymystax* and *Hucho.* Three are found in both hemispheres, including Canada: *Salmo,* the trouts and the AT-LANTIC SALMON; *Oncorhynchus,* the PACIFIC SALMON; and *Salvelinus,* the chars. Salmoninae differ from other salmonids in having well-developed teeth in large jaws, and small scales. There is one genus of subfamily Thymallinae (*Thymallus*) and 3 of subfamily Coregoninae (*Stenodus, Prosopium* and *Coregonus*), all in Canada. Grayling and whitefish have weak teeth and larger scales. All salmonids spawn in fresh water, usually in streams; many, especially Pacific salmon, are anadromous, ie, spend their adult lives in the ocean, returning to their native streams to spawn. Unlike other salmonids, Pacific salmon die after spawning. Salmonid eggs, large compared to those of most other fish, vary from yellowish pink to orange-red. Females maintain streamlined head shape throughout life; in many species, males develop a pronounced hook, called a kype, in the jaw before spawning. Salmonids are famous for their ability to home precisely to their place of birth to spawn, and for their fighting and jumping when angled.

In Canada, combined sport and commercial values make the salmonids the most economically important group of wild animals. In 1985, the marketed value of Pacific Salmon was $512 million. Pacific Salmon also support a growing aquaculture and a huge sports fishing industry. Chinook and some coho salmon stocks from SE Vancouver I are severely depressed, although stocks elsewhere in BC appear stable. The trouts, including Atlantic salmon, have a large sport fishery and a small but growing commercial AQUACULTURE industry. The chars are important as sport fish and support a small commercial industry and subsistence fishery, especially among native peo-

Kokanee salmon. Salmon are famous for their ability to home precisely to their place of birth to spawn (*photo by Tim Fitzharris*).

ples of northern Canada. There is a small sports fishery for grayling, primarily in the North. The whitefishes support a commercial fishery in central Canada and a subsistence fishery of considerable importance to native people in the North.

E.D. LANE

Salmon Arm, BC, District Municipality, pop 11 199 (1986c), is located at the head of the SW arm of Shuswap Lk, also called Salmon Arm, 525 km E of Vancouver and 110 km E of Kamloops. Best known for its fruit and dairy farming and as a vacation spot, the area was settled relatively recently. It was originally the home of Shuswap Indians. A GOLD RUSH in the 1860s brought prospectors into the region briefly, but exploration did not begin until 1871 when a route was surveyed for the CPR. Settlement came in the late 1880s with the railway, mixed and fruit farming, and logging and lumbering. Settlement boomed from 1905 to 1912 – the year it was incorporated as a city. Today lumber, tourism, fruit and dairy farming and provincial and federal government agencies are the major employers. A satellite campus of Okanagan College is located here, and the municipality has a museum, a historical society and an active theatre group with a winter and summer season.

JOHN R. STEWART

Salmonella, genus of bacteria of the family Enterobacteriaceae, members of which are commonly found in the intestinal tract of humans and other animals. It is named after D.E. Salmon, the American bacteriologist who described it in 1885. For 100 years salmonellae have been recognized as important in causing food-borne disease and water-borne disease. The salmonellae can be divided into 3 groups based on host preference. Those primarily adapted to humans include the typhoid and paratyphoid organisms which have long incubation periods (10-21 days), cause high fever, invade the bloodstream, require a slow convalescence, and have a higher proportion of carriers (ie, asymptomatic victims who excrete the organism) than salmonellae in other groups. Those primarily adapted to animal hosts include *S. choleraesuis* (pigs), *S. dublin* (cattle) and *S. pullorum* (chickens). Only the first 2 serotypes are significant for human illness. Salmonellae not adapted to any specific host include the more than 1700 serotypes with the potential for causing human salmonellosis, a form of gastroenteritis. *S. typhimurium* is the serotype causing most salmonellosis in Canada and other countries. Diarrhea, abdominal cramps, fever, nausea and vomiting occur 8-48 hours after consumption of as few as 100 organisms. Patients typically recover after a few days, but infants and elderly persons can be seriously ill and occasionally may die.

Salmonellosis probably costs Canadians as much as $1 billion annually in total medical care and economic loss. Increased foreign trade and travel have brought in serotypes from other countries and the increased demand for highly processed animal products and interprovincial distribution have made salmonellae widespread in the Canadian environment (eg, about 60% of poultry carcasses contain the organism). Foods associated with salmonellosis in Canada have been turkeys, chickens, salami, products made with cracked eggs, chocolate candy, pepper and cream pies. Salmonellae are difficult to eliminate from the environment and, once they come in contact with suitable food, can multiply rapidly, provided the temperature is suitable. Prevention of illness depends on decreasing the source of the organism (eg, salmonellae-free animal feed), reducing the chances of cross-contamination in the processing plant or kitchen, and not allowing growth to take place by keeping the food either cold (4°C or less) or hot (60°C or more).

EWEN TODD

Salt Neither sodium nor chlorine can exist alone in natural form, but together they form the stable compound sodium chloride (NaCl), or common salt, known to geologists as halite. Salt crystallizes as colourless cubes. In 1866, Samuel Platt drilled for oil near Goderich, Ont. Although oil eluded him, he struck a thick bed of clean, white salt, part of the geological formation now known as the Michigan Basin, which underlies much of southwestern Ontario. In western Canada, salt beds extend in a broad belt from southwestern Manitoba to northern Alberta. The Atlantic provinces are underlain by a sedimentary basin containing thick pockets of salt. Underground deposits of rock salt are recovered either by conventional room and pillar MINING, with subsequent milling and refining at the surface, or by the brine method, where water is injected into deposits at depth and the resulting saturated solution is pumped to the surface.

Salt is an essential part of the human and animal diet, aiding digestion, but over-consumption is widely held to be a cause of hypertension and heart disease. It is used as a seasoning and in curing meats and preserving fish. Manufacture of salt is one of the oldest chemical industries and salt was used as currency in ancient times. Canada is the world's largest per capita consumer of salt, largely because it is widely used to improve winter driving conditions (it melts ice and snow). The CHEMICAL INDUSTRY uses NaCl to manufacture chlorine, caustic soda and soda ash, which are used in the production of soaps, fibres, PETRO-CHEMICALS, etc. Canada's 1986 production was 11 088 000 t, valued at $241 million. Canada could easily supply the total Canadian requirement, but the expense of transporting such a high-bulk product over great distances makes trade, particularly with the US, more economical in some areas. However, exports are consistently higher than imports.

HELEN R. WEBSTER

Salter, Robert Bruce, orthopedic surgeon, teacher (b at Stratford, Ont 15 Dec 1924). One of the most respected and best-known orthopedic surgeons in the world, Salter has lectured in 35 countries and is recognized for innovative methods of orthopedic treatment, including the Salter operation for children and young adults with abnormal hip joints. Appointed to Toronto's Hospital for Sick Children and U of T in 1955, he became chief of orthopedic surgery in 1957 and surgeon in chief in 1966. In 1976 he was appointed head of orthopedics at U of T. In the late 1970s he originated the revolutionary concept of continuous passive motion (CPM) of joints to stimulate the regeneration of cartilage. He has written over 130 scientific articles and a textbook on the musculoskeletal system. His honours include fellowship of the RSC, the Nicolas Andry Award and the Gairdner Foundation International Award for Medical Science. He is an Officer of the Order of Canada.

J. KNELMAN

Saltspring Island is the largest of the GULF IS-LANDS, a group lying in the Str of Georgia off the SE corner of VANCOUVER I, BC. Before the arrival of Europeans, several Indian groups gathered a variety of foods among the islands. The first permanent settlers were black immigrants from the US who arrived in the 1850s and began one of the earliest agricultural communities in the region. The island became known for its sheep, fruit and dairy products. Today it has a permanent population of about 4000, with many more enjoying its beautiful coastal waters each summer. Ganges, at the head of Ganges Harbour on the E coast, is the largest town in the Gulf Is. Bruce Peak, at 690 m the highest mountain in the group of islands, towers above the W coast. The island is named for brine pools in its interior.

DANIEL FRANCIS

Salut Galarneau! (1967), by Jacques GODBOUT, is cast in the first person as the diary of François Galarneau, a working-class rebel who owns and operates a hot-dog stand in the Montréal suburb of Île-Perrot. Interweaving the story of his "failed" personal life, narrated piecemeal and randomly, and his "naïve" observations about his society, conveyed by the author with satiric insight and poetic power, Galarneau's diary is begun as a pastime suggested by his mistress but soon acquires the resilient humour of an existential act. Jilted and feeling increasingly alienated from his surroundings, the hot-dog king conceals himself behind a brick wall of his own fabrication, but finally cannot resist keeping a ladder, if only to renew his supply of notebooks. A warm and witty allegory of Québec and of the artist's role in Québec society, *Salut Galarneau!* won the Gov Gen's Award and was translated by Alan Brown as *Hail Galarneau!* (1970). MICHÈLE LACOMBE

Salutin, Rick, playwright and journalist (b at Toronto 30 Aug 1942). After studying at Brandeis U, Columbia U and New York's New School for Social Research, Salutin returned to Toronto in 1970 to work as a trade-union organizer. He found effective outlets for his strong nationalist and socialist views through his writing. After his first play, *Fanshen* (1971), he began collaborating with Toronto's Theatre Passe Muraille in the techniques of collective creation, calling himself "the writer on, but not of" *1837: The Farmers' Revolt* (1973), a vivid popularization of Canadian history which won the Chalmers Outstanding Play award. He pursued his political analysis of Canadian history in other collective plays such as *I.W.A.* (1976) with Newfoundland's Mummers Troupe, and in his own *Les Canadiens* (1977), an account of nationalism and hockey in Québec, which won a second Chalmers. As playwright, free lance journalist, editor of *This Magazine* and scriptwriter for TV docudramas, Salutin remains an important interpreter of Canada's social and political development. JERRY WASSERMAN

Salvation Army "Soup to Salvation" was the response of disaffected METHODIST preacher William Booth in 1865 to "the bitter cry of outcast London." From it emerged the Salvation Army, dedicated to the physical and spiritual reclamation of lost humanity: "soup" soon included men's hostels, women's shelters, farm colonies and other similar institutions; "salvation" was preached along Methodist lines by an army of officers – with flags, bands and war songs – seeking out their congregations in the slums. By century's end the Army had become a permanent feature of English society and had invaded many other countries as well. The Army came to Canada in 1882. Introduced by such zealots as Mr and Mrs William Freer (Toronto) and Jack Addie and Joe Ludgate (London), Army Corps sprang up in every major Ontario town. By 1886 the "army" religion was being practised from Victoria to St John's, although its unusual methods of worship – "hallelujah joy-jigs," free-and-easy meetings, noisy open-airs – raised considerable ire and resulted in some legal battles. But eventually, through persistent social welfare work, the Army won nationwide respect. In 1886 the Rescue Home for "fallen" girls opened in Toronto, followed by similar homes in Winnipeg, Montréal and Victoria. In 1891 the Army opened its first Prison Gate Home to rehabilitate released prisoners, and soon children's shelters, prison farms and men's hostels were added. In 1904 the first Grace Hospital opened in Winnipeg; in 1905 an Army officer became the first Dominion Parole Officer and the Army's first emigrants sailed from England; by 1914 more than 150 000 had settled in Canada under its sponsorship.

Today the Army maintains its dual social and evangelical purpose. It is a recognized church, with some 125 000 members who, though less evangelical than their forebears, still espouse a Methodist theology with strong adherence to teetotalism and withdrawal from "worldliness." Bands and timbrels still make feet tap and hearts stir. The Social Wing offers language classes for new Canadians, new development programs on behalf of the CANADIAN INTERNATIONAL DEVELOPMENT AGENCY, parole supervision, Harbour Light centres for alcoholics, Sunset lodges, Grace hospitals, fresh air camps for underprivileged children, drug addiction counselling and a willing hand in times of need. The Army's motto still is "With heart to God, and hand to man." R.G. MOYLES

Reading: R.G. Moyles, *The Blood and Fire in Canada* (1977).

Salverson, Laura, née Goodman, novelist (b at Winnipeg 9 Dec 1890; d at Toronto 13 July 1970). Daughter of Icelandic immigrants, she lived throughout western Canada after her marriage to George Salverson in 1913. Nurtured on Icelandic sagas and legends, she celebrated the cultural heritage of Scandinavian settlers, most memorably in her first and best novel, *The Viking Heart* (1923), but also in *When Sparrows Fall* (1925), *Johann Lind* (1928) and *The Dark Weaver* (1937, Gov Gen's Award). She also wrote a volume of verse, *Wayside Gleams* (1924-25), 2 minor romances, *The Dove* (1933) and *Black Lace* (1938), and 2 historical novels about Norse explorers, *Lord of the Silver Dragon* (1927) and *Immortal Rock* (1954, All-Canada Fiction Award). She won her second Gov Gen's Award for her autobiography, *Confessions of an Immigrant's Daughter* (1939), a sensitive record of conflict and assimilation. Salverson was a member of the Paris Institute of Arts and Sciences, which awarded her a gold medal for literary merit. HALLVARD DAHLIE

Samson, first locomotive in N America to burn coal and the first to run over all-iron rails. Built in New Shildon, Eng, it was shipped to Pictou, NS, to haul coal from the Albion Mines 9.6 km over a tramway to Dunbar Point on Pictou Harbour. The railway, built of cast-iron rails believed to be the first rails manufactured in N America, was officially opened 19 Sept 1839. The *Samson* was one of 3 locomotives and it was in service for nearly 30 years. Exhibited at the Chicago World's Fair in 1893, it was eventually returned to NS and is on display in New Glasgow. JAMES MARSH

Samuel, Lewis, merchant, philanthropist (b at Kingston upon Hull, Eng 1827; d at Victoria 10 May 1887). He founded the organized Jewish community of Toronto, and was a prime mover in establishing in 1856 the first synagogue in Canada W – the Toronto Hebrew Congregation (now Holy Blossom Temple). An orthodox Jew, he served almost continuously as its president 1862-80, fighting to maintain traditional practices, then under attack from reformers. With his brother Mark and A.D. Benjamin, he operated a wholesale metals firm, M. & L. Samuel, Benjamin and Co, which exported a variety of Canadian raw materials in exchange for gas chandeliers, metals, chemicals, glass and marble. An enthusiastic supporter of the British connection, he belonged to the Sons of England Benefit Soc and the St George's Soc. He also served as president of the MECHANICS' INSTITUTE, precursor of the Toronto Public Library (late 1870s). STEPHEN A. SPEISMAN

Reading: Stephen A. Speisman, *The Jews of Toronto* (1979).

Sand and Gravel, unconsolidated, granular mineral materials produced by the natural disin-tegration of rock caused by weathering. The terms sand, gravel, clay and silt relate to grain size rather than composition. Sand is material passing a number 4 (4.76 mm) sieve and remaining on a number 200 (74 μm) sieve. Gravel is granular material remaining on a number 4 sieve and ranging up to about 9 cm. Material finer than 200 mesh is called silt or clay.

Sand and gravel are used as fill, base and finish material for highway construction, as coarse and fine aggregates in concrete and asphalt production, and as fine aggregates in mortar and concrete blocks. They are also used as backfill in mines, along with cement and mill tailings. Sand is also used in the manufacture of glass, pottery and bricks and in water filtration. "Sandy" soils are favourable to certain types of agriculture. Deposits are widespread throughout Canada and large producers have established plants as close to major consuming centres as possible. In addition to large aggregate operations, usually associated with some phase of the CONSTRUCTION INDUSTRY, many small producers serve local markets. Exploitation is generally by power shovel or loader and trucks or conveyor systems; processing consists of washing, crushing and screening. In 1986 production in Canada was valued at $546.3 million. *See also* CEMENT INDUSTRY. D.H. STONEHOUSE

Sandon, BC, Ghost Town, pop 3 (1987e), is located in the Slocan Valley, West Kootenay, 13 km E of New Denver. Known as the "Silver City of the Slocan" when a prosperous mining community, it was once the centre of one of the richest silver-lead producing regions in the province. Set in a narrow gulch, split by a fast-flowing creek and surrounded by high, steep mountains, it was vulnerable to avalanches, fire and floods. But the mountains contained silver-lead mines, the base of its economy and source of its origin in 1892. Founded by prospectors, the small camp was made the terminus of 2 railway branch lines in 1895 and boomed in 1896. It was incorporated as a city 1898, peaked in 1900 (pop 2000) and disincorporated in 1920. During WWII it was a relocation centre for Japanese from the coast. For the few remaining residents, the end came in 1955 when the creek overflowed, causing much damage. A few buildings remain; one is now a museum. Though some mines are still being worked, most of the mine employees live elsewhere. C.M. YOUNG

Sandpiper, common name for family (Scolopacidae) of SHOREBIRDS that includes true sandpipers, SNIPE, TURNSTONES, WOODCOCKS, curlews (*see* ENDANGERED ANIMALS), dunlin, geese, knots, sanderling, surfbirds, tattlers, yellowlegs and willets. Typical sandpipers have been classified recently in a separate tribe, Calidridini (23 species). Species commonly seen in Canada include spotted, solitary, semipalmated, whiterumped and pectoral sandpipers (*Actitis macularia, Tringa solitaria, Calidris pusilla, C. fuscicollis, C. melanotos,* respectively) and dunlin (*C. alpina*). Sandpipers are distinguished from PLOVERS by their proportionately longer and thinner bills, elongated legs, cryptically coloured plumage, and hind toe (in all but sanderling, *C. alba*). They range in size from the 21 g least sandpiper (*C. minutilla*) to the 200 g great knot (*C. tenuirostris*). True sandpipers breed at high latitudes in the Northern Hemisphere and undertake long MIGRATIONS, wintering in Australia, New Zealand, Asia, Africa and S America. After breeding season they gather in flocks of one or more species. In flight these flocks are remarkable for the precision with which they wheel and turn. The alternate flashing of white ventral plumage and grey dorsal plumage seems to confuse BIRDS OF PREY by making it difficult to single out an individual for at-

Spotted sandpiper (*artwork by Claire Tremblay*).

tack. Sandpipers have various soft calls that have earned them the popular name "peeps" in N America. No other group of birds has such diverse breeding systems. Most sandpipers are monogamous, laying 1-2 clutches per breeding season; some (eg, dunlin) are polyandrous with different males incubating successive clutches laid by one female; others (eg, white-rumped sandpipers) are polygynous with one male mating with more than one female. A clutch usually contains 4 eggs (range 2-5). Incubation takes 18-32 days, depending on species. Young leave the nest soon after hatching. Like plovers, sandpipers guard young and often use distraction displays to lure predators away from eggs or chicks. A.J. BAKER

Sandwell, Bernard Keble, editor and essayist (b at Ipswich, Eng 1876; d at Toronto 7 Dec 1954). Sandwell will forever be identified as the editor, 1932-51, of SATURDAY NIGHT, a magazine he made the ears and voice of Canadian liberalism. Sandwell has been characterized by Robert FUL-FORD, a later editor of the same journal, as "progressive but not too progressive, tolerant but not too tolerant." But for his time, Sandwell's championing of civil liberties, his belief in Canadian nationalism within an imperial framework, and his instinctive anti-Americanism made him an important figure in a broader movement. His pen was prolific and seemingly adaptable to any task, from corporate panegyrics to a history of music in Montréal. But his best and most representative books are *The Privacity Agent and Other Modest Proposals* (1928) and *The Diversions of Duchesstown and Other Essays* (publ posthumously 1955). DOUGLAS FETHERLING

Sangster, Charles, editor, poet (b at Kingston, UC 16 July 1822; d there 9 Dec 1893). Sangster's first job was with the Ordnance in Kingston. Simultaneously he held a position with the local *British Whig.* In 1849 he became full-time editor of the Amherstburg *Courier* but soon returned to the *Whig* as subeditor. At this time he published his first poetry, in the *Literary Garland,* followed by publication of his only 2 volumes, *The St Lawrence and the Saguenay and Other Poems* (1856) and *Hesperus and Other Poems and Lyrics* (1860).

With his appointment to the Ottawa Post Office (1868) Sangster's life became characterized by overwork, ill health and scant literary output. He published 16 poems during the 1870s, most of which display a distraught, melancholy introspection. Between his 1886 retirement and his death he laboured on revised editions of his 2 volumes and prepared 2 others, *Norland Echoes and Other Strains and Lyrics* and *The Angel Guest.* His poetry distinguishes him as a lover and keen observer of the natural world. He displays overwhelming passion in some poems and equally extreme melancholy in others. Whatever his mood he is consistently and intensely serious and deeply religious. MARLENE ALT

Sanikiluaq, NWT, Hamlet, pop 422 (1986c), 383 (1981c), is located on the BELCHER ISLANDS in HUDSON BAY, 2092 air km SE of Yellowknife. The original INUIT inhabitants of the barren Belcher Islands were expert kayak men. Because there were few caribou, they made frequent use of eider duck skins for clothing. The first European in the area was Henry HUDSON, who sighted the islands in 1610. Today the Inuit residents of Sanikiluaq have an economy based on domestic fishing, trapping and the production of distinctive soapstone carvings. ANNELIES POOL

Sapir, Edward, anthropologist, linguist, essayist (b at Lauenburg, Ger 26 Jan 1884; d at New Haven, Conn 4 Feb 1939). A brilliant anthropologist, Sapir pioneered studies of language and culture and of the psychology of culture. He was the first chief of the GEOLOGICAL SURVEY OF CANADA's division of anthropology, the only professional base for anthropological research in Canada 1910-25.

While he was training at Columbia under Franz BOAS, anthropology and linguistics were in their early stages of professional maturity. Sapir brought to this formative period a scope of interest, expertise and depth of intuition that are unequalled. He combined an extraordinarily fine analysis with an awareness of the vital unity of all aspects of communication and culture and of the essentially human nature in which all languages and cultures are firmly rooted. For him, anthropology did not describe the exotic, but rather rediscovered, in a new idiom, the normal, the human. His book *Language* (1921) presents to general readers and specialists alike the scope, nature and cultural contributions of speech and writing; it is still authoritative. He left Canada for university posts in 1925, but his career was cut short by illness and his major work, to have been titled "The Psychology of Culture," was never written. He published over 400 articles, reviews and poems, and international recognition came during his lifetime. He was a fascinating teacher, and his writings have inspired later generations of scholars with the central importance of understanding the human condition as a historical whole. R.J. PRESTON

Reading: D.G. Mandelbaum, ed, *Selected Writings of Edward Sapir in Language, Culture, and Personality* (1949) and *Edward Sapir: Culture, Language and Personality: Selected Essays* (1958).

Sapp, Allen, artist (b at Red Pheasant IR, Sask 2 Jan 1929). As a child, his favourite activity was drawing and sketching. He moved from the Plains Cree reserve to N Battleford, Sask, in 1960 to pursue a career as a professional artist. In 1966 Dr A.B. Gonor arranged for him to be tutored by Wynona Mulcaster of Saskatoon. Many regard Sapp as one of Canada's foremost native painters because of the sense of melancholic emotion that infuses his paintings, which portray the Plains Cree people in their daily activities of the 1930s and 1940s. He sees his people as poor, but with a sense of awareness about themselves. In 1987 his work was included at a show of native art at the Museum of

Allen Sapp, *Where I Used to Live* (1969), acrylic on canvas (*courtesy Glenbow Museum, Calgary*).

Civilization in Los Angeles. JOHN ANSON WARNER

Reading: John Anson Warner and Thecla Bradshaw, *A Cree Life: The Art of Allen Sapp* (1977).

Sarah Binks, by U of Manitoba professor Paul HIEBERT, was published 1947 in Toronto. That the "Sweet Songstress of Saskatchewan" never drew breath has not prevented Hiebert's imaginary poet from holding in thrall the hearts of those for whom she has immortalized the "Saskatchewan-esque" voice in Canadian letters. Sarah's accomplishments are legend: founder of the influential "geo-literary" school of Canadian verse; creator of such heart-rending lyrics as "Hiawatha's Milking"; winner of Saskatchewan's highest poetic honour – the Wheat Pool Medal – for her epic "Up From the Magma and Back Again"; dead, tragically young, of mercury poisoning from a cracked thermometer. Fortunately, by the time of her death her charming lyrical gifts, her sharp eye for natural detail, her acute ear for tripping metre, and her unerring sense of clinching rhyme had already secured her reputation; consider, for example, the oft-quoted opening of "My Garden":

> A little blade of grass I see,
> Its banner waving wild and free,
> And I wonder if in time to come
> 'Twill be a great big onion;

Which of our real poets of the prairies has rivalled the verse of Hiebert's sweet creation? Hiebert judiciously traces the complex and subtle interweaving of Binksian life and art; his definitive biography memorialized the imperishable power, beauty, and grace of the Binksian oeuvre.
NEIL BESNER

Sarcee, an Athapaskan or DENE tribe whose reserve adjoins the SW city limits of Calgary. Their name is believed to have originated from a Blackfoot word meaning boldness and hardiness. The Sarcee people call themselves *tsúùt'ínà*, translated literally as "many people" or "every one (in the tribe)." Following the signing of Treaty No 7 in 1877, the Sarcee moved to their present 280 km² reserve (*see* INDIAN RESERVE). According to legend, the Sarcee split from a northern tribe, probably the BEAVER, and moved to the plains, where they have maintained close contact with the BLACK-FOOT, CREE and STONEY. Their acculturation to the Plains culture distinguishes them from other northern Dene people, but they have retained their Athapaskan language. Capt PALLISER estimated the Sarcee population at 1400 during his journey of 1857 to 1860. Epidemics of smallpox (1837), scarlet fever (1864) and other diseases as well as wars, reduced the number to 400-450 by the time they settled on the reserve. By 1924 the population had decreased to about 160. In 1986 there were 804 Sarcee.

When Diamond JENNESS visited the reserve in 1921 the tribe consisted of 5 bands: Big Plumes, Crow Childs, Crow Chiefs, Old Sarcees and Many Horses. Before they were confined to the reserve, each BAND, led by a chief, camped in TIPIS and hunted along the edge of the forest during the winter. During summer all bands met in the open prairie to hunt buffalo, collect berries and engage in ceremonies, dances and festivals (*see* BUFFALO HUNT; SUN DANCE). The Sarcee believed in supernatural power that could be obtained through a vision or dream and was enshrined in a medicine object (beaver bundle, pipe bundle) or a tipi painting (*see* MEDICINE BUNDLE). The quest for supernatural power, for bravery (men) and chastity (women) was highly valued. Marriages were usually arranged by the family and the gifts exchanged reflected family status.

Well-known leaders include Chief Bull Head, who reluctantly signed Treaty No 7, and Chief David Crowchild, a distinguished contemporary leader. The band is governed by an elected chief

Sarcee with travois (*courtesy McCord Museum, McGill University*).

Saskatchewan

Capital: Regina
Motto: None
Flower: Western red lily (also known as prairie lily)
Largest Cities: Saskatoon, Regina, Moose Jaw, Prince Albert, North Battleford, Swift Current, Yorkton
Population: 1 009 613 (1986c); rank sixth, 4% of Canada; 61.4% urban; 38.6% rural; 1.8 per km² density; 3.8% increase from 1981-86; 9.6% increase from 1976-86
Languages: 80.7% English; 2.1% French; 13.2% Other; 4% English plus one or more languages
Entered Confederation: 1 Sept 1905
Government: Provincial – Lieutenant-Governor, Executive Council, Legislative Assembly of 64 members; federal – 6 senators, 14 members of the House of Commons
Area: 651 900 km²; including 81 631 km² of inland water; 6.6% of Canada
Elevation: Highest point – Cypress Hills (1392 m); lowest point – Lake Athabasca shore (64.9 m)
Gross Domestic Product: $17.4 billion (1986)
Farm Cash Receipts: $ 4.1 billion (1986)
Electric Power Produced: 11 816 GWh
Sales Tax: 5% (1987)

and counsellors. Though Sarcees have in recent years taken an active part in modern industries, and in cattle raising and real estate, efforts are being made to revive the traditional culture and lifestyle. The Sarcee Culture Program records historical, folkloric and linguistic material. Although many people attend one of the 2 churches (Anglican and Catholic) on the reserve, and children attend public or separate schools in Calgary, they observe native ceremonies and feasts, such as the Beaver Bundle Ceremony (spring), the Rock Pile Feast (summer) and the Christmas Powwow. Their annual Indian Days celebration draws people from across the continent, and their participation has become an integral part of the CALGARY STAMPEDE. *See also* NATIVE PEOPLE: PLAINS and general articles under NATIVE PEOPLE.   EUNG-DO COOK

Reading: D. Jenness, *The Sarcee Indians of Alberta* (1938).

Sardine, name applied to various small fishes packed in oil. The true sardine from France, Spain and Portugal is usually the young pilchard. In Canada small HERRING are used.

Sarlos, Andrew, financier, Bay Street power broker (b in Budapest, Hungary 24 Nov 1931). Imprisoned for his liberal views while studying economics at U of Budapest, he was part of the Petofi Circle which became vanguard of Hungary's anti-Soviet 1956 revolution; he escaped to Austria, and eventually Canada. After qualifying as a CA and becoming a Canadian citizen, he spent 17 years in administrative positions with Canadian Bechtel and Acres Ltd, eventually heading their merchant banking group. He went on his own in 1974 and has since become one of the Toronto financial community's most sought-after investment counsellors, running a private trust fund with assets of more than $500 million. One of the few Canadian financiers with impressive intellectual and international credentials, he is contributing editor of the *Money Letter*, has served as governor of U of Waterloo and is currently on the board of Toronto's Central Hospital, Toronto General and Western Foundation and the Canadian Institute of International Affairs. He is also a director of several public companies, including the Toronto Zoological Society, and International Polaris and The Horsham Corp.
                                PETER C. NEWMAN

Sarnia, Ont, City, pop 49 033 (1986c), 50 892 (1981c), inc 1914. Population of the surrounding area is 85 700 (1986c). It is located at the convergence of the St Clair R and Lk Huron, 100 km W of London. A railway tunnel beneath the St Clair, car ferries and a highway bridge from nearby Point Edward connect Sarnia with Port Huron,

Mich. Sarnia is a petrochemical centre and the southern terminus of an oil pipeline from Alberta. Its government is of the city-manager type, with mayor and council elected every 3 years.

History Father HENNEPIN recorded that La Salle's expedition lay becalmed near here in 1679. Some 120 years later French settlers began to arrive. After the crown settlement with local Ojibwa in 1827, an English-speaking community formed, called The Rapids until 1836 when it was named Port Sarnia after Sarnia Township. Sir John Colborne is said to have named the township Sarnia because that is the Latin name for Guernsey where he had been governor before his appointment to Canada. "Port" was dropped from the name when the town was incorporated in 1857. In 1858 the GREAT WESTERN RY extended its line from London to Sarnia and ran ferries across the St Clair. The GRAND TRUNK RY put a line into Point Edward in 1859. When the St Clair Tunnel opened in 1891, the car ferries stopped running for some years, and Point Edward declined as a rail centre.

Primitive oil refining started in Sarnia after the first commercial oil well on the continent went into production in 1858 at Oil Springs, 36 km SE. In 1898 Imperial Oil Co moved to Sarnia from Petrolia, 26 km SE, and built a refinery. During WWII POLYMER CORP, now Polysar, built a synthetic-rubber plant here. In its wake numerous petrochemical plants were built, the latest being Petrosar, opened in 1978. The population of 18 000 before Polysar was almost tripled in the next decade. In 1951 the city annexed part of Sarnia Township and all of the St Clair Indian Reserve.

Economy The PETROCHEMICAL INDUSTRY depends on oil and gas from Alberta, local salt, abundant fresh water and the Great Lks shipping facilities. Products include gasoline, fuels, components for plastics and textiles, rubber, chemicals and insulation. During peak construction in the 1970s, the work force numbered over 7000; by the mid-1980s, partly as a result of the slump in oil prices that hit the West, it was reduced to 2200. The city lies in an agricultural district, and because of its location attracts tourists.

Townscape The shores of Sarnia Bay, an inlet of the St Clair R formerly devoted to lumbering and

salt wells, were changed by dredging and filling in 1927 to provide for grain elevators. Docks are accessible to the largest ships on the lakes. Most public buildings are recent, including the public library, which houses over 300 pieces of Canadian art. Sarnia was the home of Alexander MACKENZIE, first Liberal prime minister of Canada.
                                JEAN ELFORD

Sarrazin, Michel, surgeon, physician, naturalist (b at Nuits-sous-Beaune, France 5 Sept 1659; d at Québec C 8 Sept 1734). He came to NEW FRANCE in 1685 and the following year was appointed surgeon-major to the colonial regular troops. He later studied medicine in France for 3 years and returned to Québec in 1697 as king's physician. Keenly interested in natural history by this time – he had been introduced to BOTANY by scientist Joseph Pitton de Tournefort – he spent the next 30-odd years collecting specimens of plants and minerals, and dissecting and reporting on Canadian animals and natural life to Tournefort and other members of the Académie royale des sciences of Paris. Sarrazin became a corresponding member of the Académie in 1699. He was the first to collect and catalogue plant specimens systematically and his HERBARIUM, which did not survive, may have reached 800 in number. Duplicates of most are found, however, in various collections in Paris. *See also* FLORAS AND BOTANICAL JOURNALS.
                                BERNARD BOIVIN

Saskatchewan is the only province with entirely man-made boundaries; it lies between the 49th and 60th parallels of latitude, bordered by the US and the Northwest Territories; and between long 101° 30' and 102°W and 110°W, bordered by Manitoba and Alberta. It was created from the North-West Territories in 1905, at the same time as Alberta, and shares with that province the distinction of having no coast on salt water. The name, which was first used officially for a district of the North-West Territories in 1882, is derived from an anglicized version of a Cree word denoting a swiftly flowing river, which appears in a variety of spellings in early records. When the prairie region was being made into provinces, the largest part of the old district bearing the name was incorporated into the new province. Saskatchewan, unlike the 3 provinces immediately E

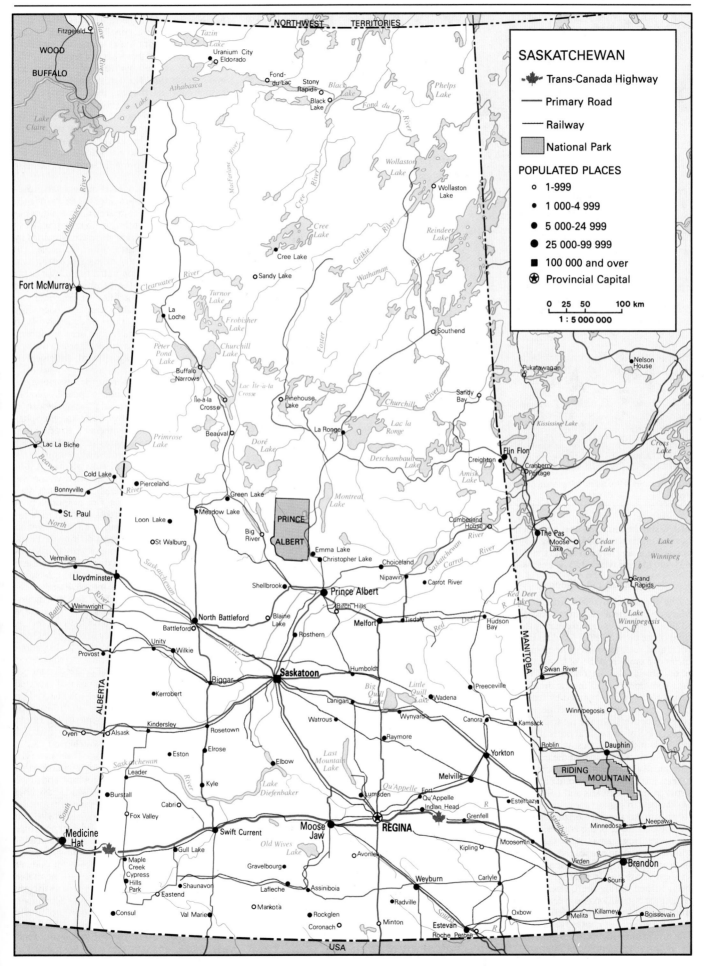

NORTHWEST TERRITORIES

WOOD
BUFFALO

SASKATCHEWAN

🍁 Trans-Canada Highway
── Primary Road
─·─ Railway
▨ National Park

POPULATED PLACES
○ 1-999
● 1 000-4 999
● 5 000-24 999
● 25 000-99 999
■ 100 000 and over
✪ Provincial Capital

0 25 50 100 km
1 : 5 000 000

Fitzgerald

Uranium City
Eldorado
Fond-du-Lac
Stony Rapids
Black Lake
Phelps Lake

Lake Claire

Athabasca Lake

Tazin Lake

Wollaston Lake
Wollaston Lake

Fort McMurray

Cree Lake
Sandy Lake

La Loche

Turnor Lake
Frobisher Lake

Southend

Peter Pond Lake
Churchill Lake

Buffalo Narrows
Île-à-la-Crosse
Lac Île-à-la-Crosse

Pinehouse Lake

Beauval

Doré Lake
La Ronge
Lac la Ronge

Pukatawagan
Nelson House

Sandy Bay

Kississine Lake

Lac La Biche

Cold Lake
Pierceland

Green Lake

Montreal Lake

Flin Flon
Creighton
Cranberry Portage

Bonnyville

Loon Lake

Meadow Lake

Amisk Lake

Cross Lake

St. Paul

St Walburg

Big River

PRINCE
ALBERT

Emma Lake
Christopher Lake

Cumberland House

The Pas
Moose Lake

Cedar Lake

Lake Winnipeg

Vermilion

Choiceland

Saskatchewan River
Carrot River

Grand Rapids

Lloydminster

Shellbrook

Nipawin

Carrot River

Red Deer Lake

Wainwright

Birch Hills

Prince Albert

Tisdale

Hudson Bay

Lake Winnipegosis

North Battleford
Battleford
Blaine Lake
Rosthern

Melfort

Red Deer R.

Unity
Wilkie

Swan River

Provost

Humboldt

Biggar

Saskatoon

Preeceville

Little Quill Lake
Big Quill Lake

Kerrobert

Lanigan

Wadena

Winnipegosis

Kindersley

Rosetown

Wynyard

Canora

Kamsack

Oyen
Alsask

Eston

Elrose

Watrous

Raymore

Yorkton

Roblin

Dauphin

Leader

Elbow

Last Mountain Lake

Melville

RIDING
MOUNTAIN

Kyle

Lake Diefenbaker

Qu'Appelle

Fort Qu'Appelle

Esterhazy

Minnedosa

Neepawa

Burstall

Cabri

Indian Head
Lumsden

Grenfell

Fox Valley

REGINA

Medicine Hat

Swift Current

Gull Lake

Moose Jaw

Avonlea

Kipling

Moosomin

Virden

Brandon

Maple Creek
Cypress Hills Park

Gravelbourg

Old Wives Lake

Weyburn

Carlyle

Souris

Shaunavon

Lafleche

Assiniboia

Radville

Oxbow

Melita

Killarney

Boissevain

Eastend

Mankota

Rockglen

Minton

Estevan
Roche Percée

Consul

Val Marie

Coronach

ALBERTA

MANITOBA

USA

Grain elevators at Broderick, Sask (*courtesy Colour Library Books*).

of it, is still the same size as it was when created: in round numbers, 1225 km long, 630 km wide across the S, and 445 km across the N. Its area is 651 900 km², of which 12% is fresh water.

Land and Resources

The Precambrian SHIELD, running diagonally SE across Saskatchewan, from above 57° latitude to almost 54°, covers approximately the northern third of the province. The Shield is characterized by rugged rock exposures and many lakes, and includes a sandy region S of Lk Athabasca. South of the Shield, also diagonal from W to E, is the area commonly called the "grain belt," level or gently rolling plains marked by fertile soils that make Saskatchewan one of the world's great wheat producers. On the western boundary and across the SW corner is another plains region of generally higher altitudes, with rolling and hilly terrain distinct from that of the grain belt. In the extreme SW the province shares with Alberta the CYPRESS HILLS, the highest point of land in Canada between the Rocky Mts and Labrador. Much of Saskatchewan's landscape consists of undulating slopes, unlike the flat horizons featured in the stereotyped image of the Prairies.

Geology Large areas of Saskatchewan once formed the bottom of a sea that departed millions of years ago. In geological terms much of the modern landscape is relatively young, having been shaped during the Quaternary period, ie, within the last million or so years. The oldest formations, the Precambrian, predated the sea, and there is evidence of impressive mountain ranges that eroded over time into the plains characteristic of today. Erosion, molten uprisings, the ebb and flow of the sea and its attendant water courses

all contributed in different geological eras to the development of the formations in which are now found the grain belt, gas and oil fields, and deposits of salt, clays, coals, potash and other valuable minerals. The main geological influence of the Quaternary period in Saskatchewan was GLACIATION, which variously polished and scarred substantial areas of exposed rock, and left rich sediments elsewhere. The glaciers moved SW across the land, leaving behind lakes that at their largest covered most of the province, and marking the landscape with drumlins, eskers and moraines. (The buildings on U of Saskatchewan's campus are made largely of multicoloured stone deposited by the glaciers.) At one time or another the glaciers touched all of Saskatchewan except for two small pockets of high land in the extreme S, which still have flora and fauna showing significant variations from their counterparts in the rest of the province. The last glaciers melted in the S approximately 16 to 18 000 years ago, and further N as recently as 8000 years ago.

Surface Generally inhospitable to agriculture because of the climate and thin soil, the northern third of the province is marked by swamp and muskeg, lichened rock, and forest characteristic of the Shield. The altitudes of the grain belt drop markedly from W to E, and from S to N; levels of 600 and 900 m above sea level, common in the W and S, slope to 150 and 300 m in the E and N, causing the province's extensive river systems to flow to Hudson Bay. The soils permit agricultural settlement in what is roughly the southern half of the province; in the northern half the climate is inimical to the use of what little arable land there is. The cultivated areas of the southern portion depend on a variety of soils, predominantly brown and black, whose texture ranges from loamy sands to clays.

Saskatchewan's natural vegetation is divided

from N to S into 6 fairly distinct zones, all of which cross the province diagonally SE. A band of subarctic forest tundra exists along the northern boundary, and S of that is a broad region of northern coniferous forest, with a third band of mixed woods below that. The northern agricultural belt is aspen parkland, the central is mid-grass prairie, and the southernmost is short grass prairie. Each of the 6 zones corresponds roughly to particular soil deposits. Soil erosion is a continuing problem in the province, the broad river systems providing one type, the winds, so well known that they are a familiar element in prairie literature, creating another.

Water A superficial view of maps of Saskatchewan suggests that the province has an abundance of WATER, both on the surface and in aquifers occurring at varying depths, and in important ways the abundance is real. The province is drained by parts of 4 major basins, the Mackenzie and Churchill in the north, the Saskatchewan and Qu'Appelle-Assiniboine in the south. The larger aquifers are estimated to be capable of yielding about 10% of the annual flow of the South SASKATCHEWAN R. But aquifers can be tapped only through technology that may be expensive, with individual wells generally not large producers; and much of the most accessible surface water is in the north, where agricultural settlement is minimal.

Both agriculture and industrial development (particularly the production of potash) require large amounts of water, and Saskatchewan is heavily dependent on river flows and precipitation, neither of which is amenable to provincial control. The river systems in the agricultural sector utilize water that comes mainly from snow melt in the Rocky Mts, and snowfall there is subject to wide variations. Precipitation within the province is similarly unreliable, and what does arrive may suffer high rates of evaporation. A characteristic feature of the Saskatchewan farming landscape is the dugout, a large excavation designed to catch the spring runoff from the fields.

Annual precipitation in the province varies enormously, both for the province as a whole and for the differing zones within it. The celebrated drought of the 1930s was intensive and widespread, but it was most severe in the S and diminished northwards into the parkland. The average annual precipitation runs from a few centimetres to about 50, the fall generally becoming increasingly heavy from the SW to the NE. Irrigation, although the province's terrain in many areas seems adaptable to it, has not progressed far beyond the experimental stage; much was expected from the elongated Diefenbaker Lake backed up behind the Gardiner Dam on the South Saskatchewan R, but irrigation developments have been small.

Climate The climate of Saskatchewan can in one year include many extremes. Three main climatic zones, corresponding roughly to the main zones of vegetation, cross the province, and range from cold snowy areas in the N, which have brief summers, through more moderate areas in the grain belt, to semi-arid steppes in the SW. Jan temperatures below -50°C and July temperatures above 40°C have been recorded, as have Jan temperatures well above freezing and July temperatures well below. Days free of frost can number from 60 to over 100 in any year. In the arable sections the last spring frost usually comes in early June, and the first in autumn in early September. The relatively short growing season profoundly affects what agriculture can produce in Saskatchewan, for grains are sensitive to frost from germination until harvest. In one sense the number of frost-free days is a misleading indicator of the

Potash plant at Esterhazy, Sask (*photo by Richard Vroom*).

growing season, as the province's northern setting also produces in the summer early sunrises and late sunsets. In the grain belt, on June 21, the sun rises before 5 am and sets after 9:30 pm. For the same reason winter days are short: on Dec 21 sunrise is after 9 am and sunset at 5 pm. Blizzards in winter and thunderstorms in summer are common features of the climate, and the southern half of the province is occasionally visited by tornadoes. Saskatchewan's climate is often given part of the credit for the province's vigorous communal and co-operative life, the long winters allegedly obliging the population to provide offsetting social developments. Winter also produces a unique export: disproportionately large numbers of gifted hockey players.

Resources Soils and water are the fundamental resources of any heavily agricultural region, but to them in recent decades have been added increasingly important discoveries and developments of a nonagricultural nature. The most spectacular of these have been in minerals. Saskatchewan in the 1980s ranked fifth among the provinces in mineral production, although its wealth in metallic resources, abundant elsewhere in Canada, was generally negligible. But the province contains immensely valuable deposits of POTASH and URANIUM, whose use depends on factors beyond provincial jurisdiction, and of fossil fuels that can to some degree be refined and consumed locally. Saskatchewan contains Canada's largest potash resources, and ranks second in uranium and petroleum. It has significant deposits of fuels, especially natural gas, and clays.

The forest resources are limited by soil and climate. Even so, over half the province is wooded, and roughly one-third of the stands yield a harvest; Saskatchewan ranks eighth among provincial forest inventories, and it has more soft than hard woods. In dry years losses from fire are high, not only in the immediate destruction of potential pulp and lumber, but in the loss of habitat for wildlife, which variously supports recreational and commercial fishing, trapping and other hunting, which in the N are essential to the native peoples. Saskatchewan's mammals include most of those familiar on the Canadian landscape, although two of the largest in the W are rarely sighted; the COUGAR is still seen, but evidence of the GRIZZLY BEAR has all but disappeared. The province is a main flyway for an abundance of waterfowl and songbirds, and supports a lush insect life which both impedes and helps agriculture. The

wildlife is a major factor in attracting hunters and fishermen, and the province usually ranks around fifth in the value of wild pelts taken. The commercial freshwater fisheries, although valuable locally where they exist, are among the smallest in Canada.

Conservation Saskatchewan has for decades assumed that CONSERVATION principles applied not just to "natural resources" but to human as well, and its government pioneered in publicly supported medical care, advanced labour legislation, and the protection of civil rights. Human occupations have led to further conservation of such essentials as water, and the province is the chief beneficiary of a major federal statute, the PRAIRIE FARM REHABILITATION ACT, which, with amendments, has since 1935 facilitated the transformation of the agricultural landscape through the creation of dams and dugouts. The need for conserving water on the prairies is a subject about which there can be little serious disagreement, and federal policy is supplemented by related provincial policies.

The conservation of most other natural resources is more controversial. Hunters, for example, may be willing to accept bag limits on waterfowl, to ensure the continuation of hunting; but the maintenance of large flocks may also mean that some farmers have to tolerate substantial destruction of grain each fall. Pesticides and herbicides are necessary for large crops of weed-free grain, and their use is officially encouraged; but the chemicals used sometimes show up in disturbing quantities in foods consumed by humans and livestock. Even that most traditional of prairie conservation policies, leaving arable fields idle in summerfallow to reduce weeds and conserve moisture, has been shown to be in important ways more wasteful than continual cropping from the soil. The inevitable tensions brought by modern technology have not prevented Saskatchewan from adopting comprehensive programs aimed at preserving its environment. Lookout towers and patrol aircraft in the N, controlled harvesting of wildlife everywhere, game preserves, fish hatcheries, and bird sanctuaries are all familiar parts of provincial life.

People

Evidence of aboriginal occupation of Saskatchewan can be traced to at least 10 000 BC, when hunters followed the migratory herds of bison, leaving behind arrowheads and ashes. The first European explorers, most of them seeking routes for the fur trade, appeared late in the 17th centu-

ry, and were in time joined by more scientific travellers who expanded knowledge of the area throughout the 19th century. Actual settlement was preceded in most sections by the establishment in 1873 of the North-West Mounted Police; and thereafter homesteaders, attracted by land that was all but free, poured in at an accelerated rate. The census of 1881 revealed 19 114 inhabitants, that of 1911, 492 432, and that of 1931, 921 785. Thereafter the population levelled off and even declined considerably, partly because WWII drained off people to the armed forces and industrial plants elsewhere; after 1961 the population fluctuated between 920 000 and 955 000 and the census of 1981 revealed the largest population yet, 968 313; by 1986 the population reached 1 009 613. The first immigrants naturally chose to live in farming areas, and most residents still live in the southern half of Saskatchewan. But towns and villages were always necessary as supply depots for farm implements and related service industries, and with the rise of nonagricultural production rural areas have steadily lost population to urban ones.

Urban Centres Saskatchewan has no metropolitan centre, but its urban population grew from a negligible early beginning to 61.5% by 1986, while the rural farm population declined from a dominant position to less than a quarter of the total. Even so, only 2 cities are of even moderate size: SASKATOON (1986 census population 177 641) and REGINA (175 064), with MOOSE JAW (35 073), PRINCE ALBERT (33 686), North Battleford (14 876), SWIFT CURRENT (15 666), and YORKTON (15 574) following far behind. The cities are joined by a grid of E-W, N-S highways, and each serves a surrounding rural area as a market town and shipping centre. Regina and Saskatoon, especially, serve respectively as southern and northern economic "capitals," containing the wholesale houses that provide surrounding retailers with the multitude of consumer goods necessary to the late 20th century. Prince Albert, as the province's most northerly city, performs a special function as a "gateway to the north," of particular importance as the point of departure for recreational and forest areas. Despite its large urban population, Saskatchewan's vast expanses of open landscape, combined with the conspicuous architecture of GRAIN ELEVATORS in the villages and towns, continue to convey the impression of a predominantly agricultural province.

Labour Force Saskatchewan's labour force (500 000 in 1987) has naturally reflected the changes in the provincial economy, as urban workers have steadily replaced farmers and their helpers. Union organization began around the turn of the century in Moose Jaw and Regina, principally among skilled tradesmen in printing and railways; but the development of the economy did not encourage influential union activity of the kind familiar in heavily industrialized communities. The largest single unions of the 1980s are not primarily of steelworkers or automobile makers, but of teachers and public servants, although unions are active in such areas as the retail and wholesale trades, and in oil and potash. Provincial governments under the CCF and NDP were perceived as being particularly friendly to organized labour.

Although the province was one of the chief sufferers during the GREAT DEPRESSION and drought of the 1930s, the technology of later decades has been more conducive to sustaining its labour force. One factor is that Saskatchewan has been an exporter of labour to other provinces, but whatever the reasons the province in the 1980s, in sharp contrast to the 1930s, had one of the lowest unemployment rates in Canada. Saskatche-

Saskatchewan is Canada's foremost wheat-growing area and one of the great wheat-growing regions of the world (*photo by Brian Milne/First Light*).

wan also has one of the highest proportions of married women in the labour force.

Language and Ethnicity Modern Saskatchewan has a population over 80% of whose members, when asked about Canada's official languages, claimed to speak English only, with 2.1% speaking French only. The same population, however, offered a striking variety of mother tongues, the languages first spoken in the home, and in the 1980s over 13% learned a mother tongue other than English or French. The current situation is in marked contrast to the beginnings. When the settlement of Saskatchewan began in earnest, residents of French origin slightly outnumbered those of British, but both comprised less than 11% of the population; almost all the rest were aboriginal peoples. The influx of settlers brought few new French (migration from Québec to the West was considered by some influential clergy to be a form of exile), but it did bring large numbers of British and other Europeans whose descendants, in one or two generations, also became English speaking. The result was that by 1981 citizens of French origin had dropped to barely 6% of the population, ranking behind the British (40%), German and Austrian (20%), Ukrainian (10%) and Scandinavian (7%). Below those of French origin numerically were Russian, Polish, native Indian and Dutch. Significant numbers of people of Asian origin appeared in the 1970s and 1980s.

Saskatchewan GDP 1986 at Factor Cost ($Millions)

Agriculture	2155
Forestry	38
Mining	2182
Manufacturing	989
Construction	748
Utilities	477
Goods Producing Industries	6589
Transportation	1345
Trade (Wholesale & Retail)	1692
Finance	2957
Service	3098
Public Administration and Defence	1735
Service Producing Industries	10 827
Total	17 416

The high ratio of British to French has had important implications for provincial policies on language and education, for English has always been unquestionably the dominant language, and those interested in the teaching of other languages, or in conducting regular schooling in other languages, always faced formidable obstacles. The use of French was at one time confined to primary courses, and in 1931 French was prohibited as a medium of instruction; other languages fared less well. In the 1960s, however, the province began to take a more relaxed view towards French in the schools, and public schools teaching the regular curriculum in French began to appear. Saskatchewan, paradoxically, has not since the 1926 census had a population at least half British in origin.

Religion Religion in Saskatchewan has always been connected with language and ethnicity, as the incoming settlers naturally tended to congregate in communities where they hoped to practise their religion and, if possible, to have their children educated in their own language. The largest Protestant denomination in modern Saskatchewan is the United Church (32% of adherents), followed closely by the Roman Catholic (26%). Considerably smaller are the Lutheran and Anglican (about 10% each), and then the Ukrainian Catholic, Greek Orthodox, Mennonite, Presbyterian and Baptist, ranging from 4% down to less than 2%. The advent of television gave numerous fundamentalist religions access to the population, and in the 1980s they appeared to be the most rapidly growing churches.

Throughout the province's history, religious groups have been active in expressing their views on such varied social issues as prohibition, immigration, education and the language used in schools. Religious factors lie behind the division of the province's public schools into Protestant and Roman Catholic systems, and a particularly bitter confrontation occurred in the late 1920s when the KU KLUX KLAN took the lead in inflaming the electorate over religious symbols (specifically Catholic) in the schools. The Conservative Party was perceived at the time to have Klan support, and hence some Catholic voters thereafter were thought to be supporters of the party's opponents; but in 1982 the party, led by a Roman Catholic, won an overwhelming victory.

Economy

Saskatchewan's economy, since settlement began, has been heavily dependent on influences that lie outside the province's boundaries. The earliest inhabitants of the area, nomads and hunters, were able to rely on creatures as indigenous as themselves. The earliest settlers, when favoured with good weather, were able to produce grains, and especially wheat, in far larger quantities than they could consume, and from the start of the modern era the province has been an exporter of a few staples, often unprocessed, to markets throughout the world.

Commonly the province has had little control over the transportation of its own products, or the financing of it, and this situation did not change as wheat was supplemented by natural gas, petroleum and potash. A high percentage of the consumer goods used in Saskatchewan, on the other hand, from canned food to automobiles and farm implements, come from outside. A recurring feeling among sections of the population is that the province's economy is the victim of outside forces that are not always benign.

This feeling provides one reason for the remarkable success of the CO-OPERATIVE MOVEMENT in Saskatchewan, through which citizens have banded together to satisfy numerous economic needs. Saskatchewan contains nearly 20% of all the co-operative associations in Canada, with individual memberships numbering over a half of the population. The co-operatives are found in virtually every segment of the retailing and distributing trades, and in many service industries; in 1986 56% of the population belonged to 1313 associations whose total assets amounted to more than $55 billion.

Agriculture Although nonagricultural production constitutes over half of Saskatchewan's annual output, agriculture remains the largest single industry. The settled era began almost exclusively as a farm economy, with nearly 460 000 hectares planted to wheat in the year of the province's creation, yielding 26 million bushels. With setbacks occasioned by the depression years of the 1930s, when drought helped reduce all rural activities, and WWII, when some overseas markets for wheat almost disappeared, wheat acreage has grown steadily throughout the province's history and now tops 8 million hectares annually. Saskatchewan is incomparably the largest wheat producer in Canada and one of the largest in the world: in 1986 the province grew 12 710 t of wheat (compared with about half that amount in the other provinces combined). The province is also a leader in the production of canola (1542 t in 1986) and rye (205 t), and is always among the largest producers of oats (682 t), barley (3636 t), flaxseed (315 t), and forage crops and pasturage for livestock, which, since they do not all enter the market, are harder to measure.

The province's livestock industry, though not comparable to its grains, is always an important element in the agricultural economy, farms reporting significant sales of cattle and hogs constituting roughly one-fifth of the number reporting significant wheat sales.

Like all modern agricultural economies, Saskatchewan's is characterized by a diminution in the number of farms and a growth in the size of those surviving. Saskatchewan has the smallest proportion of small to moderate sized farms in Canada, while those yielding annual sales of $25 000 or more number about 30 000. The same dwindling number of farms continues to provide one of the country's largest markets for farm vehicles and machinery, and the total net income from farming in Saskatchewan remains the largest in Canada.

Industry Saskatchewan is not in a conventional sense a manufacturing centre, commonly ranking eighth or ninth in the value of shipped goods of its own manufacture; in 1985 these goods totalled $2.9 billion. Manufacturing establishments, most

Battle Creek, in the Cypress Hills, Sask (*photo by Menno Fieguth*).

of them employing fewer than 100 workers, numbered over 1000 in 1986. Most manufactured goods that are exported go to other parts of Canada.

Saskatchewan's industrial economy has always been affected by the relatively small provincial market. What the province produces well it produces in enormous quantities. The Saskatchewan internal market is in many ways more economically served by imports. While a number of attempts were made to establish major industries (Regina obtained an automobile assembly plant in 1928), the province was in the wrong location, and with the wrong resources, to share in the huge industrial expansion of WWII. Nonagricultural production in the 1980s was larger and more varied than it had ever been, but Saskatchewan is still a long way from posing a threat to central Canada as an industrial heartland.

Mining From the 1950s the development of mining in Saskatchewan was almost as spectacular, though not as conspicuous, as that of agricultural settlement half a century earlier. In 1950 the total value of all mineral production was barely $34 million, of which nearly 80% was of metals, mostly copper and zinc; 15% fuels, mostly coal; and most of the rest was sodium sulphate. By the 1980s mining ranked second to agriculture as a contributor to the province's production; the three largest items, oil, potash and uranium, had been of negligible importance in 1950. Crude petroleum accounted for 3.3% of all mineral production in 1950, and 50% in 1986. In 1985 the province exported 4 million m³ of crude oil to the rest of Canada and 7.2 million m³ to the US. In 1950 no potash was mined; it accounted for over 25% of mineral production in 1986. In 1985 potash exports totalled $586 million. In 1950 uranium was not being mined; by the 1980s one large mine had already been, in economic terms, worked out, but remarkably rich deposits remained elsewhere. By 1986 uranium accounted for over 15% of annual mineral production, and in 1986 Saskatchewan produced 6 532 000 kg ($450 million) of the metal. These rising statistics were offset by another relevant factor: in regard to both capital invested and gross production, none of the big 3 prairie minerals employs large labour forces.

Forestry Forestry does not provide one of Saskatchewan's largest industries, although where it exists it is of great local significance. The rapid opening of the prairies for settlement created a demand for building materials, not just for farm buildings but also for railway ties and telegraph poles; the closer settlement moved to the northern forest, the more local wood could be used. Pulpwood, which utilizes smaller growth than lumber, was cut for export as early as the 1920s, but the province's first pulp mill was not built until the 1960s, and then with substantial assistance from the government.

Saskatchewan wood is used for lumber, parti-

cle board and plywood, poles and fence posts, and pulp, but the total cut, in statistical terms, makes a minor contribution to the province's economy. In 1985, for example, Saskatchewan's exports of lumber were valued at only $40 million, barely 2% of grain exports, and 7% of those of potash. The forest industries are nonetheless sufficiently active that Indian leaders frequently express concern over the damage caused to wildlife habitat.

Fisheries Fisheries rank well below forestry as a contributor to the province's economy, competing for rank with wildlife trapping and fur farming, for an annual production of $3-4 million, chiefly in walleye, whitefish, lake trout and pike. Three-quarters of the commercial activity is in the north, while in the grain belt a fairly common sight is the rainbow trout dugout, a licensed artificial pond in which individual farmers, several hundred a year, raise fish for their own use. Of unknown commercial value, but significant to the tourist industry, is the province's rich supply of game fish and edible wild animals. From 5% to 10% of the sportfishing and hunting licences issued annually go to visitors, most of them from neighbouring American states.

Finance Farming and mining both require a great amount of capital, and Saskatchewan has always had to supplement what it could create with heavy inflows from financial centres elsewhere. No major Canadian bank or trust company has its head office in the province, and the provincial government routinely floats loans in American money markets. The net public debt outstanding in Mar 1987 was over $9 billion; total liabilities amounted to approximately the same.

In 1985 there were only about 400 branches of chartered banks throughout the province, each village serving a farming area ordinarily having one. It is part of the province's traditional beliefs that banks exploit as well as serve those in debt to them; this response, together with the citizens' confidence in co-operative ventures, led to a widespread network of credit unions, in effect banks owned by their own local customers. In 1985 there were 272 chartered credit unions, with 566 867 members (nearly half the provincial population) and assets of $3.95 billion.

The provincial government pioneered in its own financial enterprises when in 1944 the legislature passed the Government Insurance Act. The Saskatchewan Government Insurance office handles most kinds of property insurance, including fire, and is particularly involved in automobile insurance, in which Saskatchewan also pioneered in 1944 by making it compulsory. Profits from the public insurance operations are reinvested within the province whenever possible. In 1985 the insurance office's assets were over $450 million, about half of which was in bonds of the province and its municipalities.

Transportation Saskatchewan is peculiarly vulnerable to transportation problems. The least difficult usually are in air transport, for the province is served by the usual network of major and minor airlines, none of which are involved in moving its bulkiest products. In the north, where some communities are readily accessible only by air, unpredictable weather is the worst factor to be dealt with. On the surface, on the other hand, the long distances between points, the absence of navigable waters, and the sheer quantities of wheat and potash to be hauled make both highways and railways of overwhelming importance. Potash can be moved directly from the mines to the railways, but grains must be carried by truck from each farm before entering the elevator for subsequent shipment by rail. Mainline railway track in Saskatchewan accounts for 12% of the total in Canada (over 4000 km).

Saskatchewan roads under provincial jurisdiction are the longest in Canada per capita, and when municipal responsibilities are added, many of which include rural roads essential to farms, the province's road total is in absolute terms the longest in Canada: over 200 000 km. Railways are under federal jurisdiction, but roads and highways are provincial: a major item in every provincial budget, vying for position behind health and education, is transportation. Combined provincial and municipal expenditures on roads in 1986 were over $200 million. A special problem of Saskatchewan transportation, often vexatious enough in itself but also entirely beyond the province's jurisdiction, arises from work stoppages elsewhere in the system. Saskatchewan farmers are aware that they are landlocked; it is a hazard of their occupation that their grain is sometimes held up by labour-management disputes in ports far away.

Energy Generously endowed with real and potential sources of energy, Saskatchewan exports what it does in forms other than electricity. Through the Saskatchewan Power Corporation, established in 1949 out of a provincial commission 20 years older, the province generates large amounts of power in conventional ways, but not nuclear, and it neither imports nor exports significant quantities.

Domestically the governmental agency enjoys a monopoly over power production and natural gas distribution; and farms, homes and mines are supplied at rates that compare favourably with those elsewhere. The province's total installed capacity for generating electricity in 1986 was 2735 megawatts. Nearly 31% of the electricity produced in 1986 was from hydroelectric plants, and the long lines of transmission towers from sites in the north are conspicuous on the landscape. Thermal units producing power are primarily fired by coal, which accounts for nearly 70% of the provincial total. Generation from oil is negligible, but oil still heats many homes, particularly in rural areas. Urban homes are more likely to be warmed by natural gas, piped to each one by the power corporation.

Government and Politics

The Government of Saskatchewan in form resembles that of the other provinces. The executive consists of the lieutenant-governor and an executive council called the Cabinet, which in the name of the Crown exercises the real powers of government, with the aid of a public service organized into departments and crown corporations. The legislature is unicameral, and its members are elected in 64 single-member constituencies; the support of a majority of the members of the legislature is necessary for the continued life of a particular Cabinet.

The leader of the majority is the premier, and his Cabinet colleagues are ministers, each with assigned responsibilities; the Leader of the Opposition is paid as if he were a minister. The province's judicial system is the usual hierarchy, with a Court of Appeal and a Court of Queen's Bench at the summit, and provincial courts (formerly magistrate's courts) below. The federal authority appoints all judges except for those of the provincial courts.

The parliamentary tradition is strong, and Saskatchewan is unique among the western provinces in that its legislature has never supported coalition governments for prolonged periods nor been dominated by one party to the virtual exclusion of an Opposition. Even during the life of the lone coalition, the Co-operative Government of 1929-34, the largest single party was the opposition. Since 1905, when the assembly had 25 members of whom 3 had urban seats, to 1986, when the assembly's 64 members included 27 urban seats, there has always been a vigorous Opposition, even though sometimes small numerically. A second major tradition of government in Saskatchewan depends on a blurring of the line between public and private sectors: the government, no matter what party was in power, has not only encouraged citizens to develop co-operatives that competed with private enterprise but has not hesitated to go into business itself, as in the creation of a telephone system and a power corporation.

Local Government Saskatchewan has developed its own municipal system, in which townships and counties are not known as governing units, although a measured area may be called a township. There are urban municipalities (in 1987, 12 cities, 143 towns, 2 northern towns and 355 villages) and rural (299), the latter having been created originally through provincial policy rather than through local demand. There are also 10 northern villages and 14 northern hamlets. The remainder of the north receives municipal services through provincial initiatives. The municipal governments provide the usual housekeeping facilities: streets, police, water, sewage disposal and hospitals in the urban areas; roads, help with problems of drainage and weed control in the rural. Municipal governments, often reluctantly, also collect taxes for other local spending authorities, the largest of which are school districts. Total municipal revenues in 1985 were $1.6 billion; expenditures were $1.8 billion. The Saskatchewan Urban Municipalities Association and the Saskatchewan Association of Rural Municipalities are respected political forces.

Federal Representation Saskatchewan has never loomed large in numbers in Parliament, but its representatives have included many notably vocal individuals. The province usually has at least one Cabinet member at Ottawa; 2 prime ministers, King and Diefenbaker, sat for Saskatchewan seats for prolonged periods. One federal minister, James GARDINER, held a portfolio (Agriculture) for a longer consecutive period than any other individual in Canadian history.

In 1905 the province had 4 senators, which rose to 6 in 1915, where it has stayed. Its Commons delegation has never exceeded 8.6% of the total membership (in 1925-35, when it had 21 MPs) and is now, barring a constitutional amendment, pegged at 14 in a House whose total membership will rise after each decennial census. On one occasion (1952), when the rules for dividing parliamentary seats among the provinces would have dropped Saskatchewan's share from 20 to 15, a change was enacted to drop it to 17 only. The influence of the province's parliamentary representation has never depended primarily on numbers but on the quality of those elected.

Public Finance Governmental expenditures in Saskatchewan, as elsewhere, grew rapidly after WWII and in 1981 for the first time passed $2 billion. The main sources of taxation in 1986 were individual income tax (21% of the consolidated fund budgetary revenue), sales tax (13%), gasoline tax (1%) and corporation income tax (4%). The Saskatchewan Heritage Fund provided another 25% and receipts from other governments (almost all of them from federal sources) 22%. The Heritage Fund, established in the 1970s and drawing its income from nonrenewable resources, received 81% of its income from oil and 8% from potash and uranium. Total provincial revenue from all sources in 1986 was $2.95 billion. The main expenditures were in public health (30% of the total), education (19%), social services (10%) and highways (9%).

Lieutenant-Governors of Saskatchewan 1905-87	
	Term
Amédée Emmanuel Forget	1905-10
George William Brown	1910-15
Richard Stuart Lake	1915-21
Henry William Newlands	1921-31
Hugh Edwin Munroe	1931-36
Archibald Peter McNab	1936-45
Thomas Miller	1945
Reginal John Marsden Parker	1945-48
John Michael Uhrich	1948-51
William John Patterson	1951-58
Frank Lindsay Bastedo	1958-63
Robert Leith Hanbidge	1963-70
Dr Stephen Worobetz	1970-76
George Porteous	1976-78
Cameron Irwin McIntosh	1978-83
Fred W. Johnson	1983-

Health Public health policies in Saskatchewan predate the province's creation in 1905, but the province nonetheless pioneered in comprehensive extensions of health care. The hospital services plan, which became effective in 1947, provided universal hospital care insurance throughout the province: every qualified citizen has since 1947 been provided with a card assuring hospital care when needed, at public expense. The hospital plan provided part of the foundation for universal prepaid medical care, as did the establishment of a medical faculty and teaching hospital at the University of Saskatchewan. Medicare was enacted in 1961 and inaugurated in 1962, after considerable tension between the government and the medical profession, which resulted in many doctors withdrawing their services for a month. Since 1962 the hospital and medicare plans have been supplemented by a dental plan (1974) and a prescription plan (1975). In the 1980s the dental plan was not universal but was limited to categories of school children, and the prescription service was not fully prepaid but imposed a standard dispensing fee for each prescription.

Politics The recent lively partisan traditions of Saskatchewan are reflected in its election results: in the last 7 general elections to 1986, the winning party won over 50% of the vote only twice. The Liberals were chosen to form the first administration in 1905 and won the first 6 elections handily, although always facing Opposition groups with considerable support. The Liberals' early successes, in keeping with the mores of the day, produced a public service weighted with patronage appointments, an issue used against the party in 1929. The basic issue of the 1929 election, however, about which vast ill-feeling was generated, turned on the use of the schools for religious purposes, and a loose coalition of Conservatives, Progressives and Independents defeated the government. The Co-operative government then formed fell in turn a victim to drought and depression, and not one of its candidates was elected in 1934. After another decade of Liberal rule, the province in 1944 elected North America's first socialist government, in the CO-OPERATIVE COMMONWEALTH FEDERATION, or CCF. The CCF (known later in Saskatchewan as the CCF-NDP and finally as the NEW DEMOCRATIC PARTY) lasted 20 years, after which the Liberals returned for the years 1964-71. The NDP came back for 1971-82, and in 1982 the Progressive CONSERVATIVES, who had all but disappeared between 1934 and the 1970s, won their first victory in their own right and were returned to power again in 1986.

The volatility of the Saskatchewan electorate is less evidence of a capacity to swing from left to right than it is of the parties' practices in rarely differing fundamentally in what they offer. The CCF was plainly the furthest left of the parties, with the Liberals and Conservatives on the right; but the Liberals after 1964, for example, did not dismantle the health and welfare policies or the public enterprises of the preceding CCF, which had in turn built on foundations laid by the Liberals. In a similar way, the province's relations with Ottawa, generally good, have depended primarily not on which parties were in power in each place but on the provincial government's perception, regardless of its partisan outlook, of the province's needs.

Education

The province inherited the beginnings of a public school system, as well as the idea for a university, from its territorial days. The rapid expansion of the population during the early settlement gave to the provision of teachers and schools a sense of urgency felt almost everywhere, and the upgrading of inadequately trained teachers and the replacement of makeshift premises were major preoccupations of Saskatchewan's first years. Many of the teachers at the start came from provinces to the east, but the new province created Normal Schools, whose work was in 1927 supplemented by a College of Education at the UNIVERSITY OF SASKATCHEWAN; in due course the college absorbed the Normal Schools. The university itself was established in 1909, with a solitary faculty of arts, a teaching staff of 5, and 70 students. By the 1980s the university had 14 faculties, a teaching staff of over 1000, and over 16 000 students. In 1974 UNIVERSITY OF REGINA was created out of the Regina campus of University of Saskatchewan. In 1986 it had over 8000 students. The universities are nonsectarian, although they have affiliated theological colleges. A striking feature of Saskatchewan's public and high school systems is that both Protestant and Roman Catholic systems are public, ie, they are managed by separate elected boards of education and financed by taxes collected by the relevant municipal authority. In the 1970s a series of community colleges, emphasizing non-academic post-secondary education, was also begun and now consists of 16 schools with an enrolment of 86 014 in 1986.

The basic instruments of educational policy are two related departments of government, Education and Continuing Education, which usually have the same minister. Locally, the chief unit is the school district, whose elected board is in effect a municipal council with a single responsibility, schools. The schools are financed primarily by local taxes and provincial grants; education annually provides one of the largest items in the provincial budget. In 1985-86 Saskatchewan had 202 600 students in public schools, and 2900 in private, not counting several thousands in federal institutions, the latter chiefly for Indian and Inuit peoples.

Cultural Life

Much of the artistic energy of the indigenous peoples went into artifacts connected with the

Premiers of Saskatchewan 1905-87		
	Party	*Term*
T. Walter Scott	Liberal	1905-16
William M. Martin	Liberal	1916-22
Charles A. Dunning	Liberal	1922-26
James G. Gardiner	Liberal	1926-29
James T. M. Anderson	Conservative	1929-34
James G. Gardiner	Liberal	1934-35
William J. Patterson	Liberal	1935-44
Thomas C. Douglas	CCF/NDP	1944-61
Woodrow S. Lloyd	CCF/NDP	1961-64
W. Ross Thatcher	Liberal	1964-71
Allan E. Blakeney	NDP	1971-82
D. Grant Devine	Conservative	1982-

hunt, and the making of decorated leather clothing and moccasins has survived. There are petroglyphs on outcrops at Roche Percée, in the southeast. The Europeans brought their own crafts with them, and the significance of handicrafts in Saskatchewan's development is reflected in the seriousness with which they are still taken. When in 1948 the Saskatchewan Arts Board was created, the first governmental body of its kind on the continent, it treated crafts from the start as art forms, and the provincial crafts exhibition held each summer under official auspices is a highlight of the cultural year. The arts board is an independent organization that encourages and funds a wide variety of artistic endeavours, and it reports through the minister of culture and youth. The board has a valuable collection of work by provincial artists; its expenditures in 1986 were $2.65 million.

Arts Individual Saskatchewan artists have excelled in every branch of the arts. Musicians raised in the province have gone on to national and international fame, including performances with leading orchestras and opera companies. Visual artists of both Indian and European origin have earned outstanding reputations. The province's rich deposits of clays have given rise to an unusually active community of ceramicists. Many Saskatchewan artists, like their fellow Canadians generally, have had to leave home to find listeners and viewers, but the domestic scene continues to be extremely active. There are symphony orchestras in Regina and Saskatoon, and the universities there have well-developed arts departments. Workshops for singers, writers, painters et al are available to large numbers of participants, and the Emma Lake campus of University of Saskatchewan each summer becomes a camp for artists. Publishing also flourishes, and one house, the property of the Wheat Pool's weekly newspaper, is a successful commercial enterprise specializing in prairie works.

Communications Absentee ownership is a striking characteristic of the media in the province, but since all the outlets in both print and broadcasting have to cater to local communities the effect of so much external ownership is not conspicuous. Only the major cities support daily newspapers, and smaller centres are served by journals published less frequently, most of them weeklies. Several articulate magazines of literary or political bent struggle constantly for existence, and there are also periodicals that express the particular interests of Indian and Métis associations. A variety of learned journals emanate from the universities.

Radio is as important in the north as the telegraph was formerly throughout the Prairies. Few communities in the 1980s, however remote, are beyond the reach of radio, and the national services of the CBC are distributed through stations in Regina and La Ronge, the latter being one of the most northerly villages accessible by road. Television signals, their distribution facilitated by microwave towers and satellite stations, reach all the settled areas; and cable TV, beginning in the late 1970s, widened the range of domestic outlets and also, for the first time, made programs originating in the United States available to most viewers in Saskatchewan.

Historic Sites Saskatchewan's native peoples found a renewed interest in their history, as their awareness of their common aspirations grew in the 1970s and 1980s. The descendants of the European settlers, whose occupation was so recent, have also been sensitive to their past. The province is dotted with national and provincial historic sites, the most northerly of them marking early missions, the rest variously celebrating fur posts, the first newspaper, Mounted Police

Tommy Douglas (centre) standing under CCF billboard shortly after his election as premier of Saskatchewan, 1944, with C.M. Fines (left) and Clarence Gillis (right) (*courtesy Saskatchewan Archives Board/R-B2895*).

depots, colonies of settlers, old trails, the founding of a grain growers' organization, or a steamship landing. Hundreds of local histories were written around the province's diamond jubilee in 1980, most of them with the help of the Saskatchewan Archives Board, a co-operative university-government venture established in 1945. Between the records around the historic sites and those of the homestead applications and the land titles office, more detailed information is available about Saskatchewan since its European settlement than about most places.

History

The earliest human inhabitants of the area that became Saskatchewan, who left almost no written records, were Indians grouped roughly from N to S as follows: 3 tribes of the Athapaskan linguistic group, the CHIPEWYAN and, to the west of them, the Amisk (or BEAVER), N of whom were the SLAVEY; 2 tribes speaking Algonquian, the CREE and, W and S of them, the BLACKFOOT; 2 tribes of the Siouan group, the ASSINIBOINE and, W of them, the Gros Ventres. Each of the 3 main language groups occupied approximately a third of the area, those in the N depending heavily on caribou and moose as a staple food, those in the southern third (ie, that part which is now the agricultural belt) on the buffalo. All of them had a considerable influence in providing place-names throughout the province.

To this day some of the northern Indians have limited contact with people of European descent. Others, especially those close to waterways, were in contact with whites as early as 1690 when Henry KELSEY, an employee of the Hudson's Bay Company, followed the Saskatchewan R west to the area that is now Prince Albert and then proceeded S into the plains. Thereafter exploration continued throughout the 18th and 19th centuries, and by 1870 not only were the main water routes well known, but the prairie was crisscrossed by well-worn trails, some of whose routes are still visible from the air.

Exploration The earliest European explorers travelled the prairies for no more laudable reason than moneymaking: the felt hat was fashionable in the late 17th century, and the best felt came from beaver. Even before the first fur traders the plains were well known to many, for the various Indian tribes moved about following the migrations of caribou and buffalo herds, and the boundaries of the regions occupied by the main tribes were never clearly defined. Paradoxically, the Indians are rarely thought of as explorers, perhaps because they had different motives from the Europeans, but also because they did not need maps and left no records.

The Europeans, once they had discovered the usefulness of the plains for their purposes, wast-

ed little time in moving in. The HUDSON'S BAY COMPANY was two decades old when Kelsey first saw Saskatchewan in 1690. LA VÉRENDRYE then explored some of SE Saskatchewan in the late 1730s and he was followed by several more of English extraction, of whom the best known is probably Peter POND. None penetrated north of the Churchill R until 1796, when David THOMPSON explored the area before heading to Lk Athabasca. At that time little was known of the southern third of the province, but in 1800 Peter FIDLER crossed the area using the S Saskatchewan. The primary interest of most of the early explorers was exploitation of the fur resources, and that, unfortunately, often included exploitation of the aboriginal peoples.

Not all the Indians cared about the fur trade, the Plains Cree especially having few opportunities for trapping. Indians who were in the trade often became increasingly dependent on one particular fort or post – by the late 18th century such settlements dotted the fur-bearing areas – and often also on alcohol, which was used shamelessly as an element in competition between white traders.

Not all exploration had selfish motives, and men interested in the land and the environment entered the region a century behind the traders. The best known of the early observers were Sir John FRANKLIN and Dr John RICHARDSON, between 1819 and 1827, and John PALLISER, 1857-58; and coincidentally with the PALLISER EXPEDITION, which was British, the Province of Canada despatched Henry HIND with a colleague to assess agricultural possibilities. By the middle of the 19th century the domination of the prairies by the fur trade was being threatened.

Settlement A sequence of events in the 19th century determined that the Prairies were to be settled primarily by peoples of European ancestry. The foundation was laid by the acquisition of Rupert's Land from the HBC and its subsequent transfer to Canada shortly after Confederation in 1870. A series of treaties with the Indians, beginning in 1871, established the natives on reserves in a manner that suggested that the rest of the land was for somebody else. The treaties were negotiated with the help of the North-West Mounted Police, an adaptation to the plains of a European institution. The defeat of the Métis under RIEL in 1885, in a rebellion in which land was a major issue, meant among other things that the Métis were not the chosen people. Concurrently with this period Parliament in 1872 passed the first Dominion Lands Act, a provision for homesteaders, and an Act to stimulate immigration. In 1882-83 the first railway lines crossed the area, in a southern route through Regina and Moose Jaw. The prerequisites for immigration and settlement were thus all in place well before 1900.

The impact of their combined influence shows dramatically in the statistics. In 1885 the population of the area was 32 097, of whom half were British and 44% were Indian. Three censuses later, in 1911, the population was 492 432, of which half was still British, but the Indians had dropped to 2.4%. The British element by then had consolidated its hold on familiar political institutions: the principles of responsible government, which held the Cabinet responsible to a majority of the legislature, had been settled in 1897. Provincial status, first sought in 1900, came in 1905, and with it the relevant apparatus of parliamentary government. The province's size and shape were important; although many leading prairie politicians favoured one large western province, the federal authorities always insisted that the western plains were too large to be made into a single constitutional entity. Depending on where one settled its northern boundary, such a province could have been the largest in Canada, a potential economic threat to the central heartland. In any event, in 1905 the federal government retained in federal hands the jurisdiction over crown lands in Saskatchewan.

Alienation of the land which, shortly after 1905, included over 6 million hectares for railway grants and 1.6 million for the support of schools, proceeded for settlement in a generally northwesterly direction, most of the arable area being occupied by the 1930s. The pattern of settlement itself profoundly affected the nature of Saskatchewan society. Identifiable groups of immigrants, varying from English people desiring to set up a temperance colony to DOUKHOBORS escaping persecution with the aid of Leo Tolstoy and the Society of Friends (see QUAKERS), established communities which in the 1980s still reflected their origins. Time, social mobility and intermarriage have blurred the lines separating the original settlements, but many parts of the province were still discernibly French and German, Ukrainian and Scandinavian, Hutterite and Mennonite.

Development Immigration en masse into Saskatchewan had ended at least temporarily by the 1930s, although a high turnover in the population did not stop. A population of barely a million can absorb only limited numbers of artisans, artists and other professionals, and the province's modern history is marked by the steady departure of energetic people born and educated in Saskatchewan. Sometimes, as in the two world wars, thousands left over a short period to enlist or to work in war industries, and many did not return. At the same time, migration inwards of trained people did not end, as the universities grew and as industries attracted professionals and administrators.

The maturing of the population meant also a slackening of the hold of the English-speaking Protestant establishment on political institutions. In the early years, citizens of non-British origin did not often seek election to Parliament or the assembly, and even more rarely were they elected. By the 1970s people with names that were recognizably continental European were working successfully at all levels of politics and administration, often attaining high office. In earlier times religion or national origin frequently decided how sides were chosen over such varied issues as languages in the schools, women's suffrage, or prohibition; and similar divisions can still occur over, for example, abortion. But in the 1980s citizens of every origin are more likely to be found on both sides of most controversies.

Economically, the most significant single event of Saskatchewan's modern history was the transfer of jurisdiction over crown lands to the province in 1930. Without this authority, the province was still able to become a great agricultural producer, and it would still have been able to make the remarkable contribution to the war effort that it did from 1939 to 1945. But with it the province did not merely have access to lucrative sources of taxation; it also had new sources of power which affected its influence within Canada in the 1970s and after, and gave it, despite its small population, a formidable voice in national affairs. Wheat, once the plains were settled, was always a large factor in Canada's international dealings. In modern Saskatchewan wheat has been joined by potash and several forms of precious energy. The province's economy since the drought and depression decade of the 1930s has shown an impressive capacity for diversification in both agricultural and nonagricultural production. In all this it has been assisted by a sequence of lively and progressive governments supported and trusted by a lively and progressive electorate.   NORMAN WARD

Reading: John H. Archer, *Saskatchewan: A History* (1980); D.H. Bocking, ed, *Pages from the Past: Essays on Saskatchewan History* (1970); G. Friesen, *Prairie Road* (1984); Edward McCourt, *Saskatchewan* (1968); J. Howard Richards and K.I. Fung, *Atlas of Saskatchewan* (1969).

Saskatchewan Doctors' Strike In 1959, Premier T.C. DOUGLAS announced his intention to provide medical care insurance, based on prepayment, universal coverage, quality service and government administration, and through a scheme acceptable to both doctors and patients. The election of 1960 was fought on this issue, the doctors campaigning against it. A commission, established to recommend a plan, reported in Sept 1961. Members of the Saskatchewan College of Physicians and Surgeons met with the government, stating that they could not work with a compulsory, government-controlled scheme.

The Saskatchewan Medical Care Insurance Bill was introduced in the Legislature 13 Oct 1961, and received royal assent 17 Nov 1961, after Woodrow S. LLOYD had replaced Douglas as premier. It was to come into force April 1, but this was amended, later, to 1 July 1962. While the bill was still being debated, the college emphasized its refusal to co-operate with the scheme, claiming that it would bring regimentation and would interfere with the doctor-patient relationship. At a meeting in May 1962, the doctors resolved not to practise should the Act come into force. In Regina, a group of mothers formed a committee to support their doctors. Similar committees were organized throughout the province, encouraged by doctors and joined by political opponents of the government. These KOD (Keep Our Doctors) Committees, with support from the media, launched a well-organized campaign against the government and the medicare plan. Rallies, petitions, panels and advertisements raised the emotional climate to a white heat.

On 1 July 1962, when the Act came into force, most doctors closed their offices, some took holidays or educational leave, while some staffed emergency centres. A few left the province for good. The Medical Care Insurance Commission brought doctors from Britain and encouraged others to come from the US and other parts of Canada to meet the emergency. Local citizens groups organized medical clinics and hired doctors to attend them. By mid-July much of the KOD support had dissipated. Some doctors were returning to work; the force of the strike was spent. Lord Taylor, a physician who had been active in introducing Britain's health-care scheme, was brought to Saskatchewan by the government. He acted as mediator and the 2 sides signed an agreement in Saskatoon 23 July 1962.

On 2 Aug 1962, amendments to the Act were passed allowing doctors to practise outside the plan. Payments by the government would be 85% of the college fee schedule, as was common in

doctor-sponsored insurance schemes. In addition, the number of doctors on the Medical Care Insurance Commission was increased to at least 3. The powers of the commission were more limited, and certain other sections and phrases were amended or omitted to relieve the doctors' fears of interference.

The doctors returned to work after the Saskatoon agreement, but hostilities long remained. Patients resented their doctors' desertion, while doctors objected to government involvement in medical care. Nevertheless, a 1965 survey found that most doctors favoured continuing the plan.   JEAN LARMOUR

Saskatchewan Legislative Building, Regina, was built 1908-12, following the plans of Montréal architects Edward and William MAXWELL. The symmetrical design of the façades, the classical details and the interior all show the influence of the beaux-arts style, an architectural movement that deeply marked Canadian public architecture of this era. Divided into 5 sections, the façade has in its central section a huge portico consisting of Doric columns and a pediment. The floor plan, in the shape of a Latin cross, is based on a system of axes housing the building's major functions. *See also* GOVERNMENT BUILDING.   NATHALIE CLERK

Saskatchewan Research Council (SRC) After an unsuccessful attempt to form a research council in 1930, the Saskatchewan government established SRC in 1947. The council served primarily as an agency for grants and scholarships to university researchers until 1954; its mandate then expanded to include independent research in natural and management sciences directed towards improving the provincial economy. Its own laboratories were opened in 1958, expanding in 1963. Special expertise has developed in slurry pipelines, uranium-ore genesis, GROUNDWATER management and various aspects of AGRICULTURE. The Board of Directors, appointed by the Lieutenant-Governor-in-Council, are from government, industry and the universities. Laboratories, including the Canadian Centre for Advanced Instrumentation, are located at Innovation Place on UNIVERSITY OF SASKATCHEWAN's Saskatoon campus, with the exception of the Petroleum Division laboratory in Regina which specializes in developing the province's heavy oil resources. Over 240 staff members, in 4 branches, report to a vice-president. Seventy percent of the council's funding comes from private industry, provincial and federal contracts; most of the remainder from provincial grants. In addition to conducting and funding research, SRC issues free technical advice to small businesses, informs the public on SCIENCE POLICY issues and advises the government.
                MARTIN K. McNICHOLL

Saskatchewan River, 1939 km long, formed by the confluence of the North Saskatchewan

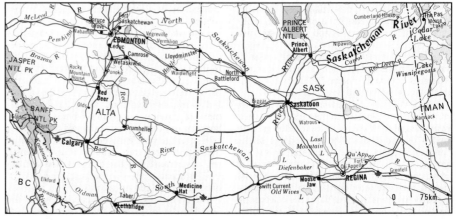

(1287 km) and the South Saskatchewan (1392 km) rivers about 50 km E of PRINCE ALBERT, Sask. The system of waters has a combined length greater than the St Lawrence R and drains much of the western prairie. The N Saskatchewan rises in the COLUMBIA ICEFIELD at the foot of Mt Columbia and flows E to ROCKY MOUNTAIN HOUSE, where it takes in the Clearwater R, on through EDMONTON, Alta, where much of its valley has been preserved as parkland, and then past North Battleford and Prince Albert. The river cuts a deep, wide valley in the prairie and like all prairie streams carries a heavy load of silt. The S Saskatchewan is formed in southern Alberta by the junction of the BOW and OLDMAN rivers. It flows E past MEDICINE HAT, Alta, then NE into Saskatchewan, past SASKA-TOON, and continues a course roughly parallel to the N Saskatchewan to the confluence some 130 km downstream. The S Saskatchewan has been dammed about 100 km S of Saskatoon, creating a long broad reservoir, called DIEFENBAKER LK, which provides hydroelectric power and irrigation for SW Saskatchewan. From the confluence, the river continues nearly 600 km eastward through Tobin Lk and Cumberland Lk, Sask, into Manitoba, where it trends SE past THE PAS and into CEDAR LK. The waters of the Saskatchewan enter Lk WINNIPEG at Grand Rapids and are carried to Hudson Bay by the NELSON R.

Called *Kisiskatchewani Sipi*, "swift-flowing river," by the Indians, Henry KELSEY (1690) and the LA VÉRENDRYE family (*c*1741) were the first Europeans to see it. The modern rendering of the name was adopted in 1882 when part of the present-day province was made a district of the NWT. The section between Grand Rapids and CUMBERLAND HOUSE (built in 1774 by Samuel HEARNE), was hotly contested by the HBC and NWC. From Cumberland House to Edmonton, there are no rapids that could not be lined up or run down, although shifting gravel bars were a menace. This was a much-travelled route of the HBC traders and made Edmonton an early focal point of trade. The southern branch carried traders SW to Wyoming and into the Rockies by Bow Pass. In years when the sovereignty of the North-West was in question, the Saskatchewan made possible an E-W highway tying the area to English commercial enterprise on Hudson Bay and, via the Great Lakes, to Canadian interests centered in Montréal. JAMES MARSH

Saskatchewan Roughriders, FOOTBALL team. They were founded as the Regina Rugby Club in 1910, adopting the Roughrider nickname in 1924 and becoming the Saskatchewan Roughriders in 1948. Until 1936 they were the West's dominant team, winning 16 championships. Although defeated in their 7 early GREY CUP attempts (1923, 1928-32, 1934), the Roughriders won respect for western football, introducing the forward pass to the Grey Cup in 1929 and scoring the West's first Grey Cup touchdown in 1930. Except for a 1951 Cup loss to Ottawa, they did not return to the national final until the 1960s. In 1956 tragedy struck the team when 4 players were killed in a plane crash when returning from the All-Star Game in Vancouver. A rebuilding program began in 1962 and the team made the playoffs in each of the next 15 years. Led by quarterback Ron LANCASTER and indomitable running back George REED, the team made 5 Grey Cup appearances (1966, 1967, 1969, 1972, 1976) – its sole victory occurring over Ottawa in 1966. The community-owned team has not made the playoffs since 1977 and has survived only with strong fan support. Home games are played at Regina's Taylor Field, named in 1946 for former quarterback N.J. "Piffles" Taylor. DEREK DRAGER

Saskatchewan Sports Hall of Fame, in Regina, captures the rich sports history of the province. It was established in 1966 to honour outstanding athletes, championship teams and sports personalities. Its present location, the old land titles building, is protected as a heritage site by the province. The hall features pictures and information on the inducted individuals and teams, and a collection of artifacts, trophies and memorabilia related to the history of sport in the province. It is open to the public 7 days a week. MARGARET J. SANDISON

Saskatchewan Wheat Pool, Canada's largest grain-handling company and largest farmer-owned co-operative, began operations in 1924. Its purpose was to market WHEAT in an orderly and stable manner directly to importers, rather than through the grain exchange and futures markets (*see* GRAIN HANDLING AND MARKETING). Returns were "pooled" and divided annually among members after expenses were paid (a function assumed by the CANADIAN WHEAT BOARD upon its formation in 1935). The company originally contracted with existing elevator companies to handle grain delivered by members. In 1926 it purchased the Saskatchewan Co-operative Elevator Co and its 451 elevators and 4 terminals. By 1928-29 the Pool owned 970 elevators and was handling 158 million bu (57.5 million hL) of wheat annually. The Pool was an early casualty of the GREAT DEPRESSION, falling deeply into debt, but it emerged after WWII as the foremost organization of its kind in Canada.

In 1974 the Pool operated 1000 country elevators as well as export terminals in Thunder Bay and one in Vancouver, but the number of elevators has been progressively reduced (to about 600 in 1984 and a target of 425 in 1987). It has diversified into virtually every agricultural activity, including fertilizer, oilseed processing, margarine, salad oil and livestock. It also publishes the *West-*

Population: 177 641 (1986c), 154 217 (1981c A); 200 665 (1986 CMA) 175 058 (1981 ACMA)

Rate of Increase (1981-86): (City) 15.2%; (CMA) 14.6%

Rank in Canada: Seventeenth (by CMA)

Date of Incorporation: 1906

Land Area: 132.2 km² (CMA); 4749.35 km²

Elevation: 515 m

Climate: Average daily temp, July 18.7°C, Jan -18.8°C; Yearly precip 345.0 mm; Hours of sunshine 2449.7 per year

Looking north at the downtown core of Saskatoon, showing 6 of the 7 bridges that span the South Saskatchewan R (*courtesy Saskatoon City Hall/photo by Ron Garnett*).

ern Producer newspaper (circulation 132 625) and has published books since 1954 under the name Western Producer Prairie Books. Equally important are the Pool's activities in public policy. Its elected officials lobby all levels of government for policies favourable to agriculture and are involved in international farm-policy discussions. The Pool ranked 50th among Canadian corporations (1986) with sales of $1.7 billion; it employed 3513 and was wholly owned by its 70 000 farmer members. JAMES MARSH

Saskatoon, largest city in Saskatchewan, is situated in rolling parklands on the banks of the

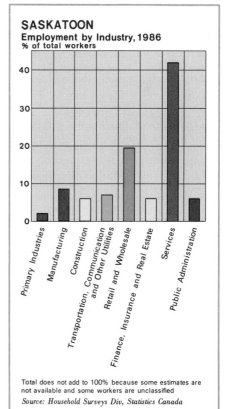

SASKATOON
Employment by Industry, 1986
% of total workers

Total does not add to 100% because some estimates are not available and some workers are unclassified

Source: Household Surveys Div, Statistics Canada

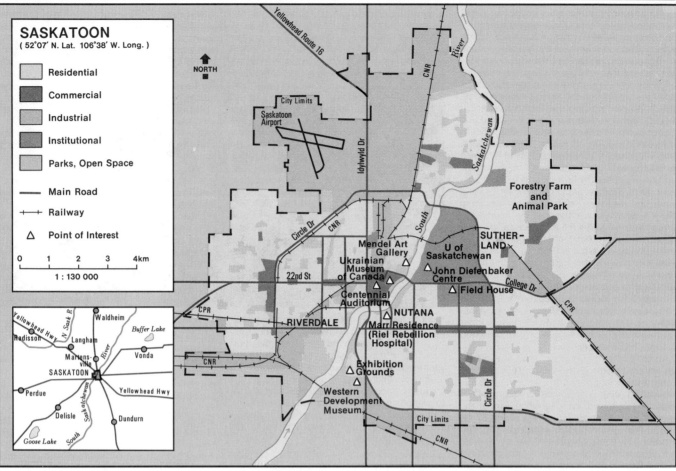

SASKATOON
(52°07' N. Lat. 106°38' W. Long.)

Residential

Commercial

Industrial

Institutional

Parks, Open Space

Main Road

Railway

△ Point of Interest

0   1   2   3   4km

1 : 130 000

northward-flowing S SASKATCHEWAN R, 235 km (by air) NW of REGINA. It serves as regional centre for the northern prairies and for central and northern Saskatchewan.

Settlement The 2 Gowen sites give evidence that hunting tribes were here 6000 years ago. Stratified settlement sites at Tipperary Cr indicate regular winter habitation by Indians. The region was occupied primarily by Cree and Métis, with Sioux at Moose Woods. White settlement began when the area was chosen for a TEMPERANCE colony by a Toronto society. John Lake's survey party selected an E bank site 1882, and the first settlers arrived 1883.

Development Construction of a railway from Regina in 1890 caused the commercial centre to shift to the flatter W bank. The new community appropriated the name Saskatoon (from the Cree word for a local red berry), while the original settlement became Nutana. A third, Riverdale, arose S of the railway yards. All 3 incorporated as villages (1901-05) and in 1906 they combined to form the city of Saskatoon. During the ensuing 7 years, Saskatoon became a hub of western Canada's railway network and underwent a boom, becoming a major distributive centre and, in 1909, gaining the provincial university. Inflated land values and overambitious land-subdivision schemes resulted, and a trade recession (1913) brought a "bust." Not until 1919 did growth recommence, to be stunted anew by the Depression years. Only after WWII did significant development resume. During the 1950s, a healthy farm economy and population shift from the countryside made Saskatoon one of Canada's fastest-growing cities. The opening of POTASH mines nearby and of uranium mines in northern Saskatchewan meant continuing expansion during the 1960s and 1970s. Development slowed for a while as world demand for uranium declined, then took off again as high-tech industry moved in during the 1980s.

Cityscape Located on glacial deposits within the meander belt of a large river, Saskatoon has an attractively variable topography, with oxbow lakes (Moon and Pike) providing recreational opportunities close by. The river is spanned by 7 bridges, including the Traffic Bridge (1907) and the 42nd-Street Bridge, which completes a ring road. Prominent on the low W bank are the château-style Bessborough Hotel, St John's Anglican and St Paul's Roman Catholic cathedrals and Knox United Church. Attractive residences and university buildings line the higher E bank. Notable buildings from the boom period include the land titles office and CPR station; among new structures are the Centennial Auditorium and Provincial Building.

The city acquired a land bank through forfeiture of holdings during 2 depressions. Development is under tight control, reinforced by agreements with the surrounding RM of Corman Park. Citizen action during the early 1970s brought establishment of the Meewasin Valley Authority to conserve the riverbank.

Population Initially, settlement was from eastern Canada and the British Isles, but later immigrants came from most parts of Europe, notably Ukraine and Scandinavia. Changing agricultural practices caused a progressive population shift from prairie farms into the city; and boundary expansion, notably the incorporation of the town of Sutherland (1956), also added citizens. Recent features are rapid growth in the native Indian population and the arrival of East Indians, Filipinos, Vietnamese and Chileans.

Economy and Labour Force Saskatoon is a centre for health and education services, commercial banking, food processing, mining and manufacturing, and research. The largest employers are the university, the city and Intercontinental Packers Ltd.

Transportation The CNR and CPR retain freight yards here and VIA Rail operates minimal passenger services. The airport handles national and international flights. Local bus services are operated by the city, long-distance service by Saskatchewan Transportation Co.

Government and Politics The city charter (1906) specified a commission government, the city's officers being the mayor and at least one appointed commissioner. The strong rule of Commissioner C.J. Yorath (1913-21) gave permanency to this system, much criticized initially. In early aldermanic elections, men voted in each ward where they owned property. The ward system was abolished and female suffrage was introduced in 1920. The ward system was reintroduced by the province in 1973, though not approved by voters until 1979. At present, each of 10 wards elects one alderman. The city has 3 standing committees of aldermen, plus several others, notably the Municipal Planning Commission, which include citizens; these are advisory to council and have no separate authority. Relations between the civic and provincial governments are defined by the Urban Municipalities Act (1984). Their fiscal relationships include extensive revenue sharing and unconditional grants.

Cultural Life The UNIVERSITY OF SASKATCHEWAN and its associated religious colleges, Kelsey Institute, Saskatoon Region Community College and the Co-operative College of Canada, are the city's key educational institutions. Important also are the Ukrainian Museum of Canada, Western Development Museum, Mendel Art Gallery and John G. Diefenbaker Centre. There is a daily newspaper (*Star-Phoenix*) and a weekly agricultural paper (*Western Producer*), 3 TV and 5 radio stations and a publishing house (Western Producer Prairie Books). Ethnic organizations operate through the Saskatoon Multicultural Council. The Yevshan Ukrainian Folk-Ballet is the most prominent among numerous dance groups; there are theatres, a symphony orchestra, an opera group and a jazz society. Sports facilities include the Arena, the Field House, Gordie Howe Park and the Harry Bailey Aquatic Centre.

A. MARGARET SARJEANT AND WILLIAM A.S. SARJEANT

Reading: S.P. Clubb, *Saskatoon: The Serenity and the Surge* (1966); W.P. Delainey, J.H. Duerkop and William A.S. Sarjeant, *Saskatoon: A Century in Pictures* (1982); Delainey and Sarjeant, *Saskatoon: The Growth of A City* (1975); D. Kerr and S. Hanson, *Saskatoon: The First Half-Century* (1982); G. McConnell, *Saskatoon: Hub City of the West* (1983).

Saskatoon Berry, *see* BERRIES, WILD.

Sasquatch [Salish, "wild man" or "hairy man"], the name of the mysterious, apelike creature said to inhabit the remoter regions of the Pacific Northwest. In northern California the giant creature is called "Big Foot." Evidence for the existence of the Sasquatch in BC and Alberta is based on references in Indian legend and myth, in passages from journals kept by early travellers and on modern sightings.   JOHN ROBERT COLOMBO

Satellite, Artificial The Space Age was inaugurated in 1957 by the launching of Sputnik 1; in 1962 Alouette 1 signalled Canada's entry into this era. Canada's early interest in the use of space is not accidental. The country's vast area and sparse population militate against the establishment of viable COMMUNICATIONS systems using traditional terrestrial techniques (eg, telephone lines, microwave systems). Communications satellites are not distance sensitive and, from a single location, can provide service over large areas. Recognition of this potential led to the establishment in 1969 of Telesat Canada as a purveyor of satellite communications on a viable commercial basis. Since then, 9 Anik-series satellites have been launched.

Canada is endowed with generous natural resources, many of them located in remote areas. Identification, exploitation and management of these resources (eg, mineral deposits, petroleum, forests, agricultural lands) can be greatly assisted by resource satellites, eg, the US Landsat series which Canada has used since 1972 and the Radarsat system which the Canadian government approved in June 1987 at a cost of $725 million over a 10-year period. Radarsat will be a Canadian-led international joint project to design, construct and operate Canada's first Earth observation satellite system. The satellite is scheduled to be launched in 1994 and is to operate for 5 years. WEATHER satellites also provide increasingly reliable information upon which many activities (including resource exploration) depend. Because of its size and position, Canada is an area where weather systems affecting much of the planet are generated and developed. It is thus important that Canada participate in developing weather-information systems. Since 1963 Canada has been receiving and analysing data from the American NOAA and GOES satellites.

Briefly defined, a satellite is a body that revolves about another; thus, the MOON is a satellite of Earth; Earth, a satellite of the SUN. Objects which are lofted into space by man and which continue to revolve around Earth or another planet are referred to as "artificial" or "manmade" satellites. The track repeatedly described by the satellite is called its orbit. Orbits can be relatively low, with an altitude of 200-300 nautical miles and an orbit period of 90-100 minutes for one revolution (eg, those of early US manned flights or the current Shuttle). The forces that keep a satellite aloft can be likened to those affecting an object twirled around at the end of a string: the object's velocity creates a force which tends to propel it away from the source of its initial impulse; the string, like gravity, tends to draw it back

towards the source; the 2 forces create a balance which causes the object to remain in a given trajectory (orbit).

The time required for one revolution increases with the height of the orbit. Eventually, an orbital altitude is found at which the satellite takes exactly 24 hours per revolution. Then, if the satellite is moving in the same direction as Earth's rotation and if it remains above the equator (ie, its orbital plane is the same as that of Earth), it will appear to remain immobile above a certain spot on the equator and will be referred to as a geosynchronous or stationary satellite. Most communications satellites are stationary. Such a satellite may be used without requiring constant changes in the pointing of the user's antenna. One disadvantage, a minor one in many applications, is the lack of coverage over the poles. Polar coverage can be improved by using satellites with orbits inclined relative to the equator; at 90° inclination a polar orbit is described. Such orbits are not only useful in providing polar coverage but, since the satellites are in motion relative to Earth's surface, they will travel, through successive orbits, over Earth's entire surface. These moving satellites are thus useful for the REMOTE SENSING of natural resources, ice and ocean conditions, etc, but they require highly sophisticated antenna systems on the ground to locate and follow them.

The useful lifetime of a satellite can range from a few months to 7-8 years or more. This rarely depends on the quality of the mission-related equipment; usually, it is limited by the amount of fuel on board or, in some cases, by degradation of solar cells or loss in battery capacity. Fuel is expended to change or correct orbit or to change the attitude (ie, direction) of the satellite relative to the Earth or the sun, etc. Even nominally "stationary" satellites can move from their initial positions under the influence of sun, moon, planets, particle bombardment, etc. Corrections are made by activating small jets or nozzles.

The most advanced technologies contribute to the success of today's relatively sophisticated space systems, and yet the Space Age is in its infancy. Many novel and ambitious concepts, some still found only in the pages of science fiction, are attracting the attention of the scientific community and of industry and social scientists. The 1990s will probably see the realization of large space stations and improved means of transport between Earth and space.   J.R. MARCHAND

Satellite Communications In 1945 Arthur C. Clarke proposed that a man-made Earth SATELLITE could be used for communication by radio microwaves between distant locations on Earth. The satellite would be positioned in space at an altitude of about 35 900 km so that its speed of revolution around the Earth would be the same as the speed of the Earth's rotation. This synchronous satellite would always appear in the same place in the sky. It would be in geostationary orbit.

Characteristics A typical satellite consists of a number of repeaters (transponders), each of which provides a large capacity communication channel. Each transponder has a receiver tuned to a frequency channel that has been allocated for uplink communication signals from Earth to the satellite; a frequency shifter to lower the received signals to a downlink frequency; and a power amplifier to transmit signals back to Earth. The communication capacity of a satellite is determined by the number of transponder channels and the volume of communication that can be transmitted on each channel. Although this varies from one type of satellite to another, the most commonly used satellite in 1984 has 12 transponders. Each can carry a colour TV signal or at least 1200 telephone voice signals in one direc-

tion. Each new generation of satellites tends to have increased communication capability.

The transmitting and receiving stations on Earth (earth stations) range in size from sophisticated, expensive stations that send and receive all types of communication signals to relatively simple and less costly stations (dish-shaped TV antennas) used only to receive television signals. The size and cost of Earth stations depend upon the power built into the satellite, as well as the frequencies used. The stronger the signal from the satellite, the smaller and less costly the receiving station. Direct Broadcast Satellites (DBS) are designed specifically to minimize size and cost.

Satellites have significant advantages over other modes of transmission such as cable and landline microwave for certain kinds of communication. The cost of transmission is independent of geographical terrain or distance, as long as both sender and receiver are within line of sight of the satellite (about one-third of the Earth's surface). Communication links can be extended to remote areas that could not otherwise be reached. Satellites are less costly for transmission over extremely long distances – especially for relatively small volumes of communication. A communication signal can be sent to any number of reception points simultaneously, making satellites ideal for television and other forms of point-to-multipoint communication. Satellites are also extremely flexible because the sending and receiving points can be changed on short notice to meet changes in demand. Although satellites are used for voice communication, they are considered to be qualitatively inferior to land-line transmission systems because of the delay (almost 0.3 second) required for the signal to travel to the satellite and return to Earth. Echoes of a speaker's voice are heard 0.6 second after speaking. When echo suppressors are used they sometimes cause the speech of the other party to be clipped.

History The earliest satellite communication experiments were sponsored by the US government. Under project SCORE (Signal Communication by Orbiting Relay Equipment), the first communication satellite was launched by the National Aeronautics and Space Administration (NASA) on 18 Dec 1958 and worked for 13 days. Echo 1, launched 12 Aug 1960, was a passive satellite that simply reflected signals sent from ground transmitters back to Earth. Telstar, launched 10 July 1962, was the first active satellite with a microwave receiver and transmitter. The first synchronous satellite, Syncom 1, was launched on 14 Feb 1963; it failed after a few days and was followed by a more successful version, Syncom 2, on July 26. During this period, the USSR also began a program of satellite experimentation, soon followed by Canada.

The US Congress passed the Communication Satellite Act in 1962, creating the Comsat Corporation with a monopoly on US international satellite communication. An International Satellite Organization (Intelsat) was created in Aug 1964 when 11 Western countries agreed to establish a global satellite communication system. By the early 1980s more than 100 countries were members of Intelsat. It had earth stations in about 150 countries and had successfully launched 24 satellites. (Not all of these satellites continue to be used, since the average useful life of a communication satellite is about 8-10 years.)

Within the Soviet bloc, satellite communication is managed by an organization called Intersputnik. By 1980 the Soviets had launched 14 synchronous satellites (Stationar) and at least 75 Molniya satellites, placed in elliptical orbits to serve the Far North, where synchronous satellites would be below the horizon.

Canadian Developments On 29 Sept 1962 Canada's first satellite was launched into orbit by NASA, making Canada the third nation in space. Alouette 1 was designed and built by the Defence Research and Telecommunications Establishment (now the Communications Research Centre), and was used for scientific experiments in the ionosphere. From 1963 to 1969 Canada participated in a joint experimental program with the US called ISIS (International Satellites for Ionospheric Studies). A major objective of this program was to transfer the skills and knowledge developed by government scientists and technicians in the early phase of space communication activity to private industry. RCA Victor, DE HAVILLAND AIRCRAFT and Spar Aerospace were the major companies participating (*see* SPACE TECHNOLOGY).

By 1967 the prime Canadian objective had shifted from scientific experimentation to applications, with emphasis on domestic TELECOMMUNICATIONS and surveys of natural resources. In 1969 Parliament created Telesat Canada to operate a domestic commercial satellite system. Anik A-1 was launched in Nov 1972, followed by Anik A-2 in April 1973, when Canada became the first country to employ satellites for domestic COMMUNICATIONS. A third satellite, Anik A-3, was launched in May 1975. The Anik A system used satellites originally developed in the US for the Intelsat IV program. Two Canadian companies, Spar Aerospace and Northern Telecom, were subcontractors. Each satellite had 12 transponder channels in the 6/4 GHz band. Over 100 earth stations were installed across Canada.

An experimental communication satellite system, the Communications Technology Satellite (CTS), renamed Hermes, was developed parallel to the commercial system. The main objective was the opening up of the higher radio frequency 14/12 GHz band that had been allocated for the exclusive use of space communication services. However, the higher frequencies required new technical systems and components, and higher satellite power levels to compensate for the expected increase in signal attenuation, caused primarily by rainfall. The development of new components and the increased weight made necessary by higher power levels meant that major expenditures would have to be incurred on an unproven satellite. Since private firms were unwilling to take these risks, the federal government undertook the project. The Hermes program (1970-80) was a Canada-US collaborative effort: the Dept of Communications was responsible for the design, construction and operation of the spacecraft; NASA provided the launching and other specialized space facilities, and developed a high-power transmitting tube. Use of the satellite was shared equally. The European Space Research Organization (ESRO) joined the program in 1972.

Hermes was launched on 17 Jan 1976, the most powerful communications satellite at that time and the first to operate in the 14/12 GHz band. The exclusive use of the frequency band and the higher power of the transponders made possible the use of parabolic (dish) antennas as small as 0.6 m in diameter, especially suited for direct broadcasting of television signals to homes. The Hermes program also included experiments in tele-health, tele-education, community communications, delivery of administrative services, and scientific applications. In addition to experiments conducted over Canada and the US, Hermes was used to demonstrate direct broadcasting in Peru, Australia, and Papua New Guinea. The latter 2 demonstrations were conducted after moving the satellite to a different orbital position over the Pacific. New components developed in government laboratories, such as Field Effect Transistor amplifiers, were

Hermes communications satellite (*courtesy Communications Research Centre/Dept of Communications*).

subsequently transferred to private industry and are now commonplace in commercial satellites. Major Canadian contractors for Hermes included Spar Aerospace, RCA Ltd, and SED Systems.

NASA launched Anik B for Telesat Canada in Dec 1978. It had 12 commercial radio frequency channels in the 6/4 GHz band and 4 experimental channels in the 14/12 GHz band. The experimental channels were leased to the Dept of Communications for field trials continuing from the Hermes program. Anik C-3 was placed in orbit in Nov 1982 by the US space shuttle *Columbia*. It has 16 channels, operates in the 14/12 GHz band, and represents a major step toward direct satellite broadcasting to small, rooftop receiving antenna dishes. A second satellite in the same series, Anik C-2, was launched in June 1983 and a third, Anik C-3 was launched in Dec 1985. These new satellites will operate with 4 regional beams across Canada, producing television signals of sufficient strength that they can be received on smaller (1.2-1.8 m) rooftop receiving dishes. A fourth generation of satellites was then planned. Anik D-1 was launched on 26 Aug 1982, replacing the aging Anik A and B satellites. Anik D-2 was placed in orbit by the US space shuttle *Discovery* in Nov 1984. The next series of commercial communications satellites, Anik E, is being planned for launch in the 1990s.

With the completion of the Hermes program, government development activity has focused on the Remote Manipulator System (RMS) or the CANADARM for use in the American Space Shuttle Program. The armlike device was designed to deploy and retrieve objects in space and would be carried in the US space shuttle cargo bay. The Canadian government funded the development of the SRMS by an industrial team led by Spar Aerospace Ltd. In return, NASA agreed to procure production systems for the shuttle fleet from Canada. The Canadarm was successfully tested for the first time in 1981 on the US space shuttle *Columbia*. Current experimentation is also directed toward the use of satellites for mobile communications. This is made difficult because of the problem of placing satellite microwave antennas on moving vehicles. The first commercial mobile satellite service was to ships at sea. The Marisat system was established in 1976, and the International Maritime Satellite Organization (INMARSAT) in 1979. Canada, with several other countries including the US,

France and the Soviet Union, participates in the SARSAT program directed to use satellite technology for locating aircraft and ships in distress. Spar Aerospace is designing and building specialized transponders for 3 US Tiros weather satellites under this program. By the 1990s Canada expects to have completed its mobile MSAT, which will further reduce the size of satellite receiving dishes.

Long-term Implications Despite many technical accomplishments, satellites have not provided the benefits to Canadians that were anticipated. Telesat has become a member of Telecom Canada, the consortium of Canadian telephone companies, and has severely restricted access to its system (*see* TELEPHONES). Telesat's public stock shares were never issued, leaving dominant control of Telesat with the telephone companies. A high proportion of satellite capacity has gone unused. The 1984 satellite was launched into a "parking orbit" because Telesat will have no use for it, at least for several years. Telecommunication service to the North has improved, but many locations do not have satellite service. Television service to the North has expanded by providing northerners with access to television programs of southern Canadian and US stations, but little has been done to promote communication from or between northern communities, or in the languages of native Canadians.

Similarly, satellites, especially direct broadcast satellites, have increased dramatically the number of US television signals that Canadians can receive. But this has had detrimental effects on the Canadian television and FILM production industries. In 1980, for entertainment/drama programs, only 4% of the programs available were Canadian (*see* TELEVISION PROGRAMMING). Satellites have promoted a wider choice of TV programs for Canadians, but they have not promoted increased opportunities for Canadian expression through its mass media.

Many countries that do not yet have satellites are concerned that the new technology might be detrimental to both sovereignty and the preservation of national cultures. The expansion of satellite systems in the future will be accompanied by discussion at both national and international levels directed to methods of obtaining the benefits of satellites while avoiding the potential disadvantages. WILLIAM H. MELODY

Reading: Dept of Communications, *Direct-to-Home Satellite Broadcasting for Canada* (1983) and *The Canadian Space Program: Five Year Plan C80181-84185* (1980); Science Council of Canada, *A Space Program for Canada*, Report No 1 (1967).

Saturday Night began its life as *Toronto Saturday Night* in 1887 under the editorship of E.E. Sheppard. It was initially published weekly in newspaper format, and literally went on sale at 6 PM Saturday. There was a dedicated snobbishness about the magazine as it sought readers among Toronto's high society, but as the desire for circulation and ADVERTISING grew, the snobbishness turned toward a critical and opinionated review of life with a heavy Canadian content. During the 1920s, most notably when Hector Charlesworth was editor, the message was optimism and conservatism, a faithful reflection of the Canadian mood. The magazine first became a genuine critical success when B.K. SANDWELL became editor in 1932. Sandwell, who stayed at the helm until 1951, was a man of strong interests, most notably in civil libertarian questions, and he made *Saturday Night* a force. He found good writers on politics and the arts, gave space to profiles of Canadian leaders in government and the arts, and published splendid photographic portraits. By the late 1930s *Saturday Night* had built its advertising lineage to the third largest in N America.

Once Sandwell was gone, *Saturday Night* entered a long decline. Arnold Edinborough was editor for most of the decade after 1958, but it was not until Robert FULFORD became editor in 1968 that *Saturday Night* began to find its critical niche. Under Fulford's lead, the magazine gave ample space to the arts (notably Fulford's film reviews published under the pseudonym of Marshall Delaney) and presented long and sometimes brilliant political reportage, often by Christina McCall. Over the years, *Saturday Night* has featured short stories and poems. It was here that authors such as Dennis LEE and Margaret ATWOOD received their first national exposure.

There were serious financial problems through the 1970s, resolved in 1979 when the Webster family – led by Norman Webster, now editor of the *Globe and Mail* – bought the magazine and provided its first secure backing since the early 1950s. In 1987 financier Conrad BLACK bought *Saturday Night*. Fulford resigned, to be replaced by John FRASER of the *Globe and Mail*. The life of a general magazine is perilous at best in Canada, but in 1987 *Saturday Night* celebrated its centenary, the longest surviving magazine in the country. J.L. GRANATSTEIN

Sault Ste Marie, Ont, City, seat of Algoma Dist, pop 80 905 (1986c), 82 687 (1981c), popularly called the "Soo," inc as town 1887 and city 1912, located adjacent to the rapids of the ST MARY'S R between Lks SUPERIOR and HURON and across the river from the American settlement of the same name. The Algonquian tribes who originally occupied the site called it Bawating ("place of the rapids") and valued it for its control of the upper Great Lks water routes and as a source of abundant whitefish and maple sugar. Étienne BRÛLÉ was probably the first European to visit the area (1622). The site is called Sault (Fr, "falls") de Gaston on Champlain's map of 1632. It became Ste-Marie du Sault when a Jesuit mission was established 1668. The NORTH WEST CO built a post here 1783, developed the fishery as a major food source for the fur trade and dug the first canal past the rapids in 1798. Charles Ermatinger's house, built 1814-23, the oldest stone house in Canada W of Toronto, survives from that period. The original canal was destroyed in the WAR OF 1812, but lake and ocean shipping, with cargoes of grain and iron ore, now bypasses the rapids through a Canadian canal, opened in 1895, and 4 American locks that regularly handle more traffic than any comparable system in the world.

Industrial development was initiated by American-born businessman Francis CLERGUE who built an electric-power plant and pulp mill, the Algoma Steel Co (1900) and the Algoma Central Ry (1899-1914), which runs to iron-ore reserves nearby. Clergue went into bankruptcy and the Ontario government was forced to step in and rescue some of the businesses. Algoma Steel Co is still the major economic force in the area, employing at peak some 9000 workers. The Soo is Canada's second-largest steel producer after Hamilton, Ont. The forests of the Algoma region also support 2 pulp-and-paper companies in the city. The Ontario Air Service, centered here, maintains the world's largest fleet of planes for fighting forest fires. In its position as a focal point for E-W transportation routes, Sault Ste Marie has become an important regional centre for federal and provincial services, recreation and tourism and post-secondary education.
DAVID D. KEMP

Saumur v City of Québec The Supreme Court, by a 5-4 majority, upheld (1953) the province of Québec's power, challenged by JEHOVAH'S WITNESS Laurier Saumur, to authorize municipalities to prohibit distribution, without police permission, of all publications in the streets. But one majority judge held that, by an Act guaranteeing "free exercise and enjoyment of Religious Profession and Worship," the Québec legislature had precluded application of such bylaws to religious publications; on narrow grounds, the court barred Québec City's interference with Witnesses' pamphleteering, which had been characterized by harsh attacks on Roman Catholicism. John DIEFENBAKER supported the Witnesses' petition for a Bill of Rights, which became the Canadian Bill of Rights (1960). STEPHEN A. SCOTT

Saunders, Albert Charles, lawyer, politician, judge, premier of PEI (b at Summerside, PEI 12 Oct 1874; d there 18 Oct 1943). Saunders, having completed 4 terms as mayor of Summerside, became the Liberal Party leader in 1923, winning the 1927 election by supporting continuing liquor prohibition. In 1931 he became a provincial Supreme Court judge. LEONARD CUSACK

Saunders, Sir Charles Edward, public servant, plant breeder (b at London, Ont 2 Feb 1867; d at Toronto 25 July 1937), third son of William SAUNDERS. He selected, tested and introduced MARQUIS WHEAT to the Canadian West, the foundation for the large commercial production of high-quality bread wheat in Canada. Like his 4 brothers, Charles assisted his father in his many varied interests of plant hybridization, entomology and music. Charles was the least robust of them all but perhaps had the highest standards. Educated at U of T and Johns Hopkins U, he was a professor of chemistry at Central U, Ky, in 1892-93 and then devoted 1894-1903 to the study of music and teaching of voice. In 1903 his father, recognizing his meticulous standards and perseverence, appointed him to the Experimental Farms Service as experimentalist. (The title became cerealist in 1905 and Dominion cerealist in 1910.)

Saunders immediately applied scientific methods to his new task and spent summers selecting individual heads of wheat from breeding material that previously had been selected in mass. From a cross of Hard Red Calcutta by RED FIFE, made in 1892 by his brother A.P. Saunders, a new variety, Markham, resulted. Markham did not produce uniform offspring, however, even though many plants had desirable characteristics. Saunders carefully selected individual heads from early plants that had stiff straw. He emphasized that seed from each plant was grown separately with no mixing of strains. Selection was rigorous, only the top lines being kept. He determined which lines had strong gluten by chewing a sample of

Sir Charles Edward Saunders, the plant breeder who developed Marquis wheat (*courtesy National Archives of Canada/C-9071*).

kernels, and he introduced the baking of small loaves to measure volume. The best strain was named Marquis. In 1907 all surplus seed was sent to Indian Head, Sask, for further testing.

According to Saunders' annual reports, the response of Marquis to Saskatchewan conditions was phenomenal. It was a week earlier than Red Fife, produced high yields and made excellent bread. Marquis remains the standard for bread making. By 1909 sufficient seed had been produced to permit its distribution to 407 farmers. The following year 2112 farmers received samples. Wheat could now be grown confidently in Saskatchewan and Alberta, where Red Fife frequently matured too late and was damaged by frost. By 1920, 90% of the wheat grown in western Canada was Marquis and a large acreage was grown in the US. Marquis was the variety that matured early, thus avoiding damage from frost. It yielded as well as, or better than, any other early variety. It produced a "strong" flour and therefore was in demand by the millers and bakers of the world. Marquis was the variety that made Canada famous for its hard red spring wheat and annually produced millions of dollars in export revenue for Canadian farmers and Canada. Saunders also applied his single-line selection methods to barley, oats, peas, beans and flax and introduced several new excellent varieties of each kind of crop.

In 1922, after 19 years as a plant breeder, Saunders suffered a physical breakdown and resigned his position. He went to Paris where he studied French literature at the Sorbonne for 3 years. He returned to Ottawa but moved to Toronto in 1928. He was knighted in 1934. He continued to lecture on both Marquis wheat and the French language. Music was his major consolation until his death. T.H. ANSTEY

Saunders, John, judge and politician (b at Virginia Beach, Virginia 1 June 1754; d at Fredericton, NB 24 May 1834). Saunders served with distinction in the Queen's Rangers during the American Revolutionary War, and later studied law in England. Appointed a judge of the Supreme Court of New Brunswick in 1790, he became, in 1791, the only member of that body to hold a seat in the House of Assembly. In 1793 he was appointed a member of the Council and in 1822 became chief justice, a position he held until his death. He supported the Church of England, the imperial connection and the control of authority by the loyalist elite, and he tried to keep alive the dream of establishing a landed aristocracy in the province, becoming one of the largest landowners in the province. Although Saunders remained firmly opposed to the new political and social order emerging in New Brunswick, he attempted to do his duty until the day he died.

WILLIAM A. SPRAY

Saunders, Margaret Marshall, writer (b at Milton, NS 13 Apr 1861; d at Toronto 15 Feb 1947). She moved with her family to Halifax at age 6. At 15 she attended boarding school in Edinburgh, then studied French at Orléans. On her return home she taught school for a short time. Her first novel, a romance, *My Spanish Sailor,* was published in 1889. She wrote *Beautiful Joe* (1894), the story of an abused dog, for an American Humane Soc competition. It won first prize and became a best-seller, was translated into more than 14 languages and was reportedly the first Canadian book to sell more than a million copies. Saunders travelled widely in the US, setting her children's stories of domestic animals and birds in the locales she visited. Her romantic novels include *Esther de Warren* (1927), her own favourite, based on her experiences in Scotland. In 1914 she moved to Toronto. In the 1920s she and her sister toured Canada and the US giving illustrated lectures. A woman of charm and humour, she had an ever-growing interest in humanitarian concerns (especially regarding children) and the treatment of animals. Her stories of pets, while sentimental and didactic, are gracefully written and entertaining.

LORRAINE MCMULLEN

Saunders, William, druggist, naturalist, agriculturalist (b at Crediton, Eng 16 June 1836; d at London, Ont 13 Sept 1914). Saunders established the Experimental Farms Service (now Research Branch) of the federal Dept of AGRICULTURE. He moved with his family from England to Canada in 1848 and apprenticed as a druggist, opening his own store in 1855. His concern about insects attacking pharmaceutical plants led him to help found the Entomological Soc of Canada in 1863. An avid gardener and orchardist, he introduced many new varieties of fruit. In 1874 he was made a fellow of the American Assn for the Advancement of Science; he was president of the Ontario College of Pharmacy 1879-82, as well as of the Huron and Erie Mortgage Co; in 1881 he became a fellow of the RSC; and in 1882 he was president of the Fruit Growers' Assn of Ontario. In 1886 Parliament passed legislation establishing the Dominion Experimental Farms and Stations, partly based on Saunders's report of his 1885 investigation of US stations, and he was appointed director. He pursued his new task with vigour, personally selecting sites for each of the original 5 farms, choosing staff and continuing his interests in cereal breeding, horticulture and forestry. He commenced the wheat-breeding program that resulted in his son Sir Charles Edward SAUNDERS's development of MARQUIS, the variety that opened the Canadian West. He received honorary degrees from Queen's and U of T; his many technical writings are in Dept of Agriculture libraries.

T.H. ANSTEY

Sauvé, Jeanne-Mathilde, née Benoît, journalist, politician, governor general of Canada (b at Prud'homme, Sask 26 Apr 1922). She studied at Collège Notre-Dame-du-Rosaire in Ottawa, U d'Ottawa and U de Paris. She was national president of the Young Catholic Students Group 1942-47. She married Maurice SAUVÉ in 1948 and began a brilliant career as a free-lance journalist in print, radio and television. Her participation in

Jeanne Sauvé, the first woman in Canada to be appointed governor general (*courtesy Canapress Photo Service*).

discussions of political and social issues, her role in the improvement in the status of women and her commitment in a variety of domains all contributed to the development of ideas and the evolution of Canadian society. Elected as an MP from Montréal in 1972, she was re-elected in 1974, 1979 and 1980. She was the first female French Canadian Cabinet member, minister of state for science and technology, minister of the environment and of communications; it was largely because of initiatives taken during her tenure that Canada joined the world leaders in advanced technologies. The first female Speaker of the House of Commons (14 Apr 1980), she won respect through a combination of competence and authority. In less than 3 years, she completely reformed the administration of the House. The first female governor general of Canada (14 May 1984), she proceeded to put in place a management system suitable to modern needs. Thanks to her prestige and leadership, she commands respect for her attitude, opinions and pronouncements on major domestic and foreign issues of the day. As head of state, she has been a rallying point for her compatriots and has become a leading example of Canadian unity.

JEAN-NOËL TREMBLAY

Sauvé, Joseph-Mignault-Paul, premier of Québec (b at St-Benoît, Qué 24 Mar 1907; d at St-Eustache, Qué 2 Jan 1960). Though he was premier for only a short time, Sept 1959 to his death, he inaugurated a period of major political and social change for Québec. A member of the reserve from 1931 he served overseas during WWII, and was second-in-command of the Fusiliers de Mont-Royal during the Normandy landing. Promoted brigadier in 1947 he was also able to maintain an active political career throughout. Elected Conservative member of the Québec legislature for Deux-Montagnes during the 1930 by-elections, he was defeated in 1935, but played an important role in the creation of the UNION NATIONALE Party and was repeatedly elected for that party from 1936 to 1956. He was chosen successor to Maurice DUPLESSIS and quickly served notice that things would not be the same by pronouncing a single word that became famous throughout Québec: *Désormais* ("henceforth"). Sauvé's "hundred days" are seen as the start of the QUIET REVOLUTION because they brought new life and settled several matters that were "on hold," including hospital insurance and university subsidies.

DANIEL LATOUCHE

Sauvé, Maurice, economist, politician, businessman (b at Montréal 20 Sept 1923). Maurice Sauvé received his PhD from U de Paris in 1952

and returned to Montréal to work for the Canadian and Catholic Confederation of Labour. A Liberal, he was closely associated with the construction of the economic base for Québec's QUIET REVOLUTION. In 1962 he was elected to the House of Commons and served as minister of forestry and rural development 1964-68. Leaving politics for business, he joined Consolidated-Bathurst Inc and held a number of directorships. In 1985 he was named chancellor of U d'Ottawa. He is married to Gov Gen Jeanne SAUVÉ.

HARRIET GORHAM

Savage, Alfred, veterinarian, teacher, researcher (b at Montréal 10 Aug 1889; d at Winnipeg 14 Jan 1970). After serving in the Canadian Army Veterinary Corps 1915-19, he became professor of animal pathology at U Man 1921-64. He was also head of the dept of animal pathology and bacteriology 1930-45 and dean of agriculture 1933-37, and was animal pathologist for the Manitoba Dept of Agriculture 1937-57. Savage conducted early investigations of semen evaluation and agglutination tests for brucellosis, and developed surgical instruments and improved techniques for anesthesia. He was an outstanding lecturer and teacher, and was influential in the formation of the Canadian Veterinary Medical Assn, of which he was president 1951-52.

R.G. THOMSON

Savage, Anne Douglas, painter (b at Montréal 27 July 1896; d there 25 Mar 1971). Best known during her lifetime as a pioneer in teaching children's art along progressive lines, Anne Savage's early paintings were initially strongly influenced by the GROUP OF SEVEN. Later her work showed a lyrical quality of its own, characterized by muted colour, sound rhythm and a late-in-life foray into abstraction. Trained by William BRYMNER, she was a member of the Beaver Hall Hill group and president of the Canadian Group of Painters (1949, 1960). Savage taught at Baron Byng High School 1922-48 and had a far-reaching influence on Montréal artists of the next generation.

ANNE MCDOUGALL

Savard, Félix-Antoine, priest, writer, educator (b at Québec C 31 Aug 1896; d there 24 Aug 1982). After spending his childhood and youth in the Saguenay, Savard discovered and fell in love with the Charlevoix region, which he called Québec's metaphysical county. Ordained a priest in 1922, he started teaching the humanities. He subsequently became curate of several parishes and founding curé of St-Philippe-de-Clermont. He also was active in colonizing the Abitibi region in the 1930s. During these years of pastoral work, Savard's knowledge of humanism deepened through an intensive study of Greek, Latin and French authors of the medieval and classical periods, as well as his contemporaries Mistral, Claudel and Valéry.

In 1937 MENAUD, MAÎTRE-DRAVEUR was published and assured Savard a place among the leading authors of his time. His novel moves like an epic poem in which symbol, image and metaphor abound; its vibrant character, a truly mythical hero, is presented against the magnificent Charlevoix landscape and the cyclical unfolding of the seasons, and his suffering and tragic end provide a grave and urgent warning to future generations.

From the 1940s Savard was closely associated with Laval. Dean of its Faculty of Arts for 7 years, he taught literature and played an important role in FOLKLORE discoveries and research. He was elected to the RSC in 1945 and to the Académie canadienne-française in 1954. A masterful and often highly controversial speaker, Savard spent most of his active retirement in his chosen region of St-Joseph-de-la-Rive, in Charlevoix.

Savard devoted his life to writing. He published 3 collections, mainly composed of poetry and prose: *L'Abatis* (1943), *Le Barachois* (1959), *Le Bouscueil* (1972); 2 plays, *La Folle* (1960) and *La Dalle-des-morts* (1965), and narrative works in the form of short stories and parables, eg, *La Minuit* (1948) and *Martin et le pauvre* (1959). He also was the author of personal notebooks, journals and memoirs in which, while he promotes and defends keeping faith with sacred national traditions, he reveals himself to be an artist in words, a sculptor of form, always searching for new images and finding pleasure in the language.

But it is *Menaud, maître-draveur*, a work that took 30 years to complete, that firmly established his literary renown. It was published in 5 versions (3 of which are distinctly different). It remains a fine example of a patiently crafted, successful literary work. RÉJEAN ROBIDOUX

Savijarvi, Lisa, alpine skier (b at Bracebridge, Ont 29 Dec 1963). Off to an early start at age 14 months, she began racing at 8 and was competing nationally by 14. In a sport increasingly dominated by specialists, she excelled in all of the alpine disciplines, as demonstrated by her 1985 Canadian championship results: champion in Giant Slalom, second in Super Giant Slalom; third in Slalom and Downhill, and therefore a decisive winner of the Overall Alpine championship. Too large and powerful for international slalom competition, she concentrated on the other 3 events, achieving 10 World Cup top 10 finishes in 1986, including a win in the Super Giant Slalom (Furano), a second in the Downhill (Badgastein) and a fourth in the Giant Slalom (Banff). Despite a serious fall in a World Cup Downhill training run at Vail in March 1987, which shattered her right knee and crushed a vertebra, she hoped to return to competitive skiing in 1988. MURRAY C. SHAW

Savile, Douglas Barton Osborne, botanist, ecologist (b at Dublin, Ire 19 July 1909). After studies at McGill (1933, 1934), Savile began a career with the federal Dept of Agriculture (1936) while studying for his doctorate at U of Mich (1939). His interdisciplinary approach is shown by his wide range of publications on taxonomy, ecology and parasitology of fungi, vascular plants, birds and mammals, including expertise on bird flight. Much of his botanical research was conducted in the Arctic, with a 3-year interlude in coastal BC, eventually resulting in a monograph, *Arctic Adaptations in Plants* (1972). A 1962 monograph on collection and care of plant specimens remains popular with botanists. Savile rose through various government positions to the post of principal mycologist (1957), becoming emeritus research associate of the Biosystematics Research Inst upon "retirement" in 1975. MARTIN K. McNICHOLL

Sawchuk, Terrence Gordon, hockey goalkeeper (b at Winnipeg 28 Dec 1929; d at New York 31 May 1970). He played junior hockey in Winnipeg and Galt, Ont, turning professional at age 17 with Omaha. He joined Detroit Red Wings 1951 and won the CALDER TROPHY (best rookie). Acrobatic, fearless, he had exceptional reflexes and for the first 5 years of his career played brilliantly, winning the VÉZINA TROPHY (fewest goals allowed) 3 times, recording 56 shutouts and allowing fewer than 2 goals a game. However, physical and psychological strains shattered his health and career. He suffered nervous exhaustion, arthritis, mononucleosis, severe back injuries, innumerable cuts, as well as a collapsed lung in a car accident. He was traded from team to team and briefly regained his former glory with TORONTO MAPLE LEAFS, sharing the Vézina Trophy (1965) and leading the team to a Stanley Cup vic-

tory (1967) with spectacular play. He compiled 103 shutouts, a record unlikely to be surpassed. He died of injuries suffered accidentally in a scuffle with teammate Ron Stewart. JAMES MARSH

Sawfly, common name for members of insect order Hymenoptera, which resemble wasps and are characterized by the lack of a marked constriction between first and second abdominal segments. Common name is derived from the sawlike ovipositor used by females to slit open host plants and lay eggs. In Canada sawflies are found everywhere, especially in boreal regions. About 10 000 species are known worldwide; about 600 in Canada. Larvae and most adults are herbivorous; adults of some species feed partly on other insects. Their plant-feeding habit may make sawflies important defoliators; however, surprisingly few species are recognized as regular threats to crops and forests. Most species feed on plants of little economic importance (eg, willows, sedges, wild grasses) or show irregular population explosions of limited extent. Larvae are caterpillarlike but are distinguished from true caterpillars by having smooth prolegs (false legs) on abdomen. Most species reproduce bisexually; in some, males are rare or unknown and reproduction is by parthenogenesis (development of offspring from unfertilized eggs). HENRI GOULET

Sawmill, a common feature of 19th-century eastern Canadian landscapes. Early sawmills were simple structures: water-powered and cheaply built, usually with a single reciprocating blade and a hand-operated ratchet carriage to feed logs into the blade. They were used for cutting local logs for local consumption. Sawing was slow: a day's work might produce 500 boards. Built alongside or in conjunction with a gristmill and near a blacksmith shop, such mills might be the focus of a growing village, though work was seasonal and often part-time.

Far more significant were the fewer, larger mills cutting logs for export. Equipped with gang saws and ancillary machinery, they produced better lumber faster. After 1840 new technologies increased their size and efficiency. Circular saws were used for edging and trimming. The continuous-cutting band saw largely replaced the reciprocating gang after 1890. Rollers and log chains moved material through the mill quickly. Steam power, increasingly common after mid-century, meant faster, more continuous cutting and locational freedom. Electric lighting reduced the fire hazard of night work. In 1830 a large mill might have produced 7500 m/day; by 1850, 18 000 m was unexceptional; in 1900 the figure might be 180 000 m. Massive investment lay behind these increases, and with it came concentration in fewer locations and the pre-eminence of a relatively small number of firms. GRAEME WYNN

Saxifrage, common name for several herbaceous plants of family Saxifragaceae, primarily genus *Saxifraga* [from Lat *saxifragus,* "stonebreaking," describing the ability of roots to burrow into rocks via cracks]. Thirty-three species occur in Canada; 370 worldwide. Some Canadian species, eg, *S. aizoides* and *S. oppositifolia,* are circumpolar and are also found in Iceland, Spitsbergen, northern Europe and Siberia. Most Canadian saxifrages are found in western alpine regions from the YT to BC and Alberta. Flowers, mostly small, commonly white or yellow, are borne as terminal clusters on hairy stalks. Plants form tufted, spreading cushions, frequently giving striking patches of colour. *S. oppositifolia* (purple mountain saxifrage), forming low mats covered by cup-shaped, rosy-purple flowers, is among northernmost growing plants (found on Ellesmere I). Other well-known Canadian mem-

Virginia Saxifrage (*artwork by Claire Tremblay*).

bers of the family include genera: *Ribes* (currants and gooseberries), *Philadelphus* (mock orange), *Mitella* (mitrewort or bishop's cap) and *Tiarella* (false mitrewort or foam flower). Introduced plants include *Bergenia* (elephant ear) with deep pink flowers. PATRICK SEYMOUR

Sayer Trial Pierre Guillaume Sayer and 3 other MÉTIS in the RED RIVER COLONY were brought to trial on 17 May 1849 in the General Quarterly Court of Assiniboia on charges of violating the HUDSON'S BAY CO's charter by illegally trafficking in furs. Led by a "committee" or "council" including Louis Riel, *pére*, 300 armed Métis assembled outside the court. Styled "Chief of the Halfbreeds," a prominent merchant and former free trader, James Sinclair, acted as Sayer's counsel. A jury of 7 English speakers and 5 French speakers heard evidence proving Sayer's guilt but indicating HBC encouragement to itinerant traders in border regions. Following recorder Adam Thom's summation, the jury retired to find the defendant guilty, but it recommended mercy. Chief factor John Ballenden, HBC, satisfied with the verdict, asked that there be no punishment and withdrew charges against the other 3. When Sayer and his supporters emerged "free" from court, gunfire as a *feu de joie* and shouts of "*le commerce est libre*" greeted them. To the dismay of the HBC their legal victory dissolved into commercial setback. Henceforth they would have to meet the free traders with effective competition and not with the legal canons of their charter. JOHN E. FOSTER

Scadding, Henry, clergyman, scholar (b at Dunkeswell, Eng 29 July 1813; d at Toronto 6 May 1901). Educated at Upper Canada College and St John's College, Cambridge, Scadding became a Church of England clergyman in 1838. After teaching several years at Upper Canada College, he was appointed by Bishop John STRACHAN to be rector of the newly built Holy Trinity Church 1847, where he remained until 1875. Throughout his life, Scadding was a strong supporter of Strachan. He produced numerous pamphlets and articles, but his passion for Toronto's history dominated: in 1873 he produced *Toronto of Old;* in 1884 he and J.C. DENT published *Toronto, Past and Present.* In 1891 he and G. Mercer Adam wrote *Toronto, Old and New.* Scadding's house is now a Toronto landmark. VICTOR RUSSELL

Scale Insect, highly specialized insect belonging to order Hemiptera, suborder Homoptera, superfamily Coccoidea. Scale insects are diverse in habit and structure. Females are wingless, legless and obscurely segmented, have poorly developed eyes and antennae, and may be protected by a waxy, cottony or hard, scalelike covering. Males are tiny, lack mouthparts, and are short-lived. Crawlers, the first juvenile stage, are mobile and function in dispersal. Most species are 0.5-2.0 mm long, but one measures over 25 mm. Many cause serious damage to plants. In Canada, major pests include oystershell scale, pine needle scale, and San José scale; they are controlled by predators, parasites, insecticides and fumigants. Cottony maple scale, which occurs throughout the US and Canada, was introduced from Europe. Some species are beneficial: one produces lac, from which shellac is made; several have been dye sources; one produces Indian wax, used for medicinal purposes; another produces China wax, formerly used for candles.   A.M. HARPER

Scallan, Thomas, Roman Catholic bishop of Nfld (b at Churchtown, Ire 1766?; d at St John's 28 May 1830). A leading Franciscan priest in Ireland, Scallan transferred to Newfoundland in 1812, became coadjutor bishop in 1816 and succeeded Bishop Patrick Lambert that same year. Scallan had to deal with major problems, including poverty arising from massive IRISH immigration, attempts to introduce laws restricting the right of Catholic priests to perform marriages, and the British government's failure to extend civil liberties (including the right to hold public office) to Newfoundland Catholics. Scallan promoted religious harmony in Newfoundland, and, unusual for his time, even attended occasional services in the Anglican church. Though handicapped by illness from 1823, Scallan did much to strengthen the Roman Catholic church and to build up good relations within the community.
RAYMOND J. LAHEY

Scallop, bivalve (hinged shell) MOLLUSC of suborder Pectinina. Scallops are found in all seas. Their rounded or fan-shaped SHELLS are among the most beautiful and colourful of mollusc shells. Larger species are fished worldwide. Scallops usually lie free on the bottom, or may be attached to a solid object by byssal threads (tough filaments secreted by the scallop) or cementlike substance. Many species are present in all Canadian seas, but only sea scallops (*Placopecten magellanicus*) occur in sufficient numbers to be trawled off the East Coast. Weathervane scallops (*Patinopecten caurinus*) are sporadically present on the West Coast but are usually too scarce to fish. Other species, taken recreationally on the Pacific coast, include red scallop (*Chlamys rubida*) and large rock scallop (*Hinnites giganteus*). Iceland scallop (*C. islandica*) is taken in small numbers on the East Coast.   FRANK R. BERNARD

Scammell, Arthur Reginald, teacher, writer (b at Change Is, Nfld 12 Feb 1913). He taught school in outport Newfoundland 1932-39 and in Montréal 1942-70, retiring in 1970 to St John's. At age 15 he wrote what was to be his most famous poem, "The Squid-Jiggin' Ground," featuring a wonderful collection of characters participating in a traditional Newfoundland outport activity. A collection of his prose and verse, *My Newfoundland*, appeared in print in 1966 and on record in 1973; featured Scammell reciting and singing his own works. He became a Member of the Order of Canada in 1987.   JAMES G.G. MOORE

Scarlett, Earle Parkhill, physician (b at High Bluff, Man 27 June 1896; d at Calgary 14 June 1982). He received his BA from U Man in 1916 and then served in WWI with the Canadian Machine Gun Corps, was gassed in 1917 and severely wounded in 1918. After medical studies at U of

T and practice in the US, he joined the Calgary Associate Clinic in 1930 and was a leading Calgary physician until he retired in 1958. A writer of elegance, he was author of over 450 papers, a collection of which, edited by C.G. Roland, was published as *In Sickness and in Health* (1972). A man of culture, he was chancellor of U of A, 1952-58. His honours include doctorates from U of T, U of A and U of Calgary; he was one of the most respected Canadians of his time.   WALTER H. JOHNS

Schaefer, Carl Fellman, artist, teacher (b at Hanover, Ont 30 Apr 1903). A vigorous yet sensitive interpreter of rural southern Ontario scenery, Schaefer is typical of regionalist Canadian artists who chose to concentrate on agrarian and social rather than wilderness themes during the 1930s. His best work was inspired by the farm environment of his native Grey County. He studied at the Ontario Coll of Art 1921-24, where his teachers included Arthur LISMER and J.E.H. MACDONALD. His introduction to northern Ontario came in 1926 with a canoe trip to the Pickerel and French rivers, but he was forced by the Depression to reestablish himself and his family at Hanover, where he took up watercolour painting. His first "Hanover period" (1932-42) was marked by a transition from a decorative and geometric to a starkly realistic, occasionally allegorical approach to landscape and still life. His experience as an official war artist with the RCAF (1943-46) darkened his vision, but by the 1950s he was again painting in a broad, lyrical spirit in the countryside around Hanover and in neighbouring Wellington and Waterloo counties. Schaefer began teaching in 1930 and taught at OCA 1948-70. His paintings in the show "Canadian Landscape" toured European galleries (1983-85). He has received numerous awards and honours.
ROBERT STACEY

Reading: G. Johnston, *Carl: Portrait of a Painter* (1986).

Schafer, Raymond Murray, composer, writer, educator (b at Sarnia, Ont 18 July 1933). R. Murray Schafer has earned an international reputation for his musical compositions, innovative educational theories and outspoken opinions. His early career led him in 1956 from Toronto to Austria and England and back to Canada in 1961, where he became artist-in-residence at Memorial (1963-64) and SFU (1965-75). Since 1975 he has lived on a farm near Bancroft, Ont.

Schafer first drew wide attention through his radical experiments in elementary music education in the late 1960s, which resulted in a series of imaginative educational booklets and several compositions designed for performance by youth orchestras and choirs. His intense interest in soundscape ecology led to his forming the WORLD SOUNDSCAPE PROJECT (1969, fully functional by 1971), an organization devoted to the critical study of the social and aesthetic aspects of the sonic environment. His musical compositions reveal many concerns, ranging from themes of alienation and political oppression to a fascination with eastern mysticism and the sounds of the environment. His recent music reflects a strong sense of Canadian identity, one man's response to the Canadian landscape and his search for the myth without which, as he wrote in 1983, "the nation dies.   ALAN M. GILLMOR

Reading: S. Adams, *R. Murray Schafer* (1983).

Schefferville, Qué, Town, pop 322 (1986c), 1997 (1981c), inc 1955, is located between Knob and Pearce lakes, in the heart of the Québec-Labrador peninsula, 576 km N of SEPT-ÎLES. Father Louis Babel, on a mission to the MONTAGNAIS-NASKAPI 1866-70, made a map of the Ungava region showing mineral-rich areas. In 1895 a Montréal geologist, A.P. LOW, did detailed survey

and mapping work showing the presence of major iron-ore deposits in the Knob Lk region. In 1938 the research results of a Laval geologist, J.A. Retty, attracted the interest of financiers, and in 1942 the Hollinger North Shore Exploration Co won some land concessions. In 1950 the QUEBEC NORTH SHORE AND LABRADOR RY, a subsidiary of IRON ORE CO OF CANADA, started building a rail line to Knob Lk. The first shipment of minerals arrived in Sept-Îles in 1954. Schefferville, built in 1953 by the Iron Ore Co, was named by Prem Maurice DUPLESSIS in honour of Mgr Lionel Scheffer (1903-66), first bishop of Labrador.

The area's economic activity basically depends on its IRON ORE. Initial reserves were estimated at 420 million t; the company yearly extracted about 8 million t. In 1979 iron production at Schefferville topped $282 million, but in 1983 Iron Ore Co ceased operations completely, causing the near shutdown of the town. By 1986 the town had suffered a -83.9% population change since 1981.   CLAUDINE PIERRE-DESCHÊNES

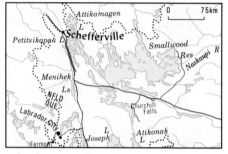

Schenley Awards, emblematic of excellence in Canadian professional football, were originally created to honour the most outstanding player in the CANADIAN FOOTBALL LEAGUE in 1953. That year Billy Vessels of the Edmonton Eskimos became the first recipient. New categories were added in 1954 (most outstanding Canadian player) and 1955 (most outstanding defensive player). In 1972 another category was added, the most outstanding rookie, and the most outstanding offensive lineman category was included in 1974. Russ JACKSON was 3 times outstanding player and 4 times outstanding Canadian. Jackie PARKER was also outstanding player 3 times, while Calgary Stampeder Wayne HARRIS was 4 times outstanding defensive player. The winners are chosen by members of the Football Reporters of Canada.   PETER WONS

Schmidt, Milton Conrad, Milt, hockey player (b at Kitchener, Ont 5 Mar 1918). He played for Boston Bruins from 1936 to 1955, except for 3 years when he served with the RCAF during WWII. He centered the "Kraut Line," one of the NHL's most famous ensembles, with Woody Dumart and Bobby Bauer on the wings. He led the league in scoring 1939-40, won the HART TROPHY (MVP) in 1951-52 and was first all-star centre 3 times. He scored 229 goals and 346 assists in 16 seasons, adding 24 goals and 25 assists in playoffs. After retirement he was coach and then general manager of the Bruins.   JAMES MARSH

Schneider, Julius Gustav Albert, Bert, boxer (b at Cleveland, Ohio 1 July 1897). Schneider's family moved to Montréal when he was 9 and he took up boxing in high school. He later joined the Montreal Amateur Athletic Assn and became its welterweight champion. Slim in the legs but heavily muscled in the upper body, he was not a stylish boxer. A mixer and scrapper, he capitalized on his ability to move quickly. He was chosen for the 1920 Canadian Olympic team, though still an American citizen, and won the welterweight title. After 75 professional fights he joined the US Border Patrol. He eventually retired to Montréal.
J. THOMAS WEST

Schneider, William George, scientist, scientific administrator (b at Wolseley, Sask 1 June 1915). Schneider received his BSc and MS from U Sask (1937, 1939) and his PhD from McGill (1941). From 1943 to 1946 he was employed by the Woods Hole Oceanographic Institute, leaving it to join the NATIONAL RESEARCH COUNCIL (1946-80). There he was successively director of the division of pure chemistry (1963-65), vice-president, scientific (1965-67) and president (1967-80). Since 1980 he has been a chemical consultant. He has published extensively in molecular forces, critical phenomena, ultrasonics, nuclear magnetic resonance and organic semiconductors. He has also received many honours and awards, including fellowship in the Royal Soc (London), the RSC and the Chemical Inst of Canada. He was president of the International Union of Pure and Applied Chemistry 1983-85.
LEO YAFFE

Schofield, Francis William, veterinarian, teacher, researcher (b at Rugby, Eng 15 Mar 1889; d at Seoul, S Korea 12 Apr 1970). Schofield joined the faculty of the Ontario Veterinary Coll in 1910. He was a teacher and missionary in Korea 1916-19, and returned there in 1955 at retirement. From 1924 to 1956 he was professor of veterinary pathology at OVC. He was nationally and internationally known for his research in animal disease, in particular sweet-clover poisoning of cattle, infections in young animals and viral mink enteritis. An outstanding lecturer and teacher, he provided philosophy and religion with his teaching, and demonstrated his profoundly intuitive intellect through excellent oratorical ability and a sense of the dramatic.
R.G. THOMSON

School Boards, groups of elected (with exceptions) members of a community to whom the provinces have delegated authority over some aspects of education. There are about 900 school boards in Canada, although the number is steadily decreasing as small jurisdictions are combined into larger ones. A variety of publicly supported school boards exist, generally organized according to religion or language, or both. The 2 largest groups of school boards are the public boards, providing schools open to all children, and the separate boards, providing educational services for children of Roman Catholic parents. In sparsely populated areas and in the territories schools are operated directly by the provincial or federal governments; in these places there are school committees but no formally elected school boards.

The degree to which local school boards, as opposed to the provincial governments, control education is an important issue. Local boards are primarily responsible for personnel matters and for providing facilities and supplies. For example, local boards may hire any professional personnel they wish, although the provinces require that such personnel have completed a certain amount of specific training. Local boards have the power to dismiss teachers (they rarely do so) for just cause if proper procedures are followed. Teachers can generally appeal a dismissal to a board of reference, established by but independent of the minister of education and the local school board. Unless the provincial authorities revoke the teaching certificate, however, the teacher can be hired by another board or rehired by the first. There is some shared authority with the province in many other areas, eg, curriculum, textbook selection and courses of study. In curriculum, for example, guidelines are produced by the provincial authorities. Within these guidelines, however, the boards can exercise wide discretionary powers. Sometimes provincial rules, regulations and statutes are ignored, sometimes they are interpreted liberally. Provincial governments generally produce lists of approved books as well, and local boards may choose to use them, may approve others, or may ask for the approval of others. It seems that generally boards can prohibit the use of books not approved by provincial authorities. School boards have taxing powers, although in all jurisdictions the provincial treasury provides a significant amount of funding. Local boards are legislated by various statutes and regulations.

School business is conducted primarily at school-board meetings, which are scheduled regularly, usually once or twice a month. By law, these are open meetings to which the public is invited; the meetings are run by a chairperson, generally elected by other trustees for a one-year term. Professional staff are also involved in the meetings. Usually the chief executive officer (most commonly the superintendent) submits information for the board's consideration. While the audience is seldom very large (unless a controversial issue arises), it is not uncommon for delegations from the community to appear and present opinions or arguments about various issues, and representatives from the media are often in attendance. It is only the elected trustees, however, who vote on any motion or business before the board.

School-board operation in Canada is distinguished by the use of committees to work out the details of the business. Occasionally members of the public are appointed as well, although this is usually only true for special committees established to study some major problem. Large boards sometimes have more than 20 committees, which are responsible for a variety of areas such as curriculum, personnel, salary negotiations, long-range planning and special education. There is a slight trend toward reducing the number of committees and some boards use only 2 – one for business concerns and one for academic concerns. According to conventional wisdom, school boards establish policy and administrators carry it out. In reality, the situation is much more complex. While the board has final authority in matters not affected by provincial regulation, most issues are debated by a variety of interest groups and the final policy is the result of extensive consultation. Teachers, for example, are highly organized and often influence a board's policy decisions, as do parents and taxpayers. Although each school board is uniquely a part of a local community, school boards in general discuss the same issues and carry out similar tasks across the country. Usually a great amount of effort is expended approving and spending the budget, which can run into several hundreds of millions of dollars. In connection with the budget, the board negotiates regularly, often annually, with various categories of staff about salary and work conditions, except in certain provinces, eg, New Brunswick and Québec, where bargaining is conducted by provincial authorities.

Language instruction, special education, curriculum versus enrichment programs, multiculturalism, technical versus liberal education, the role of computers and computer technology, and problems associated with declining enrolments are all issues with which school boards must contend. School boards have formed provincial organizations in each province for purposes of communication, in-service training and effective representation to the legislatures. The Canadian School Trustees Association is the national organization, with offices in Ottawa.

School boards are a phenomenon rather peculiar to Canada and the US. Some other countries, such as Britain, have school committees, but these are really subgroupings of municipal bodies. Other countries, eg, Australia, have no local governing bodies but are administered from the central governments. While often criticized for inefficiency, parochial points of view and lack of expertise in educational technology, school boards are among the most democratic institutions, responsive to local demands. They provide a lively and sometimes vibrant vehicle for grassroots participation in educational policies and practice.
EDWARD S. HICKCOX

School Facilities have been an integral part of SCHOOL SYSTEMS since the beginning of European settlement in the early 17th century. The first schools were established shortly after the French settled Québec in 1608. The few *petits écoles* organized by the Roman Catholic clergy and other missionaries in French Canada to teach reading, writing, arithmetic and religion appear to have been the first and, for many decades, the only schools in Canada.

Because the parish priest was often the initial organizer and only teacher until a lay person or someone from a teaching order could be recruited from France, these early schools were located close to the local church. The earliest schools probably reflected notions about function and structure that the clergy and settlers had brought with them from their native regions, especially Normandy, Île-de-France and Poitou. Glass and other fittings were not available in Canada at this time and during the winter months the poorly lit rooms could only be used a few hours each day. Only the larger centres, such as Québec and Trois-Rivières, had substantial buildings; most were one-room schools that were small in comparison to the one-room schools of the present century, because population concentrations were small and the finished building materials required considerable manual labour. The only secondary education available was at the Collège de Québec, founded in 1635. As the culturally isolated French Canadian population increased in the 17th and 18th centuries, schools opened where there was a parish priest and a suitable building.

The prerevolutionary PLANTERS and the post-revolutionary LOYALISTS who came first to Nova Scotia and later to Ontario from New England brought their own ideas about schools, including the notion of public sectarian schools financed from the sale of crown lands, an idea that was repeated later throughout the upper St Lawrence-Great Lakes region and even later in western Canada. The New Englanders also wanted to establish SECONDARY SCHOOLS, or grammar schools, as they had already done in Boston, Salem and other prosperous New England coastal towns. Among the first of such schools were King's College, the Halifax Grammar School, the College of New Brunswick and Prince of Wales College in PEI.

The architecture of school buildings in the 19th century varied considerably. In Québec City, Trois-Rivières and Montréal, school buildings developed according to a "French Provincial" style. The SÉMINAIRE DE QUÉBEC and Collège de Montréal are well-known examples. In Halifax and Windsor, NS, they represented the "American Colonial" style, as evident in King's College and the Halifax Grammar School (see ARCHITECTURAL STYLES). In contrast, the school facilities in the small, remote frontier settlements were the simplest buildings that would serve the purpose, and authorities used whatever local skills and materials were available at the time. In many cases these buildings were nothing more than log cabins or sheds. During the early 19th century, tiny wooden schools were still being built in frontier settlements, such as those begun by the Hudson's Bay Company on the N Saskatchewan R in 1808 for

The traditional one-room schoolhouse of rural Canada, c1900-25 (*courtesy Archives of Ontario*).

the children of company employees, but in the older and larger communities more substantial schools, including some secondary schools, were being constructed. Generally, these buildings facilitated learning only in the sense that they provided relatively comfortable shelter, and the larger of them organized students into groups of manageable size and levels of achievement.

The simple buildings of earlier times began to disappear in the second half of the century as architects imitated American or British schools, with their impressive neoclassical entrances. Brick and stone were widely used. Furnishings, equipment and books were distributed from rapidly growing commercial centres such as Montréal and Toronto; some were imported. School sites, or school grounds as they were usually called, were cleared and levelled so that school gardens could be planted and playgrounds could be reserved. Unfortunately, inside these massive buildings the plan was often the same. The larger schools generally had a corridor running down the centre of each of the 2- or even 3-storey buildings with identical classrooms on both sides, a design pejoratively referred to as an "egg carton." The typical classroom was a large squarish compartment with a high ceiling and a raised platform at one end for the teacher's desk. The intention was no doubt to awe the students by the sheer scale of their surroundings and by the importance attached to education.

In the first quarter of the 20th century, the number of schools increased at a phenomenal rate as the population of Canada mushroomed from 5.3 million in 1901 to approximately 9 million in 1926. During this period, compulsory attendance legislation was stringently enforced wherever possible and recalcitrant families were obliged to send their children to school. As an example of the increase in school building activity, the number of school districts in the new province of Saskatchewan increased from 896 to 3702 from 1905 to 1915, a large proportion of which operated only a one-room rural elementary school. Such a demand for one-room schools developed that The T. EATON COMPANY advertised what amounted to school building kits in the Winnipeg edition of its 1917-18 catalogue. These kits contained school building plans along with the necessary lumber, nails, fittings and other materials. The school became the ubiquitous public building on the Canadian landscape.

Most schools of the first quarter of this century consisted largely of classrooms, corridors and cloakrooms. However, attempts were made to improve their appearances, especially in rural Ontario. The Ontario Department of Education's *Plans for Rural School Building* commented that "everyone connected with school work should endeavour to improve school architecture so that the present buildings, which are devoid of architectural beauty, should be replaced within the next generation by modern structures."

Little improvement was made during the GREAT DEPRESSION or WWII, though as a result of the emerging "human relations" approach in various disciplines, the heavy wood and iron desks that had been bolted to the floor were replaced by lighter materials so that children no longer had to be seated in rows but could be arranged in rings, blocks and other patterns to facilitate various instructional techniques.

Some of the school buildings in use through WWII were either physically or functionally obsolete, or both, by 1951. Many of the older buildings needed substantial repair or replacement. Furthermore, because of farm consolidation and mechanization, and in some cases farm abandonment, population drifted from rural to urban areas leaving many small schools virtually empty while tending to overcrowd schools in the larger towns and cities. Simultaneously, the consolidation of small school districts and the accompanying school busing and other school services required that larger, more centralized buildings be provided. A special feature of this period was the separation of elementary and high-school students in small towns, villages and farming areas, for it created a need for large central or regional high schools.

Different approaches to instruction and new approaches to the planning of educational facilities originating in the US and western Europe also helped render the old "egg carton" schools obsolete. A large study of educational facilities (SEF) undertaken by the Toronto Metropolitan Board of Education was used in school planning across Canada.

Fresh ideas about organizing students for instruction, including small and large group instruction, team teaching, differentiated staffing, individualized instruction and continuous progress, required flexible space and sophisticated support functions. This period also marked the beginning of the democratization of architecture: buildings were designed for public use and with public advice. The use of educational specifications ("Ed Spec"), prepared after consultations with teachers and others who might be affected by the new facilities, resulted in flexible but complex school buildings with specialized learning spaces for sciences, languages, home economics,

industrial arts and occasionally others. A new and radical type of building, the "open-area" or "open-plan school," was the most controversial innovation through the 1970s and beyond. These schools had few enclosed spaces and the floor plan was organized around a learning resource centre, or library, with teaching stations and services areas surrounding it. Soon there were complaints by teachers about noise, confusion and inadequate wall space for display purposes; consequently, second and third generation open-area schools were modified to include more closed spaces, including a few traditional classrooms.

Many of the new high-school facilities of this era still contained the traditional classrooms and science laboratories but also included new features. Larger more diversified instructional resource centres replaced the small school libraries. Gymnasiums were expanded to meet official standards and to accommodate more activities. In some instances swimming pools were added to the facilities. Specialized facilities such as language laboratories, cafeterias and guidance centres became regular features. Consequently the new high school became a very complex and very costly public facility that attracted more use by the general public.

During this period of economic and population growth, Canadian architects produced some notable examples of modern architecture, including some distinctive educational buildings. Most of the educational showpieces were buildings at post-secondary institutions, particularly some of the newer universities such as SIMON FRASER UNIVERSITY, UNIVERSITY OF LETHBRIDGE and TRENT UNIVERSITY, but a few exemplary school buildings were also designed, eg, the Mayland Heights Elementary School in Calgary designed by architect Gordon Atkins, and Douglas CARDINAL's Cumberland Elementary School at La Ronge, Sask. The floor plan of the latter is shaped like an Indian Chief's ceremonial headdress and has a kindergarten room with one-way glass so that parents may monitor the initial adjustment of their children to the classroom.

During this period school sites began to attract attention again. The old school garden virtually disappeared, but playgrounds were retained and recreational facilities and landscaping were added. While provincial governments and boards of education might have suggested or even imposed limits on the size of all school sites, some of the high schools built during this period had cam-

The larger "consolidated" school of the late 19th and early 20th centuries classified students according to age, achievement and sex. The school bus was already part of school life (*courtesy National Archives of Canada*).

pus settings, including improved facilities for football, soccer, and track and field.

Some of the newer schools reflect the same trends as other buildings being designed for the workplace: post-modern architecture, concern for personal environments and accommodation of high-tech equipment, particularly computers.

As a result of spending restraints, fewer new schools are being built in the 1980s. Provincial departments and school boards have settled for a "no-frills" approach. Energy efficiency has also become a major concern. Furthermore, with so many comparatively new schools being closed because of decreasing enrolments, boards of education are reluctant to build new facilities except where long-term need can be clearly demonstrated. For this century at least, the golden age of school construction seems to have passed.

ALLAN GUY

School Systems In most modern societies, the young are educated within schools which are generally part of systems organized by the state. The schools within these systems are universal, compulsory, publicly controlled and tax supported. The state not only finances the schools but determines their goals and values. In independent nonsystem schools, the parents and not the state pay for the cost of educating the students.

Constitutional and Political Context The Canadian education system has been shaped by the federal nature of the country. The CONSTITUTION ACT, 1867, allotted exclusive responsibility for education to the provinces (exceptions are noted in subsections of the Constitution), stating that "in and for each province, the Legislature may exclusively make laws in relation to education." In exercising its sovereign power with respect to education, each province has developed a distinctive system of education. Provincial power over education is only restricted with respect to the rights of denominational schools that existed at the time the province entered Confederation (s93 says nothing about language rights; s33 speaks of language rights but significantly not in relation to education). Under the Constitution, the rights guaranteed to schools by a province when it joined Confederation may not be abrogated by the province, although the powers of the provinces to do as they see fit regarding education have been strengthened by historical and political precedents. For example, Manitoba has denied or abridged the denominational rights of minorities in its school systems in contravention of those constitutional provisions regarding educational rights of minorities, but arguably it has not contravened the provisions of the Constitution regarding language rights.

The systems of education established by the provinces are public and most often nonsectarian, ie, they are open to all citizens. A SEPARATE SCHOOL is a special kind of public school open to those of a minority religious faith, usually Catholic. Tax-supported separate schools exist in Ontario, Saskatchewan, Alberta, the Yukon and the NWT. Québec has a dual confessional system divided between Protestants and Catholics, and Newfoundland has an exclusively denominational system that recognizes several religious groups for the purpose of organizing school systems. Recently, in Newfoundland, the major Protestant groups joined together in the larger centres to establish amalgamated school systems. The result is that Newfoundland's system is becoming similar to that of other provinces, in which the major dividing line is between public nonsectarian schools and Catholic separate schools. BC has a nondenominational system of schools. In addition to these formal mechanisms for recognizing religion as a basis for organizing educational systems, some provinces make infor-

mal arrangements that accomplish the same ends. For example, in NS some schools are designated as serving Catholic students.

Although the provinces are primarily responsible for education, the federal government also has responsibilities in this area, for example, for the education of Indian and Inuit children, and for the education of children of members of the Armed Forces. The federal government also provides subventions to the provinces to support post-secondary education, adult labour training, official SECOND-LANGUAGE INSTRUCTION and cultural development activities, and is drawn into education through its jurisdiction over external affairs. When the Organization for Economic Cooperation and Development surveyed Canadian education in the mid-1970s, the voice of the federal government joined those of the provinces in preparing a statement about the problems, priorities and needs of Canadian education.

The Expansion of Educational Systems in Canada The rapid growth of Canada's population, which by 1987 was more than 25 million, strained educational systems considerably. To meet new demands across the country both for more education and for new kinds of education, these systems had to grow both quantitatively and qualitatively. By the 1985-86 school year, there were nearly 5 million students in Canadian pre-elementary, elementary and secondary schools and another 790 000 students in post-secondary institutions. The number of students overall had increased by 34% from 1956: the increase in the number of post-secondary students was even larger. These increases were caused by the BABY BOOM and the influx of immigrants between 1945 and 1960. By the mid-1980s, the number of students in the education systems other than post-secondary had declined because of falling birthrates and reduced immigration.

From the 1950s to the 1970s, Canadians spent generously on their school systems. Standards for training teachers were increased and an enormous amount of capital was invested in buildings and equipment. Salaries of teachers and administrators rose steadily, the ratio of students to teachers dropped markedly, and the curriculum and the organization of schools were continually modified to increase their scope and effectiveness. During this period of expansion, some observers claimed that contemporary education was long on quantity but short on quality. "So little for the mind" was the stinging phrase critic Hilda NEATBY used to argue that the expanded system at the secondary levels had abandoned traditional values and the fundamentals of education. On the other hand, the view that there was nothing much wrong with Canadian education that a great deal of money, properly applied, could not cure was supported by surveys of the resources, personnel and facilities devoted to education. For example, Statistics Canada reported in 1951 that 15% of elementary teachers had not met the minimum requirements of secondary-school graduation followed by a year of professional training; 40% of secondary teachers did not have a university degree and professional training, and at the university level 15% of teachers had no more than a bachelor's degree.

During the years of expansion, massive resources were directed into educational systems, resources that helped ensure, by the 1960s and 1970s, that virtually all those who could benefit from schools were in educational systems. The systems provided increasingly complex and diversified programs, and students were taught by more experienced, better trained and better paid teachers. Participation rates are still high, particularly in western Canada and Ontario. In 1985-86, 99-100% of Canadian elementary-school-age

children were in elementary schools, 87% of secondary-school-age children were in secondary schools and 23% of university-age students were attending post-secondary institutions. Fifty-six percent of this last group were in universities.

Organization and Structure of Systems Canadian educational systems provide successive programs for children from ages 3 and 4 in nursery schools and kindergartens, and on through elementary and secondary schools. Education is compulsory from ages 6 for about 10 years and covers the elementary grades and most – but usually not all – of high school. Public-school systems may provide one or more years of education prior to grade one. This service is now quite common in urban schools, but there are also many private kindergartens and nursery schools that operate under varying, but usually nonrestrictive, provincial supervision. Elementary schools often offer 8 grades of study (45% of the provinces have junior-high schools) and secondary another 4, but this pattern varies considerably among the provincial school systems. The length of high school varies as well, eg, in some provinces students graduate after grade 11, in others after grade 13. Newfoundland's schools are organized on a 6-2-3 plan; in BC it is 6-5, in BC, 7-5 or 7-3-2; and in Ontario, 8-4 or 8-5. The view reflected in most provincial systems of education is that all children are entitled to a period of 12 to 14 years of publicly funded schooling.

Provincial authorities govern all educational systems within their boundaries, but sharp differences exist even among the systems of a single province with regard to administrative structures. Public, compulsory education is administered by SCHOOL BOARDS, most of whose members are elected and who have the power to levy taxes against local property. Post-secondary institutions, on the other hand, while funded from the public treasury, are established by charter, are governed by appointed boards and with the general exception of community colleges are relatively autonomous, although some provincial governments have now moved to create unified ministries that are responsible for education at all levels of schooling, including post-secondary.

The Financing of Education Constitutionally, only the federal and provincial governments enjoy the authority to levy taxes for the support of public services, but provincial governments have delegated certain taxing powers to local authorities, the most important of which is the real-property tax. Traditionally, elementary- and secondary-school costs were met by municipal authorities through property taxes while universities were funded through private sources, including tuition fees. The growth of the system after WWII destroyed this pattern as the demand for education expanded rapidly and costs skyrocketed. In 1947 total expenditure on education exceeded $1 billion for the first time; for 1985-86 it totalled about $34 billion. From 1950 the cost of education rose from 2.5% of gross domestic product to 7.3% by 1985-86.

A colonial statistician estimated in 1882 that it cost parents about $10 annually in fees to keep a child in school and that this was more than most parents could afford. By 1984 the average amount spent in Canada per full-time student was $4211. In that year, Québec spent the highest amount per pupil, at $5024, and Nfld the lowest at $2957. However, although citizens in the Atlantic provinces appear to spend generally less on education, they spend a larger part of their incomes on education, since their average income is less than that in other provinces.

Most of the money spent on education in Canada is public money. Around 5% of Canadian children attend PRIVATE SCHOOLS (where the cost is

Standardization and conformity have been heavily emphasized in school systems. Here, all pupils sit in rows, hands in the same position. Each student has drawn the same boat (*courtesy National Archives of Canada*).

borne largely by fees), but some provincial governments – notably Québec, Manitoba, Saskatchewan, Alberta and BC – provide some financial support to private schools. The decision to fund private institutions with public money represents a crack in the monolith of public education. Strong voices in Canadian society are opposing the vision of a universal, free and compulsory school system. For those who oppose public-school systems, values (and money to support them) are the heart of the educational question. These critics demand the right to pursue their own values through education, but with the model of the publicly supported common school vividly before them, they now demand public money to pursue private values through private schools. They wish to educate only those who choose their values, raising the spectre of one of Egerton RYERSON's critics who complained that he was under no obligation to educate "every brat on the street." The opinion that private money is better spent than public money has also been resurrected, allied once again to the view that "that which costs nothing is likely to be valued at nothing." These ideas challenge the fundamentals of a public-school system.

The Future of Educational Systems in Canada In the postwar period, larger numbers of children were in school and were there for longer periods of time, and comprehensive and diversified programs had been designed to serve their needs and interests. In some deep sense Canadians have always shown faith in their institutions, otherwise they would not have built such elaborate and costly systems of education. Despite the fact that major questions are being asked about the Canadian school systems, that there are declining enrolments, a sharper competition for the funds that support the systems and a declining faith in the value of education itself and in the policies and programs that shape it, the systems as a whole represent an enduring and substantial achievement. A relatively small proportion of school-age children in Canada attend private and independent schools. The majority's choice in this matter bespeaks an extraordinary and continuing faith in the idea of common schools based on compulsory attendance and public tax support.

School Trustee, member of a board of education elected (a few are appointed) for terms ranging from 2 to 4 years. Membership varies from 5 to more than 20 on some large boards. There are roughly 6000 to 8000 trustees in Canada; the number is decreasing in accordance with a trend toward fewer boards. SCHOOL BOARDS in some provinces pay a stipend to trustees, from a few hundred dollars to more than $20 000 in wealthy jurisdictions. Most boards include a number of professional people and business executives. Increasingly, in recent years, educators (from other

jurisdictions) have become trustees and it is not uncommon to have students elected. Although it is commonly held that school trustees are not politically oriented, the governance of education is a political process and many trustees move on to higher office in municipal, provincial and federal politics.   EDWARD S. HICKCOX

Schreiber, Charlotte Mount Brock, née Morrell, painter (b at Woodham, Eng 1834; d at Paignton, Eng 1922). Schreiber was the only female charter member of the ROYAL CANADIAN ACADEMY in 1880 and was the only woman elected full academician until 1933. She studied in London, Eng, and exhibited at the Paris Salon and at the Royal Academy, London. She moved to Toronto in 1875 when she married Weymouth Schreiber. She painted figures, landscapes and genre in a sentimental Victorian manner. *The Croppy Boy,* oil on canvas, was her RCA diploma piece and she exhibited regularly at the RCA until her return to England in 1898. She was one of the first female book illustrators in Canada and 3 children's books with Schreiber illustrations were published in Toronto. She was the sole woman on the board of the Ontario School of Art and Design (later Ontario Coll of Art). Ernest Thompson SETON was her protégé.   DOROTHY FARR

Schreyer, Edward Richard, politician, premier of Manitoba, governor general of Canada 1979-84, diplomat (b at Beauséjour, Man 21 Dec 1935). Educated at United College and U Man he became the youngest member of the Manitoba legislature at age 22. He served there 1958-65 and in the federal Commons 1965-69. Returning to Manitoba politics, he swept to the leadership of the Manitoba NEW DEMOCRATIC PARTY in 1969 and within months was premier. It was a Schreyer-dominated government: moderate, honest, mildly progressive. An advocate of bilingualism and a strong central government, he got along well with PM Pierre TRUDEAU. It was Trudeau who named Schreyer governor general, rescuing him from an unhappy period as Manitoba Opposition leader, 1977-78. He was determined as head of state to speak his mind and to democratize the office. He and his popular wife Lily made RIDEAU HALL more accessible to ordinary Canadians and travelled prodigiously. But a governor general's words, he discovered, were easily misunderstood and he was forced to tailor his speeches accordingly. A stiff, earnest public manner conflicted with his desire to be open and friendly, and made him an easy media target.

Schreyer caused political controversy by hesitating before allowing PM Joe CLARK to call an election in 1979, and by suggesting that he might have dissolved Parliament if Trudeau had attempted to impose his constitutional proposals unilaterally in 1981-82. Through it all, Schreyer indulged an intense curiosity about a wide range of subjects, from topography to native peoples. Before taking up his duties as Canadian high commissioner to Australia in 1984, he announced that until age 65 his pension would be directed to scientific research into problems faced by farmers and foresters. In Feb 1988 he returned to Canada as a private citizen.   NORMAN HILLMER

Schull, Joseph, historian (b at Watertown, S Dakota 6 Feb 1906; d at Montréal 19 May 1980). Schull grew up in Moose Jaw, Sask, and began writing professionally after WWII, primarily as a radio dramatist and journalist, though his first book publications were as a poet. Work on the official history of the Royal Canadian Navy in the war (*The Far Distant Ships,* 1950; repr 1987) led him to many other commissioned histories, including *100 Years of Banking in Canada: A History of the Toronto-Dominion Bank* (1958) and *Edward*

Blake (1975-76), an impressive 2-vol biography of the 19th-century Liberal leader commissioned by Blake's old law firm. *Laurier: The First Canadian* (1965) is a first-rate political biography. Other works include *Rebellion: The Rising in French Canada 1837* (1971), a concise and readable narrative, as well as works for children.   D. FETHERLING

Schultz, Sir John Christian, businessman, medical practitioner, politician (b at Amherstburg, UC 1 Jan 1840; d at Monterey, Mexico 13 Apr 1896). Schultz settled at the RED RIVER COLONY in 1861. He practised medicine but increasingly occupied himself with furs, retail trade and real estate. During 1865-68 he was owner of the *Nor'-Wester,* and in its columns attacked the "tyranny" of the HUDSON'S BAY CO. He became the leader of the small but noisy Canadian party which demanded annexation to Canada and which roused Métis fears. Imprisoned by Louis RIEL's provisional government 7 Dec 1869, Schultz escaped 23 Jan 1870 and later made his way to Ontario where he and others of the CANADA FIRST movement raised Protestant ire over the execution of Orangeman Thomas SCOTT. No mention was made of the deaths of Hugh Sutherland and Norbert Parisien for which Schultz and others were responsible. Shrewd and acquisitive, Schultz became a wealthy businessman. He was an MP 1871-82, a Senator 1882-88 and lieutenant-governor of Manitoba 1888-95. A figure of controversy, he played a key role in the troubles of 1869-70 and left a legacy of bitterness.   LOVELL CLARK

Science, the rational study of nature, rose to prominence in European civilization at almost the same time as the first European EXPLORATION of what is now Canada and was, from the beginning, an element in those explorations. From the time of John CABOT, scientific navigation and GEOGRAPHY were essential to enable explorers to reach and penetrate Canada. During the 19th century and, more particularly, the 20th century, science, increasingly closely linked with TECHNOLOGY, assumed a central place in Canadian life and culture, providing the basis of national wealth and well-being.

The practical uses of science have always been foremost in Canada. From the earliest times, scientific observers noted and catalogued the natural RESOURCES of the country. The Jesuit missionaries, the first organized group with both a scientific education and an interest in nature, sent back to Europe reports of the new land (*see* JESUIT RELATIONS). From the mid-17th century, they taught general science in Québec and trained navigators. During the following century, the Jesuits were joined by civil and military authorities with a taste for science. Physicians J.F. GAULTIER and Michel SARRAZIN, the marquis de la Galissonière and engineer Michel Chartier de Lotbinière made forays into BOTANY and GEOLOGY, but their contributions were transient; after 1759, only the Jesuit-inspired education survived. A procession of foreign visitors, such as Pehr KALM, André Michaux, Capt John PALLISER and J.J. Bigsby, noted Canada's geology, botany and ZOOLOGY well into the 19th century. The native Canadian development of science did not begin until the early 19th century, with the coming of colleges, government agencies and locally sponsored expeditions. Important contributors such as Adam Henry Bayfield, Lt Frederick Baddeley, Capt Richard Bonnycastle, Lt Edward Ashe and Capt John Lefroy were British military men with an appetite for science. As the British military presence in Canada diminished during the second half of the century, Canadian-born and educated men, both professional and amateur, replaced them and gave Canadian science its own flavour. The structure of modern Canadian science began to form during the last quarter of the century. It was slower to develop than its American counterpart and while similar in many ways, is distinguishable from it. One major difference, which retains much of its original impact, is the strong role of government in Canadian science.

Government Involvement Because of Canada's small population, few universities and industries, government has long been an important supporter of science. The PROVINCE OF CANADA took the lead in 1842 by creating the GEOLOGICAL SURVEY OF CANADA under Montréal-born William (later Sir William) LOGAN. Modelled on the British survey and American state surveys, it was intended to be a short-lived project aimed at the discovery of economic MINERALS, but so vast was Canada and so adroit were Logan, his colleagues and successors that the survey has survived to the present as the second-oldest national survey in the world, and one of the most distinguished. Although the survey was officially limited to Upper and Lower Canada, Logan's assistant, Alexander Murray, who became provincial geologist in Newfoundland, and Logan's correspondents in the Maritimes, such as Charles Hartt and G.F. Matthew of Saint John, and James Robb and Loring BAILEY of Fredericton, ensured, before Confederation, the foundations of a systematic study of Canadian geology. After 1867, the survey was faced with the exploration of virtually all the territories now comprising Canada. A succession of visionary directors, such as A.R.C. SELWYN, George M. DAWSON, Albert P. LOW and Reginald Brock nurtured the survey into a large and multifaceted organization. The collections of the survey, first housed in Logan's home, evolved into the National Museum (now NATIONAL MUSEUM OF NATURAL SCIENCES), by the 1890s. The more economic aspects of geology called forth the creation of different organizations such as the federal Department of Mines (1907). Some provinces had moved earlier, eg, NS had established a Commissioner of Mines before Confederation, and Ontario set up a Bureau of Mines in 1891. After the turn of the century, most provinces maintained government bureaus devoted to MINING.

The imperial government initiated little in science beyond creating the Toronto Magnetic Observatory in 1840 as a link in an international chain of institutions for the study of geomagnetism. On the British withdrawal of support in 1853, the provincial government assumed its operation. The small astronomical OBSERVATORY in Québec, established in 1850 and built in 1854 to provide TIME for shipping, and small observatories in Saint John, Montréal and Kingston were linked together with Toronto by the federal Dept of Marine and Fisheries in the 1870s as the Canadian Meteorological Service, which survives as the Atmospheric Environment Service (*see* CLIMATOLOGY). The Dept of the Interior pursued practical ASTRONOMY in the 1880s as part of the transcontinental railway surveys. The need for a permanent observatory for geographic and timekeeping purposes led to the establishment of Ottawa's Dominion Observatory, which opened in 1905. Not only was the observatory an important centre for practical astronomy but it was also the birthplace of Canadian astrophysics, in the hands of J.S. PLASKETT and his colleagues. As a result of Plaskett's efforts, the Dominion Astrophysical Observatory, which briefly possessed the world's largest telescope, commenced work in 1918. It has remained one of the most important international astrophysical centres.

Federal government scientific programs nearly always grew from practical and economic considerations. Because AGRICULTURE was so central to the 19th-century economy, the Central Experimental Farm was founded in Ottawa in 1886 under the direction of William SAUNDERS (*see* RESEARCH STATIONS). The staff, including the Dominion cerealist, entomologist, chemist and others, were responsible for new varieties of CROPS and for pest control. The Experimental Farm system rapidly opened branches across the country. The Dept of Agriculture's research staff has, during the present century, carried on the traditions of research of the pioneers such as John MACOUN, William and Charles SAUNDERS, C.J.S. BETHUNE, Frank Shutt and others.

Zoological research was initiated by the government in the mid-19th century with Pierre FORTIN's fisheries studies in the Gulf of St Lawrence; by 1899, the Marine Biological Station at St Andrew's, NB, directed by E.E. PRINCE, was in operation, followed by a number of other marine stations (*see* OCEANOGRAPHY). The Biological Board of Canada, first appointed in 1912, oversaw this research; by 1937 it had become the Fisheries Research Board. The Canadian COMMISSION OF CONSERVATION, established in 1909 and dismantled in 1921, took a wider view of Canada's natural heritage. Contemporary government agencies for the natural sciences, mostly grouped within the departments of Environment and Agriculture, consume the largest portion of the federal science budget.

The most important government initiative in science was the appointment, in 1916, of the Honorary Advisory Council for Scientific and Industrial Research, a group similar to the British wartime scientific advisory council. It soon became the NATIONAL RESEARCH COUNCIL. Obtaining its own laboratories for industrial research in 1932, the NRC, under the leadership of such men as H.M. TORY, C.J. MACKENZIE and E.W.R. STEACIE, expanded to become one of the most diversified and successful governmental research organizations in the world. Before WWII, its endeavours were largely in aid of INDUSTRIAL RESEARCH AND DEVELOPMENT, but, with a tenfold increase in staff during and after the war, its work branched into many new fields including RADAR, NUCLEAR ENERGY, aeronautics and radio astronomy (*see* DEFENCE RESEARCH). Its pure science component continues to be strong, complementing applied research in TRANSPORTATION, northern environments, ENERGY, building technology, materials science and CHEMISTRY. Along with its laboratory work, the NRC has, since its early days, been a primary contributor to university science with its grants, scholarships and fellowships. From a modest $13 000 in 1918, its subventions grew to nearly $70 million annually by the early 1970s. More recently, research and educational grants for the sciences have been disbursed by the NATURAL SCIENCES AND ENGINEERING RESEARCH COUNCIL of Canada and by the MEDICAL RESEARCH COUNCIL.

Other government agencies, such as the Defence Research Board, the departments of National Defence, Communications, Transport and others, have, since 1945, become important in Canadian science. One branch of the NRC wartime operation, the nuclear research at CHALK RIVER, Ont, grew into the crown corporation, ATOMIC ENERGY OF CANADA LTD (1952) which, with ONTARIO HYDRO, a world leader in electrical technology since early in the century, developed the CANDU reactor. The reactor employs Canada's natural uranium and Canadian-manufactured heavy water. Another crown corporation, the Polymer Corp, has been an important leader in the PETROCHEMICAL INDUSTRY. The provinces have also participated in science: beginning with the precursor to the ALBERTA RESEARCH COUNCIL in 1919 and the ONTARIO RESEARCH FOUNDATION in 1928, nearly all the provinces have created more modest versions of the NRC (*see* RESEARCH, PROVINCIAL ORGANIZATIONS).

Education Early EDUCATION in Canada was in private or church hands and, although elementary MATHEMATICS appeared in all curricula, elementary science was rare. From the 1840s, provincially supported schools included only a smattering of science. During the latter part of the 19th century, the prevailing ideology of science education held that only natural history was suitable for children, they being unable to grasp the complexities of physical science. This view, then also current in Britain and the US, has survived almost to the present; biological studies, complemented by environmental studies, remain the core of elementary science. Ontario SECONDARY SCHOOLS led the way in science courses as a preparation for university matriculation examinations. The church-run classical colleges of Québec, following the original French pattern, taught science to few students and only in the last 2 years of study. By the mid-19th century, the francophone student was as knowledgeable in science as an anglophone liberal arts student in a 3- or 4-year college program. The curriculum froze, however, and the gap between anglophone and francophone science education continued to grow. Dissatisfaction in the state-supported universities and the conservatism of the church-run colleges combined to produce a widespread debate in the late 1920s and early 1930s which was led, on the scientific side, by U de M biologist Frère MARIE-VICTORIN and U Laval chemist Adrien Pouliot. Progress was slow and science began to take its proper place in the secondary curriculum in Québec only in the 1960s.

Science teaching in Canadian universities was a mixture of various elements, with the Scottish and American predominating. From the founding until after the turn of the 20th century, most of the small liberal arts colleges offered general science as part of a general education. For most of the century, 2 reasons for teaching science were commonly given: science aided the student in learning to think logically, and it exhibited to the student the wonders of God's creation. Little thought was given to preparing future scientists, and those Canadians who became professionals had either to resort to schools overseas (usually German or American) or virtually to train themselves with the help of sympathetic professors. The state of science was such, however, that practical work in geology, botany or zoology required far less formal training than it would a century later. Typically, 2 professors, one for natural history and geology, the other for PHYSICS, chemistry and perhaps astronomy, covered the entire range of science. Laboratory practice was unknown until the present century.

The few 19th-century universities to develop curricula beyond the introductory level were those possessing ENGINEERING or medical faculties. McGill, Toronto and, to a lesser extent, Dalhousie, New Brunswick and Queen's, were the sources of science graduates and the employers of the best-known academic scientists. McGill, under the inspired leadership of paleontologist Sir William Dawson, and Toronto, with the physicist James LOUDON as president, moved away from the liberal arts tradition to more professionally oriented education during the last 2 decades of the 19th century. This modernization included the creation of specialized degrees (the Bachelor of Science, BSc), research laboratories for chemistry, physics, biology and engineering, larger staffs and the adoption of the earned doctorate (PhD). The science PhD, an earlier German innovation, required independent research on the part of the student rather than preparation for examinations. American schools adopted doctoral programs from 1876, but Toronto did not award its first, to J.C. MCLENNAN, until 1900.

McGill followed soon after and was quickly emulated by others, such as Queen's, where engineering had developed in the 1890s. This modernization was costly and was borne, in most cases, by provincial authorities eager for economic benefits of scientific training. McGill, which was the object of the private philanthropy of Peter Redpath and Sir William C. MACDONALD, was able to create excellent laboratory facilities and, consequently, could attract a younger generation of scientists such as Ernest RUTHERFORD, Frederick Soddy and Otto Hann, who would become international stars after their Canadian apprenticeships.

Despite the lack of funds, books, laboratories and research students, and the lack of understanding on the part of college councils and provincial legislatures, several college teachers distinguished themselves in their researches. Among them were the natural historian James Robb, biologist and geologist L.W. Bailey and astronomer W.B. JACK in UNB; geologist William Dawson, biologist J.F. Whiteaves and geologist Frank ADAMS at McGill; mathematician Nathan Dupuis and botanist George LAWSON at Queen's (later at Dalhousie); chemist Henry CROFT, at U of T. They were largely self-made scientists and were superseded by a better-educated generation which created the science education format that, with changes, still exists.

In Canada's colleges and universities, science evolved slowly from the liberal arts tradition to the research-oriented system. A strong influence in the West was H.M. Tory, a McGill mathematician and physicist and later president of the NRC, who was not only the outstanding institution builder of the interwar years but also one convinced of the importance of science in the university curriculum. The western schools were thus able to attract first-rate staffs, including physicist Gordon Shrum (a co-worker of Sir John McLennan's at Toronto) at UBC, chemist John SPINKS and astrophysicist Gerhard HERZBERG at Saskatchewan, and physicist R.W. BOYLE at Alberta.

The end of WWII signalled a massive influx of students, the availability of many young scientists who had been involved in the war effort and greater financial resources from governments. These developments led to a new phase in university science, one devoted to larger faculties, new specialties and facilities and, from the 1960s, a stronger emphasis on the importance of science for society. Older schools became centres of excellence: Western Ontario became noted for biomedical research, SPECTROSCOPY and astronomy, McMaster for nuclear science and engineering, Manitoba for agricultural science and biology. At the same time, the tremendous increase in students and interest in higher education during the 1960s and 1970s resulted in establishment of new universities, distinguished from the outset by scientific specialization, including York in biology and space science, Waterloo in COMPUTER SCIENCE and engineering, and Victoria in physics.

The relative lack of interest in science as a profession in French Canada meant that the move to modern laboratory-oriented science was slower in Québec. Laval created a FORESTRY school in 1910, followed a decade later with its École supérieure de chimie (1920); at the same time, U de M became independent of Laval and inaugurated its faculty of sciences. The École polytechnique de Montréal, founded on a small scale by U.E. Archambault in 1873, became linked to the new university as its faculty of engineering. Real expansion in the sciences, in terms of facilities, faculty and student numbers, did not occur until the 1960s. Even by the late 1960s,

Debates over the nature of the universe are full of philosophical implications for humanity. The concept of black holes has challenged the long-standing theories of gravitation and quantum mechanics – and may provide the long-sought link between the 2 (*artist's conception by Helmut K. Wimmer*).

McGill was producing nearly twice as many PhDs and first degrees in science as Laval and Montréal together.

Scientific Organizations The pattern of growth of Canada's scientific organizations, institutions and publications is unique, because of the nature of Canadian government, education, population mixture and distribution and economic patterns. Professional societies were late in emerging; their predecessors were strongly oriented towards amateurs and those for whom science was a cultural outlet or entertainment. The first of these societies, the LITERARY AND HISTORICAL SOCIETY OF QUEBEC (1824), enrolled amateurs and a small band of military men of the Québec garrison with a penchant for geology or exploration. The Natural History Society of Montreal (1827) was dominated by amateurs until after mid-century when William Dawson, together with his scientific colleagues at McGill, raised the level of professionalism. The Geological Survey's paleontologist, Elkanah BILLINGS, founded in 1856 Canada's first scientific journal, the *Canadian Naturalist and Geologist*, which became the official organ of the society. It remained the most important outlet for papers on geology, botany and zoology until the turn of the century. No francophone scientific society of any size emerged before the 20th century, although Abbé Léon Provancher published the *Naturaliste canadien* from 1868.

In the Maritimes, Saint John geologists Charles Hartt and G.F. Matthew created the Natural History Society of New Brunswick (est 1863) and published its *Transactions*, while a group centered at Dalhousie University directed the Nova Scotian Institute of Science (est 1862) and produced its *Transactions*. In Ontario, the Canadian Institute was formed by engineers and university scientists in 1849, launching the *Canadian Journal* in 1852, the primary outlet for Toronto science until the end of the century. Smaller organizations, some devoted to natural history, others to more general scientific and cultural ends, appeared in Fredericton; Kingston, Ottawa, Belleville, Hamilton and London, Ont; and Winnipeg.

By the time of Confederation, the first societies devoted to one science appeared: the Toronto Astronomical Club (1868), which evolved into the ROYAL ASTRONOMICAL SOCIETY OF CANADA, and the Entomological Society of Ontario. None of these

societies were for professionals, still too few in number, and many faded and disappeared in the early years of the 20th century. The marquess of LORNE was instrumental in founding the first organization for distinguished scientists, the ROYAL SOCIETY OF CANADA, in 1882. The Royal Society, with so few specialists in any one field, failed to provide the institutional basis for professional scientists. It has never found a clearly defined role and its journal, the *Proceedings and Transactions,* already marginal in the 19th century, ceased to be of much value for the scientific community in the 20th. The 20th century brought the rise of professional, disciplinary organizations and the demise of most of the amateur and general societies. The largest single discipline, chemistry, has been served by a series of organizations dating from the mid-19th century; in 1920, the nationwide Canadian Institute of Chemistry was formed, which evolved into the Chemical Institute of Canada in 1945, launching *Chemistry in Canada* 4 years later. With more than 10 000 members, the CIC, with its subdisciplinary and regional branches, represents the scientific area most closely allied with the Canadian economy. Other large disciplines followed: the Geological Association of Canada, 1947; Canadian Association of Physicists, 1946, sponsor of the journal *Physics in Canada* from 1949; and several smaller groups in the life sciences which formed the Canadian Federation of Biological Societies in 1957. A number of newer specialties have become foci of societies and journals, mostly dating from the late 1950s to the present. The first truly international journal in Canada, the *Canadian Journal of Research*, established by the NRC in 1929, was successively split into NRC-published specialist journals, as the quantity of papers in new disciplines grew.

The style and aims of scientific organizations differed in French Canada during the 20th century. Attempts to form scientific societies for Francophones late in the 19th century had mostly failed but, by the 1920s and 1930s, several professional groups began to emerge, particularly the Association canadienne-française pour l'avancement des sciences (ACFAS), which affiliated local and specialist societies. ACFAS, like its British, French and American counterparts, successfully grouped scientists from all disciplines and took special pains to popularize science in Québec. No anglophone organization has ever seriously attempted either function; consequently, the association's popular journal, *Québec Science*, has no English-language equivalent. The defunct *Science Forum* appealed more narrowly to those with SCIENCE POLICY interests. The need for a voice in government circles led to the formation by Canadian scientific and engineering societies of SCITEC (Association of Scientific, Engineering and Technical Community of Canada) in 1970 but, as an organization of organizations rather than of individuals, it has primarily restricted its activities to lobbying.

Before the 1960s, popular interest in science had few outlets, besides scientific collections in federal or provincial museums. The great stimulus of space exploration has, as in the US, added new dimensions to popular awareness of science. Most major cities possess planetariums or science-oriented museums such as Ottawa's National Museum of Science and Technology, Toronto's ONTARIO SCIENCE CENTRE and Winnipeg's Manitoba Museum of Man and Nature, attracting millions of visitors annually (*see* SCIENCE CENTRES). The Canadian media have been more conservative in their attempts to popularize science (*see* SCIENCE AND SOCIETY). Amateur societies and clubs for geology and natural history exist across the country, while astronomy, perhaps the most popular amateur science, is represented by the 3000-

strong ROYAL ASTRONOMICAL SOCIETY OF CANADA.

The outstanding feature of 20th-century Canadian science is specialization. In the last century, Canadian contributions to areas other than the earth sciences were few, but a sign of maturity of science is its broadening into new areas, followed by a steady stream of results. The Canadian population has been small in relation to that of world scientific leaders and its scientific manpower numbers only a few thousand; therefore, excellence is possible only in a few areas. The earth sciences have continued to grow in strength, not only in practical work but also in the theoretical, as J.T. WILSON's contributions to PLATE TECTONICS show. The demands for mining and energy sustain the importance of applied research. Chemistry, too, despite fundamental research in the universities and the NRC, has retained its strong practical orientation because of our essentially resource-based economy. The forestry research centres at Laval and Toronto, and the Pulp and Paper Research Institute of Canada at McGill are internationally known; research in METALLURGY by International Nickel (INCO LTD), Falconbridge, DOMINION FOUNDRIES AND STEEL, LTD and STELCO is necessary to maintain a competitive place in the metals markets; PHARMACEUTICAL chemistry in Montréal and biomedical and GENETIC research in centres in Toronto, Montréal, London and Saskatoon have placed Canada in the vanguard of life science research. AGRICULTURAL RESEARCH has a long and illustrious history, dating from the production of Marquis WHEAT by Saunders. Researches on new grains such as TRITICALE, on new uses for older plants such as rapeseed (CANOLA) and on pest control methods and widespread work on plant breeding and ANIMAL BREEDING in government laboratories, research councils and universities, especially Saskatchewan, Guelph and Manitoba, have created a pool of expertise and products employed throughout the world.

As a result of the small communities of researchers and the lack of financial resources, the glamour areas of contemporary science (such as astrophysics, radio astronomy, nuclear particle research, solid state physics, recombinant DNA research and theoretical work in general) are cultivated on a much more modest scale in Canada than in the US, the USSR or Britain. Canadian scientists in these specialties have built up relationships with colleagues in other English- and French-speaking nations, which have allowed them access to facilities impossible to obtain at home. These links ensure that Canadian scientists will not be restricted to practical, economically oriented research but, in small numbers, can share in the excitement at the cutting edge of modern research.

The concepts and methods of science are universal, but its social relations, politics and structure are unique to each nation. In a country as large as Canada, these aspects of science also have a regional flavour. Canadian science has strong similarities to American science but has its special properties: the strong and central role of the NRC in its laboratories and funding; the federal-provincial division of science funding and policy making; and the specialization of science strengths in areas tied closely to the economy. The "big science" element in American science, ie, large teams, huge financial resources and extensive facilities, are lacking in Canada, where no substantial industrial research effort is undertaken and where a small defence establishment has not required large-scale projects of science-based technology. Nonetheless, Canadian science has made significant contributions to knowledge and, during the 20th century, has become an integral part of the international scientific effort.

RICHARD A. JARRELL

Reading: R.A. Jarrell and N.R. Ball, eds, *Science, Technology and Canadian History* (1980); T.H. Levere and Jarrell, eds, *A Curious Field-Book: Science and Society in Canadian History* (1974); G.F.G. Stanley, *Pioneers of Canadian Science* (1966).

Science and Society Most Canadians are unaware of the profound effect SCIENCE has on their daily lives. While politicians, labour leaders and business people take actions which influence our lives, most of these actions pale in significance when compared to the long-term effects of experiments going on in laboratories around the world. Consider the impact of a few of the discoveries that have occurred in a single generation: polio vaccine, kidney and heart transplants, transistors, jet planes, space travel, nuclear weapons, GENETIC ENGINEERING, cloning, antibiotics, tranquillizers, microwave heating, computers, LASERS, PLASTICS, TELEVISION, contraceptives, test-tube babies and the extinction of smallpox.

N American society exhibits a puzzling dichotomy: we have the highest level of LITERACY, the most widely available higher EDUCATION and the broadest exposure to information (via print and electronic media) in history, yet there is a remarkable ignorance of science and TECHNOLOGY. Only a handful of NEWSPAPERS and MAGAZINES employ full-time science or medical reporters, while primetime television is virtually devoid of science. Tabloids that publish sensational stories of monsters, UFO landings and miracle cancer cures are much more widely circulated than science magazines. In fact, Canada lacks a national science magazine of interest to the general reader. Québec is the exception, with the popular *Québec Science*. This broad ignorance of science and technology is reflected in our elected representatives: over 80% of all members of Parliament come from the law or business – 2 professions whose members are notoriously ignorant of science. Yet these leaders daily make decisions in which a considerable amount of scientific and technical expertise is required. Our society readily accepts the products of scientific innovation but remains virtually ignorant of their source. In order to understand how this situation has arisen, we must look back to our evolutionary roots.

Human Evolution Our prehistoric, protohuman ancestors were not gifted with the survival attributes of many of their mammalian contemporaries (speed, strength, size, armour, fangs, camouflage or claws). Their genetically dictated survival strategy rested primarily on a complex brain which, with its capacity to remember, imagine and think in abstract terms, freed early humans from the tight constraints of instinct and gave them choice. Nevertheless, there were numerous situations in which the rational, analytical functions of the brain were too slow and the capacity to react instantly, without conscious thought, had an important survival value. The imprint of both evolutionary developments remains with us as we struggle with the duality of human personality: the rational, analytical side that often conflicts with the emotional, nonrational, visceral impulse. The power of the human brain was unprecedented in the history of life on the planet. *Homo sapiens* evolved language and the ability to transmit knowledge from generation to generation. Not only did this ability compensate for the lack of other physical attributes but it also enabled human beings to develop CULTURE. Cultural evolution was thousands of times more rapid than biological evolution.

In their attempts to impose order on the apparent chaos of events, early humans began with the recognizable regularities in the world: day and night, the seasons, TIDES, plant succession, animal MIGRATION. Their explanations of these regularities and other, more unusual events were embodied in mythologies and usually referred to divine forces as the ultimate cause. World views had to be all-embracing and, therefore, were vulnerable to disruption by events which simply could not be explained.

Our complex brain has been a spectacularly "successful" survival strategy, based on the numbers of our species and the territory we occupy. However, while we as a species have transcended the constraints of day-to-day survival, we nevertheless behave as if that remains our dominant priority. We are still compelled to reproduce, accumulate material goods and fight rivals as if we lived under the same conditions that existed tens of thousands of years back. In the Western world, the ultimate expression of the human brain is its technological inventions, which have become so powerful and fast that they now exceed the brain's ability to control them.

Evolution of Science In the 17th century, Francis Bacon recognized that "knowledge [*scientia*] is power." Through science, Bacon thought, we could come to understand how God works and, armed with these insights, could carry out the biblical injunction to dominate and subdue nature. Bacon saw science in the service of God and foresaw no conflict with the established church. Early scientists perceived that nature reflects an overall design, obeys recognizable principles and laws, and follows a wonderful regularity – all of which pointed to the divine work of God. Thus, understanding nature only increased one's sense of the greatness of God. The scientific method admits to the impossibility of making sense of the entire cosmos with a single, all-inclusive explanation. Instead, science concentrates on a very small part of nature, isolating it as fully as possible from everything else. The power of this way of knowing soon became apparent as astronomers, such as Copernicus, Kepler and Galileo, began to question cosmic dogma. Their work led to the heliocentric theory of planetary movement, which clashed with the notion of Earth as the centre of the universe. In the 19th century, geologist Charles Lyell countered church estimates of Earth's age by proposing that the planet might be tens of millions, if not billions, of years old. In 19th-century Canada, the descriptive approach of natural history provided an ideal activity for the deeply religious English communities. There was no history of experimental investigation in this young country but there was a strong sense of colonial status. However, N America was a new frontier with untold and untapped "resources." Science was valued insofar as it could aid directly in the exploitation of these resources; eg, by identifying the locations of ore deposits, geological surveys provided valuable information for a mining industry, just as descriptions of plants and animals became an inventory of potentially useful biological organisms. The thrust of Canadian "science" thus was highly descriptive and was based on the conviction that by meticulous cataloguing of God's works, unexpected insights would be obtained.

Charles Darwin then shook the Christian notion of man's special place on Earth with the proposal that, like all other life forms, humans had evolved from ancestral species. In each instance (the heliocentric theory, geological age, evolution, etc) the battle which took place between church dogma and scientific theory ended with the confirmation of the validity of scientific insights, while having a secondary effect of reducing the church's sphere of influence. Science came to be freed not only from the constricting bonds of dogma but also from considerations of morality.

In Canada, one of the leading opponents of Darwin's ideas was Sir J.W. DAWSON, an eminent geologist and principal of McGill University. Dawson vigorously attacked Darwin's key proposal that evolution proceeded by the gradual accumulation of genetic change over long periods of time. Dawson argued that the fossil record did not support this notion – the changes in fossils seemed to occur suddenly. Ironically, Dawson's arguments lost to the forces of Darwinism, yet today his very evidence is accepted and used to support a modern theory that evolution does occur suddenly in major jumps, rather than by slow incremental change.

The scientific method, of necessity, is "reductionist" in that its power comes from focusing on a small part of nature. The success of this approach suggested that the whole could be inferred from the sum of its parts. For example, researchers in PHYSICS were driven by Newton's faith that, as the layers of complexity in nature were stripped away, we would ultimately arrive at the fundamental particle of which all matter is made, and from that elementary entity, the entire cosmos would eventually be comprehensible. But early in the 20th century, physics underwent a profound philosophical upheaval when Albert Einstein introduced the "Alice-in-Wonderland" concept of relativity, where mass and energy are interchangeable, and a universe in which what we see depends on our point of view. Werner Karl Heisenberg further clouded the Newtonian dream by pointing out that, in studying nature, the investigator intrudes in a way that alters the phenomenon under observation; ie, we alter even subatomic particles in the attempt to measure them. Niels Bohr's new theory of the atom altered the picture of electrons orbiting nuclei like planets around a sun, to one of clouds of electrons in which the density of the cloud reflected the probability that an electron would be found in that region. Thus, the behaviour of subatomic particles is neither absolute nor fixed. Furthermore, at each increase in complexity of matter, new properties emerge which could not have been predicted from the properties of the constituent parts. Thus, while a great deal is known about the atomic properties of oxygen and hydrogen, very little of that information is useful for predicting what their properties will be when combined in a water molecule.

Clearly, a reductionist approach cannot provide adequate information about the structure or properties of matter; still less does it allow for the control of natural phenomena. Unfortunately, these philosophical insights have not percolated from physics to the other natural sciences. Much of BIOLOGY, both cellular and ecological, is still predicated on the principle of understanding the whole by studying its isolated parts. The limitations of the reductionism of science become apparent when the theory is applied. The untenable notion that we can "manage" SALMON or FORESTS, as if they were cows or tomatoes, is an expression of faith in the reductionism of science, yet the results of our attempts put the lie to that faith.

Modern Science One of the most important aspects of modern science has been its close association with industrial and military activities; the primary stimuli for its growth and support have been global crises. This pattern is especially true in Canada where, as we have already noted, "science" had been concerned primarily with cataloguing the wondrous storehouse of nature. While most technology was imported, there were exceptions, such as the breeding of Marquis WHEAT at the turn of the century. As Omond SOLANDT has noted, modern Canadian INDUSTRIAL RESEARCH, innovations and development were closely tied to the needs of the Allies in WWII. The growth of HIGH TECHNOLOGY industries in nuclear power, telecommunications, computers and aerospace was possible because of the support of military interests through the Defence Research Board.

From its origins as an indulgence by aristocrats or as the pure curiosity of university scholars, science has become the source of ideas for technology and INDUSTRY, a multibillion-dollar activity spewing forth a cornucopia of weapons and consumer items. The enormous proliferation of the scientific profession in the latter part of this century is illustrated by the fact that "of all scientists who ever lived, 90% are still alive and publishing today." Before this century, the interval between a discovery and its application was usually measured in decades; that interval has now been reduced practically to zero. The rapidity with which innovations such as chemically modified female hormones (eg, ESTROGEN) for oral consumption, lasers and transistors have been adapted for use attests to the speed of application of new ideas. In some cases, systems for using phenomena precede their actual discovery. For example, while BLACK HOLES have been extensively discussed by theoretical physicists and none has yet been proved to exist, already a proposal has been made to harness them to produce energy. Because of the intricate relationship between industry, jobs and the economy, it is often found that upon detection of a potential hazard (such as an environmental carcinogen or occupational risk), the burden of proof rests with the potential victim. Usually this means that there must be a convincing body of proof before corrective action is taken. Canada's difficulty in stimulating action on US-caused ACID RAIN illustrates the problems of taking political action, even when the data are very clear.

In society, the impact of television, birth-control pills or computers ripples far beyond the immediate value of the technology itself. In this century, science and technology are creating problems for which there are no precedents and which are altering our very concepts of society and humanity. For example, in MEDICINE, the major health problems of malnutrition, infection and sepsis have been effectively controlled in N America. Medical research, therefore, is turning to the treatment of non-life-threatening problems (psychiatric disorders, herpes, cosmetic surgery, etc) and the consequences of effective medical treatment (eg, retinal detachment in diabetics, congenital defects, diseases of old age). Hearts were transplanted before there was an accepted definition of DEATH, while sophisticated life-support technologies raise the dilemma of quality of life, medical priorities and euthanasia. The ability to recover human eggs, fertilize them *in vitro* and implant the embryos into a recipient womb now bypasses all biological constraints to parenthood and introduces hitherto undreamed-of legal and moral questions.

Our ability to escape the pull of Earth's gravity has brought outer space within human reach. To whom does this new frontier belong? Can we claim new bodies, such as asteroids or the MOON, in the same way that explorers claimed new continents, by setting foot or capsule and planting a flag? Is outer space a zone to be fought over and in which any nation can park industrial debris or establish new generations of weapons?

The explorations of astrophysicists, eg, the debate over whether the universe is closed or open, are full of philosophical implications for humanity as well. In a closed universe, there is sufficient mass to bring expansion of the universe to a halt 30 billion years after a big bang and to induce its collapse back in another 30 billion. Thus, our present universe would be only the latest in a series of explosions and contractions extending back forever. In an open universe the big bang could only have occurred once, so the universe will continue to expand forever. Of equal philosophical importance is the search for signals indicating the existence of intelligent life elsewhere in the universe. SETI, the Search for Extra-Terrestrial Intelligence, has been prompted by speculations on the statistical probability that, given the number of planets in the universe with conditions comparable to those in the early history of Earth, the evolution of life is highly probable. But demonstration of intelligent life elsewhere will have enormous repercussions for those who accept that human beings were specially created in the image of God or those who hold the notion that we are unique.

Given the limited view provided by scientific insights, we should have learned to be extremely cautious when applying new knowledge to manipulate nature. In this half of the century this caution is becoming especially necessary in the field of GENETICS. We have come to identify DNA as the actual chemical material of heredity, the blueprint that dictates the hereditary properties of all organisms. The structure of DNA has been discovered and the principles whereby it stores and transmits information delineated. Molecular biologists have developed tools to isolate specific sequences of DNA, to read the information contained in them, to synthesize identical replicas and to insert them into virtually any living organism. Genetic engineering, the ability to manipulate the very stuff that determines our special qualities, is now a reality, fraught with potential benefits and hazards.

Perhaps no greater challenge exists than in the creation, by humans, of a technology that could conceivably exceed the intelligence of its creators. Computers with ARTIFICIAL INTELLIGENCE (AI) are now accepted by computer scientists as a real possibility. With the arrival of genuine thinking machines, we shall reach a new stage in evolution – from biological to cultural to machine intelligence. For, just as human intellect produced an acceleration in cultural evolution, AI will accelerate information processing because of its enormous storage capacity and speed. Human neurons transmit signals at about 100 m/s; computer commands travel at the speed of light. Human performance is disrupted by fatigue, sleep, illness, memory loss, emotional upset and hunger; computers can perform continuously 24 hours a day. Humans must begin each new generation with a prolonged period of education and training; computers will be able to transfer all of their accumulated knowledge to improved machines at the speed of light. The long-term implications of AI become staggering for it will be a technology that will rapidly evolve and will soon exceed our comprehension.

Nothing illustrates more the terrible dilemma of human inventiveness than nuclear weapons. The release of vast amounts of energy by splitting the atom was an exciting corroboration of the predictions of fundamental physics. The controlled release of energy by atomic fission was a dramatic demonstration of the potential of basic research to contribute to society in a practical way. However, the Allied effort in harnessing the atom was motivated by the fear that German physicists would use it to produce a bomb. Canada played a major role in the development of the first atomic bomb as a full partner with Britain and the US (many British scientists worked with Canadian colleagues at Chalk River, Ont, and after the war became part of the daring venture to develop the CANDU reactor). The successful detonation of the first atomic bomb at Alamogordo, New Mexico, 16 July 1945, ushered in a new era of destruction that depended on the inventive abilities of scientists and engineers.

Today the nuclear arsenal contains weapons that operate on the same principle that allows the sun to burn (NUCLEAR FUSION). Now, the nuclear arsenal contains enough explosive potential to destroy every human being on the planet. The arms race has been "rationalized" by military planners with an appropriate acronym, MAD (Mutual Assured Destruction). Yet the reality of nuclear weapons is that if even a small proportion perform as expected and hit their targets, neither side will be able to claim a victory as an electromagnetic surge knocks out most electrical systems to create chaos, while the resulting debris will so blacken the atmosphere that the surface temperature of the planet will plummet (thus creating a so-called "nuclear winter").

What becomes clear is that, while the scientific analytical part of the brain has created terrible weapons, we are impelled to use them by more primitive impulses of self-defence, territoriality and emotion. Each leader of a country, however articulate and reasonable normally, is ultimately a complex individual whose biases, fears and areas of ignorance will affect the way the weapons are used. Modern technology, the crowning achievement of the human brain, has reached a scale of size and speed that is literally out of human control. Thus, nuclear-tipped missiles can now hit targets anywhere on the planet within 10-15 minutes. Even with a perfect defence system that detects and identifies an enemy missile within seconds of its launch, the problems of human reaction time, complex emotional responses to the event, and the need to assimilate the information and formulate a response at several levels of command preclude a rational, considered decision in the response time allowed by the weapons. Thus, as US President Ronald Reagan admitted in Apr 1984, weapons such as his proposed "star-wars" machines in outer space act too fast for human control and will have to be trusted to computers. As the technology increases in speed and complexity, not only do we lose control, but the probability of an accidental firing of a weapon through human or machine error increases proportionately. Nuclear weapons graphically illustrate the dilemma of technology – once invented and used, there is no going back; the situation is irreversible. Profound consequences usually become apparent only much later.

Science and Morality How, then, are we to deal with science and its applications in a way that will maximize the quality of our lives, while minimizing detrimental effects on the environment and other people? Victory on any specific issue, such as acid rain, nuclear weapons or PCBs (polychlorinated biphenyls), will not have affected the primary factor generating the problem in the first place. There must be a fundamental shift in perspective that will come from a recognition that as long as we see ourselves as separate from nature, superior to all other beings, compelled to use every "resource" and capable of understanding and controlling all of nature through science and technology, we will never escape the cycle of harmful or destructive results. Scientific research provides powerful insights that lead to the capacity to interfere with and control a part of nature. But the necessity of seeing nature in bits and pieces precludes any ability to evaluate the effect of a manipulation on the rest of nature. Science is a way of knowing, but there are many others (music, art, literature, etc). Science is not in the business of finding absolute truth; instead, it is constantly disproving or modifying its current theories. The assumption that human control is not subject to unpredictable or uncontrollable natural forces or human fallibility dooms us.

All technological designs and plans are predicated on the notion that human beings will respond rationally in all predictable situations. Yet anyone who has participated in a debate over ABORTION, nuclear power, political ideology or religion realizes that rationality plays a small role in shaping our actions. Technologies cannot be "foolproof" unless they eliminate the "fool" who, as HAL the computer in the movie *2001* realized, is any fallible human being. People get sick, emotionally disturbed, intoxicated, tired; in short, we are distractable and no one can predict the foolish behaviour that may result. Unless technology is designed with that insight, it will remain prone to breakdown. It is not clear how that can be done; however, without a shift in perspective before examination of the challenge, it will not be possible.

The way to change profoundly thinking about science and technology must come from a broad public understanding of the foundations of the scientific enterprise, its basic methodology and its limitations, and of the social context within which it is used. As long as science is effectively removed from the social reality of most people, that change will not take place. As long as society continues to fragment its activities into spheres of expertise distinguished by special knowledge and jargon, we are effectively barred from affecting those activities. Science must not continue to remain in the jurisdiction of experts and people with vested interests, for theirs is a severely restricted perspective. Just as military leaders must, in a democracy, submit to the dictates of the popularly elected government, so those who apply science should come under the control of our political representatives who, in turn, must be capable of understanding the scientific and technical counsel of experts. The process of making science a political priority comes from the bottom up, impressed on candidates for office by an informed and concerned electorate.

Science Education Canada's educational system pays little attention to the need to educate future lay citizens as well as prospective science students in science and technology. In the first national survey of science education in Canada, the SCIENCE COUNCIL OF CANADA documented serious deficits from elementary to high schools. The study pointed to problems in both teaching personnel and facilities. Across Canada, over half of all early (grades 1-6) schoolteachers have had no university level MATHEMATICS courses, while three-quarters had no science. In the middle years (grades 7-9), one-third of all teachers have had no math or science since high school. In the senior years, while 95% of teachers have had some university level science, over one-third had taken their last course over a decade ago. In science, experimental observation is a critical part of the activity, yet in elementary schools, fewer than one in 5 teachers even have occasional access to a science room. In consequence, science is taught sporadically, often varying from school to school. These conditions are in striking contrast to the Japanese school system, in which science is a priority subject from primary school on. In Canadian high schools, science courses are designed for the small percentage of graduates who will go on to enrol in science programs in universities and technical schools. There is considerable emphasis on mathematics as a prerequisite for doing science, with the result that students who have difficulty with math often conclude that science is simply beyond their grasp. Eventually, being unable to do math leads to the conclusion that science does not affect one in daily life.

The results of the above deficiencies and others, such as inadequate textbooks, lab equipment, etc, are that science is rarely taught adequately (if at all) in elementary schools across Canada; students who are high achievers and science enthusiasts are not challenged by science courses; very

little is taught about the interactions among science, technology and society; Canadian students are taught very little about scientific and technological advances made in this country; from an early age, girls are turned away from science and do not see career opportunities in science and technology. This situation has led the Science Council to endorse a concept of science for all, stated by the US National Science Teachers Association: "Every child shall study science every day of every year." In order to achieve a scientifically literate society, the Science Council warns of the hazards of the current situation and strongly urges the adoption of 47 recommendations which would radically change the teaching of science without requiring major overhauling of the educational system. The lack of scientific literacy reflects itself in the priorities of upper management in the electronic and print media as well as in politicians. If a society is to consider seriously the place of science and technology, then it must have an aware public. Although all the recommendations have been widely accepted by both federal and provincial governments, only low-cost changes have been implemented

Science education should not be restricted to knowing the definition of terms, principles and the latest theories. The greatest lesson from science for all aspects of culture is its skepticism, its demand for a rigorous presentation and analysis of data. Canadians today consume information at an astonishing rate. By the criteria of hours of television watched, newspapers, books and magazines purchased and years of schooling, we have access to information to an unprecedented degree, although most of this information will ultimately be judged wrong, trivial or unimportant. Scientific skepticism demands more than repeating an anecdote or referring to something "I saw on TV" or "I read." Science does not accept as truth a statement based simply on a television program or a printed source. The profound thrust of science education must be to inculcate this rigour and skepticism in the INFORMATION AGE. *See also* ASTRONOMY; BIOCHEMISTRY; BIOETHICS; ELECTRONICS; IMMUNOLOGY; INVENTORS AND INNOVATION; MEDICAL ETHICS; MOLECULAR BIOLOGY; PHILOSOPHY; POLLUTION; ROBOTICS; SCIENCE POLICY; SCIENTIFIC RESEARCH AND DEVELOPMENT. DAVID T. SUZUKI

Reading: Carl Berger, *Science, God and Nature in Victorian Canada* (1983); Science Council of Canada, *Science Education in Canada* (3 vols, 1984).

Science Centre, establishment devoted to the popular exposition of science by means of participatory exhibits. For example, an elementary PHYSICS gallery might invite visitors to push handles to test the effects of leverage, to swing on merry-go-rounds to experience changes in moments of inertia, to pump air or water to demonstrate the principles of fluid dynamics and to crank handles to generate electricity. While science museums, with static displays of scientific and technological objects, have existed for many years, science centres are a contemporary phenomenon aimed at making science subjects more accessible to the general public. The movement to popularize science has been fueled in many Western societies by the perceived economic threat of newly industrialized nations such as Japan. Japan's success in producing quality manufactured goods at lower prices is partly attributed to better scientific and technological education.

Most physical-science subjects are difficult to display. The first to succeed in building participatory exhibits were German industrialists at the Deutsches Museum in Munich in 1906. Later, other museums of the history of science (eg, in London, Chicago, Philadelphia, Boston) added some working exhibits to their historical artifacts.

Only after 1960 did the Philips Company in Amsterdam, Frank Oppenheimer in San Francisco and the Ontario government in Toronto establish museums devoted predominantly to experiments in modern science rather than to the display of historical objects.

The ONTARIO SCIENCE CENTRE, designed by Toronto architect Raymond MORIYAMA, is the oldest in Canada and opened in Toronto in 1969. The Ontario government founded it as a museum of the history of technology but, when it was discovered that historical exhibits of the highest quality were almost unobtainable, the Cabinet ordered the centre to abandon its traditional objectives and to build working exhibits. It has 400 "hands-on" exhibits, more than any other institution. The centre caters to organized groups (168 541 students and teachers in 1986) and to the general public (787 835 people in 1986). In 1982, in collaboration with the Chinese, the OSC staged an exhibition on Chinese science that attracted visitors who paid over $3 million in fees. It was the largest temporary exhibition of a cultural nature ever held in Canada, and it toured the US. On 20 Sept 1983 the OSC opened a return exhibition in Beijing. Copies of OSC exhibits were sold to the Chinese by Ontario industry for $400 000. On 8 Oct 1983 the centre opened a tour in Japan; the Japanese paid $780 000 for the Canadian-made exhibits. Delegates from the UK, the US and France have also visited Canada to investigate science centres and purchase exhibits.

Today, Canada is fortunate in having more science centres, in various stages of development, than any other country, except perhaps the US. These developments are the result of local initiatives across the country. In Vancouver a world-class, full-facility science centre, SCIENCE WORLD, will open in 1989 at the Expo Centre, the geodesic dome designed by Bruno Freschi. In Alberta, contributions from the provincial government ($5 million), the city of Edmonton ($5 million) and private and corporate donors allowed construction of the Edmonton Space Sciences Centre. The striking building was designed by Douglas J. CARDINAL. Zeiss Jena produced the star projector for the planetarium (Margaret Ziedler Star Theatre) and IMAX, the curved-screen film projector for the Devonian Theatre. The centre has 2 large galleries to be devoted to largely participatory exhibits. Edmonton also boasts a smaller centre, the Alberta Energy Natural Science Centre, which has many computer exhibits. In Regina volunteers have acquired the shell of an abandoned power plant in Wascana Park in the city centre for a science centre. In Sudbury Inco, Falconbridge Mines, the Ontario government and many citizens made possible the renovation of a working mine and have built a pavilion for a science centre, Science North, at a cost of $15 million. The centre, designed by Raymond Moriyama, opened in May 1984. In London, Ont, the London Regional Children's Museum is now operating in a downtown school. The museum has participatory experiments and programs, which enable students to dig and reassemble the casts of dinosaur bones, dress up and re-enact the past, or perform scientific experiments on their own. In Niagara Falls, Ontario Hydro and the Niagara Parks Commission are planning to convert the powerhouse above the falls into a museum and information centre. Prohibitive costs forced the cessation of similar plans in 1983. The building is the finest conspicuous example of architecture in the region. On 13 Nov 1983 Prem René Lévesque announced that Québec intended to build a science centre on Île Ste-Hélène, Montréal, on the 1967 world's fair site. Other centres are planned for Calgary, Winnipeg and the Atlantic provinces.

J. TUZO WILSON

Edmonton Space Sciences Centre, designed by architect Douglas Cardinal (*photo by J.A. Kraulis*).

Science Council of Canada, organization created by federal statute in 1966 to advise the government on SCIENCE and TECHNOLOGY policy. The original membership was 25 appointed scientists and senior federal civil servants, later altered to 30 appointed scientists, from the natural and SOCIAL SCIENCES, and no civil servants. While the statute provided that the council would undertake specific studies at ministerial request, its practice has been to determine its own study program, with virtual autonomy from ministerial direction. The council's published work consists of signed background studies expressing the views of the authors, but certified by council for reliability and methodology; formal council reports and statements, expressing the consensus of members, and usually recommending actions to governments and other parties; and proceedings of workshops and conferences. The council's judgements derive their legitimacy from the fact that its members are broadly representative of the Canadian scientific community, in both the academic and private sectors.

Over the first 17 years of its work, the council has held different perceptions of its primary role, depending on the beliefs of its various chairmen and members. It has most often seen itself as a national adviser, transcending purely federal considerations. It has also assumed an early warning function, to alert governments and society to emerging opportunities and problems. It has championed university research, especially basic research, against government predispositions to cut budgets. Occasionally, it has essayed an international role. Under its responsibility for enhancing public awareness of science and technology policy, it has undertaken a public discussion role through stimulating or organizing conferences and other meetings aimed at professionals.

Probably its most enduring preoccupation and greatest contribution has been in advocating a national industrial strategy. The council has argued against the mainstream of advice from other agencies, public and private, and against the apparent inclinations of federal ministers. By 1983 it seemed to have begun to turn the tide, at least in general terms. Indeed, the council's recommen-

dations have more often been effective in helping to create a policy climate than in providing specific blueprints for government action. Since its inception, the council's chairmen have been Omond SOLANDT, Roger Gaudry, Joseph Kates, Claude Fortier, Stuart L. Smith and Geraldine Kenney-Wallace.

LESLIE MILLIN

Science Fiction explores possible alternative realities, usually placed in the future. Most Canadian SF deals with the near future on Earth. *The Handmaid's Tale* (1986) by Margaret ATWOOD, *Voices in Time* (1980) by Hugh MACLENNAN and *Starmaggedon* (1986) by Richard ROHMER are prime examples. Computers are a popular theme of Canadian SF, beginning with *The Adolescence of P-1* (1977) by Thomas J. Ryan and further explored in *Planiverse* (1984) by A.K. Dewdney. The computer novel *Neuromancer* (1984) by William Gibson spawned a raft of American imitators called the Cyberpunk Movement.

Canadian novels about other planets appear occasionally, including *Courtship Rite* (1982) by Donald Kingsbury and *Station Gehenna* (1987) by Andrew Weiner, but these often involve human outposts on harsh worlds, a subject that has its roots in the survival theme of mainstream Canadian literature. Phyllis GOTLIEB is Canada's reigning queen of far-future, outer-space SF. She has published 6 novels since 1964, including *A Judgment of Dragons* (1980).

Canada has one SF magazine, the French *Solaris* (fd 1974), edited and published by Elisabeth Vonarburg, a leading Québecois SF writer who is the author of *Le silence de la Cité* (1981). *Other Canadas* (1979), edited by John Robert COLOMBO was the first Canadian SF anthology. Judith Merrill edited *Tesseracts* (1985), the first anthology of strictly modern Canadian SF. Both contain French-language work in translation. *Visions from the Edge* (1981) is a collection of Atlantic Canadian SF edited by John Bell and Lesley Choyce.

Canadian publishers release single-author SF short-story collections from time to time. The first was *North by 2000* (1976) by H.A. Hargreaves. Also noteworthy are *Melancholy Elephants* (1984) by Spider Robinson and *The Woman who is the Midnight Wind* (1987) by Terence M. Green.

Canadians do well with the 2 English-language international SF awards, the Nebula (presented by the Science Fiction Writers of America, which has 21 Canadians among its 900 members) and the Hugo (a readers' choice award). Spider and Jeanne Robinson shared both awards for the 1977 novella *Stardance* and Spider won the short story Hugo for his 1982 *Melancholy Elephants*. William Gibson won both best novel awards for *Neuromancer*. Phyllis Gotlieb's 1972 novella *Son of the Morning* was a Nebula nominee. Donald Kingsbury received Hugo nominations for *Courtship Rite* and his 1979 novella *The Moon Goddess and the Son*. Margaret Atwood was a Nebula nominee for *The Handmaid's Tale*.

ROBERT J. SAWYER

Science Policy, term which came into use in the 1960s to denote the co-ordinated measures that should be taken by governments to promote the development of scientific and technological research and, especially, to guide the exploitation of research results to further national economic growth and welfare. State patronage of SCIENCE and TECHNOLOGY was not new; indeed it has a long history. What was new was the growing sense, among the public and political leaders, of the central importance of science and technology in the modern world and of the need for more systematic action by governments to direct and control their use. A 1963 Organization for Economic Co-operation and Development report stated: "To say that a government needs an articulated science policy is simply to note that there has devolved upon that government a major and continuing responsibility to make choices about issues that involve science." Science had become a "national asset" (*see* INVENTORS AND INNOVATION).

The need for national science policy was widely promoted in the 1960s and early 1970s by international agencies (eg, OECD) and by a multiplicity of official and unofficial bodies in many countries; however, there were serious disagreements about the precise form science policy should take and the appropriate governmental institutions for making it. The most important institutional developments in Canada were the creation of a Science Secretariat (1964) in the PRIVY COUNCIL OFFICE, establishment of the SCIENCE COUNCIL OF CANADA (1966), and creation of the Ministry of State for Science and Technology (1971). The most important documents to emerge in the debate were reports by the Science Council, especially its 4th report, *Towards a National Science Policy in Canada* (Oct 1968), the *Review of Science Policy, Canada* by OECD (1969), and the 3 comprehensive reports from the Senate Special Committee on Science Policy (the Lamontagne Committee), which was set up in 1967 and sat for more than 5 years.

Science policy can be said to have 2 complementary aspects: policy for promoting science, ie, the provision by governments of an environment that fosters growth of scientific and technological knowledge; and policy for using science, ie, the exploitation of this knowledge in development and innovation. The former might be taken to mean a collection of policies that are pursued, more or less independently, by government agencies to sponsor research relating solely to their specific functional responsibilities. In this sense, most "advanced" nations (and certainly Canada) could be said to have had a policy for promoting science for more than a century. However, more than this minimal definition is intended: namely, a comprehensive and coherent policy for government support of science and technology generally. This point was made by the Glassco Commission (*see* GOVERNMENT ORGANIZATION, ROYAL COMMISSION ON) in a report published in 1962. The commission was strongly critical of what it regarded as the unco-ordinated and policyless expansion of science and technology in Canada after WWII, and this criticism led directly to the establishment of the Science Secretariat. Moreover, in an era in which advances in scientific knowledge were creating many more opportunities for exploitation than could be satisfied with the resources that were available, there was need for establishment of priorities.

In a "small-science" country like Canada, especially, there were severe limits on what kinds of science and technology could be supported. Thus, it was argued that a policy for promoting science must be based on carefully specified "criteria for scientific choice"; ie, on principles for deciding how much support in the form of public money and other resources (eg, trained personnel) should go to the nation's science and technology as a whole; how this "pool" should then be distributed sector by sector (ie, among university research, "in-house" research done by government agencies, and research done by industry); and, lastly, how each of these sectoral allocations should be distributed among the various scientific and technological disciplines. The implementation of these criteria would have an indirect effect on the rate of growth and the direction taken by the various sciences and technologies, and a direct effect on the balance between basic science, applied science and development through technological innovation. The Science Council, OECD and the Lamontagne Committee all ar-

gued strongly that the promotion of Canadian science had been too heavily weighted towards basic research and that both basic and applied research were too far removed from the point where development could take place (namely INDUSTRY). Much has been done since the 1970s to correct this imbalance, although problems persist, since so much Canadian industry is "branch-plant industry," for which the research and development is done in the laboratories of parent companies in the US.

A government could pursue a coherent policy for promoting basic and applied science using criteria that make little or no reference to the relevance of the research to specific social needs or national priorities. Such a policy could support those areas of research that seem to promise the most important results from a scientific point of view, and those scientists who were demonstrably the most competent and productive. Indeed, this policy was pursued for many years by the NATIONAL RESEARCH COUNCIL, the objective of which was to build a viable "science base" in Canada and to create a body of competent scientists who could take their place in the international science community. If, however, science policy is also to relate directly to the use of science, criteria of social "relevance" must necessarily be invoked. There are then 3 possibilities. In deciding how government support is to be allocated, public agencies responsible for supporting projects may simply be given a directive to ensure that priority is given to those projects that can demonstrate a direct relevance to specific social needs or to the solution of important social problems. Canadian science policy eventually took this route.

The second possibility, explored by the Science Council in its 4th report, requires that at least a major portion of the nation's scientific and technological effort should be pursued through very large "mission-oriented" projects involving government science agencies, universities and industry. The prototype scientific "mission" was the Manhattan Project in WWII, which produced the first atomic bombs. Postwar examples are the Canadian NUCLEAR-ENERGY program that developed the CANDU reactor, and the American and Soviet space programs. The Science Council recommended "that most new undertakings in Canadian science be organized as large, multidisciplinary, mission-oriented projects having as a goal the solution of some important economic or social problem in which all the sectors of the scientific community . . . must participate on an equal footing." These "major programs" would each contain components of basic and applied research, development and innovation. The council foresaw future basic research as being done principally in fields allied to these programs, but stressed that it should also be supported as a possible source of new theoretical discoveries and as a means of providing the necessary body of expertise for understanding and absorbing advances made in other countries (notably the US). The council suggested several broad areas in which "missions" would be appropriate, including upper atmosphere and SPACE, WATER resources, TRANSPORTATION, the URBAN environment, and development of the Canadian NORTH and of new ENERGY sources. These proposals were not entirely without effect on the subsequent progress of government support for science and technology in Canada, but the basic idea of a series of major multidisciplinary missions has never been implemented.

The third possibility for structuring policy for the use of science was hinted at, perhaps unwittingly, in the 1963 OECD report which suggested that science policy should lead to "national decisions about where and how fast science will go,

and about the national goals to which it will contribute." Implicit in this statement is the idea of the comprehensive planning of science, according to state-prescribed objectives, such as is supposed to occur in the USSR. The pursuit of science policy within a framework of national goals was given some attention by the Science Council in its 4th report, but there was little apparent relationship between the very general goals it suggested (national prosperity, personal freedom, etc) and the programs it actually prescribed. The notion that science can be comprehensively planned in a free society has now been abandoned by all countries that may have contemplated it, even by France with its long tradition of *dirigisme* and its (post-WWII) adoption of *planification*. In a totalitarian state like the USSR the central planning of science is in principle possible (although in practice it is frequently attended by unfortunate consequences), but in highly pluralistic and decentralized democracies, such as Canada, the idea is now recognized as unattainable, except, perhaps, in the highly unlikely circumstance of a conventional world war in the future. This situation does not solely, or even primarily, arise from inadequacies in governmental machinery; rather, it results from the fact that it is impossible, in Western democracies, to establish by fiat broad societal objectives towards which scientific and technological progress must be directed.

In the course of the international debate about science policy, 3 major options emerged respecting the governmental machinery that might be adopted. The first was the creation of a minister for science, with executive responsibilities, who would head a department for running at least the major government scientific establishments, for funding and other support of the nation's scientific and technological research and development, and (through the minister) for advising on science policy (in the case of parliamentary, cabinet systems of government like Britain and Canada, directly to the Cabinet). The second option was the creation of a minister of scientific affairs or a minister for science policy (possibly heading a department or assisted by an appropriately sized ministerial staff), who would have no executive functions but would serve in an advisory capacity to other departments and agencies and to the Cabinet, and who might also be given certain co-ordinating functions (eg, chairmanship of a Cabinet science-policy committee). The third option was to establish a nonministerial advisory agency in the central core of government (ie, in the Cabinet office or, possibly, in the department responsible for authorizing all government spending). Such an agency would be responsible for advising on the science policy aspects of all government policies and programs, and might be headed by a chief scientific adviser to the government, with direct access to the chief executive (in a parliamentary cabinet system, to the prime minister).

The option of a minister for science was rejected for Canada, chiefly on the grounds that a minister with direct responsibilities for the performance of research in agencies of his own department would not be an impartial adviser on government science policy in general and that the concentration of so many science functions in one place would create an overcentralized and unwieldy administration. The idea was particularly disliked by scientists, who have traditionally been jealous of their autonomy, preferring to operate within a decentralized and pluralistic system. The advisory agency option was adopted, at least in part, by the creation of a Science Secretariat within the Privy Council Office in 1964, and the appointment in 1968 of its director as principal science adviser to the Cabinet. This promising move was abandoned in 1971 when the government shifted to the second option and set up the Ministry of State for Science and Technology. This option has proved to be weak, given the political realities of the Canadian Cabinet and bureaucratic system, and there has been a succession of short-lived incumbents of the office of minister of state, none of whom has been particularly effective. Between 1971 and 1986 the ministry had 13 incumbents and it was reorganized 5 times. In this system, a minister without executive responsibilities tends to have little influence in Cabinet, and this lack of influence means that the office is usually filled either by a prominent political figure for whom the office is simply a stepping-stone to more important posts, or by a lesser figure who is unlikely to advance much farther. On the other hand, if the post is filled by a minister who is given a second (executive) portfolio (as has happened on several occasions), the duties of this portfolio tend to take precedence, to the neglect of the science policy advisory functions.

A further effort to produce a national science and technology policy was initiated in 1986 when, at the request of the federal minister of state for science and technology, the Science Council convened a conference of representatives from industry, labour, the universities and governments. This was part of an ongoing process which included several federal-provincial meetings and a series of conferences between federal officials and provincial officials on a bilateral basis. These steps resulted in the creation of a Council of Science and Technology Ministers in Dec 1986 and the signing of a federal-provincial-territorial agreement on 12 Mar 1987, the purpose of which was, for the first time, to work towards a co-ordinated nationwide strategy to "promote entrepreneurial activity, recognize the critical importance of R & D to Canada's economic, social, cultural and regional development and address the impediments to research, development and innovations." In Jan 1988 PM Mulroney pledged an additional $1.3 billion over 5 years for science and technology. One-quarter was to go towards 2 new initiatives: "centres of excellence" and a national scholarship program.

J.W. GROVE

Reading: G.B. Doern, *Science and Politics in Canada* (1972); N.H. Lithwick, *Canada's Science Policy and the Economy* (1969); Science Council of Canada Background Study No 31, *Knowledge, Power and Public Policy* (1974); Science Council of Canada, *The National Science and Technology Forum* (1986); Senate Special Committee on Science Policy, *A Science Policy for Canada* 3 vols (1970, 1972, 1973).

Scientific Research and Development "Research and Development" is a phrase used to denote activities the overall goal of which is to gain and use knowledge. These activities are normally well organized, making use of the methods of various branches of knowledge and the services of highly trained personnel. Scientific research and development (referred to in this article as "R & D") signifies activities focused on the natural sciences rather than the humanities and social sciences. R & D is usually classified, according to its aims, into 3 broad categories: pure research, applied research and development. Pure research is curiosity oriented, undertaken to advance knowledge for its own sake; applied research is carried out in anticipation that its results will be useful to TECHNOLOGY; development is concerned with transforming technological knowledge into concrete operational hardware. The R & D process is often described by linking the 3 categories. Applied research is said to use the ideas generated by pure research in making inventions which, in turn, are made commercially viable through development. This description, while suggestive of how knowledge is applied, is too simplistic to be of much use in understanding R & D efforts.

R & D in Canada has many similarities with R & D in other countries. An awareness of the general development and chief features of R & D is important for understanding its state in Canada.

R & D, as a formal activity, began to emerge in the second half of the 19th century and grew very rapidly in the 20th. The quickening pace of industrialization in such countries as Germany and the US and the increasing utility of science were important factors in its rise. The growth of R & D occurred within an institutional context, composed of higher education, INDUSTRY and the state. Universities in many countries strove to follow the lead of those in Germany by introducing laboratory science and higher degrees for research, and by coming to see research as one of their duties. Certain industries, the ELECTRIC-POWER and CHEMICAL industries being the best examples, were created or revolutionized by scientific knowledge. These science-based industries were also the first to establish research laboratories as part of their business, with the aim of institutionalizing innovation. By engaging in research, firms attempted to gain security in the face of changing technology, to restrict competition and to control markets. The state, too, began to engage in scientific activities on a more formal basis, according to perceived national goals. Scientific agencies were established to deal with such areas as AGRICULTURE, the MILITARY, PUBLIC HEALTH, STANDARDS, the exploitation of natural RESOURCES and MANUFACTURING. Furthermore, new links, based on scientific research, were formed among universities, industries and governments, reflecting the importance being attached to R & D by society.

A significant proportion of national resources are now devoted to R & D by developed countries, and the level of funding has become a major policy concern. R & D is valued primarily as a source of technological change. However, little is known about the effectiveness of expenditures on R & D, in part because R & D encompasses activities with a wide range of goals, is found in many areas (eg, medical, military, SPACE) and is pursued for many purposes (eg, health and welfare, prestige, security and the advancement of knowledge). Hence, aggregate measures of R & D, such as the ratio of gross expenditures on R & D to gross domestic product, are very difficult to interpret. Another factor is our lack of knowledge about the efficiency of R & D systems. A third area of difficulty is that the effectiveness of R & D is measured in terms of social and economic consequences to which many factors besides R & D-induced technology contribute. For example, INDUSTRIAL RESEARCH AND DEVELOPMENT (ie, R & D devoted to economic objectives) is performed with the expectation that it will contribute to economic growth, by improving products and processes or developing new ones. Yet the exact role of industrial R & D is difficult to substantiate because many other factors, including market forces, management and labour skills, and financing, play an important part in determining whether the results of industrial R & D will lead to economic growth. In fact, R & D costs are usually a small fraction of the total costs of launching a new product or process.

Although much remains to be learned about R & D and especially its economics, some of its features have been identified. Expenditures on R & D are concentrated in the most economically developed countries, with the US spending by far the most. In all these countries governments provide extensive support, funding their own work and a high proportion of university R & D,

and also contributing significantly to industrial R & D. Universities tend to focus their activities on pure research and on training scientists and engineers, performing very little development work. Industries, because of the high risks and uncertainties involved in R & D, devote most of their efforts to development and, within this area, to short-term improvements. Nearly all industrial R & D is devoted to capital and intermediate goods, not consumer goods. Industrial R & D expenditures are heavily concentrated in a few industries (AEROSPACE, ELECTRICAL ENGINEERING, chemicals, ELECTRONICS and scientific instruments). Large firms undertake most industrial R & D but many smaller ones are equally research intensive. The determinants of research intensity are difficult to identify and evaluate because of differences between industries and the lack of proper data.

The history of scientific research and development in Canada has barely been examined. Some studies have been devoted to federal government activities, in particular those of the NATIONAL RESEARCH COUNCIL; however, much less work has been done on university research, and practically none on industrial R & D. Nevertheless the general historical outlines may still be sketched. The Canadian government established scientific agencies in the 19th century to deal with primary industries such as MINING, agriculture, FORESTRY and FISHERIES. The support and organization of scientific and industrial research in Canada gained momentum in the early decades of the 20th century, when a movement arose promoting such research. The movement was both a reaction to similar efforts in other industrialized countries, in particular following the outbreak of WWI, and a response to developments within Canada. Many Canadian universities attempted to improve and expand their science and engineering programs, to foster graduate studies and promote the ideal of research. The federal government founded the NRC in 1916 to encourage R & D in Canada. The ALBERTA RESEARCH COUNCIL was formed in 1921; the ONTARIO RESEARCH FOUNDATION in 1928; and other provincial RESEARCH organizations followed, especially after WWII.

In Canadian industry, the turn of the century witnessed a trend towards industrial concentration, specialization, and the growing dominance of large corporations, all of which fostered the emergence of industrial R & D. The CANADIAN MANUFACTURERS' ASSOCIATION was an important advocate of increased R & D in Canada. Several firms, such as Shawinigan Chemicals Ltd and Riordon Pulp and Paper, engaged in research. The amount of industrial R & D expanded very rapidly following WWI: approximately 37 Canadian firms had research laboratories in 1917-18; by 1939 there were 998 industrial laboratories. The exponential rate of growth of gross expenditures on R & D after WWII reflects the rapid development of R & D activities in Canada. Accompanying this increase in the late 1960s and 1970s was a widespread concern about the lack of an explicit SCIENCE POLICY and about the performance of industrial innovation in Canada. As a result, the federal government created a number of study and advisory groups, among them the SCIENCE COUNCIL OF CANADA (est 1966) and the Ministry of State for Science and Technology (1971).

According to Statistics Canada, in 1987 an estimated $7.1 billion was spent on scientific R & D in Canada (approximately another $860 million was spent on the humanities and social sciences). Of the $7.1 billion, the federal government funded 34%; the provincial governments, 6%; business, 42%; higher education, 9%; private non-profit organizations, and foreign sources, 9%. In terms of performance, the federal government's share of the $7.1 billion was 20%; the provincial governments', 3.2%; business's, 51%; higher education's, 247%; private nonprofit organizations', 1.3%. The federal government spent 66% of its R & D funds on its own programs; 15.2% was contributed to business; 21.4%, to higher education.

Of the R & D performed by business, 69.5% was funded by business; 10.9%, by the federal government; 11.1%, by other Canadian sources, including provincial governments; 8.5%, by foreign sources. As in other countries, industrial R & D in Canada is concentrated in manufacturing, mostly in electrical products, PETROLEUM products, MACHINERY, chemicals and other products, transportation equipment (aerospace), primary metals, and paper and allied products. For R & D performed by HIGHER EDUCATION, the federal government contributed 45.1%; provincial governments, 11.7%; business, 3.5%; private nonprofit organizations, 12.3%; higher education, 26.3%; foreign sources, 1.1%. Regionally, in 1985, 52% of R & D expenditures were in Ontario; 21%, in the western provinces; 22%, in Québec; 5%, in the Atlantic provinces.

Gross expenditure on R & D (GERD) in the natural sciences and engineering in Canada was an estimated 1.35% of the gross domestic product (GDP) in 1986, about half the percentage of the leading country, the US. After rising from 1979 to 1982, GERD/GDP has been stable since then. There is no theoretical basis for determining the optimum ratio of GERD/GDP and this ratio must be interpreted in the light of the individual country's economic and scientific goals and structures. Thus, while Canada's GERD/GDP has consistently been among the lowest major industrialized countries, Canada is classified by the Organization for Economic Cooperation and Development as a medium R & D country along with others who have higher ratios. The level of funding for R & D in Canada has long been thought to be too low, although in Jan 1988 the federal government pledged additional funding – $1.3 billion over 5 years – for science and technology.

The major concern about the state of R & D in Canada, aside from its level of funding, has been its distribution. Here, the dominant problem has been industrial R & D. Critics have argued (often without much understanding of the role of government in science) that in the past the federal government overemphasized basic research to the detriment of development and spent too much of its R & D funds intramurally. Universities have also been criticized for being too insulated from the needs of business. In the late 1960s, and especially in the 1970s, the federal government began to take some steps towards contracting out R & D, supporting R & D performed by industry, and establishing links to foster the transfer of ideas and technology from government and university to industry. Industry's funding and performance of R & D has also been a source of considerable unease. Both are held to be too low and, thus, to affect the Canadian economy adversely. There has been much debate over the role of FOREIGN INVESTMENT in truncating industrial R & D in Canada. Foreign subsidiaries are said to decrease the amount of research in Canada and to increase reliance on foreign technology; others argue it is unlikely that Canada would have been able to achieve the growth rates it did without subsidiaries; and, through them, Canada gains invisible inflows of technology. The evidence for either of these views is mixed and, although it does now appear that Canadian-owned firms are more research intensive than their foreign-owned counterparts, it is still not known if this situation is the result of ownership or of other factors, such as structural differences within industries. *See also* INVENTORS AND INNOVATION.　PHILIP C. ENROS

Reading: G.B. Doern, *Science and Politics in Canada* (1972); C. Freeman, *The Economics of Industrial Innovation* (2nd ed, 1982); K. Green and C. Morphet, *Research and Technology as Economic Activities* (1977).

Scobie, Stephen, poet, critic, professor, publisher (b at Carnoustie, Scot 31 Dec 1943). Typical of his 12 volumes of poetry are *The Birken Tree* (1973), *The Rooms We Are* (1974), *A Grand Memory for Forgetting* (1981) and *Expecting Rain* (1984). In these, open verse forms, extensive historical and literary references commemorate, sometimes nostalgically, people and places. *McAlmon's Chinese Opera* (1980), dramatic monologues in the voice of Robert McAlmon, won Scobie a Governor General's Award. He collaborates with Douglas BARBOUR in the sound-poetry duo *re:sounding* and co-authored with him the "homolinguistic translations," *The Pirates of Pen's Chance* (1981). Scobie has authored 3 critical monographs: *Leonard Cohen* (1978), *What History Teaches* (1984, on bp Nichol) and *Sheila Watson* (1984). His writing reflects his interest in Gertrude Stein, in Cubism, and, recently, in deconstruction. Scobie was a founding editor of Longspoon Press.　SHIRLEY NEUMAN

Scorpion, carnivorous arthropod of class ARACHNIDA, order Scorpiones. Known from fossils 400 million years old, scorpions are among the oldest terrestrial animals. They have front appendages modified into claws for catching and holding prey, a 7-segmented preabdomen and a 5-segmented posterior with a tail ending in a stinger. Ventrally, they have 2 comblike appendages, thought to be sensory organs. Although they have up to 12 eyes, scorpions can only distinguish dark from light. The largest living species are about 15 cm long. About 1000 species are found worldwide, throughout tropical and warmer desert regions; only one species occurs in Canada (southern Sask, Alta and BC). It is about 5 cm long and has a 2-year life cycle. Although many scorpions have poisonous stings for defence or killing prey, most are harmless to humans. The effect of the sting is like that of a bee. Scorpions are nocturnal, living under logs, bark or rocks. The young are usually born alive; shortly after birth, they crawl onto the mother's back for protection.　ROBIN LEECH

Scorpionfish, or rockfish (Scorpaenidae), family of bottom-dwelling, marine fishes with large heads, mouths and eyes, stout bodies and large pectoral fins. Over 300 species are distributed worldwide, in temperate and tropical waters. The greatest variety of forms is found in the Indo-Australian region, where several bizarrely shaped, deceptively coloured and often venomous species exist. The highly venomous lionfish and turkeyfish can inflict painful injuries. Like SCULPINS, scorpionfish belong to the "mail-cheeked fishes," characterized by a bony stay or splint extending from the eye to the cheekbone. The head and fins exhibit many spines, and the body frequently has cirri and skin flaps, thought to help in camouflage. Many forms have internal fertilization and bear live young, but a few egg-laying species are known. The family has been divided into several subgroups, based on various criteria. In Canadian waters, it is represented by over 30 forms on the Pacific coast; fewer than 5 on the Atlantic. Many are important commercial food fishes, eg, Pacific ocean perch and rockfish, and Atlantic redfish – all members of genus *Sebastes*. Rockfishes range in size from about 15 cm in dwarf forms to almost 100 cm in some Alaskan representatives. Depending upon the species, young are born from winter to late spring. Young rockfish drift with and feed upon PLANKTON. After several weeks they settle, becoming bottom dwellers. The mechanism triggering settling is unknown.

Many young rockfish are differently coloured from adults of the same species. Recent analyses indicate that rockfish are among the longest-lived marine fishes, frequently surviving for 80-90 years. Scorpionfishes occur from subtidal waters to depths of over 500 m. Some live close inshore, among rocks and kelp, in small groups or associations. Others, including the commercially important species, live in massive schools in offshore waters at mid-depths. Offshore populations undergo diurnal and seasonal movements. They are generally fished by trawl, and are competed for by several nations on both Canadian coasts.　NORMAN J. WILIMOVSKY

Scotian Shelf, a 700 km section of the Continental Shelf off Nova Scotia. Bounded by the Laurentian Channel on the NE, and Northeast Channel and the Gulf of Maine on the SW, it varies in width from 120 to 240 km; the average depth is 90 m. Deep basins and channels, separating shallow offshore banks (dry land during the ice age), characterize its irregular bathymetry. Only SABLE I remains above water today. Circulation over the inner shelf is dominated by a southwesterly longshore current that varies seasonally with freshwater runoff from the Gulf of ST LAWRENCE. Over the banks the circulation is weaker and more variable, under the influence of storms, tides and the Gulf Stream several hundred km S. Strong tidal streams around southwestern NS produce vertical mixing and enrichment of the herring and lobster fisheries; offshore an international fleet annually removes around half a million tonnes of fish and squid. Recent discoveries of natural gas near Sable I have stimulated further hydrocarbon explorations, creating potential conflict between renewable and nonrenewable resources on the shelf.　P.C. SMITH AND R.J. CONOVER

Scots Although often considered Anglo-Canadians, the Scots have always regarded themselves as a separate people. The connection between Scotland and Canada dates to the 17th century. The Scots have been immigrating in steady and substantial numbers for over 200 years. In 1961, the last census for which the category was recorded, 1 894 000 Canadians, or 10.4% of the population, listed themselves as of Scottish origin.

The kingdom of Scotland established one of the earliest colonies in Canada in 1621, when Sir William Alexander was granted a charter for Nova Scotia. Alexander established small settlements on Cape Breton and on the Bay of FUNDY, but they did not flourish and Scottish claims were surrendered to France in 1632. A few Scots immigrated to NEW FRANCE, but the major early movement of Scots to Canada was a small flow of men from Orkney – beginning about 1720 – recruited by the HUDSON'S BAY COMPANY for service in the West. Soldiers from the Highlands of Scotland comprised the crack regiments of the British army that defeated the French in the SEVEN YEARS' WAR. Many soldiers remained in N America, and Scots merchants moved on to Québec after 1759 where they dominated commercial life and the fur trade.

Between 1770 and 1815 some 15 000 Highland Scots came to Canada, settling mainly in PEI, NS (*see* HECTOR) and Upper Canada. Most of these immigrants came from the western Highlands and the islands of Scotland. They were almost exclusively Gaelic speaking and many were Roman Catholics. They congregated in agrarian communities in the new land and, in the early years of the 19th century, Gaelic was the third most common European language spoken in Canada. A few Highlanders were brought to the RED RIVER COLONY by the earl of SELKIRK, and other Scots from the fur trade moved with their Indian families to Red River after 1821. In all these communities Highland traditions were preserved and for many

Antigonish games, Nova Scotia (*photo by Sherman Hines/ Masterfile*).

years they remained distinctive ethnic enclaves.

After 1815 Scottish immigration increased in numbers, and the pattern altered. Scots from the Lowlands area, encouraged by the British government, joined Highlanders in coming to Canada. Some 170 000 Scots crossed the Atlantic between 1815 and 1870, roughly 14% of the total British migration of this period. By the 1850s most of the newcomers were settling in the PROVINCE OF CANADA rather than in the Maritime colonies. According to the 1871 census, 157 of every 1000 Canadians were of Scottish origin, ranging from 4.1% in Québec to 33.7% in NS. The immigrants of this period represented a cross section of the Scottish population. Most were farmers and artisans, although large numbers of business and professional people were included, especially teachers and clergymen. Most of the newcomers were Presbyterians and most spoke English. They tended to live and fraternize together and were particularly active in establishing schools (eg, the St John's College in Red River) that emphasized training for the talented.

Scots were highly visible in politics and business; men such as James Glenie and John Neilsen often led the criticism of elitist political structures, although other Scots such as John STRACHAN were members of the ELITE. The first 2 Canadian prime ministers – John A. MACDONALD and Alexander MACKENZIE – were born in Scotland. Scots dominated the fur trade, the timber trade, banking and railway management; nearly 50% of the nation's industrial leaders in the 1880s had recent Scottish origins.

Scots in Canada increasingly found themselves in an ambivalent position, both part of the dominant British culture and yet insistent on maintaining their own identity. It was largely because of their influence that the preponderant culture in Canada was British, rather than ENGLISH, and distinctive Scottish patterns can be discerned in Canadian education and moral attitudes, eg, Sabbath observance and TEMPERANCE. Scottish moral philosophers strongly influenced philosophical teaching in Canada.

Since 1870 patterns of Scottish immigration and settlement have altered significantly, reflecting shifts in both Scotland and Canada. When population pressures in the Highland region lessened, Highlanders no longer immigrated to Canada in substantial numbers. In the Scottish Lowlands, urbanization and industrialization reduced the agricultural component of the population, and the percentage of farmers among immigrants to Canada fell correspondingly. Meanwhile, in Canada burgeoning factories and cities were attracting Scottish immigrants, although many made their way to the last great agricultural frontier in western Canada. The flow of people from Scotland to Canada continued unabated, however. From 1871 to 1901, 80 000 Scots entered Canada seeking a better future: 240 000 arrived in the first years of the century before WWI, 200 000

more between 1919 and 1930 and another 147 000 between 1946 and 1960.

Like most immigrant groups, the Scots since 1870 have shunned the Atlantic region and Québec in favour of Ontario and the West. A substantial population of Scottish origin in the Maritime provinces is native-born. Newfoundland, like Québec, has never had a significant Scottish population. Scots are widely distributed across the remaining provinces and territories in both urban and rural communites. Like most ethnic groups in Canada, the Scots have become increasingly assimilated into Canadian society, although still retaining an awareness of their distinctive heritage. Like other ethnic groups as well, the Scots have tended to focus on a few highly visible symbols of their origins, such as clans, tartans and Highland dancing. The number of Gaelic speakers has declined in Canada as in Scotland itself, and only a few thousand people, mainly in Cape Breton, keep the language alive in Canada.

Scots have been involved in every aspect of Canada's development as explorers, educators, businessmen, politicians, writers, artists, etc. A few of many well-known Canadians of Scottish descent include Sir A.T. GALT, Lord ELGIN, Donald SMITH (Lord Strathcona), William Lyon MACKENZIE, Harold INNIS, Sir William MACKENZIE, Maxwell AITKEN (Lord Beaverbrook), W.L. MORTON, Blair Fraser, Norman BETHUNE, Farley MOWAT, Douglas CAMPBELL and Norman MCLAREN.

The history and culture of Scots developed quite differently from that of other groups from the British Isles and Scots have always regarded themselves as distinctive from – indeed superior to – their English, WELSH and IRISH cousins. Their pattern of immigration to and development in Canada is clearly unlike that of most other ethnic peoples, for it has been protracted over several centuries rather than being chronologically or regionally specific. Scots have never been sufficiently numerous to dominate, nor sufficiently lacking in numbers to vanish. Their Scottish background has on the whole served them well as successful Canadian settlers. Sufficiently close culturally to the English to become part of the dominant society, their Scottish background has provided them with skills and aspirations well suited to a developing country.   J.M. BUMSTED

Reading: R. Connor, *Glengarry School Days* (1902); J.K. Galbraith, *The Scotch* (1964); M. Laurence, *The Diviners* (1974); F.J. Niven, *The Flying Years* (1935) and *The Transplanted* (1944); W.S. Reid, *The Scottish Tradition in Canada* (1976).

Scott, Anthony Dalton, professor of economics (b at Vancouver 2 Aug 1923). Scott is perhaps best known for his pioneering contributions to the economics of natural resource use and management. His thesis, published as *Natural Resources: The Economics of Conservation* (1955, repr 1973), is considered a classic in the field, as is his book with Francis Christy, *The Commonwealth in Ocean Fisheries* (1965). He is also noted for work on human capital flows (the "brain drain") and for work on the economics of FEDERALISM. He has served with several government bodies and many professional associations. He was a commissioner on the INTERNATIONAL JOINT COMMISSION 1968-72. More recently he edited and contributed to *Progress in Natural Resource Economics* (1985) and *Economics of Water Exports* (1985).

Scott, Barbara Ann, figure skater (b at Ottawa 9 May 1928). One of Canada's best-remembered athletes, Scott endeared herself to Canadians in winning the 1948 St Moritz Olympics figure-skating title. At age 9, she had begun a daily 7-hour training routine; a year later, she became the youngest Canadian to earn a gold medal for figures. She was Canadian senior women's champi-

Barbara Ann Scott's gold medal in figure skating at the 1948 St Moritz winter Olympics made her a celebrity (*courtesy Canada's Sports Hall of Fame*).

on 1944-48, N American champion 1945-48, and European and world champion 1947-48. Her capture of the coveted Olympic gold medal made her a celebrity; in Ottawa she was honoured by adoring crowds and showered with gifts; she was the object of endless media attention. Scott received the LOU MARSH TROPHY as Canada's athlete of the year in 1945, 1947 and 1948. She toured in an ice show as a professional 1949-54. On retirement, she began training show horses, and in her mid-40s was rated among the top equestrians in the US.   BARBARA SCHRODT

Scott, Duncan Campbell, poet, short-story writer, civil servant (b at Ottawa 2 Aug 1862; d there 19 Dec 1947). Scott's ambition was to become a doctor, but family finances were precarious and in 1879 he joined the federal Dept of Indian Affairs. He became its deputy superintendent in 1913, a post he held until retirement in 1932. Scott is commonly placed with the "poets of the Confederation," but although the contemporary of Archibald LAMPMAN, Bliss CARMAN and C.G.D. ROBERTS he was personally close only to Lampman, who in the 1880s had sparked him to try poetry. By the late 1880s he was a regular contributor to *Scribner's Magazine*. In 1893 he published his first volume of poetry, *The Magic House and Other Poems*. This was followed in 1896 by *In the Village of Viger*, a collection of delicate sketches of French Canadian life. Two later collections, *The Witching of Elspie* (1923) and *The Circle of Affection* (1947), contained many fine short stories about Indians and traders in wilderness settings. But as a spare-time writer Scott found the pursuit of poetry more manageable than fiction. Seven collections of poems followed: *The Magic House: Labor and the Angel* (1898), *New World Lyrics and Ballads* (1905), *Via Borealis* (1906), *Lundy's Lane and Other Poems* (1916), *Beauty and Life* (1921), *The Poems of Duncan Campbell Scott* (1926) and *The Green Cloister* (1935). *The Circle of Affection*, chiefly a collection of prose, included a number of poems not previously published.

Although Scott complained of critical neglect, his literary reputation has never been in doubt. He has been well represented in virtually all major anthologies of Canadian poetry published since 1900. His "Indian" poems, in which he drew on his experiences in the field, have been widely recognized and valued. There is some conflict here between Scott's views as an administrator committed to an assimilation policy, and his sensibilities as a poet saddened by the waning of an ancient culture. Precise in imagery, intense yet disciplined, flexible in metre and form, Scott's poems weathered well the transition from traditional to modern poetry in Canada.

Scott valued music even above poetry and was

Poet Duncan Campbell Scott (*courtesy National Archives of Canada/C-3187*).

an accomplished pianist. Murray ADASKIN was a friend, as were painters Homer WATSON and Edmund Morris and later Lawren HARRIS and Clarence GAGNON. Scott was a prime mover in the establishment of the Ottawa Little Théatre and the Dominion Drama Festival. A one-act play, *Pierre*, was first performed at the Ottawa Little Theatre in 1923 and subsequently published in *Canadian Plays from Hart House Theatre* (1926).

There is ample evidence of Scott's engagement as a writer. He contributed (with Lampman and Wilfred CAMPBELL) informal essays to the Toronto *Globe* in 1892-93, published as *At the Mermaid Inn* (1979). He wrote a novel which did not go to press until it was brought out in 1979 as *The Untitled Novel*. For the Makers of Canada series, which he directed with Pelham Edgar, he wrote a biography of John Graves SIMCOE (1905). In 1947 he published a book on Walter J. PHILLIPS. Perhaps most impressive was Scott's lifelong concern for Lampman's literary reputation. This loyalty to his good friend was expressed mainly by Scott's editions of Lampman's poems (1900-47).

R.L. McDOUGALL

Scott, Edward Walter, Ted, Anglican clergyman (b at Edmonton, 30 Apr 1919). Educated at UBC and Anglican Theological College, Vancouver. As bishop of Kootenay (1966-71) and archbishop and primate of the ANGLICAN CHURCH OF CANADA (1971-86) Scott encouraged ecumenical and social expressions of Christian faith. He was an active participant in the movement for Anglican-United Church union, which failed in 1975, and was moderator of the Central Committee of the World Council of Churches (1975-83). He became a Companion of the Order of Canada in 1978. In 1986 Scott was a member of a committee which sought means of bringing an end to apartheid in South Africa. Scott's commitment to ecumenism and social justice have given him wide influence. MARGARET PRANG

Scott, Francis Reginald, poet, professor of constitutional law, founding member of the socialist movement in Canada (b at Québec City 1 Aug 1899; d at Montréal 30 Jan 1985). As a man of letters and social commitment, Scott profoundly influenced the evolution of modern Canada's

artistic and political culture. He was the sixth of 7 children of Amy and Canon Frederick George Scott, an Anglican priest, minor poet and staunch advocate of the civilizing tradition of imperial Britain, who instilled in his son a commitment to serve mankind, a love for the regenerative balance of the Laurentian landscape and a firm respect for the social order. His mother's quiet presence figures in various of his poems. Scott passed a peaceful childhood and adolescence in Québec, his pastoral upbringing disturbed only slightly by WWI, though the war claimed the life of an older brother and took Canon Scott to Europe as pastor to the Canadian troops. Scott was first exposed to social disorder through the CONSCRIPTION riots in Québec. The carnage and social upheaval brought by WWI did not affect him until the mid-1920s when he began reading modern poetry. After graduating from Québec High School and Bishop's Coll (1919), Scott went as a Rhodes scholar to Magdalen Coll, Oxford, and as a member of the Student Christian Movement began to explore socialist theory through the works of R.H. Tawney.

He returned to Canada in 1923, largely ignorant of his own country. Montréal seemed to him singularly ugly, bereft of the ancient beauty of Europe. Scott settled down to teach at Lower Canada Coll and to write poetry. In 1924 he enrolled in the McGill law faculty, where H.A. Smith was to spark his interest in constitutional law. In 1924-25, as a contributor to the *McGill Daily Literary Supplement,* he met the poet/critic A.J.M. SMITH, who became a lifelong friend; they founded the *McGill Fortnightly Review* in 1925. Under Smith's influence Scott began to introduce to his poetry a more contemporary diction, leading eventually to poetic portraits of the austere Laurentian landscape – an inspiration comparable to the antiquity of Europe. His progress into such landscapes matched his intellectual movement away from a self-regarding universe and towards the social environment. In 1927-28 he undertook a year's legal practice, joined McGill's law faculty as a professor, and married Montréal painter Marian Dale SCOTT. He also continued to participate in "The Group," an informal, socially aware discussion group composed of Oxford graduates. By the end of the 1920s, as illustrated by *The Canadian Mercury*, which he helped to found, Scott was chastising his fellow Canadians for genuflecting to the cultural values of imperial Britain.

The onset of the Depression led him to probe the economic causes of the ugliness and social deprivation that surrounded him. Inspired by J.S. WOODSWORTH, Scott and historian Frank UNDERHILL founded the LEAGUE FOR SOCIAL RECONSTRUCTION (LSR) in 1931-32, a socialist study group which drafted national economic and social policies to combat the misery caused by the Depression, and which became the brain trust for the new CO-OPERATIVE COMMONWEALTH FEDERATION. Scott helped to frame the now-famous Regina Manifesto of the CCF and to write *Social Planning for Canada* (1935). Over the years he was a stalwart of the CCF, both nationally and in Québec. The goal of the LSR and the CCF to create a more egalitarian society was to shape the satiric poetry and the constitutional and socialist essays that Scott published during the Depression, often in the *Canadian Forum*, of which he was an editor. During the late 1930s he was consumed by such issues as the Spanish Civil War and his campaign for Canadian neutrality in the face of the threatening war, earned him much criticism.

WWII, seeming to prove that collective man could not peacefully resolve problems, profoundly disturbed Scott. In his poems of the period, he swings from deep anxiety to a reawakened faith in mankind. He finally convinced himself that

collective man could prosper in the postwar era. In such magazines as *Preview* and *Northern Review,* in the philanthropic Canada Foundation, and in artists' organizations, Scott urged artists to cultivate a socially critical intelligence and to abandon narrow regional and artistic perspectives in favour of a democratic national culture. As national chairman of the CCF (1942-50), his renewed interest in socialism brought him into conflict with McGill authorities who refused to appoint him dean of the law faculty.

In 1950-51 Scott cofounded Recherches sociales, a study group concerned with the relationship between English and French Canada. He also became an active translator of French Canadian poets such as Anne HÉBERT and Saint-Denys GARNEAU. In 1952 he went to Burma as a UN technical assistant to help build a co-operative, socialist state. In the mid-1950s he successfully completed 2 landmark legal cases before the Supreme Court, the PADLOCK ACT and RONCARELLI V DUPLESSIS, in which he battled autocratic Québec Premier Maurice DUPLESSIS. Scott's poetry of the 1950s shows a singularly critical eye turned to his national society and to man in general.

In 1962, with the CCF having transformed itself into the NEW DEMOCRATIC PARTY, a process in which Scott participated actively, he retired from partisan politics. McGill appointed him dean of law (1961-64) and he began to devote increasing attention to the survival of Canadian Confederation. He was a member of the Royal Commission on BILINGUALISM AND BICULTURALISM and an ardent defender of the civil order of Confederation, supporting the invocation of the War Measures Act in 1970. In later years Scott produced a retrospective series of largely summary volumes, including *Poems of French Canada* (1977), which won the Canada Council's translation prize; *Essays on the Constitution* (1977), which won the Gov Gen's Award for nonfiction; and *Collected Poems* (1981), which won the Gov Gen's Award for poetry. Scott worked to help develop Canada into an international model of co-operation. His social vision sought to realize the best of both the individual and the community, though his loyalty to the social whole might limit the freedom to be enjoyed by the individual. His political commitments and his poetry illustrated the continuing tension between the needs of the individual and those of the potentially homogeneous society. KEITH RICHARDSON

Reading: S. Djwa, *Politics of the Imagination: A Life of F.R. Scott* (1987); David Lewis and F.R. Scott, *Make This "Your" Canada ...* (1943).

Scott, Marian Mildred Dale, painter (b at Montréal 26 June 1906). For 50 years Scott has experimented with fresh art forms, reaching for symmetry, often through repetition of small abstract forms. After study at the École des beaux-arts, Montréal, and the Slade School of Art, London, she painted landscapes, later plant life, buds and pods, organized geometrically. A series of human faces, influenced by Modigliani, show strong linear forms set ambiguously in a background of heavy black paint. During the Depression years, Scott depicted the people of urban Montréal, up against machines, bureaucracy and hard times, showing them in pictures like *Tenants* and *Escalator*. She taught 1935-38 with Fritz BRANDTNER at the Children's Art Centre set up by Norman Bethune, and joined the Contemporary Arts Soc in 1939. In 1941 she gave a one-man show at Boston's Grace Horne Gallery, and from 1948-77 held 9 solo exhibitions at Queen's U; Dominion Gallery, Montréal; Laing Gallery, Toronto; L'atelier Renée le Sieur, Québec City; and the McGill Art Education Department. In 1983 she exhibited in London, Ont, with the show "Visions and Victories: 10 Canadian Women Artists,

1914-1945." She was married to poet and lawyer F.R. SCOTT. ANNE McDOUGALL

Scott, Robert Austin, painter (b at Melfort, Sask 16 May 1941). Scott studied fine art at the Alberta College of Art, Calgary (1969) and U of A (1976). He is one of a group of prairie abstract artists whose work is characterized by experimentation with the formal qualities of painting. Influenced by New York abstract expressionism and abstract colour-field painting, Scott has developed a style of drawing with his fingers through the top layer of paint to expose the underpainted colours. The incising can be highly controlled and patterned, or random. The resulting rhythm creates visual tension, a quality comparable to Jackson Pollock's automatic style. Scott also explores visual textures by painting with thick acrylic gel and by using a spraying technique. KATHLEEN LAVERTY

Kittiwake Rift (1986), acrylic on canvas, by Robert Scott (*courtesy Woltjen/Udell Gallery*).

Scott, Robert Balgarnie Young, biblical scholar (b at Toronto 16 July 1899). After serving in the RCN Volunteer Reserve in WWI, he studied Greek and Hebrew at U of T (PhD 1928). He spent a year studying in Britain and Palestine, and was appointed professor of Old Testament studies at Union Coll, Vancouver, in 1928 and at United Theological Coll, Montréal, in 1931, becoming in 1948 first dean of the McGill Faculty of Divinity. From 1955 until retirement in 1968 he taught at Princeton, being annual professor at the American School of Oriental Research in Jerusalem in 1962-63. A prolific writer, Scott published 5 books on the Old Testament, innumerable articles, book chapters and reference works, as well as lyrics for 10 hymns. He was a founder and first secretary-treasurer of the Canadian Soc of Biblical Studies and its president in 1972. He has received 5 honorary degrees for his biblical scholarship. JOHN S. MOIR

Scott, Thomas, adventurer (b at Clandeboye, Ire *c*1842; d at Red River Colony, Man 4 Mar 1870). Immigrating to Canada in 1863, Scott was "a violent and boisterous" individual with Protestant and Orange sympathies. He drifted to the RED RIVER COLONY in 1869. Captured and imprisoned several times by the Métis, he was court-martialled and executed with Louis RIEL's approval; he became an anglophone-Protestant martyr and his execution became a symbol of Métis hostility to Ontario. J.M. BUMSTED

Scott, Thomas Seaton, architect (b at Birkenhead, Eng 16 July 1826; d at Ottawa 15 June 1895). Scott immigrated to Montréal in the mid-1850s, and became best known for his work in the Gothic style, which included churches in Ontario and Québec and an 1874 design for the Mackenzie Tower on the W block of the PARLIAMENT BUILDINGS. From 1871 until 1881 he was the first chief architect of the federal Dept of Public Works. He directed the post-Confederation building program, which produced some of Canada's finest examples of public building in the Second Empire style. JANET WRIGHT

Scott, Thomas Walter, politician, journalist, printer, premier of Saskatchewan (b at London Twp, Ont 27 Oct 1867; d at Guelph, Ont 23 Mar 1938). As the first premier of Saskatchewan, he played a key role in the province's early development. Scott went to PORTAGE LA PRAIRIE in 1885 and apprenticed as a printer. He moved to REGINA in 1886 and by 1896 had become an influential journalist and owner of the Regina *Leader* and the Moose Jaw *Times*. As the Liberal member for Assiniboia West in 1900 and 1904, he participated in the autonomy debates. In 1905 he was chosen leader of the Saskatchewan Liberal Party and asked to form the first provincial government. Under his leadership, the party won the elections of 1905, 1908 and 1912. Ill health forced him to resign in Oct 1916 and he retired from public life. D.H. BOCKING

Scouine, La, by Albert LABERGE (1918), a series of discrete, interlocking sketches forming a novel, is French Canada's first example of naturalism. Demythologizing the romantic portrait of 19th-century peasant life promoted by the church, it blends close descriptive detail, local speech and humour, and a pessimistic attitude toward human nature. Paulima, the daughter of Urgèle and Maco Deschamps, is nicknamed "La Scouine" because of her strong, unpleasant odour; the sobriquet reflects her character as a avaricious, gossipy spinster. Traditional scenes such as harvest, the fall fair and the pastoral visit are introduced with Christian imagery which is immediately undermined by the peasant's unsavoury earthiness. The publication of excerpts in 1903 resulted in censorship and a private edition (1918) of only 60 copies. Gérard Bessette's anthology of Laberge's writing led to a facsimile edition (1968), which was withdrawn from circulation at the insistence of Laberge's son. Finally published in 1972, the underground classic *La Scouine* was then translated by C. Dion as *Bitter Bread* (1977). MICHÈLE LACOMBE

Scouts Canada The scouting movement was founded in England in 1907 by Robert Baden-Powell, then a lt-gen in the British army, after a successful boys camp. Canadian author and naturalist Ernest Thompson SETON was co-founder of Boy Scouts of America in 1910 and the official scout manual was based on his work. Scouting came to Canada in early 1908 and in 1912 the Boy Scout Assn was granted a royal charter throughout the Commonwealth by King George V. The Canadian General Council of the Boy Scout Assn, incorporated 12 June 1914, was a branch of the Boy Scout Assn until 30 Oct 1946 when it became an independent member of the Boy Scout World Conference. The name was changed to Boy Scouts of Canada and to Scouts Canada in 1976. Every governor general since Earl Grey in 1910 has been "Chief Scout."

The stated aim of Scouts Canada is to help boys and young adults develop their character as resourceful and responsible members of the community. There are 5 programs: Beavers (for boys aged 5-7 years); Cubs (boys 8-10); Scouts (boys 11-14); Venturers (boys and girls 14-17); and Rovers (young adults 17-26). Sponsors include churches, service clubs, professional and business associations, the Canadian Forces, etc. In 1987 there were over 280 000 members.

SCTV, the call letters for a fictional Second City television station, was written and performed by primarily Canadian artists from 1976 through 1983, and seen across the US and Canada. It eventually produced 72 half-hour shows, 42 ninety-minute shows, 18 forty-five-minute shows, and it was honoured with 13 Emmy award nominations, 2 Emmy awards for best writing, 3 Actra nominations and 2 Actra awards. It is in syndication across N America and around the world.

The origins of this remarkable satire of the very media on which it appeared can be found in the original Second City, a comedy cabaret which opened in Chicago in 1959, and, since 1985, has been owned by Canadian entertainment entrepreneur Andrew Alexander. In 1973, the Toronto-based Alexander bought Canadian rights to Second City from its Chicago founder for one dollar, its first show opening in Feb 1974 at The Old Firehall in downtown Toronto. Soon a respected theatrical institution in that city, SCTV grew out of the stage show.

By 1976 Alexander and his partner, Len Stuart, began to produce a half-hour format TV show, initially produced by and airing on Global Television to good ratings and excellent critical response. From 1977 through 1981, jointly produced by Old Firehall TV Productions Ltd and Allarcom Ltd, SCTV was taped in Edmonton, then back in Toronto, syndicated in the US as well as in Canada, and moved to CBC and eventually NBC. Most of the performers also wrote the superb comic and satiric material. They included Andrea Martin, Eugene Levy, John Candy, Joe Flaherty, Catherine O'Hara, Dave Thomas, Rick Moranis and latecomer Martin Short. All but Martin and Flaherty were born in Canada.

Moranis and Thomas both dropped out of SCTV early, owing to the phenomenal success of their parody of 2 Canadian hicks, the McKenzie brothers, and others also left and returned during its brief reign. They and most of the others found success in Hollywood films (Candy has appeared in some 2 dozen) and American TV comedy, both weekly and pay-TV specials. Many of the characters ("Edith Prickly," "Guy Caballero," "Ed Grimley") and impersonations of the SCTV performers have entered international television history. ALLAN M. GOULD

Sculpin, one of many common names given to the fish family Cottidae and its close relatives. The group, comprising over 400 species, is one of the dominant faunal components of the N Pacific Ocean, where it is believed to have evolved. Sculpins also occur in the Arctic and N Atlantic oceans; a few have penetrated to the SW Pacific, S American and southern African waters. Freshwater forms occur in temperate and arctic waters of N America, Europe and Asia. Sculpins and related families (eg, stonefish, SCORPIONFISH) are characterized by a bony stay extending from below the eye to the cheekbone. This brace, often armoured with spines, gave rise to the name "mail-cheeked fishes."

Sculpins are generally small (5-20 cm), although some species approach 100 cm. Marine sculpins are found from intertidal waters to depths of several hundred metres; most inhabit relatively shallow waters (100 m or less). Freshwater forms generally live in shallow water.

Most sculpins are bottom living; a few occupy pelagic or mid-water habitats. About 50 species occur in Canadian waters, mostly on the West Coast; a few in rivers and lakes throughout the country. Sculpins are generally scaleless; a few groups have a narrow band of scales down the upper back. Others exhibit platelike structures on the body; still others have extensive patches of small cirri covering the skin, giving them a furry appearance. Spines and other "armour" on head and body make them spectacular objects. Reproduction varies: most exhibit external fertilization, laying eggs in masses or clumps under or among rocks; others show internal fertilization; some bear live young. Sculpins are found singly or in small groups, although "schooling" has been reported in at least one species. Some intertidal forms exhibit restricted ranges and "home" to their resident pool. Sculpins, important as food for other fishes, are not generally eaten by humans.   NORMAN J. WILIMOVSKY

Sculpture The first sculpture in NEW FRANCE was in wood and was the work of craftsmen who were imported from France. In 1671 Intendant Jean TALON asked the French government to send him sculptors to do the decorative work on a merchant vessel, the *Canadien,* he had commissioned. Religious communities and local leading citizens imported sculpture from Europe, though a tabernacle ordered for the Hôtel-Dieu in Québec in 1704 took 12 years to arrive. In 1675 the SÉMINAIRE DE QUÉBEC brought the 2 sculptors Samuel Genner and Michel Fauchois from France, who, during their 3- or 4-year stay, did the ornamentation for the séminaire's various chapels. Thereafter a steady stream of sculptors immigrated to New France. The best known are Denis Mallet from Alençon, Charles Chaboulié from St-Rémi de Troyes and Jan Jacques Bloem (better known as Jean Jacquiès dit Leblond) from Brussels. This first group of sculptors met the colony's needs and, by establishing an apprenticeship system, trained the first local sculptors.

Other sculptors arrived during the 18th century: Gilles Bolvin from St-Nicholas d'Avesnes in Flanders, François Guernon *dit* Belleville from Paris and Philippe Liébert from Nemours. Local sculptors emerged as well. In 1651 the brothers Jean and Pierre LEVASSEUR settled as carpenters in New France; their grandsons Noël and Pierre-Noël became sculptors; they were the first of several generations of indigenous sculptors prominent in New France, who also had cordial contacts with new arrivals in their trade such as Chaboulié and Jacquiès dit Leblond. Little remains from that century, either in religious or secular sculpture.

The splendid baldachin (ornamental canopy)

One of the statues (St Simon), representing Christ and the Apostles, by Louis-Philippe Hébert (*courtesy Musée du Québec/photo by Patrick Altman*).

in the choir of the church of Neuville near Québec City is the oldest sculpture ensemble in Canada. Created between 1690 and 1700 for the chapel of the episcopal palace of Mgr de St-Vallier, this baldachin is a scaled-down copy of one in the chapel of Val-de-Grâce in Paris and shows the importance of European models to the colony (*see* ARCHITECTURE; ART; PAINTING). In 1712 Jacquiès dit Leblond, a protégé of Noël Levasseur, created the altar-piece (screen located behind an altar) of the chapel of the Recollet convent in Montréal, now in the choir of the church of St-Grégoire-de-Nicolet opposite Trois-Rivières. The altar-piece in the Ursuline Chapel in Québec City, created by Noël Levasseur between 1732 and 1737, recalls a triumphal arch; even though mostly in relief, it creates a 3-dimensional illusion, heightened by the play of white decorated surfaces, black columns and gilded narrative panels, and statues in the round. In complexity, monumentality and latent baroque style it favourably echoes French prototypes.

Sculptors of the French regime did not limit themselves to religious work. Around 1725 one of the Levasseurs was commissioned to carve the royal arms to be placed over doors of official buildings in the colony. The example preserved in the Musée du Québec is the oldest surviving non-religious sculpture in Canada. In 1700 Denis Mallet carved a ship's figurehead of a lion for Sieur Brouve; in 1704 a captain from Québec, Louis Prat, commissioned an anonymous sculptor to carve a figurehead of the archangel Saint Michael in armour for the bow of his ship, the *Joybert,* and a VOTIVE PAINTING preserved in Ste-Anne-de-Beaupré shows us this figure. This same Prat in 1715 hired Noël Levasseur to sculpt the decorations for his new ship, the *Raudot.*

The establishment of a royal shipyard in the colony encouraged naval sculpture. Noël, Pierre and Jean-Baptiste Levasseur won handsome contracts to decorate the vessels of the French navy. The frigate *Castor* was decorated with a figurehead of a beaver and of a shield of the arms of France. The rear escutcheon of the supply ship *Caribou* was given a bas-relief of this native Canadian animal. The different Amerindian tribes were also honoured; the *Algonquin* was launched

in 1750, the *Abénaquise* in 1754, the *Iroquoise* and the *Outaouaise* in 1759. Unfortunately, no examples survive, and we know of their existence only through archival records. An agent responsible for the royal shipyards frequently complained about the poor quality of local sculptors; he was probably the one who sent Pierre-Noël Levasseur II to the sculpture workshop of the French arsenal in Rochefort in 1743, though the apprentice chose not to return.

While the wood sculptors of New France acknowledged the fashions prevalent in 17th-century France, from the few surviving examples it can be assumed that stylistically sculpture in the colony was somewhat different. The rich, round forms of the French baroque were usually subdued by a robustness which makes them essentially Canadian. This robustness was to linger in the sculpture of French Canada until well into the 19th century; it was probably also tied to the qualities and limitations of the material used by the sculptors of New France, that is, wood. In contrast to France, sculptors in New France almost never worked in stone.

The change in administration after 1760, the poor economy exacerbated by wartime destruction and the departure of French officials ushered in a lean time for sculptors in the colony. With the American War of Independence, warships were constructed in St-Jean-sur-Richelieu in 1775-77, some of which, including the schooner *Maria* and the frigate the *Royal George,* were given figureheads.

The economic situation improved in Canada in the last quarter of the century and steady population growth forced ecclesiastical authorities to open new parishes. The resulting wave of church construction was a boon to sculptors and a new dynasty, the BAILLAIRGÉ family, arose. François Baillairgé studied in France, 1778-81, visited London, and on his return introduced a fusion of 2 great artistic traditions and many new trends to the colony. He sculptured a huge baldachin leaning against the choir walls and a high altar for Notre-Dame-de-Québec. From 1816 he worked for more than 10 years on what was to be his finest work in the little church of St-Joachim near Ste-Anne-de-Beaupré: the placing and embellishment of the 4 monumental columns were inspired by the theoretician Jérôme Demers. Baillairgé was also involved with secular sculpture, including more than one-third of all ship figureheads made in Québec. He became sculptor of the king's shipyards in St-Jean-sur-Richelieu and in Kingston. His plans for 2 military vessels have been preserved: the *Royal Edward* and the *Earl of Moira.* He also sculpted signboards for Québec merchants, and the mace of Lower Canada's legislative assembly.

This was the time when Philippe Liébert rose to the height of his career. In 1790 he made his reputation by carving the high altar for the chapel of the Grey Nuns in Montréal. Soon after, other parishes in the area (Sault-au-Recollet, Ste-Rose, Vaudreuil) commissioned similar work from Liébert. Louis QUÉVILLON became the most important sculptor of the Montréal region in the early 19th century; and his models came from Liébert. In almost all the churches built between 1800 and 1825 works can be found by Quévillon and his associates, including Joseph Pépin, René St-James, Paul Rollin and many apprentices. In order to keep up with demand, Quévillon standardized his works, and his altars systematically followed the Liébert model. The best-preserved example of work by the Quévillon group is in the little church of St-Mathias, near Chambly.

Secular works continued to be important in the early 19th century. England needed ships for its merchant marine, which had suffered heavy loss-

Sunlife (1984), bronze sculpture weighing 12 t, by Sorel Etrog (*courtesy Sun Life Assurance Co of Canada*).

es in the Napoleonic Wars. The shipyards of British North America now included Québec City, and Yarmouth, Lunenburg and Halifax in NS, various yards in the Saint John Valley and on the Miramichi R in NB, and Bath (near Kingston) and Niagara-on-the-Lake in Upper Canada. Of the 2112 ships built in Québec City during the period from 1762 to 1897, 1651 were embellished with figureheads. Probably 10 000 figureheads were sculpted in Canada during the 19th century, and almost all of the sculptors in the country were involved, including Louis-Xavier Leprohon, Louis-Thomas BERLINGUET, André Giroux and Jean-Baptiste Côté. Scotsmen like John Rogerson worked out of NB. Many carvers of ship ornamentations in wood were anonymous. Figureheads in the bows of ships were modelled on historic personages, local notables, Amerindians and members of the shipowner's family. There were also generalized images, such as women, animals (especially native creatures such as the bear, caribou, beaver) or simple scrolls. The sterns of ships were also ornamented, mostly with coats of arms or shields with armorial bearings, often amplified with other types of decorative devices. But it was the end of the age of traditional shipbuilding; as of the mid-19th century, sails were replaced by the steam engine, and metal plates gradually replaced the old wooden hull. New decorative solutions made obsolete the once lucrative business of ship decorators (*see* SAILING SHIPS; FOLK ART).

Sculptors were also involved in the woodworking business. Parts of FURNITURE such as chair backs were often ornamented with sculpture, and merchants, especially tobacconists, tavern keepers and sellers of navigation instruments, sometimes called on sculptors to make their shop signs.

The second half of the 19th century saw the appearance of a phenomenon that was to shatter the traditional wood-sculptor's market – plaster statuary. In 1824 the Italian Donati made a copy in plaster of François Baillairgé's carvings on the panelled vaults of the cathedral of Québec. Thirty years earlier Liébert had already used molds to make decorative elements for his altars; Quévillon also did so, probably using some molds that had belonged to Liébert. In 1846 Mgr Bourget, on his return from a trip to Italy, introduced Hector Vacca to the Montréal market. Carlo Catteli arrived at the same time and made plaster statues for Montréal churches. Around 1855, 2 French sculptors, G.H. Sohier and Alexis Michelot, set up an "Académie des beaux-arts" which, though it

lasted less than a year, heralded the arrival of academic sculpture, made in plaster, in Canada.

Wood sculptors reacted slowly; they failed to see the extent of the change taking place or the impact of new techniques. As the Industrial Revolution took hold of Canada, wood sculptors gradually became obsolete. One of the most important wood sculptors of the time, Jean-Baptiste Côté, summed up the situation in a sentence: "My time is over." By scrounging whatever commissions they could, a few sculptors managed to survive.

Louis JOBIN, a sculptor who had trained in the workshop of François-Xavier Berlinguet, had to go to New York to complete his studies. He then worked for 5 years in Montréal and in late 1875 moved to Québec City. He carved the neogothic statues of the church of St-Henri in Lévis and in 1880 worked on the allegorical floats for the St-Jean-Baptiste parade; the agriculture float is preserved in the Musée du Québec. He was among the original carvers of ice sculptures at the early Québec winter carnivals. At the end of the century Jobin left Québec City for Ste-Anne-de-Beaupré, the last bastion of religious wood sculpture, where he tried to imitate in wood what a new generation of sculptors was doing in other materials such as bronze. His death in 1928 was also the death of traditional wood sculpture. On a much smaller scale, often created with a deep feeling for a lost past and mostly attractive to tourists, aspects of the wood-carving tradition in Québec have survived, particularly in the town of St-Jean-Port-Joli; however, these carvings have little in common with the monumental art forms in wood which once embellished the churches and ships of the New World.   JEAN BÉLISLE

Sculpture 1880-1950

It was fashionable for critics considering Canadian sculpture between 1880 and 1950 to mourn the demise of traditional wooden sculpture and the invasion of plaster and bronze, as though wood possessed certain authentic virtues missing in the other 2 materials. However, it was because of the limits of wood that the sculptors of the period, inspired by the needs of a new realism, often preferred bronze. Wood, like stone, sculpture is referred to as a subtractive method; also it is difficult to dissociate the finished sculpture from the tree trunk. The preparations for a bronze object are called additive sculpture; a model is built in flexible material, such as clay, from which a mold is made into which molten bronze is cast. This technique provided much greater flexibility, offering sculptors almost unlimited opportunities for expression. Since there were no specific facilities in Canada to cast bronze art objects until the 1960s, sculptures, especially large monuments, had to be cast in the US or Europe and shipped back to Canada.

Stylistically the sculpture of this period may be considered under 3 headings, each corresponding to similar European movements of the period: realism, art nouveau, art deco. Canadian sculpture did not develop in isolation, and yet it showed a certain originality.

Realism In Québec realism is represented by Napoléon BOURASSA (a multitalented artist who distinguished himself in architecture and painting as well as in sculpture) and by Anatole Partenais and Louis-Philippe HÉBERT. Hébert was the most important, and it is thought that he learned his art from Bourassa when they collaborated around 1870 on the Notre-Dame-de-Lourdes chapel in Montréal. The dominating ideology of this period in Québec attempted to define the people of French Canada in terms of their French Catholic origins; this too was important for

Hébert. In sculpture he created memorable examples of his countrymen's history.

Hébert was also influenced by the French realist tradition, which he combined with his robust talent. His works included a number of bronze sculptures of Indians (including the famous *Pêcheur à la nigogue* beside a fountain) which he produced for the legislative building in Québec City; the statue of *Maisonneuve* at Place d'Armes in Montréal; and his proud monument *Madeleine de Verchères*, located in the middle of the Québec village of Verchères. Those of his works devoted to English rulers (*Queen Victoria* in Ottawa) or to contemporary personages are less inspired. Historical subjects stimulated his imagination, and it is here that he produced his best work (*see* PUBLIC ART). Hamilton MacCarthy is also known for his historical monuments, in particular his *Sieur de Monts* at ANNAPOLIS ROYAL (1904). The historical works of Henri BEAU and Charles HUOT have been largely forgotten.

The late 19th century was a period of expansion which saw the settlement of the Canadian West. It is therefore not surprising that many N American artists, English Canadian sculptors as well, concentrated with deep, often romantic feelings on Indians and subjects involving Indians. Emmanuel Otto Hahn, a German sculptor who immigrated to Canada early in his life and married the sculptor Elizabeth WYN WOOD, is noted for his Indian subjects; Alexander Phimister Proctor, although known primarily for his animals, also included Indians in his sculptures. These "noble savages" were nostalgically perceived as the descendants of a vanishing race whose characteristics had to be captured before they disappeared under the wheel of civilization. Realism was the preferred style.

WW1 greatly stimulated sculpture in the 1920s, as everywhere there was a call for monuments to commemorate Canada's participation in the war. Walter Seymour Allward was commissioned to create a memorial on site in France to the Canadians who died at Vimy Ridge; Alfred Howell was responsible for monuments in Saint John, NB, and Guelph, Ont; Frances Norma LORING for a memorial in Galt, Ont, and R. Tait MCKENZIE for works in the US, England and Scotland. Each contract afforded the opportunity to illustrate the courage of Canadian troops and to express pride in the achievements of the country's sons. Loring dealt with women's participation in the war effort on the "home front" in *Girls with a Rail*, which is part of a series preserved at the Canadian War Memorial in Ottawa.

Art Nouveau Canadian sculptors did not escape the influence of art nouveau. The works of Alfred LALIBERTÉ illustrate the problems raised by applying to sculpture a style initially conceived to decorate flat surfaces. He broke away from the French academic influence of Gabriel-Jules Thomas and Antoine Injalbert to explore new avenues, and explored the possibilities of art nouveau's fluid line when, ceasing to be merely decorative, it animates interior space and sets it in wave-shaped relief. His romantic imagination may be seen in his 1920 monument *Dollard des Ormeaux* in Lafontaine Park, Montréal. His works also display a late 19th-century sensuality, and portray women as figures to be both feared and exalted. Woman – muse and source of the artist's inspiration – is also seductress! Laliberté worked in a variety of subjects, from the historical monument (*Louis Hébert* in Québec and *Tomb of Sir Wilfrid Laurier* in Ottawa) to jewels of the purest art-nouveau style, to self-portraits and folk scenes. The Musée de la province de Québec has 215 of his sculptures on the trades, customs and legends of French Canada.

Other Canadian sculptors were influenced by

art nouveau. Marc-Aurèle de Foy SUZOR-COTÉ, whose sculpture cannot be neglected even though he is better known as a painter, was touched by it. His *Indiennes de Caughnawaga* appears to be sculpted by the wind, which the figures in their large coats are fighting. The wind theme of *The Storm* enabled Allward to drape the human anatomy of his figure, thus creating freer and more fluid forms. In *Sun Worshipper* by academic sculptor Florence WYLE, the figure is bent backward, its arm extended beyond the limit of the sculpture.

Art Deco The influence of art deco appeared in the work of a number of sculptors in the 1930s, artists such as Elizabeth Wyn Wood of Toronto (whose bas-relief, *Passing Rain,* is famous) and Sylvia Daoust of Montréal. Two prolific sculptors of lesser talent were Émile Brunet, who produced the bas-reliefs and ornamental façade of the Musée de la province in Québec City, and Marius Plamondon.

The influence of art deco on sculpture may be seen in the elimination of surface detail and in giving space a more massive presence, making joints more defined and replacing the spiral art-nouveau line with straight or curved lines. It may be seen in the work of Phyllis Jacobine Jones, who produced the bronze doors of the Bank of Canada in Ottawa in 1938; in Orson Wheeler's works; in some of the later works of Florence Wyle; and in the larger-than-life-sized *Chemin de Croix,* sculpted by Louis-Joseph Parent in 1959 for the St-Joseph's Oratory in Montréal.

In Europe during this period, modernism was to lead from cubism to constructivism. Canadian sculpture was awakened to modern styles only later. It was not until the work of Louis ARCHAMBAULT and Anne KAHANE in the early 1950s that the influence of Julio Gonzalez, Pablo Picasso and Jacques Lipchitz began to be felt in Canadian sculpture.   FRANÇOIS-MARC GAGNON

Contemporary Sculpture

Some of the most inventive art made in Canada since WWII is in the realm of sculpture. The period exposed sculptors to a great variety of new materials, and they responded with new kinds of constructions, multimedia works, installations and site-specific inventions, along with more traditional freestanding objects (*see* ART, CONTEMPORARY TRENDS).

The new vigour of sculpture in Canada is part of a widespread cultural coming of age, owing something to improved communications and transportation. Artists today have far more experience of works of art than their predecessors, because of colour photography, ease of travel and the frequency of touring exhibitions. The CANADA COUNCIL and related provincial agencies support artists and assist their travel, and encourage the growth and programs of galleries and museums across the country. There is no simple explanation for the recent burgeoning of Canadian sculpture. A new climate of experiment at art schools and universities has been both a cause and an effect. Particular exhibitions, teachers and critics, symposia and major purchases have stimulated sculptors of various regions. For some, reaction against influences has been as important as response to them. Whatever the reasons, the proliferation of serious sculptors is a new phenomenon (*see* ARTISTS' ORGANIZATIONS).

In Canada, as in Europe, the development of advanced sculpture lagged behind that of advanced painting. For centuries, sculpture had meant carved or modelled figurative objects, usually upright on pedestals or part of an architectural complex, and made of wood, stone or bronze. Gradually, as in other art forms, sculpture

Kosso Eloul, *Time* (1973), aluminum, 6.4 x 38.1 m (*courtesy Kosso Eloul*).

also challenged traditional notions of form, content and technique, sharing in the aesthetic revolution known as "modernism."

At first, even the most adventurous Canadian sculptors (who were largely removed from the mainstream of innovative art) joined this revolution cautiously. While undoubtedly modernists, Québecois sculptors such as Louis Archambault and Charles DAUDELIN used more or less traditional techniques to make nontraditional images in the 1940s. By the 1950s these pioneers had been joined by others, but much of the most successful modernist sculpture retained a strong preference for the figure. John Ivor Smith, Anne Kahane, George Wallace and William McElcheran all used the figure as a starting point, but simplified and stylized it, smoothing or elaborating its surfaces. Kahane worked in many materials, while the others preferred bronze.

In the late 1950s and early 1960s relatively traditional techniques still prevailed, even among those who departed from literal figurative reference. The use of smooth, carved or cast masses suggests an awareness of the British sculptor, Henry Moore, as in the meticulously finished marbles of Hans Schleeh. Even among those interested in alternatives, there was a conservative quality related to British and European sculpture of the time. Robert ROUSSIL's works seem to amalgamate both Moore and a spiky expressionism. David Partridge developed an idiosyncratic type of relief made by driving nails of various sizes into wood. Ulysse COMTOIS, known for his brilliant, optically active paintings, also made elegantly crafted sculpture with geometric movable parts. Armand VAILLANCOURT attracted attention for aggressively textured abstract castings. A peculiarly self-contained movement, structurism, has flourished since the 1950s, particularly on the Prairies, under the influence of Eli BORNSTEIN. Structurists such as Gino Lorcini and Ron Kostyniuk explore geometric permutations in shallow, elegantly crafted reliefs.

Since there were no indigenous models for advanced sculpture, it is not surprising that Canadians should have looked to Europe, especially to England, for inspiration. Many had studied in England or with British artists in Canadian art schools, but more importantly, Henry Moore was internationally acclaimed by the 1950s. His amalgam of natural and invented forms seemed a pattern for carrying the great tradition of sculpture into the 20th century. But another "new tradition," dating from the late 1920s, was becoming just as powerful: drawinglike, abstract sculpture constructed out of iron, steel and found objects. This radical rethinking of what sculpture could be, begun by Pablo Picasso and Julio Gonzalez in France, was being continued in New York, as were equally radical notions about painting. By the late 1950s and the 1960s it was obvious that the centre of important innovative art had shifted from Europe to N America, and Canadians began to find great stimulation on their own continent.

Art of the late 1960s was characterized by a new openness, a willingness to accept new ideas, new materials and techniques, and we see these expanded possibilities clearly reflected in Canadian art. A new generation of Canadian sculptors came to maturity in the 1960s, with far more adventurous ideas than their predecessors. Some, such as Les Levine and Michael SNOW, were painters as well as multimedia artists, but their 3-dimensional work established their reputations. Levine's vacuum-formed plastic modules introduced a generation of Canadians to the then most modish kind of environmental sculpture, and the thick stainless-steel versions of Snow's "cookie cutter" walking-woman image were greeted with enthusiasm. Others, such as Gord Smith, were exclusively sculptors. Smith, Yves TRUDEAU, Gerald Gladstone and Vaillancourt were all testing the possibilities of welded-steel construction.

Modernist sculpture gradually gained adherents across the country. If an earlier generation of Canadians responded most to Henry Moore's example, many sculptors of the 1960s and 1970s looked to the work of the American sculptor in

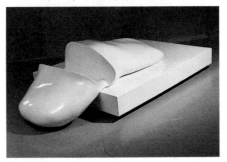
Walter Redinger, *Spermatogenesis II* (1968), fibreglass and wood (*courtesy Art Gallery of Ontario*).

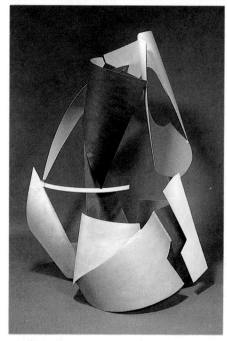

Douglas Bentham, *Saraband* (1984), steel paint (*courtesy Douglas Bentham*).

steel, David Smith, and his younger British colleague, Anthony Caro. Otto ROGERS in Saskatoon has continued to work with equal facility as a painter of landscape-derived abstractions and as a sculptor of vigorous, linear steel pieces. John Nugent in Regina was an early admirer of David Smith and an ambitious sculptor in steel. In Calgary, Katie Von Der Ohe exhibited complex pilings of interlocking forms. In Toronto, Ted Bieler received numerous public commissions and Sorel ETROG became known for a signature style of "knotted" bronze which owed a great deal to the later work of the French Cubist Jacques Lipchitz. In Québec, Françoise Sullivan, a modern dancer, choreographer and visual artist, abandoned her other activities to make painted steel constructions. Robert MURRAY is probably the most significant Canadian sculptor of his generation, internationally recognized for his severe metal constructions. He works with fabricators to produce large-scale structures of inflected planes, richly coloured with industrial finishes.

The most exciting aspect of Canadian sculpture in the 1970s and 1980s is its diversity. Approaches vary from "orthodox" object making to a stretching of the limits of the discipline. The object makers range from Kosso ELOUL, whose modular constructions of rectangular solids can be seen on many public sites, to Roland Poulin and Peter Kolisnyk, whose works are the sparest possible indicators of sculptural notions, threatening to disappear into pure idea.

The "new tradition" of constructed sculpture in various materials is especially strong on the Prairies, although it has gifted practitioners elsewhere, such as Ontario's André FAUTEUX and Louis Stokes. In the West, Douglas Bentham, Alan REYNOLDS and Peter HIDE have all developed intensely personal, potent ways of working in welded metal. Each is distinct, but collectively they seem less interested in sculpture as "drawing in space" and more concerned with finding new ways of appropriating the mass and volume of the traditional monolith for abstract construction. Michael Bigger, Tommie Gallie, Haydn Davies, Patrick Thibert and Henry Saxe testify to the range of the tradition across Canada, from Gallie's piled timbers to Thibert's suggestive "tables."

Saxe has worked in both orthodox steel construction and complex multisection works. David RABINOWITCH further extends the range with inquiries into the expressive possibilities of the weight and mass of steel, while Royden RABINOWITCH explores horizontality and layering. In Toronto, John McEwen comments on the new tradition of sculpture in steel with naturalistic images, flame cut from massive metal slabs. In Québec, Claude Mongrain, Roland Poulin and Jean-Serge Champagne have evolved variations on the ideas of construction, incorporating unexpected combinations of materials. Catherine Burgess, Don Foulds, John McKinnon, Anthony Massett and Delio Fonseca belong to an even younger generation of constructors in steel.

Many recent sculptors have been fascinated by new technology and media: Michael Hayden has used neon tubing in both static and kinetic works; Walter Redinger and Ed Zelenak use fiberglass; Don Proch uses molded fiberglass, often covered with drawing, along with elements in other media. Mark Prent's nightmare images depend upon combinations of made and recycled objects in technical *tours de forces*. Richard Prince's delicate, improbable machines are intimate kinetic constructions. For other sculptors, the single discrete object seems too restrictive. They make structures which respond to particular settings and sites, often on a scale which demands that we enter or move through the work. Like architecture, these sculptures depend upon physical participation as well as upon visual perception, but unlike architecture, they are without specific function. George TRAKAS and Melvin CHARNEY make arresting, often poetic, parodies of man-made structures. Robert Bowers and Mark Gomes also use everyday, often banal, objects as points of departure in more self-contained works. Roland Brener expands this notion, employing stock materials in systematic ways; angle iron and industrial scaffolding have been used with equal success.

While these sculptors explore challenging new ideas, they are still makers of objects, albeit unconventional ones. Other artists are more interested in process than in result, and their "sculptures" are often simply the by-product of an event or the symbol of an idea. Documentation of the event can become part of the final structure, as in Colette WHITEN's works. Mowry Baden's environmental constructions exist more for the physical sensations they create in the "viewer" who moves through them than for their appearance. The size and shape of Robin Peck's objects are dictated by the proportions of their settings. For others, ephemeral moments or phenomena take precedence over the object. The work of these artists can incorporate film projections, sound, temporary or perishable structures, and the passage of time itself. While their works often involve a great deal of 3-dimensional equipment, and for this reason often get termed "sculpture," they seem to have little to do with sculptural notions; they belong to some other category, closer to literature or theatre, to the "happenings" of the 1960s.

The recent resurgence of interest in public art, as evidenced by programs allocating a percentage of building costs for art projects, in certain new constructions, has led many sculptors to reconsider their attitudes towards the self-contained object. They are beginning to think in terms of collaboration with architects to make publicly scaled works of art that represent a true integration of disciplines. Montréal's competition for the design of fountains to enhance the reclaimed lakefront, Toronto's art component for its new covered stadium and many similar projects across the country are good examples of this new way of thinking.

Relatively traditional sculpture continues to have adherents. While not very large, because of the constraints of the medium, the best work of ceramic artists such as Victor Cikansky and Joe FAFARD recalls the tradition of portrait sculpture. Among the younger generation, Evan Penny's haunting nudes and torsos are noteworthy. Ric Gomez's abstract bronzes are elegant, precious objects.

In the 1980s just about anything can be considered sculpture. There is no "official" approach, no single method or medium which guarantees success or seriousness. The antithesis of the traditional academy has been reached, with its preconceived standards of excellence and measurable levels of achievement. Recent Canadian sculpture is a history of individuals who speak an international sculptural language, probably with a Canadian accent. It is difficult to isolate their Canadianness easily. The bewildering variety of contemporary Canadian sculpture may be a sign of health and strength. *See also* INDIAN ART; INUIT ART; NORTHWEST COAST INDIAN ART.

KAREN WILKIN

Reading: *Artmagazine*, Sculpture Issue (May/June 1978); D. Burnett and M. Schiff, *Contemporary Canadian Art* (1983); Dalhousie Art Gallery, *Sculpture '81* (1981); The Guildhall, *Contemporary Outdoor Sculpture at The Guild* (1982); N. Karczmar, ed, *Canadian Sculpture Expo 67* (1967); Musée d'art contemporain, *Panorama de la sculpture au Québec, 1945-1970* (1970); Musée du Québec, *Profil de la sculpture québecoise: XVIIe-XIXe siècle* (1969); National Gallery of Canada, *Pluralities 1980/Pluralités 1980* (1980); Winnipeg Art Gallery, *Sculpture on the Prairies* (1977); *S/10 Sculpture Today/Sculpture d'aujourd'hui* (1978).

Scurvy is a disease caused by a dietary deficiency of vitamin C (ascorbic acid). The disease has occurred with regular frequency throughout human history and prehistory in populations lacking fresh foods, especially vegetables and meat. Deficiency in vitamin C may accompany wars and famine, but it is most commonly associated with post-Renaissance European EXPLORATION, particularly ocean voyages.

Vitamin C was first isolated in 1928 by the Hungarian scientist Albert Szent-Györgyi, and synthesized by a Swiss group in 1933. It is important in maintaining the healthy condition of the body's mesenchyma, specifically connective tissues (which bind together and support body structures), osteoid (the organic part of bone) and dentin (the bone-like portion of teeth). Deficiency of the vitamin causes a breakdown in the binding function of these tissues, producing a series of characteristic signs and symptoms: weakness, lethargy, irritability, anemia, purple spongy gums which bleed freely, loosening teeth, the reopening of healed scars (including refracturing of bone) and hemorrhaging in the mucous membranes and skin. In severe cases the mortality rate is high.

Scurvy was a serious problem throughout the whole period of exploration and settlement in Canada. In 1535 Jacques CARTIER's voyage to the New World brought him to the present location of Québec City (STADACONA) where he and his men spent the winter. Signs of scurvy soon appeared among the crew. By Feb 1536 only 10 of the 110 men on the expedition were in good health. Also, Cartier noted that many people in the local native population succumbed to the disease before the end of 1535. Many of Cartier's men were saved by drinking a native concoction of ground coniferous needles and bark (called "anneda," probably white cedar) boiled in water. In 1542 a party of 200 French under ROBERVAL wintered near Cartier's earlier camp. During that winter about 50 died of the disease, and it appears they did not employ the cure that had saved Cartier's men.

Subsequent explorations and settlements in the New World met regularly with the catastrophic effects of scurvy during long and cold winters and food shortages.

During the 18th century scurvy caused more losses in the British navy than were suffered in enemy action. A surgeon with the Royal Navy, James Lind, conducted an extensive controlled experiment on the effects of diet on sailors with scurvy, and the results were published in 1753 in the landmark book *A Treatise of the Scurvy*. Lind recommended the use of citrus fruits in treating and preventing scurvy during ocean voyages, advice which was not heeded by the Royal Navy until 1795.

Scurvy was a major problem on nearly all of the 19th-century polar expeditions, and the tragic loss of John FRANKLIN's third arctic expedition in 1847 has been partly attributed to the disease. Though foods known to be antiscorbutic (antiscurvy) were carried by these expeditions, the effectiveness diminished over a period of months as the vitamin C oxidized, leaving the explorers without protection. Many armies during WWI also suffered very severe outbreaks; by WWII the problem of scurvy was monitored closely and all but eliminated. In Canada the years 1945-65 were marked by outbreaks of scurvy in bottle-fed infants given evaporated milk (then lacking in vitamin C).

Today scurvy is rare and is usually related to poor attention to diet, or to diets heavily weighted towards a single food low in vitamin C.

OWEN BEATTIE

Sea Ice, any ICE formed by the freezing of seawater. As it varies widely in thickness, strength, behaviour and appearance, it is classified in several ways. In bays, inlets and shallow COASTAL WATERS, one usually encounters fast ice, a smooth, even layer from 30-40 cm to 2-3 m thick. Fast ice remains where formed until spring thaw, or until melting or the action of wind and current causes it to break up and become drift ice. Each winter, fast ice covers most of the waterways of the ARCTIC ARCHIPELAGO and significant coastal areas of BAFFIN BAY, HUDSON BAY and the Labrador Sea.

Drift ice is found in oceanic areas and broad expanses like the Gulf of ST LAWRENCE, BEAUFORT SEA, FOXE BASIN and Hudson Bay. It is in more or less continual motion as a result of ocean currents, WINDS and TIDES and is composed of floes ranging in size from a few metres up to 10 km or more. Its thickness varies from 5-30 cm in the case of new and young ice, up to 30-200 cm for first-year ice and up to 2-4 m for old ice. First-year ice is formed in winter, having grown progressively from the young stage. In summer it becomes covered with puddles of melted snow and ice and, in temperate areas, eventually melts completely. In the Arctic, complete melting may not occur and, once summer ends, the ice floes "graduate" to become second-year or eventually multiyear ice, collectively called old ice. These terms related to thickness and age can be applied to either pack or fast ice. Because they are formed from seawater, young and first-year ice contain a small percentage of salt. During the melting process, this brine drains out of the floes and, if melting is not complete, the resulting old floes are much fresher and stronger than in their first year. They then become an increased hindrance to mariners.

Old ice predominates in the northernmost passages of the QUEEN ELIZABETH IS, the Arctic Ocean and the western part of PARRY CHANNEL. First-year ice prevails in southern Beaufort Sea, from Amundsen Gulf to Boothia Pen, from LANCASTER SOUND and Baffin Bay to Foxe Basin, Hudson Bay and HUDSON STR, and to the Gulf of St Lawrence and the northern GRAND BANKS E of Newfoundland. Because first-year ice predominates, it follows that all sea ice clears from this vast area every summer. In old ice areas, clearing is unusual, if it occurs at all.

Drift ice is continually deformed by its motion, in some cases merely by having one floe bump into another, but more often by wind and current forcing floes together to form pressure ridges and hummocks. These mounds of deformed ice fragments rise 1-5 m above level surfaces and can occur 100 m apart. Below each pressure ridge an ice keel extends downward 4-5 times as far as the ridge projects upward. This mass of ice provides the buoyancy to support the ridge. It is these underwater features that cause most of the problems for ship operation through drift ice. Keels under ridges of old ice are even more of a hindrance than those under first-year ice. In Canada, an ice information and forecasting service is provided by the Atmospheric Environment Service, Environment Canada. Terminology and chart symbols used were developed by the World Meteorological Organization. Canada participated in developing and establishing these procedures. *See also* ICEBERG. WILLIAM E. MARKHAM

Sea Lion The northern sea lion (*Eumetopias jubata*), the largest eared SEAL, occurs on the N Pacific coast from Japan to California. There are 2 large breeding colonies on the BC coast. In winter sea lions migrate southward and inshore. Bulls average 3 m long and weigh up to 900 kg; cows are less than half that weight. The short, coarse pelage lacks underfur. There is a blubber layer. Both sexes are reddish brown, the bulls with buff upperparts. Cows are slender and streamlined but adult bulls have massive necks and foreparts. The flippers are large and hairless; those of the forelimbs are used for propulsion. The hind flippers are turned forward on land and permit the animal to move at a hobbling run. Sea lions are powerful and graceful swimmers. Food is a wide variety of fish and invertebrates. Breeding is polygamous; the harem master bulls defend 5-20 cows. Pups arrive in May-June and cows mate again in about a week. The gestation period is about 51 weeks. Some fishermen accuse sea lions of stealing salmon from lines and nets and urge control of their numbers. IAN McTAGGART-COWAN

Northern sea lions breed in 2 large colonies on the BC coast (*photo by Tim Fitzharris*).

Sea Otter (*Enhydra lutris*), largest and most marine WEASEL, lives exclusively in shallow seas of the N Pacific, formerly from Japan to California. Ruthless hunting for their valuable pelts almost exterminated sea otters before 1900. A few survived in Alaska and California. Protection has permitted them to increase and reoccupy some former range. Transplants to SE Alaska and BC have been successful. Males reach 1.6 m in length and 36 kg in weight; females about 3/4 of this. The body is long; tail and legs short. Forefeet are pad-like and have sharp claws; hindfeet are flippers and fully furred. The head is broad, flattish with small ears. The animal is dark brown, frequently with a whitish face. Fur so dense that water cannot penetrate provides insulation; there is no blubber. Food, mainly urchins, molluscs and fish obtained during dives to 80 m, is consumed at the surface. The sea otter is known to use a stone as a hammer to break shells. Although concentrated in June, some breeding occurs in all months; most births occur in summer. The single pup may be born ashore (Alaska) or at sea (California) and is nursed about 11 months. Pups are carried on the female's chest as she swims belly up. They are groomed frequently to maintain waterproofing. Females breed in alternate years. *See also* ENDANGERED ANIMALS; FUR TRADE.

IAN McTAGGART-COWAN

Sea Urchin, radially symmetrical marine INVERTEBRATE. Sea urchins and near relatives, the sand dollars and heart urchins, belong to class Echinoidea of phylum ECHINODERMATA; about 900 species are known worldwide. A characteristic external covering of movable spines serves for protection and locomotion. In some tropical forms, spines can be 30 cm long and, being poisonous, can inflict painful wounds on swimmers. The body wall contains an internal skeleton that gives characteristic shapes: sea urchins, spherical; heart urchins, heart-shaped; sand dollars, flattened discs. Sea urchins have the mouth on the undersurface and the anus directed upwards. Usually, 5 double rows of tube feet encircle the body. These are the principal means of locomotion and attachment. Like other echinoderms, sea urchins have a water-vascular system to operate tube feet. Pedicellariae (small, pincerlike appendages) cover the body surface at the base of spines. These often have a poison sac with a hypodermiclike fang, used to deter predators. Sea urchins are common in Canada, intertidally and subtidally. They are usually associated with rocky bottoms. They feed on algae. In some countries they are harvested for eggs, eaten like caviar.

R.D. BURKE

Seabird, bird that spends a large proportion of its life at sea. Primary seabirds (AUKS, GULLS, GANNETS, SHEARWATERS, FULMARS, etc) belong to families of which all members are adapted to life at sea; secondary seabirds (eg, eider DUCKS, PHALAROPES) belong to families that otherwise live in terrestrial habitats. The more specialized species have a long life expectancy and adolescent period, and lay only one egg. They can adjust only with difficulty to increased mortality, eg, from HUNTING and oil POLLUTION, and their populations have recently declined sharply. One Canadian seabird, the GREAT AUK, is extinct. Forty-five primary seabird species breed in Canada today, including 16 gulls and 11 auks. They number well over 4 million pairs with the largest colonies in Hudson Str and SE Nfld. The best-known site is the northern gannet (*Sula bassanus*) colony on Bonaventure I, Qué, a federal migratory BIRD SANCTUARY, PROVINCIAL PARK and major tourist attraction.

R.G.B. BROWN

Seaborn, James Blair, public servant (b at Toronto 18 Mar 1924). Seaborn joined the Dept of External Affairs in 1948. In 1964-65, while the Canadian member of the International Commission for Supervision and Control (Vietnam), he visited Hanoi 5 times in an effort by Ottawa to establish communications between the US and North Vietnam. The "Seaborn Mission," undertaken with the active involvement of the US, was one of the most controversial aspects of Canadian diplomacy during the Vietnam War. Seaborn was subsequently assistant deputy minister of consumer and corporate affairs 1970-74 and deputy minister of Environment Canada 1975-82. He was appointed Canadian chairman of the INTER-

NATIONAL JOINT COMMISSION 1982 to 1985, when he became intelligence and security co-ordinator at the Privy Council Office. NORMAN HILLMER

Seafarers' International Union In 1949, supported by the federal government and some union leaders and shipping executives, an unsavoury ex-convict was allowed into Canada to destroy the powerful, communist-dominated Canadian Seamen's Union. Within a few months, Hal BANKS and the "goons" he brought with him, through beatings, threats and even murder, had replaced the CSU with the American Seafarers' International Union. Although the union was expelled from the CANADIAN LABOUR CONGRESS, its practices condemned by a royal commission, and Banks arrested and forced to flee the country, the SIU remains Canada's dominant seamen's union.
IRVING ABELLA

Seagram, Joseph Emm, distiller, turfman, politician (b at Fisher Mills [near Cambridge], Ont 15 Apr 1841; d at Waterloo, Ont 18 Aug 1919). Founder of the world's largest producers and marketers of distilled spirits and wines, owner and breeder of an unprecedented 15 QUEEN'S/KING'S PLATE horse-race winners, and Conservative MP for Waterloo North 1896-1908, Seagram was one of Canada's most prominent gentleman entrepreneurs. He realized the market potential of high-quality, brand-name products. In 1883 he became sole owner of a Waterloo distillery and created Seagram's '83, which became one of Canada's most popular whiskies. Seagram's VO, first blended in 1907, is now the largest-selling Canadian whisky worldwide. The Seagram commitment to product excellence permitted the BRONFMAN FAMILY, which acquired controlling interest in 1928, to mold the company into a corporate empire. Noted for his physical likeness to King Edward VII, Seagram was a racing enthusiast. The Seagram Stables, begun in 1888, won 8 consecutive Queen's Plates 1891-98. Seagram was president of the Ontario Jockey Club 1906-17 and a founder of the Canadian Racing Assn in 1908. DON SPENCER

Reading: P.C. Newman, *Bronfman Dynasty: The Rothschilds of the New World* (1978); W.F. Rannie, *Canadian Whisky* (1976).

Seagram Company Limited is a producer of distilled spirits and wines, with head offices in Montréal. The company was incorporated in 1928 as Distillers Corporation-Seagrams Ltd, as a holding company to acquire the capital stocks of Distillers Corp Ltd and Joseph E. Seagram & Sons Ltd, and adopted its present name in 1975. It gained a certain notoriety in the PROHIBITION era and enjoyed a certain celebrity thanks to the colourful nature of its owner, Samuel Bronfman (*see* BRONFMAN FAMILY). The company has continued to expand in the liquor business and in other areas, although in 1980 it sold its oil, gas and related properties in the US to Sun Co, Inc. In 1987 it held a 22.5% interest in E.I. DuPont de Nemours and Co, the largest chemical company in N America. Today, its principal business and products are the manufacture and marketing of distilled spirits and wines through its subsidiaries and affiliates in 29 countries on 6 continents. As of Jan 1987, it had annual sales of $3.3 billion (ranking 27th in Canada), assets of $9.2 billion (2nd) and 14 400 employees. The Bronfman family owns 38%. *See also* DISTILLING INDUSTRY.
DEBORAH C. SAWYER

Seal, carnivorous, marine MAMMAL with streamlined body, limbs developed into flippers, eyes adapted for vision under and out of water, and valved nostrils. The respiratory, circulatory and excretory systems are adapted to diving and to life without fresh water. Nine species, classified in 3

Nine species of seal occur in Canadian waters. The young of the harp seal (*Phoca groenlandica*) was long hunted for its white fur (*photo by Norman R. Lightfoot*).

families, occur in Canadian seas: elephant seals and northern fur seals (*Mirounga angustirostris, Callorhinus ursinus,* respectively) are Pacific; ribbon, bearded and ringed seals (*Phoca fasciata, Erignathus barbatus, P. hispida*), exclusively Arctic; harp, hooded and grey seals (*P. groenlandica, Cystophora cristata, Halichoerus grypus*), N Atlantic; common or harbour seal (*P. vitulina*), all 3 oceans and a few lakes. All are fish, crustacean or squid eaters. Eared seals (eg, northern fur seal) can run on land using fore and hind limbs and swim with the large fore flippers. They breed on the Pribilof Is, Alaska, and migrate to winter off BC. The young are helpless with a long nursing period.

Elephant seal are winter visitors from the south. The 7 species of earless seals (family Phocidae) move on land by undulating, swim with the hind flippers and have precocious young that nurse for a few weeks only. Best known is the harp seal. Many thousands of its newborn, white-furred young were taken each year off Québec and Labrador for the FUR INDUSTRY until seal products were banned by many European countries, causing the market to collapse. *See also* SEALING.
IAN MCTAGGART-COWAN

Seal hunt *c*1900 (*courtesy National Archives of Canada/PA 129900*).

Sealing Fourteen species of SEALS, SEA LIONS and WALRUS inhabit the waters surrounding continental N America. Most of these may be found within Canadian boundaries for at least part of each year. Seals are taken by Canadian native people in subsistence hunts for food and clothing. Coastal Inuit communities in the Canadian Arctic have long relied on ringed seals (*Phoca hispida*) for food, clothing and fuel. Pelts may also be sold directly to the processors.

The plush pelt of the northern fur seal (*Callorhi-*

nus ursinus) has been the object of a commercial hunt since discovery of the species's Pribilof Is breeding grounds in the late 18th century. By 1910, there were concerns that the herds had been seriously depleted by intensive pelagic (high-seas) sealing. Representatives from the US, Russia, Japan and Great Britain (on behalf of Canada) met and signed the North Pacific Fur Seal Convention (1911). Under the terms of this treaty, pelagic hunting of fur seals ceased and a regulated land hunt was maintained (*see* BERING SEA DISPUTE). Canada and the other member countries signed a revised treaty in 1957. Together, these countries form the North Pacific Fur Seal Commission, which co-ordinates fur-seal management and research. While Canada takes no active part in the hunt, profits from the sale of pelts are shared by the 4 nations. In spite of active management programs, there are indications that this herd may be decreasing.

Each spring a large-scale commercial hunt takes place off Canada's East Coast and in the Gulf of ST LAWRENCE. Two species are hunted: harp seals (*Phoca groenlandica*) and hooded seals (*Cystophora cristata*). In the past 2 decades, this commercial hunt has come under considerable public scrutiny. Consequently, although seals are commercially hunted in other countries, when they hear of sealing many people think first of the annual Canadian hunt.

Seals have long provided man with food and clothing. Bones unearthed in archaeological digs show that Stone Age men caught harp seals off the coasts of Western Europe 10 000 years ago. The indigenous peoples of N America hunted seals long before the arrival of Europeans. When the first European colonists arrived in Newfoundland in the 16th century, they evidently caught seals in nets placed under water; the Inuit had long used this method. In the mid- to late 1700s, the European demand for oil and skins led to the development of a commercial seal fishery, based in Newfoundland. Seal oil produced an almost smokeless light, particularly useful in miners' headlamps. At first, an offshore hunt was carried out from small boats, and wooden sailing ships first left St John's harbour in 1794 in search of seals. The industry grew, bringing foreign investment and employing not only sealers but shipbuilders, carpenters, sailmasters, and refiners who extracted the prized oil from seal blubber. Between 1800 and 1840, more people from more ports worked in the sealing industry than at any other time. This era culminated in 1831 when 300 ships are reported to have returned from the hunt with over 680 000 pelts. Only the celebrated cod fishery was more important to the colonial economy. In the sealing industry, wooden sailing ships gradually gave way to those powered by steam (1863) and made of steel (1906). The advantage of heavier vessels lay in their speed and ease of handling and also in their ability to force a passage through ice.

By the late 19th century, production of PETROLEUM had cut the demand for seal oil. The industry continued to decline through the world wars (when sealing ships were claimed for other pursuits) and the Depression. Markets reopened after WWII, when the hunt again became profitable, primarily because of demands for fur and leather. Norway, Québec and NS joined the offshore hunt. Between 1949 and 1961 an average of 310 000 seals were taken annually off the East Coast. More than 400 000 seals were caught in 1951. The NW Atlantic harp seal population declined by up to 50% between 1952 and the early 1970s. Today, sealing is part of a national Canadian FISHERIES industry, under the jurisdiction of the Department of Fisheries and Oceans. The Seal Protection Regulations (first established in 1966 and amended annually) set down rules governing issuance of sealing permits, annual seal quotas, and opening and closing dates of the hunt (first introduced in 1961). Only those holding a valid permit may hunt.

Seals often migrate great distances; therefore, their pursuit must be governed by international agreements. Outside Canada's 200-nautical-mile (370 km) territorial zone, sealing comes under the jurisdiction of the Northwest Atlantic Fisheries Organization (NAFO), which includes countries using major aquatic resources of the region. The Canadian Atlantic Fisheries Scientific Advisory Committee (CAFSAC) advises on matters concerning fisheries within the 370 km zone, as does the independent Committee on Seals and Sealing (COSS), established by the federal government in 1971 to monitor the hunt and advise on sealing policy. The quota of seals that may be caught in the NW Atlantic each year is established initially by the Canadian government. Subsequently, negotiations take place with other sealing nations, particularly Norway and the European Economic Community (EEC), which represents Denmark (Greenland).

The commercial hunt is divided between those who travel to the hunt on foot or in boats under 20 m (landsmen) and those hunting from vessels longer than 20 m (large vessel hunt). Recently, the landsmen's catch has exceeded the large-vessel catch, particularly in the Gulf of St Lawrence. Sealers in the Gulf may not take hooded seals. Farther east sealers sail from ports in Newfoundland and NS to hunt amid the ice floes off the NE coast of Newfoundland-Labrador (the Front). On the ice, sealers carry a hardwood club (bat), curved knife and sharpening steel. Those hunting from large vessels may carry a long-handled iron weapon (hakapik) with a curved head. Fisheries officers, members of COSS and other observers travel to the hunt to ensure that it is carried out humanely and according to regulations. The pelt from a newborn (whitecoat) or fully molted harp seal pup (beater) is of great economic value to the sealer, although that of a young hooded seal (blueback) is more highly prized.

Canada imposed a partial quota on its sealers in the gulf in 1965; quotas limiting catch at the gulf and the Front were introduced by the federal government in 1971. In 1982 hunters were permitted to take up to 186 000 harp and 15 000 hooded seals in Canadian waters. Approximately 164 000 harp and 10 000 hooded seals were caught. In 1983, the total allowable catch was not met; in 1984 only 30 000 harp and 250 hooded seals were taken because of the failure of the commercial market. In 1987, the overall Canadian quota was unchanged, except that 57 000 non-

whitecoated seals were allotted to large vessels. Two large vessels prosecuted the hunt off Newfoundland and Labrador, but took less than 4000 seals. Young-of-the-year (including whitecoats) were taken in comparatively small numbers by landsmen. Large vessels have now been restricted from the hunt, although all other activities will continue.

Pelts are graded and sold to processors directly or through an agent. While initial pelt processing (eg, removal of blubber and oil) is done in Canada, the final processing and sale of skins usually takes place abroad. Seal oil is still sold for use in tanneries and in food. Seal meat is popular in Newfoundland-Labrador; the flippers are an eagerly awaited delicacy.

Since the early 1960s, intense opposition to the commercial hunt has arisen from both national and international groups. This is countered by the equally fierce desire of the sealers and their supporters to preserve not only a source of income but what they regard as their heritage. There are about 1-2 million harp seals and 300 000 hooded seals in the NW Atlantic. The harp seal is not an ENDANGERED ANIMAL; the hooded seal's status is still curiously unknown. These marine mammals may be potentially more threatened by environmental changes (eg, biochemical contamination and the search for and transportation of fossil fuels) than by a regulated commercial hunt. Although harp and hooded seals travel great distances and theoretically could avoid highly contaminated areas, an oil spill could have disastrous consequences, particularly at breeding or whelping grounds or in northern waters, where biodegradation is slow and cleanup difficult. Man is also placing considerable pressure on fish stocks, including species on which seals depend. Clearly the management of any species must owe a greater debt to reason, caution and sound scientific knowledge than to emotionalism or to human overconfidence in our ability to predict the future.　　　　　K. RONALD AND J.L. DOUGAN

Sears Canada Inc, headquartered in Toronto, is a Canadian retailer incorporated in 1952. In 1953 operating under the name Simpsons-Sears Ltd, it acquired the mail-order agency and order office of SIMPSONS, LIMITED and its subsidiaries and today operates over 1400 catalogue sales units, 3 customer merchandise service centres and 75 retail stores. In 1986, Sears had sales of $3.9 billion and 51 732 employees. Sears, Roebuck and Co of Chicago is the principal shareholder with a 60% interest in the company.

Seashell Shell is a hard covering made primarily of calcium carbonate, secreted by invertebrate animals (eg, MOLLUSCS, BARNACLES, SEA URCHINS). Some shells grow with the animal; others are shed and replaced periodically. The shell provides protection, a site for muscle insertion and, in a few cases, buoyancy. In most molluscs it consists of 3 layers secreted by the mantle and its marginal lobes. The outer layer (periostracum) consists of an organic material, conchiolin. It may be thin and glossy or coarse, flaky or spiny. The underlying prismatic layer, usually the thickest part of the shell, consists of calcium carbonate crystals laid down in an organic matrix, obliquely or at right angles to the periostracum. The inner layer is of similar composition but is laid down as flat plates. This often iridescent, nacreous layer is called mother of pearl because if a sand grain or a parasite becomes trapped between mantle and shell, nacreous material secreted around it forms a pearl. Many bivalves, including common freshwater MUSSELS (*Lampsilis* and *Anodonta*) and bay mussel (*Mytilus*), can make pearls; the valuable forms are secreted by members of tropical genera of pearl OYSTERS (*Pinctada* and *Pteria*).

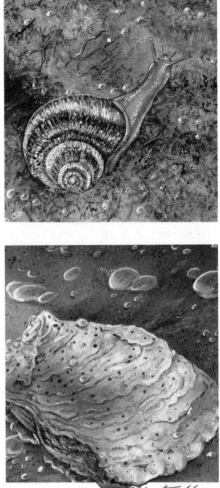

Seashells: snail (*Helix sp*) and American oyster (*Crassostrea virginica*). Shell is a hard covering made primarily of calcium carbonate, which is secreted by invertebrate animals (*artwork by Claire Tremblay*).

The 3 forms of crystalline calcium carbonate forming the shell are calcite, aragonite and vaterite. Calcium is less abundant in fresh water than in the ocean; consequently, pond snails have thin, fragile shells, which can be partly regenerated following injury.

The study of shells, conchology, dates to the 17th century when merchants and explorers brought back tropical shells for the "curiosity cabinets" of the wealthy. Until Linnaeus's system of taxonomy was accepted in the late 18th century, conchology was relatively unscientific. It flourished during the Victorian era when popular interest in natural history was fueled by such voyages of discovery as the CHALLENGER EXPEDITION (1872-76). This great oceanographic enterprise, which visited Halifax briefly, pioneered deep-sea dredging for marine organisms, including molluscs. Modern conchologists place as much emphasis on the BIOLOGY and ecology of the organism as on the structure of its shell.

Beach specimens may be collected as souvenirs. Although sometimes worn or damaged, they indicate which species may be found alive in the vicinity. If a collection is intended to have scientific or commercial value, the animals should be collected live at low tide or by diving and dredging. The collector must make sure in advance that harvesting is permitted (some countries have strict conservation programs and ban export of rare species). Joining a malacological or shell club, through which shells are exchanged or bought, allows collectors to acquire exotic species such as beautifully shaped and coloured cones, cowries, tuns, conches, strombids and olives. Satisfactory examples of these are often found in souvenir shops at museums and aquaria, or through dealers and catalogues. Shells may be conical, planispiral, spiral cones, dome shaped, plain or sculptured. Shells have been collected since prehistoric times for use in adornment and mosaics, as fertility symbols, money, dishes, trumpets, sources of mortar, and adzes for constructing dugout canoes. Crusaders and pilgrims wore scallops or "coquilles St Jacques." FOSSIL shells are used as a means of determining the age of SEDIMENTARY ROCKS. The shells most likely to be found on beaches belong to one of the 5 classes of the phylum Mollusca described below.

Gastropoda, including snails, whelks, limpets, cone shells, cowries and conches, are the most numerous class. Some species bear a horny or shelly covering on the foot (operculum), which can seal the opening for protection against predators or desiccation.

Amphineura, the chitons, have cradle or coat-of-mail shells, divided into 8 overlapping butterfly-shaped plates.

Bivalvia, the clams, cockles, oysters and mussels, have 2 convex valves joined dorsally by an elastic hinge ligament. Hinge teeth help lock the valves along the hinge line. Concentric lines in the shell sculpture may be "growth checks," so-called since they result from variations in growth rate. Sculpturing may consist of spines, plates, knobs or corrugations.

Scaphopoda, the tusk or tooth shells, have a conical, tubular shell open at both ends. They were used as currency by the Northwest Coast Indians.

Cephalopoda In octopus, cuttlefish and squid, the shell is lost or much reduced, except in *Nautilus, Spirula* and *Argonauta* (paper nautilus). *Nautilus* is an Indo-Pacific genus; its large, white, coiled shell, decorated with russet stripes, is common in collections. *Spirula* has a white, coiled shell that is washed up on Atlantic beaches as far N as Cape Cod; its shell, like that of *Nautilus,* is known as a chambered cone. The female *Argonauta* secretes a delicate, frilled pseudo-shell to protect her eggs. A.M. REID AND R.G.B. REID

Reading: Tucker R. Abbott, *Seashells of North America* (1968); Peter S. Dance, *Sea Shells* (1973).

Seaweed, Willie, or the formal address Hiamas, meaning "right maker," or more commonly Kwaxitola, meaning "smoky-top," Northwest Coast artist, singer, dancer (b at Nugent Sound, BC *c* 1873; d at Blunden Harbour, BC 1967). Seaweed participated in the development of southern Kwakiutl art from the "restrained" style of the 19th century to what Bill Holm describes as the "baroque period which reached its culmination in the cannibal bird masks of the 1940s and 1950s." The years during which Seaweed practised his art were times of great change. Most of his carving was done for traditional uses. One of his best-known works is a memorial Dzoonokwa and Thunderbird pole, in the graveyard at Alert Bay. The work was executed with a contemporary of Seaweed, Mungo MARTIN, in 1931. Seaweed never signed his work, but it remains identifiable because of his consistent use of 3 circles placed within one another with evenly spaced centres and black and white paint. GERALD R. MCMASTER

Seaweeds are multicellular marine ALGAE, visible to the naked eye. They extend from the uppermost reaches of sea spray on the shore to the lower limits of light beneath the surface of the water. They fringe all ocean coastlines, with few species

found below 30-40 m depth. Seaweeds are most abundant in lower intertidal and shallower subtidal zones. Some are small filaments, barely visible; others are large and complex in structure. There are reports of giant kelp (*Macrocystis*) attaining 100 m in length, and single plants of bull kelp (*Durvillaea,* genus of Southern Hemisphere) weighing more than 100 kg. Seaweeds, as algae, are classified as "greens," "browns" and "reds." Most seaweeds belong to the red or brown algae, most green algae occurring as planktonic or freshwater forms (*see* PLANKTON). Many species of seaweeds occur along Canadian coasts: about 175 are reported for the Arctic; 350 in the Atlantic; nearly 500 in the Pacific.

The use of seaweed as food is largely restricted to the Orient. The Japanese include many species in their diet, the most noteworthy being nori (*Porphyra*), which is "farmed," the annual crop valued at about $1 billion. The Chinese still consume kelp (*Laminaria*) to prevent goitre. In the West, only purple laver (*Porphyra*), IRISH MOSS (*Chondrus crispus*) and dulse (*Palmaria palmata*) are eaten routinely, the latter 2 in Atlantic Canada. Seaweeds are included in animal rations and used as soil conditioners and fertilizers. Hydrocolloids (water-soluble gums) are employed in industry, particularly food and textile sectors. These include agar and carrageenin from "reds" and algin from "browns." Irish moss is harvested in the Maritime provinces and exported for processing of carrageenin. In NS, knotted wrack (*Ascophyllum nodosun*) is harvested for alginate. Seaweeds are little used in BC. Some species, especially "reds," are beautiful and have been collected and mounted. J. McLACHLAN

Sechelt Peninsula, approximately 35 000 ha, pop 4505 (1986c), is part of a coastal area known as the "Sunshine Coast," isolated from nearby VANCOUVER, BC, by both Howe Sound and the COAST MTS. The name, meaning "place of shelter from the sea," is that of an Indian village and band. Settlement by Europeans began in 1870. Now linked by ferries with Saltery Bay and Horseshoe Bay, the peninsula still attracts settlers and is a popular cottage, tourist and yachting area. PETER GRANT

Second-Language Instruction The language that children first acquire naturally in the home is known as a first language (also as "mother tongue" and "native language"); any language learned after the first language has been acquired is a second language. Most children appear to learn their first language without any special instruction or formal teaching. Some linguists have attributed this facility to an innate, specific language-learning capacity; others believe it to be attributable to general cognitive capacities. Even in the first language, however, reading and writing must be taught, and thus first-language and second-language teaching and learning have much in common.

Languages in Canada

There are 3 major classes of languages in Canada: official or "charter" languages (French and English) which are recognized under the federal OFFICIAL LANGUAGES ACT (under provincial legislation, however, only in Québec and New Brunswick is French an official language); immigrant languages, which enjoy no official status in Canada but which are spoken as national or regional languages elsewhere; and ancestral languages of native peoples, which are not protected legally at the federal level (*see* NATIVE PEOPLE, LANGUAGES). The language issues of particular significance in Canada include the learning of French as a second language (FSL) by English-speaking Canadians and by immigrants to Québec; the

learning of English (ESL) as a second language by Francophones in Québec, by native people and by immigrants to English-speaking Canada; and the maintenance of other ethnic languages, ie, languages of immigrants and of native people.

French as a Second Language

The great importance attached to the teaching of French reflects changes in the long history of FRANCOPHONE-ANGLOPHONE RELATIONS. Until recently, because economic power was largely in the hands of the English, the French language did not enjoy the same status in Canada as English, despite the historical significance of French, its demographic significance, and the fact that French is one of the world's major languages. This was true even in Québec, where the vast majority of the population speaks French. In response to the discontent of francophone Quebeckers with this situation, successive Québec governments since the 1960s have taken measures to protect the French language, culminating in legislation such as BILL 101, which was passed to promote the use of the French language.

In the early 1960s some members of the English community of St Lambert, Qué (the St Lambert Bilingual School Study Group) reacted to the evolving importance of French and to the isolation of the French and English communities from each other by questioning methods of FSL instruction in English schools. Searching for better methods, this group consulted Wallace Lambert of McGill University, who had studied the sociopsychological and cognitive aspects of BILINGUALISM, and Wilder PENFIELD of the Montreal Neurological Institute, who had studied brain mechanisms underlying language functions. At this parents' initiative, an experimental kinder garten French-immersion program was established in St Lambert in 1965. In this kind of program, participating children receive the same type of education they would receive in the regular English program, except that the material is all taught in French. The teachers are generally native speakers of French who understand English, and children are generally treated as though they too were native speakers. By 1986-87 close to 200 000 anglophone students were enrolled in French immersion programs in over 860 schools in 434 boards of education across Canada. There are 3 main types of such programs in existence.

Early Total Immersion Programs are divided into a monolingual phase (usually kindergarten to grade 2 or 3) when all curriculum materials are presented in the second language but children may speak among themselves or to the teacher in English; a bilingual phase (usually grade 2 or 3 to grade 6) when English and French are used equally for instruction; and a maintenance phase (usually from grade 7 to the end of secondary school) when 3 to 5 subjects are offered in French.

Delayed Immersion Programs are those in which the use of French as a major medium of instruction is delayed until the middle elementary grades.

Late Immersion Programs postpone intensive use of FSL until the end of primary school or the beginning of secondary school.

Immersion education, pioneered in Canada, is internationally recognized as one of the few successful experiments in second-language instruction. A distinguishing feature of this movement has been the active involvement of parents' groups across Canada. In 1977 a national association, Canadian Parents for French (CPF), was created to promote increased opportunities for FSL of all types. CPF has become a powerful lobby group at all levels of government.

Although immersion is a widespread and popular option across Canada, the majority of English-speaking students in elementary and secondary schools still learn French as a second language in classes where French is taught as a subject (so-called "core" French) and is not the medium of instruction. Because of the success of immersion, core French is less popular and is regarded as a less successful "Cinderella" language course and improvements in core French instruction are widely demanded.

English as a Second Language

If French LANGUAGE POLICIES raise questions about Canadian unity and francophone-anglophone relations, the debate over English as a second language (ESL) has been less political. For immigrants to English-speaking Canada, for example, learning English is a necessary prerequisite for economic survival. It was not until after WWII that provincial governments created language and citizenship programs for adult newcomers, that school boards established language classes for immigrant children, and that the growth of community colleges led to the development of post-secondary ESL programs. By the early 1970s teachers of ESL had founded a number of provincial ESL associations, and in 1978, TESL Canada, a nationwide federation of associations involved in teaching ESL, was created.

No coherent national strategy concerned with the problems of immigrant adaptation has yet been formulated, and immigrant services are still provided by a complex network of school boards, universities and community colleges, and by agencies of the federal and provincial governments. A wide variety of approaches has been developed to meet the needs of ESL students, but the field is beset by problems (which also beset FSL), such as insufficient numbers of teachers and consultants, inadequate teacher training, a paucity of appropriate curricula and materials, and the lack of clear goals. In the late 1970s, with the wave of refugees from Southeast Asia, the inadequacies of the language-training system and of settlement services became apparent. In 1981, after a national symposium on the problems of adult refugees, the TESL Canada Action Committee urged the development of a national policy of refugee settlement. The committee recommended a 2-stage approach in which a basic 3-month program would be followed by a variety of vocational options, with special provision being made for literacy training, for English in the workplace and English as a second dialect, and for special groups such as young adults, senior citizens, women and people in remote areas.

Language-Training Program

Because any federal public service must be available in either official language, many federal public servants must be bilingual. The federal public service has established its own language-training program. Since the early 1970s, over 2000 public servants annually have received language training in French or English in language centres across Canada.

Teaching Methods

A century ago, the most popular method of second-language instruction was *grammar translation*, ie, the teaching and practice of grammar rules through translation exercises. Around 1900, the moderately successful *direct method* was created. It involved teaching without translation and dispensing with the mother tongue completely in class. In the 1960s, the *audiolingual method* (ie, speaking and listening in rapid drills) was popular. Since then, a number of new methods have been advocated. One of these empha-

sized the training of listening abilities through actions (*total physical response*); another the use of psychological relaxation (*suggestopedia*); and a third the use of techniques based on group therapy (*counselling learning*). In the 1970s other second-language instruction reformers suggested that more emphasis be paid to the curriculum and to the practical needs and specific purposes of language learners. There has been an accompanying attempt to ground second-language instruction more thoroughly in the language sciences, eg, linguistics, psycholinguistics, sociolinguistics and applied linguistics. The most widely used method of language teaching in the 1980s is *communicative language teaching*, ie, teachers involve students as much as possible in realistic language use. New technologies have also been recruited in the search for better instructional techniques. In the 1950s, the language laboratory was created; in the 1980s microcomputers and videocassette recorders are commonly used as teaching resources. None of these innovations, however, has resulted in a radical breakthrough in second-language instruction.

Maintenance of Nonofficial Languages

The 1963 Royal Commission on BILINGUALISM AND BICULTURALISM took the view that linguistic diversity is an important personal and social resource. In 1977 Ontario initiated its Heritage Languages Program, which provided funds for the teaching of "heritage" languages, ie, languages other than English or French. Similar programs have been started in Québec, Manitoba, Alberta, BC and the NWT.

Native Indian Languages Linguists generally recognize 11 major groups of Canadian native languages, some of which contain a number of languages and dialects. Some native peoples (particularly in the North) have strongly retained their languages, but the medium of instruction in northern native schools is usually French or English (which most students must learn as a second language) and recently there has been a growing interest in developing ESL and FSL curriculum materials for native students and in conducting research into the conditions under which these students learn second languages. However, few teachers of native children have had second-language training, and appropriate methods of second-language instruction are not yet widely employed. Some bilingual education programs have been designed to maintain ancestral languages while allowing native children to acquire a knowledge of French or English. Here, as in other areas of second-language instruction, much still remains to be done in order to provide satisfactory programs. H.H. STERN

Reading: B. Burnaby, *Languages and their Roles in Educating Native Children* (1980); J.K. Chambers, ed, *The Languages of Canada* (1979); Commissioner of Official Languages, *Annual Reports* (since 1971); S. Lapkin, M. Swain and V. Argue, *French Immersion: The Trial Balloon That Flew* (1983); W.R. McGillivray, ed, *More French, s'il vous plaît!* (1985); B. Mlacak and E. Isabelle, eds, *So You Want Your Child to Learn French! A Handbook for Parents* (1979); H.H. Stern, *Fundamental Concepts of Language Teaching* (1983); R. Wardhaugh, *Language and Nationhood: The Canadian Experience* (1983).

Secondary School Originally established as schools offering a narrow, classical curriculum to the sons of gentlemen, secondary schools became coeducational, offering a widened variety of programs and courses to all children who had completed the elementary school program.

In English-speaking Canada the first secondary schools, modelled after the English grammar schools, were usually operated by comparatively well-educated Church of England clergy. The ruling group considered these training schools for

future leaders to be of greater importance to the colony than schools for the children of the common people, an "official" view reflected in the earlier provision for the establishment and generous public support of secondary schools for the few. These schools, however, were forced to offer elementary instruction as well because many of their students were not prepared to undertake secondary-school work. When publicly supported elementary schools were established, there were then 2 types of schools offering elementary instruction, a "necessary" duplication at a time when few aristocrats were prepared to send their children to the common schools.

Despite the financial advantage enjoyed by the grammar schools, they did not prosper, largely because they were looked upon as elitist and were unsuited to a sparsely populated region. Proving more acceptable to a growing number of people were the later academies, coeducational institutions offering a more varied program to a wider segment of society. These academies flourished because they offered what an increasing number of parents demanded for their children, namely less emphasis on the classics and more emphasis on commercial and work-related studies.

In Ontario, Egerton RYERSON, superintendent of public instruction during an important period (1844-76) in Canada's development, concentrated his attention on setting up a system of common (elementary) schools before turning to the problems of the secondary schools. Noting that the grammar-school enrolment had remained low and that many of the smaller grammar schools were concerned more about ways of obtaining increased government grants than on ways of improving instruction, Ryerson introduced central control of these schools (1853). As a part of this centralization, he established a system of regular inspection (1855) and a short-lived system of "payment by results" (in effect 1875-82), under which the government grant was, in part, based on the examination results obtained by students. Through the introduction of an entrance examination to secondary schools (1853), Ryerson removed the problem of duplication of programs in common (elementary) and secondary schools, the elementary school becoming the first division of the school system extending from the earliest grade to university.

Even after the elementary and secondary schools were made into a single public system within each province, there was much controversy about the role to be played by the secondary school. To those who considered it an upward extension of the elementary school, it was obvious that the secondary school's program should not be primarily university-oriented. As the compulsory school attendance age was raised over the years (for Ontario, eg, from age 12 in 1871 to age 16 in 1919), the need to offer a variety of programs in addition to the academic, university-oriented program became evident, especially when it was noted that a high proportion of the students entering high school were not completing their program or moving on to university studies.

The curriculum of the secondary school and the methods of instruction used therein have tended to reflect the university orientation. For example, when provincial secondary-school graduation examinations were in general use, they were prepared by subject committees usually dominated by university professors. The great importance attached to these examinations by both the educational authorities and the public helped to increase the universities' role in determining the secondary-school curriculum, largely as a result of the schools' "teaching to the exams," a widespread practice that has been of decreasing importance in recent years. Another result of this close association of secondary schools with the universities has been the long-delayed provision for the professional training of secondary-school teachers. Because university instructors were ready to support the widely held view that the secondary-school teacher did not need training in methods of teaching but only intensive preparation in his specific subject area, provision for the training of secondary-school teacher candidates tended to come much later than that for elementary teachers. Ontario's Provincial School of Pedagogy for the training of secondary school teachers was established in 1890; its first NORMAL SCHOOL for the training of elementary teachers was opened in 1847.

As a result of the higher academic qualifications required of secondary teachers, salary scales for secondary teachers have generally been considerably higher than those for elementary teachers, thereby tending to create barriers between the 2 groups.

Among the recent developments that have affected secondary schools in Canada has been the attempt by provincial authorities to tear down the long-standing wall between elementary and secondary schools. Significant progress toward this objective has been made by placing within university faculties of education the teacher education programs for all teachers, a noteworthy change from the earlier arrangement whereby elementary teachers were trained in normal schools (or teachers' colleges) while secondary teachers were enrolled in university faculties of education.

This change, together with the move requiring all teachers to hold a university degree, will undoubtedly lead to a lessening of the old distinctions, academic and financial. Another recent change related to secondary schools in Ontario was that province's decision, in Sept 1985, to extend public funding of SEPARATE SCHOOLS to grades 11, 12 and 13, thereby reversing a policy, of more than a century, of nonsupport for the upper grades of such schools. One of the most serious problems in secondary education in Canada has been that of providing equal educational opportunities in rural and urban areas. Because the cost of providing the academic program is less than the cost of programs requiring expensive shop equipment, the smaller rural secondary schools found themselves unable to offer the more expensive work-related programs and, as a result, tended to offer academic programs to be taken by a relatively small proportion of students. This problem has usually been dealt with by enlarging the secondary-school unit of administration to permit the offering of a variety of programs and courses to a larger pool of secondary students.

In western Canada, for example, the high schools established in rural areas before the advent of large school units in the 1940s were often one-room, one-teacher schools, offering a limited curriculum, largely academic. The creation of large units of school administration, however, made possible the establishment of large regional secondary schools offering programs to accommodate students who wished to enter university as well as those with vocational interests. In this, as in other areas of development, the western provinces showed greater readiness to introduce change than the eastern provinces did.

Another means of making secondary education more readily available to students in smaller communities was legislation that enabled common (or elementary) schools to add secondary grades in a combination known in some provinces (eg, Ontario) as a continuation school. In certain regions, especially in the Atlantic provinces, one-room rural schools often conducted classes from grades 1 to 10, with larger

communities adding grades 11 and 12 to their offerings.

Although education is constitutionally a provincial responsibility (there are exceptions; *see* NATIVE PEOPLE, EDUCATION), there have been periods in Canada's history when the federal government has poured large amounts of money into education, especially in areas considered to be of national importance (eg, agricultural education, vocational and technical training). Such infusions have tended to occur during national crises, eg, in 1960 when the federal government, responding to the urgent need for trained workers in Canada's labour force, introduced a program which provided many millions of dollars to the provinces for the building and equipping of secondary vocational and technical schools.

Marked differences characterize secondary education in Québec, notably in the early establishment of COLLÈGES CLASSIQUES, which combined secondary and college education in an 8-year program. Affiliated with the French-language universities, these institutions were for males only during the greater part of their existence. Unlike the English-style grammar schools, the classical colleges admitted boys from all social levels and had a notable impact on all sectors of French Canadian society.

During Québec's QUIET REVOLUTION the reform of secondary education moved that province from the position of having one of the lowest secondary-school retention rates in Canada to having one of the highest. This great leap forward resulted from the introduction, in 1967, of a new type of post-secondary general and vocational community college (collège d'enseignement général et professionel [CEGEP]). A most important part of the planned democratization of education in Québec, the CEGEPs made post-secondary education more easily available to more people, thereby increasing the student retention rate of the secondary schools. At the same time, the role of the Church in the control of education at all levels was reduced, as evidenced by the fact that the classical college was no longer practically the only avenue leading to the French-language universities and no longer were students to pay fees in public secondary schools.

In all Canadian provinces, secondary education aims to prepare students for tertiary-level education at university or community college and to prepare them to live and work in society.

Because the teaching of citizenship has long been one of the objectives of Canadian secondary schools, A.B. Hodgetts's widely discussed analysis of the shortcomings of the civic-education programs in Canada received careful attention from curriculum planners, administrators and teachers at the elementary- and secondary-school levels. Among the shortcomings noted by Hodgetts were the lack of any contemporary meaning in the courses of study in Canadian history, the narrowness of the program ("confined to constitutional and political history"), the lack of controversy ("a bland, unrealistic consensus version of our past") and the use of uninspiring teaching methods. The report of this inquiry, *What Culture? What Heritage?* (1968), caused nationwide soul-searching that led to the creation in 1970 of the Canada Studies Foundation, an independent, nonprofit organization designed to find ways of improving the quality of Canadian studies in both elementary and secondary schools.

For a variety of reasons, a number of students have found the traditional secondary-school program unsuited to their interests. In some instances, this has led to the "dropout problem" which received much public attention at various periods, particularly during the late 1950s and 1960s. Largely in response to this problem, cer-

tain kinds of alternative education were established, usually for secondary-school students in urban areas who were seeking an approach to teaching and learning different from that normally found in the larger, more traditional, schools. The fact that these alternative schools have been publicly supported for several years indicates that they have been accepted as filling an important need in Canadian education.

WILLARD BREHAUT

Reading: F.H. Johnson, *A Brief History of Canadian Education* (1968); R.M. Stamp, *The Schools of Ontario 1876-1976* (1982); J.D. Wilson, R.M. Stamp, L.P. Audet, *Canadian Education: A History* (1970).

Secord, Laura, née Ingersoll, heroine of the WAR OF 1812 (b at Great Barrington, Mass 13 Sept 1775; d at Chippawa [Niagara Falls], Ont 17 Oct 1868). During the War of 1812, Laura walked 30 km from Queenston to Beaver Dams to warn the British officer, James FitzGibbon, that the Americans were planning to attack his outpost. She had overheard some American officers discussing their plan while dining at her house. Two days later, 24 June 1813, the Americans were ambushed by Indians at Beaver Dams and surrendered to FitzGibbon. Years later, historians questioned Laura's story, but found confirmation of it in 3 testimonials by FitzGibbon. Monuments to Laura Secord stand in Lundy's Lane, Niagara Falls and on Queenston Heights.   RUTH MCKENZIE

Reading: Ruth McKenzie, *Laura Secord* (1971).

Secret Societies are sometimes seen as religious, philosophical or spiritual sects that confer upon their initiates a certain mystery; the mystery is patiently and meticulously maintained and gradually made accessible, in succeeding stages, through the performance of secret rites designed to purify the fortunate elect. At other times, secret societies are seen as seditious political organizations, clandestine economic associations, criminal groups, ideological movements with revolutionary intentions, or occult interest groups. They may also be viewed as agencies for mutual aid, support, brotherhood, charity or good works.

In order to attract the attention of the curious or the spiritualistic, a group generally need only indulge in clandestine activities (eg, the FREEMASONS), have an unusual series of rites and customs (many social clubs), or maintain a certain secrecy around initiation ceremonies (some native groups). Myth-makers capitalize on man's interest in the immaterial and supernatural to maintain in initiates and aspirants the superrational element necessary for any lasting socialization.

Historically, all secret societies, whether brotherhoods, trade guilds, mystery societies, initiating associations and spiritualist societies or, more simply, closed associations with specific economic, political or religious purpose, have or have had their own oaths, rituals, customs and secret languages to promote and maintain necessary group solidarity. All have adopted signs of recognition and passwords, rhythmic chants and other ways of reminding one another of their society's moral conditions of behaviour. All have developed and followed successive stages to the attainment of secret knowledge or power, periods of apprenticeship and trial, and an often intricate hierarchy. All have evolved internal ceremonies capable of separating the neophyte from the member of long standing, the profane from the chosen. All have identified themselves with certain moral principles and beliefs that distinguish them from that which surrounds them and is therefore foreign or subordinate to them. All have given a sacred significance to their existence.

It is therefore not very helpful to attempt to differentiate between secret societies and other organizations on the basis of distinctions of place (primitive societies, Western societies), culture (Caribbean, Germanic, Slavic or American Protestant societies), religion (ORDRE DE JACQUES-CARTIER, ORANGE ORDER), nationality (Amerindian, Spanish, Italian, Irish or French) or sex (witches or high priests).

Secret societies have been in existence at least since the date of the earliest known writings. Some have served utilitarian ends, others speculative; some have been visible, others invisible, except to government information services, which have always been aware of their existence. Each has based its existence on a secret, the secret of its mystery, purpose, direction, ritual or, more generally, its organization. Ultimately, what has at all times and in all places distinguished secret societies from other associations is that the former are organized in a manner parallel to, but often above, official forms of government, whatever those forms may be.

In Canada, secret societies were often founded by ethnic groups, particularly the Irish; the Whiteboys and the United Irishmen were active before 1812 and the FENIANS (Irish Republican Brotherhood) during the Confederation period. Farm and labour organizations like the Grange and KNIGHTS OF LABOR began as secret societies. Today, the best-known societies are the Freemasons, Orange Order, Ordre de Jacques-Cartier, Opus Dei and, at certain periods, the KU KLUX KLAN. *See also* NEW RELIGIOUS MOVEMENTS.

G.-RAYMOND LALIBERTÉ

Secretary of State, Department of One of the oldest departments of the federal government, it was established in 1867 as the official channel of communication between the Dominion of Canada and the imperial government. Its diverse responsibilities have at times included Indian affairs, crown lands, the RCMP, the civil service and government printing and stationery. It has always had responsibility for state and ceremonial occasions. Present responsibilities include encouraging the use of the 2 official languages of Canada, state protocol and ceremonies and events, education policies and funding translation services, promotion of MULTICULTURALISM and the granting of Canadian citizenship. The department reports to Parliament for the PUBLIC SERVICE COMMISSION's Advisory Council on the Status of Women, and for the Public Service Commission. The Multicultural Directorate is part of the administrative apparatus of the department. The department's total expenditures for 1986-87 were $3.1 billion.

Section 94 BC Vehicle Act Reference By virtue of par 94(2) of the Motor Vehicle Act of British Columbia, anyone who drives his vehicle without a valid permit or while his permit is suspended commits an infraction for which the minimum penalty is a prison sentence. It is a case of an absolute liability offence, that is, the individual is guilty whether or not he is aware of the ban or suspension. On 17 Dec 1985 the Supreme Court handed down the ruling that "a law that has the potential to convict a person who has not really done anything wrong" offends the principles of fundamental justice and, if it carries a prison sentence with it, violates the liberty guaranteed under s7 of the CANADIAN CHARTER OF RIGHTS AND FREEDOMS which says that "Everyone has the right to life, liberty and security of the person and the right not to be deprived thereof except in accordance with the principles of fundamental justice." The Court added that s7 is not limited to procedural guarantees; it applies also to SUBSTANTIVE LAW. There is a violation of s7 if an absolute liability offence can lead to the deprivation of life, freedom and security. GÉRALD-A. BEAUDOIN

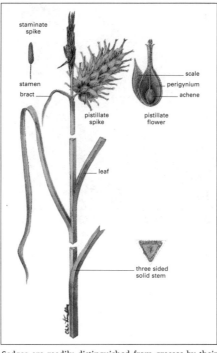

Sedges are readily distinguished from grasses by their 3-sided, solid stems (*artwork by Claire Tremblay*).

Sedge, grasslike plant common throughout temperate and cold regions. The genus name, *Carex* (family *Cyperaceae*), is probably derived from *keiro* [Gk, "to cut"], referring to the sharp leaf margins. Worldwide this taxonomically involved complex is represented by some 2000 species; in Canada by about 270, plus others of subspecific rank and several hybrids. Sedges are readily distinguished from GRASSES by their 3-sided, solid stems and by leaves with 3 ranks instead of 2. Within the spike, the minute individual flowers are solitary in the axils of scales. Male flowers normally have 3 stamens; female flowers (enclosed in a sac, the perigynium) have 2 or 3 stigmas. The seed, surrounded by the persistent perigynium, may be lens shaped or three angled. Flower spikes and mature seeds are needed for accurate identification to specific or lower rank. The position of male and female spikes on the plant is another important identification characteristic. In milder climates *C. pendula,* grown as a garden ORNAMENTAL (usually near water), is prized for its bold effect (up to 1.5 m tall) and long, drooping spikes. Also grown is Japanese sedge grass (*C. morrowii* var *expallida*), which has leaves striped white.

The hardier *C. plantaginea,* found wild in deciduous woods from NB to Manitoba (and south), is conspicuous with its broad evergreen leaves and purple sheaths. While sedges are of limited garden value, they are sometimes planted for erosion control. The ancient Egyptians cultivated *Cyperus papyrus* to provide the earliest form of paper. Today the value of sedge is most evident in its native habitat, bordering sloughs and other wet places, where it provides cover and food for waterfowl. ROGER VICK

Sedgewick, Robert, lawyer, jurist (b at Aberdeen, Scot 10 May 1848; d at Chester, NS 4 Aug 1906). Sedgewick was the prime mover in the establishment of Dalhousie U's law school in 1883, the first school to teach common law in the British Empire. He was appointed municipal judge for Halifax in 1883 and also lectured in equity jurisprudence at Dalhousie. In 1886 he was appointed deputy minister of justice for Canada. In

1890 he drafted both the Bills of Exchange Act, the first codified legislation in Canada, and with Judge BURBIDGE, the Canadian CRIMINAL CODE, the first legislation of its kind in the British Empire. With Sir John THOMPSON, he planned the strategy whereby the bill became law in 1892. In 1893 he was appointed to the bench of the Supreme Court of Canada. D.H. BROWN

Sedimentary Rock, one of the 3 major classes of rock comprising the Earth's crust (the others being IGNEOUS and metamorphic), is made up of loose, unconsolidated sediment that has been transformed into rock (ie, lithified) during GEOLOGICAL HISTORY. Only about 5% of the Earth's crust is composed of sedimentary rocks, but they cover 70-75% of the exposed surface and contain many economically important MINERALS, as well as COAL and PETROLEUM. As exposed at the surface, the most important types by volume are shale 50%, sandstone 30% and limestone 20%. Calculations suggest that total surface plus subsurface proportions may be shale 79%, sandstone 13% and limestone 8%. Sedimentary rocks are classified by their mineral and chemical composition and by the source of the sediment. The 4 main classes are discussed below.

Terrigenous Rocks result from the erosion of older rocks, transport of the debris to the depositional site and slow lithification during geological time. EROSION produces particles of different sizes, and terrigenous rocks are classified by grain size. Shales are composed mostly of CLAY minerals smaller than 0.004 mm diameter. The plate-shaped clays allow shales to split easily into thin layers. Shales are prominent in the Cretaceous rocks of Alberta outcropping along the FOOTHILLS of the Rockies, particularly the Blackstone and Wapiabi formations. Siltstones contain particles of 0.004-0.062 mm, with quartz grains and clays as the commonest particle types. Sandstones (particles 0.062-2 mm) are composed mostly of quartz and feldspar, weathered from older igneous and metamorphic rocks (or from pre-existing sandstones). There are 3 main families of sandstones: orthoquartzites (90% of the sand-sized fraction composed of quartz plus chert), arkoses (more than 25% feldspar grains); and greywackes (high proportion of muddy matrix and commonly more rock fragments than orthoquartzites and arkoses). Sandstones form the reservoir at Pembina, Alta, Canada's largest single oilfield. Conglomerates contain particles larger than 2 mm, ranging from small pebbles to boulders metres in diameter. Spaces between pebbles and boulders are usually filled with sand, silt and mud. Composition of the coarse fraction is varied, commonly with pebbles of pre-existing rocks such as granite, limestone, sandstone and basalt. URANIUM deposits in the Elliot Lk area of Ontario are confined to conglomerate beds.

After deposition as loose sediment, the particles may become lithified. Individual particles can be cemented together by calcareous or siliceous cements deposited in pore spaces from percolating water. Particles can also be held together by materials that either were deposited with the larger particles or grew in the pore spaces during burial of the sediment.

Carbonate Rocks Almost all particles in carbonate rocks are formed of the hard parts of marine organisms that lived close to the final depositional site. The main minerals are calcite, aragonite and dolomite. Aragonite precipitates most easily in warm water and maximum carbonate productivity occurs in shallow tropical seas. The particles commonly accumulate where they are formed, or may be swept by currents toward the shoreline or out into deeper water. Carbonate rocks consist of

3 basic types of material: discrete coarse grains; microcrystalline calcite ooze, called micrite; and sparry calcite cement. The discrete grains may be composed of ALGAE and whole or broken skeletons of INVERTEBRATE animals. Other grains, called pellets, are fecal in origin, consisting of rounded aggregates of carbonate mud excreted by mud-eating organisms. Ooliths are grains consisting of concentric layers of fine carbonate particles around a nucleus, commonly a skeletal fragment. The nucleus is rolled on the seafloor by strong currents and layers of inorganic precipitates are built up around it. Skeletal fragments, pellets and ooliths can clump together to form aggregates known as grapestones. All these particles can act as a surface for BLUE-GREEN ALGAE, which may coat them with a sticky layer that traps fine, carbonate sediment. The fine sediment micrite is mostly formed by calcareous algae. The algae contain minute aragonite needles that are released on death and accumulate as carbonate mud. Sparry calcite is an inorganically precipitated cement that grows in the pore spaces between discrete grains. It commonly forms from dissolved skeletal or micritic material, moved in solution by fluids in the pore spaces and reprecipitated as cement.

The naming of carbonate rocks derives from their composition and is based on the type of discrete grains and type of pore filling (micrite or sparry calcite). Thus a pelmicrite is composed of pellets with a micrite matrix, and an ocsparite consists of ooliths with a sparry calcite cement. Carbonate rocks undergo mineralogical changes (diagenesis) during burial and lithification. For example, aragonite is frequently converted to calcite. The calcite grains are bound together as a result of the solution of some grains and the reprecipitation of the carbonate as cement, thus forming limestones. Spectacular examples dominate the scenery at BANFF NATIONAL PARK, eg, the limestone cliffs of the Palliser and Rundle formations. The other major change involves conversion of calcite to dolomite which takes place as pore waters enriched with magnesium percolate through the sediment. Dolomitization can take place molecule for molecule, preserving the textures of the original discrete grains. Alternatively, calcite can be dissolved and dolomite precipitated somewhat later, destroying the original texture. Dolomites with chert nodules form the hard capping layer of the NIAGARA ESCARPMENT.

As well as the particulate rocks described above, there are massive limestones and dolomites built up by reef-building organisms such as CORALS. The immediate fore-reef area is commonly made up of a coarse-grained talus slope composed of broken blocks of the reef itself. Pore spaces in the reef or talus can remain open, or may fill with discrete grains, micrite or sparry calcite. Important examples include the reservoir rocks of the Leduc and Redwater oil fields in Alberta.

Chemical Rocks are composed of material that has been emplaced by a chemical process (eg, evaporation, precipitation). In volume, the most important chemical rocks are the evaporites, formed in hot, arid areas by the intense evaporation of seawater. The most important minerals formed are gypsum (converted to anhydrite on burial) and halite (common salt). Both gypsum and halite make up sequences of layered rocks, commonly associated with limestones and dolomites. The evaporite rocks of southern Saskatchewan form the basis of the POTASH mining industry.

Some bedded rocks are made up of microcrystalline or cryptocrystalline silica, termed chert. Many cherts, such as those now accumulating on the deep ocean floors, are made up of the hard parts of microscopic, silica-secreting organisms (radiolarians and diatoms). Some very ancient

Graywacke rock formations on Blanchet I in Great Slave Lake. Formed beneath an ancient sea, such rocks are the most commonly found sedimentary rock in greenstone belts (*courtesy Ron Redfern, Random House Inc*).

cherts are older than the oldest known siliceous organisms and may be chemical precipitates. An example of this formation occurs in the Gunflint Chert, Lk Superior.

Coal can also be considered a chemical rock, formed as a result of the accumulation of plant material and its transformation into PEAT and then coal. There is a progression or increase in "rank" (carbon and calorific content) from peat to lignite to subbituminous and bituminous coals and, finally, to anthracite. Anthracite is darkest in colour, containing the highest proportion of carbon and lowest amounts of moisture, volatile components and oxygen. Coal is economically important in BC, Alberta and the Maritimes.

Pyroclastic Rocks are made up of volcanic-derived particles including bombs and blocks (larger than 64 mm), lapilli (or stones, 2-64 mm) and ash (finer than 2 mm). Most of the debris is transported through the air rather than by water. Pyroclastic rocks are termed agglomerates or volcanic breccias (bombs and blocks), lapilli tuffs or tuffs (mostly composed of ash). Welded tuffs contain fragments that were still hot when deposited from glowing avalanches (*nuées ardentes*); the deposits, called ignimbrites, may cover many hundred square kilometres.

Volcanic ejecta are classified compositionally as rock fragments, crystals or glass, the latter being small lumps of magma (molten rock) that cooled too quickly for development of specific minerals. Sequences of pyroclastic rocks can be thousands of metres thick; many examples occur in BC's Interior Plateau and on Vancouver I. It has been estimated that in the last 400 years alone over 320 km³ of pyroclastic materials have been ejected from the world's VOLCANOES.

R.G. WALKER

Seed Plants, the most abundant and familiar component of Earth's vegetation, comprise an estimated 250 000-300 000 species. They outnumber all other plant groups, dominate the land, thrive in bodies of fresh water and are found to a limited extent in the oceans. They include the largest (giant sequoia) and oldest (bristlecone pine) living things, and encompass tiny water-meal scarcely 1 mm long and ephemeral annuals that survive only a few weeks. Seed plants share with other vascular plants (plants with woody conducting systems) basic organs (root, stem and leaf), cell types and tissues. In response to different environments, they have evolved many forms. The common feature uniting them is the "seed habit," a unique method of sexual repro-

duction. In all vascular plants, the conspicuous plant is a spore producer (sporophyte) that alternates, in the life cycle, with a sexual phase (gametophyte). In seed plants, the spore that produces the female gametophyte is not shed to initiate an independent plant but is retained in the sporangium (reproductive structure), which is surrounded by a protective covering (integument). This is the immature seed or ovule. Spores that produce male gametophytes are released as the gametophytes begin to develop. These are the pollen grains, which are transferred to the ovules where fertilization is completed, resulting in seed development. The EVOLUTION of this method of reproduction, more than 350 million years ago, was one of the most significant steps in the adaptation of plants to life on land. MOSSES and lower vascular plants (eg, FERNS), like their aquatic ancestors, release sperm that must swim through water to effect fertilization. Seed plants are freed from this dependence on water.

Seed plants fall into 2 major groups, gymnosperms and angiosperms. Gymnosperms, the more ancient group, include CONIFERS, cycads and the maidenhair tree (*Ginkgo*). Although there are only about 700 living species, gymnosperms are important in the flora of many areas (eg, boreal forest). The FOSSIL record shows that they were much more important in the past, and included several now-extinct forms (eg, seed ferns). Pollen and ovules are produced in separate cones. Pollen grains are transferred directly to ovules, ultimately being drawn inside through an opening in the integument. Thus the ovules are exposed at the time of POLLINATION (gymnosperm means "naked seed"), although usually enclosed later by growth of the cone scales. In the mature seed, the embryo is embedded in a nutritive tissue that is actually the female gametophyte.

The angiosperms, flowering plants, have dominated Earth's vegetation since the Cretaceous period (144-64 million years ago). Their distinctive reproductive structure, the flower, occurs in diverse forms related to different methods of pollination. Pollen and ovules may be found in the same or separate flowers. Pollen is produced in stamens. Ovules are formed inside the pistil; they are not exposed at the time of pollination (angiosperm means "vessel seed"). Pollen is transferred to a receptive surface on the pistil where it germinates; sperm are carried into the ovule by growth of the pollen tube. Seeds mature inside the pistil, which becomes the fruit. Some one-seeded fruits (eg, cereal grains) are often confused with seeds.

The nutritive tissue of the angiosperm seed is a new tissue, endosperm, which with the embryo results from the fertilization process. The endosperm frequently is absorbed by the embryo before the seed is mature. There are 2 major evolutionary lines of angiosperms: monocotyledons, with flower parts usually in threes, major leaf veins parallel and only one cotyledon (embryo leaf); and dicotyledons, with flower parts usually in fours or fives, net-veined leaves and 2 cotyledons. The economic significance of seed plants cannot be overemphasized. Angiosperms provide most of our important food CROPS (*see* GRASS) and produce spices, drugs, fibres, timber and industrial raw materials. Gymnosperms (conifers) are major sources of wood products; seeds of a few (eg, pinyon pine) are minor food sources.

T.A. STEEVES

Seeman, Mary Violette, clinical psychiatrist, psychopharmacologist (b at Lódź, Poland 24 Mar 1935), married to Philip SEEMAN. She was educated in Montréal (BA, McGill) and did postgraduate training at the Sorbonne, receiving an MD and CM at McGill (1960). She received psychiatric training at the Adolf Meyer Psychiatric Hospital (New York) and Columbia U and psychopharmacological research begun in 1965 in New York was expanded during periods as registrar and researcher at Fulbourn Hospital at Cambridge, as staff psychiatrist at Toronto Western Hospital (1968), and as associate and later professor (1980) of the dept of psychiatry, U of T. Seeman became head of the Active Treatment Clinic of the Clarke Institute of Psychiatry in Toronto and co-ordinator of Studies in Schizophrenia for the Institute (1981). Her clinical research on schizophrenia has resulted in a clearer understanding of the physiological, biochemical, cellular and psychohormonal basis of schizophrenia. Her extensive knowledge of the molecular basis of, and experience in treatment of, schizophrenia is evident in an extensive record of publication in scholarly journals and books. She heads the ethics committee of the Clarke Institute and of the Ontario Psychiatric Association. In 1984 she was elected president of the Ontario branch of the American Psychiatric Association. Seeman and co-workers have rendered a seminal service by summarizing the current state of the scientific and clinical basis of schizophrenia and its management in a book for the layperson: *Living and Working with Schizophrenia* (1982).

ROSE SHEININ

Seeman, Philip, molecular neuropharmacologist, educator (b at Winnipeg 8 Feb 1934), married to Mary Violette SEEMAN. Educated at McGill and Rockefeller U he has studied the structure and function of the plasma membrane at the surface of animal cells. His special interest is in neurologically active compounds, their interaction with receptors on the periphery of nerve cells, and their effect on human behaviour and mood. Seeman's major scientific discoveries concern the nerve-cell receptor for the neurohormone L-dopamine, whose aberrant function is manifest in one or more forms of Parkinsonism. The studies of Seeman and co-workers of the interaction of L-dopamine, its analogues and its antagonists with nerve cell membranes have brought a rational basis to the understanding and treatment of Parkinson's disease and other illnesses that derive from faulty neurohormone function. Seeman was head of the dept of pharmacology, U of T, 1977-87. His publications include the text *Principles of Medical Pharmacology* (1976). ROSE SHEININ

Sefton, Lawrence Frederick, Larry, labour leader (b at Iroquois Falls, Ont 31 Mar 1917; d at Toronto 9 May 1973). A firm believer in international unions and political action, he was secretary of the mine, mill and smelter workers in KIRKLAND LK and helped lead the historic 1941 strike for union recognition. Blacklisted after the strike collapsed, he moved to Toronto and became an organizer on the steelworkers' union staff. He led the 1946 Stelco strike in Hamilton, becoming senior union representative in the Hamilton-Niagara area. In 1953 he was elected director of District 6 of the steelworkers, which covered Canada west of Québec. From 1958 he was an active VP of the Canadian Labour Congress; his greatest contribution internationally was as an initiator of the 1971 World Nickel Conference of unions. A CCF candidate for Parliament in 1949, he served on the party provincial council. LAUREL SEFTON MACDOWELL

Seguin, Fernand, biochemist and scientific popularizer (b at Montréal 9 June 1922). His MA thesis, concerning a method to determine the aminopyrine in the blood, won him the Prix Casgrain-Charbonneau. He conducted biochemical research in the late 1940s in Chicago and Paris and was professor at U de M (1945-50). In 1950

he founded the biochemical research department at Saint-Jean-de-Dieu hospital, where he specialized in research into the biological causes of schizophrenia. In 1954 he abandoned his career as a researcher and teacher and began a long series of radio and TV programs which sparked the emergence of popular scientific curiosity in Québec and inspired a number of scientific careers. Then came programs for adults: *Le Roman de la science* (1956-60), *Aux frontières de la science* (1960-61) and *L'Homme devant la science*. With *Le Sel de la semaine* (1965-70), he became more of a science critic. From 1975 to 1977 he hosted *Science Réalité* (1975-77), a weekly TV show. In 1977 he became the first Canadian to receive UNESCO's Kalinga Award, the highest award for scientific popularization, joining the ranks of Bertrand Russell (1957), Julian Huxley (1953) and Margaret Mead (1970). MARTHE LEGAULT

Seigneurial System, an institutional form of land distribution and occupation established in NEW FRANCE in 1627 and officially abolished in 1854. It was inspired by the feudal system, which involved the personal dependency of *censitaires* (tenants) on the seigneur; in New France the similarities ended with occupation of land and payment of certain dues, and the *censitaire* was normally referred to as a HABITANT. The COMPAGNIE DES CENT-ASSOCIÉS, which in 1627 was granted ownership and legal and seigneurial rights over New France, also obtained the rights to allocate the land to its best advantage. The land was therefore granted as fiefs and seigneuries to the most influential colonists who, in turn, granted tenancies.

This politically determined system of land distribution was regulated by law and had many advantages. Its purpose was to promote settlement in a systematic way. Seigneuries, which were usually 1 x 3 leagues (5 x 15 km) in size, were generally divided into river lots (*rangs*), a survey system based on the French experience in Normandy. The long, rectangular strips were particularly well adapted to the local terrain, since they facilitated interaction between neighbours and provided multiple points of access to the river, the principal communication route. Individual holdings were large enough (usually about 3 x 30 ARPENTS) to provide a reasonable living to farmers. Finally, the seigneurial system established between the seigneur and the tenant a well-defined individual relationship.

The state established regulations to govern the operation of this system and the relationship between the seigneurs and their tenants. The principal one was that the state granted to a person, who thus became seigneur, a parcel of land which he was to put into production, either directly or through concession to habitants who requested land; portions of the seigneur's land were usually leased on the basis of a duly notarized contract. These acts of concession set out the rights and obligations of each party. The seigneur had both onerous and honorary rights. He could establish a court of law, operate a mill and organize a commune. He received from the habitants various forms of rent: the *cens*, a small tithe dating from the feudal period, which reaffirmed the tenant's theoretical subjection to the seigneur; the *rente* in cash or kind; and the *banalités*, taxes levied on grain, which the tenant had to grind at his seigneur's mill. He also usually granted hunting, fishing and woodcutting licences. In the early 18th century, seigneurs began to insist that their tenants work for them a certain number of days annually (*see* CORVÉE).

The seigneurial system was central to France's colonization policy and came to play a major role in traditional Québec society. Despite the attractions of city life and the fur trade, 75-80% of the

Remote-sensing image showing the unique narrow field patterns of the seigneurial system along the St Lawrence and adjacent rivers (*courtesy Canada Centre for Remote Sensing/EMR Canada*).

population lived on seigneurial land until the mid-19th century. The roughly 200 seigneuries granted during the French regime covered virtually all the inhabited areas on both banks of the St Lawrence R between Montréal and Québec, and the Chaudière and Richelieu valleys, and they extended to the Gaspé. Seigneuries were granted to the nobility, to religious institutions (in return for education and hospital services), to military officers and to civil administrators. Other institutional organizations such as parishes, municipalities and the militia held land bordering on these seigneuries.

This method of land settlement left its mark on both the countryside and the Québec mentality. The land of the habitant was a kind of economic unit essential for survival. Everyone hoped to be the sole tenant, producing most of what he required in order to live. The system of land tenure, which placed rural inhabitants close to one another, and in the early 19th century the village, were the foundation upon which the family, neighbour relations and community spirit developed. The closeness of this agricultural society to the soil led naturally to a feeling that land was included in one's patrimony, to be passed from generation to generation.

After Canada was ceded to Britain in 1763, new British laws respected the private agreements and the property rights of francophone society, and the seigneurial system was maintained. But as new land was opened for colonization, the township system developed. As time went on, the seigneural system increasingly appeared to favour the privileged and to hinder economic development. After much political agitation it was abolished in 1854 by a law that permitted tenants to claim rights to their land. The last vestiges of this institution, which many historians believe profoundly influenced traditional Québec society, did not disappear until a century later.

JACQUES MATHIEU

Reading: R.C. Harris, *The Seigneurial System in Early Canada* (1968); Marcel Trudel, *The Seigneurial Regime* (1956).

Sekani, "people of the rocks or mountains," were first contacted by Samuel BLACK in 1824.

They consisted of several family groups or bands, each of 30-40 persons, who hunted and traded along the Finlay and Parsnip tributaries of the PEACE R. Since the band rather than the tribe was the primary unit of affiliation, identification of some bands with the Sekani is arbitrary. Sekani speak a form of the Beaver-Sarcee-Sekani branch of Athapaskan and appear to have diverged from the BEAVER only late in the 18th century.

Traditional Sekani subsistence was based primarily on hunting moose, caribou, mountain sheep, bears and, prior to the time they were excluded from the prairies, bison and wapiti. Whitefish were caught but salmon were inaccessible prior to Sekani expansion westward after contact. Most aspects of Sekani technology, including tools, shelters and food preparation, were similar to those of other western Subarctic Athapaskans. However, dogs were not used either for traction or for packing. Toboggans were adopted only in the 20th century and the dugout canoe was copied from others, although aboriginally the Sekani made spruce-bark canoes.

The Sekani had trading alliances with the SLAVEY and Beaver to the E, and the TAHLTAN and the CARRIER to the W. Their trade goods were furs and high-quality tanned skin goods. Several bands were said to have wintered at their trade locations, often in the territory of other peoples, where salmon and bison or caribou were available. Early in the 19th century, however, they were driven out of the eastern foothills of the Rocky Mts by the Beaver. They also fought with their southern neighbours, into whose territory they tried to intrude.

Trading posts were established in or near Sekani territory in 1826-27, beginning with Bear Lake Post, but the Sekani continued to obtain European goods from the coast through Carrier and TSIMSHIAN middlemen. After intermarriage with these 2 groups, the bilateral Sekani adopted many elements of matrilineal West Coast social organization, including clan crests and potlatching, but their attempts to take on the tripartite clan system failed.

During the height of the Omineca gold rush in 1871, Bear Lk (Pacific drainage) became their permanent wintering quarters. Many Sekani followed fortune seekers northward to the next major gold rush in the Cassiar area and, around the turn of the century, settled at Ft Ware; other Sekani attached themselves to Ft Grahame and Ft McLeod. Further relocation to Ingenika and nearby Mackenzie occurred in the 1960s when the Bennett Dam caused Ft Grahame to be flooded. By 1986 the Sekani numbered 685. *See also* NATIVE PEOPLE: SUBARCTIC and general articles under NATIVE PEOPLE.

Reading: J. Helm, ed, *Handbook of North American Indians,* 6: *Subarctic* (1981); D. Jenness, *The Sekani Indians of British Columbia* (1937).

Selections from Canadian Poets: *With Occasional Critical and Biographical Notes, and an Introductory Essay on Canadian Poetry.* Edited by E.H. Dewart, a clergyman of St Johns, Canada East, and printed by John Lovell of Montréal in 1864, this landmark collection of early Canadian verse is noted not only as "the first and last general anthology compiled before Confederation," but is also significant for its use of the term *Canadian* as applied to English-language verse written in Canada. The collection is representative of the poetic styles and interests of colonial writers. Dewart's introduction is a sound piece of pioneer criticism which complements the eclectic range of his selection, comprising 172 poems. It is to the credit of Dewart's taste and perspicacity as an anthologist that those poets whom he singled out for special comment have stood the test of time. Descrip-

tive, thoughtful and displaying considerable skill, the verse in this key anthology is an important measure of Canada's literary beginnings.
MICHAEL GNAROWSKI

Selke, Frank J., sport administrator and coach (b at Kitchener, Ont 7 May 1893; d at Rigaud, Qué 3 July 1985). At the age of 13, Selke became the manager of the Iroquois Bantams ice-hockey team in his hometown. By 1918 he began his long association with CONN SMYTHE in Toronto, where he helped to build the Toronto Maple Leafs. He left Toronto in 1946 and went to Montréal where he guided the Canadiens to 6 Stanley Cup victories before retiring in 1964 after 18 years as general manager. Selke was elected to the Hockey Hall of Fame in 1960.
GERALD REDMOND

Selkirk, Man, Town, pop 10 013 (1986c), 10 037 (1981c), inc 1882, is located on the W bank of the RED R, 29 km N of Winnipeg. In the mid-1800s the area was an Indian agricultural settlement. Land speculation and frenzied building began 1875 with proposals to route the CPR across the Red R here. Winnipeg gained the rail crossing, but Selkirk went on to become a river port and centre for shipbuilding, lumber, fish exports and agricultural services. Manitoba Rolling Mills (Canada) Ltd, producer of steel products and the town's major employer, was established here in 1913. Steel, light manufacturing, the service sector and government administration are key parts of Selkirk's economy today. The town has an industrial park, a shipyard, a regional mental health centre, and one of 2 companies in Canada producing high-grade silica sand for glass manufacturing. It has its own radio station and a regional secondary school. Selkirk – named for Lord SELKIRK – is near Lower Fort Garry National Historic Park and the St Andrews Locks on the Red R. The town has a marine museum and celebrates its Scottish heritage in July with the Manitoba Highland Gathering.
D.M. LYON

Reading: B. Potyondi, *Selkirk: The First Hundred Years* (1981).

Selkirk, Thomas Douglas, 5th Earl of, colonizer (b on St Mary's Isle, Scot 20 June 1771; d at Pau, France 8 Apr 1820). The youngest son in a large family, he unexpectedly became next in line to the title and upon his father's death (1799) sought to make his mark in the world. He found his place in the sponsorship of displaced Highlanders to settlements in BNA. In 1803 he settled 800 Highlanders on land he had purchased in PEI, and in 1804 he established a settlement at BALDOON, UC. Selkirk's motives were a complex mixture of humanitarianism, land improvement and personal ambition. In 1806 he was elected as one of the 16 Scottish peers to the House of Lords and in 1807 was appointed lord lieutenant of Kirkcudbright. Less than successful in politics and public life, Selkirk resumed his interest in settlement and in 1811 – he and his family having bought into the HUDSON'S BAY CO – received from the company a large land grant of ASSINIBOIA, in what is now Manitoba. An advance party, sent under Miles MACDONELL in 1811, established RED RIVER COLONY in 1812. Conflict with the NORTH WEST CO and local mixed bloods led to the colony's dispersal in 1815, and Selkirk arrived in Canada to supervise in person. On his way to Red River in 1816 with a party of disbanded Swiss soldiers, Selkirk learned of the deaths of Governor Robert SEMPLE and a number of colonists at SEVEN OAKS; accordingly he occupied the NWC depot at Ft William. Embroiled in complex litigation with the NWC and Canadian opponents of his colony, Selkirk visited Red River in 1817 before returning to Canada to battle his opponents in the courts. Selkirk regarded as a stain upon his honour his

Thomas Douglas, earl of Selkirk. His motives in founding colonies in PEI, Upper Canada and at Red R were a complex mixture of humanitarianism and personal ambition (*courtesy National Archives of Canada/C-1346*).

inability to convince either the Canadian authorities or the British government that the western disputes resulted from a conspiracy against him and the HBC. Ill with consumption, he departed for Britain in 1818. Deteriorating health inhibited his efforts at vindication and he died in France, on his way to a more congenial climate. Although his ventures were expensive failures in his lifetime, Selkirk is best remembered as an earnest and articulate advocate of the right of cultural minorities to preserve their way of life through resettlement in BNA, and as an early opponent of efforts by the British government to restrict emigration as a way of improving living standards.
J.M. BUMSTED

Selkirk Communications Limited is among Canada's largest broadcasting group owners, with 14 radio stations (Vancouver, Calgary, Edmonton, Blairmore, Lethbridge, Grande Prairie, Elkford and Vernon), television stations (CFAC-TV in Calgary-Lethbridge, CHCH-TV in Hamilton, and partial owner of CHEK-TV, CHAN-TV and CHBC-TV in BC), a half interest in CABLE-TELEVISION systems serving Winnipeg and Ottawa, and a 7.5% interest in Canadian Satellite Communications Inc (CANCOM). Selkirk's other holdings include interests in radio in the UK; cable television in the US; the marketing of broadcasting advertising in Canada and the US; and radio news services in Canada. Selkirk also owns R-Tek Corporation, an international manufacturer and distributor of phonograph records in 7 countries, and Westwood One Canada, a distributor of syndicated radio programs in Canada and the US. In 1986, total assets of Selkirk were $227 million, with revenues of $172 million. Amid controversy, SOUTHAM INC gained 47.3% of Selkirk's nonvoting shares and 20% of its voting shares in early 1988.
PETER S. ANDERSON

Selkirk Mountains are ranges in southeastern BC between the COLUMBIA R on the W and the valley of KOOTENAY LK. Around ROGERS PASS in Glacier National Park and N to the ROCKY MOUNTAIN TRENCH are many impressive peaks with spectacular relief, including Mt Sir Sandford, the highest at 3533 m. The more accessible southern ranges were settled in the 1880s, when mining activity drew prospectors from the northwestern US. Small silver mines are still operating in the Slocan Valley. Successive waves of settlers in the Kootenay and Slocan valleys have included religious groups like the DOUKHOBORS. TRAIL is the industrial centre of the Kootenay region; NELSON and CASTLEGAR are forest-products manufacturing centres.

PETER GRANT

Sellar, Robert Watson, politician (b at Huntingdon, Qué 6 Aug 1894; d at Ottawa 4 Jan 1965). Born into a prominent publishing family, Sellar tried various careers before securing a berth in Ottawa as private secretary. He became assistant deputy minister of finance in 1930 and then was treasury comptroller 1932-40. Appointed auditor general in 1940, Sellar reorganized the office, employing a system of personal cajolery and private reproaches. Retiring in 1959, Sellar became royal commissioner examining problems of government organization.

ROBERT BOTHWELL

Selwyn, Alfred Richard Cecil, geologist (b at Kilmington, Eng 28 July 1824; d at Vancouver 19 Oct 1902). A natural interest in GEOLOGY was encouraged by Selwyn's education in Switzerland. In 1845 he was assistant geologist with the Geological Survey of Great Britain, in 1852 director of the Geological Survey of Victoria, Australia, and in 1869 succeeded Sir W.E. LOGAN as director of the GEOLOGICAL SURVEY OF CANADA. Selwyn's directorship coincided with Canada's territorial expansion to the Pacific, necessitating a complex expansion of the GSC as a bureaucratic and scientific institution. In addition, Selwyn carried out much fieldwork himself, surveying southern BC in 1871 and examining the Peace R district as a possible northern route for the CPR in 1875. He also made studies of the eastern Canadian goldfields. As an outsider replacing a man of Logan's stature during a crucial period in Canadian history, Selwyn was in a difficult position, but he ably supervised the GSC's enormous growth and solved some of its theoretical problems. He retired in Jan 1895.

SUZANNE ZELLER

Reading: Morris Zaslow, *Reading the Rocks* (1975).

Selwyn Mountains straddle the Yukon-NWT border, trending northwestward. They comprise chains of glaciated mountain peaks, ridges, plateaus and U-shaped valleys, and are composed of faulted, folded and intruded sedimentary rocks. Named for A.R.C. SELWYN, director of the Geological Survey of Canada 1869-95, their peaks range in altitude from 2130 to 2740 m. The highest mountain is Keele Peak (2972 m). Major ice fields cover Keele Peak, the Itsi Range and the Ragged Range. The Selwyns were virtually unexplored and unmapped until after WWII.

LIONEL E. JACKSON, JR

Selye, Hans, endocrinologist, world-famous pioneer and popularizer of research on "biological stress" in human individuals and groups (b at Vienna, Austria 26 Jan 1907; d at Montréal 16 Oct 1982). Educated in Prague, Paris and Rome, he joined the staff of McGill in 1932. He became the first director of the Institute of Experimental Medicine and Surgery at U de M (1945) and guided its activities until his 1976 retirement. In 1977 he founded the International Institute of Stress, based in his own home.

His theorizing about a General Adaptation Syndrome based on much experimentation on rats, provoked much controversy. Briefly put, his model suggests that all stimuli are "stressors" which produce a general response of "stress" in the affected person. (Selye later claimed that he was hampered by his inadequate English and "should have called my syndrome the 'strain syndrome.'") For Selye, "stress plays some role in the development of every disease" and is "the nonspecific response of the body to any demand made upon it." This process, which he called the General Adaptation Syndrome, has 3 phases: alarm, resistance and exhaustion. Failure to "cope adequately" with stressors results in and is displayed by "diseases of adaptation" (eg, high blood pressure, gastric and duodenal ulcers, various mental disorders). Later, Selye spoke of 2 major types of "stress": "pleasant or curative stress" ("eustress") and "unpleasant or disease-producing stress" ("distress"). He also had earlier flirted with the idea that an entire "nation" could experience a General Adaptation Syndrome, whereby, in a situation of mass "frustration" and insecurity, "the incidence of all stress diseases will increase."

A prolific author and lecturer, he strove to make his ideas accessible to the general public in writings such as *The Stress of Life* (1956; rev ed 1976); *Stress without Distress* (1974), and his autobiography, *The Stress of My Life* (1977; 2nd ed 1979). He received many honours including some 20 honorary degrees and was a Companion of the Order of Canada. Selye's overly "biological" focus ignored or underestimated the role played by the person's psychology and culture in shaping and affecting the body's physiology, and his theoretical model has now been superseded by the "cognitive" models of stress and coping put forward by psychologist Richard Lazarus (U of Calif, Berkeley) and others.

D. PAUL LUMSDEN

Semaines sociales du Canada, annual conferences started in 1920 by Jesuit Fr Joseph-Papin ARCHAMBAULT and organizers from the École sociale populaire. The goal was to train an elite who would spread a Christian spirit and the church's SOCIAL DOCTRINE throughout Québec's mores, institutions and laws. Participating intellectuals applied the teachings of papal encyclicals – especially *Rerum Novarum*, the basis of Action sociale – to the social questions of trade unionism, the family, rural life, education, etc. Like the Roman Catholic Church with which it was linked, the semaines sociales were much more popular before WWII than after, although meetings continued until 1962.

FERNANDE ROY

Séminaire de Québec, an educational institution consisting of the Grand Séminaire and the Petit Séminaire. The former, fd 26 Mar 1663 by Mgr François de LAVAL, was to train priests and guarantee parish ministries and evangelization throughout the diocese. In 1665 it was affiliated with the Séminaire des Missions Étrangères de Paris. The Petit Séminaire opened Oct 1668, accepting Indian and French students who were going to study at the Collège des Jésuites. In 1692 the Séminaire de Québec was forced to give up control of parish ministries and become merely a centre for the training of priests, under the ultimate control of the bishop. The CONQUEST (1760) ended its control of the presbytery of Québec and of the missions in Illinois; in 1768 affiliation with the Séminaire des Missions Étrangères de Québec also ended. Three years earlier the Petit Séminaire had become a college, teaching the *cours classique* (liberal arts) along Jesuit lines and accepting students who did not intend to become priests. In 1852 the Séminaire de Québec was asked to found UNIVERSITÉ LAVAL and provide its first officials; it became the centre of the Faculty of Arts, with which all seminaries and colleges in the province had to be affiliated. In 1964 the liberal-arts course was divided into a secondary section and a college section (the final 3 classes). When the Québec government took over control of the entire educational system, the Séminaire de Québec remained a private institution. It was recog-

Le Séminaire de Québec (*photo © Hartill Art Associates, London, Ont*).

nized as being of public interest in 1969, and its students in the college section took the public program of general education in preparation for all university faculties. Since 1971 women have also been accepted into the college section.

Architecture The Séminaire's buildings were laid out according to 17th-century planning principles, with wings or pavilions arranged around interior courtyards reached through a covered carriageway. The principal quadrilateral, though composed of buildings ranging in age from the 17th to the early 20th centuries, displays features characteristic of French regime public architecture: rubble masonry covered with stucco, or *crépi*, casement windows with small panes of glass, steep roofs with dormers, and massive chimneys set in raised firewalls. Of particular note are the Bursar's wing, designed from 1678 to 1681 and restored in 1866 after a fire, which conserves intact its vaulted kitchen, and Mgr Briand's chapel with its delicate altarpiece carved in 1785-86 by joiner Pierre Emond.

NIVE VOISINE AND CHRISTINA CAMERON

Semlin, Charles Augustus, schoolteacher, prospector, rancher, premier of BC (b at Barrie, UC Oct 1836; d at Ashcroft, BC 3 Nov 1927). After teaching in Barrie, Semlin came to BC in 1862, buying the Dominion Ranch in 1869. Elected Conservative MLA for Yale in 1871, he was defeated in 1875. Re-elected in 1882 he became leader of the Opposition in 1894 and premier in Aug 1898, but his government was defeated in 1900. Semlin himself was defeated in the ensuing election but regained his seat in a by-election in 1903. When MCBRIDE called an election shortly after, Semlin retired to his Cariboo ranch, where he remained active in ranching and stockbreeding associations.

SYDNEY W. JACKMAN

Reading: Sydney W. Jackman, *Portraits of the Premiers* (1969).

Semple, Robert, governor in chief of Rupert's Land (b at Boston, Mass 26 Feb 1777; d at Red River Colony 19 June 1816). The son of a prominent London merchant and former Loyalist, Semple travelled extensively on his father's business and became a prolific author. His travel accounts included *Walks and Sketches at the Cape of Good Hope* (1803), *Observations on a Journey through Spain and Italy to Naples, and thence to Smyrna and Constantinople* (1807) and *Sketch of the Present State of Carcas* (1812). His commercial activities brought him to the notice of Lord SELKIRK who effected his appointment as "Governor of the Company's Territories in Hudson's Bay" in Apr 1815. He left immediately for RED RIVER COLONY and the following spring was caught up in the struggle between the HBC and the North West Co. On 19 June 1816 he unwisely challenged a party of Métis allies of the Nor'Westers led by Cuthbert GRANT. Semple and 20 of his men were quickly enveloped and slain. *See also* SEVEN OAKS INCIDENT.

J.E. REA

Senate Upper House of PARLIAMENT, appointed by the GOVERNOR GENERAL on the advice of the PRIME MINISTER. (If the spring 1987 MEECH LAKE ACCORD holds, the PM will have to select senators from lists provided by the provincial premiers.) It has 104 members; 24 from the Maritimes (NS and NB 10 each, PEI 4), 24 from Quebec, 24 from Ontario, 24 from the western provinces (6 each), 6 from Newfoundland, one from the Yukon, and one from the NWT. There is also a provision, never used, for 4 or 8 extra senators, drawn equally from the Maritimes, Québec, Ontario and the western provinces. Until 1965 appointment was for life, but is now until age 75.

Senators must be subjects of the Queen, at least 30 years old; have real property worth $4000 free of mortgage and a net worth of at least $4000; and reside in the province or territory for which they are appointed, and in Québec (divided into 24 senatorial divisions) reside or have their real property in the division for which they are appointed. Senators lose their seats if they become aliens; become bankrupt, insolvent or public defaulters; are attainted or convicted of felony or any infamous crime; lose their residence or property qualification; or are absent for 2 consecutive sessions of Parliament. They receive a sessional indemnity of $57 400 (1987) and a tax-free expense allowance of $9200 (both partially indexed for increases in the cost of living), free mail privileges, free coach-class rail transportation, and a limited amount of free air transportation.

The Senate was created under the CONSTITUTION ACT, 1867, primarily to protect regional interests but also to provide what George-Etienne CARTIER called a "power of resistance to oppose the democratic element." The HOUSE OF COMMONS was to be elected on the basis of representation by population. In 1867 Ontario was the most populous, fastest-growing province, but Québec and the Maritimes were more important to the national economy than their population suggested, and their interests were by no means identical with Ontario's. They dared not leave matters such as tariffs, taxation and railways to the mercy of an Ontario-dominated Commons, and they insisted on equal regional representation in the Upper House, without which there would have been no CONFEDERATION. The Senate was not set up to represent provincial governments or legislatures, or to protect the provinces against federal invasion of their powers. The courts protected provincial powers, and the protection of provincial interests in matters under federal jurisdiction soon fell mainly to the ministers from each province in the federal CABINET. The first Cabinet had 5 senators out of a total of 13 ministers. From 1911 to 1979, there were seldom more than 2, often only one. In 1979 the Conservatives were so short of Québec and French Canadian members in the Commons that they had to eke out their Québec and French Canadian representation in the Cabinet with 3 senators; from 1980 to 1984, the Liberals were equally short of western members and did the same.

The Senate was intended also to provide "sober second thought" on legislation (though the Commons has passed very few bills that even the Senate could consider radical) and to protect minorities, but although the Senate was responsible for establishing official BILINGUALISM in the original North-West Territories, it has not been very effective in this role, partly because the Commons has done the job so effectively.

The Senate has almost the same powers as the House of Commons, eg, bills are read 3 times in the Commons as well as the Senate. It can only delay constitutional amendments for 180 days. But no bill can become law without its consent, and it can veto any bill as often as it likes. It cannot

View of the Senate Chamber in the Parliament Buildings, Ottawa (*courtesy SSC Photocentre*).

initiate money bills (taxes or expenditures). Neither House can increase amounts in money bills. The Senate has not vetoed a bill from the Commons since 1939. It killed one (in 1961) by insisting on an amendment the Commons refused to accept. It did not proceed with the bill to remove the governor of the BANK OF CANADA, because he removed himself by resigning. The Senate now very rarely makes amendments of principle. The amendments it does make now are almost always related to drafting, ie, to clarify, simplify and tidy proposed legislation. In 1987 the Senate temporarily blocked Bill C22 (pharmaceutical patents) but eventually agreed to amendments. Much of the Senate's main work is done in COMMITTEES, which go over the bills clause by clause and often hear voluminous evidence, sometimes over a period of months. Committees are usually nonpartisan and can draw on a vast reservoir of members' knowledge and experience: former federal and provincial ministers, former members of the Commons and provincial Assemblies, veteran lawyers and business people, farmers, women and ethnic representatives, and even an occasional trade unionist. Its committees have produced careful studies on UNEMPLOYMENT, land use, SCIENCE POLICY, POVERTY, AGING, the mass media (*see* COMMUNICATIONS) and INDIAN AFFAIRS. Senate investigations have produced valuable reports, which have often led to important changes in government policy or legislation. The Senate is usually less partisan in its operations than the House of Commons, but in certain areas, eg, tax reform, the heavy representation of lawyers and businessmen, many of whom hold positions with private companies, is reflected in its reactions. The Senate's legally absolute veto was expected to be really no more than a delaying veto because, until the late 1860s, governments were usually short-lived, and none, it seemed, would be able to build up a large enough majority in the Senate to block a successor government of the opposition party. But most Canadian governments since then have been long-lived, and as appointments are almost invariably partisan, the Senate has often had a large opposition majority, and for the last 20 years a heavy preponderance of Liberals.

A traditional objection to the Senate is that PATRONAGE appointees have no right to a position of

authority in a democracy. Proposals to make the Senate more representative of regional interests were introduced by the Liberal government in 1978 but received little support. An appointed Upper House with a legal absolute veto on legislation has come to seem anomalous, and Senate reform has become more and more popular. Some provinces have proposed that Senate appointments be a provincial responsibility (*see* Task Force on CANADIAN UNITY). Senators could act as provincial delegates, although critics charge that such a system would run counter to the principles of FEDERALISM. But, under the CONSTITUTION ACT, 1982, making the Senate elective would require the consent of 7 provincial legislatures, representing at least half the population of the 10 provinces. So too would any change in the Senate's powers, or in the number of senators from any province. However, a tentative agreement reached in early May 1987 at Meech Lake, Qué, between the 10 provincial premiers and the prime minister provided for a new constitutional amending formula requiring the unanimous consent of Parliament and the provincial legislatures for changes to such institutions as the Senate. As well, provinces were to be given a voice in the selection of senators. Other recent proposals for Senate reform include Alberta premier Don Getty's Triple-E Senate, which stands for an elected body with effective powers and equal representation from the provinces. Experts feel, however, that Senate reforms may be as difficult with the Meech Lake Accord as with the previous system.

Seneca, the farthest west and most populous member of the IROQUOIS Confederacy, played a major role in the dispersal of the HURON, PETUN and NEUTRAL in the mid-17th century. Much of southern Ontario then became Seneca hunting territory, until OJIBWA expansion into this region confined Seneca influence to S of the Great Lakes. Periodically at war with New France, all Seneca villages were burned by GOV DENONVILLE in 1687. Revenge was extracted through the destruction of Lachine, outside Montréal, 2 years later (*see* LACHINE RAID). After construction of the French post at Niagara in the 1720s, the western Seneca frequently sided with the French in conflicts with the English. With the expulsion of French power from the Great Lakes, these same western Seneca in 1763 joined PONTIAC and his followers against the English, who had taken possession of the region. During the AMERICAN REVOLUTION, the full weight of Seneca arms supported the royal cause, but the Seneca, except for a small segment, chose not to follow Joseph BRANT after the war to a new homeland in Canada. They negotiated peace with the Americans, and still reside on reservations in the US guaranteed at that time. In 1799 HANDSOME LAKE experienced a vision which led to a regeneration of traditional Iroquois religion. *See also* NATIVE PEOPLE: EASTERN WOODLANDS and general articles under NATIVE PEOPLE.   THOMAS S. ABLER

Reading: B.G. Trigger, ed, *Handbook of North American Indians,* vol 15: *Northeast* (1978); A.F.C. Wallace, *Death and Rebirth of the Seneca* (1969).

Senécal, Louis-Adélard, businessman, politician (b at Varennes, LC 10 July 1829; d at Montréal 11 Oct 1887). A colourful and controversial public figure, Senécal was considered by some contemporaries as the symbol of French Canada's economic awakening and by others as dishonesty incarnate with both hands in the public purse. Beginning in the regional grain trade of the Richelieu Valley, he took advantage of opportunities offered by the 1854 Reciprocity Treaty with the US to establish himself in shipping, sawmilling and real-estate speculation. In 1867 his annual volume of business was estimated at $3 million. A Liberal, he sat in the Québec Legislative Assembly 1867-71 and as a federal MP 1867-72. Financial difficulties, however, occupied most of his time during these years. He turned his attention to railway construction in the early 1870s. With the Liberals in Opposition in Québec, he changed his allegiance to the provincial Bleus in 1874, and his assistance in returning the Bleus to power in 1879 earned for him the position of superintendent of the government-owned Quebec, Montreal, Ottawa and Occidental Railway 1880-82. In 1884 Senécal failed to gain the British and French financial support he sought for 3 multimillion-dollar projects, including a transatlantic cable, because of doubts circulated by the Canadian press as to his business ethics. He then turned to the Richelieu and Ontario Navigation Co, having replaced Sir Hugh ALLAN as president in 1882. He was named to the Senate on 25 Jan 1887.   JOHN KEYES

Senneterre, Qué, Town, pop 4017 (1986c), 4339 (1981c), is located 130 km E of Rouyn-Noranda in Québec's Abitibi region. It was founded around 1914 with the arrival of the Transcontinental Railway. At that time, it was called Nottaway, after the river that flowed alongside the railway, one of the largest rivers in the Abitibi region. Senneterre became a township municipality in 1919 and a town in 1959. Located in the eastern part of the Abitibi region, it has grown because of its sawmills and CNR station. The town took its name from Henri de Senneterre, duc de la Ferté, a commander in Montcalm's army.   BENOÎT-BEAUDRY GOURD

Separate School In both the US and Canada parents are free to choose to send their children to the state-run public SCHOOL SYSTEM or to a variety of private fee-paying schools. In Canada, several provinces, through systems of public separate schools or public support of PRIVATE SCHOOLS, allow families greater choice, usually on the basis of denominationalism. In the US, however, a strict interpretation of the doctrine of the separation of church and state restricts choice somewhat. For parents there, education ceases to be free if they decline to exercise their prior right to send their children to the public schools. In contrast to US constitutionalism, under which state aid is denied to separate schools, Canadians have used constitutional provisions to guarantee state aid to such schools.

The basic framework for Canada's use of public monies for separate and denominational schools and, more generally, for the relationship between the state and schooling was established in the 19th century. Fundamental to the creation of a system of free and universal education was the notion, then common, that education and religion were inseparable and that the state had a responsibility to foster, wherever possible, a harmonious relationship between them. Religion in education was important, even essential, to both Protestants and Catholics.

Many residents of the British N American colonies became convinced that it was essential to organize truly public common schools for all children to attend. This conviction was spurred by the fear of both denominational factionalism and US republican influence, but nondenominational public schools were also seen as an effective nation-building instrument. In Nova Scotia and New Brunswick, for example, separate denominational schools were regarded as socially divisive. In contrast, in Upper and Lower Canada the trend was to accept dissentient and separate schools as a way to maintain some publicly controlled uniformity while also recognizing the validity of certain minority rights. This pattern was duplicated elsewhere later, eg, in Saskatchewan and Alberta, with the result that the Canadi-

an practice generally became one of subsidizing the education of some religious minorities in confessional, separate and dissentient schools. The accommodation of these minorities was made for educational, not religious reasons, reflecting a consensus that the parent is an important agent of education and that schools should be responsive to parental demands in matters relating to moral and religious education.

The situation in early and mid-19th-century Canada was strikingly different from that in the US, primarily because of the great political power of those associated with the dominant Church of England in the early days of UPPER CANADA and because of the existence of a French Catholic majority in LOWER CANADA. These 2 conditions and the tensions they engendered, with non-Anglican Protestants and Catholics fighting for their legitimate rights in Upper Canada and Anglo-Protestants seeking security against French Catholic domination in Lower Canada, impelled the state to avoid establishing a nondenominational common school system and moved it instead to assume legal protection and support for denominationally based schooling. These arrangements were enshrined in the CONSTITUTION ACT, 1867, and despite a growing secularization and increased homogenization among Protestant denominations in the 20th century, the responsibility of the state to support denominational schools in some form has remained intact in most provinces. The concept that church and state are partners, not hostile and incompatible forces that must be kept at a distance, has made it possible for educational authorities in Canada to subsidize Jewish schools in Québec and Hutterite schools on the Prairies, to condone Amish schools in Ontario, and to permit the Salvation Army to develop its own public schools in Newfoundland.

By 1867 each of the 3 colonies of British N America that formed the Dominion of Canada had its own system of common schools. After Confederation, by the provisions of s93 of the Constitution Act, 1867, each province maintained exclusive jurisdiction over its own educational structure. The effect of subsection 1 of s93 was to give all legally established existing denominational schools at the time of Confederation perpetual rights to public funds. What was left unsaid, however, was that denominational schools established by custom but not by law were not guaranteed the same right to existence.

In the wake of the Constitution Act, 1867, the provinces were free to forge their own education statutes, subject to the guarantees for denominational schools already legally established. Five different administrative arrangements emerged. In Québec a dual confessional public school system developed, composed of 2 separate and independent streams, Catholic and Protestant, representing the 2 confessions of Western Christianity. In each school district, the confessional schools of the minority were known as dissentient schools, but like the majority's public common schools, they controlled their own curriculum, teacher training and inspection through their confessional section of the Council of Public Instruction (now Ministry of Education). After the establishment of a provincial ministry of education in 1964, however, confessional autonomy was considerably reduced to the point where the 2 branches now essentially share a common curriculum.

Ontario, Saskatchewan and Alberta established a separate-school system, normally Protestant or Catholic segregated confessional systems, along with the common nonsectarian public schools. Both the separate schools and the nonsectarian public schools were and are administered by either a department or ministry of educa-

tion with control over curriculum, teacher training and certification, special programs and inspection. Nova Scotia, New Brunswick, PEI and Manitoba adopted informal arrangements for funding denominational schools. (Between 1871 and 1890 Manitoba had the dual confessional system, ie, Catholic and Protestant, similar to that of Québec. From then until the late 1960s it granted no aid to any religious group.) Officially, in these provinces, there are single nonsectarian public school systems. In practice, however, political compromises and administrative leeway over the years allowed Catholic schools to receive state funds with varying degrees of state supervision attached. Thus a separate-school system has virtually come into being in all but name.

Newfoundland and BC, until quite recently, have represented the poles of Canadian funding patterns. Before the late 1960s, Newfoundland provided support exclusively for denominational schools; thus a truly denominational public school system was in operation. Then, in March 1969 the Anglican Church, United Church and Salvation Army signed a Document of Integration, which the Presbyterian Church later accepted. Each church thereby relinquished its right to operate its own schools but retained an executive secretary to advise the provincial department of education on denominational questions. The other denominations – Roman Catholic, Pentecostal Assemblies and Seventh Day Adventist – also appointed executive secretaries to the Denominational Education Commission operating outside the department but advisory to it. Until 1977, BC alone among the provinces funded no religiously based schools. The first school legislation enacted by the new province's legislature in 1872 established free nonsectarian public schools, thereby invoking the doctrine of the separation of church and state. The public system remains intact but, with the passage of Bill 33 in 1977, BC now provides funding to private denominational and nondenominational schools.

The organizational structure, assumptions and practices that emerged a century ago have been contested, often bitterly, and occasionally modified, but on the whole there was little substantive administrative change between the end of the century and the 1960s. Over the years Canadian courts have established that denominational rights with respect to schooling are based on religion, not language, and that the religion of the parent is the decisive factor. However, parents do not always have a free choice as to which school, public or separate, their children may attend, nor for which they shall be taxed. In Ontario, for example, a Catholic parent may elect the school system to which his or her taxes go; the children will then attend the system to which such taxes are paid. Although a Catholic may choose to be a public-school supporter, however, a non-Catholic may not elect to support a Catholic separate school. In Saskatchewan, if a separate school exists in a district the taxpayer has no choice but to support the school operated by members of his or her denomination. In Alberta, once a Roman Catholic separate-school district is established, all Catholic residents are separate-school supporters and all non-Catholic residents are public-school supporters. In Edmonton, Calgary and Saskatoon the school boards have arranged that non-Catholic children may attend Catholic separate schools and Catholic children may attend public schools at no cost. But it is not clear whether non-Catholics can be separate-school supporters even if they declare themselves Catholic for tax purposes. In Alberta and Saskatchewan there was equal provision of corporation taxes, larger units and secondary schools to both streams. In Ontario, however, not only were non-Catholic parents denied the right to choose Catholic schooling for their children, but equal public support for both systems soon disappeared and funding for separate schools was not extended beyond grade 10 until Sept 1985. At that time public funding was extended to separate schools and grade 11, then grades 12 and 13 one year at a time.

Despite these striking differences among the provinces, certain factors remain common: the property tax remains the basic source of all school revenue; public schools, whether separate or common, are usually tuition-free; a centralized administrative structure (though varying in power) is in place in each province and normally exercises a similar supervisory role over both public and separate schools; until the 1960s all provinces insisted upon religious instruction in all public schools and religious exercises (the Lord's Prayer, Bible reading from selected passages) to open the day; and funding arrangements are quite similar in a number of provinces.

In the past 20 years a number of significant changes have occurred and political controversy over separate school funding has intensified. The changes result from several developments. The growing importance of education as a means of access to the labour market, manifest in the conversion of the secondary school into a mass institution and the rapid expansion of post-secondary schooling, increased the financial costs of providing separate schools and raised questions about the adequacy of the secular instruction available within them. In both cases, separate-school advocates had a larger stake in gaining more public funds. The consolidation of small school districts into larger units often meant that ethnically or denominationally homogeneous schools were converted into more heterogeneous institutions, complicating or eliminating the monolithic basis of the original schools. This was particularly true in Atlantic Canada. The centralization of funding at the provincial level replaced the previous dominance of locally based financing and usually coincided with larger funding. Simultaneously, however, centralization tended to increase state supervisory powers and led to a diminution of autonomy among schools accepting provincial funds. The expansion of provincial involvement in schools and the growing importance of schooling itself affected separate-school funding and church-state relations in every province.

Atlantic Canada presents a typical picture of how efforts to modernize the public schools reduced both the informal and formal authority and autonomy previously held by the Catholic denominational schools. In Nova Scotia, New Brunswick and PEI informal agreements continue to link church and state in education, allowing, for example, teachers in public schools in Catholic areas to wear religious dress, but the effort by provincial governments to improve educational services through more efficient and economic organizational structures, by centralizing and consolidating funding so as to distribute public money more equitably and by increasing supervisory control over all schools, seriously challenged the denominational basis of schooling. Likewise, denominationalism is now confined to an advisory rather than policymaking role in Nfld.

The politics of separate-school funding in Ontario are in many ways unique. Thanks to recent large-scale immigration from Catholic Europe (from countries such as Italy and Portugal), 37% of Ontario's population is Catholic and about 34% of elementary students are in separate schools. Of the 160 elementary school boards, 57 are Catholic and only one is Protestant. From Sept 1987 all separate schools are funded on the same basis as public schools. For Francophones in some regions of the province, there was (until Sept

1985) another way to receive public funds for Catholic students in grades 11 to 13: they attended public French secondary schools. Significantly, this required a shift in emphasis from religion to ethnicity and language.

The extraordinary growth in the past 2 decades of enrolments in separate and nonpublic denominational schools and the increased political power of denominational groups attest to the importance parents attach to schooling as a means of preserving religio-cultural values and improving economic position. Other groupings of parents with language, ethnocultural or educational interests who are not currently served in public or grant-aided private schools are likely to emerge and demand support in a version of Canadian educational pluralism unmatched since the pre-public-school era of the mid-19th century. By the mid-1980s denominationalism had gained an educational prominence few would have predicted 20 years ago. J. DONALD WILSON

Separatism, the advocacy of separation or secession by a group or people of a particular subunit or section from a larger political unit to which it belongs. In modern times, separatism has frequently been identified with a desire for freedom from perceived colonial oppression. It is a term commonly associated with various movements in Québec in the 1960s. Some of these movements merged to form the PARTI QUÉBÉCOIS, which abandoned the term separatism for "independence" and for the more complex SOVEREIGNTY-ASSOCIATION. The first full-fledged secessionist movement in Canada emerged in Nova Scotia shortly after Confederation in response to economic grievances, but it was quickly defeated. No other serious separatist force appeared in an English-speaking province for another century. In Québec the Manifesto of the PATRIOTES in the REBELLIONS OF 1837 had included a declaration that the province secede from Canada. After the defeat of that rebellion, separatism no longer existed as a genuine component of the conservative FRENCH CANADIAN NATIONALISM which emerged and which was dominant for over a century in Québec. There were, however, isolated advocates of the doctrine of separatism, eg, the journalist Jules-Paul TARDIVEL, and occasional flirtations with it in the early 1920s and mid-1930s by strong nationalists such as Abbé Lionel GROULX and his followers.

The separatist movement re-emerged as a political force in modern Québec in the late 1950s and the 1960s, a time of great socioeconomic change and nationalist ferment in that province. The earliest organizational signs of this rejuvenation were the right-wing secessionist Alliance laurentienne (1957), the left-wing Action socialiste pour l'indépendance du Québec (1960) and, most important, the centre-left Rassemblement pour l'indépendance nationale (RIN) in the 1960s. The RIN first competed electorally in 1966, and together with its right-of-centre offshoot, the Ralliement national, garnered over 9% of the Québec vote. Some violent radical fringe movements committed to independence also operated during this decade, most notably the FRONT DE LIBÉRATION DU QUÉBEC (FLQ), which attained notoriety in the OCTOBER CRISIS of 1970.

Popular support for separatism in Québec and for the organizations which represented it rapidly increased in the province in the late 1960s and the 1970s, particularly after the Parti Québécois was formed in 1968. The party was able to rally most of the province's political groups to its program of political independence coupled with economic association ("sovereignty-association") with English-speaking Canada. Founded and led by the dynamic René LÉVESQUE, in 1970 the PQ gained about 23% of the popular vote in Québec

and won 7 seats. In 1973 it increased its support to 30% of the vote and, despite its reduction to 6 seats, became the official Opposition. On 15 Nov 1976 it swept to power, with 41% of the popular vote and 71 seats, on a promise to delay any move toward independence until after the people of Québec had been consulted in a referendum, which was to be held before the end of its electoral mandate. During the next 3 years Lévesque's government attempted to flesh out its separatist option, which it published in the form of a white paper on Sovereignty-Association in 1979. The white paper envisaged full exercise of sovereignty for Québec and a few institutions in common with Canada, eg, a community council, secretariat, monetary authority and court. The QUÉBEC REFERENDUM campaign was launched shortly afterwards. The people of Québec were asked for a mandate to negotiate sovereignty-association with the rest of Canada. Although this was only a mild expression of the independence option, it was decisively rejected on 20 May 1980 by about 60% of the Québec electorate, including a majority of the French-speaking population. Despite the referendum defeat, which constituted a severe setback for the separatist cause, the PQ was re-elected in 1981 on a program that included a promise to defer the independence question for at least another full term of office. Polls taken from 1981 to 1985 showed a declining interest in the independence issue among Quebeckers as well as plummeting support for the PQ. In Jan 1985 the PQ voted to shelve the independence option in the next provincial election. In the provincial election of Dec, 1985, the PQ under Pierre-Marc JOHNSON was resoundingly defeated by the Liberals. It won only 23 seats and 39% of the popular vote in comparison to the Liberals' 99 seats and 56% of the popular vote. After this defeat and Lévesque's death, Johnson resigned and in 1988 the party was expected to return to a more orthodox separatist platform.

The modern form of separatism in Québec has been particularly popular among the new middle classes, especially those linked to state structures and with aspirations for upward mobility in other expanding bureaucratic sectors of society. The principal adherents of the Parti Québécois, both within the rank and file and the leadership, have been some groups of professionals (eg, teachers, administrators and media specialists), white-collar workers and students. There has also been considerable support from trade-union members. There is relatively poor support from the business sector and from the traditional liberal professions such as law and medicine. This is not surprising, since both the ideology of independence and the social-democratic orientation of the PQ appeal to those favouring an expanding state and the strengthening of French-language institutions in Québec. Francophone businessmen and traditional professionals are more sympathetic to pan-Canadian political appeals, which are more in tune with their national economic interests.

In English Canada, disaffection with the policies of the federal government has helped spawn some separatist activity as well. The DENE people of the Mackenzie District of the NWT attracted some attention by invoking the right of self-determination in their testimony to the Berger Commission on the MACKENZIE VALLEY PIPELINE in 1976. Since that time, however, the Dene have made it clear that they are only seeking a greater measure of political autonomy within the NWT, not outright political independence.

After the failure of the negotiations on constitutional revision in Sept 1980, and the announcement of the federal government's National Energy Policy the following month, separatist sentiment rose dramatically in Alberta and moderately in BC, although it actually declined slightly in Saskatchewan and Manitoba. It was widely viewed as a more extreme manifestation of historically deep-rooted western attitudes of alienation and protest against central Canada and the federal government. Separatism was embodied in the Western Canada Concept Party, an amalgam of 2 earlier provincial political organizations. Its objectives were to rectify perceived injustices in western Canada concerning such matters as freight rates, tariff barriers, oil pricing, bilingualism and western representation in the federal governing party and, failing that, to secede from Canada. It was difficult to characterize those predisposed to western separatism by the usual indicators, eg, age, education, income or occupation. The major differences of opinion occurred among the 4 provinces and among supporters of the national political parties. Internal wrangling and splits in the separatist parties and some improvement in the climate of Ottawa-western Canada relations have since resulted in a decline in separatist support, although splinter parties, such as the REFORM PARTY continue to be established.

MICHAEL STEIN

Reading: R. Lévesque, *An Option for Québec* (1968); M. Rioux, *Québec in Question* (1978); M. Watkins, ed, *Dene Nation* (1977).

Sept-Îles, Qué, City, pop 25 637 (1986c), 29 262 (1981c), inc 1951, metropolis of the North Shore region and centre of its mining industry, is located on the ST LAWRENCE R, 230 km NE of Baie-Comeau. It is one of Canada's most important seaports. The site, visited by MONTAGNAIS-NASKAPI tribes, was known to BASQUE fishermen before 1535, when Jacques CARTIER named it – after the 7 islands that protect access to the bay. The first permanent European settlement dates from 1651: the Ange-Gardien mission founded by Father Jean de Quen. A trading and fishing post set up there in 1676 by Louis JOLLIET was ceded in the 19th century to the HUDSON'S BAY CO. At the start of the 20th century, Sept-Îles had only 200 inhabitants, mostly ACADIANS by birth, living from fishing, plus 600 Montagnais on the reserve. In 1908 development of the pulp industry at Clarke City caused an influx of new workers. The exploitation of the mining resources of the hinterland, starting in the 1950s, led to rapid expansion of the city and activities related to the mineral and IRON ORE deposits of Nouvelle Québec and Labrador. Its port was improved in 1954 and 1970 to receive the massive cargo of ore brought down the QUEBEC, NORTH SHORE AND LABRADOR RY from SCHEFFERVILLE. Sept-Îles has a mineral processing plant but its Iron Ore Co of Canada mine has been inactive since 1983. The Vieux-Poste, restored after archaeological digs, houses Sept-Îles museum.

CLAUDINE PIERRE-DESCHÊNES

Serbs are South Slavs. It is commonly believed that they migrated to the Balkans during the 6th and 7th centuries, where they constituted several independent south Slav states. United into an empire in the 1340s, these states flourished until the Turkish Conquest of the Balkans in the 14th century. From 1804, when the Serbs initiated their struggle for national independence, to 1918 the principality (later kingdom) of Serbia evolved in-

to a constitutional and democratic state. In 1918 Serbia and Montenegro, along with other south Slav territories, united to form the kingdom of Serbs, Croats and Slovenes, which became Yugoslavia in 1929. Today, Serbia is one of the 6 constituent republics comprising Yugoslavia and accounts for 42% of its population. The first immigrants to the US and Canada started arriving in the middle of the 19th century. Before the 1900s the Canadian census wrongly classified Serbs into other national groups such as Austrians, Hungarians and Turks. This was because of the complexity of the classification system in use then and because Serbs lived under several foreign sovereignties. In 1901 the term "Serbian" appeared in the census, although in succeeding years this group was again unlisted, reappearing eventually in official statistics as Serbo-Croats or Yugoslavs. Today, over 60 000 Canadians (of the quarter of a million Canadians of Yugoslavian ancestry) claim Serbian descent.

Migration and Settlement In the 1850s the first Serbs to immigrate to Canada (probably from Boka Kotorska on the southern Adriatic coast) settled in BC along the Fraser R and in Vancouver. Most of them were young, single men who worked in the mining and forest industries. The second wave arrived in the 1870s. In 1900 Serbs began to migrate to other provinces, particularly Saskatchewan where a sizable number were from the plains of Vojvodina. The Serbian community in Regina dates from this time. Between 1907 and 1908 many Serbs migrated to Canada from the US, working in coal mines around Lethbridge, Alta, building roads and working on the railway. Before WWI, Serbian communities were founded in Toronto, Hamilton and Niagara Falls, Ont. The third wave of immigration occurred between the wars, particularly 1924-29 and 1934-39. Most of these immigrants settled in industrial centres of Ontario. Of the fourth wave of immigrants (1947-53), many were highly educated. Of the fifth group (generally university educated), after 1955, many were sponsored by family or friends.

Social and Cultural Life Serbian voluntary associations and organizations were established to ease the economic hardships of new immigrants and to help them adjust to Canadian society. Serbian organizations in Canada today include the Serbian Brothers' Help; 2 organizations of the Serbian National Defence; one of which dates back to 1916; and the Serbian National Heritage Academy which has been active in inviting prominent Serbian writers and historians from Yugoslavia and other countries to Canada for public lectures. Other Serbian organizations include cultural and historical societies: "Njegos," "Karadjordje" and "Tesla Memorial Society"; several youth folklore organizations, eg, "Oplenac" and "Hajduk Veljko" dance groups of Toronto. Those Serbs talented in creative writing have joined other Yugoslav Canadians in Toronto and formed 2 literature appreciation clubs.

Several newspapers and journals have been created and published by Canadian Serbs and by Serbs who participated in other Canadian-Yugoslav organizations. These publications were intended for the Serbs in the US as well. The first Serbian newspaper in Canada (1916), *Kanadski Glasnik* (*Canadian Herald*) was published in Welland, Ont, and was followed by *Serbian Herald* and several others. As well, various publications put out by the Church, congregations, women, youth, students, business-professional groups, etc, play important roles in Serbian communities in Canada. By now, many old documents have been donated to the provincial and federal archives for public use.

The first Serbian Day was held in Canada in 1946, and annual festivals featuring singers and

dancers are sponsored by Serbian and other Yugoslav organizations. Several radio programs are available to Serbians in the metro areas of the provinces. In sports, Serbians are known for their success in organizing soccer clubs.

About 70% of the second and subsequent generations of Serbs in Canada have maintained the Serbian language. There is some variation by occupation and other aspects of the parents. Almost all Serbs adhere to the Serbian Orthodox Church. They have built some 15 churches and cultural centres across Canada. The first Serbian Orthodox Church built in Canada was Svete Trojice in Regina in 1916. Those in Toronto, Hamilton, Windsor, Niagara Falls, Kitchener and Sudbury are noteworthy for their Byzantine architectural design. It was not until 14 Oct 1984 that Canadian Serbs acquired their own bishop. On that day, Bishop Georgije arrived from Belgrade to become the first head of the newly created Canadian Diocese (Eparchy) and to lead and administer Serbian congregations in 13 cities. The Serbian Orthodox Church is an autocephalous (self-governing) part of the Universal Orthodox Church (The Churches of the Ancient East).

VLADISLAV A. TOMOVIĆ

Serpent Mound, situated on a bluff overlooking Rice Lk near Peterborough, Ont, is the only known effigy mound in Canada. It is a sinuous earthen structure, 59.1 m long and 1.5-1.8 m high. Excavation indicates that it was an accretion mound, gradually built up between 128 and 302 AD. This would suggest that Serpent Mound was a sacred place, visited periodically for religious ceremonies. Although pieces of grave furniture were not plentiful, their distribution shows they were restricted largely to individuals of higher status within the community. Those individuals were buried either at the base of the mound or in shallow, submound pits. The commoners were randomly scattered throughout the mound fill.

WALTER A. KENYON

Service, Robert William, poet, novelist (b at Preston, Eng 16 Jan 1874; d at Lancieux, France

Poet Robert Service in front of his famous Dawson cabin (*courtesy Yukon Archives/Martha Louise Black Coll*).

11 Sept 1958). Educated in Scotland, Service worked in a bank after he left school. In 1894 he immigrated to Canada, where, after wandering from California to British Columbia, he joined the Canadian Bank of Commerce. He was stationed throughout British Columbia and eventually at Whitehorse and Dawson City. In 1907 he published his first collection of poems, *Songs of a Sourdough*; an immediate success, it was followed by *Ballads of a Cheechako* (1909) and *Rhymes of a Rolling Stone* (1912). Poems such as "The Shooting of Dan McGrew" assured Service of lasting fame and gave rise to his nicknames: "the Canadian Kipling" and "the Poet of the Yukon." During WWI he was an ambulance driver, and after the war he travelled throughout Europe but lived mostly in France. His later works include *Ballads of a Bohemian* (1921), *Rhymes of a Roughneck* (1950) and his autobiographical works: *Ploughman of the Moon* (1945) and *Harper of Heaven* (1948).   DAVID EVANS

Service Industry The Canadian ECONOMY has 2 main components, the goods-producing sector and the service sector. The former includes agriculture, forestry, mining, fishing, construction and manufacturing (*see also* ECONOMICS). The latter includes noncommercial activities, such as health and welfare, EDUCATION, religion and charity; commercial services, such as restaurants, recreation, amusement, personal care, etc; trade, including wholesale and retail; TRANSPORTATION, COMMUNICATIONS and utilities; and financial and legal, including INSURANCE, REAL ESTATE, BANKING and investment.

As Canada's population has grown and its economy has expanded, and as the goods-producing sector has increased its efficiency and productivity, there has been a steady growth in the share of the working population employed in the service sector.

In 1911 about 66% of the working population were employed directly in the goods-producing sector and 33% in the service sector; by 1987 these ratios had been reversed. As the farm population has declined the number of people employed in service activities has increased. At Confederation, 50% of the workforce was employed in agriculture, but by 1987 this had dropped to less than 4%.

From Confederation, 1867, to WWII there was steady but slow growth in the service sector; but after WWII, as Canada exported more of its resource products and manufactured goods, more services could be afforded and employment in this area (particularly in education and health and welfare) mushroomed.

In addition to expansion of such personal services there has been significant growth in services provided to the goods-producing sector. This growth has resulted from increased output of that sector as well from new services that have become available through new technology. As the output of the goods sector increased, it expanded the work of providing services for transporting goods, warehousing, ACCOUNTING, communications and other supporting activities. Certain service industries now provide functions which were previously performed internally by companies themselves, such as data processing and other computer services, professional consulting, industrial design and maintenance.

Commencing with the first industrial computer installation in Canada in 1957, new technology has vastly expanded the activities of the service sector by creating new functions, eg, the provision of "on-line" information to subscribers for financial and stock market data, weather reports and general news, or by increasing the efficiency of conducting existing functions, eg,

Employment by Sector (000s) (Source: S/C 71-001 *The Labour Force*)					
	1911	*1951*	*1971*	*1981*	*1986*
Total work force	2725	5286	8627	12 005	12 870
Goods producing	1720	2773	2995	3800	3832
Public administration and unspecified	188	389	1295	1293	963
Service industries					
– transportation	192	450	671	936	965
– retail and wholesale trade	260	746	1269	1956	2274
– finance, insurance, real estate	37	144	358	621	687
– education	47	153	569		
– health and welfare	34	174	513		
– food and lodging	56	155	331	3399	4150
– personal and recreation	138	187	253		
– other services	53	115	373		
Total service industries	817	2124	4337	6912	8076

automatic tellers in banking, vastly improved productivity in worldwide transactions through the use of computers and communication satellites. In the medical field new technologies have made it possible to provide new and better services for detection, prevention and correction of ailments.

Many organizations in the service sector are owned or regulated by governments, although in the 1970s and 1980s there was some movement toward freer competition and less regulation arising to some extent from competitive pressures from the US, where a policy of deregulation was pursued during the early 1980s. During the 1970s and early 1980s, Canadian industry faced increased competition from many countries. Initially, this had little direct effect on the service sector, but with the increasing intensity of the worldwide competition in the 1980s, the service industries have felt the pressure of foreign competition not only directly in activities such as data processing, banking and tourism, but also indirectly in activities such as communications and utilities.

The bilateral trade agreement (*see* FREE TRADE) between the US and Canada, signed by Prime Minister Mulroney and President Reagan in Jan 1988 but not yet ratified, may affect Canada's service industry as trade barriers between the 2 countries are relaxed.

In the 1960s and 1970s it was predicted by many that computers and other technological advancements would replace people and destroy jobs, but new products and services have also created jobs that were not available previously. The fastest-growing occupations since the advent of computers have been the secretarial, clerical, sales and other service-industry occupations. It is expected they will continue to be the fastest-growing occupations through the remainder of the 20th century.   ROY A. PHILLIPS

Seton, Ernest Thompson, author, naturalist, artist (b Ernest Thompson at Shields, Eng 14 Aug 1860; d at Seton Village, Santa Fe, New Mexico 23 Oct 1946).

Seton is remembered for his part in the creation of a distinctively Canadian literary genre: the realistic animal story. He spent his boyhood in Ontario, graduated from the Ontario College of Arts in 1879 and then studied at the Royal Academy in England. He studied art in Paris and was soon in demand as an illustrator. His most famous painting, *The Sleeping Wolf*, won first prize at the annual competition held at the Paris Salon. He moved to the US in 1896 where he published his first collection of animal stories, *Wild Animals I Have Known* (1898). It contained his most famous story, "Lobo, the King of Currumpaw," and has since

Ernest Thompson Seton, naturalist whose prolific writings anticipated Kipling in the development of the anthropomorphic animal story (*courtesy National Archives of Canada/C-9485*).

been translated into many languages. This was followed by more than a dozen additional collections of similar stories, which won him international acclaim.

In 1906, Seton published *Two Little Savages; Being the Adventures of Two Boys Who Lived as Indians and What They Learned*. Based on his childhood experience of "playing Indian" in Ontario, it is now considered a classic of children's literature. This was followed by numerous books on woodcraft, one of which formed the basis for the *Boy Scouts of America Official Manual* (1910). In 1910, Seton joined Lord Baden-Powell (British) and Daniel Beard (American) in establishing the Boy Scouts of America. Seton's charismatic appeal made it hard for the association to get rid of him. He levelled charges of militarism and they, in turn, charged him with pacifism. Finally, in 1915, he was expelled on the pretext that he was not an American citizen.

In the meantime, Seton had intensified his scientific activities. In 1908 he published the 2-volume *The Life Histories of Northern Animals: An Account of the Mammals of Manitoba*. After a trip to the far north, he also published *The Arctic Prairies: A Canoe Journey of 2000 Miles in Search of the Caribou* (1911). Between 1925 and 1927 he published 4 volumes in a series entitled *Lives of Game Animals*, for which he was awarded the John Burroughs and Elliott Gold Medals.

Seton spent the last 16 years of his life near Santa Fe, New Mexico and took out American citizenship in 1931. With his second wife, Julia Buttree, he set up Seton Village, a study centre for naturalists which is still active. Until his death, he remained so bitter about his conflict with the Boy Scouts of America that he was persuaded to leave out all mention of it in his autobiography, *Trail of an Artist-Naturalist* (1940).   MAGDALENE REDEKOP

Reading: Magdalene Redekop, *Ernest Thompson Seton* (1979).

Seul, Lac, 1658 km², elev 357 m, 55 m deep, located in northwestern Ontario, 50 km N of Dryden, drains W via the English and WINNIPEG rivers to Lk WINNIPEG. It appears as "Lake Alone" – a literal translation of its present French name – on Peter POND's map of 1784. The Cree, who inhabited the area until the mid-18th century, were

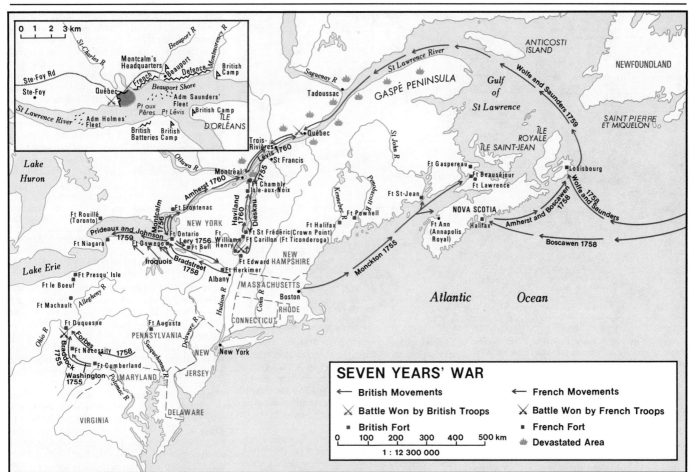

SEVEN YEARS' WAR

← British Movements   ← French Movements

✕ Battle Won by British Troops   ✕ Battle Won by French Troops

■ British Fort   ■ French Fort

Devastated Area

0   100   200   300   400   500 km

1 : 12 300 000

gradually displaced by the Ojibwa. Descendants of the latter now occupy the Lac Seul Reserve adjacent to the towns of Hudson and Sioux Lookout. Although the lake was off the main fur-trade routes, both the HBC and NWC were active in the area, and the former continues to be represented at Lac Seul Post. The lake supports a small commercial fishery, but present resource development is concentrated in the forest industry. The unspoiled environment, with its abundant fish and wildlife, also makes this one of the prime outdoor recreation areas in northwestern Ontario. The natural capacity of Lac Seul is augmented by the diversion of water from the ALBANY R watershed, allowing hydroelectric stations at Ear Falls, where the English R leaves the lake, and Manitou Falls, 30 km downstream, to generate 90 600 kW of electricity.   DAVID D. KEMP

Seven Oaks Incident Prior to the union of the North West Co and the Hudson's Bay Co in 1821, the endemic struggles between the 2 fur-trading rivals were capped by a violent incident 19 June 1816 at Seven Oaks, a few km from the HBC's Fort Douglas in the Red River Settlement. The so-called massacre of Seven Oaks provoked retaliation and led to a merger of the 2 companies.

The colony at the vital junction of the Red and Assiniboine rivers, established by Thomas Douglas, fifth earl of SELKIRK, was perceived by the Nor'Westers as the base from which the HBC was preparing to launch its penetration of the Athabaska country. It posed a threat, as well, to the annual brigades of the Montréal-based company, lying athwart their main communication route.

In the spring of 1816, the HBC officers and men seized and destroyed the Nor'Westers' Fort Gibraltar at the forks, thus exposing the latter's canoe brigades, just as the pemmican supplies were being moved down the Assiniboine to meet the Nor'Westers returning from the annual coun-

cil at Fort William. The HBC's Fort Douglas thus dominated the Red and denied passage both to the Nor'Westers and the provision boats of their Métis allies.

Brandon House, a HBC post on the upper Assiniboine, was captured by the Métis on 1 June 1816 under Cuthbert GRANT, who then organized an escort to secure the pemmican supplies. Leaving the Assiniboine near Portage la Prairie, Grant and his men struck northeast across the plain to intercept the Nor'Westers on the Red. But they were, in fact, themselves intercepted by the HBC's local governor, Robert SEMPLE, who with a score of his men, had unwisely ventured out of Fort Douglas. Although the clash was not premeditated, the Métis quickly enveloped Semple's party and he and 20 of his men were killed. The Métis suffered only one casualty.

In retaliation, Selkirk captured the Nor'Westers' primary base at Fort William and reoccupied Fort Douglas. Law suits and countersuits ensued. Only Selkirk's death in 1820 cleared the way for an end to the rivalry. As for the Métis, they came to see Red River as a place of settlement and for several decades were a permanent element in the colony.   J.E. REA

Seven Years' War, 1756-63, was the first global war. The protagonists were Britain, Prussia and Hanover against France, Austria, Sweden, Saxony, Russia and eventually Spain. Britain declined to commit its main forces on the continent, where it depended on the Prussians and German mercenaries to defend George II's Electorate of Hanover. Britain's war aims were to destroy the French navy and merchant fleet, seize its colonies, and eliminate France as a commercial rival. France found itself committed to fighting in Europe to defend Austria, which could do nothing to aid France overseas.

Hostilities began in 1754 in America's Ohio

Valley when a Virginian major of militia, George Washington, ambushed a small French detachment. He was subsequently forced to accept humiliating terms dictated by the commander of the French force sent to bring him to account. The British then ordered 2 regiments, commanded by Maj-Gen Edward Braddock, to America. Other regiments were to be raised in the colonies, and a 4-pronged attack was to be launched against the French at FORT BEAUSÉJOUR on the border of NS, against their forts on Lk Champlain, and at Niagara, and against Ft Duquesne on the Ohio R.

On learning of these movements the French ordered 6 battalions under Baron Armand Dieskau to be sent to reinforce LOUISBOURG and Canada. Vice-Adm Edward Boscawen was then ordered to sail with his squadron to intercept and capture the French convoy, although war had not been declared. He captured only 2 ships. The British had even less success on land. The army advancing on Lk Champlain was stopped by the French near Lk George but Dieskau was wounded and taken prisoner. The proposed assault on Niagara collapsed through military ineptitude, and Braddock's 1500-man army was destroyed by a small detachment of French and Indians. Only in ACADIA did the British enjoy success. Ft Beauséjour with its small garrison was captured. The Acadian settlers were subsequently rounded up by the New England forces and deported.

In Apr 1756 more French troops and a new commander, the marquis de MONTCALM, arrived in Canada, and the next month Britain declared war. The strategy of the commander in chief and governor general, the marquis de VAUDREUIL, was to keep the British on the defensive and as far from Canadian settlements as possible. He captured the British forts at Oswego on Lk Ontario and thereby gained control of the Great Lakes. At the same time Canadian and Indian war parties

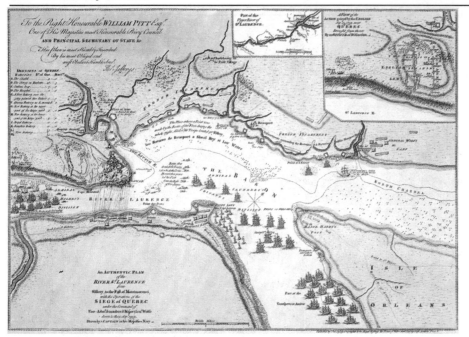

Contemporary plan of the St Lawrence R and Québec, showing British action during the siege of Québec, 1759 (*courtesy National Archives of Canada/NMC-2716*).

ravaged the American frontier settlements. The Americans could not cope with these attacks and Britain was forced to send over 23 000 troops to the colonies and commit most of its navy to blockading the French ports. The French aim was to tie down these large British forces with a small army, and the Canadians and Indian allies, thereby sparing more valuable colonies from attack.

In Aug 1757 the French captured Ft William Henry on Lk George. The next year Maj-Gen James Abercromby, with an army of over 15 000 British and American troops, suffered a crushing defeat at Ft Carillon (Ticonderoga) at the hands of Montcalm and 3500 men. The tide of war now turned against the French. On Lk Ontario, FT FRONTENAC [Kingston, Ont] was destroyed in Aug 1758 with its stock of supplies for the western posts. Elsewhere Louisbourg and Guadeloupe were taken by the British. France's Indian allies in the Ohio region concluded a separate peace with the British, forcing the French to abandon Ft Duquesne. Supply ships reached Québec every year but the French refused to send more than token troop reinforcements. They pinned their hopes on an invasion of Britain to force the British to come to terms.

In 1759, 2 British armies advanced on Canada while a third captured Niagara. The Royal Navy brought Maj-Gen James WOLFE with 9000 men to Québec and Gen Jeffery AMHERST advanced up Lk Champlain only to halt at Crown Point. After maneuvering fruitlessly all summer Wolfe induced Montcalm to give battle on Sept 13 outside Québec, and inflicted a shattering defeat in the Battle of the PLAINS OF ABRAHAM. The city surrendered a few days later. The Chevalier de LÉVIS took over command of the French army and the following Apr soundly defeated the British on the same battlefield (*see* Battle of STE-FOY). On May 16 he had to raise the siege of the city when

British frigates arrived to dash all hope of French reinforcements. Retiring to Montréal, the French army was forced to capitulate to Amherst on 8 Sept 1760 (*see* CONQUEST), freeing the British forces for service elsewhere. In 1762 Martinique was taken and only the intervention of Spain that year saved the other French islands in the W Indies.

France and Spain had organized a major expedition for the invasion of England, but the British naval victories at Lagos, Portugal, in Aug and Quiberon Bay, France, in Nov 1759 had ended that. The British, however, were now war weary and staggering under a colossal national debt. The war minister, William Pitt, was driven out of office in 1761 by the new king, George III, and peace negotiations began. The first minister in the French government, the duc de Choiseul, was determined to regain Martinique and Guadeloupe and to retain a base for the Grand Banks fisheries. He also wanted CAPE BRETON, but had to settle for St-Pierre and Miquelon. He left Canada to Britain, convinced that the American colonies, no longer needing British military pro-

tection, would soon strike out for independence. The loss to France of Canada would be as nothing compared to the loss to Britain of her American colonies. To force the stubborn Spanish king to agree to peace terms, France ceded the vast Louisiana territory as compensation for the loss of Florida. Despite some opposition in Britain from those who foresaw what Choiseul privately predicted, Guadeloupe rather than Canada was returned to France by the Treaty of PARIS (1763). Twelve years later the American colonies rose in revolt against Britain. Ironically, it was only with the military aid of the French that they finally gained their independence.   W.J. ECCLES

Reading: Sir J.S. Corbett, *England in the Seven Years' War*, 2 vols (1918); W.L. Dorn, *Competition for Empire, 1740-1763* (1940); G. Frégault, *Canada: The War of the Conquest*, trans M.M. Cameron (1969); L.H. Gipson, *The British Empire Before the American Revolution*, IV-VIII (1936-64); L. Kennett, *The French Armies in the Seven Years' War* (1967); G.F.G. Stanley, *New France* (1968); R. Waddington, *La Guerre de Sept Ans*, 5 vols (1899-1914).

Seventh-Day Adventists are heirs of the American Millerite Adventist movement of the 1840s. When Christ failed to come in 1844 as William Miller's followers expected, it was explained that He had had to cleanse the "heavenly sanctuary rather than the earthly one." This idea was confirmed by Ellen White, who then became a founder and a prophet of the Seventh-Day Adventists.

Primary doctrines of the denomination are broadly EVANGELICAL. They include the imminent return (advent) of Christ, the observance of Saturday as the sabbath (seventh day), baptism by single immersion and a fundamentalist-literalist interpretation of the Bible. The immortality of human beings is contingent on their acceptance of Christ as saviour. Many members are vegetarians and all are enjoined to abstain from alcohol and the use of tobacco. Seventh-Day Adventists are noted for high moral standards, a commitment to human rights and the promotion of medical missions in many lands. Canadian membership has increased significantly during the last decade through immigration from oriental lands, especially Korea. But the church has also recently experienced some turmoil among its members over the question of whether White's writings should be treated as the works of a true prophet.

Congregations are administered partly on a

The Death of General Wolfe by American artist Benjamin West (1770), oil on canvas. Though the content of the painting was largely apocryphal, its romantic symbolism made it one of the most famous images of its time (*courtesy National Gallery of Canada/Gift of the duke of Westminster, 1918*).

PRESBYTERIAN pattern, but ministers are assigned by conferences. Groups of local conferences form union conferences, which in turn are members of the General Conference, the worldwide administrative body of the church. With headquarters in Washington, DC, the SDA has become a worldwide movement with millions of members. Although Seventh-Day Adventists have been in Canada since the establishment of their church about 1860, they are not numerous. In 1981 there were 41 605 Adventists in the country, most of them Seventh-Day Adventists. M. JAMES PENTON

Reading: Don F. Neufeld, ed, *Seventh-Day Adventist Encyclopedia* (1976).

Severn River, 982 km long, rises in the wooded SHIELD country of NW Ontario and flows NE through Severn Lk to HUDSON BAY. Part of the territory inhabited by the Woodland CREE, it was discovered for Europeans in 1631 by Thomas JAMES while searching the bay for a NORTHWEST PASSAGE. Later in the 17th century the HBC erected a trading post at its mouth. The river was used by fur traders travelling between the bay and Lk Winnipeg. It was named after the Severn R in the British Isles. DANIEL FRANCIS

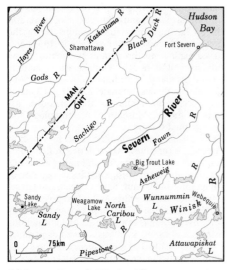

Sévigny, Joseph-Pierre-Albert, contractor, politician (b at Québec C 17 Sept 1917). Son of a prominent politician and judge, Pierre Sévigny was an early Québec supporter of John DIEFENBAKER. A Conservative candidate in a Québec dominated federally by the Liberals, he was defeated several times before his election to the House in 1958. A good speaker and strong Canadian nationalist, Sévigny was appointed deputy Speaker in May 1958 and associate minister of defence in Aug 1959. Dissatisfied with Diefenbaker's politics, particularly those relating to defence, he resigned in Feb 1963 and was defeated in the 1963 general election. He was again in the spotlight during the MUNSINGER AFFAIR. He is now associated with Concordia U in Montréal.
PATRICIA WILLIAMS

Sévilla, Jean-Paul, pianist (b at Oran, Algeria 26 Mar 1934). A graduate of the Paris Conservatoire in 1952, he won the Geneva International Competition in 1959. He first appeared in Canada at the invitation of the JEUNESSES MUSICALES DU CANADA, 1961; in 1970 he began to teach at U of O. Among his Canadian students, Angela HEWITT and Andrew Tunis have won many international competitions. His concert tours take him to the Americas, Europe and the Far East; he gives lectures and master classes as well. He dedicates himself mostly to French music, including the complete works of Ravel, but his repertoire encompasses music from Bach to contemporary

composers whose works he often premieres, including Complémentairité, a work dedicated to him by Jean PAPINEAU-COUTURE. He also has a wide knowledge of the vocal and chamber music literature. A Canada Council grant (1978-79) enabled him to begin a critical study of the piano works of Fauré. DOUGLAS VOICE

Sewell, Jonathan, judge, politician (bap at Cambridge, Mass 29 June 1766; d at Québec 11 Nov 1839). Chief justice of Lower Canada 1808-38, he was also an influential political leader of those opposing Louis-Joseph PAPINEAU's Patriote Party. The son of a Loyalist, Sewell's political views were determined by the AMERICAN REVOLUTION. He sat in the LC Assembly 1796-1808, and was president of the Executive Council 1808-30 and Speaker of the Legislative Council 1809-39. He favoured a strong imperial and executive authority, anglicization of Canadian children through the schools, eliminating the French legal code, replacing the seigneurial system by freehold tenure, and reducing the position of the Roman Catholic Church. While he shared many of the political goals of the clique of British officeholders, he was more conciliatory than his colleagues and was subtle of mind. An intellectual of many talents, he was the first president of the Literary and Historical Soc of Quebec and wrote on history, literature and law. Harvard honoured him with an LLD degree in 1832. JAMES H. LAMBERT

Sexton, Frederic Henry, educator, mining engineer (b at New Boston, NH 9 June 1879; d at Wolfville, NS 12 Jan 1955). After serving as an assistant in metallurgy at the Massachusetts Institute of Technology 1901-02, he worked for the General Electric Co as a research chemist and metallurgist. He taught mining engineering and metallurgy at Dalhousie from 1904. When the TECHNICAL UNIVERSITY OF NS was founded in 1907, he became its first principal and remained in that position until his retirement in 1947. Created CBE in 1944, he was the author of many articles and monographs on technical and industrial education as well as on mining. PHYLLIS ROSE

Sexual Abuse of Children has been defined in Ontario as abuse that includes "any sexual intercourse, sexual molestation, exhibitionism or sexual exploitation involving a child that could be a violation of the Criminal Code or render the child in need of protection under the Child Welfare Act. This includes incidents between family members and between those who are not related." More simply, child sexual abuse is the exploitation of children to meet the sexual needs of adults. For true consent to occur, 2 conditions must prevail: a person must know what it is that he or she is consenting to, and a person must be free to say yes or no. By this definition, children cannot give informed consent to sex.

The Criminal Code of Canada states that "everyone commits incest who, knowing that another person is by blood relationship his or her parent, brother, sister, grandparent or grandchild, as the case may be, has sexual intercourse with that person." Father-daughter incest is most reported, although brother-sister incest is apparently 5 times more frequent. Incestuous activity is not only a criminal offence but can be a symptom of serious family problems. It causes fear and humiliation for the victims and creates secrecy and shame in the family. A child experiences fear and guilt that "telling" may send a parent to prison. A wife fears that exposure will destroy a marriage and leave her family without support. These factors strongly hinder discovery and correction of the problem. If the criminal conduct is prosecuted through the judicial system, these same emotional responses are devastating to a child who must

testify in court to incestuous acts with a parent.

It is estimated that about 20-30% of all sexual abuse is committed by nonfamily members and that most victims are girls. The vast majority of abusers are male. The methods of sexual abuse include indecent exposure and genital contact of the children by fondling. Sexual intercourse is rarely committed and violence is seldom used. Abusers generally use threats or coercion in the form of bribes, toys, candy, money or affection. On the basis of limited evidence, some authorities believe that the actual incidence of sexual abuse is unknown but that it may be as common as one in 4 for females and one in 10 for males, if all forms of inappropriate sexual behaviour towards children from birth to 16 years are included.

As a result of changing public attitudes it is now possible to acknowledge publicly and clinically the existence of child sexual abuse in Canadian society, but more objective research is needed to examine the multifaceted issues arising from this problem. B. SCHLESINGER

Reading: B. Schlesinger, *Sexual Abuse of Children* (1982) and *Sexual Abuse of Children in the 1980s: Issues and Annotated Bibliography, 1980-84* (1986).

Sexual Assault *see* RAPE.

Sexually Transmitted Disease (STD) is the name now used to describe a group of infections previously referred to as venereal disease or VD. Primarily affecting the genital organs of the body, the organisms or germs causing these diseases are transmitted through "skin to skin" contact, ie, sexual intercourse or other intimate physical contact. Until recently only syphilis and gonorrhea were regarded as significant sexually transmitted diseases, but it is now known that at least 20 different conditions may be communicated this way, many exclusively, others only occasionally. The most common sexually transmitted diseases in Canada include nongonococcal urethritis, and cervicitis (Chlamydia), gonorrhea, genital herpes, syphilis and certain types of vaginal infections, venereal warts and infestations of pubic lice (also known as "crabs") and scabies.

Each STD is caused by a specific germ or organism. Although different in nature, most organisms can only survive in the environment of the areas of the body lined with mucous tissue, eg, the mouth or the vagina. Warmth and moisture must be present as well, to allow the organisms to multiply and produce an infection. Most germs rapidly die when removed from this environment; subsequently, they can only be transmitted when there is direct contact between an uninfected susceptible tissue and an infected one. The most common sites of infection are the cervix and vagina in women and the urethra in the male. In certain circumstances or as the result of some sexual practices, the throat, rectum and conjunctiva (eye) can also be affected.

Sexually transmitted diseases can affect anyone, regardless of age, sex, race or socioeconomic background, though the highest incidence is among sexually active individuals from their middle teens to late twenties.

The signs and symptoms of sexually transmitted diseases usually appear in or around the genital area. Although each disease produces a particular symptom, the same symptom may occur with different diseases or may resemble symptoms produced by nonsexually transmitted infections. In a sexually active person a discharge of pus from the urinary opening, vagina or rectum, burning pain on urination, the appearance of blisters, growths or sores on or around the genital organs, or itching of the genital or pubic areas may signal infection. Several STDs, however, can cause an infection without producing symptoms. This is frequently the case with women in particular, in whom signs of infection are often hidden and go unnoticed. Depending upon the disease, this can lead to the development of serious complications of the reproductive organs that can result in pelvic inflammatory disease, tubal pregnancy, sterility and chronic pelvic pain. Unborn infants or infants at the time of delivery can also be affected by STDs.

All sexually transmitted diseases can be detected and differentiated by laboratory testing utilizing either cultures or blood tests. With the exception of genital herpes, which is caused by a virus, each of the common STDs can be treated by appropriate medications (usually antibiotics), although this therapy, while curing the infection, may not reverse the damage produced by complications. However, none of these diseases will produce immunity against future infection should re-exposure occur.

The real incidence of STD in Canada is difficult to determine. Of the common infections, only cases of syphilis and gonorrhea must be reported to the federal health authorities. Some provinces have now added other STDs to their list of notifiable infections. Available statistics indicate that the incidence of STD is exceedingly high; in 1985 they comprised more than 55% of all notifiable diseases reported in Canada. Over the past 70 years the number of reported cases has varied, rising after each of the world wars and declining during the beginning of the antibiotic era in the early 1950s. Since 1981 the incidence of gonorrhea has slowly decreased, but this is offset by an equal increase in nongonococcal urethritis and cervicitis. The occurrence of the nonreportable STDs can only be estimated, but it is felt that cases of these common infections may equal or exceed those of gonorrhea.

The high incidence of STD in Canada can be attributed both to biological and social factors. The diseases have the ability to become more resistant to the treatment drugs and in many cases asymptomatic infections prevent early detection. Although changes in attitudes towards acceptance of more permissive sexual behaviour have favoured the increase of opportunities for disease transmission, this openness has not been accompanied by similar attitudes toward diseases that may be acquired through sexual activity. This stigma attached to STD results in widespread ignorance and fear and interferes with both medical and public recognition of the problems.

Each province has jurisdictional authority to establish public-health programs for the control of the notifiable STDs. Most programs make provisions for diagnostic and treatment centres and clinics, for statistical data collection and for the promotion of education programs for the medical community and the public.

The concern about STD is international, and research is being conducted worldwide to gain a better understanding of the diseases and the organisms causing them, to examine and identify patterns of incidence within given populations, to develop and explore the potential of new therapies, and to devise preventive measures such as vaccines. Scientists in Canada are conducting or participating with other countries in numerous studies examining all these issues. Continued surveillance is essential to determine changes in patterns of STD incidence, to apply new knowledge and technology, and to be alert to the emergence of new diseases, eg, acquired immunodeficiency syndrome (AIDS). This disease was first recognized in 1981 and is characterized by unusual infections and cancers resulting from failure of the body's immune system to function properly.

The existence of disease undermines the physical and emotional health and productivity of a nation. Sexually transmitted disease can only be controlled through the combined efforts of government, health-care professionals and the Canadian public. B. ROMANOWSKI AND M. STAYNER

Reading: R. Lumiere and S. Cook, *Healthy Sex and Keeping It That Way* (1983); A.S. Meltzer, *Sexually Transmitted Diseases* (1981).

Seymour, Frederick, colonial administrator, governor of BC (b at Belfast, Ire 6 Sept 1820; d at Bella Coola, BC 10 June 1869). Seymour obtained an appointment in the colonial service of Van Diemen's Land [Tasmania] in 1842, and in 1848 he was sent to the West Indies, where he spent the next 16 years in various senior administrative posts. He was appointed governor of mainland British Columbia in 1864 but he left the following year for consultations with the Colonial Office in England. He returned in 1866 as governor of the united colony of BC under an Act of union that incorporated many of his recommendations. Despite his achievements within the colony, Seymour treated the issue of CONFEDERATION with Canada with indifference. He died suddenly while returning from successful treaty talks with the Tsimshian. DAVID EVANS

Seymour, Horace Llewellyn, urban planner (b at Burford, Ont 1882; d at Ottawa 21 Apr 1940). One of the founders of modern Canadian URBAN AND REGIONAL PLANNING, Seymour was a leading exponent of the scientific approach to planning and of zoning as the best means of achieving efficient cities. Seymour worked as a land surveyor before joining the town-planning section of the COMMISSION OF CONSERVATION in 1914. His broad experience over the next quarter of a century included the reconstruction of Halifax (1918-21) and a plan for Vancouver (1926-29). He also served as a consultant to the governments of NB and NS and to many municipal governments, chiefly in Ontario. Seymour was director of town and rural planning for Alberta 1929-32, and his planning system for Alberta set a model that other provinces eventually followed. P.J. SMITH

Seymour, Berta Lynn, née Springbett, dancer, choreographer (b at Wainwright, Alta 8 Mar 1939). One of the greatest dramatic ballerinas of the century, Seymour studied at the Rosemary Deveson School and with Nicolai Svetlanoff in Vancouver before entering the Sadler's Wells School in England (1954). By 1959 she was a principal dancer with the Royal Ballet. Famed for her fluent, impetuous movement, extraordinary musicality and intense dramatic power, Seymour is best known in works created for her by Sir Frederick Ashton (*The Two Pigeons, A Month in the Country, Five Waltzes in the Manner of Isadora Duncan*) and by Sir Kenneth MacMillan (*The Burrow, The Invitation, Romeo and Juliet, Anastasia, Mayerling*). Ballerina of the Deutsche Oper Ballet (Berlin, 1966-69) and director of the Bavarian State Opera Ballet (Munich, 1978-79), Seymour is also a talented choreographer. She has appeared in Canada with the Royal Ballet, Western Dance Theatre and NATIONAL BALLET OF CANADA. Her autobiography, *Lynn* was published in 1984. PENELOPE DOOB

Reading: R. Austin, *Lynn Seymour: An Authorized Biography* (1980).

Shadbolt, Douglas, architect, teacher (b at Victoria 18 Apr 1925). Educated at Victoria Coll, UBC and McGill, Shadbolt finished his architectural studies (while also teaching and working for various architectural firms) at U of Oregon between 1955 and 1957. In 1958 he began teaching at McGill and in 1961 organized a new architecture program at Nova Scotia Technical Coll, the first Canadian program alternating periods of study with periods of training in architectural offices. In 1968 Shadbolt became head of a new architecture program at Carleton U. Since 1979 he has been head of the UBC School of Architecture. In 1987 he was invested as an Association of Collegiate Schools of Architecture Distinguished Professor, an award which recognizes sustained creative achievement in architectural education. *See also* ARCHITECTURAL PRACTICE. MICHAEL MCMORDIE

Shadbolt, Jack Leonard, artist, teacher, author, poet (b at Shoeburyness, Eng 4 Feb 1909). Best known as a painter and draftsman, he has written 3 books and many articles and has through his teaching profoundly influenced art and artists in BC and across Canada. He has lived in BC since 1912.

He studied at the Art Students' League in New York C (1928, 1948), and in London (1937) and Paris (1938). After teaching art to children in BC between 1929 and 1937, he joined the Vancouver School of Art. He served in WWII 1942-45, including 1944-45 as a Canadian war artist, and then returned to the school where he was head of painting and drawing until 1966. He has been an influential teacher and adviser across Canada and the US, having conducted workshops (he was the first artist to do so at Emma Lake in 1955) and juried exhibitions throughout N America. Some 60 solo exhibitions of his work have been mounted and his many major international exhibitions include the Venice Biennale, XXVIII and 3 major retrospective exhibitions at the Vancouver Art Gallery, the BC Museum of Anthropology and the National Gallery.

An extraordinarily prolific artist, he works in large series (or suites) which derive from his personal experiences of nature and native art in BC, his many travels in Europe and his recognition of calligraphy and OP-art; in paint slashes and in incisive lines, in butterflies and totem poles, in insect life and ritual brides, in poetry and architecture. Everything is transformed by his emotions as much as by his intellect. As well as painting many murals, he has done stage, ballet and costume designs and theatre posters. His books are *In Search of Form* (1968), *Mind's I* (1973) and *Act of Art* (1981). He continues to have an enormous output, eg, a 3-dimensional plywood relief created for the MacMillan Bloedel building in Vancouver (1987). GEORGE SWINTON

Reading: G.M. Dault, *Jack Shadbolt* (1988).

Shadd, Alfred Schmitz, black educator, physician, farmer, politician, pharmacist, editor, civic leader (b at Raleigh Township, Kent County, Ont 1870; d at Winnipeg 1915). He was from a distinguished family known for its abolitionist and equal rights stance. In 1896 Shadd moved from Chatham, Ont, to Kinistino, North-West Territories where he taught school. He returned to the U of T to complete his medical degree in 1898. Shadd practised medicine in Kinistino and later in Melfort. The "country doctor's" talents and energies became respected by the Indians and white settlers of the Carrot River parkbelt. He operated a drugstore, engaged in mixed farming and stock breeding, edited the town's newspaper, and served on town council and various boards. In 1901 he was an unsuccessful candidate in the territorial elections. In the 1905 election as the Equal Rights Party candidate he came within 52 votes of becoming the first black elected to a provincial legislature. In his forceful speeches and editorials he stressed stronger provincial government, taxes for the Canadian Pacific Ry and local control of schools. A Canadian black granite stone marks his Melfort burial place. COLIN A. THOMSON

Shaganappi [Algonquian, "flayed cord"], thongs or cord made of rawhide. During the settlement of the West, one use of shaganappi was to bind together the parts of RED RIVER CARTS. The word also means "inexperienced" or "inferior," as in "shaganappi pony," a pony that is untrained or undersized. JOHN ROBERT COLOMBO

Shaker Religion originated in the mid-18th-century religious tension among Indians of the American West which also produced the Smohalla Cult, the Ghost Dance and many prophets. In 1881 a Skokomish, John Slocum, was being prepared for burial when he "came back to life," claiming to have "been to heaven" and to have new spiritual and moral teaching for the Indians. He preached the imminent millennium of Christ. In 1882 Slocum again became ill, but his wife Mary "received the gift of healing" accompanied by trembling and shaking and cured him. This gave the name to the new religion. It is composed of Protestant, Roman Catholic and traditional Indian elements of doctrine, belief and ritual. "Getting the shake" is said to confer enlightenment, powers of healing and divination, and "second sight." Sunday worship, healing services, public confession and baptism are the main ceremonies. Not every adherent has the power of "shaking" and healing. Shakerism has extended to tribal groups in NW California, Oregon, Washington state and southern BC. Traditionally, it was indifferent, even hostile, to conventional Christian churches and traditional Indian religions, especially in its healing rituals (*see* SHAMAN). In recent years, however, in NW Washington and BC, the Shakers have accommodated both Christian and Indian religions, and many spirit dancers are also members of the Shaker congregations. There is no direct connection with the American Shakers (The United Society of Believers). Numbers of persons involved in the Shaker Religion have always been very difficult to establish. There has been a decline in activity since the 1960s. *See also* NATIVE PEOPLE, RELIGION.
DEREK G. SMITH
Reading: H.G. Barnett, *Indian Shakers* (1957).

Shaking Tent rite was widespread among the OJIBWA, MONTAGNAIS-NASKAPI, CREE, Penobscot and ABENAKI and involved the shamanistic use of a special cylindrical lodge or tent. A SHAMAN, paid by a client, would construct his tent and enter it at dark. Singing and drumming summoned the shaman's spirit helpers, whose arrival was signified by animal cries and the shaking tent. These spirit helpers were used in curing and also in antisorcery. RENÉ R. GADACZ

Shaman's drum (*courtesy National Museums of Canada/ Canadian Museum of Civilization/S77-264*).

Shaman is a religious or mystical expert (male or female) who in Indian and Inuit societies undergoes initiation experiences in altered states of consciousness (trance or possession). Initiates have frequently reported experiences of death, followed by a rebirth and total healing. The healed shaman is believed to become a bringer of health and prosperity, as a power-filled guide and technician in religion, and in magical, prophetic and mythic dramas. Some are thought to possess evil powers. Translations such as "witch doctor" are pejorative.
DEREK G. SMITH

Shandro, Alta, UP, is located 70 km NE of Edmonton. It is named for Andrew Shandro (1886-1942), its first settler and, as MLA for Whitford, Alta (1913-21), the first UKRAINIAN elected to a legislature in Canada. The Historical Living Village and Pioneer Museum recreates the pioneer life of early Ukrainian settlers. It contains Shandro's thatched log home, a granary, blacksmith shop, a gristmill, a replica of a Boorday, and one of the province's oldest Orthodox churches, St Mary's, completed in 1904. ERIC J. HOLMGREN

Shanly, Francis (Frank), engineer, railway builder (b at Stradbally, Ire 29 Oct 1820; d near Brockville, Ont 13 Sept 1882). Encouraged by H.H. KILLALY, he followed his brother Walter SHANLY into railway building. Both were employed on the Ogdensburg and Lk Champlain Railroad. Frank was responsible for building part of the GRAND TRUNK and Northern railways in Canada. With his brother in 1869 he undertook completion of the Hoosac Tunnel in Massachusetts, still the longest railway tunnel E of the Mississippi. They completed it in 1875. Shanly had just been appointed chief engineer of the INTERCOLONIAL RY when he died in a train between Kingston and Brockville. R.F. LEGGET

Shanly, Walter, civil and consulting engineer and builder (b at Stradbally, Ire 11 Oct 1817; d at Montréal 17 Dec 1899). Encouraged by H.H. KILLALY, he started work in 1840 on canal construction but moved to railways in 1848. With his brother Francis SHANLY, he worked on the Ogdensburg and Lk Champlain Railroad. He then became chief engineer of the Bytown and Prescott Ry. For 4 critical years (1858-62) he was general manager of the GRAND TRUNK RY. After completing the Hoosac Tunnel in Massachusetts with his brother in 1875, he became increasingly famous as a consulting engineer and advised on many major engineering works. In 1863 he was elected to the Legislative Assembly of the Province of Canada and, in 1867, to the House of Commons, where he remained a member until 1891. A confidant of Sir John A. MACDONALD, the last letter written by Macdonald was to Shanly. R.F. LEGGET

Shannon, Kathleen, film director, producer (b at Vancouver 11 Nov 1935). She joined the NFB in 1956. Seven years and about 115 films later, she became interested in film editing. In 1970 she participated in the celebrated Challenge for Change, a production program that dealt with social and economic change in Canada. Shannon then directed *I Don't Think It's Meant for Us* (1971), followed by *Working Mothers* (1974-75), a series of 11 films about women's work. From 1974 to 1987 she was the executive producer of Studio D, an NFB production unit primarily staffed by women, whose principal function has been to examine the role of women in society. In 1983 she returned to production with the documentary *Dream of a Free Country: A Message from Nicaraguan Women*. She was awarded the Order of Canada in 1986. PIERRE VÉRONNEAU

Shanty, winter lumber camp. Early camps were simple, made of notched pine or spruce logs with

a flat roof of rough shingles or bark and poles. By the 1840s larger "camboose" shanties could accommodate over 40 men in their 110 or 140 m^2; the central fire with its large open chimney for light and ventilation did not yield to the stove until late in the century. Men slept fully clothed in bunk beds of hay or boughs; cooking facilities, the foreman's office, barrels of wash water and grindstones occupied much of the remaining space. *See also* TIMBER TRADE HISTORY. GRAEME WYNN

Shark, marine fish with cartilaginous skeleton belonging to subclass Elasmobranchii, class Chondrichthyes, order Pleurotremata. Modern shark ancestry dates back at least 150 million years. About 340 species in 90 genera are found worldwide from arctic to antarctic waters, including ocean depths. The greatest abundance and diversity occurs in tropical and warm temperate regions. A few species invade tropical fresh waters. Twenty-five species occur in Canada's coastal and offshore waters including thresher, great white, porbeagle, mako, basking, blue, hammerhead and dogfish. A few species occur off both coasts throughout the year, especially in deep water; the large, predaceous forms appear mainly during summer and fall. Sharks range from 15 cm and a few grams (*Squaliolus laticaudas*) to over 18 m and many tonnes (whale shark, *Rhincodon typus*, the world's largest fish). They are typically elongate, cylindrical fishes with one or 2 dorsal fins, large pectoral and moderate to small pelvic fins and, usually, an anal fin and the characteristic tail fin with its enlarged upper lobe. The crescent-shaped mouth is normally ventral. The jaws have multiple rows of teeth, which are continually replaced from inside the mouth. The skin is covered with pointed, toothlike denticles. Male sharks have copulatory organs (claspers) on the pelvic fins for internal fertilization. Most species are live bearers (ovoviviparous) but a few deposit eggs in horny capsules (oviparous). The gestation period for the dogfish shark (*Squalus acanthias*), 20-22 months, is one of the longest for a vertebrate.

Sharks of family Lamnidae (eg, mako, great white) have heat-regulating mechanisms allowing maintenance of a warm body temperature and thus increasing swimming and predation efficiency. The large liver stores food reserves, allowing survival during prolonged fasting. Small species of sharks eat planktonic crustaceans and other invertebrates; large predaceous species prey on marine fishes, cephalopods, marine mammals and other vertebrates. The largest sharks (eg, basking and whale) are plankton feeders. Shark fisheries are conducted in many countries by longlines, gill nets and purse seines for food, fishmeal and leather. Shark meat is marketed fresh, frozen, salted and dried. Dogfish sharks are used extensively in biomedical research. Most sharks are harmless, but about 10% are a hazard to humans and another 10% a potential hazard. The danger of shark attack is greatly exaggerated. W.B. SCOTT

Sharp, Francis Peabody, orchardist, horticulturalist (b at Northampton, NB 1823; d at Upper Woodstock, NB 1903). When Sharp moved to Upper Woodstock in 1844, he established the first of many family orchards that developed into the major NB fruit industry. Apples and plums were exported widely to other parts of Canada and the US. At his first orchard, he imported fruit and nursery stock from England and the US. He was one of the first 2 people in N America to hybridize apple and pear varieties scientifically and was the first horticulturalist in Canada. He developed his first new apple variety, "New Brunswick," in 1853, and several followed, most notably "Early Scarlet," later known as "Crimson Beauty," produced about 1880. MARTIN K. McNICHOLL

Sharp, Mitchell William, public servant, politician (b at Winnipeg 11 May 1911). He joined the Dept of Finance in 1942 and attracted the attention of C.D. HOWE, who had him transferred to the Dept of Trade and Commerce in 1951. As associate deputy minister and then deputy minister, Sharp worked closely with Howe, providing economic analysis and writing speeches. It was made plain that the new Conservative government did not want him, and Sharp entered private business, 1958-63. Elected to Parliament for Eglinton, 1963-74, Sharp became PM PEARSON's minister of trade and commerce and then minister of finance, and was known as the leading antinationalist in the Cabinet, as well as a reformer of federal-provincial financial relations. After running unsuccessfully for the Liberal leadership, he became PM TRUDEAU's minister of external affairs, 1968-74, then president of the Privy Council. He retired from politics in 1978 and since then has been commissioner for the Northern Pipeline Agency.   ROBERT BOTHWELL

Shatford, Sidney Smith, business executive (b at Hubbards, NS 1 Dec 1864; d at Halifax 8 June 1956). In partnership with his brother, he founded NS's first oil business. He started work as a hardware clerk in Halifax, and in 1885 he and his brother established an oil-importing and wholesale business with $4000 borrowed from their father. Shatford Brothers Ltd imported kerosene and lubricating oil from New York and distributed it throughout most of NS, PEI and Newfoundland. In 1894 the business was merged with competitor Joseph Bullock of Saint John under the name of Eastern Oil Co, which was purchased by Imperial Oil 1898. Sidney Shatford then headed Imperial's operations in NS until retirement in 1930.   EARLE GRAY

Shaughnessy, Thomas George, first Baron Shaughnessy, railway executive (b at Milwaukee, Wis 6 Oct 1853; d at Montréal 10 Dec 1923). In 1869 Shaughnessy joined the Milwaukee Road as a clerk. On becoming manager in 1880, W.C. VAN HORNE promoted Shaughnessy storekeeper, and in 1882 persuaded him to join the CANADIAN PACIFIC RY as general purchasing agent in Montréal. Shaughnessy helped save the CPR from bankruptcy in 1884-85 by placating creditors, became vice-president in 1891 and president in 1899. Under Shaughnessy's leadership, the CPR became a large and profitable transportation corporation. From 1899 to 1913 its trackage in Canada increased from 11 200 km to 18 000 km and 70% of the Prairie main line was double-tracked. Shaughnessy launched the Atlantic steamship service and made the CPR a major world shipowner. Under his direction, Consolidated Mining and Smelting (now Cominco) became an important producer of lead and zinc. He retired as president in 1918 but remained chairman until his death.   JOHN A. EAGLE

Shaunavon, Sask, Town, pop 2153 (1986c), inc 1914, is located in SW Saskatchewan 70 km N of the international boundary and 110 km E of the Alberta border. With the near extinction of the buffalo during the 1870s the Plains Indians were successfully removed from the Cypress Hills-Wood Mountain area. During the late 19th and early 20th centuries ranching was the primary activity in the area and from 1910 the ranchers were forced to share the land with grain farmers. In 1913 the CPR extended its line into the area and the Shaunavon site developed. Cattle, grain and oil are the major products of the district.   DON HERPERGER

Shaw, Walter Russell, farmer, politician, premier of PEI (b at West River, PEI 20 Dec 1887; d at Charlottetown 29 May 1981). Elected leader in

1957, Shaw led the Conservatives to victory in 1959. Under Shaw, the civil service was enlarged and modernized and in 1963 the Island's electoral system was reformed. Despite the alarms over the "farm crisis" raised by Shaw when in Opposition, the number of family farms and persons engaged in farming continued to decline throughout his tenure. His government concentrated on the problems of Island development but was unable to establish resource-based secondary industry. Defeated by the Liberals under Alex CAMPBELL in 1966, he remained leader of the Opposition until 1970. Eloquent, witty and personable, Shaw remained a highly respected public figure after he retired from politics.   DAVID A. MILNE

Shaw Festival (Niagara-on-the-Lake, Ont) was founded in 1962 by lawyer/playwright/producer Brian Doherty and is the only festival in the world devoted to the production of plays by George Bernard Shaw. After an initial season of 8 amateur performances, directed by Maynard Burgess, the festival went professional. Radio producer Andrew ALLAN was appointed artistic director with Sean Mulcahy between 1963 and 1965. In 1966 Barry Morse transformed the festival into a major event, and in the decade 1967-77 Paxton Whitehead consolidated its international reputation. He broadened the repertoire to include any play falling within the long span of Shaw's life and introduced musical events and mime. Several of the productions went on tour. Housed for 11 years in the historic courthouse, this popular tourist attraction achieved permanent status when a handsome new 860-seat theatre designed by architect Ron THOM was inaugurated by Her Majesty Queen Elizabeth II on 28 June 1973. Tony Van Bridge was artistic director in 1975 during Whitehead's sabbatical. The festival faltered in 1977 with the departure of Whitehead. After interim managements by Richard Kirschner (1978) and Leslie Yeo (1979), Christopher Newton became artistic director in 1980.

Newton continued the eclectic policy begun by Whitehead, skilfully juxtaposing European farces with *Saint Joan, Camille* and even plays by Bertolt Brecht. His refreshingly offbeat seasons included revues and Edwardian musical comedies at a third festival playhouse, the Royal George, as well as unfamiliar Shavian one-act plays for lunchtime audiences. In 1982-83 the Shaw Festival enjoyed a great artistic success with Derek Goldby's production of *Cyrano de Bergerac* featuring Heath Lamberts in the title role, a Canadian actor brought to stardom by the festival. In 1983 the festival began a policy of mounting co-productions in Toronto during the winter season. The 1987 season hit was *Peter Pan*, by J.M. Barrie, with the title role played by Tom McCamus, another Canadian actor. The extensive archives of the Shaw Festival are housed at University of Guelph. *See also* THEATRE, ENGLISH-LANGUAGE.   DAVID GARDNER

Shawinigan, Qué, City, pop 21 470 (1986c), 23 011 (1981c), inc 1921, home of the Québec chemical industry, is located 30 km NW of TROIS-RIVIÈRES on the shores of the Rivière ST-MAURICE. The name derives from the Algonquin word

The hydroelectric potential of Shawinigan Falls, on the Rivière St-Maurice, led to the founding of nearby Shawinigan (*photo by John deVisser*).

Ashawenikan, meaning "portage on the crest" used to avoid the area's major waterfalls.

History After 1825 the government of Lower Canada had the territory of the Mauricie region surveyed. The first concessions were given out in 1831. Shawinigan was first the site of a waterslide (1852), built so that log booms could be sent downstream to Trois-Rivières. From 1843 to 1883 the region's very sparse population spread a little S of Shawinigan to the Grès sawmill. Shawinigan was born of the desire to exploit the hydroelectric potential of the falls. In 1899, after an extension of the Great North Ry line, Shawinigan Water & Power (SWP) built a dam and organized the development of the settlement, which then grew rapidly. Several industries, attracted by the available electricity, moved there: in 1900 Belgo-Canadian Pulp (since 1967, Consolidated-Bathurst), in 1901 Pittsburg Reduction (Alcan), and in 1903 the Carbure Co of Shawinigan (Shawinigan Chemicals).

Economy SWP began providing electricity for Montréal in 1903, but the power soon stimulated Shawinigan's own growth. The great industrial development of the early 20th century, based on paper, aluminum and chemicals, continued with the arrival of Prest-O-Lite in 1907, Shawinigan Cotton in 1909 and CIL in 1931. After the Depression of the 1930s the economy began picking up again in 1940. However, there has been a marked decline since the 1960s: the old industries have reduced or ceased activity and no significant new employer has arrived. In 1963 HYDRO-QUÉBEC took over the SWP installations.   CLAUDINE PIERRE-DESCHÊNES

Shawinigan, Lac, 3.2 km², 6.3 km long, 80 m deep, lies on Québec's Laurentian Plateau, 70 km N of Lac St-Pierre on the St Lawrence R. This lake of glacial gouging is prolonged to the E by Petit Lac Shawinigan, Lac Bernard and Lac en Croix. The Shawinigan R runs out of this last lake to meet the ST-MAURICE R at Baie-de-Shawinigan. The name comes from the Algonquin word, *Ashawenikan,* meaning "portage on the crest."   SERGE OCCHIETTI

Shawnandithit, also Nance April or Nancy, the last BEOTHUK (b *c*1801; d at St John's 6 June 1829). A member of one of the small and dwindling family groups of native Indians, Shawnandithit was the niece of DEMASDUWIT. In Mar 1823 she, her mother and her sister, all starving, were captured by English furriers at Badger Bay and taken to St John's. The authorities determined to return them, laden with presents, to their people, but no contact could be made. The other 2 women died of pulmonary consumption and Shawnandithit was taken into the household of planter John Peyton at Exploits-Burnt Is. In 1828 she was brought to the Beothuk Institution at St John's and from her its president, W.E. CORMACK, recorded valuable information about the language and customs of her unfortunate people during their last melancholy years; her deftness with pencil and sketchbook was especially useful. She too died of consumption and was buried in the military and naval cemetery.   G.M. STORY

Sheaffe, Sir Roger Hale, army officer (b at Boston, Mass 15 July 1763; d at Edinburgh, Scot 17 July 1851). Commissioned in the British army in 1778, Sheaffe was posted to Canada 1787-97, 1802-11 and 1812-13. At the Battle of Queenston Heights, 13 Oct 1812, he led the regular and militia forces to victory after Sir Isaac BROCK's death. In Apr 1813, as president and administrator of Upper Canada, he unsuccessfully defended York against an American raid.   CARL A. CHRISTIE

Shearer, John George, Presbyterian minister, social reformer (b at Bright, Canada W 9 Aug 1859; d at Toronto 27 Mar 1925). Shearer left parish work in 1900 to become secretary of the LORD'S DAY ALLIANCE, editor of the *Lord's Day Advocate* and architect of the Lord's Day Act introduced in 1906. In 1907 he became the permanent secretary of the new Committee on Temperance and Other Moral Reforms (organized in 1909 as the Board of Temperance and Reform and renamed in 1911 the Board of Social Service and Evangelism) of the Presbyterian Church in Canada. From 1918 until his death he was full-time secretary of the Social Service Council of Canada, which he helped to establish. For his speeches and articles against unsafe housing and working conditions, abuse of women and children, alcoholism, venereal disease, prostitution and political corruption, Shearer was called the mouthpiece of the social conscience of Canadian Christianity.
                                          JOHN S. MOIR

Shearwater (order Procellariiformes, family Procellariidae), medium-sized SEABIRD (up to 50 cm long) related to the albatross and FULMAR. Shearwaters are all dark or dark above and white below. They breed in large colonies which they visit only at night, and lay their single, white eggs in burrows. Only the Manx shearwater (*Puffinus puffinus*) breeds in Canada, in a small colony in Nfld. However, large numbers of Southern Hemisphere shearwaters visit Canadian waters in summer. Short-tailed shearwaters (*P. tenuirostris*) from Tasmania and sooty shearwaters (*P. griseus*) from New Zealand and Tierra del Fuego occur off BC. Some sooties and the world population of greater shearwaters (*P. gravis*) from Tristan da Cunha come up to Nfld waters; these migrants probably outnumber the local breeding population of seabirds. Shearwaters feed on squid, capelin, herring and swarms of crustaceans, and scavenge from fishing boats.   R.G.B. BROWN

Shebib, Donald, filmmaker (b at Toronto 17 Jan 1938). Shebib's *Goin' Down the Road* (1970) — perhaps the single most important film in English Canada — proved that Canadians could make feature films about English Canada that audiences would want to see. He studied cinema in Califor-

nia and returned to Canada in 1963 to direct several documentaries for the CBC. *Goin' Down the Road* built on these documentary roots as it followed the vicissitudes of 2 Maritimers in Toronto. *Between Friends* (1973) established Shebib as a major filmmaker but did poorly at the box office. He has subsequently made more commercially accessible films: *Second Wind* (1976), *Fish Hawk* (1979), *Heartaches* (1981), *Running Brave* (1983) and *The Climb* (1986). He continues to work in television between films.   PIERS HANDLING

Shediac, NB, Town, pop 4370 (1986c), 4285 (1981c), inc 1903, is located on Northumberland Str, 20 km E of MONCTON. Its name derives from a Micmac word meaning "running far back," a reference to its location on Shediac Bay at the mouth of the Scoudouc R. Although first settled by ACADIANS in the mid-1700s, it received English immigrants after 1785. Nineteenth-century prosperity was based on the export of square timber and sawn lumber to Britain, as well as on shipbuilding. Construction of a railway link with Saint John (1860) made Shediac a centre for freight and passenger traffic to and from PEI until WWI. Tourism is now the major industry in this popular summer resort, which has some of the province's finest beaches. Fishing, particularly for lobster, remains a mainstay for many residents. Each July the Shediac Lobster Festival, held annually since 1948, attracts thousands to the "lobster capital of the world."   DEAN JOBB

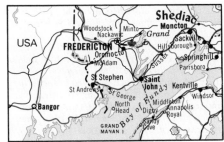

Sheep Farming Sheep (genus *Ovis*, primarily *Ovis aries*) are ruminant MAMMALS now raised in Canada primarily for their meat and milk. The French brought the first sheep to what is now Canada. In 1677 there were 85 sheep in NEW FRANCE; in 1698, nearly 1000; by the mid-18th century, just over 28 000. To the early settlers, sheep were important not only for their meat and milk but also as a source of wool for CLOTHING and TEXTILES. Today, wool production is minimal and consumption of lamb and mutton varies according to the consumer's ethnic origin, the region and season.

According to Statistics Canada, Canada's 1986 sheep and lamb population was 721 500 head, a decrease of 36% from 1985, and a decrease from a 1965 high of over one million head. Although sheep can be raised in most settled parts of the country, Canada's sheep production is so small that the demand for lamb and wool is met largely by imports. There are 3 major categories of lamb on the market: new crop lamb (about 15 kg), light lamb (about 25 kg) and heavy lamb (40 kg). Producers deal directly with consumers or sell live animals to the MEAT-PROCESSING INDUSTRY through slaughterhouses, auctions or public markets. Canadian annual per capita consumption of lamb is 0.94 kg. The promotion of fresh lamb, demand for which has risen over the past decade, should bring per capita consumption to 1.5 kg by 1990.

The breeds of sheep are categorized according to appearance, adaptation and use. Factors influencing choice of breed include type of farming operation, personal taste, availability of breeding animals, precocity, hardiness, breeding capabilities, meat quality, maternal qualities and milk production. The major breeds are grouped into 2 classes.

Breeds that pass on useful characteristics for breeder ewes (eg, climatic adaptability, maternal instinct, fertility, milk production capacity) are the so-called maternal breeds and may be used for cross-breeding purposes. Breeds that pass on useful qualities for meat-producing animals (eg, daily weight gain, food conversion, meat quality) are the paternal breeds and are also used in terminal cross-breeding with hybrid females to produce animals for meat. Some of the principal breeds in Canada are as follows.

Border Cheviot, developed in the mountainous border area between England and Scotland, is a small, cold-hardy breed, capable of surviving on poor pasture. Desirable characteristics include good mothering, good-quality meat and soft, lightweight fleece.

Dorset, developed in the English counties of Dorset and Somerset, is a prolific breed (ewes often lamb twice annually). The fleece is particularly white; ewes have a high milk-production capacity.

Hampshire, developed in England's Hampshire County, is known for its good food conversion and high daily weight gain. Hampshires are chunky sheep with a dark brown face and ears, and fine fleece.

North Country Cheviot, a cold-hardy, dark sheep with a white face, ears and legs, is native to northern Scotland. The breed yields good meat, but its fleece contains wiry fibres making it less valuable.

Oxford, a heavy breed originating in England's Oxford County, is characterized by a light body fleece and grey face, ears and legs. Ewes have good milk-production capacity.

Suffolk, a large, hardy breed originating in England's Suffolk County, is characterized by good milk production. Lambs mature early and yield high-quality meat. Head and legs have fine black hair, instead of wool.

Key technical factors influencing effective production of meat, wool and milk are selection, diet and management. Generally, a breed may be improved by working on heredity or on the environmental factors that influence heredity. Breeders at Agriculture Canada's RESEARCH STATION at Lennoxville, Qué, have been crossbreeding Dorsets, Leicesters and Suffolks for the past 15 years to produce a unique Canadian breed (the DLS breed). The Russian Romanov breed was imported in 1981 to increase lamb production in the DLS breed. The Finnish Landrace or Finnsheep is also popular in crosses because of its proneness to multiple births; litters of 3-5 lambs are not uncommon. Experiments are also taking place at the Lethbridge, Alta, research station. *See also* ANIMAL AGRICULTURE; COMMODITY INSPECTION AND GRADING.
                                          JEAN-PAUL LEMAY

Shelburne, NS, pop 2312 (1986c), 2303 (1981c), seat of Shelburne County, inc 1907, located on Shelburne harbour, lies 208 km SW of Halifax. At the close of the American Revolution some 16 000 LOYALISTS, including 2000 black Loyalists, found temporary refuge here, drawn by the magnificent harbour. Today, many 18th-century buildings remain, fishing is the mainstay of the economy and 70% of citizens trace their ancestry back to the Loyalist refugees. The historic complex on Dock Street includes 4 Loyalist houses and the John C. Williams Dory Shop built by the grandson of Loyalist Amos Williams. Shelburne was named for Lord Shelburne, prime minister of England during the American Revolution. Donald MCKAY, the famous designer and builder of clipper ships, was born in Jordan Falls, 11 km NE.
                                          MARY ARCHIBALD

Shell Canada Limited is an integrated energy resource company with head offices in Calgary. Active in Canada since 1911 (Dominion incorporation, 1925), the company is involved in natural gas and petroleum, petrochemicals and refined oil products, and alternative fuels research. Shell is the largest producer of natural gas and sulphur in Canada. The company is also working with oil sands and has constructed the first refinery in the world designed to process only synthetic crude oil; it opened in 1984. In Jan 1986 Shell Canada Ltd amalgamated with a wholly owned subsidiary, Shell Canada Resources Ltd. In 1986 the company had sales of $4.8 billion (ranking 9th in Canada), assets of $5.2 billion (ranking 17th) and 7011 employees. Shell (Netherlands/Britain) is the major shareholder, and foreign ownership stands at 72%. DEBORAH C. SAWYER

Shepherd, Francis John, anatomist, surgeon, dermatologist, medical administrator, art connoisseur and critic (b at Como, Qué 25 Nov 1851; d at Montréal 18 Jan 1929). Shepherd revolutionized the teaching of anatomy at McGill. In his time it was a common saying that McGill medical graduates "knew their anatomy." His diagnostic power, surgical judgement, technical skill and knowledge of anatomy made him one of the most successful and reliable surgeons of his generation. He was also a pioneer dermatologist. As a medical administrator, he served McGill as dean of medicine. As an art connoisseur and critic, he commanded sufficient respect to be president of the Art Association of Montréal and chairman of the board of trustees of the National Gallery at Ottawa. EDWARD H. BENSLEY

Sherbrooke, Qué, City, located 160 km E of Montréal, is the principal city of the EASTERN TOWNSHIPS. Situated in the heart of a region of lakes and mountains near Orford Provincial Park, it was for many years a commercial, industrial and railway centre. As of the 1960s, it also became a service centre. A Catholic archdiocese and headquarters of the judicial district of St-François, Sherbrooke is also the administrative centre of Québec's Region No 5.

Settlement and Development Located on ABENAKI land, Sherbrooke was initially known as Ktinéké-tolékouac or Grandes Fourches ("The Forks"), and was the site of a portage at the foot of the falls of the Magog R. The first permanent settlement was established in 1802 when American pioneers from Vermont built several mills. The village took the name of Gov Gen John Coape SHERBROOKE in 1818. The city owes its initial urban growth to industrialization, which occurred in waves from the 1840s. It became a textile centre with the establishment of Canada's first cotton manufacturing plant in 1844 and a large wool plant in 1867. The town owed its success in the 19th century as much to its dynamic anglophone businessmen, who established a regional bank and promoted railways and new industries, as to its francophone population, which supplied much of the industrial manpower.

The development of agriculture and mining in the region also enhanced Sherbrooke's role as a wholesale trade and services centre. Since the 1950s, the city has had difficulty attracting new industry and has experienced a decline in its textile and clothing industries. The founding of UNI-

Population: 74 438 (1986c) 74 075 (1981c); 129 960 (1986 CMA) 125 173 (1981A CMA)

Rate of Increase (1981-86): City 0.5%; CMA 3.8%

Rank in Canada: Twenty-second

Date of Incorporation: 1875

Land Area: City 55.42 km²; CMA 915.75 km²

Elevation: 181m

Climate: Average daily temp, July 20.0°C, Jan -9.8°C; Yearly precip 949.9 mm; Hours of sunshine 1900.8 per year

VERSITÉ DE SHERBROOKE in 1954 and the decentralization of the province's administration have helped restore much of the city's dynamism.

Cityscape Located at the confluence of the Magog and ST-FRANÇOIS rivers, Sherbrooke resembles a basin, the curved sides of which have become residential areas. After 1950 the urban community expanded along an E-W axis under the polarizing influence of the university and the outlying commercial centres. The city centre, the traditional commercial area, took on a new vitality in the 1970s. Several residential areas near the centre contain predominantly wooden buildings that display 19th-century Victorian and American architecture. The city's many open spaces, a lake located right in town and a mountain offering ski trails provide an abundant source of outdoor recreation for its citizens.

Population and Economy Because of its fluctuating industrial activity, the city's demographic growth was slow in the 19th century. It had 3000 inhabitants in 1852, 10 000 in 1891 and over 50 000 in 1951. Since 1971 (80 700) the population has declined, many people having moved to the Fleurimont, Ascot and Rock Forest suburbs. The percentage of Francophones has risen from 50% in 1871 to almost 94% today. There are 4500 Anglophones in the community.

Sherbrooke's industrial base is still dependent upon the textile and machinery industries and the food sector. Since the 1960s, however, most of the work force has been involved in the tertiary sectors of commerce, teaching, health services and regional administration.

Government and Transportation Incorporated as a city since 1852, Sherbrooke has been governed by a mayor and councillors representing 4 wards. From 1890 to 1952 the mayors were alternately francophone and anglophone. Municipal policies are now rarely the object of vehement debate and concentrate on providing sound administration and attracting new industries. Since 1908 the city has had its own electrical system, supplied by several hydroelectric dams.

For nearly a century, Sherbrooke has been a major intersection for railway lines radiating towards Montréal, Québec City, Halifax, and to Portland, Maine, and Boston, Mass. Passenger service, which had been offered since 1852 with the ST LAWRENCE AND ATLANTIC RAILROAD, ceased in 1981 but has been again offered since 1985. The city is now at the intersection of the Trans-Québec Autoroute, running N towards TROIS-RIVIÈRES and S to the US, and of the Autoroute du Canton de

Sherbrooke, Qué, owed its initial growth to industrialization after the 1840s; it became a textile centre with the establishment of Canada's first cotton factory (*courtesy City of Sherbrooke*).

l'est to Montréal. Tramways were the predominant form of urban transportation from 1897 to 1931, when trams were replaced by buses.

Cultural Life In the heart of a region that attracts many artists, Sherbrooke has an active cultural life, with the university's cultural centre, a symphony orchestra and several theatre groups. It also has a Musée des beaux-arts (1982) and Musée de sciences naturelles (1879). The city has 3 TV and 5 radio stations (one of which is English), 2 daily newspapers, the *Tribune* (French) and the *Record* (English), and 1 weekly, the *Nouvelle* (French). JEAN-PIERRE KESTEMAN

Sherbrooke, Sir John Coape, soldier, administrator, governor-in-chief of British N America (b in Eng 1764; d at Calverton, Eng 14 Feb 1830). A British army officer, Sherbrooke was stationed in Nova Scotia in 1784-85. He then saw active service in the Netherlands (1794), India (1799) and throughout the Mediterranean (1805-09). He distinguished himself while serving under Wellington in the Peninsular War (1809-10). Plagued by recurring illness, which had begun in India, Sherbrooke returned to England. In 1811 he was appointed lieutenant-governor of NS and vigorously defended the colony during the WAR OF 1812. Despite poor health, he led military campaigns, in particular an expedition up the Penobscot R through Maine which compensated partly for Sir George PREVOST's defeat at Plattsburgh in 1814. Succeeding Prevost as governor-in-chief in 1816, Sherbrooke handled his short term with competence. By 1818, however, his illness – exacerbated by a paralytic stroke – forced his retirement to England. DAVID EVANS

Sheriff In each county and judicial district in Canada sheriffs, appointed by the lieutenant-governor-in-council, serve processes (eg, writs of summonses); attend upon supreme and county court judges and maintain order in the courts (performed by constables); execute judgements, eg, seizing the judgement debtor's goods (performed by BAILIFFS); summon and supervise JURIES, and take custody of noncriminal prisoners. K.G. McSHANE

Sherman, Frank Albert, industrialist (b at Crown Point, NY 19 May 1887; d at Surfside, Fla 27 Jan 1967). Sherman worked in the steel industry at Pittsburgh, Pa, and in 1914 moved to Hamilton, Ont, to work in his brother Clifton's Dominion Steel Foundry Co (later DOFASCO), eventually becoming president and chairman. By matching salaries at the rival Stelco plant and by profit sharing, Sherman achieved labour peace and kept his plant free of unions. An active Liberal, Sherman helped raise election funds for C.D. HOWE; he was also a president of the HAMILTON TIGER-CATS. ROBERT BOTHWELL

Sherman, Frank Henry, trade unionist (b at Gloucester, Eng 10 May 1869; d at Fernie, BC 11 Oct 1909). A former chapel preacher and coal miner, he became an ardent socialist and candidate for the Alberta legislature or Parliament in 1905, 1906 and 1908. Under his unquestioned leadership as president of District 18 United Mine Workers of America (1903-09), the western miners' union expanded to a membership of over 9000 and established collective bargaining in the coalfields of Alberta and southeastern BC. Sherman was befriended by W.L. Mackenzie KING during the famous Lethbridge strike of 1906, but broke with Liberal labour policy over the application of the Industrial Disputes Investigation Act (1907) to the mining industry. When he failed to obtain adequate support from the international UMW, Sherman began discussions towards the creation of an autonomous

Canadian Miners' Federation. His policies thus anticipated the OBU and western secession by a decade. His daughter Annie Balderstone became prominent in the New Zealand miners' struggles of the 1930s; his son William succeeded to the presidency of District 18 in 1922. ALLEN SEAGER

Sheshaht, a NOOTKA Indian tribe of Barkley Sound and Alberni Inlet, Vancouver I, BC. Formerly a small independent group whose territory was confined to the outer islands of the Broken Island Group in Barkley Sound, the Sheshaht developed into a powerful tribe in the historic period through conquering and amalgamating with other groups, and taking their territories. By the mid-19th century the Sheshaht had expanded their territory to include all of the Broken Islands, most of the N shore of Barkley Sound, Alberni Inlet and the lower Somass R. Today the Sheshaht live mainly on the Tsahaheh reserve near Port Alberni. JOHN DEWHIRST

Shickluna, Louis, shipbuilder (b at Senglea, Malta 16 June 1808; d at St Catharines, Ont 24 Apr 1880). By 1835 he was engaged in ship construction at Youngstown, NY. He later moved to St Catharines and from 1838 leased a shipyard on the WELLAND CANAL which he purchased in 1845. His expanding operations significantly promoted inland navigation and contributed to the region's commercial prosperity. Between 1838 and 1880 he directed the construction of some 140 schooners, propellers, barkentines, barks and other vessels primarily designed for service on the Great Lakes. He was, in fact, perhaps the greatest 19th-century shipbuilder on the Great Lakes in Canada. He was an innovator and an original designer who was responsible for the unique Great Lakes snub-nosed schooner designed to make maximum use of the canal locks. He served as a councillor in St Catharines.
GEORGE BONAVIA AND PETER D.A. WARWICK

Shield, or Precambrian Shield, extensive structural unit of the Earth's continental crust composed of exposed Precambrian rocks (basement rocks 570 million years old or older). Shields have been unaffected by mountain-building activity since Precambrian times and, because their original mountain belts have been almost completely eroded, are slightly convex, flat, low-lying areas. The best-known examples are the Canadian Shield and the Baltic Shield in Scandinavia.

Canadian Shield The Canadian Shield covers about 4.6 million km² and extends from the arctic islands around Hudson Bay, S to the Adirondack Mts and E across Labrador. Repeated advances and retreats of ice sheets have scoured its surface and left it strewn with countless lakes, rivers, streams and ponds. Along its edge lie many of the great lakes and waterways of Canada: the eastern shores of GREAT BEAR LK, GREAT SLAVE LK, Lk ATHABASCA and Lk WINNIPEG; the northern shores of LAKE OF THE WOODS, Lk SUPERIOR and Lk HURON; and the N shore of the ST LAWRENCE R.

The origin and age of the Shield were among the great mysteries of Canadian GEOLOGY. The Shield's southern limits were traced by Alexander Murray, who examined the country below Gananoque, Bytown [Ottawa], the St Lawrence and Ottawa rivers and the perimeter from Kingston to Lk Superior in 1851-52. A.C. Lawson made an important contribution by working out the Precambrian succession in the 1880s, but a more current time scale was not developed until the 1950s, when geologists such as C.H. Stockwell had seismic and gravity measures at their disposal (*see* GEOLOGICAL HISTORY). Stockwell divided the Shield into 3 great provinces – Superior, Churchill and Grenville – and 23 subprovinces. It is now considered to fall into 9 provinces (*see* GEOLOGICAL REGIONS).

The Shield has had a profound effect on Canadian history, settlement and economic development. In pre-European times it was the home of Algonquian nomadic hunters, who developed the birchbark CANOE to travel its myriad waterways. Similar canoes were used by the COUREURS DE BOIS, VOYAGEURS and explorers to penetrate the continent. The abundant fur-bearing animals were the basis of the colonial economy until about 1810. The hegemony of MONTRÉAL was thus extended far into the wilderness, via the Ottawa R and connecting waterways into the

Typical stretch of the Shield near Coronation Gulf, NWT (*courtesy Ron Redfern, Random House Inc*).

North-West, creating the precedent for future-Canadian sovereignty over these lands.

The bare rock, thin soils, MUSKEG and insects of the Shield have presented a barrier to settlement; the agricultural frontier of eastern Canada ends abruptly at its perimeter. The railway link to the West had literally to be blasted through its rock, coincidentally exposing the Shield's great treasures: gold, silver, nickel, cobalt, zinc, copper and iron ore. Its coniferous forests and hydroelectric power support a large PULP AND PAPER industry. Gigantic power developments at CHURCHILL FALLS, Lab; JAMES BAY, Qué; Kettle Rapids, Man; and elsewhere feed electricity to the urban south. The Shield's stark and rugged beauty has attracted Canadian artists, writers, tourists and cottagers and has become almost synonymous with Canada itself. JAMES MARSH

Shields, Carol, novelist, poet (b at Oak Park, Illinois, 2 June 1935). Shields was educated at Hanover College and the U of Ottawa. The award-winning *Small Ceremonies* (1976) is the first and finest of her 4 novels to date; its narrator, biographer Judith Gill (who, like Shields, writes on Susanna MOODIE), discovers how fiction can enrich biography's more documentary account of life. Shields, who teaches at the U of Manitoba, has also written *Susanna Moodie: Voice and Vision* (1975); 2 books of poetry, *Others* (1972) and *Intersect* (1974); and a short story collection, *Various Miracles* (1985). Her latest novel, *Swann*, was published in 1987.
NEIL BESNER

Shields, Thomas Todhunter, clergyman (b at Bristol, Eng 1 Nov 1873; d at Toronto 4 Apr 1955). A self-educated man and pastor of Jarvis Street Baptist Church, Toronto, for 45 years where he edited the *Gospel Witness*, Dr Shields championed BAPTIST Christianity and British imperialism against liberal Protestantism and Roman Catholicism. He verbally abused the leaders of Catholic Québec for "slacking" in 2 world wars and was expelled from the Baptist Convention of Ontario and Quebec for his intolerant, personal attacks on professors at McMaster University. In response he founded his own denomination and seminary. TOM SINCLAIR-FAULKNER

Shilling, Arthur, artist (b at Rama IR, Orillia, Ont 19 Apr 1941; d there 4 Mar 1986). The son of Ojibwa parents, Shilling attended the Mohawk Institute Residential School (Brantford, Ont) and the Ontario College of Art. He won national acclaim at his first solo show in Ottawa in 1967. Using oil on canvas, he depicted life on the Rama Reserve, where he built an art gallery to encourage local talent. His specialty was portraits in a broad impressionist style. In May 1983 Shilling was one of 7 Canadian artists invited by Gov Gen SCHREYER to show at RIDEAU HALL, Ottawa. His paintings are in many corporate and private collections throughout N America. His life is documented in the film *The Beauty of My People* (NFB, 1978). Shilling's book *The Ojibway Dream* (1986) was posthumously published by Tundra Press, Montréal. MARY E. SOUTHCOTT

Shilo, CFB, pop 1183 (1986c), is located on the western boundary of Manitoba's Spruce Woods Provincial Forest, 195 km W of Winnipeg and 25 km E of Brandon. Most of the forest is leased to the federal government for the Shilo military reserve. Assiniboine Indians inhabited the region when the first Europeans arrived to set up trading posts along the Assiniboine R. Homesteaders followed in the 1880s but found the land unsuited to farming. Spruce Woods was created as an experimental forestry reserve 1895. Military planners soon became interested in the site and by 1910 had established Camp Sewell (later Camp

Hughes) to the NE of present-day Shilo. A busy training area during WWI, it later became a military summer camp and by 1932 a relief camp for the unemployed who began building permanent structures for a new base at Shilo. During WWII Shilo expanded into a permanent, year-round facility, and many Royal Canadian Artillery units have trained here. It became the home station of the Royal Canadian Horse Artillery in 1970 and a summer militia camp in the postwar years. Since 1974 West German troops have received tank and artillery training here under a NATO agreement. A federal-provincial monitoring committee was formed to safeguard the forest's Bald Head Hills, a rare area of sand dunes, evergreen stands and grassy plains. Military activity dominates the Shilo economy. D.M. LYON

Shiners' Wars, 1837-45, were violent outbreaks between IRISH and French Canadian lumbermen in the Ottawa Valley. After construction of the RIDEAU CANAL was completed the Irish moved to the Bytown [Ottawa] area and began displacing the French in the timber trade. Violence, primarily in the form of brawling, peaked in 1837, at the time of the highest annual Irish immigration to date and a time of financial crisis, rising prices, and increased unemployment in the lumber camps. Bytown's outraged citizens formed The Association of the Preservation of the Public Peace in Bytown, but terrorism continued until the late 1840s. The term "Shiners" may have come from the French word, *cheneur* ("oakman"); from the shiny hats worn by newcomers to the region; or from the kind of coins paid to the lumbermen.

Shinguacöuse, or Little Pine, Indian leader (b *c*1773; d at Garden R, Canada W 1854). Son of an OJIBWA woman and possibly Lavoine Barthe, a trader, Shinguacöuse became a warrior, orator and medicine man. He joined the British during the WAR OF 1812, but afterward promoted harmony between the Ojibwa and the American government. In 1832 he requested that Lt-Gov COLBORNE help establish a native settlement near Sault Ste Marie. With Allan McDonnell, a mine shareholder, Shinguacöuse devised a plan in 1849 whereby Indians might benefit, under government protection, from revenues and employment opportunities arising from mining on unsurrendered Indian territory. When the government failed to respond, Shinguacöuse, accompanied mainly by Métis and Indians, forcibly took possession of mining operations at Mica Bay that fall. Although prominent in Robinson Treaty negotiations in 1850, Shinguacöuse failed to gain recognition for his plan, since prevailing policy viewed Indians as wards, not participants, in the developing nation. JANET CHUTE

Shinplasters, 25-cent Dominion government notes that were first issued in 1870 as a temporary measure to counteract the effects of an excess of American silver coinage circulating in Canada. Shinplasters were popular and were reissued in 1900 and 1923. Over 5 million were in circulation in 1929, but in 1935 the new BANK OF CANADA began recalling them. The term may have been used initially in American revolutionary times by soldiers who used similar bills to pad their shoes.

Ship Harbour, NS, UP, pop 175 (1981c), is located 67 km E of Dartmouth. Three communities, East Ship Harbour, Head Ship Harbour and Lower Ship Harbour, share this name. Called *Tedumunaboowek* ("waterworn rock") by the Micmac, its present name is derived from a cliff in the harbour that resembled a ship under full sail. LOYALISTS from S Carolina founded the settlement in 1783. The early years were trying, owing to a shortage of supplies and the difficulty of growing crops. Fishing and lumbering remain the chief industries. JEAN PETERSON

Shipbuilding and Ship Repair are among Canada's oldest industries. The long inland waterways and coastlines, rich timber supplies, fisheries and offshore oil, together with the need to export natural resources, have generated a demand for ships. Though Canadians have demonstrated high-quality workmanship in both enterprises, and at times innovation on a world scale, success has been cyclical.

The first SAILING SHIPS built in what is now Canada were 2 small craft launched at PORT-ROYAL, Acadia, by François Gravé du Pont in 1606. The first recorded seagoing vessel, *Galiote*, was built in NEW FRANCE in 1663. Some building continued under Jean TALON and others at Québec City and a brisk industry was recorded in 1715 despite the mercantilist system which discouraged industry in the colony. As a result of encouragement by French Minister of Marine de Maurepas, Intendant Hocquart gave the industry a real impetus with the establishment of a shipyard in 1732 on the R St-Charles. The 10 merchant vessels built there that year may be termed the true start of the industry as a commercial enterprise in Canada. These merchant ships impressed French authorities and warships were also ordered for the French navy, including a ship-of-the-line mounting 70 guns built in 1750.

In 1677-78 Cavelier de LA SALLE presaged the development of a transportation system on the Great Lakes with the building on Lk Ontario of a single-decked barque of 10 tons, *Frontenac*, and 3 other vessels. This achievement was eclipsed by the construction in 1679 at Cayuga Creek on the Niagara R of the ill-fated GRIFFON, 20 m overall, perhaps 60 tons burden, to further fur-trade interests on the Upper Great Lakes. Between 1732 and 1745 a number of vessels were built, 6 for Lk Ontario and one for Lk Superior. In the Seven Years' War, the French war fleet on Lk Ontario consisted of 4 vessels, 2 rated as corsairs, *Marquise de Vaudreuil* of 14 guns and *La Hurault* of 12 guns, launched in 1756 and 1755, respectively.

The ready supply of timber for shipbuilding attracted artisans and shipwrights to the colonies after the Conquest. George HERIOT in his travels (1807) stated that vessels "from fifty to a thousand tons burthen" were constructed at Québec City and commercial vessels at Kingston. The WAR OF 1812 generated a flurry of shipbuilding. The *St Lawrence*, built in Kingston in 1814, was a 3-decker mounting 102 guns, and was larger than Nelson's *Victory*. The early years of the 19th century saw the rapid growth of ship construction in the British colonies. Vessels were built on creeks, rivers and coves in every colony of British N America – at Alma on the Bay of FUNDY; at the Ellis-Yeo property in PEI, now a historical restoration; and at shipyards extending for 20 km on both sides of the Miramichi R in NB.

The expansion of the timber trade in the early 19th century stimulated a rapid expansion of shipbuilding. The *Columbus* and *Baron of Renfrew* built in 1824 and 1825, respectively, were built of heavy timbers near Québec, sailed to England to be broken up and sold as timber in order to evade a British tax. Though freak vessels at over 90 m length, they could claim to be the largest sailing ships in the world at the time and for 30 years after. Many conventional vessels were also built, and Lévis to Lauzon in Québec became a vast timber yard and shipyard.

The construction of fishing vessels was more of a cottage industry than a commercial enterprise. A natural response to demand throughout the colonies, these vessels were built of a size and type suited to the fishery, whether inshore or off-shore. Among them was *Jenny*, built in Newfoundland in 1783, the first recorded tern (3-masted) schooner in the world.

The most colourful and profitable days of Canadian shipbuilding were from 1849 to 1895, when many famous full-rigged ships and barques were built. In 1853 some 80 ships of between 1000 and 2000 tons each were launched in the Canadas and the Maritimes. In 1858, of the 100 sailing ships of 1200 tons or more that cleared Liverpool, Eng, for Australia, 64 were Canadian built. The Shipping Register of Liverpool showed that more than 85% of the ships over 500 tons were built in British N America. In 1875, the peak year, nearly 500 ships were built in Canadian shipyards. A prominent vessel of that glorious period was MARCO POLO, built at Saint John in 1851. She was big, 1625 tons, strong, and for a time "the fastest ship in the world." Another was W.D. LAWRENCE, 2458 tons, built in 1874 at Maitland, NS, the largest Canadian-built full-rigged ship afloat. The Canadian merchant fleet in 1878 numbered 7196 vessels, of 1 333 015 aggregate tonnage, making Canada the fourth shipowning nation in the world, a position that has been regained on 2 occasions since, in 1918 and in 1944. The industry gave employment to craftsmen and lumbermen, provided bottoms for transport of goods and immigrants and, perhaps the greatest commercial advantage, had favourable influence on the balance of payments; at times ships were the most valuable exports of the colonies. Between 1786 and 1920, over 4000 wooden sailing ships exceeding 500 tons were built in eastern Canada. The fast passages made by Canadian-built ships, their great size and innovative design made them popular among British owners and contributed to Britain's commercial conquest of the seas. As iron- and steel-hulled sailing ships and steamships built in Britain, Germany and Denmark replaced wooden square-riggers, Canada found it harder and harder to compete. By 1895 the Canadian builders were out of the big-ship business, although construction of fishing schooners and coasters continued for many years. Tens of thousands of men skilled in marine iron-working, sail making, wood shaping, etc, were put out of work.

In 1809 the first Canadian STEAMBOAT, ACCOMMODATION, was built and launched in Montréal by John MOLSON adjacent to his brewery. The vessel was 26 m in length and carried passengers between Montréal and Québec City. Steam engines of greater strength were rapidly developed. The 100-hp engine of the Montréal tug *Hercules* (1823) was at the time the largest in the world. The paddle steamer ROYAL WILLIAM was built at Anse au Foulon, Qué, in 1831, with a 200-hp engine made in Montréal. In 1833 she was the first merchant vessel to make a transatlantic voyage (from Pictou to Gravesend) largely under steam. One of her owners was Samuel CUNARD of Halifax, founder of the CUNARD COMPANY. As well as pioneering the building of marine steam engines, Canada produced the first compound steam engine. The St John R steamboat *Reindeer* had a 43-hp compound engine built in Fredericton, NB, and installed in 1845.

Collingwood Shipyards (1902) now at Collingwood, Ont, was the first Canadian steel shipbuilding yard on the upper lakes. It and Canadian Vickers Ltd at Montréal, after building icebreakers and submarine sections, now concentrate on repair work. The shipyard at Pt Arthur [Thunder Bay] was built in 1912, and next year produced the passenger steamer NORONIC. By then, 1980 steamers aggregating 415 089 grt were registered in Québec and Ontario ports compared with only 598 steamers totalling 89 079 grt registered in the Maritime ports.

The Canadian shipyards of this period exhibited a versatility that remains their strength to this day, in the construction of vessels of many diverse types and special purposes, including bulk grain, coal and ore LAKE CARRIERS, passenger ships, coasters, FERRIES, ICEBREAKERS and government patrol vessels. Tugs, dredges and hopper barges, many still in service, were also built in the prewar years. The dimensions of the vessels for the St Lawrence canal system and the upper lakes were controlled by the size of the locks. As such, they were long, slender vessels efficient for that trade but unsuitable for open sea, although many of these ships did ply the N Atlantic during WWI and WWII. The need for bottoms to transport supplies overseas during WWI led the IMPERIAL MUNITIONS BOARD to place many orders for ships in Canadian yards. In 1917-18 approximately 60 steel cargo steamers of 1700-5800 grt were built, as well as submarine chasers, tugs, drifters and minesweeping trawlers. Because of urgency of demand, wooden shipbuilding was revived as well. In British Columbia alone, 134 vessels comprising 20 wooden schooners, 69 wooden steamers and 45 steel steamers were built by West Coast shipyards. Wooden steamers were also built in Montréal, Trois-Rivières, Québec and Saint John. Some steel vessels built on the lakes were constructed in halves, in order to pass through the St Lawrence canals, and then joined together at Montréal.

At the end of WWI the Canadian Government Merchant Marine Ltd was incorporated in an effort to maintain shipyard employment and to continue Canada's position in ocean shipping. As the vessels became obsolete they were not replaced, and they were sold off during the GREAT DEPRESSION. By 1936 the fleet ceased to exist. From 1930 to 1939 the Canadian shipyards built only 14 steamers exceeding 46 m in length, but in the same period many vessels for the lakes and canal trade were imported from Britain.

Canada's response to the Allies' need for ships at the outbreak of WWII was immediate, effective, and on a much larger scale than that of WWI. This quick expansion under the direction of the Dept of Munitions and Supply was managed by a cadre of resident Canadian shipbuilders and naval architects, a delegation of shipbuilders sent by the British Admiralty, and experienced managers from other Canadian industries recruited for the duration. War production peaked in 1943 and, though for a time building barely kept pace with sinkings, a stage was reached where construction had to be phased down because of a surplus of ships. At peak there were 7 shipyards building 10 000 tonners, 3 producing 4700 tonners, 10 engaged in naval work, and 62 producing tugs, lighters and landing craft. In total, 398 merchant ships and 393 naval vessels were built. The naval vessels were primarily corvettes, minesweepers, frigates, and eventually destroyers. The cargo vessels were operated by the Park Steamship Co, a crown corporation. They were sold off after the war, many to Canadian shipowners in an attempt to maintain a Canadian merchant fleet; if resold the proceeds went into escrow for the construction of new Canadian registered vessels. Most went to foreign owners (see SHIPPING INDUSTRY).

Since 1945 the Canadian shipbuilding industry has been much reduced in scale. Various subsidy programs, accelerated depreciation allowances, export development grants, and import duties helped the industry, but not sufficiently to meet the competition from abroad assisted by more generous subsidies, foreign-exchange rates, and lower wage scales.

Canadian shipyards of necessity cannot concentrate on multiple production of vessels of stan-

The Halifax shipyards, showing construction of a stern "dragger" (*photo by Barrett and MacKay/Masterfile*).

dard design or on a limited range of special service vessels, but must be capable of adapting to a very wide range of vessel types, many of them prototypes. They specialize in high-quality construction for inland and coastal trade and in government service and naval vessels. They are pre-eminent in ice-capable vessels, from the icebreaking car ferry *Abegweit*, built in 1947 for the Northumberland Strait, which established design standards for welded steel icebreakers with diesel-electric propulsion and multiple propellers, to the 23 200-hp icebreaking supply vessel *Terry Fox*, built in 1983 to support oil exploration in the Beaufort Sea. Other examples of Canadian innovation are the thorough design effort devoted to the Arctic Pilot Project; the proposed 395 m, 140 000 m³ Arctic class 10, LNG carrier; vessels for oceanographic, hydrographic and fisheries research which are of world class; the development of tug-and-barge operations on the West Coast and, in particular, self-dumping log barges. The development of hydrofoil craft, begun in Canada with the early experiments of Alexander Graham BELL in Cape Breton, was brought to success with *Bras d'Or* in 1964, a prototype of advanced design despite metallurgical faults in the foils material. Canadian shipyards have also been active in the construction of offshore oil exploration platforms, from semisubmersible rigs built by Victoria Machinery Depot Ltd in the late 1960s to jack-up rigs built at Davie Shipbuilding Co Ltd. In the 1970s Halifax Shipyards Ltd and in the early 1980s Saint John Drydock and Shipbuilding were active in semisubmersible vessel construction.

Naval construction since the war has been maintained to a degree. Canada's NATO role of submarine hunting and escort tasks has been met by a series of destroyer construction programs. From the "Tribal" class of the end of the war to the Canadian-designed "St Laurent" class of the 1950s was a quantum leap in design and production to provide an escort vessel that was the envy of other navies. "Mackenzie" class of the 1960s followed, then the new "Tribal" class and the CPF (Canadian Patrol Frigate) "City" class – of which there are 12 – currently being built. A variety of service vessels ranging from wood-and-aluminum minesweepers to replenishment vessels such as *Provider* have also been built.

Ship Repairing is a necessary service wherever

Canadian Shipbuilding and Ship Repair Assn Shipyards, 1938-86

Year	Workers Employed	Year	Workers Employed
1938	3 372	1968	9 913
1943	50 529	1973	10 654
1948	14 787	1978	10 574
1953	19 456	1983	6 821
1958	13 076	1986	7 500
1963	12 797		

ships ply and, as an exporting nation, Canada must provide such facilities. Naval strategic requirements have a bearing on the location of drydocks and repair shops on Canada's coasts; repair installations also provide employment for essential shipbuilding technical staff, managers and tradesmen during slack times between new building contracts.

On the Great Lakes are large drydocks at Pt Arthur, Collingwood and Pt Weller, all associated with shipyards and capable of docking large lake carriers. Docks at Kingston, and the St Lawrence Dry Dock and Cantin Dry Dock at Montréal for the 245-ft canalers are now gone. The major drydocks on the West Coast are at Esquimalt adjacent to Yarrows Ltd and the Burrard Dry Dock in Vancouver harbour. On the East Coast is a floating dock of 36 000-ton capacity at Halifax, and the Saint John Shipbuilding & Dry Dock Co Ltd, which when built in 1914, and for 40 years after, was the largest in the world. Lauzon has a large dock, and Montréal a floating dock similar to that at Halifax. The Newfoundland Dockyard, located virtually in the middle of the N Atlantic shipping lanes, was built of wood in 1884, and later replaced by a stone graving dock. A new ship-lift system at the same location, for the repair of deep-sea factory trawlers and offshore supply vessels, is capable of lifting 4000-ton vessels into 3 berths. Many other Canadian harbours have marine railways, ship lifts and small drydocks for repair of floating equipment and vessels. A few of these are a legacy of the wartime installations for the maintenance of frigates and corvettes and the repair of war-damaged merchant ships, but many have been built or improved since then for commercial or fishery vessel repair.

The Canadian Shipbuilding and Ship Repair Assn was formed in 1944 to ensure the continuance of a viable industry after the war and to prevent repetition of the gradual dissolution of the dearly won industry in the early 1920s. It also serves to encourage technical-information exchange within an industry where technology transfer is vital to survival. The CSSRA member shipyards currently account for over 95% of all ship construction in Canada of vessels in excess of 30 m length. Although total shipyard employment in recent "good" years is down from the peak years of 1952 and 1953 to 7500 workers in mid-1986, current manufacturing capacity is higher than at any time since WWII. An estimated 400 000 dwt tons of standard shipping could be built annually.   W.J. MILNE

Reading: Canadian Shipbuilding and Ship Repairing Assn *Annual Reports*; K. Matthews and G. Panting, eds, *Ships and Shipbuilding in the North Atlantic Region* (1977); F.W. Wallace, *The Story of Shipbuilding in Canada* (1944) and *Wooden Ships and Iron Men* (1924, repr 1973).

Shipman, Ernest G., "Ten Percent Ernie," film producer, promoter (b at either Hull, Qué, or Ottawa 16 Dec 1871; d at New York C 7 Aug 1931). The most successful film producer during the expansive period 1914-22, he was responsible for 7 feature films, all adaptations of Canadian stories and filmed on location. Educated at Ryerson, he established the Canadian Entertainment Bureau in Toronto and later became a successful promoter of theatrical stock companies in New York. Following a move to California in 1912, he became increasingly active in films as publicist, agent and then promoter. A 1918 contract for the film rights of James Oliver Curwood's stories led to the establishment in Calgary of a company to film *Back to God's Country* (1919), a major success. He then created production companies in Winnipeg, Ottawa, Sault Ste Marie and Saint John. Five of the films made were modest successes, but the last, *Blue Water* (1923), was not released. He

left Canada in 1931 and died in relative obscurity.
PETER MORRIS

Reading: Peter Morris, *Embattled Shadows* (1978).

Shippegan, NB, Town, inc 1958, pop 2801 (1986c), is located at the extreme northeastern point of mainland NB. It obtained its name from the Micmac *sepaguncheech*, meaning "duck way," the passage between the mainland and Île Lameque. The Jesuits operated a mission in the area from 1634 to 1662 and Nicolas DENYS established a trading post there in 1645. As early as 1760, Jersey fishermen visited and used the harbours and the surrounding shores and in 1777 American privateers operated in the area. The first permanent settlers who arrived after 1780 were ACADIANS, Norman French and Jerseymen, all engaged in fishing and farming. After 2 centuries, fishing and fish processing remain the main industries, although after WWII peat bogs began to be profitably exploited. BURTON GLENDENNING

Shipping Industry As one of the world's oldest transport modes, shipping, or carriage of goods by water, has played a significant role in the development of human society over the centuries. Shipping has been a crucial link by which commercial relationships have been established between widely separated parts of the world.

There are 2 major types of shipping services: shipload services, which move goods in bulk for one or 2 shippers; and liner services, which carry relatively small shipments of general cargo on a regular schedule for many shippers. Some ships are owned by firms engaged in the production or processing of goods in bulk. Examples are tankers owned by petroleum companies, and bulk carriers owned by steel companies. Most ships, however, are owned by firms whose prime business is shipping. These owners make their vessels available to importers/exporters through a highly efficient international network of shipping brokers.

History and Development Shipping is often the least expensive way of moving large quantities of goods over long distances. The existence of reliable water transportation has been a key to the economic and political well-being of most nations throughout history. For example, the merchant fleet of Great Britain during the Industrial Revolution was instrumental in the growth of that nation as a world power. Shipping services have always been an economic lifeline for Canadians. For the first settlers, ships were the source of essential supplies from the Old World, and they provided the means by which fur, agricultural, forestry and mining products could be marketed. In eastern Canada, especially in the Maritimes, a tradition based on SHIPBUILDING, fishing and trade flourished.

In 1840 Samuel CUNARD of Halifax established a transoceanic service that developed into the world-famous CUNARD CO, and by 1878 Canada ranked fourth among the shipowning nations of the world. However, in the last decades of the century, Canadian participation in shipbuilding and shipping diminished, as steel and engineering skills, which Canada lacked, became prerequisites for a successful shipbuilding industry. The 2 world wars caused temporary booms in shipping under the Canadian flag, but since 1949, when the Canadian government decided to sell off its Canadian-registered fleet, the vast majority of Canadian overseas trade has been carried in ships registered in other countries. Most Canadian-registered ships now operate on domestic routes, such as the ST LAWRENCE SEAWAY, the Great Lakes and the coastlines.

Economic Significance Shipping is especially important to Canada because of the importance of trade in the economy (in 1985, exports were

25.3% and imports 21.6% of Gross Domestic Product), and the importance of water transport in facilitating this export and import trade. About one third of exports and over a quarter of imports by value are transported by water, more than half of this by liner vessels. By weight, however, because of the volume of resource exports and oil imports, the quantity of goods carried by shipload services greatly exceeds that carried by liners.

Although the Canadian-registered deep-sea fleet is small, officers and crews are needed to operate vessels on domestic routes. Vessels arriving from abroad require a variety of services, including Canadian pilots and tugs to bring them into port, as well as repair facilities and supply services in port. The movement of the cargoes themselves also creates considerable employment. For example, longshoremen help load and unload cargoes on the docks, and many persons, such as customs and insurance agents, look after documentary and other related requirements. Shipping agents, located in many Canadian cities, strive to sell their company's shipping services to prospective customers.

Domestic and Transborder Routes Domestic shipping can be divided into 3 main categories. East Coast traffic consists primarily of fuel, pulpwood and general cargo shipments to Newfoundland and along the coastlines of the Maritime provinces and into the St Lawrence. The St Lawrence-Great Lakes traffic is by far the most important route. The main commodity movements are grain from the Lakehead to the St Lawrence ports, and IRON ORE from Canada to the US (*see also* CANALS AND INLAND WATERWAYS). West Coast shipping services include the movement of forest products and other natural resources, often by tug and barge operations. On both the East and West coasts there is an extensive network of ferry services (*see* FERRIES). Other shipping services include occasional intercoastal movements of bulk commodities, barge services on the MACKENZIE R and supply services to arctic communities. Shipping is a key to the development of Canada's North, a means by which natural resources can be reached (*see* TRANSPORTATION IN THE NORTH). The supply lines to many remote northern communities are maintained as the weather permits. In 1969 the American tanker SS *Manhattan* successfully navigated the NORTHWEST PASSAGE with the aid of a Canadian Coast Guard vessel, thereby proving that mineral and petroleum resources in remote northern areas could be reached by water (*see* ICEBREAKERS).

Overseas Shipping Canada's most important overseas trading partners are Japan, Great Britain and other western European nations, so that the busiest shipping routes are the N Atlantic and the N Pacific. One-third of Canada's trade with the US moves by water. Significant ties are maintained with all regions of the world, and bulk shipping services are available as needed. Canada's trade is carried in vessels registered in many different countries. Many of these deep-sea vessels are registered in so-called flag-of-convenience nations, such as Liberia and Panama, where favourable tax and legal environments permit lower-cost operations.

Ships and Harbour Facilities are efficiently serving Canadian trade. Specially designed ships and HARBOURS have been built to accommodate particular commodities. In eastern Canada, for example, ships called LAKE CARRIERS are built to the maximum allowable seaway dimensions. Maximum-sized lakers can carry about 29 000 tonnes (28 000 cargo capacity, 1000 fuel etc). On the West Coast, the self-dumping log barge has been developed for use in the forest industry. Roberts Bank, BC, is the site of a large coal superport, specially designed to handle the large volume of coal

which arrives by rail for export overseas.

Canadian Shipping Today Few Canadian-flag ships operate deep-sea routes. However, some Canadian-incorporated companies operate foreign-registered ships. The major Canadian companies owning deep-sea fleets are CP Ships Ltd, Cast North America Ltd, Papachristidis Maritime Inc and Fednav Ltd. Owing to government regulations that give preference in coastal waters to Canadian-flag vessels, all ships operating domestic routes are registered in Canada, unless a foreign-flag vessel is granted a waiver.

As of 30 June 1985 the Canadian-flag fleet of vessels over 100 gross registered tons (grt) was 3.3 million grt. By comparison, the Liberian fleet at 58.2 million grt was the largest, the Panamanian at 40.7 million grt was second; the US fleet at 19.5 million grt was sixth and the British fleet at 14.3 million grt was eighth (Lloyds Register of Shipping). Most Canadian-registered merchant vessels operate on domestic routes, although recent technological development has seen the introduction of several vessels constructed for the Great Lakes-St Lawrence Seaway traffic which are also capable of transoceanic voyages.

The present lack of a Canadian-flag deep-sea fleet is a source of frequent debate. Some importers and exporters argue that foreign-flag operations permit lower-cost operations and thereby help to keep Canadian trade competitive. This view is opposed by others who feel that selective employment of Canadian vessels could be efficient if the government would provide tax concessions comparable, for example, to those of Great Britain. A federal Task Force on Deep-Sea Shipping recommended in 1985 that Canadian International Shipping Corporations should not be taxed on income until distributed. The proposal has not been implemented.

Regulation Most shipping is by nature international – the carriage of goods between countries and across international waters. A ship may be owned, financed, registered, insured, and managed, each in a different country. When a ship is registered in any given country, it becomes subject to the laws of that country at all times. Each country has the right to establish its own shipping laws. International shipping conventions have been reached by a number of intergovernmental organizations, such as the International Labour Organization (ILO), the United Nations Conference on Trade and Development (UNCTAD), and the International Maritime Organization (IMO). Many of the conventions have been ratified by Canada (*see* INTERNATIONAL LAW; LAW OF THE SEA).

In Canada, shipping falls under the jurisdiction of the federal Department of TRANSPORT. The Canada Shipping Act sets out the basic rules for ships flying the Canadian flag or operating in Canadian waters. The CANADIAN COAST GUARD ensures that ships meet the requirements of the Shipping Act and follow pollution-prevention procedures. The National Transportation Agency (formerly CANADIAN TRANSPORT COMMISSION) is responsible for economic regulation: for example, shipping conferences must file their rates with the Agency. Ports Canada administers the major ports in Canada.

Recent Developments The United Nations Conference of the Law of the Sea (UNCLOS) has established a new regime of international maritime law of interest to shipowners and shippers. UNCLOS defines international maritime boundaries and, therefore, the extent of coastal state jurisdiction in environmental-protection and coastal shipping regulation. UNCTAD has tried to help developing nations participate in international shipping. The Code of Conduct for Liner Conferences was drawn up under the auspices of UNCTAD. It suggests that countries may reserve 40% of their liner cargo to national carriers.

Significant technological advances have occurred in shipping. Large specialized ships are used for bulk cargoes; general cargo is carried by liners in containers. In Canada, improvements have included the development of the self-unloading carrier for use particularly in the Great Lakes-St Lawrence Seaway trade. Liquefied-natural-gas (LNG) carriers may yet transport western natural gas to Japan. Special vessels are being discussed for the movement of petroleum and mineral resources from arctic areas. Petroleum may eventually be carried by specially strengthened vessels or even by submarine tankers. The development of trade will be linked, as always, to cost-reducing technologies in shipping. TREVOR D. HEAVER

Shoctor, Joseph Harvey, lawyer, theatrical producer (b at Edmonton 18 Aug 1922). A theatre buff and disappointed actor and Broadway impresario, Shoctor was instrumental in the establishment of Edmonton's first professional theatre, the CITADEL, in 1965, using a run-down Salvation Army building as its first venue. Concentrating on the production of commercially attractive plays, the Citadel, with Shoctor as president and executive producer, quickly gained enough public support to justify the construction of a magnificent new $6.5-million complex that opened in 1976. Although he has been criticized for using too many foreign plays and actors in his own productions, Shoctor has been active in promoting the development of Canadian theatre, and has served as vice-president of the National Theatre School of Canada. The recipient of numerous public honours, he was awarded the Order of Canada in 1986. STANLEY GORDON

Shooting As Canada was developing as a nation, the sport of shooting played an integral role in the life-style of its early settlers, both as a means for survival and for amusement and enjoyment as a recreational pastime. Firearms could be found in every home, and as the nation developed so did the sport of shooting. Today, it is one of the fastest-growing sports in the world, offering the widest appeal to men and women, young and old, and to the recreational or more competitive participant. Shooting can truly be called a lifetime sporting activity. Shooting is a diversified sport that can be practised in a variety of forms and with an array of firearms. The 3 main types of arms are the rifle, pistol and shotgun. During the 1860s, rifle associations were formed in Canada to accommodate the growing interest in shooting sports. The first record of a Canadian team representing Canada abroad was in 1871 when a full-bore team shot at Wimbledon, Eng. By 1890, shooting clubs had developed in most provinces.

Rifle shooting is divided into 3 basic categories based on the type of rifle used: smallbore, fullbore and air rifle. Further subdivisions in competitive shooting are based on the type of shooting position: prone, kneeling and standing. The average weight of a rifle is between 5 and 8 kg. Targets range in distance from 10 to 300 m. The rifle events included in the Olympics are, for men, air rifle, prone smallbore, 3-position smallbore and running game target, and for women, standard rifle and air rifle.

The pistol, designed to be light in weight, was invented by an Italian, Caminello Vitelli, in 1540 and its name derives from his home town of Pistola. Competitive pistol shooting is growing rapidly in Canada and is as popular as other forms of shooting. Some of the most common pistols used today are the rim fire, air, and centre-fire pistols. In competitive pistol shooting the targets range from 10 to 50 m, depending on the event. In the Olympics there are 3 pistol events: rapid fire and free for men and match pistol for women.

The third category of firearms, the shotgun, is used in clay pigeon shooting, where saucerlike clay targets are released into the air at various angles. There are 2 types of clay pigeon shooting – trapshooting and skeet. Trapshooting dates from the early 19th century in England. Because the supply of birds had been severely exhausted throughout the 1880s, marksmen had to find a substitute. In 1880 George Ligowsky of Cincinnati, Ohio, developed the first clay pigeon, which was made of finely ground clay mixed with water and baked. The first record of a trapshooting competition in Canada was the Canadian Clay-Pigeon Championships held in Jan 1886 at Carlton Place, Ontario. Trapshooting clubs were established throughout the country in the late 1880s and early 1890s. There are 2 types of trapshooting in Canada: International Clay Pigeon shooting (also known as Olympic Trap) and ATA (Amateur Trapshooting Assn) trapshooting. A 12-gauge shotgun is used in both. In International Clay Pigeon shooting there are 15 machines that throw the target at various angles between 0° and 45° horizontal and at different heights for a distance of 70 to 80 m. Competitors are allowed 2 shots at each clay pigeon. In ATA trapshooting one machine is used to throw the clay pigeon 50 m at various angles between 0° and 22°. Only one shot is taken by competitors. International Clay Pigeon shooting was first introduced into the Olympics in 1900.

Skeet shooting was started in the US in 1926. Intended as a way to help shooters improve their field shooting, it is now an intensely competitive and popular sport. There are 2 types of skeet shooting in Canada: International Skeet and NSSA (National Skeet Shooting Assn) or American skeet. The 3 significant differences in International and American skeet are the starting position of the gun, the variable-time release system for throwing the target, and the distance to which targets are thrown – 65 m versus 50 to 55 m. Skeet shooting was introduced into the Olympics in 1968 in Mexico City.

Shooting has been a recognized Olympic sport since the revival of the modern Olympics in 1896 and the founder, Baron Pierre de Coubertin, was a renowned French pistol champion. The International Shooting Union (ISU) was formed in 1907 to oversee and implement the rules, regulations and safe conduct of shooting competitions. Canada applied for membership in the ISU in 1908, and that same year sent a shooting team for the first time to the Olympics. Walter EWING, a trapshooter, was one of Canada's gold medallists. At the 1987 Pan-Am Games, Canada won 5 golds, 2 silvers and 7 bronzes.

A national organization was formed in Canada in 1932 under the name of the Canadian Small Bore Rifle Assn. In 1949 it became the Canadian Civilian Assn of Marksmen. The present name, the Shooting Federation of Canada (SFC) was authorized in 1964 when the trap and skeet associations affiliated to form one umbrella organization. The SFC is responsible for the co-ordination and administration of all programs regarding Olympic-style shooting sports in Canada. *See also* G. GENEREUX; B. HARTMAN; G. OUELLETTE and S. NATTRASS. SUSAN M. NATTRASS

Shooting Star (genus *Dodecatheon*), perennial herbaceous plant of Primulaceae family (primrose). Most of the 13 known species are native to western N America; 6 to Canada. *D. hendersonii* and *D. jeffreyi* occur in coastal BC; *D. dentatum* in southern BC; *D. frigidum* in northern BC, coastal YT and Mackenzie R delta. These 4 species grow on damp meadows, heaths and streambanks, in low to high elevations. *D. conjugens* ranges from southeastern BC to southwestern Saskatchewan in seepage areas, in sagebrush plains and up to alpine meadows. *D. pauciflorum,* the most widespread, is found from the Mackenzie Delta to southern Manitoba, in meadows, open woods, moist slopes and saline places.

Shoppers Drug Mart was first opened in Toronto in 1962 by Murray Koffler, a pharmacist, although he had already opened a store known as Koffler Associated Drugstore in 1952. The 1962 store became the prototype on which the Shoppers Drug Mart Limited concept was developed. At the time of the public underwriting in 1968, there were 53 retail drug outlets doing an annual sales volume of $27.8 million. A major expansion followed throughout the 1970s and 1980s, and today the company has 3 corporate divisions: Shoppers Drug Mart/Pharmaprix (450 stores operating across Canada), Howie's (10 stores in Ont and Man) and Super X Drugs (80 stores in Ont). There are 16 000 employees and total retail sales have exceeded $1.7 billion. The Shoppers Drug Mart concept provides pharmacists with an opportunity to operate their own businesses while benefiting from the management efficiencies and economies of scale inherent in being part of the Shoppers Drug Mart network of stores. Each store is owned and operated by a licensed pharmacist, called an associate, and in return for an annual royalty fee, the associate has access to a variety of exclusive umbrella services designed to enhance sales and profitability at store level. Shoppers Drug Mart Limited is a wholly owned subsidiary of Imasco Limited, a Canadian-based company with a broad range of manufacturing, retailing and investment interests.

Shopping Centre, a group of retail and service establishments developed and managed as a unit, having one or more major "anchor" tenants and usually with its own parking area. Prototypes were Market Square, Lake Forest, Ill (1916), and Country Club Plaza, Kansas City, Mo (1922). Suburban shopping centres developed rapidly after WWII to serve new residential subdivisions. Planner E.G. Faludi promoted the concept in an influential Canadian article in 1949. Norgate Shopping Centre, St-Laurent, Qué (M.M. Kalman, 1949), Dorval Shopping Centre, Dorval, Qué (Eliasoph and Bercowitz, with M.M. Kalman, 1950), and Park Royal Shopping Centre, West Vancouver, BC (C.B.K. Van Norman and J.C. Page, 1950), were among Canada's first; other early centres were York Mills and Sunnybrook near Toronto. Early shopping centres were one-storey "strips" or L-shaped with entrances facing a large parking lot. The entrances subsequently turned away from the cars and towards an internal sheltered and landscaped walkway; eg, Don Mills Shopping Centre, Don Mills, Ont (John B. Parkin and Associates, 1957) and Rockland Shopping Centres, Town of Mount Royal, Qué (Ian Martin and Victor Prus, 1958).

Walkways were next enclosed entirely to create a climate-controlled space. The first was Southdale Centre, Edina, Minnesota (Victor Gruen, 1954-56), modelled in part on European pedestrian arcades, such as the Galleria Vittoria Emanuele in Milan. An early Canadian example of an enclosed, all-weather "mall" (derived from "pall-mall," a game, and the long grass field on which it was played) was Yorkdale Shopping Centre, North York, Ont (John B. Parkin and Associates, 1960-64), the largest to that date in Canada (118 959 m², with 2 department stores, a supermarket, and 90 shops); it was an early regional mall located at the intersection of 2 superhighways. Multiple levels of shops increased density and reduced distances, as at Bayshore Shopping Centre, Nepean, Ont (Petroff and Jerulaski, 1973; enlarged from 2 to 3 storeys, 1986-87). Older shopping centres were continually upgraded and renamed to compete with newer ones. The enclosed mall has become a centre of social activity, often with recreational amenities, culminating in the mammoth WEST EDMONTON MALL (Maurice Sunderland Architecture Inc, 1981-85, 5.2 million sq ft), with more than 800 stores and services; and 7 recreation and amusement parks.

Suburban and regional shopping centres have had a detrimental impact on downtown commercial areas. NS, PEI and NB all introduced regulatory legislation in the late 1970s. Canada, more than the US, maintained its commitment to its cities. Wellington Square, London, Ont (developed by Webb & Knapp, 1958-60), was claimed to be the first downtown shopping centre in N America. Underground shopping centres were created beneath office-tower complexes, eg, PLACE VILLE MARIE, Montréal (I.M. Pei with Ray Affleck, 1956-65), and Pacific Centre, Vancouver (Victor Gruen and Associates, with McCarter, Nairne, and Partners, 1969-76); within towers, eg, Scotia Square, Halifax (Allward and Gouinlock, 1969); or as above-ground developments, eg, Midtown Plaza, Saskatoon (Gordon R. Arnott and Associates, 1969-70). The EATON CENTRE, Toronto (Zeidler Partnership and Bregman and Hamann, 1976-79), has been particularly successful at integration into the city's infrastructure and revitalizing the inner city. A recent trend has been the rehabilitation of groups of old buildings to become shopping centres, such as Market Square, Saint John, NB (Arcop Associates, with Mott, Myles, and Chatwin, 1980-83). Another is the simulation of urban design with separate buildings creating images of streets. In doing this, Sundial Square, Tsawwassen, BC (Cornerstone Architects, 1985), almost comes full circle to Lake Forest's Market Square of 1916.

Most shopping centre retail outlets are large department stores, supermarkets, chains and franchises familiar to the large national developers who build them and control the "tenant mix." A few developers have immense shopping-centre holdings; one is Trizec Corp (owned by Olympia & York Developments Ltd and Edper Investments), which has 50 large shopping centres and owns an interest in 2 large American developers of shopping centres, and another is the Oxford Development Groups Ltd, with some 100 shopping centres.   HAROLD KALMAN

Shore, Edward William, hockey player (b at Ft Qu'Appelle, Sask 25 Nov 1902; d at Springfield, Mass 16 Mar 1985). He attended the Manitoba Agricultural Coll, played senior hockey in Melville and turned professional with Regina Caps and Edmonton Eskimos of the Western Hockey League. The WHL went bankrupt and Shore was sold to the Boston Bruins in 1926. Called the "Iceman," Shore was aloof and aggressive, a fearless rushing defenceman of legendary toughness. He was a brilliant and exciting player, but combative as well, and his career was marred by controversy. In Dec 1934 he almost killed "Ace" Bailey with a vicious check, and he himself suffered numerous serious injuries as a result of violent play. He was the greatest defenceman of his day, and was awarded the HART TROPHY (most valuable player) 4 times. Tales of his eccentric, even bizarre behaviour as owner of the AHL Springfield Indians, which he purchased in 1939, have become part of hockey folklore. For example, he made his netminders practise with a belt around their necks, tied to the crossbar of the goal. However, he remained widely respected for his astute understanding of the sport's fundamentals.   JAMES MARSH

Short Fiction in English encompasses a wide range of forms, including the ESSAY, sketch and short story; and elements of all these forms may blend in individual works, as in "The Village Inside" and "Predictions of Ice" from Hugh HOOD's *Around the Mountain: Scenes from Montreal Life* (1967). Such questions of form tantalize writers and readers. Hugh MACLENNAN, for example, has composed nearly 400 essays and only one short story ("An Orange from Portugal," which he later called an essay) yet has remarked that "The secret of writing a successful personal essay ... is to turn it into a short story." There are other ways of classifying short fiction – the most time-honoured category, in which Canadian writers like Ernest Thompson SETON and Charles G.D. ROBERTS have made major contributions, being the animal story. Another category, in which Gregory CLARK, Morley CALLAGHAN, Hugh Hood, Mordecai RICHLER, W.P. KINSELLA and George BOWERING have excelled, is the sports story. A third category is the writer's story, in which authors momentarily unmask themselves as they examine their lives as writers, and sometimes even question the purposes of their fiction. The number of such subgenres is great and includes initiation stories, war stories, mystery, science-fiction and adventure stories, humorous stories, ethnic stories, etc.

Canadian short fiction has always maintained close associations with the popular markets provided by newspapers and LITERARY MAGAZINES. A pattern of first publication in periodicals and subsequent collection in book form was established in the 19th century and has continued to the present day. It began with Thomas MCCULLOCH, whose "Letters of Mephibosheth Stepsure" was first published in the *Acadian Recorder*, 1821-23, but was not collected in book form until 1862. Satirist Thomas Chandler HALIBURTON's "The Clockmaker" was first published in Joseph HOWE's *Novascotian* in 1835-36, then expanded into book form in 1836, with sequels in 1838 and 1840. In total, Haliburton published 10 collections of sketches. Portions of Susanna MOODIE's ROUGHING IT IN THE BUSH were first published in *The Literary Garland* before appearing in book form in 1852. Stephen LEACOCK published SUNSHINE SKETCHES OF A LITTLE TOWN in *The Montreal Daily Star* (Feb-June 1912), then as a book later the same year.

Since the 1920s the connections between short fiction and newspapers or magazines have remained strong, as seen in the publication of work by Raymond KNISTER, Morley Callaghan, Mavis GALLANT, Alice MUNRO, Hugh Hood, Jack HODGINS and Leon ROOKE in periodicals as diverse as *This Quarter, Toronto Star Weekly, The* TAMARACK REVIEW, *The Malahat Review, Canadian Fiction Magazine, Journal of Canadian Fiction* and *The New Yorker*. Several writers have also edited newspapers, magazines or anthologies.

Sketches Critics Carole Gerson and Kathy Mezei define the sketch as "an apparently personal anecdote or memoir which focuses on one particular place, person, or experience, and is usually intended for magazine publication." Its colloquial tone and informal structure relate it to the epistolary form employed in several early Canadian works. One common kind is the humorous or satirical sketch, as found in the works of McCulloch, Haliburton and Leacock. A second kind is the autobiographical, descriptive or travel sketch, as practised by Howe, William "Tiger" DUNLOP, Catharine Parr TRAILL, Anna Jameson, Archibald LAMPMAN, William Wilfred CAMPBELL, Duncan Campbell SCOTT, Sara Jeannette DUNCAN and Frederick Philip GROVE. Raymond Knister's country sketches about Corncob Corners represent a third kind of sketch.

The sketch had slipped into the shadow of the short story by the late 1920s, although it has continued in the works of several humorists, including Paul HIEBERT (SARAH BINKS, 1947), Robertson DAVIES (*The Diary of Samuel Marchbanks*, 1947, *The Table Talk of Samuel Marchbanks*, 1949, *Samuel Marchbanks' Almanack*, 1967, and the omnibus *The Papers of Samuel Marchbanks*, 1985) and Earle BIRNEY (*Big Bird in the Bush*, 1978), as well as in such AUTOBIOGRAPHICAL WRITING as Emily CARR's KLEE WYCK (1941) and Mordecai Richler's *The Street* (1969). Hood's *Around the Mountain* is an important late-20th-century contribution to the history of the sketch in Canada.

Animal Stories The most distinctive early contribution by Canadians to short fiction was the animal stories of Seton and Roberts. According to critic Alec Lucas, Seton's first book, WILD ANIMALS I HAVE KNOWN (1898), "established ... the realistic animal story." Roberts's first full collection was *The Kindred of the Wild* (1902). The Canadian tradition of the animal story has continued to thrive, not only in the nonfictional and fictional prose writing of naturalists and storytellers Roderick HAIG-BROWN, Fred BODSWORTH, Sheila BURNFORD and Farley MOWAT, but also in the highly literary, formally conceived short fiction of Dave GODFREY (*Death Goes Better with Coca-Cola*, 1967).

Scott, Callaghan, Wilson, Gallant and their Successors In the introduction to his pioneer anthology *Canadian Short Stories* (1928), Raymond Knister writes of the "unobtrusive influence" of D.C. Scott's story cycle *In the Village of Viger* (1896) and praises it as "a perfect flowering of art." Subsequent critics, such as Stan Dragland, have supported Knister's view. *In the Village of Viger* was followed by *The Witching of Elspie* (1923) and *The Circle of Affection* (1947). Scott's work looks back to 19th-century American gothic and romantic and local-colour writing, yet its ironic tone connects it with mid-20th-century writing, and his use of imagery anticipates the poetically conceived short stories written later in the century. Moreover, as a unit, *In the Village of Viger* is a foundation stone in the Canadian tradition of the story cycle.

In editor Robert WEAVER's view, Morley Callaghan was "the first and most important of the modern short-story writers in Canada." Callaghan was also a significant influence on writers such as Norman LEVINE, whose first book of stories, *One Way Ticket*, was published in 1961, and Hugh Hood, whose first book of stories, *Flying a Red Kite*, appeared in 1962. Callaghan's early books of short fiction were *A Native Argosy* (1929), the novella *No Man's Meat* (1931) and *Now That April's Here and Other Stories* (1936). Most of these stories were collected, with a number of more recent ones, in *Morley Callaghan's Stories* (1959). *No Man's Meat & the Enchanted Pimp* (1978) contains a slightly revised version of his 1931 novella and a new novella. Other old stories were collected in *The Lost and Found Stories of Morley Callaghan* (1985). Callaghan's stories were important for his choices of subject and situation; his modern, urban, even international outlook; his understanding of the importance and the difficulty of writing about everyday life; and the intimately human moral complexities that he explored. Furthermore, as poet Margaret AVISON has observed, the stories created a strong feeling of immediacy because of his special and new way of using words plainly. Perhaps even more important to the succeeding generation of writers was the reputation that Callaghan had made for himself.

Callaghan did not establish a standard of stylistic elegance. That achievement belonged to Ethel WILSON. Two novellas by Wilson, "Tuesday and Wednesday" and "Lilly's Story," were published as *The Equations of Love* (1952); some of her short stories, first published in magazines, appeared in *Mrs. Golightly and Other Stories* (1961); and further stories were collected posthumously in *Ethel Wilson: Stories, Essays, and Letters* (1987). Wilson's fiction – novels, novellas and short stories –

significantly influenced Canadian writers from the late 1940s to the early 1960s, including Margaret LAURENCE and Alice Munro, both major contributors to the history of short fiction in Canada. Laurence's first book of stories, *The Tomorrow-Tamer and Other Stories*, was published in 1963. Her story cycle *A Bird in the House* (1970), stands with Scott's *In the Village of Viger*, Leacock's *Sunshine Sketches of a Little Town* and Hood's *Around the Mountain* as major benchmarks for subsequent creators of story cycles (or sketchbooks) in Canada. Munro's first book of stories, *Dance of the Happy Shades* (1968), contained the best of her work from nearly 2 decades. By the 1980s, Munro had the best popular and international reputation of Canadian short story writers. She emerged as the writer most often identified with the rebirth of the Canadian short story, and as the writer most prominently concerned with trying to shape short stories into coherent books or story cycles – notably in *Who Do You Think You Are?* (1978).

The most truly international of Canadian short-story writers, however, are Mavis Gallant and Clark BLAISE. Gallant's *The Other Paris* (1956), *My Heart Is Broken* (1964), *The Pegnitz Junction* (1973), *The End of the World and Other Stories* (1974), *From the Fifteenth District* (1979), *Home Truths* (1981) and *Overhead in a Balloon: Stories of Paris* (1985) brought a more intricate internationalism, a richly textured political awareness and exquisite craft to Canadian short fiction. These remarkable features also characterized the work of Clark Blaise, in *A North American Education* (1973), *Tribal Justice* (1974) and *Resident Alien* (1986).

Leon Rooke and Hugh Hood Leon Rooke published *Last One Home Sleeps in the Yellow Bed* (1968) in the US before moving to Canada, and numerous books of his fiction have subsequently appeared in both countries. His achievement, as Blaise and John METCALF have recognized, lies in his mastery of voices, tones and especially language – from Rooke's native American South back to Renaissance England and ahead to contemporary times. This mastery, amply demonstrated in his seventh and eighth volumes of short fiction, *Sing Me No Love Songs I'll Say You No Prayers* (1984) and *A Bolt of White Cloth* (1984), sets Rooke in a class almost by himself – with the exception of Hugh Hood.

Hood's subtle explorations of the possibilities of language and form began with the publication of *Flying a Red Kite* and *Around the Mountain*, then continued in *The Fruit Man, The Meat Man & The Manager* (1971) and *Dark Glasses* (1976). His fifth and sixth collections of new work, *None Genuine Without This Signature* (1980) and *August Nights* (1985), further exemplify the union of language, feeling and form. "The Woodcutter's Third Son" is a quietly dazzling treatment of the conflicting implications for human character of magical folklore and sacred scripture. "Every Piece Different" represents a moving personal testament and an important declaration of the writer's continued commitment to 'making it new.'

Experimental Writing A number of writers of short fiction have created works that, in the words of critic W.H. New, "strive for the expression of a total linguistic gesture: the restructuring of the world in the mind of the writer/reader." As examples New cites Malcolm LOWRY's *Hear Us O Lord from Heaven Thy Dwelling Place* (1961), George Elliott's *The Kissing Man* (1962), Godfrey's *Death Goes Better with Coca-Cola*, Ray Smith's audacious collection *Cape Breton is the Thought-Control Centre of Canada* (1969) and Blaise's *A North American Education*. Smith's *Cape Breton* has been followed by 2 verbally and structurally and psychologically exciting books, *Lord Nelson Tavern* (1974) and *Century* (1986). God-

frey's *Death Goes Better* was also followed by 2 extraordinary volumes, *I Ching Kanada* (1976) and *Dark Must Yield* (1978). Other interesting experimental works published since the 1960s include Lawrence Garber's *Garber's Tales from the Quarter* (1969) and *Circuit* (1970); Matt COHEN's *Columbus and the Fat Lady and Other Stories* (1972), *Night Flights* (1978), *The Expatriate* (1982) and *Café Le Dog* (1983); Terrence Heath's *the truth & other stories* (1972); Gwendolyn MACEWEN's *Noman* (1972) and *Noman's Land* (1985); Andreas Schroeder's *The Late Man* (1972); George Bowering's *Flycatcher & Other Stories* (1974), *Protective Footwear: Stories and Fables* (1978) and *A Place to Die* (1983); John GLASSCO's *The Fatal Woman* (1974); Rudy WIEBE's *Where Is the Voice Coming From?* (1974), *Alberta/A Celebration* (1979) and *The Angel of the Tar Sands and Other Stories* (1982); bp NICHOL's *Craft Dinner* (1978); Sheila WATSON's *Four Stories* (1979), expanded to *Five Stories* (1984); David Arnason's *Fifty Stories and a Piece of Advice* (1982) and *The Circus Performer's Bar* (1984); Margaret ATWOOD's *Murder in the Dark* (1983); Phyllis GOTLIEB's *Son of the Morning and Other Stories* (1983); Stan Dragland's *Journey Through Bookland and Other Passages* (1984); and Robin SKELTON's *The Man Who Sang in His Sleep* (1984) and *Telling the Tale* (1987).

Continuing Concerns and Evolving Forms Short fiction has many forms and purposes, yet trends exist. Jack Hodgins (*Spit Delaney's Island: Selected Stories*, 1976, and *The Barclay Family Theatre*, 1981) writes, in part, to challenge "a reader's concept of reality." Like Hugh Hood, Leon Rooke and John Metcalf (from *The Lady Who Sold Furniture*, 1970, through *Adult Entertainment*, 1986), Hodgins believes that writers must recognize the moral implications of their work. Nevertheless, there are major differences between these writers and earlier moral realists such as Grove, Callaghan, Sinclair ROSS, W.O. MITCHELL, Ernest BUCKLER and Margaret Laurence. As John Metcalf states in "Editing the Best" (*Kicking Against the Pricks*, 1982), "Where twenty years ago Canadian stories stressed content – what a story was *about* – the main emphasis now is on the story as verbal and rhetorical *performance*." These differences can be perceived in the evolution of some writers' conceptions of the short story. Munro's stories, for example, move from her early narrative style towards a freer, more open, more dreamlike form evident in such collections as *The Moons of Jupiter* (1982) and *The Progress of Love* (1986). This movement is true also of the development of Canadian short-story writing in general.

New Directions Hood's "The Woodcutter's Third Son," from *None Genuine Without This Signature*, the title story of Rooke's *The Birth Control King of the Upper Volta* (1982) and Metcalf's "Gentle as Flowers Make the Stones," from *The Teeth of My Father* (1975), represent 3 important directions that late-20th-century Canadian short fiction is taking: towards allegory of the human spirit, fantasy and poetic expression. The allegorical quality of Hood's writing is also evident, to varying degrees, in works by Rooke, Blaise, Hodgins, Terence Byrnes, Guy VANDERHAEGHE and Peter Behrens. The fantastic character of Rooke's stories can be found as well, again to varying degrees, in the writing of H.R. Percy, Elliott, Hood, MacEwen, Schroeder, Wiebe, Margaret Gibson, Hodgins, Seán Virgo, Atwood and Carol SHIELDS. The poetic quality which is a mark of Metcalf's writing is apparent also in the structural and emblematic keys to stories by many of Metcalf's finest contemporaries. All 3 directions are represented in the opening paragraph of W.P. Kinsella's elegy for rock singer Janis Joplin, "First Names and Empty Pockets," from *Shoeless Joe Jackson Comes to Iowa* (1980).

Reputations Canadian writers of short fiction, like authors in other genres, are subject to fluctuations in popularity. As personal likes shift back and forth between plain style and verbal play or between realism and fantasy, individual writers' reputations rise and fall accordingly – regardless of their work's quality. Furthermore, attention is rarely given to a writer's literary development, to a writer's changing views of the form of the short story. The most unfairly neglected authors are the border crossers: the new Canadians (including Elizabeth Spencer, Eugene MacNamara, Leon Rooke, Jane RULE, Audrey THOMAS, Kent Thompson, John Metcalf and Daphne MARLATT) and the so-called expatriates (including Wallace Stegner, Mavis Gallant, for many years Norman Levine, and now Clark Blaise) – writers who have made significant contributions to Canada's literary traditions but are generally regarded as not fully belonging to them. However, several deserving authors of recently published stories, novellas or short fiction collections are gaining fine reputations. Among these writers are the 8 who participated in the "New Canadian Fiction/New Canadian Criticism" conference organized in their honour by David HELWIG and John Metcalf in Kingston, Ont, 4-6 Oct 1986: Edna Alford, Keath Fraser, Douglas Glover, Dayv James-Frenche, Janice Kulyk Keefer, Rohinton Mistry, Patrick Roscoe and Linda Svendsen. It is to be hoped that they, together with other talented newcomers, will have the breadth of vision, the determination, the energy and the good fortune to contribute significantly to the tradition of short fiction in Canada. *See also* LITERATURE IN ENGLISH. J.R. (TIM) STRUTHERS

Reading: J. Metcalf, *Kicking Against the Pricks* (1982, rev 1986); W.H. New, *Dreams of Speech and Violence: The Art of the Short Story in Canada and New Zealand* (1987).

Short Fiction in French Tales (*contes*) and POETRY lie at the origin of Québec literature, perhaps by chance, perhaps as a necessary stage in the evolution of literary genres. Whatever the reason, the specific context of the beginnings of Canadian LITERATURE IN FRENCH seems in itself to justify the preponderance of short texts. Institutional theory has it that in the 19th century, books were rare and publishers essentially operated printing houses involved in everything but literature. Authors could often publish only in journals and LITERARY PERIODICALS, and this encouraged the production of short texts. Another possible explanation is aesthetic: the influence of romanticism made a fashion of FOLKLORE, popular traditions and local colour. The third possible explanation is ideological: at a time when the novel was viewed as pernicious because of the passions it revealed (17th-century THEATRE fell into similar disrepute), the short story seemed morally less offensive.

The short story proliferated, and appeared in the form of narratives embedded in the first NOVEL published in Québec, INFLUENCE D'UN LIVRE by Philippe AUBERT DE GASPÉ, JR. It became a permanent feature of literary journals and daily newspapers and emerged as an important genre in James Huston's *Répertoire national* (1848-50). The genre encompasses various types of short narratives, including summaries, novellae, exempla, short stories, anecdotes, portraits and various types of picturesque descriptions. These texts were both naive and detailed, often containing pompous rhetoric or a heavily didactic message. Of some 1100 works published in 19th-century periodicals, roughly 200, identified as tales and legends, have been published in collections. From a literary viewpoint, these tales and legends constitute the period's most interesting production of short narrative texts.

Many imaginative tales were drawn from legends. Major recurring themes included stories about the devil in which a character who has defied or ignored religious teaching is guided back to righteousness by some exemplary punishment. But this triadic organization (prohibition, transgression, punishment) is an oversimplification of the scope of these texts throughout which the transgression described has the glamour of a voluntary action. Of the devil's various acts (seduction, pact, possession), the first 2 appear most frequently. The character coming into contact with Satan is usually not a victim but a person in search of his own destiny. Rose LATULIPPE deliberately dances on Ash Wednesday with her "handsome devil dancer," despite the alarmed looks of those close to her. In *La* CHASSE-GALERIE, 8 lumberjacks risk their lives and souls to see their girl friends on New Year's Eve. Werewolves, rough and ready characters who ignore the priest's orders, are somewhat aware of having caused their own possession. The devil himself, the unmistakable protagonist, is cowardly and impotent, his powers limited by those of the priest and of sacred objects: he flees at the sight of a few drops of holy water.

To consider these texts an attempt by triumphant 19th-century ULTRAMONTANISM to reassert its influence on literature would be to ignore the internal tensions and contradictions contained in the many levels of meaning. The content of the written tale cannot be divorced from the form it usually took in early Québec literature. A substitute for oral communication, it frequently reproduces the signs of the ORAL LITERATURE by including the festive character of the story in a 2-level narrative. The tale's introductions (prologue, preface or first narrative) proceed from a masterly description of the setting in which the relationship between storyteller and story is defined and the nature of the narrative pact established according to the form of dialogue chosen. This pact varies from one author to the next. Louis-Honoré FRÉCHETTE (*Contes I* and *II*) is more ironic, playful and freethinking than his fellow writers, taking pleasure in demystifying the supernatural and presenting as his main character Jos Violon, an unrepentant storyteller of a popular culture with which he maintains a tacit complicity. Honoré Beaugrand (*La Chasse-galerie*, 1900) is closer to myth and to the archetypal figures of the imagination, whereas Pamphile Lemay (*Contes vrais*, 1899) is at the same time more literary (craftily playing with oral/written ambiguity, truth and falsehood), digressive and moralizing. His texts cover a variety of significant themes, historical, legendary and commonplace. Others, such as Joseph-Charles Taché or N.H.É. Faucher de St-Maurice wrote documentary or moral texts. Despite these differences, the 19th-century literary tale had a certain uniformity that displayed basic characteristics: the predominance of a set exemplary narrative, explicit references to oral expression, presentation of a narrator who is also a character in the story, and a view consistent with the Christian idea of the supernatural, which in many cases precludes the possibility of the fantastic.

The short texts of the 20th century are fewer and more diverse. The relative importance of the tale has diminished. A number of writers have tried their hand at short stories before writing novels; others, such as Jean-Aubert LORANGER, Jacques FERRON and Roch CARRIER, periodically return to this genre, choosing to make it the leit-motif of their literary production. This gives rise to various types of texts. Lionel GROULX and Brother MARIE-VICTORIN wrote tales of the land, whereas Michel TREMBLAY writes fantasy; Loranger's and Ferron's tales are philosophical and ironic, and those of Félix LECLERC, Carrier, Gilles VIGNEAULT, Yves THÉRIAULT and Réal Benoît are poetic, tragic and playful. The works of Marius BARBEAU, Luc Lacourcière, Félix-Antoine SAVARD, Jean-Claude Dupont and other specialists in folklore and ethnology present transcriptions of oral narratives. Social scientists have now taken upon themselves the task of preserving this literature, something formerly the preserve of writers of the romantic generation.

The novella is more discreet than the tale. It appeared mainly as a collective expression in the 1960s when writers such as Jacques RENAUD and André MAJOR used it as a vehicle for literary and social ideas. It is making a vigorous comeback in the 1980s among authors who, following Gabrielle ROY, Madeleine Ferron, Louise MAHEUX-FORCIER and Claire Martin, are seeking to reveal the immediacy and harmonies of a situation. Suzanne Jacob, Marilu Mallet and Gaétan Brulotte represent this "post-modernist" generation of writers. The tale, although it may seem to have disappeared, has nevertheless found its way into the 20th-century novel (Yves BEAUCHEMIN's *Le Matou*, 1981, and Louis Caron's narratives), in which techniques and themes are very similar to those used by 19th-century storytellers.

A study of Québec literature through the history of its forms shows that the tale – paradoxically because of its fixed or permanent elements – lends itself to a broader range of modulations and reveals the literary profile of a period perhaps even more than the novel or the short story. If every tale is a "chasse-galerie," the adventure is made all the more fascinating by the fact that it transports the reader to another world full of reminders of the past, of everyday existence and, inevitably, of culture. LISE GAUVIN

Shortt, Adam, economist, historian (b at Kilworth, Canada W 24 Nov 1859; d at Ottawa 14 Jan 1931). Educated at Queen's U (BA 1883, MA 1885) and at Glasgow and Edinburgh, Shortt joined the staff at Queen's in 1886 and was professor of political science 1891-1908. An unusually influential teacher, he was also a pioneering scholar in Canadian economic history, and his articles on banking and his edition of *Documents Relating to Canadian Currency, Exchange and Finance During the French Regime* (1926) still have value. He co-edited, with A.G. DOUGHTY, both *Documents Relating to the Constitutional History of Canada 1759-1791* (1907, rev 1918) and, 1913-1917, the 23-volume CANADA AND ITS PROVINCES. From 1908 to 1917 he served on the first Civil Service Commission in Ottawa, and from 1918 to his death was chairman of the Board of Historical Publications at the National Archives. STANLEY GORDON

Shortt, Terence Michael, ornithologist, artist (b at Winnipeg 1 Mar 1911; d at Toronto 28 Dec 1986). He joined the ROYAL ONTARIO MUSEUM, Toronto, in 1930, and his career there spanned 46 years, during which he played an important role in the advancement of ornithology in field research and as an artist of exceptional insight. From 1948, when he became head of Biology Display, Shortt led many expeditions to places such as Galapagos, India and East Africa, collecting materials for the world-class dioramas which he created for the museum. His renderings from life of bird portraits and intimate attitudes of nearly 2000 bird species, display his exceptional powers of observation and his uncanny ability to portray a bird's essence. J.L. CRANMER-BYNG

Shoyama, Thomas Kunito, economist, public servant (b at Kamloops, BC 24 Sept 1916). Denied employment in his native BC because he was of JAPANESE ancestry, Shoyama was prominent among the young civil servants who set up the machinery for new social programs in Saskatchewan under T.C. DOUGLAS. He was economic adviser to the premier when he left in 1964 to become a senior economist with the ECONOMIC COUNCIL OF CANADA. He held many senior positions with the federal government, including deputy minister of energy, mines and resources, deputy minister of finance, special adviser to the Privy Council on the Constitution and chairman of the board of Atomic Energy of Canada Ltd. He has been a visiting professor at U of Victoria since 1980 and was a member of the ROYAL COMMISSION ON CANADA'S ECONOMIC PROSPECTS. Shoyama became an Officer of the Order of Canada in 1978. BILL CAMERON

Shrew (Soricidae), family of small insectivores represented today by approximately 250 species worldwide, 16 in Canada. Shrews are small (35-180 mm long) and have short legs; a well-developed tail; long, pointed snout; small eyes; and ears usually partially hidden in soft, often velvetlike fur. The long, narrow, somewhat conical skull lacks zygomatic arches (bone arches in skull extending beneath the eye sockets). The unique dental structure has hooklike upper incisors that, with the elongated, horizontally projecting, lower incisors, form a tweezerlike organ with shearing tips, perfectly adapted for grasping and cutting insects. The molars are suited to piercing the tough external skeleton of insects and shredding food. Shrews are continually active and, to maintain their high metabolic rate, daily may consume their own weight in insects, other small animals and vegetable matter. If deprived of food, they die quickly. Shrews occur throughout Canada except in the arctic islands. Most species live in leaf litter and dense ground cover of woods and in open grassland and tundra. Short-tailed and least shrews (*Blarina brevicauda, Cryptotis parva*) dig well and spend much time underground. Gaspé and rock shrews (*Sorex gaspensis, S. dispar*) are largely restricted to talus slopes. Water shrews (*S. palustris, S. bendirii*) are semiaquatic. Little is known about reproduction in most native shrews. Available information indicates that shrews mate from late winter or early spring to late summer or fall, and give birth to litters of from 3 to 10 naked, blind young after a gestation of 2 to 3 weeks. C.G. VAN ZYLL DE JONG

Shrike, common name for the family Laniidae of singing birds. The family, which includes 74 species, ranges widely in Africa, Europe, Asia and N America. The only 2 species found in Canada, loggerhead and northern shrike (*Lanius ludovicianus* and *L. excubitor*), are both migratory. Shrikes range from 15 to 37 cm in length. Plumage is mainly grey or brown above; white or light coloured below. Wings are black; the long tail is black and white. Both Canadian species have a bold black mask across the eyes. The black bill is strong, hooked, and toothed in many species (as in BIRDS OF PREY). Legs and feet are strong with sharp claws. Shrikes are solitary except during nesting season. Both parents co-operate in building a deep, bulky nest, usually in trees or bushes. The eggs (2-8) are incubated by the female, with assistance from the male in some species. Young are fed by both parents. Shrikes are perching songbirds, with a great variety of notes; Canadian species have a melodious song. They are predators, feeding on insects, small reptiles, birds and mammals. They watch for prey from exposed perches and are bold and aggressive, attacking swiftly. They carry their prey away, often impaling it on thornbushes before eating.

HENRI OUELLET

Shrimp, decapod ("10-footed") CRUSTACEAN, differing from other decapods (CRABS, CRAYFISH, LOBSTERS) in being adapted for swimming, a fact reflected in the large, laterally compressed abdomen and well-developed pleopods (pairs of swimming legs). All shrimp native to Canada are marine, although the large, freshwater Malaysian prawn (*Macrobrachium*) has been reared experimentally. In Canadian waters, there are more than 100 species of shrimp, of which 85 have been recorded off the Pacific coast. These vary considerably in size, ranging from less than 20 mm to well over 200 mm in length. Females are almost always larger than males; some species are protandric, ie, grow up and mature as males, then change into females for the balance of their reproductive lives. The most valuable commercial species in Canada are the prawn (*Pandalus platyceros*) on the Pacific coast, and the pink shrimp (*Pandalus borealis*) on the Atlantic coast. Although the terms "shrimp" and "prawn" are used interchangeably in N America, a culinary distinction may be made between small shrimp and large prawns. D.E. AIKEN

Shrum, Gordon Merritt, physicist (b at Smithville, Ont 14 Jan 1896; d at Vancouver 20 June 1985). After service in WWI, Shrum took a PhD under J.C. MCLENNAN at U of T, where he discovered in 1925 the "green line" in the spectrum of the aurora. He joined UBC that year and eventually became dean of graduate studies. Shrum's personality, and his membership in such bodies as the NATIONAL RESEARCH COUNCIL and Defence Research Board, gave his influence national scope. He was the apostle of research in BC (a prime promoter of the BC Research Council, created in 1944) and of the competence of scientists as public servants. After retiring from UBC at age 65, he became chairman of BC Hydro for 12 years and chancellor of Simon Fraser U; at age 80 he began work as chairman of the Robson Square redevelopment project in Vancouver. A power generating station on the Peace R is named after him. *Gordon Shrum: An Autobiography* (1986) was prepared with Peter Stursberg and edited by Clive Cocking. DONALD J.C. PHILLIPSON

Shuster, Joe, cartoonist (b at Toronto, 10 July 1914), first cousin of comedian Frank Shuster of Wayne and Shuster. Working in Cleveland, Ohio, in 1931 with writer Jerome Siegel, Shuster created Superman, the most famous hero in comic-book history. He had moved to Cleveland at the age of 9 and later attended art school there. Superman made its public debut in the monthly *Action Comics* in June, 1938. Shuster and Siegel sold this first story for $130 and inadvertently lost the rights to the character. Although Superman initially brought them wealth and fame (an estimated $75 000 in 1940), Shuster stopped drawing the character in 1947. In Shuster's original version, Superman's alter-ego, reporter Clark Kent, worked for *The Daily Star*, named after the *Toronto Star*. A comic book editor later changed the newspaper's name to *The Daily Planet* in the fictitious city of Metropolis. PETER DESBARATS

Sibbeston, Nicholas George, lawyer, MLA (b at Fort Simpson, NWT 21 Nov 1943). The first native northerner to become a lawyer (LLB 1975), and the second Métis in Canadian history to lead a constitutional government (after John Norquay of Manitoba), Sibbeston has been a determined and sometimes tempestuous advocate for native rights since he entered Territorial politics in 1970. As chairman of the Western Constitutional Forum, the group negotiating for the new territory to be created when the present NWT are divided, he has insisted that its eastern boundary must be placed so as to guarantee at least parity between the native population and the whites, most of whom live in the western region. In 1984 he was appointed to the territorial council. As government leader of the NWT (1986-87) he launched and lost a lawsuit against the federal government, claiming that the MEECH

LAKE ACCORD violated citizens' rights. In 1988, as minister of economic development and tourism, he continued to oppose the accord. STANLEY GORDON

Sicamous, BC, UP, pop 2004 (1986c), 1057 (1981c), is located at the eastern end of Shuswap Lk in S-central BC, 550 km E of Vancouver and 140 km E of Kamloops. It lies at the western end of the EAGLE PASS through the Monashee Mts on a narrow strip of land between Shuswap and Mara lakes. Its name derives from an Indian word meaning "in the middle." Sicamous is on the CPR main line and is at the junction of the TRANS-CANADA HWY and Hwy 97, which leads S to the Okanagan Valley. Tourism and the beaches and resorts on the lakes are mainstays of the local economy, along with some lumbering and agriculture. Attractions in the area are primitive rock paintings along the shores of the lakes, and CRAIGELLACHIE station, 25 km E, where the "last spike" of the CPR was driven. JOHN R. STEWART

Sicotte, Louis-Victor, lawyer, politician, judge (b at Boucherville, LC 6 Nov 1812; d at St-Hyacinthe, Qué 5 Sept 1889). He was a fervent Patriote and is considered a co-founder of the ST-JEAN-BAPTISTE SOCIETY of Montréal. He was not convinced of the wisdom of the REBELLIONS OF 1837 and opposed the Patriotes' border forays because he feared they would bring reprisals. First elected to the Assembly for St-Hyacinthe in 1851, he identified with the dissident Reformers whose position lay somewhere between LAFONTAINE's supporters and the PARTI ROUGE. In 1854 he was named Speaker over the government's candidate, George-Etienne CARTIER. Commissioner of crown lands 1857-10 Jan 1859, he resigned to become leader of the opposition from Canada East. In May 1862, Sicotte formed a new government with John Sandfield MACDONALD, but having had to lead the country in a period of deep economic and political trouble, the ministry was defeated in the Assembly on 8 May 1863. Sicotte refused a Cabinet position in the new Sandfield Macdonald-Dorion government and was named a puisne judge of the Superior Court for St-Hyacinthe on 5 Sept 1863, a post he held until 7 Nov 1887. ANDRÉE DÉSILETS

Sidbec-Dosco Limitée Inc, along with Sidbec-Feruni, is a wholly owned subsidiary of Sidbec (Siderurgie du Québec), established by the Québec government in 1964 so that the province would have an integrated steelmaking facility. There are now plants at Contrecoeur, Longueuil, Montréal and Etobicoke. Sidbec does not use conventional iron and steelmaking technology. Its plant at Contrecoeur, E of Montréal, produces sponge iron using the Midrex process, in which IRON ORE pellets are directly reduced by reformed natural gas in a shaft furnace. The sponge iron is melted with scrap steel in an electric-arc furnace to make steel. The first Midrex unit became operational in Apr 1973, the world's second plant making tonnage high-quality flat-rolled products by electric-furnace steelmaking. Power is supplied by Hydro-Québec; natural gas by Gaz-Métropolitain Inc. The company employs 3105 and in 1986 had net sales of $519 million. The Contrecoeur plant has 2 Midrex furnaces, 4 large electric melting furnaces and continuous casting facilities. The annual raw-steel capacity is about 1.2 million t, most of it processed into bars and rods. JOHN G. PEACEY

Sidney, BC, Town, pop 8982 (1986c), 7946 (1981c), inc 1967, is located on the E side of the Saanich Pen on Vancouver I, 30 km N of VICTORIA, facing Haro Str. It is the business hub of the northern part of the Saanich Pen and the gateway to Vancouver I, with 2 official ports of entry: the

Anacortes Ferry from the US and the international airport, 1.6 km W of the town. Eight km to the N is the Swartz B terminal of the BC Ferry system, which connects with the mainland. Salish first inhabited the area, and permanent settlement began only in the late 1880s, when agriculture developed. Nearby Sidney I was named 1859 for F.W. Sidney of the Royal Navy. In 1895 the Victoria-Sidney Ry opened, and by the early 1900s local industries included a roofing factory, a cannery and a large sawmill. During the 1920s a major fire and competition from the mainland destroyed Sidney's early industries. They have since been replaced by service functions, boat building, fishing and tourism. The area is popular for sailing and has a racing track. ALAN F.J. ARTIBISE

Siemens, Jacob John, farmer, teacher, farm organizer (b at Altona, Man 23 May 1896). After attending the Manitoba Normal School, he taught school 1918-29, but then assumed management of the family farm and started to re-organize his liberal Mennonite community. His organizational skills were soon transferred to co-operatives, and he established the Rhineland Consumers Co-operative Ltd, probably Manitoba's first, in 1930 or 1931. He eventually helped promote and establish 32 other co-operatives which he organized into the Federation of Southern Manitoba Co-operatives. Convinced that economic and community stability depended on diversification he promoted new crops, serving as the first president of Co-operative Vegetable Oils Ltd (1946), the first plant in N America to extract oil from sunflower seeds, and as VP of the Manitoba Sugar Beet Growers Association (1947). MARTIN K. MCNICHOLL

Sifton, Arthur Lewis, judge, politician, premier of Alberta (b at St Johns, Canada W 26 Oct 1858; d at Ottawa 21 Jan 1921). Firm, stoical and politically astute, Sifton was one of the most outstanding figures in the political life of the early West. He practised law in Brandon, Man, 1883-85 (with his brother Clifford), in Prince Albert in the North-West Territories 1885-88, and in Calgary after 1889. In 1899 he was elected to the territorial legislature for Banff and from 1901 served on HAULTAIN's Executive Council. He was an early and strong advocate of provincial status. In 1903 LAURIER appointed him territorial chief justice, and in 1907 he became the first chief justice of Alberta. As a trial judge he was excellent; he said little and gave short, sound and prompt judgement. In 1910 he resigned and became Liberal premier of Alberta, succeeding A.C. RUTHERFORD. Sifton held together a divided party and was an effective premier, a strong leader and skilled administrator. He pressed for the transfer of natural resources, finally accomplished by J.E. BROWNLEE in 1930. In 1916 women were given the vote and 2 were made magistrates. During the CONSCRIPTION crisis of 1917, PM BORDEN invited leading Liberals, including Sifton, to join a Union government. He accepted. On Oct 12 he resigned as premier and was appointed minister of customs. In the general election of 17 Dec 1917 he was elected member for Medicine Hat. Though not conspicuous in the Commons, Sifton was valuable in Cabinet and as a delegate to the Paris Peace Conference. In 1919 he became minister of public works and secretary of state, and in 1920 was named an imperial privy councillor. W.F. BOWKER

Reading: L.G. Thomas, *The Liberal Party in Alberta* (1959).

Sifton, Sir Clifford, lawyer, politician, businessman (b near Arva, Canada W 10 Mar 1861; d at New York C 17 Apr 1929) and brother of A.L. SIFTON. One of the ablest politicians of his time, he is best known for his aggressive promotion of immigration to settle the PRAIRIE WEST.

Sir Clifford Sifton (c1900), aggressive promoter of immigrant settlement in the West (*courtesy National Archives of Canada/PA-27943*).

Sifton moved to Manitoba in 1875, graduated from Victoria College (Cobourg, Ont) in 1880, and was called to the Manitoba Bar in 1882. He was first elected as a Liberal MLA for Brandon North in 1888, and on 14 May 1891 became attorney general in the government of Thomas GREENWAY. His brilliant defence of the "national school system" (est 1890) brought him to prominence. After the Laurier-Greenway compromise on the MANITOBA SCHOOLS QUESTION in 1896, Sifton became federal minister of the interior and superintendent general of Indian affairs in LAURIER'S government Nov 17.

Sifton's energy, mastery of political organization and incisive analytical capacity, his dynamic view of the role of government in stimulating development, and his broad grasp of Canada's material and economic problems all set him apart. He was the principal negotiator of the CROW'S NEST PASS AGREEMENT with the CPR. He was responsible for the administration of the Yukon during the gold rush; controversial among his policies was the endeavour to shift from individual placer-mining operations to large-scale mechanized mining for gold. He was agent in charge of presenting Canada's case to the Alaska Boundary Tribunal in 1903.

His promotion of immigration was an immense success. Taking advantage of a strong economic recovery that made farming in the West more attractive, he established a vigorous organization to seek out settlers in the US, Britain and — most controversially — east-central Europe. Against attacks by nativists, he defended the "stalwart peasants in sheep-skin coats" who were turning some of the most difficult areas of the West into productive farms.

Sifton resigned on 27 Feb 1905 following a dispute with Laurier over school policy for Alberta and Saskatchewan. He never acquired a broad view of the compromises necessary to protect minority rights in Canada. In 1911 he broke with the Liberal Party on RECIPROCITY with the US, supporting the Conservatives, though he did not run for Parliament again. He was chairman of the Canadian COMMISSION OF CONSERVATION 1909-18, promoting a wide spectrum of conservation mea-

sures. He was knighted 1 Jan 1915. Instrumental in the formation of Union Government in 1917, he subsequently preferred the PROGRESSIVES, and then the Liberals under Mackenzie KING. Sifton left an estate valued at nearly $10 million but was highly secretive about his private and business affairs. His most important acquistion was the *Manitoba Free Press;* its editor, J.W. DAFOE, became his closest confidant and eventual biographer. Sifton was a man of unusual achievement despite the deafness that afflicted him most of his life. He considered the settlement of the West a sufficient monument to his endeavours.   DAVID J. HALL

Reading: J.W. Dafoe, *Clifford Sifton in Relation to His Times* (1931); David J. Hall, *Clifford Sifton,* 2 vols (1981, 1985).

Signal Hill, overlooking the harbour of ST JOHN'S, Nfld, was for many years the centre of the town's defences. A signal cannon was placed here in the late 16th century, and stone fortifications were built in the late 18th century during the NAPOLEONIC WARS. By that time a system of flags flown from the hill warned ships of weather and sea hazards. Cabot Tower was built 1897-1900 to commemorate the 400th anniversary of John CABOT's voyage of discovery in 1497. Italian inventor Guglielmo Marconi chose this site to conduct an experiment to prove that electrical signals could be transmitted without wires, and on 12 Dec 1901 he received the world's first radio transmission, sent in Morse code from Cornwall, Eng. Signal Hill was declared a national historic park in 1958, and an interpretive centre has been developed there. *See also* HISTORIC SITE.
                                                  C.J. TAYLOR

Sigogne, Jean-Mandé, Roman Catholic missionary (b at Beaulieu-les-Loches, France 6 Apr 1763; d at Sainte-Marie [Church Point], NS 9 Nov 1844). Forced in 1792 to flee persecution in revolutionary France, he came by way of England to southwestern NS in 1799 as missionary to the ACADIANS of 2 widely separated missions. He was authoritarian by temperament and a moral rigorist, and this, coupled with his being the only man among them both learned and fluent in English, gave Sigogne an ascendancy over temporal and spiritual affairs. His most substantive legacy was the survival of the French and Catholic traditions among the Acadians of Digby and Yarmouth counties, to whom he ministered for 45 years.
                                             BERNARD POTHIER

Sikhism, a major world religion, arose through the teachings of Guru Nanak (c1469-1538) in Punjab, India. Its 15 000 000 adherents call themselves Sikhs (disciples), and like JEWS they are distinguished both as a religion and as an ethnic group. Though in principle universalistic and open to converts regardless of background, Sikhism has been identified primarily with Punjabi people, events and culture. Guru Nanak travelled widely and incorporated many ideas from the HINDU Sant (saint) tradition, some from the Hindu Bhakti (devotional) tradition and, indirectly, some from the Muslim Sufis (see ISLAM) into his own distinctive theology. He believed in monotheism and rejected Hindu notions of caste, idol worship and bodily mortification, as well as the belief in salvation through ascetic isolation from worldly affairs. Guru Nanak claimed that salvation was accessible to all through devotion to God and the maintenance of a moral, responsible and selfless everyday life. The mainstream Sikh tradition teaches that Nanak's ideas were elaborated by 9 subsequent gurus or teachers. Guru Angad (c1504-52) is said to have had Nanak's teachings written in Punjabi. He is also believed to have strengthened the unique Sikh practice of *Guru ka langar,* in which Sikhs repudiate aspects of caste by eating together. The tradi-

tion has it that Guru Amar Das (c1479-1574) further organized the church and fought against *purdah* (seclusion of women) and *sati* (widow burning); Guru Ram Das (c1534-81) founded Amritsar, Punjab, now the centre of the Sikh faith. Guru Arjun (c1563-1606) collected Sikh scriptures into a single volume, later termed the *Adi Granth,* which became the main scriptural base of Sikhism.

Oppression by the Muslim Moguls and unsettled conditions in Punjab gave rise to increasing ethnic consciousness and militancy among Sikhs. Made Guru after the martyrdom of his father, Tegh Bahadur (c1620-75), who was the tenth and last Guru, Gobind Singh (1666-1708) was both a spiritual and a military leader. In 1699 he is thought to have brought Sikh theology to its final development by creating the *Khalsa* (the pure), the community of believers who become *amritdhari* ("nectar bearing") through receiving *amrit pahul* (initiation). Men who did so took the name "Singh" (lion), while women took "Kaur" (princess). Men of the Khalsa were directed to observe the 5 *kakas* ("Ks"): to keep their hair and beard uncut (*kes*), and to wear a comb (*kangha*) symbolizing neatness, a steel bracelet (*kara*), soldier's breeches (*kach*) and a dagger (*kirpan*). While some Sikhs (Sahijdharis, "lightly burdened") have not personally accepted these conventions, among those who did (Keshadharis, "one who bears hair") are an overwhelming majority of those from whom Canadian Sikhs are drawn.

There was thus established a continuum of religious observances among Sikhs. *Amritdharis* were required to observe a more onerous devotional practice and a more restrictive moral code (*rehat maryada*) than those *Keshadharis* who had not been administered *amrit pahul,* while *Sahajdharis* were, as the term implies, religiously more lightly burdened. All were nevertheless considered Sikhs, in that they subscribed to the core teachings of the Gurus.

Seeing death impending, the mainstream Sikh tradition holds that Guru Gobind Singh permanently passed on the spiritual leadership of the faith to the *Adi Granth,* naming it the *Guru Granth Sahib.* After his death, Sikhs continued to have a turbulent history. As the Mogul empire weakened, military and political conflict in Punjab escalated, to be subdued partially by the rise to power of the Sikh, Ranjit Singh (1780-1839), who consolidated much of Punjab and Kashmir. Sikh converts increased dramatically during this period, as they did after Punjab was conquered by the British in 1846. Sikh men soon were an important part of the British Indian army, and thus migrated in small numbers throughout the British Empire.

Sikhism in Canada Canadian Sikhs practise one of Canada's best-represented non-Christian religions and form this country's largest SOUTH ASIAN ethnic group. Although census figures suggest that there were 67 710 Sikhs in Canada in 1981, this is recognized to be an undercount. Population estimates of all Canadian South Asians based primarily on immigration data show that there were roughly 370 000 South Asians in Canada at the end of 1987; of these, about 35%, or 130 000, were Sikhs.

The first Sikhs came to Canada in 1902 as part of a Hong Kong military contingent travelling to the coronation of Edward VII. Some soon returned to Canada, establishing themselves in BC. More than 5000 South Asians, over 90% of them Sikhs, came to BC before their IMMIGRATION was banned in 1908. This population was soon reduced to about 2000 through out-migration, almost all those remaining being Sikhs. Despite profound racial discrimination (*see* KOMAGATA

MARU), Sikhs quickly established their religious institutions in BC. The Vancouver Khalsa Diwan Society was created in 1907. Through its leadership Sikhs built their first permanent *gurdwara* (temple) the following year. By 1920, other gurdwaras had been established in New Westminster, Victoria, Nanaimo, Golden, Abbotsford, Fraser Mills and Paldi. Each was controlled by an independent, elected executive board.

From the beginning, gurdwaras were the central community institutions of Canadian Sikhs. Through them, Sikhs provided extensive aid to community members in need. The dramatic fight to have the immigration ban rescinded was also organized through the temples. By 1920 Vancouver Sikhs alone had contributed $300 000 to charitable causes in India and to the defence of Sikhs in Canada. Temples were also the focus of much anti-British revolutionary activity. Canadian Sikh religious institutions reached another stage of development in the 1920s, when wives and children of legal Sikh residents were allowed entry to the country. In accord with the teachings of the gurus, men, women and children participated fully in temple observances. Sikh religion provided the basis for a strong collective identity between the world wars, so that virtually no Sikhs renounced the faith or married outside it. The main religious revision of the period 1920-60 was a tendency among second-generation men to become *Sahajdharis* – to cut their hair and beards to conform to Canadian dress. Initiation into the *Khalsa* through *amrit pahul* became very rare.

Sikhism in Canada began to change its character in the 1950s as immigration resumed. Many postwar immigrants were more urbane, educated, westernized and religiously untraditional than those who had come earlier. The democratic basis of control over temples soon reflected this division in the domination of older temples by immigrant *Sahajdharis* and the establishment of alternative, more "orthodox" temples by *Keshdharis* in Vancouver and Victoria. In the 1960s and 1970s tens of thousands of skilled Sikhs, some highly educated, settled across Canada, especially in the urban corridor from Toronto to Windsor. As their numbers grew, Sikhs established temporary gurdwaras in every major city eastward to Montréal. These have been followed in many instances by permanent gurdwaras and Sikh centres. Most cities now have several gurdwaras, each reflecting a different shade of religious, social or political opinion. As before, they are the central community institutions. Through them Sikhs now have access to a full set of public observances. Central among these are Sunday prayer services followed by *langar*, a free meal provided to all by members of the *sangat* (congregation). Services are open to anyone who obeys the conventions for entering a temple: that one do so shoeless with the head covered, and refrain from smoking or drinking. Temple observances are also held to celebrate the various gurus and such traditional Sikh calendrical celebrations as Baisakhi Day. The temples are also used for marriages and funeral services.

Perhaps the most important aspects of Sikh religion in Canada are personal and devotional. A daily routine for an *Amritdhari* Sikh would include rising early for a bath and prayers. Many Sikh families have a copy of the *Guru Granth Sahib* in their homes and in the morning select a passage at random from it for inspiration. A hymn is read at sunset, and a hymn and prayer at night. All Sikhs are expected to abstain from tobacco and alcohol, stealing, adultery and gambling. They are not to make caste distinctions, worship idols or acknowledge any living religious teachers as gurus. Sikhism emphasizes the importance of family life, philanthropy, service and defence of

The Sikh "Ceremony of Bliss." The couple sits in the presence of a copy of the *Guru Granth Sahib* during a marriage ceremony in the Sikh community, Calgary (*courtesy Provincial Museum of Alberta/Folk Life Program*).

the faith. Sikh philanthropy has been extensive, especially in support of local gurdwaras and increasingly of pan-Canadian social causes and the arts. Service has been traditionally interpreted chiefly in terms of service to the religion and the community, but this notion of service is slowly broadening out to incorporate Canadian social issues. Save for a possible resident *gyanji* (priest), volunteers take on all the affairs of local gurdwaras, from administration to cooking food at the weekly *langar*.

Sikhs have gone to greater lengths to teach their children their culture and religion than virtually any other ethnoreligious group in Canada. Many temples support classes to teach religious precepts and the written language to children; most second-generation Sikhs speak Punjabi from an early age but must be formally taught the unique Sikh *gurmukhi* written script in order to read from the *Guru Granth Sahib*. There have been several attempts to develop a unitary national Sikh religious organization, but this objective had not yet been achieved by 1987. National and regional conferences to discuss Sikh issues have been held in several cities, and informal contacts between various regional temple organizations are usually maintained. The primary organizational basis of Canadian Sikhism remains, however, the local temple association. Sikh Canadians maintain strong religious ties with India. A continual stream of theologians and teachers visits Canada, and Indian religious texts are in wide circulation. Sikh Canadians visiting India often go on PILGRIMAGE to the famous Sikh shrines, especially the Darbar Sahib (commonly called the Golden Temple) in Amritsar.

Canadian Sikhs are also strongly affected by events concerning Sikhs and Sikhism in India, where a central issue in recent years has been the rise of a vocal movement in Punjab for greater Sikh rights and for an independent Sikh state, Khalistan. Many Canadian Sikhs have supported this movement financially, especially after the Indian army's attack on the extremist Sikh independence sect led by Jarnial Singh Bhindranwali, which had established itself on the grounds of the Golden Temple. This attack in 1984 left Bhindranwali and more than 1000 others dead and seriously damaged the Sikhs' most sacred shrine. In Canada the immediate consequences were militant demonstrations against the Indian government by Sikhs and a sharp deterioration in relations between Canadian Sikhs and Hindus.

Canadian Hindu-Sikh relations were further strained when Indian PM Indira Gandhi was assassinated by 2 of her Sikh security guards 31 Oct 1984; in India, over 2500 Sikhs were killed in the rioting and looting that followed. That no one was ever charged for these outrages has further alienated Canadian Sikhs from the Indian gov-

ernment and has fueled separatist sentiments. These events in India have also had a dramatic effect on general Sikh religious practice in Canada. Heightened Sikh consciousness has led to a remarkable increase in *Amritdharis* and *Keshdharis*, even among second- and third-generation Canadians. It has also led to considerable, albeit qualified, national support for separatist groups such as the World Sikh Organization of Canada and the International Sikh Youth Federation.

With its strong community institutions and group consciousness, Sikhism has found fertile ground in Canada, where many other sects and religions have fallen prey to assimilationist pressures. With continued immigration and the rise of a large second generation, Canadian Sikhs could number 200 000 by 2000 AD. *See also* PREJUDICE AND DISCRIMINATION. NORMAN BUCHIGNANI

Reading: Norman Buchignani and D. Indra, *Continuous Journey: A Social History of South Asians in Canada* (1985); W.O. Cole and P. Singh Sambhi, *The Sikhs* (1978); C.H. Loehlin, *The Sikhs and Their Scriptures* (1964); W.H. McLeod, *Guru Nanak and the Sikh Religion* (1968); H. Singh, *The Heritage of the Sikhs* (1964); K. Singh, *A History of the Sikhs*, 2 vols (1977).

Silica, or silicon dioxide (SiO_2), occurs as the MINERAL quartz and is the most abundant rock-forming compound, making up approximately 60% of the Earth's crust. Quartz forms hexagonal crystals, will change form slightly when heated, and melts at 1723°C. It is extremely resistant to weathering. Pure quartz is colourless, but GEMSTONES such as amethyst, rose quartz, cairngorm (smoky quartz) and jasper result from impurities. The term silica is used whether the silica is found as loose, unconsolidated quartz grains (eg, beach sand), sandstone, quartzite, vein quartz or pegmatitic quartz. Silica is used in the manufacture of optical glass, glass containers, tableware, window and automotive glass; as a metallurgical flux (to promote fluidity) in the base-metal industry; as glass fibre; as an ore in the manufacture of silicon metal, ferrosilicon and silicon carbide; as foundry sand for metal castings; for sandblasting and other abrasives; as filler material in tile, asbestos pipe, concrete and bricks. Very high-purity silicon is used to produce transistors and computer chips. Silica deposits occur throughout Canada. To be economically viable, a deposit should be 95-99% pure, easily mined from open pits and close to a market or transportation. A cheap power source is a consideration in beneficiation (ie, treatment to improve properties). The above factors may make it advantageous for a Canadian company to import silica from a nearby foreign source. Similarly, Canada is able to export silica to nearby US markets. *See also* MINING.
HELEN R. WEBSTER

Silk Train, the term used to describe CPR cargo trains carrying expensive shipments of Oriental raw silk. The trains sped from Vancouver to merchants in eastern Canada and the US, from 1900 to the 1930s. The valuable cargo deteriorates rapidly and the market fluctuated daily, so speed, security and safety were essential. Silk arriving by CP ship in Vancouver was loaded into airtight train cars specially lined with varnished wood, sheathed in paper and sealed so that no damaging moisture or thieves could intrude. Armed guards were the only passengers. Trains of up to 15 cars rushed from Vancouver to Ft William [Thunder Bay] in 15 hours less than the fastest passenger train. The silk trains had preference over any others on the tracks: once a train carrying Prince Albert, later King George VI, was held on a siding while a silk train went through. The trains were discontinued in the 1930s with the advent of air transportation and man-made fibres.

Sillery, first Canadian INDIAN RESERVE, was established 1637 near Québec City. It was funded by a French nobleman, Noël Brûlart de Sillery, who answered Fr Paul Le Jeune's call in the JESUIT RELATIONS to draw together in a suitable place the wandering Indians in order to convert them. It was granted as a seigneury to Christian Indians under Jesuit supervision. Alcoholism, EPIDEMICS and the difficulties of adapting to sedentary life depopulated the settlement by the 1680s. The Jesuits long maintained Sillery's celebrated house, which is now a museum.   DALE MIQUELON

Silver (Ag), metallic element with brilliant white lustre and a melting point of 962°C. It has the highest electrical and thermal conductivities of all metals and, although tarnished by sulphur, is relatively corrosion resistant. Silver is second to GOLD in malleability and ductility, being easily rolled or beaten into foil or drawn into fine wire. Its use for ornaments and utensils predates recorded history. Silver has been an important medium of exchange since very early times. Mines in the eastern Mediterranean and Spain were early sources, but the centre of production had moved to the Western Hemisphere by the 16th century. Important producing countries now are Mexico, the USSR, Peru, the US, Canada, Australia and Poland. Photographic films and papers account for about 40% of silver consumption, but silver also has applications in the electrical and electronics industries for contacts, conductors and batteries. Silver is widely used in silverware, jewellery and works of art, as sterling silver (92.5% silver, 7.5% copper) and for silver plating. Other uses are in brazing and soldering, in alloys, mirrors and catalysts, and in medicine. The use of silver in coinage is now largely confined to numismatic coins and medallions (see MINTING; COINAGE). Some silver is recovered from ores mined principally for the silver content, eg, around Cobalt, Ont; Great Bear Lk, NWT; Coeur d'Alene, Idaho; and Mexico; however, about 80% of supply is a by-product of lead-zinc-copper ores. The main producing areas in Canada are Ontario, BC, NB and the YT. In 1985 Canadian production was 1.1 million kg, over 12% of the world total. Ores at primary silver mines are concentrated by gravity and flotation, and the silver recovered by cyanidation or pyrometallurgy (see METALLURGY). Silver occurring in base-metal ores follows these metals in concentrating and smelting processes, ends up in residues and is recovered by electrolysis.   J.J. HOGAN

Silver, Church A large proportion of the silver objects surviving from Canada's colonial years were made for ecclesiastical use. This important legacy of church silver results from the early establishment of the Catholic Church in NEW FRANCE. Laws of the church required that chalices and patens used in the celebration of the mass be made of a noble metal. As gold was too expensive, SILVER was used for these sacred vessels and for as many other religious objects. Works of art were encouraged as outward expressions of faith and their beauty was regarded as inspirational.

In the 17th century, religious silver was brought to the colonies by missionaries, or sent from patrons in France. The Huron of Lorette, Qué, have an important French reliquary presented to the mission in 1679 and a monstrance of 1664 that originally belonged to the Jesuits. The Jesuits also passed on a Parisian monstrance to the Iroquois at Caughnawaga, Qué, and dispersed other, early French-made works to various parishes and institutions. Colonial churches sometimes commissioned silver objects from makers in Paris. About 1700, as new parishes appeared and prospered, and as the demand for silver works increased, French-trained silversmiths

began to immigrate to New France. They taught others the skills of their trade through an APPRENTICESHIP system and passed on their coveted tools. Soon it became faster, safer and cheaper to entrust a local maker with a church commission than to order from abroad. The scarcity of silver was a constant problem and coins or worn-out objects were saved to be melted down and fashioned into new vessels. Much Catholic silver is preserved in early Québec parishes and religious institutions. It is also exhibited at the Québec Museum, the Musée des beaux-arts in Montreal, the ROYAL ONTARIO MUSEUM, the NATIONAL GALLERY OF CANADA and other art galleries and museums.

The most sacred of the vessels are the chalice, a goblet that contains the wine for the mass, and the paten or plate, used for the blessed wafer or "host." Although these objects are made of silver, the interior surfaces that come in contact with the sacraments are usually gilt. Other church objects were often made of PEWTER, COPPER or brass; these were replaced with silver ones as soon as the parish could afford it. Important pieces include the ciborium, a goblet-shaped, lidded vessel used to hold the host, and the monstrance that displays the host at the top of its long stem in a small glass lunette surrounded by radiating rays. Other large works in silver are processional crosses, holy-water pails (stoups), sanctuary lamps, candlesticks and ewers. Small birdlike burettes or cruets on trays hold wine and water; censers on chains hold burning incense and navettes store it. Baptismal ewers are tiny, as are lidded containers (ampullae) for holy oils; these articles are often set into boxes for carrying on visitations. Other items are the pyx (a portable ciborium), crucifixes, reliquary crosses and cases. The pax, now dated, is a little plaque formerly kissed by the clergy and congregation during the mass.

The most important silversmiths during the French regime, eg, Paul Lambert, Jean-François Landron and Jacques Pagé, worked in Québec City. Roland Paradis and Ignace-François Delezenne produced religious silver for both the Québec City and Montréal areas. Early makers followed traditional Louis XIV provincial styles, perhaps using local treasures from France for inspiration, but producing their own less elaborate interpretations. Favourite motifs included simple bands of stylized leaves, beads or gadroons, usually offset by smooth surfaces. Decoration was created by embossing, chasing and engraving and sometimes by applying details that had been cast. Rounded shapes were raised with the hammer from flattened sheets of silver and soldered to bases. The stems of chalices and ciboria were made in sections, cast or raised, and screwed together with threaded rods.

Québec City remained the centre of church silver production after the British CONQUEST (1759-60). Here the exceptional Ignace François Ranvoyzé created many religious works in a free and decorative style. Among these are 4 gold objects, made for the parish at L'Islet between 1810 and 1812. Laurent Amiot, who returned to Québec in 1787 after studying in Paris, introduced neoclassical elements, reflecting France's newly popular Louis XVI style. Elegant, elongated shapes are decorated with simple reeding, fluting and circular motifs. Smooth surfaces are sometimes engraved with gentle designs; often they are left completely free of decoration. Large sheets of flat silver, introduced about this time, enabled the silversmith to cut and seam hollow parts, instead of raising and hammering them.

There is less early silver from Protestant churches and few of these works are exhibited. Eighteenth-century Anglican churches obtained silver from patrons in England, including royalty. Queen Anne sent plainly elegant chalices, patens,

Monstrance, by Laurent Amiot. The monstrance displays the Host at the top of its long stem in a small glass lunette surrounded by radiating rays (*courtesy Royal Ontario Museum*).

tankard-shaped flagons and alms basins. A communion set she gave to ANNAPOLIS ROYAL is now at St Paul's Church in Halifax. Another set went to the Mohawk in New York; it was later brought to Ontario and is preserved on the Six Nations Reserve near Brantford. George III sent silver to Saint John and Québec City; some of the Québec pieces are in the cathedral there, but 2 are at the St Armand parish in the Eastern Townships. Many forms used in the Anglican Church are similar to Catholic ones, but they tend to be simple in decoration and follow British stylistic traditions. Silver was used in other early Protestant churches but to a lesser degree. Works in the Presbyterian and Methodist churches are very plain and often resemble domestic forms. Communion plate came primarily from Great Britain and the US.

The various churches in the Maritimes received most of their silver from France and Britain, but some was made locally. An early Acadian piece is the pyx in Moncton Cathedral, made by Jean Ferment of Québec about 1751. In 1835 John Munro made a pair of silver patens for St Andrews Presbyterian Church in Saint John, NB. In Halifax, Peter Nordbeck and others made beautiful works for NS churches from 1820 into the middle of the century.

As the rest of the country was settled and churches were established, most religious silver was imported. By the middle of the 19th century new manufacturing and silver-plating techniques resulted in cheaper wares from abroad. Although Montréal's Robert Hendery and François Sasseville of Québec City made a great deal of church silver, it was increasingly difficult for the individual craftsman to compete. This is still true today, when only a small amount is Canadian made. Protestant churches rely primarily on British and American imports; Catholic churches buy silver from various parts of the world.

HONOR DE PENCIER

Silver, Domestic, has existed in Canada since colonial times. The ruling classes of the French regime owned substantial quantities of SILVER objects, which they brought with them or imported from France. The earliest known works actually made in NEW FRANCE, dating from the first quarter of the 18th century, were produced by French-trained craftsmen who passed on their skills through an APPRENTICESHIP system. Among the important silversmiths active in Québec City and Montréal during the French regime were Paul Lambert, Roland Paradis, Jacques Pagé and Jean-François Landron.

As little domestic silver has survived, it is difficult to determine how much was made in the colony. Silver, obtained by melting coins or existing silver articles, was always in short supply. Some locally made works no doubt were lost in refashioning, were converted into cash, destroyed in fires or taken back to France. Early surviving flatware indicates that tablespoons were the most numerous items made, along with forks and long-handled *ragout* spoons. Examples are of considerable weight and follow the plain, handsome 18th-century French style, with handle tips turned up. It was customary to lay spoons and forks facedown on the table and variations occur in such details as the engraved decorative drop on the back of the spoon bowl. Owner's initials are often engraved on the back near the maker's marks.

In holloware, many small tumbler cups bear the marks of Québec silversmiths. Another popular French form is the 2-handled dish or *écuelle*, for stews or soups. Plates, wine tasters, candlesticks and salt cellars are less common, although enough exist to indicate they were made locally, as were snuffboxes and buckles. These colonial domestic works, although unoriginal in form, reflect a restrained style, competently executed. Decoration consists of simple raised or engraved bands, small details such as a shell or leaf motif and, sometimes, a coat of arms or the owner's name as an integral part of the piece.

After the establishment of British rule, silversmiths continued to make domestic silver in the traditional French forms. As the colony was cut off from French sources of supply, resident craftsmen occasionally received important commissions such as soup tureens or ewers. Remaining works confirm the excellent workmanship of such smiths as Ignace-François Delezenne, Jacques Varin and Ignace François Ranvoyzé (one of Québec's greatest silversmiths).

Gradually, the influence of British and European immigrants and imports changed the colony's style of living and the silver that reflects it. With the introduction of sheet silver, a new method for making holloware emerged: the silversmith cut and joined separate parts into cylindrical forms, instead of raising a vessel into shape by hand.

From the 1780s to 1840s, Canadian silversmiths, inspired by the new techniques, produced teapots, sugar bowls, creamers, beakers and mugs in fashionable neoclassical styles from Britain and the Continent. They also created small articles such as pepper and spice casters, nutmeg graters, wine strainers, mustard pots, snuffboxes, vinaigrettes, buckles and buttons. In flatware, tablespoons and forks, as well as soup, sauce and toddy ladles, appear in the "Old English" and "Fiddle" styles, with handle tips turning down. A few spoons are decorated with a shell motif or bright-cut engraving; more often they are plain. Some have owner's initials in script on the front of the handle end. Other utensils used include teaspoons, sugar-sifting spoons and tongs; salt, mustard and marrow spoons; meat skewers and fish servers. These forms changed little until the Victo-

Domestic silver teapot, sugar bowl and creamer by Salomon Marion (*courtesy National Gallery of Canada/gift of the Henry Birks Coll of Canadian Silver, 1979*).

rian era, when more decorative styles became fashionable.

In Québec City, Laurent Amiot became the leading silversmith, after Ranvoyzé; they were followed by a line of excellent craftsmen. However, Montréal emerged as the centre for domestic silver, spurred on by a growing population and the economic success of the FUR TRADE. Important silversmiths from Britain were Robert Cruickshank, James Hanna and, later, George Savage. Among the Europeans were the Arnoldis, Schindlers and Bohles. Canadian makers followed, notably Salomon Marion and Paul Morand, both apprentices of the distinguished workshop of Pierre Huguet *dit* Latour, another locally born silversmith.

Halifax was the third major silversmithing centre in pre-Confederation Canada. By 1800 British and German immigrants and American Loyalists had established a tradition of the craft in NS. Their works closely echo those being made in Québec at the time, although their flatware is often more decorative. Rare pieces of early holloware include an epergne, an inkstand and a silvergilt clock. Among the NS silversmiths, of whom Peter Nordbeck was perhaps the most skilled, are James Langford, William Veith and, later, Julius Cornelius and Michael Septimus Brown. Many are also known for their JEWELLERY, into which they incorporated local gold, stones and shells. Among NB Loyalists were silver craftsmen who also advertised as jewellers and watchmakers. Their table silver consists primarily of flatware. Imports remained the prime source of domestic silver in all the Atlantic provinces. In Newfoundland and PEI, advertisers only occasionally mentioned making their own silverware.

Ontario produced little handmade silver before the transition to manufactured wares. The first local work may be by Loyalist Jordan Post, who settled in York [Toronto] in 1787. Early 19th-century flatware bears the marks of makers in Niagara, Kingston and Toronto. Known holloware is scarce, although large presentation cups were made by William Stennett (1829) and Henry Jackson (1838).

By the 1850s technical discoveries in England and the US had further affected the silversmith's role. New manufacturing techniques and the introduction of silver electroplating on to base-metal forms resulted in the mass production of inexpensive tableware. Imports increased and local manufacture of silver became concentrated in the hands of a few craftsmen who supplied dealers and were known as "makers to the trade." The firm of Robert Hendery, later Hendery and Leslie, became the leading manufacturer in Montréal. Their marks consist of a lion rampant in an oval and a sovereign head in a square with clipped corners. These marks appear on most Canadian silver from the last half of the 19th century, usually accompanied by the name or initials of the dealer for whom the piece was made. Over 100 dealers,

including one in BC, ordered silver from the Hendery firm. In 1899 Henry BIRKS and Sons took over Hendery and Leslie and expanded across Canada to become the country's largest silversmithing firm.

Individually created sterling presentation pieces are the most unique silver made in Canada during the era of mass production and plated wares. Cups, medals, trowels, ewers and trays were specially ordered to celebrate a victory, an occasion or a particular skill. Their engraved inscriptions date and identify the item and often name the donor and recipient. Many of these pieces and other small souvenir items were intended for display rather than use, a fact that has helped preserve them. Some examples bear decorative motifs in the form of maple leaves and beavers.

By the mid-20th century, silver craftsmen were once again producing handmade works in Canada, usually for special commissions. These orders were placed in an individual's studio and meant that the public was renewing contact with the individual silversmith. Large manufacturing firms and dealers dominate the industry, but a growing interest continues in the craftsmen who combine traditional techniques and styles to form unique designs.

No guild or official rules governed the marking or quality of silver used in Canada until the 20th century. During the French regime, silversmiths used a typical punchmark showing their initials, with a fleur-de-lis or crown above and a star or crescent-type motif below, all enclosed in an irregular-shaped cartouche. Towards the end of the 18th century, Québec makers tended to place their initials, in block capitals or script, in a rectangular or rounded cartouche. Sometimes they added a punch indicating their city. This practice was repeated in the Maritimes but with additional marks of a sovereign's head, a lion and perhaps an anchor. Similar British-type symbols were also loosely used by silversmiths in Québec from 1820 and in Ontario slightly later.

HONOR DE PENCIER

Reading: R. Derome, *Les orfèvres de Nouvelle-France* (1974); R. Fox, *Presentation Pieces and Trophies from the Henry Birks Collection of Canadian Silver* (1985) and *Quebec and Related Silver at the Detroit Institute of Arts* (1978); G. Langdon, *Canadian Silversmiths 1700-1900* (1966); D.C. MacKay, *Silversmiths and Related Craftsmen of the Atlantic Provinces* (1973); J. Trudel, *Silver in New France* (1974).

Silver, Indian Trade Silver JEWELLERY was traded to the Indians by European fur traders from the mid-17th to early 19th centuries. From the earliest exchanges (between seasonal fishermen and the Indians) SILVER played an important role. The first pieces of silver were medals and military gorgets (ie, crescent-shaped pendants symbolizing rank), presented by the French, British, Dutch and Spanish to their respective Indian allies. Then came a number of other designs, based on European fashions and traditions, such as crosses and Luckenbooth hearts, a love token popular in Scotland in the 18th century. Circular brooches of varying sizes, sometimes decorated with engravings or cutout geometric designs, were very common. Eventually, Indian designs were fashioned in silver as well, to produce such items as concave, round brooches that copied similar adornments made from shell in precontact times. Earrings, bracelets, headbands, square brooches and animal effigies were also worked in silver for the FUR TRADE.

Trade silver was made by silversmiths in Québec City, Montréal, London and various American cities, including New York, Philadelphia and Detroit. Because of the high demand between 1780 and 1820, it became a mainstay of the silversmiths' trade. Major Canadian makers included Robert Cruickshank, Charles Arnoldi, Pierre Huguet *dit* Latour, Joseph Schindler and Narcisse Roy. At times, such masters would employ up to 30 other silversmiths to help meet the demands of fur traders. Larger pieces bore the mark of the silversmith; smaller pieces usually did not. Fashioned from coin silver, usually melted down and shaped or hammered into thin sheets, trade silver was produced in large quantities (*see* COINAGE). The most important requirement from the trader's point of view was that the pieces be thin, both to reduce cost and to make the silver light for transportation into the interior.

Silver became a symbol of friendship and alliance and was first used in military alliances during the colonial wars. Later, fur traders presented gifts of silver to the chiefs of tribes with whom they wanted to trade. Viewed not as a bribe but as a token of goodwill, the practice followed an Indian tradition most commonly associated with WAMPUM exchange, and symbolized an agreement between equals. Eventually, fur traders realized that silver could be a lucrative trade item: small, easy to transport, locally made and much sought after by the Indians. An Indian hunter might as easily trade 3 beaver pelts for a silver brooch as for a blanket or iron knife blade. In the fierce competition between the HUDSON'S BAY COMPANY and the NORTH WEST COMPANY, the British-based HBC tried to avoid introducing silver into its trade because it was a fairly expensive item. However, the NOR'WESTERS were so successful that the British were forced to introduce trade silver in 1796. In 1821, when they took over control of the Montréal-based NWC, the first item dropped from the trading lists was silver.

In the mid-19th century, Indian silversmiths began to rework some of the larger pieces into smaller items. Eventually, they also fashioned pieces from new silver. Although there was a hiatus during the early part of the 20th century, the period since 1960 has brought a revival of interest in traditional designs. Today, Indian silversmiths in eastern Canada are once again producing trade-silver designs for Indian and non-native customers.   SANDRA GIBB

Silver Dart, the first powered, heavier-than-air machine to fly in Canada; designed and built by the Aerial Experiment Assn (Oct 1907-Mar 1909) under Alexander Graham BELL, a flight en-

thusiast since boyhood. After several successful flights at Hammondsport, NY, early in 1909 the *Silver Dart* was dismantled, crated and brought to Baddeck Bay, NS, the Bells' Canadian home. The "aerodrome" (Bell's preferred term) had a 14.9 m wingspan and an all-up weight of 390 kg, pilot included.

J.A.D. MCCURDY was the principal designer and pilot; Glenn H. Curtiss developed the water-cooled engine, an advance on the association's earlier experiments. Pulled on to the ice of Baddeck Bay by horsedrawn sleigh on Feb 23, the silver-winged machine rose on its second attempt after travelling about 30 m, flying at an elevation from 3 to 9 m at roughly 65 km/hr for 0.8 km. Over 100 of Bell's neighbours witnessed the first flight of a British subject anywhere in the Empire. The *Silver Dart* flew more than 200 times before being damaged beyond repair upon landing in the soft sand of Petawawa, Ont, during military trials in early Aug 1909. The engine was later retrieved and restored and is now on display at the National Museum of Science and Technology in Ottawa. A full-scale model of the *Silver Dart* may be found in Ottawa's National Aviation Museum.
                              NORMAN HILLMER

Silver Islet lies off the tip of Sibley Pen, across the harbour from THUNDER BAY, Ont. In 1868 prospectors found nuggets of pure SILVER, and from 1869 to 1884 shafts were sunk deep beneath the rock, which rose only 2.5 m above the water, and $3.2 million in silver was taken. A virtual town was erected on the rock, which is only 24 m in diameter, along with massive docks and a lighthouse. The mine shut down in 1884; its shafts are now flooded and its buildings are in ruin.   JAMES MARSH

Silverheels, Jay, professional name of Harry (Harold Jay) Smith, later legally changed to Jay Smith Silverheels, actor (b on the Six Nations Indian Reserve, Ont 26 May 1919; d at Woodland Hills, Calif 5 Mar 1980). A leading athlete on his reserve as a youth, he was a top lacrosse player and boxer. He was spotted by comedian Joe E. Brown during a Hollywood tour with a lacrosse team in 1938. Joining the Actor's Guild with Brown's help, he worked his way up from extra to starring roles in over 30 films, including *Broken Arrow* (1950), *Saskatchewan* (1954), *The Man Who Loved Cat Dancing* (1973) and of course the *Lone Ranger* films (1956, 1958), based on the TV series (1949-57) in which he immortalized the role of Tonto. He assisted many budding actors personally and through the Indian Actors Workshop which he founded in Hollywood in 1963. He was

active in sports, especially harness racing, throughout his life.   ROY WRIGHT

Silviculture, the branch of FORESTRY that deals with establishing, caring for and reproducing stands of timber, usually with the aim of a sustained yield of forest products. It requires a knowledge of how various TREE species will grow under particular conditions of SOIL, CLIMATE and spacing. The way in which a forest is harvested influences how it is regenerated. Some systems leave it to nature to provide new seedlings; others require seeding or planting by man. When seeding or planting is required, silviculturists must decide the species and tree spacing most suited to the particular area. They must also be able to predict how a stand of timber will grow and how much wood may be harvested from it.

Until recently, seedlings were grown from ordinary tree seed, but silviculturists are increasingly using seed from genetically superior trees in order to establish healthier and faster-growing forests. Ordinary seed comes directly from the forests, but genetically improved seed is grown in "seed orchards" where special trees are cultivated just to produce seed crops. Seedlings are grown in nurseries before being planted out, usually in spring or fall, on the land where they are needed. Sometimes it is necessary to clear brush or surface litter from an area before the seedlings can be planted. This site preparation may be done mechanically, with fire or with chemicals.

Once the trees are planted, several other steps may be taken to tend the stand. At all stages of growth a FOREST is vulnerable to damage by fire, INSECT PESTS or PLANT DISEASE. It is an important step in silviculture to protect timber stands from these enemies. Since young seedlings may be suffocated by weeds and brush, it is also sometimes necessary to weed or "brush" a recently regenerated area. As the young trees get taller, reaching perhaps 3 or 4 m in height, they may overcrowd each other, and the stand will stagnate. In this case, it is desirable to thin them out, either mechanically or with chemicals, in an operation known as "juvenile spacing" or "precommercial thinning." Later on, when the trees are big enough to be used commercially, the stand may be thinned out one or more times before the final harvest. Other silvicultural practices that may be used include pruning to reduce the number of knots in the lumber, fertilizing to increase growth, and sometimes "sanitation spacing" to remove diseased or undesirable trees.

Silviculture is roughly divided into "basic," comprising REFORESTATION and protection (the minimum requirements of good forest management), and "intensive," comprising the other operations that improve growth and yield. Although silviculture is practised intensively in Europe, other forested countries, including Canada, have not yet progressed as far in this field. In 1983, 25% of the area logged in Canada was planted, but intensive silviculture was practised on only 0.05% of the nation's productive forest area. *See also* MYCORRHIZAE.   M.F. PAINTER

Simcoe, Ont, Town, seat of the Regional Municipality of Haldimand-Norfolk, pop 14 290 (1986c), 14 326 (1981c), inc 1878, located on the Lynn R, 10 km N of Lk Erie. It was named after John Graves SIMCOE, first lt-gov of Upper Canada (1791-96), who visited here 1795. He granted milling privileges to Aaron Culver, a Loyalist settler, whose mill became the centre of a small hamlet. It was plundered by American soldiers during the WAR OF 1812, but a new village was laid out 1819-23. It serves the surrounding area as a retail and service centre. The flue-cured tobacco industry is a major regional enterprise, along with fruit and vegetable production.   DANIEL FRANCIS

J.A.D. McCurdy pilots the *Silver Dart* over Baddeck Bay, NS, in the first airplane flight in Canada, 23 Feb 1909 (*courtesy Library of Canapress*).

Simcoe, Elizabeth Posthuma, née Gwillim, diarist, artist (b at Whitchurch, Herefordshire, Eng Nov 1766 [she invented the date and may have invented the place of her birth – she was bap 22 Sept 1762 at Aldwickle Church, Northamptonshire]; d at Wolford Lodge, Devon, Eng 17 Jan 1850). Orphaned, she was raised by her mother's sister, receiving an education in languages, drawing and music. She married John Graves SIMCOE in 1782 and came to UC when he was appointed the first lieutenant-governor. She left a diary of her stay in Newark [Niagara-on-the-Lake] and York [Toronto], and her line and watercolour sketches of the Canadian landscape are of topographical and historical interest. JAMES MARSH

Simcoe, John Graves, army officer, lt-gov of Upper Canada (b at Cotterstock, Eng 25 Feb 1752; d at Exeter, Eng 26 Oct 1806). Commander of the Queen's Rangers in the AMERICAN REVOLUTION, he became in 1791 the first lt-gov of UPPER CANADA, where he arrived in 1792. He began the policy of granting land to American settlers, confident that they would become loyal settlers and aware that they were the main hope for rapid economic growth. He saw the southwestern peninsula as the future centre not only of the province but of trade with the interior of the continent. He founded York [TORONTO], intending it to be a temporary capital, and laid the foundation of a road system. He wanted to make the colony an example of the superiority of British institutions, and he appointed lieutenants of counties, introduced a court of king's bench and had slavery declared illegal. He also effectively defeated attempts to set up elected town meetings on the New England model. He proposed municipal councils, urged a university with preparatory schools and sought the full endowment of the Church of England. He had few critics in the province but could not persuade the imperial government to finance his projects or to exempt him from the military authority of Guy CARLETON, Lord Dorchester, at Québec. Concerned about defence and in ill health, he left the colony in 1796. He was then governor of Santo Domingo [Dominican Republic] and later commander of the Western District in England. Appointed commander in chief for India in 1806, he died before he could take up the position.
S.R. MEALING

Reading: S.R. Mealing, "The Enthusiasms of John Graves Simcoe," Canadian Historical Assn, *Report* (1958) and "John Graves Simcoe" in R.L. McDougall, ed, *Our Living Tradition,* Fourth Series (1962).

Simcoe, Lake, 743 km², elev 219 m, is situated in southern Ontario between Georgian Bay and Lk Ontario, 65 km N of Toronto. In the N, Atherley narrows divides it from Lk Couchiching at ORILLIA, and both lakes drain NW via the Severn R to Georgian Bay. On the S, it touches a fertile marshland that has developed into an extensive market-gardening area. BARRIE lies at the head of the lake's deep western arm, Kempenfelt Bay. Long frequented by Indians who hunted its shores and fished its waters, the lake was visited in 1615 by Samuel de CHAMPLAIN who was recruiting Huron allies for a campaign against the Iroquois. During the French regime it was part of a fur-trade portage route linking Georgian Bay to Lk Ontario. Originally known by the French as Lac Aux Claies, it was named by Lt-Gov John Graves SIMCOE after his father. During the latter half of the 19th century, loggers proceeded N around Lk Simcoe and the area attracted summer vacationers from the growing cities of southern Ontario. The lake is part of the Trent-Severn navigation system and a centre for recreational boating. Fishing for trout, whitefish and muskellunge has always been popular, especially today during the winter, through the ice. DANIEL FRANCIS

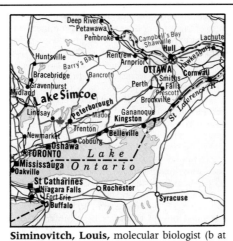

Siminovitch, Louis, molecular biologist (b at Montréal 15 May 1920). He received his undergraduate and graduate education in chemistry from McGill and he trained at the Institut Pasteur, where he shared in the discovery of bacteriophage lysogeny. Returning to U of T, Siminovitch participated in the formation of the Dept of Medical Biophysics, founded the Dept of Medical Cell Biology (now Medical Genetics) as its first chairman, established the Dept of Genetics at the Hospital for Sick Children as geneticist in chief (1970-85), and since 1983 has been director of research at the Mount Sinai Research Institute. In his unofficial capacity as Canada's chief biologist, he has served nationally and provincially on various bodies, as editor of the scientific journals *Virology* and *Molecular and Cellular Biology,* and was a founding member of the now-defunct Canadian science journal *Science Forum.* He has had a major influence on the careers of numerous Canadian molecular biologists. His research has centered on somatic cell genetics, as a founder of the field, and on the MOLECULAR BIOLOGY of mammalian cells. Some 170 publications in books and leading scientific journals have come from his work. Among numerous awards are the Centennial Medal, Gairdner Foundation International Award, Flavelle Gold Medal and membership in the Royal Society (London). He is an Officer of the Order of Canada. JAMES D. FRIESEN

Simon Fraser University, Burnaby, BC, was founded in 1963 as one of Canada's instant universities, built to meet the anticipated need for higher education in BC's Lower Mainland. Situated on top of Burnaby Mt, the award-winning campus designed by architects Arthur ERICKSON and Geoffrey Massey includes a central mall bordered by 5 main buildings. SFU's academic programs emphasize an interdisciplinary approach to traditional and newer disciplines, and the university operates year-round on a trimester system. There are over 70 programs offered by the 5 faculties: arts, business administration, education, applied sciences, and science, offering a wide range of courses and programs. In addition there are co-operative education programs in accounting (CA, CGA and RIA), biological sciences, chemistry/biochemistry, computing science, engineering science, kinesiology, management and systems science, mathematics and physics. SFU also offers correspondence courses enabling students to complete credit courses entirely by mail. Graduate studies at the master's and doctoral levels are offered in all faculties except engineering

science, and SFU is enriched by many research institutes and centres including a new Centre for Systems Science. B. BEATON

Simonds, Guy Granville, army officer (b at Bury St Edmunds, Eng 23 Apr 1903; d at Toronto 15 May 1974). Much favoured by Field Marshal Montgomery for his ruthlessness and offensive spirit, Simonds commanded the 1st Canadian Infantry Div and 5th Canadian Armoured Div in Italy before taking over the 2nd Canadian Corps in NW Europe in 1944. Credited with developing armoured personnel-carrier tactics during the NORMANDY INVASION, he also commanded the First Canadian Army while General CRERAR was ill, leading it through the Scheldt battle (Oct-Nov 1944). Chief instructor at Britain's Imperial Defence College 1946-49 (a signal honour for a Canadian), Simonds was later commandant of Canada's National Defence College (1949-51) and chief of the general staff (1951-55). He advocated peacetime conscription and close ties with Britain, criticizing the government for seeking a closer military relationship with the US. STEPHEN HARRIS

Simoneau, Léopold, tenor, teacher, administrator (b at St-Flavien, near Québec City 3 May 1918). He was widely regarded as the most elegant Mozart tenor of his time, noted for his clear and precise tone, but he was praised for performances of other parts of the lyric tenor's repertóire as well. In 1941, while studying with Salvator Issaurel, he made his debut with the Variétés lyriques. In 1943 he first interpreted a role in a Mozart opera, Basilio in *Le Nozze di Figaro.* On various occasions (the last being in 1970), he sang with his wife, Pierrette ALARIE. He recorded all the major Mozart tenor roles, notably *Così fan tutte* with Herbert von Karajan. Named assistant to the office of Québec's Ministry of Cultural Affairs, he prepared the report that led to the creation of the Opéra du Québec in 1971; that year as well he was made an Officer of the Order of Canada. He and his wife were also teachers of music, notably at the BANFF CENTRE. HÉLÈNE PLOUFFE

Simons, Beverley, née Rosen, playwright (b at Flin Flon, Man 31 Mar 1938). Simons's dramatic works, highly condensed and symbolic, have encountered production difficulties and audience resistance. Best known and most widely produced is *Crabdance,* a ritualistic treatment of women as elders, which premiered in Seattle, Wash, in 1969. Other successful stage plays – *Green Lawn Rest Home* (1969, pub 1973), *Preparing* (1962, 1969), *Crusader* (1976, pub 1975) and *Triangle* (1976, pub 1975) – show the influence of her early musical education and performance. Her study of Oriental theatre has taken her across the Pacific in 1967-68 and 1986. Simons dramatized her Jewish background in "My Torah, My Tree" (written 1956) and "The Elephant and the Jewish Question" (1968). *Leela Means to Play* (1978, pub 1976) is an orientally inspired process drama. The importance of her work was recognized by a special issue of *Canadian Theatre Review* (1976). She contributed "Hunting the Lion" to the CBC "Sextet" of Canadian plays in 1986.
ROTA HERZBERG LISTER

Simpkins, James N., cartoonist, artist (b at Winnipeg 26 Nov 1910). After army service Simpkins became a staff artist for the NATIONAL FILM BOARD. In 1948 he created "Jasper," a bear who lived in the national park for which he was named. Jasper appeared for 24 years in *Maclean's* and in syndication thereafter, and became English-Canada's best-known cartoon character; he has been described by Peter NEWMAN as the "quintessential Canadian" in the introduction to one of several books of Jasper cartoons. Jasper's success has overshadowed Simpkins's other

Full-time Undergrad	Full-time Graduate	Part-time Undergrad	Part-time Graduate
5 481	1 067	5 435	380

artistic achievements ("I was trapped by a bear," he once complained): filmstrip production, book illustration and monthly cartoons in the *Medical Post*, which have been collected in *When's the last time you cleaned your navel?* (1976).

JOHN H. THOMPSON

Simpson, Sir George, governor of the HUDSON'S BAY COMPANY (b at Lochbroom, Scot about 1787; d at Lachine, Canada E 7 Sept 1860). Simpson's knowledge of the FUR TRADE and fur traders was never before equalled. An able administrator and indefatigable traveller, he was imperious when it suited his purposes and loyal to those whose interest paralleled his. Simpson was sent by the HBC from London to N America in 1820 to take charge should the company's governor, William Williams, be arrested by the NWC. He spent his first winter on Lk Athabasca in uneasy competition with the Nor'Westers. When the 2 companies amalgamated in 1821, Simpson was made governor of the large Northern Department, and 5 years later governor of the company's trading territories in British N America. He held this position until his death. Many of his voluminous reports and correspondence have survived in the HBC Archives.

From 1833 Simpson made his headquarters at Lachine, outside Montréal, where he courted politicians, entertained lavishly and invested his money in banks and transportation projects. He was a director of the North Shore Railway Co, Montréal, and of the Champlain Railroad, and he was on the Montréal board of the Bank of British North America. He published his ghostwritten travels, *Narrative of a Journey Round the World, During the Years 1841 and 1842*, and was knighted in 1841 for his contribution to arctic discoveries. In 1830 he married his cousin Frances Ramsey Simpson. They had 2 sons and 3 daughters. Simpson, who was himself illegitimate, also had at least 5 illegitimate children. SHIRLEE ANNE SMITH

Reading: J.S. Galbraith, *The Little Emperor: Governor Simpson of the Hudson's Bay Company* (1976).

Sir George Simpson, able governor of the Hudson's Bay Co, 1821-60, and indefatigable traveller (*courtesy National Archives of Canada/C-44702*).

Simpson, James, printer, journalist, trade unionist (b at Lindal-in-Furness, Eng 14 Dec 1873; d at Toronto 24 Sept 1938). In the 1890s Simpson rose quickly from printer's "devil" to a career as a journalist for the *Toronto Star*. At the turn of the century he moved into prominence as a leader in his own printers' union, as vice-president of the Toronto and District Trades and Labor Council, and later as manager of the Labor Temple. He served 3 terms as vice-president of the TRADES AND LABOR CONGRESS OF CANADA (1904-9, 1916-17, 1924-36). He was on a federal royal commission on technical education in 1910 and was a delegate to the International Labour Organization in the 1920s and 1930s. A committed socialist, he stood as a candidate for early socialist organizations and contributed to the socialist press as writer and editor. He served as a Toronto school-board trustee (1905-10) and controller (1914 and 1930-34) and as Toronto's first labour mayor (1935). For more than 30 years Simpson remained one of Canada's best-known labour radicals. CRAIG HERON

Simpson, Robert, merchant, founder of the Robert Simpson Co (b at Morayshire, Scot 16 Sept 1834; d at Toronto 14 Dec 1897). After his apprenticeship, he arrived in Canada in 1854 and found employment as a clerk in a store in Newmarket, Ont. The following year he opened his own dry-goods store there. In 1872, seeking greater opportunities, he opened a small store in Toronto and by 1894 had erected a new 6-storey building which became a longtime competitor of T. EATON CO across Queen St. Though a fire completely destroyed the new building in March 1895, Simpson set up in temporary quarters and in early 1896 opened another building utilizing every new fire-prevention measure. It had nearly 500 employees and 35 departments. His sudden death at age 63 resulted in the sale of the store for $135 000 to a syndicate of 3 Toronto businessmen, A.E. Ames, J.W. FLAVELLE and H.H. Fudger. JOY L. SANTINK

Reading: J.W. Ferry, *A History of the Department Store* (1960).

Simpsons, Limited with head offices in Toronto, is the present-day successor to the dry-goods store opened in 1872 by Robert SIMPSON in Toronto. Originally averse to the idea of running a "department store," Simpsons eventually added shoe and specialty-food departments and a mail-order business. Catalogues were published regularly after 1894. That year a large new store was built which, because of its impressive architecture, became known as "the most copied store" on the continent. Fire destroyed it in 1895 and soon after a new building (built in the same style) opened. In 1897 Simpson died and the store was bought by a group of financiers. Over the next several decades, Simpsons expanded into a cross-Canadian enterprise. In 1953 the mail order business was acquired by the then Simpsons-Sears Limited (SEARS CANADA INC). In 1978, Simpsons was acquired by the Hudson's Bay Co and in 1986 it had sales or operating revenue of $644 million and assets of $419 million.

Sinclair, Gordon Allan, journalist, author, radio commentator, television panelist (b at Toronto 3 June 1900; d there 17 May 1984). He began a long and often controversial career when he joined the *Toronto Star* in 1922 after a modest education and various dead-end jobs. During the Depression when the country yearned for release, Sinclair, on assignment for the *Star*, transported his readers to faraway places, from war-torn China to Africa. He began his radio career on 6 June 1944 when he broadcast the news of the D-Day invasion over CFRB, Toronto. He continued to broadcast news and comment, his own feature, "Let's Be Personal" and "Showbiz," and he was an original panelist on the CBC's enduring FRONT PAGE CHALLENGE. He gained international recognition in 1973 when he broadcast on CFRB an essay that became known as "The Americans." It was subsequently recorded with a musical background and became so popular that Sinclair was revered by Americans, including Richard Nixon, John Wayne and Ronald Reagan. He was author of several books including *Footloose in India, Cannibal Quest, Khyber Caravan* and *Will the Real Gordon Sinclair Please Stand Up?* BOB HESKETH

Reading: Scott Young, *Gordon Sinclair: A Life . . . And Then Some* (1987).

Sinclair, Lister Shedden, writer, actor, critic, producer, mathematician (b at Bombay, India 9 Jan 1921). Son of a Scottish engineer, Sinclair was educated at St Paul's, London, UBC and U of T, where he lectured in mathematics before beginning his lengthy association with the CBC in 1944. A true Renaissance man, his eclectic interests include ornithology, astronomy, music, linguistics and anthropology. He is a prolific, prize-winning playwright whose plays include *The Blood Is Strong: A Drama of Early Scottish Settlement in Cape Breton* (1956) and *Socrates* (1957), and has contributed numerous plays to CBC radio, some of which are collected in *A Play on Words and Other Radio Plays* (1948). He has held key positions with the CBC, including actor, panelist, critic, commentator, executive vice-president and vice-president, program policy and development, and has been involved with such important television series as *Man at the Centre* and *The Nature of Things*. Sinclair is perhaps best known as the mellifluous host of the sophisticated *Ideas* series and its summer replacement, *A is for Aardvark*. Throughout his distinguished career, he has received many broadcasting honours, including the prestigious international George Foster Peabody Award. He holds honorary doctorates from 4 universities. In 1985, he was invested as an Officer of the Order of Canada. DONNA COATES

Sinclair, Robert William, painter (b at Saltcoats, Sask 9 Feb 1939). Sinclair continued his art studies at the universities of Manitoba and Iowa and since 1965 has taught art at U of A. He has developed a unique and distinctly western Canadian theme in his landscape paintings and sculpture. He uses the symbol of a highway as a familiar shape to draw the eye into a simplified 2-dimensional composition. The painted road device gives an immediate illusion of space, yet this is counterbalanced by strongly drawn linear elements and paradoxical unpainted areas that flatten the space. Sinclair's landscapes portray connections between 2 observed states or combinations of elements such as sky, hills and mountain peaks. Drawing dominates all of his work — watercolours, canvases and his hand-formed plexiglas landscape sculptures. KATHLEEN LAVERTY

Singh Case In this case, individuals from outside Canada tried unsuccessfully to claim from Canadian authorities and the federal Court the status of REFUGEES under the Immigration Act of 1976. On 4 April 1985, 3 justices of the Supreme Court of Canada concluded that a refugee has the right not to "be removed from Canada to a country where his life or his freedom would be threatened." To deny this right would threaten the "security of the individual" in the sense of s7 of the CANADIAN CHARTER OF RIGHTS AND FREEDOMS. This section applies to every person in Canada. The procedure for determining refugee status established in the Immigration Act of 1976 does not meet the requirements of the principle of fundamental justice proclaimed in s7. The individual must have a hearing. The Act constitutes a denial of justice which cannot be justified under s1 of the Charter.

Three other justices of the Court concluded that the procedure for the determination of refugee status violated par 2(e) of the Canadian Bill of Rights of 1960. In this instance, the individuals claiming refugee status had the right to a full oral hearing before bodies or civil servants competent to rule on their case. GÉRALD-A. BEAUDOIN

Singing is the production of musical tones by the human voice. Singing has been a vital part of the life of people in all societies and cultures. The Indians and Inuit, original inhabitants of Canada, used singing to communicate with supernatural powers and in aspects of their work, rituals, dances and recreation. The European settlers who came to Canada brought their own wealth of folk songs (13 000 texts of French-language folk songs were collected by Marius BARBEAU) as well as sacred or secular songs. As songs and masses could be sung without instrumental accompaniment, singing was a very important part of recreation and religious ceremonies. Concert programs in the late 18th century included the singing of art songs and songs with instrumental accompaniment, as well as oratorio or opera selections with instrumental or orchestral accompaniment. The chamber opera *Colas et Colinette* (1788) by Joseph QUESNEL premiered in Montréal in 1790.

Mother de St Joseph, an Ursuline who came to Canada in the mid-1630s, was one of the first to train young singers. From about 1776 to 1900 singing schools were established in various locations, usually for brief periods, by itinerant teachers from the US who stressed music reading and on-pitch singing. Many fine singers came as immigrants to Canada and taught singing, and Canadian singers went abroad to study in various centres in Italy, Germany, France and England. Travelling theatrical companies visiting Canada from the US and Europe provided opportunities to hear singers.

Voice training entails developing the human body into a musical instrument and depends on posture, breath control, producing pure vowels, focusing tone and building resonance. Notable Canadian teachers of singing over the last 150 years include Achille Fortier, Rolande Dion, Guillaume COUTURE, Bernard Diamant, Irene Jessner, Emile Larochelle, Dorothy Allan Park, George Lambert, May Lawson, Helen Davies, and Sherry and Ernesto Vinci. As a result of the varied backgrounds of singing teachers, Canadian singers have been able to perform in various styles and in several languages. Emma ALBANI became one of the world's foremost sopranos and travelled the world taking leading opera roles and performing in concerts in major centres. Other Canadian singers who have gained international fame are Lois MARSHALL, lyric soprano; Teresa STRATAS, lyric soprano; Mary MORRISON, soprano; Pauline DONALDA, soprano; Jeanne Dusseau, soprano; Phyllis Mailing, mezzo-soprano; Eva Gauthier, mezzo-soprano; Maureen FORRESTER, contralto; Jon VICKERS, dramatic tenor; Edward JOHNSON, tenor; Raoul JOBIN, tenor; Léopold SIMONEAU, lyric tenor; John Boyden, baritone; Louis QUILICO, baritone; Morley Meredith, baritone; James Milligan, baritone; Donald Bell, bass-baritone; Claude Corbeil, lyric bass; Joseph Rouleau, bass. ISABELLE MILLS

Singing Schools The 18th-century US institution of local singing classes for sacred music had its counterpart in the Maritimes and in some parts of both Lower and Upper Canada between the 1770s and Confederation. A singing master, often an itinerant and an immigrant from the New England states, would advertise "tuition in psalmody" or "lessons in sacred vocal music," conduct classes 2 or 3 evenings a week over a period of 3 months or so, collect a fee from the (mainly young-adult) participants, and then move on to another small town. Schools were usually organized on the master's initiative, but some also under community or church auspices.

Singers learned a repertoire of hymn-tunes and short anthems from a "tunebook," a combination of musical anthology and sight-singing primer. The schools were thus an instrument of informal education in both musical rudiments and Protestant "psalmody" (metrical psalms and hymns). They were also a notable social phenomenon: a scene in Haliburton's *The Clockmaker*, 1836-40, cites favourite tunes and also depicts the singing class as a venue for courting.

James Lyon, a minister and tunebook compiler from New Jersey, may have operated a singing school during his appointment in Nova Scotia, 1765-70, as he did in earlier and later appointments elsewhere. More precise records exist for the schools of Amasa Braman (Liverpool, NS, c1776), Reuben McFarlen (Halifax, 1788) and Stephen Humbert (Saint John, 1796). No doubt there were others; and after 1800 a considerable spread of the movement is documented. The first Canadian tunebook, Humbert's *Union Harmony* (1801; further editions 1816, 1831, 1840) includes an original tune entitled "Singing School," with text and music by the compiler, vividly outlining the practices and purposes of such classes and their pursuit in a Canadian environment.

As in the US, the movement in Canada inspired original tunebook publications and a modest body of original compositions. As late as 1867 one such publication in Toronto, *The Vocalist*, included 70 new tunes by the compiler, Missouri-born George W. Linton; typically, the title-page says it was "designed for the Choir, Congregation, *and Singing Class*" (italics added).

The singing schools propagated a simple repertoire and performing style and gave amateurs a genuine and active, if elementary, musical experience. They represent a significant "grass roots" aspect of early Canadian musical, religious and social history. JOHN BECKWITH

Sinnisiak (d c1930) and **Uluksuk** (d 1924), Inuit hunters from the Coppermine region of the NWT, were the first Inuit to be tried for murder under Canadian law. In 1913 they had been hired by 2 Oblate missionaries, Jean-Baptiste Rouvière and Guillaume Le Roux, to act as guides and sled drivers NE of Great Bear Lk. When Le Roux threatened and struck Sinnisiak, the 2 Inuit killed both priests, ate part of Le Roux's liver, and took some of their goods. A mounted police expedition headed by Inspector Charles Dearing La Nauze arrested both men in 1916. They were tried in Edmonton in Aug 1917 for the murder of Rouvière but were acquitted; later that month they were convicted in Calgary of murdering Le Roux. The death sentences were commuted to life imprisonment at Ft Resolution, NWT, and after 2 years they were released. W.R. MORRISON

Reading: R.G. Moyles, *British Law and Arctic Men* (1979).

Sioux, *see* DAKOTA.

Sioux Narrows, Ont, Village, pop 373 (1986c), 394 (1981c), centre of Improvement Dist, inc 1944, located on eastern shore of LAKE OF THE WOODS, 80 km SE of KENORA; traditionally considered the site of an Ojibwa victory over the Sioux. Pictographs in the Sioux Narrows area indicate early Indian occupation of the area. Some 500 Ojibwa currently live on the nearby Whitefish Bay Reserve. European settlement dates from the late 1920s, although previously there were numerous lumber camps in the area. The present economy depends on tourism and related services provided for a summer population of as many as 5000 vacationers. DAVID D. KEMP

Sise, Charles Fleetford, businessman (b at Portsmouth, NH 27 Sept 1834; d at Montréal 9 Apr 1918). Before coming to Canada, Sise had careers as a sea captain, as owner of shipping businesses and as an insurance executive. In 1880 he was appointed special agent in Canada of the National Bell Telephone Co of Boston, Mass, and promptly organized its Canadian subsidiary: The Bell Telephone Company of Canada. He became VP in 1880 and was its second president 1890-1915. Sise directed Bell's emergence into a powerful business entity, molding its very structure: he oversaw its victorious battles with independent telephone companies, its sale of territory in the Maritimes (1887-89) and on the Prairies (1908-09), and its incorporation of an equipment manufacturing subsidiary in 1895 (today known as Northern Telecom). Perhaps most importantly, he defended the company before the 1905 parliamentary Select Committee on Telephone Systems, chaired by Sir William MULOCK, deflecting popular and political agitation for nationalization of Bell into regulatory supervision by the Board of Railway Commissioners for Canada. ROBERT E. BABE

Reading: R.C. Fetherstonaugh, *Charles Fleetford Sise: 1834-1918* (1944).

Sissons, John Howard, "Jack," lawyer, judge (b at Orillia, Ont 14 July 1892; d at Edmonton 11 July 1969). As first judge of the Territorial Court of the Northwest Territories (est 1955), he took "justice to every man's door" by aircraft and dogsled. Sissons practised law in the Peace R country from 1921 and was Liberal MP for that area 1940-45. He was named a district court judge in southern Alberta in 1946 and was chief judge 1950-55. He travelled 64 000 km in twice-yearly circuit, holding trials in remote communities. Several of his decisions relating to hunting rights and to native marriage and adoption practices became legal landmarks. His views were not always popular with the bureaucracy, but he became a legend to the native people and was called *Ekoktoegee,* "the one who listens to things," by the Inuit. He retired in 1966 and wrote his memoirs, *Judge of the Far North* (1968). LEE GIBSON

Sisterhood of St John the Divine, *see* CHRISTIAN RELIGIOUS COMMUNITIES.

Sisters of Providence A female religious congregation founded in 1844 in Montréal by the widow Marie-Émilie Gamelin, née Tavernier, under the name of Daughters of Charity, Servants of the Poor (the present name has been in official usage since 1970). The congregation works in the fields of education and social services but always with emphasis on direct service to society's rejects. From 1828 on the founder was active in a variety of charitable works. Her bishop, Ignace BOURGET, tried to find French sisters to work with her and, after their negative response, asked her to establish the present foundation. In 1986 there were 2129 sisters in 159 communities in Canada and the US. MICHEL THÉRIAULT

Sisters of St Anne A female religious congregation founded in 1850 in Vaudreuil, Qué, by the Servant of God Marie-Esther Sureau, *dit* Blondin (Mother Marie-Anne), for the education of young rural girls and some activities of mercy. She had the support of Bishop Ignace BOURGET, Montréal from the beginning, but the young congregation experienced serious problems in its early years (the founder even had to relinquish her position as superior in 1854 and remain in seclusion until her death in 1890). The Congregation recovered from these trials and spread throughout Canada and the US. In 1986 there were 1369 sisters in 120 communities in Canada and the US. MICHEL THÉRIAULT

Sisters of St Joseph In 1966, 6 Canadian congregations of Sisters of St Joseph (Hamilton, London, Pembroke, Peterborough, Sault Ste Marie, Toronto), working in the fields of education and health-care activities, formed the Federation of the Sisters of St Joseph of Canada. (In a federation, each congregation preserves its autonomy and administration, but shares activities and services.) It was formed because these congregations originate from the Sisters of St Joseph of Carondelet (St Louis, Mo), who in turn had originated from the Soeurs de Saint-Joseph of Le Puy (France, 1648). The first sisters arrived in Toronto from St Louis in 1851. In 1986 there were 1470 sisters in 170 communities in Canada and the US.
MICHEL THÉRIAULT

Sisters of the Holy Names of Jesus and Mary, a religious congregation of women founded in Longueuil, Qué, by the blessed Eulalie Durocher (Mother Marie-Rose) to educate young girls. The spirituality of the congregation is Ignatian (Jesuit). The founder, closely linked with the Oblates of Mary Immaculate, had agreed in 1842 to preside over the first Canadian group of Children of Mary (a sisterhood influenced by the Oblates); in 1843, Eulalie was ordered by Ignace BOURGET, bishop of Montréal, to found a congregation to replace the French sisters (from Marseilles) who had refused to settle in Canada (she took their name, habit and constitutions). In 1986 there were 2727 members in 218 communities in Canada.
MICHEL THÉRIAULT

Sitting Bull, Ta-tanka I-yotank, Sioux chief (b somewhere in the buffalo country about 1834; d at Standing Rock, N Dak 5 Dec 1890). For a decade after the Battle of the Little Bighorn in Montana on 25 June 1876, in which the Sioux (DAKOTA) destroyed Lt-Col Custer's force, Sitting Bull was the best-known and most-feared native warrior on the continent. For 4 of those years, he and 5000 of his people were unwanted guests in Canada, in the Wood Mountain area of southern Saskatchewan.

American and Canadian authorities were unhappy with this turn of events and the Canadian government, fearful that his presence would incite intertribal or racial warfare, refused Sitting Bull's request for a reservation. The task of surveillance was assigned to Major James Morrow WALSH of the NWMP who came to sympathize with and admire the chief. But the government stood firm in refusing reservation and food, and gradually the hungry Sioux began returning to accept American promises of rations. Among the last to surrender to the threat of starvation was the old chief who was finally settled at Standing Rock Reserve in N Dakota.
GRANT MacEWAN

Sivuarapik, Charlie (Sheeguapik), sculptor (b near Povungnituk, Qué about 1911; d 26 Sept 1968 of tuberculosis). Prohibited by ill health from participating in the hunting economy, he was rescued from abject poverty by his carving skill, but he benefited only briefly from the escalation in INUIT ART prices during the 1960s. A perfectionist, he studied his own anatomy and produced powerful, elegantly realistic hunters with their prey. He was the first Inuk member of the Sculptors Soc of Canada, and was a founding member and first president (1958-67) of the Povungnituk Co-operative Soc.
MARY M. CRAIG

Six Nations, *see* IROQUOIS.

Skeena River, 580 km long, rises in the northern interior of BC and flows generally SW, draining about 54 000 km², to meet the Pacific Ocean at Chatham Sound S of PRINCE RUPERT. The second-largest river (after the FRASER) entirely within BC, its main tributaries are the Bulkley and Babine

rivers. It was called *K-shian* ("water of the clouds") by the Tsimshian ("people at the mouth of the K-shian") and Gitksan ("people who live up the K-shian"), and has always played an important role in the lives of the native people.

Non-Indian influence is relatively recent. Because of strong native control of the lower river, the first non-Indian penetration of the Skeena watershed was from the E, when the HBC established posts on Babine and Bear lakes (1822, 1826). In 1859 a reconnaissance for a transcontinental railway was made up the Skeena as far as the Bulkley R. 1871 saw a gold rush up the Skeena to the Omineca goldfields; some good strikes were made on the Skeena itself. With the establishment of Port Essington near the mouth, and Hazelton at the head of navigation at the Bulkley confluence, freight traffic on the Skeena developed rapidly.

From 1880 the HBC used the Skeena route to supply its inland posts. Salmon fishing became an important activity, as it is today. By the 1890s there were 7 canneries in the Skeena estuary. Interest in the agricultural potential of the Skeena below Hazelton grew next, and the provincial government encouraged settlement.

The Skeena provides Canada's only practical alternative rail and road outlet to the Pacific besides the Fraser. In 1914 the GRAND TRUNK PACIFIC RY (now CN) was completed from Hazelton to the coast, terminating at Prince Rupert. Following WWII the valley was reached by the Yellowhead Highway. The town of TERRACE is a regional centre today for the lumber industry.
ROSEMARY J. FOX

Reading: R.G. Large, *Skeena: River of Destiny* (1981).

Skelton, Oscar Douglas, academic, public servant (b at Orangeville, Ont 13 July 1878; d at Ottawa 28 Jan 1941). After a brilliant student career in classics at Queen's, Skelton graduated in 1908 from the U of Chicago with a PhD in political economy. He returned to Queen's, where he was John A. Macdonald Professor of Political Science and Economics, 1909-25, and dean of arts, 1919-25. Skelton was a dedicated, popular teacher and he published widely on economics and history as well as current affairs. A liberal democrat and an uncompromising nationalist who believed Canada must take control of its own affairs, he worked for the LIBERAL PARTY as early as the election of 1911 and was close to Sir Wilfrid LAURIER in his last years. Mackenzie KING engaged him as a foreign-policy consultant after winning the election of 1921, and appointed him undersecretary of state for external affairs in 1925. He held the position until his death, serving King and also Conservative PM R.B. BENNETT. Although unassuming and unaffected and not a strong administrator, Skelton was the leading civil servant of his time, with a finger in every bureaucratic pie: a key adviser on domestic as well as foreign policy, the founder of the modern Department of EXTERNAL AFFAIRS, and an architect of the Canadian public service. His major publications were *Socialism: A Critical Analysis* (1911), *Life and Times of Sir Alexander Tilloch Galt* (1920), *Life and Letters of Sir Wilfrid Laurier* (2 vols, 1921) and *Our Generation, Its Gains and Losses* (1938).
NORMAN HILLMER

Skelton, Robin, poet, critic, publisher, educator (b at Easington, East Yorkshire, Eng 12 Oct 1925). He was raised in England and educated at Leeds U (MA 1951) and taught at the U of Manchester 1951 to 1963, when he immigrated to Canada. He began teaching at U of Victoria (1963). Skelton has published 32 books of poetry, including *Patmos and Other Poems* (1955), *Selected Poems: 1947-67* (1968), *The Hunting Dark* (1971), *Wordsong: Twelve Ballads* (1983), *Distances* (1985) and *Collected Longer Poems: 1947-77* (1985). He is a meditative, personal poet adept at poetic genres from the ballad to obscure Welsh lyric forms. Skelton is also an accomplished translator (eg, *Two Hundred Poems from the Greek Anthology,* 1971) and a devotee of the occult (eg, *Talismanic Magic,* 1985), as well as an artist. His 8 critical works include *The Poet's Calling* (1975) and *Poetic Truth* (1978). A book of short stories, *Telling the Tale,* was published in 1987.
SHARON DRACHE

Ski Jumping Although informal ski jumping had taken place for decades, the first officially measured jump (30.5 m) was made by Sondre Nordheim in Norway in 1860. About 20 years later, Scandinavian miners and lumbermen brought the sport to western Canada, where it flourished. In 1891 local Scandinavians formed a ski club in Revelstoke, BC, to promote ski-jumping competition. Although it lasted only a few years, it provided excellent jumping meets in its rivalry with neighbouring Rossland, BC. The Rossland winter carnival of 1898, for example, attracted thousands to watch the local hero Olaus Jeldness win Canada's first ski-jumping championship. Over the next 25 years ski jumping was one of Canada's most popular winter spectator sports. Large crowds watched jumpers hurtle down mountainsides in the Rockies, down large wooden trestles on the Prairies, down Mont Royal in the heart of Montréal, and down the "cliffs" of Rockliffe Park in Ottawa. In 1919 Ted Devlin set up the Cliffside Ski Club in Ottawa to challenge Sigurd Lockeberg's Ottawa Ski Club. During several years of intense but friendly competition, jumping reached its all-time peak of popularity. Almost 10 000 spectators gathered at the Fairy Lake jump (near Hull, Qué), designed by Gunnar Sjelderup, to watch an international field compete in a meet presided over by the governor general. Somersaults over the jump, and even a tandem somersault performed by 2 Dartmouth College (New Hampshire) students, added a spectacular element, anticipating today's freestyle skiing.

Although the newly formed Canadian Amateur Ski Association held its first national championships in Montréal in 1921 (won by E. Sundberg), the centre of Canadian jumping soon shifted back west. Resurrected in 1914, the Revelstoke Ski Club became internationally famous through the efforts of its founder, Sigurd Halverson, and Nels Nelson, a young local athlete. After many years of near misses, Nelson set a world amateur record of 68.3 m in 1925 and went on to coach several other world-famous Canadian-born jumpers, including Bob Lymbourne, who jumped a world record 87.5 m in 1933.

From 1933 to the 1970s, ski jumping assumed a much lower profile, as alpine SKIING captured most of the public attention. Strong local programs persisted across the country, however, and suddenly pushed the sport back into prominence in 1979 when Ottawa's Horst BULAU won the world junior championship, followed closely by Thunder Bay's Steve COLLINS in 1980. Since then, the 2 have gone on to many World Cup wins and have rekindled Canadian public interest in the sport.
MURRAY SHAW

Skiing It is probable that the first skiers in Canada were the NORSE, who established several East Coast settlements about 1000 AD. Although no direct proof has been found, it would be remarkable if they had not brought their then 4000-year-old tradition of winter travel on long wooden sticks ("*skath*") with them.

The birth of modern skiing in N America, nearly 1000 years later, can be credited to their direct descendants. Scandinavian prospectors and miners participating in the gold rushes of the mid-1800s used wooden "snowshoes" or "gliding shoes" up to 4 m long as a means of travel as well as for highly competitive professional downhill racing competitions. From 1856 to 1869, the Norwegian John "Snowshoe" Thomson provided the only winter overland mail route from the East to California. He was famous throughout the American West for his 300 km round trips, accomplished in 5 days with up to 50 kg of mail. Many of Canada's Scandinavian prospectors and railway builders were probably inspired by Thomson to polish the skiing skills developed in their homelands.

While westerners were out skiing unobserved in the wilderness, the first recorded Canadian ski outing was a trip by "Mr. A. Birch, a Norwegian gentleman of Montreal," who skied from Montréal to Québec in 1879 on a 3 m pair of "patent Norwegian snowshoes" using a single pole. In 1883 the Montréal *Daily Star* published a major article, "New Winter Sport in Norway," describing in detail the use of 2.5 m wooden "snowskates" plus a single 1.5 m staff. In 1887 Frederick Hamilton, the governor general's aide-de-camp, introduced skiing to Ottawa "amidst universal derision." In Montréal, however, skis were being adopted by the most adventurous members of the many large snowshoe clubs popular at that time. As skis slowly supplanted snowshoes for social winter sporting excursions in eastern Canada (*see* SNOWSHOEING), major ski clubs sprang up in Montréal (1904), Québec and Toronto (1908) and Ottawa (1910).

Initially the popularity of the sport was largely based on SKI JUMPING competitions, featuring such famous Scandinavian immigrants as Olaus Jeldness (Rossland, BC), Andy Ohlgren (the Lakehead) and Sigurd Lockeberg (Ottawa). The large crowds attracted to these meets financed a wide variety of social activities for many fledgling ski clubs. The supremacy of jumping lasted right up to the mid-1930s in western Canada, where world ski-jumping distance records were set on the giant Revelstoke jump from 1925 (Nels Nelson, 68.3 m) to 1933 (Bob Lymbourne, 87.5 m). In the East, the emphasis shifted from nordic (jumping and cross-country) to alpine (downhill, giant slalom and slalom) disciplines during the 1920s. Open hills in the vicinity of most major cities were frequented by skiers, who packed the snow by climbing the hill sideways in the morning and then spent the day practicing Telemark and Christiania turns developed in Norway.

The first professional instructor in Canada, Emile Cochand, was brought to the LAURENTIANS from Switzerland in 1911. By 1917 he had built the first Canadian ski resort, Chalet Cochand, in Ste-Marguerite, Qué. During the 1920s and early 1930s the Laurentians, the Gatineau hills and the Collingwood area of Ontario began attracting skiers for weekend excursions to large hills. Normal equipment in those days comprised wooden skis with adjustable steel toeplates and leather heel straps, plus a pair of short bamboo poles with large baskets. When worn with flexible leather boots, this gear was also suited to ski touring on the many trails being blazed by "Jackrabbit" JOHANNSEN all across the Laurentians.

In 1932 a number of events combined to change the face of the sport completely. The Redbirds of McGill hosted an Oxford-Cambridge ski team at the first major Canadian slalom race at Ste-Marguerite. The victorious British team introduced steel edges (invented in Austria by Rudolf Lettner about 1930) and the Arlberg turning technique developed in the Austrian ski schools established by Hannes Schneider during the 1920s. A few kilometres away in Shawbridge, Qué, Alex Foster jacked up an old 4-cylinder Dodge to power the world's first rope tow. For 25 cents a half day, "Foster's Folly" enabled Canadian skiers to concentrate on the new downhill techniques without spending time and effort climbing back up. Within a few years, rope tows and downhill ski runs were found all over N America.

The 1932 Lake Placid Winter OLYMPIC GAMES marked the last time that international ski competition was restricted to nordic events, since increased resort skiing was causing a worldwide surge of interest in the alpine events. The end of old-time ski touring came with the introduction of the cable binding in 1935. The new "Kandahar" bindings, by fastening the skiers' heels down, gave them dramatically improved downhill performances but made ski touring and hill climbing unacceptably awkward. Fortunately, many ski pioneers were building just the sort of resorts the new generation required, eg, Mike Dehouck at Mont Ste-Anne, Joe Ryan at Mont Tremblant, John Clifford at Camp Fortune, Cliff White in Banff and Rudolph Verne on the West Coast. The resorts to which the new generation of skiers now flocked offered a wide variety of ski lifts and groomed slopes, as well as ski schools run by professional instructors, mostly Swiss and Austrian but including a few well-known Canadians such as Harvey Clifford, Louis Cochand and Ernie McCulloch.

Canada's international competition began rather modestly. In 1933 the McGill team took what they had learned from the British back to Europe to win the international intercollegiate relay championship. On the same trip, George Jost also won the first individual Canadian overseas title, the Roberts of Kandahar downhill. For the next 15 years, Canadian skiers remained largely unnoticed at major world competitions.

WWII had an important impact on Canadian skiing in 2 areas: it provided ski training for a number of soldiers, and it produced large quantities of solid dependable equipment which subsequently became available at very low prices as war surplus. Large heavy skis, metal-framed khaki rucksacks and bulky canvas parkas gave the sport a decidedly utilitarian air well into the 1950s but offered many young postwar families an inexpensive start. The beginning of skiing's mass popularity in Canada, however, coincided roughly with the introduction in 1955 of stretch pants, buckle boots, polyethylene bases and brightly coloured metal skis. Skiing rapidly became a fashionable way to spend an exciting and healthy winter weekend.

The glamour of the sport was sharply enhanced in 1958, when Lucile WHEELER unexpectedly won the world championship titles in both downhill and giant slalom. These wins attracted great public interest to the sport in Canada and inspired the country to send a national team to Europe the following year. A tradition of internationally competitive female skiers has been maintained ever since, featuring world champions or Olympic gold medalists Anne HEGGTVEIT (1960), Nancy GREENE (1967, 1968), Betsy CLIFFORD (1970) and Kathy KREINER (1976). Laurie GRAHAM, Lisa SAVIJARVI and Karen Percy (2 bronze medals at the 1988 Winter Olympics, Calgary) continued to provide strong international competition through the 1980s. The international stature of Canadian male skiers was slower to develop. "Jungle Jim" Hunter's alpine combined Olympic bronze medal in Sapporo, Japan, in 1972 was a remarkable individual achievement for such an inexperienced national team. In the early 1970s a decision was made to concentrate the team's resources on downhill, the international glamour event. In 1975-76 the success of the strategy became obvious. Hunter, in his last year, placed in the top 10 in 4 World Cup races but was overshadowed by the new team of Dave Irwin, Dave Murray, Steve PODBORSKI and Ken READ. They burst into prominence with Read's season-opening win at Val d'Isere, followed only a few weeks later by a win by Irwin at Schladming.

Famous for their daring assaults on the toughest, iciest courses, the "Crazy Canucks" took the international press by storm. During careers lasting well into the 1980s, these 4 skiers provided consistent excitement with 14 World Cup victories and dozens of top 10 placings. Under coaches Glenn Wurtele and former Austrian coach Heinz Stohl, a new group of men, including Rob BOYD, Brian Stemmle and Felix Belczyk, emerged in the mid-1980s, with Boyd winning at Val di Gardena, Italy, in 1987. In early 1988 Belczyk won Canada's first Alpine World Cup supergiant slalom, in Leukerbad, Switzerland.

In 1986 over 2 million Canadians own alpine ski equipment. About 900 000 ski once a week or more, providing 70% of the activity at roughly 650 ski areas, staffed by about 6000 certified instructors and 6000 ski patrollers. Their equipment normally consists of fibreglass skis rigidly fastened to stiff synthetic boots by safety-release bindings. The skis have become shorter over the last decade, to enable recreational skiers to maneuvre more easily. Use of shorter skis by competitive skiers soon led to the creation of freestyle skiing (*see* SKIING, FREESTYLE), an acrobatic branch of the sport highlighting performances in 3 new disciplines: aerial, ballet and moguls. Canadian athletes have dominated international competition from the sport's inception.

The popularity of alpine skiing has not been achieved at the expense of the original nordic disciplines. Although ski jumping does not involve great numbers of participants, it has attracted a great deal of public attention during the early 1980s through the unprecedented international victories of Horst BULAU and Steve COLLINS. Over the last decade, the most significant trend in Canadian skiing has been the tremendous growth in CROSS-COUNTRY SKIING. In 1986 over 3.5 million Canadians owned cross-country equipment, of whom almost 2 million ski once a week or more. After 50 years of increasing specialization of equipment and technique, it is interesting to observe a strong movement afoot today to return to all-purpose touring skis, flexible leather boots and bindings that leave the heels free. Using such equipment and the Telemark turning techniques of the early 1900s, skiers are again able to enjoy both the challenge and exhilaration of downhill skiing and the healthy exercise and serenity of cross-country skiing. MURRAY SHAW

Skiing, Freestyle, is the newest addition to the SKIING family of disciplines. Freestyle's distinctive 3-event format — moguls, ballet and aerials — has set it apart from its competitive skiing cousins and made it one of the most popular and spectacular winter spectator sports. The evolution of the aerials event in freestyle skiing can be traced to 1907, when the first flip on skis was recorded. It was not until the 1950s, however, that Stein Erickson, the high-profile Olympic alpine silver medalist, popularized front and back aerial somersaults during professional ski shows in Vermont and Colorado. In 1965, Austrian gymnast Herman Goellner surpassed the single somersaults achieved by Erickson by performing the first double, triple and mobius (full-twisting) flips. Sites across Vermont also bore first witness to the feats of Goellner and Tom Leroy, who performed simultaneous inverted aerials to the astonishment of large, ski-show crowds.

The ballet event was born in 1929, when Dr Fritz Reuel conceived of a form of skiing similar to figure skating and developed the Reuel Christie and other spinning maneuvres for skiers. Doug Pfeiffer's School of Exotic Skiing (1956-62) expanded Dr Reuel's premise by teaching new tricks such as the mambo, the Charleston, spinners, tip rolls and crossovers, and was the first evidence that on-hill instruction was being provided for the skiing public.

Organized freestyle skiing in Canada took shape when a group headed by John Johnston founded the Canadian Freestyle Skiers Assn in 1974. Shortly thereafter the Canadian Ski Assn adopted freestyle as a discipline within its jurisdiction and hired Johnston to administer and organize competitive freestyle programs for amateur skiers across the country. One of the most important steps in the evolution of the sport was taken when the International Olympic Committee (IOC) accepted freestyle skiing as a demonstration event in the 1988 and 1992 Winter Olympic Games. The Canadians who have dominated the international freestyle competitive circuit over the past decade have gone relatively unheralded, including 5-time world champions John Eaves and Marie-Claude Asselin, and world cup grand prix championship winners Greg Athans, Stephanie Sloan, Lauralee Bowie, Jean Corriveau, Craig Clow, Peter Judge, Bill Keenan, Yves Laroche, Anna Fraser, Meredith Gardner and Jean-Marc Rozon. Out of the first-ever International Ski Federation world championships held in Tignes, France, in 1986, came 2 Canadian world champions – Lloyd Langlois and Alain Laroche who, because of their records of accomplishment on the international level, were elected to the Canadian Amateur Sports Hall of Fame in Apr 1987. SUSAN VERDIER

Reading: R. Wieman, Freestyle Skiing: A Complete Guide to the Fundamentals (1980).

Skinner, Frank Leith, farmer, horticulturalist (b at Rosehearty, Scot 5 May 1882; d at Dropmore, Man 27 Aug 1967). After schooling in Aberdeen, he immigrated to Dropmore in 1895 and ran a large grain and stock farm with his brother. In a search for hardy varieties able to withstand the harsh climate, he pioneered horticulture on the Canadian prairie. Skinner introduced many economically important fruits and shrubs, at first as a hobby, but after 1924, as part of a nursery business. He wrote widely in popular and scientific literature and served as president of the Manitoba Horticultural Soc. MARTIN K. McNICHOLL

Skinners Pond, PEI, UP, pop 119 (1986c), 132 (1981c), 135 km NW of Charlottetown, is a fishing port on the western coast of Prince County. There are 2 suggestions for the community's distinctive name: the bay could have been the site of pelting operations or it might have been named after a shipwrecked sea captain. The ACADIANS were the first settlers to establish a permanent community, to be joined by IRISH immigrants around the mid-19th century. Thanks to the sheltered, navigable harbour, fishing has been the community's economic backbone. Beginning in the 1940s, the fishermen have supplemented their incomes by raking IRISH MOSS from the harbour beaches, from which a gelatinous substance called carrageenin is extracted for use in pharmaceutical and certain food products. As in the other

small communities on the Island's northwestern peninsula, the people of Skinners Pond are commercially tied to the centrally located town of Tignish. A recent addition to the community is a museum dedicated to the career of Canadian country-music star and former resident, Stompin' Tom CONNORS. W.S. KEIZER

Skreslet, Laurie Grant, mountaineer and guide, outdoor equipment designer (b at Calgary 25 Oct 1949). Skreslet's affinity for international MOUNTAINEERING can be traced to early hiking and camping trips in the Rockies and a 2-year, 35-country stint at sea, which followed his departure from home at age 16. He was introduced to climbing in 1970 and within 2 years was a member of a successful expedition to Huascarán (6768 m), Peru's highest mountain. He participated in expeditions nearly every year thereafter in S America, the US and the British Isles. He first climbed in Nepal in 1981 and returned with the Canadian MOUNT EVEREST EXPEDITION in 1982, where, on Oct 5, he became the first Canadian to stand atop the world. He has since been part of an attempt on Kanchenjunga (8598 m, the world's third largest peak) and the 1986 Canadian Everest Light Expedition, in which Sharon WOOD was successful in her bid to become the first woman from the Americas to reach the 8848 m summit. BART ROBINSON

Skunk, carnivorous, cat-sized member of the WEASEL family, black in colour with conspicuous white stripes or spots. Two genera occur in Canada. Skunks are notorious for a foul-smelling secretion (mercaptan) produced in a pair of anal glands. Used in self-defence, it can be projected a distance of 3-4 m. The horned OWL is one of the skunk's few natural predators. The striped skunk (*Mephitis mephitis*) occurs in every province except Newfoundland. Adults average 54 cm long and weigh 1.6 kg. Skunks are nocturnal, passing the day in burrows. They hibernate through the coldest months, frequently several animals together. Insects, vegetation, fruit, birds' eggs and small mammals are major foods. Males are polygamous and the female alone cares for young. Litters, averaging 5-6 young, are born after a 62-day gestation. Young grow rapidly and at 2 months are fully weaned and have operational scent glands. They usually stay with the mother through the winter. The smaller spotted skunk (*Spilogale putorius*) occurs in southwestern BC, and ranges south to the western US and Mexico. IAN McTAGGART-COWAN

The striped skunk (*Mephitis mephitis*) occurs in every province except Nfld (*artwork by Claire Tremblay*).

Škvorecký, Josef, novelist, editor, professor (b in Nachod, Czech 27 Sept 1924). His early involvement with literature and jazz helped him survive the successive Nazi and communist occupations of his homeland, in spite of retaliations and censorship. His first 2 novels, *The End of the*

Nylon Age (1956) and *The Cowards* (1958, tr 1970) were promptly banned, and he lost his position as editor of *World Literature* in a 1958 purge of intellectuals. After the 1968 Soviet invasion, he and his wife, the actress-novelist Zdena Salivarova, came to Toronto, where in 1971 they established Sixty Eight Publishers to make available the works of Czech exiles. Škvorecký served as writer-in-residence at U of T for a year, and in 1971 joined its English department, where he still teaches. That same year he published his first book in Canada, *All the Bright Young Men and Women,* which he called "a personal history of the Czech cinema." In Canada his reputation was firmly consolidated with the 1977 translation of his 1963 novel, *The Bass Saxophone,* and has grown steadily, reflected by his winning the Governor General's Award for *The Engineer of Human Souls* (1977, tr 1984). Other novels available in English include *The Mournful Demeanour of Lieutenant Boruvka* (1966, tr 1974; Canadian ed 1987), *Miss Silver's Past* (1968, tr 1975), *The Swell Season* (1975, tr 1982) and *Dvořak in Love* (1983, tr 1986), a fictional interpretation of Dvořak's career in America in the 1890s. Škvorecký's work reflects his essentially comic view of life, his scholarly knowledge of music, film and fictional form, and his compassion for characters like exiles, lovers and artists, drawn from societies in constant flux. He enjoys a wide reputation throughout the literary world: he won a Guggenheim Fellowship and the Neustadt International Prize for Literature in 1980, and in 1982 was nominated for the Nobel Prize. HALLVARD DAHLIE

Reading: World Literature Today (Autumn, 1980), issue devoted to Škvorecký.

Slave Lake, Alta, Town, pop 5429 (1986c). Slave Lake is about 1.6 km from the S shore of LESSER SLAVE LK, and a major transportation hub on the divide which ties the Arctic and Hudson Bay drainage systems. At the turn of the century, it was a focus for the riverboats that connected Edmonton to the Peace River country. In 1909 the telegraph came through and in 1913 the railway. By 1906 the settlement of Sawridge was in evidence; it was renamed Slave Lake in 1922. After the disastrous flood of 1935-36, the town was moved 2 km to its present location. Slave Lake experienced a boom in World War II with the construction of the ALASKA HIGHWAY, and later from the 1950s to 1980s with the development of its timber and oil resources. FRITS PANNEKOEK

Slave River, 434 km, connects the PEACE R and the drainage from Lks CLAIRE and ATHABASCA to GREAT SLAVE LK, forming the short upper reaches of the Slave-MACKENZIE R system in the NWT. It has a sinuous, often multichannelled, course traversing the flat, extensively glaciated Archean granitic terrain of the Canadian SHIELD and is currently used almost entirely as a transportation waterway and an important habitat for wildlife. The Alberta government is evaluating the possible construction of a major (2000 MW) hydroelectric-power dam at the Pelican Rapids near FORT SMITH. This controversial project may destroy nesting grounds of the white pelican, endanger breeding areas of the rare whooping crane and cause flooding in the Peace-Athabasca Delta. IAN A. CAMPBELL

Slavery in what is now Canada was practised by a number of Indian tribes, notably those on the Northwest Coast. As practised by Europeans it may have begun with the Portuguese explorer Gaspar CORTE-REAL, who enslaved 50 Indian men and women in 1500 in Newfoundland. Black slaves were introduced by the French as early as 1608. The first slave transported directly from Africa was sold in 1629. Slavery received a legal foundation in NEW FRANCE, 1689-1709, and by 1759 there were 3604 recorded slaves, of whom 1132 were black. Whereas the French preferred *panis* (Indians, so called after the often docile Pawnee), the English settlers brought in African slaves. Slavery expanded rapidly after 1783, as American LOYALISTS brought their slaves with them. The total was never high, however, as slavery was generally unsuited to Canadian agriculture or commerce, and most of the BLACKS who settled in Nova Scotia immediately following the AMERICAN REVOLUTION were free. Slavery technically remained legal in most of Canada until it was abolished for the entire British Empire in 1834 (legislation, 1833), though slavery as an institution declined steadily after 1793, when John Graves SIMCOE challenged the legality of slavery for Upper Canada. Upper Canada's Act to abolish slavery freed no slaves, however, since it proposed only gradual emancipation.

In Canada slaves generally worked as personal servants or on the wharves. A few settlers had many slaves, but more than 20 was considered unusual. This made the attack on slavery far simpler than it was in plantation economies, where their labour was more important. The most effective and sustained attack on slavery came in New Brunswick in 1800, when Ward CHIPMAN prepared an especially thorough legal, historical and moral statement against slavery. Generally, slavery was physically benign, and especially so in PEI, though there were recorded instances of harsh punishment and many advertisements for the return of runaway slaves. The UNDERGROUND RAILROAD assisted fugitive American slaves to reach Canada prior to the abolition of slavery in the US during the AMERICAN CIVIL WAR. In Canada the last surviving former slave died in Cornwall, Ont, in 1871. ROBIN W. WINKS

Reading: Robin W. Winks, *The Blacks in Canada* (1971).

Slavey (Slave) are a major group of Athapaskan-speaking (or DENE) people living in the boreal forest region of the western Canadian Subarctic. Although there is no equivalent in Dene languages, the term has been adopted by many Dene as a collective term of self-designation when speaking English. The Slavey inhabit an area dominated by lakes, mountains and river systems, which extends along the Slave, Athabasca and Mackenzie drainages S from Ft Nelson, BC, on the W and from the Hay Lakes region of Alberta on the E, N to a region near Ft Norman and the S shore of Great Bear Lk in the NWT. They are closely related linguistically and culturally to the HARE, KUTCHIN, DOGRIB, BEAVER and CHIPEWYAN. The Slavey, according to a 1978 census, number about 4000, of whom 2500 live in the NWT. The term Slavey may be a translation of the Cree word meaning captive or, as Father Petitot suggested in the 19th century, the term may indicate timidity.

Archaeological evidence suggests that the Slavey region has been inhabited from at least 3000 BC (*see* PREHISTORY). During the late precontact period, the Slavey economy was based on the harvesting of fish, small game, moose, caribou and berries. In winter the Slavey camped in groups or local bands of some 10-30 kin-related individuals. In summer these groups came together briefly near the shores of a major lake to form a regional BAND of perhaps 200 persons.

Initial European contact occurred with Alexander MACKENZIE's expedition in 1789. Soon after, trading posts were established throughout the area. After 1821 the HBC made Ft Simpson its major terminus for the Mackenzie region and in 1858 Anglican and Roman Catholic missions were established. Slavey in Alberta, BC and some parts of the NWT were incorporated into Treaty No 8 between 1899 and 1911; those in the rest of the NWT into Treaty No 11 in 1921-22 (*see* INDIAN TREATIES). Despite the influx of many non-Dene, evidence indicates that the Slavey, between contact and the end of WWII, still lived for most of the year in small, kin-based communities, harvested traditional foods, spoke their own languages, and raised children in the manner of their parents.

After WWII new government programs intended to extend benefits including health care and schooling to the Slavey, together with economic conditions which resulted in a collapse of the fur trade, brought about a major transformation in the life-style of the Slavey, as people moved into town and sent their children to school. However, recent studies show that subsistence obtained through traditional harvesting has remained a significant activity. MICHAEL I. ASCH

Reading: J. Helm, ed, *Handbook of North American Indians*, vol 6: *Subarctic* (1981) and *The Lynx People: The Dynamics of a Northern Athapaskan Band* (1961); J.J. Honigmann, *Ethnography and Acculturation of the Fort Nelson Slave* (1946).

Slemon, Charles Roy, air marshal (b at Winnipeg 7 Nov 1904). One of the first group of provisional pilot officers trained in the RCAF after its creation in 1924, Slemon spent much of the following decade as a "bush pilot in uniform" flying aerial photography operations over the North. He was senior staff officer and then commander of western air command 1938-41, and in 1942 was posted overseas. He served as senior air staff officer of No 6 (Canadian) Bomber Group 1942-44, and was deputy air officer commander in chief of the RCAF overseas in 1945. A fine administrator he was appointed chief of the air staff 1953-57, leaving to become the first deputy commander in chief of NORAD. He retired to live in Colorado Springs, Colo, in 1964. NORMAN HILLMER

Slocan, BC, Village, pop 294 (1986c), 351 (1981c), inc 1901, is located 27 km S of Silverton and 70 km by road NW of Nelson, at the S end of Slocan Lk. It was founded to service the Springer and Slocan Valley galena mining boom, and began as a transportation centre at the foot of the lake in 1895. However, it declined rapidly with the demise of Slocan Mines. It revived during WWII when 4800 JAPANESE were relocated at Lemon Cr. Today, logging and sawmilling are Slocan's main enterprises. Creation of Valhalla Park to the NW (1983) gives the area a future as a tourist centre. WILLIAM A. SLOAN

Slocum, Joshua, sea captain and author (b at Wilmot Township, NS 20 Feb 1844; d at sea sometime after 14 Nov 1909). Largely self-educated, Slocum began his deep-water career at 16, gaining experience in the American, European and Far Eastern trades. A peripatetic mariner, adventurer and sometime shipbuilder, he moved fluently among vessels, ports and cargoes; his family regularly accompanied him. His *Voyage of the Liberdade* (1890) and *Voyage of the Destroyer* (1894) highlight his early career. In 1893, having fallen on hard times in New England, Slocum rebuilt a derelict oyster sloop, the *Spray*, intending to sail it alone around the world — one of the few great marine challenges then remaining. The *Spray* was 36'9" long, 14'2" wide, 4'2" deep, and at just under 13 tons gross, it "sat on the water like a swan." Slocum left Boston, Mass, on 24 Apr 1895, and after a voyage exceeding 46 000 miles, reached Newport, RI, on 27 June 1898. *Sailing Alone Around the World* (1900) is an eloquent account of this voyage, and remains a classic in seafaring literature. The Slocum Society (US) perpetuates his memory, but in Canada his achievements have received little attention, other than a plaque erected in his boyhood community of Westport, Brier Island, NS. LOIS KERNAGHAN

Slovaks The first known Slovak immigrant to Canada was Joseph Bellon, who landed in 1878 in Toronto and started a wireworks factory. The majority of the early immigrants were manual workers from the US. According to the 1981 census, only 43 070 Canadians declared their ethnic origin as Slovak (0.00017% of Canada's population) but in fact it can be assumed that there are about 100 000 Canadians of Slovak origin. Slovaks are generally a deeply religious people; they are proud of their origin and are therefore quick to correct those who refer to them as CZECHS or Czechoslovaks.

Migration and Settlement There have been 4 main waves of Slovak immigrants, inspired mainly by economic and political conditions in their homeland. Immigrants of the first wave (1885-1914) settled on farmland in the West. Later groups went to work in Alberta and BC mines, and for the CPR. The second wave, estimated at 30 000, took place during the interwar years. Many were young skilled workers who emigrated to earn good wages in order to buy land in Slovakia. Others, however, sent for their families and went either to farming settlements in the West or to Ontario and Québec mining towns. The third wave of some 20 000 began to arrive after WWII and included war refugees as well as those fleeing the communist takeover of 1948. Many were former government officials who gave new impetus to Slovak organizations. Most settled in the major urban centres. The fourth wave was sparked by the Warsaw Pact invasion of Czechoslovakia in 1968. These refugees (some 13 000) were among the best educated to leave their homeland. Settling in urban centres, they contributed to the growth of Slovak organizations and found their place in Canadian economic, political and cultural life.

Social and Cultural Life Social stratification among Slovak Canadians today is determined by date of arrival in Canada, the position held in Slovakia, the success achieved in Canada and the willingness to participate actively in Slovak organizations. Catholic and Protestant clergy have played an important role as spiritual and community leaders, and Slovak parishioners of all denominations have helped immigrants to overcome linguistic and cultural differences. Parish life, especially for the first 3 waves, and Slovak organizations have helped to foster the Slovak language and enhance family cohesion. A notable example of the importance of parish life was the consecration of the Slovak Cathedral of the Transfiguration in Unionville, Ontario on 15 Sept 1984 by Pope John Paul II during his visit to Canada. Slovak newspapers have played an equally important role in assisting immigrants, and they have also reflected the political and economic divisions in the community.

The early immigrants created benefit societies because of difficult economic conditions and lack of state-supported welfare measures. Today the Canadian Slovak League is the most important Slovak organization. It publishes *Kanadský Slovák (The Canadian Slovak)*, and helps to maintain Slovak traditions. Literary works are fostered through Slovak publications in the Western world and by the Slovak World Congress, headquartered in Toronto.

Group Maintenance The political fate of the Slovaks in their homeland has been the main factor in preserving the group's consciousness and cohesion in Canada. Most Slovak Canadians today are concerned about their homeland and through various organizations and newspapers keep abreast of events there. STANISLAV J. KIRSCHBAUM

Slovenes are inhabitants of Slovenia, a republic of Yugoslavia. Until the 1971 census, Canadian statistics included immigrant Slovenes among Hungarians, Italians, Yugoslavs or Austrians, and some (those who had settled in France first) as French. The 1986 census preliminary estimates record 5890 Slovenes in Canada, but this figure is low, since many Slovenes declare themselves to be Yugoslavs or Canadians.

Migration and Settlement In 1830 Reverend Frederick Baraga, a Slovenian missionary, later the first bishop of Sault Ste Marie and Marquette, came to work among the Indians around Lk Superior. He learned the language of the Ottawa and Chippewa and published *A Theoretical and Practical Grammar of the Otchipwe Language* (for which he is known as the "Father of Indian Literature") and a dictionary of the Ojibwa language (1853). Large numbers of Slovenes, attracted partly by Father Baraga's reports, began to immigrate to N America 1875-1900. Those who settled in Canada worked primarily in mines, in road construction around Timmins and Kirkland Lake, and farming in the Niagara Peninsula. At Beamsville, they established the Slovenian Farmers' Co-operative and Slovenian Farmers' Home. Others settled in centres such as Nanaimo, Port Alberni, Vancouver, Rossland, Penticton and Cassidy in BC; Canmore, Bankhead, Banff and Evergreen in Alberta; Quill Lake, Sask; New Waterford and Caledonia Mines, NS; and in Montréal.

Between 1921 and 1936 (according to Yugoslav statistics) only 4281 Slovenes immigrated to Canada, primarily for economic reasons, but after 1948 large numbers immigrated (many of whom settled in Toronto) following the establishment of the communist regime in Yugoslavia. Some Slovenes also immigrated to Canada (1956-58) after the Hungarian uprising.

Social and Cultural Life Early settlers organized mutual benefit societies which also served as social and cultural centres. Cultural activities increased with the settlement of post-WWII political refugees. Slovenes are predominantly Roman Catholic, and Slovene parishes such as those in Toronto, Hamilton, Montréal and Winnipeg are major centres of religious, social, cultural and recreational activities, including Slovene language classes for children, choirs, drama societies and religious organizations.

In Toronto a religious monthly, *Božja beseda* (*God's Word*), is published. The Slovenian National Federation, established in 1952 to promote the idea of a noncommunist and democratic Slovenia, publishes the monthly *Slovenska država* (*Slovenian State*). Slovenes in the Toronto area are served by 2 Slovenian credit unions. The Research Centre for Slovenian Culture (fd 1955 in Toronto) has published 3 books. RUDOLPH ČUJEŠ

Slug, common name for several terrestrial pulmonate and numerous marine gilled species of gastropod MOLLUSCS conspicuous by the lack of an exposed shell. Terrestrial slugs have rudimentary shells, embedded in the body tissue. The mantle encapsulates a lung sack which communicates with the outside atmosphere through a single breathing pore; gills are absent. The head bears sensory tentacles and encloses a rasping feeding organ, the radula. Land slugs possess a muscular foot which employs peristaltic muscle waves, aided by mucous secretions, to creep over the substratum. Canada's introduced greyish brown European slug (*Limax maximus*) grows to about 15 cm, but most land slugs are much smaller. The most destructive slug is the black slug (*Arion ater*). Most slugs are herbivorous but *Arion ater* will, in addition, feed voraciously upon animal flesh and feces. Fortunately, this species is easily attracted to slug baits.

The sea slug (*Melibe leonina*), a predacious, semipelagic opisthobranch gastropod, inhabits open, quiet channels, eelgrass beds and kelp forests from BC to California. The genus name *Melibe* ("honeylike") refers to the resin-sweet odour that it imparts to anything touching it. This sea slug can attain 10 cm in length and resembles a diaphanous, truncated soupspoon, with several inflated, ovoid leaves on its handle. Delicate in appearance, it is often mistaken for a strange jellyfish. *Melibe* usually comes in translucent shades of yellow, brown, grey and lavender, but can be colourless. A convincing swimmer of the thrashing-twisting school, the sea slug can also trap air in its oral hood for buoyancy. The large, basket-shaped hood is fringed with a mane of slender tentacles which are used as strainers for retaining minute ZOOPLANKTON as water is forced out of the oral basket. Reproduction is a gregarious affair with hundreds of animals collecting at one site for mating. The broad, spiral ribbons of eggs are laid in summer. PETER V. FANKBONER

Small Business has many definitions, but generally it refers to the many business firms that are small compared to the relatively few giant firms (characterized by multi-locational operation, large numbers of hired employees, ownership by publicly traded stocks and management by professionally trained salaried managers). Economic activity has become concentrated in the frequently conglomerate, usually foreign-owned MULTINATIONAL CORPORATIONS, the wealth and power of which sometimes exceeds that of most nation-states. By contrast, small businesses are typically local operations owned privately by a family or by a small number of shareholders, some of whom also manage the operation, and staffed by a small number of hired workers (if any) in addition to the owner-managers. By any criterion some 90% of all businesses are small, but a further distinction can be made between small and medium-sized businesses. The international definition of a small business is one which employs fewer than 50 employees, although other sources define firms with up to 20 employees as being small. In certain sectors (eg, construction business, personal services, that do not lend themselves to standardization and centralized management), small businesses are still responsible for a large part of economic activity.

Role in the Economy Recent data suggest that small business currently accounts for about 25 to 30% of Gross Domestic Product in Canada, and this proportion is growing. An estimated 850 000 firms, equivalent to about 94% of the total number of firms in Canada, have less than 20 employees. In 1985, companies with less than 20 full-year equivalent employees maintained a labour force of around 2.5 million, representing about 30% of total private-sector employment.

Small businesses produce goods for which there is no mass market – specialty items, high-quality and hand-crafted items, custom-made goods and components that require detailed design and production. Small business does much of the wholesaling and retailing where the sales and service requirements (owing to the nature of the goods or to the absence of high-volume customer traffic) are high, and in certain cases, particularly construction, services and agriculture, where individual application is at a premium, small business continues to hold its own. The most important nonstandardized types of goods and services are those that are new and innovative; despite the commercial technological successes of gigantic, concentrated research and development efforts, a large number of the most fundamental advances have been developed by individuals working alone or in small firms.

The indispensable role of small business in the Canadian ECONOMY is likely to expand. From 1978 to 1985, businesses with less than 20 employees were responsible for as much as 81% of the 1.2 million net jobs created across Canada, and this trend is expected to continue in future years. With the long term decline in some major industries, Canada will be turning more to innovative small businesses to create new international markets for specialized goods and services.

Characteristics of Small Business Small businesses vary greatly from one another in size, lines of business and type of organization. Most businesses begin as small firms. The difficulties and myriad details of setting up require all the attention of the entrepreneur, and securing adequate financing is usually a difficulty. It is variously estimated that about 50% of all new businesses fail within 5 years of their creation and do so most often as a result of limited capital. Because smaller businesses are undercapitalized they rely heavily on banks for financing, which leaves them peculiarly vulnerable to recessions and management error. Ironically, large firms like DOME PETROLEUM or MASSEY-FERGUSON may lose millions of dollars and still survive. Nevertheless, it is vitally important to the economy that new firms are formed regularly because frequently new ideas or processes can only realize development in a new firm.

Small business has had to overcome the general feeling by both the public and the government that large businesses are more efficient and progressive. Only in the 1970s has it developed a national voice to represent its concerns before government and the general public. The Canadian Federation of Independent Business, formed in 1971, grew to 80 000 members by 1987. In addition, improved business data have revealed the growing economic role of small business. For example, small businesses continued to create jobs through the 1982-83 recession when larger companies were shedding workers in record numbers. Even in the subsequent economic recovery, large firms continued to "downsize" while small business expanded. Consequently, governments are introducing policies more favourable to entrepreneurship and small business.

PATRICIA C. JOHNSTON AND CATHERINE SWIFT

Small Claims Court, the common name of courts established by provincial legislation for civil matters involving small sums of money. In Québec, the upper limit of the small claims court is $10 000, but in the other provinces it is $1000, $2000 or $3000. The procedure in these courts is less formal than in higher courts and it is usually possible for individuals to conduct their cases without a lawyer. In Québec, lawyers are barred from appearing on behalf of clients. Most provinces have created a small claims or civil division of the provincial court, but PEI has established a small claims section of the General Division of the Supreme Court of PEI, just as in NB small claims are handled by a section of the Court of Queen's Bench. In NS, the Municipal Court in Halifax is responsible for claims of less than $500. In the Yukon Territory, claims of less than $500 can be dealt with by a small-debt official of the territorial court and a magistrate can deal with claims of less than $1000. In the NWT, the territorial court deals with actions that are for less than $5000. P.K. DOODY AND T.B. SMITH

Small Presses, publishing companies operating on a small scale, have appeared in Canada almost entirely since WWII. More than larger, commercial publishers they tend to be oriented towards furthering, by publication of appropriate material, the peculiar views and interests of their founders. Their function is largely critical and educational. In an era of social and technological change and the consequent fragmentation of lifestyles, they attempt to offer modes of thought, behaviour and expression which are alternatives to those normally encountered by readers of commercial publications. Many small presses originated as direct offshoots of little magazines (*see* LITERARY MAGAZINES), others as writers' co-operatives. Some presses specialize in genre publication; others limit themselves to promoting a certain aesthetic within genres. Some promote political causes; others try to preserve the essential flavour of a region. A few attempt a limited commercialism through the use of fine paper, hand-set printing and numbered, limited editions.

This fringe industry requires for its survival adequate financing, an educated audience and a means of reaching that audience. The postwar proliferation of universities and community colleges and a growing disillusionment with the products of mass circulation have done much to supply a potential readership. At the same time, the development of offset and computerized printing has made possible the production of relatively low-cost, attractively designed books. The establishment of the CANADA COUNCIL in 1957 prepared the way for government funding, of which small-press proprietors were quick to take advantage. Coincidentally, a postwar expansion into Canada by multinational book companies created a backlash among authors, educationalists, the Canadian public and the relatively few Canadian publishers. The Independent Publishers Association, organized in 1969, was made up largely of representatives of the small presses; it lobbied so successfully for an indigenous industry that within a decade most larger, more commercial Canadian houses joined it to form the Association of Canadian Publishers. In this organization the interests of the small presses are served by a special subdivision, the Literary Press Group.

Small presses are now scattered from coast to coast. Serving writers and audiences in the Atlantic region are Breakwater Books of St John's, Ragweed of Charlottetown, Lancelot Press of Windsor, NS, and Les Éditions d'Acadie of Moncton. They issue textbooks, literary works, regional studies, and illustrated books. Fiddlehead Poetry Books of Fredericton is best known for its poetry although it also issues fiction. In Montréal Tundra Books has gained international renown for its CHILDREN'S LITERATURE, and Véhicule Press has branched out from local authors to national and American authors. Guernica Editions issues English and Italian translations of French writers, and English translations of Italian writers. Les Éditions du Noroît and Nicole Brossard's L'Integrale issue poetry. Also active are Québec Amérique and VLB Editeur.

Tecumseh Press of Ottawa and ECW Press of Toronto concentrate on academic and bibliographical publications. In Toronto are Coach House, which in the 1960s was the leading small press for experimental poetry and handsome graphics; the House of Anansi, which publishes fiction and criticism; and Playwrights Canada, which issues plays that have been professionally produced; and Sixty Eight, which, under the management of novelist Joseph Škvorecký and his wife, publishes Czech writers. Penumbra Press of Moonbeam, Ont, is devoted to publications on the North, and Potlatch of Hamilton issues the *Canadian Children's Annual*.

The Prairies are likewise well sprinkled with vibrant firms. In Winnipeg Turnstone, Pegasus, and Mosaic Press issue fiction, poetry, and criticism. Thistledown of Saskatoon and Longspoon of Edmonton concentrate on Prairie poets. The West Coast has the liveliest publishing and diversified trade outside Toronto and Montréal. Talonbooks of Vancouver is well known for its plays; Sono Nis Press of Victoria focuses on avant-garde poetry; and Theytus Books issues works by and about

native peoples. Oolican Books on Vancouver I issues poetry and fiction.

Traditionally the little presses have published new poets or noncommercial writers, as did First Statement, CONTACT, Quarry, Alphabet Press, and Klanack Press back in the 1950s and 1960s, but today's small presses have attracted many major and commercial writers such as Hugh HOOD, Robert KROETSCH, Carol BOLT and Northrop FRYE. Several firms, notably Hurtig (Edmonton), Oberon (Ottawa), Simon & Pierre (Toronto) and Lester, Orpen & Denys (Toronto), have enlarged their businesses to move beyond the designation "little press."

The circumstances governing library purchases and the bookstore trade in Canada have made the distribution and sale of small-press books difficult compared to that by the mass-market commercial publishers. However, the small presses have largely avoided the high costs of national distribution by concentrating on regional and local markets. A number of small publishers have gained access to national and foreign markets through participation in the *Literary Press Group Catalogue*, published since 1975 with the financial assistance of the Ontario Arts Council. Such subsidies, from both provincial and federal governments, are needed to maintain the small-press industry. Despite their precarious financial circumstances, however, the regional publishers awakened a new interest in regional literature, and by the 1980s had demonstrated the vigour of publishing outside Toronto. *See also* BOOK PUBLISHING; PRIVATE PRESSES; REGIONALISM IN LITERATURE.

FRED COGSWELL AND GEORGE L. PARKER

Small Presses in French Small publishing houses are closely linked to the birth and growth of distinct Québec literature. Living on the fringe of the big houses (themselves dependent on the educational market), they publish and thus help assure the survival of certain types of more marginal material and ideas. Always at odds with the mainstream, they are the experimental laboratories. One of the oldest, La Maison Déom (1895), played an extraordinary role in the publication of Québec poetry.

During the economic crisis of the 1930s, market concentration in the hands of the educational institutions discouraged publishers through the elimination of competition and thus of diversity. The era saw the birth of new publishing houses whose survival depended on their close ties with groups or associations or even magazines. Les Éditions du Totem were, eg, linked to Albert Lévesque's *Les Idées* and Les Éditions de l'Arbre to *La Nouvelle Relève*. The magazines guaranteed a degree of circulation which the few and localized bookstores could not. In truth, Québec literature was born in these small houses independent of both church and school.

The small publishing houses did not take on their present form until after WWII. The crisis facing Québec publishing in 1947 led to the closing of a number of commercial houses and the arrival of French ones anxious to establish themselves in a country which they saw primarily as a market for their books. Squeezed between French publishers and religious presses, independent Québec publishing almost disappeared.

And so in the late 1940s and early 1950s an intellectual circle developed for whom publications served as a literary movement as well. The entire history of Québec poetry is to be found in these presses where the poet sometimes doubled as the typographer (Roland GIGUÈRE at Les Éditions Erta), where the press run was often extremely small (75 or 100 copies) and where circulation depended on the subscription approach of the 19th century: Erta, 1949; L'Hexagone, 1953;

Les Éditions de Malte, 1954; Les Éditions d'Orphée, 1955.

After 1960, the small publishing houses instead became linked with political activities (Les Éditions coopératives Albert Saint-Martin), or feminist ones (Les Éditions du Remue-Ménage and Les Éditions de la Pleine Lune). Poetry magazines also published authors' works which could be assimilated into books: eg, *Les Herbes rouges* and *La Nouvelle Barre du Jour*. Other presses specialized in literature for ethnic minorities (Guernica) or regional ones (Les Éditions du Royaume). Most of these houses were heavily subsidized.

While some of these presses in time became true institutions (Déom, L'Hexagone), most had a brief life, just enough time to carry out the project that had sparked their existence in the first place or to exhaust their resources. In comparison with the large publishing houses, they are distinguished by their originality and the sometimes exceptional quality of their graphics (eg, Éditions du Noroît). LUCIE ROBERT

Smallboy, Johnny Bob (also Robert), or Apitchitchiw, community leader (b on Peigan Reserve, SW of Ft Macleod, Alta 7 Nov 1898, d at Smallboy Camp near Nordegg, Alta, 8 July 1984). Chief Smallboy focused national attention on urban and reserve Indian problems when he "returned to the land" with followers from troubled Indian settlements. Born of a traditional Cree family who were among the last to settle on their allotted reserve at Hobbema in central Alberta, Smallboy became a hunter, trapper, farmer, and eventually chief of the Ermineskin Band from 1959 to 1969. In 1968, to escape deteriorating social and political conditions on the reserve, he moved to a bush camp on the Kootenay Plains, accompanied by some 125 people. Despite factional splits, the return of many residents to Hobbema, and the group's failure to obtain permanent land tenure, Smallboy Camp persisted into the 1980s as a working community used as a retreat by Plains and Woodlands Indians from western Canada and the US. BENNETT McCARDLE

Smallpox (variola) is an infectious disease caused by a DNA virus of the genus *orthopox*. The smallpox virus is distinct from that of cowpox, a disease of the udders of cows, but infection with cowpox virus ("vaccination," from *vaccus*, a cow) confers immunity against smallpox without significant illness. Smallpox is spread by droplets from the nose and throat or by dried viral particles on blankets and clothing. After infection, the nonimmune subject is well for an incubation period of about 12 days. The illness usually begins with backache, fever and prostration, followed by a pustular rash affecting chiefly the face and limbs. During the phase of the rash, which lasts a few weeks, the patient is likely to infect from 3 to 5 close contacts. The rash leaves pitted scars or pocks. Complications include pneumonia, blindness, infection of joints or bones. A haemorrhagic form is invariably fatal. In variola major the mortality rate is 30-40%, whereas in variola minor the rate is only 1-2%.

Smallpox may have been prevalent in Asia in ancient times but was first described for certain by Rhazes in the 9th century AD in Asia Minor. The disease was brought to America by Spaniards visiting and conquering Caribbean islands (1507) and Mexico (1519). It was reported first in New France in 1616 near Tadoussac, brought by French settlers to the St Lawrence and Saguenay R regions. Because the Indians were totally devoid of immunity, they were ravaged by smallpox, which quickly spread to tribes in the Maritimes, James Bay and Great Lakes area. Between 1636 and 1640 Jesuit priests introduced smallpox into HURONIA W of Lk Simcoe and S of Georgian

Bay. Because priests baptized the sick and dying Indians their visits spread the disease which Indians perceived as the evil "medicine of the black robes."

Smallpox played a significant role in the struggles of French, British and Americans to dominate the St Lawrence area. The worst epidemic in French Canada occurred between 1755 and 1757 and spread to New England. De Vaudreuil, the French commander, was forced to abandon his invasion of New England. In 1757 Montcalm reported 2500 cases in Québec City of whom 20% died. British troops besieging Louisbourg and attempting to invade Québec were affected. In 1763 the British used blankets exposed to smallpox as germ warfare in their attempt to subdue the Indian uprising led by PONTIAC. In 1775 during the AMERICAN REVOLUTION American troops besieging Québec City were stricken with smallpox.

Vaccination was introduced into N America in 1798 by the Rev John Clinch, a classmate of Edward Jenner who first proved that vaccination prevented smallpox. The widespread use of vaccination, advocated by public-health leaders, met with much resistance by anti-vaccinationists. Although provincial legislation was passed making vaccination of school children mandatory and empowering municipalities and townships to carry out general vaccination when an epidemic threatened, passive resistance was widespread. In Montréal in 1885 a major outbreak occurred, ultimately resulting in over 3000 deaths. Many French Canadians in Montréal opposed vaccination. The attempts to enforce control measures, plus the announcement in Sept 1885 that Louis Riel, leader of the North-West Rebellion, had been sentenced to death, resulted in street rioting which could only be suppressed by calling out the militia.

Smallpox smouldered in Canada during the first half of the 20th century. In 1924 in Windsor, Ont, there were 67 cases with 32 deaths, all in unvaccinated persons. The disease was finally eradicated in 1979 by a vigorous vaccination campaign in S America, Africa and Asia carried out by the World Health Organization. Smallpox is the first major disease to have been wiped out by public-health measures. W.B. SPAULDING

Smallwood, Charles, physician, professor of meteorology, founder of the McGill Observatory (b at Birmingham, Eng 1812; d at Montréal 22 Dec 1873). Arriving in Montréal in 1833, he later set up medical practice in St-Martin. There he kept a weather notebook and built an observatory for astronomy and meteorology. The astronomy had practical application: for "time from the stars," the observatory was connected by the Montréal telegraph with major US cities. Smallwood examined and photographed snow crystals through a microscope, surely one of the first to do so. Fifteen of his scientific articles and 11 weather reviews appeared in the *Canadian Naturalist* between 1857 and 1872. In 1856 McGill granted him an honorary LLD and appointed him professor of meteorology (without salary). The work of this pioneering Victorian scientist foreshadowed modern CLOUD physics. J.S. MARSHALL

Smallwood, Joseph Roberts, journalist, politician, premier of Newfoundland 1949-72 (b at Gambo, Nfld 24 Dec 1900). As a bright young man, he became a journalist and covered the 1919 transatlantic flights. In New York, 1920-25, he worked for a left-wing daily and campaigned for the Progressive Party; ever since, he has called himself a "socialist." Back in Newfoundland, he became a union organizer, radio broadcaster, an unsuccessful candidate in the 1932 election, and during WWII he ran a piggery at the air base at GANDER. His chance came when Britain's new

Joseph Smallwood signing the agreement admitting Newfoundland to Confederation. On the right is Hon A.J. Walsh, chairman of the delegation, Ottawa (*courtesy National Archives of Canada/PA-128080/NFB*).

Labour government announced that Newfoundlanders, then ruled by an appointed COMMISSION OF GOVERNMENT, could elect representatives to a convention which was to advise the government on the choice to be put to the electorate in a referendum about their political future. Smallwood, who favoured CONFEDERATION with Canada, was elected to the Convention in 1946. For the next 3 years, he demonstrated the willpower, courage, ruthlessness and mastery of populist propaganda that made him one of the most remarkable of contemporary politicians. Despite opposition from influential St John's merchants who accused him of betraying Newfoundland for arguing that it should not retain its independence, he dominated the convention debates, there delivering his finest speech in which he told Newfoundlanders the bitter truth: "We are not a nation. We are a medium-sized municipality . . . left far behind the march of time." With the bait of family allowances, welcome hard cash for many Newfoundlanders, he won the second of 2 hard-fought and close referenda on 22 July 1948. He was appointed premier of the interim government 1 Apr 1949, elected leader of the Liberal Party, and won the first provincial election in May 1949. He was not seriously challenged for 2 decades.

Smallwood's early years in power alternated between farce and tragedy. An attempt at forced industrialization ended in bankruptcy for most of his manufacturing plants and in the imprisonment for embezzlement of his economic adviser, the mysterious Latvian Alfred A. Valdmanis. The tragedy happened in Mar 1959 at the small town of Badger where striking loggers clashed with police officers; in the melee, one member of the Newfoundland constabulary was clubbed and later died. Smallwood, who had opposed the strike and decertified the union a few days before, made him into a martyr. No longer a socialist, except in his rhetoric, Smallwood from then on consorted with corporate tycoons such as John C. DOYLE and John Shaheen and devoted himself to large industrial endeavours like the CHURCHILL FALLS power project, at the same time encouraging Newfoundlanders to leave isolated outports for new "resettlement" communities. He retained power through the 1960s because he, and Newfoundlanders, benefited from lavish new federal spending schemes. The progress proved his undoing as a new, educated and relatively affluent generation of Newfoundlanders came of age. He survived his first challenge, by disaffected Cabinet minister John CROSBIE, at the 1969 Liberal leadership convention. But in the Oct 1971 election, the Conservatives led by Frank MOORES won 21 seats, Smallwood 20, and the New Labrador Party one.

He resigned 18 Jan 1972 after 3 tense and intrigue-ridden months.

Characteristically, Smallwood refused to give up. He tried to win back the Liberal leadership in 1974 and to form a new party, the Liberal Reform Party. Only after both attempts failed did he give up politics. He resigned his seat in 1977 to take on a new role as elder statesman and return to writing, most notably in his planned, 4-vol *Encyclopedia of Newfoundland* (vol 1, 1981; vol 2, 1984). He was made a Companion of the Order of Canada in 1986. RICHARD J. GWYN

Reading: Richard J. Gwyn, *Smallwood: the Unlikely Revolutionary* (1968).

Smallwood Reservoir, 6527 km², elev 472 m, tenth-largest freshwater body in Canada, is situated on the remote Labrador Plateau, near the Québec border. It was created in the 1960s for hydroelectric-power production by damming the CHURCHILL R at CHURCHILL FALLS and diking other rivers. The water level varies by 8.7 m, giving a usable water reserve of 28 billion m³. MICHIKAMAU and Lobstick lakes were the largest of hundreds of lakes that now make up the reservoir, named for Joseph R. SMALLWOOD, first premier of Newfoundland. Originally inhabited by Naskapi, the area was first visited by Europeans John MCLEAN and Erland Erlandson in 1839. The area was first mapped by the Oblate missionary Father Babel, and later, in detail, by Albert LOW of the Dominion Geological Survey (1895). IAN MACCALLUM

Smart, Elizabeth, novelist, poet (b at Ottawa 27 Dec 1913; d at London, Eng 4 Mar 1986). Smart was educated at Hartfield House, a private school in Cobourg, Ont. At the age of 19, she travelled to London, Eng, to study piano. She returned to Canada to work briefly for the *Ottawa Journal*, writing society news. During the 1930s, Smart travelled extensively and through contact with Lawrence Durrell she met George Barker, the British poet who was to become the father of her 4 children. She worked at the British Embassy in Washington during WWII and moved to England in 1943 where she worked to support herself and her family for the next 2 decades writing advertising copy and working for *Queen* (as literary editor) and *House and Garden*.

Smart's first work, *By Grand Central Station I Sat Down and Wept* (1945), immediately established a cult following. Republished in 1966, 1975, 1977 and in Canada in 1982, it has been critically hailed as a masterpiece of poetic prose and a homage to love unique in its style and sensibility. In 1977, following 32 years of silence, 2 new works appeared: *A Bonus*, a collection of sharp and witty poems, and *The Assumption of Rogues and Rascals*, a prose-poem that is both a continuation of and a comment on her early work. Smart returned to Canada in 1982 as the writer-in-residence at the U of Alberta in Edmonton for a year. In 1984 followed a collection of previously unpublished poetry and prose, *In the Mean Time*. In 1986, *Necessary Secrets*, a volume of her early journals appeared, further establishing and enhancing her literary reputation. In 1984, after a brief stay in Toronto, Smart returned to England and her cottage in The Dell, Suffolk. ALICE VAN WART

Smellie, Elizabeth Lawrie, nurse (b at Port Arthur, Ont 22 Mar 1884; d at Toronto 5 Mar 1968), first woman promoted colonel in the Canadian Army (1944). A graduate of Johns Hopkins Training School for Nurses, she joined the Canadian Army Nursing Service in WWI, served in France and Britain (mentioned in dispatches, 1916; awarded Royal Red Cross, 1917), and on her return to Canada was appointed assistant matron in chief (1918-20). During the following years she helped build the VICTORIAN ORDER OF

NURSES into a thriving nationwide organization and was its chief superintendent in Canada 1923-47. Taking leave of absence from the VON during WWII, she served as matron in chief in Canada of the Royal Canadian Army Medical Corps (1940-44) and in 1941 laid the foundations of the Canadian Women's Army Corps. CARLOTTA HACKER

Smelt (Osmeridae), family of small, iridescent fishes of class Osteichthyes, found in coastal seas, streams and lakes of the Northern Hemisphere. Worldwide, 6 genera, 11 named and 2 unnamed species are known; in Canada, 6 genera and 9 species. Rainbow smelt and capelin occur on all 3 coasts; pond smelt on the Arctic coast and drainage; pygmy smelt in Québec and NB lakes; the others on the Pacific coast and drainage. Some smelts are marine fishes; some live in fresh water; others live in the sea but spawn in fresh water (anadromous). The family name derives from their characteristic, cucumberlike odour. Their shape and fins are much like those of a slender SALMON, but they lack the tiny, triangular structure found just above the pelvic fins on the abdomen of salmonids. Like salmon, they have a small, tablike, adipose (fleshy) fin on the back, just in front of the tail fin. Smelts seldom exceed 41 cm. At spawning time, the male develops granulations on the scales and fins to help maintain contact with the female while fertilizing eggs on sand or gravel. The egg membrane peels back, sticking the egg to the bottom. Spawning occurs in spring or summer; the eggs are left unguarded. Smelts are excellent to eat and are sought by fishermen angling through ice or dip netting, seining or gill netting during spawning, and by commercial trawlers. They are also an important food for many animals, including Atlantic cod, beluga whales and aquatic birds. The famed eulachon (candlefish) was and is used by native Canadians for food, especially for its nutritious oil. Formerly, it was also burned like a candle. Most young smelts eat PLANKTON; adults of some species (eg, rainbow smelt) eat small fishes and shrimp. D.E. MCALLISTER

Smith, Sir Albert James, lawyer, politician, premier of NB (b at Shediac, NB 12 Mar 1822; d at Dorchester, NB 30 June 1883). Smith was the anti-Confederation leader of NB who almost wrecked the movement in 1865. Entering politics as a radical in 1852 and a member of the reform government that took office 1854, he was appointed attorney general in 1861 when S.L. TILLEY became premier. The 2 divided over government railway policies in 1862 and battled over CONFEDERATION, which Smith regarded as a devious scheme from the "oily brains of Canadian politicians." The "antis" trounced the Confederation forces in the 1865 election. Smith failed to suppress the unionists as premier 1865-66 and was eventually driven from office by an arbitrary lieutenant-governor. After Confederation, Smith went to Ottawa, becoming minister of fisheries under PM Alexander MACKENZIE. In 1877 he was the "ruling spirit throughout" the Halifax Fisheries Commission which awarded Canada $5.5 million, the first diplomatic victory over the US. For his efforts Smith became the first native-born New Brunswicker to be knighted, an ironic twist not lost on those who supported Confederation. CARL M. WALLACE

Smith, Andrew, veterinarian, educator (b at Dalrymple, Scot 12 July 1834; d at 15 Aug Toronto 1910). A graduate of Edinburgh Veterinary Coll in 1881, he came to Canada that year. In 1862 he started lectures on veterinary science leading to the founding of the Upper Canada Veterinary School (later Ontario Veterinary Coll), the oldest such college in N America. He graduated over 3000 veterinarians during his 40-year tenure as principal. A pioneer of VETERINARY MEDICINE and education in N America, Smith was a great promoter of his profession. He was first president of the Ontario Veterinary Assn and a prime mover for its organization (1874) and incorporation (1879). He was a founder of what is now the CANADIAN NATIONAL EXHIBITION. R.G. THOMSON

Smith, Arnold Cantwell, diplomat (b at Toronto 18 Jan 1915). A Rhodes scholar who joined the Dept of External Affairs in 1943, he was posted to Russia, 1943-45, and he acted as secretary to the Kellock-Taschereau Royal Commission (see GOUZENKO). His subsequent service included stints in Brussels, New York, Cambodia and London, and culminated in terms as ambassador to Cairo, 1958-61, and to Moscow, 1961-63. From 1965 to 1975 he was an enthusiastic, creative, deeply committed first secretary-general of the COMMONWEALTH, a period he recalls in *Stitches in Time* (1981). He is also the author of *The We-They Frontier: From International Relations to World Politics* (1983) and, with Arthur Lall, *Multilateral Negotiation and Mediation: Instruments and Methods* (1985). He became an Officer of the Order of Canada in 1984. NORMAN HILLMER

Smith, Arthur James Marshall, poet, critic, anthologist (b at Montréal 8 Nov 1902; d at East Lansing, Mich 21 Nov 1980). A.J.M. Smith was educated at McGill and U of Edinburgh. In 1925, while a graduate student in Montréal, he founded and edited the *McGill Fortnightly Review* with F.R. SCOTT, the first journal to publish modernist poetry and critical opinion in Canada. This began a period of significant activities amid the staid provincialism of contemporary Canadian letters. In 1936 he coedited *New Provinces*, followed in 1943 by publication of both Smith's own first collection, *News of the Phoenix* (Gov Gen's Award) and *A Book of Canadian Poetry*, in which he distinguished a separate national voice. He continued to edit numerous anthologies and produce his own poetry and, in 1973, published a collection of critical essays, *Towards a View of Canadian Letters*. Early in his career Smith moved to Lansing, Mich, to teach at Michigan State U although he spent most of his summers near Magog, Qué. In 1966 the RSC awarded him the Lorne Pierce Medal. In 1972 Smith retired and the university created the A.J.M. Smith Award, given annually for a noteworthy volume by a Canadian poet. MARLENE ALT

Smith, David Laurence Thomson, veterinarian, teacher (b at Regina 18 Apr 1914; d at Saskatoon 15 Nov 1983). After serving in the Royal Canadian Army Medical Corps in WWII, he joined the faculty of the Ontario Veterinary College in 1946, and was head of pathology and bacteriology there 1955-63. Smith is best known as the founder of the Western College of Veterinary Medicine at U of Sask, where he was dean 1963-74 and professor of pathology 1974-81. Highly regarded in the profession for his leadership and integrity, he was president of the Canadian Veterinary Medical Assn in 1980-81. After retirement, he was heavily involved in CANADIAN INTERNATIONAL DEVELOPMENT AGENCY projects related to veterinary colleges in Uganda, Malaysia and Somalia. R.G. THOMSON

Smith, Donald Alexander, 1st Baron Strathcona and Mount Royal, fur trader, railroad financier, diplomat (b at Forres, Scot 6 Aug 1820; d at London, Eng 21 Jan 1914). The son of a tradesman, Smith joined the HUDSON'S BAY COMPANY in 1838 and worked his way through the ranks from apprentice clerk to chief commissioner in 1871. By 1883 he was a director of the com-

Donald Smith's financial backing was essential to the completion of the CPR, and he was given the honour of driving the "last spike" (*courtesy National Archives of Canada/C-3841*).

pany and, through careful investments, its largest shareholder. In 1889 he was chosen governor, or chief executive officer, of the company. Smith came to public attention in 1869 when sent to Ft Garry to assist in settling the terms of union between Louis RIEL's provisional government and Canada. The mission was successful and Smith began a political career, representing Winnipeg-St John in the Manitoba legislature 1870-74 and Selkirk in the House of Commons 1871-78. In 1874, when dual representation was abolished, he elected to sit in the Dominion Parliament. A Conservative, he voted against the Macdonald government in the PACIFIC SCANDAL, and thereafter relations between Macdonald and Smith were cool. After a 9-year absence Smith returned to Parliament, representing Montréal W 1887-96. In 1873-74 Smith joined his cousin George STEPHEN, J.J. HILL and others in acquiring the depreciated bonds of the St Paul, Minneapolis and Manitoba Ry, a line running through Minnesota to the Canadian border. He was an enthusiastic supporter of the CANADIAN PACIFIC RY, and his financial backing was essential to its progress. He was therefore invited to drive the last spike when the railway was completed in 1885. Smith was a principal shareholder and, in 1887, president of the BANK OF MONTREAL, which was closely associated with the CPR. In April 1896 Sir Mackenzie BOWELL appointed Smith high commissioner for Canada in the UK, a post he held, along with the HBC governorship, until his death. He became prominent in British public affairs and spokesman in London for the self-governing colonies. During the SOUTH AFRICAN WAR he personally maintained Strathcona's Horse, a regiment of over 500 mounted riflemen which later became Lord Strathcona's Horse (Royal Canadians). He was elevated to the peerage in 1897 and served as chancellor of McGill, where he founded Royal Victoria College for women in 1896. D.M.L. FARR

Smith, Donald Graham, swimmer (b at Edmonton, Alta 9 May 1958). A breaststroke specialist, Graham Smith became the youngest Canadian male to win 2 national titles in one meet, winning both the 100 m and 200 m breaststroke events in 1974. At the 1976 Montréal Olympics, he was on the 2nd-place 400 m medley relay team, and in 1977 and 1978 he set world records in the 200 m individual medley over the 25 m course. At the 1978 Commonwealth Games, Smith won an unprecedented 6 gold medals – in the 100 m and 200 m breaststroke, the 200 m and 400 m individual medley, and the 400 m freestyle and medley relays. Later that year he won the 200 m individual medley at the World Aquatic Games. Smith received the LOU MARSH TROPHY as Canada's outstanding athlete for 1978 and was honoured with the Order of Canada that same year.   BARBARA SCHRODT

Smith, Ernest John, architect (b at Winnipeg 17 Dec 1919). A founding member of Smith Carter Partners (1972), Smith studied architecture at U Man and MIT. Smith, Carter, Parkin was founded in 1947 with Dennis Carter and John C. PARKIN, co-principals. The firm's work included major projects, public and private, in Manitoba, the Prairies and later abroad. Many of the projects Smith directed changed the urban character of Winnipeg; these included Winnipeg Square and the underground concourse at Portage and Main, the Woodsworth Bldg on Broadway and the Monarch Life Insurance Bldg. Major international work under Smith's direction includes the Warsaw Chancery. In 1985 Smith Carter Partners and Number Ten Architectural Group were selected to design an 18 600 m² retail commercial complex in downtown Winnipeg.
                              WILLIAM P. THOMPSON

Smith, George Isaac, lawyer, politician, premier of NS (b at Stewiacke, NS 6 Apr 1909; d at Truro, NS 19 Dec 1982). He began his career as a lawyer and served with the army in WWII. He then became politically involved, helping to recruit R.L. STANFIELD as Progressive Conservative Party leader in NS in 1948. Smith entered the legislature in 1949 and occupied various strategic Cabinet posts, until 1967 when he replaced Stanfield as premier. He supported regional equalization and federal-provincial conferences, and was praised for decisiveness in the government takeover of Sydney Steel in 1968. After his administration was defeated in 1970, he resigned as party leader in 1971. He remained an MLA until 1974 and was appointed a senator in 1975.   LOIS KERNAGHAN

Smith, Goldwin, "Annexation" to his opponents, historian, journalist (b at Reading, Eng 13 Aug 1823; d at Toronto 7 June 1910). An acknowledged historian and journalist when he settled permanently in Canada in 1871, Smith became best known to Canadians as the advocate of union with the US as a prerequisite to moral unification of the Anglo-Saxon race. Smith was educated at Eton and Oxford, where his liberal stand against the conservative Tractarian movement led to his appointment to 2 royal commissions on the university. He befriended Richard Cobden and John Bright of the Manchester School, who taught that abolition of tariffs and introduction of free trade between nations would lead to interdependence and make war impossible. Smith supported this creed, derived from Adam Smith, in contributions to the *Morning Chronicle, Daily News* and *Saturday Review.* In 1858 he was appointed Regius Professor of Modern History at Oxford, and in his *Lectures on Modern History* (1861) preached the gospel of the "invisible hand": man as an economic being wresting a living from nature is in an unfallen world which, naturally harmonious, should be left unregulated.

In 1866 Smith resigned to nurse his ailing father. After his father's death, Smith moved to the US to teach at Cornell. He settled in Toronto in 1871 to be near relatives. In 1875 he married Henry Boulton's widow and moved into The Grange, where as a self-declared bystander he wrote extensively on Canadian and international affairs. Initially he supported the CANADA FIRST movement, but its collapse convinced him that Canada was not viable as a nation – a view he expressed in *Canada and the Canadian Question* (1891). As a journalist Smith wrote for the *Liberal,* the *Nation,* the *Canadian Monthly and National Review,* the *Week,* which he founded in 1883 with Charles G.D. ROBERTS as literary editor, *The Bystander* and the *Weekly Sun.* He opposed Canadian participation in the SOUTH AFRICAN WAR and the imperial federation movement. His *Reminiscences* and a selected *Correspondence* were published after his death.   TOM MIDDLEBRO'

Smith, Gordon Appelbe, painter, teacher (b at Hove, Eng 18 June 1919). In 1934 Smith immigrated to Winnipeg where he studied under L.L. FITZGERALD. Wounded during WWII, he moved to Vancouver in 1944, where he joined his wife and completed his studies at the Vancouver School of Art. He taught at the VSA 1946-56, and at the Faculty of Education, UBC, as professor of fine arts 1956-82. Smith attracted national attention for his award-winning *Structure with Red Sun* at the First Biennial of Canadian Painting in 1955. His work is a form of romantic lyric abstraction that balances the pervasive influence of the West Coast landscape with a gestural, nonobjective manner of painting. In 1976 the Vancouver Art Gallery mounted a 30-year retrospective of his work. He also designed the Expo 86 poster.
                              PETER MALKIN

Smith, Harold Greville, industrialist (b at Sheffield, Eng 25 Jan 1902; d at Montréal 19 Feb 1974). After graduating from Oxford, Smith was hired by a chemical firm later absorbed by Imperial Chemical Industries. ICI sent Smith to Canada in 1932 to direct chemical development in Canadian Industries Limited (CIL). In 1939 he became a VP of CIL and VP and general manager of Defence Industries Ltd, a CIL subsidiary (and not, as is commonly believed, a crown corporation) engaged in defence work for the government. In 1951 he became president of CIL and was confronted by an antitrust judgement against its 2 parent companies, ICI and DuPont. With the agreement of C.D. HOWE, Smith supervised division of the company into CIL (ICI) and DuPont of Canada. He was president of CIL until 1958; he was chairman and chief executive officer of Brinco 1960-63.   ROBERT BOTHWELL

Smith, Irving Norman, journalist, author (b at Ottawa 28 Oct 1909). He was a newspaperman for more than 40 years, mostly with the Ottawa *Journal,* where he began 1928. In the 1960s, following his father, E. Norman Smith, he became editor, then president, of the paper and did much to make it more than the party organ it had been. Also interested in the North, Smith served for a time on the NWT Council and edited *The Unbelievable Land,* a collection of essays about the Arctic.

Smith, Joseph Leopold, Leo, composer, cellist, writer, teacher (b at Birmingham, Eng 26 Nov 1881; d at Toronto 18 Apr 1952). At a crucial period in Canada's musical development, Smith influenced many of the country's future leaders in performance, composition, writing and teaching. A child prodigy in England, he later played cello in the Halle and Covent Garden orchestras before coming to Canada in 1910. He joined the Toronto Symphony and was its principal cellist 1917-18 and 1932-40. He taught at the Toronto Conservatory from 1911 and was a professor of music at U of T 1938-50. Smith wrote 3 widely used textbooks: *Musical Rudiments* (1920), *Music of the 17th and 18th Centuries* (1931) and *Elementary Part-Writing* (1939). His compositions, sensitive impressionistic works, included Québec folk material, West Coast Indian songs and settings of verse by Canadian poets.   BARCLAY McMILLAN

Smith, Lois, ballet dancer (b at Vancouver 8 Oct 1929). Dancing with the NATIONAL BALLET OF CANADA 1951-69, she was Canada's first prima ballerina. She began her formal ballet training in Vancouver at age 15, and her early performance experience was in musicals and light opera. Celia FRANCA, recognizing her potential, invited her to join the National Ballet at its inception in 1951 as principal dancer. Smith performed in a wide range of ballets, from comedy to drama, but was most acclaimed for her roles in the great classic ballets. After an injury forced her retirement in 1969, she opened her own school in Toronto. She is an Officer of the Order of Canada.   JILLIAN M. OFFICER

Smith, Mary Ellen, née Spear, politician (b at Tavistock, Eng 11 Oct 1863; d at Vancouver 3 May 1933). Smith was the first woman member of BC's Legislative Assembly and the first woman Cabinet minister in the British Empire. As an independent, she won a Jan 1918 Vancouver by-election called after the death of her husband Ralph SMITH, finance minister in the BC Liberal government. Re-elected as a Liberal in 1920 and 1924, she served as minister without portfolio from Mar to Nov 1921. She was an advocate of BC's first Mothers' Pensions and Female Minimum Wage Acts.   DIANE CROSSLEY

Smith, Ralph, labour politician (b at Newcastle-on-Tyne, Eng 8 Aug 1858; d at Victoria 12 Feb 1917). Starting as a secretary of a miners' union in Nanaimo, Smith later served as president of the Dominion Trades and Labor Congress from 1900 to 1902. He also was elected to the BC legislature in 1898 and from 1900 to 1911 sat in the House of Commons. A devoted Laurier Liberal, Smith tried to nationalize the Canadian labour movement by removing American unions and organizers. At the famous TLC convention in 1902 in Berlin [Kitchener], Ont, his policies were defeated by the forces of American labour boss Samuel Gompers. In 1916 he returned to BC provincial politics and became minister of finance. On his death the following year, his wife Mary Ellen SMITH was elected to his Vancouver riding.   IRVING ABELLA

Smith, Sidney Earle, lawyer, professor, politician (b at Port Hood, NS 9 Mar 1897; d at Ottawa 17 Mar 1959). He lectured at Dalhousie and Osgoode Hall before becoming dean of the Dalhousie Law School in 1929. In 1934 he began a successful tenure as president of U of Man and in 1945 was appointed president of U of T, where he was a strong supporter of liberal-arts education. In Sept 1957 he was sworn in as John DIEFENBAKER's minister of external affairs. After an initial period of adjustment, Smith was gaining respect in the international community and had just hit his stride as minister when he died suddenly.

                              PATRICIA WILLIAMS

Smith, Titus, naturalist, surveyor, traveller, agriculturist (b at Granby, Mass 4 Sept 1768; d at Dutch Village near Halifax 4 Jan 1850). To his innate interest in all natural studies, Smith brought a mind well schooled in botany and a keen interest in the conservation of animal and plant life. He became well known to his contemporaries first through his one-man expedition around NS reporting to Gov WENTWORTH on the colony's resources. Later he acclimatized seeds and sold improved varieties that he introduced into British N America. Smith testified before Lord DURHAM's investigation in 1839 concerning conditions in NS, and served 1841-50 as secretary to the Central Board of Agriculture. With his writings in the press and his lectures to the Mechanics' Institute, his name became a household word and his advice was sought on diverse subjects. Smith advocated careful use of resources and a commonsense approach to problems of agriculture and forest management.   TERRENCE M. PUNCH

Smith, William, fourth chief justice of the Province of Quebec (b at New York C 18 June 1728; d at Quebec C 6 Dec 1793). Smith, a Yale graduate (1745), succeeded his father as a judge in New York (1767) and was subsequently chief justice there (1780). He remained loyal to the British Crown during the American Revolution. He was a friend of Governor Guy CARLETON and was named chief justice of Quebec (1786). He is now remembered for his interpretation of the QUEBEC ACT (1774) and his view that English or French law applied according to whether the litigants were of French or English expression. That position is now seen as having been motivated by political considerations. Smith is also known as an historian of NY state.   JOHN E.C. BRIERLEY

Smith-Shortt, Elizabeth, née Smith, physician, feminist (b at Winona, Canada W 18 Jan 1859; d at Ottawa 14 Jan 1949). She belonged to the prosperous LOYALIST family that founded the E.D. Smith preserves company. After teaching for a short time she almost single-handedly stimulated Queen's to introduce medical coeducation. After Elizabeth and others were forced out of medical school by jealous male students, the Canadian Women's Medical Coll was opened in fall 1883. Next year 3 women graduated and Dr Elizabeth Smith entered general practice in Hamilton, Ont. In 1886 she married Queen's professor Adam Shortt and returned to Kingston as a lecturer and later professor in medical jurisprudence in the Women's Medical Coll. Thereafter she became an enthusiastic champion of women's rights. When her husband became Canada's first civil service commissioner in Ottawa, Elizabeth battled unsuccessfully for numerous women's causes which led to her election as VP of the National Council of Women.   A.A. TRAVILL

Smithe, William, politician, premier of BC (b at Matfen, Eng 30 June 1842; d at Victoria, 28 Mar 1887). In 1862 Smithe settled as a farmer in southern Vancouver I. Elected in 1871 to BC's first provincial legislature, he had by 1875 become leader of the loosely organized opposition to G.A. WALKEM's government, a post he gave up to A.C. ELLIOTT. Smithe was a Cabinet minister in the Elliott government of 1876-78 and then again led the Opposition until he replaced BEAVEN as premier in 1883. Smithe remained in office until his death, initiating the "Great Potlatch" era, during which successive administrations made generous grants of crown-owned resources to entrepreneurs. By settling with Ottawa intergovernmental issues outstanding from the construction of the CPR, Smithe cleared the way for the development boom.   H. KEITH RALSTON

Smitheram, Henry Arthur, "Butch," politician, public servant (b at Penticton, BC 8 Jan 1918; d at Keremeos, BC 14 Mar 1982). Smitheram was a nonstatus Indian, his Okanagan mother having lost her status upon marrying her English father. In the late 1950s he resigned his position as an assistant Indian agent, completed high school graduation, attended university and became active in the Indian Eskimo Assn of Canada. He travelled throughout BC organizing Métis and nonstatus Indians into what became, in 1969, under his presidency, the BC Association of Non-Status Indians. Advocating personal and community self-help programs, Smitheram induced

lasting political awareness among BC's Métis and nonstatus Indians. He played the major part in founding the Native Council of Canada, calling the first organizational meeting in Victoria in 1970 and then drafting the NCC's first constitution. He was made a Member of the Order of Canada in 1982.   PAUL TENNANT

Smithers, BC, Town, pop 4713 (1986c), located on the Bulkley R in central BC, on Highway 16, 334 km W of Prince George and 351 km E of Prince Rupert. The town was named after Sir Alfred Waldron Smithers, a director of the Grand Trunk Pacific Ry (now the CNR) when a divisional point was established there in 1913. The original inhabitants were the Babine Indians who were largely dependent on the salmon runs. Settlement was sparse in the area until after the railway was completed. Smithers became the first incorporated village in BC in 1921 and changed its status to a town in 1967. Growth has been a result of thriving forest. Other major industries in the town are government services and the railway.
          JOHN STEWART

Smiths Falls, Ont, Town, pop 9163 (1986c), 8831 (1981c), inc 1882, located on the Rideau R, 60 km SW of Ottawa. The site was granted to Major Thomas Smyth, a LOYALIST, and named for him, but active settlement awaited Abel Russel Ward (1826), and was much expanded with the building of the RIDEAU CANAL. The town is an important lockport on the waterway. The waterfalls provided power for early industries, such as farm implements. Now machinery, electrical instruments, food and beverages, and printing are the main industries.

The town is a CPR divisional point, tourist centre for the RIDEAU LAKES, and houses the Rideau Regional Centre for Retarded Children. Smiths Falls was among the first municipalities in Ontario to have an official plan for development.
          K.L. MORRISON

Smoking is a universal health hazard. All forms of TOBACCO smoking are potentially risky, depending on the amount of smoke inhaled and the duration of the habit. Canadian consumption of 2500 manufactured cigarettes per capita per year is among the highest in the industrialized world. About 34% of men and 28% of women smoke cigarettes regularly; however, there is no sex difference in consumption in the 12-29 age group.

Cigarette smoke contains more than 3000 substances, many of which have a deleterious effect on biological systems. Among the immediate undesirable consequences of smoke inhalation include contraction of the airways of the lung, an increase in heart rate, a generalized constriction of blood vessels and an elevation of blood pressure and heart rate. Carbon monoxide in the blood of smokers deprives tissues of oxygen, a fact of potential critical importance for individuals with severe HEART DISEASE. Chronic elevation of blood carbon monoxide contributes to the gradual narrowing of arteries (arteriosclerosis). The inhalation of cigarette smoke by pregnant women subjects the circulation of the fetus to the same stresses as the smoker, which leads to a higher rate of certain obstetrical complications, perinatal mortality and the birth of slightly smaller, less mature infants.

In addition to vascular diseases, there are 2 other serious long-term effects from smoking. The first is emphysema (commonly found in older smokers), a disease in which the air sacs of the lung break down. This disease and chronic bronchitis account for the symptoms of cough, sputum production and shortness of breath in most long-term smokers.

The second is lung CANCER, the major cause of death from smoking. Lung cancer is difficult to detect in an early stage and only a small minority of cases are curable. The age-corrected incidence of lung cancer in Canada has reached about 68 per 100 000 in males and 22 per 100 000 in females annually. The increase has been greater in women, as the proportion of smokers who are female increases. Cancers of the tongue, pharynx, larynx, esophagus and even remote organs such as the bladder are all more common among smokers than nonsmokers. The hazards of exposure to carcinogenic substances, such as asbestos, uranium and certain industrial products, are enormously increased for smokers. Most smokers are strongly habituated or addicted, and the heaviest smokers are least likely to quit smoking. Those smokers wishing help can be assisted by a variety of educational, psychological and pharmacological techniques.

Studies have shown that switching to low-tar cigarettes, or reducing consumption is ineffective because smokers tend to unknowingly compensate for the reduction by altering their smoking techniques.

The substitution of smokeless tobacco in the form of snuff or chewing tobacco has been increasing in N America, especially among young males. These products also constitute a major health risk of cancerous and noncancerous oral conditions, and can also result in nicotine dependence and addiction.

A general awareness of the consequences of involuntary or passive smoking has led to the development of powerful antismoking groups among the public. Concerns raised by such groups and the scientific community have resulted in legislation controlling smoking in public places, the work site and on public transportation, including aircraft flights of short duration. Furthermore the federal government has indicated that it will extend its restrictions on all forms of tobacco advertising in Canada. Accordingly, in early 1988 the government introduced Bill C-51, which proposed to discourage tobacco sales to minors, to ensure that responsibility for their products rested with the tobacco companies and to require warnings on the inside as well as on the outside of cigarette packages.
          ALEC HERBERT

Reading: W.J. Millar, *Smoking Behaviour of Canadians* (1981).

Smucker, Barbara, née Claasen, author (b at Newton, Kansas 1 Sept 1915). A New Order Mennonite, Smucker graduated in journalism from Kansas State U (1936) and has worked as a reporter, teacher and librarian. Basically an historical novelist, she began writing books to teach Mennonite children their heritage. In 1969 she moved to Canada. Her books follow a pattern in which children are dragged into a conflict between a minority group and outsiders, forcing them to undertake journeys that lead to self-discovery and an affirmation of humane values. She has portrayed black slaves in *Underground to Canada* (1977) and dispossessed Indians in her time fantasy, *White Mist* (1985), but her best novel, *Days of Terror* (1979), is a moving account of the violence that drove the pacifist Mennonites from revolutionary Russia to Canada.
          RAYMOND E. JONES

Smuggling, clandestine transportation of goods or persons across a boundary in such a way as to evade the payment of CUSTOMS duties or internal taxes, or to evade a prohibition on import or export. In Canada, smuggling has always been of considerable importance because of the long land frontier with the US, and because the Atlantic and Pacific coasts are extensive and poorly policed. Traditionally, smuggling in Canada was a business: it is at least as old as European settlement, and occasionally in coastal communities it has been almost a way of life.

Most smuggling is international, but there can be interprovincial smuggling because the provinces tax goods at different rates and apply differing markups within their liquor monopolies. Every nation, including Canada, attempts to stop smugglers. The provinces, however, do not, so interprovincial smuggling cannot be prevented. International smugglers have always been especially interested in valuable commodities that are not bulky and that government tends to tax heavily – liquor, tobacco products, wine and jewels. In the 1920s and 1930s, because of the American prohibition on the import or consumption of alcoholic drinks, a great deal of liquor was smuggled from Canada into the US, allowing some large fortunes to be made. Professional smugglers now concern themselves chiefly with prohibited drugs or druglike substances – heroin, cocaine, marijuana and various chemicals. More recently, because the Canadian government controls the exports of arms and other strategic materials, there have been more or less successful attempts to smuggle such goods out of Canada. In addition, a new kind of smuggling has developed, in which importers or exporters attach fictitiously low values to the goods they are trading so that customs duties will be lower than they should be.

The smuggling of traditional products by amateurs has obviously become much more tempting insofar as many more Canadians than previously are travelling between countries and provinces. However, because the costs of travel are high in comparison with the amount that can be saved, amateur smuggling rarely makes economic sense unless one is travelling for some other reason. There are no reliable statistics on the volume or value of smuggled goods, but the practice produces an understatement of the volume and value of Canada's INTERNATIONAL TRADE and a loss of government customs revenue. IAN M. DRUMMOND

Smyth, Sir Edward Selby, military officer (b at Belfast, Ire 31 Mar 1819; d in Eng 22 Sept 1896). He was adjutant general and general officer commanding the Canadian militia 1874-80, an appointment capping a British service career in India, Africa, Ireland and Mauritius. Economic depression and decreased militia expenditures forced Selby Smyth to concentrate on the survival of the militia as an institution. Although many of his proposals were rejected by the government, his relations with his Canadian political masters were better than those of his successors. In 1875 Selby Smyth undertook an 11 000 mile (18 333 km) tour through the Canadian West to inspect NWMP and militia units. His timely arrival in Batoche with 50 policemen forestalled declaration of a Métis republic. O.A. COOKE

Smythe, Constantine Falkland Cary, "Conn," sports entrepreneur (b at Toronto 1 Feb 1895; d there 18 Nov 1980). He was awarded the Military Cross in WWI and was severely injured by shrapnel in WWII. His reputation for hockey acumen derived from his success coaching U of T Varsity Grads to the Allan Cup (1927), and from the success of the original New York Ranger team, which he assembled in 1926. In 1927 he and associates raised $160 000 and bought Toronto St Pats, changing their name to TORONTO MAPLE LEAFS. Maple Leaf Gardens was built largely owing to his efforts (1931). He sold his controlling interest in the Gardens and the team in 1961 to his son Stafford and others. His autobiography, *Conn Smythe: If you can't beat 'em in the alley,* with Scott Young, appeared in 1981. JAMES MARSH

Snag, YT, UP, is located at the mouth of Snag Cr, 465 km NW of Whitehorse. The creek was so named in 1898 by members of the US Geological Survey, possibly because it was choked with dead trees. In 1942 the federal Dept of Transport established an emergency-landing strip and a weather station, which were maintained until 1966. On 3 Feb 1947 the station recorded a temperature of -62.8°C, the lowest official temperature ever measured in Canada. This small Indian village is accessible by road from Snag Junction at kilometre 1895 of the ALASKA HIGHWAY. H. GUEST

Snail, common name for members of several groups of gastropod MOLLUSCS. Snails inhabit all moist habitats, but most forms are marine. Typically, snails possess a protective spiral shell secreted by the mantle, a muscular foot for locomotion, a definable head region, housing both sensory structures, and a rasping ribbon of minute, chitinous teeth (the radula) for feeding. Gills are present in most snails (orders Prosobranchia and Opisthobranchia), but in the lung-breathing forms (Pulmonata) the mantle cavity forms the respiratory exchange surface. The common terrestrial snail (genus *Helix*) is edible. When prepared with seasoned garlic butter, this pulmonate is more familiar as the escargot of French cuisine. Other edible snails include the ABALONE and the conch. Freshwater snails are especially abundant in the Great Lakes region; in the temperature extremes of the more northern latitudes, species' numbers are reduced. Gastropod feeding processes range from filter feeding and grazing to predation on organisms much larger than themselves (eg, sea slugs feed upon coelenterate anemones). The sexes are often separate, but snails such as the slipper limpet (genus *Crepidula*) may change from male to male-female to female in the course of a lifetime. PETER V. FANKBONER

Snake, long, slender REPTILE of suborder Serpentes, order Squamata (which also includes LIZARDS). Snakes are limbless; however, primitive forms have a pelvic girdle and spurs, which are vestiges of hind limbs (eg, Canadian rubber boa). As with other reptiles, the body is covered by large scales which help reduce water loss in dry environments and provide mechanical protection. This epidermis is shed, usually as a single piece, a few times a year. About 2267 species occur worldwide, mostly in the tropics. One species reaches N of the Arctic Circle (to 68° N) in Scandinavia; another reaches 50° S in S America. In Canada, 25 species, classified in 3 families, are native: Boidae (1), Viperidae (3) and Colubridae (21). Boids and viperids feed mainly on warm-blooded prey. Canadian colubrids are harmless, although larger species can give painful bites. Larger colubrids prey on small mammals; medium-sized species take amphibians and fish; smaller species eat insects, invertebrates and smaller amphibians. Most occur in southern Canada, but the common GARTER SNAKE reaches about 60° N near Fort Smith, NWT. Although some tropical snakes attain great lengths (eg, reticulated python and anaconda, at 10 m the longest snakes known), Canadian species range from about 40 cm (northern redbelly snake) to over 180 cm (black rat snake and bullsnake). Snakes live in various ways and include burrowing, tree-dwelling, freshwater and marine forms; most Ca-

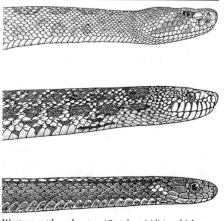

Western rattlesnake, top (*Crotalus viridis*), which may produce a brood only every 2 years or more; bullsnake, centre (*Pituophis melanoleucus*), which grows to lengths of more than 180 cm; and redbelly snake, bottom (*Storeria occipitomaculata*), a smaller snake of only c40 cm (*courtesy National Museums of Canada/National Museum of Natural Sciences/Charles Douglas*).

nadian species are terrestrial ground dwellers but some are semiaquatic or aquatic, mainly in fresh water.

Although limbless, snakes can move in different ways. In the most common method, lateral undulation, the body is formed into a series of horizontal curves, the back of each curve pressing against irregularities in the ground; this technique is also used in swimming. Heavy-bodied snakes can also exhibit rectilinear (straight line) locomotion, propulsion being provided by the forward movement and anchoring of the relatively loose skin, followed by the body within. Concertina movement is used by some species in confined spaces; the snake anchors its posterior end by a few horizontal curves, extends and reanchors its anterior end, then brings the posterior part forward. The most specialized form of locomotion, sidewinding, is used on soft (and hot) substrates such as desert sands, and is not practised regularly by any Canadian species.

All snakes are carnivores; most species are adapted to swallowing large prey whole. The many joints between bones of the skull and the elastic ligament joining the 2 lower jaw bones allow the various parts of skull and lower jaws to move independently. While back-curved teeth hold prey, snakes "walk" the 4 quadrants of the jaws over their prey when swallowing. Elastic skin and a windpipe opening in the mouth are also adaptations to the often lengthy process of swallowing large food whole. Most species detect prey visually and chemically. Snakes' main chemosensory organ is Jacobson's organ, in the roof of the mouth; molecules are delivered to this organ by the forked tongue, which is continually flicked out of the mouth when the snake examines potential prey.

Pit vipers (eg, RATTLESNAKES) feed mainly on warm-blooded animals and can accurately locate prey even in darkness via the thermosensory pit below the eye; many boas and pythons have thermosensory organs along the lips. Although snakes can detect earthborne vibrations, their hearing is poorly developed and is probably of no importance to predation.

Many species simply grab prey and swallow it live, usually head first; however, the risk of injury is relatively high with some prey. More specialized modes involve killing before eating. Constrictors coil around prey, preventing it from breathing but rarely crushing it. Although the boas and pythons are the most famous constrictors, constriction is practised by many other spe-

Snakes of Canada

Common Name	Scientific Name	Range
Family Viperidae:		
timber rattlesnake	*Crotalus horridus*	southwestern Ont; possibly extirpated in Canada
western rattlesnake	*C. viridis*	southern Sask, Alta, BC
massasauga rattlesnake	*Sistrurus catenatus*	southwestern Ont
Family Boidae:		
rubber boa	*Charina bottae*	southern BC
Family Colubridae:		
(black) rat snake	*Elaphe obsoleta*	southern Ont
fox snake	*E. vulpina*	southwestern Ont
bull (gopher) snake	*Pituophis melanoleucus*	southern BC, Alta, Sask
milk snake	*Lampropeltis triangulum*	southern Ont, Qué
eastern hognose snake	*Heterodon platyrhinos*	southern Ont
western hognose snake	*H. nasicus*	southern Prairies
common garter snake	*Thamnophis sirtalis*	coast to coast, except Nfld, N to Fort Smith, NWT
Butler's garter snake	*T. butleri*	southwestern Ont
eastern ribbon snake	*T. sauritus*	southern Ont, southwestern NS
plains garter snake	*T. radix*	Alta, Sask, Man
western terrestrial garter snake	*T. elegans*	central Sask to BC
northwestern garter snake	*T. ordinoides*	Vancouver I and southwestern mainland
northern water snake	*Nerodia sipedon*	southern Ont, Qué
queen snake	*Regina septemvittata*	southwestern Ont
redbelly snake	*Storeria occipitomaculata*	Sask to Maritimes
brown snake	*S. dekayi*	southern Ont, Qué
racer snake	*Coluber constrictor*	southern BC, Sask, Ont
ringneck snake	*Diadophis punctatus*	southern Ont to Maritimes
smooth green snake	*Opheodrys vernalis*	central southern Sask to Maritimes
sharptail snake	*Contia tenuis*	Vancouver I, Gulf Is, Chase, BC
night snake	*Hypsiglena torquata*	extreme southcentral BC

cies, eg, bullsnake and black rat snake in Canada. The most effective and least risky means of handling prey is by envenomation. Venomous snakes have a venom gland above the upper jaw, connected by a duct to a tubular fang at the front of the mouth. Injected venom kills prey and begins its digestion while the snake waits for it to die. In vipers and pit vipers, the fang is so long that it is hinged back along the roof of the mouth when not in use. The 3 rattlesnakes native to Canada are pit vipers. Other highly venomous snakes have shorter, permanently erect fangs. The most primitive have grooved teeth at the rear of the jaw and "chew" venom into prey. The only Canadian rear-fanged snake is the secretive night snake, recently found to reach its northern limit in BC.

Like other reptiles, snakes are ectotherms (having body temperature governed mainly by external conditions) and can regulate body temperature to some extent by moving in and out of shade. While northern snakes are generally more cold tolerant than tropical species, the extreme seasonality of north temperate regions means that they are regularly faced with conditions too cold for continued activity or survival. Snakes in Canada must therefore hibernate below the frost line. In areas with very cold winters, sites which allow snakes to go deep enough to avoid subfreezing temperatures may be scarce, and available sites are used by many snakes. Communal

hibernation is demonstrated particularly well in western Canada by the western rattlesnake and the common garter snake; hibernating groups of the latter may number in the thousands. Because overwintering sites are often concentrated in particular areas, communal hibernation is sometimes accompanied by migrations of several km between hibernating site and summer habitat.

In Canada, most species of snakes mate in spring shortly after hibernation. Western rattlesnakes, however, mate in late summer or fall and the female retains sperm over winter; fertilization occurs the following spring. Fertilization in snakes is always internal and sperm are transferred into the female by a copulatory organ. Each male has 2 such organs (hemipenes) housed in the base of the tail. Snakes include egg-laying and live-bearing species. While egg-laying species are more numerous worldwide, the proportion of live-bearing species is higher in cooler environments (eg, 14 of the 25 species in Canada are live-bearers). Live bearing is, presumably, a useful adaptation where summers are short because the female can better regulate the temperature at which the young develop than if eggs were simply laid in the ground. Females may give birth late in summer and be unable to feed enough before hibernation to reproduce again the following summer. Consequently, females of live-bearing species at high altitudes or latitudes may produce a brood only every 2 or more years (eg, the western rattlesnake). In Canada, as elsewhere, litters or clutches usually include 3-16 young, although some species occasionally produce broods of 50 or more. PATRICK T. GREGORY

Snipe, name given to 16 species of small to medium-sized SHOREBIRDS (254-406 mm) of the SANDPIPER family. Like WOODCOCKS, snipes have long bills with flexible tips and eyes set well back on the skull, allowing almost all-round vision. They are renowned for courtship and territorial displays known as winnowing – birds circle over their territory and dive with a loud "bleating" noise caused by air rushing past the extended outer tail feathers. Hence, they are sometimes called "goat of the bogs." The common or Wilson's snipe (*Gallinago gallinago*) nests from Alaska to California, E across Canada and the northern US to Newfoundland, and winters S to Venezuela and Colombia. A.J. BAKER

Snow, Clarence Eugene, "Hank," singer, songwriter, guitarist (b at Liverpool, NS 9 May 1914), one of the fathers of Canadian COUNTRY AND WESTERN MUSIC. His singing style, with its clear enunciation, influenced scores of artists in Canada and the US. He ran away to sea and was soon entertaining crew members with his singing. By 1929 he was singing professionally and by 1935 had a radio show in Halifax. In 1936 he signed with RCA Victor and recorded his first hits. He tried to break into the US market in the late 1940s, but with slight success. In 1950 RCA released "I'm Movin' On," the song that established his career in the US, and Snow became one of the top stars of country music in the 1950s. He eventually moved to Nashville and became an American citizen, though he still appeared in Canada regularly. He was selected for the Country Music Hall of Fame in 1976 and the Juno (Awards) Hall of Fame in 1979. In 1985 "I'm Moving' On" won the Millionaire Award for having been played on the radio 1 million times, an all-time country music record. In 1986 he made a 7-day concert tour of NS and Nfld; NS Prem Buchanan declared "Hank Snow Week" in NS (20-27 July 1986). RICHARD GREEN

Snow, John, or *Îtebiian Mânii,* meaning "Walking Seal," Indian spokesman, philosopher, states-

man, spiritual leader (b at Morley, Alta 31 Jan 1933). Snow was the first Stoney Indian ordained in the United Church of Canada (1963). After serving parishes in Saskatchewan and Alberta, he returned to his home reserve at Morley (1968). In 1969 he became chief of the Wesley band. When the government tabled the 1969 Indian assimilationist policy, "The White Paper," Snow in 1970 presented the Alberta chiefs' response, "The Red Paper," asserting aboriginal and treaty rights (*see* NATIVE PEOPLE, GOVERNMENT POLICY). In 1975 Snow was named chairman of the Indian Ecumenical Conference, a continent-wide gathering of Indian traditional elders, youth and church leaders concerned about their spiritual heritage. Snow's 1977 book, *These Mountains Are Our Sacred Places,* presents his philosophy on Indian culture and spirituality. IAN A.L. GETTY

Snow, Michael James Aleck, painter, sculptor, photographer, filmmaker, musician (b at Toronto 10 Dec 1929). After study at the Ontario Coll of Art (1948-52) and a visit to Europe (1953-54), he worked for a small Toronto film company until 1956, during which time he produced his first independent film. In 1956 Snow held his first solo exhibition at Avrom Isaacs's Greenwich Gallery in Toronto. Following extended stays in New York (1962-64), he settled there in 1964, returning to Toronto in 1972. Between 1961 and 1967 his work in all media was based on the silhouette of a young woman. This important series of works, titled the *Walking Woman Works,* culminated in an 11-part sculpture for the Ontario Pavillion at EXPO 67. In 1970 Snow represented Canada at the Venice Biennale and was also given a retrospective exhibition of his work at the Art Gallery of Ontario. In 1979 a comprehensive survey of his work was shown in Lucerne, Bonn and Munich. The same year, he received a sculptural commission, *Flight Stop,* for Toronto's EATON CENTRE. For Expo 86 he was commissioned to produce a major work in holography; *The Spectral Image* is a grouping of installation pieces involving 48 holographic images.

Film has occupied a major place in his work from the mid-1960s with works such as *Wavelength* (1967), *La Région centrale* (1971), *Rameau's Nephew by Diderot (Thanx to Dennis Young) by Wilma Schoen* (1974) and *Presents* (1981). Snow has received critical acclaim in the US and Europe as an experimental filmmaker. His work has been continually concerned with defining and redefining the relationships between media themselves, the acts and interpretations of perception and the complex of sound, language and meaning. He is also an accomplished pianist and trumpet player. He played professionally, was a member of the Artists' Jazz Band in Toronto and founder of the Canadian Creative Music Collective. DAVID BURNETT

Reading: R. Cornwell, *Snow Seen* (1980); L. Dompierre, *Walking Woman Works, 1961-1967* (1983).

Venus Simultaneous (1962), oil on canvas and wood, by Michael Snow (*courtesy Art Gallery of Ontario/Purchase, 1964/photo by James Chambers*).

Snow Lake, Man, Town, inc 1976, pop 1837 (1986c). Located 705 km NW of Winnipeg on the Canadian SHIELD, the town owes its existence to mining and milling operations in the vicinity. Gold was first discovered at nearby Wekusko Lake in 1914 and by C.R. (Lew) Parres in 1927 at what is now Snow Lake. The townsite was laid out in 1945 after Howe Sound Exploration Co Ltd decided to develop the Snow Lake property. In 1958 Hudson's Bay Mining and Smelting Co took over and began a major expansion program. Mines currently operating at Chisel Lake, Stall Lake, Anderson Lake, Spruce Point and the Rod Mine produce primarily copper for the concentrator at nearby Stall Lake.   H. JOHN SELWOOD

Snowbirds, successors to the Canadian Armed Forces' aerobatics teams of the 1950s and 1960s, the Golden Hawks and the Centennaires, were formed in 1971 by Col O.B. Philp, base commander at CFB Moose Jaw. Later known as 431 Air Demonstration Squadron, Snowbirds, they are the only 9-plane aerobatic flight demonstration team outside Europe. The team performs annually to over 5 million people at 65 airshows in the US and Canada. The 21-man team of pilots and technical crew changes half of its members each year, so that the entire team revolves every 2 years. Flying the Canadian-designed and built Canadair CL-41 Tutor jet painted red, white and blue, they have become the pride of the CAF.   ROBERT M. MUMMERY

Reading: Robert M. Mummery, *Snowbirds* (1983).

Snowmobile, automotive vehicle for travel on snow. As with most technical innovations, the development of the snowmobile is obscure. Joseph-Armand BOMBARDIER, a mechanic from Valcourt, Qué, developed the first of many oversnow vehicles – a propeller-driven sled – in 1922. A moderately successful motor toboggan was developed in Wisconsin in 1927, but it was Bombardier who incorporated the motive sprocket wheel and double, endless track that made the vehicle practical. In 1937 he sold 50 of his B-7 model as buses and medical transport, and he designed vehicles used in WWII; by 1948 about 1000 B-12s had been produced. Bombardier patented many other improvements to suspension, transmission and braking systems to make the snowmobile more reliable, and in the mid-1950s the introduction of the air-cooled, 2-stroke engine made possible the small sport models common today.

From sales of 225 recreational snowmobiles in 1959, about 250 000 were being bought per year in North America by the 1970s. In 1987 there were about 700 000 households in Canada with at least one snowmobile, ranging from 3.2% of households in BC to 7.5% in Ontario, 11.1% in Saskatchewan, 15.3% in Québec and 23.5% in NB. In 1970 there were 129 manufacturers in N

America, 26 in Canada – of which 20 were in Québec. Bombardier never yielded its lead, and after the number of companies shrank by the 1980s to a half dozen, it remained the world's largest.

Most innovations in transportation have been adapted to recreation, eg, the bicycle, boat and car, and widespread use of the snowmobile was a logical development in Canada. Over snow-covered ground it provides transportation previously impossible except on skis, snowshoes or dogsled. It has provided a means for Canadians to enjoy winter in an unprecedented way and has enabled year-round use of recreational facilities such as cottages. Unlike other recreation equipment, ownership of snowmobiles is more heavily rural than urban, since the vehicle is very useful in farm work. A small number of vehicles are used for racing, but the main attraction seems to be enjoyment of the outdoors and socializing; there are an estimated 10 000 clubs in N America.

The explosion of snowmobiling brought serious concerns, particularly in the early years, about noise disturbance, ecological damage and safety (100 deaths in 1970). The snowmobile was misused for vandalism, habitat destruction and chasing game. By 1972 all provinces except PEI had legislation governing and restricting the use of snowmobiles. The provision of extensive trails, notably in Québec, overcame many of the objections. Although other forms of winter recreation, such as CROSS-COUNTRY SKIING, gained in popularity in the late 1970s and early 1980s, snowmobiling remains popular in North America. In the North the snowmobile has changed the hunting, herding and trapping patterns of the Inuit, although dogsleds continue to be used in extreme conditions.   CHRIS DEBRESSON

Snowshoeing is a form of physical activity that utilizes 2 wooden-frame "shoes," each strung together with interlaced webbing, to walk or run over snow. A common form of transport, and probably of sport, among native peoples prior to European settlement in N America, the "encumbrance" was first embraced by fur trappers. Twelve English-speaking men from Montréal met regularly around 1840 to tramp or hike on snowshoes on Saturday afternoons. In 1843, these men, some of whom were Montréal's most prominent businessmen, formed the Montreal Snow Shoe Club (MSSC) – the first of its kind in the world. Nicholas "Evergreen" Hughes was a key figure in organizing the club and in the growth of snowshoeing itself.

Long-distance "tramps" were the most common form of the activity for almost 20 years. Men from the MSSC and a handful of other clubs would rendezvous near McGill College to tramp 19 km or more, following the club's senior officer in single file. At the rear of the line was the "whipper-in," an accomplished snowshoer whose job was to keep the pack together. Halfway through, or after these tramps, the snowshoers rested their feet at a local chophouse or tavern in the city or atop Mount Royal. Meals were eaten, songs such as "Rise, Ye Sons of Canada" and "Partant pour la Syrie" were sung, poems were recited and cotillions were danced. Race meetings were held as early as 1843 and featured dashes, 2-mi (3.2 km) events and hurdles over 4-ft (1.2 m)-high barriers. There is good evidence that the hurdle race in snowshoeing preceded its summer counterpart by almost a decade. (Similarly, the word "jogged" was used to describe the slow, chugging motion of trampers during the early 1870s.) Prior to WWII, track athletes used the snowshoe as a winter training device.

By the late 1860s, the number of snowshoe clubs and race meetings in Montréal had prolifer-

Man Strapping on Snow Shoes (1884), watercolour and gouache over pencil by R.W. Rutherford (*courtesy National Archives of Canada/C-98974*).

ated. The increased interest in competition was also reflected in prestigious trophies such as the Tecumseh Cup; in new events such as the mountain steeplechase; in the appearance of outstanding competitors, especially the fleet-footed Keraronwe and W.L. Maltby; in improved times in all events (1.6 km in 6 min became common); in the introduction of the 1.5-pound (0.68 kg) racing shoe that replaced the old regulation "four-pounder"; in the birth of competitive clubs in Ottawa, Toronto and Québec City; in the snowshoe races featured by skating rinks as their premier event at annual races; and in the development of a snowshoe-racing vocabulary, for example, the "brush," connoting a successful acceleration of one racer past another. By the early 1880s, snowshoeing was clearly the most popular winter amusement.

Clubs were in evidence from Winnipeg to Terra Nova, Nfld. The MSSC was instrumental in forming the multi-sport Montreal Amateur Athletic Assn in 1881 and, along with other Montréal snowshoe clubs, organized, promoted and staged the world-famous, week-long winter Mardi Gras or carnival from 1883 to 1889.

Snowshoers also gave concerts, engaged in campaigns to raise charity funds and organized pedestrian clubs in the summer. In facing the rigours of long tramps, frostbite, bleeding toes and the ever-present side stitch, snowshoers displayed a particularly Canadian example of the 19th-century sporting phenomenon called "muscular Christianity."

A skating resurgence in the 1890s and fanatical interest in a new winter sport, ICE HOCKEY, halted and reversed the growth and development of snowshoeing. Winnipeg became the centre of the sport during the early 20th century, and the Canadian Snowshoe Union, the current governing body for the sport's 70 modern clubs, was formed in 1907.   DON MORROW

Reading: H.W. Becket, *The Montreal Snow Shoe Club* (1882).

Snowshoes for winter travel were almost universal among native people in Canada outside the Pacific and Arctic coasts. The Athapaskans of the West and Algonquians of the northeast made the most sophisticated snowshoes. Frames were generally made of durable, flexible ash wood, and lacing from deer, caribou and moose hide. The toe and tail sections of the shoe were laced with a light BABICHE and the central body with a heavy babiche for better weight suspension. The Indian-style MOCCASIN is the traditional snowshoe footwear. Much Indian FOLKLORE centered on the snowshoe. The OJIBWA, for example, celebrated the first snowfall of the winter with a snowshoe dance. During the early historic period the snowshoe was as important as the canoe, the wagon or the railway in opening up the country. *See also* SNOWSHOEING.   RENÉ R. GADACZ

Soapstone, a metamorphic rock composed essentially of talc with varying amounts of mineral

J.A. Bombardier's use of a motive sprocket wheel and double, endless track created the snowmobile industry in 1937. By the 1980s, Bombardier Inc was the world's largest producer (*courtesy Bombardier Inc*).

Soapstone quarry, Fleur de Lys, NE Newfoundland (*courtesy Ron Redfern, Random House Inc*).

impurities, including mica, chlorite, pyroxene, amphibole, serpentine, quartz, calcite and iron oxides. The rock may be massive or schistose (ie, strongly foliated and capable of being split into thinner sheets). In commercial usage the term refers to the primary product, block soapstone, and talc refers to the processed (ground) product. Colour varies from white to greenish grey and dark green. It is soft (1-2 on the Mohs scale), with a specific gravity of 2.2-2.8, but these properties vary with type and amount of impurities. Soapstone has a greasy feel (hence the name), can be ground to a powder or carved, has a high fusion point, low electrical and thermal conductivity, superior heat retention and high lubricating power. It is chemically inert.

Soapstone's use dates back to antiquity: early Egyptians carved it into scarabs and seals; in China and India it was used for ornaments, implements and domestic utensils. It was similarly used at various times over the past 7500 years by Indians, Inuit and Norse in Canada (*see* INUIT ART). In recent years, soapstone has been used to produce purely decorative, rather than functional, objects. The term soapstone carving is often used for sculptures carved from other soft, compact carving mediums, including serpentine and the talc-like mineral pyrophyllite. Block soapstone is used as refractory material, for metalworkers' crayons, sculpture and the recently revived griddle plates. It was used infrequently as a building stone. The ground material talc is used mainly as a filler in paper, plastic, rubber and paint industries and for cosmetics and pharmaceuticals.

Soapstone occurs in Québec, Ontario, BC, Alberta, Saskatchewan and NS. Canada's first production was in 1871 from a deposit in the Eastern Townships, Qué. The 1985 Canadian production of soapstone, talc and pyrophyllite of 127 000 t came from underground and open-pit mines in Québec (Broughton and South Bolton) and Ontario (Madoc and Timmins). Canada is a minor producer, far behind the world leaders, Japan and the US. Block soapstone for the northern carving industry is quarried from deposits adjacent to Baffin I (Markham Bay and Broughton I) and scattered localities in the North. Annual production of 500-1000 t is supplemented by sculpture-grade soapstone from Québec producers who also supply hobby shops and sculptors in southern regions.   ANN P. SABINA

Soaring, or gliding is the sport of flying a sailplane or glider for a sustained period of time by utilizing currents of rising air to stay aloft. The term "soaring" means ascending, high flying or mounting upward, while "gliding" describes the more basic flying which is performed during take-off, circuit patterns and landings. Some sailplanes are motorized and self-launching, but the majority are launched by aero-tow, winch or car-tow from about 50 airfields across the country. Instruction in the art and science of soaring is given freely by volunteer instructors qualified to national standards and operating within a club structure. As a rule, students pay for club membership and for the use of aircraft; once licenced, pilots can opt for private ownership.

Glider design and development has often been at the forefront of aviation technology. The first powered aircraft were developed by the Wright brothers in the US and J.A.D. MCCURDY and others in Canada from gliders. For example, some remarkable gliders were designed, built and briefly flown in Europe during the second half of the 19th century. In 1902 the general problem of lack of control in flight was solved when the first glider with 3-axis flight control (pilot control in pitch, yaw and roll) was built in the US by the Wright brothers; only after achieving equilibrium in the air could they safely add an engine and develop the first successful powered aircraft. While sleek aircraft profiles may seem to be a recent innovation, soaring pilots have long known that only smooth well-profiled wings could ensure the efficiency and higher speeds needed to win sailplane races. This has meant that fibreglass, carbon fibres and other space-age composites have been used in the construction of sailplanes decades before their acceptance by commercial aviation companies. The first all fibreglass sailplane to be built in Canada was designed as long ago as 1960. In addition to promoting the practical use of advanced materials, the unique ability of the glider pilot to fly at low speeds has helped in the first hand analysis of flutter and structural instability, while an intimate understanding of air currents – particularly in thunderstorms and around and over mountain ranges – continues to enrich our knowledge of meteorology.

The first gliders in Canada were built by adventurous individuals early in the 20th century. Most were copied from magazine diagrams and were more akin to kites and hang gliders. As gliding became popular in Germany and the US in the 1920s, the idea of "airmindedness" spread to Canada and by 1930, Halifax, New Glasgow, Montréal, Ottawa, Toronto, Windsor, North Battleford, Lethbridge, Calgary and Vancouver all had gliding clubs. By the mid-1930s, successful clubs had sprung up all over the Prairies where the terrain was ideal, and where dust-bowl conditions and the Depression had given a lot of young people free time to get involved in an affordable do-it-yourself type of flying. At that time, little was known about thermal updrafts and the sport consisted of being towed up to 30 m or less (by horse, car, winch and occasionally aeroplane) and gliding down to the take-off point with a turn or 2 if there was enough height. The first planned distance flight in which the pilot landed 10 miles from home after climbing to a height of 1200 m was done by a Lethbridge woman, Evelyn Fletcher, in 1939.

In the 1940s, a new breed of pilots emerged from the armed forces and saw the need to organize the gliding movement so that safety, instruction and competition could be encouraged and standardized, and lines of communication opened across the country; the Soaring Association of Canada (SAC) was incorporated in 1945 and the first issue of the national magazine *Free Flight* was printed in 1949. In 1947 Ovila "Shorty" Boudreault of Ottawa earned an international soaring badge, and Canadian pilots began to measure their standards against those of the rest of the world. In 1949, Canada held its first national contest. However, by 1952 a Canadian team was ready to compete internationally in Spain and since that time has been represented at most World Soaring Contests sponsored by the Fédération Aeronautique Internationale (FAI). Several Canadians have had daily placings in the top 10, but the best result was by Wolf Mix of Toronto who in 1970 came fourth overall in the standard class.

Pins are awarded for reaching several international levels of soaring proficiency from the basic 5 hours duration, and 1000 m altitude gain to completing a 1000 km triangle. Records are maintained at national and world levels for distance, altitude and speed around courses of set length. (Duration record attempts were stopped after pilot endurance became the limiting safety factor over pilot skill.) Some of the Canadian records recognized by the FAI are 115.4 km/h around a 500 km out and return, H. Werneburg, 1984; 108.8 km/h around a 750 km triangle, W. Krug, 1982; 1093 km straight distance, M. Apps and D. Marsden 1984. The highest altitude attained so far is 10 485 m by B. Hea in 1982.
                                        CHRISTINE FIRTH

Sobey, William Macdonald, executive (b at New Glasgow, NS 9 June 1927). As chairman of the board of Sobeys Stores Ltd, he continues the family control of the Nova Scotia-based chain of food stores founded in 1907 by his grandfather, John William Sobey. The retail and wholesale company operates 100 supermarkets and has a market that extends beyond the Atlantic provinces into the Gaspé and southern Ontario. Sobey was mayor of Stellarton, NS, for 5 years. In 1987 the Sobey family and another NS family lost a 5-year legal battle for Nova Scotia Savings & Loan Co. The Sobeys have a 20% interest in PROVIGO Inc which operates food stores and owns Consumers Distributing.   MARY HALLORAN

Soccer (Association Football) is a sport played by 2 teams of 11 players each, using a round ball, usually on a grass field called the "pitch." Only the 2 goalkeepers may intentionally handle the ball, which is moved from player to player by kicking, and a goal may be scored by kicking or heading the ball into the opponent's goal. Association Football, the traditional name of the game, has now been shortened to "football," while the term "soccer" is derived from the second syllable of the word "association." In Canada and the US the game is usually referred to as soccer to distinguish it from other forms of FOOTBALL.

Soccer in Canada was played under a variety of rules from the early years of the 19th century. The first game played as we would play it today seems to have taken place in Toronto in Oct 1876 between 2 local clubs. From 1876 on, the game grew and spread across the country. The Dominion Football Assn was organized in Montréal in 1878 and operated a loosely arranged cup competition largely involving college teams from southern Ontario. The Western Football Assn of Ontario was formed in Jan 1880 in Berlin [Kitchener] and had 19 clubs in membership by April of that year. Its formation led to the first international soccer match in N America, with Canada defeating the US 1-0 in Nov 1885 in Newark, NJ; the following year, Canada lost 3-2. On the Canadian side in both games was David Forsyth, a teacher at Berlin High School, who was instrumental in founding the WFA, playing the first internationals and organizing a tour to Britain in 1888. In Britain the Canadian touring team won 9 games, tied 5 and lost 9 against some of the finest opposition of the day. A similar tour took place in 1891; the touring party this time was made up of both Canadian and American players, with disastrous results.

Represented by the Galt Football Club, Canada entered Olympic competition for the first time in 1904 and came away with the gold medal at the Olympic Games in St Louis, Mo. Faced with 2 American teams in a competition abbreviated because of travel problems, Canada won its first game 7-0 and the second 4-0. By 1912, when the Dominion of Canada Football Assn (forerunner of today's national governing body, the Canadian Soccer Assn) was formed, there were leagues and associations across the country. In 1914 Canada gained full membership in the Fédération internationale de football association (FIFA), the governing body of world soccer. A national championship came into being in 1913 when the Connaught Cup (presented by the duke of CON- NAUGHT) was offered for competition. The first winners were the Norwood Wanderers of Winnipeg. In 1926 the Connaught Cup was succeeded by a new trophy, donated by the Football Assn of England and still played for today. The most successful national champions have been the New Westminster Royals, who have appeared in 10 finals, winning 8 times. A Canadian national team toured Australia in 1924 and New Zealand in 1927, while in the 1920s and 1930s numerous teams from Britain toured Canada. One member of the Canadian team in New Zealand was Dave TURNER; another notable player of this era, Joe Kennaway, played for Canada and Scotland, and in his day was one of the finest goalkeepers in the world.

The influx of immigrants from around the world following WWII changed the face of Canadian soccer. In the prewar years the influence had been largely British, but it rapidly became international, particularly in the 1950s and 1960s. As the immigrants were assimilated into Canadian life, the emphasis began to shift to the development of Canadian players. As a result, Canada's status as a soccer power is steadily improving, and Canada has regularly fielded teams in World Cup (world professional championship), Olympic, Pan-American, youth and womens competition.

Canada first entered for the World Cup in 1957 but did not pass beyond the first preliminary round until 1978, when the team narrowly missed qualifying for the final rounds. Similarly, in 1982 only one goal prevented the team from reaching the objective that was finally achieved in 1986. Canada reached the finals of the World Cup for the first time in 1986, under coach Tony Waiters, and despite losing to France, Hungary and the Soviet Union, all long-established world-class powers, the team distinguished itself by the quality of its play.

In Olympic competition Canada played in the final rounds of the Montréal Olympics in 1976, losing narrowly to the Soviet Union and North Korea. In the final of this competition East Germany defeated Poland 3-1 before a Canadian record crowd of 71 619 in Montréal's Olympic Stadium. Canada went one step farther in the 1984 Los Angeles Olympics, reaching the quarter finals before being beaten by Brazil. In this game the score was tied 1-1 after 90 minutes of regulation time and 30 minutes of overtime. Canada lost its bid for a place in the semi-final in the subsequent penalty kick shoot out.

Canada's national youth team has qualified for the world finals 3 times in the last decade, the first time being in Japan in 1979, followed by the Soviet Union in 1985 and Chile in 1987.

An increasing involvement in international competition has produced a number of outstanding Canadian players, among them fullback Bruce Wilson, who captained the Canadian team in the 1984 Olympics and 1986 World Cup finals and who played a record 57 times for his country before retiring. Playing alongside Wilson in many

of those games was Bobby Lenarduzzi, who also had a notable career with the Vancouver Whitecaps of the NASL. During the 1986 World Cup finals, centre back Randy Samuel played so well that he was offered a lucrative contract with a famous Dutch team, while midfielder Randy Ragan has emerged as one of the best players at his position anywhere in the world. In addition Sam Lenarduzzi, older brother of Bob, Buzz Parsons, Jimmy Douglas and Robert Iarusci, who also played for the world famous New York Cosmos, made their mark on the Canadian and international game some years earlier.

Most of the players who have represented Canada in recent years played at one time in the North American Soccer League. The NASL, which folded early in 1985, at one time boasted 5 Canadian teams: the Calgary Boomers, Edmonton Drillers, Montreal Manic, Toronto Blizzard and Vancouver Whitecaps. The Blizzard were the fourth NASL franchise in Toronto following the Falcons, Metros and the Metros-Croatia. The Metros-Croatia won the NASL championship in 1976, a feat duplicated by the Vancouver Whitecaps in 1979, while the Blizzard were beaten finalists in 1983 and 1984. Prior to the NASL's formation in 1968, there were few Canadians playing professionally, and even those leagues classed as professional, such as the National Soccer League, employed few full-time professionals. The first attempt to form a professional league in Canada came in 1913 and was short lived. Other attempts have been made, with the NSL (formed in 1926) being the longest running.

Following the collapse of the NASL the Canadian Soccer Association replaced it with a league of its own. This league, known as the Canadian Soccer League, began play in the spring of 1987 with teams in Vancouver, Edmonton, Calgary, Winnipeg, Hamilton, Toronto, Ottawa and North York. Canada also hosted the second FIFA World Under 16 Championship in 1987.

In contrast to Canadian and American football, soccer has spread to every nation in the world, and over 150 nations are members of FIFA. Although on uncertain grounds as a professional sport in Canada, soccer continues to grow in popularity as a recreational sport for both men and women, and ranks second only to hockey in numbers of participants. COLIN JOSE

Reading: R. Henshaw, *The Encyclopedia of World Soccer* (1979); Colin Jose and B. Rannie, *The Story of Soccer in Canada* (1982); Desmond Morris, *The Soccer Tribe* (1981).

Social and Welfare Services There is a general division, in Canada, between SOCIAL SECURITY programs and social and welfare services. Social security programs, which are the responsibility of all levels of government, provide direct economic assistance in one form or another to individuals or families. Included in this category are programs such as FAMILY ALLOWANCES, OLD AGE PENSIONS and provincial and municipal social-assistance programs. Social and welfare service programs, on the other hand, have been developed in an attempt to respond to personal, social and emotional needs. Included are the services for the residential care of people in government-run or private residences, care of people in their own homes, and a wide range of community-based services such as DAY CARE, home-delivered meals and counselling. These services are now often referred to as the "personal" social services and have been developed and expanded primarily during the 20th century, particularly during the last 2 decades.

In the past, the family was expected to care for its members with assistance from the church, private charity and workplace associations when the

family's own resources were insufficient. With industrialization, there was a shift in emphasis from farm labour to industrial labour. As manufacturing expanded, the cities attracted more wage earners, which resulted in congested living conditions and new social needs. The state responded initially by financing the expansion of private and church charities but then began to administer social and welfare services itself.

There are still many residential services provided for people in need, but in addition a great variety of noninstitutional social and welfare services have been developed. The growth of state-run services has not eliminated the role of the more informal sources of help, such as the family and the church, but it has shifted the primary responsibility for financing, administration and direct provision of services to the 3 levels of government. In some provinces various private social-service organizations, funded in part by government and in part by United Way campaigns, also exist, as do a number of alternative services that function outside both government and established private organizations.

Purpose and Range of Services Social and welfare services are organized primarily around the populations they serve, eg, children and families, youth, the elderly, the physically handicapped and the developmentally handicapped. However, no matter what population they serve, these services exist for a number of different purposes. Some provide daily, 24-hour care; others support the family (particularly mothers, who are in most cases responsible for meeting the social and emotional needs of the family); others provide protection for those in jeopardy, eg, neglected or abused children. For children who may require temporary or permanent removal from their own family, a range of foster homes, group homes and residential services are provided. Included in the general child-welfare system are services for ADOPTION of children. For children with psychological problems, counselling services are available and MENTAL HEALTH centres for residential care have been established. A limited number of day-care services have been established in each jurisdiction, primarily for preschool children. There are very few spaces for children of school age and for children with special needs; indeed, the availability of day-care spaces of any kind falls short of the actual need.

There are a number of smaller, and in some cases, more recent programs designed to support the family, including homemaker services, which provide help in the home; parent-education programs; and respite services that allow mothers a break from the daily demands of caring for young children. Family-planning programs across the country provide information and counselling to families. There are also a small number of alternative services for women, established at the initiation of local groups of women in the absence of state activity. The services include local women's centres which provide information, advice, counselling and referral; rape crisis centres; and a number of interval or transitional houses for battered women and their children. These services, while they respond to pressing needs, suffer from inadequate and insecure funding.

To meet the needs of the elderly, residential homes, including large centres for long-term care and an expanding network of smaller community-based nursing homes, have been established. In some areas community-based services for the elderly include drop-in centres, home-delivered meal services and homemaker services.

A network of services has been developed for the physically and mentally handicapped (see DISABILITIES), including large-scale institutions and smaller, community-based residential services such as foster homes and group homes. Some jurisdictions have established sheltered workshops to provide training to facilitate the integration of the handicapped person into the community. Local associations for the mentally retarded, which advocate on behalf of the developmentally handicapped and also provide some services in their local communities, have been founded in many parts of Canada. Services for the mentally ill have been set up outside the general health system (*see* PSYCHIATRY). In some areas there are community-based rehabilitation programs that help the mentally ill who have been institutionalized to integrate themselves back into the community; in others, emergency housing facilities and drop-in services are provided to assist people recently released from hospital.

Jurisdiction Under the Canadian CONSTITUTION, the responsibility for social and welfare services rests with the provincial and territorial governments. The services are operated primarily under provincial and territorial legislation. Each province and territory has established its own variety of services. Some provinces delegate partial responsibility for the administration of social and welfare services to the local or municipal level of government and in some instances the municipal governments also contribute to the financing of some of these services.

The federal government, through its cost-sharing agreements with the provinces and territories, is also involved in social and welfare services. For example, through the federal Canada Assistance Plan, the cost for many services is split on a 50-50 basis with the provinces.

A small percentage of social and welfare services are under the jurisdiction of private or church organizations. In many cases these organizations receive some financing from the government bodies and the remainder is solicited through private donations, including the annual campaigns of United Way appeals. In some jurisdictions the private agencies have essentially been taken over by the government; in others these agencies (essentially semipublic organizations) have been maintained, although they operate primarily on government funding and frequently under the mandates legislated by the provincial government.

Regional Variation During the past 20 years most jurisdictions in Canada have reviewed their pattern of social services. For example, Alberta initiated a preventive social service program in 1966; Québec launched an inquiry into health and social welfare services in 1966; Manitoba began some integration of health and welfare services in 1968; NB established a task force on social development in 1970; BC began a review of social services in 1972; and Ontario established a task force on social services in 1979. In most provinces these developments have resulted in an increase in the control of the provincial government over social and welfare services. The now terminated experience with community resource boards in BC represented a move towards decentralization of decision making. Québec is the only province which integrates health and welfare services; all others maintain separate health and welfare services in different ministries. Generally the reorganization has bypassed the local level of government.

Over this period some provinces, eg, Québec and BC, have assumed wide control over private agencies, while others, eg, Ontario, have continued to support some private agencies. Most of the jurisdictions have established some form of decentralization of responsibility for the actual administration of services, while maintaining central government control of policy and financing. Québec, for example, has established regional bodies, community-service centres, and local neighbourhood organizations called "local community service centres." Alberta and Québec have both established regional offices and in some cases local area offices for their provincial social and welfare services. Newfoundland's regionalized services reflect its geography and the number of isolated communities. The NEWFOUNDLAND RESETTLEMENT PROGRAM of the early 1960s, however, disrupted family and community life by forcing the closure of small industries in an attempt to centralize economic activity. This resulted in a shift of population to the larger centres and a concentration of social and welfare services.

The provision of social and welfare services for native people is complicated by a debate over jurisdiction (*see* NATIVE PEOPLE, HEALTH). The federal government has overall responsibility for native people and their lands under the Constitution Act, 1867, in general, and under the Indian Act in particular. Certain services, such as child welfare, have been delegated to the provincial governments but not all provinces have willingly assumed this responsibility. In other areas of social and welfare services it is not clear who is responsible. Indian organizations, eg, band councils, have sometimes taken on responsibility for the actual administration of child-welfare services. In addition, native people are demanding more direct control over the development and administration of their social and welfare services. In 1982, under an agreement signed by the federal government, the Manitoba government and the Four Nations Confederacy, child-welfare services were to be administered by native organizations, but in other regions there has been little such direct participation in administration.

Recent Developments One of the most important developments affecting social and welfare services is the general cutback in state expenditure on these services by the federal and provincial governments. For welfare recipients, this has exacerbated the problem of the erosion of real purchasing power which they have suffered since about 1975 and which worsened in the economic recession of the early 1980s.

In addition to curtailing any needed expansion and actually cutting back on the amount of money spent on social services, a number of additional strategies have been developed. The first is de-institutionalization, which involves both the removal of people from institutions and the prevention of institutionalization in the first place. This is resulting in the closing of some large institutions across the country, eg, institutions for the handicapped, the mentally ill, the elderly, and children. Related to this is the second strategy of community care, ie, an emphasis on caring for people in their own community and in many cases in their own family. Part of this strategy is focused on receiving people back into the community from institutional settings; part is focused on trying to provide some services in the community so that people will not have to be institutionalized. It appears that considerable emphasis in this strategy is on having women take care of children, handicapped persons and old people in their own homes. At present serious problems exist as a result of a lack of adequate community facilities and services in response to the de-institutionalization of a great many people across the country. A third strategy of transferring the responsibility for the administration of social services to the private sector has been more pronounced in some parts of the country than others. It is particularly conspicuous in the development of profit-making nursing homes for the elderly.   JIM ALBERT

Reading: A. Armitage, *Social Welfare in Canada* (1975).

Social Class refers to persistent social inequalities. Two distinct types of social inequality have been identified by researchers working with 2 different sociological theories. One theory is derived from the work of Karl Marx, the other from writings by Max Weber, which are somewhat critical of Marx's work. The Weberian approach became popular in Canadian and American sociology in the 1940s to 1960s, but currently the Marxian approach is in ascendancy.

In the Marxian approach, social classes, which are defined by ownership of the means of production and labour power (*see also* ECONOMICS, RADICAL) exist in all capitalist societies. Means of production include the machines, buildings, land and materials used in the production of goods and services. Labour power (the physical and mental capacity of people to work) is bought and sold for wages (or salary) by the owners of the means of production or by their agents.

Marxists identify 3 main classes: the *petite bourgeoisie*, who own businesses (the means of production), work for themselves, and do not employ others; the *proletariat* or working class, who do not own the means of production and who sell their labour power for wages; and the *bourgeoisie* or capitalist class, owners of the means of production, who purchase labour power and acquire a living and accumulate wealth from surplus value provided through workers' labour. (The theory of surplus value is based on the premise that part of the value of goods or services that people produce is determined by the labour power that goes into them.) Surplus value is the total value of commodities when exchanged in the marketplace, minus the value of labour power and the value of the means of production. The rate of surplus value is surplus value divided by total wages. This rate is used by Marxist researchers as an indicator of the rate of class exploitation, ie, the rate at which value is being extracted from the labour power of the working class by the bourgeoisie.

The Marxian social class distinctions do not refer to types of occupation or levels of income. For example, a plumber could be a member of the working class (because he sells labour power and does not own a business), or he could be a small capitalist who owns a company and purchases the labour of several plumbers, or a member of the petite bourgeoisie. Also, members of different classes may have similar, or overlapping, incomes. An owner of a small engineering firm with a few employees may in one year earn less than a worker, eg, a successful engineer employed by a large firm. However, capitalists generally have more power than workers to determine the distribution of wealth, because capitalists own and control the means of production and because the working class is not fully organized in opposition (eg, in unions or political organizations). Marxists believe that a conflict of interests (eg, wage disputes, and opposition by capitalists to the formation of unions) between capitalists and the working class is an inherent feature of capitalism. Capitalists try to keep wages low and productivity high to maximize their proportion in the distribution of wealth; workers attempt to increase their share of wealth through higher wages and to improve their working conditions.

The non-Marxists claim that social classes can be defined through inequalities in income, educational attainment, power and occupational prestige, and they often study these forms of social inequality to the neglect of social class in the Marxian sense. They have identified different kinds of social classes depending, for example, on which of the other dimensions of social inequality has been selected for study. People are categorized and given ranks according to their income, occupational prestige, power or education, the difficulty being that the same people may fall into different ranks according to different dimensions of social class. For example, the very rich, the middle class and the poor can be easily distinguished from one another by using standards of income and wealth, but those in the middle-income category, eg, white-collar and blue-collar workers, will be accorded quite different degrees of prestige for their different jobs. By the same token, although white-collar jobs usually carry more prestige and income, this is not always the case. The same is true of differences in educational levels. Those with secondary-school diplomas more often have white-collar jobs and higher incomes than those with less education, but some skilled blue-collar workers, such as electricians, earn comparatively high wages without high-school training. Finally, the respective amounts of power attached to different jobs, incomes and educational credentials are difficult to discern.

Non-Marxists emphasize the distribution patterns of scarce rewards, ie, the numbers and social backgrounds of the people who acquire university educations or high prestige jobs, while Marxists emphasize the social activities and interactions of the classes, eg, who purchases labour power from whom and what is the rate of exploitation of one class by another. Non-Marxists are concerned with explaining the patterns of social inequality, while Marxists study the way class relations explain social change. Because of the attention to change, Marxist research generally has a historical dimension.

Marxist-oriented researchers in Canada have studied the development and consequences of Canada's branch-plant ECONOMY, the process of "de-industrialization," the heavy investment of both foreign multinationals and Canadian-owned corporations in the Third World and the exploitation, in Canada, of staple raw materials for export, which incurred a dependence on export markets beyond the control of local capitalists and workers. Other research of this kind indicates that there has been a long-term trend in industrialized countries of a rise in the rate of surplus value, and that owners in various industries have stood together to try to enforce low wages. Studies have also shown that Canada's petite bourgeoisie has declined to a small proportion of the labour force (eg, from 12% in 1951 to about 6% in 1986), that the working class has remained fairly stable over recent years (approximately 86% in 1951 and 90% in 1986), and that the capitalist class has grown slightly (2% in 1951 to about 3% in 1986). There is also evidence that the capitalist class has evolved into a class of investment capitalists, with stock ownership but limited managerial control. At the same time, a large category of top-level managers has been formed.

Non-Marxist researchers have discovered that, by the occupational criterion, Canada has a large and growing middle class of white-collar workers (eg, 25% of workers in 1921, 55% in 1986); a smaller and rather stable blue-collar sector (eg, 31% in 1921, 40% in 1986); and fewer workers in the primary sector (fishing, logging and mining) and in agriculture (the number of workers in agriculture declined from 33% in 1921 to 4% in 1986). In education, the middle category of those with some secondary-school education is the largest (48% for males and 51% for females in 1986). The category of those with some post-secondary training had grown to 21% for males and 22% for females in 1986. Studies of income distribution reveal that the top 20% of individual income earners receive about 40% of all earned income while the bottom 20% receive only about 4% of all income (*see* INCOME DISTRIBUTION). Further studies have shown that the attainment of income, education and occupational prestige are related to the social class of parents and to region

and ethnic origin. Also, it has been found that people with better occupations, income and education have better life expectancies, better health, use medical facilities more, belong to more clubs and organizations, vote more frequently and have fewer children. A study by Wigle and Mao has found, from data on 21 metropolitan areas in Canada, that the life expectancies at birth of men living in the most affluent areas of the cities were 6.2 years longer than those for males from the least affluent areas. The comparable figures for females showed less difference, however, at 2.9 years. What accounts for the income-life expectancy association is still a matter of debate.

A synthesis of Marxist and non-Marxist approaches to social class may eventually emerge because researchers from each tradition are now beginning to study the types of inequality emphasized by the other. This should result, fortunately, in different terms being used for the categories identified in each approach. "Social class" or "class" is increasingly being reserved for the types of distinction described by Marx, while the term "socioeconomic status" will likely apply to differences in income and occupational prestige.

JAMES E. CURTIS

Reading: C.J. Cuneo, "Class, Stratification and Mobility," in R. Hagedorn, ed, *Sociology* (1980); J.E. Curtis, E. Grabb, N. Guppy and S. Gilbert, eds, *Social Inequality in Canada* (1988); D. Forcese, *The Canadian Class Structure* (1986); A.A. Hunter, *Class Tells: On Social Inequality in Canada* (1986); D.J. Wigle and Y. Mao, *Mortality by Income Level in Urban Canada* (1980).

Social Credit is an economic doctrine that for a time was influential in Canada as the touchstone of a significant political party. Its principles were formulated by an English engineer, Maj C.H. Douglas (1879-1952), who argued that economic hardships resulted from an inefficient capitalist economy which failed to provide people with sufficient purchasing power for them to enjoy the fruits of a well-developed productive capacity. He advocated the distribution of money, or "social credit," so that people might purchase the goods and services readily produced by capitalist enterprise. He believed that the total wages paid to individuals who produced goods (which he called "A") would always be less than the total costs of production ("B"). This meant that, without social credit, there would be insufficient money in the community for the purchase of all the goods and services produced. This was known as the "A plus B theorem."

Douglas's doctrine had little political impact elsewhere in the world and likely would have remained relatively unknown in Canada, except that in 1932 Alberta evangelist William ABERHART became converted to it. He used his radio program to encourage other Albertans to adopt social cred-

Prosperity certificate issued by the Alberta Social Credit government, 1936 (*courtesy Glenbow Archives, Calgary*).

it as the means of rescuing the province and Canada from the drastic effects of the GREAT DEPRESSION. In 1935 Aberhart led the new Social Credit Party to victory in Alberta, capturing 56 of 63 seats with 54% of the popular vote. Social Credit, first under Aberhart and then, after his death in 1943, under Ernest C. MANNING, won 9 successive elections and governed the province until 1971. This remarkable success was purchased in part by the replacement of social credit fundamentalism with conservative financial and social policies which even bankers could applaud. Success was also purchased by judicious use of massive oil revenues which flowed to provincial coffers after 1947.

In 1952 a Social Credit government under W.A.C. BENNETT was elected in British Columbia. Bennett paid no attention to social credit doctrine but combined a mixture of conservative financial policies with aggressive development schemes. He governed BC in the name of Social Credit for 20 years, and his son, William R. BENNETT, became premier in 1975, succeeded by William VANDER ZALM as a "Socred" premier in 1986. During the 1950s and early 1960s the party was successful also in sending a few members to the Saskatchewan and Manitoba legislatures.

In 1935 the federal Social Credit Party won 17 seats in the House of Commons – 15 from Alberta, where it received 46.6% of the popular vote. The federal party's support gradually declined in Alberta until 1968, when it became insignificant. During the 1950s and early 1960s the party won a handful of federal seats in BC. Under the Québec leadership of Réal CAOUETTE, the federal Social Credit Party obtained 26 seats from that province in the 1962 general election. The national leader, Robert THOMPSON, was responsible for a scant 4 more seats from English Canada including his own. Tensions created by this imbalance among the MPs and exacerbated by the party's pivotal position in a minority Parliament led to a split in 1963 with Caouette forming his own group, the Ralliement des CREDITISTES. This party, in regional and federal guises, continued to have representation in Parliament until 1980.

Social Credit had disappeared as a viable political force by the early 1980s, voting to disband as a party in Alberta. The BC government continues to use the name, but has severed its links with "Socreds" in the rest of the country and remains a relatively mainstream conservative government.

J.T. MORLEY

Social Darwinism generally refers to the extension of Charles Darwin's theories of natural selection in EVOLUTION, as used in his *Origin of Species* (1859), into the realm of social relations. Darwin had not intended his theories to be extended by analogy into the examination of racial groups, societies or nations. But certain British and American social theorists, notably Herbert Spencer and William Graham Sumner, made the analogy. The result was a social theory that provided late Victorians with a "scientific" explanation and social justification of racial inequality, cultural exploitation and laissez-faire capitalist activity. Canada produced few such extreme social theorists during the Darwinian revolution. The critic William Dawson LESUEUR sought to explain the theories of both Darwin and Spencer to Canadians in the *Canadian Monthly and National Review* during the 1870s and 1880s, but he consistently rejected the metaphoric extension of Darwin's phrase into the study of society. The logic of Darwin's notion of competition within and between species led instead, he argued, to the necessity of mutual aid and co-operation. Other Canadian observers agreed, with the exception of Goldwin SMITH, whose social views were more akin to those of Spencer. The dependent nature of Canadian economic and political life pointed most Canadian commentators toward ideas similar to those of Peter Kropotkin in *Mutual Aid, a Factor of Evolution* (1902).   A.B. McKILLOP

Social Democracy, historically, is a term that has been used by individuals on both the far and moderate left to describe their beliefs, but in recent years the latter have embraced the term almost exclusively (indeed radical left-wing critics often use the term disparagingly). For many adherents, the term "social democracy" is interchangeable with the term "democratic socialism." By the beginning of the 20th century, workers in many industrial countries had acquired the vote and the right to organize in unions and parties. Many socialists were thus led to believe that the working class, the largest group in modern society, could increasingly direct the STATE towards abolishing POVERTY, inequality and class exploitation, ie, capitalism could be transformed through legislation. The German socialist Eduard Bernstein (1850-1932) pioneered the idea that all-out class struggle was not inevitable and that a peaceful, nonrevolutionary road to socialism was both possible and desirable.

The Russian Revolution of 1917 and the founding of the Communist International (Comintern) in 1919 precipitated an irrevocable split between the revolutionary and evolutionary wings – with the former emerging as communist parties and the latter as social democratic parties.

After this date, social democracy could be defined by its opposition not only to capitalism but also to communism. Social democrats are resolute in their defence of individual rights and constitutional methods, and in their repudiation of the Marxist concept of the dictatorship of the proletariat. They also argue that political democracy (eg, equal right to vote) needs to be expanded to include social and economic democracy (ie, equal right to an education, medical care, pensions, employment and safe working conditions). Believing in the power of education and persuasion, and the potentially benevolent power of the state to redistribute wealth, social democrats have encouraged the emergence of an activist, interventionist state that provides extensive SOCIAL SECURITY assistance to the less privileged.

In Canada, one of the earliest exponents of reformism was the Social Democratic Party of Canada, founded in 1911 out of frustration with the more doctrinaire and revolutionary Socialist Party of Canada, established in 1904. Later, the LEAGUE FOR SOCIAL RECONSTRUCTION (1932-42),

closely patterned after Britain's Fabian Society, provided the most visible intellectual expression in Canada of democratic socialism. Through the journal the *Canadian Forum* and the book *Social Planning for Canada*, individuals such as F.R. SCOTT, Frank UNDERHILL, Eugene FORSEY, Leonard MARSH and Harry Cassidy communicated their ideas on social democracy. The CO-OPERATIVE COMMONWEALTH FEDERATION (CCF) and its successor, the NEW DEMOCRATIC PARTY (NDP), have been the political parties which have most consistently expressed a social democratic vision. Accordingly, the NDP belongs to the Socialist International, a confederation of social democratic parties. Several CCF-NDP manifestos provide detailed illustrations of the social democratic philosophy: the Regina Manifesto (1933), the Winnipeg Declaration (1956), the New Party Declaration (1961) and the New Regina Manifesto (1983). Leading political practitioners of social democracy have included J.S. WOODSWORTH, T.C. DOUGLAS, "M.J." COLDWELL, Stanley KNOWLES, David LEWIS, Ed BROADBENT and Allan BLAKENEY. The PARTI QUÉBÉCOIS, in addition to being nationalist and separatist, also lays claim to being a social democratic party and has sought and received observer status in the Socialist International.

Social democratic thought in Canada inspired legislation such as WORKERS' COMPENSATION, MINIMUM WAGE, OLD-AGE PENSION, UNEMPLOYMENT INSURANCE, FAMILY ALLOWANCE, subsidized housing (Canada Mortgage and Housing Corporation) and medicare (*see* HEALTH POLICY). The WELFARE STATE has largely been the product of joint action by social democrats and reform-minded liberals. Certainly, the birth of the CCF in 1932 and its rapid growth in the early 1940s induced the LIBERAL PARTY to shift to the left lest it be displaced like its counterpart in England. However, social democracy appears to have had its greatest impact in the provincial governments formed by the CCF-NDP in BC, Saskatchewan and Manitoba. Most notable was the Douglas regime in Saskatchewan, N America's first socialist government, which pioneered medicare. While the party has never formed the government federally, it has had considerable influence on the policy of MINORITY GOVERNMENTS. Internationally, social democracy's greatest advances occurred in the postwar era of the late 1940s and 1950s when it seemed to offer a moderate alternative to the extremes of capitalism and communism.

However, as socialists came to power, the practical problems of governing led many to question important socialist assumptions about methods employed. Unlike the communists, social democrats do not believe that wholesale nationalization of the means of production is a panacea to the ills of capitalism. Instead, they propose selected expansion of PUBLIC OWNERSHIP (eg, co-operatives, CROWN CORPORATIONS and state enterprises) in a mixed economy. In the past, social democrats have favoured the creation of public enterprises such as the Canadian Broadcasting Corporation and Air Canada and state institutions such as the Bank of Canada. With the emergence of KEYNESIAN ECONOMICS, social democrats had begun to argue that government FISCAL POLICY and MONETARY POLICY (eg, TAXATION rates, government expenditure, regulation of the money supply) could regulate the market economy in a socially beneficial manner; for example, full employment, greater equality and economic growth could be achieved through a combination of government planning and legislation, public enterprises and use of the market mechanism.

Social democrats have not only advocated the lessening of inequalities between SOCIAL CLASSES but also between regions (*see* REGIONALISM). They have thus supported government actions to redis-

tribute wealth from the richer to the poorer provinces and have encouraged Canadianization of the economy through greater public ownership (eg, PETRO-CANADA) and state regulation (eg, FOREIGN INVESTMENT REVIEW AGENCY) which would lessen Canada's dependency on other countries.

In recent years, social democratic doctrine has come under increasing criticism from both the left and the right. The more radical and revolutionary left charges that social democratic reforms are too eclectic and produce only cosmetic changes, making capitalism appear more humane and workable, and delaying needed structural change. These critics claim that social democrats have nationalized too few and mostly unprofitable industries and question whether social democracy can ever lead to socialism. They cite detailed statistical analyses of Canadian society which reveal that the welfare state has not altered class inequality to the degree expected and that poverty is more firmly entrenched than the optimistic social reformers suspected. The welfare state is also under attack by neo-conservatives. Critical of large increases in government expenditure and the size of the civil service, conservatives question both the desirability of increasing state power and the growing cost of that power. They note that economic growth, a premise of Keynesian economics and past social democratic thought, is now slowing down. STAGFLATION raises the spectre of reduced funds with which to finance social programs, and the universality of some programs (eg, pensions and medicare) has been challenged. Several additional problems have arisen as well. Social democratic theory has long had a predisposition towards central government planning, and in a country such as Canada that has strong concerns about provincial rights, particularly in Québec, such centralizing policies have hindered the spread of social democratic thought. Indeed, there is a significant gulf between the social democratic forces in English and French Canada, represented by the NDP and the PQ respectively. In the mid-1980s many European social democratic parties seem to be faltering electorally. In Canada, the NDP, despite varied levels of support in public-opinion polls, has yet to come to power federally; however, in 1988 it formed the governments of Manitoba and the Yukon and was the official Opposition in BC, Alberta, Saskatchewan and Ontario.

Critics have suggested a need to reformulate its social democratic doctrine. Social democrats seem less certain today than in the 1950s about the most effective way of pursuing their goals. To survive, any ideology must be an evolving doctrine which provides more effective answers to problems. As Canada moves into the postindustrial era, social democrats will need to deal with the growing concern about ecology, the danger of nuclear war, the changing composition of the work force, technical innovation in the workplace, the decline in economic growth, high unemployment, the plight of the Third World, the growing power of the state and the quest for greater industrial democracy.   ALAN WHITEHORN

Social Doctrine of the Roman Catholic Church, defined particularly in 2 papal encyclicals: *Rerum Novarum*, by Leo XIII (1891), and *Quadragesimo Anno*, by Pius XI (1931). The church wished to show its preoccupation with the fate of the working classes, often victims of unbridled capitalism. Both documents preached a Christian humanism, decried the insufficiencies of capitalism, and warned against the evils inherent in socialism and in the doctrine of class struggle. The church clarified its teachings concerning employers' responsibilities and workers' rights, as well as related duties of the state. Leo XIII wrote that workers had a right to fair wages and that they could form Catholic unions whose existence should be protected by governments.

Through various organizations, study sessions and publications, the Catholic Church, in Canada as elsewhere, publicized and applied pontifical doctrine. In Québec, however, a conservative clergy rooted in rural society was ill-prepared to confront urban problems. Catholic trade unions were slow to be established and it was 1921 before the Canadian Catholic Confederation of Labour emerged (*see* CONFEDERATION OF NATIONAL TRADE UNIONS). The École sociale populaire, a Jesuit organization charged with interpreting the church's social doctrine and with preparing an elite to put it into practice, was founded in 1911, 20 years after *Rerum Novarum*. The group proved particularly influential in the 1930s with the "Programme de restauration sociale," which in 1934-36 became the basis of the radical electoral platforms of the ACTION LIBÉRALE NATIONALE and the UNION NATIONALE. After WWII the social doctrine underwent considerable modernization, thanks in part to the work of the Sacerdotal Commission on Social Studies, which in 1950 published a pastoral letter on social conditions. During the 1950s, however, with the increasing secularization of Québec Society, the church's social role declined markedly. *See also* CATHOLICISM; SOCIAL GOSPEL.   RICHARD JONES

Social Gospel, an attempt to apply Christianity to the collective ills of an industrializing society, and a major force in Canadian religious, social and political life from the 1890s through the 1930s. It drew its unusual strength from the remarkable expansion of Protestant, especially EVANGELICAL, churches in the latter part of the 19th century. For several decades the prevalent expression of evangelical nationalism, the Social Gospel was equally a secularizing force in its readiness to adopt such contemporary ideas as liberal progressivism, reform Darwinism, biblical criticism and philosophical idealism as vehicles for its message of social salvation. It developed, however, a distinctive spirituality elevating social involvement to a religious significance expressed in prayers, hymns, poems and novels of "social awakening." Its central belief was that God was at work in social change, creating moral order and social justice. It held an optimistic view of human nature and entertained high prospects for social reform. Leaders reworked such traditional Christian doctrines as sin, atonement, salvation and the Kingdom of God to emphasize a social content relevant to an increasingly collective society. The Social Gospel at large gave birth to the new academic discipline of social ethics and in Canada contributed most of the impetus to the first sociology programs.

It appeared in Canada in the 1880s, a decade of materialism, political corruption, economic distress and a growing sense of urban disorder. Moved by the difficulties of the time, by Protestant negativism and otherworldliness, and enthused by such social prophets as Carlyle, Ruskin, Tolstoy and Henry George, young Protestants such as J.W. BENGOUGH and Salem BLAND, together with idealist philosophers such as John WATSON at Queen's, precipitated a movement that by the mid-1890s had become the stuff of church journalism, ministerial institutes, college alumni conferences and youth movements. Early evidence of the church's expanding role came with the founding of city missions and institutional churches such as the St Andrew's Institute (Toronto, 1890) and the Fred Victor Mission (Toronto, 1894), followed by a chain of church settlement houses (1901-19). Whereas METHODISM probably fielded the Social Gospel most easi-

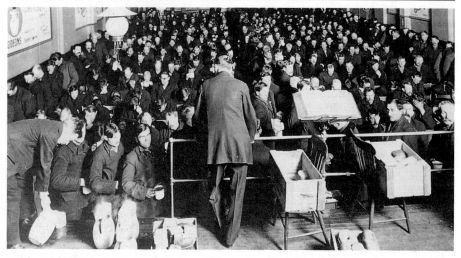

Social Gospel meeting, Yonge Street Mission, *c*1915 (*courtesy City of Toronto Archives/James 1964*).

ly, between 1894 and 1910 all the major Protestant denominations created board structures to handle its mushrooming concerns. Older moral causes – TEMPERANCE, sabbath observance and social purity (against prostitution) – were reinterpreted, reinvigorated and incorporated into the progressive reforms.

Joined nationally and provincially in 1908 under Presbyterian J.G. SHEARER in the Moral and Social Reform Council, the churches readily aligned these concerns with others: the child, health, housing and urban reform.

In 1912 the council was reorganized as the Social Service Council of Canada, and the churches began sponsoring comprehensive surveys of urban conditions. In 1914 the council sponsored the first national congress on social problems. With notable exceptions, the male leadership did not give a high place to WOMEN'S SUFFRAGE, but many women of the National Council of Women, the WOMAN'S CHRISTIAN TEMPERANCE UNION and the suffrage organizations found in the Social Gospel a convenient vehicle for articulating the needed reforms based on their maternal feminist creed.

Although the Social Gospel is often categorized as an urban middle-class phenomenon, it did attract agrarian and labour reformers. W.C. GOOD of the UNITED FARMERS OF ONTARIO, R.C. Henders of the Manitoba GRAIN GROWERS' ASSOCIATION, E.A. PARTRIDGE of the Saskatchewan Grain Growers' Association and H.W. WOOD of the UNITED FARMERS OF ALBERTA were all enthusiasts, as were labour leaders, including James Simpson in Ontario, A.W. PUTTEE in Manitoba and Elmer Roper in Alberta. By WWI it had become a primary informing principle of social reform. The increase in social purpose occasioned by the war brought the movement to a height of influence as reforms it espoused – direct legislation, prohibition, women's suffrage, civil service reform, bureaus of social research, expansion of co-operatives, the decline of party government and, for some, state direction of the economy for national efficiency – all made immense strides.

Postwar unrest gave the Social Gospel further prominence through association with the WINNIPEG GENERAL STRIKE of 1919 and the PROGRESSIVE PARTY campaign, 1919-21. Radical social gospellers such as J.S. WOODSWORTH and William IRVINE became increasingly alienated from the church-based Social Gospel. In turn, its hopes and accomplishments were compromised by economic decline, the secularizing of social work and the backlash against PROHIBITION, while labour and agrarian factional strife undermined the basis of

radical Social Gospel action. The formation of the UNITED CHURCH in 1925, itself in part a product of the Social Gospel, did not stem the growing crises in the movement, whose fortunes plummeted.

The reasons for decline in the 1920s were manifold: the accomplishment of many reforms; a delayed disillusionment with the war, a weariness with doing good and a general abandonment of moral earnestness for a new hedonism; and the decline of idealism as a reigning philosophy. The Social Gospel, ideologically bound to the primacy of reason in a being vitally attuned to a benevolent God, could hardly survive in a world apparently animated by power and unreason on the one hand and frivolity on the other.

However, under the impact of the GREAT DEPRESSION, a new younger generation combined the insights of Alfred North Whitehead, Reinhold Niebuhr and Karl Marx to fashion what some termed a new Social Gospel, others a form of "radical Christianity," which recognized the need for personal as well as social renewal, accepted the importance of class struggle and sought a society of "mutuality."

Associated in the Fellowship for a Christian Social Order (later complemented by the Anglican Fellowship for Social Action), most of this younger leadership (J.W.A. Nicholson in the Maritimes, King GORDON and Eugene FORSEY in central Canada, T.C. DOUGLAS and J.H. Horricks on the Prairies and Harold Allen in BC) contributed to the creation of the CO-OPERATIVE COMMONWEALTH FEDERATION (1932).

A broadly diffused older Social Gospel played a less obvious role in the creation of the SOCIAL CREDIT and Reconstruction parties and in the Depression attempts to transform the Conservative and Liberal parties. After WWII the Social Gospel could be given much credit for public readiness to maintain Canada's new welfare state and its international posture as a PEACEKEEPING nation. Sons and daughters of the Social Gospel could be found critically placed throughout both enterprises. That an almost apocalyptic age of the later 1960s and 1970s has overtaken the grandly progressive, if somewhat vaguely entertained, social hopes of a residual social gospel is evident in the limited objectives of church-based coalitions on native rights, corporate responsibility and the environment. Nonetheless, Third World Christianity, Marxist-Christian dialogue and Catholic liberation theology have had some effect in regenerating a body of Canadian Christian social thought and action reminiscent of the radical Social Gospel. *See also* ECUMENICAL SOCIAL ACTION.

A. RICHARD ALLEN

Reading: Richard Allen, *The Social Passion* (1971).

Social History is a way of looking at how a society organizes itself and how this organization changes over time. It is an approach, not a subject. The ultimate goal of social historians is to write the complete history of social relations, but this goal is unlikely ever to be achieved. Nevertheless the goal serves as a constant reminder to historians that aspects of history cannot be considered in isolation and that social history is an integrative study concerned with building towards a global picture of society. Any aspect of society can usefully be studied, but what is important is that it be studied within its relationships to other social institutions.

Social history began as the garbage collector of the discipline. With some notable exceptions, social history, as practised earlier in the 20th century, was usually seen as what was left over after political and ECONOMIC HISTORY had been written. The result was purely descriptive accounts of "daily life in pioneer days" or administrative histories of welfare agencies and the like. This began to change after about 1960 as the influence of new approaches, developed in France and Britain, rippled across the historical world. A group of French scholars, dubbed the *Annales* school for the journal in which their work appeared, showed the potential of truly integrative approaches. They brought together insights from the social sciences, "quantitative" or statistical studies, at times an extravagantly literary style, and an interest in "material culture" – the objects of everyday life – in their attempt to write complete history. Equally influential has been the "new social history" from Britain, which is in large part an attempt to view the working class as a group with its own dynamics, distinctive customs and ideologies.

Canada presents some particular problems for the social historian, since it is a complex mosaic of ethnic groups, cultures, traditions and institutions. In Canada's history the French and English cultural backgrounds made themselves felt in political institutions, in the "established" Anglican and Roman Catholic churches and in elite cultural activities; but at the popular level of entertainment, architectural styles, marriage customs, etc, the social forms and institutions have come from the US, Ireland, Ukraine and elsewhere. Once imported, these diverse forms have sunk roots into the different regions of Canada, there to develop in ways that have been sometimes markedly, sometimes subtly, different.

Geography thus influenced social development through the sharply regionalized character of Canada (*see* REGIONALISM). It did so in other ways as well. The relationship between geography and government was very different from that in the US. Americans have often explained their social and political uniqueness by the impact of the "frontier," that meeting point between civilization and wilderness that moved W across the US as settlement advanced; at the frontier Americans were cast upon their own resources and learned to be independent and inventive. However well the FRONTIER THESIS applies to American development, Canada had a very different experience, although the theory was popular during the interwar years among Canadian historians such as A.R.M. LOWER and Frank UNDERHILL. Whereas a frontier line moved W across the American colonies and the US for over 250 years, making the frontier experience a pervasive one, Canada had such a continuous frontier only during the French regime, before 1763. Thereafter the wilderness was quickly pushed back in eastern Canada, the arable land rapidly occupied. The frontier experience lapsed, to be renewed 2 generations later on the PRAIRIE WEST, where a similarly rapid settlement process occurred. For most Canadians the frontier was transitory; for most, in fact, the American-style frontier never existed. Canadians were rarely far from authority and social institutions, rarely divorced from social solutions to problems. Government moved out onto the frontier with, sometimes before, the population, in the form of the British military, colonial officials and later the NORTH-WEST MOUNTED POLICE.

Theories of Canadian social development involve disciplines other than geography. The STAPLE THESIS, formulated in the 1920s by economic historians H.A. INNIS and W.A. MacIntosh asserted that Canada's export of staples influenced its social and political systems. The LAURENTIAN THESIS, expounded from the 1930s to 1950s, argued in favour of the influence of the St Lawrence Valley on the Canadian development; its most sophisticated presentation was in D.G. CREIGHTON's *The* COMMERCIAL EMPIRE OF THE ST. LAWRENCE. Since the 1950s the METROPOLITAN-HINTERLAND THESIS, presented by historians such as J.M.S. CARELESS, has been used to explain the development of Canada's economy and regional tensions.

Government has helped to give shape to Canadian social structure. NEW FRANCE has been called an "aristocratic welfare state," with a tiny population protected by the French military, supported by enlightened laws and sustained by government expenditures. After the CONQUEST, 1759-60, British aristocratic pretensions were imported into Canada with the structure of colonial government, which created such local elites as Upper Canada's FAMILY COMPACT. Government initiative helped launch the CANADIAN PACIFIC RAILWAY and western settlement; immigration policy determined the Prairies' ethnic mix.

Social history is concerned with how all of these influences shape social structure. It shares many interests and some methodology with other SOCIAL SCIENCES, especially historical SOCIOLOGY. In fact, if anyone could claim to be the parent of Canadian social history it is sociologist S.D. CLARK, in his many works, beginning with *The Social Development of Canada* (1942). Clark assessed the impact of the frontier, social movements and Canadian economic activities on our society, and he demonstrated the possibilities of an integrated social approach. Even where sociology and history overlap in content and concern, however, differences are apparent. Traditional historians are more concerned with chronology and tend to be less comfortable with general theories that approximate "laws" of development; they are likely to be conscious of the individual and the idiosyncratic, even when they generalize to groups. Nevertheless, sociology continues to influence and to stimulate social history. Beginning in the 1970s, as Canadian scholars drew on the example of British historian E.P. Thompson and "cultural history," ANTHROPOLOGY also began to influence historians. A good example of disciplinary cross-fertilization is *Modern Canada, 1930-1980* (1984), vol V of *Readings in Social History*, ed M.S. Cross and G. Kealey: the authors include 5 historians, 2 sociologists, 2 economists and a political scientist. The computer has begun to be applied in historical analysis and has permitted generalizations from the experience of large groups. Québec historians have been particularly active in large-scale demographic studies of population characteristics, but the most polished printed account is Michael Katz's *The People of Hamilton, Canada West* (1975), which reports the results of a massive computer-aided analysis of that city.

Two ongoing series of books in social history give some sense of the interests of Canadian historians working in the field. The Social History of Canada series (University of Toronto Press) and the Canadian Social History series (McClelland and Stewart) were both launched in the early 1970s. The M&S collection has presented studies of poverty in Montréal, the ideology of 19th-century businessmen, attitudes towards immigrants, educational reform, working-class history, and the history of childhood, of medicine and of women. The UTP series was begun to reprint important books and documents, such as Mackenzie KING's 1918 musings on industrial relations, *Industry and Humanity* (1973), and H.B. AMES's pioneering sociological study of working-class Montréal, *The City Below the Hill* (1897; repr 1972). In the 1980s the series began to publish original monographs, including Geoffrey Bilson's *A Darkened House* (1980) on cholera epidemics and Judith Fingard's study of the life of 19th-century sailors, *Jack in Port* (1982).

In the first generation of Canadian social history some long-neglected areas came to prominence. One was the history of women. A natural interest for those pursuing an integrated history of society, the study of women was given additional impetus by the growth of feminism and by the entry of increasing numbers of women into the academic world. Themes from WOMEN'S SUFFRAGE to the ideology of reproduction to women's work were explored in early collections on women's history such as *Women at Work: Ontario, 1850-1930* (1974) and *The Neglected Majority* (1977), ed by S.M. Trofimenkoff and A. Prentice. The history of childhood has been studied in works such as Joy Parr, ed, *Childhood and Family in Canadian History* (1982). The practices and politics of reproduction have been discussed in Angus and Arlene Tigar McLaren, *The Bedroom and the State* (1986). An excellent sampler of articles on women's history is Veronica Strong-Boag and Anita Clair Fellman, eds, *Rethinking Canada: The Promise of Women's History* (1986). Other previously neglected areas drawing new attention were the immigrant experience (*see* IMMIGRATION), ethnic groups, COMMUNICATIONS, urban history (*see* URBAN STUDIES), NATIVE PEOPLE and the history of VIOLENCE in Canada.

Since the 1960s some of the most significant social history has been written in Québec on a wide variety of topics by historians such as Fernand OUELLET (*Histoire économique et sociale du Québec, 1760-1850*, 1966; trans *Economic and Social History of Quebec, 1760-1850*, 1980), Jean Hamelin (ed, *Histoire du Québec*, 1976), Louise Dechêne (*Habitants et marchands de Montréal au XVII siècle*, 1974) and Jean-Pierre Wallot. S.M. Trofimenkoff's *The Dream of Nation* (1983) is a major contribution to Québec social history.

More than any other area, WORKING-CLASS HISTORY prospered both in Québec and in the rest of Canada. The study of unions already had a strong tradition and it waxed further in the work of labour historians such as Irving Abella, David Bercuson (*Confrontation at Winnipeg*, 1974) and Jacques Rouillard (*Les Syndicats nationaux au Québec de 1900 à 1930*, 1979). More of a departure were the forays into working-class life and culture by historians such as Gregory Kealey (*Toronto Workers Respond to Industrial Capitalism*, 1980), and Bryan Palmer, whose works include *Working-Class Experience* (1983); both were strongly influenced by E.P. Thompson. Kealey and Palmer combined to write an ambitious and integrative study of the Knights of Labor, *Dreaming of What Might Be* (1982).

Historical Outline Geography, economy, class, sex, ethnicity and institutions are the major themes of the new social history. They can be seen interplaying in Canadian history, with particular clarity at the beginning of European penetration. The aboriginal population was divided into hundreds of tribal units. Regional splintering made impossible any unified response to European threats; instead, it created intertribal animosities (such as that between the HURON of central Ontario and the IROQUOIS of northern New York) which could be exploited by whites seeking to use native peoples in European struggles for supremacy (*see* IROQUOIS WARS). These struggles, in turn, sprang from both political rivalries and the needs of the European economies for American resources. Marked differences in the institutional structures of Indian and European societies contributed to the eventual outcome of their contact. Native concepts of citizenship and ownership were usually flexible and accommodating, and their religious beliefs were tolerant. As a result, most native groups accepted French visitors, and they were prepared to share land and resources with the newcomers and to consider French religious and social practices sympathetically. In contrast, the whites tended to have rigid, proselytizing religious beliefs, which they were anxious to impose on the aborigines, and exclusive concepts of ownership and of appropriate social behaviour to which all had to conform.

The flexibility of Indian societies was indicated by the skill with which some nations learned to conduct the FUR TRADE with Europeans and with other tribes. Ultimately, however, native societies buckled under the combined pressure of European economic demands, constant warfare, and the European diseases that swept through Indian communities. By the time of the British Conquest, the Indians of eastern Canada had been so reduced in numbers and power that they were no longer a key factor in either the economy or politics. As native power waned, it was replaced by that of the French and British, whose empires had competed for dominance from the beginning of the 17th century until the fall of Québec in 1759. Each had reached out to the New World with its own imperial forms and its peculiar institutions. Economic motivations were primary and, as a result, the initial form of social organization was essentially that of a business. Until 1663 the control of New France was granted to a series of private companies, each charged with developing the fur trade and settling the colony. The English, for their part, rested their imperial hopes in Canada on the HUDSON'S BAY COMPANY (chartered 1670). The French pursued an intrusive fur-trade policy, sending traders into native villages to conduct their business, whereas the English company required natives to come to its posts on Hudson Bay to trade. One consequence of this difference was that French traders more often established marriages with native women "in the style of the country," a practice that the HBC actively discouraged. In addition, relations between the many traders in the West and native women created a whole new society, the MÉTIS. After the Conquest removed France from competition in the fur trade, rivalries arose between the HBC and other traders of British background, particularly those who formed the Montréal-based NORTH WEST COMPANY. Alcohol and violence were used more frequently to gain furs, with profound effects on the cohesion of native social organization.

New France had been a controlled society, at least in design. The basic institution of the colony was the SEIGNEURIAL SYSTEM, a quasi-feudal form of landholding in which large lots were granted to lords, or seigneurs, who in turn provided farms to peasants. But few lower-class French migrated to Canada (no more than 10 000 in the entire history of the colony). These few always had alternatives to seigneurial farming, particularly in the fur trade. The government needed to keep its people on the farms in the St Lawrence Valley to supply food for the army and to help defend New France, but it had difficulty coercing the people into giving up the fur trade and had to make seigneurial

Settlers moving back to Cardston, summer 1924. These settlers came from the dried-out area of southeastern Alberta, where they had lost the battle against drought (*courtesy Glenbow Archives, Calgary/NA-114-17*).

life attractive. Strict limits were placed on the dues and taxes that seigneurs could levy, and a state legal system (*see* CIVIL CODE) protected the peasants against feudal oppression. As a result, the Canadian peasant retained far more of the product of his labour than the European peasant did, and he was far freer. A symbol of this was that the farmers in New France rejected the traditional appellation *paysan* and instead called themselves HABITANTS.

The British N America that succeeded New France grew quickly, and its social patterns became more complex. Although the patterns became more difficult to discern, as in New France the social structure emerged from the interplay of institutions, geography, economy, ethnicity and class. The most obvious elements were geography and its adjunct, climate. BNA existed on a large continent which, after the AMERICAN REVOLUTION, it shared with an aggressive rival, the US. This geographical fact helped to give contradictory conservative and progressive casts to Canadian society. Many of the LOYALIST refugees who resettled in BNA carried with them a powerful bitterness against the US, republicanism and democracy. The WAR OF 1812 reinforced TORY belief in the duplicity, irrationality and menace of the US and in the need to protect Canada from "infection" by American ideas. The colonial form of government imported from Britain was a suitably conservative instrument for the purpose. So were institutions such as the Church of England (*see* ANGLICANISM) and a highly stratified class system. Elites emerged to implement this Tory ethos, groups such as the Family Compact in Upper Canada [Ontario], the CHÂTEAU CLIQUE in Lower Canada [Québec] and the COUNCIL OF TWELVE in NS.

At the same time, American ideas and practices were permeating Canada despite the best Tory efforts. Many Americans who came to BNA before 1812 were not Loyalists but simply landseekers with no political motivation. Even the Loyalists were as much American as British; Britain found them as likely as non-Loyalists to cling to American concepts of local self-government. The Canadian colonial period was marked by a conscious rejection of the political hegemony of the US but, equally, by an instinctive refusal to become a facsimile of Britain. The American phase of settlement had passed by 1812, and after 1818 a new wave of British migration broke over Canada. The values and customs of the British settlers intermixed with those of the Americans to produce the essential compromise that was "English" Canada. Geography continued to be a powerful influence, so that the economic assumptions, business forms and TECHNOLOGY of Canada remained predominantly American, and the economic success of the US was the brass ring pursued by English Canadians. Social institutions, however, were often a blend of the 2 cultures. American individualism influenced Canadians, but it was coloured by a British sense of group and class solidarities and a more explicit class system.

French Canada, too, was influenced by American and British migration. In some respects, however, this influence worked to emphasize the unique characteristics of French Canadian society. Again geography played a major role. The Conquest left French Canada surrounded by the "English." By the early 19th century the growing population was already bursting the seams of the seigneuries, producing overcrowding and overcultivated farms, with a resultant decline in the standard of living. The seigneurial system was finally abolished in 1854, but this was too late to solve the problem of Québec agriculture or to prevent the economic retardation of French Canada. The end of seigneurialism put even greater emphasis on 2 other institutions which helped French Canadians to retain their distinctiveness: the Roman Catholic Church (*see* CATHOLICISM) and the FRENCH LANGUAGE.

The church remained central in the Québecois identity until the 1960s. Its decline then, under the force of modern secularism, left language as the key mark of distinctiveness. The often fervid attempts by successive Québec governments in the 1960s, 1970s and 1980s to compel the use of French in schools and workplaces and on public signs demonstrated the significance of this last great distinction in an increasingly homogeneous N American continent.

In Canada's cultural mix, ETHNICITY and RELIGION assumed special importance, for English as well as French Canadians. From the 1830s, for example, the ORANGE ORDER played a major, bloody role in the life of Ontario, Québec and New Brunswick. Militantly Protestant and ostentatiously loyal to the British Crown, the order was a focus of identity and reassurance for many immigrants, especially Protestant Irishmen (*see* SHINERS' WARS). Unhappily for social peace, Orangemen expressed their identity in verbal abuse of Catholics (and often French Canadians), in provocative parades and in frequent riots with Catholic opponents. Yet the Orange Order was an important institution of social adjustment for hundreds of thousands of Protestant immigrants. Ethnic and religious bonding papered over class differences in Canada, obscuring socioeconomic conflicts that might have been even more productive of social conflict.

The transition to an industrial society altered many social patterns. Mechanized industry began to emerge in Canada in the 1840s; it was dominant by the 1890s and produced widespread concentration of economic power before WWI. The old elites, created by British economic and political needs, gave way to elites of industrialists and financiers who were represented politically by professional men, especially lawyers. Industrialism also created a working class and an organized response – trade unionism – to the new economic order. Unions sprang up in the 1870s and were a permanent feature of the social environment by the end of the 19th century. As with the economic system itself, unions were heavily influenced by American ideology and example. By 1902 "international" unions with headquarters in the US had become dominant in the Canadian labour movement. Their espousal of moderate, apolitical approaches helped to prevent class conflicts in industrial Canada. Exceptional conditions could cast light on class differences, which were given sharper outlines by the gulf between capital and labour in an industrial setting. The unrest that grew out of WWI produced the labour upheaval of 1919, focused on the WINNIPEG GENERAL STRIKE (much as Québec's QUIET REVOLUTION would trigger unprecedented labour militancy in that province in the 1960s and 1970s). For the most part, however, Canadian labour remained moderate, committed to peaceful collective bargaining. The American example, N American ideology and the influence of institutions, such as schools and the mass media, which cut across class lines and inculcated a classless ideology, minimized social group conflict (*see* SOCIAL CLASS).

Industrialism had a homogenizing effect. Mass markets were created for mass-produced products, railways sped goods and ideas across the country, and NEWSPAPERS (later radio and TV) helped to reduce regional differences. Geography continued to resist these tendencies, however. Confederation was, in many ways, a logical political response to the needs of the railway, or industrial, age (*see* RAILWAY HISTORY). It erected a larger political and economic structure, which could press forward with grander economic programs. But the continuing reality of regional economic and social communities required that Confederation, like Canada itself, be a compromise. It was a federal not a unitary state; it was a parliamentary system on the British model, but one operated by political parties whose style was more American than British (*see* FEDERALISM).

Industrialism also demanded a larger labour force. After 1897 a booming Canadian economy supplemented its familiar American and British sources of immigrants with large numbers of continental Europeans. Canadians who in the 19th century had defined theirs as either an American or a British society – but certainly an Anglo-Saxon-dominated one – in the 20th century had to deal with a cultural mosaic. What is striking is how little the basic social institutions had to adjust to ethnic diversity. Political and economic forms continued to evolve within the same broadly Anglo-American patterns, and leadership continued to be exercised by those of British stock. Geographic proximity to the United States, the maintenance of a modified free-enterprise economy and the inertia of social institutions allowed Canadian society to absorb and assimilate immigrants.

Québec, the most rapidly modernizing part of Canada after 1960, was also the most troubled by the social implications of a mass N American society. Among other groups, as well, there were somewhat paradoxical reactions. If institutions such as the media helped inculcate a stabilizing common ideology, it also became clear to some disadvantaged elements that they were not receiving an equitable share of the bounty promised by those institutions. Native people began to demand, especially after 1960, compensation for economic and social losses they had suffered. More influential were the demands of women, who formed a majority of the population. As in Québec and among the native peoples, women began during the 1960s to insist on the removal of some of their disadvantages. The economic system had delivered the promised improvement in wages and working conditions to male workers, and the media had become pervasive and pervasively successful in publicizing the triumphs of the society. Women began to demand a place in the mainstream, and social institutions slowly responded. A royal commission on the STATUS OF WOMEN was appointed in 1967; divorce reform was introduced in 1968; and traditionally all-male professions began to open to women. However, the basic institutions of society were resilient enough to survive the adjustment with little disruption.

The pace of 20th-century change seemed very great. A predominantly rural country until about 1940, Canada became thereafter an overwhelmingly urban one (*see* RURAL SOCIETY). In 1941, for example, 41% of Québec Francophones lived on farms, in 1971 only 6%; the Quiet Revolution was stimulated in significant measure by the upheaval produced by this shift. The family, always

the rhetorical focus of social ideology, seemed to be challenged. Canadian divorce rates soared after WWII, especially after the divorce law reform of 1968, while birth rates, especially in Québec, declined. Yet the patterns remained remarkably stable. Although many more women worked outside the home in the 1980s, the gap between male and female wages had not narrowed. Far more marriages ended in divorce, but most Canadians still chose to marry. Although agricultural employment was replaced by urban employment, the distribution of wealth in Canada changed little and wealth continued to be maldistributed geographically, with the Atlantic region lagging behind other regions economically.

Geography remained a solid anchor for society, sheltering regional and economic differences. Social classes and institutions evolved, and growing importance was attached to the educated professionals who serviced more complicated social needs. Yet studies such as John PORTER's *The* VERTICAL MOSAIC (1965) and Wallace Clement's *The Canadian Corporate Elite* (1975) suggested a remarkable continuity in the groups that wielded social and economic power in Canada. The relative influence of organized religion in Canadian life declined, again most dramatically in Québec. Fraternal groups and SECRET SOCIETIES lost prominence after WWII as the religious and imperial causes they espoused became less significant. The visit of a pope to Canada in 1900 would have set off religious riots; in 1984 it produced celebrations in a country whose population was by then almost half Roman Catholic. Part of the reason for the decreasing influence of voluntary organizations, as well, was the WELFARE STATE, in which government assumed responsibility for charity, job placement and training, education, social adjustment and a myriad other social roles once filled by voluntary organizations and religious and ethnic communities. Still, the social and institutional patterns in which these changes were worked out were those of the Anglo-American compromise that was at the base of Canadian society.

For a treatment of specific themes in social history, *see also* CHILDHOOD, HISTORY OF; DISEASES, HUMAN; EPIDEMIC; GREAT DEPRESSION; POLITICAL PROTEST; SOCIAL DOCTRINE OF THE ROMAN CATHOLIC CHURCH; SOCIAL GOSPEL; TEMPERANCE.   MICHAEL S. CROSS

Social Impact Assessment (SIA), a set of procedures designed to identify social changes likely to occur because of a major project or new program. In Canada a social impact assessment is usually conducted as part of an environmental impact assessment. In 1973 a federal Cabinet decision established the Environmental Assessment and Review Process to ensure that both biophysical and social consequences are considered in the planning of major projects and programs. Most provinces have similar legislation or regulations, and Canada is a signatory of a 1972 international declaration on the human environment. Federal procedures involve several steps. Initial screening and evaluation predicts potentially significant effects. If any are identified, a panel is formed, guidelines are established for an EIA and its SIA component, studies are conducted to produce environmental and social impact statements, a public review is held, and the panel makes recommendations to the federal minister of the environment. The review panel may recommend and the minister may decide that the project proceed as proposed, proceed with modifications to mitigate undesirable effects, be postponed or be cancelled. The environmental assessment and review process is similar to a judicial process, considering testimony and direct evidence, including social impact assessment research reports, and opinions

and information provided through the participation of the public.   ROY T. BOWLES

Reading: Roy T. Bowles, *Social Impact Assessment in Small Communities* (1981); K. Finsterbusch, *Understanding Social Impacts* (1980).

Social Insurance Number (SIN) Almost every Canadian who pays money to, or receives benefits from, the federal government has a 9-digit Social Insurance Number (SIN). The numbers are used in addition to names and addresses so that computers may more easily keep unique records of certain transactions between Canadians and their federal and provincial governments.

The Unemployment Insurance Commission (UIC) invented the SIN in 1964. The UIC, created under the Unemployment Insurance Act (1940), began in 1942 to issue numbered cards to both insured and uninsured persons. Twenty years later the UIC master index contained information on 7.5 million persons holding UIC cards. However, a new numbering system was needed to promote accuracy in computer processing of data and because adequate combinations of numbers and letters could no longer be generated under the old numbering system. Two additional factors contributed to the adoption of the SIN. In 1962 the report of the Royal Commission on GOVERNMENT ORGANIZATION (the Glassco Commission) concluded that a unique personal identifier was necessary to increase administrative efficiency in federal government services as large computers came into widespread use. In 1963, the Canada Pension Plan (CPP) was proposed. About 80% of those who would be covered by the pension plan were already registered with the UIC. Thus, it seemed logical that a single number should be used for both purposes.

Although the use of SINs is a source of continuing political controversy, Parliament has never been given the opportunity to vote on the issue. The regulations governing the issuance of SINs were authorized by an order-in-council and took effect in April 1964. Employers were required at the time to ensure that their employees and any employees subsequently hired had SINs. By June 1964, 6.3 million SINs had been issued. Since its inception, more than 25 million numbers have been issued; virtually every adult residing in Canada, and many children, have a SIN.

The use of the SIN was initially restricted in practice to the UIC and CPP. Anyone with insurable employment or anyone over the age of 18 and making CPP contributions was required to obtain a number. But since there were no restrictions placed on further uses of the SIN, it gradually came into service as a unique personal identifier in all sectors of society and is now used, for example, on income tax returns, family allowances, school records and even on permits for wheat farming. Anyone filing an income tax return must provide a SIN on the return. Similarly a parent applying for a family allowance must furnish his or her SIN. Basically, most financial and service program transactions between governments and Canadian citizens are controlled by means of a SIN.

It seems reasonable to suggest that at least nongovernmental use of the SIN is improper, though it is not illegal. It is arguable that to request a SIN as identification to cash a cheque is an example of abuse. Similar examples of abuse include requiring a SIN to obtain a telephone or burial permit or to rent an apartment. In addition, both provincial and municipal governments use SINs to establish and record the identity of individuals involved in their programs. A person choosing not to furnish their SIN on demand risks denial of services.

Another aspect of abuse of SINs involves data

linkage or record matching. If all interactions with the federal government are recorded using an individual's SIN, then checking government data banks for information associated with that number can reveal all available information on that person, such as whether a family allowance was declared on an income tax return. Clearly, it is useful to have controlled access to such information. On the other hand, indiscriminate use of this technique is obviously an invasion of PRIVACY, and many people fear that personal information in government data banks can and will be used for social control. The federal Privacy Act (1982) is silent on the uses of SINs, even though these numbers are the most frequent source of complaint to the federal privacy commissioner.

Abuse of the SIN is less likely to occur if those with a number make sure that they only use the number when they are required to do so by law. Moreover, the use of SINs may decline as sophisticated new computers become able to identify persons and link their records without relying on such numbers.   D. FLAHERTY AND P. HARTE

Social Mobility, the movement of individuals, families and groups from one social position to another. The theory of social mobility attempts to explain the frequency of these movements, and the ways people became distributed into various social positions (social selection). Scholars were first attracted to the study of social mobility by the regularity with which people end up in roughly the same social position as their parents. Despite some intergenerational movement up and down the social ladder, people born into wealthy and important families are likely to live their lives as wealthy and important people, while those born into the working class are not. In our society, this regularity is the result of inherited wealth, useful social contacts and education – not superior intelligence and judgement as some thought originally. Societies have been characterized as "open" or "closed" according to the degree to which the fortune of children depends on that of the parents. Late 18th- and 19th-century writers, in criticizing their societies, were concerned with the institutional factors affecting mobility. They advocated a society in which merit and talent were rewarded and opportunities for developing them were freely available. Unfortunately, contemporary writers have been more inclined to substitute summary statistical measures of mobility for critical analysis of the entire society.

Sociologists usually distinguish "structural mobility" (all people are doing better than they used to, or better than their parents did) from "exchange mobility" (some people are changing their positions relative to others). In the 20th century, structural mobility has increased in Canada, the US, Britain and other industrialized countries, but exchange mobility has changed very little.

Changes in Structural Mobility With industrialization, agricultural labour declined and labour in factories and offices increased. As certain jobs become more common, the opportunity to enter these jobs (as compared to other jobs) increases. Thus, mobility into growing sectors of the economy outstrips mobility into declining sectors. This is one kind of structural mobility. At the same time, the opportunity to enter a job is greatest when competition for the job is least; this is the other kind of structural mobility. Rates of structural mobility are thus determined by both the number of jobs and the number of competitors for these jobs. When the economy booms, UNEMPLOYMENT declines, new jobs are created and old jobs are often improved. Higher salaries and benefits are paid to attract the best workers. In times of economic stagnation few new jobs are available, upgrading is less frequent and mobility deceler-

ates. This boom-and-bust cycle is particularly evident in Canada. Because the economy is largely owned by foreign investors (*see* FOREIGN INVESTMENT) and dominated by the export of raw resources to foreign consumers, Canada is particularly susceptible to fluctuations in foreign economies. Economic growth and technological change are also largely determined by outside forces.

Generally, the size of the LABOUR FORCE and competition for jobs within it is determined by natural population growth, the migration of workers and change in the rates of adult participation. During the GREAT DEPRESSION birthrates fell dramatically, but afterward, particularly between 1946 and 1962, birthrates rose to very high levels. The BABY BOOM generation crowded schools in the 1950s, universities in the 1960s and the market for entry-level jobs during the 1970s. Since the baby boom, birthrates have fallen once again, although some observers believe 40-year cycles of strong and weak competition will result from future demographic booms and busts.

Since the Depression, IMMIGRATION into Canada has remained consistently high. The Canadian government has generally encouraged the immigration of workers who will accept jobs that native-born Canadians will not or cannot do; therefore, a rise in immigration rates does not necessarily indicate increased competition for all jobs. Nevertheless, in the mid-1960s the altered immigration laws favoured those with more education, resulting in an increase of urban, educated migrants who competed successfully for white-collar jobs. As migrants arrive, competition for jobs intensifies and rates of mobility may decline. On the other hand, emigration of capital and highly skilled people to the US has continued; however, the numbers leaving are too few to have significantly influenced mobility among those who remained.

Participation rates, particularly those of women, also influence the numbers of competitors for positions. Public education, urbanization, the development of office work and economic need have all resulted in increasing numbers of entrants to the labour force. More young women are planning careers, having fewer children and returning to work shortly after childbearing.

Other kinds of social mobility are apparently less affected by changes in the size and composition of the work force. For example, the social characteristics of the Canadian elite have changed little in the last half century or more, despite changes in the general population. Members of the elite still tend to be male, white, Anglo-Saxon Protestants born into upper- or upper-middle-class families. However, there is some variation from one part of Canada to another; for example, more francophone Catholics would be found in the Québec BUSINESS ELITE or the federal political elite than in the Ontario business or political elite. Otherwise excluded social groups enter the elite and the upper class in growing areas of the economy, eg, Italians and Jews in real estate and construction. Multinational corporations also seem more likely to provide opportunities for mobility into elite positions than indigenous Canadian corporations. In general, however, social characteristics that limit the extent and rate of occupational mobility overall – characteristics such as gender, race, religion and class of origin – also appear to hinder entry into the elite.

Forms of Unequal Opportunity Rates of mobility are also affected by prevailing recruitment rules and barriers. Average individuals are most able to enter positions in agencies that recruit outsiders and are committed to impartial recruitment, such as the federal civil service. Outside these organizations, elite positions are generally filled by the

children of elite parents. For example, positions in medical schools are disproportionately filled by the children of doctors, and even in many skilled trades the right or opportunity to enter is passed from parent to child. Parental social class largely determines early educational opportunities and choices that are important to later mobility. By and large, people do not make radical changes in their occupational or social position after entering the work force; they advance beyond their parents right away or not at all. Once they have started on a particular job ladder, they advance largely by seniority, so they can hardly change their position relative to their workmates. The labour market is also split into many segments, eg, jobs entered by means of credentials, jobs entered by means of union membership and jobs entered by anyone. People starting out in one segment will rarely, if ever, compete with people in another; eg, casual labourers will rarely compete with licensed skilled workers or accredited professionals. Outside of structural mobility, and because little exchange mobility and free competition occurs, Canadians do not enjoy equal opportunity to advance. Leaving wealth and status aside, Canadians also compete unequally for power because Canadian society protects power in various ways. Family power is preserved in wealth. Many occupations and positions of authority are closed to people without credentials, eg, university degrees. Those who can obtain such credentials are drawn disproportionately from the middle and upper classes.

Attempts to Equalize Opportunity The attempt to redistribute wealth through TAXATION and TRANSFER PAYMENTS has failed to reduce inequality of wealth significantly. However, antidiscrimination laws or affirmative-action efforts are especially valuable for traditionally excluded groups, such as women and racial minorities. Evidence suggests these efforts are beginning to affect occupational mobility. Likewise, the widening of educational opportunity – more universities, increased admittance of students, the provision of more scholarships – has weakened the original value of the credentials and has led to demands by employers for rarer credentials. Still, higher education has helped many children of poorer families to obtain better jobs than they might otherwise have obtained even if top positions are closed to them.

Collective mobility has been an effective means of equalizing opportunity. Increasingly, groups of people with a common goal, eg, unions or associations of professionals, have co-operated to advance themselves. But other, less obvious groups have also mobilized collectively, including ethnic groups, such as the Toronto Italian community, language groups, such as Canadian Francophones, regional or provincial groups, and networks comprising personal acquaintances, friends or family. In many instances collective mobilization has advanced both group and individual interests. Yet the collective mobilization of everyone would ensure a new stalemate – an indirect, inefficient way of eliminating social inequality.

Trends in Canadian Research and Writing Summarizing the state of mobility research in Canada, one observer commented that "Canadian studies have led to a fuller understanding of the origins of elite groups than has been achieved in the US." On the other hand, valuable census data have been available, but they have not been fully exploited and Canadians have not been innovative in applying quantitative methodology to the study of social mobility. Canadian research continues to emulate American mobility research based on occupational and status attainment. Research initiated by John PORTER and his colleagues at Carleton set out to replicate in Canada the studies of P. Blau and O.D. Duncan. Results to date (Boyd et al, 1984) suggest a continuing importance of gender and a declining importance of ethnicity and language group in status attainment. The limited mobility of women is also documented in other studies, using other data. Other research on the experience of ethnic minorities confirms that Porter's image of Canada as a VERTICAL MOSAIC (1965) of ethnic groups is less valid today and that social mobility in Canada more closely resembles mobility in the US and other modern industrial nations. Class origin or parental occupation strongly influences the level of education a person attains, and thus the increased rate of university attendance is not as likely to equalize opportunity as once believed.

Recent research on social mobility is following fairly traditional lines, with few modifications. Research on the mobility of women has paid increasing attention to economic theories of labour-market segmentation and to effects of the introduction of new technologies. Unlike the traditional mass survey studies that focused on occupational mobility, recent research has examined the major structural changes in the incidence of service sector work. Of particular interest have been changes in the popularity of part-time work and changed patterning of careers by married women. Research on the mobility of language and ethnic groups has focused on actual work settings and the centre of control in these settings; and on the economic rationality of racism. Research on elites, which examined national and international networks of interlocking directorships throughout the 1970s, has become less common in the 1980s. **L. TEPPERMAN**

Reading: M. Boyd et al, *Ascription and Achievement* (1984); W. Clement, *The Canadian Corporate Elite* (1975); J. Porter, *The Vertical Mosaic* (1965).

Social Science, in general, has come to refer to the specialized teaching and research conducted in disciplines characterized by their concern with human beings, their culture and their economic, political and social relationship with the environment. Academicians generally categorize knowledge into 4 main areas: physical sciences, biological sciences (or natural sciences), humanities and social sciences, although others recognize only 2 categories – natural sciences and social sciences. Social sciences are included in various disciplines in different universities and there is no clear demarcation between a number of the member disciplines within these areas. Generally, the social sciences include ANTHROPOLOGY, ECONOMICS, POLITICAL SCIENCE, PSYCHOLOGY, SOCIOLOGY and sometimes CRIMINOLOGY, EDUCATION, GEOGRAPHY, LAW, PSYCHIATRY, PHILOSOPHY, RELIGION and history.

The beginnings of modern social science can be traced to the 18th-century Enlightenment. The rise of capitalist society and attendant phenomena inspired social inquiry. In France, through the work of the physiocrats, economics was launched as an empirical science. Moral philosophy also made substantial advances, laying the foundations for modern sociology, psychology and anthropology. During the 19th century, social science became diversified, but some thinkers (Comte, Marx) in an opposing trend tried to construct a synthesis. Five changes characterize the 20th-century advances in the social sciences. First, the development of modest theorizing and high standards of empirical testing; second, the recognition of the interdependence of social, political and economic forces; third, the rise of several branches of psychology important to the analysis of social behaviour; fourth, the improvement of quantitative methods; and fifth, the incorporation of social sciences into society.

In the 1950s the term "behavioural sciences" came into widespread use, usually in reference to anthropology, sociology and psychology. As an attempt to emphasize the method of scientific process, behavioural science concentrates on those aspects of the social sciences that can be explored, recorded and interpreted. Social scientists generally, however, are as much concerned with method as with results. English economist John Maynard Keynes, speaking of economics, described all social sciences when he said that "it is a method rather than a doctrine, an apparatus of the mind, a technique of thinking, which helps its possessor to draw correct conclusions." However, unlike much natural-science research, only a very small part of research in social science is conducted in controlled, laboratory settings.

Social Sciences in Canada The changes in higher education in Canada from 1663 to 1960 and the retarded development of social-science subjects relative to those closely connected with the humanities and natural sciences have been documented, but each of the social-science disciplines has its own history, its own periods of gestation, birth and growth to adulthood as a distinctive profession. Some, eg, history, economics, political science and psychology, were approaching adulthood while others, eg, geography, anthropology and sociology, were still in their infancy. These latecomers were not firmly established until the 1950s.

Growth in the social sciences was encouraged by the recognized need to resolve or understand the many problems associated with the increasing size and complexity of Canada and its institutions. Outside of Québec, much of the growth during the first 40 years of this century was promoted by spokesmen who argued that universities should provide training for the expanding public service, as well as for institutions in the private sector. In contrast, the first Québec social-science programs in the 1930s were sponsored by the Roman Catholic Church in an attempt to shape the changing society according to the social doctrines set forth in the papal encyclicals; the orientation stressed social service in the interest of French Canadian society as a whole. The social sciences helped prepare the way for the formation of co-operatives, credit unions, workers' syndicates and other institutions. The social sciences in Québec have since been secularized, but they remain strongly committed to participation in the shaping of Québec society.

From 1945 to the early 1960s, earlier gains made by the social sciences throughout Canada were consolidated. Many new departments in universities were founded and older ones expanded at a steady rate. Unfortunately, in most of the social sciences, graduate study programs were only feebly developed so that it was impossible to meet from within Canada the surge in demand for professional social scientists that occurred in the 1960s. Many prospective social scientists had to leave Canada to earn their professional degrees elsewhere, particularly in the US.

The tidal wave of students that engulfed the universities in the 1960s and early 1970s had an enormous impact on the social sciences. There was also a growing demand for the teaching of social-science subjects in community colleges and high schools. Within many universities the growing strength of social-science disciplines was accompanied by their fusion into divisions or, in some universities, into faculties of social science. The increasing importance of social science is reflected as well in the application, both directly and indirectly, of its perspectives and methods to many areas in society. Although a large number of social scientists teach in universities, thousands work in the private sector and in government and

in their jobs apply social-science knowledge and methods of research. Furthermore, social-science theories and findings are applied by many who do not have advanced social-science degrees, eg, those employed in such fields as administration, commerce, education, health, leisure, social work, etc.

Social scientists are primarily concerned with research, although it is true that social-science research does not have the impact, prestige or the same degree of financial support as research in the natural sciences. As well, the findings of social-science research do not reach a very wide audience and are often difficult to understand because they are couched in jargon. Those it does reach may be disappointed and frustrated with the contradictory and biased analyses, and lack of certainty in the predictions, which often reflect the difficulties and uncertainties of human life itself, and not the failure of the discipline.

Some social-science research is conducted for corporations, school boards, government agencies and other institutions; in such cases the client poses the questions. At the other extreme, research is generated by the scholars themselves, by universities, private foundations, or by a government-sponsored body like the SOCIAL SCIENCES AND HUMANITIES RESEARCH COUNCIL OF CANADA.

Contributions of social science to public policy are channelled through a number of streams, eg, the ECONOMIC COUNCIL OF CANADA and the Institute for Research on Public Policy. Social scientists of many specialties have played an important part on scores of task forces, committees of inquiry and royal commissions. For example, the Royal Commission on BILINGUALISM AND BICULTURALISM involved both English- and French-speaking demographers, economists, historians, linguists, political scientists and sociologists.

The spectacular growth in the social sciences in Canada is reflected in the number of national and regional associations and journals established since 1950, before which time fewer than 10 associations and no more than 7 journals existed. By the late 1980s there were 37 associations and at least 32 journals catering entirely or partly to the social-science community.

Individual social-science disciplines have developed an impressive capacity to organize, but less impressive has been the capacity for the social sciences to create and sustain a strong collective organization that transcends the boundaries of the disciplines. The first attempt to bring together the various social sciences under an umbrella organization was the founding (1940) of the Social Science Research Council (later changed to SOCIAL SCIENCE FEDERATION OF CANADA). This voluntary association was organized by a small group of distinguished scholars to promote research, the training of social scientists, the publication of studies and the holding of conferences. Almost all of the funding for these activities derived from American sources – the Carnegie, Ford and Rockefeller foundations. The council was able to function on only a small scale without government support. With the establishment of the CANADA COUNCIL in 1957, government support for the social sciences as well as the humanities was instituted, although on a more modest scale than for the natural sciences. In 1978 the functions of the Canada Council relating to the social sciences were taken over by the Social Sciences and Humanities Research Council, a federal agency. Its role is to promote the interests of the social-science community vis-à-vis the public and the state. **FRANK G. VALLEE**

Reading: Encyclopedia of the Social Sciences (1965).

Social Science Federation of Canada (SSFC) was established in 1940 as the Social Science Research Council of Canada. A nonprofit organization with registered charity status, the federation was incorporated under its present name in 1977. It unites academic social-science associations and related organizations representing more than 14 000 Canadians working in various disciplines in the SOCIAL SCIENCES. The federation has been a driving force behind many Canadian academic and cultural activities. From 1940 to 1957, it was the only Canadian funding agency for social-science research. The federation, with other organizations, worked for the establishment of the Massey Commission and later the CANADA COUNCIL, from which was derived the present granting council for the social sciences, the SOCIAL SCIENCES AND HUMANITIES RESEARCH COUNCIL OF CANADA (SSHRC).

In recent years, the SSFC has concentrated on fulfilling 4 major roles. It acts as an interest group, enabling the Canadian academic social-science community to convey its needs to the government and its agencies. It serves as an information gathering and dissemination organization among the government, university and federation and in addition, aims at increasing public awareness of the contributions of the SOCIAL SCIENCES to Canadian society. A third SSFC role is to act as a forum for associations of researchers in the social sciences through frequent seminars and meetings. Finally, the SSFC serves as a funding organization by administering the Aid to Scholarly Publications Programme in collaboration with the Canadian Federation for the Humanities. The funds for this program are provided by the SSHRC.

The SSFC is governed by an executive committee, a board of directors and a general assembly. The permanent secretariat of the federation is located in Ottawa and has a small professional staff.

ALAN F.J. ARTIBISE

Social Sciences and Humanities Research Council of Canada (SSHRC), created 29 June 1977 by an Act of Parliament. It began operations 1 Apr 1978, taking over the programs previously administered by the CANADA COUNCIL's humanities and social sciences division. With the Medical Research Council and the Natural Sciences and Engineering Research Council, SSHRC administers federal funds for university-based research. It is governed by a 22-member appointed council selected from the academic community and other groups.

SSHRC's mandate, defined in section 5 of the Government Organization (Scientific Activities) Act, 1976, is to assist research and scholarship in the social sciences and humanities and to advise the minister on matters referred to it by the minister. SSHRC enhances the advancement of knowledge by assisting research; advises on maintaining and developing the national capacity for research; facilitates the dissemination of research results; and increases Canada's international presence and recognition in the social sciences and humanities.

SSHRC has a staff of 95, based in Ottawa. Its annual budget (voted by Parliament) is approximately $70 million. The type of research funded ranges from proposals of individual scholars to major national projects such as the *Canadian Historical Atlas* and the DICTIONARY OF CANADIAN BIOGRAPHY. In 1986-87 it awarded $64.4 million in grants and fellowships.

JEFFREY HOLMES

Social Security denotes public programs intended to maintain, protect and raise basic living standards. Specifically the term covers publicly financed and administered programs that replace income that has been lost because of pregnancy, illness, accident, disability, the death or absence of a family's breadwinner, unemployment, old age or retirement, or other factors. Since WWII social security in Canada has been expanded to protect the adequacy of individual and family incomes threatened by the costs of medical and hospital care, of family size or of shelter (although Canada, unlike many western European countries, provides only limited help to ensure that a disproportionate share of people's income is not spent on shelter). Governments have also introduced MINIMUM WAGE legislation and have provided help for workers to upgrade job skills or to relocate. Federal and provincial governments have recently been experimenting with programs to supplement the incomes of working people when their earned income falls below a level that is considered adequate.

The history of social security in Canada can be divided into the colonial era (from the arrival of the first European settlers in the 17th century to 1867); from Confederation to WWI; 1919-39; and the post-WWII era. The settlers who colonized NEW FRANCE introduced the 17th-century French practice of assigning the care of the elderly, sick and orphaned to the Catholic Church and its institutions. The British who established Halifax in the mid-18th century introduced the English poor law enacted by the English Parliament in 1598, which assigned the care of the poor to the smallest unit of government, the parish, financed by property taxes raised there. The British legislation introduced the idea of public responsibility for the care of the destitute, replacing a much older tradition of licensed begging and reliance on voluntary donations.

The English poor-law model was also imported into the American colonies and from there to what is now NB by the LOYALISTS. In 1763 NS enacted legislation modelled on the English poor law, as did NB in 1786. Money raised locally was supplemented occasionally by a provincial grant to meet an extraordinary emergency, eg, serious fire or an outbreak of typhoid fever. In other parts of British North America the poor law model was not as closely copied. In PEI, for example, where there were only 1 or 2 towns of any size, all emergency help was dispensed from there; in Newfoundland (where the Colonial Office in London had actively discouraged settlement and the development of municipal institutions), charity organizations, friends and family were the principal sources of help. UPPER CANADA failed to enact a poor law in 1792 when the main body of English civil law was introduced into the new province; one result was the encouragement of voluntary charities. LOWER CANADA, with its French traditions, relied upon voluntary charitable collections to finance the welfare work of the Catholic Church. English Protestants settling in Lower Canada formed their own charitable agencies to take care of English-speaking poor.

In the colonial era, people who lived primarily in small, rural communities were more self-sufficient than Canadians today, not only from necessity but because it was more feasible. They produced most of their own food on small family farms and obtained many other necessities through barter; in emergencies neighbours helped each other. However, for those without friends and family, the only recourse was charity, considered proof of personal failure in many instances. In French Canada even asking for help from the churches was resisted. The help offered by charitable agencies was often paternalistic and meagre, and frequently administered in a harsh and demeaning manner. The classic example of this was the municipal poorhouse, a poor-law institution found in larger towns and cities. It housed the destitute of all ages, the sick, the senile, the mentally ill, the unemployed, children and infants. Its reputation was so fearsome that only those facing starvation would seek such help. In NB some of the smaller communities that could not afford the cost of such institutions auctioned off the care of the poor to local families, an utterly demeaning practice which continued until the latter part of the 19th century.

Under the BRITISH NORTH AMERICA ACT (now Constitution Act, 1867) the relatively minor roles of government were assigned to the provinces, among them the exclusive right to legislate regarding "the establishment, maintenance and management of hospitals, asylums, charities and charitable institutions," a succinct description of existing organizations. The implicit judgement was that health and welfare were matters of purely local interest and control and that the provinces should reassign much of the responsibility to the municipalities or to voluntary charities. Provincial governments, however, became increasingly involved in a range of health and welfare programs, particularly in western provinces, where municipal organizations were rudimentary or nonexistent.

After 1867, industrialization drew people to the towns and cities in search of greater economic opportunity. Many discovered they had traded the relative security of the family farm for the insecurity of a factory job. People were now dependent upon a regular cash income, and any event which interrupted it gravely threatened their livelihood. In the years following Confederation, peoples' attitudes toward the appropriate government role regarding the economic security of the individual were still shaped by the pioneer values of independence and individualism, reflected in furious public debates about the necessity for, and value of, public schools, public-health measures and government regulation of working conditions. Poor relief was still delivered in a stigmatizing manner, and POVERTY, which was still related in the public mind to individual failure, was commonly blamed on excessive drinking. To avoid dependence on charity, 19th-century workers organized fraternal societies, each member contributing a small, regular amount to a special fund from which he could draw if sickness or accident prevented him from working. Trade unions, many of which originated at this time, struggled to raise standards of living and to provide income protection against the risk of wage loss, but these limited protections were available only to a minority of the work force. With the increasing industrialization of the late 19th century the number of work accidents rose. Trade unions and other groups made this a public issue, and the result in 1914 was the first modern social-security program, the Workmen's Compensation Act of Ontario. Injured workers could now claim a regular cash income as a right. Ontario's example was soon copied by other provinces.

Social insurance, based on the assumption that risks to income security are a normal aspect of life in an urban-industrial society and not the result of individual shortcomings, was pioneered in Germany in the 1880s. Britain introduced the world's first UNEMPLOYMENT INSURANCE scheme in 1911. Nearly all workers contributed to a fund from which all could draw; employers were also asked to contribute, and government could contribute toward administration costs. Workers' contributions provided a sense of entitlement to help, which the old poor law had never done.

WWI accelerated the processes of urbanization and industrialization and led to increased agitation for OLD-AGE PENSIONS and allowances for civilian widows, deserted wives and their children. In 1916 Manitoba was the first province to pass a Mothers' Pensions Act to provide a small but assured income to widows and divorced or deserted wives with children to support. Within 5 years, all provinces from Ontario west had passed similar legislation. Called public assistance, the help was based on a means test and constituted a modern version of the English poor law. In 1919 the Liberal Party pledged to pass legislation on health insurance, contributory old-age pensions and unemployment insurance. To circumvent the BNA Act, the federal government devised the conditional grant, which enabled it to initiate programs by offering to share the cost of provincially administered social-security programs, provided they met certain federal guidelines (*see* INTERGOVERNMENTAL FINANCE). Under this arrangement the first old-age pension program was introduced in 1927. In its first major entry into the social-security field, the federal government paid 50% of a $20 monthly pension to needy citizens age 70 and over. The pension was subject, however, to a strict and often humiliating means test – proof that poor-law attitudes still influenced Canadian political leaders in the 1920s.

The GREAT DEPRESSION seared Canadian society. Thousands of formerly independent Canadians joined the public-welfare rolls. The federal government was compelled to become involved in the massive problem of unemployment relief, previously a purely local concern. The 1930 programs to relieve poverty and destitution were essentially left over from the 19th-century poor-relief systems of municipal aid supplemented by voluntary charitable agencies. Rather than cash, assistance was granted in the form of grocery, fuel and clothing orders. Single, unemployed men were herded into military-style camps, reminiscent of the 19th-century poorhouse (*see* UNEMPLOYMENT RELIEF CAMPS). In Alberta nonstatus Indians and Métis could only collect welfare on "halfbreed" agricultural colonies. By 1939 a majority of Canadians realized that it was the economic and social systems that had failed and not the individuals.

WWII temporarily solved the unemployment problem, but Canadians demanded more economic security and an end to stigmatizing health and welfare programs. In 1940 the federal government introduced the Unemployment Insurance Act; in 1943, as part of its envisaged postwar planning, it published the *Report on Social Security for Canada*, by Leonard C. MARSH, which created a public sensation and provided a blueprint for a comprehensive social-security system. It emphasized the use of contributory social insurance and a universal system of family allowances and health care. Although the report had caught the imagination of the country, the federal government selected only some of its ideas and ignored its central advice – the need for comprehensive, co-ordinated planning. In 1944 the government introduced the Family Allowances Act, under which, without a means test, all Canadian mothers, on behalf of their children under the age of 16, would receive an allowance. The gross cost of the program, estimated at $250 million for the first year, was until then the largest expenditure on a social-security program. In 1945 the federal government offered a social-security plan to the provinces involving a cost-shared medical and hospital insurance scheme, federal assumption of old-age pensions for Canadians over the age of 70 and a cost-shared plan for pensions for people 65-69, plus federal responsibility for the unemployed, but in a squabble over revenue sharing the 2 levels of government abandoned the plan. In 1951 a universal old-age pension system was instituted. All Canadians, at the age of 70, were now entitled to receive a pension, an acknowledgement that upon retirement the majority of Canadians had little or no income or savings.

Canadians were also aware that access to health care was blocked for many by their inabili-

Christmas food and clothing hampers presented to a poor Winnipeg family (*courtesy United Church Archives*).

ty to afford it and that public-health insurance offered a solution. Saskatchewan's highly successful hospital insurance plan, which covered every Saskatchewan resident, was launched in 1945. It prompted residents in other provinces to seek similar protection. In 1957 the federal government agreed to share in the cost of provincial hospital insurance programs, and by 1961 all 10 provinces had provided them. The charity ward of hospitals vanished overnight, but doctors' bills were still beyond the means of many people. The Saskatchewan government, again a pioneer, introduced a universal, tax-supported, publicly administered medical-care insurance plan, the first province or state in N America to do so. In 1966, the federal government passed the Medical Care Act, according to which it would contribute to provincial medical-care insurance plans provided that such plans met the central federal goal of ensuring universal coverage to provincial residents for a comprehensive range of general practitioner and specialist services, available to all regardless of age or condition, or ability to pay and upon uniform terms and conditions. By 1971 all provinces were participating under the terms of the legislation (*see* HEALTH POLICY).

Earlier, in 1965, the federal government had passed the CANADA PENSION PLAN, which provided social-insurance protection for retirement, disability and the provision of survivors' benefits. The plan, designed to improve the adequacy of old-age pensions, was also an acknowledgement that a majority of workers were not protected by an occupational pension plan. A national program (with the exception of Québec, which legislated the equivalent QUÉBEC PENSION PLAN), it meant that workers did not lose their membership when changing jobs or moving to another province. The compulsory plan covers almost the entire labour force. It was also the first Canadian social-security program to provide for automatic increases in benefits in accordance with increases in the cost of living.

A Senate inquiry (1969) revealed that 1 in 4 Canadians lived below the poverty line and that close to 2 million of these were working poor – people whose income from employment was insufficient to lift them out of poverty. Saskatchewan (1974), Québec (1979) and Manitoba (1980) began to supplement the income of working-poor families. A 1975 federal proposal, the result of a 3-year, federal-provincial, social-security review, offered to share the cost of an income-supplement scheme for working-poor families, but it was rejected by the provinces as being too expensive. In 1967 the Guaranteed Income Supplement program provided an income-tested supplement to pensioners with little or no income other than their universal old-age-security pension. In 1975 the federal government also introduced the Spouses' Allowance, paid to old-age pensioners' spouses aged 60-64 when other in-

come is less than adequate. Family allowances were raised in 1973, and in 1978 the federal government introduced a child tax credit that paid $200 for each child under 18 to families where total family income did not exceed $18 000 annually, but this credit was raised by reducing family allowances. Under the Canada Assistance Plan (1966), another federal cost-sharing program, the federal government supports provincial social-assistance programs which provide both financial and other services. During the 1970s the provinces also began providing supplements to their most needy pensioners and offering tax credits for housing costs.

The 1980s have proved to be a testing time for Canada's social security system. The decade began with double-digit inflation followed by the most severe economic recession since the 1930s. The result was high unemployment, reduced economic growth, a sharp decline in the tax revenue with a corresponding increase in government deficits. These circumstances have led provincial and federal governments to carefully scrutinize spending on social security programs and to put forward cost-containment proposals. Medicare, old age pensions, family allowances, and unemployment insurance were particularly singled out for attention. Concern about the future of the Canadian economy also resulted in a proposal to radically redesign Canadian social security.

In the opinion of many observers, the medicare system's goal of providing unfettered access to a comprehensive range of medical services was being increasingly jeopardized in the early 1980s by the practice of extra billing by doctors and the imposition of hospital user fees by some provinces. These practices represented an attempt to compensate for the increasing stringency of both federal and provincial health budgets. In 1984, with the support of all political parties, the federal government acted to stem the erosion of universal accessibility by passing the Canada Health Act which reasserted the principle of universal access by requiring the provinces, as a condition for receiving the federal share of provincial health care costs, to eliminate hospital user fees and extra billing by physicians within 3 years or suffer a financial penalty equal to the amount collected in extra charges. By 1987, the Canada Health Act had largely achieved its aim. Although the proponents of extra billing and hospital user fees claimed that health care costs were out of control and additional revenue was needed, a review of public spending on health care by a federal royal commission in 1984 revealed the relative stability of public spending in this sector since the inception of medicare.

The impact of double-digit inflation beginning first in the mid-1970s and continuing until the early 1980s had a serious impact on people living on fixed incomes. As one result, old-age pension policy became a major public issue. A variety of concerns were nationally debated: a reported increase in poverty among the elderly and particularly among single, elderly women; concern for the cost of future pensions given the aging of the Canadian population; the need for pension policy to recognize the changing role of women; and, perhaps the most contentious issue, the failure of a great majority of the more than 14 000 private pension plans, covering some 4.1 million workers, to index pension benefits to the cost of living as do public pensions. Labour unions, welfare organizations, women's groups, the Québec and Saskatchewan governments and a report by a senate committee advocated improvements in the public pension system and the adoption of higher standards of performance for private pensions including full indexing to the cost of living. Business groups, the pension industry, and the

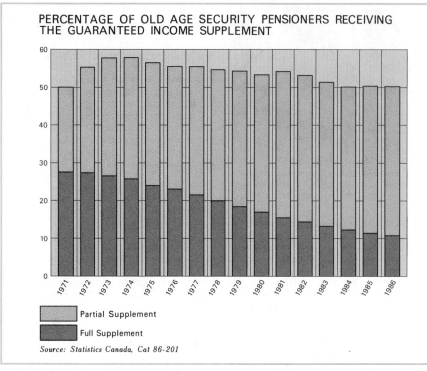

PERCENTAGE OF OLD AGE SECURITY PENSIONERS RECEIVING THE GUARANTEED INCOME SUPPLEMENT

Partial Supplement
Full Supplement

Source: Statistics Canada, Cat 86-201

provinces of Ontario and British Columbia supported a private market approach to retirement pensions and opposed any expansion of the public pension system. Private pension representatives also disagreed on the amount of regulation required by private pension plans and suggestions that they be indexed to the cost of living were firmly rejected. When the rate of inflation declined in 1983, the pressure for reform of the pension system eased and no substantive changes occurred. A federal government attempt to reduce its deficit in 1984 by partially de-indexing the Old Age Security benefit failed when pensioner organizations successfully lobbied Ottawa in opposition. To deal with the issue of old age pensioners living in poverty, the federal government raised the Guaranteed Income Supplement by $50 a month. A similar strategy of partially de-indexing Family Allowances and the Child Tax Credit and raising the income-tested Child Tax Credit was implemented by the federal government in 1985 (*see* FAMILY ALLOWANCES).

Unemployment insurance was the subject of a federal commission of inquiry in the 1980s. Unusually high rates of unemployment magnified the costs of this program while concern was expressed by representatives of business that the very existence of UI was contributing to the unemployment rate. The majority report of the commission took a similar view and recommended a series of changes aimed at cutting back on benefits which, it argued, encouraged people to remain on UI longer than necessary. The majority report also recommended that some of the $3 billion to be saved by cutting benefits be transferred into worker retraining and relocation programs as well as wage subsidy programs. A minority report took an opposing view and argued that the unemployment rate reflected a scarcity of jobs and slow economic growth and was unrelated to individual motivation. It urged that UI should be made easier to qualify for and that benefits should be increased. The commission's report was issued in Nov 1986 but as the majority report's main proposals were so contentious the report was subsequently shelved.

A plan to comprehensively redesign Canada's social security system emerged in 1984 as part of the report of the Royal Commission on the ECO-NOMIC UNION AND DEVELOPMENT PROSPECTS FOR CANADA. The report contended that in the years remaining in the 20th century, Canada would be forced to undergo major economic changes resulting in dislocation for many Canadian workers and the social security system should be redesigned to reflect this eventuality. The commission recommended a comprehensive guaranteed income plan, called the Universal Income Security Program, to be financed and administered by the federal government and which would pay, as one option, $3875 per year for all adults and for the first child of a single parent family, and $765 for other children (providing a family of 4, with no other income, $9150 per year). The program would be financed by eliminating some existing social security programs as well as certain tax concessions. As an income of $9150 is 50% below the poverty line for all except those living in the most rural parts of Canada, the provinces would be expected to add to the guarantee for those individuals and families without other means of supplementing their federal benefit. Earned income, it was suggested, might be taxed back at a 20% rate. These proposals, termed "radical, not cosmetic" by the commission, have encountered the same political problems of all such proposals and have not been acted upon.

From the perspective of the 1980s Canadians can look back to 1874 when the bill for public welfare for all of Canada was a scant $4 million. In 1985, federal and provincial expenditure on social security programs, including assistance through the tax system, to assist Canada's families, the elderly, the unemployed and the poor totalled $61.6 billion. This increase reflects not only the expansion in social security coverage and the growth in the population generally but also the more recent social and economic developments in our history such as the inflationary period of the late 1970s and early 1980s; the recession of 1981-82 with its high unemployment; and the growing number of Canadians over the age of 65. Although the 1980s has witnessed considerable questioning and criticism of social security programs and expenditure, the Canadian public is strongly supportive of the social safety net. Comparative studies of social security spending among Western industrialized nations indicate that Canada is in the middle rank in terms of spending on social security, and current expenditures are fully consistent with the country's wealth and resources. Despite the sizeable budgets allocated to social security, an estimated 3 951 000 Canadian, or 1 in 6, including more than 1 million children, lived on low incomes in 1985, a substantial increase over estimates made in 1980. Since 1982 so-called FOOD BANKS, where once a week people line up for a bag of groceries, have become a common feature of many Canadian towns and cities. Food banks demonstrate that without a policy of full employment and a comprehensive income guarantee, the existing Canadian social security system does not adequately protect all people from the depredations of poverty. Correcting these inadequacies will present Canadians in the 1990s with a very significant challenge. DENNIS GUEST

Reading: Dennis Guest, *The Emergence of Social Security in Canada* (2nd ed, rev, 1985); National Welfare Council, *Pension Primer* (1984); Health and Welfare Canada, *Better Pensions for Canadians* (1982); Emett M. Hall, *Canada's National-Provincial Health Program for the 1980's* (1980); Canada, *Commission of Enquiry on Unemployment Insurance*, Report (1986); Canada, *Royal Commission on the Economic Union and Development Prospects for Canada* (1985).

Social Work is intended to assist individuals, families and communities in understanding and solving their personal and social problems. Historically social work was associated with charities and volunteer assistance to the needy. The professionalization of social work was a consequence of industrialization and the conviction that rational solutions to social problems were possible.

Prior to 1867 social work in Canada meant, as it did in England and the US, relief of the poor, whose situation was generally believed to result from weakness of character, exemplified in a publication of the London Charity Organization Society: "If the head of the family makes no provision in case of his death part of the responsibility falls on his wife and it is doubtful whether the widow ought to be relieved of the consequences by charitable aid."

The Associated Charities, part of a movement originating in England in 1869, was established in Canada in 1881. It differed from similar organizations of the time in stressing the importance of systematic investigation rather than the simple provision of relief. By 1912 the Associated Charities were being replaced by municipal social-service commissions; simultaneously the social casework method of investigation was being popularized in Canada by followers of Mary Richmond, one of America's social-work pioneers. In 1914 a training program for social workers was established at U of T, followed (1918) by a similar program at McGill. In 1926 the Canadian Association of Social Workers was formed. The first charter members were drawn principally from child and family welfare agencies, municipal departments and settlement houses. Social work grew slowly during the 1920s and 1930s. The GREAT DEPRESSION years placed heavy demands on social-work agencies, but governments were reluctant to promote the advancement of trained social workers in universities. Only 2 new training programs opened during this period – one at UBC (1928) and the other at U de Montréal (1939). After WWII the profession expanded, along with the development of medicare, hospital insurance, old-age PENSIONS, SOCIAL SECURITY, homes for the aged and special services for the handicapped; many agencies supplying these services employed social workers. In 1941 the census reported 1767 social workers in Canada; by 1981 there were over 27 590.

Some of Canada's principal social reformers

have been associated with the social-work profession, including J.S. WOODSWORTH, founder of the CCF; Charlotte WHITTON, child-welfare activist and mayor of Ottawa; Leonard MARSH, author of an influential report on social security; and Harry Cassidy, writer and director of University of Toronto School of Social Work for many years.

Training and Specialization At the undergraduate level (BSW), courses include human behaviour and social development, social services, social security, and social intervention (eg, counselling, group work, community organizations, administration, etc). At the graduate level (MSW, DSW or PhD), students specialize in various fields of study (eg, family and child welfare, mental health, corrections, etc). Masters' programs in social work are offered at UBC, U of Calgary, Carleton, Dalhousie, Laval, McGill, McMaster, U of Manitoba, Memorial, U of Regina, U of T, Wilfrid Laurier, U of Windsor, York; and doctoral programs are offered at Wilfrid Laurier and U of T. New specialties of social work develop in response to personal and social problems created by changes in society. Across Canada, at least 4 specializations are recognized: counselling, group work, community development and social administration, although they share a common body of theory and practice integral to the profession as a whole. As counsellors, social workers work with individuals and families suffering difficulties from problems such as marital breakdown, parenting inadequacies, CHILD ABUSE, ALCOHOLISM and drug abuse, as well as those that may arise in schools or in the workplace. Group work generally refers to programs in which participants are not necessarily closely related. Sometimes the groups are organized around social-recreational programs, eg, senior-citizen centres or day care; sometimes they are formed to deal with personal problems or simply to share common experiences. Community development refers to activities aimed at improving social conditions, co-ordinating services or promoting public-policy changes. Emphasis is on the development of community leaders and self-help initiatives. Finally, with the growth of public and voluntary services, social workers are increasingly required to specialize in social administration, ie, the management of a wide range of services and the direction of large bureaucracies.

Field of Practice Many social workers are employed in public social services contributing to the care and rehabilitation of the physically and mentally ill, the young, the aged, the mentally handicapped or the disabled. SCHOOL BOARDS engage social workers to counsel students with emotional and social problems. Settlement houses, community centres, senior-citizen centres and hostels hire social workers to work with groups. Some social workers are employed in industry to assist employees with personal problems. In the corrections field, social workers counsel offenders, prisoners and parolees. Some are employed as organizers in social-planning agencies, community organizations and trade unions, while others work as administrators for government or voluntary associations. Some teach in universities and community colleges. A few are self-employed as private practitioners.

Institutions, Societies and Journals The Canadian Assn of Social Workers (CASW), a national, professional organization, is a federation of provincial and territorial associations representing about 9700 members (1987). The CASW establishes a code of ethics, issues guidelines for practice and publishes books on social-work/social-welfare systems. The federal and provincial associations have been active in helping to develop social-service and social-security programs in Canada. The Canadian Assn of Schools of Social

Work (CASSW) is the accreditation body for schools of social work. It promotes research and scholarly publications. A bachelor's degree (BSW) is a prerequisite for professional practice. Principal professional journals in Canada include *The Social Worker/Le Travailleur social, Canadian Social Work Review/Revue canadienne de travail social, Service Social* and *Intervention*.

Future of Social Work Despite the significant changes in the discipline over the last 80 years, and its evolution from a residual function in early industrial society to an institutional function in advanced industrial society, controversy still prevails within the profession, as within the larger society, about the extent to which welfare services should be institutionally integrated into society. Some social workers, for example, believe social services should be universally available to all Canadians as a right, while others believe that programs should be offered selectively. Some social workers are persuaded that social security helps to safeguard the dignity of the individual; others believe that there is too much government intrusion into the daily lives of people. The resolution of these debates will inevitably affect the future development of social work in Canada.
GLENN DROVER

Socialism, a political doctrine focusing on the economic order in society and on the broad differences in the people's circumstances produced by economic factors. It proposes STATE intervention to lessen inequality of conditions in society, with social and economic planning as the key. Socialism has enjoyed such a wide expression in so many countries by so many parties and governments that many politicians today eschew the term to avoid confusion. What was "socialism" in 1940 is often now "SOCIAL DEMOCRACY" or, among the bolder, "democratic socialism." Socialism did not originate with Karl Marx and not all socialism is MARXISM. Marx, however, gave the idea its most forceful and elaborate expression, postulating not only that a revolution of the workers was necessary but that it was historically inevitable. Many interpreters have elaborated and reinterpreted Marx's ideas. A democratic socialist today would believe in an evolutionary path and in the active involvement of the state to ensure an equitable society – one in which the major means of production, distribution and supply are either owned or closely controlled by the state. Socialism places more emphasis on the goals of the community than on those of the individual. Diversity is the nature of the modern socialist movement. In Canada the most important socialist political party began in 1932 as the CO-OPERATIVE COMMONWEALTH FEDERATION, which in 1961 became the NEW DEMOCRATIC PARTY. The first socialist government in N America was Saskatchewan's CCF government, formed in 1944 by T.C. DOUGLAS. In recent years, NDP governments have been elected in BC, Sask, Man and YT.
WALTER D. YOUNG

Reading: D. Wilson, ed, Democratic Socialism: The Challenge of the Eighties (1985).

Socialist Party of Canada (SPC) emerged in 1904 when the Socialist Party of British Columbia, a group of Marxists influential in BC mining camps and among BC trade unionists, merged with the Canadian Socialist League. By 1910 it had spread from coast to coast. Members of the SPC held the revolutionary view (known as "impossiblism") that attempts to reform the capitalist system were useless and that militant political action was necessary in order to destroy the wage system and usher in the co-operative commonwealth. The party's support waned after the collapse of the general strikes of 1919 when most workers adopted a reformist stance and their organizations a gradualist strategy. Many of the

activists in the SPC who continued to reject reformism and labourism later joined the COMMUNIST PARTY OF CANADA.
J.T. MORLEY

Société des missions étrangères de la province de Québec The bishops of Québec decided during a conference held in Québec City in 1921 to respond to the appeal for the propagation of the faith launched by Pope Benedict XV (apostolic letter *Maximum illud* of 30.XI.1919) and to play a collective role in the Catholic missionary movement by founding a society of French Canadian diocesan priests dedicated to foreign missions. Canon Avila Roch, parish priest of the cathedral in Joliette, Qué, was put in charge of the new society and served as its superior general until his death (1940). The first missionaries departed in 1925 for China (Manchuria). The society spread as well to Argentina, Chile, Colombia, Cuba, Honduras, Japan, Peru and the Philippines. In 1986 there were 247 members.
MICHEL THÉRIAULT

Society of Contemporary Music of Québec (SCMQ)/Société de musique contemporaine du Québec Founded in Montréal in 1966 by Wilfrid PELLETIER, Jean PAPINEAU-COUTURE, Maryvonne Kendergi, Serge GARANT, Hugh Davidson, Jean Vallerand and Pierre Mercure, SCMQ exists to promote contemporary music, international as well as Canadian, and to inspire the creation of new works. Each season it organizes 6 to 8 concerts presented in Montréal by the Ensemble of the SCMQ or by guest artists. Thus, a number of great composers and interpreters, such as Luciaco Berio, Olivier Messiaen, Yvonne Loriod, Karlheinz Stockhausen, Mauricio Kagel, Xavier Darasse, the Percussions of Strasbourg and Cathy Berberian, have all taken part. The ensemble appears in other Canadian cities, the US and Europe. It has commissioned and presented a number of Canadian works, including *Souffles (Champs II)* by Gilles TREMBLAY, *Cycle* op 16 by Jacques Hétu, *IIKKII (Froidure)* by François MOREL, *Ishuma* by Micheline Saint-Marcoux, *Uraufführung* by Otto Joachim and *Interactions* by Clermont PÉPIN.
HÉLÈNE PLOUFFE

Society of Friends, *see* QUAKERS.

Sociology is the study of human relationships, the rules and norms that guide them, and the development of institutions and movements that conserve and change society. Sociological methodology includes the analysis of data obtained through questionnaires and surveys, the analysis of official statistics, the observation of human interaction and the study of historical records. Theories developed from the analysis of such data are subjected to testing, modification and further verification by continuing research. Within the discipline of sociology there are numerous specializations and subspecializations. Sociology of the FAMILY, of WORK and the professions, of education, and of political, economic and labour organizations are among the major specializations in the discipline today. Others include CRIMINOLOGY, statistics, social DEMOGRAPHY, and sociology of religion, of ETHNIC AND RACE RELATIONS, of sport, of sex roles, of AGING and of knowledge.

Between 1940 and 1960, when sociology was being established in N America as an academic discipline, the drive toward scientific status led to the separation of sociology from the humanistic disciplines and the greater internal specialization of fields within the discipline, although since its emergence sociology has been closely allied for some purposes with social PSYCHOLOGY and social ANTHROPOLOGY. The 1970s witnessed a strong interdisciplinary movement, a broadening of the scope of sociological inquiry toward the inclusion of historical, economic and political aspects of human relationships. Hence the work of many sociologists has overlapped with that of scholars outside their discipline. Sociologists now study the historical development of class relations and its relationship to economic, political and ideological processes.

Origins of the Discipline and Historical Development in Canada The intellectual origins of sociology are numerous, but as a special science it originated in France. Auguste Comte gave the name "sociology" to the new discipline and outlined a philosophy (positivism) that shaped its development. Positivism holds that only actual phenomena and facts constitute knowledge. Émile Durkheim contributed most to the emergence of sociology in France by combining empirical research and theories in the development of a general set of propositions about social relations. The 2 other traditions that have significantly shaped modern sociology are grounded in the works of the German sociologists Max Weber and Karl Marx. The common problem that Durkheim, Weber and Marx confronted was the historical transition from feudalism to capitalism and its effects on social integration, the organization of power and SOCIAL CLASS relations. Coincident with this transition were the rapid and profound changes, often involving individual and social disorganization, that resulted from the Industrial Revolution.

In N America, the first academic course in sociology was introduced at Yale in 1876; in 1893 University of Chicago was the first to offer a doctorate in sociology. Sociology had not made an appearance in Canada as an academic discipline in the 1890s, but by 1920 courses in sociology were being offered in a number of disciplines and were included in theology curricula. The Canadian Political Science Association, formed in 1913, accepted sociologists as members. The association was inactive during WWI and was not reactivated until 1929. The first academic appointment in sociology in Canada was that of Carl A. Dawson in 1922 at McGill. Honours programs were established at McGill in 1926 and at U of T in 1932. Still, in 1941, Harold INNIS, one of the founding figures in Canadian social science, described sociology as the "Cinderella of the social sciences." The work of S.D. CLARK at U of T at this time was important to the subsequent recognition of sociology as a legitimate field of study, despite opposition from the entrenched disciplines. Significant SOCIAL SCIENCE research had been under way from the late 1880s to the late 1930s. This included the work of Marius BARBEAU, Carl Dawson, Léon GÉRIN, Diamond JENNESS and Everett Hughes on Canada's indigenous peoples; the human ecological approach to urban growth and planning; and studies of ethnic groups in the West, of education and Québec's rural population, and of ethnic relations (particularly FRANCOPHONE-ANGLOPHONE RELATIONS). By 1940 a substantial body of material on Canadian economic, political and social development existed.

While the social problems of the times were common to all parts of Canada, sociology developed differently in the anglophone and francophone academic communities. Francophone sociology in Québec originally took its inspiration from the encyclical *Rerum Novarum* (1891). The Roman Catholic Church defined the limits and content of early francophone sociology, and the Catholic Action movement became the vehicle for a Catholic sociology in Québec. By the early 1930s, Catholic sociology was taught at Laval and U de M. From the outset sociology was viewed as an instrument of "national" development in Québec and helped foster ideological self-awareness and critical debate.

During the 1940s, Father Georges-Henri Lévesque of Laval was a leading force in a movement to establish a secularized sociology in Québec. He encouraged a greater scientific sophistication and directed the attention of francophone sociologists away from "la survivance" of French Canadian traditions and towards the aim of aiding the INDUSTRIALIZATION and modernization of the Québec economy and society. This secularized view of sociology and its role in Québec reinforced a profederalist ideology. In the 1960s a new nationalism appeared in Québec sociology in support of an ideology of self-determination and sovereignty for Québec society. With the growth of the state bureaucracy in Québec during the 1960s and 1970s, sociologists became directly involved in the programming and administration of the new society.

Both anglophone and francophone sociology share stylistic similarities, but certain traditions are more influential in one than the other. For instance, in Québec, perspectives from Europe (and from France in particular) are more evident than they are elsewhere in Canada, where American influence is relatively stronger.

Beginning in the 1960s, sociology underwent a spectacular expansion everywhere in Canada. In 1960-61 there were 61 sociologists in Canadian universities, no doctorates were awarded in sociology and only 2 had been awarded up to that date. During the next 2 decades, sociology was established in virtually every academic institution; in 1985, 46 doctorates and 171 masters degrees in sociology were conferred by Canadian universities. In 1960 sociology had been organized at the departmental level in only 4 universities in Canada: Carleton, McMaster, Saskatchewan and U de M. In 1985, 44 institutions had enrolments in sociology, although not all of them had sociology departments.

Applications Sociological knowledge is used indirectly in teaching and in everyday work of many kinds, and is applied directly to policy issues either through research conducted during the course of officially sponsored inquiries or through independent research. Sociology is taught primarily at the university level, although since the 1970s sociological content has permeated courses at the community-college and high-school levels. In teaching, research is used not so much as an end in itself but as a means of conveying the perspectives of sociology. Indirectly, sociological research also informs the everyday activities of people in certain jobs, eg, those employed in administration, education, marketing, recreation, SOCIAL WORK and other sectors – although it is impossible to gauge the extent of such practical applications.

It is easier to determine how sociological research feeds directly into the deliberations of those responsible for shaping social policy. For example, the recommendations of the Royal Commission on Health Services (1964-65) were strongly influenced by sociological research (4 studies and numerous submissions) conducted on behalf of the commission. The reports of this commission helped shape Canadian HEALTH POLICY. Of similar importance, in the shaping of LANGUAGE POLICIES and cultural policies, were the recommendations of the Royal Commission on BILINGUALISM AND BICULTURALISM (1963-69). Sociologists contributed to the Royal Commission on the STATUS OF WOMEN IN CANADA (1967-70); some of the recommendations have been accepted as public policy. Research by sociologists was significant in developing the recommendations of La Commission d'enquête sur l'enseignement au Québec (1963-66), often referred to as the Parent Commission after its chairman. The educational reforms based on these recommendations drastically altered Québec's educational system. Sociological research in the early 1970s helped shape many of the recommendations of the Gendron Commission (Commission d'enquête sur la situation de la langue française au Québec), the policy implications of which have been profound.

Other public inquiries to which sociologists have made significant contributions include the Senate committees on poverty and on aging, and institutional research under independent and quasi-governmental sponsorship. In this latter category are the projects undertaken by the former Saskatchewan Centre for Community Studies at U Sask; by the Institute of Social and Economic Research at Memorial U; and by the Bureau d'aménagement de l'est du Québec at Laval.

As these examples show, much social research and planning in Canada has been conducted collectively under the auspices of government and university research institutes. Canada has also been the subject of significant research and writing by independent scholars. On the relationship between culture and environment and their effects on social and economic life in Québec, 2 pioneer studies were particularly important: Léon Gérin's *Le Type économique et social des canadiens* (1937) and Everett C. Hughes's *French Canada in Transition* (1943). French sociologist Marcel Giraud's *Le Métis canadien* (1947) remains the most comprehensive study of the Métis. S.D. Clark's *Church and Sect in Canada* (1948) was a major study of religious and political movements. American sociologist S.M. Lipset's *Agrarian Socialism* (1950) was a definitive study of the rise of the socialist movement and the rise of the CO-OPERATIVE COMMONWEALTH FEDERATION. John PORTER's *The Vertical Mosaic* (1965) challenged the conventional view of Canada as an egalitarian society. More than any other scholar of his time, Porter influenced the theoretical, empirical and critical directions of modern Canadian sociology. Many contemporary scholars have turned their attention to the effects of a resource-based economy on national and regional social organization. Rex Lucas's *Minetown, Milltown, Railtown* (1971) has influenced the direction of many of these studies.

Fields of Work Most of the professional sociologists in Canada have master's or doctoral degrees in the subject. Of course, not all who have taken advanced degrees in sociology are professional sociologists; many are employed as administrators, executives, entrepreneurs and in other capacities. Because precise figures are lacking, it is impossible to say how many people in Canada are working as professional sociologists, but it is safe to assume that the majority who do so are full-time university teachers. According to one report, the number of full-time university teachers of sociology in Canada for the 1979-80 academic year was 962. Perhaps scores of others teach full-time at the community-college level. The number of professional sociologists working in research in government and other public and private agencies has been estimated at about 400.

Until 1956, when the Sociology-Anthropology Chapter of the Canadian Political Science Association was formed, there was no national organization that brought sociologists together. A decade later, this chapter was transformed into an officially bilingual independent organization, the Canadian Sociology and Anthropology Association. Several affiliated regional associations represent sociologists in western Canada, Ontario, Québec and the Atlantic provinces. One of these, l'Association canadienne des sociologues et anthropologues de la langue française, caters especially to Francophones.

Sociologists in Canada publish their scholarly work within and outside Canada. Within Canada their articles are published primarily in 4 journals: the *Canadian Journal of Sociology; Canadian Review of Sociology and Anthropology; Récherches sociographiques;* and *Sociologie et sociétés.* Besides these outlets, the publications of sociologists often appear in such journals as *Cahiers québécois de démographie; Canadian Ethnic Studies; Canadian Journal of Criminology; Canadian Studies in Population; Canadian Women's Studies;* and *Studies in Political Economy,* to mention a few.

DONALD R. WHYTE AND FRANK G. VALLEE

Reading: Donald Whyte, "Sociology and the Nationalist Challenge in Canada," *Journal of Canadian Studies* 19, 4 (1984-85).

Sod Houses, built primarily before WWI in the PRAIRIE WEST, where sod was the only construction material at hand. Sod buildings were inexpensive, the only cost being for windows, hinges and perhaps boards for a door and framing. First, long, straight furrows generally 30-40 cm wide were ploughed, preferably in dry sloughs since fibrous grass roots there prevented soil from crumbling. Sods, some 10 cm deep, were cut into 60-80 cm lengths. Placed grass-side down they were used like bricks, usually with 2 courses side by side making thick, tight walls. Spaces were left for the door and windows. For the roof, boards or light poplar poles, extending from the side walls to a ridge pole, were covered with hay, then with a layer of thinner sod. The average house was 18' by 24' (5.5 by 7.3 m), the minimum size required under HOMESTEADING law. The interior walls might be covered by paper or cloth, or plastered with a clay mixture and whitewashed. Houses were often partitioned with blankets or poles; many women, by using curtains and other touches, made their sod houses attractive and homey. Unfortunately, sod roofs leaked; one day's rain outside resulted in 2 inside. However, sod houses were warm in winter and cool in summer, and served their purpose well. SHEILAGH S. JAMESON

Reading: T.B. Dennis, *Albertans Built* (1986).

Soft-Drink Industry comprises companies that manufacture nonalcoholic beverages and carbonated mineral waters or concentrates and syrups for the manufacture of carbonated beverages. Naturally occurring bubbling or sparkling mineral waters have been popular for thousands of years: the ancient Greeks believed that such waters had medicinal properties and bathed in them regularly; the Romans established resorts around mineral springs throughout Europe. In the 1500s the village of Spa in Belgium became famous for its waters, which by the early 1600s were sold, in bottles, as far away as London, Eng.

Development of the first man-made sparkling or carbonated water is credited to Joseph Priestley, the British scientist who discovered oxygen. In 1772 he invented a method of "pushing" carbon dioxide into water by dissolving it under pressure, thus creating fairly long-lasting bubbles. The technique led to development of the soft-drink industry. By the beginning of the 19th century, carbonated water was being made commercially in France and N America; shortly thereafter, flavours (normally fruit concentrates) were added to enliven the taste. In the 1820s, small carbonated bottling operations were established in Canada, producing carbonated drinks in refillable bottles which were merchandised as medicinal elixirs or tonics. Most soft drinks are still carbonated to give drinks a "tangy bite" and to stimulate the tongue. Furthermore, because scent is an important part of taste, the flavours carried as vapours in the bubbles enhance taste.

The principle of "pushing" carbon dioxide is still used, but now the water is first purified in a process known as "polishing." Cooled carbon dioxide is then injected at pressures of 275-550 kilopascals. Some of the early drinks bottled in Canada were called Birch Beer, Ginger Beer, Sarsaparilla, Sour Lemon, None-Such Soda Water and Cream Soda. The first carbonated beverage or "pop" bottles were sealed with corks held tightly in place with a wire binding. Because they had to be stored neck down so that the cork would not dry and allow the carbonation to leak away, they were manufactured with rounded bottoms. By the mid-1800s, soft drinks sold in Canada were packaged in 8-ounce (227.2 ml) round-bottom bottles for about 25 cents a dozen, except ginger beer, which was sold in draught form from wooden kegs. Wired cork closures were used until about 1884 with Codd's Patented Globe Stoppers (25 types in all). Such closures were replaced by the Hutcheson Spring Stopper. The crown cap was introduced around 1905 and improved versions are still widely used, although they are gradually being replaced, especially on larger containers, with reclosable screw caps.

Other packaging innovations since the mid-1960s include canned carbonated beverages, nonreturnable glass bottles and containers made from rigid plastics. However, an effort is being made, often through provincial legislation, to increase the use of returnable glass containers.

In the industry's early years the number of carbonated-beverage plants increased steadily, most serving small regional markets. In 1929 the industry was made up of 345 production plants and the value of shipments reached $12.3 million. By 1960 the number of plants had increased to 502 and the value of sales to $172.7 million. Subsequently, consolidation began, prompted by improved production, packaging and distribution facilities. By 1973, 337 plants were in production and the value of shipments was $484 million. In 1985, with sales of about $1.8 billion, the industry had 187 plants in production: Nfld had 3; PEI, 1; NS, 7; NB, 8; Qué, 66; Ont, 58; Man, 7; Sask, 10; Alta, 13; and BC, 14. Production volume has also increased dramatically: in 1939, soft-drink bottlers produced about 162 million litres of carbonated beverages; by 1967, production passed 758 million litres; in 1986, shipments were estimated at over 2.1 billion litres.

The industry is regulated by both federal and provincial agencies, 3 of the most important being Consumer and Corporate Affairs (responsible for the Consumer Packaging and Labelling Act), Health and Welfare Canada (which administers the Food and Drugs Act) and Environment Canada (which focuses on environmental matters). The industry is represented by the Canadian Soft Drink Association in Toronto and by several provincial associations.

The introduction of diet carbonated beverages has changed the industry's profile. Several years ago, in response to increasing consumer diet consciousness, the industry introduced the first successful sugar-free diet drinks using the artificial sweetener cyclamate. But questions were raised about the safety of this additive and, based on existing scientific data, Health and Welfare Canada banned its use in Canadian commercial FOODS AND BEVERAGES. This decision, estimated to have cost the industry more than $15 million, was a setback to diet-drink development. The industry turned to saccharin, but this too was eventually banned. Now, a new sugar-free additive, aspartame, has been approved for use in diet soft drinks, and the cyclamate/saccharin situation is not expected to recur because aspartame consists of amino acids, which occur naturally. Aspartame-sweetened diet drinks have had a dramatic effect on the Canadian carbonated-beverage industry. Just before the saccharin ban in 1977, diet drinks accounted for about 10% of the soft-drink market; following the ban the diet share dropped to about 2%, con-sisting of beverages partially sweetened with small amounts of sugar. In 1982, the first full year that aspartame was used in Canada, diet drinks increased by 15.2% of total soft-drink sales, while the total soft-drink industry grew 8%. In 1987 total soft-drink sales increased 5.3% over 1986, while diet soft-drink sales increased by 10.7%. This single development has encouraged strong growth in the industry. ROBERT F. BARRATT

Softball, *see* BASEBALL.

Softwood Lumber Dispute first arose in 1982 with a complaint by the US lumber industry that low Canadian stumpage rates constituted an unfair advantage. In Canada, provinces own most of the forest resource and administer the rates whereas in the US rates are set at an auction. The US Commerce Dept turned down the application for countervailing duties in 1983, but by 1985 the Canadian industry had captured more than one-third of the US market. In June 1985, US producers set up the Coalition for Fair Lumber Imports, lobbied Washington again and sought redress through the Int Trade Commission (ITC).

Negotiations between Canada and the US began in Jan 1986, with added pressure from US President Ronald Reagan, who promised to take action on the US producers' behalf if bilateral negotiations failed. On 19 May 1986 the Coalition filed a countervail petition seeking an import duty of 27%. On June 26 the ITC determined that Canadian policies had injured US producers. Meanwhile, Prem William VANDER ZALM of BC stunned the Canadian producers by declaring that stumpage rates were too low, in effect admitting the validity of the US complaint. In Sept, Trade Minister Pat CARNEY offered concessions amounting to a 10% increase. Meanwhile, the US Commerce Dept handed down a decision imposing a 15% duty. Canadians then undertook to avoid the duty by a "suspension agreement" by which the amount of any subsidy alleged by the US could be kept in Canada; however, the US would have considerable control over how the penalty would be imposed. BC and Québec supported the suspension. The result was an agreement, signed 30 Dec 1986, in which Canada agreed to impose a tax of 15% – amounting to $600 million a year – on Canadian softwood exports to the US. It was the largest self-imposed penalty in the history of world trade.

The case underscored the problems Canada faces in trade negotiations with the US (*see* FREE TRADE). Federal positions can easily undercut the provinces. Canadian producers argued that their success was the result of efficiency and good management, and that they were being victimized in the negotiations. Canadian reactions were a turmoil of fear at the American actions, outrage at the threat to Canadian sovereignty, and pessimism over the ability of federal representatives to negotiate in the face of provincial willingness to capitulate. In late 1987 the federal government reached agreements with BC and Québec whereby higher provincial stumpage charges were to be substituted for the 15% federal export tax on softwood lumber originating in these provinces.

Soil, upper, unconsolidated, usually weathered layer of planet Earth. Seldom more than a metre thick, soils constitute a skin on Earth resembling, in relative thickness, a paper cover on a beach ball. Soils influence air and water quality and are the basis for most food and fibre production. Linking cycles of nutrients with the hydrologic cycle, soils are central to all terrestrial ecosystems. Unlike other parts of the solid Earth, soil is characterized by life: most energy trapped in terrestrial ecosystems is dissipated by organisms forming part of soil. Soils form over many centuries and are often destroyed in just decades.

Soil Classification Classification involves arranging individual units with similar characteristics into groups. Soil classification contributes to organizing and communicating information about soils and to showing relationships among soils and environments. It also provides a means for showing on maps the varieties of soils within the landscape.

The land area of Canada (excluding inland waters) is approximately 9 180 000 km², of which about 1 375 000 km² (15%) is rock land. The remainder is classified according to the Canadian system of soil classification, which groups soils into sets of classes at 5 levels or categories, ie, from most general to most specific: order, great group, subgroup, family, series. There are 9 orders, several thousand series. Thus the system makes it possible to consider soils in different degrees of detail. The classes are defined as specifically as possible to permit uniformity of classification. Limits between classes are arbitrary as there are few sharp divisions of the soil continuum in nature. The classification system will change as soil knowledge grows through soil mapping and research in Canada and elsewhere. It is hoped that ultimately all national systems will give way to an international one.

Order The 9 classes in this category are based on properties of the pedon, reflecting major soil environment factors (especially climatic factors) and dominant soil-forming processes.

Great Group classes are formed by subdividing order classes on the basis of soil properties that reflect differences in soil-forming processes (eg, kinds and amounts of organic matter in surface soil horizons).

Subgroup classes are formed by subdividing great group classes according to the kinds of horizons present in the pedon, and their arrangement.

Family classes are formed by subdividing subgroup classes on the basis of parent material characteristics (eg, proportions of SAND and CLAY) and soil temperature and moisture regimes.

Series classes are formed by subdividing family classes according to detailed properties of the pedon (eg, horizon thickness and structure).

Orders and Great Groups

The orders are discussed according to the sequence followed in classifying a pedon.

Cryosolic Order includes soils having PERMA-FROST (permanently frozen material) within one metre of the surface (2 m if the soil is strongly cryoturbated, ie, disturbed by frost action). As permafrost is a barrier to roots and water, the active layer (seasonally thawed material) above it may become a saturated, semifluid material in spring. Commonly the permafrost layer near the surface contains abundant ICE. Melting of ice and frozen materials, resulting from disturbance of the surface vegetation (boreal forest or TUNDRA), may cause slumping of the soil and disruption of roads, pipelines and buildings. Cryosolic soils, occupying about 3 672 000 km² (about 40%) of Canada's land area, are dominant in much of the YT and the NWT and occur in northern areas of all but the Atlantic provinces.

The order, containing 3 great groups, was defined in 1973, after soil and terrain surveys in the Mackenzie Valley yielded new knowledge about the properties, genesis and significance of these soils. Turbic Cryosols have a patterned surface (hummocks, stone nets, etc) and mixed horizons or other evidence of cryoturbation (*see* PERI-GLACIAL LANDFORMS). Static Cryosols lack marked evidence of cryoturbation; they are associated with sandy or gravelly materials. Organic Cryosols are composed dominantly of organic materials (eg, PEAT). Because organic material acts as an insulator, Organic Cryosols occur farther S than the boundary of continuous permafrost.

Organic Order soils are composed predominantly of organic matter in the upper half metre (over 30% organic matter by weight) and do not have permafrost near the surface. They are the major soils of peatlands (eg, SWAMP, bog, fen). Most organic soils develop by the accumulation of plant materials from species that grow well in areas usually saturated with water. Some organic soils are composed largely of plant materials deposited in lakes; others, mainly of forest leaf litter on rocky slopes in areas of high rainfall. Organic soils cover almost 374 000 km² (4.1%) of Canada's land area: large areas occur in Manitoba, Ontario and northern Alberta, smaller areas in humid regions of Canada.

Organic soils are subdivided into 4 great groups. Fibrisols, common in Canada, consist predominantly of relatively undecomposed organic material with clearly visible plant fragments; resistant fibres account for over 40% by volume. Most soils derived from *Sphagnum* mosses are Fibrisols. Mesisols are more highly decomposed and contain less fibrous material than Fibrisols (10-40% by volume). Humisols consist mainly of humified organic materials and may contain up to 10% fibre by volume. Folisols consist mainly of thick deposits of forest litter overlying bedrock or fractured bedrock. They occur commonly in wet mountainous areas of coastal British Columbia.

Podzolic Order soils have a B horizon containing accumulations of amorphous materials composed of humified organic matter associated with aluminum and iron. They develop most commonly in sandy materials in areas of cold, humid climate under forest or shrub vegetation. Water moving downward through the relatively porous material leaches out basic elements (eg, calcium), and acidic conditions develop. Soluble organic substances formed by decomposition of the forest litter attack soil minerals in surface horizons, and much of the iron and aluminum released combines with this organic material. When the proportion of aluminum and iron to organic matter reaches a certain level, the organic complexes become insoluble and are deposited in the B horizon. Silicon-aluminum complexes and iron oxides also occur. An Ae (light grey, strongly leached) horizon usually overlies the podzolic B horizon.

Podzolic soils occupy about 1 429 000 km² (15.6%) of Canada's land area and are dominant in vast areas of the humid Appalachian and Canadian Shield regions and in the humid coastal region of BC. They are divided among 3 great groups on the basis of the kind of podzolic B horizon. Humic Podzols have a dark B horizon with a low iron content. They occur mainly in wet sites under humid climates and are much less common than other Podzolic soils. Ferro-Humic Podzols have a dark reddish brown or black B horizon containing at least 5% organic carbon and appreciable amounts (often 2% or more) of aluminum and iron in organic complexes. They occur commonly in the more humid parts of the area of Podzolic soils, eg, coastal BC and parts of Newfoundland and southern Québec. Humo-Ferric Podzols, the most common Podzolic soils in Canada, have a reddish brown B horizon containing less than 5% organic carbon associated with aluminum and iron complexes.

Gleysolic Order soils are periodically or permanently saturated with water and depleted of oxygen. They occur commonly in shallow depressions and level areas of subhumid and humid climate in association with other classes of soil on slopes and hills. After snowmelt or heavy rains, depressions in the landscape may be flooded. If flooding occurs when the soil temperature is above approximately 5°C, microbial activity results in depletion of oxygen within a few days. Under such conditions, oxidized soil components (eg, nitrate, ferric oxide) are reduced. Depletion of ferric oxide removes the brownish colour of many soils, leaving them grey. As the soil dries and oxygen re-enters, the reduced iron may be oxidized locally to bright yellow-brown spots (mottles). Thus, Gleysolic soils are usually identified by their poor drainage and drab grey colour, sometimes accompanied by brown mottles. Gleysolic soils cover about 117 000 km² (1.3%) of Canada's land area.

Three great groups of Gleysolic soils are defined. Humic Gleysols have a dark A horizon enriched in organic matter. Gleysols lack such a horizon. Luvic Gleysols have a leached (Ae) horizon underlain by a B horizon in which the clay has accumulated; they may have a dark surface horizon.

Solonetzic Order soils have B horizons that are very hard when dry, swelling to a sticky, compact mass when wet. They usually develop in saline parent materials in semiarid and subhumid regions. Properties of the B horizons are associated with sodium ions that cause the clay to disperse readily and swell on wetting, thus closing the large pores and preventing water flow. Solonetzic soils cover almost 73 000 km² (0.7%) of Canada's land area; most occur in southern Alberta, because of the large areas of saline parent material and semiarid climate.

The 3 great groups of Solonetzic soils are based on properties reflecting the degree of leaching. Solonetz have an Ah (dark, organically enriched) horizon overlying the solonetzic B, which occurs usually at a depth of 20 cm or less. The Ae (grey, leached) horizon is very thin or absent. Solodized Solonetz have a distinct Ae horizon between the Ah and the solonetzic B. Solods have a transitional AB or BA horizon formed by degradation of the upper part of the solonetzic B horizon. The developmental sequence of Solonetzic soils is from saline parent material to Solonetz, Solodized Solonetz and Solod. As leaching progresses, the salts and sodium ions may be translocated downward. If leaching proceeds for long enough and salts are removed completely, the solonetzic B may disintegrate completely. The soil would then be classified in another order.

Chernozemic Order soils have an A horizon darkened by the addition of organic matter, usually from the decay of grass roots. The A horizon is neutral to slightly acid and is well supplied with bases such as calcium. The C horizon usually contains calcium carbonate (lime); it may contain salts. Chernozemic soils have mean annual soil temperatures above 0°C and occur in regions of semiarid and subhumid climates. Covering about 468 000 km² (5.1%) of Canada's land area, they are the major class of soils in the southern Interior Plains, where grass was the major type of native vegetation.

The 4 great groups of Chernozemic soils are based upon surface horizon colour, associated with the relative dryness of the soil. Brown soils have brownish A horizons and occur in the driest area of the Chernozemic region. Dark Brown soils have a darker A horizon than Brown soils, reflecting a somewhat higher precipitation and associated higher organic-matter content. Black soils, associated with subhumid climates and tall-grass native vegetation, have a black A horizon which is usually thicker than that of Brown or Dark Brown soils. Dark Gray soils are transitional between grassland Chernozemic soils and the more strongly leached soils of forested regions.

Luvisolic Order soils have eluvial horizons (ie, from which clay has been leached after snowmelt

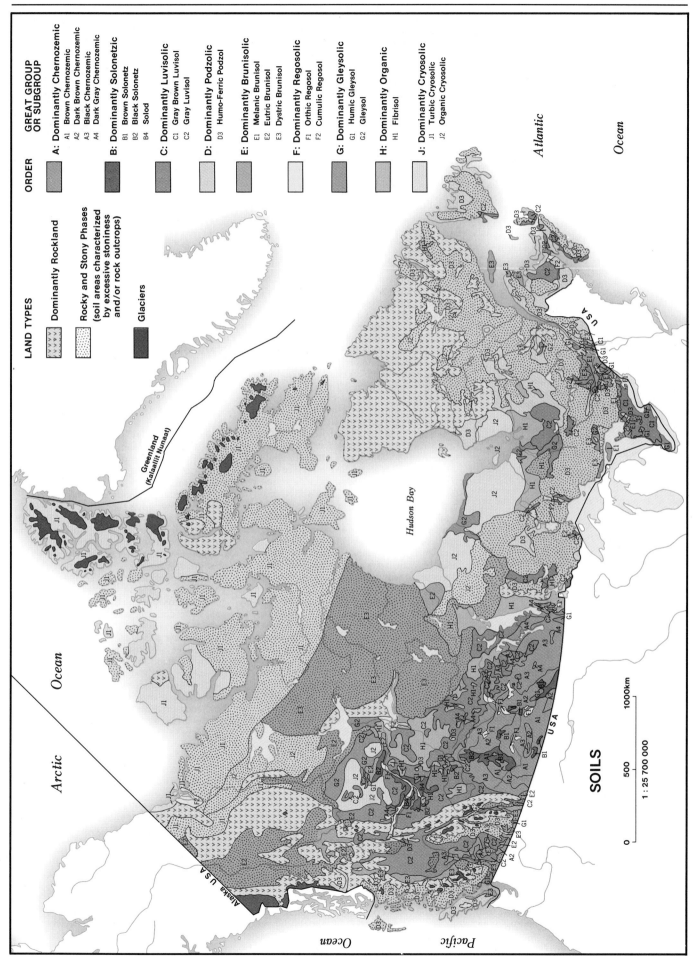

LAND TYPES

Dominantly Rockland

Rocky and Stony Phases
(soil areas characterized
by excessive stoniness
and/or rock outcrops)

Glaciers

ORDER

GREAT GROUP
OR SUBGROUP

A: Dominantly Chernozemic
A1 Brown Chernozemic
A2 Dark Brown Chernozemic
A3 Black Chernozemic
A4 Dark Gray Chernozemic

B: Dominantly Solonetzic
B1 Brown Solonetz
B2 Black Solonetz
B4 Solod

C: Dominantly Luvisolic
C1 Gray Brown Luvisol
C2 Gray Luvisol

D: Dominantly Podzolic
D3 Humo-Ferric Podzol

E: Dominantly Brunisolic
E1 Melanic Brunisol
E2 Eutric Brunisol
E3 Dystric Brunisol

F: Dominantly Regosolic
F1 Orthic Regosol
F2 Cumulic Regosol

G: Dominantly Gleysolic
G1 Humic Gleysol
G2 Gleysol

H: Dominantly Organic
H1 Fibrisol

J: Dominantly Cryosolic
J1 Turbic Cryosolic
J2 Organic Cryosolic

Arctic   Ocean

Greenland
(Kalaallit Nunaat)

Alaska U.S.A

Atlantic   Ocean

Hudson Bay

U.S.A

U.S.A

Pacific   Ocean

SOILS

1 : 25 700 000

0   500   1000 km

or heavy rains) and illuvial horizons (ie, in which clay has been deposited), designated Ae and Bt, respectively. In saline or calcareous materials clay translocation is preceded by leaching of salts and carbonates. Luvisolic soils occur typically in forested areas of subhumid to humid climate where the parent materials contain appreciable clay. Luvisolic soils cover about 809 000 km² (8.8%) of Canada's land area: large areas occur in the central to northern Interior Plains; smaller areas in all regions S of the permafrost zone.

The 2 great groups of Luvisolic soils are distinguished mainly on the basis of soil temperature. Gray Brown Luvisols have an Ah horizon in which organic matter has been mixed with the mineral material (commonly by earthworm activity), an eluvial (Ae) horizon and an illuvial (Bt) horizon. The mean annual soil temperature is 8°C or higher. The major area of Gray Brown Luvisols is found in the southern part of the Great Lakes-St Lawrence Lowlands. Gray Luvisols have eluvial and illuvial horizons and may have an Ah horizon if the mean annual soil temperature is below 8°C. Vast areas of Gray Luvisols in the Boreal Forest Zone of the Interior Plains have thick, light grey eluvial horizons underlying the forest litter and thick Bt horizons with clay coating the surface of aggregates.

Brunisolic Order soils include all soils that have developed B horizons but do not conform to any of the orders described previously. Many Brunisolic soils have brownish B horizons without much evidence of clay accumulation, as in Luvisolic soils, or of amorphous materials, as in Podzolic soils. With time and stable environmental conditions, some Brunisolic soils will evolve to Luvisolic soils; others, to Podzolic soils. Covering almost 790 000 km² (8.6%) of Canada's land area, Brunisolic soils occur in association with other soils in all regions S of the permafrost zone.

Four great groups are distinguished on the basis of organic matter enrichment in the A horizon and acidity. Melanic Brunisols have an Ah horizon at least 10 cm thick; they are not strongly acidic, their pH being above 5.5. They occur commonly in southern Ontario and Québec. Eutric Brunisols have the same basic properties as Melanic Brunisols, but do not have an Ah horizon 10 cm thick. Sombric Brunisols have an Ah horizon at least 10 cm thick and are acid, with pH below 5.5. Dystric Brunisols are acidic and do not have an Ah horizon 10 cm thick.

Regosolic Order soils are too weakly developed to meet the limits of any other order. The absence or weak development of genetic horizons may result from a lack of time for development or from instability of material. The properties of Regosolic soils are essentially those of the parent material. Two great groups are defined. Regosols consist essentially of C horizons; they may have an Ah horizon less than 10 cm thick. Humic Regosols have an Ah horizon at least 10 cm thick. Regosolic soils cover about 73 000 km² (0.8%) of Canada's land area.

Subgroups, Families and Series

Subgroups are based on the sequence of horizons; many subgroups intergrade to other soil orders. For example, the Gray Luvisol great group includes 12 subgroups, of which the Orthic Gray Luvisol is most typical, the others being defined by additional features. Transitional Gray Luvisols are also defined, eg, Gleyed Gray Luvisol, with rusty mottles indicating an intergrade to Gleysolic soils.

Families Subgroups are divided into families according to parent material properties and soil climate. For example, the Orthic Gray Luvisol subgroup includes soils of a wide range of texture (gravelly sandy loam to clay), different mineralogy and different temperature and water regimes. The soil family designation is much more specific, eg, Orthic Gray Luvisol, clayey, mixed (mineralogy), cold, subhumid.

Series have a vast array of properties (eg, horizon thickness and colour, gravel content, structure) that fall within narrow ranges. Thus, for example, the series name Breton implies all the basic properties of the Luvisolic order, the Gray Luvisol great group, the Orthic Gray Luvisol subgroup and the clayey, mixed, cold, subhumid family of that subgroup as well as series-specific properties. A series name implies so much specific information about soil properties that a wide range of interpretations can be made on the probable suitability of the soil for various uses.

J.A. McKeague

When unprotected, soils, crops and homesteads alike may suffer much damage from the ravages of wind (*courtesy Charles S. Baldwin/Ontario Ministry of Agriculture and Food*).

Soil Conservation The agricultural industry of Canada is perhaps the only resource-based industry that can be guaranteed to continue its dominant and indispensable role in the economy of the country provided the quality of the resource base on which it is dependent, the soils, can be maintained. In 1981 for example, Canada's agricultural trade surplus was $3.2 billion, or 151% of the nonagricultural trade surplus. In 1986, the agricultural trade surplus was $1.87 billion (down from $4.3 billion in 1983 and $2.9 billion in 1985). This surplus provides an essential support for the Canadian dollar so indispensable in our trade relations around the world.

One in 5 Canadian jobs is based in agriculture. The AGRICULTURAL FOOD POLICY in Canada has made the provision of cheap food for all a high priority, and Canadians have continued to enjoy the world's cheapest food supplies. This is not fortuitous or an accident of fate but a direct result of agricultural policy and a highly efficient agricultural industry. Canadians in general take the accomplishments of the agricultural sector for granted; regrettably the efficiency of the agricultural industry has in part resulted from cultural practices which are known to result in rapid degradation of the agricultural soils.

Two recent but sobering studies, *Soil at Risk* (Sparrow, 1984) and *Will the Bounty End* (1984), have concluded that the limited soil resource on which Canada's agricultural industry is so dependent is being destroyed by the combined impacts of poor husbandry and agricultural policies which perpetuate the use of soil-degrading farm practices. The latter book drew upon the vast knowledge and expertise of the Agriculture Institute of Canada and the Canadian Society of Soil Science. The former was a product of a series of public hearings across Canada and meetings with leading agricultural scientists. Although both have been criticized for what is termed exaggerating the degradation that has occurred in the agricultural soils, they are a must for everyone even remotely interested in soil conservation.

Western Canada

For almost a century farmers in the brown, dark brown and black soil zones of the Prairie Provinces have followed an amazingly simple cereal fallow rotation. The fallow, which in many cases appeared in a rotation every other year, has given a measure of weed control and has caught a limited amount of total precipitation during the 20-month fallow period (5 - 25% of the total precipitation). However, its main benefit has been to accelerate mineralization of nutrients bound up in the soil humus, primarily nitrogen. It was not unusual for fallow soils to contain in the 0-60 cm sod depth from 100-150 kg N/ha. However, this simple cropping system has resulted in rapid soil degradation which has led in some cases to a dramatic decline in soil quality.

Erosion As might be expected, the incidence of wind erosion in the agricultural regions of BC is insignificant. However, water erosion is serious in the Peace Region, medium in the mainland areas of the province, and relatively low elsewhere.

Wind erosion has been the dominant process responsible for the decline in soil quality in the drier regions of the Prairie Provinces. It has been a major concern in the Palliser Triangle region since the 1920s and has resulted in extensive areas suffering total loss of topsoil. The incidence of wind erosion, after being quiescent for a number of years, has increased sharply in the 1980s. The severity of water erosion throughout the prairies has been increasing rapidly; perhaps as a consequence of the decline in the stability of the surface soil structure.

In the prairie region, the popular practice of summerfallowing has been identified as a major cause of both wind and water erosion. While precise estimates of the amount of topsoil loss that has occurred are not available, recent information has shown that over a relatively large region of Saskatchewan, there are major differences in amount of topsoil lost within very short distances. These data, in general, confirm the visual evidence of erosion, which is so dramatic on the knolls and not evident at all in the lower slope positions.

Salinization Salinization is a process that is much easier for the casual observer to recognize, because it results in a whitish, "salty" colour of the surface soil and can dramatically reduce yields. Salts in productive agricultural soils have spread at an alarming rate in Alberta and Saskatchewan in particular. Saline soils are a product of semi- arid and arid climates where evaporation exceeds precipitation. There were extensive areas of salt-affected soils in the prairie region prior to settlement of the West. Recent estimates of new or "man-made" salinity in Alberta and Saskatchewan total 1.67 million kg/ha/yr. A very much smaller area of salt-affected soils is under cultivation in Manitoba, and the majority of this area is considered to have developed owing to natural salinization processes. In contrast, the incidence of salinity in the agriculturally developed soils of BC is essentially nonexistent.

Organic Matter Organic matter depletion has occurred almost universally in BC, Alberta and Saskatchewan, but to a very much lesser extent in Manitoba. The rapid rate at which organic matter has disappeared is largely owing to intensive tillage and, of course, to erosion. Depletion of organic matter is directly accompanied by a sharp drop in nitrogen mineralization. To the farmer, this drastic change means that the soils which for so long fully met the nitrogen requirements of his crop are no longer capable of doing it. He then is faced with the purchase of large amounts of fertilizer nitrogen in order to maintain economic yields.

Acidification, owing to the use of nitrogen and phosphorous fertilizers and ACID RAIN, is customarily expressed by the amount of calcium carbonate required to neutralize the acids formed. Acidification is most serious in the Fraser Valley, the Lower Mainland and on Vancouver I, BC. In the prairies, it is primarily restricted to the Gray Luvisolic, Gray Brown, Black Chernozemic and Solonetzic soils. It can be estimated that the acidity derived from the mineralization of soil organic nitrogen in Saskatchewan, in particular, has been several times more significant than fertilizer nitrogen. However, the well-buffered soils have not experienced any measurable decrease in soil pH.

Drainage and Compaction The 2 remaining degradation processes, drainage, and compaction and subsidence, are primarily of significance in BC. In that province, the areas of glysolic and organic soils under cultivation are, on a relative basis, significant. A typical example is the high-productivity soils found in the flood plain and delta of the Fraser R.

Controlled drainage plays a major role in the subsidence of organic soils; as the organic soils subside, bulk density increases and drainage problems are accelerated because porosity and water movement decrease.

Although poorly drained glysolic soils are not "man-made," drainage is still considered a degradation process and one that can be overcome with the installation of tile drains. This is accompanied by a major increase in yield of food crops.

Costs of Soil Degradation On the basis of present information and local expertise, the annual costs of soil degradation in BC, Alberta, Saskatchewan and Manitoba amount to $45.9 million, $429.2 million, $560 million and $43.7 million, respectively. All indices generally agree that degradation has been accelerated in recent years. These values clearly support G.L. Fairbairn's observation that the wealth of agriculture, and the long-enjoyed cheap food policy, has been built on lost soil.

Eastern Canada

The perception of soil degradation in eastern Canada ranges from those who insist it is not sufficiently severe to be of concern to the agricultural industry through those who argue that from an economic viewpoint, the current degree of degradation can be categorized as a near crisis situation. Notwithstanding differing views on the impact of soil degradation, there is general unanimity that the main degradation processes are erosion, compaction, loss of organic matter and acidification.

Many of the advances in agricultural productivity in central Canada during the past 25 years have accelerated soil degradation. One of the major causes is the increase in row-crop production, which has taken place largely at the expense of spring cereals and hay. The trend is almost identical in both Ontario and Québec, and it has resulted in a 4.7-fold increase in area seeded to corn between 1961 and 1981. This increase has been accompanied by a 43% and 25% decrease in acreage of spring cereals and hay, respectively. The introduction in recent years of short-season corn hybrids has been a major stimuli for these changes. While the profitability of agriculture in the regions suitable for corn has increased, and the agricultural economy of eastern Canada in general has benefited, these have been associated with serious soil degradation.

Erosion and soil loss from spring runoff (*courtesy K.D. Switzer-Howse/Agriculture Canada*).

Increased corn production has been accompanied by a general decrease in livestock numbers, which in turn has resulted in a further decrease in demand for hay and pasture. The decreased livestock population means a reduction in the amount of manure returned to the land. Decreased manure combined with reduced area devoted to hay and pasture, and increased intensity of cultivation associated with corn, have led directly to reduced organic matter content in the soil and increased risk of erosion and compaction. Corn has a high requirement for nitrogen, and in the absence of manure use or legume production, acidification has been increased.

Associated with the above change has been a trend towards larger farm operations. The concomitant increase in machinery size and demand on operator's time has resulted in tillage under other than ideal soil moisture conditions, the direct result of which has been increased production problems associated with compaction.

The increase in row-crop production in Atlantic Canada has not been so marked. While corn production has increased rather markedly, the area involved is still small relative to the main row-crop, potatoes. The area devoted to potatoes has not increased greatly, but the topographic conditions on which this is produced are very conducive to erosion.

Erosion The most serious degradation problem in Ontario and the Atlantic provinces is erosion. Water erosion is the dominant component, although wind erosion is significant on certain selected soils such as the light- textured sandy soils of PEI, the organic soils in Québec and selected sandy soils in Ontario.

Compaction Large areas of fine textured soils in the ST LAWRENCE LOWLANDS are affected and this is the prime reason why soil compaction is considered the dominant degradation problem in Québec. Compaction ranks second in importance in Ontario and third in Atlantic Canada. There are, however, many soils in eastern Canada with naturally compact subsoils which restrict drainage and which limit root penetration. It is frequently difficult to separate this natural compaction from that caused by excessive tillage or tillage when the soil is most vulnerable.

Soil Organic Matter Although not well docu-

mented, decreases in organic matter levels in the vicinity of 30% are considered typical, even under ideal conditions such as where cereals are in rotation with hay crops.

Further sharp declines occur with more intensive cultivation associated with row-crop production, and such declines are associated with a reduction of nutrient supplying power and, hence, fertilizer input needs are increased. Notwithstanding this, the major impact throughout eastern Canada is deterioration of soil structure and increased erosion which is associated with a decline in soil organic matter.

Acidification Eastern Canadian soils are naturally acid, particularly in Atlantic Canada and Québec. The major "man-made" causes of soil acidification are acid rain and fertilizer use, particularly nitrogen. These effects are much more severe on the naturally acid soils with a lower buffering capacity. It has been estimated that it would require 30, 35 and 33 kg/ha/yr calcium carbonate to neutralize the acidity caused by acid rain in the Atlantic provinces, Québec, and Ontario respectively. The acidity resulting from the application of nitrogen fertilizers would require an average of 80, 151 and 90 kg/ha/yr for the respective regions.

Costs of Soil Degradation Annual costs of soil degradation in Ontario, Québec and Atlantic Canada have been estimated at $90 million, $114 million and $23 million, respectively. These estimates do not include the impact of soil degradation on the surrounding environment which in many ways is much more difficult to determine, partly because of the diffuse nature of the impact but also because of the subjectivity. Notwithstanding these restraints, the recent increase in funding for soil conservation in Ontario is reportedly because, at least in part, of the need to reduce phosphorus input to Lake Erie from agricultural lands.

Soil Conservation Technology

Most of the impressive gains in soil conservation technology have occurred in the area of land management. Preliminary information suggests that it is now technically possible to improve most Canadian agricultural land through cropping systems uniquely adapted to local conditions and through fertilization, timely cultivation, use of improved tillage practices and equipment, terracing, land levelling, drainage, etc. Soil erosion can be held to acceptable levels or, in some cases, reduced to zero. These practices may even lead to an improvement in soil quality.

The obstacles that impede adoption of "conservation farming" are not restricted to a lack of capital. Extensive educational programs are required to enable farmers to benefit from new tools and techniques, and enable agricultural policymakers to establish a socioeconomic environment offering incentives for efficient production. For example, in western Canada, newer, water-efficient soil-conserving farming systems will lead to levels of production ranging from 75% to 100% or more above present levels.

Conservation Legislation

There are many Acts and regulations relating to soil and water conservation in Canada, but few directly address the loss of soil or productivity through erosion or degradation. Those that impinge directly on soil erosion were developed primarily to support farm planning, conservation districts, land use, water resources, conservation and development, watersheds, drainage, irrigation, water rights and agricultural zoning. Federal Acts such as the Agricultural Land Rural Development Act and the Prairie Farm Rehabilitation Act address some aspects of soil conservation, particularly on the prairies. However, only the provinces can directly legislate the management or disposition of provincial land resources within their boundaries. Thus in Alberta the control and prevention of erosion and land degradation is embodied in the Soil Conservation Act and the Agricultural Services Board Act. Other provinces have similar legislation which encourages adoption of soil conservation practices and addresses the loss of soil and soil productivity through negligence and misuse. Many, but not all, such Acts embody the principle of ownership responsibility. In general, the major responsibility for land use planning, and particularly as it pertains to soil conservation, is left to the local (municipal) authority.

In Canada soil conservation has traditionally been subject to a laissez-faire policy from governments. All levels of government are responsible, but provincial governments undoubtedly bear the greatest responsibility. In many instances (eg, the Lift Program, 1970), government intervention encouraged practices leading to accelerated erosion, salinity and organic matter loss. While Canada is perhaps unique among developed nations in having no clearly defined soil conservation legislation, this deficiency cannot be criticized unduly since legislation inevitably is a reaction to the problem of soil degradation after it has become serious, rather than a means of addressing prevention before degradation occurs. Thus society's increasing concern for conservation of soils can best be met by providing research, extension education and financial incentive programs which will encourage, but not legislate, conservation farming. *See also* ENVIRONMENTAL LAW; HAZARDOUS WASTES; PRAIRIE FARM REHABILITATION ADMINISTRATION.   D.A. RENNIE

Reading: G.L. Fairbairn, *Will the Bounty End? The Uncertain Future of Canada's Food Supply* (1984); Lands Directorate, Environment Canada, *Stress on Land* (1983); H.O. Sparrow, *Soil at Risk* (1984).

Soil Science, the science that deals with soils as a natural RESOURCE. It studies soil formation, classification and mapping, and the physical, chemical and biological properties and fertility of soils as such and in relation to their management for CROP production. This definition, adopted by the Canadian Society of Soil Science, is somewhat dated. In the last 20 years, soil science has expanded to include the study of soil resources in relation to ecology, FORESTRY, Quaternary GEOLOGY, HYDROLOGY, watershed management, ENGINEERING, ARCHAEOLOGY, renewable RESOURCE MANAGEMENT and land-use planning. Biometeorology and REMOTE SENSING are very closely allied to soil science.

Soil has been studied scientifically for approximately 2 centuries. The major concepts were developed over the past 100 years, following the contributions of V.V. Dokuchaiev and others in Russia. These scientists demonstrated that soils are natural bodies, developing as a result of environmental factors. Two important concepts have emerged: pedology considers soil as a natural body, placing less emphasis on its immediate use; edaphology studies soil from the standpoint of higher plants. Pedologists study and classify soil as it occurs in the natural environment; edaphologists consider soil properties as they relate to food and fibre production.

History In Canada soil has been studied systematically for approximately 100 years. The first work, written by Dominion Chemist F.T. Shutt and published in 1893, originated from the Experimental Farms Service of the federal Department of Agriculture. During this early period, work on soils was begun at the Ontario Agricultural College (Department of Agricultural Chemistry; *see* UNIVERSITY OF GUELPH) and at Macdonald College, McGill (Department of Agricultural Physics). Soil surveying was initiated in 1914 by A.J. Galbraith of the OAC. F.A. Wyatt began soil-survey work in Alberta in 1920; R. Hansen in Saskatchewan 1921. Surveys began in BC in 1931; Qué and NS, 1934; NB, 1938; PEI, 1943; NWT, 1944; Nfld, following its entry into Confederation, 1949. The earliest surveys, financed by provincial governments, were conducted under co-operative programs among the federal and provincial departments of agriculture and the universities.

Many individuals contributed to the development of soil science in Canada, but its founders were professors F.A. Wyatt (Alta), A.H. Joel and R. Hansen (Sask), J.H. Ellis (Man) and G.N. Ruhnke (Ont). E.S. Archibald, director of the Dominion Experimental Farms Service, played an important role in reviving the soil survey in the 1930s.

Training Professional education is offered mainly through departments of soil science at the universities of BC, Alberta, Saskatchewan, Manitoba and Laval. In Ontario, U of Guelph offers the degree from the Dept of Land Resources science. In Québec, professional education is given at Macdonald College, McGill, by the Dept of Renewable Resources. In addition, universities which do not have departments specializing in soil science often have professors of soil science in departments of GEOGRAPHY.

Most universities offering soil-science programs award bachelors', masters' and doctoral degrees. Although there is some variation in the designation of specialization, some of the major areas of study include soil BIOLOGY, chemistry, physics and fertility; soil classification, genesis, mineralogy and conservation; land classification; and FOREST soils. Often specialization occurs only at the postgraduate level. Students require a background in biology, chemistry, mathematics and physics, and also study agronomy, botany, computer science, ecology, economics, English, geology, geomorphology, hydrology, land-use planning, meteorology, microbiology, mineralogy, photogrammetry, remote sensing, resource management, etc. Soil-science education is useful to botanists, plant scientists, and civil and agricultural engineers.

Research Research is carried out by various federal agencies, notably Agriculture Canada (through Land Resource Research Institute), ENVIRONMENT Canada, NATIONAL RESEARCH COUNCIL and Canadian Forestry Service. Some provincial departments of agriculture, notably those in Alberta and Ontario, also conduct research. In some provinces (eg, BC) departments of forestry are beginning to do research. University departments conduct research along with teaching. Private companies are supporting work in such areas as forestry, MINING and PETROLEUM resources. Mining and petroleum research also focuses on land reclamation.

Research concerned with SURVEYING, mapping and classification remains a joint effort of federal and provincial governments and universities. Several universities (eg, Alberta, Saskatchewan, Guelph, Laval) have established institutes of pedology to co-ordinate these activities. Much of the research conducted in Canada has international applications.

The early work carried out by the Dept of Soil Science, UBC, on organic matter decomposition led the country in soil microbiology. The U of Alberta's Dept of Soil Science carried out innovative research on the management and genesis of Gray Wooded (Gray Luvisol) soils. The use of radioactive isotopes in relation to soil fertility and phosphorus was pioneered at the U of Saskatchewan. Study of the effects of application of sewage sludge to soil was initiated at Guelph. Fundamental research on soil properties relating them to the physical behaviour of soils (eg, correlation of shear strength with the electrochemical properties of clays and forces involved in clay swelling) was carried out at the Macdonald College. Researchers from Agriculture Canada have taken a leading role in understanding the reclamation and management of solonetzic soils, and have pioneered studies of soil organic matter, its properties, its characteristics and its functions in the soil system. The Canada Soil Survey Committee, composed of federal and provincial scientists and university professors, has developed a soil-classification system and unique approaches to soil-survey and soil-information data banks. Québec researchers were in the forefront of farm drainage for intensive agriculture. Soil scientists from Atlantic Canada have developed management techniques for the important potato industry.

Agencies involved in soil research have developed testing procedures for better crop growth on Canadian soils. This process is endless as new varieties of crops, with different requirements, are steadily being developed or introduced into Canada. Research efforts focus on soil EROSION, salinity and conservation, and make use of remote sensing and computer-assisted laboratory and field techniques, computer-assisted information systems, and automatic graphic and cartographic displays.

Application Most soil research is applied to agriculture, especially to improving crop yields. Thus, much research has focused on the nutrients and trace elements essential for plant growth. Knowledge of soil properties has helped to develop irrigation and drainage projects, promote proper use of fertilizers and PESTICIDES and explain the effect that soil management has on the resource. The availability of soil surveys for much of the country allows planners to make choices, depending on the capability of soils, among agriculture, forestry, recreation and wildlife uses. Highway engineers are beginning to use soil surveys for siting roadways. Other engineers and planners use soil information for locating septic tank disposal fields, effluent irrigation, urban subdivisions, PIPELINE and TRANSPORTATION corridors and for regulating and predicting water supply. Regional planners make use of soil science in developing plans for municipalities and counties. Land appraisers must know soil productivity to make fair assessments of value. Soil properties and genesis are important in understanding terrestrial ecology and groundwater flow. Knowledge of soil genesis aids better understanding of the events that have taken place during the Quaternary, and soils hold the record of facts important in archaeology. Rangeland managers must take into account the productive potential of soil so that range deterioration will not accelerate. Increasingly, agencies involved with land restoration (eg, mining and petroleum exploration companies) are making use of soil-science principles. Soil scientists are employed by federal and provincial governments and consulting firms, forest companies, mining and petroleum companies, banks, real-estate firms and large corporate farms.

Societies and Institutions In Canada the recognized society fostering soil science is the Canadian Society of Soil Science. The CSSS was founded in 1955 from an earlier organization, the Soils Group, which had been formed in 1932 and was closely affiliated with the Canadian Society of Technical Agriculturists. Today the society has 506 members. The CSSS is affiliated with the Agricultural Institute of Canada (AIC), the

Canadian Geoscience Council and the International Society of Soil Science. The CSSS holds annual meetings and technical sessions and in collaboration with the Agricultural Institute of Canada publishes the quarterly *Canadian Journal of Soil Science.* The CSSS honours distinguished soil scientists by bestowing fellowships in the society. Over 35 fellowships have been awarded since 1962, when the program was initiated.

L.M. LAVKULICH

Sointula, BC, pop 692 (1986c), 567 (1981c), UP, is situated on the S shore of Malcolm I between Vancouver I and the BC mainland, in the Regional Dist of Mt Waddington. Sointula was started at the turn of the century as a utopian community by Finnish political refugee Mattii Kurikka (1862-1915). Sointula means "a place of harmony." The colony was to be an independent enterprise based on logging, fishing and agriculture. By 1902 there were 127 inhabitants, and a sawmill was in operation. But prosperity did not materialize and by 1905 the colony was liquidated. A community remained but its socialistic ideals were discontinued. Today, only a few descendants of the original settlers still live there. Once a totally Finnish-speaking community, Sointula is now mainly English speaking. A few buildings date back to the original settlement, including the "Finnish Order" hall, a firehall and a school. Since 1905 the majority of the population has engaged in fishing. A few small businesses exist on Malcolm I. Many artists also reside here.

ALAN F.J. ARTIBISE

Reading: A. Anderson, *History of Sointula* (1969).

Soirées canadiennes, Les, magazine fd 1861 by H.R. CASGRAIN, A. GÉRIN-LAJOIE, F.A.H. LaRue and J.C. Taché, which published assorted "collection[s] of national literature" in monthly instalments. *Les Soirées canadiennes* followed the spirit of James Huston's *Le Répertoire national* (1848-50) and welcomed all original writing as long as it was Canadien: legends, poetry, studies of society, novels (which were serialized), travel accounts, historical sketches, biographies, topographies, etc. It attracted such writers as P.J.O. CHAUVEAU, Octave CRÉMAZIE, J.B.A. Ferland, Louis-Honoré FRÉCHETTE, François-Xavier GARNEAU and Étienne PARENT. Five volumes appeared, 1861-65. A dispute with the printers in late 1862 provoked a break between Taché and the others, who quit *Les Soirées* to found an equivalent publication, *Le Foyer canadien.* It appeared until 1866, publishing 4 annual collections, 4 bonus volumes for subscribers and 5 other works, including *Les Anciens Canadiens* and *Mémoires* by Philippe AUBERT DE GASPÉ. The so-called "Literary Movement of 1860" revolved around *Soirées* and *Foyer.*

RÉJEAN ROBIDOUX

Solandt, Omond McKillop, research director (b at Winnipeg 2 Sept 1909). He studied at Toronto and began a research career in physiology under C.H. BEST before winning a scholarship to England for advanced training in 1939. When running a London blood bank in 1940 Solandt was asked to investigate why army tank crews were fainting in action. It turned out to be because, when the gun fired, its gases went back into the tank rather than outside. His success led to his becoming one of the chief British army advisers on scientific methods, and he became superintendent of the British Army Operational Research Group, with the rank of colonel.

In 1946 Solandt was recruited by the Canadian government to plan postwar military research, and he became in 1947 the founding chairman of the DEFENCE RESEARCH Board. He later was VP for research and development at CANADIAN NATIONAL RAILWAYS, 1956-63, at DE HAVILLAND AIRCRAFT,

1963-66, and he was chancellor of U of T, 1965-71. From 1966 to 1972, Solandt was chairman of the SCIENCE COUNCIL OF CANADA and thus one of the most influential voices in the SCIENCE POLICY debate of those years. His last annual report as chairman proposed the foundations of the CONSERVER SOCIETY movement. In retirement, Solandt remained active as a company director and consultant, specializing in agricultural research in a number of developing countries (eg, Peru, Kenya and Bangladesh). *See also* INDUSTRIAL RESEARCH AND DEVELOPMENT. DONALD J.C. PHILLIPSON

Solar Energy is electromagnetic radiation (including infrared, visible and ultraviolet light) released by thermonuclear reactions in the core of the sun. With a few exceptions (eg, NUCLEAR ENERGY; GEOTHERMAL ENERGY), solar energy is the source of all ENERGY used by mankind. Indirect forms include HYDROELECTRICITY, ocean thermal energy, TIDAL ENERGY and WIND ENERGY; the sun also powers the process of photosynthesis that is the original source of the energy contained in BIOMASS, PEAT, COAL and PETROLEUM. Usually, however, the term solar energy refers to the portion of the sun's radiant energy harnessed for a specific purpose by man-made devices. A further distinction is often made between "active" and "passive" solar systems: active systems capture energy by mechanical means (eg, rooftop collectors, focusing mirrors); passive systems incorporate solar principles (eg, into the design of buildings through south-facing windows), without special mechanical systems. Most energy statistics refer only to active solar-energy systems, thus vastly understating the importance of solar energy. Active solar energy accounts for only a tiny fraction of Canada's energy use, but some studies have indicated that it could meet as much as 5% of the country's energy needs by the year 2025.

Low intensity and high variability have limited the use of active solar energy in Canada. Most purposes demand that the energy be concentrated into useful quantities and require either a storage system or a supplemental energy source for nighttime and cloudy days. Technologies have been developed for these purposes, but until recently most of them have been too expensive and too untried for widespread use. The main applications of solar-energy technology in Canada have been for space heating, domestic hot water, and for drying crops and lumber. Photovoltaic cells are used in some remote areas of Canada to power radio transmitters and navigational aids but have been too expensive for widespread use. Photovoltaic cells are used in many consumer electronic products, such as calculators and watches. Other countries have developed solar systems that produce steam to run conventional electrical generators, but this work has not been pursued in Canada. At northern latitudes, the solar resource is too seasonally variable for exploitation of many energy applications developed elsewhere. North of the ARCTIC CIRCLE, there are periods during the winter when the sun remains below the horizon.

The Future The sun delivers solar energy to all parts of Canada. Direct use of this ambient energy minimizes the need for expensive and inefficient transmission and delivery systems. The remote expanses of Canada, where costs of conventional nonrenewable energy are high, offer opportunities for developing and using many cost-effective solar technologies. Although the continuing supply of solar energy is free, the capital cost of capture hardware can be expensive, but if compared to marginal cost of conventional sources it can be cost competitive. However, simple passive-heating systems may only increase the cost of buildings by 1-5%. Active systems usually require several years of operation to recover the initial cost of

operation in fuel savings. Until economic support structures match those for conventional energy sources, solar energy will have difficulty competing in all but remote or small applications. However, once the system is in place, delivery energy costs are stable and immune to market fluctuations that affect conventional nonrenewable energy resources. The Solar Energy Soc of Canada is the national technical organization that promotes education and the dissemination of information on all aspects of solar-energy use. It is affiliated with the International Solar Energy Soc. The Canadian Solar Industries Assn is a manufacturers' organization promoting industrial development.

RICHARD KADULSKI

Reading: J.F. Kreider and F. Kreith, *Solar Energy Handbook* (1979).

Soldiers of Fortune, a term used to describe those ready to serve in a military or police capacity under any state or person outside their own country. Often confused with mercenaries who are motivated chiefly by gain, monetary or otherwise, soldiers of fortune seek adventure or serve for idealistic reasons and have existed from the earliest times. Columbus, for example, was a Genoese in the Spanish Navy. In the 19th century Lord Byron joined the Philhellenes to free Greece from Turkish rule, and "Chinese" Gordon's "Ever-Victorious Army" attracted soldiers of fortune during the Taiping Revolution in China in the 1860s, as has the French Foreign Legion since its inception in 1831. In this century, the Spanish Foreign Legion, the "Flying Tigers" in China, and the International Brigades of the Spanish Civil War have drawn soldiers of fortune to their banners.

Canadian soldiers of fortune have often been professional soldiers or entrepreneurs who have become adventurers by chance as, for example, Sir William Fenwick WILLIAMS of NS, commander of a Turkish army in the Crimean War of 1854-1856, and Torontonian Alexander Roberts DUNN who won a VC at the Charge of the Light Brigade at Balaclava during the same conflict. Elsewhere, Daniel O'Connor (d 1858) of Ottawa was a volunteer in the Irish Legion against Spanish colonial troops in Panama in the early 1820s, John RICHARDSON fought from 1834 to 1837 in the British Auxiliary Legion during the Carlist Wars in Spain, and Col George Mason Green (1836-1912) and Narcisse Faucher de Saint-Maurice served respectively with Juarez and Emperor Maximilian during the French occupation of Mexico in the 1860s.

Some 45 000 Canadians are estimated to have served in the AMERICAN CIVIL WAR. Several hundred French Canadians joined the Canadian Pontifical ZOUAVES of the Papal Army to prevent reunion of Italy by the forces of King Victor Emmanuel in 1868-70, while Arthur BUIES had served in the forces of Giuseppi Garibaldi that opposed them. Toronto-born Civil War veteran Brig William Ryan, who joined the Cuban revolutionary army, was captured aboard the filibustering vessel *Virginius* in 1873 and was executed by the Spanish in Cuba. Another Civil War veteran, Indian fighter Lt William Winer Cooke (b 1845) of Mt Pleasant, Ont, was adjutant to Col George Armstrong Custer and among the 14 Canadians in the Seventh Cavalry; at least 4 of them died with Custer at the Little Big Horn in 1876. In the NORTH-WEST REBELLION OF 1885, Martin Waters Kirwan (1841-99), a veteran of the French Foreign Legion, served as a staff officer under Maj-Gen Frederick MIDDLETON, while William Henry JACKSON joined the Métis forces as secretary to Louis RIEL. William Grant STAIRS seized Katanga (Shaba) for Belgium in the early 1890s. Commandante Joseph Chapleau died in action in 1897 in an attack on a

Spanish garrison, and 9 Canadians served in Teddy Roosevelt's "Rough Riders" in Cuba in the SPANISH-AMERICAN WAR of 1898, which was reported on by one of Canada's most celebrated early war correspondents, Kathleen (Kit) Coleman. George Charette, of Ste-Élisabeth, Qué, was a US navy volunteer during the same conflict, who helped in sinking a barge at the mouth of Santiago harbour. Henry Herbert STEVENS was a member of the US Army in the Philippines and later in China during the Boxer Rebellion. Col Charles James Townsend Stewart (1874-1918), of Halifax, killed while commanding the PPCLI on the Western Front in WWI, was a soldier of fortune in China and Peru as well as an NWMP trooper in the Yukon and a railway foreman in BC.

James Kennedy CORNWALL served in a Venezuelan revolution at the turn of the century, and Frederic Franklin WORTHINGTON commanded 3 ships of the Nicaraguan navy against one Salvadorian ship of Frederick William Thompson (1888-1985) in a 1906 boundary war; both men later served in the Borden Machine Gun Battery on the Western Front. Aloha Wanderwell BAKER was a soldier-pilot-photojournalist who served in the French Foreign Legion against the Riffs, and was an adviser to a Chinese army during the "Warlord Years" of the 1920s, while Morris Abraham COHEN commanded another Chinese army during the same period. Leon Bedat (1881-1961) of Huntsville, Ont, and Jan Van den Berg (1884-1961) were among several dozen Canadian volunteers in the Mexican revolutions of 1911-20; later, both men served on the Western Front in WWI and in S Russia (see RUSSIAN CIVIL WAR, CANADIAN INTERVENTION IN). Raymond COLLISHAW, Joseph Whiteside ("Klondike Joe") BOYLE, John Edwards LECKIE and Walter Sussan (1892-1969) of Ottawa participated in the Russian Civil War.

T.V. McCallum of Toronto was killed while a member of the Kosciusko Squadron in Poland flying against the Bolsheviks in 1920. Hilliard Lyle (1878-1931) of Allenford, Ont, served with the Greek Army against Turkey in 1920-22, while Sussan flew as a fighter-pilot with Greece's Air Force; in 1925 Sussan joined the Escadrille de la Garde chérifienne in Morocco and flew bombers against the Riffian rebels of Abdel Krim on behalf of the French. Bert Levy (1897-1965) of Hamilton, Ont, and Alfred Batson (1900-77) of Vancouver were gunnery officers under Augusto Sandino in Nicaragua during the mid-1920s, while Ralph Beardsley (1899-1982) and Ted Huestis (1909-61) fought for the government alongside the US Marines and the Guardia Nacional. Huestis was an adviser to the Chinese Army and a pilot in the Ecuadorian Air Force, and Levy the first Canadian to join the International Brigades (British Battalion) in the Spanish Civil War (1936-39).

Toronto labour journalist and playwright Edward Cecil-Smith, a former adventurer in S America, commanded the MACKENZIE-PAPINEAU BATTALION in Spain. In the same conflict, Henry Norman BETHUNE ran the celebrated Canadian blood-transfusion service for the Spanish Army. Members of his staff were Hazen Sise and Ted Allan of Montréal, Henning SORENSEN of Vancouver and Allen R. May of Toronto. Ralph Linton of London, Ont, who had fought the Japanese in a Chinese guerrilla army, also served in Spain, as did writers Alain GRANDBOIS and Hugh GARNER. BC adventurer and journalist Sir Michael Bruce (1894-1957) led 2 Brazilian rebellions and authorized several books of autobiography.

Fighter ace George Frederick "Buzz" BEURLING died in the crash of a plane which he was ferrying to Palestine during Israel's War of Independence in 1948. That same year, Sherman "Snark" Wilson, former chief pilot for BWIA, was shot down during a Salvadoran revolution. In Israel, WORLD WAR II RCAF veteran Dennis Wilson of Hamilton, Ont, shot down 2 Egyptian Spitfires, while Joseph John Doyle and John McElroy of London downed 3 and 4 Arab aircraft, respectively, while Flying Officer Leonard Fitchett was killed during a bomber attack on an Egyptian-held fortress. Several hundred other Canadians volunteered for service in the Israeli forces, among them Ben Dunkelman, Lee Sinclair, Morris Pearce, and John (Jack) Blanc of Toronto, the latter a veteran of the Spanish Civil War shot while attempting to foil a bank robbery in 1964. RCAF flier, writer and Korean War veteran Tony Foster (b 1932) participated in the overthrow of Arbenz of Guatemala in 1954 and of Villeda Morales of Honduras in 1957. Canadians have served in the Congo, Biafra, Rhodesia and Angola and in other African and Latin American conflicts of the 1960s and 1970s, and as many as 35 000 of them have served alongside British, Irish, German, Korean and other foreign volunteers in the US forces during the VIETNAM WAR. Richard Dextraze, son of Gen Jacques DEXTRAZE, Canadian Army (Ret) was among the 56 Canadians listed as killed or missing in action in that conflict. Toronto adventurer and free-lance writer Peter Bertie was killed in action in Nicaragua in Mar 1987, while working with anti-Communist "Contra" guerrillas.

ALLAN LEVINE

Soleil, Le, a French daily newspaper published in Québec City, was founded as *L'Electeur* in July 1880 by a group of moderate Liberals including Wilfrid LAURIER. Ernest Pacaud, editor for the first 2 decades, is regarded as the true founder, and in Dec 1896 he changed the name to *Le Soleil*. With the advent of Maurice DUPLESSIS in 1936, *Le Soleil* abandoned its Liberal stance and adopted the policy of "reporting only news." In 1974 the paper was bought by UNIMÉDIA. Average paid Monday-Friday circulation in 1986 was 116 688; 145 545 on Saturday; and 92 753 on Sunday. Once a national newspaper with reporters across Canada, *Le Soleil* has become a regional newspaper of fluctuating quality. Its principal reporting focuses on the politics, economics and social life of Québec City, with only 5% allotted to international news. *Le Soleil* has always responded to technological change. In 1984 it became a morning newspaper, including a Sunday edition, with a special tabloid sport section. *See also* NEWSPAPERS.

ANDRÉ DONNEUR AND ONNIG BEYLERIAN

Solicitor, a lawyer who advises on legal problems and whose work – contracts of sale, real-estate transactions, wills and trusts – normally does not require court appearance. The term has a distinct legal definition in England, but in Canada's common-law provinces, lawyers are called to the bar (see BARRISTER) and admitted as solicitors simultaneously. There is no exact corresponding designation under Québec civil law, where the legal profession is divided into *notaires* (see NOTARY) and *avocats*.

K.G. McSHANE

Solicitor General The office of the solicitor general has its historic roots in England. In Canada the office varies substantially from jurisdiction to jurisdiction. In some provinces the office of the solicitor general is subsumed under one or more different portfolios, but in most it is separate and distinct. In the former situation, functions of the solicitor general are likely to be assumed by the office of the ATTORNEY GENERAL. Federally the office of the solicitor general is separate and distinct from other Cabinet portfolios.

Generally speaking, a provincial solicitor general is responsible for matters relating to POLICING in the province, corrections, motor vehicles and liquor licensing. However, the functions assigned to the solicitor general's office differ from province to province. Federally, the solicitor general of Canada is responsible for the Correctional Service of Canada, the Royal Canadian Mounted Police and the National Parole Board. As of July 1984 the federal solicitor general was made responsible for the CANADIAN SECURITY INTELLIGENCE SERVICE, now established separate and apart from the RCMP; however, one of the controversies concerning the enactment of the new security legislation relates to considerable independence of the service from the minister responsible.

Federally, there is a close working relationship between the offices of the attorney general and the solicitor general as their functions somewhat overlap.

G. GALL

Solicitor General, Department of Before 1936, the department was either a Cabinet post or a ministerial post outside Cabinet. Between 1936 and 1945, the solicitor general's responsibilities were handled by the attorney general. The Solicitor General Act of 1945 re-established the Cabinet pqst and in 1966 the department was created, making the solicitor general responsible for federal prisons and penitentiaries, (eg, Correctional Service of Canada), parole and remissions, law enforcement (eg, the ROYAL CANADIAN MOUNTED POLICE). The solicitor general reports to Parliament for the National Parole Board.

Solid Waste, general term for all discarded materials other than fluids. Solid wastes, including some HAZARDOUS WASTES, are by-products of industrial, MINING and agricultural operations as well as being the garbage and sewage produced by society. The first 3 categories of wastes involve special disposal techniques which are, or should be, integral parts of the operation that produces them. The by-products of human activities become more and more a problem as concentrations of population increase; in Canada, they are largely the responsibility of the municipalities. Municipalities must cope with 2 general categories of solid waste: garbage and sewage sludge.

Garbage Most Canadian communities probably produce domestic, commercial and urban industrial waste at a rate near the N American average of 2.5 kg per person per day, with considerable seasonal variation. This high rate is attributed to N American affluence, with a preoccupation with exploitation of virgin RESOURCES and a high level of subsidization of garbage disposal. The disposal of this volume of garbage is expensive; costs are estimated to average $25 per person per year. Traditional open garbage dumps are now generally illegal because they attract large mammals, rodents and birds which may be hazards to health and safety. If properly operated, sanitary landfills reduce POLLUTION problems (air and groundwater contamination, odour, litter). Garbage collection and disposal is generally a local government responsibility, whether carried out by municipal employees or by private contractors. Federal and provincial laws relate to health, clean air and water supply.

Solid-waste management should adhere to 3 priorities: to reduce the volume of waste generated, through control of packaging and emphasis on durability and repairability as design criteria for products; to direct the recycling of materials through separation at source (business or home), where volumes of garbage and population densities allow; to provide economic incentives to reduce waste and to encourage recycling and the use of recycled products.

Sewage Any concentration of humans will eventually encounter problems with disposal of human wastes. On average, each human adult produces approximately 0.5 L of urine per day and 115 g of feces. Safe return of body wastes to the ecosystem maintains the natural cycles of nutrients and moisture. However, population concentrations soon create problems which lead to disease, pollution of natural systems and a generally offensive environment. The development of sewage handling and treatment technologies has reduced or eliminated sewage-related diseases and has made our cities much more pleasant places to live in (*see* WATER TREATMENT; WATERBORNE DISEASE). Most communities dump their treated or untreated sewage into bodies of water, creating special WATER POLLUTION problems, including the incorporation of toxic materials and disease-causing organisms, and the accelerated growth of unwanted vegetation and algae. Many towns now use sewage lagoons, large-scale equivalents of the septic tanks used in less densely populated areas. Composting toilets are a dry alternative to septic tanks.

Sewage Sludge Where more sophisticated primary, secondary and tertiary sewage-treatment plants are used, sewage sludge is generated. The city of Calgary leads Canada in sludge utilization by disposing of the liquid sludge in a safe, odourless way by injecting it as fertilizer into agricultural land. Otherwise the sludge is incinerated or disposed of in land fills.

Another solution to water pollution problems from sewage is land disposal where soil conditions are suitable. This practice is followed throughout the world, especially in countries which cannot afford the loss of the valuable nutrients. In Canada some ecologists advocate using sewage for fertilizer. Where soils are suitable, especially on the prairies, use of liquid effluent in farm IRRIGATION eliminates the water pollution problem and provides water and nutrients for crops. In 1983 the number of land-application sites for treatment of municipal wastewater was as follows: NWT, one; BC, 31; Alta, 26; Sask, 15-20; Man, 10; Ont, 3; Qué, one; Nfld, one. In addition, there were 20 industrial wastewater irrigation projects. A large city, eg, Calgary, would require about 50 000 ha of land to dispose of its effluent.   DIXON THOMPSON

Solidarity In May 1983 British Columbians voted the Social Credit Party, headed by William BENNETT, into office. Two months later, on July 7, the Socreds introduced their so-called Restraint Budget, accompanied by 26 prospective bills. The crucial legislation fell into 3 categories: those that abolished watchdog-type bodies; those that undermined trade-union practices and the status of collective bargaining, especially in the public sector; and those that cut social services. The Bennett legislation threatened labour and a host of underprivileged groups, including welfare recipients, women and children, the handicapped and ethnic minorities. In response, the BC Federation of Labour, led by Arthur Kube, allied with community and advocacy groups and organized a massive protest movement, known as Solidarity. It was composed of a trade-union wing, Operation Solidarity, and the Solidarity Coalition, made up of the various "people's organizations." Funded and staffed by the trade-union movement, Solidarity gave the appearance of a democratic, grassroots movement; in fact it was carefully controlled by a narrow stratum of labour leaders.

For 3 months Solidarity protested the proposed legislation. Huge marches and rallies were staged, bringing tens of thousands into the streets of Vancouver and onto the lawns of the provincial legislature, a weekly newspaper was launched, and the Vancouver offices of the Cabinet were occupied. There were rumours of a general strike. By late Oct many of the Restraint Bills had been passed into law. Parliamentary debate was stifled by CLOSURE and all-night sittings were used by the Socreds to force through certain pieces of legisla-

tion. The leader of the Opposition, NDP head Dave BARRETT, was ejected from the House.

Many government workers were scheduled to be fired on Oct 31 with the lapsing of the BC Government Employees Union contract. That date thus became associated with strike action. When the BCGEU did indeed take action on Nov 1, Solidarity organized an escalating series of strikes in the public sector which threatened to put 200 000 workers in the streets. In the second week of November, a teachers' walkout seemed to tip the balance in Solidarity's direction. With thousands of pivotal public-sector workers ready to leave their employment in political protest, the labour leaders at the helm of BC Fed began to get uneasy at the prospect of an all-out confrontation which might force Bennett to introduce repressive back-to-work orders which, in turn, would necessitate promised private-sector job action.

Solidarity was thus stopped by the very trade-union officials who had led it. They abandoned the movement's broad aims of repeal of the entire legislative package for the narrower end of a contract for the BCGEU. When that was secured, on Nov 13, Jack Munro, vice-president of BC Fed, flew to Bennett's Kelowna home, shook hands with the architect of restraint, and ended the most massive protest movement in the history of Canada's West Coast province.   BRYAN D. PALMER

Solitaire, common name for 11 species of New World THRUSHES, one of which occurs in Canada. Ornithologists also use the term for 2 species belonging to an extinct family related to the dodo and the modern pigeon family. Townsend's solitaire (*Myadestes townsendi*) summers in open mountain forests N to YT and winters at lower elevations N to southern BC. Males and females are similar in appearance, being brownish grey overall with longish tails and short bills. They nest on or near the ground or in rock crevices and lay dull white eggs, spotted with brown. In summer, solitaires feed on insects; in winter, as much as half their diet is fruit. Their clear, sweet, loud warbling notes are among the most beautiful of bird songs.   R.D. JAMES

Solomon's Seal (genus *Polygonatum*), herbaceous plant of lily family (Liliaceae). About 50 species occur in the Northern Hemisphere. Two are found in Canada, *P. biflorum* and *P. pubescens*, in moist woods and thickets from southeastern Saskatchewan to the Maritimes. Stems, up to 1 m high, have greenish white, pendant flowers and alternate leaves. Berries are blue to blue-black. Both native species were a source of food, cosmetics and medicines (eg, for bruises, headaches) for Indian peoples. Both native and introduced species are good garden plants (easily propagated by division). Introduced species have flowers and habit of growth similar to native species, except for *P. hookeri*, a good alpine garden plant, 2 cm high, with small, lilac flowers in leaf axils. Common name refers to marks on the rhizomes (underground stems) which resemble seals used on legal documents. *Smilacina*, false Solomon's seal, also a member of lily family, may be confused with *Polygonatum*.   PATRICK SEYMOUR

Somers, Harry Stewart, composer (b at Toronto 11 Sept 1925). Somers began studying piano and classical guitar, but working first with John WEINZWEIG and then with Darius Milhaud in Paris led to his career as a composer. He supported himself by ushering, driving a taxi and copying music, acquiring his meticulous handwriting in the process. By 1960, after further study in Paris, he was able to live on his commission fees. He is one of Canada's most productive and original composers and a keen promoter of contemporary Canadian music; he was a founding member in 1951 of

the Canadian League of Composers. Concerned about the teaching and performance of Canadian music in schools, he became involved in 1963 in the John Adaskin Project to introduce Canadian composers and hosted several youth concerts on CBC. A grant from the Canadian Cultural Institute in Rome permitted him to study there (1969-71), completing works that reveal his interest in new vocal techniques. Eastern music and philosophy have also influenced him considerably. Somers's music is internationally respected and is performed throughout the Western world. He has received major commissions from most of Canada's musical and theatrical organizations. His opera *Louis Riel* was commissioned for Canada's Centennial by the Floyd S. CHALMERS Foundation and was subsequently performed in Washington, DC, for the US Bicentennial. Always associated with intense feeling, his work is simple, eloquent and forceful, often employing dramatic juxtaposition of styles, dramatic silences and sharp fluctuations in volume, which he calls "dramatic unrest." Somers in 1972 became a Companion of the Order of Canada. In 1986 he was the subject of a half-hour documentary, "The Music of Harry Somers."   MABEL H. LAINE

Somerset Island, 24 786 km², ninth-largest island in the ARCTIC ARCHIPELAGO. Its western part is on Precambrian bedrock, reaching an elevation of 503 m, but the larger part is an elevated plateau of sedimentary rocks. Vegetation is scant, except in some depressions and lowlands where Peary caribou are common. Muskoxen are making a comeback after having been decimated by whalers around the turn of the century. Hundreds of thousands of birds nest on the sheer cliffs of Prince Leopold I, off the NE tip of Somerset. The island was named by Lt W.E. PARRY, who discovered it in 1819, after the county in England.   S.C. ZOLTAI

Somme, Battle of the, 1 July-late Nov 1916, during WORLD WAR I, saw British, Imperial, and French troops hammering German defence lines N of the Somme R in one of the most futile and bloody battles in history. The 1st Newfoundland Regiment was virtually wiped out at Beaumont Hamel on the first day of the battle. The Canadian Corps entered the battle on Aug 30, and during its attacks in Sept was supported by the first tanks used in action on the Western Front. The machine guns, barbed wire, trenches and massive use of artillery resulted in hard fighting and heavy casualties, especially in the capture of Regina Trench, Courcelette, Thiepval and Ancre Heights. Rain, snow, and sleet brought the battle to an end. After 5 months' fighting the Allies had penetrated about 13 km along a 35 km front. Allied losses were estimated at 623 907, of whom 24 713 were Canadians and Newfoundlanders. German losses were estimated at 660 000.   R.H. ROY

Sonar (*so*und *n*avigation *a*nd *r*anging), method for locating objects by the reflection of sound waves. It is used naturally by such animals as BATS and DOLPHINS to locate food and obstacles. Sonar was first developed – as a practical method of detecting underwater hazards (eg, submarines, icebergs) and for measuring water depths – by Constantin Chilowsky and Paul Langevin in France during WWI, with the collaboration of the Canadian R.W. BOYLE. During WWII the Royal Canadian Navy, specializing in convoy escort and in antisubmarine activities, called on Canadian oceanographers to assess water-stratification conditions and to study the behaviour of sound under water. J.P. TULLY and W.M. CAMERON worked with G.S. Field of the NATIONAL RESEARCH COUNCIL on ways of improving sonar detection of submarines. Sonar has since been further developed for civilian, scientific and military uses.

Because sonar techniques can be used to locate and map changes in the medium through which sound waves travel, they can be used to determine variations in the sedimentary structure of the Earth beneath the sea, through a method known as seismic reflection, and to map the seafloor surface. Seafloor sediments absorb normal high-sonar frequencies very rapidly, so that early application of seismic-reflection techniques at sea used repeated detonation of explosives as a low-frequency sound source (*see* SURVEYING).

Seismic Deeptow In marine seismic exploration the acoustic sound source and receiver are normally towed behind the survey vessel at a shallow depth below the sea surface.

In Canada, 2 deep-towed seismic systems have been developed to provide the high resolution required for mapping unconsolidated seabed sediments. In both systems the sound source and receiving hydrophones are on or are towed from a hydrodynamically designed "fish," itself towed at depths of 200-600 m and at speeds up to 6-8 knots by a survey vessel. The Nova Scotia Research Foundation (NSRF) system uses a 1.2 m V-fin underwater vehicle as the deep-towed stable platform to house the source and receiver. The Deep Tow Seismic System was developed by Huntec '70 Ltd in Toronto as part of the joint Government/Industry Seabed Project (1975-80) and it uses a specially designed hydrodynamic tow body to house power supplies and transducers. The Seabed Project brought together the scientists and engineers required to develop the technology to quantify the acoustic response of marine sediments and to apply seismic deep-tow techniques to the mapping of the surficial sediments over the Canadian Continental Shelf.

Recent Canadian developments in sonar have attempted to improve the image quality or information content in the reflected signal through the use of pattern-recognition techniques, initially developed for processing satellite and space vehicle photographic images; multi-frequency source/receiver systems for improved signal redundancy and target identification; broad-band swept or parametric sources for improved beam geometry and resolution; and high-speed digital processors for real-time beam forming and image processing. These techniques have led to several new developments with enhanced capability for fish finding, mine and submarine detection, as well as sea floor mapping and sediment property delineation. DAVID I. ROSS

Songs and Songwriting Song may be described as a tonal vocalization of words and emotions. It can be fragmentary or extended and can range from a simple, unaffected statement to a highly complex linear and harmonic structure. What determines its character is the situation that elicits the music, the text being treated (or the emotion being expressed) and the vocal and instrumental resources used. Song is usually thought of as text set to music, and it is frequently the nature and purpose of the words that form the basis for categorizing song types; thus, there are such familiar divisions as folksong, religious song, patriotic song, children's song and art song. Music can heighten the meaning of words, and the combination of text and tone can enhance the emotional statement. The presence of peoples from many lands and cultural backgrounds has contributed to the growth of Canadian songwriting. In addition, technology now makes available music from around the world. Artistic influences are no longer simply those from native traditions, from patterns of privileged travel or from emigration. Influences are as varied as international touring, broadcasting and recording allow.

Predating and contemporary with immigration

of people from western Europe were the songs of the native people, conveyed by oral tradition and often associated with dance. In this century indigenous music has been the subject of extensive study and has also been a source of material for composers working within the Western tradition. The early French Canadian settlers brought with them their own melodic and stylistic material, dependent on oral tradition, and subsequently evolved forms, such as rhythmical paddling songs, that were often related to the occupation of the singer. The Anglo-Canadian folksong tradition was equally vigorous, and examples of both musical streams have been collected and preserved and have formed the basis of new works. Every national group of any size represented in Canada's population has brought its own tradition with it.

Like the paddling songs of the voyageurs and fur traders, the shanties were sailors' work songs and served to provide not only a lifting of the spirit but a measured pulse for the task. Most of the shanties and sea songs of Canadian heritage or adoption come from the East Coast, mainly from NS and Newfoundland, and to a lesser degree from the Great Lakes region. W. Roy Mackenzie, the first to collect Anglo-Canadian songs, gathered work songs from old Nova Scotia seamen, including shanties such as "Santy Anna," "Sally Brown" and "We're Homeward Bound." There were other sea songs with texts describing activities, events and superstitions; the vocal narratives of such ballads tell of sealing and fishing trips and voyages ("The Ferryland Sealer," "The *Greenland* Disaster"). Even the dance songs reflect the Maritimers' dependence on the sea, as in "I'se the B'y That Builds the Boat" and "The Feller from Fortune." The land itself also offered opportunities for work-related song. The lumber camps of NB and Ontario, agricultural areas from the Maritimes to the Prairies and, to a lesser degree, the mining regions of both coasts and Ontario have contributed songs ("Cobalt Song," "The Scarborough Settler's Lament"). Though tunes were at times shared between regions or even occupations, texts often possessed a local focus; thus the tune of "The Lumbercamp Song," patterned after an English ditty, is found, with various texts, among East Coast fishermen as well as loggers. Hardships endured by the workers are recounted in songs such as "Canaday-I-O" and "The Rock Island Line." Ballads describing death in the woods or on the rivers are numerous ("Peter Amberley," "The Haggertys and Young Mulvanny"). In the West both homesteaders and cowboys borrowed songs from the US. Cowboys were often hired from the US and brought with them popular songs like "The Streets of Laredo" and "Bury Me Not on the Lone Prairie." "Dakota Land" and other parodies of the old hymn "Beulah Land" were rewritten in Canada as "Prairie Land," "Alberta Land" and "Saskatchewan." It is easy to dismiss such material as unsophisticated and unimportant, but the texts provide insight into Canada's history. The nature and use of melody can reveal much about taste and about the transmission of artistic ideas and the movement of people across the country and across borders.

Together with occupational songs may be categorized the limited number of trade-union and political songs. The body of material is small and some of it is adaptive in nature, making use of existing tunes, and much of it is related to specific events. Political or labour songs have sometimes suffered the same fate as many clever political cartoons – the particular relevance is lost, though the principle involved may be taken up at another time. A similar fate might have overtaken the shanties after the demise of sail, but the larger body of material and the effects of nostalgia and

romantic notions have served to sustain their popularity. Examples of political songs survive in the form of 18th-century satirical material from Québec ("Chanson sur les élections") and songs stemming from 19th-century crises and elections. In this century, world wars and other events and issues such as working conditions in mining and lumbering ("Hard, Hard Times," "The Loggers' Plight") and the aspirations of the Acadians and the Québecois have given rise to protest songs.

The distinction between songs that are political and those that are patriotic often depends on the views and emotions of one group or another. Nevertheless, Canada has a considerable list of songs that display national sentiment. These works often owe their creation and popularity to an event, eg, Confederation, or to an idea such as the preservation of the entity and spirit of a region, culture and language. Hence, in Québec we find "Canada, terre d'espérance," "O Canada! beau pays, ma patrie," along with "À la claire fontaine" and "Vive la Canadienne"; in NB and NS, "Un Acadien errant"; and in English Canada, works like "The Maple Leaf for Ever," "Canada for Ever," and "O Canada, Dear Canada." LAVALLÉE's "O Canada, terre de nos aïeux" (original text by A.B. Routhier) is the country's national anthem.

Children have their own songs. Here, again, pieces are handed from one generation to another and like occupational songs are often associated with particular activities such as bridge games ("Trois fois passera"), ring games ("The Farmer in the Dell") or skipping ("On Yonder Mountain Stands a Lady"). Camp and campfire songs are popular with some adults, and children frequently share these, for example, rounds like "Row, Row, Row Your Boat," parodies like "Found a Peanut" (sung to the "Clementine" melody) and others. Once more, there is a universality to such material; we can hear many of these songs in NS or BC; some of them have their origin outside Canada or outside our range of history ("Three Blind Mice" was printed by Thomas Ravenscroft in *Deuteromelia*, 1609). Among Canadian composers, Lionel Daunais has written at least 30 chansons, popular pieces and songs for children.

There is a considerable wealth of Canadian songs, though most are relatively neglected and unknown beyond circles of devotees and concert and recital goers. The chansons of Québec have an interesting history and again reflect the merging of imported cultural influences and, more recently, folksong and modern trends in popular music and developments in audio electronics. English Canadian popular music has lately followed the same path, though it is not as concerned with the stimulation and preservation of a linguistic and cultural heritage. The works of Ernest Whyte, Clarence Lucas and W.O. Forsyth rested, until the mid-1980s, in undeserved shade, along with those of Achille Fortier and Calixa Lavallée. Some mid-20th-century composers who have contributed to Canadian song are Violet ARCHER, Michael Baker, John BECKWITH, Jean Coulthard, Lionel Daunais, Kelsey Jones, Ernest MACMILLAN, Oskar MORAWETZ, Jean PAPINEAU-COUTURE, Barbara PENTLAND, Clermont PÉPIN, André Prévost, Leo Smith, Healey WILLAN and Charles Wilson. Notable is the extent to which vocal music has attracted Canadian composers over the years (*see* CHORAL MUSIC). The output often reflects broad trends in technique and style in serious music but also bears the mark of individual character and taste. Composers have frequently found inspiration in words by Canadian writers, a tendency that is likely to continue as both arts flourish. Further, many Canadian composers (MacMillan and Willan, for example) have written some remarkable and unique arrangements of existing songs, some of which have origins in other lands. Such arrangements, like original works, form a proper part of Canadian music.

If there is a problem for the Canadian writer of serious songs, it lies not in a lack of something to say but in the difficulty of getting the musical statement to the potential audience in Canada. Recitals are still too few, and though radio, especially the CBC, has offered many opportunities to composers, TV has not used the wealth of available material. Both radio and TV have assisted popular song, but though Canadian-content requirements offer a measure of comfort, more must be done. In evaluating songs and songwriting, it is not enough to reflect on melody and harmony: the texts will tell us about our life and our land as well. Any art must also be considered in a larger context – against trends and styles in other arts, and against political and social movements, economic conditions, geography, climate and other factors, both within the country and internationally. *See also* MUSIC HISTORY; FOLK MUSIC; POPULAR MUSIC; SINGING.   BRYAN N.S. GOOCH

Reading: H. Kallmann et al, eds, *Encyclopedia of Music in Canada* (1981).

Songs of the Great Dominion: *Voices from the Forests and Waters, the Settlements and Cities of Canada* (1889). Selected and edited by W.D. Lighthall, a writer and barrister of Montréal, and intended as one of the Windsor Series of "Poetical Anthologies" published by Walter Scott of London who also issued it under the title *Canadian Songs and Poems* in 1892, this late 19th-century collection of Canadian verse is animated by the high ideals and the greater British Empire loyalties of its compiler. Supplied with a ringing introduction which echoes with patriotic sentiment and lyrical praise for Canada, this is a collection of confident poetry truly representative of the national and literary self-respect of the emergent Dominion. The anthology is noteworthy for its attempt to include some French Canadian poetry in the appendix as well as some folksongs in translation, and for its recognition of a distinct Indian element in Canadian writing.

MICHAEL GNAROWSKI

Soper, Joseph Dewey, naturalist, explorer, writer (b near Guelph, Ont 5 May 1893; d at Edmonton 2 Nov 1982). Soper exemplified the quiet, unpretentious men who, surveying for the Dominion government, established the outline and substance of Canada. The wilderness of western Canada attracted him before WWI. After the war, he opened new territory in the eastern Arctic (1923-31) and discovered the breeding grounds of the blue goose. Later he contributed important knowledge about bison in Wood Buffalo National Pk. He also ranged the prairies, (especially along the international boundary), the Rocky Mt parks, the NWT and the Yukon. His more than 100 scientific and popular articles and books were illustrated often with his own pen sketches and watercolours. The names of several mammals (eg, Soper's ringed seal) and geographical features on Baffin I (eg, Soper R) testify to his work. In 1960 he received an LLD from U of A.

J.R. NURSALL

Sorel, Qué, City, pop 19 522 (1986c), 20 347 (1981c), inc 1889, is located on the S shore of the St Lawrence R, at the mouth of the Rivière RICHELIEU, 76 km NE of Montréal. Pierre de Saurel, a captain in the CARIGNAN-SALIÈRES REGIMENT, gave his name to the seigneury granted in 1672. In 1781 Sir Frederick HALDIMAND, the governor of Québec, built a manor on the Richelieu (later used as a summer residence for governors general of Canada) and made plans to build a town he hoped would be populated by Loyalists. However, few such settlers came to the area. From 1787 the town was called William Henry, after a son of George III. It was renamed Sorel in 1845, with a slightly changed spelling. In 1784 the first Anglican mission was established.

In the mid-19th century, the rapidly growing town was a terminal for river shipping originating in Lac CHAMPLAIN and profited from the trade between Montréal and Québec City. The lumber industry and shipyards also prospered. In the 20th century, Sorel has remained a busy year-round seaport and is the commercial centre for agriculture in the Richelieu Valley. In WWII, as a centre for wartime industry, it employed 20 000 workers. Today, shipbuilding and heavy industry are its principal activities. It also has textile plants, clothing, plastics, concrete and light manufacturing industries.   SYLVIE TASCHEREAU

Sorensen, Henning Ingeman, adventurer, translator (b at Copenhagen, Den 14 May 1901; d at Vancouver 3 Aug 1986). Sorensen abandoned a promising banking career in Copenhagen in 1922 to travel and work through Europe, Africa and N America, finally arriving at Montréal in 1929. In 1937, during the SPANISH CIVIL WAR, he went to Spain to report on medical conditions for the Committee to Aid Spanish Democracy, a Canadian organization supporting the Republicans, and there became the chief assistant and interpreter to Norman BETHUNE, the Canadian doctor who was providing mobile blood transfusions and emergency surgery to republican troops and soldiers of the International Brigades. During WWII he worked for Canadian naval intelligence, and subsequently for the international service of the CBC; and finally, during the early 1960s, he served as a translator in the Cuban foreign ministry.   STANLEY GORDON

Souris, PEI, Town, pop 1379 (1986c), 1413 (1981c), is a port located 80 km NE of Charlottetown. The town is likely named, after the French word for mouse, for the plagues of mice that appeared in the area around 1750, devouring the Acadians' crops. With the demise of the Island's shipbuilding industry in the late 19th century, the seaport's economy was buoyed by the harvests of land and sea. Today Souris remains one of the province's main ports; its harbour is not only the site of the Îles de la Madeleine ferry terminal, but it has the only offshore fishing fleet on PEI. It is also noted for its lobster industry and fine beach on NORTHUMBERLAND STR. The town is the commercial centre of northeastern Kings County.

W.S. KEIZER

Souris, Man, Town, pop 1751 (1986c), 1731 (1981c), inc 1903, is located at the junction of Plum Cr and the SOURIS R, 45 km by road SW of Brandon. Souris is known for its semiprecious agate stones, used in costume jewellery, and for one of the longest (177 m) suspension footbridges in Canada. The Souris area has seen Indian warfare, fur-trading rivalries, Red River brigade buffalo hunts, and feudallike settlements under English and French landowners. The townsite's first permanent settlers arrived 1880, followed in 1881 by a group of Ontarians. Souris, then called Plum Creek, was soon a developing agricultural centre. During WWII the town had a large Commonwealth air school. Souris services the surrounding agricultural region (grain production, dairying, purebred stock breeding) and has a few small industries.   D.M. LYON

Souris River, about 720 km long, rises in the Yellow Grass marshes N of Weyburn, Sask, flows SE past ESTEVAN and wanders S across the N Dakota border before entering Manitoba. Near the town of Souris it swirls through a series of deep gorges, then makes an abrupt NE turn to join the ASSINIBOINE R. Much of its drainage basin is fertile silt and clay deposited by former glacial Lk Souris, and much of the river's course follows the cut of the lake's outfall. The river's name, French for mouse, aptly describes its meandering course, which from a distant vantage resembles the track of a mouse. The river was an ancillary route of the fur trade, and at least 7 posts were built along its gentle banks between 1785 and 1832. It is still a popular canoe route, but the dominant feature around it now is wheat.   JAMES MARSH

Sourkes, Theodore Lionel, biochemist, neuropsychopharmacologist (b at Montréal 21 Feb 1919). One of Canada's great scholars, he became professor of PSYCHIATRY at McGill in 1965 and director of the neurochemistry laboratory at the Allan Memorial Inst of Psychiatry; in 1970 he was appointed professor of biochemistry as well. He has been a prime mover in the establishment of biochemical psychiatry as an accurate discipline. He is a brilliant scientist, internationally known as a pioneer in nutrition, particularly the role of vitamins in the nervous system and the metabolism of brain neurotransmitters. He was one of the originators of the studies that led to the use of L-DOPA in the treatment of Parkinson's disease, and his introduction of α-methylDOPA into the pharmacological literature resulted in its widespread use to combat hypertension. He received the senior award of the Parkinson's Disease Foundation 1963-66, became a fellow of the Royal Soc of Canada in 1971 and was honoured with the first Heinz-Lehmann Award in neuropsychopharmacology in 1982. Esteemed by students and colleagues, he is the author of more than 300 publications, among them a landmark study of the biochemistry of mental disease (1962) and an account of the Nobel Prize winners in medicine and physiology. LEONHARD S. WOLFE

Souster, Raymond Holmes, poet and editor (b at Toronto 15 Jan 1921). Souster has spent his entire life in his native city except for wartime service in the RCAF. In civilian life he has been employed by the Canadian Imperial Bank of Commerce. Souster's literary activities began with an association with John Sutherland and his FIRST STATEMENT group in Montréal which led him to launch *Direction* (1943-46), the first of a series of LITTLE MAGAZINES which would place him in the forefront of the literary avant-garde in Canada. Souster was represented with 21 poems in Ronald Hambleton's anthology, *Unit of Five* (1944), and had his first independent collection, *When we are Young* (1946), published by the First Statement Press. This was followed by *Go to Sleep World* (1947). In the early poems, Souster showed himself to be an idealist with a working-class voice, a strong belief in youthful love and a naïve sense of the lyrical quality of nature to which were opposed the shabbiness of the inner city, the squalor of the industrial landscape and the destruction of war. In 1952 his "friendship-by-letter" with Louis DUDEK crystallized into an active co-operation with Dudek and Irving LAYTON in the activities of CONTACT magazine (1952-54) and Contact Press (1952-67). His *Selected Poems* (1956), chosen by Dudek, brought Souster serious critical attention. In the 1960s he entered into a prolific and distinguished period in his writing, the highlight of which was the Governor General's Award for *The Colour of the Times* (1964). In 1967 he received the Centennial Medal, and in 1968-69 he served as president of the League of Canadian Poets, which he had been instrumental in founding.

Souster brought several young poets to Contact Press, and gave an important boost to the new poetry with *New Wave Canada: The New Explosion in Canadian Poetry* (1966). He embarked, as well, on the reworking of some of his earlier poetry with a view to republication, leading up to *Collected Poems* (4 vols) which began to appear in 1980, confirming his colloquial voice, the low-strung, city-bred images and the modest nostalgias of a middle-class vision. Souster has also tried his hand at fiction, publishing *The Winter of Time* (1949) and *On Target* (1972) under the pseudonyms of Raymond Holmes and John Holmes respectively.   MICHAEL GNAROWSKI

Reading: F. Davey, *Louis Dudek and Raymond Souster* (1981).

South African War (Boer War), 11 Oct 1899 to 31 May 1902 between Britain and the 2 Afrikaner republics of South Africa (SAR, or Transvaal) and the Orange Free State. When war began, Canadian opinion was already sharply divided on the question of sending troops to aid the British. French Canadians led by Henri BOURASSA, seeing growing British imperialism as a threat to their survival, sympathized with the Afrikaners, whereas English Canadians, with some notable exceptions, rallied to the British cause. Under intense public pressure, Wilfrid Laurier's government reluctantly authorized recruitment of a token 1000 infantrymen, designated the 2nd (Special Service) Battalion, Royal Canadian Regiment, commanded by Lt-Col William D. OTTER. They sailed Oct 30 from Québec. With British reverses and mounting casualties, Canada had no difficulty procuring 6000 more volunteers, all mounted men, including 3 batteries of field artillery which accompanied Canada's 2nd contingent, the 1st Regiment, Canadian Mounted Rifles; another 1000 men, the 3rd Battalion, RCR, were raised to relieve regular British troops garrisoned at Halifax, NS. Only the 1st, 2nd and Halifax contingents, 12 instructional officers, 6 chaplains, 8 nurses and 22 artificers (mostly blacksmiths) were recruited under the authority of the Canadian MILITIA ACT and were organized, clothed, equipped, transported and partially paid by the Canadian government, at a cost of $2 830 965. The 3rd contingent, Strathcona's Horse, was funded entirely by Lord Strathcona (Donald SMITH), Canada's wealthy high commissioner to the UK. The rest, the South African Constabulary, the 2nd, 3rd, 4th, 5th and 6th Regiments of CMR and the 10th Canadian Field Hospital, were recruited and paid by Britain. All volunteers agreed to serve for up to one year, except in the Constabulary, which insisted on 3 years' service. Canadians also served in imperial, irregular units, such as the Canadian Scouts and Brabant's Horse.

The war can be divided into 3 phases. Euphoria marked the start of hostilities and ended in Britain's "Black Week" of mid-Dec 1899. This first period, characterized by British blunders and defeats, startled Canadians as the more numerous Afrikaner soldiers, highly mobile and armed with modern weapons and the determination to de-

Rifle drill on board the SS *Monterey* for members of the Strathcona Horse en route to the South African War (*by permission of the British Library*).

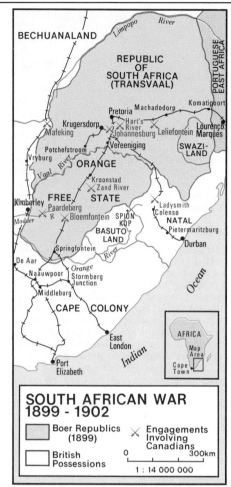

SOUTH AFRICAN WAR 1899 - 1902

- ▨ Boer Republics (1899)
- ☐ British Possessions
- ✕ Engagements Involving Canadians

0   300km

1 : 14 000 000

fend their homeland, confounded the British. The second phase, Feb-Aug 1900, reversed the trend. During this period the British reorganized and reinforced, and under new leadership began their steady march to Bloemfontein and Pretoria, the capitals of the OFS and the SAR. After Paul Kruger, SAR president, fled to Europe 3 months following Pretoria's fall, the war continued another 2 years. But it had become dull, dirty guerrilla warfare, with the British resorting to blockhouses, farm burning and concentration camps to subdue the "bitter-enders."

Only the 1st and 2nd contingents, Lord Strathcona's Horse, the 2nd Canadian Mounted Rifles and the Constabulary saw active service; the rest arrived around the Peace of Vereeniging, signed 31 May 1902. In battles at PAARDEBERG, Zand River, Mafeking, LELIEFONTEIN, Lydengur, Hart's River and elsewhere, Canadian troops had distinguished themselves. Their tenacity, stamina and initiative seemed especially suited to the Afrikaners' unorthodox, guerrilla tactics. Four Canadians received the VICTORIA CROSS, 19 the Distinguished Service Order and 17 the Distinguished Conduct Medal; 117 were mentioned in dispatches, and Canada's senior nursing sister, Georgina POPE, was awarded the Royal Red Cross. During the final months of the war 40 Canadian teachers went to South Africa as part of Milner's reconstruction plans.

Canadians at home viewed their soldiers' martial success with pride and marked their victories by massive parades and demonstrations lasting several days. They insured the men's lives upon their enlistment, showered them with gifts upon their departure and during their service, and feted them upon their return. They formed a Patriotic Fund and a Canadian branch of the Soldiers' Wives' League to care for their dependants, and a Canadian South African Memorial

Association to mark the graves of the 244 Canadian casualties, over half of them victims of diseases, principally enteric fever. After the war they erected monuments to the men who fought. The wounded, men such as the celebrated trooper L.W. Mulloy, who had been blinded, remained for years a living testimony to the war's human cost.

The success of Canada's soldiers and their criticism of British leadership and social values fed a new sense of Canadian self-confidence, which loosened rather than cemented the ties of empire. Many of Canada's young South African War veterans, such as R.E.W. TURNER, E.W.B. Morrison, A.C. MACDONNELL, E.H. Burstall and V.A.S. Williams, played a prominent part in WWI. The war also damaged relations between French and English Canadians. Once during the war the bitterness created by the conflict erupted into a 3-day riot in Montréal. Consequently, although the war undoubtedly sharpened English Canada's identity, it left distrust and resentment in its wake.   CARMAN MILLER

Reading: S. Evans, *The Canadian Contingents and Canadian Imperialism* (1901); Carman Miller, "Canada and the Boer War," *Canada's Visual History*, vol 24 (1978); Thomas Pakenham, *The Boer War* (1979).

South Asians Those people referred to as South Asians or East Indians are easily the most diverse ethnocultural population in Canada. They trace their origins to South Asia, which encompasses India (where 55% of immigrants were born), Pakistan (8%), Bangladesh and Sri Lanka (formerly Ceylon). Most South Asian Canadians are immigrants or descendants of immigrants from these countries, but about 35% are from South Asian communities established during British colonial times in East and South Africa (13%), the Caribbean (15%), Fiji (5%) and Mauritius. Others come from Britain, the US and Europe. Although revised census figures suggest that there were 221 085 South Asian Canadians in 1981, immigration figures show this to be an undercount. The roughly 370 000 South Asians in Canada at the end of 1987 comprise 1.5% of the total population.

People who are called "South Asian" view the term in the way that those from European countries might view the label "European." While they acknowledge that South Asians share cultural and historical characteristics, their basic identification is with more specific ethnocultural roots. In cities such as Toronto, over 20 distinct ethnic groups can be identified within the large (130 000) South Asian population.

Origins The ethnic diversity of South Asian Canadians reflects the enormous cultural variability of South Asia's 800 million people. About 40-50% of South Asian Canadians emigrated from India (and more were born there), where 14 major languages are spoken and where there are hundreds of discrete ethnic groups. This pluralism extends to religion, for though 83% of Indians are Hindus, over 50 million practise Islam, and 15 million practise Sikhism. Many others are Christian or Jain. Islam is the predominant religion in Pakistan and Bangladesh, yet both countries are culturally diverse. A third major world religion (BUDDHISM) is practised by most Sri Lankans, but large Hindu, Christian and Muslim religious minority groups exist there as well. Communities established outside South Asia are much more homogeneous, but in each community people have developed a unique identity and way of life which is distinct from any in South Asia.

Migration The first South Asian migrants to Canada were Sikhs who arrived in Vancouver in 1903. The great majority of them were Sikhs who had heard of Canada from British Indian troops in Hong Kong, who had travelled through Canada the previous year on their way to the coronation celebrations of Edward VII. Attracted by high Canadian wages, they soon found work. Immigration thereafter increased quickly and reached 5209 by the end of 1908; all of these immigrants were men who had temporarily left their families to find employment in Canada. Perhaps 90% were Sikhs, primarily from Punjab farming backgrounds. Virtually all of them remained in BC.

Seeing in them the same racial threat as in JAPANESE and CHINESE immigrants before them, the BC government quickly limited South Asian rights and privileges. In 1907 South Asians were provincially disenfranchised, which denied them the federal vote and access to political office, jury duty, the professions, public-service jobs and labour on public works. In the following year the federal government enacted an immigration regulation which specified that immigrants had to travel to Canada with continuous ticketing arrangements from their country of origin. There were no such arrangements between India and Canada and, as was its intent, the continuous-passage provision consequently precluded further South Asian immigration. This ban separated men from their families and made further growth of the community impossible. Vigorous court challenges of the regulations proved ineffective and in 1913 frustration with government treatment culminated in the evolution of the Ghadar Party, an organization which aimed at the overthrow of British rule in India. The immigration ban was directly challenged in 1914, when the freighter KOMAGATA MARU sailed from Hong Kong to Canada with 376 prospective South Asian immigrants. Immigration officials isolated the ship in Vancouver harbour for 2 months, and it was forced to return to Asia. Revolutionary sentiment thereafter reached a high pitch, and many men returned to India to work for Ghadar.

The federal government's continuous-journey provision remained law until 1947, as did most BC anti-South Asian legislation. Because of community pressure and representations by the government of India, Canada allowed the wives and dependent children of South Asian Canadian residents to immigrate in 1919, and by the mid-1920s a small flow of wives and children had been established. This did not counter the effect of migration by South Asian Canadians to India and the US, which by the mid-1920s had reduced the South Asian population in Canada to about 1300.

During the 1920s South Asian economic security increased, primarily through work in the lumber industry and the sale of wood and sawdust as home heating fuel. In addition, a number of lumber mills were acquired by South Asians, 2 of which employed over 300 people. The effects of the GREAT DEPRESSION on the community were severe but were mitigated by extensive mutual aid. By WWII South Asians in BC had gained much local support in their drive to secure the vote, especially from the CO-OPERATIVE COMMONWEALTH FEDERATION. In 1947 the BC ban against voting and other restrictions were removed. Faced with the coming independence of India, the federal government removed the continuous-passage regulation in the same year, replacing it in 1951 by an annual immigration quota for India (150 a year), Pakistan (100) and Ceylon (50). There were then only 2148 South Asians in Canada, 1937 of them in BC. Moderate expansion of immigration increased the Canadian total to 6774 in 1961.

As racial and national restrictions were removed from the immigration regulations in the 1960s, South Asian immigration mushroomed. It also became much more culturally diverse; a high proportion of immigrants in the 1950s were the Sikh relatives of pioneer South Asian settlers, while the 1960s also saw sharp increases in immigration from other parts of India and from Pakistan. By the early 1960s, two-thirds of South Asian immigrant men were professionals – teachers, doctors, university professors and scientists. Canadian preferences for highly skilled immigrants during 1960-70 broadened the ethnic range of South Asians and hence decreased the proportion who were Sikh. Nondiscriminatory immigration regulations enacted in 1967 resulted in a further, dramatic increase in South Asian immigration. South Asian Canadians numbered 67 925 in 1971.

In 1972 all South Asians were expelled from Uganda. Canada accepted 7000 of them (many of whom were Ismailis) as political REFUGEES. Thereafter a steady flow of South Asians have come to Canada from Kenya, Tanzania and Zaire, either directly or via Britain. The 1970s also marked the beginning of migration from Fiji, Guyana, Trinidad and Mauritius. Since 1978 a weaker Canadian economy has significantly reduced South Asian immigration, but it will likely remain above 10 000 a year for the foreseeable future.

Settlement Patterns Virtually all South Asians lived in BC until the late 1950s, when professional South Asian immigrants began to settle across the country. The South Asian population of the urban corridor from Metro Toronto to Windsor grew dramatically to a present total of about 170 000. BC's South Asian population is now some 100 000, most of which (63 000) is concentrated in the Vancouver area. Virtually all South Asian Canadians live in urban contexts, and 95% of South Asians reside in Ontario (180 000), BC (100 000), Alberta (40 000) and Québec (30 000). In addition, some ethnic South Asian populations are quite localized, primarily as the result of chain migration. For example, Sikhs are heavily overrepresented in Vancouver, as are those from Fiji; those from Guyana and Trinidad in Toronto; and Ismailis in Vancouver, Edmonton and Calgary.

Economic Life Early Sikhs in BC were almost entirely involved in the lumber industry. They are still active in this industry, both as workers and millowners. Skilled South Asian professionals of various ethnocultural backgrounds who arrived between 1960 and 1975 are now well established. The occupational distribution broadened in the 1970s with the arrival of an increasing proportion of South Asian blue- and white-collar workers. The exodus of Ugandan South Asians brought many business people to Canada, and a number have taken up entrepreneurial activities ranging from the ownership of taxis to the control of corporations. The participation of other South Asians in businesses has also been high. In South Asia few women worked outside the home, but Canadian South Asian women have been very active participants in the economy in a variety of blue- and white-collar jobs; 70% of women aged 20-45 had paid work according to the 1981 census, compared with 52% of all Canadian women in this age bracket. South Asians have also been involved in farming, especially in BC.

Social Life and Community South Asian Canadians have such widely varying backgrounds that few generalities can be made about their social and community life. One critical cultural commonality is that they all come from places where extended families, kinship and community relations are extremely important. Immigrants from South Asia quickly accept most Canadian cultural patterns, but they have tried to maintain a core of continuity in family and community practice. Parents generally attempt, often quite unsuccessfully, to instill in their children key South Asian family values. This goes hand in hand with massive acculturation among the Canadian born. Husband-wife relations are changing, especially as wives acquire access to economic and social resources. Future family changes are likely, particularly in regard to intermarriage, as the second generation matures.

As a rule, informal social links between individuals of similar backgrounds are strong. South Asians do not usually form strongly geographically concentrated communities, and relationships are supported chiefly by continual visiting. In contrast, links between the various South Asian communities are extremely weak and are chiefly restricted to contacts among leaders. As a consequence, it is inaccurate to speak of "the" South Asian community of a given place, for there are likely to be many. Contacts between communities most frequently arise when communities are small or where culture, language or religion are shared.

Religious and Cultural Life South Asian communities vary widely in the emphasis they place on extra-familial cultural activities. As a rule, groups with high ethnic consciousness, eg, Sikhs, maintain a quite full round of these activities, whereas groups such as Fijians and Guyanese, and South Asians of the professional classes do not. A similar degree of variability exists in regard to religious institutions. Sikhs are numerous, their identity is both ethnic and religious, and their religious institutions have been in place since the first Canadian Sikh temple was founded in 1908. They have consequently been very successful in establishing and preserving their religion in Canada. Ismaili Muslims, whose spiritual leader is the Aga Khan, are also both an ethnic and a religious group, and they have founded strong religious institutions wherever they have gone. Sunni Muslims (chiefly from Pakistan and India) have generally allied themselves with other Sunnis in support of pan-ethnic mosques, and they too seem to be effectively transmitting their religion to their children. In Hindu populations of sufficient size, people have established Hindu temples, which are used by a range of different ethnic groups for prayer, for the presentation of annual ceremonies, and for important rituals linked to marriage and death. Sinhalese, who practise BUDDHISM, have established a temple in Toronto. Most communities support a variety of other activities and institutions. Nominally religious organizations frequently support language classes for children and cultural activities such as South Asian music and dance. In addition, there are now over 250 South Asian sociocultural associations in Canada, most formed in the past 15 years. Folk and classical music and dance traditions are popular. In addition, South Asian Canadians now support a number of newspapers and newsletters. South Asian programming on radio and cable television is expanding rapidly, especially in major centres (*see* HINDUISM; ISLAM; SIKHISM).

Politics Until 1965, South Asian politics were devoted primarily to lobbying for elimination of the legal restrictions enacted by the BC Legislature and to changing immigration laws. Over the past 20 years, South Asians have become increasingly involved on other political fronts. Their associations now actively lobby for government support for cultural programs, for greater access to immigration, and for government action to reduce PREJUDICE AND DISCRIMINATION. South Asians have frequently held local level offices, but their participation has not yet been extensive at higher levels. South Asians are sometimes involved in home country politics, the key recent example being the rising post-1983 Canadian Sikh support for greater rights for Sikhs in Punjab.

Basic South Asian Canadian Ethnocultural Categories, 1987				
Group	*Primary place of origin*	*Majority religion*	*Major languages*	*Number*
Sikhs	Punjab, India	Sikh	Punjabi	130 000
Pakistanis	Pakistan	Sunni Muslim	Urdu	130 000
Trinida-dians	Trinidad	Christian Hindu	English	25 000
Ismailis	East Africa	Ismaili Muslim	Gujarati	25 000
Northern Indians	Uttar Pradesh India, etc	Hindu	Hindi Punjabi	30 000
Fijians	Fiji	Hindu	English Hindi	15 000
Gujaratis	Gujarat, India, East Africa	Hindu	Gujarati	20 000
Guyanese	Guyana	mixed	English	25 000
Southern Indians	Kerala and Madras, India	Hindu	Malayalam Tamil Telugu	7 000
Sinhalese	Sri Lanka	Buddhist	Sinhala	5 000
Bengalis	Bengal, India	Hindu	Bengali	3 000
Bangla-deshis	Bangla-desh	Sunni Muslim	Bengali	2 000

Group Maintenance In 1981 the census showed that 76% of South Asian Canadians were immigrants. 90% of the Canadian born were then 19 years old or less. Only the Sikhs have been in Canada long enough to have demonstrated a clear pattern of group maintenance through the generations. Strong group consciousness and minority-group status resulted in high rates of cultural retention among BC Sikhs. Virtually all of the second generation are knowledgeable of Sikh culture and language and marry other Sikhs.

Other groups, eg, Ismailis, Pakistanis and other Sunni Muslims, have stressed religious above cultural and linguistic maintenance. For most South Asian groups, acculturation in the second generation will be extensive, the universal South Asian exception being in regard to patterns of marriage and the family. Whether social integration will be equally thorough will depend chiefly on the future development of relations between South Asians and others. Increases in South Asian immigration were met by some racial prejudice in the mid-1970s, especially in Toronto and Vancouver. It has since decreased.

NORMAN BUCHIGNANI

Reading: Norman Buchignani and Doreen Indra, with R. Srivastava, *Continuous Journey* (1985); R. Kanungo, ed, *South Asians in the Canadian Mosaic* (1984); G. Kurian and R. Srivastava, eds, *Overseas Indians: A Study in Adaptation* (1983); S. Sugunasiri, ed, *The Search for Meaning: The Literature of South Asian Canadian Writers* (1983).

South Moresby, 145 000 ha wilderness archipelago of the QUEEN CHARLOTTE ISLANDS, including Moresby I, south of Tangil Peninsula, reserved for a NATIONAL PARK in 1987. Inaccessible by land, South Moresby has become popular (est 2000 visitors in 1987) for summer sailing and kayaking in the sheltered passages on its east side, hiking in the San Cristobal Mts and visiting the cedar ruins of HAIDA Indian villages, particularly Ninstints on ANTHONY ISLAND. South Moresby's intact wildlands are widely known for their old forests of cedar and spruce that harbour rare mosses and unusual animal subspecies (providing evidence it was a North Pacific refuge from glaciation *c*75 000 to 10 000 years ago). In its intertidal zone

are spectacular clusters of ocean life. On the water are huge seabird colonies, their raptor predators in nearby aeries. Sea lions make colonies on rocks and islets, and large whales migrate through HECATE STRAIT. This rugged, storm-wracked setting was inhabited for many centuries, and as many as 40 Haida villages were in South Moresby when Europeans arrived (first landing 1789). Contact for trade, initially in sea otter pelts, led to smallpox epidemics which totally depopulated the area, and extractive industries moved in. Copper mines operated at Jedway and Ikeda intermittently from 1906; a whaling station at Rose Harbour (1910-48); A-frame logging from *c* 1925 on slopes handy to tidewater. BC licenced 56 168 ha of South Moresby to a forest company in 1958, and clearcut logging proceeded on Lyell Island from 1975. The 1987 Canada-BC agreement for the national park followed 13 years of controversy, even civil disobedience, over the exclusion of logging from South Moresby. Canada's $106-million investment will compensate for cancelled tenures and lost work as well as building park facilities and developing tourism in the Queen Charlottes. The area's future still hangs on settlement of the Haida nation's claim, opened in 1984, to possession of the islands. PETER GRANT

South Nahanni River, 563 km long, flows SE out of the Ragged Range of the Selwyn Mts, cuts across successive spines of the Mackenzie Mts and empties into the LIARD R. In 1972 the federal government formed NAHANNI NATIONAL PK to enclose the lower two-thirds of the S Nahanni and the lower half of its main tributary, the Flat R. The area's geological diversity is unexcelled: hot springs, glaciers, KARST landscape with bottomless sinkhole lakes, marshes, desertscapes, tundra plateaus, towering hoodoos and thick forests. Through it plunges the river called *Nahadeh* by the SLAVEY, "powerful river," with its whirlpool rapids, waterfalls and the 3 most spectacular river canyons in Canada. The name "Nahanni" is Athapaskan for "people of the west," referring to the NAHANI. The gorges of Five Mile Canyon, Fig-

The South Nahanni River flows through canyons of unexcelled natural beauty. Gate Pulpit Rock is shown (*courtesy Environment Canada, Parks*).

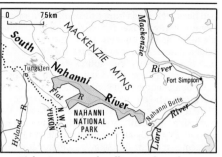

ure Eight Canyon and Hell's Gate have been cut by the river through the spine of the Mackenzie Mts and remain sharp and narrow because this is one of the few spots in Canada that escaped the gouging of the last continental ice sheets. About 150 km from the confluence with the Liard, the river constricts to one-fifth its previous width, forms a jet called the Chutes and flares out into a waterfall – almost half again as high as Niagara – called Virginia Falls for the daughter of Fenley Hunter, who first measured it in 1928. NAHANNI BUTTE, an Indian village, is practically the only settlement in the area. The first whites to see the river were the passing traders on their way to the Klondike. JAMES MARSH

South Porcupine, Ont, subdivision of the city of TIMMINS, located about 300 km NW of Sudbury. Although traces of gold in the Porcupine district had been discovered earlier, serious prospecting began 1906 and culminated in the rush of 1909. South Porcupine, inc 1911, and named for an island in a local river reportedly shaped like the animal, stood on the S shore of Porcupine Lk at a point intersecting a branch line of the Temiskaming and Northern Ont Ry, then under construction. This position, along with the town's accessibility to a major producer, Dome mine, gave it an initial advantage over rivals such as Golden City. In June 1911, however, the town was destroyed by fire and Noah TIMMINS, owner of the Hollinger mine, established a new townsite, also on the railway, that was closer to his own property. Though rebuilt, South Porcupine lost its advantage and thereafter Timmins emerged as the chief urban centre, as acknowledged by the town's 1973 incorporation into Timmins. MATT BRAY

South Sea Company, chartered in 1711 by the British Parliament, with a monopoly over the W coast of the Americas to a distance of 300 leagues out to sea. In 1720 it assumed a large part of the British national debt and almost collapsed that year in a stock market crash known as the South Sea Bubble. However, until 1833 British vessels trading on the NORTHWEST COAST were obliged to carry licences from the company, as well as from the EAST INDIA COMPANY. BARRY M. GOUGH

Southam, William, newspaper publisher (b near Montréal 23 Aug 1843; d at Hamilton 27 Feb 1932). He was a typical 19th-century printer-publisher who lived to see a modern newspaper chain bearing the name he shared with the 6 sons who were the instruments of his dream. Southam had spent years on the *London Free Press* when, in 1877, he and a partner took over the ailing Hamilton *Spectator*, hoping a return to Conservative government in Ottawa would improve its health; it did. Despite comparatively low start-up costs, he continued to buy existing dailies rather than begin his own, acquiring the Ottawa *Citizen*, Calgary *Herald*, Edmonton *Journal*, Windsor *Star* and Montréal *Gazette*. Subsequent diversification into broadcasting, magazines and business publications has not prevented Southam Inc, still family controlled, from retaining a high-quality and devoutly Conservative flavour traceable to its founder's influence. DOUGLAS FETHERLING

Southam Inc is the oldest and largest cross-media-group owner in Canada. With 16 daily newspapers and its own news service (Southam News, with 6 Canadian and 7 foreign bureaus), Southam is the largest Canadian NEWSPAPER-group owner in terms of circulation. Total daily circulation average for 1986 was 1 547 000 and in 1987 was 1 541 200. Southam also owns a 30% equity interest in TORSTAR CORP, publishers of the *Toronto Star*; a 47.3% interest in SELKIRK COMMUNICATIONS; 35% of Telemedia Publishing (publishers of *TV Guide* and *Canadian Living*); and 48% of JEMCOM Inc, formerly Kitchener-Waterloo Record Ltd.

Southam also publishes 53 business publications, 1 special-interest and consumer publication, 24 annuals and directories, 10 newsletters and looseleaf services, and it operates 62 trade shows and exhibitions and 18 related service companies. Southam also owns Infomart, an electronic publishing firm which markets Canadian and US databases. In printing operations, Southam operates 17 commercial printing plants across Canada and the US as well as 2 specialized printing divisions for the production of lottery tickets and promotional card games. Southam Inc assets totalled $1.145 billion in 1987, with revenues of $1.479 billion.

Southampton Island, 41 214 km², is situated between FOXE BASIN and HUDSON BAY. It combines the 2 basic regional relief types. Its north and northeast consist of undulating highlands of Precambrian SHIELD rocks, reaching elevations of 400 m and terminating in steep cliffs on Foxe Channel. In complete contrast, its south and southwest are made up of gently sloping flat-lying Paleozoic rocks, forming limestone plains and plateaus of low relief (less than 200 m). Frost-shattered boulders and clayey gravels give the surface a desert-like appearance. Exposures of ancient reefs hint at the possible presence of hydrocarbons, but economically significant accumulations more likely lie offshore. The island was named for the earl of Southampton (1573-1624).   DOUG FINLAYSON

Southeast Asians Southeast Asia includes Indonesia, Brunei, Singapore, the Philippines, Burma, Malaysia, Thailand, Vietnam, Kampuchea and Laos. This article only concerns those from Indochina: the Vietnamese (estimated Canadian population at the end of 1986: 64 000), Vietnamese Chinese (44 000), Lao (15 500) and Khmer or Kampucheans (17 000).

Migration and Settlement Indochinese have come to Canada in 4 waves. Some arrived as students during the 1950s and 1960s and remained, so that by 1970 there were about 1200 Vietnamese and a few hundred Lao and Khmer living primarily in Québec. The American defeat in Vietnam and the fall of the Thieu regime in early 1975 led to a mass flight of Vietnamese, about 6500 of whom were admitted to Canada as political REFUGEES. By 1978 there were 10 000 Indochinese in Canada; most were in Montréal, Toronto, Calgary, Edmonton and Vancouver. Almost all were ethnic Vietnamese, and most men were professionals, bureaucrats, military personnel or students. In late 1978 the exodus of "boat people" (Vietnamese and Vietnamese Chinese), increased dramatically and in Nov 1978 Canada accepted 604 refugees from the freighter *Hai Hong*. The situation of the boat people and of Lao, Khmer and Vietnamese "land people" who fled to Thailand thereafter grew increasingly severe, and in response Canada took in 59 970 refugee and designated class immigrants during the next 2 years (1979-80). Over 32 000 were sponsored by 6887 private groups or churches, and 65% of these sponsorship groups were organized through religious organizations: Catholic, Mennonite, Chris-

tian Reformed, and United Church groups together supported 48% of all privately sponsored refugees.

Sponsorship dispersed Indochinese across the country, but many subsequently migrated to the cities, especially to Toronto, Ottawa, Montréal, Edmonton, Calgary and Vancouver. Thereafter (1981-86), many Indochinese continued to come as refugees and designated class immigrants: 24 240 from Vietnam, 3395 from Laos and 8906 from Kampuchea. At the same time, an increasing number of people have come from Vietnam through normal immigration channels: 16 553 in 1984-86 alone. At the end of 1986, 134 000 Indochinese, or 95%, were immigrants; 103 000 from Vietnam, 16 000 from Kampuchea and 17 000 from Laos.

Economic Life The ethnic Vietnamese refugees of the 1975-76 exodus were typically well educated and occupationally skilled. Many were fluent in English or French. Despite some downward economic mobility, they were soon established economically. The economic backgrounds of Indochinese arriving since 1977 have been more varied, and so have their Canadian economic prospects. Among more recent arrivals from Vietnam about 75% of workers have blue-collar occupational experience; 15% are white collar workers and 10% are professionals, managers or owners of businesses. Many Vietnamese Chinese own small businesses. Lao and Khmer often have farming backgrounds.

Post-1976 refugees have shown great flexibility in adapting to Canadian economic life. In this, a strong dependence on family and informal community support systems has been of great assistance. Nevertheless, many Indochinese today can be found in low-paying and uncertain jobs in the service and industrial sectors. Many are underemployed. As a response to the post-1980 Canadian economic downturn thousands have migrated to Ontario and secondarily to Québec from other parts of the country.

Social and Cultural Life As Indochinese emigrated under traumatic circumstances, their efforts were initially directed towards employment, English- and French-language training and family unification. For Indochinese the family has traditionally been the central social institution, and this centrality has been maintained in Canada — at least for those who have been able to reconstitute their family life here. Most families in Canada are incomplete, especially among the Khmer, many of whose family members died during the reign of Pol Pot. Informal community networks are important, providing psychological support, association with others having common roots and much useful information. Each group forms almost entirely separate local ethnocultural communities, even at the informal level. This is also true in terms of community institutions.

Most Vietnamese practise Mahayana BUDDHISM, and have formed Buddhist associations across Canada to perform required religious rites at birth, marriage and death. Vietnamese Catholics usually affiliate with extant Canadian Catholic congregations, but sometimes have their own religious organizations and congregations, as do those of other Christian denominations. The Vietnamese have actively developed formal community organizations across Canada, which have become important foci for cultural celebrations, recreational activities and sociocultural maintenance. Nationally, the Canadian Federation of Vietnamese Associations has 19 local member associations and is concerned primarily with maintaining Vietnamese culture and facilitating social integration into Canadian life. The vast majority of Vietnamese are fiercely antithetical to the present Vietnamese regime, and many support

Canadian political groups such as the United National Front for the Liberation of Vietnam, and the Movement for Support of the Liberation of Vietnam.

Chinese migrants from Vietnam share many cultural and linguistic commonalities with other CHINESE in Canada whose ultimate origins are Canton. Hence, Vietnamese Chinese have made heavy use of extant Chinese Canadian community institutions. Most of the religious observances of Mahayana Buddhists, Confucianists, Taoists and ancestor worshippers are done in the home; for life cycle-based religious events they make use of Chinese Canadian institutions. Vietnamese Chinese nevertheless strongly identify with their unique heritage and have formed cultural associations in most cities.

The Lao and the Khmer are both Theravada Buddhists, and as such are quite religiously distinct from Buddhists from Vietnam. Few in number, neither group has yet established its own permanent religious institutions outside Québec; Lao and Khmer monks and religious organizations in various parts of the country perform an increasing range of religious ceremonies important to Khmer personal and collective identities. Lao and Khmer cultural associations are not yet as well developed as those of their Vietnamese counterparts.   DOREEN INDRA

Reading: K. Chan and D. Indra, Uprooting, Loss and Adaptation: The Resettlement of Indochinese in Canada (1987); E. Tepper, ed, Southeast Asian Exodus: From Tradition to Resettlement (1980).

Southern Indian Lake, 2248 km², elev 255 m, max length 146 km, is located in N-central Manitoba, 40 km NE of Leaf Rapids and 94 km E of Lynn Lake. Together with its eastern neighbour, the much smaller Northern Indian Lk, Southern Indian Lk is an expansion of the CHURCHILL R, which drains it in a northeasterly direction and eventually empties into the W side of HUDSON BAY. The lake has heavily indented shoreline. It is dotted with many small islands. An HBC post was established at South Indian Lk, a settlement on the S shore, as the river and the lakes it joined became one of the most important arteries in the FUR TRADE. The community was flooded in 1980 when the lake was dammed by Manitoba Hydro. The lake appears on Peter FIDLER's map (1814) and is probably named after the "southern Indians" or Cree.   DAVID EVANS

Sovereign, the head of STATE who reigns by hereditary right, as opposed to the elected head of GOVERNMENT. In Canada, a constitutional monarchy, the sovereign is one of the 3 components of Parliament. Since the 16th century some 32 French and British kings and queens have reigned over Canada. In 1867 the FATHERS OF CONFEDERATION vested executive authority and many statutory responsibilities in Queen Victoria, her heirs and successors. In 1947, under Letters Patent issued by George VI, all of the sovereign's powers and authorities in Canada were delegated to the GOVERNOR GENERAL. Contrary to popular belief, the sovereign's presence in Canada does not supersede this delegation except when the sovereign is actually asked to perform specific royal functions, eg, the opening of Parliament. George VI was the first reigning sovereign to visit Canada. In the spring of 1939 he toured with his consort, Elizabeth (now the Queen Mother), and on May 19 gave royal assent to several Canadian Bills in the Senate Chamber.

On 6 Feb 1952 Elizabeth II became sovereign, and in 1953 the Canadian Royal Style and Titles Act officially entitled her Queen of Canada. Her full title is "Elizabeth II, by the Grace of God, of the United Kingdom, Canada, and her other Realms and Territories Queen, Head of the Common-

Sovereigns Who Have Reigned Over Canadian Territory

British Isles

(1485)-1509	Henry VII	1702-1714	Anne
1509-1547	Henry VIII	1714-1727	George I
1547-1553	Edward VI	1727-1760	George II
1553-1558	Mary I	1760-1820	George III
1558-1603	Elizabeth I	1820-1830	George IV
1603-1625	James I	1830-1837	William IV
1625-1649	Charles I	1837-1901	Victoria
1649-1660	(Republic)	1901-1910	Edward VII
1660-1685	Charles II	1910-1936	George V
1685-1688	James II	1936	Edward VIII
1689-1702	William III	1936-1952	George VI
1689-1694	and Mary II	1952-	Elizabeth II

France

(1515)-1547	François I	1589-1610	Henri IV
1547-1559	Henri II	1610-1643	Louis XIII
1559-1560	François II	1643-1715	Louis XIV
1560-1574	Charles IX	1715-(1775)	Louis XV
1574-1589	Henri III		

wealth, Defender of the Faith." In 1957 she was the first sovereign to open the Canadian Parliament. She opened Parliament again for her Silver Jubilee in 1977, and on 17 Apr 1982 she proclaimed the Canadian CONSTITUTION. *See also* CROWN; ROYAL TOURS.   JACQUES MONET, S.J.

Sovereign Council In early NEW FRANCE a governing council was created, comprising the GOUVERNEUR (governor), the bishop and representatives ("syndics") of Québec, Trois-Rivières and Montréal. In 1663 Louis XIV equipped the colony with a complete administrative system modelled on those used to govern French provinces. The Sovereign Council, which in 1703 became the Superior Council, was comparable to the *parlements* of those provinces.

The council initially comprised the governor, the bishop, the INTENDANT and 5 councillors. In 1703 membership grew to 12, to which 4 associated judges were added in 1742. Members, usually recruited from the French gentry, were nominated initially by the governor and the bishop and later by the king.

The council acted also as a court of appeal for civil and criminal matters originating in the lower courts. Its decisions could be reversed only by the King's Council, under which a judicial structure was established in each government of the colony: the provost marshal of Québec City (1663), the royal courts of Trois-Rivières (1665) and Montréal (1693), and the Admiralty (1717). The council also played an administrative role in regulating trade and public order, in registering the king's edicts, ordinances and commissions, and in promulgating them in the colony. After the CONQUEST of 1760 its appeal-court functions were taken over by a board of British military officers.
JACQUES MATHIEU

Sovereignty is an abstract legal concept which has also, today, some nonlegal (political, social and economic) implications. In strictly legal terms it denotes the supreme power or authority in the state – the ultimate source of legality. For Canadians, the historical-legal roots go back to the early 17th-century English constitutional battles between king and Parliament, colourfully rendered in the rebuke by Chief Justice Sir Edward Coke to the Royalist claims that executive (Prerogative) powers were immune from legal control or review by other authority (judicial or legislative) in the state. In Coke's celebrated remark (rooted in the words of 13th-century cleric and legist Henry de Braxton), that while the king was not under any man, he was, nevertheless, "under God and the Law." There is a forerunner, here, of late 17th-century social contract theories of the limits of the ultimate duty of obedience to

the law in the case of an unjust ruler or unjust commands stemming from the state.

In its constitutional application in Canada, the concept of sovereignty is addressed, first, to the relations between the different institutions of government – executive, legislative and judicial. The English constitutional theory, deriving historically from Coke but much refined and elaborated and elevated to constitutional dogma by the late-Victorian jurist, Albert Venn Dicey, proclaimed the sovereignty of Parliament. Literally, this meant that there was no law that Parliament could not make or unmake; hence, no distinction between the law of the constitution and any other law; and no power of the courts to refuse to apply any law on constitutional grounds. The political justification for Dicey's theory was the establishment of Parliament as the ultimate democratic institution through the progressive extension of the franchise and the eventual achievement of universal, adult suffrage. While the sovereignty of Parliament was "received" or carried over, without any serious question, into Canadian constitutional theory after the enactment by the British Parliament of the British North America Act, 1867, there were some legal anomalies created by the fact that the new Canadian Parliament was still legally subordinate to the British (Imperial) Parliament and that Canadian courts were subject to review, on appeal, by an imperial tribunal, the JUDICIAL COMMITTEE OF THE PRIVY COUNCIL, sitting in London. These contradictions were resolved, in legal terms, by the further notion of imperial (British) sovereignty and the consequent legal paramountcy of imperial (British) institutions in regard to the overseas British colonies of which Canada was, in 1867, a constituent part.

With the political changes within the British Empire in the 1920s and the 1930s, and the evolution of what was called Dominion status – legal sovereignty and self-government within the new British COMMONWEALTH – legal concepts marched in step with changing political realities. By 1949, when the British Commonwealth gave way to a plain, unprefixed Commonwealth of Nations, Canada had become fully independent in legal terms – sovereign – in relation to Great Britain. Henceforward, legal relations between Canada and Great Britain would be regulated by INTERNATIONAL LAW – the law between sovereign states – and not, as heretofore, by (imperial) CONSTITUTIONAL LAW. The Constitution Act, 1982 (the "patriation package," sponsored by the Trudeau government), for these purposes, simply swept away some final, vestigial footnotes remaining from the imperial constitutional-legal past.

In Canadian constitutional law today, the concept of sovereignty presents 2 distinct and different problems. The first relates to the federal character of the Canadian constitution and the division, for these purposes, of constitutional law-making competence between the central, federal government and regional, PROVINCIAL GOVERNMENTS. In theoretical terms, the notion of a divided sovereignty is represented by saying that within the respective powers allocated to them under the Constitution Act (the contemporary, renamed British North America Act), the federal legislature and the provincial legislatures each have plenary, sovereign law-making capacity, with the courts available, in case of conflicts over federal-provincial legislative jurisdiction, to arbitrate and rule on the ultimate location of sovereign power (federal or provincial, as the case may be). A second problem relates to the continued legal applicability and relevance of the "received" English notion of the sovereignty of Parliament in an era when, with the enactment of the CANADIAN CHARTER OF RIGHTS AND FREEDOMS in 1982, the constitutional charter now entrenches certain funda-

mental, "higher law," principles that are supposed to limit all law-makers. "Received" in the American colonies after their War of Independence against Great Britain – also from Coke, but by way of Sir William Blackstone's famous *Commentaries* – the notion of a Constitution itself as the "supreme law of the land" binding on executive and legislative authority alike, enters into the Constitution of the US adopted in 1787 and is proclaimed as constitutional truth by the Supreme Court of the US in Chief Justice John Marshall's celebrated judgement in *Marbury v Madison* at the opening of the 19th century. It may be suggested that Canadian constitutionalism, by the close of the 20th century, now essentially rejects the "received" English concept of the sovereignty of Parliament in favour of a "received" US concept of the supremacy (sovereignty) of the law (Constitution).

In international law terms, sovereignty denotes the international legal personality of a state. Only states are persons (legal actors) at international law; and the state's sovereignty, for these purposes, is projected in its legal control of territory, territorial waters and national air space, and its legal power to exclude other states from these domains; its legal power to represent and vindicate the claims and interests of its citizens with other states; and its own representation in international legal arenas such as the UNITED NATIONS and international diplomatic conferences, and before international tribunals such as the World Court. These theories of state sovereignty in international law are the products of the period after the Thirty Years' War, Westphalia peace settlement of 1648 and the emergence of the new nation state as the master institution of modern international relations, in displacement of the old, medieval theory of political and religious, and hence legal, unity in western Europe. State sovereignty is itself subject to challenge, at the close of the 20th century, as a viable theoretical base for international relations, when new concepts of supra-nationalism and world government are developing. It also poses problems of minimum correspondence to the ultimate realities of world public order today, as new trans-national political, social and economic actors, far more powerful, sometimes, than individual nation states (multinational corporations, international political parties and cultural or religious movements, even international terrorist organizations) emerge. Yet these new actors have no legal status at international law, other than what they may wish to claim vicariously through attachment to or sponsorship by one or more nation state. We are, in this sense, in an era of transition in international relations and international law; and the notion of state sovereignty is under attack today and may be in a long-range decline, in both political and legal terms.

The strictly legal meaning of the term sovereignty should be differentiated from more popular usages which are sometimes employed out of intellectual fuzziness and sometimes to extract the extra public-relations mileage deriving from a presumedly ancient and hallowed concept like sovereignty. Recurring Canada-US differences over Canada's claims to sovereignty over the arctic waters and the Northwest Passage (*see* ARCTIC SOVEREIGNTY), and contentions that "economic sovereignty" or "cultural sovereignty" may be endangered in any Canada-US FREE TRADE negotiations, can be seen from this point of view to have a high rhetorical-political content. Disputes over the legal extension of state sovereignty in territorial matters turn on issues of legal fact-finding that are most sensibly resolved by independent, third-party arbitration or judicial settlement. International diplomatic negotiations, on the other hand, are essentially exercises in political bargaining and give-and-take, with the dynamic factor in producing consensus being mutuality and reciprocity of interest and benefit: such matters turn, then, on political and not legal considerations, and the introduction of the abstract concept of sovereignty may bring confusion and not reason to the public dialogue involved.

EDWARD McWHINNEY

Sovereignty-Association First used as a slogan by the Mouvement Souveraineté-Association (MSA), forerunners of the PARTI QUÉBÉCOIS, the phrase became the PQ's cornerstone and main objective. Introduced in the document *Option-Québec*, written by party leader René LÉVESQUE, the expression replaced the word independence and implied the idea of an association which would evolve from an agreement under international law and be limited to the economic domain (1967). In the 1970 péquiste program, La Solution (1970), it is not presented as a necessary condition for Québec's accession to sovereignty. With time, however, association came to be viewed as the equal and necessary other half of sovereignty.

In Oct 1978, Premier Lévesque declared in the National Assembly that Québec had to transform radically its union with the rest of Canada, and that sovereignty and association should come about "smoothly and simultaneously." In what came to be called the White Paper on Sovereignty-Association (La nouvelle entente Québec-Canada), the péquiste government claimed that "sovereignty is indissolubly linked with association." The document went on to describe the doctrine more fully: it foresaw a common monetary system with the rest of Canada, coupled with a reorganization of the tasks of the present Bank of Canada into new common institutions, including a central monetary authority. It also presupposed a joint free-trade zone and a common external tariff (though each of the 2 communities could protect its own agriculture). It allowed for the free passage of goods and persons between Québec and Canada, and a variety of special agreements concerning jobs and immigration. A community council, composed of an equal number of ministers from each side and presided over alternately by a Canadian and a Québecois, would settle any disputes that might arise. Three other Québec-Canada institutions were proposed: a committee of experts to serve (under the council) as general secretariat to the community; a court of justice consisting of an equal number of Québec and Canadian judges with exclusive jurisdiction over the interpretation and workings of the association treaty; and a joint monetary authority responsible for the management of the single exchange rate, but not for the debt of the 2 sovereign partners (each would handle its own). Sovereignty-association, in the view of the White Paper, was not an end in itself, but a means by which Québec could freely direct its own affairs. Québec would thus enjoy the economic advantages of the federal union and the benefits of political independence.

In May 1980, the Parti Québécois government used a REFERENDUM to ask the people of Québec for a mandate to negotiate sovereignty-association, thus defined, with the federal and other provincial authorities. The PQ lost the vote (60% to 40%). Early in 1985, after consultation with its membership, the PQ decided to put aside this option, and not make it the party's platform in the next election. This led to internal dissent and a group of the dissidents including Jacques PARIZEAU, faithful to the party's basic objective, decided to leave. The PQ subsequently lost the Québec election of 1985. *See also* FRENCH CANADIAN NATIONALISM.

CLINTON ARCHIBALD

Soward, Frederic Hubert, historian, educator (b at Minden, Ont 10 Apr 1899; d at Vancouver 1 Jan 1985). Educated at Toronto, Edinburgh and Oxford, he taught history at UBC 1922-64 (head of department, 1953-63). As founder and director (1946-64) of the program in international studies at UBC he was a pioneer of academic study in this area in Canada. A consultant in the Dept of External Affairs during WWII, he helped to plan its rapid expansion during those years. Through his teaching, publications and popular lectures, and by his promotion of the League of Nations Society, the Canadian Institute of International Affairs, the Institute of Pacific Relations and the United Nations Assn he promoted among Canadians a more informed interest in the world beyond their borders.

MARGARET E. PRANG

Soybean (*Glycine max*), herbaceous annual belonging to the legume family, grown as an OILSEED CROP in Canada. The soybean, among the oldest of cultivated crops, probably originated in East Asia. Introduced into the US as a hay crop about 1800, it was not recognized as a valuable source of edible oil until the early 1900s. During and immediately after WWII, soybean production expanded rapidly, with the US, China and Brazil accounting for over 90% of world production. In processing, the seed is crushed and the oil extracted. The oil, a high-quality cooking oil, is used in the production of margarine, shortening and salad oils. The meal remaining after the oil is extracted is a high-protein livestock and poultry feed. As a legume, the soybean plant can fix atmospheric nitrogen in its root nodules. The nodules are formed early in the growth of the plant, as a result of an interaction between the roots and a soilborne bacterium, *Rhizobium japonicum*. Soybeans are a warm-season crop, requiring a mean summer temperature of 21°C and a frost-free period of 120-150 days for optimum production; therefore, most of Canada's annual production (*c* 988 000 t) is grown in southern Ontario.

E.N. LARTER

Space Technology Canada's entry into the Space Age was prompted by an interest, which increased markedly during WWII, in the investigation of the properties of Earth's upper atmosphere and, in particular, the ionosphere, ie, the layer of charged particles which reflects shortwave radio signals. An agreement signed with the US National Aeronautics and Space Administration (NASA) led to the launching of a series of 4 Canadian SATELLITES, beginning with Alouette 1 (on 29 Sept 1962) from the Western Test Range in Vandenburg, California, by a Thor-Agena rocket. Alouette 1 carried 2 Canadian-developed spacecraft antennae with tip-to-tip lengths of 23 and 45 m, respectively, which were deployed after the satellite was in orbit. Alouette 1 was followed by Alouette 2 (1965) and by ISIS (International Satellites for Ionospheric Studies) 1 (1969) and 2 (1971). These satellites were designed and built at the Defence Research Telecommunications Establishment in Ottawa (in 1969 this became the Communications Research Centre of the Dept of Communications), which had previous experience in using rockets for upper-atmosphere research. Each was increasingly complex in design and measurement capability and each involved greater participation by the then developing Canadian AEROSPACE INDUSTRY. Other Canadian and foreign organizations contributed equipment and experiments to the program, and studies were carried out using the results from the satellite investigations in conjunction with ground-based measurements in various countries. In its time, Alouette 1 established a longevity record for operation of a complex satellite. Alouette 1 and ISIS 2 were launched into near-circular orbits, at about 1000 km and 1400 km above Earth, respectively;

Alouette 2 and ISIS 1 were launched into elliptical orbits with perigees of 500 km and apogees of 3000 and 3500 km, respectively. ISIS 1 and 2 were still providing data regularly in 1987.

Canada's attention soon turned to applying space technology to serve the requirements imposed by the country's widely dispersed population, its vast distances, harsh terrain and severe CLIMATE. In 1964 Canada joined with several other nations in establishing an international system (Intelsat) for the exchange of commercial international telecommunications traffic. Following a 1968 White Paper on the possibility of establishing a domestic SATELLITE COMMUNICATIONS system, the Telesat Canada Corp was established by Act of Parliament in 1969. The corporation is owned jointly by the federal government and Canadian telecommunications carriers. With the launch of the first of Telesat's 3 Anik A satellites in late 1972, Canada became the first country to implement a commercial domestic satellite system operating in geostationary orbit (35 700 km above the equator). The satellites were stabilized in orbit by the technique known as spin-stabilization, in which the communications antenna and associated platform are de-spun so that the antenna points continually towards Earth. This series was built by a US prime contractor but involved major participation by Canadian industry. These satellites transmitted at frequencies of 4 GHz (billion Hertz) and received at 6 GHz and were located at 104°W, 109°W and 114°W longitude.

Anik B, which followed in late 1978, was somewhat higher powered and was 3-axis stabilized to maintain a precisely controlled fixed orientation in space. The Anik D series replaced the capacity of the now failing Anik A and aging Anik B satellites. Anik D1, launched in Aug 1982, was the first commercial satellite built by a Canadian prime contractor, Spar Aerospace Limited. Anik D2 was launched in Nov 1984. The first of the Anik C satellites, which operate in the higher 12 and 14 GHz frequency bands, was one of 2 satellites launched to inaugurate the operational use of the US Space Shuttle in Nov 1982. The other satellites in the Anik C series were launched in June 1983 and Apr 1985. In 1987, Telesat Canada awarded a prime contract to Spar Aerospace for the provision of 2 Anik E satellites to be launched about 1990 and which will operate in both sets of frequency bands, replacing both the Anik C and Anik D satellites.

In 1971 Canada entered into an agreement with NASA for the development and launch of an experimental Communications Technology Satellite (CTS). CTS, known as Hermes in Canada, was launched on 17 Jan 1976. Hermes had several objectives: to develop and flight-test a high-power, high-efficiency travelling-wave-tube amplifier (wide band power amplifier such as those used in RADAR or communications transmitters) operating at 12 GHz; to develop and flight-test a 3-axis stabilization system to maintain accurate antenna pointing; and to conduct communications experiments in the newly allocated 12 and 14 GHz frequency bands using small, transportable Earth stations. The satellite was designed and built in Canada at the Communications Research Centre (CRC) of the Dept of Communications by a joint government/industry team of scientists and engineers. Use of the satellite permitted investigation of a number of innovative approaches to the delivery of new communications services and extension of existing services to remote and rural regions. Hermes was the first satellite capable of broadcasting television and radio programs directly to inexpensive home receivers and was equipped with spot-beam antennae which could be directed to any point on Earth that was visible from the satellite.

Hermes was built to last 2 years but operated for nearly 4.

To test various subsystems of the satellite in a simulated space environment, the federal government established the satellite assembly, integration and test facilities of the David Florida Laboratory at CRC. These were later expanded to permit testing of complete spacecraft of a shuttle class in the simulated thermal, vacuum, vibration and electromagnetic environment of space. Techniques for computer simulation and analysis of spacecraft motions were also developed.

Because of the success of the Hermes program and under an arrangement between Telesat and the federal government, Anik B was equipped with 4 transponders operating at 12 and 14 GHz, in addition to transponders at the 4 and 6 GHz frequencies used by the earlier Anik A satellites. A transponder is an electronic device which receives a signal and retransmits it at a different frequency. Anik B thus became the world's first satellite to operate simultaneously in both of these pairs of frequency bands.

In 1975 Canada signed an agreement with the US to participate in the Space Transportation System (Shuttle) by providing a unique remote-manipulator system, later named the CANADARM, to be mounted on the shuttle to move payloads in and out of the shuttle bay. This work was carried out by a Canadian industry team led by Spar Aerospace under contract to the NATIONAL RESEARCH COUNCIL OF CANADA. A general-purpose simulation facility (called SIMFAC) was designed, using mathematical modelling techniques, to verify Canadarm's operability in a zero-gravity environment and to train ASTRONAUTS to operate the Canadarm in space. While the arm cannot support its own weight on Earth, it is capable of manipulating a payload of nearly 30 000 kg in space, maneuvering it at 3 cm/s and placing it in any position with an accuracy of about 5 cm. The Canadarm was declared operational in Nov 1982, after having been flown successfully on the second, third and fourth shuttle launches, and having been used in maneuvering and handling exercises. NASA procured 3 additional systems directly from Spar Aerospace. All have been deployed successfully on subsequent shuttle flights.

Another area in which Canadian space and related technology has also pioneered is in the application of space techniques to assist in search and rescue. All aircraft in Canada are equipped with emergency locator transmitters (ELTs) which may be turned on manually or are activated automatically on impact. A concept was developed to use satellites in low orbits highly inclined to the equator to detect aircraft and ships in distress. Canada joined with France and the US and several other countries to demonstrate the operational use of the concept through the SARSAT (Search and Rescue Satellite Aided Tracking) Project. Canada supplied the satellite transponders operating at frequencies of 121.5, 243 and 406 MHz, and designed and built the ground station for reception of the satellite-relayed signals. France provided the on-board signal processor and the US contributed the spacecraft antennae and tested, integrated and launched the SARSAT space hardware on board the NOAA series of meteorological satellites. First launch of a SARSAT-equipped spacecraft was in Mar 1983. To allow more frequent coverage of Earth's surface, an arrangement was concluded with the USSR for the launch of a compatible system, called COSPAS. The first satellite equipped with the COSPAS system was launched in June 1982. In 1984, a memorandum of understanding was signed among Canada, France, the USA, and the USSR which established COSPAS and SARSAT as an interim operational search and rescue satellite system to

Two astronauts working outside the Space Shuttle with Earth in the background (*courtesy SSC Photocentre*).

the end of 1990. By the end of 1986, the combined COSPAS-SARSAT system had contributed to the saving of more than 700 lives worldwide of which more than 200 were in Canada.

Canada has also been involved in applications of satellite technology to REMOTE SENSING of the Earth's surface. Readout stations are used for the reception of signals from various US satellites and for ground-based processing of sensor data. In addition, design studies are being carried out in preparation for the possible implementation by Canada of a remote-sensing satellite, Radarsat, equipped with synthetic aperture radar to provide all-weather information on ice coverage in the Canadian Arctic, and to assist in surveillance of oceans and land resources. Other sensors are being considered for inclusion on Radarsat. Canadian industry will supply part of the radar and ground-based data-processing systems for the European Space Agency's European Remote Sensing Satellite, to be launched in 1989. The satellite will provide information on ice and ocean conditions.

The use of large spacecraft to provide data communications to terminals on board ships and aircraft and on land, as well as improved service to mobile radio and radio telephones, is also being planned. Such a system would use highly efficient narrow-bandwidth voice and data transmissions. Called MSAT, for Mobile Satellite, such a satellite would be launched about 1992 and would operate in the ultra high frequency band (0.8 GHz or 1.5 GHz). It is expected that the satellite would be built under contract to, and be operated on a commercial basis by, Telesat Canada.

Based on capabilities developed over 20 years in space, Canadian industry is participating in the Olympus program (previously called L-SAT) of the European Space Agency which involves the design and development of a large spacecraft platform to carry various payloads, eg, direct television broadcasting. Canada is contributing the critical extendible solar array subsystem and certain payload elements, and will have major responsibilities in the final integration and test of the spacecraft. Spar Aerospace as prime contractor also supplied a domestic communications satellite system to Brazil, based on the Anik D satellites. Called Brazilsat, 2 satellites were launched, one in 1985 and one in 1986.

Space-science activities are co-ordinated by the Canada Centre for Space Science of the NRC. The major element of current activity is a co-operative program with NASA to place a number of instruments in the shuttle, primarily to study plasmas in space. The program will include a network of ground stations to obtain complementary infor-

mation and a data-processing system. In a co-operative program with Sweden, Canada provided an ultraviolet imager for the Swedish Viking satellite, launched in 1984, to obtain images of the Aurora to support studies of the magnetosphere (*see* NORTHERN LIGHTS; PHYSICS).

In 1984 the space industry employed over 3200 people and, as a result of further investment promised by the federal government, was expected to involve 3700 people by 1987. Canada's exports of space technology represent over 70% of total sales. In fact, industry sales generate more money than government investment does, a situation unique in the world. In recognition of Canada's contributions to the US space program, NASA has made places available to Canadian astronauts on various shuttle flights, and Canadian engineers are planning for participation in the US Space Station Program through the provision of a Mobile Servicing System (MSS). The MSS would help assemble and maintain the Space Station as well as manipulate and service visiting spacecraft and payloads.

In the Speech from the Throne on 1 Oct 1986, the Canadian government announced its intention to create a Canadian Space Agency to promote the peaceful use and development of space and to ensure that space science and technology provide social and economic benefits for Canadians. The agency will incorporate and co-ordinate many of the space activities now being carried out in various departments and agencies of government. As of the spring of 1987, the 25th anniversary of Canada in space, legislation was being prepared for consideration by Parliament and an implementation plan was being drawn up. *See also* John Herbert CHAPMAN.   B.C. BLEVIS

Spallumcheen, BC, District Municipality, pop 4310 (1986c), area 26 585 ha, inc 1892, about 7 km N of VERNON, completely encloses the city of ARMSTRONG. The name derives from the Shuswap Indian word "spalmtsin" meaning "flat area along edge." Among the first settlers were members of the famous OVERLANDERS, who had trekked across Canada in 1862 to reach the gold-diggings of the Cariboo but who gave up prospecting for farming. The first settlers raised vegetables, grain and a few cattle, but when the CPR arrived, giving transportation to markets, wheat became the main crop. In the drier southern part of the district agriculturalists use dryland farming techniques to produce grain, hay, field peas and beans, while in the northern part, where rainfall is somewhat heavier, dairy farming predominates. In recent years the overflow of residential development from Vernon and development of other industries such as a plywood mill have somewhat reduced the importance of agriculture.   DUANE THOMSON

Spaniard's Bay, Nfld, Town, pop 2190 (1986c), inc 1965, is located N of Bay Roberts on the W side of Conception Bay. The name is first recorded in the area in the early 1800s and probably commemorates the early Spanish or Basque fishermen who visited the area as early as the 1500s. Settlers may have been in the area in the early 1600s after the breakup of John Guy's colony. The fishing community recorded more than 1000 residents by 1857 and prospered, with other nearby communities, in the Labrador fishery during the 1800s. Today it is largely a residential community between the larger towns of Bay Roberts and Harbour Grace.   ROBERT PITT

Spanish Canada's relations with Spain date back several centuries to the voyages of the BASQUE fishermen to the Atlantic coast and to Spanish exploration of the Pacific coast. Basque expeditions are recalled in names such as Channel-Port aux Basques and Île aux Basques. Archaeologists have uncovered traces of a 16th-century Basque whaling station at RED BAY, Labrador. The numerous Spanish explorations on the Pacific coast between 1542 and 1792 are recalled in names such as Alberni, Laredo Strait, Carmelo Strait, Mazaredo Sound, Mount Bodega, Quadra Rocks and Narvaez Bay. At one time Vancouver I was called Quadra and Vancouver's I to commemorate the friendship between the Spanish navigator BODEGA Y QUADRA and English Captain George VANCOUVER.

Migration and Settlement Significant Spanish settlement did not occur in Canada until the 20th century. Between 1913 and 1914 about 2000 Spaniards arrived in Canada. A small trickle immigrated during the interwar period. Just over 1000 had immigrated 1946-55, but the figure rose to 11 000, 1956-67, to 5000 in the years 1970 to 1977 and to 4800 in the years 1978-84.

Spanish-speaking people have immigrated to Canada from Spain and from several S American countries. They have immigrated for a number of reasons, including a desire for greater economic opportunities and a desire to escape political oppression. Because of improvements in Spain's economic and political climate, emigration has decreased dramatically. In 1986, some 78% of the estimated 57 125 people of Spanish origin lived in Ont and Qué. The balance was sparsely scattered across the country, with concentration in Alta, BC and Man. In Canada the Spanish have overwhelmingly settled in cities, particularly Montréal, Toronto and Vancouver.

Social and Cultural Life Many Spanish immigrants are skilled workers, eg, welders, technicians, professionals; some are farmers who immigrated to Canada in 1957 under an agreement between Canada and Spain; others are labourers. Most Spanish immigrants are Roman Catholic, but there is also a very small group of active Protestants. Religion is one important basis of social organization. In areas of Spanish concentration there are recreational and social organizations to help immigrants adjust to Canadian life and to provide language instruction.

Several Spanish newspapers are published in Toronto and Montréal. In the smaller settlements the Spanish and Latin Americans are involved in joint publishing ventures. Dance groups, especially of the flamboyant flamenco variety, flourish in several centres and soccer is a popular sport.

Group Maintenance Spanish immigrants tend to maintain their former regional allegiances. The Basques openly express their desire for the independence of their homeland from Spain. Other areas of Spain are distinguished by regional languages, eg, the Gallegos from Galicia in the NW and the people from Valencia in the SE of Spain speak their separate, though related, languages. Many northerners are of Gaelic ancestry, whereas some of the southerners are of Moorish background. Small settlements of Sephardic Jews from Spain in both Toronto and Montréal form separate enclaves.

Spanish is generally not spoken past the second generation, although Spanish-language classes are frequently available. The immigrants assimilate readily in French communities, with whom they identify more easily than with English-speaking areas. GRACE M. ANDERSON

Reading: Grace M. Anderson, "Spanish- and Portuguese-speaking Immigrants in Canada," in *Two Nations, Many Cultures: Ethnic Groups in Canada* (1979).

Spanish-American War, the 1898 conflict between the US and Spain, during which the US removed Cuba, Puerto Rico, Guam and the Philippines from Spain, annexing the last 3. During the war, US consular officials in Canada reported on Spanish espionage, Canadian opinion, movements of ships and Spanish efforts to pur-

chase coal. Spain upgraded posts in Halifax, Québec City and Victoria and redeployed consuls previously based in the US. The staff at Spain's legation in Washington moved to Toronto and Montréal, where it engaged in espionage and public relations. Canadian shipping profited from suppliers and passengers anxious to avoid attacks by the Spanish Navy. Canadian vessels, financed through the Bank of Montreal, ran US blockades around Cuba and Puerto Rico.

Canadian opinion was largely sympathetic to the US, and Canadian support helped the US. Spanish spies based in Montréal had to leave Canada, but the US agents who had stolen the incriminating evidence did not. While media pressure forced Spaniards from Canada, Canadian officials exchanged information with American agents. Spain could not buy coal for its navy, despite middlemen willing to circumvent the Canadian embargo against sales to belligerents; the US Navy had no such difficulty.

Yet British neutrality laws prevented Canadians from serving in either belligerent's armed forces. The Montréal-based Beaver Line's *Lake Ontario* could not ferry troops to Cuba, and Halifax sheltered the Spanish vessel, *San Ignacio de Loyola.*

Despite Canadian support for the US war effort, Canadian trade with Puerto Rico subsequently declined, and the US refused to soften its stand on the ALASKA BOUNDARY DISPUTE. However, Sudbury benefited as foreign navies, impressed by the effectiveness of nickel alloys in protecting the US Navy from Spanish fire, offered new markets. GRAEME S. MOUNT

Spanish Exploration Following the global circumnavigation of Magellan's expedition, 1519-22, Holy Roman Emperor Charles V wished to locate a N American strait into Asian waters. The Spaniards possessed information on the Newfoundland and Labrador coasts from Portuguese voyages and from BASQUE fishermen and whalers. In 1524 Spain, which had previously focused on Central and S America, dispatched Esteban Gómez to explore the New England coast. On the Pacific, the California and Oregon coasts were explored from Mexican ports in the 1540s, but Spain's claim to the entire Pacific littoral of America was not based upon actual exploration. To confuse the situation, apocryphal voyages such as those of Juan de FUCA, Lorenzo FERRER MALDONADO and Bartholomew de Fonte caused cartographers to place imaginary passages and inland seas in present-day Canada.

During the 1770s reports of Russian expansion from Kamchatka into N America forced Spanish exploration of the NORTHWEST COAST. Within Spanish administrative structure the viceroyalty of Mexico was responsible for Pacific operations north of San Blas. In 1774 Juan PÉREZ HERNÁNDEZ sailed north from Mexico, reaching the Queen Charlotte Is, where the HAIDA paddled out in their canoes to trade. Fearful of shipwreck, Pérez did not land to take possession, although he did anchor off Nootka Sd, Vancouver I. The inconclusive results caused the Mexican viceroy to dispatch another expedition. In 1775 Juan Francisco de la BODEGA Y QUADRA reached Alaska with 2 ships at about 58°30′N. He took possession and located excellent ports in Prince of Wales I. The Spaniards were impressed by the civilization of NW Coast Indians. Their maritime, artistic, commercial, architectural and military capabilities had not been anticipated by Spanish observers familiar with northern Mexico and California.

When reports reached Madrid about James COOK's third Pacific voyage (1776-79), King Charles III of Spain, concerned with imperial expansion and scientific discovery, ordered new ef-

forts to counter the foreign challenge. Short of ships and personnel, the Spaniards missed Cook entirely. In 1779 Ignacio de Arteaga and Bodega y Quadra sailed to Bucareli Bay and explored as far as Cook Inlet. The expedition produced scientific charts and ethnological data, but Spain did not publish the results. Cook's journal became the handbook for those who would pursue exploration or commerce in the N Pacific.

In 1788 the controversial Esteban José Martínez led an expedition back to Alaska and as far west as Unalaska I. He visited Russian posts and returned to Mexico with information that in 1789 Russian traders planned to occupy Nootka Sd. Unaware that British and American FUR TRADERS were active in the sea-otter trade along the NW Coast, the Mexican viceroy ordered Martínez to occupy Nootka Sd. The resulting clash produced the NOOTKA SOUND CONTROVERSY with Britain. In 1791 the scientific expedition of Alejandro Malaspina (*see* MALASPINA EXPEDITION) was diverted into the N Pacific to search for a NORTHWEST PASSAGE. Other Spanish expeditions were dispatched from Yuquot (Friendly Cove) at Nootka Sd and from Mexico. Bodega y Quadra and other explorers, including Francisco de Eliza, Jacinto Caamaño, Manuel Quimper, Dionisio Alcalá-Galiano and Cayetano Valdés, explored the coast from Alaska to California. With the final settlement of the Nootka Sd issues in 1795, Spain withdrew from the North Pacific. *See also* SUTIL AND MEXICANA. CHRISTON I. ARCHER

Reading: W. L. Cook, *Flood Tide of Empire* (1973); Iris H.W. Engstrand, *Spanish Scientists in the New World* (1981).

Spar Aerospace Limited, *see* ELECTRONICS INDUSTRY.

Sparling, Gordon, filmmaker (b at Toronto 13 Aug 1900), pioneer director, writer and producer of some 200 films, especially the Canadian Cameo series of short films (1932-55). These were Canada's first major films with sound and in the 1930s represented virtually the only reflection of Canada on its own and the world's screens. Sparling graduated from U of T and joined the Ontario Motion Picture Bureau in 1924. After a brief period as assistant director on the feature *Carry on Sergeant!* (1928) and with the federal Motion Picture Bureau, he moved to New York in 1929. He returned to Canada in 1931 to make sponsored films for Associated Screen News in Montréal on condition that he could also produce short films for theatrical release. During the war, he supervised newsreels and training films for the Canadian Army, rejoining ASN in 1946 and remaining until its production department closed in 1957. He later worked for the NFB. PETER MORRIS

Sparrow, name given to several unrelated groups of birds. Sparrows are classified in 3 families: Emberizidae, which includes New World sparrows; Estrildidae; and Passeridae, which includes the familiar HOUSE SPARROW. About 34 species of the subfamily Emberizinae occur in Canada. They are primarily ground feeders, eating mostly seeds, although insects are eaten in summer. Adults of most species feed insects to young. They are small- to medium-sized, ranging in length from LeConte's sparrow (*Ammodramus lecontei*), as small as 11 cm, to the rufous-sided towhee (*Pipilo erythrophthalmus*), up to 22 cm. Generally, sparrows have dull plumage with distinctive head markings; the exceptions are the brightly coloured towhees and the sharply patterned juncos and longspurs. Males and females of most species are similar in size and plumage; eg, male and female song sparrows (*Melospiza melodia*), widespread in Canada, are virtually in-

White-throated sparrow (*Zonotrichia albicollis*) (*artwork by Claire Tremblay*).

distinguishable by plumage alone. Usually, only males sing; thus a singing song sparrow is almost certainly male. Songs differ considerably among species. Lark sparrows (*Chondestes grammacus*), of dry fields with scattered bushes and trees, sing long, melodious songs containing many trills. White-throated sparrows (*Zonotrichia albicollis*), of coniferous and mixed forests, utter songs of pure tone; one rendition, paraphrased as "Oh sweet Canada Canada Canada," has given them the local name Canada bird. Grasshopper sparrows (*A. savannarum*), of grassy fields in the extreme southern prairies and Ontario, give tuneless, insectlike reelings. Henslow's sparrow (*A. henslowii*), of weedy fields of southern Ontario, gives one of the poorest vocal efforts of any bird, a hiccoughing "tsi-lick." All species of sparrows in Canada are migratory to some extent. American tree sparrows (*Spizella arborea*) nest in scrub willow of the Subarctic and winter in southern Canada and northern US. Clay-coloured sparrows (*S. pallida*), of brush-covered prairies, winter in Mexico. The Ipswich sparrow (*Passerculus s. princeps*), a well-marked subspecies of the widely distributed savannah sparrow (*P. sandwichensis*), breeds only on SABLE I and winters on the Atlantic seaboard. RICHARD W. KNAPTON

Sparshott, Francis Edward, professor of philosophy, poet (b at Chatham, Eng 19 May 1926). Sparshott is Canada's leading philosopher of the arts (aesthetics) with an international reputation among scholars. His philosophy career started at U of T in 1950 and continues at Victoria College, U of T. He has written 6 major works in philosophy, his latest on the aesthetics of dance, and 7 books of poetry. His interest in discovering connections that are not evident pervades his philosophy and poetry and is most evidenced in his CBC award-winning poem, 1981, *The Cave of Trophonius*. He aspires to write a "drier sort of Horace," and though many poems are dark and brooding, others are witty and comically poignant as are his famous footnotes in his philosophy texts. ELIZABETH A. TROTT

Sparwood, BC, District Municipality, pop 4540 (1986c), 4167 (1981c), inc 1966, is located 30 km NE of Fernie in the Elk R valley. The local timber was considered "suitable for spars" by early railway builders. Recently developed after the historic mining towns of Michel, Natal and Middletown were levelled, Sparwood is a centre for coal mining and processing, as well as for outdoor recreation. It has experienced rapid growth in the 1970s, with the development of the Line Creek Mine and the nearby Byron Creek Collieries. WILLIAM A. SLOAN

Speaker, the presiding officer of the HOUSE OF COMMONS, elected by the members after each general election. Until 1986 the Speaker was nomi-

nated by the prime minister, usually after consultation with the leader of the Opposition. On 30 Sept 1986 the members selected a new speaker by secret ballot from among several candidates. The Speaker represents the House and speaks for it. At the opening of each Parliament the Speaker requests confirmation of the privileges of the Commons, and at royal assent presents appropriation bills on its behalf. To be disrespectful of the Speaker is to be disrespectful of the House. The Speaker, who is responsible, as chairman, umpire and manager, for House proceedings, is expected to be fair, patient and understanding, but also to prevent obstructive members from frustrating the House. With the 4 other Commissioners of Internal Economy, the Speaker applies to the CROWN for money to pay the indemnities of members, expenses for summoned witnesses, and salaries for pages, cooks and secretaries. He or she appoints HANSARD staff, constables, etc. After being forced to the Chair – nominees feign resistance out of modesty – the Speaker severs party ties. In 1963 PM John Diefenbaker appointed the Hon Marcel Lambert, the 1962-63 Speaker, to the Cabinet, and in 1980 PM Pierre Trudeau moved the Hon Jeanne SAUVÉ from the Cabinet to the Chair – 2 moves criticized by those favouring a strong, independent Speaker. All recent Speakers have been bilingual. Speakers vote only to break a tie and then not according to their views but so as to leave the substance of the question to be decided later by the House. In Britain, the House of Lords has no Speaker, and a minister, the Lord Chancellor, presides, but at Ottawa the Senate has a "speaker," appointed by the Crown and permitted to vote. The Speakers of provincial assemblies follow the pattern of the Commons Speaker. JOHN B. STEWART

Newly elected Speaker of the House of Commons Jeanne Sauvé is taken to the Speaker's chair by PM Pierre Trudeau and Opposition Leader Joe Clark during opening of Parliament ceremonies 14 Apr 1980. The Speaker shows the traditional "reluctance" to assume her duties (*courtesy Canapress Photo Service*).

Speck, Frank Gouldsmith, anthropologist (b at Brooklyn, NY 8 Nov 1881; d at Philadelphia, Pa 6 Feb 1950). He pioneered study of the Algonquian peoples of eastern Canada and New England. After studying under Franz BOAS at Columbia, he taught at University of Pennsylvania from 1909 and began a lifelong project of recording the changing cultures of the Algonquians and their neighbours. He collected Algonquian artifacts for the National Museum of Canada, recorded their myths and customs, and mapped their hunting territories. His maps of individual and band hunting territories documented Algonquian land rights. Research of this kind has become crucial to native LAND CLAIMS, as Speck predicted. BRUCE COX

Reading: F. Speck, "The Family Hunting Band as the Basis of Algonquian Social Organization," *Cultural Ecology*, ed Bruce Cox (1973); and *Naskapi* (1935, repr 1977).

Spectroscopy is the field of study that examines, measures and interprets the electromagnetic spectra produced when radiant energy is emitted or absorbed by a substance. Spectroscopic methods are important in performing chemical analyses of substances and are used in astronomical studies. Spectroscopy started in 1666 when Sir Isaac Newton passed rays of light from the SUN through a glass prism and observed the colours of the visible spectrum. Light is composed of electromagnetic waves, each colour corresponding to a different wavelength. The separation of light into the individual wavelengths by means of a device, such as a prism or a diffraction grating, forms the basis of optical spectroscopy. However, the visible segment comprises only a small fraction of the complete electromagnetic spectrum. The ultraviolet region begins at wavelengths shorter than the violet and extends eventually into the X-ray region; the infrared portion starts at wavelengths longer than the red and extends into the microwave and radio regions. In these regions it is more usual to characterize the radiation by its frequency rather than its wavelength, although the 2 are interconnected by the relation: wavelength times frequency equals velocity of light (299 792 458 m/s).

All substances emit or absorb radiation at their own characteristic frequencies or wavelengths; therefore the spectrum of a substance provides a "fingerprint" by which it can be identified. When light from a star is spread out according to colour, many fine details, called spectral lines, can be seen. A study of the frequencies and intensities of these lines gives information on the amounts of the various substances present and about the temperature, pressure and radiation within the emitting gas. An early example of this research involved Joseph von Fraunhofer's observation of dark absorption lines in the visible spectrum of the sun, caused by the presence of sodium, calcium and other elements in the solar atmosphere. Helium was discovered in the spectrum of the sun before it was found on Earth.

A detailed understanding of the spectra of atoms and molecules originated with the introduction of the quantum theory by Max Planck in 1900. According to this theory, energy is emitted or absorbed in discrete units called quanta. In 1913 Niels Bohr was able to give a detailed explanation of the spectrum of the hydrogen atom by postulating that the atom can exist in a series of discrete energy levels and that emission or absorption of radiation only occurs when there is a change from one energy level to another. The introduction of quantum mechanics by Werner Heisenberg and Erwin Schrödinger in 1925-26 was another important development. Spectra associated with a change of the rotational quantum numbers of a molecule are normally studied in the microwave and adjoining regions of the spectrum; those associated with a change in the vibrational quantum numbers occur in the infrared region. Electronic spectra are usually studied in the visible and ultraviolet regions. In 1925 S.A. Goudsmit and G.E. Uhlenbeck postulated that the electron possesses an intrinsic angular momentum (or spin) with which is associated a magnetic moment. This idea was introduced to explain some groups of lines found in the spectra of the alkali and alkaline earth metals. A similar multiplicity of lines is found in the spectra of molecules containing one or more unpaired electron spins. Such species are often called free radicals. Similarly, many nuclei have magnetic moments the energies of which depend on their orientation in a magnetic field. The study of nuclear magnetic resonance (NMR) spectroscopy has yielded valuable information on the structures of molecules.

Since the advent of LASERS in 1960 many new forms of spectroscopy have evolved. With fixed-frequency lasers, molecules and free radicals can be tuned into resonance by applying electrical or magnetic fields. With tunable lasers many types of high-resolution spectroscopy have been developed. All these techniques yield very precise measurements of the properties of atoms and molecules. Lasers have also extended the use of Raman spectroscopy, in which molecules are excited by strong monochromatic radiation and the scattered radiation is found to contain extra frequencies which are characteristic of the molecule excited. Spectroscopy has numerous applications. Atomic emission and absorption spectroscopy is used to identify elements present in MINERALS or to determine traces of impurities of the order of one part per million or even one part per billion. Nuclear magnetic resonance spectroscopy and infrared spectroscopy are used routinely by chemists to identify materials and to monitor reactions. Various forms of spectroscopy are used to measure the concentrations of pollutants in the atmosphere. Optical spectroscopy has identified many molecules present in the atmospheres of the stars and planets, while microwave spectroscopy has identified over 50 molecular species in the interstellar medium.

In Canada research in spectroscopy has taken place at the NATIONAL RESEARCH COUNCIL; in university departments of chemistry, physics and astronomy; and at observatories across the country. The spectroscopy section of NRC's Physics Division received world recognition through the work of Gerhard HERZBERG and his many colleagues. At the University of Toronto H.L. WELSH has done significant work on the Raman spectra of molecules. Early workers at the Dominion Astrophysical Observatory include J.S. PLASKETT, J.A. PEARCE, A. MCKELLAR and C.S. BEALS. *See also* PHYSICS. D.A. RAMSAY

Speech from the Throne reveals to the SENATE and the HOUSE OF COMMONS the work the ministers propose for the session of Parliament then beginning. Historically, in England, the speech sometimes explained why Parliament had been called into session when many years had elapsed between sessions. Now, with Parliament doing very much the same kinds of business year after year

Governor General Edward Schreyer reading the Speech from the Throne during the opening of Parliament in Ottawa. Her Excellency Lily Schreyer is on the right (*courtesy SSC Photocentre*).

and in session almost constantly, few speeches arouse great curiosity. The speech contains comments on the state of the nation and outlines the measures on which the government will seek parliamentary action. Although delivered by the queen or her representative (usually the GOVERNOR GENERAL) the speech is entirely the work of ministers; consequently the opposition parties feel obliged to dismiss the speech as vacuous or misconceived. Normally the first business of the House of Commons – and of the Senate – is to authorize a response to the speech. This is the "Address in Reply to the Speech from the Throne." A government backbencher moves for a thankful Address; then members in opposition move amendments lamenting the content of the speech and usually declaring their nonconfidence in the ministers. In the House of Commons the debate on the Address is limited to 8 days. Given the very general nature of the motions, a member can speak on almost any subject and remain relevant. To demonstrate that the House can initiate business other than what has been proposed in the speech the first bill introduced in a session always deals with a matter not mentioned in the speech. JOHN B. STEWART

Speed Skating races are held for men and women both indoors and outdoors. Outdoor races are held on open-air oval tracks 400 m in length. Two competitors race in separate lanes against the clock, changing lanes on each lap so that both skaters go the same distance. For men, there are races of 500, 1500, 5000 and 10 000 m. Women race distances of 500, 1000, 1500 and 3000 m. A fifth event is added for the Olympics: 1000 m for men and 5000 m for women. This is commonly regarded as the European style of speed skating; in N America, mass start races, where more than 2 compete, and indoor racing have always been popular. Indoor skating is practised on shorter rinks (111 m) sheltered from the weather and has slightly different rules: departures are made in groups, distances are shorter, and, as there are no defined lanes, skaters come into contact with one another. Short-track speed skating first became an Olympic demonstration event in 1988.

Although there is evidence of the appearance of ICE SKATING in 1250, the first organized race was not recorded until 1763 in England. The first race in Canada is believed to have taken place in 1854, and the first organized competitions were held at the Victoria Rink in Saint John, NB, in 1883. Four years later, the Amateur Skating Assn of Canada was formed and held its first official Canadian championships. In 1894 the ASAC joined the International Skating Union, bringing Canadian skating on to the international scene. In those formative years, speed skating and FIGURE SKATING were both under the auspices of one organization, with the concerns of the speed skaters predominating. Figure skaters did not form their own association until 1939.

Speed skating, at the world level, has largely been the preserve of Dutch and Scandinavian skaters. The Russians and Americans have also enjoyed considerable success; the most notable of the Americans, Eric Heiden, won 5 gold medals at the 1980 Winter Olympics. Canada, however, has also produced many outstanding speed skaters. In 1897 Jack McCulloch of Winnipeg won the ISU world championships held in Montréal. Fred Robson, Gladys Robinson and Lela BROOKS, all of Toronto, were prominent in N American skating competitions and set a number of world records in the first 3 decades of this century. Another prominent skater of that time was Charles I. GORMAN of Saint John. Jean WILSON of Toronto won gold and silver medals at the 1932

The greatest speedskater in Canada's history is Gaéten Boucher, who captured 2 gold medals at the Sarajevo Olympics in 1984 (*courtesy Canapress Photo Service*).

Olympics, where women's speed skating was a demonstration event.

From then until the 1970s, Canada's main speed skating achievement was Gordon Audley's bronze medal in the 500 m event at the 1952 Olympics. Twenty-four years later, Cathy Priestner won a silver medal in Innsbruck, Austria. In 1973 Sylvia BURKA became the unofficial world junior ladies' champion and won the women's world championship in 1976. The following year she won the world sprint championship. For men, Gaétan BOUCHER of Québec was second only to Heiden in world competition in 1980, and set a world record for the 1000 m event. In the 1984 Olympics at Sarajevo, Boucher stimulated interest in speed skating with 2 gold medals and one bronze. In the same year he won the World Sprint Championships. In 1988 the 16-person Canadian team skated on the newly constructed $39-million Olympic Oval in Calgary. J. THOMAS WEST

Reading: J. Hurdis, Speed Skating in Canada – 1854-1981: A Chronological History (1981).

Spence, George, homesteader, politician, civil servant (b at Birsey, Orkney I, Scot 25 Oct 1879; d at Regina 4 Mar 1975). As first director of PRAIRIE FARM REHABILITATION ADMINISTRATION (PFRA), Spence initiated land rehabilitation, soil conservation and water development programs in the Prairie region. He immigrated to Canada in 1900 after receiving his education in England and Edinburgh. He staked a gold claim in the Yukon, farmed near MacGregor, Man and worked as a survey engineer for the CPR before homesteading S of Swift Current, Sask in 1912.

Spence's political career began in 1917, when he won the provincial riding of Notukeu for the Liberals. He held the seat until 1925, when he resigned to successfully seek federal election as the member from Maple Creek. He attended one session of Parliament. When the federal government resigned, Spence returned to Saskatchewan and re-entered provincial politics. He won a provincial by-election in Maple Creek in 1926. He remained in the legislature until 1937, serving as minister of highways, labour and industry 1926-29; as a member of the Opposition 1929-34; and as minister of Public Works 1934-39. In 1938 he was appointed director of PFRA, a post he held for 9 years. From 1947 to 1957 he served on the INTERNATIONAL JOINT COMMISSION. His many awards and recognitions included Commander of the Order of the British Empire (CBE) in 1946.

Spence Bay, NWT, UP, is located in a narrow inlet on the W side of the BOOTHIA PENINSULA, 1231 air km NE of YELLOWKNIFE. Inuit settled at the site in 1947. Spence Bay was the location of a well-known legal case in 1966, when 2 Inuit were tried after executing an insane woman. The execution had been carried out according to traditional custom. The outcome of the trial blended Western law with Inuit tradition, with one man acquitted and the other receiving a suspended sentence. Most of the Inuit residents subsist on trapping, hunting and fishing.   ANNELIES POOL

Spence-Sales, Harold, urban planner (b at Lahore, India 22 Oct 1907). Professor of architecture at McGill 1947-70, he led the first Canadian university program in town planning and in the later 1940s and the 1950s frequently advised governments on policy measures for land use and planning legislation. His more notable works relate to the planning of new towns (eg, Oromocto, NB, and Préville [now part of St-Lambert], Qué) and to master-plan schemes for Moncton, NB; Charlottetown; Sudbury, Ont; Prince Albert, Sask; and other towns. His teaching and consulting work emphasized not only the aesthetics of urban planning but sensitivity to the environment, treating town planning as both an art form and a social mission. His writings include *How to Subdivide* (1949), *A Guide to Urban Dispersal* (1956) and *Beautifying Towns* (1967). Two generations of Canadian planners have been influenced by his original thought and imaginative style of planning.   WILLIAM T. PERKS

Spencer, David, merchant (b at St Athan, Wales 9 Aug 1837; d at Victoria 2 Mar 1920). A farmer's son, he was apprenticed to a dry-goods merchant in Wales and came to Victoria in 1862. After operating a book and stationery business, in 1873 he bought a dry-goods store from which developed the department store which bore his name. Branches were established in Nanaimo in 1889, Vancouver in 1907 and other BC centres. Spencer, a local preacher for the Methodist Church, was cofounder of the first TEMPERANCE society on Vancouver I and a benefactor of Victoria's Protestant Orphanage and other philanthropies. His eldest child, Christopher (1868-1953), was active in the firm until it was sold to The T. Eaton Co in 1948.   PATRICIA E. ROY

Sphagnum, *see* MOSS; PEAT; SWAMP, MARSH AND BOG.

Spice-Box of Earth, The Published in 1961, *The Spice-Box of Earth* was the volume which established Leonard COHEN's reputation as a lyric poet; it remains the most popular single volume of his verse. The language is rich, sensuous and beautiful, but many of Cohen's darker themes – victimization, loss, cruelty – are nonetheless present. The poems deal with the role of the poet, with his inheritance of the Jewish tradition, and of course with love. Among the best-known poems are "As the Mist Leaves No Scar" and the lovely "For Anne," which Cohen nominates as his own favourite poem. But perhaps the most searching poem in the volume is the darkly symbolic "You Have the Lovers," which sets out in concise form the themes later explored in Cohen's novel *Beautiful Losers*.   STEPHEN SCOBIE

Spider, carnivorous arthropod (segmented, jointed-limbed animal) of class ARACHNIDA, order Araneae. About 30 000 species are known of an estimated 50 000 world total. Spiders occur throughout the world excluding Antarctica, inhabiting terrestrial and aquatic environments. Almost 1300 species are known from Canada, including 9 species of tarantulas from Ontario and BC. Thirteen species of spiders occur on Ellesmere I, the northernmost point in Canada. Spiders have 8 legs and 2 body parts, abdomen and cephalothorax (fused head and thorax). Spinnerets on the abdomen produce silk, used for making webs and draglines, and for wrapping prey and protecting eggs. Some spiders build a new web daily, eating the old one and recycling the silk. Although most spiders have 8 eyes, they

The black widow spider (with its distinctive hour-glass pattern) is among the most poisonous of all creatures. Its venom is 200 times as poisonous as that of a rattlesnake (*photo by Stephen J. Krasemann/DRK Photo*).

can only distinguish light and dark. Jumping and wolf spiders have good, binocular vision for about 15-20 cm. Most spiders in Canada produce young annually, or once in 2 years. Dwarf spiders may lay only 8-10 eggs; black widow spiders, 1000 or more. The smallest adults are about 0.4 mm long; the largest, about 25 cm (total leg span). In grassy fields, spider populations may reach over 2 million per hectare. Some spiders have amazing powers of dispersal. Large spiders may crawl only a few metres per day, but small ones "balloon" through the air 50 km or more in a day.

Spiders can ingest only liquids. After catching prey, they suck its blood. Then they exude enzymes into and onto prey, converting its tissues to a soup, which is then sucked up. All spiders are poisonous to some degree, even those few species that have poison glands partly modified into glue-spitting glands. Black widow spiders, which are among the most poisonous of animals, are found in southern Ontario, Saskatchewan, Alberta and BC. Their venom is about 200 times as poisonous as that of a rattlesnake. Spiders are important predators, eating many destructive insects, and helping to control INSECT PESTS.   ROBIN LEECH

Spinach (*Spinacia oleracea*), leafy, cool-season VEGETABLE belonging to the Chenopodiaceae family. First cultivated in Persia over 2000 years ago, spinach was introduced to Europe in the 12th century. The plant consists of a leafy rosette formed around a crown (compressed stem). One variety, with smooth leaves, is used in the processing industry; another, with wrinkled foliage, is used solely for the fresh market. First sown in early spring, spinach requires only 40 days to mature and will produce several crops if sowing is staggered. The crop is usually harvested mechanically. Spinach is susceptible to VIRUS diseases, mildew and attacks by burrowing insects. It is rich in iron and contains vitamins A and C. Traditionally used in salads, spinach is now used increasingly in various food products (eg, purées). In Canada only a few hundred hectares are devoted to commercial production; however, spinach is popular in home gardens.   PIERRE SAURIOL

Spinks, John William Tranter, chemist, educator (b in Norfolk, Eng 1 Jan 1908). He moved to Canada in 1930 to join the staff of U Sask and has since earned an international reputation as a teacher and researcher. While on leave in Germany in 1933 he worked with Gerhard HERZBERG, and he was instrumental in bringing him to Canada. During WWII Spinks developed search-and-rescue operations for the RCAF and took part in the early work on atomic energy. Later he pioneered the use of radioactive isotopes in research, coauthored with R.J. Woods the first textbook on the chemical effects of high-energy radiation, and represented Canada at meetings on the peaceful uses of atomic energy. Appointed dean of graduate studies at U Sask in 1949 and president in 1959, he has been a member of many national and international groups concerned with university education. He is the author of more than 250 scientific and other works and has been honoured by universities and governments alike. He is a Companion of the Order of Canada.   R.J. WOODS

Reading: John Spinks, *Two Blades of Grass: An Autobiography* (1980).

Spiraea (*Spiraea*) is a genus of small shrubs of the family Rosaceae (rose). The genus consists of some 70-80 species, as well as many horticultural varieties of garden origin that have resulted from hybridization. Probably the most noteworthy of these hybrids is *S. vanhouttei* (bridal wreath spiraea), derived from 2 Asiatic species, *S. trilobata* and *S. cantoniensis*, which is widely cultivated in Canada and elsewhere for its spectacular spring blossoms. Spiraeas are deciduous, with simple leaves and generally dense clusters of small, white, pink or purple flowers. They are native to the N temperate zones of Eurasia and N America, generally growing on moist, wooded slopes and meadows. Canada has 7 native species, none of which is found all across the country. The most widespread, *S. alba*, occurs from Alberta to Newfoundland. One species, the western *S. beauverdiana*, extends northward to the Arctic Ocean.

Spiritualism, *see* NEW RELIGIOUS MOVEMENTS.

Spit Delaney's Island (1976), a short-story collection by Jack HODGINS, creates memorable characters in and against the varied landscape of Vancouver I, at once a place of isolation and community. The stories focus on the effects of change or the process of transformation; they are characterized by a combination of high-spirited humour, grotesque detail, and understated pathos, all of which complement the essential integrity of the protagonists. Concrete, descriptive language, lively dialogue, and sometimes violent action create vivid portraits of people caught between illusion and reality, the fantastic and the mundane. Resolution, however, is possible and the depiction of Spit Delaney, the folksy, eccentric protagonist of the first and last stories, is paradigmatic: the bizarre is seen in a comprehensive and sympathetic light; the transcending ordinary is revealed in the everyday extraordinary.   JOHN LENNOX

Spitsbergen, a bleak Norwegian island group only 965 km from the North Pole. It became strategically significant in WWII when Germany attacked the USSR in June 1941. Weather reports broadcast from the island were inadvertently useful to the Germans in the northern USSR, and a German occupation would have threatened the vital arctic supply route to the Russian port of Murmansk. Consequently, some 600 Canadian troops were sent from Britain in a top-secret raid to evacuate the 2800 inhabitants and lay waste the island's 4 settlements. Between 25 Aug and 3 Sept 1941 the raiders disabled Spitsbergen's coal mines and machinery, destroyed the power house, set fire to 450 000 tons of coal and wrecked wharves, loading tipples and railway spurs. The raiders also broadcast false weather broadcasts, halting German reconnaisance flights. However, both German and Anglo-Norwegian weather stations were subsequently established there.

BRERETON GREENHOUS

Spohr, Arnold Theodore, dancer, choreographer, teacher, director (b at Rhein, Sask 26 Dec 1927). One of the most respected figures in Canadian BALLET, Spohr was responsible for leading the ROYAL WINNIPEG BALLET to its position as an internationally acclaimed troupe. Spohr trained in London (Eng), New York C and Hollywood. He danced with the then Winnipeg Ballet, 1945-54, becoming a principal dancer. In London he partnered the famous ballerina Alicia Markova. Interim director of the Royal Winnipeg Ballet in 1957, Spohr was officially appointed artistic director in 1958. He set about restoring the company's vitality following a period of crisis after its premises were destroyed by fire in 1954. Through frequent travel at home and abroad Spohr sought choreographers to construct skilfully blended programs that would show off the dancers to advantage and please audiences. Under Spohr, the company has undertaken many successful foreign tours and has become arguably the most popular ballet troupe in Canada. Spohr's concern for the training of dancers led him in 1970 to establish a professional division of the Royal Winnipeg Ballet School. For many years he helped direct the ballet summer school of the BANFF CENTRE SCHOOL FOR CONTINUING EDUCATION. In June 1988 he retired as artistic director of the Royal Winnipeg Ballet. Among Spohr's honours are the MOLSON PRIZE (1970), the Dance Magazine Award (1982), the Diplôme d'honneur of the Canadian Conference of the Arts (1983) and the ROYAL BANK AWARD (1987).

MICHAEL CRABB

Sponge (Porifera), phylum of bottom-dwelling, attached, aquatic organisms which, as adults, generate vigorous water currents through their porous bodies by action of internal fields of microscopic flagella (whiplike structures). Sponges are the most primitive multicelled animals. The 5000-10 000 known species are distributed worldwide in marine and freshwater habitats (98% and 2% of species, respectively). They are common in Canadian waters, but a thorough inventory has not been made. The phylum is usually divided into 4 classes (Hexactinellida, Calcarea, Demospongiae and Sclerospongiae), according to the form and chemical nature of the skeleton. Living tissues of common, shallow-water sponges consist of loosely organized cells. Deepsea hexactinellids (glass sponges) are syncytial, ie, lack division of living tissues into separate cells. In both types, water pulled into small surface pores and distributed through internal canals provides oxygen, food (caught by filtration), waste removal (by water leaving the larger body pores) and distribution of sperm and eggs. Sponges are important in the bath sponge industry, as boring organisms which damage oysters and limestone coastlines, as sources of bioactive compounds in the PHARMACEUTICALS INDUSTRY, and for their use in studies of cell specialization and intercommunication.

H.M. REISWIG

Sportfishing The presence of anglers shown in 5000-year-old Egyptian drawings suggests that fishing for pleasure emerged when time became available for activities other than the acquisition of food and shelter. In Canada, sportfishing ranks among the most popular and enduring forms of outdoor recreation and dates back to the first Europeans, who brought with them well-established sportfishing interests and traditions, and

laws relating to FISHERIES. Species such as salmon played an important role in the life and culture of coastal Indians, but the enjoyment of Indian and Inuit youths in emulating the fisheries exploits of elders is shared by youths the world over. Succeeding settlers and visiting writers sent back reports of unlimited abundance of fish, thus laying the foundation for Canada's international image as a sportfishing mecca.

The appeal of sportfishing is universal, although it has always had a special attraction for the very young and old. A national survey in 1985 showed that 6.5 million anglers fished for pleasure in Canada, about 25% of them under 16 years of age. About 5.5 million were Canadians, 21% of the total population. The other million were visitors (primarily from the US). Catches ranged from MINNOW, SMELT and other smaller fishes sometimes counted by the bucket, to bluefin TUNA (the bluefin tuna record was caught off PEI, and weighed 679 kg). Total weight provides one measure of the angler's overall catch. Results showed that in 1985 a conservatively estimated 114 000 t were landed by anglers. This represented about 8.4% of the weight of Canada's total combined commercial and sport catch of finfish for the year.

For anglers, however, the sport centres on the fish and the experience. Traditionally, anglers use lure, bait and fly, but gear and methods vary by species, season, place and preference, ranging from the most primitive gear to boats outfitted with the most modern electronic equipment and conveniences. Among the 100 or so species that are sought, many rank the SALMON, on both coasts, supreme. Atlantic salmon, historically, has been esteemed as the king of gamefish. Rivers such as the MIRAMICHI in New Brunswick, and the RESTIGOUCHE, shared by Québec and NB, are known to fly-fishermen worldwide. Canada's 5 species of Pacific salmon are far more numerous, with 2 (coho and chinook), weighing up to 40 kg, providing the main focus for BC ocean sport fisheries. Thousands of anglers are drawn to YT and NWT in search of wilderness solitude and opportunities to fish for trophy-sized lake TROUT, northern PIKE, arctic CHAR and arctic GRAYLING. Elsewhere, anglers enjoy wide choice. Northern pike, WALLEYE and lake trout are widely distributed. However, there are major regional differences and preferences: brook trout are favoured in Newfoundland; lake trout and northern pike are main attractions for fly-in fishing in northern Sask, Man, Ont and Qué. In overall landings, however, 4 species, yellow PERCH, walleye, brook trout and northern pike, head the list. Winter adds another dimension to the sport, when anglers go ice fishing (see FISHING, ICE).

Responsibility for protection and management is shared by the federal and provincial governments. Tidal fisheries are exclusively under federal jurisdiction. In inland fresh waters, there is an overlap based on court interpretations of provisions of the BNA Act (1867). All laws for fisheries regulation, as such, are federally enacted. Provinces, however, possess and exercise proprietary rights over fresh waters, largely through setting and collecting licence fees. While there is a mosaic of federal-provincial arrangements for the administration of fisheries laws, there is a further anomaly regarding public access. Two provinces, NB and Québec, have retained riparian ownership in their fresh waters and the exclusive right to fish can be privately owned. All tidal fisheries are common property and, with a few exceptions, so are freshwater fisheries of the territories and the other 8 provinces.

Governments face increasingly complex fisheries problems. Much of Canada's treasure of relatively unfished northern waters is in areas vul-

Sportfishing on the Miramichi River. A 1985 survey showed that 6.5 million people fish for pleasure each year in Canada (*courtesy Tourism New Brunswick*).

nerable to ACID RAIN. POLLUTION, in the form of industrial and natural contaminants (eg, mercury), does not necessarily kill fish, as does acid rain, but these and an ever-increasing list of man-made compounds tend to become concentrated in larger, predator gamefish and, in certain instances, are a health threat to all who eat them. Some fish stocks, like the salmons, are depleted and overfished, and with the prospect of ever-growing numbers of anglers, there is intensified competition with other users of fish and the habitat, as well as problems of funding fisheries restoration and enhancement.

Support for the role and welfare of sport fisheries comes from many sources. Organized anglers are Canada's prototypal consumer advocates. Some Atlantic salmon clubs were organized over a century ago, and organized anglers in nationally affiliated provincial fish and game federations are in the forefront of endeavours to protect and enhance sport fisheries. According to the 1985 survey, anglers spent and invested $4.4 billion in sportfishing in Canada, directly attributable to their angling activity. Thanks to the nearly $600 million spent the same year by visiting anglers, Canada leads the world in foreign exchange earnings from sportfishing. From an environmental viewpoint, the continuing natural abundance of gamefish is regarded by many as a key measure of the quality of the aquatic habitat. With 21% of the population fishing every year, the extent of public goodwill and support for sportfishing is not surprising. However, Canada has also been blessed by the contributions made to sportfishing literature by individuals such as Roderick HAIG-BROWN, the Izaak Walton of this era.

A.L.W. TUOMI

Reading: D.E. McAllister and E.J. Crossman, Guide to the Freshwater Sport Fishes of Canada (1973).

Sporting-Goods Industry The Canadian sporting-goods industry has grown and diversified a great deal in the past 60 years, as a result of the increasing amount of leisure time available to Canadians. As early as 1929, 30 manufacturers, employing 1212 people, produced goods (eg, skates, lacrosse equipment, snowshoes) worth $4.8 million. The GREAT DEPRESSION of the 1930s severely curtailed the infant industry, and by the beginning of WWII production had declined by over 50%. The war years spurred recovery and output increased from $5 million in 1940 to $8.6 million in 1945. The industry reacted positively to the buoyant economy of the 1950s and to the first signs of changes in living patterns that favoured active and outdoor life-styles. Shipments increased from $9.4 million to $31.6 million during the 1950s; the number of manufacturers grew from 70 to 107. Throughout the 1960s, the industry grew steadily, as nonwork activities took on even greater importance for Canadians and as family outdoor recreation and physical fitness activities became more attractive. Industry shipments increased during the 1960s from $31.6 million to $81.7 million and employment in the industry rose by 45% to 5463 persons.

The greatest period of growth occurred in the 1970s, when significant export markets opened up for ice HOCKEY and CAMPING equipment, and for sports goods ranging from swimming pools to fitness and gymnasium equipment. Domestic shipments increased about 400% in this decade, from $81.7 million to $321.3 million. Exports rose over the same period from $22 million to $96 million. The number of manufacturers grew from 123 to 189 and employment increased 24% to 6798. By 1984 employment reached 7341 and there were 202 manufacturers, of which 82 were in Ontario and 66 in Québec. Most of the rest were in BC, Alberta and Manitoba. Manufacturers are equally divided between large-city and small-town locations. Most (68%) are small operations, employing less than 20 workers and usually specializing in one product area. They account for only 10% of total shipments and only 9% of employment.

Pressure from trading nations in Asia, Europe and the US has resulted in increasing rationalization of the Canadian industry in the past 20 years, and several large manufacturers (more than 100 employees) have emerged. They represent only 8% of establishments, but they produce 60% of all shipments and employ 61% of workers. Most Canadian sporting-goods firms are domestically controlled. The main sectors of the industry are ice sports, bicycles, swimming pools and skiing, gym and golf equipment. Canada exports about 24% of total domestic shipments. Although 75% goes to the US, significant new markets have developed in Europe, Australia and Japan. Total sports exports grew from $22 million in 1970 to $116.3 million in 1986. The market for sporting-goods equipment grew 183% in Canada in the first half of the 1970s. Domestic suppliers could not meet the demand for more and newer products; therefore, imports increased 200% from 1970 to 1975, while domestic production increased 133%. By 1975, imports represented $146 million in shipments, while domestic production represented $190 million. In the latter 1970s, the total market increased by 68%, as did imports, and domestic shipments increased by 94%, reflecting increased export activity by domestic manufacturers. By the mid-1980s Canada imported $300 million in sporting goods, while domestic shipments averaged $500 million annually. Recently, several European suppliers of equipment, such as hockey sticks and cross-country skis, have established plants in Canada to serve growing US and Japanese as well as Canadian markets. *A.J. RENNIE*

Sports History Canadian sport is indebted to the Indian for the TOBOGGAN, snowshoe, lacrosse stick

Snowshoeing, 1910. By the 1880s snowshoeing was the favourite winter sport, though it was soon overtaken by both skating and ice hockey (*by permission of the British Library*).

and CANOE. The COUREURS DE BOIS and the VOYAGEURS, through their close contact with the Indians, helped introduce into European settlements the activities that resulted from the use of these pieces of equipment. Many Indian games had utilitarian purposes related to survival (eg, wrestling, jousting, archery, spear throwing, and foot and canoe racing), while activities such as dancing and baggattaway (*see* LACROSSE) had religious significance. The Indians also developed a great variety of games, such as awl games, ring and pole, snow snake, cat's cradle, dice and birchbark cards, partly for the sheer love of play and sometimes for the purpose of gambling. The games of the Inuit were similarly related to preparing youth for co-operative existence in a harsh environment where one also needed to know one's tolerance limits. Blanket toss, tug-of-war, dogsled races, drum dances, spear throwing and ball games, as well as self-testing games such as arm-pull, hand-wrestling and finger-pull, helped to fulfil this purpose. Gambling was common and even useful, as it served to redistribute surplus goods.

In the pioneer settlements of the Europeans, play was relatively unimportant compared with the serious work of survival, yet social and recreational activities were necessary and did occur. From France, the French Canadian inherited his love of social gatherings, and N America's first social club, the ORDRE DE BON TEMPS, was formed at PORT-ROYAL. Social gatherings in pioneer societies, in the form of "bees" (husking, quilting and barn raising), also had a utilitarian basis, as participants could benefit from co-operative labours. Such gatherings usually offered music and dancing, wrestling and horse racing, and in French Canada provided opportunity for the "strong man" tradition to develop, exemplified later in Louis CYR. Where pioneer settlements consolidated into rural communities, a more organized form of recreation developed, largely from British migration in the 19th century. The formation of agricultural societies within these communities provided the administrative structure for regular competitions in plowing and horse racing. Rural regattas followed in which settlers plied their

skills against voyageur and Indian since, even to the farmer, the canoe often provided the swiftest and easiest method of transportation.

The ubiquitous SCOTS played a major role in transporting British sporting traditions to N America. GOLF was played by some of Gen Wolfe's Scottish officers, though it did not become an established sport before Confederation. CURLING, by contrast, after its introduction under similar circumstances, thrived in Canada; the first sporting club, founded in 1807, was the Montreal Curling Club. In 1865 curling became one of the select group of sports to enter international competition. Golf's initial failure and curling's success serve to demonstrate the relationship between sport and society. In the early period, the large tracts of land required to maintain a small number of golfers were an unaffordable luxury, whereas in the Canadian winter ice was plentiful and accessible to all. Also, scattered throughout the provinces after 1760 were the British military garrisons whose soldiers perpetuated 2 traditional loves, CRICKET and EQUESTRIAN SPORTS.

Games introduced by Scotsmen or Englishmen soon found adherents among the mixture of cultures developing in the colony. In addition, sports that owed little traditional allegiance to a particular ethnic origin were emerging and growing in popularity. These ranged from simple and useful sports such as tobogganing, sleighing, ICE SKATING and sailing, through individual sports advocated for their general health values (GYMNASTICS, TRACK AND FIELD, and swimming), to such highly complex sports as ROWING, where the skill of the rowers was combined with the science of the boat builders. In 1867 a Saint John crew won the world rowing championship at the Paris Exposition in France. In the early 19th century, the majority of the active sportsmen were gentlemen players from the merchant or upper strata of society and officers of the garrison. Not only did these officers re-establish in their new environment the sporting traditions of their homeland, but they were also eager to adopt and sponsor new activities. Their love of horse racing, along with their leisured existence, gave impetus to such allied sports as hunting, trotting and steeplechasing. They also added colour to the skating rink, the toboggan slide, the sleigh ride and the ballroom. Their all-encompassing interest and enthusiasm, allied with their managerial expertise, resulted in a broad spectrum of sport being established within the communities.

In theory, skating, SNOWSHOEING, cricket, FOOTBALL and similar activities were available for the workingman, but he lacked time and organizational experience. Those for whom Sunday provided the only leisure time were deterred from sporting activities on that day by religious groups, and by the law after the Lord's Day Act was passed in 1845 in the Province of Canada. It was not until early closing hours for shop and factory became more widespread in the mid-1860s that the workingman's participation in sport became possible. In this context, the advent of lacrosse and BASEBALL was timely, although even these sports tended to exclude members of the lower class, or "rowdies" as they were called, from organized teams. Where an activity was dependent upon organization, it still remained largely the prerogative of the affluent members of society.

Most pioneer women were far too busy to enjoy much leisure, but even when the opportunity presented itself, the conventions of the time prevented their active participation in most of the outdoor recreational activities followed by men. In the cities, their passive involvement was always encouraged through attendance at horse races, regattas, cricket matches and other spectator sports. It was permissible for them to be pas-

Members of the Grand Trunk Ry Amateur Athletic Association "Wheelmen" Toronto, Sept 1898 (*courtesy National Archives of Canada/PA-60593/John Boyd*).

Capt Robert Pearson of the YMCA umpiring behind the plate at a baseball match held in the Canadian lines, Sept 1917 (*courtesy National Archives of Canada/PA-1921*).

sengers in carrioles, iceboats and yachts; the more fortunate and independent were allowed to ride horses, skate or play croquet. The 1850s witnessed a change in attitude towards women engaging in sport that was also aided by changes in sporting attire. Female participation in fox hunting, the Ladies' Prince of Wales Snowshoe Club (1861), the Montreal Ladies Archery Club (1858), rowing regattas, FIGURE SKATING championships and foot races at social picnics was evidence of growing emancipation.

Probably the greatest role sporting competition played prior to 1867 was as social gathering and mixing ground. City and country dwellers could meet at the agricultural-social events; voyageurs could compete with Indians and settlers at canoe regattas; Indians could engage townsfolk in lacrosse. Race meetings were very popular and attracted thousands of spectators in the large urban centres. Horse racing provided a social as well as sporting environment for the townsfolk and was the setting for the greatest social mingling of 19th-century society. The upper classes tended to resist this mingling, however, and made unsuccessful efforts to preserve horse races for themselves by erecting fences around the courses and charging admission. This exclusion policy may also be seen in the appearance of events for "gentlemen amateurs" in regattas and horse races, ensuring that the practised fisherman rower or the skilled farmhand could not compete with the social elite.

The greatest impact upon sports came from advances in TECHNOLOGY. The steamboat, railway locomotive and steam-powered printing press made it possible for sport to be brought before the public. Steamboats carried sporting teams and spectators on excursions that had previously been highly impractical by stagecoach. They even followed the boats and yachts during regattas. The rapid expansion of railways made the one-day excursion for match play feasible (*see* RAILWAY HISTORY). More widely represented team meetings and bonspiels could be arranged, provincial associations formed and rules of play made more uniform. The larger newspapers, made possible by steam-powered printing presses, carried greater sports coverage, and the invention of the telegraph brought quicker reporting of results.

Sport, by Confederation, 1867, was approaching a new era. Old activities such as cricket, rowing and horse racing continued to be important, while the emergence of new ones, such as lacrosse and baseball, were the mark of a country with expanding sporting interests. Urbanization advanced liberal attitudes among civic leaders towards the population's need for healthy diversion and exercise. As these 2 forces gathered strength and allied with advancing technology, increased organization of sporting activities was the natural result. Of even more importance was an emerging Canadian identity in sport. Sport played an integral part in the development of national feeling, at least among English-speaking Canadians. This

trend is clearly seen in the phenomenal growth of lacrosse from 6 to 80 clubs during the summer of 1867, as George BEERS urged – unsuccessfully, despite popular support – that this sport be proclaimed Canada's national game. The unifying force of sport was also clearly shown when all of Canada basked in the glory achieved by the Saint John crew in Paris.   PETER L. LINDSAY

Sport from 1867 to 1900

On 26 Sept 1867, at a convention in Kingston, Ont, the National Lacrosse Assn was formed – the first of many such SPORTS ORGANIZATIONS to be established in Canada before the turn of the century. During the last 3 decades of the 19th century, sport in Canada matured and established the foundations that would carry it through much of the 20th century. It came under the influence of men who sought to rationalize and codify their games as they brought form and order to their sporting pursuits. Moreover, sport became a means for Canadians to express their feelings of pride in their new nation, aggressively searching for international competition and finding considerable success on the playing fields of the world.

This was a time when sport was intensely creative and exciting. Canadians were at the forefront of the development and popularization of 3 sports: lacrosse, HOCKEY and BASKETBALL. In 1874 in football, Canadians introduced to their American neighbours the oval ball and the rules of RUGBY. Lacrosse was so popular in the 1880s that the myth grew that it had been declared, by Act of Parliament, to be the national game. By the 1880s the game had been introduced to England and was spreading to western Canada. Eventually baseball would challenge lacrosse for public support and interest as a summer sport. The Canadian Baseball Assn was formed in 1876 and the first baseball leagues shortly thereafter. Much of baseball's early success occurred in southwestern Ontario, where the proximity of the US was enhanced by railway links.

Football, too, had a rapid evolution. The year 1874 marked the beginning of a series of annual matches between McGill and Harvard universities. As a result, the Americans shifted away from association football, called SOCCER today in N America, and adopted the oval ball and scrum of rugby. The links of the game to the universities and colleges of both countries, well established during this time, contributed to its longstanding success. In 1884 the first national championship for this largely Ontario- and Québec-based sport was held. By the turn of the century, through numerous rule changes, play had evolved away from rugger to the unique game of Canadian football. Both rugby and lacrosse contributed to hockey's evolution from an ill-defined version of British stick and ball games. Many of its practices,

including the face-off, its regulations concerning offsides, and the use of goals to score points owe a debt to one or other of the former games.

Montréal was the cradle for most of these dynamic developments of the late 19th century in Canada. The Montreal Amateur Athletic Assn (est 1881) was the first club of its kind, and acted as an umbrella for many sports clubs in that city. It was a social as well as a sports centre, with a large building providing reading and meeting rooms, a gymnasium and, eventually, a swimming pool. This club was the driving force behind the formation of the Amateur Athletic Assn of Canada, the first attempt to unify and regulate all sport in the country.

It is clear that the thrust behind the organization of sports in Canada's cities at this time came from members of the professional and business classes, who had the contacts, organizational skills and time to devote to this development. Faith in a scientific approach to all matters in life helped shape their attitudes to sport. One result of this approach, besides the development of sports organizations, was a fervent belief in amateurism and amateur codes. At the beginning of the 19th century, sport was largely controlled by the upper classes, and restrictive codes were established to segregate undesirables; the earliest forms were often racially based, restricting Indians and blacks from competing with whites. Eventually, as the working classes gained more free time, there arose the need to restrict them too. Having the time to develop strength and skills became a determinant, but eventually it was money, which released one from having to find other means of livelihood, that separated the amateurs from the professionals. The Amateur Athletic Union of Canada, in 1895, defined an amateur as being "one who has never pursued or assisted in the practice of manly exercise as a means of obtaining a livelihood."

There was more than social exclusivity behind the development of amateur codes. The desire for order moved Canadian sportsmen of the period to end a system of sporadic challenge matches which had open gambling and paid, imported athletes. Professionals were highly suspect and held in very low regard. The man who contributed most to changing these attitudes was Toronto's great Ned HANLAN, the world's professional sculling champion 1880-84. Thousands travelled great distances on special excursions arranged by railway promoters to watch him row against the world's best. He became the focus of a growing national spirit and helped to create a broad public acceptance, indeed adulation, for those who possessed great athletic skills. Deriving com-

Curling on the Kaministikwia R, Thunder Bay, *c* 1893 (*courtesy Provincial Archives of Ontario*).

Members of McGill's first hockey team in 1881 (*courtesy National Archives of Canada/C-81739*).

mercial benefit from his talent was simple affirmation of his ability.

Those who continued in the amateur tradition included Louis RUBENSTEIN and George ORTON. Rubenstein won the unofficial world championship in figure skating in 1890 and eventually became a pillar in the development of that sport, and in others like cycling. Orton became the first Canadian champion in the modern OLYMPIC GAMES, the great forum for the amateur athletic ideal. Canada sent no representative to the first Olympics, held in Greece in 1896, but Orton won the 1500 m steeplechase event as a member of the US team at the second Olympics in 1900.

As Canada entered the 20th century, it had regionally and nationally based structures for the governing of sports that provided the means of athletic competition. The amateur ethic was strong and would remain the basis for much athletic participation, but the door was open for professional sports where public interest made it commercially viable. Moreover, Canadians had found success and pride in challenging athletes from other parts of the world. It is little wonder that historians have regarded the years from Confederation to the turn of the century as the golden age of sport in Canada.   J. THOMAS WEST

Sport from 1900 to the Present

The twin processes of urbanization and industrialization, which had helped sow the seeds of modern sport in the 19th century, continued into the 20th century with even greater impact. One result was the full maturing of professional sports into great commercial spectator attractions. A second development, as the world was made smaller by air travel, was the growth of competitive opportunities for Canadians against athletes from around the world. As success in international events became of increasing importance, it came to be seen as part of the "national interest" to support athletes with government assistance.

By the turn of the century, hockey's roots were firmly planted in Canada and it was rapidly replacing lacrosse as the "national game." By 1908 it epitomized the divergent trends of sports towards amateurism and professionalism. The STANLEY CUP became emblematic of the professional championship and the Allen Cup and Memorial Cup of the amateur championships. After WWII, first through Foster HEWITT's radio broadcasts and later through television, professional hockey gained an almost mesmerized national audience. At the same time, small communities across the country were linked through the Allen Cup, the symbol of the national senior amateur title. Until 1952 Canada could count on its amateur champions to win the world title, but that changed after 1952 with the emergence of the Soviet Union as a hockey power.

The belief that hockey's professionals were the

world's best was shattered through various competitions in the 1970s (*see* CANADA-SOVIET HOCKEY SERIES). Nevertheless, professional hockey continued to be Canada's most popular sport and the sport most associated with the national identity. Lacrosse, in contrast, had dropped from being by far the most popular sport of the first decade, in number of spectators and press attention, into a state of serious decline by the 1920s. The press of the day was critical of the recurring violence in lacrosse matches. The game failed to develop a system of minor leagues that could produce future talent. Furthermore, it was a summer sport and the arrival of the automobile enabled people to escape the hot cities to other forms of recreation. Finally the media lost interest in lacrosse, turning their attention to baseball, with its "big league" glamour.

Despite baseball's popularity as a summer sport, however, it took nearly 70 years before a major league franchise was established in the country, although Montréal and Toronto had teams in the "Triple A" International League. There were several variations of the game played throughout the country. As well as hardball, softball in fast-pitch and slow-pitch versions have been popular. The Toronto Tip Tops claimed the world softball championship in 1949 and the Richmond Hill Dynes repeated this feat in 1972. With the formation of the MONTREAL EXPOS in 1969 and the TORONTO BLUE JAYS in 1977, 2 Canadian cities had franchises in the American-based professional major leagues of baseball. However, only a few Canadians have starred in professional baseball since WWII.

Football was another sport that experienced healthy growth in the 20th century, evolving from a game with a large amateur base into one that was played by professionals in a highly commercialized milieu. Until the 1920s the game was played and watched by a small but relatively well-educated and wealthy group of Canadians. It was based mainly in the country's large eastern universities and it used these roots to ensure its long-term survival. In the 1920s western teams began to use American players, and in 1936 the Canadian Rugby Union passed its first "residency" rule to curb such practices. Still, the pattern had been set so that, by the late 1960s, most of the key playing and coaching positions were held by Americans, with Canadians playing supporting roles. (Since the retirement of Russ JACKSON no Canadian has played quarterback regularly for a CFL team.) Nevertheless, Canadian football has retained its unique flavour and has enjoyed, in its own season, a major commercial endeavour capable of drawing widespread public interest. One of the reasons for this is the East versus West rivalry that the game has generated. This began in 1921, when the EDMONTON ESKIMOS first provided a western challenge for the GREY CUP. In 1935 Winnipeg won the national championship, a first for a western team. In 1948, the antics of Calgary fans in Toronto started the idea for a full-blown festival associated with the Grey Cup game – perhaps the closest thing to a national sports celebration Canada has.

While certain team sports enjoyed growing popularity and professionalization, the sector of Canadian sport that is broadly regarded as amateur survived and grew slowly, first under the broad umbrella of the Olympic movement and finally with government support. Canada has entered an official team at the Olympic Games since 1908 (except for the boycott of the 1980 Moscow games). Hamilton, Ont, was the host for the first British Empire Games (later the COMMONWEALTH GAMES) in 1930 and the PAN-AMERICAN GAMES were started in 1951. All 3 multi-sport festivals provide a highly visible international

stage for amateur athletes to focus their training programs and aspirations for success. In the 1920s Canada produced some of the world's finest amateur boxers, oarsmen and track and field competitors. However, by 1936, when Canada's gold medal success at the Olympics was limited to Frank Amyot's victory in canoeing, it was apparent that the world was beginning to leave Canadians behind, and a long period of feelings of national failure in athletics set in. Since the arrival of a strong Soviet team at the 1952 Olympic Games, the world of international sport has become increasingly the focus of political and national rivalries. Athletes have come to be seen as national spear carriers, increasingly under pressure to perform well in order to defend their country's honour. These pressures weighed heavily on nations such as Canada, which in 1960 returned from the Rome Olympics with but one silver medal.

As in other nations that come to consider sports to be wrapped up in the "national interest," Canadian sport sought the aid of the federal government. In 1961 the Fitness and Amateur Sport Act was passed. It was intended to provide $5 million annually to amateur sport and fitness-related activities. Growth was slow, however, and it was only after the stimulation provided by the findings of the Task Force on Sport for Canadians in 1969 that the federal government took a more aggressive approach to funding amateur sport. By the 1980s, the annual budget of the Fitness and Amateur Sport Program exceeded $50 million. One result of this government support was the growing bureaucratization of sport. Most of the affairs of national and regional sports organizations became the responsibility of paid administrators instead of long-time volunteers. However, another result has been increasing international success. Since 1980 Canadians have won world championships or held world records in alpine skiing, speed skating, figure skating, yachting, track and field, equestrianism, swimming, trap shooting, boxing, wrestling and modern pentathlon. In Sarajevo in 1984, Canada produced its most successful winter Olympian in speedskater Gaëtan BOUCHER, who won 3 medals: 2 gold and a bronze. In sharp contrast to the 1976 Montréal games in which Canadians won 11 medals, none of them gold, in the 1984 Los Angeles Olympics Canadians won 44 medals, including 10 gold. The 1984 triumph included 2 gold medals and Olympic records in swimming by Alex BAUMANN; the first woman in history to win an Olympic shooting gold medal (Linda THOM); the first Canadian woman swimmer to win a gold medal (Anne OTTENBRITE); and the first Canadian diver to take an Olympic gold (Sylvie BERNIER). Although the medal count was somewhat inflated by the boycott of Soviet bloc nations, Canada still placed a surprising fourth among the 140 nations that did attend.

Elite sport is not the only area enjoying growth and success in Canada. Under the urgings of the government-funded organization, ParticipAction, more and more Canadians are pursuing FITNESS and finding enjoyment through sports activities. Golf and curling always had widespread popularity as participation sports for Canadians of all ages. Cycling enjoyed a great boom in the 1970s. Joggers number in the hundreds of thousands. Events such as the Ottawa Capital Marathon annually attract thousands of competitors, most of whom took up running for their personal fitness and are trying to meet the challenge of finishing the 26 mile (43.3 km) distance. The development of Canadian sport in the 8 decades of this century have given it a vital place in the Canadian cultural mosaic. *See also* entries under individual sports.   J. THOMAS WEST

Reading: D. Fisher and S.F. Wise, *Canada's Sporting Heroes* (1974); T. Frayne and P. Gzowski, *Great Canadian Sport Stories* (1965); B. Schrodt, G. Redmond and R. Baka, *Sport Canadiana* (1980).

Sports Medicine and sports sciences are terms used by physiologists, physicians, psychologists, physiotherapists, trainers, coaches and physical educators, all of whom are interested in the sociological, psychological and physiological aspects of sports. The area also includes the prevention of injury to athletes and the treatment of injured athletes, and awareness of the needs of Canadians (particularly young children, adolescents, women, the handicapped and the elderly) who participate in some form of active pastime. Only a few hundred physicians and specialists in Canada, however, are qualified in all aspects of sports medicine and sports science.

Sports medicine practitioners help serious athletes plan preseason training and testing, provide early treatment for injuries, identify groups that may be susceptible to risk, and record frequencies in patterns of injuries. The study of safety equipment and modification of rules to preclude injuries have also become integral to sports medicine. The evolution of sports medicine in Canada was somewhat haphazard until 1965, when a joint subcommittee of the Canadian Medical Assn and the Canadian Assn of Health, Physical Education and Recreation was established to investigate problems relating to sports medicine and national fitness. This led to the formation of the Canadian Association of Sports Sciences in 1967.

Groups specializing in motor learning and the sociology, physiology and psychology of sport have also emerged. Since the early 1970s the Medical Committee of the Canadian Olympic Association, the Canadian Academy of Sports Medicine, the Sports Medicine Division of the Canadian Physiotherapy Association and the Canadian Athletic Therapists Association have helped develop a system to aid top Canadian athletes. In 1978 the Sports Medicine Council was founded to advance the development of medical, paramedical and scientific services and their provision to Canadian amateur athletes, and specifically to establish policies to safeguard high-quality care; to promote education and research in the fields of sports science and sports medicine; to develop an information bank on epidemiology and management of sports injuries and illnesses; and to stimulate and provide for applied research related to the training, treatment and evaluation of athletes. The council is associated with the Sports Information and Resource Centre, a documentation centre headquartered in Ottawa for sports, physical education, recreation and sports sciences. The major sports-medicine clinics are in universities across Canada. In the US, by contrast, many of the largest sports-medicine clinics are private enterprises.

Sports and Drugs According to most sports-governing bodies, the performance of athletes should reflect their inborn ability, training techniques, perseverance, dedication and skill. Unfortunately, success for athletes has become synonymous with the success of a training system, a country and even an ideology (*see* CANADA-SOVIET HOCKEY SERIES); pressure on international athletes is enormous and the use of drugs common. Canada is not exempt from these practices. Many of these drugs are dangerous during their immediate use and because of their long-term side effects. They can be broadly divided into anabolic substances capable of enhancing body bulk and mass; stimulants that alter states of alertness and awareness; and drugs that alter the body's metabolism, allowing more rapid recovery of oxygen or enhancing its supply to muscles. At present, more money is spent policing drug abuse than is spent on injured athletes, and it is really only the athletes who bear the punishment for drug abuse. DAVID C. REID

Reading: L. Peterson and P. Renström, *Sports Injuries: Their Prevention and Treatment* (1986).

Sports Organization, Amateur The earliest athletic body organized to administer sport was the Montreal Amateur Athletic Assn (MAAA). Formed in 1881, it comprised clubs for lacrosse, swimming and bicycling. The first national organization was the Amateur Athletic Assn of Canada, founded in 1884. It was later named the Canadian Amateur Athletic Union. In 1907 the MAAA formed its own group, the Amateur Athletic Federation of Canada. In 1909, the Amateur Athletic Union of Canada was formed, comprising the MAAA and the CAAU. This group encouraged the entry of individual sports groups and became the thread from which Canadian sport organizations grew. Dr A.S. Lamb of McGill had a strong role in its development.

The Canadian Olympic Committee emerged in 1909 from an earlier 1907 Central Olympic Committee. This committee was empowered to select teams and secure finances for travel to the Olympic Games, and was part of the larger AAUC organization. Sir John Handbury Williams was appointed Canada's first representative to the International Olympic Committee. In 1913 the COC became the Canadian Olympic Assn, a member of the AAUC. Finally, in 1949, the Canadian Olympic Assn was formed, independent of the AAUC.

The AAUC controlled amateur sport in Canada throughout the first half of the 20th century. On 1 Oct 1943 the Canada National Physical Fitness Act (NPFA) was passed. Although it did not compete with the AAUC, it recognized the importance of physical fitness for Canadians through physical education, sports and athletics. Most significantly, it brought the federal government into the sphere of amateur sport. In 1951, the NPFA brought into being the Canadian Sports Advisory Council, later to become the Sports Federation of Canada, which became the official lobbyist for national sport-governing bodies in Ottawa. The Fitness and Amateur Sport Act was passed on 29 Sept 1961, to promote and to develop fitness and amateur sport in Canada. For the first time, sport was to be actively supported by the federal government; the Fitness and Amateur Sport Directorate was formed as the administrative body.

A significant year for amateur sport in Canada was 1969. The Task Force on Sport for Canadians made numerous recommendations to the federal government, many of which were implemented. The most important consequence for amateur sport organizations was that in 1970 the Centre for Sport and Recreation became a reality, incorporated in 1974 as the National Sport and Recreation Centre. In return for locating in Ottawa, the federal government offered to amateur sport groups financial support for technical, executive and program staff, office expenses and secretarial help, and use of the centre's services at a reduced cost. By 1988, those services included graphics, printing, mail and shipping, computer, audio visual and personnel. Today, 65 amateur sport groups reside in Ottawa; another 19 organizations are affiliated as nonresident sports. Associations receive contributions for their annual budgets from Fitness and Amateur Sport based upon their needs, popularity and status in the international competitive arena. The COA, Sport Federation of Canada, Coaching Assn of Canada, Athlete Information Bureau and Fitness and Amateur Sport work together with organizations to provide one of the most comprehensive systems in the world. The growth of support for amateur sport associations has been acknowledged by the creation of a federal ministry for Fitness and Amateur Sport. LORNE SAWULA

Spraggett, Kevin, Canadian chess grandmaster (b at Montréal 10 Nov 1954). His chess career gained momentum with a second-place showing at the 1973 Canadian Open. With the influence of Soviet dissident Igor Ivanov, Spraggett's chess became stronger and in 1983 he entered foreign competitions, winning the prestigious New York Open and 2 Commonwealth championships. At the world championship at Toluca Interzonal, Mexico (1985), he became the first Canadian to qualify for the candidates cycle. The next year he played top board in the Chess Olympiad at Dubai. At the 1988 World Chess festival in Saint John, he defeated Soviet Andrei Sokolov and became the first Canadian to advance to the quarterfinals of this competition.

Spremo, Boris, press photographer (b at Susak, Yugoslavia 20 Oct 1935). A graduate of Belgrade's Cinematographic Institute, Spremo immigrated to Canada in 1957. He began his career in newspaper PHOTOGRAPHY in Toronto 5 years later when he joined the *Globe and Mail.* In 1966 he switched to the *Toronto Star.* In addition to photographing many politicians, entertainers and sports personalities, Spremo has covered the FLQ crisis in Québec, drought and famine in central Africa, the end of the war in Vietnam, the first Cruise missile launching in Alaska, and the pope's tour of Canada. His photographs have appeared in magazines such as *Maclean's* and his books include *Boris Spremo: Twenty Years of Photojournalism* (1983). Spremo was among the 100 photojournalists chosen to contribute to *A Day in the Life of Canada* (1985). LOUISE ABBOTT

Spring, a point of natural, concentrated GROUNDWATER discharge from soil or rock. Some springs are located in river or lake beds (subaqueous springs) or below mean sea level along the coast (submarine springs), but many are found some distance from surface water bodies. Springs with water temperatures near the local mean-annual air temperature are commonly called cold springs. Springs with higher temperatures are known as thermal springs: warm springs have temperatures up to 37°C; hot springs between 37°C and the boiling temperature of water at the spring location (often well below 100°C at higher elevations in mountainous areas); boiling springs have a temperature equal to the boiling temperature. Intermittent hot springs that eject columns of hot water and steam into the air, at more or less regular intervals, are called geysers (after Stora Geysir, Iceland). All spring waters contain dissolved minerals, derived from slow dissolution of rocks which the groundwater contacts during its movement to the spring. Freshwater springs produce water with under 1 g dissolved mineral content per litre. Mineral springs have dissolved mineral contents of 1-35 g/L (the approximate salt concentration in seawater). Brine springs have concentrations ranging to over 300 g/L. The minerals dissolved in spring waters include carbonates, sulphates, chlorides and sulphides (of calcium, magnesium, sodium, potassium and iron). Spring waters contain small quantities of gases, including carbon dioxide, nitrogen, oxygen and methane, and minute quantities of helium, radon, neon, argon, krypton and xenon.

All thermal springs known in Canada occur in the western mountain region of Alberta, in BC, in the YT and in the NWT, where high relief permits deep circulation of rain and snowmelt, leading to GEOTHERMAL heating of the water. Some of these springs are only warm (eg, Cave and Basin Springs in BANFF NATIONAL PARK, Alta; Rabbitkettle

Hot Springs in NAHANNI NATIONAL PARK, NWT). Many are true hot springs (eg, Upper Hot Spring in Banff; Fairmont Hot Springs and Harrison Hot Springs, BC; Takhini Hot Spring, YT). These hot springs are also mineral springs. The notable exception is the McArthur Hot Springs, YT, with a dissolved mineral content of under 0.2 g/L. Cold mineral springs are found in other parts of Canada. Cold brine springs occur in areas with marine SEDIMENTARY ROCKS (eg, limestone, dolomite, gypsum, rock salt) near the eastern edge of the Interior Plains in Alberta and Manitoba, and in sedimentary basins in the St Lawrence Lowland and Appalachian regions in Québec, NB and NS. Some thermal and mineral springs produce spring deposits at or near their outlets through precipitation of part of their mineral content. The mineral composition of a spring deposit reflects the chemical composition of the spring water. For example, the Cave and Basin Springs deposit mainly calcium carbonate, through loss of CO_2 and evaporation; the McArthur Hot Springs produce small amounts of silica, through cooling and evaporation; the Paint Pots, in KOOTENAY NATIONAL PARK, BC, produce iron sulphates and iron oxyhydroxides, through evaporation, oxidation and hydrolysis; and the cold Fly-by Springs in the Mackenzie Mts deposit barium sulphate. The most spectacular spring deposit is the terraced calcium-carbonate cone of Rabbitkettle Hot Springs in Nahanni National Park.

R.O. VAN EVERDINGEN

Springfield, Man, Rural Municipality, pop 9836 (1986c), 8986 (1981c), was formed when Springfield and Sunnyside (Dugald) jointly incorporated 1873. It covers 105 866 ha immediately E of Winnipeg, with Birds Hill Provincial Park in the NW, and Agassiz and Sandilands provincial forests to the E. Its largest communities are the villages of Oakbank, Dugald and Anola. The municipality is governed by a reeve and 6 councillors. Large-scale settlement by Ontario, British and American farmers occurred in the area in the early 1870s. Subsequent settlers included French Canadians, German, Ukrainian, Polish, Belgian and Danish immigrants, and more recently Hutterites. Mixed farming and gravel extraction have dominated Springfield's economy. Since the 1960s the area has experienced migration from Winnipeg of families wishing to combine urban employment with a country life-style.

D.M. LYON

Springhill, NS, Town, pop 4712 (1986c), 4896 (1981c), inc 1889, located in the heart of Cumberland County on the Chignecto Isthmus, is so named because the hill on which it is situated once contained numerous springs. Once noted for its coalfields, Springhill is now famous as the hometown of pop singer Anne MURRAY. The town

John Totten (left) tells his brother William of progress in the search for victims of the coal mine disaster in Springhill, NS, 23 Oct 1958. 74 men died (*courtesy Canapress Photo Service*).

was first settled about 1820 by LOYALISTS. Coal was soon discovered and a small mine opened in 1834. Mining began on a large scale in 1872 when the Springhill and Parrsboro Coal and Ry Co Ltd sank shafts and opened a rail line. Several mining DISASTERS have plagued the town, the worst occurring in 1958 when 74 men died in the deepest mine in N America. After this, the DOSCO-owned mines were shut down. Small coal seams have been mined only intermittently since then. There is high unemployment and little secondary industry here. The Springhill Miners Museum, opened in 1972, and the Springhill Medium Security Institution (1960) provide some employment for residents.

HEATHER MacDONALD

Sproatt and Rolph, architectural firm (est 1899) of Henry Sproatt (b at Toronto 14 June 1866; d there 4 Oct 1934), and Ernest Ross Rolph (b at Toronto 21 Jan 1871; d there 4 May 1958). Sproatt, an authority on Gothic architecture, served as the principal designer. He was trained in New York C 1886-89 and commenced architectural practice in Toronto in 1890. He was in partnership with Frank Darling in the 1890s. Rolph, the pragmatic designer and builder, trained with David Roberts, an early Toronto architect (Gooderham Mansion, York Club), and then worked as an architect and engineer for the Canadian Pacific Ry in BC. The firm Sproatt and Rolph was responsible for numerous institutional, commercial and residential buildings in Toronto, including Hart House and the Memorial Tower at U of T (American Inst of Architects Gold Medal, 1926); Bishop Strachan School, Manufacturer's Life Building, Ontario Club and National Club. Both men were widely recognized as patrons of the arts and were elected fellows of the Royal Institute of British Architects.

ANDREA KRISTOF

Spruce, evergreen CONIFER (genus *Picea*) of PINE family (Pinaceae). About 40 species occur worldwide, in circumpolar distribution in the Northern Hemisphere; 5 are native to Canada. White spruce (*P. glauca*) and black spruce (*P. mariana*) are found nearly from coast to coast in the boreal forest; Sitka spruce (*P. sitchensis*) in a narrow

White, or "Canadian," spruce (*Picea glauca*), with female flowers, male flowers and cones, bottom right (*artwork by Claire Tremblay*).

band along the West Coast; Engelmann spruce (*P. engelmannii*) in interior BC to the Rockies; red spruce (*P. rubens*) in the Great Lakes-St Lawrence and Acadian forest regions. Norway spruce (*P. abies*) and blue spruce (*P. pungens*) have been introduced. Trunks are long and straight; crowns dense and narrow. Evergreen leaves are needlelike, usually 4-sided, often sharply pointed and borne on woody pegs or stalks. Seed cones are 2-10 cm long, nonwoody with rounded scales and small bracts. POLLINATION occurs in spring. Winged seeds are shed in fall. Spruces, used for pulp, paper and lumber, are the most important commercial conifers.

JOHN N. OWENS

Spruce Grove, Alta, City, pop 11 918 (1986c), 10 326 (1981c), inc 1971, is located W of Edmonton. Named for the spruce trees once common in the area, the town grew up around a station on the Grand Trunk Pacific Ry. Spruce Grove became Alberta's 16th city on 1 Mar 1986. It is governed by a mayor and 6 aldermen. It serves an agricultural district, and since the 1960s many residents commute to Edmonton.

ERIC J. HOLMGREN

Spry, Graham, journalist, diplomat, international business executive, political organizer, advocate of public broadcasting (b at St Thomas, Ont 20 Feb 1900; d at Ottawa 24 Nov 1983). As cofounder with Alan PLAUNT in 1930 of the Canadian Radio League he was instrumental in mobilizing popular and political support for public broadcasting in Canada. A Rhodes scholar in history at Oxford, Spry began his career as a reporter and editorial writer for the *Manitoba Free Press* (1920-22). He was chairman of the Canadian Radio League 1930-34 (and years later of the Canadian Broadcasting League 1968-73). The CRL campaigned for the general recommendation of the 1929 royal commission on broadcasting – the establishment and the support of a national system operated as a public undertaking. Spry's famous 1932 aphorism, "The State or the United States," is apt even today (*see* CANADIAN BROADCASTING CORPORATION).

A political activist, he published the *Farmers' Sun,* renamed the *New Commonwealth* (1932-34); was coauthor of *Social Planning for Canada,* published by the LEAGUE FOR SOCIAL RECONSTRUCTION (1935); and was chairman of the Ontario Co-operative Commonwealth Federation (1934-36). He then joined Standard Oil of California, becoming director (1940-46) of UK-based subsidiaries engaged in Arabian and other operations. At the same time he was personal assistant to Sir Stafford Cripps of the British War Cabinet (1942-45), accompanying him on his mission to India, and served in the Home Guard. As agent general for Saskatchewan in the UK, Europe and the Near East (1946-68), among other duties he recruited doctors, nurses and other skilled personnel. He was instrumental in neutralizing the 1962 SASKATCHEWAN DOCTORS' STRIKE against medicare. In Canada 1968-83, he continued to work for public broadcasting until the end of his life.

ROBERT E. BABE

Spry, Irene Mary, née Biss, economic historian (b at Standerton, Transvaal, S Africa 28 Aug 1907; daughter of Evan E. and Amelia Bagshaw Johnstone). Student of the "great transformation" in 19th-century western Canada, and of natural resource economics, she has written books and articles and made valuable contributions to the maintenance of humane values in many communities. Her works on the PALLISER EXPEDITION 1857-60 and the reminiscences of Peter Erasmus are marked by an appreciation of the imperial context and the economic factors underlying Canadian history in this era. She was a member of the LEAGUE FOR SOCIAL RECONSTRUCTION in the 1930s, worked with H.A. INNIS while he was engaged in his studies of the cod fishery and pulp and paper, and examined the development of electric power in Canada. She represented the Federated Women's Institutes of Canada with the Associated Country Women of the World from 1954 to 1967, acting as executive chairman 1959-65 and deputy president 1968-74. With her late husband Graham SPRY, Saskatchewan's agent general in the United Kingdom and Europe for 2 decades, she has been an untiring supporter of Canada and of a social democratic approach to public policy. GERALD FRIESEN

Spying, *see* INTELLIGENCE AND ESPIONAGE.

Squamish, BC, District Municipality, pop 10 157 (1986c), 10 272 (1981c), inc 1964, is located 70 km N of Vancouver at the head of Howe Sound. The municipality is governed by a mayor and 6 aldermen. It is the service centre for a richly endowed recreational area, with road, rail and water access to Vancouver. Some of BC's best skiing is available at nearby Whistler Mt, and Garibaldi Park, alpine meadows, waterfalls and glacier-fed lakes are close by. Nearby Squamish Chief, the 2nd-largest granite monolith in the Commonwealth, attracts rock climbers. Squamish holds the largest loggers' sports show in Canada, including world championship events. Squamish is the winter home for hundreds of American Bald Eagles, which spend late December, January and February on the river banks during the annual salmon spawn.

The area was originally inhabited by the Squohomish, a tribe of Coast Salish; Squamish is the Indian word for "strong wind." The first Europeans settled in the Squamish Valley about 1888. Though their settlement was known for a while as Newport, the older name was eventually restored. In the early years, hop farming was the valley's main industry, and Squamish hops were some of the finest shipped to England. The primary industries in the area are logging, milling, and chemical and pulp production. Squamish is serviced by a year-round, fog-free, deep-sea port and is close to rail and road transport. BC Railway has 500 employees in its main shops in Squamish. ALAN F.J. ARTIBISE

Squash (genus *Cucurbita*), annual plant belonging to the Cucurbitaceae family and native to the New World. Squash may have been domesticated as early as 7000 to 5000 BC in the Tehuacan Valley in Mexico; evidence suggests that it was cultivated in present-day Ontario by the HURON and related groups by about 1400 AD. Both running and bush types occur. Squashes have large yellow flowers which attract bees; each plant carries male and female flowers. Squashes are classified as either summer or winter varieties, depending on when they are harvested. Summer squashes (mainly *C. pepo*) are harvested before maturity, when they are still small and tender; common varieties are zucchini and yellow crookneck. Winter squashes (mainly *C. maxima*, but also *C. pepo, C. moschata* or *C. mixta*) are harvested at full maturity (3-4 months after planting), when the rind is hard; common varieties are acorn squash and butternut squash. Winter squashes have a higher carbohydrate content and are more nutritious. Squash grows rapidly, producing abundant foliage and a well-developed but rather superficial root system. Summer squash is normally seeded directly in the field, as is winter squash if the growing season is long enough. Winter squash can be stored at about 10°C, under dry, well-ventilated conditions. Squash species crossbreed readily; numerous cultivars vary enormously in shape, colour, size and texture. Squash has a low commercial value, although it is found in most family gardens and is grown by a few specialized growers. *See also* PUMPKIN. ROGER BÉDARD

Squash Racquets is played with a long-handled, small-headed racquet in an enclosed court that resembles a giant, lidded shoebox. Each player (or pair in doubles) takes turns hitting the ball to the front wall – rather like lawn TENNIS but with both players on one side of the court. The game is an offshoot of racquets but is played with a soft, "squashy" ball, hence the name. There are 2 versions of the game: the International game, which is played worldwide, including in America, where it is becoming increasingly popular; and the American game, which is played almost solely in Canada and the US. Although squash courts may have existed in Vancouver as early as the 1880s, it was the Montreal Racquet Club, Toronto Racquet Club and Hamilton Squash Racquets Club that formed the Canadian Squash Racquets Assn (CSRA) in 1913 – the world's first national squash organization.

Canadians who have excelled at the game include Ernest Howard of Toronto, the first Canadian to win the US singles championship (1953); Colin Adair of Montréal, the only Canadian to win the US title twice; Michael Desaulniers, who won the US title twice; and S. McElhinney, S. Murray and J. Maycock, all winners of the North American Women's Open Championships. In recent years, the fact that many-times world champions Sharif Khan and Heather McKay lived and played in Canada helped to develop the game in this country, as did the advent of nationally televised matches.

Until the 1970s most squash courts in Canada were privately owned, or were found in social clubs, sports clubs, universities or private schools. Recently many new commercial courts are being constructed with large galleries and facilities for televising games. This business approach has opened the game to increasing numbers of spectators and participants. Although facing stiff competition in some centres from other racquet sports, the intense competition and high levels of skill and fitness demanded by the game, together with the fact that people of all ages and fitness levels can play, guarantee its popularity. BRIAN T.P. MUTIMER

Squid, decapod ("10-footed") MOLLUSC of class Cephalopoda. Squid are usually of the order Teuthoidea, but only an expert could distinguish a slow squid from a fast CUTTLEFISH (order Sepioidea). Generally the term is applied to fast-swimming, streamlined forms in which a powerful jet-propulsion system provides the "squirt" by which the squid moves. Squid are the only INVERTEBRATE competitors of pelagic (open sea) fish; some are even capable of brief, jet-powered flight. Thirty teuthids occur in Canadian waters including *Gonatus fabricii*, found on all 3 coasts, and the giant squid *Architeuthis dux*. The former has commercial potential. The largest fishery is for Atlantic squid (*Illex illecebrosus*). These squid migrate hundreds of km to warm waters to spawn and die after growing to 500 g in 9 to 12 months. Their schools have some social structure and they communicate by changing colour patterns. The flying squid (*Ommastrephes bartramii*) of the Pacific is taken by Japanese fishermen using driftnet sets up to 45 km long. There is a potential fishery for this squid off the BC coast. R.K. O'DOR

Squires, Sir Richard Anderson, lawyer, politician, prime minister of Newfoundland 1919-23 and 1928-32 (b at Harbour Grace, Nfld 18 Jan 1880; d at St John's 26 Mar 1940). Squires entered the Newfoundland Assembly in 1909. Defeated in 1913, he was appointed to the Legislative Council and the Cabinet by Sir Edward MORRIS as a reward for his electoral battle against the Fishermen's Protective Union. He lost his Cabinet post when Sir William Lloyd formed the second National Government in 1918. On its 1919 collapse, Squires founded the Liberal Reform Party, which, in alliance with the FPU, won the election that year. His administration had to deal with postwar chaos in the fishing industry. In July 1923 Squires resigned in the face of corruption charges, later substantiated. He rebounded to win the 1928 election, but his government proved virtually helpless as the economic crisis of the period deepened. Corruption charges were again levelled against him in 1932, sparking a riot in St John's in Apr. In the June election his party was decimated. A Tory government was elected to preside over the end of responsible government in 1934, a debacle to which Squires contributed. *See also* COMMISSION OF GOVERNMENT. J.K. HILLER

Squirrel, common name for family (Sciuridae) of RODENTS, comprising 261 species, found in N and S America, Eurasia and Africa. Twenty-two species occur in Canada: 6 are tree species (*Sciurus carolinensis, S. niger, Tamiasciurus hudsonicus T. douglasii, Glaucomys volans, G. sabrinus*), the latter 2 flying squirrels; and 16 are ground-dwelling species, of which 6 are ground squirrels (*Spermophilus richardsonii, S. columbianus, S. parryii, S. tridecemlineatus, S. franklinii, S. lateralis*), 5 are CHIPMUNKS, 4 are MARMOTS and one a PRAIRIE DOG. Squirrels have 4 toes on forefeet; 5 on hindfeet. Tree squirrels have bushy tails and small, agile feet; ground species have less bushy tails and more robust forefeet. Ground squirrels and chipmunks carry food in cheek pouches. The flying squirrel has a skin fold along its flanks and attached to its feet that enables it to glide. There is great variation in size: the largest Canadian squirrel, the hoary marmot, is 80 cm long and weighs 6 kg; the smallest, the least chipmunk, 22 cm and 50 g. In Canada, most species reproduce once annually. Mating occurs in spring; gestation lasts 24-44 days and litters average 3-8 young, depending on species. At birth, young are hairless and poorly developed; growth is rapid. All Canadian species, except flying squirrels, are diurnal. While most ground squirrels hibernate, tree squirrels are active year round. Certain species are found throughout Canada; others only inhabit specific areas. Preferred habitats are varied, including forests, prairies, mountains and arctic regions. Primarily herbivorous, squirrels sometimes eat insects, eggs and even small birds. Some are gregarious; others, solitary. Tree squirrels generally build nests; ground-dwelling species dig burrows. Squirrels can damage cereal crops, maple-tapping equipment and telephone wires; burrows and hillocks can harm livestock and agricultural machinery. JEAN FERRON

Stabilization refers to government MONETARY POLICY, FISCAL POLICY, or other actions taken with the goal of minimizing BUSINESS CYCLE fluctuations in important economy-wide variables – especially employment, output and INFLATION. For example, a cyclical decline in output might be cushioned by fiscal initiatives such as tax cuts or increased government expenditures, or by a monetary policy generating lower INTEREST rates to stimulate investment expenditures. The reverse of these policies, accompanied by the introduction of WAGE AND PRICE CONTROLS, may be adopted to forestall any acceleration of inflation.

The development of the modern idea of stabilization policy can be attributed to the British economist John Maynard Keynes. During the GREAT DEPRESSION, Keynes argued forcefully that cyclical fluctuations were not sufficiently self-correcting, and that active government intervention might be needed to prevent a repetition of such a severe and prolonged economic downturn. Although this principle is now generally well accepted, critics assert that the effectiveness of stabilization policy is limited by conflicts among objectives (eg, actions to reduce inflation may increase unemployment) and by inconsistencies between short-term and long-term effects – especially when the pressures of political expediency are considered. These issues continue to be debated both at theoretical and practical levels.

RONALD G. WIRICK

Stacey, Charles Perry, historian (b at Toronto 30 July 1906). Stacey was a Princeton PhD and taught there 1934-40. He had been a committed part-time soldier since his student days at U of T and Oxford, and he served as the Canadian Army's historical officer in London 1940-45 and chief army historian 1945-59. A lively teacher possessed of a mischievous wit, he was a professor at U of T, 1959-76, briefly returning to preside over National Defence's newly unified triservice directorate of history 1965-66. Canada's first historical craftsman, a superb researcher and easy stylist, Stacey has written, among other books, *Canada and the British Army, 1846-71* (1936); *The Military Problems of Canada* (1940); *The Canadian Army, 1939-45* (1948); *Six Years of War* (1955); *Quebec, 1759* (1959); *The Victory Campaign* (1960); *Arms, Men and Governments* (1970); *A Very Double Life* (1976); *Canada and the Age of Conflict* (2 vols, 1977-81); *The Half Million: Canadians in Britain 1939-1946* (1987, with Barbara Wilson); and his memoirs, *A Date with History* (1983).

NORMAN HILLMER

Stadacona, IROQUOIS village located at the present site of QUÉBEC CITY, had an estimated population of about 500. Jacques CARTIER was led to the village on his second voyage in 1535 and wintered at a safe distance, across the St Charles R. In midwinter more than 50 Stadaconans died, likely of European diseases to which they had no immunity, and 25 French died of scurvy before the Indians provided them with a cure – a potion made from fronds of white cedar. Cartier unwittingly offended the Stadaconans by establishing a base without their permission and by travelling upriver to HOCHELAGA. He kidnapped DONNACONA, his 2 sons and 7 others and returned to France, but all except a young girl perished before Cartier returned to Stadacona in 1541. He established a second base at Cap Rouge, upstream from Stadacona, but increasing hostility and his belief that he had found gold and diamonds prompted his retreat. Jean-François ROBERVAL arrived at Stadacona shortly after and though relations with the Indians improved, he abandoned the fledgling colony. By the time the French returned to the site in 1603, the Stadaconans and the St Lawrence Iroquois had vanished. Various theories about their fate have been put forward: that they were driven out by the Montagnais and ALGONQUIN; that they suffered poor harvests brought on by climatic changes; that they succumbed to European diseases; that they were dispersed by the southern Iroquois, eg, the Mohawk. There is some evidence that refugees from Stadacona and Hochelaga were adopted by the HURON. By Samuel de CHAMPLAIN's time, the St Lawrence Valley was a no-man's-land travelled only by war parties of the Montagnais and Iroquois.

JAMES MARSH

Stage and Costume Design in Canada reflected the practices and standards of London and New York. The American influence was absorbed through visits to NY, contact with theatre departments in American universities, and touring productions. British standards were introduced by talented individuals who visited or chose to live here. Until the 1950s there were no true stage designers; there was minimal recognition of scenic and costume design as an art. At the DOMINION DRAMA FESTIVAL, the amateur competition formed in 1932 and held annually from 1933 to the 1970s, there was no travel allowance for designers and initially no design award was made. Though this was later rectified with an award honouring Martha Jamieson, the producing group and not the designer's name went onto the plaque. Established amateur companies copied sets of the original productions or asked local artists to provide them. In the 1920s and 1930s some well-known painters, particularly the GROUP OF SEVEN, designed sets and costumes for Hart House Theatre and the Arts and Letters Club in Toronto. Firms which rented formal wear introduced costume departments; Mallabar's, now an international concern, began this way. The costumes were the work of anonymous sewers and pattern drafters, not designers.

As professional theatre, ballet and opera companies were established and the CBC began TV broadcasting in the 1950s, opportunities for designers were suddenly provided, though there were few designers and fewer technicians (*see* BROADCASTING; TELEVISION PROGRAMMING). Initially many of the CBC set designers were European. But it was the STRATFORD FESTIVAL, and Tanya Moiseiwitsch, who designed its stage and first productions, that made Canadian artists aware of the possibilities in theatrical design. Young Canadians, many still at art schools and universities, were employed as technicians, and with their Stratford training became the core of the designers working at the regional and festival theatres established in the 1960s and 1970s.

Moiseiwitsch continued to work at Stratford for the next 30 years. Other British designers followed. Leslie Hurry contributed most of his important designs to the festival: some of his best work was done in Canada. His vision was singular and painterly but capable of rendering a fine barbarism, as in *Pericles*. Desmond Heeley's spare yet exotic designs have made their mark on this country. Susan Benson brought a control of texture and palette that has influenced many younger designers. In recent years Canadian designers, trained in this country, have assumed the principal design role at the festival. Prominent among them are Michael Egan, Philip Silver, Christina Poddubiuk and Debra Hanson.

By the 1970s theatrical design was an established profession in Canada. The Associated Designers of Canada, founded in 1965, now has some 120 members employed at most of the theatres in the country. Outstanding practitioners include Murray Laufer, whose architectural settings established the house style of the St Lawrence Centre in Toronto; Suzanne Mess, prominent as a costume designer for grand opera in N America; François Barbeau, pre-eminent in Montréal; Philip Silver, the pioneer designer at the Citadel in Edmonton; Jack King, whose designs for new Canadian works with the NATIONAL BALLET have been notable; and Cameron Porteous, who has done impressive work as head of design at both the SHAW FESTIVAL and the VANCOUVER PLAYHOUSE.

Stratford's influence was felt beyond Canada. Tyrone GUTHRIE's demonstration of the effectiveness of the thrust stage was widely imitated. A style of design consisting of carefully lit and detailed costumes and properties on an elaborate scale against a plain background offered an exciting alternative to proscenium-arch settings.

Nationwide there are now about 60 schools, in addition to the National Theatre School, offering training for the theatre, and over 100 professional companies producing plays. The regional and institutional theatres provide varied employment, and the small alternative theatres encourage experimentation. Designers are no longer restricted to individual productions but are actively involved with architects in the design of new buildings and restoration of old structures. Canada is recognized for the ingenuity with which its architectural and theatrical designers transform 19th-century industrial and public buildings to new use in the 20th century. In less than 30 years Canadian theatrical design has begun to earn international recognition.

Canadian designers now work outside Canada, and at the Prague Quadrennial, the juried exhibition of the best in theatrical design from around the world, the Canadian exhibition has received an honourable mention in every competition since 1975. Two Canadian designers, Murray Laufer in 1975 and Roy Robitschek in 1983, received special commendations. *See also* TELEVISION DRAMA.

MARTHA MANN

Stagecoach The principal means of public overland transportation in Canada and the US in the first half of the 19th century, the stagecoach was a 4-wheeled vehicle pulled by 4 or more horses. Six or more passengers sat in the suspended carriage protected from the elements; parcels were fastened to racks on its roof; and the driver sat in an exposed, forward position. Regular routes were travelled which took passengers and mail by stages from station to station. Developed in England in the 17th century, the stagecoach was displaced by the railway coach in the 1840s. Today it is principally associated with the Western movie and the Wild West.

JOHN ROBERT COLOMBO

Stagflation, the combination of high unemployment and high rates of INFLATION. Prior to the late 1960s, variations in economic activity were caused primarily by "demand shocks" (fluctuations in aggregate demand or total expenditure). Increases in aggregate demand led to increased output, employment and prices, while reductions resulted in reduced output, higher unemployment and lower inflation. Stagflation in the 1970s and 1980s has been caused partly by "supply shocks" (increases in price). If governments respond to a large supply shock by maintaining total expenditure, a severe RECESSION will result because the increased expenditure on energy or food means reduced expenditure on other goods and services, and therefore reduced output and employment. If governments increase total expenditure, inflation will result. Most Western governments have chosen a policy between these 2 extremes, creating both higher inflation and unemployment. Expectations can also affect stagflation. If people expect inflation to continue, they will set wages and prices accordingly, giving inflation a momentum that cannot quickly be halted.

W.C. RIDDELL

Stairs, John Fitz-William, merchant, shipper, politician (b at Halifax 19 Jan 1848; d there 24 Sept 1904). Eldest son of William Stairs, MLA and a leading merchant, Stairs studied at Dalhousie. Elected to the NS Legislative Assembly in 1879, he resigned in 1882. From 1883 until 1896 he sat as a Conservative in the House of Commons. President of many companies, including Nova Scotia Steel, Eastern Trust, Trinidad Electric and Royal Securities, Stairs was also director of the Dartmouth and Halifax Steamboat Co, Nova Scotia Sugar Refining, the Union Bank of Halifax, Consumer Cordage, and dominated the financial elite of the Maritimes during the last 15 years of his life. He also employed Max AITKEN (Lord Beaverbrook) at the beginning of Aitken's business career, hiring him in 1902 when he set up Royal Securities, the first investment firm in eastern Canada.

JORGE NIOSI

Artist's rendition of Canada as seen from far above the Arctic Archipelago. Courtesy Northern Transportation Company Limited.